KU-733-245

FOR
REFERENCE ONLY

# British Pharmacopoeia 2010

Volume I

*Withdrawn from stock*
*UCC Library*

Ref

HS 615·1 BRIT
v.1

# British Pharmacopoeia 2010

**Volume I**

Published on the recommendation of the Commission on Human Medicines pursuant to the Medicines Act 1968 and notified in draft to the European Commission in accordance with Directive 98/34/EEC.

The monographs of the Sixth Edition of the European Pharmacopoeia (2007), as amended by Supplements 6.1 to 6.5 published by the Council of Europe, are reproduced either in this edition of the British Pharmacopoeia or in the associated edition of the British Pharmacopoeia (Veterinary).

*See General Notices*

Effective date: 1 January 2010

*see Notices*

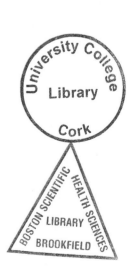

London: The Stationery Office

In respect of Great Britain:

THE DEPARTMENT OF HEALTH

In respect of Northern Ireland:

THE DEPARTMENT OF HEALTH, SOCIAL SERVICES AND PUBLIC SAFETY

© Crown Copyright 2009

Published by The Stationery Office on behalf of the Medicines and Healthcare products Regulatory Agency (MHRA) except that:

European Pharmacopoeia monographs are reproduced with the permission of the Council of Europe and are not Crown Copyright. These are identified in the publication by a chaplet of stars.

This publication is a 'value added' product. If you wish to re-use the Crown Copyright material from this publication, applications must be made in writing, clearly stating the material requested for re-use, and the purpose for which it is required. Applications should be sent to: Dr M G Lee, MHRA, Market Towers, 1 Nine Elms Lane, London SW8 5NQ or by e-mailing: ged.lee@mhra.gsi.gov.uk.

First Published 2009

ISBN 978 0 11 322828 7

*British Pharmacopoeia Commission Office:*
Market Towers
1 Nine Elms Lane
London SW8 5NQ
Telephone: +44 (0)20 7084 2561
Fax: +44 (0)20 7084 2566
E-mail: bpcom@mhra.gsi.gov.uk
Web site: www.pharmacopoeia.gov.uk

*Laboratory:*
British Pharmacopoeia Commission Laboratory
Queen's Road
Teddington
Middlesex TW11 0LY
Telephone: +44 (0)20 8943 8960
Fax: +44 (0)20 8943 8962
E-mail: bpcrs@mhra.gsi.gov.uk
Web site: www.pharmacopoeia.gov.uk

Printed in the United Kingdom by The Stationery Office
N5977690    C34    8/2009

**MHRA**

# FOREWORD

Since 1864, the British Pharmacopoeia has been providing authoritative official standards for pharmaceutical substances and medicinal products. The 2010 edition (BP 2010) continues this tradition. It makes an important contribution, therefore, to the role of the Medicines and Healthcare products Regulatory Agency in protecting public health by setting publicly available standards for the quality of medicines.

In addition to expanding the numbers of monographs for licensed formulated products, this edition continues to support regulatory work in the fields of herbal and complementary medicines by providing new monographs and guidance on the elaboration of BP monographs for traditional herbal medicines. The 2010 edition continues to improve the control of the quality of unlicensed medicines by providing standards for extensively used unlicensed formulations together with guidance on preservative-free unlicensed medicines and bioequivalence of oral suspensions.

The launch of a new website, www.pharmacopoeia.gov.uk, has improved the regulatory transparency of the British Pharmacopoeia in line with the principles contained in the Hampton Review and the central government's initiative on Better Regulation. It also increases the scope of information available to stakeholders and allows the BP Secretariat to move towards increased electronic working.

The British Pharmacopoeia maintains close ties with the work of the European Pharmacopoeia and continues to play a significant role in the standard-setting process in Europe, participating in the activities of the European Directorate for the Quality of Medicines and HealthCare, and influencing the decisions of the European Pharmacopoeia Commission through the United Kingdom Delegation. The texts and monographs of the European Pharmacopoeia form an integral part of the BP 2010.

Published annually, with the introduction of in-year electronic updates for this new edition, the British Pharmacopoeia is the only comprehensive collection of standards for UK medicinal substances. It is essential for all individuals and organisations involved in pharmaceutical research, development, manufacture, quality control and analysis.

Sir Alasdair Breckenridge
Chairman, MHRA

# Contents

**Contents of Volume IV**

NOTICES

GENERAL NOTICES

INFRARED REFERENCE SPECTRA

APPENDICES

Contents of the Appendices

SUPPLEMENTARY CHAPTERS

Contents of the Supplementary Chapters

INDEX

# Notices

Monographs of the European Pharmacopoeia are distinguished by a chaplet of stars against the title. The term European Pharmacopoeia, used without qualification, means the sixth edition of the European Pharmacopoeia comprising, unless otherwise stated, the main volume, published in 2007 as amended by any subsequent supplements and revisions.

**Patents**    In this Pharmacopoeia certain drugs and preparations have been included notwithstanding the existence of actual or potential patent rights. In so far as such substances are protected by Letters Patent their inclusion in this Pharmacopoeia neither conveys, nor implies, licence to manufacture.

**Effective dates**    New and revised monographs of national origin enter into force on 1 January 2010. Monographs of the European Pharmacopoeia have previously been published by the Council of Europe and have been brought into effect by means of Notices published in the Belfast, Edinburgh and London Gazettes.

# Preface

The British Pharmacopoeia 2010 is published for the Health Ministers on the recommendation of the Commission on Human Medicines in accordance with section 99(6) of the Medicines Act 1968.

The Commission on Human Medicines believes that the British Pharmacopoeia contributes significantly to the overall control of the quality of medicinal products by providing an authoritative statement of the quality that a product, material or article is expected to meet at any time during its period of use. The Pharmacopoeial standards, which are publicly available and legally enforceable, are designed to complement and assist the licensing and inspection processes and are part of the system for safeguarding purchasers and users of medicinal products.

The Commission on Human Medicines wishes to record its appreciation of the services of all those who have contributed to this important work.

# British Pharmacopoeia Commission

The British Pharmacopoeia Commission is appointed, on behalf of the Secretary of State for Health, by the Appointments Commission, the body responsible for appointments to all of the Medicines Act 1968 Advisory Bodies.

The duties of the British Pharmacopoeia Commission are as follows:

(a) the preparation under section 99(1) of the Act of any new edition of the British Pharmacopoeia;

(b) the preparation under section 99(1) of the Act, as given effect by section 102(1) thereof, of any amendments of the edition of the British Pharmacopoeia published in 1968 or any new edition of it;

(c) the preparation under section 100 of the Act (which provides for the preparation and publication of lists of names to be used as headings to monographs in the British Pharmacopoeia) of any list of names and the preparation under that section as given effect by section 102(3) of the Act of any amendments of any published list;

(d) the preparation under section 99(6) of the Act, of any compendium, or any new edition thereof, containing information relating to substances and articles which are or may be used in the practice of veterinary medicine or veterinary surgery;

(e) to frame clear and unequivocal technical advice in order to discharge the Commission's responsibilities both for the British Pharmacopoeia, the British Pharmacopoeia (Veterinary) and British Approved Names and as the national pharmacopoeial authority with respect to the European Pharmacopoeia.

Members of the British Pharmacopoeia Commission are appointed for a (renewable) term of 4 years and, under the requirements laid down by the Office of the Commissioner for Public Appointments, can serve for a maximum of 10 years.

# Expert Advisory Groups, Panels of Experts and Working Parties

Members of Expert Advisory Groups, Panels of Experts and Working Parties are appointed by the British Pharmacopoeia Commission.

The duties of the members are as follows:

(a) To collaborate in the preparation and revision of Monographs, Appendices and Supplementary Chapters for inclusion in the British Pharmacopoeia and British Pharmacopoeia (Veterinary).

(b) To collaborate in the preparation and revision of Monographs, Methods and General Chapters of the European Pharmacopoeia.

(c) To collaborate in the preparation and revision of the list of names to be used as titles for monographs of the British Pharmacopoeia and British Pharmacopoeia (Veterinary).

Members of Expert Advisory Groups, Panels of Experts and Working Parties are usually appointed for a (renewable) term of 4 years.

# Membership of the British Pharmacopoeia Commission

The list below includes those members who served during the period 2008 to 2009.

*Chairman* — Professor David Woolfson BSc PhD CChem FRSC FPSNI
*Professor of Pharmaceutics, Queens University of Belfast*

*Vice-Chairman* — Mr V'Iain Fenton-May BPharm MI PharmM FRPharmS
*Former Specialist Quality Controller to the Welsh Hospitals*

Professor Graham Buckton BPharm PhD DSc AKC FRPharmS CChem FRSC
*Professor of Pharmaceutics; School of Pharmacy, University of London*

Professor Donald Cairns BSc PhD MRPharmS CSci CChem FRSC
*Associate Head, School of Pharmacy and Life Sciences, Robert Gordon University, Aberdeen*

Mr Barry Capon CBE MA DL (*Lay representative*)
*Non-executive Director, Norfolk and Waveney Mental Health NHS Foundation Trust*

Professor Alastair Davidson BSc PhD FRPharmS
*Visiting Professor of Pharmaceutical Sciences, University of Strathclyde*

Mrs Margaret A Dow MSc PhC
*Consultant in the registration of biological and biotechnological products*

Dr Thomas D Duffy BSc PhD FRPharmS CChem MRSC FCQI CQP MRQA
*Director, Lowden International (providing consultancy and training to pharmaceutical organisations)*

Mr Christopher Goddard BSc DIS CSci EurChem CChem FRSC
*Quality Control Manager, Recipharm Limited*

Dr Keith Helliwell BPharm PhD MRPharmS
*Senior Technical Adviser, William Ransom & Son PLC*

Dr Rodney L Horder BPharm PhD MRPharmS
*Divisional Vice President, European Quality and Regulatory Strategy, Abbott*

Dr Aileen M T Lee BVMS PhD MRCVS
*Member of the Veterinary Medicines Directorate*
*Specialism: Regulation of Veterinary Immunological Products*

Dr Lincoln Tsang BPharm LLB PhD FRSC FIBiol FRSA FRPharmS
Solicitor
*Life Sciences Lawyer; Partner, Arnold & Porter LLP*

Mrs Josephine Turnbull LLB (*Lay representative*)
*Chairman of Tees, Esk and Wear Valley NHS Trust*

Professor Elizabeth Williamson BPharm PhD MRPharmS
*Professor of Pharmacy, University of Reading*

Professor Peter York BSc PhD DSc FRPharmS CChem FRSC
*Professor of Physical Pharmaceutics, University of Bradford*

*Secretary and Scientific Director*    Dr Gerard Lee BPharm PhD FRPharmS MRSC CChem

# Membership of Expert Advisory Groups, Panels of Experts and Working Parties

The Commission appointed the following Expert Advisory Groups, Panels of Experts and Working Parties to advise it in carrying out its duties. Membership has changed from time to time; the lists below include all who have served during the period 2008 to 2009.

## EXPERT ADVISORY GROUPS

**ABS: Antibiotics**
R L Horder (*Chairman*), P York (*Vice-Chairman*), A Ambrose, A H Andrews, J F Chissell, P Ellis, S Green, R Harryman, A Livingstone, W Mann, S Patel, B White, I R Williams

**HCM: Herbal and Complementary Medicines**
E Williamson (*Chairman*), L A Anderson (*Vice-Chairman*), M Berry, P Bremner, K Chan, T Chapman, A Charvill, K Helliwell, C Leon, A C Moffat, J D Phillipson, M Pires, J Sumal

(*Corresponding member* B P Jackson)

**MC1: Medicinal Chemicals**
A G Davidson (*Chairman*), D Cairns (*Vice-Chairman*), M Ahmed, L Anderson, J C Berridge, M Broughton, A J Caws, P Fleming, W J Lough, D Malpas

**MC2: Medicinal Chemicals**
T D Duffy (*Chairman*), C T Goddard (*Vice-Chairman*), M Cole, B M Everett, S Jones, M A Lee, J Lim, K McKiernan, P Murray, M Turgoose

**MC3: Medicinal Chemicals**
V Fenton-May (*Chairman*), E Williamson (*Vice-Chairman*), S Arkle, J F Chissell, C T Goddard, W K L Pugh, W H Smith, R Tomlinson, R Torano, M Tubby, I R Williams

**NOM: Nomenclature**
J K Aronson (*Chairman*), L Tsang (*Vice-Chairman*), M Ahmed, G Gallagher, P W Golightly, A D McNaught, G P Moss, C Preston, R Thorpe, B Warner

(*Corresponding members* R G Balocco Mattavelli, E M Cortés Montejano, J Robertson)

**PCY: Pharmacy**
R L Horder (*Chairman*), A D Woolfson (*Vice-Chairman*), M Aulton, E Baker, S Branch, G Buckton, G Davison, G Eccleston, D Elder, R Lowe, B R Matthews, J F McGuire, S C Nichols

**ULM: Unlicensed Medicines**
V Fenton-May (*Chairman*), T D Duffy (*Vice-Chairman*), I Beaumont, A Charvill, P Forsey, W Goddard, S Jones, M A Oldcorne, A Pandya, N J Precious, J Rothwell, J Smith

# PANELS OF EXPERTS

**BIO: Biological and Biotechnological Products**  M A Dow (*Chairman*), L Tsang (*Vice-Chairman*), A F Bristow, D H Calam, J Cook, J Lawrence, B Mason, A Onadipe, A M Pickett, S Poole, D Sesardic, P Sheppard, W J Tarbit, J N A Tettey, A H Thomas, R Thorpe

**BLP: Blood Products**  B Cuthbertson, A R Hubbard, S Jenkins, J Lawrence, P Varley

**IGC: Inorganic and General Chemicals**  C T Goddard (*Chairman*), A C Cartwright, B M Everett, P Henrys, D Malpas, C Mroz, I D Newton

**MIC: Microbiology**  V Fenton-May (*Chairman*), S Denyer, D P Hargreaves, B R Matthews, P Newby

**RAD: Radioactive Materials**  S R Hesslewood, A M Millar, R D Pickett, S Waters

**VIP: Veterinary Immunological Products**  A M T Lee (*Chairman*), A H Andrews, A M Brady, K Redhead, J Salt, P W Wells

# WORKING PARTIES

**CX: Excipients**  G Buckton (*Chairman*), C Mroz (*Vice-Chairman*), E Anno, R Cawthorne, B R Matthews, M I Robertson

# Current British Pharmacopoeia Staff

**Secretariat**   M Vallender (*Editor-in-Chief*)

S Young (*Head of Science*)

M Barrett, L Caller, A Evans, J Francomb, P Holland, R A Pask-Hughes, J Pound, F J Swanson, R L Turner, M Whaley

**Administrative**   M Cumberbatch, B F Delahunty, W Jeffries, D Myburgh, J Paine

ISO 9001
FS 27268

# Current British Pharmacopoeia Laboratory Staff

J Gan, P Hansal, K Harper, M Kram, R Mannan, A Panchal, H Patel, K Patel, M Patel, N Patel, C Provis-Evans, P Webb

ISO 9001
FS 27613

# Introduction

The British Pharmacopoeia 2010 supersedes the British Pharmacopoeia 2009. It has been prepared by the British Pharmacopoeia Commission, with the collaboration and support of its Expert Advisory Groups and Panels of Experts, and contains approximately 3300 monographs for substances, preparations and articles used in the practice of medicine. Some of these monographs are of national origin while others have been reproduced from the 6th edition of the European Pharmacopoeia. This edition, together with its companion edition, the British Pharmacopoeia (Veterinary) 2010, incorporates all the monographs of the 6th edition of the European Pharmacopoeia as amended by Supplements 6.1 to 6.5. The user of the British Pharmacopoeia thereby benefits by finding within this one, comprehensively indexed, compendium all current United Kingdom pharmacopoeial standards for medicines for human use. The new edition comprises five volumes as follows.

| Volumes I and II | Medicinal Substances |
|---|---|
| Volume III | Formulated Preparations, Blood-related Products, Immunological Products, Radiopharmaceutical Preparations, Surgical Materials, Herbal Drugs, Herbal Drug Preparations and Herbal Medicinal Products and Materials for use in the Manufacture of Homoeopathic Preparations |
| Volume IV | Infrared Reference Spectra, Appendices, Supplementary Chapters and Index |
| Volume V | British Pharmacopoeia (Veterinary) 2010 |

**Book Format**    The formats of the British Pharmacopoeia are regularly reviewed. For this new edition, the weight of the book format has been reduced with the use of a lighter weight paper.

**Effective Date**    The effective date for this edition is 1 January 2010.

Where a monograph which appeared previously in an earlier edition of the British Pharmacopoeia has not been included in this edition, it remains effective in accordance with Section 65(4) of the Medicines Act 1968.

**General Notices**    The British Pharmacopoeia General Notices (Parts I, II and III) have been amended as follows.

### European Pharmacopoeia

A review of the presentation, within the British Pharmacopoeia, of texts harmonised between the European Pharmacopoeia, Japanese Pharmacopoeia and United States Pharmacopeia, will be made for a future edition of the British Pharmacopoeia. In the meantime, the statement explaining the significance of the triangle within the chaplet of stars has been deleted from this General Notice in Part I.

### Crude Drugs: Traditional Herbal and Complementary Medicines; Homoeopathic Medicines

These General Notices in Part II have been amended to clarify the use of the acronyms 'THM' and 'THMP' and to provide a definition of the term 'Potentisation' when used in homoeopathic medicines.

### Part III

The British Pharmacopoeia General Notices (Part III) have been amended to harmonise with the changes published in Supplement 6.5 of the 6<sup>th</sup> edition of the European Pharmacopoeia.

**Additions** A list of monographs included for the first time in the British Pharmacopoeia 2010 is given at the end of this introduction. It includes 40 new monographs of national origin and 42 new monographs reproduced from the 6<sup>th</sup> Edition of the European Pharmacopoeia as amended by Supplements 6.3 to 6.5.

### Traditional Herbal Medicines

Work is continuing on the development of monographs for herbal materials and processed herbs used in Traditional Chinese Medicines. This new edition sees the publication of a new monograph for Phyllanthus Emblica Pericarp for use in THMP and a new General Monograph to cover the requirements for processed herbal drugs. It is emphasized that, although requirements for the *quality* of the material are provided in the monograph to assist the registration scheme by the UK Licensing Authority, the British Pharmacopoeia Commission has not assessed the safety of the material in traditional use.

### Homoeopathic Preparations

A further 2 new monographs for homoeopathic stocks and mother tinctures, that support the simplified registration scheme by the UK Licensing Authority, have been added to this edition.

### Unlicensed Medicines

With this new edition, 9 individual monographs for unlicensed formulations have been added. These individual monographs are characterised by a statement that they are unlicensed in the United Kingdom. The general and individual monographs are intended to apply to all types of Unlicensed Medicines, that is, those formulations manufactured under a specials licence and those prepared extemporaneously under the supervision of a pharmacist.

**Revisions** National monographs which have been amended technically by means of this edition are also listed at the end of this introduction. For the benefit of the reader this list indicates the section, or sections, of each monograph which has/have been revised. A pilot service identifying all types of revisions for national monographs (see below) will be introduced for subscribers on the new British Pharmacopoeia website, www.pharmacopoeia.gov.uk.

The list of revisions appended to this Introduction is as comprehensive as practicable. However, to ensure that the reader uses the current standard, it is essential to refer to the full text of each individual monograph.

### Bacterial Endotoxins

A statement relating to the use of a suitably diluted solution has been deleted from 41 monographs in this new edition since this aspect is covered by the methods in the relevant Appendix. In line with the BP policy on refinement of methods, 2 monographs have been revised to replace the test for Pyrogens with a test for Bacterial endotoxins.

### Reference Substances

A number of monographs for medicinal substances and formulated preparations of the BP have been amended to refer to new British Pharmacopoeia Chemical Reference Substances established by the British Pharmacopoeia Laboratory.

**Infrared Reference Spectra**

As with the previous edition, the reference spectra are placed in alphabetical order within this edition. 7 new spectra have been added to the collection.

**Appendices**

The Appendix on Apparent Volume (Appendix XVII D; *Ph Eur method 2.9.15*) has been omitted to harmonise with the European Pharmacopoeia.

A new Appendix XVII T (Wettability of Porous Solids Including Powders) has been created to incorporate the methods of the European Pharmacopoeia.

**Supplementary Chapters**

Four new Supplementary Chapters are published in this edition of the British Pharmacopoeia as follows.

### Traditional Herbal Medicines

The Supplementary Chapter for Traditional Herbal Medicines (Supplementary Chapter VII) provides information to help users of the British Pharmacopoeia to understand the process in the elaboration of BP monographs for traditional herbal medicines.

### Guidelines for Using the Test for Sterility

This Supplementary Chapter (Supplementary Chapter IV P) incorporates the European Pharmacopoeia Guidelines for using the Test for Sterility.

### Unlicensed Medicines

Two Supplementary Chapters, the first for Preservative-free Unlicensed Medicines (Supplementary Chapter V A) and the second for Bioequivalence of Oral Suspensions (Supplementary Chapter V B), have been introduced.

**Editorial Changes**

### Chromatographic tests

The new format for chromatographic tests, introduced in the BP 2008, to delineate sample preparation, chromatographic conditions, system suitability and acceptance criteria has been refined and applied to a further 106 monographs. The format will continue to be harmonised in future editions for all BP monographs.

### Dissolution tests

A new format, similar to the one for chromatographic tests, has been applied to tests for Dissolution in BP monographs. The new format will continue to be harmonised in future editions for all BP monographs.

### Herbal Medicines

The reorganisation of the monographs for herbal and complementary medicines has been refined in Volume III of the new edition. The section is retitled 'Herbal Drugs, Herbal Drug Preparations and Herbal Medicinal Products'.

**European Pharmacopoeia**

In accordance with previous practice, all monographs and requirements of the European Pharmacopoeia are reproduced in this edition of the British Pharmacopoeia or, where appropriate, within its companion edition, the British Pharmacopoeia (Veterinary) 2010.

Where a monograph has been reproduced from the European Pharmacopoeia, this is signified by the presence of a European chaplet of stars alongside its title. Additionally, reference to the European Pharmacopoeia monograph number is included immediately below the title in italics in the form '*Ph Eur monograph xxxx*'. Where the title in the British Pharmacopoeia is different from that in the European Pharmacopoeia, an approved synonym has been created (see Appendix XXI B) and the Ph Eur title is included before the monograph number. The entire European Pharmacopoeia text is then bounded by two horizontal lines bearing the symbol '*Ph Eur*'.

The European Pharmacopoeia texts have been reproduced in their entirety but, where deemed appropriate, additional statements of relevance to UK usage have been added (e.g. action and use statement, a list of BP preparations). It should be noted, however, that in the event of doubt of interpretation in any text of the European Pharmacopoeia, the text published in English under the direction of the Council of Europe should be consulted.

Correspondence between the general methods of the European Pharmacopoeia and the appendices of the British Pharmacopoeia is indicated in each appendix and by inclusion of a check list at the beginning of the appendices section.

**Pharmacopoeial Requirements**

It should be noted that any article intended for medicinal use which is described by a name at the head of a monograph in the current edition of the Pharmacopoeia must comply with that monograph '*whether or not it is referred to as BP*'.

It is also important to note that no requirement of the Pharmacopoeia can be taken in isolation. A valid interpretation of any particular requirement depends upon it being read in the context of (i) the monograph as a whole, (ii) the specified method of analysis, (iii) the relevant General Notices and (iv) where appropriate, the relevant general monograph(s). Familiarity with the General Notices of the Pharmacopoeia will facilitate the correct application of the requirements. Additional guidance and information on the basis of pharmacopoeial requirements is provided in Supplementary

Chapter I. This non-mandatory text describes the general underlying philosophy and current approaches to particular aspects of pharmacopoeial control.

**Websites**  The primary functions of the two official websites associated with the work of the British Pharmacopoeia are outlined below.

**www.pharmacopoeia.gov.uk** This new website is intended to increase the scope of information available to British Pharmacopoeia stakeholders and to improve the regulatory transparency of the British Pharmacopoeia.

A pilot service for subscribers to identify revisions in British Pharmacopoeia monographs has been launched to coincide with the publication of this new edition and to support users of the website involved in regulatory affairs. Feedback for this pilot service is sought from users and can be provided to the BP Secretariat either using the feedback forms available at the end of Volume IV of the BP or through the website.

Chromatograms for information to support new monographs published in the British Pharmacopoeia 2010 have been added to the Image Gallery on the website. This service will increase year on year to support British Pharmacopoeia monographs and to allow users to examine chromatograms obtained during the practical evaluation of new monographs by the British Pharmacopoeia Commission Laboratory.

**www.pharmacopoeia.co.uk** This website provides subscribers with access to the *British Pharmacopoeia 2010 and British Pharmacopoeia (Veterinary) 2010 online* and access to the current edition and Supplements of the *British Approved Names*. Concurrent access to the previous edition of the BP and the new edition is maintained for a short period. This website is administered by the publisher of the British Pharmacopoeia.

**Forward Look**  The processes for the publication of each edition of the British Pharmacopoeia are reviewed and refined annually to maximise efficiency and to improve the service for users. For this edition, a new in-year update service will be introduced on the website, www.pharmacopoeia.co.uk, to enable users to keep up to date with monographs published in Supplements of the European Pharmacopoeia. These updates will be integrated annually with the publication of the main edition of the British Pharmacopoeia.

**Acknowledgements**  The British Pharmacopoeia Commission is greatly indebted to the members of its Expert Advisory Groups, Panels of Experts and Working Parties whose dedicated enthusiasm and assistance enabled this edition to be published.

Close co-operation has continued with many organisations at home and overseas. These include the Medicines and Healthcare products Regulatory Agency, the National Institute for Biological Standards and Control, the Veterinary Medicines Directorate, the Royal Pharmaceutical Society of Great Britain, the Association of the British Pharmaceutical Industry, the British Association of Homoeopathic Manufacturers, the European Pharmacopoeia Commission and the European Directorate for the Quality of Medicines & HealthCare, the Therapeutic Goods Administration (Australia), the Health Protection Branch of the Canadian Department of Health and Welfare, the Committee of Revision of the United States

Pharmacopeia, the Essential Drugs and Other Medicines Department of the World Health Organization (WHO) and the WHO Collaborating Centre for Chemical Reference Substances.

The British Pharmacopoeia Commission appreciates the help and advice of the Medicines and Healthcare products Regulatory Agency Communications Division and, in particular, Diane Leakey and Jane Viner and their teams, in the launch of the new British Pharmacopoeia website.

The British Pharmacopoeia Commission is grateful for the contribution of Holly Douglas and Daniel Hopkins, of the Medicines and Healthcare products Regulatory Agency Laboratory, for their collaboration and advice in the practical evaluation of a number of monographs in this edition. The Commission also acknowledges the contribution to this edition of Alan Bentley, a former member of the BP Secretariat.

The British Pharmacopoeia Commission acknowledges the contribution of Professor Frederick A Senese, Department of Chemistry, Frostburg State University, USA, for his kind permission to reproduce the indicator colour chart.

The British Pharmacopoeia Commission also acknowledges and appreciates the advice of the publishing team at The Stationery Office, in particular, Mr Robert Bullen, in the production of this edition.

**Additions**  The following monographs of the British Pharmacopoeia 2010 were not included in the British Pharmacopoeia 2009.

### Medicinal and Pharmaceutical Substances
Aluminium Sodium Silicate*
Benazepril Hydrochloride*
Anhydrous Calcium Gluconate*
Ceftazidime Pentahydrate with Sodium Carbonate for Injection*
Citalopram Hydrobromide*
Citalopram Hydrochloride*
Farmed Cod-liver Oil*
Drospirenone*
Dydrogesterone*
Esomeprazole Magnesium Trihydrate*
Filgrastim Concentrated Solution*
Fluvastatin Sodium*
Gestodene*
Interferon Beta-1a Concentrated Solution*
Iopromide*
Lamotrigine*
Lauromacrogol 400*
Losartan Potassium*
Meloxicam*
Methylphenidate Hydrochloride*
Omeprazole Magnesium*
Rifaximin*
Saquinavir Mesilate*
Sevoflurane*

---

* denotes a monograph of the European Pharmacopoeia

Stanozolol* (deleted on 1 April 2008; re-instated on 10 June 2008)
Pea Starch*
Teicoplanin*
Zinc Gluconate*

**Formulated Preparations: Specific Monographs**
Allopurinol Oral Suspension
Budesonide Aqueous Nasal Spray
Budesonide Nebuliser Suspension
Budesonide Powder for Inhalation
Budesonide Pressurised Inhalation
Bupivacaine and Fentanyl Injection
Chewable Calcium Carbonate and Heavy Magnesium Carbonate Tablets
Ceftazidime Injection
Chloral Hydrate Oral Solution
Clonazepam Tablets
Co-amoxiclav Oral Suspension
Dispersible Co-amoxiclav Tablets
Ephedrine Injection
Gastro-resistant Erythromycin Capsules
Erythropoietin Injection
Goserelin Implants
Prolonged-release Ibuprofen Capsules
Prolonged-release Ibuprofen Tablets
Gastro-resistant Lansoprazole Capsules
Gastro-resistant Lansoprazole Tablets
Loratadine Tablets
Magnesium Glycerophosphate Oral Solution
Chewable Magnesium Glycerophosphate Tablets
Prolonged-release Metoprolol Tartrate Tablets
Midazolam Oral Solution
Mirtazapine Tablets
Orodispersible Mirtazapine Tablets
Paediatric Paracetamol Oral Suspension
Phosphate Oral Solution
Propylene Glycol Solution
Prolonged-release Salbutamol Capsules
Prolonged-release Salbutamol Tablets
Prolonged-release Tamsulosin Capsules
Tibolone Tablets
Trazodone Capsules
Trazodone Tablets
Warfarin Oral Suspension

**Immunological Products**
Rotavirus Vaccine (Live, Oral)*
Shingles (Herpes Zoster) Vaccine (Live)*

**Radiopharmaceutical Preparations**
Medronic Acid for Radiopharmaceutical Preparations*
Pentetate Sodium Calcium for Radiopharmaceutical Preparations*
Technetium [$^{99m}$Tc] Mebrofenin Injection*
Tetra-O-Acetyl-Mannose Triflate for Radiopharmaceutical Preparations*

---

* denotes a monograph of the European Pharmacopoeia

**Herbal Drugs, Herbal Drug Preparations and Herbal Medicinal Products**
Processed Herbal Drugs
Artichoke Leaf Dry Extract*
Dandelion Herb with Root*
Bitter-Fennel Herb Oil*
Spike Lavender Oil*
Mallow Leaf*
Olive Leaf Dry Extract*
Peppermint Leaf Dry Extract*
Phyllanthus Emblica Pericarp for use in THMP
Schisandra Fruit*
Valerian Dry Aqueous Extract*

**Materials for use in the Manufacture of Homoeopathic Preparations**
Cineraria Maritima for Homoeopathic Preparations
Cydonia Oblonga for Homoeopathic Preparations

**Omissions**  The following monographs of the British Pharmacopoeia 2009 are not included in the British Pharmacopoeia 2010.

**Medicinal and Pharmaceutical Substances**
Lindane[1]

**Technical Changes**  The following monographs in the British Pharmacopoeia 2010 have been technically amended since the publication of the British Pharmacopoeia 2009. This list does not include revised monographs of the European Pharmacopoeia. An indication of the nature of the change or the section of the monograph that has been changed is given in *italic type* in the right hand column.

**Medicinal and Pharmaceutical Substances**

| | |
|---|---|
| Fluocinolone Acetonide Dihydrate | *Related substances* |
| Menotrophin | *Water* |
| Sumatriptan | *Related substances* |
| Tioguanine | *Related substances; Assay* |
| Trazodone Hydrochloride | *Related substances; Assay* |

**Formulated Preparations: Specific Monographs**

| | |
|---|---|
| Amikacin Injection | *Related substances* |
| Amiodarone Intravenous Infusion | *Iodides* |
| Betahistine Dihydrochloride Tablets | *Identification; Related substances* |
| Benzylpenicillin Injection | *Pyrogens → Bacterial endotoxins* |
| Caffeine Citrate Injection | *Removal of unlicensed status* |
| Caffeine Citrate Oral Solution | *Removal of unlicensed status* |
| Chloramphenicol Sodium Succinate Injection | *Pyrogens → Bacterial endotoxins* |
| Co-amoxiclav Tablets | *Related substances* |
| Colistin Tablets | *Content of colistin suphate; Related substances; Assay* |
| Dacarbazine Injection | *Identification test B* |

---

* denotes a monograph of the European Pharmacopoeia.
[1] Monograph suppressed by European Pharmacopoeia Commission on 1 April 2009.

| | |
|---|---|
| Desmopressin Intranasal Solution | *Acidity* |
| Doxepin Capsules | *Content of doxepin; Related substances; Assay* |
| Erythromycin Estolate Capsules | *Related substances* |
| Erythromycin Ethyl Succinate Tablets | *Related substances* |
| Estradiol and Norethisterone Acetate Tablets | *Content of estradiol and norethisterone acetate; Estrone and norethisterone* |
| Glibenclamide Tablets | *Production; Dissolution* |
| Heparin Injection | *Production* |
| Hypromellose Eye Drops | *Content (deleted); Assay (deleted)* |
| Isotretinoin Gel | *Identification test B* |
| Levobunolol Eye Drops | *Related substances* |
| Levomepromazine Tablets | *Identification test B* |
| Lisinopril Tablets | *Dissolution; Related substances* |
| Menotrophin Injection | *Water* |
| Methotrexate Injection | *Related substances* |
| Methotrexate Tablets | *Related substances* |
| Metoprolol Injection | *Related substances* |
| Metoprolol Tartrate Tablets | *Related substances* |
| Paroxetine Tablets | *Related substances* |
| Sodium Valproate Oral Solution | *Identification* |
| Sodium Valproate Tablets | *Identification test A* |
| Gastro-resistant Sodium Valproate Tablets | *Identification* |
| Sulpiride Tablets | *Related substances* |
| Tioguanine Tablets | *Related substances; Assay* |
| Vincristine Injection | *Content of vincristine sulphate* |

### Materials for use in the Manufacture of Homoeopathic Preparations

| | |
|---|---|
| Artemisia Cina for Homoeopathic Preparations | *Identification tests A and B* |
| Toxicodendron Quercifolium for Homoeopathic Preparations | *Identification* |
| Urtica Urens Herb for Homoeopathic Preparations | *Identification* |

**Changes in Title**  The following list gives the alterations in the titles of monographs of the British Pharmacopoeia 2009 that have been retained in the British Pharmacopoeia 2010.

| **BRITISH PHARMACOPOEIA 2009** | **BRITISH PHARMACOPOEIA 2010** |
|---|---|
| **Medicinal and Pharmaceutical Substances** | |
| Ceftazidime | Ceftazidime Pentahydrate |

**Reference Substances**   A number of formulated preparation monographs of the British Pharmacopoeia 2010 have been revised to refer to British Pharmacopoeia Chemical Reference Substances (BPCRS). The following is a list of those reference standards that have been revised.

Allopurinol Impurity A
Allopurinol Impurity B
Amikacin Sulphate
Ascorbic Acid
Bisacodyl
Cefaclor
Cefalexin
Chloramphenicol
2-(4-Chloro-3-sulphamoylbenzoyl)benzoic acid
Chlorothiazide
Chlorpromazine Hydrochloride
Cisplatin
Clonazepam
Demeclocycline Hydrochloride
Dibenzosuberone
Diclofenac Impurity A
Dicloxacillin Sodium
Diethylstilbestrol
Digitoxin
Diltiazem Hydrochloride
Estrone
Gentamicin Sulphate
Hydrocortisone Hydrogen Succinate
D-α-(4-Hydroxyphenyl)glycine
Hydroxyzine Hydrochloride
Kanamycin Monosulphate
Lincomycin Hydrochloride
Minocycline Hydrochloride
Nortriptyline Hydrochloride
Oxytetracycline
Oxytetracycline Hydrochloride
Quinidine Sulphate
Quinine Sulphate
Sulfasalazine+

# General Notices

# CONTENTS OF THE GENERAL NOTICES

# General Notices

# Part I

*The British Pharmacopoeia comprises the entire text within this publication.*
*The word 'official' is used in the Pharmacopoeia to signify 'of the Pharmacopoeia'.*
*It applies to any title, substance, preparation, method or statement included in the*
*general notices, monographs and appendices of the Pharmacopoeia.*
*The abbreviation for British Pharmacopoeia is BP.*

**European Pharmacopoeia**

Monographs of the European Pharmacopoeia are reproduced in this edition of the British Pharmacopoeia by incorporation of the text published under the direction of the Council of Europe (Partial Agreement) in accordance with the Convention on the Elaboration of a European Pharmacopoeia (Treaty Series No. 32 (1974) CMND 5763) as amended by the Protocol to the Convention (Treaty Series No. MISC16 (1990) CMND 1133).

They are included for the convenience of users of the British Pharmacopoeia. In cases of doubt or dispute reference should be made to the Council of Europe text.

Monographs of the European Pharmacopoeia are distinguished by a chaplet of stars against the title and by reference to the European Pharmacopoeia monograph number included immediately below the title in italics. The beginning and end of text from the European Pharmacopoeia are denoted by means of horizontal lines with the symbol '*Ph Eur*' ranged left and right, respectively.

The general provisions of the European Pharmacopoeia relating to different types of dosage form are included in the appropriate general monograph in that section of the British Pharmacopoeia entitled Monographs: Formulated Preparations. These general provisions apply to all dosage forms of the type defined, whether an individual monograph is included in the British Pharmacopoeia or not.

Texts of the European Pharmacopoeia are governed by the General Notices of the European Pharmacopoeia. These are reproduced as Part III of these notices.

# Part II

*The following general notices apply to the statements made in the monographs of the British Pharmacopoeia other than those reproduced from the European Pharmacopoeia and to the statements made in the Appendices of the British Pharmacopoeia other than when a method, test or other matter described in an appendix is invoked in a monograph reproduced from the European Pharmacopoeia.*

**Official Standards**

The requirements stated in the monographs of the Pharmacopoeia apply to articles that are intended for medicinal use but not necessarily to articles that may be sold under the same name for other purposes. An article intended for medicinal use that is described by means of an official title must comply with the requirements of the relevant monograph. A formulated preparation must comply throughout its assigned shelf-life (period of validity). The subject of any other monograph must comply throughout its period of use.

A monograph is to be construed in accordance with any general monograph or notice or any appendix, note or other explanatory material that is contained in this edition and that is applicable to that monograph. All statements contained in the monographs, except where a specific general notice indicates otherwise and with the exceptions given below, constitute standards for the official articles. An article is not of pharmacopoeial quality unless it complies with all of the requirements stated. This does not imply that a manufacturer is obliged to perform all the tests in a monograph in order to assess compliance with the Pharmacopoeia before release of a product. The manufacturer may assure himself that a product is of pharmacopoeial quality by other means, for example, from data derived from validation studies of the manufacturing process, from in-process controls or from a combination of the two. Parametric release in appropriate circumstances is thus not precluded by the need to comply with the Pharmacopoeia. The general notice on Assays and Tests indicates that analytical methods other than those described in the Pharmacopoeia may be employed for routine purposes.

Requirements in monographs have been framed to provide appropriate limitation of potential impurities rather than to provide against all possible impurities. Material found to contain an impurity not detectable by means of the prescribed tests is not of pharmacopoeial quality if the nature or amount of the impurity found is incompatible with good pharmaceutical practice.

The status of any statement given under the headings Definition, Production, Characteristics, Storage, Labelling or Action and use is defined within the general notice relating to the relevant heading. In addition to any exceptions indicated by one of the general notices referred to above, the following parts of a monograph do not constitute standards: (a) a graphic or molecular formula given at the beginning of a monograph; (b) a molecular weight; (c) a Chemical Abstracts Service Registry Number; (d) any information given at the end of a monograph concerning impurities known to be limited by that monograph; (e) information in any annex to a monograph. Any statement containing the word 'should' constitutes non-mandatory advice or recommendation.

The expression 'unless otherwise justified and authorised' means that the requirement in question has to be met, unless a competent authority authorises a modification or exemption where justified in a particular case. The term 'competent authority' means the national, supranational or international body or organisation vested with the authority for making decisions concerning the issue in question. It may, for example, be a licensing authority or an official control laboratory. For a formulated preparation that is the subject of monograph in the British Pharmacopoeia any justified and authorised modification to, or exemption from, the requirements of the relevant general monograph of the European Pharmacopoeia is stated in the individual monograph. For example, the general monograph for Tablets requires that Uncoated Tablets, except for chewable tablets, disintegrate within 15 minutes; for Calcium Lactate Tablets a time of 30 minutes is permitted.

Many of the general monographs for formulated preparations include statements and requirements additional to those of the European Pharmacopoeia that are applicable to the individual monographs of the British Pharmacopoeia. Such statements and requirements apply to all monographs for that dosage form included in the Pharmacopoeia unless otherwise indicated in the individual monograph.

Where a monograph on a biological substance or preparation refers to a strain, a test, a method, a substance, etc., using the qualifications 'suitable' or 'appropriate' without further definition in the text, the choice of such strain, test, method, substance, etc., is made in accordance with any international agreements or national regulations affecting the subject concerned.

**Definition of Terms**

Where the term "about" is included in a monograph or test it should be taken to mean approximately (fairly correct or accurate; near to the actual value).

Where the term "corresponds" is included in a monograph or test it should be taken to mean similar or equivalent in character or quantity.

Where the term "similar" is included in a monograph or test it should be taken to mean alike though not necessarily identical.

Further qualifiers (such as numerical acceptance criteria) for the above terms are not included in the BP. The acceptance criteria for any individual case is set based on the range of results obtained from known reference samples, the level of precision of the equipment or apparatus used and the level of accuracy required for the particular application. The user should determine the variability seen in his/her own laboratory and set in-house acceptance criteria that he/she judges to be appropriate based on the local operating conditions.

**Expression of Standards**

Where the standard for the content of a substance described in a monograph is expressed in terms of the chemical formula for that substance an upper limit exceeding 100% may be stated. Such an upper limit applies to the result of the assay calculated in terms of the equivalent content of the specified chemical formula. For example, the statement 'contains not less than 99.0% and not more than 101.0% of $C_{20}H_{24}N_2O_2,HCl$' implies that the result of the assay is not less than 99.0% and not more than 101.0%, calculated in terms of the equivalent content of $C_{20}H_{24}N_2O_2,HCl$.

Where the result of an assay or test is required to be calculated with reference to the dried, anhydrous or ignited substance, the substance free from a specified solvent or to the peptide content, the determination of loss on drying, water content, loss on ignition, content of the specified solvent or peptide content is carried out by the method prescribed in the relevant test in the monograph.

**Temperature**    The Celsius thermometric scale is used in expressing temperatures.

**Weights and Measures**    The metric system of weights and measures is employed; SI Units have generally been adopted. Metric measures are required to have been graduated at 20°C and all measurements involved in the analytical operations of the Pharmacopoeia are intended, unless otherwise stated, to be made at that temperature. Graduated glass apparatus used in analytical operations should comply with Class A requirements of the appropriate International Standard issued by the International Organization for Standardization.

**Atomic Weights**    The atomic weights adopted are the values given in the Table of Relative Atomic Weights 2001 published by the International Union of Pure and Applied Chemistry (Appendix XXV).

**Constant Weight**    The term 'constant weight', used in relation to the process of drying or the process of ignition, means that two consecutive weighings do not differ by more than 0.5 mg, the second weighing being made after an additional period of drying or ignition under the specified conditions appropriate to the nature and quantity of the residue (1 hour is usually suitable).

**Expression of Concentrations**    The term 'per cent' or more usually the symbol '%' is used with one of four different meanings in the expression of concentrations according to circumstances. In order that the meaning to be attached to the expression in each instance is clear, the following notation is used:

Per cent w/w (% w/w) (percentage weight in weight) expresses the number of grams of solute in 100 g of product.

Per cent w/v (% w/v) (percentage weight in volume) expresses the number of grams of solute in 100 ml of product.

Per cent v/v (% v/v) (percentage volume in volume) expresses the number of millilitres of solute in 100 ml of product.

Per cent v/w (% v/w) (percentage volume in weight) expresses the number of millilitres of solute in 100 g of product.

Usually the strength of solutions of solids in liquids is expressed as percentage weight in volume, of liquids in liquids as percentage volume in volume and of gases in liquids as percentage weight in weight.

When the concentration of a solution is expressed as parts per million (p.p.m.), it means weight in weight, unless otherwise specified.

When the concentration of a solution is expressed as parts of dissolved substance in parts of the solution, it means parts by weight (g) of a solid in parts by volume (ml) of the final solution; or parts by volume (ml) of a liquid in parts by volume (ml) of the final solution; or parts by weight (g) of a gas in parts by weight (g) of the final solution.

When the concentration of a solution is expressed in molarity designated by the symbol M preceded by a number, it denotes the number of moles of the stated solute contained in sufficient Purified Water (unless otherwise stated) to produce 1 litre of solution.

**Water Bath**  The term 'water bath' means a bath of boiling water, unless water at some other temperature is indicated in the text. An alternative form of heating may be employed providing that the required temperature is approximately maintained but not exceeded.

**Reagents**  The reagents required for the assays and tests of the Pharmacopoeia are defined in appendices. The descriptions set out in the appendices do not imply that the materials are suitable for use in medicine.

**Indicators**  Indicators, the colours of which change over approximately the same range of pH, may be substituted for one another but in the event of doubt or dispute as to the equivalence of indicators for a particular purpose, the indicator specified in the text is alone authoritative.

The quantity of an indicator solution appropriate for use in acid-base titrations described in assays or tests is 0.1 ml unless otherwise stated in the text.

Any solvent required in an assay or test in which an indicator is specified is previously neutralised to the indicator, unless a blank test is prescribed.

**Caution Statements**  A number of materials described in the monographs and some of the reagents specified for use in the assays and tests of the Pharmacopoeia may be injurious to health unless adequate precautions are taken. The principles of good laboratory practice and the provisions of any appropriate regulations such as those issued in the United Kingdom in accordance with the Health and Safety at Work etc. Act 1974 should be observed at all times in carrying out the assays and tests of the Pharmacopoeia.

Attention is drawn to particular hazards in certain monographs by means of an italicised statement; the absence of such a statement should not however be taken to mean that no hazard exists.

**Titles**  Subsidiary titles, where included, have the same significance as the main titles. An abbreviated title constructed in accordance with the directions given in Appendix XXI A has the same significance as the main title.

Titles that are derived by the suitable inversion of words of a main or subsidiary title, with the addition of a preposition if appropriate, are also official titles. Thus, the following are all official titles: Aspirin Tablets, Tablets of Aspirin; Ginger Tincture, Tincture of Ginger; Atropine Injection, Injection of Atropine.

A title of a formulated preparation that includes the full nonproprietary name of the active ingredient or ingredients, where this is not included in the title of the monograph, is also an official title. For example, the title Promethazine Hydrochloride Oral Solution has the same significance as Promethazine Oral Solution and the title Brompheniramine Maleate Tablets has the same significance as Brompheniramine Tablets.

Where the English title at the head of a monograph in the European Pharmacopoeia is different from that at the head of the text incorporated into the British Pharmacopoeia, an Approved Synonym has been declared in accordance with section 65(8) of the Medicines Act 1968. The titles and subsidiary titles, if any, are thus official titles. A cumulative list of such Approved Synonyms is provided in Appendix XXI B.

Where the names of pharmacopoeial substances, preparations and other materials occur in the text they are printed with capital initial letters and this indicates that materials of Pharmacopoeial quality must be used. Words in the text that name a reagent or other material, a physical characteristic or a process that is described or defined in an appendix are printed in italic type, for example, *methanol, absorbance, gas chromatography*, and these imply compliance with the requirements specified in the appropriate appendix.

**Chemical Formulae**   When the chemical composition of an official substance is known or generally accepted, the graphic and molecular formulae, the molecular weight and the Chemical Abstracts Service Registry Number are normally given at the beginning of the monograph for information. This information refers to the chemically pure substance and is not to be regarded as an indication of the purity of the official material. Elsewhere, in statements of standards of purity and strength and in descriptions of processes of assay, it is evident from the context that the formulae denote the chemically pure substances.

Where the absolute stereochemical configuration is specified, the International Union of Pure and Applied Chemistry (IUPAC) *R/S* and *E/Z* systems of designation have been used. If the substance is an enantiomer of unknown absolute stereochemistry the sign of the optical rotation, as determined in the solvent and under the conditions specified in the monograph, has been attached to the systematic name. An indication of sign of rotation has also been given where this is incorporated in a trivial name that appears on an IUPAC preferred list.

All amino acids, except glycine, have the L-configuration unless otherwise indicated. The three-letter and one-letter symbols used for amino acids in peptide and protein sequences are those recommended by the Joint Commission on Biochemical Nomenclature of the International Union of Pure and Applied Chemistry and the International Union of Biochemistry.

In the graphic formulae the following abbreviations are used:

| | | | |
|---|---|---|---|
| Me | $-CH_3$ | Bu$^s$ | $-CH_3(CH_3)CH_2CH_3$ |
| Et | $-CH_2CH_3$ | Bu$^n$ | $-CH_2CH_2CH_2CH_3$ |
| Pr$^i$ | $-CH(CH_3)$ | Bu$^t$ | $-C(CH_3)_3$ |
| Pr$^n$ | $-CH_2CH_2CH_3$ | Ph | $-C_6H_5$ |
| Bu$^i$ | $-CH_2CH(CH_3)_2$ | Ac | $-COCH_3$ |

**Definition**   Statements given under the heading Definition constitute an official definition of the substance, preparation or other article that is the subject of the monograph. They constitute instructions or requirements and are mandatory in nature.

Certain medicinal or pharmaceutical substances and other articles are defined by reference to a particular method of manufacture. A statement that a substance or article *is* prepared or obtained by a certain method constitutes part of the official definition and implies that other methods are not permitted. A statement that a substance *may be* prepared or obtained by a certain method, however, indicates that this is one possible method and does not imply that other methods are proscribed.

Additional statements concerning the definition of formulated preparations are given in the general notice on Manufacture of Formulated Preparations.

**Production**  Statements given under the heading Production draw attention to particular aspects of the manufacturing process but are not necessarily comprehensive. They constitute mandatory instructions to manufacturers. They may relate, for example, to source materials, to the manufacturing process itself and its validation and control, to in-process testing or to testing that is to be carried out by the manufacturer on the final product (bulk material or dosage form) either on selected batches or on each batch prior to release. These statements cannot necessarily be verified on a sample of the final product by an independent analyst. The competent authority may establish that the instructions have been followed, for example, by examination of data received from the manufacturer, by inspection or by testing appropriate samples.

The absence of a section on Production does not imply that attention to features such as those referred to above is not required. A substance, preparation or article described in a monograph of the Pharmacopoeia is to be manufactured in accordance with the principles of good manufacturing practice and in accordance with relevant international agreements and supranational and national regulations governing medicinal products.

Where in the section under the heading Production a monograph on a vaccine defines the characteristics of the vaccine strain to be used, any test methods given for confirming these characteristics are provided as examples of suitable methods. The use of these methods is not mandatory.

Additional statements concerning the production of formulated preparations are given in the general notice on Manufacture of Formulated Preparations.

**Manufacture of Formulated Preparations**  Attention is drawn to the need to observe adequate hygienic precautions in the preparation and dispensing of pharmaceutical formulations. The principles of good pharmaceutical manufacturing practice should be observed.

The Definition in certain monographs for pharmaceutical preparations is given in terms of the principal ingredients only. Any ingredient, other than those included in the Definition, must comply with the general notice on Excipients and the product must conform with the Pharmacopoeial requirements.

The Definition in other monographs for pharmaceutical preparations is presented as a full formula. No deviation from the stated formula is permitted except those allowed by the general notices on Colouring Agents and Antimicrobial Preservatives. Where additionally directions are given under the heading Extemporaneous Preparation these are intended for the extemporaneous preparation of relatively small quantities for short-term supply and use. When so prepared, no deviation from the stated directions is permitted. If, however, such a pharmaceutical preparation is manufactured on a larger scale with the intention that it may be stored, deviations from the stated directions are permitted provided that the final product meets the following criteria:

(1) compliance with all of the requirements stated in the monograph;

(2) retention of the essential characteristics of the preparation made strictly in accordance with the directions of the Pharmacopoeia.

Monographs for yet other pharmaceutical preparations include both a Definition in terms of the principal ingredients and, under the side-heading Extemporaneous Preparation, a full formula together with, in some cases, directions for their preparation. Such full formulae and directions are intended for the extemporaneous preparation of relatively small quantities for short-term supply and use. When so prepared, no deviation from the stated formula and directions is permitted. If, however, such a pharmaceutical preparation is manufactured on a larger scale with the intention that it may be stored, deviations from the formula and directions stated under the heading Extemporaneous Preparation are permitted provided that any ingredient, other than those included in the Definition, complies with the general notice on Excipients and that the final product meets the following criteria:

(1)  accordance with the Definition stated in the monograph;

(2)  compliance with all of the requirements stated in the monograph;

(3)  retention of the essential characteristics of the preparation made strictly in accordance with the formula and directions of the Pharmacopoeia.

In the manufacture of any official preparation on a large scale with the intention that it should be stored, in addition to following any instruction under the heading Production, it is necessary to ascertain that the product is satisfactory with respect to its physical and chemical stability and its state of preservation over the claimed shelf-life. This applies irrespective of whether the formula of the Pharmacopoeia and any instructions given under the heading Extemporaneous Preparation are followed precisely or modified. Provided that the preparation has been shown to be stable in other respects, deterioration due to microbial contamination may be inhibited by the incorporation of a suitable antimicrobial preservative. In such circumstances the label states appropriate storage conditions, the date after which the product should not be used and the identity and concentration of the antimicrobial preservative.

**Freshly and Recently Prepared**  The direction, given under the heading Extemporaneous Preparation, that a preparation must be freshly prepared indicates that it must be made not more than 24 hours before it is issued for use. The direction that a preparation should be recently prepared indicates that deterioration is likely if the preparation is stored for longer than about 4 weeks at 15°C to 25°C.

**Methods of Sterilisation**  The methods of sterilisation used in preparing the sterile materials described in the Pharmacopoeia are given in Appendix XVIII. For aqueous preparations, steam sterilisation (heating in an autoclave) is the method of choice wherever it is known to be suitable. Any method of sterilisation must be validated with respect to both the assurance of sterility and the integrity of the product and to ensure that the final product complies with the requirements of the monograph.

**Water**  The term water used without qualification in formulae for formulated preparations means either potable water freshly drawn direct from the public supply and suitable for drinking or freshly boiled and cooled Purified Water. The latter should be used if the public supply is from a local storage tank or if the potable water is unsuitable for a particular preparation.

**Excipients**  Where an excipient for which there is a pharmacopoeial monograph is used in preparing an official preparation it shall comply with that monograph. Any substance added in preparing an official preparation shall be innocuous, shall have no adverse influence on the therapeutic efficacy of the active ingredients and shall not interfere with the assays and tests of the Pharmacopoeia. Particular care should be taken to ensure that such substances are free from harmful organisms.

**Colouring Agents**  If in a monograph for a formulated preparation defined by means of a full formula a specific colouring agent or agents is prescribed, suitable alternatives approved in the country concerned may be substituted.

**Antimicrobial Preservatives**  When the term 'suitable antimicrobial preservative' is used it is implied that the preparation concerned will be effectively preserved according to the appropriate criteria applied and interpreted as described in the test for *efficacy of antimicrobial preservation* (Appendix XVI C). In certain monographs for formulated preparations defined by means of a full formula, a specific antimicrobial agent or agents may be prescribed; suitable alternatives may be substituted provided that their identity and concentration are stated on the label.

**Characteristics**  Statements given under the heading Characteristics are not to be interpreted in a strict sense and are not to be regarded as official requirements. Statements on taste are provided only in cases where this property is a guide to the acceptability of the material (for example, a material used primarily for flavouring). The status of statements on solubility is given in the general notice on Solubility.

**Solubility**  Statements on solubility given under the heading Characteristics are intended as information on the approximate solubility at a temperature between 15°C and 25°C, unless otherwise stated, and are not to be considered as official requirements.

Statements given under headings such as Solubility in ethanol express exact requirements and constitute part of the standards for the substances under which they occur.

The following table indicates the meanings of the terms used in statements of approximate solubilities.

| Descriptive term | Approximate volume of solvent in millilitres per gram of solute |
| --- | --- |
| very soluble | less than 1 |
| freely soluble | from 1 to 10 |
| soluble | from 10 to 30 |
| sparingly soluble | from 30 to 100 |
| slightly soluble | from 100 to 1000 |
| very slightly soluble | from 1000 to 10,000 |
| practically insoluble | more than 10,000 |

The term 'partly soluble' is used to describe a mixture of which only some of the components dissolve.

**Identification**  The tests described or referred to under the heading Identification are not necessarily sufficient to establish absolute proof of identity. They provide a means of verifying that the identity of the material being examined is in accordance with the label on the container.

Unless otherwise prescribed, identification tests are carried out at a temperature between 15°C and 25°C.

**Reference spectra** Where a monograph refers to an infrared reference spectrum, this spectrum is provided in a separate section of the Pharmacopoeia. A sample spectrum is considered to be concordant with a reference spectrum if the transmission minima (absorption maxima) of the principal bands in the sample correspond in position, relative intensities and shape to those of the reference. Instrumentation software may be used to calculate concordance with a previously recorded reference spectrum.

When tests for infrared absorption are applied to material extracted from formulated preparations, strict concordance with the specified reference spectrum may not always be possible, but nevertheless a close resemblance between the spectrum of the extracted material and the specified reference spectrum should be achieved.

**Assays and Tests**

The assays and tests described are the official methods upon which the standards of the Pharmacopoeia depend. The analyst is not precluded from employing alternative methods, including methods of micro-analysis, in any assay or test if it is known that the method used will give a result of equivalent accuracy. Local reference materials may be used for routine analysis, provided that these are calibrated against the official reference materials. In the event of doubt or dispute, the methods of analysis, the reference materials and the reference spectra of the Pharmacopoeia are alone authoritative.

Where the solvent used for a solution is not named, the solvent is Purified Water.

Unless otherwise prescribed, the assays and tests are carried out at a temperature between 15°C and 25°C.

A temperature in a test for Loss on drying, where no temperature range is given, implies a range of ±2°C about the stated value.

Visual comparative tests, unless otherwise prescribed, are carried out using identical tubes of colourless, transparent, neutral glass with a flat base. The volumes of liquid prescribed are for use with tubes 16 mm in internal diameter; tubes with a larger internal diameter may be used but the volume of liquid examined must be increased so that the depth of liquid in the tubes is not less than that obtained when the prescribed volume of liquid and tubes 16 mm in internal diameter are used. Equal volumes of the liquids to be compared are examined down the vertical axis of the tubes against a white background or, if necessary, against a black background. The examination is carried out in diffuse light.

Where a direction is given that an analytical operation is to be carried out 'in subdued light', precautions should be taken to avoid exposure to direct sunlight or other strong light. Where a direction is given that an analytical operation is to be carried out 'protected from light', precautions should be taken to exclude actinic light by the use of low-actinic glassware, working in a dark room or similar procedures.

For preparations other than those of fixed strength, the quantity to be taken for an assay or test is usually expressed in terms of the active ingredient. This means that the quantity of the active ingredient expected to be present and the quantity of the preparation to be taken are calculated from the strength stated on the label.

In assays the approximate quantity to be taken for examination is indicated but the quantity actually used must not deviate by more than

10% from that stated. The quantity taken is accurately weighed or measured and the result of the assay is calculated from this exact quantity. Reagents are measured and the procedures are carried out with an accuracy commensurate with the degree of precision implied by the standard stated for the assay.

In tests the stated quantity to be taken for examination must be used unless any divergence can be taken into account in conducting the test and calculating the result. The quantity taken is accurately weighed or measured with the degree of precision implied by the standard or, where the standard is not stated numerically (for example, in tests for Clarity and colour of solution), with the degree of precision implied by the number of significant figures stated. Reagents are measured and the procedures are carried out with an accuracy commensurate with this degree of precision.

The limits stated in monographs are based on data obtained in normal analytical practice; they take account of normal analytical errors, of acceptable variations in manufacture and of deterioration to an extent considered acceptable. No further tolerances are to be applied to the limits prescribed to determine whether the article being examined complies with the requirements of the monograph.

In determining compliance with a numerical limit, the calculated result of a test or assay is first rounded to the number of significant figures stated, unless otherwise prescribed. The last figure is increased by 1 when the part rejected is equal to or exceeds one half-unit, whereas it is not modified when the part rejected is less than a half-unit.

In certain tests, the concentration of impurity is given in parentheses either as a percentage or in parts per million by weight (ppm). In chromatographic tests such concentrations are stated as a percentage irrespective of the limit. In other tests they are usually stated in ppm unless the limit exceeds 500 ppm. In those chromatographic tests in which a secondary spot or peak in a chromatogram obtained with a solution of the substance being examined is described as corresponding to a named impurity and is compared with a spot or peak in a chromatogram obtained with a reference solution of the same impurity, the percentage given in parentheses indicates the limit for that impurity. In those chromatographic tests in which a spot or peak in a chromatogram obtained with a solution of the substance being examined is described in terms other than as corresponding to a named impurity (commonly, for example, as any (other) *secondary spot* or *peak*) but is compared with a spot or peak in a chromatogram obtained with a reference solution of a named impurity, the percentage given in parentheses indicates an impurity limit expressed in terms of a nominal concentration of the named impurity. In chromatographic tests in which a comparison is made between spots or peaks in chromatograms obtained with solutions of different concentrations of the substance being examined, the percentage given in parentheses indicates an impurity limit expressed in terms of a nominal concentration of the medicinal substance itself. In some monographs, in particular those for certain formulated preparations, the impurity limit is expressed in terms of a nominal concentration of the active moiety rather than of the medicinal substance itself. Where necessary for clarification the terms in which the limit is expressed are stated within the monograph.

In all cases where an impurity limit is given in parentheses, the figures given are approximations for information only; conformity with the requirements is determined on the basis of compliance or otherwise with the stated test.

The use of a proprietary designation to identify a material used in an assay or test does not imply that another equally suitable material may not be used.

**Biological Assays and Tests**

Methods of assay described as Suggested methods are not obligatory, but when another method is used its precision must be not less than that required for the Suggested method.

For those antibiotics for which the monograph specifies a microbiological assay the potency requirement is expressed in the monograph in International Units (IU) per milligram. The material is not of pharmacopoeial quality if the upper fiducial limit of error is less than the stated potency. For such antibiotics the required precision of the assay is stated in the monograph in terms of the fiducial limits of error about the estimated potency.

For other substances and preparations for which the monograph specifies a biological assay, unless otherwise stated, the precision of the assay is such that the fiducial limits of error, expressed as a percentage of the estimated potency, are within a range not wider than that obtained by multiplying by a factor of 10 the square roots of the limits given in the monograph for the fiducial limits of error about the stated potency.

In all cases fiducial limits of error are based on a probability of 95% ($P = 0.95$).

Where the biological assay is being used to ascertain the purity of the material, the stated potency means the potency stated on the label in terms of International Units (IU) or other Units per gram, per milligram or per millilitre. When no such statement appears on the label, the stated potency means the fixed or minimum potency required in the monograph. This interpretation of stated potency applies in all cases except where the monograph specifically directs otherwise.

Where the biological assay is being used to determine the total activity in the container, the stated potency means the total number of International Units (IU) or other Units stated on the label or, if no such statement appears, the total activity calculated in accordance with the instructions in the monograph.

Wherever possible the primary standard used in an assay or test is the respective International Standard or Reference Preparation established by the World Health Organization for international use and the biological activity is expressed in International Units (IU).

In other cases, where Units are referred to in an assay or test, the Unit for a particular substance or preparation is, for the United Kingdom, the specific biological activity contained in such an amount of the respective primary standard as the appropriate international or national organisation indicates. The necessary information is provided with the primary standard.

Unless otherwise directed, animals used in an assay or a test are healthy animals, drawn from a uniform stock, that have not previously been treated with any material that will interfere with the assay or test. Unless otherwise stated, guinea-pigs weigh not less than 250 g or, when used in systemic toxicity tests, not less than 350 g. When used in skin tests they are white or light coloured. Unless otherwise stated, mice weigh not less than 17 g and not more than 22 g.

Certain of the biological assays and tests of the Pharmacopoeia are such that in the United Kingdom they may be carried out only in accordance with the Animals (Scientific Procedures) Act 1986. Instructions included in such assays and tests in the Pharmacopoeia, with respect to the handling of animals, are therefore confined to those concerned with the accuracy and reproducibility of the assay or test.

**Reference Substances and Reference Preparations**  Certain monographs require the use of a reference substance, a reference preparation or a reference spectrum. These are chosen with regard to their intended use as prescribed in the monographs of the Pharmacopoeia and are not necessarily suitable in other circumstances.

Any information necessary for proper use of the reference substance or reference preparation is given on the label or in the accompanying leaflet or brochure. Where no drying conditions are stated in the leaflet or on the label, the substance is to be used as received. No certificate of analysis or other data not relevant to the prescribed use of the product are provided. The products are guaranteed to be suitable for use for a period of three months from dispatch when stored under the appropriate conditions. The stability of the contents of opened containers cannot be guaranteed. The current lot is listed in the BP Laboratory website catalogue. Additional information is provided in Supplementary Chapter III E.

**Chemical Reference Substances**  The abbreviation BPCRS indicates a Chemical Reference Substance established by the British Pharmacopoeia Commission. The abbreviation CRS or EPCRS indicates a Chemical Reference Substance established by the European Pharmacopoeia Commission. Some Chemical Reference Substances are used for the microbiological assay of antibiotics and their activity is stated, in International Units, on the label or on the accompanying leaflet and defined in the same manner as for Biological Reference Preparations.

**Biological Reference Preparations**  The majority of the primary biological reference preparations referred to are the appropriate International Standards and Reference Preparations established by the World Health Organisation. Because these reference materials are usually available only in limited quantities, the European Pharmacopoeia has established Biological Reference Preparations (indicated by the abbreviation BRP or EPBRP) where appropriate. Where applicable, the potency of the Biological Reference Preparations is expressed in International Units. For some Biological Reference Preparations, where an international standard or reference preparation does not exist, the potency is expressed in European Pharmacopoeia Units.

**Storage**  Statements under the side-heading Storage constitute non-mandatory advice. The substances and preparations described in the Pharmacopoeia are to be stored under conditions that prevent contamination and, as far as possible, deterioration. Unless otherwise stated in the monograph, the substances and preparations described in the Pharmacopoeia are kept in well-closed containers and stored at a temperature not exceeding 25°. Precautions that should be taken in relation to the effects of the atmosphere, moisture, heat and light are indicated, where appropriate, in the monographs. Further precautions may be necessary when some materials are stored in tropical climates or under other severe conditions.

The expression 'protected from moisture' means that the product is to be stored in an airtight container. Care is to be taken when the container is opened in a damp atmosphere. A low moisture content may be maintained, if necessary, by the use of a desiccant in the container provided that direct contact with the product is avoided.

The expression 'protected from light' means that the product is to be stored either in a container made of a material that absorbs actinic light sufficiently to protect the contents from change induced by such light or in a container enclosed in an outer cover that provides such protection or stored in a place from which all such light is excluded.

The expression 'tamper-evident container' means a closed container fitted with a device that reveals irreversibly whether the container has been opened, whereas, the expression 'tamper-proof container' means a closed container in which access to the contents is prevented under normal conditions of use. The two terms are considered to be synonymous by the European Pharmacopoeia Commission.

**Labelling**  The labelling requirements of the Pharmacopoeia are not comprehensive, and the provisions of regulations issued in accordance with the requirements of the territory in which the medicinal product is to be used should be met.

Licensed medicines intended for use within the United Kingdom must comply with the requirements of the Medicines Act 1968 and EU Directive 2001/83/EC, Title V (as amended) in respect of their labelling and package leaflets, together with those regulations for the labelling of hazardous materials.

Best practice guidance on the labelling and packaging of medicines for use in the United Kingdom advises that certain items of information are deemed critical for the safe use of the medicine (see MHRA Guidance Note No. 25: Best Practice Guidance on Labelling and Packaging of Medicines). Further information and guidance on the labelling of medicinal products can be found in Supplementary Chapter I G.

Such matters as the exact form of wording to be used and whether a particular item of information should appear on the primary label and additionally, or alternatively, on the package or exceptionally in a leaflet are, in general, outside the scope of the Pharmacopoeia. When the term 'label' is used in Labelling statements of the Pharmacopoeia, decisions as to where the particular statement should appear should therefore be made in accordance with relevant legislation.

The label of every official formulated preparation other than those of fixed strength also states the content of the active ingredient or ingredients expressed in the terms required by the monograph. Where the content of active ingredient is required to be expressed in terms other than the weight of the official medicinal substance used in making the formulation, this is specifically stated under the heading Labelling. Unless otherwise stated in the monograph, the content of the active ingredient is expressed in terms of the official medicinal substance used in making the formulation.

These requirements do not necessarily apply to unlicensed preparations supplied in accordance with a prescription. For requirements for unlicensed medicines see the general monograph on Unlicensed Medicines.

**Action and Use**  The statements given under this heading in monographs are intended only as information on the principal pharmacological actions or the uses of the materials in medicine or pharmacy. It should not be assumed that the substance has no other action or use. The statements are not intended to be binding on prescribers or to limit their discretion.

**Crude Drugs; Traditional Herbal and Complementary Medicines**

*Herbal and complementary medicines are classed as medicines under European Directive 2001/83/EC as amended. It is emphasised that, although requirements for the quality of the material are provided in the monograph to assist the registration scheme by the UK Licensing Authority, the British Pharmacopoeia Commission has not assessed the safety or efficacy of the material in traditional use.*

**Monograph Title** For traditional herbal medicines, the monograph title is a combination of the binomial name together with a description of use. Monographs for the material that has not been processed (the herbal drug) and the processed material (the herbal drug preparation) are published where possible. To distinguish between the two, the word 'Processed' is included in the relevant monograph title. The acronym 'THM' is used in the title to indicate a monograph on the unprocessed herbal drug when it is only the processed herbal drug which is incorporated into herbal medicinal products and the unprocessed herbal drug is used solely to produce the processed herbal drug. The acronym 'THMP' is used in the title to indicate a monograph on a herbal drug which is incorporated into a herbal medicinal product, this acronym may be applied to either the unprocessed or processed herbal drug.

**Definition** Under the heading Definition, the botanical name together with any synonym is given. Where appropriate, for material that has not been processed, information on the collection/harvesting and/or treatment/drying of the whole herbal drug may be given. For processed materials, the method of processing, where appropriate, will normally be given in a separate section.

**Characteristics** References to odour are included only where this is highly characteristic. References to taste are not included.

**Control methods** Where applicable, the control methods to be used in monographs are:

(a) macroscopical and microscopical descriptions and chemical/chromatographic tests for identification

(b) tests for absence of any related species

(c) microbial test to assure microbial quality

(d) tests for inorganic impurities and non-specific purity tests, including extractive tests, sulphated ash and heavy metals where appropriate

(e) test for Loss on drying or Water

(f) wherever possible, a method for assaying the active constituent(s) or suitable marker constituent(s).

The macroscopical characteristics include those features that can be seen by the unaided eye or by the use of a hand lens. When two species/subspecies of the same plant are included in the Definition, individual differences between the two are indicated where possible.

The description of the microscopical characteristics of the powdered drug includes information on the dominant or the most specific characters. Where it is considered to be an aid to identification, illustrations of the powdered drug may be provided.

The following aspects are controlled by the general monograph for Herbal Drugs, that is, they are required to be free from moulds, insects, decay, animal matter and animal excreta. Unless otherwise prescribed the amount of foreign matter is not more than 2% w/w. Microbial contamination should be minimal.

In determining the content of the active constituents or the suitable marker substances measurements are made with reference to the dried or anhydrous herbal drug. In the tests for Acid-insoluble ash, Ash, Extractive soluble in ethanol, Loss on drying, Sulphated ash, Water, Water-soluble ash and Water-soluble extractive of herbal drugs, the calculations are made with reference to the herbal drug that has not been specifically dried unless otherwise prescribed in the monograph.

**Homoeopathic Medicines**

*Homoeopathic medicines are classed as medicines under European Directive 2001/83/EC as amended. It is emphasised that, although requirements for the quality of the material are provided in the relevant monograph in order to assist the simplified registration scheme by the UK Licensing Authority, the British Pharmacopoeia Commission has not assessed the safety or efficacy of the material in use.*

All materials used for the production of homoeopathic medicines, including excipients, must comply with European Pharmacopoeia or British Pharmacopoeia monographs for those materials. Where such European Pharmacopoeia or British Pharmacopoeia monographs do not exist, each material used for the production of homoeopathic medicines must comply with an official national pharmacopoeia of a Member State.

British Pharmacopoeia monographs for homoeopathic medicines apply to homoeopathic stocks and mother tinctures only, but may be prefaced by a section which details the quality requirements applicable to the principle component where there is no European Pharmacopoeia or British Pharmacopoeia monograph for the material. These monographs also include either general statements on the methods of preparation or refer to specific methods of preparation given in the European Pharmacopoeia. Homoeopathic stocks and mother tinctures undergo the further process referred to as potentisation. Potentisation is a term specific to homoeopathic medicine and is a process of dilution of stocks and mother tinctures to produce the final product.

Identification tests are established for the components in homoeopathic stocks and usually relate to those applied to the materials used in the production of the homoeopathic stocks. An assay is included for the principal component(s) where possible. For mother tinctures, an identification test, usually chromatographic, is established and, where applicable, an assay for the principle component(s); where appropriate, other tests, related to the solvent, dry matter or known adulterants, are included.

Specifications have not been set for final homoeopathic products due to the high dilution used in their preparation and the subsequent difficulty in applying analytical methodology.

Statements under Crude Drugs; Traditional Herbal and Complementary Medicines also apply to homoeopathic stocks and mother tinctures, when appropriate.

**Unlicensed Medicines**

The General Monograph for Unlicensed Medicines applies to those formulations used in human medicine that are prepared under a manufacturing specials licence or prepared extemporaneously under the supervision of a pharmacist, whether or not there is a published monograph for the specific dosage form.

An article intended for medicinal use that is described by means of an official title must comply with the requirements of the relevant monograph. A formulated preparation must comply throughout its assigned shelf-life (period of validity). The subject of any other monograph must comply throughout its period of use.

Unlicensed medicines that are prepared under a manufacturing specials licence comply with the requirements of the general monograph and, where applicable, the requirements of the individual monograph for the specific dosage form.

Unlicensed medicines prepared extemporaneously under the supervision of a pharmacist comply with the requirements of the general monograph and, where applicable, the requirements of the individual monograph for the specific dosage form. While it is expected that extemporaneous preparations will demonstrate pharmacopoeial compliance when tested, it is recognised that it might not be practicable to carry out the pharmacopoeial tests routinely on such formulations. In the event of doubt or dispute, the methods of analysis, the reference materials and the reference spectra of the Pharmacopoeia are alone authoritative.

# Part III

*Monographs and other texts of the European Pharmacopoeia that are incorporated in this edition of the British Pharmacopoeia are governed by the general notices of the European Pharmacopoeia; these are reproduced below.*

## GENERAL NOTICES OF THE EUROPEAN PHARMACOPOEIA

### 1.1. GENERAL STATEMENTS

The General Notices apply to all monographs and other texts of the European Pharmacopoeia.

The official texts of the European Pharmacopoeia are published in English and French. Translations in other languages may be prepared by the signatory States of the European Pharmacopoeia Convention. In case of doubt or dispute, the English and French versions are alone authoritative.

In the texts of the European Pharmacopoeia, the word 'Pharmacopoeia' without qualification means the European Pharmacopoeia. The official abbreviation Ph. Eur. may be used to indicate the European Pharmacopoeia.

The use of the title or the subtitle of a monograph implies that the article complies with the requirements of the relevant monograph. Such references to monographs in the texts of the Pharmacopoeia are shown using the monograph title and reference number in *italics*.

A preparation must comply throughout its period of validity; a distinct period of validity and/or specifications for opened or broached containers may be decided by the competent authority. The subject of any other monograph must comply throughout its period of use. The period of validity that is assigned to any given article and the time from which that period is to be calculated are decided by the competent authority in light of experimental results of stability studies.

Unless otherwise indicated in the General Notices or in the monographs, statements in monographs constitute mandatory requirements. General chapters become mandatory when referred to in a monograph, unless such reference is made in a way that indicates that it is not the intention to make the text referred to mandatory but rather to cite it for information.

The active substances, excipients, pharmaceutical preparations and other articles described in the monographs are intended for human and veterinary use (unless explicitly restricted to one of these uses). An article is not of Pharmacopoeia quality unless it complies with all the requirements stated in the monograph. This does not imply that performance of all the tests in a monograph is necessarily a prerequisite for a manufacturer in assessing compliance with the Pharmacopoeia before release of a product. The manufacturer may obtain assurance that a product is of Pharmacopoeia quality from data derived, for example, from validation studies of the manufacturing process and from in-process controls. Parametric release in circumstances deemed appropriate by the competent authority is thus not precluded by the need to comply with the Pharmacopoeia.

The tests and assays described are the official methods upon which the standards of the Pharmacopoeia are based. With the agreement of the competent authority, alternative methods of analysis may be used for control purposes, provided that the methods used enable an unequivocal decision to be made as to whether compliance with the standards of the monographs would be achieved if the official methods were used. In the event of doubt or dispute, the methods of analysis of the Pharmacopoeia are alone authoritative.

Certain materials that are the subject of a pharmacopoeial monograph may exist in different grades suitable for different purposes. Unless otherwise indicated in the monograph, the requirements apply to all grades of the material. In some monographs, particularly those on excipients, a list of functionality-related characteristics that are relevant to the use of the substance may be appended to the monograph for information. Test methods for determination of one or more of these characteristics may be given, also for information.

**Quality Systems**  The quality standards represented by monographs are valid only where the articles in question are produced within the framework of a suitable quality system.

**General Monographs**  Substances and preparations that are the subject of an individual monograph are also required to comply with relevant, applicable general monographs. Cross-references to applicable general monographs are not normally given in individual monographs.

General monographs apply to all substances and preparations within the scope of the Definition section of the general monograph, except where a preamble limits the application, for example to substances and preparations that are the subject of a monograph of the Pharmacopoeia.

General monographs on dosage forms apply to all preparations of the type defined. The requirements are not necessarily comprehensive for a given specific preparation and requirements additional to those prescribed in the general monograph may be imposed by the competent authority.

General monographs and individual monographs are complementary. If the provisions of a general monograph do not apply to a particular product, this is expressly stated in the individual monograph.

**Validation of Pharmacopoeial Methods**  The test methods given in monographs and general chapters have been validated in accordance with accepted scientific practice and current recommendations on analytical validation. Unless otherwise stated in the monograph or general chapter, validation of the test methods by the analyst is not required.

**Conventional Terms**  The term 'competent authority' means the national, supranational or international body or organisation vested with the authority for making decisions concerning the issue in question. It may, for example, be a national pharmacopoeia authority, a licensing authority or an official control laboratory.

The expression 'unless otherwise justified and authorised' means that the requirements have to be met, unless the competent authority authorises a modification or an exemption where justified in a particular case.

Statements containing the word 'should' are informative or advisory.

In certain monographs or other texts, the terms 'suitable' and 'appropriate' are used to describe a reagent, micro-organism, test method etc.; if criteria for suitability are not described in the monograph, suitability is demonstrated to the satisfaction of the competent authority.

*Medicinal product.* (a) Any substance or combination of substances presented as having properties for treating or preventing disease in human beings and/or animals; or (b) any substance or combination of substances that may be used in or administered to human beings and/or animals with a view either to restoring, correcting or modifying physiological functions by exerting a pharmacological, immunological or metabolic action, or to making a medical diagnosis.

*Active substance.* Any substance intended to be used in the manufacture of a medicinal product and that, when so used, becomes an active ingredient of the medicinal product. Such substances are intended to furnish a pharmacological activity or other direct effect in the diagnosis, cure, mitigation, treatment or prevention of disease, or to affect the structure and function of the body.

*Excipient* (auxiliary substance). Any constituent of a medicinal product that is not an active substance. Adjuvants, stabilisers, antimicrobial preservatives, diluents, antioxidants, for example, are excipients.

**Interchangeable Methods**

Certain general chapters contain a statement that the text in question is harmonised with the corresponding text of the Japanese Pharmacopoeia and/or the United States Pharmacopeia and that these texts are interchangeable. This implies that if a substance or preparation is found to comply with a requirement using an interchangeable method from one of these pharmacopoeias it complies with the requirements of the European Pharmacopoeia. In the event of doubt or dispute, the text of the European Pharmacopoeia is alone authoritative.

**References to Regulatory Documents**

Monographs and general chapters may contain references to documents issued by regulatory authorities for medicines, for example directives and notes for guidance of the European Union. These references are provided for information for users for the Pharmacopoeia. Inclusion of such a reference does not modify the status of the documents referred to, which may be mandatory or for guidance.

## 1.2. OTHER PROVISIONS APPLYING TO GENERAL CHAPTERS AND MONOGRAPHS

**Quantities**

In tests with numerical limits and assays, the quantity stated to be taken for examination is approximate. The amount actually used, which may deviate by not more than 10 per cent from that stated, is accurately weighed or measured and the result is calculated from this exact quantity. In tests where the limit is not numerical, but usually depends upon comparison with the behaviour of a reference substance in the same conditions, the stated quantity is taken for examination. Reagents are used in the prescribed amounts.

Quantities are weighed or measured with an accuracy commensurate with the indicated degree of precision. For weighings, the precision corresponds to plus or minus 5 units after the last figure stated (for example, 0.25 g is to be interpreted as 0.245 g to 0.255 g). For the measurement of volumes, if the figure after the decimal point is a zero or ends in a zero (for example, 10.0 ml or 0.50 ml), the volume is measured using a pipette, a volumetric flask or a burette, as appropriate; otherwise, a graduated measuring cylinder or a graduated pipette may be used. Volumes stated in microlitres are measured using a micropipette or microsyringe.

It is recognised, however, that in certain cases the precision with which quantities are stated does not correspond to the number of significant figures stated in a specified numerical limit. The weighings and measurements are then carried out with a sufficiently improved accuracy.

**Apparatus and Procedures**  Volumetric glassware complies with Class A requirements of the appropriate International Standard issued by the International Organisation for Standardisation.

Unless otherwise prescribed, analytical procedures are carried out at a temperature between 15 °C and 25 °C.

Unless otherwise prescribed, comparative tests are carried out using identical tubes of colourless, transparent, neutral glass with a flat base; the volumes of liquid prescribed are for use with tubes having an internal diameter of 16 mm, but tubes with a larger internal diameter may be used provided the volume of liquid used is adjusted *(2.1.5)*. Equal volumes of the liquids to be compared are examined down the vertical axis of the tubes against a white background, or if necessary against a black background. The examination is carried out in diffuse light.

Any solvent required in a test or assay in which an indicator is to be used is previously neutralised to the indicator, unless a blank test is prescribed.

**Water Bath**  The term 'water-bath' means a bath of boiling water unless water at another temperature is indicated. Other methods of heating may be substituted provided the temperature is near to but not higher than 100 °C or the indicated temperature.

**Drying and Ignition to Constant Mass**  The terms "dried to constant mass" and "ignited to constant mass" mean that 2 consecutive weighings do not differ by more than 0.5 mg, the $2^{nd}$ weighing following an additional period of drying or of ignition respectively appropriate to the nature and quantity of the residue.

Where drying is prescribed using one of the expressions 'in a desiccator' or '*in vacuo*', it is carried out using the conditions described in chapter *2.2.32. Loss on drying*.

**Reagents**  The proper conduct of the analytical procedures described in the Pharmacopoeia and the reliability of the results depend, in part, upon the quality of the reagents used. The reagents are described in general chapter 4. It is assumed that reagents of analytical grade are used; for some reagents, tests to determine suitability are included in the specifications.

**Solvents**  Where the name of the solvent is not stated, the term 'solution' implies a solution in water.

Where the use of water is specified or implied in the analytical procedures described in the Pharmacopoeia or for the preparation of reagents, water complying with the requirements of the monograph *Purified water (0008)* is used, except that for many purposes the requirements for bacterial endotoxins (*Purified water in bulk*) and microbial contamination (*Purified water in containers*) are not relevant. The term 'distilled water' indicates purified water prepared by distillation.

The term 'ethanol' without qualification means anhydrous ethanol. The term 'alcohol' without qualification means ethanol (96 per cent). Other dilutions of ethanol are indicated by the term 'ethanol' or 'alcohol' followed by a statement of the percentage by volume of ethanol ($C_2H_6O$) required.

**Expression of Content**

In defining content, the expression 'per cent' is used according to circumstances with one of 2 meanings:

— per cent *m/m* (percentage, mass in mass) expresses the number of grams of substance in 100 grams of final product;

— per cent *V/V* (percentage, volume in volume) expresses the number of millilitres of substance in 100 millilitres of final product.

The expression 'parts per million' (or ppm) refers to mass in mass, unless otherwise specified.

**Temperature**

Where an analytical procedure describes temperature without a figure, the general terms used have the following meaning:

— in a deep-freeze:  below − 15 °C;

— in a refrigerator:  2 °C to 8 °C;

— cold or cool:  8 °C to 15 °C;

— room temperature: 15 °C to 25 °C.

## 1.3. GENERAL CHAPTERS

**Containers**

Materials used for containers are described in general chapter *3.1*. General names used for materials, particularly plastic materials, each cover a range of products varying not only in the properties of the principal constituent but also in the additives used. The test methods and limits for materials depend on the formulation and are therefore applicable only for materials whose formulation is covered by the preamble to the specification. The use of materials with different formulations, and the test methods and limits applied to them, are subject to agreement by the competent authority.

The specifications for containers in general chapter *3.2* have been developed for general application to containers of the stated category, but in view of the wide variety of containers available and possible new developments, the publication of a specification does not exclude the use, in justified circumstances, of containers that comply with other specifications, subject to agreement by the competent authority.

Reference may be made within the monographs of the Pharmacopoeia to the definitions and specifications for containers provided in chapter *3.2. Containers*. The general monographs for pharmaceutical dosage forms may, under the heading Definition/Production, require the use of certain types of container; certain other monographs may, under the heading Storage, indicate the type of container that is recommended for use.

## 1.4. MONOGRAPHS

**Titles**

Monograph titles are in English and French in the respective versions and there is a Latin subtitle.

**Relative Atomic and Molecular Masses**

The relative atomic mass ($A_r$) or the relative molecular mass ($M_r$) is shown, as and where appropriate, at the beginning of each monograph. The relative atomic and molecular masses and the molecular and graphic formulae do not constitute analytical standards for the substances described.

**Chemical Abstracts Service (CAS) Registry Number** CAS registry numbers are included for information in monographs, where applicable, to provide convenient access to useful information for users. CAS Registry Number® is a Registered Trademark of the American Chemical Society.

**Definition** Statements under the heading Definition constitute an official definition of the substance, preparation or other article that is the subject of the monograph.

**Limits of content** Where limits of content are prescribed, they are those determined by the method described under Assay.

**Herbal drugs** In monographs on herbal drugs, the definition indicates whether the subject of the monograph is, for example, the whole drug or the drug in powdered form. Where a monograph applies to the drug in several states, for example both to the whole drug and the drug in powdered form, the definition states this.

**Production** Statements under the heading Production draw attention to particular aspects of the manufacturing process but are not necessarily comprehensive. They constitute mandatory requirements for manufacturers, unless otherwise stated. They may relate, for example, to source materials; to the manufacturing process itself and its validation and control; to in-process testing; or to testing that is to be carried out by the manufacturer on the final article, either on selected batches or on each batch prior to release. These statements cannot necessarily be verified on a sample of the final article by an independent analyst. The competent authority may establish that the instructions have been followed, for example, by examination of data received from the manufacturer, by inspection of manufacture or by testing appropriate samples.

The absence of a Production section does not imply that attention to features such as those referred to above is not required.

**Choice of Vaccine Strain, Choice of Vaccine Composition** The Production section of a monograph may define the characteristics of a vaccine strain or vaccine composition. Unless otherwise stated, test methods given for verification of these characteristics are provided for information as examples of suitable methods. Subject to approval by the competent authority, other test methods may be used without validation against the method shown in the monograph.

**Characters** The statements under the heading Characters are not to be interpreted in a strict sense and are not requirements.

**Solubility** In statements of solubility in the Characters section, the terms used have the following significance, referred to a temperature between 15 °C and 25 °C.

| Descriptive term | Approximate volume of solvent in millilitres per gram of solute | | |
|---|---|---|---|
| Very soluble | less than | 1 | |
| Freely soluble | from | 1 | to 10 |
| Soluble | from | 10 | to 30 |
| Sparingly soluble | from | 30 | to 100 |
| Slightly soluble | from | 100 | to 1000 |
| Very slightly soluble | from | 1000 | to 10 000 |
| Practically insoluble | more than | | 10 000 |

The term 'partly soluble' is used to describe a mixture where only some of the components dissolve. The term 'miscible' is used to describe a liquid that is miscible in all proportions with the stated solvent.

## Identification

**Scope** The tests given in the Identification section are not designed to give a full confirmation of the chemical structure or composition of the product; they are intended to give confirmation, with an acceptable degree of assurance, that the article conforms to the description on the label.

**First and second identifications** Certain monographs have subdivisions entitled 'First identification' and 'Second identification'. The test or tests that constitute the 'First identification' may be used in all circumstances. The test or tests that constitute the 'Second identification' may be used in pharmacies provided it can be demonstrated that the substance or preparation is fully traceable to a batch certified to comply with all the other requirements of the monograph.

Certain monographs give two or more sets of tests for the purpose of the first identification, which are equivalent and may be used independently. One or more of these sets usually contain a cross-reference to a test prescribed in the Tests section of the monograph. It may be used to simplify the work of the analyst carrying out the identification and the prescribed tests. For example, one identification set cross-refers to a test for enantiomeric purity while the other set gives a test for specific optical rotation: the intended purpose of the two is the same, that is, verification that the correct enantiomer is present.

**Powdered herbal drugs** Monographs on herbal drugs may contain schematic drawings of the powdered drug. These drawings complement the description given in the relevant identification test.

## Tests and Assays

**Scope** The requirements are not framed to take account of all possible impurities. It is not to be presumed, for example, that an impurity that is not detectable by means of the prescribed tests is tolerated if common sense and good pharmaceutical practice require that it be absent. See also below under Impurities.

**Calculation** Where the result of a test or assay is required to be calculated with reference to the dried or anhydrous substance or on some other specified basis, the determination of loss on drying, water content or other property is carried out by the method prescribed in the relevant test in the monograph. The words 'dried substance' or 'anhydrous substance' etc. appear in parentheses after the result.

**Limits** The limits prescribed are based on data obtained in normal analytical practice; they take account of normal analytical errors, of acceptable variations in manufacture and compounding and of deterioration to an extent considered acceptable. No further tolerances are to be applied to the limits prescribed to determine whether the article being examined complies with the requirements of the monograph.

In determining compliance with a numerical limit, the calculated result of a test or assay is first rounded to the number of significant figures stated, unless otherwise prescribed. The last figure is increased by one when the part rejected is equal to or exceeds one half-unit, whereas it is not modified when the part rejected is less than a half-unit.

**Indication of permitted limit of impurities** For comparative tests, the approximate content of impurity tolerated, or the sum of impurities, may be indicated for information only. Acceptance or rejection is determined on the basis of compliance or non-compliance with the stated test. If the use of a reference substance for the named impurity is not prescribed, this content may be expressed as a nominal concentration of the substance used to prepare the reference solution specified in the monograph, unless otherwise described.

**Herbal drugs** For herbal drugs, the sulphated ash, total ash, water-soluble matter, alcohol-soluble matter, water content, content of essential oil and content of active principle are calculated with reference to the drug that has not been specially dried, unless otherwise prescribed in the monograph.

**Equivalents** Where an equivalent is given, for the purposes of the Pharmacopoeia only the figures shown are to be used in applying the requirements of the monograph.

**Culture media** The culture media described in monographs and general chapters have been found to be satisfactory for the intended purpose. However, the components of media, particularly those of biological origin, are of variable quality, and it may be necessary for optimal performance to modulate the concentration of some ingredients, notably:

— peptones and meat or yeast extracts, with respect to their nutritive properties;

— buffering substances;

— bile salts, bile extract, deoxycholate, and colouring matter, depending on their selective properties;

— antibiotics, with respect to their activity.

**Storage** The information and recommendations given under the heading Storage do not constitute a pharmacopoeial requirement but the competent authority may specify particular storage conditions that must be met.

The articles described in the Pharmacopoeia are stored in such a way as to prevent contamination and, as far as possible, deterioration. Where special conditions of storage are recommended, including the type of container (see section 1.3. General chapters) and limits of temperature, they are stated in the monograph.

The following expressions are used in monographs under Storage with the meaning shown.

*In an airtight container* means that the product is stored in an airtight container (*3.2*). Care is to be taken when the container is opened in a damp atmosphere. A low moisture content may be maintained, if necessary, by the use of a desiccant in the container provided that direct contact with the product is avoided.

*Protected from light* means that the product is stored either in a container made of a material that absorbs actinic light sufficiently to protect the contents from change induced by such light, or in a container enclosed in an outer cover that provides such protection, or is stored in a place from which all such light is excluded.

**Labelling** In general, labelling of medicines is subject to supranational and national regulation and to international agreements. The statements under the heading Labelling are not therefore comprehensive and, moreover, for the purposes of the Pharmacopoeia only those statements that are necessary to demonstrate compliance or non-compliance with the monograph are mandatory. Any other labelling statements are included as recommendations. When the term 'label' is used in the Pharmacopoeia, the labelling statements may appear on the container, the package, a leaflet accompanying the package, or a certificate of analysis accompanying the article, as decided by the competent authority.

**Warnings**　Materials described in monographs and reagents specified for use in the Pharmacopoeia may be injurious to health unless adequate precautions are taken. The principles of good quality control laboratory practice and the provisions of any appropriate regulations are to be observed at all times. Attention is drawn to particular hazards in certain monographs by means of a warning statement; absence of such a statement is not to be taken to mean that no hazard exists.

**Impurities**　A list of all known and potential impurities that have been shown to be detected by the tests in a monograph may be given. See also chapter *5.10. Control of impurities in substances for pharmaceutical use*. The impurities are designated by a letter or letters of the alphabet. Where a letter appears to be missing, the impurity designated by this letter has been deleted from the list during monograph development prior to publication or during monograph revision.

**Functionality-Related Characteristics of Excipients**　Monographs on excipients may have a section on functionality-related characteristics. The characteristics, any test methods for determination and any tolerances are not mandatory requirements; they may nevertheless be relevant for use of the excipient and are given for information (see also section 1.1. General statements).

**Reference Standards**　Certain monographs require the use of reference standards (chemical reference substances, biological reference preparations, reference spectra). See also chapter *5.12. Reference standards*. The European Pharmacopoeia Commission establishes the official reference standards, which are alone authoritative in case of arbitration. These reference standards are available from the European Directorate for the Quality of Medicines & HealthCare (EDQM). Information on the available reference standards and a batch validity statement can be obtained via the EDQM website.

# 1.5. ABBREVIATIONS AND SYMBOLS

| | | | |
|---|---|---|---|
| $A$ | Absorbance | mp | Melting point |
| $A_{1\,cm}^{1\,per\,cent}$ | Specific absorbance | $n_D^{20}$ | Refractive index |
| $A_r$ | Relative atomic mass | Ph. Eur. U. | European Pharmacopoeia Unit |
| $[\alpha]_D^{20}$ | Specific optical rotation | ppm | Parts per million |
| bp | Boiling point | R | Substance or solution defined under *4. Reagents* |
| BRP | Biological Reference Preparation | | |
| CRS | Chemical Reference Substance | $R_f$ | Used in chromatography to indicate the ratio of the distance travelled by a substance to the distance travelled by the solvent front |
| $d_{20}^{20}$ | Relative density | | |
| IU | International Unit | $R_{st}$ | Used in chromatography to indicate the ratio of the distance travelled by a substance to the distance travelled by a reference substance |
| $\lambda$ | Wavelength | | |
| M | Molarity | | |
| $M_r$ | Relative molecular mass | RV | Substance used as a primary standard in volumetric analysis (chapter *4.2.1*) |

## Abbreviations used in the monographs on immunoglobulins, immunosera and vaccines

| | | | |
|---|---|---|---|
| $LD_{50}$ | The statistically determined quantity of a substance that, when administered by the specified route, may be expected to cause the death of 50 per cent of the test animals within a given period | Lo/10 dose | The largest quantity of a toxin that, in the conditions of the test, when mixed with 0.1 IU of antitoxin and administered by the specified route, does not cause symptoms of toxicity in the test animals within a given period |
| MLD | Minimum lethal dose | Lf dose | The quantity of toxin or toxoid that flocculates in the shortest time with 1 IU of antitoxin |
| L+/10 dose | The smallest quantity of a toxin that, in the conditions of the test, when mixed with 0.1 IU of antitoxin and administered by the specified route, causes the death of the test animals within a given period | $CCID_{50}$ | The statistically determined quantity of virus that may be expected to infect 50 per cent of the cell cultures to which it is added |
| L+ dose | The smallest quantity of a toxin that, in the conditions of the test, when mixed with 1 IU of antitoxin and administered by the specified route, causes the death of the test animals within a given period | $EID_{50}$ | The statistically determined quantity of virus that may be expected to infect 50 per cent of fertilised eggs into which it is inoculated |
| lr/100 dose | The smallest quantity of a toxin that, in the conditions of the test, when mixed with 0.01 IU of antitoxin and injected intracutaneously causes a characteristic reaction at the site of injection within a given period | $ID_{50}$ | The statistically determined quantity of a virus that may be expected to infect 50 per cent of the animals into which it is inoculated |
| | | $PD_{50}$ | The statistically determined dose of a vaccine that, in the conditions of the test, may be expected to protect 50 per cent of the animals against a challenge dose of the micro-organisms or toxins against which it is active |
| Lp/10 dose | The smallest quantity of toxin that, in the conditions of the test, when mixed with 0.1 IU of antitoxin and administered by the specified route, causes paralysis in the test animals within a given period | $ED_{50}$ | The statistically determined dose of a vaccine that, in the conditions of the test, may be expected to induce specific antibodies in 50 per cent of the animals for the relevant vaccine antigens |
| | | PFU | Pock-forming units or plaque-forming units |
| | | SPF | Specified-pathogen-free. |

## Collections of micro-organisms

ATCC    American Type Culture Collection
        10801 University Boulevard
        Manassas, Virginia 20110-2209, USA

C.I.P.  Collection de Bactéries de l'Institut Pasteur
        B.P. 52, 25 rue du Docteur Roux
        75724 Paris Cedex 15, France

IMI     International Mycological Institute
        Bakeham Lane
        Surrey TW20 9TY, Great Britain

I.P.    Collection Nationale de Culture de
        Microorganismes (C.N.C.M.)
        Institut Pasteur
        25, rue du Docteur Roux
        75724 Paris Cedex 15, France

NCIMB   National Collection of Industrial and Marine
        Bacteria Ltd
        23 St Machar Drive
        Aberdeen AB2 1RY, Great Britain

NCPF    National Collection of Pathogenic Fungi
        London School of Hygiene and Tropical
        Medicine
        Keppel Street
        London WC1E 7HT, Great Britain

NCTC    National Collection of Type Cultures
        Central Public Health Laboratory
        Colindale Avenue
        London NW9 5HT, Great Britain

NCYC    National Collection of Yeast Cultures
        AFRC Food Research Institute
        Colney Lane
        Norwich NR4 7UA, Great Britain

S.S.I.  Statens Serum Institut
        80 Amager Boulevard, Copenhagen, Denmark

## 1.6. UNITS OF THE INTERNATIONAL SYSTEM (SI) USED IN THE PHARMACOPOEIA AND EQUIVALENCE WITH OTHER UNITS

**International System Of Units (SI)**

The International System of Units comprises 3 classes of units, namely base units, derived units and supplementary units[1]. The base units and their definitions are set out in Table 1.6-1.

The derived units may be formed by combining the base units according to the algebraic relationships linking the corresponding quantities. Some of these derived units have special names and symbols. The SI units used in the Pharmacopoeia are shown in Table 1.6-2.

Some important and widely used units outside the International System are shown in Table 1.6-3.

The prefixes shown in Table 1.6-4 are used to form the names and symbols of the decimal multiples and submultiples of SI units.

---

[1] *The definitions of the units used in the International System are given in the booklet "Le Système International d'Unités (SI)" published by the Bureau International des Poids et Mesures, Pavillion de Breteuil, F-92310 Sèvres.*

**Notes**

1. In the Pharmacopoeia, the Celsius temperature is used (symbol $t$). This is defined by the equation:

$$t = T - T_0$$

where $T_0 = 273.15$ K by definition. The Celsius or centigrade temperature is expressed in degree Celsius (symbol °C). The unit 'degree Celsius' is equal to the unit 'kelvin'.

2. The practical expressions of concentrations used in the Pharmacopoeia are defined in the General Notices.

3. The radian is the plane angle between two radii of a circle that cut off on the circumference an arc equal in length to the radius.

4. In the Pharmacopoeia, conditions of centrifugation are defined by reference to the acceleration due to gravity ($g$):

$$g = 9.806\,65\ m \cdot s^{-2}$$

5. Certain quantities without dimensions are used in the Pharmacopoeia: relative density *(2.2.5)*, absorbance *(2.2.25)*, specific absorbance *(2.2.25)* and refractive index *(2.2.6)*.

6. The microkatal is defined as the enzymic activity that, under defined conditions, produces the transformation (e.g. hydrolysis) of 1 micromole of the substrate per second.

Table 1.6.-1. – *SI base units*

| Quantity | | Unit | | Definition |
|---|---|---|---|---|
| Name | Symbol | Name | Symbol | |
| Length | $l$ | metre | m | The metre is the length of the path travelled by light in a vacuum during a time interval of 1/299 792 458 of a second. |
| Mass | $m$ | kilogram | kg | The kilogram is equal to the mass of the international prototype of the kilogram. |
| Time | $t$ | second | s | The second is the duration of 9 192 631 770 periods of the radiation corresponding to the transition between the two hyperfine levels of the ground state of the caesium-133 atom. |
| Electric current | $I$ | ampere | A | The ampere is that constant current which, maintained in two straight parallel conductors of infinite length, of negligible circular cross-section and placed 1 metre apart in vacuum would produce between these conductors a force equal to $2 \times 10^{-7}$ newton per metre of length. |
| Thermodynamic temperature | $T$ | kelvin | K | The kelvin is the fraction 1/273.16 of the thermodynamic temperature of the triple point of water. |
| Amount of substance | $n$ | mole | mol | The mole is the amount of substance of a system containing as many elementary entities as there are atoms in 0.012 kilogram of carbon-12*. |
| Luminous intensity | $I_v$ | candela | cd | The candela is the luminous intensity in a given direction of a source emitting monochromatic radiation with a frequency of $540 \times 10^{12}$ hertz and whose energy intensity in that direction is 1/683 watt per steradian. |
| * When the mole is used, the elementary entities must be specified and may be atoms, molecules, ions, electrons, other particles or specified groups of such particles. | | | | |

Table 1.6.-2. – *SI units used in the European Pharmacopoeia and equivalence with other units*

| Quantity | | Unit | | | | Conversion of other units into SI units |
|---|---|---|---|---|---|---|
| **Name** | **Symbol** | **Name** | **Symbol** | **Expression in SI base units** | **Expression in other SI units** | |
| Wave number | $\nu$ | one per metre | 1/m | $m^{-1}$ | | |
| Wavelength | $\lambda$ | micrometre | µm | $10^{-6}m$ | | |
| | | nanometre | nm | $10^{-9}m$ | | |
| Area | $A, S$ | square metre | $m^2$ | $m^2$ | | |
| Volume | $V$ | cubic metre | $m^3$ | $m^3$ | | $1 \text{ ml} = 1 \text{ cm}^3 = 10^{-6} \text{ m}^3$ |
| Frequency | $\nu$ | hertz | Hz | $s^{-1}$ | | |
| Density | $\rho$ | kilogram per cubic metre | $kg/m^3$ | $kg{\cdot}m^{-3}$ | | $1 \text{ g/ml} = 1 \text{ g/cm}^3 = 10^3 \text{ kg}{\cdot}\text{m}^{-3}$ |
| Velocity | $v$ | metre per second | m/s | $m{\cdot}s^{-1}$ | | |
| Force | $F$ | newton | N | $m{\cdot}kg{\cdot}s^{-2}$ | | $1 \text{ dyne} = 1 \text{ g}{\cdot}\text{cm}{\cdot}\text{s}^{-2} = 10^{-5} \text{ N}$ |
| Pressure | $p$ | pascal | Pa | $m^{-1}{\cdot}kg{\cdot}s^{-2}$ | $N{\cdot}m^{-2}$ | $1 \text{ kp} = 9.806\ 65 \text{ N}$ <br> $1 \text{ dyne/cm}^2 = 10^{-1} \text{ Pa} = 10^{-1} \text{ N}{\cdot}\text{m}^{-2}$ <br> $1 \text{ atm} = 101\ 325 \text{ Pa} = 101.325 \text{ kPa}$ <br> $1 \text{ bar} = 10^5 \text{ Pa} = 0.1 \text{ MPa}$ <br> $1 \text{ mm Hg} = 133.322\ 387 \text{ Pa}$ <br> $1 \text{ Torr} = 133.322\ 368 \text{ Pa}$ <br> $1 \text{ psi} = 6.894\ 757 \text{ kPa}$ |
| Dynamic viscosity | $\eta$ | pascal second | Pa·s | $m^{-1}{\cdot}kg{\cdot}s^{-1}$ | $N{\cdot}s{\cdot}m^{-2}$ | $1 \text{ P} = 10^{-1} \text{ Pa}{\cdot}\text{s} = 10^{-1} \text{ N}{\cdot}\text{s}{\cdot}\text{m}^{-2}$ <br> $1 \text{ cP} = 1 \text{ mPa}{\cdot}\text{s}$ |
| Kinematic viscosity | $\nu$ | square metre per second | $m^2/s$ | $m^2{\cdot}s^{-1}$ | $Pa{\cdot}s{\cdot}m^3{\cdot}kg^{-1}$ <br> $N{\cdot}m{\cdot}s{\cdot}kg^{-1}$ | $1 \text{ St} = 1 \text{ cm}^2{\cdot}\text{s}^{-1} = 10^{-4} \text{ m}^2{\cdot}\text{s}^{-1}$ |
| Energy | $W$ | joule | J | $m^2{\cdot}kg{\cdot}s^{-2}$ | $N{\cdot}m$ | $1 \text{ erg} = 1 \text{ cm}^2{\cdot}\text{g}{\cdot}\text{s}^{-2} =$ <br> $1 \text{ dyne}{\cdot}\text{cm} = 10^{-7} \text{ J}$ <br> $1 \text{ cal} = 4.1868 \text{ J}$ |
| Power <br> Radiant flux | $P$ | watt | W | $m^2{\cdot}kg{\cdot}s^{-3}$ | $N{\cdot}m{\cdot}s^{-1}$ <br> $J{\cdot}s^{-1}$ | $1 \text{ erg/s} = 1 \text{ dyne}{\cdot}\text{cm}{\cdot}\text{s}^{-1} =$ <br> $10^{-7} \text{ W} = 10^{-7} \text{ N}{\cdot}\text{m}{\cdot}\text{s}^{-1} =$ <br> $10^{-7} \text{ J}{\cdot}\text{s}^{-1}$ |
| Absorbed dose (of radiant energy) | $D$ | gray | Gy | $m^2{\cdot}s^{-2}$ | $J{\cdot}kg^{-1}$ | $1 \text{ rad} = 10^{-2} \text{ Gy}$ |
| Electric potential, electromotive force | $U$ | volt | V | $m^2{\cdot} kg{\cdot}s^{-3}{\cdot}A^{-1}$ | $W{\cdot}A^{-1}$ | |
| Electric resistance | $R$ | ohm | $\Omega$ | $m^2{\cdot} kg{\cdot}s^{-3}{\cdot}A^{-2}$ | $V{\cdot}A^{-1}$ | |
| Quantity of electricity | $Q$ | coulomb | C | $A{\cdot}s$ | | |
| Activity of a radionuclide | $A$ | becquerel | Bq | $s^{-1}$ | | $1 \text{ Ci} = 37{\cdot}10^9 \text{ Bq} = 37{\cdot}10^9 \text{ s}^{-1}$ |
| Concentration (of amount of substance), molar concentration | $c$ | mole per cubic metre | $mol/m^3$ | $mol{\cdot}m^{-3}$ | | $1 \text{ mol/l} = 1\text{M} = 1 \text{ mol/dm}^3 = 10^3 \text{ mol}{\cdot}\text{m}^{-3}$ |
| Mass concentration | $\rho$ | kilogram per cubic metre | $kg/m^3$ | $kg{\cdot}m^{-3}$ | | $1 \text{ g/l} = 1 \text{ g/dm}^3 = 1 \text{ kg}{\cdot}\text{m}^{-3}$ |

Table 1.6.-3. – *Units used with the International System*

| Quantity | Unit | | Value in SI units |
|---|---|---|---|
| | **Name** | **Symbol** | |
| Time | minute | min | 1 min = 60 s |
| | hour | h | 1 h = 60 min = 3600 s |
| | day | d | 1 d = 24 h = 86 400 s |
| Plane angle | degree | ° | 1° = ($\pi$/180) rad |
| Volume | litre | l | 1 l = 1 dm$^3$ = 10$^{-3}$ m$^3$ |
| Mass | tonne | t | 1 t = 10$^3$ kg |
| Rotational frequency | revolution per minute | r/min | 1 r/min = (1/60) s$^{-1}$ |

Table 1.6.-4. – *Decimal multiples and sub-multiples of units*

| Factor | Prefix | Symbol | Factor | Prefix | Symbol |
|---|---|---|---|---|---|
| 10$^{18}$ | exa | E | 10$^{-1}$ | deci | d |
| 10$^{15}$ | peta | P | 10$^{-2}$ | centi | c |
| 10$^{12}$ | tera | T | 10$^{-3}$ | milli | m |
| 10$^9$ | giga | G | 10$^{-6}$ | micro | µ |
| 10$^6$ | mega | M | 10$^{-9}$ | nano | n |
| 10$^3$ | kilo | k | 10$^{-12}$ | pico | p |
| 10$^2$ | hecto | h | 10$^{-15}$ | femto | f |
| 10$^1$ | deca | da | 10$^{-18}$ | atto | a |

# Monographs


# Medicinal and Pharmaceutical Substances A to I

# MEDICINAL AND PHARMACEUTICAL SUBSTANCES

## Substances for Pharmaceutical Use

(*Ph Eur monograph 2034*)

*Ph Eur* _____

### DEFINITION

Substances for pharmaceutical use are any organic or inorganic substances that are used as active substances or excipients for the production of medicinal products for human or veterinary use. They may be obtained from natural sources or produced by extraction from raw materials, fermentation or synthesis.

This general monograph does not apply to herbal drugs, herbal drugs for homoeopathic preparations, herbal drug preparations, extracts, or mother tinctures for homoeopathic preparations, which are the subject of separate general monographs (*Herbal drugs (1433)*, *Herbal drugs for homoeopathic preparations (2045)*, *Herbal drug preparations (1434)*, *Extracts (0765)*, *Mother tinctures for homoeopathic preparations (2029)*). It does not apply to raw materials for homoeopathic preparations, except where there is an individual monograph for the substance in the non-homoeopathic part of the Pharmacopoeia.

Where a substance for pharmaceutical use not described in an individual monograph of the Pharmacopoeia is used in a medicinal product prepared for the special needs of individual patients, the need for compliance with the present general monograph is decided in the light of a risk assessment that takes account of the available quality of the substance and its intended use.

Where medicinal products are manufactured using substances for pharmaceutical use of human or animal origin, the requirements of chapter *5.1.7. Viral safety* apply.

Substances for pharmaceutical use may be used as such or as starting materials for subsequent formulation to prepare medicinal products. Depending on the formulation, certain substances may be used either as active substances or as excipients. Solid substances may be compacted, coated, granulated, powdered to a certain fineness, or processed in other ways. A monograph is applicable to a substance processed with an excipient only where such processing is mentioned in the definition section of the monograph.

*Substance for pharmaceutical use of special grade*  Unless otherwise indicated or restricted in the individual monographs, a substance for pharmaceutical use is intended for human and veterinary use, and is of appropriate quality for the manufacture of all dosage forms in which it can be used.

*Polymorphism*  Individual monographs do not usually specify crystalline or amorphous forms, unless bioavailability is affected. All forms of a substance for pharmaceutical use comply with the requirements of the monograph, unless otherwise indicated.

### PRODUCTION

Substances for pharmaceutical use are manufactured by procedures that are designed to ensure a consistent quality and comply with the requirements of the individual monograph or approved specification.

The provisions of general chapter *5.10* apply to the control of impurities in substances for pharmaceutical use.

Whether or not it is specifically stated in the individual monograph that the substance for pharmaceutical use:
— is a recombinant protein or another substance obtained as a direct gene product based on genetic modification, where applicable, the substance also complies with the requirements of the general monograph *Products of recombinant DNA technology (0784)*;
— is obtained from animals susceptible to transmissible spongiform encephalopathies other than by experimental challenge, where applicable, the substance also complies with the requirements of the general monograph *Products with risk of transmitting agents of animal spongiform encephalopathies (1483)*;
— is a substance derived from a fermentation process, whether or not the micro-organisms involved are modified by traditional procedures or recombinant DNA (rDNA) technology, where applicable, the substance also complies with the requirements of the general monograph *Products of fermentation (1468)*.

If solvents are used during production, they are of suitable quality. In addition, their toxicity and their residual level are taken into consideration (*5.4*). If water is used during production, it is of suitable quality.

If substances are produced or processed to yield a certain form or grade, that specific form or grade of the substance complies with the requirements of the monograph. Certain functionality-related tests may be described to control properties that may influence the suitability of the substance and subsequently the properties of dosage forms prepared from it.

*Powdered substances* may be processed to obtain a certain degree of fineness (*2.9.35*).

*Compacted substances* are processed to increase the particle size or to obtain particles of a specific form and/or to obtain a substance with a higher bulk density.

*Coated active substances* consist of particles of the active substance coated with one or more suitable excipients.

*Granulated active substances* are particles of a specified size and/or form produced from the active substance by granulation directly or with one or more suitable excipients.

If substances are processed with excipients, these excipients comply with the requirements of the relevant monograph or, where no such monograph exists, the approved specification.

Where active substances have been processed with excipients to produce, for example, coated or granulated substances, the processing is carried out under conditions of good manufacturing practice and the processed substances are regarded as intermediates in the manufacture of a medicinal product.

### CHARACTERS

The statements under the heading Characters (e.g. statements about the solubility or a decomposition point) are not to be interpreted in a strict sense and are not requirements. They are given for information.

Where a substance may show polymorphism, this may be stated under Characters in order to draw this to the attention of the user who may have to take this characteristic into consideration during formulation of a preparation.

Table 2034.-1. – *Reporting, identification and qualification of organic impurities in active substances*

| Use | Maximum daily dose | Reporting threshold | Identification threshold | Qualification threshold |
|---|---|---|---|---|
| Human use or human and veterinary use | ≤ 2 g/day | > 0.05 per cent | > 0.10 per cent or a daily intake of > 1.0 mg (whichever is the lower) | > 0.15 per cent or a daily intake of > 1.0 mg (whichever is the lower) |
| Human use or human and veterinary use | > 2 g/day | > 0.03 per cent | > 0.05 per cent | > 0.05 per cent |
| Veterinary use only | Not applicable | > 0.1 per cent | > 0.2 per cent | > 0.5 per cent |

## IDENTIFICATION

Where under Identification an individual monograph contains subdivisions entitled 'First identification' and 'Second identification', the test or tests that constitute the 'First identification' may be used in all circumstances. The test or tests that constitute the 'Second identification' may be used in pharmacies provided it can be demonstrated that the substance or preparation is fully traceable to a batch certified to comply with all the other requirements of the monograph.

Certain monographs give two or more sets of tests for the purpose of the first identification, which are equivalent and may be used independently. One or more of these sets usually contain a cross-reference to a test prescribed in the Tests section of the monograph. It may be used to simplify the work of the analyst carrying out the identification and the prescribed tests. For example, one identification set cross-refers to a test for enantiomeric purity while the other set gives a test for specific optical rotation: the intended purpose of the two is the same, that is, verification that the correct enantiomer is present.

## TESTS

### Polymorphism (5.9)

If the nature of a crystalline or amorphous form imposes restrictions on its use in preparations, the nature of the specific crystalline or amorphous form is identified, its morphology is adequately controlled and its identity is stated on the label.

### Related substances

Unless otherwise prescribed or justified and authorised, organic impurities in active substances are to be reported, identified wherever possible, and qualified as indicated in Table 2034.-1 or in Table 2034.-2 for peptides obtained by chemical synthesis.

Table 2034.-2. – *Reporting, identification and qualification of organic impurities in peptides obtained by chemical synthesis*

| Reporting threshold | Identification threshold | Qualification threshold |
|---|---|---|
| > 0.1 per cent | > 0.5 per cent | > 1.0 per cent |

Specific thresholds may be applied for impurities known to be unusually potent or to produce toxic or unexpected pharmacological effects.

If the individual monograph does not provide suitable control for a new impurity, a suitable test for control must be developed and included in the specification for the substance.

The requirements above do not apply to biological and biotechnological products, oligonucleotides, radiopharmaceuticals, products of fermentation and semi-synthetic products derived therefrom, to crude products of animal or plant origin or herbal products.

### Residual solvents

Are limited according to the principles defined in chapter 5.4, using general method 2.4.24 or another suitable method. Where a quantitative determination of a residual solvent is carried out and a test for loss on drying is not carried out, the content of residual solvent is taken into account for calculation of the assay content of the substance, the specific optical rotation and the specific absorbance.

### Microbiological quality

Individual monographs give acceptance criteria for microbiological quality wherever such control is necessary. Table 5.1.4.-2. – *Acceptance criteria for microbiological quality of non-sterile substances for pharmaceutical use in chapter 5.1.4. Microbiological quality of non-sterile pharmaceutical preparations and substances for pharmaceutical use* gives recommendations on microbiological quality that are of general relevance for substances subject to microbial contamination. Depending on the nature of the substance and its intended use, different acceptance criteria may be justified.

### Sterility (2.6.1)

If intended for use in the manufacture of sterile dosage forms without a further appropriate sterilisation procedure, or if offered as sterile grade, the substance for pharmaceutical use complies with the test for sterility.

### Bacterial endotoxins (2.6.14)

If offered as bacterial endotoxin-free grade, the substance for pharmaceutical use complies with the test for bacterial endotoxins. The limit and test method (if not gelation method A) are stated in the individual monograph. The limit is calculated in accordance with *Test for bacterial endotoxins: guidelines in chapter* 2.6.14. Bacterial endotoxins, unless a lower limit is justified from results from production batches or is required by the competent authority. Where a test for bacterial endotoxins is prescribed, a test for pyrogens is not required.

### Pyrogens (2.6.8)

If the test for pyrogens is justified rather than the test for bacterial endotoxins and if a pyrogen-free grade is offered, the substance for pharmaceutical use complies with the test for pyrogens. The limit and test method are stated in the individual monograph or approved by the competent authority. Based on appropriate test validation for bacterial endotoxins and pyrogens, the test for bacterial endotoxins may replace the test for pyrogens.

### Additional properties

Control of additional properties (e.g. physical characteristics, functionality-related characteristics) may be necessary for individual manufacturing processes or formulations. Grades (such as sterile, endotoxin-free, pyrogen-free) may be produced with a view to manufacture of preparations for parenteral administration or other dosage forms and appropriate requirements may be specified in an individual monograph.

## ASSAY

Unless justified and authorised, contents of substances for pharmaceutical use are determined. Suitable methods are used.

## LABELLING

In general, labelling is subject to supranational and national regulation and to international agreements. The statements under the heading Labelling therefore are not comprehensive and, moreover, for the purposes of the Pharmacopoeia only those statements that are necessary to demonstrate compliance or non-compliance with the monograph are mandatory. Any other labelling statements are included as recommendations. When the term 'label' is used in the Pharmacopoeia, the labelling statements may appear on the container, the package, a leaflet accompanying the package or a certificate of analysis accompanying the article, as decided by the competent authority.

Where appropriate, the label states that the substance is:
— intended for a specific use;
— of a distinct crystalline form;
— of a specific degree of fineness;
— compacted;
— coated;
— granulated;
— sterile;
— free from bacterial endotoxins;
— free from pyrogens;
— containing gliding agents.

Where applicable, the label states:
— the degree of hydration;
— the name and concentration of any excipient.

_____ _Ph Eur_

# Acacia

(_Ph Eur monograph 0307_)

## Action and use
Bulk-forming laxative; excipient.

When Powdered Acacia is prescribed or demanded, material complying with the requirements below with the exception of Identification test A shall be dispensed or supplied.

_Ph Eur_ _____

## DEFINITION

Air-hardened, gummy exudate flowing naturally from or obtained by incision of the trunk and branches of _Acacia senegal_ L. Willdenow, other species of _Acacia_ of African origin and _Acacia seyal Del._

## CHARACTERS

Acacia is almost completely but very slowly soluble, after about 2 h, in twice its mass of water leaving only a very small residue of vegetable particles; the liquid obtained is colourless or yellowish, dense, viscous, adhesive, translucent and weakly acid to blue litmus paper. Acacia is practically insoluble in ethanol (96 per cent).

## IDENTIFICATION

A. Acacia occurs as yellowish-white, yellow or pale amber, sometimes with a pinkish tint, friable, opaque, spheroidal, oval or reniform pieces (tears) of a diameter from about 1-3 cm, frequently with a cracked surface, easily broken into irregular, whitish or slightly yellowish angular fragments with conchoidal fracture and a glassy and transparent appearance.

In the centre of an unbroken tear there is sometimes a small cavity.

B. Reduce to a powder (355) (_2.9.12_). The powder is white or yellowish-white. Examine under a microscope using a 50 per cent _V/V_ solution of _glycerol R_. The powder shows the following diagnostic characters: angular, irregular, colourless, transparent fragments. Only traces of starch or vegetable tissues are visible. No stratified membrane is apparent.

C. Examine the chromatograms obtained in the test for glucose and fructose.

_Results_   The chromatogram obtained with the test solution shows 3 zones due to galactose, arabinose and rhamnose. No other important zones are visible, particularly in the upper part of the chromatogram.

D. Dissolve 1 g of the powdered drug (355) (_2.9.12_) in 2 ml of _water R_ by stirring frequently for 2 h. Add 2 ml of _ethanol (96 per cent) R_. After shaking, a white, gelatinous mucilage is formed which becomes fluid on adding 10 ml of _water R_.

## TESTS
### Solution S
Dissolve 3.0 g of the powdered drug (355) (_2.9.12_) in 25 ml of _water R_ by stirring for 30 min. Allow to stand for 30 min and dilute to 30 ml with _water R_.

### Insoluble matter
Maximum 0.5 per cent.

To 5.0 g of the powdered drug (355) (_2.9.12_) add 100 ml of _water R_ and 14 ml of _dilute hydrochloric acid R_, boil gently for 15 min, shaking frequently and filter while hot through a tared sintered-glass filter (_2.1.2_). Wash with hot _water R_ and dry at 100-105 °C. The residue weighs a maximum of 25 mg.

### Glucose and fructose
Thin-layer chromatography (_2.2.27_).

_Test solution_   To 0.100 g of the powdered drug (355) (_2.9.12_) in a thick-walled centrifuge tube add 2 ml of a 100 g/l solution of _trifluoroacetic acid R_, shake vigorously to dissolve the forming gel, stopper the tube and heat the mixture at 120 °C for 1 h. Centrifuge the hydrolysate, transfer the clear supernatant carefully into a 50 ml flask, add 10 ml of _water R_ and evaporate the solution to dryness under reduced pressure. To the resulting clear film add 0.1 ml of _water R_ and 0.9 ml of _methanol R_. Centrifuge to separate the amorphous precipitate. Dilute the supernatant, if necessary, to 1 ml with _methanol R_.

_Reference solution_   Dissolve 10 mg of _arabinose R_, 10 mg of _galactose R_, 10 mg of _glucose R_, 10 mg of _rhamnose R_ and 10 mg of _xylose R_ in 1 ml of _water R_ and dilute to 10 ml with _methanol R_.

_Plate_   TLC silica gel plate R.

_Mobile phase_   16 g/l solution of _sodium dihydrogen phosphate R, butanol R, acetone R_ (10:40:50 _V/V/V_).

_Application_   10 µl as bands.

_Development A_   Over a path of 10 cm.

_Drying A_   In a current of warm air for a few minutes.

_Development B_   Over a path of 15 cm using the same mobile phase.

_Drying B_   At 110 °C for 10 min.

_Detection_   Spray with a_nisaldehyde solution R_ and heat at 110 °C for 10 min.

_Results_   The chromatogram obtained with the reference solution shows 5 clearly separated coloured zones due to galactose (greyish-green or green), glucose (grey), arabinose (yellowish-green), xylose (greenish-grey or yellowish-grey) and rhamnose (yellowish-green), in order of increasing $R_F$ value. The chromatogram obtained with the test solution shows no grey zone and no greyish-green zone between the zones corresponding to galactose and arabinose in the chromatogram obtained with the reference solution.

### Starch, dextrin and agar

To 10 ml of solution S previously boiled and cooled add 0.1 ml of *0.05 M iodine*. No blue or reddish-brown colour develops.

### Sterculia gum

A. Place 0.2 g of the powdered drug (355) (*2.9.12*) in a 10 ml ground-glass-stoppered cylinder graduated in 0.1 ml. Add 10 ml of *ethanol (60 per cent V/V) R* and shake. Any gel formed occupies a maximum of 1.5 ml.

B. To 1.0 g of the powdered drug (355) (*2.9.12*) add 100 ml of *water R* and shake. Add 0.1 ml of *methyl red solution R*. Not more than 5.0 ml of *0.01 M sodium hydroxide* is required to change the colour of the indicator.

### Tannins

To 10 ml of solution S add 0.1 ml of *ferric chloride solution R1*. A gelatinous precipitate is formed, but neither the precipitate nor the liquid are dark blue.

### Tragacanth

Examine the chromatograms obtained in the test for glucose and fructose.

*Results* The chromatogram obtained with the test solution shows no greenish-grey or yellowish-grey zone corresponding to the zone of xylose in the chromatogram obtained with the reference solution.

### Loss on drying (*2.2.32*)

Maximum 15.0 per cent, determined on 1.000 g of the powdered drug (355) (*2.9.12*) by drying in an oven at 105 °C.

### Total ash (*2.4.16*)

Maximum 4.0 per cent.

### Microbial contamination

TAMC: acceptance criterion $10^4$ CFU/g (*2.6.12*).

TYMC: acceptance criterion $10^2$ CFU/g (*2.6.12*).

Absence of *Escherichia coli* (*2.6.13*).

Absence of *Salmonella* (*2.6.13*).

### FUNCTIONALITY-RELATED CHARACTERISTICS

*This section provides information on characteristics that are recognised as being relevant control parameters for one or more functions of the substance when used as an excipient (see chapter 5.15). This section is a non-mandatory part of the monograph and it is not necessary to verify the characteristics to demonstrate compliance. Control of these characteristics can however contribute to the quality of a medicinal product by improving the consistency of the manufacturing process and the performance of the medicinal product during use. Where control methods are cited, they are recognised as being suitable for the purpose, but other methods can also be used. Wherever results for a particular characteristic are reported, the control method must be indicated.*

*The following characteristic may be relevant for acacia used as a viscosity-increasing agent and/or suspending agent in aqueous preparations.*

### Apparent viscosity

Determine the dynamic viscosity using a capillary viscometer (*2.2.9*) or a rotating viscometer (*2.2.10*) on a 100 g/l solution of acacia (dried substance).

*Ph Eur*

# Spray-dried Acacia

(*Ph Eur monograph 0308*)

*Ph Eur*

### DEFINITION

Spray-dried acacia is obtained from a solution of acacia.

### CHARACTERS

It dissolves completely and rapidly, after about 20 min, in twice its mass of water. The liquid obtained is colourless or yellowish, dense, viscous, adhesive, translucent and weakly acid to blue litmus paper. Spray-dried acacia is practically insoluble in ethanol (96 per cent).

### IDENTIFICATION

A. Examined under a microscope, in *ethanol (96 per cent) R*, the powder is seen to consist predominantly of spheroidal particles about 4-40 μm in diameter, with a central cavity containing 1 or several air-bubbles; a few minute flat fragments are present. Only traces of starch granules are visible. No vegetable tissue is seen.

B. Examine the chromatograms obtained in the test for glucose and fructose.

*Results* The chromatogram obtained with the test solution shows 3 zones due to galactose, arabinose and rhamnose. No other important zones are visible, particularly in the upper part of the chromatogram.

C. Dissolve 1 g of the drug to be examined in 2 ml of *water R* by stirring frequently for 20 min. Add 2 ml of *ethanol (96 per cent) R*. After shaking a white gelatinous mucilage is formed which becomes fluid on adding 10 ml of *water R*.

### TESTS

#### Solution S

Dissolve 3.0 g of the drug to be examined in 25 ml of *water R* by stirring for 10 min. Allow to stand for 20 min and dilute to 30 ml with *water R*.

#### Glucose and fructose

Thin-layer chromatography (*2.2.27*).

*Test solution* To 0.100 g in a thick-walled centrifuge tube add 2 ml of a 100 g/l solution of *trifluoroacetic acid R*, shake vigorously to dissolve the forming gel, stopper the tube and heat the mixture at 120 °C for 1 h. Centrifuge the hydrolysate, transfer the clear supernatant carefully into a 50 ml flask, add 10 ml of *water R* and evaporate to dryness under reduced pressure. To the resulting clear film add 0.1 ml of *water R* and 0.9 ml of *methanol R*. Centrifuge to separate the amorphous precipitate. Dilute the supernatant, if necessary, to 1 ml with *methanol R*.

*Reference solution* Dissolve 10 mg of *arabinose R*, 10 mg of *galactose R*, 10 mg of *glucose R*, 10 mg of *rhamnose R* and 10 mg of *xylose R* in 1 ml of *water R* and dilute to 10 ml with *methanol R*.

*Plate* *TLC silica gel plate R*.

*Mobile phase* 16 g/l solution of *sodium dihydrogen phosphate R*, butanol R, acetone R (10:40:50 V/V/V).

*Application* 10 μl as bands.

*Development A* Over a path of 10 cm.

*Drying A* In a current of warm air for a few minutes.

*Development B* Over a path of 15 cm using the same mobile phase.

*Detection* Spray with *anisaldehyde solution R* and heat at 110 °C for 10 min.

*Results* The chromatogram obtained with the reference solution shows 5 clearly separated coloured zones due to galactose (greyish-green or green), glucose (grey), arabinose (yellowish-green), xylose (greenish-grey or yellowish-grey) and rhamnose (yellowish-green), in order of increasing $R_F$ value. The chromatogram obtained with the test solution shows no grey zone and no greyish-green zone between the zones corresponding to galactose and arabinose in the chromatogram obtained with the reference solution.

**Starch, dextrin and agar**
To 10 ml of solution S previously boiled and cooled add 0.1 ml of *0.05 M iodine*. No blue or reddish-brown colour develops.

**Sterculia gum**
A. Place 0.2 g in a 10 ml ground-glass-stoppered cylinder graduated in 0.1 ml. Add 10 ml of *ethanol (60 per cent V/V) R* and shake. Any gel formed occupies not more than 1.5 ml.

B. To 1.0 g add 100 ml of *water R* and shake. Add 0.1 ml of *methyl red solution R*. Not more than 5.0 ml of *0.01 M sodium hydroxide* is required to change the colour of the indicator.

**Tannins**
To 10 ml of solution S add 0.1 ml of *ferric chloride solution R1*. A gelatinous precipitate is formed, but neither the precipitate nor the liquid shows a dark blue colour.

**Tragacanth**
Examine the chromatograms obtained in the test for Glucose and fructose.

*Results* The chromatogram obtained with the test solution shows no greenish-grey or yellowish-grey zone corresponding to the zone of xylose in the chromatogram obtained with the reference solution.

**Loss on drying** (*2.2.32*)
Maximum 10.0 per cent, determined on 1.000 g by drying in an oven at 105 °C.

**Total ash** (*2.4.16*)
Maximum 4.0 per cent.

**Microbial contamination**
TAMC: acceptance criterion $10^4$ CFU/g (*2.6.12*).
TYMC: acceptance criterion $10^2$ CFU/g (*2.6.12*).
Absence of Escherichia coli (*2.6.13*).
Absence of *Salmonella* (*2.6.13*).

**FUNCTIONALITY-RELATED CHARACTERISTICS**
*This section provides information on characteristics that are recognised as being relevant control parameters for one or more functions of the substance when used as an excipient (see chapter 5.15). This section is a non-mandatory part of the monograph and it is not necessary to verify the characteristics to demonstrate compliance. Control of these characteristics can however contribute to the quality of a medicinal product by improving the consistency of the manufacturing process and the performance of the medicinal product during use. Where control methods are cited, they are recognised as being suitable for the purpose, but other methods can also be used. Wherever results for a particular characteristic are reported, the control method must be indicated.*

*The following characteristic may be relevant for spray-dried acacia used as a viscosity-increasing agent and/or suspending agent in aqueous preparations.*

**Apparent viscosity**
Determine the dynamic viscosity using a capillary viscometer (*2.2.9*) or a rotating viscometer (*2.2.10*) on a 100 g/l solution of spray-dried acacia (dried substance).

# Acamprosate Calcium

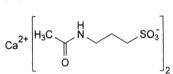

(*Ph Eur monograph 1585*)

$C_{10}H_{20}CaN_2O_8S_2$      400.5      77337-73-6

**Action and use**
Treatment of alcoholism.

*Ph Eur* _____

**DEFINITION**
Calcium bis[3-(acetylamino)propane-1-sulphonate].

*Content* 98.0 per cent to 102.0 per cent (dried substance).

**CHARACTERS**
**Appearance**
White or almost white powder.

**Solubility**
Freely soluble in water, practically insoluble in alcohol and in methylene chloride.

**IDENTIFICATION**
A. Infrared absorption spectrophotometry (*2.2.24*).

*Comparison* Ph. Eur. *reference spectrum of acamprosate calcium.*

B. It gives reaction (a) of calcium (*2.3.1*).

**TESTS**
**Solution S**
Dissolve 5.0 g in *carbon dioxide-free water R* and dilute to 100 ml with the same solvent.

**Appearance of solution**
Solution S is clear (*2.2.1*) and colourless (*2.2.2, Method II*).

**pH** (*2.2.3*)
5.5 to 7.0 for solution S.

**Impurity A**
Liquid chromatography (*2.2.29*).

*Test solution* Dissolve 0.40 g of the substance to be examined in *distilled water R* and dilute to 20.0 ml with the same solvent. Dilute 10.0 ml of this solution to 100.0 ml with *borate buffer solution pH 10.4 R*. Place 3.0 ml of the solution obtained in a 25 ml ground-glass-stoppered tube. Add 0.15 ml of a freshly prepared 5 g/l solution of *fluorescamine R* in *acetonitrile R*. Shake immediately and vigorously for 30 s. Place in a water-bath at 50 °C for 30 min. Cool under a stream of cold water. Centrifuge and filter the supernatant through a suitable membrane filter (0.45 µm), 25 mm in diameter.

*Reference solution* Dissolve 50 mg of *acamprosate impurity A CRS* in *distilled water R* and dilute to 200.0 ml with the same solvent. Dilute 0.4 ml of the solution to 100.0 ml with *borate buffer solution pH 10.4 R*. Treat 3.0 ml of this solution in the same way as the test solution

*Column:*
— *size: l* = 0.15 m, Ø = 4.6 mm,
— *stationary phase: spherical octadecylsilyl silica gel for chromatography R* (5 µm) with a specific surface area of 170 m2/g and a pore size of 12 nm.

*Mobile phase* acetonitrile R, methanol R, 0.1 M phosphate buffer solution pH 6.5 R (10:10:80 V/V/V).

*Flow rate* 1 ml/min.

*Detection* Spectrophotometer at 261 nm.

*Injection* 20 μl.

*Run time* 6 times the retention time of impurity A

*Retention times* Fluorescamine = about 4 min; impurity A = about 8 min; acamprosate is not detected by this system.

*Limits:*
— *impurity A*: not more than the area of the corresponding peak in the chromatogram obtained with the reference solution (0.05 per cent).

## Heavy metals (2.4.8)
Maximum 10 ppm.

Dissolve 2.0 g in *distilled water R* and dilute to 20 ml with the same solvent. 12 ml of the solution complies with limit test A. Prepare the standard using 10 ml of *lead standard solution (1 ppm Pb) R*.

## Loss on drying (2.2.32)
Maximum 0.4 per cent, determined on 1.000 g by drying in an oven at 105 °C.

## ASSAY
To 4 g of *cation exchange resin R* (75-150 μm) add 20 ml of *distilled water R* and stir magnetically for 10 min. Introduce this suspension into a glass column, 45 cm long and 2.2 cm in internal diameter, equipped with a polytetrafluoroethylene flow cap covered by a glass-wool plug. Allow a few millilitres of this solution to flow, then place a plug of glass wool over the resin. Pass 50 ml of *1 M hydrochloric acid* through the column. The pH of the eluate is close to 1. Wash with 3 quantities, each of 200 ml, of *distilled water R* to obtain an eluate at pH 6. Dissolve 0.100 g of the substance to be examined in 15 ml of *distilled water R*. Pass through the column and wash with 3 quantities, each of 25 ml, of *distilled water R*, collecting the eluate. Allow to elute until an eluate at pH 6 is obtained. Titrate the solution obtained with *0.1 M sodium hydroxide*, determining the end-point potentiometrically (2.2.20).

1 ml of *0.1 M sodium hydroxide* corresponds to 20.02 mg of $C_{10}H_{20}CaN_2O_8S_2$.

## IMPURITIES

$H_2N$‿‿$SO_3H$

A. 3-aminopropane-1-sulphonic acid (homotaurine).

_____ *Ph Eur*

# Acarbose

(*Ph Eur monograph 2089*)

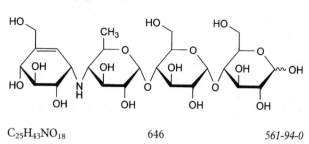

$C_{25}H_{43}NO_{18}$   646   561-94-0

## Action and use
Alpha-glucosidase inhibitor; treatment of diabetes mellitus.

*Ph Eur* _____

## DEFINITION
O-4,6-Dideoxy-4-[[(1S,4R,5S,6S)-4,5,6-trihydroxy-3-(hydroxymethyl)cyclohex-2-enyl]amino]-α-D-glucopyranosyl-(1→4)-O-α-D-glucopyranosyl-(1→4)-D-glucopyranose, which is produced by certain strains of *Actinoplanes utahensis*.

## Content
95.0 per cent to 102.0 per cent (anhydrous substance).

## CHARACTERS
### Appearance
White or yellowish, amorphous powder, hygroscopic.

### Solubility
Very soluble in water, soluble in methanol, practically insoluble in methylene chloride.

## IDENTIFICATION
A. Infrared absorption spectrophotometry (2.2.24).

*Comparison* acarbose for identification CRS.

B. Examine the chromatograms obtained in the assay.

*Results* The principal peak in the chromatogram obtained with the test solution is similar in retention time and size to the principal peak in the chromatogram obtained with reference solution (a).

## TESTS
### Solution S
Dissolve 1.00 g in *carbon dioxide-free water R* and dilute to 20.0 ml with the same solvent.

### pH (2.2.3)
5.5 to 7.5 for solution S.

### Specific optical rotation (2.2.7)
+ 168 to + 183 (anhydrous substance).

Dilute 2.0 ml of solution S to 10.0 ml with *water R*.

### Absorbance (2.2.25)
Maximum 0.15 at 425 nm for solution S.

### Related substances.
Liquid chromatography (2.2.29).

*Test solution* Dissolve 0.200 g of the substance to be examined in *water R* and dilute to 10.0 ml with the same solvent.

*Reference solution (a)* Dissolve the contents of a vial of acarbose CRS in 5.0 ml of *water R*.

*Reference solution (b)* Dissolve 20 mg of acarbose for peak identification CRS (acarbose containing impurities A, B, C, D, E, F, G and H) in 1 ml of *water R*.

*Reference solution (c)* Dilute 1.0 ml of the test solution to 100.0 ml with *water R*.

**Column:**
— *size*: l = 0.25 m, Ø = 4 mm,
— *stationary phase*: aminopropylsilyl silica gel for chromatography R (5 μm),
— *temperature*: 35 °C.

*Mobile phase* Mix 750 volumes of *acetonitrile R1* and 250 volumes of a solution containing 0.60 g/l of *potassium dihydrogen phosphate R* and 0.35 g/l of *disodium hydrogen phosphate dihydrate R*.

*Flow rate* 2.0 ml/min.

*Detection* Spectrophotometer at 210 nm.

*Injection* 10 μl of the test solution and reference solutions (b) and (c).

*Run time* 2.5 times the retention time of acarbose.

*Identification of impurities* Use the chromatogram supplied with *acarbose for peak identification CRS* and the chromatogram obtained with reference solution (b) to identify the peaks due to impurities A, B, C, D, E, F, G and H.

*Relative retention* With reference to acarbose (retention time = about 16 min): impurity D = about 0.5; impurity H = about 0.6; impurity B = about 0.8; impurity A = about 0.9; impurity C = about 1.2; impurity E = about 1.7; impurity F = about 1.9; impurity G = about 2.2.

*System suitability* Reference solution (b):
— *peak-to-valley ratio*: minimum 1.2, where $H_p$ = height above the baseline of the peak due to impurity A and $H_v$ = height above the baseline of the lowest point of the curve separating this peak from the peak due to acarbose,
— the chromatogram obtained is similar to the chromatogram supplied with *acarbose for peak identification CRS*.

*Limits*:
— *correction factors*: for the calculation of contents, multiply the peak areas of the following impurities by the corresponding correction factor: impurity B = 0.63; impurity D = 0.75; impurity E = 1.25; impurity F = 1.25; impurity G = 1.25;
— *impurity A*: not more than 0.6 times the area of the principal peak in the chromatogram obtained with reference solution (c) (0.6 per cent);
— *impurity B*: not more than 0.5 times the area of the principal peak in the chromatogram obtained with reference solution (c) (0.5 per cent);
— *impurity C*: not more than 1.5 times the area of the principal peak in the chromatogram obtained with reference solution (c) (1.5 per cent);
— *impurity D*: not more than the area of the principal peak in the chromatogram obtained with reference solution (c) (1.0 per cent);
— *impurity E*: not more than 0.2 times the area of the principal peak in the chromatogram obtained with reference solution (c) (0.2 per cent);
— *impurities F, G*: for each impurity, not more than 0.3 times the area of the principal peak in the chromatogram obtained with reference solution (c) (0.3 per cent);
— *impurity H*: not more than 0.2 times the area of the principal peak in the chromatogram obtained with reference solution (c) (0.2 per cent);
— *any other impurities*: for each impurity, not more than 0.2 times the area of the principal peak in the chromatogram obtained with reference solution (c) (0.2 per cent);

— *total*: not more than 3 times the area of the principal peak in the chromatogram obtained with reference solution (c) (3.0 per cent);
— *disregard limit*: 0.1 times the area of the principal peak in the chromatogram obtained with reference solution (c) (0.1 per cent).

**Heavy metals** (*2.4.8*)
Maximum 20 ppm.

Dissolve 1.5 g in *water R* and dilute to 15 ml with the same solvent. If the solution is not clear, carry out prefiltration and use the filtrate. 10 ml complies with limit test E. Prepare the reference solution using 20 ml of *lead standard solution (1 ppm Pb) R*.

**Water** (*2.5.12*)
Maximum 4.0 per cent, determined on 0.300 g.

**Sulphated ash** (*2.4.14*)
Maximum 0.2 per cent, determined on 1.0 g.

**ASSAY**
Liquid chromatography (*2.2.29*) as described in the test for related substances with the following modification.

*Injection* Test solution and reference solution (a).

Calculate the percentage content of $C_{25}H_{43}NO_{18}$ from the areas of the peaks and the declared content of *acarbose CRS*.

**STORAGE**
In an airtight container.

**IMPURITIES**
*Specified impurities* A, B, C, D, E, F, G, H.

A. O-4,6-dideoxy-4-[[(1S,4R,5S,6S)-4,5,6-trihydroxy-3-(hydroxymethyl)cyclohex-2-enyl]amino]-α-D-glucopyranosyl-(1→4)-O-α-D-glucopyranosyl-(1→4)-D-*arabino*-hex-2-ulopyranose,

B. (1R,4R,5S,6R)-4,5,6-trihydroxy-2-(hydroxymethyl)cyclohex-2-enyl 4-O-[4,6-dideoxy-4-[[(1S,4R,5S,6S)-4,5,6-trihydroxy-3-(hydroxymethyl)cyclohex-2-enyl]amino]-α-D-glucopyranosyl]-α-D-glucopyranoside,

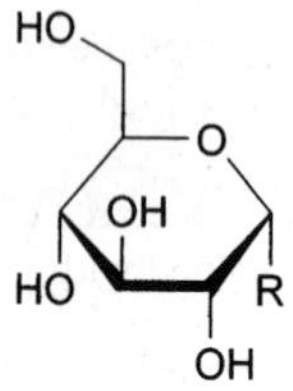

C. α-D-glucopyranosyl 4-O-[4,6-dideoxy-4-[[(1S,4R,5S,6S)-4,5,6-trihydroxy-3-(hydroxymethyl)cyclohex-2-enyl]amino]-α-D-glucopyranosyl]-α-D-glucopyranoside,

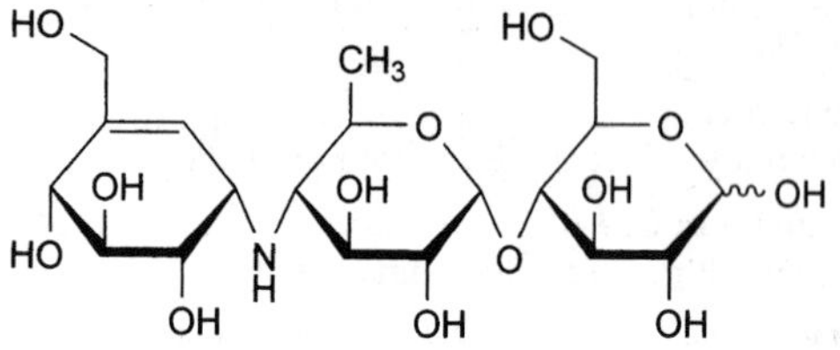

D. 4-O-[4,6-dideoxy-4-[[(1S,4R,5S,6S)-4,5,6-trihydroxy-3-(hydroxymethyl)cyclohex-2-enyl]amino]-α-D-glucopyranosyl]-D-glucopyranose,

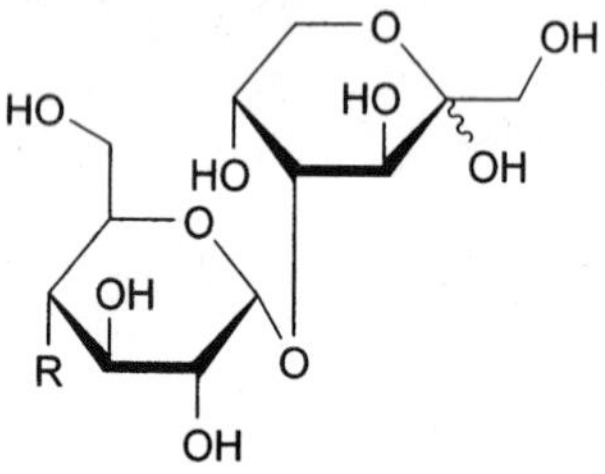

E. O-4,6-dideoxy-4-[[(1S,4R,5S,6S)-4,5,6-trihydroxy-3-(hydroxymethyl)cyclohex-2-enyl]amino]-α-D-glucopyranosyl-(1→4)-O-α-D-glucopyranosyl-(1→4)-O-α-D-glucopyranosyl-(1→4)-D-arabino-hex-2-ulopyranose (4-O-α-acarbosyl-D-fructopyranose),

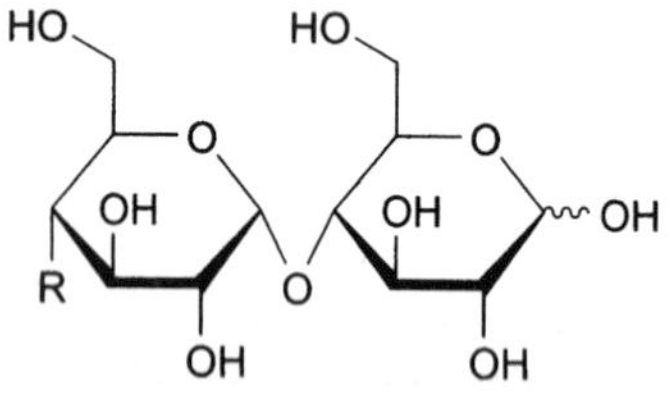

F. O-4,6-dideoxy-4-[[(1S,4R,5S,6S)-4,5,6-trihydroxy-3-(hydroxymethyl)cyclohex-2-enyl]amino]-α-D-glucopyranosyl-(1→4)-O-α-D-glucopyranosyl-(1→4)-O-α-D-glucopyranosyl-(1→4)-D-glucopyranose (4-O-α-acarbosyl-D-glucopyranose),

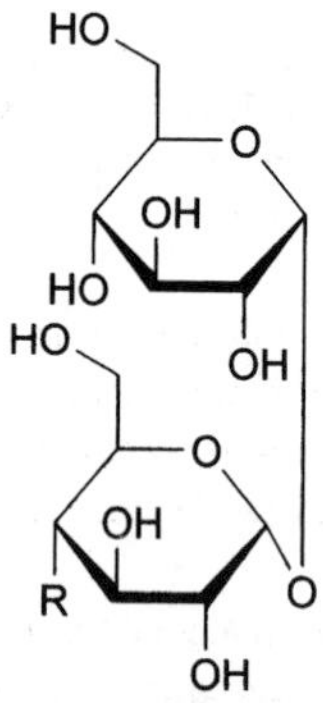

G. α-D-glucopyranosyl O-4,6-dideoxy-4-[[(1S,4R,5S,6S)-4,5,6-trihydroxy-3-(hydroxymethyl)cyclohex-2-enyl]amino]-α-D-glucopyranosyl-(1→4)-O-α-D-glucopyranosyl-(1→4)-O-α-D-glucopyranoside (α-D-glucopyranosyl α-acarboside),

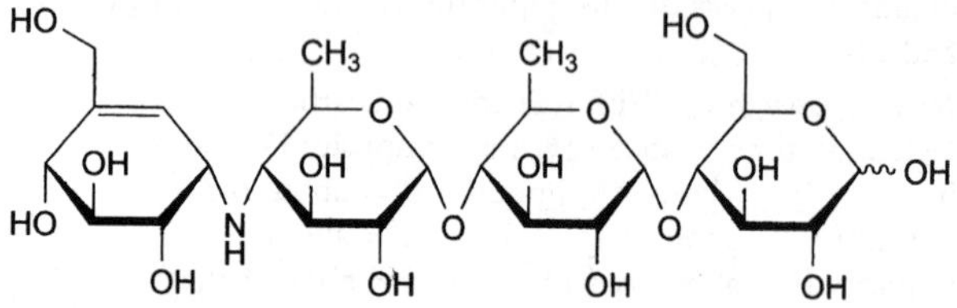

H. O-4,6-dideoxy-4-[[(1S,4R,5S,6S)-4,5,6-trihydroxy-3-(hydroxymethyl)cyclohex-2-enyl]amino]-α-D-glucopyranosyl-(1→4)-O-6-deoxy-α-D-glucopyranosyl-(1→4)-D-glucopyranose.

_____ *Ph Eur*

# Acebutolol Hydrochloride

(*Ph Eur monograph 0871*)

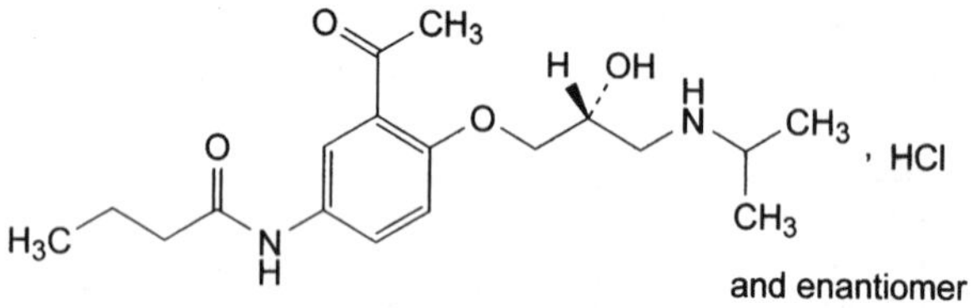

and enantiomer

$C_{18}H_{28}N_2O_4,HCl$      372.9      *34381-68-5*

**Action and use**
Beta-adrenoceptor antagonist.

**Preparations**
Acebutolol Capsules
Acebutolol Tablets

*Ph Eur* _____

## DEFINITION
N-[3-Acetyl-4-[(2RS)-2-hydroxy-3-[(1-methylethyl)amino]propoxy]phenyl]butanamide hydrochloride.

## Content
99.0 per cent to 101.0 per cent (dried substance).

## CHARACTERS
**Appearance**
White or almost white, crystalline powder.

**Solubility**

Freely soluble in water and in ethanol (96 per cent), very slightly soluble in acetone and in methylene chloride.

**mp**

About 143 °C.

## IDENTIFICATION

*First identification   B, D.*

*Second identification   A, C, D.*

A. Ultraviolet and visible absorption spectrophotometry (*2.2.25*).

*Test solution*   Dissolve 20.0 mg in a 0.1 per cent *V/V* solution of *hydrochloric acid R* and dilute to 100.0 ml with the same acid solution. Dilute 5.0 ml of this solution to 100.0 ml with a 0.1 per cent *V/V* solution of *hydrochloric acid R*.

*Spectral range*   220-350 nm.

*Absorption maxima*   At 233 nm and 322 nm.

*Specific absorbance at the absorption maximum*   555 to 605 at 233 nm.

B. Infrared absorption spectrophotometry (*2.2.24*).

*Preparation*   Discs.

*Comparison*   *acebutolol hydrochloride CRS.*

C. Thin-layer chromatography (*2.2.27*).

*Test solution*   Dissolve 20 mg of the substance to be examined in *methanol R* and dilute to 20 ml with the same solvent.

*Reference solution (a)*   Dissolve 20 mg of *acebutolol hydrochloride CRS* in *methanol R* and dilute to 20 ml with the same solvent.

*Reference solution (b)*   Dissolve 20 mg of *pindolol CRS* in *methanol R* and dilute to 20 ml with the same solvent. To 1 ml of this solution add 1 ml of reference solution (a).

*Plate*   TLC silica gel F$_{254}$ *plate R*.

*Mobile phase*   Perchloric acid *R*, methanol *R*, water *R* (5:395:600 *V/V/V*).

*Application*   10 µl.

*Development*   Over 3/4 of the plate.

*Drying*   In air.

*Detection*   Examine in ultraviolet light at 254 nm.

*System suitability*   The chromatogram obtained with reference solution (b) shows 2 clearly separated principal spots.

*Results*   The principal spot in the chromatogram obtained with the test solution is similar in position and size to the principal spot in the chromatogram obtained with reference solution (a).

D It gives reaction (a) of chlorides (*2.3.1*).

## TESTS

### Appearance of solution

The solution is not more opalescent than reference suspension II (*2.2.1*) and not more intensely coloured than reference solution BY$_5$ (*2.2.2, Method II*).

Dissolve 0.5 g in *water R* and dilute to 10 ml with the same solvent.

**pH** (*2.2.3*)

5.0 to 7.0.

Dissolve 0.20 g in *carbon dioxide-free water R* and dilute to 20 ml with the same solvent.

**Related substances**

Liquid chromatography (*2.2.29*).

*Test solution*   Dissolve 0.100 g of the substance to be examined in mobile phase A and dilute to 50.0 ml with mobile phase A.

*Reference solution (a)*   Dissolve 20.0 mg of the substance to be examined in mobile phase A and dilute to 100.0 ml with mobile phase A. Dilute 0.5 ml of this solution to 50.0 ml with mobile phase A.

*Reference solution (b)*   Dissolve the contents of a vial of *acebutolol impurity I CRS* in 1.0 ml of mobile phase A.

*Reference solution (c)*   Mix 2.0 ml of reference solution (a) and 1.0 ml of reference solution (b) and dilute to 10.0 ml with mobile phase A.

*Reference solution (d)*   Dissolve 5.0 mg of *acebutolol impurity C CRS* in 10 ml of *acetonitrile R* and dilute to 25.0 ml with mobile phase A. Dilute 0.5 ml of this solution to 50.0 ml with mobile phase A.

*Reference solution (e)*   Dissolve 5.0 mg of *acebutolol impurity B CRS* in 10.0 ml of *acetonitrile R* and dilute to 25.0 ml with mobile phase A. Dilute 1.0 ml of this solution to 50.0 ml with mobile phase A.

*Column:*
— *size:* $l = 0.125$ m, Ø = 4 mm,
— *stationary phase:* end-capped octadecylsilyl silica gel for chromatography *R* (5 µm),
— *temperature*: 40 °C.

*Mobile phase:*
— *mobile phase A*: mix 2.0 ml of *phosphoric acid R*, and 3.0 ml of *triethylamine R* and dilute to 1000 ml with water *R*;
— *mobile phase B*: mix equal volumes of *acetonitrile R* and mobile phase A;

| Time (min) | Mobile phase A (per cent *V/V*) | Mobile phase B (per cent *V/V*) |
|---|---|---|
| 0 - 2 | 98 | 2 |
| 2 - 30.5 | 98 → 10 | 2 → 90 |
| 30.5 - 41 | 10 | 90 |
| 41 - 42 | 10 → 98 | 90 → 2 |
| 42 - 50 | 98 | 2 |

*Flow rate*   1.2 ml/min.

*Detection*   Spectrophotometer at 240 nm.

*Injection*   25 µl.

*System suitability*   Reference solution (c):
— *resolution*: minimum 7.0 between the peaks due to impurity I and acebutolol.

*Limits:*
— *impurity B*: not more than the area of the principal peak in the chromatogram obtained with reference solution (e) (0.2 per cent);
— *impurity C*: not more than the area of the principal peak in the chromatogram obtained with reference solution (d) (0.1 per cent);
— *impurity I*: not more than twice the area of the principal peak in the chromatogram obtained with reference solution (a) (0.2 per cent);
— *any other impurity*: for each impurity, not more than the area of the principal peak in the chromatogram obtained with reference solution (a) (0.1 per cent);
— *total*: not more than 5 times the area of the principal peak in the chromatogram obtained with reference solution (a) (0.5 per cent);

— *disregard limit*: 0.5 times the area of the principal peak in the chromatogram obtained with reference solution (a) (0.05 per cent).

**Heavy metals** *(2.4.8)*

Maximum 20 ppm.

Dissolve 0.50 g in 20.0 ml of *water R*. The solution complies with test E. Prepare the reference solution by diluting 10.0 ml of *lead standard solution (1 ppm Pb) R* to 20.0 ml with *water R*.

**Loss on drying** *(2.2.32)*

Maximum 0.5 per cent, determined on 1.000 g by drying in an oven at 105 °C for 3 h.

**Sulphated ash** *(2.4.14)*

Maximum 0.1 per cent, determined on 1.0 g.

**ASSAY**

Dissolve 0.300 g in 50 ml of *ethanol (96 per cent) R* and add 1 ml of *0.1 M hydrochloric acid*. Carry out a potentiometric titration *(2.2.20)*, using *0.1 M sodium hydroxide*. Read the volume added between the 2 points of inflexion.

1 ml of *0.1 M sodium hydroxide* is equivalent to 37.29 mg of $C_{18}H_{29}ClN_2O_4$.

**STORAGE**

Protected from light.

**IMPURITIES**

*Specified impurities*   A, B, C, D, E, F, G, H, I, J, K.

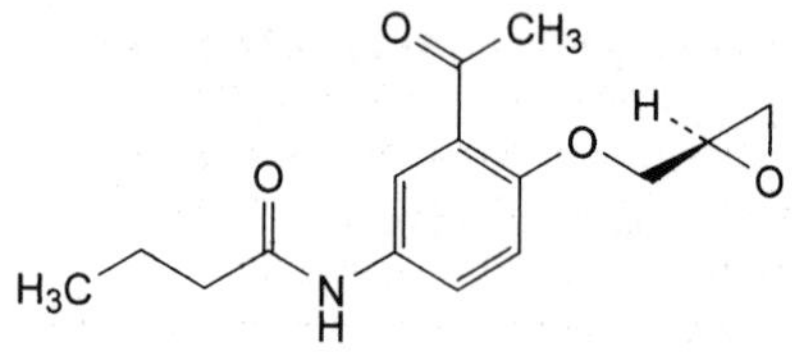

A. *N*-[3-acetyl-4-[(2*RS*)-oxiran-2-ylmethoxy]phenyl]butanamide,

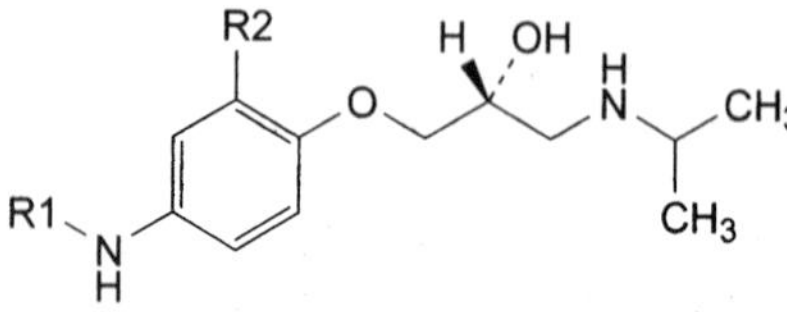

B. R1 = R2 = CO-CH$_3$: *N*-[3-acetyl-4-[(2*RS*)-2-hydroxy-3-[(1-methylethyl)amino]propoxy]phenyl]acetamide (diacetolol),

D. R1 = H, R2 = CO-CH$_3$: 1-[5-amino-2-[(2*RS*)-2-hydroxy-3-[(1-methylethyl)amino]propoxy]phenyl]ethanone,

E. R1 = CO-CH$_2$-CH$_2$-CH$_3$, R2 = H: *N*-[4-[(2*RS*)-2-hydroxy-3-[(1-methylethyl)amino]propoxy]phenyl]butanamide,

J. R1 = CO-CH$_2$-CH$_3$, R2 = CO-CH$_3$: *N*-[3-acetyl-4-[(2*RS*)-2-hydroxy-3-[(1-methylethyl)amino]propoxy]phenyl]propanamide,

K. R1 = R2 = CO-CH$_2$-CH$_2$-CH$_3$: *N*-[3-butanoyl-4-[(2*RS*)-2-hydroxy-3-[(1-methylethyl)amino]propoxy]phenyl]butanamide,

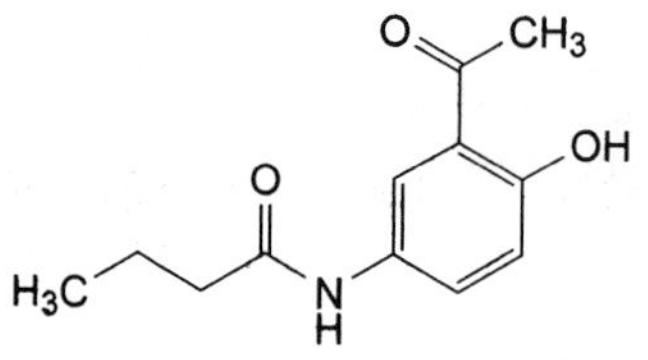

C. *N*-(3-acetyl-4-hydroxyphenyl)butanamide,

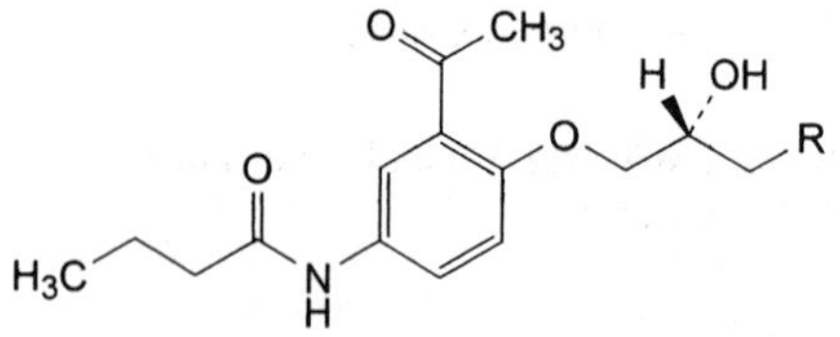

F. R = OH: *N*-[3-acetyl-4-[(2*RS*)-2,3-dihydroxypropoxy]phenyl]butanamide,

I. R = NH-CH$_2$-CH$_3$: *N*-[3-acetyl-4-[(2*RS*)-3-(ethylamino)-2-hydroxypropoxy]phenyl]butanamide,

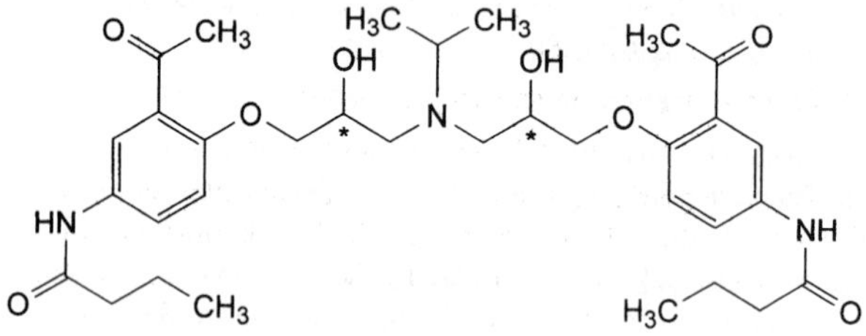

G. *N*,*N'*-[[(1-methylethyl)imino]bis[(2-hydroxypropane-1,3-diyl)oxy(3-acetyl-1,4-phenylene)]]dibutanamide (biamine),

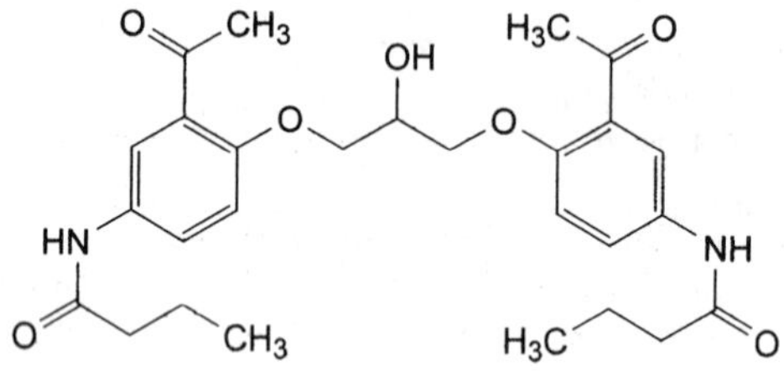

H. *N*,*N'*-[(2-hydroxypropane-1,3-diyl)bis[oxy(3-acetyl-1,4-phenylene)]]dibutanamide.

*Ph Eur*

# Aceclofenac

*(Ph Eur monograph 1281)*

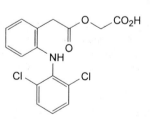

$C_{16}H_{13}Cl_2NO_4$          354.2          *89796-99-6*

**Action and use**

Cyclo-oxygenase inhibitor; analgesic; anti-inflammatory.

Ph Eur

## DEFINITION

[[[2-[(2,6-Dichlorophenyl)amino]phenyl]acetyl]oxy]acetic acid.

## Content

99.0 per cent to 101.0 per cent (dried substance).

## CHARACTERS

### Appearance

White or almost white, crystalline powder.

### Solubility

Practically insoluble in water, freely soluble in acetone, soluble in ethanol (96 per cent).

## IDENTIFICATION

*First identification  B.*

*Second identification  A, C.*

A. Dissolve 50.0 mg in *methanol R* and dilute to 100.0 ml with the same solvent. Dilute 2.0 ml of the solution to 50.0 ml with *methanol R*. Examined between 220 nm and 370 nm (*2.2.25*), the solution shows an absorption maximum at 275 nm. The specific absorbance at the absorption maximum is 320 to 350.

B. Infrared absorption spectrophotometry (*2.2.24*).

*Comparison  Ph. Eur. reference spectrum of aceclofenac.*

C. Dissolve about 10 mg in 10 ml of *ethanol (96 per cent) R*. To 1 ml of the solution, add 0.2 ml of a mixture, prepared immediately before use, of equal volumes of a 6 g/l solution of *potassium ferricyanide R* and a 9 g/l solution of *ferric chloride R*. Allow to stand protected from light for 5 min. Add 3 ml of a 10.0 g/l solution of *hydrochloric acid R*. Allow to stand protected from light for 15 min. A blue colour develops and a precipitate is formed.

## TESTS

### Related substances

Liquid chromatography (*2.2.29*). *Prepare the solutions immediately before use.*

*Test solution*  Dissolve 50.0 mg of the substance to be examined in a mixture of 30 volumes of mobile phase A and 70 volumes of mobile phase B and dilute to 25.0 ml with the same mixture of solvents.

*Reference solution (a)*  Dissolve 21.6 mg of *diclofenac sodium CRS* (impurity A) in a mixture of 30 volumes of mobile phase A and 70 volumes of mobile phase B and dilute to 50.0 ml with the same mixture of solvents.

*Reference solution (b)*  Dilute 2.0 ml of the test solution to 10.0 ml with a mixture of 30 volumes of mobile phase A and 70 volumes of mobile phase B.

*Reference solution (c)*  Mix 1.0 ml of reference solution (a) and 1.0 ml of reference solution (b) and dilute to 100.0 ml with a mixture of 30 volumes of mobile phase A and 70 volumes of mobile phase B.

*Reference solution (d)*  Dissolve 4.0 mg of *aceclofenac impurity F CRS* and 2.0 mg of *aceclofenac impurity H CRS* in a mixture of 30 volumes of mobile phase A and 70 volumes of mobile phase B then dilute to 10.0 ml with the same mixture of solvents.

*Reference solution (e)*  Mix 1.0 ml of reference solution (b) and 1.0 ml of reference solution (d) and dilute to 100.0 ml with a mixture of 30 volumes of mobile phase A and 70 volumes of mobile phase B.

*Reference solution (f)*  Dissolve the contents of a vial of *diclofenac impurity A CRS* (aceclofenac impurity I) in 1.0 ml of a mixture of 30 volumes of mobile phase A and 70 volumes of mobile phase B, add 1.5 ml of the same mixture of solvents and mix.

*Reference solution (g)*  Dissolve 4 mg of *aceclofenac for peak identification CRS* (containing impurities B, C, D, E and G) in 2.0 ml of a mixture of 30 volumes of mobile phase A and 70 volumes of mobile phase B.

*Column:*
— *size: l* = 0.25 m, Ø = 4.6 mm;
— *stationary phase*: spherical *end-capped octadecylsilyl silica gel for chromatography R* (5 μm) with a pore size of 10 nm and a carbon loading of 19 per cent;
— *temperature*: 40 °C.

*Mobile phase:*
— *mobile phase A*: 1.12 g/l solution of *phosphoric acid R* adjusted to pH 7.0 using a 42 g/l solution of *sodium hydroxide R*;
— *mobile phase B: water R, acetonitrile R* (1:9 *V/V*);

| Time (min) | Mobile phase A (per cent *V/V*) | Mobile phase B (per cent *V/V*) |
|---|---|---|
| 0 - 25 | 70 → 50 | 30 → 50 |
| 25 - 30 | 50 → 20 | 50 → 80 |
| 30 - 50 | 20 | 80 |

*Flow rate*  1.0 ml/min.

*Detection*  Spectrophotometer at 275 nm.

*Injection*  10 μl of the test solution and reference solutions (c), (e), (f) and (g).

*Identification of impurities*  Use the chromatogram supplied with *aceclofenac for peak identification CRS* and the chromatogram obtained with reference solution (g) to identify the peaks due to impurities B, C, D, E and G.

*Relative retention*  With reference to aceclofenac (retention time = about 11 min): impurity A = about 0.8; impurity G = about 1.3; impurity H = about 1.5; impurity I = about 2.3; impurity D = about 3.1; impurity B = about 3.2; impurity E = about 3.3; impurity C = about 3.5; impurity F = about 3.7.

*System suitability*  Reference solution (c):
— *resolution*: minimum 5.0 between the peaks due to impurity A and aceclofenac.

*Limits:*
— *impurity A*: not more than the area of the corresponding peak in the chromatogram obtained with reference solution (c) (0.2 per cent);
— *impurities B, C, D, E, G*: for each impurity, not more than the area of the peak due to aceclofenac in the chromatogram obtained with reference solution (e) (0.2 per cent);
— *impurity F*: not more than the area of the corresponding peak in the chromatogram obtained with reference solution (e) (0.2 per cent);
— *impurity H*: not more than the area of the corresponding peak in the chromatogram obtained with reference solution (e) (0.1 per cent);
— *impurity I*: not more than the area of the corresponding peak in the chromatogram obtained with reference solution (f) (0.1 per cent);
— *unspecified impurities*: not more than 0.5 times the area of the peak due to aceclofenac in the chromatogram obtained with reference solution (e) (0.10 per cent);
— *total*: not more than 0.7 per cent;
— *disregard limit*: 0.1 times the area of the peak due to aceclofenac in the chromatogram obtained with reference solution (e) (0.02 per cent).

**Heavy metals** (*2.4.8*)
Maximum 10 ppm.

To 2.0 g in a silica crucible, add 2 ml of *sulphuric acid R* to wet the substance. Heat progressively to ignition and continue heating until an almost white or at most a greyish residue is obtained. Carry out the ignition at a temperature not exceeding 800 °C. Allow to cool. Add 3 ml of *hydrochloric acid R* and 1 ml of *nitric acid R*. Heat and evaporate slowly to dryness. Cool and add 1 ml of a 100 g/l solution of *hydrochloric acid R* and 10.0 ml of *distilled water R*. Neutralise with a 1.0 g/l solution of *ammonia R* using 0.1 ml of *phenolphthalein solution R* as indicator. Add 2.0 ml of a 60 g/l solution of *anhydrous acetic acid R* and dilute to 20 ml with *distilled water R*. 12 ml of the solution complies with test A. Prepare the reference solution using *lead standard solution (1 ppm Pb) R*.

**Loss on drying** (*2.2.32*)
Maximum 0.5 per cent, determined on 1.000 g by drying in an oven at 105 °C.

**Sulphated ash** (*2.4.14*)
Maximum 0.1 per cent, determined on 1.0 g.

## ASSAY
Dissolve 0.300 g in 40 ml of *methanol R*. Titrate with *0.1 M sodium hydroxide*, determining the end-point potentiometrically (*2.2.20*).

1 ml of *0.1 M sodium hydroxide* is equivalent to 35.42 mg of $C_{16}H_{13}Cl_2NO_4$.

## STORAGE
In an airtight container, protected from light.

## IMPURITIES
*Specified impurities* A, B, C, D, E, F, G, H, I.

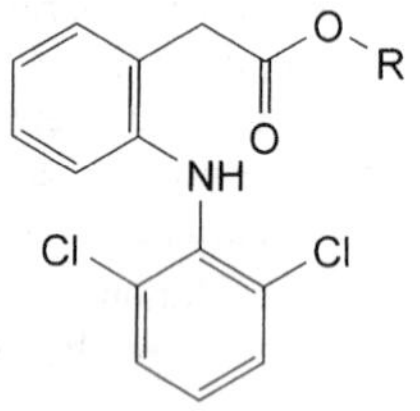

A. R = H: [2-[(2,6-dichlorophenyl)amino]phenyl]acetic acid (diclofenac),

B. R = CH₃: methyl [2-[(2,6-dichlorophenyl)amino]phenyl]acetate (methyl ester of diclofenac),

C. R = C₂H₅: ethyl [2-[(2,6-dichlorophenyl)amino]phenyl]acetate (ethyl ester of diclofenac),

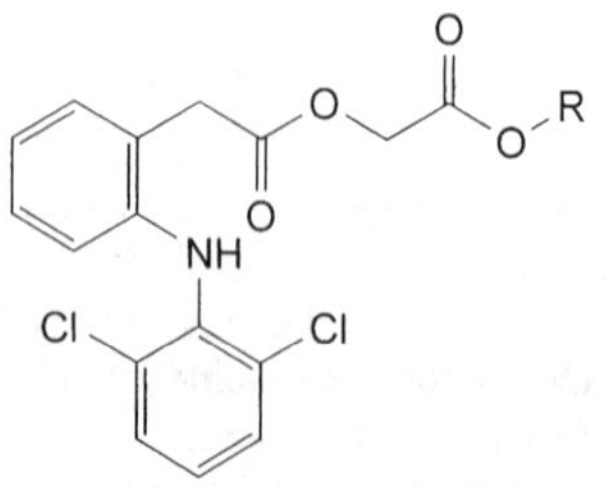

D. R = CH₃: methyl [[[2-[(2,6-dichlorophenyl)amino]phenyl]acetyl]oxy]acetate (methyl ester of aceclofenac),

E. R = C₂H₅: ethyl [[[2-[(2,6-dichlorophenyl)amino]phenyl]acetyl]oxy]acetate (ethyl ester of aceclofenac),

F. R = CH₂-C₆H₅: benzyl [[[2-[(2,6-dichlorophenyl)amino]phenyl]acetyl]oxy]acetate (benzyl ester of aceclofenac),

G. R = CH₂-CO₂H: [[[[[2-[(2,6-dichlorophenyl)amino]phenyl]acetyl]oxy]acetyl]oxy]acetic acid (acetic aceclofenac),

H. R = CH₂-CO-O-CH₂-CO₂H: [[[[[[[2-[(2,6-dichlorophenyl)amino]phenyl]acetyl]oxy]acetyl]oxy]acetyl]oxy]acetic acid (diacetic aceclofenac),

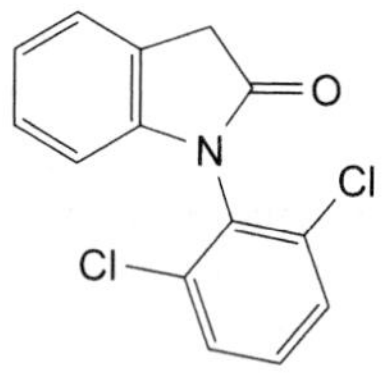

I. 1-(2,6-dichlorophenyl)-1,3-dihydro-2H-indol-2-one.

*Ph Eur*

# Acemetacin

(*Ph Eur monograph 1686*)

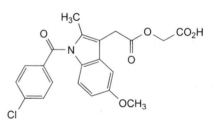

$C_{21}H_{18}ClNO_6$         415.8         *53164-05-9*

**Action and use**
Cyclo-oxygenase inhibitor; analgesic; anti-inflammatory.

*Ph Eur*

## DEFINITION
[[[1-(4-Chlorobenzoyl)-5-methoxy-2-methyl-1H-indol-3-yl]acetyl]oxy]acetic acid.

**Content**
99.0 per cent to 101.0 per cent (dried substance).

## CHARACTERS
**Appearance**
Yellow or greenish-yellow, crystalline powder.

**Solubility**
Practically insoluble in water, soluble in acetone, slightly soluble in anhydrous ethanol.

It shows polymorphism (*5.9*).

## IDENTIFICATION
Infrared absorption spectrophotometry (*2.2.24*).

*Comparison* acemetacin CRS.

If the spectra obtained in the solid state show differences, dissolve the substance to be examined and the reference substance separately in *acetone R*, evaporate to dryness and record new spectra using the residues.

## TESTS
### Related substances
Liquid chromatography (2.2.29).

*Test solution*   Dissolve 0.100 g of the substance to be examined in *acetonitrile for chromatography R* and dilute to 20.0 ml with the same solvent.

*Reference solution (a)*   Dilute 5.0 ml of the test solution to 50.0 ml with *acetonitrile for chromatography R*. Dilute 1.0 ml of this solution to 100.0 ml with *acetonitrile for chromatography R*.

*Reference solution (b)*   Dissolve 5.0 mg of *acemetacin impurity A CRS* and 10.0 mg of *indometacin CRS* (impurity B) in *acetonitrile for chromatography R*, and dilute to 50.0 ml with the same solvent.

*Reference solution (c)*   Dilute 1.0 ml of reference solution (b) to 20.0 ml with *acetonitrile for chromatography R*.

*Reference solution (d)*   To 1 ml of reference solution (b), add 10 ml of the test solution and dilute to 20 ml with *acetonitrile for chromatography R*.

*Reference solution (e)*   Dissolve the contents of a vial of *acemetacin impurity mixture CRS* (containing impurities C, D, E and F) in 1.0 ml of the test solution.

*Column:*
— *size: l* = 0.25 m, Ø = 4 mm;
— *stationary phase: spherical end-capped octadecylsilyl silica gel for chromatography R* (5 µm);
— *temperature:* 40 °C.

*Mobile phase:*
— *mobile phase A:* dissolve 1.0 g of *potassium dihydrogen phosphate R* in 900 ml of *water R*, adjust to pH 6.5 with *1 M sodium hydroxide* and dilute to 1000 ml with *water R*;
— *mobile phase B: acetonitrile for chromatography R*;

| Time (min) | Mobile phase A (per cent *V/V*) | Mobile phase B (per cent *V/V*) |
|---|---|---|
| 0 - 5 | 95 | 5 |
| 5 - 9 | 95 → 65 | 5 → 35 |
| 9 - 16 | 65 | 35 |
| 16 - 28 | 65 → 20 | 35 → 80 |
| 28 - 34 | 20 | 80 |

*Flow rate*   1.0 ml/min.

*Detection*   Spectrophotometer at 235 nm.

*Injection*   20 µl.

*Identification of impurities:*
— use the chromatogram supplied with *acemetacin impurity mixture CRS* and the chromatogram obtained with reference solution (e) to identify the peaks due to impurities C, D, E and F;
— use the chromatogram obtained with reference solution (b) to identify the peak due to impurity B.

*Relative retention*   With reference to acemetacin (retention time = about 15 min): impurity A = about 0.7; impurity B = about 0.9; impurity F = about 1.2; impurity C = about 1.3; impurity D = about 1.5; impurity E = about 2.2.

*System suitability*   Reference solution (d):
— *peak-to-valley ratio:* minimum 15, where $H_p$ = height above the baseline of the peak due to impurity B and $H_v$ = height above the baseline of the lowest point of the curve separating this peak from the peak due to acemetacin.

*Limits:*
— *correction factors:* for the calculation of content, multiply the peak areas of the following impurities by the corresponding correction factor: impurity C = 1.3; impurity D = 1.4; impurity F = 1.3;
— *impurity E:* not more than 3 times the area of the principal peak in the chromatogram obtained with reference solution (a) (0.3 per cent);
— *impurity B:* not more than the area of the corresponding peak in the chromatogram obtained with reference solution (c) (0.2 per cent);
— *impurity A:* not more than the area of the corresponding peak in the chromatogram obtained with reference solution (c) (0.1 per cent);
— *impurities C, D, F:* for each impurity, not more than the area of the principal peak in the chromatogram obtained with reference solution (a) (0.1 per cent);
— *unspecified impurities:* for each impurity, not more than the area of the principal peak in the chromatogram obtained with reference solution (a) (0.10 per cent);
— *total:* not more than 4 times the area of the principal peak in the chromatogram obtained with reference solution (a) (0.4 per cent);
— *disregard limit:* 0.5 times the area of the principal peak in the chromatogram obtained with reference solution (a) (0.05 per cent).

### Heavy metals
Maximum 20 ppm.

*Solvent mixture*   methanol R, acetone R (10:90 *V/V*).

*Test solution*   Dissolve 0.250 g of the substance to be examined in 20 ml of the solvent mixture.

*Reference solution*   Dilute 0.5 ml of *lead standard solution (10 ppm Pb) R* to 20 ml with the solvent mixture.

*Blank solution*   20 ml of the solvent mixture.

*Monitor solution*   Dissolve 0.250 g of the substance to be examined in 0.5 ml of *lead standard solution (10 ppm Pb) R* and dilute to 20 ml with the solvent mixture.

To each solution, add 2 ml of *buffer solution pH 3.5 R*. Mix and add to 1.2 ml of *thioacetamide reagent R*. Mix immediately. Filter the solutions through a membrane filter (nominal pore size 0.45 µm) (2.4.8). Compare the spots on the filters obtained with the different solutions. The test is invalid if the reference solution does not show a slight brown colour compared to the blank solution. The substance to be examined complies with the test if the brown colour of the spot resulting from the test solution is not more intense than that of the spot resulting from the reference solution.

### Loss on drying (2.2.32)
Maximum 0.5 per cent, determined on 1.000 g by drying in an oven at 105 °C.

### Sulphated ash (2.4.14)
Maximum 0.1 per cent, determined on 1.0 g.

## ASSAY
Dissolve 0.350 g in 20 ml of *acetone R* and add 10 ml of *water R*. Titrate with *0.1 M sodium hydroxide*, determining the end-point potentiometrically (2.2.20).

1 ml of *0.1 M sodium hydroxide* is equivalent to 41.58 mg of $C_{21}H_{18}ClNO_6$.

## STORAGE
Protected from light.

## IMPURITIES
*Specified impurities* *A, B, C, D, E, F.*

A. 4-chlorobenzoic acid,

B. R1 = R2 = R3 = H: indometacin,

C. R1 = Cl, R2 = H, R3 = CH$_2$-CO$_2$H:
[[[1-(3,4-dichlorobenzoyl)-5-methoxy-2-methyl-1*H*-indol-3-yl]acetyl]oxy]acetic acid,

D. R1 = H, R2 = C(CH$_3$)$_3$, R3 = CH$_2$-CO$_2$H:
[[[1-(4-chlorobenzoyl)-6-(1,1-dimethylethyl)-5-methoxy-2-methyl-1*H*-indol-3-yl]acetyl]oxy]acetic acid,

E. R1 = R2 = H, R3 = CH$_2$-CO-O-C(CH$_3$)$_3$:
1,1-dimethylethyl [[[1-(4-chlorobenzoyl)-5-methoxy-2-methyl-1*H*-indol-3-yl]acetyl]oxy]acetate,

F. R1 = R2 = H, R3 = CH$_2$-CO-O-CH$_2$-CO$_2$H:
[[[[[1-(4-chlorobenzoyl)-5-methoxy-2-methyl-1*H*-indol-3-yl]acetyl]oxy]acetyl]oxy]acetic acid.

*Ph Eur*

# Acenocoumarol

and enantiomer

C$_{19}$H$_{15}$NO$_6$        353.3        *152-72-7*

## Action and use
Vitamin K epoxide reductase inhibitor; oral anticoagulant.

## Preparation
Acenocoumarol Tablets

## DEFINITION
Acenocoumarol is (*RS*)-4-hydroxy-3-(1-*p*-nitrophenyl-3-oxobutyl)coumarin. It contains not less than 98.5% and not more than 100.5% of C$_{19}$H$_{15}$NO$_6$, calculated with reference to the dried substance.

## CHARACTERISTICS
An almost white to buff powder.

Practically insoluble in *water* and in *ether*; slightly soluble in *ethanol (96%)*. It dissolves in aqueous solutions of the alkali hydroxides. It exhibits polymorphism.

## IDENTIFICATION
The *infrared absorption spectrum*, Appendix II A, is concordant with the *reference spectrum* of acenocoumarol *(RS 001)*. If the spectra are not concordant, dissolve 0.1 g of the substance being examined in 10 ml of *acetone* and add *water* drop wise until the solution becomes turbid. Heat on a water bath until the solution is clear and allow to stand. Filter, wash the crystals with a mixture of equal volumes of *acetone* and *water* and dry at 100° at a pressure of 2 kPa for 30 minutes. Prepare a new spectrum of the residue.

## TESTS
### Clarity and colour of solution
A. A 2.0% w/v solution in *acetone* is *clear*, Appendix IV A.

B. The *absorbance* of a 4-cm layer of a 2.0% w/v solution in *acetone* at 460 nm is not more than 0.12, Appendix II B.

C. A 2.0% w/v solution in 0.1M *sodium hydroxide* is *clear*, Appendix IV A, and yellow.

### Light absorption
*Absorbance* of a 0.001% w/v solution in a mixture of 1 volume of 1M *hydrochloric acid* and 9 volumes of *methanol* at the maximum at 306 nm, 0.50 to 0.54, calculated with reference to the dried substance, Appendix II B.

### Related substances
Carry out the method for *thin-layer chromatography*, Appendix III A, using *silica gel GF$_{254}$* as the coating substance and a mixture of 50 volumes of *dichloromethane*, 50 volumes of *cyclohexane* and 20 volumes of *glacial acetic acid* as the mobile phase. Apply separately to the plate 20 µl of each of two solutions of the substance being examined in *acetone* containing (1) 2.0% w/v and (2) 0.0020% w/v. After removal of the plate, allow it to dry in air and immediately examine under *ultraviolet light (254 nm)*. Any *secondary spot* in the chromatogram obtained with solution (1) is not more intense than the spot in the chromatogram obtained with solution (2) (0.1%).

### Loss on drying
When dried to constant weight at 105°, loses not more than 0.5% of its weight. Use 1 g.

### Sulphated ash
Not more than 0.1%, Appendix IX A.

## ASSAY
Dissolve 0.6 g in 50 ml of *acetone* and titrate with 0.1M *sodium hydroxide VS* using *bromothymol blue solution R3* as indicator. Repeat the operation without the substance being examined. The difference between the titrations represents the amount of sodium hydroxide required. Each ml of 0.1M *sodium hydroxide VS* is equivalent to 35.33 mg of C$_{19}$H$_{15}$NO$_6$.

# Acesulfame Potassium

(*Ph Eur monograph 1282*)

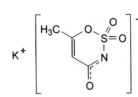

C$_4$H$_4$KNO$_4$S            201.2            *55589-62-3*

**Action and use**
Sweetening agent.

*Ph Eur*

## DEFINITION
Potassium 6-methyl-1,2,3-oxathiazin-4-olate 2,2-dioxide.

## Content
99.0 per cent to 101.0 per cent (dried substance).

## CHARACTERS
**Appearance**
White or almost white, crystalline powder or colourless crystals.

**Solubility**
Soluble in water, very slightly soluble in acetone and in ethanol (96 per cent).

## IDENTIFICATION
*First identification*   A, C.

*Second identification*   B, C.

A. Infrared absorption spectrophotometry (*2.2.24*).

*Comparison*   acesulfame potassium CRS.

B. Thin-layer chromatography (*2.2.27*).

*Test solution*   Dissolve 5 mg of the substance to be examined in *water R* and dilute to 5 ml with the same solvent.

*Reference solution (a)*   Dissolve 5 mg of *acesulfame potassium CRS* in *water R* and dilute to 5 ml with the same solvent.

*Reference solution (b)*   Dissolve 5 mg of *acesulfame potassium CRS* and 5 mg of *saccharin sodium R* in *water R* and dilute to 5 ml with the same solvent.

*Plate*   *Cellulose for chromatography R* as the coating substance.

*Mobile phase*   *Concentrated ammonia R, acetone R, ethyl acetate R* (10:60:60 *V/V/V*).

*Application*   5 μl as bands.

*Development*   Twice over a path of 15 cm.

*Drying*   In a current of warm air.

*Detection*   Examine in ultraviolet light at 254 nm.

*System suitability*   Reference solution (b):
— the chromatogram shows 2 clearly separated bands.

*Results*   The principal band in the chromatogram obtained with the test solution is similar in position and size to the principal band in the chromatogram obtained with reference solution (a).

C. 0.5 ml of solution S (see Tests) gives reaction (b) of potassium (*2.3.1*).

## TESTS
**Solution S**
Dissolve 10.0 g in *carbon dioxide-free water R* and dilute to 50 ml with the same solvent.

**Appearance of solution**
Solution S is clear (*2.2.1*) and colourless (*2.2.2, Method II*).

**Acidity or alkalinity**
To 20 ml of solution S add 0.1 ml of *bromothymol blue solution R1*. Not more than 0.2 ml of *0.01 M hydrochloric acid* or *0.01 M sodium hydroxide* is required to change the colour of the indicator.

**Impurity A**
Thin-layer chromatography (*2.2.27*).

*Test solution*   Dissolve 0.80 g of the substance to be examined in *water R* and dilute to 10 ml with the same solvent.

*Reference solution (a)*   Dissolve 50 mg of *acetylacetamide R* (impurity A) in *water R* and dilute to 25 ml with the same solvent. To 5 ml of the solution add 45 ml of *water R* and dilute to 100 ml with *methanol R*.

*Reference solution (b)*   To 10 ml of reference solution (a) add 1 ml of the test solution and dilute to 20 ml with *methanol R*.

*Plate*   *TLC silica gel plate R*.

*Mobile phase*   *water R, ethanol (96 per cent) R, ethyl acetate R* (2:15:74 *V/V/V*).

*Application*   5 μl.

*Development*   Over a path of 15 cm.

*Drying*   In air until the solvents are completely removed.

*Detection*   Spray with *phosphoric vanillin solution R* and heat at 120 °C for about 10 min; examine in daylight.

*System suitability*   The chromatogram obtained with reference solution (a) shows a clearly visible spot and the chromatogram obtained with reference solution (b) shows 2 clearly separated spots.

*Limit:*
— *impurity A*: any spot due to impurity A is not more intense than the spot in the chromatogram obtained with reference solution (a) (0.125 per cent).

**Related substances**
Liquid chromatography (*2.2.29*).

*Test solution*   Dissolve 0.100 g of the substance to be examined in *water R* and dilute to 10.0 ml with the same solvent.

*Reference solution (a)*   Dissolve 4.0 mg of *acesulfame potassium impurity B CRS* in *water R* and dilute to 100.0 ml with the same solvent. Dilute 1.0 ml of this solution to 200.0 ml with *water R*.

*Reference solution (b)*   Dissolve 0.100 g of the substance to be examined in reference solution (a) and dilute to 10.0 ml with the same solution.

*Reference solution (c)*   Dilute 1.0 ml of the test solution to 100.0 ml with *water R*. Dilute 1.0 ml of this solution to 10.0 ml with *water R*.

*Column:*
— *size: l* = 0.25 m, Ø = 4.6 mm,
— *stationary phase: octadecylsilyl silica gel for chromatography R* (3 μm).

*Mobile phase*   Mix 40 volumes of *acetonitrile R* and 60 volumes of a 3.3 g/l solution of *tetrabutylammonium hydrogen sulphate R*.

*Flow rate*   1 ml/min.

*Detection*   Spectrophotometer at 234 nm.

*Injection*   20 μl.

*Run time*   3 times the retention time of acesulfame.

*Relative retention* With reference to acesulfame (retention time = about 5.3 min): impurity B = about 1.6.

*System suitability:*
— *peak-to-valley ratio*: minimum 1.2, where $H_p$ = height above the baseline of the peak due to impurity B and $H_v$ = height above the baseline of the lowest point of the curve separating this peak from the peak due to acesulfame in the chromatogram obtained with reference solution (b).

*Limits:*
— *impurity B*: not more than the area of the principal peak in the chromatogram obtained with reference solution (a) (20 ppm),
— *unspecified impurities*: for each impurity, not more than the area of the principal peak in the chromatogram obtained with reference solution (c) (0.1 per cent),
— *total*: not more than the area of the principal peak in the chromatogram obtained with reference solution (c) (0.1 per cent),
— *disregard limit*: 0.5 times the area of the principal peak in the chromatogram obtained with reference solution (c) except for the peak due to impurity B (0.05 per cent).

**Fluorides**

Maximum 3 ppm.

Potentiometry (*2.2.36, Method I*).

*Test solution* Dissolve 3.000 g of the substance to be examined in *distilled water R*, add 15.0 ml of *total-ionic-strength-adjustment buffer R1* and dilute to 50.0 ml with *distilled water R*.

*Reference solutions* To 0.5 ml, 1.0 ml, 1.5 ml and 3.0 ml of *fluoride standard solution (10 ppm F) R* add 15.0 ml of *total-ionic-strength-adjustment buffer R1* and dilute to 50.0 ml with *distilled water R*.

*Indicator electrode* Fluoride-selective.

*Reference electrode* Silver-silver chloride.

**Heavy metals** (*2.4.8*)
Maximum 5 ppm.

12 ml of solution S complies with test A. Prepare the reference solution using *lead standard solution (1 ppm Pb) R*.

**Loss on drying** (*2.2.32*)
Maximum 1.0 per cent, determined on 1.000 g by drying in an oven at 105 °C for 3 h.

**ASSAY**

Dissolve 0.150 g in 50 ml of *anhydrous acetic acid R*. Titrate with *0.1 M perchloric acid*, determining the end-point potentiometrically (*2.2.20*).

1 ml of *0.1 M perchloric acid* is equivalent to 20.12 mg of $C_4H_4KNO_4S$.

**IMPURITIES**

*Specified impurities* A, B.

A. 3-oxobutanamide (acetylacetamide),

B. 5-chloro-6-methyl-1,2,3-oxathiazin-4(3*H*)-one 2,2-dioxide.

*Ph Eur*

# Acetazolamide

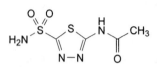

(*Ph Eur monograph 0454*)

$C_4H_6N_4O_3S_2$      222.2      59-66-5

**Action and use**
Carbonic anhydrase inhibitor; diuretic; treatment of glaucoma and ocular hypertension; treatment of mountain sickness.

**Preparation**
Acetazolamide Tablets

*Ph Eur*

**DEFINITION**
*N*-(5-Sulphamoyl-1,3,4-thiadiazol-2-yl)acetamide.

**Content**
98.5 per cent to 101.0 per cent (dried substance).

**CHARACTERS**

**Appearance**
White or almost white, crystalline powder.

**Solubility**
Very slightly soluble in water, slightly soluble in ethanol (96 per cent). It dissolves in dilute solutions of alkali hydroxides.

It shows polymorphism (*5.9*).

**IDENTIFICATION**
*First identification* A, B.
*Second identification* A, C, D.

A. Ultraviolet and visible absorption spectrophotometry (*2.2.25*).

*Solution A* Dissolve 30.0 mg in *0.01 M sodium hydroxide* and dilute to 100.0 ml with the same solvent. Dilute 10.0 ml of the solution to 100.0 ml with *0.01 M sodium hydroxide*.

*Solution B* Dilute 25.0 ml of solution A to 100.0 ml with *0.01 M sodium hydroxide*.

*Spectral range* 230-260 nm for solution A; 260-350 nm for solution B.

*Absorption maximum* At 240 nm for solution A; at 292 nm for solution B.

*Specific absorbance at the absorption maximum* 162 to 176 for solution A; 570 to 620 for solution B.

B. Infrared absorption spectrophotometry (*2.2.24*).

*Comparison* acetazolamide CRS.

If the spectra obtained in the solid state show differences, dissolve the substance to be examined and the reference substance separately in *ethanol (96 per cent) R*, evaporate to dryness and record new spectra using the residues.

C. Introduce about 20 mg into a test-tube and add 4 ml of *dilute hydrochloric acid R* and 0.2 g of *zinc powder R*. Immediately place a piece of *lead acetate paper R* over the mouth of the tube. The paper shows a brownish-black colour.

D. Dissolve about 25 mg in a mixture of 0.1 ml of *dilute sodium hydroxide solution R* and 5 ml of *water R*. Add 0.1 ml of *copper sulphate solution R*. A greenish-blue precipitate is formed.

## TESTS

### Appearance of solution
The solution is not more opalescent than reference suspension II (*2.2.1*) and not more intensely coloured than reference solution $Y_5$ or $BY_5$ (*2.2.2, Method II*).

Dissolve 1.0 g in 10 ml of *1 M sodium hydroxide*.

### Related substances
Liquid chromatography (*2.2.29*).

*Test solution*    Dissolve 40 mg of the substance to be examined in the mobile phase and dilute to 100.0 ml with the mobile phase.

*Reference solution (a)*    Dilute 1.0 ml of the test solution to 100.0 ml with the mobile phase. Dilute 1.0 ml of this solution to 10.0 ml with the mobile phase.

*Reference solution (b)*    Dissolve the contents of a vial of *acetazolamide for system suitability CRS* (containing impurities A, B, C, D, E and F) in 1.0 ml of the mobile phase.

*Column:*
— *size*: $l$ = 0.15 m, Ø = 4.6 mm;
— *stationary phase*: *end-capped propoxybenzene silica gel for chromatography R* (4 μm).

*Mobile phase*    *acetonitrile for chromatography R*, 6.8 g/l solution of *potassium dihydrogen phosphate R* (10:90 *V/V*).

*Flow rate*    1.0 ml/min.

*Detection*    Spectrophotometer at 265 nm.

*Injection*    25 μl.

*Run time*    3.5 times the retention time of acetazolamide.

*Identification of impurities*    Use the chromatogram supplied with *acetazolamide for system suitability CRS* and the chromatogram obtained with reference solution (b) to identify the peaks due to impurities A, B, C, D, E and F.

*Relative retention*    With reference to acetazolamide (retention time = about 8 min): impurity E = about 0.3; impurity D = about 0.4; impurity B = about 0.6; impurity C = about 1.4; impurity A = about 2.1; impurity F = about 2.6.

*System suitability*    Reference solution (b):
— *resolution*: minimum 2.0 between the peaks due to impurities E and D.

*Limits:*
— *correction factors*: for the calculation of content, multiply the peak areas of the following impurities by the corresponding correction factor: impurity B = 2.3; impurity C = 2.6; impurity D = 1.6;
— *impurities A, B, C, D, E, F*: for each impurity, not more than 1.5 times the area of the principal peak in the chromatogram obtained with reference solution (a) (0.15 per cent);
— *unspecified impurities*: for each impurity, not more than the area of the principal peak in the chromatogram obtained with reference solution (a) (0.10 per cent);

— *total*: not more than 6 times the area of the principal peak in the chromatogram obtained with reference solution (a) (0.6 per cent);
— *disregard limit*: 0.5 times the area of the principal peak in the chromatogram obtained with reference solution (a) (0.05 per cent).

### Sulphates (*2.4.13*)
Maximum 500 ppm.

To 0.4 g add 20 ml of *distilled water R* and dissolve by heating to boiling. Allow to cool with frequent shaking and filter.

### Heavy metals (*2.4.8*)
Maximum 20 ppm.

1.0 g complies with test C. Prepare the reference solution using 2 ml of *lead standard solution (10 ppm Pb) R*.

### Loss on drying (*2.2.32*)
Maximum 0.5 per cent, determined on 1.000 g by drying in an oven at 105 °C.

### Sulphated ash (*2.4.14*)
Maximum 0.1 per cent, determined on 1.0 g.

## ASSAY
Dissolve 0.200 g in 25 ml of *dimethylformamide R*. Titrate with *0.1 M ethanolic sodium hydroxide*, determining the end-point potentiometrically (*2.2.20*).

1 ml of *0.1 M ethanolic sodium hydroxide* is equivalent to 22.22 mg of $C_4H_6N_4O_3S_2$.

## IMPURITIES
*Specified impurities*    *A, B, C, D, E, F.*

*Other detectable impurities*    (The following substances would, if present at a sufficient level, be detected by one or other of the tests in the monograph. They are limited by the general acceptance criterion for other/unspecified impurities and/or by the general monograph *Substances for pharmaceutical use (2034)*. It is therefore not necessary to identify these impurities for demonstration of compliance. See also *5.10. Control of impurities in substances for pharmaceutical use*): G.

A. R1 = CO-CH$_3$, R2 = Cl: *N*-(5-chloro-1,3,4-thiadiazol-2-yl)acetamide,

B. R1 = CO-CH$_3$, R2 = H: *N*-(1,3,4-thiadiazol-2-yl)acetamide,

C. R1 = CO-CH$_3$, R2 = SH: *N*-(5-sulphanyl-1,3,4-thiadiazol-2-yl)acetamide,

D. R1 = H, R2 = SO$_2$-NH$_2$: 5-amino-1,3,4-thiadiazole-2-sulphonamide,

E. R1 = CO-CH$_3$, R2 = SO$_2$-OH: 5-acetamido-1,3,4-thiadiazole-2-sulphonic acid,

F. *N*-[5-[(5-acetamido-1,3,4-thiadiazol-2-yl)sulphonyl]sulphamoyl-1,3,4-thiadiazol-2-yl]acetamide,

G. 5-amino-1,3,4-thiadiazole-2-thiol.

*———————————————————————— Ph Eur*

# Glacial Acetic Acid

*(Ph Eur monograph 0590)*

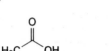

| C₂H₄O₂ | 60.1 | 64-19-7 |
|---|---|---|

$C_2H_4O_2$      60.1      *64-19-7*

*Ph Eur* ————————————————————————

## DEFINITION
**Content**
99.0 per cent *m/m* to 100.5 per cent *m/m*.

## CHARACTERS
**Appearance**
Crystalline mass or clear, colourless, volatile liquid.

**Solubility**
Miscible with water, with ethanol (96 per cent) and with methylene chloride.

## IDENTIFICATION
A. A 100 g/l solution is strongly acid (*2.2.4*).

B. To 0.03 ml add 3 ml of *water R* and neutralise with *dilute sodium hydroxide solution R*. The solution gives reaction (b) of acetates (*2.3.1*).

## TESTS
**Solution S**
Dilute 20 ml to 100 ml with *distilled water R*.

**Appearance**
The substance to be examined is clear (*2.2.1*) and colourless (*2.2.2, Method II*).

**Freezing point** (*2.2.18*)
Minimum 14.8 °C.

**Reducing substances**
To 5.0 ml add 10.0 ml of *water R* and mix. To 5.0 ml of this solution add 6 ml of *sulphuric acid R*, cool and add 2.0 ml of *0.0167 M potassium dichromate*. Allow to stand for 1 min and add 25 ml of *water R* and 1 ml of a freshly prepared 100 g/l solution of *potassium iodide R*. Titrate with *0.1 M sodium thiosulphate*, using 1.0 ml of *starch solution R* as indicator. Not less than 1.0 ml of *0.1 M sodium thiosulphate solution* is required.

**Chlorides** (*2.4.4*)
Maximum 25 mg/l.

Dilute 10 ml of solution S to 15 ml with *water R*.

**Sulphates** (*2.4.13*)
Maximum 50 mg/l, determined on solution S.

**Iron** (*2.4.9*)
Maximum 5 ppm.

Dilute 5.0 ml of solution A obtained in the test for heavy metals to 10.0 ml with *water R*.

**Heavy metals** (*2.4.8*)
Maximum 5 ppm.

Dissolve the residue obtained in the test for residue on evaporation by heating with 2 quantities, each of 15 ml, of *water R* and dilute to 50.0 ml (solution A). 12 ml of solution A complies with test A. Prepare the reference solution using *lead standard solution (2 ppm Pb) R*.

**Residue on evaporation**
Maximum 0.01 per cent.

Evaporate 20 g to dryness on a water-bath and dry at 100-105 °C. The residue weighs a maximum of 2.0 mg.

## ASSAY
Weigh accurately a conical flask with a ground-glass stopper containing 25 ml of *water R*. Add 1.0 ml of the substance to be examined and weigh again accurately. Add 0.5 ml of *phenolphthalein solution R* and titrate with *1 M sodium hydroxide*.

1 ml of *1 M sodium hydroxide* is equivalent to 60.1 mg of $C_2H_4O_2$.

## STORAGE
In an airtight container.

*———————————————————————— Ph Eur*

# Acetic Acid (6 per cent)

Dilute Acetic Acid

## DEFINITION
Acetic Acid (6 per cent) contains not less than 5.7% and not more than 6.3% w/w of acetic acid, $C_2H_4O_2$. It may be prepared by mixing 182 g of Acetic Acid (33 per cent) with 818 g of Purified Water.

## IDENTIFICATION
A. Strongly acidic.

B. When neutralised, yields the reactions characteristic of *acetates*, Appendix VI.

## TESTS
**Weight per ml**
About 1.005 g, Appendix V G.

**Heavy metals**
Evaporate 20.0 ml to dryness and add 20 ml of *water*. 12 ml of the resulting solution complies with *limit test A for heavy metals*, Appendix VII. Use *lead standard solution (1 ppm Pb)* to prepare the standard (1 ppm).

**Chloride**
Dilute 5.0 ml with sufficient *water* to produce 100 ml. 15 ml of the resulting solution complies with the *limit test for chlorides*, Appendix VII (70 ppm).

**Sulphate**
12.5 ml of the solution used in the test for Chloride, diluted to 15 ml with *water*, complies with the *limit test for sulphates*, Appendix VII (240 ppm).

**Aldehydes**
Distil 75 ml. To the first 5 ml of the distillate add 10 ml of a 5% w/v solution of *mercury(II) chloride*, make alkaline with 5M *sodium hydroxide*, allow to stand for 5 minutes and acidify with 1M *sulphuric acid*. The solution shows not more than a faint turbidity.

**Formic acid and oxidisable impurities**
Mix 5 ml with 6 ml of *sulphuric acid* and cool to 20°. Add 0.4 ml of 0.0167M *potassium dichromate VS*, allow to stand for

1 minute, add 25 ml of *water* and 1 ml of freshly prepared *dilute potassium iodide solution* and titrate the liberated iodine with 0.1M *sodium thiosulphate VS* using *starch mucilage* as indicator. Not less than 0.2 ml of 0.1M *sodium thiosulphate VS* is required.

**Readily oxidisable impurities**

To 25 ml add 0.2 ml of 0.02M *potassium permanganate VS* and allow to stand for 1 minute. The pink colour is not entirely discharged.

**Non-volatile matter**

When evaporated to dryness and dried at 105°, leaves not more than 0.01% w/w of residue.

**ASSAY**

Add 30 ml of *water* to 20 g in a stopper flask and titrate with 1M *sodium hydroxide VS* using *phenolphthalein solution R1* as indicator. Each ml of 1M *sodium hydroxide VS* is equivalent to 60.05 mg of $C_2H_4O_2$.

# Acetic Acid (33 per cent)

Acetic Acid

**Preparation**

Acetic Acid (6 per cent)

**DEFINITION**

Acetic Acid (33 per cent) contains not less than 32.5% and not more than 33.5% w/w of acetic acid, $C_2H_4O_2$.

**CHARACTERISTICS**

A clear, colourless liquid.

Miscible with *water*, with *ethanol (96%)* and with *glycerol*.

**IDENTIFICATION**

A. Strongly acidic, even when diluted freely.

B. When neutralised, yields the reactions characteristic of *acetates*, Appendix VI.

**TESTS**

**Weight per ml**

1.040 to 1.042 g, Appendix V G.

**Heavy metals**

Evaporate 10.0 ml to dryness and add 20 ml of *water*. 12 ml of the resulting solution complies with *limit test A for heavy metals*, Appendix VII. Use *lead standard solution (1 ppm Pb)* to prepare the standard (2 ppm).

**Chloride**

Dilute 5.0 ml with sufficient *water* to produce 100 ml. 15 ml of the resulting solution complies with the *limit test for chlorides*, Appendix VII (70 ppm).

**Sulphate**

12.5 ml of the solution used in the test for Chloride, diluted to 15 ml with *water*, complies with the *limit test for sulphates*, Appendix VII (240 ppm).

**Aldehydes**

Distil 15 ml. To the first 5 ml of the distillate add 10 ml of a 5% w/v solution of *mercury(II) chloride*, make alkaline with 5M *sodium hydroxide*, allow to stand for 5 minutes and make acidic with 1M *sulphuric acid*. The solution shows not more than a faint turbidity.

**Formic acid and oxidisable impurities**

Mix 5 ml with 6 ml of *sulphuric acid* and cool to 20°. Add 2 ml of 0.0167M *potassium dichromate VS*, allow to stand for 1 minute, add 25 ml of *water* and 1 ml of freshly prepared *dilute potassium iodide solution* and titrate the liberated iodine

with 0.1M *sodium thiosulphate VS* using *starch mucilage* as indicator. Not less than 1.0 ml of 0.1M *sodium thiosulphate VS* is required.

**Readily oxidisable impurities**

To 5.0 ml add 20 ml of *water* and 0.2 ml of 0.02M *potassium permanganate VS* and allow to stand for 1 minute. The pink colour is not entirely discharged.

**Non-volatile matter**

When evaporated to dryness and dried at 105°, leaves not more than 0.01% w/w of residue.

**ASSAY**

Weigh 5 g into a stopper flask containing 50 ml of *water* and titrate with 1M *sodium hydroxide VS* using *phenolphthalein solution R1* as indicator. Each ml of 1M *sodium hydroxide VS* is equivalent to 60.05 mg of $C_2H_4O_2$.

# Acetone

(*Ph Eur monograph 0872*)

$$H_3C \overset{\overset{\text{O}}{\|}}{\underset{}{C}} CH_3$$

| $C_3H_6O$ | 58.08 | 67-64-1 |
|---|---|---|

*Ph Eur*

**DEFINITION**

Propanone.

**CHARACTERS**

**Appearance**

Volatile, clear, colourless liquid.

**Solubility**

Miscible with water and with ethanol (96 per cent).

The vapour is flammable.

**IDENTIFICATION**

A. It complies with the test for relative density (see Tests).

B. To 1 ml, add 3 ml of *dilute sodium hydroxide solution R* and 0.3 ml of a 25 g/l solution of *sodium nitroprusside R*. An intense red colour is produced which becomes violet with the addition of 3.5 ml of *acetic acid R*.

C. To 10 ml of a 0.1 per cent *V/V* solution of the substance to be examined in *ethanol (50 per cent V/V) R*, add 1 ml of a 10 g/l solution of *nitrobenzaldehyde R* in *ethanol (50 per cent V/V) R* and 0.5 ml of *strong sodium hydroxide solution R*. Allow to stand for about 2 min and acidify with *acetic acid R*. A greenish-blue colour is produced.

**TESTS**

**Appearance of solution**

To 10 ml add 10 ml of *water R*. The solution is clear (*2.2.1*) and colourless (*2.2.2, Method II*).

**Acidity or alkalinity**

To 5 ml add 5 ml of *carbon dioxide-free water R*, 0.15 ml of *phenolphthalein solution R* and 0.5 ml of *0.01 M sodium hydroxide*. The solution is pink. Add 0.7 ml of *0.01 M hydrochloric acid* and 0.05 ml of *methyl red solution R*. The solution is red or orange.

**Relative density** (*2.2.5*)

0.790 to 0.793.

## Reducing substances

To 30 ml add 0.1 ml of *0.02 M potassium permanganate* and allow to stand in the dark for 2 h. The mixture is not completely decolourised.

## Related substances

Gas chromatography (*2.2.28*).

*Test solution* The substance to be examined.

*Reference solution (a)* To 0.5 ml of *methanol R* add 0.5 ml of *2-propanol R* and dilute to 100.0 ml with the test solution. Dilute 1.0 ml of this solution to 10.0 ml with the test solution.

*Reference solution (b)* Dilute 100 μl of *benzene R* to 100.0 ml with the test solution. Dilute 0.20 ml of this solution to 100.0 ml with the test solution.

*Column:*
— *material*: fused silica,
— *size*: $l = 50$ m, Ø = 0.3 mm,
— *stationary phase*: macrogol 20 000 R (film thickness 1 μm).

*Carrier gas* helium for chromatography *R*.

*Linear velocity* 21 cm/s.

*Split ratio* 1:50.

*Temperature:*

|  | Time (min) | Temperature (°C) |
|---|---|---|
| Column | 0 - 11 | 45 → 100 |
|  | 11 - 20 | 100 |
| Injection port |  | 150 |
| Detector |  | 250 |

*Detection* Flame ionisation.

*Injection* 1 μl.

*Retention time* Impurity C = about 7.5 min.

*System suitability:*
— *resolution*: minimum 5.0 between the peak due to impurity A (2nd peak) and the peak due to impurity B (3rd peak) in the chromatogram obtained with reference solution (a),
— *signal-to-noise ratio*: minimum 5 for the peak due to impurity C in the chromatogram obtained with reference solution (b).

*Limits:*
— *impurities A, B*: for each impurity, not more than the difference between the areas of the corresponding peaks in the chromatogram obtained with reference solution (a) and the areas of the corresponding peaks in the chromatogram obtained with the test solution (0.05 per cent *V/V*),
— *impurity C*: not more than the difference between the area of the peak due to impurity C in the chromatogram obtained with reference solution (b) and the area of the corresponding peak in the chromatogram obtained with the test solution (2 ppm *V/V*),
— *any other impurity*: for each impurity, not more than the difference between the area of the peak due to impurity A in the chromatogram obtained with reference solution (a) and the area of the corresponding peak in the chromatogram obtained with the test solution (0.05 per cent *V/V*).

## Matter insoluble in water

Dilute 1.0 ml to 20 ml with *water R*. The solution is clear (*2.2.1*).

## Residue on evaporation

Maximum 50 ppm.

Evaporate 20.0 g to dryness on a water-bath and dry at 100-105 °C. The residue weighs a maximum of 1 mg.

## Water (*2.5.12*)

Maximum 3 g/l, determined on 10.0 ml. Use 20 ml of *anhydrous pyridine R* as solvent.

## STORAGE

Protected from light.

## IMPURITIES

*Specified impurities* *A, B, C*.

A. $CH_3$-OH: methanol,

B. $CH_3$-CHOH-$CH_3$: propan-2-ol (isopropanol),

C. $C_6H_6$: benzene.

*Ph Eur*

# Acetylcholine Chloride

(*Ph Eur monograph 1485*)

$C_7H_{16}ClNO_2$      181.7      *60-31-1*

## Action and use

Cholinoceptor agonist.

*Ph Eur*

## DEFINITION

2-(Acetyloxy)-*N,N,N*-trimethylethanaminium chloride.

## Content

98.5 per cent to 101.5 per cent (dried substance).

## CHARACTERS

### Appearance

White or almost white crystalline powder or colourless crystals, very hygroscopic.

### Solubility

Very soluble in water, freely soluble in alcohol, slightly soluble in methylene chloride.

## IDENTIFICATION

*First identification* B, E.

*Second identification* A, C, D, E.

A. Melting point (*2.2.14*): 149 °C to 152 °C.

Introduce the substance to be examined into a capillary tube. Dry in an oven at 100-105 °C for 3 h. Seal the tube and determine the melting point.

B. Infrared absorption spectrophotometry (*2.2.24*).

*Comparison* acetylcholine chloride CRS.

C. Examine the chromatograms obtained in the test for related substances.

*Results* The principal band in the chromatogram obtained with test solution (b) is similar in position, colour and size to the principal band in the chromatogram obtained with reference solution (b).

D. To 15 mg add 10 ml of *dilute sodium hydroxide solution R*, 2 ml of *0.02 M potassium permanganate* and heat. The vapours formed change the colour of *red litmus paper R* to blue.

E. 0.5 ml of solution S (see Tests) gives reaction (a) of chlorides (2.3.1).

## TESTS

### Solution S
Dissolve 5.0 g in *carbon dioxide-free water R* and dilute to 50 ml with the same solvent.

### Appearance of solution
Solution S is clear (2.2.1) and not more intensely coloured than reference solution $Y_6$ or $BY_6$ (2.2.2, *Method II*).

### Acidity
Dilute 1 ml of solution S to 10 ml with *carbon dioxide-free water R*. Add 0.05 ml of *phenolphthalein solution R*. Not more than 0.4 ml of *0.01 M sodium hydroxide* is required to change the colour of the indicator to pink.

### Related substances
Thin-layer chromatography (2.2.27). *Prepare the solutions immediately before use.*

*Test solution (a)* Dissolve 0.30 g of the substance to be examined in *methanol R* and dilute to 3.0 ml with the same solvent.

*Test solution (b)* Dilute 1 ml of test solution (a) to 10 ml with *methanol R*.

*Reference solution (a)* Dilute 1 ml of test solution (a) to 100 ml with *methanol R*.

*Reference solution (b)* Dissolve 20.0 mg of *acetylcholine chloride CRS* in *methanol R* and dilute to 2.0 ml with the same solvent.

*Reference solution (c)* Dissolve 20 mg of *choline chloride R* in *methanol R*, add 0.4 ml of test solution (a) and dilute to 2.0 ml with *methanol R*.

*Plate* TLC silica gel plate R.

*Mobile phase* Mix 20 volumes of a 40 g/l solution of *ammonium nitrate R*, 20 volumes of *methanol R* and 60 volumes of *acetonitrile R*.

*Application* 5 µl as bands of 10 mm by 2 mm.

*Development* Over 2/3 of the plate.

*Detection* Spray with *potassium iodobismuthate solution R3*.

*System suitability* The chromatogram obtained with reference solution (c) shows 2 clearly separated bands.

*Limits:*
— *any impurity*: any bands in the chromatogram obtained with test solution (a), apart from the principal band, are not more intense than the principal band in the chromatogram obtained with reference solution (a) (1 per cent).

### Trimethylamine
Dissolve 0.1 g in 10 ml of *sodium carbonate solution R* and heat to boiling. No vapours appear which turn *red litmus paper R* blue.

### Heavy metals (2.4.8)
Maximum 10 ppm.

12 ml of solution S complies with limit test A. Prepare the standard using *lead standard solution (1 ppm Pb) R*.

### Loss on drying (2.2.32)
Maximum 1.0 per cent, determined on 1.000 g by drying in an oven at 105 °C for 3 h.

### Sulphated ash (2.4.14)
Maximum 0.1 per cent, determined on the residue obtained in the test for loss on drying.

## ASSAY
Dissolve 0.200 g in 20 ml of *carbon dioxide-free water R*. Neutralise with *0.01 M sodium hydroxide* using 0.15 ml of *phenolphthalein solution R* as indicator. Add 20.0 ml of *0.1 M sodium hydroxide* and allow to stand for 30 min. Titrate with *0.1 M hydrochloric acid*.

1 ml of *0.1 M sodium hydroxide* is equivalent to 18.17 mg of $C_7H_{16}ClNO_2$.

## STORAGE
In ampoules, protected from light.

## IMPURITIES

A. 2-hydroxy-*N,N,N*-trimethylethanaminium chloride (choline chloride),

B. 2-(acetyloxy)-*N,N*-dimethylethanaminium chloride,

C. *N,N*-dimethylmethanamine.

*Ph Eur*

# Acetylcysteine

(*Ph Eur monograph 0967*)

$C_5H_9NO_3S$          163.2          *616-91-1*

## Action and use
Sulphydryl donor; antidote to paracetamol poisoning; mucolytic.

## Preparation
Acetylcysteine Injection

*Ph Eur* ___

## DEFINITION
(2R)-2-(Acetylamino)-3-sulfanylpropanoic acid.

## Content
98.0 per cent to 101.0 per cent (dried substance).

## CHARACTERS

### Appearance
White or almost white, crystalline powder or colourless crystals.

### Solubility
Freely soluble in water and in ethanol (96 per cent), practically insoluble in methylene chloride.

## IDENTIFICATION

*First identification*  A, C.

*Second identification*  A, B, D, E.

A. Specific optical rotation (see Tests).

B. Melting point (*2.2.14*): 104 °C to 110 °C.

C. Infrared absorption spectrophotometry (*2.2.24*).

*Preparation*  Discs of *potassium bromide R*.

*Comparison*  acetylcysteine CRS.

D. Examine the chromatograms obtained in the test for related substances.

*Results*  The principal peak in the chromatogram obtained with test solution (b) is similar in retention time and size to the principal peak in the chromatogram obtained with reference solution (b).

E. To 0.5 ml of solution S (see Tests) add 0.05 ml of a 50 g/l solution of *sodium nitroprusside R* and 0.05 ml of *concentrated ammonia R*. A dark violet colour develops.

## TESTS
### Solution S

Dissolve 1.0 g in *carbon dioxide-free water R* and dilute to 20 ml with the same solvent.

### Appearance of solution

Solution S is clear (*2.2.1*) and colourless (*2.2.2, Method II*).

### pH (*2.2.3*)

2.0 to 2.8.

To 2 ml of solution S add 8 ml of *carbon dioxide-free water R* and mix.

### Specific optical rotation (*2.2.7*)

+ 21.0 to + 27.0 (dried substance).

In a 25 ml volumetric flask, mix 1.25 g with 1 ml of a 10 g/l solution of *sodium edetate R*. Add 7.5 ml of a 40 g/l solution of *sodium hydroxide R*, mix and dissolve. Dilute to 25.0 ml with *phosphate buffer solution pH 7.0 R2*.

### Related substances

Liquid chromatography (*2.2.29*). *Except where otherwise prescribed, prepare the solutions immediately before use.*

*Test solution (a)*  Suspend 0.80 g of the substance to be examined in 1 ml of *1 M hydrochloric acid* and dilute to 100.0 ml with *water R*.

*Test solution (b)*  Dilute 5.0 ml of test solution (a) to 100.0 ml with *water R*. Dilute 5.0 ml of this solution to 50.0 ml with *water R*.

*Test solution (c)*  Use test solution (a) after storage for at least 1 h.

*Reference solution (a)*  Suspend 4.0 mg of *acetylcysteine CRS*, 4.0 mg of *L-cystine R* (impurity A), 4.0 mg of *L-cysteine R* (impurity B), 4.0 mg of *acetylcysteine impurity C CRS* and 4.0 mg of *acetylcysteine impurity D CRS* in 1 ml of *1 M hydrochloric acid* and dilute to 100.0 ml with *water R*.

*Reference solution (b)*  Suspend 4.0 mg of *acetylcysteine CRS* in 1 ml of *1 M hydrochloric acid* and dilute to 100.0 ml with *water R*.

*Column:*
— *size: l* = 0.25 m, Ø = 4 mm;
— *stationary phase: octadecylsilyl silica gel for chromatography R* (5 µm).

*Mobile phase*  Stir 3 volumes of *acetonitrile R* and 97 volumes of *water R* in a beaker; adjust to pH 3.0 with *phosphoric acid R*.

*Flow rate*  1.0 ml/min.

*Detection*  Spectrophotometer at 220 nm.

*Injection*  20 µl, 3 times; inject *0.01 M hydrochloric acid* as a blank.

*Run time*  5 times the retention time of acetylcysteine (about 30 min).

*Retention time*  Impurity A = about 2.2 min; impurity B = about 2.4 min; 2-methyl-2-thiazoline-4-carboxylic acid, originating in test solution (c) = about 3.3 min; acetylcysteine = about 6.4 min; impurity C = about 12 min; impurity D = about 14 min.

*System suitability*  Reference solution (a):
— *resolution*: minimum 1.5 between the peaks due to impurities A and B and minimum 2.0 between the peaks due to impurities C and D.

From the chromatogram obtained with test solution (a), calculate the percentage content of the known impurities ($T_1$) and the unknown impurities ($T_2$) using the following equations:

$$T_1 = \frac{A_1 \times m_2 \times 100}{A_2 \times m_1}$$

$$T_2 = \frac{A_3 \times m_3 \times 100}{A_4 \times m_1}$$

$A_1$ = peak area of individual impurity (impurity A, impurity B, impurity C and impurity D) in the chromatogram obtained with test solution (a);

$A_2$ = peak area of the corresponding individual impurity (impurity A, impurity B, impurity C and impurity D) in the chromatogram obtained with reference solution (a);

$A_3$ = peak area of unknown impurity in the chromatogram obtained with test solution (a);

$A_4$ = peak area of acetylcysteine in the chromatogram obtained with reference solution (b);

$m_1$ = mass of the substance to be examined in test solution (a);

$m_2$ = mass of the individual impurity in reference solution (a);

$m_3$ = mass of acetylcysteine in reference solution (b).

*Limits:*
— *impurities A, B, C, D*: for each impurity, maximum 0.5 per cent;
— *any other impurity*: for each impurity, maximum 0.5 per cent;
— *total*: maximum 0.5 per cent;
— *disregard limit*: 0.1 times the area of the principal peak in the chromatogram obtained with reference solution (b) (0.05 per cent); disregard any peak with a retention time of about 3.3 min due to 2-methyl-2-thiazoline-4-carboxylic acid.

### Heavy metals (*2.4.8*)

Maximum 10 ppm.

2.0 g complies with test C. Prepare the reference solution using 2 ml of *lead standard (10 ppm Pb) R*.

### Zinc

Maximum 10.0 ppm.

Atomic absorption spectrometry (*2.2.23, Method II*).

*Test solution*  Dissolve 1.00 g in *0.001 M hydrochloric acid* and dilute to 50.0 ml with the same acid.

*Reference solutions*  Prepare the reference solutions using *zinc standard solution (5 mg/ml Zn) R*, diluting with *0.001 M hydrochloric acid*.

*Source*  Zinc hollow-cathode lamp.

*Wavelength* 213.8 nm.

*Atomisation device* Air-acetylene flame.

Use a correction procedure for non-specific absorption.

**Loss on drying** (*2.2.32*)
Maximum 1.0 per cent, determined on 1.000 g by drying in an oven *in vacuo* at 70 °C for 3 h.

**Sulphated ash** (*2.4.14*)
Maximum 0.2 per cent, determined on 1.0 g.

**ASSAY**
Dissolve 0.140 g in 60 ml of *water R* and add 10 ml of *dilute hydrochloric acid R*. After cooling in iced water, add 10 ml of *potassium iodide solution R* and titrate with *0.05 M iodine*, using 1 ml of *starch solution R* as indicator.

1 ml of *0.05 M iodine* is equivalent to 16.32 mg of $C_5H_9NO_3S$.

**STORAGE**
Protected from light.

**IMPURITIES**
*Specified impurities* *A, B, C, D.*

A. L-cystine,

B. L-cysteine,

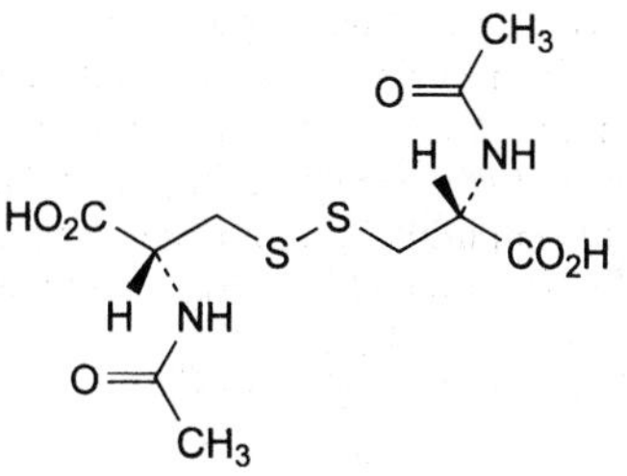

C. *N,N'*-diacetyl-l-cystine,

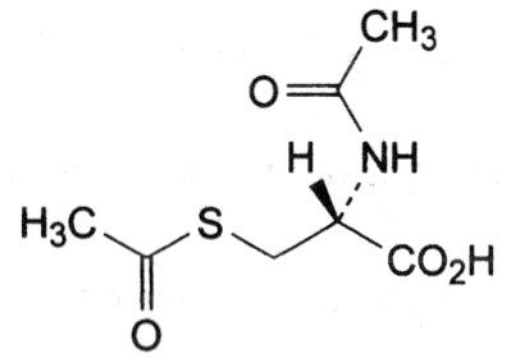

D. *N,S*-diacetyl-l-cysteine.

─────────────── *Ph Eur*

# Acetyldigoxin

(*β-Acetyldigoxin, Ph Eur monograph 2168*)

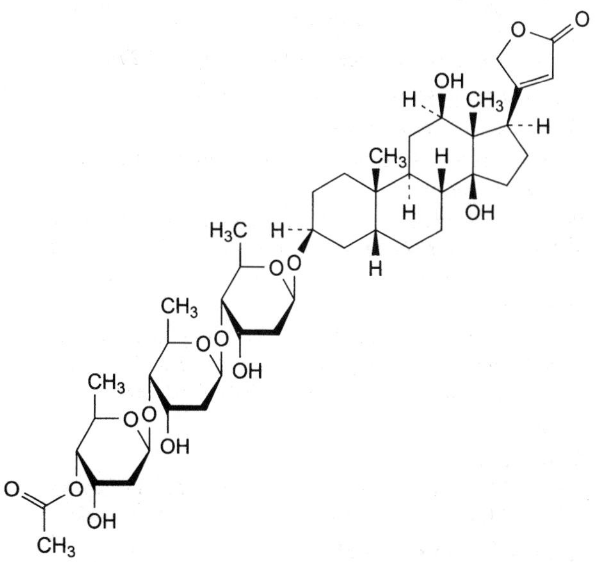

$C_{43}H_{66}O_{15}$          823          *5355-48-6*

**Action and use**
Cardiac Glycoside.

*Ph Eur* ─────────────────

**DEFINITION**
3β-[(4-*O*-Acetyl-2,6-dideoxy-β-D-*ribo*-hexopyranosyl-(1→4)-2,6-dideoxy-β-D-*ribo*-hexopyranosyl-(1→4)-2,6-dideoxy-β-D-*ribo*-hexopyranosyl)oxy]-12β,14-dihydroxy-5β-card-20(22)-enolide.

**Content**
97.0 per cent to 102.0 per cent (dried substance).

**CHARACTERS**
**Appearance**
White or almost white powder.

**Solubility**
Practically insoluble in water, sparingly soluble in methylene chloride, slightly soluble in ethanol (96 per cent).

**IDENTIFICATION**
Infrared absorption spectrophotometry (*2.2.24*).

*Comparison* β-acetyldigoxin CRS.

**TESTS**
**Specific optical rotation** (*2.2.7*)
+ 26.2 to + 28.2 (dried substance).

Dissolve 0.50 g in a mixture of equal volumes of *methanol R* and *methylene chloride R* and dilute to 25.0 ml with the same mixture of solvents.

**Related substances**
Liquid chromatography (*2.2.29*). *Prepare the solutions immediately before use.*

*Solvent mixture* Mix equal volumes of *methanol R2* and *acetonitrile for chromatography R*.

*Test solution* Dissolve 50.0 mg of the substance to be examined in the solvent mixture and dilute to 100.0 ml with the solvent mixture.

*Reference solution (a)* Dissolve 10.0 mg of β-acetyldigoxin CRS in the solvent mixture and dilute to 20.0 ml with the solvent mixture.

*Reference solution (b)* Dilute 1.0 ml of the test solution to 20.0 ml with the solvent mixture. Dilute 1.0 ml of this solution to 10.0 ml with the solvent mixture.

*Reference solution (c)* Dissolve 5 mg of *gitoxin CRS* (impurity D) in the solvent mixture and dilute to 100.0 ml with the solvent mixture. To 5.0 ml of this solution, add 0.5 ml of reference solution (a) and dilute to 100.0 ml with the solvent mixture.

*Reference solution (d)* Dissolve 5.0 mg of *β-acetyldigoxin for peak identification CRS* (containing impurities A and B) in 10.0 ml of the solvent mixture.

*Column:*
— *size: l* = 0.125 m, Ø = 4.0 mm;
— *stationary phase:* octadecylsilyl silica gel for chromatography R (4 μm).

*Mobile phase:*
— *mobile phase A:* water for chromatography R;
— *mobile phase B:* acetonitrile for chromatography R;

| Time (min) | Mobile phase A (per cent *V/V*) | Mobile phase B (per cent *V/V*) |
|---|---|---|
| 0 - 10 | 70 | 30 |
| 10 - 20 | 70 → 35 | 30 → 65 |
| 20 - 20.1 | 35 → 70 | 65 → 30 |
| 20.1 - 25 | 70 | 30 |

*Flow rate* 1.5 ml/min.

*Detection* Spectrophotometer at 225 nm.

*Injection* 10 μl of the test solution and reference solutions (b), (c) and (d).

*Identification of impurities* Use the chromatograms obtained with reference solutions (c) and (d) to identify the peaks due to impurities A, B and D.

*Relative retention* With reference to β-acetyldigoxin (retention time = about 9 min): impurity about 0.3; impurity A = about 0.7; impurity D = about 1.2.

*System suitability* Reference solution (c):
— *resolution:* minimum 1.5 between the peaks due to β-acetyldigoxin and impurity D;
— *symmetry factor:* maximum 2.5 for the peak due to β-acetyldigoxin.

*Limits:*
— *impurities A, B:* for each impurity, not more than the area of the principal peak in the chromatogram obtained with reference solution (b) (0.5 per cent);
— *impurity D:* not more than 0.6 times the area of the principal peak in the chromatogram obtained with reference solution (b) (0.3 per cent);
— *any other impurity:* for each impurity, not more than 0.4 times the area of the principal peak in the chromatogram obtained with reference solution (b) (0.2 per cent);
— *sum of impurities other than A, B and D:* not more than 1.2 times the area of the principal peak in the chromatogram obtained with reference solution (b) (0.6 per cent);
— *total:* not more than 3 times the area of the principal peak in the chromatogram obtained with reference solution (b) (1.5 per cent);

— *disregard limit:* 0.1 times the area of the principal peak in the chromatogram obtained with reference solution (b) (0.05 per cent).

The thresholds indicated under Related substances (Table 2034.-1) in the general monograph *Substances for pharmaceutical use (2034)* do not apply.

**Loss on drying** (*2.2.32*)
Maximum 1.5 per cent, determined on 1.000 g by drying in an oven at 105 °C.

**Sulphated ash** (*2.4.14*)
Maximum 0.1 per cent, determined on the residue obtained in the test for loss on drying.

**ASSAY**
Liquid chromatography (*2.2.29*) as described in the test for related substances with the following modification.

*Injection* Test solution and reference solution (a).

Calculate the percentage content of $C_{43}H_{66}O_{15}$ from the declared content of *β-acetyldigoxin CRS*.

**STORAGE**
Protected from light.

**IMPURITIES**
*Specified impurities* *A, B, D.*

*Other detectable impurities* (the following substances would, if present at a sufficient level, be detected by one or other of the tests in the monograph. They are limited by the general acceptance criterion for other/unspecified impurities and/or by the general monograph *Substances for pharmaceutical use (2034)*. It is therefore not necessary to identify these impurities for demonstration of compliance. See also *5.10. Control of impurities in substances for pharmaceutical use*): *C, E, F, G, H.*

A. R1 = OH, R2 = R4 = H, R3 = CO-CH$_3$: 3β-[(3-*O*-acetyl-2,6-dideoxy-β-D-*ribo*-hexopyranosyl-(1→4)-2,6-dideoxy-β-D-*ribo*-hexopyranosyl-(1→4)-2,6-dideoxy-β-D-*ribo*-hexopyranosyl)oxy]-12β,14-dihydroxy-5β-card-20(22)-enolide (α-acetyldigoxin),

B. R1 = OH, R2 = R3 = R4 = H: digoxin,

D. R1 = R3 = R4 = H, R2 = OH: 3β-[(2,6-dideoxy-β-D-*ribo*-hexopyranosyl-(1→4)-2,6-dideoxy-β-D-*ribo*-hexopyranosyl-(1→4)-2,6-dideoxy-β-D-*ribo*-hexopyranosyl)oxy]-14,16β-dihydroxy-5β-card-20(22)-enolide (gitoxin),

E. R1 = R2 = R3 = R4 = H: digitoxin,

H. R1 = R2 = R3 = H, R4 = CO-CH₃: β-acetyldigitoxin,

F. R1 = OH, R2 = H, R3 = R4 = CO-CH₃: 3β-[(3,4-*O*-diacetyl-2,6-dideoxy-β-D-*ribo*-hexopyranosyl-(1→4)-2,6-dideoxy-β-D-*ribo*-hexopyranosyl-(1→4)-2,6-dideoxy-β-D-*ribo*-hexopyranosyl)oxy]-12β,14-dihydroxy-5β-card-20(22)-enolide (diacetyldigoxin),

G. R1 = R2 = R4 = H, R3 = CO-CH₃: 3β-[(3-*O*-acetyl-2,6-dideoxy-β-D-*ribo*-hexopyranosyl-(1→4)-2,6-dideoxy-β-D-*ribo*-hexopyranosyl-(1→4)-2,6-dideoxy-β-D-*ribo*-hexopyranosyl)oxy]-14-hydroxy-5β-card-20(22)-enolide (α-acetyldigitoxin),

C. 3β,12β,14-trihydroxy-5β-card-20(22)-enolide (digoxigenin).

*Ph Eur*

# Acetyltryptophan

(*N-Acetyltryptophan*, Ph Eur monograph 1383)

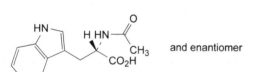

and enantiomer

C₁₃H₁₄N₂O₃          246.3          87-32-1

*Ph Eur*

## DEFINITION
(*RS*)-2-Acetylamino-3-(1*H*-indol-3-yl)propanoic acid.

## Content
99.0 per cent to 101.0 per cent (dried substance).

## PRODUCTION
Tryptophan used for the production of *N*-acetyltryptophan complies with the test for impurity A and other related substances in the monograph on *Tryptophan (1272)*.

## CHARACTERS
### Appearance
White or almost white, crystalline powder, or colourless crystals.

### Solubility
Slightly soluble in water, very soluble in ethanol (96 per cent). It dissolves in dilute solutions of alkali hydroxides.

### mp
About 205 °C.

## IDENTIFICATION
*First identification*   A, B.

*Second identification*   A, C, D, E.

A. Optical rotation (see Tests).

B. Infrared absorption spectrophotometry (*2.2.24*).

*Comparison*   N-acetyltryptophan CRS.

C. Thin-layer chromatography (*2.2.27*).

*Test solution*   Dissolve 50 mg of the substance to be examined in 0.2 ml of *concentrated ammonia R* and dilute to 10 ml with *water R*.

*Reference solution (a)*   Dissolve 50 mg of *N*-acetyltryptophan CRS in 0.2 ml of *concentrated ammonia R* and dilute to 10 ml with *water R*.

*Reference solution (b)*   Dissolve 10 mg of *tryptophan R* in the test solution and dilute to 2 ml with the test solution.

*Plate*   TLC silica gel F₂₅₄ plate R.

*Mobile phase*   glacial acetic acid R, water R, butanol R (25:25:40 *V/V/V*).

*Application*   2 µl.

*Development*   Over a path of 10 cm.

*Drying*   In an oven at 100-105 °C for 15 min.

*Detection*   Examine in ultraviolet light at 254 nm.

*System suitability*   Reference solution (b):
— the chromatogram shows 2 clearly separated spots.

*Results*   The principal spot in the chromatogram obtained with the test solution is similar in position and size to the principal spot in the chromatogram obtained with reference solution (a).

D. Dissolve about 2 mg in 2 ml of *water R*. Add 2 ml of *dimethylaminobenzaldehyde solution R6*. Heat on a water-bath. A blue or greenish-blue colour develops.

E. It gives the reaction of acetyl (*2.3.1*). Proceed as described for substances hydrolysable only with difficulty.

## TESTS
### Appearance of solution
The solution is clear (*2.2.1*) and not more intensely coloured than reference solution Y₇ or GY₇ (*2.2.2, Method II*).

Dissolve 1.0 g in a 40 g/l solution of *sodium hydroxide R* and dilute to 100 ml with the same alkaline solution.

### Optical rotation (*2.2.7*)
− 0.1° to + 0.1°.

Dissolve 2.50 g in a 40 g/l solution of *sodium hydroxide R* and dilute to 25.0 ml with the same alkaline solution.

### Related substances
Liquid chromatography (*2.2.29*). *Prepare the test and reference solutions immediately before use.*

*Buffer solution pH 2.3*   Dissolve 3.90 g of *sodium dihydrogen phosphate R* in 1000 ml of *water R*. Add about 700 ml of a 2.9 g/l solution of *phosphoric acid R* and adjust to pH 2.3 with the same acidic solution.

*Solvent mixture*   acetonitrile R, water R (10:90 *V/V*).

*Test solution*   Dissolve 0.10 g of the substance to be examined in a mixture of 50 volumes of *acetonitrile R* and 50 volumes of *water R* and dilute to 20.0 ml with the same mixture of solvents.

*Reference solution (a)*   Dilute 1.0 ml of the test solution to 100.0 ml with the solvent mixture.

*Reference solution (b)*   Dilute 4.0 ml of reference solution (a) to 100.0 ml with the solvent mixture.

*Reference solution (c)* Dissolve the contents of a vial of *1,1'-ethylidenebistryptophan CRS* in 1 ml of reference solution (b).

*Column:*
— *size:* $l = 0.25$ m, $\varnothing = 4.6$ mm;
— *stationary phase:* octadecylsilyl silica gel for chromatography R (5 μm);
— *temperature:* 40 °C.

*Mobile phase:*
— *mobile phase A:* acetonitrile R, buffer solution pH 2.3 (115:885 V/V);
— *mobile phase B:* acetonitrile R, buffer solution pH 2.3 (350:650 V/V);

| Time (min) | Mobile phase A (per cent *V/V*) | Mobile phase B (per cent *V/V*) |
|---|---|---|
| 0 - 10 | 100 | 0 |
| 10 - 45 | 100 → 0 | 0 → 100 |
| 45 - 65 | 0 | 100 |
| 65 - 66 | 0 → 100 | 100 → 0 |
| 66 - 80 | 100 | 0 |

*Flow rate* 0.7 ml/min.

*Detection* Spectrophotometer at 220 nm.

*Injection* 20 μl of the test solution and reference solutions (a) and (c).

*Retention time* N-acetyltryptophan = about 29 min; 1,1'-ethylidenebis(tryptophan) = about 34 min.

*System suitability* Reference solution (c):
— *resolution:* minimum 8.0 between the peaks due to N-acetyltryptophan and 1,1'-ethylidenebis(tryptophan); if necessary, adjust the time programme for the elution gradient (an increase in the duration of elution with mobile phase A produces longer retention times and a better resolution);
— *symmetry factor:* maximum 3.5 for the peak due to 1,1'-ethylidenebistryptophan in the chromatogram obtained with reference solution (c).

*Limits:*
— *impurities A, B, C, D, E, F, G, H, I, J, K, L:* for each impurity, not more than 0.25 times the area of the principal peak in the chromatogram obtained with reference solution (a) (0.25 per cent);
— *total:* not more than 0.5 times the area of the principal peak in the chromatogram obtained with reference solution (a) (0.5 per cent);
— *disregard limit:* 0.01 times the area of the principal peak the chromatogram obtained with reference solution (a) (0.01 per cent).

**Ammonium** (*2.4.1, Method B*)
Maximum 200 ppm, determined on 0.10 g.

Prepare the standard using 0.2 ml of *ammonium standard solution (100 ppm NH₄) R*.

**Iron** (*2.4.9*)
Maximum 10 ppm.

Dissolve 1.0 g in 50 ml of *hydrochloric acid R1*, with heating at 50 °C. Allow to cool. In a separating funnel, shake with 3 quantities, each of 10 ml, of *methyl isobutyl ketone R1*, shaking for 3 min each time. To the combined organic layers add 10 ml of *water R* and shake for 3 min. Examine the aqueous layer.

**Heavy metals** (*2.4.8*)
Maximum 10 ppm.

2.0 g complies with test C. Prepare the reference solution using 2 ml of *lead standard solution (10 ppm Pb) R*.

**Loss on drying** (*2.2.32*)
Maximum 0.5 per cent, determined on 1.000 g by drying in an oven at 105 °C.

**Sulphated ash** (*2.4.14*)
Maximum 0.1 per cent, determined on 1.0 g.

**ASSAY**
Dissolve 0.200 g in 5 ml of *methanol R*. Add 50 ml of *anhydrous ethanol R*. Titrate with *0.1 M sodium hydroxide*, determining the end-point potentiometrically (*2.2.20*).

1 ml of *0.1 M sodium hydroxide* is equivalent to 24.63 mg of $C_{13}H_{14}N_2O_3$.

**STORAGE**
Protected from light.

**IMPURITIES**
*Specified impurities* A, B, C, D, E, F, G, H, I, J, K, L.
A. tryptophan,

and epimer at C*

B. (S)-2-amino-3-[(3RS)-3-hydroxy-2-oxo-2,3-dihydro-1H-indol-3-yl]propanoic acid (dioxyindolylalanine),

C. R = H: (S)-2-amino-4-(2-aminophenyl)-4-oxobutanoic acid (kynurenine),

E. R = CHO: (S)-2-amino-4-[2-(formylamino)phenyl]-4-oxobutanoic acid (N-formylkynurenine),

D. (S)-2-amino-3-(5-hydroxy-1H-indol-3-yl)propanoic acid (5-hydroxytryptophan),

F. (S)-2-amino-3-(phenylamino)propanoic acid (3-phenylaminoalanine),

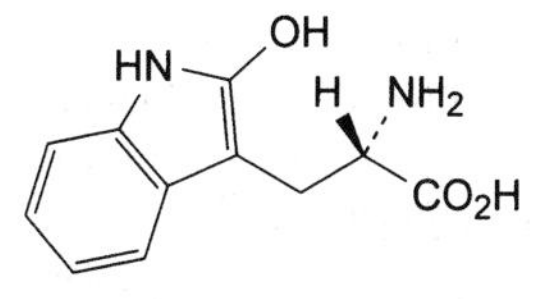

G. (S)-2-amino-3-(2-hydroxy-1H-indol-3-yl)propanoic acid (2-hydroxytryptophan),

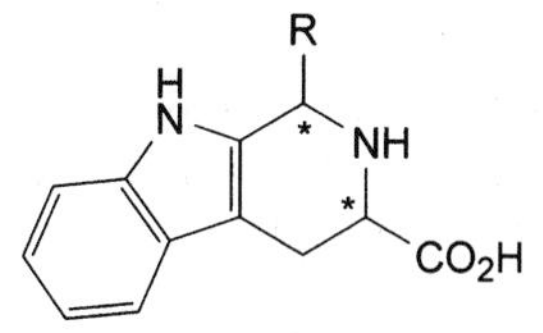

H. R = H: (3RS)-1,2,3,4-tetrahydro-9H-β-carboline-3-carboxylic acid,

I. R = CH₃: 1-methyl-1,2,3,4-tetrahydro-9H-β-carboline-3-carboxylic acid,

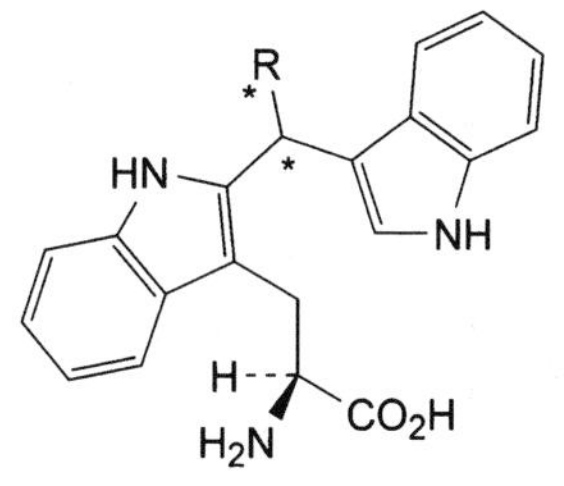

J. R = CHOH-CH₂-OH: (S)-2-amino-3-[2-[2,3-dihydroxy-1-(1H-indol-3-yl)propyl]-1H-indol-3-yl]propanoic acid,

K. R = H: (S)-2-amino-3-[2-(1H-indol-3-ylmethyl)-1H-indol-3-yl]propanoic acid,

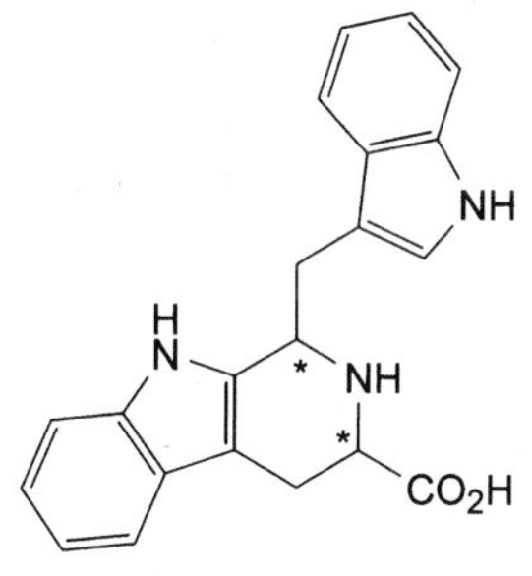

L. 1-(1H-indol-3-ylmethyl)-1,2,3,4-tetrahydro-9H-β-carboline-3-carboxylic acid.

*Ph Eur*

# Acetyltyrosine

(*N-Acetyltyrosine, Ph Eur monograph 1384*)

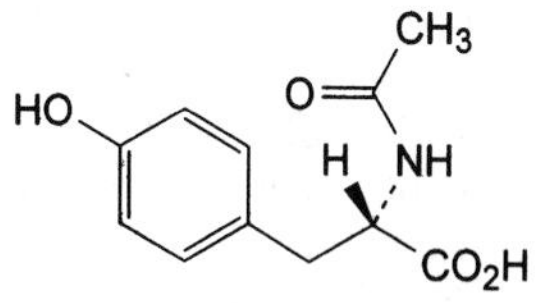

C₁₁H₁₃NO₄           223.2           *537-55-3*

*Ph Eur*

## DEFINITION

*N*-Acetyltyrosine contains not less than 98.5 per cent and not more than the equivalent of 101.0 per cent of (2S)-2-(acetylamino)-3-(4-hydroxyphenyl)propanoic acid, calculated with reference to the dried substance.

## CHARACTERS

A white or almost white, crystalline powder or colourless crystals, freely soluble in water, practically insoluble in cyclohexane.

## IDENTIFICATION

*First identification   A, B.*

*Second identification   A, C, D.*

A. It complies with the test for specific optical rotation (see Tests).

B. Examine by infrared absorption spectrophotometry (*2.2.24*), comparing with the spectrum obtained with *N*-acetyltyrosine CRS. Examine the substances prepared as discs.

C. Examine the chromatograms obtained in the test for related substances in ultraviolet light at 254 nm. The principal spot obtained with test solution (b) is similar in position and size to the principal spot in the chromatogram obtained with reference solution (a).

D. Solution S (see Tests) is strongly acid (*2.2.4*).

## TESTS

**Solution S**

Dissolve 2.50 g in *water R* and dilute to 100.0 ml with the same solvent.

**Appearance of solution**

Solution S is clear (*2.2.1*) and colourless (*2.2.2, Method II*).

**Specific optical rotation (*2.2.7*)**

Dilute 10.0 ml of solution S to 25.0 ml with *water R*. The specific optical rotation is + 46 to + 49, calculated with reference to the dried substance.

**Related substances**

Examine by thin-layer chromatography (*2.2.27*), using a *TLC silica gel F₂₅₄ plate R*.

*Test solution (a)*   Dissolve 0.80 g of the substance to be examined in 6 ml of a mixture of equal volumes of *glacial acetic acid R* and *water R* and dilute to 10 ml with *ethanol R*.

*Test solution (b)*   Dilute 1 ml of test solution (a) to 10 ml with *ethanol R*.

*Reference solution (a)*   Dissolve 80 mg of *N*-acetyltyrosine CRS in a mixture of 3 volumes of *water R*, 3 volumes of *glacial acetic acid R* and 94 volumes of *ethanol R* and dilute to 10 ml with the same mixture of solvents.

*Reference solution (b)*   Dilute 0.5 ml of test solution (b) to 10 ml with *ethanol R*.

*Reference solution (c)* Dissolve 40 mg of *tyrosine CRS* in 20 ml of a mixture of equal volumes of *water R* and *glacial acetic acid R* and dilute to 50 ml with *ethanol R*.

Apply separately to the plate 5 μl of each solution. Develop over a path of 10 cm using a mixture of 10 volumes of *water R*, 15 volumes of *glacial acetic acid R* and 75 volumes of *ethyl acetate R*. Allow the plate to dry in air. Examine in ultraviolet light at 254 nm. Any spot in the chromatogram obtained with test solution (a), apart from the principal spot, is not more intense than the spot in the chromatogram obtained with reference solution (b) (0.5 per cent). Spray with *ninhydrin solution R* and heat at 100 °C to 105 °C for 10 min. Examine in daylight. Any spot corresponding to tyrosine is not more intense that the spot in the chromatogram obtained with reference solution (c) (1 per cent).

### Chlorides (2.4.4)
Dilute 10 ml of solution S to 15 ml with *water R*. The solution complies with the limit test for chlorides (200 ppm).

### Sulphates (2.4.13)
Dissolve 1.0 g in *distilled water R* and dilute to 20 ml with the same solvent. The solution complies with the limit test for sulphates (200 ppm).

### Ammonium
Prepare a cell consisting of two watch-glasses 60 mm in diameter placed edge to edge. To the inner wall of the upper watch-glass stick a piece of *red litmus paper R* 5 mm square and wetted with a few drops of *water R*. Finely powder the substance to be examined, place 50 mg in the lower watch-glass and dissolve in 0.5 ml of *water R*. To the solution add 0.30 g of *heavy magnesium oxide R*. Briefly triturate with a glass rod. Immediately close the cell by putting the two watch-glasses together. Heat at 40 °C for 15 min. The litmus paper is not more intensely blue coloured than a standard prepared at the same time and in the same manner using 0.1 ml of *ammonium standard solution (100 ppm NH4) R*, 0.5 ml of *water R* and 0.30 g of *heavy magnesium oxide R* (200 ppm).

### Iron (2.4.9)
In a separating funnel, dissolve 0.5 g in 10 ml of *dilute hydrochloric acid R*. Shake with three quantities, each of 10 ml, of *methyl isobutyl ketone R1*, shaking for 3 min each time. To the combined organic layers add 10 ml of *water R* and shake for 3 min. The aqueous layer complies with the limit test for iron (20 ppm).

### Heavy metals (2.4.8)
Dissolve 2.0 g in *water R* and dilute to 20 ml with the same solvent. 12 ml of the solution complies with limit test A for heavy metals (10 ppm). Prepare the standard using *lead standard solution (1 ppm Pb) R*.

### Loss on drying (2.2.32)
Not more than 0.5 per cent, determined on 1.000 g by drying in an oven at 105 °C.

### Sulphated ash (2.4.14)
Not more than 0.1 per cent, determined on 1.0 g.

### Pyrogens (2.6.8)
If intended for use in the manufacture of parenteral dosage forms without a further appropriate procedure for the removal of pyrogens, it complies with the test for pyrogens. Inject per kilogram of the rabbit's mass 1.0 ml of a freshly prepared solution in *water for injections R* containing per millilitre 10.0 mg of the substance to be examined and 9.0 mg of *pyrogen-free sodium chloride R*.

### ASSAY
Dissolve 0.180 g in 50 ml of *carbon dioxide-free water R*. Titrate with *0.1 M sodium hydroxide*, determining the end-point potentiometrically (2.2.20).

1 ml of *0.1 M sodium hydroxide* is equivalent to 22.32 mg of $C_{11}H_{13}NO_4$.

### STORAGE
Store protected from light. If the substance is sterile, store in a sterile, airtight, tamper-proof container.

### IMPURITIES
A. tyrosine,

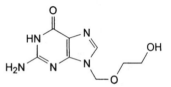

B. (2*S*)-2-(acetylamino)-3-[4-(acetoxy)phenyl]propanoic acid (diacetyltyrosine).

*Ph Eur*

# Aciclovir

(*Ph Eur monograph 0968*)

$C_8H_{11}N_5O_3$     225.2     59277-89-3

### Action and use
Purine nucleoside analogue; antiviral (herpesviruses).

### Preparations
Aciclovir Cream

Aciclovir Eye Ointment

Aciclovir Intravenous Infusion

Aciclovir Oral Suspension

Aciclovir Tablets

Dispersible Aciclovir Tablets

*Ph Eur*

### DEFINITION
Aciclovir contains not less than 98.5 per cent and not more than the equivalent of 101.0 per cent of 2-amino-9-[(2-hydroxyethoxy)methyl]-1,9-dihydro-6*H*-purin-6-one, calculated with reference to the anhydrous substance.

### CHARACTERS
A white or almost white, crystalline powder, slightly soluble in water, freely soluble in dimethyl sulphoxide, very slightly soluble in ethanol (96 per cent). It dissolves in dilute solutions of mineral acids and alkali hydroxides.

### IDENTIFICATION
Examine by infrared absorption spectrophotometry (2.2.24), comparing with the spectrum obtained with *aciclovir CRS*.

## TESTS

### Appearance of solution

Dissolve 0.25 g in *0.1 M sodium hydroxide* and dilute to 25 ml with the same solvent. The solution is clear (*2.2.1*) and not more intensely coloured than reference solution $Y_7$ (*2.2.2, Method II*).

### Related substances

A. Examine by thin-layer chromatography (*2.2.27*), using *silica gel GF$_{254}$ R* as the coating substance.

*Prepare the solutions immediately before use.*

*Test solution*   Dissolve 0.1 g of the substance to be examined in *dimethyl sulphoxide R* and dilute to 10 ml with the same solvent.

*Reference solution*   Dissolve 5 mg of *aciclovir impurity A CRS* in *dimethyl sulphoxide R* and dilute to 10 ml with the same solvent. Dilute 1 ml of the solution to 10 ml with *dimethyl sulphoxide R*.

Apply to the plate 10 µl of each solution. Keep the spots compact by drying in a current of warm air. Allow the plate to cool and develop over a path of 10 cm with a mixture of 2 volumes of *concentrated ammonia R*, 20 volumes of *methanol R* and 80 volumes of *methylene chloride R*. Allow the plate to dry in air and examine in ultraviolet light at 254 nm. In the chromatogram obtained with the test solution, any spot with an $R_F$ value greater than that of the principal spot is not more intense than the spot in the chromatogram obtained with the reference solution (0.5 per cent).

B. Examine by liquid chromatography (*2.2.29*).

*Test solution*   Dissolve 50.0 mg of the substance to be examined in 10 ml of a mixture of 20 volumes of *glacial acetic acid R* and 80 volumes of *water R* and dilute to 100.0 ml with the mobile phase.

*Reference solution (a)*   Dilute 1.0 ml of the test solution to 200.0 ml with the mobile phase.

*Reference solution (b)*   Dissolve 5 mg of *aciclovir CRS* and 5 mg of *aciclovir impurity A CRS* in a mixture of 20 volumes of *glacial acetic acid R* and 80 volumes of *water R* and dilute to 25.0 ml with the same mixture of solvents. Dilute 1.0 ml of the solution to 10.0 ml with the mobile phase.

*Reference solution (c)*   Dissolve 7 mg of *guanine R* in *0.1 M sodium hydroxide* and dilute to 100.0 ml with the same solution. Dilute 1.0 ml to 20.0 ml with the mobile phase.

The chromatographic procedure may be carried out using:
— a stainless steel column 0.10 m long and 4.6 mm in internal diameter packed with *octadecylsilyl silica gel for chromatography R* (3 µm),
— as mobile phase at a flow rate of 2 ml/min a mixture prepared as follows: dissolve 6.0 g of *sodium dihydrogen phosphate R* and 1.0 g of *sodium decanesulphonate R* in 900 ml of *water R* and adjust to pH 3 ± 0.1 with *phosphoric acid R*; add 40 ml of *acetonitrile R* and dilute to 1 litre with *water R*,
— as detector a spectrophotometer set at 254 nm,
— a loop injector.

Inject 20 µl of each solution. Record the chromatograms for 7 times the retention time of aciclovir. The test is not valid unless in the chromatogram obtained with reference solution (b), the number of theoretical plates calculated for the peak due to impurity A is at least 1500 and its mass distribution ratio is at least 7 ($V_0$ can be calculated using *dimethyl sulphoxide R*). In the chromatogram obtained with the test solution: the area of any peak corresponding to guanine is not greater than that of the peak in the chromatogram obtained with reference solution (c) (0.7 per cent); the area

of any peak apart from the principal peak and any peak corresponding to guanine is not greater than the area of the peak in the chromatogram obtained with reference solution (a) (0.5 per cent) and the sum of the areas of such peaks is not greater than twice the area of the peak in the chromatogram obtained with reference solution (a) (1 per cent). Disregard any peak with an area less than 0.05 times that of the principal peak in the chromatogram obtained with reference solution (a).

### Water (*2.5.12*)

Not more than 6.0 per cent, determined on 0.500 g.

### Sulphated ash (*2.4.14*)

Not more than 0.1 per cent, determined on 1.0 g.

## ASSAY

Dissolve 0.150 g in 60 ml of *anhydrous acetic acid R*. Titrate with *0.1 M perchloric acid*, determining the end-point potentiometrically (*2.2.20*). Carry out a blank titration.

1 ml of *0.1 M perchloric acid* is equivalent to 22.52 mg of $C_8H_{11}N_5O_3$.

## IMPURITIES

A. R = CH$_3$: 2-[(2-amino-6-oxo-1,6-dihydro-9*H*-purin-9-yl)methoxy]ethyl acetate,

D. R = C$_6$H$_5$: 2-[(2-amino-6-oxo-1,6-dihydro-9*H*-purin-9-yl)methoxy]ethyl benzoate,

B. R = H: 2-amino-1,7-dihydro-6*H*-purin-6-one (guanine),

C. R = CH$_2$-O-CH$_2$-CH$_2$-OH: 2-amino-7-[(2-hydroxyethoxy)methyl]-1,7-dihydro-6*H*-purin-6-one,

E. 6-amino-9-[(2-hydroxyethoxy)methyl]-1,9-dihydro-2*H*-purin-2-one,

F. R = H: *N*-[9-[(2-hydroxyethoxy)methyl]-6-oxo-6,9-dihydro-1*H*-purin-2-yl]acetamide,

G. R = CO-CH$_3$: 2-[[2-(acetylamino)-6-oxo-1,6-dihydro-9*H*-purin-9-yl]methoxy]ethyl acetate,

H. R = CO-C₆H₅: 2-[[2-(acetylamino)-6-oxo-1,6-dihydro-9*H*-purin-9-yl]methoxy]ethyl benzoate.

*Ph Eur*

# Acitretin

(*Ph Eur monograph 1385*)

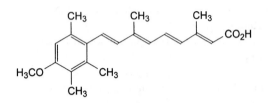

C₂₁H₂₆O₃           326.4           55079-83-9

## Action and use
Vitamin A analogue (retinoid); treatment of psoriasis; ichthyosis; Darier's disease.

*Ph Eur*

## DEFINITION
(all-*E*)-9-(4-Methoxy-2,3,6-trimethylphenyl)-3,7-dimethylnona-2,4,6,8-tetraenoic acid.

## Content
98.0 per cent to 102.0 per cent (dried substance).

## CHARACTERS
### Appearance
Yellow or greenish-yellow, crystalline powder.

### Solubility
Practically insoluble in water, sparingly soluble in tetrahydrofuran, slightly soluble in acetone and in ethanol (96 per cent), very slightly soluble in cyclohexane.

It is sensitive to air, heat and light, especially in solution.

*Carry out all operations as rapidly as possible and avoid exposure to actinic light; use freshly prepared solutions.*

## IDENTIFICATION
*First identification*  B.

*Second identification*  A, C.

A. Ultraviolet and visible absorption spectrophotometry (*2.2.25*).

*Test solution*  Dissolve 15.0 mg in 10 ml of *tetrahydrofuran R* and dilute immediately to 100.0 ml with the same solvent. Dilute 2.5 ml of this solution to 100.0 ml with *tetrahydrofuran R*.

*Spectral range*  300-400 nm.

*Absorption maximum*  At 358 nm.

*Specific absorbance at the absorption maximum*  1350 to 1475.

B. Infrared absorption spectrophotometry (*2.2.24*).

*Preparation*  Discs.

*Comparison*  acitretin CRS.

C. Examine the chromatograms obtained in the assay.

*Results*  The principal peak in the chromatogram obtained with test solution (b) is similar in retention time to the principal peak in the chromatogram obtained with reference solution (a).

## TESTS
### Related substances
Liquid chromatography (*2.2.29*). Maintain the sampler at 4 °C.

*Test solution (a)*  Dissolve 25.0 mg of the substance to be examined in 5 ml of *tetrahydrofuran R* and dilute immediately to 100.0 ml with *anhydrous ethanol R*.

*Test solution (b)*  Dilute 10.0 ml of test solution (a) to 25.0 ml with *anhydrous ethanol R*.

*Reference solution (a)*  Dissolve 25.0 mg of *acitretin CRS* in 5 ml of *tetrahydrofuran R* and dilute immediately to 100.0 ml with *anhydrous ethanol R*. Dilute 10.0 ml of this solution to 25.0 ml with *anhydrous ethanol R*.

*Reference solution (b)*  Dissolve 1.0 mg of *tretinoin CRS* in *anhydrous ethanol R* and dilute to 20.0 ml with the same solvent. Mix 5.0 ml of this solution with 2.5 ml of reference solution (a) and dilute to 100.0 ml with *anhydrous ethanol R*.

*Reference solution (c)*  Dilute 2.5 ml of reference solution (a) to 50.0 ml with *anhydrous ethanol R*. Dilute 3.0 ml of this solution to 20.0 ml with *anhydrous ethanol R*.

*Column*:
— *size l* = 0.25 m, Ø = 4 mm;
— *stationary phase*: microparticulate *octadecylsilyl silica gel for chromatography R* (5 µm) with a specific surface area of 200 m²/g, a pore size of 15 nm and a carbon loading of 20 per cent;
— *temperature*: 25 °C.

*Mobile phase*  A 0.3 per cent *V/V* solution of *glacial acetic acid R* in a mixture of 8 volumes of *water R* and 92 volumes of *anhydrous ethanol R*.

*Flow rate*  0.6 ml/min.

*Detection*  Spectrophotometer at 360 nm.

*Injection*  10 µl of test solution (a) and reference solutions (b) and (c).

*Run time*  2.5 times the retention time of acitretin.

*Retention time*  Impurity A = about 4.8 min; tretinoin = about 5.2 min; acitretin = about 6.2 min; impurity B = about 10.2 min.

*System suitability*  Reference solution (b):
— *resolution*: minimum 2.0 between the peaks due to acitretin and tretinoin; if necessary, adjust the concentration of *anhydrous ethanol R*.

*Limits*:
— *impurities A, B*: for each impurity, not more than the area of the peak due to acitretin in the chromatogram obtained with reference solution (c) (0.3 per cent);
— *total*: not more than the area of the peak due to acitretin in the chromatogram obtained with reference solution (b) (1.0 per cent);
— *disregard limit*: 0.1 times the area of the principal peak in the chromatogram obtained with reference solution (c).

### Palladium
Maximum 10.0 ppm.

Atomic absorption spectrometry (*2.2.23, Method I*).

*Test solution*  Introduce 2.0 g into a quartz beaker and add 3 ml of *magnesium nitrate solution R*. Heat in a muffle furnace to 350 °C at a rate of 40 °C/min to incinerate the content. Ignite at about 450 °C for 8 h and then at 550 ± 50 °C for a further hour. Dissolve the residue in a mixture of 0.75 ml of *hydrochloric acid R* and 0.25 ml of *nitric acid R*, warming gently. Cool, then transfer the solution into a volumetric flask containing *water R* and dilute to 50.0 ml with the same solvent.

*Reference solution* Dissolve 0.163 g of *heavy magnesium oxide R* in a mixture of 0.5 ml of *nitric acid R*, 1.5 ml of *hydrochloric acid R* and 50 ml of *water R*, add 2.0 ml of *palladium standard solution (20 ppm Pd R)* and dilute to 100.0 ml with *water R*.

*Source* Palladium hollow-cathode lamp.

*Wavelength* 247.6 nm.

*Atomisation device* Air-acetylene flame.

**Heavy metals** (*2.4.8*)
Maximum 20 ppm.

2.0 g complies with test C. Prepare the reference solution using 2 ml of *lead standard solution (10 ppm Pb) R*.

**Loss on drying** (*2.2.32*)
Maximum 0.5 per cent, determined on 1.000 g by drying *in vacuo* at 100 °C for 4 h.

**Sulphated ash** (*2.4.14*)
Maximum 0.1 per cent, determined on 1.0 g.

**ASSAY**
*Carry out the assay protected from light, use amber volumetric flasks and prepare the solutions immediately before use.*

Liquid chromatography (*2.2.29*) as described in the test for related substances with the following modifications.

*Injection* Test solution (b) and reference solution (a).

*System suitability:*
— *repeatability*: maximum relative standard deviation of 1.0 per cent after 6 injections of reference solution (a); if necessary, adjust the integration parameters.

Calculate the percentage content of $C_{21}H_{26}O_3$ from the declared content of *acitretin CRS*.

**STORAGE**
In an airtight container, protected from light, at a temperature of 2 °C to 8 °C.

It is recommended that the contents of an opened container be used as soon as possible and any unused part be protected by an atmosphere of inert gas.

**IMPURITIES**
*Specified impurities* A, B.

A. (2Z,4E,6E,8E)-9-(4-methoxy-2,3,6-trimethylphenyl)-3,7-dimethylnona-2,4,6,8-tetraenoic acid,

B. ethyl (all-*E*)-9-(4-methoxy-2,3,6-trimethylphenyl)-3,7-dimethylnona-2,4,6,8-tetraenoate.

# Adenine

(*Ph Eur monograph 0800*)

$C_5H_5N_5$                  135.1                  *73-24-5*

**Action and use**
Constituent of anticoagulant and preservative solutions for blood.

*Ph Eur*

**DEFINITION**
Adenine contains not less than 98.5 per cent and not more than the equivalent of 101.0 per cent of 7*H*-purin-6-amine, calculated with reference to the dried substance.

**CHARACTERS**
A white or almost white powder, very slightly soluble in water and in alcohol. It dissolves in dilute mineral acids and in dilute solutions of alkali hydroxides.

**IDENTIFICATION**
*First identification* A.

*Second identification* B, C.

A. Examine by infrared absorption spectrophotometry (*2.2.24*), comparing with the spectrum obtained with *adenine CRS*. Examine the substances prepared as discs.

B. Examine the chromatograms obtained in the test for related substances. The principal spot in the chromatogram obtained with test solution (b) is similar in position and size to the principal spot in the chromatogram obtained with reference solution (a).

C. To 1 g add 3.5 ml of *propionic anhydride R* and boil for 15 min with stirring. Cool. To the resulting crystalline mass add 15 ml of *light petroleum R* and heat to boiling with vigorous stirring. Cool and filter. Wash the precipitate with two quantities, each of 5 ml, of *light petroleum R*. Dissolve the precipitate in 10 ml of *water R* and boil for 1 min. Filter the mixture at 30 °C to 40 °C. Allow to cool. Filter, and dry the precipitate at 100 °C to 105 °C for 1 h. The melting point (*2.2.14*) of the precipitate is 237 °C to 241 °C.

**TESTS**
**Solution S**
Suspend 2.5 g in 50 ml of *distilled water R* and boil for 3 min. Cool and dilute to 50 ml with *distilled water R*. Filter. Use the filtrate as solution S.

**Appearance of solution**
Dissolve 0.5 g in *dilute hydrochloric acid R* and dilute to 50 ml with the same acid. The solution is clear (*2.2.1*) and colourless (*2.2.2, Method II*).

**Acidity or alkalinity**
To 10 ml of solution S add 0.1 ml of *bromothymol blue solution R1* and 0.2 ml of *0.01 M sodium hydroxide*. The solution is blue. Add 0.4 ml of *0.01 M hydrochloric acid*. The solution is yellow.

## Related substances

Examine by thin-layer chromatography (2.2.27), using *silica gel GF₂₅₄ R* as the coating substance.

*Test solution (a)* Dissolve 0.10 g of the substance to be examined in *dilute acetic acid R*, with heating if necessary, and dilute to 10 ml with the same acid.

*Test solution (b)* Dilute 1 ml of test solution (a) to 10 ml with *dilute acetic acid R*.

*Reference solution (a)* Dissolve 10 mg of *adenine CRS* in *dilute acetic acid R*, with heating if necessary, and dilute to 10 ml with the same acid.

*Reference solution (b)* Dilute 1 ml of test solution (b) to 20 ml with *dilute acetic acid R*.

*Reference solution (c)* Dissolve 10 mg of *adenine CRS* and 10 mg of *adenosine R* in *dilute acetic acid R*, with heating if necessary, and dilute to 10 ml with the same acid.

Apply to the plate 5 μl of each solution. Develop over a path of 12 cm using a mixture of 20 volumes of *concentrated ammonia R*, 40 volumes of *ethyl acetate R* and 40 volumes of *propanol R*. Dry the plate in a current of warm air and examine in ultraviolet light at 254 nm. Any spot in the chromatogram obtained with test solution (a), apart from the principal spot, is not more intense than the spot in the chromatogram obtained with reference solution (b) (0.5 per cent). The test is not valid unless the chromatogram obtained with reference solution (c) shows two clearly separated spots.

## Chlorides (2.4.4)

To 10 ml of solution S add 1 ml of *concentrated ammonia R* and 3 ml of *silver nitrate solution R2*. Filter. Wash the precipitate with a little *water R* and dilute the filtrate to 15 ml with *water R*. The solution complies with the limit test for chlorides (100 ppm). When carrying out the test, add 2 ml of *dilute nitric acid R* instead of 1 ml of *dilute nitric acid R*.

## Sulphates (2.4.13)

Dilute 10 ml of solution S to 15 ml with *distilled water R*. The solution complies with the limit test for sulphates (300 ppm).

## Ammonium

Prepare a cell consisting of two watch-glasses 60 mm in diameter placed edge to edge. To the inner wall of the upper watch-glass stick a piece of *red litmus paper R* 5 mm square and wetted with a few drops of *water R*. Finely powder the substance to be examined, place 0.5 g in the lower watch-glass and suspend in 0.5 ml of *water R*. To the suspension add 0.30 g of *heavy magnesium oxide R*. Briefly triturate with a glass rod. Immediately close the cell by putting the two watch-glasses together. Heat at 40 °C for 15 min. The litmus paper is not more intensely blue coloured than a standard prepared at the same time and in the same manner using 0.05 ml of *ammonium standard solution (100 ppm NH₄) R*, 0.5 ml of *water R* and 0.30 g of *heavy magnesium oxide R* (10 ppm).

## Heavy metals (2.4.8)

1.0 g complies with limit test C for heavy metals (20 ppm). Prepare the standard using 2 ml of *lead standard solution (10 ppm Pb) R*.

## Loss on drying (2.2.32)

Not more than 0.5 per cent, determined on 1.000 g by drying in an oven at 105 °C.

## Sulphated ash (2.4.14)

Not more than 0.1 per cent, determined on 1.0 g.

## ASSAY

Dissolve 0.100 g in a mixture of 20 ml of *acetic anhydride R* and 30 ml of *anhydrous acetic acid R*. Titrate with *0.1 M perchloric acid*, determining the end-point potentiometrically (2.2.20).

1 ml of *0.1 M perchloric acid* is equivalent to 13.51 mg of $C_5H_5N_5$.

*Ph Eur*

# Adenosine

(*Ph Eur monograph 1486*)

$C_{10}H_{13}N_5O_4$          267.2          58-61-7

## Action and use

Antiarrhythmic.

*Ph Eur*

## DEFINITION

9-β-D-Ribofuranosyl-9*H*-purin-6-amine.

## Content

99.0 per cent to 101.0 per cent (dried substance).

## CHARACTERS

### Appearance

White or almost white, crystalline powder.

### Solubility

Lightly soluble in water, soluble in hot water, practically insoluble in ethanol (96 per cent) and in methylene chloride. It dissolves in dilute mineral acids.

### mp

About 234 °C.

## IDENTIFICATION

Infrared absorption spectrophotometry (2.2.24).

*Comparison* adenosine CRS.

## TESTS

### Solution S

Suspend 5.0 g in 100 ml of distilled *water R* and heat to boiling. Allow to cool, filter with the aid of vacuum and dilute to 100 ml with *distilled water R*.

### Appearance of solution

Solution S is colourless (2.2.2, Method II).

### Acidity or alkalinity

To 10 ml of solution S, add 0.1 ml of *bromocresol purple solution R* and 0.1 ml of *0.01 M hydrochloric acid*. The solution is yellow. Add 0.4 ml of *0.01 M sodium hydroxide*. The solution is violet-blue.

**Specific optical rotation** (*2.2.7*)
− 45 to − 49 (dried substance).

Dissolve 1.25 g in *1 M hydrochloric acid* and dilute to 50.0 ml with the same acid. Examine within 10 min of preparing the solution.

**Related substances**
Liquid chromatography (*2.2.29*).

*Solvent mixture*   Dissolve 6.8 g of *potassium hydrogen sulphate R* and 3.4 g of *tetrabutylammonium hydrogen sulphate R* in *water R*, adjust to pH 6.5 with a 60 g/l solution of *potassium hydroxide R* and dilute to 1000 ml with the same solvent. Use a freshly prepared solvent mixture.

*Test solution*   Dissolve 20 mg of the substance to be examined in the mobile phase and dilute to 20 ml with the mobile phase.

*Reference solution (a)*   Dilute 1.0 ml of the test solution to 100.0 ml with the mobile phase. Dilute 1.0 ml of this solution to 10.0 ml with the mobile phase.

*Reference solution (b)*   Dissolve 5 mg of *adenine R* (impurity A) and 5 mg of *inosine R* (impurity G) in the mobile phase and dilute to 50 ml with the mobile phase. Dilute 4 ml of this solution to 100 ml with the mobile phase.

*Column:*
— *size*: $l = 0.25$ m, $\varnothing = 4.6$ mm;
— *stationary phase*: end-capped octadecylsilyl silica gel for chromatography R (5 μm).

*Mobile phase*   *water R*, solvent mixture (40:60 *V/V*).

*Flow rate*   1.5 ml/min.

*Detection*   Spectrophotometer at 254 nm.

*Injection*   20 μl.

*Run time*   1.5 times the retention time of adenosine.

*Relative retention*   With reference to adenosine (retention time = about 13 min): impurity A = about 0.3; impurity G = about 0.4.

*System suitability*   Reference solution (b):
— *resolution*: minimum 1.5 between the peaks due to impurities A and G.

*Limits:*
— *correction factors*: for the calculation of content, multiply the peak areas of the following impurities by the corresponding correction factor: impurity A = 0.6; impurity G = 1.4;
— *impurity A*: not more than twice the area of the principal peak in the chromatogram obtained with reference solution (a) (0.2 per cent);
— *impurity G*: not more than the area of the principal peak in the chromatogram obtained with reference solution (a) (0.1 per cent);
— *unspecified impurities*: for each impurity, not more than the area of the principal peak in the chromatogram obtained with reference solution (a) (0.10 per cent);
— *total*: not more than 5 times the area of the principal peak in the chromatogram obtained with reference solution (a) (0.5 per cent);
— *disregard limit*: 0.5 times the area of the principal peak in the chromatogram obtained with reference solution (a) (0.05 per cent).

**Chlorides** (*2.4.4*)
Maximum 100 ppm.

Dilute 10 ml of solution S to 15 ml with *water R*.

**Sulphates** (*2.4.13*)
Maximum 200 ppm, determined on solution S.

**Ammonium** (*2.4.1, Method B*)
Maximum 10 ppm, determined on 0.5 g.

Prepare the standard using 5 ml of *ammonium standard solution (1 ppm NH₄) R*.

**Loss on drying** (*2.2.32*)
Maximum 0.5 per cent, determined on 1.000 g by drying in an oven at 105 °C.

**Sulphated ash** (*2.4.14*)
Maximum 0.1 per cent, determined on 1.0 g.

**ASSAY**

Dissolve 0.200 g, warming slightly if necessary, in a mixture of 20 ml of *acetic anhydride R* and 30 ml of *anhydrous acetic acid R*. Titrate with *0.1 M perchloric acid*, determining the end-point potentiometrically (*2.2.20*).

1 ml of *0.1 M perchloric acid* is equivalent to 26.72 mg of $C_{10}H_{13}N_5O_4$.

**IMPURITIES**

*Specified impurities*   A, G.

*Other detectable impurities*   (The following substances would, if present at a sufficient level, be detected by one or other of the tests in the monograph. They are limited by the general acceptance criterion for other/unspecified impurities and/or by the general monograph *Substances for pharmaceutical use (2034)*. It is therefore not necessary to identify these impurities for demonstration of compliance. See also *5.10*. *Control of impurities in substances for pharmaceutical use*): F, H.

A. adenine,

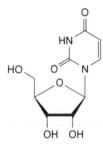

F. 1-β-D-ribofuranosylpyrimidine-2,4(1*H*,3*H*)-dione (uridine),

G. R = H: 9-β-D-ribofuranosyl-1,9-dihydro-6*H*-purin-6-one (inosine),

H. R = NH₂: 2-amino-9-β-D-ribofuranosyl-1,9-dihydro-6*H*-purin-6-one (guanosine).

*Ph Eur*

# Adipic Acid

*(Ph Eur monograph 1586)*

$C_6H_{10}O_4$                146.1                *124-04-9*

**Action and use**
Excipient.

*Ph Eur*

## DEFINITION
Hexanedioic acid.

## Content
99.0 per cent to 101.0 per cent (dried substance).

## CHARACTERS
**Appearance**
White or almost white, crystalline powder.

**Solubility**
Sparingly soluble in water, soluble in boiling water, freely soluble in alcohol and in methanol, soluble in acetone.

## IDENTIFICATION
A. Melting point (*2.2.14*): 151 °C to 154 °C.

B. Infrared absorption spectrophotometry (*2.2.24*).

*Comparison*    adipic acid CRS.

## TESTS
**Solution S**
Dissolve 5.0 g with heating in *distilled water R* and dilute to 50 ml with the same solvent. Allow to cool and to crystallise. Filter through a sintered-glass filter (40) (*2.1.2*). Wash the filter with *distilled water R*. Collect the filtrate and the washings until a volume of 50 ml is obtained.

**Appearance of solution**
The solution is clear (*2.2.1*) and colourless (*2.2.2*, *Method II*).

Dissolve 1.0 g in *methanol R* and dilute to 20 ml with the same solvent.

**Related substances**
Liquid chromatography (*2.2.29*).

*Test solution*    Dissolve 0.20 g of the substance to be examined in the mobile phase and dilute to 10.0 ml with the mobile phase.

*Reference solution (a)*    Dissolve 20 mg of *glutaric acid R* in 1.0 ml of the test solution and dilute to 10.0 ml with the mobile phase.

*Reference solution (b)*    Dilute 1.0 ml of the test solution to 100.0 ml with the mobile phase, dilute 1.0 ml of the solution to 10.0 ml with the mobile phase.

*Column:*
— *size: l* = 0.125 m, Ø = 4.0 mm,
— *stationary phase*: spherical octadecylsilyl silica gel for chromatography R (5 µm) with a specific surface area of 350 m²/g and a pore size of 10 nm,
— *temperature*: 30 °C.

*Mobile phase*    Mix 3 volumes of *acetonitrile R* and 97 volumes of a 24.5 g/l solution of *dilute phosphoric acid R*.

*Flow rate*    1 ml/min.

*Detection*    Spectrophotometer at 209 nm.

*Injection*    20 µl.

*Run time*    3 times the retention time of adipic acid.

*System suitability*    Reference solution (a):
— *resolution*: minimum 9.0 between the peaks due to glutaric acid and adipic acid.

*Limits:*
— *any impurity*: not more than the area of the principal peak in the chromatogram obtained with reference solution (b) (0.1 per cent),
— *total*: not more than 5 times the area of the principal peak in the chromatogram obtained with reference solution (b) (0.5 per cent),
— *disregard limit*: 0.5 times the area of the principal peak in the chromatogram obtained with reference solution (b) (0.05 per cent).

**Chlorides** (*2.4.4*)
Maximum 200 ppm.

2.5 ml of solution S diluted to 15 ml with *water R* complies with the limit test for chlorides.

**Nitrates**
Maximum 30 ppm.

To 1 ml of solution S add 2 ml of *concentrated ammonia R*, 0.5 ml of a 10 g/l solution of *manganese sulphate R*, 1 ml of a 10 g/l solution of *sulfanilamide R* and dilute to 20 ml with *water R*. Add 0.10 g of *zinc powder R* and cool in iced water for 30 min; shake from time to time. Filter and cool 10 ml of the filtrate in iced water. Add 2.5 ml of *hydrochloric acid R1* and 1 ml of a 10 g/l solution of *naphthylethylenediamine dihydrochloride R*. Allow to stand at room temperature. After 15 min the mixture is not more intensely coloured than a standard prepared at the same time and in the same manner, using 1.5 ml of *nitrate standard solution (2 ppm NO₃) R* instead of 1 ml of solution S. The test is invalid if a blank solution prepared at the same time and in the same manner, using 1 ml of *water R* instead of 1 ml of solution S, is more intensely coloured than a 2 mg/l solution of *potassium permanganate R*.

**Sulphates** (*2.4.13*)
Maximum 500 ppm.

3 ml of solution S diluted to 15 ml with *distilled water R* complies with the limit test for sulphates.

**Iron** (*2.4.9*)
Maximum 10 ppm.

10 ml of solution S complies with the limit test for iron.

**Heavy metals** (*2.4.8*)
Maximum 10 ppm.

12 ml of solution S complies with limit test A. Prepare the standard using *lead standard solution (1 ppm Pb) R*.

**Loss on drying** (*2.2.32*)
Maximum 0.2 per cent, determined on 1.000 g by drying in an oven at 105 °C.

**Sulphated ash** (*2.4.14*)
Maximum 0.1 per cent.

Melt 1.0 g completely over a gas burner, then ignite the melted substance with the burner. After ignition, lower or remove the flame in order to prevent the substance from boiling and keep it burning until completely carbonised. Carry out the test for sulphated ash using the residue.

## ASSAY
Dissolve 60.0 mg in 50 ml of *water R*. Add 0.2 ml of *phenolphthalein solution R* and titrate with *0.1 M sodium hydroxide*.

1 ml of *0.1 M sodium hydroxide* is equivalent to 7.31 mg of $C_6H_{10}O_4$.

## IMPURITIES

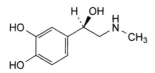

A. R = CH₂-CO₂H: pentanedioic acid (glutaric acid),

B. R = CO₂H: butanedioic acid (succinic acid),

C. R = [CH₂]₃-CO₂H: heptanedioic acid (pimelic acid).

_____ *Ph Eur*

# Adrenaline
# Epinephrine

(*Ph Eur monograph 2303*)

C₉H₁₃NO₃      183.2      *51-43-4*

### Action and use
Adrenoceptor agonist.

### Preparations
Adrenaline Eye Drops/Epinephrine Eye Drops

Dilute Adrenaline Injection (1 in 10,000)/Dilute Epinephrine Injection (1 in 10,000)

*Ph Eur* _____

## DEFINITION
4-[(1$R$)-1-Hydroxy-2-(methylamino)ethyl]benzene-1,2-diol. Synthetic product.

## Content
99.0 per cent to 101.0 per cent (dried substance).

## CHARACTERS
### Appearance
White or almost white crystalline powder, becoming coloured on exposure to air and light.

### Solubility
Practically insoluble in water, in ethanol (96 per cent) and in methylene chloride. It dissolves in hydrochloric acid.

## IDENTIFICATION
A. Infrared absorption spectrophotometry (*2.2.24*).

*Comparison*   adrenaline CRS.

B. Specific optical rotation (see Tests).

## TESTS
### Solution S
Dissolve 1.000 g in a 25.75 g/l solution of *hydrochloric acid R* and dilute to 50.0 ml with the same solvent. Examine the solution immediately.

### Appearance of solution
Solution S is not more opalescent than reference suspension II (*2.2.1*) and not more intensely coloured than reference solution BY₅ (*2.2.2, Method II*).

### Specific optical rotation (*2.2.7*)
− 50.0 to − 54.0 (dried substance), determined on solution S.

## Related substances
Liquid chromatography (*2.2.29*). *Prepare the solutions protected from light.*

*Solvent mixture A*   Dissolve 5.0 g of *potassium dihydrogen phosphate R* and 2.6 g of *sodium octanesulphonate R* in *water for chromatography R* and dilute to 1000 ml with the same solvent (it is usually necessary to stir for at least 30 min to achieve complete dissolution). Adjust to pH 2.8 with *phosphoric acid R*.

*Solvent mixture B*   acetonitrile R1, solvent mixture A (13:87 *V/V*).

*Test solution*   Dissolve 40 mg of the substance to be examined in 5 ml of *0.1 M hydrochloric acid* and dilute to 50.0 ml with solvent mixture B.

*Reference solution (a)*   Dilute 1.0 ml of the test solution to 100.0 ml with solvent mixture B. Dilute 1.0 ml of this solution to 10.0 ml with solvent mixture B.

*Reference solution (b)*   Dissolve 1.5 mg of noradrenaline tartrate CRS (impurity B) and 1.5 mg of *adrenalone hydrochloride R* (impurity C) in solvent mixture B, add 1.0 ml of the test solution and dilute to 100 ml with solvent mixture B.

*Reference solution (c)*   Dissolve the contents of a vial of *adrenaline impurity mixture CRS* (containing impurities D and E) in 1.0 ml of the blank solution.

*Reference solution (d)*   Dissolve 4 mg of *adrenaline with impurity F CRS* in 0.5 ml of *0.1 M hydrochloric acid* and dilute to 5 ml with solvent mixture B.

*Blank solution*   0.1 M hydrochloric acid, solvent mixture B (1:9 *V/V*).

*Column:*
— *size:* $l$ = 0.10 m, Ø = 4.6 mm;
— *stationary phase:* end-capped octadecylsilyl silica gel for chromatography R (3 µm);
— *temperature:* 50 °C.

*Mobile phase:*
— *mobile phase A:* acetonitrile R1, solvent mixture A (5:95 *V/V*);
— *mobile phase B:* acetonitrile R1, solvent mixture A (45:55 *V/V*);

| Time (min) | Mobile phase A (per cent *V/V*) | Mobile phase B (per cent *V/V*) |
|---|---|---|
| 0 - 15 | 92 → 50 | 8 → 50 |
| 15 - 20 | 50 → 92 | 50 → 8 |
| 20 - 25 | 92 | 8 |

*Flow rate*   2.0 ml/min.

*Detection*   Spectrophotometer at 210 nm.

*Injection*   20 µl.

*Identification of impurities*   Use the chromatogram supplied with *adrenaline impurity mixture CRS* and the chromatogram obtained with reference solution (c) to identify the peaks due to impurities D and E; use the chromatogram supplied with *adrenaline with impurity F CRS* and the chromatogram obtained with reference solution (d) to identify the peak due to impurity F.

*Relative retention*   With reference to adrenaline (retention time = about 4 min): impurity F = about 0.2; impurity B = about 0.8; impurity C = about 1.3; impurity D = about 3.3; impurity E = about 3.7.

*System suitability*   Reference solution (b):
— *resolution:* minimum 3.0 between the peaks due to impurity B and adrenaline.

*Limits:*
— *correction factors*: for the calculation of content, multiply the peak areas of the following impurities by the corresponding correction factor: impurity D = 0.7; impurity E = 0.6;
— *impurities B, C, F*: for each impurity, not more than twice the area of the principal peak in the chromatogram obtained with reference solution (a) (0.2 per cent);
— *impurities D, E*: for each impurity, not more than the area of the principal peak in the chromatogram obtained with reference solution (a) (0.1 per cent);
— *unspecified impurities*: for each impurity, not more than the area of the principal peak in the chromatogram obtained with reference solution (a) (0.10 per cent);
— *total*: not more than 5 times the area of the principal peak in the chromatogram obtained with reference solution (a) (0.5 per cent);
— *disregard limit*: 0.5 times the area of the principal peak in the chromatogram obtained with reference solution (a) (0.05 per cent).

**Loss on drying** *(2.2.32)*
Maximum 0.5 per cent, determined on 1.000 g by drying over *diphosphorus pentoxide R* at a pressure not exceeding 0.7 kPa for 18 h.

**Sulphated ash** *(2.4.14)*
Maximum 0.1 per cent, determined on 1.0 g.

**ASSAY**
Dissolve 0.150 g in 50 ml of *anhydrous acetic acid R*. Titrate with *0.1 M perchloric acid*, determining the end-point potentiometrically *(2.2.20)*.

1 ml of *0.1 M perchloric acid* is equivalent to 18.32 mg of $C_9H_{13}NO_3$.

**STORAGE**
Under nitrogen, protected from light.

**IMPURITIES**
*Specified impurities*   *B, C, D, E, F.*

B. noradrenaline,

C. R = H: 1-(3,4-dihydroxyphenyl)-2-(methylamino)ethanone (adrenalone),
E. R = CH$_2$-C$_6$H$_5$: 2-(benzylmethylamino)-1-(3,4-dihydroxyphenyl)ethanone,

D. R = OH, R' = CH$_2$-C$_6$H$_5$: 4-[(1R)-2-(benzylmethylamino)-1-hydroxyethyl]benzene-1,2-diol,
F. R = SO$_3$H, R' = H: (1R)-1-(3,4-dihydroxyphenyl)-2-(methylamino)ethanesulphonic acid.

*Ph Eur*

# Adrenaline Acid Tartrate
# Epinephrine Acid Tartrate
*(Adrenaline Tartrate, Ph Eur monograph 0254)*

$C_9H_{13}NO_3,C_4H_6O_6$          333.3          *51-42-3*

**Action and use**
Adrenoceptor agonist.

**Preparations**
Adrenaline Injection/Epinephrine Injection

Dilute Adrenaline Injection (1 in 10,000)/Dilute Epinephrine Injection (1 in 10,000)

Adrenaline Solution/Epinephrine Solution

Adrenaline and Cocaine Intranasal Solution

Bupivacaine and Adrenaline Injection/Bupivacaine and Epinephrine Injection

Lidocaine and Adrenaline Injection/Lidocaine and Epinephrine Injection

*Ph Eur*

**DEFINITION**
(1R)-1-(3,4-Dihydroxyphenyl)-2-(methylamino)ethanol hydrogen (2R,3R)-2,3-dihydroxybutanedioate.

**Content**
98.5 per cent to 101.0 per cent (dried substance).

**CHARACTERS**
**Appearance**
White or greyish-white, crystalline powder.

**Solubility**
Freely soluble in water, slightly soluble in ethanol (96 per cent).

**IDENTIFICATION**
A. Dissolve 5 g in 50 ml of a 5 g/l solution of *sodium metabisulphite R* and make alkaline by addition of *ammonia R*. Keep the mixture at room temperature for at least 15 min and filter. Reserve the filtrate for identification test C. Wash the precipitate with 3 quantities, each of 10 ml, of *methanol R*. Dry at 80 °C. The specific optical rotation *(2.2.7)* of the residue (adrenaline base) is − 50 to − 53.5, determined using a 20.0 g/l solution in *0.5 M hydrochloric acid*.

B. Infrared absorption spectrophotometry *(2.2.24)*.

*Preparation*   Discs of adrenaline base prepared as described under identification test A.

*Comparison*   Use adrenaline base prepared as described under identification test A from 50 mg of *adrenaline tartrate CRS* dissolved in 5 ml of a 5 g/l solution of *sodium metabisulphite R*. Keep the mixture at room temperature for at least 30 min. Filter through a sintered-glass filter *(2.1.2)*.

C. 0.2 ml of the filtrate obtained in identification test A gives reaction (b) of tartrates *(2.3.1)*.

## TESTS

### Appearance of solution

The solution is not more opalescent than reference suspension II (*2.2.1*) and not more intensely coloured than reference solution $BY_5$ (*2.2.2, Method II*).

Dissolve 0.5 g in *water R* and dilute to 10 ml with the same solvent. Examine the solution immediately.

### Related substances

Liquid chromatography (*2.2.29*). *Prepare the solutions protected from light.*

*Solvent mixture A*   Dissolve 5.0 g of *potassium dihydrogen phosphate R* and then 2.6 g of *sodium octanesulphonate R* in *water for chromatography R*, and dilute to 1000 ml with the same solvent (it is usually necessary to stir for at least 30 min to achieve complete dissolution). Adjust to pH 2.8 with *phosphoric acid R*.

*Solvent mixture B*   *acetonitrile R1*, solvent mixture A (130:870 *V/V*).

*Test solution*   Dissolve 75 mg of the substance to be examined in 5 ml of *0.1 M hydrochloric acid* and dilute to 50 ml with solvent mixture B.

*Reference solution (a)*   Dilute 1.0 ml of the test solution to 100.0 ml with solvent mixture B. Dilute 1.0 ml of this solution to 10.0 ml with solvent mixture B.

*Reference solution (b)*   Dissolve 1.5 mg of *noradrenaline tartrate CRS* (impurity B) and 1.5 mg of *adrenalone hydrochloride R* (impurity C) in solvent mixture B, add 1.0 ml of the test solution and dilute to 100.0 ml with solvent mixture B.

*Reference solution (c)*   Dissolve the contents of a vial of *adrenaline impurity mixture CRS* (impurities D and E) in 0.1 ml of *0.1 M hydrochloric acid* and 0.9 ml of solvent mixture B.

*Reference solution (d)*   Dissolve 7.5 mg of *adrenaline tartrate with impurity A CRS* in 0.5 ml of *0.1 M hydrochloric acid* and dilute to 5.0 ml with solvent mixture B.

*Blank solution*   *0.1 M hydrochloric acid*, solvent mixture B (1:9 *V/V*).

*Column:*
— *size: l* = 0.10 m, Ø = 4.6 mm;
— *stationary phase: end-capped octadecylsilyl silica gel for chromatography R* (3 μm);
— *temperature*: 50 °C.

*Mobile phase:*
— *mobile phase A: acetonitrile R1*, solvent mixture A (5:95 *V/V*);
— *mobile phase B: acetonitrile R1*, solvent mixture A (45:55 *V/V*);

| Time (min) | Mobile phase A (per cent *V/V*) | Mobile phase B (per cent *V/V*) |
|---|---|---|
| 0 - 15 | 92 → 50 | 8 → 50 |
| 15 - 20 | 50 → 92 | 50 → 8 |
| 20 - 25 | 92 | 8 |

*Flow rate*   2.0 ml/min.

*Detection*   Spectrophotometer at 210 nm.

*Injection*   20 μl.

*Identification of impurities*   Use the chromatogram supplied with *adrenaline impurity mixture CRS* and the chromatogram obtained with reference solution (c) to identify the peaks due to impurities D and E; use the chromatogram supplied with *adrenaline tartrate with impurity A CRS* and the chromatogram obtained with reference solution (d) to identify the peak due to impurity A.

*Relative retention*   With reference to adrenaline (retention time = about 4 min): impurity B = about 0.8; impurity C = about 1.3; impurity A = about 3.2; impurity D = about 3.3; impurity E = about 3.7.

*System suitability*   Reference solution (b):
— *resolution*: minimum 3.0 between the peaks due to impurity B and adrenaline.

*Limits:*
— *correction factors*: for the calculation of content, multiply the peak areas of the following impurities by the corresponding correction factor: impurity D = 0.7; impurity E = 0.6;
— *impurity A*: not more than 3 times the area of the principal peak in the chromatogram obtained with reference solution (a) (0.3 per cent);
— *impurities B, C*: for each impurity, not more than twice the area of the principal peak in the chromatogram obtained with reference solution (a) (0.2 per cent);
— *impurities D, E*: for each impurity, not more than the area of the principal peak in the chromatogram obtained with reference solution (a) (0.1 per cent);
— *unspecified impurities*: for each impurity, not more than the area of the principal peak in the chromatogram obtained with reference solution (a) (0.10 per cent);
— *total*: not more than 6 times the area of the principal peak in the chromatogram obtained with reference solution (a) (0.6 per cent);
— *disregard limit*: 0.5 times the area of the principal peak in the chromatogram obtained with reference solution (a) (0.05 per cent).

### Loss on drying (*2.2.32*)

Maximum 0.5 per cent, determined on 1.000 g by drying *in vacuo* for 18 h.

### Sulphated ash (*2.4.14*)

Maximum 0.1 per cent, determined on 1.0 g.

## ASSAY

Dissolve 0.300 g in 50 ml of *anhydrous acetic acid R*, heating gently if necessary. Titrate with *0.1 M perchloric acid* until a bluish-green colour is obtained, using 0.1 ml of *crystal violet solution R* as indicator.

1 ml of *0.1 M perchloric acid* is equivalent to 33.33 mg of $C_{13}H_{19}NO_9$.

## STORAGE

In an airtight container, or preferably in a sealed tube under vacuum or under an inert gas, protected from light.

## IMPURITIES

*Specified impurities*   A, B, C, D, E.

A. unknown structure,

B. noradrenaline,

C. R = H: 1-(3,4-dihydroxyphenyl)-2-(methylamino)ethanone (adrenalone),

E. R = $CH_2$-$C_6H_5$: 2-(benzylmethylamino)-1-(3,4-dihydroxyphenyl)ethanone,

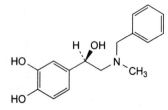

D. (1*R*)-2-(benzylmethylamino)-
1-(3,4-dihydroxyphenyl)ethanol.

_____ *Ph Eur*

# Agar

(*Ph Eur monograph 0310*)

**Action and use**
Excipient.

*Ph Eur* _____

## DEFINITION
Polysaccharides from various species of Rhodophyceae mainly belonging to the genus *Gelidium*. It is prepared by treating the algae with boiling water; the extract is filtered whilst hot, concentrated and dried.

## CHARACTERS
**Appearance**
Powder or crumpled strips 2-5 mm wide or sometimes flakes, colourless or pale yellow, translucent, somewhat tough and difficult to break, becoming more brittle on drying.
Mucilaginous taste.

## IDENTIFICATION
A. Examine under a microscope. When mounted in *0.005 M iodine*, the strips or flakes are partly stained brownish-violet. Magnified 100 times, they show the following diagnostic characters: numerous minute, colourless, ovoid or rounded grains on an amorphous background; occasional brown, round or ovoid spores with a reticulated surface, measuring up to 60 μm, may be present. Reduce to a powder, if necessary. The powder is yellowish-white. Examine under a microscope using *0.005 M iodine*. The powder presents angular fragments with numerous grains similar to those seen in the strips and flakes; some of the fragments are stained brownish-violet.

B. Dissolve 0.1 g with heating in 50 ml of *water R*. Cool. To 1 ml of the mucilage carefully add 3 ml of *water R* so as to form 2 separate layers. Add 0.1 ml of *0.05 M iodine*. A dark brownish-violet colour appears at the interface. Mix. The liquid becomes pale yellow.

C. Heat 5 ml of the mucilage prepared for identification test B on a water-bath with 0.5 ml of *hydrochloric acid R* for 30 min. Add 1 ml of *barium chloride solution R1*. A white turbidity develops within 30 min.

D. Heat 0.5 g with 50 ml of *water R* on a water-bath until dissolved. Only a few fragments remain insoluble. During cooling, the solution gels between 35 °C and 30 °C. Heat the gel thus obtained on a water-bath; it does not liquefy below 80 °C.

## TESTS
**Swelling index** (*2.8.4*)
Minimum 10 and within 10 per cent of the value stated on the label, determined on the powdered drug (355) (*2.9.12*).

**Insoluble matter**
Maximum 1.0 per cent.

To 5.00 g of the powdered drug (355) (*2.9.12*) add 100 ml of *water R* and 14 ml of dilute *hydrochloric acid R*. Boil gently for 15 min with frequent stirring. Filter the hot liquid through a tared, sintered-glass filter (160) (*2.1.2*), rinse the filter with hot *water R* and dry at 100-105 °C. The residue weighs a maximum of 50 mg.

**Gelatin**
To 1.00 g add 100 ml of *water R* and heat on a water-bath until dissolved. Allow to cool to 50 °C. To 5 ml of this solution add 5 ml of *picric acid solution R*. No turbidity appears within 10 min.

**Loss on drying** (*2.2.32*)
Maximum 20.0 per cent, determined on 1.000 g of the powdered drug (355) (*2.9.12*) by drying in an oven at 105 °C.

**Total ash** (*2.4.16*)
Maximum 5.0 per cent.

**Microbial contamination**
TAMC: acceptance criterion $10^3$ CFU/g (*2.6.12*).
TYMC: acceptance criterion $10^2$ CFU/g (*2.6.12*).
Absence of *Escherichia coli* (*2.6.13*).
Absence of *Salmonella* (*2.6.13*).

## LABELLING
The label states the swelling index.

_____ *Ph Eur*

# Medical Air

(*Medicinal Air, Ph Eur monograph 1238*)
*When Medical Air is intended for use in a room in which magnetic resonance imaging (MRI) is being performed, the cylinder and fittings should be made from suitable non-ferromagnetic materials and labelled accordingly.*

*Ph Eur* _____

## DEFINITION
Compressed ambient air.

**Content**
20.4 per cent *V/V* to 21.4 per cent *V/V* of oxygen ($O_2$).

## CHARACTERS
**Appearance**
Colourless gas.

**Solubility**
At 20 °C at a pressure of 101 kPa, 1 volume dissolves in about 50 volumes of water.

## PRODUCTION
**Carbon dioxide**
Maximum 500 ppm *V/V*, determined using an infrared analyser (*2.5.24*).

*Gas to be examined* Filter the substance to be examined to avoid stray light phenomena.

*Reference gas (a)* Use a mixture of 21 per cent *V/V* of oxygen *R* and 79 per cent *V/V* of *nitrogen R1*, containing less than 1 ppm *V/V* of *carbon dioxide R1*.

*Reference gas (b)* Use a mixture of 21 per cent *V/V* of oxygen *R* and 79 per cent *V/V* of *nitrogen R1*, containing 500 ppm *V/V* of *carbon dioxide R1*.

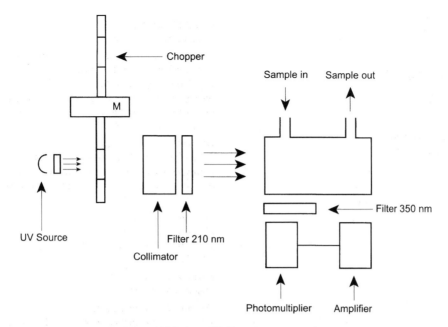

Figure 1238.-1. – *UV fluorescence analyser*

Calibrate the apparatus and set the sensitivity using reference gases (a) and (b). Measure the content of carbon dioxide in the gas to be examined.

**Carbon monoxide**

Maximum 5 ppm *V/V*, determined using an infrared analyser (2.5.25).

*Gas to be examined*   Filter the substance to be examined to avoid stray light phenomena.

*Reference gas (a)*   Use a mixture of 21 per cent *V/V* of oxygen R and 79 per cent *V/V* of *nitrogen R1*, containing less than 1 ppm *V/V* of *carbon monoxide R*.

*Reference gas (b)*   Use a mixture of 21 per cent *V/V* of oxygen R and 79 per cent *V/V* of *nitrogen R1*, containing 5 ppm *V/V* of *carbon monoxide R*.

Calibrate the apparatus and set the sensitivity using reference gases (a) and (b). Measure the content of carbon monoxide in the gas to be examined.

**Sulphur dioxide**

Maximum 1 ppm *V/V*, determined using an ultraviolet fluorescence analyser (Figure 1238.-1).

The apparatus consists of the following:

— a system generating ultraviolet radiation with a wavelength of 210 nm, made up of an ultraviolet lamp, a collimator, and a selective filter; the beam is blocked periodically by a chopper rotating at high speeds;

— a reaction chamber, through which flows the gas to be examined;

— a system that detects radiation emitted at a wavelength of 350 nm, made up of a selective filter, a photomultiplier tube and an amplifier.

*Gas to be examined*   Filter the substance to be examined.

*Reference gas (a)*   Use a mixture of 21 per cent *V/V* of oxygen R and 79 per cent *V/V* of *nitrogen R1*.

*Reference gas (b)*   Use a mixture of 21 per cent *V/V* of oxygen R and 79 per cent *V/V* of *nitrogen R1*, containing 0.5 ppm *V/V* to 2 ppm *V/V* of *sulphur dioxide R1*.

Calibrate the apparatus and set the sensitivity using reference gases (a) and (b). Measure the content of sulphur dioxide in the gas to be examined.

**Oil**

Maximum 0.1 mg/m³, determined using an oil detector tube (2.1.6), when an oil-lubricated compressor is used for the production.

**Nitrogen monoxide and nitrogen dioxide**

Maximum 2 ppm *V/V* in total, determined using a chemiluminescence analyser (2.5.26).

*Gas to be examined*   The substance to be examined.

*Reference gas (a)*   Use a mixture of 21 per cent *V/V* of oxygen R and 79 per cent *V/V* of *nitrogen R1*, containing less than 0.05 ppm *V/V* of nitrogen monoxide and nitrogen dioxide.

*Reference gas (b)*   Use a mixture of 2 ppm *V/V* of *nitrogen monoxide R* in *nitrogen R1*.

Calibrate the apparatus and set the sensitivity using reference gases (a) and (b). Measure the content of nitrogen monoxide and nitrogen dioxide in the gas to be examined.

**Water**

Maximum 67 ppm *V/V*, determined using an electrolytic hygrometer (2.5.28), except where the competent authority decides that the following limit applies to medicinal air generated on-site and distributed in pipe-line systems operating at a pressure not greater than 10 bars and a temperature not less than 5 °C: maximum 870 ppm *V/V*, determined using an electrolytic hygrometer (2.5.28).

**Assay**

Determine the concentration of oxygen in air using a paramagnetic analyser (2.5.27).

**IDENTIFICATION**

*First identification*   C.

*Second identification*   A, B.

A. In a conical flask containing the substance to be examined, place a glowing wood splinter. The splinter remains glowing.

B. Use a gas burette (Figure 1238.-2) of 25 ml capacity in the form of a chamber in the middle of which is a tube graduated in 0.2 per cent between 19.0 per cent and 23.0 per cent, and isolated at each end by a tap with a conical barrel. The lower tap is joined to a tube with an

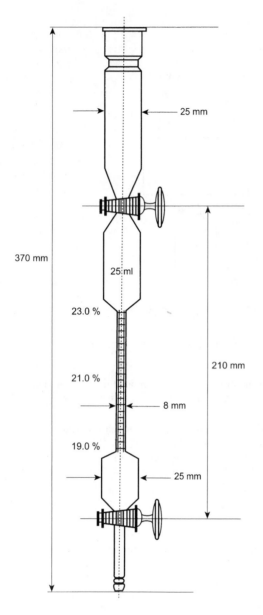

Figure 1238.-2. – *Gas burette*

25 mm

370 mm

25 ml

23.0 %

210 mm

21.0 %

8 mm

19.0 %

25 mm

olive-shaped nozzle and is used to introduce the gas into the apparatus. A cylindrical funnel above the upper tap is used to introduce the absorbent solution. Wash the burette with *water R* and dry. Open the 2 taps. Connect the nozzle to the source of the gas to be examined and set the flow rate to 1 litre/min. Flush the burette by passing the gas to be examined through it for 1 min. Close the lower tap of the burette and immediately afterwards the upper tap. Rapidly disconnect the burette from the source of the gas to be examined. Rapidly give a half turn to the upper tap to eliminate any excess pressure in the burette. Keeping the burette vertical, fill the funnel with a freshly prepared mixture of 21 ml of a 560 g/l solution of *potassium hydroxide R* and 130 ml of a 200 g/l solution of *sodium dithionite R*. Open the upper tap slowly. The solution absorbs the oxygen and enters the burette. Allow to stand for 10 min without shaking. Read the level of the liquid meniscus on the graduated part of the burette. This figure represents the percentage *V/V* of oxygen. The value read is 20.4 to 21.4.

C. It complies with the limits of the assay.

## TESTS

### Carbon dioxide
Maximum 500 ppm *V/V*, determined using a carbon dioxide detector tube (*2.1.6*).

### Sulphur dioxide
Maximum 1 ppm *V/V*, determined using a sulphur dioxide detector tube (*2.1.6*).

### Oil
Maximum 0.1 mg/m$^3$, determined using an oil detector tube (*2.1.6*), when an oil-lubricated compressor is used for the production.

### Nitrogen monoxide and nitrogen dioxide
Maximum 2 ppm *V/V*, determined using a nitrogen monoxide and nitrogen dioxide detector tube (*2.1.6*).

### Carbon monoxide
Maximum 5 ppm *V/V*, determined using a carbon monoxide detector tube (*2.1.6*).

### Water vapour
Maximum 67 ppm *V/V*, determined using a water vapour detector tube (*2.1.6*), except where the competent authority decides that the following limit applies to medicinal air generated on-site and distributed in pipe-line systems operating at a pressure not greater than 10 bars and a temperature not less than 5 °C: maximum 870 ppm *V/V*, determined using a water vapour detector tube (*2.1.6*).

## STORAGE
As a gas, in suitable containers complying with the legal regulations or as a gas supplied by a pipe network.

## LABELLING
Where applicable, the label states the production method, as regards to the use of an oil - lubricated compression.

## IMPURITIES
A. carbon dioxide,

B. sulphur dioxide,

C. nitrogen monoxide,

D. nitrogen dioxide,

E. oil,

F. carbon monoxide,

G. water.

*Ph Eur*

# Synthetic Air

(*Synthetic Medicinal Air, Ph Eur monograph 1684*)
*When Synthetic Air is intended for use in a room in which magnetic resonance imaging (MRI) is being performed, the cylinder and fittings should be made from suitable non-ferromagnetic materials and labelled accordingly.*

*Ph Eur*

## DEFINITION
Mixture of *Nitrogen (1247)* and *Oxygen (0417)*.

### Content
95.0 per cent to 105.0 per cent of the nominal value which is between 21.0 per cent *V/V* to 22.5 per cent *V/V* of oxygen ($O_2$).

## CHARACTERS
Colourless and odourless gas.

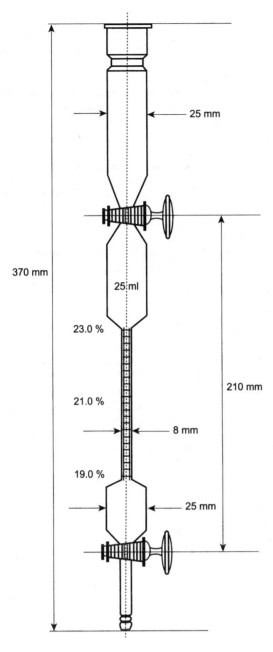

Figure 1684.-1.– *Gas burette*

**Solubility**

At a temperature of 20 °C and a pressure of 101 kPa, 1 volume dissolves in about 50 volumes of water.

## PRODUCTION

**Water** (*2.5.28*)

Maximum 67 ppm *V/V*.

**Assay** (*2.5.27*)

Carry out the determination of oxygen in gases.

## IDENTIFICATION

*First identification   C.*

*Second identification   A, B.*

A. In a conical flask containing the substance to be examined, place a glowing splinter of wood. The splinter remains glowing.

B. Use a gas burette (Figure 1684.-1) of 25 ml capacity in the form of a chamber, in the middle of which is a tube

graduated in 0.2 per cent between 19.0 per cent and 23.0 per cent, and isolated at each end by a tap with a conical barrel. The lower tap is joined to a tube with an olive-shaped nozzle and is used to introduce the gas into the apparatus. A cylindrical funnel above the upper tap is used to introduce the absorbent solution. Wash the burette with *water R* and dry. Open both taps. Connect the nozzle to the source of the substance to be examined and set the flow rate to 1 litre/min. Flush the burette by passing the substance to be examined through it for 1 min. Close the lower tap of the burette and immediately afterwards the upper tap. Rapidly disconnect the burette from the source of the substance to be examined. Rapidly give a half turn of the upper tap to eliminate any excess pressure in the burette. Keeping the burette vertical, fill the funnel with a freshly prepared mixture of 21 ml of a 560 g/l solution of *potassium hydroxide R* and 130 ml of a 200 g/l solution of *sodium dithionite R*. Open the upper tap slowly. The solution absorbs the oxygen and enters the burette. Allow to stand for 10 min without shaking. Read the level of the liquid meniscus on the graduated part of the burette. This figure represents the percentage *V/V* of oxygen. The value read is 95.0 per cent to 105.0 per cent of the nominal value.

C. It complies with the limits of the assay.

## TESTS

**Water vapour**

Maximum 67 ppm *V/V*, determined using a water vapour detector tube (*2.1.6*).

## STORAGE

As a compressed gas in suitable containers complying with the legal regulations or as a compressed gas supplied by a pipe network, after mixing of the components.

## LABELLING

The label states the nominal content of $O_2$ in per cent *V/V*.

## IMPURITIES

A. water.

*Ph Eur*

# Alanine

(*Ph Eur monograph 0752*)

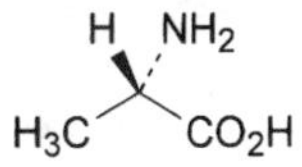

$C_3H_7NO_2$                   89.1                   *56-41-7*

**Action and use**

Amino acid.

*Ph Eur*

## DEFINITION

Alanine contains not less than 98.5 per cent and not more than the equivalent of 101.0 per cent of (*S*)-2-aminopropanoic acid, calculated with reference to the dried substance.

## CHARACTERS

White or almost white, crystalline powder or colourless crystals, freely soluble in water, very slightly soluble in alcohol.

## IDENTIFICATION

*First identification* A, B.

*Second identification* A, C, D.

A. It complies with the test for specific optical rotation (see Tests).

B. Examine by infrared absorption spectrophotometry (2.2.24), comparing with the spectrum obtained with *alanine CRS*. Examine the substances prepared as discs.

C. Examine the chromatograms obtained in the test for ninhydrin-positive substances. The principal spot in the chromatogram obtained with test solution (b) is similar in position, colour and size to the principal spot in the chromatogram obtained with reference solution (a).

D. Dissolve 0.5 g in a mixture of 1 ml of *water R*, 0.5 ml of a 100 g/l solution of *sodium nitrite R* and 0.25 ml of *hydrochloric acid R1*. Shake. Gas is given off. Add 2 ml of *dilute sodium hydroxide solution R*, followed by 0.25 ml of *iodinated potassium iodide solution R*. After about 30 min, a yellow precipitate with a characteristic odour is formed.

## TESTS

### Solution S

Dissolve 2.5 g in *distilled water R* and dilute to 50 ml with the same solvent.

### Appearance of solution

Dilute 10 ml of solution S to 20 ml with *water R*. The solution is clear (2.2.1) and not more intensely coloured than reference solution $BY_6$ (2.2.2, Method II).

### Specific optical rotation (2.2.7)

Dissolve 2.50 g in *hydrochloric acid R1* and dilute to 25.0 ml with the same acid. The specific optical rotation is + 13.5 to + 15.5, calculated with reference to the dried substance.

### Ninhydrin-positive substances

Examine by thin-layer chromatography (2.2.27), using a *TLC silica gel plate R*.

*Test solution (a)* Dissolve 0.10 g in *water R* and dilute to 10 ml with the same solvent.

*Test solution (b)* Dilute 1 ml of test solution (a) to 50 ml with *water R*.

*Reference solution (a)* Dissolve 10 mg of *alanine CRS* in *water R* and dilute to 50 ml with the same solvent.

*Reference solution (b)* Dilute 5 ml of test solution (b) to 20 ml with *water R*.

*Reference solution (c)* Dissolve 10 mg of *alanine CRS* and 10 mg of *glycine CRS* in *water R* and dilute to 25 ml with the same solvent.

Apply separately to the plate 5 µl of each solution. Allow the plate to dry in air. Develop over a path of 15 cm with a mixture of 20 volumes of *glacial acetic acid R*, 20 volumes of *water R* and 60 volumes of *butanol R*. Allow the plate to dry in air. Spray with *ninhydrin solution R*. Heat the plate at 100 °C to 105 °C for 15 min. Any spot in the chromatogram obtained with test solution (a), apart from the principal spot, is not more intense than the spot in the chromatogram obtained with reference solution (b) (0.5 per cent). The test is not valid unless the chromatogram obtained with reference solution (c) shows two clearly separated spots.

### Chlorides (2.4.4)

Dilute 5 ml of solution S to 15 ml with *water R*. The solution complies with the limit test for chlorides (200 ppm).

### Sulphates (2.4.13)

Dilute 10 ml of solution S to 15 ml with *distilled water R*. The solution complies with the limit test for sulphates (300 ppm).

### Ammonium (2.4.1)

50 mg complies with limit test B for ammonium (200 ppm). Prepare the standard using 0.1 ml of *ammonium standard solution (100 ppm NH4) R*.

### Iron (2.4.9)

In a separating funnel, dissolve 1.0 g in 10 ml of *dilute hydrochloric acid R*. Shake with three quantities, each of 10 ml, of *methyl isobutyl ketone R1*, shaking for 3 min each time. To the combined organic layers add 10 ml of *water R* and shake for 3 min. The aqueous layer complies with the limit test for iron (10 ppm).

### Heavy metals (2.4.8)

Dissolve 2.0 g in *water R* and dilute to 20 ml with the same solvent. 12 ml of the solution complies with limit test A for heavy metals (10 ppm). Prepare the standard using *lead standard solution (1 ppm Pb) R*.

### Loss on drying (2.2.32)

Not more than 0.5 per cent, determined on 1.000 g by drying in an oven at 105 °C.

### Sulphated ash (2.4.14)

Not more than 0.1 per cent, determined on 1.0 g.

## ASSAY

Dissolve 80.0 mg in 3 ml of *anhydrous formic acid R*. Add 30 ml of *anhydrous acetic acid R*. Using 0.1 ml of *naphtholbenzein solution R* as indicator, titrate with *0.1 M perchloric acid*, until the colour changes from brownish-yellow to green.

1 ml of *0.1 M perchloric acid* is equivalent to 8.91 mg of $C_3H_7NO_2$.

## STORAGE

Store protected from light.

*Ph Eur*

# Albendazole

*(Ph Eur monograph 1386)*

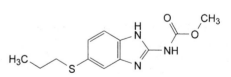

$C_{12}H_{15}N_3O_2S$          265.3          54965-21-8

### Action and use

Benzimidazole antihelminthic.

### Preparations

Albendazole Oral Suspension

Albendazole Oral Suspension with Minerals

*Ph Eur*

## DEFINITION

Methyl [5-(propylsulphanyl)-1*H*-benzimidazol-2-yl]carbamate.

### Content

98.0 per cent to 102.0 per cent (dried substance).

## CHARACTERS

### Appearance

White or slightly yellowish powder.

### Solubility

Practically insoluble in water, freely soluble in anhydrous formic acid, very slightly soluble in methylene chloride, practically insoluble in ethanol (96 per cent).

## IDENTIFICATION

Infrared absorption spectrophotometry (2.2.24).

*Preparation*   Discs.

*Comparison*   albendazole CRS.

## TESTS

### Appearance of solution

The solution is clear (2.2.1) and not more intensely coloured than reference solution $BY_6$ (2.2.2, Method II).

Dissolve 0.10 g in a mixture of 1 volume of *anhydrous formic acid R* and 9 volumes of *methylene chloride R* and dilute to 10 ml with the same mixture of solvents.

### Related substances

Liquid chromatography (2.2.29).

*Test solution*   Dissolve 25.0 mg of the substance to be examined in 5 ml of *methanol R* containing 1 per cent V/V of *sulphuric acid R* and dilute to 50.0 ml with the mobile phase.

*Reference solution (a)*   Dissolve 10.0 mg of the substance to be examined in 10 ml of *methanol R* containing 1 per cent V/V of *sulphuric acid R* and dilute to 100.0 ml with the mobile phase. Dilute 0.5 ml of this solution to 20.0 ml with the mobile phase.

*Reference solution (b)*   Dissolve 50.0 mg of the substance to be examined and 50 mg of *oxibendazole CRS* in 5 ml of *methanol R* containing 1 per cent V/V of *sulphuric acid R* and dilute to 100.0 ml with the mobile phase.

*Column:*
— *size*: $l$ = 0.25 m, Ø = 4.6 mm;
— *stationary phase*: spherical end-capped octadecylsilyl silica gel for chromatography R (5 μm) with a pore size of 10 nm and a carbon loading of 19 per cent.

*Mobile phase*   Mix 300 volumes of a 1.67 g/l solution of *ammonium dihydrogen phosphate R* and 700 volumes of *methanol R*.

*Flow rate*   0.7 ml/min.

*Detection*   Spectrophotometer at 254 nm.

*Injection*   20 μl.

*Run time*   1.5 times the retention time of albendazole.

*Relative retention*   With reference to albendazole: impurity D = about 0.40; impurities B and C = about 0.43; impurity E = about 0.47; impurity F = about 0.57; impurity A = about 0.80.

*System suitability*   Reference solution (b):
— *resolution*: minimum 3.0 between the peaks due to albendazole and oxibendazole.

*Limits:*
— *impurities A, B, C, D, E, F*: for each impurity, not more than 1.5 times the area of the principal peak in the chromatogram obtained with reference solution (a) (0.75 per cent);
— *total*: not more than 3 times the area of the principal peak in the chromatogram obtained with reference solution (a) (1.5 per cent);
— *disregard limit*: 0.1 times the area of the principal peak in the chromatogram obtained with reference solution (a) (0.05 per cent).

### Loss on drying (2.2.32)

Maximum 0.5 per cent, determined on 1.000 g by drying in an oven at 105 °C for 4 h.

### Sulphated ash (2.4.14)

Maximum 0.2 per cent, determined on 1.0 g.

## ASSAY

*In order to avoid overheating during the titration, mix thoroughly throughout and stop the titration immediately after the end-point has been reached.*

Dissolve 0.250 g in 3 ml of *anhydrous formic acid R* and add 40 ml of *anhydrous acetic acid R*. Titrate with *0.1 M perchloric acid*, determining the end-point potentiometrically (2.2.20).

1 ml of *0.1 M perchloric acid* is equivalent to 26.53 mg of $C_{12}H_{15}N_3O_2S$.

## STORAGE

Protected from light.

## IMPURITIES

*Specified impurities   A, B, C, D, E, F.*

A. R = S-CH$_2$-CH$_2$-CH$_3$: 5-(propylsulphanyl)-1H-benzimidazol-2-amine,

D. R = SO$_2$-CH$_2$-CH$_2$-CH$_3$: 5-(propylsulphonyl)-1H-benzimidazol-2-amine,

B. R = SO-CH$_2$-CH$_2$-CH$_3$: methyl [5-(propylsulphinyl)-1H-benzimidazol-2-yl]carbamate,

C. R = SO$_2$-CH$_2$-CH$_2$-CH$_3$: methyl [5-(propylsulphonyl)-1H-benzimidazol-2-yl]carbamate,

E. R = H: methyl (1H-benzimidazol-2-yl)carbamate,

F. R = S-CH$_3$: methyl [5-(methylsulphanyl)-1H-benzimidazol-2-yl]carbamate.

*Ph Eur*

# Alcuronium Chloride

*(Ph Eur monograph 1285)*

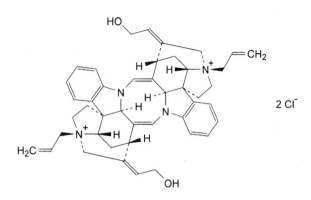

$C_{44}H_{50}Cl_2N_4O_2$      738.0      *151180-03-7*

## Action and use
Non-depolarizing neuromuscular blocker.

*Ph Eur*

## DEFINITION
(1*R*,3a*S*,10*S*,11a*S*,12*R*,14a*S*,19a*S*,20b*S*,21*S*,22a*S*,23*E*,26*E*)-23,26-bis(2-Hydroxyethylidene)-1,12-bis(prop-2-enyl)-2,3,11,11a,13,14,22,22a-octahydro-10*H*,21*H*-1,21:10,12-diethano-19a*H*,20b*H*-[1,5]diazocino[1,2,3-*lm*:5,6,7-*l'm'*]dipyrrolo[2',3'-*d*:2'',3''-*d'*]dicarbazolediium dichloride (4,4'-didesmethyl-4,4'-bis(prop-2-enyl)toxiferin I dichloride).

## Content
98.0 per cent to 102.0 per cent (anhydrous substance).

## CHARACTERS
### Appearance
White or slightly greyish-white, crystalline powder.

### Solubility
Freely soluble in water and in methanol, soluble in ethanol (96 per cent), practically insoluble in cyclohexane.

*Carry out the identification, tests and assay as rapidly as possible avoiding exposure to actinic light.*

## IDENTIFICATION
*First identification* A, C.

*Second identification* B, C.

A. Infrared absorption spectrophotometry (*2.2.24*).

*Comparison* alcuronium chloride CRS.

B. Thin-layer chromatography (*2.2.27*).

*Test solution* Dissolve 10 mg of the substance to be examined in *methanol R* and dilute to 10 ml with the same solvent.

*Reference solution* Dissolve 10 mg of *alcuronium chloride CRS* in *methanol R* and dilute to 10 ml with the same solvent.

*Plate* TLC silica gel plate R.

*Mobile phase* Mix 15 volumes of a 58.4 g/l solution of *sodium chloride R*, 35 volumes of *dilute ammonia R2* and 50 volumes of *methanol R*.

*Application* 10 μl.

*Development* Over a path of 15 cm.

*Drying* In air for 10 min.

*Detection* Spray with *0.1 M ammonium and cerium nitrate*.

*Results* The principal spot in the chromatogram obtained with the test solution is similar in position, colour and size to the principal spot in the chromatogram obtained with the reference solution.

C. It gives reaction (a) of chlorides (*2.3.1*).

## TESTS
### Solution S
Dissolve 0.250 g in *carbon dioxide-free water R* and dilute to 25.0 ml with the same solvent.

### Appearance of solution
Solution S is clear (*2.2.1*) and not more intensely coloured than reference solution $Y_6$, $BY_6$ or $B_6$ (*2.2.2, Method I*).

### Acidity or alkalinity
To 10 ml of solution S add 0.1 ml of *methyl red solution R* and 0.2 ml of *0.01 M hydrochloric acid*. The solution is red. Add 0.4 ml of *0.01 M sodium hydroxide*. The solution is yellow.

### Specific optical rotation (*2.2.7*)
− 430 to − 451 (anhydrous substance), determined on solution S.

### Propan-2-ol (*2.4.24, System A*)
Maximum 1.0 per cent.

### Related substances
Liquid chromatography (*2.2.29*).

*Solvent mixture* Mix 100 ml of *methanol R*, 200 ml of *acetonitrile R* and 200 ml of a 6.82 g/l solution of *potassium dihydrogen phosphate R*. Dissolve 1.09 g of *sodium laurylsulphonate for chromatography R* in the mixture and adjust the apparent pH to 8.0 with a 100 g/l solution of *sodium hydroxide R*.

*Test solution* Dissolve 0.20 g of the substance to be examined in the solvent mixture and dilute to 100.0 ml with the solvent mixture.

*Reference solution (a)* Dilute 0.5 ml of the test solution to 100.0 ml with the solvent mixture.

*Reference solution (b)* Dilute 4.0 ml of reference solution (a) to 10.0 ml with the solvent mixture.

*Reference solution (c)* Dilute 1.0 ml of reference solution (a) to 10.0 ml with the solvent mixture.

*Reference solution (d)* To 5.0 ml of the test solution add 5.0 mg of *allylstrychnine bromide CRS*, dissolve in the solvent mixture and dilute to 100.0 ml with the solvent mixture.

*Column:*
— size: $l = 0.25$ m, Ø = 4 mm;
— stationary phase: octylsilyl silica gel for chromatography R (5 μm).

*Mobile phase* Mix 200 ml of *methanol R*, 400 ml of *acetonitrile R* and 400 ml of a 6.82 g/l solution of *potassium dihydrogen phosphate R*. Dissolve 2.18 g of *sodium laurylsulphonate for chromatography R* in the mixture and adjust the apparent pH to 5.4 with a 100 g/l solution of *phosphoric acid R*.

*Flow rate* 1.2 ml/min.

*Detection* Spectrophotometer at 254 nm.

*Injection* 10 μl.

*Run time* Twice the retention time of alcuronium.

*System suitability* Reference solution (d):
— resolution: minimum 4.0 between the peaks due to N-allylstrychnine and alcuronium.

*Limits:*
— impurities A, B: for each impurity, not more than the area of the principal peak in the chromatogram obtained with reference solution (a) (0.5 per cent) and not more than one of the peaks has an area greater than the area of the

principal peak in the chromatogram obtained with reference solution (b) (0.2 per cent);

— *total*: not more than twice the area of the principal peak in the chromatogram obtained with reference solution (a) (1 per cent);

— *disregard limit*: the area of the principal peak in the chromatogram obtained with reference solution (c) (0.05 per cent).

**Water** (*2.5.12*)

Maximum 5.0 per cent, determined on 0.500 g.

**Sulphated ash** (*2.4.14*)

Maximum 0.1 per cent, determined on 1.0 g.

## ASSAY

Dissolve 0.300 g by stirring in 70 ml of *acetic anhydride R* for 1 min. Titrate with *0.1 M perchloric acid* until the colour changes from violet-blue to greenish-blue, using 0.1 ml of *crystal violet solution R* as indicator.

1 ml of *0.1 M perchloric acid* is equivalent to 36.9 mg of $C_{44}H_{50}Cl_2N_4O_2$.

## STORAGE

In an airtight container under nitrogen, protected from light, at a temperature of 2 °C to 8 °C.

## IMPURITIES

*Specified impurities   A, B.*

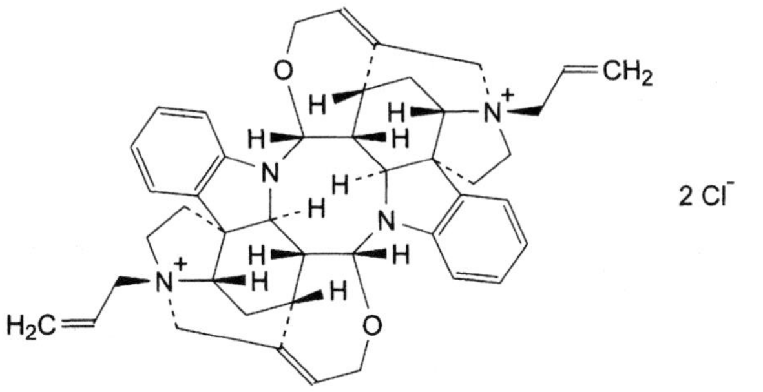

A. (1*R*,3a*S*,9*R*,9a*R*,10*R*,11a*S*,12*R*,14a*S*,19a*S*,20*R*, 20a*R*,20b*S*,21*R*,22a*S*)-1,12-bis(prop-2-enyl)-2,3,9a,11,11a,13,14,19a,20a,21,22,22a-dodecahydro-10*H*,20b*H*-1,23:12,27-dimethano-9,10:20,21-bis(epoxyprop[2]eno)-9*H*,20*H*-[1,5]diazocino[1,2,3-*lm*:5,6,7-*l'm'*]dipyrrolo[2',3'-*d*:2'',3'':*d'*]dicarbazolediium dichloride (4,4'-diallylcaracurin V dichloride),

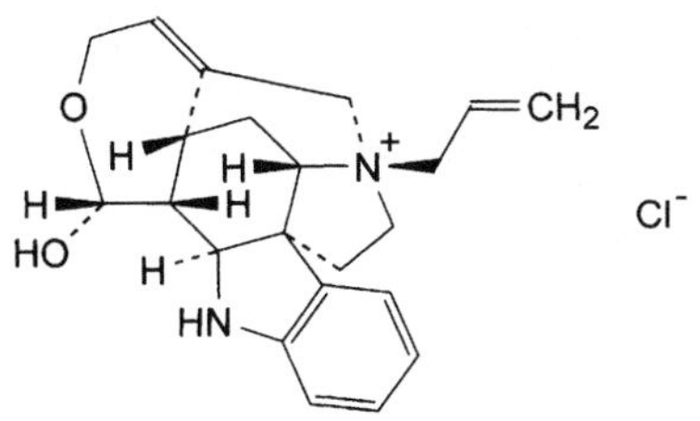

B. (4b*S*,7*R*,7a*S*,8a*R*,13*R*,13a*R*,13b*S*)-13-hydroxy-7-(prop-2-enyl)-5,6,7a,8,8a,11,13,13a,13b,14-decahydro-7,9-methano-7*H*-oxepino[3,4-*a*]pyrrolo[2,3-*d*]carbazolium chloride ((4*R*,17*R*)-4-allyl-17,18-epoxy-17-hydroxy-19,20-didehydrocuranium chloride).

_____ *Ph Eur*

# Alfacalcidol

(*Ph Eur monograph 1286*)

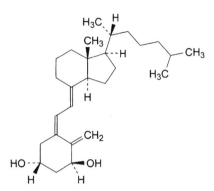

$C_{27}H_{44}O_2$         400.6         *41294-56-8*

**Action and use**

Vitamin D analogue.

*Ph Eur* _____

## DEFINITION

(5*Z*,7*E*)-9,10-Secocholesta-5,7,10(19)-triene-1α,3β-diol.

**Content**

97.0 per cent to 102.0 per cent.

## CHARACTERS

**Appearance**

White or almost white crystals.

**Solubility**

Practically insoluble in water, freely soluble in ethanol (96 per cent), soluble in fatty oils.

It is sensitive to air, heat and light.

A reversible isomerisation to pre-alfacalcidol takes place in solution, depending on temperature and time. The activity is due to both compounds.

## IDENTIFICATION

A. Infrared absorption spectrophotometry (*2.2.24*).

*Comparison   Ph. Eur. reference spectrum of alfacalcidol.*

B. Examine the chromatograms obtained in the test for related substances.

*Results*   The principal peak in the chromatogram obtained with the test solution is similar in retention time and size to the principal peak in the chromatogram obtained with reference solution (a).

## TESTS

**Related substances**

Liquid chromatography (*2.2.29*): use the normalisation procedure. *Carry out the test as rapidly as possible, avoiding exposure to actinic light and air.*

*Test solution*   Dissolve 1.0 mg of the substance to be examined without heating in 10.0 ml of the mobile phase.

*Reference solution (a)*   Dissolve 1.0 mg of *alfacalcidol CRS* without heating in 10.0 ml of the mobile phase.

*Reference solution (b)*   Dilute 1.0 ml of reference solution (a) to 100.0 ml with the mobile phase.

*Reference solution (c)*   Heat 2 ml of reference solution (a) in a water-bath at 80 °C under a reflux condenser for 2 h and cool.

*Column:*
— *size:* l = 0.25 m, Ø = 4.0 mm;
— *stationary phase:* octadecylsilyl silica gel for chromatography R2 (5 μm).

*Mobile phase*  ammonia R, water R, acetonitrile R (1:200:800 *V/V/V*).

*Flow rate*  2.0 ml/min.

*Detection*  Spectrophotometer at 265 nm.

*Injection*  100 μl of the test solution and reference solutions (b) and (c).

*Run time*  Twice the retention time of alfacalcidol.

*Relative retention*  With reference to alfacalcidol: pre-alfacalcidol = about 1.3.

*System suitability*  Reference solution (c):
— *resolution*: minimum 4.0 between the peaks due to pre-alfacalcidol and alfacalcidol; if necessary, adjust the proportions of the constituents of the mobile phase.

*Limits:*
— *impurities A, B, C*: for each impurity, maximum 0.5 per cent;
— *total*: maximum 1.0 per cent;
— *disregard limit*: 0.1 times the area of the principal peak in the chromatogram obtained with reference solution (b) (0.1 per cent); disregard the peak due to pre-alfacalcidol.

## ASSAY

Liquid chromatography (*2.2.29*) as described in the test for related substances with the following modification.

*Injection*  The test solution and reference solutions (a) and (c).

*System suitability*  Reference solution (c):
— *repeatability*: maximum relative standard deviation of 1 per cent for the peak due to alfacalcidol after 6 injections.

Calculate the percentage content of $C_{27}H_{44}O_2$ from the declared content of *alfacalcidol CRS*.

## STORAGE

Under nitrogen, in an airtight container, protected from light, at a temperature of 2 °C to 8 °C.

The contents of an opened container are to be used immediately.

## IMPURITIES

*Specified impurities  A, B, C.*

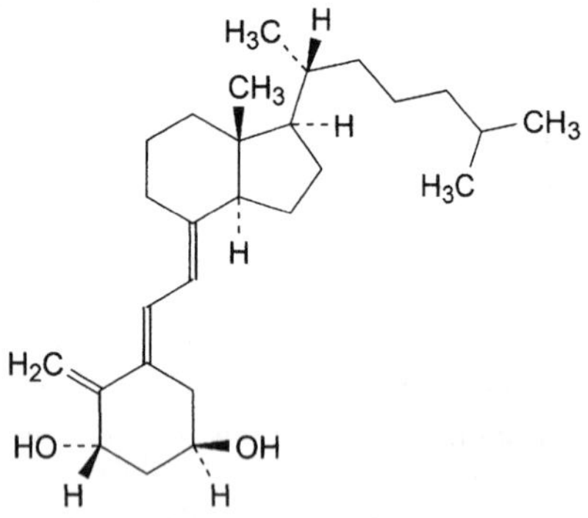

A. (5E,7E)-9,10-secocholesta-5,7,10(19)-triene-1α,3β-diol (*trans*-alfacalcidol),

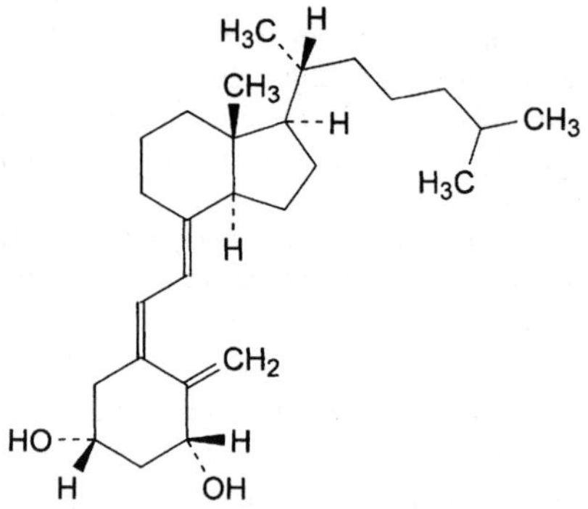

B. (5Z,7E)-9,10-secocholesta-5,7,10(19)-triene-1β,3β-diol (1β-calcidol),

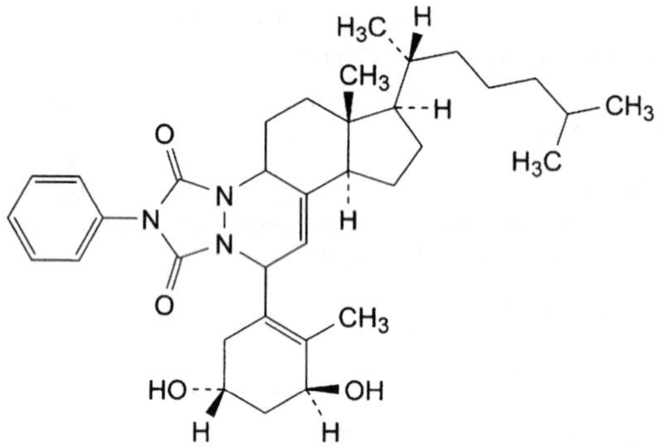

C. triazoline adduct of pre-alfacalcidol.

*Ph Eur*

# Alfadex

Alphacyclodextrin

(*Ph Eur monograph 1487*)

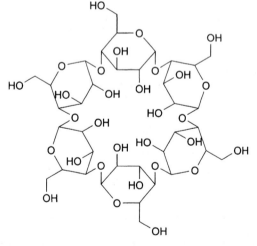

[$C_6H_{10}O_5$]₆          973          *10016-20-3*

## Action and use

Cyclodextran; carrier molecule for drug delivery systems.

*Ph Eur*

## DEFINITION

Cyclohexakis-(1→4)-(α-D -glucopyranosyl) (cyclomaltohexaose or α-cyclodextrin).

**Content**

98.0 per cent to 101.0 per cent (dried substance).

## CHARACTERS

**Appearance**

White or almost white, amorphous or crystalline powder.

**Solubility**

Freely soluble in water and in propylene glycol, practically insoluble in anhydrous ethanol and in methylene chloride.

## IDENTIFICATION

A. Specific optical rotation (see Tests).

B. Examine the chromatograms obtained in the assay.

*Results*   The principal peak in the chromatogram obtained with test solution (b) is similar in retention time and size to the principal peak in the chromatogram obtained with reference solution (c).

C. Dissolve 0.2 g in 2 ml of *iodine solution R4* by warming on a water-bath, and allow to stand at room temperature; a yellowish-brown precipitate is formed.

## TESTS

**Solution S**

Dissolve 1.000 g in *carbon dioxide-free water R* and dilute to 100.0 ml with the same solvent.

**Appearance of solution**

Solution S is clear (*2.2.1*).

**pH** (*2.2.3*)

5.0 to 8.0.

Mix 1 ml of a 223.6 g/l solution of *potassium chloride R* and 30 ml of solution S.

**Specific optical rotation** (*2.2.7*)

+ 147 to + 152 (dried substance), determined on solution S.

**Reducing sugars**

Maximum 0.2 per cent.

*Test solution*   To 1 ml of solution S add 1 ml of *cupri-tartaric solution R4*. Heat on a water-bath for 10 min, cool to room temperature. Add 10 ml of *ammonium molybdate reagent R1* and allow to stand for 15 min.

*Reference solution*   Prepare a reference solution at the same time and in the same manner as the test solution, using 1 ml of a 0.02 g/l solution of *glucose R*.

Measure the absorbance (*2.2.25*) of the test solution and the reference solution at the absorption maximum at 740 nm using *water R* as the compensation liquid. The absorbance of the test solution is not greater than that of the reference solution.

**Light-absorbing impurities**

Examine solution S between 230 nm and 750 nm. Between 230 nm and 350 nm, the absorbance (*2.2.25*) is not greater than 0.10. Between 350 nm and 750 nm, the absorbance (*2.2.25*) is not greater than 0.05.

**Related substances**

Liquid chromatography (*2.2.29*).

*Test solution (a)*   Dissolve 0.25 g of the substance to be examined in *water R* with heating, cool and dilute to 25.0 ml with the same solvent.

*Test solution (b)*   Dilute 5.0 ml of test solution (a) to 50.0 ml with *water R*.

*Reference solution (a)*   Dissolve 25.0 mg of *betadex CRS* (impurity A), 25.0 mg of *gammacyclodextrin CRS* (impurity B) and 50.0 mg of *alfadex CRS* in *water R*, then dilute to 50.0 ml with the same solvent.

*Reference solution (b)*   Dilute 5.0 ml of reference solution (a) to 50.0 ml with *water R*.

*Reference solution (c)*   Dissolve 25.0 mg of *alfadex CRS* in *water R* and dilute to 25.0 ml with the same solvent.

*Column:*

— size: $l$ = 0.25 m, Ø = 4.6 mm;

— stationary phase: *octadecylsilyl silica gel for chromatography R* (10 μm).

*Mobile phase*   methanol R, water R (10:90 *V/V*).

*Flow rate*   1.5 ml/min.

*Detection*   Differential refractometer.

*Equilibration*   With the mobile phase for about 3 h.

*Injection*   50 μl of test solution (a) and reference solutions (a) and (b).

*Run time*   3.5 times the retention time of alfadex.

*Relative retention*   With reference to alfadex (retention time = about 10 min): impurity B = about 0.7; impurity A = about 2.2.

*System suitability*   Reference solution (a):

— resolution: minimum 1.5 between the peaks due to impurity B and alfadex; if necessary, adjust the concentration of methanol in the mobile phase.

*Limits:*

— impurities A, B: for each impurity, not more than 0.5 times the area of the corresponding peak in the chromatogram obtained with reference solution (b) (0.25 per cent);

— sum of impurities other than A and B: not more than 0.5 times the area of the peak due to alfadex in the chromatogram obtained with reference solution (b) (0.5 per cent).

**Heavy metals** (*2.4.8*)

Maximum 10 ppm.

2.0 g complies with test C. Prepare the reference solution using 2 ml of *lead standard solution (10 ppm Pb) R*.

**Loss on drying** (*2.2.32*)

Maximum 11 per cent, determined on 1.000 g by drying in an oven at 120 °C for 2 h.

**Sulphated ash** (*2.4.14*)

Maximum 0.1 per cent, determined on 1.0 g.

## ASSAY

Liquid chromatography (*2.2.29*) as described in the test for related substances with the following modifications.

*Injection*   Test solution (b) and reference solutions (a) and (c).

*System suitability*   Reference solution (a):

— repeatability: maximum relative standard deviation of 2.0 per cent for the peak due to alfadex after 5 injections.

Calculate the percentage content of $[C_6H_{10}O_5]_6$ from the declared content of *alfadex CRS*.

## STORAGE

In an airtight container.

## IMPURITIES

*Specified impurities*   A, B.

A. betadex,

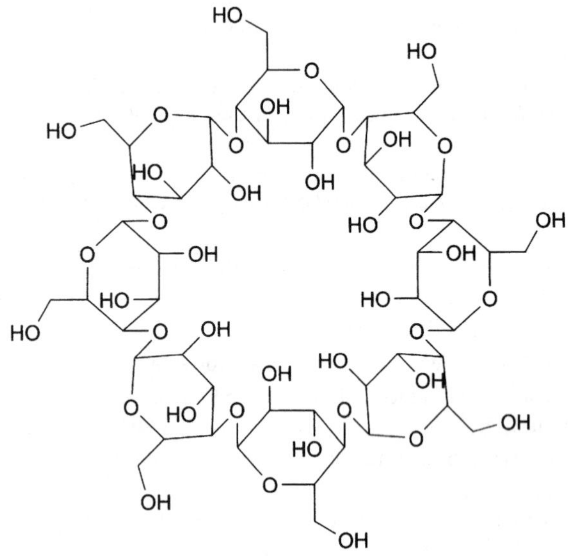

B. cyclooctakis-(1→4)-(α-D-glucopyranosyl)
(cyclomaltooctaose or γ-cyclodextrin).

*Ph Eur*

# Alfentanil Hydrochloride

*(Ph Eur monograph 1062)*

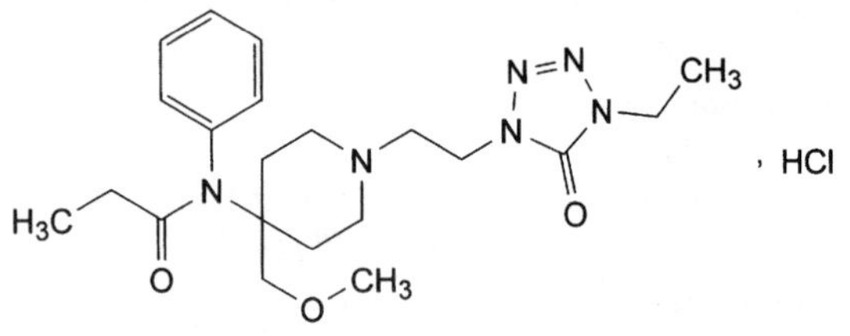

$C_{21}H_{32}N_6O,HCl$         453.0         69049-06-5

## Action and use
Opioid receptor agonist; analgesic.

*Ph Eur*

## DEFINITION
N-[1-[2-(4-Ethyl-4,5-dihydro-5-oxo-1H-tetrazol-1-yl)ethyl]-
4-(methoxymethyl)piperidin-4-yl]-N-phenylpropanamide
hydrochloride.

## Content
98.5 per cent to 101.5 per cent (anhydrous substance).

## CHARACTERS
### Appearance
White or almost white powder.

### Solubility
Freely soluble in water, in ethanol (96 per cent) and in
methanol.

### mp
About 140 °C, with decomposition.

## IDENTIFICATION
A. Infrared absorption spectrophotometry (*2.2.24*).

*Comparison*   Ph. Eur. reference spectrum of alfentanil
hydrochloride.

B. Dissolve 50 mg in a mixture of 0.4 ml of *ammonia R* and
2 ml of *water R*. Mix, allow to stand for 5 min and filter.
Acidify the filtrate with *dilute nitric acid R*. It gives reaction
(a) of chlorides (*2.3.1*).

## TESTS
### Appearance of solution
The solution is clear (*2.2.1*) and colourless (*2.2.2*,
*Method II*).

Dissolve 0.2 g in *water R* and dilute to 20 ml with the same
solvent.

### Related substances
Liquid chromatography (*2.2.29*).

*Test solution*   Dissolve 0.100 g of the substance to be
examined in *methanol R* and dilute to 10.0 ml with the same
solvent.

*Reference solution (a)*   In order to produce impurity E *in situ*,
dissolve 10 mg of the substance to be examined in 10.0 ml of
*dilute hydrochloric acid R*. Heat on a water-bath under a reflux
condenser for 4 h. Neutralise with 10.0 ml of *dilute sodium
hydroxide solution R*. Evaporate to dryness on a water-bath.
Cool and take up the residue in 10 ml of *methanol R*. Filter.

*Reference solution (b)*   Dilute 1.0 ml of the test solution to
100.0 ml with *methanol R*. Dilute 5.0 ml of this solution to
20.0 ml with *methanol R*.

*Column:*
— *size: l* = 0.1 m, Ø = 4.6 mm;
— *stationary phase: octadecylsilyl silica gel for chromatography R*
   (3 µm).

*Mobile phase:*
— mobile phase A: 5 g/l solution of *ammonium carbonate R* in
   a mixture of 10 volumes of *tetrahydrofuran R* and
   90 volumes of *water R*;
— mobile phase B: *acetonitrile R*;

| Time (min) | Mobile phase A (per cent V/V) | Mobile phase B (per cent V/V) |
|---|---|---|
| 0 - 15 | 90 → 40 | 10 → 60 |
| 15 - 20 | 40 | 60 |
| 20 - 25 | 90 | 10 |

*Flow rate*   1.5 ml/min.

*Detection*   Spectrophotometer at 220 nm.

*Equilibration*   With *acetonitrile R* for at least 30 min and then
with the mobile phase at the initial composition for at least
5 min.

*Injection*   10 µl; inject *methanol R* as a blank.

*Retention time*   Impurity E = about 6 min;
alfentanil = about 7 min.

*Identification of impurities*   Use the chromatogram obtained
with reference solution (a) to identify the peak due to
impurity E; disregard any other peak.

*System suitability*   Reference solution (a):
— *resolution*: minimum 4.0 between the peaks due to
   alfentanil and impurity E; if necessary, adjust the
   concentration of acetonitrile in the mobile phase or adjust
   the time programme for the linear-gradient elution.

*Limits:*
— impurities A, B, C, D, E, F, G, H: for each impurity, not
   more than the area of the principal peak in the
   chromatogram obtained with reference solution (b)
   (0.25 per cent);

— *total*: not more than twice the area of the principal peak in the chromatogram obtained with reference solution (b) (0.5 per cent);

— *disregard limit*: 0.2 times the area of the principal peak in the chromatogram obtained with reference solution (b) (0.05 per cent); disregard any peak due to the blank.

**Water** *(2.5.12)*

3.0 per cent to 4.0 per cent, determined on 0.500 g.

## ASSAY

Dissolve 0.350 g in 50 ml of a mixture of 1 volume of *ethanol (96 per cent) R* and 4 volumes of *water R* and add 5.0 ml of *0.01 M hydrochloric acid*. Titrate with *0.1 M sodium hydroxide*, determining the end-point potentiometrically *(2.2.20)*. Read the volume added between the 2 points of inflexion.

1 ml of *0.1 M sodium hydroxide* is equivalent to 45.30 mg of $C_{21}H_{33}ClN_6O_3$.

## STORAGE

Protected from light.

## IMPURITIES

*Specified impurities   A, B, C, D, E, F, G, H.*

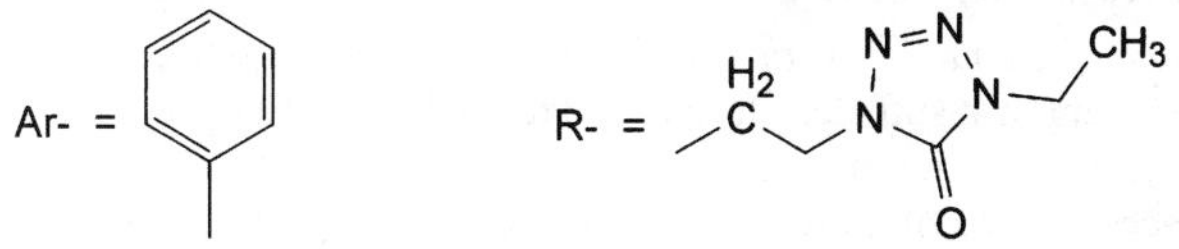

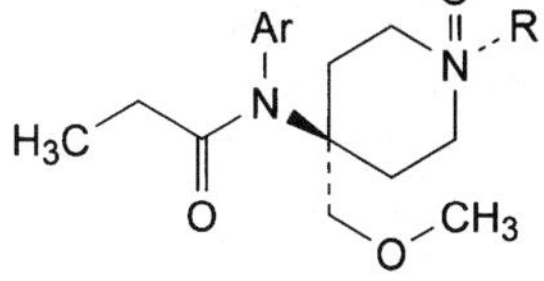

A. *cis*-N-[1-[2-(4-ethyl-4,5-dihydro-5-oxo-1H-tetrazol-1-yl)ethyl]-4-(methoxymethyl)piperidin-4-yl]-N-phenylpropanamide N-oxide,

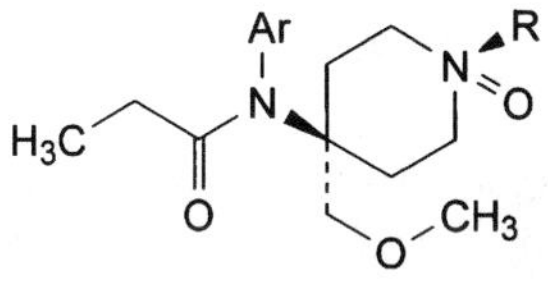

B. *trans*-N-[1-[2-(4-ethyl-4,5-dihydro-5-oxo-1H-tetrazol-1-yl)ethyl]-4-(methoxymethyl)piperidin-4-yl]-N-phenylpropanamide N-oxide,

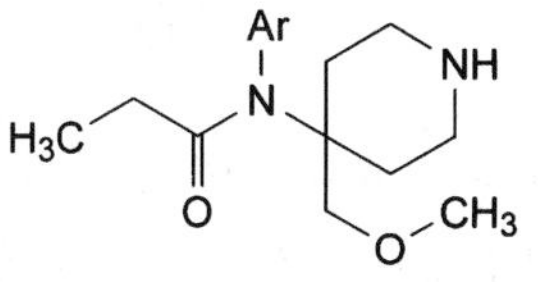

C. N-[4-(methoxymethyl)piperidin-4-yl]-N-phenylpropanamide,

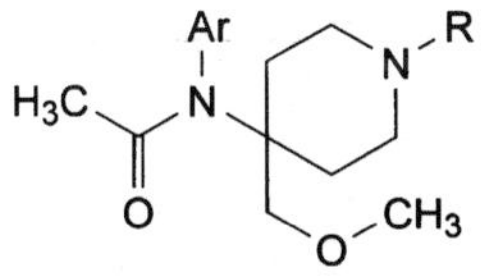

D. N-[1-[2-(4-ethyl-4,5-dihydro-5-oxo-1H-tetrazol-1-yl)ethyl]-4-(methoxymethyl)piperidin-4-yl]-N-phenylacetamide,

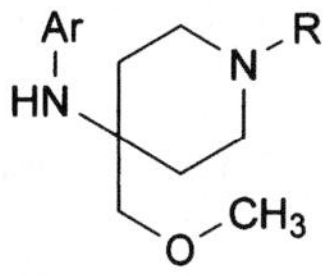

E. 1-ethyl-1,4-dihydro-4-[2-[[4-(methoxymethyl)-4-phenylamino]piperidin-1-yl]ethyl]-5H-tetrazol-5-one,

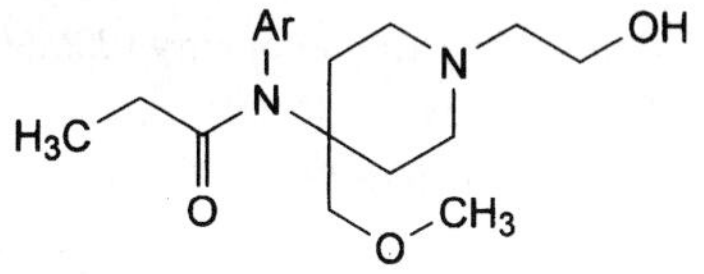

F. N-[1-(2-hydroxyethyl)-4-(methoxymethyl)piperidin-4-yl]-N-phenylpropanamide,

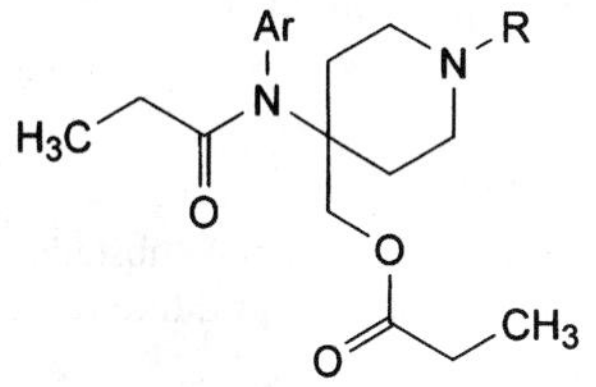

G. N-[1-[2-(4-ethyl-4,5-dihydro-5-oxo-1H-tetrazol-1-yl)ethyl]-4-(propanoyloxymethyl)piperidin-4-yl]-N-phenylpropanamide,

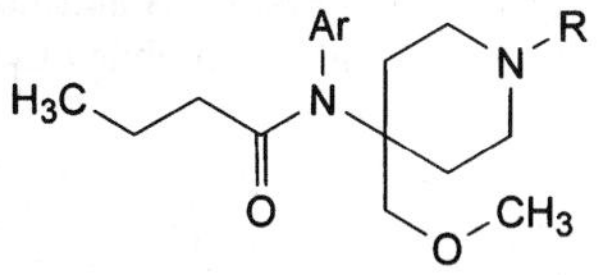

H. N-[1-[2-(4-ethyl-4,5-dihydro-5-oxo-1H-tetrazol-1-yl)ethyl]-4-(methoxymethyl)piperidin-4-yl]-N-phenylbutanamide.

*Ph Eur*

# Alfuzosin Hydrochloride

*(Ph Eur monograph 1287)*

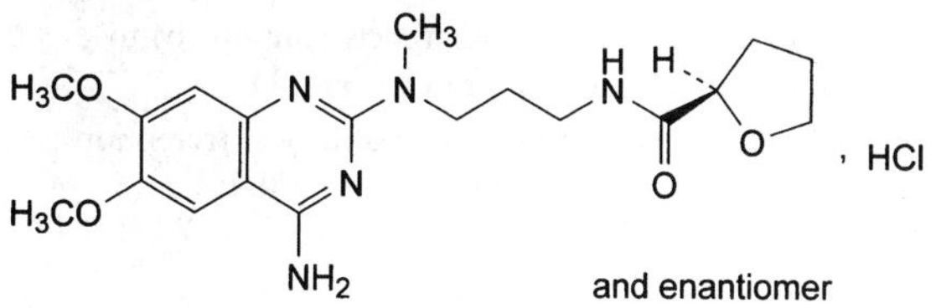

and enantiomer

$C_{19}H_{27}N_5O_4,HCl$     425.9     *81403-68-1*

**Action and use**

Alpha$_1$-adrenoceptor antagonist.

*Ph Eur*

## DEFINITION

(2RS)-N-[3-[(4-Amino-6,7-dimethoxyquinazolin-2-yl)methylamino]propyl]tetrahydrofuran-2-carboxamide hydrochloride.

**Content**

99.0 per cent to 101.0 per cent (anhydrous substance).

## CHARACTERS

### Appearance
White or almost white, crystalline powder, slightly hygroscopic.

### Solubility
Freely soluble in water, sparingly soluble in ethanol (96 per cent), practically insoluble in methylene chloride.

## IDENTIFICATION

A. Infrared absorption spectrophotometry (2.2.24).

*Comparison*   *alfuzosin hydrochloride CRS.*

B. It gives reaction (a) of chlorides (2.3.1).

## TESTS

### pH (2.2.3)
4.0 to 5.5.

Dissolve 0.500 g in *carbon dioxide-free water R* and dilute to 25.0 ml with the same solvent. Use a freshly prepared solution.

### Related substances
Liquid chromatography (2.2.29).

*Test solution*   Dissolve 40 mg of the substance to be examined in the mobile phase and dilute to 100.0 ml with the mobile phase.

*Reference solution (a)*   Dilute 1.0 ml of the test solution to 100.0 ml with the mobile phase. Dilute 1.0 ml of this solution to 10.0 ml with the mobile phase.

*Reference solution (b)*   Dissolve 4 mg of *alfuzosin for system suitability CRS* (containing impurities A and D) in the mobile phase and dilute to 10 ml with the mobile phase.

*Column:*
— *size*: $l = 0.15$ m, $\emptyset = 4.6$ mm;
— *stationary phase*: end-capped octadecylsilyl silica gel for chromatography R (5 µm).

*Mobile phase*   Mix 1 volume of *tetrahydrofuran R*, 20 volumes of *acetonitrile R* and 80 volumes of a solution prepared as follows: dilute 5.0 ml of *perchloric acid R* in 900 ml of *water R*, adjust to pH 3.5 with *dilute sodium hydroxide solution R* and dilute to 1000 ml with *water R*.

*Flow rate*   1.5 ml/min.

*Detection*   Spectrophotometer at 254 nm.

*Injection*   10 µl.

*Run time*   Twice the retention time of alfuzosin.

*Identification of impurities*   Use the chromatogram supplied with alfuzosin for system suitability CRS and the chromatogram obtained with reference solution (b) to identify the peaks due to impurities A and D.

*Relative retention*   With reference to alfuzosin (retention time = about 8 min): impurity D = about 0.4; impurity A = about 1.2.

*System suitability*   Reference solution (b):
— *peak-to-valley ratio*: minimum 5.0, where $H_p$ = height above the baseline of the peak due to impurity A and $H_v$ = height above the baseline of the lowest point of the curve separating this peak from the peak due to alfuzosin.

*Limits:*
— *impurity D*: not more than twice the area of the principal peak in the chromatogram obtained with reference solution (a) (0.2 per cent);
— *unspecified impurities*: for each impurity, not more than the area of the principal peak in the chromatogram obtained with reference solution (a) (0.10 per cent);

— *total*: not more than 3 times the area of the principal peak in the chromatogram obtained with reference solution (a) (0.3 per cent);
— *disregard limit*: 0.5 times the area of the principal peak in the chromatogram obtained with reference solution (a) (0.05 per cent).

### Water (2.5.12)
Maximum 0.5 per cent, determined on 1.000 g.

### Sulphated ash (2.4.14)
Maximum 0.1 per cent, determined on 1.0 g.

## ASSAY
Dissolve 0.300 g in a mixture of 40 ml of *anhydrous acetic acid R* and 40 ml of *acetic anhydride R*. Titrate with *0.1 M perchloric acid*, determining the end-point potentiometrically (2.2.20).

1 ml of *0.1 M perchloric acid* is equivalent to 42.59 mg of $C_{19}H_{28}ClN_5O_4$.

## STORAGE
In an airtight container, protected from light.

## IMPURITIES
*Specified impurities*   *D.*

*Other detectable impurities* (the following substances would, if present at a sufficient level, be detected by one or other of the tests in the monograph. They are limited by the general acceptance criterion for other/unspecified impurities and/or by the general monograph *Substances for pharmaceutical use* (2034). It is therefore not necessary to identify these impurities for demonstration of compliance. See also 5.10. Control of impurities in substances for pharmaceutical use): A, B, C, E.

A. *N*-[3-[(4-amino-6,7-dimethoxyquinazolin-2-yl)methylamino]propyl]furan-2-carboxamide,

B. R = Cl: 2-chloro-6,7-dimethoxyquinazolin-4-amine,

D. R = N(CH₃)-[CH₂]₃-NH₂: *N*-(4-amino-6,7-dimethoxyquinazolin-2-yl)-*N*-methylpropane-1,3-diamine,

E. R = N(CH₃)-[CH₂]₃-NH-CO-H: *N*-[3-[(4-amino-6,7-dimethoxyquinazolin-2-yl)methylamino]propyl]formamide,

C. (2RS)-N-[3-[(4-amino-6,7-dimethoxyquinazolin-2-yl)amino]propyl]-N-methyltetrahydrofuran-2-carboxamide.

——————————————————— Ph Eur

# Alginic Acid

(Ph Eur monograph 0591)

**Action and use**
Treatment of gastro-oesophageal reflux disease; excipient; thickening agent.

Ph Eur _____

## DEFINITION
Mixture of polyuronic acids $[(C_6H_8O_6)_n]$ composed of residues of D-mannuronic and L-guluronic acids, obtained mainly from algae belonging to the Phaeophyceae. A small proportion of the carboxyl groups may be neutralised.

## Content
19.0 per cent to 25.0 per cent of carboxyl groups (-CO₂H) (dried substance).

## CHARACTERS
**Appearance**
White or pale yellowish-brown, crystalline or amorphous powder.

**Solubility**
Very slightly soluble or practically insoluble in ethanol (96 per cent), practically insoluble in organic solvents. It swells in water but does not dissolve; it dissolves in solutions of alkali hydroxides.

## IDENTIFICATION
A. To 0.2 g add 20 ml of *water R* and 0.5 ml of *sodium carbonate solution R*. Shake and filter. To 5 ml of the filtrate add 1 ml of *calcium chloride solution R*. A voluminous gelatinous mass is formed.

B. To 5 ml of the filtrate obtained in identification test A add 0.5 ml of a 123 g/l solution of *magnesium sulphate R*. No voluminous gelatinous mass is formed.

C. To 5 mg add 5 ml of *water R*, 1 ml of a freshly prepared 10 g/l solution of *1,3-dihydroxynaphthalene R* in *ethanol (96 per cent) R* and 5 ml of *hydrochloric acid R*. Boil gently for 3 min, cool, add 5 ml of *water R*, and shake with 15 ml of *di-isopropyl ether R*. Carry out a blank test. The upper layer obtained with the substance to be examined exhibits a deeper bluish-red colour than that obtained with the blank.

## TESTS
**Chlorides**
Maximum 1,0 per cent.

To 2.50 g add 50 ml of *dilute nitric acid R*, shake for 1 h and dilute to 100.0 ml with *dilute nitric acid R*. Filter. To 50.0 ml of the filtrate add 10.0 ml of *0.1 M silver nitrate* and 5 ml of *toluene R*. Titrate with *0.1 M ammonium thiocyanate*, using 2 ml of *ferric ammonium sulphate solution R2* as indicator and shaking vigorously towards the end-point.

1 ml of *0.1 M silver nitrate* is equivalent to 3.545 mg of Cl.

**Heavy metals** (2.4.8)
Maximum 20 ppm.

1.0 g complies with test F. Prepare the reference solution using 2 ml of *lead standard solution (10 ppm Pb) R*.

**Loss on drying** (2.2.32)
Maximum 15.0 per cent, determined on 0.1000 g by drying in an oven at 105 °C for 4 h.

**Sulphated ash** (2.4.14)
Maximum 8.0 per cent (dried substance), determined on 0.100 g.

**Microbial contamination**
TAMC: acceptance criterion $10^2$ CFU/g (2.6.12).
Absence of *Escherichia coli* (2.6.13).
Absence of *Salmonella* (2.6.13).

## ASSAY
To 0.2500 g add 25 ml of *water R*, 25.0 ml of *0.1 M sodium hydroxide* and 0.2 ml of *phenolphthalein solution R*. Titrate with *0.1 M hydrochloric acid*.

1 ml of *0.1 M sodium hydroxide* is equivalent to 4.502 mg of carboxyl groups (-CO₂H).

## FUNCTIONALITY-RELATED CHARACTERISTICS
*This section provides information on characteristics that are recognised as being relevant control parameters for one or more functions of the substance when used as an excipient (see chapter 5.15). This section is a non-mandatory part of the monograph and it is not necessary to verify the characteristics to demonstrate compliance. Control of these characteristics can however contribute to the quality of a medicinal product by improving the consistency of the manufacturing process and the performance of the medicinal product during use. Where control methods are cited, they are recognised as being suitable for the purpose, but other methods can also be used. Wherever results for a particular characteristic are reported, the control method must be indicated.*

*The following characteristics may be relevant for alginic acid used as disintegrant and/or binder.*

**Particle-size distribution** (2.9.31 or 2.9.38).

**Settling volume**
Place 75 ml of *water R* in a 100 ml graduated cylinder and add 1.5 g of the substance to be examined in 0.5 g portions, shaking vigorously after each addition. Dilute to 100.0 ml with *water R* and shake again until the substance is homogeneously distributed. Allow to stand for 4 h and determine the volume of the settled mass.

*The following characteristic may be relevant for alginic acid used as gelling agent or viscosity-increasing agent.*

**Apparent viscosity**
Determine the dynamic viscosity using a rotating viscometer (2.2.10).

Prepare a 20 g/l suspension of alginic acid (dried substance) and add *0.1 M sodium hydroxide* until a solution is obtained.

——————————————————— Ph Eur

# Alimemazine Tartrate

$(C_{18}H_{22}N_2S)_2,C_4H_6O_6$    747.0    4330-99-8

**Action and use**
Histamine $H_1$ receptor antagonist; antihistamine.

**Preparations**
Paediatric Alimemazine Oral Solution
Strong Paediatric Alimemazine Oral Solution
Alimemazine Tablets

## DEFINITION
Alimemazine Tartrate is (RS)-dimethyl (2-methyl-
3-phenothiazin-10-ylpropyl)amine (2R,3R)-tartrate. It
contains not less than 99.0% and not more than 101.0% of
$(C_{18}H_{22}N_2S)_2,C_4H_6O_6$, calculated with reference to the
dried substance.

## CHARACTERISTICS
A white or slightly cream powder. It darkens on exposure
to light.

Freely soluble in *water*; sparingly soluble in *ethanol (96%)*;
very slightly soluble in *ether*.

## IDENTIFICATION
A. Dissolve 0.1 g in 10 ml of *water* and add 2 ml of
1M *sodium hydroxide*. Extract with 25 ml of *ether*, wash the
extract with 5 ml of *water*, dry over *anhydrous sodium sulphate*,
evaporate to dryness and dissolve the residue in 1 ml of
*dichloromethane*. The *infrared absorption spectrum* of the
resulting solution, Appendix II A, is concordant with the
reference spectrum of alimemazine *(RS 005)*.

B. *Melting point*, 159° to 163°, Appendix V A.

## TESTS
**Acidity**
pH of a 2% w/v solution, 5.0 to 6.5, Appendix V L.

**Related substances**
Complies with the test for *related substances in phenothiazines*,
Appendix III A, using *mobile phase A*.

**Loss on drying**
When dried to constant weight at 100° at a pressure not
exceeding 0.7 kPa, loses not more than 0.5% of its weight.
Use 1 g.

**Sulphated ash**
Not more than 0.1%, Appendix IX A.

## ASSAY
Carry out Method I for *non-aqueous titration*,
Appendix VIII A, using 1 g and *crystal violet solution* as
indicator. Each ml of 0.1M *perchloric acid VS* is equivalent to
37.35 mg of $(C_{18}H_{22}N_2S)_2,C_4H_6O_6$.

## STORAGE
Alimemazine Tartrate should be protected from light.

# Allantoin
*(Ph Eur monograph 1288)*

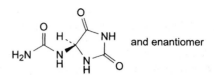

$C_4H_6N_4O_3$    158.1    97-59-6

**Action and use**
Astringent; keratolytic.

*Ph Eur*

## DEFINITION
Allantoin contains not less than 98.5 per cent and not more
than the equivalent of 101.0 per cent of
(RS)-(2,5-dioxoimidazolidin-4-yl)urea.

## CHARACTERS
A white or almost white, crystalline powder, slightly soluble
in water, very slightly soluble in alcohol.

It melts at about 225 °C, with decomposition.

## IDENTIFICATION
*First identification   A.*

*Second identification   B, C, D.*

A. Examine by infrared absorption spectrophotometry
*(2.2.24)*, comparing with the spectrum obtained with
*allantoin CRS*.

B. Examine the chromatograms obtained in the test for
related substances. The principal spot in the chromatogram
obtained with test solution (b) is similar in position, colour
and size to the principal spot in the chromatogram obtained
with reference solution (a).

C. Boil 20 mg with a mixture of 1 ml of *dilute sodium
hydroxide solution R* and 1 ml of *water R*. Allow to cool. Add
1 ml of *dilute hydrochloric acid R*. To 0.1 ml of the solution
add 0.1 ml of a 100 g/l solution of *potassium bromide R*,
0.1 ml of a 20 g/l solution of *resorcinol R* and 3 ml of
*sulphuric acid R*. Heat for 5 min to 10 min on a water-bath.
A dark blue colour develops, which becomes red after
cooling and pouring into about 10 ml of *water R*.

D. Heat about 0.5 g. Ammonia vapour is evolved, which
turns *red litmus paper R* blue.

## TESTS
**Solution S**
Dissolve 0.5 g in *carbon dioxide-free water R*, with heating if
necessary, and dilute to 100 ml with the same solvent.

**Acidity or alkalinity**
To 5 ml of solution S add 5 ml of *carbon dioxide-free water R*,
0.1 ml of *methyl red solution R* and 0.2 ml of *0.01 M sodium
hydroxide*. The solution is yellow. Add 0.4 ml of *0.01 M
hydrochloric acid*. The solution is red.

**Optical rotation** *(2.2.7)*
The angle of optical rotation, determined on solution S, is
− 0.10° to + 0.10°.

**Reducing substances**
Shake 1.0 g with 10 ml of *water R* for 2 min. Filter. Add
1.5 ml of *0.02 M potassium permanganate*. The solution must
remain violet for at least 10 min.

**Related substances**

Examine by thin-layer chromatography (2.2.27), using a suitable *cellulose for chromatography R* as the coating substance.

*Test solution (a)* Dissolve 0.10 g of the substance to be examined in 5.0 ml of *water R* with heating. Allow to cool. Dilute to 10 ml with *methanol R*. *Use the solution immediately after preparation.*

*Test solution (b)* Dilute 1 ml of test solution (a) to 10 ml with a mixture of 1 volume of *methanol R* and 1 volume of *water R*.

*Reference solution (a)* Dissolve 10 mg of *allantoin CRS* in a mixture of 1 volume of *methanol R* and 1 volume of *water R* and dilute to 10 ml with the same mixture of solvents.

*Reference solution (b)* Dissolve 10 mg of *urea R* in 10 ml of *water R*. Dilute 1 ml of this solution to 10 ml with *methanol R*.

*Reference solution (c)* Mix 1 ml of reference solution (a) and 1 ml of reference solution (b).

Apply to the plate 10 µl of test solution (a) and 5 µl each of test solution (b), reference solution (a), reference solution (b) and reference solution (c). Develop over a path of 10 cm using a mixture of 15 volumes of *glacial acetic acid R*, 25 volumes of *water R* and 60 volumes of *butanol R*. Allow the plate to dry in air. Spray the plate with a 5 g/l solution of *dimethylaminobenzaldehyde R* in a mixture of 1 volume of *hydrochloric acid R* and 3 volumes of *methanol R*. Dry the plate in a current of hot air. Examine in daylight after 30 min. Any spot in the chromatogram obtained with test solution (a), apart from the principal spot, is not more intense than the spot in the chromatogram obtained with reference solution (b) (0.5 per cent). The test is not valid unless the chromatogram obtained with reference solution (c) shows two clearly separated principal spots.

**Loss on drying** (2.2.32)

Not more than 0.1 per cent, determined on 1.000 g by drying in an oven at 105 °C.

**Sulphated ash** (2.4.14)

Not more than 0.1 per cent, determined on 1.0 g.

**ASSAY**

Dissolve 120.0 mg in 40 ml of *water R*. Titrate with *0.1 M sodium hydroxide*, determining the end-point potentiometrically (2.2.20).

1 ml of *0.1 M sodium hydroxide* is equivalent to 15.81 mg of $C_4H_6N_4O_3$.

**IMPURITIES**

$$H \diagdown \diagup CO_2H$$
$$\vert$$
$$O$$

A. glyoxylic acid,

B. urea.

_____ Ph Eur

# Allergen Products

(*Ph Eur monograph 1063*)

*Ph Eur*

## DEFINITION

Allergen products are pharmaceutical preparations derived from extracts of naturally occurring source materials containing allergens, which are substances that cause or provoke allergic (hypersensitivity) disease. The allergenic components are most often of a proteinaceous nature. Allergen products are intended for *in vivo* diagnosis or treatment of allergic (hypersensitivity) diseases attributed to these allergens.

Allergen products are available as finished products, as bulk preparations in dried form, solutions or suspensions intended to be further concentrated or diluted prior to use or as final preparations in solutions, suspensions or freeze-dried. Allergen products intended for parenteral, bronchial and conjunctival administration are sterile.

For *diagnostic use*, allergen products are usually prepared as unmodified extracts in a 50 per cent *V/V* solution of glycerol for skin-prick testing. For intradermal diagnosis or for provocation tests by nasal, ocular or bronchial routes, suitable dilutions of allergen products may be prepared by dilution of aqueous or glycerinated extracts, or by reconstitution immediately before use of unmodified freeze-dried extracts.

For *immunotherapy*, allergen products may be either unmodified extracts or extracts modified chemically and/or by adsorption onto different carriers (for example, aluminium hydroxide, calcium phosphate or tyrosine).

*This monograph does not apply to: chemicals that are used solely for diagnosis of contact dermatitis; chemically synthesised products; allergens derived by rDNA technology; finished products used on a named-patient basis. It does not necessarily apply to allergen products for veterinary use.*

## PRODUCTION

Allergen products are derived from a wide range of allergenic source materials. They are often prepared as bulk products intended to be further diluted or concentrated prior to use. They may be treated to modify or reduce the allergenic activity or remain unmodified.

Where allergen products are manufactured using materials of human or animal origin, the requirements of chapter *5.1.7. Viral safety* apply.

### SOURCE MATERIALS

Source materials for the preparation of allergen products are mostly pollens, moulds, mites, animal epithelia, hymenoptera venoms and certain foods.

They are described by their origin, nature, method of collection or production and pretreatment, and are stored under defined conditions that minimise deterioration.

The collection or production, as well as the handling of the source materials are such that uniform qualitative and quantitative composition is ensured as far as possible from batch to batch.

**Pollens**

Potential chemical contaminants, such as pesticides and heavy metals, must be minimised. Pollens contain not more than 1 per cent of foreign pollens as determined by microscopic examination. Pollens contain not more than 1 per cent of mould spores as determined by microscopic examination.

## Mites and moulds

Biologically active contaminants such as mycotoxins in moulds must be minimised and any presence justified. Care must be taken to minimise any allergenic constituents of the media used for the cultivation of mites and moulds as source materials. Culture media that contain substances of human or animal origin must be justified and, when required must be suitably treated to ensure the inactivation or elimination of possible transmissible agents of disease.

## Animal epithelia

Animal epithelia must be obtained from healthy animals selected to avoid possible transmissible agents of disease.

### MANUFACTURING PROCESS

Allergen products are generally obtained by extraction, and may be purified, from the source materials using appropriate methods shown to preserve the biological properties of the allergenic components. Allergen products are manufactured under conditions designed to minimise microbial growth and enzymatic degradation.

A purification procedure, if any, is designed to minimise the content of any potential irritant low-molecular-mass components or other non-allergenic components.

Allergen products may contain a suitable antimicrobial preservative. The nature and the concentration of the antimicrobial preservative have to be justified.

*The manufacturing process comprises various stages.*

**Native allergen extracts** result after separation from the extracted source materials.

**Intermediate allergen products** are obtained by further processing or modification of the native allergen extracts. The modification may be achieved by chemical processes (chemical conjugation) or physical processes (physical adsorption onto different carriers, for example, aluminium hydroxide, calcium phosphate or tyrosine). They may also be modified by inclusion into such vehicles as liposomes or microspheres, or by the addition of other biologically active agents to enhance efficacy or safety. Intermediate allergen products may be freeze-dried.

**Bulk allergen preparations** consist of products in solution or suspension which will not be further processed or modified, and are ready for dilution or filling into final containers.

### IN-HOUSE REFERENCE PREPARATION

An appropriate representative preparation is selected as the In-House Reference Preparation (IHRP), characterised and used to verify batch-to-batch consistency. The IHRP is stored in suitably sized aliquots under conditions ensuring its stability, usually freeze-dried.

### Characterisation of the In-House Reference Preparation

*The extent of characterisation of the IHRP depends on the nature of the allergenic source material, knowledge of the allergenic components and availability of suitable reagents, as well as the intended use. The characterised IHRP is used as reference in the batch control of native allergen extracts or intermediate allergen products and, if possible, in the batch control of final allergen preparations.*

The In-House Reference Preparation (IHRP) is characterised by the protein content determination and a protein profile using relevant methods (such as isoelectric focusing, polyacrylamide gel electrophoresis, immunoelectrophoresis or molecular-mass profiling). Allergenic components may be detected by appropriate methods (for example, immunoblotting or crossed radio-immunoelectrophoresis).

Characterisation of the allergenic components may include identification of relevant allergens based on serological or other techniques using a pool or individual sera from allergic patients, or allergen-specific polyclonal or monoclonal antibodies. When allergen reference substances are available, determination of the content of individual allergens may be performed. Individual allergens are identified according to internationally established nomenclature whenever possible.

Where possible, the biological potency of the IHRP is established by *in vivo* techniques such as skin testing, and expressed in units of biological activity. If not, for certain extracts, potency may be established by suitable immunoassays (for example, those based on the inhibition of the binding capacity of specific immunoglobulin E antibodies) or by quantitative techniques for a single major component.

### IDENTIFICATION

Identity is confirmed at the intermediate or other applicable stage by comparison with the IHRP using protein profiling by appropriate methods (for example, isoelectric focusing, sodium dodecyl sulphate-polyacrylamide gel electrophoresis or immunoelectrophoresis).

### TESTS

*Various biochemical and immunological tests have been developed in order to characterise allergens qualitatively and quantitatively. However, some of the methods, particularly for the determination of allergenic activity and allergen profile, are not applicable to all products at present. This is because knowledge of the allergenic components or the required reagents is not available. Accordingly, allergen products have been classified in different categories with increasing test requirements, according to quality and intended use.*

*Where possible the following tests are applied to the final preparations. If not, they must be performed on the extracts as late as possible in the manufacturing process, for example, at the stage immediately prior to that stage (modification, dilution etc.) which renders the test not feasible on the final preparation.*

**Water** (*2.5.12*)
Not more than 5 per cent for freeze-dried products.

**Sterility** (*2.6.1*)
Allergen products intended for parenteral, bronchial and conjunctival administration comply with the test for sterility.

**Protein content**
80 per cent to 120 per cent of the stated content of a given batch. If the biological potency can be determined then the test for protein content may be omitted.

**Protein profile**
The protein composition determined by suitable methods corresponds to that of the IHRP.

**Abnormal toxicity** (*2.6.9*)
Allergen products obtained from moulds and intended for parenteral administration (except skin-prick tests) comply with the test for abnormal toxicity for immunosera and vaccines for human use.

*Various additional tests, some with increasing selectivity, depending on the allergen product concerned can be applied, but in any case for allergen products intended for therapeutic use, a validated test measuring the potency (total allergenic activity, determination of individual allergens or any other justified tests) must be applied.*

**Aluminium** (*2.5.13*)
Not less than 80 per cent and not more than 120 per cent of the stated amount but in any case not more than 1.25 mg per human dose unless otherwise justified and authorised,

when aluminium hydroxide or aluminium phosphate is used as adsorbent.

**Calcium** (*2.5.14*)

Not less than 80 per cent and not more than 120 per cent of the stated amount when calcium phosphate is used as adsorbent.

**Antigen profile**

The antigens are identified by means of suitable techniques using antigen-specific animal antibodies.

**Allergen profile**

Relevant allergenic components are identified by means of suitable techniques using allergen-specific human antibodies.

**Total allergenic activity**

The activity is 50 per cent to 200 per cent of the stated amount as assayed by inhibition of the binding capacity of specific immunoglobulin E antibodies or a suitable equivalent *in vitro* method.

**Individual allergens**

50 per cent to 200 per cent of the stated amount, determined by a suitable method.

**STORAGE**

Adsorbed allergen products should not be frozen.

**LABELLING**

The label states:
— the biological potency and/or the protein content and/or the extraction concentration;
— the route of administration and the intended use;
— the storage conditions;
— where applicable, the name and amount of added antimicrobial preservative;
— for freeze-dried preparations:
  — the name, composition and volume of the reconstituting liquid to be added
  — the period of time within which the preparation is to be used after reconstitution;
— where applicable, that the preparation is sterile;
— where applicable, the name and amount of adsorbent.

*Ph Eur*

# Allopurinol

(*Ph Eur monograph 0576*)

C$_5$H$_4$N$_4$O          136.1          *315-30-0*

**Action and use**

Xanthine oxidase inhibitor; treatment of gout and hyperuricaemia.

**Preparations**

Allopurinol Oral Suspension

Allopurinol Tablets

*Ph Eur*

**DEFINITION**

1,5-Dihydro-4*H*-pyrazolo[3,4-*d*]pyrimidin-4-one.

**Content**

97.0 per cent to 102.0 per cent (dried substance).

**CHARACTERS**

**Appearance**

White or almost white powder.

**Solubility**

Very slightly soluble in water and in ethanol (96 per cent). It dissolves in dilute solutions of alkali hydroxides.

**IDENTIFICATION**

*First identification    B.*

*Second identification    A, C, D.*

A. Ultraviolet and visible absorption spectrophotometry (*2.2.25*).

*Test solution*    Dissolve 10 mg in 1 ml of a 4 g/l solution of *sodium hydroxide R* and dilute to 100.0 ml with a 10.3 g/l solution of *hydrochloric acid R*. Dilute 10.0 ml of this solution to 100.0 ml with a 10.3 g/l solution of *hydrochloric acid R*.

*Spectral range*    220-350 nm.

*Absorption maximum*    At 250 nm.

*Absorption minimum*    At 231 nm.

*Absorbance ratio*    A$_{231}$/A$_{250}$ = 0.52 to 0.62.

B. Infrared absorption spectrophotometry (*2.2.24*).

*Comparison*    allopurinol CRS.

C. Dissolve 0.3 g in 2.5 ml of *dilute sodium hydroxide solution R* and add 50 ml of *water R*. Add slowly and with shaking 5 ml of *silver nitrate solution R1*. A white precipitate is formed which does not dissolve on the addition of 5 ml of *ammonia R*.

D. Thin-layer chromatography (*2.2.27*).

*Test solution*    Dissolve 20 mg of the substance to be examined in *concentrated ammonia R* and dilute to 10 ml with the same solvent.

*Reference solution*    Dissolve 20 mg of *allopurinol CRS* in concentrated *ammonia R* and dilute to 10 ml with the same solvent.

*Plate*    TLC silica gel F$_{254}$ plate R.

*Mobile phase*    anhydrous ethanol R, methylene chloride R (40:60 *V/V*).

*Application*    10 µl.

*Development*    Over 2/3 of the plate.

*Drying*    In air.

*Detection*    Examine in ultraviolet light at 254 nm.

*Results*    The principal spot in the chromatogram obtained with the test solution is similar in position and size to the principal spot in the chromatogram obtained with the reference solution.

**TESTS**

**Related substances**

Liquid chromatography (*2.2.29*). *Use freshly prepared solutions. Store and inject them at 8 °C, using a cooled autosampler.*

*Test solution (a)*    Dissolve 25.0 mg of the substance to be examined in 2.5 ml of a 4 g/l solution of *sodium hydroxide R* and dilute immediately to 50.0 ml with the mobile phase.

*Test solution (b)*    Dissolve 20.0 mg of the substance to be examined in 5.0 ml of a 4 g/l solution of *sodium hydroxide R* and dilute immediately to 250.0 ml with the mobile phase.

*Reference solution (a)* Dilute 2.0 ml of test solution (a) to 100.0 ml with the mobile phase. Dilute 5.0 ml of this solution to 100.0 ml with the mobile phase.

*Reference solution (b)* Dissolve 5 mg of *allopurinol impurity A CRS*, 5 mg of *allopurinol impurity B CRS* and 5.0 mg of *allopurinol impurity C CRS* in 5.0 ml of a 4 g/l solution of *sodium hydroxide R* and dilute immediately to 100.0 ml with the mobile phase. Dilute 1.0 ml of this solution to 100.0 ml with the mobile phase.

*Reference solution (c)* Dissolve 20.0 mg of *allopurinol CRS* in 5.0 ml of a 4 g/l solution of *sodium hydroxide R* and dilute immediately to 250.0 ml with the mobile phase.

*Column:*
— *size:* $l = 0.25$ m, $\emptyset = 4.6$ mm;
— *stationary phase: octadecylsilyl silica gel for chromatography R* (5 µm).

*Mobile phase* 1.25 g/l solution of *potassium dihydrogen phosphate R.*

*Flow rate* 1.4 ml/min.

*Detection* Spectrophotometer at 230 nm.

*Injection* 20 µl of test solution (a) and reference solutions (a) and (b).

*Run time* Twice the retention time of allopurinol.

*Elution order* Impurity A, impurity B, impurity C, allopurinol.

*Retention time* allopurinol = about 10 min.

*System suitability* Reference solution (b):
— *resolution:* minimum 1.1 between the peaks due to impurities B and C.

*Limits:*
— *impurity A:* not more than twice the area of the principal peak in the chromatogram obtained with reference solution (a) (0.2 per cent);
— *impurity B:* not more than the area of the principal peak in the chromatogram obtained with reference solution (a) (0.1 per cent);
— *impurity C:* not more than the area of the corresponding peak in the chromatogram obtained with reference solution (b) (0.1 per cent);
— *unspecified impurities:* for each impurity, not more than the area of the principal peak in the chromatogram obtained with reference solution (a) (0.10 per cent);
— *sum of impurities other than A, B and C:* not more than 3 times the area of the principal peak in the chromatogram obtained with reference solution (a) (0.3 per cent);
— *disregard limit:* 0.5 times the area of the principal peak in the chromatogram obtained with reference solution (a) (0.05 per cent).

**Impurities D and E**

Liquid chromatography (*2.2.29*). *Use freshly prepared solutions. Store and inject them at 8 °C, using a cooled autosampler.*

*Solution A* 1.25 g/l solution of *potassium dihydrogen phosphate R.*

*Test solution* Dissolve 50.0 mg of the substance to be examined in 5.0 ml of a 4 g/l solution of *sodium hydroxide R* and dilute immediately to 100.0 ml with solution A.

*Reference solution* Dissolve 5.0 mg of *allopurinol impurity D CRS* and 5.0 mg of *allopurinol impurity E CRS* in 5.0 ml of a 4 g/l solution of *sodium hydroxide R* and dilute immediately to 100.0 ml with solution A. Dilute 1.0 ml of this solution to 100.0 ml with solution A.

*Column:*
— *size:* $l = 0.05$ m, $\emptyset = 4.6$ mm;
— *stationary phase: base-deactivated octadecylsilyl silica gel for chromatography R* (3 µm).

*Mobile phase* methanol R, 1.25 g/l solution of *potassium dihydrogen phosphate R* (10:90 V/V).

*Flow rate* 2 ml/min.

*Detection* Spectrophotometer at 230 nm.

*Injection* 20 µl.

*Run time* 1.5 times the retention time of impurity E.

*Retention times* Impurity D = about 3.6 min; impurity E = about 4.5 min.

*System suitability* Reference solution:
— *resolution:* minimum 2.0 between the peaks due to impurities D and E.

*Limits:*
— *impurity D:* not more than the area of the corresponding peak in the chromatogram obtained with the reference solution (0.1 per cent);
— *impurity E:* not more than the area of the corresponding peak in the chromatogram obtained with the reference solution (0.1 per cent).

**Impurity F**

Liquid chromatography (*2.2.29*).

Under the following conditions, any hydrazine in the sample reacts with benzaldehyde to give benzaldehyde azine.

*Solvent mixture* Mix equal volumes of *dilute sodium hydroxide solution R* and *methanol R.*

*Solution A* Dissolve 2.0 g of *benzaldehyde R* in the solvent mixture and dilute to 50.0 ml with the solvent mixture. Prepare immediately before use.

*Test solution* Dissolve 250.0 mg of the substance to be examined in 5 ml of the solvent mixture. Add 4 ml of solution A, mix and allow to stand for 2.5 h at room temperature. Add 5.0 ml of *hexane R* and shake for 1 min. Allow the layers to separate and use the upper layer.

*Reference solution* Dissolve 10.0 mg of *hydrazine sulphate R* in the solvent mixture by sonicating for about 2 min and dilute to 50.0 ml with the solvent mixture. Dilute 1.0 ml to 20.0 ml with the solvent mixture. Dilute 1.0 ml of this solution to 20.0 ml with the solvent mixture. To 5.0 ml of the solution obtained, add 4 ml of solution A, mix and allow to stand for 2.5 h at room temperature. Add 5.0 ml of *hexane R* and shake for 1 min. Allow the layers to separate and use the upper layer.

*Blank solution* To 5 ml of the solvent mixture add 4 ml of solution A, mix and allow to stand for 2.5 h at room temperature. Add 5.0 ml of *hexane R* and shake for 1 min. Allow the layers to separate and use the upper layer.

*Column:*
— *size:* $l = 0.25$ m, $\emptyset = 4.0$ mm;
— *stationary phase: cyanosilyl silica gel for chromatography R* (5 µm) with a pore size of 100 nm;
— *temperature:* 30 °C.

*Mobile phase* 2-propanol R, hexane R (5:95 V/V).

*Flow rate* 1.5 ml/min.

*Detection* Spectrophotometer at 310 nm.

*Injection* 20 µl.

*Relative retention* With reference to benzaldehyde (retention time = about 2.8 min): benzaldehyde azine = about 0.8.

*System suitability* Reference solution:
— *resolution*: minimum 2 between the peaks due to benzaldehyde azine and benzaldehyde;
— *signal-to-noise ratio*: minimum 20 for the peak due to benzaldehyde azine.

*Limit*:
— *impurity F*: the area of the peak due to benzaldehyde azine in the chromatogram obtained with the test solution is not more than the area of the corresponding peak in the chromatogram obtained with the reference solution (10 ppm of hydrazine sulphate equivalent to 2.5 ppm of hydrazine).

**Heavy metals** (*2.4.8*)
Maximum 20 ppm.

1.0 g complies with test C. Prepare the reference solution using 2 ml of *lead standard solution (10 ppm Pb) R*.

**Loss on drying** (*2.2.32*)
Maximum 0.5 per cent, determined on 1.000 g by drying in an oven at 105 °C.

**Sulphated ash** (*2.4.14*)
Maximum 0.1 per cent, determined on 1.0 g.

**ASSAY**
Liquid chromatography (*2.2.29*) as described in the test for related substances with the following modification.

*Injection* Test solution (b) and reference solution (c).

Calculate the percentage content of $C_5H_4N_4O$ from the declared content of *allopurinol CRS*.

**IMPURITIES**
*Specified impurities* A, B, C, D, E, F.

A. R1 = NH$_2$, R2 = H:
5-amino-1*H*-pyrazole-4-carboxamide,

B. R1 = NH$_2$, R2 = CHO:
5-(formylamino)-1*H*-pyrazole-4-carboxamide,

D. R1 = O-C$_2$H$_5$, R2 = H:
ethyl 5-amino-1*H*-pyrazole-4-carboxylate,

E. R1 = O-C$_2$H$_5$, R2 = CHO:
ethyl 5-(formylamino)-1*H*-pyrazole-4-carboxylate,

C. 5-(4*H*-1,2,4-triazol-4-yl)-1*H*-pyrazole-4-carboxamide,

F. H$_2$N-NH$_2$: diazane (hydrazine).

*Ph Eur* _____

# Almagate

(*Ph Eur monograph 2010*)

$Al_2Mg_6C_2O_{20}H_{14},4H_2O$      630      *66827-12-1*

**Action and use**
Antacid.

*Ph Eur* _____

**DEFINITION**
Hydrated aluminium magnesium hydroxycarbonate.

*Content*:
— *aluminium*: 15.0 per cent to 17.0 per cent (calculated as $Al_2O_3$),
— *magnesium*: 36.0 per cent to 40.0 per cent (calculated as MgO),
— *carbonic acid*: 12.5 per cent to 14.5 per cent (calculated as $CO_2$).

**CHARACTERS**
**Appearance**
White or almost white, fine, crystalline powder.

**Solubility**
Practically insoluble in water, in ethanol (96 per cent) and in methylene chloride. It dissolves with effervescence and heating in dilute mineral acids.

**IDENTIFICATION**
A. Infrared absorption spectrophotometry (*2.2.24*).

*Comparison* Ph. Eur. reference spectrum of almagate.

B. Dissolve 0.15 g in *dilute hydrochloric acid R* and dilute to 20 ml with the same acid. 2 ml of the solution gives the reaction of aluminium (*2.3.1*).

C. 2 ml of the solution prepared under identification test B gives the reaction of magnesium (*2.3.1*).

**TESTS**
**pH** (*2.2.3*)
9.1 to 9.7.

Disperse 4.0 g in 100 ml of *carbon dioxide-free water R*, stir for 2 min and filter.

**Neutralising capacity**
*Carry out the test at 37 °C*. Disperse 0.5 g in 100 ml of *water R*, heat, add 100.0 ml of *0.1 M hydrochloric acid*, previously heated and stir continuously; the pH (*2.2.3*) of the solution between 5 min and 20 min is not less than 3.0 and not greater than 4.5. Add 10.0 ml of *0.5 M hydrochloric acid*, previously heated, stir continuously for 1 h and titrate with *0.1 M sodium hydroxide* to pH 3.5; not more than 20.0 ml of *0.1 M sodium hydroxide* is required.

**Chlorides** (*2.4.4*)
Maximum 0.1 per cent.

Dissolve 0.33 g in 5 ml of *dilute nitric acid R* and dilute to 100 ml with *water R*. 15 ml of the solution complies with the limit test for chlorides. Prepare simultaneously the standard by diluting 0.7 ml of *dilute nitric acid R* to 5 ml with *water R* and adding 10 ml of *chloride standard solution (5 ppm Cl) R*.

**Sulphates** (*2.4.13*)
Maximum 0.4 per cent.

Dissolve 0.25 g in 5 ml of *dilute hydrochloric acid R* and dilute to 100 ml with *distilled water R*. 15 ml of the solution complies with the limit test for sulphates. Prepare simultaneously the standard by adding 0.8 ml of *dilute hydrochloric acid R* to 15 ml of *sulphate standard solution (10 ppm SO$_4$) R*.

**Sodium**

Maximum $1.50 \times 10^2$ ppm.

Atomic absorption spectrometry (*2.2.23, Method I*).

*Test solution*  Dissolve 0.25 g in 50 ml of a 103 g/l solution of *hydrochloric acid R*.

*Reference solutions*  Prepare the reference solutions using *sodium standard solution (200 ppm Na) R*, diluted as necessary with a 103 g/l solution of *hydrochloric acid R*.

**Heavy metals** (*2.4.8*)

Maximum 20 ppm.

Dissolve 1.0 g in *dilute hydrochloric acid R* and dilute to 20.0 ml with the same acid. 12 ml of the solution complies with limit test A. Prepare the reference solution using *lead standard solution (1 ppm Pb) R*.

**Loss on ignition**

43.0 per cent to 49.0 per cent, determined on 1.000 g by ignition at $900 \pm 50$ °C.

**Microbial contamination**

TAMC: acceptance criterion $10^3$ CFU/g (*2.6.12*).

TYMC: acceptance criterion $10^2$ CFU/g (*2.6.12*).

Absence of *Escherichia coli* (*2.6.13*).

Absence of *Pseudomonas aeruginosa* (*2.6.13*).

## ASSAY

**Aluminium**

Dissolve 1.000 g in 5 ml of *hydrochloric acid R*, heating if necessary. Allow to cool to room temperature and dilute to 100.0 ml with *water R* (solution A). Introduce 10.0 ml of solution A into a 250 ml conical flask, add 25.0 ml of *0.05 M sodium edetate*, 20 ml of *buffer solution pH 3.5 R*, 40 ml of *ethanol R* and 2 ml of a freshly prepared 0.25 g/l solution of *dithizone R* in *ethanol R*. Titrate the excess of sodium edetate with *0.05 M zinc sulphate* until the colour changes from greenish-violet to pink.

1 ml of *0.05 M sodium edetate* is equivalent to 2.549 mg of $Al_2O_3$.

**Magnesium**

Introduce 10.0 ml of solution A prepared in the assay of aluminium into a 500 ml conical flask, add 200 ml of *water R*, 20 ml of *triethanolamine R* with shaking, 10 ml of *ammonium chloride buffer solution pH 10.0 R* and 50 mg of *mordant black 11 triturate R*. Titrate with *0.05 M sodium edetate* until the colour changes from violet to pure blue.

1 ml of *0.05 M sodium edetate* is equivalent to 2.015 mg of MgO.

**Carbonic acid**

12.5 per cent to 14.5 per cent.

*Test sample*  Place 7.00 mg of the substance to be examined in a tin capsule. Seal the capsule.

*Reference sample*  Place 7.00 mg of *almagate CRS* in a tin capsule. Seal the capsule.

Introduce separately the test sample and the reference sample into a combustion chamber of a CHN analyser purged with *helium for chromatography R* and maintained at a temperature of 1020 °C. Simultaneously, introduce *oxygen R* at a pressure of 40 kPa and a flow rate of 20 ml/min and allow complete combustion of the sample. Sweep the combustion gases through a reduction reactor and separate the gases formed by gas chromatography (*2.2.28*).

*Column:*
— *size: l = 2 m, Ø = 4 mm*;
— *stationary phase: ethylvinylbenzene-divinylbenzene copolymer R1*.

*Carrier gas*  *helium for chromatography R*.

*Flow rate*  100 ml/min.

*Temperature:*
— *column*: 65 °C;
— *detector*: 190 °C.

*Detection*  Thermal conductivity.

*Run time*  16 min.

*System suitability:*
— average percentage of carbon in 5 reference samples must be within $\pm$ 0.2 per cent of the value assigned to the CRS; the difference between the upper and the lower values of the percentage of carbon in these samples must be below 0.2 per cent.

Calculate the percentage content of carbonic acid in the test sample according to the following formula:

$$C \times K \times \frac{A}{m}$$

$C$ = percentage content of carbonic acid in the reference sample;

$K$ = mean value for the 5 reference samples of the ratio of the mass in milligrams to the area of the peak due to carbonic acid;

$A$ = area of the peak due to carbonic acid in the chromatogram obtained with the test sample;

$m$ = sample mass, in milligrams.

## STORAGE

In an airtight container.

*Ph Eur*

# Aloxiprin

*9014-67-9*

**Action and use**

Salicylate; non-selective cyclo-oxygenase inhibitor; antipyretic; analgesic; anti-inflammatory.

**Preparation**

Aloxiprin Tablets

## DEFINITION

Aloxiprin is a polymeric condensation product of aluminium oxide and *O*-acetylsalicylic acid. It contains not less than 7.5% and not more than 8.5% of aluminium, Al, and not less than 79.0% and not more than 87.4% of total salicylates, calculated as *O*-acetylsalicylic acid, $C_9H_8O_4$, both calculated with reference to the dried substance.

## CHARACTERISTICS

A fine, white or slightly pink powder.

Practically insoluble in *water*; practically insoluble in *ethanol (96%)* and in *ether*.

## IDENTIFICATION

A. Boil 1 g with 20 ml of 2M *hydrochloric acid*, cool, filter and reserve the filtrate. Dissolve the residue in 10 ml of 0.1M *sodium hydroxide* and neutralise with 1M *acetic acid*. 1 ml of the resulting solution yields reaction A characteristic of *salicylates*, Appendix VI.

B. The filtrate reserved in test A yields the reaction characteristic of *aluminium salts*, Appendix VI.

## TESTS

### Heavy metals

Carefully ignite 2.0 g at a low temperature until completely charred, cool, add 2 ml of *nitric acid* and 0.25 ml of *sulphuric acid*, heat cautiously until white fumes are evolved and ignite at 500° to 600°. Cool, add 2 ml of *hydrochloric acid*, evaporate to dryness on a water bath and carry out the procedure for *limit test C for heavy metals*, Appendix VII, beginning at the words 'Dissolve the residue...'. Use 2 ml of *lead standard solution (10 ppm Pb)* to prepare the standard (10 ppm).

### Free acetylsalicylic acid

To a quantity containing the equivalent of 1.0 g of total salicylates add 50 ml of dry *ether* and shake for 30 minutes. Filter quickly through fluted filter paper, wash the paper with several portions of dry *ether* and dilute the combined filtrate and washings to 100 ml with dry *ether*. The *absorbance* of the solution at the maximum at 278 nm is not more than 0.36, Appendix II B (0.5%, calculated with reference to the content of total salicylates).

### Salicylic acid

The *absorbance* of the solution used in the test for Free acetylsalicylic acid at the maximum at 308 nm is not more than 0.50, Appendix II B (0.15%, calculated with reference to the content of total salicylates).

### Combined salicylate

Not more than 9.5%, calculated as salicylic acid, $C_7H_6O_3$, with reference to the content of total salicylates calculated as *O*-acetylsalicylic acid when determined in the following manner. To 0.1 g add 40 ml of a 0.5% w/v solution of *sodium fluoride* in 0.1M *hydrochloric acid* and shake for 5 minutes. Allow the solution to stand for 10 minutes, shaking at frequent intervals. Extract with six 20 ml quantities of *dichloromethane*, filter the combined extracts through a layer of *anhydrous sodium sulphate*, wash with 30 ml of *dichloromethane* and dilute the combined filtrate and washings to 200 ml with *dichloromethane*. Dilute 20 ml of the solution to 50 ml with *dichloromethane* and measure the *absorbance* of the resulting solution at the maximum at 308 nm, Appendix II B. Calculate the content of $C_7H_6O_3$ taking 293 as the value of A(1%, 1 cm) at the maximum at 308 nm.

### Loss on drying

When dried to constant weight over *phosphorus pentoxide* at a pressure not exceeding 0.7 kPa, loses not more than 2.0% of its weight. Use 1 g.

## ASSAY

### For aluminium

Ignite 2 g in a tared silica crucible, heat gently until the organic matter is destroyed and then ignite to constant weight at 1000°. Each g of residue is equivalent to 0.5292 g of Al.

### For total salicylates

To 0.25 g add 50 ml of 1M *sodium hydroxide* and boil gently until dissolved. Cool, add 50 ml of *water*, adjust the pH to between 2.40 and 2.50 with 1M *hydrochloric acid* and dilute to 500 ml with *water*. To 5 ml add 4 ml of *iron(III) chloride solution*, allow to stand for 30 minutes, dilute to 50 ml with *water* and measure the *absorbance* of the resulting solution at the maximum at 530 nm, Appendix II B, using in the reference cell a solution prepared by diluting 4 ml of *iron(III) chloride solution* to 50 ml with *water*. Calculate the content of total salicylates as $C_9H_8O_4$ from the *absorbance* obtained by repeating the procedure using 4 ml of a 0.05% w/v solution

of *salicylic acid* in place of the solution being examined and beginning at the words 'add 4 ml of *iron(III) chloride solution...*'. Each g of salicylic acid is equivalent to 1.305 g of $C_9H_8O_4$.

# Alprazolam

(*Ph Eur monograph 1065*)

$C_{17}H_{13}ClN_4$      308.8      *28981-97-7*

### Action and use

Benzodiazepine.

*Ph Eur* _____

## DEFINITION

8-Chloro-1-methyl-6-phenyl-4*H*-[1,2,4]triazolo[4,3-*a*][1,4]-benzodiazepine.

### Content

99.0 per cent to 101.0 per cent (dried substance).

## CHARACTERS

### Appearance

White or almost white, crystalline powder.

### Solubility

Practically insoluble in water, freely soluble in methylene chloride, sparingly soluble in acetone and in ethanol (96 per cent).

It shows polymorphism (*5.9*).

## IDENTIFICATION

*First identification*   B.

*Second identification*   A, C.

A. Dissolve the substance to be examined in the smallest necessary quantity of *ethyl acetate R* and evaporate to dryness on a water-bath. Thoroughly mix 5.0 mg of the substance to be examined with 5.0 mg of *alprazolam CRS*. The melting point (*2.2.14*) of the mixture does not differ by more than 2 °C from the melting point of the substance to be examined.

B. Infrared absorption spectrophotometry (*2.2.24*).

*Preparation*   Discs.

*Comparison*   *alprazolam CRS* .

If the spectra obtained in the solid state show differences, dissolve the substance to be examined and the reference substance separately in the minimum volume of *ethyl acetate R*, evaporate to dryness on a water-bath and record new spectra using the residues.

C. Thin-layer chromatography (*2.2.27*).

*Test solution*   Dissolve 10 mg of the substance to be examined in *methanol R* and dilute to 10 ml with the same solvent.

*Reference solution (a)* Dissolve 10 mg of *alprazolam CRS* in *methanol R* and dilute to 10 ml with the same solvent.

*Reference solution (b)* Dissolve 10 mg of *alprazolam CRS* and 10 mg of *midazolam CRS* in *methanol R* and dilute to 10 ml with the same solvent.

*Plate* *TLC silica gel GF$_{254}$ plate R.*

*Mobile phase* glacial acetic acid R, water R, methanol R, ethyl acetate R (2:15:20:80 V/V/V/V).

*Application* 5 µl.

*Development* Over a path of 12 cm.

*Drying* In air.

*Detection* Examine in ultraviolet light at 254 nm.

*System suitability* Reference solution (b):
— the chromatogram shows 2 clearly separately spots.

*Results* The principal spot in the chromatogram obtained with the test solution is similar in position and size to the principal spot in the chromatogram obtained with reference solution (a).

## TESTS

### Related substances
Liquid chromatography (2.2.29).

*Buffer solution* Dissolve 7.7 g of *ammonium acetate R* in 1000 ml of *water R* and adjust to pH 4.2 with *glacial acetic acid R*.

*Test solution* Dissolve 0.100 g of the substance to be examined in *dimethylformamide R* and dilute to 10.0 ml with the same solvent.

*Reference solution (a)* Dissolve 2 mg of *alprazolam CRS* and 2 mg of *triazolam CRS* in *dimethylformamide R* and dilute to 100.0 ml with the same solvent.

*Reference solution (b)* Dilute 5.0 ml of the test solution to 100.0 ml with *dimethylformamide R*. Dilute 0.5 ml of this solution to 10.0 ml with *dimethylformamide R*.

*Column:*
— *size: l* = 0.25 m, Ø = 4.6 mm;
— *stationary phase: phenylsilyl silica gel for chromatography R1* (5 µm).

*Mobile phase:*
— *mobile phase A*: buffer solution, *methanol R* (44:56 V/V);
— *mobile phase B*: buffer solution, *methanol R* (5:95 V/V);
— *temperature*: 40 °C;

| Time (min) | Mobile phase A (per cent V/V) | Mobile phase B (per cent V/V) |
|---|---|---|
| 0 - 15 | 98 | 2 |
| 15 - 35 | 98 → 1 | 2 → 99 |
| 35 - 40 | 1 | 99 |

*Flow rate* 2 ml/min.

*Detection* Spectrophotometer at 254 nm.

*Injection* 10 µl; inject *dimethylformamide R* as a blank.

*Retention time* triazolam = about 9 min; alprazolam = about 10 min.

*System suitability* Reference solution (a):
— *resolution*: minimum 1.5 between the peaks due to triazolam and alprazolam.

*Limits:*
— *total*: not more than the area of the principal peak in the chromatogram obtained with reference solution (b) (0.25 per cent);

— *disregard limit*: 0.2 times the area of the principal peak in the chromatogram obtained with reference solution (b) (0.05 per cent).

**Loss on drying** (2.2.32)
Maximum 0.5 per cent, determined on 1.000 g by drying in an oven at 105 °C.

**Sulphated ash** (2.4.14)
Maximum 0.1 per cent, determined on 1.0 g.

## ASSAY
Dissolve 0.140 g in 50 ml of a mixture of 2 volumes of *acetic anhydride R* and 3 volumes of *anhydrous acetic acid R*. Titrate with *0.1 M perchloric acid*, determining the end-point potentiometrically (2.2.20). Titrate to the 2$^{nd}$ point of inflexion.

1 ml of *0.1 M perchloric acid* is equivalent to 15.44 mg of $C_{17}H_{13}ClN_4$.

## STORAGE
Protected from light.

## IMPURITIES

A. (4RS)-3-amino-6-chloro-2-methyl-4-phenyl-3,4-dihydroquinazolin-4-ol,

B. R = CH$_2$OH: [5-chloro-2-[3-(hydroxymethyl)-5-methyl-4H-1,2,4-triazol-4-yl]phenyl]phenylmethanone,

C. R = H: [5-chloro-2-[3-methyl-4H-1,2,4-triazol-4-yl]phenyl]phenylmethanone,

F. R = CH$_2$Cl: [5-chloro-2-[3-(chloromethyl)-5-methyl-4H-1,2,4-triazol-4-yl]phenyl]phenylmethanone,

D. 8-chloro-1-ethenyl-6-phenyl-4H-[1,2,4]triazolo[4,3-a][1,4]benzodiazepine,

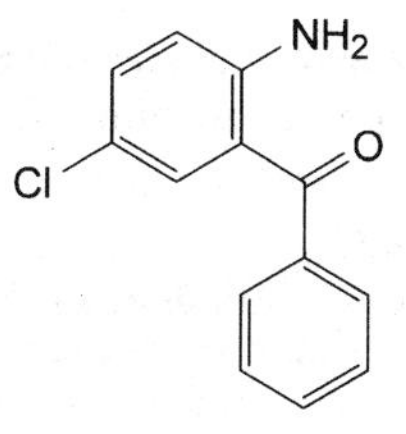

E. (2-amino-5-chlorophenyl)phenylmethanone,

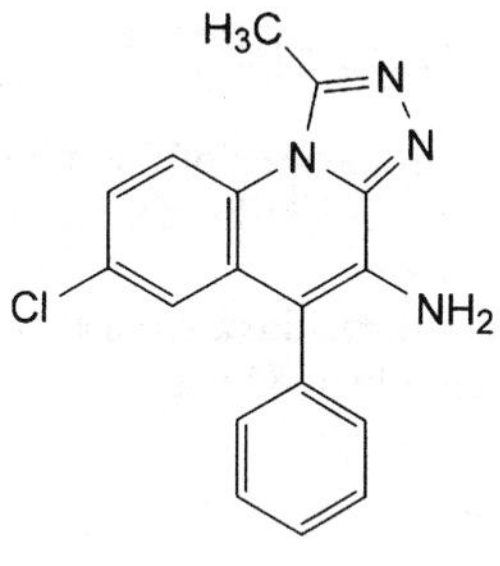

G. 7-chloro-1-methyl-5-phenyl[1,2,4]triazolo[4,3-a]quinolin-4-amine,

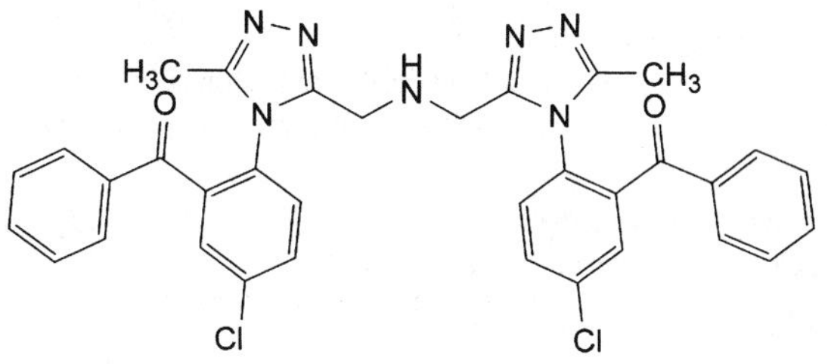

H. bis[[4-(2-benzoyl-4-chlorophenyl)-5-methyl-4H-1,2,4-triazol-3-yl]methyl]amine,

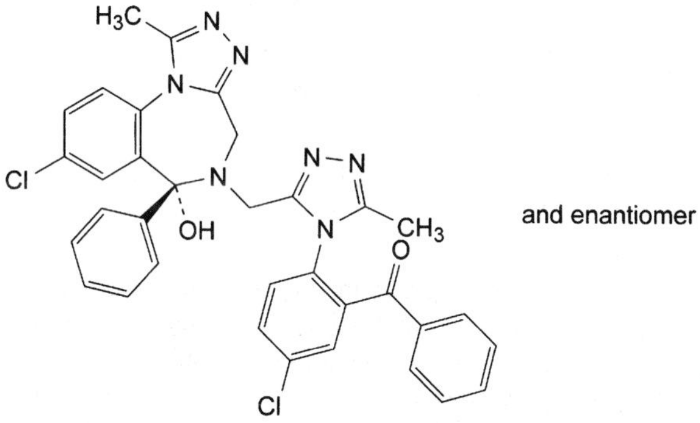

and enantiomer

I. [5-chloro-2-[3-[[(6RS)-8-chloro-6-hydroxy-1-methyl-6-phenyl-4H-[1,2,4]triazolo[4,3-a][1,4]benzodiazepin-5(6H)-yl]methyl]-5-methyl-4H-1,2,4-triazol-4-yl]phenyl]phenylmethanone,

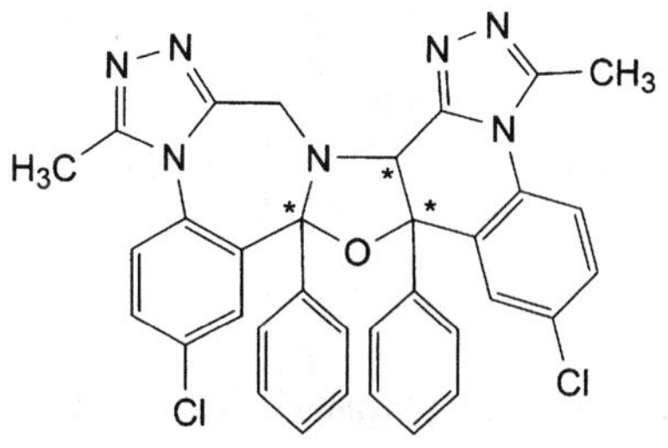

J. 2,17-dichloro-6,13-dimethyl-18b,19a-diphenyl-8b,19adihydro-10H,18bH-[1,2,4]triazolo[4′′′,3′′′:1″,2″]

quinolo[3″,4″:4′,5′]oxazolo[3′,2′-d]-1,2,4-triazolo[4,3-a][1,4]benzodiazepine.

*Ph Eur*

# Alprenolol Hydrochloride

(*Ph Eur monograph 0876*)

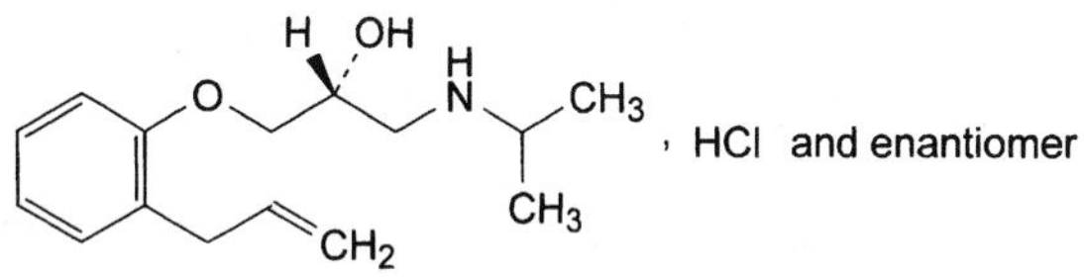

, HCl and enantiomer

C₁₅H₂₃NO₂,HCl        285.8        *13707-88-5*

**Action and use**
Beta-adrenoceptor antagonist.

*Ph Eur*

**DEFINITION**
(2RS)-1-[(1-Methylethyl)amino]-3-[2-(prop-2-enyl)phenoxy]propan-2-ol hydrochloride.

**Content**
99.0 per cent to 101.0 per cent (dried substance).

**CHARACTERS**

**Appearance**
White or almost white, crystalline powder or colourless crystals.

**Solubility**
Very soluble in water, freely soluble in ethanol (96 per cent) and in methylene chloride.

**IDENTIFICATION**
*First identification*    B, D.
*Second identification*    A, C, D.

A. Melting point (*2.2.14*): 108 °C to 112 °C.

B. Infrared absorption spectrophotometry (*2.2.24*).

*Comparison*    alprenolol hydrochloride CRS.

C. Examine the chromatograms obtained in test A for related substances.

*Detection*    Examine in daylight, after exposure to iodine vapour for 30 min.

*Results*    The principal spot in the chromatogram obtained with test solution (b) is similar in position, colour and size to the principal spot in the chromatogram obtained with reference solution (a).

D. It gives reaction (a) of chlorides (*2.3.1*).

**TESTS**

**Solution S**
Dissolve 1.0 g in *carbon dioxide-free water R* and dilute to 50 ml with the same solvent.

**Appearance of solution**
Solution S is clear (*2.2.1*) and not more intensely coloured than reference solution B₉ (*2.2.2, Method II*).

**Acidity or alkalinity**
To 10 ml of solution S add 0.2 ml of *methyl red solution R* and 0.2 ml of *0.01 M hydrochloric acid*; the solution is red. Add 0.4 ml of *0.01 M sodium hydroxide*; the solution is yellow.

**Impurity C**

Maximum 0.1 per cent.

Dissolve 0.25 g in *ethanol (96 per cent) R* and dilute to 25 ml with the same solvent. The absorbance (*2.2.25*) measured at 297 nm is not greater than 0.20.

**Related substances**

A. Thin-layer chromatography (*2.2.27*).

*Test solution (a)* Dissolve 0.50 g of the substance to be examined in *methanol R* and dilute to 10 ml with the same solvent.

*Test solution (b)* Dilute 1 ml of test solution (a) to 50 ml with *methanol R*.

*Reference solution (a)* Dissolve 10 mg of *alprenolol hydrochloride CRS* in *methanol R* and dilute to 10 ml with the same solvent.

*Reference solution (b)* Dissolve 10 mg of *alprenolol hydrochloride CRS* and 10 mg of *oxprenolol hydrochloride CRS* in *methanol R* and dilute to 10 ml with the same solvent.

*Reference solution (c)* Dilute 5 ml of test solution (b) to 50 ml with *methanol R*.

*Plate* *TLC silica gel G plate R*.

*Mobile phase* Place 2 beakers each containing 30 ml of *ammonia R* at the bottom of the tank containing a mixture of 5 volumes of *methanol R* and 95 volumes of *ethyl acetate R*.

*Application* 5 µl.

*Development* Over a path of 15 cm in a tank saturated for at least 1 h.

*Drying* At 100 °C for 15 min.

*Detection* Expose to iodine vapour for up to 6 h.

*System suitability* Reference solution (b):
— the chromatogram shows 2 clearly separated spots.

*Limits* Test solution (a):
— *impurity D*: any spot with an $R_F$ value greater than that of the principal spot is not more intense than the principal spot in the chromatogram obtained with reference solution (c) (0.2 per cent).

B. Liquid chromatography (*2.2.29*).

*Test solution* Dissolve 20.0 mg of the substance to be examined in the mobile phase and dilute to 10.0 ml with the mobile phase.

*Reference solution (a)* Dissolve 4.0 mg of *alprenolol hydrochloride CRS* and 0.8 mg of *4-isopropylphenol R* in the mobile phase and dilute to 100.0 ml with the mobile phase.

*Reference solution (b)* Dilute 4.0 ml of the test solution to 100.0 ml with the mobile phase. Dilute 1.0 ml of this solution to 10.0 ml with the mobile phase.

*Column:*
— *size: l* = 0.15 m, Ø = 4 mm;
— *stationary phase*: *octylsilyl silica gel for chromatography R* (5 µm).

*Mobile phase* Mix 0.656 g of *sodium octanesulphonate R* with 150 ml of *acetonitrile R* and dilute to 500 ml with phosphate buffer pH 2.8 prepared as follows: mix 1.78 g of *phosphoric acid R* and 15.6 g of *sodium dihydrogen phosphate R* and dilute to 2000 ml with *water R*.

*Flow rate* 1 ml/min.

*Detection* Spectrophotometer at 280 nm.

*Equilibration* With the mobile phase for about 1 h.

*Injection* 20 µl.

*Run time* Twice the retention time of alprenolol.

*Retention time* Alprenolol = about 11 min; 4-isopropylphenol = about 18 min.

*System suitability* Reference solution (a):
— *resolution*: minimum 5 between the peaks due to alprenolol and 4-isopropylphenol; if necessary, adjust the concentration of sodium octanesulphonate and/or acetonitrile in the mobile phase (increase the concentration of sodium octanesulphonate to increase the retention time of alprenolol and increase the concentration of acetonitrile to decrease the retention times of both compounds).

*Limits:*
— *total*: not more than the area of the principal peak in the chromatogram obtained with reference solution (b) (0.4 per cent);
— *disregard limit*: 0.1 times the area of the principal peak in the chromatogram obtained with reference solution (b) (0.04 per cent).

**Heavy metals** (*2.4.8*)

Maximum 10 ppm.

Dissolve 2.0 g in 20 ml of *water R*. 12 ml of the solution complies with test A. Prepare the reference solution using *lead standard solution (1 ppm Pb) R*.

**Loss on drying** (*2.2.32*)

Maximum 0.5 per cent, determined on 1.000 g by drying over *diphosphorus pentoxide R* at a pressure not exceeding 2.7 kPa.

**Sulphated ash** (*2.4.14*)

Maximum 0.1 per cent, determined on 1.0 g.

**ASSAY**

Dissolve 0.400 g in 25 ml of a mixture of equal volumes of *anhydrous ethanol R* and *water R*. Add 10 ml of *0.01 M hydrochloric acid*. Carry out a potentiometric titration (*2.2.20*), using *0.1 M sodium hydroxide*. Read the volume added between the 2 points of inflexion.

1 ml of *0.1 M sodium hydroxide* is equivalent to 28.58 mg of $C_{15}H_{24}ClNO_2$.

**STORAGE**

Protected from light.

**IMPURITIES**

*Specified impurities* *C, D.*

*Other detectable impurities* (the following substances would, if present at a sufficient level, be detected by one or other of the tests in the monograph. They are limited by the general acceptance criterion for other/unspecified impurities and/or by the general monograph *Substances for pharmaceutical use (2034)*. It is therefore not necessary to identify these impurities for demonstration of compliance. See also *5.10*. *Control of impurities in substances for pharmaceutical use*): *A, B.*

*By thin-layer chromatography* *D.*

*By liquid chromatography* *A, B.*

A. R1 = OH, R2 = CH$_2$-CH=CH$_2$: (2*RS*)-3-[2-(prop-2-enyl)phenoxy]propan-1,2-diol,

C. R1 = NH-CH(CH$_3$)$_2$, R2 = CH=CH-CH$_3$: (2*RS*)-1-[(1-methylethyl)amino]-3-[2-(prop-1-enyl)phenoxy] propan-2-ol,

B. 2-(prop-2-enyl)phenol,

D. 1,1′-[(1-methylethyl)imino]bis[3-[2-(prop-2-enyl)phenoxy]propan-2-ol].

*Ph Eur*

# Alprostadil

(*Ph Eur monograph 1488*)

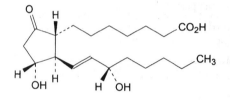

$C_{20}H_{34}O_5$      354.5      745-65-3

## Action and use
Prostaglandin $E_1$ ($PGE_1$).

*Ph Eur*

## DEFINITION
7-[(1R,2R,3R)-3-Hydroxy-2-[(1E,3S)-3-hydroxyoct-1-enyl]-5-oxocyclopentyl]heptanoic acid.

## Content
95.0 per cent to 102.5 per cent (anhydrous substance).

## CHARACTERS
### Appearance
White or slightly yellowish, crystalline powder.

### Solubility
Practically insoluble in water, freely soluble in alcohol, soluble in acetone, slightly soluble in ethyl acetate.

## IDENTIFICATION
A. Specific optical rotation (*2.2.7*): − 60 to − 70 (anhydrous substance).

Immediately before use, dissolve 50 mg in *alcohol R* and dilute to 10.0 ml with the same solvent.

B. Infrared absorption spectrophotometry (*2.2.24*).

*Preparation* Discs.

*Comparison* alprostadil CRS.

C. Examine the chromatograms obtained in the assay.

*Results* The principal peak in the chromatogram obtained with the test solution is similar in retention time and size to the principal peak in the chromatogram obtained with the reference solution.

## TESTS
### Related substances
Liquid chromatography (*2.2.29*). *Prepare the solutions protected from light.*

*Test solution* Dissolve 10.0 mg of the substance to be examined in a mixture of equal volumes of *acetonitrile R1* and *water R* and dilute to 10.0 ml with the same mixture of solvents.

*Reference solution (a)* Dilute 100 µl of the test solution to 20.0 ml with a mixture of equal volumes of *acetonitrile R1* and *water R*.

*Reference solution (b)* Dissolve 1.0 mg of *dinoprostone impurity C CRS* (alprostadil impurity H) and 1.0 mg of *alprostadil CRS* in a mixture of equal volumes of *acetonitrile R1* and *water R* and dilute to 20.0 ml with the same mixture of solvents.

*Reference solution (c)* In order to prepare in situ the degradation compounds (impurity A and impurity B), dissolve 1 mg of the substance to be examined in 100 µl of *1 M sodium hydroxide* (the solution becomes brownish-red), wait for 3 min and add 100 µl of *1 M phosphoric acid* (yellowish-white opalescent solution); dilute to 5.0 ml with a mixture of equal volumes of *acetonitrile R1* and *water R*.

### System A
*Column:*
— size: $l$ = 0.25 m, Ø = 4.0 mm,
— stationary phase: octylsilyl base-deactivated silica gel for chromatography R (4 µm) with a pore size of 6 nm,
— temperature: 35 °C.

*Mobile phase:*
— mobile phase A. Dissolve 3.9 g of *sodium dihydrogen phosphate R* in *water R* and dilute to 1000.0 ml with the same solvent; adjust to pH 2.5 with a 2.9 g/l solution of *phosphoric acid R* (approximately 600 ml is required); to 740 ml of the buffer solution add 260 ml of *acetonitrile R1*;
— mobile phase B. Dissolve 3.9 g of *sodium dihydrogen phosphate R* in *water R* and dilute to 1000.0 ml with the same solvent; adjust to pH 2.5 with a 2.9 g/l solution of *phosphoric acid R* (approximately 600 ml is required); to 200 ml of the buffer solution add 800 ml of *acetonitrile R1*;

| Time (min) | Mobile phase A (per cent V/V) | Mobile phase B (per cent V/V) |
|---|---|---|
| 0 - 75 | 100 | 0 |
| 75 - 76 | 100 → 0 | 0 → 100 |
| 76 - 86 | 0 | 100 |
| 86 - 87 | 0 → 100 | 100 → 0 |
| 87 - 102 | 100 | 0 |

*Flow rate* 1 ml/min.

*Detection* Spectrophotometer at 200 nm.

*Injection* 20 µl loop injector.

*System suitability:*
— retention time: alprostadil = about 63 min,
— resolution: minimum of 1.5 between the peaks due to impurity H and alprostadil in the chromatogram obtained with reference solution (b).

### System B
Use the same conditions as for system A with the following mobile phase and elution programme:
— mobile phase A. Dissolve 3.9 g of *sodium dihydrogen phosphate R* in *water R* and dilute to 1000.0 ml with the

same solvent; adjust to pH 2.5 with a 2.9 g/l solution of *phosphoric acid R* (approximately 600 ml is required); to 600 ml of the buffer solution add 400 ml of *acetonitrile R1*;
— *mobile phase B.* Use mobile phase B as described under system A;

| Time (min) | Mobile phase A (per cent *V/V*) | Mobile phase B (per cent *V/V*) |
|---|---|---|
| 0 - 50 | 100 | 0 |
| 50 - 51 | 100 → 0 | 0 → 100 |
| 51 - 61 | 0 | 100 |
| 61 - 62 | 0 → 100 | 100 → 0 |
| 62 - 72 | 100 | 0 |

*System suitability:*
— *relative retentions* with reference to alprostadil (retention time = about 7 min): impurity A = about 2.4; impurity B = about 2.6,
— *resolution*: minimum of 1.5 between the peaks due to impurity A and impurity B in the chromatogram obtained with reference solution (c).

Carry out the test according to system A and B.

*Limits:*
— *correction factors*: multiply the areas of the corresponding peaks using the correction factors in Table 1488.-1 to obtain the corrected areas,

Table 1488.-1

| Impurity | Relative retention (system A) | Relative retention (system B) | Correction factor |
|---|---|---|---|
| impurity G | 0.80 | - | 0.7 |
| impurity F | 0.88 | - | 0.8 |
| impurity D | 0.90 | - | 1.0 |
| impurity H | 0.96 | - | 0.7 |
| impurity E | 1.10 | - | 0.7 |
| impurity C | - | 1.36 | 1.9 |
| impurity K | - | 1.85 | 0.06 |
| impurity A | - | 2.32 | 0.7 |
| impurity B | - | 2.45 | 1.5 |
| impurity I | - | 4.00 | 1.0 |
| impurity J | - | 5.89 | 1.0 |

— *impurity A (corrected area)*: not more than 3 times the area of the principal peak in the chromatogram obtained with reference solution (a) (1.5 per cent),
— *impurity B (corrected area)*: not more than the area of the principal peak in the chromatogram obtained with reference solution (a) (0.5 per cent),
— *any other impurity (corrected area)*: not more than 1.8 times the area of the principal peak in the chromatogram obtained with reference solution (a) (0.9 per cent), and not more than 1 such peak has an area greater than the area of the principal peak in the chromatogram obtained with reference solution (a) (0.5 per cent). Evaluate impurities appearing at relative retentions less than 1.2 by system A and impurities appearing at relative retentions greater than 1.2 by system B,

— *total (corrected area)*: not more than 3 times the area of the principal peak in the chromatogram obtained with reference solution (a) (1.5 per cent),
— *disregard limit*: 0.1 times the area of the principal peak in the chromatogram obtained with reference solution (a) (0.05 per cent).

**Water** (*2.5.32*)
Maximum 0.5 per cent, determined on 50 mg.

**ASSAY**
Liquid chromatography (*2.2.29*) as described in the test for related substances, system A. *Prepare the solutions protected from light.*

*Test solution* Dissolve 10.0 mg of the substance to be examined in a mixture of equal volumes of *acetonitrile R1* and *water R* and dilute to 25.0 ml with the same mixture of solvents. Dilute 3.0 ml of the solution to 20.0 ml with a mixture of equal volumes of *acetonitrile R1* and *water R*.

*Reference solution* Dissolve 10.0 mg of *alprostadil CRS* in a mixture of equal volumes of *acetonitrile R1* and *water R* and dilute to 25.0 ml with the same mixture of solvents. Dilute 3.0 ml of the solution to 20.0 ml with a mixture of equal volumes of *acetonitrile R1* and *water R*.

*Injection* 20 µl.

Calculate the percentage content of $C_{20}H_{34}O_5$.

**STORAGE**
At a temperature of 2 °C to 8 °C.

**IMPURITIES**

A. 7-[(1R,2S)-2-[(1E,3S)-3-hydroxyoct-1-enyl]-5-oxocyclopent-3-enyl]heptanoic acid (prostaglandin $A_1$),

B. 7-[2-[(1E,3S)-3-hydroxyoct-1-enyl]-5-oxocyclopent-1-enyl]heptanoic acid (prostaglandin $B_1$),

C. 7-[(1R,2R,3R)-3-hydroxy-2-[(1E)-3-oxooct-1-enyl]-5-oxocyclopentyl]heptanoic acid (15-oxoprostaglandin $E_1$),

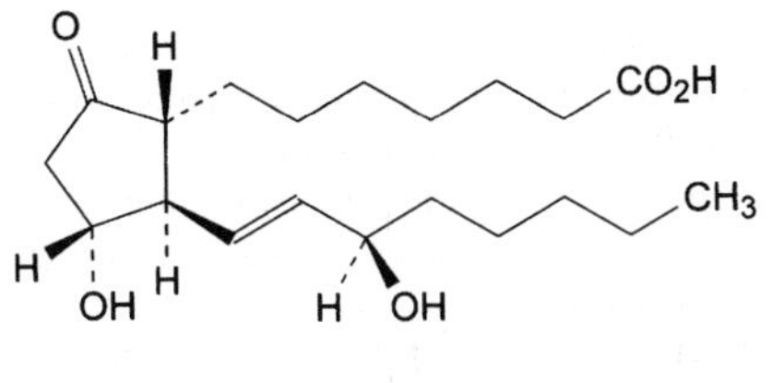

D. 7-[(1*R*,2*R*,3*R*)-3-hydroxy-2-[(1*E*,3*R*)-3-hydroxyoct-1-enyl]-5-oxocyclopentyl]heptanoic acid (15-epiprostaglandin E$_1$),

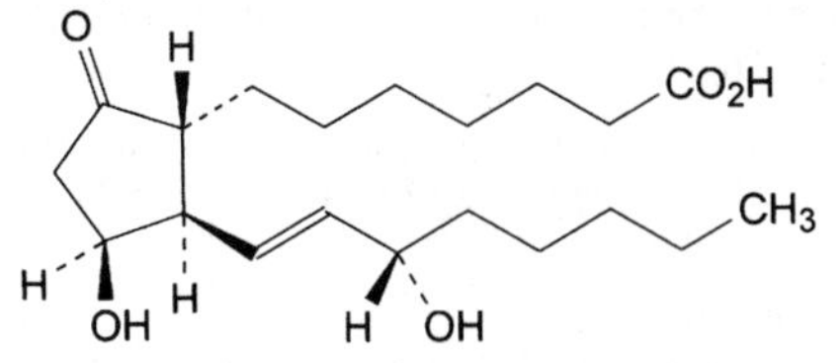

E. 7-[(1*R*,2*R*,3*S*)-3-hydroxy-2-[(1*E*,3*S*)-3-hydroxyoct-1-enyl]-5-oxocyclopentyl]heptanoic acid (11-epiprostaglandin E$_1$),

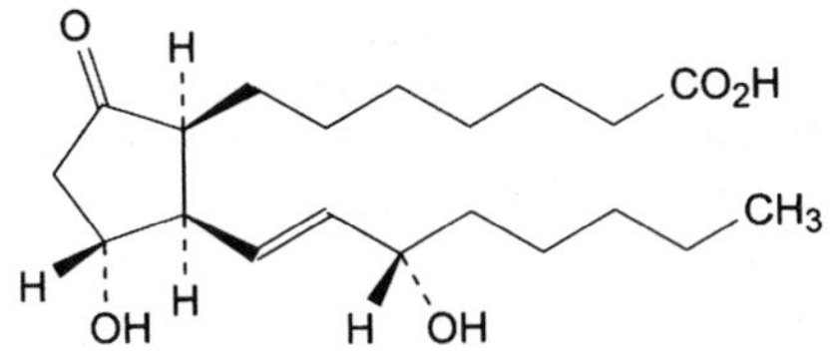

F. 7-[(1*S*,2*R*,3*R*)-3-hydroxy-2-[(1*E*,3*S*)-3-hydroxyoct-1-enyl]-5-oxocyclopentyl]heptanoic acid (8-epiprostaglandin E$_1$),

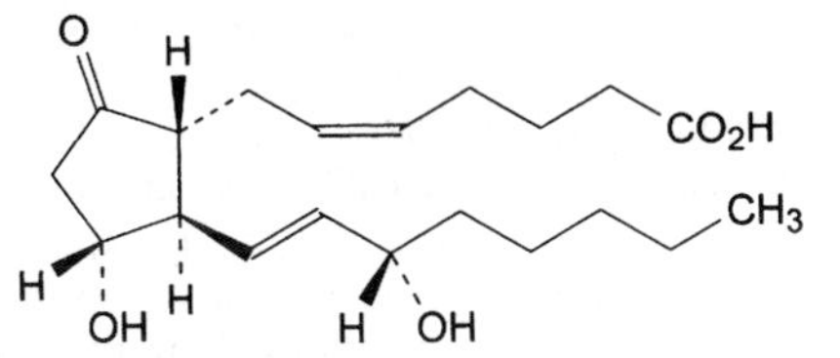

G. (5*Z*)-7-[(1*R*,2*R*,3*R*)-3-hydroxy-2-[(1*E*,3*S*)-3-hydroxyoct-1-enyl]-5-oxocyclopentyl]hept-5-enoic acid (dinoprostone),

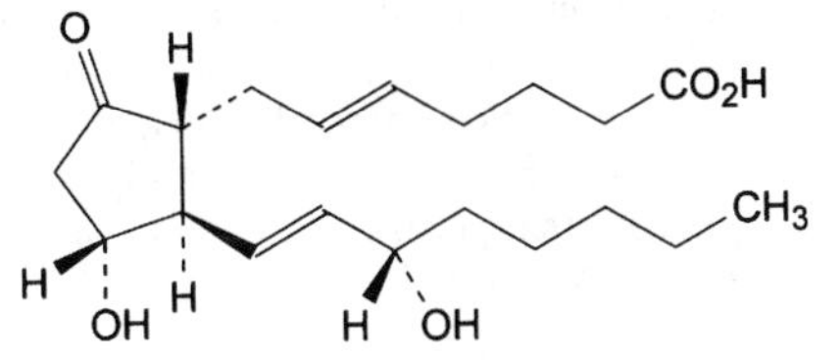

H. (5*E*)-7-[(1*R*,2*R*,3*R*)-3-hydroxy-2-[(1*E*,3*S*)-3-hydroxyoct-1-enyl]-5-oxocyclopentyl]hept-5-enoic acid ((5*E*)-prostaglandin E$_2$),

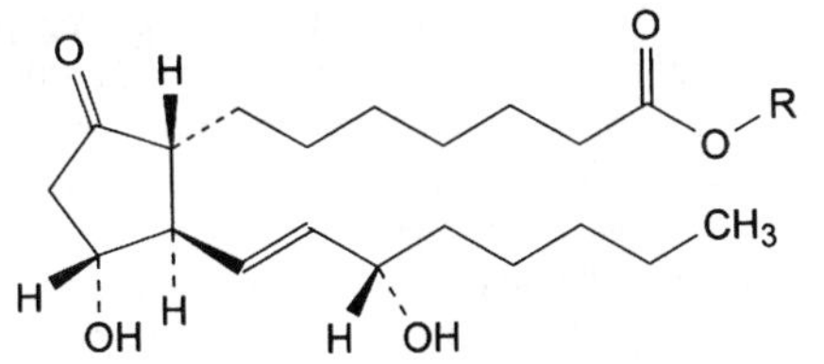

I. R = CH$_2$-CH$_3$: ethyl 7-[(1*R*,2*R*,3*R*)-3-hydroxy-2-[(1*E*,3*S*)-3-hydroxyoct-1-enyl]-5-oxocyclopentyl]heptanoate (prostaglandin E$_1$, ethyl ester),

J. R = CH(CH$_3$)$_2$: 1-methylethyl 7-[(1*R*,2*R*,3*R*)-3-hydroxy-2-[(1*E*,3*S*)-3-hydroxyoct-1-enyl]-5-oxocyclopentyl]heptanoate (prostaglandin E$_1$, isopropyl ester),

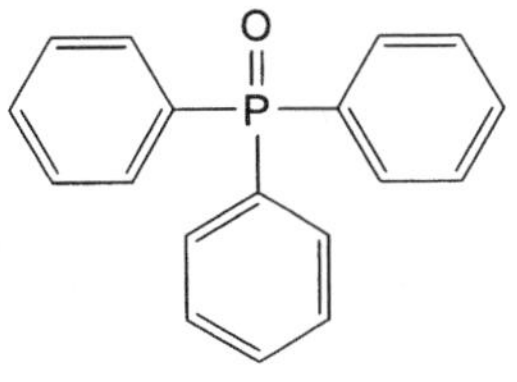

K. triphenylphosphine oxide.

*Ph Eur*

# Alteplase for Injection

(*Ph Eur monograph 1170*)

```
SYQVICRDEK  TQMIYQQHQS  WLRPVLRSNR  VEYCWCNSGR
AQCHSVPVKS  CSEPRCFNGG  TCQQALYFSD  FVCQCPEGFA
GKCCEIDTRA  TCYEDQGISY  RGTWSTAESG  AECTNWNSSA
LAQKPYSGRR  PDAIRLGLGN  HNYCRNPDRD  SKPWCYVFKA
GKYSSEFCST  PACSEGNSDC  YFGNGSAYRG  THSLTESGAS
CLPWNSMILI  GKVYTAQNPS  AQALGLGKHN  YCNRPDGDAK
PWCHVLKNRR  LTWEYCDVPS  CSTCGLRQYS  QPQFR

                                          IKGGL

FADIASHPWQ  AAIFAKHRRS  PGERFLCGGI  LISSCWILSA
AHCFQERFPP  HHLTVILGRT  YRVVPGEEEQ  KFEVEKYIVH
KEFDDDTYDN  DIALLQLKSD  SSRCAQESSV  VRTVCLPPAD
LQLPDWTECE  LSGYGKHEAL  SPFYSERLKE  AHVRLYPSSR
CTSQHLLNRT  VTDNMLCAGD  TRSGGPQANL  HDACQGDSGG
PLVCLNDGRM  TLVGIISWGL  GCGQKDVPGV  YTKVTNYLDW
IRDNMRP
```

C$_{2736}$H$_{4174}$N$_{914}$O$_{824}$S$_{45}$ (non-glycosylated protein)

*105857-23-6*

### Action and use

Tissue-type plasminogen activator; fibrinolytic.

*Ph Eur*

### DEFINITION

Alteplase for injection is a sterile, freeze-dried preparation of alteplase, a tissue plasminogen activator produced by recombinant DNA technology. It has a potency of not less than 500 000 IU per milligram of protein.

Tissue plasminogen activator binds to fibrin clots and activates plasminogen, leading to the generation of plasmin and to the degradation of fibrin clots or blood coagulates.

Alteplase consists of 527 amino acids with a calculated relative molecular mass of 59 050 without consideration of the carbohydrate moieties attached at positions Asn 117, Asn 184 and Asn 448. The total relative molecular mass is approximately 65 000. Alteplase is cleaved by plasmin between amino-acids 275 and 276 into a two-chain form (A chain and B chain) that are connected by a disulphide bridge between Cys 264 and Cys 395. The single-chain form and the two-chain form show comparable fibrinolytic activity *in vitro*.

## PRODUCTION

Alteplase is produced by recombinant DNA synthesis in cell culture; the fermentation takes place in serum-free medium.

The purification process is designed to remove efficiently potential impurities, such as antibiotics, DNA and protein contaminants derived both from the host cell and from the production medium, and potential viral contaminants.

If alteplase is stored in bulk form, stability (maintenance of potency) in the intended storage conditions must be demonstrated.

The production, purification and product consistency are checked by a number of analytical methods described below, carried out routinely as in-process controls.

### Protein content

The protein concentration of alteplase solutions is determined by measuring the absorbance (*2.2.25*) of the protein solution at 280 nm and at 320 nm, using formulation buffer as the compensation liquid. If dilution of alteplase samples is necessary, the samples are diluted in formulation buffer. For the calculation of the alteplase concentration the absorbance value ($A_{280} - A_{320}$) is divided by the specific absorption coefficient for alteplase of 1.9.

### Potency

The potency of alteplase is determined in an *in-vitro* clot-lysis assay as described under Assay. The specific activity of bulk alteplase is approximately 580 000 IU per milligram of alteplase.

### *N*-terminal sequence

*N*-terminal sequencing is applied to determine the correct *N*-terminal sequence and to determine semiquantitatively additional cleavage sites in the alteplase molecule, for example at position AA 275-276 or at position AA 27-28. The *N*-terminal sequence must conform with the sequence of human tissue plasminogen activator.

### Isoelectric focusing

The consistency in the microheterogeneity of glycosylation of the alteplase molecule can be demonstrated by isoelectric focusing (IEF). A complex banding pattern with ten major and several minor bands in the pH range 6.5-8.5 is observed. Denaturing conditions are applied to achieve a good separation of differently charged variants of alteplase. The broad charge distribution observed is due to a population of molecules, which differ in the fine structure of biantenary and triantenary complex-type carbohydrate residues, with different degrees of substitution with sialic acids. The banding pattern of alteplase test samples must be consistent with the pattern of alteplase reference standard.

### Single-chain alteplase content

The alteplase produced by CHO (Chinese hamster ovary) cells in serum-free medium is predominantly single-chain alteplase. The single-chain form can be separated from the two-chain form by gel-permeation liquid chromatography under reducing conditions as described under Single-chain content (see Tests). The single-chain alteplase content in bulk samples must be higher than 60 per cent.

### Tryptic-peptide mapping

The primary structure of the alteplase molecule is verified by tryptic-peptide mapping as described under Identification B. The reduced and carboxymethylated molecule is cleaved by trypsin into about fifty peptides, which are separated by reverse-phase liquid chromatography. A characteristic chromatogram (fingerprint) is obtained. The identity of the tryptic-peptide map of a given alteplase sample with the profile of a well-characterised reference standard is an indirect confirmation of the amino-acid sequence, because even single amino-acid exchanges in individual peptides can be detected by this sensitive technique. In addition, complex peaks of the glycopeptides can be isolated from the tryptic-peptide map and separated in a second dimension, either by reverse-phase liquid chromatography under modified conditions or by capillary electrophoresis. By this two-dimensional separation of glycopeptide variants, lot-to-lot consistency of the microheterogeneity of glycosylation can be demonstrated.

The tryptic-peptide map of alteplase samples must be consistent with the tryptic-peptide map of alteplase reference standard.

### Monomer content

The monomer content of alteplase is measured by gel-permeation liquid chromatography under non-reduced conditions as described under Monomer content (see Tests). The monomer content of alteplase bulk samples must be higher than 95 per cent.

### Type I/Type II alteplase content

CHO cells produce two glycosylation variants of alteplase. Type I alteplase contains one polymannose-type glycosylation at position Asn 117 and two complex-type glycosylation sites at positions Asn 184 and Asn 448. Type II alteplase is only glycosylated at positions Asn 117 and Asn 448.

The ratio of Type I/Type II alteplase is constant in the range of 45 to 65 per cent of Type I and 35 to 55 per cent of Type II. The content of alteplase Type I and Type II can be determined by a densitometric scan of SDS-PAGE (sodium dodecyl sulphate polyacrylamide gel electrophoresis) gel. Plasmin-treated samples of alteplase, which are reduced and carboxymethylated before loading on the gel, are separated into three bands: Type I alteplase A-chain (AA 1-275), Type II alteplase A-chain (AA 1-275) and alteplase B-chain (AA 276-527). The ratio of Type I/Type II alteplase is determined from a calibration curve, which is obtained by a densitometric scan of defined mixtures of purified Type I alteplase and Type II alteplase standards.

### SDS-PAGE

SDS-PAGE (silver staining) is used to demonstrate purity of the alteplase bulk material and the integrity of the alteplase molecule. For alteplase bulk samples, no additional protein bands compared to reference standard or degradation products must occur in SDS-PAGE gels at a loading amount of 2.5 µg alteplase protein per lane and a limit of detection of 5 ng per protein (BSA) band.

### Bacterial endotoxins (*2.6.14*)

Less than 1 IU per milligram of alteplase.

### Sialic acids

Dialyse samples and alteplase reference standard against enzyme buffer (8.9 g/l *sodium chloride R*, 4.1 g/l *sodium acetate R*, pH 5.5) using a membrane with a cut-off point corresponding to a relative molecular mass of 10 000 for globular proteins. After dialysis, determine the protein concentration. Add 5 µl of calcium chloride solution (19.98 per cent *m/m calcium chloride R*) to 1 ml of protein solution. Add 10 milliunits of neuraminidase per milligram of protein. Incubate this solution at 37 °C for about 17 h.

Prepare standard dilutions between 1.56 mg/ml and 25.0 mg/ml from an *N-acetylneuraminic acid R* reference stock solution with a concentration of 50 mg/ml. Pipette 0.2 ml of the sample and of the protein reference standard in duplicate into reagent tubes. Pipette also 0.2 ml of the standard dilutions into reagent tubes. Add 0.25 ml of periodate reagent (5.4 g/l solution of *sodium periodate R* in a 1.25 per cent *V/V* solution of *sulphuric acid R*), mix and incubate for 30 min at 37 °C. Add 0.2 ml of arsenite reagent (20 g/l solution of *sodium arsenite R* in a 1.55 per cent *V/V* solution of *hydrochloric acid R*) and mix. A yellowish-brown colour develops and disappears. Add 2.0 ml of a 28.9 g/l solution of *thiobarbituric acid R* and mix. Heat the closed tubes in boiling water for 7.5 min and then cool them in an ice-bath for 5 min. Add 2.0 ml of a mixture of *butanol R* and *hydrochloric acid R* (95:5) and mix. Centrifuge the tubes at 3000 r/min for 3 min. Measure the absorbance of the butanol-HCl layer at 552 nm within 30 min using the butanol-HCl mixture as the compensation solution. Perform a linear-regression analysis for the *N*-acetylneuraminic acid standard. The molar content of *N*-acetylneuraminic acid for the samples and for alteplase reference standard is calculated from the calibration curve. The sialic acids content for the test samples must be within the range 70 to 130 per cent of alteplase reference standard, which contains about 3 moles of sialic acids per mole of alteplase.

**Neutral sugars**

Dilute alteplase samples and the reference standard in the assay buffer, containing 34.8 g/l of *arginine R*, 0.1 g/l of *polysorbate 80 R* and adjusted to pH 7.4 with *phosphoric acid R*, to a protein concentration of 50 µg/ml. Prepare the following concentrations of mannose in the same assay buffer for a calibration curve: 20, 30, 40, 50 and 60 µg/ml. Pipette 2 ml of alteplase samples and reference standard, as well as 2 ml of each mannose concentration in duplicate in reagent tubes. Add 50 µl of *phenol R*, followed by 5 ml of *sulphuric acid R* in each reagent tube. Incubate the mixture for 30 min at room temperature. Measure the absorbance at 492 nm for each tube. Read the content of neutral sugars from the mannose calibration curve. The neutral sugar content is expressed in moles of neutral sugar per mole of alteplase, taking into account the dilution factor for alteplase samples and reference standard and using a relative molecular mass of 180.2 for mannose and a relative molecular mass of 59 050 for the alteplase protein moiety. The neutral sugar content of the alteplase samples must be in the range of 70 to 130 per cent compared to alteplase reference standard, which contains about 12 moles of neutral sugar per mole of alteplase.

**CHARACTERS**

A white or slightly yellow powder or solid friable mass.

*Reconstitute the preparation as stated on the label immediately before carrying out the Identification, Tests (except those for solubility and water) and Assay.*

**IDENTIFICATION**

A. The assay serves also to identify the preparation.

B. Tryptic-peptide mapping. Examine by liquid chromatography (*2.2.29*).

*Test solution* Dilute the preparation to be examined with *water R* to obtain a solution containing about 1 mg of alteplase per millilitre. Dialyse about 2.5 ml of the solution for at least 12 h into a solution containing 480 g/l of *urea R*, 44 g/l of *tris(hydroxymethyl)aminomethane R* and 1.5 g/l of *disodium edetate R* and adjusted to pH 8.6, using a membrane with a cut-off point corresponding to a relative molecular mass of 10 000 for globular proteins. Measure the volume of the solution, transfer it to a clean test-tube and add per millilitre 10 µl of a 156 g/l solution of *dithiothreitol R*. Allow

to stand for 4 h, cool in iced water and add per millilitre of solution 25 µl of a freshly prepared 190 g/l solution of *iodoacetic acid R*. Allow to stand in the dark for 30 min. Add per millilitre 50 µl of dithiothreitol solution to stop the reaction. Dialyse for 24 h against an 8 g/l solution of *ammonium hydrogen carbonate R*. Add 1 part of *trypsin for peptide mapping R* to 100 parts of the protein and allow to stand for 6 h to 8 h. Repeat the addition of trypsin and allow to stand for a total of 24 h.

*Reference solution* Prepare as for the test solution using a suitable reference standard instead of the preparation to be examined.

The chromatographic procedure may be carried out using:
— a column 0.1 m long and 4.6 mm in internal diameter packed with *octadecylsilyl silica gel for chromatography R* (5 µm to 10 µm);

*Mobile phase A* A 8 g/l solution of *sodium dihydrogen phosphate R*, adjusted to pH 2.85 with *phosphoric acid R*, filtered and degassed;

*Mobile phase B* *Acetonitrile R* 75 per cent *V/V* in mobile phase A;
— as detector a spectrophotometer set at 210 nm.

Equilibrate the system with mobile phase A at a flow rate of 1 ml/min. After injection of the solution, increase the proportion of mobile phase B at a rate of 0.44 per cent per minute until the ratio of mobile phase A to mobile phase B is 60:40, then increase the proportion of mobile phase B at a rate of 1.33 per cent per minute until the ratio of mobile phase A to mobile phase B is 20:80 and then continue elution with this mixture for a further 10 min. Record the chromatogram for the reference solution: the test is not valid unless the resolution of peaks 6 (peptides 268-275) and 7 (peptides 1-7) is at least 1.5; $b_{0.5a}$ and $b_{0.5b}$ are not more than 0.4 min. Inject about 100 µl of the test solution and record the chromatogram. Verify the identity of the peaks by comparison with the chromatograms of the reference solution. There should not be any additional significant peaks or shoulders, a significant peak or shoulder being defined as one with an area response equal to or greater than 5 per cent of peak 19 (peptides 278-296); no significant peak is missing. A type chromatogram for identification of the peaks cited is given at the end of the monograph (see Figure 1170.-1).

**TESTS**

**Appearance of solution**

The reconstituted preparation is clear (*2.2.1*) and not more intensely coloured than reference solution $Y_7$ (*2.2.2, Method II*).

**pH** (*2.2.3*)

7.1 to 7.5.

**Solubility**

Add the volume of the liquid stated on the label. The preparation dissolves completely within 2 min at 20 °C to 25 °C.

**Protein content**

Prepare a solution of the substance to be examined with an accurately known concentration of about 1 g/l. Using a 34.8 g/l solution of *arginine R* adjusted to pH 7.3 with *phosphoric acid R*, dilute an accurately measured volume of the solution of the substance to be examined so that the absorbance measured at the maximum at about 280 nm is 0.5 to 1.0 (*test solution*). Measure the absorbance (*2.2.25*) of the solution at the maximum at about 280 nm and at 320 nm using the arginine solution as the compensation

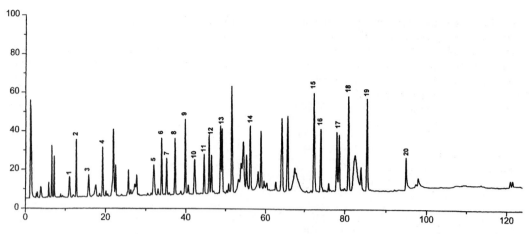

Figure 1170.-1. – *Chromatogram for tryptic-peptide mapping of alteplase*

liquid. Calculate the protein content in the portion of alteplase taken from the following expression:

$$\frac{V\left(A_{280} - A_{320}\right)}{1.9}$$

in which $V$ is the volume of arginine solution required to prepare the test solution, $A_{280}$ is the absorbance at the maximum at about 280 nm and $A_{320}$ is the absorbance at 320 nm.

**Single-chain content**

Examine by liquid chromatography(2.2.29).

*Test solution*  Dissolve the preparation to be examined in *water R* to obtain a solution containing about 1 mg of alteplase per millilitre. Place about 1 ml of the solution in a tube, add 3 ml of a 3 g/l solution of *dithiothreitol R* in the mobile phase, place a cap on the tube and heat at about 80 °C for 3 min to 5 min.

The chromatographic procedure may be carried out using:
— a column 0.6 m long and 7.5 mm in internal diameter packed with silica-based rigid, hydrophilic gel with spherical particles 10 μm to 13 μm in diameter, suitable for size-exclusion chromatography;
— as mobile phase at a flow rate of 0.5 ml/min a solution containing 30 g/l of *sodium dihydrogen phosphate R* and 1 g/l of *sodium dodecyl sulphate R*, adjusted to pH 6.8 with *dilute sodium hydroxide solution R*;
— as detector a spectrophotometer set at 214 nm.

Inject about 50 μl of the test solution and record the chromatogram. The chromatogram shows two major peaks corresponding to single-chain and two-chain alteplase. Calculate the relative amount of single-chain alteplase from the peak area values.

The test is not valid unless: the number of theoretical plates calculated on the basis of the single-chain alteplase peak is at least 1000. The content of single-chain alteplase is not less than 60 per cent of the total amount of alteplase-related substances found.

**Monomer content**

Examine by liquid chromatography (2.2.29).

*Test solution*  Reconstitute the preparation to be examined to obtain a solution containing about 1 mg per millilitre.

The chromatographic procedure may be carried out using:
— a column 0.6 m long and 7.5 mm in internal diameter packed with silica-based rigid, hydrophilic gel with

spherical particles 10 μm to 13 μm in diameter, suitable for size-exclusion chromatography;
— as mobile phase at a flow rate of 0.5 ml/min a solution containing 30 g/l of *sodium dihydrogen phosphate R* and 1 g/l of *sodium dodecyl sulphate R*, adjusted to pH 6.8 with *dilute sodium hydroxide solution R*;
— as detector a spectrophotometer set at 214 nm.

Inject the test solution and record the chromatogram. The test is not valid unless the number of theoretical plates calculated for the alteplase monomer peak is at least 1000. Measure the response for all peaks, i.e. peaks corresponding to alteplase species of different molecular masses. Calculate the relative content of monomer from the area values of these peaks. The monomer content for alteplase must be at least 95 per cent.

**Water** (2.5.12)

Not more than 4.0 per cent, determined by the semi-micro determination of water.

**Bacterial endotoxins** (2.6.14)

Less than 1 IU per milligram of protein.

**Sterility** (2.6.1)

It complies with the test for sterility.

**ASSAY**

The potency of alteplase is determined by comparing its ability to activate plasminogen to form plasmin with the same capacity of a reference preparation calibrated in International Units. The formation of plasmin is measured by the determination of the lysis time of a fibrin clot in given conditions.

The International Unit is the activity of a stated quantity of the International Standard of alteplase. The equivalence in International Units of the International Standard is stated by the World Health Organisation.

*Solvent buffer*  A solution containing 1.38 g/l of *sodium dihydrogen phosphate monohydrate R*, 7.10 g/l of *anhydrous disodium hydrogen phosphate R*, 0.20 g/l of *sodium azide R* and 0.10 g/l of *polysorbate 80 R*.

*Human thrombin solution*  A solution of *human thrombin R* containing 33 IU/ml in solvent buffer.

*Human fibrinogen solution*  A 2 g/l solution of *fibrinogen R* in solvent buffer.

*Human plasminogen solution*  A 1 g/l solution of *human plasminogen R* in solvent buffer.

*Test solutions*   Using a solution of the substance to be examined containing 1 g/l, prepare serial dilutions using solvent buffer, for example 1:5000, 1:10 000, 1:20 000.

*Reference solutions*   Using a solution of a suitable reference standard having an accurately known concentration of about 1 g/l (580 000 IU of alteplase per millilitre), prepare five serial dilutions using *water R* to obtain reference solutions having known concentrations in the range 9.0 IU/ml to 145 IU/ml.

To each of a set of labelled glass test-tubes, add 0.5 ml of human thrombin solution. Allocate each test and reference solution to a separate tube and add to each tube 0.5 ml of the solution allocated to it. To each of a second set of labelled glass tubes, add 20 μl of human plasminogen solution, and 1 ml of human fibrinogen solution, mix and store on ice. Beginning with the reference/thrombin mixture containing the lowest number of International Units per millilitre, record the time and separately add 200 μl of each of the thrombin mixtures to the test tubes containing the plasminogen-fibrinogen mixture. Using a vortex mixture, intermittently mix the contents of each tube for a total of 15 s and carefully place in a rack in a circulating water-bath at 37 °C. A visibly turbid clot forms within 30 s and bubbles subsequently form within the clot. Record the clot-lysis time as the time between the first addition of alteplase solution and the moment when the last bubble rises to the surface. Using a least-squares fit, determine the equation of the line using the logarithms of the concentrations of the reference preparation in International Units per millilitre versus the logarithms of the values of their clot-lysis times in seconds, according to the following equation:

$$\log t = a + b \, (\log U_s)$$

in which $t$ is the clot-lysis time, $U_S$ the activity in International Units per millilitre of the reference preparation, $b$ is the slope and $a$ the $y$-intercept of the line. The test is not valid unless the correlation coefficient is − 0.9900 to − 1.0000. From the line equation and the clot-lysis time for the test solution, calculate the logarithm of the activity $U_A$ from the following equation:

$$\log U_A = \frac{[(\log t) - a]}{b}$$

Calculate the alteplase activity in International Units per millilitre from the following expression:

$$D \times U_A$$

in which $D$ is the dilution factor for the test solution. Calculate the specific activity in the portion of the substance to be examined from the following expression:

$$\frac{U_A}{P}$$

in which $P$ is the concentration of protein obtained in the test for protein content.

The estimated potency is not less than 90 per cent and not more than 110 per cent of the stated potency.

## STORAGE

Store in a colourless, glass container, under vacuum or under an inert gas, protected from light, at a temperature of 2 °C to 30 °C.

## LABELLING

The label states:
— the number of International Units per container;
— the amount of protein per container.

_____ *Ph Eur*

# Altizide

*(Ph Eur monograph 2185)*

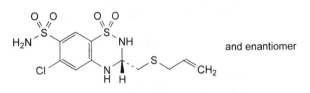

and enantiomer

$C_{11}H_{14}CIN_3O_4S_3$          383.9          *5588-16-9*

## Action and Use
Thiazide diuretic.

*Ph Eur* _____

## DEFINITION
(3*RS*)-6-Chloro-3-[(prop-2-enylsulphanyl)methyl]-3,4-dihydro-2*H*-1,2,4-benzothiadiazine-7-sulphonamide 1,1-dioxide.

## Content
97.5 per cent to 102.0 per cent (anhydrous substance).

## CHARACTERS
### Appearance
White or almost white powder.

### Solubility
Practically insoluble in water, soluble in methanol, practically insoluble in dichloromethane.

It shows polymorphism (*5.9*).

## IDENTIFICATION
Infrared absorption spectrophotometry (*2.2.24*).

*Comparison*   altizide CRS.

If the spectra obtained show differences, dissolve 50 mg of the substance to be examined and 50 mg of the reference substance separately in 2 ml of *acetone R* and evaporate the solvent. Precipitate by adding 1 ml of *methylene chloride R*. Evaporate to dryness and record new spectra using the residues.

## TESTS
### Impurity B
Thin-layer chromatography (*2.2.27*).

*Test solution*   Dissolve 0.200 g of the substance to be examined in *acetone R* and dilute to 2.0 ml with the same solvent.

*Reference solution (a)*   Dissolve 10.0 mg of *altizide impurity B CRS* in *acetone R* and dilute to 25.0 ml with the same solvent.

*Reference solution (b)*   To 1.0 ml of reference solution (a) add 1.0 ml of the test solution.

*Reference solution (c)*   Dilute 5.0 ml of reference solution (a) to 10.0 ml with *acetone R*.

*Plate*   TLC silica gel $F_{254}$ *plate R*.

*Mobile phase* acetone R, methylene chloride R
(25:75 V/V).

*Application* 10 µl of the test solution and reference solutions (b) and (c).

*Development* Over 2/3 of the plate.

*Drying* In air.

*Detection* Spray with a mixture of equal volumes of a 10 g/l solution of *potassium permanganate R* and a 50 g/l solution of *sodium carbonate R*, prepared immediately before use. Allow to stand for 30 min and examine in daylight.

*System suitability* Reference solution (b):
— the chromatogram shows 2 clearly separated spots.

*Limit* Any spot due to impurity B is not more intense than the principal spot in the chromatogram obtained with reference solution (c) (0.2 per cent).

### Related substances

Liquid chromatography (2.2.29). *Prepare the solutions immediately before use, except reference solution (b).*

*Test solution* Dissolve 50 mg of the substance to be examined in 5 ml of *acetonitrile R* and dilute to 25 ml with the mobile phase.

*Reference solution (a)* Dilute 1.0 ml of the test solution to 100.0 ml with the mobile phase. Dilute 1.0 ml of this solution to 10.0 ml with the mobile phase.

*Reference solution (b)* In order to produce impurity A in situ, dissolve 50 mg of the substance to be examined in 5 ml of *acetonitrile R* and dilute to 25 ml with *water R*. Allow to stand for 30 min.

*Reference solution (c)* Dissolve 4 mg of *furosemide CRS* in 2 ml of *acetonitrile R*, add 2 ml of the test solution and dilute to 100 ml with the mobile phase.

*Column:*
— *size: l = 0.15 m, Ø = 3.9 mm;*
— *stationary phase: end-capped octadecylsilyl silica gel for chromatography R (5 µm);*
— *temperature: 30 °C.*

*Mobile phase* acetonitrile R, water R previously adjusted to pH 2.0 with *perchloric acid R* (25:75 V/V).

*Flow rate* 0.7 ml/min.

*Detection* Spectrophotometer at 270 nm.

*Injection* 5 µl.

*Run time* Twice the retention time of altizide.

*Relative retention* With reference to altizide (retention time = about 25 min): impurity A = about 0.15; furosemide = about 1.05.

*System suitability* Reference solution (c):
— *resolution:* minimum 1.0 between the peaks due to altizide and furosemide.

*Limits:*
— *impurity A:* not more than 3 times the area of the principal peak in the chromatogram obtained with reference solution (a) (0.3 per cent);
— *unspecified impurities:* for each impurity, not more than the area of the principal peak in the chromatogram obtained with reference solution (a) (0.10 per cent);
— *total:* not more than 5 times the area of the principal peak in the chromatogram obtained with reference solution (a) (0.5 per cent);
— *disregard limit:* 0.5 times the area of the principal peak in the chromatogram obtained with reference solution (a) (0.05 per cent).

**Water** (2.5.32)
Maximum 0.5 per cent, determined on 50.0 mg.

**Sulphated ash** (2.4.14)
Maximum 0.1 per cent, determined on 1.0 g.

### ASSAY

Liquid chromatography (2.2.29) as described in the test for related substances, with the following modifications.

*Test solution* Dissolve 25.0 mg of the substance to be examined in 2 ml of *acetonitrile R* and dilute to 25.0 ml with the mobile phase.

*Reference solution* Dissolve 25.0 mg of *altizide CRS* in 2 ml of *acetonitrile R* and dilute to 25.0 ml with the mobile phase.

Calculate the percentage content of $C_{11}H_{14}ClN_3O_4S_3$ from the declared content of *altizide CRS*.

### IMPURITIES

*Specified impurities* A, B.

A. 4-amino-6-chlorobenzene-1,3-disulphonamide,

B. 3-[(2,2-dimethoxyethyl)sulphanyl]prop-1-ene.

*Ph Eur*

# Alum

Potash Alum; Aluminium Potassium Sulphate
(*Ph Eur monograph 0006*)

AlK(SO$_4$)$_2$,12H$_2$O    474.4    7784-24-9

**Action and use**
Astringent.

*Ph Eur*

### DEFINITION

**Content**
99.0 per cent to 100.5 per cent of AlK(SO$_4$)$_2$,12H$_2$O.

### CHARACTERS

**Appearance**
Granular powder or colourless, transparent, crystalline masses.

**Solubility**
Freely soluble in water, very soluble in boiling water, soluble in glycerol, practically insoluble in ethanol (96 per cent).

### IDENTIFICATION

A. Solution S (see Tests) gives the reactions of sulphates (2.3.1).

B. Solution S gives the reaction of aluminium (2.3.1).

C. Shake 10 ml of solution S with 0.5 g of *sodium bicarbonate R* and filter. The filtrate gives reaction (a) of potassium (2.3.1).

## TESTS

**Solution S**

Dissolve 2.5 g in *water R* and dilute to 50 ml with the same solvent.

**Appearance of solution**

Solution S is clear (*2.2.1*) and colourless (*2.2.2, Method II*).

**pH** (*2.2.3*)

3.0 to 3.5.

Dissolve 1.0 g in *carbon dioxide-free water R* and dilute to 10 ml with the same solvent.

**Ammonium** (*2.4.1*)

Maximum 0.2 per cent.

To 1 ml of solution S add 4 ml of *water R*. Dilute 0.5 ml of this solution to 14 ml with *water R*.

**Iron** (*2.4.9*)

Maximum 100 ppm.

Dilute 2 ml of solution S to 10 ml with *water R*. Use in this test 0.3 ml of *thioglycollic acid R*.

**Heavy metals** (*2.4.8*)

Maximum 20 ppm.

12 ml of solution S complies with test A. Prepare the reference solution using *lead standard solution (1 ppm Pb) R*.

## ASSAY

Dissolve 0.900 g in 20 ml of *water R* and carry out the complexometric titration of aluminium (*2.5.11*).

1 ml of *0.1 M sodium edetate* is equivalent to 47.44 mg of $AlK(SO_4)_2,12H_2O$.

*———————————————————— Ph Eur*

# Aluminium Chloride Hexahydrate

(*Ph Eur monograph 0971*)

| | | |
|---|---|---|
| $AlCl_3,6H_2O$ | 241.4 | *7784-13-6* |

**Action and use**

Astringent.

**Preparation**

Aluminium Chloride Solution

*Ph Eur* _____

## DEFINITION

**Content**

95.0 per cent to 101.0 per cent.

## CHARACTERS

**Appearance**

White or slightly yellow, crystalline powder or colourless crystals, deliquescent.

**Solubility**

Very soluble in water, freely soluble in ethanol (96 per cent), soluble in glycerol.

## IDENTIFICATION

A. Dilute 0.1 ml of solution S2 (see Tests) to 2 ml with *water R*. The solution gives reaction (a) of chlorides (*2.3.1*).

B. Dilute 0.3 ml of solution S2 to 2 ml with *water R*. The solution gives the reaction of aluminium (*2.3.1*).

## TESTS

**Solution S1**

Dissolve 10.0 g in *distilled water R* and dilute to 100 ml with the same solvent.

**Solution S2**

Dilute 50 ml of solution S1 to 100 ml with *water R*.

**Appearance of solution**

Solution S2 is clear (*2.2.1*) and not more intensely coloured than reference solution $B_7$ (*2.2.2, Method II*).

**Sulphates** (*2.4.13*)

Maximum 100 ppm, determined on solution S1.

**Iron** (*2.4.9*)

Maximum 10 ppm, determined on solution S1.

**Alkali and alkaline-earth metals**

Maximum 0.5 per cent.

To 20 ml of solution S2 add 100 ml of *water R* and heat to boiling. To the hot solution add 0.2 ml of *methyl red solution R*. Add *dilute ammonia R1* until the colour of the indicator changes to yellow and dilute to 150 ml with *water R*. Heat to boiling and filter. Evaporate 75 ml of the filtrate to dryness on a water-bath and ignite to constant mass. The residue weighs a maximum of 2.5 mg.

**Heavy metals** (*2.4.8*)

Maximum 20 ppm.

12 ml of solution S1 complies with test A. Prepare the reference solution using *lead standard solution (2 ppm Pb) R*.

**Water** (*2.5.12*)

42.0 per cent to 48.0 per cent, determined on 50.0 mg.

## ASSAY

Dissolve 0.500 g in 25.0 ml of *water R*. Carry out the complexometric titration of aluminium (*2.5.11*). Titrate with *0.1 M zinc sulphate* until the colour of the indicator changes from greyish-green to pink. Carry out a blank titration.

1 ml of *0.1 M sodium edetate* is equivalent to 24.14 mg of $AlCl_3,6H_2O$.

## STORAGE

In an airtight container.

*———————————————————— Ph Eur*

# Aluminium Glycinate

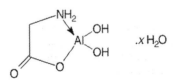

| | | |
|---|---|---|
| $C_2H_6AlNO_4,xH_2O$ | 135.1 | *41354-48-7* |

**Action and use**

Antacid.

## DEFINITION

Aluminium Glycinate is a basic aluminium monoglycinate, partly hydrated. It contains not less than 34.5% and not more than 38.5% of $Al_2O_3$ and not less than 9.9% and not more than 10.8% of N, both calculated with reference to the dried substance.

## CHARACTERISTICS

A white or almost white powder.

Practically insoluble in *water* and in organic solvents. It dissolves in dilute mineral acids and in aqueous solutions of the alkali hydroxides.

## IDENTIFICATION

A. Add 0.1 g to 10 ml of a solution prepared by dissolving 0.84 g of *citric acid* in 8 ml of *1M sodium hydroxide* and diluting to 20 ml with *water*. Add 0.5 ml of a 0.1% w/v solution of *ninhydrin* in *methanol* and warm. A purple colour is produced.

B. Suspend 1 g in 25 ml of *0.5M hydrochloric acid* and heat gently until a clear solution is produced. Reserve half of the solution. To 2 ml of the solution add 0.15 ml of *liquefied phenol*, shake and add carefully without shaking 5 ml of *dilute sodium hypochlorite solution*. A blue colour is produced.

C. The solution reserved in test B yields the reaction characteristic of *aluminium salts*, Appendix VI.

## TESTS

### Acidity or alkalinity
pH of a suspension of 1 g in 25 ml of *carbon dioxide-free water*, 6.5 to 7.5, Appendix V L.

### Neutralising capacity
Shake 0.2 g vigorously with 25 ml of *0.1M hydrochloric acid* for 5 minutes and allow to stand for 5 minutes. The pH of the mixture is greater than 3.0, Appendix V L.

### Arsenic
Dissolve 2.0 g in 18 ml of *brominated hydrochloric acid* and 32 ml of *water*. 25 ml of the resulting solution complies with the *limit test for arsenic*, Appendix VII (1 ppm).

### Heavy metals
Dissolve 1.5 g in 20 ml of *2M hydrochloric acid* and 10 ml of *water*, add 0.5 ml of *nitric acid* and boil for about 30 seconds. Cool, add 2 g of *ammonium chloride* and 2 g of *ammonium thiocyanate* and extract with two 10 ml quantities of a mixture of equal parts of *isoamyl alcohol* and *ether*. To the aqueous layer add 2 g of *citric acid*. 12 ml of the resulting solution complies with *limit test A for heavy metals*, Appendix VII. Use *lead standard solution (1 ppm Pb)* to prepare the standard (20 ppm).

### Mercuric salts
Dissolve 2.0 g in 10 ml of *1M sulphuric acid*, transfer to a separating funnel with the aid of *water*, dilute to about 50 ml with *water* and add 50 ml of *0.5M sulphuric acid*. Add 100 ml of *water*, 2 g of *hydroxylamine hydrochloride*, 1 ml of *0.05M disodium edetate* and 1 ml of *glacial acetic acid*. Add 5 ml of *chloroform*, shake, allow to separate and discard the chloroform layer. Titrate the aqueous layer with a solution of *dithizone* in *chloroform* containing 8 μg per ml until the chloroform layer remains green. After each addition, shake vigorously, allow the layers to separate and discard the chloroform layer. Repeat the operation using a solution prepared by diluting 1 ml of *mercury standard solution (5 ppm Hg)* to 100 ml with *0.5M sulphuric acid* and beginning at the words 'Add 100 ml of *water* ...'. The volume of the dithizone solution required by the substance being examined does not exceed that required by the mercury standard solution.

### Chloride
Dissolve 1.0 g in 10 ml of *2M nitric acid* and dilute to 100 ml with *water*. 15 ml of the resulting solution complies with the *limit test for chlorides*, Appendix VII (330 ppm).

### Loss on drying
When dried to constant weight at 130°, loses not more than 12.0% of its weight. Use 1 g.

## ASSAY

### For Al₂O₃
Dissolve 0.25 g in a mixture of 3 ml of *1M hydrochloric acid* and 50 ml of *water*, add 50 ml of *0.05M disodium edetate VS* and neutralise with *1M sodium hydroxide* using *methyl red solution* as indicator. Heat the solution to boiling, allow to stand for 10 minutes on a water bath, cool rapidly, add about 50 mg of *xylenol orange triturate* and 5 g of *hexamine* and titrate the excess of disodium edetate with *0.05M lead nitrate VS* until the solution becomes red. Each ml of *0.05M disodium edetate VS* is equivalent to 2.549 mg of Al₂O₃.

# Hydrated Aluminium Hydroxide for Adsorption

*(Ph Eur monograph 1664)*

[AlO(OH)],$n$H₂O

*Ph Eur*

## DEFINITION

### Content
90.0 per cent to 110.0 per cent of the content of aluminium stated on the label.

*NOTE: shake the gel vigorously for at least 30 s immediately before examining.*

## CHARACTERS

### Appearance
White or almost white, translucent, viscous, colloidal gel. A supernatant may be formed upon standing.

### Solubility
A clear or almost clear solution is obtained with alkali hydroxide solutions and mineral acids.

## IDENTIFICATION

Solution S (see Tests) gives the reaction of aluminium.

To 10 ml of solution S add about 0.5 ml of *dilute hydrochloric acid R* and about 0.5 ml of *thioacetamide reagent R*. No precipitate is formed. Add dropwise 5 ml of *dilute sodium hydroxide solution R*. Allow to stand for 1 h. A gelatinous white precipitate is formed which dissolves upon addition of 5 ml of *dilute sodium hydroxide solution R*. Gradually add 5 ml of *ammonium chloride solution R* and allow to stand for 30 min. The gelatinous white precipitate is re-formed.

## TESTS

### Solution S
Add 1 g to 4 ml of *hydrochloric acid R*. Heat at 60 °C for 1 h, cool, dilute to 50 ml with *distilled water R* and filter if necessary.

### pH *(2.2.3)*
5.5 to 8.5.

### Adsorption power
Dilute the substance to be examined with *distilled water R* to obtain an aluminium concentration of 5 mg/ml. Prepare *bovine albumin R* solutions with the following concentrations of bovine albumin: 0.5 mg/ml, 1 mg/ml, 2 mg/ml, 3 mg/ml, 5 mg/ml and 10 mg/ml. If necessary, adjust the gel and the *bovine albumin R* solutions to pH 6.0 with *dilute hydrochloric acid R* or *dilute sodium hydroxide solution R*.

For adsorption, mix 1 part of the diluted gel with 4 parts of each of the solutions of *bovine albumin R* and allow to stand at room temperature for 1 h. During this time shake the mixture vigorously at least 5 times. Centrifuge or filter through a non-protein-retaining filter. Immediately determine the protein content (*2.5.33, Method 2*) of either the supernatant or the filtrate.

It complies with the test if no bovine albumin is detectable in the supernatant or filtrate of the 2 mg/ml *bovine albumin R* solution (maximum level of adsorption) and in the supernatant or filtrate of *bovine albumin R* solutions of lower concentrations. Solutions containing 3 mg/ml, 5 mg/ml and 10 mg/ml *bovine albumin R* may show bovine albumin in the supernatant or filtrate, proportional to the amount of bovine albumin in the solutions.

### Sedimentation

If necessary, adjust the substance to be examined to pH 6.0 using *dilute hydrochloric acid R* or *dilute sodium hydroxide solution R*. Dilute with *distilled water R* to obtain an aluminium concentration of approximately 5 mg/ml. If the aluminium content of the substance to be examined is lower than 5 mg/ml, adjust to pH 6.0 and dilute with a 9 g/l solution of *sodium chloride R* to obtain an aluminium concentration of about 1 mg/ml. After shaking for at least 30 s, place 25 ml of the preparation in a 25 ml graduated cylinder and allow to stand for 24 h.

It complies with the test if the volume of the clear supernatant is less than 5 ml for the gel with an aluminium content of about 5 mg/ml.

It complies with the test if the volume of the clear supernatant is less than 20 ml for the gel with an aluminium content of about 1 mg/ml.

### Chlorides (*2.4.4*)

Maximum 0.33 per cent.

Dissolve 0.5 g in 10 ml of *dilute nitric acid R* and dilute to 500 ml with *water R*.

### Nitrates

Maximum 100 ppm.

Place 5 g in a test-tube immersed in ice-water, add 0.4 ml of a 100 g/l solution of *potassium chloride R*, 0.1 ml of *diphenylamine solution R* and, dropwise with shaking, 5 ml of *sulphuric acid R*. Transfer the tube to a water-bath at 50 °C. After 15 min, any blue colour in the solution is not more intense than that in a standard prepared at the same time and in the same manner using 5 ml of *nitrate standard solution (100 ppm NO₃) R*.

### Sulphates (*2.4.13*)

Maximum 0.5 per cent.

Dilute 2 ml of solution S to 20 ml with *water R*.

### Ammonium (*2.4.1, Method B*)

Maximum 50 ppm, determined on 1.0 g.

Prepare the standard using 0.5 ml of *ammonium standard solution (100 ppm NH₄) R*.

### Arsenic (*2.4.2, Method A*)

Maximum 1 ppm, determined on 1 g.

### Iron (*2.4.9*)

Maximum 15 ppm, determined on 0.67 g.

### Heavy metals (*2.4.8*)

Maximum 20 ppm.

Dissolve 2.0 g in 10 ml of *dilute nitric acid R* and dilute to 20 ml with *water R*. The solution complies with test A. Prepare the reference solution using *lead standard solution (2 ppm Pb) R*.

### Bacterial endotoxins (*2.6.14*)

Less than 5 IU of endotoxin per milligram of aluminium, if intended for use in the manufacture of an adsorbed product without a further appropriate procedure for the removal of bacterial endotoxins.

### ASSAY

Dissolve 2.50 g in 10 ml of *hydrochloric acid R*, heating for 30 min at 100 °C on a water-bath. Cool and dilute to 20 ml with *water R*. To 10 ml of the solution, add *concentrated ammonia R* until a precipitate is obtained. Add the smallest quantity of *hydrochloric acid R* needed to dissolve the precipitate and dilute to 20 ml with *water R*. Carry out the complexometric titration of aluminium (*2.5.11*). Carry out a blank titration.

### STORAGE

At a temperature not exceeding 30 °C. Do not allow to freeze. If the substance is sterile, store in a sterile, airtight, tamper-proof container.

### LABELLING

The label states the declared content of aluminium.

*Ph Eur*

# Dried Aluminium Hydroxide

(*Hydrated Aluminium Oxide,
Ph Eur monograph 0311*)

**Action and use**
Antacid.

**Preparations**
Aluminium Hydroxide Tablets

Aluminium Hydroxide Oral Suspension

Co-magaldrox Oral Suspension

Co-magaldrox Tablets

Compound Magnesium Trisilicate Tablets

*Ph Eur*

### DEFINITION

Content: 47.0 per cent to 60.0 per cent of $Al_2O_3$ ($M_r$ 102.0).

### CHARACTERS

**Appearance**
White or almost white, amorphous powder.

**Solubility**
Practically insoluble in water. It dissolves in dilute mineral acids and in solutions of alkali hydroxides.

### IDENTIFICATION

Solution S (see Tests) gives the reaction of aluminium (*2.3.1*).

### TESTS

**Solution S**
Dissolve 2.5 g in 15 ml of *hydrochloric acid R*, heating on a water-bath. Dilute to 100 ml with *distilled water R*.

**Appearance of solution**
Solution S is not more opalescent than reference suspension II (*2.2.1*) and not more intensely coloured than reference solution GY₆ (*2.2.2, Method II*).

**Alkaline impurities**
Shake 1.0 g with 20 ml of *carbon dioxide-free water R* for 1 min and filter. To 10 ml of the filtrate add 0.1 ml of *phenolphthalein solution R*. Any pink colour disappears on the addition of 0.3 ml of *0.1 M hydrochloric acid*.

### Neutralising capacity

Carry out the test at 37 °C. Disperse 0.5 g in 100 ml of *water R*, heat, add 100.0 ml of *0.1 M hydrochloric acid*, previously heated, and stir continuously; the pH (*2.2.3*) of the solution after 10 min, 15 min and 20 min is not less than 1.8, 2.3 and 3.0 respectively and is at no time greater than 4.5. Add 10.0 ml of *0.5 M hydrochloric acid*, previously heated, stir continuously for 1 h and titrate with *0.1 M sodium hydroxide* to pH 3.5; not more than 35.0 ml of *0.1 M sodium hydroxide* is required.

### Chlorides (*2.4.4*)

Maximum 1 per cent.

Dissolve 0.1 g with heating in 10 ml of *dilute nitric acid R* and dilute to 100 ml with *water R*. Dilute 5 ml of the solution to 15 ml with *water R*.

### Sulphates (*2.4.13*)

Maximum 1 per cent.

Dilute 4 ml of solution S to 100 ml with *distilled water R*.

### Arsenic (*2.4.2, Method A*)

Maximum 4 ppm, determined on 10 ml of solution S.

### Heavy metals (*2.4.8*)

Maximum 60 ppm.

Neutralise 20 ml of solution S with *concentrated ammonia R*, using *metanil yellow solution R* as an external indicator. Filter, if necessary, and dilute to 30 ml with *water R*. 12 ml of the solution complies with test A. Prepare the reference solution using 10 ml of *lead standard solution (1 ppm Pb) R*.

### Microbial contamination

TAMC: acceptance criterion $10^3$ CFU/g (*2.6.12*).

TYMC: acceptance criterion $10^2$ CFU/g (*2.6.12*).

Absence of bile-tolerant gram-negative bacteria (*2.6.13*).

Absence of *Escherichia coli* (*2.6.13*).

### ASSAY

Dissolve 0.800 g in 10 ml of *hydrochloric acid R1*, heating on a water-bath. Cool and dilute to 50.0 ml with *water R*. To 10.0 ml of the solution add *dilute ammonia R1* until a precipitate begins to appear. Add the smallest quantity of *dilute hydrochloric acid R* needed to dissolve the precipitate and dilute to 20 ml with *water R*. Carry out the complexometric titration of aluminium (*2.5.11*).

1 ml of *0.1 M sodium edetate* is equivalent to 5.098 mg of $Al_2O_3$.

### STORAGE

In an airtight container, at a temperature not exceeding 30 °C.

_____ *Ph Eur*

# Aluminium Magnesium Silicate

(*Ph Eur monograph 1388*)

12511-31-8

### Action and use

Excipient.

*Ph Eur* _____

### DEFINITION

Mixture of particles with colloidal particle size of montmorillonite and saponite, free from grit and non-swellable ore.

*Content:*
— *aluminium* (Al; $A_r$ 26.98): 95.0 per cent to 105.0 per cent of the value stated on the label;
— *magnesium* (Mg; $A_r$ 24.30): 95.0 per cent to 105.0 per cent of the value stated on the label.

## CHARACTERS

### Appearance

Almost white powder, granules or plates.

### Solubility

Practically insoluble in water and in organic solvents.

It swells in water to produce a colloidal dispersion.

## IDENTIFICATION

A. Fuse 1 g with 2 g of *anhydrous sodium carbonate R*. Warm the residue with *water R* and filter. Acidify the filtrate with *hydrochloric acid R* and evaporate to dryness on a water-bath. 0.25 g of the residue gives the reaction of silicates (*2.3.1*).

B. Dissolve the remainder of the residue obtained in identification test A in a mixture of 5 ml of *dilute hydrochloric acid R* and 10 ml of *water R*. Filter and add *ammonium chloride buffer solution pH 10.0 R*. A white, gelatinous precipitate is formed. Centrifuge and keep the supernatant for identification C. Dissolve the remaining precipitate in *dilute hydrochloric acid R*. The solution gives the reaction of aluminium (*2.3.1*).

C. The supernatant liquid obtained after centrifugation in identification test B gives the reaction of magnesium (*2.3.1*).

## TESTS

### pH (*2.2.3*)

9.0 to 10.0.

Disperse 5.0 g in 100 ml of *carbon dioxide-free water R*.

### Arsenic (*2.4.2, Method A*)

Maximum 3 ppm.

Transfer 16.6 g to a 250 ml beaker containing 100 ml of *dilute hydrochloric acid R*. Mix, cover with a watch glass and boil gently, with occasional stirring, for 15 min. Allow the insoluble matter to settle and decant the supernatant liquid through a rapid-flow filter paper into a 250 ml volumetric flask, retaining as much sediment as possible in the beaker. To the residue in the beaker add 25 ml of hot *dilute hydrochloric acid R*, stir, heat to boiling, allow the insoluble matter to settle and decant the supernatant liquid through the filter into the volumetric flask. Repeat the extraction with 4 additional quantities, each of 25 ml, of hot *dilute hydrochloric acid R*, decanting each supernatant liquid through the filter into the volumetric flask. At the last extraction, transfer as much of the insoluble matter as possible onto the filter. Allow the combined filtrates to cool to room temperature and dilute to 250.0 ml with *dilute hydrochloric acid R*. Dilute 5.0 ml of this solution to 25.0 ml with *dilute hydrochloric acid R*.

### Lead

Maximum 15.0 ppm.

Atomic absorption spectrometry (*2.2.23, Method I*).

*Test solution*  Transfer 10.0 g to a 250 ml beaker containing 100 ml of *dilute hydrochloric acid R*. Mix, cover with a watch glass and boil for 15 min. Allow to cool to room temperature and allow the insoluble matter to settle. Decant the supernatant liquid through a rapid-flow filter paper into a 400 ml beaker. To the insoluble matter in the 250 ml beaker add 25 ml of hot *water R*. Stir, allow the insoluble matter to settle and decant the supernatant liquid through the filter into the 400 ml beaker. Repeat the extraction with 2 additional quantities, each of 25 ml, of *water R*, decanting each time the supernatant liquid through the filter into the 400 ml beaker. Wash the filter with 25 ml of hot *water R*, collecting this filtrate in the 400 ml beaker. Concentrate the combined filtrates to about 20 ml by gently boiling. If a precipitate appears, add about 0.1 ml of *nitric acid R*, heat to boiling and allow to cool to room temperature. Filter the concentrated extracts through a rapid-flow filter paper into a 50 ml volumetric flask. Transfer the remaining contents of the 400 ml beaker through the filter paper and into the flask with *water R*. Dilute this solution to 50.0 ml with *water R*.

*Reference solutions* Prepare the reference solutions using *lead standard solution (10 ppm Pb) R*, diluted as necessary with *water R*.

*Source* Lead hollow-cathode lamp.

*Wavelength* 217 nm.

*Atomisation device* Oxidising air-acetylene flame.

**Loss on drying** (*2.2.32*)
Maximum 8.0 per cent, determined on 1.000 g by drying in an oven at 105 °C.

**Microbial contamination**
TAMC: acceptance criterion $10^3$ CFU/g (*2.6.12*).
TYMC: acceptance criterion $10^2$ CFU/g (*2.6.12*).
Absence of *Escherichia coli* (*2.6.13*).

**ASSAY**
**Aluminium**
Atomic absorption spectrometry (*2.2.23, Method I*).

*Test solution* In a platinum crucible mix 0.200 g with 1.0 g of *lithium metaborate R*. Heat slowly at first and ignite at 1000-1200 °C for 15 min. Allow to cool, then place the crucible in a 100 ml beaker containing 25 ml of *dilute nitric acid R* and add an additional 50 ml of *dilute nitric acid R*, filling and submerging the crucible. Place a polytetrafluoroethylene-coated magnetic stirring bar in the crucible and stir gently with a magnetic stirrer until dissolution is complete. Pour the contents into a 250 ml beaker and remove the crucible. Warm the solution and transfer through a rapid-flow filter paper into a 250 ml volumetric flask, wash the filter and beaker with *water R* and dilute to 250.0 ml with *water R* (solution A). To 20.0 ml of solution A add 20 ml of a 10 g/l solution of *sodium chloride R* and dilute to 100.0 ml with *water R*.

*Reference solutions* Dissolve, with gentle heating, 1.000 g of *aluminium R* in a mixture of 10 ml of *hydrochloric acid R* and 10 ml of *water R*. Allow to cool, then dilute to 1000.0 ml with *water R* (1 mg of aluminium per millilitre). Into 3 identical volumetric flasks, each containing 0.20 g of *sodium chloride R*, introduce 2.0 ml, 5.0 ml and 10.0 ml of this solution respectively, and dilute to 100.0 ml with *water R*.

*Source* Aluminium hollow-cathode lamp.

*Wavelength* 309 nm.

*Atomisation device* Oxidising acetylene-nitrous oxide flame.

**Magnesium**
Atomic absorption spectrometry (*2.2.23, Method I*).

*Test solution* Dilute 25.0 ml of solution A, prepared in the assay for aluminium, to 50.0 ml with *water R*. To 5.0 ml of this solution add 20.0 ml of *lanthanum nitrate solution R* and dilute to 100.0 ml with *water R*.

*Reference solutions* Place 1.000 g of *magnesium R* in a 250 ml beaker containing 20 ml of *water R* and carefully add 20 ml of *hydrochloric acid R*, warming if necessary to dissolve. Transfer the solution to a volumetric flask and dilute to 1000.0 ml with *water R* (1 mg of magnesium per millilitre).

Dilute 5.0 ml of this solution to 250.0 ml with *water R*. Into 4 identical volumetric flasks, introduce 5.0 ml, 10.0 ml, 15.0 ml and 20.0 ml of the solution respectively. To each flask add 20.0 ml of *lanthanum nitrate solution R* and dilute to 100.0 ml with *water R*.

*Source* Magnesium hollow-cathode lamp.

*Wavelength* 285 nm.

*Atomisation device* Reducing air-acetylene flame.

**LABELLING**
The label states the content of aluminium and magnesium.

———————————————————————— *Ph Eur*

# Dried Aluminium Phosphate

(*Hydrated Aluminium Phosphate,*
*Ph Eur monograph 1598*)

| AlPO$_4$,$x$H$_2$O | 122.0 | 7784-30-7 |
| | (anhydrous) | (anhydrous) |

**Action and use**
Antacid.

*Ph Eur* ————————————————————————

**DEFINITION**
**Content**
94.0 per cent to 102.0 per cent of AlPO$_4$ ($M_r$ 122.0) (ignited substance).

**CHARACTERS**
**Appearance**
White or almost white powder.

**Solubility**
Very slightly soluble in water, practically insoluble in alcohol. It dissolves in dilute solutions of mineral acids and alkali hydroxides.

**IDENTIFICATION**
A. Solution S (see Tests) gives reaction (b) of phosphates (*2.3.1*).

B. Solution S gives the reaction of aluminium (*2.3.1*).

**TESTS**
**Solution S**
Dissolve 2.00 g in *dilute hydrochloric acid R* and dilute to 100 ml with the same acid.

**Appearance of solution**
Solution S is clear (*2.2.1*) and colourless (*2.2.2, Method II*).

**pH** (*2.2.3*)
5.5 to 7.2

Shake 4.0 g with *carbon dioxide-free water R* and dilute to 100 ml with the same solvent.

**Chlorides** (*2.4.4*)
Maximum 1.3 per cent.

Dissolve 50.0 mg in 10 ml of *dilute nitric acid R* and dilute to 200 ml with *water R*. 15 ml of the solution complies with the limit test for chlorides.

**Soluble phosphates**
Maximum 1.0 per cent, calculated as PO$_4^{3-}$.

*Test solution* Stir 5.0 g with 150 ml of *water R* for 2 h. Filter and wash the filter with 50 ml of *water R*. Combine the filtrate and the washings and dilute to 250.0 ml with *water R*. Dilute 10.0 ml of this solution to 100.0 ml with *water R*.

*Reference solution (a)* Dissolve 2.86 g of *potassium dihydrogen phosphate R* in *water R* and dilute to 100 ml with the same solvent.

*Reference solution (b)* Dilute 1 ml of reference solution (a) to 5 ml with *water R*.

*Reference solution (c)* Dilute 3 ml of reference solution (a) to 5 ml with *water R*.

Treat each solution as follows. To 5.0 ml add 4 ml of *dilute sulphuric acid R*, 1 ml of *ammonium molybdate solution R*, 5 ml of *water R* and 2 ml of a solution containing 0.10 g of *4-methylaminophenol sulphate R*, 0.5 g of *anhydrous sodium sulphite R* and 20.0 g of *sodium metabisulphite R* in 100 ml of *water R*. Shake and allow to stand for 15 min. Dilute to 25.0 ml with *water R* and allow to stand for a further 15 min. Measure the absorbance (*2.2.25*) at 730 nm. Calculate the content of soluble phosphates from a calibration curve prepared using reference solutions (a), (b) and (c) after treatment.

**Sulphates** (*2.4.13*)
Maximum 0.6 per cent.

Dilute 8 ml of solution S to 100 ml with *distilled water R*. 15 ml of the solution complies with the limit test for sulphates.

**Arsenic** (*2.4.2*)
Maximum 1 ppm.

1.0 g complies with limit test A.

**Heavy metals** (*2.4.8*)
Maximum 20 ppm.

Dissolve 1.0 g in *dilute hydrochloric acid R* and dilute to 20 ml with the same acid. 12 ml of the solution complies with limit test A. Prepare the standard using *lead standard solution (1 ppm Pb) R*.

**Loss on ignition**
10.0 per cent to 20.0 per cent, determined on 1.000 g at 800 ± 50 °C.

**Neutralising capacity**
Add 0.50 g to 30 ml of *0.1 M hydrochloric acid* previously heated to 37 °C and maintain at this temperature for 15 min while stirring. The pH (*2.2.3*) of the mixture after 15 min at 37 °C is 2.0 to 2.5.

**ASSAY**
Dissolve 0.400 g in 10 ml of *dilute hydrochloric acid R* and dilute to 100.0 ml with *water R*. To 10.0 ml of the solution, add 10.0 ml of *0.1 M sodium edetate* and 30 ml of a mixture of equal volumes of *ammonium acetate solution R* and *dilute acetic acid R*. Boil for 3 min, then cool. Add 25 ml of *alcohol R* and 1 ml of a freshly prepared 0.25 g/l solution of *dithizone R* in *alcohol R*. Titrate the excess of sodium edetate with *0.1 M zinc sulphate* until the colour changes to pink.

1 ml of *0.1 M sodium edetate* is equivalent to 12.20 mg of $AlPO_4$.

**STORAGE**
In an airtight container.

_____ *Ph Eur*

# Aluminium Phosphate Gel

★★★
★ ○ ★
★ ★
★★★

(*Ph Eur monograph 2166*)

$Al(OH)x(PO_4)y$      122.0      7784-30-7

         (anhydrous)      (anhydrous)

**Action and use**
Antacid; vaccine adjuvant.

*Ph Eur* _____

**DEFINITION**
Hydrated $AlPO_4$ in gel form.

**Content**
19.0 per cent to 21.0 per cent of $AlPO_4$.

**CHARACTERS**

**Appearance**
Gel.

**Solubility**
Practically insoluble in water, in ethanol (96 per cent) and in methylene chloride. It dissolves in dilute solutions of mineral acids.

**IDENTIFICATION**
A. Solution S (see Tests) gives reaction (b) of phosphates (*2.3.1*).

B. Solution S gives the reaction of aluminium (*2.3.1*).

C. It complies with the assay.

**TESTS**

**Solution S**
Dissolve 2.00 g in *dilute hydrochloric acid R* and dilute to 100 ml with the same acid.

**pH** (*2.2.3*)
6.0 to 8.0.

**Peroxides**
Maximum 150 ppm, expressed as hydrogen peroxide.

*Test solution* Dissolve with heating 1.0 g of the substance to be examined in 5 ml of *dilute hydrochloric acid R*, then add 5 ml of *water R* and 2 ml of *divanadium pentoxide solution in sulphuric acid R*.

*Reference solution* Dilute 1.0 ml of *dilute hydrogen peroxide solution R* to 200.0 ml with *water R*. To 1 ml of this solution add 9 ml of *water R* and 2 ml of *divanadium pentoxide solution in sulphuric acid R*.

The test solution is not more intensely coloured than the reference solution.

**Chlorides** (*2.4.4*)
Maximum 500 ppm.

Dissolve 1.3 g in 5 ml of *dilute nitric acid R* and dilute to 200 ml with *water R*.

**Soluble phosphates**
Maximum 0.5 per cent, expressed as $PO_4$.

*Test solution* Centrifuge 10.0 g until a clear supernatant is obtained. To 2.00 ml of the supernatant add 20.0 ml of a 10.3 g/l solution of *hydrochloric acid R* and dilute to 100.0 ml with *water R*. To 10.0 ml of this solution add 10.0 ml of *nitro-molybdovanadic reagent R* and dilute to 50.0 ml with *water R*. Allow to stand protected from light for 15 min.

*Reference solution* Add 10.0 ml of *nitro-molybdovanadic reagent R* to 10.0 ml of a 143 mg/l solution of *potassium dihydrogen phosphate R* and dilute to 50.0 ml with *water R*. Allow to stand protected from light for 15 min.

Measure the absorbances (*2.2.25*) of the 2 solutions at 400 nm. The absorbance of the test solution is not greater than that of the reference solution.

### Sulphates (*2.4.13*)
Maximum 0.2 per cent.

Dilute 25 ml of solution S to 100 ml with *distilled water R*.

### Soluble aluminium
Maximum 50 ppm.

To 16.0 g add 50 ml of *water R*. Heat to boiling for 5 min. Cool and centrifuge. Separate the supernatant. Wash the residue with 20 ml of *water R* and centrifuge. Separate the supernatant and add to the first supernatant. To the combined supernatants add 5 ml of *hydrochloric acid R* and 20 ml of *water R*. Introduce all of this solution into a 500 ml conical flask and carry out the complexometric titration of aluminium (*2.5.11*) using *0.01 M sodium edetate*.

### Arsenic (*2.4.2, Method A*)
Maximum 1 ppm, determined on 1.0 g.

### Heavy metals (*2.4.8*)
Maximum 10 ppm.

Dissolve 4.0 g in *dilute hydrochloric acid R* and dilute to 20 ml with the same acid. 12 ml of the solution complies with test A. Prepare the reference solution using *lead standard solution (2 ppm Pb) R*.

### Acid neutralising capacity
Add 2.0 g to 30 ml of *0.1 M hydrochloric acid R* heated to 37 °C and maintain at 37 °C while shaking. Determine the pH after 15 min. The pH (*2.2.3*) of the mixture is 2.0 to 2.5.

### Residue on ignition
19.0 per cent to 23.0 per cent.

Heat 0.500 g at 50 °C for 5 hours, then ignite at 500 ± 50 °C until constant mass.

### Microbial contamination
TAMC: acceptance criterion $10^3$ CFU/g (*2.6.12*).

TYMC: acceptance criterion $10^2$ CFU/g (*2.6.12*).

Absence of bile-tolerant gram-negative bacteria (*2.6.13*).

Absence of *Escherichia coli* (*2.6.13*).

### ASSAY
Dissolve with heating 0.300 g in 5 ml of *dilute hydrochloric acid R*. Add 45 ml of *water R*, 10.0 ml of *0.1 M sodium edetate* and 30 ml of a mixture of equal volumes of *ammonium acetate solution R* and *dilute acetic acid R*. Heat to boiling and maintain boiling for 3 min. Cool, then add 25 ml of *ethanol (96 per cent) R*. Titrate with *0.1 M zinc sulphate*, determining the end-point potentiometrically (*2.2.20*).

1 ml of *0.1 M zinc sulphate* is equivalent to 12.2 mg of $AlPO_4$.

### STORAGE
In an airtight container.

_____ *Ph Eur*

# Aluminium Powder

Al             26.98           7429-90-5

### Action and use
Topical protective.

### Preparation
Compound Aluminium Paste

### DEFINITION
Aluminium Powder consists mainly of metallic aluminium in the form of very small flakes, usually with an appreciable proportion of aluminium oxide; it is lubricated with stearic acid to prevent oxidation. It contains not less than 86.0% of Al, calculated with reference to the substance freed from lubricant and volatile matter.

### CHARACTERISTICS
A silvery grey powder.

Practically insoluble in *water* and in *ethanol (96%)*. It dissolves in dilute acids and in aqueous solutions of alkali hydroxides, with the evolution of hydrogen.

### IDENTIFICATION
A solution in *2M hydrochloric acid* yields the reaction characteristic of *aluminium salts*, Appendix VI.

### TESTS
#### Surface-covering power
Not less than 4000 cm² per g when determined by the following method. Fill with *water* a shallow trough measuring approximately 60 cm × 12 cm × 1.5 cm, fitted with a movable partition so constructed that it is a sliding fit and can be used to divide the trough into two rectangular areas. Place the movable partition near one end and sprinkle 50 mg of the substance being examined on the surface of the liquid confined in the smaller area. Using a glass rod, spread the powder evenly over the liquid surface until an unbroken film covers the entire surface. Move the partition so as to increase the area confined and again spread the powder to cover the increased surface. Continue this process and determine the maximum unbroken surface area obtained. The surface-covering power is the area covered per g of the powder at the breaking point of the film.

#### Iron
Dissolve 10 mg in 20 ml of *2M hydrochloric acid* and dilute to 100 ml with *water*. 10 ml of the resulting solution complies with the *limit test for iron*, Appendix VII (1.0%).

#### Lead
Use two solutions prepared in the following manner. For solution (1) boil 0.40 g with 20 ml of *2M hydrochloric acid* and 10 ml of *water* until effervescence ceases, add 0.5 ml of *nitric acid*, boil for 30 seconds and cool; add 2 g of *ammonium chloride* and 2 g of *ammonium thiocyanate*, extract with three 10 ml quantities of a mixture of equal volumes of *amyl alcohol* and *ether*, discard the extracts and add 2 g of *citric acid*. For solution (2) dissolve 2 g of *citric acid* in 10 ml of *2M hydrochloric acid* and add 4 ml of *lead standard solution (10 ppm Pb)*. Make solutions (1) and (2) alkaline with *5M ammonia* and to each add 1 ml of *potassium cyanide solution PbT*. The solutions should be not more than faintly opalescent. If the colours of the solutions differ, equalise by the addition of about 0.2 ml of a highly diluted solution of burnt sugar or other non-reactive substance. Dilute each solution to 50 ml with *water*, add 0.1 ml of a 10% w/v solution of *sodium sulphide* to each and mix thoroughly. The colour produced in solution (1) is not more intense than that

produced in solution (2), when viewed against a white background (100 ppm).

### Other metals

Dissolve 2 g in 40 ml of 2M *hydrochloric acid*. Dilute 20 ml of the solution to 100 ml with *water*, make alkaline to *litmus paper* by the addition of 5M *ammonia*, boil and filter. Evaporate the filtrate to dryness, add 0.05 ml of *sulphuric acid* and ignite. The residue weighs not more than 2 mg.

### Lubricant

To 2 g add 100 ml of hot *water*, cover and add, drop wise, sufficient of a mixture of equal volumes of *hydrochloric acid* and *water* to dissolve the metal almost completely. Heat to complete dissolution, cool, filter through a hardened filter paper and wash the vessel and filter paper thoroughly with *water*; dry both the vessel and paper at room temperature. Extract the paper with three 100-ml quantities of boiling, freshly distilled *acetone*, using the original vessel to contain the solvent and then wash the paper with five 10-ml quantities of freshly distilled *acetone*. Evaporate the combined filtrate and washings to dryness using a rotary evaporator. The residue, after drying at 105° for 30 minutes and allowing to cool, weighs 10 to 60 mg.

When the basin containing the residue is floated in a beaker of water suitably stirred and heated, the residue melts between 40° and 60°. The residue is almost completely soluble, with effervescence, in hot *dilute sodium carbonate solution*.

### Volatile matter

When heated to constant weight at 105°, loses not more than 0.5% of its weight. Use 1 g.

### ASSAY

Transfer 0.2 g, previously freed from lubricant by successive washing with *acetone* and drying, to a three-necked 500 ml flask fitted with a 150 ml dropping funnel, an inlet tube connected to a cylinder of *carbon dioxide* and an outlet tube dipping into a water trap. Add 60 ml of *water* and disperse the substance being examined; replace the air by *carbon dioxide* and add 100 ml of a solution containing 56 g of *ammonium iron(III) sulphate* and 7.5 ml of *sulphuric acid* in *water*. While maintaining an atmosphere of *carbon dioxide* in the flask, heat to boiling, boil for 5 minutes after the sample has dissolved, cool rapidly to 20° and dilute to 250 ml with *water*. To 50 ml add 15 ml of *orthophosphoric acid* and titrate with 0.02M *potassium permanganate VS*. Each ml of 0.02M *potassium permanganate VS* is equivalent to 0.8994 mg of Al.

# Aluminium Sodium Silicate

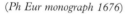

(*Ph Eur monograph 1676*)

*Ph Eur*

## DEFINITION

Silicic acid aluminium sodium salt of synthetic origin.

*Content:*
— *aluminium* (Al; $M_r$ 26.98): 2.7 per cent to 7.9 per cent (dried substance);
— *sodium* (Na; $M_r$ 22.99): 3.7 per cent to 6.3 per cent (dried substance).

## CHARACTERS

### Appearance

White or almost white, fine, light, amorphous powder.

### Solubility

Practically insoluble in water and in organic solvents.

## IDENTIFICATION

A. Transfer 1.0 g to a 100 ml beaker and add 10 ml of *dilute hydrochloric acid R*. Mix, cover with a watch glass and boil for 15 min. Allow to cool to room temperature, mix and centrifuge the solution. 2 ml of the supernatant gives the reaction of aluminium (*2.3.1*).

B. 2 ml of the supernatant obtained in identification test A gives reaction (a) of sodium (*2.3.1*).

C. 0.2 g gives the reaction of silicates (*2.3.1*).

## TESTS

### pH (*2.2.3*)
9.5 to 11.5.

Disperse 5.0 g in 100 ml of *carbon dioxide-free water R*.

### Arsenic (*2.4.2, Method A*)
Maximum 3 ppm.

Transfer 8.3 g to a 250 ml beaker containing 50 ml of *dilute hydrochloric acid R*. Mix, cover with a watch glass and boil gently, with occasional stirring, for 15 min. Centrifuge, and decant the supernatant through a rapid-flow filter paper into a 250 ml volumetric flask. To the residue in the beaker, add 25 ml of hot *dilute hydrochloric acid R*, stir, centrifuge, and decant the supernatant through the same filter into the volumetric flask. Repeat the extraction with 3 additional quantities, each of 25 ml, of hot *dilute hydrochloric acid R*, filtering each supernatant through this filter into the volumetric flask. Allow the combined filtrates to cool to room temperature and dilute to 250.0 ml with *dilute hydrochloric acid R*. Dilute 10.0 ml of the solution to 25.0 ml with *water R*.

### Lead
Maximum 5.0 ppm.

Atomic absorption spectrometry (*2.2.23, Method I*).

*Test solution* Transfer 5.0 g to a 250 ml beaker containing 50 ml of *dilute hydrochloric acid R*. Mix, cover with a watch glass and boil for 15 min. Allow to cool to room temperature. Centrifuge, and decant the supernatant through a rapid-flow filter paper into a 250 ml beaker. To the insoluble matter add 25 ml of hot *water R*. Stir vigorously, centrifuge, and decant the supernatant through the same filter into the beaker. Repeat the extraction with 2 additional quantities, each of 25 ml, of hot *water R*, decanting each supernatant through the filter into the beaker. Wash the filter with 25 ml of hot *water R*, collecting the filtrate in the beaker. Concentrate the combined filtrates by gently boiling to about 15 ml. Add about 0.05 ml of *heavy metal-free nitric acid R*, heat to boiling and allow to cool to room temperature. Filter the concentrated extracts through a rapid-flow filter paper into a 25 ml volumetric flask. Transfer the remaining contents of the beaker through the filter paper and into the volumetric flask with *water R* and dilute to 25.0 ml with the same solvent.

*Reference solutions* Into 4 separate 100 ml volumetric flasks, introduce respectively 3.0 ml, 5.0 ml, 10.0 ml and 15.0 ml of *lead standard solution (10 ppm Pb) R*, add 0.20 ml of *heavy metal-free nitric acid R* and dilute to 100.0 ml with *water R*.

*Source* Lead hollow-cathode lamp.

*Wavelength* 217.0 nm.

*Atomisation device* Air-acetylene flame.

### Loss on drying (*2.2.32*)
Maximum 8.0 per cent, determined on 1.000 g by drying in an oven at 105 °C for 4 h.

## Loss on ignition

5.0 per cent to 11.0 per cent (dried substance), determined on 1.000 g by ignition in a platinum crucible to constant mass at 1000 ± 25 °C.

## Microbial contamination

TAMC: acceptance criterion $10^3$ CFU/g (*2.6.12*).

TYMC: acceptance criterion $10^2$ CFU/g (*2.6.12*).

Absence of *Escherichia coli* (*2.6.13*).

## ASSAY

### Aluminium

Atomic absorption spectrometry (*2.2.23, Method I*).

*Acid mixture*   Add 50 ml of *nitric acid R* to 500 ml of *water R*. Dissolve in this solution 17 g of *tartaric acid R* and dilute to 1000 ml with *water R*.

*Blank solution*   Dissolve 1.4 g of *anhydrous lithium metaborate R* in 60 ml of the acid mixture and dilute to 200 ml with *water R*.

*Test solution*   In a platinum crucible mix 0.200 g with 1.4 g of *anhydrous lithium metaborate R*. Heat slowly at first and ignite at 1100 ± 25 °C for 15 min. Cool, then place the crucible in a 100 ml beaker containing 60 ml of the acid mixture. Place a polytetrafluoroethylene-coated magnetic stirring bar in the crucible and stir gently with a magnetic stirrer for 16 h. Transfer the contents of the crucible into a 200 ml volumetric flask. Wash the crucible, the magnetic stirring bar and the beaker with *water R* and dilute to 200.0 ml with the same solvent (solution A). To 10.0 ml of this solution, add 1.0 ml of *lanthanum chloride solution R* and dilute to 50.0 ml with *water R*.

*Reference solutions*   Into 5 separate 50 ml volumetric flasks, introduce respectively 1.0 ml, 2.5 ml, 5.0 ml, 7.5 ml and 10.0 ml of *aluminium standard solution (100 ppm Al) R*, add 1 ml of *lanthanum chloride solution R* and 10 ml of the blank solution, and dilute to 50.0 ml with *water R*.

*Source*   Aluminium hollow-cathode lamp.

*Wavelength*   309.3 nm.

*Atomisation device*   Acetylene-nitrous oxide flame.

### Sodium

Atomic emission spectrometry (*2.2.22, Method I*).

*Test solution*   To 2.0 ml of solution A, prepared in the assay of aluminium, add 1 ml of a 12.5 g/l solution of *caesium chloride R* and dilute to 20.0 ml with *water R*.

*Reference solutions*   Into 5 separate 200 ml volumetric flasks, each containing 10 ml of a 12.5 g/l solution of *caesium chloride R*, introduce respectively 1.0 ml, 2.0 ml, 4.0 ml, 6.0 ml and 10.0 ml of *sodium standard solution (200 ppm Na) R* and dilute to 200.0 ml with *water R*.

*Wavelength*   589.0 nm.

*Ph Eur*

---

# Aluminium Sulphate

(*Ph Eur monograph 0165*)

**Preparation**

Aluminium Acetate Ear Drops

*Ph Eur* _____

## DEFINITION

### Content

51.0 per cent to 59.0 per cent of $Al_2(SO_4)_3$.

It contains a variable quantity of water of crystallisation.

## CHARACTERS

### Appearance

Colourless, lustrous crystals or crystalline masses.

### Solubility

Soluble in cold water, freely soluble in hot water, practically insoluble in ethanol (96 per cent).

## IDENTIFICATION

A. Solution S (see Tests) gives reaction (a) of sulphates (*2.3.1*).

B. Solution S gives the reaction of aluminium (*2.3.1*).

## TESTS

### Solution S

Dissolve 2.5 g in *water R* and dilute to 50 ml with the same solvent.

### Appearance of solution

Solution S is not more opalescent than reference suspension III (*2.2.1*) and is colourless (*2.2.2, Method II*).

### pH (*2.2.3*)

2.5 to 4.0.

Dissolve 0.5 g in *carbon dioxide-free water R* and dilute to 25 ml with the same solvent.

### Alkali and alkaline-earth metals

Maximum 0.4 per cent.

To 20 ml of solution S add 100 ml of *water R*, heat and add 0.1 ml of *methyl red solution R*. Add *dilute ammonia R1* until the colour of the indicator changes to yellow. Dilute to 150 ml with *water R*, heat to boiling and filter. Evaporate 75 ml of the filtrate to dryness on a water-bath and ignite. The residue weighs a maximum of 2 mg.

### Ammonium (*2.4.1*)

Maximum 500 ppm.

Dilute 0.4 ml of solution S to 14 ml with *water R*.

### Iron (*2.4.9*)

Maximum 100 ppm.

Dilute 2 ml of solution S to 10 ml with *water R*. Use 0.3 ml of *thioglycollic acid R* in this test.

### Heavy metals (*2.4.8*)

Maximum 50 ppm.

Dilute 8 ml of solution S to 20 ml with *water R*. 12 ml of the solution complies with test A. Prepare the reference solution using *lead standard solution (1 ppm Pb) R*.

## ASSAY

Dissolve 0.500 g in 20 ml of *water R*. Carry out the complexometric titration of aluminium (*2.5.11*).

1 ml of *0.1 M sodium edetate* is equivalent to 17.11 mg of $Al_2(SO_4)_3$.

## STORAGE

In an airtight container.

_____ *Ph Eur*

# Alverine Citrate

*(Ph Eur monograph 2156)*

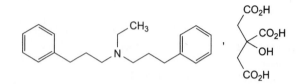

$C_{20}H_{27}N, C_6H_8O_7$       473.6       5560-59-8

**Action and use**
Smooth muscle relaxant; antispasmodic.

**Preparation**
Alverine Capsules

*Ph Eur*

## DEFINITION
*N*-Ethyl-3-phenyl-*N*-(3-phenylpropyl)propan-1-amine dihydrogen 2-hydroxypropane-1,2,3-tricarboxylate.

## Content
99.0 per cent to 101.0 per cent (dried substance).

## CHARACTERS
**Appearance**
White or almost white, crystalline powder.

**Solubility**
Slightly soluble in water and in methylene chloride, sparingly soluble in ethanol (96 per cent).

**mp**
About 104 °C.

## IDENTIFICATION
Infrared absorption spectrophotometry (*2.2.24*).

*Comparison*   alverine citrate CRS.

## TESTS
**pH** (*2.2.3*)
3.5 to 4.5.

Dissolve 0.250 g in *carbon dioxide-free water R* and dilute to 50.0 ml with the same solvent.

**Related substances**
Gas chromatography (*2.2.28*): use the normalisation procedure. *Use freshly prepared solutions.*

*Test solution*   Dissolve 0.250 g of the substance to be examined in *water R* and dilute to 20 ml with the same solvent. Add 2 ml of *concentrated ammonia R* and shake with 3 quantities, each of 15 ml, of *methylene chloride R*. To the combined lower layers add *anhydrous sodium sulphate R*, shake, filter, and evaporate the filtrate at a temperature not exceeding 30 °C, using a rotary evaporator. Take up the residue with *methylene chloride R* and dilute to 10.0 ml with the same solvent.

*Reference solution (a)*   Dissolve 5 mg of *alverine impurity D CRS* (impurity D citrate) in 5 ml of *water R*, add 1 ml of *concentrated ammonia R* and shake with 3 quantities, each of 5 ml, of *methylene chloride R*. To the combined lower layers add *anhydrous sodium sulphate R*, shake, filter, and evaporate the filtrate at a temperature not exceeding 30 °C, using a rotary evaporator. Take up the residue with *methylene chloride R*, add 0.2 ml of the test solution and dilute to 2 ml with *methylene chloride R*.

*Reference solution (b)*   Dilute 1.0 ml of the test solution to 100.0 ml with *methylene chloride R*. Dilute 1.0 ml of this solution to 20.0 ml with *methylene chloride R*.

*Reference solution (c)*   Dissolve the contents of a vial of *alverine for peak identification CRS* (containing impurities C and E) in 1 ml of *methylene chloride R*.

*Column:*
— *material*: fused silica;
— *size*: l = 25 m, Ø = 0.32 mm;
— *stationary phase*: poly(dimethyl)(diphenyl)siloxane R (film thickness 0.45 µm).

*Carrier gas*   helium for chromatography R.

*Flow rate*   2.2 ml/min.

*Split ratio*   1:11.

*Temperature:*

|  | Time (min) | Temperature (°C) |
|---|---|---|
| Column | 0 - 7 | 120 |
|  | 7 - 13 | 120 → 240 |
|  | 13 - 21 | 240 |
|  | 21 - 24 | 240 → 290 |
|  | 24 - 39 | 290 |
| Injection port |  | 290 |
| Detector |  | 290 |

*Detection*   Flame ionisation.

*Injection*   1 µl.

*Identification of impurities*   Use the chromatogram supplied with *alverine for peak identification CRS* and the chromatogram obtained with reference solution (c) to identify the peaks due to impurities C and E.

*Relative retention*   With reference to alverine (retention time = about 16 min): impurity A = about 0.28; impurity B = about 0.29; impurity C = about 0.46; impurity D = about 0.97; impurity E = about 1.7.

*System suitability*   Reference solution (a):
— *resolution*: minimum 3.0 between the peaks due to impurity D and alverine.

*Limits:*
— *impurities A, B*: for each impurity, maximum 0.1 per cent;
— *impurity C*: maximum 0.2 per cent;
— *impurities D, E*: for each impurity, maximum 0.3 per cent;
— *unspecified impurities*: for each impurity, maximum 0.10 per cent;
— *total*: maximum 1.0 per cent;
— *disregard limit*: the area of the principal peak in the chromatogram obtained with reference solution (b) (0.05 per cent).

**Heavy metals** (*2.4.8*)
Maximum 20 ppm.

0.5 g complies with test G. Prepare the reference solution using 1 ml of *lead standard solution (10 ppm Pb) R*.

**Loss on drying** (*2.2.32*)
Maximum 0.5 per cent, determined on 1.000 g by drying in an oven at 80 °C for 2 h.

**Sulphated ash** (*2.4.14*)
Maximum 0.1 per cent, determined on 1.0 g.

## ASSAY

Dissolve 0.375 g in 50 ml of *anhydrous acetic acid R*. Titrate with *0.1 M perchloric acid*, determining the end-point potentiometrically (*2.2.20*).

1 ml of *0.1 M perchloric acid* is equivalent to 47.36 mg of $C_{26}H_{35}NO_7$.

## STORAGE

Protected from light.

## IMPURITIES

*Specified impurities   A, B, C, D, E.*

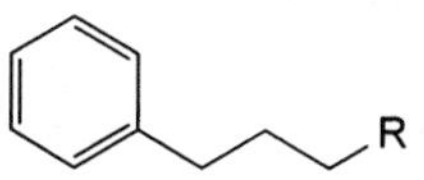

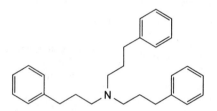

A. R = Cl: 1-chloro-3-phenylpropane,

B. R = OH: 3-phenylpropan-1-ol,

C. R = NH-$C_2H_5$: *N*-ethyl-3-phenylpropan-1-amine,

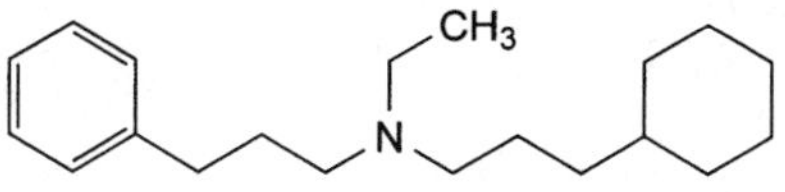

D. *N*-(3-cyclohexylpropyl)-*N*-ethyl-3-phenylpropan-1-amine,

E. 3-phenyl-*N,N*-bis(3-phenylpropyl)propan-1-amine.

*_____ Ph Eur*

# Amantadine Hydrochloride

(*Ph Eur monograph 0463*)

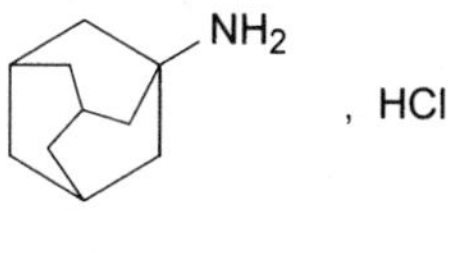

$C_{10}H_{17}N,HCl$          187.7          665-66-7

## Action and use

Viral replication inhibitor (influenza A); dopamine receptor agonist; treatment of influenza and Parkinson's disease.

## Preparations

Amantadine Capsules

Amantadine Oral Solution

*Ph Eur _____*

## DEFINITION

Tricyclo[3.3.1.1$^{3,7}$]decan-1-amine hydrochloride.

## Content

98.5 per cent to 101.0 per cent (anhydrous substance).

## CHARACTERS

### Appearance

White or almost white, crystalline powder.

### Solubility

Freely soluble in water and in ethanol (96 per cent).

It sublimes on heating.

## IDENTIFICATION

*First identification   A, D.*

*Second identification   B, C, D.*

A. Infrared absorption spectrophotometry (*2.2.24*).

*Preparation   Discs.*

*Comparison   amantadine hydrochloride CRS.*

B. To 0.1 g add 1 ml of *pyridine R*, mix and add 0.1 ml of *acetic anhydride R*. Heat to boiling for about 10 s. Pour the hot solution into 10 ml of *dilute hydrochloric acid R*, cool to 5 °C and filter. The precipitate, washed with *water R* and dried *in vacuo* at 60 °C for 1 h, melts (*2.2.14*) at 147 °C to 151 °C.

C. Dissolve 0.2 g in 1 ml of *0.1 M hydrochloric acid*. Add 1 ml of a 500 g/l solution of *sodium nitrite R*. A white precipitate is formed.

D. 1 ml of solution S (see Tests) gives reaction (a) of chlorides (*2.3.1*).

## TESTS

### Solution S

Dissolve 2.5 g in *carbon dioxide-free water R* and dilute to 25 ml with the same solvent.

### Appearance of solution

Solution S is clear (*2.2.1*) and not more intensely coloured than reference solution $Y_7$ (*2.2.2, Method II*).

### Acidity or alkalinity

Dilute 2 ml of solution S to 10 ml with *carbon dioxide-free water R*. Add 0.1 ml of *methyl red solution R* and 0.2 ml of *0.01 M sodium hydroxide*. The solution is yellow. Add 0.4 ml of *0.01 M hydrochloric acid*. The solution is red.

### Related substances

Gas chromatography (*2.2.28*): use the normalisation procedure.

*Test solution   Dissolve 0.10 g of the substance to be examined in 2 ml of water R. Add 2 ml of a 200 g/l solution of sodium hydroxide R and 2 ml of chloroform R. Shake for 10 min. Separate the chloroform layer, dry over anhydrous sodium sulphate R and filter.*

*Column:*

— *material: glass;*

— *size: l = 1.8 m, Ø = 2 mm;*

— *stationary phase: mix 19.5 g of silanised diatomaceous earth for gas chromatography R with 60 ml of a 3.3 g/l solution of potassium hydroxide R in methanol R and evaporate the solvent under reduced pressure while rotating the mixture slowly (support); dissolve 0.4 g of low-vapour-pressure hydrocarbons (type L) R in 60 ml of toluene R (dissolution requires up to 5 h), add this solution to the support and evaporate the solvent under reduced pressure while rotating the mixture slowly.*

*Carrier gas   nitrogen for chromatography R.*

*Flow rate   30 ml/min.*

*Temperature:*

| | Time (min) | Temperature (°C) |
|---|---|---|
| Column | 0 - 16.7 | 100 → 200 |
| Injection port | | 220 |
| Detector | | 300 |

*Detection*  Flame ionisation.

*Injection*  1 µl or the chosen volume.

*Run time*  At least 2.5 times the retention time of amantadine.

*Limits:*
— *any impurity*: for each impurity, maximum 0.3 per cent;
— *total*: maximum 1 per cent;
— *disregard limit*: disregard the peak due to the solvent.

**Heavy metals** *(2.4.8)*
Maximum 20 ppm.

12 ml of solution S complies with test A. Prepare the reference solution using *lead standard solution (2 ppm Pb) R*.

**Water** *(2.5.12)*
Maximum 0.5 per cent, determined on 2.000 g.

**Sulphated ash** *(2.4.14)*
Maximum 0.1 per cent, determined on 1.0 g.

## ASSAY
Dissolve 0.150 g in a mixture of 5.0 ml of *0.01 M hydrochloric acid* and 50 ml of *ethanol (96 per cent) R*. Carry out a potentiometric titration *(2.2.20)*, using *0.1 M sodium hydroxide*. Read the volume added between the 2 points of inflexion.

1 ml of *0.1 M sodium hydroxide* is equivalent to 18.77 mg of $C_{10}H_{18}ClN$.

*_____ Ph Eur*

# Ambroxol Hydrochloride

*(Ph Eur monograph 1489)*

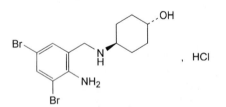

$C_{13}H_{18}Br_2N_2O,HCl$        414.6        *23828-92-4*

**Action and use**
Mucolytic expectorant.

*Ph Eur* _____

## DEFINITION
*trans*-4-[(2-Amino-3,5-dibromobenzyl)amino]cyclohexanol hydrochloride.

## Content
99.0 per cent to 101.0 per cent (dried substance).

## CHARACTERS
**Appearance**
White or yellowish crystalline powder.

**Solubility**
Sparingly soluble in water, soluble in methanol, practically insoluble in methylene chloride.

## IDENTIFICATION
*First identification*  B, D.

*Second identification*  A, C, D.

A. Dissolve 20.0 mg in *0.05 M sulphuric acid* and dilute to 100.0 ml with the same acid. Dilute 2.0 ml of the solution to 10.0 ml with *0.05 M sulphuric acid*. Examined between 200 nm and 350 nm *(2.2.25)*, the solution shows two absorption maxima at 245 nm and 310 nm. The ratio of the absorbance measured at 245 nm to that measured at 310 nm is 3.2 to 3.4.

B. Infrared absorption spectrophotometry *(2.2.24)*.

*Comparison*  ambroxol hydrochloride CRS .

C. Examine by thin-layer chromatography *(2.2.27)*.

*Test solution*  Dissolve 50 mg of the substance to be examined in *methanol R* and dilute to 5 ml with the same solvent.

*Reference solution*  Dissolve 50 mg of *ambroxol hydrochloride CRS* in *methanol R* and dilute to 5 ml with the same solvent.

*Plate*  TLC silica gel $F_{254}$ plate R.

*Mobile phase*  concentrated ammonia R, 1-propanol R, ethyl acetate R, hexane R (1:10:20:70 *V/V/V/V*).

*Application*  10 µl.

*Development*  Over 2/3 of the plate.

*Drying*  In air.

*Detection*  Examine in ultraviolet light at 254 nm.

*Results*  The principal spot in the chromatogram obtained with the test solution is similar in position and size to the principal spot in the chromatogram obtained with the reference solution.

D. Dissolve 25 mg in 2.5 ml of *water R*, mix with 1.0 ml of *dilute ammonia R1* and allow to stand for 5 min. Filter and acidify the filtrate with *dilute nitric acid R*. The filtrate gives reaction (a) of chlorides *(2.3.1)*.

## TESTS
**Solution S**
Dissolve 0.75 g in *methanol R* and dilute to 15 ml with the same solvent.

**Appearance of solution**
Solution S is clear *(2.2.1)* and not more intensely coloured than reference solution $Y_6$ *(2.2.2, Method II)*.

**pH** *(2.2.3)*
4.5 to 6.0.

Dissolve 0.2 g in *carbon dioxide-free water R* and dilute to 20 ml with the same solvent.

**Related substances**
Liquid chromatography *(2.2.29)*. *Prepare the solutions immediately before use.*

*Test solution*  Dissolve 50.0 mg of the substance to be examined in *water R* and dilute to 50.0 ml with the same solvent.

*Reference solution (a)*  Dilute 5.0 ml of the test solution to 250.0 ml with *water R*. Dilute 1.0 ml of this solution to 20.0 ml with the mobile phase.

*Reference solution (b)*  Dissolve 5 mg of the substance to be examined in 0.2 ml of *methanol R* and add 0.04 ml of a mixture of 1 volume of *formaldehyde solution R* and 99 volumes of *water R*. Heat at 60 °C for 5 min. Evaporate to dryness under a current of nitrogen. Dissolve the residue in 5 ml of *water R* and dilute to 20 ml with the mobile phase.

*Column:*
— *size:* $l = 0.25$ m, Ø $= 4.0$ mm,
— *stationary phase:* octadecylsilyl silica gel for chromatography R (5 µm).

*Mobile phase* A mixture of equal volumes of *acetonitrile R* and a solution prepared as follows: dissolve 1.32 g of *ammonium phosphate R* in 900 ml of *water R*, adjust to pH 7.0 with *phosphoric acid R* and dilute to 1000 ml with *water R*.

*Flow rate* 1 ml/min.

*Detection* Spectrophotometer at 248 nm.

*Injection* 20 µl.

*Sensitivity* Reference solution (a).

*Run time* 3 times the retention time of the principal peak in the chromatogram obtained with the test solution.

*System suitability:*
— *resolution:* minimum of 4.0 between the peaks due to impurity B and ambroxol in the chromatogram obtained with reference solution (b).

*Limits:*
— *any impurity:* not more than the area of the principal peak in the chromatogram obtained with reference solution (a) (0.1 per cent),
— *total:* not more than 3 times the area of the principal peak in the chromatogram obtained with reference solution (a) (0.3 per cent),
— *disregard limit:* 0.1 times the area of the principal peak in the chromatogram obtained with reference solution (a).

**Heavy metals** (*2.4.8*)
Maximum 20 ppm.

1.0 g complies with limit test C. Prepare the standard using 2 ml of *lead standard solution (10 ppm Pb) R*.

**Loss on drying** (*2.2.32*)
Maximum 0.5 per cent, determined on 1.000 g by drying in an oven at 105 °C.

**Sulphated ash** (*2.4.14*)
Maximum 0.1 per cent, determined on 1.0 g.

**ASSAY**
Dissolve 0.300 g in 70 ml of *alcohol R* and add 5 ml of *0.01 M hydrochloric acid*. Carry out a potentiometric titration (*2.2.20*), using *0.1 M sodium hydroxide*. Read the volume added between the two points of inflexion.

1 ml of *0.1 M sodium hydroxide* is equivalent to 41.46 mg of $C_{13}H_{19}Br_2ClN_2O$.

**STORAGE**
Store protected from light.

**IMPURITIES**

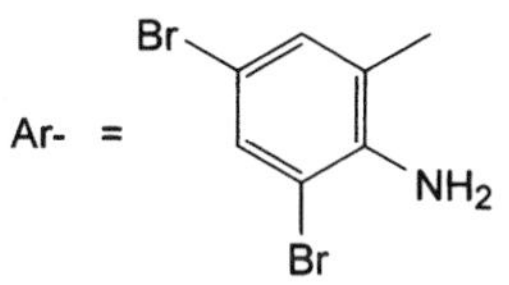

Ar- =

A. Ar-CH$_2$OH: (2-amino-3,5-dibromophenyl)methanol,

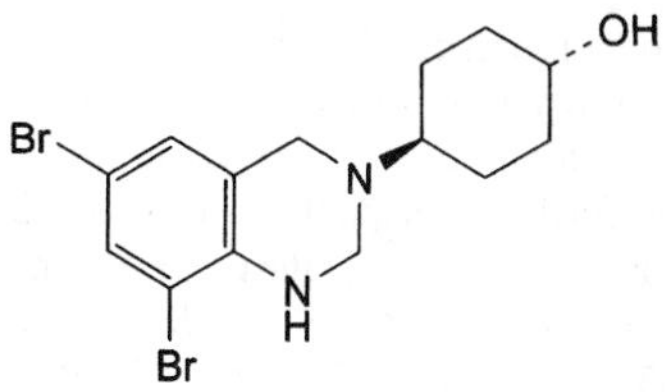

B. *trans*-4-(6,8-dibromo-1,4-dihydroquinazolin-3(2*H*)-yl)cyclohexanol,

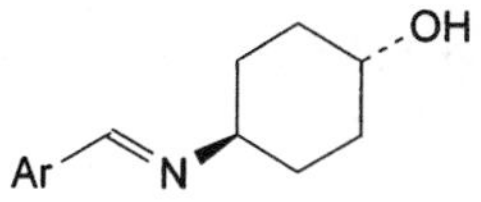

C. *trans*-4-[[(*E*)-2-amino-3,5-dibromobenzyliden]amino]cyclohexanol,

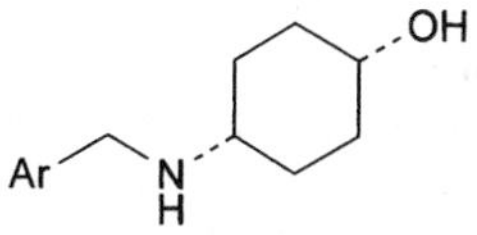

D. *cis*-4-[(2-amino-3,5-dibromobenzyl)amino]cyclohexanol,
E. Ar-CH=O: 2-amino-3,5-dibromobenzaldehyde.

*_____ Ph Eur*

# Amfetamine Sulphate

(*Ph Eur monograph 0368*)

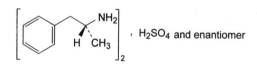

, H$_2$SO$_4$ and enantiomer

$C_{18}H_{26}N_2,H_2SO_4$       368.5       *60-13-9*

**Action and use**
Releases dopamine; central nervous system stimulant.

*Ph Eur* _____

**DEFINITION**
Bis[(2*RS*)-1-phenylpropan-2-amine] sulphate.

**Content**
99.0 per cent to 100.5 per cent (dried substance).

**CHARACTERS**
**Appearance**
White or almost white powder.

**Solubility**
Freely soluble in water, slightly soluble in ethanol (96 per cent).

**IDENTIFICATION**
*First identification* A, B, E.

*Second identification* A, C, D, E.

A Optical rotation (*2.2.7*): $- 0.04°$ to $+ 0.04°$ (measured in a 2 dm tube), determined on solution S (see Tests).

B. Infrared absorption spectrophotometry (*2.2.24*).

*Preparation* Mulls in *liquid paraffin R*.

*Comparison* Ph. Eur. reference spectrum of amfetamine sulphate.

C. To 50 ml of solution S add 5 ml of *strong sodium hydroxide solution R* and 0.5 ml of *benzoyl chloride R* and shake. Continue to add *benzoyl chloride R* in portions of 0.5 ml until no further precipitate is formed. Filter, wash the precipitate with *water R*, recrystallise twice from a mixture of equal volumes of *ethanol (96 per cent) R* and *water R*, then dry at 100-105 °C. The crystals melt (*2.2.14*) at 131 °C to 135 °C.

D. To about 2 mg add 1 ml of *sulphuric acid-formaldehyde reagent R*. An orange colour develops and quickly becomes dark-brown.

E. Solution S gives reaction (a) of sulphates (*2.3.1*).

## TESTS
### Solution S
Dissolve 2.0 g in *carbon dioxide-free water R* and dilute to 100 ml with the same solvent.

### Appearance of solution
Solution S is clear (*2.2.1*) and colourless (*2.2.2, Method II*).

### Acidity or alkalinity
To 25 ml of solution S add 0.1 ml of *methyl red solution R*. Not more than 0.1 ml of *0.01 M hydrochloric acid* or *0.01 M sodium hydroxide* is required to change the colour of the indicator.

### Loss on drying (*2.2.32*)
Maximum 1.0 per cent, determined on 1.00 g by drying in an oven at 105 °C.

### Sulphated ash (*2.4.14*)
Maximum 0.1 per cent, determined on 1.0 g.

## ASSAY
Dissolve 0.300 g in 30 ml of *anhydrous acetic acid R*. Titrate with *0.1 M perchloric aci*d, determining the end-point potentiometrically (*2.2.20*).

1 ml of *0.1 M perchloric acid* is equivalent to 36.85 mg of $C_{18}H_{28}N_2O_4S$.

## STORAGE
Protected from light.

*Ph Eur*

---

# Amidotrizoic Acid Dihydrate

★ ★ ★
★       ★
★       ★
★ ★ ★

(*Ph Eur monograph 0873*)

, 2 H₂O

$C_{11}H_9I_3N_2O_4,2H_2O$          650          *50978-11-5*

### Action and use
Iodinated contrast medium.

### Preparation
Meglumine Amidotrizoate Injection

*Ph Eur* _____

## DEFINITION
Amidotrizoic acid dihydrate contains not less than 98.5 per cent and not more than the equivalent of

101.0 per cent of 3,5-bis(acetylamino)-2,4,6-triiodobenzoic acid, calculated with reference to the dried substance.

## CHARACTERS
A white or almost white, crystalline powder, very slightly soluble in water and in alcohol. It dissolves in dilute solutions of alkali hydroxides.

## IDENTIFICATION
*First identification   A.*

*Second identification   B, C.*

A. Examine by infrared absorption spectrophotometry (*2.2.24*), comparing with the spectrum obtained with *amidotrizoic acid dihydrate CRS* .

B. Examine the chromatograms obtained in the test for related substances (see Tests). The principal spot in the chromatogram obtained with test solution (b) is similar in position and size to the principal spot in the chromatogram obtained with reference solution (b).

C. Heat 50 mg gently in a small porcelain dish over a naked flame. Violet vapour is evolved.

## TESTS
### Appearance of solution
Dissolve 1.0 g in *dilute sodium hydroxide solution R* and dilute to 20 ml with the same solvent. The solution is clear (*2.2.1*) and colourless (*2.2.2, Method II*).

### Related substances
Examine by thin-layer chromatography (*2.2.27*), using *silica gel GF₂₅₄ R* as the coating substance.

*Test solution (a)*   Dissolve 0.50 g of the substance to be examined in a 3 per cent *V/V* solution of *ammonia R* in *methanol R* and dilute to 10 ml with the same solvent.

*Test solution (b)*   Dilute 1 ml of test solution (a) to 10 ml with a 3 per cent *V/V* solution of *ammonia R* in *methanol R*.

*Reference solution (a)*   Dilute 1 ml of test solution (b) to 50 ml with a 3 per cent *V/V* solution of *ammonia R* in *methanol R*.

*Reference solution (b)*   Dissolve 50 mg of a*midotrizoic acid dihydrate CRS* in a 3 per cent *V/V* solution of *ammonia R* in *methanol R* and dilute to 10 ml with the same solvent.

Apply separately to the plate 2 µl of each solution. Develop over a path of 15 cm using a mixture of 20 volumes of *anhydrous formic acid R*, 25 volumes of *methyl ethyl ketone R* and 60 volumes of *toluene R*. Allow the plate to dry until the solvents have evaporated and examine in ultraviolet light at 254 nm. Any spot in the chromatogram obtained with test solution (a), apart from the principal spot, is not more intense than the spot in the chromatogram obtained with reference solution (a) (0.2 per cent).

### Halides
Dissolve 0.55 g in a mixture of 4 ml of *dilute sodium hydroxide solution R* and 15 ml of *water R*. Add 6 ml of *dilute nitric acid R* and filter. 15 ml of the filtrate complies with the limit test for chlorides (*2.4.4*) (150 ppm expressed as chloride).

### Free aromatic amines
*Maintain the solutions and reagents in iced water protected from bright light.* To 0.50 g in a 50 ml volumetric flask add 15 ml of *water R*. Shake and add 1 ml of *dilute sodium hydroxide solution R*. Cool in iced water, add 5 ml of a freshly prepared 5 g/l solution of *sodium nitrite R* and 12 ml of *dilute hydrochloric acid R*. Shake gently and allow to stand for exactly 2 min after adding the hydrochloric acid. Add 10 ml of a 20 g/l solution of *ammonium sulphamate R*. Allow to stand for 5 min, shaking frequently, and add 0.15 ml of a

100 g/l solution of α-*naphthol R* in *alcohol R*. Shake and allow to stand for 5 min. Add 3.5 ml of *buffer solution pH 10.9 R*, mix and dilute to 50.0 ml with *water R*. The absorbance (*2.2.25*), measured within 20 min at 485 nm using as the compensation liquid a solution prepared at the same time and in the same manner but omitting the substance to be examined, is not greater than 0.30.

**Heavy metals** (*2.4.8*)
Dissolve 2.0 g in 4 ml of *dilute sodium hydroxide solution R* and dilute to 20 ml with *water R*. 12 ml of this solution complies with limit test A for heavy metals (20 ppm). Prepare the standard using *lead standard solution (2 ppm Pb) R*.

**Loss on drying** (*2.2.32*)
4.5 per cent to 7.0 per cent, determined on 0.500 g by drying in an oven at 105 °C.

**Sulphated ash** (*2.4.14*)
Not more than 0.1 per cent, determined on 1.0 g.

**ASSAY**
To 0.150 g in a 250 ml round-bottomed flask add 5 ml of *strong sodium hydroxide solution R*, 20 ml of *water R*, 1 g of *zinc powder R* and a few glass beads. Boil under a reflux condenser for 30 min. Allow to cool and rinse the condenser with 20 ml of *water R*, adding the rinsings to the flask. Filter through a sintered-glass filter (*2.1.2*) and wash the filter with several quantities of *water R*. Collect the filtrate and washings. Add 40 ml of *dilute sulphuric acid R* and titrate immediately with *0.1 M silver nitrate*. Determine the end-point potentiometrically (*2.2.20*), using a suitable electrode system such as silver-mercurous sulphate.

1 ml of *0.1 M silver nitrate* is equivalent to 20.47 mg of $C_{11}H_9I_3N_2O_4$.

**STORAGE**
Store protected from light.

**IMPURITIES**

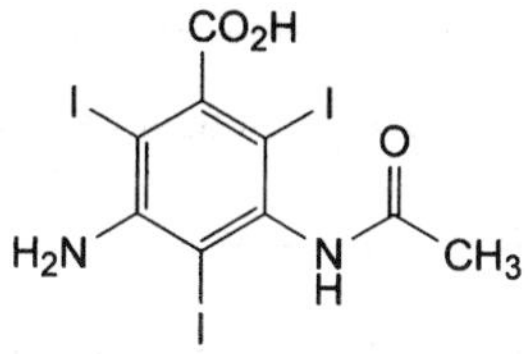

A. 3-(acetylamino)-5-amino-2,4,6-triiodobenzoic acid.

_____ *Ph Eur*

# Amikacin

(*Ph Eur monograph 1289*)

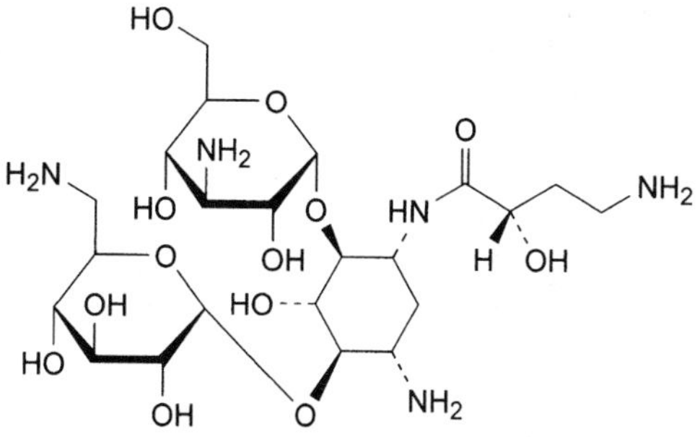

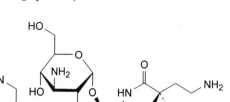

$C_{22}H_{43}N_5O_{13}$      585.6      *37517-28-5*

**Action and use**
Aminoglycoside antibacterial.

*Ph Eur* _____

## DEFINITION
6-*O*-(3-Amino-3-deoxy-α-D-glucopyranosyl)-4-*O*-(6-amino-6-deoxy-α-D-glucopyranosyl)-1-*N*-[(2*S*)-4-amino-2-hydroxybutanoyl]-2-deoxy-D-streptamine.

Antimicrobial substance obtained from kanamycin A.

Semi-synthetic product derived from a fermentation product.

**Content**
96.5 per cent to 102.0 per cent (anhydrous substance).

## CHARACTERS
**Appearance**
White or almost white powder.

**Solubility**
Sparingly soluble in water, slightly soluble in methanol, practically insoluble in acetone and in ethanol (96 per cent).

## IDENTIFICATION
A. Infrared absorption spectrophotometry (*2.2.24*).

*Comparison*    amikacin CRS.

B. Thin-layer chromatography (*2.2.27*).

*Test solution*    Dissolve 25 mg of the substance to be examined in *water R* and dilute to 10 ml with the same solvent.

*Reference solution (a)*    Dissolve 25 mg of *amikacin CRS* in *water R* and dilute to 10 ml with the same solvent.

*Reference solution (b)*    Dissolve 5 mg of *kanamycin monosulphate CRS* in 1 ml of the test solution and dilute to 10 ml with *water R*.

*Plate*    TLC silica gel plate R.

*Mobile phase*    The lower layer of a mixture of equal volumes of *concentrated ammonia R*, *methanol R* and *methylene chloride R*.

*Application*    5 μl.

*Development*    Over a path of 15 cm.

*Drying*    In air.

*Detection*    Spray with *ninhydrin solution R1* and heat at 110 °C for 5 min.

*System suitability*    Reference solution (b):
— the chromatogram shows 2 clearly separated spots.

*Results*    The principal spot in the chromatogram obtained with the test solution is similar in position, colour and size to

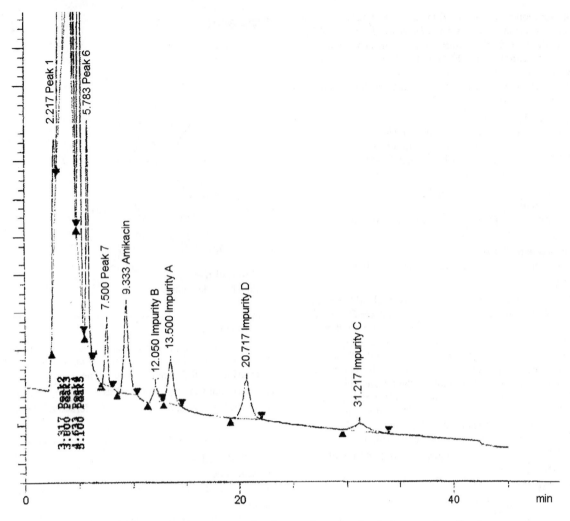

Figure 1289.-1. – *Chromatogram for the test for related substances of amikacin*

the principal spot in the chromatogram obtained with reference solution (a).

## TESTS
### pH (2.2.3)
9.5 to 11.5.

Dissolve 0.1 g in *carbon dioxide-free water R* and dilute to 10 ml with the same solvent.

### Specific optical rotation (2.2.7)
+ 97 to + 105 (anhydrous substance).

Dissolve 0.50 g in *water R* and dilute to 25.0 ml with the same solvent.

### Related substances
Liquid chromatography (2.2.29). *Maintain the solutions at 10 °C.*

*Test solution (a)* Dissolve 0.100 g of the substance to be examined in *water R* and dilute to 10.0 ml with the same solvent. In a ground-glass-stoppered vial, add 0.2 ml of this solution to 2.0 ml of a 10 g/l solution of *2,4,6-trinitrobenzene sulphonic acid R*. Then add 3.0 ml of *pyridine R* and close the vial tightly. Shake vigorously for 30 s and heat in a water-bath at 75 °C for 45 min. Cool in cold water for 2 min and add 2 ml of *glacial acetic acid R*. Shake vigorously for 30 s.

*Test solution (b)* Dissolve 50.0 mg of the substance to be examined in *water R* and dilute to 50.0 ml with the same solvent. Then prepare as prescribed for test solution (a).

*Reference solution (a)* Dissolve 5.0 mg of *amikacin impurity A CRS* in *water R* and dilute to 50.0 ml with the same solvent. Then prepare as prescribed for test solution (a).

*Reference solution (b)* Dissolve 50.0 mg of *amikacin CRS* in *water R* and dilute to 50.0 ml with the same solvent. Then prepare as prescribed for test solution (a).

*Reference solution (c)* Dissolve 2 mg of *amikacin CRS* and 2 mg of *amikacin impurity A CRS* in *water R* and dilute to 20 ml with the same solvent. Then prepare as prescribed for test solution (a).

*Blank solution* Prepare as described for test solution (a) using 0.2 ml of *water R*.

*Column:*
— *size*: $l$ = 0.25 m, Ø = 4.6 mm;
— *stationary phase*: *octadecylsilyl silica gel for chromatography R* (5 µm);
— *temperature*: 30 °C.

*Mobile phase* Mix 30 volumes of a 2.7 g/l solution of *potassium dihydrogen phosphate R*, adjusted to pH 6.5 with a 22 g/l solution of *potassium hydroxide R*, and 70 volumes of *methanol R*.

*Flow rate*   1 ml/min.

*Detection*   Spectrophotometer at 340 nm.

*Injection*   20 μl of test solution (a) and reference solutions (a) and (c).

*Run time*   4 times the retention time of amikacin.

*System suitability*   Reference solution (c):
— *resolution*: minimum 3.5 between the peaks due to amikacin and impurity A (see Figure 1289.-1).

*Limits:*
— *impurity A*: not more than the area of the principal peak in the chromatogram obtained with reference solution (a) (1 per cent);
— *any other impurity*: for each impurity, not more than 0.5 times the area of the principal peak in the chromatogram obtained with reference solution (a) (0.5 per cent);
— *sum of impurities other than A*: not more than 1.5 times the area of the principal peak in the chromatogram obtained with reference solution (a) (1.5 per cent);
— *disregard limit*: 0.1 times the area of the principal peak in the chromatogram obtained with reference solution (a) (0.1 per cent); disregard any peak due to the blank.

**Water** (*2.5.12*)
Maximum 8.5 per cent, determined on 0.200 g.

**Sulphated ash** (*2.4.14*)
Maximum 0.5 per cent, determined on 1.0 g.

**ASSAY**
Liquid chromatography (*2.2.29*) as described in the test for related substances with the following modifications.

*Injection*   Test solution (b) and reference solution (b).

*System suitability:*
— *repeatability*: maximum relative standard deviation of 2.0 per cent after 6 injections of reference solution (b).

Calculate the percentage content of $C_{22}H_{43}N_5O_{13}$ from the declared content of *amikacin CRS*.

**IMPURITIES**

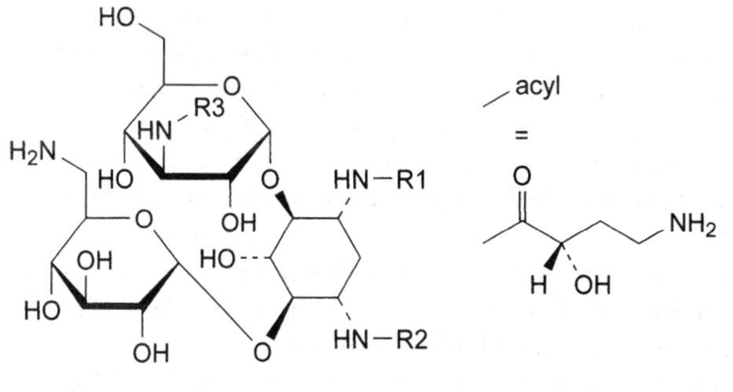

A. R1 = R3 = H, R2 = acyl: 4-*O*-(3-amino-3-deoxy-α-D-glucopyranosyl)-6-*O*-(6-amino-6-deoxy-α-D-glucopyranosyl)-1-*N*-[(2*S*)-4-amino-2-hydroxybutanoyl]-2-deoxy-L-streptamine,

B. R1 = R2 = acyl, R3 = H: 4-*O*-(3-amino-3-deoxy-α-D-glucopyranosyl)-6-*O*-(6-amino-6-deoxy-α-D-glucopyranosyl)-1,3-*N*-bis[(2*S*)-4-amino-2-hydroxybutanoyl]-2-deoxy-L-streptamine,

C. R1 = R2 = H, R3 = acyl: 4-*O*-(6-amino-6-deoxy-α-D-glucopyranosyl)-6-*O*-[3-[[(2S)-4-amino-2-hydroxybutanoyl]amino]-3-deoxy-α-D-glucopyranosyl]-2-deoxy-D-streptamine,

D. R1 = R2 = R3 = H: kanamycin.

_____ *Ph Eur*

# Amikacin Sulphate

*(Ph Eur monograph 1290)*

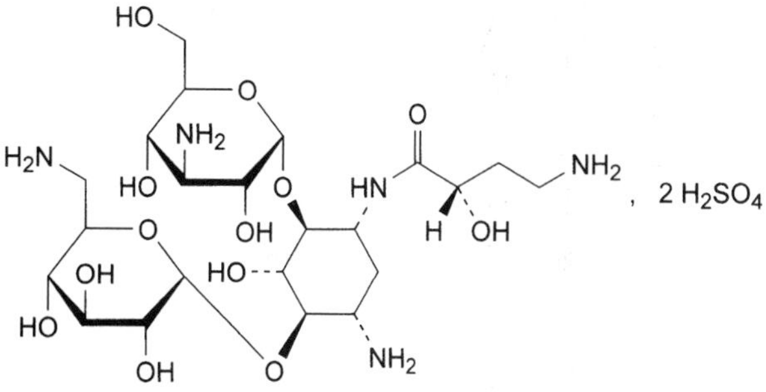

$C_{22}H_{43}N_5O_{13},2H_2SO_4$   782   *149022-22-0*

**Action and use**
Aminoglycoside antibacterial.

**Preparation**
Amikacin Injection

*Ph Eur* _____

**DEFINITION**
6-*O*-(3-Amino-3-deoxy-α-D-glucopyranosyl)-4-*O*-(6-amino-6-deoxy-α-D-glucopyranosyl)-1-*N*-[(2*S*)-4-amino-2-hydroxybutanoyl]-2-deoxy-D-streptamine sulphate.

Antimicrobial substance obtained from kanamycin A.

Semi-synthetic product derived from a fermentation product.

**Content**
96.5 per cent to 102.0 per cent (dried substance).

**CHARACTERS**
**Appearance**
White or almost white powder.

**Solubility**
Freely soluble in water, practically insoluble in acetone and in ethanol (96 per cent).

**IDENTIFICATION**
A. Infrared absorption spectrophotometry (*2.2.24*).

*Comparison*   amikacin sulphate CRS.

B. Thin-layer chromatography (*2.2.27*).

*Test solution*   Dissolve 25 mg of the substance to be examined in *water R* and dilute to 10 ml with the same solvent.

*Reference solution (a)*   Dissolve 25 mg of *amikacin sulphate CRS* in *water R* and dilute to 10 ml with the same solvent.

*Reference solution (b)*   Dissolve 5 mg of *kanamycin monosulphate CRS* in 1 ml of the test solution and dilute to 10 ml with *water R*.

*Plate*   TLC silica gel plate R.

*Mobile phase*   The lower layer of a mixture of equal volumes of *concentrated ammonia R*, *methanol R* and *methylene chloride R*.

*Application*   5 μl.

*Development*   Over a path of 15 cm.

*Drying*   In air.

*Detection*   Spray with *ninhydrin solution R1* and heat at 110 °C for 5 min.

*System suitability*   Reference solution (b):
— the chromatogram shows 2 clearly separated spots.

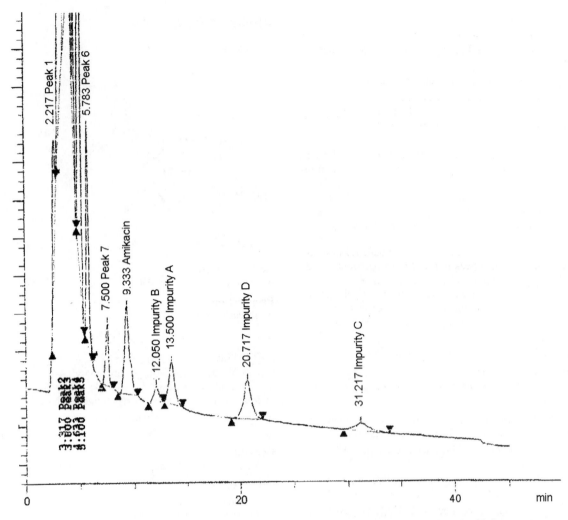

Figure 1290.-1. – *Chromatogram for the test for related substances of amikacin sulphate*

*Results*   The principal spot in the chromatogram obtained with the test solution is similar in position, colour and size to the principal spot in the chromatogram obtained with reference solution (a).

C. It gives reaction (a) of sulphates (*2.3.1*).

### TESTS

**pH** (*2.2.3*)
2.0 to 4.0.

Dissolve 0.1 g in *carbon dioxide-free water R* and dilute to 10 ml with the same solvent.

**Specific optical rotation** (*2.2.7*)
+ 76 to + 84 (dried substance).

Dissolve 0.50 g in *water R* and dilute to 25.0 ml with the same solvent.

### Related substances

Liquid chromatography (*2.2.29*). *Maintain the solutions at 10 °C.*

*Test solution (a)*   Dissolve 0.100 g of the substance to be examined in *water R* and dilute to 10.0 ml with the same solvent. In a ground-glass-stoppered vial, add 0.2 ml of this solution to 2.0 ml of a 10 g/l solution of *2,4,6-trinitrobenzene sulphonic acid R*. Then add 3.0 ml of *pyridine R* and close the vial tightly. Shake vigorously for 30 s and heat on a water-bath at 75 °C for 2 h. Cool in cold water for 2 min and add 2 ml of *glacial acetic acid R*. Shake vigorously for 30 s.

*Test solution (b)*   Dissolve 50.0 mg of the substance to be examined in *water R* and dilute to 50.0 ml with the same solvent. Then prepare as prescribed for test solution (a).

*Reference solution (a)*   Dissolve 5.0 mg of *amikacin impurity A CRS* in *water R* and dilute to 50.0 ml with the same solvent. Then prepare as prescribed for test solution (a).

*Reference solution (b)*   Dissolve 50.0 mg of *amikacin sulphate CRS* in *water R* and dilute to 50.0 ml with the same solvent. Then prepare as prescribed for test solution (a).

*Reference solution (c)*   Dissolve 2 mg of *amikacin sulphate CRS* and 2 mg of *amikacin impurity A CRS* in *water R* and dilute to 20 ml with the same solvent. Then prepare as prescribed for test solution (a).

*Blank solution*   Prepare as described for test solution (a) using 0.2 ml of water R.

*Column:*
— *size*: l = 0.25 m, Ø = 4.6 mm;
— *stationary phase*: octadecylsilyl silica gel for chromatography R (5 μm);
— *temperature*: 30 °C.

*Mobile phase*   Mix 30 volumes of a 2.7 g/l solution of *potassium dihydrogen phosphate R*, adjusted to pH 6.5 with a 22 g/l solution of *potassium hydroxide R*, and 70 volumes of *methanol R*.

*Flow rate*   1 ml/min.

*Detection*   Spectrophotometer at 340 nm.

*Injection*   20 µl of test solution (a) and reference solutions (a) and (c).

*Run time*   4 times the retention time of amikacin.

*System suitability*   Reference solution (c):
— *resolution*: minimum 3.5 between the peaks due to amikacin and impurity A (see Figure 1290.-1).

*Limits:*
— *impurity A*: not more than the area of the principal peak in the chromatogram obtained with reference solution (a) (1.0 per cent);
— *any other impurity*: for each impurity, not more than 0.5 times the area of the principal peak in the chromatogram obtained with reference solution (a) (0.5 per cent);
— *sum of impurities other than A*: not more than 1.5 times the area of the principal peak in the chromatogram obtained with reference solution (a) (1.5 per cent);
— *disregard limit*: 0.1 times the area of the principal peak in the chromatogram obtained with reference solution (a) (0.1 per cent); disregard any peak due to the blank and any peak eluting before the principal peak.

## Sulphate

23.3 per cent to 25.8 per cent (dried substance).

Dissolve 0.250 g in 100 ml of *water R* and adjust the solution to pH 11 using *concentrated ammonia R*. Add 10.0 ml of *0.1 M barium chloride* and about 0.5 mg of *phthalein purple R*. Titrate with *0.1 M sodium edetate* adding 50 ml of *ethanol (96 per cent) R* when the colour of the solution begins to change and continue the titration until the violet-blue colour disappears.

1 ml of *0.1 M barium chloride* is equivalent to 9.606 mg of sulphate ($SO_4$).

## Loss on drying (2.2.32)

Maximum 13.0 per cent, determined on 0.500 g by drying in an oven at 105 °C at a pressure not exceeding 0.7 kPa for 3 h.

## Pyrogens (2.6.8)

If intended for use in the manufacture of parenteral dosage forms without a further appropriate procedure for the removal of pyrogens, it complies with the test for pyrogens. Inject per kilogram of the rabbit's mass 5 ml of a solution containing 25 mg of the substance to be examined in *water for injections R*.

## ASSAY

Liquid chromatography (*2.2.29*) as described in the test for related substances with the following modifications.

*Injection*   Test solution (b) and reference solution (b).

*System suitability:*
— *repeatability*: maximum relative standard deviation of 2.0 per cent after 6 injections of reference solution (b).

Calculate the percentage content of $C_{22}H_{47}N_5O_{21}S_2$ from the declared content of *amikacin sulphate CRS*.

## STORAGE

If the substance is sterile, store in a sterile, airtight, tamper-proof container.

## IMPURITIES

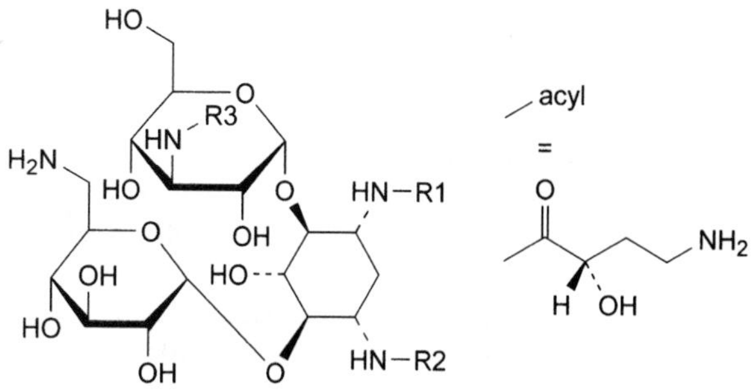

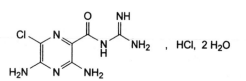

A. R1 = R3 = H, R2 = acyl: 4-*O*-(3-amino-3-deoxy-α-D-glucopyranosyl)-6-*O*-(6-amino-6-deoxy-α-D-glucopyranosyl)-1-*N*-[(2*S*)-4-amino-2-hydroxybutanoyl]-2-deoxy-L-streptamine,

B. R1 = R2 = acyl, R3 = H: 4-*O*-(3-amino-3-deoxy-α-D-glucopyranosyl)-6-*O*-(6-amino-6-deoxy-α-D-glucopyranosyl)-1,3-*N*-bis[(2*S*)-4-amino-2-hydroxybutanoyl]-2-deoxy-L-streptamine,

C. R1 = R2 = H, R3 = acyl: 4-*O*-(6-amino-6-deoxy-α-D-glucopyranosyl)-6-*O*-[3-[[(2*S*)-4-amino-2-hydroxybutanoyl]amino]-3-deoxy-α-D-glucopyranosyl]-2-deoxy-D-streptamine,

D. R1 = R2 = R3 = H: kanamycin.

*Ph Eur*

# Amiloride Hydrochloride

(*Ph Eur monograph 0651*)

$C_6H_8ClN_7O,HCl,2H_2O$       302.1       *17440-83-4*

## Action and use

Sodium channel blocker; potassium-sparing diuretic.

## Preparations

Amiloride Tablets

Co-amilofruse Tablets

Co-amilozide Oral Solution

Co-amilozide Tablets

*Ph Eur*

## DEFINITION

3,5-Diamino-*N*-carbamimidoyl-6-chloropyrazine-2-carboxamide hydrochloride dihydrate.

## Content

98.0 per cent to 101.0 per cent (anhydrous substance).

## CHARACTERS

### Appearance

Pale yellow or greenish-yellow powder.

### Solubility

Slightly soluble in water and in anhydrous ethanol.

## IDENTIFICATION

*First identification* A, D.

*Second identification* B, C, D.

A. Infrared absorption spectrophotometry (2.2.24).

*Comparison* amiloride hydrochloride CRS.

B. Thin-layer chromatography (2.2.27).

*Test solution* Dissolve 40 mg of the substance to be examined in *methanol R* and dilute to 10 ml with the same solvent.

*Reference solution* Dissolve 40 mg of *amiloride hydrochloride CRS* in *methanol R* and dilute to 10 ml with the same solvent.

*Plate* TLC silica gel plate R.

*Mobile phase* dilute ammonia R1, water R, dioxan R (6:6:88 *V/V/V*); freshly prepared mixture.

*Application* 5 μl.

*Development* Over a path of 12 cm.

*Drying* In air.

*Detection* Examine in ultraviolet light at 365 nm.

*Results* The principal spot in the chromatogram obtained with the test solution is similar in position, fluorescence and size to the principal spot in the chromatogram obtained with the reference solution.

C. Dissolve about 10 mg in 10 ml of *water R*. Add 10 ml of a 200 g/l solution of *cetrimide R*, 0.25 ml of *dilute sodium hydroxide solution R* and 1 ml of *bromine water R*. A greenish-yellow colour is produced. Add 2 ml of *dilute hydrochloric acid R*. The solution becomes deep yellow and shows blue fluorescence in ultraviolet light at 365 nm.

D. It gives reaction (b) of chlorides (2.3.1).

## TESTS

### Free acid

Dissolve 1.0 g in a mixture of 50 ml of *methanol R* and 50 ml of *water R* and titrate with *0.1 M sodium hydroxide*, determining the end-point potentiometrically (2.2.20). Not more than 0.3 ml of *0.1 M sodium hydroxide* is required to reach the end-point.

### Related substances

Liquid chromatography (2.2.29).

*Test solution* Dissolve 20.0 mg of the substance to be examined in a mixture of 1 volume of *acetonitrile R* and 3 volumes of *water R* and dilute to 10.0 ml with the same mixture of solvents.

*Reference solution (a)* Dilute 1.0 ml of the test solution to 100.0 ml with a mixture of 1 volume of *acetonitrile R* and 3 volumes of *water R*.

*Reference solution (b)* Dilute 1.0 ml of reference solution (a) to 10.0 ml with a mixture of 1 volume of *acetonitrile R* and 3 volumes of *water R*.

*Reference solution (c)* Dissolve 5.0 mg of *amiloride impurity A CRS* in a mixture of 1 volume of *acetonitrile R* and 3 volumes of *water R* and dilute to 5.0 ml with the same mixture of solvents. Dilute 1.0 ml of this solution to 100.0 ml with a mixture of 1 volume of *acetonitrile R* and 3 volumes of *water R*.

*Column:*
— *size:* l = 0.25 m, Ø = 4.6 mm;
— *stationary phase:* octadecylsilyl silica gel for chromatography R (5 μm).

*Mobile phase* Mix 5 volumes of *tetramethylammonium hydroxide solution R*, 250 volumes of *acetonitrile R* and 745 volumes of *water R*; adjust to pH 7.0 with a mixture of 1 volume of *phosphoric acid R* and 9 volumes of *water R*. Adjust the concentration of acetonitrile in the mobile phase so that the retention time of impurity A is 5-6 min (an increase in the concentration of acetonitrile results in a shorter retention time). Adjust the concentration of tetramethylammonium hydroxide and of phosphoric acid keeping the pH at 7.0 so that the retention time of amiloride is 9-12 min (an increase in the concentration results in a shorter retention time for amiloride).

*Flow rate* 1 ml/min.

*Detection* Spectrophotometer at 254 nm.

*Injection* 20 μl.

*Run time* 5 times the retention time of amiloride.

*System suitability* Reference solution (b):
— *signal-to-noise ratio:* minimum 5.0 for the peak due to amiloride.

*Limits:*
— *total:* not more than the area of the peak due to impurity A in the chromatogram obtained with reference solution (c) (0.5 per cent);
— *disregard limit:* 0.1 times the area of the peak due to impurity A in the chromatogram obtained with reference solution (c) (0.05 per cent).

**Water** (2.5.12)

11.0 per cent to 13.0 per cent, determined on 0.200 g.

**Sulphated ash** (2.4.14)

Maximum 0.1 per cent, determined on 1.0 g.

## ASSAY

Dissolve 0.200 g in a mixture of 5.0 ml of *0.01 M hydrochloric acid* and 50 ml of *ethanol (96 per cent) R*. Carry out a potentiometric titration (2.2.20), using *0.1 M sodium hydroxide*. Read the volume added between the 2 points of inflexion.

1 ml of *0.1 M sodium hydroxide* is equivalent to 26.61 mg of $C_6H_9Cl_2N_7O$.

## STORAGE

Protected from light.

## IMPURITIES

A. methyl 3,5-diamino-6-chloropyrazine-2-carboxylate.

# Aminobenzoic Acid

*(4-Aminobenzoic Acid, Ph Eur monograph 1687)*

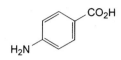

C$_7$H$_7$NO$_2$         137.1         *150-13-0*

## Action and use
Skin protective.

*Ph Eur*

## DEFINITION
4-Aminobenzoic acid.

## Content
99.0 per cent to 101.0 per cent (anhydrous substance).

## CHARACTERS
### Appearance
White or slightly yellow, crystalline powder.

### Solubility
Slightly soluble in water, freely soluble in alcohol. It dissolves in dilute solutions of alkali hydroxides.

## IDENTIFICATION
*First identification*   B.

*Second identification*   A, C.

A. Melting point (*2.2.14*): 186 °C to 189 °C.

B. Infrared absorption spectrophotometry (*2.2.24*).

*Comparison*   4-aminobenzoic acid CRS .

C. Thin-layer chromatography (*2.2.27*).

*Test solution*   Dissolve 20 mg of the substance to be examined in *methanol R* and dilute to 20 ml with the same solvent.

*Reference solution (a)*   Dissolve 20 mg of *4-aminobenzoic acid CRS* in *methanol R* and dilute to 20 ml with the same solvent.

*Reference solution (b)*   Dissolve 10 mg of *4-nitrobenzoic acid R* in 10 ml of reference solution (a).

*Plate*   Suitable silica gel with a fluorescent indicator having an optimal intensity at 254 nm as the coating substance.

*Mobile phase*   glacial acetic acid R, hexane R, methylene chloride R (5:20:75 V/V/V).

*Application*   1 µl.

*Development*   Over a path of 10 cm.

*Drying*   In air.

*Detection*   Examine in ultraviolet light at 254 nm.

*System suitability*   The chromatogram obtained with reference solution (b) shows 2 clearly separated spots.

*Results*   The principal spot in the chromatogram obtained with the test solution is similar in position and size to the principal spot in the chromatogram obtained with reference solution (a).

## TESTS
### Appearance of solution
The solution is clear (*2.2.1*) and not more intensely coloured than reference solution B$_5$ (*2.2.2, Method II*).

Dissolve 1.0 g in *alcohol R* and dilute to 20 ml with the same solvent.

### Related substances
Liquid chromatography (*2.2.29*).

*Test solution*   Dissolve 25.0 mg of the substance to be examined in the mobile phase and dilute to 100.0 ml with the mobile phase.

*Reference solution*   Dissolve 25.0 mg of *4-nitrobenzoic acid R* and 25.0 mg of *benzocaine R* in *methanol R* and dilute to 100.0 ml with the same solvent. Dilute 1.0 ml to 50.0 ml with the mobile phase. Dilute 1.0 ml of this solution to 10.0 ml with the mobile phase.

*Column:*
— *size: l* = 0.12 m, Ø = 4.0 mm,
— *stationary phase*: octylsilyl silica gel for chromatography R (5 µm).

*Mobile phase*   Mix 20 volumes of a mixture of 70 volumes of *acetonitrile R* and 80 volumes of *methanol R*, and 80 volumes of a solution containing 1.5 g/l of *potassium dihydrogen phosphate R* and 2.5 g/l of *sodium octanesulphonate R* adjusted to pH 2.2 with *phosphoric acid R*.

*Flow rate*   1.0 ml/min.

*Detection*   Spectrophotometer at 270 nm.

*Injection*   20 µl.

*Run time*   11 times the retention time of 4-aminobenzoic acid.

*Relative retention*   With reference to 4-aminobenzoic acid (retention time = about 3 min): impurity A = about 4; impurity B = about 9.

*Limits:*
— *impurity A*: not more than the area of the corresponding peak in the chromatogram obtained with the reference solution (0.2 per cent),
— *impurity B*: not more than the area of the corresponding peak in the chromatogram obtained with the reference solution (0.2 per cent),
— *any other impurity*: not more than 0.5 times the area of the peak due to impurity A in the chromatogram obtained with the reference solution (0.1 per cent),
— *total*: not more than 2.5 times the area of the peak due to impurity A in the chromatogram obtained with the reference solution (0.5 per cent),
— *disregard limit*: 0.1 times the area of the peak due to impurity A in the chromatogram obtained with the reference solution (0.02 per cent).

### Impurity C and impurity D
Gas chromatography (*2.2.28*).

*Internal standard solution*   Dissolve 20.0 mg of *lauric acid R* in *methylene chloride R* and dilute to 100.0 ml with the same solvent.

*Test solution*   Dissolve 1.000 g of the substance to be examined in 10.0 ml of an 84 g/l solution of *sodium hydroxide R* and extract with 2 quantities, each of 10 ml, of *methylene chloride R*. Combine and wash with 5 ml of *water R*; filter through *anhydrous sodium sulphate R*. Wash the filter with *methylene chloride R*. Evaporate in a water-bath at 50-60 °C to obtain a volume of about 1-5 ml. Add 1.0 ml of the internal standard solution and dilute to 10.0 ml with *methylene chloride R*.

*Reference solution (a)*   Dissolve 20.0 mg of *aniline R* in *methylene chloride R* and dilute to 100.0 ml with the same solvent.

*Reference solution (b)*   Dissolve 20.0 mg of *p-toluidine R* in *methylene chloride R* and dilute to 100.0 ml with the same solvent.

*Reference solution (c)*   Dilute 0.50 ml of reference solution (a), 0.50 ml of reference solution (b) and 10.0 ml of the internal standard solution to 100.0 ml with *methylene chloride R*.

*Column:*
— *material:* fused silica,
— *size: l* = 30 m, Ø = 0.32 mm,
— *stationary phase: poly[methyl(95)phenyl(5)] siloxane R* (film thickness 0.5 μm).

*Carrier gas   helium for chromatography R.*

*Flow rate*   1.0 ml/min.

*Split ratio*   1:10.

*Temperature:*

|               | Time (min) | Temperature (°C) |
|---------------|-----------|------------------|
| Column        | 0 - 4     | 130              |
|               | 4 - 6.5   | 130 → 180        |
|               | 6.5 - 11.5| 180              |
| Injection port|           | 280              |
| Detector      |           | 300              |

*Detection*   Flame ionisation.

*Injection*   2 μl; inject the test solution and reference solution (c).

*Retention time*   Internal standard = about 9.5 min.

*Limits:*
— *impurity C*: calculate the ratio (*R*) of the area of the peak due to impurity C to the area of the peak due to the internal standard from the chromatogram obtained with reference solution (c); calculate the ratio of the area of the peak due to impurity C to the area of the peak due to the internal standard from the chromatogram obtained with the test solution: this ratio is not greater than *R* (10 ppm),
— *impurity D*: calculate the ratio (*R*) of the area of the peak due to impurity D to the area of the peak due to the internal standard from the chromatogram obtained with reference solution (c); calculate the ratio of the area of the peak due to impurity D to the area of the peak due to the internal standard from the chromatogram obtained with the test solution: this ratio is not greater than *R* (10 ppm).

**Iron** (*2.4.9*)
Maximum 40 ppm.
Dissolve 0.250 g in 3 ml of *alcohol R* and dilute to 10.0 ml with *water R*.

**Heavy metals** (*2.4.8*)
Maximum 20 ppm.
1.0 g complies with limit test C. Prepare the standard using 2 ml of *lead standard solution (10 ppm Pb) R*.

**Water** (*2.5.12*)
Maximum 0.2 per cent, determined on 1.00 g.

**Sulphated ash** (*2.4.14*)
Maximum 0.1 per cent, determined on 1.0 g.

**ASSAY**
Dissolve 0.100 g with heating in 50 ml of *carbon dioxide-free water R*. Titrate with *0.1 M sodium hydroxide* determining the end-point potentiometrically (*2.2.20*).

1 ml of *0.1 M sodium hydroxide* is equivalent to 13.71 mg of $C_7H_7NO_2$.

**STORAGE**
Protected from light.

**IMPURITIES**

A. R = $CO_2H$, R' = $NO_2$: 4-nitrobenzoic acid,
B. R = $CO$-O-$C_2H_5$, R' = $NH_2$: benzocaine,
C. R = H, R' = $NH_2$: aniline,
D. R = $CH_3$, R' = $NH_2$: 4-methylaniline (*p*-toluidine).

_____ *Ph Eur*

# Aminocaproic Acid

*(Ph Eur monograph 0874)*

$$H_2N \diagdown\diagup\diagdown\diagup\diagdown CO_2H$$

$C_6H_{13}NO_2$          131.2          *60-32-2*

**Action and use**
Antifibrinolytic.

*Ph Eur* _____

**DEFINITION**
Aminocaproic acid contains not less than 98.5 per cent and not more than the equivalent of 101.0 per cent of 6-aminohexanoic acid, calculated with reference to the dried substance.

**CHARACTERS**
A white or almost white, crystalline powder or colourless crystals, freely soluble in water, slightly soluble in alcohol.
It melts at about 205 °C with decomposition.

**IDENTIFICATION**
*First identification   A.*
*Second identification   B, C, D.*

A. Examine by infrared absorption spectrophotometry (*2.2.24*), comparing with the spectrum obtained with *aminocaproic acid CRS* . Examine the substances prepared as discs.

B. Examine the chromatograms obtained in the test for ninhydrin-positive substances. The principal spot in the chromatogram obtained with the test solution (b) is similar in position, colour and size to the principal spot in the chromatogram obtained with reference solution (a).

C. Dissolve 0.5 g in 4 ml of a mixture of equal volumes of *dilute hydrochloric acid R* and *water R*. Evaporate to dryness by heating on a water-bath. Dry the residue in a desiccator. Dissolve the residue in about 2 ml of boiling *ethanol R*. Allow to cool and maintain at 4 °C to 8 °C for 3 h. Filter under reduced pressure. The residue washed with about 10 ml of *acetone R* and dried at 60 °C for 30 min, melts (*2.2.14*) at 131 °C to 133 °C.

D. Dissolve about 5 mg in 0.5 ml of *distilled water R*. Add 3 ml of *dimethylformamide R* and 2 ml of *ascorbic acid solution R*. Heat on a water-bath. An orange colour develops.

## TESTS

### Solution S

Dissolve 10.0 g in *carbon dioxide-free water R* and dilute to 50.0 ml with the same solvent.

### Appearance of solution

Solution S is colourless (*2.2.2, Method II*) and remains clear (*2.2.1*) on standing for 24 h.

### pH (*2.2.3*)

The pH of solution S is 7.5 to 8.0.

### Absorbance (*2.2.25*).

A. The absorbance of solution S at 287 nm is not more than 0.10 and at 450 nm is not more than 0.03.

B. Place 2.0 g in an even layer in a shallow dish 9 cm in diameter, cover and allow to stand at 98 °C to 102 °C for 72 h. Dissolve in *water R* and dilute to 10.0 ml with the same solvent. The absorbance of the solution at 287 nm is not more than 0.15 and at 450 nm is not more than 0.03.

### Ninhydrin-positive substances

Examine by thin-layer chromatography (*2.2.27*), using a suitable silica gel as the coating substance.

*Test solution (a)*   Dissolve 0.10 g of the substance to be examined in *water R* and dilute to 10 ml with the same solvent.

*Test solution (b)*   Dilute 1 ml of test solution (a) to 50 ml with *water R*.

*Reference solution (a)*   Dissolve 10 mg of *aminocaproic acid CRS* in *water R* and dilute to 50 ml with the same solvent.

*Reference solution (b)*   Dilute 5 ml of test solution (b) to 20 ml with *water R*.

*Reference solution (c)*   Dissolve 10 mg of *aminocaproic acid CRS* and 10 mg of *leucine CRS* in *water R* and dilute to 25 ml with the same solvent.

Apply separately to the plate 5 µl of each solution. Allow the plate to dry in air. Develop over a path of 15 cm using a mixture of 20 volumes of *glacial acetic acid R*, 20 volumes of *water R* and 60 volumes of *butanol R*. Dry the plate in a current of warm air. Spray with *ninhydrin solution R* and heat at 100 °C to 105 °C for 15 min. Any spot in the chromatogram obtained with the test solution (a), apart from the principal spot, is not more intense than the spot in the chromatogram obtained with reference solution (b) (0.5 per cent). The test is not valid unless the chromatogram obtained with reference solution (c) shows two clearly separated principal spots.

### Heavy metals (*2.4.8*)

12 ml of solution S complies with limit test A for heavy metals (10 ppm). Prepare the standard using *lead standard solution (2 ppm Pb) R*.

### Loss on drying (*2.2.32*)

Not more than 0.5 per cent, determined on 1.000 g by drying in an oven at 105 °C.

### Sulphated ash (*2.4.14*)

Not more than 0.1 per cent, determined on 1.0 g.

## ASSAY

Dissolve 0.100 g in 20 ml of *anhydrous acetic acid R*. Using 0.1 ml of *crystal violet solution R* as indicator, titrate with *0.1 M perchloric acid* until the colour changes from bluish-violet to bluish-green.

1 ml of *0.1 M perchloric acid* is equivalent to 13.12 mg of $C_6H_{13}NO_2$.

# Aminoglutethimide

(*Ph Eur monograph 1291*)

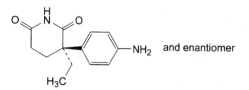

and enantiomer

$C_{13}H_{16}N_2O_2$          232.3          *125-84-8*

### Action and use

Inhibitor of adrenal corticosteroid synthesis; used in chemical adrenalectomy.

### Preparation

Aminoglutethimide Tablets

*Ph Eur*

## DEFINITION

(*3RS*)-3-(4-Aminophenyl)-3-ethylpiperidine-2,6-dione.

### Content

98.0 per cent to 101.5 per cent (dried substance).

## CHARACTERS

### Appearance

White or slightly yellow, crystalline powder.

### Solubility

Practically insoluble in water, freely soluble in acetone, soluble in methanol.

## IDENTIFICATION

*First identification*   B.

*Second identification*   A, C.

A. Melting point (*2.2.14*): 150 °C to 154 °C.

B. Infrared absorption spectrophotometry (*2.2.24*).

*Preparation*   Discs.

*Comparison*   aminoglutethimide CRS .

C. Thin-layer chromatography (*2.2.27*).

*Test solution*   Dissolve 25 mg of the substance to be examined in *acetone R* and dilute to 5 ml with the same solvent.

*Reference solution (a)*   Dissolve 25 mg of *aminoglutethimide CRS* in *acetone R* and dilute to 5 ml with the same solvent.

*Reference solution (b)*   Dissolve 25 mg of *aminoglutethimide CRS* and 25 mg of *glutethimide CRS* in *acetone R* and dilute to 5 ml with the same solvent.

*Plate*   TLC silica gel $F_{254}$ plate R.

*Mobile phase*   glacial acetic acid R, methanol R, ethyl acetate R (0.5:15:85 *V/V/V*).

*Application*   5 µl.

*Development*   Over a path of 15 cm.

*Drying*   In air.

*Detection*   Examine in ultraviolet light at 254 nm.

*System suitability*   Reference solution (b):
— the chromatogram shows 2 clearly separed spots.

*Results*   The principal spot in the chromatogram obtained with the test solution is similar in position and size to the principal spot in the chromatogram obtained with reference solution (a).

## TESTS

### Solution S

Dissolve 1.0 g in *methanol R* and dilute to 20.0 ml with the same solvent.

### Appearance of solution

Solution S is clear (*2.2.1*) and not more intensely coloured than reference solution $Y_7$ (*2.2.2, Method II*).

### Optical rotation (*2.2.7*)

$-0.10°$ to $+0.10°$, determined on solution S.

### Related substances

Liquid chromatography (*2.2.29*).

*Test solution* Dissolve 0.10 g of the substance to be examined in a mixture of equal volumes of *methanol R* and *acetate buffer solution pH 5.0 R* and dilute to 50.0 ml with the same mixture of solvents.

*Reference solution (a)* Dissolve 5.0 mg of *aminoglutethimide impurity A CRS* in a mixture of equal volumes of *methanol R* and *acetate buffer solution pH 5.0 R* and dilute to 25.0 ml with the same mixture of solvents.

*Reference solution (b)* Dilute 1.0 ml of reference solution (a) to 10.0 ml with a mixture of equal volumes of *methanol R* and *acetate buffer solution pH 5.0 R*.

*Reference solution (c)* Dilute 1.0 ml of the test solution to 100.0 ml with a mixture of equal volumes of *methanol R* and *acetate buffer solution pH 5.0 R*.

*Reference solution (d)* Dilute 1.0 ml of the test solution to 10.0 ml with reference solution (a).

*Column:*
— *size: l* = 0.15 m, Ø = 3.9 mm;
— *stationary phase: octadecylsilyl silica gel for chromatography R* (4 μm);
— *temperature*: 40 °C.

*Mobile phase* Mix 27 volumes of *methanol R* and 73 volumes of *acetate buffer solution pH 5.0 R*.

*Flow rate* 1.3 ml/min.

*Detection* Spectrophotometer at 240 nm.

*Injection* 10 μl of the test solution and reference solutions (b), (c) and (d).

*Run time* 4 times the retention time of aminoglutethimide.

*Retention time* aminoglutethimide = about 9 min; impurity A = about 12 min.

*System suitability* Reference solution (d):
— *resolution*: minimum 2.0 between the peaks due to aminoglutethimide and impurity A.

*Limits:*
— *impurity A*: not more than twice the area of the principal peak in the chromatogram obtained with reference solution (b) (2 per cent);
— *sum of impurities other than A*: not more than the area of the principal peak in the chromatogram obtained with reference solution (c) (1 per cent);
— *total*: maximum 2.0 per cent for the sum of the contents of all impurities;
— *disregard limit*: 0.05 times the area of the principal peak in the chromatogram obtained with reference solution (c) (0.05 per cent).

### Impurity D

Liquid chromatography (*2.2.29*). *Carry out the test protected from light. Use shaking, not sonication or heat, to dissolve the reference substance and the substance to be examined.*

*Test solution* Dissolve 0.100 g of the substance to be examined in *dimethyl sulphoxide R* and dilute to 100.0 ml with the same solvent.

*Reference solution* Dissolve 3.0 mg of *aminoglutethimide impurity D CRS* in *dimethyl sulphoxide R* and dilute to 100.0 ml with the same solvent. Dilute 1.0 ml of this solution to 100.0 ml with *dimethyl sulphoxide R*.

*Column:*
— *size: l* = 0.12 m, Ø = 4 mm;
— *stationary phase: octadecylsilyl silica gel for chromatography R* (5 μm).

*Mobile phase* Dissolve 0.285 g of *sodium edetate R* in *water R*, add 7.5 ml of *dilute acetic acid R* and 50 ml of *0.1 M potassium hydroxide* and dilute to 1000 ml with *water R*; adjust to pH 5.0 with *glacial acetic acid R*; mix 350 ml of this solution with 650 ml of *methanol R*.

*Flow rate* 1.0 ml/min.

*Detection* Spectrophotometer at 328 nm.

*Injection* 10 μl.

*System suitability* Test solution:
— *number of theoretical plates*: minimum 3300, calculated for the principal peak;
— *mass distribution ratio*: 2.0 to 5.0 for the principal peak;
— *symmetry factor*: maximum 1.2 for the principal peak.

*Limit:*
— *impurity D*: not more than the area of the principal peak in the chromatogram obtained with the reference solution (300 ppm).

### Sulphates (*2.4.13*)

Maximum 500 ppm.

Dilute 6 ml of solution S to 15 ml with *distilled water R*.

### Heavy metals (*2.4.8*)

Maximum 10 ppm.

Dissolve 2.0 g in 15 ml of *acetone R* and dilute to 20 ml with *water R*. 12 ml of the solution complies with test B. Prepare the reference solution using lead standard solution (1 ppm Pb) obtained by diluting *lead standard solution (100 ppm Pb) R* with a mixture of 15 ml of *acetone R* and 5 ml of *water R*.

### Loss on drying (*2.2.32*)

Maximum 0.5 per cent, determined on 1.000 g by drying in an oven at 105 °C.

### Sulphated ash (*2.4.14*)

Maximum 0.1 per cent, determined on 1.0 g.

## ASSAY

Dissolve 0.180 g in 50 ml of *anhydrous acetic acid R* and titrate with *0.1 M perchloric acid*, determining the end-point potentiometrically (*2.2.20*).

1 ml of *0.1 M perchloric acid* is equivalent to 23.23 mg of $C_{13}H_{16}N_2O_2$.

## IMPURITIES

*Specified impurities* A, D.

*Other detectable impurities* (the following substances would, if present at a sufficient level, be detected by one or other of the tests in the monograph. They are limited by the general acceptance criterion for other/unspecified impurities and/or by the general monograph *Substances for pharmaceutical use (2034)*. It is therefore not necessary to identify these impurities for demonstration of compliance. See also *5.10. Control of impurities in substances for pharmaceutical use*)

B, C.

A. R3 = NH₂, R4 = H: (3RS)-3-(3-aminophenyl)-3-ethylpiperidine-2,6-dione (3-aminoglutethimide),

B. R3 = NO₂, R4 = H: (3RS)-3-ethyl-3-(3-nitrophenyl)piperidine-2,6-dione,

C. R3 = H, R4 = NO₂: (3RS)-3-ethyl-3-(4-nitrophenyl)piperidine-2,6-dione,

D. 3,3'-[diazenediylbis(4,1-phenylene)]bis(3-ethylpiperidine-2,6-dione) (azoglutethimide).

*Ph Eur*

# Aminophylline

*(Theophylline-ethylenediamine, Ph Eur monograph 0300)*

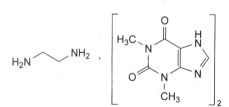

C₁₆H₂₄N₁₀O₄          420.4          *317-34-0*

## Action and use
Non-selective phosphodiesterase inhibitor; treatment of reversible airways obstruction.

## Preparations
Aminophylline Injection

Aminophylline Tablets

Prolonged-release Aminophylline Tablets

*Ph Eur*

## DEFINITION
Theophylline-ethylenediamine contains not less than 84.0 per cent and not more than the equivalent of 87.4 per cent of theophylline (C₇H₈N₄O₂; $M_r$ 180.2) and not less than 13.5 per cent and not more than the equivalent of 15.0 per cent of ethylenediamine (C₂H₈N₂; $M_r$ 60.1), both calculated with reference to the anhydrous substance.

## CHARACTERS
A white or slightly yellowish powder, sometimes granular, freely soluble in water (the solution becomes cloudy through absorption of carbon dioxide), practically insoluble in ethanol.

## IDENTIFICATION
*First identification   B, C, E.*

*Second identification   A, C, D, E, F.*

Dissolve 1.0 g in 10 ml of *water R* and add 2 ml of *dilute hydrochloric acid R* dropwise with shaking. Filter. Use the precipitate for identification tests A, B, D and F and the filtrate for identification test C.

A. The precipitate, washed with *water R* and dried at 100 °C to 105 °C, melts (*2.2.14*) at 270 °C to 274 °C.

B. Examine the precipitate, washed with *water R* and dried at 100 °C to 105 °C, by infrared absorption spectrophotometry (*2.2.24*), comparing with the spectrum obtained with *theophylline CRS*.

C. To the filtrate add 0.2 ml of *benzoyl chloride R*, make alkaline with *dilute sodium hydroxide solution R* and shake vigorously. Filter the precipitate, wash with 10 ml of *water R*, dissolve in 5 ml of hot *alcohol R* and add 5 ml of *water R*. A precipitate is formed, which when washed and dried at 100 °C to 105 °C, melts (*2.2.14*) at 248 °C to 252 °C.

D. Heat about 10 mg of the precipitate with 1.0 ml of a 360 g/l solution of *potassium hydroxide R* in a water-bath at 90 °C for 3 min, then add 1.0 ml of *diazotised sulphanilic acid solution R*. A red colour slowly develops. Carry out a blank test.

E. It complies with the test for water (see Tests).

F. The precipitate gives the reaction of xanthines (*2.3.1*).

## TESTS
### Appearance of solution
Dissolve 0.5 g with gentle warming in 10 ml of *carbon dioxide-free water R*. The solution is not more opalescent than reference suspension II (*2.2.1*) and not more intensely coloured than reference solution GY₆ (*2.2.2, Method II*).

### Related substances
Examine by thin-layer chromatography (*2.2.27*), using as the coating substance a suitable silica gel with a fluorescent indicator having an optimal intensity at 254 nm.

*Test solution*   Dissolve 0.2 g of the substance to be examined in 2 ml of *water R* with heating and dilute to 10 ml with *methanol R*.

*Reference solution*   Dilute 0.5 ml of the test solution to 100 ml with *methanol R*.

Apply to the plate 10 µl of each solution. Develop over a path of 15 cm using a mixture of 10 volumes of *concentrated ammonia R*, 30 volumes of *acetone R*, 30 volumes of *chloroform R* and 40 volumes of *butanol R*. Allow the plate to dry in air and examine in ultraviolet light at 254 nm. Any spot in the chromatogram obtained with the test solution, apart from the principal spot, is not more intense than the spot in the chromatogram obtained with the reference solution (0.5 per cent).

### Heavy metals (*2.4.8*)
1.0 g complies with limit test C for heavy metals (20 ppm). Prepare the standard using 2 ml of *lead standard solution (10 ppm Pb) R*.

### Water (*2.5.12*)
Not more than 1.5 per cent, determined on 2.00 g dissolved in 20 ml of *anhydrous pyridine R*, by the semi-micro determination of water.

### Sulphated ash (*2.4.14*)
Not more than 0.1 per cent, determined on 1.0 g.

## ASSAY

### Ethylenediamine

Dissolve 0.250 g in 30 ml of *water R*. Add 0.1 ml of *bromocresol green solution R*. Titrate with *0.1 M hydrochloric acid* until a green colour is obtained.

1 ml of *0.1 M hydrochloric acid* is equivalent to 3.005 mg of $C_2H_8N_2$.

### Theophylline

Heat 0.200 g to constant mass in an oven at 135 °C. Dissolve the residue with heating in 100 ml of *water R*, allow to cool, add 20 ml of *0.1 M silver nitrate* and shake. Add 1 ml of *bromothymol blue solution R1*. Titrate with *0.1 M sodium hydroxide*.

1 ml of *0.1 M sodium hydroxide* is equivalent to 18.02 mg of $C_7H_8N_4O_2$.

## STORAGE

Store in airtight container, protected from light.

*———————————— Ph Eur*

# Aminophylline Hydrate

(*Theophylline-ethylenediamine Hydrate,*
*Ph Eur monograph 0301*)

5877-66-5

## Action and use

Non-selective phosphodiesterase inhibitor; treatment of reversible airways obstruction.

## Preparation

Aminophylline Injection

*Ph Eur* ————————————————————————

## DEFINITION

Theophylline-ethylenediamine hydrate contains not less than 84.0 per cent and not more than the equivalent of 87.4 per cent of theophylline ($C_7H_8N_4O_2$; $M_r$ 180.2) and not less than 13.5 per cent and not more than the equivalent of 15.0 per cent of ethylenediamine ($C_2H_8N_2$; $M_r$ 60.1), both calculated with reference to the anhydrous substance.

## CHARACTERS

A white or slightly yellowish powder, sometimes granular, freely soluble in water (the solution becomes cloudy through absorption of carbon dioxide), practically insoluble in ethanol.

## IDENTIFICATION

*First identification* B, C, E.

*Second identification* A, C, D, E, F.

Dissolve 1.0 g in 10 ml of *water R* and add 2 ml of *dilute hydrochloric acid R* dropwise with shaking. Filter. Use the precipitate for identification tests A, B, D and F and the filtrate for identification test C.

A. The precipitate, washed with *water R* and dried at 100 °C to 105 °C, melts (*2.2.14*) at 270 °C to 274 °C.

B. Examine the precipitate, washed with *water R* and dried at 100 °C to 105 °C, by infrared absorption spectrophotometry (*2.2.24*), comparing with the spectrum obtained with *theophylline CRS* .

C. To the filtrate add 0.2 ml of *benzoyl chloride R*, make alkaline with *dilute sodium hydroxide solution R* and shake vigorously. Filter the precipitate, wash with 10 ml of *water R*, dissolve in 5 ml of hot *alcohol R* and add 5 ml of *water R*.

A precipitate is formed, which when washed and dried at 100 °C to 105 °C, melts (*2.2.14*) at 248 °C to 252 °C.

D. Heat about 10 mg of the precipitate with 1.0 ml of a 360 g/l solution of *potassium hydroxide R* in a water-bath at 90 °C for 3 min, then add 1.0 ml of *diazotised sulphanilic acid solution R*. A red colour slowly develops. Carry out a blank test.

E. It contains 3.0 per cent to 8.0 per cent of water (see Tests).

F. The precipitate gives the reaction of xanthines (*2.3.1*).

## TESTS

### Appearance of solution

Dissolve 0.5 g with gentle warming in 10 ml of *carbon dioxide-free water R*. The solution is not more opalescent than reference suspension II (*2.2.1*) and not more intensely coloured than reference solution $GY_6$ (*2.2.2, Method II*).

### Related substances

Examine by thin-layer chromatography (*2.2.27*), using as the coating substance a suitable silica gel with a fluorescent indicator having an optimal intensity at 254 nm.

*Test solution* Dissolve 0.2 g of the substance to be examined in 2 ml of *water R* with heating and dilute to 10 ml with *methanol R*.

*Reference solution* Dilute 0.5 ml of the test solution to 100 ml with *methanol R*.

Apply separately to the plate 10 μl of each solution. Develop over a path of 15 cm using a mixture of 10 volumes of *concentrated ammonia R*, 30 volumes of *acetone R*, 30 volumes of *chloroform R* and 40 volumes of *butanol R*. Allow the plate to dry in air and examine in ultraviolet light at 254 nm. Any spot in the chromatogram obtained with the test solution, apart from the principal spot, is not more intense than the spot in the chromatogram obtained with the reference solution (0.5 per cent).

### Heavy metals (*2.4.8*)

1.0 g complies with limit test C for heavy metals (20 ppm). Prepare the standard using 2 ml of *lead standard solution (10 ppm Pb) R*.

### Water (*2.5.12*)

3.0 per cent to 8.0 per cent, determined on 0.50 g dissolved in 20 ml of *pyridine R*, by the semi-micro determination of water.

### Sulphated ash (*2.4.14*)

Not more than 0.1 per cent, determined on 1.0 g.

## ASSAY

### Ethylenediamine

Dissolve 0.250 g in 30 ml of *water R*. Add 0.1 ml of *bromocresol green solution R*. Titrate with *0.1 M hydrochloric acid* until a green colour is obtained.

1 ml of *0.1 M hydrochloric acid* is equivalent to 3.005 mg of $C_2H_8N_2$.

### Theophylline

Heat 0.200 g to constant mass in an oven at 135 °C. Dissolve the residue with heating in 100 ml of *water R*, allow to cool, add 20 ml of *0.1 M silver nitrate* and shake. Add 1 ml of *bromothymol blue solution R1*. Titrate with *0.1 M sodium hydroxide*.

1 ml of *0.1 M sodium hydroxide* is equivalent to 18.02 mg of $C_7H_8N_4O_2$.

## STORAGE

Store in a well-filled airtight container, protected from light.

*———————————— Ph Eur*

# Amiodarone Hydrochloride

(*Ph Eur monograph 0803*)

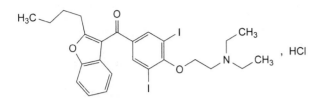

C₂₅H₂₉I₂NO₃,HCl        682        *19774-82-4*

**Action and use**

Potassium channel blocker; class III antiarrhythmic.

**Preparations**

Amiodarone Intravenous Infusion

Amiodarone Tablets

*Ph Eur* _____

## DEFINITION

(2-Butylbenzofuran-3-yl)[4-[2-(diethylamino)ethoxy]-3,5-diiodophenyl]methanone hydrochloride.

**Content**

98.5 per cent to 101.0 per cent (dried substance).

## CHARACTERS

**Appearance**

White or almost white, fine, crystalline powder.

**Solubility**

Very slightly soluble in water, freely soluble in methylene chloride, soluble in methanol, sparingly soluble in ethanol (96 per cent).

## IDENTIFICATION

A. Infrared absorption spectrophotometry (*2.2.24*).

*Comparison*    amiodarone hydrochloride CRS.

B. It gives reaction (b) of chlorides (*2.3.1*).

## TESTS

**Appearance of solution**

The solution is clear (*2.2.1*) and not more intensely coloured than reference solution GY₅ or BY₅ (*2.2.2, Method II*).

Dissolve 1.0 g in *methanol R* and dilute to 20 ml with the same solvent.

**pH** (*2.2.3*)

3.2 to 3.8.

Dissolve 1.0 g in *carbon dioxide-free water R*, heating at 80 °C, cool and dilute to 20 ml with the same solvent.

**Impurity H**

Thin-layer chromatography (*2.2.27*). *Prepare the solutions immediately before use and keep protected from bright light.*

*Test solution*    Dissolve 0.500 g of the substance to be examined in *methylene chloride R* and dilute to 5.0 ml with the same solvent.

*Reference solution (a)*    Dissolve 10.0 mg of (2-chloroethyl)diethylamine hydrochloride R (impurity H) in *methylene chloride R* and dilute to 50.0 ml with the same solvent. Dilute 2.0 ml of this solution to 20.0 ml with *methylene chloride R*.

*Reference solution (b)*    Mix 2.0 ml of the test solution and 2.0 ml of reference solution (a).

*Plate*    *TLC silica gel F₂₅₄ plate R*.

*Mobile phase*    anhydrous formic acid R, methanol R, methylene chloride R (5:10:85 *V/V/V*).

*Application*    50 µl of the test solution and reference solution (a); 100 µl of reference solution (b).

*Development*    Over 2/3 of the plate.

*Drying*    In a current of cold air.

*Detection*    Spray with *potassium iodobismuthate solution R1* and then with *dilute hydrogen peroxide solution R*; examine immediately in daylight.

*System suitability*    Reference solution (b):

— the spot due to impurity H is clearly visible.

*Limit:*

— *impurity H*: any spot with the same $R_F$ as the spot due to impurity H in the chromatogram obtained with reference solution (b), is not more intense than the spot in the chromatogram obtained with reference solution (a) (0.02 per cent).

**Related substances**

Liquid chromatography (*2.2.29*).

*Buffer solution pH 4.9*    To 800 ml of *water R* add 3.0 ml of *glacial acetic acid R*, adjust to pH 4.9 with *dilute ammonia R1* and dilute to 1000 ml with *water R*.

*Test solution*    Dissolve 0.125 g of the substance to be examined in a mixture of equal volumes of *acetonitrile R* and *water R* and dilute to 25.0 ml with the same mixture of solvents.

*Reference solution*    Dissolve 5 mg of *amiodarone impurity D CRS*, 5 mg of *amiodarone impurity E CRS* and 5.0 mg of *amiodarone hydrochloride CRS* in *methanol R* and dilute to 25.0 ml with the same solvent. Dilute 1.0 ml of this solution to 20.0 ml with a mixture of equal volumes of *acetonitrile R* and *water R*.

*Column:*

— *size:* l = 0.15 m, Ø = 4.6 mm;

— *stationary phase:* octadecylsilyl silica gel for chromatography R (5 µm);

— *temperature:* 30 °C.

*Mobile phase*    Buffer solution pH 4.9, *methanol R*, *acetonitrile R* (30:30:40 *V/V/V*).

*Flow rate*    1 ml/min.

*Detection*    Spectrophotometer at 240 nm.

*Injection*    10 µl.

*Run time*    Twice the retention time of amiodarone.

*Relative retention*    With reference to amiodarone (retention time = about 24 min): impurity A = about 0.26; impurity D = about 0.29; impurity E = about 0.37; impurity B = about 0.49; impurity C = about 0.55; impurity G = about 0.62; impurity F = about 0.69.

*System suitability*    Reference solution:

— *resolution:* minimum 3.5 between the peaks due to impurities D and E.

*Limits:*

— *impurities A, B, C, D, E, F, G:* for each impurity, not more than the area of the peak due to amiodarone in the chromatogram obtained with the reference solution (0.2 per cent);

— *unspecified impurities:* for each impurity, not more than 0.5 times the area of the peak due to amiodarone in the chromatogram obtained with the reference solution (0.10 per cent);

— *total:* not more than 2.5 times the area of the peak due to amiodarone in the chromatogram obtained with the reference solution (0.5 per cent);

— *disregard limit*: 0.25 times the area of the peak due to amiodarone in the chromatogram obtained with the reference solution (0.05 per cent).

## Iodides
Maximum 150 ppm.

*Prepare the test and reference solutions simultaneously.*

*Solution A* Add 1.50 g of the substance to be examined to 40 ml of *water R* at 80 °C and shake until completely dissolved. Cool and dilute to 50.0 ml with *water R*.

*Test solution* To 15.0 ml of solution A add 1.0 ml of *0.1 M hydrochloric acid* and 1.0 ml of *0.05 M potassium iodate*. Dilute to 20.0 ml with *water R*. Allow to stand protected from light for 4 h.

*Reference solution* To 15.0 ml of solution A add 1.0 ml of *0.1 M hydrochloric acid*, 1.0 ml of an 88.2 mg/l solution of *potassium iodide R* and 1.0 ml of *0.05 M potassium iodate*. Dilute to 20.0 ml with *water R*. Allow to stand protected from light for 4 h.

Measure the absorbances (*2.2.25*) of the solutions at 420 nm, using a mixture of 15.0 ml of solution A and 1.0 ml of *0.1 M hydrochloric acid* diluted to 20.0 ml with *water R* as the compensation liquid. The absorbance of the test solution is not greater than half the absorbance of the reference solution.

## Heavy metals (*2.4.8*)
Maximum 20 ppm.

1.0 g complies with test C. Prepare the reference solution using 2 ml of *lead standard solution (10 ppm Pb) R*.

## Loss on drying (*2.2.32*)
Maximum 0.5 per cent, determined on 1.000 g by drying at 50 °C at a pressure not exceeding 0.3 kPa for 4 h.

## Sulphated ash (*2.4.14*)
Maximum 0.1 per cent, determined on 1.0 g.

## ASSAY
Dissolve 0.600 g in a mixture of 5.0 ml of *0.01 M hydrochloric acid* and 75 ml of *ethanol (96 per cent) R*. Carry out a potentiometric titration (*2.2.20*), using *0.1 M sodium hydroxide*. Read the volume added between the 2 points of inflexion.

1 ml of *0.1 M sodium hydroxide* is equivalent to 68.18 mg of $C_{25}H_{30}ClI_2NO_3$.

## STORAGE
Protected from light, at a temperature not exceeding 30 °C.

## IMPURITIES
*Specified impurities A, B, C, D, E, F, G, H.*

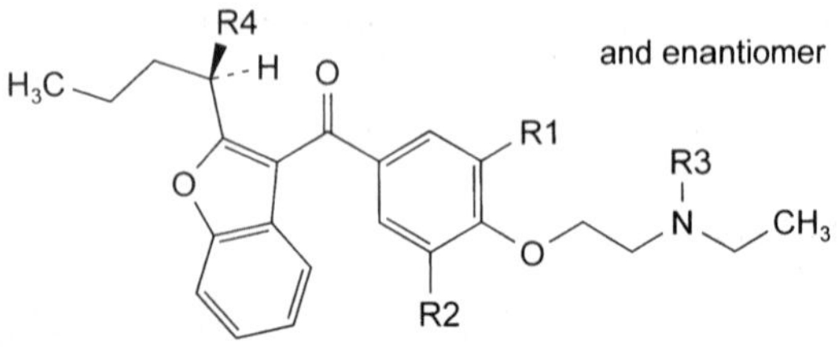

A. R1 = R2 = R4 = H, R3 = $C_2H_5$: (2-butylbenzofuran-3-yl)[4-[2-(diethylamino)ethoxy]phenyl]methanone,

B. R1 = R2 = I, R3 = R4 = H: (2-butylbenzofuran-3-yl)[4-[2-(ethylamino)ethoxy]-3,5-diiodophenyl]methanone,

C. R1 = I, R2 = R4 = H, R3 = $C_2H_5$: (2-butylbenzofuran-3-yl)[4-[2-(diethylamino)ethoxy]-3-iodophenyl]methanone,

G. R1 = R2 = I, R3 = $C_2H_5$, R4 = $OCH_3$: [4-[2-(diethylamino)ethoxy]-3,5-diiodophenyl][2-[(1*RS*)-1-methoxybutyl]benzofuran-3-yl]methanone,

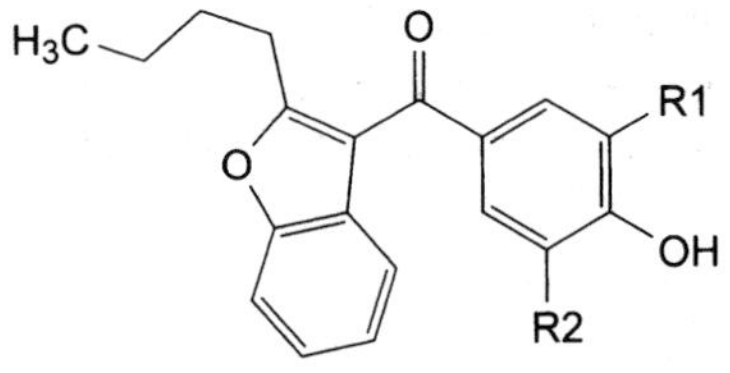

D. R1 = R2 = I: (2-butylbenzofuran-3-yl)(4-hydroxy-3,5-diiodophenyl)methanone,

E. R1 = R2 = H: (2-butylbenzofuran-3-yl)(4-hydroxyphenyl)methanone,

F. R1 = I, R2 = H: (2-butylbenzofuran-3-yl)(4-hydroxy-3-iodophenyl)methanone,

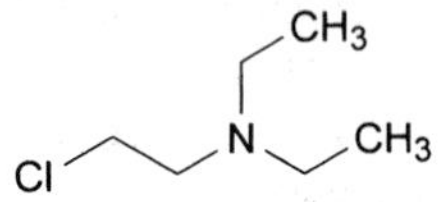

H. 2-chloro-*N,N*-diethylethanamine (2-chlorotriethylamine, (2-chloroethyl)diethylamine).

*_____ Ph Eur*

# Amisulpride

(*Ph Eur monograph 1490*)

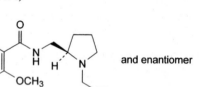

$C_{17}H_{27}N_3O_4S$       369.5       71675-85-9

## Action and use
Dopamine receptor antagonist; neuroleptic.

*Ph Eur _____*

## DEFINITION
4-Amino-*N*-[[(2*RS*)-1-ethylpyrrolidin-2-yl]methyl]-5-(ethylsulphonyl)-2-methoxybenzamide.

## Content
99.0 per cent to 101.0 per cent (dried substance).

## CHARACTERS
### Appearance
White or almost white, crystalline powder.

### Solubility
Practically insoluble in water, freely soluble in methylene chloride, sparingly soluble in anhydrous ethanol.

### mp
About 126 °C.

## IDENTIFICATION
Infrared absorption spectrophotometry (*2.2.24*).

*Comparison amisulpride CRS .*

## TESTS

### Appearance of solution

The solution is not more opalescent than reference suspension II (*2.2.1*) and not more intensely coloured than reference solution $Y_6$ (*2.2.2, Method II*).

Dissolve 1.0 g in 3 ml of a mixture of 1 volume of *acetic acid R* and 4 volumes of *water R* and dilute to 20 ml with *water R*.

### Optical rotation (*2.2.7*)

$- 0.10°$ to $+ 0.10°$.

Dissolve 5.0 g in *dimethylformamide R* and dilute to 50.0 ml with the same solvent.

### Impurity A

Thin-layer chromatography (*2.2.27*).

*Test solution*   Dissolve 0.20 g in *methanol R* and dilute to 10 ml with the same solvent.

*Reference solution (a)*   Dissolve 5 mg of *sulpiride impurity A CRS* (amisulpride impurity A) in *methanol R* and dilute to 25 ml with the same solvent. Dilute 2 ml of the solution to 20 ml with *methanol R*.

*Reference solution (b)*   Dilute 1 ml of the test solution to 10 ml with reference solution (a).

*Plate*   TLC *silica gel G plate R*.

*Mobile phase*   The upper layer obtained after shaking a mixture of a 50 per cent *V/V* solution of *concentrated ammonia R*, *anhydrous ethanol R* and *di-isopropyl ether R* (10:25:65 *V/V/V*).

*Application*   10 μl.

*Development*   Over a path of 12 cm.

*Drying*   In air.

*Detection*   Spray with *ninhydrin solution R* and heat at 100-105 °C for 15 min.

*System suitability*   The chromatogram obtained with reference solution (b) shows 2 clearly separated spots.

*Limit:*

— *impurity A*: any spot corresponding to impurity A is not more intense than the spot in the chromatogram obtained with reference solution (a) (0.1 per cent).

### Related substances

Examine by liquid chromatography (*2.2.29*).

*Test solution*   Dissolve 0.10 g in 30 ml of *methanol R* and dilute to 100.0 ml with mobile phase B.

*Reference solution (a)*   Dilute 5.0 ml of the test solution to 100.0 ml with a mixture of 30 volumes of mobile phase A and 70 volumes of mobile phase B. Dilute 1.0 ml of the solution to 25.0 ml with a mixture of 30 volumes of mobile phase A and 70 volumes of mobile phase B.

*Reference solution (b)*   Dissolve 5 mg of *amisulpride impurity B CRS* in 5 ml of the test solution and dilute to 50 ml with a mixture of 30 volumes of mobile phase A and 70 volumes of mobile phase B. Dilute 1 ml of the solution to 10 ml with a mixture of 30 volumes of mobile phase A and 70 volumes of mobile phase B.

*Column:*

— *size: l* = 0.25 m, Ø = 4.6 mm,

— *stationary phase: octylsilyl silica gel for chromatography R* (5 μm) with a carbon loading of 16 per cent, a specific surface area of 330 m2/g and a pore size of 7.5 nm.

*Mobile phase:*

— *mobile phase A: methanol R*,

— *mobile phase B*: 0.7 g/l solution of *sodium octanesulphonate R* in a 0.25 per cent *V/V* solution of *dilute sulphuric acid R*,

| Time (min) | Mobile phase A (per cent *V/V*) | Mobile phase B (per cent *V/V*) |
|---|---|---|
| 0 - 18 | 30 → 36 | 70 → 64 |
| 18 - 35 | 36 → 52 | 64 → 48 |
| 35 - 45 | 52 | 48 |
| 45 - 46 | 52 → 30 | 48 → 70 |
| 46 - 56 | 30 | 70 |

*Flow rate*   1.5 ml/min.

*Detection*   Spectrophotometer at 225 nm.

*Injection*   10 μl.

*System suitability*   Reference solution (b):

— *resolution*: minimum 2.0 between the peaks due to amisulpride and impurity B.

*Limits:*

— *any impurity*: not more than 0.5 times the area of the principal peak in the chromatogram obtained with reference solution (a) (0.1 per cent),

— *total*: not more than 1.5 times the area of the principal peak in the chromatogram obtained with reference solution (a) (0.3 per cent),

— *disregard limit*: 0.1 times the area of the principal peak in the chromatogram obtained with reference solution (a) (0.02 per cent).

### Chlorides (*2.4.4*)

Maximum 200 ppm.

Shake 0.5 g with 30 ml of *water R* for 10 min. Filter. 15 ml of the filtrate complies with the test.

### Heavy metals (*2.4.8*)

Maximum 10 ppm.

Dissolve 4.0 g by gently heating in 5 ml of *dilute acetic acid R*. Allow to cool and dilute to 20 ml with *water R*. 12 ml of the solution complies with test A. Prepare the reference solution using *lead standard solution (2 ppm Pb) R*.

### Loss on drying (*2.2.32*)

Maximum 0.5 per cent, determined on 1.000 g by drying in an oven at 105 °C for 3 h.

### Sulphated ash (*2.4.14*)

Maximum 0.1 per cent, determined on 1.0 g.

## ASSAY

Dissolve 0.300 g with shaking in a mixture of 5 ml of *acetic anhydride R* and 50 ml of *anhydrous acetic acid R*. Titrate with *0.1 M perchloric acid*, determining the end-point potentiometrically (*2.2.20*).

1 ml of *0.1 M perchloric acid* is equivalent to 36.95 mg of $C_{17}H_{27}N_3O_4S$.

## IMPURITIES

and enantiomer

A. [(2*RS*)-1-ethylpyrrolidin-2-yl]methanamine,

B. R1 = OH, R2 = SO$_2$-CH$_2$-CH$_3$:
4-amino-N-[[(2RS)-1-ethylpyrrolidin-2-yl]methyl]-5-(ethylsulphonyl)-2-hydroxybenzamide,

C. R1 = OCH$_3$, R2 = I: 4-amino-N-[[(2RS)-1-ethylpyrrolidin-2-yl]methyl]-5-iodo-2-methoxybenzamide,

D. R1 = OCH$_3$, R2 = SO$_2$-CH$_3$:
4-amino-N-[[(2RS)-1-ethylpyrrolidin-2-yl]methyl]-2-methoxy-5-(methylsulphonyl)benzamide,

E. 4-amino-5-(ethylsulphonyl)-2-methoxybenzoic acid.

*Ph Eur*

# Amitriptyline Embonate

$(C_{20}H_{23}N)_2, C_{23}H_{16}O_6$     943.2     *17086-03-2*

## Action and use
Monoamine reuptake inhibitor; tricyclic antidepressant.

## DEFINITION
Amitriptyline Embonate is 3-(10,11-dihydro-5H-dibenzo[a,d]cyclohept-5-ylidene)propyldimethylamine 4,4'-methylenebis(3-hydroxy-2-naphthoate). It contains not less than 98.5% and not more than 101.0% of $(C_{20}H_{23}N)_2, C_{23}H_{16}O_6$, calculated with reference to the anhydrous substance.

## CHARACTERISTICS
A pale yellow to brownish yellow powder.

Practically insoluble in *water*; slightly soluble in *ethanol (96%)*.

## IDENTIFICATION
A. Dissolve 40 mg in 100 ml of *methanol*. To 1 ml of the solution add 1 ml of a 2.5% w/v solution of *sodium hydrogen carbonate*, 1 ml of a 2.0% w/v solution of *sodium periodate* and 1 ml of a 0.3% w/v solution of *potassium permanganate*, shake and allow to stand for 15 minutes. Acidify with 1M *sulphuric acid*, extract with 10 ml of *2,2,4-trimethylpentane* and filter. The *light absorption* of the filtrate, Appendix II B, in the range 230 to 350 nm exhibits a maximum only at 265 nm.

B. Dissolve 0.2 g in 10 ml of *dichloromethane*, add 5 ml of 1.25M *sodium hydroxide* and shake. The aqueous layer exhibits a green fluorescence when examined under *ultraviolet light (365 nm)*.

## TESTS
### Chloride
Not more than 0.2% when determined by the following method. Dissolve 1 g in a mixture of 50 ml of *acetone* and 50 ml of *water*, add 2 ml of *nitric acid* and 75 ml of *acetate buffer pH 5.0* and titrate with 0.01M *silver nitrate VS* determining the end point potentiometrically. Each ml of 0.01M *silver nitrate VS* is equivalent to 0.3545 mg of Cl.

### Related substances
Carry out the method for *thin-layer chromatography*, Appendix III A, protected from light, using *silica gel G* as the coating substance and a mixture of 3 volumes of *diethylamine*, 15 volumes of *ethyl acetate* and 85 volumes of *cyclohexane* as the mobile phase but allowing the solvent front to ascend 14 cm above the line of application in an unlined tank. Apply separately to the plate 10 µl of each of three solutions in *chloroform* containing (1) 3.3% w/v of the substance being examined, (2) 0.0010% w/v of *dibenzosuberone BPCRS* and (3) 0.0040% w/v of *cyclobenzaprine hydrochloride EPCRS*. After removal of the plate, allow it to dry in air, spray with a freshly prepared mixture of 4 volumes of *formaldehyde* and 96 volumes of *sulphuric acid*, heat at 100° to 105° for 10 minutes and examine under *ultraviolet light (365 nm)*. Any spot corresponding to dibenzosuberone in the chromatogram obtained with solution (1) is not more intense than the spot in the chromatogram obtained with solution (2) (0.05%, with reference to amitriptyline). Examine the plate under *ultraviolet light (254 nm)*. Any other *secondary spot* in the chromatogram obtained with solution (1) is not more intense than the spot in the chromatogram obtained with solution (3) (0.2%, with reference to amitriptyline).

### Sulphated ash
Not more than 0.2%, Appendix IX A.

### Water
Not more than 5.0% w/w, Appendix IX C. Use 0.5 g.

## ASSAY
Dissolve 0.6 g in 50 ml of *acetic anhydride* and carry out Method I for *non-aqueous titration*, Appendix VIII A, using *1-naphtholbenzein solution* as indicator. Each ml of 0.1M *perchloric acid VS* is equivalent to 47.16 mg of $(C_{20}H_{23}N)_2, C_{23}H_{16}O_6$.

## STORAGE
Amitriptyline Embonate should be protected from light.

## IMPURITIES

A. dibenzosuberone

B. cyclobenzaprine.

# Amitriptyline Hydrochloride

(*Ph Eur monograph 0464*)

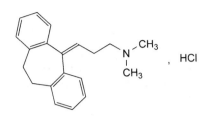

C₂₀H₂₃N,HCl       313.9       *549-18-8*

$C_{20}H_{23}N,HCl$     313.9     *549-18-8*

## Action and use
Monoamine reuptake inhibitor; tricyclic antidepressant.

## Preparation
Amitriptyline Tablets

*Ph Eur*

## DEFINITION
3-(10,11-Dihydro-5*H*-dibenzo[*a,d*][7]annulen-5-ylidene)-*N,N*-dimethylpropan-1-amine hydrochloride.

## Content
99.0 per cent to 101.0 per cent (dried substance).

## CHARACTERS
### Appearance
White or almost white powder or colourless crystals.

### Solubility
Freely soluble in water, in ethanol (96 per cent) and in methylene chloride.

## IDENTIFICATION
A. Infrared absorption spectrophotometry (*2.2.24*).

*Comparison*   amitriptyline hydrochloride CRS.

B. 20 mg gives reaction (a) of chlorides (*2.3.1*).

## TESTS
### Appearance of solution
The solution is clear (*2.2.1*) and not more intensely coloured than reference solution B₇ (*2.2.2, Method II*).

Dissolve 1.25 g in *water R* and dilute to 25 ml with the same solvent.

### Acidity or alkalinity
Dissolve 0.20 g in *carbon dioxide-free water R* and dilute to 10 ml with the same solvent. Add 0.1 ml of *methyl red solution R* and 0.2 ml of *0.01 M sodium hydroxide*. The solution is yellow. Add 0.4 ml of *0.01 M hydrochloric acid*. The solution is red.

### Related substances
Liquid chromatography (*2.2.29*).

*Test solution*   Dissolve 50.0 mg of the substance to be examined in the mobile phase and dilute to 50.0 ml with the mobile phase.

*Reference solution (a)*   Dissolve 5.0 mg of *dibenzosuberone CRS* (impurity A) and 5.0 mg of *cyclobenzaprine hydrochloride CRS* (impurity B) in 5.0 ml of the test solution and dilute to 100.0 ml with the mobile phase.

*Reference solution (b)*   Dilute 1.0 ml of reference solution (a) to 50.0 ml with the mobile phase.

*Column:*
— *size: l* = 0.15 m, Ø = 4.6 mm;

— *stationary phase*: end-capped polar-embedded octadecylsilyl amorphous organosilica polymer *R* (5 µm);
— *temperature*: 40 °C.

*Mobile phase*   Mix 35 volumes of *acetonitrile R* and 65 volumes of a 5.23 g/l solution of *dipotassium hydrogen phosphate R* previously adjusted to pH 7.0 with *phosphoric acid R*.

*Flow rate*   1.2 ml/min.

*Detection*   Spectrophotometer at 220 nm.

*Injection*   10 µl.

*Run time*   3 times the retention time of amitriptyline.

*Relative retention*   With reference to amitriptyline (retention time = about 14 min): impurity B = about 0.9; impurity A = about 2.2.

*System suitability*   Reference solution (a):
— *resolution*: minimum 2.0 between the peaks due to impurity B and amitriptyline.

*Limits:*
— *impurity B*: not more than the area of the corresponding peak in the chromatogram obtained with reference solution (b) (0.1 per cent);
— *impurity A*: not more than 0.5 times the area of the corresponding peak in the chromatogram obtained with reference solution (b) (0.05 per cent);
— *unspecified impurities*: for each impurity, not more than the area of the peak due to amitriptyline in the chromatogram obtained with reference solution (b) (0.10 per cent);
— *total*: not more than 3 times the area of the peak due to amitriptyline in the chromatogram obtained with reference solution (b) (0.3 per cent);
— *disregard limit*: 0.5 times the area of the peak due to amitriptyline in the chromatogram obtained with reference solution (b) (0.05 per cent).

### Heavy metals (*2.4.8*)
Maximum 20 ppm.

1.0 g complies with test F. Prepare the reference solution using 2 ml of *lead standard solution (10 ppm Pb) R*.

### Loss on drying (*2.2.32*)
Maximum 0.5 per cent, determined on 1.000 g by drying in an oven at 105 °C for 2 h.

### Sulphated ash (*2.4.14*)
Maximum 0.1 per cent, determined on 1.0 g.

## ASSAY
Dissolve 0.250 g in 30 ml of *ethanol (96 per cent) R*. Titrate with *0.1 M sodium hydroxide*, determining the end-point potentiometrically (*2.2.20*).

1 ml of *0.1 M sodium hydroxide* is equivalent to 31.39 mg of $C_{20}H_{24}ClN$.

## STORAGE
Protected from light.

## IMPURITIES

*Specified impurities  A, B.*

*Other detectable impurities*  (The following substances would, if present at a sufficient level, be detected by one or other of the tests in the monograph. They are limited by the general acceptance criterion for other/unspecified impurities and/or by the general monograph *Substances for pharmaceutical use (2034)*. It is therefore not necessary to identify these impurities for demonstration of compliance. See also *5.10. Control of impurities in substances for pharmaceutical use): C, D, E, F, G.*

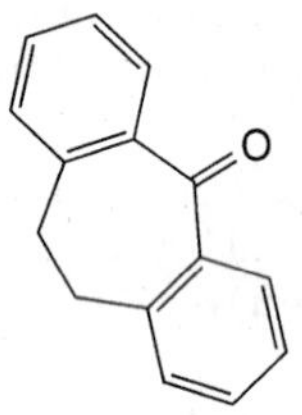

A. 10,11-dihydro-5*H*-dibenzo[*a,d*][7]annulen-5-one (dibenzosuberone),

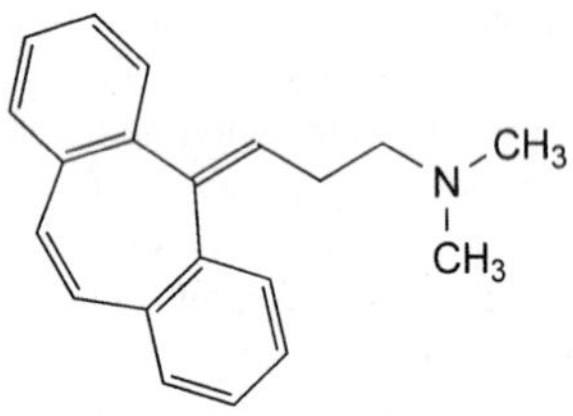

B. 3-(5*H*-dibenzo[*a,d*][7]annulen-5-ylidene)-*N,N*-dimethylpropan-1-amine (cyclobenzaprine),

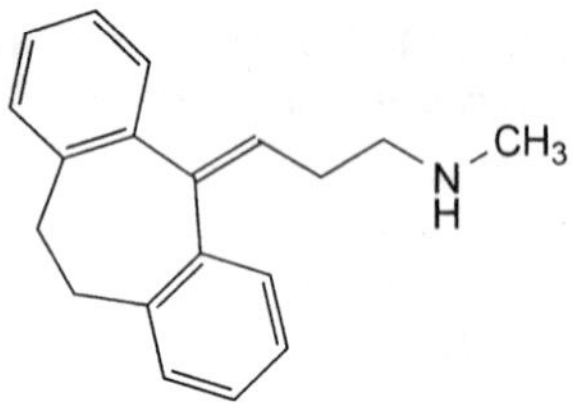

C. 3-(10,11-dihydro-5*H*-dibenzo[*a,d*][7]annulen-5-ylidene)-*N*-methylpropan-1-amine (nortriptyline),

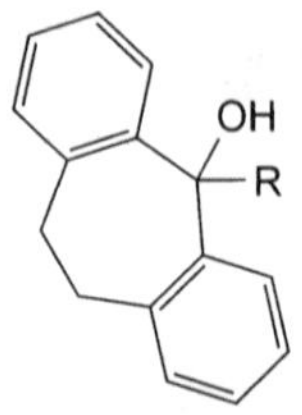

D. R = CH$_2$-CH$_2$-CH$_2$-N(CH$_3$)$_2$:
5-[3-(dimethylamino)propyl]-10,11-dihydro-5*H*-dibenzo[*a,d*][7]annulen-5-ol,

G. R = H: 10,11-dihydro-5*H*-dibenzo[*a,d*][7]annulen-5-ol (dibenzosuberol),

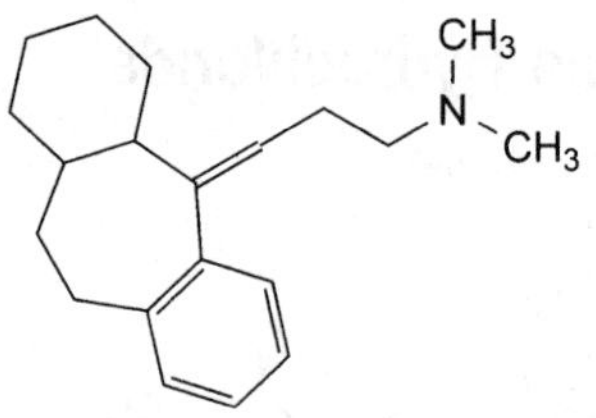

E. *N,N*-dimethyl-3-(1,2,3,4,4a,10,11,11a-octahydro-5*H*-dibenzo[*a,d*][7]annulen-5-ylidene)propan-1-amine,

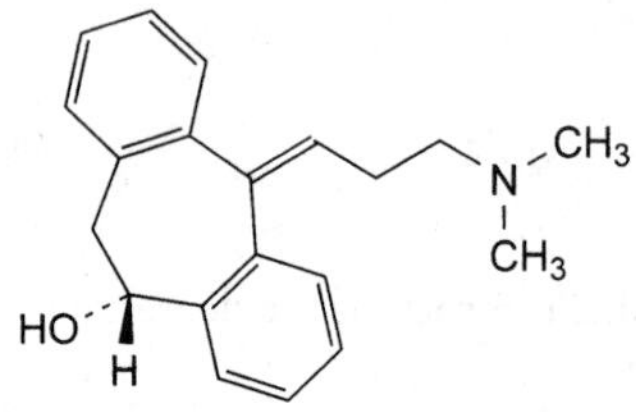

its (*E*)-isomer and their enantiomers

F. (5*EZ*,10*RS*)-5-[3-(dimethylamino)propylidene]-10,11-dihydro-5*H*-dibenzo[*a,d*][7]annulen-10-ol.

*Ph Eur*

---

# Amlodipine Besilate

(*Ph Eur monograph 1491*)

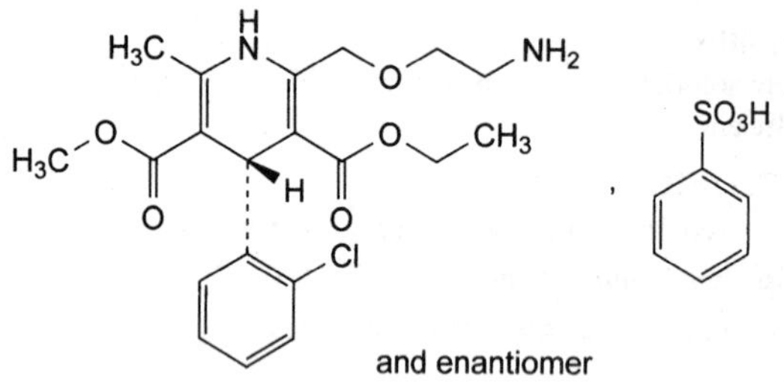

C$_{20}$H$_{25}$ClN$_2$O$_5$,C$_6$H$_6$O$_3$S    567.1        *111470-99-6*

## Action and use
Calcium channel blocker.

*Ph Eur*

## DEFINITION
3-Ethyl 5-methyl (4*RS*)-2-[(2-aminoethoxy)methyl]-4-(2-chlorophenyl)-6-methyl-1,4-dihydropyridine-3,5-dicarboxylate benzenesulphonate.

## Content
97.0 per cent to 102.0 per cent (anhydrous substance).

## CHARACTERS
### Appearance
White or almost white powder.

### Solubility
Slightly soluble in water, freely soluble in methanol, sparingly soluble in anhydrous ethanol, slightly soluble in 2-propanol.

## IDENTIFICATION
Infrared absorption spectrophotometry (*2.2.24*).

*Comparison  amlodipine besilate CRS.*

## TESTS
### Optical rotation (*2.2.7*)
− 0.10° to + 0.10°.

Dissolve 0.250 g in *methanol R* and dilute to 25.0 ml with the same solvent.

**Related substances**

Liquid chromatography (*2.2.29*). *Carry out the test protected from light.*

*Test solution (a)* Dissolve 50.0 mg of the substance to be examined in *methanol R* and dilute to 50.0 ml with the same solvent.

*Test solution (b)* Dilute 5.0 ml of test solution (a) to 100.0 ml with *methanol R*.

*Reference solution (a)* Dilute 1.0 ml of test solution (a) to 10.0 ml with *methanol R*. Dilute 1.0 ml of this solution to 100.0 ml with *methanol R*.

*Reference solution (b)* Dissolve 5 mg of *amlodipine impurity B CRS* and 5 mg of *amlodipine impurity G CRS* in *methanol R* and dilute to 50.0 ml with the same solvent. Dilute 1.0 ml of this solution to 10.0 ml with *methanol R*.

*Reference solution (c)* Dissolve 5 mg of *amlodipine for peak identification CRS* (containing impurities D, E and F) in 10 ml of *methanol R*.

*Reference solution (d)* Dissolve 5.0 mg of *amlodipine impurity A CRS* in *methanol R* and dilute to 5.0 ml with the same solvent. Dilute 1.0 ml of the solution to 100.0 ml with *methanol R*. Dilute 1.0 ml of this solution to 10.0 ml with *methanol R*.

*Reference solution (e)* Dissolve 50.0 mg of *amlodipine besilate CRS* in *methanol R* and dilute to 50.0 ml with the same solvent. Dilute 5.0 ml of this solution to 100.0 ml with *methanol R*.

*Column:*
— *size*: $l$ = 0.25 m, Ø = 4.0 mm;
— *stationary phase*: octadecylsilyl silica gel for chromatography R (5 µm);
— *temperature*: 30 °C.

*Mobile phase* 2.3 g/l solution of *ammonium acetate R*, *methanol R* (30:70 *V/V*).

*Flow rate* 1.5 ml/min.

*Detection* Spectrophotometer at 237 nm.

*Injection* 20 µl of test solution (a) and reference solutions (a), (b), (c) and (d).

*Run time* Twice the retention time of amlodipine.

*Identification of impurities* Use the chromatogram supplied with *amlodipine for peak identification CRS* and the chromatogram obtained with reference solution (c) to identify the peaks due to impurities D, E and F; use the chromatogram obtained with reference solution (d) to identify the peak due to impurity A.

*Relative retention* With reference to amlodipine (retention time = about 20 min): impurity G = about 0.15; impurity B = about 0.2; impurity A = about 0.3; impurity D = about 0.5; impurity F = about 0.8; impurity E = about 1.3.

*System suitability* Reference solution (b):
— *resolution*: minimum 2.0 between the peaks due to impurities B and G.

*Limits:*
— *correction factors*: for the calculation of content, multiply the peak areas of the following impurities by the corresponding correction factor: impurity D = 1.7; impurity F = 0.7;
— *impurity D*: not more than 3 times the area of the principal peak in the chromatogram obtained with reference solution (a) (0.3 per cent);

— *impurity A*: not more than 1.5 times the area of the corresponding peak in the chromatogram obtained with reference solution (d) (0.15 per cent);
— *impurities E, F*: for each impurity, not more than 1.5 times the area of the principal peak in the chromatogram obtained with reference solution (a) (0.15 per cent);
— *unspecified impurities*: for each impurity, not more than the area of the principal peak in the chromatogram obtained with reference solution (a) (0.10 per cent);
— *total*: not more than 8 times the area of the principal peak in the chromatogram obtained with reference solution (a) (0.8 per cent);
— *disregard limit*: 0.5 times the area of the principal peak in the chromatogram obtained with reference solution (a) (0.05 per cent). Disregard any peak due to benzene sulphonate (relative retention = about 0.14).

**Water** (*2.5.12*)
Maximum 0.5 per cent, determined on 1.000 g.

**Sulphated ash** (*2.4.14*)
Maximum 0.2 per cent, determined on 1.0 g.

**ASSAY**

Liquid chromatography (*2.2.29*) as described in the test for related substances with the following modification.

*Injection* Test solution (b), reference solution (e).

Calculate the percentage content of $C_{26}H_{31}ClN_2O_8S$ from the declared content of *amlodipine besilate CRS*.

**STORAGE**

In an airtight container, protected from light.

**IMPURITIES**

*Specified impurities* A, D, E, F.

*Other detectable impurities* (The following substances would, if present at a sufficient level, be detected by one or other of the tests in the monograph. They are limited by the general acceptance criterion for other/unspecified impurities and/or by the general monograph *Substances for pharmaceutical use* (*2034*). It is therefore not necessary to identify these impurities for demonstration of compliance. See also *5.10.* *Control of impurities in substances for pharmaceutical use*): B, G, H.

and enantiomer

A. 3-ethyl 5-methyl (4*RS*)-4-(2-chlorophenyl)-2-[[2-(1,3-dioxo-1,3-dihydro-2*H*-isoindol-2-yl)ethoxy]methyl]-6-methyl-1,4-dihydropyridine-3,5-dicarboxylate,

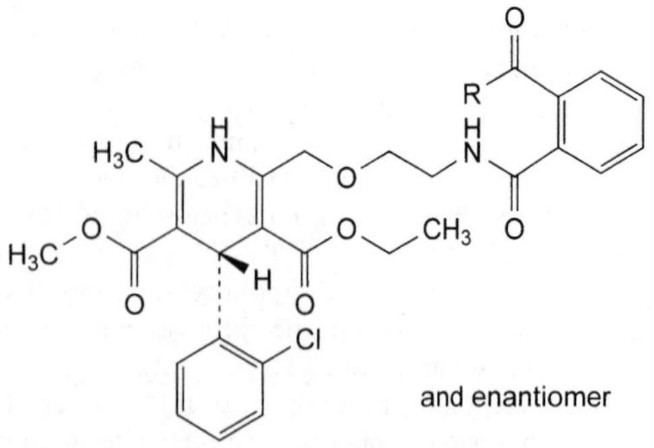

B. R = NHCH₃: 3-ethyl 5-methyl (4RS)-4-
(2-chlorophenyl)6-methyl-2-[[2-[[2-
(methylcarbamoyl)benzoyl]amino]ethoxy]methyl]-1,4-
dihydropyridine-3,5-dicarboxylate,

H. R = OH: 2-[[2-[[(4RS)-4-(2-chlorophenyl)-3-
(ethoxycarbonyl)-5-methoxycarbonyl)-6-methyl-1,4-
dihydropyridin-2-yl]methoxy]ethyl]carbamoyl]benzoic acid,

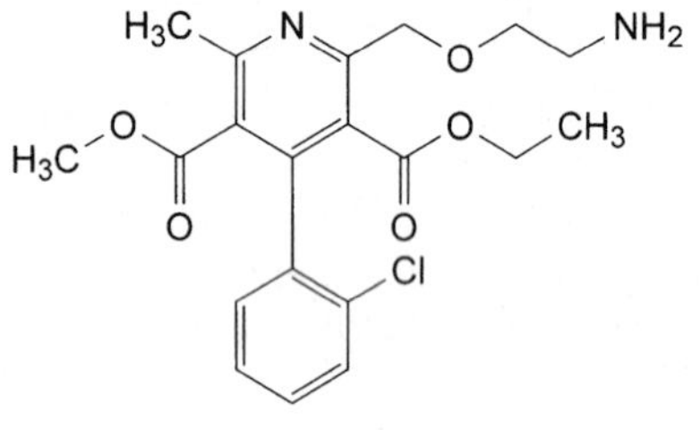

D. 3-ethyl 5-methyl 2-[(2-aminoethoxy)methyl]-4-
(2-chlorophenyl)-6-methylpyridine-3,5-dicarboxylate,

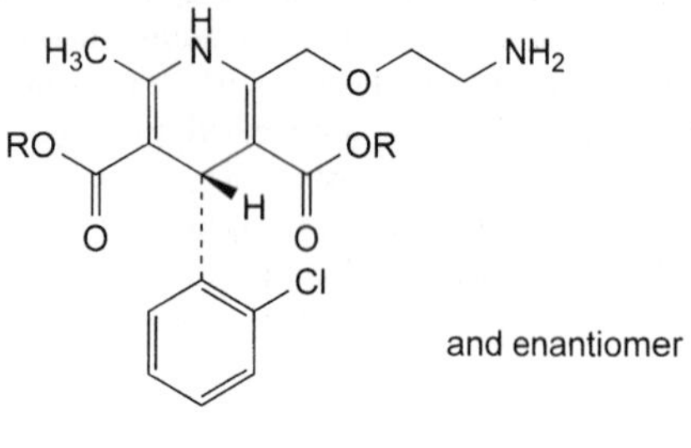

E. R = C₂H₅: diethyl (4RS)-2-[(2-aminoethoxy)methyl]-4-
(2-chlorophenyl)-6-methyl-1,4-dihydropyridine-3,5-
dicarboxylate,

F. R = CH₃: dimethyl (4RS)-2-[(2-aminoethoxy)methyl]-4-
(2-chlorophenyl)-6-methyl-1,4-dihydropyridine-3,5-
dicarboxylate,

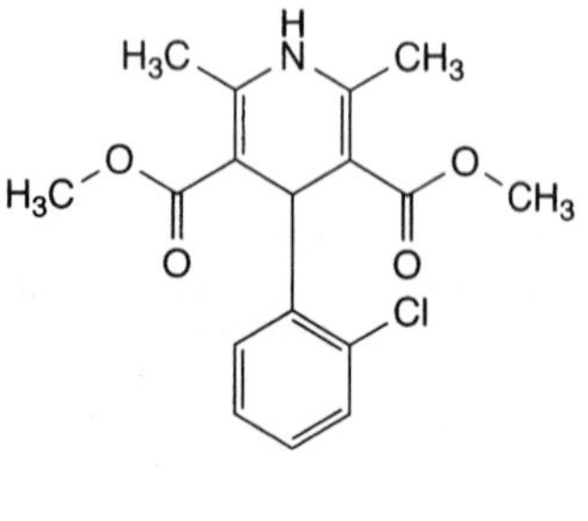

G. dimethyl 4-(2-chlorophenyl)-2,6-dimethyl-1,4-
dihydropyridine-3,5-dicarboxylate.

*Ph Eur*

---

# Strong Ammonia Solution

(*Concentrated Ammonia Solution,*
*Ph Eur monograph 0877*)

**Preparation**
Dilute Ammonia Solution

*Ph Eur*

## DEFINITION
### Content
25.0 per cent m/m to 30.0 per cent *m/m*.

## CHARACTERS
### Appearance
Clear, colourless liquid, very caustic.

### Solubility
Miscible with water and with ethanol (96 per cent).

## IDENTIFICATION
A. Relative density (*2.2.5*): 0.892 to 0.910.

B. It is strongly alkaline (*2.2.4*).

C. To 0.5 ml add 5 ml of *water R*. Bubble air through the solution and lead the gaseous mixture obtained over the surface of a solution containing 1 ml of *0.1 M hydrochloric acid* and 0.05 ml of *methyl red solution R*. The colour changes from red to yellow. Add 1 ml of *sodium cobaltinitrite solution R*. A yellow precipitate is formed.

## TESTS
### Solution S
Evaporate 220 ml almost to dryness on a water-bath. Cool, add 1 ml of *dilute acetic acid R* and dilute to 20 ml with *distilled water R*.

### Appearance of solution
The solution is clear (*2.2.1*) and colourless (*2.2.2, Method II*).

To 2 ml add 8 ml of *water R*.

### Oxidisable substances
Cautiously add, whilst cooling, 8.8 ml to 100 ml of *dilute sulphuric acid R*. Add 0.75 ml of *0.002 M potassium permanganate*. Allow to stand for 5 min. The solution remains faintly pink.

### Pyridine and related substances
Maximum 2 ppm, calculated as pyridine.

Measure the absorbance (*2.2.25*) at 252 nm using *water R* as the compensation liquid. The absorbance is not greater than 0.06.

### Carbonates
Maximum 60 ppm.

To 10 ml in a test-tube with a ground-glass neck add 10 ml of *calcium hydroxide solution R*. Stopper immediately and mix. Any opalescence in the solution is not more intense than that in a standard prepared at the same time and in the same manner using 10 ml of a 0.1 g/l solution of *anhydrous sodium carbonate R*.

### Chlorides (*2.4.4*)
Maximum 1 ppm.

Dilute 5 ml of solution S to 15 ml with *water R*.

### Sulphates (*2.4.13*)
Maximum 5 ppm.

Dilute 3 ml of solution S to 15 ml with *distilled water R*.

### Iron (*2.4.9*)
Maximum 0.25 ppm.

Dilute 4 ml of solution S to 10 ml with *water R*.

**Heavy metals** (*2.4.8*)

Maximum 1 ppm.

Dilute 4 ml of solution S to 20 ml with *water R*. 12 ml of the solution complies with test A. Prepare the reference solution using *lead standard solution (2 ppm Pb) R*.

### Residue on evaporation

Maximum 20 mg/l.

Evaporate 50 ml to dryness on a water-bath and dry at 100-105 °C for 1 h. The residue weighs a maximum of 1 mg.

### ASSAY

Weigh accurately a flask with a ground-glass neck containing 50.0 ml of *1 M hydrochloric acid*. Add 2 ml of the substance to be examined and re-weigh. Add 0.1 ml of *methyl red solution R* as indicator. Titrate with *1 M sodium hydroxide* until the colour changes from red to yellow.

1 ml of *1 M hydrochloric acid* is equivalent to 17.03 mg of $NH_3$.

### STORAGE

Protected from air, at a temperature not exceeding 20 °C.

_____ *Ph Eur*

# Ammonio Methacrylate Copolymer (Type A)

(*Ph Eur monograph 2081*)

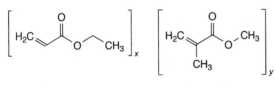

### Action and use

Excipient.

*Ph Eur* _____

### DEFINITION

Poly(ethyl propenoate-co-methyl 2-methylpropenoate-co-2-(trimethylammonio)ethyl 2-methylpropenoate) chloride having a mean relative molecular mass of about 150 000.

The ratio of ethyl propenoate groups to methyl 2-methylpropenoate groups to 2-(trimethylammonio)ethyl 2-methylpropenoate groups is about 1:2:0.2.

*Content of ammonio methacrylate groups* 8.9 per cent to 12.3 per cent (dried substance).

### CHARACTERS

### Appearance

Colourless to white or almost white granules or powder.

### Solubility

Practically insoluble in water, freely soluble in anhydrous ethanol and in methylene chloride giving clear to cloudy solutions. Due to the polymeric nature of the substance, a stirring time of up to 5 h may be necessary.

### IDENTIFICATION

A. Infrared absorption spectrophotometry (*2.2.24*).

*Comparison Ph. Eur. reference spectrum of ammonio methacrylate copolymer (type A).*

B. Viscosity (see Tests).

C. It complies with the limits of the assay.

### TESTS

### Solution S

Dissolve a quantity of the substance to be examined corresponding to 12.5 g of the dried substance in a mixture of 35.0 g of *acetone R* and 52.5 g of *2-propanol R*.

**Viscosity** (*2.2.10*)

Maximum 15 mPa·s, determined on solution S.

*Apparatus* Rotating viscometer.

*Dimensions:*
— *spindle*: diameter = 25.15 mm; height = 90.74 mm; shaft diameter = 4.0 mm;
— *cylinder*: diameter = 27.62 mm; height = 0.135 m.

*Stirring speed* 30 r/min.

*Volume of solution* 16 ml of solution S.

*Temperature* 20 °C.

### Appearance of a film

Spread 2 ml of solution S evenly on a glass plate. Upon drying a clear film is formed.

### Monomers

Liquid chromatography (*2.2.29*).

*Solution A* Dissolve 3.5 g of *sodium perchlorate R* in *water for chromatography R* and dilute to 100 ml with the same solvent.

*Test solution* Dissolve 5.00 g of the substance to be examined in *methanol R* and dilute to 50.0 ml with the same solvent. To 10.0 ml of this solution add 5.0 ml of solution A, dropwise, while continuously stirring. Remove the precipitated polymer by centrifugation. Use the clear supernatant solution.

*Reference solution* Dissolve 50.0 mg of *ethyl acrylate R* and 10.0 mg of *methyl methacrylate R* in *methanol R* and dilute to 50.0 ml with the same solvent. Dilute 1.0 ml of the solution to 100.0 ml with *methanol R*. Add 10 ml of this solution to 5 ml of solution A.

*Column:*
— *size: l* = 0.12 m, Ø = 4.6 mm;
— *stationary phase: octadecylsilyl silica gel for chromatography R* (7 µm).

*Mobile phase* Dilute *phosphoric acid R* with *water for chromatography R* to obtain a solution at pH 2.0; mix 800 ml of this solution and 200 ml of *methanol R*, filter and degas.

*Flow rate* 2.0 ml/min.

*Detection* Spectrophotometer at 202 nm.

*Injection* 50 µl.

*System suitability* Reference solution:
— *resolution*: minimum 1.5 between the peaks due to impurity A and impurity B.

*Limits:*
— *impurity A*: not more than the area of the corresponding peak in the chromatogram obtained with the reference solution (100 ppm);
— *impurity B*: not more than 2.5 times the area of the corresponding peak in the chromatogram obtained with the reference solution (50 ppm).

**Methanol** (*2.4.24, System A*)

Maximum 1.5 per cent.

**Heavy metals** (2.4.8)

Maximum 20 ppm.

1.0 g complies with test C. Prepare the reference solution using 2.0 ml of *lead standard solution (10 ppm Pb) R.*

**Loss on drying** (2.2.32)

Maximum 3.0 per cent, determined on 1.000 g by drying *in vacuo* at 80 °C for 5 h.

## ASSAY

Dissolve 1.000 g in a mixture of 3 ml of *anhydrous formic acid R* and 30 ml of *anhydrous acetic acid R* and heat to dissolve. Add 20 ml *of acetic anhydride R.* Titrate with *0.1 M perchloric acid*, determining the end-point potentiometrically (2.2.20).

1 ml of *0.1 M perchloric acid* is equivalent to 20.77 mg of $C_9H_{18}O_2NCl$ (ammonio methacrylate groups).

## IMPURITIES

*Specified impurities    A, B.*

A. R = H, R′ = $C_2H_5$: ethyl propenoate (ethyl acrylate),

B. R = R′ = $CH_3$: methyl 2-methylpropenoate (methyl methacrylate).

*Ph Eur*

# Ammonio Methacrylate Copolymer (Type B)

(*Ph Eur monograph 2082*)

**Action and use**

Excipient.

*Ph Eur*

## DEFINITION

Poly(ethyl propenoate-co-methyl 2-methylpropenoate-co-2-(trimethylammonio)ethyl 2-methylpropenoate) chloride having a mean relative molecular mass of about 150 000.

The ratio of ethyl propenoate groups to methyl 2-methylpropenoate groups to 2-(trimethylammonio)ethyl 2-methylpropenoate groups is about 1:2:0.1.

*Content of ammonio methacrylate groups*    4.5 per cent to 7.0 per cent (dried substance).

## CHARACTERS

**Appearance**

Colourless to white or almost white granules or powder.

**Solubility**

Practically insoluble in water, freely soluble in anhydrous ethanol and in methylene chloride giving clear to cloudy solutions. Due to the polymeric nature of the substance, a stirring time of up to 5 h may be necessary.

## IDENTIFICATION

A. Infrared absorption spectrophotometry (2.2.24).

*Comparison    Ph. Eur. reference spectrum of ammonio methacrylate copolymer (type B)* .

B. Viscosity (see Tests).

C. It complies with the limits of the assay.

## TESTS

**Solution S**

Dissolve a quantity of the substance to be examined corresponding to 12.5 g of the dried substance in a mixture of 35.0 g of *acetone R* and 52.5 g of *2-propanol R.*

**Viscosity** (2.2.10)

Maximum 15 mPa·s, determined on solution S.

*Apparatus    Rotating viscometer.*

*Dimensions:*
— *spindle*: diameter = 25.15 mm; height = 90.74 mm; shaft diameter = 4.0 mm;
— *cylinder*: diameter = 27.62 mm; height = 0.135 m.

*Stirring speed    30 r/min.*

*Volume of solution    16 ml of solution S.*

*Temperature    20 °C.*

**Appearance of a film**

Spread 2 ml of solution S evenly on a glass plate. Upon drying a clear film is formed.

**Monomers**

Liquid chromatography (2.2.29).

*Solution A*    Dissolve 3.5 g of *sodium perchlorate R* in *water for chromatography R* and dilute to 100 ml with the same solvent.

*Test solution*    Dissolve 5.00 g of the substance to be examined in *methanol R* and dilute to 50.0 ml with the same solvent. To 10.0 ml of this solution add 5.0 ml of solution A, dropwise, while continuously stirring. Remove the precipitated polymer by centrifugation. Use the clear supernatant solution.

*Reference solution*    Dissolve 50.0 mg of *ethyl acrylate R* and 10.0 mg of *methyl methacrylate R* in *methanol R* and dilute to 50.0 ml with the same solvent. Dilute 1.0 ml of the solution to 100.0 ml with *methanol R.* Add 10 ml of this solution to 5 ml of solution A.

*Column:*
— *size: l* = 0.12 m, Ø = 4.6 mm;
— *stationary phase: octadecylsilyl silica gel for chromatography R* (7 μm).

*Mobile phase*    Dilute *phosphoric acid R* with *water for chromatography R* to obtain a solution at pH 2.0; mix 800 ml of this solution and 200 ml of *methanol R*, filter and degas.

*Flow rate    2.0 ml/min.*

*Detection    Spectrophotometer at 202 nm.*

*Injection    50 μl.*

*System suitability    Reference solution:*
— *resolution*: minimum 1.5 between the peaks due to impurity A and impurity B.

*Limits:*
— *impurity A*: not more than the area of the corresponding peak in the chromatogram obtained with the reference solution (100 ppm);

— *impurity B*: not more than 2.5 times the area of the corresponding peak in the chromatogram obtained with the reference solution (50 ppm).

**Methanol** (*2.4.24, System A*)
Maximum 1.5 per cent.

**Heavy metals** (*2.4.8*)
Maximum 20 ppm.

1.0 g complies with test C. Prepare the reference solution using 2.0 ml of *lead standard solution (10 ppm Pb) R*.

**Loss on drying** (*2.2.32*)
Maximum 3.0 per cent, determined on 1.000 g by drying *in vacuo* at 80 °C for 5 h.

## ASSAY

Dissolve 2.000 g in a mixture of 3 ml of *anhydrous formic acid R* and 30 ml of *anhydrous acetic acid R* and heat to dissolve. Add 20 ml of *acetic anhydride R*. Titrate with *0.1 M perchloric acid*, determining the end-point potentiometrically (*2.2.20*).

1 ml of *0.1 M perchloric acid* is equivalent to 20.77 mg of $C_9H_{18}O_2NCl$ (ammonio methacrylate groups).

## IMPURITIES

*Specified impurities*   *A, B*.

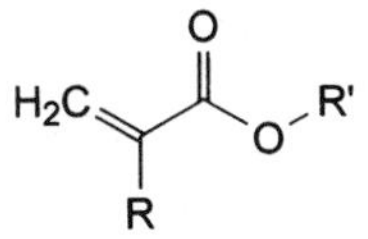

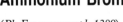

A. R = H, R′ = $C_2H_5$: ethyl propenoate (ethyl acrylate),
B. R = R′ = $CH_3$: methyl 2-methylpropenoate (methyl methacrylate).

*Ph Eur*

# Ammonium Bicarbonate

(*Ammonium Hydrogen Carbonate,
Ph Eur monograph 1390*)

| $NH_4HCO_3$ | 79.1 | *1066-33-7* |
|---|---|---|

**Action and use**
Expectorant.

**Preparations**
Aromatic Ammonia Solution
Strong Ammonium Acetate Solution
Aromatic Ammonia Spirit

*Ph Eur*

## DEFINITION
**Content**
98.0 per cent to 101.0 per cent.

## CHARACTERS
**Appearance**
Fine, white or almost white, crystalline powder or white or almost white crystals, slightly hygroscopic.

**Solubility**
Freely soluble in water, practically insoluble in ethanol (96 per cent).

It volatilises rapidly at 60 °C. The volatilisation takes place slowly at ambient temperatures if the substance is slightly

moist. It is in a state of equilibrium with ammonium carbamate.

## IDENTIFICATION
A. It gives the reaction of carbonates and bicarbonates (*2.3.1*).

B. Dissolve 50 mg in 2 ml of *water R*. The solution gives the reaction of ammonium salts (*2.3.1*).

## TESTS
**Solution S**
Dissolve 14.0 g in 100 ml of *distilled water R*. Boil to remove the ammonia, allow to cool and dilute to 100.0 ml with *distilled water R*.

**Chlorides** (*2.4.4*)
Maximum 70 ppm.

Dilute 5 ml of solution S to 15 ml with *water R*.

**Sulphates** (*2.4.13*)
Maximum 70 ppm, determined on solution S.

**Iron** (*2.4.9*)
Maximum 40 ppm.

Dilute 1.8 ml of solution S to 10 ml with *water R*.

**Heavy metals** (*2.4.8*)
Maximum 10 ppm.

Dissolve cautiously 2.5 g in 25 ml of *1 M hydrochloric acid*. 12 ml of the solution complies with test A. Prepare the reference solution using *lead standard solution (1 ppm Pb) R*.

## ASSAY
Dissolve cautiously 1.0 g in 20.0 ml of *0.5 M sulphuric acid* and dilute to 50 ml with *water R*. Boil, cool and titrate the excess of acid with *1 M sodium hydroxide*, using 0.1 ml of *methyl red solution R* as indicator.

1 ml of *0.5 M sulphuric acid* is equivalent to 79.1 mg of $NH_4HCO_3$.

## STORAGE
In an airtight container.

*Ph Eur*

# Ammonium Bromide

(*Ph Eur monograph 1389*)

| $NH_4Br$ | 97.9 | *12124-97-9* |
|---|---|---|

*Ph Eur*

## DEFINITION
**Content**
98.5 per cent to 100.5 per cent (dried substance).

## CHARACTERS
**Appearance**
White or almost white, crystalline powder or colourless crystals, hygroscopic.

**Solubility**
Freely soluble in water, sparingly soluble in alcohol.

It becomes yellow when exposed to light or air.

## IDENTIFICATION
A. It gives reaction (a) of bromides (*2.3.1*).

B. 10 ml of solution S (see Tests) gives the reaction of ammonium salts (*2.3.1*).

## TESTS

### Solution S
Dissolve 10.0 g in *carbon dioxide-free water R* prepared from *distilled water R* and dilute to 100 ml with the same solvent.

### Appearance of solution
Solution S is clear (*2.2.1*) and colourless (*2.2.2, Method II*).

### Acidity or alkalinity
To 10 ml of solution S add 0.05 ml of *methyl red solution R*. Not more than 0.5 ml of *0.01 M hydrochloric acid* or *0.01 M sodium hydroxide* is required to change the colour of the indicator.

### Bromates
To 10 ml of solution S add 1 ml of *starch solution R*, 0.1 ml of a 100 g/l solution of *potassium iodide R* and 0.25 ml of *0.5 M sulphuric acid* and allow to stand protected from light for 5 min. No blue or violet colour develops.

### Chlorides
Maximum 0.6 per cent.

In a conical flask, dissolve 1.000 g in 20 ml of *dilute nitric acid R*. Add 5 ml of *strong hydrogen peroxide solution R* and heat on a water-bath until the solution is completely decolorised. Wash down the sides of the flask with a little *water R* and heat on a water-bath for 15 min. Allow to cool, dilute to 50 ml with *water R* and add 5.0 ml of *0.1 M silver nitrate* and 1 ml of *dibutyl phthalate R*. Shake and titrate with *0.1 M ammonium thiocyanate* using 5 ml of *ferric ammonium sulphate solution R2* as indicator. Not more than 1.7 ml of *0.1 M silver nitrate* is used. Note the volume of *0.1 M silver nitrate* used (see Assay). Carry out a blank test.

### Iodides
To 5 ml of solution S add 0.15 ml of *ferric chloride solution R1* and 2 ml of *methylene chloride R*. Shake and allow to separate. The lower layer is colourless (*2.2.2, Method I*).

### Sulphates (*2.4.13*)
Maximum 100 ppm.

15 ml of solution S complies with the limit test for sulphates.

### Iron (*2.4.9*)
Maximum 20 ppm.

5 ml of solution S diluted to 10 ml with *water R* complies with the limit test for iron.

### Magnesium and alkaline-earth metals (*2.4.7*)
Maximum 200 ppm, calculated as Ca.

10.0 g complies with the limit test for magnesium and alkaline-earth metals. The volume of *0.01 M sodium edetate* used does not exceed 5.0 ml.

### Heavy metals (*2.4.8*)
Maximum 10 ppm.

12 ml of solution S complies with limit test A. Prepare the standard using *lead standard solution (1 ppm Pb) R*.

### Loss on drying (*2.2.32*)
Maximum 1.0 per cent, determined on 1.000 g by drying in an oven at 105 °C.

### Sulphated ash (*2.4.14*)
Maximum 0.1 per cent, determined on 1.0 g.

## ASSAY
Dissolve 1.500 g in *water R* and dilute to 100.0 ml with the same solvent. To 10.0 ml of the solution add 50 ml of *water R*, 5 ml of *dilute nitric acid R*, 25.0 ml of *0.1 M silver nitrate* and 2 ml of *dibutyl phthalate R*. Shake. Titrate with *0.1 M ammonium thiocyanate* using 2 ml of *ferric ammonium sulphate solution R2* as indicator and shaking vigorously towards the end-point.

1 ml of *0.1 M silver nitrate* is equivalent to 9.794 mg of $NH_4Br$.

Calculate the percentage content of $NH_4Br$ from the expression:

$$a - 2.763\ b$$

$a$ = percentage content of $NH_4Br$ and $NH_4Cl$ obtained in the assay and calculated as $NH_4Br$,

$b$ = percentage content of Cl obtained in the test for chlorides.

## STORAGE
In an airtight container, protected from light.

*Ph Eur*

# Ammonium Chloride

(*Ph Eur monograph 0007*)

| | | |
|---|---|---|
| $NH_4Cl$ | 53.49 | 12125-02-9 |

### Action and use
Used for the acidification of urine and to correct metabolic alkalosis.

### Preparation
Ammonium Chloride Mixture

*Ph Eur*

## DEFINITION
### Content
99.0 per cent to 100.5 per cent (dried substance).

## CHARACTERS
### Appearance
White or almost white, crystalline powder or colourless crystals.

### Solubility
Freely soluble in water.

## IDENTIFICATION
A. It gives the reactions of chlorides (*2.3.1*).

B. 10 ml of solution S (see Tests) gives the reaction of ammonium salts (*2.3.1*).

## TESTS
### Solution S
Dissolve 10.0 g in *carbon dioxide-free water R* prepared from *distilled water R* and dilute to 100 ml with the same solvent.

### Appearance of solution
Solution S is clear (*2.2.1*) and colourless (*2.2.2, Method II*).

### Acidity or alkalinity
To 10 ml of solution S add 0.05 ml of *methyl red solution R*. Not more than 0.5 ml of *0.01 M hydrochloric acid* or *0.01 M sodium hydroxide* is required to change the colour of the indicator.

### Bromides and iodides
To 10 ml of solution S add 0.1 ml of *dilute hydrochloric acid R* and 0.05 ml of *chloramine solution R*. After 1 min, add 2 ml of *chloroform R* and shake vigorously. The chloroform layer remains colourless (*2.2.2, Method I*).

### Sulphates (*2.4.13*)
Maximum 150 ppm.

Dilute 10 ml of solution S to 15 ml with *distilled water R*.

### Calcium (*2.4.3*)
Maximum 200 ppm.

Dilute 5 ml of solution S to 15 ml with *distilled water R.*

**Iron** (*2.4.9*)

Maximum 20 ppm.

Dilute 5 ml of solution S to 10 ml with *water R.*

**Heavy metals** (*2.4.8*)

Maximum 10 ppm.

12 ml of solution S complies with test A. Prepare the reference solution using *lead standard solution (1 ppm Pb) R.*

**Loss on drying** (*2.2.32*)

Maximum 1.0 per cent, determined on 1.00 g by drying in an oven at 105 °C for 2 h.

**Sulphated ash** (*2.4.14*)

Maximum 0.1 per cent, determined on 2.0 g.

## ASSAY

Dissolve 1.000 g in 20 ml of *water R* and add a mixture of 5 ml of *formaldehyde solution R*, previously neutralised to *phenolphthalein solution R*, and 20 ml of *water R*. After 1-2 min, titrate slowly with *1 M sodium hydroxide*, using a further 0.2 ml of the same indicator.

1 ml of *1 M sodium hydroxide* is equivalent to 53.49 mg of $NH_4Cl$.

*Ph Eur*

# Ammonium Glycyrrhizinate

(*Ammonium Glycyrrhizate, Ph Eur monograph 1772*)

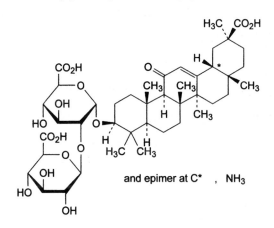

H₃C CO₂H

and epimer at C*   , NH₃

$C_{42}H_{65}NO_{16}$        840        53956-04-0

*Ph Eur*

## DEFINITION

Mixture of ammonium 18α- and 18β-glycyrrhizate (ammonium salt of (20β)-3β-[[2-O-(β-D-glucopyranosyluronic acid)-α-D-glucopyranosyluronic acid]oxy]-11-oxoolean-12-en-29-oic acid), the 18β-isomer being the main component.

## Content

98.0 per cent to 102.0 per cent (anhydrous substance).

## CHARACTERS

**Appearance**

White or yellowish-white, hygroscopic powder.

**Solubility**

Slightly soluble in water, very slightly soluble in anhydrous ethanol, practically insoluble in acetone. It dissolves in dilute solutions of acids and of alkali hydroxides.

## IDENTIFICATION

A. Infrared absorption spectrophotometry (*2.2.24*).

*Comparison   ammonium glycyrrhizate CRS.*

B. Dissolve 0.1 g in 20 ml of *water R*, add 2 ml of *dilute sodium hydroxide solution R* and heat cautiously. On heating, the solution gives off vapours that may be identified by the alkaline reaction of wet litmus paper (*2.3.1*).

## TESTS

**Appearance of solution**

The solution is clear (*2.2.1*) and not more intensely coloured than reference solution BY₇ (*2.2.2, Method I*).

Dissolve 1.0 g in *ethanol (20 per cent V/V) R* and dilute to 100.0 ml with the same solvent.

**Specific optical rotation** (*2.2.7*)

+ 49.0 to + 54.0 (anhydrous substance).

Dissolve 0.5 g in *ethanol (50 per cent V/V) R* and dilute to 50.0 ml with the same solvent.

*Related substances*   Liquid chromatography (*2.2.29*).

*Test solution*   Dissolve 0.100 g of the substance to be examined in the mobile phase and dilute to 100.0 ml with the mobile phase.

*Reference solution (a)*   Dilute 1.0 ml of the test solution to 20.0 ml with the mobile phase.

*Reference solution (b)*   Dissolve 50 mg of *ammonium glycyrrhizate CRS* in the mobile phase and dilute to 50.0 ml with the mobile phase. Dilute 1.0 ml of the solution to 20.0 ml with the mobile phase.

*Column:*
— *size: l = 0.25 m, Ø = 4.0 mm,*
— *stationary phase: octadecylsilyl silica gel for chromatography R* (5-10 μm).

*Mobile phase   glacial acetic acid R, acetonitrile R, water R* (6:380:614 *V/V/V*).

*Flow rate*   1.2 ml/min.

*Detection*   Spectrophotometer at 254 nm.

*Injection*   10 μl.

*Run time*   3 times the retention time of 18β-glycyrrhizic acid.

*Relative retention*   With reference to 18β-glycyrrhizic acid (retention time = about 8 min): impurity A = about 0.8; 18α-glycyrrhizic acid = about 1.2.

*System suitability*   Reference solution (b):
— *resolution*: minimum 2.0 between the peaks due to 18β-glycyrrhizic acid and 18α-glycyrrhizic acid.

*Limits:*
— *18α-glycyrrhizic acid*: not more than twice the sum of the areas of the peaks in the chromatogram obtained with reference solution (a) (10.0 per cent),
— *impurity A*: not more than the sum of the areas of the peaks in the chromatogram obtained with reference solution (a) (5.0 per cent),
— *any other impurity*: for each impurity, not more than 0.4 times the sum of the areas of the peaks in the chromatogram obtained with reference solution (a) (2.0 per cent),
— *sum of other impurities*: not more than 1.4 times the sum of the areas of the peaks in the chromatogram obtained with reference solution (a) (7.0 per cent),
— *disregard limit*: 0.04 times the sum of the areas of the peaks in the chromatogram obtained with reference solution (a) (0.2 per cent).

**Heavy metals** (*2.4.8*)

Maximum 20 ppm.

1.0 g complies with limit test C. Prepare the reference solution using 2 ml of *lead standard solution (10 ppm Pb) R*.

**Water** (*2.5.12*)

Maximum 6.0 per cent, determined on 0.250 g.

**Sulphated ash** (*2.4.14*)

Maximum 0.2 per cent, determined on 1.0 g.

**ASSAY**

Dissolve 0.600 g in 60 ml of *anhydrous acetic acid R* heating at 80 °C if necessary. Cool. Titrate with *0.1 M perchloric acid*, determining the end-point potentiometrically (*2.2.20*).

1 ml of *0.1 M perchloric acid* is equivalent to 84.0 mg of $C_{42}H_{65}NO_{16}$.

**STORAGE**

In an airtight container.

**IMPURITIES**

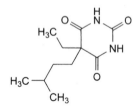

A. (4β,20β)-3β-[[2-O-(β-D-glucopyranosyluronic acid)-α-D-glucopyranosyluronic acid]oxy]-23-hydroxy-11-oxoolean-12-en-29-oic acid (24-hydroxyglycyrrhizinic acid).

*Ph Eur*

# Amobarbital

(*Ph Eur monograph 0594*)

$C_{11}H_{18}N_2O_3$          226.3          57-43-2

**Action and use**

Barbiturate.

*Ph Eur*

**DEFINITION**

Amobarbital contains not less than 99.0 per cent and not more than the equivalent of 101.0 per cent of 5-ethyl-5-(3-methylbutyl)pyrimidin-2,4,6(1*H*,3*H*,5*H*)-trione, calculated with reference to the dried substance.

**CHARACTERS**

A white or almost white, crystalline powder, very slightly soluble in water, freely soluble in alcohol, soluble in methylene chloride. It forms water-soluble compounds with alkali hydroxides and carbonates and with ammonia.

**IDENTIFICATION**

*First identification*   A, B.

*Second identification*   A, C, D.

A. Determine the melting point (*2.2.14*) of the substance to be examined. Mix equal parts of the substance to be examined and *amobarbital CRS* and determine the melting point of the mixture. The difference between the melting points (which are about 157 °C) is not greater than 2 °C.

B. Examine by infrared absorption spectrophotometry (*2.2.24*), comparing with the spectrum obtained with *amobarbital CRS* .

C. Examine by thin-layer chromatography (*2.2.27*), using *silica gel GF$_{254}$ R* as the coating substance.

*Test solution*   Dissolve 0.1 g of the substance to be examined in *alcohol R* and dilute to 100 ml with the same solvent.

*Reference solution*   Dissolve 0.1 g of *amobarbital CRS* in *alcohol R* and dilute to 100 ml with the same solvent.

Apply separately to the plate 10 µl of each solution. Develop over a path of 18 cm using the lower layer from a mixture of 5 volumes of *concentrated ammonia R*, 15 volumes of *alcohol R* and 80 volumes of *chloroform R*. Examine immediately in ultraviolet light at 254 nm. The principal spot in the chromatogram obtained with the test solution is similar in position and size to the principal spot in the chromatogram obtained with the reference solution.

D. It gives the reaction of non-nitrogen substituted barbiturates (*2.3.1*).

**TESTS**

**Appearance of solution**

Dissolve 1.0 g in a mixture of 4 ml of *dilute sodium hydroxide solution R* and 6 ml of *water R*. The solution is clear (*2.2.1*) and not more intensely coloured than reference solution $Y_6$ (*2.2.2, Method II*).

**Acidity or alkalinity**

To 1.0 g add 50 ml of *water R* and boil for 2 min. Allow to cool and filter. To 10 ml of the filtrate add 0.15 ml of *methyl red solution R* and 0.1 ml of *0.01 M sodium hydroxide*. The solution is yellow. Add 0.2 ml of *0.01 M hydrochloric acid*. The solution is red.

**Related substances**

Examine by thin-layer chromatography (*2.2.27*), using *silica gel GF$_{254}$ R* as the coating substance.

*Test solution*   Dissolve 1.0 g of the substance to be examined in *alcohol R* and dilute to 100 ml with the same solvent.

*Reference solution*   Dilute 0.5 ml of the test solution to 100 ml with *alcohol R*.

Apply separately to the plate 20 µl of each solution. Develop over a path of 15 cm using the lower layer from a mixture of 5 volumes of *concentrated ammonia R*, 15 volumes of *alcohol R* and 80 volumes of *chloroform R*. Examine the plate immediately in ultraviolet light at 254 nm. Any spot in the chromatogram obtained with the test solution, apart from the principal spot, is not more intense than the spot in the chromatogram obtained with the reference solution. Spray with *diphenylcarbazone mercuric reagent R*. Allow the plate to dry in air and spray with freshly prepared *alcoholic potassium hydroxide solution R* diluted 1 in 5 with *aldehyde-free alcohol R*. Heat at 100 °C to 105 °C for 5 min and examine immediately. Any spot in the chromatogram obtained with the test solution, apart from the principal spot, is not more intense than the spot in the chromatogram obtained with the reference solution (0.5 per cent).

**Loss on drying** (2.2.32)
Not more than 0.5 per cent, determined on 1.000 g by drying in an oven at 105 °C.

**Sulphated ash** (2.4.14)
Not more than 0.1 per cent, determined on 1.0 g.

**ASSAY**
Dissolve 0.100 g in 5 ml of *pyridine R*. Add 0.5 ml of *thymolphthalein solution R* and 10 ml of *silver nitrate solution* in *pyridine R*. Titrate with *0.1 M ethanolic sodium hydroxide* until a pure blue colour is obtained. Carry out a blank titration.

1 ml of *0.1 M ethanolic sodium hydroxide* is equivalent to 11.31 mg of $C_{11}H_{18}N_2O_3$.

*Ph Eur*

# Amobarbital Sodium

(*Ph Eur monograph 0166*)

$C_{11}H_{17}N_2NaO_3$          248.3          *64-43-7*

**Action and use**
Barbiturate.

*Ph Eur*

## DEFINITION
Amobarbital sodium contains not less than 98.5 per cent and not more than the equivalent of 102.0 per cent of sodium derivative of 5-ethyl-5-(3-methylbutyl)pyrimidin-2,4,6(1*H*,3*H*,5*H*)-trione, calculated with reference to the dried substance.

## CHARACTERS
A white or almost white, granular powder, hygroscopic, very soluble in carbon dioxide-free water (a small fraction may be insoluble), freely soluble in alcohol.

## IDENTIFICATION
*First identification* A, B, E.

*Second identification* A, C, D, E.

A. Acidify 10 ml of solution S (see Tests) with *dilute hydrochloric acid R* and shake with 20 ml of *ether R*. Separate the ether layer, wash with 10 ml of *water R*, dry over *anhydrous sodium sulphate R* and filter. Evaporate the filtrate to dryness and dry the residue at 100 °C to 105 °C (test residue). Repeat the operations using 0.1 g of *amobarbital sodium CRS* (reference residue). Determine the melting point (2.2.14) of the test residue. Mix equal parts of the test residue and the reference residue and determine the melting point of the mixture. The difference between the melting points (which are about 157 °C) is not greater than 2 °C.

B. Examine by infrared absorption spectrophotometry (2.2.24), comparing the spectrum obtained with the reference residue prepared from *amobarbital sodium CRS* with that obtained with the test residue (see identification test A).

C. Examine by thin-layer chromatography (2.2.27), using *silica gel GF₂₅₄ R* as the coating substance.

*Test solution* Dissolve 0.1 g of the substance to be examined in *alcohol R* and dilute to 100 ml with the same solvent.

*Reference solution* Dissolve 0.1 g of *amobarbital sodium CRS* in *alcohol R* and dilute to 100 ml with the same solvent.

Apply separately to the plate 10 µl of each solution. Develop over a path of 18 cm using the lower layer of a mixture of 5 volumes of *concentrated ammonia R*, 15 volumes of *alcohol R* and 80 volumes of *chloroform R*. Examine immediately in ultraviolet light at 254 nm. The principal spot in the chromatogram obtained with the test solution is similar in position and size to the principal spot in the chromatogram obtained with the reference solution.

D. It gives the reaction of non-nitrogen substituted barbiturates (2.3.1).

E. It gives reaction (a) of sodium (2.3.1).

## TESTS
### Solution S
Dissolve 5.0 g in *alcohol (50 per cent V/V) R* and dilute to 50 ml with the same solvent.

### Appearance of solution
Solution S is clear (2.2.1) and not more intensely coloured than reference solution Y₇ (2.2.2, *Method II*).

### pH (2.2.3)
Dissolve 5.0 g in *carbon dioxide-free water R* and dilute to 50 ml with the same solvent. Disregard any slight residue. The pH of the solution is not more than 11.0.

### Related substances
Examine by thin-layer chromatography (2.2.27), using *silica gel GF₂₅₄ R* as the coating substance.

*Test solution* Dissolve 1.0 g of the substance to be examined in *alcohol R* and dilute to 100 ml with the same solvent.

*Reference solution* Dilute 0.5 ml of the test solution to 100 ml with *alcohol R*.

Apply separately to the plate 20 µl of each solution. Develop over a path of 15 cm using the lower layer of a mixture of 5 volumes of *concentrated ammonia R*, 15 volumes of *alcohol R* and 80 volumes of *chloroform R*. Examine the plate immediately in ultraviolet light at 254 nm. Spray with *diphenylcarbazone mercuric reagent R*. Allow the plate to dry in air and spray with freshly prepared *alcoholic potassium hydroxide solution R* diluted 1 in 5 with *aldehyde-free alcohol R*. Heat at 100 °C to 105 °C for 5 min and examine immediately. When examined in ultraviolet light and after spraying, any spot in the chromatogram obtained with the test solution, apart from the principal spot, is not more intense than the spot in the chromatogram obtained with the reference solution (0.5 per cent). Disregard any spot at the starting-point.

### Loss on drying (2.2.32)
Not more than 3.0 per cent, determined on 0.50 g by drying in an oven at 130 °C.

## ASSAY

Dissolve 0.200 g in 5 ml of *ethanol R*. Add 0.5 ml of *thymolphthalein solution R* and 10 ml of *silver nitrate solution in pyridine R*. Titrate with *0.1 M ethanolic sodium hydroxide* until a pure blue colour is obtained. Carry out a blank titration.

1 ml of *0.1 M ethanolic sodium hydroxide* is equivalent to 24.83 mg of $C_{11}H_{17}N_2NaO_3$.

## STORAGE

Store in an airtight container.

*Ph Eur*

# Amoxicillin Sodium

*(Ph Eur monograph 0577)*

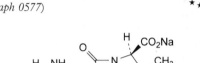

$C_{16}H_{18}N_3NaO_5S$        387.4        *34642-77-8*

### Action and use
Penicillin antibacterial.

### Preparations
Amoxicillin Injection

Co-amoxiclav Injection

*Ph Eur*

## DEFINITION

Sodium (2S,5R,6R)-6-[[(2R)-2-amino-2-(4-hydroxyphenyl)acetyl]amino]-3,3-dimethyl-7-oxo-4-thia-1-azabicyclo[3.2.0]heptane-2-carboxylate.

Semi-synthetic product derived from a fermentation product.

### Content
89.0 per cent to 102.0 per cent (anhydrous substance).

## CHARACTERS

### Appearance
White or almost white, very hygroscopic, powder.

### Solubility
Very soluble in water, sparingly soluble in anhydrous ethanol, very slightly soluble in acetone.

## IDENTIFICATION

*First identification*   A, D.

*Second identification*   B, C, D.

A. Infrared absorption spectrophotometry (2.2.24).

*Preparation*   Dissolve 0.250 g in 5 ml of *water R*, add 0.5 ml of *dilute acetic acid R*, swirl and allow to stand for 10 min in iced water. Filter the crystals and wash with 2-3 ml of a mixture of 1 volume of *water R* and 9 volumes of *acetone R*, then dry in an oven at 60 °C for 30 min.

*Comparison*   amoxicillin trihydrate CRS.

B. Thin-layer chromatography (2.2.27).

*Test solution*   Dissolve 25 mg of the substance to be examined in 10 ml of *sodium hydrogen carbonate solution R*.

*Reference solution (a)*   Dissolve 25 mg of *amoxicillin trihydrate CRS* in 10 ml of *sodium hydrogen carbonate solution R*.

*Reference solution (b)*   Dissolve 25 mg of *amoxicillin trihydrate CRS* and 25 mg of *ampicillin trihydrate CRS* in 10 ml of *sodium hydrogen carbonate solution R*.

*Plate*   TLC silanised silica gel plate R.

*Mobile phase*   Mix 10 volumes of *acetone R* and 90 volumes of a 154 g/l solution of *ammonium acetate R* previously adjusted to pH 5.0 with *glacial acetic acid R*.

*Application*   1 μl.

*Development*   Over a path of 15 cm.

*Drying*   In air.

*Detection*   Expose to iodine vapour until the spots appear and examine in daylight.

*System suitability*   Reference solution (b):
— the chromatogram shows 2 clearly separated spots.

*Results*   The principal spot in the chromatogram obtained with the test solution is similar in position, colour and size to the principal spot in the chromatogram obtained with reference solution (a).

C. Place about 2 mg in a test-tube about 150 mm long and about 15 mm in diameter. Moisten with 0.05 ml of *water R* and add 2 ml of *sulphuric acid-formaldehyde reagent R*. Mix the contents of the tube by swirling; the solution is practically colourless. Place the test-tube in a water-bath for 1 min; a dark yellow colour develops.

D. It gives reaction (a) of sodium (2.3.1).

## TESTS

### Appearance of solution

The solution is not more opalescent than reference suspension II (2.2.1), it may show an initial, but transient, pink colour, and after 5 min, its absorbance (2.2.25) at 430 nm is not greater than 0.20.

Dissolve 1.0 g in *water R* and dilute to 10.0 ml with the same solvent. Examine immediately after dissolution.

### pH (2.2.3)
8.0 to 10.0.

Dissolve 2.0 g in *carbon dioxide-free water R* and dilute to 20 ml with the same solvent.

### Specific optical rotation (2.2.7)
+ 240 to + 290 (anhydrous substance).

Dissolve 62.5 mg in a 4 g/l solution of *potassium hydrogen phthalate R* and dilute to 25.0 ml with the same solution.

### Related substances
Liquid chromatography (2.2.29).

*Test solution (a)*   Dissolve 30.0 mg of the substance to be examined in mobile phase A and dilute to 50.0 ml with mobile phase A.

*Test solution (b)*   Dissolve 30.0 mg of the substance to be examined in mobile phase A and dilute to 20.0 ml with mobile phase A. *Prepare immediately before use.*

*Reference solution (a)*   Dissolve 30.0 mg of *amoxicillin trihydrate CRS* in mobile phase A and dilute to 50.0 ml with mobile phase A.

*Reference solution (b)*   Dissolve 4.0 mg of *cefadroxil CRS* in mobile phase A and dilute to 50 ml with mobile phase A. To 5.0 ml of this solution add 5.0 ml of reference solution (a) and dilute to 100 ml with mobile phase A.

*Reference solution (c)*   Dilute 2.0 ml of reference solution (a) to 20.0 ml with mobile phase A. Dilute 5.0 ml of this solution to 20.0 ml with mobile phase A.

*Reference solution (d)*   To 0.20 g of *amoxicillin trihydrate R* add 1.0 ml of *water R*. Shake and add dropwise *dilute sodium hydroxide solution R* to obtain a solution. The pH of the solution is about 8.5. Store the solution at room temperature for 4 h. Dilute 0.5 ml of this solution to 50.0 ml with mobile phase A.

*Column:*
— *size*: $l = 0.25$ m, Ø = 4.6 mm;
— *stationary phase*: octadecylsilyl silica gel for chromatography R (5 μm).

*Mobile phase:*
— *mobile phase A*: mix 1 volume of *acetonitrile R* and 99 volumes of a 25 per cent *V/V* solution of *0.2 M potassium dihydrogen phosphate R* adjusted to pH 5.0 with *dilute sodium hydroxide solution R*;
— *mobile phase B*: mix 20 volumes of *acetonitrile R* and 80 volumes of a 25 per cent *V/V* solution of *0.2 M potassium dihydrogen phosphate R* adjusted to pH 5.0 with *dilute sodium hydroxide solution R*;

| Time (min) | Mobile phase A (per cent *V/V*) | Mobile phase B (per cent *V/V*) |
|---|---|---|
| $0 - t_R$ | 92 | 8 |
| $t_R - (t_R + 25)$ | $92 \rightarrow 0$ | $8 \rightarrow 100$ |
| $(t_R + 25) - (t_R + 40)$ | 0 | 100 |
| $(t_R + 40) - (t_R + 55)$ | 92 | 8 |

$t_R$ = retention time of amoxicillin determined with reference solution (c)

If the mobile phase has been adjusted to achieve the required resolution, the adjusted composition will apply at time zero in the gradient and in the assay.

*Flow rate*   1.0 ml/min.

*Detection*   Spectrophotometer at 254 nm.

*Injection*   50 μl of reference solutions (b) and (c) with isocratic elution at the initial mobile phase composition and 50 μl of test solution (b) and reference solution (d) according to the elution gradient described under Mobile phase; inject mobile phase A as a blank according to the elution gradient described under Mobile phase.

*Identification of impurities*   Use the chromatogram obtained with reference solution (d) to identify the 3 principal peaks eluted after the main peak corresponding to impurity C, amoxicillin dimer (impurity J; $n = 1$) and amoxicillin trimer (impurity J; $n = 2$).

*Relative retention*   With reference to amoxicillin: impurity C = about 3.4; impurity J ($n = 1$) = about 4.1; impurity J ($n = 2$) = about 4.5.

*System suitability*   Reference solution (b):
— *resolution*: minimum 2.0 between the peaks due to amoxicillin and cefadroxil; if necessary, adjust the ratio A:B of the mobile phase.

*Limits:*
— *impurity J ($n = 1$)*: not more than 3 times the area of the principal peak in the chromatogram obtained with reference solution (c) (3 per cent);
— *any other impurity*: for each impurity, not more than twice the area of the principal peak in the chromatogram obtained with reference solution (c) (2 per cent);
— *total*: not more than 9 times the area of the principal peak in the chromatogram obtained with reference solution (c) (9 per cent);

— *disregard limit*: 0.1 times the area of the principal peak in the chromatogram obtained with reference solution (c) (0.1 per cent).

**N,N-Dimethylaniline** (*2.4.26, Method A or B*)
Maximum 20 ppm.

**2-Ethylhexanoic acid** (*2.4.28*)
Maximum 0.8 per cent m/m.

**Heavy metals** (*2.4.8*)
Maximum 20 ppm.

1.0 g complies with test C. Prepare the reference solution using 2 ml of *lead standard solution (10 ppm Pb) R*.

**Water** (*2.5.12*)
Maximum 3.0 per cent, determined on 0.400 g.

**Bacterial endotoxins** (*2.6.14*)
Less than 0.25 IU/mg, if intended for use in the manufacture of parenteral dosage forms without a further appropriate procedure for the removal of bacterial endotoxins.

**ASSAY**
Liquid chromatography (*2.2.29*) as described in the test for related substances with the following modifications.

*Mobile phase*   Initial composition of the mixture of mobile phases A and B, adjusted where applicable.

*Injection*   Test solution (a) and reference solution (a).

*System suitability*   Reference solution (a):
— *repeatability*: maximum relative standard deviation of 1.0 per cent after 6 injections.

Calculate the percentage content of amoxicillin sodium by multiplying the percentage content of amoxicillin by 1.060.

**STORAGE**
In an airtight container. If the substance is sterile, store in a sterile, airtight, tamper-proof container.

**IMPURITIES**

A. (2*S*,5*R*,6*R*)-6-amino-3,3-dimethyl-7-oxo-4-thia-1-azabicyclo[3.2.0]heptane-2-carboxylic acid (6-aminopenicillanic acid),

B. (2*S*,5*R*,6*R*)-6-[[(2*S*)-2-amino-2-(4-hydroxyphenyl)acetyl]amino]-3,3-dimethyl-7-oxo-4-thia-1-azabicyclo[3.2.0]heptane-2-carboxylic acid (L-amoxicillin),

C. (4S)-2-[5-(4-hydroxyphenyl)-3,6-dioxopiperazin-2-yl]-5,5-dimethylthiazolidine-4-carboxylic acid (amoxicillin diketopiperazines),

D. (4S)-2-[[[(2R)-2-amino-2-(4-hydroxyphenyl)acetyl]amino]carboxymethyl]-5,5-dimethylthiazolidine-4-carboxylic acid (penicilloic acids of amoxicillin),

and epimer at C*

E. (2RS,4S)-2-[[[(2R)-2-amino-2-(4-hydroxyphenyl)acetyl]amino]methyl]-5,5-dimethylthiazolidine-4-carboxylic acid (penilloic acids of amoxicillin),

F. 3-(4-hydroxyphenyl)pyrazin-2-ol,

G. (2S,5R,6R)-6-[[(2R)-2-[[(2R)-2-amino-2-(4-hydroxyphenyl)acetyl]amino]2-(4-hydroxyphenyl)acetyl]amino]-3,3-dimethyl-7-oxo-4-thia-1-azabicyclo[3.2.0]heptane2-carboxylic acid (D-(4-hydroxyphenyl)glycylamoxicillin),

H. (2R)-2-[(2,2-dimethylpropanoyl)amino]-2-(4-hydroxyphenyl)acetic acid,

I. (2R)-2-amino-2-(4-hydroxyphenyl)acetic acid,

J. co-oligomers of amoxicillin and penicilloic acids of amoxicillin,

K. oligomers of penicilloic acids of amoxicillin.

# Amoxicillin Trihydrate

*(Ph Eur monograph 0260)*

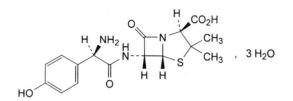

$C_{16}H_{19}N_3O_5S,3H_2O$     419.4     *61336-70-7*

### Action and use
Penicillin antibacterial.

### Preparations
Amoxicillin Capsules

Amoxicillin Oral Suspension

Co-amoxiclav Oral Suspension

Co-amoxiclav Tablets

Dispersible Co-amoxiclav Tablets

*Ph Eur* _____

## DEFINITION
(2S,5R,6R)-6-[[(2R)-2-Amino-2-(4-hydroxyphenyl)acetyl]amino]-3,3-dimethyl-7-oxo-4-thia-1-azabicyclo[3.2.0]heptane-2-carboxylic acid trihydrate.

Semi-synthetic product derived from a fermentation product.

### Content
95.0 per cent to 102.0 per cent (anhydrous substance).

## CHARACTERS
### Appearance
White or almost white, crystalline powder.

### Solubility
Slightly soluble in water, very slightly soluble in ethanol (96 per cent), practically insoluble in fatty oils. It dissolves in dilute acids and dilute solutions of alkali hydroxides.

## IDENTIFICATION
*First identification   A.*

*Second identification   B, C.*

A. Infrared absorption spectrophotometry (2.2.24).

*Comparison   amoxicillin trihydrate CRS.*

B. Thin-layer chromatography (2.2.27).

*Test solution*   Dissolve 25 mg of the substance to be examined in 10 ml of *sodium hydrogen carbonate solution R.*

*Reference solution (a)*   Dissolve 25 mg of *amoxicillin trihydrate CRS* in 10 ml of *sodium hydrogen carbonate solution R.*

*Reference solution (b)*   Dissolve 25 mg of *amoxicillin trihydrate CRS* and 25 mg of *ampicillin trihydrate CRS* in 10 ml of *sodium hydrogen carbonate solution R.*

*Plate*   TLC silanised silica gel plate R.

*Mobile phase*   Mix 10 volumes of *acetone R* and 90 volumes of a 154 g/l solution of *ammonium acetate R* previously adjusted to pH 5.0 with *glacial acetic acid R.*

*Application*   1 µl.

*Development*   Over a path of 15 cm.

*Drying*   In air.

*Detection*   Expose to iodine vapour until the spots appear and examine in daylight.

*System suitability*   Reference solution (b):
— the chromatogram shows 2 clearly separated spots.

*Results*   The principal spot in the chromatogram obtained with the test solution is similar in position, colour and size to the principal spot in the chromatogram obtained with reference solution (a).

C. Place about 2 mg in a test-tube about 150 mm long and about 15 mm in diameter. Moisten with 0.05 ml of *water R* and add 2 ml of *sulphuric acid-formaldehyde reagent R.* Mix the contents of the tube by swirling; the solution is practically colourless. Place the test-tube in a water-bath for 1 min; a dark yellow colour develops.

## TESTS
### Solution S
With the aid of ultrasound or gentle heating, dissolve 0.100 g in *carbon dioxide-free water R* and dilute to 50.0 ml with the same solvent.

### Appearance of solution
The solutions are not more opalescent than reference suspension II (2.2.1).

Dissolve 1.0 g in 10 ml of *0.5 M hydrochloric acid.* Dissolve separately 1.0 g in 10 ml of *dilute ammonia R2.* Examine immediately after dissolution.

### pH (2.2.3)
3.5 to 5.5 for solution S.

### Specific optical rotation (2.2.7)
+ 290 to + 315 (anhydrous substance), determined on solution S.

### Related substances
Liquid chromatography (2.2.29).

*Buffer solution pH 5.0*   To 250 ml of *0.2 M potassium dihydrogen phosphate R* add *dilute sodium hydroxide solution R* to pH 5.0 and dilute to 1000.0 ml with *water R.*

*Test solution (a)*   Dissolve 30.0 mg of the substance to be examined in mobile phase A and dilute to 50.0 ml with mobile phase A.

*Test solution (b)*   Dissolve 30.0 mg of the substance to be examined in mobile phase A and dilute to 20.0 ml with mobile phase A. *Prepare immediately before use.*

*Reference solution (a)*   Dissolve 30.0 mg of *amoxicillin trihydrate CRS* in mobile phase A and dilute to 50.0 ml with mobile phase A.

*Reference solution (b)*   Dissolve 4.0 mg of *cefadroxil CRS* in mobile phase A and dilute to 50 ml with mobile phase A. To 5.0 ml of this solution add 5.0 ml of reference solution (a) and dilute to 100 ml with mobile phase A.

*Reference solution (c)*   Dilute 2.0 ml of reference solution (a) to 20.0 ml with mobile phase A. Dilute 5.0 ml of this solution to 20.0 ml with mobile phase A.

*Column:*
— size: l = 0.25 m, Ø = 4.6 mm;
— stationary phase: octadecylsilyl silica gel for chromatography R (5 µm).

*Mobile phase:*
— mobile phase A: acetonitrile R, buffer solution pH 5.0 (1:99 V/V);
— mobile phase B: acetonitrile R, buffer solution pH 5.0 (20:80 V/V);

| Time (min) | Mobile phase A (per cent V/V) | Mobile phase B (per cent V/V) |
|---|---|---|
| 0 - $t_R$ | 92 | 8 |
| $t_R$ - ($t_R$ + 25) | 92 → 0 | 8 → 100 |
| ($t_R$ + 25) - ($t_R$ + 40) | 0 | 100 |
| ($t_R$ + 40) - ($t_R$ + 55) | 92 | 8 |

$t_R$ = retention time of amoxicillin determined with reference solution (c)

If the mobile phase composition has been adjusted to achieve the required resolution, the adjusted composition will apply at time zero in the gradient and in the assay.

*Flow rate*   1.0 ml/min.

*Detection*   Spectrophotometer at 254 nm.

*Injection*   50 μl of reference solutions (b) and (c) with isocratic elution at the initial mobile phase composition and 50 μl of test solution (b) according to the elution gradient described under Mobile phase; inject mobile phase A as a blank according to the elution gradient described under Mobile phase.

*System suitability*   Reference solution (b):
— *resolution*: minimum 2.0 between the peaks due to amoxicillin and cefadroxil; if necessary, adjust the ratio A:B of the mobile phase.

*Limit:*
— *any impurity*: for each impurity, not more than the area of the principal peak in the chromatogram obtained with reference solution (c) (1 per cent).

**N,N-Dimethylaniline** (*2.4.26, Method A or B*)
Maximum 20 ppm.

**Water** (*2.5.12*)
11.5 per cent to 14.5 per cent, determined on 0.100 g.

**Sulphated ash** (*2.4.14*)
Maximum 1.0 per cent, determined on 1.0 g.

**ASSAY**
Liquid chromatography (*2.2.29*) as described in the test for related substances with the following modifications.

*Mobile phase*   Initial composition of the mixture of mobile phases A and B, adjusted where applicable.

*Injection*   Test solution (a) and reference solution (a).

*System suitability*   Reference solution (a):
— *repeatability*: maximum relative standard deviation of 1.0 per cent after 6 injections.

Calculate the percentage content of $C_{16}H_{19}N_3O_5S$ from the declared content of *amoxicillin trihydrate CRS*.

**STORAGE**
In an airtight container.

**IMPURITIES**

A. (2S,5R,6R)-6-amino-3,3-dimethyl-7-oxo-4-thia-1-azabicyclo[3.2.0]heptane-2-carboxylic acid (6-aminopenicillanic acid),

B. (2S,5R,6R)-6-[[(2S)-2-amino-2-(4-hydroxyphenyl)acetyl]amino]-3,3-dimethyl-7-oxo-4-thia-1-azabicyclo[3.2.0]heptane-2-carboxylic acid (L-amoxicillin),

C. (4S)-2-[5-(4-hydroxyphenyl)-3,6-dioxopiperazin-2-yl]-5,5-dimethylthiazolidine-4-carboxylic acid (amoxicillin diketopiperazines),

D. R = CO$_2$H: (4S)-2-[[[(2R)-2-amino-2-(4-hydroxyphenyl)acetyl]amino]carboxymethyl]-5,5-dimethylthiazolidine-4-carboxylic acid (penicilloic acids of amoxicillin),

E. R = H: (2RS,4S)-2-[[[(2R)-2-amino-2-(4-hydroxyphenyl)acetyl]amino]methyl]-5,5-dimethylthiazolidine-4-carboxylic acid (penilloic acids of amoxicillin),

F. 3-(4-hydroxyphenyl)pyrazin-2-ol,

G. (2S,5R,6R)-6-[[(2R)-2-[[(2R)-2-amino-2-(4-hydroxyphenyl)acetyl]amino]-2-(4-hydroxyphenyl)acetyl]amino]-3,3-dimethyl-7-oxo-4-thia-1-azabicyclo[3.2.0]-heptane-2-carboxylic acid (D-(4-hydroxyphenyl)glycylamoxicillin),

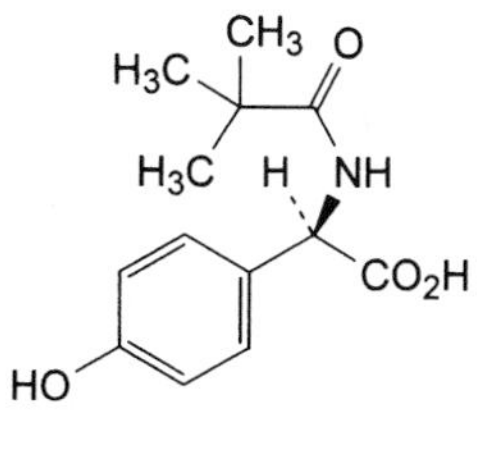

H. (2R)-2-[(2,2-dimethylpropanoyl)amino]-2-(4-hydroxyphenyl)acetic acid,

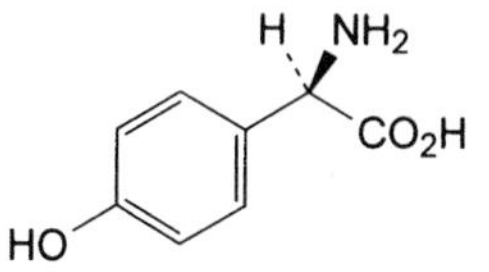

I. (2R)-2-amino-2-(4-hydroxyphenyl)acetic acid,

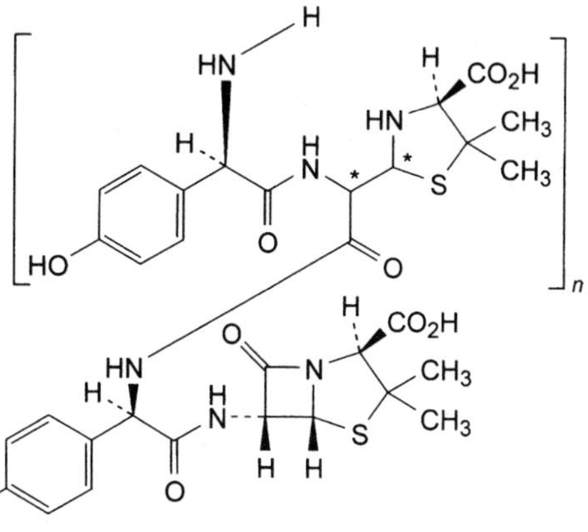

J. co-oligomers of amoxicillin and of penicilloic acids of amoxicillin,

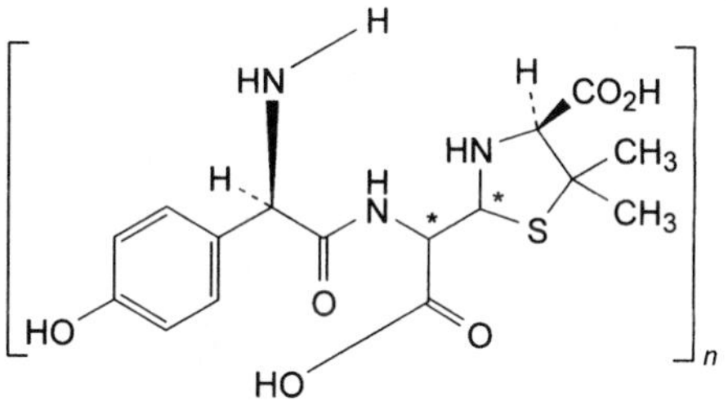

K. oligomers of penicilloic acids of amoxicillin,

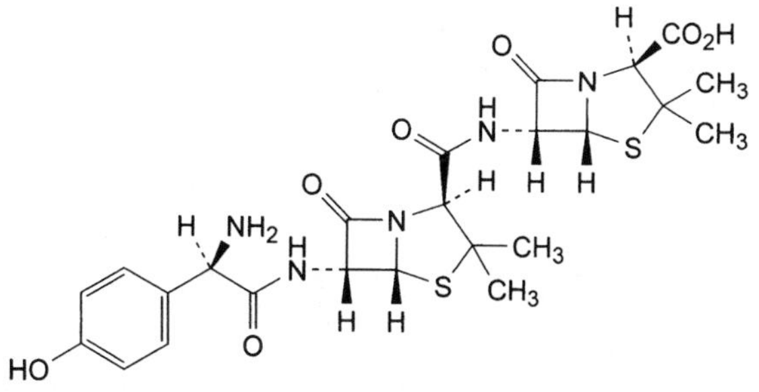

L. (2S,5R,6R)-6-[[(2S,5R,6R)-6-[[(2R)-2-amino-2-(4-hydroxyphenyl)acetyl]amino]-3,3-dimethyl-7-oxo-4-thia-1-azabicyclo[3.2.0]heptane-2-carbonyl]amino]-3,3-dimethyl-7-oxo-4-thia-1-azabicyclo[3.2.0]heptane-2-carboxylic acid (6-APA amoxicillin amide).

Ph Eur

# Amphotericin

(*Amphotericin B, Ph Eur monograph 1292*)

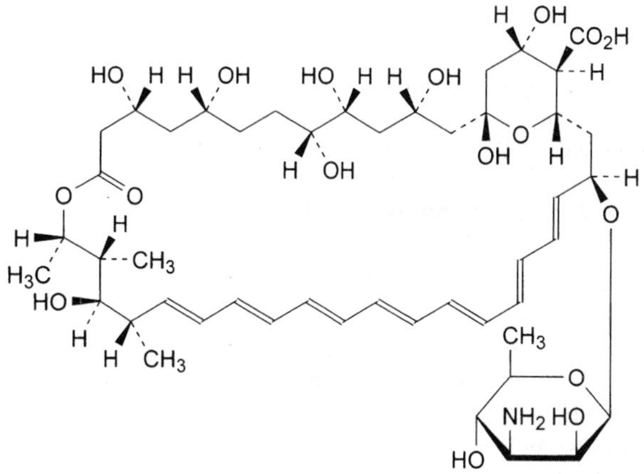

C$_{47}$H$_{73}$NO$_{17}$     924     *1397-89-3*

**Action and use**
Antifungal.

**Preparation**
Amphotericin Lozenges
Amphotericin Oral Suspension

Ph Eur

## DEFINITION
Mixture of antifungal polyenes produced by the growth of certain strains of *Streptomyces nodosus* or obtained by any other means. It consists mainly of amphotericin B which is (1R,3S,5R,6R,9R,11R,15S,16R,17R,18S,19E,21E,23E,25E,27E,29E,31E,33R,35S,36R,37S)-33-[(3-amino-3,6-dideoxy-β-D-mannopyranosyl)oxy]-1,3,5,6,9,11,17,37-octahydroxy-15,16,18-trimethyl-13-oxo-14,39-dioxabicyclo[33.3.1]nonatriaconta-19,21,23,25,27,29,31-heptaene-36-carboxylic acid.

**Content**
Minimum 750 IU/mg (dried substance).

## CHARACTERS
**Appearance**
Yellow or orange, hygroscopic powder.

**Solubility**
Practically insoluble in water, soluble in dimethyl sulphoxide and in propylene glycol, slightly soluble in dimethylformamide, very slightly soluble in methanol, practically insoluble in ethanol (96 per cent).

It is sensitive to light in dilute solutions.

## IDENTIFICATION
*First identification*   B, D.

*Second identification*   A, C.

A. Ultraviolet and visible absorption spectrophotometry (*2.2.25*).

*Test solution*   Dissolve 25 mg in 5 ml of *dimethyl sulphoxide R* and dilute to 50 ml with *methanol R*. Dilute 2 ml of the solution to 200 ml with *methanol R*.

*Spectral range*   300-450 nm.

*Absorption maxima*   At 362 nm, 381 nm and 405 nm.

*Absorbance ratios:*
— A$_{362}$/A$_{381}$ = 0.57 to 0.61;

— $A_{381}/A_{405} = 0.87$ to $0.93$.

B. Infrared absorption spectrophotometry (2.2.24).

*Comparison amphotericin B CRS.*

If the spectra obtained show differences, dry the substance to be examined and reference substance at 60 °C at a pressure not exceeding 0.7 kPa for 1 h and record new spectra.

C. To 1 ml of a 0.5 g/l solution in *dimethyl sulphoxide R*, add 5 ml of *phosphoric acid R* to form a lower layer, avoiding mixing the 2 liquids. A blue ring is immediately produced at the junction of the liquids. Mix, an intense blue colour is produced. Add 15 ml of *water R* and mix; the solution becomes pale yellow.

D. Examine the chromatograms obtained in the test for related substances.

*Results*  The principal peak in the chromatogram obtained with the test solution at 383 nm is similar in retention time to the principal peak in the chromatogram obtained with reference solution (a).

## TESTS
### Related substances
Liquid chromatography (2.2.29). *Protect the solutions from light and use within 24 h of preparation, except for reference solution (c) which should be injected immediately after its preparation.*

*Solvent mixture*  10 g/l solution of *ammonium acetate R*, *N-methylpyrrolidone R*, *methanol R* (1:1:2 *V/V/V*).

*Test solution*  Dissolve 20.0 mg of the substance to be examined in 15 ml of *N-methylpyrrolidone R* and within 2 h dilute to 50.0 ml with the solvent mixture. Dilute 5.0 ml of this solution to 25.0 ml with the solvent mixture.

*Reference solution (a)*  Dissolve 20.0 mg of *amphotericin B CRS* in 15 ml of *N-methylpyrrolidone R* and within 2 h dilute to 50.0 ml with the solvent mixture. Dilute 5.0 ml of this solution to 25.0 ml with the solvent mixture.

*Reference solution (b)*  Dilute 1.0 ml of reference solution (a) to 100.0 ml with the solvent mixture.

*Reference solution (c)*  Dissolve 20.0 mg of *nystatin CRS* in 15 ml of *N-methylpyrrolidone R* and within 2 h dilute to 50.0 ml with the solvent mixture. Dilute 5.0 ml of the solution to 25.0 ml with solution A. Dilute 2.0 ml of this solution to 100.0 ml with the solvent mixture.

*Reference solution (d)*  In order to prepare impurities B and C, dissolve 10 mg of the substance to be examined in 5 ml of *N-methylpyrrolidone R* and within 2 h add 35 ml of a mixture of 1 volume of *methanol R* and 4 volumes of *anhydrous ethanol R*. Add 0.10 ml of *dilute hydrochloric acid R*, mix and incubate at 25 °C for 2.5 h. Add 10 ml of 10 g/l solution of *ammonium acetate R* and mix.

*Reference solution (e)*  Dissolve 4 mg of *amphotericin B for peak identification CRS* (containing impurities A and B) in 5 ml of *N-methylpyrrolidone R* and within 2 h dilute to 50 ml with the solvent mixture.

*Blank solution*  The solvent mixture.

*Column:*
— size: $l = 0.15$ m, $\varnothing = 4.6$ mm;
— stationary phase: base-deactivated end-capped octadecylsilyl silica gel for chromatography R (3 µm);
— temperature: 20 °C.

*Mobile phase:*
— mobile phase A: mix 1 volume of *methanol R*, 3 volumes of *acetonitrile R* and 6 volumes of a 4.2 g/l solution of *citric acid R* previously adjusted to pH 4.7 using *concentrated ammonia R*;

— mobile phase B: mix 12 volumes of *methanol R*, 20 volumes of a 4.2 g/l solution of *citric acid R* previously adjusted to pH 3.9 using *concentrated ammonia R* and 68 volumes of *acetonitrile R*;

| Time (min) | Mobile phase A (per cent V/V) | Mobile phase B (per cent V/V) |
|---|---|---|
| 0 - 3 | 100 | 0 |
| 3 - 23 | 100 → 70 | 0 → 30 |
| 23 - 33 | 70 → 0 | 30 → 100 |
| 33 - 40 | 0 | 100 |

*Flow rate*  0.8 ml/min.

*Detection*  Spectrophotometer:
— at 303 nm: detection of tetraenes;
— at 383 nm: detection of heptaenes.

*Injection*  20 µl of the test solution and reference solutions (b), (c), (d) and (e).

*Identification of impurities*  Use the chromatograms supplied with *amphotericin B for peak identification CRS* and the chromatograms obtained with reference solution (e) to identify the peaks due to impurities A and B.

*Relative retention*  With reference to amphotericin B (retention time = about 16 min): impurity B = about 0.75; impurity A = about 0.8; nystatin = about 0.85.

*System suitability at 383 nm*  Reference solution (d):
— resolution: minimum 1.5 between the 2 peaks presenting a relative retention of about 0.7.

*Limits:*
— impurity A at 303 nm: not more than 2.5 times the area of the principal peak in the chromatogram obtained with reference solution (c) (5.0 per cent); if intended for use in the manufacture of parenteral preparations: not more than the area of the principal peak in the chromatogram obtained with reference solution (c) (2.0 per cent);
— any other impurity at 303 nm: for each impurity, not more than 0.5 times the area of the principal peak in the chromatogram obtained with reference solution (c) (1.0 per cent);
— impurity B at 383 nm: not more than 4 times the area of the principal peak in the chromatogram obtained with reference solution (b) (4.0 per cent);
— any other impurity at 383 nm: for each impurity, not more than 2 times the area of the principal peak in the chromatogram obtained with reference solution (b) (2.0 per cent);
— total at 303 and 383 nm: maximum 15.0 per cent;
— disregard limit at 303 nm: 0.05 times the area of the principal peak in the chromatogram obtained with reference solution (c) (0.1 per cent);
— disregard limit at 383 nm: 0.1 times the area of the principal peak in the chromatogram obtained with reference solution (b) (0.1 per cent).

**Loss on drying** (2.2.32)
Maximum 5.0 per cent, determined on 1.000 g by drying in an oven at 60 °C at a pressure not exceeding 0.7 kPa.

**Sulphated ash** (2.4.14)
Maximum 3.0 per cent, determined on 1.0 g; if intended for use in the manufacture of parenteral preparations: maximum 0.5 per cent.

**Bacterial endotoxins** (2.6.14)
Less than 1.0 IU/mg, if intended for use in the manufacture of parenteral preparations without a further appropriate procedure for the removal of bacterial endotoxins.

## ASSAY

*Protect all solutions from light throughout the assay.* Dissolve 25.0 mg in *dimethyl sulphoxide R* and dilute, with shaking, to 25.0 ml with the same solvent. Under constant stirring of this stock solution, dilute with *dimethyl sulphoxide R* to obtain solutions of appropriate concentrations (the following concentrations have been found suitable: 44.4, 66.7 and 100 IU/ml). Prepare final solutions by diluting 1:20 with 0.2 M phosphate buffer solution pH 10.5 so that they all contain 5 per cent *V/V* of dimethyl sulphoxide. Prepare the reference and the test solutions simultaneously. Carry out the microbiological assay of antibiotics (*2.7.2*).

## STORAGE

Protected from light, at a temperature of 2 °C to 8 °C in an airtight container. If the substance is sterile, store in a sterile, tamper-proof container.

## LABELLING

The label states, where applicable, that the substance is suitable for use in the manufacture of parenteral preparations.

## IMPURITIES

*Specified impurities  A, B.*

*Other detectable impurities*  (The following substances would, if present at a sufficient level, be detected by one or other of the tests in the monograph. They are limited by the general acceptance criterion for other/unspecified impurities and/or by the general monograph *Substances for pharmaceutical use (2034)*. It is therefore not necessary to identify these impurities for demonstration of compliance. See also *5.10. Control of impurities in substances for pharmaceutical use*): *C*.

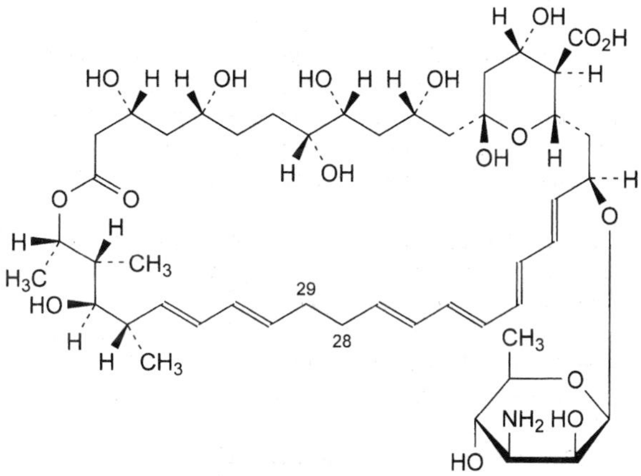

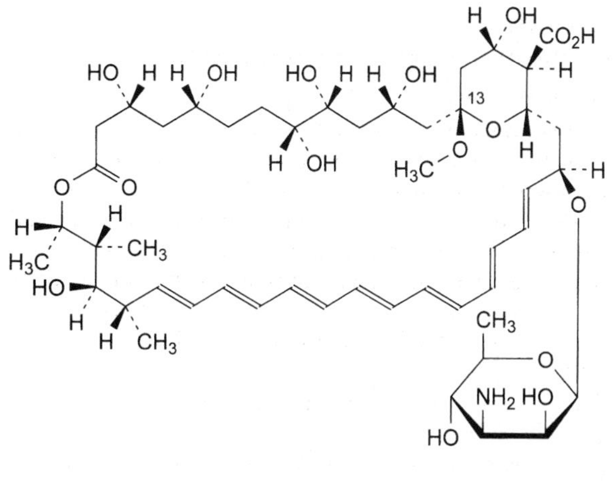

B. amphotericin X1 (13-*O*-methyl-amphotericin B),

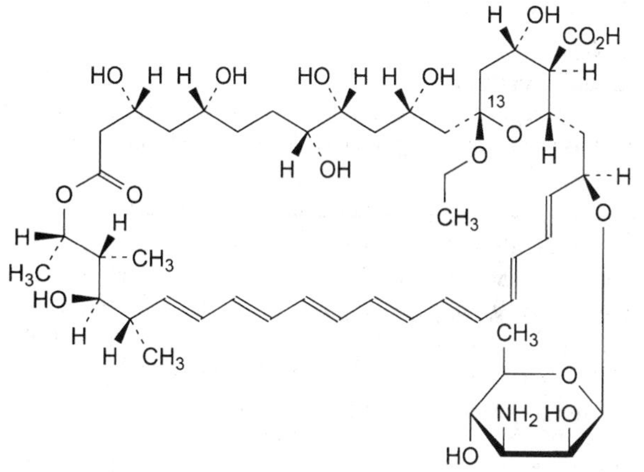

C. amphotericin X2 (13-*O*-ethyl-amphotericin B).

*Ph Eur*

A. amphotericin A (28,29-dihydro-amphotericin B),

# Ampicillin

(*Anhydrous Ampicillin, Ph Eur monograph 0167*)

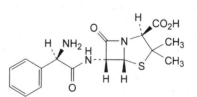

C₁₆H₁₉N₃O₄S          349.4          69-53-4

**Action and use**
Penicillin antibacterial.

**Preparations**
Ampicillin Capsules
Ampicillin Oral Suspension

*Ph Eur*

## DEFINITION

(2*S*,5*R*,6*R*)-6-[[(2*R*)-2-Amino-2-phenylacetyl]amino]-3,3-dimethyl-7-oxo-4-thia-1-azabicyclo[3.2.0]heptane-2-carboxylic acid.

Semi-synthetic product derived from a fermentation product.

## Content

96.0 per cent to 102.0 per cent (anhydrous substance).

## CHARACTERS

### Appearance

White or almost white, crystalline powder.

### Solubility

Sparingly soluble in water, practically insoluble in acetone, in ethanol (96 per cent) and in fatty oils. It dissolves in dilute solutions of acids and of alkali hydroxides.

It shows polymorphism (5.9).

## IDENTIFICATION

*First identification*  A, D.

*Second identification*  B, C, D.

A. Infrared absorption spectrophotometry (2.2.24).

*Preparation*  Discs of *potassium bromide R*.

*Comparison*  anhydrous ampicillin CRS.

B. Thin-layer chromatography (2.2.27).

*Test solution*  Dissolve 25 mg of the substance to be examined in 10 ml of *sodium hydrogen carbonate solution R*.

*Reference solution (a)*  Dissolve 25 mg of *anhydrous ampicillin CRS* in 10 ml of *sodium hydrogen carbonate solution R*.

*Reference solution (b)*  Dissolve 25 mg of *amoxicillin trihydrate CRS* and 25 mg of *anhydrous ampicillin CRS* in 10 ml of *sodium hydrogen carbonate solution R*.

*Plate*  TLC *silanised silica gel plate R*.

*Mobile phase*  Mix 10 volumes of *acetone R* and 90 volumes of a 154 g/l solution of *ammonium acetate R* previously adjusted to pH 5.0 with *glacial acetic acid R*.

*Application*  1 µl.

*Development*  Over a path of 15 cm.

*Drying*  In air.

*Detection*  Expose to iodine vapour until the spots appear and examine in daylight.

*System suitability*  Reference solution (b):
— the chromatogram shows 2 clearly separated spots.

*Results*  The principal spot in the chromatogram obtained with the test solution is similar in position, colour and size to the principal spot in the chromatogram obtained with reference solution (a).

C. Place about 2 mg in a test-tube about 150 mm long and about 15 mm in diameter. Moisten with 0.05 ml of *water R* and add 2 ml of *sulphuric acid-formaldehyde reagent R*. Mix the contents of the tube by swirling; the solution is practically colourless. Place the test-tube in a water-bath for 1 min; a dark yellow colour develops.

D. Water (see Tests).

## TESTS

### Appearance of solution

The solutions are not more opalescent than reference suspension II (2.2.1).

Dissolve 1.0 g in 10 ml of *1 M hydrochloric acid*. Separately dissolve 1.0 g in 10 ml of *dilute ammonia R2*. Examine immediately after dissolution.

### pH (2.2.3)

3.5 to 5.5.

Dissolve 0.1 g in *carbon dioxide-free water R* and dilute to 40 ml with the same solvent.

### Specific optical rotation (2.2.7)

+ 280 to + 305 (anhydrous substance).

Dissolve 62.5 mg in *water R* and dilute to 25.0 ml with the same solvent.

### Related substances

Liquid chromatography (2.2.29).

*Test solution (a)*  Dissolve 27.0 mg of the substance to be examined in mobile phase A and dilute to 50.0 ml with mobile phase A.

*Test solution (b)*  Dissolve 27.0 mg of the substance to be examined in mobile phase A and dilute to 10.0 ml with mobile phase A. *Prepare immediately before use.*

*Reference solution (a)*  Dissolve 27.0 mg of *anhydrous ampicillin CRS* in mobile phase A and dilute to 50.0 ml with mobile phase A.

*Reference solution (b)*  Dissolve 2.0 mg of *cefradine CRS* in mobile phase A and dilute to 50 ml with mobile phase A. To 5.0 ml of this solution add 5.0 ml of reference solution (a).

*Reference solution (c)*  Dilute 1.0 ml of reference solution (a) to 20.0 ml with mobile phase A.

*Column:*
— *size: l* = 0.25 m, Ø = 4.6 mm;
— *stationary phase: octadecylsilyl silica gel for chromatography R* (5 µm).

*Mobile phase:*
— *mobile phase A*: mix 0.5 ml of *dilute acetic acid R*, 50 ml of *0.2 M potassium dihydrogen phosphate R* and 50 ml of *acetonitrile R*, then dilute to 1000 ml with *water R*;
— *mobile phase B*: mix 0.5 ml of *dilute acetic acid R*, 50 ml of *0.2 M potassium dihydrogen phosphate R* and 400 ml of *acetonitrile R*, then dilute to 1000 ml with *water R*;

| Time (min) | Mobile phase A (per cent $V/V$) | Mobile phase B (per cent $V/V$) |
|---|---|---|
| 0 - $t_R$ | 85 | 15 |
| $t_R$ - ($t_R$ + 30) | 85 → 0 | 15 → 100 |
| ($t_R$ + 30) - ($t_R$ + 45) | 0 | 100 |
| ($t_R$ + 45) - ($t_R$ + 60) | 85 | 15 |

$t_R$ = retention time of ampicillin determined with reference solution (c)

If the mobile phase composition has been adjusted to achieve the required resolution, the adjusted composition will apply at time zero in the gradient and in the assay.

*Flow rate*  1.0 ml/min.

*Detection*  Spectrophotometer at 254 nm.

*Injection*  50 µl of reference solutions (b) and (c) with isocratic elution at the initial mobile phase composition and 50 µl of test solution (b) according to the elution gradient described under Mobile phase; inject mobile phase A as a blank according to the elution gradient described under Mobile phase.

*System suitability*  Reference solution (b):
— *resolution*: minimum 3.0 between the peaks due to ampicillin and cefradin; if necessary, adjust the ratio A:B of the mobile phase.

*Limit:*
— *any impurity*: for each impurity, not more than the area of the principal peak in the chromatogram obtained with reference solution (c) (1.0 per cent).

### N,N-Dimethylaniline (2.4.26, *Method B*)

Maximum 20 ppm.

### Water (2.5.12)

Maximum 2.0 per cent, determined on 0.300 g.

### Sulphated ash (2.4.14)

Maximum 0.5 per cent, determined on 1.0 g.

## ASSAY

Liquid chromatography (*2.2.29*) as described in the test for related substances with the following modifications.

*Mobile phase* Initial composition of the mixture of mobile phases A and B, adjusted where applicable.

*Injection* Test solution (a) and reference solution (a).

*System suitability* Reference solution (a):
— *repeatability*: maximum relative standard deviation of 1.0 per cent after 6 injections.

Calculate the percentage content of $C_{16}H_{19}N_3O_4S$ from the declared content of *anhydrous ampicillin CRS*.

## STORAGE

In an airtight container, at a temperature not exceeding 30 °C.

## IMPURITIES

A. (2*S*,5*R*,6*R*)-6-amino-3,3-dimethyl-7-oxo-4-thia-1-azabicyclo[3.2.0]heptane-2-carboxylic acid (6-aminopenicillanic acid),

B. (2*S*,5*R*,6*R*)-6-[[(2*S*)-2-amino-2-phenylacetyl]amino]-3,3-dimethyl-7-oxo-4-thia-1-azabicyclo[3.2.0]heptane-2-carboxylic acid (L-ampicillin),

C. (4*S*)-2-(3,6-dioxo-5-phenylpiperazin-2-yl)-5,5-dimethylthiazolidine-4-carboxylic acid (diketopiperazines of ampicillin),

D. R = CO₂H: (4*S*)-2-[[[(2*R*)-2-amino-2-phenylacetyl]amino]carboxymethyl]-5,5-dimethylthiazolidine-4-carboxylic acid (penicilloic acids of ampicillin),

F. R = H: (2*RS*,4*S*)-2-[[[(2*R*)-2-amino-2-phenylacetyl]amino]methyl]-5,5-dimethylthiazolidine-4-carboxylic acid (penilloic acids of ampicillin),

E. (2*R*)-2-[[[(2*S*,5*R*,6*R*)-6-[[(2*R*)-2-amino-2-phenylacetyl]amino]-3,3-dimethyl-7-oxo-4-thia-1-azabicyclo[3.2.0]hept-2-yl]carbonyl]amino]-2-phenylacetic acid (ampicillinyl-d-phenylglycine),

G. (3*R*,6*R*)-3,6-diphenylpiperazine-2,5-dione,

H. 3-phenylpyrazin-2-ol,

I. (2*S*,5*R*,6*R*)-6-[[(2*R*)-2-[[(2*R*)-2-amino-2-phenylacetyl]amino]-2-phenylacetyl]amino]-3,3-dimethyl-7-oxo-4-thia-1-azabicyclo[3.2.0]heptane-2-carboxylic acid (D-phenylglycylampicillin),

J. (2*S*,5*R*,6*R*)-6-[(2,2-dimethylpropanoyl)amino]-3,3-dimethyl-7-oxo-4-thia-1-azabicyclo[3.2.0]heptane-2-carboxylic acid,

K. (2*R*)-2-[(2,2-dimethylpropanoyl)amino]-2-phenylacetic acid,

L. (2R)-2-amino-2-phenylacetic acid (D-phenylglycine),

M. co-oligomers of ampicillin and of penicilloic acids of ampicillin.

_____ *Ph Eur*

# Ampicillin Sodium

*(Ph Eur monograph 0578)*

$C_{16}H_{18}N_3NaO_4S$          371.4          69-52-3

## Action and use
Penicillin antibacterial.

## Preparation
Ampicillin Injection

*Ph Eur* _____

## DEFINITION
Sodium (2S,5R,6R)-6-[[(2R)-2-amino-2-phenylacetyl]amino]-3,3-dimethyl-7-oxo-4-thia-1-azabicyclo[3.2.0]heptane-2-carboxylate.

Semi-synthetic product derived from a fermentation product.

## Content
91.0 per cent to 102.0 per cent (anhydrous substance).

## CHARACTERS

### Appearance
White or almost white powder, hygroscopic.

### Solubility
Freely soluble in water, sparingly soluble in acetone, practically insoluble in fatty oils and in liquid paraffin.

## IDENTIFICATION
*First identification*   A, D.

*Second identification*   B, C, D.

A. Infrared absorption spectrophotometry (*2.2.24*).

*Preparation*   Dissolve 0.250 g in 5 ml of *water R*, add 0.5 ml of *dilute acetic acid R*, swirl and allow to stand for 10 min in iced water. Filter the crystals through a small sintered-glass filter (40) (*2.1.2*), applying suction, wash with 2-3 ml of a mixture of 1 volume of *water R* and 9 volumes of *acetone R*, then dry in an oven at 60 °C for 30 min.

*Comparison*   ampicillin trihydrate CRS.

B. Thin-layer chromatography (*2.2.27*).

*Test solution*   Dissolve 25 mg of the substance to be examined in 10 ml of *sodium hydrogen carbonate solution R*.

*Reference solution (a)*   Dissolve 25 mg of *ampicillin trihydrate CRS* in 10 ml of *sodium hydrogen carbonate solution R*.

*Reference solution (b)*   Dissolve 25 mg of *amoxicillin trihydrate CRS* and 25 mg of *ampicillin trihydrate CRS* in 10 ml of *sodium hydrogen carbonate solution R*.

*Plate*   TLC silanised silica gel plate R.

*Mobile phase*   Mix 10 volumes of *acetone R* and 90 volumes of a 154 g/l solution of *ammonium acetate R* previously adjusted to pH 5.0 with *glacial acetic acid R*.

*Application*   1 µl.

*Development*   Over a path of 15 cm.

*Drying*   In air.

*Detection*   Expose to iodine vapour until the spots appear and examine in daylight.

*System suitability*   Reference solution (b):
— the chromatogram shows 2 clearly separated spots.

*Results*   The principal spot in the chromatogram obtained with the test solution is similar in position, colour and size to the principal spot in the chromatogram obtained with reference solution (a).

C. Place about 2 mg in a test-tube about 150 mm long and about 15 mm in diameter. Moisten with 0.05 ml of *water R* and add 2 ml of *sulphuric acid-formaldehyde reagent R*. Mix the contents of the tube by swirling; the solution is practically colourless. Place the test-tube in a water-bath for 1 min; a dark yellow colour develops.

D. It gives reaction (a) of sodium (*2.3.1*).

## TESTS
### Appearance of solution
Solutions A and B are not more opalescent than reference suspension II (*2.2.1*) and the absorbance (*2.2.25*) of solution B at 430 nm is not greater than 0.15.

Place 1.0 g in a conical flask and add slowly and with continuous swirling 10 ml of *1 M hydrochloric acid* (solution A). Separately dissolve 1.0 g in *water R* and dilute to 10.0 ml with the same solvent (solution B). Examine immediately after dissolution.

### pH (*2.2.3*)
8.0 to 10.0.

Dissolve 2.0 g in *carbon dioxide-free water R* and dilute to 20 ml with the same solvent. Measure 10 min after dissolution.

### Specific optical rotation (*2.2.7*)
+ 258 to + 287 (anhydrous substance).

Dissolve 62.5 mg in a 4 g/l solution of *potassium hydrogen phthalate R* and dilute to 25.0 ml with the same solvent.

### Related substances
Liquid chromatography (*2.2.29*).

*Test solution (a)* Dissolve 31.0 mg of the substance to be examined in mobile phase A and dilute to 50.0 ml with mobile phase A.

*Test solution (b)* Dissolve 31.0 mg of the substance to be examined in mobile phase A and dilute to 10.0 ml with mobile phase A. *Prepare immediately before use.*

*Reference solution (a)* Dissolve 27.0 mg of *anhydrous ampicillin CRS* in mobile phase A and dilute to 50.0 ml with mobile phase A.

*Reference solution (b)* Dissolve 2.0 mg of *cefradine CRS* in mobile phase A and dilute to 50 ml with mobile phase A. To 5.0 ml of this solution add 5.0 ml of reference solution (a).

*Reference solution (c)* Dilute 1.0 ml of reference solution (a) to 20.0 ml with mobile phase A.

*Reference solution (d)* To 0.20 g of the substance to be examined add 1.0 ml of *water R*. Heat the solution at 60 °C for 1 h. Dilute 0.5 ml of this solution to 50.0 ml with mobile phase A.

*Column:*
— *size: l* = 0.25 m, Ø = 4.6 mm;
— *stationary phase*: octadecylsilyl silica gel for chromatography R (5 µm).

*Mobile phase:*
— *mobile phase A*: mix 0.5 ml of *dilute acetic acid R*, 50 ml of *0.2 M potassium dihydrogen phosphate* R and 50 ml of *acetonitrile R*, then dilute to 1000 ml with *water R*;
— *mobile phase B*: mix 0.5 ml of *dilute acetic acid R*, 50 ml of *0.2 M potassium dihydrogen phosphate* R and 400 ml of *acetonitrile R*, then dilute to 1000 ml with *water R;*

| Time (min) | Mobile phase A (per cent $V/V$) | Mobile phase B (per cent $V/V$) |
|---|---|---|
| $0 - t_R$ | 85 | 15 |
| $t_R - (t_R + 30)$ | 85 → 0 | 15 → 100 |
| $(t_R + 30) - (t_R + 45)$ | 0 | 100 |
| $(t_R + 45) - (t_R + 60)$ | 85 | 15 |

$t_R$ = retention time of ampicillin determined with reference solution (c)

If the mobile phase composition has been adjusted to achieve the required resolution, the adjusted composition will apply at time zero in the gradient and in the assay.

*Flow rate* 1.0 ml/min.

*Detection* Spectrophotometer at 254 nm.

*Injection* 50 µl of reference solutions (b) and (c) with isocratic elution at the initial mobile phase composition and 50 µl of test solution (b) and reference solution (d) according to the elution gradient described under Mobile phase; inject mobile phase A as a blank according to the elution gradient described under Mobile phase.

*Identification of peaks* Use the chromatogram obtained with reference solution (d) to identify the peaks due to ampicillin and ampicillin dimer.

*Relative retention* With reference to ampicillin: ampicillin dimer = about 2.8.

*System suitability* Reference solution (b):
— *resolution*: minimum 3.0 between the peaks due to ampicillin and cefradin; if necessary adjust the ratio A:B of the mobile phase.

*Limits:*
— *ampicillin dimmer*: not more than 4.5 times the area of the principal peak in the chromatogram obtained with reference solution (c) (4.5 per cent);

— *any other impurity*: for each impurity, not more than twice the area of the principal peak in the chromatogram obtained with reference solution (c) (2 per cent).

**N,N-Dimethylaniline** (*2.4.26, Method B*)
Maximum 20 ppm.

**2-Ethylhexanoic acid** (*2.4.28*)
Maximum 0.8 per cent m/m.

**Methylene chloride**
Gas chromatography (*2.2.28*).

*Internal standard solution* Dissolve 1.0 ml of *ethylene chloride R* in *water R* and dilute to 500.0 ml with the same solvent.

*Test solution (a)* Dissolve 1.0 g of the substance to be examined in *water R* and dilute to 10.0 ml with the same solvent.

*Test solution (b)* Dissolve 1.0 g of the substance to be examined in *water R*, add 1.0 ml of the internal standard solution and dilute to 10.0 ml with *water R*.

*Reference solution* Dissolve 1.0 ml of *methylene chloride R* in *water R* and dilute to 500.0 ml with the same solvent. To 1.0 ml of this solution add 1.0 ml of the internal standard solution and dilute to 10.0 ml with *water R*.

*Column:*
— *material*: glass;
— *size: l* = 1.5 m, Ø = 4 mm;
— *stationary phase*: *diatomaceous earth for gas chromatography R* impregnated with 10 per cent *m/m* of *macrogol 1000 R*.

*Carrier gas* *nitrogen for chromatography R*.

*Flow rate* 40 ml/min.

*Temperature:*
— *column*: 60 °C;
— *injection port*: 100 °C;
— *detector*: 150 °C.

*Detection* Flame ionisation.

Calculate the content of methylene chloride taking its density at 20 °C to be 1.325 g/ml.

*Limit:*
— *methylene chloride*: maximum 0.2 per cent m/m.

**Heavy metals** (*2.4.8*)
Maximum 20 ppm.

1.0 g complies with test C. Prepare the reference solution using 2 ml of *lead standard solution (10 ppm Pb) R*.

**Water** (*2.5.12*)
Maximum 2.0 per cent, determined on 0.300 g.

**Bacterial endotoxins** (*2.6.14*)
Less than 0.15 IU/mg, if intended for use in the manufacture of parenteral dosage forms without a further appropriate procedure for the removal of bacterial endotoxins.

**ASSAY**

Liquid chromatography (*2.2.29*) as described in the test for related substances with the following modifications.

*Mobile phase* Initial composition of the mixture of mobile phases A and B, adjusted where applicable.

*Injection* Test solution (a) and reference solution (a).

*System suitability* Reference solution (a):
— *repeatability*: maximum relative standard deviation of 1.0 per cent after 6 injections.

Calculate the percentage content of ampicillin sodium by multiplying the percentage content of ampicillin by 1.063.

**STORAGE**

In an airtight container. If the substance is sterile, store in a sterile, airtight, tamper-proof container.

**IMPURITIES**

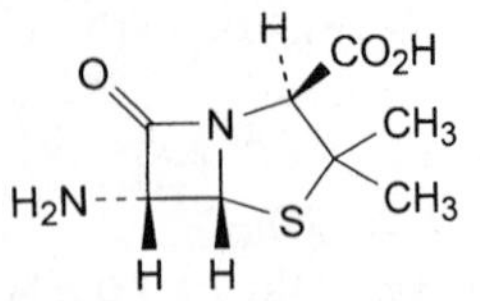

A. (2S,5R,6R)-6-amino-3,3-dimethyl-7-oxo-4-thia-1-azabicyclo[3.2.0]heptane-2-carboxylic acid (6-aminopenicillanic acid),

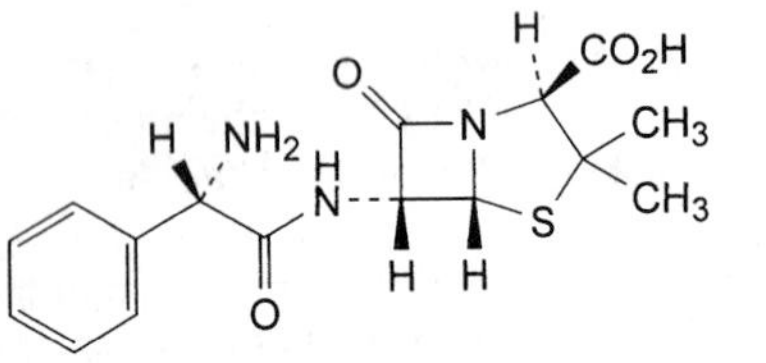

B. (2S,5R,6R)-6-[[(2S)-2-amino-2-phenylacetyl]amino]-3,3-dimethyl-7-oxo-4-thia-1-azabicyclo[3.2.0]heptane-2-carboxylic acid (L-ampicillin),

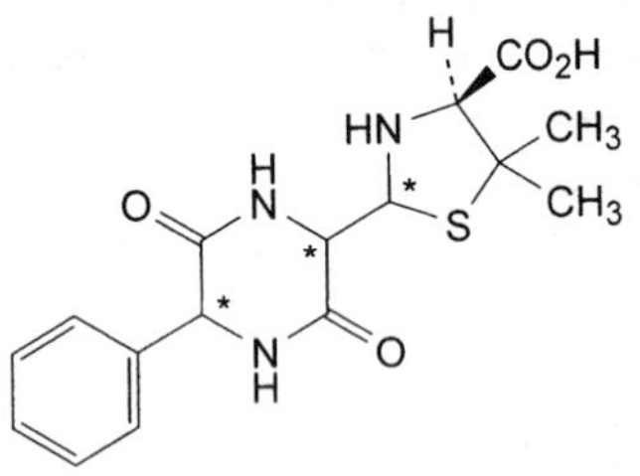

C. (4S)-2-(3,6-dioxo-5-phenylpiperazin-2-yl)-5,5-dimethylthiazolidine-4-carboxylic acid (diketopiperazines of ampicillin),

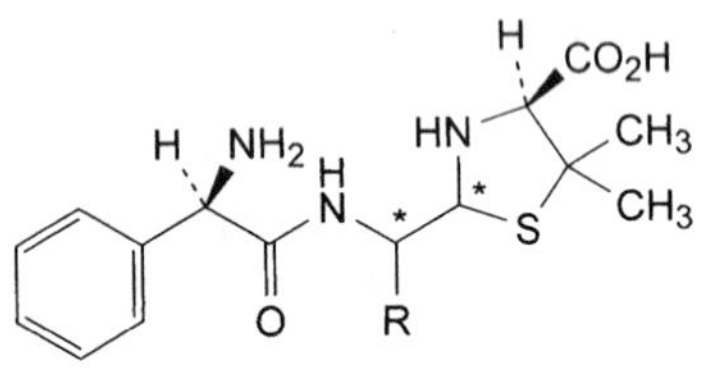

D. R = CO$_2$H: (4S)-2-[[[(2R)-2-amino-2-phenylacetyl]amino]carboxymethyl]-5,5-dimethylthiazolidine-4-carboxylic acid (penicilloic acids of ampicillin),

F. R = H: (2RS,4S)-2-[[[(2R)-2-amino-2-phenylacetyl]amino]methyl]-5,5-dimethylthiazolidine-4-carboxylic acid (penilloic acids of ampicillin),

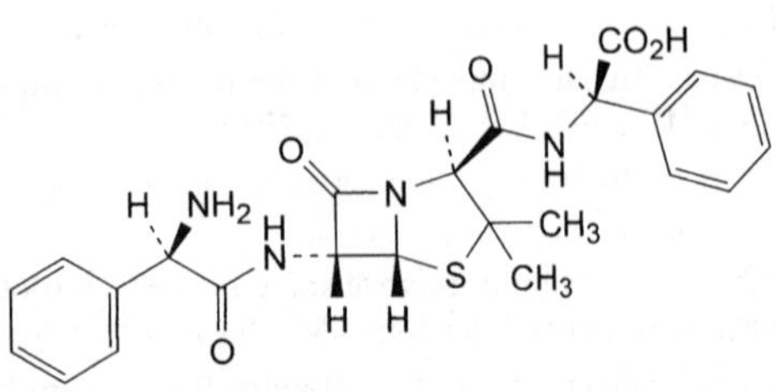

E. (2R)-2-[[[(2S,5R,6R)-6-[[(2R)-2-amino-2-phenylacetyl]amino]-3,3-dimethyl-7-oxo-4-thia-1-azabicyclo[3.2.0]hept-2-yl]carbonyl]amino]-2-phenylacetic acid (ampicillinyl-D-phenylglycine),

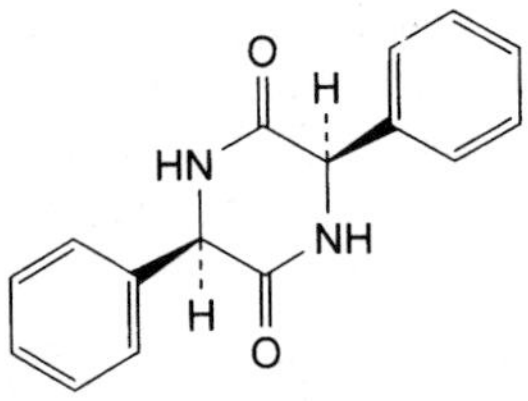

G. (3R,6R)-3,6-diphenylpiperazine-2,5-dione,

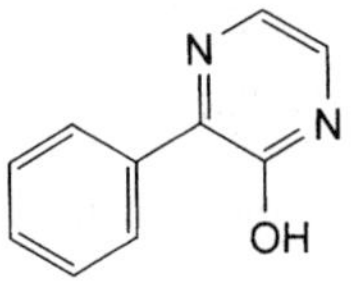

H. 3-phenylpyrazin-2-ol,

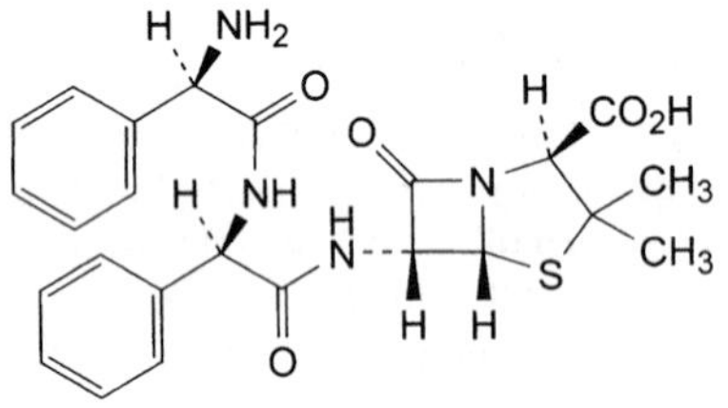

I. (2S,5R,6R)-6-[[(2R)-2-[[(2R)-2-amino-2-phenylacetyl]amino]-2-phenylacetyl]amino]-3,3-dimethyl-7-oxo-4-thia1-azabicyclo[3.2.0]heptane-2-carboxylic acid (D-phenylglycylampicillin),

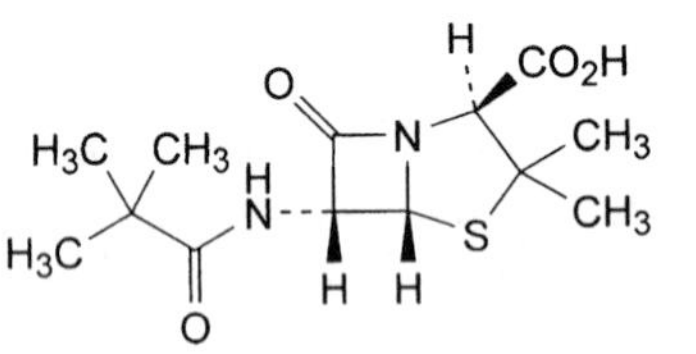

J. (2S,5R,6R)-6-[(2,2-dimethylpropanoyl)amino]-3,3-dimethyl-7-oxo-4-thia-1-azabicyclo[3.2.0]heptane-2-carboxylic acid,

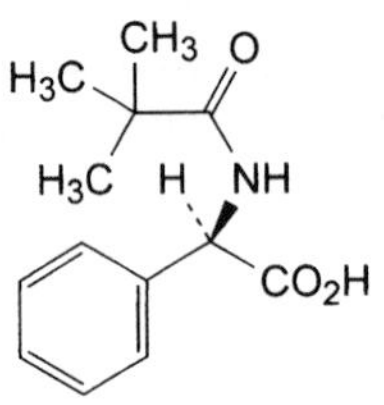

K. (2R)-2-[(2,2-dimethylpropanoyl)amino]-2-phenylacetic acid,

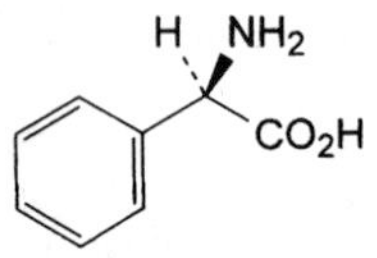

L. (2R)-2-amino-2-phenylacetic acid (D-phenylglycine),

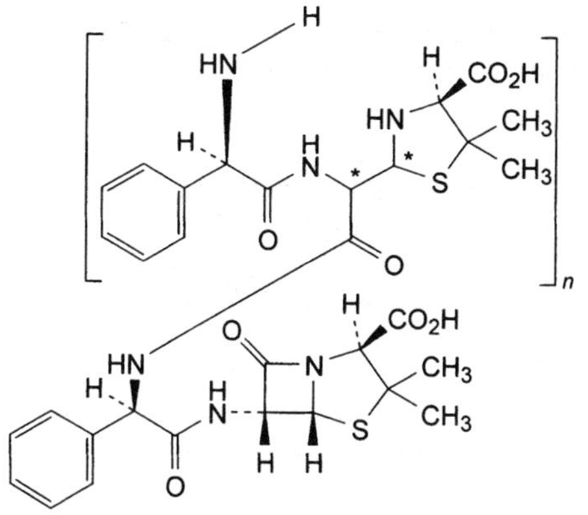

M. co-oligomers of ampicillin and of penicilloic acids of ampicillin,

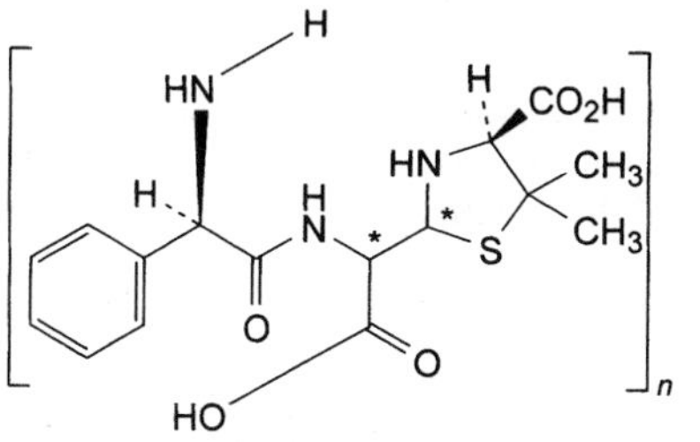

N. oligomers of penicilloic acids of ampicillin.

*Ph Eur*

# Ampicillin Trihydrate

*(Ph Eur monograph 0168)*

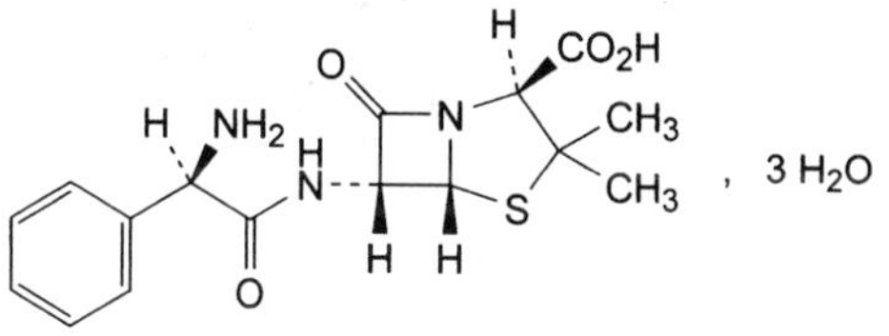

C$_{16}$H$_{19}$N$_3$O$_4$S,3H$_2$O    403.5    *7177-48-2*

**Action and use**
Penicillin antibacterial.

**Preparations**
Ampicillin Capsules
Ampicillin Oral Suspension
Co-fluampicil Capsules
Co-fluampicil Oral Suspension

*Ph Eur*

## DEFINITION

(2S,5R,6R)-6-[[(2R)-2-Amino-2-phenylacetyl]amino]-3,3-dimethyl-7-oxo-4-thia-1-azabicyclo[3.2.0]heptane-2-carboxylic acid trihydrate.

Semi-synthetic product derived from a fermentation product.

## Content
96.0 per cent to 102.0 per cent (anhydrous substance).

## CHARACTERS
**Appearance**
White or almost white, crystalline powder.

**Solubility**
Slightly soluble in water, practically insoluble in ethanol (96 per cent) and in fatty oils. It dissolves in dilute solutions of acids and of alkali hydroxides.

## IDENTIFICATION
*First identification   A, D.*

*Second identification   B, C, D.*

A. Infrared absorption spectrophotometry (2.2.24).

*Comparison   ampicillin trihydrate CRS .*

B. Thin-layer chromatography (2.2.27).

*Test solution*   Dissolve 25 mg of the substance to be examined in 10 ml of *sodium hydrogen carbonate solution R*.

*Reference solution (a)*   Dissolve 25 mg of *ampicillin trihydrate CRS* in 10 ml of *sodium hydrogen carbonate solution R*.

*Reference solution (b)*   Dissolve 25 mg of *amoxicillin trihydrate CRS* and 25 mg of *ampicillin trihydrate CRS* in 10 ml of *sodium hydrogen carbonate solution R*.

*Plate   TLC silanised silica gel plate R.*

*Mobile phase*   Mix 10 volumes of *acetone R* and 90 volumes of a 154 g/l solution of *ammonium acetate R* previously adjusted to pH 5.0 with *glacial acetic acid R*.

*Application*   1 µl.

*Development*   Over a path of 15 cm.

*Drying*   In air.

*Detection*   Expose to iodine vapour until the spots appear and examine in daylight.

*System suitability*   Reference solution (b):
— the chromatogram shows 2 clearly separated spots.

*Results*   The principal spot in the chromatogram obtained with the test solution is similar in position, colour and size to the principal spot in the chromatogram obtained with reference solution (a).

C. Place about 2 mg in a test-tube about 150 mm long and about 15 mm in diameter. Moisten with 0.05 ml of *water R* and add 2 ml of *sulphuric acid-formaldehyde reagent R*. Mix the contents of the tube by swirling; the solution is practically colourless. Place the test-tube in a water-bath for 1 min; a dark yellow colour develops.

D. Water (see Tests).

## TESTS
**Appearance of solution**
The solutions are not more opalescent than reference suspension II (2.2.1).

Dissolve 1.0 g in 10 ml of *1 M hydrochloric acid*. Separately dissolve 1.0 g in 10 ml of *dilute ammonia R2*. Examine immediately after dissolution.

**pH** (2.2.3)
3.5 to 5.5.

Dissolve 0.1 g in *carbon dioxide-free water R* and dilute to 40 ml with the same solvent.

**Specific optical rotation** (2.2.7)
+ 280 to + 305 (anhydrous substance).

Dissolve 62.5 mg in *water R* and dilute to 25.0 ml with the same solvent.

**Related substances**
Liquid chromatography (2.2.29).

*Test solution (a)* Dissolve 31.0 mg of the substance to be examined in mobile phase A and dilute to 50.0 ml with mobile phase A.

*Test solution (b)* Dissolve 31.0 mg of the substance to be examined in mobile phase A and dilute to 10.0 ml with mobile phase A. *Prepare immediately before use.*

*Reference solution (a)* Dissolve 27.0 mg of *anhydrous ampicillin CRS* in mobile phase A and dilute to 50.0 ml with mobile phase A.

*Reference solution (b)* Dissolve 2 mg of *cefradine CRS* in mobile phase A and dilute to 50 ml with mobile phase A. To 5 ml of this solution, add 5 ml of reference solution (a).

*Reference solution (c)* Dilute 1.0 ml of reference solution (a) to 20.0 ml with mobile phase A.

*Column:*
— *size: l = 0.25 m, Ø = 4.6 mm;*
— *stationary phase:* octadecylsilyl silica gel for chromatography R (5 µm).

*Mobile phase:*
— *mobile phase A:* mix 0.5 ml of *dilute acetic acid R*, 50 ml of *0.2 M potassium dihydrogen phosphate R* and 50 ml of *acetonitrile R*, then dilute to 1000 ml with *water R*;
— *mobile phase B:* mix 0.5 ml of *dilute acetic acid R*, 50 ml of *0.2 M potassium dihydrogen phosphate R* and 400 ml of *acetonitrile R*, then dilute to 1000 ml with *water R*;

| Time (min) | Mobile phase A (per cent V/V) | Mobile phase B (per cent V/V) |
|---|---|---|
| $0 - t_R$ | 85 | 15 |
| $t_R - (t_R + 30)$ | 85 → 0 | 15 → 100 |
| $(t_R + 30) - (t_R + 45)$ | 0 | 100 |
| $(t_R + 45) - (t_R + 60)$ | 85 | 15 |

$t_R$ = retention time of ampicillin determined with reference solution (c)

If the mobile phase composition has been adjusted to achieve the required resolution, the adjusted composition will apply at time zero in the gradient and in the assay.

*Flow rate* 1.0 ml/min.

*Detection* Spectrophotometer at 254 nm.

*Injection* 50 µl of reference solutions (b) and (c) with isocratic elution at the initial mobile phase composition and 50 µl of test solution (b) according to the elution gradient described under Mobile phase; inject mobile phase A as a blank according to the elution gradient described under Mobile phase.

*System suitability* Reference solution (b):
— *resolution:* minimum 3.0 between the peaks due to ampicillin and cefradin; if necessary, adjust the ratio A:B of the mobile phase.

*Limit:*
— *any impurity:* for each impurity, not more than the area of the principal peak in the chromatogram obtained with reference solution (c) (1.0 per cent).

**N,N-Dimethylaniline** (*2.4.26, Method B*)
Maximum 20 ppm.

**Water** (*2.5.12*)
12.0 per cent to 15.0 per cent, determined on 0.100 g.

**Sulphated ash** (*2.4.14*)
Maximum 0.5 per cent, determined on 1.0 g.

**ASSAY**
Liquid chromatography (*2.2.29*) as described in the test for related substances with the following modifications.

*Mobile phase* Initial composition of the mixture of mobile phases A and B, adjusted where applicable.

*Injection* Test solution (a) and reference solution (a).

*System suitability* Reference solution (a):
— *repeatability:* maximum relative standard deviation of 1.0 per cent after 6 injections.

Calculate the percentage content of ampicillin from the declared content of *anhydrous ampicillin CRS* .

**STORAGE**
In an airtight container.

**IMPURITIES**

A. (2S,5R,6R)-6-amino-3,3-dimethyl-7-oxo-4-thia-1-azabicyclo[3.2.0]heptane-2-carboxylic acid (6-aminopenicillanic acid),

B. (2S,5R,6R)-6-[[(2S)-2-amino-2-phenylacetyl]amino]-3,3-dimethyl-7-oxo-4-thia-1-azabicyclo[3.2.0]heptane-2-carboxylic acid (L-ampicillin),

C. (4S)-2-(3,6-dioxo-5-phenylpiperazin-2-yl)-5,5-dimethylthiazolidine-4-carboxylic acid (diketopiperazines of ampicillin),

D. R = CO₂H: (4S)-2-[[[(2R)-2-amino-2-phenylacetyl]amino]carboxymethyl]-5,5-dimethylthiazolidine-4-carboxylic acid (penicilloic acids of ampicillin),

F. R = H: (2RS,4S)-2-[[[(2R)-2-amino-2-phenylacetyl]amino]methyl]-5,5-dimethylthiazolidine-4-carboxylic acid (penilloic acids of ampicillin),

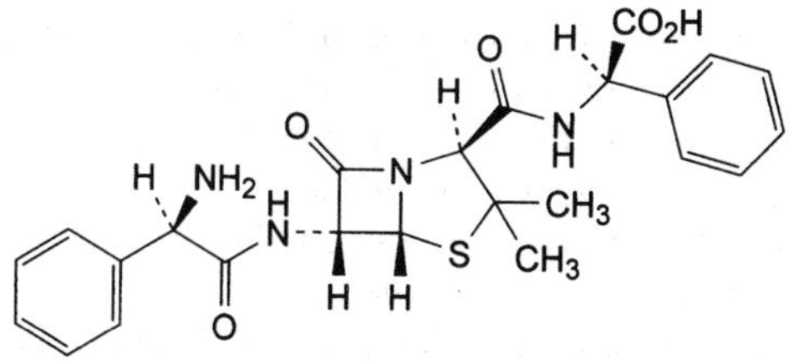

E. (2R)-2-[[[(2S,5R,6R)-6-[[(2R)-2-amino-2-
phenylacetyl]amino]-3,3-dimethyl-7-oxo-4-thia-1-
azabicyclo[3.2.0]hept-2-yl]carbonyl]amino]-2-phenylacetic
acid (ampicillinyl-D-phenylglycine),

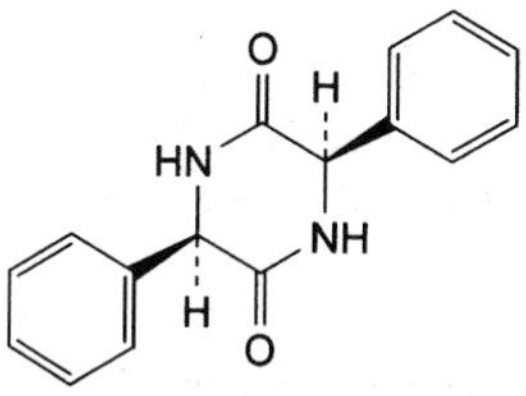

G. (3R,6R)-3,6-diphenylpiperazine-2,5-dione,

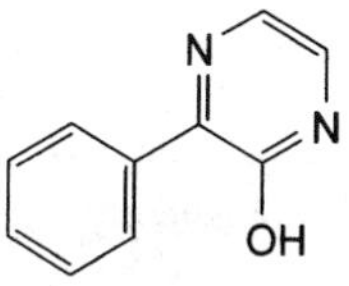

H. 3-phenylpyrazin-2-ol,

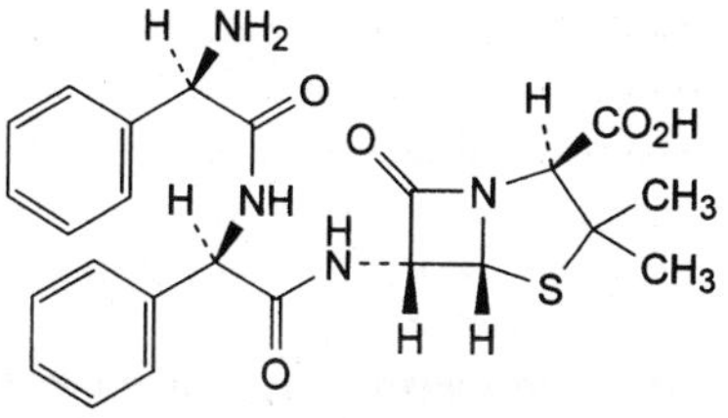

I. (2S,5R,6R)-6-[[(2R)-2-[[(2R)-2-amino-2-
phenylacetyl]amino]-2-phenylacetyl]amino]-3,3-dimethyl-7-
oxo-4-thia-1-azabicyclo[3.2.0]heptane-2-carboxylic acid
(D-phenylglycylampicillin),

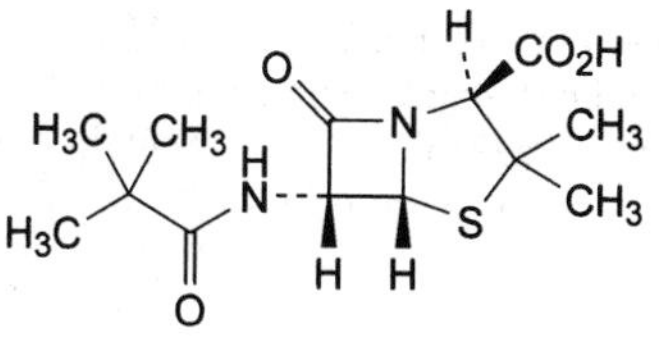

J. (2S,5R,6R)-6-[(2,2-dimethylpropanoyl)amino]-3,3-
dimethyl-7-oxo-4-thia-1-azabicyclo[3.2.0]heptane-2-
carboxylic acid,

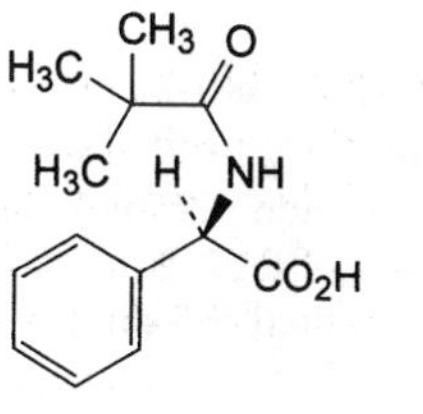

K. (2R)-2-[(2,2-dimethylpropanoyl)amino]-
2-phenylacetic acid,

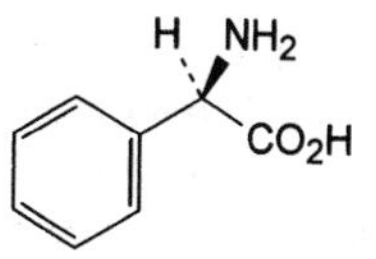

L. (2R)-2-amino-2-phenylacetic acid (D-phenylglycine),

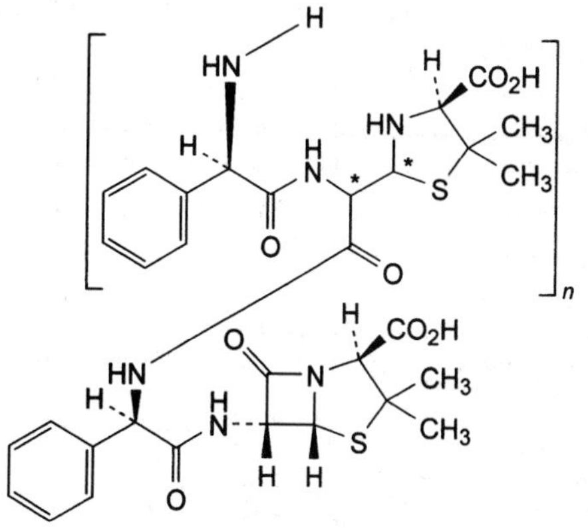

M. co-oligomers of ampicillin and of penicilloic acids of
ampicillin,

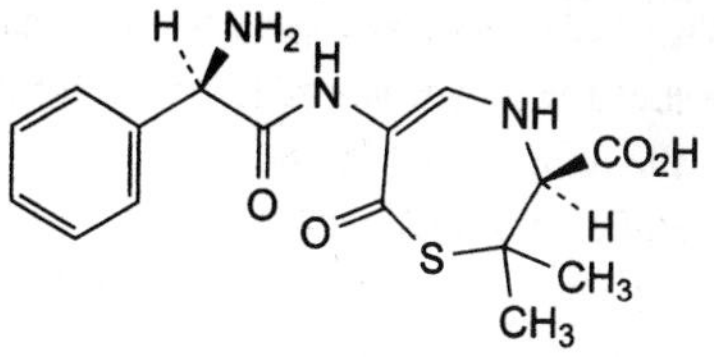

N. (3S)-6-[[(2R)-2-amino-2-phenylacetyl]amino]-2,2-
dimethyl-7-oxo-2,3,4,7-tetrahydro-1,4-thiazepine-
3-carboxylic acid.

_____ *Ph Eur*

# Amylmetacresol

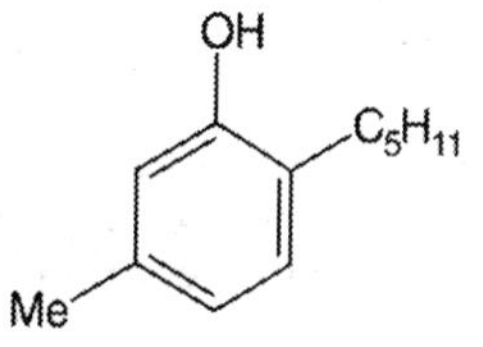

$C_{12}H_{18}O$                178.3                *1300-94-3*

**Action and use**
Antiseptic.

**DEFINITION**
Amylmetacresol is 5-methyl-2-pentylphenol. It contains not
less than 96.0% and not more than 104.0% of $C_{12}H_{18}O$.

**CHARACTERISTICS**
A clear or almost clear liquid or a solid crystalline mass,
colourless or slightly yellow when freshly prepared, which
darkens on storage.

Practically insoluble in *water*; soluble in *ethanol (96%)*, in
*ether* and in fixed and volatile oils.

## IDENTIFICATION

A. The *infrared absorption spectrum*, Appendix II A, is concordant with the *reference spectrum* of amylmetacresol (*RS 014*).

B. The *light absorption*, Appendix II B, in the range 230 to 350 nm of a 0.004% w/v solution in *absolute ethanol* containing 2% v/v of *0.1M hydrochloric acid* exhibits a maximum at 278 nm and a less well-defined maximum at 286 nm. The *absorbance* at the maximum at 278 nm is about 0.53.

C. To 5 ml of a 0.5% v/v solution in *methanol* add 5 ml of *bromine water*. A yellow precipitate is produced.

D. *Freezing point*, about 22°, Appendix V B.

## TESTS

### Weight per ml
0.947 to 0.953 g, Appendix V G.

### Related substances
Carry out the method for *gas chromatography*, Appendix III B.

(1) The substance being examined.

(2) 1% w/v of the substance being examined in *chloroform*.

CHROMATOGRAPHIC CONDITIONS

(a) Use a glass column (1.8 m × 3 mm) packed with *acid-washed, silanised diatomaceous support* (80 to 100 mesh) coated with 10% w/w of silicone grease (Apiezon L is suitable).

(b) Use *helium* as the carrier gas at 1.7 ml per minute.

(c) Maintain the temperature at 180°.

(d) Inject 1 μl of each solution.

LIMITS

In the chromatogram obtained with solution (1) the area of any *secondary peak* is not greater than 2% by *normalisation*; the sum of the areas of any *secondary peaks* is not greater than 3% by *normalisation*.

### Sulphated ash
Not more than 0.1%, Appendix IX A.

## ASSAY

Dissolve 0.2 g in *absolute ethanol* containing 2% v/v of *0.1M hydrochloric acid* and dilute to 100 ml with the same solvent. Dilute 2 ml of the solution to 100 ml with the same solvent and measure the *absorbance* of the resulting solution at the maximum at 278 nm, Appendix II B. Calculate the content of $C_{12}H_{18}O$ taking 132 as the value of A(1%, 1 cm) at the maximum at 278 nm.

## STORAGE

Amylmetacresol should be protected from light.

# Antazoline Hydrochloride

*(Ph Eur monograph 0972)*

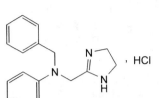

$C_{17}H_{19}N_3,HCl$        301.8        *2508-72-7*

### Action and use
Histamine $H_1$ receptor antagonist; antihistamine.

*Ph Eur*

## DEFINITION

Antazoline hydrochloride contains not less than 99.0 per cent and not more than the equivalent of 101.0 per cent of *N*-benzyl-*N*-[(4,5-dihydro-1*H*-imidazol-2-yl)methyl]aniline hydrochloride, calculated with reference to the dried substance.

## CHARACTERS

A white or almost white, crystalline powder, sparingly soluble in water, soluble in alcohol, slightly soluble in methylene chloride.

It melts at about 240 °C, with decomposition.

## IDENTIFICATION

*First identification*   A, D.

*Second identification*   B, C, D.

A. Examine by infrared absorption spectrophotometry (*2.2.24*), comparing with the spectrum obtained with *antazoline hydrochloride CRS* . Examine the substances as discs prepared using *potassium chloride R*.

B. Examine the chromatograms obtained in the test for related substances in daylight after spraying. The principal spot in the chromatogram obtained with test solution (b) is similar in position, colour and size to the principal spot in the chromatogram obtained with reference solution (b).

C. To 5 ml of solution S (see Tests) add, drop by drop, *dilute sodium hydroxide solution R* until an alkaline reaction is produced. Filter. The precipitate, washed with two quantities, each of 10 ml, of *water R* and dried in a desicator under reduced pressure, melts (*2.2.14*) at 119 °C to 123 °C.

D. It gives reaction (a) of chlorides (*2.3.1*).

## TESTS

### Solution S
Dissolve 2.0 g in *carbon dioxide-free water R* prepared from *distilled water R*, heating at 60 °C if necessary. Allow to cool and dilute to 100 ml with the same solvent.

### Appearance of solution
Solution S is clear (*2.2.1*) and not more intensely coloured than reference solution $Y_7$ (*2.2.2, Method II*).

### Acidity or alkalinity
To 10 ml of solution S add 0.2 ml of *methyl red solution R*. Not more than 0.1 ml of *0.01 M hydrochloric acid* or *0.01 M sodium hydroxide* is required to change the colour of the indicator.

## Related substances

Examine by thin-layer chromatography (2.2.27), using *silica gel GF*$_{254}$ *R* as the coating substance. Heat the plate at 110 °C for 15 min before using.

*Test solution (a)*   Dissolve 0.10 g of the substance to be examined in *methanol R* and dilute to 5 ml with the same solvent.

*Test solution (b)*   Dilute 1 ml of test solution (a) to 5 ml with *methanol R*.

*Reference solution (a)*   Dilute 0.5 ml of test solution (a) to 100 ml with *methanol R*.

*Reference solution (b)*   Dissolve 20 mg of *antazoline hydrochloride CRS* in *methanol R* and dilute to 5 ml with the same solvent.

*Reference solution (c)*   Dissolve 20 mg of *xylometazoline hydrochloride CRS* in 1 ml of test solution (a) and dilute to 5 ml with *methanol R*.

Apply to the plate 5 µl of each solution. Develop over a path of 15 cm using a mixture of 5 volumes of *diethylamine R*, 10 volumes of *methanol R* and 85 volumes of *ethyl acetate R*. Dry the plate in a current of warm air for 15 min. Examine in ultraviolet light at 254 nm. The test is not valid unless the chromatogram obtained with reference solution (c) shows two clearly separated principal spots. Spray with a mixture of equal volumes of a 200 g/l solution of *ferric chloride R* and a 5 g/l solution of *potassium ferricyanide R*. Examine immediately in daylight. Any spot in the chromatogram obtained with test solution (a), apart from the principal spot, is not more intense than the spot in the chromatogram obtained with reference solution (a) (0.5 per cent).

## Heavy metals (2.4.8)

1.0 g complies with limit test C for heavy metals (20 ppm). Prepare the standard using 2 ml of *lead standard solution (10 ppm Pb) R*.

## Loss on drying (2.2.32)

Not more than 0.5 per cent, determined on 1.000 g by drying in an oven at 105 °C for 3 h.

## Sulphated ash (2.4.14)

Not more than 0.1 per cent, determined on the residue obtained in the test for loss on drying.

## ASSAY

Dissolve 0.250 g in 100 ml of *alcohol R*. Add 0.1 ml of *phenolphthalein solution R1*. Titrate with *0.1 M alcoholic potassium hydroxide*.

1 ml of *0.1 M alcoholic potassium hydroxide* is equivalent to 30.18 mg of $C_{17}H_{20}ClN_3$.

## IMPURITIES

A. *N*-(2-aminoethyl)-2-(benzylphenylamino)acetamide.

*Ph Eur*

# Apomorphine Hydrochloride

(*Ph Eur monograph 0136*)

$C_{17}H_{17}NO_2,HCl,\frac{1}{2}H_2O$       312.8       *41372-20-7*

## Action and use

Dopamine receptor agonist; treatment of Parkinson's disease.

## Preparation

Apomorphine Hydrochloride for Homoeopathic Preparations

*Ph Eur*

## DEFINITION

(6a*R*)-6-Methyl-5,6,6a,7-tetrahydro-4*H*-dibenzo[*de,g*]quinoline-10,11-diol hydrochloride hemihydrate.

## Content

99.0 per cent to 101.0 per cent (dried substance).

## CHARACTERS

### Appearance

White or slightly yellowish-brown or green-tinged greyish, crystalline powder or crystals; on exposure to air and light, the green tinge becomes more pronounced.

### Solubility

Sparingly soluble in water and in alcohol, practically insoluble in toluene.

## IDENTIFICATION

*First identification   B, D.*

*Second identification   A, C, D.*

A. Dissolve 10.0 mg in *0.1 M hydrochloric acid* and dilute to 100.0 ml with the same acid. Dilute 10.0 ml of the solution to 100.0 ml with *0.1 M hydrochloric acid*. Examined between 230 nm and 350 nm (2.2.25), the solution shows an absorption maximum at 273 nm and a shoulder at 300 nm to 310 nm. The specific absorbance at the maximum is 530 to 570.

B. Infrared absorption spectrophotometry (2.2.24).

*Comparison   Ph. Eur. reference spectrum of apomorphine hydrochloride* .

C. To 5 ml of solution S (see Tests) add a few millilitres of *sodium hydrogen carbonate solution R* until a permanent, white precipitate is formed. The precipitate slowly becomes greenish. Add 0.25 ml of *0.05 M iodine* and shake. The precipitate becomes greyish-green. Collect the precipitate. The precipitate dissolves in *ether R* giving a purple solution, in *methylene chloride R* giving a violet-blue solution and in *alcohol R* giving a blue solution.

D. To 2 ml of solution S add 0.1 ml of *nitric acid R*. Mix and filter. The filtrate gives reaction (a) of chlorides (2.3.1).

## TESTS

### Solution S

Dissolve 0.25 g without heating in *carbon dioxide-free water R* and dilute to 25 ml with the same solvent.

### Appearance of solution

Solution S is clear (2.2.1) and not more intensely coloured than reference solution $BY_5$ or $GY_5$(2.2.2, *Method II*).

**pH** (2.2.3)

4.0 to 5.0 for solution S.

**Specific optical rotation** (2.2.7)

− 48 to − 52 (dried substance).

Dissolve 0.25 g in *0.02 M hydrochloric acid* and dilute to 25.0 ml with the same acid.

**Related substances**

Liquid chromatography (2.2.29).

*Test solution*   Dissolve 0.25 g of the substance to be examined in a 1 per cent V/V solution of *glacial acetic acid R* and dilute to 100.0 ml with the same solution.

*Reference solution (a)*   Dilute 1.0 ml of the test solution to 10.0 ml with a 1 per cent V/V solution of *glacial acetic acid R*. Dilute 1.0 ml to 100.0 ml with a 1 per cent V/V solution of *glacial acetic acid R*.

*Reference solution (b)*   Dissolve 25 mg of *boldine R* in a 1 per cent V/V solution of *glacial acetic acid R* and dilute to 10.0 ml with the same solvent. To 1 ml of this solution, add 1 ml of the test solution and dilute to 10.0 ml with a 1 per cent V/V solution of *glacial acetic acid R*.

*Column:*

— *size*: l = 0.15 m, Ø = 4.6 mm,

— *stationary phase*: octadecylsilyl silica gel for chromatography R (5 μm),

— *temperature*: 35 °C.

*Mobile phase:*

— *mobile phase A*: 1.1 g/l solution of *sodium octanesulphonate R*, adjusted to pH 2.2 using a 50 per cent m/m solution of *phosphoric acid R*,

— *mobile phase B*: acetonitrile R,

| Time (min) | Mobile phase A (per cent V/V) | Mobile phase B (per cent V/V) |
|---|---|---|
| 0 - 30 | 85 → 68 | 15 → 32 |
| 30 - 35 | 68 | 32 |
| 35 - 45 | 68 → 85 | 32 → 15 |

*Flow rate*   1.5 ml/min.

*Detection*   Spectrophotometer at 280 nm.

*Injection*   10 μl.

*System suitability*   Reference solution (b):

— *resolution*: minimum 2.5 between the peaks due to boldine and apomorphine.

*Limits:*

— *any impurity*: not more than twice the area of the principal peak in the chromatogram obtained with reference solution (a) (0.2 per cent),

— *total*: not more than 8 times the area of the principal peak in the chromatogram obtained with reference solution (a) (0.8 per cent),

— *disregard limit*: 0.2 times the area of the principal peak in the chromatogram obtained with reference solution (a) (0.02 per cent).

**Heavy metals** (2.4.8)

Maximum 20 ppm.

1.0 g complies with limit test C. Prepare the standard using 2 ml of *lead standard solution (10 ppm Pb) R*.

**Loss on drying** (2.2.32)

2.5 per cent to 4.2 per cent, determined on 1.000 g by drying in an oven at 105 °C.

**Sulphated ash** (2.4.14)

Maximum 0.1 per cent, determined on 1.0 g.

**ASSAY**

Dissolve 0.250 g in a mixture of 5.0 ml of *0.01 M hydrochloric acid* and 50 ml of *alcohol R*. Carry out a potentiometric titration (2.2.20), using *0.1 M sodium hydroxide*. Read the volume added between the first 2 points of inflexion.

1 ml of *0.1 M sodium hydroxide* is equivalent to 30.38 mg of $C_{17}H_{18}ClNO_2$.

**STORAGE**

In an airtight container, protected from light.

**IMPURITIES**

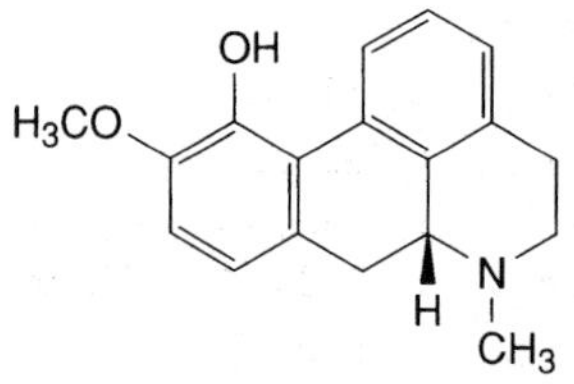

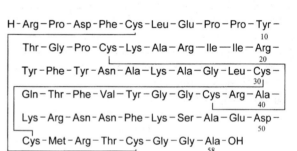

A. (6aR)-10-methoxy-6-methyl-5,6,6a,7-tetrahydro-4H-dibenzo[de,g]quinolin-11-ol (apocodeine),

B. morphine.

*Ph Eur*

# Aprotinin

(*Ph Eur monograph 0580*)

```
H - Arg - Pro - Asp - Phe - Cys - Leu - Glu - Pro - Pro - Tyr -
                                                          10
  Thr - Gly - Pro - Cys - Lys - Ala - Arg — Ile — Ile - Arg -
                                                          20
  Tyr - Phe - Tyr - Asn - Ala - Lys - Ala - Gly - Leu - Cys -
                                                          30
  Gln - Thr - Phe - Val - Tyr - Gly - Gly - Cys - Arg - Ala -
                                                          40
  Lys - Arg - Asn - Asn - Phe - Lys - Ser - Ala - Glu - Asp -
                                                          50
  Cys - Met - Arg - Thr - Cys - Gly - Gly - Ala - OH
                                                   58
```

$C_{284}H_{432}N_{84}O_{79}S_7$    6511

**Action and use**

Antifibrinolytic.

**Preparation**

Aprotinin Injection

*Ph Eur*

**DEFINITION**

Aprotinin is a polypeptide consisting of a chain of 58 amino acids. It inhibits stoichiometrically the activity of several proteolytic enzymes such as chymotrypsin, kallikrein, plasmin and trypsin. It contains not less than 3.0 Ph. Eur. U. of aprotinin activity per milligram, calculated with reference to the dried substance.

**PRODUCTION**

The animals from which aprotinin is derived must fulfil the requirements for the health of animals suitable for human consumption to the satisfaction of the competent authority.

The method of manufacture is validated to demonstrate that the product, if tested, would comply with the following tests.

**Abnormal toxicity** (*2.6.9*)

Inject into each mouse a quantity of the substance to be examined containing 2 Ph. Eur. U. dissolved in a sufficient quantity of *water for injections R* to give a volume of 0.5 ml.

**Histamine** (*2.6.10*)

Maximum 0.2 μg of histamine base per 3 Ph. Eur. U.

## CHARACTERS

### Appearance

Almost white hygroscopic powder.

### Solubility

Soluble in water and in isotonic solutions, practically insoluble in organic solvents.

## IDENTIFICATION

A. Thin-layer chromatography (*2.2.27*).

*Test solution*  Solution S (see Tests).

*Reference solution*  Dilute *aprotinin solution BRP* in *water R* to obtain a concentration of 15 Ph. Eur. U./ ml.

*Plate*  TLC silica gel G plate R.

*Mobile phase*  *water R*, *glacial acetic acid R* (80:100 *V/V*) containing 100 g/l of *sodium acetate R*.

*Application*  10 μl.

*Development*  Over a path of 12 cm.

*Drying*  In air.

*Detection*  Spray with a solution of 0.1 g of *ninhydrin R* in a mixture of 6 ml of a 10 g/l solution of *cupric chloride R*, 21 ml of *glacial acetic acid R* and 70 ml of *anhydrous ethanol R*. Dry the plate at 60 °C.

*Results*  The principal spot in the chromatogram obtained with the test solution is similar in position, colour and size to the principal spot in the chromatogram obtained with the reference solution.

B. Determine the ability of the substance to be examined to inhibit trypsin activity using the method described below.

*Test solution*  Dilute 1 ml of solution S to 50 ml with *buffer solution pH 7.2 R*.

*Trypsin solution*  Dissolve 10 mg of *trypsin BRP* in *0.002 M hydrochloric acid* and dilute to 100 ml with the same acid.

*Casein solution*  Dissolve 0.2 g of *casein R* in *buffer solution pH 7.2 R* and dilute to 100 ml with the same buffer solution.

*Precipitating solution*  *glacial acetic acid R*, *water R*, *anhydrous ethanol R* (1:49:50 *V/V/V*).

Mix 1 ml of the test solution with 1 ml of the trypsin solution. Allow to stand for 10 min and add 1 ml of the casein solution. Incubate at 35 °C for 30 min. Cool in iced water and add 0.5 ml of the precipitating solution. Shake and allow to stand at room temperature for 15 min. The solution is cloudy. Carry out a blank test under the same conditions using *buffer solution pH 7.2 R* instead of the test solution. The solution is not cloudy.

## TESTS

### Solution S

Prepare a solution of the substance to be examined containing 15 Ph. Eur. U./ml, calculated from the activity stated on the label.

### Appearance of solution

Solution S is clear (*2.2.1*).

### Absorbance (*2.2.25*)

Maximum 0.80 by measuring at the absorption maximum at 277 nm.

Prepare a solution of the substance to be examined containing 3.0 Ph. Eur. U./ml.

### Des-Ala-aprotinin and des-Ala-des-Gly-aprotinin

Capillary zone electrophoresis (*2.2.47*): use the normalisation procedure.

*Test solution*  Prepare a solution of the substance to be examined in *water R* containing not less than 1 Ph. Eur. U./ml.

*Reference solution*  Dilute *aprotinin solution BRP* in *water R* to obtain the same concentration as the test solution.

*Capillary:*
— *material*: uncoated fused silica;
— *size*: effective length = 45-60 cm, Ø = 75 μm.

*Temperature*  25 °C.

*CZE buffer*  Dissolve 8.21 g of *potassium dihydrogen phosphate R* in 400 ml of *water R*, adjust to pH 3.0 with *phosphoric acid R*, dilute to 500.0 ml with *water R* and filter through a membrane filter (nominal pore size 0.45 μm).

*Detection*  Spectrophotometer at 214 nm.

*Between-run rinsing*  Rinse the capillary for at least 1 min with *0.1 M sodium hydroxide* filtered through a membrane filter (nominal pore size 0.45 μm) and for 2 min with the CZE buffer.

*Injection*  Under pressure or vacuum (for example, 3 s at a differential pressure of 3.5 kPa).

*Migration*  Apply a field strength of 0.2 kV/cm, using the CZE buffer as the electrolyte in both buffer reservoirs.

*Run time*  30 min.

*Identification of impurities*  Use the electropherogram supplied with *aprotinin solution BRP* and the electropherogram obtained with the reference solution to identify the peaks due to impurities A and B.

*Relative migration*  With reference to aprotinin (migration time = about 22 min): impurity A = about 0.98; impurity B = about 0.99.

*System suitability*  Reference solution after at least 6 injections:
— *migration time*: aprotinin = 19.0 min to 25.0 min;
— *resolution*: minimum 0.8 between the peaks due to impurities A and B; minimum 0.5 between the peaks due to impurity B and aprotinin;
— *peak distribution*: the electrophoregram obtained is qualitatively and quantitatively similar to the electropherogram supplied with *aprotinin solution BRP*;
— *height of the principal peak*: at least 1000 times the height of the baseline noise. If necessary, adjust the sample load to give peaks of sufficient height.

*Limits:*
— *impurity A*: maximum 8.0 per cent;
— *impurity B*: maximum 7.5 per cent.

### Pyroglutamyl-aprotinin and related compounds

Liquid chromatography (*2.2.29*): use the normalisation procedure.

*Test solution*  Prepare a solution of the substance to be examined in mobile phase A, containing about 5 Ph. Eur. U./ml.

*Reference solution*  Dissolve the contents of a vial of *aprotinin for system suitability CRS* in mobile phase A to obtain the same concentration as the test solution.

*Column:*
— *size*: l = 0.075 m, Ø = 7.5 mm;
— *stationary phase*: *strong cation-exchange silica gel for chromatography R* (10 μm);
— *temperature*: 40 °C.

*Mobile phase:*
— *mobile phase A*: Dissolve 3.52 g of *potassium dihydrogen phosphate R* and 7.26 g of *disodium hydrogen phosphate dihydrate R* in 1000 ml of water; filter and degas;
— mobile phase B: Dissolve 3.52 g of *potassium dihydrogen phosphate R*, 7.26 g of *disodium hydrogen phosphate dihydrate R* and 66.07 g of *ammonium sulphate R* in 1000 ml of water; filter and degas;

| Time (min) | Mobile phase A (per cent *V/V*) | Mobile phase B (per cent *V/V*) |
|---|---|---|
| 0 - 21 | 92 → 64 | 8 → 36 |
| 21 - 30 | 64 → 0 | 36 → 100 |
| 30 - 31 | 0 → 92 | 100 → 8 |
| 31 - 40 | 92 | 8 |

*Flow rate* 1.0 ml/min.

*Detection* Spectrophotometer at 210 nm.

*Injection* 40 µl.

*Relative retention* With reference to aprotinin (retention time = 17.0 min to 20.0 min): impurity C = about 0.9.

*System suitability* Reference solution:
— *resolution*: minimum 1.5 between the peaks due to impurity C and aprotinin;
— *symmetry factor*: maximum 1.3 for the peak due to aprotinin.

*Limits:*
— *impurity C*: maximum 1.0 per cent;
— *any other impurity*: maximum 0.5 per cent;
— *sum of impurities other than C*: maximum 1.0 per cent.

**Aprotinin oligomers**

Size-exclusion chromatography (*2.2.30*): use the normalisation procedure.

*Test solution* Prepare a solution of the substance to be examined in *water R* containing about 5 Ph. Eur. U./ml.

*Reference solution* Treat the substance to be examined to obtain about 2 per cent aprotinin oligomers. For example, heat freeze-dried aprotinin at about 110 °C for about 4 h. Then dissolve in *water R* to obtain a concentration of about 5 Ph. Eur. U./ml.

*Column* 3 columns coupled in series:
— *size*: l = 0.30 m, Ø = 7.8 mm;
— *stationary phase*: *hydrophilic silica gel for chromatography R* of a grade suitable for fractionation of globular proteins in the relative molecular mass range of 20 000 to 10 000 000 (8 µm).

*Mobile phase* *acetonitrile R, glacial acetic acid R, water R* (2:2:6 *V/V/V*); filter and degas.

*Flow rate* 1.0 ml/min.

*Detection* Spectrophotometer at 277 nm.

*Injection* 100 µl.

*Run time* 40 min.

*Relative retention* With reference to aprotinin monomer (retention time = 24.5 min to 25.5 min): aprotinin dimmer = about 0.9.

*System suitability* Reference solution:
— *resolution*: minimum 1.3 between the peaks due to aprotinin dimer and monomer;
— *symmetry factor*: maximum 2.5 for the peak due to aprotinin monomer.

*Limit:*
— *total*: maximum 1.0 per cent.

**Loss on drying** (*2.2.32*)
Maximum 6.0 per cent, determined on 0.100 g by drying *in vacuo.*

**Bacterial endotoxins** (*2.6.14*)
Less than 0.14 IU per European Pharmacopoeia Unit of aprotinin, if intended for use in the manufacture of parenteral preparations without a further appropriate procedure for the removal of bacterial endotoxins.

**ASSAY**

The activity of aprotinin is determined by measuring its inhibitory action on a solution of trypsin of known activity. The inhibiting activity of the aprotinin is calculated from the difference between the initial activity and the residual activity of the trypsin.

The inhibiting activity of aprotinin is expressed in European Pharmacopoeia Units. 1 Ph. Eur. U. inhibits 50 per cent of the enzymatic activity of 2 microkatals of trypsin.

Use a reaction vessel with a capacity of about 30 ml, provided with:
— a device that will maintain a temperature of 25 ± 0.1 °C;
— a stirring device, such as a magnetic stirrer;
— a lid with 5 holes for accommodating the electrodes, the tip of a burette, a tube for the admission of nitrogen and the introduction of the reagents.

An automatic or manual titration apparatus may be used. In the latter case the burette is graduated in 0.05 ml and the pH-meter is provided with a wide reading scale and glass and calomel or glass-silver-silver chloride electrodes.

*Test solution* Prepare a solution of the substance to be examined in *0.0015 M borate buffer solution pH 8.0 R* expected to contain 1.67 Ph. Eur. U./ml (about 0.6 mg (m mg) per millilitre).

*Trypsin solution* Prepare a solution of *trypsin BRP* containing about 0.8 microkatals per millilitre (about 1 mg/ml), using *0.001 M hydrochloric acid* as the solvent. Use a freshly prepared solution and keep in iced water.

*Trypsin and aprotinin solution* To 4.0 ml of the trypsin solution add 1.0 ml of the test solution. Dilute immediately to 40.0 ml with *0.0015 M borate buffer solution pH 8.0 R*. Allow to stand at room temperature for 10 min and then keep in iced water. Use within 6 h of preparation.

*Dilute trypsin solution* Dilute 0.5 ml of the trypsin solution to 10.0 ml with *0.0015 M borate buffer solution pH 8.0 R*. Allow to stand at room temperature for 10 min and then keep in iced water.

Maintain an atmosphere of nitrogen in the reaction flask and stir continuously; introduce 9.0 ml of *0.0015 M borate buffer solution pH 8.0 R* and 1.0 ml of a freshly prepared 6.9 g/l solution of *benzoylarginine ethyl ester hydrochloride R*. Adjust to pH 8.0 with *0.1 M sodium hydroxide*. When the temperature has reached equilibrium at 25 ± 0.1 °C, add 1.0 ml of the trypsin and aprotinin solution and start a timer. Maintain at pH 8.0 by the addition of *0.1 M sodium hydroxide* and note the volume added every 30 s. Continue the reaction for 6 min. Determine the number of millilitres of *0.1 M sodium hydroxide* used per second ($n_1$ ml). Carry out, under the same conditions, a titration using 1.0 ml of the dilute trypsin solution. Determine the number of millilitres of *0.1 M sodium hydroxide* used per second ($n_2$ ml).

Calculate the aprotinin activity in European Pharmacopoeia Units per milligram using the following expression:

$$\frac{4000\,(2n_2 - n_1)}{m}$$

The estimated activity is not less than 90 per cent and not more than 110 per cent of the activity stated on the label.

## STORAGE

In an airtight, tamper-proof container, protected from light.

## LABELLING

The label states:
— the number of European Pharmacopoeia Units of aprotinin activity per milligram;
— where applicable, that the substance is suitable for use in the manufacture of parenteral preparations.

## IMPURITIES

A. Ra = H, Rb = OH: aprotinin-(1-56)-peptide,

B. Ra = H, Rb = Gly-OH: aprotinin-(1-57)-peptide,

C. Ra = Glp, Rb = Gly-Ala-OH: (5-oxoprolyl)aprotinin (pyroglutamylaprotinin).

_____ *Ph Eur*

# Aprotinin Concentrated Solution

*(Ph Eur monograph 0579)*

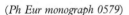

$C_{284}H_{432}N_{84}O_{79}S_7$        6511

**Action and use**
Antifibrinolytic.

**Preparation**
Aprotinin Injection

*Ph Eur* _____

## DEFINITION

Aprotinin concentrated solution is a solution of aprotinin, a polypeptide consisting of a chain of 58 amino acids, which inhibits stoichiometrically the activity of several proteolytic enzymes such as chymotrypsin, kallikrein, plasmin and trypsin. It contains not less than 15.0 Ph. Eur. U. of aprotinin activity per millilitre.

## PRODUCTION

The animals from which aprotinin is derived must fulfil the requirements for the health of animals suitable for human consumption to the satisfaction of the competent authority.

The method of manufacture is validated to demonstrate that the product, if tested, would comply with the following tests.

**Abnormal toxicity** *(2.6.9)*
Inject into each mouse a quantity of the preparation to be examined containing 2 Ph. Eur. U. diluted with a sufficient quantity of *water for injections R* to give a volume of 0.5 ml.

**Histamine** *(2.6.10)*
Maximum 0.2 µg of histamine base per 3 Ph. Eur. U.

## CHARACTERS

**Appearance**
Clear, colourless liquid.

## IDENTIFICATION

A. Thin-layer chromatography *(2.2.27)*.

*Test solution*    Solution S (see Tests).

*Reference solution*    Dilute *aprotinin solution BRP* in *water R* to obtain a concentration of 15 Ph. Eur. U./ ml.

*Plate*    *TLC silica gel G plate R.*

*Mobile phase*    *water R, glacial acetic acid R* (80:100 *V/V*) containing 100 g/l of *sodium acetate R.*

*Application*    10 µl.

*Development*    Over a path of 12 cm.

*Drying*    In air.

*Detection*    Spray with a solution of 0.1 g of *ninhydrin R* in a mixture of 6 ml of a 10 g/l solution of *cupric chloride R*, 21 ml of *glacial acetic acid R* and 70 ml of *anhydrous ethanol R*. Dry the plate at 60 °C.

*Results*    The principal spot in the chromatogram obtained with the test solution is similar in position, colour and size to the principal spot in the chromatogram obtained with the reference solution.

B. Determine the ability of the preparation to be examined to inhibit trypsin activity using the method described below.

*Test solution*    Dilute 1 ml of solution S to 50 ml with *buffer solution pH 7.2 R.*

*Trypsin solution*    Dissolve 10 mg of *trypsin BRP* in *0.002 M hydrochloric acid* and dilute to 100 ml with the same acid.

*Casein solution*    Dissolve 0.2 g of *casein R* in *buffer solution pH 7.2 R* and dilute to 100 ml with the same buffer solution.

*Precipitating solution*    *glacial acetic acid R, water R, anhydrous ethanol R* (1:49:50 *V/V/V*).

Mix 1 ml of the test solution with 1 ml of the trypsin solution. Allow to stand for 10 min and add 1 ml of the casein solution. Incubate at 35 °C for 30 min. Cool in iced water and add 0.5 ml of the precipitating solution. Shake and allow to stand at room temperature for 15 min. The solution is cloudy. Carry out a blank test under the same conditions using *buffer solution pH 7.2 R* instead of the test solution. The solution is not cloudy.

## TESTS

**Solution S**
Prepare a solution containing 15 Ph. Eur. U./ml, if necessary by dilution, on the basis of the activity stated on the label.

**Appearance of solution**
Solution S is clear *(2.2.1)*.

**Absorbance** *(2.2.25)*
Maximum 0.80 by measuring at the absorption maximum at 277 nm.

Prepare a solution containing 3.0 Ph. Eur. U./ml.

**Des-Ala-aprotinin and des-Ala-des-Gly-aprotinin**
Capillary zone electrophoresis (2.2.47): use the normalisation procedure.

*Test solution* Dilute the preparation to be examined in *water R* to obtain a concentration of not less than 1 Ph Eur. U./ml.

*Reference solution* Dilute *aprotinin solution BRP* in *water R* to obtain the same concentration as the test solution.

*Capillary:*
— *material*: uncoated fused silica;
— *size*: effective length = 45-60 cm, Ø = 75 μm.

*Temperature* 25 °C.

*CZE buffer* Dissolve 8.21 g of *potassium dihydrogen phosphate R* in 400 ml of *water R*, adjust to pH 3.0 with *phosphoric acid R*, dilute to 500.0 ml with *water R* and filter through a membrane filter (nominal pore size 0.45 μm).

*Detection* Spectrophotometer at 214 nm.

*Between-run rinsing* Rinse the capillary for at least 1 min with *0.1 M sodium hydroxide* filtered through a membrane filter (nominal pore size 0.45 μm) and for 2 min with the CZE buffer.

*Injection* Under pressure or vacuum (for example, 3 s at a differential pressure of 3.5 kPa).

*Migration* Apply a field strength of 0.2 kV/cm, using the CZE buffer as the electrolyte in both buffer reservoirs.

*Run time* 30 min.

*Identification of impurities* Use the electropherogram supplied with *aprotinin solution BRP* and the electropherogram obtained with the reference solution to identify the peaks due to impurities A and B.

*Relative migration* With reference to aprotinin (migration time = about 22 min): impurity A = about 0.98; impurity B = about 0.99.

*System suitability* Reference solution after at least 6 injections:
— *migration time*: aprotinin = 19.0 min to 25.0 min;
— *resolution*: minimum 0.8 between the peaks due to impurities A and B; minimum 0.5 between the peaks due to impurity B and aprotinin;
— *peak distribution*: the electrophoregram obtained is qualitatively and quantitatively similar to the electropherogram supplied with *aprotinin solution BRP*;
— *height of the principal peak*: at least 1000 times the height of the baseline noise. If necessary, adjust the sample load to give peaks of a sufficient height.

*Limits:*
— *impurity A*: maximum 8.0 per cent;
— *impurity B*: maximum 7.5 per cent.

**Pyroglutamyl-aprotinin and related compounds**
Liquid chromatography (2.2.29): use the normalisation procedure.

*Test solution* Dilute the preparation to be examined in mobile phase A to a concentration of about 5 Ph. Eur. U./ml.

*Reference solution* Dissolve the contents of a vial of *aprotinin for system suitability CRS* in mobile phase A to obtain the same concentration as the test solution.

*Column:*
— *size*: l = 0.075 m, Ø = 7.5 mm;
— *stationary phase*: *strong cation-exchange silica gel for chromatography R* (10 μm);
— *temperature*: 40 °C.

*Mobile phase:*
— *mobile phase A*: Dissolve 3.52 g of *potassium dihydrogen phosphate R* and 7.26 g of *disodium hydrogen phosphate dihydrate R* in 1000 ml of water; filter and degas;
— *mobile phase B*: Dissolve 3.52 g of *potassium dihydrogen phosphate R*, 7.26 g of *disodium hydrogen phosphate dihydrate R* and 66.07 g of *ammonium sulphate R* in 1000 ml of water; filter and degas;

| Time (min) | Mobile phase A (per cent V/V) | Mobile phase B (per cent V/V) |
|---|---|---|
| 0 - 21 | 92 → 64 | 8 → 36 |
| 21 - 30 | 64 → 0 | 36 → 100 |
| 30 - 31 | 0 → 92 | 100 → 8 |
| 31 - 40 | 92 | 8 |

*Flow rate* 1.0 ml/min.

*Detection* Spectrophotometer at 210 nm.

*Injection* 40 μl.

*Relative retention* With reference to aprotinin (retention time = 17.0 min to 20.0 min): impurity C = about 0.9.

*System suitability* Reference solution:
— *resolution*: minimum 1.5 between the peaks due to impurity C and aprotinin;
— *symmetry factor*: maximum 1.3 for the peak due to aprotinin.

*Limits:*
— *impurity C*: maximum 1.0 per cent;
— *any other impurity*: maximum 0.5 per cent;
— *sum of impurities other than C*: maximum 1.0 per cent.

**Aprotinin oligomers**
Size-exclusion chromatography (2.2.30): use the normalisation procedure.

*Test solution* Dilute the preparation to be examined in *water R* to obtain a concentration of about 5 Ph. Eur. U./ml.

*Reference solution* Treat the substance to be examined to obtain about 2 per cent aprotinin oligomers. For example, heat freeze-dried aprotinin at about 110 °C for about 4 h. Then dissolve in *water R* to obtain a concentration of about 5 Ph. Eur. U./ml.

*Column* 3 columns coupled in series:
— *size*: l = 0.30 m, Ø = 7.8 mm;
— *stationary phase*: *hydrophilic silica gel for chromatography R* of a grade suitable for fractionation of globular proteins in the relative molecular mass range of 20 000 to 10 000 000 (8 μm).

*Mobile phase* *acetonitrile R*, *glacial acetic acid R*, *water R* (2:2:6 V/V/V); filter and degas.

*Flow rate* 1.0 ml/min.

*Detection* Spectrophotometer at 277 nm.

*Injection* 100 μl.

*Run time* 40 min.

*Relative retention* With reference to aprotinin monomer (retention time = 24.5 min to 25.5 min): aprotinin dimer = about 0.9.

*System suitability* Reference solution:
— *resolution*: minimum 1.3 between the peaks due to aprotinin dimer and monomer;
— *symmetry factor*: maximum 2.5 for the peak due to aprotinin monomer.

*Limit:*
— *total*: maximum 1.0 per cent.

**Specific activity of the dry residue**

Minimum 3.0 Ph. Eur. U. of aprotinin activity per milligram of dry residue.

Evaporate 25.0 ml to dryness in a water-bath, dry the residue at 110 °C for 15 h and weigh. From the mass of the residue and the activity determined as described below, calculate the number of European Pharmacopoeia Units per milligram of dry residue.

**Bacterial endotoxins** (*2.6.14*)

Less than 0.14 IU per European Pharmacopoeia Unit of aprotinin, if intended for use in the manufacture of parenteral preparations without a further appropriate procedure for the removal of bacterial endotoxins.

## ASSAY

The activity of aprotinin is determined by measuring its inhibitory action on a solution of trypsin of known activity. The inhibiting activity of the aprotinin is calculated from the difference between the initial activity and the residual activity of the trypsin.

The inhibiting activity of aprotinin is expressed in European Pharmacopoeia Units. 1 Ph. Eur. U. inhibits 50 per cent of the enzymatic activity of 2 microkatals of trypsin.

Use a reaction vessel with a capacity of about 30 ml, provided with:
— a device that will maintain a temperature of 25 $\pm$ 0.1 °C;
— a stirring device, such as a magnetic stirrer;
— a lid with 5 holes for accommodating the electrodes, the tip of a burette, a tube for the admission of nitrogen and the introduction of the reagents.

An automatic or manual titration apparatus may be used. In the latter case the burette is graduated in 0.05 ml and the pH-meter is provided with a wide reading scale and glass and calomel or glass-silver-silver chloride electrodes.

*Test solution*   With *0.0015 M borate buffer solution pH 8.0 R* prepare an appropriate dilution (D) of the aprotinin concentrated solution expected, on the basis of the stated potency, to contain 1.67 Ph. Eur. U./ml.

*Trypsin solution*   Prepare a solution of *trypsin BRP* containing about 0.8 microkatals per millilitre (about 1 mg/ml), using *0.001 M hydrochloric acid* as the solvent. Use a freshly prepared solution and keep in iced water.

*Trypsin and aprotinin solution*   To 4.0 ml of the trypsin solution add 1.0 ml of the test solution. Dilute immediately to 40.0 ml with *0.0015 M borate buffer solution pH 8.0 R*. Allow to stand at room temperature for 10 min and then keep in iced water. Use within 6 h of preparation.

*Dilute trypsin solution*   Dilute 0.5 ml of the trypsin solution to 10.0 ml with *0.0015 M borate buffer solution pH 8.0 R*. Allow to stand at room temperature for 10 min and then keep in iced water.

Maintain an atmosphere of nitrogen in the reaction flask and stir continuously; introduce 9.0 ml of *0.0015 M borate buffer solution pH 8.0 R* and 1.0 ml of a freshly prepared 6.9 g/l solution of *benzoylarginine ethyl ester hydrochloride R*. Adjust to pH 8.0 with *0.1 M sodium hydroxide*. When the temperature has reached equilibrium at 25 $\pm$ 0.1 °C, add 1.0 ml of the trypsin and aprotinin solution and start a timer. Maintain at pH 8.0 by the addition of *0.1 M sodium hydroxide* and note the volume added every 30 s. Continue the reaction for 6 min. Determine the number of millilitres of *0.1 M sodium hydroxide* used per second ($n_1$ ml). Carry out, under the same conditions, a titration using 1.0 ml of the dilute trypsin solution. Determine the number of millilitres of *0.1 M sodium hydroxide* used per second ($n_2$ ml).

Calculate the aprotinin activity in European Pharmacopoeia Units per millilitre using the following expression:

$$4000\,(2n_2 - n_1) \times D$$

$D =$ dilution factor of the aprotinin concentrated solution to be examined in order to obtain a solution containing 1.67 Ph. Eur. U./ml.

The estimated activity is not less than 90 per cent and not more than 110 per cent of the activity stated on the label.

## STORAGE

In an airtight, tamper-proof container, protected from light.

## LABELLING

The label states:
— the number of European Pharmacopoeia Units of aprotinin activity per millilitre;
— where applicable, that the substance is suitable for use in the manufacture of parenteral preparations.

## IMPURITIES

```
Ra – Arg – Pro – Asp – Phe – Cys – Leu – Glu – Pro – Pro – Tyr –
      1                                                      10
   Thr – Gly – Pro – Cys – Lys – Ala – Arg — Ile — Ile – Arg –
                                                       20
   Tyr – Phe – Tyr – Asn – Ala – Lys – Ala – Gly – Leu – Cys –
                                                    30
   Gln – Thr – Phe – Val – Tyr – Gly – Gly – Cys – Arg – Ala –
                                                         40
   Lys – Arg – Asn – Asn – Phe – Lys – Ser – Ala – Glu – Asp –
                                                          50
   Cys – Met – Arg – Thr – Cys – Gly – Rb
                       56
```

A. Ra = H, Rb = OH: aprotinin-(1-56)-peptide,

B. Ra = H, Rb = Gly-OH: aprotinin-(1-57)-peptide,

C. Ra = Glp, Rb = Gly-Ala-OH: (5-oxoprolyl)aprotinin (pyroglutamylaprotinin).

*Ph Eur*

# Arginine

(*Ph Eur monograph 0806*)

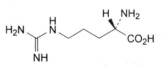

$C_6H_{14}N_4O_2$                    174.2                    74-79-3

**Action and use**

Amino acid; nutrient.

*Ph Eur*

## DEFINITION

Arginine contains not less than 98.5 per cent and not more than the equivalent of 101.0 per cent of (*S*)-2-amino-5-guanidinopentanoic acid, calculated with reference to the dried substance.

## CHARACTERS

A white or almost white, crystalline powder or colourless crystals, freely soluble in water, very slightly soluble in alcohol.

## IDENTIFICATION

*First identification   A, C.*

*Second identification   A, B, D, E.*

A. It complies with the test for specific optical rotation (see Tests).

B. Solution S (see Tests) is strongly alkaline (*2.2.4*).

C. Examine by infrared absorption spectrophotometry (*2.2.24*), comparing with the spectrum obtained with *arginine CRS* . Examine the substances prepared as discs.

D. Examine the chromatograms obtained in the test for ninhydrin-positive substances. The principal spot in the chromatogram obtained with test solution (b) is similar in position, colour and size to the principal spot in the chromatogram obtained with reference solution (a).

E. Dissolve about 25 mg in 2 ml of *water R*. Add 1 ml of α-*naphthol solution R* and 2 ml of a mixture of equal volumes of *strong sodium hypochlorite solution R* and water. A red colour develops.

## TESTS

### Solution S

Dissolve 2.5 g in *distilled water R* and dilute to 50 ml with the same solvent.

### Appearance of solution

Solution S is clear (*2.2.1*) and not more intensely coloured than reference solution $BY_6$ (*2.2.2, Method II*).

### Specific optical rotation (*2.2.7*)

Dissolve 2.00 g in *hydrochloric acid R1* and dilute to 25.0 ml with the same acid. The specific optical rotation is + 25.5 to + 28.5, calculated with reference to the dried substance.

### Ninhydrin-positive substances

Examine by thin-layer chromatography (*2.2.27*), using a *TLC silica gel plate R*.

*Test solution (a)*   Dissolve 0.10 g of the substance to be examined in *dilute hydrochloric acid R* and dilute to 10 ml with the same acid.

*Test solution (b)*   Dilute 1 ml of test solution (a) to 50 ml with *water R*.

*Reference solution (a)*   Dissolve 10 mg of *arginine CRS* in *0.1 M hydrochloric acid* and dilute to 50 ml with the same acid.

*Reference solution (b)*   Dilute 5 ml of test solution (b) to 20 ml with *water R*.

*Reference solution (c)*   Dissolve 10 mg of *arginine CRS* and 10 mg of *lysine hydrochloride CRS* in *0.1 M hydrochloric acid* and dilute to 25 ml with the same acid.

Apply to the plate 5 µl of each solution. Allow the plate to dry in air. Develop over a path of 15 cm using a mixture of 30 volumes of *concentrated ammonia R* and 70 volumes of *2-propanol R*. Dry the plate at 100 °C to 105 °C until the ammonia disappears completely. Spray with *ninhydrin solution R* and heat at 100 °C to 105 °C for 15 min. Any spot in the chromatogram obtained with test solution (a), apart from the principal spot, is not more intense than the spot in the chromatogram obtained with reference solution (b) (0.5 per cent). The test is not valid unless the chromatogram obtained with reference solution (c) shows two clearly separated spots.

### Chlorides (*2.4.4*)

To 5 ml of solution S add 0.5 ml of *dilute nitric acid R* and dilute to 15 ml with *water R*. The solution complies with the limit test for chlorides (200 ppm).

### Sulphates (*2.4.13*)

To 10 ml of solution S, add 1.7 ml of *dilute hydrochloric acid R* and dilute to 15 ml with *distilled water R*. The solution complies with the limit test for sulphates (300 ppm).

### Ammonium (*2.4.1*)

50 mg complies with limit test B for ammonium (200 ppm). Prepare the standard using 0.1 ml of *ammonium standard solution (100 ppm NH4) R*.

### Iron (*2.4.9*)

In a separating funnel, dissolve 1.0 g in 10 ml of *dilute hydrochloric acid R*. Shake with three quantities, each of 10 ml, of *methyl isobutyl ketone R1*, shaking for 3 min each time. To the combined organic layers add 10 ml of *water R* and shake for 3 min. The aqueous layer complies with the limit test for iron (10 ppm).

### Heavy metals (*2.4.8*)

Dissolve 2.0 g in *water R* and dilute to 20 ml with the same solvent. 12 ml of the solution complies with limit test A for heavy metals (10 ppm). Prepare the standard using *lead standard solution (1 ppm Pb) R*.

### Loss on drying (*2.2.32*)

Not more than 0.5 per cent, determined on 1.000 g by drying in an oven at 105 °C.

### Sulphated ash (*2.4.14*)

Not more than 0.1 per cent, determined on 1.0 g.

## ASSAY

Dissolve 0.150 g in 50 ml of *water R*. Using 0.2 ml of *methyl red mixed solution R* as indicator, titrate with *0.1 M hydrochloric acid* until the colour changes from green to violet-red.

1 ml of *0.1 M hydrochloric acid* is equivalent to 17.42 mg of $C_6H_{14}N_4O_2$.

## STORAGE

Store protected from light.

*Ph Eur*

# Arginine Aspartate

(*Ph Eur monograph 2096*)

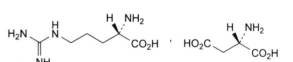

$C_6H_{14}N_4O_2,C_4H_7NO_4$          307.3          7675-83-4

**Action and use**

Amino acid; nutrient.

*Ph Eur*

## DEFINITION

(2*S*)-2-Amino-5-guanidinopentanoic acid (2*S*)-2-aminobutanedioate.

### Content

99.0 per cent to 101.0 per cent (dried substance).

## CHARACTERS

### Appearance

White or almost white granules or powder.

**Solubility**

Very soluble in water, practically insoluble in alcohol and in methylene chloride.

## IDENTIFICATION

A. It complies with the test for specific optical rotation (see Tests).

B. Infrared absorption spectrophotometry (2.2.24).

*Comparison  arginine aspartate CRS*.

C. Examine the chromatograms obtained in the test for ninhydrin-positive substances.

*Results*  The 2 principal spots in the chromatogram obtained with test solution (b) are similar in position, colour and size to the 2 principal spots in the chromatogram obtained with reference solution (a).

## TESTS

**Solution S**

Dissolve 5.0 g in *carbon dioxide-free water R* and dilute to 50 ml with the same solvent.

**Appearance of solution**

Solution S is clear (2.2.1) and not more intensely coloured than reference solution $Y_7$ (2.2.2, *Method II*).

**pH** (2.2.3)

6.0 to 7.0 for solution S.

**Specific optical rotation** (2.2.7)

+ 25 to + 27 (dried substance).

Dissolve 2.50 g in *dilute hydrochloric acid R* and dilute to 25.0 ml with the same acid.

**Ninhydrin-positive substances**

Thin-layer chromatography (2.2.27).

*Test solution (a)*  Dissolve 0.20 g of the substance to be examined in *water R* and dilute to 10 ml with the same solvent.

*Test solution (b)*  Dilute 1 ml of test solution (a) to 10 ml with *water R*.

*Reference solution (a)*  Dissolve 25 mg of *arginine R* and 25 mg of *aspartic acid R* in *water R* and dilute to 25 ml with the same solvent.

*Reference solution (b)*  Dilute 2 ml of reference solution (a) to 50 ml with *water R*.

*Plate*  TLC silica gel G plate R.

*Mobile phase*  ammonia R, propanol R (36:64 *V/V*).

*Application*  5 μl.

*Development*  Over 2/3 of the plate.

*Drying*  At 100-105 °C for 10 min.

*Detection*  Spray with *ninhydrin solution R* and heat at 100-105 °C for 10 min.

*System suitability*  Reference solution (b):
— the chromatogram shows 2 clearly separated principal spots.

*Limit*  Test solution (a):
— *any impurity*: any spots, apart from the 2 principal spots, are not more intense than each of the 2 principal spots in the chromatogram obtained with reference solution (b) (0.2 per cent).

**Chlorides** (2.4.4)

Maximum 200 ppm.

Dilute 2.5 ml of solution S to 15 ml with *water R*.

**Sulphates** (2.4.13)

Maximum 300 ppm.

To 0.5 g add 2.5 ml of *dilute hydrochloric acid R* and dilute to 15 ml with *distilled water R*. Examine after 30 min.

**Ammonium** (2.4.1)

Maximum 100 ppm, determined on 100 mg.

**Heavy metals** (2.4.8)

Maximum 20 ppm.

12 ml of solution S complies with limit test A. Prepare the standard using *lead standard solution (2 ppm Pb) R*.

**Loss on drying** (2.2.32)

Maximum 0.5 per cent, determined on 1.000 g by drying in an oven at 60 °C for 24 h.

**Sulphated ash** (2.4.14)

Maximum 0.1 per cent, determined on 1.0 g.

## ASSAY

Dissolve 80.0 mg in 2 ml of *anhydrous formic acid R*. Add 50 ml of anhydrous acetic acid R. Titrate with *0.1 M perchloric acid*, determining the end-point potentiometrically (2.2.20).

1 ml of *0.1 M perchloric acid* is equivalent to 10.24 mg of $C_{10}H_{21}N_5O_6$.

*———————————— Ph Eur*

# Arginine Hydrochloride

(*Ph Eur monograph 0805*)

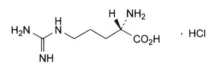

$C_6H_{14}N_4O_2,HCl$          210.7          *1119-34-2*

**Action and use**

Amino acid; nutrient.

**Preparation**

Arginine Hydrochloride Intravenous Infusion

*Ph Eur ————————————*

## DEFINITION

Arginine hydrochloride contains not less than 98.5 per cent and not more than the equivalent of 101.0 per cent of the hydrochloride of (*S*)-2-amino-5-guanidinopentanoic acid, calculated with reference to the dried substance.

## CHARACTERS

A white or almost white, crystalline powder or colourless crystals, freely soluble in water, very slightly soluble in alcohol.

## IDENTIFICATION

*First identification  A, B, E.*

*Second identification  A, C, D, E.*

A. It complies with the test for specific optical rotation (see Tests).

B. Examine by infrared absorption spectrophotometry (2.2.24), comparing with the spectrum obtained with *arginine hydrochloride CRS*. Examine the substances prepared as discs.

C. Examine the chromatograms obtained in the test for ninhydrin-positive substances. The principal spot in the chromatogram obtained with test solution (b) is similar in position, colour and size to the principal spot in the chromatogram obtained with reference solution (a).

D. Dissolve about 25 mg in 2 ml of *water R*. Add 1 ml of α-*naphthol solution R* and 2 ml of a mixture of equal volumes of *strong sodium hypochlorite solution R* and *water R*. A red colour develops.

E. It gives reaction (a) of chlorides (*2.3.1*).

## TESTS
### Solution S
Dissolve 2.5 g in *distilled water R* and dilute to 50 ml with the same solvent.

### Appearance of solution
Solution S is clear (*2.2.1*) and not more intensely coloured than reference solution $BY_6$ (*2.2.2, Method II*).

### Specific optical rotation (*2.2.7*)
Dissolve 2.00 g in *hydrochloric acid R1* and dilute to 25.0 ml with the same acid. The specific optical rotation is + 21.0 to + 23.5, calculated with reference to the dried substance.

### Ninhydrin-positive substances
Examine by thin-layer chromatography (*2.2.27*), using a *TLC silica gel plate R*.

*Test solution (a)* Dissolve 0.10 g of the substance to be examined in *water R* and dilute to 10 ml with the same solvent.

*Test solution (b)* Dilute 1 ml of test solution (a) to 50 ml with *water R*.

*Reference solution (a)* Dissolve 10 mg of *arginine hydrochloride CRS* in *water R* and dilute to 50 ml with the same solvent.

*Reference solution (b)* Dilute 5 ml of test solution (b) to 20 ml with *water R*.

*Reference solution (c)* Dissolve 10 mg of *arginine hydrochloride CRS* and 10 mg of *lysine hydrochloride CRS* in *water R* and dilute to 25 ml with the same solvent.

Apply to the plate 5 µl of each solution. Allow the plate to dry in air. Develop over a path of 15 cm using a mixture of 30 volumes of *concentrated ammonia R* and 70 volumes of *2-propanol R*. Dry the plate at 100 °C to 105 °C until the ammonia disappears completely. Spray with *ninhydrin solution R* and heat at 100 °C to 105 °C for 15 min. Any spot in the chromatogram obtained with test solution (a), apart from the principal spot, is not more intense than the spot in the chromatogram obtained with reference solution (b) (0.5 per cent). The test is not valid unless the chromatogram obtained with reference solution (c) shows two clearly separated spots.

### Sulphates (*2.4.13*)
Dilute 10 ml of solution S to 15 ml with *distilled water R*. The solution complies with the limit test for sulphates (300 ppm).

### Ammonium (*2.4.1*)
50 mg complies with limit test B for ammonium (200 ppm). Prepare the standard using 0.1 ml of *ammonium standard solution (100 ppm $NH_4$) R*.

### Iron (*2.4.9*)
In a separating funnel, dissolve 1.0 g in 10 ml of *dilute hydrochloric acid R*. Shake with three quantities, each of 10 ml, of *methyl isobutyl ketone R1*, shaking for 3 min each time. To the combined organic layers add 10 ml of *water R* and shake for 3 min. The aqueous layer complies with the limit test for iron (10 ppm).

### Heavy metals (*2.4.8*)
Dissolve 2.0 g in *water R* and dilute to 20 ml with the same solvent. 12 ml of the solution complies with limit test A for heavy metals (10 ppm). Prepare the standard using *lead standard solution (1 ppm Pb) R*.

### Loss on drying (*2.2.32*)
Not more than 0.5 per cent, determined on 1.000 g by drying in an oven at 105 °C.

### Sulphated ash (*2.4.14*)
Not more than 0.1 per cent, determined on 1.0 g.

## ASSAY
Dissolve 0.180 g in 3 ml of *anhydrous formic acid R*. Add 30 ml of *anhydrous acetic acid R*. Using 0.1 ml of *naphtholbenzein solution R* as indicator, titrate with *0.1 M perchloric acid* until the colour changes from brownish-yellow to green.

1 ml of *0.1 M perchloric acid* is equivalent to 21.07 mg of $C_6H_{15}ClN_4O_2$.

## STORAGE
Store protected from light.

_____ *Ph Eur*

# Articaine Hydrochloride

(*Ph Eur monograph 1688*)

H3C—O—C(=O) ... thiophene structure with CH3, S, N—H, CH3, N—H, CH3 , HCl

and enantiomer

$C_{13}H_{20}N_2O_3S,HCl$          320.8          *23964-57-0*

**Action and use**
Local anaesthetic.

*Ph Eur* _____

## DEFINITION
Methyl 4-methyl-3-[[(2*RS*)-2-(propylamino)propanoyl]amino]thiophene-2-carboxylate hydrochloride.

### Content
98.5 per cent to 101.0 per cent (dried substance).

## CHARACTERS
### Appearance
White or almost white, crystalline powder.

### Solubility
Freely soluble in water and in alcohol.

## IDENTIFICATION
*First identification* B, D.

*Second identification* A, C, D.

A. Dissolve 50.0 mg in a 1 g/l solution of *hydrochloric acid R* and dilute to 100.0 ml with the same acid. Dilute 5.0 ml of the solution to 100.0 ml with a 1 g/l solution of *hydrochloric acid R*. Examined between 200 nm and 350 nm (*2.2.25*), the solution shows an absorption maximum at 272 nm. The specific absorbance at the maximum is 290 to 320.

B. Infrared absorption spectrophotometry (*2.2.24*).

*Preparation*   Place dropwise 20 µl of the test solution on 300 mg discs.

*Test solution*   Dissolve 0.1 g in 5 ml of *water R*, add 3 ml of a saturated solution of *sodium hydrogen carbonate R* and shake twice with 2 ml of *methylene chloride R*. Combine the methylene chloride layers, dilute to 5.0 ml with *methylene chloride R* and dry over *anhydrous sodium sulphate R*.

*Comparison*   articaine hydrochloride CRS .

C. Thin-layer chromatography (*2.2.27*).

*Test solution*   Dissolve 20 mg of the substance to be examined in 5 ml of *alcohol R*.

*Reference solution*   Dissolve 20 mg of *articaine hydrochloride CRS* in 5 ml of *alcohol R*.

*Plate*   TLC silica gel $F_{254}$ plate R.

*Mobile phase*   triethylamine R, ethyl acetate R, heptane R (10:35:65 *V/V/V*).

*Application*   5 µl.

*Development*   Over a path of 15 cm.

*Drying*   In air.

*Detection*   .Examine in ultraviolet light at 254 nm.

*Results*   The principal spot in the chromatogram obtained with the test solution is similar in position and size to the principal spot in the chromatogram obtained with the reference solution.

D. It gives reaction (a) of chlorides (*2.3.1*).

## TESTS
### Solution S
Dissolve 0.50 g in *water R* and dilute to 10 ml with the same solvent.

### Appearance of solution
Solution S is clear (*2.2.1*) and not more intensely coloured than reference solution $BY_6$ (*2.2.2, Method I*).

### pH (*2.2.3*)
4.2 to 5.2.

Dissolve 0.20 g in *carbon dioxide-free water R* and dilute to 20.0 ml with the same solvent.

### Related substances
Liquid chromatography (*2.2.29*).

*Test solution*   Dissolve 10.0 mg of the substance to be examined in the mobile phase and dilute to 10.0 ml with the mobile phase.

*Reference solution (a)*   Dilute 1.0 ml of the test solution to 100.0 ml with the mobile phase. Dilute 1.0 ml of this solution to 10.0 ml with the mobile phase.

*Reference solution (b)*   Dissolve 10.0 mg of *articaine impurity A CRS* and 5.0 mg of *articaine impurity E CRS* in the mobile phase and dilute to 100.0 ml with the mobile phase.

*Reference solution (c)*   Add 1.0 ml of reference solution (b) to 50.0 mg of *articaine hydrochloride CRS* and dilute to 50 ml with the mobile phase.

*Reference solution (d)*   Dilute 1.0 ml of reference solution (b) to 50.0 ml with the mobile phase.

*Column:*
— *size: l* = 0.25 m, Ø = 4.6 mm,
— *stationary phase*: spherical *end-capped octadecylsilyl silica gel for chromatography R* (5 µm) with a specific surface area of 335 m2/g and a carbon loading of 19 per cent,
— *temperature*: 45 °C.

*Mobile phase*   Mix 25 volumes of *acetonitrile R* and 75 volumes of a solution prepared as follows: dissolve 2.02 g of *sodium heptanesulphonate R* and 4.08 g of *potassium dihydrogen phosphate R* in *water R* and dilute to 1000 ml with the same solvent. Adjust to pH 2.0 with *phosphoric acid R*.

*Flow rate*   1 ml/min.

*Detection*   Spectrophotometer at 276 nm.

*Injection*   10 µl; inject the test solution and reference solutions (a), (c) and (d).

*Run time*   5 times the retention time of articaine.

*Relative retentions*   With reference to articaine (retention time = about 9.3 min): impurity B = about 0.6; impurity D = about 0.7; impurity A = about 0.8; impurity E = about 0.86; impurity F = about 0.9; impurity G = about 1.7; impurity H = about 2.1; impurity I = about 2.6; impurity C = about 3.6; impurity J = about 4.0.

*System suitability*   Reference solution (c):
— *resolution*: minimum 1.2 between the peaks due to impurity A and impurity E.

*Limits:*
— *impurity A*: not more than the area of the corresponding peak in the chromatogram obtained with reference solution (d) (0.2 per cent),
— *any other impurity*: not more than the area of the principal peak in the chromatogram obtained with reference solution (a) (0.1 per cent),
— *total of other impurities*: not more than 5 times the area of the principal peak in the chromatogram obtained with reference solution (a) (0.5 per cent),
— *disregard limit*: half the area of the principal peak in the chromatogram obtained with reference solution (a) (0.05 per cent).

### Heavy metals (*2.4.8*)
Maximum 5 ppm.

Dissolve 4.0 g in 20.0 ml of wa*ter R*. 12 ml of the solution complies with limit test A. Prepare the standard using *lead standard solution (1 ppm Pb) R*.

### Loss on drying (*2.2.32*)
Maximum 0.5 per cent, determined on 1.000 g by drying in an oven at 105 °C for 5 h.

### Sulphated ash (*2.4.14*)
Maximum 0.1 per cent, determined on 1.0 g.

## ASSAY
Dissolve 0.250 g in a mixture of 5.0 ml of *0.01 M hydrochloric acid* and 50 ml of *alcohol R*. Carry out a potentiometric titration (*2.2.20*) using *0.1 M sodium hydroxide*. Read the volume added between the 2 points of inflexion.

1 ml of *0.1 M sodium hydroxide* is equivalent to 32.08 mg of $C_{13}H_{21}ClN_2O_3S$.

## STORAGE
Protected from light.

## IMPURITIES
*Specified impurities*   A, B, C.

*Other detectable impurities*

D, E, F, G, H, I, J.

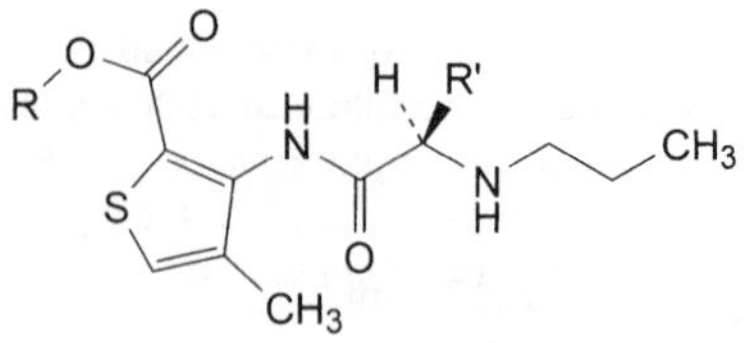

A. R = CH₃, R′ = H:
methyl 3-[[2-(propylamino)acetyl]amino]-4-methylthiophene-2-carboxylate (acetamidoarticaine),

B. R = H, R′ = CH₃:
4-methyl-3-[[(2RS)-2-(propylamino)propanoyl]amino]thiophene-2-carboxylic acid (articaine acid),

C. R = CH(CH₃)₂, R′ = CH₃: 1-methylethyl 4-methyl-3-[[(2RS)-2-(propylamino)propanoyl]amino]thiophene-2-carboxylate (articaine isopropyl ester),

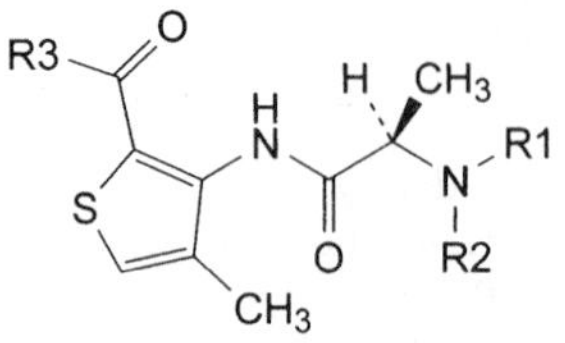

D. R1 = CH₂-CH₃, R2 = H, R3 = OCH₃:
methyl 3-[[(2RS)-2-(ethylamino)propanoyl]amino]-4-methylthiophene-2-carboxylate (ethylarticaine),

E. R1 = CH(CH₃)₂, R2 = H, R3 = OCH₃:
methyl 4-methyl-3-[[(2RS)-2-[(1-methylethyl)amino]propanoyl]amino]thiophene-2-carboxylate (isopropylarticaine),

F. R1 = CH₂-CH₂-CH₃, R2 = H, R3 = NH-CH₂-CH₂-CH₃: 4-methyl-N-propyl-3-[[(2RS)-2-(propylamino)propanoyl]amino]thiophene-2-carboxamide (articaine acid propionamide),

G. R1 = (CH₂)₃-CH₃, R2 = H, R3 = OCH₃:
methyl 3-[[(2RS)-2-(butylamino)propanoyl]amino]-4-methylthiophene-2-carboxylate (butylarticaine),

H. R1 = R2 = CH₂-CH₂-CH₃, R3 = OCH₃:
methyl 3-[[(2RS)-2-(dipropylamino)propanoyl]amino]-4-methylthiophene-2-carboxylate (dipropylarticaine),

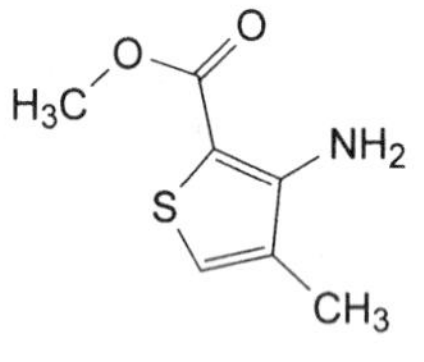

I. methyl 3-amino-4-methylthiophene-2-carboxylate (3-aminoarticaine),

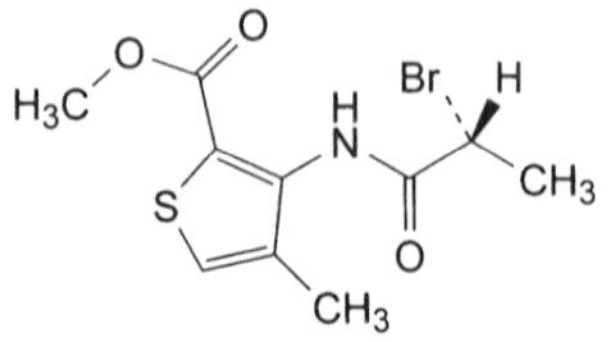

J. methyl 3-[[(2RS)-2-bromopropanoyl]amino]-4-methylthiophene-2-carboxylate (bromo compound).

_____ Ph Eur

# Ascorbic Acid

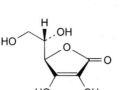

(*Ph Eur monograph 0253*)

C₆H₈O₆          176.1          *50-81-7*

**Action and use**
Vitamin C.

**Preparations**
Ascorbic Acid Injection

Ascorbic Acid Tablets

Paediatric Vitamins A, C and D Oral Drops

Vitamins B and C Injection

When Vitamin C is prescribed or demanded, Ascorbic Acid shall be dispensed or supplied.

*Ph Eur* _____

**DEFINITION**
(5R)-5-[(1S)-1,2-Dihydroxyethyl]-3,4-dihydroxyfuran-2(5H)-one.

**Content**
99.0 per cent to 100.5 per cent.

**CHARACTERS**

**Appearance**
White or almost white, crystalline powder or colourless crystals, becoming discoloured on exposure to air and moisture.

**Solubility**
Freely soluble in water, soluble in ethanol (96 per cent).

**mp**
About 190 °C, with decomposition.

**IDENTIFICATION**
*First identification*  B, C.

*Second identification*  A, C, D.

A. Ultraviolet and visible absorption spectrophotometry (*2.2.25*).

*Test solution*  Dissolve 0.10 g in *water R* and dilute immediately to 100.0 ml with the same solvent. Add 1.0 ml of this solution to 10 ml of *0.1 M hydrochloric acid* and dilute to 100.0 ml with *water R*.

*Absorption maximum*  At 243 nm, determined immediately after dissolution.

*Specific absorbance at the absorption maximum*  545 to 585.

B. Infrared absorption spectrophotometry (*2.2.24*).

*Comparison*  ascorbic acid CRS.

C. pH (*2.2.3*): 2.1 to 2.6 for solution S (see Tests).

D. To 1 ml of solution S add 0.2 ml of *dilute nitric acid R* and 0.2 ml of *silver nitrate solution R2*. A grey precipitate is formed.

**TESTS**

**Solution S**
Dissolve 1.0 g in *carbon dioxide-free water R* and dilute to 20 ml with the same solvent.

**Appearance of solution**

Solution S is clear (2.2.1) and not more intensely coloured than reference solution BY₇ (2.2.2, Method II).

**Specific optical rotation** (2.2.7)

$+ 20.5$ to $+ 21.5$.

Dissolve 2.50 g in *water R* and dilute to 25.0 ml with the same solvent.

**Impurity E**

Maximum 0.2 per cent.

*Test solution*  Dissolve 0.25 g in 5 ml of *water R*. Neutralise to *red litmus paper R* using *dilute sodium hydroxide solution R* and add 1 ml of *dilute acetic acid R* and 0.5 ml of *calcium chloride solution R*.

*Reference solution*  Dissolve 70 mg of *oxalic acid R* in *water R* and dilute to 500 ml with the same solvent; to 5 ml of this solution add 1 ml of *dilute acetic acid R* and 0.5 ml of *calcium chloride solution R*.

Allow the solutions to stand for 1 h. Any opalescence in the test solution is not more intense than that in the reference solution.

**Related substances**

Liquid chromatography (2.2.29). *Prepare the solutions immediately before use.*

*Phosphate buffer solution*  Dissolve 6.8 g of *potassium dihydrogen phosphate R* in *water R* and dilute to about 175 ml with the same solvent. Filter (porosity 0.45 μm) and dilute to 1000 ml with *water R*.

*Test solution*  Dissolve 0.500 g of the substance to be examined in the mobile phase and dilute to 10.0 ml with the mobile phase.

*Reference solution (a)*  Dissolve 10.0 mg of *ascorbic acid impurity C CRS* in the mobile phase and dilute to 5.0 ml with the mobile phase.

*Reference solution (b)*  Dilute 2.5 ml of reference solution (a) to 100.0 ml with the mobile phase.

*Reference solution (c)*  Dilute 1.0 ml of the test solution to 200.0 ml with the mobile phase. Mix 1.0 ml of this solution with 1.0 ml of reference solution (a).

*Column:*
— *size*: l = 0.25 m, Ø = 4.6 mm;
— *stationary phase*: aminopropylsilyl silica gel for chromatography R (5 μm);
— *temperature*: 45 °C.

*Mobile phase*  Phosphate buffer solution, *acetonitrile R1* (30:70 V/V).

*Flow rate*  1.0 ml/min.

*Detection*  Spectrophotometer at 210 nm.

*Injection*  20 μl of the test solution and reference solutions (b) and (c).

*Run time*  Twice the retention time of ascorbic acid.

*Relative retention*  With reference to ascorbic acid (retention time = about 8 min): impurity C = about 1.4.

*System suitability*  Reference solution (c):
— *resolution*: minimum 3.0 between the peaks due to ascorbic acid and impurity C.

*Limits:*
— *impurity C*: not more than the area of the corresponding peak in the chromatogram obtained with reference solution (b) (0.1 per cent);
— *unspecified impurities*: for each impurity, not more than the area of the peak due to impurity C in the chromatogram obtained with reference solution (b) (0.10 per cent);

— *total*: not more than twice the area of the peak due to impurity C in the chromatogram obtained with reference solution (b) (0.2 per cent);
— *disregard limit*: 0.5 times the area of the peak due to impurity C in the chromatogram obtained with reference solution (b) (0.05 per cent).

**Copper**

Maximum 5.0 ppm.

Atomic absorption spectrometry (2.2.23, Method I).

*Test solution*  Dissolve 2.0 g in *0.1 M nitric acid* and dilute to 25.0 ml with the same acid.

*Reference solutions*  Prepare the reference solutions (0.2 ppm, 0.4 ppm and 0.6 ppm) by diluting *copper standard solution (10 ppm Cu) R* with *0.1 M nitric acid*.

*Source*  Copper hollow-cathode lamp.

*Wavelength*  324.8 nm.

*Atomisation device*  Air-acetylene flame.

Adjust the zero of the apparatus using *0.1 M nitric acid*.

**Iron**

Maximum 2.0 ppm.

Atomic absorption spectrometry (2.2.23, Method I).

*Test solution*  Dissolve 5.0 g in *0.1 M nitric acid* and dilute to 25.0 ml with the same acid.

*Reference solutions*  Prepare the reference solutions (0.2 ppm, 0.4 ppm and 0.6 ppm) by diluting *iron standard solution (20 ppm Fe) R* with *0.1 M nitric acid*.

*Source*  Iron hollow-cathode lamp.

*Wavelength*  248.3 nm.

*Atomisation device*  Air-acetylene flame.

Adjust the zero of the apparatus using *0.1 M nitric acid*.

**Heavy metals** (2.4.8)

Maximum 10 ppm.

Dissolve 2.0 g in *water R* and dilute to 20 ml with the same solvent. 12 ml of the solution complies with test A. Prepare the reference solution using *lead standard solution (1 ppm Pb) R*.

**Sulphated ash** (2.4.14)

Maximum 0.1 per cent, determined on 1.0 g.

**ASSAY**

Dissolve 0.150 g in a mixture of 10 ml of *dilute sulphuric acid R* and 80 ml of *carbon dioxide-free water R*. Add 1 ml of *starch solution R*. Titrate with *0.05 M iodine* until a persistent violet-blue colour is obtained.

1 ml of *0.05 M iodine* is equivalent to 8.81 mg of $C_6H_8O_6$.

**STORAGE**

In a non-metallic container, protected from light.

## IMPURITIES

*Specified impurities* C, E.

*Other detectable impurities* (The following substances would, if present at a sufficient level, be detected by one or other of the tests in the monograph. They are limited by the general acceptance criterion for other/unspecified impurities and/or by the general monograph *Substances for pharmaceutical use (2034)*. It is therefore not necessary to identify these impurities for demonstration of compliance. See also *5.10. Control of impurities in substances for pharmaceutical use*): A, B, D.

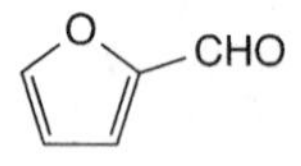

A. 2-furaldehyde,

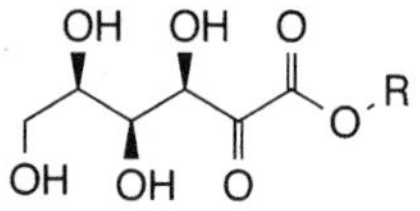

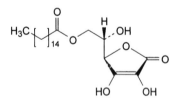

B. R = [CH₂]₃-CH₃: butyl d-sorbosonate,

C. R = H: D-sorbosonic acid,

D. R = CH₃: methyl d-sorbosonate,

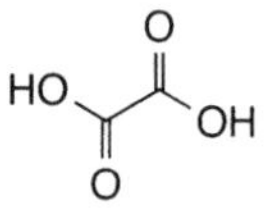

E. oxalic acid.

*——————————————— Ph Eur*

# Ascorbyl Palmitate

(*Ph Eur monograph 0807*)

$C_{22}H_{38}O_7$      414.5      137-66-3

## Action and use
Excipient.

*Ph Eur*

## DEFINITION
(2S)-2-[(5R)-3,4-Dihydroxy-5-oxo-2,5-dihydrofuran-2-yl]-2-hydroxyethyl hexadecanoate.

## Content
98.0 per cent to 100.5 per cent (dried substance).

## CHARACTERS
### Appearance
White or yellowish-white powder.

### Solubility
Practically insoluble in water, freely soluble in ethanol (96 per cent) and in methanol, practically insoluble in methylene chloride and in fatty oils.

## IDENTIFICATION
A. Specific optical rotation (see Tests).

B. Infrared absorption spectrophotometry (*2.2.24*).

*Comparison* ascorbyl palmitate CRS .

C. Dissolve about 10 mg in 5 ml of *methanol R*. The solution decolourises *dichlorophenolindophenol standard solution R*.

## TESTS
### Solution S
Dissolve 2.50 g in *methanol R* and dilute to 25.0 ml with the same solvent.

### Appearance of solution
Solution S is clear (*2.2.1*) and not more intensely coloured than reference solution $BY_4$ (*2.2.2, Method I*).

### Specific optical rotation (*2.2.7*)
+ 21 to + 24 (dried substance), determined on solution S.

### Related substances
The thresholds indicated under Related substances (Table 2034.-1) in the general monograph *Substances for pharmaceutical use (2034)* do not apply.

### Heavy metals (*2.4.8*)
Maximum 10 ppm.

2.0 g complies with test C. Prepare the reference solution using 2 ml of *lead standard solution (10 ppm Pb) R*.

### Loss on drying (*2.2.32*)
Maximum 1.0 per cent, determined on 1.000 g by drying *in vacuo* at 60 °C for 5 h.

### Sulphated ash (*2.4.14*)
Maximum 0.1 per cent, determined on 1.0 g.

## ASSAY
Dissolve 0.160 g in 50 ml of *methanol R*. Add 30 ml of *water R* and 1 ml of *starch solution R*. Titrate with *0.05 M iodine* until a persistent violet-blue colour is obtained.

1 ml of *0.05 M iodine* is equivalent to 20.73 mg of $C_{22}H_{38}O_7$.

## STORAGE
In an airtight container, protected from light.

*——————————————— Ph Eur*

# Asparagine Monohydrate

(*Ph Eur monograph 2086*)

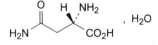

$C_4H_8N_2O_3,H_2O$      150.1      5794-13-8

## Action and use
Amino acid.

*Ph Eur*

## DEFINITION
(2S)-2,4-Diamino-4-oxobutanoic acid monohydrate.

## Content
99.0 per cent to 101.0 per cent (dried substance).

## CHARACTERS

### Appearance

White or almost white crystalline powder or colourless crystals.

### Solubility

Slightly soluble in water, practically insoluble in alcohol and in methylene chloride.

## IDENTIFICATION

*First identification   A, B.*

*Second identification   A, C.*

A. It complies with the test for specific optical rotation (see Tests).

B. Infrared absorption spectrophotometry (*2.2.24*).

*Comparison   asparagine monohydrate CRS .*

C. Examine the chromatograms obtained in the test for ninhydrin-positive substances.

*Results*   The principal spot in the chromatogram obtained with test solution (b) is similar in position, colour and size to the principal spot in the chromatogram obtained with reference solution (c).

## TESTS

### Solution S

Dissolve with heating 2.0 g in *carbon dioxide-free water R* and dilute to 100 ml with the same solvent.

### Appearance of solution

Solution S is clear (*2.2.1*) and colourless (*2.2.2, Method II*).

### pH (*2.2.3*)

4.0 to 6.0 for solution S.

### Specific optical rotation (*2.2.7*)

+ 33.7 to + 36.0 (dried substance).

Dissolve 2.50 g in a 309.0 g/l solution of *hydrochloric acid R* and dilute to 25.0 ml with the same acid.

### Ninhydrin-positive substances

Thin-layer chromatography (*2.2.27*).

*Test solution (a)*   Dissolve 0.25 g of the substance to be examined in *water R*, heating to not more than 40 °C, and dilute to 10 ml with the same solvent.

*Test solution (b)*   Dilute 1 ml of test solution (a) to 10 ml with *water R*.

*Reference solution (a)*   Dilute 1.0 ml of test solution (a) to 200 ml with *water R*.

*Reference solution (b)*   Dissolve 25 mg of *glutamic acid R* in *water R*, add 1 ml of test solution (a) and dilute to 10 ml with *water R*.

*Reference solution (c)*   Dissolve 25 mg of *asparagine monohydrate CRS* in *water R* and dilute to 10 ml with the same solvent.

*Plate*   TLC silica gel G plate R.

*Mobile phase*   glacial acetic acid R, water R, butanol R (25:25:50 *V/V/V*).

*Application*   5 µl.

*Development*   Over half of the plate.

*Drying*   At 110 °C for 15 min.

*Detection*   Spray with *ninhydrin solution R* and heat at 110 °C for 10 min.

*System suitability*   Reference solution (b):
— the chromatogram shows 2 clearly separated principal spots.

*Limit*   Test solution (a):

— *any impurity*: any spot, apart from the principal spot, is not more intense than the principal spot in the chromatogram obtained with reference solution (a) (0.5 per cent).

### Chlorides (*2.4.4*)

Maximum 200 ppm.

Dilute 12.5 ml of solution S to 15 ml with *water R*.

### Sulphates (*2.4.13*)

Maximum 200 ppm.

To 0.75 g add 2.5 ml of *dilute hydrochloric acid R* and dilute to 15 ml with *distilled water R*. Examine after 30 min.

### Ammonium (*2.4.1, Method B*)

Maximum 0.1 per cent, determined on 10 mg.

### Iron (*2.4.9*)

Maximum 10 ppm.

Dissolve 1.0 g in *dilute hydrochloric acid R* and dilute to 10 ml with the same acid. Shake 3 times with 10 ml of *methyl isobutyl ketone R1* for 3 min. Wash the combined organic phases with 10 ml of *water R* for 3 min. The aqueous phase complies with the limit test for iron.

### Heavy metals (*2.4.8*)

Maximum 10 ppm.

Dissolve 2.0 g in a mixture of 3 ml of *dilute hydrochloric acid R* and 15 ml of *water R* with gentle warming if necessary. Dilute to 20 ml with *water R*. 12 ml of the solution complies with limit test A. Prepare the standard using *lead standard solution (1 ppm Pb) R*.

### Loss on drying (*2.2.32*)

10.5 per cent to 12.5 per cent, determined on 1.000 g by drying in an oven at 60 °C for 24 h.

### Sulphated ash (*2.4.14*)

Maximum 0.1 per cent, determined on 1.0 g.

## ASSAY

Dissolve 0.110 g in 5 ml of *anhydrous formic acid R*. Add 50 ml of *anhydrous acetic acid R*. Titrate with *0.1 M perchloric acid*, determining the end-point potentiometrically (*2.2.20*).

1 ml of *0.1 M perchloric acid* is equivalent to 13.21 mg of $C_4H_8N_2O_3$.

## IMPURITIES

*Specified impurities   A, B.*

A. aspartic acid,

B. glutamic acid.

*Ph Eur*

# Aspartame

*(Ph Eur monograph 0973)*

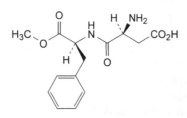

C₁₄H₁₈N₂O₅          294.3          53906-69-7

## Action and use
Sweetening agent.

*Ph Eur* _____

## DEFINITION
(3*S*)-3-Amino-4-[[(1*S*)-1-benzyl-2-methoxy-2-oxoethyl]amino]-4-oxobutanoic acid.

## Content
98.0 per cent to 102.0 per cent (dried substance).

## CHARACTERS
### Appearance
White or almost white, slightly hygroscopic, crystalline powder.

### Solubility
Sparingly soluble or slightly soluble in water and in ethanol (96 per cent), practically insoluble in hexane and in methylene chloride.

## IDENTIFICATION
*First identification*  B.

*Second identification*  A, C, D.

A. Ultraviolet and visible absorption spectrophotometry (*2.2.25*).

*Test solution*  Dissolve 0.1 g in *ethanol (96 per cent) R* and dilute to 100 ml with the same solvent.

*Spectral range*  230-300 nm.

*Absorption maxima*  At 247 nm, 252 nm, 258 nm and 264 nm.

B. Infrared absorption spectrophotometry (*2.2.24*).

*Preparation*  Discs.

*Comparison*  aspartame CRS .

C. Thin-layer chromatography (*2.2.27*).

*Test solution*  Dissolve 15 mg of the substance to be examined in 2.5 ml of *water R* and dilute to 10 ml with *acetic acid R*.

*Reference solution*  Dissolve 15 mg of *aspartame CRS* in 2.5 ml of *water R* and dilute to 10 ml with *acetic acid R*.

*Plate*  *TLC silica gel G plate R*.

*Mobile phase*  water R, anhydrous formic acid R, methanol R, methylene chloride R (2:4:30:64 V/V/V/V).

*Application*  20 μl.

*Development*  Over a path of 15 cm.

*Drying*  In air.

*Detection*  Spray with *ninhydrin solution R* and heat at 100-105 °C for 15 min.

*Results*  The spot in the chromatogram obtained with the test solution is similar in position, colour and size to the spot in the chromatogram obtained with the reference solution.

D. Dissolve about 20 mg in 5 ml of *methanol R* and add 1 ml of *alkaline hydroxylamine solution R1*. Heat on a water-bath for 15 min. Allow to cool and adjust to about pH 2 with *dilute hydrochloric acid R*. Add 0.1 ml of *ferric chloride solution R1*. A brownish-red colour is produced.

## TESTS
### Solution S
Dissolve 0.8 g in *carbon dioxide-free water R* and dilute to 100 ml with the same solvent.

### Appearance of solution
Solution S is clear (*2.2.1*) and not more intensely coloured than reference solution GY₆ (*2.2.2, Method II*).

### Conductivity (*2.2.38*)
Maximum 30 μS·cm⁻¹.

Dissolve 0.80 g in *carbon dioxide-free water R* prepared from *distilled water R* and dilute to 100.0 ml with the same solvent. Measure the conductivity of the solution ($C_1$) and that of the water used for preparing the solution ($C_2$). The readings must be stable within 1 per cent over a period of 30 s.

Calculate the conductivity of the solution of the substance to be examined using the following expression:

$$C_1 - 0.992\ C_2$$

### Specific optical rotation (*2.2.7*)
+ 14.5 to + 16.5 (dried substance).

Dissolve 2.00 g in a 690 g/l solution of *anhydrous formic acid R* and dilute to 50.0 ml with the same solution. Measure within 30 min of preparation.

### Related substances
Liquid chromatography (*2.2.29*).

*Test solution*  Dissolve 0.60 g of the substance to be examined in a mixture of 1.5 volumes of *glacial acetic acid R* and 98.5 volumes of *water R* and dilute to 100.0 ml with the same mixture of solvents.

*Reference solution (a)*  Dissolve 4.5 mg of *aspartame impurity A CRS* in a mixture of 1.5 volumes of *glacial acetic acid R* and 98.5 volumes of *water R* and dilute to 50.0 ml with the same mixture of solvents.

*Reference solution (b)*  Dissolve 30.0 mg of *phenylalanine R* (impurity C) in a mixture of 15 volumes of *glacial acetic acid R* and 85 volumes of *water R* and dilute to 100.0 ml with the same mixture of solvents. Dilute 1.0 ml of this solution to 10.0 ml with *water R*.

*Reference solution (c)*  Dilute 5.0 ml of the test solution to 10.0 ml with *water R*. Dilute 3.0 ml of this solution to 100.0 ml with *water R*.

*Reference solution (d)*  Dissolve 30.0 mg of L-aspartyl-L-phenylalanine R (impurity B) in a mixture of 15 volumes of *glacial acetic acid R* and 85 volumes of *water R* and dilute to 100.0 ml with the same mixture of solvents. Dilute 1.0 ml of the solution to 10.0 ml with *water R*. Mix 1.0 ml of this solution with 1.0 ml of reference solution (b).

*Column*:
— *size*: l = 0.25 m, Ø = 4.0 mm;
— *stationary phase*: octadecylsilyl silica gel for chromatography R (5-10 μm).

*Mobile phase*  Mix 10 volumes of *acetonitrile R* and 90 volumes of a 6.8 g/l solution of *potassium dihydrogen phosphate R* previously adjusted to pH 3.7 with *phosphoric acid R*.

*Flow rate*  1 ml/min.

*Detection*  Spectrophotometer at 220 nm.

*Injection* 20 μl.

*Run time* Twice the retention time of aspartame.

*System suitability* Reference solution (d):
— *resolution*: minimum 3.5 between the peaks due to impurities B and C.

*Limits:*
— *impurity A*: not more than the area of the principal peak in the chromatogram obtained with reference solution (a) (1.5 per cent);
— *impurity C*: not more than the area of the principal peak in the chromatogram obtained with reference solution (b) (0.5 per cent);
— *sum of impurities other than A and C*: not more than the area of the principal peak in the chromatogram obtained with reference solution (c) (1.5 per cent);
— *disregard limit*: disregard any peak due to the solvent.

**Heavy metals** (*2.4.8*)
Maximum 10 ppm.

1.0 g complies with test C. Prepare the reference solution using 1 ml of *lead standard solution (10 ppm Pb) R*.

**Loss on drying** (*2.2.32*)
Maximum 4.5 per cent, determined on 1.000 g by drying in an oven at 105 °C.

**Sulphated ash** (*2.4.14*)
Maximum 0.2 per cent, determined on 1.0 g.

**ASSAY**
Dissolve 0.250 g in 1.5 ml of *anhydrous formic acid R* and 60 ml of *anhydrous acetic acid R*. Titrate immediately with *0.1 M perchloric acid*, determining the end-point potentiometrically (*2.2.20*).

1 ml of *0.1 M perchloric acid* is equivalent to 29.43 mg of $C_{14}H_{18}N_2O_5$.

**STORAGE**
In an airtight container.

**IMPURITIES**
*Specified impurities* A, C.

*Other detectable impurities* (the following substances would, if present at a sufficient level, be detected by one or other of the tests in the monograph. They are limited by the general acceptance criterion for other/unspecified impurities and/or by the general monograph *Substances for pharmaceutical use (2034)*. It is therefore not necessary to identify these impurities for demonstration of compliance. See also *5.10*. *Control of impurities in substances for pharmaceutical use*): B.

A. 2-(5-benzyl-3,6-dioxopiperazin-2-yl)acetic acid (diketopiperazine),

B. L-aspartyl-L-phenylalanine,

C. phenylalanine.

_____ *Ph Eur*

# Aspartic Acid

(*Ph Eur monograph 0797*)

| $C_4H_7NO_4$ | 133.1 | *6899-03-2* |

**Action and use**
Amino acid.

*Ph Eur* _____

**DEFINITION**
Aspartic acid contains not less than 98.5 per cent and not more than the equivalent of 101.5 per cent of (2S)-2-aminobutanedioic acid, calculated with reference to the dried substance.

**CHARACTERS**
A white or almost white, crystalline powder or colourless crystals, slightly soluble in water, practically insoluble in alcohol. It dissolves in dilute mineral acids and in dilute solutions of alkali hydroxides.

**IDENTIFICATION**
*First identification* A, C.

*Second identification* A, B, D.

A. It complies with the test for specific optical rotation (see Tests).

B. A suspension of 1 g in 10 ml of *water R* is strongly acid (*2.2.4*).

C. Examine by infrared absorption spectrophotometry (*2.2.24*), comparing with the spectrum obtained with *aspartic acid CRS*. Examine the substances prepared as discs.

D. Examine the chromatograms obtained in the test for ninhydrin-positive substances. The principal spot in the chromatogram obtained with test solution (b) is similar in position, colour and size to the principal spot in the chromatogram obtained with reference solution (a).

**TESTS**
**Appearance of solution**
Dissolve 0.5 g in *1 M hydrochloric acid* and dilute to 10 ml with the same acid. The solution is clear (*2.2.1*) and not more intensely coloured than reference solution $BY_6$ (*2.2.2, Method II*).

**Specific optical rotation** (*2.2.7*)
Dissolve 2.000 g in *hydrochloric acid R1* and dilute to 25.0 ml with the same acid. The specific optical rotation is + 24.0 to + 26.0, calculated with reference to the dried substance.

**Ninhydrin-positive substances**
Examine by thin-layer chromatography (*2.2.27*), using a *TLC silica gel plate R*.

*Test solution (a)* Dissolve 0.10 g of the substance to be examined in 2 ml of *ammonia R* and dilute to 10 ml with *water R*.

*Test solution (b)* Dilute 1 ml of test solution (a) to 50 ml with *water R*.

*Reference solution (a)* Dissolve 10 mg of *aspartic acid CRS* in 2 ml of *dilute ammonia R1* and dilute to 50 ml with *water R*.

*Reference solution (b)* Dilute 5 ml of test solution (b) to 20 ml with *water R*.

*Reference solution (c)*    Dissolve 10 mg of *aspartic acid CRS* and 10 mg of *glutamic acid CRS* in 2 ml of *dilute ammonia R1* and dilute to 25 ml with *water R*.

Apply separately to the plate 5 µl of each solution. Allow the plate to dry in air. Develop over a path of 15 cm using a mixture of 20 volumes of *glacial acetic acid R*, 20 volumes of *water R* and 60 volumes of *butanol R*. Allow the plate to dry in air, spray with *ninhydrin solution R*. Heat at 100-105 °C for 15 min. Any spot in the chromatogram obtained with test solution (a), apart from the principal spot, is not more intense than the spot in the chromatogram obtained with reference solution (b) (0.5 per cent). The test is not valid unless the chromatogram obtained with reference solution (c) shows 2 clearly separated principal spots.

**Chlorides** *(2.4.4)*
Dissolve 0.25 g in 3 ml of *dilute nitric acid R* and dilute to 15 ml with *water R*. The solution, to which 1 ml of *water R* is added instead of *dilute nitric acid R*, complies with the limit test for chlorides (200 ppm).

**Sulphates** *(2.4.13)*
Dissolve 0.5 g in 4 ml of *hydrochloric acid R* and dilute to 15 ml with *distilled water R*. The solution complies with the limit test for sulphates (300 ppm). Carry out the evaluation of the test after 30 min.

**Ammonium.***(2.4.1)*
50 mg complies with limit test B (200 ppm). Prepare the standard using 0.1 ml of *ammonium standard solution (100 ppm NH4) R*.

**Iron** *(2.4.9)*
In a separating funnel, dissolve 1.0 g in 10 ml of *dilute hydrochloric acid R*. Shake with 3 quantities, each of 10 ml, of *methyl isobutyl ketone R1*, shaking for 3 min each time. To the combined organic layers add 10 ml of *water R* and shake for 3 min. The aqueous layer complies with the limit test for iron (10 ppm).

**Heavy metals** *(2.4.8)*
2.0 g complies with limit test D (10 ppm). Prepare the standard using 2 ml of *lead standard solution (10 ppm Pb) R*.

**Loss on drying** *(2.2.32)*
Not more than 0.5 per cent, determined on 1.000 g by drying in an oven at 105 °C.

**Sulphated ash** *(2.4.14)*
Not more than 0.1 per cent, determined on 1.0 g.

**ASSAY**
Dissolve 0.100 g in 50 ml of *carbon dioxide-free water R*, with slight heating if necessary. Cool and add *0.1 ml of bromothymol blue solution R1*. Titrate with *0.1 M sodium hydroxide* until the colour changes from yellow to blue.

1 ml of *0.1 M sodium hydroxide* is equivalent to 13.31 mg of $C_4H_7NO_4$.

**STORAGE**
Protected from light.

———————————————— *Ph Eur*

# Aspirin

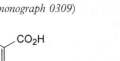

*(Acetylsalicylic Acid, Ph Eur monograph 0309)*

$C_9H_8O_4$                    180.2                    50-78-2

**Action and use**
Salicylate; non-selective cyclo-oxygenase inhibitor;antipyretic; analgesic; anti-inflammatory.

**Preparations**
Aspirin Tablets
Dispersible Aspirin Tablets
Effervescent Soluble Aspirin Tablets
Gastro-resistant Aspirin Tablets
Aspirin and Caffeine Tablets
Co-codaprin Tablets
Dispersible Co-codaprin Tablets

*Ph Eur* _____

**DEFINITION**
2-(Acetyloxy)benzoic acid.

**Content**
99.5 per cent to 101.0 per cent (dried substance).

**CHARACTERS**
**Appearance**
White or almost white, crystalline powder or colourless crystals.

**Solubility**
Slightly soluble in water, freely soluble in ethanol (96 per cent).

**mp**
About 143 °C (instantaneous method).

**IDENTIFICATION**
*First identification    A, B.*

*Second identification    B, C, D.*

A. Infrared absorption spectrophotometry *(2.2.24)*.

*Comparison    acetylsalicylic acid CRS.*

B. To 0.2 g add 4 ml of *dilute sodium hydroxide solution R* and boil for 3 min. Cool and add 5 ml of *dilute sulphuric acid R*. A crystalline precipitate is formed. Filter, wash the precipitate and dry at 100-105 °C. The melting point *(2.2.14)* is 156 °C to 161 °C.

C. In a test tube mix 0.1 g with 0.5 g of *calcium hydroxide R*. Heat the mixture and expose to the fumes produced a piece of filter paper impregnated with 0.05 ml of *nitrobenzaldehyde solution R*. A greenish-blue or greenish-yellow colour develops on the paper. Moisten the paper with *dilute hydrochloric acid R*. The colour becomes blue.

D. Dissolve with heating about 20 mg of the precipitate obtained in identification test B in 10 ml of *water R* and cool. The solution gives reaction (a) of salicylates *(2.3.1)*.

# TESTS

## Appearance of solution

The solution is clear (2.2.1) and colourless (2.2.2, Method II).

Dissolve 1.0 g in 9 ml of *ethanol (96 per cent) R*.

## Related substances

Liquid chromatography (2.2.29). *Prepare the solutions immediately before use.*

*Test solution*   Dissolve 0.10 g of the substance to be examined in *acetonitrile for chromatography R* and dilute to 10.0 ml with the same solvent.

*Reference solution (a)*   Dissolve 50.0 mg of *salicylic acid R* in the mobile phase and dilute to 50.0 ml with the mobile phase. Dilute 1.0 ml of this solution to 100.0 ml with the mobile phase.

*Reference solution (b)*   Dissolve 10.0 mg of *salicylic acid R* in the mobile phase and dilute to 10.0 ml with the mobile phase. To 1.0 ml of this solution add 0.2 ml of the test solution and dilute to 100.0 ml with the mobile phase.

*Column:*
— size: $l$ = 0.25 m, Ø = 4.6 mm;
— stationary phase: octadecylsilyl silica gel for chromatography R (5 μm).

*Mobile phase*   phosphoric acid R, acetonitrile for chromatography R, water R (2:400:600 *V/V/V*).

*Flow rate*   1 ml/min.

*Detection*   Spectrophotometer at 237 nm.

*Injection*   10 μl.

*Run time*   7 times the retention time of acetylsalicylic acid.

*System suitability*   Reference solution (b):
— resolution: minimum 6.0 between the 2 principal peaks.

*Limits:*
— any impurity: for each impurity, not more than the area of the principal peak in the chromatogram obtained with reference solution (a) (0.1 per cent);
— total: not more than 2.5 times the area of the principal peak in the chromatogram obtained with reference solution (a) (0.25 per cent);
— disregard limit: 0.25 times the area of the principal peak in the chromatogram obtained with reference solution (a) (0.025 per cent).

## Heavy metals (2.4.8)

Maximum 20 ppm.

Dissolve 1.0 g in 12 ml of *acetone R* and dilute to 20 ml with *water R*. 12 ml of this solution complies with test B. Prepare the reference solution using lead standard solution (1 ppm Pb) obtained by diluting *lead standard solution (100 ppm Pb) R* with a mixture of 6 volumes of *water R* and 9 volumes of *acetone R*.

## Loss on drying (2.2.32)

Maximum 0.5 per cent, determined on 1.000 g by drying *in vacuo*.

## Sulphated ash (2.4.14)

Maximum 0.1 per cent, determined on 1.0 g.

## ASSAY

In a flask with a ground-glass stopper, dissolve 1.000 g in 10 ml of *ethanol (96 per cent) R*. Add 50.0 ml of *0.5 M sodium hydroxide*. Close the flask and allow to stand for 1 h. Using 0.2 ml of *phenolphthalein solution R* as indicator, titrate with *0.5 M hydrochloric acid*. Carry out a blank titration.

1 ml of *0.5 M sodium hydroxide* is equivalent to 45.04 mg of $C_9H_8O_4$.

# STORAGE

In an airtight container.

# IMPURITIES

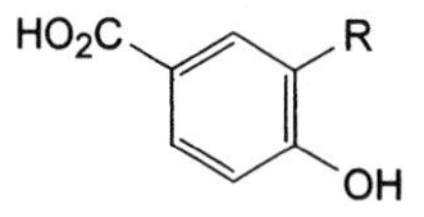

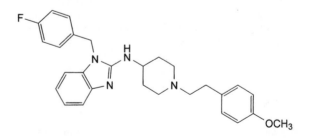

A. R = H: 4-hydroxybenzoic acid,

B. R = $CO_2H$: 4-hydroxybenzene-1,3-dicarboxylic acid (4-hydroxyisophthalic acid),

C. salicylic acid,

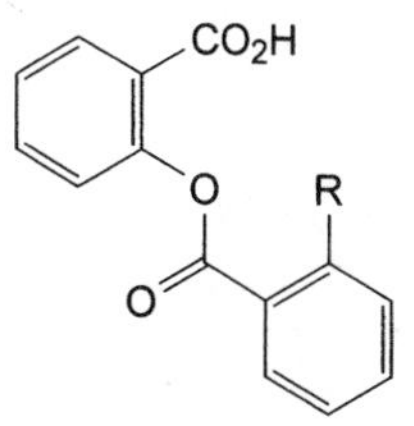

D. R = O-CO-$CH_3$: 2-[[2-(acetyloxy)benzoyl]oxy]benzoic acid (acetylsalicylsalicylic acid),

E. R = OH: 2-[(2-hydroxybenzoyl)oxy]benzoic acid (salicylsalicylic acid),

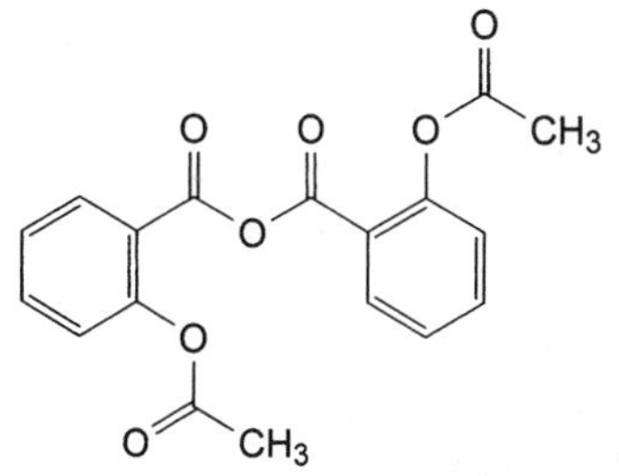

F. 2-(acetyloxy)benzoic anhydride (acetylsalicylic anhydride).

*Ph Eur*

# Astemizole

*(Ph Eur monograph 1067)*

$C_{28}H_{31}FN_4O$         458.6         *68844-77-9*

## Action and use

Histamine $H_1$ receptor antagonist.

*Ph Eur*

# DEFINITION

1-(4-Fluorobenzyl)-*N*-[1-[2-(4-methoxyphenyl)ethyl] piperidin-4-yl]-1*H*-benzimidazol-2-amine.

## Content
99.0 per cent to 101.0 per cent (dried substance).

## CHARACTERS

### Appearance
White or almost white powder.

### Solubility
Practically insoluble in water, freely soluble in methylene chloride and in methanol, soluble in ethanol (96 per cent).

## IDENTIFICATION

*First identification*   A, B.

*Second identification*   A, C, D.

A. Melting point (*2.2.14*): 175 °C to 178 °C.

B. Infrared absorption spectrophotometry (*2.2.24*).

*Preparation*   Discs.

*Comparison*   astemizole CRS.

C. Thin layer chromatography (*2.2.27*).

*Test solution*   Dissolve 30 mg of the substance to be examined in *methanol R* and dilute to 5 ml with the same solvent.

*Reference solution (a)*   Dissolve 30 mg of *astemizole CRS* in *methanol R* and dilute to 5 ml with the same solvent.

*Reference solution (b)*   Dissolve 30 mg of *astemizole CRS* and 30 mg of *ketoconazole CRS* in *methanol R* and dilute to 5 ml with the same solvent.

*Plate*   TLC octadecylsilyl silica gel plate R.

*Mobile phase*   ammonium acetate solution R, dioxan R, methanol R (20:40:40 *V/V/V*).

*Application*   5 μl.

*Development*   Over a path of 15 cm.

*Drying*   In a current of warm air for 15 min.

*Detection*   Expose the plate to iodine vapour until the spots appear and examine in daylight.

*System suitability*   Reference solution (b):
— the chromatogram shows 2 clearly separated spots.

*Results*   The principal spot in the chromatogram obtained with the test solution is similar in position and size to the principal spot in the chromatogram obtained with reference solution (a).

D. Mix about 5 mg with 45 mg of *heavy magnesium oxide R* and ignite in a crucible until an almost white residue is obtained (usually less than 5 min). Allow to cool, add 1 ml of *water R*, 0.05 ml of *phenolphthalein solution R1* and about 1 ml of *dilute hydrochloric acid R* to render the solution colourless. Filter. To a freshly prepared mixture of 0.1 ml of *alizarin S solution R* and 0.1 ml of *zirconyl nitrate solution R*, add 1 ml of the filtrate. Mix, allow to stand for 5 min and compare the colour of the solution with that of a blank solution prepared in the same manner. The test solution is yellow and the blank solution is red.

## TESTS

### Appearance of solution
The solution is clear (*2.2.1*) and is not more intensely coloured than reference solution $Y_7$ (*2.2.2, Method II*).

Dissolve 0.2 g in *methanol R* and dilute to 20 ml with the same solvent.

### Related substances
Liquid chromatography (*2.2.29*). *Prepare the solutions immediately before use.*

*Test solution*   Dissolve 0.100 g of the substance to be examined in *methanol R* and dilute to 10.0 ml with the same solvent.

*Reference solution (a)*   Dissolve 2.5 mg of *astemizole CRS* and 25 mg of *ketoconazole CRS* in *methanol R* and dilute to 100.0 ml with the same solvent.

*Reference solution (b)*   Dilute 1.0 ml of the test solution to 100.0 ml with *methanol R*. Dilute 5.0 ml of this solution to 20.0 ml with *methanol R*.

*Column:*
— *size*: $l$ = 0.1 m, Ø = 4.6 mm;
— *stationary phase*: base-deactivated octadecylsilyl silica gel for chromatography R (3 μm).

*Mobile phase:*
— *mobile phase A*: a 17 g/l solution of *tetrabutylammonium hydrogen sulphate R*;
— *mobile phase B*: acetonitrile R;

| Time (min) | Mobile phase A (per cent *V/V*) | Mobile phase B (per cent *V/V*) |
|---|---|---|
| 0 - 15 | 95 → 80 | 5 → 20 |
| 15 - 18 | 80 → 0 | 20 → 100 |
| 18 - 23 | 0 → 95 | 100 → 5 |
| 23 - 28 | 95 | 5 |

*Flow rate*   1.5 ml/min.

*Detection*   Spectrophotometer at 278 nm.

*Equilibration*   With *acetonitrile R* for at least 30 min then with the mobile phase at the initial composition for at least 5 min.

*Injection*   10 μl; inject *methanol R* as a blank.

*Retention time*   ketoconazole = about 8 min; astemizole = about 9 min.

*System suitability*   Reference solution (a):
— *resolution*: minimum 1.5 between the peaks due to ketoconazole and astemizole; if necessary, adjust the final concentration of acetonitrile or the percentage of tetrabutylammonium hydrogen sulphate in the mobile phase or adjust the time programme for the linear gradient elution.

*Limits:*
— *impurities A, B, C, D, E, F, G, H*: for each impurity, not more than the area of the principal peak in the chromatogram obtained with reference solution (b) (0.25 per cent);
— *total*: not more than twice the area of the principal peak in the chromatogram obtained with reference solution (b) (0.5 per cent);
— *disregard limit*: 0.2 times the area of the principal peak in the chromatogram obtained with reference solution (b) (0.05 per cent); disregard any peak obtained with the blank.

### Loss on drying (*2.2.32*)
Maximum 0.5 per cent, determined on 1.000 g by drying in an oven at 105 °C.

### Sulphated ash (*2.4.14*)
Maximum 0.1 per cent, determined on 1.0 g.

## ASSAY
Dissolve 0.200 g in 50 ml of a mixture of 1 volume of *anhydrous acetic acid R* and 7 volumes of *methyl ethyl ketone R*. Titrate with *0.1 M perchloric acid*, using 0.2 ml of *naphtholbenzein solution R* as indicator.

1 ml of *0.1 M perchloric acid* is equivalent to 22.93 mg of $C_{28}H_{31}FN_4O$.

**STORAGE**

Protected from light.

**IMPURITIES**

*Specified impurities*   *A, B, C, D, E, F, G, H.*

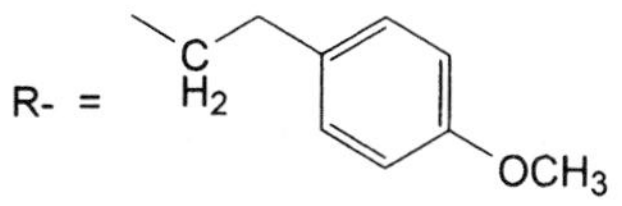

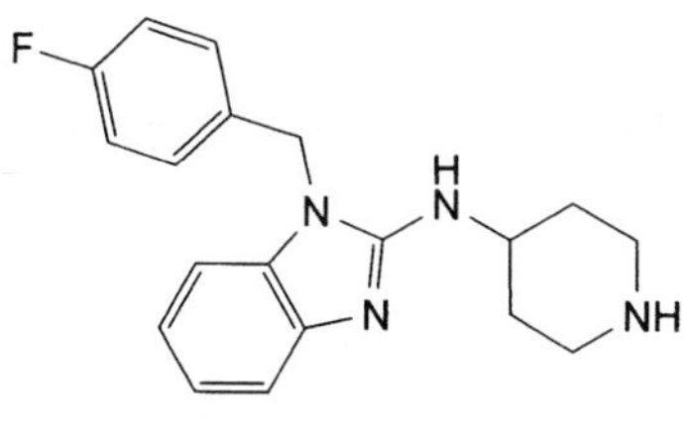

R- =

A. 1-(4-fluorobenzyl)-*N*-(piperidin-4-yl)-1*H*-benzimidazol-2-amine,

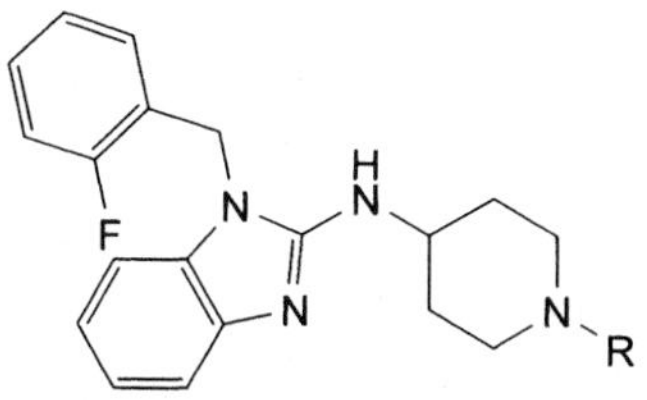

B. 1-(2-fluorobenzyl)-*N*-[1-[2-(4-methoxyphenyl)ethyl]piperidin-4-yl]-1*H*-benzimidazol-2-amine,

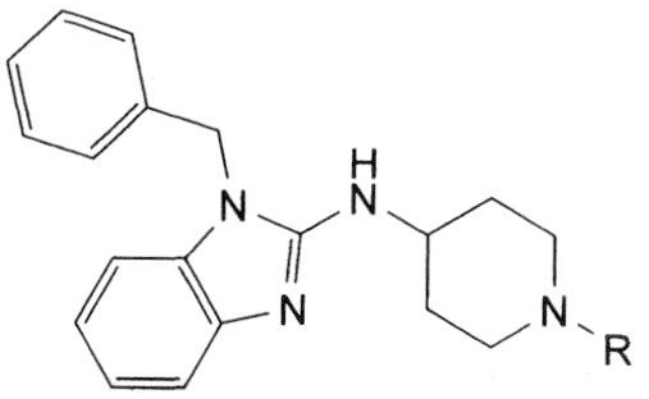

C. 1-benzyl-*N*-[1-[2-(4-methoxyphenyl)ethyl]piperidin-4-yl]-1*H*-benzimidazol-2-amine,

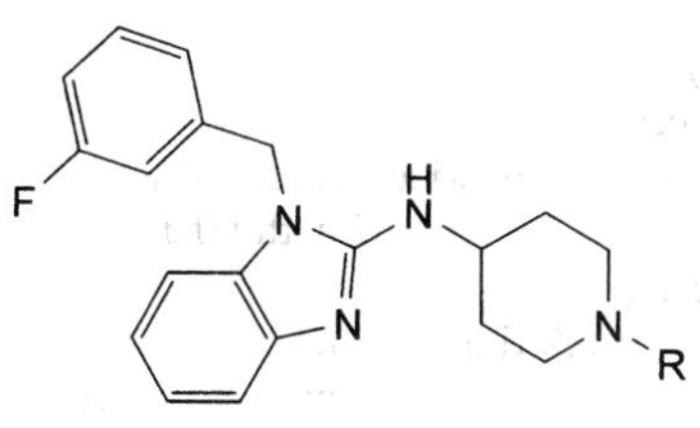

D. 1-(3-fluorobenzyl)-*N*-[1-[2-(4-methoxyphenyl)ethyl]piperidin-4-yl]-1*H*-benzimidazol-2-amine,

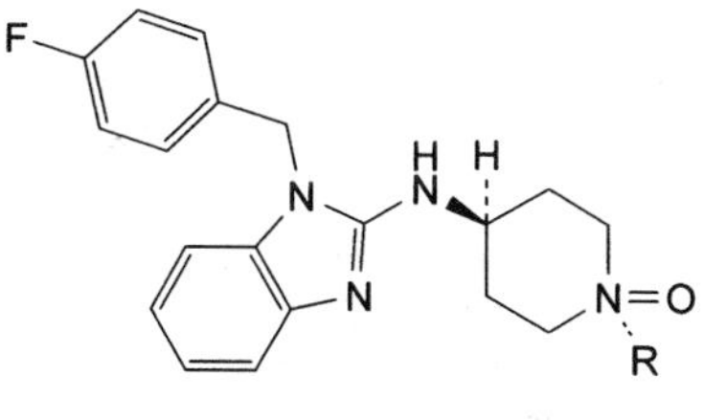

E. 1-(4-fluorobenzyl)-*N*-[*cis*-1-[2-(4-methoxyphenyl)ethyl]piperidin-4-yl 1-oxide]-1*H*-benzimidazol-2-amine,

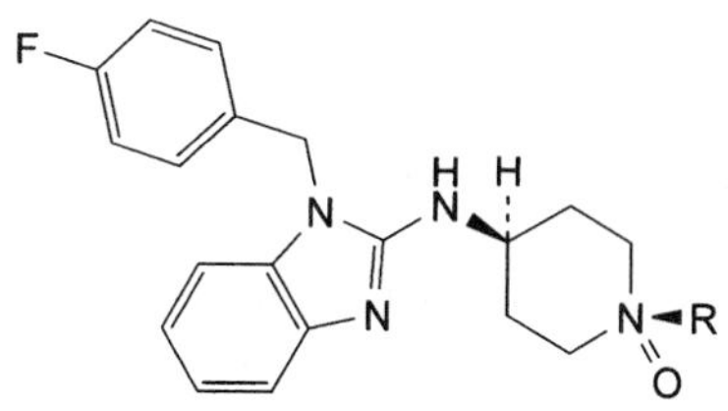

F. 1-(4-fluorobenzyl)-*N*-[*trans*-1-[2-(4-methoxyphenyl)ethyl]piperidin-4-yl 1-oxide]-1*H*-benzimidazol-2-amine,

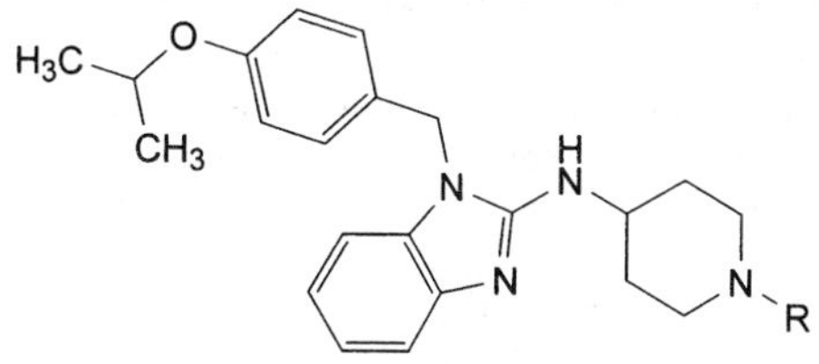

G. *N*-[1-[2-(4-methoxyphenyl)ethyl]piperidin-4-yl]-1-[4-(1-methylethoxy)benzyl]-1*H*-benzimidazol-2-amine,

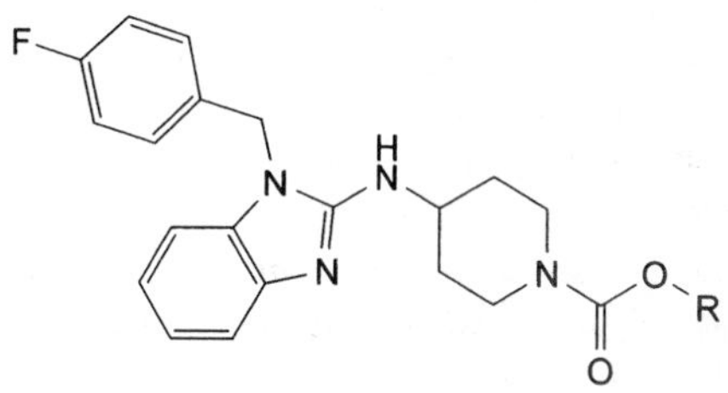

H. 2-(4-methoxyphenyl)ethyl 4-[[1-(4-fluorobenzyl)-1*H*-benzimidazol-2-yl]amino]piperidin-1-carboxylate.

*Ph Eur*

# Atenolol

*(Ph Eur monograph 0703)*

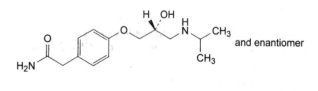

and enantiomer

$C_{14}H_{22}N_2O_3$        266.3        *29122-68-7*

**Action and use**

Beta-adrenoceptor antagonist.

**Preparations**

Atenolol Injection

Atenolol Oral Solution

Atenolol Tablets

Co-tenidone Tablets

*Ph Eur*

**DEFINITION**

2-[4-[(2*RS*)-2-Hydroxy-3-[(1-methylethyl)amino]propoxy]phenyl]acetamide.

**Content**

99.0 per cent to 101.0 per cent (dried substance).

## CHARACTERS
### Appearance
White or almost white powder.

### Solubility
Sparingly soluble in water, soluble in anhydrous ethanol, slightly soluble in methylene chloride.

## IDENTIFICATION
*First identification* C.

*Second identification* A, B, D.

A. Melting point (*2.2.14*): 152 °C to 155 °C.

B. Ultraviolet and visible absorption spectrophotometry (*2.2.25*).

*Test solution* Dissolve 0.100 g in *methanol R* and dilute to 100 ml with the same solvent. Dilute 10.0 ml of this solution to 100 ml with *methanol R*.

*Spectral range* 230-350 nm.

*Absorption maxima* At 275 nm and 282 nm.

*Absorbance ratio* $A_{275}/A_{282}$ = 1.15 to 1.20.

C. Infrared absorption spectrophotometry (*2.2.24*).

*Comparison* atenolol CRS.

D. Thin-layer chromatography (*2.2.27*).

*Test solution* Dissolve 10 mg of the substance to be examined in 1 ml of *methanol R*.

*Reference solution* Dissolve 10 mg of *atenolol CRS* in 1 ml of *methanol R*.

*Plate* TLC silanised silica gel $F_{254}$ plate R.

*Mobile phase* concentrated ammonia R1, methanol R (1:99 *V/V*).

*Application* 10 µl.

*Drying* In air.

*Detection* Examine in ultraviolet light at 254 nm.

*Results* The principal spot in the chromatogram obtained with the test solution is similar in position and size to the principal spot in the chromatogram obtained with the reference solution.

## TESTS
### Solution S
Dissolve 0.10 g in *water R* and dilute to 10 ml with the same solvent.

### Appearance of solution
Solution S is clear (*2.2.1*) and not more intensely coloured than degree 6 of the range of reference solutions of the most appropriate colour (*2.2.2, Method II*).

### Optical rotation (*2.2.7*)
+ 0.10° to − 0.10°, determined on solution S.

### Related substances
Liquid chromatography (*2.2.29*).

*Test solution* Dissolve 50 mg of the substance to be examined in 20 ml of the mobile phase and dilute to 25.0 ml with the mobile phase.

*Reference solution (a)* Dissolve 2 mg of *atenolol for system suitability CRS* (containing impurities B, F, G, I and J) in 1.0 ml of the mobile phase.

*Reference solution (b)* Dilute 1.0 ml of the test solution to 100.0 ml with the mobile phase. Dilute 1.0 ml of this solution to 10.0 ml with the mobile phase.

*Column:*
— *size: l* = 0.125 m, Ø = 4.0 mm;
— *stationary phase:* end-capped octadecylsilyl silica gel for chromatography R (5 µm).

*Mobile phase* Dissolve 1.0 g of *sodium octanesulphonate R* and 0.4 g of *tetrabutylammonium hydrogen sulphate R* in 1 litre of a mixture of 20 volumes of *tetrahydrofuran R*, 180 volumes of *methanol R2*, and 800 volumes of a 3.4 g/l solution of *potassium dihydrogen phosphate R*; adjust the apparent pH to 3.0 with *phosphoric acid R*.

*Flow rate* 0.6 ml/min.

*Detection* Spectrophotometer at 226 nm.

*Injection* 10 µl.

*Run time* 5 times the retention time of atenolol.

*Identification of impurities* Use the chromatogram supplied with *atenolol for system suitability CRS* and the chromatogram obtained with reference solution (a) to identify the peaks due to impurities B, F, G, I and J.

*Relative retention* With reference to atenolol (retention time = about 8 min): impurity B = about 0.3; impurity J = about 0.7; impurity I = about 0.8; impurity F = about 2.0 (pair of peaks); impurity G = about 3.5.

*System suitability* Reference solution (a):
— *resolution:* minimum 1.4 between the peaks due to impurities J (unidentified impurity) and I.

*Limits:*
— *correction factor:* for the calculation of content, multiply the peak area of impurity I by 1.5;
— *impurity B:* not more than twice the area of the principal peak in the chromatogram obtained with reference solution (b) (0.2 per cent);
— *impurities F, G, I:* for each impurity, not more than 1.5 times the area of the principal peak in the chromatogram obtained with reference solution (b) (0.15 per cent);
— *unspecified impurities:* for each impurity, not more than the area of the principal peak in the chromatogram obtained with reference solution (b) (0.10 per cent);
— *total:* not more than 5 times the area of the principal peak in the chromatogram obtained with reference solution (b) (0.5 per cent);
— *disregard limit:* 0.5 times the area of the principal peak in the chromatogram obtained with reference solution (b) (0.05 per cent).

### Chlorides (*2.4.4*)
Maximum 0.1 per cent.

Dissolve 50 mg in a mixture of 1 ml of *dilute nitric acid R* and 15 ml of *water R*. The solution, without further addition of *dilute nitric acid R*, complies with the test.

### Loss on drying (*2.2.32*)
Maximum 0.5 per cent, determined on 1.000 g by drying in an oven at 105 °C.

### Sulphated ash (*2.4.14*)
Maximum 0.1 per cent, determined on 1.0 g.

## ASSAY
Dissolve 0.200 g in 80 ml of *anhydrous acetic acid R*. Titrate with *0.1 M perchloric acid*, determining the end-point potentiometrically (*2.2.20*).

1 ml of *0.1 M perchloric acid* is equivalent to 26.63 mg of $C_{14}H_{22}N_2O_3$.

## IMPURITIES

*Specified impurities*   *B, F, G, I.*

*Other detectable impurities*   (The following substances would, if present at a sufficient level, be detected by one or other of the tests in the monograph. They are limited by the general acceptance criterion for other/unspecified impurities and/or by the general monograph *Substances for pharmaceutical use (2034)*. It is therefore not necessary to identify these impurities for demonstration of compliance. See also *5.10. Control of impurities in substances for pharmaceutical use):* A, D, E, H.

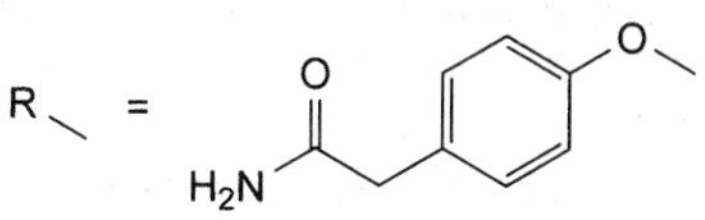

A. R-H: 2-(4-hydroxyphenyl)acetamide,

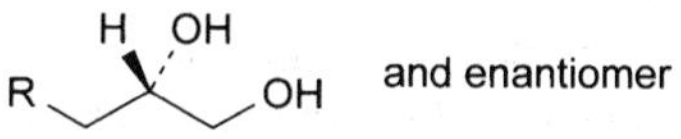

B. 2-[4-[(2RS)-2,3-dihydroxypropoxy]phenyl]acetamide,

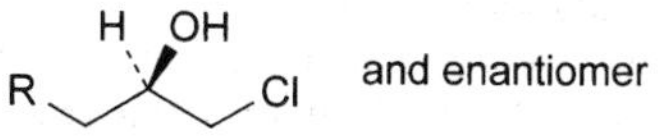

D. 2-[4-[(2RS)-3-chloro-2-hydroxypropoxy]phenyl]acetamide,

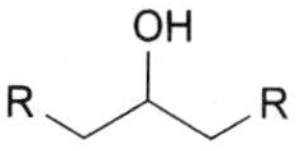

E. 2,2′-[(2-hydroxypropane-1,3-diyl)bis(oxy-4,1-phenylene)]diacetamide,

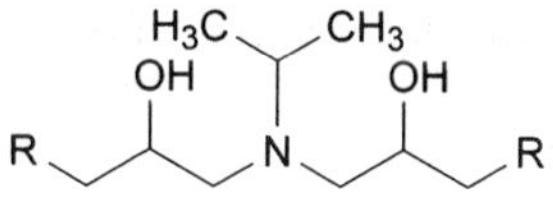

F. 2,2′-[[(1-methylethyl)imino]bis[(2-hydroxypropane-3,1-diyl)oxy-4,1-phenylene]]diacetamide,

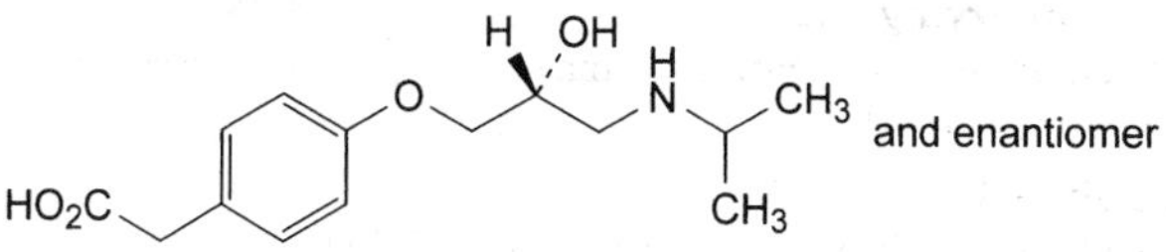

G. 2-[4-[(2RS)-2-hydroxy-3-[(1-methylethyl)amino]propoxy]phenyl]acetic acid,

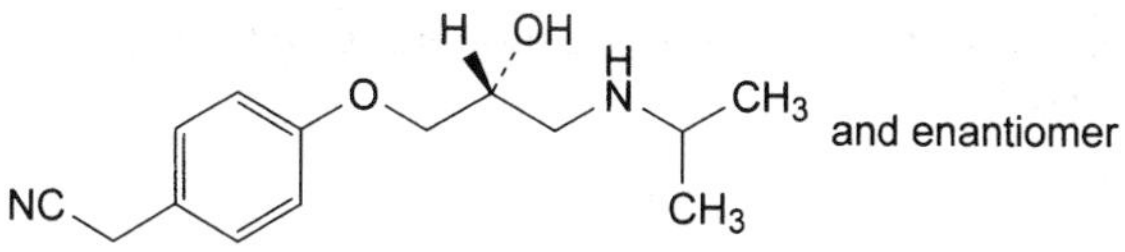

H. 2-[4-[(2RS)-2-hydroxy-3-[(1-methylethyl)amino]propoxy]phenyl]acetonitrile,

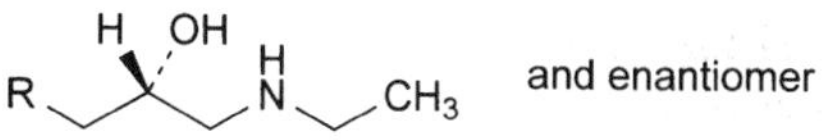

I. 2-[4-[(2RS)-3-(ethylamino)-2-hydroxypropoxy]phenyl]acetamide.

*Ph Eur*

# Atracurium Besilate

(*Ph Eur monograph 1970*)

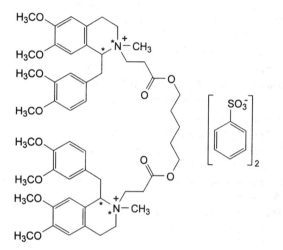

$C_{65}H_{82}N_2O_{18}S_2$          1243          *64228-81-5*

### Action and use
Non-depolarizing neuromuscular blocker.

*Ph Eur*

## DEFINITION
Mixture of the *cis-cis, cis-trans* and *trans-trans* isomers of 2,2′-[pentane-1,5-diylbis[oxy(3-oxopropane-1,3-diyl)]]bis[1-(3,4-dimethoxybenzyl)-6,7-dimethoxy-2-methyl-1,2,3,4-tetrahydroisoquinolinium] dibenzenesulphonate.

### Content
96.0 per cent to 102.0 per cent (anhydrous substance).

## CHARACTERS
### Appearance
White to yellowish-white powder, slightly hygroscopic.

### Solubility
Soluble in water, very soluble in acetonitrile, in ethanol (96 per cent) and in methylene chloride.

## IDENTIFICATION
A. Infrared absorption spectrophotometry (*2.2.24*).

*Comparison*   atracurium besilate CRS.

B. Examine the chromatograms obtained in the assay.

*Results*   The 3 principal isomeric peaks in the chromatogram obtained with test solution (a) are similar in retention time to those in the chromatogram obtained with reference solution (a).

## TESTS
### Solution S
Dissolve 1.00 g in *water R* and dilute to 100 ml with the same solvent.

**Appearance of solution**

Solution S is clear (*2.2.1*) and not more intensely coloured than reference solution $Y_7$ (*2.2.2, Method II*).

**Related substances**

Liquid chromatography (*2.2.29*).

*Test solution (a)*   Dissolve 50.0 mg of the substance to be examined in mobile phase A and dilute to 50.0 ml with mobile phase A.

*Test solution (b)*   Dissolve 0.100 g of the substance to be examined in mobile phase A and dilute to 10.0 ml with mobile phase A.

*Reference solution (a)*   Dissolve 50.0 mg of *atracurium besilate CRS* in mobile phase A and dilute to 50.0 ml with mobile phase A.

*Reference solution (b)*   Dilute 1.0 ml of test solution (a) to 100.0 ml with mobile phase A.

*Reference solution (c)*   Dissolve 20.0 mg of *methyl benzenesulphonate R* in *acetonitrile R* and dilute to 100.0 ml with the same solvent. Dilute 50 µl of the solution to 100.0 ml with mobile phase A.

*Reference solution (d)*   Dissolve 2.0 mg of *atracurium for peak identification CRS* (containing impurities A1, A2, B, C1, C2, D1, D2, E, G and K) in 2.0 ml of mobile phase A.

*Reference solution (e)*   Dissolve 2.0 mg of *atracurium for impurity F identification CRS* in 2.0 ml of mobile phase A.

*Column:*
— *size:* $l = 0.25$ m, Ø = 4.6 mm,
— *stationary phase:* base-deactivated octadecylsilyl silica gel for chromatography R (5 µm).

*Mobile phase:*
— *mobile phase A:* mix 5 volumes of *methanol R*, 20 volumes of *acetonitrile R* and 75 volumes of a 10.2 g/l solution of *potassium dihydrogen phosphate R* previously adjusted to pH 3.1 with *phosphoric acid R*,
— *mobile phase B:* mix 20 volumes of *acetonitrile R*, 30 volumes of *methanol R* and 50 volumes of a 10.2 g/l solution of *potassium dihydrogen phosphate R* previously adjusted to pH 3.1 with *phosphoric acid R*,

| Time (min) | Mobile phase A (per cent *V/V*) | Mobile phase B (per cent *V/V*) |
|---|---|---|
| 0 - 5 | 80 | 20 |
| 5 - 15 | 80 → 40 | 20 → 60 |
| 15 - 25 | 40 | 60 |
| 25 - 30 | 40 → 0 | 60 → 100 |
| 30 - 45 | 0 | 100 |
| 45 - 50 | 0 → 80 | 100 → 20 |

*Flow rate*   1 ml/min.

*Detection*   Spectrophotometer at 280 nm.

*Injection*   20 µl of test solution (a) and reference solutions (a), (b), (d) and (e).

*Relative retention*   With reference to the atracurium *cis-cis* isomer (retention time = about 30 min):
impurity E = about 0.2; impurity F = about 0.25;
impurity G = about 0.3; impurity D1 = about 0.45;
impurity D2 = about 0.5; atracurium *trans-trans* isomer = about 0.8; atracurium *cis-trans* isomer = about 0.9; impurity A1 = about 1.04;
impurity I1 = about 1.07; impurity H1 = about 1.07 (shoulder on the front of peak A2);
impurity A2 (major isomer) = about 1.08;
impurity K1 = about 1.09 (shoulder on the tail of peak A2);

impurity I2 (major isomer) = about 1.12; impurity H2 (major isomer) = about 1.12;
impurity K2 (major isomer) = about 1.12;
impurity B = about 1.15; impurity C1 = about 1.2;
impurity C2 (major isomer) = about 1.3.

*Identification of impurities:*
— use the chromatogram obtained with reference solution (d) and the chromatogram supplied *with atracurium for peak identification CRS* to identify the peaks due to impurities A1, A2, B, C1, C2, D1, D2, E, G and K;
— use the chromatogram obtained with reference solution (e) and the chromatogram supplied with *atracurium for impurity F identification CRS* to identify the peak due to impurity F.

*System suitability*   Reference solution (a):
— *resolution:* minimum 1.5 between the peaks due to the atracurium *trans-trans* isomer and the atracurium *cis-trans* isomer, and minimum 1.5 between the peaks due to the atracurium *cis-trans* isomer and the atracurium *cis-cis* isomer.

*Limits:*
— *correction factor:* for the calculation of content, multiply the peak area of impurity G by 0.5,
— *impurity E:* not more than 1.5 times the sum of the areas of the peaks due to the atracurium *cis-cis*, *trans-trans* and *cis-trans* isomers in the chromatogram obtained with reference solution (b) (1.5 per cent),
— *impurities A, D:* for each impurity, for the sum of the areas of the 2 isomer peaks, not more than 1.5 times the sum of the areas of the peaks due to the atracurium *cis-cis*, *trans-trans* and *cis-trans* isomers in the chromatogram obtained with reference solution (b) (1.5 per cent),
— *impurity C:* for the sum of the areas of the 2 isomer peaks, not more than the sum of the areas of the peaks due to the atracurium *cis-cis*, *trans-trans* and *cis-trans* isomers in the chromatogram obtained with reference solution (b) (1.0 per cent),
— *impurities F, G:* for each impurity, not more than the sum of the areas of the peaks due to the atracurium *cis-cis*, *trans-trans* and *cis-trans* isomers in the chromatogram obtained with reference solution (b) (1.0 per cent),
— *impurities H, I, K:* for the sum of the areas of the isomer peaks of these impurities, not more than the sum of the areas of the peaks due to the atracurium *cis-cis*, *trans-trans* and *cis-trans* isomers in the chromatogram obtained with reference solution (b) (1.0 per cent),
— *any other impurity:* for each impurity, not more than 0.1 times the sum of the areas of the peaks due to the atracurium *cis-cis*, *trans-trans* and *cis-trans* isomers in the chromatogram obtained with reference solution (b) (0.1 per cent),
— *total:* not more than 3.5 times the sum of the areas of the peaks due to the atracurium *cis-cis*, *trans-trans* and *cis-trans* isomers in the chromatogram obtained with reference solution (b) (3.5 per cent),
— *disregard limit:* 0.05 times the sum of the areas of the peaks due to the atracurium *cis-cis*, *trans-trans* and *cis-trans* isomers in the chromatogram obtained with reference solution (b) (0.05 per cent).

**Impurity J**

Liquid chromatography (*2.2.29*) as described in the test for related substances with the following modifications.

*Mobile phase:*

| Time (min) | Mobile phase A (per cent V/V) | Mobile phase B (per cent V/V) |
|---|---|---|
| 0 - 5 | 80 | 20 |
| 5 - 15 | 80 → 75 | 20 → 25 |
| 15 - 25 | 75 | 25 |
| 25 - 30 | 75 → 55 | 25 → 45 |
| 30 - 38 | 55 → 0 | 45 → 100 |
| 38 - 45 | 0 | 100 |
| 45 - 50 | 0 → 80 | 100 → 20 |

*Detection*   Spectrophotometer at 217 nm.

*Injection*   100 µl of test solution (b) and reference solution (c).

*Retention time*   Impurity J = about 25 min; atracurium *trans-trans* isomer = about 38 min.

*Limit:*
— *impurity J*: not more than the area of the principal peak in the chromatogram obtained with reference solution (c) (10 ppm).

**Isomer composition**
Liquid chromatography (*2.2.29*) as described in the test for related substances with the following modifications. Use the normalisation procedure.

*Injection*   Test solution (a).

*Limits:*
— *atracurium cis-cis isomer*: 55.0 per cent to 60.0 per cent,
— *atracurium cis-trans isomer*: 34.5 per cent to 38.5 per cent,
— *atracurium trans-trans isomer*: 5.0 per cent to 6.5 per cent.

**Water** (*2.5.12*)
Maximum 5.0 per cent, determined on 1.000 g.

**Sulphated ash** (*2.4.14*)
Maximum 0.1 per cent, determined on 1.0 g.

**ASSAY**
Liquid chromatography (*2.2.29*) as described in the test for related substances with the following modification.

*Injection*   Test solution (a) and reference solution (a).

Calculate the percentage content of $C_{65}H_{82}N_2O_{18}S_2$ from the sum of the areas of the peaks due to the 3 isomers in test solution (a) and reference solution (a).

**STORAGE**
In an airtight container, protected from light, at a temperature of 2 °C to 8 °C.

**IMPURITIES**
*Specified impurities*   A, C, D, E, F, G, H, I, J, K.

*Other detectable impurities* (the following substances would, if present at a sufficient level, be detected by one or other of the tests in the monograph. They are limited by the general acceptance criterion for other/unspecified impurities and/or by the general monograph *Substances for pharmaceutical use* (*2034*). It is therefore not necessary to identify these impurities for demonstration of compliance. See also *5.10*. *Control of impurities in substances for pharmaceutical use*): B.

A. 1-(3,4-dimethoxybenzyl)-2-[13-[1-(3,4-dimethoxybenzyl)-6,7-dimethoxy-3,4-dihydroisoquinolin-2(1H)-yl]-3,11-dioxo-4,10-dioxatridecyl]-6,7-dimethoxy-2-methyl-1,2,3,4-tetrahydroisoquinolinium
(A1 = *cis-trans* isomer, A2 = *cis-cis* isomer),

B. pentane-1,5-diyl bis[3-[1-(3,4-dimethoxybenzyl)-6,7-dimethoxy-3,4-dihydroisoquinolin-2(1H)-yl]propanoate],

C. 1-(3,4-dimethoxybenzyl)-2-(3,11-dioxo-4,10-dioxatridec-12-enyl)-6,7-dimethoxy-2-methyl-1,2,3,4-tetrahydroisoquinolinium
(C1 = *trans* isomer, C2 = *cis* isomer),

D. 1-(3,4-dimethoxybenzyl)-2-[3-[(5-hydroxypentyl)oxy]-3-oxopropyl]-6,7-dimethoxy-2-methyl-1,2,3,4-tetrahydroisoquinolinium
(D1 = *trans* isomer, D2 = *cis* isomer),

E. 3-[1-(3,4-dimethoxybenzyl)-6,7-dimethoxy-2-methyl-1,2,3,4-tetrahydroisoquinolinio]propanoate,

F. R+-CH₃: 1-(3,4-dimethoxybenzyl)-6,7-dimethoxy-2,2-dimethyl-1,2,3,4-tetrahydroisoquinolinium,

G. R-CH₃: 1-(3,4-dimethoxybenzyl)-6,7-dimethoxy-2-methyl-1,2,3,4-tetrahydroisoquinoline,

H. 2,2′-[hexane-1,6-diylbis[oxy(3-oxopropane-1,3-diyl)]]bis[1-(3,4-dimethoxybenzyl)-6,7-dimethoxy-2-methyl-1,2,3,4-tetrahydroisoquinolinium]
(H1 = *cis-trans* isomer, H2 = *cis-cis* isomer),

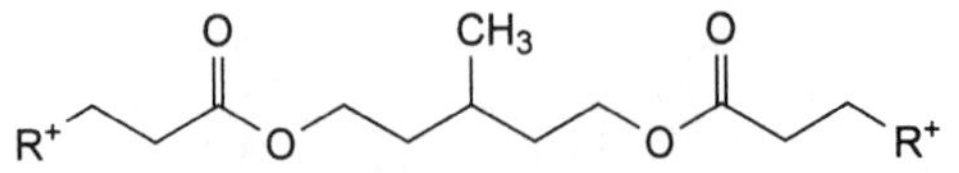

I. 2,2′-[(3-methylpentane-1,5)-diylbis[oxy(3-oxopropane-1,3-diyl)]]bis[1-(3,4-dimethoxybenzyl)-6,7-dimethoxy-2-methyl-1,2,3,4-tetrahydroisoquinolinium]
(I1 = *cis-trans* isomer, I2 = *cis-cis* isomer),

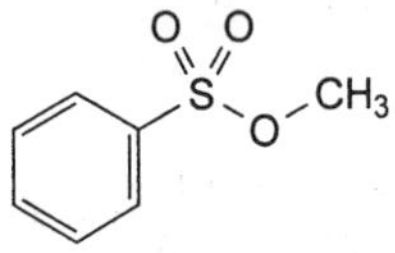

J. methyl benzenesulphonate,

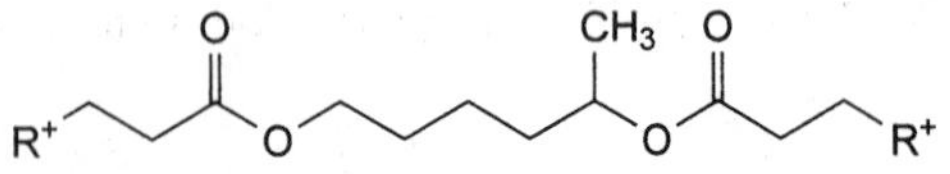

K. 2,2′-[(hexane-1,5)-diylbis[oxy(3-oxopropane-1,3-diyl)]]bis[1-(3,4-dimethoxybenzyl)-6,7-dimethoxy-2-methyl-1,2,3,4-tetrahydroisoquinolinium]).

_____ *Ph Eur*

# Atropine

(*Ph Eur monograph 2056*)

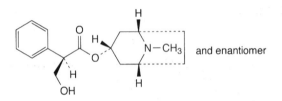

and enantiomer

$C_{17}H_{23}NO_3$      289.4      51-55-8

**Action and use**

Anticholinergic.

*Ph Eur* _____

## DEFINITION

(1R,3r,5S)-8-Methyl-8-azabicyclo[3.2.1]oct-3-yl (2RS)-3-hydroxy-2-phenylpropanoate.

## Content

99.0 per cent to 101.0 per cent (dried substance).

## CHARACTERS

**Appearance**

White or almost white, crystalline powder or colourless crystals.

**Solubility**

Very slightly soluble in water, freely soluble in ethanol (96 per cent) and in methylene chloride.

## IDENTIFICATION

*First identification*  A, B, E.

*Second identification*  A, C, D, E.

A. Melting point (*2.2.14*): 115 °C to 119 °C.

B. Infrared absorption spectrophotometry (*2.2.24*).

*Comparison*  atropine CRS.

C. Thin-layer chromatography (*2.2.27*).

*Test solution*  Dissolve 10 mg of the substance to be examined in *methanol R* and dilute to 10 ml with the same solvent.

*Reference solution*  Dissolve 10 mg of *atropine CRS* in *methanol R* and dilute to 10 ml with the same solvent.

*Plate*  TLC silica gel plate R.

*Mobile phase*  concentrated ammonia R, water R, acetone R (3:7:90 *V/V/V*).

*Application*  10 µl.

*Development*  Over half of the plate.

*Drying*  At 100-105 °C for 15 min.

*Detection*  After cooling, spray with *dilute potassium iodobismuthate solution R*.

*Results*  The principal spot in the chromatogram obtained with the test solution is similar in position, colour and size to the principal spot in the chromatogram obtained with the reference solution.

D. Place about 3 mg in a porcelain crucible and add 0.2 ml of *fuming nitric acid R*. Evaporate to dryness on a water-bath. Dissolve the residue in 0.5 ml of a 30 g/l solution of *potassium hydroxide R* in *methanol R*; a violet colour develops.

E. Optical rotation (see Tests).

## TESTS

**Optical rotation** (*2.2.7*)

– 0.70° to + 0.05° (measured in a 2 dm tube).

Dissolve 1.25 g in *ethanol (96 per cent) R* and dilute to 25.0 ml with the same solvent.

**Related substances**

Liquid chromatography (*2.2.29*).

*Test solution*  Dissolve 24 mg of the substance to be examined in mobile phase A and dilute to 100.0 ml with mobile phase A.

*Reference solution (a)*  Dilute 1.0 ml of the test solution to 100.0 ml with mobile phase A. Dilute 1.0 ml of this solution to 10.0 ml with mobile phase A.

*Reference solution (b)*  Dissolve 5 mg of *atropine impurity B CRS* in the test solution and dilute to 20 ml with the test solution. Dilute 5 ml of this solution to 25 ml with mobile phase A.

*Reference solution (c)*  Dissolve the contents of a vial of *atropine for peak identification CRS* (containing impurities A, B, D, E, F, G and H) in 1 ml of mobile phase A.

*Reference solution (d)*  Dissolve 5 mg of *tropic acid R* (impurity C) in mobile phase A and dilute to 10 ml with mobile phase A. Dilute 1 ml of the solution to 100 ml with mobile phase A. Dilute 1 ml of this solution to 10 ml with mobile phase A.

*Column:*

— size: $l$ = 0.10 m, Ø = 4.6 mm;

— stationary phase: octadecylsilyl silica gel for chromatography R (3 µm).

*Mobile phase:*

— mobile phase A: dissolve 3.5 g of *sodium dodecyl sulphate R* in 606 ml of a 7.0 g/l solution of *potassium dihydrogen phosphate R* previously adjusted to pH 3.3 with *0.05 M phosphoric acid*, and mix with 320 ml of *acetonitrile R1*;

— mobile phase B: *acetonitrile R1*;

| Time (min) | Mobile phase A (per cent *V/V*) | Mobile phase B (per cent *V/V*) |
|---|---|---|
| 0 - 2 | 95 | 5 |
| 2 - 20 | 95 → 70 | 5 → 30 |

*Flow rate*    1 ml/min.

*Detection*    Spectrophotometer at 210 nm.

*Injection*    10 µl.

*Identification of impurities*    Use the chromatogram supplied with *atropine for peak identification CRS* and the chromatogram obtained with reference solution (c) to identify the peaks due to impurities A, B, D, E, F, G and H. Use the chromatogram obtained with reference solution (d) to identify the peak due to impurity C.

*Relative retention*    With reference to atropine (retention time = about 11 min): impurity C = about 0.2; impurity E = about 0.67; impurity D = about 0.73; impurity F = about 0.8; impurity B = about 0.89; impurity H = about 0.93; impurity G = about 1.1; impurity A = about 1.7.

*System suitability*    Reference solution (b):
— *resolution*: minimum 2.5 between the peaks due to impurity B and atropine.

*Limits*:
— *correction factors*: for the calculation of content, multiply the peak areas of the following impurities by the corresponding correction factor: impurity A = 0.6; impurity C = 0.6;
— *impurities E, H*: for each impurity, not more than 3 times the area of the principal peak in the chromatogram obtained with reference solution (a) (0.3 per cent);
— *impurities A, B, C, D, F, G*: for each impurity, not more than twice the area of the principal peak in the chromatogram obtained with reference solution (a) (0.2 per cent);
— *unspecified impurities*: for each impurity, not more than the area of the principal peak in the chromatogram obtained with reference solution (a) (0.10 per cent);
— *total*: not more than 5 times the area of the principal peak in the chromatogram obtained with reference solution (a) (0.5 per cent);
— *disregard limit*: 0.5 times the area of the principal peak in the chromatogram obtained with reference solution (a) (0.05 per cent).

**Loss on drying** (2.2.32)
Maximum 0.2 per cent, determined on 1.000 g by drying in an oven at 105 °C for 2 h.

**ASSAY**
Dissolve 0.250 g in 40 ml of *anhydrous acetic acid R*, warming if necessary. Allow the solution to cool. Titrate with *0.1 M perchloric acid*, determining the end-point potentiometrically (2.2.20).

1 ml of *0.1 M perchloric acid* is equivalent to 28.94 mg of $C_{17}H_{23}NO_3$.

**STORAGE**
Protected from light.

**IMPURITIES**
*Specified impurities*    A, B, C, D, E, F, G, H.

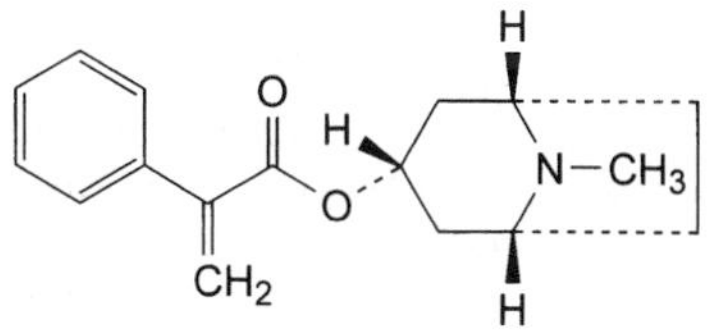

A. (1R,3r,5S)-8-methyl-8-azabicyclo[3.2.1]oct-3-yl 2-phenylpropenoate (apoatropine),

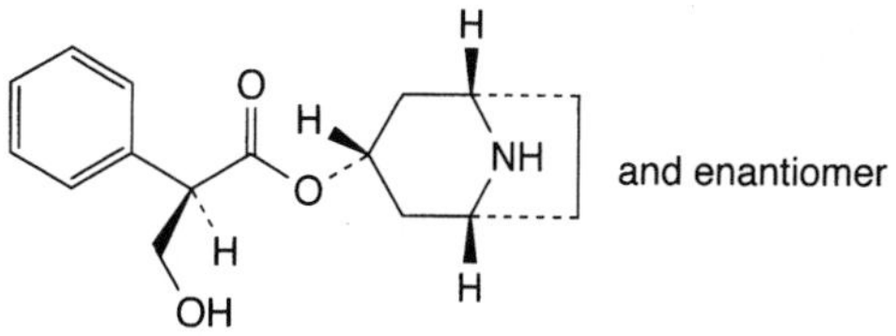

B. (1R,3r,5S)-8-azabicyclo[3.2.1]oct-3-yl (2RS)-3-hydroxy-2-phenylpropanoate (noratropine),

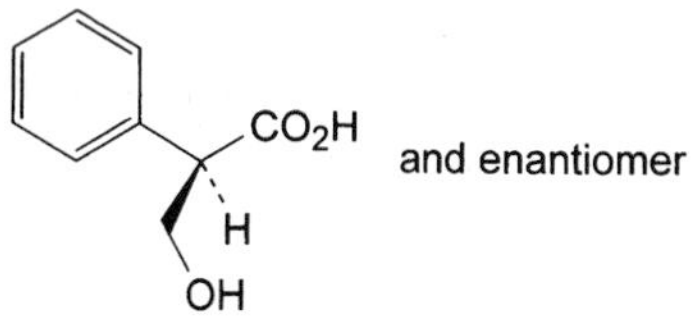

C. (2RS)-3-hydroxy-2-phenylpropanoic acid (tropic acid),

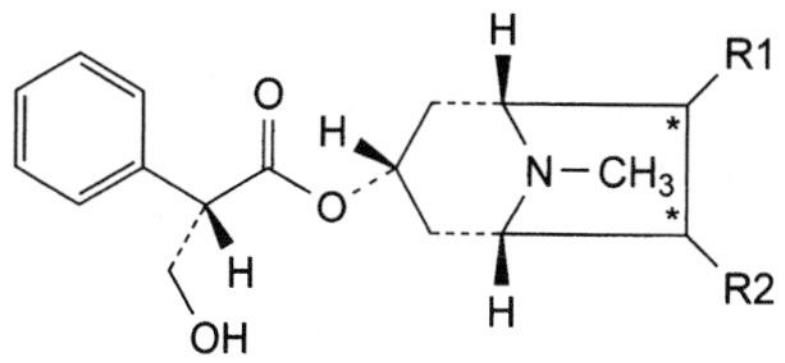

D. R1 = OH, R2 = H: (1R,3S,5R,6RS)-6-hydroxy-8-methyl-8-azabicyclo[3.2.1]oct-3-yl (2S)-3-hydroxy-2-phenylpropanoate (6-hydroxyhyoscyamine),

E. R1 = H, R2 = OH: (1S,3R,5S,6RS)-6-hydroxy-8-methyl-8-azabicyclo[3.2.1]oct-3-yl (2S)-3-hydroxy-2-phenylpropanoate (7-hydroxyhyoscyamine),

F. hyoscine,

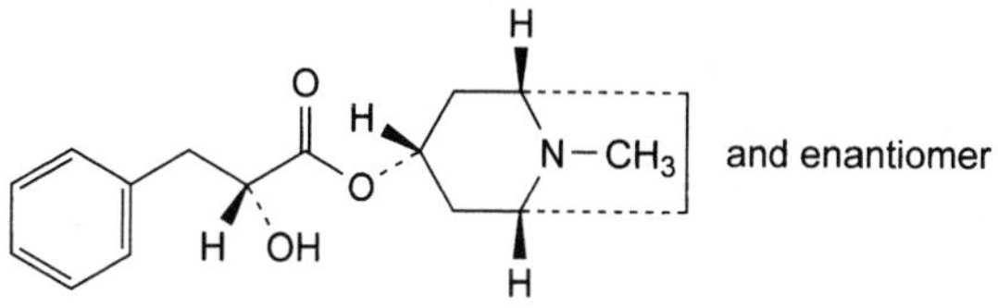

G. (1R,3r,5S)-8-methyl-8-azabicyclo[3.2.1]oct-3-yl (2RS)-2-hydroxy-3-phenylpropanoate (littorine),

H. unknown structure.

*Ph Eur*

# Atropine Methobromide

*(Methylatropine Bromide, Ph Eur monograph 0511)*

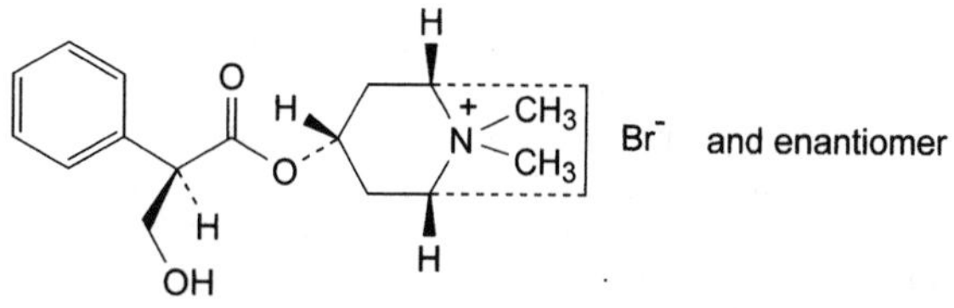

$C_{18}H_{26}BrNO_3$          384.3          *2870-71-5*

**Action and use**
Anticholinergic.

*Ph Eur* _____

**DEFINITION**
Methylatropine bromide contains not less than 99.0 per cent and not more than the equivalent of 101.0 per cent of (1R,3r,5S)-3-[[(2RS)-3-hydroxy-2-phenylpropanoyl]oxy]-8,8-

dimethyl-8-azoniabicyclo[3.2.1]octane bromide, calculated with reference to the dried substance.

## CHARACTERS

A white or almost white, crystalline powder or colourless crystals, freely soluble in water, sparingly soluble in alcohol.

It melts at about 219 °C, with decomposition.

## IDENTIFICATION

*First identification  B, E.*

*Second identification   A, C, D, E.*

A. It complies with the test for optical rotation (see Tests).

B. Examine by infrared absorption spectrophotometry (*2.2.24*), comparing with the spectrum obtained with *methylatropine bromide CRS.*

C. To 5 ml of solution S (see Tests) add 2 ml of *dilute sodium hydroxide solution R.* No precipitate is formed.

D. To about 1 mg add 0.2 ml of *fuming nitric acid R* and evaporate to dryness on a water-bath. Dissolve the residue in 2 ml of *acetone R* and add 0.1 ml of a 30 g/l solution of *potassium hydroxide R* in *methanol R.* A violet colour develops.

E. It gives reaction (a) of bromides (*2.3.1*).

## TESTS

### Solution S

Dissolve 1.25 g in *carbon dioxide-free water R* and dilute to 25 ml with the same solvent.

### Appearance of solution

Solution S is clear (*2.2.1*) and not more intensely coloured than reference solution $B_9$ (*2.2.2, Method II*).

### Acidity or alkalinity

To 10 ml of solution S add 0.1 ml of *phenolphthalein solution R*; the solution is colourless. Add 0.5 ml of *0.01 M sodium hydroxide*; the solution is red.

### Optical rotation (*2.2.7*)

Dissolve 2.50 g in *water R* and dilute to 25.0 ml with the same solvent. The angle of optical rotation, measured in a 2 dm tube, is − 0.25° to + 0.05°.

### Related substances

Examine by thin-layer chromatography (*2.2.27*), using a *TLC silica gel G plate R.*

*Test solution*   Dissolve 0.2 g of the substance to be examined in a mixture of 1 volume of *water R* and 9 volumes of *methanol R* and dilute to 5 ml with the same mixture of solvents.

*Reference solution*   Dilute 0.5 ml of the test solution to 100 ml with a mixture of 1 volume of *water R* and 9 volumes of *methanol R.*

Apply to the plate 5 μl of each solution. Develop over a path of 15 cm using a mixture of 10 volumes of *methanol R,* 15 volumes of *anhydrous formic acid R,* 15 volumes of *water R* and 60 volumes of *ethyl acetate R.* Dry the plate at 100 °C to 105 °C until the solvent has evaporated, allow to cool and spray with *dilute potassium iodobismuthate solution R* until the spots appear. Any spot in the chromatogram obtained with the test solution, apart from the principal spot, is not more intense than the spot in the chromatogram obtained with the reference solution (0.5 per cent).

### Apomethylatropine

Dissolve 0.10 g in *0.01 M hydrochloric acid* and dilute to 100.0 ml with the same acid. Measure the absorbances (*2.2.25*) at the maxima at 252 nm and 257 nm. The ratio of the absorbance at 257 nm to that at 252 nm is at least 1.19.

### Loss on drying (*2.2.32*)

Not more than 0.5 per cent, determined on 0.500 g by drying in an oven at 105 °C.

### Sulphated ash (*2.4.14*)

Not more than 0.1 per cent, determined on the residue obtained in the test for loss on drying.

## ASSAY

Dissolve 0.300 g in 50 ml of *anhydrous acetic acid R*, warming slightly if necessary. Titrate with *0.1 M perchloric acid*, determining the end-point potentiometrically (*2.2.20*).

1 ml of *0.1 M perchloric acid* is equivalent to 38.43 mg of $C_{18}H_{26}BrNO_3$.

## STORAGE

Store protected from light.

_____ Ph Eur

# Atropine Methonitrate

(*Methylatropine Nitrate, Ph Eur monograph 0512*)

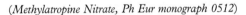

| $C_{18}H_{26}N_2O_6$ | 366.4 | 52-88-0 |

## Action and use

Anticholinergic.

*Ph Eur*

## DEFINITION

Methylatropine nitrate contains not less than 99.0 per cent and not more than the equivalent of 101.0 per cent of (1R,3r,5S)-3-[[(2RS)-3-hydroxy-2-phenylpropanoyl]oxy]-8,8-dimethyl-8-azoniabicyclo[3.2.1]octane nitrate, calculated with reference to the dried substance.

## CHARACTERS

A white or almost white, crystalline powder or colourless crystals, freely soluble in water, soluble in alcohol.

It melts at about 167 °C.

## IDENTIFICATION

*First identification   B, E.*

*Second identification   A, C, D, E.*

A. It complies with the test for optical rotation (see Tests).

B. Examine by infrared absorption spectrophotometry (*2.2.24*), comparing with the spectrum obtained with *methylatropine nitrate CRS.*

C. To a mixture of 2.5 ml of solution S (see Tests) and 2.5 ml of *water R* add 2 ml of *dilute sodium hydroxide solution R.* No precipitate is formed.

D. To about 1 mg add 0.2 ml of *fuming nitric acid R* and evaporate to dryness on a water-bath. Dissolve the residue in 2 ml of *acetone R* and add 0.25 ml of a 30 g/l solution of *potassium hydroxide R* in *methanol R.* A violet colour develops.

E. To 0.05 ml of *diphenylamine solution R* add 0.05 ml of a 1 in 10 dilution of solution S. An intense blue colour is produced.

## TESTS

### Solution S

Dissolve 1.25 g in *carbon dioxide-free water R* and dilute to 25 ml with the same solvent.

### Appearance of solution

Solution S is clear (*2.2.1*) and not more intensely coloured than reference solution B₉ (*2.2.2, Method II*).

### Acidity or alkalinity

To 10 ml of solution S add 0.1 ml of *phenolphthalein solution R*; the solution is colourless. Add 0.5 ml of *0.01 M sodium hydroxide*; the solution is red.

### Optical rotation (*2.2.7*)

Dissolve 2.50 g in *water R* and dilute to 25.0 ml with the same solvent. The angle of optical rotation, measured in a 2 dm tube, is − 0.25° to + 0.05°.

### Related substances

Examine by thin-layer chromatography (*2.2.27*), using *silica gel G R* as the coating substance.

*Test solution*   Dissolve 0.2 g of the substance to be examined in a mixture of 1 volume of *water R* and 9 volumes of *methanol R* and dilute to 5 ml with the same mixture of solvents.

*Reference solution*   Dilute 0.5 ml of the test solution to 100 ml with a mixture of 1 volume of *water R* and 9 volumes of *methanol R*.

Apply to the plate 5 µl of each solution. Develop over a path of 15 cm using a mixture of 10 volumes of *methanol R*, 15 volumes of *anhydrous formic acid R*, 15 volumes of *water R* and 60 volumes of *ethyl acetate R*. Dry the plate at 100 °C to 105 °C until the solvent has evaporated, allow to cool and spray with *dilute potassium iodobismuthate solution R* until the spots appear. Any spot in the chromatogram obtained with the test solution, apart from the principal spot, is not more intense than the spot in the chromatogram obtained with reference solution (0.5 per cent).

### Apomethylatropine

Dissolve 0.10 g in *0.01 M hydrochloric acid* and dilute to 100.0 ml with the same acid. Measure the absorbances (*2.2.25*) at the maxima at 252 nm and 257 nm. The ratio of the absorbance at 257 nm to that at 252 nm is not less than 1.17.

### Halides

15 ml of solution S complies with the limit test for chlorides (*2.4.4*). Prepare the standard using 1.5 ml of *chloride standard solution (5 ppm Cl) R* (10 ppm).

### Silver

Dissolve 1.0 g in 10 ml of *water R* and add 0.1 ml of *sodium sulphide solution R*. Allow to stand for 2 min. The solution is not more intensely coloured than reference solution B₈ (*2.2.2, Method II*) (10 ppm).

### Loss on drying (*2.2.32*)

Not more than 0.5 per cent, determined on 0.500 g by drying in an oven at 105 °C.

### Sulphated ash (*2.4.14*)

Not more than 0.1 per cent, determined on the residue obtained in the test for loss on drying.

## ASSAY

Dissolve 0.300 g in 50 ml of *anhydrous acetic acid R*. Titrate with *0.1 M perchloric acid* determining the end-point potentiometrically (*2.2.20*).

1 ml of *0.1 M perchloric acid* is equivalent to 36.64 mg of $C_{18}H_{26}N_2O_6$.

## STORAGE

Store protected from light.

*_____ Ph Eur*

# Atropine Sulphate

(*Ph Eur monograph 0068*)

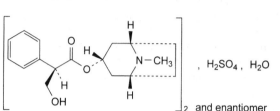

$C_{34}H_{46}N_2O_6,H_2SO_4,H_2O$       695       5908-99-6

### Action and use

Anticholinergic.

### Preparations

Atropine Eye Drops

Atropine Eye Ointment

Atropine Injection

Atropine Tablets

Morphine and Atropine Injection

*Ph Eur* _____

## DEFINITION

Bis[(1*R*,3*r*,5*S*)-8-methyl-8-azabicyclo[3.2.1]oct-3-yl (2*RS*)-3-hydroxy-2-phenylpropanoate] sulphate monohydrate.

### Content

99.0 per cent to 101.0 per cent (anhydrous substance).

## CHARACTERS

### Appearance

White or almost white, crystalline powder or colourless crystals.

### Solubility

Very soluble in water, freely soluble in ethanol (96 per cent).

## IDENTIFICATION

*First identification*   A, B, E.

*Second identification*   C, D, E, F.

A. Optical rotation (see Tests).

B. Infrared absorption spectrophotometry (*2.2.24*).

*Comparison*   atropine sulphate CRS.

C. Dissolve about 50 mg in 5 ml of *water R* and add 5 ml of *picric acid solution R*. The precipitate, washed with *water R* and dried at 100-105 °C for 2 h, melts (*2.2.14*) at 174 °C to 179 °C.

D. To about 1 mg add 0.2 ml of *fuming nitric acid R* and evaporate to dryness in a water-bath. Dissolve the residue in 2 ml of *acetone R* and add 0.1 ml of a 30 g/l solution of *potassium hydroxide R* in *methanol R*. A violet colour develops.

E. It gives the reactions of sulphates (2.3.1).

F. It gives the reaction of alkaloids (2.3.1).

## TESTS

**pH** (2.2.3)

4.5 to 6.2.

Dissolve 0.6 g in *carbon dioxide-free water R* and dilute to 30 ml with the same solvent.

**Optical rotation** (2.2.7)

− 0.50° to + 0.05° (measured in a 2 dm tube).

Dissolve 2.50 g in *water R* and dilute to 25.0 ml with the same solvent.

**Related substances**

Liquid chromatography (2.2.29).

*Test solution*   Dissolve 24 mg of the substance to be examined in mobile phase A and dilute to 100.0 ml with mobile phase A.

*Reference solution (a)*   Dilute 1.0 ml of the test solution to 100.0 ml with mobile phase A. Dilute 1.0 ml of this solution to 10.0 ml with mobile phase A.

*Reference solution (b)*   Dissolve 5 mg of *atropine impurity B CRS* in the test solution and dilute to 20 ml with the test solution. Dilute 5 ml of this solution to 25 ml with mobile phase A.

*Reference solution (c)*   Dissolve the contents of a vial of *atropine for peak identification CRS* (containing impurities A, B, D, E, F, G and H) in 1 ml of mobile phase A.

*Reference solution (d)*   Dissolve 5 mg of *tropic acid R* (impurity C) in mobile phase A and dilute to 10 ml with mobile phase A. Dilute 1 ml of the solution to 100 ml with mobile phase A. Dilute 1 ml of this solution to 10 ml with mobile phase A.

*Column:*

— *size:* l = 0.10 m, Ø = 4.6 mm;

— *stationary phase: octadecylsilyl silica gel for chromatography R* (3 μm).

*Mobile phase:*

— *mobile phase A*: dissolve 3.5 g of *sodium dodecyl sulphate R* in 606 ml of a 7.0 g/l solution of *potassium dihydrogen phosphate R* previously adjusted to pH 3.3 with *0.05 M phosphoric acid*, and mix with 320 ml of *acetonitrile R1*;

— *mobile phase B: acetonitrile R1*;

| Time (min) | Mobile phase A (per cent V/V) | Mobile phase B (per cent V/V) |
|---|---|---|
| 0 - 2 | 95 | 5 |
| 2 - 20 | 95 → 70 | 5 → 30 |

*Flow rate*   1 ml/min.

*Detection*   Spectrophotometer at 210 nm.

*Injection*   10 μl.

*Identification of impurities*   Use the chromatogram supplied with *atropine for peak identification CRS* and the chromatogram obtained with reference solution (c) to identify the peaks due to impurities A, B, D, E, F, G and H. Use the chromatogram obtained with reference solution (d) to identify the peak due to impurity C.

*Relative retention*   With reference to atropine (retention time = about 11 min): impurity C = about 0.2; impurity E = about 0.67; impurity D = about 0.73; impurity F = about 0.8; impurity B = about 0.89; impurity H = about 0.93; impurity G = about 1.1; impurity A = about 1.7.

*System suitability*   Reference solution (b):

— *resolution*: minimum 2.5 between the peaks due to impurity B and atropine.

*Limits:*

— *correction factors*: for the calculation of content, multiply the peak areas of the following impurities by the corresponding correction factor: impurity A = 0.6; impurity C = 0.6;

— *impurities E, H*: for each impurity, not more than 3 times the area of the principal peak in the chromatogram obtained with reference solution (a) (0.3 per cent);

— *impurities A, B, C, D, F, G*: for each impurity, not more than twice the area of the principal peak in the chromatogram obtained with reference solution (a) (0.2 per cent);

— *unspecified impurities*: for each impurity, not more than the area of the principal peak in the chromatogram obtained with reference solution (a) (0.10 per cent);

— *total*: not more than 5 times the area of the principal peak in the chromatogram obtained with reference solution (a) (0.5 per cent);

— *disregard limit*: 0.5 times the area of the principal peak in the chromatogram obtained with reference solution (a) (0.05 per cent).

**Water** (2.5.12)

2.0 per cent to 4.0 per cent, determined on 0.500 g.

**Sulphated ash** (2.4.14)

Maximum 0.1 per cent, determined on 1.0 g.

## ASSAY

Dissolve 0.500 g in 30 ml of *anhydrous acetic acid R*, warming if necessary. Cool the solution. Titrate with *0.1 M perchloric acid*, determining the end-point potentiometrically (2.2.20).

1 ml of *0.1 M perchloric acid* is equivalent to 67.68 mg of $C_{34}H_{48}N_2O_{10}S$.

## STORAGE

Protected from light.

## IMPURITIES

*Specified impurities*   A, B, C, D, E, F, G, H.

A. (1R,3r,5S)-8-methyl-8-azabicyclo[3.2.1]oct-3-yl 2-phenylpropenoate (apoatropine),

B. (1R,3r,5S)-8-azabicyclo[3.2.1]oct-3-yl (2RS)-3-hydroxy-2-phenylpropanoate (noratropine), and enantiomer

C. (2*RS*)-3-hydroxy-2-phenylpropanoic acid (tropic acid),

D. R1 = OH, R2 = H: (1*R*,3*S*,5*R*,6*RS*)-6-hydroxy-8-methyl-8-azabicyclo[3.2.1]oct-3-yl (2*S*)-3-hydroxy-2-phenylpropanoate (6-hydroxyhyoscyamine),

E. R1 = H, R2 = OH: (1*S*,3*R*,5*S*,6*RS*)-6-hydroxy-8-methyl-8-azabicyclo[3.2.1]oct-3-yl (2*S*)-3-hydroxy-2-phenylpropanoate (7-hydroxyhyoscyamine),

F. hyoscine,

and enantiomer

G. (1*R*,3*r*,5*S*)-8-methyl-8-azabicyclo[3.2.1]oct-3-yl (2*RS*)-2-hydroxy-3-phenylpropanoate (littorine).

H. unknown structure.

*Ph Eur*

# Attapulgite

## Action and use
Excipient.

## DEFINITION
Attapulgite is a purified native hydrated magnesium aluminium silicate essentially consisting of the clay mineral palygorskite.

## CHARACTERISTICS
A light, cream or buff, very fine powder, free or almost free from gritty particles.

## IDENTIFICATION
A. Ignite 0.5 g with 2 g of *anhydrous sodium carbonate* for 20 minutes, cool and extract with 25 ml of boiling *water*. Cool, filter, wash the residue with *water* and add the washings to the filtrate. Reserve the residue for test B. Cautiously acidify the combined filtrate and washings with *hydrochloric acid*, evaporate to dryness, moisten the residue with 0.2 ml of *hydrochloric acid*, add 10 ml of *water* and stir. A white, gelatinous precipitate is produced.

B. Wash the residue reserved in test A with *water* and dissolve in 10 ml of *2M hydrochloric acid*. To 2 ml of the solution add a 10% w/v solution of *ammonium thiocyanate*. An intense red colour is produced.

C. To 2 ml of the solution obtained in test B add 1 ml of *strong sodium hydroxide solution* and filter. To the filtrate add 3 ml of *ammonium chloride solution*. A gelatinous white precipitate is produced.

D. To 2 ml of the solution obtained in test B add *ammonium chloride* and an excess of *13.5M ammonia* and filter. To the filtrate add 0.15 ml of *magneson reagent* and an excess of *5M sodium hydroxide*. A blue precipitate is produced.

## TESTS
### Acidity or alkalinity
pH of a 5% w/v suspension in *carbon dioxide-free water*, after shaking for 5 minutes, 7.0 to 9.5, Appendix V L.

### Adsorptive capacity
Moisture adsorption, 5 to 14% when determined by the following method. Dry in air and powder a sufficient quantity of the substance being examined and pass through a sieve with a nominal mesh aperture of 150 µm. Spread 0.5 g as a thin layer on a previously weighed piece of aluminium foil (60 mm × 50 mm) of nominal gauge 17.5 µm and transfer to a desiccator containing a dish of sodium chloride crystals partially immersed in saturated brine at 25°. After 4 hours, remove from the desiccator and weigh immediately. Dry in an oven at 110° for 4 hours, allow to cool in a desiccator and weigh. The *moisture adsorption* is the gain in weight of the substance being examined expressed as a percentage of its oven-dried weight.

### Arsenic
To 0.13 g add 5 ml of *water*, 2 ml of *sulphuric acid* and 10 ml of *sulphur dioxide solution* and evaporate on a water bath until the sulphur dioxide solution is removed and the volume reduced to about 2 ml. Transfer the solution to the generator flask with the aid of 5 ml of *water*. The resulting solution complies with the *limit test for arsenic*, Appendix VII (8 ppm).

### Heavy metals
A. Not more than 20 ppm when determined by the following method. Shake 6.0 g with 40 ml of *0.5M hydrochloric acid* at 37° for 30 minutes, cool and filter. Wash the residue with *water* and dilute the combined filtrate and washings to 50 ml with *water*. To 20 ml add 2 g each of *ammonium chloride* and *ammonium thiocyanate* and dissolve. Shake the solution with 80 ml of a mixture of equal volumes of *ether* and *isoamyl alcohol* and separate, retaining the aqueous layer. Extract with a further 80 ml of the mixture. To the aqueous layer add 2 g of *citric acid*, neutralise with *13.5M ammonia* and dilute to 25 ml with *water*. 12 ml of the resulting solution complies with *limit test A for heavy metals*, Appendix VII. Use *lead standard solution (2 ppm Pb)* to prepare the standard.

B. Not more than 10 ppm when determined by the following method. Shake 6.0 g with 40 ml of *0.5M sodium hydroxide* at 37° for 30 minutes, cool and filter. Wash the residue with *water* and dilute the combined filtrate and washings to 50 ml with *water*. Neutralise 20 ml of the solution with *hydrochloric acid* and dilute to 25 ml with *water*. 12 ml of the resulting solution complies with *limit test A for heavy metals*, Appendix VII. Use *lead standard solution (1 ppm Pb)* to prepare the standard.

### Acid-soluble matter
Boil 2 g with 100 ml of *0.2M hydrochloric acid* under a reflux condenser for 5 minutes, cool and filter. Evaporate 50 ml of the filtrate to dryness. The residue, after ignition at about 600° for 30 minutes, weighs not more than 0.25 g.

### Water-soluble matter
Boil 10 g with 100 ml of *water* under a reflux condenser for 5 minutes, cool and filter. Evaporate 50 ml of the filtrate to

dryness. The residue, after ignition at 600° for 30 minutes, weighs not more than 50 mg.

**Loss on drying**
When dried to constant weight at 105°, loses not more than 17.0% of its weight. Use 1 g.

**Loss on ignition**
When ignited at 600°, loses 15.0 to 27.0% of its weight. Use 1 g.

# Activated Attapulgite

**Action and use**
Antidiarrhoeal.

## DEFINITION
Activated Attapulgite is a purified native hydrated magnesium aluminium silicate essentially consisting of the clay mineral palygorskite that has been carefully heated to increase its adsorptive capacity.

## CHARACTERISTICS
A light, cream or buff, very fine powder, free or almost free from gritty particles.

## IDENTIFICATION
A. Ignite 0.5 g with 2 g of *anhydrous sodium carbonate* for 20 minutes, cool and extract with 25 ml of boiling *water*. Cool, filter, wash the residue with *water* and add the washings to the filtrate. Reserve the residue for test B. Cautiously acidify the combined filtrate and washings with *hydrochloric acid*, evaporate to dryness, moisten the residue with 0.2 ml of *hydrochloric acid*, add 10 ml of *water* and stir. A white, gelatinous precipitate is produced.

B. Wash the residue reserved in test A with *water* and dissolve in 10 ml of *2M hydrochloric acid*. To 2 ml of the solution add a 10% w/v solution of *ammonium thiocyanate*. An intense red colour is produced.

C. To 2 ml of the solution obtained in test B add 1 ml of *strong sodium hydroxide solution* and filter. To the filtrate add 3 ml of *ammonium chloride solution*. A gelatinous white precipitate is produced.

D. To 2 ml of the solution obtained in test B add *ammonium chloride* and an excess of *13.5M ammonia* and filter. To the filtrate add 0.15 ml of *magneson reagent* and an excess of *5M sodium hydroxide*. A blue precipitate is produced.

## TESTS
**Acidity or alkalinity**
pH of a 5% w/v suspension in *carbon dioxide-free water*, after shaking for 5 minutes, 7.0 to 9.5, Appendix V L.

**Arsenic**
To 0.13 g add 5 ml of *water*, 2 ml of *sulphuric acid* and 10 ml of *sulphur dioxide solution* and evaporate on a water bath until the sulphur dioxide solution is removed and the volume reduced to about 2 ml. Transfer the solution to the generator flask with the aid of 5 ml of *water*. The resulting solution complies with the *limit test for arsenic*, Appendix VII (8 ppm).

**Heavy metals**
A. Not more than 20 ppm when determined by the following method. Shake 6.0 g with 40 ml of *0.5M hydrochloric acid* at 37° for 30 minutes, cool and filter. Wash the residue with *water* and dilute the combined filtrate and washings to 50 ml with *water*. To 20 ml add 2 g each of *ammonium chloride* and *ammonium thiocyanate* and dissolve. Shake the solution with

80 ml of a mixture of equal volumes of *ether* and *isoamyl alcohol* and separate, retaining the aqueous layer. Extract with a further 80 ml of the mixture. To the aqueous layer add 2 g of *citric acid*, neutralise with *13.5M ammonia* and dilute to 25 ml with *water*. 12 ml of the resulting solution complies with *limit test A for heavy metals*, Appendix VII. Use *lead standard solution (2 ppm Pb)* to prepare the standard.

B. Not more than 10 ppm when determined by the following method. Shake 6.0 g with 40 ml of *0.5M sodium hydroxide* at 37° for 30 minutes, cool and filter. Wash the residue with *water* and dilute the combined filtrate and washings to 50 ml with *water*. Neutralise 20 ml of the solution with *hydrochloric acid* and dilute to 25 ml with *water*. 12 ml of the resulting solution complies with *limit test A for heavy metals*, Appendix VII. Use *lead standard solution (1 ppm Pb)* to prepare the standard.

**Acid-soluble matter**
Boil 2 g with 100 ml of *0.2M hydrochloric acid* under a reflux condenser for 5 minutes, cool and filter. Evaporate 50 ml of the filtrate to dryness. The residue, after ignition at about 600° for 30 minutes, weighs not more than 0.25 g.

**Water-soluble matter**
Boil 10 g with 100 ml of *water* under a reflux condenser for 5 minutes, cool and filter. Evaporate 50 ml of the filtrate to dryness. The residue, after ignition at 600° for 30 minutes, weighs not more than 50 mg.

**Adsorptive capacity**
In a stoppered bottle shake 1.0 g, in *very fine powder*, with 50 ml of a 0.12% w/v solution of *methylene blue* for 5 minutes, allow to settle and centrifuge. The colour of the clear supernatant solution is not more intense than that of a 0.0012% w/v solution of *methylene blue*.

**Loss on drying**
When dried to constant weight at 105°, loses not more than 4.0% of its weight. Use 1 g.

**Loss on ignition**
When ignited at 600°, loses not more than 9.0% of its weight. Use 1 g.

# Azapropazone

$C_{16}H_{20}N_4O_2,2H_2O$        336.4        *13539-59-8 (anhydrous)*

**Action and use**
Cyclo-oxygenase inhibitor; analgesic; anti-inflammatory.

**Preparations**
Azapropazone Capsules
Azapropazone Tablets

## DEFINITION
Azapropazone is 5-dimethylamino-9-methyl-2-propylpyrazolo[1,2-a][1,2,4]benzotriazine-1,3(2H)-dione dihydrate. It contains not less than 99.0% and not more than

101.0% of $C_{16}H_{20}N_4O_2$, calculated with reference to the anhydrous substance.

## CHARACTERISTICS

A white to pale yellow, crystalline powder.

Very slightly soluble in *water*; soluble in *ethanol (96%)*; it dissolves in solutions of alkali hydroxides.

## IDENTIFICATION

A. The *infrared absorption spectrum*, Appendix II A, is concordant with the *reference spectrum* of azapropazone *(RS 016)*.

B. The *light absorption*, Appendix II B, in the range 230 to 350 nm of a 0.0008% w/v solution in 0.1M *sodium hydroxide* exhibits two maxima, at 255 nm and 325 nm. The *absorbances* at 255 nm and 325 nm are about 0.86 and 0.18 respectively.

## TESTS

### Acetic acid

Not more than 0.2%, determined by the following method. Dissolve 10 g in 25 ml of *methanol*, add 75 ml of *water* and carry out a *potentiometric titration*, Appendix VIII B, using *0.1M sodium hydroxide VS* as titrant to a pH of 5.9. Each ml of *0.1M sodium hydroxide VS* is equivalent to 6.005 mg of acetic acid, $C_2H_4O_2$.

### Related substances

Carry out the following operations in subdued light using low-actinic glassware without delay. Carry out the method for *liquid chromatography*, Appendix III D, using the following solutions in a mixture of 1 volume of *phosphate buffer pH 4.0* and 3 volumes of *methanol*.

(1) 0.10% w/v of the substance being examined.

(2) 0.00010% w/v of *azapropazone impurity A BPCRS*.

(3) 0.00025% w/v of *azapropazone impurity B BPCRS*.

(4) 0.00025% w/v of *azapropazone impurity C BPCRS*.

(5) 0.0001% w/v of the substance being examined.

(6) 0.00005% w/v of the substance being examined.

(7) 0.1% w/v of *azapropazone impurity standard BPCRS*.

CHROMATOGRAPHIC CONDITIONS

(a) Use a stainless steel column (30 cm × 3.9 mm) packed with *octadecylsilyl silica gel for chromatography* (10 μm) (μBondapak C18 is suitable).

(b) Use isocratic elution and the mobile phase described below.

(c) Use a flow rate of 2.5 ml per minute.

(d) Use ambient column temperature.

(e) Use a detection wavelength of 254 nm.

(f) Inject 20 μl of each solution.

MOBILE PHASE

1 volume of *glacial acetic acid*, 36 volumes of *methanol* and 63 volumes of a 0.068% w/v solution of *sodium butanesulphonate* in *water*.

SYSTEM SUITABILITY

Inject solution (7) and continue the chromatography for 5 times the retention time of the principal peak.

The test is not valid unless the chromatogram obtained with solution (7) closely resembles the reference chromatogram supplied with the azapropazone impurity standard. If necessary adjust the proportion of methanol in the mobile phase to give the required retention times.

LIMITS

In the chromatogram obtained with solution (1):

the area of any peak corresponding to azapropazone impurity A is not greater than the area of the corresponding peak in the chromatogram obtained with solution (2) (0.1%);

the area of any peak corresponding to azapropazone impurity B is not greater than the area of the corresponding peak in the chromatogram obtained with solution (3) (0.25%);

the area of any peak corresponding to azapropazone impurity C is not greater than the area of the corresponding peak in the chromatogram obtained with solution (4) (0.25%);

the area of any other *secondary peak* is not greater than the area of the peak in the chromatogram obtained with solution (5) (0.1%).

Calculate the content of impurities A, B and C using the respective reference solutions and the content of any unnamed impurities using solution (5). The total nominal content of impurities is not greater than 0.5%.

Disregard any peak with an area less than the area of the principal peak in the chromatogram obtained with solution (6) (0.05%).

### Heavy metals

Dissolve 3.125 g in 20 ml of *water*, boil for 10 minutes, dilute to 50 ml and filter (solution A). 12 ml of solution A complies with *limit test A for heavy metals*, Appendix VII. Use 10 ml of *lead standard solution (1 ppm Pb)* to prepare the standard (16 ppm).

### Chloride

A mixture of 10 ml of solution A and 5 ml of *water* complies with the limit *test for chlorides*, Appendix VII (80 ppm).

### Sulphate

A mixture of 10 ml of solution A and 5 ml of *water* complies with the *limit test for sulphates*, Appendix VII (240 ppm).

### Water

10.0 to 11.5% w/w, Appendix IX C. Use 0.25 g.

### Sulphated ash

Not more than 0.1%, Appendix IX A.

## ASSAY

Carry out Method I for *non-aqueous titration*, Appendix VIII A, using 0.25 g and determining the end point potentiometrically. Each ml of *0.1M perchloric acid VS* is equivalent to 30.04 mg of $C_{16}H_{20}N_4O_2$.

## IMPURITIES

1. 3-dimethylamino-7-methyl-1,2,4-benzotriazine *(impurity A)*,

2. 3-dimethylamino-1,2-dihydro-7-methyl-2-valeryl-1,2,4-benzotriazine,

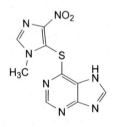

3. 5-hydroxy-9-methyl-2-propylpyrazolo[1,2-a][1,2,4]benzotriazine-1,3(2*H*)-dione *(impurity B)*,

4. α-(3-dimethylamino-7-methyl-1,2-dihydro-1,2,4-benzotriazin-2-ylcarbonyl)valeric acid *(impurity C)*.

# Azathioprine

*(Ph Eur monograph 0369)*

$C_9H_7N_7O_2S$     277.3     446-86-6

**Action and use**
Immunosuppressant.

**Preparation**
Azathioprine Tablets

*Ph Eur* _____

## DEFINITION
6-[(1-Methyl-4-nitro-1*H*-imidazol-5-yl)sulfanyl]-7*H*-purine.

**Content**
98.5 per cent to 101.0 per cent (dried substance).

## CHARACTERS
**Appearance**
Pale yellow powder.

**Solubility**
Practically insoluble in water and in ethanol (96 per cent). It is soluble in dilute solutions of alkali hydroxides and sparingly soluble in dilute mineral acids.

## IDENTIFICATION
A. Ultraviolet and visible absorption spectrophotometry *(2.2.25)*.

*Test solution* Dissolve 0.150 g in 30 ml of *dimethyl sulphoxide R* and dilute to 500.0 ml with *0.1 M hydrochloric acid*. Dilute 25.0 ml of the solution to 1000.0 ml with *0.1 M hydrochloric acid*.

*Spectral range* 230-350 nm.

*Absorption maximum* At 280 nm.

*Specific absorbance at the absorption maximum* 600 to 660.

B. Infrared absorption spectrophotometry *(2.2.24)*.

*Comparison azathioprine CRS* .

C. To about 20 mg add 100 ml of *water R*, heat and filter. To 5 ml of the filtrate add 1 ml of *hydrochloric acid R* and about 10 mg of *zinc powder R*. Allow to stand for 5 min. The solution becomes yellow. Filter, cool in iced water, add 0.1 ml of *sodium nitrite solution R* and 0.1 g of *sulphamic acid R* and shake until the bubbles disappear. Add 1 ml of *β-naphthol solution R*. A pale pink precipitate is formed.

## TESTS
**Acidity or alkalinity**
To 0.5 g add 25 ml of *carbon dioxide-free water R*, shake for 15 min and filter. To 20 ml of the filtrate add 0.1 ml of *methyl red solution R*. Not more than 0.2 ml of *0.01 M hydrochloric acid* or *0.01 M sodium hydroxide* is required to change the colour of the indicator.

**Chloromethylnitroimidazole and mercaptopurine**
Thin-layer chromatography *(2.2.27)*. *Prepare the solutions immediately before use.*

*Test solution* Dissolve 0.2 g of the substance to be examined in *dilute ammonia R1* and dilute to 10 ml with the same solvent.

*Reference solution (a)* Dissolve 10 mg of *chloromethylnitroimidazole CRS* in *dilute ammonia R1* and dilute to 50 ml with the same solvent.

*Reference solution (b)* Dissolve 10 mg of *mercaptopurine R* in *dilute ammonia R1* and dilute to 50 ml with the same solvent.

*Plate cellulose for chromatography F₂₅₄ R* as the coating substance.

*Mobile phase butanol R* saturated with *dilute ammonia R1*.

*Application* 5 μl.

*Development* Over a path of 15 cm.

*Drying* At 50 °C.

*Detection* Examine in ultraviolet light at 254 nm.

*Limits:*
— *chloromethylnitroimidazole:* any spot due to chloromethylnitroimidazole is not more intense than the spot in the chromatogram obtained with reference solution (a) (1.0 per cent);
— *mercaptopurine:* any spot due to mercaptopurine is not more intense than the spot in the chromatogram obtained with reference solution (b) (1.0 per cent).

**Loss on drying** *(2.2.32)*
Maximum 1.0 per cent, determined on 0.50 g by drying in an oven at 105 °C.

**Sulphated ash** *(2.4.14)*
Maximum 0.1 per cent, determined on 1.0 g.

## ASSAY
Dissolve 0.250 g in 25 ml of *dimethylformamide R*. Titrate with *0.1 M tetrabutylammonium hydroxide*, determining the end-point potentiometrically *(2.2.20)*.

1 ml of *0.1 M tetrabutylammonium hydroxide* is equivalent to 27.73 mg of $C_9H_7N_7O_2S$.

## STORAGE
Protected from light.

_____ *Ph Eur*

# Azelastine Hydrochloride

(*Ph Eur monograph 1633*)

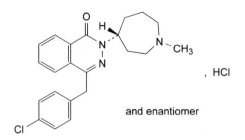

C$_{22}$H$_{24}$ClN$_3$O,HCl          418.4          79307-93-0

## Action and use

Histamine H$_1$ receptor antagonist; antihistamine.

*Ph Eur* _____

## DEFINITION

4-(4-Chlorobenzyl)-2-[(4*RS*)-1-methylhexahydro-1*H*-azepin-4-yl]phthalazin-1(2*H*)-one hydrochloride.

## Content

99.0 per cent to 101.0 per cent (dried substance).

## CHARACTERS

### Appearance

White or almost white, crystalline powder.

### Solubility

Sparingly soluble in water, soluble in ethanol and in methylene chloride.

## IDENTIFICATION

A. Infrared absorption spectrophotometry (*2.2.24*).

*Comparison*   azelastine hydrochloride CRS .

B. Solution S (see Tests) gives reaction (a) of chlorides (*2.3.1*).

## TESTS

### Solution S

Dissolve 1.0 g in *carbon dioxide-free water R* and dilute to 100 ml with the same solvent.

### Appearance of solution

Solution S is clear (*2.2.1*) and colourless (*2.2.2, Method II*).

### Acidity or alkalinity

To 10 ml of solution S add 0.2 ml of *bromothymol blue solution R1*. Not more than 0.1 ml of *0.01 M hydrochloric acid* or *0.01 M sodium hydroxide* is required to change the colour of the solution.

### Related substances

Liquid chromatography (*2.2.29*).

*Solvent mixture*   acetonitrile for chromatography R, water R (45:55 *V/V*).

*Test solution*   Dissolve 0.125 g of the substance to be examined in the solvent mixture and dilute to 50.0 ml with the solvent mixture.

*Reference solution (a)*   Dilute 1.0 ml of the test solution to 100.0 ml with the solvent mixture. Dilute 1.0 ml of this solution to 10.0 ml with the solvent mixture.

*Reference solution (b)*   Dissolve 1 mg of *azelastine impurity B CRS* , 1 mg of *azelastine impurity D CRS* and 1 mg of *azelastine impurity E CRS* in the test solution and dilute to 20 ml with the test solution.

*Column:*
— *size*: *l* = 0.25 m, Ø = 4.6 mm,
— *stationary phase*: *nitrile silica gel for chromatography R* (10 μm),
— *temperature*: 30°C.

*Mobile phase*   Dissolve 2.16 g of *sodium octanesulphonate R* and 0.68 g of *potassium dihydrogen phosphate R* in 740 ml of *water for chromatography R*, adjust to pH 3.0-3.1 with *dilute phosphoric acid R*, add 260 ml of *acetonitrile for chromatography R* and mix.

*Flow rate*   2.0 ml/min.

*Detection*   Spectrophotometer at 210 nm.

*Injection*   10 μl.

*Run time*   Twice the retention time of azelastine.

*Relative retention*   With reference to azelastine (retention time = about 8-9 min): impurity A = about 0.2; impurity B = about 0.3; impurity C = about 0.4; impurity D = about 0.6; impurity E = about 1.4.

*System suitability*   Reference solution (b):
— *resolution*: minimum 4.0 between the peaks due to impurity B and impurity D,
— the peaks due to impurity D and impurity E are baseline separated from the principal peak.

*Limits*:
— *correction factors*: for the calculation of contents, multiply the peak areas of the following impurities by the corresponding correction factor: impurity B = 3.6; impurity D = 0.7; impurity E = 2.1;
— *impurities A, B, C, D, E*: for each impurity, not more than the area of the principal peak in the chromatogram obtained with reference solution (a) (0.1 per cent);
— *any other impurity*: for each impurity, not more than the area of the principal peak in the chromatogram obtained with reference solution (a) (0.1 per cent);
— *total*: not more than twice the area of the principal peak in the chromatogram obtained with reference solution (a) (0.2 per cent);
— *disregard limit*: 0.5 times the area of the principal peak in the chromatogram obtained with reference solution (a) (0.05 per cent).

## Loss on drying (*2.2.32*)

Maximum 0.5 per cent, determined on 1.000 g by drying in an oven at 105 °C.

## ASSAY

*In order to avoid overheating in the reaction medium, mix thoroughly throughout and stop the titration immediately after the end-point has been reached.*

Dissolve 0.300 g in 5 ml of *anhydrous formic acid R*. Add 30 ml of *acetic anhydride R*. Titrate quickly with *0.1 M perchloric acid*, determining the end-point potentiometrically (*2.2.20*).

1.0 ml of *0.1 M perchloric acid* is equivalent to 41.84 mg of C$_{22}$H$_{25}$Cl$_2$N$_3$O.

## IMPURITIES

*Specified impurities*   A, B, C, D, E.

A. benzoyldiazane (benzohydrazide),

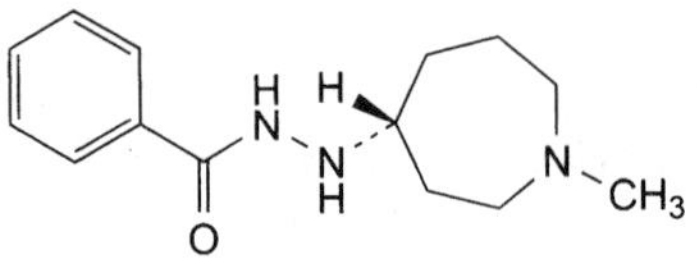

B. 1-benzoyl-2-[(4RS)-1-methylhexahydro-1H-azepin-4-yl]diazane,

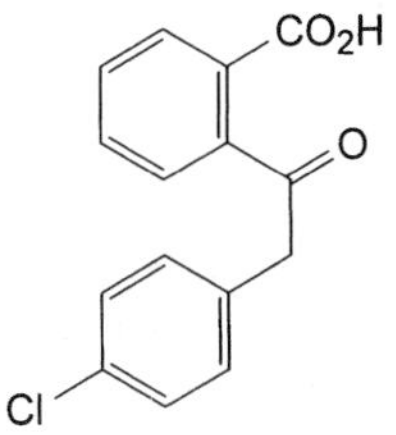

and enantiomer

C. 2-[(4-chlorophenyl)acetyl]benzoic acid,

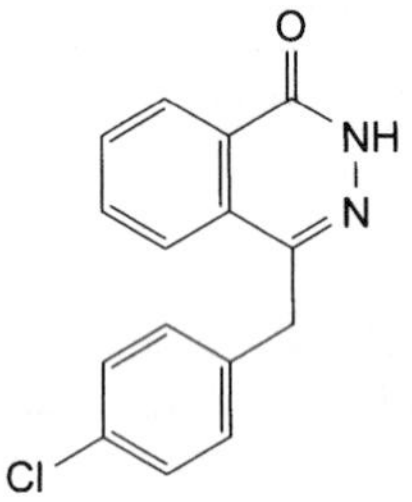

D. 4-(4-chlorobenzyl)phthalazin-1(2H)-one,

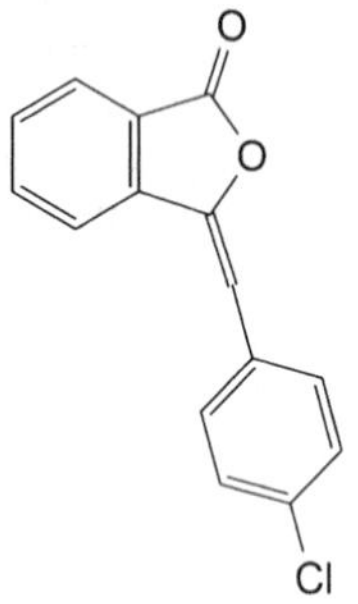

E. 3-(4-chlorobenzylidene)isobenzofuran-1(3H)-one.

_____ Ph Eur

# Azithromycin

*(Ph Eur monograph 1649)*

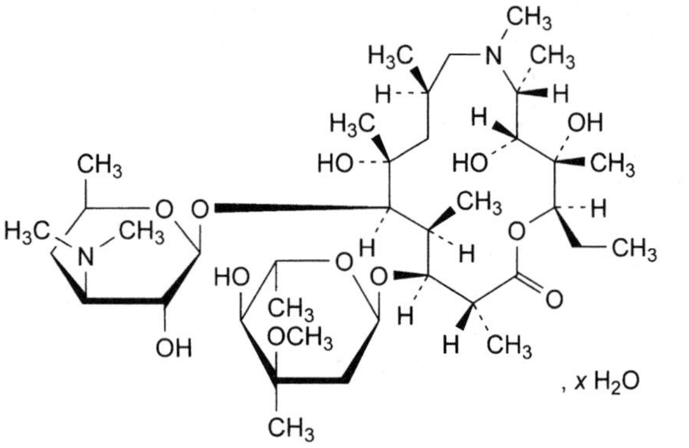

, x H₂O

$C_{38}H_{72}N_2O_{12},xH_2O$   749   *83905-01-5*

With $x = 1$ or $2$     (anhydrous)

## Action and use
Macrolide antibacterial.

*Ph Eur* _____

## DEFINITION
(2R,3S,4R,5R,8R,10R,11R,12S,13S,14R)-13-[(2,6-Dideoxy-3-C-methyl-3-O-methyl-α-L-*ribo*-hexopyranosyl)oxy]-2-ethyl-3,4,10-trihydroxy-3,5,6,8,10,12,14-heptamethyl-11-[[3,4,6-trideoxy-3-(dimethylamino)-β-D-*xylo*-hexopyranosyl]oxy]-1-oxa-6-azacyclopentadecan-15-one. The degree of hydration is 1 or 2.

Semi-synthetic product derived from a fermentation product.

## Content
96.0 per cent to 102.0 per cent (anhydrous substance).

## CHARACTERS
### Appearance
White or almost white powder.

### Solubility
Practically insoluble in water, freely soluble in anhydrous ethanol and in methylene chloride.

## IDENTIFICATION
Infrared absorption spectrophotometry (*2.2.24*).

*Comparison   azithromycin CRS.*

If the spectra obtained in the solid state show differences, prepare further spectra using 90 g/l solutions in *methylene chloride R*.

## TESTS
### Solution S
Dissolve 0.500 g in *anhydrous ethanol R* and dilute to 50.0 ml with the same solvent.

### Appearance of solution
Solution S is clear (*2.2.1*) and colourless (*2.2.2, Method II*).

### pH (*2.2.3*)
9.0 to 11.0.

Dissolve 0.100 g in 25.0 ml of *methanol R* and dilute to 50.0 ml with *carbon dioxide-free water R*.

### Specific optical rotation (*2.2.7*)
− 45 to − 49 (anhydrous substance), determined on solution S.

**Related substances**

Liquid chromatography (2.2.29).

*Solvent mixture* Prepare a 1.73 g/l solution of *ammonium dihydrogen phosphate R* adjusted to pH 10.0 with *ammonia R*. Transfer 350 ml of this solution to a suitable container. Add 300 ml of *acetonitrile R1* and 350 ml of *methanol R1*. Mix well.

*Test solution* Dissolve 0.200 g of the substance to be examined in the solvent mixture and dilute to 25.0 ml with the solvent mixture.

*Reference solution (a)* Dilute 1.0 ml of the test solution to 100.0 ml with the solvent mixture.

*Reference solution (b)* Dissolve the contents of a vial of *azithromycin for system suitability CRS* (containing impurities F, H and J) in 1.0 ml of the solvent mixture and sonicate for 5 min.

*Reference solution (c)* Dissolve 8.0 mg of *azithromycin for peak identification CRS* (containing impurities A, B, C, E, F, G, I, J, L, M, N, O, P) in 1.0 ml of the solvent mixture.

*Column:*
— *size:* $l$ = 0.25 m, Ø = 4.6 mm;
— *stationary phase:* end-capped octadecylsilyl amorphous organosilica polymer for mass spectrometry R (5 μm);
— *temperature:* 60 °C.

*Mobile phase:*
— *mobile phase A:* 1.80 g/l solution of *anhydrous disodium hydrogen phosphate R* adjusted to pH 8.9 with *dilute phosphoric acid R* or with *dilute sodium hydroxide solution R*;
— *mobile phase B: methanol R1, acetonitrile R1* (250:750 V/V);

| Time (min) | Mobile phase A (per cent V/V) | Mobile phase B (per cent V/V) |
|---|---|---|
| 0 - 25 | 50 → 45 | 50 → 55 |
| 25 - 30 | 45 → 40 | 55 → 60 |
| 30 - 80 | 40 → 25 | 60 → 75 |
| 80 - 81 | 25 → 50 | 75 → 50 |
| 81 - 93 | 50 | 50 |

*Flow rate* 1.0 ml/min.

*Detection* Spectrophotometer at 210 nm.

*Injection* 50 μl.

*Relative retention* With reference to azithromycin (retention time = 45-50 min): impurity L = about 0.29; impurity M = about 0.37; impurity E = about 0.43; impurity F = about 0.51; impurity D = about 0.54; impurity J = about 0.54; impurity I = about 0.61; impurity C = about 0.73; impurity N = about 0.76; impurity H = about 0.79; impurity A = about 0.83; impurity P = about 0.92; impurity O = about 1.23; impurity G = about 1.26; impurity B = about 1.31.

*Identification of impurities* Use the chromatogram supplied with *azithromycin for peak identification CRS* and the chromatogram obtained with reference solution (c) to identify the peaks due to impurities A, B, C, E, F, G, I, J, L, M, N, O and P and the chromatogram obtained with reference solution (b) to identify the peak due to impurity H.

*System suitability* Reference solution (b):
— *peak-to-valley ratio:* minimum 1.4, where $H_p$ = height above the baseline of the peak due to impurity J and $H_v$ = height above the baseline of the lowest point of the curve separating this peak from the peak due to impurity F.

*Limits:*
— *correction factors:* for the calculation of content, multiply the peak areas of the following impurities by the corresponding correction factor: impurity F = 0.3; impurity H = 0.1; impurity L = 2.3; impurity M = 0.6; impurity N = 0.7;
— *impurity B:* not more than twice the area of the principal peak in the chromatogram obtained with reference solution (a) (2.0 per cent);
— *impurities A, C, E, F, G, H, I, L, M, N, O, P:* for each impurity, not more than 0.5 times the area of the principal peak in the chromatogram obtained with reference solution (a) (0.5 per cent);
— *sum of impurities D and J:* not more than 0.5 times the area of the principal peak in the chromatogram obtained with reference solution (a) (0.5 per cent);
— *any other impurity:* for each impurity, not more than 0.2 times the area of the principal peak in the chromatogram obtained with reference solution (a) (0.2 per cent);
— *total:* not more than 3 times the area of the principal peak in the chromatogram obtained with reference solution (a) (3.0 per cent);
— *disregard limit:* 0.1 times the area of the principal peak in the chromatogram obtained with reference solution (a) (0.1 per cent); disregard the peaks eluting before impurity L and after impurity B.

**Heavy metals** (2.4.8)

Maximum 25 ppm.

Dissolve 2.0 g in a mixture of 15 volumes of *water R* and 85 volumes of *anhydrous ethanol R* and dilute to 20 ml with the same mixture of solvents. 12 ml of the solution complies with test B. Prepare the reference solution using lead standard solution (2.5 ppm Pb) obtained by diluting *lead standard solution (100 ppm Pb) R* with a mixture of 15 volumes of *water R* and 85 volumes of *anhydrous ethanol R*.

**Water** (2.5.12)

1.8 per cent to 6.5 per cent, determined on 0.200 g.

**Sulphated ash** (2.4.14)

Maximum 0.2 per cent, determined on 1.0 g.

**ASSAY**

Liquid chromatography (2.2.29).

*Solution A* Mix 60 volumes of *acetonitrile R1* and 40 volumes of a 6.7 g/l solution of *dipotassium hydrogen phosphate R* adjusted to pH 8.0 with *phosphoric acid R*.

*Test solution* Dissolve 53.0 mg of the substance to be examined in 2 ml of *acetonitrile R1* and dilute to 100.0 ml with solution A.

*Reference solution (a)* Dissolve 53.0 mg of *azithromycin CRS* in 2 ml of *acetonitrile R1* and dilute to 100.0 ml with solution A.

*Reference solution (b)* Dissolve 5 mg of the substance to be examined and 5 mg of *azithromycin impurity A CRS* in 0.5 ml of *acetonitrile R1* and dilute to 10 ml with solution A.

*Column:*
— *size:* $l$ = 0.25 m, Ø = 4.6 mm;
— *stationary phase:* octadecylsilyl vinyl polymer for chromatography R (5 μm);
— *temperature:* 40 °C.

*Mobile phase* Mix 60 volumes of *acetonitrile R1* and 40 volumes of a 6.7 g/l solution of *dipotassium hydrogen phosphate R* adjusted to pH 11.0 with a 560 g/l solution of *potassium hydroxide R*.

*Flow rate*   1.0 ml/min.

*Detection*   Spectrophotometer at 210 nm.

*Injection*   10 µl.

*Run time*   1.5 times the retention time of azithromycin.

*Retention time*   Azithromycin = about 10 min.

*System suitability*   Reference solution (b):
— *resolution*: minimum 3.0 between the peaks due to impurity A and azithromycin.

Calculate the percentage content of $C_{38}H_{72}N_2O_{12}$ from the declared content of *azithromycin CRS*.

## STORAGE
In an airtight container.

## IMPURITIES
*Specified impurities*   A, B, C, D, E, F, G, H, I, J, L, M, N, O, P.

*Other detectable impurities*   (The following substances would, if present at a sufficient level, be detected by one or other of the tests in the monograph. They are limited by the general acceptance criterion for other/unspecified impurities and/or by the general monograph *Substances for pharmaceutical use (2034)*. It is therefore not necessary to identify these impurities for demonstration of compliance. See also *5.10. Control of impurities in substances for pharmaceutical use*): K.

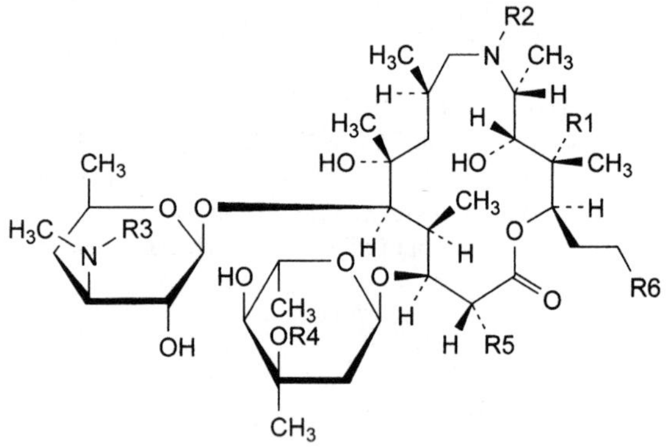

A. R1 = OH, R2 = R6 = H, R3 = R4 = R5 = CH₃: 6-demethylazithromycin,

B. R1 = R6 = H, R2 = R3 = R4 = R5 = CH₃: 3-deoxyazithromycin (azithromycin B),

C. R1 = OH, R2 = R3 = R5 = CH₃, R4 = R6 = H: 3″-O-demethylazithromycin (azithromycin C),

D. R1 = OH, R2 = R3 = R4 = CH₃, R5 = CH₂OH, R6 = H: 14-demethyl-14-(hydroxymethyl)azithromycin (azithromycin F),

F. R1 = OH, R2 = R4 = R5 = CH₃, R3 = CHO, R6 = H: 3′-N-demethyl-3′-N-formylazithromycin,

I. R1 = OH, R2 = R4 = R5 = CH₃, R3 = R6 = H: 3′-N-demethylazithromycin,

O. R1 = OH, R2 = R3 = R4 = R5 = R6 = CH₃: 2-desethyl-2-propylazithromycin,

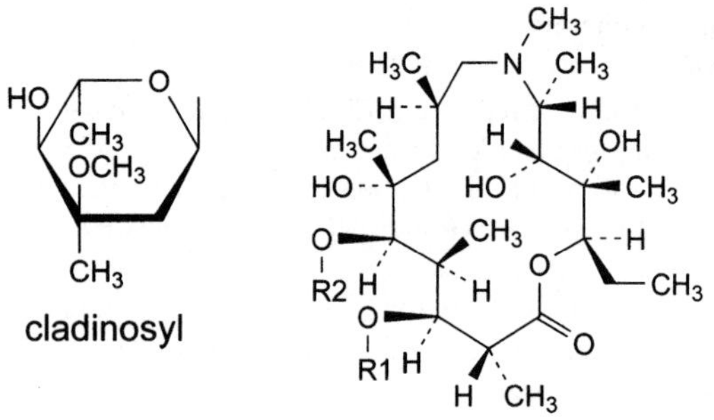

cladinosyl

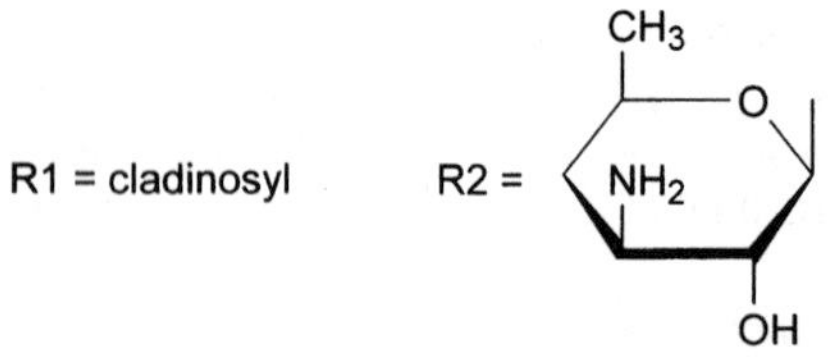

R1 = cladinosyl   R2 =

E. 3′-(N,N-didemethyl)azithromycin (aminoazithromycin),

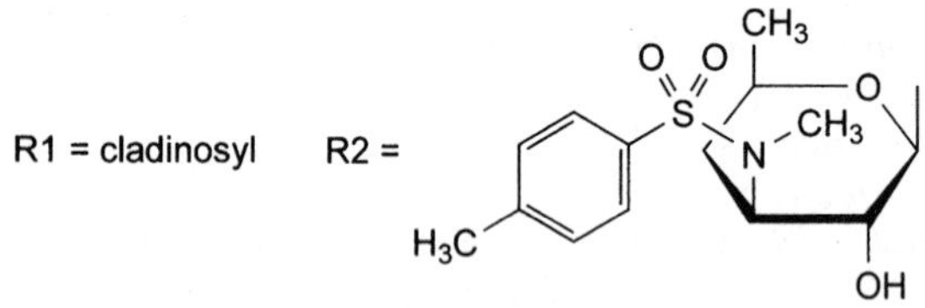

R1 = cladinosyl   R2 =

G. 3′-N-demethyl-3′-N-[(4-methylphenyl)sulphonyl]azithromycin,

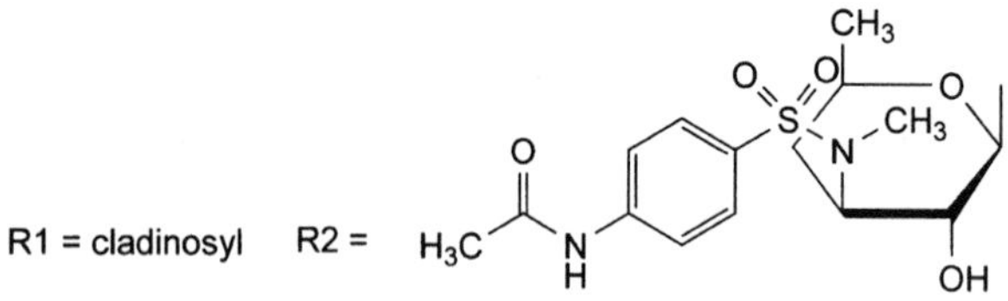

R1 = cladinosyl   R2 =

H. 3′-N-[[4-(acetylamino)phenyl]sulphonyl]-3′-N-demethylazithromycin,

R1 = H   R2 =

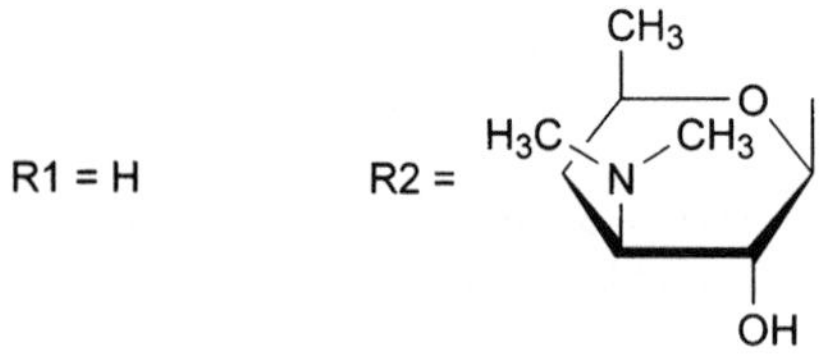

J. 13-O-decladinosylazithromycin,

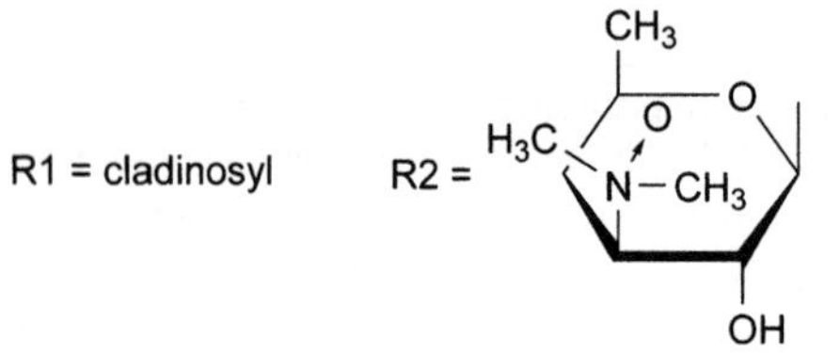

R1 = cladinosyl   R2 =

L. azithromycin 3′-N-oxide,

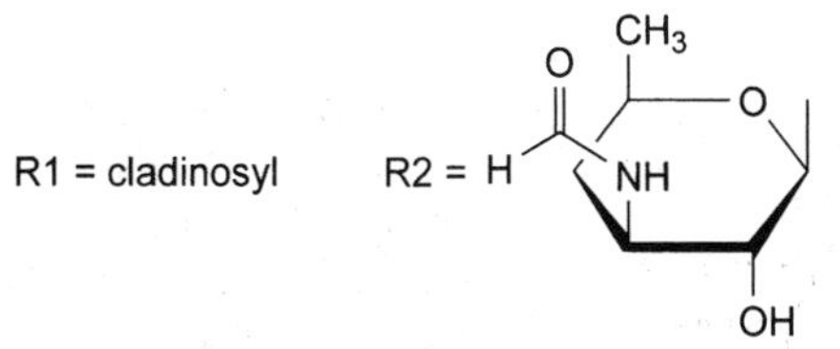

R1 = cladinosyl   R2 = H

M. 3'-(N,N-didemethyl)-3'-N-formylazithromycin,

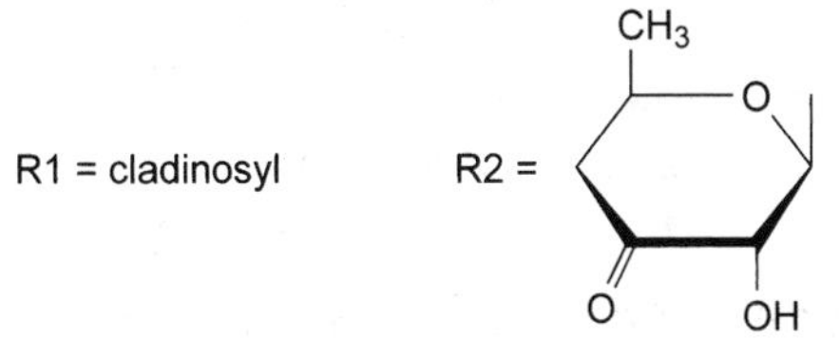

R1 = cladinosyl   R2 =

N. 3'-de(dimethylamino)-3'-oxoazithromycin,

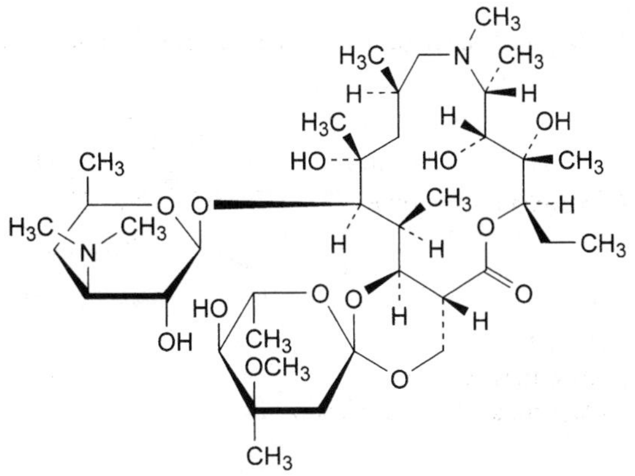

K. $C^{14},1''$-epoxyazithromycin (azithromycin E),

P. unknown structure.

*Ph Eur*

# Bacampicillin Hydrochloride

(*Ph Eur monograph 0808*)

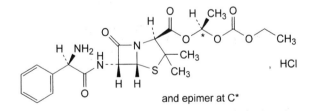

C₂₁H₂₇N₃O₇S, HCl        502.0        *37661-08-8*

$C_{21}H_{27}N_3O_7S$, HCl        502.0        *37661-08-8*

and epimer at C*

**Action and use**

Penicillin antibacterial.

*Ph Eur*

## DEFINITION

(1*RS*)-1-[(Ethoxycarbonyl)oxy]ethyl (2*S*,5*R*,6*R*)-6-[[(2*R*)-2-amino-2-phenylacetyl]amino]-3,3-dimethyl-7-oxo-4-thia-1-azabicyclo[3.2.0]heptane-2-carboxylate hydrochloride.

Semi-synthetic product derived from a fermentation product.

**Content**

95.0 per cent to 102.0 per cent (anhydrous substance).

## CHARACTERS

**Appearance**

White or almost white powder or granules, hygroscopic.

**Solubility**

Soluble in water, freely soluble in ethanol (96 per cent), soluble in methylene chloride.

## IDENTIFICATION

*First identification   A, D.*

*Second identification   B, C, D.*

A. Infrared absorption spectrophotometry (*2.2.24*).

*Comparison   bacampicillin hydrochloride CRS.*

B. Thin-layer chromatography (*2.2.27*).

*Test solution   Dissolve 10 mg of the substance to be examined in 2 ml of methanol R.*

*Reference solution (a)   Dissolve 10 mg of bacampicillin hydrochloride CRS in 2 ml of methanol R.*

*Reference solution (b)   Dissolve 10 mg of bacampicillin hydrochloride CRS, 10 mg of talampicillin hydrochloride CRS and 10 mg of pivampicillin CRS in 2 ml of methanol R.*

*Plate   TLC silanised silica gel plate R.*

*Mobile phase   Mix 10 volumes of a 272 g/l solution of sodium acetate R adjusted to pH 5.0 with glacial acetic acid R, 40 volumes of water R and 50 volumes of ethanol (96 per cent) R.*

*Application   1 μl.*

*Development   Over a path of 15 cm.*

*Drying   In a current of warm air.*

*Detection   Spray with ninhydrin solution R1 and heat at 60 °C for 10 min.*

*System suitability   Reference solution (b):*

— the chromatogram shows 3 clearly separated spots.

*Results   The principal spot in the chromatogram obtained with the test solution is similar in position, colour and size to the principal spot in the chromatogram obtained with reference solution (a).*

C. Place about 2 mg in a test-tube about 150 mm long and 15 mm in diameter. Moisten with 0.05 ml of *water R* and add 2 ml of *sulphuric acid-formaldehyde reagent R*. Mix the contents of the tube by swirling; the solution is practically colourless. Place the test-tube on a water-bath for 1 min; a dark yellow colour develops.

D. Dissolve about 25 mg in 2 ml of *water R*. Add 2 ml of *dilute sodium hydroxide solution R* and shake. Wait a few minutes and add 3 ml of *dilute nitric acid R* and 0.5 ml of *silver nitrate solution R1*. A white precipitate is formed. Add 0.5 ml of *concentrated ammonia R*. The precipitate dissolves.

## TESTS

**Appearance of solution**

Dissolve 0.200 g in 20 ml of *water R*; the solution is not more opalescent than reference suspension II (*2.2.1*).

Dissolve 0.500 g in 10 ml of *water R*; the absorbance (*2.2.25*) of the solution at 430 nm is not greater than 0.10.

**pH** (*2.2.3*)

3.0 to 4.5.

Dissolve 1.0 g in *carbon dioxide-free water R* and dilute to 50 ml with the same solvent.

**Specific optical rotation** (*2.2.7*)

+ 175 to + 195 (anhydrous substance).

Dissolve 0.250 g in *water R* and dilute to 25.0 ml with the same solvent.

## Related substances

Liquid chromatography (2.2.29). *Prepare the test solution and reference solutions (a), (b) and (d) immediately before use.*

*Phosphate buffer A*  Dissolve 1.4 g of *sodium dihydrogen phosphate monohydrate R* in *water R* and dilute to about 800 ml with the same solvent. Adjust to pH 3.0 with *dilute phosphoric acid R* and dilute to 1000.0 ml with *water R*.

*Phosphate buffer B*  Dissolve 2.75 g of *sodium dihydrogen phosphate monohydrate R* and 2.3 g of *disodium hydrogen phosphate dihydrate R* in *water R* and dilute to about 1800 ml with the same solvent. Adjust to pH 6.8, if necessary, using *dilute phosphoric acid R* or *dilute sodium hydroxide solution R* and dilute to 2000.0 ml with *water R*.

*Test solution*  Dissolve 30.0 mg of the substance to be examined in phosphate buffer A and dilute to 100.0 ml with phosphate buffer A.

*Reference solution (a)*  Dissolve 30.0 mg of *bacampicillin hydrochloride CRS* in phosphate buffer A and dilute to 100.0 ml with phosphate buffer A.

*Reference solution (b)*  Dilute 1.0 ml of reference solution (a) to 100.0 ml with phosphate buffer A.

*Reference solution (c)*  Dissolve 30 mg of the substance to be examined in phosphate buffer B and dilute to 100 ml with phosphate buffer B. Heat at 80 °C for about 30 min.

*Reference solution (d)*  Dissolve 20 mg of *ampicillin trihydrate CRS* (impurity I) in phosphate buffer A and dilute to 250 ml with phosphate buffer A. Dilute 5 ml of this solution to 100 ml with phosphate buffer A.

*Column:*
— *size*: $l = 0.05$ m, $\emptyset = 3.9$ mm;
— *stationary phase*: octadecylsilyl silica gel for chromatography R (5 µm).

*Mobile phase*  Mix 30 volumes of *acetonitrile R1* and 70 volumes of a 0.06 per cent *m/m* solution of *tetrahexylammonium hydrogen sulphate R* in phosphate buffer B.

*Flow rate*  1.0 ml/min.

*Detection*  Spectrophotometer at 220 nm.

*Injection*  20 µl of the test solution and reference solutions (b), (c) and (d).

*Run time*  3.5 times the retention time of bacampicillin.

*System suitability:*
— the peak due to impurity I is separated from the peaks due to the solvent in the chromatogram obtained with reference solution (d);
— *relative retention* with reference to bacampicillin: degradation product eluting just after bacampicillin = 1.12 to 1.38 in the chromatogram obtained with reference solution (c); if necessary, adjust the concentration of tetrahexylammonium hydrogen sulphate in the mobile phase.

*Limits:*
— *any impurity*: for each impurity, not more than 1.5 times the area of the principal peak in the chromatogram obtained with reference solution (b) (1.5 per cent);
— *total*: not more than 3 times the area of the principal peak in the chromatogram obtained with reference solution (b) (3 per cent);
— *disregard limit*: 0.1 times the area of the principal peak in the chromatogram obtained with reference solution (b) (0.1 per cent).

**Butyl acetate and ethyl acetate** (2.4.24, System A)
Maximum 2.0 per cent of butyl acetate, maximum 4.0 per cent of ethyl acetate and maximum 5.0 per cent for the sum of the contents.

*Sample solution*  Dissolve 50.0 mg of the substance to be examined in *water R* and dilute to 10.0 ml with the same solvent.

Use the method of standard additions.

*Static head-space conditions that may be used:*
— equilibration temperature: 60 °C;
— equilibration time: 20 min.

**N,N-Dimethylaniline** (2.4.26, Method A)
Maximum 20 ppm.

**Water** (2.5.12)
Maximum 0.8 per cent, determined on 0.300 g.

**Sulphated ash** (2.4.14)
Maximum 1.5 per cent, determined on 1.0 g.

## ASSAY

Liquid chromatography (2.2.29) as described in the test for related substances with the following modifications.

*Injection*  Test solution and reference solution (a).

*System suitability*  Reference solution (a):
— *repeatability*: maximum relative standard deviation of 1.0 per cent after 6 injections.

Calculate the percentage content of $C_{21}H_{28}ClN_3O_7S$ from the declared content of *bacampicillin hydrochloride CRS*.

## STORAGE

In an airtight container.

## IMPURITIES

A. (2S,5R,6R)-6-amino-3,3-dimethyl-7-oxo-4-thia-1-azabicyclo[3.2.0]heptane-2-carboxylic acid (6-aminopenicillanic acid),

B. R = H: (2R)-2-amino-2-phenylacetic acid (D-phenylglycine),

G. R = CH3: methyl (2R)-2-amino-2-phenylacetate (methyl D-phenylglycinate),

C. R = H: (2RS,4S)-2-[[[(2R)-2-amino-2-phenylacetyl]amino]methyl]-5,5-dimethylthiazolidine-4-carboxylic acid (penilloic acids of ampicillin),

D. R = CO$_2$H: (4S)-2-[[[(2R)-2-amino-2-phenylacetyl]amino]carboxymethyl]-5,5-dimethylthiazolidine-4-carboxylic acid (penicilloic acids of ampicillin),

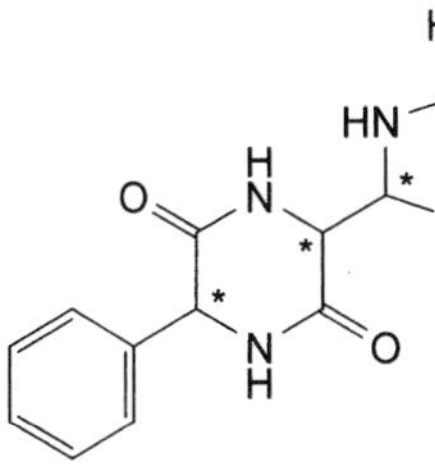

E. (4S)-2-(3,6-dioxo-5-phenylpiperazin-2-yl)-5,5-dimethylthiazolidine-4-carboxylic acid (diketopiperazines of ampicillin),

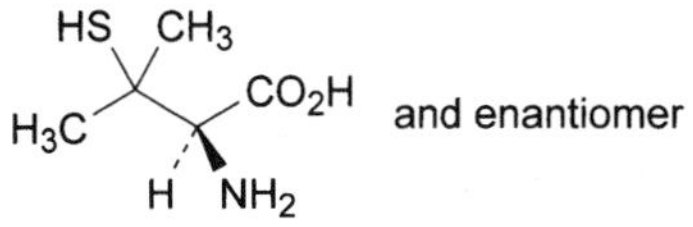

F. (2RS)-2-amino-3-methyl-3-sulphanylbutanoic acid (DL-penicillamine),

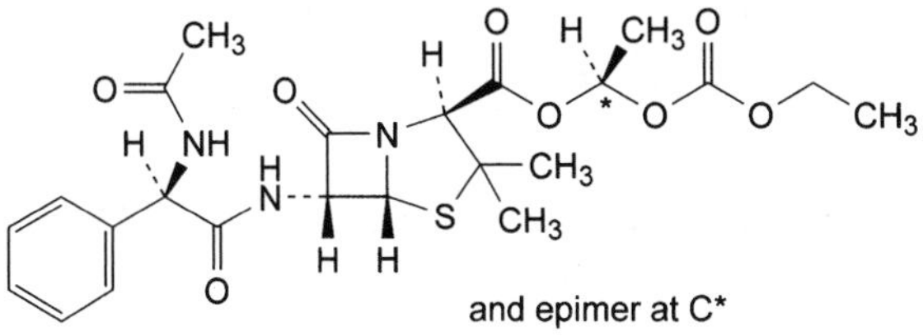

H. (1RS)-1-[(ethoxycarbonyl)oxy]ethyl (2S,5R,6R)-6-[[(2R)-2-(acetylamino)-2-phenylacetyl]amino]-3,3-dimethyl-7-oxo-4-thia-1-azabicyclo[3.2.0]heptane-2-carboxylate (N-acetylbacampicillin),

I. ampicillin.

_____ Ph Eur

# Bacitracin

(Ph Eur monograph 0465)

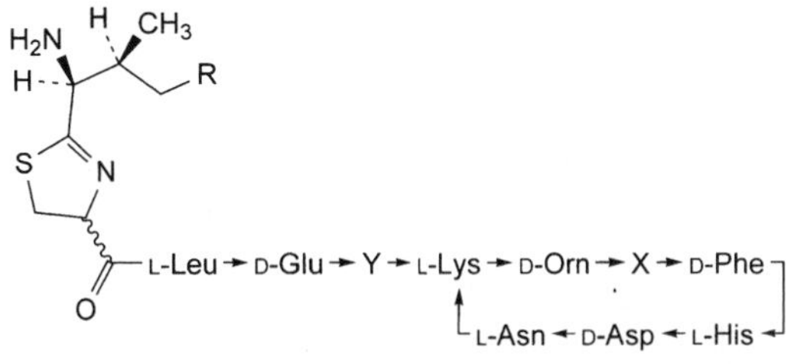

| Name | Mol. Formula | X | Y | R |
|---|---|---|---|---|
| Bacitracin A | C$_{66}$H$_{103}$N$_{17}$O$_{16}$S | L-Ile | L-Ile | CH$_3$ |
| Bacitracin B1 | C$_{65}$H$_{101}$N$_{17}$O$_{16}$S | L-Ile | L-Ile | H |
| Bacitracin B2 | C$_{65}$H$_{101}$N$_{17}$O$_{16}$S | L-Val | L-Ile | CH$_3$ |
| Bacitracin B3 | C$_{65}$H$_{101}$N$_{17}$O$_{16}$S | L-Ile | L-Val | CH$_3$ |

*1405-87-4*

### Action and use
Polypeptide antibacterial.

*Ph Eur* _____

## DEFINITION
Mixture of antimicrobial polypeptides produced by certain strains of *Bacillus licheniformis* or *Bacillus subtilis*, the main components being bacitracins A, B1, B2 and B3.

### Content
Minimum 60 IU/mg (dried substance).

## CHARACTERS
### Appearance
White or almost white powder, hygroscopic.

### Solubility
Freely soluble in water and in alcohol.

## IDENTIFICATION
*First identification   B, C.*

*Second identification   A, C.*

A. Thin-layer chromatography (2.2.27).

*Test solution*   Dissolve 10 mg of the substance to be examined in a 3.4 g/l solution of *hydrochloric acid R* and dilute to 1.0 ml with the same solution.

*Reference solution*   Dissolve 10 mg of *bacitracin zinc CRS* in a 3.4 g/l solution of *hydrochloric acid R* and dilute to 1.0 ml with the same solution.

*Plate*   TLC silica gel plate R.

*Mobile phase*   glacial acetic acid R, water R, butanol R (1:2:4 V/V/V).

*Application*   10 µl.

*Development*   Over half of the plate.

*Drying*   At 100-105 °C.

*Detection*   Spray with *ninhydrin solution R1* and heat at 110 °C for 5 min.

*Results*   The spots in the chromatogram obtained with the test solution are similar in position, size and colour to the spots in the chromatogram obtained with the reference solution.

B. It complies with the test for composition (see Tests).

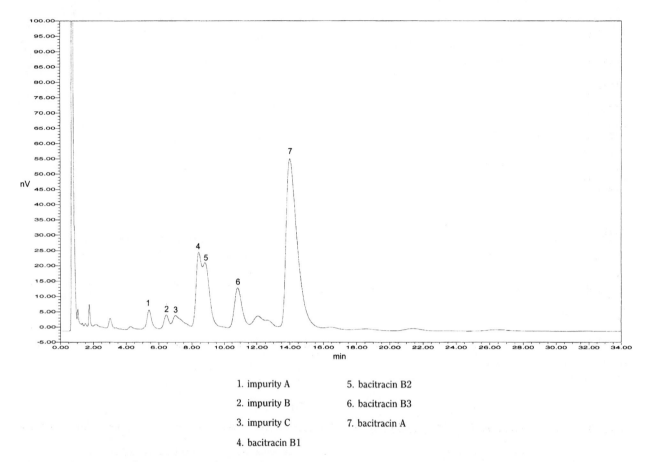

1. impurity A
2. impurity B
3. impurity C
4. bacitracin B1

5. bacitracin B2
6. bacitracin B3
7. bacitracin A

Figure 0465.-1. – *Chromatogram of the test for composition in bacitracin obtained with the test solution at 254 nm*

C. Ignite 0.2 g. An insignificant residue remains which is not yellow at high temperature. Allow to cool. Dissolve the residue in 0.1 ml *of dilute hydrochloric acid R*. Add 5 ml of *water R* and 0.2 ml of *strong sodium hydroxide solution R*. No white precipitate is formed.

## TESTS

**Solution S**
Dissolve 0.25 g in *carbon dioxide-free water R* and dilute to 25 ml with the same solvent.

**Appearance of solution**
Solution S is clear (*2.2.1*).

**pH** (*2.2.3*)
6.0 to 7.0 for solution S.

**Composition**
Liquid chromatography (*2.2.29*): use the normalisation procedure. *Prepare the solutions immediately before use.*

*Test solution* Dissolve 0.100 g of the substance to be examined in 50.0 ml of the mobile phase.

*Reference solution (a)* Suspend 20.0 mg of *bacitracin zinc CRS* in *water R*, add 0.2 ml of *dilute hydrochloric acid R* and dilute to 10.0 ml with *water R*.

*Reference solution (b)* Dilute 5.0 ml of the test solution to 100.0 ml with the mobile phase.

*Reference solution (c)* Dilute 1.0 ml of reference solution (b) to 10.0 ml with the mobile phase.

*Reference solution (d)* Dissolve 50.0 mg of the substance to be examined in 25.0 ml of a 40 g/l solution of *sodium edetate R* adjusted to pH 7.0 with *dilute sodium hydroxide R*.

Heat in a boiling water-bath for 30 min. Cool to room temperature.

*Blank solution* A 40 g/l solution of *sodium edetate R* adjusted to pH 7.0 with *dilute sodium hydroxide R*.

*Column:*
— size: $l$ = 0.25 m, Ø = 4.6 mm,
— *stationary phase: end-capped octadecylsilyl silica gel for chromatography R* (5 μm).

*Mobile phase* Add 520 volumes of *methanol R1*, 40 volumes of *acetonitrile R* and 300 volumes of *water R* to 100 volumes of a 34.8 g/l solution of *dipotassium hydrogen phosphate R* adjusted to pH 6.0 with a 27.2 g/l solution of *potassium dihydrogen phosphate R*.

*Flow rate* 1.0 ml/min.

*Detection* Spectrophotometer at 254 nm.

*Injection* 100 μl; inject the blank, the test solution and reference solutions (a) and (c).

*Run time* 3 times the retention time of bacitracin A.

*Relative retention* with reference to bacitracin A (retention time = 15 min to 25 min): bacitracin B1 = about 0.6; bacitracin B3 = about 0.8; impurity E = about 2.5.

If necessary, adjust the composition of the mobile phase by changing the amount of organic modifier whilst keeping the ratio constant between methanol and acetonitrile.

*System suitability* Reference solution (a):
— *peak-to-valley ratio*: minimum of 1.2, where $H_p$ = height above the baseline of the peak due to bacitracin B1 and $H_v$ = height above the baseline of the lowest point of the curve separating this peak from the peak due to bacitracin B2.

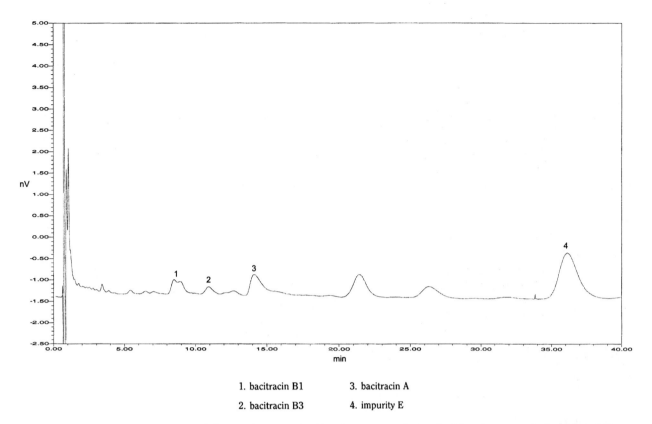

1. bacitracin B1    3. bacitracin A
2. bacitracin B3    4. impurity E

Figure 0465.-2. – *Chromatogram of the test for impurity E in bacitracin obtained with reference solution (d) at 300 nm*

*Limits:*
— *bacitracin A*: minimum 40.0 per cent,
— *sum of bacitracins A, B1, B2 and B3*: minimum 70.0 per cent,
— *disregard limit*: the area of the peak due to bacitracin A in the chromatogram obtained with reference solution (c) (0.5 per cent); disregard any peak observed in the blank run.

**Related peptides**
Liquid chromatography (*2.2.29*) as described in the test for composition.
See Figure 0465.-1.
*Limit:*
— *sum of the areas of all peaks eluting before the peak due to bacitracin B1*: maximum 20.0 per cent.

**Impurity E**
Liquid chromatography (*2.2.29*) as described in the test for composition.
*Detection* Spectrophotometer at 254 nm; spectrophotometer at 300 nm for reference solution (d).
*Injection* Test solution and reference solutions (b) and (d).
*Limit:*
— *impurity E*: not more than 1.2 times the area of the principal peak in the chromatogram obtained with reference solution (b) (6.0 per cent).

**Loss on drying** (*2.2.32*)
Maximum 5.0 per cent, determined on 1.000 g by drying at 60 °C over *diphosphorus pentoxide R* at a pressure not exceeding 0.1 kPa for 3 h.

**Sulphated ash** (*2.4.14*)
Maximum 1.0 per cent, determined on 1.0 g.

**Sterility** (*2.6.1*)
If intended for the preparation of ophthalmic dosage forms without a further appropriate sterilisation procedure, it complies with the test for sterility.

**Bacterial endotoxins** (*2.6.14*)
Less than 0.8 IU/mg, if intended for use in the manufacture of ophthalmic dosage forms without a further appropriate procedure for the removal of bacterial endotoxins.

**ASSAY**
Carry out the microbiological assay of antibiotics (*2.7.2*). Use *bacitracin zinc CRS* as the reference substance.

**STORAGE**
In an airtight container at 2 °C to 8 °C. If the substance is sterile, store in a sterile, airtight, tamper-proof container.

**IMPURITIES**

A. X = L-Val, Y = L-Ile, R = H: bacitracin C1,
B. X = L-Ile, Y = L-Val, R = H: bacitracin C2,
C. X = Y = L-Val, R = CH$_3$: bacitracin C3,
D. X = Y = L-Val, R = H: bacitracin E,

E. X = Y = L-Ile, R = CH₃: bacitracin F,

F. X = Y = L-Ile, R = H: bacitracin H1,

G. X = L-Val, Y = L-Ile, R = CH₃: bacitracin H2,

H. X = L-Ile, Y = L-Val, R = CH₃: bacitracin H3,

I. X = L-Val, Y = L-Ile, R = H: bacitracin I1,

J. X = L-Ile, Y = L-Val, R = H: bacitracin I2,

K. X = Y = L-Val, R = CH₃: bacitracin I3.

_____ *Ph Eur*

# Bacitracin Zinc

(*Ph Eur monograph 0466*)

1405-49-6

## Action and use
Polypeptide antibacterial.

## Preparation
Polymyxin and Bacitracin Eye Ointment

*Ph Eur* _____

## DEFINITION
Zinc complex of bacitracin, which consists of a mixture of antimicrobial polypeptides produced by certain strains of *Bacillus licheniformis* or *Bacillus subtilis*, the main components being bacitracins A, B1, B2 and B3.

## Content
Minimum 60 IU/mg (dried substance).

## CHARACTERS

### Appearance
White or light yellowish-grey powder, hygroscopic.

### Solubility
Slightly soluble in water and in alcohol.

## IDENTIFICATION
*First identification* B, C.

*Second identification* A, C.

A. Thin-layer chromatography (*2.2.27*).

*Test solution* Dissolve 10 mg of the substance to be examined in 0.5 ml of *dilute hydrochloride acid R* and dilute to 1.0 ml with *water R*.

*Reference solution* Dissolve 10 mg of *bacitracin zinc CRS* in 0.5 ml of *dilute hydrochloric acid R* and dilute to 1.0 ml with *water R*.

*Plate* TLC silica gel plate R.

*Mobile phase* glacial acetic acid R, water R, butanol R (1:2:4 *V/V/V*).

*Application* 10 µl.

*Development* Over half of the plate.

*Drying* At 100-105 °C.

*Detection* Spray with *ninhydrin solution R1* and heat at 110 °C for 5 min.

*Results* The spots in the chromatogram obtained with the test solution are similar in position, size and colour to the spots in the chromatogram obtained with the reference solution.

B. It complies with the test for composition (see Tests).

C. Ignite about 0.15 g, allow to cool and dissolve the residue in 1 ml of *dilute hydrochloric acid R*. Add 4 ml of *water R*. The solution gives the reaction of zinc (*2.3.1*).

## TESTS

### pH (*2.2.3*)
6.0 to 7.5.

Shake 1.0 g for about 1 min with 10 ml of *carbon dioxide-free water R* and filter.

### Composition
Liquid chromatography (*2.2.29*): use the normalisation procedure. *Prepare the solutions immediately before use.*

*Test solution* Dissolve 0.100 g of the substance to be examined in 50.0 ml of a 40 g/l solution of *sodium edetate R* adjusted to pH 7.0 with *dilute sodium hydroxide R*.

*Reference solution (a)* Dissolve 20.0 mg of *bacitracin zinc CRS* in 10.0 ml of a 40 g/l solution of *sodium edetate R* adjusted to pH 7.0 with *dilute sodium hydroxide R*.

*Reference solution (b)* Dilute 5.0 ml of the test solution to 100.0 ml with *water R*.

*Reference solution (c)* Dilute 1.0 ml of reference solution (b) to 10.0 ml with *water R*.

*Reference solution (d)* Dissolve 50.0 mg of the substance to be examined in 25.0 ml of a 40 g/l solution of *sodium edetate R* adjusted to pH 7.0 with *dilute sodium hydroxide R*. Heat in a boiling water-bath for 30 min. Cool to room temperature.

*Blank solution* A 40 g/l solution of *sodium edetate R* adjusted to pH 7.0 with dilute *sodium hydroxide R*.

*Column:*
— size: $l$ = 0.25 m, Ø = 4.6 mm,
— stationary phase: end-capped octadecylsilyl silica gel for chromatography R (5 µm).

*Mobile phase* Add 520 volumes of *methanol R1*, 40 volumes of *acetonitrile R* and 300 volumes of *water R* to 100 volumes of a 34.8 g/l solution of *dipotassium hydrogen phosphate R*, adjusted to pH 6.0 with a 27.2 g/l solution of *potassium dihydrogen phosphate R*.

*Flow rate* 1.0 ml/min.

*Detection* Spectrophotometer at 254 nm.

*Injection* 100 µl; inject the blank, the test solution and reference solutions (a) and (c).

*Run time* 3 times the retention time of bacitracin A.

*Relative retention* With reference to bacitracin A (retention time = 15 min to 25 min):
bacitracin B1 = about 0.6; bacitracin B3 = about 0.8; impurity E = about 2.5.

If necessary, adjust the composition of the mobile phase by changing the amount of organic modifier whilst keeping the ratio constant between methanol and acetonitrile.

*System suitability* Reference solution (a):
— peak-to-valley ratio: minimum of 1.2, where $H_p$ = height above the baseline of the peak due to bacitracin B1 and $H_v$ = height above the baseline of the lowest point of the curve separating this peak from the peak due to bacitracin B2.

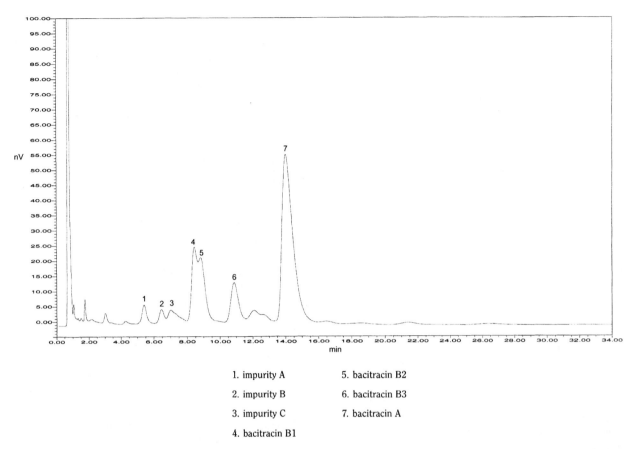

1. impurity A
2. impurity B
3. impurity C
4. bacitracin B1

5. bacitracin B2
6. bacitracin B3
7. bacitracin A

Figure 0466.-1. – *Chromatogram of the test for composition in bacitracin zinc obtained with the test solution at 254 nm*

*Limits:*
— *bacitracin A*: minimum 40.0 per cent,
— *sum of bacitracins A, B1, B2 and B3*: minimum
   70.0 per cent.
— *disregard limit*: the area of the peak due to bacitracin A in
   the chromatogram obtained with reference solution (c)
   (0.5 per cent); disregard any peak observed in the blank
   run.

**Related peptides**
Liquid chromatography (*2.2.29*) as described in the test for
composition.
See Figure 0466.-1.
*Limit:*
— *sum of the areas of all peaks eluting before the peak due to
   bacitracin B1*: maximum 20.0 per cent.

**Impurity E**
Liquid chromatography (*2.2.29*) as described in the test for
composition.
See Figure 0466.-2.

*Detection*   Spectrophotometer at 254 nm; spectrophotometer
at 300 nm for reference solution (d).

*Injection*   Test solution and reference solutions (b) and (d).

*Limit:*
— *impurity E*: not more than 1.2 times the area of the
   principal peak in the chromatogram obtained with
   reference solution (b) (6.0 per cent).

**Zinc**
4.0 per cent to 6.0 per cent (dried substance).

Dissolve 0.200 g in a mixture of 2.5 ml of *dilute acetic acid R*
and 2.5 ml of water. Add 50 ml of *water R*, 50 mg of *xylenol*

*orange triturate R* and sufficient *hexamethylenetetramine R* to
produce a red colour. Add 2 g of *hexamethylenetetramine R* in
excess. Titrate with *0.01 M sodium edetate* until a yellow
colour is obtained.

1 ml of *0.01 M sodium edetate* is equivalent to 0.654 mg of
Zn.

**Loss on drying** (*2.2.32*)
Maximum 5.0 per cent, determined on 1.000 g by drying at
60 °C over *diphosphorus pentoxide R* at a pressure not
exceeding 0.1 kPa for 3 h.

**Sterility** (*2.6.1*)
If intended for administration by spraying into internal body
cavities without a further appropriate sterilisation procedure,
it complies with the test for sterility.

**Pyrogens** (*2.6.8*)
If intended for administration by spraying into internal body
cavities without a further appropriate procedure for the
removal of pyrogens, it complies with the test for pyrogens.
Inject per kilogram of the rabbit's mass 1 ml of the
supernatant liquid obtained by centrifuging a suspension
containing 11 mg per millilitre in a 9 g/l solution of *sodium
chloride R*.

**ASSAY**
Suspend 50.0 mg in 5 ml of *water R*, add 0.5 ml of *dilute
hydrochloric acid R* and dilute to 100.0 ml with *water R*.
Allow the solution to stand for 30 min. Carry out the
microbiological assay of antibiotics (*2.7.2*).

**STORAGE**
In an airtight container. If the substance is sterile, store in a
sterile, airtight, tamper-proof container.

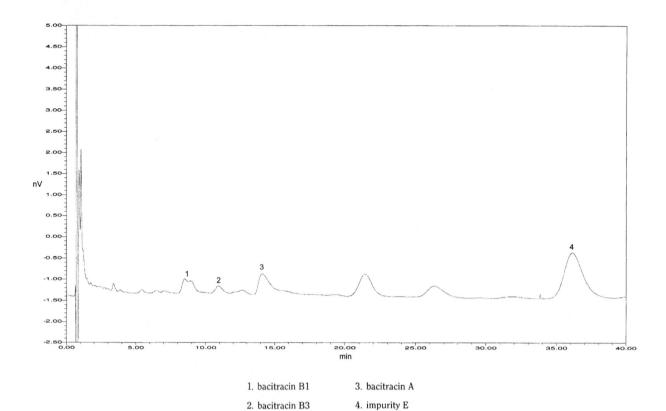

1. bacitracin B1          3. bacitracin A

2. bacitracin B3          4. impurity E

Figure 0466.-2. — *Chromatogram of the test for impurity E in bacitracin zinc obtained with reference solution (d) at 300 nm*

## IMPURITIES

A. X = L-Val, Y = L-Ile, R = H: bacitracin C1,

B. = L-Ile, Y = L-Val, R = H: bacitracin C2,

C. = Y = L-Val, R = CH₃ bacitracin C3,

D. X = Y = L-Val, R = H: bacitracin E,

E. = Y = L-Ile, R = CH₃: bacitracin F,

F. X = Y = L-Ile, R = H: bacitracin H1,

G. X = L-Val, Y = L-Ile, R = CH₃: bacitracin H2,

H. X = L-Ile, Y = L-Val, R = CH₃: bacitracin H3,

I. = L-Val, Y = L-Ile, R = H: bacitracin I1,

J. X = L-Ile, Y = L-Val, R = H: bacitracin I2,

K. X = Y = L-Val, R = CH₃: bacitracin I3.

_____ *Ph Eur*

# Baclofen

(*Ph Eur monograph 0653*)

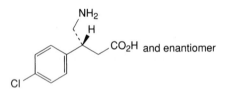

and enantiomer

$C_{10}H_{12}ClNO_2$            213.7            *1134-47-0*

## Action and use
Skeletal muscle relaxant.

## Preparations
Baclofen Oral Solution

Baclofen Tablets

*Ph Eur* _____

## DEFINITION
(3RS)-4-Amino-3-(4-chlorophenyl)butanoic acid.

## Content
98.0 per cent to 101.0 per cent (anhydrous substance).

## CHARACTERS
### Appearance
White or almost white powder.

### Solubility
Slightly soluble in water, very slightly soluble in ethanol (96 per cent), practically insoluble in acetone. It dissolves in dilute mineral acids and in dilute solutions of alkali hydroxides.

It shows polymorphism (5.9).

## IDENTIFICATION

*First identification* B.

*Second identification* A, C.

A. Ultraviolet and visible absorption spectrophotometry (*2.2.25*).

*Test solution* Dissolve 70 mg in *water R* and dilute to 100.0 ml with the same solvent.

*Spectral range* 220-320 nm.

*Absorption maxima* At 259 nm, 266 nm and 275 nm.

*Resolution (2.2.25)* Minimum 1.5 for the absorbance ratio.

*Specific absorbance at the absorption maxima:*
— at 259 nm: 9.8 to 10.8;
— at 266 nm: 11.5 to 12.7;
— at 275 nm: 8.4 to 9.3.

B. Infrared absorption spectrophotometry (*2.2.24*).

*Preparation* Discs prepared using 3 mg of substance and 300 mg of *potassium bromide R*.

*Comparison* baclofen CRS.

If the spectra obtained in the solid state show differences, dissolve 0.1 g of each of the substances separately in 1 ml of *dilute sodium hydroxide solution R* and add 10 ml of *ethanol (96 per cent) R* and 1 ml of *dilute acetic acid R*. Allow to stand for 1 h. Filter, wash the precipitate with *ethanol (96 per cent) R* and dry *in vacuo*. Prepare new discs and record the spectra.

C. Thin-layer chromatography (*2.2.27*).

*Test solution* Dissolve 10 mg of the substance to be examined in the mobile phase and dilute to 10 ml with the mobile phase.

*Reference solution* Dissolve 10 mg of *baclofen CRS* in the mobile phase and dilute to 10 ml with the mobile phase.

*Plate* TLC silica gel G plate R.

*Mobile phase* anhydrous formic acid R, water R, methanol R, chloroform R, ethyl acetate R (5:5:20:30:40 *V/V/V/V/V*).

*Application* 5 μl.

*Development* Over a path of 12 cm.

*Drying* Allow the solvents to evaporate.

*Detection* Spray with *ninhydrin solution R3* until the plate is slightly wet. Place in an oven maintained at 100 °C for 10 min. Examine in daylight.

*Results* The principal spot in the chromatogram obtained with the test solution is similar in position, colour and size to the principal spot in the chromatogram obtained with the reference solution.

## TESTS

### Appearance of solution

The solution is not more opalescent than reference suspension II (*2.2.1*) and not more intensely coloured than reference solution $BY_5$ (*2.2.2, Method II*).

Dissolve 0.50 g in *1 M sodium hydroxide* and dilute to 25 ml with the same solvent.

### Related substances

Liquid chromatography (*2.2.29*).

*Test solution* Dissolve 25.0 mg of the substance to be examined in the mobile phase and dilute to 10.0 ml with the mobile phase.

*Reference solution (a)* Dissolve 25.0 mg of *baclofen impurity A CRS* in the mobile phase and dilute to 10.0 ml with the mobile phase.

*Reference solution (b)* Dilute 1.0 ml of reference solution (a) to 100.0 ml with the mobile phase.

*Reference solution (c)* Dilute 2.0 ml of the test solution to 100.0 ml with the mobile phase.

*Reference solution (d)* Dilute 2.0 ml of the test solution and 2.0 ml of reference solution (a) to 100.0 ml with the mobile phase.

*Column:*
— *size:* $l$ = 0.25 m, Ø = 4.0 mm;
— *stationary phase: octadecylsilyl silica gel for chromatography R* (10 μm).

*Mobile phase* Dissolve 1.822 g of *sodium hexanesulphonate R* in 1 litre of a mixture of 560 volumes of *water R*, 440 volumes of *methanol R* and 5 volumes of *glacial acetic acid R*.

*Flow rate* 2.0 ml/min.

*Detection* Spectrophotometer at 266 nm.

*Injection* 20 μl of the test solution and reference solutions (b), (c) and (d).

*Run time* 5 times the retention time of baclofen.

*System suitability* Reference solution (d):
— *resolution:* minimum 2.0 between the peaks due to baclofen and impurity A.

*Limits:*
— *impurity A*: not more than the area of the principal peak in the chromatogram obtained with reference solution (b) (1.0 per cent);
— *total*: not more than the area of the principal peak in the chromatogram obtained with reference solution (c) (2.0 per cent).

### Water (*2.5.12*)

Maximum 1.0 per cent, determined on 1.000 g.

### Sulphated ash (*2.4.14*)

Maximum 0.1 per cent, determined on 1.0 g.

## ASSAY

Dissolve 0.1500 g in 50 ml of *anhydrous acetic acid R*. Titrate with *0.1 M perchloric acid*, determining the end-point potentiometrically (*2.2.20*).

1 ml of *0.1 M perchloric acid* is equivalent to 21.37 mg of $C_{10}H_{12}ClNO_2$.

## IMPURITIES

*Specified impurities* A.

*Other detectable impurities* (The following substances would, if present at a sufficient level, be detected by one or other of the tests in the monograph. They are limited by the general acceptance criterion for other/unspecified impurities and/or by the general monograph *Substances for pharmaceutical use (2034)*. It is therefore not necessary to identify these impurities for demonstration of compliance. See also *5.10. Control of impurities in substances for pharmaceutical use*):B.

and enantiomer

A. (4RS)-4-(4-chlorophenyl)pyrrolidin-2-one,

B. (3RS)-5-amino-3-(4-chlorophenyl)-5-oxopentanoic acid.

*Ph Eur*

# Bambuterol Hydrochloride

(*Ph Eur monograph 1293*)

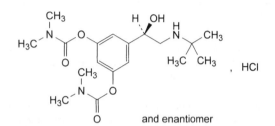

and enantiomer

$C_{18}H_{29}N_3O_5,HCl$        403.9        81732-46-9

### Action and use

Beta$_2$-adrenoceptor agonist; bronchodilator.

*Ph Eur*

## DEFINITION

5-[(1RS)-2-[(1,1-Dimethylethyl)amino]-1-hydroxyethyl]-1,3-phenylene bis(dimethylcarbamate) hydrochloride.

### Content

98.5 per cent to 101.5 per cent (anhydrous substance).

## CHARACTERS

### Appearance

White or almost white, crystalline powder.

### Solubility

Freely soluble in water, soluble in ethanol (96 per cent).

It shows polymorphism (5.9).

## IDENTIFICATION

A. Infrared absorption spectrophotometry (2.2.24).

*Preparation*   Discs.

*Comparison*   *bambuterol hydrochloride CRS.*

If the spectra obtained show differences, dissolve the substance to be examined and the reference substance separately in a mixture of 1 volume of *water R* and 6 volumes of *acetone R*, cool in ice to precipitate and dry both precipitates *in vacuo* at 50 °C to constant weight. Record new spectra using the residues.

B. It gives reaction (a) of chlorides (2.3.1).

## TESTS

### Solution S

Dissolve 4.0 g in *carbon dioxide-free water R* and dilute to 20.0 ml with the same solvent.

### Acidity or alkalinity

To 10 ml of solution S add 0.2 ml of *methyl red solution R* and 0.2 ml of *0.01 M hydrochloric acid*. The solution is red. Add 0.4 ml of *0.01 M sodium hydroxide*. The solution is yellow.

### Optical rotation (2.2.7)

– 0.10° to + 0.10°.

Dilute 1 ml of solution S to 10 ml with *carbon dioxide-free water R.*

### Related substances

Liquid chromatography (2.2.29).

*Test solution*   Dissolve 5.0 mg of the substance to be examined in the mobile phase and dilute to 10.0 ml with the mobile phase.

*Reference solution (a)*   Dissolve 1.0 mg of *formoterol fumarate dihydrate CRS* in the mobile phase and dilute to 10.0 ml with the mobile phase. Mix 0.8 ml of this solution with 0.4 ml of the test solution and dilute to 100.0 ml with the mobile phase.

*Reference solution (b)*   Dilute 1.0 ml of the test solution to 50.0 ml with the mobile phase. Dilute 2.0 ml of this solution to 20.0 ml with the mobile phase.

*Column:*
— *size: l = 0.15 m, Ø = 4.6 mm;*
— *stationary phase: base-deactivated octadecylsilyl silica gel for chromatography R (5 μm).*

*Mobile phase*   Dissolve 1.3 g of *sodium octanesulphonate R* in 430 ml of a mixture of 25 volumes of *acetonitrile R1* and 75 volumes of *methanol R*; then mix this solution with 570 ml of 0.050 M phosphate buffer pH 3.0 prepared as follows: dissolve 6.90 g of *sodium dihydrogen phosphate monohydrate R* in *water R* and dilute to 1000 ml with *water R*, adjust to pH 3.0 with a 50 g/l solution of *dilute phosphoric acid R.*

*Flow rate*   1.5 ml/min.

*Detection*   Spectrophotometer at 214 nm.

*Injection*   20 μl; inject the mobile phase as a blank.

*Run time*   1.5 times the retention time of bambuterol.

*Retention time*   formoterol = about 7 min; bambuterol = about 9 min. If necessary, adjust the composition of the mobile phase; increase the content of phosphate buffer to increase the retention time.

*System suitability*   Reference solution (a):
— *resolution*: minimum 5.0 between the peaks due to bambuterol and formoterol.

*Limits:*
— *impurities A, B, C, D, E, F*: for each impurity, not more than the area of the principal peak in the chromatogram obtained with reference solution (b) (0.2 per cent);
— *total*: not more than 3 times the area of the principal peak in the chromatogram obtained with reference solution (b) (0.6 per cent);
— *disregard limit*: 0.25 times the area of the principal peak in the chromatogram obtained with reference solution (b) (0.05 per cent); disregard any peak due to the mobile phase.

### Water (2.5.12)

Maximum 0.5 per cent, determined on 0.500 g.

### Sulphated ash (2.4.14)

Maximum 0.1 per cent, determined on 1.0 g.

## ASSAY

Dissolve 0.320 g in 50 ml of *ethanol (96 per cent) R* and add 5 ml of *0.01 M hydrochloric acid*. Carry out a potentiometric titration (2.2.20), using *0.1 M sodium hydroxide*. Read the volume added between the 2 points of inflexion.

1 ml of *0.1 M sodium hydroxide* is equivalent to 40.39 mg of $C_{18}H_{30}ClN_3O_5$.

## IMPURITIES

*Specified impurities: A, B, C, D, E, F.*

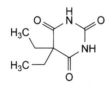

and enantiomer

A. R1 = NH-C(CH₃)₃, R2 = R3 = H: (1RS)-1-(3,5-dihydroxyphenyl)-2-[(1,1-dimethylethyl)amino]ethanol (terbutaline),

B. R1 = OH, R2 = R3 = CO-N(CH₃)₂: 5-[(1RS)-1,2-dihydroxyethyl]-1,3-phenylene bis(dimethylcarbamate),

C. R1 = NH-C(CH₃)₃, R2 = H, R3 = CO-N(CH₃)₂: 3-[(1RS)-2-[(1,1-dimethylethyl)amino]-1-hydroxyethyl]-5-hydroxyphenyl dimethylcarbamate,

D. R1 = H, R2 = R3 = CO-N(CH₃)₂: 5-[(1RS)-1-hydroxyethyl]-1,3-phenylene bis(dimethylcarbamate),

E. R = H: 5-acetyl-1,3-phenylene bis(dimethylcarbamate),

F. R = NH-C(CH₃)₃: 5-[[(1,1-dimethylethyl)amino]acetyl]-1,3-phenylene bis(dimethylcarbamate).

*Ph Eur*

# Barbital

*(Ph Eur monograph 0170)*

C₈H₁₂N₂O₃          184.2          *57-44-3*

## Action and use

Barbiturate.

*Ph Eur*

## DEFINITION

Barbital contains not less than 99.0 per cent and not more than the equivalent of 101.0 per cent of 5,5-diethylpyrimidine-2,4,6(1H,3H,5H)-trione, calculated with reference to the dried substance.

## CHARACTERS

A white or almost white, crystalline powder or colourless crystals, slightly soluble in water, soluble in boiling water and in alcohol. It forms water-soluble compounds with alkali hydroxides and carbonates and with ammonia.

## IDENTIFICATION

*First identification   A, B.*

*Second identification   A, C, D.*

A. Determine the melting point (2.2.14) of the substance to be examined. Mix equal parts of the substance to be examined and *barbital CRS* and determine the melting point of the mixture. The difference between the melting points (which are about 190 °C) is not greater than 2 °C.

B. Examine by infrared absorption spectrophotometry (2.2.24), comparing with the spectrum obtained with *barbital CRS*.

C. Examine by thin-layer chromatography (2.2.27), using *silica gel GF₂₅₄ R* as the coating substance.

*Test solution*   Dissolve 75 mg of the substance to be examined in *alcohol R* and dilute to 25 ml with the same solvent.

*Reference solution*   Dissolve 75 mg of *barbital CRS* in alcohol R and dilute to 25 ml with the same solvent.

Apply separately to the plate 10 μl of each solution. Develop over a path of 18 cm using the lower layer of a mixture of 5 volumes of *concentrated ammonia R*, 15 volumes of *alcohol R* and 80 volumes of *chloroform R*. Examine immediately in ultraviolet light at 254 nm. The principal spot in the chromatogram obtained with the test solution is similar in position and size to the principal spot in the chromatogram obtained with the reference solution.

D. It gives the reaction of non-nitrogen substituted barbiturates (2.3.1).

## TESTS

### Appearance of solution

Dissolve 1.0 g in a mixture of 4 ml of *dilute sodium hydroxide solution R* and 6 ml of *water R*. The solution is clear (2.2.1) and not more intensely coloured than reference solution Y₆ (2.2.2, Method II).

### Acidity

Boil 1.0 g with 50 ml of *water R* for 2 min, allow to cool and filter. To 10 ml of the filtrate add 0.15 ml of *methyl red solution R*. The solution is orange-yellow. Not more than 0.1 ml of *0.1 M sodium hydroxide* is required to produce a pure yellow colour.

### Related substances

Examine by thin-layer chromatography (2.2.27), using *silica gel GF₂₅₄ R* as the coating substance.

*Test solution*   Dissolve 1.0 g of the substance to be examined in *alcohol R* and dilute to 100 ml with the same solvent.

*Reference solution*   Dilute 0.5 ml of the test solution to 100 ml with *alcohol R*.

Apply separately to the plate 20 μl of each solution. Develop over a path of 15 cm using the lower layer of a mixture of 5 volumes of *concentrated ammonia R*, 15 volumes of *alcohol R* and 80 volumes of *chloroform R*. Examine immediately in ultraviolet light at 254 nm. Spray with *diphenylcarbazone mercuric reagent R*. Allow the plate to dry in air and spray with freshly prepared *alcoholic potassium hydroxide solution R* diluted 1 in 5 with *aldehyde-free alcohol R*. Heat at 100 °C to 105 °C for 5 min and examine immediately. When examined in ultraviolet light and after spraying, any spot in the chromatogram obtained with the test solution, apart from the principal spot, is not more intense than the spot in the chromatogram obtained with the reference solution (0.5 per cent).

**Loss on drying** (2.2.32)

Not more than 0.5 per cent, determined on 1.00 g by drying in an oven at 105 °C.

**Sulphated ash** (2.4.14)

Not more than 0.1 per cent, determined on 1.0 g.

## ASSAY

Dissolve 85.0 mg in 5 ml of *pyridine R*. Add 0.5 ml of *thymolphthalein solution R* and 10 ml of *silver nitrate solution in pyridine R*. Titrate with 0.1 M *ethanolic sodium hydroxide* until a pure blue colour is obtained. Carry out a blank titration.

1 ml of *0.1 M ethanolic sodium hydroxide* is equivalent to 9.21 mg of $C_8H_{12}N_2O_3$.

*———— Ph Eur*

# Barium Sulphate

(*Ph Eur monograph 0010*)

BaSO$_4$              233.4              *7727-43-7*

## Action and use
Radio-opaque substance used in the investigation of the gastro-intestinal tract.

## Preparation
Barium Sulphate for Suspension

*Ph Eur ————*

## CHARACTERS

**Appearance**

Fine, white or almost white powder, free from gritty particles.

**Solubility**

Practically insoluble in water and in organic solvents. It is very slightly soluble in acids and in solutions of alkali hydroxides.

## IDENTIFICATION

A. Boil a suspension of 0.2 g with 5 ml of a 500 g/l solution of *sodium carbonate R* for 5 min, add 10 ml of *water R*, filter and acidify a part of the filtrate with *dilute hydrochloric acid R*. The solution gives the reactions of sulphates (*2.3.1*).

B. Wash the residue collected in the preceding test with 3 successive small quantities of *water R*. To the residue add 5 ml of *dilute hydrochloric acid R*, filter and add to the filtrate 0.3 ml of *dilute sulphuric acid R*. A white precipitate is formed that is insoluble in *dilute sodium hydroxide solution R*.

## TESTS

**Solution S**

To 20.0 g add 40 ml of *distilled water R* and 60 ml of *dilute acetic acid R*. Boil for 5 min, filter and dilute the cooled filtrate to 100 ml with *distilled water R*.

**Acidity or alkalinity**

Heat 5.0 g with 20 ml of *carbon dioxide-free water R* on a water-bath for 5 min and filter. To 10 ml of the filtrate add 0.05 ml of *bromothymol blue solution R1*. Not more than 0.5 ml of *0.01 M hydrochloric acid* or *0.01 M sodium hydroxide* is required to change the colour of the indicator.

**Acid-soluble substances**

Maximum 0.3 per cent.

Evaporate 25 ml of solution S to dryness on a water-bath and dry to constant mass at 100-105 °C. The residue weighs a maximum of 15 mg.

**Oxidisable sulphur compounds**

Shake 1.0 g with 5 ml of *water R* for 30 s and filter. To the filtrate add 0.1 ml of *starch solution R*, dissolve 0.1 g of *potassium iodide R* in the mixture, add 1.0 ml of a freshly prepared 3.6 mg/l solution of *potassium iodate R* and 1 ml of *1 M hydrochloric acid* and shake well. The colour of the solution is more intense than that of a standard prepared at the same time and in the same manner, but omitting the potassium iodate.

**Soluble barium salts**

Maximum 10 ppm.

To 2.5 ml of a 0.2 mg/l solution of *barium nitrate R* in a mixture of 30 volumes of *ethanol (96 per cent) R* and 70 ml of *water R*, add 10 ml of *dilute sulphuric acid R*. Shake and allow to stand for 5 min. To 1 ml of this solution, add 10 ml of solution S. Prepare a standard in the same manner using 10 ml of *barium standard solution (2 ppm Ba) R* instead of solution S.

After 10 min, any opalescence in the test solution is not more intense than that in the standard.

**Heavy metals** (2.4.8)

Maximum 10 ppm.

Dilute 10 ml of solution S to 20 ml with *water R*. 12 ml of the solution complies with test A. Prepare the reference solution using *lead standard solution (1 ppm Pb) R*.

**Loss on ignition**

Maximum 2.0 per cent, determined on 1.0 g at 600 ± 50 °C.

*———— Ph Eur*

# Barium Sulphate for Suspension

## Action and use
Radio-opaque preparation used in the investigation of the gastro-intestinal tract.

## Preparation
Barium Sulphate Oral Suspension

## DEFINITION
Barium Sulphate for Suspension is a dry mixture of Barium Sulphate with a suitable dispersing agent and may contain suitable flavours and suitable antimicrobial preservatives.

**Content of barium sulphate, BaSO$_4$**

90.0 to 110.0% of the stated amount.

## CHARACTERISTICS
A fine, white or creamy white powder.

## IDENTIFICATION

A. Ignite 1 g to constant weight. To 0.2 g of the residue add 5 ml of a 50% w/v solution of *sodium carbonate* and boil for 5 minutes. Add 10 ml of *water* and filter. Reserve the residue for test B. Acidify a portion of the filtrate with *2M hydrochloric acid*. The solution yields the reactions characteristic of *sulphates*, Appendix VI.

B. Wash the residue reserved in test A with *water*, add 5 ml of *2M hydrochloric acid*, mix well and filter. Add 0.3 ml of *1M sulphuric acid* to the filtrate. A white precipitate is produced which is insoluble in *2M hydrochloric acid*.

## TESTS

**Acidity or alkalinity**

pH of an aqueous suspension containing the equivalent of 60% w/w of Barium Sulphate or, for lower strengths, the aqueous suspension at the strength of intended use, 3.5 to 8.5, Appendix V L.

**Loss on drying**

When dried at 105° for 4 hours, loses not more than 1.0% of its weight. Use 1 g.

**ASSAY**

To a quantity containing 0.6 g of Barium Sulphate in a platinum dish add 5 g of *sodium carbonate* and 5 g of *potassium carbonate sesquihydrate* and mix. Heat to 1000° and maintain at this temperature for 15 minutes. Allow to cool and suspend the residue in 150 ml of *water*. Wash the dish with 2 ml of *6M acetic acid* and add the washings to the suspension. Cool in ice and decant the supernatant liquid, transferring as little of the solid matter as possible to the filter. Wash the residue with successive quantities of a 2% w/v solution of *sodium carbonate* until the washings are free from sulphate and discard the washings. Add 5 ml of *2M hydrochloric acid* to the filter, wash through into the vessel containing the bulk of the solid matter with *water*, add 5 ml of *hydrochloric acid* and dilute to 100 ml with *water*. Add 10 ml of a 40% w/v solution of *ammonium acetate*, 25 ml of a 10% w/v solution of *potassium dichromate* and 10 g of *urea*. Cover and digest in a hot-air oven at 80° to 85° for 16 hours. Filter whilst still hot through a sintered-glass filter (ISO 4793, porosity grade 4, is suitable), washing the precipitate initially with a 0.5% w/v solution of *potassium dichromate* and finally with 2 ml of *water*. Dry to constant weight at 105°. Each g of the residue is equivalent to 0.9213 g of barium sulphate, $BaSO_4$.

# Anhydrous Beclometasone Dipropionate

*(Ph Eur monograph 0654)*

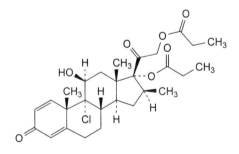

$C_{28}H_{37}ClO_7$       521.1       *5534-09-8*

**Action and use**

Glucocorticoid.

**Preparations**

Beclometasone Cream

Beclometasone Nasal Spray

Beclometasone Ointment

Beclometasone Powder for Inhalation

Beclometasone Pressurised Inhalation

*Ph Eur* _____

**DEFINITION**

9-Chloro-11β-hydroxy-16β-methyl-3,20-dioxopregna-1,4-diene-17,21-diyl dipropanoate.

**Content**

96.0 per cent to 102.0 per cent (dried substance).

**CHARACTERS**

**Appearance**

White or almost white, crystalline powder.

**Solubility**

Practically insoluble in water, freely soluble in acetone, sparingly soluble in ethanol (96 per cent).

**IDENTIFICATION**

A. Infrared absorption spectrophotometry *(2.2.24)*.

*Comparison* anhydrous beclometasone dipropionate CRS.

B. Treat 25 mg by the oxygen-flask method *(2.5.10)*. Use a mixture of 1 ml of *1 M sodium hydroxide* and 20 ml of *water R* to absorb the combustion products. The solution gives reaction (a) of chlorides *(2.3.1)*.

C. Loss on drying (see Tests).

**TESTS**

**Specific optical rotation** *(2.2.7)*

+ 108 to + 115 (dried substance).

Dissolve 0.100 g in *ethanol (96 per cent) R* and dilute to 10.0 ml with the same solvent.

**Related substances**

Liquid chromatography *(2.2.29)*.

*Solvent mixture* Mobile phase A, mobile phase B (45:55 *V/V*).

*Test solution (a)* Dissolve 50.0 mg of the substance to be examined in 28 ml of mobile phase B and dilute to 50.0 ml with mobile phase A.

*Test solution (b)* Dilute 1.0 ml of test solution (a) to 50.0 ml with the solvent mixture.

*Reference solution (a)* Dilute 5.0 ml of test solution (b) to 100.0 ml with the solvent mixture.

*Reference solution (b)* Dissolve 5 mg of *beclometasone dipropionate for system suitability CRS* (containing impurity D) in 3 ml of mobile phase B and dilute to 5 ml with mobile phase A.

*Reference solution (c)* Dissolve 5 mg of *beclometasone dipropionate for peak identification CRS* (containing impurities A, B, C, L and M) in 3 ml of mobile phase B and dilute to 5 ml with mobile phase A. Use 1 ml of this solution to dissolve the contents of a vial of *beclometasone dipropionate impurities F and N CRS*.

*Reference solution (d)* Dissolve 50.0 mg of *anhydrous beclometasone dipropionate CRS* in 28 ml of mobile phase B and dilute to 50.0 ml with mobile phase A. Dilute 1.0 ml of this solution to 50.0 ml with the solvent mixture.

*Column:*

— *size*: l = 0.25 m, Ø = 4.6 mm;

— *stationary phase*: spherical difunctional bonded *end-capped octadecylsilyl silica gel for chromatography R* (5 μm);

— *temperature*: 50 °C.

*Mobile phase:*

— *mobile phase A*: 2.72 g/l solution of *potassium dihydrogen phosphate R* adjusted to pH 2.35 with *phosphoric acid R*;

— *mobile phase B*: *tetrahydrofuran R*, *acetonitrile R*, *methanol R* (5:23:25 *V/V/V*);

| Time (min) | Mobile phase A (per cent V/V) | Mobile phase B (per cent V/V) |
|---|---|---|
| 0 - 4 | 40 | 60 |
| 4 - 12 | 40 → 45 | 60 → 55 |
| 12 - 59 | 45 | 55 |

*Flow rate*   1.4 ml/min.

*Detection*   Spectrophotometer at 254 nm.

*Injection*   20 µl of test solution (a) and reference solutions (a), (b) and (c).

*Identification of impurities*   Use the chromatogram supplied with *beclometasone dipropionate for peak identification CRS* and the chromatogram obtained with reference solution (c) to identify the peaks due to impurities A, B, C, F, L, M and N; use the chromatogram supplied with *beclometasone dipropionate for system suitability CRS* and the chromatogram obtained with reference solution (b) to identify the peak due to impurity D.

*Relative retention*   With reference to beclometasone dipropionate (retention time = about 25 min):
impurity A = about 0.3; impurity B = about 0.6;
impurity D = about 1.1; impurity M = about 1.2;
impurity L = about 1.3; impurity C = about 1.8;
impurity N = about 2.0; impurity F = about 2.2.

*System suitability*   Reference solution (b):
— peak-to-valley ratio: minimum 1.5, where $H_p$ = height above the baseline of the peak due to impurity D and $H_v$ = height above the baseline of the lowest point of the curve separating this peak from the peak due to beclometasone dipropionate.

*Limits:*
— *correction factors*: for the calculation of content, multiply the peak areas of the following impurities by the corresponding correction factor: impurity F = 1.3; impurity M = 2.0;
— *impurity L*: not more than 6 times the area of the principal peak in the chromatogram obtained with reference solution (a) (0.6 per cent);
— *impurities B, F, M*: for each impurity, not more than 5 times the area of the principal peak in the chromatogram obtained with reference solution (a) (0.5 per cent);
— *impurities A, D, N*: for each impurity, not more than twice the area of the principal peak in the chromatogram obtained with reference solution (a) (0.2 per cent);
— *impurity C*: not more than 1.5 times the area of the principal peak in the chromatogram obtained with reference solution (a) (0.15 per cent);
— *unspecified impurities*: for each impurity, not more than the area of the principal peak in the chromatogram obtained with reference solution (a) (0.10 per cent);
— *total*: not more than 15 times the area of the principal peak in the chromatogram obtained with reference solution (a) (1.5 per cent);
— *disregard limit*: 0.5 times the area of the principal peak in the chromatogram obtained with reference solution (a) (0.05 per cent).

**Loss on drying** (2.2.32)
Maximum 0.5 per cent, determined on 1.000 g by drying in an oven at 105 °C for 3 h.

**ASSAY**
Liquid chromatography (2.2.29) as described in the test for related substances with the following modification.

*Injection*   Test solution (b) and reference solution (d).

Calculate the percentage content of $C_{28}H_{37}ClO_7$ from the declared content of *beclometasone dipropionate anhydrous CRS*.

**IMPURITIES**
*Specified impurities*   A, B, C, D, F, L, M, N.

*Other detectable impurities*   (The following substances would, if present at a sufficient level, be detected by one or other of the tests in the monograph. They are limited by the general acceptance criterion for other/unspecified impurities and/or by the general monograph *Substances for pharmaceutical use (2034)*. It is therefore not necessary to identify these impurities for demonstration of compliance. See also *5.10*. *Control of impurities in substances for pharmaceutical use*): E, H, I, J, O, Q, R, S, U, V.

A. R1 = R3 = H, R2 = Cl, R4 = CO-C₂H₅: 9-chloro-11β,17-dihydroxy-16β-methyl-3,20-dioxopregna-1,4-dien-21-yl propanoate (beclometasone 21-propionate),

B. R1 = H, R2 = Cl, R3 = CO-C₂H₅, R4 = CO-CH₃: 21-(acetyloxy)-9-chloro-11β-hydroxy-16β-methyl-3,20-dioxopregna-1,4-dien-17-yl propanoate (beclometasone 21-acetate 17-propionate),

C. R1 = H, R2 = Cl, R3 = CO-C₂H₅, R4 = CO-CH₂-CH₂-CH₃: 9-chloro-11β-hydroxy-16β-methyl-3,20-dioxo-17-(propanoyloxy)-pregna-1,4-dien-21-yl butanoate (beclometasone 21-butyrate 17-propionate),

D. R1 = H, R2 = Br, R3 = R4 = CO-C₂H₅: 9-bromo-11β-hydroxy-16β-methyl-3,20-dioxopregna-1,4-diene-17,21-diyl dipropanoate,

F. R1 = Br, R2 = Cl, R3 = R4 = CO-C₂H₅: 6α-bromo-9-chloro-11β-hydroxy-16β-methyl-3,20-dioxopregna-1,4-diene-17,21-diyl dipropanoate,

E. R1 = Cl, R2 = CO-C₂H₅: 6α,9-dichloro-11β-hydroxy-16β-methyl-3,20-dioxopregna-1,4-diene-17,21-diyl dipropanoate,

H. R1 = R2 = H: 9-chloro-11β,21-dihydroxy-16β-methyl-3,20-dioxopregna-1,4-dien-17-yl propanoate (beclometasone 17-propionate),

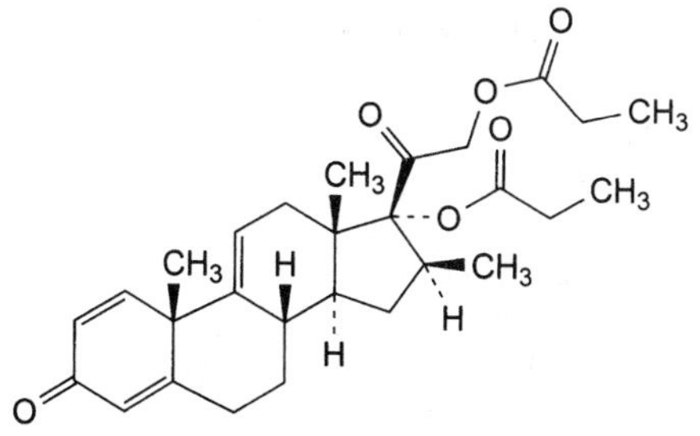

I. 16β-methyl-3,20-dioxopregna-1,4,9(11)-triene-17,21-diyl dipropanoate,

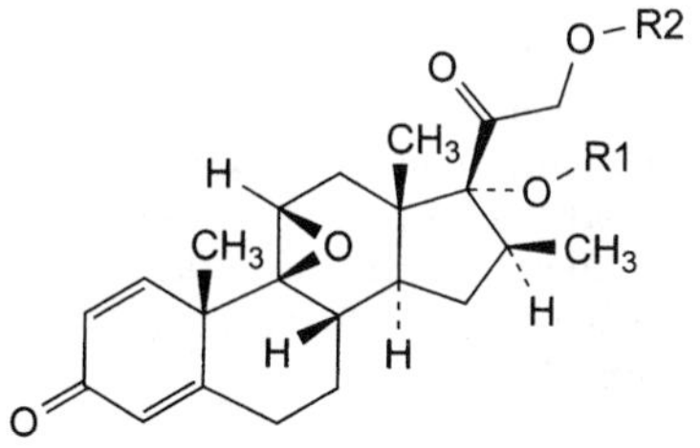

J. R1 = R2 = CO-C₂H₅: 9,11β-epoxy-16β-methyl-3,20-dioxo-9β-pregna-1,4-diene-17,21-diyl dipropanoate,

R. R1 = R2 = H: 9,11β-epoxy-17,21-dihydroxy-16β-methyl-9β-pregna-1,4-diene-3,20-dione,

U. R1 = H, R2 = CO-C₂H₅: 9,11β-epoxy-21-hydroxy-16β-methyl-3,20-dioxo-9β-pregna-1,4-dien-17-yl propanoate,

V. R1 = CO-C₂H₅, R2 = H: 9,11β-epoxy-17-hydroxy-16β-methyl-3,20-dioxo-9β-pregna-1,4-dien-21-yl propanoate,

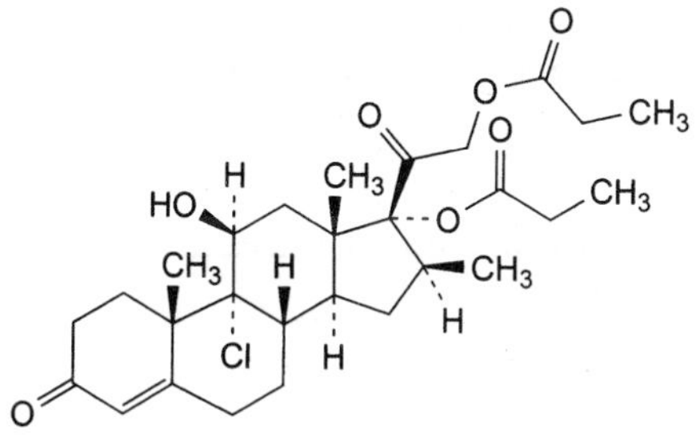

L. 9-chloro-11β-hydroxy-16β-methyl-3,20-dioxopregn-4-ene-17,21-diyl dipropanoate,

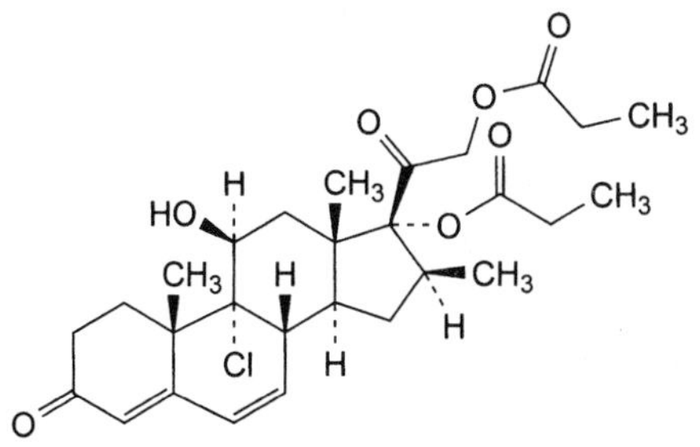

M. 9-chloro-11β-hydroxy-16β-methyl-3,20-dioxopregna-4,6-diene-17,21-diyl dipropanoate,

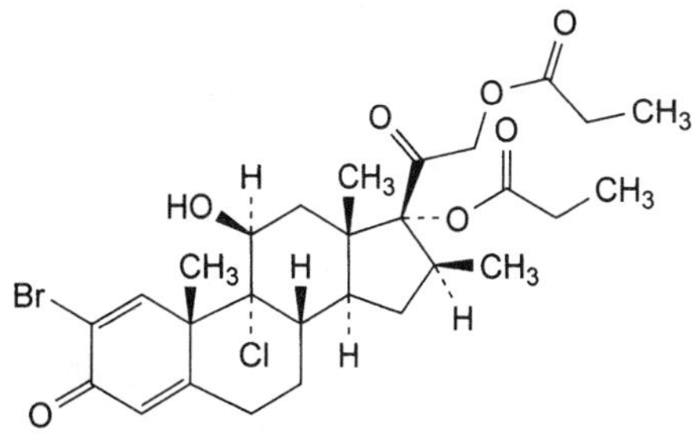

N. 2-bromo-9-chloro-11β-hydroxy-16β-methyl-3,20-dioxopregna-1,4-diene-17,21-diyl dipropanoate,

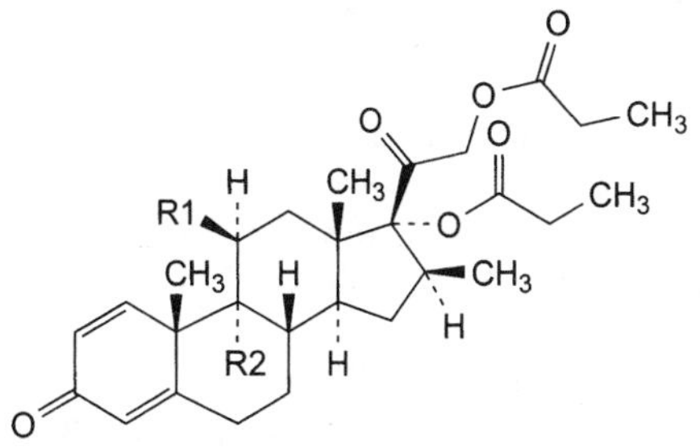

O. R1 = R2 = Cl: 9,11β-dichloro-16β-methyl-3,20-dioxopregna-1,4-diene-17,21-diyl dipropanoate,

Q. R1 = R2 = H: 16β-methyl-3,20-dioxopregna-1,4-diene-17,21-diyl dipropanoate,

S. R1 = O-CO-C₂H₅, R2 = Cl: 9-chloro-16β-methyl-3,20-dioxopregna-1,4-diene-11β,17,21-triyl tripropanoate (beclometasone tripropionate).

*Ph Eur*

# Beclometasone Dipropionate Monohydrate

(*Ph Eur monograph 1709*)

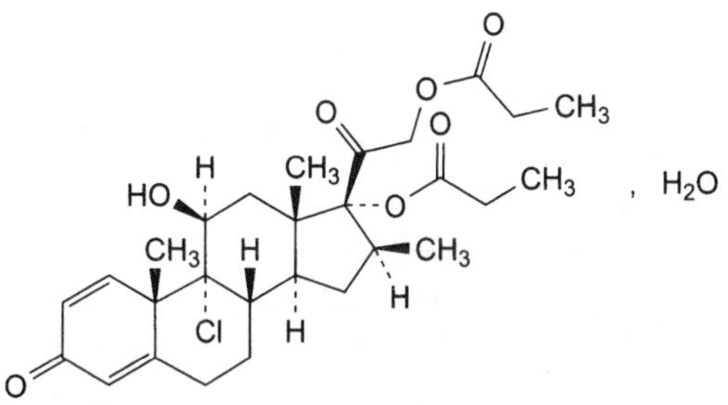

C₂₈H₃₇ClO₇,H₂O          539.1          *5534-09-8*

**Action and use**
Glucocorticoid.

*Ph Eur*

**DEFINITION**
9-Chloro-11β-hydroxy-16β-methyl-3,20-dioxopregna-1,4-diene-17,21-diyl dipropanoate monohydrate.

**Content**
97.0 per cent to 102.0 per cent (dried substance).

## CHARACTERS

### Appearance

White or almost white powder.

### Solubility

Practically insoluble in water, freely soluble in acetone, sparingly soluble in ethanol (96 per cent).

## IDENTIFICATION

A. Infrared absorption spectrophotometry (2.2.24).

*Comparison* beclometasone dipropionate monohydrate CRS.

B. Treat 25 mg by the oxygen-flask method (2.5.10). Use a mixture of 1 ml of *1 M sodium hydroxide* and 20 ml of *water R* to absorb the combustion products. The solution gives reaction (a) of chlorides (2.3.1).

C. Loss on drying (see Tests).

## TESTS

### Specific optical rotation (2.2.7)

+ 108 to + 115 (dried substance).

Dissolve 0.100 g in *ethanol (96 per cent) R* and dilute to 10.0 ml with the same solvent.

### Related substances

Liquid chromatography (2.2.29).

*Solvent mixture* Mobile phase A, mobile phase B (45:55 V/V).

*Test solution (a)* Dissolve 50.0 mg of the substance to be examined in 28 ml of mobile phase B and dilute to 50.0 ml with mobile phase A.

*Test solution (b)* Dilute 1.0 ml of test solution (a) to 50.0 ml with the solvent mixture.

*Reference solution (a)* Dilute 5.0 ml of test solution (b) to 100.0 ml with the solvent mixture.

*Reference solution (b)* Dissolve 5 mg of *beclometasone dipropionate for system suitability CRS* (containing impurity D) in 3 ml of mobile phase B and dilute to 5 ml with mobile phase A.

*Reference solution (c)* Dissolve 5 mg of *beclometasone dipropionate for peak identification CRS* (containing impurities B, C and L) in 3 ml of mobile phase B and dilute to 5 ml with mobile phase A. Use 1 ml of this solution to dissolve the contents of a vial of *beclometasone dipropionate impurities F and N CRS*.

*Reference solution (d)* Dissolve 50.0 mg of *beclometasone dipropionate anhydrous CRS* in 28 ml of mobile phase B and dilute to 50.0 ml with mobile phase A. Dilute 1.0 ml of this solution to 50.0 ml with the solvent mixture.

*Column:*
— *size:* $l = 0.25$ m, $\emptyset = 4.6$ mm;
— *stationary phase:* spherical difunctional bonded *end-capped octadecylsilyl silica gel for chromatography R* (5 μm);
— *temperature:* 50 °C.

*Mobile phase:*
— *mobile phase A:* 2.72 g/l solution of *potassium dihydrogen phosphate R* adjusted to pH 2.35 with *phosphoric acid R*;
— *mobile phase B:* tetrahydrofuran R, acetonitrile R, methanol R (5:23:25 V/V/V);

| Time (min) | Mobile phase A (per cent V/V) | Mobile phase B (per cent V/V) |
|---|---|---|
| 0 - 4 | 40 | 60 |
| 4 - 12 | 40 → 45 | 60 → 55 |
| 12 - 59 | 45 | 55 |

*Flow rate* 1.4 ml/min.

*Detection* Spectrophotometer at 254 nm.

*Injection* 20 μl of test solution (a) and reference solutions (a), (b) and (c).

*Identification of impurities* Use the chromatogram supplied with *beclometasone dipropionate for peak identification CRS* and the chromatogram obtained with reference solution (c) to identify the peaks due to impurities B, C, F and L; use the chromatogram supplied with *beclometasone dipropionate for system suitability CRS* and the chromatogram obtained with reference solution (b) to identify the peak due to impurity D.

*Relative retention* With reference to beclometasone dipropionate (retention time = about 25 min):
impurity B = about 0.6; impurity D = about 1.1;
impurity L = about 1.3; impurity C = about 1.8;
impurity F = about 2.2.

*System suitability* Reference solution (b):
— *peak-to-valley ratio:* minimum 1.5, where $H_p$ = height above the baseline of the peak due to impurity D and $H_v$ = height above the baseline of the lowest point of the curve separating this peak from the peak due to beclometasone dipropionate.

*Limits:*
— *correction factor:* for the calculation of content, multiply the peak area of impurity F by 1.3;
— *impurity B:* not more than 5 times the area of the principal peak in the chromatogram obtained with reference solution (a) (0.5 per cent);
— *impurities C, F, L:* for each impurity, not more than 1.5 times the area of the principal peak in the chromatogram obtained with reference solution (a) (0.15 per cent);
— *unspecified impurities:* for each impurity, not more than the area of the principal peak in the chromatogram obtained with reference solution (a) (0.10 per cent);
— *total:* not more than 10 times the area of the principal peak in the chromatogram obtained with reference solution (a) (1.0 per cent);
— *disregard limit:* 0.5 times the area of the principal peak in the chromatogram obtained with reference solution (a) (0.05 per cent).

### Loss on drying (2.2.32)

2.8 per cent to 3.8 per cent, determined on 1.000 g by drying in an oven at 105 °C for 3 h.

## ASSAY

Liquid chromatography (2.2.29) as described in the test for related substances with the following modification.

*Injection* Test solution (b) and reference solution (d).

Calculate the percentage content of $C_{28}H_{37}ClO_7$ from the declared content of *anhydrous beclometasone dipropionate CRS*.

## IMPURITIES

*Specified impurities* B, C, F, L.

*Other detectable impurities* (The following substances would, if present at a sufficient level, be detected by one or other of the tests in the monograph. They are limited by the general acceptance criterion for other/unspecified impurities and/or by the general monograph *Substances for pharmaceutical use (2034)*. It is therefore not necessary to identify these impurities for demonstration of compliance. See also *5.10. Control of impurities in substances for pharmaceutical use*): A, D, E, H, I, J, M, N, O, Q, R, S, U, V.

I. 16β-methyl-3,20-dioxopregna-1,4,9(11)-triene-17,21-diyl dipropanoate,

A. R1 = R3 = H, R2 = Cl, R4 = CO-C$_2$H$_5$: 9-chloro-11β,17-dihydroxy-16β-methyl-3,20-dioxopregna-1,4-dien-21-yl propanoate (beclometasone 21-propionate),

D. R1 = H, R2 = Br, R3 = R4 = CO-C$_2$H$_5$: 9-bromo-11β-hydroxy-16β-methyl-3,20-dioxopregna-1,4-diene-17,21-diyl dipropanoate,

E. R1 = R2 = Cl, R3 = R4 = CO-C$_2$H$_5$: 6α,9-dichloro-11β-hydroxy-16β-methyl-3,20-dioxopregna-1,4-diene-17,21-diyl dipropanoate,

H. R1 = R4 = H, R2 = Cl, R3 = CO-C$_2$H$_5$: 9-chloro-11β,21-dihydroxy-16β-methyl-3,20-dioxopregna-1,4-dien-17-yl propanoate (beclometasone 17-propionate),

J. R1 = R2 = CO-C$_2$H$_5$: 9,11β-epoxy-16β-methyl-3,20-dioxo-9β-pregna-1,4-diene-17,21-diyl dipropanoate,

R. R1 = R2 = H: 9,11β-epoxy-17,21-dihydroxy-16β-methyl-9β-pregna-1,4-diene-3,20-dione,

U. R1 = H, R2 = CO-C$_2$H$_5$: 9,11β-epoxy-21-hydroxy-16β-methyl-3,20-dioxo-9β-pregna-1,4-dien-17-yl propanoate,

V. R1 = CO-C$_2$H$_5$, R2 = H: 9,11β-epoxy-17-hydroxy-16β-methyl-3,20-dioxo-9β-pregna-1,4-dien-21-yl propanoate,

B. R1 = H, R2 = CO-CH$_3$: 21-(acetyloxy)-9-chloro-11β-hydroxy-16β-methyl-3,20-dioxopregna-1,4-dien-17-yl propanoate (beclometasone 21-acetate 17-propionate),

C. R1 = H, R2 = CO-CH$_2$-CH$_2$-CH$_3$: 9-chloro-11β-hydroxy-16β-methyl-3,20-dioxo-17-(propanoyloxy)-pregna-1,4-dien-21-yl butanoate (beclometasone 21-butyrate 17-propionate),

F. R1 = Br, R2 = CO-C$_2$H$_5$: 6α-bromo-9-chloro-11β-hydroxy-16β-methyl-3,20-dioxopregna-1,4-diene-17,21-diyl dipropanoate,

L. 9-chloro-11β-hydroxy-16β-methyl-3,20-dioxopregn-4-ene-17,21-diyl dipropanoate,

M. 9-chloro-11β-hydroxy-16β-methyl-3,20-dioxopregna-4,6-diene-17,21-diyl dipropanoate,

N. R1 = Br, R2 = OH, R3 = Cl:
2-bromo-9-chloro-11β-hydroxy-16β-methyl-3,20-
dioxopregna-1,4-diene-17,21-diyl dipropanoate,

O. R1 = H, R2 = R3 = Cl: 9,11β-dichloro-16β-methyl-
3,20-dioxopregna-1,4-diene-17,21-diyl dipropanoate,

Q. R1 = R2 = R3 = H: 16β-methyl-3,20-dioxopregna-1,4-
diene-17,21-diyl dipropanoate,

S. R1 = H, R2 = O-CO-C₂H₅, R3 = Cl: 9-chloro-16β-
methyl-3,20-dioxopregna-1,4-diene-11β,17,21-triyl
tripropanoate (beclometasone tripropionate).

*Ph Eur*

# White Beeswax

(*Ph Eur monograph 0069*)

**Action and use**
Excipient.

*Ph Eur*

## DEFINITION
Wax obtained by bleaching yellow beeswax.

## CHARACTERS
**Appearance**
White or yellowish-white pieces or plates, translucent when
thin, with a fine-grained, matt and non-crystalline fracture;
when warmed in the hand they become soft and malleable.

It has an odour similar to that of yellow beeswax, though
fainter and never rancid. It is tasteless and does not stick to
the teeth.

**Solubility**
Practically insoluble in water, partially soluble in hot ethanol
(90 per cent *V/V*) and completely soluble in fatty and
essential oils.

**Relative density**
About 0.960.

## TESTS
**Drop point** (*2.2.17*)
61 °C to 66 °C.

Melt the beeswax by heating on a water-bath, pour onto a
glass plate and allow to cool to a semi-solid mass. Fill the
metal cup by inserting the wider end into the beeswax and
repeating the procedure until beeswax extrudes from the
narrow opening. Remove the excess with a spatula and insert
the thermometer immediately. Remove the beeswax
displaced. Allow to stand at room temperature for at least
12 h before determining the drop point.

**Acid value**
17.0 to 24.0.

To 2.00 g (m g), in a 250 ml conical flask fitted with a reflux
condenser, add 40 ml of *xylene R* and a few glass beads. Heat

until the substance is dissolved. Add 20 ml of *ethanol
(96 per cent) R* and 0.5 ml of *phenolphthalein solution R1* and
titrate the hot solution with *0.5 M alcoholic potassium
hydroxide* until a red colour persists for at least 10 s ($n_1$ ml).
Carry out a blank test ($n_2$ ml).

$$\text{Acid value} = \frac{28.05\,(n_1 - n_2)}{m}$$

**Ester value** (*2.5.2*)
70 to 80.

**Saponification value**
87 to 104.

To 2.00 g (m g), in a 250 ml conical flask fitted with a reflux
condenser, add 30 ml of a mixture of equal volumes of
*ethanol (96 per cent) R* and *xylene R* and a few glass beads.
Heat until the substance is dissolved. Add 25.0 ml of 0.5 M
*alcoholic potassium hydroxide* and heat under a reflux
condenser for 3 h. Titrate the hot solution immediately with
*0.5 M hydrochloric acid*, using 1 ml of *phenolphthalein
solution R1* as indicator ($n_1$ ml). Reheat the solution to
boiling several times during the course of the titration. Carry
out a blank test ($n_2$ ml).

$$\text{Saponification value} = \frac{28.05\,(n_2 - n_1)}{m}$$

**Ceresin, paraffins and certain other waxes**
To 3.0 g, in a 100 ml round-bottomed flask, add 30 ml of a
40 g/l solution of *potassium hydroxide R* in *aldehyde-free
alcohol R* and boil gently under a reflux condenser for 2 h.
Remove the condenser and immediately insert a
thermometer. Place the flask in a water-bath at 80 °C and
allow to cool, swirling the solution continuously. No
precipitate is formed until 65 °C, although the solution may
be slightly opalescent. Beginning at 65 °C, the solution may
become cloudy and precipitates may be formed. At 59 °C,
the solution is cloudy.

**Glycerol and other polyols**
Maximum 0.5 per cent *m/m*, calculated as glycerol.

To 0.20 g add 10 ml of *alcoholic potassium hydroxide
solution R* and heat on a water-bath under a reflux condenser
for 30 min. Add 50 ml of *dilute sulphuric acid R*, cool and
filter. Rinse the flask and the filter with *dilute sulphuric acid R*.
Combine the filtrate and washings and dilute to 100.0 ml
with *dilute sulphuric acid R*. Place 1.0 ml of the solution in a
test-tube, add 0.5 ml of a 10.7 g/l solution of *sodium
periodate R*, mix and allow to stand for 5 min. Add 1.0 ml of
*decolorised fuchsin solution R* and mix. Any precipitate
disappears. Place the tube in a beaker containing water at
40 °C. During cooling observe for 10-15 min. Any violet-
blue colour in the solution is not more intense than that in a
standard prepared at the same time and in the same manner
using 1.0 ml of a 10 mg/l solution of *glycerol R* in *dilute
sulphuric acid R*.

*Ph Eur*

# Yellow Beeswax

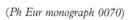

(*Ph Eur monograph 0070*)

**Action and use**

Excipient.

*Ph Eur*

## DEFINITION

Wax obtained by melting the walls of the honeycomb made by the honey-bee, *Apis mellifera* L., with hot water and removing foreign matter.

## CHARACTERS

**Appearance**

Yellow or light brown pieces or plates with a fine-grained, matt and non-crystalline fracture; when warmed in the hand they become soft and malleable.

It has a faint odour, characteristic of honey. It is tasteless and does not stick to the teeth.

**Solubility**

Practically insoluble in water, partially soluble in hot ethanol (90 per cent *V/V*) and completely soluble in fatty and essential oils.

Relative density: about 0.960.

## TESTS

**Drop point** (*2.2.17*)

61 °C to 66 °C.

Melt the beeswax by heating on a water-bath, pour onto a glass plate and allow to cool to a semi-solid mass. Fill the metal cup by inserting the wider end into the beeswax and repeating the procedure until beeswax extrudes from the narrow opening. Remove the excess with a spatula and insert the thermometer immediately. Remove the beeswax displaced. Allow to stand at room temperature for at least 12 h before determining the drop point.

**Acid value**

17.0 to 22.0.

To 2.00 g (*m* g), in a 250 ml conical flask fitted with a reflux condenser, add 40 ml of *xylene R* and a few glass beads. Heat until the substance is dissolved. Add 20 ml of *ethanol (96 per cent) R* and 0.5 ml of *phenolphthalein solution R1* and titrate the hot solution with *0.5 M alcoholic potassium hydroxide* until a red colour persists for at least 10 s ($n_1$ ml). Carry out a blank test ($n_2$ ml).

$$\text{Acid value} = \frac{28.05\,(n_1 - n_2)}{m}$$

**Ester value** (*2.5.2*)

70 to 80.

**Saponification value**

87 to 102.

To 2.00 g (*m* g), in a 250 ml conical flask fitted with a reflux condenser, add 30 ml of a mixture of equal volumes of *ethanol (96 per cent) R* and *xylene R* and a few glass beads. Heat until the substance is dissolved. Add 25.0 ml of *0.5 M alcoholic potassium hydroxide* and heat under a reflux condenser for 3 h. Titrate the hot solution immediately with *0.5 M hydrochloric acid*, using 1 ml of *phenolphthalein solution R1* as indicator ($n_1$ ml). Reheat the solution to boiling several times during the course of the titration. Carry out a blank test ($n_2$ ml).

$$\text{Saponification value} = \frac{28.05\,(n_2 - n_1)}{m}$$

**Ceresin, paraffins and certain other waxes**

To 3.0 g, in a 100 ml round-bottomed flask, add 30 ml of a 40 g/l solution of *potassium hydroxide R* in *aldehyde-free alcohol R* and boil gently under a reflux condenser for 2 h. Remove the condenser and immediately insert a thermometer. Place the flask in a water-bath at 80 °C and allow to cool, swirling the solution continuously. No precipitate is formed until 65 °C, although the solution may be slightly opalescent. Beginning at 65 °C, the solution may become cloudy and precipitates may be formed. At 59 °C, the solution is cloudy.

**Glycerol and other polyols**

Maximum 0.5 per cent *m/m*, calculated as glycerol.

To 0.20 g add 10 ml of *alcoholic potassium hydroxide solution R* and heat on a water-bath under a reflux condenser for 30 min. Add 50 ml of *dilute sulphuric acid R*, cool and filter. Rinse the flask and the filter with *dilute sulphuric acid R*. Combine the filtrate and washings and dilute to 100.0 ml with *dilute sulphuric acid R*. Place 1.0 ml of the solution in a test-tube, add 0.5 ml of a 10.7 g/l solution of *sodium periodate R*, mix and allow to stand for 5 min. Add 1.0 ml of *decolorised fuchsin solution R* and mix. Any precipitate disappears. Place the tube in a beaker containing water at 40 °C. During cooling observe for 10-15 min. Any violet-blue colour in the solution is not more intense than that in a standard prepared at the same time and in the same manner using 1.0 ml of a 10 mg/l solution of *glycerol R* in *dilute sulphuric acid R*.

*Ph Eur*

# Benazepril Hydrochloride

(*Ph Eur monograph 2388*)

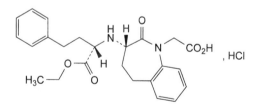

$C_{24}H_{29}ClN_2O_5$       461.0       *86541-74-4*

**Action and use**

Angiotensin converting enzyme inhibitor.

*Ph Eur*

## DEFINITION

[(3*S*)-3-[[(1*S*)-1-(Ethoxycarbonyl)-3-phenylpropyl]amino]-2-oxo-2,3,4,5-tetrahydro-1*H*-1-benzazepin-1-yl]acetic acid hydrochloride.

**Content**

97.5 per cent to 102.0 per cent (dried substance).

## CHARACTERS

**Appearance**

White or almost white, crystalline powder.

**Solubility**

Slightly soluble in water, freely soluble in anhydrous ethanol, very slightly soluble in ethyl acetate, practically insoluble in cyclohexane.

It shows polymorphism (5.9).

**IDENTIFICATION**

Carry out either tests A, B, D or tests B, C, D.

A. Specific optical rotation (2.2.7): − 136 to − 141 (dried substance).

Dissolve 1.000 g in *anhydrous ethanol R* and dilute to 50.0 ml with the same solvent.

B. Infrared absorption spectrophotometry (2.2.24).

*Comparison*   benazepril hydrochloride CRS.

If the spectra obtained in the solid state show differences, dissolve the substance to be examined and the reference substance separately in *methanol R*, evaporate to dryness and record new spectra using the residues.

C. Enantiomeric purity (see Tests).

D. It gives reaction (a) of chlorides (2.3.1).

**TESTS**

**Related substances**

Liquid chromatography (2.2.29).

*Test solution (a)*   Dissolve 50.0 mg of the substance to be examined in the mobile phase and dilute to 50.0 ml with the mobile phase.

*Test solution (b)*   Dilute 10.0 ml of test solution (a) to 100.0 ml with the mobile phase.

*Reference solution (a)*   Dissolve 50.0 mg of *benazepril hydrochloride CRS* in the mobile phase and dilute to 50.0 ml with the mobile phase. Dilute 10.0 ml of this solution to 100.0 ml with the mobile phase.

*Reference solution (b)*   Dissolve the contents of a vial of *benazepril for system suitability CRS* (containing impurities B, C, D, E, F and G) in 1.0 ml of test solution (a).

*Reference solution (c)*   Dilute 1.0 ml of reference solution (a) to 50.0 ml with the mobile phase.

*Column:*
— *size: l* = 0.30 m, Ø = 3.9 mm;
— *stationary phase: end-capped octadecylsilyl silica gel for chromatography R* (10 μm).

*Mobile phase*   Add 0.2 ml of *glacial acetic acid R* to 1000 ml of a mixture of 360 volumes of *water R* and 640 volumes of *methanol R2*; add 0.81 g of *tetrabutylammonium bromide R* and stir to dissolve.

*Flow rate*   1.0 ml/min.

*Detection*   Spectrophotometer at 240 nm.

*Injection*   25 μl of test solution (a) and reference solutions (b) and (c).

*Run time*   3 times the retention time of benazepril.

*Relative retention*   With reference to benazepril (retention time = about 6 min): impurity E = about 0.3; impurity F = about 0.4; impurity C = about 0.5; impurity B = about 1.8; impurity D = about 2.0; impurity G = about 2.5.

*Identification of impurities*   Use the chromatogram supplied with *benazepril for system suitability CRS* and the chromatogram obtained with reference solution (b) to identify the peaks due to impurities B, C, D, E, F and G.

*System suitability*   Reference solution (b):

— *resolution*: minimum 2.5 between the peaks due to benazepril and impurity B and minimum 1.5 between the peaks due to impurities E and F.

*Limits:*

— *correction factors*: for the calculation of content, multiply the peak areas of the following impurities by the corresponding correction factor: impurity E = 0.5; impurity F = 0.7;

— *impurity B*: not more than 2.5 times the area of the principal peak in the chromatogram obtained with reference solution (c) (0.5 per cent);

— *impurity C*: not more than 1.5 times the area of the principal peak in the chromatogram obtained with reference solution (c) (0.3 per cent);

— *impurities D, E, F, G*: for each impurity, not more than the area of the principal peak in the chromatogram obtained with reference solution (c) (0.2 per cent);

— *unspecified impurities*: for each impurity, not more than 0.5 times the area of the principal peak in the chromatogram obtained with reference solution (c) (0.10 per cent);

— *total*: not more than 10 times the area of the principal peak in the chromatogram obtained with reference solution (c) (2.0 per cent);

— *disregard limit*: 0.25 times the area of the principal peak in the chromatogram obtained with reference solution (c) (0.05 per cent).

**Enantiomeric purity**

Liquid chromatography (2.2.29).

*Buffer solution pH 6.0*   Dissolve 3.58 g of *disodium hydrogen phosphate R* and 9.66 g of *potassium dihydrogen phosphate R* in *water R* and dilute to 1000.0 ml with the same solvent.

*Test solution*   Dissolve 50.0 mg of the substance to be examined in the mobile phase and dilute to 50.0 ml with the mobile phase.

*Reference solution (a)*   Dissolve 5.0 mg of *benazepril impurity A CRS* in the mobile phase and dilute to 50.0 ml with the mobile phase.

*Reference solution (b)*   Dilute 1.0 ml of reference solution (a) to 100.0 ml with the mobile phase.

*Reference solution (c)*   Dilute 1.0 ml of reference solution (a) to 10.0 ml with the mobile phase. Dilute 1.0 ml of this solution to 10.0 ml with the test solution.

*Column:*
— *size: l* = 0.10 m, Ø = 4.0 mm;
— *stationary phase*: spherical *silica gel AGP for chiral chromatography R* (5 μm);
— *temperature*: 30 °C.

*Mobile phase*   methanol R2, buffer solution pH 6.0 (20:80 V/V).

*Flow rate*   0.9 ml/min.

*Detection*   Spectrophotometer at 240 nm.

*Injection*   50 μl of the test solution and reference solutions (b) and (c).

*Run time*   3.5 times the retention time of benazepril.

*Relative retention*   With reference to benazepril (retention time = about 6 min): impurity A = about 1.9.

*System suitability*   Reference solution (c):

— *peak-to-valley ratio*: minimum 2.5, where $H_p$ = height above the baseline of the peak due to impurity A and $H_v$ = height above the baseline of the lowest point of the curve separating this peak from the peak due to benazepril.

*Limit:*

— *impurity A*: not more than the area of the corresponding peak in the chromatogram obtained with reference solution (b) (0.1 per cent).

**Heavy metals** *(2.4.8)*

Maximum 20 ppm.

1.0 g complies with test C. Prepare the reference solution using 2 ml of *lead standard solution (10 ppm Pb) R*.

**Loss on drying** *(2.2.32)*

Maximum 0.50 per cent, determined on 1.000 g by drying *in vacuo* at 105 °C for 3 h.

**Sulphated ash** *(2.4.14)*

Maximum 0.1 per cent, determined on 1.0 g.

**ASSAY**

Liquid chromatography *(2.2.29)* as described in the test for related substances with the following modification.

*Injection*   Test solution (b) and reference solution (a).

Calculate the percentage content of $C_{24}H_{29}ClN_2O_5$ from the declared content of *benazepril hydrochloride CRS*.

**STORAGE**

Protected from light.

**IMPURITIES**

*Specified impurities*   *A, B, C, D, E, F, G.*

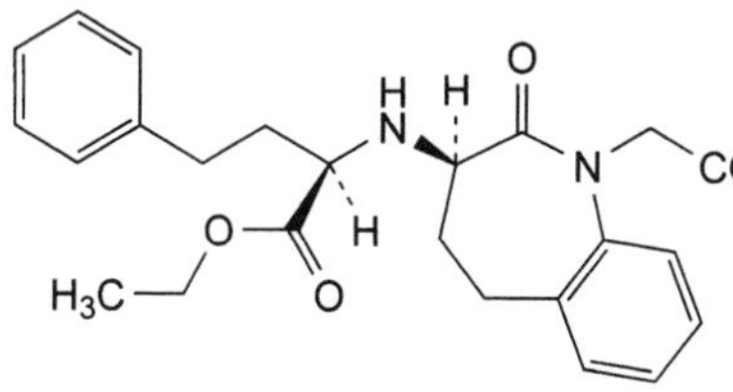

A. [(3*R*)-3-[[(1*R*)-1-(ethoxycarbonyl)-3-phenylpropyl]amino]-2-oxo-2,3,4,5-tetrahydro-1*H*-1-benzazepin-1-yl]acetic acid,

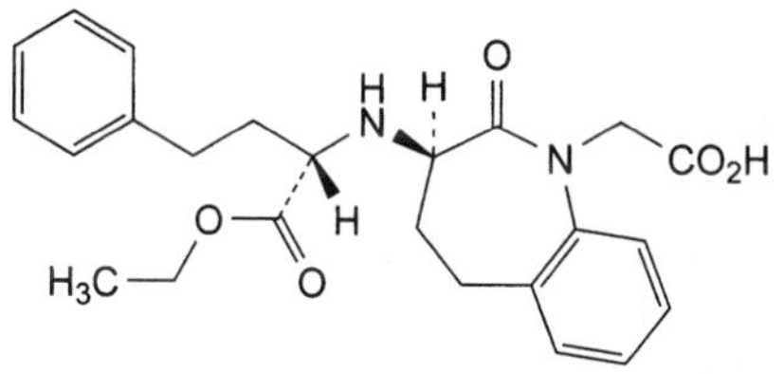

B. [(3*RS*)-3-[[(1*SR*)-1-(ethoxycarbonyl)-3-phenylpropyl]amino]-2-oxo-2,3,4,5-tetrahydro-1*H*-1-benzazepin-1-yl]acetic acid,

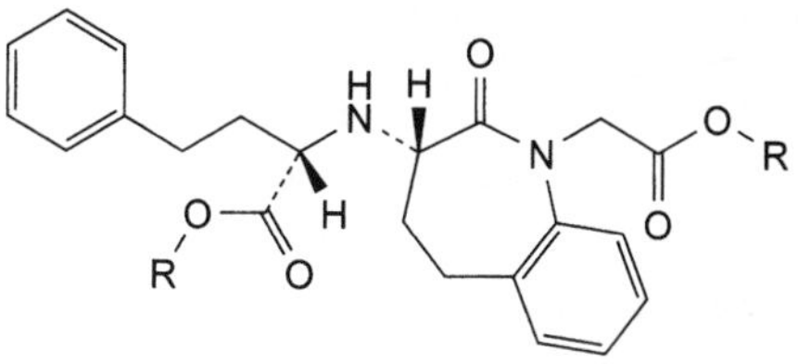

C. R = H: (2*S*)-2-[[(3*S*)-1-(carboxymethyl)-2-oxo-2,3,4,5-tetrahydro-1*H*-1-benzazepin-3-yl]amino]-4-phenylbutanoic acid,

G. R = $C_2H_5$: ethyl (2*S*)-2-[[(3*S*)-1-(2-ethoxy-2-oxoethyl)-2-oxo-2,3,4,5-tetrahydro-1*H*-1-benzazepin-3-yl]amino]-4-phenylbutanoate,

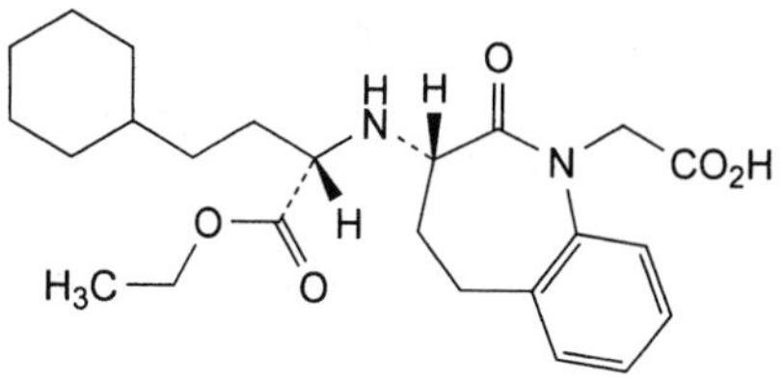

D. [(3*S*)-3-[[(1*S*)-3-cyclohexyl-1-(ethoxycarbonyl)propyl]amino]-2-oxo-2,3,4,5-tetrahydro-1*H*-1-benzazepin-1-yl]acetic acid,

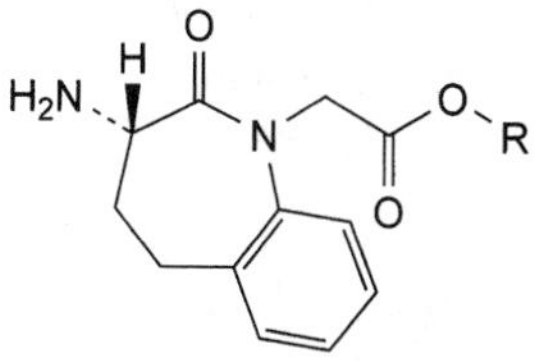

E. R = H: [(3*S*)-3-amino-2-oxo-2,3,4,5-tetrahydro-1*H*-1-benzazepin-1-yl]acetic acid,

F. R = $C(CH_3)_3$: 1,1-dimethylethyl [(3*S*)-3-amino-2-oxo-2,3,4,5-tetrahydro-1*H*-1-benzazepin-1-yl]acetate.

*Ph Eur*

# Bendroflumethiazide

*(Ph Eur monograph 0370)*

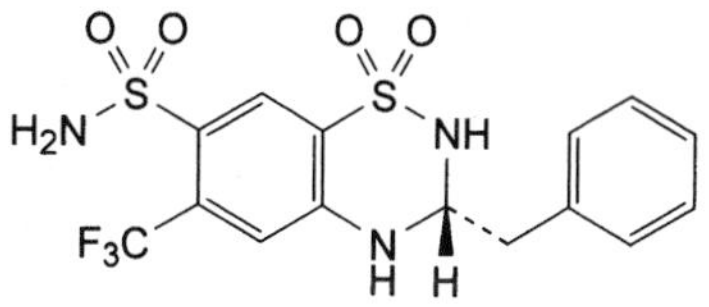

and enantiomer

$C_{15}H_{14}F_3N_3O_4S_2$     421.4     *73-48-3*

**Action and use**

Thiazide diuretic.

**Preparation**

Bendroflumethiazide Tablets

*Ph Eur*

**DEFINITION**

(3*RS*)-3-Benzyl-6-(trifluoromethyl)-3,4-dihydro-2*H*-1,2,4-benzothiadiazine-7-sulphonamide 1,1-dioxide.

**Content**

98.0 per cent to 102.0 per cent (dried substance).

**CHARACTERS**

**Appearance**

White or almost white, crystalline powder.

**Solubility**

Practically insoluble in water, freely soluble in acetone, soluble in ethanol (96 per cent).

**IDENTIFICATION**

Infrared absorption spectrophotometry *(2.2.24)*.

*Comparison*   bendroflumethiazide CRS.

**TESTS**

**Related substances**

Liquid chromatography *(2.2.29)*.

*Prepare the solutions immediately before use.*

*Solvent mixture* Mix 40 volumes of *methanol R* and 60 volumes of a 2.0 g/l solution of *citric acid R*.

*Test solution* Dissolve 10.0 mg of the substance to be examined in the solvent mixture and dilute to 50.0 ml with the solvent mixture.

*Reference solution (a)* Dissolve 2 mg of *bendroflumethiazide impurity A CRS* and 2.5 mg of *altizide CRS* in the solvent mixture and dilute to 10 ml with the solvent mixture. Mix 1 ml of this solution with 1 ml of the test solution and dilute to 100 ml with the solvent mixture.

*Reference solution (b)* Dilute 1.0 ml of the test solution to 100.0 ml with the solvent mixture. Dilute 1.0 ml of this solution to 10.0 ml with the solvent mixture.

*Column:*
— *size*: $l = 0.15$ m, $\varnothing = 3.0$ mm;
— *stationary phase*: end-capped octadecylsilyl silica gel for chromatography R (5 μm);
— *temperature*: 40 °C.

*Mobile phase* Mix 15 volumes of *tetrahydrofuran R*, 25 volumes of *methanol R* and 60 volumes of a 2.0 g/l solution of *citric acid R*.

*Flow rate* 0.8 ml/min.

*Detection* Spectrophotometer at 273 nm.

*Injection* 20 μl.

*Run time* Twice the retention time of bendroflumethiazide.

*Relative retention* With reference to bendroflumethiazide (retention time = about 8 min): impurity A = about 0.2; altizide = about 0.5.

*System suitability* Reference solution (a):
— *resolution*: minimum 10 between the peaks due to altizide and bendroflumethiazide.

*Limits:*
— *impurity A*: not more than the area of the principal peak in the chromatogram obtained with reference solution (b) (0.1 per cent);
— *unspecified impurities*: for each impurity, not more than the area of the principal peak in the chromatogram obtained with reference solution (b) (0.10 per cent);
— *total*: not more than twice the area of the principal peak in the chromatogram obtained with reference solution (b) (0.2 per cent);
— *disregard limit*: 0.5 times the area of the principal peak in the chromatogram obtained with reference solution (b) (0.05 per cent).

**Loss on drying** (*2.2.32*)
Maximum 0.5 per cent, determined on 1.000 g by drying in an oven at 105 °C.

**Sulphated ash** (*2.4.14*)
Maximum 0.1 per cent, determined on 1.0 g.

**ASSAY**
Dissolve 0.150 g in 50 ml of *dimethyl sulphoxide R*. Titrate to the 2$^{nd}$ point of inflexion with *0.1 M tetrabutylammonium hydroxide in 2-propanol*, determining the end-point potentiometrically (*2.2.20*). Carry out a blank titration.

1 ml of *0.1 M tetrabutylammonium hydroxide in 2-propanol* is equivalent to 21.07 mg of $C_{15}H_{14}F_3N_3O_4S_2$.

**IMPURITIES**

*Specified impurities* A.

A. 4-amino-6-(trifluoromethyl)benzene-1,3-disulphonamide.

*Ph Eur*

---

# Benfluorex Hydrochloride

(*Ph Eur monograph 1601*)

and enantiomer

$C_{19}H_{20}F_3NO_2,HCl$      387.8      23642-66-2

**Action and use**
Lipid-regulating drug.

*Ph Eur*

**DEFINITION**
2-[[(1*RS*)-1-Methyl-2-[3-(trifluoromethyl)phenyl]ethyl]amino]ethyl benzoate hydrochloride.

**Content**
98.5 per cent to 101.0 per cent (dried substance).

**CHARACTERS**

**Appearance**
White or almost white powder.

**Solubility**
Slightly soluble in water, freely soluble in methanol, soluble in methylene chloride, sparingly soluble or soluble in alcohol.

It shows polymorphism (*5.9*).

**IDENTIFICATION**
A. Infrared absorption spectrophotometry (*2.2.24*).

*Preparation* Mulls in *liquid paraffin R*.

*Comparison* benfluorex hydrochloride CRS.

If the spectra obtained show differences, heat the substance to be examined and the reference substance separately in an oven at 150 °C for 3 h and record new spectra.

B. It gives reaction (a) of chlorides (*2.3.1*).

**TESTS**

**Optical rotation** (*2.2.7*)
− 0.10° to + 0.10°.

Dissolve 0.2 g in *ethanol R* and dilute to 20.0 ml with the same solvent.

**Impurity B**
Gas chromatography (*2.2.28*): use the normalisation procedure.

*Test solution* Dissolve 0.30 g of the substance to be examined in *methylene chloride R* and dilute to 20 ml with the same solvent. Transfer to a separating funnel, add 10 ml of a 40 g/l solution of *sodium hydroxide R*. Shake the flask vigorously and allow the phases to separate. Collect the organic layer.

*Reference solution* Dissolve 0.30 g of *benfluorex hydrochloride for system suitability CRS* in *methylene chloride R* and dilute to 20 ml with the same solvent. Transfer to a separating funnel and add 10 ml of a 40 g/l solution of *sodium hydroxide R*. Shake the flask vigorously and allow the phases to separate. Collect the organic layer.

*Column:*
— *material*: fused silica,
— *size*: $l = 25$ m, $\emptyset = 0.32$ mm,
— *stationary phase*: *macrogol 20 000 R* (film thickness 0.2 µm).

*Carrier gas* *hydrogen for chromatography R*.

*Linear velocity* 75 cm/s.

*Split ratio* 1:35.

*Temperature:*
— *column*: 220 °C,
— *injection port and detector*: 250 °C.

*Detection* Flame ionisation.

*Injection* 1 µl.

*Run time* 1.5 times the retention time of benfluorex.

*Relative retention* With reference to benfluorex (retention time = about 4.5 min): impurity B = about 1.1.

*System suitability:*
— *peak-to-valley ratio*: minimum 2.5, where $H_p$ = height above the baseline of the peak due to impurity B, and $H_v$ = height above the baseline of the lowest point of the curve separating this peak from the peak due to benfluorex.

*Limit:*
— *impurity B*: maximum 0.1 per cent.

**Related substances, other than impurity B**
Liquid chromatography (*2.2.29*).

*Test solution* Dissolve 60.0 mg of the substance to be examined in 50 ml of *acetonitrile R* and dilute to 100.0 ml with *water R*.

*Reference solution (a)* Dissolve 60.0 mg of *benfluorex hydrochloride for system suitability CRS* in 50 ml of *acetonitrile R* and dilute to 100.0 ml with *water R*.

*Reference solution (b)* Dilute 1.0 ml of the test solution to 100.0 ml with a mixture of equal volumes of *acetonitrile R* and *water R*. Dilute 5.0 ml of this solution to 50.0 ml with the same mixture of solvents.

*Column:*
— *size*: $l = 0.15$ m, $\emptyset = 4.6$ mm,
— *stationary phase*: *silica gel bonded with alkylamide groups* (5 µm),
— *temperature*: 60 °C.

*Mobile phase* A mixture of equal volumes of *acetonitrile R* and a solution containing 2.18 g/l of *potassium dihydrogen phosphate R* adjusted to pH 2.5 with *phosphoric acid R* and 6.5 g/l of *sodium decyl sulphate R*.

*Flow rate* 1.4 ml/min.

*Detection* Spectrophotometer at 210 nm.

*Injection* 10 µl.

*Run time* 3 times the retention time of benfluorex.

*Relative retention* With reference to benfluorex (retention time = about 5 min): impurity A = about 0.9.

*System suitability:*
— *signal-to-noise ratio*: minimum 20 for the principal peak in the chromatogram obtained with reference solution (b),
— *peak-to-valley ratio*: minimum 2.5, where $H_p$ = height above the baseline of the peak due to impurity A, and $H_v$ = height above the baseline of the lowest point of the curve separating this peak from the peak due to benfluorex in the chromatogram obtained with reference solution (a).

*Limits:*
— *any impurity*: not more than the area of the principal peak in the chromatogram obtained with reference solution (b) (0.1 per cent),
— *total*: not more than twice the area of the principal peak in the chromatogram obtained with reference solution (b) (0.2 per cent),
— *disregard limit*: 0.5 times the area of the principal peak in the chromatogram obtained with reference solution (b) (0.05 per cent).

**Heavy metals** (*2.4.8*)
Maximum 20 ppm.

1.0 g complies with limit test C. Prepare the standard using 2 ml of *lead standard solution (10 ppm Pb) R*.

**Loss on drying** (*2.2.32*)
Maximum 0.5 per cent, determined on 1.000 g by drying in an oven at 105 °C.

**Sulphated ash** (*2.4.14*)
Maximum 0.1 per cent, determined on 1.0 g.

**ASSAY**
*In order to avoid overheating in the reaction medium, mix thoroughly throughout and stop the titration immediately after the end-point has been reached.*

Dissolve 0.250 g rapidly in 2.0 ml of *anhydrous formic acid R* and add 50.0 ml of *acetic anhydride R*. Titrate immediately with *0.1 M perchloric acid*, determining the end-point potentiometrically (*2.2.20*).

1 ml of *0.1 M perchloric acid* is equivalent to 38.78 mg of $C_{19}H_{21}ClF_3NO_2$.

**IMPURITIES**

and enantiomer

A. R = CF$_3$, R$'$ = H: 2-[[(1RS)-1-methyl-2-[2-(trifluoromethyl)phenyl]ethyl]amino]ethyl benzoate,
B. R = H, R$'$ = CF$_3$: 2-[[(1RS)-1-methyl-2-[4-(trifluoromethyl)phenyl]ethyl]amino]ethyl benzoate,
C. benzoic acid,

and enantiomer

D. R = CH$_2$-CH$_2$-OH, R$'$ = H: 2-[[(1RS)-1-methyl-2-[3-(trifluoromethyl)phenyl]ethyl]amino]ethanol,

E. R = CH₂-CH₂-OH, R′ = CO-C₆H₅: *N-(2-hydroxyethyl)-N-[(1RS)-1-methyl-2-[3-(trifluoromethyl)phenyl]ethyl]benzamide*,

F. R = CH₂-CH₂-O-CO-C₆H₅, R′ = CO-C₆H₅: *2-[benzoyl[(1RS)-1-methyl-2-[3-(trifluoromethyl)phenyl]ethyl]amino]ethyl benzoate*.

_____ *Ph Eur*

# Benorilate

C₁₇H₁₅NO₅      313.3      *5003-48-5*

### Action and use
Salicylate-paracetamol derivative; antipyretic; analgesic; anti-inflammatory.

### Preparations
Benorilate Oral Suspension

Benorilate Tablets

## DEFINITION
Benorilate is 4-acetamidophenyl *O*-acetylsalicylate. It contains not less than 99.0% and not more than 100.5% of C₁₇H₁₅NO₅, calculated with reference to the dried substance.

## CHARACTERISTICS
A white or almost white, crystalline powder.

Practically insoluble in *water*; soluble in *acetone*; sparingly soluble in *ethanol (96%)* and in *methanol*.

## IDENTIFICATION
A. The *infrared absorption spectrum*, Appendix II A, is concordant with the *reference spectrum* of benorilate *(RS 023)*.

B. To 10 mg add 10 ml of 6M *hydrochloric acid* and boil until completely dissolved. To 5 ml of the resulting solution add 0.1 ml of *strong 1-naphthol solution*, mix and add sufficient 1M *sodium hydroxide* to make the solution just alkaline. A blue colour is produced which is extracted into *butan-1-ol*.

C. The *light absorption*, Appendix II B, in the range 230 to 350 nm of a 0.001% w/v solution in *absolute ethanol* exhibits a maximum only at 240 nm. The *absorbance* at 240 nm is about 0.74.

## TESTS
### Melting point
178° to 181°, Appendix V A.

### Heavy metals
1.0 g complies with *limit test C for heavy metals*, Appendix VII. Use 2 ml of *lead standard solution (10 ppm Pb)* to prepare the standard (20 ppm).

### 4-Aminophenol
Shake 2.5 g with 100 ml of *water* for 15 minutes and filter. To 20 ml of the filtrate add 0.2 ml of *sodium nitroprusside-carbonate solution*, mix and allow to stand for 30 minutes. The solution is not more intensely coloured than a solution prepared at the same time and in the same manner but using 2 ml of a solution of *4-aminophenol* containing 5 µg per ml and 18 ml of *water* in place of the filtrate (20 ppm).

### Salicylic acid
Shake 0.50 g with 20 ml of *water* for 15 minutes and filter. Transfer 10 ml of the filtrate to a *Nessler cylinder*, dilute to 50 ml with *water*, add 0.2 ml of a 0.5% w/v solution of *iron(III) chloride* and allow to stand for 1 minute. The colour obtained is not more intense than that of a solution prepared at the same time by adding 0.2 ml of a 0.5% w/v solution of *iron(III) chloride* to a mixture of 1 ml of a 0.025% w/v solution of *salicylic acid* in *ethanol (96%)* and sufficient *water* to produce 50 ml (0.1%).

### Related substances
Carry out the method for *thin-layer chromatography*, Appendix III A, using the following solutions in a mixture of 1 volume of *methanol* and 9 volumes of *dichloromethane*.

(1) 4.0% w/v of the substance being examined.

(2) 0.040% w/v of the substance being examined.

(3) 0.0080% w/v of the substance being examined.

(4) 0.0080% w/v of *paracetamol*.

CHROMATOGRAPHIC CONDITIONS

Develop the plate in the first mobile phase (mobile phase A). After development dry in air and develop in the second mobile phase (mobile phase B).

(a) Use a silica gel HF₂₅₄ precoated plate (Analtech plates are suitable).

(b) Use mobile phase A as described below.

(c) Apply 10 µl of each solution.

(d) Develop the plate to 15 cm.

(e) After removal of the plate, dry in air and examine under *ultraviolet light (254 nm)*.

MOBILE PHASE

*Mobile phase A*    5 volumes of *glacial acetic acid*, 15 volumes of *ether*, and 80 volumes of *dichloromethane*.

*Mobile phase B*    10 volumes of *formic acid*, 45 volumes of *ether*, and 45 volumes of *2,2,4-trimethylpentane*.

LIMITS

In the chromatogram obtained with solution (1):

any spot corresponding to paracetamol is not more intense than the spot in the chromatogram obtained with solution (4) (0.2%);

any *secondary spot* with an Rf value slightly higher than that of the principal spot is not more intense than the principal spot in the chromatogram obtained with solution (2) (1%);

any other *secondary spot* is not more intense than the spot in the chromatogram obtained with solution (3) (0.2%).

### Loss on drying
When dried to constant weight at 105°, loses not more than 0.5% of its weight. Use 1 g.

### Sulphated ash
Not more than 0.1%, Appendix IX A.

## ASSAY
Carry out Method I for the *determination of nitrogen*, Appendix VIII H, using 0.6 g and 10 ml of *nitrogen-free sulphuric acid*. Each ml of 0.05M *sulphuric acid VS* is equivalent to 31.33 mg of C₁₇H₁₅NO₅.

# Benperidol

*(Ph Eur monograph 1172)*

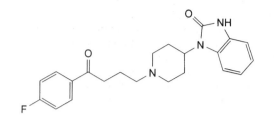

C₂₂H₂₄FN₃O₂    381.4    *2062-84-2*

$C_{22}H_{24}FN_3O_2$    381.4    *2062-84-2*

## Action and use
Dopamine receptor antagonist; neuroleptic.

*Ph Eur* _____

## DEFINITION
1-[1-[4-(4-Fluorophenyl)-4-oxobutyl]piperidin-4-yl]-1,3-
dihydro-2*H*-benzimidazol-2-one.

## Content
99.0 per cent to 101.0 per cent (dried substance).

## CHARACTERS
### Appearance
White or almost white powder.

### Solubility
Practically insoluble in water, freely soluble in
dimethylformamide, soluble in methylene chloride, slightly
soluble in ethanol (96 per cent).

It shows polymorphism (*5.9*).

## IDENTIFICATION
*First identification*  A.

*Second identification*  B, C, D.

A. Infrared absorption spectrophotometry (*2.2.24*).

*Preparation*  Discs.

*Comparison*  benperidol CRS.

If the spectra obtained in the solid state show differences,
dissolve the substance to be examined and the reference
substance separately in the minimum volume of *methyl
isobutyl ketone R*, evaporate to dryness and record new
spectra using the residues.

B. Thin-layer chromatography (*2.2.27*).

*Test solution*  Dissolve 30 mg of the substance to be
examined in the mobile phase and dilute to 10 ml with the
mobile phase.

*Reference solution (a)*  Dissolve 30 mg of *benperidol CRS* in
the mobile phase and dilute to 10 ml with the mobile phase.

*Reference solution (b)*  Dissolve 30 mg of *benperidol CRS* and
30 mg of *droperidol CRS* in the mobile phase and dilute to
10 ml with the mobile phase.

*Plate*  TLC silica gel F₂₅₄ plate R.

*Mobile phase*  acetone R, methanol R (1:9 *V/V*).

*Application*  10 µl.

*Development*  Over a path of 15 cm.

*Drying*  In air.

*Detection*  Examine in ultraviolet light at 254 nm.

*System suitability*  Reference solution (b)
— the chromatogram shows 2 clearly separated spots.

*Results*  The principal spot in the chromatogram obtained
with the test solution is similar in position and size to the
principal spot in the chromatogram obtained with reference
solution (a).

C. Dissolve about 10 mg in 5 ml of *anhydrous ethanol R*. Add
0.5 ml of *dinitrobenzene solution R* and 0.5 ml of *2 M alcoholic
potassium hydroxide R*. A violet colour is produced which
becomes brownish-red after 20 min.

D. Mix about 5 mg with 45 mg of heavy *magnesium oxide R*
and ignite in a crucible until an almost white residue is
obtained (usually less than 5 min). Allow to cool, add 1 ml
of *water R*, 0.05 ml of *phenolphthalein solution R1* and about
1 ml of *dilute hydrochloric acid R* to render the solution
colourless. Filter. To a freshly prepared mixture of 0.1 ml of
*alizarin S solution R* and 0.1 ml of *zirconyl nitrate solution R*,
add 1.0 ml of the filtrate. Mix, allow to stand for 5 min and
compare the colour of the solution with that of a blank
prepared in the same manner. The test solution is yellow and
the blank is red.

## TESTS
### Related substances
Liquid chromatography (*2.2.29*). *Prepare the solutions
immediately before use.*

*Test solution*  Dissolve 0.10 g of the substance to be
examined in *dimethylformamide R* and dilute to 10.0 ml with
the same solvent.

*Reference solution (a)*  Dissolve 2.5 mg of *benperidol CRS* and
2.5 mg of *droperidol CRS* in *dimethylformamide R* and dilute to
100.0 ml with the same solvent.

*Reference solution (b)*  Dilute 1.0 ml of the test solution to
100.0 ml with *dimethylformamide R*. Dilute 5.0 ml of this
solution to 20.0 ml with *dimethylformamide R*.

*Column*:
— *size*: l = 0.1 m, Ø = 4.6 mm;
— *stationary phase*: base-deactivated octadecylsilyl silica gel for
  chromatography R (3 µm).

*Mobile phase*:
— *mobile phase A*: 10 g/l solution of *tetrabutylammonium
  hydrogen sulphate R*;
— *mobile phase B*: *acetonitrile R*;

| Time (min) | Mobile phase A (per cent *V/V*) | Mobile phase B (per cent *V/V*) |
|---|---|---|
| 0 - 15 | 100 → 60 | 0 → 40 |
| 15 - 20 | 60 | 40 |
| 20 - 25 | 100 | 0 |

*Flow rate*  1.5 ml/min.

*Detection*  Spectrophotometer at 275 nm.

*Equilibration*  With *acetonitrile R* for at least 30 min and then
with the mobile phase at the initial composition for at least
5 min.

*Injection*  10 µl; inject *dimethylformamide R* as a blank.

*Retention time*  Benperidol = about 6.5 min;
droperidol = about 7 min.

*System suitability*  Reference solution (a)
— *resolution*: minimum 2.0 between the peaks due to
  benperidol and droperidol; if necessary, adjust the
  concentration of acetonitrile in the mobile phase or adjust
  the time programme for the linear gradient.

*Limits:*
— *impurities A, B, C, D, E*: for each impurity, not more than the area of the principal peak in the chromatogram obtained with reference solution (b) (0.25 per cent);
— *total*: not more than twice the area of the principal peak in the chromatogram obtained with reference solution (b) (0.5 per cent);
— *disregard limit*: 0.2 times the area of the principal peak in the chromatogram obtained with reference solution (b) (0.05 per cent); disregard any peak due to the blank.

**Loss on drying** (*2.2.32*)
Maximum 0.5 per cent, determined on 1.000 g by drying in an oven at 105 °C.

**Sulphated ash** (*2.4.14*)
Maximum 0.1 per cent, determined on 1.0 g in a platinum crucible.

**ASSAY**
Dissolve 0.300 g in 50 ml of a mixture of 1 volume of *anhydrous acetic acid R* and 7 volumes of *methyl ethyl ketone R* and titrate with *0.1 M perchloric acid*, using 0.2 ml of *naphtholbenzein solution R* as indicator.

1 ml of *0.1 M perchloric acid* is equivalent to 38.14 mg of $C_{22}H_{24}FN_3O_2$.

**STORAGE**
Protected from light.

**IMPURITIES**
*Specified impurities*   *A, B, C, D, E.*

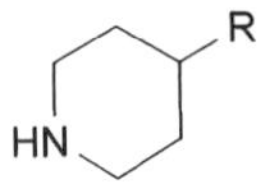

Ar- = [structure: 4-fluoro-methylphenyl]

R- = [structure: benzimidazol-2-one]

[structure: piperidine with R]

A. 1-(piperidin-4-yl)-1,3-dihydro-2*H*-benzimidazol-2-one,

[structure]

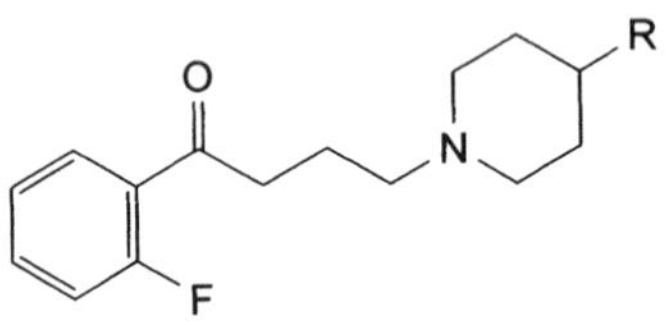

B. 1-[1-[4-(2-fluorophenyl)-4-oxobutyl]piperidin-4-yl]-1,3-dihydro-2*H*-benzimidazol-2-one,

[structure]

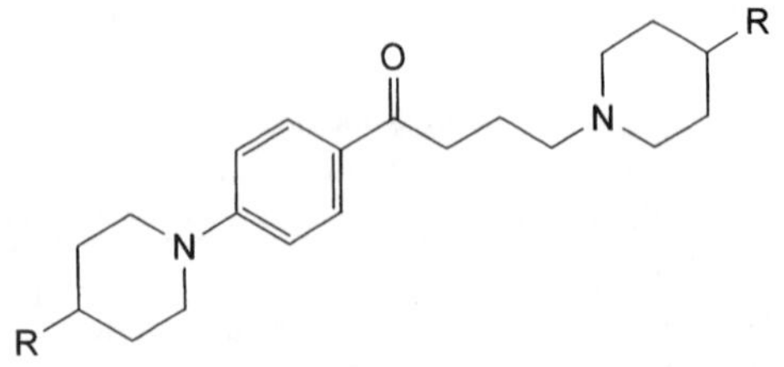

C. 1-[1-[4-oxo-4-[4-[4-(2-oxo-2,3-dihydro-1*H*-benzimidazol-1-yl)piperidin-1-yl]phenyl]butyl]piperidin-4-yl]-1,3-dihydro-2*H*-benzimidazol-2-one,

[structure]

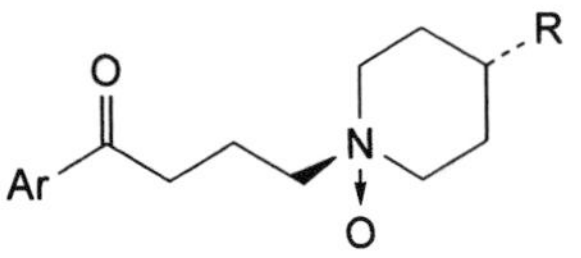

D. *cis*-1-[1-[4-(4-fluorophenyl)-4-oxobutyl]piperidin-4-yl 1-oxide]-1,3-dihydro-2*H*-benzimidazol-2-one,

[structure]

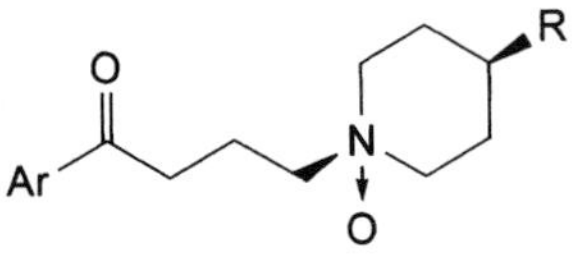

E. *trans*-1-[1-[4-(4-fluorophenyl)-4-oxobutyl]piperidin-4-yl 1-oxide]-1,3-dihydro-2*H*-benzimidazol-2-one.

*_____ Ph Eur*

# Benserazide Hydrochloride

(*Ph Eur monograph 1173*)

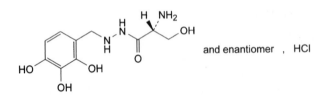

and enantiomer , HCl

$C_{10}H_{15}N_3O_5,HCl$          293.7          *14919-77-8*

**Action and use**
Dopa decarboxylase inhibitor.

**Preparations**
Co-beneldopa Capsules
Dispersible Co-beneldopa Tablets

*Ph Eur* _____

**DEFINITION**
(2*RS*)-2-Amino-3-hydroxy-2′-(2,3,4-trihydroxybenzyl)propanohydrazide hydrochloride.

**Content**
98.5 per cent to 101.0 per cent (anhydrous substance).

**CHARACTERS**
**Appearance**
White or yellowish-white or orange-white, crystalline powder.

**Solubility**
Freely soluble in water, very slightly soluble in anhydrous ethanol, practically insoluble in acetone.

It shows polymorphism (*5.9*).

**IDENTIFICATION**
A. Infrared absorption spectrophotometry (*2.2.24*).

*Comparison   benserazide hydrochloride CRS.*

If the spectra obtained show differences, dissolve the substance to be examined and the reference substance separately in hot *methanol R*, evaporate to dryness and record new spectra using the residues.

B. Solution S (see Tests) gives reaction (b) of chlorides (*2.3.1*).

## TESTS

### Solution S

Dissolve 1.0 g in *carbon dioxide-free water R* and dilute to 100 ml with the same solvent.

### Appearance of solution

Solution S is clear (*2.2.1*) and not more intensely coloured than reference solution $BY_6$ (*2.2.2, Method II*).

### pH (*2.2.3*)

4.0 to 5.0 for solution S.

### Related substances

Liquid chromatography (*2.2.29*).

*All solutions must be injected immediately or stored at 4 °C.*

*Test solution*   Dissolve 0.100 g of the substance to be examined in *methanol R2* and dilute to 50.0 ml with the same solvent.

*Reference solution (a)*   Dissolve 5.0 mg of *benserazide impurity A CRS*, 5.0 mg of *benserazide impurity C CRS* and 5.0 mg of *benserazide hydrochloride CRS* in *methanol R2* and dilute to 50.0 ml with the same solvent. Dilute 5.0 ml of this solution to 50.0 ml with *methanol R2*.

*Reference solution (b)*   Dilute 2.0 ml of reference solution (a) to 10.0 ml with *methanol R2*.

*Reference solution (c)*   Dissolve 5 mg of *benserazide for peak identification CRS* (containing impurities A, B and C) in *methanol R2* and dilute to 5.0 ml with the same solvent.

*Column:*
— *size*: $l = 0.25$ m, $\varnothing = 4$ mm;
— *stationary phase*: octylsilyl silica gel for chromatography R (5 µm);
— *temperature*: 30 °C.

*Mobile phase:*
— *mobile phase A*: dissolve 2.2 g of *sodium heptanesulphonate monohydrate R* and 6.8 g of *potassium dihydrogen phosphate R* in 900 ml of *water R*, add 50 ml of *methanol R2* and adjust to pH 3.5 with *phosphoric acid R*;
— *mobile phase B*: dissolve 2.2 g of *sodium heptanesulphonate monohydrate R* and 6.8 g of *potassium dihydrogen phosphate R* in 500 ml of *water R*, adjust to pH 3.5 with *phosphoric acid R* and add 500 ml of *methanol R2*;

| Time (min) | Mobile phase A (per cent V/V) | Mobile phase B (per cent V/V) |
|---|---|---|
| 0 - 15 | $100 \rightarrow 0$ | $0 \rightarrow 100$ |
| 15 - 25 | 0 | 100 |

*Flow rate*   1.3 ml/min.

*Detection*   Spectrophotometer at 210 nm.

*Injection*   5 µl.

*Identification of impurities*   Use the chromatogram supplied with *benserazide for peak identification CRS* and the chromatogram obtained with reference solution (c) to identify the peaks due to impurities A, B and C; doubling of the peak due to impurity C, related to separation of the (*EZ*)-isomers, may be observed.

*Relative retention*   With reference to benserazide (retention time = about 9 min): impurity A = about 0.6; impurity C = about 1.2; impurity B = about 1.5.

*System suitability*   Reference solution (a):
— *resolution*: minimum 5.0 between the peaks due to benserazide and impurity C; use the 1<sup>st</sup> peak of impurity C if 2 peaks occur.

*Limits:*
— *correction factor*: for the calculation of content, multiply the peak area of impurity B by 0.7;

— *impurity A*: not more than the area of the corresponding peak in the chromatogram obtained with reference solution (a) (0.5 per cent);
— *impurity B*: not more than the area of the peak due to benserazide in the chromatogram obtained with reference solution (a) (0.5 per cent);
— *impurity C*: not more than the area of the corresponding peak or pair of peaks in the chromatogram obtained with reference solution (a) (0.5 per cent);
— *unspecified impurities*: for each impurity, not more than the area of the peak due to benserazide in the chromatogram obtained with reference solution (b) (0.10 per cent);
— *sum of impurities other than A*: not more than twice the area of the peak due to benserazide in the chromatogram obtained with reference solution (a) (1.0 per cent);
— *disregard limit*: 0.5 times the area of the peak due to benserazide in the chromatogram obtained with reference solution (b) (0.05 per cent).

### Heavy metals (*2.4.8*)

Maximum 20 ppm.

1.0 g complies with test C. Prepare the reference solution using 2 ml of *lead standard solution (10 ppm Pb) R*.

### Water (*2.5.12*)

Maximum 1.0 per cent, determined on 0.500 g.

### Sulphated ash (*2.4.14*)

Maximum 0.1 per cent, determined on 1.0 g.

## ASSAY

*In order to avoid overheating during the titration, mix thoroughly throughout and stop the titration immediately after the end-point has been reached.*

Dissolve 0.250 g in 5 ml of *anhydrous formic acid R*. Add 70 ml of *anhydrous acetic acid R*. Titrate immediately with *0.1 M perchloric acid*, determining the end-point potentiometrically (*2.2.20*).

1 ml of *0.1 M perchloric acid* is equivalent to 29.37 mg of $C_{10}H_{16}ClN_3O_5$.

## STORAGE

Protected from light.

## IMPURITIES

*Specified impurities*   A, B, C.

A. (2RS)-2-amino-3-hydroxypropanohydrazide,

B. (2RS)-2-amino-3-hydroxy-2′,2′-bis(2,3,4-trihydroxybenzyl)propanohydrazide,

its (Z)-isomer and their enantiomers

C. (2RS)-2-amino-3-hydroxy-2'-[(1EZ)-(2,3,4-trihydroxybenzylidene)]propanohydrazide.

*Ph Eur*

# Bentonite

(*Ph Eur monograph 0467*)

1302-78-9

*Ph Eur*

## DEFINITION

Natural clay containing a high proportion of montmorillonite, a native hydrated aluminium silicate in which some aluminium and silicon atoms may be replaced by other atoms such as magnesium and iron.

## CHARACTERS

**Appearance**

Very fine, homogeneous, greyish-white powder with a more or less yellowish or pinkish tint.

**Solubility**

Practically insoluble in water and in aqueous solutions.

It swells with a little water forming a malleable mass.

## IDENTIFICATION

A. To 0.5 g in a metal crucible add 1 g of *potassium nitrate R* and 3 g of *sodium carbonate R* and heat until the mixture melts. Allow to cool. To this residue add 20 ml of boiling *water R*, mix and filter. Wash the insoluble residue with 50 ml of *water R*. To this residue add 1 ml of *hydrochloric acid R* and 5 ml of *water R*. Filter. To the filtrate add 1 ml of *strong sodium hydroxide solution R* and filter. To this filtrate add 3 ml of *ammonium chloride solution R*. A gelatinous white precipitate is formed.

B. Add 2.0 g in 20 portions to 100 ml of a 10 g/l solution of *sodium laurilsulfate R* in a 100 ml graduated cylinder about 30 mm in diameter. Allow 2 min between additions for each portion to settle. Allow to stand for 2 h. The apparent volume of the sediment is not less than 22 ml.

C. 0.25 g gives the reaction of silicates (*2.3.1*).

## TESTS

**Alkalinity**

To 2 g add 100 ml of *carbon dioxide-free water R* and shake for 5 min. To 5 ml of this suspension add 0.1 ml of *thymolphthalein solution R*. The liquid becomes bluish. Add 0.1 ml of *0.1 M hydrochloric acid*. The liquid is decolourised within 5 min.

**Coarse particles**

Maximum 0.5 per cent.

To 20 g add 1000 ml of *water R* and mix for 15 min using a high-speed mixer capable of operating at not less than 5000 r/min. Transfer the suspension to a wet sieve (75), tared after drying at 100-105 °C. Wash with 3 quantities, each of 500 ml, of *water R*, ensuring that any agglomerates have been dispersed. Dry the sieve at 100-105 °C and weigh. The particles on the sieve weigh a maximum of 0.1 g.

**Heavy metals** (*2.4.8*)

Maximum 50 ppm.

To 5.0 g add 7.5 ml of *dilute hydrochloric acid R* and 27.5 ml of *water R*. Boil for 5 min. Centrifuge and filter the supernatant liquid. Wash the centrifugation residue with *water R* and filter. Dilute the combined filtrates to 50.0 ml with *water R*. To 5 ml of this solution add 5 ml of *water R*, 10 ml of *hydrochloric acid R* and 25 ml of *methyl isobutyl ketone R* and shake for 2 min. Separate the layers. Evaporate the aqueous layer to dryness on a water-bath. Dissolve the residue in 1 ml of *acetic acid R*, dilute to 25 ml with *water R* and filter. 12 ml of the filtrate complies with test A. Prepare the reference solution using *lead standard solution (1 ppm Pb) R*.

**Loss on drying** (*2.2.32*)

Maximum 15 per cent, determined on 1.000 g by drying in an oven at 105 °C.

**Microbial contamination**

TAMC: acceptance criterion $10^3$ CFU/g (*2.6.12*).

## FUNCTIONALITY-RELATED CHARACTERISTICS

*This section provides information on characteristics that are recognised as being relevant control parameters for one or more functions of the substance when used as an excipient (see chapter 5.15). This section is a non-mandatory part of the monograph and it is not necessary to verify the characteristics to demonstrate compliance. Control of these characteristics can however contribute to the quality of a medicinal product by improving the consistency of the manufacturing process and the performance of the medicinal product during use. Where control methods are cited, they are recognised as being suitable for the purpose, but other methods can also be used. Wherever results for a particular characteristic are reported, the control method must be indicated.*

*The following characteristics may be relevant for bentonite used as viscosity-increasing agent or suspending agent.*

**Sedimentation volume**

To 6.0 g add 200 ml of *water R* and mix for 20 min using a high-speed mixer capable of operating at 10 000 r/min. Transfer 100 ml of this suspension to a graduated cylinder. Allow to stand for 24 h. The volume of the clear supernatant liquid is not greater than 2 ml.

**Swelling power with water**

See Identification B.

*Ph Eur*

# Benzaldehyde

CHO

C₇H₆O      106.1      100-52-7

**Action and use**

Flavour.

## DEFINITION

Benzaldehyde contains not less than 98.0% w/w and not more than 100.5% w/w of $C_7H_6O$.

## CHARACTERISTICS

A clear, colourless liquid.

Slightly soluble in *water*, miscible with *ethanol (96%)* and with *ether*.

## TESTS

### Refractive index
1.544 to 1.546, Appendix V E.

### Weight per ml
1.043 to 1.049 g, Appendix V G.

### Free acid
Not more than 1.0% w/v, calculated as benzoic acid, $C_7H_6O_2$, when determined by the following method. To 10 ml add 20 ml of *ethanol (96%)* previously neutralised to *phenolphthalein solution R1* and titrate with *0.1M sodium hydroxide VS* using *phenolphthalein solution R1* as indicator. Each ml of *0.1M sodium hydroxide VS* is equivalent to 12.21 mg of $C_7H_6O_2$.

### Chlorinated compounds
Not more than 0.05% w/v, calculated as Cl, when determined by the following method. To 5 ml add 50 ml of *isoamyl alcohol* and 3 g of *sodium* and boil under a reflux condenser for 1 hour. Cool, add 50 ml of *water* and 15 ml of *nitric acid*, cool, add 5 ml of *0.1M silver nitrate VS*, shake and titrate the excess silver nitrate with *0.1M ammonium thiocyanate VS* using *ammonium iron(III) sulphate solution R2* as indicator. Repeat the procedure without the substance being examined. The difference between the titrations represents the amount of silver nitrate required. Each ml of *0.1M silver nitrate VS* is equivalent to 3.545 mg of Cl.

## ASSAY
Carry out the method for *determination of aldehydes*, Appendix X K, using 0.5 g. Each ml of *0.5M potassium hydroxide in ethanol (60%) VS* is equivalent to 53.06 mg of $C_7H_6O$.

## STORAGE
Benzaldehyde should be kept in a well-filled container, protected from light and stored at a temperature not exceeding 15°.

# Benzalkonium Chloride

*(Ph Eur monograph 0372)*

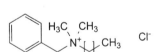

*8001-54-5*

## Action and use
Antiseptic.

*Ph Eur*

## DEFINITION
Mixture of alkylbenzyldimethylammonium chlorides, the alkyl groups mainly having chain lengths of $C_{12}$, $C_{14}$ and $C_{16}$.

## Content
95.0 per cent to 104.0 per cent of alkylbenzyldimethylammonium chlorides (anhydrous substance) calculated using the average relative molecular mass (see Tests).

## CHARACTERS
### Appearance
White or yellowish-white powder or gelatinous, yellowish-white fragments, hygroscopic. On heating it forms a clear molten mass.

### Solubility
Very soluble in water and in ethanol (96 per cent). An aqueous solution froths copiously when shaken.

## IDENTIFICATION
*First identification    B, E.*

*Second identification    A, C, D, E.*

A. Ultraviolet and visible absorption spectrophotometry (2.2.25).

*Test solution*    Dissolve 80 mg in *water R* and dilute to 100.0 ml with the same solvent.

*Spectral range*    220-350 nm.

*Absorption maxima*    At 257 nm, 263 nm and 269 nm.

*Shoulder*    At about 250 nm.

B. Examine the chromatograms obtained in the test for average relative molecular mass and ratio of alkyl components.

*Results*    The principal peaks in the chromatogram obtained with the test solution are similar in retention time to the principal peaks in the chromatogram obtained with reference solution.

C. To 2 ml of solution S (see Tests) add 0.1 ml of *glacial acetic acid R* and, dropwise, 1 ml of *sodium tetraphenylborate solution R*. A white precipitate is formed. Filter. Dissolve the precipitate in a mixture of 1 ml of *acetone R* and 5 ml of *ethanol (96 per cent) R*, heating to not more than 70 °C. Add *water R* dropwise to the warm solution until a slight opalescence forms. Heat gently until the solution is clear and allow to cool. White crystals separate. Filter, wash with 3 quantities, each of 10 ml, of *water R* and dry *in vacuo* over *diphosphorus pentoxide R* or *anhydrous silica gel R* at a temperature not exceeding 50 °C. The crystals melt (2.2.14) at 127 °C to 133 °C.

D. To 5 ml of *dilute sodium hydroxide solution R* add 0.1 ml of *bromophenol blue solution R1* and 5 ml of *methylene chloride R* and shake. The methylene chloride layer is colourless. Add 0.1 ml of solution S and shake. The methylene chloride layer becomes blue.

E. To 2 ml of solution S add 1 ml of *dilute nitric acid R*. A white precipitate is formed which dissolves on the addition of 5 ml of *ethanol (96 per cent) R*. The solution gives reaction (a) of chlorides (2.3.1).

## TESTS
### Solution S
Dissolve 1.0 g in *carbon dioxide-free water R* and dilute to 100 ml with the same solvent.

### Appearance of solution
Solution S is clear (2.2.1) and not more intensely coloured than reference solution $Y_6$ (2.2.2, Method II).

### Acidity or alkalinity
To 50 ml of solution S add 0.1 ml of *bromocresol purple solution R*. Not more than 0.1 ml of *0.1 M hydrochloric acid* or *0.1 M sodium hydroxide* is required to change the colour of the indicator.

### Average relative molecular mass and ratio of alkyl components
Liquid chromatography (2.2.29).

*Test solution* Dissolve 0.400 g of the substance to be examined in *water R* and dilute to 100.0 ml with the same solvent.

*Reference solution* Dissolve 40 mg of *benzalkonium chloride for system suitability CRS* in *water R* and dilute to 10.0 ml with the same solvent.

*Column:*
— *size: l = 0.25 m, Ø = 4.6 mm;*
— *stationary phase: end-capped nitrile silica gel for chromatography R (5 μm).*

*Mobile phase* Mix 45 volumes of *acetonitrile R* and 55 volumes of a 13.6 g/l solution of *sodium acetate R* previously adjusted to pH 5.0 with *glacial acetic acid R*.

*Flow rate* 2.0 ml/min.

*Detection* Spectrophotometer at 254 nm.

*Injection* 10 μl.

*Identification of homologues* Use the chromatogram supplied with *benzalkonium chloride for system suitability CRS* and the chromatogram obtained with the reference solution to identify the peaks due to $C_{12}$, $C_{14}$ and $C_{16}$.

*Relative retention* With reference to $C_{12}$ homologue (retention time = about 6 min): $C_{14}$ homologue = about 1.1; $C_{16}$ homologue = about 1.3.

*System suitability* Reference solution:
— *resolution:* minimum 1.5 between the peaks due to the $C_{12}$ and $C_{14}$ homologues.

Calculate the average relative molecular mass of the sample by summing the products for each homologue, using the following expression:

$$W \left( \frac{A}{B} \right)$$

$A$ = area of the peak due to the given homologue in the chromatogram obtained with the test solution;

$B$ = sum of the areas of the peaks due to all homologues in the chromatogram obtained with the test solution;

$W$ = relative molecular mass for the given homologue: 340, 368 and 396 for the $C_{12}$, $C_{14}$ and $C_{16}$ homologues, respectively.

Calculate the percentage of each homologue, using the following expression:

$$100 \left( \frac{C}{D} \right)$$

$C$ = product of the relative molecular mass of the given homologue and the area of the corresponding peak in the chromatogram obtained with the test solution;

$D$ = sum of the $C$ values for all homologues quantified.

*Limits:*
— $C_{12}$ homologue: minimum 40 per cent;
— $C_{14}$ homologue: minimum 20 per cent;
— sum of $C_{12}$ and $C_{14}$ homologues: minimum 70 per cent.

**Impurities A, B and C**
Liquid chromatography (2.2.29). *Prepare the solutions immediately before use.*

*Test solution* Dissolve 0.50 g of the substance to be examined in *methanol R1* and dilute to 10.0 ml with the same solvent.

*Reference solution (a)* Dissolve 25.0 mg of *benzyl alcohol CRS* (impurity A) in *methanol R1* and dilute to 100.0 ml with the same solvent.

*Reference solution (b)* Dissolve 75.0 mg of *benzaldehyde CRS* (impurity B) in *methanol R1* and dilute to 100.0 ml with the same solvent. Dilute 1.0 ml of this solution to 10.0 ml with *methanol R1*.

*Reference solution (c)* Dilute 1.0 ml of reference solution (a) to 10.0 ml with *methanol R1*.

*Column:*
— *size: l = 0.15 m, Ø = 4.6 mm;*
— *stationary phase: end-capped octadecylsilyl silica gel for chromatography R (5 μm);*
— *temperature:* 30 °C.

*Mobile phase:*
— *mobile phase A:* dissolve 1.09 g of *sodium hexanesulphonate R* and 6.9 g of *sodium dihydrogen phosphate monohydrate R* in *water R*; adjust to pH 3.5 with *concentrated phosphoric acid R* and dilute to 1000.0 ml with the same solvent;
— *mobile phase B: methanol R1;*

| Time (min) | Mobile phase A (per cent *V/V*) | Mobile phase B (per cent *V/V*) |
|---|---|---|
| 0 - 10 | 80 | 20 |
| 10 - 14 | 80 → 50 | 20 → 50 |
| 14 - 35 | 50 | 50 |
| 35 - 36 | 50 → 20 | 50 → 80 |
| 36 - 55 | 20 | 80 |
| 55 - 56 | 20 → 80 | 80 → 20 |
| 56 - 65 | 80 | 20 |

*Flow rate* 1.0 ml/min.

*Detection* Spectrophotometer at 210 nm for impurities A and C, and at 257 nm for impurity B.

*Injection* 20 μl.

*Relative retention* With reference to impurity A (retention time = about 10 min): impurity B = about 1.3; impurity C = 2.4.

*System suitability* At 210 nm:
— *signal-to-noise ratio:* minimum 10 for the principal peak in the chromatogram obtained with reference solution (c);
— *symmetry factor:* minimum 0.6 for the peak due to impurity A in the chromatogram obtained with reference solution (a).

*Limits:*
— *correction factor:* for the calculation of content, multiply the peak area of impurity C by 0.7;
— *impurity A:* not more than the area of the corresponding peak in the chromatogram obtained with reference solution (a) (0.5 per cent);
— *impurity B:* not more than the area of the corresponding peak in the chromatogram obtained with reference solution (b) (0.15 per cent);
— *impurity C:* not more than 0.1 times the area of the principal peak in the chromatogram obtained with reference solution (a) (0.05 per cent).

**Amines and amine salts**
Dissolve 5.0 g with heating in 20 ml of a mixture of 3 volumes of *1 M hydrochloric acid* and 97 volumes of *methanol R* and add 100 ml of *2-propanol R*. Pass a stream of *nitrogen R* slowly through the solution. Titrate with up to 12.0 ml of *0.1 M tetrabutylammonium hydroxide* and record

the potentiometric titration curve (*2.2.20*). If the curve shows 2 points of inflexion, the volume of titrant added between the 2 points is not greater than 5.0 ml. If the curve shows no point of inflexion, the substance to be examined does not comply with the test. If the curve shows 1 point of inflexion, repeat the test but add 3.0 ml of a 25.0 g/l solution of *dimethyldecylamine R* in *2-propanol R* before the titration. If the titration curve after addition of 12.0 ml of the titrant shows only 1 point of inflexion, the substance to be examined does not comply with the test.

**Water** (*2.5.12*)

Maximum 10 per cent, determined on 0.300 g.

**Sulphated ash** (*2.4.14*)

Maximum 0.1 per cent, determined on 1.0 g.

## ASSAY

Dissolve 2.00 g in *water R* and dilute to 100.0 ml with the same solvent. Transfer 25.0 ml of the solution to a separating funnel, add 25 ml of *methylene chloride R*, 10 ml of *0.1 M sodium hydroxide* and 10.0 ml of a freshly prepared 50 g/l solution of *potassium iodide R*. Shake well, allow to separate and discard the methylene chloride layer. Shake the aqueous layer with 3 quantities, each of 10 ml, of *methylene chloride R* and discard the methylene chloride layers. To the aqueous layer add 40 ml of *hydrochloric acid R*, allow to cool and titrate with *0.05 M potassium iodate* until the deep-brown colour is almost discharged. Add 5 ml of *methylene chloride R* and continue the titration, shaking vigorously, until the methylene chloride layer no longer changes colour. Carry out a blank titration on a mixture of 10.0 ml of the freshly prepared 50 g/l solution of *potassium iodide R*, 20 ml of *water R* and 40 ml of *hydrochloric acid R*.

1 ml of *0.05 M potassium iodate* is equivalent to $\frac{x}{10}$ mg of benzalkonium chloride where $x$ is the average relative molecular mass of the sample.

## STORAGE

In an airtight container.

## IMPURITIES

*Specified impurities   A, B, C.*

A. R = $CH_2OH$: benzyl alcohol,

B. R = CHO: benzaldehyde,

C. R = $CH_2Cl$: (chloromethyl)benzene.

_____ *Ph Eur*

# Benzalkonium Chloride Solution

(*Ph Eur monograph 0371*)

**Action and use**

Antiseptic.

*Ph Eur* _____

## DEFINITION

Aqueous solution of a mixture of alkylbenzyldimethylammonium chlorides, the alkyl groups mainly having chain lengths of $C_{12}$, $C_{14}$ and $C_{16}$.

**Content**

475 g/l to 525 g/l of alkylbenzyldimethylammonium chlorides, calculated using the average relative molecular mass (see Tests). The solution may contain ethanol (96 per cent).

## CHARACTERS

**Appearance**

Clear, colourless or slightly yellowish liquid.

**Solubility**

Miscible with water and with ethanol (96 per cent).

It froths copiously when shaken.

## IDENTIFICATION

*First identification   B, E.*

*Second identification   A, C, D, E.*

A. Ultraviolet and visible absorption spectrophotometry (*2.2.25*).

*Test solution*   Dilute 0.3 ml to 100.0 ml with *water R*.

*Spectral range*   220-350 nm.

*Absorption maxima*   At 257 nm, 263 nm and 269 nm.

*Shoulder*   At about 250 nm.

B. Examine the chromatograms obtained in the test for average relative molecular mass and ratio of alkyl components.

*Results*   The principal peaks in the chromatogram obtained with the test solution are similar in retention time to the principal peaks in the chromatogram obtained with the reference solution.

C. To 0.05 ml add 2 ml of *water R*, 0.1 ml of *glacial acetic acid R* and, dropwise, 1 ml of *sodium tetraphenylborate solution R*. A white precipitate is formed. Filter. Dissolve the precipitate in a mixture of 1 ml of *acetone R* and 5 ml of *ethanol (96 per cent) R*, heating to not more than 70 °C. Add *water R* dropwise to the warm solution until a slight opalescence forms. Heat gently until the solution is clear and allow to cool. White crystals separate. Filter, wash with 3 quantities, each of 10 ml, of *water R* and dry *in vacuo* over *diphosphorus pentoxide R* or *anhydrous silica gel R* at a temperature not exceeding 50 °C. The crystals melt (*2.2.14*) at 127 °C to 133 °C.

D. To 5 ml of *dilute sodium hydroxide solution R* add 0.1 ml of *bromophenol blue solution R1* and 5 ml of *methylene chloride R* and shake. The methylene chloride layer is colourless. Add 0.05 ml of the solution to be examined and shake. The methylene chloride layer becomes blue.

E. To 0.05 ml add 1 ml of *dilute nitric acid R*. A white precipitate is formed which dissolves on the addition of 5 ml of *ethanol (96 per cent) R*. The solution gives reaction (a) of chlorides (*2.3.1*).

## TESTS

**Solution S**

Dilute 2.0 g to 100 ml with *carbon dioxide-free water R*.

**Appearance of solution**

Solution S is clear (*2.2.1*) and not more intensely coloured than reference solution $Y_6$ (*2.2.2, Method II*).

**Acidity or alkalinity**

To 50 ml of solution S add 0.1 ml of *bromocresol purple solution R*. Not more than 0.1 ml of *0.1 M hydrochloric acid* or *0.1 M sodium hydroxide* is required to change the colour of the indicator.

**Average relative molecular mass and ratio of alkyl components**

Liquid chromatography (2.2.29).

*Test solution*  Determine the density (2.2.5) of the solution to be examined. Dilute a quantity of the solution to be examined equivalent to about 0.400 g of benzalkonium chloride to 100.0 ml with *water R*.

*Reference solution*  Dissolve 40 mg of *benzalkonium chloride for system suitability CRS* in *water R* and dilute to 10.0 ml with the same solvent.

*Column:*
— *size: l* = 0.25 m, Ø = 4.6 mm;
— *stationary phase: end-capped nitrile silica gel for chromatography R* (5 µm).

*Mobile phase*  Mix 45 volumes of *acetonitrile R* and 55 volumes of a 13.6 g/l solution of *sodium acetate R* previously adjusted to pH 5.0 with *glacial acetic acid R*.

*Flow rate*  2.0 ml/min.

*Detection*  Spectrophotometer at 254 nm.

*Injection*  10 µl.

*Identification of homologues*  Use the chromatogram supplied with *benzalkonium chloride for system suitability CRS* and the chromatogram obtained with the reference solution to identify the peaks due to homologues $C_{12}$, $C_{14}$ and $C_{16}$.

*Relative retention*  With reference to $C_{12}$ homologue (retention time = about 6 min): $C_{14}$ homologue = about 1.1; $C_{16}$ homologue = about 1.3.

*System suitability*  Reference solution:
— *resolution*: minimum 1.5 between the peaks due to the $C_{12}$ and $C_{14}$ homologues.

Calculate the average relative molecular mass of the sample by summing the products for each homologue, using the following expression:

$$ W\left(\frac{A}{B}\right) $$

$A$ = area of the peak due to the given homologue in the chromatogram obtained with the test solution;

$B$ = sum of the areas of the peaks due to all homologues in the chromatogram obtained with the test solution;

$W$ = relative molecular mass for the given homologue: 340, 368 and 396 for the $C_{12}$, $C_{14}$ and $C_{16}$ homologues, respectively.

Calculate the percentage of each homologue, using the following expression:

$$ 100\left(\frac{C}{D}\right) $$

$C$ = product of the relative molecular mass of the given homologue and the area of the corresponding peak in the chromatogram obtained with the test solution;

$D$ = sum of the $C$ values for all homologues quantified.

*Limits:*
— $C_{12}$ *homologue*: minimum 40 per cent.
— $C_{14}$ *homologue*: minimum 20 per cent.
— *sum of* $C_{12}$ *and* $C_{14}$ *homologues*: minimum 70 per cent.

**Impurities A, B and C**

Liquid chromatography (2.2.29). *Prepare the solutions immediately before use.*

*Test solution*  Determine the density (2.2.5) of the solution to be examined. Dilute a quantity of the solution to be examined equivalent to 2.5 g of benzalkonium chloride to 50.0 ml with *methanol R1*.

*Reference solution (a)*  Dissolve 25.0 mg of *benzyl alcohol CRS* (impurity A) in *methanol R1* and dilute to 100.0 ml with the same solvent.

*Reference solution (b)*  Dissolve 75.0 mg of *benzaldehyde CRS* (impurity B) in *methanol R1* and dilute to 100.0 ml with the same solvent. Dilute 1.0 ml of this solution to 10.0 ml with *methanol R1*.

*Reference solution (c)*  Dilute 1.0 ml of reference solution (a) to 10.0 ml with *methanol R1*.

*Column:*
— *size: l* = 0.15 m, Ø = 4.6 mm;
— *stationary phase: end-capped octadecylsilyl silica gel for chromatography R* (5 µm);
— *temperature*: 30 °C.

*Mobile phase:*
— *mobile phase A*: dissolve 1.09 g of sodium hexanesulphonate R and 6.9 g of *sodium dihydrogen phosphate monohydrate R* in *water R*; adjust to pH 3.5 with *concentrated phosphoric acid R* and dilute to 1000.0 ml with the same solvent;
— *mobile phase B*: methanol R1;

| Time (min) | Mobile phase A (per cent V/V) | Mobile phase B (per cent V/V) |
|---|---|---|
| 0 - 10 | 80 | 20 |
| 10 - 14 | 80 → 50 | 20 → 50 |
| 14 - 35 | 50 | 50 |
| 35 - 36 | 50 → 20 | 50 → 80 |
| 36 - 55 | 20 | 80 |
| 55 - 56 | 20 → 80 | 80 → 20 |
| 56 - 65 | 80 | 20 |

*Flow rate*  1.0 ml/min.

*Detection*  Spectrophotometer at 210 nm for impurities A and C, and at 257 nm for impurity B.

*Injection*  20 µl.

*Relative retention*  With reference to impurity A (retention time = about 10 min): impurity B = about 1.3; impurity C = about 2.4.

*System suitability*  At 210 nm:
— *signal-to-noise ratio*: minimum 10 for the principal peak in the chromatogram obtained with reference solution (c);
— *symmetry factor*: minimum 0.6 for the peak due to impurity A in the chromatogram obtained with reference solution (a).

*Limits:*
— *correction factor*: for the calculation of content, multiply the peak area of impurity C by 0.7;
— *impurity A*: not more than the area of the corresponding peak in the chromatogram obtained with reference solution (a) (0.5 per cent),
— *impurity B*: not more than the area of the corresponding peak in the chromatogram obtained with reference solution (b) (0.15 per cent),
— *impurity C*: not more than 0.1 times the area of the principal peak in the chromatogram obtained with reference solution (a) (0.05 per cent).

**Amines and amine salts**

Mix 10.0 g, while heating, with 20 ml of a mixture of 3 volumes of *1 M hydrochloric acid* and 97 volumes of *methanol R* and add 100 ml of *2-propanol R*. Pass a stream of *nitrogen R* slowly through the solution. Titrate with up to 12.0 ml of *0.1 M tetrabutylammonium hydroxide* and record the potentiometric titration curve (*2.2.20*). If the curve shows 2 points of inflexion, the volume of titrant added between the 2 points is not greater than 5.0 ml. If the curve shows no point of inflexion, the solution to be examined does not comply with the test. If the curve shows 1 point of inflexion, repeat the test but add 3.0 ml of a 25.0 g/l solution of *dimethyldecylamine R* in *2-propanol R* before the titration. If the titration curve after the addition of 12.0 ml of the titrant shows only 1 point of inflexion, the solution to be examined does not comply with the test.

**Sulphated ash** (*2.4.14*)

Maximum 0.1 per cent, determined on 1.0 g.

**ASSAY**

Determine the density (*2.2.5*) of the solution to be examined. Dilute 4.00 g to 100.0 ml with *water R*. Transfer 25.0 ml of the solution to a separating funnel, add 25 ml of *methylene chloride R*, 10 ml of *0.1 M sodium hydroxide* and 10.0 ml of a freshly prepared 50 g/l solution of *potassium iodide R*. Shake well, allow to separate and discard the methylene chloride layer. Shake the aqueous layer with 3 quantities, each of 10 ml, of *methylene chloride R* and discard the methylene chloride layers. To the aqueous layer add 40 ml of *hydrochloric acid R*, allow to cool and titrate with *0.05 M potassium iodate* until the deep-brown colour is almost discharged. Add 5 ml of *methylene chloride R* and continue the titration, shaking vigorously, until the methylene chloride layer no longer changes colour. Carry out a blank titration on a mixture of 10.0 ml of the freshly prepared 50 g/l solution of *potassium iodide R*, 20 ml of *water R* and 40 ml of *hydrochloric acid R*.

1 ml of *0.05 M potassium iodate* is equivalent to $\frac{x}{10}$ mg of benzalkonium chloride where $x$ is the average relative molecular mass of the sample.

**LABELLING**

The label states the content of ethanol (96 per cent), if any.

**IMPURITIES**

*Specified impurities   A, B, C.*

A. R = CH$_2$OH: benzyl alcohol,

B. R = CHO: benzaldehyde,

C. R = CH$_2$Cl: (chloromethyl)benzene.

_____ *Ph Eur*

# Benzathine Benzylpenicillin

(*Ph Eur monograph 0373*)

(C$_{16}$H$_{18}$N$_2$O$_4$S)$_2$C$_{16}$H$_{20}$N$_2$   909   1538-09-6

**Action and use**

Penicillin antibacterial.

*Ph Eur* _____

**DEFINITION**

N,N'-Dibenzylethane-1,2-diamine compound (1:2) with (2S,5R,6R)-3,3-dimethyl-7-oxo-6-[(phenylacetyl)amino]-4-thia-1-azabicyclo[3.2.0]heptane-2-carboxylic acid.

Substance produced by the growth of certain strains of *Penicillium notatum* or related organisms, or obtained by any other means.

**Content**

— *benzathine benzylpenicillin*: 96.0 per cent to 102.0 per cent (anhydrous substance);

— *N,N'-dibenzylethylenediamine* (benzathine C$_{16}$H$_{20}$N$_2$; $M_r$ 240.3): 24.0 per cent to 27.0 per cent (anhydrous substance).

It contains a variable quantity of water. Dispersing or suspending agents may be added.

**CHARACTERS**

**Appearance**

White or almost white powder.

**Solubility**

Very slightly soluble in water, freely soluble in dimethylformamide and in formamide, slightly soluble in ethanol (96 per cent).

**IDENTIFICATION**

*First identification   A.*

*Second identification   B, C, D.*

A. Infrared absorption spectrophotometry (*2.2.24*).

*Comparison   benzathine benzylpenicillin CRS.*

B. Thin-layer chromatography (*2.2.27*).

*Test solution   Dissolve 25 mg of the substance to be examined in 5 ml of methanol R.*

*Reference solution   Dissolve 25 mg of benzathine benzylpenicillin CRS in 5 ml of methanol R.*

*Plate   TLC silanised silica gel plate R.*

*Mobile phase   Mix 30 volumes of acetone R and 70 volumes of a 154 g/l solution of ammonium acetate R adjusted to pH 7.0 with ammonia R.*

*Application   1 µl.*

*Development   Over a path of 15 cm.*

*Drying   In air.*

*Detection   Expose to iodine vapour until the spots appear and examine in daylight.*

*System suitability   Reference solution*

— The chromatogram shows 2 clearly separated spots.

*Results* The 2 principal spots in the chromatogram obtained with the test solution are similar in position, colour and size to the 2 principal spots in the chromatogram obtained with the reference solution.

C. Place about 2 mg in a test-tube about 150 mm long and 15 mm in diameter. Moisten with 0.05 ml of *water R* and add 2 ml of *sulphuric acid-formaldehyde reagent R*. Mix the contents of the tube by swirling; the solution is practically colourless. Place the test-tube on a water-bath for 1 min; a reddish-brown colour develops.

D. To 0.1 g add 2 ml of *1 M sodium hydroxide* and shake for 2 min. Shake the mixture with 2 quantities, each of 3 ml, of *ether R*. Evaporate the combined ether layers to dryness and dissolve the residue in 1 ml of *ethanol (50 per cent V/V) R*. Add 5 ml of *picric acid solution R*, heat at 90 °C for 5 min and allow to cool slowly. Separate the crystals and recrystallise from *ethanol (25 per cent V/V) R* containing 10 g/l of *picric acid R*. The crystals melt (*2.2.14*) at about 214 °C.

## TESTS

### Acidity or alkalinity

To 0.50 g add 100 ml of *carbon dioxide-free water R* and shake for 5 min. Filter through a sintered-glass filter (2.1.2). To 20 ml of the filtrate add 0.1 ml of *bromothymol blue solution R1*. The solution is green or yellow. Not more than 0.2 ml of *0.02 M sodium hydroxide* is required to change the colour of the indicator to blue.

### Related substances

Liquid chromatography (*2.2.29*). *Prepare the solutions immediately before use, using sonication (for about 2 min) to dissolve the samples. Avoid any overheating during the sample preparation.*

*Test solution* Dissolve 70.0 mg of the substance to be examined in 25 ml of *methanol R* and dilute to 50.0 ml with a solution containing 6.8 g/l of *potassium dihydrogen phosphate R* and 1.02 g/l of *disodium hydrogen phosphate R*.

*Reference solution (a)* Dissolve 70.0 mg of *benzathine benzylpenicillin CRS* in 25 ml of *methanol R* and dilute to 50.0 ml with a solution containing 6.8 g/l of *potassium dihydrogen phosphate R* and 1.02 g/l of *disodium hydrogen phosphate R*.

*Reference solution (b)* Dilute 1.0 ml of reference solution (a) to 100.0 ml with mobile phase A.

*Column:*
— *size*: $l$ = 0.25 m, Ø = 4.0 mm;
— *stationary phase: end-capped octadecylsilyl silica gel for chromatography R (5 µm);*
— *temperature*: 40 °C.

*Mobile phase:*
— *mobile phase A*: mix 10 volumes of a 34 g/l solution of *potassium dihydrogen phosphate R* adjusted to pH 3.5 with *phosphoric acid R*, 30 volumes of *methanol R* and 60 volumes of *water R*;
— *mobile phase B*: mix 10 volumes of a 34 g/l solution of *potassium dihydrogen phosphate R* adjusted to pH 3.5 with *phosphoric acid R*, 30 volumes of *water R* and 60 volumes of *methanol R*;

| Time (min) | Mobile phase A (per cent V/V) | Mobile phase B (per cent V/V) |
|---|---|---|
| 0 - 10 | 75 | 25 |
| 10 - 20 | 75 → 0 | 25 → 100 |
| 20 - 55 | 0 | 100 |
| 55 - 70 | 75 | 25 |

*Flow rate* 1 ml/min.

*Detection* Spectrophotometer at 220 nm.

*Injection* 20 µl.

*System suitability* Reference solution (a):
— *relative retention* with reference to benzylpenicillin: benzathine = 0.3 to 0.4 impurity C = about 2.4; if necessary, adjust the concentration of methanol in the mobile phase.

*Limits:*
— *impurity C*: not more than twice the sum of the areas of the 2 principal peaks in the chromatogram obtained with reference solution (b) (2 per cent);
— *any other impurity*: for each impurity, not more than the sum of the areas of the 2 principal peaks in the chromatogram obtained with reference solution (b) (1 per cent);
— *disregard limit*: 0.05 times the sum of the areas of the 2 principal peaks in the chromatogram obtained with reference solution (b) (0.05 per cent).

**Water** (*2.5.12*)
5.0 per cent to 8.0 per cent, determined on 0.300 g.

**Bacterial endotoxins** (*2.6.14, Method E*)
Less than 0.13 IU/ml, if intended for use in the manufacture of parenteral dosage forms without a further appropriate procedure for the removal of bacterial endotoxins.

Suspend 20 mg in 20 ml of a solution of *0.1 M sodium hydroxide* diluted 1 to 100, shake thoroughly and centrifuge. Examine the supernatant.

## ASSAY

Liquid chromatography (*2.2.29*) as described in the test for related substances with the following modifications.

*Mobile phase phosphate buffer solution pH 3.5 R, methanol R, water R (10:35:55 V/V/V).*

*Injection* Test solution and reference solution (a).

Calculate the percentage contents of benzathine and benzathine benzylpenicillin. Calculate the percentage content of benzathine benzylpenicillin by multiplying the percentage content of benzylpenicillin by 1.36.

## STORAGE

In an airtight container. If the substance is sterile, store in a sterile, airtight, tamper-proof container.

## IMPURITIES

*Specified impurities* C.

*Other detectable impurities* (the following substances would, if present at a sufficient level, be detected by one or other of the tests in the monograph. They are limited by the general acceptance criterion for other/unspecified impurities and/or by the general monograph *Substances for pharmaceutical use (2034)*. It is therefore not necessary to identify these impurities for demonstration of compliance. See also *5.10*. *Control of impurities in substances for pharmaceutical use): A, B, D, E, F.*

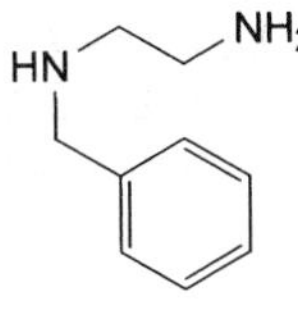

A. monobenzylethylenediamine,

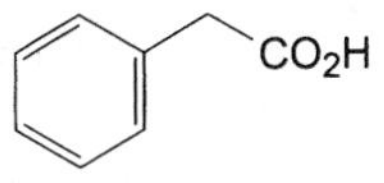

B. phenylacetic acid,

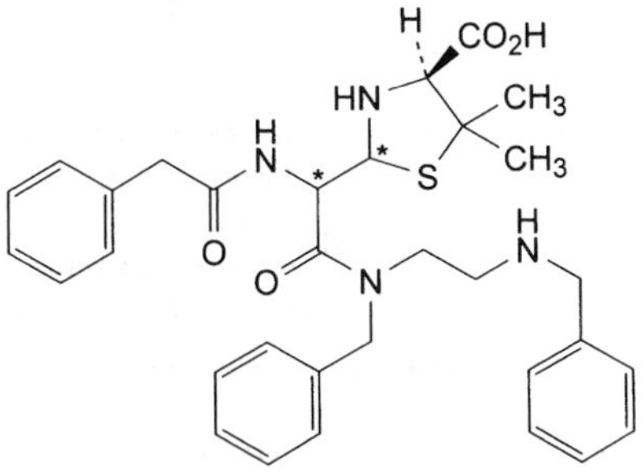

C. benzylpenicilloic acids benzathide,

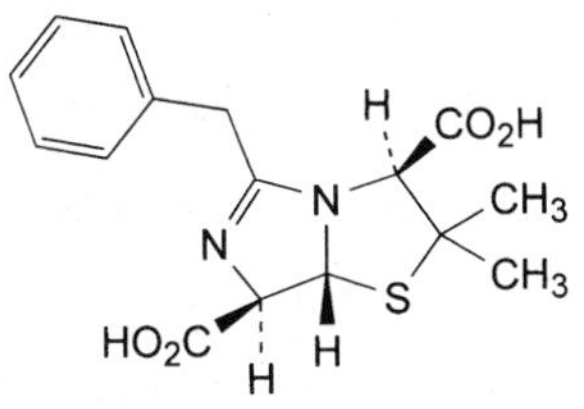

D. (3S,7R,7aR)-5-benzyl-2,2-dimethyl-2,3,7,7a-tetrahydroimidazo[5,1-b]thiazole-3,7-dicarboxylic acid (penillic acid of benzylpenicillin),

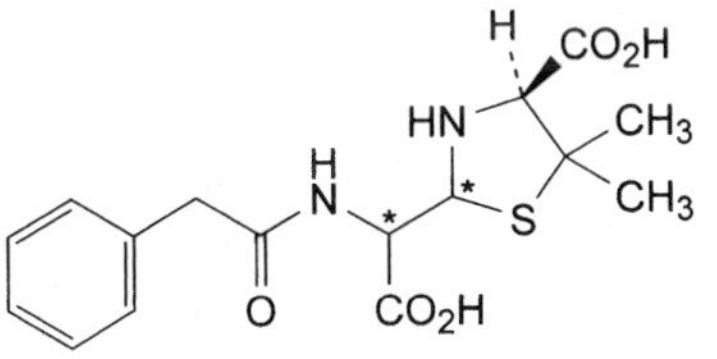

E. (4S)-2-[carboxy[(phenylacetyl)amino]methyl]-5,5-dimethylthiazolidine-4-carboxylic acid (penicilloic acids of benzylpenicillin),

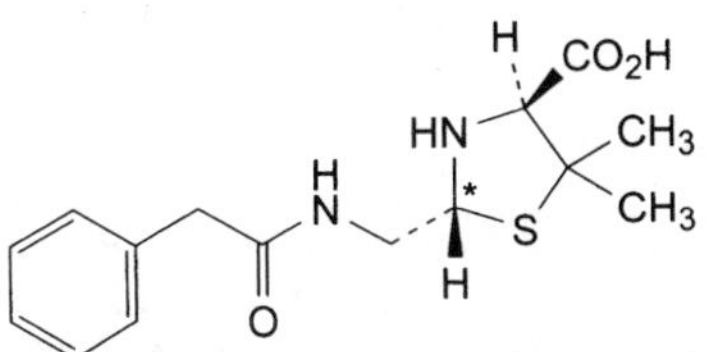

and epimer at C*

F. (2RS,4S)-2-[[(phenylacetyl)amino]methyl]-5,5-dimethylthiazolidine-4-carboxylic acid (penilloic acids of benzylpenicillin).

_____ *Ph Eur*

# Benzatropine Mesilate

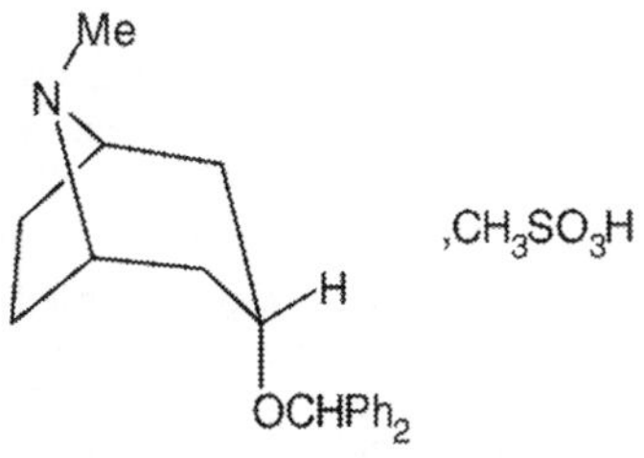

$C_{21}H_{25}NO,CH_4O_3S$    403.5    *132-17-2*

**Action and use**
Anticholinergic.

**Preparations**
Benzatropine Injection
Benzatropine Tablets

## DEFINITION
Benzatropine Mesilate is (1R,3R,5S)-3-benzhydryloxytropane methanesulphonate. It contains not less than 98.0% and not more than 100.5% of $C_{21}H_{25}NO,CH_4O_3S$, calculated with reference to the dried substance.

## CHARACTERISTICS
A white, crystalline powder. It melts at about 144°.

Very soluble in *water*; freely soluble in *ethanol (96%)*; practically insoluble in *ether*.

## IDENTIFICATION
A. Dry the substance at 105° for 3 hours. The *infrared absorption spectrum*, Appendix II A, is concordant with the *reference spectrum* of benzatropine mesilate (*RS 026*).

B. The *light absorption*, Appendix II B, in the range 230 to 350 nm of a 0.1% w/v solution in *2M hydrochloric acid* exhibits two maxima, at 253 and 258 nm. The *absorbance* at 253 nm is about 0.96 and at 258 nm is about 1.1.

C. Dissolve 10 mg in 2 ml of *water*, pour into 5 ml of hot *picric acid solution R1* and allow to cool. The *melting point* of the precipitate, after drying at 105°, is about 185°, Appendix V A.

## TESTS
**Tropine**
Carry out the method for *thin-layer chromatography*, Appendix III A, using *silica gel G* as the coating substance and a mixture of 75 volumes of *ethanol (96%)* and 15 volumes of *13.5M ammonia* as the mobile phase. Apply separately to the plate 10 μl of each of two solutions in *acetone* containing (1) 4.0% w/v of the substance being examined and (2) 0.020% w/v of *tropine*. After removal of the plate, allow it to dry in air and spray with *sodium iodobismuthate solution* and then with a 0.4% w/v solution of *sulphuric acid*. Any spot corresponding to tropine in the chromatogram obtained with solution (1) is not more intense than the spot in the chromatogram obtained with solution (2).

**Related substances**
Carry out the method for *liquid chromatography*, Appendix III D, using the following solutions. For solution (1) mix with the aid of ultrasound 50 mg of the substance being examined with 15 ml of mobile phase A, dilute to 50 ml with the same solvent and filter. For solution (2) dilute 1 volume of solution (1) to 100 volumes with mobile phase

A and further dilute 1 volume of the resulting solution to
5 volumes with the same solvent. For solution (3) mix with
the aid of ultrasound 50 mg of *desmethyl benzatropine
hydrochloride BPCRS* with 15 ml of mobile phase A, dilute to
100 ml and dilute 1 volume of the resulting solution to
100 volumes with the same solvent. Solution (4) contains
0.01% w/v each of *benzatropine mesilate BPCRS* and *desmethyl
benzatropine hydrochloride BPCRS* in mobile phase A.

The chromatographic procedure may be carried out using
(a) a stainless steel column (25 cm × 4.6 mm) packed with
*phenylsilyl silica gel for chromatography* (5 μm) (Zorbax
SB-Phenyl 5μ is suitable). Carry out a linear gradient elution
with a flow rate of 1 ml per minute using the following
conditions. Use a detection wavelength of 220 nm.

*Mobile phase A*   A mixture of 5 volumes of a 1M potassium
phosphate buffer prepared as described for mobile phase B,
20 volumes of *acetonitrile* and 75 volumes of *water*.

*Mobile phase B*   A mixture of 35 volumes of *water*,
60 volumes of *acetonitrile* and 5 volumes of a 1M potassium
phosphate buffer prepared in the following manner: dissolve
136.1 g of *potassium dihydrogen orthophosphate* in 900 ml of
*water*, add 5 ml of *orthophosphoric acid (85%)* and dilute to
1000 ml.

| Time (minutes) | Mobile phase A % v/v | Mobile phase B % v/v |
|---|---|---|
| 0 | 70 | 30 |
| 20 | 30 | 70 |
| 30 | 0 | 100 |
| 50 | 0 | 100 |
| 55 | 70 | 30 |
| 65 | 70 | 30 |

Inject 20 μl of solution (4). The test is not valid unless the
*resolution factor* between the two principal peaks is at least 1.
If necessary adjust the concentration of acetonitrile or adjust
the time program of the linear gradient elution.

Inject separately 20 μl of mobile phase A as a blank and
20 μl each of solutions (1), (2) and (3). In the chromatogram
obtained with solution (1) the area of any peak
corresponding to desmethyl benzatropine is not greater than
the area of the principal peak in the chromatogram obtained
with solution (3) (0.5%), the area of any other *secondary peak*
is not greater that the area of the principal peak in the
chromatogram obtained with solution (2) (0.2%) and the
sum of the areas of any such peaks is not greater than
2.5 times the area of the principal peak in the chromatogram
obtained with solution (2) (0.5%). In solution (1) disregard
any peaks corresponding to the peaks in the chromatogram
obtained with the blank solution.

**Loss on drying**
When dried to constant weight at 105°, loses not more than
5.0% of its weight. Use 1 g.

**Sulphated ash**
Not more than 0.1%, Appendix IX A.

**ASSAY**
Dissolve 0.6 g in 25 ml of *water*, add 5 ml of *dilute sodium
carbonate solution* and extract with four 10 ml quantities of
*chloroform*. Wash the combined extracts with 10 ml of *water*,
extract the washings with 5 ml of *chloroform* and add the
chloroform to the combined extracts. Filter and wash the
filter with 5 ml of *chloroform*. To the combined filtrate and
washings add 25 ml of *1,4-dioxan* and titrate with

*0.1M perchloric acid VS* using 0.15 ml of a 0.1% w/v solution
of *methyl red* in *methanol* as indicator. Each ml of *0.1M
perchloric acid VS* is equivalent to 40.35 mg of
$C_{21}H_{25}NO,CH_4O_3S$.

# Benzbromarone

*(Ph Eur monograph 1393)*

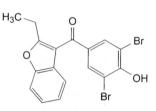

$C_{17}H_{12}Br_2O_3$          424.1          *3562-84-3*

**Action and use**
Uricosuric; treatment of hyperuricaemia.

*Ph Eur*

## DEFINITION
(3,5-Dibromo-4-hydroxyphenyl)(2-ethylbenzofuran-3-
yl)methanone.

## Content
98.0 per cent to 101.0 per cent (dried substance).

## CHARACTERS
**Appearance**
White or almost white, crystalline powder.

**Solubility**
Practically insoluble in water, freely soluble in acetone and in
methylene chloride, sparingly soluble in ethanol
(96 per cent).

mp: about 152 °C.

## IDENTIFICATION
A. Infrared absorption spectrophotometry (*2.2.24*).

*Comparison*   benzbromarone CRS.

B. By means of a copper wire, previously ignited, introduce a
small amount of the substance to be examined into the
non-luminous part of a flame. The colour of the flame
becomes green.

## TESTS
**Appearance of solution**
The solution is clear (*2.2.1*) and not more intensely coloured
than reference solution $Y_5$ (*2.2.2, Method II*).

Dissolve 1.25 g in *dimethylformamide R* and dilute to 25 ml
with the same solvent.

**Acidity or alkalinity**
Shake 0.5 g with 10 ml of *carbon dioxide-free water R* for
1 min and filter. To 2.0 ml of the filtrate add 0.1 ml of
*methyl red solution R* and 0.1 ml of *0.01 M hydrochloric acid*.
The solution is red. Add 0.3 ml of *0.01 M sodium hydroxide*.
The solution is yellow.

**Related substances**
Liquid chromatography (*2.2.29*).

*Test solution*   Dissolve 0.125 g of the substance to be
examined in 30 ml of *methanol R* and dilute to 50.0 ml with
the mobile phase.

*Reference solution (a)* Dilute 1.0 ml of the test solution to 100.0 ml with the mobile phase. Dilute 1.0 ml of this solution to 10.0 ml with the mobile phase.

*Reference solution (b)* Dissolve 10 mg of *benzarone CRS* (impurity C) in the mobile phase and dilute to 20 ml with the mobile phase. To 5 ml of this solution add 1 ml of the test solution and dilute to 100 ml with the mobile phase.

*Column:*
— *size*: $l$ = 0.25 m, Ø = 4.6 mm;
— *stationary phase*: octadecylsilyl silica gel for chromatography R (5 µm).

*Mobile phase* glacial acetic acid R, acetonitrile R, water R, methanol R (5:25:300:990 V/V/V/V).

*Flow rate* 1.5 ml/min.

*Detection* Spectrophotometer at 231 nm.

*Injection* 20 µl.

*Run time* 2.5 times the retention time of benzbromarone.

*Relative retention* With reference to benzbromarone: impurity A = about 0.6; impurity B = about 2.

*System suitability* Reference solution (b).
— *resolution*: minimum 10.0 between the peaks due to impurity C (1st peak) and benzbromarone (2nd peak).

*Limits:*
— *impurity A*: not more than 4 times the area of the principal peak in the chromatogram obtained with reference solution (a) (0.4 per cent);
— *impurity B*: not more than 10 times the area of the principal peak in the chromatogram obtained with reference solution (a) (1.0 per cent);
— *unspecified impurities*: for each impurity, not more than the area of the principal peak in the chromatogram obtained with reference solution (a) (0.10 per cent);
— *sum of impurities* other than A and B: not more than twice the area of the principal peak in the chromatogram obtained with reference solution (a) (0.2 per cent);
— *disregard limit*: 0.2 times the area of the principal peak in the chromatogram obtained with reference solution (a) (0.02 per cent).

**Halides expressed as chlorides** *(2.4.4)*
Maximum 400 ppm.

Shake 1.25 g with a mixture of 5 ml of *dilute nitric acid R* and 15 ml of *water R*. Filter. Rinse the filter with *water R* and dilute the filtrate to 25 ml with the same solvent. Dilute 2.5 ml of this solution to 15 ml with *water R*.

**Iron** *(2.4.9)*
Maximum 125 ppm.

Moisten the residue obtained in the test for sulphated ash with 2 ml of *hydrochloric acid R* and evaporate to dryness on a water-bath. Add 0.05 ml of *hydrochloric acid R* and 10 ml of *water R*, heat to boiling and maintain boiling for 1 min. Allow to cool. Rinse the crucible with *water R*, collect the rinsings and dilute to 25 ml with *water R*. Dilute 2 ml of this solution to 10 ml with *water R*.

**Heavy metals** *(2.4.8)*
Maximum 20 ppm.

0.5 g complies with test C. Prepare the reference solution using 1 ml of *lead standard solution (10 ppm Pb) R*.

**Loss on drying** *(2.2.32)*
maximum 0.5 per cent, determined on 1.000 g by drying *in vacuo* at 50 °C for 4 h.

**Sulphated ash** *(2.4.14)*
Maximum 0.1 per cent, determined on 1.0 g.

**ASSAY**
Dissolve 0.300 g in 60 ml of *methanol R*. Stir until completely dissolved and add 10 ml of *water R*. Titrate with *0.1 M sodium hydroxide*, determining the end-point potentiometrically *(2.2.20)*.

1 ml of *0.1 M sodium hydroxide* is equivalent to 42.41 mg of $C_{17}H_{12}Br_2O_3$.

**STORAGE**
Protected from light.

**IMPURITIES**
*Specified impurities* A, B.

*Other detectable impurities* (the following substances would, if present at a sufficient level, be detected by one or other of the tests in the monograph. They are limited by the general acceptance criterion for other/unspecified impurities and/or by the general monograph *Substances for pharmaceutical use (2034)*. It is therefore not necessary to identify these impurities for demonstration of compliance. See also *5.10. Control of impurities in substances for pharmaceutical use)*: C.

A. R1 = R2 = H, R3 = Br: (3-bromo-4-hydroxyphenyl)(2-ethylbenzofuran-3-yl)methanone,

B. R1 = R2 = R3 = Br: (6-bromo-2-ethylbenzofuran-3-yl)(3,5-dibromo-4-hydroxyphenyl)methanone,

C. R1 = R2 = R3 = H: (2-ethylbenzofuran-3-yl)(4-hydroxyphenyl)methanone (benzarone).

*Ph Eur*

# Benzethonium Chloride

*(Ph Eur monograph 0974)*

$C_{27}H_{42}ClNO_2$ 448.1 *121-54-0*

**Action and use**
Antiseptic.

*Ph Eur*

**DEFINITION**
*N*-Benzyl-*N,N*-dimethyl-2-[2-[4-(1,1,3,3-tetramethylbutyl)phenoxy]ethoxy]ethanaminium chloride.

**Content**
97.0 per cent to 103.0 per cent (dried substance).

## CHARACTERS

### Appearance
White or yellowish-white powder.

### Solubility
Very soluble in water and in ethanol (96 per cent), freely soluble in methylene chloride.

An aqueous solution froths copiously when shaken.

## IDENTIFICATION
A. Melting point (2.2.14): 158 °C to 164 °C, after drying at 105 °C for 4 h.

B. Thin-layer chromatography (2.2.27).

*Test solution*   Dissolve 25 mg of the substance to be examined in *water R* and dilute to 5 ml with the same solvent.

*Reference solution*   Dissolve 25 mg of *benzethonium chloride CRS* in *water R* and dilute to 5 ml with the same solvent.

*Plate*   *TLC silica gel F₂₅₄ plate R.*

*Mobile phase*   *glacial acetic acid R, water R, methanol R* (5:5:100 *V/V/V*).

*Application*   20 µl.

*Development*   Over a path of 12 cm.

*Drying*   In a current of warm air.

*Detection*   Examine in ultraviolet light at 254 nm.

*Results*   The principal spot in the chromatogram obtained with the test solution is similar in position and size to the principal spot in the chromatogram obtained with the reference solution.

C. To 5 ml of *dilute sodium hydroxide solution R* add 0.1 ml of *bromophenol blue solution R1* and 5 ml of *methylene chloride R* and shake. The lower layer is colourless. Add 0.1 ml of solution S (see Tests) and shake. A blue colour develops in the lower layer.

D. To 2 ml of solution S add 1 ml of *dilute nitric acid R*. A white precipitate is formed which dissolves upon addition of 5 ml of *ethanol (96 per cent) R*. The solution gives reaction (a) of chlorides (2.3.1).

## TESTS

### Solution S
Dissolve 5.0 g in *carbon dioxide-free water R* and dilute to 50 ml with the same solvent.

### Appearance of solution
Solution S is clear (2.2.1) and not more intensely coloured than reference solution $Y_6$ (2.2.2, Method II).

### Acidity or alkalinity
To 25 ml of solution S add 0.1 ml of *phenolphthalein solution R*. The solution is colourless. Add 0.3 ml of *0.01 M sodium hydroxide*. The solution is pink. Add 0.1 ml of *methyl red solution R* and 0.5 ml of *0.01 M hydrochloric acid*. The solution is orange-red.

### Volatile bases and salts of volatile bases (2.4.1,
*Method B*)

Maximum 50 ppm, determined on 0.20 g.

Prepare the standard using 0.1 ml of *ammonium standard solution (100 ppm NH₄) R*. Replace heavy magnesium oxide by 2.0 ml of *strong sodium hydroxide solution R*.

### Loss on drying (2.2.32)
Maximum 5.0 per cent, determined on 1.000 g by drying in an oven at 105 °C for 4 h.

### Sulphated ash (2.4.14)
Maximum 0.1 per cent, determined on 1.0 g.

## ASSAY
Dissolve 2.000 g in *water R* and dilute to 100.0 ml with the same solvent. Transfer 25.0 ml of the solution to a separating funnel, add 10 ml of a 4 g/l solution of *sodium hydroxide R*, 10.0 ml of a freshly prepared 50 g/l solution of *potassium iodide R* and 25 ml of *methylene chloride R*. Shake vigorously, allow to separate and discard the lower layer. Shake the upper layer with 3 quantities, each of 10 ml, of *methylene chloride R* and discard the lower layers. To the upper layer add 40 ml of *hydrochloric acid R*, allow to cool and titrate with *0.05 M potassium iodate* until the deep brown colour is almost discharged. Add 4 ml of *methylene chloride R* and continue the titration, shaking vigorously, until the lower layer is no longer brown. Carry out a blank titration using a mixture of 10.0 ml of a freshly prepared 50 g/l solution of *potassium iodide R*, 20 ml of *water R* and 40 ml of *hydrochloric acid R*.

1 ml of *0.05 M potassium iodate* is equivalent to 44.81 mg of $C_{27}H_{42}ClNO_2$.

## STORAGE
Protected from light.

_____ *Ph Eur*

# Benzocaine

*(Ph Eur monograph 0011)*

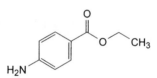

$C_9H_{11}NO_2$                165.2                94-09-7

### Action and use
Local anaesthetic.

*Ph Eur* _____

## DEFINITION
Ethyl 4-aminobenzoate.

### Content
99.0 per cent to 101.0 per cent (dried substance).

## CHARACTERS

### Appearance
White or almost white, crystalline powder or colourless crystals.

### Solubility
Very slightly soluble in water, freely soluble in ethanol (96 per cent).

## IDENTIFICATION
*First identification*   A, B.

*Second identification*   A, C, D.

A. Melting point (2.2.14): 89 °C to 92 °C.

B. Infrared absorption spectrophotometry (2.2.24).

*Comparison*   benzocaine CRS.

C. To about 50 mg in a test tube add 0.2 ml of a 500 g/l solution of *chromium trioxide R*. Cover the mouth of the tube with a piece of filter paper moistened with a freshly prepared mixture of equal volumes of a 50 g/l solution of *sodium nitroprusside R* and a 200 g/l solution of *piperazine hydrate R*.

Boil gently for at least 30 s. A blue colour develops on the filter paper.

D. Dissolve about 50 mg in *ethanol (96 per cent) R* and dilute to 100 ml with the same solvent. 2 ml of the solution gives the reaction of primary aromatic amines (*2.3.1*).

## TESTS
### Appearance of solution
The solution is clear (*2.2.1*) and colourless (*2.2.2*, *Method II*).

Dissolve 1.0 g in *ethanol (96 per cent) R* and dilute to 20 ml with the same solvent.

### Acidity or alkalinity
Dissolve 0.5 g in 10 ml of *ethanol (96 per cent) R* previously neutralised to 0.05 ml of *phenolphthalein solution R*. Add 10 ml of *carbon dioxide-free water R*. The solution remains colourless and not more than 0.5 ml of *0.01 M sodium hydroxide* is required to change the colour of the indicator.

### Loss on drying (*2.2.32*)
Maximum 0.5 per cent, determined on 1.00 g by drying *in vacuo*.

### Sulphated ash (*2.4.14*)
Maximum 0.1 per cent, determined on 1.0 g.

## ASSAY
Carry out the determination of primary aromatic amino-nitrogen (*2.5.8*), using 0.400 g dissolved in a mixture of 25 ml of *hydrochloric acid R* and 50 ml of *water R*.

1 ml of *0.1 M sodium nitrite* is equivalent to 16.52 mg of $C_9H_{11}NO_2$.

## STORAGE
Protected from light.

*Ph Eur*

# Benzoic Acid

(*Ph Eur monograph 0066*)

$C_7H_6O_2$ 122.1 65-85-0

### Action and use
Antimicrobial preservative.

### Preparations
Compound Benzoic Acid Ointment

Benzoic Acid Solution

*Ph Eur*

## DEFINITION
Benzenecarboxylic acid.

### Content
99.0 per cent to 100.5 per cent.

## CHARACTERS
### Appearance
White or almost white, crystalline powder or colourless crystals.

### Solubility
Slightly soluble in water, soluble in boiling water, freely soluble in ethanol (96 per cent) and in fatty oils.

## IDENTIFICATION
A. Melting point (*2.2.14*): 121 °C to 124 °C.

B. Solution S (see Tests) gives reaction (a) of benzoates (*2.3.1*).

## TESTS
### Solution S
Dissolve 5.0 g in *ethanol (96 per cent) R* and dilute to 100 ml with the same solvent.

### Appearance of solution
Solution S is clear (*2.2.1*) and colourless (*2.2.2*, *Method II*).

### Carbonisable substances
Dissolve 0.5 g with shaking in 5 ml of *sulphuric acid R*. After 5 min, the solution is not more intensely coloured than reference solution $Y_5$ (*2.2.2*, *Method I*).

### Oxidisable substances
Dissolve 0.2 g in 10 ml of boiling *water R*. Cool, shake and filter. To the filtrate add 1 ml of *dilute sulphuric acid R* and 0.2 ml of *0.02 M potassium permanganate*. After 5 min, the solution is still coloured pink.

### Halogenated compounds and halides
Maximum 300 ppm.

*All glassware used must be chloride-free and may be prepared by soaking overnight in a 500 g/l solution of nitric acid R, rinsed with water R and stored full of water R. It is recommended that glassware be reserved for this test.*

*Solution (a)* Dissolve 6.7 g in a mixture of 40 ml of *1 M sodium hydroxide* and 50 ml of *ethanol (96 per cent) R* and dilute to 100.0 ml with *water R*. To 10.0 ml of this solution add 7.5 ml of *dilute sodium hydroxide solution R* and 0.125 g of *nickel-aluminium alloy R* and heat on a water-bath for 10 min. Allow to cool to room temperature, filter into a 25 ml volumetric flask and wash with 3 quantities, each of 2 ml, of *ethanol (96 per cent) R*. Dilute the filtrate and washings to 25.0 ml with *water R*. This solution is used to prepare solution A.

*Solution (b)* In the same manner, prepare a similar solution without the substance to be examined. This solution is used to prepare solution B.

In four 25 ml volumetric flasks, place separately 10 ml of solution (a), 10 ml of solution (b), 10 ml of *chloride standard solution (8 ppm Cl) R* (used to prepare solution C) and 10 ml of *water R*. To each flask add 5 ml of *ferric ammonium sulphate solution R5*, mix and add dropwise and with swirling 2 ml of *nitric acid R* and 5 ml of *mercuric thiocyanate solution R*. Shake. Dilute the contents of each flask to 25.0 ml with *water R* and allow the solutions to stand in a water-bath at 20 °C for 15 min. Measure at 460 nm the absorbance (*2.2.25*) of solution A using solution B as the compensation liquid, and the absorbance of solution C using the solution obtained with 10 ml of *water R* as the compensation liquid. The absorbance of solution A is not greater than that of solution C.

### Heavy metals (*2.4.8*)
Maximum 10 ppm.

12 ml of solution S complies with test B. Prepare the reference solution using a mixture of 5 ml of *lead standard solution (1 ppm Pb) R* and 5 ml of *ethanol (96 per cent) R*.

### Sulphated ash (*2.4.14*)
Maximum 0.1 per cent, determined on 1.0 g.

## ASSAY

Dissolve 0.200 g in 20 ml of *ethanol (96 per cent) R* and titrate with *0.1 M sodium hydroxide*, using 0.1 ml of *phenol red solution R* as indicator, until the colour changes from yellow to violet-red.

1 ml of *0.1 M sodium hydroxide* is equivalent to 12.21 mg of $C_7H_6O_2$.

*_____ Ph Eur*

# Hydrous Benzoyl Peroxide

(*Ph Eur monograph 0704*)

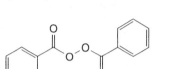

| $C_{14}H_{10}O_4$ | 242.2 | 94-36-0 |

## Action and use
Used topically in the treatment of acne.

## Preparations
Benzoyl Peroxide Cream

Benzoyl Peroxide Gel

Benzoyl Peroxide Lotion

Potassium Hydroxyquinoline Sulphate and Benzoyl Peroxide Cream

*Ph Eur _____*

## DEFINITION
*Content:*
— dibenzoyl peroxide: 70.0 per cent to 77.0 per cent,
— water: minimum 20.0 per cent.

## CHARACTERS
### Appearance
White or almost white, amorphous or granular powder.

### Solubility
Practically insoluble in water, soluble in acetone, soluble in methylene chloride with the separation of water, slightly soluble in alcohol.

It loses water rapidly on exposure to air with a risk of explosion.

*Mix the entire sample thoroughly before carrying out the following tests.*

## IDENTIFICATION
*First identification   B.*

*Second identification   A, C, D.*

A. Dissolve 80.0 mg in *alcohol R* and dilute to 100.0 ml with the same solvent. Dilute 10.0 ml of the solution to 100.0 ml with *alcohol R* (solution A). Dilute 10.0 ml of solution A to 100.0 ml with *alcohol R* (solution B). Examined between 250 nm and 300 nm (*2.2.25*), solution A shows an absorption maximum at 274 nm and a shoulder at about 282 nm. Examined between 220 nm and 250 nm, solution B shows an absorption maximum at 235 nm. The ratio of the absorbance at the maximum at 235 nm (solution B) to that at the maximum at 274 nm (solution A) is 1.17 to 1.21.

B. Infrared absorption spectrophotometry (*2.2.24*).

*Comparison   Ph. Eur. reference spectrum of hydrous benzoyl peroxide.*

C. Dissolve about 25 mg in 2 ml of *acetone R*. Add 1 ml of a 10 g/l solution of *diethylphenylenediamine sulphate R* and mix. A red colour develops which quickly darkens and becomes dark violet within 5 min.

D. To 1 g add 5 ml of *alcohol R*, 5 ml of *dilute sodium hydroxide solution R* and 10 ml of *water R*. Boil the mixture under reflux for 20 min. Cool. The solution gives reaction (c) of benzoates (*2.3.1*).

## TESTS
### Acidity
Dissolve a quantity of the substance to be examined containing the equivalent of 1.0 g of dibenzoyl peroxide in 25 ml of *acetone R*, add 75 ml of *water R* and filter. Wash the residue with two quantities, each of 10 ml, of *water R*. Combine the filtrate and the washings and add 0.25 ml of *phenolphthalein solution R1*. Not more than 1.25 ml of *0.1 M sodium hydroxide* is required to change the colour of the indicator. Carry out a blank test.

### Related substances
Liquid chromatography (*2.2.29*). *Prepare the solutions immediately before use.*

*Test solution   *Dissolve a quantity of the substance to be examined containing the equivalent of 0.10 g of dibenzoyl peroxide in *acetonitrile R* and dilute to 50 ml with the same solvent.

*Reference solution (a)   *Dilute 1.0 ml of the test solution to 100.0 ml with *acetonitrile R*. Dilute 1.0 ml of this solution to 10.0 ml with *acetonitrile R*.

*Reference solution (b)   *Dissolve 30.0 mg of *benzoic acid R* in the mobile phase and dilute to 100.0 ml with the mobile phase. Dilute 1.0 ml of the solution to 10.0 ml with the mobile phase.

*Reference solution (c)   *Dissolve 50.0 mg of *ethyl benzoate R* in the mobile phase and dilute to 100.0 ml with the mobile phase. Dilute 1.0 ml of the solution to 100.0 ml with the mobile phase.

*Reference solution (d)   *Dissolve 50.0 mg of *benzaldehyde R* in the mobile phase and dilute to 100.0 ml with the mobile phase. Dilute 1.0 ml of the solution to 100.0 ml with the mobile phase.

*Reference solution (e)   *Dissolve 30.0 mg of *benzoic acid R* and 30.0 mg of *benzaldehyde R* in the mobile phase and dilute to 100.0 ml with the mobile phase. Dilute 1.0 ml of the solution to 10.0 ml with the mobile phase.

*Column:*
— size: $l$ = 0.25 m, Ø = 4.6 mm,
— stationary phase: *octadecylsilyl silica gel for chromatography R* (10 μm),

*Mobile phase   glacial acetic acid R, acetonitrile R, water R* (1:500:500 *V/V/V*).

*Flow rate   *1 ml/min.

*Detection   *Spectrophotometer at 235 nm.

*Injection   *20 μl loop injector.

*Run time   *2 times the retention time of dibenzoyl peroxide.

*Relative retention* with reference to dibenzoyl peroxide (retention time = about 28.4 min): impurity B = about 0.15; impurity A = about 0.2; impurity C = about 0.4.

*System suitability   *Reference solution (e):
— *resolution*: minimum 6 between the peaks corresponding to benzoic acid and benzaldehyde.

*Limits:*
— *impurity A*: not more than the area of the principal peak in the chromatogram obtained with reference solution (d) (0.25 per cent),
— *impurity B*: not more than the area of the principal peak in the chromatogram obtained with reference solution (b) (1.5 per cent),
— *impurity C*: not more than the area of the principal peak in the chromatogram obtained with reference solution (c) (0.25 per cent),
— *any other impurity*: not more than the area of the principal peak in the chromatogram obtained with reference solution (a) (0.1 per cent),
— *disregard limit*: 0.2 times the area of the principal peak in the chromatogram obtained with reference solution (a) (0.02 per cent).

### Chlorides (2.4.4)
Maximum 0.4 per cent.

Dissolve a quantity of the substance to be examined containing the equivalent of 0.5 g of dibenzoyl peroxide in 15 ml of *acetone R*. Add, while stirring, 50 ml of *0.05 M nitric acid*. Allow to stand for 10 min and filter. Wash the residue with 2 quantities, each of 10 ml, of *0.05 M nitric acid*. Combine the filtrate and the washings and dilute to 100 ml with *0.05 M nitric acid*. 2.5 ml of the solution diluted to 15.0 ml with *water R* complies with the limit test for chlorides.

### ASSAY
*Solution (a)*   Dissolve 2.500 g immediately before use in 75 ml of *dimethylformamide R* and dilute to 100.0 ml with the same solvent.

### Dibenzoyl peroxide
To 5.0 ml of solution (a) add 20 ml of *acetone R* and 3 ml of a 500 g/l solution of *potassium iodide R* and mix. Allow to stand for 1 min. Titrate with *0.1 M sodium thiosulphate* using 1 ml of *starch solution R*, added towards the end of the titration, as indicator. Carry out a blank titration.

1 ml of *0.1 M sodium thiosulphate* is equivalent to 12.11 mg of $C_{14}H_{10}O_4$.

### Water (2.5.12)
Carry out the semi-micro determination of water, using 5.0 ml of solution (a). Use as the solvent a mixture of 20.0 ml of *anhydrous methanol R* and 3.0 ml of a 100 g/l solution of *potassium iodide R* in *dimethylformamide R*. After adding solution (a), stir for 5 min before starting the titration. Carry out a blank determination.

Calculate the percentage content of water using the expression:

$$\frac{(n_1 - n_2) \times w \times 2}{m} + (p \times 0.0744)$$

$n_1$ = number of millilitres of *iodosulphurous reagent R* used in the sample determination,
$n_2$ = number of millilitres of *iodosulphurous reagent R* used in the blank determination,
$w$ = water equivalent of *iodosulphurous reagent R* in milligrams of water per millilitre of reagent,
$m$ = mass of the substance to be examined used for the preparation of solution (a) in grams,
$p$ = percentage content of dibenzoyl peroxide.

### STORAGE
In a container that has been treated to reduce static discharge and that has a device for release of excess pressure, at a temperature of 2 °C to 8 °C, protected from light.

### IMPURITIES

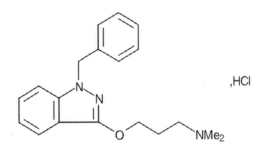

A. R = H: benzaldehyde,
B. R = OH: benzoic acid,
C. R = O-CH$_2$-CH$_3$: ethyl benzoate.

_____ *Ph Eur*


# Benzydamine Hydrochloride

$C_{19}H_{23}N_3O,HCl$                     345.9                     *132-69-4*

### Action and use
Cyclo-oxygenase inhibitor; analgesic; anti-inflammatory.

### Preparations
Benzydamine Cream
Benzydamine Mouthwash
Benzydamine Oromucosal Spray

### DEFINITION
Benzydamine Hydrochloride is 3-(1-benzylindazol-3-yloxy)propyldimethylamine hydrochloride. It contains not less than 99.0% and not more than 101.0% of $C_{19}H_{23}N_3O,HCl$, calculated with reference to the dried substance.

### PRODUCTION
The method of manufacture is such that the level of 3-chloropropyl(dimethyl)amine hydrochloride is not more than 5 ppm when determined by a suitable method.

### CHARACTERISTICS
A white crystalline powder.

Very soluble in *water*; freely soluble in *ethanol (96%)*; practically insoluble in *ether*.

### IDENTIFICATION
A. The *infrared absorption spectrum*, Appendix II A, is concordant with the *reference spectrum* of benzydamine hydrochloride *(RS 027)*.

B. Yields reaction A characteristic of *chlorides*, Appendix VI.

## TESTS

### Clarity and colour of solution

A 10.0% w/v solution is *clear*, Appendix IV A, and not more intensely coloured than *reference solution $Y_6$*, Appendix IV B, Method II.

### Acidity

pH of a 10% w/v solution, 4.0 to 5.5, Appendix V L.

### Heavy metals

12 ml of a 10% w/v solution complies with *limit test A for heavy metals*, Appendix VII (10 ppm). Use 1 ml of *lead standard solution (10 ppm Pb)* to prepare the standard.

### Related substances

Carry out the method for *liquid chromatography*, Appendix III D, using the following solutions in *methanol (50%)*. Solution (1) contains 0.25% w/v of the substance being examined. Solution (2) contains 0.0005% w/v of *3-dimethylaminopropyl 2-benzylaminobenzoate hydrochloride BPCRS* (impurity A) and 0.00125% w/v of *3-(1,5-dibenzyl-1*H*-indazole-3-yl)oxypropyldimethylamine hydrochloride BPCRS* (impurity B). Solution (3) contains 0.00025% w/v of *1-benzyl-1*H*-indazol-3-ol BPCRS* (impurity C). Solution (4) contains 0.00025% w/v of the substance being examined. Solution (5) contains equal volumes of solutions (1), (2) and (3).

The chromatographic procedure may be carried out using a stainless steel column (25 cm × 4.6 mm) packed with *end-capped octadecylsilyl silica gel for chromatography* (5 μm) (Suplex pKB-100 is suitable), fitted with a stainless steel guard column (2 cm × 4.6 mm) packed with the same material. Use as the initial mobile phase with a flow rate of 1.5 ml per minute, a mixture of 50 volumes of solution A and 50 volumes of *methanol*. Solution A contains *0.01*M *potassium dihydrogen orthophosphate* and *0.005*M *sodium octyl sulphate* in *water*, adjusted to pH 3.0 ± 0.1 with *orthophosphoric acid*. Carry out a linear gradient elution increasing the percentage of *methanol* to 70% over 20 minutes from the moment of injection and then decreasing the percentage of *methanol* to 50% over 2 minutes and maintain the final mobile phase until the completion of that run. Use a detection wavelength of 320 nm.

Inject 20 μl of solution (5) and modify the rate of change of the mobile phase, if necessary, to obtain a retention time of about 10 minutes for the substance being examined.

The test is not valid unless, in the chromatogram obtained with solution (5), the *resolution factor* between any two adjacent peaks is at least 2.5.

Inject 20 μl of solution (1) and allow the chromatography to proceed for 30 minutes. In the chromatogram obtained the areas of any peak corresponding to impurity A or impurity B is not greater than the area of the corresponding peak in the chromatogram obtained with solution (2) (0.2% of impurity A and 0.5% of impurity B), the area of any peak corresponding to impurity C is not greater than the area of the peak in the chromatogram obtained with solution (3) (0.1%) and the area of any other *secondary peak* is not greater than the area of the peak in the chromatogram obtained with solution (4) (0.1%). The sum of the areas of any such peaks is not greater than 1%.

### Primary amines

Dissolve 50 mg of the substance being examined in 10 ml of *ethanol (96%)*, add 0.1 ml of *hydrochloric acid* and 2 ml of a 5% w/v solution of *4-dimethylaminobenzaldehyde* in *ethanol (96%)*. The yellow colour obtained is not more intense than that obtained by treating 10 ml of a 0.00005% w/v solution of *2-aminobenzoic acid* in *ethanol (96%)* in the same manner.

### Loss on drying

When dried for 3 hours at 100° to 105° at a pressure not exceeding 0.7 kPa, loses not more than 0.5% of its weight. Use 1 g.

### Sulphated ash

Not more than 0.1%, Appendix IX A. Use 1 g.

## ASSAY

Dissolve 0.3 g in 100 ml of *anhydrous acetic acid* and carry out Method I for *non-aqueous titration*, Appendix VIII A, determining the end point potentiometrically. Each ml of *0.1*M *perchloric acid VS* is equivalent to 34.59 mg of $C_{19}H_{23}N_3O,HCl$.

## IMPURITIES

A.  3-dimethylaminopropyl 2-benzylaminobenzoate

B.  3-(1,5-dibenzyl-1*H*-indazol-3-yl)oxypropyldimethylamine

C.  1-benzyl-1*H*-indazol-3-ol

# Benzyl Alcohol

(*Ph Eur monograph 0256*)

C₇H₈O       108.1       *100-51-6*

## Action and use
Local anaesthetic; disinfectant.

*Ph Eur*

## DEFINITION
Phenylmethanol.

## Content
98.0 per cent to 100.5 per cent.

## CHARACTERS
### Appearance
Clear, colourless, oily liquid.

### Solubility
Soluble in water, miscible with ethanol (96 per cent) and with fatty and essential oils.

### Relative density
1.043 to 1.049.

## IDENTIFICATION
Infrared absorption spectrophotometry (*2.2.24*).

*Comparison*   benzyl alcohol CRS.

## TESTS
### Appearance of solution
Shake 2.0 ml with 60 ml of *water R*. It dissolves completely. The solution is clear (*2.2.1*) and colourless (*2.2.2, Method II*).

### Acidity
To 10 ml add 10 ml of *ethanol (96 per cent) R* and 1 ml of *phenolphthalein solution R*. Not more than 1 ml of *0.1 M sodium hydroxide* is required to change the colour of the indicator to pink.

### Refractive index (*2.2.6*)
1.538 to 1.541.

### Peroxide value (*2.5.5*)
Maximum 5.

### Related substances
Gas chromatography (*2.2.28*).

*Test solution*   The substance to be examined.

*Standard solution (a)*   Dissolve 0.100 g of *ethylbenzene R* in the test solution and dilute to 10.0 ml with the same solution. Dilute 2.0 ml of this solution to 20.0 ml with the test solution.

*Standard solution (b)*   Dissolve 2.000 g of *dicyclohexyl R* in the test solution and dilute to 10.0 ml with the same solution. Dilute 2.0 ml of this solution to 20.0 ml with the test solution.

*Reference solution (a)*   Dissolve 0.750 g of *benzaldehyde R* and 0.500 g of *cyclohexylmethanol R* in the test solution and dilute to 25.0 ml with the test solution. Add 1.0 ml of this solution to a mixture of 2.0 ml of standard solution (a) and 3.0 ml of standard solution (b) and dilute to 20.0 ml with the test solution.

*Reference solution (b)*   Dissolve 0.250 g of *benzaldehyde R* and 0.500 g of *cyclohexylmethanol R* in the test solution and dilute to 25.0 ml with the test solution. Add 1.0 ml of this solution to a mixture of 2.0 ml of standard solution (a) and 2.0 ml of standard solution (b) and dilute to 20.0 ml with the test solution.

*Column:*
— *material*: fused silica;
— *size: l* = 30 m, Ø = 0.32 mm;
— *stationary phase: macrogol 20 000 R* (film thickness 0.5 µm).

*Carrier gas*   helium for chromatography R.

*Linear velocity*   25 cm/s.

*Temperature:*

| | Time (min) | Temperature (°C) |
|---|---|---|
| Column | 0 - 34 | 50 → 220 |
| | 34 - 69 | 220 |
| Injection port | | 200 |
| Detector | | 310 |

*Detection*   Flame ionisation.

*Benzyl alcohol not intended for parenteral use*

*Injection*   Without air-plug, 0.1 µl of the test solution and reference solution (a).

*Relative retention*   With reference to benzyl alcohol (retention time = about 26 min): ethylbenzene = about 0.28; dicyclohexyl = about 0.59; impurity A = about 0.68; impurity B = about 0.71.

*System suitability*   Reference solution (a):
— *resolution*: minimum 3.0 between the peaks due to impurities A and B.

If any peaks in the chromatogram obtained with the test solution have the same retention time as the peaks due to ethyl benzene or dicyclohexyl, substract the areas of any such peaks from the peak areas at these retention times in the chromatograms obtained with reference solutions (a) or (b) (corrected peak areas of ethyl benzene and dicyclohexyl). Any such peaks in the chromatogram obtained with the test solution are to be included in the assessments for the sum of other peaks.

*Limits:*
— *impurity A*: not more than the difference between the area of the peak due to impurity A in the chromatogram obtained with reference solution (a) and the area of the peak due to impurity A in the chromatogram obtained with the test solution (0.15 per cent);
— *impurity B*: not more than the difference between the area of the peak due to impurity B in the chromatogram obtained with reference solution (a) and the area of the peak due to impurity B in the chromatogram obtained with the test solution (0.10 per cent);
— *sum of other peaks with a relative retention less than that of benzyl alcohol*: not more than 4 times the area of the peak due to ethylbenzene in the chromatogram obtained with reference solution (a) corrected if necessary as described above (0.04 per cent);
— *sum of peaks with a relative retention greater than that of benzyl alcohol*: not more than the area of the peak due to dicyclohexyl in the chromatogram obtained with reference solution (a) corrected if necessary as described above (0.3 per cent);

— *disregard limit*: 0.01 times the area of the peak due to ethylbenzene in the chromatogram obtained with reference solution (a) corrected if necessary as described above (0.0001 per cent).

*Benzyl alcohol intended for parenteral use*

*Injection*　Without air-plug, 0.1 µl of the test solution and reference solution (b).

*Relative retention*　With reference to benzyl alcohol (retention time = about 26 min): ethylbenzene = about 0.28; dicyclohexyl = about 0.59; impurity A = about 0.68; impurity B = about 0.71.

*System suitability*　Reference solution (b):
— *resolution*: minimum 3.0 between the peaks due to impurities A and B.

If any peaks in the chromatogram obtained with the test solution have the same retention times as the peaks due to ethyl benzene or dicyclohexyl, substract the areas of any such peaks from the peak areas at these retention times in the chromatograms obtained with reference solutions (a) or (b) (corrected peak areas of ethyl benzene and dicyclohexyl). Any such peaks in the chromatogram obtained with the test solution are to be included in the assessments for the sum of other peaks.

*Limits:*
— *impurity A*: not more than the difference between the area of the peak due to impurity A in the chromatogram obtained with reference solution (b) and the area of the peak due to impurity A in the chromatogram obtained with the test solution (0.05 per cent);
— *impurity B*: not more than the difference between the area of the peak due to impurity B in the chromatogram obtained with reference solution (b) and the area of the peak due to impurity B in the chromatogram obtained with the test solution (0.10 per cent);
— *sum of other peaks with a relative retention less than that of benzyl alcohol*: not more than twice the area of the peak due to ethylbenzene in the chromatogram obtained with reference solution (b) corrected if necessary as described above (0.02 per cent);
— *sum of peaks with a relative retention greater than that of benzyl alcohol*: not more than the area of the peak due to dicyclohexyl in the chromatogram obtained with reference solution (b) corrected if necessary as described above (0.2 per cent);
— *disregard limit*: 0.01 times the area of the peak due to ethylbenzene in the chromatogram obtained with reference solution (b) corrected if necessary as described above (0.0001 per cent).

**Residue on evaporation**

Maximum 0.05 per cent.

After ensuring that the substance to be examined complies with the test for peroxide value, evaporate 10.0 g to dryness in a tared quartz or porcelain crucible or platinum dish on a hot plate at a temperature not exceeding 200 °C. Ensure that the substance to be examined does not boil during evaporation. Dry the residue on the hot plate for 1 h and allow to cool in a desiccator. The residue weighs a maximum of 5 mg.

**ASSAY**

To 0.900 g (*m* g) add 15.0 ml of a freshly prepared mixture of 1 volume of *acetic anhydride R* and 7 volumes of *pyridine R* and boil under a reflux condenser on a water-bath for 30 min. Cool and add 25 ml of *water R*. Using 0.25 ml of

*phenolphthalein solution R* as indicator, titrate with *1 M sodium hydroxide* ($n_1$ ml). Carry out a blank titration ($n_2$ ml).

Calculate the percentage content of $C_7H_8O$ using the following expression:

$$\frac{10.81\left(n_2 - n_1\right)}{m}$$

**STORAGE**

In an airtight container, under nitrogen, protected from light and at a temperature between 2 °C and 8 °C.

**LABELLING**

The label states, where applicable, that the substance is suitable for use in the manufacture of parenteral preparations.

**IMPURITIES**

*Specified impurities*　A, B.

A. benzaldehyde,

B. cyclohexylmethanol.

_____ *Ph Eur*

# Benzyl Benzoate

*(Ph Eur monograph 0705)*

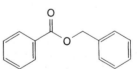

C$_{14}$H$_{12}$O$_2$　　　212.2　　　*120-51-4*

**Action and use**

Used topically in the treatment of scabies.

**Preparation**

Benzyl Benzoate Application

*Ph Eur* _____

**DEFINITION**

Phenylmethyl benzoate.

**Content**

99.0 per cent to 100.5 per cent.

**CHARACTERS**

**Appearance**

Colourless or almost colourless crystals or colourless or almost colourless, oily liquid.

**Solubility**

Practically insoluble in water, miscible with ethanol (96 per cent), with methylene chloride and with fatty and essential oils.

Eb: about 320 °C.

## IDENTIFICATION

*First identification   A.*

*Second identification   B, C.*

A. Infrared absorption spectrophotometry (*2.2.24*).

*Comparison   Ph. Eur. reference spectrum of benzyl benzoate.*

B. To 2 g add 25 ml of *alcoholic potassium hydroxide solution R* and boil under a reflux condenser for 2 h. Remove the ethanol on a water-bath, add 50 ml of *water R* and distill. Collect about 25 ml of distillate and use it for identification test C. Acidify the liquid remaining in the distillation flask with *dilute hydrochloric acid R*. A white precipitate is formed that, when washed with *water R* and dried in vacuo melts (*2.2.14*) at 121 °C to 124 °C.

C. To the distillate obtained in identification test B add 2.5 g of *potassium permanganate R* and 5 ml of *dilute sodium hydroxide solution R*. Boil under a reflux condenser for 15 min, cool and filter. Acidify the filtrate with *dilute hydrochloric acid R*. A white precipitate is formed that, when washed with *water R* and dried *in vacuo*, melts (*2.2.14*) at 121 °C to 124 °C.

## TESTS

**Acidity**

Dissolve 2.0 g in *ethanol (96 per cent) R* and dilute to 10 ml with the same solvent. Titrate with *0.1 M sodium hydroxide* using *phenolphthalein solution R* as indicator. Not more than 0.2 ml is required to change the colour of the indicator to pink.

**Relative density** (*2.2.5*)

1.118 to 1.122.

**Refractive index** (*2.2.6*)

1.568 to 1.570.

**Freezing point** (*2.2.18*)

Minimum 17.0 °C.

**Sulphated ash** (*2.4.14*)

Maximum 0.1 per cent, determined on 1.0 g.

## ASSAY

To 2.000 g add 50.0 ml of *0.5 M alcoholic potassium hydroxide* and boil gently under a reflux condenser for 1 h. Titrate the hot solution with *0.5 M hydrochloric acid* using 1 ml of *phenolphthalein solution R* as indicator. Carry out a blank determination.

1 ml of *0.5 M alcoholic potassium hydroxide* is equivalent to 106.1 mg of $C_{14}H_{12}O_2$.

## STORAGE

In an airtight, well-filled container, protected from light.

*Ph Eur*

# Benzyl Hydroxybenzoate

Benzylparaben

$C_{14}H_{12}O_3$                   228.3                   94-18-8

**Action and use**

Antimicrobial preservative.

## DEFINITION

Benzyl Hydroxybenzoate is benzyl 4-hydroxybenzoate. It contains not less than 99.0% and not more than 101.0% of $C_{14}H_{12}O_3$.

## CHARACTERISTICS

A white to creamy white, crystalline powder.

Practically insoluble in *water*; freely soluble in *ethanol (96%)* and in *ether*. It dissolves in solutions of alkali hydroxides.

## IDENTIFICATION

A. The *infrared absorption spectrum*, Appendix II A, is concordant with the *reference spectrum* of benzyl hydroxybenzoate (*RS 028*).

B. The *light absorption*, Appendix II B, in the range 230 to 350 nm of a 0.001% w/v solution in *ethanol (96%)* exhibits a maximum only at 260 nm. The *absorbance* at the maximum at 260 nm is about 0.76.

C. Dissolve 0.1 g in 2 ml of *ethanol (96%)*, boil and add 0.5 ml of *nitric acid solution of mercury*. A precipitate is produced slowly and the supernatant liquid becomes red.

D. *Melting point*, about 112°, Appendix V A.

## TESTS

**Acidity**

Dissolve 0.2 g in 10 ml of *ethanol (50%)* previously neutralised to *methyl red solution* and titrate with 0.1M *sodium hydroxide VS* using *methyl red solution* as indicator. Not more than 0.1 ml of *0.1M sodium hydroxide VS* is required to change the colour of the solution.

**Related substances**

Carry out the method for *thin-layer chromatography*, Appendix III A, using a plate precoated with silica gel $F_{254}$, the surface of which has been modified with chemically-bonded octadecylsilyl groups (Whatman KC18F plates are suitable) and a mixture of 70 volumes of *methanol*, 30 volumes of *water* and 1 volume of *glacial acetic acid* as the mobile phase. Apply separately to the plate 2 µl of each of two solutions of the substance being examined in *acetone* containing (1) 1.0% w/v and (2) 0.010% w/v. After removal of the plate, allow it to dry in air and examine under *ultraviolet light (254 nm)*. Any *secondary spot* in the chromatogram obtained with solution (1) is not more intense than the spot in the chromatogram obtained with solution (2).

**Sulphated ash**

Not more than 0.1%, Appendix IX A.

## ASSAY

Gently boil 0.12 g under a reflux condenser with 20 ml of 2M *sodium hydroxide* for 30 minutes. Cool and extract with three

20-ml quantities of *1,2-dichloroethane*. Wash the combined extracts with 20 ml of *0.1M sodium hydroxide* and add the washings to the main aqueous phase, discarding the organic layer. To the aqueous solution add 25 ml of *0.0333M potassium bromate VS*, 5 ml of a 12.5% w/v solution of *potassium bromide* and 10 ml of *hydrochloric acid* and immediately stopper the flask. Shake for 15 minutes and allow to stand for 15 minutes. Add 25 ml of *dilute potassium iodide solution* and shake vigorously. Titrate the liberated iodine with *0.1M sodium thiosulphate VS* using *starch mucilage*, added towards the end of the titration, as indicator. Repeat the operation without the substance being examined. The difference between the titrations represents the amount of potassium bromate required. The volume of *0.0333M potassium bromate VS* used is equivalent to half of the volume of *0.1M sodium thiosulphate VS* required for the titration. Each ml of *0.0333M potassium bromate VS* is equivalent to 7.608 mg of $C_{14}H_{12}O_3$.

# Benzylpenicillin Potassium

(*Ph Eur monograph 0113*)

C$_{16}$H$_{17}$KN$_2$O$_4$S          372.5          *113-98-4*

**Action and use**
Penicillin antibacterial.

**Preparation**
Benzylpenicillin Injection

*Ph Eur* _____

## DEFINITION
Potassium (2S,5R,6R)-3,3-dimethyl-7-oxo-6-[(phenylacetyl)amino]-4-thia-1-azabicyclo[3.2.0]heptane-2-carboxylate.

Substance produced by the growth of certain strains of *Penicillium notatum* or related organisms, or obtained by any other means.

**Content**
96.0 per cent to 102.0 per cent (dried substance).

## CHARACTERS
**Appearance**
White or almost white, crystalline powder.

**Solubility**
Very soluble in water, practically insoluble in fatty oils and in liquid paraffin.

## IDENTIFICATION
*First identification   A, D.*
*Second identification   B, C, D.*

A. Infrared absorption spectrophotometry (*2.2.24*).

*Comparison   benzylpenicillin potassium CRS.*

B. Thin-layer chromatography (*2.2.27*).

*Test solution*   Dissolve 25 mg of the substance to be examined in 5 ml of *water R*.

*Reference solution (a)*   Dissolve 25 mg of *benzylpenicillin potassium CRS* in 5 ml of *water R*.

*Reference solution (b)*   Dissolve 25 mg of *benzylpenicillin potassium CRS* and 25 mg of *phenoxymethylpenicillin potassium CRS* in 5 ml of *water R*.

*Plate*   TLC silanised silica gel plate R.

*Mobile phase*   Mix 30 volumes of *acetone R* and 70 volumes of a 154 g/l solution of *ammonium acetate R* previously adjusted to pH 5.0 with *glacial acetic acid R*.

*Application*   1 µl.

*Development*   Over a path of 15 cm.

*Drying*   In air.

*Detection*   Expose to iodine vapour until the spots appear and examine in daylight.

*System suitability*   Reference solution (b):
— the chromatogram shows 2 clearly separated spots.

*Results*   The principal spot in the chromatogram obtained with the test solution is similar in position, colour and size to the principal spot in obtained with reference solution (a).

C. Place about 2 mg in a test-tube about 150 mm long and 15 mm in diameter. Moisten with 0.05 ml of *water R* and add 2 ml of *sulphuric acid-formaldehyde reagent R*. Mix the contents of the tube by swirling; the solution is practically colourless. Place the test-tube on a water-bath for 1 min; a reddish-brown colour develops.

D. It gives reaction (a) of potassium (*2.3.1*).

## TESTS
**pH** (*2.2.3*)
5.5 to 7.5.

Dissolve 2.0 g in *carbon dioxide-free water R* and dilute to 20 ml with the same solvent.

**Specific optical rotation** (*2.2.7*)
+ 270 to + 300 (dried substance).

Dissolve 0.500 g in *carbon dioxide-free water R* and dilute to 25.0 ml with the same solvent.

**Absorbance** (*2.2.25*)
Dissolve 94.0 mg in *water R* and dilute to 50.0 ml with the same solvent. Measure the absorbance of the solution at 325 nm, 280 nm and at the absorption maximum at 264 nm, diluting the solution, if necessary, for the measurement at 264 nm. The absorbances at 325 nm and 280 nm do not exceed 0.10 and that at the absorption maximum at 264 nm is 0.80 to 0.88, calculated on the basis of the undiluted (1.88 g/l) solution. Verify the resolution of the apparatus (*2.2.25*); the ratio of the absorbances is at least 1.7.

**Related substances**
Liquid chromatography (*2.2.29*).

*Prepare the solutions immediately before use.*

*Test solution (a)*   Dissolve 50.0 mg of the substance to be examined in *water R* and dilute to 50.0 ml with the same solvent.

*Test solution (b)*   Dissolve 80.0 mg of the substance to be examined in *water R* and dilute to 20.0 ml with the same solvent.

*Reference solution (a)*   Dissolve 50.0 mg of *benzylpenicillin sodium CRS* in *water R* and dilute to 50.0 ml with the same solvent.

*Reference solution (b)*   Dissolve 10 mg of *benzylpenicillin sodium CRS* and 10 mg of *phenylacetic acid R* (impurity B) in *water R*, then dilute to 50 ml with the same solvent.

*Reference solution (c)* Dilute 4.0 ml of reference solution (a) to 100.0 ml with *water R*.

*Column:*
— *size: l* = 0.25 m, Ø = 4.6 mm;
— *stationary phase: octadecylsilyl silica gel for chromatography R* (5 µm).

*Mobile phase:*
— *mobile phase A*: mix 10 volumes of a 68 g/l solution of *potassium dihydrogen phosphate R* adjusted to pH 3.5 with a 500 g/l solution of *dilute phosphoric acid R*, 30 volumes of *methanol R* and 60 volumes of *water R*;
— *mobile phase B*: mix 10 volumes of a 68 g/l solution of *potassium dihydrogen phosphate R* adjusted to pH 3.5 with a 500 g/l solution of *dilute phosphoric acid R*, 40 volumes of *water R* and 50 volumes of *methanol R*;

| Time (min) | Mobile phase A (per cent *V/V*) | Mobile phase B (per cent *V/V*) |
|---|---|---|
| 0 - $t_R$ | 70 | 30 |
| $t_R$ - ($t_R$ + 20) | 70 → 0 | 30 → 100 |
| ($t_R$ + 20) - ($t_R$ + 35) | 0 | 100 |
| ($t_R$ + 35) - ($t_R$ + 50) | 70 | 30 |

$t_R$ = retention time of benzylpenicillin determined with reference solution (c)

If the mobile phase composition has been adjusted to achieve the required resolution, the adjusted composition will apply at time zero in the gradient and in the assay.

*Flow rate* 1.0 ml/min.

*Detection* Spectrophotometer at 225 nm.

*Injection* 20 µl of reference solutions (b) and (c) with isocratic elution at the initial mobile phase composition and 20 µl of test solution (b) according to the elution gradient described under Mobile phase; inject *water R* as a blank according to the elution gradient described under Mobile phase.

*System suitability* Reference solution (b):
— *resolution*: minimum 6.0 between the peaks due to impurity B and benzylpenicillin; if necessary, adjust the ratio A:B of the mobile phase.

*Limit:*
— *any impurity*: for each impurity, not more than the area of the principal peak in the chromatogram obtained with reference solution (c) (1 per cent).

**Loss on drying** (*2.2.32*)
Maximum 1.0 per cent, determined on 1.000 g by drying in an oven at 105 °C.

**Bacterial endotoxins** (*2.6.14, Method E*)
Less than 0.16 IU/mg, if intended for use in the manufacture of parenteral dosage forms without a further appropriate procedure for the removal of bacterial endotoxins.

**ASSAY**
Liquid chromatography (*2.2.29*) as described in the test for related substances with the following modifications.

*Mobile phase* Initial composition of the mixture of mobile phases A and B, adjusted where applicable.

*Injection* Test solution (a) and reference solution (a).

Calculate the percentage content of $C_{16}H_{17}KN_2O_4S$ by multiplying the percentage content of benzylpenicillin sodium by 1.045.

**STORAGE**
In an airtight container. If the substance is sterile, store in a sterile, airtight, tamper-proof container.

**IMPURITIES**

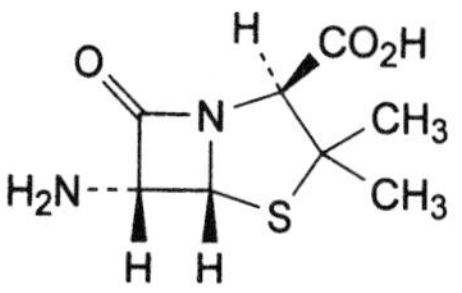

A. (2*S*,5*R*,6*R*)-6-amino-3,3-dimethyl-7-oxo-4-thia-1-azabicyclo[3.2.0]heptane-2-carboxylic acid (6-aminopenicillanic acid),

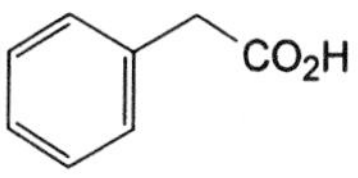

B. phenylacetic acid,

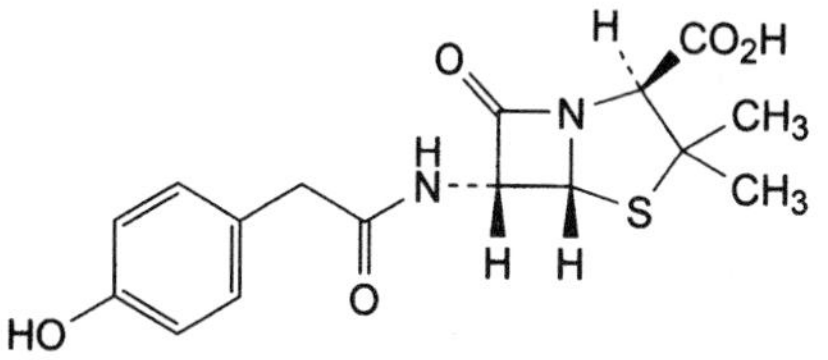

C. (2*S*,5*R*,6*R*)-6-[[(4-hydroxyphenyl)acetyl]amino]-3,3-dimethyl-7-oxo-4-thia-1-azabicyclo[3.2.0]heptane-2-carboxylic acid,

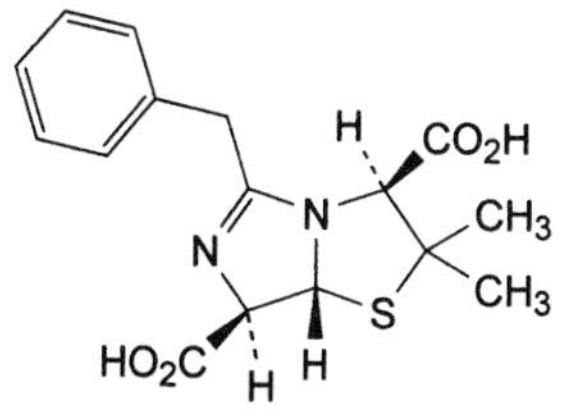

D. (3*S*,7*R*,7a*R*)-5-benzyl-2,2-dimethyl-2,3,7,7a-tetrahydroimidazo[5,1-*b*]thiazole-3,7-dicarboxylic acid (penillic acid of benzylpenicillin),

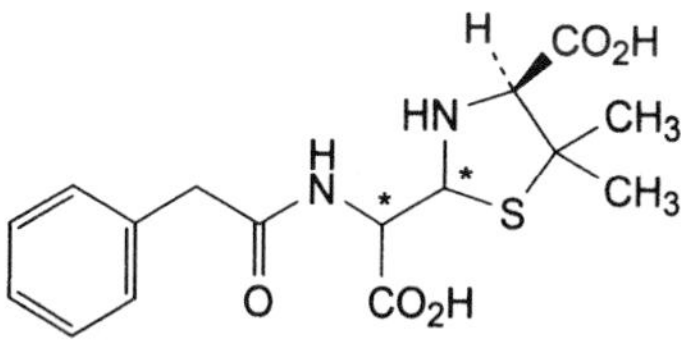

E. (4*S*)-2-[carboxy[(phenylacetyl)amino]methyl]-5,5-dimethylthiazolidine-4-carboxylic acid (penicilloic acids of benzylpenicillin),

and epimer at C*

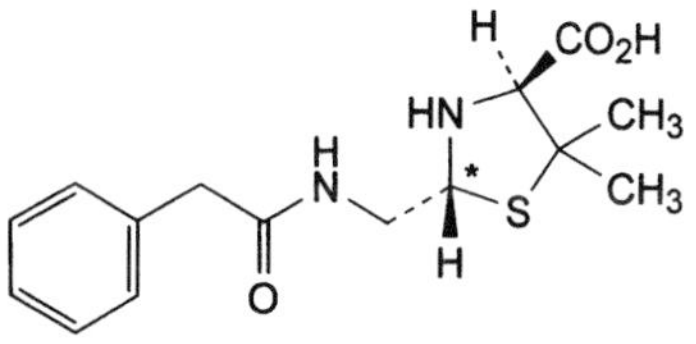

F. (2*RS*,4*S*)-2-[[(phenylacetyl)amino]methyl]-5,5-dimethylthiazolidine-4-carboxylic acid (penilloic acids of benzylpenicillin).

# Benzylpenicillin Sodium

(*Ph Eur monograph 0114*)

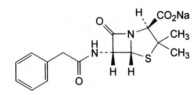

C$_{16}$H$_{17}$N$_2$NaO$_4$S      356.4      69-57-8

## Action and use

Penicillin antibacterial.

## Preparation

Benzylpenicillin Injection

*Ph Eur*

## DEFINITION

Sodium (2*S*,5*R*,6*R*)-3,3-dimethyl-7-oxo-6-
[(phenylacetyl)amino]-4-thia-1-azabicyclo[3.2.0]heptane-2-
carboxylate.

Substance produced by the growth of certain strains of
*Penicillium notatum* or related organisms, or obtained by
any other means.

## Content

96.0 per cent to 102.0 per cent (dried substance).

## CHARACTERS

### Appearance

White or almost white, crystalline powder.

### Solubility

Very soluble in water, practically insoluble in fatty oils and
in liquid paraffin.

## IDENTIFICATION

*First identification*  A, D.

*Second identification*  B, C, D.

A. Infrared absorption spectrophotometry (*2.2.24*).

*Comparison*  benzylpenicillin sodium CRS.

B. Thin-layer chromatography (*2.2.27*).

*Test solution*  Dissolve 25 mg of the substance to be
examined in 5 ml of *water R*.

*Reference solution (a)*  Dissolve 25 mg of *benzylpenicillin
sodium CRS* in 5 ml of *water R*.

*Reference solution (b)*  Dissolve 25 mg of *benzylpenicillin
sodium CRS* and 25 mg of *phenoxymethylpenicillin
potassium CRS* in 5 ml of *water R*.

*Plate*  TLC silanised silica gel plate R.

*Mobile phase*  Mix 30 volumes of *acetone R* and 70 volumes
of a 154 g/l solution of *ammonium acetate R* previously
adjusted to pH 5.0 with *glacial acetic acid R*.

*Application*  1 μl.

*Development*  Over a path of 15 cm.

*Drying*  In air.

*Detection*  Expose to iodine vapour until the spots appear
and examine in daylight.

*System suitability*  Reference solution (b):
— the chromatogram shows 2 clearly separated spots.

### Results

The principal spot in the chromatogram obtained with the
test solution is similar in position, colour and size to the
principal spot in the chromatogram obtained with reference
solution (a).

C. Place about 2 mg in a test-tube about 150 mm long and
15 mm in diameter. Moisten with 0.05 ml of *water R* and
add 2 ml of *sulphuric acid-formaldehyde reagent R*. Mix the
contents of the tube by swirling; the solution is practically
colourless. Place the test-tube on a water-bath for 1 min; a
reddish-brown colour develops.

D. It gives reaction (a) of sodium (*2.3.1*).

## TESTS

**pH** (*2.2.3*)

5.5 to 7.5.

Dissolve 2.0 g in *carbon dioxide-free water R* and dilute to
20 ml with the same solvent.

**Specific optical rotation** (*2.2.7*)

+ 285 to + 310 (dried substance).

Dissolve 0.500 g in *carbon dioxide-free water R* and dilute to
25.0 ml with the same solvent.

**Absorbance** (*2.2.25*)

Dissolve 90.0 mg in *water R* and dilute to 50.0 ml with the
same solvent. Measure the absorbance of the solution at
325 nm, at 280 nm and at the absorption maximum at
264 nm, diluting the solution, if necessary, for the
measurement at 264 nm. The absorbances at 325 nm and
280 nm are not greater than 0.10 and the absorbance at the
absorption maximum at 264 nm is 0.80 to 0.88, calculated
on the basis of the undiluted (1.80 g/l) solution. Verify the
resolution of the apparatus (*2.2.25*); the ratio of the
absorbances is at least 1.7.

**Related substances**

Liquid chromatography (*2.2.29*). *Prepare the solutions
immediately before use.*

*Test solution (a)*  Dissolve 50.0 mg of the substance to be
examined in *water R* and dilute to 50.0 ml with the same
solvent.

*Test solution (b)*  Dissolve 80.0 mg of the substance to be
examined in *water R* and dilute to 20.0 ml with the same
solvent.

*Reference solution (a)*  Dissolve 50.0 mg of *benzylpenicillin
sodium CRS* in *water R* and dilute to 50.0 ml with the same
solvent.

*Reference solution (b)*  Dissolve 10 mg of *benzylpenicillin
sodium CRS* and 10 mg of *phenylacetic acid R* (impurity B) in
*water R*, then dilute to 50 ml with the same solvent.

*Reference solution (c)*  Dilute 4.0 ml of reference solution (a)
to 100.0 ml with *water R*.

*Column:*
— *size: l* = 0.25 m, Ø = 4.6 mm;
— *stationary phase*: octadecylsilyl silica gel for chromatography R
(5 μm).

*Mobile phase:*
— *mobile phase A*: mix 10 volumes of a 68 g/l solution of
*potassium dihydrogen phosphate R* adjusted to pH 3.5 with
a 500 g/l solution of *dilute phosphoric acid* R, 30 volumes
of *methanol R* and 60 volumes of *water R*;
— *mobile phase B*: mix 10 volumes of a 68 g/l solution of
*potassium dihydrogen phosphate R* adjusted to pH 3.5 with
a 500 g/l solution of *dilute phosphoric acid* R, 40 volumes
of *water R* and 50 volumes of *methanol R*;

| Time (min) | Mobile phase A (per cent $V/V$) | Mobile phase B (per cent $V/V$) |
|---|---|---|
| $0 - t_R$ | 70 | 30 |
| $t_R - (t_R + 20)$ | $70 \rightarrow 0$ | $30 \rightarrow 100$ |
| $(t_R + 20) - (t_R + 35)$ | 0 | 100 |
| $(t_R + 35) - (t_R + 50)$ | 70 | 30 |

$t_R$ = retention time of benzylpenicillin determined with reference solution (c)

If the mobile phase composition has been adjusted to achieve the required resolution, the adjusted composition will apply at time zero in the gradient and in the assay.

*Flow rate* 1.0 ml/min.

*Detection* Spectrophotometer at 225 nm.

*Injection* 20 µl of reference solutions (b) and (c) with isocratic elution at the initial mobile phase composition and 20 µl of test solution (b) according to the elution gradient described under Mobile phase; inject *water R* as a blank according to the elution gradient described under Mobile phase.

*System suitability* Reference solution (b):
— *resolution*: minimum 6.0 between the peaks due to impurity B and benzylpenicillin; if necessary, adjust the ratio A:B of the mobile phase.

*Limit:*
— *any impurity*: for each impurity, not more than the area of the principal peak in the chromatogram obtained with reference solution (c) (1 per cent).

**2-Ethylhexanoic acid** (*2.4.28*)
Maximum 0.5 per cent *m/m*.

**Loss on drying** (*2.2.32*)
Maximum 1.0 per cent, determined on 1.000 g by drying in an oven at 105 °C.

**Bacterial endotoxins** (*2.6.14, Method E*)
Less than 0.16 IU/mg, if intended for use in the manufacture of parenteral dosage forms without a further appropriate procedure for the removal of bacterial endotoxins.

## ASSAY

Liquid chromatography (*2.2.29*) as described in the test for related substances with the following modifications.

*Mobile phase* Initial composition of the mixture of mobile phases A and B, adjusted where applicable.

*Injection* Test solution (a) and reference solution (a).

Calculate the percentage content of $C_{16}H_{17}N_2NaO_4S$ from the declared content of *benzylpenicillin sodium CRS*.

## STORAGE

In an airtight container. If the substance is sterile, store in a sterile, airtight, tamper-proof container.

## IMPURITIES

A. (2S,5R,6R)-6-amino-3,3-dimethyl-7-oxo-4-thia-1-azabicyclo[3.2.0]heptane-2-carboxylic acid (6-aminopenicillanic acid),

B. phenylacetic acid,

C. (2S,5R,6R)-6-[[(4-hydroxyphenyl)acetyl]amino]-3,3-dimethyl-7-oxo-4-thia- 1-azabicyclo[3.2.0]heptane-2-carboxylic acid,

D. (3S,7R,7aR)-5-benzyl-2,2-dimethyl-2,3,7,7a-tetrahydroimidazo[5,1-*b*]thiazole-3,7-dicarboxylic acid (penillic acid of benzylpenicillin),

E. (4S)-2-[carboxy[(phenylacetyl)amino]methyl]-5,5-dimethylthiazolidine-4-carboxylic acid (penicilloic acids of benzylpenicillin),

F. (2RS,4S)-2-[[(phenylacetyl)amino]methyl]-5,5-dimethylthiazolidine-4-carboxylic acid (penilloic acids of benzylpenicillin).

# Betacarotene

*(Ph Eur monograph 1069)*

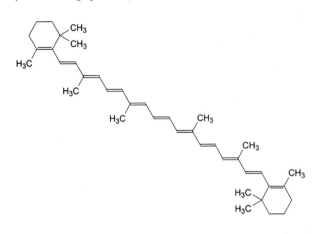

$C_{40}H_{56}$            536.9            *7235-40-7*

## Action and use
Precursor of vitamin A.

*Ph Eur*

## DEFINITION
(all-*E*)-3,7,12,16-Tetramethyl-1,18-bis(2,6,6-trimethylcyclohex-1-enyl)octadeca-1,3,5,7,9,11,13,15,17-nonaene.

## Content
96.0 per cent to 101.0 per cent (dried substance).

## CHARACTERS
### Appearance
Brown-red or brownish-red, crystalline powder.

### Solubility
Practically insoluble in water, slightly soluble in cyclohexane, practically insoluble in anhydrous ethanol.

It is sensitive to air, heat and light, especially in solution.

*Carry out all operations as rapidly as possible avoiding exposure to actinic light; use freshly prepared solutions.*

## IDENTIFICATION
Ultraviolet and visible absorption spectrophotometry (*2.2.25*).

*Test solution (a)* Dissolve 50.0 mg in 10 ml of *chloroform R* and dilute immediately to 100.0 ml with *cyclohexane R*. Dilute 5.0 ml of this solution to 100.0 ml with *cyclohexane R*.

*Test solution (b)* Dilute 5.0 ml of test solution (a) to 50.0 ml with *cyclohexane R*.

*Absorption maximum* At 455 nm for test solution (b).

*Absorbance ratio* $A_{455} / A_{483} = 1.14$ to 1.18 for test solution (b).

## TESTS
### Related substances
Determine the absorbance (*2.2.25*) of test solutions (b) and (a) used in Identification, at 455 nm and at 340 nm respectively.

*Absorbance ratio* $A_{455} / A_{340}$: minimum 1.5.

The thresholds indicated under Related substances (Table 2034.-1) in the general monograph *Substances for pharmaceutical use (2034)* do not apply.

### Heavy metals (*2.4.8*)
Maximum 10 ppm.

2.0 g complies with test D. Prepare the reference solution using 2 ml of *lead standard solution (10 ppm Pb) R*.

### Loss on drying (*2.2.32*)
Maximum 0.2 per cent, determined on 1.000 g by drying *in vacuo* over *diphosphorus pentoxide R* at 40 °C for 4 h.

### Sulphated ash (*2.4.14*)
Maximum 0.2 per cent, determined on 1.0 g, moistened with a mixture of 2 ml of *dilute sulphuric acid R* and 5 ml of *ethanol (96 per cent) R*.

## ASSAY
Measure the absorbance (*2.2.25*) of test solution (b) used in Identification at the absorption maximum at 455 nm, using *cyclohexane R* as the compensation liquid.

Calculate the content of $C_{40}H_{56}$ taking the specific absorbance to be 2500.

## STORAGE
In an airtight container, protected from light, at a temperature not exceeding 25 °C.

*Ph Eur*

# Betadex

Betacyclodextrin

*(Ph Eur monograph 1070)*

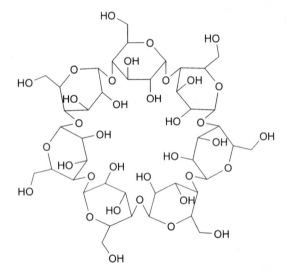

$[C_6H_{10}O_5]_7$            1135            *68168-23-0*

(monohydrate)

## Action and use
Carrier molecule for drug delivery systems.

*Ph Eur*

## DEFINITION
Cyclo-α-(1→4)-D-heptaglucopyranoside (betacyclodextrin).

## Content
98.0 per cent to 101.0 per cent (dried substance).

## CHARACTERS
### Appearance
White or almost white, amorphous or crystalline powder.

**Solubility**

Sparingly soluble in water, freely soluble in propylene glycol, practically insoluble in anhydrous ethanol and in methylene chloride.

**IDENTIFICATION**

A. Specific optical rotation (see Tests).

B. Examine the chromatograms obtained in the assay.

*Results* The principal peak in the chromatogram obtained with test solution (b) is similar in retention time and size to the principal peak in the chromatogram obtained with reference solution (c).

C. Dissolve 0.2 g in 2 ml of *iodine solution R4* by warming on a water-bath, and allow to stand at room temperature. A yellowish-brown precipitate is formed.

**TESTS**

**Solution S**

Dissolve 1.000 g in *carbon dioxide-free water R* with heating, allow to cool and dilute to 100.0 ml with the same solvent.

**Appearance of solution**

Solution S is clear (*2.2.1*).

**pH** (*2.2.3*)

5.0 to 8.0.

To 10 ml of solution S add 0.1 ml of a saturated solution of *potassium chloride R*.

**Specific optical rotation** (*2.2.7*)

+ 160 to + 164 (dried substance), determined on solution S.

**Reducing sugars**

Maximum 0.2 per cent.

*Test solution* To 1 ml of solution S add 1 ml of *cupri-tartaric solution R4*. Heat on a water-bath for 10 min, cool to room temperature. Add 10 ml of *ammonium molybdate reagent R1* and allow to stand for 15 min.

*Reference solution* Prepare a reference solution at the same time and in the same manner as the test solution, using 1 ml of a 0.02 g/l solution of *glucose R*.

Measure the absorbance (*2.2.25*) of the test solution and the reference solution at the absorption maximum at 740 nm using *water R* as the compensation liquid. The absorbance of the test solution is not greater than that of the reference solution.

**Light-absorbing impurities**

Examine solution S between 230 nm and 750 nm. Between 230 nm and 350 nm, the absorbance (*2.2.25*) is not greater than 0.10. Between 350 nm and 750 nm, the absorbance (*2.2.25*) is not greater than 0.05.

**Related substances**

Liquid chromatography (*2.2.29*).

*Test solution (a)* Dissolve 0.25 g of the substance to be examined in *water R* with heating, cool and dilute to 25.0 ml with the same solvent.

*Test solution (b)* Dilute 5.0 ml of test solution (a) to 50.0 ml with *water R*.

*Reference solution (a)* Dissolve 25.0 mg of *alfadex CRS* (impurity A), 25.0 mg of *gammacyclodextrin CRS* (impurity B) and 50.0 mg of *betadex CRS* in *water R*, then dilute to 50.0 ml with the same solvent.

*Reference solution (b)* Dilute 5.0 ml of reference solution (a) to 50.0 ml with *water R*.

*Reference solution (c)* Dissolve 25.0 mg of *betadex CRS* in *water R* and dilute to 25.0 ml with the same solvent.

*Column:*
— *size*: $l$ = 0.25 m, Ø = 4.6 mm;
— *stationary phase: octadecylsilyl silica gel for chromatography R* (10 μm).

*Mobile phase* methanol R, water R (10:90 V/V).

*Flow rate* 1.5 ml/min.

*Detection* Differential refractometer.

*Equilibration* With the mobile phase for about 3 h.

*Injection* 50 μl of test solution (a) and reference solutions (a) and (b).

*Run time* 1.5 times the retention time of betadex.

*Relative retention* With reference to betadex (retention time = about 10 min): impurity B = about 0.3; impurity A = about 0.45.

*System suitability* Reference solution (a):
— *resolution*: minimum 1.5 between the peaks due to impurities B and A; if necessary, adjust the concentration of methanol in the mobile phase.

*Limits:*
— *impurities A, B*: for each impurity, not more than 0.5 times the area of the corresponding peak in the chromatogram obtained with reference solution (b) (0.25 per cent);
— *sum of impurities other than A and B*: not more than 0.5 times the area of the peak due to betadex in the chromatogram obtained with reference solution (b) (0.5 per cent).

**Residual solvents**

Head-space gas chromatography (*2.2.28*): use the standard additions method.

*Internal standard ethylene chloride R.*

*Test solutions* In each of 4 identical 20 ml flasks, dissolve 0.5 g of the substance to be examined in *water R* and add 0.10 g of *calcium chloride R* and 30 μl of *α-amylase solution R*. Add 1 ml of reference solutions (a), (b), (c) and (d), adding a different solution to each flask. Dilute to 10 ml with *water R*.

*Reference solutions* Prepare a 10 μl/l solution of *ethylene chloride R* (reference solution (a)). Prepare reference solutions (b), (c) and (d) from reference solution (a) to contain respectively, per litre, 5 μl, 10 μl and 15 μl of both *trichloroethylene R* and *toluene R*.

*Column:*
— *material*: fused silica;
— *size*: $l$ = 25 m, Ø = 0.32 mm;
— *stationary phase: macrogol 20 000 R* (film thickness 1 μm).

*Carrier gas helium for chromatography R.*

*Static head-space conditions which may be used:*
— *equilibration temperature: 45 °C;*
— *equilibration time: 2 h.*

*Temperature:*
— *column*: 50 °C;
— *injection port*: 140 °C;
— *detector*: 280 °C.

*Detection* Flame ionisation.

*Injection* 200 μl of the head space, at least 3 times.

*Retention time* toluene = about 10 min.

*System suitability:*
— *resolution*: minimum 1.1 between the peaks due to trichloroethylene and toluene; minimum 1.1 between the peaks due to toluene and ethylene chloride;

— *repeatability*: maximum relative standard deviations of the ratios of the areas of the peaks due to trichloroethylene and toluene to that of the peak due to ethylene chloride of 5 per cent.

Calculate the content of trichloroethylene and of toluene taking their relative densities to be 1.46 and 0.87, respectively.

*Limits*:
— *trichloroethylene*: maximum 10 ppm;
— *toluene*: maximum 10 ppm.

**Heavy metals** (*2.4.8*)
Maximum 10 ppm.

1.0 g complies with test C. Prepare the reference solution using 1 ml of *lead standard solution (10 ppm Pb) R*.

**Loss on drying** (*2.2.32*)
Maximum 16.0 per cent, determined on 1.000 g by drying in an oven at 120 °C for 2 h.

**Sulphated ash** (*2.4.14*)
Maximum 0.1 per cent, determined on 1.0 g.

## ASSAY
Liquid chromatography (*2.2.29*) as described in the test for related substances with the following modifications.

*Injection* Test solution (b) and reference solutions (a) and (c).

*System suitability* Reference solution (a):
— *repeatability*: maximum relative standard deviation of the area of the peak due to betadex of 2.0 per cent.

Calculate the percentage content of $[C_6H_{10}O_5]_7$ from the declared content of *betadex CRS*.

## STORAGE
In an airtight container.

## IMPURITIES
*Specified impurities* A, B.

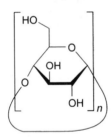

A. *n* = 6: alfadex,
B. *n* = 8: gammacyclodextrin.

_____ *Ph Eur*

# Betahistine Dihydrochloride
(*Ph Eur monograph 1665*)

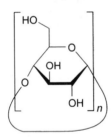

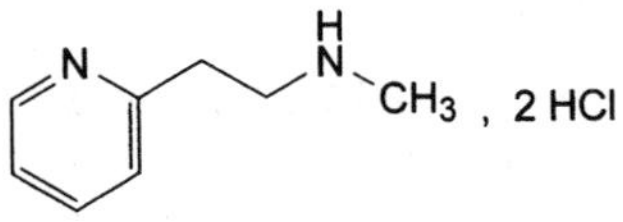

$C_8H_{12}N_2,2HCl$      209.1      *5579-84-0*

**Action and use**
Histamine $H_1$ receptor antagonist; antihistamine.

**Preparation**
Betahistine Dihydrochloride Tablets

*Ph Eur* _____

## DEFINITION
*N*-Methyl-2-(pyridin-2-yl)ethanamine dihydrochloride.

**Content**
99.0 per cent to 101.0 per cent (dried substance).

## CHARACTERS
**Appearance**
White to slightly yellow powder, very hygroscopic.

**Solubility**
Very soluble in water, soluble in ethanol (96 per cent), practically insoluble in 2-propanol.

## IDENTIFICATION
*First identification* B, D.

*Second identification* A, C, D.

A. Melting point (*2.2.14*): 150 °C to 154 °C.

B. Infrared absorption spectrophotometry (*2.2.24*).

*Comparison* betahistine dihydrochloride CRS.

C. Thin-layer chromatography (*2.2.27*).

*Test solution* Dissolve 10 mg of the substance to be examined in 2 ml of *ethanol (96 per cent) R*.

*Reference solution* Dissolve 10 mg of *betahistine dihydrochloride CRS* in 2 ml of *ethanol (96 per cent) R*.

*Plate* TLC silica gel GF_{254} plate R.

*Mobile phase* concentrated ammonia R, ethyl acetate R, methanol R (0.75:15:30 *V/V/V*).

*Application* 2 µl.

*Development* Over 2/3 of the plate.

*Drying* At 110 °C for 10 min.

*Detection* Examine in ultraviolet light at 254 nm.

*Results* The principal spot in the chromatogram obtained with the test solution is similar in position and size to the principal spot in the chromatogram obtained with the reference solution.

D. It gives reaction (a) of chlorides (*2.3.1*).

## TESTS
**Solution S**
Dissolve 5.0 g in *carbon dioxide-free water R*, and dilute to 50 ml with the same solvent.

**Appearance of solution**
Solution S is clear (*2.2.1*) and not more intensely coloured than reference solution $B_8$ (*2.2.2, Method II*).

**pH** (*2.2.3*)
2.0 to 3.0 for solution S.

## Related substances

Liquid chromatography (2.2.29).

*Test solution*   Dissolve 25 mg of the substance to be examined in the mobile phase and dilute to 25.0 ml with the mobile phase.

*Reference solution (a)*   Dissolve 10 mg of *betahistine dihydrochloride CRS* and 10 mg of *2-vinylpyridine R* in the mobile phase and dilute to 50.0 ml with the mobile phase. Dilute 2.0 ml of the solution to 50.0 ml with the mobile phase.

*Reference solution (b)*   Dilute 1.0 ml of the test solution to 100.0 ml with the mobile phase.

*Reference solution (c)*   Dilute 2.0 ml of reference solution (b) to 10.0 ml with the mobile phase.

*Column:*
— *size:* $l = 0.15$ m, Ø = 3.0 mm,
— *stationary phase:* end-capped octadecylsilyl base deactivated silica gel for chromatography R (5 μm).

*Mobile phase*   Dissolve 2.0 g of *sodium dodecyl sulphate R* in a mixture of 15 ml of a 10 per cent *V/V* solution of *sulphuric acid R*, 35 ml of a 17 g/l solution of *tetrabutylammonium hydrogen sulphate R* and 650 ml of *water R*; adjust to pH 3.3 using *dilute sodium hydroxide solution R* and mix with 300 ml of *acetonitrile R*.

*Flow rate*   1 ml/min.

*Detection*   Spectrophotometer at 260 nm.

*Injection*   20 μl.

*Run time*   4 times the retention time of betahistine.

*Relative retention*   With reference to betahistine (retention time = about 7 min): impurity B = about 0.2; impurity A = about 0.3; impurity C = about 3.

*System suitability:*   reference solution (a):
— *resolution:* minimum 3.5 between the peaks due to 2-vinylpyridine and betahistine.

*Limits:*
— *correction factor:* for the calculation of content, multiply the peak area of impurity B by 0.4;
— *impurities A, B, C:* for each impurity, not more than the area of the principal peak in the chromatogram obtained with reference solution (c) (0.2 per cent);
— *any other impurity:* for each impurity, not more than 0.5 times of the area of the principal peak in the chromatogram obtained with reference solution (c) (0.1 per cent);
— *total:* not more than 0.5 times the area of the principal peak in the chromatogram obtained with reference solution (b) (0.5 per cent);
— *disregard limit:* 0.25 times the area of the principal peak in the chromatogram obtained with reference solution (c) (0.05 per cent).

## Loss on drying (2.2.32)

Maximum 1.0 per cent, determined on 1.000 g by drying in an oven at 105 °C.

## Sulphated ash (2.4.14)

Maximum 0.1 per cent, determined on 1.0 g.

## ASSAY

Dissolve 80.0 mg in 50 ml of *ethanol (96 per cent) R*. Titrate with *0.1 M sodium hydroxide*, determining the end-point potentiometrically (2.2.20). Read the volume added to reach the second point of inflexion.

1 ml of *0.1 M sodium hydroxide* is equivalent to 10.46 mg of $C_8H_{14}Cl_2N_2$.

STORAGE

In an airtight container.

## IMPURITIES

*Specified impurities   A, B, C.*

A. 2-ethenylpyridine (2-vinylpyridine),

B. 2-(pyridin-2-yl)ethanol,

C. *N*-methyl-2-(pyridin-2-yl)-*N*-[2-(pyridin-2-yl)ethyl]ethanamine.

_____ *Ph Eur*

# Betahistine Mesilate

(*Ph Eur monograph 1071*)

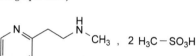

$C_8H_{12}N_2,2CH_3SO_3H$        328.4        54856-23-4

## Action and use

Histamine $H_1$ receptor antagonist; antihistamine.

*Ph Eur* _____

## DEFINITION

*N*-Methyl-2-(pyridin-2-yl)ethanamine bis(methanesulphonate).

## Content

98.0 per cent to 101.0 per cent (anhydrous substance).

## PRODUCTION

The production method must be evaluated to determine the potential for formation of alkyl mesilates, which is particularly likely to occur if the reaction medium contains lower alcohols. Where necessary, the production method is validated to demonstrate that alkyl mesilates are not detectable in the final product.

## CHARACTERS

### Appearance

White or almost white, crystalline powder, very hygroscopic.

### Solubility

Very soluble in water, freely soluble in ethanol (96 per cent), very slightly soluble in 2-propanol.

## IDENTIFICATION

*First identification   B.*

*Second identification*   *A, C, D.*

A. Melting point (*2.2.14*): 108 °C to 112 °C.

B. Infrared absorption spectrophotometry (*2.2.24*).

*Preparation*   Discs.

*Comparison*   *betahistine mesilate CRS.*

C. Thin-layer chromatography (*2.2.27*).

*Test solution*   Dissolve 10 mg of the substance to be examined in *ethanol (96 per cent) R* and dilute to 2 ml with the same solvent.

*Reference solution*   Dissolve 10 mg of *betahistine mesilate CRS*, in *ethanol (96 per cent) R* and dilute to 2 ml with the same solvent.

*Plate*   *TLC silica gel $F_{254}$ plate R.*

*Mobile phase*   *concentrated ammonia R, ethyl acetate R, methanol R* (0.75:15:30 *V/V/V*).

*Application*   2 µl.

*Development*   Over a path of 15 cm.

*Drying*   At 110 °C for 10 min.

*Detection*   Examine in ultraviolet light at 254 nm.

*Results*   The principal spot in the chromatogram obtained with the test solution is similar in position and size to the principal spot in the chromatogram obtained with the reference solution.

D. To 0.1 g add 5 ml of *dilute hydrochloric acid R* and shake for about 5 min. Add 1 ml of *barium chloride solution R1*. The solution remains clear. To a further 0.1 g add 0.5 g of *anhydrous sodium carbonate R*, mix and ignite until a white residue is obtained. Allow to cool and dissolve the residue in 7 ml of *water R*. The solution gives reaction (a) of sulphates (*2.3.1*).

## TESTS

### Solution S

Dissolve 5.0 g in *carbon dioxide-free water R* prepared from *distilled water R*, and dilute to 50 ml with the same solvent.

### Appearance of solution

Solution S is clear (*2.2.1*) and colourless (*2.2.2, Method II*).

### pH (*2.2.3*)

2.0 to 3.0 for solution S.

### Related substances

Liquid chromatography (*2.2.29*).

*Test solution*   Dissolve 50 mg of the substance to be examined in the mobile phase and dilute to 10.0 ml with the mobile phase.

*Reference solution (a)*   Dissolve 10 mg of *betahistine mesilate CRS* and 10 mg of *2-vinylpyridine R* (impurity A) in the mobile phase and dilute to 50.0 ml with the mobile phase. Dilute 2.0 ml of this solution to 50.0 ml with the mobile phase.

*Reference solution (b)*   Dilute 1.0 ml of the test solution to 100.0 ml with the mobile phase.

*Reference solution (c)*   Dilute 2.0 ml of reference solution (b) to 10.0 ml with the mobile phase.

*Column:*
— *size: l* = 0.25 m, Ø = 4.6 mm;
— *stationary phase: octadecylsilyl silica gel for chromatography R* (5 µm).

*Mobile phase*   Dissolve 2.0 g of *sodium dodecyl sulphate R* in a mixture of 15 volumes of a 10 per cent V/V solution of *sulphuric acid R*, 35 volumes of a 17 g/l solution of *tetrabutylammoniumhydrogen sulphate R* and 650 volumes of *water R*; adjust to pH 3.3 using *dilute sodium hydroxide solution R* and mix with 300 volumes of *acetonitrile R*.

*Flow rate*   1 ml/min.

*Detection*   Spectrophotometer at 260 nm.

*Injection*   20 µl.

*Run time*   3 times the retention time of betahistine mesilate.

*Retention time*   betahistine mesilate = about 8 min.

*System suitability*   Reference solution (a):
— *resolution*: minimum 3.5 between the peaks due to impurity A and betahistine mesilate.

*Limits:*
— *impurity A*: not more than the area of the principal peak in the chromatogram obtained with reference solution (c) (0.2 per cent);
— *total*: not more than 0.5 times the area of the principal peak in the chromatogram obtained with reference solution (b) (0.5 per cent);
— *disregard limit*: 0.025 times the area of the principal peak in the chromatogram obtained with reference solution (b) (0.025 per cent).

### 2-Propanol (*2.4.24*)

Maximum 0.5 per cent.

### Chlorides (*2.4.4*)

Maximum 35 ppm.

To 14 ml of solution S add 1 ml of *water R*.

### Sulphates (*2.4.13*)

Maximum 250 ppm.

Dilute 6 ml of solution S to 15 ml with *distilled water R*.

### Heavy metals (*2.4.8*)

Maximum 20 ppm.

12 ml of solution S complies with test A. Prepare the reference solution using *lead standard solution (2 ppm Pb) R*.

### Water (*2.5.12*)

Maximum 2.0 per cent, determined on 0.50 g.

## ASSAY

Dissolve 0.140 g in 50 ml of a mixture of 1 volume of *anhydrous acetic acid R* and 7 volumes of *acetic anhydride R*. Titrate with *0.1 M perchloric acid*, determining the end-point potentiometrically (*2.2.20*).

1 ml of *0.1 M perchloric acid* is equivalent to 16.42 mg of $C_{10}H_{20}N_2O_6S_2$.

## STORAGE

In an airtight container.

## IMPURITIES

*Specified impurities*   *A.*

A. 2-ethenylpyridine.

# Betamethasone

(Ph Eur monograph 0312)

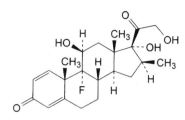

$C_{22}H_{29}FO_5$      392.5      378-44-9

**Action and use**
Glucocorticoid.

**Preparation**
Betamethasone Tablets

Ph Eur

## DEFINITION

9-Fluoro-11β,17,21-trihydroxy-16β-methylpregna-1,4-diene
3,20-dione.

## Content

97.0 per cent to 103.0 per cent (dried substance).

## CHARACTERS

**Appearance**
White or almost white, crystalline powder.

**Solubility**
Practically insoluble in water, sparingly soluble in anhydrous
ethanol, very slightly soluble in methylene chloride.

## IDENTIFICATION

*First identification*   B, C.

*Second identification*   A, C, D, E.

A. Dissolve 10.0 mg in *anhydrous ethanol R* and dilute to
100.0 ml with the same solvent. Place 2.0 ml of this solution
in a stoppered tube, add 10.0 ml of *phenylhydrazine-sulphuric
acid solution R*, mix and heat in a water-bath at 60 °C for
20 min. Cool immediately. The absorbance (2.2.25)
measured at 419 nm is not greater than 0.10.

B. Infrared absorption spectrophotometry (2.2.24).

*Comparison*   betamethasone CRS.

If the spectra obtained in the solid state show differences,
dissolve the substance to be examined and the reference
substance separately in the minimum volume of *methylene
chloride R*, evaporate to dryness on a water-bath and record
new spectra using the residues.

C. Thin-layer chromatography (2.2.27).

*Solvent mixture*   methanol R, methylene chloride R (1:9 V/V).

*Test solution*   Dissolve 10 mg of the substance to be
examined in the solvent mixture and dilute to 10 ml with the
solvent mixture.

*Reference solution (a)*   Dissolve 20 mg of *betamethasone CRS*
in the solvent mixture and dilute to 20 ml with the solvent
mixture.

*Reference solution (b)*   Dissolve 10 mg of *dexamethasone CRS*
in reference solution (a) and dilute to 10 ml with reference
solution (a).

*Plate*   TLC silica gel $F_{254}$ plate R.

*Mobile phase*   butanol R saturated with water R, toluene R,
ether R (5:10:85 V/V/V).

*Application*   5 µl.

*Development*   Over a path of 15 cm.

*Drying*   In air.

*Detection A*   Examine in ultraviolet light at 254 nm.

*Results A*   The principal spot in the chromatogram obtained
with the test solution is similar in position and size to the
principal spot in the chromatogram obtained with reference
solution (a).

*Detection B*   Spray with *alcoholic solution of sulphuric acid R*.
Heat at 120 °C for 10 min or until the spots appear. Allow
to cool. Examine in daylight and in ultraviolet light at
365 nm.

*Results*   The principal spot in the chromatogram obtained
with the test solution is similar in position, colour in daylight,
fluorescence in ultraviolet light at 365 nm and size to the
principal spot in the chromatogram obtained with reference
solution (a).

*System suitability*   Reference solution (b):
— the chromatogram shows 2 spots which may, however,
   not be completely separated.

D. Mix about 5 mg with 45 mg of *heavy magnesium oxide R*
and ignite in a crucible until an almost white residue is
obtained (usually less than 5 min). Allow to cool, add 1 ml
of *water R*, 0.05 ml of *phenolphthalein solution R1* and about
1 ml of *dilute hydrochloric acid R* to render the solution
colourless. Filter. Add 1.0 ml of the filtrate to a freshly
prepared mixture of 0.1 ml of *alizarin S solution R* and 0.1 ml
of *zirconyl nitrate solution R*. Mix, allow to stand for 5 min
and compare the colour of the solution with that of a blank
prepared in the same manner. The test solution is yellow and
the blank is red.

E. Add about 2 mg to 2 ml of *sulphuric acid R* and shake to
dissolve. Within 5 min, a deep reddish-brown colour
develops. Add this solution to 10 ml of *water R* and mix.
The colour is discharged and a clear solution remains.

## TESTS

**Specific optical rotation** (2.2.7)
+ 118 to + 126 (dried substance).

Dissolve 0.125 g in *methanol R* and dilute to 25.0 ml with the
same solvent.

**Related substances**
Liquid chromatography (2.2.29).

*Test solution*   Dissolve 25.0 mg of the substance to be
examined in a mixture of equal volumes of *acetonitrile R* and
*methanol R* and dilute to 10.0 ml with the same mixture of
solvents.

*Reference solution (a)*   Dissolve 2 mg of *betamethasone CRS*
and 2 mg of *methylprednisolone CRS* in mobile phase A, then
dilute to 100.0 ml with mobile phase A.

*Reference solution (b)*   Dilute 1.0 ml of the test solution to
100.0 ml with mobile phase A.

*Column:*
— size: $I$ = 0.25 m, Ø = 4.6 mm;
— stationary phase: octadecylsilyl silica gel for chromatography R
   (5 µm);
— temperature: 45 °C.

*Mobile phase:*
— mobile phase A: in a 1000 ml volumetric flask mix 250 ml
   of acetonitrile R with 700 ml of water R and allow to
   equilibrate; dilute to 1000 ml with water R and mix again;
— mobile phase B: acetonitrile R;

| Time (min) | Mobile phase A (per cent V/V) | Mobile phase B (per cent V/V) |
|---|---|---|
| 0 - 15 | 100 | 0 |
| 15 - 40 | 100 → 0 | 0 → 100 |
| 40 - 41 | 0 → 100 | 100 → 0 |
| 41 - 46 | 100 | 0 |

*Flow rate*    2.5 ml/min.

*Detection*    Spectrophotometer at 254 nm.

*Equilibration*    With mobile phase B for at least 30 min and then with mobile phase A for 5 min. For subsequent chromatograms, use the conditions described from 40 min to 46 min.

*Injection*    20 µl; inject the mixture of equal volumes of *acetonitrile R* and *methanol R* as a blank.

*Retention time*    methylprednisolone = about 11.5 min; betamethasone = about 12.5 min.

*System suitability*    Reference solution (a):
— *resolution*: minimum 1.5 between the peaks due to methylprednisolone and betamethasone; if necessary, adjust the concentration of acetonitrile in mobile phase A.

*Limits:*
— *impurities A, B, C, D, E, F, G, H, I, J*: for each impurity, not more than the area of the principal peak in the chromatogram obtained with reference solution (b) (1.0 per cent), and not more than 1 such peak has an area greater than 0.5 times the area of the principal peak in the chromatogram obtained with reference solution (b) (0.5 per cent);
— *total*: not more than twice the area of the principal peak in the chromatogram obtained with reference solution (b) (2.0 per cent);
— *disregard limit*: 0.05 times the area of the principal peak in the chromatogram obtained with reference solution (b) (0.05 per cent).

**Loss on drying** (2.2.32)
Maximum 0.5 per cent, determined on 0.500 g by drying in an oven at 105 °C.

**ASSAY**
Dissolve 0.100 g in *ethanol (96 per cent) R* and dilute to 100.0 ml with the same solvent. Dilute 2.0 ml of this solution to 100.0 ml with *ethanol (96 per cent) R*. Measure the absorbance (2.2.25) at the absorption maximum at 238.5 nm.

Calculate the content of $C_{22}H_{29}FO_5$ taking the specific absorbance to be 395.

**STORAGE**
Protected from light.

**IMPURITIES**
*Specified impurities*    A, B, C, D, E, F, G, H, I, J.

A. dexamethasone,

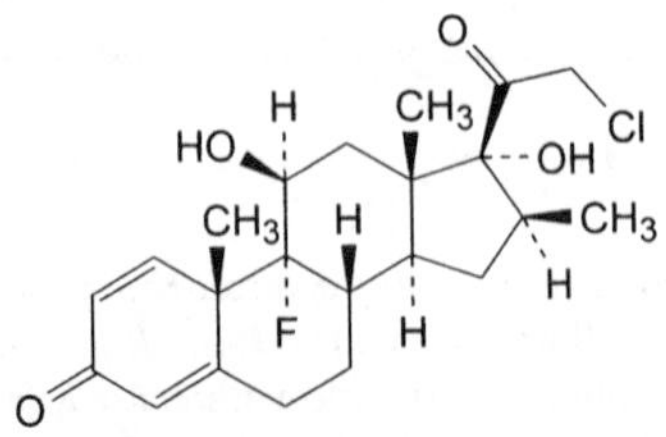

B. 21-chloro-9-fluoro-11β,17-dihydroxy-16β-methylpregna-1,4-diene-3,20-dione,

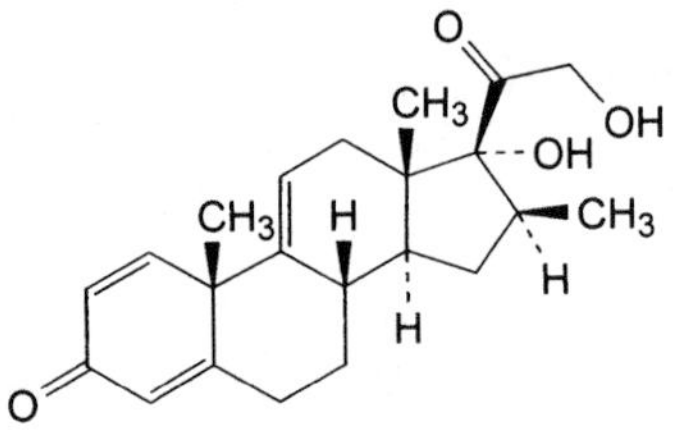

C. 17,21-dihydroxy-16β-methylpregna-1,4,9(11)-triene-3,20-dione,

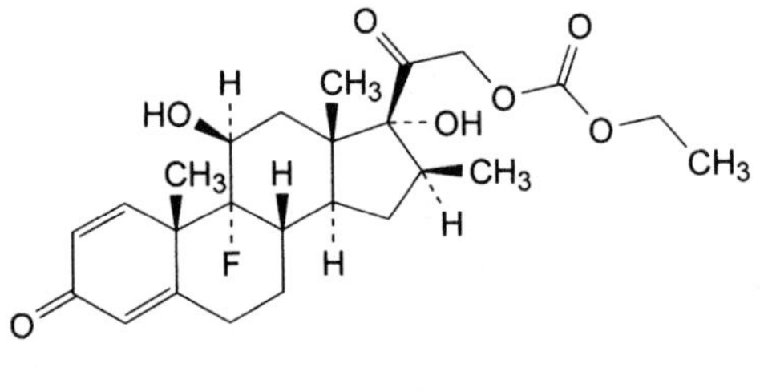

D. 9-fluoro-11β,17-dihydroxy-16β-methyl-3,20-dioxopregna-1,4-dien-21-yl ethoxycarboxylate,

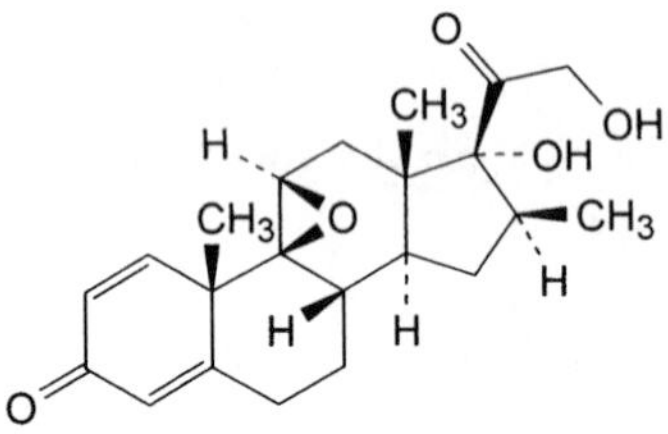

E. 9,11β-epoxy-17,21-dihydroxy-16β-methyl-9β-pregna-1,4-diene-3,20-dione,

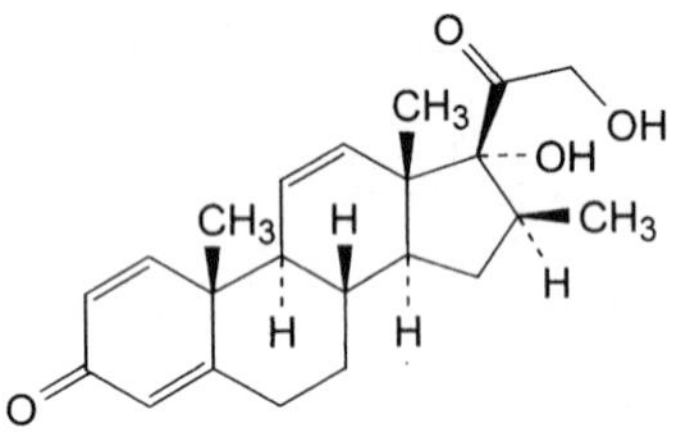

F. 17,21-dihydroxy-16β-methylpregna-1,4,11-triene-3,20-dione,

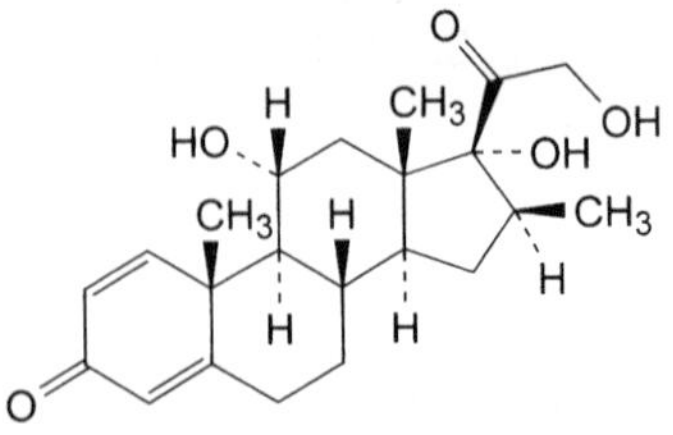

G. 11α,17,21-trihydroxy-16β-methylpregna-1,4-diene-3,20-dione,

H. 14-fluoro-11β,17,21-trihydroxy-16β-methyl-8α,9β,14β-pregna-1,4-diene-3,20-dione,

I. 8-fluoro-11β,17,21-trihydroxy-16β-methyl-8α,9β-pregna-1,4-diene-3,20-dione,

J. 17,21-dihydroxy-16β-methylpregna-1,4-diene-3,20-dione.

_____ *Ph Eur*

# Betamethasone Acetate

(*Ph Eur monograph 0975*)

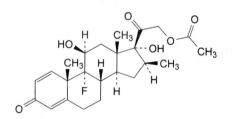

$C_{24}H_{31}FO_6$      434.5      *987-24-6*

## Action and use
Glucocorticoid.

*Ph Eur* _____

## DEFINITION
9-Fluoro-11β,17-dihydroxy-16β-methyl-3,20-dioxopregna-1,4-diene-21-yl acetate.

## Content
97.0 per cent to 103.0 per cent (anhydrous substance).

## CHARACTERS
### Appearance
White or almost white, crystalline powder.

### Solubility
Practically insoluble in water, freely soluble in acetone, soluble in ethanol (96 per cent) and in methylene chloride.

It shows polymorphism (*5.9*).

## IDENTIFICATION
*First identification*   B, C.

*Second identification*   A, C, D, E, F.

A. Dissolve 10.0 mg in *anhydrous ethanol R* and dilute to 100.0 ml with the same solvent. Place 2.0 ml of this solution in a ground-glass-stoppered tube, add 10.0 ml of *phenylhydrazine-sulphuric acid solution R*, mix and heat in a water-bath at 60 °C for 20 min. Cool immediately. The absorbance (*2.2.25*) measured at 419 nm is not greater than 0.10.

B. Infrared absorption spectrophotometry (*2.2.24*).

*Comparison*   betamethasone acetate CRS.

If the spectra obtained in the solid state show differences, dissolve the substance to be examined and the reference substance separately in the minimum volume of *methanol R*, evaporate to dryness on a water-bath and record new spectra using the residues.

C. Thin-layer chromatography (*2.2.27*).

*Solvent mixture*   methanol R, methylene chloride R (1:9 *V/V*).

*Test solution*   Dissolve 10 mg of the substance to be examined in the solvent mixture and dilute to 10 ml with the solvent mixture.

*Reference solution (a)*   Dissolve 20 mg of *betamethasone acetate CRS* in the solvent mixture and dilute to 20 ml with the solvent mixture.

*Reference solution (b)*   Dissolve 10 mg of *prednisolone acetate CRS* in reference solution (a) and dilute to 10 ml with reference solution (a).

*Plate*   TLC silica gel $F_{254}$ plate R.

*Mobile phase*   Add a mixture of 1.2 volumes of *water R* and 8 volumes of *methanol R* to a mixture of 15 volumes of *ether R* and 77 volumes of *methylene chloride R*.

*Application*   5 μl.

*Development*   Over a path of 15 cm.

*Drying*   In air.

*Detection A*   Examine in ultraviolet light at 254 nm.

*Results A*   The principal spot in the chromatogram obtained with the test solution is similar in position and size to the principal spot in the chromatogram obtained with reference solution (a).

*Detection B*   Spray with *alcoholic solution of sulphuric acid R*. Heat at 120 °C for 10 min or until the spots appear. Allow to cool. Examine in daylight and in ultraviolet light at 365 nm.

*Results B*   The principal spot in the chromatogram obtained with the test solution is similar in position, colour in daylight, fluorescence in ultraviolet light at 365 nm and size to the principal spot in the chromatogram obtained with reference solution (a).

*System suitability*   Reference solution (b):
— the chromatogram shows 2 clearly separated spots.

D. Add about 2 mg to 2 ml of *sulphuric acid R* and shake to dissolve. Within 5 min, a deep reddish-brown colour develops. Add this solution to 10 ml of *water R* and mix. The colour is discharged and a clear solution remains.

E. Mix about 5 mg with 45 mg of *heavy magnesium oxide R* and ignite in a crucible until an almost white residue is obtained (usually less than 5 min). Allow to cool, add 1 ml of *water R*, 0.05 ml of *phenolphthalein solution R1* and about 1 ml of *dilute hydrochloric acid R* to render the solution colourless. Filter. To a freshly prepared mixture of 0.1 ml of *alizarin S solution R* and 0.1 ml of *zirconyl nitrate solution R*, add 1.0 ml of the filtrate. Mix, allow to stand for 5 min and compare the colour of the solution with that of a blank prepared in the same manner. The test solution is yellow and the blank is red.

F. About 10 mg gives the reaction of acetyl (*2.3.1*).

## TESTS

**Specific optical rotation** (*2.2.7*)
+ 120 to + 128 (anhydrous substance).

Dissolve 0.250 g in *dioxan R* and dilute to 25.0 ml with the same solvent.

**Related substances**
Liquid chromatography (*2.2.29*).

*Test solution*   Dissolve 25.0 mg of the substance to be examined in 4 ml of *acetonitrile R* and dilute to 10.0 ml with the same solvent.

*Reference solution (a)*   Dissolve 2 mg of *betamethasone acetate CRS* and 2 mg of *dexamethasone acetate CRS* (impurity B) in the mobile phase, then dilute to 100.0 ml with the mobile phase.

*Reference solution (b)*   Dilute 1.0 ml of the test solution to 100.0 ml with the mobile phase.

*Column:*
— *size: l = 0.25 m, Ø = 4.6 mm;*
— *stationary phase: octadecylsilyl silica gel for chromatography R* (5 μm).

*Mobile phase*   In a 1000 ml volumetric flask mix 380 ml of acetonitrile R with 550 ml of *water R* and allow to equilibrate; dilute to 1000 ml with *water R* and mix again.

*Flow rate*   1 ml/min.

*Detection*   Spectrophotometer at 254 nm.

*Equilibration*   With the mobile phase for about 30 min.

*Injection*   20 μl.

*Run time*   2.5 times the retention time of betamethasone acetate.

*Retention time*   betamethasone acetate = about 19 min; impurity B = about 22 min.

*System suitability*   Reference solution (a):
— *resolution*: minimum 3.3 between the peaks due to betamethasone acetate and impurity B; if necessary, adjust slightly the concentration of acetonitrile in the mobile phase.

*Limits:*
— *impurities A, B, C, D*: for each impurity, not more than 0.5 times the area of the principal peak in the chromatogram obtained with reference solution (b) (0.5 per cent);
— *total*: not more than 1.25 times the area of the principal peak in the chromatogram obtained with reference solution (b) (1.25 per cent);
— *disregard limit*: 0.05 times the area of the principal peak in the chromatogram obtained with reference solution (b) (0.05 per cent).

**Water** (*2.5.12*)
Maximum 4.0 per cent, determined on 0.100 g.

## ASSAY

Dissolve 0.100 g in *ethanol (96 per cent) R* and dilute to 100.0 ml with the same solvent. Dilute 2.0 ml of this solution to 100.0 ml with *ethanol (96 per cent) R*. Measure the absorbance (*2.2.25*) at the absorption maximum at 240 nm.

Calculate the content of $C_{24}H_{31}FO_6$ taking the specific absorbance to be 350.

## STORAGE
Protected from light.

## IMPURITIES
*Specified impurities*   *A, B, C, D.*

A. betamethasone,

B. dexamethasone acetate,

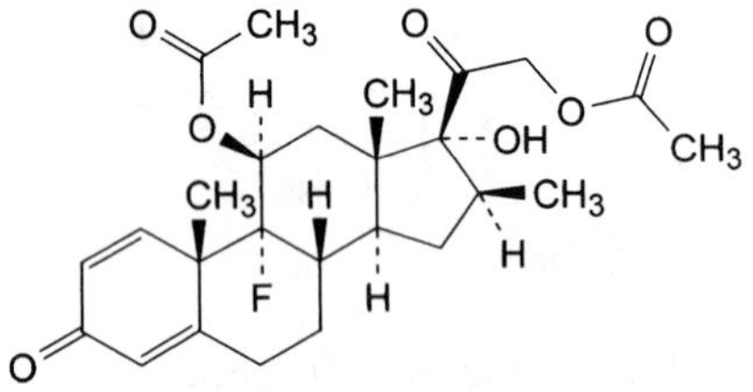

C. betamethasone 11,21-diacetate,

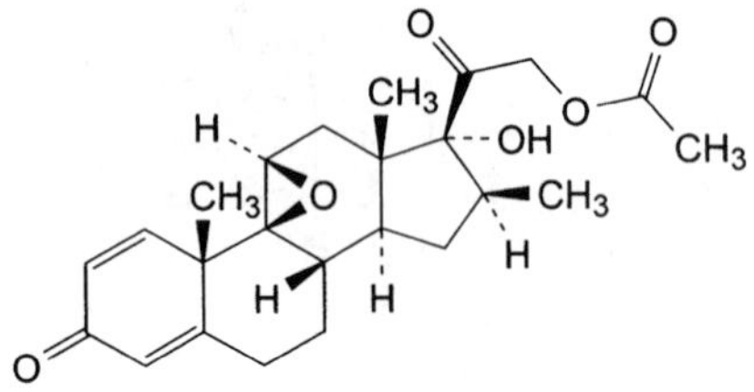

D. 9,11β-epoxy-17-hydroxy-16β-methyl-3,20-dioxo-9β-pregna-1,4-diene-21-yl acetate.

_____ *Ph Eur*

# Betamethasone Dipropionate

(*Ph Eur monograph 0809*)

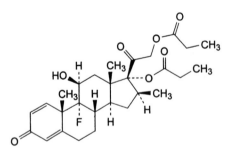

$C_{28}H_{37}FO_7$                 504.6                 5593-20-4

**Action and use**
Glucocorticoid.

*Ph Eur* _____

## DEFINITION
9-Fluoro-11β-hydroxy-16β-methyl-3,20-dioxopregna-1,4-diene-17,21-diyl dipropanoate.

**Content**
97.0 per cent to 103.0 per cent (dried substance).

## CHARACTERS

### Appearance

White or almost white, crystalline powder.

### Solubility

Practically insoluble in water, freely soluble in acetone and in methylene chloride, sparingly soluble in ethanol (96 per cent).

## IDENTIFICATION

*First identification*   B, C.

*Second identification*   A, D, E, F.

A. Dissolve 10.0 mg in *anhydrous ethanol R* and dilute to 100.0 ml with the same solvent. Place 2.0 ml of this solution in a ground-glass-stoppered tube, add 10.0 ml of *phenylhydrazine-sulphuric acid solution R*, mix and heat in a water-bath at 60 °C for 20 min. Cool immediately. The absorbance (*2.2.25*) measured at 419 nm is not more than 0.10.

B. Infrared absorption spectrophotometry (*2.2.24*).

*Comparison*   betamethasone dipropionate CRS.

C. Thin-layer chromatography (*2.2.27*).

*Solvent mixture*   methanol R, methylene chloride R (1:9 *V/V*).

*Test solution*   Dissolve 10 mg of the substance to be examined in the solvent mixture and dilute to 10 ml with the solvent mixture.

*Reference solution (a)*   Dissolve 10 mg of *betamethasone dipropionate CRS* in the solvent mixture and dilute to 10 ml with the solvent mixture.

*Reference solution (b)*   Dissolve 10 mg of *desoxycortone acetate CRS* in the solvent mixture and dilute to 10 ml with the solvent mixture. Dilute 5 ml of this solution to 10 ml with reference solution (a).

*Plate*   TLC silica gel $F_{254}$ plate R.

*Mobile phase*   Add a mixture of 1.2 volumes of *water R* and 8 volumes of *methanol R* to a mixture of 15 volumes of *ether R* and 77 volumes of *methylene chloride R*.

*Application*   5 µl.

*Development*   Over a path of 15 cm.

*Drying*   In air.

*Detection A*   Examine in ultraviolet light at 254 nm.

*Results A*   The principal spot in the chromatogram obtained with the test solution is similar in position and size to the principal spot in the chromatogram obtained with reference solution (a).

*Detection B*   Spray with *alcoholic solution of sulphuric acid R*. Heat at 120 °C for 10 min or until the spots appear. Allow to cool. Examine in daylight and in ultraviolet light at 365 nm.

*Results B*   The principal spot in the chromatogram obtained with the test solution is similar in position, colour in daylight, fluorescence in ultraviolet light at 365 nm and size to the principal spot in the chromatogram obtained with reference solution (a).

*System suitability*   Reference solution (b):
— the chromatogram shows 2 clearly separated spots.

D. Thin-layer chromatography (*2.2.27*).

*Test solution (a)*   Dissolve 25 mg of the substance to be examined in *methanol R* with gentle heating and dilute to 5 ml with the same solvent (solution A). Dilute 2 ml of this solution to 10 ml with *methylene chloride R*.

*Test solution (b)*   Transfer 2 ml of solution A to a 15 ml glass tube with a ground-glass stopper or a polytetrafluoroethylene cap. Add 10 ml of *saturated methanolic potassium hydrogen carbonate solution R* and immediately pass a current of *nitrogen R* briskly through the solution for 5 min. Stopper the tube. Heat in a water-bath at 45 °C, protected from light, for 2 h. Allow to cool.

*Reference solution (a)*   Dissolve 25 mg of *betamethasone dipropionate CRS* in *methanol R* with gentle heating and dilute to 5 ml with the same solvent (solution B). Dilute 2 ml of this solution to 10 ml with *methylene chloride R*.

*Reference solution (b)*   Transfer 2 ml of solution B to a 15 ml glass tube with a ground-glass stopper or a polytetrafluoroethylene cap. Add 10 ml of *saturated methanolic potassium hydrogen carbonate solution R* and immediately pass a current of *nitrogen R* briskly through the solution for 5 min. Stopper the tube. Heat in a water-bath at 45 °C, protected from light, for 2 h. Allow to cool.

*Plate*   TLC silica gel $F_{254}$ plate R.

*Mobile phase*   Add a mixture of 1.2 volumes of *water R* and 8 volumes of *methanol R* to a mixture of 15 volumes of *ether R* and 77 volumes of *methylene chloride R*.

*Application*   5 µl.

*Development*   Over a path of 15 cm.

*Drying*   In air.

*Detection A*   Examine in ultraviolet light at 254 nm.

*Results A*   The principal spot in each of the chromatograms obtained with the test solutions is similar in position and size to the principal spot in the chromatogram obtained with the corresponding reference solution.

*Detection B*   Spray with *alcoholic solution of sulphuric acid R*. Heat at 120 °C for 10 min or until the spots appear. Allow to cool. Examine in daylight and in ultraviolet light at 365 nm.

*Results B*   The principal spot in each of the chromatograms obtained with the test solutions is similar in position, colour in daylight, fluorescence in ultraviolet light at 365 nm and size to the principal spot in the chromatogram obtained with the corresponding reference solution. The principal spot in each of the chromatograms obtained with test solution (b) and reference solution (b) has an $R_F$ value distinctly lower than that of the principal spots in each of the chromatograms obtained with test solution (a) and reference solution (a).

E. Add about 2 mg to 2 ml of *sulphuric acid R* and shake to dissolve. Within 5 min, a deep reddish-brown colour develops. Add this solution to 10 ml of *water R* and mix. The colour is discharged and a clear solution remains.

F. Mix about 5 mg with 45 mg of *heavy magnesium oxide R* and ignite in a crucible until an almost white residue is obtained (usually less than 5 min). Allow to cool, add 1 ml of *water R*, 0.05 ml *of phenolphthalein solution R1* and about 1 ml of *dilute hydrochloric acid R* to render the solution colourless. Filter. Add 1.0 ml of the filtrate to a freshly prepared mixture of 0.1 ml of *alizarin S solution R* and 0.1 ml of *zirconyl nitrate solution R*. Mix, allow to stand for 5 min and compare the colour of the solution with that of a blank prepared in the same manner. The test solution is yellow and the blank is red.

## TESTS

**Specific optical rotation** (*2.2.7*)

+ 63 to + 70 (dried substance).

Dissolve 0.250 g in *dioxan R* and dilute to 25.0 ml with the same solvent.

**Related substances**

Liquid chromatography (*2.2.29*).

*Test solution*   Dissolve 62.5 mg of the substance to be examined in the mobile phase and dilute to 25.0 ml with the mobile phase.

*Reference solution (a)*   Dissolve 2.5 mg of *betamethasone dipropionate CRS* and 2.5 mg of *anhydrous beclometasone dipropionate CRS* in the mobile phase and dilute to 50.0 ml with the same solvent.

*Reference solution (b)*   Dilute 1.0 ml of the test solution to 50.0 ml with the mobile phase.

*Column:*
— *size: l* = 0.25 m, Ø = 4.6 mm;
— *stationary phase: octadecylsilyl silica gel for chromatography R* (5 μm).

*Mobile phase*   Mix carefully 350 ml of *water R* with 600 ml of *acetonitrile R* and allow to equilibrate; dilute to 1000 ml with *water R* and mix again.

*Flow rate*   1 ml/min.

*Detection*   Spectrophotometer at 254 nm.

*Equilibration*   With the mobile phase for about 45 min.

*Injection*   20 μl.

*Run time*   2.5 times the retention time of betamethasone dipropionate.

*Retention time*   betamethasone dipropionate = about 9 min; beclometasone dipropionate = about 10.7 min.

*System suitability*   Reference solution (a):
— *resolution*: minimum 2.5 between the peaks due to betamethasone dipropionate and beclometasone dipropionate; if necessary, adjust the concentration of acetonitrile in the mobile phase.

*Limits:*
— *any impurity*: for each impurity, not more than 0.75 times the area of the principal peak in the chromatogram obtained with reference solution (b) (1.5 per cent), and not more than 1 such peak has an area greater than 0.5 times the area of the principal peak in the chromatogram obtained with reference solution (b) (1 per cent);
— *total*: not more than 1.25 times the area of the principal peak in the chromatogram obtained with reference solution (b) (2.5 per cent);
— *disregard limit*: 0.025 times the area of the principal peak in the chromatogram obtained with reference solution (b) (0.05 per cent).

**Loss on drying** (*2.2.32*)
Maximum 1.0 per cent, determined on 0.500 g by drying in an oven at 105 °C.

**ASSAY**
Dissolve 50.0 mg in *ethanol (96 per cent) R* and dilute to 100.0 ml with the same solvent. Dilute 2.0 ml of this solution to 50.0 ml with *ethanol (96 per cent) R*. Measure the absorbance (*2.2.25*) at the absorption maximum at 240 nm. Calculate the content of $C_{28}H_{37}FO_7$ taking the specific absorbance to be 305.

**STORAGE**
Protected from light.

_____ *Ph Eur*

# Betamethasone Sodium Phosphate

(*Ph Eur monograph 0810*)

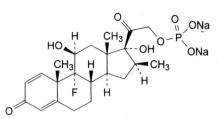

$C_{22}H_{28}FNa_2O_8P$          516.4          *151-73-5*

**Action and use**
Glucocorticoid.

**Preparations**
Betamethasone Eye Drops
Betamethasone Injection
Betamethasone Sodium Phosphate Tablets

*Ph Eur* _____

**DEFINITION**
9-Fluoro-11β,17-dihydroxy-16β-methyl-3,20-dioxopregna-1,4-diene-21-yl disodium phosphate.

**Content**
96.0 per cent to 103.0 per cent (anhydrous substance).

**CHARACTERS**
**Appearance**
White or almost white powder, very hygroscopic.

**Solubility**
Freely soluble in water, slightly soluble in ethanol (96 per cent), practically insoluble in methylene chloride.

**IDENTIFICATION**
*First identification*   B, C.

*Second identification*   A, C, D, E, F.

A. Dissolve 10.0 mg in 5 ml of *water R* and dilute to 100.0 ml with *anhydrous ethanol R*. Place 2.0 ml of this solution in a ground-glass-stoppered tube, add 10.0 ml of *phenylhydrazine-sulphuric acid solution R*, mix and heat in a water-bath at 60 °C for 20 min. Cool immediately. The absorbance (*2.2.25*) measured at the absorption maximum at 450 nm is not more than 0.10.

B. Infrared absorption spectrophotometry (*2.2.24*).

*Comparison*   betamethasone sodium phosphate CRS.

If the spectra obtained in the solid state show differences, dissolve the substance to be examined and the reference substance separately in the minimum volume of *ethanol (96 per cent) R*, evaporate to dryness on a water-bath and record new spectra using the residues.

C. Thin-layer chromatography (*2.2.27*).

*Test solution*   Dissolve 10 mg of the substance to be examined in *methanol R* and dilute to 10 ml with the same solvent.

*Reference solution (a)*   Dissolve 10 mg of *betamethasone sodium phosphate CRS* in *methanol R* and dilute to 10 ml with the same solvent.

*Reference solution (b)*   Dissolve 10 mg of *prednisolone sodium phosphate CRS* in *methanol R* and dilute to 10 ml with the same solvent. Dilute 5 ml of this solution to 10 ml with reference solution (a).

*Plate* TLC silica gel $F_{254}$ plate R.

*Mobile phase* glacial acetic acid R, water R, butanol R (20:20:60 V/V/V).

*Application* 5 µl.

*Development* Over a path of 15 cm.

*Drying* In air.

*Detection A* Examine in ultraviolet light at 254 nm.

*Results A* The principal spot in the chromatogram obtained with the test solution is similar in position and size to the principal spot in the chromatogram obtained with reference solution (a).

*Detection B* Spray with alcoholic solution of sulphuric acid R. Heat at 120 °C for 10 min or until the spots appear. Allow to cool. Examine in daylight and in ultraviolet light at 365 nm.

*Results B* The principal spot in the chromatogram obtained with the test solution is similar in position, colour in daylight, fluorescence in ultraviolet light at 365 nm and size to the principal spot in the chromatogram obtained with reference solution (a).

*System suitability* Reference solution (b):
— the chromatogram shows 2 spots which may, however, not be completely separated.

D. Add about 2 mg to 2 ml of *sulphuric acid R* and shake to dissolve. Within 5 min, an intense reddish-brown colour develops. Add the solution to 10 ml of *water R* and mix. The colour is discharged and a clear solution remains.

E. Mix about 5 mg with 45 mg of *heavy magnesium oxide R* and ignite in a crucible until an almost white residue is obtained (usually less than 5 min). Allow to cool, add 1 ml of *water R*, 0.05 ml of *phenolphthalein solution R1* and about 1 ml of *dilute hydrochloric acid R* to render the solution colourless. Filter. Add 1.0 ml of the filtrate to a freshly prepared mixture of 0.1 ml *of alizarin S solution R* and 0.1 ml of *zirconyl nitrate solution R*. Mix, allow to stand for 5 min and compare the colour of the solution with that of a blank prepared in the same manner. The test solution is yellow and the blank is red.

F. To about 40 mg add 2 ml of *sulphuric acid R* and heat gently until white fumes are evolved. Add *nitric acid R* dropwise, continue the heating until the solution is almost colourless and cool. Add 2 ml of *water R*, heat until white fumes are again evolved, cool, add 10 ml of *water R* and neutralise to *red litmus paper R* with *dilute ammonia R1*. The solution gives reaction (a) of sodium (*2.3.1*) and reaction (b) of phosphates (*2.3.1*).

## TESTS
### Solution S
Dissolve 1.0 g in *carbon dioxide-free water R* and dilute to 20 ml with the same solvent.

### Appearance of solution
Solution S is clear (*2.2.1*) and not more intensely coloured than reference solution $B_7$ (*2.2.2, Method II*).

### pH (*2.2.3*)
7.5 to 9.0.

Dilute 1 ml of solution S to 5 ml with *carbon dioxide-free water* R.

### Specific optical rotation (*2.2.7*)
+ 98 to + 104 (anhydrous substance).

Dissolve 0.250 g in *water R* and dilute to 25.0 ml with the same solvent.

### Related substances
Liquid chromatography (*2.2.29*).

*Test solution* Dissolve 62.5 mg of the substance to be examined in the mobile phase and dilute to 25.0 ml with the mobile phase.

*Reference solution (a)* Dissolve 25 mg of *betamethasone sodium phosphate CRS* and 25 mg of *dexamethasone sodium phosphate CRS* in the mobile phase and dilute to 25.0 ml with the mobile phase. Dilute 1.0 ml of this solution to 25.0 ml with the mobile phase.

*Reference solution (b)* Dilute 1.0 ml of the test solution to 50.0 ml with the mobile phase.

*Column:*
— *size:* $l = 0.25$ m, $\varnothing = 4.6$ mm;
— *stationary phase: octadecylsilyl silica gel for chromatography R* (5 µm).

*Mobile phase* In a 250 ml conical flask, weigh 1.360 g of *potassium dihydrogen phosphate R* and 0.600 g of *hexylamine R*, mix and allow to stand for 10 min and then dissolve in 185 ml of *water R*; add 65 ml of *acetonitrile R*, mix and filter (0.45 µm).

*Flow rate* 1 ml/min.

*Detection* Spectrophotometer at 254 nm.

*Equilibration* With the mobile phase for about 45 min.

*Injection* 20 µl.

*Run time* Twice the retention time of betamethasone sodium phosphate.

*Retention time* Betamethasone sodium phosphate = about 14 min; dexamethasone sodium phosphate = about 15.5 min.

*System suitability* Reference solution (a):
— *resolution:* minimum 2.0 between the peaks due to betamethasone sodium phosphate and dexamethasone sodium phosphate; if necessary, increase the concentration of acetonitrile or increase the concentration of water in the mobile phase.

*Limits:*
— *any impurity:* for each impurity, not more than the area of the principal peak in the chromatogram obtained with reference solution (b) (2 per cent), and not more than 1 such peak has an area greater than 0.5 times the area of the principal peak in the chromatogram obtained with reference solution (b) (1 per cent);
— *total:* not more than 1.5 times the area of the principal peak in the chromatogram obtained with reference solution (b) (3 per cent);
— *disregard limit:* 0.025 times the area of the principal peak in the chromatogram obtained with reference solution (b) (0.05 per cent).

*Inorganic phosphate* Maximum 1 per cent.

Dissolve 50 mg in *water R* and dilute to 100 ml with the same solvent. To 10 ml of this solution add 5 ml of *molybdovanadic reagent R*, mix and allow to stand for 5 min. Any yellow colour in the solution is not more intense than that in a standard prepared at the same time and in the same manner using 10 ml of *phosphate standard solution (5 ppm PO4) R*.

### Water (*2.5.12*)
Maximum 8.0 per cent, determined on 0.200 g.

## ASSAY
Dissolve 0.100 g in *water R* and dilute to 100.0 ml with the same solvent. Dilute 5.0 ml of this solution to 250.0 ml with

*water R*. Measure the absorbance (*2.2.25*) at the absorption maximum at 241 nm.

Calculate the content of $C_{22}H_{28}FNa_2O_8P$ taking the specific absorbance to be 297.

## STORAGE
In an airtight container, protected from light.

_____ *Ph Eur*

# Betamethasone Valerate

*(Ph Eur monograph 0811)*

$C_{27}H_{37}FO_6$          476.6          *2152-44-5*

## Action and use
Glucocorticoid.

## Preparations
Betamethasone Valerate Scalp Application

Betamethasone Valerate Cream

Betamethasone and Clioquinol Cream

Betamethasone Valerate Lotion

Betamethasone Valerate Ointment

Betamethasone and Clioquinol Ointment

*Ph Eur* _____

## DEFINITION
9-Fluoro-11β,21-dihydroxy-16β-methyl-3,20-dioxopregna-1,4-dien-17-yl pentanoate.

## Content
97.0 per cent to 103.0 per cent (dried substance).

## CHARACTERS
### Appearance
White or almost white, crystalline powder.

### Solubility
Practically insoluble in water, freely soluble in acetone and in methylene chloride, soluble in ethanol (96 per cent).

### mp
About 192 °C, with decomposition.

## IDENTIFICATION
A. Infrared absorption spectrophotometry (*2.2.24*).

*Comparison   betamethasone 17-valerate CRS.*

If the spectra obtained in the solid state show differences, dissolve the substance to be examined and the reference substance separately in the minimum volume of *methylene chloride R*, evaporate to dryness on a water-bath and record new spectra using the residues.

B. Liquid chromatography (*2.2.29*).

Examine the chromatograms obtained in the test for related substances.

*Results*   The principal peak in the chromatogram obtained with the test solution is similar in retention time and size to the principal peak in the chromatogram obtained with reference solution (b).

## TESTS
### Specific optical rotation (*2.2.7*)
+ 77 to + 83 (dried substance).

Dissolve 0.250 g in *anhydrous ethanol R* and dilute to 25.0 ml with the same solvent.

### Related substances
Liquid chromatography (*2.2.29*). *Carry out the test protected from light. Prepare the solutions immediately before use.*

*Solvent mixture   glacial acetic acid R*, mobile phase (1:1000 *V/V*).

*Test solution*   Dissolve 50 mg of the substance to be examined in the solvent mixture and dilute to 20.0 ml with the solvent mixture.

*Reference solution (a)*   Dilute 1.0 ml of the test solution to 100.0 ml with the solvent mixture. Dilute 1.0 ml of this solution to 10.0 ml with the solvent mixture.

*Reference solution (b)*   Dissolve 12.5 mg of *betamethasone valerate for system suitability CRS* (containing impurities D and G) in 5.0 ml of the solvent mixture. Use 1.0 ml of this solution to dissolve the contents of a vial of *betamethasone valerate impurity mixture CRS* (containing impurities C, H and I).

*Reference solution (c)*   Dissolve 6 mg of *betamethasone CRS* (impurity A) and 3 mg of *betamethasone 21-valerate CRS* (impurity E) in 30.0 ml of the solvent mixture. Dilute 1.0 ml of this solution to 10.0 ml with the solvent mixture.

*Column:*
— *size: l* = 0.25 m, Ø = 4.6 mm;
— *stationary phase: end-capped octadecylsilyl silica gel for chromatography R* (5 μm);
— *temperature*: 20 °C.

*Mobile phase   acetonitrile R, water R* (50:50 *V/V*).

*Flow rate*   1 ml/min.

*Detection*   Spectrophotometer at 239 nm.

*Injection*   20 μl.

*Run time*   2.5 times the retention time of betamethasone valerate.

*Identification of impurities*   Use the chromatogram supplied with *betamethasone valerate for system suitability CRS* and the chromatogram obtained with reference solution (b) to identify the peaks due to impurities C, D, G, H and I; use the chromatogram obtained with reference solution (c) to identify the peaks due to impurities A and E.

*Relative retention*   With reference to betamethasone valerate (retention time = about 20 min): impurity A = about 0.3; impurity I = about 0.6; impurity C = about 0.8; impurity H = about 1.3; impurity D = about 1.4; impurity E = about 1.6; impurity G = about 2.0.

*System suitability*   Reference solution (b):
— *resolution*: minimum 1.7 between the peaks due to impurities H and D.

*Limits:*
— *impurity A*: not more than 7 times the area of the principal peak in the chromatogram obtained with reference solution (a) (0.7 per cent);
— *impurities E, G*: for each impurity, not more than 3 times the area of the principal peak in the chromatogram obtained with reference solution (a) (0.3 per cent);

— *impurities C, H, I*: for each impurity, not more than 1.5 times the area of the principal peak in the chromatogram obtained with reference solution (a) (0.15 per cent);

— *unspecified impurities*: for each impurity, not more than the area of the principal peak in the chromatogram obtained with reference solution (a) (0.10 per cent);

— *total*: not more than 15 times the area of the principal peak in the chromatogram obtained with reference solution (a) (1.5 per cent);

— *disregard limit*: 0.5 times the area of the principal peak in the chromatogram obtained with reference solution (a) (0.05 per cent).

**Loss on drying** (*2.2.32*)
Maximum 0.5 per cent, determined on 1.000 g by drying in an oven at 105 °C.

**ASSAY**
Dissolve 50.0 mg in *ethanol (96 per cent) R* and dilute to 100.0 ml with the same solvent. Dilute 2.0 ml of this solution to 50.0 ml with *ethanol (96 per cent) R*. Measure the absorbance (*2.2.25*) at the absorption maximum at 240 nm.

Calculate the content of $C_{27}H_{37}FO_6$ taking the specific absorbance to be 325.

**STORAGE**
Protected from light.

**IMPURITIES**
*Specified impurities  A, C, E, G, H, I.*

*Other detectable impurities*  (The following substances would, if present at a sufficient level, be detected by one or other of the tests in the monograph. They are limited by the general acceptance criterion for other/unspecified impurities and/or by the general monograph *Substances for pharmaceutical use (2034)*. It is therefore not necessary to identify these impurities for demonstration of compliance. See also *5.10. Control of impurities in substances for pharmaceutical use*): B, D, F.

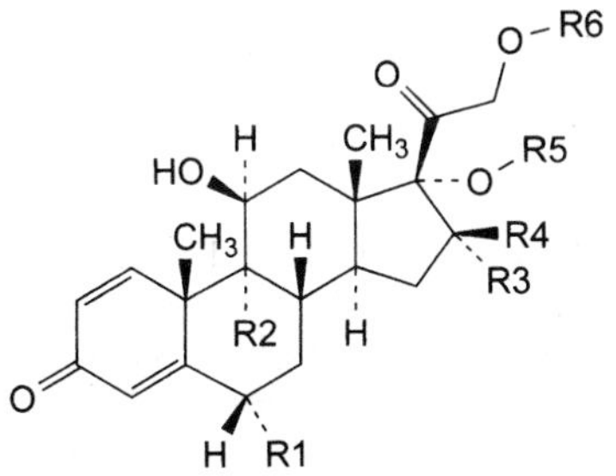

A. R1 = R3 = R5 = R6 = H, R2 = F, R4 = CH₃: betamethasone,

C. R1 = R4 = R6 = H, R2 = F, R3 = CH₃, R5 = CO-[CH₂]₃-CH₃: 9-fluoro-11β,21-dihydroxy-16α-methyl-3,20-dioxopregna-1,4-dien-17-yl pentanoate (dexamethasone 17-valerate),

E. R1 = R3 = R5 = H, R2 = F, R4 = CH₃, R6 = CO-[CH₂]₃-CH₃: 9-fluoro-11β,17-dihydroxy-16β-methyl-3,20-dioxopregna-1,4-dien-21-yl pentanoate (betamethasone 21-valerate),

G. R1 = Br, R2 = F, R3 = R6 = H, R4 = CH₃, R5 = CO-[CH₂]₃-CH₃: 6α-bromo-9-fluoro-11β,21-dihydroxy-16βmethyl-3,20-dioxopregna-1,4-dien-17-yl pentanoate (6α-bromo-betamethasone valerate),

H. R1 = R3 = R6 = H, R2 = Cl, R4 = CH₃, R5 = CO-[CH₂]₃-CH₃: 9-chloro-11β,21-dihydroxy-16β-methyl-3,20-dioxopregna-1,4-dien-17-yl pentanoate (beclomethasone 17-valerate),

I. R1 = R3 = R4 = R6 = H, R2 = F, R5 = CO-[CH₂]₃-CH₃: 9-fluoro-11β,21-dihydroxy-3,20-dioxopregna-1,4-dien-17-yl pentanoate (9-fluoro-prednisolone 17-valerate),

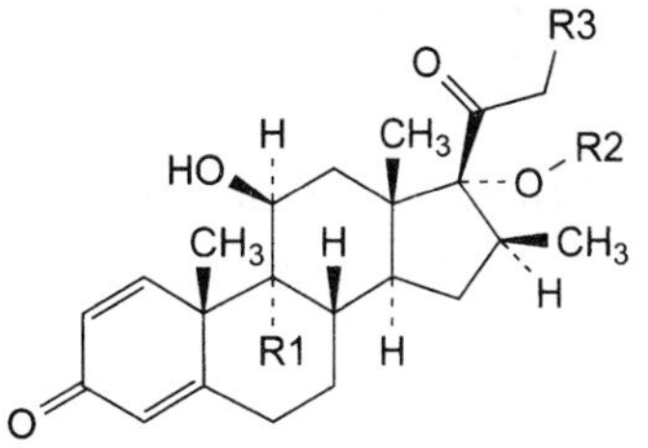

B. R1 = F, R2 = R3 = H: 9-fluoro-11β,17-dihydroxy-16β-methylpregna-1,4-diene-3,20-dione (21-deoxy-betamethasone),

D. R1 = Br, R2 = CO-[CH₂]₃-CH₃, R3 = OH: 9-bromo-11β,21dihydroxy-16β-methyl-3,20-dioxopregna-1,4-dien-17-yl pentanoate (9-bromo-betamethasone valerate),

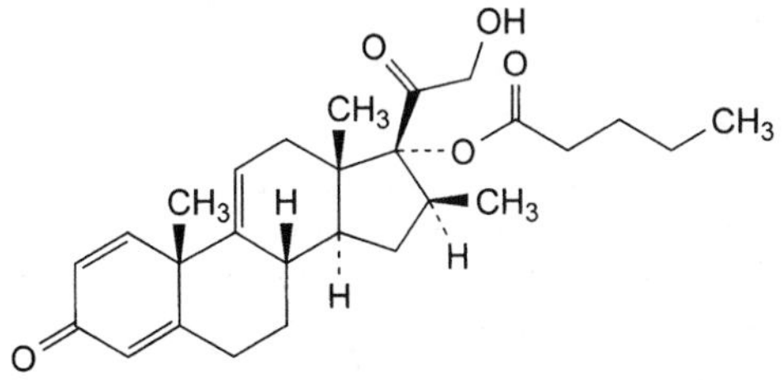

F. 21-hydroxy-16β-methyl-3,20-dioxopregna-1,4,9(11)-trien-17-yl pentanoate (betamethasone valerate δ-9(11)).

*Ph Eur*

# Betaxolol Hydrochloride

*(Ph Eur monograph 1072)*

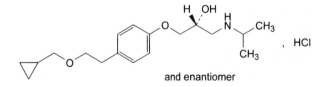

and enantiomer

$C_{18}H_{29}NO_3$, HCl          343.9          *63659-19-8*

**Action and use**
Beta-adrenoceptor antagonist.

**Preparations**
Betaxolol Eye Drops, Solution
Betaxolol Eye Drops, Suspension

*Ph Eur*

**DEFINITION**
(2RS)-1-[4-[2-(Cyclopropylmethoxy)ethyl]phenoxy]-3-[(1-methylethyl)amino]propan-2-ol hydrochloride.

**Content**
98.5 per cent to 101.5 per cent (dried substance).

## CHARACTERS

### Appearance
White or almost white, crystalline powder.

### Solubility
Very soluble in water, freely soluble in ethanol (96 per cent), soluble in methylene chloride.

## IDENTIFICATION

*First identification*   B, D.

*Second identification*   A, C, D.

A. Melting point (*2.2.14*): 113 °C to 117 °C.

B. Infrared absorption spectrophotometry (*2.2.24*).

*Comparison*   betaxolol hydrochloride CRS.

C. Thin-layer chromatography (*2.2.27*).

*Test solution*   Dissolve 10 mg of the substance to be examined in 1 ml of *methanol R*.

*Reference solution (a)*   Dissolve 20 mg of *betaxolol hydrochloride CRS* in 2 ml of *methanol R*.

*Reference solution (b)*   Dissolve 10 mg of *oxprenolol hydrochloride CRS* in 1 ml of reference solution (a).

*Plate*   TLC octadecylsilyl silica gel $F_{254}$ plate R.

*Mobile phase*   perchloric acid R, methanol R, water R (0.5:50:50 *V/V/V*).

*Application*   2 µl.

*Development*   Over a path of 10 cm.

*Drying*   In air.

*System suitability*   Reference solution (b):
— the chromatogram shows 2 clearly separated spots.

*Detection A*   Examine in ultraviolet light at 254 nm.

*Results A*   The principal spot in the chromatogram obtained with the test solution is similar in position and size to the principal spot in the chromatogram obtained with reference solution (a).

*Detection B*   Spray with a 50 g/l solution of *vanillin R* in a mixture of 5 volumes of *sulphuric acid R*, 10 volumes of *glacial acetic acid R* and 85 volumes of *methanol R*. Heat at 100-105 °C until the colour of the spots reaches maximum intensity (10-15 min). Examine in daylight.

*Results B*   The principal spot in the chromatogram obtained with the test solution is similar in position, colour and size to the principal spot in the chromatogram obtained with reference solution (a).

D. It gives reaction (a) of chlorides (*2.3.1*).

## TESTS

### Appearance of solution
The solution is clear (*2.2.1*) and colourless (*2.2.2*, *Method II*).

Dissolve 0.5 g in *water R* and dilute to 25 ml with the same solvent.

### Acidity or alkalinity
Dissolve 0.20 g in *carbon dioxide-free water R* and dilute to 20 ml with the same solvent. Add 0.2 ml of *methyl red solution R* and 0.2 ml of *0.01 M hydrochloric acid*. The solution is red. Add 0.4 ml of *0.01 M sodium hydroxide*. The solution is yellow.

### Related substances
Liquid chromatography (*2.2.29*).

*Test solution*   Dissolve 10.0 mg of the substance to be examined in the mobile phase and dilute to 5.0 ml with the mobile phase.

*Reference solution (a)*   Dissolve 8 mg of the substance to be examined and 4 mg of *betaxolol impurity A CRS* in 20.0 ml of the mobile phase.

*Reference solution (b)*   Dilute 1.0 ml of the test solution to 100.0 ml with the mobile phase.

*Column:*
— *size: l* = 0.25 m, Ø = 4 mm;
— *stationary phase: octylsilyl silica gel for chromatography R (5 µm)*.

*Mobile phase*   Mix 175 ml of *acetonitrile R* with 175 ml of *methanol R* and dilute the mixture to 1 litre with a 3.4 g/l solution of *potassium dihydrogen phosphate R*, previously adjusted to pH 3.0 with *phosphoric acid R*.

*Flow rate*   1.5 ml/min.

*Detection*   Spectrophotometer at 273 nm.

*Injection*   20 µl.

*Run time*   4 times the retention time of betaxolol.

*System suitability*   Reference solution (a):
— *resolution*: minimum 2.0 between the peaks due to impurity A and betaxolol.

*Limits:*
— *impurities A, B, C, D, E*: for each impurity, not more than 0.3 times the area of the peak in the chromatogram obtained with reference solution (b) (0.3 per cent);
— *total*: not more than the area of the peak in the chromatogram obtained with reference solution (b) (1.0 per cent);
— *disregard limit*: 0.025 times the area of the peak in the chromatogram obtained with reference solution (b) (0.025 per cent).

### Heavy metals (*2.4.8*)
Maximum 10 ppm.

Dissolve 2.0 g in 20 ml of *water R*. 12 ml of the solution complies with test A. Prepare the reference solution using 10 ml of *lead standard solution (1 ppm Pb) R*.

### Loss on drying (*2.2.32*)
Maximum 0.5 per cent, determined on 1.000 g by drying in an oven at 105 °C.

### Sulphated ash (*2.4.14*)
Maximum 0.1 per cent, determined on 1.0 g.

## ASSAY
Dissolve 0.300 g in a mixture of 10.0 ml of *0.01 M hydrochloric acid* and 50 ml of *ethanol (96 per cent) R*. Carry out a potentiometric titration (*2.2.20*), using *0.1 M sodium hydroxide*. Read the volume added between the 2 points of inflexion.

1 ml of *0.1 M sodium hydroxide* is equivalent to 34.39 mg of $C_{18}H_{30}ClNO_3$.

## STORAGE
Protected from light.

## IMPURITIES
*Specified impurities*   A, B, C, D, E.

A. R = H: (2*RS*)-1-(4-ethylphenoxy)-3-[(1-methylethyl)amino]propan-2-ol,

B. R = OH: (2RS)-1-[4-(2-hydroxyethyl)phenoxy]-3-[(1-methylethyl)amino]propan-2-ol,

E. R = O-CH₂-CH₂-C_{H2}-CH₃:
(2RS)-1-[4-(2-butoxyethyl)phenoxy]-3-[(1-methylethyl)amino]propan-2-ol,

and enantiomer

C. 2-[[4-[2-(cyclopropylmethoxy)ethyl]phenoxy]methyl]oxirane,

D. 4-[2-(cyclopropylmethoxy)ethyl]phenol.

*Ph Eur*

# Bezafibrate

*(Ph Eur monograph 1394)*

$C_{19}H_{20}ClNO_4$      361.8      *41859-67-0*

**Action and use**

Fibrate; lipid-regulating drug.

**Preparations**

Bezafibrate Tablets

Prolonged-release Bezafibrate Tablets

*Ph Eur*

**DEFINITION**

2-[4-[2-[(4-Chlorobenzoyl)amino]ethyl]phenoxy]-2-methylpropanoic acid.

**Content**

98.0 per cent to 102.0 per cent (dried substance).

**CHARACTERS**

**Appearance**

White or almost white crystalline powder.

**Solubility**

Practically insoluble in water, freely soluble in dimethylformamide, sparingly soluble in acetone and in ethanol (96 per cent). It dissolves in dilute solutions of alkali hydroxides.

It shows polymorphism (*5.9*).

**IDENTIFICATION**

*First identification* A, B.

*Second identification* A, C.

A. Melting point (*2.2.14*): 181 °C to 185 °C.

B. Infrared absorption spectrophotometry (*2.2.24*).

*Preparation* Discs.

*Comparison* bezafibrate CRS.

If the spectra obtained show differences, dissolve the substance to be examined and the reference substance separately in *methanol R* and evaporate to dryness. Dry the residues in vacuo at 80 °C for 1 h and record new spectra using the residues.

C. Thin-layer chromatography (*2.2.27*).

*Test solution* Dissolve 10 mg of the substance to be examined in *methanol R* and dilute to 5 ml with the same solvent.

*Reference solution* Dissolve 10 mg of *bezafibrate CRS* in *methanol R* and dilute to 5 ml with the same solvent.

*Plate* TLC silica gel $F_{254}$ plate R.

*Mobile phase* glacial acetic acid R, methyl ethyl ketone R, xylene R (2.7:30:60 *V/V/V*).

*Application* 5 μl.

*Development* Over a path of 10 cm.

*Drying* At 120 °C for at least 15 min.

*Detection* Examine in ultraviolet light at 254 nm.

*Results* The principal spot in the chromatogram obtained with the test solution is similar in position and size to the principal spot in the chromatogram obtained with reference solution.

**TESTS**

**Solution S**

Dissolve 1.0 g in *dimethylformamide R* and dilute to 20 ml with the same solvent.

**Appearance of solution**

Solution S is clear (*2.2.1*) and not more intensely coloured than reference solution $BY_5$ (*2.2.2, Method II*).

**Related substances**

Liquid chromatography (*2.2.29*).

*Test solution* Dissolve 50.0 mg of the substance to be examined in the mobile phase and dilute to 100.0 ml with the mobile phase.

*Reference solution (a)* Dilute 10.0 ml of the test solution to 100.0 ml with the mobile phase. Dilute 5.0 ml of this solution to 100.0 ml with the mobile phase.

*Reference solution (b)* Dilute 5.0 ml of reference solution (a) to 50.0 ml with the mobile phase.

*Reference solution (c)* To 1 ml of the test solution, add 1 ml of *0.1 M hydrochloric acid* and evaporate to dryness on a hot plate. Dissolve the residue in 20 ml of the mobile phase.

*Column:*

— size: l = 0.125 m, Ø = 4 mm;

— stationary phase: octadecylsilyl silica gel for chromatography R (5 μm).

*Mobile phase* Mix 40 volumes of a 2.72 g/l solution of *potassium dihydrogen phosphate R* adjusted to pH 2.3 with *phosphoric acid R*, and 60 volumes of *methanol R*.

*Flow rate* 1 ml/min.

*Detection* Spectrophotometer at 228 nm.

*Injection* 20 μl.

*Run time* The time necessary to detect the ester, which, depending on the route of synthesis, may be impurity C, D or E.

*Retention time* Impurity A = about 3 min; impurity B = about 3.5 min; bezafibrate = about 6.0 min; impurity C = about 9 min; impurity D = about 14 min; impurity E = about 37 min.

*System suitability:*
— *resolution*: minimum 5.0 between the 2 principal peaks in the chromatogram obtained with reference solution (c);
— *signal-to-noise ratio*: minimum 5 for the principal peak in the chromatogram obtained with reference solution (b).

*Limits:*
— *impurities A, B, C, D, E*: for each impurity, not more than the area of the principal peak in the chromatogram obtained with reference solution (a) (0.5 per cent);
— *total*: not more than 1.5 times the area of the principal peak in the chromatogram obtained with reference solution (a) (0.75 per cent);
— *disregard limit*: 0.1 times the area of the principal peak in the chromatogram obtained with reference solution (a) (0.05 per cent).

**Chlorides** (2.4.4)
Maximum 300 ppm.

Dilute 10 ml of solution S to 50 ml with *water R*. Filter the resultant suspension through a wet filter previously washed with *water R* until free from chlorides. Prepare the standard using 9 ml of *chloride standard solution (5 ppm Cl) R* and 6 ml of *water R*.

**Heavy metals** (2.4.8)
Maximum 10 ppm.

2.0 g complies with test C. Prepare the reference solution using 2 ml of *lead standard solution (10 ppm Pb) R*.

**Loss on drying** (2.2.32)
Maximum 0.5 per cent, determined on 1.000 g by drying in an oven at 105 °C.

**Sulphated ash** (2.4.14)
Maximum 0.1 per cent, determined on 1.0 g.

**ASSAY**
Dissolve 0.300 g in 50 ml of a mixture of 25 volumes of *water R* and 75 volumes of *ethanol (96 per cent) R*. Using 0.1 ml of *phenolphthalein solution R* as indicator, titrate with *0.1 M sodium hydroxide* until a pink colour is obtained. Carry out a blank titration.

1 ml *of 0.1 M sodium hydroxide* is equivalent to 36.18 mg of $C_{19}H_{20}ClNO_4$.

**IMPURITIES**
*Specified impurities   A, B, C, D, E.*

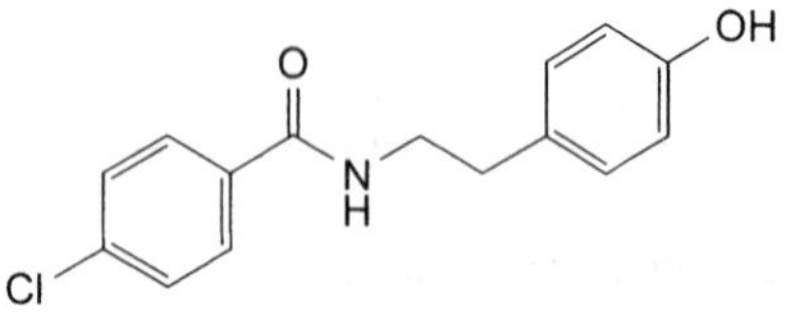

A. 4-chloro-*N*-[2-(4-hydroxyphenyl)ethyl]benzamide (chlorobenzoyltyramine),

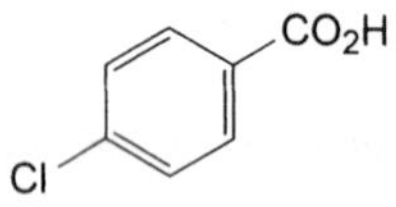

B. 4-chlorobenzoic acid,

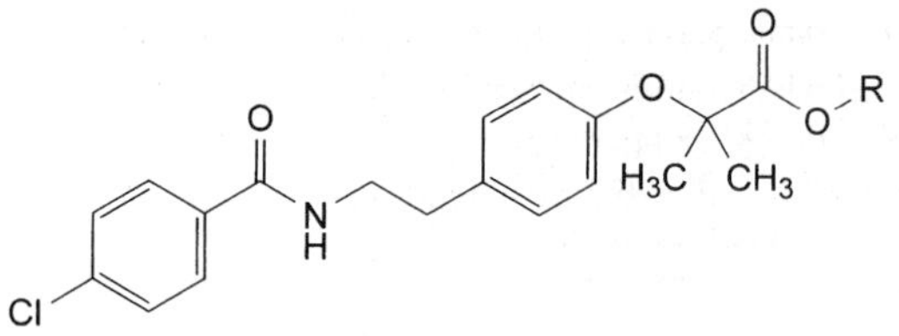

C. R = CH$_3$: methyl 2-[4-[2-[(4-chlorobenzoyl) amino]ethyl]phenoxy]-2 methylpropanoate,
D. R = CH$_2$-CH$_3$: ethyl 2-[4-[2-[(4-chlorobenzoyl) amino]ethyl]phenoxy]-2-methylpropanoate,
E. R = CH$_2$-CH$_2$-CH$_2$-CH$_3$: butyl 2-[4-[2-[(4-chlorobenzoyl) amino]ethyl]phenoxy]-2-methylpropanoate.

_____ *Ph Eur*

# Bifonazole

*(Ph Eur monograph 1395)*

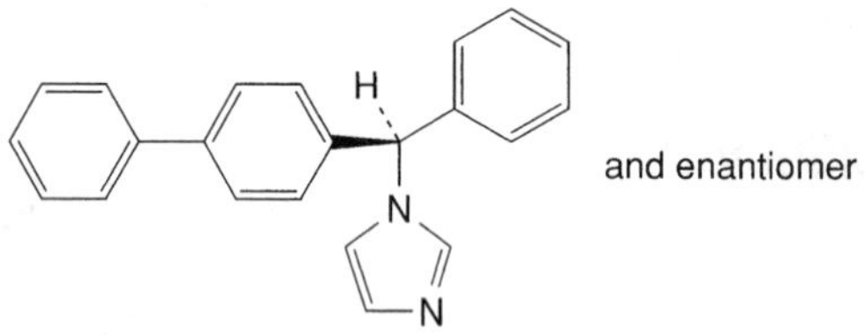

$C_{22}H_{18}N_2$        310.4        *60628-96-8*

**Action and use**
Antifungal.

*Ph Eur* _____

**DEFINITION**
1-[(*RS*)-(Biphenyl-4-yl)phenylmethyl]-1*H*-imidazole.

**Content**
98.0 per cent to 100.5 per cent (dried substance).

**CHARACTERS**
**Appearance**
White or almost white, crystalline powder.

**Solubility**
Practically insoluble in water, sparingly soluble in anhydrous ethanol.

It shows polymorphism (5.9).

**IDENTIFICATION**
Infrared absorption spectrophotometry (2.2.24).
*Comparison   bifonazole CRS.*

If the spectra obtained in the solid state show differences, dissolve the substance to be examined and the reference substance separately in the minimum volume of *2-propanol R*, evaporate to dryness and record new spectra using the residues.

**TESTS**
**Optical rotation** (2.2.7)
− 0.10° to + 0.10°.

Dissolve 0.20 g in 20.0 ml of *methanol R*.

**Related substances**
Liquid chromatography (2.2.29).

*Buffer solution pH 3.2*   Mix 2.0 ml of *phosphoric acid R* with *water R* and dilute to 1000.0 ml with the same solvent. Adjust to pH 3.2 (*2.2.3*) with *triethylamine R*.

*Test solution*   Dissolve 50.0 mg of the substance to be examined in 25 ml of *acetonitrile R* and dilute to 50.0 ml with buffer solution pH 3.2.

*Reference solution (a)*   Dilute 0.25 ml of the test solution to 50.0 ml with buffer solution pH 3.2.

*Reference solution (b)*   Dissolve 25.0 mg of *imidazole R* (impurity C) in *acetonitrile R* and dilute to 25.0 ml with the same solvent. Dilute 0.25 ml of this solution to 100.0 ml with buffer solution pH 3.2.

*Reference solution (c)*   Dissolve 5.0 mg of *bifonazole impurity B CRS* in *acetonitrile R* and dilute to 5.0 ml with the same solvent.

*Reference solution (d)*   Mix 0.25 ml of the test solution and 0.25 ml of reference solution (c) and dilute to 50.0 ml with buffer solution pH 3.2.

*Column:*
— *size: l* = 0.125 m, Ø = 4.6 mm;
— *stationary phase*: *octadecylsilyl silica gel for chromatography R* (5 μm);
— *temperature*: 40 °C.

*Mobile phase:*
— *mobile phase A*: *acetonitrile R1*, buffer solution pH 3.2 (20:80 *V/V*);
— *mobile phase B*: buffer solution pH 3.2, *acetonitrile R1* (20:80 *V/V*);

| Time (min) | Mobile phase A (per cent *V/V*) | Mobile phase B (per cent *V/V*) |
| --- | --- | --- |
| 0 - 8 | 60 | 40 |
| 8 - 12 | 60 → 10 | 40 → 90 |
| 12 - 30 | 10 | 90 |

*Flow rate*   1 ml/min.

*Detection*   Spectrophotometer at 210 nm.

*Injection*   50 μl of the test solution and reference solutions (a), (b) and (d).

*Retention time*   Impurity B = about 4 min; bifonazole = about 4.5 min.

*System suitability*   Reference solution (d):
— *resolution*: minimum 2.5 between the peaks due to impurity B and bifonazole.

*Limits:*
— *impurity B*: not more than 3 times the area of the principal peak in the chromatogram obtained with reference solution (a) (1.5 per cent);
— *impurity C*: not more than the area of the corresponding peak in the chromatogram obtained with reference solution (b) (0.25 per cent);
— *impurities A, D*: for each impurity, not more than the area of the principal peak in the chromatogram obtained with reference solution (a) (0.5 per cent);
— *total*: not more than 4 times the area of the principal peak in the chromatogram obtained with reference solution (a) (2 per cent);
— *disregard limit*: 0.1 times the area of the principal peak in the chromatogram obtained with reference solution (a) (0.05 per cent).

**Loss on drying** (*2.2.32*)
Maximum 0.5 per cent, determined on 1.000 g by drying in an oven at 105 °C.

**Sulphated ash** (*2.4.14*)
Maximum 0.1 per cent, determined on 1.0 g.

**ASSAY**
Dissolve 0.250 g in 80 ml of *anhydrous acetic acid R*. Titrate with *0.1 M perchloric acid*, determining the end-point potentiometrically (*2.2.20*).

1 ml of *0.1 M perchloric acid* is equivalent to 31.04 mg of $C_{22}H_{18}N_2$.

**IMPURITIES**
*Specified impurities   A, B, C, D.*

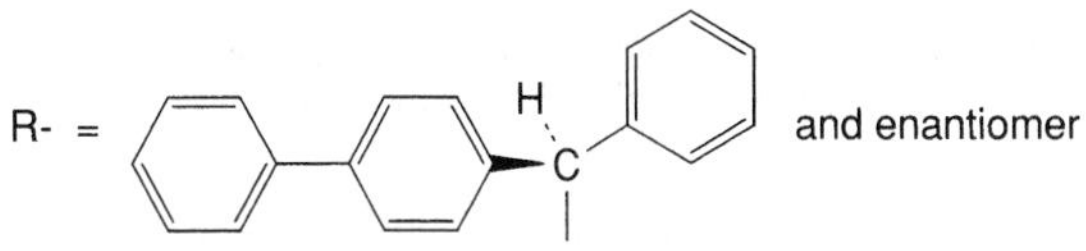

R- =   and enantiomer

A. R-OH: (*RS*)-(biphenyl-4-yl)phenylmethanol,

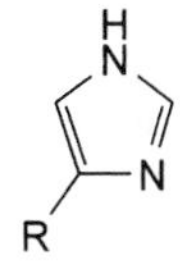

B. 4-[(*RS*)-(biphenyl-4-yl)phenylmethyl]-1*H*-imidazole,

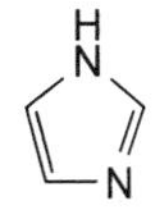

C. 1*H*-imidazole,

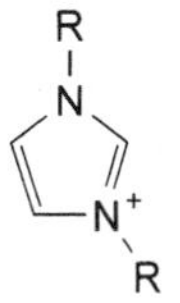

D. 1,3-bis[(biphenyl-4-yl)phenylmethyl]-1*H*-imidazolium ion.

*_____ Ph Eur*

# Biotin

(*Ph Eur monograph 1073*)

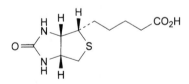

$C_{10}H_{16}N_2O_3S$          244.3          58-85-5

**Action and use**
Vitamin.

*Ph Eur* _____

**DEFINITION**
Biotin contains not less than 98.5 per cent and not more than the equivalent of 101.0 per cent of

5-[(3aS,4S,6aR)-2-oxohexahydrothieno[3,4-d]imidazol-4-yl]pentanoic acid, calculated with reference to the dried substance.

## CHARACTERS

A white or almost white crystalline powder or colourless crystals, very slightly soluble in water and in alcohol, practically insoluble in acetone. It dissolves in dilute solutions of alkali hydroxides.

## IDENTIFICATION

*First identification   A.*

*Second identification   B, C.*

A. Examine by infrared absorption spectrophotometry (2.2.24), comparing with the spectrum obtained with *biotin CRS.*

B. Examine the chromatograms obtained in the test for related substances (see Tests). The principal spot in the chromatogram obtained with test solution (b) is similar in position and size to the principal spot in the chromatogram obtained with reference solution (a).

C. Dissolve about 10 mg in 20 ml of *water R* with heating. Allow to cool. Add 0.1 ml of *bromine water R.* The bromine water is decolourised.

## TESTS

### Solution S

Dissolve 0.250 g in a 4 g/l solution of *sodium hydroxide R* and dilute to 25.0 ml with the same alkaline solution.

### Appearance of solution

Solution S is clear (2.2.1) and colourless (2.2.2, Method II).

### Specific optical rotation (2.2.7)

The specific optical rotation is + 89 to + 93, determined on solution S and calculated with reference to the dried substance.

### Related substances

Examine by thin-layer chromatography (2.2.27), using as the coating substance a suitable silica gel (5 µm). *Prepare the solutions immediately before use and keep protected from bright light.*

*Test solution (a)*   Dissolve 50 mg of the substance to be examined in *glacial acetic acid R* and dilute to 10 ml with the same solvent.

*Test solution (b)*   Dilute 1 ml of test solution (a) to 10 ml with *glacial acetic acid R.*

*Reference solution (a)*   Dissolve 5 mg of *biotin CRS* in *glacial acetic acid R* and dilute to 10 ml with the same solvent.

*Reference solution (b)*   Dilute 1 ml of test solution (b) to 20 ml with *glacial acetic acid R.*

*Reference solution (c)*   Dilute 1 ml of test solution (b) to 40 ml with *glacial acetic acid R.*

Apply to the plate 10 µl of each solution. Develop over a path of 15 cm using a mixture of 5 volumes of *methanol R,* 25 volumes of *glacial acetic acid R* and 75 volumes of *toluene R.* Dry the plate in a current of warm air. Allow to cool and spray with *4-dimethylaminocinnamaldehyde solution R.* Examine immediately in daylight. Any spot in the chromatogram obtained with test solution (a), apart from the principal spot, is not more intense than the spot in the chromatogram obtained with reference solution (b) (0.5 per cent) and at most one such spot is more intense than the spot in the chromatogram obtained with reference solution (c) (0.25 per cent).

## Heavy metals (2.4.8)

1.0 g complies with limit test C for heavy metals (10 ppm). Prepare the standard using 10 ml of *lead standard solution (1 ppm Pb) R.*

## Loss on drying (2.2.32)

Not more than 1.0 per cent, determined on 1.000 g by drying in an oven at 105 °C.

## Sulphated ash (2.4.14)

Not more than 0.1 per cent, determined on 1.0 g.

## ASSAY

Suspend 0.200 g in 5 ml of *dimethylformamide R.* Heat until the substance has dissolved completely. Add 50 ml of *ethanol R* and titrate with 0.1 M *tetrabutylammonium hydroxide,* determining the end-point potentiometrically (2.2.20).

1 ml of *0.1 M tetrabutylammonium hydroxide* is equivalent to 24.43 mg of $C_{10}H_{16}N_2O_3S$.

## STORAGE

Store protected from light.

## IMPURITIES

A. di[3-[(3aS,4S,6aR)-2-oxohexahydrothieno[3,4-d]imidazol-4-yl]propyl]acetic acid,

B. 4-[(3aS,4S,6aR)-2-oxohexahydrothieno[3,4-d]imidazol-4-yl]butane-1,1-dicarboxylic acid,

C. 5-(3,4-diamino-2-thienyl)pentanoic acid,

D. 2-methyl-5-[(3aS,4S,6aR)-2-oxohexahydrothieno[3,4-d]imidazol-4-yl]pentanoic acid,

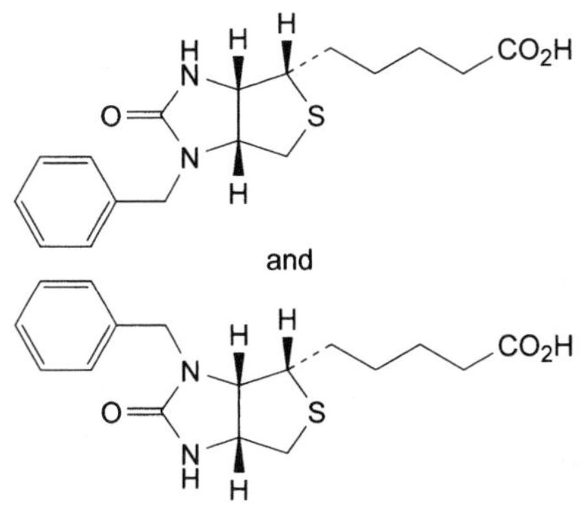

E. 5-[(3aS,4S,6aR)-3-benzyl-2-oxohexahydrothieno[3,4-
d]imidazol-4-yl]pentanoic acid and 5-[(3aS,4S,6aR)-1-benzyl-
2-oxohexahydrothieno[3,4-d]imidazol-4-yl]pentanoic acid.

———————————————————————————————— Ph Eur

# Biperiden Hydrochloride

(Ph Eur monograph 1074)

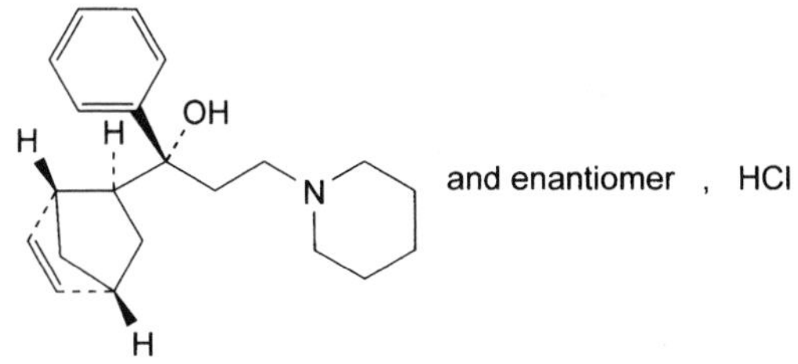

and enantiomer  ,  HCl

C$_{21}$H$_{29}$NO, HCl          347.9          1235-82-1

## Action and use
Anticholinergic.

Ph Eur ————————————————————————————————

## DEFINITION
(1RS)-1-[(1RS,2SR,4RS)-Bicyclo[2.2.1]hept-5-en-2-yl]-1-
phenyl-3-(piperidin-1-yl)propan-1-ol hydrochloride.

## Content
99.0 per cent to 101.0 per cent (dried substance).

## CHARACTERS
### Appearance
White or almost white, crystalline powder.

### Solubility
Slightly soluble in water and in alcohol, very slightly
soluble in methylene chloride.

### mp
About 280 °C, with decomposition.

## IDENTIFICATION
First identification    A, D.

Second identification    B, C, D.

A. Infrared absorption spectrophotometry (2.2.24).

Comparison    biperiden hydrochloride CRS.

B. Thin-layer chromatography (2.2.27).

Test solution    Dissolve 25 mg of the substance to be
examined in methanol R and dilute to 5 ml with the same
solvent.

Reference solution (a)    Dissolve 25 mg of biperiden
hydrochloride CRS in methanol R and dilute to 5 ml with the
same solvent.

Reference solution (b)    Dissolve 5 mg of biperiden
impurity A CRS in reference solution (a) and dilute to 2 ml
with the same solution.

Plate    TLC silica gel F$_{254}$ plate R.

Mobile phase    diethylamine R, methanol R, toluene R
(1:1:20 V/V/V).

Application    5 µl.

Development    Over a path of 15 cm.

Drying    In air.

Detection A    Examine in ultraviolet light at 254 nm.

Results A    The principal spot in the chromatogram obtained
with the test solution is similar in position and size to the
principal spot in the chromatogram obtained with reference
solution (a).

Detection B    Spray with dilute potassium iodobismuthate
solution R and then with sodium nitrite solution R and examine
in daylight.

Results B    The principal spot in the chromatogram obtained
with the test solution is similar in position, colour and size to
the principal spot in the chromatogram obtained with
reference solution (a).

System suitability    Reference solution (b):
— the chromatogram shows 2 clearly separated spots.

C. To about 20 mg add 5 ml of phosphoric acid R. A green
colour develops.

D. It gives reaction (a) of chlorides (2.3.1).

## TESTS
### Solution S
Dissolve 0.10 g in carbon dioxide-free water R, heating gently if
necessary, and dilute to 50 ml with the same solvent.

### Appearance of solution
Solution S is not more opalescent than reference suspension
II (2.2.1) and is colourless (2.2.2, Method II).

### pH (2.2.3)
5.0 to 6.5 for solution S.

### Related substances
Gas chromatography (2.2.28).

Test solution    Dissolve 0.10 g of the substance to be
examined in methanol R and dilute to 10 ml with the same
solvent.

Reference solution (a)    Dilute 0.5 ml of the test solution to
100 ml with methanol R. Dilute 10 ml of this solution to
50 ml with methanol R.

Reference solution (b)    Dissolve 5 mg of the substance to be
examined and 5 mg of biperiden impurity A CRS in
methanol R and dilute to 5 ml with the same solvent. Dilute
1 ml of the solution to 10 ml with methanol R.

Column:
— material: fused silica,
— size: l = 50 m, Ø = 0.25 mm,
— stationary phase: poly(dimethyl)(diphenyl)(divinyl)siloxane R
 (film thickness 0.25 µm).

Carrier gas    nitrogen for chromatography R.

Flow rate    0.4 ml/min.

Split ratio    1:250.

*Temperature:*

| | Time (min) | Temperature (°C) |
|---|---|---|
| Column | 0 - 5 | 200 |
| | 5 - 40 | 200 → 270 |
| Injection port | | 250 |
| Detector | | 300 |

*Detection*   Flame ionisation.

*Injection*   2 µl.

*Run time*   Twice the retention time of biperiden.

*Relative retention*   With reference to biperiden:
impurities A, B and C = between 0.95 and 1.05.

*System suitability:*
— *resolution*: minimum 2.5 between the peak due to
    biperiden (1st peak) and the peak due to impurity A (2nd
    peak) in the chromatogram obtained with reference
    solution (b),
— *signal-to-noise ratio*: minimum 6 for the principal peak in
    the chromatogram obtained with reference solution (a).

*Limits:*
— *impurities A, B, C*: for each impurity, maximum
    0.50 per cent of the area of the principal peak,
— *any other impurity*: for each impurity, maximum
    0.10 per cent of the area of the principal peak,
— *total of impurities A, B and C*: maximum 1.0 per cent of
    the area of the principal peak,
— *total of impurities other than A, B and C*: maximum
    0.50 per cent of the area of the principal peak,
— *disregard limit*: 0.05 per cent of the area of the principal
    peak.

**Impurity F** *(2.4.24)*
Maximum 2 ppm.

**Heavy metals** *(2.4.8)*
Maximum 20 ppm.

1.0 g complies with limit test D. Prepare the standard using
2 ml of *lead standard solution (10 ppm Pb) R*.

**Loss on drying** *(2.2.32)*
Maximum 0.5 per cent, determined on 1.000 g by drying in
an oven at 105 °C for 2 h.

**Sulphated ash** *(2.4.14)*
Maximum 0.1 per cent, determined on 1.0 g.

**ASSAY**
Dissolve 0.200 g in 60 ml of *alcohol R*. In a closed vessel,
titrate with *0.1 M alcoholic potassium hydroxide*, determining
the end-point potentiometrically *(2.2.20)*.

1 ml of *0.1 M alcoholic potassium hydroxide* is equivalent to
34.79 mg of $C_{21}H_{30}ClNO$.

**STORAGE**
In an airtight container, protected from light.

**IMPURITIES**
*Specified impurities*   A, B, C, F.
*Other detectable impurities: D, E.*

A. (1*RS*)-1-[(1*SR*,2*SR*,4*SR*)-bicyclo[2.2.1]hept-5-en-2-yl]-1-
phenyl-3-(piperidin-1-yl)propan-1-ol (*endo* form),

B. (1*RS*)-1-[(1*SR*,2*RS*,4*SR*)-bicyclo[2.2.1]hept-5-en-2-yl]-1-
phenyl-3-(piperidin-1-yl)propan-1-ol,

C. (1*RS*)-1-[(1*RS*,2*RS*,4*RS*)-bicyclo[2.2.1]hept-5-en-2-yl]-1-
phenyl-3-(piperidin-1-yl)propan-1-ol,

D. 1-[(1*RS*,2*SR*,4*RS*)-bicyclo[2.2.1]hept-5-en-2-yl]-3-
(piperidin-1-yl)propan-1-one,

E. 1-[(1*RS*,2*RS*,4*RS*)-bicyclo[2.2.1]hept-5-en-2-yl]-3-
(piperidin-1-yl)propan-1-one,

F. benzene.

# Bisacodyl

(Ph Eur monograph 0595)

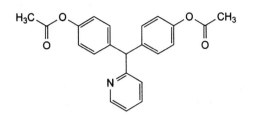

C$_{22}$H$_{19}$NO$_4$        361.4        603-50-9

## Action and use
Stimulant laxative.

## Preparations
Bisacodyl Suppositories

Bisacodyl Tablets

Ph Eur

## DEFINITION
4,4'-(Pyridin-2-ylmethylene)diphenyl diacetate.

## Content
98.0 per cent to 101.0 per cent (dried substance).

## CHARACTERS
### Appearance
White or almost white, crystalline powder.

### Solubility
Practically insoluble in water, soluble in acetone, sparingly soluble in ethanol (96 per cent). It dissolves in dilute mineral acids.

## IDENTIFICATION
*First identification*   C.

*Second identification*   A, B, D.

A. Melting point (2.2.14): 131 °C to 135 °C.

B. Ultraviolet and visible absorption spectrophotometry (2.2.25).

*Test solution*   Dissolve 10.0 mg in a 6 g/l solution of *potassium hydroxide R* in *methanol R* and dilute to 100.0 ml with the same solution. Dilute 10.0 ml of this solution to 100.0 ml with a 6 g/l solution of *potassium hydroxide R* in *methanol R*.

*Spectral range*   220-350 nm.

*Absorption maximum*   At 248 nm.

*Shoulder*   At 290 nm.

*Specific absorbance at the absorption maximum*   632 to 672.

C. Infrared absorption spectrophotometry (2.2.24).

*Comparison*   bisacodyl CRS.

If the spectra obtained in the solid state show differences, dissolve the substance to be examined and the reference substance separately in *chloroform R*, evaporate to dryness and record new spectra using the residues.

D. Thin-layer chromatography (2.2.27).

*Test solution*   Dissolve 20 mg of the substance to be examined in *acetone R* and dilute to 10 ml with the same solvent.

*Reference solution*   Dissolve 20 mg of *bisacodyl CRS* in *acetone R* and dilute to 10 ml with the same solvent.

*Plate*   TLC silica gel GF$_{254}$ plate R.

*Mobile phase*   methyl ethyl ketone R, xylene R (50:50 V/V).

*Application*   10 µl.

*Development*   Over a path of 10 cm.

*Drying*   In air, if necessary heating at 100-105 °C.

*Detection*   Spray with a mixture of equal volumes of *0.05 M iodine* and *dilute sulphuric acid R*.

*Results*   The principal spot in the chromatogram obtained with the test solution is similar in position and size to the principal spot in the chromatogram obtained with the reference solution.

## TESTS
### Acidity or alkalinity
To 1.0 g add 20 ml of *carbon dioxide-free water R*, shake, heat to boiling, cool and filter. Add 0.2 ml of 0.01 M *sodium hydroxide* and 0.1 ml of *methyl red solution R*. The solution is yellow. Not more than 0.4 ml of *0.01 M hydrochloric acid* is required to change the colour of the indicator to red.

### Related substances
Liquid chromatography (2.2.29).

*Prepare the solutions immediately before use.*

*Solvent mixture*   glacial acetic acid R, acetonitrile R, water R (4:30:66 V/V/V).

*Test solution*   Dissolve 50 mg of the substance to be examined in 25 ml of *acetonitrile R* and dilute to 50.0 ml with the solvent mixture.

*Reference solution (a)*   Dilute 1.0 ml of the test solution to 100.0 ml with the solvent mixture. Dilute 1.0 ml of this solution to 10.0 ml with the solvent mixture.

*Reference solution (b)*   Dissolve 2.0 mg of *bisacodyl for system suitability CRS* (containing impurities A, B, C, D and E) in 1.0 ml of *acetonitrile R* and dilute to 2.0 ml with the solvent mixture.

*Reference solution (c)*   Dissolve 5.0 mg of *bisacodyl for peak identification CRS* (containing impurity F) in 2.5 ml of *acetonitrile R* and dilute to 5.0 ml with the solvent mixture.

*Column:*
— *size: l* = 0.25 m, Ø = 4.6 mm;
— *stationary phase: end-capped octadecylsilyl silica gel for chromatography R* (5 µm).

*Mobile phase*   Mix 45 volumes of *acetonitrile R* and 55 volumes of a 1.58 g/l solution of *ammonium formate R* previously adjusted to pH 5.0 with *anhydrous formic acid R*.

*Flow rate*   1.5 ml/min.

*Detection*   Spectrophotometer at 265 nm.

*Injection*   20 µl.

*Run time*   3.5 times the retention time of bisacodyl.

*Identification of impurities*   Use the chromatogram supplied with *bisacodyl for system suitability CRS* and the chromatogram obtained with reference solution (b) to identify the peaks due to impurities A, B, C, D and E.

*Relative retention*   With reference to bisacodyl (retention time = about 13 min): impurity A = about 0.2; impurity B = about 0.4; impurity C = about 0.45; impurity D = about 0.8; impurity E = about 0.9; impurity F = about 2.6.

*System suitability*   Reference solution (b):
— *peak-to-valley ratio*: minimum 1.5, where $H_p$ = height above the baseline of the peak due to impurity E and $H_v$ = height above the baseline of the lowest point of the curve separating this peak from the peak due to bisacodyl.

*Limits:*
— *correction factor*: for the calculation of content, multiply the peak area of impurity A by 0.7;

— *impurities A, B*: for each impurity, not more than the area of the principal peak in the chromatogram obtained with reference solution (a) (0.1 per cent);

— *impurities C, E*: for each impurity, not more than 5 times the area of the principal peak in the chromatogram obtained with reference solution (a) (0.5 per cent);

— *impurity D*: not more than twice the area of the principal peak in the chromatogram obtained with reference solution (a) (0.2 per cent);

— *impurity F*: not more than 3 times the area of the principal peak in the chromatogram obtained with reference solution (a) (0.3 per cent);

— *unspecified impurities*: for each impurity, not more than the area of the principal peak in the chromatogram obtained with reference solution (a) (0.10 per cent);

— *total*: not more than 10 times the area of the principal peak in the chromatogram obtained with reference solution (a) (1.0 per cent);

— *disregard limit*: 0.5 times the area of the principal peak in the chromatogram obtained with reference solution (a) (0.05 per cent).

**Loss on drying** (2.2.32)
Maximum 0.5 per cent, determined on 0.500 g by drying in an oven at 105 °C.

**Sulphated ash** (2.4.14)
Maximum 0.1 per cent, determined on 1.0 g.

**ASSAY**
Dissolve 0.300 g in 60 ml of *anhydrous acetic acid R*. Titrate with *0.1 M perchloric acid* determining the end-point potentiometrically (2.2.20).

1 ml of *0.1 M perchloric acid* is equivalent to 36.14 mg of $C_{22}H_{19}NO_4$.

**STORAGE**
Protected from light.

**IMPURITIES**
*Specified impurities   A, B, C, D, E, F.*

A. R1 = R3 = OH, R2 = H: 4,4′-(pyridin-2-ylmethylene)diphenol,

B. R1 = H, R2 = R3 = OH: 2-[(RS)-(4-hydroxyphenyl)(pyridin-2-yl)methyl]phenol,

C. R1 = OH, R2 = H, R3 = O-CO-CH₃: 4-[(RS)-(4-hydroxyphenyl)(pyridin-2-yl)methyl]phenyl acetate,

E. R1 = H, R2 = R3 = O-CO-CH₃: 2-[(RS)-[4-(acetyloxy)phenyl](pyridin-2-yl)methyl]phenyl acetate,

D. unknown structure,

F. unknown structure.

——————————————————————— *Ph Eur*

# Bismuth Subcarbonate

Bismuth Carbonate

*(Ph Eur monograph 0012)*

*Ph Eur* _____

**DEFINITION**
**Content**
80.0 per cent to 82.5 per cent of Bi ($A_r$ 209.0) (dried substance).

**CHARACTERS**
**Appearance**
White or almost white powder.

**Solubility**
Practically insoluble in water and in ethanol (96 per cent). It dissolves with effervescence in mineral acids.

**IDENTIFICATION**
A. It gives the reaction of carbonates (2.3.1).
B. It gives the reactions of bismuth (2.3.1).

**TESTS**
**Solution S**
Shake 5.0 g with 10 ml of *water R* and add 20 ml of *nitric acid R*. Heat to dissolve, cool and dilute to 100 ml with *water R*.

**Appearance of solution**
Solution S is not more opalescent than reference suspension II (2.2.1) and is colourless (2.2.2, *Method II*).

**Chlorides** (2.4.4)
Maximum 500 ppm. To 6.6 ml of solution S add 4 ml of *nitric acid R* and dilute to 50 ml with *water R*.

**Nitrates**
Maximum 0.4 per cent.

To 0.25 g in a 125 ml conical flask, add 20 ml of *water R*, 0.05 ml of *indigo carmine solution R1* and then, as a single addition but with caution, 30 ml of *sulphuric acid R*. Titrate immediately with *indigo carmine solution R1* until a stable blue colour is obtained. Not more than *n* ml of the titrant is required, *n* being the volume corresponding to 1 mg of $NO_3$.

**Alkali and alkaline-earth metals**
Maximum 1.0 per cent.

To 1.0 g add 10 ml of *water R* and 10 ml of *acetic acid R*. Boil for 2 min, cool and filter. Wash the residue with 20 ml of *water R*. To the combined filtrate and washings add 2 ml of *dilute hydrochloric acid R* and 20 ml of *water R*. Boil and pass *hydrogen sulphide R* through the boiling solution until no further precipitate is formed. Filter, wash the residue with *water R*, evaporate the combined filtrate and washings to dryness on a water-bath and add 0.5 ml of *sulphuric acid R*. Ignite gently and allow to cool. The residue weighs a maximum of 10 mg.

**Arsenic** (2.4.2, *Method A*)
Maximum 5 ppm.

To 0.5 g in a distillation flask add 5 ml of *water R* and 7 ml of *sulphuric acid R*, allow to cool and add 5 g of *reducing mixture R* and 10 ml of *hydrochloric acid R*. Heat the contents of the flask to boiling gradually over 15-30 min and continue heating at such a rate that the distillation proceeds steadily until the volume in the flask is reduced by half or until 5 min after the air-condenser has become full of steam. It is important that distillation be discontinued before fumes of sulphur trioxide appear. Collect the distillate in a tube containing 15 ml of *water R* cooled in ice-water. Wash down the condenser with *water R* and dilute the distillate to 25 ml with the same solvent. Prepare the standard using a mixture of 2.5 ml of *arsenic standard solution (1 ppm As) R* and 22.5 ml of *water* R.

**Copper**

Maximum 50 ppm.

To 5 ml of solution S, add 2 ml of *ammonia R* and dilute to 50 ml with *water R*. Filter. To 10 ml of the filtrate add 1 ml of a 1 g/l solution of *sodium diethyldithiocarbamate R*. The solution is not more intensely coloured than a standard prepared at the same time in the same manner using a mixture of 0.25 ml of *copper standard solution (10 ppm Cu) R* and 9.75 ml of *water R* instead of 10 ml of the filtrate.

**Lead**

Maximum 20.0 ppm.

Atomic absorption spectrometry (*2.2.23, Method II*).

*Test solution* Dissolve 12.5 g in 75 ml of a mixture of equal volumes of *lead-free nitric acid R* and *water R*. Boil for 1 min, cool and dilute to 100.0 ml with *water R*.

*Reference solutions* Prepare the reference solutions using appropriate quantities of lead standard solution and a 37 per cent *V/V* solution of *lead-free nitric acid R*.

*Source* Lead hollow-cathode lamp.

*Wavelength* 283.3 nm (depending on the apparatus, the line at 217.0 nm may be used).

*Atomisation device* Air-acetylene flame.

**Silver**

Maximum 25 ppm.

To 2.0 g add 1 ml of *water R* and 4 ml of *nitric acid R*. Heat gently until dissolved and dilute to 11 ml with *water R*. Cool and add 2 ml of *1 M hydrochloric acid*. Allow to stand protected from light for 5 min. Any opalescence in the solution is not more intense than that in a standard prepared at the same time in the same manner using a mixture of 10 ml of *silver standard solution (5 ppm Ag) R*, 1 ml of *nitric acid R* and 2 ml of *1 M hydrochloric acid*.

**Loss on drying** (*2.2.32*)

Maximum 1.0 per cent, determined on 1.000 g by drying in an oven at 105 °C.

**ASSAY**

Dissolve 0.500 g in 3 ml of *nitric acid R* and dilute to 250 ml with *water R*. Carry out the complexometric titration of bismuth (*2.5.11*).

1 ml of *0.1 M sodium edetate* is equivalent to 20.90 mg of Bi.

**STORAGE**

Protected from light.

_____ *Ph Eur*

# Bismuth Subgallate

*(Ph Eur monograph 1493)*

| | | |
|---|---|---|
| C₇H₅BiO₆ | 394.1 | 99-26-3 |

C$_7$H$_5$BiO$_6$        394.1        99-26-3

*Ph Eur* _____

**DEFINITION**

Complex of bismuth and gallic acid.

**Content**

48.0 per cent to 51.0 per cent of Bi ($A_r$ 209.0) (dried substance).

**CHARACTERS**

**Appearance**

Yellow powder.

**Solubility**

Practically insoluble in water and in ethanol (96 per cent). It dissolves in mineral acids with decomposition and in solutions of alkali hydroxides, producing a reddish-brown liquid.

**IDENTIFICATION**

A. Mix 0.1 g with 5 ml of *water R* and 0.1 ml of *phosphoric acid R*. Heat to boiling and maintain boiling for 2 min. Cool and filter. To the filtrate, add 1.5 ml of *ferric chloride solution R1*; a blackish-blue colour develops.

B. It gives reaction (b) of bismuth (*2.3.1*).

**TESTS**

**Solution S**

In a porcelain or quartz dish, ignite 1.0 g, increasing the temperature very gradually. Heat in a muffle furnace at 600 ± 50 °C for 2 h. Cool and dissolve the residue with warming in 4 ml of a mixture of equal volumes of *lead-free nitric acid R* and *water R* and dilute to 20 ml with *water R*.

**Acidity**

Shake 1.0 g with 20 ml of *water R* for 1 min and filter. To the filtrate add 0.1 ml of *methyl red solution R*. Not more than 0.15 ml of *0.1 M sodium hydroxide* is required to change the colour of the indicator to yellow.

**Chlorides** (*2.4.4*)

Maximum 200 ppm.

To 0.5 g add 10 ml of *dilute nitric acid R*. Heat on a water-bath for 5 min and filter. Dilute 5 ml of the filtrate to 15 ml with *water R*.

**Nitrates**

Maximum 0.2 per cent.

To 1.0 g add 25 ml of *water R* then 25 ml of a mixture of 2 volumes of *sulphuric acid R* and 9 volumes of *water R*. Heat at about 50 °C for 1 min with stirring and filter. To 10 ml of the filtrate, carefully add 30 ml of *sulphuric acid R*. The solution is not more intensely brownish-yellow than a reference solution prepared at the same time as follows: to 0.4 g of *gallic acid R*, add 20 ml of *nitrate standard solution (100 ppm NO₃) R* and 30 ml of a mixture of 2 volumes of *sulphuric acid R* and 9 volumes of *water R*, then filter; to 10 ml of the filtrate, carefully add 30 ml of *sulphuric acid R*.

**Copper**

Maximum 50.0 ppm.

Atomic absorption spectrometry (*2.2.23, Method I*).

*Test solution*   Solution S.

*Reference solutions*   Prepare the reference solutions using *copper standard solution (10 ppm Cu) R* and diluting with a 6.5 per cent *V/V* solution of *lead-free nitric acid R*.

*Source*   Copper hollow-cathode lamp.

*Wavelength*   324.7 nm.

*Atomisation device*   Air-acetylene flame.

**Lead**

Maximum 20.0 ppm.

Atomic absorption spectrometry (*2.2.23, Method II*).

*Test solution*   Solution S.

*Reference solutions*   Prepare the reference solutions using *lead standard solution (10 ppm Pb) R* and diluting with a 6.5 per cent *V/V* solution of *lead-free nitric acid R*.

*Source*   Lead hollow-cathode lamp.

*Wavelength*   283.3 nm (depending on the apparatus, the line at 217.0 nm may be used).

*Atomisation device*   Air-acetylene flame.

**Silver**

Maximum 25.0 ppm.

Atomic absorption spectrometry (*2.2.23, Method I*).

*Test solution*   Solution S.

*Reference solutions*   Prepare the reference solutions using *silver standard solution (5 ppm Ag) R* and diluting with a 6.5 per cent *V/V* solution of *lead-free nitric acid R*.

*Source*   Silver hollow-cathode lamp.

*Wavelength*   328.1 nm.

*Atomisation device*   Air-acetylene flame.

**Substances not precipitated by ammonia**

Maximum 1.0 per cent.

In a porcelain or quartz dish, ignite 2.0 g, increasing the temperature very gradually to 600 $\pm$ 50 °C; allow to cool. Moisten the residue with 2 ml of *nitric acid R*, evaporate to dryness on a water-bath and carefully heat and ignite once more at 600 $\pm$ 50 °C. After cooling, dissolve the residue in 5 ml of *nitric acid R* and dilute to 20 ml with *water R*. To 10 ml of this solution, add *concentrated ammonia R* until alkaline and filter. Wash the residue with *water R* and evaporate the combined filtrate and washings to dryness on a water-bath. Add 0.3 ml of *dilute sulphuric acid R* and ignite. The residue weighs a maximum of 10 mg.

**Loss on drying** (*2.2.32*)

Maximum 7.0 per cent, determined on 1.000 g by drying in an oven at 105 °C for 3 h.

**ASSAY**

To 0.300 g add 10 ml of a mixture of equal volumes of *nitric acid R* and *water R*, heat to boiling and maintain boiling for 2 min. Add 0.1 g of *potassium chlorate R*, heat to boiling and maintain boiling for 1 min. Add 10 ml of *water R* and heat until the solution becomes colourless. To the hot solution, add 200 ml of *water R* and 50 mg of *xylenol orange triturate R*. Titrate with *0.1 M sodium edetate* until a yellow colour is obtained.

1 ml of *0.1 M sodium edetate* is equivalent to 20.90 mg of Bi.

**STORAGE**

Protected from light.

# Heavy Bismuth Subnitrate

(*Ph Eur monograph 1494*)

4[BiNO$_3$(OH)$_2$],BiO(OH)     1462          1304-85-4

*Ph Eur*
——————————————————————————————

**DEFINITION**

**Content**

71.0 per cent to 74.0 per cent of Bi (*A$_r$* 209.0) (dried substance).

**CHARACTERS**

**Appearance**

White or almost white powder.

**Solubility**

Practically insoluble in water and in ethanol (96 per cent). It dissolves in mineral acids with decomposition.

**IDENTIFICATION**

A. Dilute 1 ml of solution S1 (see Tests) to 5 ml with *water R* and add 0.3 ml of *potassium iodide solution R*. A black precipitate is formed which dissolves into an orange solution with the addition of 2 ml *of potassium iodide solution R*.

B. It gives reaction (b) of bismuth (*2.3.1*).

C. It gives the reaction of nitrates (*2.3.1*).

D. pH (*2.2.3*): maximum 2.0 for solution S2 (see Tests).

**TESTS**

**Solution S1**

Shake 5.0 g by gently heating in 10 ml of *water R* and add 20 ml of *nitric acid R*. Heat until dissolution, cool and dilute to 100 ml with *water R*.

**Solution S2**

Place 1.00 g in a 20 ml volumetric flask and add 2.0 ml of *lead-free nitric acid R*. Allow acid attack to take place without heating and if necessary warm slightly at the end to completely dissolve the test sample. Add 10 ml of *water R*, shake and add, in small fractions, 4.5 ml of *lead-free ammonia R*; shake and allow to cool. Dilute to 20.0 ml with *water R*, shake again and allow the solids to settle. The clear supernatant solution is solution S2.

**Acidity**

Suspend 1.0 g in 15 ml of *water R* and shake several times. Allow to stand for 5 min and filter. To 10 ml of the filtrate, add 0.5 ml of *phenolphthalein solution R1*. Not more than 0.5 ml of *0.1 M sodium hydroxide* is required to change the colour of the indicator to pink.

**Chlorides** (*2.4.4*)

Maximum 200 ppm.

To 5.0 ml of solution S1, add 3 ml of *nitric acid R* and dilute to 15 ml with *water R*.

**Copper**

Maximum 50.0 ppm.

Atomic absorption spectrometry (*2.2.23, Method I*).

*Test solution*   Solution S2.

*Reference solutions*   Prepare the reference solutions using *copper standard solution (10 ppm Cu) R* and diluting with a 37 per cent *V/V* solution of *lead-free nitric acid R*.

*Source*   Copper hollow-cathode lamp.

*Wavelength*   324.7 nm.

*Atomisation device*   Air-acetylene flame.

**Lead**

Maximum 20.0 ppm.

Atomic absorption spectrometry (*2.2.23, Method II*).

*Test solution* Solution S2.

*Reference solutions* Prepare the reference solutions using *lead standard solution (10 ppm Pb) R* and diluting with a 37 per cent *V/V* solution of *lead-free nitric acid R*.

*Source* Lead hollow-cathode lamp.

*Wavelength* 283.3 nm (depending on the apparatus, the line at 217.0 nm may be used).

*Atomisation device* Air-acetylene flame.

**Silver**

Maximum 25.0 ppm.

Atomic absorption spectrometry (*2.2.23, Method I*).

*Test solution* Solution S2.

*Reference solutions* Prepare the reference solutions using *silver standard solution (5 ppm Ag) R* and diluting with a 37 per cent *V/V* solution *of lead-free nitric acid R*.

*Source* Silver hollow-cathode lamp.

*Wavelength* 328.1 nm.

*Atomisation device* Air-acetylene flame.

**Substances not precipitated by ammonia**

Maximum 1.0 per cent.

To 20 ml of solution S1, add *concentrated ammonia R* until an alkaline reaction is produced and filter. Wash the residue with *water R*, and evaporate the combined filtrate and washings to dryness on a water-bath. To the residue, add 0.3 ml of *dilute sulphuric acid R* and ignite. The residue weighs a maximum of 10 mg.

**Loss on drying** (*2.2.32*)

Maximum 3.0 per cent, determined on 1.000 g by drying in an oven at 105 °C.

**ASSAY**

Dissolve with heating 0.250 g in 10 ml of a mixture of 2 volumes of *perchloric acid R* and 5 volumes of *water R*. To the hot solution, add 200 ml of *water R* and 50 mg of *xylenol orange triturate R*. Titrate with *0.1 M sodium edetate* until a yellow colour is obtained.

1 ml of *0.1 M sodium edetate* is equivalent to 20.90 mg of Bi.

*Ph Eur*

# Bismuth Subsalicylate

★ ★ ★
★　　★
★　　★
★ ★ ★

(*Ph Eur monograph 1495*)

$C_7H_5BiO_4$        362.1        *14882-18-9*

*Ph Eur*

**DEFINITION**

Complex of bismuth and salicylic acid.

**Content**

56.0 per cent to 59.4 per cent of Bi ($A_r$ 209.0) (dried substance).

**CHARACTERS**

**Appearance**

White or almost white powder.

**Solubility**

Practically insoluble in water and in alcohol. It dissolves in mineral acids with decomposition.

**IDENTIFICATION**

A. To 0.5 g add 10 ml *of hydrochloric acid R1*. Heat on a boiling water-bath for 5 min. Cool and filter. Retain the filtrate for identification test B. Wash the residue with *dilute hydrochloric acid R* and then with *water R*. Dissolve the residue in 0.5-1 ml of *dilute sodium hydroxide solution R*. Add 15 ml of *water R*. Neutralise with *dilute hydrochloric acid R*. The solution gives reaction (a) of salicylates (*2.3.1*).

B. The filtrate obtained in identification test A gives reaction (b) of bismuth (*2.3.1*).

**TESTS**

**Solution S**

In a porcelain or quartz dish, ignite 1.0 g, increasing the temperature very gradually. Heat in a muffle furnace at 600 ± 25 °C for 2 h. Cool and dissolve the residue with warming in 4 ml of a mixture of equal volumes of *lead-free nitric acid R* and *water R* and dilute to 20 ml with *water R*.

**Acidity**

Shake 2.0 g with 30 ml of *ether R* for 1 min and filter. To the filtrate add 30 ml of *alcohol R* and 0.1 ml of *thymol blue solution R*. Not more than 0.35 ml of *0.1 M sodium hydroxide* is required to change the colour of the indicator to blue.

**Chlorides** (*2.4.4*)

Maximum 200 ppm.

Dissolve 0.250 g in a mixture of 2 ml of *nitric acid R*, 5 ml of *water R* and 8 ml of *methanol R*.

**Nitrates**

Maximum 0.4 per cent.

To 0.1 g add 10 ml of *water R* and, with caution, 20 ml of *sulphuric acid R* and stir. The solution is not more intensely yellow coloured than a reference solution prepared at the same time using 0.1 g of *salicylic acid R*, 6 ml of *water R*, 4 ml of *nitrate standard solution* (100 ppm $NO_3$) R and 20 ml of *sulphuric acid R*.

**Copper**

Maximum 50.0 ppm.

Atomic absorption spectrometry (*2.2.23, Method I*).

*Test solution* Solution S.

*Reference solutions* Prepare the reference solutions using *copper standard solution (10 ppm Cu) R* and diluting with a 6.5 per cent *V/V* solution of *lead-free nitric acid R*.

*Source* Copper hollow-cathode lamp.

*Wavelength* 324.7 nm.

*Atomisation device* Air-acetylene flame.

**Lead**

Maximum 20.0 ppm.

Atomic absorption spectrometry (*2.2.23, Method II*).

*Test solution* Solution S.

*Reference solutions* Prepare the reference solutions using *lead standard solution (10 ppm Pb) R* and diluting with a 6.5 per cent *V/V* solution of *lead-free nitric acid R*.

*Source* Lead hollow-cathode lamp.

*Wavelength* 283.3 nm (depending on the apparatus, the line at 217.0 nm may be used).

*Atomisation device* Air-acetylene flame.

**Silver**

Maximum 25.0 ppm.

Atomic absorption spectrometry (*2.2.23, Method I*).

*Test solution* Solution S.

*Reference solutions* Prepare the reference solutions using *silver standard solution (5 ppm Ag) R* and diluting with a 6.5 per cent *V/V* solution of *lead-free nitric acid R*.

*Source* Silver hollow-cathode lamp.

*Wavelength* 328.1 nm.

*Atomisation device*   Air-acetylene flame.

**Soluble bismuth**
Maximum 40.0 ppm.

Atomic absorption spectrometry (*2.2.23, Method I*).

*Test solution*   Suspend 5.0 g in 100 ml of *water R*. Stir constantly for 2 h at 20-23 °C. Filter through filter paper (slow filtration) then through a cellulose micropore membrane filter (0.1 µm). To 10.0 ml of clear filtrate, add 0.1 ml of *nitric acid R*.

*Reference solutions*   Prepare the reference solutions using *bismuth standard solution (100 ppm Bi) R* and diluting with a mixture of equal volumes of *dilute nitric acid R* and *water R*.

*Source*   Bismuth hollow-cathode lamp.

*Wavelength*   223.06 nm.

*Atomisation device*   Air-acetylene flame.

**Loss on drying** (*2.2.32*)
Maximum 1.0 per cent, determined on 1.000 g by drying in an oven at 105 °C.

**ASSAY**
Dissolve with heating 0.300 g in 10 ml of a mixture of 2 volumes of *perchloric acid R* and 5 volumes of *water R*. To the hot solution, add 200 ml of water R and 50 mg of *xylenol orange triturate R*. Titrate with *0.1 M sodium edetate* until a yellow colour is obtained.

1 ml of *0.1 M sodium edetate* is equivalent to 20.90 mg of Bi.

**STORAGE**
Protected from light.

*Ph Eur*

# Bisoprolol Fumarate

*(Ph Eur monograph 1710)*

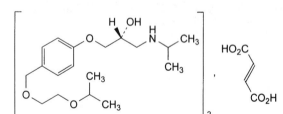

and enantiomer

$C_{40}H_{66}N_2O_{12}$          767          *104344-23-2*

**Action and use**
Beta-adrenoceptor antagonist.

*Ph Eur*

**DEFINITION**
(*RS*)-1-[4-[[2-(1-Methylethoxy)ethoxy]methyl]phenoxy]-3-[(1-methylethyl)amino]propan-2-ol fumarate.

**Content**
99.0 per cent to 101.0 per cent (anhydrous substance).

**CHARACTERS**

**Appearance**
White or almost white, slightly hygroscopic powder.

**Solubility**
Very soluble in water, freely soluble in methanol.

It shows polymorphism (*5.9*).

**IDENTIFICATION**
Infrared absorption spectrophotometry (*2.2.24*).

*Comparison*   bisoprolol fumarate CRS.

If the spectra obtained in the solid state show differences, dissolve the substance to be examined and the reference substance separately in *methanol R*, evaporate and dry the residue at 60 °C at a pressure not exceeding 0.7 kPa and record new spectra using the residues.

**TESTS**
**Related substances**
A. Impurities A and E. Liquid chromatography (*2.2.29*).

*Test solution*   Dissolve 25 mg of the substance to be examined in mobile phase A and dilute to 25.0 ml with mobile phase A.

*Reference solution (a)*   Dilute 1.0 ml of the test solution to 100.0 ml with mobile phase A. Dilute 1.0 ml of this solution to 10.0 ml with mobile phase A.

*Reference solution (b)*   Dissolve the contents of a vial of *bisoprolol for system suitability method A CRS* (containing impurities A, B and E) in 1.0 ml of mobile phase A.

*Column:*
— *size: l* = 0.25 m, Ø = 4.6 mm;
— *stationary phase: octadecylsilyl silica gel for chromatography R* (5 µm);
— *temperature*: 30 °C.

*Mobile phase:*
— *mobile phase A*: mix 10 volumes of *acetonitrile R1* and 90 volumes of a solution containing 0.4 ml/l of *triethylamine R1* and 3.12 g/l of *sodium dihydrogen phosphate R*, previously adjusted to pH 4.2 with *dilute phosphoric acid R*;
— *mobile phase B*: mix 25 volumes of a solution containing 0.4 ml/l of *triethylamine R1* and 3.12 g/l of *sodium dihydrogen phosphate R*, previously adjusted to pH 4.2 with *dilute phosphoric acid R* and 75 volumes of *acetonitrile R1*;

| Time (min) | Mobile phase A (per cent *V/V*) | Mobile phase B (per cent *V/V*) |
|---|---|---|
| 0 - 40 | 95 → 10 | 5 → 90 |
| 40 - 45 | 10 | 90 |
| 45 - 50 | 10 → 95 | 90 → 5 |
| 50 - 60 | 95 | 5 |

*Flow rate*   1.0 ml/min.

*Detection*   Spectrophotometer at 225 nm.

*Injection*   10 µl.

*Identification of impurities*   Use the chromatogram supplied with *bisoprolol for system suitability method A CRS* and the chromatogram obtained with reference solution (b) to identify the peaks due to fumaric acid and impurities A, B and E.

*Relative retention*   With reference to bisoprolol (retention time = about 14.5 min): impurity A = about 0.25; impurity G = about 1.05; impurity B = about 1.1; impurity E = about 1.3.

*System suitability*   Reference solution (b):
— *resolution*: minimum 5.0 between the peaks due to bisoprolol and impurity B.

*Limits:*
— *impurity A*: not more than 3 times the area of the principal peak in the chromatogram obtained with reference solution (a) (0.3 per cent);

— *impurity E*: not more than twice the area of the principal peak in the chromatogram obtained with reference solution (a) (0.2 per cent);

— *unspecified impurities*: for each impurity, not more than the area of the principal peak in the chromatogram obtained with reference solution (a) (0.10 per cent);

— *total*: not more than 3 times the area of the principal peak in the chromatogram obtained with reference solution (a) (0.3 per cent);

— *disregard limit*: 0.5 times the area of the principal peak in the chromatogram obtained with reference solution (a) (0.05 per cent); disregard the peak due to fumaric acid and any peak due to impurity G.

B. Impurities A and G. Liquid chromatography (*2.2.29*).

*Solvent mixture*  acetonitrile R1, water for chromatography R (20:80 *V/V*).

*Test solution*  Dissolve 25 mg of the substance to be examined in the solvent mixture and dilute to 25.0 ml with the solvent mixture.

*Reference solution (a)*  Dilute 1.0 ml of the test solution to 100.0 ml with the solvent mixture. Dilute 2.0 ml of this solution to 10.0 ml with the solvent mixture.

*Reference solution (b)*  Dissolve the contents of a vial of *bisoprolol for system suitability method B CRS* (containing impurities A and G) in 1.0 ml of the solvent mixture.

*Column*:
— *size*: *l* = 0.25 m, Ø = 4.6 mm;
— *stationary phase*: octadecylsilyl silica gel for chromatography R (5 μm);
— *temperature*: 30 °C.

*Mobile phase*:
— *mobile phase A*: 10 g/l solution of *phosphoric acid R*;
— *mobile phase B*: 10 g/l solution of *phosphoric acid R* in *acetonitrile R1*;

| Time (min) | Mobile phase A (per cent *V/V*) | Mobile phase B (per cent *V/V*) |
|---|---|---|
| 0 - 35 | 90 → 20 | 10 → 80 |
| 35 - 40 | 20 → 90 | 80 → 10 |
| 40 - 50 | 90 | 10 |

*Flow rate*  1.0 ml/min.

*Detection*  Spectrophotometer at 225 nm.

*Injection*  10 μl.

*Identification of impurities*  Use the chromatogram supplied with *bisoprolol for system suitability method B CRS* and the chromatogram obtained with reference solution (b) to identify the peaks due to fumaric acid and impurities A and G.

*Relative retention*  With reference to bisoprolol (retention time = about 13.4 min): impurity A = about 0.4; impurity G = about 1.02; impurity E = about 1.2.

*System suitability*  Reference solution (b):
— *peak-to-valley ratio*: minimum 2.5, where $H_p$ = height above the baseline of the peak due to impurity G, and $H_v$ = height above the baseline of the lowest point of the curve separating this peak from the peak due to bisoprolol.

*Limits*:
— *impurity G*: not more than 2.5 times the area of the principal peak in the chromatogram obtained with reference solution (a) (0.5 per cent);

— *impurity A*: not more than 1.5 times the area of the principal peak in the chromatogram obtained with reference solution (a) (0.3 per cent);

— *unspecified impurities*: for each impurity, not more than 0.5 times the area of the principal peak in the chromatogram obtained with reference solution (a) (0.10 per cent);

— *total*: not more than 2.5 times the area of the principal peak in the chromatogram obtained with reference solution (a) (0.5 per cent);

— *disregard limit*: 0.25 times the area of the principal peak in the chromatogram obtained with reference solution (a) (0.05 per cent); disregard the peak due to fumaric acid and any peak due to impurity E.

**Water** (*2.5.12*)
Maximum 0.5 per cent, determined on 1.000 g.

**Sulphated ash** (*2.4.14*)
Maximum 0.1 per cent, determined on 1.0 g.

**ASSAY**
Dissolve 0.300 g in 50 ml of *anhydrous acetic acid R*. Titrate with *0.1 M perchloric acid*, determining the end-point potentiometrically (*2.2.20*).

1 ml of *0.1 M perchloric acid* is equivalent to 38.35 mg of $C_{40}H_{66}N_2O_{12}$.

**STORAGE**
In an airtight container, protected from light.

**IMPURITIES**
*Specified impurities*   A, E, G.

*Other detectable impurities*  (The following substances would, if present at a sufficient level, be detected by one or other of the tests in the monograph. They are limited by the general acceptance criterion for other/unspecified impurities and/or by the general monograph *Substances for pharmaceutical use* (*2034*). It is therefore not necessary to identify these impurities for demonstration of compliance. See also *5.10*. *Control of impurities in substances for pharmaceutical use*):
— *by method A*: B, C, D, F;
— *by method B*: B, K, L, N, Q, R, S, T, U.

A. R = H: (*RS*)-1-(4-hydroxymethyl-phenoxy)-3-isopropylaminopropan-2-ol,

B. R = CH₂-CH₂-O-[CH₂]₂-CH₃: (*RS*)-1-isopropylamino-3-[4-(2-propoxy-ethoxymethyl)phenoxy]propan-2-ol,

C. Ar-CH₂-Ar: (*RS*)-1-[4-[4-(2-hydroxy-3-isopropylamino-propoxy)benzyl]phenoxy]-3-isopropylaminopropan-2-ol,

D. Ar-CH₂-O-CH₂-Ar: (*RS*)-1-[4-[4-(2-hydroxy-3-isopropylaminopropoxy)benzyloxylmethyl]phenoxy]-3-isopropylaminopropan-2-ol,

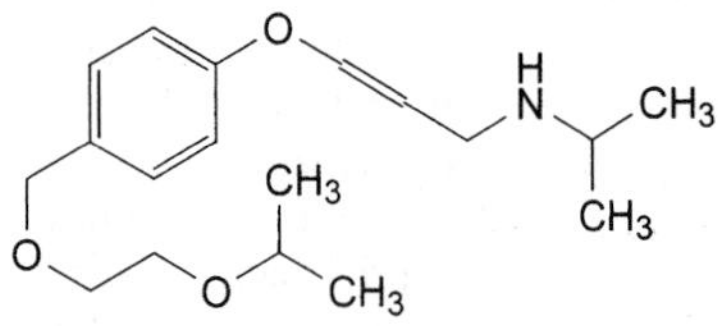

E. (*EZ*)-[3-[4-(2-isopropoxy-ethoxymethyl)phenoxy]allyl]isopropylamine,

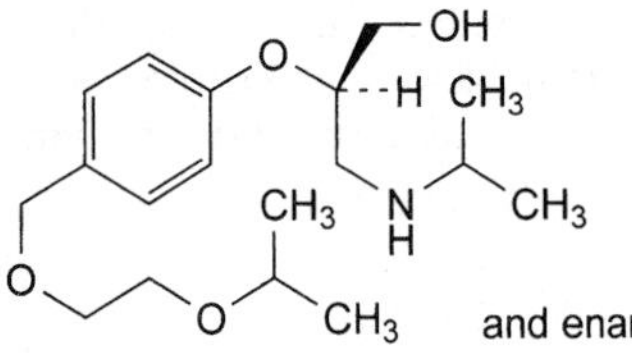

and enantiomer

F. (*RS*)-2-[4-(2-isopropoxy-ethoxymethyl)phenoxy]-3-isopropylaminopropan-2-ol,

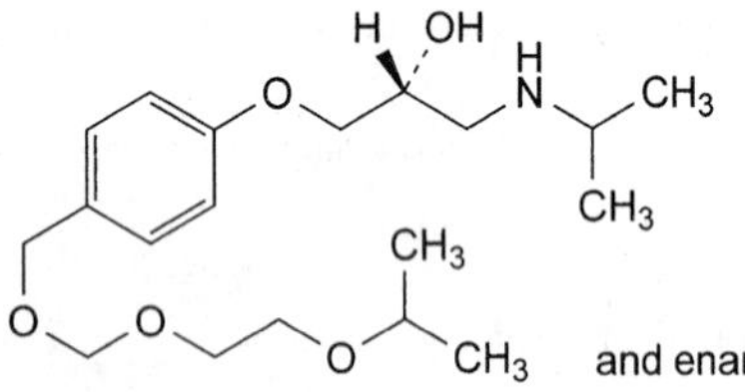

and enantiomer

G. (2*RS*)-1-[4-[[(2-isopropoxyethoxy)methoxy]methyl]phenoxy]-3-isopropylaminopropan-2-ol,

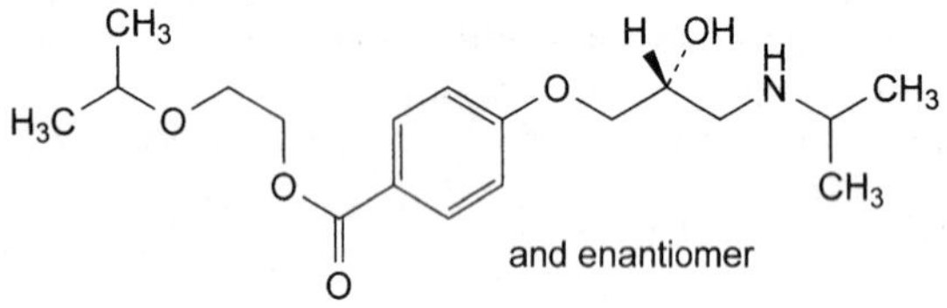

and enantiomer

K. 2-isopropoxyethyl 4-[[(2*RS*)-2-hydroxy-3-(isopropylamino)propyl]oxy]benzoate,

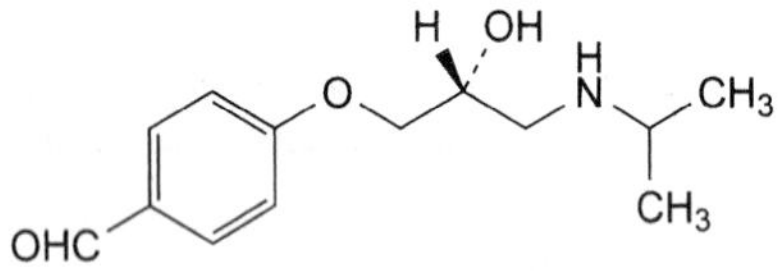

and enantiomer

L. 4-[[(2*RS*)-2-hydroxy-3-(isopropylamino)propyl]oxy]benzaldehyde,

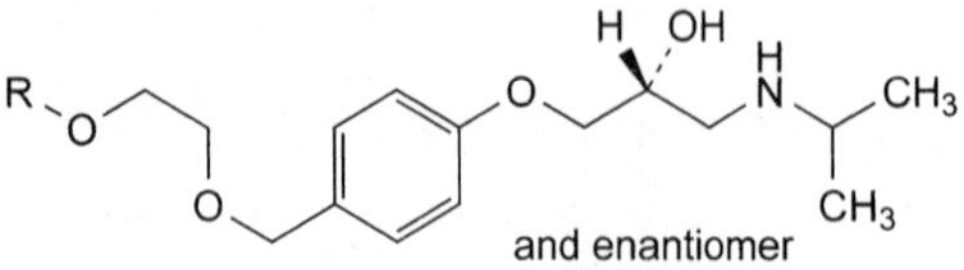

and enantiomer

N. R = $C_2H_5$: [(2*RS*)-1-[4-[(2-ethoxyethoxy)methyl]phenoxy]-3-isopropylaminopropan-2-ol,

Q. R = $CH_3$: (2*RS*)-1-(isopropylamino)-3-[4-(2-methoxyethoxy)methyl]phenoxypropan-2-ol,

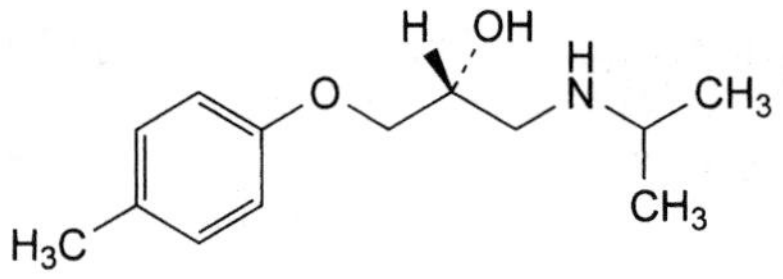

and enantiomer

R. (2*RS*)-1-(isopropylamino)-3-(4-methylphenoxy)propan-2-ol,

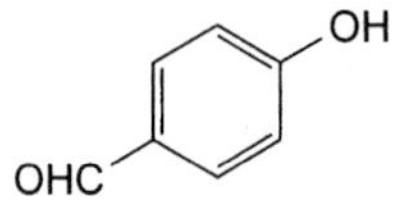

S. 4-hydroxybenzaldehyde,

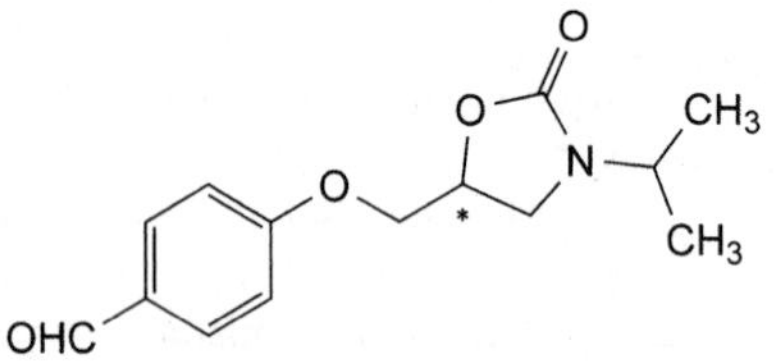

T. 4-[(3-isopropyl-2-oxo-1,3-oxazolidin-5-yl)methoxy]benzaldehyde,

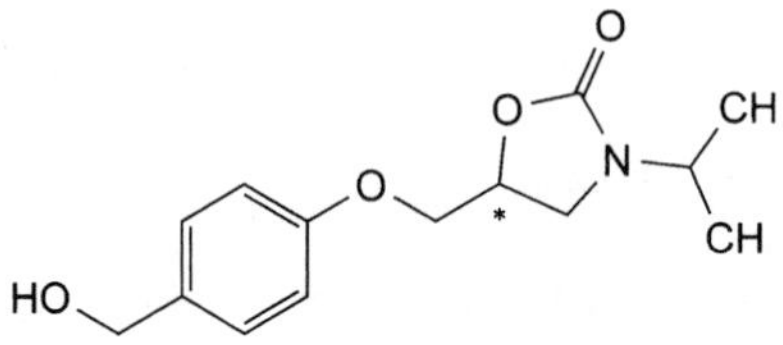

U. 5-[[4-(hydroxymethyl)phenoxy]methyl]-3-isopropyl-1,3-oxazolidin-2-one.

*Ph Eur*

# Bleomycin Sulphate

*(Ph Eur monograph 0976)*

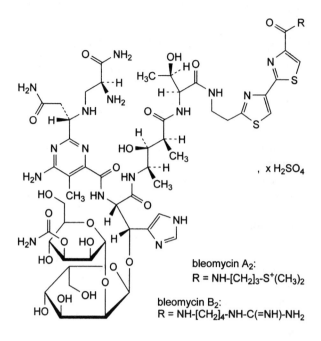

bleomycin A₂:
R = NH-[CH₂]₃-S⁺(CH₃)₂

bleomycin B₂:
R = NH-[CH₂]₄-NH-C(=NH)-NH₂

, x H₂SO₄

*9041-93-4*

**Action and use**

Cytotoxic antibacterial.

**Preparation**

Bleomycin Injection

*Ph Eur* ___

## DEFINITION

Sulphate of a mixture of glycopeptides produced by *Streptomyces verticillus* or by any other means; the 2 principal components of the mixture are *N*-[3-(dimethylsulphonio)propyl]bleomycinamide (bleomycin A₂) and *N*-[4-(carbamimidoylamino)butyl]bleomycinamide (bleomycin B₂).

*Potency* Minimum 1500 IU/mg (dried substance).

## CHARACTERS

**Appearance**

White or yellowish-white, very hygroscopic powder.

**Solubility**

Very soluble in water, slightly soluble in anhydrous ethanol, practically insoluble in acetone.

## IDENTIFICATION

A. Examine the chromatograms obtained in the test for composition.

*Results* The 2 principal peaks in the chromatogram obtained with the test solution are similar in retention time and size to the 2 principal peaks in the chromatogram obtained with reference solution (a).

B. It gives the reactions of sulphates (*2.3.1*).

## TESTS

**Appearance of solution**

The solution is clear (*2.2.1*) and its absorbance (*2.2.25*) at 430 nm is not greater than 0.10.

Dissolve 0.200 g in *water R* and dilute to 10.0 ml with the same solvent.

**pH** (*2.2.3*)

4.5 to 6.0.

Dissolve 50 mg in *carbon dioxide-free water R* and dilute to 10 ml with the same solvent.

**Composition**

Liquid chromatography (*2.2.29*): use the normalisation procedure.

*Test solution* Dissolve 25.0 mg of the substance to be examined in *water R* and dilute to 50.0 ml with the same solvent.

*Reference solution (a)* Dissolve 25.0 mg of *bleomycin sulphate CRS* in *water R* and dilute to 50.0 ml with the same solvent.

*Reference solution (b)* Dilute 1.5 ml of reference solution (a) to 100.0 ml with *water R*.

*Column:*
— *size: l* = 0.25 m, Ø = 4.6 mm;
— *stationary phase: octadecylsilyl silica gel for chromatography R* (7 μm).

*Mobile phase:*
— *mobile phase A: methanol R*;
— *mobile phase B*: dissolve 0.960 g of *sodium pentanesulphonate R* in 900 ml of acetic acid (4.8 g/l C₂H₄O₂), add 1.86 g of *sodium edetate R*, dilute to 1000 ml with the same solvent and adjust to pH 4.3 with *ammonia R*;

| Time (min) | Mobile phase A (per cent *V/V*) | Mobile phase B (per cent *V/V*) |
|---|---|---|
| 0 - 60 | 10 → 40 | 90 → 60 |
| 60 - end | 40 | 60 |

*Flow rate* 1.2 ml/min.

*Detection* Spectrophotometer at 254 nm.

*Injection* 20 μl.

*Run time* Until impurity D is eluted (about 80 min).

*Relative retention* With reference to bleomycin A₂: impurity D = 1.5 to 2.5.

*System suitability:*
— *resolution*: minimum 5 between the peaks due to bleomycin A₂ (1ˢᵗ principal peak) and bleomycin B₂ (2ⁿᵈ principal peak) in the chromatogram obtained with reference solution (a);
— *signal-to-noise ratio*: minimum 20 for the principal peak in the chromatogram obtained with reference solution (b);
— *repeatability*: maximum relative standard deviation of 2 per cent for the principal peak after 6 injections of reference solution (a).

*Limits:*
— *bleomycin A₂*: 55 per cent to 70 per cent;
— *bleomycin B₂*: 25 per cent to 32 per cent;
— *sum of bleomycin A₂ and B₂*: minimum 85 per cent;
— *impurity D*: maximum 5.5 per cent;
— *sum of impurities other than D*: maximum 9.5 per cent;
— *disregard limit*: 0.1 per cent of the total.

**Copper**

Maximum $2.00 \times 10^2$ ppm.

Atomic absorption spectrometry (*2.2.23, Method I*).

*Test solution* Dissolve 50 mg in *water R* and dilute to 10.0 ml with the same solvent.

*Reference solution* Dilute 1.0 ml of *copper standard solution (10 ppm Cu) R* to 10.0 ml with *water R*.

*Source* Copper hollow-cathode lamp.

*Wavelength*   324.7 nm.

*Atomisation device*   Air-acetylene flame.

**Loss on drying** (*2.2.32*)
Maximum 3.0 per cent, determined on 50 mg by drying at 60 °C at a pressure not exceeding 0.67 kPa for 3 h.

**Bacterial endotoxins** (*2.6.14*)
Less than 5 IU/mg, if intended for use in the manufacture of parenteral dosage forms without a further appropriate procedure for the removal of bacterial endotoxins.

## ASSAY
Carry out the microbiological assay of antibiotics (*2.7.2*), using the diffusion method. Use *bleomycin sulphate CRS* as the chemical reference substance.

## STORAGE
In an airtight container, at a temperature of 2 °C to 8 °C. If the substance is sterile, store in a sterile, airtight, tamper-proof container.

## IMPURITIES
*Specified impurities*   D.

*Other detectable impurities* (the following substances would, if present at a sufficient level, be detected by one or other of the tests in the monograph. They are limited by the general acceptance criterion for other/unspecified impurities and/or by the general monograph *Substances for pharmaceutical use* (*2034*). It is therefore not necessary to identify these impurities for demonstration of compliance. See also *5.10. Control of impurities in substances for pharmaceutical use*): A, B, C.

A. R = OH: bleomycinic acid,

B. R = NH-[CH$_2$]$_3$-NH-[CH$_2$]$_4$-NH$_2$: bleomycin A$_5$,

C. R = NH-[CH$_2$]$_4$-NH-C(=NH)-NH-[CH$_2$]$_4$-NH-C(=NH)-NH$_2$: bleomycin B$_4$,

D. R = NH-[CH$_2$]$_3$-S-CH$_3$: demethylbleomycin A$_2$.

_____ *Ph Eur*

# Borax

Sodium Borate; Sodium Tetraborate

(*Ph Eur monograph 0013*)

| | | |
|---|---|---|
| Na$_2$B$_4$O$_7$,10H$_2$O | 381.4 | 1303-96-4 |

*Ph Eur* _____

## DEFINITION
Disodium tetraborate decahydrate.

**Content**
99.0 per cent to 103.0 per cent of Na$_2$B$_4$O$_7$,10H$_2$O.

## CHARACTERS
**Appearance**
White or almost white, crystalline powder, colourless crystals or crystalline masses, efflorescent.

**Solubility**
Soluble in water, very soluble in boiling water, freely soluble in glycerol.

## IDENTIFICATION
A. To 1 ml of solution S (see Tests) add 0.1 ml of *sulphuric acid R* and 5 ml of *methanol R* and ignite. The flame has a green border.

B. To 5 ml of solution S add 0.1 ml of *phenolphthalein solution R*. The solution is red. On the addition of 5 ml of *glycerol (85 per cent) R* the colour disappears.

C. Solution S gives the reactions of sodium (*2.3.1*).

## TESTS
**Solution S**
Dissolve 4.0 g in *carbon dioxide-free water R* prepared from *distilled water R* and dilute to 100 ml with the same solvent.

**Appearance of solution**
Solution S is clear (*2.2.1*) and colourless (*2.2.2, Method II*).

**pH** (*2.2.3*)
9.0 to 9.6 for solution S.

**Sulphates** (*2.4.13*)
Maximum 50 ppm, determined on solution S.

Use in this test 1.0 ml of *acetic acid R*. Prepare the standard using a mixture of 3 ml of *sulphate standard solution (10 ppm SO$_4$) R* and 12 ml of *distilled water R*.

**Ammonium** (*2.4.1*)
Maximum 10 ppm.

Dilute 6 ml of solution S to 14 ml with *water R*. Prepare the standard using a mixture of 2.5 ml of *ammonium standard solution (1 ppm NH$_4$) R* and 7.5 ml of *water R*.

**Arsenic** (*2.4.2, Method A*)
Maximum 5 ppm, determined on 5 ml of solution S.

**Calcium** (*2.4.3*)
Maximum 100 ppm, determined on solution S.

Prepare the standard using a mixture of 6 ml of *calcium standard solution (10 ppm Ca) R* and 9 ml of *distilled water R*.

**Heavy metals** (*2.4.8*)
Maximum 25 ppm.

12 ml of solution S complies with test A. Prepare the reference solution using *lead standard solution (1 ppm Pb) R*.

## ASSAY
Dissolve 20 g of *mannitol R* in 100 ml of *water R*, heating if necessary, cool and add 0.5 ml of *phenolphthalein solution R* and neutralise with 0.1 M *sodium hydroxide* until a pink colour is obtained. Add 3.00 g of the substance to be examined, heat until dissolution is complete, cool, and titrate with 1 M *sodium hydroxide* until the pink colour reappears.

1 ml of *1 M sodium hydroxide* is equivalent to 0.1907 g of Na$_2$B$_4$O$_7$,10H$_2$O.

_____ *Ph Eur*

# Boric Acid

(*Ph Eur monograph 0001*)

| | | |
|---|---|---|
| H$_3$BO$_3$ | 61.8 | 10043-35-3 |

*Ph Eur* _____

## DEFINITION
**Content**
99.0 per cent to 100.5 per cent.

## CHARACTERS
**Appearance**
White or almost white, crystalline powder, colourless, shiny plates greasy to the touch, or white or almost white crystals.

**Solubility**
Soluble in water and in ethanol (96 per cent), freely soluble in boiling water and in glycerol (85 per cent).

## IDENTIFICATION

A. Dissolve 0.1 g by gently heating in 5 ml of *methanol R*, add 0.1 ml of *sulphuric acid R* and ignite the solution. The flame has a green border.

B. Solution S (see Tests) is acid (*2.2.4*).

## TESTS

**Solution S**

Dissolve 3.3 g in 80 ml of boiling *distilled water R*, cool and dilute to 100 ml with *carbon dioxide-free water R* prepared from *distilled water R*.

**Appearance of solution**

Solution S is clear (*2.2.1*) and colourless (*2.2.2, Method II*).

**pH** (*2.2.3*)

3.8 to 4.8 for solution S.

**Solubility in ethanol (96 per cent)**

The solution is not more opalescent than reference suspension II (*2.2.1*) and is colourless (*2.2.2, Method II*).

Dissolve 1.0 g in 10 ml of boiling *ethanol (96 per cent) R*.

**Organic matter**

It does not darken on progressive heating to dull redness.

**Sulphates** (*2.4.13*)

Maximum 450 ppm.

Dilute 10 ml of solution S to 15 ml with *distilled water R*.

**Heavy metals** (*2.4.8*)

Maximum 15 ppm.

12 ml of solution S complies with test A. Prepare the reference solution using a mixture of 2.5 ml of *lead standard solution (2 ppm Pb) R* and 7.5 ml of *water R*.

## ASSAY

Dissolve 1.000 g with heating in 100 ml of *water R* containing 15 g of *mannitol R*. Titrate with *1 M sodium hydroxide*, using 0.5 ml of *phenolphthalein solution R* as indicator, until a pink colour is obtained.

1 ml of *1 M sodium hydroxide* is equivalent to 61.8 mg of $H_3BO_3$.

*Ph Eur*

# Botulinum Toxin Type A For Injection

(*Ph Eur monograph 2113*)

*Ph Eur*

## DEFINITION

Botulinum toxin type A for injection is a dried preparation containing purified botulinum neurotoxin type A which may be present in the form of a complex with haemagglutinins and non-toxic proteins. Botulinum neurotoxin type A or its haemagglutinin complex is prepared by a suitable purification process of the liquid supernatant from a broth-culture of a suitable strain of *Clostridium botulinum* type A.

The purified complexes consist of several proteins and can be of various sizes. The largest complex (relative molecular mass of about 900 000) consists of a 150 000 relative molecular mass neurotoxin, a 130 000 relative molecular mass non-toxic protein and various haemagglutinins ranging between relative molecular mass 14 000 and 43 000. The purified toxin moiety is composed of only the same 150 000 relative molecular mass neurotoxin as is found in the 900 000

relative molecular mass neurotoxin complex, which is initially produced as a single chain and further cleaved (nicked) by endogenous proteases into a fully active, disulphide-linked, 54 000 relative molecular mass light chain and a 97 000 relative molecular mass heavy chain.

The preparation is reconstituted before use, as stated on the label.

## PRODUCTION

### GENERAL PROVISIONS

Production of the toxin is based on seed cultures, managed in a defined seed-lot system in which the ability to produce toxin is conserved. The production method must be shown to yield consistently product of activity and profile comparable to that of lots shown in clinical studies to be of adequate safety and efficacy.

The production method is validated to demonstrate that the product, if tested, would comply with the general test of abnormal toxicity (*2.6.9*) using not less than the maximum human clinical dose, in the presence of a suitable amount of specific botulinum type A antitoxin used for neutralisation.

The production method and stability of the finished product and relevant intermediates are evaluated using the tests below. Such tests include the specific toxin activity per milligram of protein of purified toxin in an appropriate functional model of toxin activity and may be supported by tests confirming the presence of botulinum toxin type A, and, if appropriate, associated non-toxic proteins.

### BACTERIAL SEED LOTS

A highly toxigenic strain of *C. botulinum* of known toxin type A and confirmed absence of genes encoding other botulinum toxins (particularly botulinum toxin type B), with known origin and history, is grown using suitable media. The bacterial strain, used for the master seed lot, shall be identified by historical records that include information on its origin and the tests used to characterise the strain. These will include morphological, cultural, biochemical, genetic and serological properties of the strain. The master seed lot and the working seed lot, where applicable, must be demonstrated to have identical profiles. Only a seed lot that complies with the following requirements may be used.

**Identification**

Each seed lot is identified as containing pure cultures of *C. botulinum* type A bacteria with no extraneous bacterial or fungal contamination.

**Microbial purity**

Each seed lot complies with the requirements for absence of contaminating micro-organisms. The purity of bacterial cultures is verified by methods of suitable sensitivity. These may include inoculation into suitable media and examination of colony morphology.

**Phenotypic parameters**

Each seed lot must have a known fatty acid profile, sugar fermentation profile (glucose, lactose, mannose, etc.) and proteolytic activity and must demonstrate relevant lipase, lecithinase and gelatinase activity.

**Genetic purity**

Each seed lot must have information on the toxin gene sequence and comply with requirements for the absence of other genes encoding other toxin serotypes.

**Production of active toxin**

A bacterial strain producing a high yield of active toxin, as determined by an acute toxicity assay, is suitable. Seed lots should demonstrate a capability of producing at least a minimum toxicity level appropriate for the manufacturing process and scale.

**MANUFACTURER'S REFERENCE PREPARATIONS**
During development, reference preparations are established for subsequent verification of batch consistency during production and for control of the bulk purified toxin and finished product. They are derived from representative batches of botulinum toxin type A that are characterised as described under Bulk Purified Toxin.

The reference preparations are suitably characterised for their intended purpose and are stored in suitably sized aliquots under conditions ensuring their suitability.

**BULK PURIFIED TOXIN**
C. botulinum type A strain is grown anaerobically, in suitable media, from which cultures are selected for step-up incubations under a suitably controlled anaerobic atmosphere through the seed culture and bulk fermentation stages to allow maximum production of toxin. The toxin is purified by suitable methods to remove nucleic acids and components likely to cause adverse reactions.

Only a purified toxin that complies with the following requirements may be used in the preparation of the final bulk. For each test and for each product, limits of acceptance are established and each new purified toxin must comply with these limits.

**Residual reagents**
Removal of residual reagents used in purification steps is confirmed by suitable limit tests or by validation of the process.

**Nucleic acids**
Removal of nucleic acids is confirmed by suitable limit tests or by validation of the process.

**Immunological identity**
The presence of specific type A toxin is confirmed by a suitable immunochemical method (2.7.1).

**Specific activity**
The specific activity is confirmed in a mouse model of toxicity or by in vivo/ex vivo methods validated with respect to the LD50 assay and expressed in mouse LD50 units per milligram of protein. Specific activity must not be less than $1 \times 10^8$ mouse LD50 units per milligram of protein for the 150 000 relative molecular mass neurotoxin and must not be less than $1 \times 10^7$ mouse LD50 units per milligram of protein for the 900 000 relative molecular mass neurotoxin complex.

**Protein**
The total protein concentration is determined by a suitable method. An acceptable value is established for the product and each batch must be shown to comply with the limits.

**Protein profile**
Identity and protein composition are determined by polyacrylamide gel electrophoresis (2.2.31) under reducing or non-reducing conditions or by other suitable physicochemical methods such as size-exclusion chromatography (2.2.30), comparing with suitable reference standards.

**Total viable count**
It complies with the limits approved for the particular product.

**FINAL BULK**
The final bulk is prepared by adding approved excipients to the bulk purified toxin. The solution is filtered through a bacteria-retentive filter. If human albumin is added, it complies with the monograph on *Human albumin solution (0255)*.

**FINAL LOT**
The final bulk is distributed aseptically into sterile, tamper-proof containers. Uniformity of fill is verified during filling and the test for uniformity of content (2.9.6) is not required. The containers are closed so as to prevent contamination.

Only a final lot that is within the limits approved for the particular product and is satisfactory with respect to each of the requirements given below under Identification, Tests and Assay may be released for use.

**pH** (2.2.3)
The pH of the reconstituted product is within $\pm$ 0.5 pH units of the limit approved for the particular product.

**Water**
Not more than the limit approved for the particular product.

**IDENTIFICATION**
The presence of botulinum toxin type A is confirmed by a suitable immunochemical method (2.7.1).

**TESTS**
**Sterility** (2.6.1)
It complies with the test for sterility.

**Bacterial endotoxins** (2.6.14)
Less than 10 IU per vial.

**ASSAY**
The potency of the reconstituted product is determined by an LD50 assay in mice or by a method validated with respect to the LD50 assay. The potency is expressed in terms of the LD50 for mice or relative to the reference preparation.

For determination of the LD50, graded doses of the product are injected intraperitoneally into groups of mice and the LD50 is calculated by the usual statistical methods (5.3) from the mouse lethality in each group. A suitable reference preparation is assayed in parallel; the potency of the toxin is expressed relative to the reference or the value found for the reference is within suitable limits defined in terms of the assigned potency.

After validation with respect to the LD50 assay (reference method), the product may also be assayed by other methods that are preferable in terms of animal welfare, including 1 of the following:

1. endopeptidase assay *in vitro*;
2. *ex vivo* assay using the mouse phrenic nerve diaphragm;
3. mouse bioassay using paralysis as the end-point.

For these other methods, the potency is calculated with respect to a suitable reference preparation calibrated in mouse LD50 units.

The estimated potency is not less than 80 per cent and not more than 125 per cent of the stated potency. The confidence limits ($P = 0.95$) are not less than 80 per cent and not more than 125 per cent of the estimated potency.

The test may be repeated but when more than 1 test is performed, the results of all valid tests must be combined in the estimate of potency.

**LABELLING**
The label states:
— the number of units of toxin per vial with a statement that units are product specific and not applicable to other preparations containing botulinum toxin type A;

— the name and the volume of the diluent to be added for reconstitution of a dried product.

*Ph Eur*

# Bovine Serum

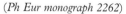

*(Ph Eur monograph 2262)*

*Ph Eur*

## DEFINITION
Liquid fraction of blood obtained from the ox (*Bos taurus* L.) and from which cells, fibrin and clotting factors have been removed.

Different types of bovine serum are used:
— *adult bovine serum* obtained at slaughter from cattle that are declared fit for human consumption;
— *calf serum* obtained at slaughter from animals, fit for human consumption, before the age of 12 months;
— *new-born calf serum* obtained at slaughter from animals before the age of 20 days;
— *foetal bovine serum* obtained from normal foetuses from dams fit for human consumption;
— *donor bovine serum* obtained by repeated bleeding of donor animals from controlled donor herds.

*This monograph provides a general quality specification for bovine serum. Various measures are applied during the production of bovine serum aimed at obtaining a product that is acceptable as regards viral safety. No single measure, nor the combination of measures outlined below can guarantee complete viral safety but they rather reduce the risk involved in the use of serum in the manufacture of medicinal products. It is therefore necessary for the manufacturer of a medicinal product to take account of this when choosing the serum for a particular use by making a risk assessment.*

## PRODUCTION
All stages of serum production are submitted to a suitable quality assurance system.

Traceability of serum is maintained from the final container to the abattoir of origin (for blood collected from slaughtered animals) or to the herd of origin (for blood collected from donor animals).

Further guarantee of the safety and quality of serum may be ensured by the use of a controlled donor herd. Where serum is obtained from such a herd, the animals are subjected to regular veterinary examination to ascertain their health status. Animals introduced into the herd are traceable as regards source, breeding and rearing history. The introduction of animals into the herd follows specified procedures, including defined quarantine measures. During the quarantine period the animals are observed and tested to establish that they are free from all agents and antibodies from which the donor herd is claimed to be free. It may be necessary to test the animals in quarantine for freedom from additional agents, depending on factors such as information available on their breeding and rearing history. It is recommended that animals in the herd should not be vaccinated against bovine viral diarrhoea virus. Tests are carried out for any agent and/or antibody from which the herd is claimed to be free.

Serum is obtained by separation of the serum from blood cells and clot under conditions designed to minimise microbial contamination. Serum from a number of animals is pooled and a batch number is allocated to the pool. Appropriate steps are taken to ensure homogeneity of the harvested material, intermediate pools and the final batch. Suitable measures (for example filtration) are taken to ensure sterility or a low bioburden. Before further processing, the serum is tested for sterility or bioburden. General and specific tests for viral contaminants are carried out as described below.

A step or steps for virus inactivation/removal are applied to serum intended for production of immunological veterinary medicinal products. Unless otherwise justified and authorised for a particular medicinal product, a step or steps for virus inactivation/removal are applied to serum intended for production of human and non-immunological veterinary medicinal products.

### INACTIVATION
The inactivation procedure applied is validated with respect to a suitable representative range of viruses covering different types (enveloped, non-enveloped, DNA, RNA viruses). The optimal choice of relevant and model viruses depends strongly on the specific inactivation/removal procedure; representative viruses with different degrees of resistance to the type of treatment must be included. Bovine viral diarrhoea virus must be included in the viruses used for validation. Serum free from antibodies against bovine viral diarrhoea virus is used in part or all of the validation studies.

For bovine serum intended for use in immunological veterinary medicinal products, for inactivation by gamma irradiation a minimum dose of 30 kGy is applied, unless otherwise justified and authorised.

Critical parameters for the method of virus inactivation/removal are established and the parameters used in the validation study are strictly adhered to during subsequent application of the procedures to each batch of serum.

For inactivation by gamma irradiation, critical parameters include:
— the temperature;
— packaging configuration;
— distribution of dosimeters to assess the effective dose received by the product whatever its position;
— the minimum and maximum dose received.

### QUALITY CONTROL TESTS APPLIED TO EACH BATCH
A suitable sample size for each batch is established. Specific tests for viral contaminants are validated with respect to sensitivity and specificity. The cell cultures used for general tests for viral contaminants are shown to be sensitive to a suitable range of potential contaminants. Control cells used in the tests are cultivated, where relevant, with a bovine serum controlled and inactivated as described in this monograph. Serum free from antibodies to bovine viral diarrhoea virus is required for validation of the effect of antibodies on the detection limits for bovine viral diarrhoea virus.

**Tests carried out on the batch prior to treatment**
The following tests are carried out on the serum (before any virus inactivation/removal steps, where applicable).

*Tests for viral contaminants*   General tests supplemented by specific tests are carried out.

*General tests*   Validated tests are carried out by inoculation of the serum on at least 2 distinct cell lines, one of which is of bovine origin. The cell lines used are suitable for detecting haemadsorbing viruses such as bovine parainfluenza virus 3 and cytopathic agents such as bovine herpesvirus 1.

*Specific tests*   For viral contaminants (if not detected by general tests), where relevant in view of the country of origin of the serum:

bluetongue virus, bovine adenovirus, bovine parvovirus, bovine respiratory syncytial virus, bovine viral diarrhoea virus, rabies virus and reovirus. Depending on the country of origin, specific tests for other viruses may be needed. The animal health status of countries is defined by the 'Office International des Epizooties' (OIE).

For serum to be subjected to a virus inactivation/removal procedure, if evidence of viral contamination is found in any of the tests described above, the serum is acceptable only if the virus is identified and shown to be present in an amount that has been shown in a validation study to be effectively inactivated.

For serum that is not to be subjected to a virus inactivation/removal procedure, if evidence of viral contamination is found in any of the tests described above, the serum is not acceptable.

A test for bovine viral diarrhoea virus antibodies is carried out; an acceptance criterion for the titre is established taking account of the risk assessment.

*Composition* The content of a suitable selection of the following components is determined and shown to be within the expected range for the type of serum: cholesterol, α-, β- and γ-globulin, albumin, creatinine, bilirubin, glucose, serum aspartate transaminase (SAST, formerly SGOT - serum glutamic-oxaloacetic transaminase), serum alanine transaminase (SALT, formerly SGPT - glutamic-pyruvic transaminase), phosphorus, potassium, calcium, sodium and pH.

**Tests carried out on the batch post-treatment**
If bovine viral diarrhoea virus was detected before virus inactivation/removal, the following test for bovine viral diarrhoea virus is carried out after virus inactivation/removal.

*Test for bovine viral diarrhoea virus* A validated test for bovine viral diarrhoea virus is carried out, for example by inoculation into susceptible cell cultures, followed by not fewer than 3 subcultures and detection by immunostaining. No evidence of the presence of bovine viral diarrhoea virus is found.

## IDENTIFICATION

A. The electrophoretic pattern corresponds to that for serum and is consistent with the type (foetal or other) of bovine serum.

B. Bovine origin is confirmed by a suitable immunochemical method (2.7.1).

## TESTS

**Osmolality** (2.2.35)
280 mosmol/kg to 365 mosmol/kg for foetal bovine serum and 240 mosmol/kg to 340 mosmol/kg for other types.

**Total protein** (2.5.33)
30 mg/ml to 45 mg/ml for foetal bovine serum and minimum 35 mg/ml for other types.

**Haemoglobin**
Maximum 4 mg/ml, determined by a validated method, such as spectrophotometry.

**Bacterial endotoxins** (2.6.14)
Less than 10 IU/ml for donor bovine serum, less than 25 IU/ml for foetal bovine serum, less than 100 IU/ml for other types.

**Sterility** (2.6.1)
It complies with the test. Use 10 ml for each medium.

**Mycoplasmas** (2.6.7)
It complies with the test.

## STORAGE
Frozen at − 10 °C or below.

## LABELLING
The label states:
— the type of serum;
— where applicable, that the serum has been inactivated and the inactivation method;
— where the serum has been inactivated by gamma irradiation, the target minimum dose of the irradiation procedure.

*Ph Eur*

# Bretylium Tosilate

$C_{18}H_{24}BrNO_3S$     414.4     *61-75-6*

**Action and use**
Antiarrhythmic.

**Preparation**
Bretylium Injection

## DEFINITION
Bretylium Tosilate is 2-bromobenzyl-*N*-ethyldimethylammonium-*p*-toluenesulphonate. It contains not less than 99.0% and not more than 101.0% of $C_{18}H_{24}BrNO_3S$, calculated with reference to the dried substance.

## CHARACTERISTICS
A white, crystalline powder. It melts at about 98°. It exhibits polymorphism.

Freely soluble in *water*, in *ethanol (96%)* and in *methanol*.

## IDENTIFICATION
A. The *infrared absorption spectrum*, Appendix II A, is concordant with the *reference spectrum* of bretylium tosilate *(RS 030)*. If the spectra are not concordant, dissolve a quantity of the substance being examined in the minimum volume of *acetone* by heating on a water bath at 50°, evaporate to dryness at room temperature under a current of nitrogen and prepare a new spectrum of the residue.

B. Carry out the method for *thin-layer chromatography*, Appendix III A, using the following solutions in *water*.

(1) 0.5% w/v of the substance being examined.

(2) 0.5% w/v of *bretylium tosilate BPCRS*.

CHROMATOGRAPHIC CONDITIONS

(a) Use a *silica gel F₂₅₄ precoated plate* (Merck plates are suitable).

(b) Use the mobile phase as described below.

(c) Apply 10 μl of each solution.

(d) Develop the plate to 15 cm.

(e) After removal of the plate, dry it in a current of air and examine under *ultraviolet light (254 nm)*.

*MOBILE PHASE*

15 volumes of *glacial acetic acid*, 30 volumes of *water* and 75 volumes of *butan-1-ol*.

CONFIRMATION

The two principal spots in the chromatogram obtained with solution (1) correspond to those in the chromatogram obtained with solution (2).

## TESTS

### Acidity

pH of a 5.0% w/v solution, 5.0 to 6.5, Appendix V L.

### Clarity and colour of solution

A 5.0% w/v solution is *clear*, Appendix IV A, and *colourless*, Appendix IV B, Method II.

### Related substances

Carry out the method for *liquid chromatography*, Appendix III D, using the following solutions in mobile phase.

(1) 0.20% w/v of the substance being examined.

(2) 0.002% w/v of the substance being examined.

(3) 0.05% w/v of *bretylium tosilate BPCRS* and 0.05% w/v of *2-bromobenzyldimethylamine hydrochloride BPCRS*.

CHROMATOGRAPHIC CONDITIONS

(a) Use a stainless steel column (25 cm × 4.6 mm) packed with particles of silica the surface of which has been modified by chemically bonded phenyl groups (5 μm) (Spherisorb Phenyl is suitable).

(b) Use isocratic elution and the mobile phase described below.

(c) Use a flow rate of 2 ml per minute.

(d) Use an ambient column temperature.

(e) Use a detection wavelength of 265 nm.

(f) Inject 20 μl of each solution.

*MOBILE PHASE*

0.5 volume of *triethylamine*, 2 volumes of *glacial acetic acid*, 19 volumes of *acetonitrile* and 81 volumes of *0.01M sodium octanesulphonate*.

SYSTEM SUITABILITY

The test is not valid unless, in the chromatogram obtained with solution (3), the *resolution factor* between the two principal peaks is at least 6.0.

LIMITS

In the chromatogram obtained with solution (1):

the area of any *secondary peak* is not greater than half the area of the peak in the chromatogram obtained with solution (2) (0.5%);

the sum of the areas of all such peaks is not greater than the area of the principal peak in the chromatogram obtained with solution (2) (1%).

Disregard the peak due to tosilate (retention time, about 2 minutes) and any peak with an area less than 0.05 times the area of the principal peak in the chromatogram obtained with solution (2) (0.05%).

### Loss on drying

When dried to constant weight over *phosphorus pentoxide* at 60° at a pressure not exceeding 0.7 kPa, loses not more than 3.0% of its weight. Use 1 g.

### Sulphated ash

Not more than 0.1%, Appendix IX A. Use 1 g.

## ASSAY

Dissolve 0.2 g in 50 ml of *1,4-dioxan* and carry out Method I for *non-aqueous titration*, Appendix VIII A, using *0.025M perchloric acid VS* as titrant and determining the end-point potentiometrically. Each ml of *0.025M perchloric acid VS* is equivalent to 10.36 mg of $C_{18}H_{24}BrNO_3S$.

## STORAGE

Bretylium Tosilate should be kept in an airtight container and protected from light.

## IMPURITIES

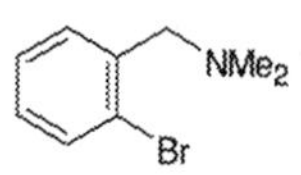

A. 2-bromobenzyldimethylamine

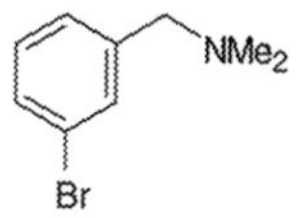

B. 3-bromobenzyldimethylamine

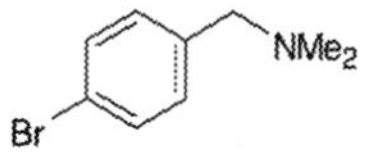

C. 4-bromobenzyldimethylamine

# Bromazepam

*(Ph Eur monograph 0879)*

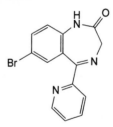

$C_{14}H_{10}BrN_3O$     316.2     *1812-30-2*

**Action and use**

Benzodiazepine.

*Ph Eur*

## DEFINITION

7-Bromo-5-(pyridin-2-yl)-1,3-dihydro-2*H*-1,4-benzodiazepin-2-one.

### Content

99.0 per cent to 101.0 per cent (dried substance).

## CHARACTERS

### Appearance

White or yellowish, crystalline powder.

### Solubility

Practically insoluble in water, slightly soluble or sparingly soluble in ethanol (96 per cent) and in methylene chloride.

## IDENTIFICATION

Infrared absorption spectrophotometry (2.2.24).

*Comparison* bromazepam CRS.

## TESTS

### Related substances

Liquid chromatography (2.2.29). *Prepare the solutions immediately before use.*

*Test solution* Dissolve 10.0 mg of the substance to be examined in 9 ml of a mixture of 1 volume of *acetonitrile R* and 8 volumes of *methanol R*. Dilute to 20.0 ml with an 11.33 g/l solution of *potassium dihydrogen phosphate R* previously adjusted to pH 7.0 with a 100 g/l solution of *potassium hydroxide R*.

*Reference solution (a)* Dilute 1.0 ml of the test solution to 100.0 ml with the mobile phase. Dilute 1.0 ml of this solution to 10.0 ml with the mobile phase.

*Reference solution (b)* Dissolve 5 mg of *bromazepam for system suitability* CRS (containing impurities A, B, C, D and E) in 5 ml of a mixture of 1 volume of *acetonitrile R* and 8 volumes of *methanol R*. Dilute to 10.0 ml with an 11.33 g/l solution of *potassium dihydrogen phosphate R* previously adjusted to pH 7.0 with a 100 g/l solution of *potassium hydroxide R*.

*Column:*
— *size: l* = 0.15 m, Ø = 4.6 mm;
— *stationary phase: end-capped octadecylsilyl silica gel for chromatography R (3.5 μm);*
— temperature: 50 °C.

*Mobile phase* Mix 5 volumes of *acetonitrile R*, 45 volumes of *methanol R* and 50 volumes of an 11.33 g/l solution of *potassium dihydrogen phosphate R* previously adjusted to pH 7.0 with a 100 g/l solution of *potassium hydroxide R*.

*Flow rate* 1.0 ml/min.

*Detection* Spectrophotometer at 235 nm.

*Injection* 20 μl.

*Run time* 4 times the retention time of bromazepam.

*Identification of impurities* Use the chromatogram supplied with *bromazepam for system suitability* CRS and the chromatogram obtained with reference solution (b) to identify the peaks due to impurities A, B, C, D and E.

*Relative retention* With reference to bromazepam (retention time = about 5 min): impurity D = about 1.4; impurity A = about 1.5; impurity C = about 1.6; impurity E = about 2.1; impurity B = about 2.2.

*System suitability* Reference solution (b):
— *resolution*: minimum 4.0 between the peaks due to bromazepam and impurity D and minimum 1.2 between the peaks due to impurities A and C.

*Limits:*
— *correction factors*: for the calculation of content, multiply the peak areas of the following impurities by the corresponding correction factor: impurity A = 1.3; impurity B = 1.8; impurity E = 2.1;
— *impurities A, B, E*: for each impurity, not more than the area of the principal peak in the chromatogram obtained with reference solution (a) (0.1 per cent);
— *unspecified impurities*: for each impurity, not more than the area of the principal peak in the chromatogram obtained with reference solution (a) (0.10 per cent);
— *total*: not more than twice the area of the principal peak in the chromatogram obtained with reference solution (a) (0.2 per cent);

— *disregard limit*: 0.5 times the area of the principal peak in the chromatogram obtained with reference solution (a) (0.05 per cent).

### Loss on drying (2.2.32)

Maximum 0.2 per cent, determined on 1.000 g by drying at 80 °C at a pressure not exceeding 2.7 kPa for 4 h.

### Sulphated ash (2.4.14)

Maximum 0.1 per cent, determined on 1.0 g.

## ASSAY

Dissolve 0.250 g in 20 ml of *anhydrous acetic acid R*. Add 50 ml of *acetic anhydride R*. Titrate with *0.1 M perchloric acid*, determining the end-point potentiometrically (2.2.20).

1 ml of *0.1 M perchloric acid* is equivalent to 31.62 mg of $C_{14}H_{10}BrN_3O$.

## STORAGE

Protected from light.

## IMPURITIES

*Specified impurities* A, B, E.

*Other detectable impurities* (the following substances would, if present at a sufficient level, be detected by one or other of the tests in the monograph. They are limited by the general acceptance criterion for other/unspecified impurities and/or by the general monograph *Substances for pharmaceutical use* (2034). It is therefore not necessary to identify these impurities for demonstration of compliance. See also 5.10. *Control of impurities in substances for pharmaceutical use*): C, D.

A. R = H: (2-amino-5-bromophenyl)(pyridin-2-yl)methanone,

B. R = CO-CH$_2$-Cl: *N*-[4-bromo-2-(pyridin-2-ylcarbonyl)phenyl]-2-chloroacetamide,

E. R = CO-CH$_2$-Br: 2-bromo-*N*-[4-bromo-2-(pyridin-2-ylcarbonyl)phenyl]acetamide,

C. 7-bromo-5-(6-methylpyridin-2-yl)-1,3-dihydro-2*H*-1,4-benzodiazepin-2-one,

D. 3-amino-6-bromo-4-(pyridin-2-yl)quinolin-2(1*H*)-one.

_____ *Ph Eur*

# Bromhexine Hydrochloride

*(Ph Eur monograph 0706)*

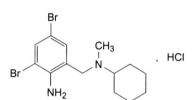

C$_{14}$H$_{20}$Br$_2$N$_2$,HCl          412.6          *611-75-6*

**Action and use**
Mucolytic.

*Ph Eur* _____

## DEFINITION
*N*-(2-Amino-3,5-dibromobenzyl)-*N*-methylcyclohexanamine hydrochloride.

**Content**
98.5 per cent to 101.5 per cent (dried substance).

## CHARACTERS
**Appearance**
White or almost white, crystalline powder.

**Solubility**
Very slightly soluble in water, slightly soluble in alcohol and in methylene chloride.

It shows polymorphism (*5.9*).

## IDENTIFICATION
*First identification   A, E.*

*Second identification   B, C, D, E.*

A. Infrared absorption spectrophotometry (*2.2.24*).

*Comparison   bromhexine hydrochloride CRS.*

If the spectra obtained in the solid state show differences, dissolve the substance to be examined and the reference substance separately in *methanol R*, evaporate to dryness and record new spectra using the residues.

B. Thin-layer chromatography (*2.2.27*).

*Test solution   Dissolve 20 mg of the substance to be examined in *methanol R* and dilute to 10 ml with the same solvent.

*Reference solution   Dissolve 20 mg of *bromhexine hydrochloride CRS* in *methanol R* and dilute to 10 ml with the same solvent.

*Plate   TLC silica gel F$_{254}$ plate R.*

*Mobile phase   glacial acetic acid R, water R, butanol R* (17:17:66 *V/V/V*).

*Application   20 µl.*

*Development   Over 3/4 of the plate.*

*Drying   In air.*

*Detection   Examine in ultraviolet light at 254 nm.*

*Results   The principal spot in the chromatogram obtained with the test solution is similar in position and size to the principal spot in the chromatogram obtained with the reference solution.

C. Dissolve about 25 mg in a mixture of 1 ml of *dilute sulphuric acid R* and 50 ml of *water R*. Add 2 ml of *methylene chloride R* and 5 ml of *chloramine solution R* and shake. A brownish-yellow colour develops in the lower layer.

D. Dissolve about 1 mg in 3 ml of *0.1 M hydrochloric acid*. The solution gives the reaction of primary aromatic amines (*2.3.1*).

E. Dissolve about 20 mg in 1 ml of *methanol R* and add 1 ml of *water R*. The solution gives reaction (a) of chlorides (*2.3.1*).

## TESTS
**Appearance of solution**
The solution is clear (*2.2.1*) and not more intensely coloured than reference solution Y$_6$ (*2.2.2, Method II*).

Dissolve 0.6 g in *methanol R* and dilute to 20 ml with the same solvent.

**Related substances**
Liquid chromatography (*2.2.29*).

*Test solution   Dissolve 50 mg of the substance to be examined in *methanol R* and dilute to 10.0 ml with the same solvent.

*Reference solution (a)   Dissolve 5 mg of *bromhexine impurity C CRS* in *methanol R*, add 1.0 ml of the test solution and dilute to 10.0 ml with the same solvent.

*Reference solution (b)   Dilute 1.0 ml of the test solution to 100.0 ml with *methanol R*. Dilute 1.0 ml of this solution to 10.0 ml with *methanol R*.

*Column:*
— *size: l* = 0.12 m, Ø = 4.6 mm;
— *stationary phase: end-capped octadecylsilyl silica gel for chromatography R (3 µm).*

*Mobile phase   Mix 0.50 ml of *phosphoric acid R* in 950 ml of *water R*, adjust to pH 7.0 with *triethylamine R* (about 1.5 ml) and dilute to 1000 ml with *water R*; mix 20 volumes of this solution with 80 volumes of *acetonitrile R*.

*Flow rate   1.0 ml/min.*

*Detection   Spectrophotometer at 248 nm.*

*Injection   10 µl.*

*Run time   2.5 times the retention time of bromhexine.*

*Relative retention   With reference to bromhexine (retention time = about 11 min): impurity A = about 0.1; impurity B = about 0.2; impurity C = about 0.4; impurity D = about 0.5.

*System suitability   Reference solution (a):*
— *resolution*: minimum 12.0 between the peaks due to impurity C and bromhexine.

*Limits:*
— *any impurity*: not more than twice the area of the principal peak in the chromatogram obtained with reference solution (b) (0.2 per cent), and not more than 1 such peak has an area greater than the area of the principal peak in the chromatogram obtained with reference solution (b) (0.1 per cent);

— *total*: not more than 3 times the area of the principal peak in the chromatogram obtained with reference solution (b) (0.3 per cent);

— *disregard limit*: 0.5 times the area of the principal peak in the chromatogram obtained with reference solution (b) (0.05 per cent).

**Loss on drying** (*2.2.32*)
Maximum 1.0 per cent, determined on 1.000 g by drying in an oven at 105 °C.

**Sulphated ash** (*2.4.14*)
Maximum 0.1 per cent, determined on 1.0 g.

**ASSAY**
Dissolve 0.300 g in 70 ml of *alcohol R* and add 1 ml of *0.1 M hydrochloric acid*. Carry out a potentiometric titration (*2.2.20*), using *0.1 M sodium hydroxide*. Read the volume between the 2 points of inflexion.

1 ml of *0.1 M sodium hydroxide* is equivalent to 41.26 mg of $C_{14}H_{21}Br_2ClN_2$.

**STORAGE**
Protected from light.

**IMPURITIES**
*Specified impurities* A, B, C, D.

*Other detectable impurities* (the following substances would, if present at a sufficient level, be detected by one or other of the tests in the monograph. They are limited by the general acceptance criterion for other/unspecified impurities and/or by the general monograph *Substances for pharmaceutical use (2034)*. It is therefore not necessary to identify these impurities for demonstration of compliance. See also *5.10. Control of impurities in substances for pharmaceutical use*): E.

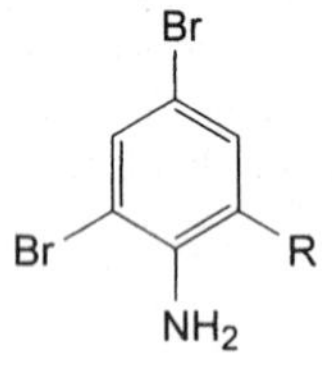

A. R = CH$_2$OH: (2-amino-3,5-dibromophenyl)methanol,
B. R = CHO: 2-amino-3,5-dibromobenzaldehyde,

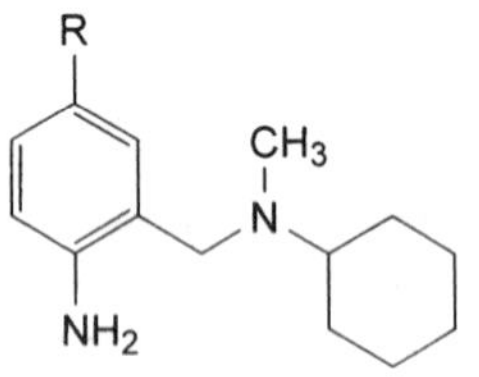

C. R = H: *N*-(2-aminobenzyl)-*N*-methylcyclohexanamine,
D. R = Br: *N*-(2-amino-5-bromobenzyl)-*N*-methylcyclohexanamine,

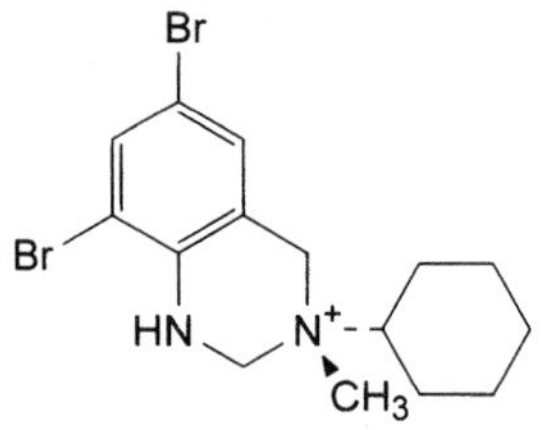

E. (3*RS*)-6,8-dibromo-3-cyclohexyl-3-methyl-1,2,3,4-tetrahydroquinazolin-3-ium.

*Ph Eur*

# Bromocriptine Mesilate

(*Ph Eur monograph 0596*)

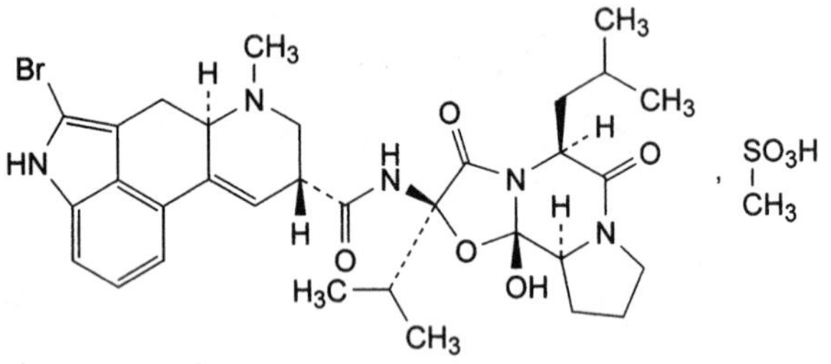

$C_{32}H_{40}BrN_5O_5S,CH_4SO_3$      751      *22260-51-1*

**Action and use**
Dopamine receptor agonist.

**Preparations**
Bromocriptine Capsules
Bromocriptine Tablets

*Ph Eur*

**DEFINITION**
(6a*R*,9*R*)-5-Bromo-*N*-[(2*R*,5*S*,10a*S*,10b*S*)-10b-hydroxy-2-(1-methylethyl)-5-(2-methylpropyl)-3,6-dioxooctahydro-8*H*-oxazolo[3,2-*a*]pyrrolo[2,1-*c*]pyrazin-2-yl]-7-methyl-4,6,6a,7,8,9-hexahydroindolo[4,3-*fg*]quinoline-9-carboxamide monomethanesulphonate.

**Content**
98.0 per cent to 101.0 per cent (dried substance).

**PRODUCTION**
The production method must be evaluated to determine the potential for formation of alkyl mesilates, which is particularly likely to occur if the reaction medium contains lower alcohols. Where necessary, the production method is validated to demonstrate that alkyl mesilates are not detectable in the final product.

**CHARACTERS**
**Appearance**
White or slightly coloured, fine crystalline powder.

**Solubility**
Practically insoluble in water, freely soluble in methanol, soluble in ethanol (96 per cent), sparingly soluble in methylene chloride.

It is very sensitive to light.

*The identification, tests and assay are to be carried out as rapidly as possible, protected from light.*

**IDENTIFICATION**

*First identification* B.

*Second identification* A, C, D, E.

A. Ultraviolet and visible absorption spectrophotometry (2.2.25).

*Test solution* Dissolve 10.0 mg in 10 ml of *methanol R* and dilute to 200.0 ml with 0.01 M hydrochloric acid.

*Spectral range* 250-380 nm.

*Absorption maximum* At 305 nm.

*Absorption minimum* At 270 nm.

*Specific absorbance at the absorption maximum* 120 to 135 (dried substance).

B. Infrared absorption spectrophotometry (2.2.24).

*Comparison* bromocriptine mesilate CRS.

C. Thin-layer chromatography (2.2.27). *Prepare the solutions immediately before use.*

*Solvent mixture* ethanol (96 per cent) R, methanol R, methylene chloride R (30:30:40 V/V/V).

*Test solution* Dissolve 10 mg of the substance to be examined in the solvent mixture and dilute to 10 ml with the solvent mixture.

*Reference solution* Dissolve 10 mg of *bromocriptine mesilate CRS* in the solvent mixture and dilute to 10 ml with the solvent mixture.

*Plate* TLC silica gel G plate R.

*Mobile phase* concentrated ammonia R, water R, 2-propanol R, methylene chloride R, ether R (0.1:1.5:3:88:100 V/V/V/V/V).

*Application* 10 μl.

*Development* Immediately in an unsaturated tank, over a path of 15 cm.

*Drying* In a current of cold air for 2 min.

*Detection* Spray with *ammonium molybdate solution R3* and dry at 100 °C until the spots appear (about 10 min).

*Results* The principal spot in the chromatogram obtained with the test solution is similar in position, colour and size to the principal spot in the chromatogram obtained with the reference solution.

D. To 0.1 g add 5 ml of *dilute hydrochloric acid R* and shake for about 5 min. Filter and add 1 ml of *barium chloride solution R1*. The filtrate remains clear. To a further 0.1 g add 0.5 g of *anhydrous sodium carbonate R*, mix and ignite until a white residue is obtained. Allow to cool and dissolve the residue in 7 ml of *water R* (solution A). Solution A gives reaction (a) of sulphates (2.3.1).

E. Solution A obtained in identification test D gives reaction (a) of bromides (2.3.1).

**TESTS**

**Appearance of solution**

The solution is clear (2.2.1) and not more intensely coloured than reference solution $B_5$, $BY_5$ or $Y_5$ (2.2.2, Method II).

Dissolve 0.25 g in *methanol R* and dilute to 25 ml with the same solvent.

**pH** (2.2.3)

3.1 to 3.8.

Dissolve 0.2 g in a mixture of 2 volumes of *methanol R* and 8 volumes of *carbon dioxide-free water R* and dilute to 20 ml with the same mixture of solvents.

**Specific optical rotation** (2.2.7)

+ 95 to + 105 (dried substance).

Dissolve 0.100 g in a mixture of equal volumes of *methanol R* and *methylene chloride R* and dilute to 10.0 ml with the same mixture of solvents.

**Related substances.**

Liquid chromatography (2.2.29).

*Solvent mixture* buffer solution pH 2.0 R, methanol R (50:50 V/V).

*Test solution* Dissolve 0.500 g of the substance to be examined in 5.0 ml of *methanol R* and dilute to 10.0 ml with *buffer solution pH 2.0 R*.

*Reference solution (a)* Dilute 1.0 ml of the test solution to 100.0 ml with the solvent mixture.

*Reference solution (b)* Dilute 1.0 ml of reference solution (a) to 10.0 ml with the solvent mixture.

*Reference solution (c)* Dissolve the contents of a vial of *bromocriptine mesilate for system suitability CRS* (containing impurities A and B) in 1.0 ml of the solvent mixture.

*Column:*
— size: $l$ = 0.12 m, Ø = 4 mm;
— stationary phase: octadecylsilyl silica gel for chromatography R (5 μm).

*Mobile phase:*
— mobile phase A: 0.791 g/l solution of *ammonium carbonate R*;
— mobile phase B: *acetonitrile R*;

| Time (min) | Mobile phase A (per cent V/V) | Mobile phase B (per cent V/V) |
|---|---|---|
| 0 - 30 | 90 → 40 | 10 → 60 |
| 30 - 45 | 40 | 60 |

*Flow rate* 2 ml/min.

*Detection* Spectrophotometer at 300 nm.

*Injection* 20 μl.

*Identification of impurities* Use the chromatogram supplied with *bromocriptine mesilate for system suitability CRS* and the chromatogram obtained with reference solution (c) to identify the peaks due to impurities A and B.

*Relative retention* With reference to bromocriptine: impurity C = about 1.2.

*System suitability* Reference solution (c):
— resolution: minimum 1.1 between the peaks due to impurities A and B.

*Limits:*
— impurity A: not more than 0.2 times the area of the principal peak in the chromatogram obtained with reference solution (b) (0.02 per cent);
— impurity C: not more than 4 times the area of the principal peak in the chromatogram obtained with reference solution (b) (0.4 per cent);
— impurities B, D, E, F, G: for each impurity, not more than twice the area of the principal peak in the chromatogram obtained with reference solution (b) (0.2 per cent) and not more than 1 such peak has an area greater than the area of the principal peak in the chromatogram obtained with reference solution (b) (0.1 per cent);
— total: not more than 1.5 times the area of the principal peak in the chromatogram obtained with reference solution (a) (1.5 per cent);
— disregard limit: 0.5 times the area of the principal peak in the chromatogram obtained with reference solution (b) (0.05 per cent), apart from the peak due to impurity A.

**Loss on drying** (*2.2.32*)

Maximum 3.0 per cent, determined on 0.500 g by drying *in vacuo* at 80 °C for 5 h.

**ASSAY**

Dissolve 0.500 g in 80 ml of a mixture of 10 volumes of *anhydrous acetic acid R* and 70 volumes of *acetic anhydride R*. Titrate with *0.1 M perchloric acid*, determining the end-point potentiometrically (*2.2.20*).

1 ml of *0.1 M perchloric acid* is equivalent to 75.1 mg of $C_{33}H_{44}BrN_5O_8S$.

**STORAGE**

In an airtight container, protected from light, at a temperature not exceeding − 15 °C.

**IMPURITIES**

*Specified impurities*  A, B, C, D, E, F, G.

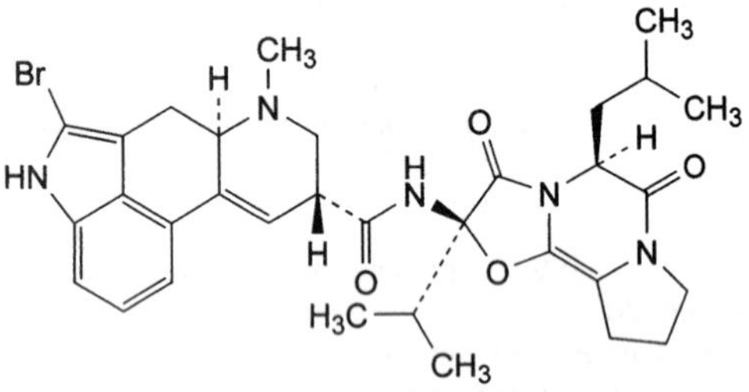

A. (6aR,9R)-5-bromo-N-[(2R,5S)-2-(1-methylethyl)-5-(2-methylpropyl)-3,6-dioxo-2,3,5,6,9,10-hexahydro-8H-oxazolo[3,2-a]pyrrolo[2,1-c]pyrazin-2-yl]-7-methyl-4,6,6a,7,8,9-hexahydroindolo[4,3-fg]quinoline-9-carboxamide (2-bromodehydro-α-ergocriptine),

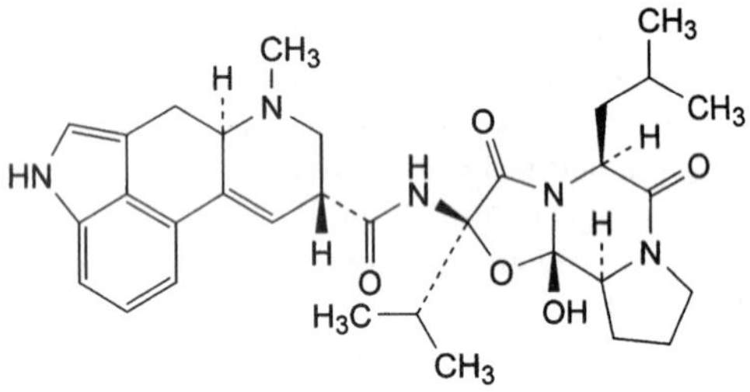

B. (6aR,9R)-N-[(2R,5S,10aS,10bS)-10b-hydroxy-2-(1-methylethyl)-5-(2-methylpropyl)-3,6-dioxooctahydro-8H-oxazolo[3,2-a]pyrrolo[2,1-c]pyrazin-2-yl]-7-methyl-4,6,6a,7,8,9-hexahydroindolo[4,3-fg]quinoline-9-carboxamide (α-ergocriptine),

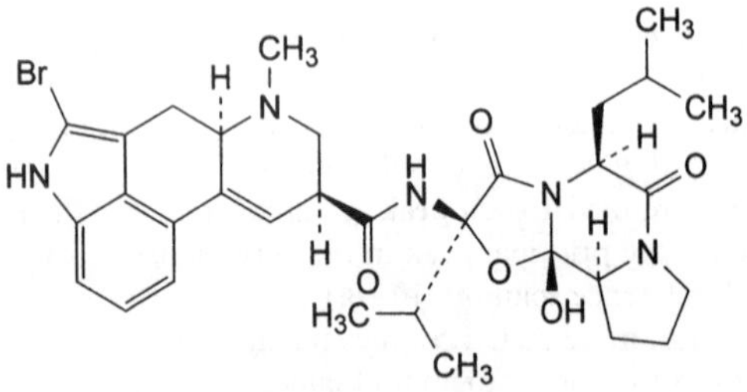

C. (6aR,9S)-5-bromo-N-[(2R,5S,10aS,10bS)-10b-hydroxy-2-(1-methylethyl)-5-(2-methylpropyl)-3,6-dioxooctahydro-8H-oxazolo[3,2-a]pyrrolo[2,1-c]pyrazin-2-yl]-7-methyl-4,6,6a,7,8,9-hexahydroindolo[4,3-fg]quinoline-9-carboxamide ((9S)-2-bromo-α-ergocriptine),

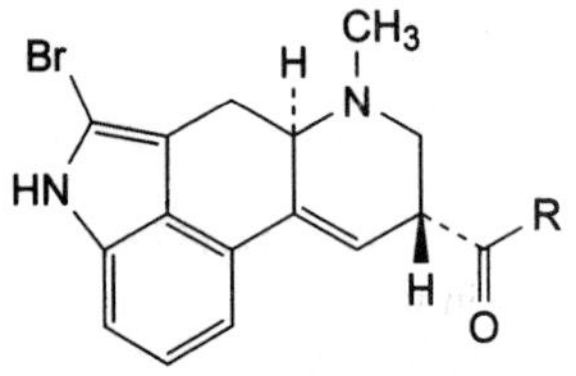

D. R = OH: (6aR,9R)-5-bromo-7-methyl-4,6,6a,7,8,9-hexahydroindolo[4,3-fg]quinoline-9-carboxylic acid,

E. R = NH₂: (6aR,9R)-5-bromo-7-methyl-4,6,6a,7,8,9-hexahydroindolo[4,3-fg]quinoline-9-carboxamide,

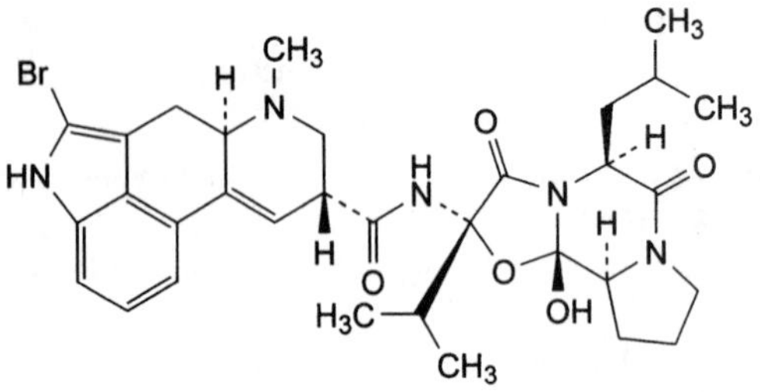

F. (6aR,9R)-5-bromo-N-[(2S,5S,10aS,10bS)-10b-hydroxy-2-(1-methylethyl)-5-(2-methylpropyl)-3,6-dioxooctahydro-8H-oxazolo[3,2-a]pyrrolo[2,1-c]pyrazin-2-yl]-7-methyl-4,6,6a,7,8,9-hexahydroindolo[4,3-fg]quinoline-9-carboxamide ((2'S)-2-bromo-α-ergocriptine),

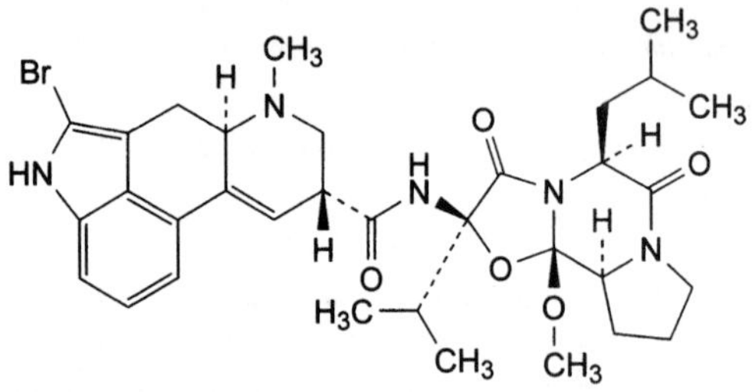

G. (6aR,9R)-5-bromo-N-[(2R,5S,10aS,10bS)-10b-methoxy-2-(1-methylethyl)-5-(2-methylpropyl)-3,6-dioxooctahydro-8H-oxazolo[3,2-a]pyrrolo[2,1-c]pyrazin-2-yl]-7-methyl-4,6,6a,7,8,9-hexahydroindolo[4,3-fg]quinoline-9-carboxamide (2-bromo-10'b-O-methyl-α-ergocriptine).

*Ph Eur*

# Bromperidol

(Ph Eur monograph 1178)

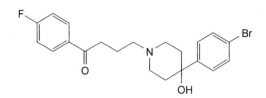

C₂₁H₂₃BrFNO₂ $\quad$ 420.3 $\quad$ 10457-90-6

## Action and use

Dopamine receptor antagonist; neuroleptic.

*Ph Eur*

## DEFINITION

4-[4-(4-Bromophenyl)-4-hydroxypiperidin-1-yl]-1-(4-fluorophenyl)butan-1-one.

## Content

99.0 per cent to 101.0 per cent (dried substance).

## CHARACTERS

### Appearance

White or almost white powder.

### Solubility

Practically insoluble in water, sparingly soluble in methanol and in methylene chloride, slightly soluble in ethanol (96 per cent).

## IDENTIFICATION

*First identification*  B, E.

*Second identification*  A, C, D, E.

A. Melting point (*2.2.14*): 156 °C to 159 °C.

B. Infrared absorption spectrophotometry (*2.2.24*).

*Preparation*  Discs.

*Comparison*  bromperidol CRS.

C. Thin layer chromatography (*2.2.27*).

*Test solution*  Dissolve 10 mg of the substance to be examined in *methanol R* and dilute to 10 ml with the same solvent.

*Reference solution (a)*  Dissolve 10 mg of *bromperidol CRS in methanol R* and dilute to 10 ml with the same solvent.

*Reference solution (b)*  Dissolve 10 mg of *bromperidol CRS* and 10 mg of *haloperidol CRS* in *methanol R* and dilute to 10 ml with the same solvent.

*Plate*  TLC octadecylsilyl silica gel plate R.

*Mobile phase*  tetrahydrofuran R, methanol R, 58 g/l solution of *sodium chloride R* (10:45:45 *V/V/V*).

*Application*  1 µl.

*Development*  In an unsaturated tank over a path of 15 cm.

*Drying*  In air.

*Detection*  Examine in ultraviolet light at 254 nm.

*System suitability*  Reference solution (b):
— the chromatogram shows 2 spots which may, however, not be completely separated.

*Results*  The principal spot in the chromatogram obtained with the test solution is similar in position and size to the principal spot in the chromatogram obtained with reference solution (a).

D. Dissolve about 10 mg in 5 ml of *anhydrous ethanol R*. Add 0.5 ml of *dinitrobenzene solution R* and 0.5 ml of *2 M alcoholic potassium hydroxide solution R*. A violet colour is produced that becomes brownish-red after 20 min.

E. To 0.1 g in a porcelain crucible add 0.5 g of *anhydrous sodium carbonate R*. Heat over an open flame for 10 min. Allow to cool. Take up the residue with 5 ml of *dilute nitric acid R* and filter. To 1 ml of the filtrate add 1 ml of *water R*. The solution gives reaction (a) of bromides (*2.3.1*).

## TESTS

### Appearance of solution

The solution is clear (*2.2.1*) and not more intensely coloured than reference solution Y₇ (*2.2.2, Method II*).

Dissolve 0.2 g in 20 ml of a 1 per cent *V/V* solution of *lactic acid R*.

### Related substances

Liquid chromatography (*2.2.29*).

*Test solution*  Dissolve 0.100 g of the substance to be examined in *methanol R* and dilute to 10.0 ml with the same solvent.

*Reference solution (a)*  Dissolve 2.5 mg of *bromperidol CRS* and 5.0 mg of *haloperidol CRS* in *methanol R* and dilute to 50.0 ml with the same solvent.

*Reference solution (b)*  Dilute 5.0 ml of the test solution to 100.0 ml with *methanol R*. Dilute 1.0 ml of this solution to 10.0 ml with *methanol R*.

*Column:*
— size: $l$ = 0.1 m, Ø = 4.0 mm;
— stationary phase: base-deactivated octadecylsilyl silica gel for chromatography R (3 µm).

*Mobile phase:*
— mobile phase A: 17 g/l solution of *tetrabutylammonium hydrogen sulphate R*;
— mobile phase B: acetonitrile R;

| Time (min) | Mobile phase A (per cent *V/V*) | Mobile phase B (per cent *V/V*) |
|---|---|---|
| 0 - 15 | 90 → 50 | 10 → 50 |
| 15 - 20 | 50 | 50 |
| 20 - 25 | 90 | 10 |

*Flow rate*  1.5 ml/min.

*Detection*  Spectrophotometer at 230 nm.

*Equilibration*  With *acetonitrile R* for at least 30 min and then with the mobile phase at the initial composition for at least 5 min.

*Injection*  10 µl; inject *methanol R* as a blank.

*Retention time*  haloperidol = about 5.5 min; bromperidol = about 6 min.

*System suitability*  Reference solution (a):
— resolution: minimum 3.0 between the peaks due to haloperidol and bromperidol; if necessary, adjust the concentration of acetonitrile in the mobile phase or adjust the time programme for the linear gradient elution.

*Limits:*
— impurities A, B, C, D, E, F: for each impurity, not more than the area of the principal peak in the chromatogram obtained with reference solution (b) (0.5 per cent);
— total: not more than twice the area of the principal peak in the chromatogram obtained with reference solution (b) (1 per cent);
— disregard limit: 0.1 times the area of the principal peak in the chromatogram obtained with reference solution (b) (0.05 per cent); disregard any peak due to the blank.

**Loss on drying** (*2.2.32*)

Maximum 0.5 per cent, determined on 1.000 g by drying in an oven at 105 °C.

**Sulphated ash** (*2.4.14*)

Maximum 0.1 per cent, determined on 1.0 g in a platinum crucible.

## ASSAY

Dissolve 0.300 g in 50 ml of a mixture of 1 volume of *anhydrous acetic acid R* and 7 volumes *of methyl ethyl ketone R*. Titrate with *0.1 M perchloric acid*, using 0.2 ml *of naphtholbenzein solution R* as indicator.

1 ml of *0.1 M perchloric acid* is equivalent to 42.03 mg of $C_{21}H_{23}BrFNO_2$.

## STORAGE

Protected from light.

## IMPURITIES

*Specified impurities*   *A, B, C, D, E, F.*

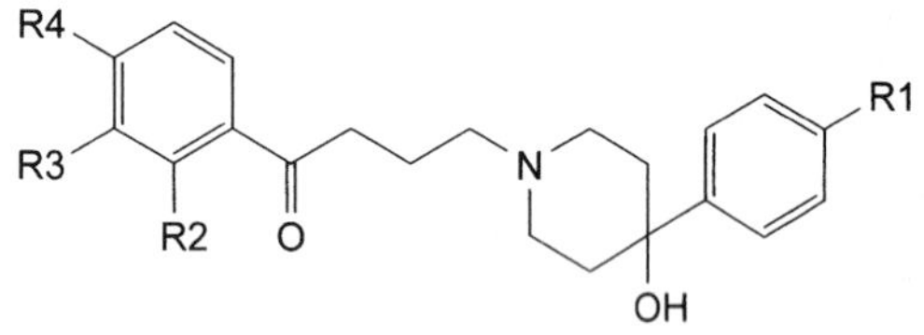

A. R1 = R2 = R3 = H, R4 = F: 1-(4-fluorophenyl)-4-(4-hydroxy-4-phenylpiperidin-1-yl)butan-1-one,

B. R1 = Br, R2 = F, R3 = R4 = H: 4-[4-(4-bromophenyl)-4-hydroxypiperidin-1-yl]-1-(2-fluorophenyl)butan-1-one,

C. R1 = $C_6H_5$, R2 = R3 = H, R4 = F: 4-[4-(biphenyl-4-yl)-4-hydroxypiperidin-1-yl]-1-(4-fluorophenyl)butan-1-one,

D. R1 = Br, R2 = H, R3 = $C_2H_5$, R4 = F: 4-[4-(4-bromophenyl)-4-hydroxypiperidin-1-yl]-1-(3-ethyl-4-fluorophenyl)butan-1-one,

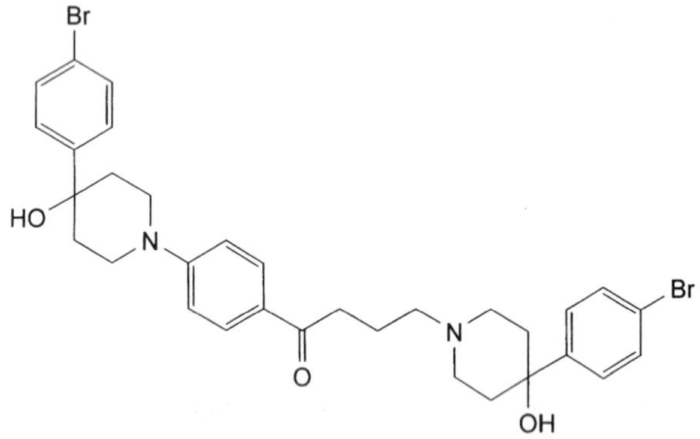

E. 4-[4-(4-bromophenyl)-4-hydroxypiperidin-1-yl]-1-[4-[4-(4-bromophenyl)-4-hydroxypiperidin-1-yl]phenyl]butan-1-one,

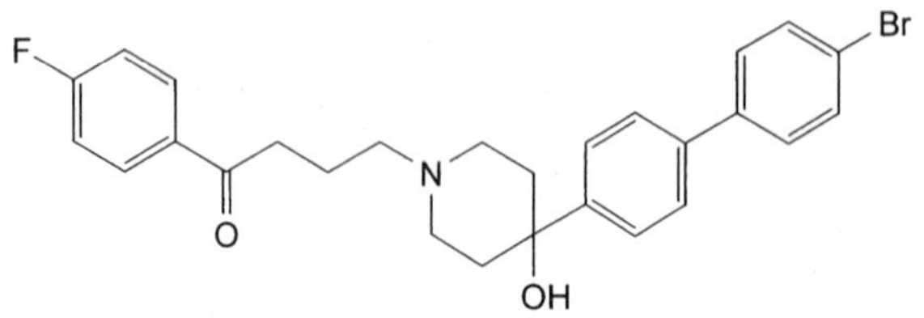

F. 4-[4-(4′-bromobiphenyl-4-yl)-4-hydroxypiperidin-1-yl]-1-(4-fluorophenyl)butan-1-one.

# Bromperidol Decanoate

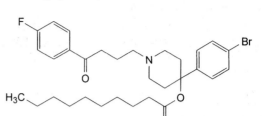

(*Ph Eur monograph 1397*)

$C_{31}H_{41}BrFNO_3$          574.6          *75067-66-2*

## Action and use

Dopamine receptor antagonist; neuroleptic.

## DEFINITION

4-(4-Bromophenyl)-1-[4-(4-fluorophenyl)-4-oxobutyl]piperidin-4-yl decanoate.

## Content

98.5 per cent to 101.0 per cent (dried substance).

## CHARACTERS

**Appearance**

White or almost white powder.

**Solubility**

Practically insoluble in water, very soluble in methylene chloride, soluble in ethanol (96 per cent).

mp: about 60 °C.

## IDENTIFICATION

A. Infrared absorption spectrophotometry (*2.2.24*).

*Preparation*   Mulls in *liquid paraffin R*.

*Comparison*   bromperidol decanoate CRS.

B. To 0.1 g in a porcelain crucible add 0.5 g of *anhydrous sodium carbonate R*. Heat over an open flame for 10 min. Allow to cool. Take up the residue with 5 ml of *dilute nitric acid R* and filter. To 1 ml of the filtrate add 1 ml of *water R*. The solution gives reaction (a) of bromides (*2.3.1*).

## TESTS

**Appearance of solution**

The solution is clear (*2.2.1*) and not more intensely coloured than reference solution $B_5$ (*2.2.2, Method II*).

Dissolve 2.0 g in *methylene chloride R* and dilute to 20 ml with the same solvent.

**Related substances**

Liquid chromatography (*2.2.29*). *Prepare the solutions immediately before use and protect from light.*

*Test solution*   Dissolve 0.100 g of the substance to be examined in *methanol R* and dilute to 10.0 ml with the same solvent.

*Reference solution (a)*   Dissolve 2.5 mg *of bromperidol decanoate CRS* and 2.5 mg of *haloperidol decanoate CRS* in *methanol R* and dilute to 50.0 ml with the same solvent.

*Reference solution (b)*   Dilute 5.0 ml of the test solution to 100.0 ml with *methanol R*. Dilute 1.0 ml of this solution to 10.0 ml with *methanol R*.

*Column:*

— *size: l* = 0.1 m, Ø = 4.0 mm;

— *stationary phase: base-deactivated octadecylsilyl silica gel for chromatography R* (3 μm).

*Mobile phase:*
— *mobile phase A*: 27 g/l solution of *tetrabutylammonium hydrogen sulphate R;*
— *mobile phase B: acetonitrile R;*

| Time (min) | Mobile phase A (per cent *V/V*) | Mobile phase B (per cent *V/V*) |
|---|---|---|
| 0 - 30 | 80 → 40 | 20 → 60 |
| 30 - 35 | 40 | 60 |
| 35 - 40 | 40 → 80 | 60 → 20 |

*Flow rate*   1.5 ml/min.

*Detection*   Spectrophotometer at 230 nm.

*Equilibration*   With *acetonitrile R* for at least 30 min and then with the mobile phase at the initial composition for at least 5 min.

*Injection*   10 μl; inject *methanol R* as a blank.

*Retention time*   Haloperidol decanoate = about 24 min; bromperidol decanoate = about 24.5 min.

*System suitability*   Reference solution (a):
— *resolution*: minimum 1.5 between the peaks due to haloperidol decanoate and bromperidol decanoate; if necessary, adjust the gradient or the time programme for the linear gradient elution.

*Limits:*
— *impurities A, B, C, D, E, F, G, H, I, J, K*: for each impurity, not more than the area of the principal peak in the chromatogram obtained with reference solution (b) (0.5 per cent);
— *total*: not more than 3 times the area of the principal peak in the chromatogram obtained with reference solution (b) (1.5 per cent);
— *disregard limit*: 0.1 times the area of the principal peak in the chromatogram obtained with reference solution (b) (0.05 per cent); disregard any peak due to the blank.

**Loss on drying** (2.2.32)
Maximum 0.5 per cent, determined on 1.000 g by drying *in vacuo* at 30 °C.

**Sulphated ash** (2.4.14)
Maximum 0.1 per cent, determined on 1.0 g in a platinum crucible.

**ASSAY**
Dissolve 0.450 g in 50 ml of a mixture of 1 volume of *anhydrous acetic acid R* and 7 volumes of *methyl ethyl ketone R*. Titrate with *0.1 M perchloric acid* using 0.2 ml of *naphtholbenzein solution R* as indicator.

1 ml of *0.1 M perchloric acid* is equivalent to 57.46 mg of $C_{31}H_{41}BrFNO_3$.

**STORAGE**
At a temperature below 25 °C, protected from light.

**IMPURITIES**
*Specified impurities   A, B, C, D, E, F, G, H, I, J, K.*

*Other detectable impurities* (the following substances would, if present at a sufficient level, be detected by one or other of the tests in the monograph. They are limited by the general acceptance criterion for other/unspecified impurities and/or by the general monograph *Substances for pharmaceutical use (2034)*. It is therefore not necessary to identify these impurities for demonstration of compliance. See also 5.10. *Control of impurities in substances for pharmaceutical use): L.*

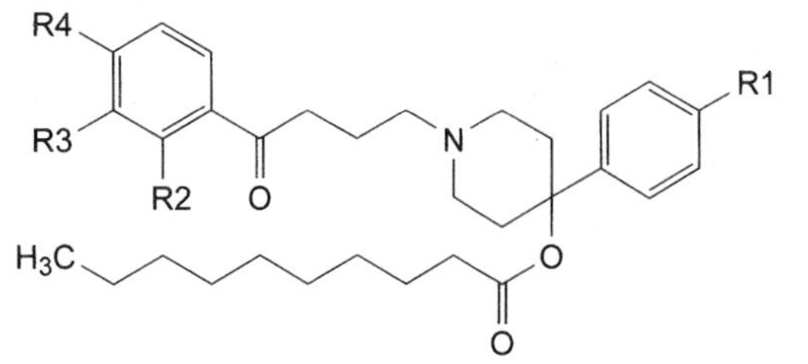

A. R1 = R2 = R3 = H, R4 = F: 1-[4-(4-fluorophenyl)-4-oxobutyl]-4-phenylpiperidin-4-yl decanoate,

B. R1 = Br, R2 = F, R3 = R4 = H: 4-(4-bromophenyl)-1-[4-(2-fluorophenyl)-4-oxobutyl]-piperidin-4-yl decanoate,

C. R1 = Br, R2 = H, R3 = $C_2H_5$, R4 = F: 4-(4-bromophenyl)-1-[4-(3-ethyl-4-fluorophenyl)-4-oxobutyl]-piperidin-4-yl decanoate,

F. R1 = $C_6H_5$, R2 = R3 = H, R4 = F: 4-(biphenyl-4-yl)-1-[4-(4-fluorophenyl)-4-oxobutyl]piperidin-4-yl decanoate,

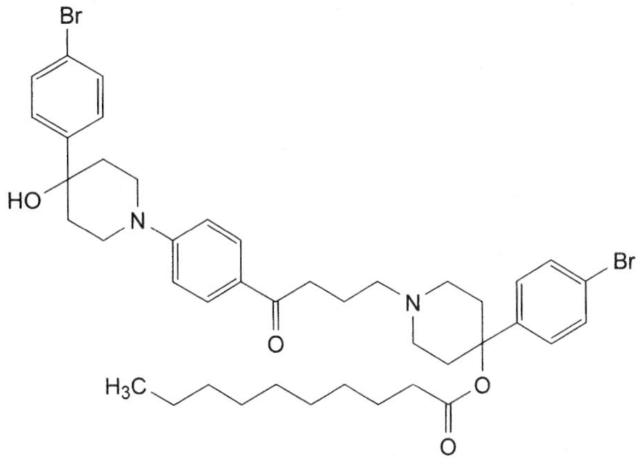

D. 4-(4-bromophenyl)-1-[4-[4-[4-(4-bromophenyl)-4-hydroxypiperidin-1-yl]phenyl]-4-oxobutyl]piperidin-4-yl decanoate,

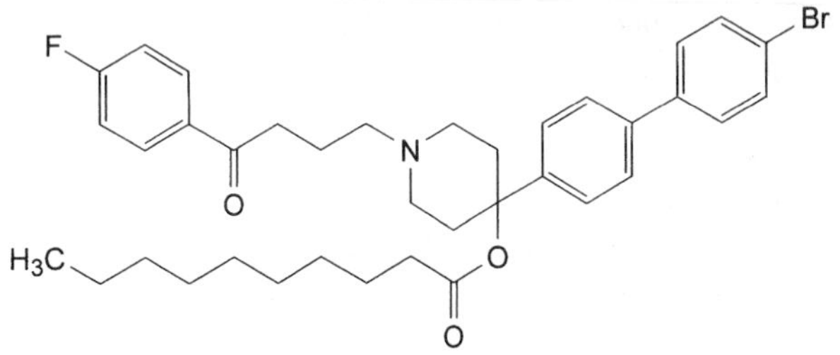

E. 4-(4'-bromobiphenyl-4-yl)-1-[4-(4-fluorophenyl)-4-oxobutyl]piperidin-4-yl decanoate,

G. bromperidol,

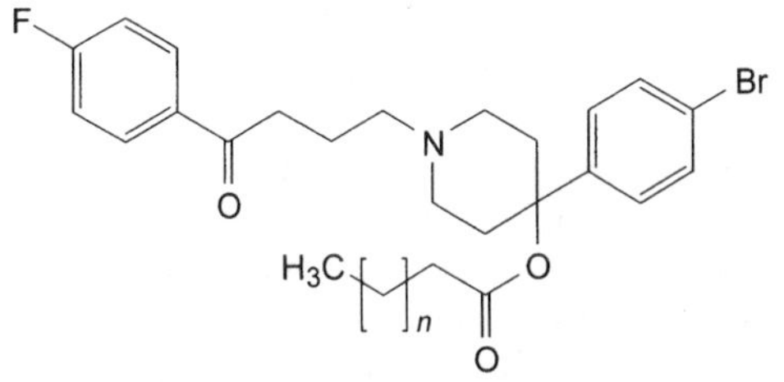

H. *n* = 5: 4-(4-bromophenyl)-1-[4-(4-fluorophenyl)-4-oxobutyl]piperidin-4-yl octanoate,

I. *n* = 6: 4-(4-bromophenyl)-1-[4-(4-fluorophenyl)-4-oxobutyl]piperidin-4-yl nonanoate,

J. n = 8: 4-(4-bromophenyl)-1-[4-(4-fluorophenyl)-4-oxobutyl]piperidin-4-yl undecanoate,

K. n = 9: 4-(4-bromophenyl)-1-[4-(4-fluorophenyl)-4-oxobutyl]piperidin-4-yl dodecanoate,

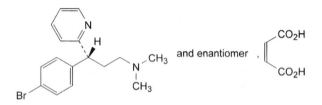

L. 1-(4-fluorophenyl)ethanone.

_____ Ph Eur

# Brompheniramine Maleate

*(Ph Eur monograph 0977)*

C₂₀H₂₃BrN₂O₄       435.3       *980-71-2*

**Action and use**
Histamine H₁ receptor antagonist; antihistamine.

**Preparation**
Brompheniramine Tablets

*Ph Eur* _____

## DEFINITION
(3RS)-3-(4-Bromophenyl)-N,N-dimethyl-3-(pyridin-2-yl)propan-1-amine (Z)-butenedioate.

## Content
98.0 per cent to 101.0 per cent (dried substance).

## CHARACTERS
**Appearance**
White or almost white, crystalline powder.

**Solubility**
Soluble in water, freely soluble in ethanol (96 per cent), in methanol and in methylene chloride.

## IDENTIFICATION
*First identification*  A, B, C, D, E.

*Second identification*  A, B, E, F.

A. Melting point (*2.2.14*): 130 °C to 135 °C.

B. Ultraviolet and visible absorption spectrophotometry (*2.2.25*).

*Test solution*  Dissolve 65 mg in *0.1 M hydrochloric acid* and dilute to 100.0 ml with the same acid. Dilute 5.0 ml of this solution to 100.0 ml with *0.1 M hydrochloric acid*.

*Spectral range*  220-320 nm.

*Absorption maximum*  At 265 nm.

*Specific absorbance at the absorption maximum*  190 to 210.

C. Infrared absorption spectrophotometry (*2.2.24*).

*Preparation*  Discs of *potassium bromide R*.

*Comparison*  *brompheniramine maleate CRS*.

D. Examine the chromatograms obtained in the test for related substances.

*System suitability*  Reference solution (c):
— the chromatogram shows 2 principal peaks with retention times corresponding to the retention times of the peaks obtained with reference solutions (a) and (b).

*Results*  The principal peak in the chromatogram obtained with the test solution is similar in retention time and size to the principal peak in the chromatogram obtained with reference solution (a).

E. Thin-layer chromatography (*2.2.27*).

*Test solution*  Dissolve 0.10 g of the substance to be examined in *methanol R* and dilute to 5.0 ml with the same solvent.

*Reference solution*  Dissolve 56 mg of *maleic acid R* in *methanol R* and dilute to 10 ml with the same solvent.

*Plate*  *TLC silica gel F₂₅₄ plate R*.

*Mobile phase*  water R, anhydrous formic acid R, methanol R, di-isopropyl ether R (3:7:20:70 V/V/V/V).

*Application*  5 µl.

*Development*  Over a path of 12 cm.

*Drying*  In a current of air for a few minutes.

*Detection*  Examine in ultraviolet light at 254 nm.

*Results*  The chromatogram obtained with the test solution shows 2 clearly separated spots. The upper spot is similar in position and size to the spot in the chromatogram obtained with the reference solution.

F. To 0.15 g in a porcelain crucible add 0.5 g of *anhydrous sodium carbonate R*. Heat over an open flame for 10 min. Allow to cool. Take up the residue in 10 ml of *dilute nitric acid R* and filter. To 1 ml of the filtrate add 1 ml of *water R*. The solution gives reaction (a) of bromides (*2.3.1*).

## TESTS
**Appearance of solution**
The solution is clear (*2.2.1*) and not more intensely coloured than reference solution BY₆ *2.2.2, Method II*).

Dissolve 2.0 g in *methanol R* and dilute to 20 ml with the same solvent.

**pH** (*2.2.3*)
4.0 to 5.0.

Dissolve 0.20 g in 20 ml of *carbon dioxide-free water R*.

**Optical rotation** (*2.2.7*)
− 0.2° to + 0.2° (measured in a 2 dm tube).

Dissolve 2.5 g in *water R* and dilute to 25.0 ml with the same solvent.

**Related substances**
Gas chromatography (*2.2.28*).

*Test solution*  Dissolve 0.10 g of the substance to be examined in 10 ml of *methylene chloride R*.

*Reference solution (a)*  Dissolve 10 mg of *brompheniramine maleate CRS* in *methylene chloride R* and dilute to 1 ml with the same solvent.

*Reference solution (b)*  Dissolve 5 mg of *chlorphenamine maleate CRS* (impurity A) in *methylene chloride R* and dilute to 1 ml with the same solvent.

*Reference solution (c)*  To 0.5 ml of the test solution add 0.5 ml of reference solution (b).

*Column:*
— *material*: glass;
— *size*: l = 2.3 m, Ø = 2 mm;

— *stationary phase*: acid- and base-washed *silanised diatomaceous earth for gas chromatography R* (135-175 μm) impregnated with 3 per cent *m/m* of *polymethylphenylsiloxane R*.

*Carrier gas*    nitrogen for chromatography R.

*Flow rate*    20 ml/min.

*Temperature*:
— *column*: 205 °C;
— *injection port and detector*: 250 °C.

*Detection*    Flame ionisation.

*Injection*    1 μl.

*Run time*    2.5 times the retention time of brompheniramine.

*System suitability*    Reference solution (c):
— *resolution*: minimum 1.5 between the peaks due to brompheniramine and impurity A.

*Limits*:
— *impurities A, B, C*: for each impurity, maximum 0.4 per cent of the area of the principal peak;
— *total*: maximum 1 per cent of the area of the principal peak;
— *disregard limit*: 0.1 per cent of the area of the principal peak.

**Heavy metals** *(2.4.8)*
Maximum 20 ppm.

1.0 g complies with test C. Prepare the reference solution using 2 ml of *lead standard solution (10 ppm Pb) R*.

**Loss on drying** *(2.2.32)*
Maximum 0.5 per cent, determined on 1.000 g by drying in an oven at 105 °C for 3 h.

**Sulphated ash** *(2.4.14)*
Maximum 0.1 per cent, determined on 1.0 g.

**ASSAY**
Dissolve 0.260 g in 50 ml of *anhydrous acetic acid R*. Titrate with *0.1 M perchloric acid*, determining the end-point potentiometrically (2.2.20).

1 ml of *0.1 M perchloric acid* is equivalent to 21.77 mg of $C_{20}H_{23}BrN_2O_4$.

**STORAGE**
Protected from light.

**IMPURITIES**
*Specified impurities*    A, B, C.

A. chlorphenamine,

B. dexchlorpheniramine,

and enantiomer

C. (3RS)-N,N-dimethyl-3-phenyl-3-(pyridin-2-yl)propan-1-amine (pheniramine).

_____ *Ph Eur*

# Bronopol

$C_3H_6BrNO_4$                    200.0                    52-51-7

**Action and use**
Antibacterial preservative.

**DEFINITION**
Bronopol is 2-bromo-2-nitropropane-1,3-diol. It contains not less than 99.0% and not more than 101.0% of $C_3H_6BrNO_4$, calculated with reference to the anhydrous substance.

**CHARACTERISTICS**
White or almost white crystals or crystalline powder.

Freely soluble in *water* and in *ethanol (96%)*; slightly soluble in *glycerol* and in *liquid paraffin*.

**IDENTIFICATION**
A. The *infrared absorption spectrum*, Appendix II A, is concordant with the *reference spectrum* of bronopol *(RS 031)*.

B. Dissolve 0.1 g in 10 ml of *water*, add 10 ml of 7.5M *sodium hydroxide* and, carefully with constant stirring and cooling, 0.5 g of *nickel-aluminium alloy*. Allow the reaction to subside, filter and carefully neutralise with *nitric acid*. The resulting solution yields reaction A characteristic of *bromides*, Appendix VI.

C. *Melting point*, after drying over *phosphorus pentoxide* at a pressure not exceeding 0.7 kPa, about 130°, Appendix V A.

**TESTS**
**Acidity or alkalinity**
pH of a 1% w/v solution, 5.0 to 7.0, Appendix V L.

**Related substances**
Carry out the method for *liquid chromatography*, Appendix III D, using the following solutions. Solution (1) contains 0.2% w/v of the substance being examined in the mobile phase. For solution (2) dilute a volume of solution (1) with sufficient mobile phase to produce a solution containing 0.0002% w/v of the substance being examined. Solution (3) contains 0.001% w/v each of *2-methyl-2-nitropropan-1,3-diol* and *tris(hydroxymethyl)nitromethane* in the mobile phase. Solution (4) contains 0.0002% w/v each of *2-methyl-2-nitropropane-1,3-diol, 2-nitroethanol, sodium bromide* and *tris(hydroxymethyl)nitromethane* and 0.2% w/v of the substance being examined in the mobile phase.

The chromatographic procedure may be carried out using (a) a stainless steel column (15 cm × 4.6 mm) packed with *octadecylsilyl silica gel for chromatography* (5 μm) (Phenomenex Luna C18 (2) is suitable) and maintained at 35°, (b) as the mobile phase with a flow rate of 1 ml per minute a mixture of 189 volumes of *water*, 10 volumes of *acetonitrile* and 1 volume of a 10% v/v solution of *orthophosphoric acid*, adjusting the pH to 3.0 using 2M *sodium hydroxide* and (c) a detection wavelength of 214 nm.

The test is not valid unless, in the chromatogram obtained with solution (4), the *resolution factor* between the peaks due to sodium bromide and tris(hydroxymethyl)nitromethane is at least 1.0 and the *resolution factor* between the peaks due to tris(hydroxymethyl)nitromethane and 2-nitroethanol is at least 1.5.

For solution (1) continue the chromatography for 3 times the retention time of the principal peak. In the chromatogram obtained with solution (1) the areas of any peaks corresponding to 2-methyl-2-nitropropane-1,3-diol and tris(hydroxymethyl)nitromethane are not greater than the area of the corresponding peaks in the chromatogram obtained with solution (3) (0.5% of each) and the area of any other *secondary peak* is not greater than the area of the principal peak in the chromatogram obtained with solution (2).

### Sulphated ash

Not more than 0.1%, Appendix IX A.

### Water

Not more than 0.5% w/w, Appendix IX C, Method I B. Use 5 g.

### ASSAY

In a flask fitted with a reflux condenser dissolve 0.4 g in 15 ml of *water* and add 15 ml of *7.5M sodium hydroxide*. Slowly, with caution, add 2 g of *nickel-aluminium alloy* through the reflux condenser, agitating the flask whilst cooling under running water. Allow the mixture to stand for 10 minutes and boil for 1 hour. Cool and filter under reduced pressure, washing the condenser, flask and residue with 150 ml of *water*. Combine the filtrate and washings, add 25 ml of *nitric acid* and 40 ml of *0.1M silver nitrate VS*, shake vigorously and titrate with *0.1M ammonium thiocyanate VS* using *ammonium iron(III) sulphate solution R2* as indicator. Repeat the operation without the substance being examined. The difference between the titrations represents the amount of silver nitrate required. Each ml of *0.1M silver nitrate VS* is equivalent to 20.00 mg of $C_3H_6BrNO_4$.

### STORAGE

Bronopol should be protected from light.

# Brotizolam

*(Ph Eur monograph 2197)*

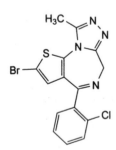

$C_{15}H_{10}BrClN_4S$      393.7      *57801-81-7*

### Action and use

Benzodiazepine.

*Ph Eur*

### DEFINITION

2-Bromo-4-(2-chlorophenyl)-9-methyl-6*H*-thieno-[3,2-*f*][1,2,4]-triazolo[4,3-*a*][1,4]diazepine.

### Content

99.0 per cent to 101.0 per cent (dried substance).

### CHARACTERS

### Appearance

White or yellowish powder.

### Solubility

Practically insoluble in water, sparingly soluble or slightly soluble in methanol, slightly soluble in ethanol (96 per cent).

### IDENTIFICATION

Infrared absorption spectrophotometry (*2.2.24*).

*Comparison*    brotizolam CRS.

### TESTS

### Related substances

Liquid chromatography (*2.2.29*). *Carry out the test protected from light and prepare the solutions immediately before use.*

*Test solution*    Dissolve 50.0 mg of the substance to be examined in *acetonitrile R* and dilute to 50.0 ml with the same solvent.

*Reference solution (a)*    Dilute 1.0 ml of the test solution to 100.0 ml of *acetonitrile R*. Dilute 1.0 ml of this solution to 10.0 ml with *acetonitrile R*.

*Reference solution (b)*    Dissolve 5 mg of the substance to be examined and 5 mg of *brotizolam impurity B CRS* in 50 ml of *acetonitrile R*. Dilute 2 ml of this solution to 20 ml with *acetonitrile R*.

*Column:*
— *size:* $l = 0.15$ m, Ø = 4.6 mm;
— *stationary phase:* octylsilyl silica gel for chromatography R (5 µm);
— *temperature:* 40 °C.

*Mobile phase:*
— *mobile phase A:* 2 g/l solution of *sodium heptanesulphonate monohydrate R;*
— *mobile phase B:* mix 25 volumes of a 2 g/l solution of *sodium heptanesulphonate R* and 75 volumes of *acetonitrile R;*

| Time (min) | Mobile phase A (per cent *V/V*) | Mobile phase B (per cent *V/V*) |
|---|---|---|
| 0 - 4 | 63 | 37 |
| 4 - 15 | 63 → 12 | 37 → 88 |
| 15 - 16 | 12 → 63 | 88 → 37 |
| 16 - 20 | 63 | 37 |

*Flow rate*    2.0 ml/min.

*Detection*    Spectrophotometer at 242 nm.

*Injection*    5 µl.

*Relative retention*    With reference to brotizolam (retention time = about 7.4 min): impurity A = about 0.5; impurity B = about 0.9.

*System suitability*    Reference solution (b):
— — *resolution:* minimum 5.0 between the peaks due to impurity B and brotizolam.

*Limits:*
— *impurity B:* not more than the area of the principal peak in the chromatogram obtained with reference solution (a) (0.1 per cent);
— *unspecified impurities:* for each impurity, not more than the area of the principal peak in the chromatogram obtained with reference solution (a) (0.10 per cent);
— *total:* not more than twice the area of the principal peak in the chromatogram obtained with reference solution (a) (0.2 per cent);
— *disregard limit:* 0.5 times the area of the principal peak in the chromatogram obtained with reference solution (a) (0.05 per cent).

### Chlorides (*2.4.4*)

Maximum 100 ppm.

Dissolve 0.67 g in 20.0 ml of *methanol R*, mix and filter.

**Loss on drying** (*2.2.32*)
Maximum 0.5 per cent, determined on 1.000 g by drying in an oven at 105 °C.

**Sulphated ash** (*2.4.14*)
Maximum 0.1 per cent, determined on 1.0 g.

## ASSAY
Dissolve 0.150 g in a mixture of 25 ml of *glacial acetic acid R* and 50 ml of *acetic anhydride R*. Titrate to the second point of inflexion with *0.1 M perchloric acid*, determining the end-point potentiometrically (*2.2.20*).

1 ml of *0.1 M perchloric acid* is equivalent to 19.68 mg of $C_{15}H_{10}BrClN_4S$.

## IMPURITIES
*Specified impurities* B.

*Other detectable impurities* (the following substances would, if present at a sufficient level, be detected by one or other of the tests in the monograph. They are limited by the general acceptance criterion for other/unspecified impurities and/or by the general monograph *Substances for pharmaceutical use (2034)*. It is therefore not necessary to identify these impurities for demonstration of compliance. See also *5.10. Control of impurities in substances for pharmaceutical use*): A.

A. R1 = CH$_3$, R2 = H: 4-(2-chlorophenyl)-9-methyl-6*H*-thieno[3,2-*f*][1,2,4]triazolo[4,3-*a*][1,4]diazepine (desbromobrotizolam),

B. R1 = H, R2 = Br: 2-bromo-4-(2-chlorophenyl)-6*H*-thieno[3,2-*f*][1,2,4]triazolo[4,3-*a*][1,4]diazepine (desmethylbrotizolam).

*Ph Eur*

# Buclizine Hydrochloride

$C_{28}H_{33}ClN_2,2HCl$          506.0          *129-74-8*

**Action and use**
Histamine H$_1$ receptor antagonist; antiemetic.

## DEFINITION
Buclizine Hydrochloride is (*RS*)-1-(4-*tert*-butylbenzyl)-4-(4-chlorobenzhydryl)piperazine dihydrochloride. It contains not less than 99.0% and not more than 100.5% of $C_{28}H_{33}ClN_2,2HCl$, calculated with reference to the dried substance.

## CHARACTERISTICS
A white or slightly yellowish, crystalline powder.

Practically insoluble in *water*; sparingly soluble in *propane-1,2-diol*; very slightly soluble in *ethanol (96%)*.

## IDENTIFICATION
A. The *infrared absorption spectrum*, Appendix II A, is concordant with the *reference spectrum* of buclizine hydrochloride (*RS 032*).

B. A 0.25% w/v solution in *ethanol (50%)* yields reaction A characteristic of *chlorides*, Appendix VI.

## TESTS
**Related substances**
Carry out the method for *liquid chromatography*, Appendix III D, using four solutions in the initial mobile phase containing (1) 0.0010% w/v of the substance being examined, (2) 0.50% w/v of the substance being examined, (3) 0.0010% w/v of *1,4-bis(4-chlorobenzhydryl)piperazine BPCRS* and (4) 0.50% w/v of *buclizine hydrochloride impurity standard BPCRS*.

The chromatographic procedure may be carried out using a stainless steel column (20 cm × 4 mm) packed with *octadecylsilyl silica gel for chromatography* (10 μm) (Nucleosil C18 is suitable). Use as the initial mobile phase *0.01M sodium heptanesulphonate* in a mixture of 55 volumes of *water* and 45 volumes of *acetonitrile* and as the final mobile phase *0.01M sodium heptanesulphonate* in a mixture of 20 volumes of *water* and 80 volumes of *acetonitrile*. Before use, adjust the pH of both the initial and final mobile phases to 4.0 with *1M orthophosphoric acid*. Carry out a linear gradient elution with a flow rate of 2 ml per minute for 30 minutes and maintain the final mobile phase for 10 minutes with the same flow rate. Use a detection wavelength of 230 nm.

The test is not valid unless the chromatogram obtained with solution (4) closely resembles the chromatogram supplied with *buclizine hydrochloride impurity standard BPCRS*.

In the chromatogram obtained with solution (2) the area of any peak corresponding to 1,4-bis(4-chlorobenzhydryl)-piperazine is not greater than the area of the peak obtained in the chromatogram with solution (3) and the area of any other *secondary peak* is not greater than the area of the peak in the chromatogram obtained with solution (1).

**Loss on drying**
When dried to constant weight at 100° to 105°, loses not more than 1.0% of its weight. Use 1 g.

**Sulphated ash**
Not more than 0.1%, Appendix IX A.

## ASSAY
Carry out Method I for *non-aqueous titration*, Appendix VIII A, using 0.4 g and determining the end point potentiometrically. Each ml of *0.1M perchloric acid VS* is equivalent to 25.30 mg of $C_{28}H_{33}ClN_2,2HCl$.

## IMPURITIES
A. 1,4-bis(4-chlorobenzhydryl)piperazine,

B. 4-chlorobenzhydrol, 1-(4-chlorobenzhydryl)piperazine, 4-chlorobenzophenone.

# Budesonide

*(Ph Eur monograph 1075)*

and epimer at C*

$C_{25}H_{34}O_6$      430.5      *51333-22-3*

## Action and use
Glucocorticoid.

## Preparations
Budesonide Aqueous Nasal Spray

Budesonide Nebuliser Suspension

Budesonide Powder for Inhalation

Budesonide Pressurised Inhalation

*Ph Eur*

## DEFINITION
Budesonide contains not less than 98.0 per cent and not more than the equivalent of 102.0 per cent of a mixture of the C-22S (epimer A) and the C-22R (epimer B) epimers of 16α,17-[(1RS)-butylidenebis(oxy)]-11β,21-dihydroxypregna-1,4-diene-3,20-dione, calculated with reference to the dried substance.

## CHARACTERS
A white or almost white, crystalline powder, practically insoluble in water, freely soluble in methylene chloride, sparingly soluble in alcohol.

## IDENTIFICATION
*First identification   A.*

*Second identification   B, C, D.*

A. Examine by infrared absorption spectrophotometry *(2.2.24)*, comparing with the spectrum obtained with *budesonide CRS*. Examine the substances prepared as discs.

B. Examine by thin-layer chromatography *(2.2.27)*, using as the coating substance a suitable silica gel with a fluorescent indicator having an optimal intensity at 254 nm.

*Test solution.*   Dissolve 25 mg of the substance to be examined in a mixture of 1 volume of *methanol R* and 9 volumes of *methylene chloride R* and dilute to 10 ml with the same mixture of solvents.

*Reference solution (a)*   Dissolve 25 mg *budesonide CRS* in a mixture of 1 volume of *methanol R* and 9 volumes of *methylene chloride R* and dilute to 10 ml with the same mixture of solvents.

*Reference solution (b)*   Dissolve 12.5 mg *triamcinolone acetonide CRS* in reference solution (a) and dilute to 5 ml with the same solution.

Apply separately to the plate 5 µl of each solution. Prepare the mobile phase by adding a mixture of 1.2 volumes of *water R* and 8 volumes of *methanol R* to a mixture of 15 volumes of *ether R* and 77 volumes of *methylene chloride R*. Develop over a path of 15 cm. Allow the plate to dry in air and examine in ultraviolet light at 254 nm. The principal spot in the chromatogram obtained with the test solution is similar in position and size to the principal spot in the

chromatogram obtained with reference solution (a). Spray with *alcoholic solution of sulphuric acid R*. Heat at 120 °C for 10 min or until spots appear. Allow to cool. Examine in daylight and in ultraviolet light at 365 nm. The principal spot in the chromatogram obtained with the test solution is similar in position, colour in daylight, fluorescence in ultraviolet light at 365 nm and size to the principal spot in the chromatogram obtained with the reference solution (a). The test is not valid unless the chromatogram obtained with reference solution (b) shows two clearly separated spots.

C. Dissolve about 2 mg in 2 ml of *sulphuric acid R*. Within 5 min, a yellow colour develops. Within 30 min, the colour changes to brown or reddish-brown. Add cautiously the solution to 10 ml of *water R* and mix. The colour fades and a clear solution remains.

D. Dissolve about 1 mg in 2 ml of a solution containing 2 g of *phosphomolybdic acid R* dissolved in a mixture of 10 ml of dilute *sodium hydroxide solution R*, 15 ml of *water R* and 25 ml of *glacial acetic acid R*. Heat for 5 min on a water-bath. Cool in iced water for 10 min and add 3 ml of dilute *sodium hydroxide solution R*. The solution is blue.

## TESTS
### Related substances
Examine by liquid chromatography *(2.2.29)* as described under Assay.

Inject 20 µl of reference solution (a). Adjust the sensitivity of the system so that the height of the peak corresponding to epimer B (the first of the two principal peaks) in the chromatogram obtained is not less than 50 per cent of the full scale of the recorder. Inject 20 µl of the test solution, 20 µl of reference solution (a) and 20 µl of reference solution (b). Continue the chromatography for 1.5 times the retention time of epimer B. In the chromatogram obtained with the test solution: the area of any peak, apart from the peaks corresponding to epimer A and epimer B, is not greater than the sum of the areas of the epimer peaks in the chromatogram obtained with reference solution (b) (0.5 per cent); the sum of the areas of any such peaks is not greater than the sum of the areas of the epimer peaks in the chromatogram obtained with reference solution (a) (1.5 per cent). Disregard any peak with an area less than 0.1 times the sum of the areas of the epimer peaks in the chromatogram obtained with reference solution (b).

### Epimer A
Examine by liquid chromatography *(2.2.29)* as described under Assay.

Inject 20 µl of the test solution. The content of epimer A (second peak) is 40.0 per cent to 51.0 per cent of the sum of the areas of the two epimer peaks of budesonide.

### Methanol
Not more than 0.1 per cent, determined by head-space gas chromatography using the standard addition method *(2.2.28)*.

*Test solution*   Dissolve 2.000 g of the substance to be examined in *dimethylacetamide R* and dilute to 20.0 ml with the same solvent.

*Reference solution*   Dilute 0.500 g of *methanol R* in *dimethylacetamide R* and dilute to 100.0 ml with the same solvent.

The following head-space conditions may be used:
— equilibration temperature: 80 °C,
— equilibration time: 30 min,
— transfer-line temperature: 85 °C,
— pressurisation time: 10 s,

— injection time: 10 s.

The chromatographic procedure may be carried out using:
— a fused-silica capillary column 30 m long and 0.32 mm in internal diameter coated with *macrogol 20 000 R* (film thickness 1 μm),
— *nitrogen for chromatography R* as the carrier gas at a pressure of 55 kPa,
— a flame-ionisation detector,

Maintaining the temperature of the column at 50 °C for 5 min, then raising the temperature at a rate of 30 °C per minute to 220 °C and maintaining at 220 °C for 2 min, and maintaining the temperature of the injection port at 250 °C and that of the detector at 300 °C.

**Loss on drying** (*2.2.32*)
Not more than 0.5 per cent, determined on 1.000 g by drying in an oven at 105 °C.

**ASSAY**
Examine by liquid chromatography (*2.2.29*). *Protect the solutions from light throughout the assay.*

*Test solution* Dissolve 25.0 mg of the substance to be examined in 15 ml of *acetonitrile R* and dilute to 50.0 ml with *phosphate buffer solution pH 3.2 R*. Allow to stand for at least 15 min before use.

*Reference solution (a)* Dilute 15.0 ml of the test solution to 100.0 ml with the mobile phase. Dilute 1.0 ml of the solution to 10.0 ml with the mobile phase.

*Reference solution (b)* Dilute 5.0 ml of the test solution to 100.0 ml with the mobile phase. Dilute 1.0 ml of the solution to 10.0 ml with the mobile phase.

*Reference solution (c)* Dissolve 25.0 mg of *budesonide CRS* in 15 ml of *acetonitrile R* and dilute to 50.0 ml with *phosphate buffer solution pH 3.2 R*.

The chromatographic procedure may be carried out using:
— a stainless steel column 0.12 m long and 4.6 mm in internal diameter packed with *octadecylsilyl silica gel for chromatography R* (5 μm),
— as mobile phase at a flow rate of 1.5 ml/min a mixture of 32 volumes of *acetonitrile R* and 68 volumes of *phosphate buffer solution pH 3.2 R*,
— as detector a spectrophotometer set at 240 nm.

Inject 20 μl of reference solution (c). Adjust the sensitivity of the system so that the height of the peak corresponding to epimer B (the first of the two principal peaks) in the chromatogram obtained is not less than 50 per cent of the full scale of the recorder. When the chromatograms are recorded in the prescribed conditions, the retention time for epimer B is about 16 min. If necessary, adjust the concentration of acetonitrile in the mobile phase (increasing the concentration to decrease the retention time). The test is not valid unless: in the chromatogram obtained with reference solution (c), the resolution between the peaks corresponding to epimer A and epimer B is not less than 1.5; the number of theoretical plates determined from the epimer B peak is at least 4000; the symmetry factor for the same peak is less than 1.5.

Inject 20 μl of reference solution (c) six times. The assay is not valid unless the relative standard deviation of the sum of the peak areas of the two epimers is at most 1.0 per cent. Inject alternatively the test solution and reference solution (c).

Calculate the percentage content of $C_{25}H_{34}O_6$ from the sum of the areas of the two epimer peaks.

**IMPURITIES**

A. 11β,16α,17,21-tetrahydroxypregna-1,4-diene-3,20-dione,

B. R = CH₃, R′ = H: 16α,17-[(1*RS*)-ethylidenebis(oxy)]-11β,21-dihydroxypregna-1,4-diene-3,20-dione,

F. R = R′ = CH₃: 16α,17-[1-methylethylidenebis(oxy)]-11β,21-dihydroxypregna-1,4-diene-3,20-dione,

C. 16α,17-[(1*RS*)-butylidenebis(oxy)]-11β-hydroxy-17-(hydroxymethyl)-*D*-homoandrosta-1,4-diene-3,17a-dione,

D. 16α,17-[(1*RS*)-butylidenebis(oxy)]-11β-hydroxy-3,20-dioxopregna-1,4-dien-21-al,

E. 16α,17-[(1*RS*)-butylidenebis(oxy)]-11β,21-dihydroxypregna-1,4,14-triene-3,20-dione,

G. 16α,17-[(1RS)-butylidenebis(oxy)]-11β,21-dihydroxypregn-4-ene-3,20-dione.

*Ph Eur*

# Bufexamac

*(Ph Eur monograph 1179)*

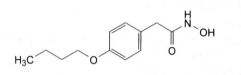

$C_{12}H_{17}NO_3$       223.3       2438-72-4

**Action and use**
Cyclo-oxygenase inhibitor; analgesic; anti-inflammatory.

*Ph Eur*

## DEFINITION
2-(4-Butoxyphenyl)-*N*-hydroxyacetamide.

**Content**
98.5 per cent to 101.5 per cent (dried substance).

## CHARACTERS
**Appearance**
White or almost white, crystalline powder.

**Solubility**
Practically insoluble in water, soluble in dimethylformamide, slightly soluble in ethyl acetate and in methanol.

## IDENTIFICATION
*First identification* B.

*Second identification* A, C.

A. Ultraviolet and visible absorption spectrophotometry (2.2.25).

*Test solution* Dissolve 20 mg in *methanol R* and dilute to 20 ml with the same solvent. Dilute 1 ml of this solution to 50 ml with *methanol R*.

*Spectral range* 210-360 nm.

*Absorption maxima* At 228 nm, 277 nm and 284 nm.

B. Infrared absorption spectrophotometry (2.2.24).

*Preparation* Discs.

*Comparison* bufexamac CRS.

C. Thin-layer chromatography (2.2.27).

*Test solution* Dissolve 10 mg of the substance to be examined in *methanol R* and dilute to 5 ml with the same solvent.

*Reference solution (a)* Dissolve 20 mg of *bufexamac CRS* in *methanol R* and dilute to 10 ml with the same solvent.

*Reference solution (b)* Dissolve 10 mg of *salicylic acid R* in reference solution (a) and dilute to 5 ml with the same solution.

*Plate* TLC silica gel $F_{254}$ plate R.

*Mobile phase* glacial acetic acid R, dioxan R, toluene R (4:20:90 V/V/V).

*Application* 10 µl.

*Development* Over a path of 15 cm.

*Drying* In a current of warm air.

*Detection* Examine in ultraviolet light at 254 nm.

*System suitability* Reference solution (b):
— the chromatogram shows 2 clearly separated spots.

*Results* The principal spot in the chromatogram obtained with the test solution is similar in position and size to the principal spot in the chromatogram obtained with reference solution (a).

## TESTS
**Related substances**
Liquid chromatography (2.2.29).

*Test solution* Dissolve 50.0 mg of the substance to be examined in the mobile phase and dilute to 20.0 ml with the mobile phase.

*Reference solution (a)* Dilute 5.0 ml of the test solution to 25.0 ml with the mobile phase. Dilute 1.0 ml of this solution to 100.0 ml with the mobile phase.

*Reference solution (b)* Dissolve 5 mg of *bufexamac CRS* and 5 mg of *salicylic acid R* in the mobile phase and dilute to 10 ml with the mobile phase. Dilute 1 ml of this solution to 10 ml with the mobile phase.

*Column:*
— *size*: l = 0.25 m, Ø = 4.6 mm;
— *stationary phase*: octadecylsilyl silica gel for chromatography R (5 µm) with a specific surface area of 350 m²/g and a pore size of 10 nm.

*Mobile phase* Mix 30 volumes of a 1.4 g/l solution of *dipotassium hydrogen phosphate R* and 70 volumes of *methanol R*, then adjust to pH 3.6 with *dilute phosphoric acid R*.

*Flow rate* 1 ml/min.

*Detection* Spectrophotometer at 275 nm.

*Injection* 20 µl.

*Run time* 4 times the retention time of bufexamac.

*System suitability* Reference solution (b):
— *resolution*: minimum 2.0 between the peaks due to salicylic acid and bufexamac.

*Limits:*
— *impurities A, B, C, D*: for each impurity, not more than the area of the principal peak in the chromatogram obtained with reference solution (a) (0.2 per cent);
— *total*: not more than 2.5 times the area of the principal peak in the chromatogram obtained with reference solution (a) (0.5 per cent);
— *disregard limit*: 0.05 times the area of the principal peak in the chromatogram obtained with reference solution (a) (0.01 per cent).

**Loss on drying** (2.2.32)
Maximum 0.5 per cent, determined on 1.000 g by drying in vacuo at 80 °C for 3 h.

**Sulphated ash** (2.4.14)
Maximum 0.1 per cent, determined on 1.0 g.

## ASSAY
Dissolve 0.200 g in 50 ml of *dimethylformamide R*. Titrate with *0.1 M lithium methoxide*, determining the end-point potentiometrically (2.2.20).

1 ml of *0.1 M lithium methoxide* is equivalent to 22.33 mg of $C_{12}H_{17}NO_3$.

## STORAGE

Protected from light.

## IMPURITIES

*Specified impurities   A, B, C, D.*

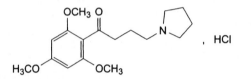

A. R = OH: 2-(4-butoxyphenyl)acetic acid,

B. R = OCH₃: methyl 2-(4-butoxyphenyl)acetate,

C. R = OC₄H₉: butyl 2-(4-butoxyphenyl)acetate,

D. R = NH₂: 2-(4-butoxyphenyl)acetamide.

*———————————————————————————— Ph Eur*

# Buflomedil Hydrochloride

*(Ph Eur monograph 1398)*

$C_{17}H_{25}NO_4,HCl$          343.9          *35543-24-9*

**Action and use**
Vasodilator.

*Ph Eur ——————————————————————————*

## DEFINITION

4-(Pyrrolidin-1-yl)-1-(2,4,6-trimethoxyphenyl)butan-1-one hydrochloride.

## Content

98.5 per cent to 101.5 per cent (dried substance).

## CHARACTERS

**Appearance**
White or almost white, microcrystalline powder.

**Solubility**
Freely soluble in water, soluble in alcohol, very slightly soluble in acetone.

## mp

About 195 °C, with decomposition.

## IDENTIFICATION

*First identification   B, D.*

*Second identification   A, C, D.*

A. Dissolve 25.0 mg in *alcohol R* and dilute to 50.0 ml with the same solvent. Dilute 2.0 ml to 20.0 ml with *alcohol R.* Examined between 220 nm and 350 nm (*2.2.25*), the solution shows an absorption maximum at 275 nm. The specific absorbance at the maximum is 143 to 149.

B. Infrared absorption spectrophotometry (*2.2.24*).

*Preparation   Discs.*

*Comparison   buflomedil hydrochloride CRS.*

C. Thin-layer chromatography (*2.2.27*).

*Test solution*   Dissolve 40 mg of the substance to be examined in *methanol R* and dilute to 2 ml with the same solvent.

*Reference solution*   Dissolve 40 mg of *buflomedil hydrochloride CRS* in *methanol R* and dilute to 2 ml with the same solvent.

*Plate*   TLC silica gel $F_{254}$ *plate R.*

*Mobile phase*   *triethylamine R, 2-propanol R, toluene R* (5:50:50 *V/V/V*).

*Application*   10 µl.

*Development*   Over a path of 15 cm.

*Drying*   In air.

*Detection*   Examine in ultraviolet light at 254 nm.

*Results*   The principal spot in the chromatogram obtained with the test solution is similar in position and size to the principal spot in the chromatogram obtained with the reference solution.

D. It gives reaction (a) of chlorides (*2.3.1*).

## TESTS

Solution S. Dissolve 2.5 g in *carbon dioxide-free water R* and dilute to 50 ml with the same solvent.

**Appearance of solution**
Solution S is clear (*2.2.1*) and colourless (*2.2.2, Method II*).

**pH** (*2.2.3*)
5.0 to 6.5 for solution S.

**Related substances**
Liquid chromatography (*2.2.29*).

*Test solution*   Dissolve 0.10 g of the substance to be examined in the mobile phase and dilute to 10.0 ml with the mobile phase.

*Reference solution (a)*   Dilute 0.5 ml of the test solution to 100.0 ml with the mobile phase. Dilute 5.0 ml of this solution to 10.0 ml with the mobile phase.

*Reference solution (b)*   Dissolve 2 mg of *buflomedil impurity B CRS* in the mobile phase. Add 0.5 ml of the test solution and dilute to 100 ml with the mobile phase.

*Column:*
— *size*: $l$ = 0.25 m, Ø = 4.6 mm,
— *stationary phase*: end-capped octadecylsilyl silica gel for chromatography *R* (5 µm),
— *temperature*: 40 °C.

*Mobile phase*   Mix 45 volumes of *acetonitrile R* and 55 volumes of a 9.25 g/l solution of *potassium dihydrogen phosphate R* adjusted to pH 2.5 with *phosphoric acid R*.

*Flow rate*   1 ml/min.

*Detection*   Spectrophotometer at 210 nm.

*Injection*   10 µl.

*Run time*   Twice the retention time of buflomedil.

*Retention time*   buflomedil = about 5 min.

*System suitability*   Reference solution (b):
— *resolution*: minimum 5.0 between the peaks due to buflomedil and impurity B.

*Limits:*
— *any impurity*: not more than the area of the principal peak in the chromatogram obtained with reference solution (a) (0.25 per cent),
— *total*: not more than twice the area of the principal peak in the chromatogram obtained with reference solution (a) (0.5 per cent),

— *disregard limit*: 0.2 times the area of the principal peak in the chromatogram obtained with reference solution (a) (0.05 per cent).

**Heavy metals** (*2.4.8*)
Maximum 10 ppm.

2.0 g complies with limit test C. Prepare the standard using 2 ml of *lead standard solution (10 ppm Pb) R*.

**Loss on drying** (*2.2.32*)
Maximum 0.5 per cent, determined on 1.000 g by drying in an oven at 105 °C for 2 h.

**Sulphated ash** (*2.4.14*)
Maximum 0.1 per cent, determined on 1.0 g.

**ASSAY**
Dissolve 0.300 g in 15 ml of *anhydrous acetic acid* R and add 35 ml of *acetic anhydride R*. Titrate with *0.1 M perchloric acid*, determining the end-point potentiometrically (*2.2.20*).

1 ml of *0.1 M perchloric acid* is equivalent to 34.39 mg of $C_{17}H_{26}ClNO_4$.

**IMPURITIES**

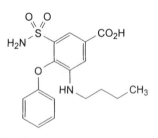

A. R1 = OH, R2 = OCH₃: 4-(pyrrolidin-1-yl)-1-(2-hydroxy-4,6-dimethoxyphenyl)butan-1-one,

B. R1 = OCH₃, R2 = OH: 4-(pyrrolidin-1-yl)-1-(4-hydroxy-2,6-dimethoxyphenyl)butan-1-one,

C. R1 = R2 = OH: 4-(pyrrolidin-1-yl)-1-(2,4-dihydroxy-6-methoxyphenyl)butan-1-one.

_____ *Ph Eur*

# Bumetanide

(*Ph Eur monograph 1076*)

$C_{17}H_{20}N_2O_5S$      364.4      *28395-03-1*

**Action and use**
Loop diuretic.

**Preparations**
Bumetanide Injection
Bumetanide Oral Solution
Bumetanide Tablets
Bumetanide and Slow Potassium Tablets

*Ph Eur* _____

**DEFINITION**
3-(Butylamino)-4-phenoxy-5-sulphamoylbenzoic acid.

**Content**
99.0 per cent to 101.0 per cent (dried substance).

**CHARACTERS**
**Appearance**
White or almost white, crystalline powder.

**Solubility**
Practically insoluble in water, soluble in acetone and in alcohol, slightly soluble in methylene chloride. It dissolves in dilute solutions of alkali hydroxides.

It shows polymorphism (*5.9*).

**mp**
About 233 °C.

**IDENTIFICATION**
Infrared absorption spectrophotometry (*2.2.24*).

*Comparison*    bumetanide CRS.

If the spectra obtained in the solid state show differences, dissolve the substance to be examined and the reference substance separately in *acetone R*, evaporate to dryness and record new spectra using the residues.

**TESTS**
**Appearance of solution**
The solution is clear (*2.2.1*) and colourless (*2.2.2, Method II*).

Dissolve 0.1 g in a 6 g/l solution of *potassium hydroxide R* and dilute to 20 ml with the same solution.

**Related substances**
Liquid chromatography (*2.2.29*).

*Test solution*    Dissolve 50 mg of the substance to be examined in the mobile phase and dilute to 25.0 ml with the mobile phase.

*Reference solution (a)*    Dilute 1.0 ml of the test solution to 100.0 ml with the mobile phase. Dilute 1.0 ml of this solution to 10.0 ml with the mobile phase.

*Reference solution (b)*    Dissolve 2 mg of *bumetanide impurity A CRS* and 2 mg of *bumetanide impurity B CRS* in the mobile phase and dilute to 10.0 ml with the mobile phase. Dilute 1.0 ml of this solution to 100.0 ml with the mobile phase.

*Column:*
— *size*: $l$ = 0.15 m, Ø = 4.6 mm,
— *stationary phase: end-capped octylsilyl silica gel for chromatography R* (3.5 μm).

*Mobile phase*    Mix 70 volumes of *methanol R*, 25 volumes of water for *chromatography R* and 5 volumes of a 27.2 g/l solution of *potassium dihydrogen phosphate R* previously adjusted to pH 7.0 with a 280 g/l solution of *potassium hydroxide R*; add *tetrahexylammonium bromide R* to this mixture to obtain a concentration of 2.17 g/l.

*Flow rate*    1.0 ml/min.

*Detection*    Spectrophotometer at 254 nm.

*Injection*    10 μl.

*Run time*    5 times the retention time of bumetanide.

*Relative retention*    With reference to bumetanide (retention time = about 6 min): impurity B = about 0.4; impurity A = about 0.6; impurity D = about 2.5; impurity C = about 4.4.

*System suitability*    Reference solution (b):
— *resolution*: minimum 2.0 between the peaks due to impurity A and impurity B.

*Limits:*
— *impurities A, B, C, D*: for each impurity, not more than the area of the principal peak in the chromatogram obtained with reference solution (a) (0.1 per cent),
— *other impurities*: for each impurity, not more than the area of the principal peak in the chromatogram obtained with reference solution (a) (0.1 per cent),
— *total*: not more than twice the area of the principal peak in the chromatogram obtained with reference solution (a) (0.2 per cent),
— *disregard limit*: 0.5 times the area of the principal peak in the chromatogram obtained with reference solution (a) (0.05 per cent).

**Loss on drying** (*2.2.32*)
Maximum 0.5 per cent, determined on 1.000 g by drying in an oven at 105 °C for 4 h.

**Sulphated ash** (*2.4.14*)
Maximum 0.1 per cent, determined on 1.0 g.

**ASSAY**
Dissolve 0.300 g in 50 ml of *alcohol R*. Add 0.1 ml of *phenol red solution R*. Titrate with *0.1 M sodium hydroxide* until a violet-red colour is obtained. Carry out a blank titration.

1 ml of *0.1 M sodium hydroxide* is equivalent to 36.44 mg of $C_{17}H_{20}N_2O_5S$.

**STORAGE**
Protected from light.

**IMPURITIES**
*Specified impurities    A, B, C, D.*

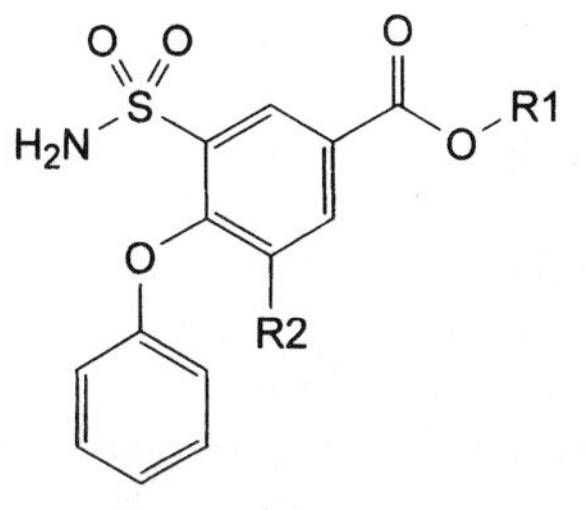

A. R1 = H, R2 = $NO_2$:
3-nitro-4-phenoxy-5-sulphamoylbenzoic acid,

B. R1 = H, R2 = $NH_2$:
3-amino-4-phenoxy-5-sulphamoylbenzoic acid,

C. R1 = $C_4H_9$, R2 = NH-$C_4H_9$: butyl 3-(butylamino)-4-phenoxy-5-sulphamoylbenzoate,

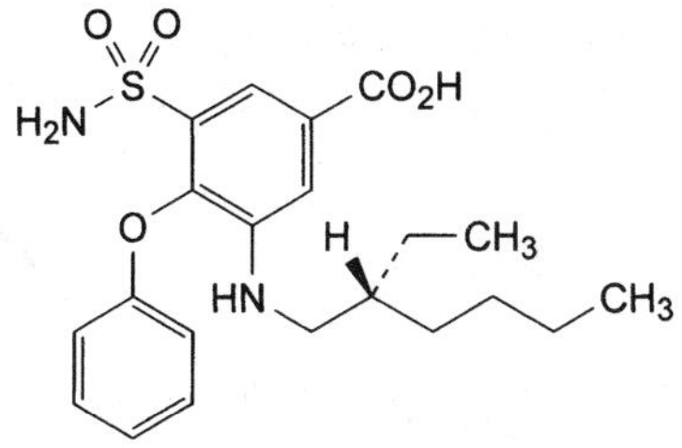

and enantiomer

D. 3-[[(2RS)-2-ethylhexyl]amino]-4-phenoxy-5-sulphamoylbenzoic acid.

*Ph Eur*

# Bupivacaine Hydrochloride

*(Ph Eur monograph 0541)*

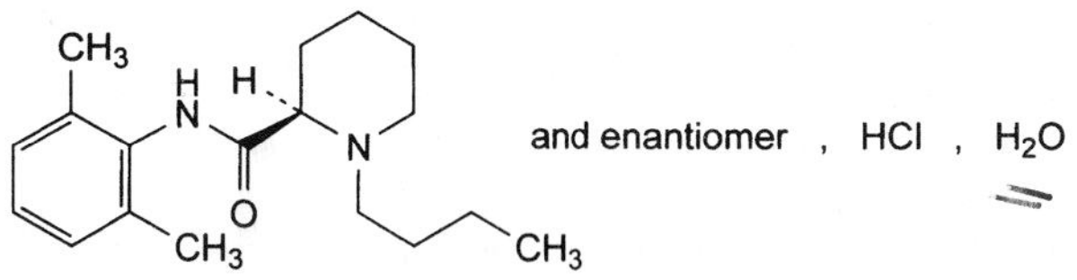

and enantiomer , HCl , $H_2O$

$C_{18}H_{28}N_2O,HCl,H_2O$          342.9          *14252-80-3*

**Action and use**
Local anaesthetic.

**Preparations**
Bupivacaine Injection
Bupivacaine Heavy Injection
Bupivacaine and Adrenaline Injection/Bupivacaine and Epinephrine Injection
Bupivacaine and Fentanyl Injection

*Ph Eur*

**DEFINITION**
(2RS)-1-Butyl-N-(2,6-dimethylphenyl)piperidine-2-carboxamide hydrochloride monohydrate.

**Content**
98.5 per cent to 101.0 per cent (dried substance).

**CHARACTERS**
**Appearance**
White or almost white, crystalline powder or colourless crystals.

**Solubility**
Soluble in water, freely soluble in alcohol.

**mp**
About 254 °C, with decomposition.

**IDENTIFICATION**
*First identification    A, D.*
*Second identification    B, C, D.*

A. Infrared absorption spectrophotometry (*2.2.24*).

*Preparation*    Discs of *potassium bromide R*.

*Comparison    bupivacaine hydrochloride CRS.*

B. Thin-layer chromatography (*2.2.27*).

*Test solution*    Dissolve 25 mg of the substance to be examined in *methanol R* and dilute to 5 ml with the same solvent.

*Reference solution*    Dissolve 25 mg of *bupivacaine hydrochloride CRS* in *methanol R* and dilute to 5 ml with the same solvent.

*Plate*    TLC silica gel G plate R.

*Mobile phase    concentrated ammonia R, methanol R* (0.1:100 *V/V*).

*Application*    5 µl.

*Development*    Over a path of 10 cm.

*Drying*    In air.

*Detection*    Spray with *dilute potassium iodobismuthate solution R*.

*Results*    The principal spot in the chromatogram obtained with the test solution is similar in position, colour and size to the principal spot in the chromatogram obtained with the reference solution.

C. Dissolve 0.1 g in 10 ml of *water R*, add 2 ml of *dilute sodium hydroxide solution R* and shake with 2 quantities, each of 15 ml, of *ether R*. Dry the combined ether layers over *anhydrous sodium sulphate R* and filter. Evaporate the ether, recrystallise the residue from *alcohol (90 per cent V/V) R* and dry under reduced pressure. The crystals melt (*2.2.14*) at 105 °C to 108 °C.

D. It gives reaction (a) of chlorides (*2.3.1*).

## TESTS

### Solution S

Dissolve 1.0 g in *carbon dioxide-free water R* and dilute to 50 ml with the same solvent.

### Appearance of solution

Solution S is clear (*2.2.1*) and colourless (*2.2.2, Method II*).

### Acidity or alkalinity

To 10 ml of solution S add 0.2 ml of *0.01 M sodium hydroxide*; the pH (*2.2.3*) is not less than 4.7. Add 0.4 ml of *0.01 M hydrochloric acid*; the pH is not greater than 4.7.

### Related substances

Gas chromatography (*2.2.28*).

*Internal standard solution*  Dissolve 25 mg of *methyl behenate R* in *methylene chloride R* and dilute to 500 ml with the same solvent.

*Test solution*  Dissolve 50.0 mg of the substance to be examined in 2.5 ml of *water R*, add 2.5 ml of *dilute sodium hydroxide solution R* and extract with 2 quantities, each of 5 ml, of the internal standard solution. Filter the lower layer.

*Reference solution (a)*  Dissolve 10 mg of the substance to be examined, 10 mg of *bupivacaine impurity B CRS* and 10 mg of *bupivacaine impurity E CRS* in 2.5 ml of *water R*, add 2.5 ml of *dilute sodium hydroxide solution R* and extract with 2 quantities, each of 5 ml, of the internal standard solution. Filter the lower layer and dilute to 20 ml with the internal standard solution.

*Reference solution (b)*  Dilute 1.0 ml of the test solution to 100.0 ml with the internal standard solution.

*Reference solution (c)*  Dilute 5.0 ml of reference solution (b) to 10.0 ml with the internal standard solution.

*Reference solution (d)*  Dilute 1.0 ml of reference solution (b) to 10.0 ml with the internal standard solution.

*Column:*
— *material*: fused silica,
— *size*: $l$ = 30 m, Ø = 0.32 mm,
— *stationary phase*: *poly(dimethyl)(diphenyl)siloxane R* (film thickness 0.25 µm).

*Carrier gas*  *helium for chromatography R*.

*Flow rate*  2.5 ml/min.

*Split ratio*  1:12.

*Temperature:*

|  | Time (min) | Temperature (°C) |
|---|---|---|
|  | 0 | 180 |
| Column | 0 - 10 | 180 → 230 |
|  | 10 - 15 | 230 |
| Injection port |  | 250 |
| Detector |  | 250 |

*Detection*  Flame ionisation.

*Injection*  1 µl.

*Relative retention*  With reference to bupivacaine (retention time = about 10 min): impurity C = about 0.5;

impurity A = about 0.6; impurity B = about 0.7; impurity D = about 0.8; impurity E = about 1.1; internal standard = about 1.4.

*System suitability*  Reference solution (a):
— *resolution*: minimum 3.0 between the peaks due to bupivacaine and impurity E.

*Limits:*
— *impurity B*: calculate the ratio (R) of the area of the principal peak to the area of the peak due to the internal standard from the chromatogram obtained with reference solution (c); from the chromatogram obtained with the test solution, calculate the ratio of the area of the peak due to impurity B to the area of the peak due to the internal standard: this ratio is not greater than R (0.5 per cent),
— *any other impurity*: calculate the ratio (R) of the area of the principal peak to the area of the peak due to the internal standard from the chromatogram obtained with reference solution (d); from the chromatogram obtained with the test solution, calculate the ratio of the area of any peak, apart from the principal peak, the peak due to impurity B and the peak due to the internal standard, to the area of the peak due to the internal standard: this ratio is not greater than R (0.1 per cent),
— *total*: calculate the ratio (R) of the area of the principal peak to the area of the peak due to the internal standard from the chromatogram obtained with reference solution (b); from the chromatogram obtained with the test solution, calculate the ratio of the sum of the areas of any peaks, apart from the principal peak and the peak due to the internal standard, to the area of the peak due to the internal standard: this ratio is not greater than R (1.0 per cent),
— *disregard limit*: ratio less than 0.01 times R (0.01 per cent).

### 2,6-Dimethylaniline

Maximum 100 ppm.

Dissolve 0.50 g in *methanol R* and dilute to 10 ml with the same solvent. To 2 ml of the solution add 1 ml of a freshly prepared 10 g/l solution of *dimethylaminobenzaldehyde R* in *methanol R* and 2 ml of *glacial acetic acid R* and allow to stand for 10 min. Any yellow colour in the solution is not more intense than that in a standard prepared at the same time and in the same manner using 2 ml of a 5 mg/l solution of *2,6-dimethylaniline R* in *methanol R*.

### Heavy metals (*2.4.8*)

Maximum 10 ppm.

Dissolve 2.0 g in a mixture of 15 volumes of *water R* and 85 volumes of *methanol R* and dilute to 20 ml with the same mixture of solvents. 12 ml of the solution complies with limit test B. Prepare the standard using lead standard solution (1 ppm Pb) obtained by diluting *lead standard solution (100 ppm Pb) R* with a mixture of 15 volumes of *water R* and 85 volumes of *methanol R*.

### Loss on drying (*2.2.32*)

4.5 per cent to 6.0 per cent, determined on 1.000 g by drying in an oven at 105 °C.

### Sulphated ash (*2.4.14*)

Maximum 0.1 per cent, determined on 1.0 g.

## ASSAY

Dissolve 0.250 g in a mixture of 20 ml of *water R* and 25 ml of *alcohol R*. Add 5.0 ml of *0.01 M hydrochloric acid*. Carry out a potentiometric titration (*2.2.20*), using *0.1 M ethanolic sodium hydroxide.* Read the volume added between the 2 points of inflexion.

1 ml of *0.1 M ethanolic sodium hydroxide* is equivalent to 32.49 mg of $C_{18}H_{29}ClN_2O$.

## STORAGE

Protected from light.

## IMPURITIES

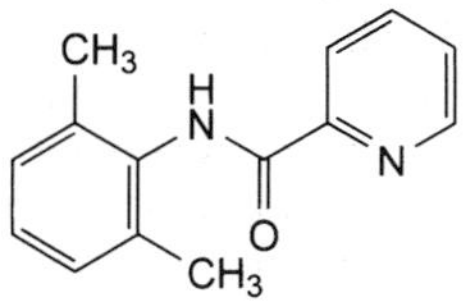

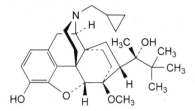

A. *N*-(2,6-dimethylphenyl)pyridine-2-carboxamide,

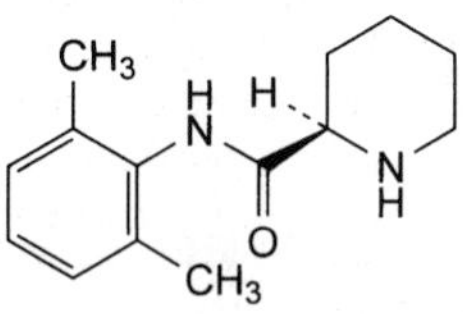

and enantiomer

B. (2*RS*)-*N*-(2,6-dimethylphenyl)piperidine-2-carboxamide,

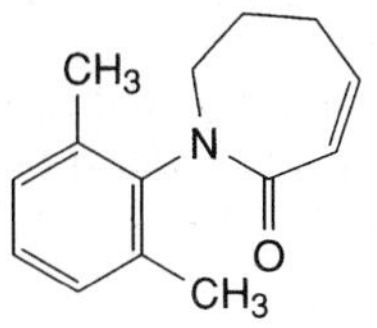

C. 1-(2,6-dimethylphenyl)-1,5,6,7-tetrahydro-2*H*-azepin-2-one,

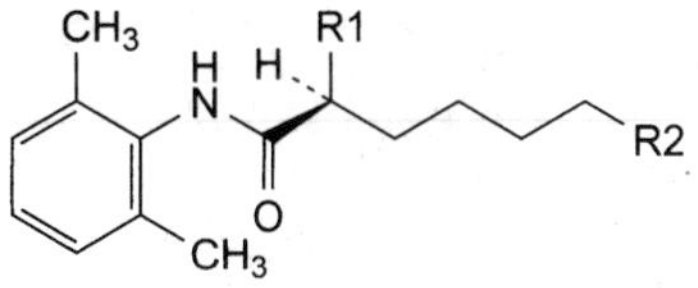

R1 and enantiomer R2

D. R1 = R2 = Cl: (2*RS*)-2,6-dichloro-*N*-(2,6-dimethylphenyl)hexanamide,

E. R1 = H, R2 = NH-$(CH_2)_3$-$CH_3$: 6-(butylamino)-*N*-(2,6-dimethylphenyl)hexanamide,

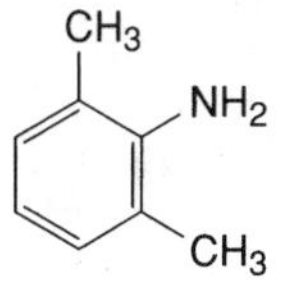

F. 2,6-dimethylaniline.

_____ *Ph Eur*

# Buprenorphine

(*Ph Eur monograph 1180*)

$C_{29}H_{41}NO_4$      467.6      *52485-79-7*

### Action and use

Opioid receptor partial agonist; analgesic.

*Ph Eur* _____

## DEFINITION

(2*S*)-2-[17-(Cyclopropylmethyl)-4,5α-epoxy-3-hydroxy-6-methoxy-6α,14-ethano-14α-morphinan-7α-yl]-3,3-dimethylbutan-2-ol.

### Content

98.5 per cent to 101.5 per cent (dried substance).

## CHARACTERS

### Appearance

White or almost white, crystalline powder.

### Solubility

Very slightly soluble in water, freely soluble in acetone, soluble in methanol, slightly soluble in cyclohexane. It dissolves in dilute solutions of acids.

### mp

About 217 °C.

## IDENTIFICATION

Infrared absorption spectrophotometry (*2.2.24*).

*Comparison* buprenorphine CRS.

## TESTS

### Solution S

Dissolve 0.250 g in *ethanol 96 per cent R* and dilute to 25.0 ml with the same solvent.

### Appearance of solution

Solution S is clear (*2.2.1*) and colourless (*2.2.2, Method II*).

### Specific optical rotation (*2.2.7*)

− 103 to − 107 (dried substance), determined on solution S.

### Related substances

Liquid chromatography (*2.2.29*).

*Test solution*   Dissolve 50.0 mg of the substance to be examined in *methanol R* and dilute to 10.0 ml with the same solvent.

*Reference solution (a)*   Dilute 1.0 ml of the test solution to 100.0 ml with *methanol R*. Dilute 1.0 ml of this solution to 10.0 ml with *methanol R*.

*Reference solution (b)*   Dissolve 5 mg of *buprenorphine for system suitability CRS* (containing impurities A, B, F, G, H and J) in 1.0 ml of *methanol R*.

*Column:*
— *size: l* = 0.05 m, Ø = 4,6 mm;
— *stationary phase: end-capped octadecylsilyl silica gel for chromatography R* (3.5 µm);
— *temperature*: 30 °C.

*Mobile phase:*
— *mobile phase A*: dissolve 5.44 g of *potassium dihydrogen phosphate R* in 900 ml of *water R*, adjust to pH 4.5 with a 5 per cent *V/V* solution of *phosphoric acid R* and dilute to 1000 ml with *water R*; mix 90 volumes of this solution and 10 volumes of *acetonitrile R*;
— *mobile phase B*: *acetonitrile R*;

| Time (min) | Mobile phase A (per cent *V/V*) | Mobile phase B (per cent *V/V*) |
|---|---|---|
| 0 - 2 | 89 | 11 |
| 2 - 12 | 89 → 64 | 11 → 36 |
| 12 - 15 | 64 → 41 | 36 → 59 |
| 15 - 20 | 41 → 39 | 59 → 61 |

*Flow rate*   1.3 ml/min.

*Detection*   Spectrophotometer at 240 nm.

*Injection*   5 μl.

*Identification of impurities*   Use the chromatogram supplied with *buprenorphine for system suitability CRS* and the chromatogram obtained with reference solution (b) to identify the peaks due to impurities A, B, F, G, H and J.

*Relative retention*   With reference to buprenorphine (retention time = about 8.5 min): impurity B = about 0.4; impurity J = about 1.1; impurity F = about 1.27; impurity H = about 1.33; impurity A = about 1.40; impurity G = about 1.8.

*System suitability*   Reference solution (b):
— *resolution*: minimum 2.0 between the peaks due to buprenorphine and impurity J.

*Limits:*
— *correction factor*: for the calculation of content, multiply the peak area of impurity G by 0.3;
— *impurity H*: not more than 2.5 times the area of the principal peak in the chromatogram obtained with reference solution (a) (0.25 per cent);
— *impurities A, B, F, J*: for each impurity, not more than twice the area of the principal peak in the chromatogram obtained with reference solution (a) (0.2 per cent);
— *impurity G*: not more than 1.5 times the area of the principal peak in the chromatogram obtained with reference solution (a) (0.15 per cent);
— *unspecified impurities*: for each impurity, not more than the area of the principal peak in the chromatogram obtained with reference solution (a) (0.10 per cent);
— *total*: not more than 7 times the area of the principal peak in the chromatogram obtained with reference solution (a) (0.7 per cent);
— *disregard limit*: 0.5 times the area of the principal peak in the chromatogram obtained with reference solution (a) (0.05 per cent).

**Loss on drying** (*2.2.32*)
Maximum 1.0 per cent, determined on 1.000 g by drying in an oven at 105 °C.

**ASSAY**
Dissolve 0.400 g in 40 ml of *anhydrous acetic acid R*. Titrate with *0.1 M perchloric acid*, determining the end-point potentiometrically (*2.2.20*).

1 ml of *0.1 M perchloric acid* is equivalent to 46.76 mg of $C_{29}H_{41}NO_4$.

**STORAGE**
Protected from light.

**IMPURITIES**
*Specified impurities*   A, B, F, G, H, J.

*Other detectable impurities*   (The following substances would, if present at a sufficient level, be detected by one or other of the tests in the monograph. They are limited by the general acceptance criterion for other/unspecified impurities and/or by the general monograph Substances for pharmaceutical use (2034). It is therefore not necessary to identify these impurities for demonstration of compliance. See also *5.10. Control of impurities in substances for pharmaceutical use*): C, D, E, I.

A. R = CH$_2$-CH$_2$-CH=CH$_2$: (2*S*)-2-[17-(but-3-enyl)-4,5α-epoxy-3-hydroxy-6-methoxy-6α,14-ethano-14α-morphinan-7α-yl]-3,3-dimethylbutan-2-ol,

B. R = H: (2*S*)-2-(4,5α-epoxy-3-hydroxy-6-methoxy-6α,14-ethano-14α-morphinan-7α-yl)-3,3-dimethylbutan-2-ol (norbuprenorphine),

H. R = CH$_2$-CH$_2$-CH$_2$-CH$_3$: (2*S*)-2-[17-butyl-4,5α-epoxy-3-hydroxy-6-methoxy-6α,14-ethano-14α-morphinan-7α-yl]3,3-dimethylbutan-2-ol,

C. 4,5α-epoxy-7α-[(1*S*)-1-hydroxy-1,2,2-trimethylpropyl]-3,6-dimethoxy-6α,14-ethano-14α-morphinan-17-carbonitrile,

D. R1 = R2 = CH$_3$: (2*S*)-2-[17-(cyclopropylmethyl)-4,5α-epoxy-3,6-dimethoxy-6α,14-ethano-14α-morphinan-7α-yl]-3,3-dimethylbutan-2-ol (3-*O*-methylbuprenorphine),

E. R1 = R2 = H: (2*S*)-2-[17-(cyclopropylmethyl)-4,5α-epoxy-3,6-dihydroxy-6α,14-ethano-14α-morphinan-7α-yl]-3,3-dimethylbutan-2-ol (6-*O*-desmethylbuprenorphine),

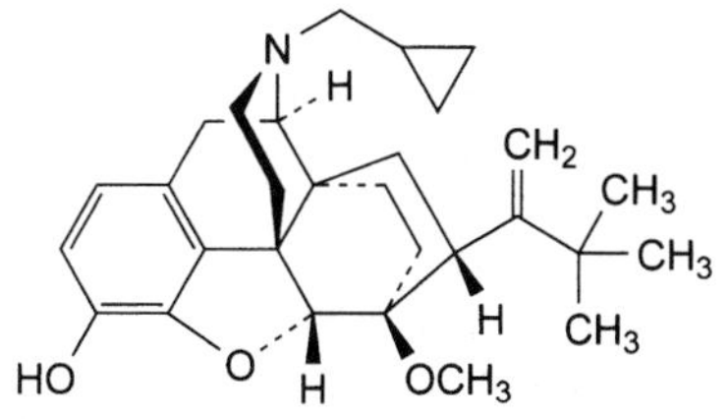

F. 17-(cyclopropylmethyl)-4,5α-epoxy-6-methoxy-7α-[1-(1,1-dimethylethyl)ethenyl]-6α,14-ethano-14α-morphinan-3-ol,

—R =

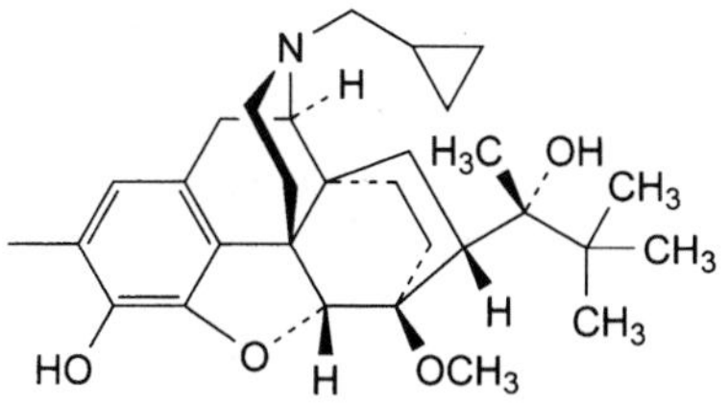

G. R-R: 17,17′-di(cyclopropylmethyl)-4,5α;4′,5α′-diepoxy-7α,7α′-di[(1S)-1-hydroxy-1,2,2-trimethylpropyl]-6,6′-dimethoxy-2,2′-bi(6α,14-ethano-14α-morphinan)-3,3′-diol (2,2′-bibuprenorphine),

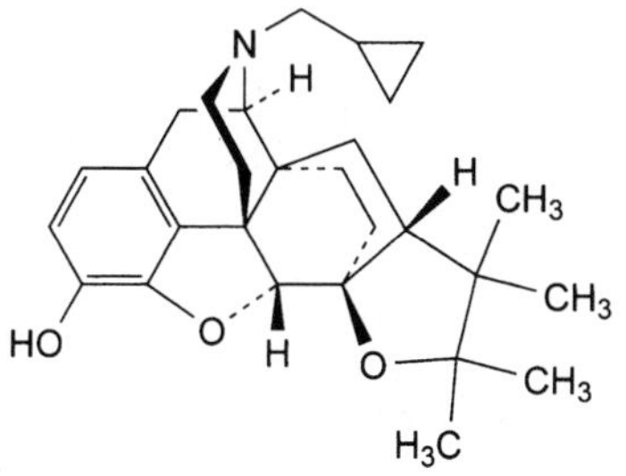

I. 17-(cyclopropylmethyl)-4″,4″,5″,5″-tetramethyl-4″,5″-dihydro-(7βH)-6α,14-ethanol-(5βH)-difurano-[2′,3′,4′,5′:4,12,13,5;2″,3″:6,7]-14α-morphinan-3-ol,

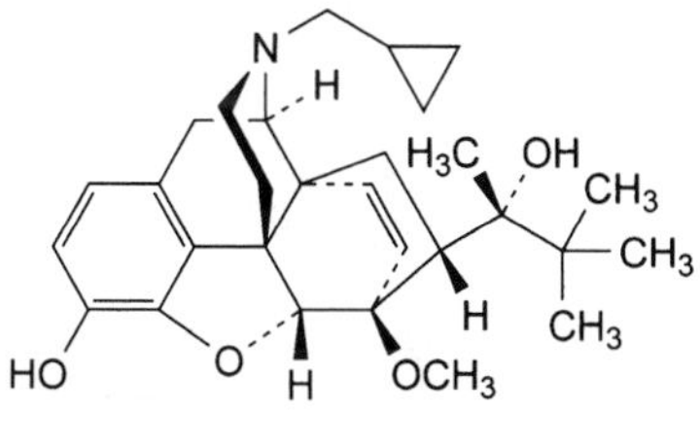

J. (2S)-2-[17-(cyclopropylmethyl)-4,5α-epoxy-3-hydroxy-6-methoxy-6α,14-etheno-14α-morphinan-7α-yl]-3,3-dimethylbutan-2-ol.

*Ph Eur*

# Buprenorphine Hydrochloride

(*Ph Eur monograph 1181*)

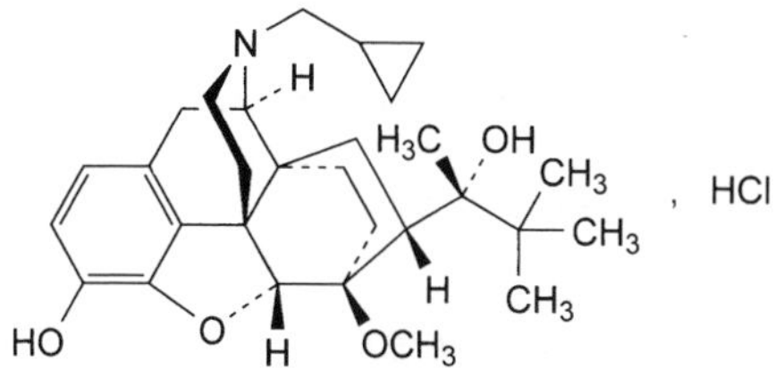

C$_{29}$H$_{41}$NO$_4$,HCl    504.1    *53152-21-9*

**Action and use**

Opioid receptor partial agonist; analgesic.

*Ph Eur*

## DEFINITION

(2S)-2-[17-(Cyclopropylmethyl)-4,5α-epoxy-3-hydroxy-6-methoxy-6α,14-ethano-14α-morphinan-7α-yl]-3,3-dimethylbutan-2-ol hydrochloride.

**Content**

98.5 per cent to 101.5 per cent (dried substance).

## CHARACTERS

**Appearance**

White or almost white, crystalline powder.

**Solubility**

Sparingly soluble in water, freely soluble in methanol, soluble in ethanol (96 per cent), practically insoluble in cyclohexane.

## IDENTIFICATION

A. Infrared absorption spectrophotometry (*2.2.24*).

*Comparison*   buprenorphine hydrochloride CRS.

B. 3 ml of solution S (see Tests) gives reaction (a) of chlorides (*2.3.1*).

## TESTS

**Solution S**

Dissolve 0.250 g in 5.0 ml of *methanol R* and, while stirring, dilute to 25.0 ml with *carbon dioxide-free water R*.

**Appearance of solution**

Solution S is clear (*2.2.1*) and colourless (*2.2.2, Method II*).

**Acidity or alkalinity**

To 10.0 ml of solution S add 0.05 ml of *methyl red solution R*. Not more than 0.2 ml of *0.02 M sodium hydroxide* or *0.02 M hydrochloric acid* is required to change the colour of the indicator.

**Specific optical rotation** (*2.2.7*)

– 92 to – 98 (dried substance).

Dissolve 0.200 g in *methanol R* and dilute to 20.0 ml with the same solvent.

**Related substances**

Liquid chromatography (*2.2.29*).

*Test solution*   Dissolve 50.0 mg of the substance to be examined in *methanol R* and dilute to 10.0 ml with the same solvent.

*Reference solution (a)*   Dilute 1.0 ml of the test solution to 100.0 ml with *methanol R*. Dilute 1.0 ml of this solution to 10.0 ml with *methanol R*.

*Reference solution (b)*   Dissolve 5 mg of *buprenorphine for system suitability CRS* (containing impurities A, B, F, G, H and J) in 1.0 ml of *methanol R*.

**Column:**
— *size:* l = 0.05 m, Ø = 4,6 mm;
— *stationary phase: end-capped octadecylsilyl silica gel for chromatography R* (3.5 μm);
— *temperature:* 30 °C.

**Mobile phase:**
— *mobile phase A*: dissolve 5.44 g of *potassium dihydrogen phosphate R* in 900 ml of *water R*, adjust to pH 4.5 with a 5 per cent *V/V* solution of *phosphoric acid R* and dilute to 1000 ml with *water R*; mix 90 volumes of this solution and 10 volumes of *acetonitrile R*;
— *mobile phase B*: *acetonitrile R*;

| Time (min) | Mobile phase A (per cent *V/V*) | Mobile phase B (per cent *V/V*) |
|---|---|---|
| 0 - 2 | 89 | 11 |
| 2 - 12 | 89 → 64 | 11 → 36 |
| 12 - 15 | 64 → 41 | 36 → 59 |
| 15 - 20 | 41 → 39 | 59 → 61 |

*Flow rate*   1.3 ml/min.

*Detection*   Spectrophotometer at 240 nm.

*Injection*   5 μl.

*Identification of impurities*   Use the chromatogram supplied with *buprenorphine for system suitability CRS* and the chromatogram obtained with reference solution (b) to identify the peaks due to impurities A, B, F, G, H and J.

*Relative retention*   With reference to buprenorphine (retention time = about 8.5 min): impurity B = about 0.4; impurity J = about 1.1; impurity F = about 1.27; impurity H = about 1.33; impurity A = about 1.40; impurity G = about 1.8.

*System suitability*   Reference solution (b):
— *resolution*: minimum 2.0 between the peaks due to buprenorphine and impurity J.

*Limits:*
— *correction factor*: for the calculation of content, multiply the peak area of impurity G by 0.3;
— *impurity H*: not more than 2.5 times the area of the principal peak in the chromatogram obtained with reference solution (a) (0.25 per cent);
— *impurities A, B, F, J*: for each impurity, not more than twice the area of the principal peak in the chromatogram obtained with reference solution (a) (0.2 per cent);
— *impurity G*: not more than 1.5 times the area of the principal peak in the chromatogram obtained with reference solution (a) (0.15 per cent);
— *unspecified impurities*: for each impurity, not more than the area of the principal peak in the chromatogram obtained with reference solution (a) (0.10 per cent);
— *total*: not more than 7 times the area of the principal peak in the chromatogram obtained with reference solution (a) (0.7 per cent);
— *disregard limit*: 0.5 times the area of the principal peak in the chromatogram obtained with reference solution (a) (0.05 per cent).

**Loss on drying** (2.2.32)
Maximum 1.0 per cent, determined on 1.000 g by heating in an oven at 115-120 °C.

**ASSAY**
Dissolve 0.400 g in a mixture of 5 ml of *0.01 M hydrochloric acid* and 50 ml of *ethanol (96 per cent) R*. Carry out a potentiometric titration (2.2.20), using *0.1 M sodium hydroxide*. Read the volume added between the 2 points of inflexion. Carry out a blank titration.

1 ml of 0.1 M sodium hydroxide is equivalent to 50.41 mg of $C_{29}H_{42}ClNO_4$.

**STORAGE**
Protected from light.

**IMPURITIES**
*Specified impurities*   A, B, F, G, H, J.

*Other detectable impurities*   (The following substances would, if present at a sufficient level, be detected by one or other of the tests in the monograph. They are limited by the general acceptance criterion for other/unspecified impurities and/or by the general monograph *Substances for pharmaceutical use (2034)*. It is therefore not necessary to identify these impurities for demonstration of compliance. See also 5.10. Control of impurities in substances for pharmaceutical use): C, D, E, I.

A. R = CH₂-CH₂-CH=CH₂: (2S)-2-[17-(but-3-enyl)-4,5α-epoxy-3-hydroxy-6-methoxy-6α,14-ethano-14α-morphinan-7α-yl]-3,3-dimethylbutan-2-ol,

B. R = H: (2S)-2-(4,5α-epoxy-3-hydroxy-6-methoxy-6α,14-ethano-14α-morphinan-7α-yl)-3,3-dimethylbutan-2-ol (norbuprenorphine),

H. R = CH₂-CH₂-CH₂-CH₃: (2S)-2-[17-butyl-4,5α-epoxy-3-hydroxy-6-methoxy-6α,14-ethano-14α-morphinan-7α-yl]3,3-dimethylbutan-2-ol,

C. 4,5α-epoxy-7α-[(1S)-1-hydroxy-1,2,2-trimethylpropyl]-3,6-dimethoxy-6α,14-ethano-14α-morphinan-17-carbonitrile,

D. R1 = R2 = CH₃: (2S)-2-[17-(cyclopropylmethyl)-4,5α-epoxy-3,6-dimethoxy-6α,14-ethano-14α-morphinan-7α-yl]-3,3-dimethylbutan-2-ol (3-O-methylbuprenorphine),

E. R1 = R2 = H: (2S)-2-[17-(cyclopropylmethyl)-4,5α-epoxy-3,6-dihydroxy-6α,14-ethano-14α-morphinan-7α-yl]-3,3-dimethylbutan-2-ol (6-O-desmethylbuprenorphine),

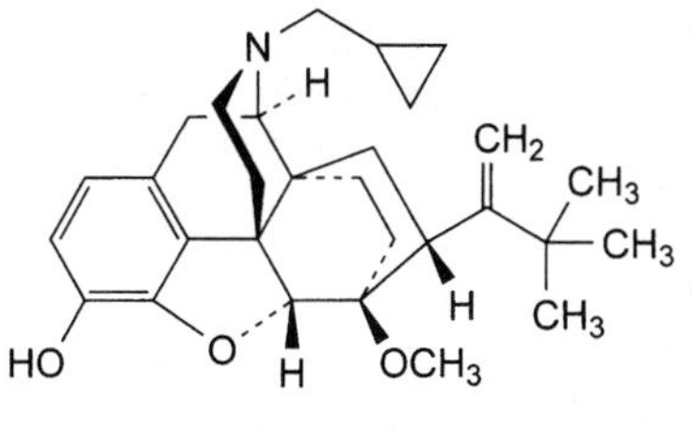

F. 17-(cyclopropylmethyl)-4,5α-epoxy-6-methoxy-7α-[1-(1,1-dimethylethyl)ethenyl]-6α,14-ethano-14α-morphinan-3-ol,

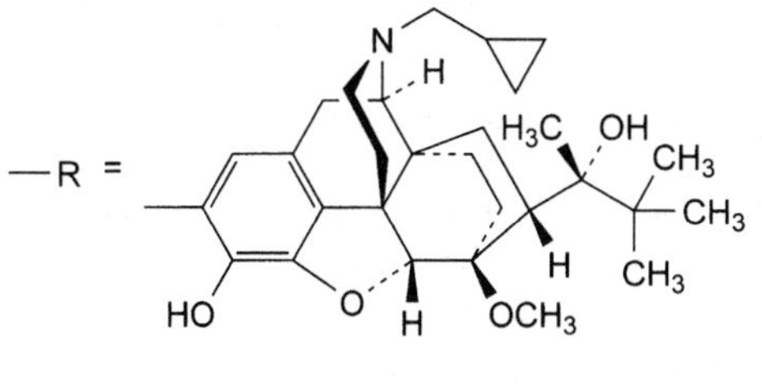

$-R =$

G. R-R: 17,17′-di(cyclopropylmethyl)-4,5α;4′,5α′-diepoxy-7α,7α′-di[(1S)-1-hydroxy-1,2,2-trimethylpropyl]-6,6′-dimethoxy-2,2′-bi(6α,14-ethano-14α-morphinan)-3,3′-diol (2,2′-bibuprenorphine),

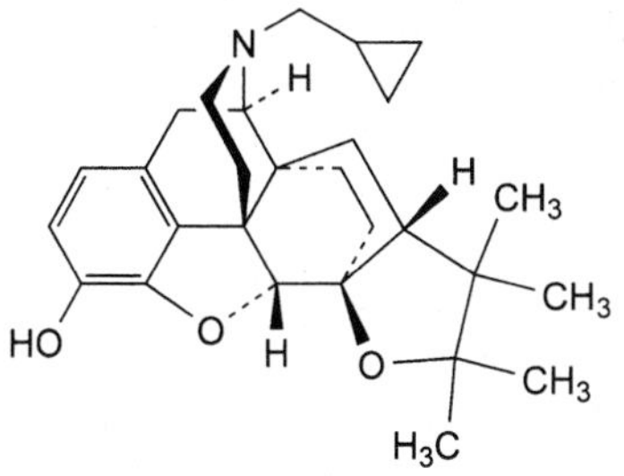

I. 17-(cyclopropylmethyl)-4″,4″,5″,5″-tetramethyl-4″,5″-dihydro-(7βH)-6α,14-ethano-(5βH)-difurano-[2′,3′,4′,5′:4,12,13,5;2″,3″:6,7]-14α-morphinan-3-ol,

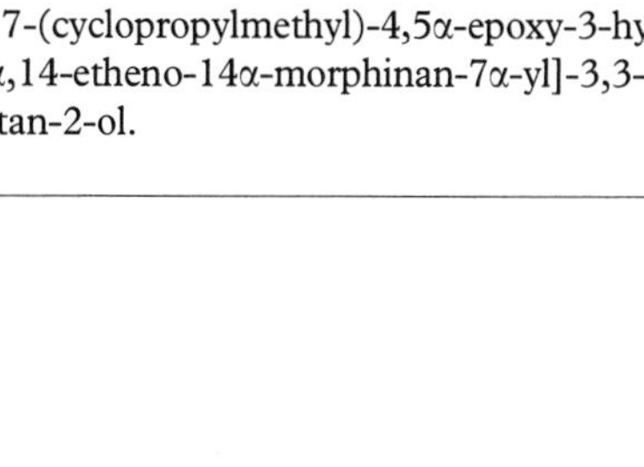

J. (2S)-2-[17-(cyclopropylmethyl)-4,5α-epoxy-3-hydroxy-6-methoxy-6α,14-etheno-14α-morphinan-7α-yl]-3,3-dimethylbutan-2-ol.

——————— Ph Eur

# Buserelin

*(Ph Eur monograph 1077)*

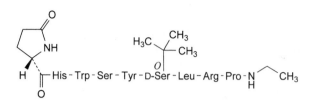

$C_{60}H_{86}N_{16}O_{13}$　　　　1239　　　　*57982-77-1*

## Action and use

Gonadotrophin releasing hormone (gonadorelin) analogue; treatment of prostate cancer.

*Ph Eur* ——————————————————————

## DEFINITION

5-Oxo-L-prolyl-L-histidyl-L-tryptophyl-L-seryl-L-tyrosyl-*O*-(1,1-dimethylethyl)-D-seryl-L-leucyl-L-arginyl-*N*-ethyl-L-prolinamide.

Synthetic nonapeptide analogue of human gonadotrophin-releasing hormone GnRH with agonistic activity to gonadorelin. It is obtained by chemical synthesis and is available as an acetate.

## Content

95.0 per cent to 102.0 per cent (anhydrous, acetic acid-free substance).

## CHARACTERS

### Appearance

White or slightly yellowish powder, hygroscopic.

### Solubility

Sparingly soluble in water and in dilute acids.

## IDENTIFICATION

A. Examine the chromatograms obtained in the assay.

*Results* The principal peak in the chromatogram obtained with the test solution is similar in retention time and size to the principal peak in the chromatogram obtained with reference solution (b).

B. Nuclear magnetic resonance spectrometry (*2.2.33*).

*Preparation* 4 mg/ml solution in a mixture of 20 volumes of *deuterated acetic acid R* and 80 volumes of *deuterium oxide R*.

*Comparison* 4 mg/ml solution of *buserelin CRS* in a mixture of 20 volumes of *deuterated acetic acid R* and 80 volumes of *deuterium oxide R* (dissolve the contents of a vial of *buserelin CRS* in this solvent mixture to obtain the desired concentration).

*Operating conditions* Field strength: minimum 300 MHz.

*Results* The ¹H NMR spectrum obtained is qualitatively similar to the ¹H NMR spectrum obtained with *buserelin CRS*.

C. Amino acid analysis (*2.2.56*). For protein hydrolysis use Method 1 and for analysis use Method 1.

Express the content of each amino acid in moles. Calculate the relative proportions of the amino acids, taking 1/6 of the sum of the number of moles of glutamic acid, histidine, tyrosine, leucine, arginine and proline as equal to 1. The values fall within the following limits: serine 1.4 to 2.0; proline 0.8 to 1.2; glutamic acid 0.9 to 1.1; leucine 0.9 to 1.1; tyrosine 0.9 to 1.1; histidine 0.9 to 1.1; arginine 0.9 to

1.1. Not more than traces of other amino acids are present, with the exception of tryptophan.

## TESTS

### Appearance of solution

A 10 g/l solution is clear (2.2.1) and not more intensely coloured than reference solution $Y_7$ (2.2.2, Method II).

### Specific optical rotation (2.2.7)

− 49 to − 58 (anhydrous, acetic acid-free substance), determined on a 10 g/l solution.

### Specific absorbance (2.2.25)

49 to 56, measured at the absorption maximum at 278 nm (anhydrous, acetic acid-free substance).

Dissolve 10.0 mg in 100.0 ml of 0.01 M hydrochloric acid.

### Related substances

Liquid chromatography (2.2.29).

*Test solution*   Dissolve 5.0 mg of the substance to be examined in 5.0 ml of the mobile phase.

*Reference solution (a)*   Dissolve the contents of a vial of D-His-buserelin CRS in the mobile phase. Dilute an appropriate volume of this solution in the mobile phase to obtain a final concentration of 1 mg/ml. Add 1.0 ml of the test solution to 1.0 ml of this solution.

*Reference solution (b)*   Dissolve the contents of a vial of buserelin CRS in the mobile phase. Dilute an appropriate volume of this solution in the mobile phase to obtain a final concentration of 1.0 mg/ml.

*Reference solution (c)*   Dilute 1.0 ml of the test solution to 100.0 ml with the mobile phase.

*Column:*
— size: $l$ = 0.25 m, Ø = 4 mm;
— stationary phase: octadecylsilyl silica gel for chromatography R (5 µm).

*Mobile phase*   Mix 200 ml of acetonitrile R and 700 ml of an 11.2 g/l solution of phosphoric acid R and adjust to pH 2.5 with triethylamine R.

*Flow rate*   0.8 ml/min.

*Detection*   Spectrophotometer at 220 nm.

*Injection*   10 µl of the test solution, reference solution (a) and reference solution (c).

*Relative retention*   With reference to buserelin (retention time = about 36 min): impurity B = about 0.76; impurity C = about 0.83; impurity A = about 0.90; impurity D = about 0.94; impurity E = about 0.94.

*System suitability*   Reference solution (a):
— resolution: minimum 1.5 between the peaks due to impurity A and buserelin.

*Limits:*
— sum of impurities D and E: not more than 3 times the area of the principal peak in the chromatogram obtained with reference solution (c) (3 per cent);
— any other impurity: for each impurity, not more than 3 times the area of the principal peak in the chromatogram obtained with reference solution (c) (3 per cent);
— total: not more than 5 times the area of the principal peak in the chromatogram obtained with reference solution (c) (5 per cent);
— disregard limit: 0.1 times the area of the principal peak in the chromatogram obtained with reference solution (c) (0.1 per cent).

### Acetic acid (2.5.34)

3.0 per cent to 7.0 per cent.

*Test solution*   Dissolve 20.0 mg of the substance to be examined in a mixture of 5 volumes of mobile phase B and 95 volumes of mobile phase A and dilute to 10.0 ml with the same mixture of solvents.

### Water (2.5.12)

Maximum 4.0 per cent, determined on 80.0 mg.

### Bacterial endotoxins (2.6.14)

Less than 55.5 IU/mg, if intended for use in the manufacture of parenteral dosage forms without a further appropriate procedure for the removal of bacterial endotoxins.

## ASSAY

Liquid chromatography (2.2.29) as described in the test for related substances with the following modification.

*Injection*   10 µl of the test solution and reference solution (b).

Calculate the content of buserelin ($C_{60}H_{86}N_{16}O_{13}$) using the areas of the peaks in the chromatograms obtained and the declared content of $C_{60}H_{86}N_{16}O_{13}$ in buserelin CRS.

## STORAGE

In an airtight container, protected from light, at a temperature of 2 °C to 8 °C. If the substance is sterile, store in an airtight, sterile, tamper-proof container.

## LABELLING

The label states the mass of peptide in the container.

## IMPURITIES

*Specified impurities*   A, B, C, D, E.

A. X2 = D-His, X4 = L-Ser, X5 = L-Tyr: [2-D-histidine]buserelin,

B. X2 = L-His, X4 = D-Ser, X5 = L-Tyr: [4-D-serine]buserelin,

D. X2 = L-His, X4 = L-Ser, X5 = D-Tyr: [5-D-tyrosine]buserelin,

C. buserelin-(3-9)-peptide,

E. [1-(5-oxo-D-proline)]buserelin.

# Buspirone Hydrochloride

*(Ph Eur monograph 1711)*

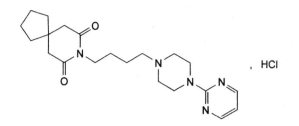

$C_{21}H_{31}N_5O_2,HCl$        422.0        *33386-08-2*

## Action and use

Non-benzodiazepine hypnotic; treatment of anxiety.

*Ph Eur*

## DEFINITION

8-[4-[4-(Pyrimidin-2-yl)piperazin-1-yl]butyl]-8-
azaspiro[4.5]decane-7,9-dione hydrochloride.

## Content

99.0 per cent to 101.0 per cent (dried substance).

## CHARACTERS

### Appearance

White or almost white, crystalline powder.

### Solubility

Freely soluble in water and in methanol, practically insoluble
in acetone.

It shows polymorphism (*5.9*).

## IDENTIFICATION

A. Infrared absorption spectrophotometry (*2.2.24*).

*Comparison*   buspirone hydrochloride CRS.

If the spectra obtained in the solid state show differences,
dissolve the substance to be examined and the reference
substance separately in *methanol R*, evaporate to dryness on a
water-bath and record new spectra using the residues.

B. It gives reaction (a) of chlorides (*2.3.1*).

## TESTS

### Related substances

Liquid chromatography (*2.2.29*).

*Test solution*   Dissolve 25.0 mg of the substance to be
examined in mobile phase A and dilute to 25.0 ml with
mobile phase A.

*Reference solution (a)*   Dilute 1.0 ml of the test solution to
100.0 ml with mobile phase A. Dilute 1.0 ml of this solution
to 10.0 ml with mobile phase A.

*Reference solution (b)*   Dissolve the contents of a vial of
*buspirone for system suitability CRS* (containing impurities E,
G, J, L and N) in 2.0 ml of mobile phase A and sonicate for
10 min.

*Column:*
— *size*: $l$ = 0.15 m, Ø = 4.6 mm,
— *stationary phase: octadecylsilyl silica gel for chromatography R*
   *(5 µm)*,
— *temperature*: 40 °C.

*Mobile phase:*
— *mobile phase A*: mix 950 volumes of a solution containing
   6.8 g/l of *potassium dihydrogen phosphate R* and 0.93 g/l of
   *sodium hexanesulphonate monohydrate R*, previously

adjusted to pH 3.4 with *phosphoric acid R* and 50 volumes
of *acetonitrile R1;*
— *mobile phase B*: mix 250 volumes of a solution containing
   3.4 g/l of *potassium dihydrogen phosphate R* and 3.52 g/l of
   *sodium hexanesulphonate monohydrate R*, previously
   adjusted to pH 2.2 with *phosphoric acid R* and
   750 volumes of *acetonitrile R1,*

| Time (min) | Mobile phase A (per cent V/V) | Mobile phase B (per cent V/V) |
|---|---|---|
| 0 - 6 | 90 | 10 |
| 6 - 34 | 90 → 42 | 10 → 58 |
| 34 - 45 | 42 | 58 |
| 45 - 55 | 42 → 0 | 58 → 100 |
| 55 - 56 | 0 → 100 | 100 → 0 |
| 56 - 60 | 100 | 0 |
| 60 - 61 | 100 → 90 | 0 → 10 |

*Flow rate*   1 ml/min.

*Detection*   Variable wavelength spectrophotometer capable of
operating at 240 nm and at 210 nm.

*Injection*   20 µl.

*Identification of impurities*   Use the chromatogram supplied
with *buspirone for system suitability CRS* and the
chromatogram obtained with reference solution (b) to
identify the peaks due to impurities E, G, J, L and N.

*Relative retention at 240 nm*   with reference to buspirone
(retention time = about 25 min): impurity A = about 0.2;
impurity B = about 0.3; impurity C = about 0.6;
impurity D = about 0.7; impurity E = about 0.8;
impurity F = about 0.9; impurity G = about 1.05;
impurity H = about 1.1; impurity I = about 1.2;
impurity J = about 1.5.

*Relative retention at 210 nm*   with reference to buspirone
(retention time = about 25 min): impurity K = about 0.6;
impurity L = about 1.7; impurity M = about 1.8;
impurity N = about 1.9.

*System suitability*   Reference solution (b):
— *peak-to-valley ratio at 240 nm*: minimum 5.0, where
   $H_p$ = height above the baseline of the peak due to
   impurity G and $H_v$ = height above the baseline of the
   lowest point of the curve separating this peak from the
   peak due to buspirone;
— *resolution at 210 nm*: minimum 4.0 between the peaks
   due to impurity L and impurity N;
— the chromatograms obtained are similar to the
   chromatograms supplied with *buspirone for system
   suitability CRS.*

*Limits*   Spectrophotometer at 240 nm:
— *correction factor*: for the calculation of content, multiply
   the peak area of impurity J by 2,
— *impurity E*: not more than 3 times the area of the
   principal peak in the chromatogram obtained with
   reference solution (a) (0.3 per cent),
— *impurity J*: not more than twice the area of the principal
   peak in the chromatogram obtained with reference
   solution (a) (0.2 per cent),
— *any other impurity*: for each impurity, not more than the
   area of the principal peak in the chromatogram obtained
   with reference solution (a) (0.1 per cent),
— *total*: not more than 4 times the area of the principal peak
   in the chromatogram obtained with reference solution (a)
   (0.4 per cent),

— *disregard limit*: 0.5 times the area of the principal peak in the chromatogram obtained with reference solution (a) (0.05 per cent).

*Limits* Spectrophotometer at 210 nm:
— *impurity K*: not more than the area of the principal peak in the chromatogram obtained with reference solution (a) (0.1 per cent),
— *any other impurity eluting with a relative retention greater than 1.6*: for each impurity, not more than the area of the principal peak in the chromatogram obtained with reference solution (a) (0.1 per cent),
— *total*: not more than twice the area of the principal peak in the chromatogram obtained with reference solution (a) (0.2 per cent),
— *disregard limit*: 0.5 times the area of the principal peak in the chromatogram obtained with reference solution (a) (0.05 per cent).

**Loss on drying** (*2.2.32*)
Maximum 0.5 per cent, determined on 1.000 g by drying at 105 °C.

**Sulphated ash** (*2.4.14*)
Maximum 0.1 per cent, determined on 1.0 g.

**ASSAY**
Dissolve 0.150 g in 10 ml of *glacial acetic acid R* and add 50 ml of *acetic anhydride R*. Titrate with *0.1 M perchloric acid*, determining the end-point potentiometrically (*2.2.20*).

1 ml of *0.1 M perchloric acid* is equivalent to 21.10 mg of $C_{21}H_{32}ClN_5O_2$.

**STORAGE**
Protected from light.

**IMPURITIES**
*Specified impurities* E, J, K.

*Other detectable impurities* (the following substances would, if present at a sufficient level, be detected by one or other of the tests in the monograph. They are limited by the general acceptance criterion for other/unspecified impurities and/or by the general monograph *Substances for pharmaceutical use (2034)*. It is therefore not necessary to identify these impurities for demonstration of compliance. See also *5.10*. *Control of impurities in substances for pharmaceutical use)*: A, B, C, D, F, G, H, I, L, M, N.

A. 2-(piperazin-1-yl)pyrimidine,

B. 8-(pyrimidin-2-yl)-8-aza-5-azoniaspiro[4.5]decane,

C. X = [CH$_2$]$_4$: 2,2′-[butane-1,4-diylbis(piperazine-1,4-diyl)]dipyrimidine,
D. X = [CH$_2$]$_4$-O-[CH$_2$]$_4$: 2,2′-[oxybis[butane-1,4-diyl(piperazine-1,4-diyl)]]dipyrimidine,

E. [1-[2-oxo-2-[[4-[4-(pyrimidin-2-yl)piperazin-1-yl]butyl]amino]ethyl]cyclopentyl]acetic acid,

F. X = NH: 4-[4-(pyrimidin-2-yl)piperazin-1-yl]butyl [1-[2-oxo-2-[[4-[4-(pyrimidin-2-yl)piperazin-1-yl]butyl]amino]ethyl]cyclopentyl]acetate,
H. X = O: bis[4-[4-(pyrimidin-2-yl)piperazin-1-yl]butyl] (cyclopentane-1,1-diyl)diacetate,

G. 2,2′-(piperazine-1,4-diyl)dipyrimidine,

I. 8-[4-[4-(5-chloropyrimidin-2-yl)piperazin-1-yl]butyl]-8-azaspiro[4.5]decane-7,9-dione,

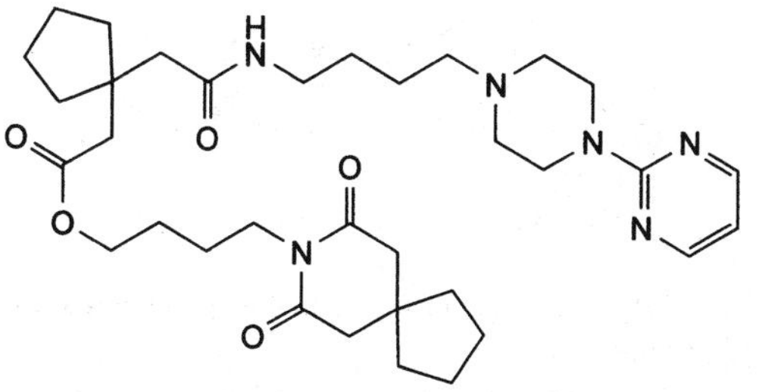

J. 4-(7,9-dioxo-8-azaspiro[4.5]dec-8-yl)butyl [1-[2-oxo-2-[[4-[4-(pyrimidin-2-yl)piperazin-1-yl]butyl]amino]ethyl]cyclopentyl]acetate,

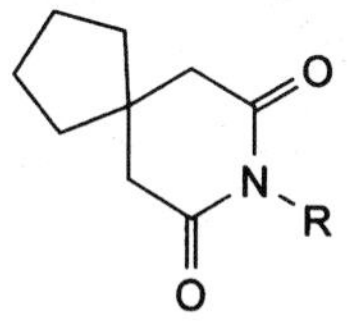

K. R = H: 8-azaspiro[4.5]decane-7,9-dione,

L R = [CH₂]₄-Cl:
8-(4-chlorobutyl)-8-azaspiro[4.5]decane-7,9-dione,

M. R = [CH₂]₄-Br:
8-(4-bromobutyl)-8-azaspiro[4.5]decane-7,9-dione,

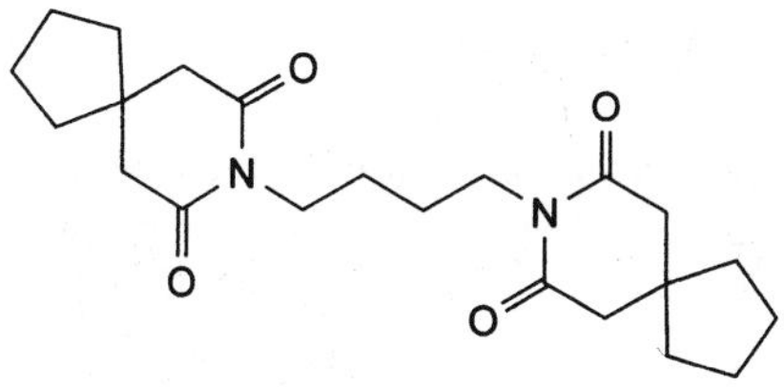

N. 8,8'-(butane-1,4-diyl)bis(8-azaspiro[4.5]decane-7,9-dione).

*Ph Eur*

# Busulfan

(*Ph Eur monograph 0542*)

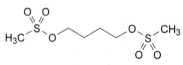

C₆H₁₄O₆S₂          246.3          55-98-1

**Action and use**
Cytotoxic alkylating agent.

**Preparation**
Busulfan Tablets

*Ph Eur*

**DEFINITION**
Butane-1,4-diyl di(methanesulphonate).

**Content**
99.0 per cent to 100.5 per cent (dried substance).

**CHARACTERS**
**Appearance**
White or almost white, crystalline powder.

**Solubility**
Very slightly soluble in water, freely soluble in acetone and in acetonitrile, very slightly soluble in ethanol (96 per cent).

mp: about 116 °C.

**IDENTIFICATION**
*First identification*   A.
*Second identification*   B, C, D.

A. Infrared absorption spectrophotometry (*2.2.24*).
*Comparison*   busulfan CRS.

B. Thin-layer chromatography (*2.2.27*).

*Test solution*   Dissolve 20 mg of the substance to be examined in 2 ml of *acetone R*.

*Reference solution*   Dissolve 20 mg of *busulfan CRS* in 2 ml of *acetone R*.

*Plate*   TLC silica gel G plate R.

*Mobile phase*   acetone R, toluene R (50:50 V/V).

*Application*   5 μl.

*Development*   Over a path of 15 cm.

*Drying*   In a current of warm air.

*Detection*   Spray with *anisaldehyde solution R* and heat at 120 °C.

*Results*   The principal spot in the chromatogram obtained with the test solution is similar in position, colour and size to the principal spot in the chromatogram obtained with the reference solution.

C. To 0.1 g add 5 ml of *1 M sodium hydroxide*. Heat until a clear solution is obtained. Allow to cool. To 2 ml of the solution add *0.1 ml of potassium permanganate solution R*. The colour changes from purple through violet to blue and finally to green. Filter and add *1 ml of ammoniacal silver nitrate solution R*. A precipitate is formed.

D. To 0.1 g add 0.1 g of *potassium nitrate R* and 0.25 g of *sodium hydroxide R*, mix and heat to fusion. Allow to cool and dissolve the residue in 5 ml of *water R*. Adjust to pH 1-2 using *dilute hydrochloric acid R*. The solution gives reaction (a) of sulphates (*2.3.1*).

**TESTS**
**Appearance of solution**
The solution is clear (*2.2.1*) and not more intensely coloured than reference solution B₇ (*2.2.2, Method II*).

Dissolve 0.25 g in 20 ml of *acetonitrile R*, dilute to 25 ml with *water R* and examine immediately.

**Acidity**
Dissolve 0.20 g with heating in 50 ml of *anhydrous ethanol R*. Add 0.1 ml of *methyl red solution R*. Not more than 0.05 ml of *0.1 M sodium hydroxide* is required to change the colour of the indicator.

**Loss on drying** (*2.2.32*)
Maximum 2.0 per cent, determined on 1.000 g by drying *in vacuo* at 60 °C.

**Sulphated ash** (*2.4.14*)
Maximum 0.1 per cent, determined on 1.0 g.

**ASSAY**
To 0.250 g add 50 ml of *water R*. Shake. Boil under a reflux condenser for 30 min and, if necessary, make up to the initial volume with *water R*. Allow to cool. Using 0.3 ml of *phenolphthalein solution R* as indicator, titrate with *0.1 M sodium hydroxide* until a pink colour is obtained.

1 ml of 0.1 M sodium hydroxide is equivalent to 12.32 mg of C₆H₁₄O₆S₂.

**STORAGE**
In an airtight container, protected from light.

*Ph Eur*

# Butyl Hydroxybenzoate

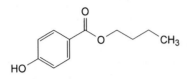

Butylparaben

*(Butyl Parahydroxybenzoate, Ph Eur monograph 0881)*

$C_{11}H_{14}O_3$        194.2        94-26-8

**Action and use**

Excipient.

*Ph Eur*

## DEFINITION

Butyl 4-hydroxybenzoate.

**Content**

98.0 per cent to 102.0 per cent.

## CHARACTERS

**Appearance**

White or almost white, crystalline powder or colourless crystals.

**Solubility**

Very slightly soluble in water, freely soluble in alcohol and in methanol.

## IDENTIFICATION

*First identification* A, B.

*Second identification* A, C, D.

A. Melting point (*2.2.14*)

68 °C to 71 °C.

B. Infrared absorption spectrophotometry (*2.2.24*).

*Comparison* butyl parahydroxybenzoate CRS.

C. Examine the chromatograms obtained in the test for related substances.

*Results* The principal spot in the chromatogram obtained with test solution (b) is similar in position and size to the principal spot in the chromatogram obtained with reference solution (b).

D. To about 10 mg in a test-tube add 1 ml of *sodium carbonate solution R*, boil for 30 s and cool (solution A). To a further 10 mg in a similar test-tube add 1 ml of *sodium carbonate solution R*; the substance partly dissolves (solution B). Add at the same time to solution A and solution B 5 ml of *aminopyrazolone solution R* and 1 ml of *potassium ferricyanide solution R* and mix. Solution B is yellow to orange-brown. Solution A is orange to red, the colour being clearly more intense than any similar colour which may be obtained with solution B.

## TESTS

**Solution S**

Dissolve 1.0 g in *alcohol R* and dilute to 10 ml with the same solvent.

**Appearance of solution**

Solution S is clear (*2.2.1*) and not more intensely coloured than reference solution $BY_6$ (*2.2.2, Method II*).

**Acidity**

To 2 ml of solution S add 3 ml of *alcohol R*, 5 ml of *carbon dioxide-free water R* and 0.1 ml of *bromocresol green solution R*.

Not more than 0.1 ml of *0.1 M sodium hydroxide* is required to change the colour of the indicator to blue.

**Related substances**

Thin-layer chromatography (*2.2.27*)

*Test solution (a)* Dissolve 0.10 g of the substance to be examined in *acetone R* and dilute to 10 ml with the same solvent.

*Test solution (b)* Dilute 1 ml of test solution (a) to 10 ml with *acetone R*.

*Reference solution (a)* Dilute 0.5 ml of test solution (a) to 100 ml with *acetone R*.

*Reference solution (b)* Dissolve 10 mg of *butyl parahydroxybenzoate CRS* in *acetone R* and dilute to 10 ml with the same solvent.

*Reference solution (c)* Dissolve 10 mg of *propyl parahydroxybenzoate R* in 1 ml of test solution (a) and dilute to 10 ml with *acetone R*.

*Plate* Suitable octadecylsilyl silica gel with a fluorescent indicator having an optimal intensity at 254 nm as the coating substance.

*Mobile phase* glacial acetic acid R, water R, methanol R (1:30:70 *V/V/V*).

*Application* 2 μl.

*Development* Over a path of 15 cm.

*Drying* In air.

*Detection* Examine in ultraviolet light at 254 nm.

*System suitability* The chromatogram obtained with reference solution (c) shows 2 clearly separated principal spots.

*Limits:*

— *any impurity*: any spot in the chromatogram obtained with test solution (a), apart from the principal spot, is not more intense than the spot in the chromatogram obtained with reference solution (a) (0.5 per cent).

**Sulphated ash** (*2.4.14*)

Maximum 0.1 per cent, determined on 1.0 g.

## ASSAY

To 1.000 g add 20.0 ml of 1 M sodium hydroxide. Heat at about 70 °C for 1 h. Cool rapidly in an ice bath. Prepare a blank in the same manner. Carry out the titration on the solutions at room temperature. Titrate the excess sodium hydroxide with *0.5 M sulphuric acid, continuing the titration until the second point of inflexion and determining the end-point potentiometrically (2.2.20)*.

1 ml of 1 M sodium hydroxide is equivalent to 194.2 mg of $C_{11}H_{14}O_3$.

## IMPURITIES

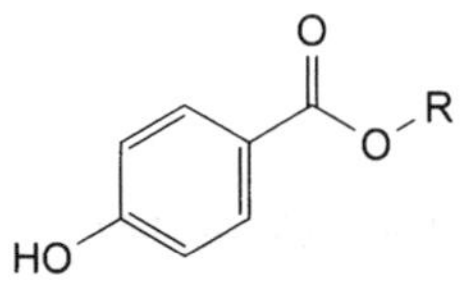

A. R = H: 4-hydroxybenzoic acid,

B. R = $CH_3$: methyl 4-hydroxybenzoate,

C. R = $CH_2$-$CH_3$: ethyl 4-hydroxybenzoate,

D. R = $CH_2$-$CH_2$-$CH_3$: propyl 4-hydroxybenzoate.

*Ph Eur*

# Butylated Hydroxyanisole

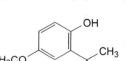

(*Butylhydroxyanisole, Ph Eur monograph 0880*)

$C_{11}H_{16}O_2$        180.3        *25013-16-5*

## Action and use
Antioxidant.

*Ph Eur*

## DEFINITION
Butylhydroxyanisole is 2-(1,1-dimethylethyl)-4-methoxyphenol containing not more than 10 per cent of 3-(1,1-dimethylethyl)-4-methoxyphenol.

## CHARACTERS
A white, yellowish or slightly pinkish, crystalline powder, practically insoluble in water, very soluble in methylene chloride, freely soluble in alcohol and in fatty oils. It dissolves in dilute solutions of alkali hydroxides.

## IDENTIFICATION
A. Examine the chromatograms obtained in the test for related substances. The principal spot in the chromatogram obtained with test solution (b) is similar in position, colour and size to the principal spot in the chromatogram obtained with reference solution (a).

B. To 0.5 ml of solution S (see Tests) add 10 ml of *aminopyrazolone solution R* and 1 ml of *potassium ferricyanide solution R*. Mix and add 10 ml of *methylene chloride R*. Shake vigorously. After separation, the organic layer is red.

C. Dissolve about 10 mg in 2 ml of *alcohol R*. Add 1 ml of a 1 g/l solution of *testosterone propionate R* in *alcohol R* and 2 ml of *dilute sodium hydroxide solution R*. Heat in a water-bath at 80 °C for 10 min and allow to cool. A red colour develops.

## TESTS
### Solution S
Dissolve 2.5 g in *alcohol R* and dilute to 25 ml with the same solvent.

### Appearance of solution
Solution S is clear (*2.2.1*) and not more intensely coloured than intensity 5 of the range of reference solutions of the most appropriate colour (*2.2.2, Method II*).

### Related substances
Examine by thin-layer chromatography (*2.2.27*), using *silica gel G R* as the coating substance.

*Test solution (a)* Dissolve 0.25 g of the substance to be examined in *methylene chloride R* and dilute to 10 ml with the same solvent.

*Test solution (b)* Dilute 1 ml of test solution (a) to 10 ml with *methylene chloride R*.

*Reference solution (a)* Dissolve 25 mg of butylhydroxyanisole CRS in *methylene chloride R* and dilute to 10 ml with the same solvent.

*Reference solution (b)* Dilute 1 ml of reference solution (a) to 20 ml with *methylene chloride R*.

*Reference solution (c)* Dissolve 50 mg of *hydroquinone R* in 5 ml of *alcohol R* and dilute to 100 ml with *methylene*

chloride R. Dilute 1 ml of this solution to 10 ml with *methylene chloride R*.

Apply separately to the plate 5 µl of each solution. Develop over a path of 10 cm using *methylene chloride R*. Allow the plate to dry in air and spray with a freshly prepared mixture of 10 volumes of *potassium ferricyanide solution R*, 20 volumes of *ferric chloride solution R1* and 70 volumes of *water R*. In the chromatogram obtained with test solution (a): any violet-blue spot with an $R_F$ value of about 0.35 (corresponding to 3-(1,1-dimethylethyl)-4-methoxyphenol) is not more intense than the principal spot in the chromatogram obtained with reference solution (a) (10 per cent); any spot corresponding to hydroquinone is not more intense than the principal spot in the chromatogram obtained with reference solution (c) (0.2 per cent); any spot, apart from the principal spot and any spots corresponding to 3-(1,1-dimethylethyl)-4-methoxyphenol and hydroquinone, is not more intense than the principal spot in the chromatogram obtained with reference solution (b) (0.5 per cent).

### Heavy metals (*2.4.8*)
1.0 g complies with limit test C for heavy metals (10 ppm). Prepare the standard using 1 ml of *lead standard solution (10 ppm Pb) R*.

### Sulphated ash (*2.4.14*)
Not more than 0.1 per cent, determined on 1.0 g.

## STORAGE
Store protected from light.

## IMPURITIES

benzene-1,4-diol (hydroquinone).

*Ph Eur*

# Butylated Hydroxytoluene

(*Butylhydroxytoluene, Ph Eur monograph 0581*)

$C_{15}H_{24}O$        220.4        *128-37-0*

## Action and use
Antioxidant.

*Ph Eur*

## DEFINITION
Butylhydroxytoluene is 2,6-bis(1,1-dimethylethyl)-4-methylphenol.

## CHARACTERS
A white or yellowish-white, crystalline powder, practically insoluble in water, very soluble in acetone, freely soluble in alcohol and in vegetable oils.

## IDENTIFICATION

*First identification*    A, C.

*Second identification*    A, B, D.

A. It complies with the test for the freezing-point (see Tests).

B. Dissolve 0.500 g in *ethanol R* and dilute to 100.0 ml with the same solvent. Dilute 1.0 ml of this solution to 100.0 ml with *ethanol R*. Examined between 230 nm and 300 nm (*2.2.25*), the solution shows an absorption maximum at 278 nm. The specific absorbance at the maximum is 80 to 90.

C. Examine by infrared absorption spectrophotometry (*2.2.24*), comparing with the spectrum obtained with *butylhydroxytoluene CRS*.

D. Dissolve about 10 mg in 2 ml of *alcohol R*. Add 1 ml of a 1 g/l solution of *testosterone propionate R* in *alcohol R* and 2 ml of *dilute sodium hydroxide solution R*. Heat in a water-bath at 80 °C for 10 min and allow to cool. A blue colour develops.

## TESTS

### Appearance of solution

Dissolve 1.0 g in *methanol R* and dilute to 10 ml with the same solvent. The solution is clear (*2.2.1*) and not more intensely coloured than reference solution $Y_5$ or $BY_5$ (*2.2.2, Method II*).

### Freezing-point (*2.2.18*)

69 °C to 70 °C.

### Related substances

Examine by thin-layer chromatography (*2.2.27*), using *silica gel G R* as the coating substance.

*Test solution*    Dissolve 0.2 g of the substance to be examined in *methanol R* and dilute to 10.0 ml with the same solvent.

*Reference solution*    Dilute 1 ml of the test solution to 200 ml with *methanol R*.

Apply separately to the plate 10 µl of each solution. Develop over a path of 15 cm using *methylene chloride R*. Dry the plate in air and spray with a freshly prepared mixture of 10 volumes of *potassium ferricyanide solution R*, 20 volumes of *ferric chloride solution R1* and 70 volumes of *water R*. Any spot in the chromatogram obtained with the test solution, apart from the principal spot, is not more intense than the spot in the chromatogram obtained with the reference solution (0.5 per cent).

### Sulphated ash (*2.4.14*)

Not more than 0.1 per cent, determined on 1.0 g.

*Ph Eur*

# Cabergoline

(*Ph Eur monograph 1773*)

$C_{26}H_{37}N_5O_2$              451.6              *81409-90-7*

### Action and use

Dopamine D2 receptor agonist.

*Ph Eur*

## DEFINITION

1-Ethyl-3-[3-(dimethylamino)propyl]-3-[[(6aR,9R,10aR)-7-(prop-2-enyl)-4,6,6a,7,8,9,10,10a-octahydroindolo[4,3-*fg*]quinolin-9-yl]carbonyl]urea.

### Content

98.0 per cent to 102.0 per cent (anhydrous substance).

## CHARACTERS

### Appearance

White or almost white, crystalline powder.

### Solubility

Practically insoluble in water, freely soluble in ethanol (96 per cent), very slightly soluble in hexane. It is slightly soluble in *0.1 M hydrochloric acid*.

It shows polymorphism (*5.9*).

## IDENTIFICATION

A. Specific optical rotation (see Tests).

B. Infrared absorption spectrophotometry (*2.2.24*).

*Comparison*    cabergoline CRS.

If the spectra obtained in the solid state show differences, dissolve 50 mg of the substance to be examined and 50 mg of the reference substance separately in 1 ml of *ethanol (96 per cent) R*, evaporate to dryness and record new spectra using the residues.

## TESTS

### Specific optical rotation (*2.2.7*)

− 77 to − 83 (anhydrous substance).

Dissolve 0.100 g in *ethanol (96 per cent) R* and dilute to 50.0 ml with the same solvent.

### Related substances

Liquid chromatography (*2.2.29*). *Prepare the solutions immediately before use and protected from light.*

*Test solution*    Dissolve 30.0 mg of the substance to be examined in the mobile phase and dilute to 25.0 ml with the mobile phase.

*Reference solution (a)*    Dissolve 30.0 mg of *cabergoline CRS* in the mobile phase and dilute to 25.0 ml with the mobile phase.

*Reference solution (b)*    Dilute 1.0 ml of the test solution to 100.0 ml with the mobile phase. Dilute 10.0 ml of this solution to 50.0 ml with the mobile phase.

*Reference solution (c)*    Suspend 50 mg of the substance to be examined in 10 ml of *0.1 M sodium hydroxide*. Stir for about

15 min. To 1 ml of the suspension add 1 ml of *0.1 M hydrochloric acid* and dilute to 10 ml with the mobile phase. Sonicate until dissolution is complete. The main degradation product obtained is impurity A.

*Column:*
— *size*: $l = 0.25$ m, $\emptyset = 4.6$ mm,
— *stationary phase*: octadecylsilyl silica gel for chromatography R (10 μm).

*Mobile phase*  Mix 16 volumes of *acetonitrile R* and 84 volumes of a freshly prepared 6.8 g/l solution of *potassium dihydrogen phosphate R* previously adjusted to pH 2.0 with *phosphoric acid R*. Add 0.2 volumes of *triethylamine R*.

*Flow rate*  1.2 ml/min.

*Detection*  Spectrophotometer at 280 nm.

*Injection*  20 μl of the test solution and reference solutions (b) and (c).

*Run time*  4 times the retention time of cabergoline.

*Relative retention*  With reference to cabergoline (retention time = about 12 min): impurity D = about 0.3; impurity B = about 0.6; impurity A = about 0.8; impurity C = about 2.9.

*System suitability*  Reference solution (c):
— *resolution*: minimum 3.0 between the peaks due to cabergoline and impurity A.

*Limits:*
— *impurities A, C*: for each impurity, not more than 1.5 times the area of the principal peak in the chromatogram obtained with reference solution (b) (0.3 per cent);
— *impurities B, D*: for each impurity, not more than 0.5 times the area of the principal peak in the chromatogram obtained with reference solution (b) (0.1 per cent);
— *any other impurity*: for each impurity, not more than 0.5 times the area of the principal peak in the chromatogram obtained with reference solution (b) (0.1 per cent);
— *total*: not more than 4 times the area of the principal peak in the chromatogram obtained with reference solution (b) (0.8 per cent);
— *disregard limit*: 0.25 times the area of the principal peak in the chromatogram obtained with reference solution (b) (0.05 per cent).

**Water** (*2.5.12*)
Maximum 0.5 per cent, determined on 1.000 g.

**ASSAY**
Liquid chromatography (*2.2.29*) as described in the test for related substances with the following modification.

*Injection*  Test solution and reference solution (a).

Calculate the percentage content of $C_{26}H_{37}N_5O_2$ from the areas of the peaks and the declared content of *cabergoline CRS*.

**STORAGE**
Protected from light.

**IMPURITIES**
*Specified impurities  A, B, C, D.*

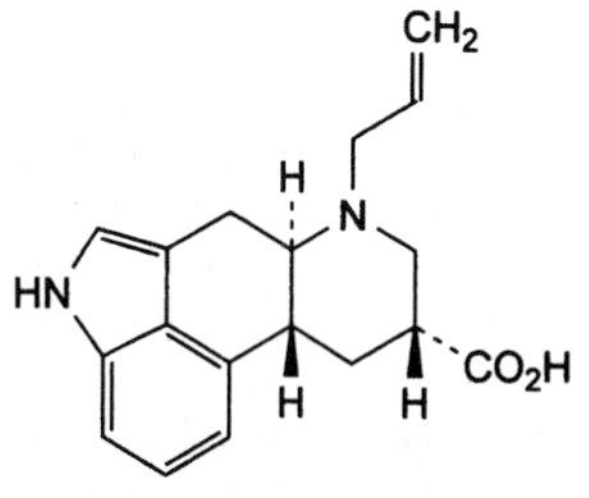

A. (6a*R*,9*R*,10a*R*)-7-(prop-2-enyl)-4,6,6a,7,8,9,10,10a-octahydroindolo[4,3-*fg*]quinoline-9-carboxylic acid,

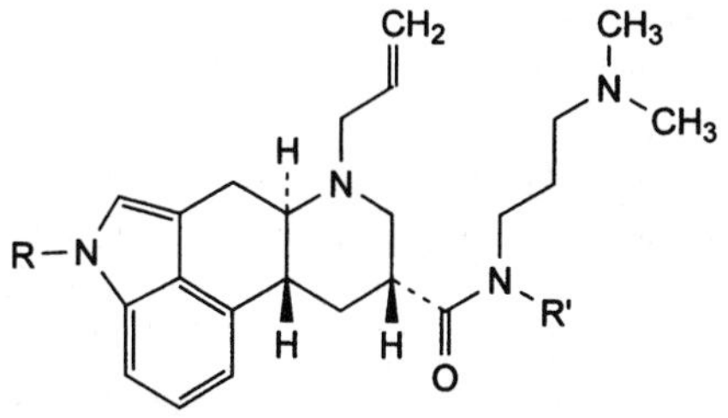

B. R = CO-NH-C$_2$H$_5$, R′ = H: (6a*R*,9*R*,10a*R*)-*N*$^9$-[3-(dimethylamino)propyl]-*N*$^4$-ethyl-7-(prop-2-enyl)-6a,7,8,9,10,10a-hexahydroindolo[4,3-*fg*]quinoline-4,9(6*H*)-dicarboxamide,

C. R = R′ = CO-NH-C$_2$H$_5$: (6a*R*,9*R*,10a*R*)-*N*$^9$-[3-(dimethylamino)propyl]-*N*$^4$-ethyl-*N*$^9$-(ethylcarbamoyl)-7-(prop-2-enyl)-6a,7,8,9,10,10a-hexahydroindolo[4,3-*fg*]quinoline-4,9(6*H*)-dicarboxamide,

D. R = R′ = H: (6a*R*,9*R*,10a*R*)-*N*-[3-(dimethylamino)propyl]-7-(prop-2-enyl)-4,6,6a,7,8,9,10,10a-octahydroindolo[4,3-*fg*]quinoline-9-carboxamide.

*———— Ph Eur*

# Caffeine

Anhydrous Caffeine
(*Ph Eur monograph 0267*)

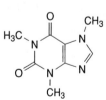

$C_8H_{10}N_4O_2$          194.2          *58-08-2*

**Action and use**
Central nervous system stimulant.

**Preparations**
Aspirin and Caffeine Tablets
Caffeine Citrate Injection
Caffeine Citrate Oral Solution
Paracetamol, Codeine Phosphate and Caffeine Capsules
Paracetamol, Codeine Phosphate and Caffeine Tablets

Ph Eur

## DEFINITION

1,3,7-Trimethyl-3,7-dihydro-1*H*-purine-2,6-dione.

## Content

98.5 per cent to 101.5 per cent (dried substance).

## CHARACTERS

### Appearance

White or almost white, crystalline powder or silky, white or almost white, crystals.

### Solubility

Sparingly soluble in water, freely soluble in boiling water, slightly soluble in ethanol (96 per cent). It dissolves in concentrated solutions of alkali benzoates or salicylates.

It sublimes readily.

## IDENTIFICATION

*First identification*   A, B, E.

*Second identification*   A, C, D, E, F.

A. Melting point (*2.2.14*): 234 °C to 239 °C.

B. Infrared absorption spectrophotometry (*2.2.24*).

*Comparison*   caffeine CRS.

C. To 2 ml of a saturated solution add 0.05 ml of *iodinated potassium iodide solution R*. The solution remains clear. Add 0.1 ml of *dilute hydrochloric acid R*; a brown precipitate is formed. Neutralise with *dilute sodium hydroxide solution R*; the precipitate dissolves.

D. In a ground-glass-stoppered tube, dissolve about 10 mg in 0.25 ml of a mixture of 0.5 ml of *acetylacetone R* and 5 ml of *dilute sodium hydroxide solution R*. Heat in a water-bath at 80 °C for 7 min. Cool and add 0.5 ml of *dimethylaminobenzaldehyde solution R2*. Heat again in a water-bath at 80 °C for 7 min. Allow to cool and add 10 ml of *water R*; an intense blue colour develops.

E. Loss on drying (see Tests).

F. It gives the reaction of xanthines (*2.3.1*).

## TESTS

### Solution S

Dissolve 0.5 g with heating in 50 ml of *carbon dioxide-free water R* prepared from *distilled water R*, cool and dilute to 50 ml with the same solvent.

### Appearance of solution

Solution S is clear (*2.2.1*) and colourless (*2.2.2, Method II*).

### Acidity

To 10 ml of solution S add 0.05 ml of *bromothymol blue solution R1*; the solution is green or yellow. Not more than 0.2 ml of *0.01 M sodium hydroxide* is required to change the colour of the indicator to blue.

### Related substances

Liquid chromatography (*2.2.29*).

*Test solution*   Dissolve 0.100 g of the substance to be examined in the mobile phase and dilute to 50.0 ml with the mobile phase. Dilute 1.0 ml of this solution to 10.0 ml with the mobile phase.

*Reference solution (a)*   Dilute 2.0 ml of the test solution to 100.0 ml with the mobile phase. Dilute 1.0 ml of this solution to 10.0 ml with the mobile phase.

*Reference solution (b)*   Dissolve 5 mg of *caffeine for system suitability CRS* (containing impurities A, C, D and F) in the mobile phase and dilute to 5 ml with the mobile phase. Dilute 2 ml of this solution to 10 ml with the mobile phase.

*Column:*
— *size*: *l* = 0.15 m, Ø = 4.6 mm;

— *stationary phase*: *base-deactivated end-capped octadecylsilyl silica gel for chromatography R* (5 µm).

*Mobile phase*   Dissolve 1.64 g of *anhydrous sodium acetate R* in *water R* and dilute to 2000 ml with the same solvent. Adjust 1910 ml of this solution to pH 4.5 with *glacial acetic acid R* and add 50 ml of *acetonitrile R* and 40 ml of *tetrahydrofuran R*.

*Flow rate*   1.0 ml/min.

*Detection*   Spectrophotometer at 275 nm.

*Injection*   10 µl.

*Run time*   1.5 times the retention time of caffeine.

*Identification of impurities*   Use the chromatogram supplied with *caffeine for system suitability CRS* and the chromatogram obtained with reference solution (b) to identify the peaks due to impurities A, C, D and F.

*Retention time*   Caffeine = about 8 min.

*System suitability*   Reference solution (b):
— *resolution*: minimum 2.5 between the peaks due to impurities C and D and minimum 2.5 between the peaks due to impurities F and A.

*Limits:*
— *unspecified impurities*: for each impurity, not more than 0.5 times the area of the principal peak in the chromatogram obtained with reference solution (a) (0.10 per cent);
— *total*: not more than 0.5 times the area of the principal peak in the chromatogram obtained with reference solution (a) (0.1 per cent);
— *disregard limit*: 0.25 times the area of the principal peak in the chromatogram obtained with reference solution (a) (0.05 per cent).

### Sulphates (*2.4.13*)

Maximum 500 ppm, determined on 15 ml of solution S.

Prepare the standard using a mixture of 7.5 ml of *sulphate standard solution (10 ppm SO$_4$) R* and 7.5 ml of *distilled water R*.

### Heavy metals (*2.4.8*)

Maximum 20 ppm.

1.0 g complies with test C. Prepare the reference solution using 2 ml of *lead standard solution (10 ppm Pb) R*.

### Loss on drying (*2.2.32*)

Maximum 0.5 per cent, determined on 1.000 g by drying in an oven at 105 °C for 1 h.

### Sulphated ash (*2.4.14*)

Maximum 0.1 per cent, determined on 1.0 g.

## ASSAY

Dissolve 0.170 g with heating in 5 ml of *anhydrous acetic acid R*. Allow to cool, add 10 ml of *acetic anhydride R* and 20 ml of *toluene R*. Titrate with *0.1 M perchloric acid*, determining the end-point potentiometrically (*2.2.20*).

1 ml of *0.1 M perchloric acid* is equivalent to 19.42 mg of $C_8H_{10}N_4O_2$.

## IMPURITIES

*Other detectable impurities* (The following substances would, if present at a sufficient level, be detected by one or other of the tests in the monograph. They are limited by the general acceptance criterion for other/unspecified impurities and/or by the general monograph *Substances for pharmaceutical use (2034)*. It is therefore not necessary to identify these impurities for demonstration of compliance. See also *5.10. Control of impurities in substances for pharmaceutical use)*: A, B, C, D, E, F.

A. theophylline,

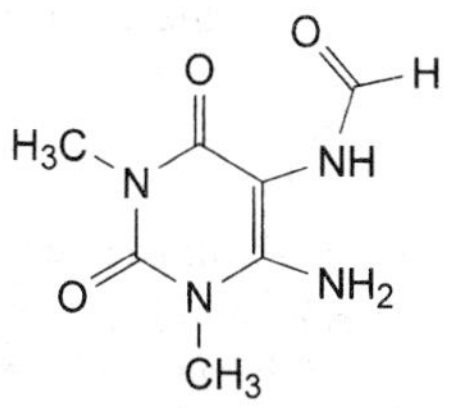

B. *N*-(6-amino-1,3-dimethyl-2,4-dioxo-1,2,3,4-tetrahydropyrimidin-5-yl)formamide,

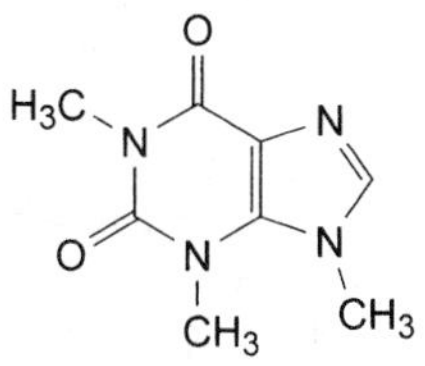

C. 1,3,9-trimethyl-3,9-dihydro-1*H*-purine-2,6-dione (isocaffeine),

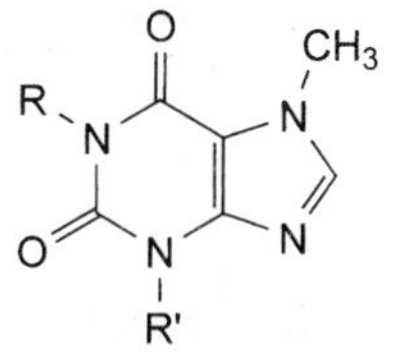

D. R = H, R′ = CH₃: theobromine,
F. R = CH₃, R′ = H:
1,7-dimethyl-3,7-dihydro-1*H*-purine-2,6-dione,

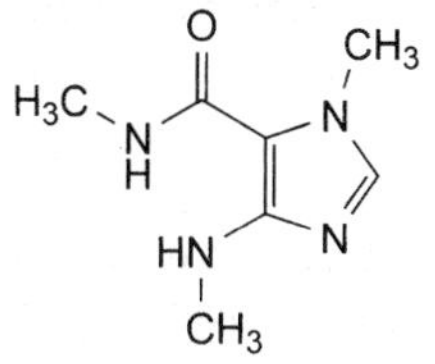

E. *N*,1-dimethyl-4-(methylamino)-1*H*-imidazole-5-carboxamide (caffeidine).

*Ph Eur*

# Caffeine Hydrate

(*Caffeine Monohydrate, Ph Eur monograph 0268*)

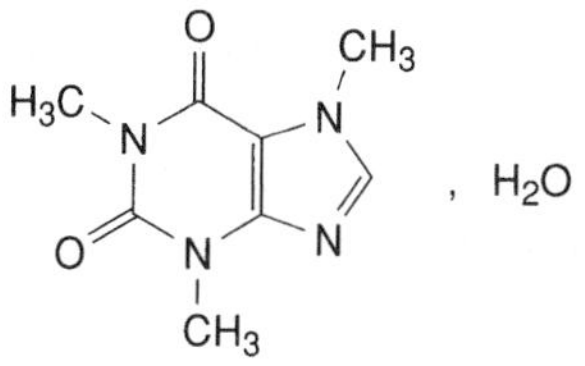

C₈H₁₀N₄O₂,H₂O          212.2          *5743-12-4*

### Action and use
Central nervous system stimulant.

*Ph Eur*

### DEFINITION
1,3,7-Trimethyl-3,7-dihydro-1*H*-purine-2,6-dione monohydrate.

### Content
98.5 per cent to 101.5 per cent (dried substance).

### CHARACTERS
#### Appearance
White or almost white, crystalline powder or silky, white or almost white crystals.

#### Solubility
Sparingly soluble in water, freely soluble in boiling water, slightly soluble in ethanol (96 per cent). It dissolves in concentrated solutions of alkali benzoates or salicylates.

It sublimes readily.

### IDENTIFICATION
*First identification* A, B, E.

*Second identification* A, C, D, E, F.

A. Melting point (*2.2.14*): 234 °C to 239 °C, determined after drying at 100-105 °C.

B. Infrared absorption spectrophotometry (*2.2.24*).

*Preparation* Dry the substance to be examined at 100-105 °C before use.

*Comparison* caffeine CRS.

C. To 2 ml of a saturated solution add 0.05 ml of *iodinated potassium iodide solution R*; the solution remains clear. Add 0.1 ml of *dilute hydrochloric acid R*; a brown precipitate is formed. Neutralise with *dilute sodium hydroxide solution R*; the precipitate dissolves.

D. In a glass-stoppered tube, dissolve about 10 mg in 0.25 ml of a mixture of 0.5 ml of *acetylacetone R* and 5 ml of *dilute sodium hydroxide solution R*. Heat in a water-bath at 80 °C for 7 min. Cool and add 0.5 ml of *dimethylaminobenzaldehyde solution R2*. Heat again in a water-bath at 80 °C for 7 min. Allow to cool and add 10 ml of *water R*; an intense blue colour develops.

E. Loss on drying (see Tests).

F. It gives the reaction of xanthines (*2.3.1*).

### TESTS
#### Solution S
Dissolve 0.5 g with heating in 50 ml of *carbon dioxide-free water R* prepared from *distilled water R*, cool, and dilute to 50 ml with the same solvent.

#### Appearance of solution
Solution S is clear (*2.2.1*) and colourless (*2.2.2, Method II*).

**Acidity**

To 10 ml of solution S add 0.05 ml of *bromothymol blue solution R1*; the solution is green or yellow. Not more than 0.2 ml of *0.01 M sodium hydroxide* is required to change the colour of the indicator to blue.

**Related substances**

Liquid chromatography (2.2.29).

*Test solution* Dissolve 0.110 g of the substance to be examined in the mobile phase and dilute to 50.0 ml with the mobile phase. Dilute 1.0 ml of this solution to 10.0 ml with the mobile phase.

*Reference solution (a)* Dilute 2.0 ml of the test solution to 100.0 ml with the mobile phase. Dilute 1.0 ml of this solution to 10.0 ml with the mobile phase.

*Reference solution (b)* Dissolve 5 mg of *caffeine for system suitability CRS* (containing impurities A, C, D and F) in the mobile phase and dilute to 5.0 ml with the mobile phase. Dilute 2.0 ml of this solution to 10.0 ml with the mobile phase.

*Column:*
— *size: l = 0.15 m, Ø = 4.6 mm;*
— *stationary phase: base-deactivated end-capped octadecylsilyl silica gel for chromatography R (5 µm).*

*Mobile phase* Mix 20 volumes of *tetrahydrofuran R*, 25 volumes of *acetonitrile R* and 955 volumes of a solution containing 0.82 g/l of *anhydrous sodium acetate R* previously adjusted to pH 4.5 with *glacial acetic acid R*.

*Flow rate* 1.0 ml/min.

*Detection* Spectrophotometer at 275 nm.

*Injection* 10 µl.

*Run time* 1.5 times the retention time of caffeine.

*Identification of impurities* Use the chromatogram supplied with *caffeine for system suitability CRS* and the chromatogram obtained with reference solution (b) to identify the peaks due to impurities A, C, D and F.

*Retention time* Caffeine = about 8 min.

*System suitability* Reference solution (b):
— *resolution*: minimum 2.5 between the peaks due to impurities C and D; minimum 2.5 between the peaks due to impurities F and A.

*Limits:*
— *unspecified impurities*: for each impurity, not more than 0.5 times the area of the principal peak in the chromatogram obtained with reference solution (a) (0.10 per cent);
— *total*: not more than 0.5 times the area of the principal peak in the chromatogram obtained with reference solution (a) (0.1 per cent);
— *disregard limit*: 0.25 times the area of the principal peak in the chromatogram obtained with reference solution (a) (0.05 per cent).

**Sulphates** (2.4.13)

Maximum 500 ppm, determined on 15 ml of solution S.

Prepare the standard using a mixture of 7.5 ml of *sulphate standard solution (10 ppm SO₄) R* and 7.5 ml of *distilled water R*.

**Heavy metals** (2.4.8)

Maximum 20 ppm.

1.0 g complies with test C. Prepare the reference solution using 2 ml of *lead standard solution (10 ppm Pb) R*.

**Loss on drying** (2.2.32)

5.0 per cent to 9.0 per cent, determined on 1.000 g by drying in an oven at 105 °C for 1 h.

**Sulphated ash** (2.4.14)

Maximum 0.1 per cent, determined on 1.0 g.

**ASSAY**

Dissolve 0.170 g, previously dried at 100-105 °C, with heating in 5 ml of *anhydrous acetic acid R*. Allow to cool, and add 10 ml of *acetic anhydride R* and 20 ml of *toluene R*. Titrate with *0.1 M perchloric acid*, determining the end-point potentiometrically (2.2.20).

1 ml of *0.1 M perchloric acid* is equivalent to 19.42 mg of $C_8H_{10}N_4O_2$.

**IMPURITIES**

*Other detectable impurities* (The following substances would, if present at a sufficient level, be detected by one or other of the tests in the monograph. They are limited by the general acceptance criterion for other/unspecified impurities and/or by the general monograph *Substances for pharmaceutical use (2034)*. It is therefore not necessary to identify these impurities for demonstration of compliance. See also 5.10. *Control of impurities in substances for pharmaceutical use*): A, B, C, D, E, F.

A. theophylline,

B. *N*-(6-amino-1,3-dimethyl-2,4-dioxo-1,2,3,4-tetrahydropyrimidin-5-yl)formamide,

C. 1,3,9-trimethyl-3,9-dihydro-1*H*-purine-2,6-dione (isocaffeine),

D. theobromine,

E. *N*,1-dimethyl-4-(methylamino)-1*H*-imidazole-5-carboxamide (caffeidine),

F. 1,7-dimethyl-3,7-dihydro-1*H*-purine-2,6-dione.

*Ph Eur*

# Calamine

Prepared Calamine

**Action and use**
Antipruritic.

**Preparations**
Aqueous Calamine Cream
Calamine Lotion
Calamine Ointment
Calamine and Coal Tar Ointment

## DEFINITION
Calamine is a basic zinc carbonate suitably coloured with iron(III) oxide.

## CHARACTERISTICS
An amorphous, impalpable, pink or reddish brown powder, the colour depending on the variety and amount of iron(III) oxide present and the process by which it is incorporated.

Practically insoluble in *water*. It dissolves with effervescence in *hydrochloric acid*.

## IDENTIFICATION
A. Yields the reactions characteristic of *carbonates*, Appendix VI.

B. To 2 g add 5 ml of *hydrochloric acid* and heat to boiling; if necessary, add *hydrochloric acid* drop wise until a bright yellow solution is obtained. Cool and add *13.5M ammonia* until the first sign of precipitate (solution A). The solution yields reaction B characteristic of *iron salts*, Appendix VI. Dilute 1 ml of solution A to 5 ml with *water*; the solution yields the reaction characteristic of *zinc salts*, Appendix VI.

## TESTS
**Calcium**
Dissolve 0.50 g in a mixture of 10 ml of *water* and 2.5 ml of *glacial acetic acid* and filter. To 0.5 ml of the filtrate add 15 ml of *5M ammonia* and 2 ml of a 2.5% w/v solution of *ammonium oxalate* and allow to stand for 2 minutes. The solution remains clear.

**Soluble barium salts**
To the remainder of the filtrate obtained in the test for Calcium add 2 ml of *1M sulphuric acid* and allow to stand for 5 minutes. The solution remains clear.

**Lead**
Not more than 150 ppm when determined by *atomic absorption spectrophotometry*, Appendix II D, Method II, measuring at 283.3 nm or 217 nm and using an air-acetylene flame. Carefully add 5 g of the substance being examined to 25 ml of *hydrochloric acid* and allow to stand for 18 hours. Add 5 ml of *nitric acid* and sufficient *water* to produce 200 ml. Use *lead standard solution (100 ppm Pb)* suitably diluted with a 3.5% v/v solution of *nitric acid* to prepare the standard solution.

**Chloride**
Dissolve 0.15 g in *water* with the addition of 1 ml of *nitric acid*, filter and dilute to 30 ml with *water*. The resulting solution complies with the *limit test for chlorides*, Appendix VII (0.07%).

**Sulphate**
Dissolve 0.1 g in *water* with the addition of 3 ml of *2M hydrochloric acid*, filter and dilute to 60 ml with *water*. The resulting solution complies with the *limit test for sulphates*, Appendix VII (0.6%).

**Ethanol-soluble dyes**
Shake 1.0 g with 10 ml of *ethanol (90%)* and filter. The filtrate is *colourless*, Appendix IV B, Method II.

**Matter insoluble in hydrochloric acid**
Dissolve 1 g in 20 ml of warm *2M hydrochloric acid* and filter. The residue, when washed with *water* and dried to constant weight at 105°, weighs not more than 10 mg.

**Water-soluble dyes**
Shake 1.0 g with 10 ml of *water* and filter. The filtrate is *colourless*, Appendix IV B, Method II.

**Residue on ignition**
68.0 to 74.0%, when ignited at a temperature not lower than 900° until, after further ignition, two successive weighings do not differ by more than 0.2% of the weight of the residue. Use 1 g.

# Calcifediol

(*Ph Eur monograph 1295*)

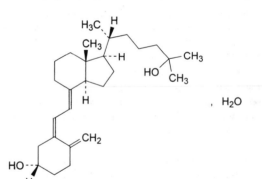

C₂₇H₄₄O₂,H₂O        418.7        *63283-36-3*

**Action and use**
Vitamin D analogue.

*Ph Eur*

## DEFINITION
(5Z,7E)-9,10-Secocholesta-5,7,10(19)-triene-3β,25-diol monohydrate.

**Content**
97.0 per cent to 102.0 per cent (anhydrous substance).

## CHARACTERS
**Appearance**
White or almost white crystals.

**Solubility**
Practically insoluble in water, freely soluble in ethanol (96 per cent), soluble in fatty oils.

It is sensitive to air, heat and light.

A reversible isomerisation to pre-calcifediol takes place in solution, depending on temperature and time. The activity is due to both compounds.

## IDENTIFICATION

A. Infrared absorption spectrophotometry (2.2.24).

*Preparation*   Mix 2 mg of the substance to be examined and 225 mg of *potassium bromide R*.

*Comparison*   *Ph. Eur. reference spectrum of calcifediol.*

B. Examine the chromatograms obtained in the assay.

*Results*   The principal peak in the chromatogram obtained with the test solution is similar in retention time and size to the principal peak in the chromatogram obtained with reference solution (a).

## TESTS

### Related substances

Liquid chromatography (2.2.29): use the normalisation procedure. *Carry out the test as rapidly as possible, avoiding exposure to actinic light and air.*

*Test solution*   Dissolve 1.0 mg of the substance to be examined without heating in 10.0 ml of the mobile phase.

*Reference solution (a)*   Dissolve 1.0 mg of *calcifediol CRS* without heating in 10.0 ml of the mobile phase.

*Reference solution (b)*   Dilute 1.0 ml of reference solution (a) to 100.0 ml with the mobile phase.

*Reference solution (c)*   Heat 2 ml of reference solution (a) in a water-bath at 80 °C under a reflux condenser for 2 h and cool.

*Column:*
— size: $l = 0.15$ m, $\varnothing = 4.6$ mm;
— stationary phase: *octylsilyl silica gel for chromatography R1* (5 µm).

*Mobile phase*   *water R, methanol R* (200:800 *V/V*).

*Flow rate*   1.5 ml/min.

*Detection*   Spectrophotometer at 265 nm.

*Injection*   50 µl of the test solution and reference solutions (b) and (c).

*Run time*   Twice the retention time of calcifediol.

*Relative retention*   With reference to calcifediol (retention time = about 11 min): pre-calcifediol = about 1.3.

*System suitability*   Reference solution (c):
— resolution: minimum 5.0 between the peaks due to pre-calcifediol and calcifediol; if necessary, adjust the proportions of the constituents in the mobile phase.

*Limits:*
— impurities A, B, C, D: for each impurity, maximum 0.5 per cent;
— total: maximum 1.0 per cent;
— disregard limit: 0.1 times the area of the principal peak in the chromatogram obtained with reference solution (b) (0.1 per cent); disregard the peak due to pre-alfacalcidiol.

### Water (2.5.32)

3.8 per cent to 5.0 per cent, determined on 10.0 mg.

## ASSAY

Liquid chromatography (2.2.29) as described in the test for related substances with the following modifications.

*Injection*   The test solution and reference solutions (a) and (c).

*System suitability*   Reference solution (c):
— repeatability: maximum relative standard deviation of 1 per cent for the peak due to calcifediol after 6 injections.

Calculate the percentage content of $C_{27}H_{44}O_2$ from the declared content of *calcifediol CRS*.

## STORAGE

Under nitrogen, in an airtight container, protected from light, at a temperature of 2 °C to 8 °C.

The contents of an opened container are to be used immediately.

## IMPURITIES

*Specified impurities*   *A, B, C, D.*

A. 9β,10α-cholesta-5,7-diene-3β,25-diol,

B. cholesta-5,7-diene-3β,25-diol,

C. (6E)-9,10-secocholesta-5(10),6,8-triene-3β,25-diol,

D. (5E,7E)-9,10-secocholesta-5,7,10(19)-triene-3β,25-diol.

# Anhydrous Calcipotriol

(*Ph Eur monograph 2011*)

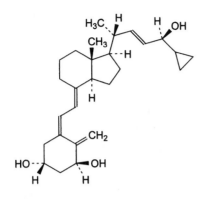

$C_{27}H_{40}O_3$      412.6      *112828-00-9*

## Action and use

Vitamin D analogue.

*Ph Eur*

## DEFINITION

(5Z,7E,22E,24S)-24-Cyclopropyl-9,10-secochola-5,7,10(19),22-tetraene-1α,3β,24-triol.

## Content

95.5 per cent to 102.0 per cent (dried substance).

## CHARACTERS

### Appearance

White or almost white, crystalline powder.

### Solubility

Practically insoluble in water, freely soluble in ethanol (96 per cent), slightly soluble in methylene chloride.

It is sensitive to heat and light.

A reversible isomerisation to pre-calcipotriol takes place in solution, depending on temperature and time. The activity is due to both compounds.

## IDENTIFICATION

A. Infrared absorption spectrophotometry (*2.2.24*).

*Comparison*  Ph. Eur. reference spectrum of anhydrous calcipotriol.

B. Loss on drying (see Tests).

*Carry out the tests for related substances and the assay as rapidly as possible and protected from actinic light and air.*

## TESTS

### Related substances

A. Thin-layer chromatography (*2.2.27*).

*Solution A*  To 1 ml of *triethylamine R* add 9 ml of *chloroform R*.

*Test solution*  Dissolve 1 mg of the substance to be examined in 100 µl of solution A.

*Reference solution (a)*  To 10 µl of the test solution add 990 µl of solution A.

*Reference solution (b)*  To 250 µl of reference solution (a) add 750 µl of solution A.

*Reference solution (c)*  To 100 µl of reference solution (a) add 900 µl of solution A.

*Reference solution (d)*  Place 2 mg of the substance to be examined in a vial and dissolve in 200 µl of solution A. Close the vial and keep it in a water bath at 60 °C for 2 h.

*Plate*  TLC silica gel $F_{254}$ plate R.

*Mobile phase*  2-methylpropanol R, methylene chloride R (20:80 V/V).

*Application*  10 µl of the test solution and reference solutions (b), (c) and (d).

*Development*  Over 2/3 of the plate.

*Drying*  In air, then at 140 °C for 10 min.

*Detection*  Spray the hot plate with an *alcoholic solution of sulphuric acid R*, dry at 140 °C for not more than 1 min and examine in ultraviolet light at 366 nm.

*Relative retention*  With reference to calcipotriol ($R_F$ = about 0.4): impurity G = about 0.4; impurity H = about 0.4; pre-calcipotriol = about 0.9; impurity A = about 1.2.

*System suitability*  Reference solution (d):
— the chromatogram shows a secondary spot due to pre-calcipotriol.

*Limits:*
— *impurity A*: any spot due to impurity A is not more intense than the spot in the chromatogram obtained with reference solution (b) (0.25 per cent),
— *impurities G, H*: any spot due to impurity G or H is not more intense than the spot in the chromatogram obtained with reference solution (b) (0.25 per cent for the sum),
— *any other impurity*: any other spot is not more intense than the spot in the chromatogram obtained with reference solution (c) (0.1 per cent).

B. Liquid chromatography (*2.2.29*).

*Solution A.*  Dissolve 1.32 g of *ammonium phosphate R* in *water R* and dilute to 10.0 ml with the same solvent.

*Solvent mixture*  solution A, water R, methanol R (3:297:700 V/V/V).

*Test solution (a)*  Dissolve 2.00 mg of the substance to be examined in the solvent mixture and dilute to 5.0 ml with the solvent mixture.

*Test solution (b)*  Dissolve 2.00 mg of the substance to be examined in the solvent mixture and dilute to 20.0 ml with the same solvent mixture.

*Reference solution (a)*  Dilute 1.0 ml of test solution (a) to 100.0 ml with the solvent mixture.

*Reference solution (b)*  Dilute 1.0 ml of reference solution (a) to 10.0 ml with the solvent mixture.

*Reference solution (c)*  Dissolve 1.0 mg of *calcipotriol monohydrate CRS* (containing impurities B, C and D) in the solvent mixture and dilute to 2.5 ml with the solvent mixture.

*Reference solution (d)*  Dissolve 2.00 mg of *calcipotriol monohydrate CRS* in the solvent mixture and dilute to 20.0 ml with the solvent mixture.

*Column:*
— size: l = 0.10 m, Ø = 4.0 mm,
— stationary phase: octadecylsilyl silica gel for chromatography R (3 µm).

*Mobile phase*  water R, methanol R (30:70 V/V).

*Flow rate*  1.0 ml/min.

*Detection*  Spectrophotometer at 264 nm.

*Injection*  20 µl of test solution (a) and reference solutions (a), (b) and (c).

*Run time*  Twice the retention time of calcipotriol.

*Relative retention*  With reference to calcipotriol (retention time = about 13.5 min): impurity B = about 0.86; impurity C = about 0.92; impurity D = about 1.3.

*System suitability* Reference solution (c):
— *peak-to-valley ratio*: minimum 1.5, where $H_p$ = height
above the baseline of the peak due to impurity C and
$H_v$ = height above the baseline of the lowest point of the
curve separating this peak from the peak due to
calcipotriol,
— the chromatogram obtained is similar to the
chromatogram supplied with *calcipotriol monohydrate CRS*.

*Limits:*
— *impurity B*: not more than 0.5 times the area of the
principal peak in the chromatogram obtained with
reference solution (a) (0.5 per cent),
— *impurities C, D*: for each impurity, not more than the area
of the principal peak in the chromatogram obtained with
reference solution (a) (1.0 per cent),
— *any other impurity*: for each impurity, not more than the
area of the principal peak in the chromatogram obtained
with reference solution (b) (0.1 per cent),
— *total*: not more than 2.5 times the area of the principal
peak in the chromatogram obtained with reference
solution (a) (2.5 per cent),
— *disregard limit*: 0.5 times the area of the principal peak in
the chromatogram obtained with reference solution (b)
(0.05 per cent).

**Loss on drying**
Maximum 1.0 per cent, determined on 5 mg by
thermogravimetry (*2.2.34*). Heat to 105 °C at a rate of
10 °C/min and maintain at 105 °C for 60 min.

**ASSAY**
Liquid chromatography (*2.2.29*) as described in the test for
related substances with the following modification.

*Injection* Test solution (b) and reference solution (d).

Calculate the percentage content of $C_{27}H_{40}O_3$ from the areas
of the peaks and the declared content of *calcipotriol
monohydrate CRS*.

**STORAGE**
In an airtight container, protected from light at − 20 °C or
below.

**IMPURITIES**
*Specified impurities A, B, C, D, G, H.*

*Other detectable impurities* (the following substances would, if
present at a sufficient level, be detected by one or other of
the tests in the monograph. They are limited by the general
acceptance criterion for other/unspecified impurities and/or
by the general monograph *Substances for pharmaceutical use
(2034)*. It is therefore not necessary to identify these
impurities for demonstration of compliance. See also *5.10.
Control of impurities in substances for pharmaceutical use*):
*E, F, I.*

*By thin-layer chromatography A, G, H, I.*
*By liquid chromatography B, C, D, E, F.*

A. R + R′ = O: (*5Z,7E,22E*)-24-cyclopropyl-1α,3β-
dihydroxy-9,10-secochola-5,7,10(19),22-tetraen-24-one,

D. R = OH, R′ = H: (*5Z,7E,22E,24R*)-24-cyclopropyl-9,10-
secochola-5,7,10(19),22-tetraene-1α,3β,24-triol
(24-*epi*-calcipotriol),

B. (*5Z,7Z,22E,24S*)-24-cyclopropyl-9,10-secochola-
5,7,10(19),22-tetraene-1α,3β,24-triol ((*7Z*)-calcipotriol),

C. (*5E,7E,22E,24S*)-24-cyclopropyl-9,10-secochola-
5,7,10(19),22-tetraene-1α,3β,24-triol ((*5E*)-calcipotriol),

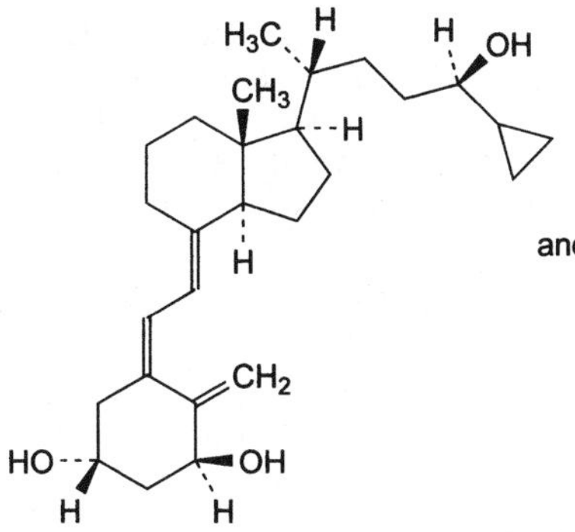

E. *rac*-(5*Z*,7*E*,22*E*,24*S*)-24-cyclopropyl-9,10-secochola-5,7,10(19)-triene-1α,3β,24-triol,

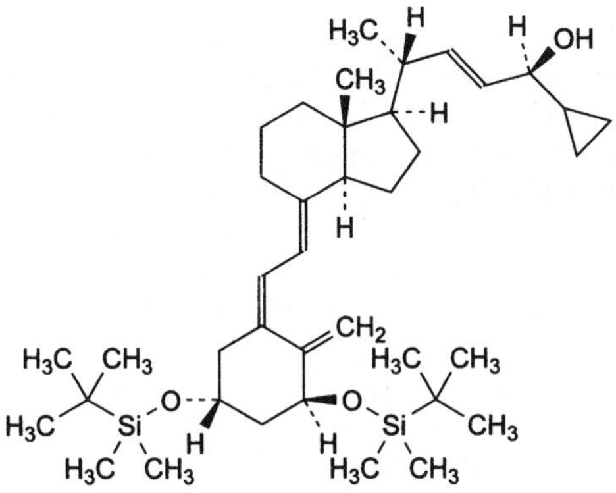

F. (5*Z*,7*E*,22*E*,24*S*)-24-cyclopropyl-1α,3β-bis[[(1,1-dimethylethyl)dimethylsilyl]oxy]-9,10-secochola-5,7,10(19),22-tetraen-24-ol,

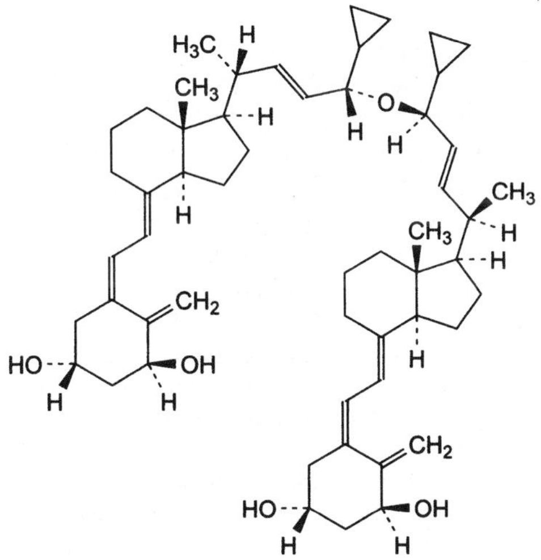

G. 24,24′-oxybis[(5*Z*,7*E*,22*E*,24*S*)-24-cyclopropyl-9,10-secochola-5,7,10(19),22-tetraene-1α,3β-diol],

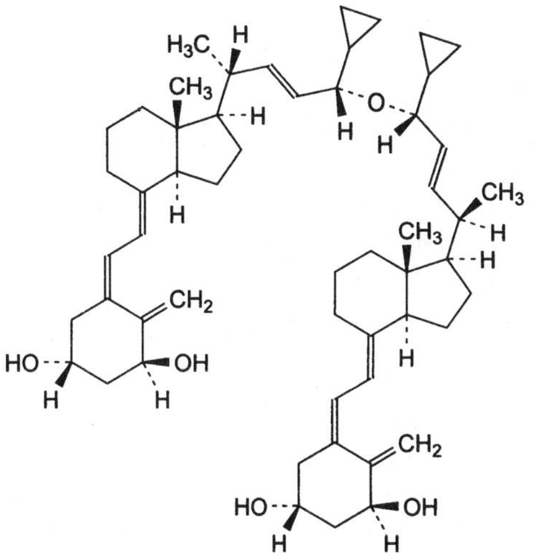

H. (5*Z*,7*E*,22*E*,24*R*)-24-cyclopropyl-24-[[(5*Z*,7*E*,22*E*,24*S*)-24-cyclopropyl-1α,3β-dihydroxy-9,10-secochola-5,7,10(19),22-tetraen-24-yl]oxy]-9,10-secochola-5,7,10(19),22-tetraene-1α,3β-diol,

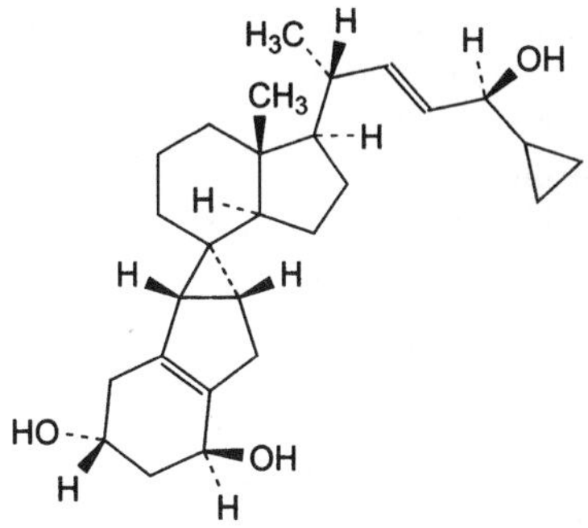

I. (6*S*,7*R*,8*R*,22*E*,24*S*)-24-cyclopropyl-6,8:7,19-dicyclo-9,10-secochola-5(10),22-diene-1α,3β,24-triol (suprasterol of calcipotriol).

*Ph Eur*

# Calcipotriol Monohydrate

(*Ph Eur monograph 2284*)

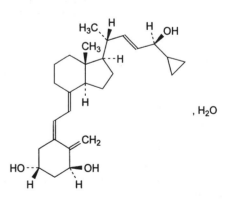

, H₂O

$C_{27}H_{40}O_3,H_2O$     430.6     *112965-21-6*

**Action and use**
Vitamin D analogue.

*Ph Eur*

## DEFINITION

(5Z,7E,22E,24S)-24-Cyclopropyl-9,10-secochola-5,7,10(19),22-tetraene-1α,3β,24-triol monohydrate.

**Content:**
95.5 per cent to 102.0 per cent (anhydrous substance).

## CHARACTERS

**Appearance**
White or almost white, crystalline powder.

**Solubility**
Practically insoluble in water, freely soluble in ethanol (96 per cent), slightly soluble in methylene chloride.

It is sensitive to light.

A reversible isomerisation to pre-calcipotriol takes place in solution, depending on temperature and time. The activity is due to both compounds.

## IDENTIFICATION

A. Infrared absorption spectrophotometry (*2.2.24*).

*Comparison* Ph. Eur. reference spectrum of calcipotriol monohydrate.

B. Water (see Tests).

*Carry out the tests for related substances and the assay as rapidly as possible and protected from actinic light and air.*

## TESTS

**Related substances**
A. Thin-layer chromatography (*2.2.27*).

*Solution A* To 1 ml of *triethylamine R* add 9 ml of *chloroform R*.

*Test solution* Dissolve 1 mg of the substance to be examined in 100 µl of solution A.

*Reference solution (a)* To 10 µl of the test solution add 990 µl of solution A.

*Reference solution (b)* To 250 µl of reference solution (a) add 750 µl of solution A.

*Reference solution (c)* To 100 µl of reference solution (a) add 900 µl of solution A.

*Reference solution (d)* Place 2 mg of the substance to be examined in a vial and dissolve in 200 µl of solution A. Close the vial and keep it in a water bath at 60 °C for 2 h.

*Plate* TLC silica gel $F_{254}$ plate R.

*Mobile phase* 2-methylpropanol R, methylene chloride R (20:80 V/V).

*Application* 10 µl of the test solution and reference solutions (b), (c) and (d).

*Development* Over 2/3 of the plate.

*Drying* In air, then at 140 °C for 10 min.

*Detection* Spray the hot plate with an *alcoholic solution of sulphuric acid R*, dry at 140 °C for not more than 1 min and examine in ultraviolet light at 366 nm.

*Relative retention* With reference to calcipotriol ($R_F$ = about 0.4): impurity G = about 0.4; impurity H = about 0.4; pre-calcipotriol = about 0.9; impurity A = about 1.2.

*System suitability* Reference solution (d):
— the chromatogram shows a secondary spot due to pre-calcipotriol.

*Limits:*
— *impurity A:* any spot due to impurity A is not more intense than the spot in the chromatogram obtained with reference solution (b) (0.25 per cent),

— *impurities G, H:* any spot due to impurity G or H is not more intense than the spot in the chromatogram obtained with reference solution (b) (0.25 per cent for the sum),
— *any other impurity:* any other spot is not more intense than the spot in the chromatogram obtained with reference solution (c) (0.1 per cent).

B. Liquid chromatography (*2.2.29*).

*Solution A* Dissolve 1.32 g of *ammonium phosphate R* in *water R* and dilute to 10.0 ml with the same solvent.

*Solvent mixture* solution A, *water R*, *methanol R* (3:297:700 V/V/V).

*Test solution (a)* Dissolve 2.00 mg of the substance to be examined in the solvent mixture and dilute to 5.0 ml with the solvent mixture.

*Test solution (b)* Dissolve 2.00 mg of the substance to be examined in the solvent mixture and dilute to 20.0 ml with the same solvent mixture.

*Reference solution (a)* Dilute 1.0 ml of test solution (a) to 100.0 ml with the solvent mixture.

*Reference solution (b)* Dilute 1.0 ml of reference solution (a) to 10.0 ml with the solvent mixture.

*Reference solution (c)* Dissolve 1.0 mg of *calcipotriol monohydrate CRS* (containing impurities B, C and D) in the solvent mixture and dilute to 2.5 ml with the solvent mixture.

*Reference solution (d)* Dissolve 2.00 mg of *calcipotriol monohydrate CRS* in the solvent mixture and dilute to 20.0 ml with the solvent mixture.

*Column:*
— size: l = 0.10 m, Ø = 4.0 mm,
— stationary phase: *octadecylsilyl silica gel for chromatography R* (3 µm).

*Mobile phase* water R, methanol R (30:70 V/V).

*Flow rate* 1.0 ml/min.

*Detection* Spectrophotometer at 264 nm.

*Injection* 20 µl of test solution (a) and reference solutions (a), (b) and (c).

*Run time* Twice the retention time of calcipotriol.

*Relative retention* With reference to calcipotriol (retention time = about 13.5 min): impurity B = about 0.86; impurity C = about 0.92; impurity D = about 1.3.

*System suitability* Reference solution (c):
— *peak-to-valley ratio:* minimum 1.5, where $H_p$ = height above the baseline of the peak due to impurity C and $H_v$ = height above the baseline of the lowest point of the curve separating this peak from the peak due to calcipotriol,
— the chromatogram obtained is similar to the chromatogram supplied with *calcipotriol monohydrate CRS*.

*Limits:*
— *impurity B:* not more than 0.5 times the area of the principal peak in the chromatogram obtained with reference solution (a) (0.5 per cent),
— *impurities C, D:* for each impurity, not more than the area of the principal peak in the chromatogram obtained with reference solution (a) (1.0 per cent),
— *any other impurity:* for each impurity, not more than the area of the principal peak in the chromatogram obtained with reference solution (b) (0.1 per cent),
— *total:* not more than 2.5 times the area of the principal peak in the chromatogram obtained with reference solution (a) (2.5 per cent),

— *disregard limit*: 0.5 times the area of the principal peak in the chromatogram obtained with reference solution (b) (0.05 per cent).

**Water** (*2.5.12*)

3.3 per cent to 5.0 per cent, determined on 0.100 g.

**ASSAY**

Liquid chromatography (*2.2.29*) as described in the test for related substances with the following modification.

*Injection*   Test solution (b) and reference solution (d).

Calculate the percentage content of $C_{27}H_{40}O_3$ from the areas of the peaks and the declared content of *calcipotriol monohydrate CRS*.

**STORAGE**

In an airtight container, protected from light.

**IMPURITIES**

*Specified impurities*   *A, B, C, D, G, H.*

*Other detectable impurities* (the following substances would, if present at a sufficient level, be detected by one or other of the tests in the monograph. They are limited by the general acceptance criterion for other/unspecified impurities and/or by the general monograph *Substances for pharmaceutical use (2034)*. It is therefore not necessary to identify these impurities for demonstration of compliance. See also *5.10*. *Control of impurities in substances for pharmaceutical use*): *E, F, I.*

*By thin-layer chromatography*   *A, G, H, I.*

*By liquid chromatography*   *B, C, D, E, F.*

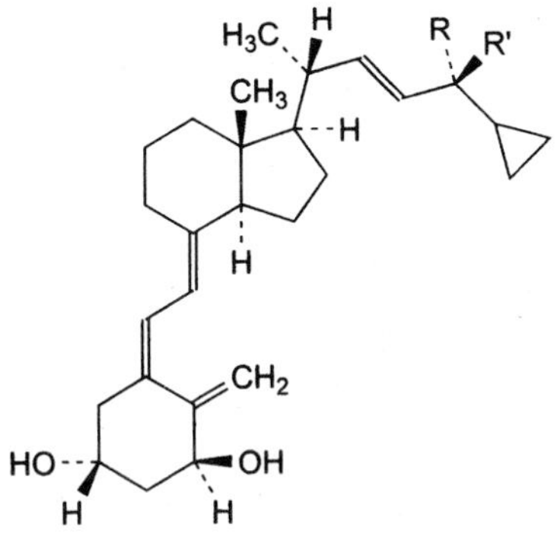

A. R + R′ = O: (5Z,7E,22E)-24-cyclopropyl-1α,3β-dihydroxy-9,10-secochola-5,7,10(19),22-tetraen-24-one,

D. R = OH, R′ = H: (5Z,7E,22E,24R)-24-cyclopropyl-9,10-secochola-5,7,10(19),22-tetraene-1α,3β,24-triol (24-*epi*-calcipotriol),

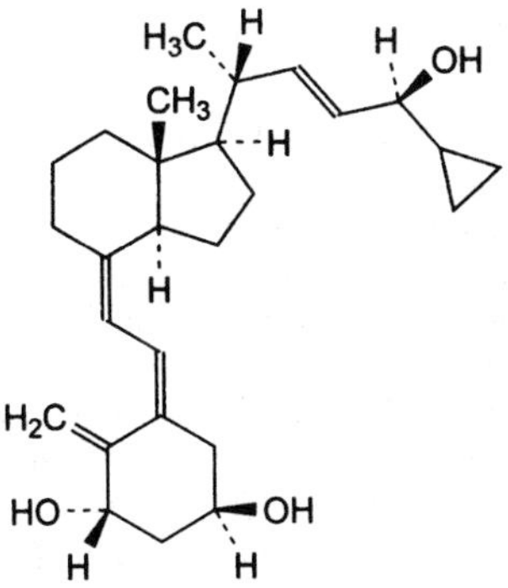

B. (5Z,7Z,22E,24S)-24-cyclopropyl-9,10-secochola-5,7,10(19),22-tetraene-1α,3β,24-triol ((7Z)-calcipotriol),

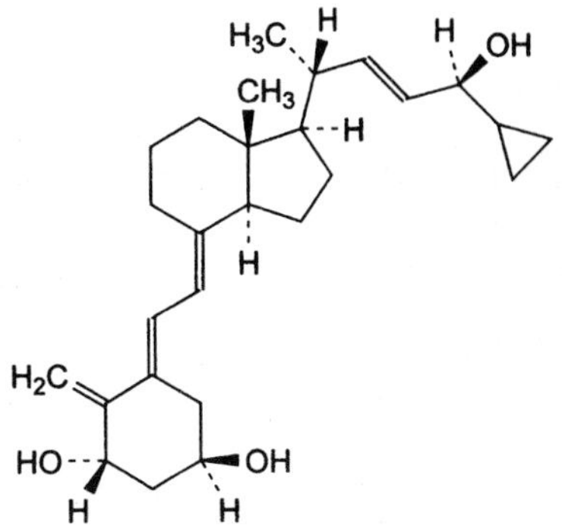

C. (5E,7E,22E,24S)-24-cyclopropyl-9,10-secochola-5,7,10(19),22-tetraene-1α,3β,24-triol ((5E)-calcipotriol),

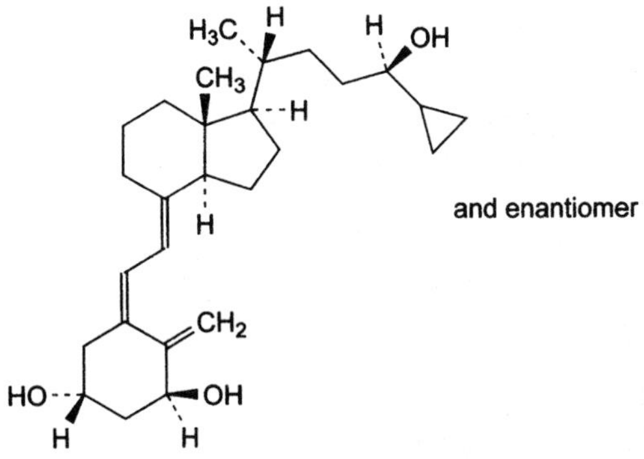

and enantiomer

E. *rac*-(5Z,7E,22E,24S)-24-cyclopropyl-9,10-secochola-5,7,10(19)-triene-1α,3β,24-triol,

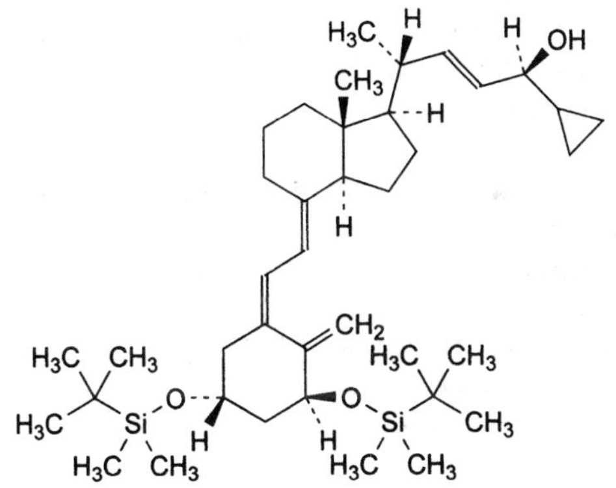

F. (5Z,7E,22E,24S)-24-cyclopropyl-1α,3β-bis[[(1,1-dimethylethyl)dimethylsilyl]oxy]-9,10-secochola-5,7,10(19),22-tetraen-24-ol,

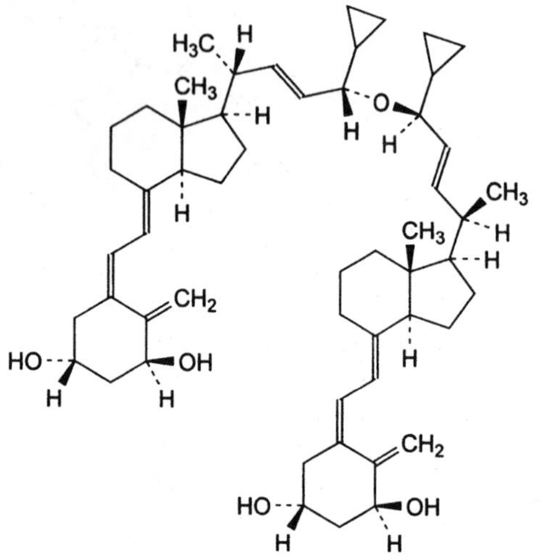

G. 24,24'-oxybis[(5Z,7E,22E,24S)-24-cyclopropyl-9,10-secochola-5,7,10(19),22-tetraene-1α,3β-diol],

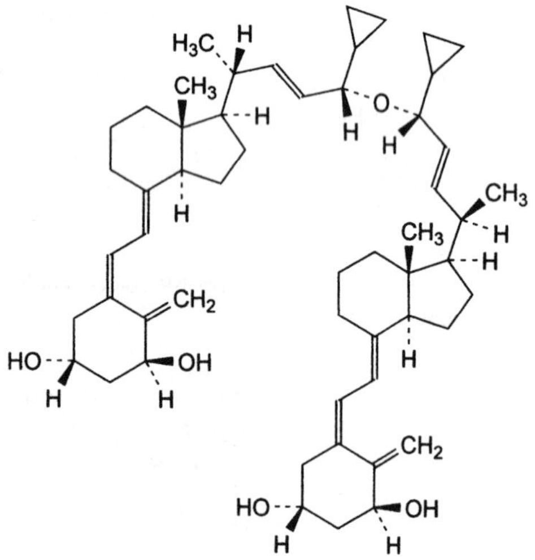

H. (5Z,7E,22E,24R)-24-cyclopropyl-24-[[(5Z,7E,22E,24S)-24-cyclopropyl-1α,3β-dihydroxy-9,10-secochola-5,7,10(19),22-tetraen-24-yl]oxy]-9,10-secochola-5,7,10(19),22-tetraene-1α,3β-diol,

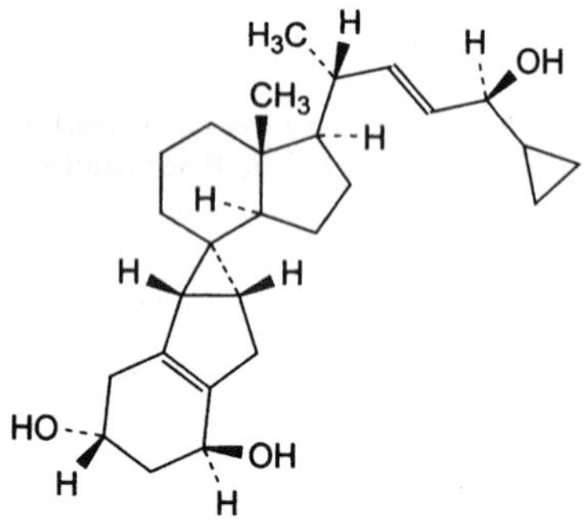

I. (6S,7R,8R,22E,24S)-24-cyclopropyl-6,8:7,19-dicyclo-9,10-secochola-5(10),22-diene-1α,3β,24-triol (suprasterol of calcipotriol).

*Ph Eur*

# Calcitonin (Salmon)

(*Ph Eur monograph 0471*)

H–Cys–Ser–Asn–Leu–Ser–Thr–Cys–Val–Leu–Gly–
Lys–Leu–Ser–Gln–Glu–Leu–His–Lys–Leu–Gln–
Thr–Tyr–Pro–Arg–Thr–Asn–Thr–Gly–Ser–Gly–
Thr–Pro–NH$_2$

$C_{145}H_{240}N_{44}O_{48}S_2$       3432       *47931-85-1*

**Action and use**

Hormone.

**Preparation**

Calcitonin (Salmon) Injection

*Ph Eur*

## DEFINITION

Polypeptide having the structure determined for salmon calcitonin I. It lowers the calcium concentration in plasma of mammals by diminishing the rate of bone resorption. It is obtained by chemical synthesis or by a method based on recombinant DNA (rDNA) technology. It is available as an acetate.

**Content**

90.0 per cent to 105.0 per cent of the peptide $C_{145}H_{240}N_{44}O_{48}S_2$ (anhydrous and acetic acid-free substance).

By convention, for the purpose of labelling calcitonin (salmon) preparations, 1 mg of calcitonin (salmon) ($C_{145}H_{240}N_{44}O_{48}S_2$) is equivalent to 6000 IU of biological activity.

## PRODUCTION

*The following requirements apply only to calcitonin (salmon) produced by a method based on rDNA technology.*

*Prior to release the following tests are carried out on each batch of final bulk product unless exemption has been granted by the competent authority.*

**Host-cell-derived proteins**

The limit is approved by the competent authority.

**Host-cell or vector-derived DNA**

The limit is approved by the competent authority.

## CHARACTERS

**Appearance**

White or almost white powder.

**Solubility**

Freely soluble in water.

## IDENTIFICATION

A. examine the chromatograms obtained in the assay.

*Results* The principal peak in the chromatogram obtained with the test solution is similar in retention time and size to the principal peak in the chromatogram obtained with the reference solution.

*The following requirement applies only to calcitonin (salmon) obtained by chemical synthesis.*

B. Amino acid analysis (*2.2.56*).

Express the content of each amino acid in moles. Calculate the relative proportions of the amino acids taking as equivalent to 1 the sum, divided by 20, of the number of moles of aspartic acid, glutamic acid, proline, glycine, valine, leucine, histidine, arginine and lysine. The values fall within the following limits: aspartic acid: 1.8 to 2.2; glutamic acid: 2.7 to 3.3; proline: 1.7 to 2.3; glycine: 2.7 to 3.3; valine: 0.9 to 1.1; leucine: 4.5 to 5.3; histidine: 0.9 to 1.1; arginine: 0.9 to 1.1; lysine: 1.8 to 2.2; serine: 3.2 to 4.2; threonine: 4.2 to 5.2; tyrosine: 0.7 to 1.1; half-cystine: 1.4 to 2.1.

*The following requirement applies only to calcitonin (salmon) produced by a method based on rDNA technology.*

C. Peptide mapping (2.2.55).

*SELECTIVE CLEAVAGE OF THE PEPTIDE BONDS*

*Test solution* Prepare a 1 mg/ml solution of the substance to be examined. Transfer 1.0 ml to a clean tube. Add 100 µl of *1 M tris-hydrochloride buffer solution pH 8.0 R* and 20 µl of a freshly prepared 1.0 mg/ml solution of *trypsin for peptide mapping R*. Allow to stand at 2-8 °C for 16-20 h. Stop the reaction by adding 10 µl of a 50 per cent *V/V* solution of *trifluoroacetic acid R*. Cap the vial and mix. Centrifuge the vials to remove air bubbles.

*Reference solution* Prepare at the same time and in the same manner as for the test solution but using *calcitonin (salmon) CRS* instead of the substance to be examined.

*CHROMATOGRAPHIC SEPARATION*

Liquid chromatography (2.2.29).

*Column:*
— *size*: $l = 0.25$ m, Ø = 4.6 mm;
— *stationary phase: octadecylsilyl silica gel for chromatography R* (5 µm) with a pore size of 30 nm.

*Mobile phase:*
— *mobile phase A*: mix 1 ml of *trifluoroacetic acid R* and 1000 ml of *water R*; filter and degas;
— *mobile phase B*: mix 0.850 ml of *trifluoroacetic acid R*, 200 ml of *water R* and 800 ml of *acetonitrile for chromatography R*; filter and degas;

| Time (min) | Mobile phase A (per cent *V/V*) | Mobile phase B (per cent *V/V*) |
|---|---|---|
| 0 - 50 | 100 → 65 | 0 → 35 |
| 50 - 60 | 65 → 40 | 35 → 60 |
| 60 - 60.1 | 40 → 0 | 60 → 100 |
| 60.1 - 65.1 | 0 | 100 |
| 65.1 - 65.2 | 0 → 100 | 100 → 0 |
| 65.2 - 80.2 | 100 | 0 |

*Flow rate* 1.2 ml/min.

*Detection* Spectrophotometer at 214 nm.

*Equilibration* At initial conditions for at least 15 min. Carry out a blank run using the above-mentioned gradient.

*Injection* 20 µl.

*System suitability* The chromatograms obtained with the test solution and the reference solution are qualitatively similar to the chromatogram of calcitonin (salmon) digest supplied with *calcitonin (salmon) CRS*.

*Results* The profile of the chromatogram obtained with the test solution corresponds to that of the chromatogram obtained with the reference solution: the retention times of the fragment peaks in the chromatogram obtained with the test solution are within 5 per cent of the retention times of the fragments obtained with the reference solution; the peak area ratios of the fragment peaks in the chromatogram obtained with the test solution, normalised to the area of peak $T_2$, are within 5 per cent of the corresponding peak

ratios in the chromatogram obtained with the reference solution.

**TESTS**

**Acetic acid** (2.5.34)

4.0 per cent to 15.0 per cent.

*Test solution* Dissolve 10.0 mg of the substance to be examined in a mixture of 5 volumes of mobile phase B and 95 volumes of mobile phase A and dilute to 10.0 ml with the same mixture of mobile phases.

**Related substances**

Liquid chromatography (2.2.29): use the normalisation procedure.

*The following requirement applies to calcitonin (salmon), whether obtained by chemical synthesis or by a method based on rDNA technology.*

A. *Test solution*

Prepare a 1.0 mg/ml solution of the substance to be examined in mobile phase A.

*Reference solution* Dissolve the contents of a vial of *calcitonin (salmon) CRS* in mobile phase A to obtain a concentration of 1.0 mg/ml.

*Resolution solution* Dissolve the contents of a vial of *N-acetyl-Cys¹-calcitonin CRS* in 400 µl of mobile phase A and add 100 µl of the test solution.

*Column:*
— *size*: $l = 0.25$ m, Ø = 4.6 mm;
— *stationary phase: octadecylsilyl silica gel for chromatography R* (5 µm);
— *temperature*: 65 °C.

*Mobile phase*
— *mobile phase A*: dissolve 3.26 g of *tetramethylammonium hydroxide R* in 900 ml of *water R*, adjust to pH 2.5 with *phosphoric acid R* and mix with 100 ml of *acetonitrile for chromatography R*; filter and degas;
— *mobile phase B*: dissolve 1.45 g of *tetramethylammonium hydroxide R* in 400 ml of *water R*, adjust to pH 2.5 with *phosphoric acid R* and mix with 600 ml of acetonitrile for *chromatography R;* filter and degas;

| Time (min) | Mobile phase A (per cent *V/V*) | Mobile phase B (per cent *V/V*) |
|---|---|---|
| 0 - 30 | 72 → 48 | 28 → 52 |
| 30 - 32 | 48 → 72 | 52 → 28 |
| 32 - 55 | 72 | 28 |

*Flow rate* 1.0 ml/min.

*Detection* Spectrophotometer at 220 nm.

*Injection* 20 µl.

*Relative retention* With reference to calcitonin (salmon) (retention time = about 20 min): impurity B = about 0.8; impurity C = about 0.9; impurity D = about 1.05; impurity A = about 1.15.

*System suitability* Resolution solution:
— *resolution*: minimum 5.0 between the peaks due to calcitonin (salmon) and impurity A,
— *symmetry factor*: maximum 2.5 for the peak due to impurity A .

*Limits:*
— *impurities A, B, C, D*: for each impurity, maximum 3.0 per cent; other unidentified, specified impurities may occur that co-elute with impurities A, B, C and D; the

acceptance criterion applies irrespective of whether these impurities co-elute;
— *total*: maximum 5.0 per cent;
— *disregard limit*: 0.1 per cent.

*The following requirement applies only to calcitonin (salmon) produced by a method based on rDNA technology.*

B. *Test solution*. Prepare a 0.5 mg/ml solution of the substance to be examined. To 1.0 ml of this solution add 100 µl of *0.25 M citrate buffer solution pH 3.0 R*.

*Resolution solution* Prepare a 1 mg/ml solution of the substance to be examined. Mix 1 volume of the solution and 1 volume of *calcitonin-Gly CRS*. To 1.0 ml of this mixture add 100 µl of *0.25 M citrate buffer solution pH 3.0 R*.

*Column*:
— *size*: $l$ = 0.20 m, Ø = 4.6 mm;
— *stationary phase*: a suitable polysulphoethylaspartamide ion-exchange gel (5 µm).

*Mobile phase*:
— *mobile phase A*: mix 15 volumes of *acetonitrile for chromatography R* and 85 volumes of a 2.72 g/l solution of *potassium dihydrogen phosphate R* adjusted to pH 5.0 with a 600 g/l solution of *potassium hydroxide R*;
— *mobile phase B*: mix 15 volumes of *acetonitrile for chromatography R* and 85 volumes of a solution containing 2.72 g/l of *potassium dihydrogen phosphate R* and 29.22 g/l of *sodium chloride R* adjusted to pH 4.6 with a 600 g/l solution of *potassium hydroxide R*;

| Time (min) | Mobile phase A (per cent *V/V*) | Mobile phase B (per cent *V/V*) |
|---|---|---|
| 0 - 10 | 100 → 0 | 0 → 100 |
| 10 - 15 | 0 | 100 |
| 15 - 15.1 | 0 → 100 | 100 → 0 |
| 15.1 - 22.1 | 100 | 0 |

*Flow rate* 1.2 ml/min.

*Detection* Spectrophotometer at 220 nm.

*Injection* 50 µl; rinse the injector with a 40 per cent *V/V* solution of *acetonitrile for chromatography R*.

*Relative retention* With reference to calcitonin (salmon) (retention time = about 9 min): impurity G = about 0.4; impurity F = about 0.6; impurity E = about 0.9.

*System suitability* Resolution solution:
— *resolution*: minimum 3.0 between the peaks due to impurity E and calcitonin (salmon).

*Limits*:
— *impurity E*: maximum 0.6 per cent;
— *impurities F, G*: for each impurity, maximum 0.2 per cent.

**Water** (*2.5.32*)
Maximum 10.0 per cent.

**Acetic acid and water**
Maximum 20 per cent, calculated by adding together the percentage contents of acetic acid and water determined by the methods described above.

**Bacterial endotoxins** (*2.6.14*)
Less than 25 IU/mg, if intended for use in the manufacture of parenteral dosage forms without a further appropriate procedure for the removal of bacterial endotoxins.

**ASSAY**
Liquid chromatography (*2.2.29*) as described in the test for related substances. Use method A for calcitonin (salmon) obtained by chemical synthesis and method B for calcitonin (salmon) obtained by a method based on rDNA technology.

Calculate the content of calcitonin (salmon) ($C_{145}H_{240}N_{44}O_{48}S_2$) from the area of the principal peak in each of the chromatograms obtained with the test solution and the reference solution and the declared content of $C_{145}H_{240}N_{44}O_{48}S_2$ in *calcitonin (salmon) CRS*. Proceed with tangential integration of the peak areas.

**STORAGE**
Protected from light at a temperature between 2 °C and 8 °C. If the substance is sterile, store in a sterile, airtight, tamper-proof container.

**LABELLING**
The label states:
— the calcitonin peptide content ($C_{145}H_{240}N_{44}O_{48}S_2$);
— the origin: synthetic or rDNA technology.

**IMPURITIES**
*Specified impurities*   *A, B, C, D, E, F, G.*

```
R1- Cys - Ser - Asn - Leu - Ser - Thr - Cys - Val — X — Gly -
                                                        10
     Lys — Leu - Ser - Gln - Glu — Leu — His — Lys - Leu - Gln -
                                                        20
     Thr - Tyr - Pro - Arg - Thr - Asn - Thr - Gly - Ser - Gly -
                                                        30
     Thr - Pro - R2
```

A. R1 = CO-CH₃, R2 = NH₂, X = L-Leu: acetylcalcitonin (salmon),

B. R1 = H, R2 = NH₂, X = D-Leu: [9-D-leucine]calcitonin (salmon),

E. R1 = H, R2 = NH-CH₂-CO₂H, X = L-Leu: salmon calcitoninylglycine,

```
H - Cys - Ser - Asn - Leu - Ser - Thr - Cys - Val — Leu — Gly -
                                                        10
    Lys — Leu - Ser - Gln - Glu — Leu — His — Lys - Leu - Gln -
                                                        20
    Thr - Pro - Arg - Thr - Asn - Thr - Gly - Ser - Gly - Thr -
                                                        30
    Pro - NH₂
```

C. des-22-tyrosine-calcitonin (salmon),
D. *O*-acetylated calcitonin (salmon),

```
      SO₃H                            SO₃H
       3|                              3|
H - Ala - Ser - Asn - Leu - Ser - Thr - Ala - Val - Leu - Gly -
                                                        10
    Lys — Leu - Ser - Gln - Glu — Leu — His - Lys - Leu - Gln -
                                                        20
    Thr - Tyr - Pro - Arg - Thr - Asn - Thr - Gly - Ser - Gly -
                                                        30
    Thr - Pro - R
```

F. R = NH₂: [1,7-bis(3-sulpho-L-alanine)]calcitonin (salmon),

G. R = NH-CH₂-CO₂H: [1,7-bis(3-sulpho-L-alanine)]calcitoninylglycine (salmon).

# Calcitriol

(Ph Eur monograph 0883)

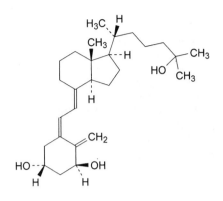

C₂₇H₄₄O₃          416.6          32222-06-3

## Action and use
Vitamin D analogue.

## Preparation
Calcitriol Capsules

*Ph Eur*

## DEFINITION
(5Z,7E)-9,10-Secocholesta-5,7,10(19)-triene-1α,3β,25-triol.

## Content
97.0 per cent to 103.0 per cent.

## CHARACTERS
### Appearance
White or almost white crystals.

### Solubility
Practically insoluble in water, freely soluble in ethanol (96 per cent), soluble in fatty oils.

It is sensitive to air, heat and light.

A reversible isomerisation to pre-calcitriol takes place in solution, depending on temperature and time. The activity is due to both compounds.

## IDENTIFICATION
A. Infrared absorption spectrophotometry (2.2.24).

*Comparison*   Ph. Eur. reference spectrum of calcitriol.

B. Examine the chromatograms obtained in the assay.

*Results*   The principal peak in the chromatogram obtained with the test solution is similar in retention time and size to the principal peak in the chromatogram obtained with reference solution (a).

## TESTS
### Related substances
Liquid chromatography (2.2.29): use the normalisation procedure. *Carry out the test as rapidly as possible, avoiding exposure to actinic light and air.*

*Test solution*   Dissolve 1.000 mg of the substance to be examined without heating in 10.0 ml of the mobile phase.

*Reference solution (a)*   Dissolve 1.000 mg of *calcitriol CRS* without heating in 10.0 ml of the mobile phase.

*Reference solution (b)*   Dilute 1.0 ml of reference solution (a) to 100.0 ml with the mobile phase.

*Reference solution (c)*   Heat 2 ml of reference solution (a) at 80 °C for 30 min.

*Column:*
— *size*: l = 0.25 m, Ø = 4.6 mm;
— *stationary phase*: octylsilyl silica gel for chromatography R1 (5 μm);
— *temperature*: 40 °C.

*Mobile phase*   Mix 450 volumes of a 1.0 g/l solution of *tris(hydroxymethyl)aminomethane R* adjusted to pH 7.0-7.5 with *phosphoric acid R*, and 550 volumes of *acetonitrile R*.

*Flow rate*   1.0 ml/min.

*Detection*   Spectrophotometer at 230 nm.

*Injection*   50 μl.

*Run time*   Twice the retention time of calcitriol.

*Relative retention*   With reference to calcitriol (retention time = about 14 min): pre-calcitriol = about 0.9.

*System suitability:*
— *resolution*: minimum 3.5 between the peaks due to calcitriol and pre-calcitriol in the chromatogram obtained with reference solution (c);
— *number of theoretical plates*: minimum 10 000, calculated for the peak due to calcitriol in the chromatogram obtained with reference solution (a).

*Limits:*
— *impurities A, B, C*: for each impurity, maximum 0.5 per cent;
— *total*: maximum 1.0 per cent;
— *disregard limit*: 0.1 times the area of the principal peak in the chromatogram obtained with reference solution (b) (0.1 per cent); disregard the peak due to pre-calcitriol.

## ASSAY
Liquid chromatography (2.2.29) as described in the test for related substances with the following modifications.

*Injection*   The test solution and reference solution (a).

*System suitability*   Reference solution (a):
— *repeatability*: maximum relative standard deviation of 1 per cent for the peak due to calcitriol after 6 injections.

Calculate the percentage content of C₂₇H₄₄O₃ from the declared content of *calcitriol CRS*.

## STORAGE
Under nitrogen, in an airtight container, protected from light, at a temperature of 2 °C to 8 °C.

The contents of an opened container are to be used immediately.

## IMPURITIES
*Specified impurities*   A, B, C.

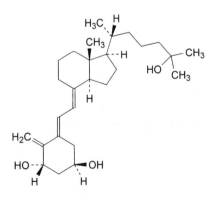

A. (5E,7E)-9,10-secocholesta-5,7,10(19)-triene-1α,3β,25-triol (*trans*-calcitriol),

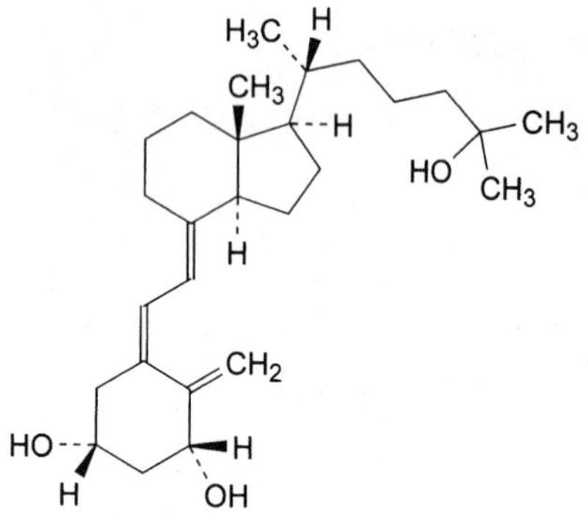

B. (5Z,7E)-9,10-secocholesta-5,7,10(19)-triene-1β,3β,25-triol (1β-calcitriol),

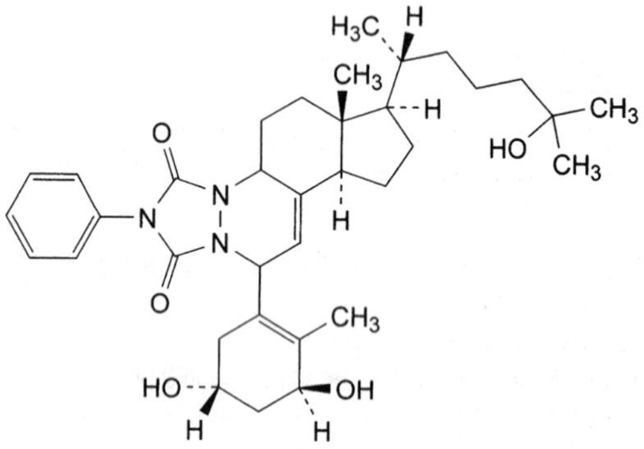

C. (6aR,7R,9aR)-11-[(3S,5R)-3,5-dihydroxy-2-methylcyclohex-1-enyl]-7-[(1R)-5-hydroxy-1,5-dimethylhexyl]-6a-methyl-2-phenyl-5,6,6a,7,8,9,9a,11-octahydro-1H,4aH-cyclopenta[f]1,2,4]triazolo[1,2-a]cinnoline-1,3(2H)-dione (triazoline adduct of pre-calcitriol).

_____ Ph Eur

# Calcium Acetate

(Ph Eur monograph 2128)

C₄H₆CaO₄      158.2      62-54-4

**Action and use**
Used in solutions for haemodialysis and peritoneal dialysis.

Ph Eur _____

**DEFINITION**
Calcium diacetate.

**Content**
98.0 per cent to 102.0 per cent (anhydrous substance).

**CHARACTERS**

**Appearance**
White or almost white, hygroscopic powder.

**Solubility**
Freely soluble in water, slightly soluble in ethanol (96 per cent).

**IDENTIFICATION**

A. It gives reaction (b) of calcium (2.3.1).

B. It gives reaction (b) of acetates (2.3.1).

**TESTS**

**pH** (2.2.3)
7.2 to 8.2.

Dissolve 0.50 g in 10.0 ml of carbon dioxide-free water R.

**Readily oxidisable substances**
Dissolve 2.0 g in boiling water R and dilute to 100 ml with boiling water R, add a few glass beads, 6 ml of 5 M sulphuric acid and 0.3 ml of 0.02 M potassium permanganate, mix, boil gently for 5 min and allow the precipitate to settle. The pink colour in the supernatant is not completely discharged.

**Chlorides** (2.4.4)
Maximum 330 ppm.

Dissolve 0.15 g in water R and dilute to 15 ml with the same solvent.

**Nitrates**
Dissolve 1.0 g in water R and dilute to 10 ml with the same solvent. Add 5 mg of sodium chloride R, 0.05 ml of indigo carmine solution R and add with stirring, 10 ml of nitrogen-free sulphuric acid R. The blue colour remains for at least 10 min.

**Sulphates** (2.4.13)
Maximum 600 ppm.

Dissolve 0.25 g in distilled water R and dilute to 15 ml with the same solvent.

**Aluminium** (2.4.17)
Maximum 1 ppm.

Test solution   Dissolve 4.0 g of the substance to be examined in 100 ml of water R and add 10 ml of acetate buffer solution pH 6.0 R.

Reference solution   Mix 2 ml of aluminium standard solution (2 ppm Al) R, 10 ml of acetate buffer solution pH 6.0 R and 98 ml of water R.

Blank solution   Mix 10 ml of acetate buffer solution pH 6.0 R and 100 ml of water R.

**Arsenic** (2.4.2)
Maximum 2 ppm.

0.5 g complies with limit test A.

**Barium**
Maximum 50.0 ppm.

Atomic emission spectrometry (2.2.22, Method II).

Test solution   Dissolve 5.00 g of the substance to be examined in water R and dilute to 100.0 ml with the same solvent.

Reference solutions   Prepare the reference solutions using barium standard solution (0.1 per cent Ba) R, diluted as necessary with water R.

Wavelength   455.4 nm.

**Magnesium**
Maximum $5.00 \times 10^2$ ppm.

Atomic absorption spectrometry (2.2.23, Method II).

Test solution   Dissolve 50.0 mg of the substance to be examined in water R and dilute to 100.0 ml with the same solvent.

Reference solutions   Prepare the reference solutions using magnesium standard solution (0.1 per cent Mg) R, diluted as necessary with water R.

Source   Magnesium hollow-cathode lamp.

Wavelength   285.2 nm.

Atomisation device   Air-acetylene flame.

**Potassium**

Maximum 0.10 per cent.

Atomic emission spectrometry (*2.2.22, Method II*).

*Test solution*   Dissolve 1.00 g of the substance to be examined in *water R* and dilute to 25.0 ml with the same solvent.

*Reference solutions*   Prepare the reference solutions using *potassium standard solution (0.2 per cent K) R*, diluted as necessary with *water R*.

*Wavelength*   766.7 nm.

**Sodium**

Maximum 0.50 per cent.

Atomic emission spectrometry (*2.2.22, Method II*).

*Test solution*   Dissolve 1.00 g of the substance to be examined in *water R* and dilute to 100.0 ml with the same solvent.

*Reference solutions*   Prepare the reference solutions using *sodium standard solution (200 ppm Na) R*, diluted as necessary with *water R*.

*Wavelength*   589.0 nm.

**Strontium**

Maximum $5.00 \times 10^2$ ppm.

Atomic emission spectrometry (*2.2.22, Method II*).

*Test solution*   Dissolve 2.00 g of the substance to be examined in *water R* and dilute to 100.0 ml with the same solvent.

*Reference solutions*   Prepare the reference solutions using *strontium standard solution (1.0 per cent Sr) R*, diluted as necessary with *water R*.

*Wavelength*   460.7 nm.

**Heavy metals** (*2.4.8*)

Maximum 20 ppm.

Dissolve 2.0 g in *water R* and dilute to 20 ml with the same solvent. 12 ml of the solution complies with limit test A. Prepare the reference solution using *lead standard solution (2 ppm Pb) R*.

**Water** (*2.5.12*)

Maximum 7.0 per cent, determined on 0.100 g. Add 2 ml of *anhydrous acetic acid R* to the titration vessel in addition to the methanol. Clean the titration vessel after each determination.

**ASSAY**

Dissolve 0.150 g in 15 ml of *water R*, add 5 ml of *diethylamine R*. Titrate with *0.1 M sodium edetate*, determining the end-point using *methylthymol blue mixture R*.

1 ml of *0.1 M sodium edetate* is equivalent to 15.82 mg of $C_4H_6CaO_4$.

**STORAGE**

In an airtight container.

——————————————————————— *Ph Eur*

# Calcium Ascorbate

(*Ph Eur monograph 1182*)

| | | |
|---|---|---|
| $C_{12}H_{14}CaO_{12},2H_2O$ | 426.3 | *5743-28-2* |

**Action and use**

Excipient.

*Ph Eur* ——————————————————————————————

**DEFINITION**

Calcium di[($R$)-2-[($S$)-1,2-dihydroxyethyl]-4-hydroxy-5-oxo-2$H$-furan-3-olate] dihydrate.

**Content**

99.0 per cent to 100.5 per cent of $C_{12}H_{14}CaO_{12},2H_2O$.

**CHARACTERS**

**Appearance**

White or slightly yellowish, crystalline powder.

**Solubility**

Freely soluble in water, practically insoluble in ethanol (96 per cent).

**IDENTIFICATION**

*First identification*   A, B, E.

*Second identification*   A, C, D, E.

A. Specific optical rotation (see Tests).

B. Infrared absorption spectrophotometry (*2.2.24*).

*Comparison*   Ph. Eur. reference spectrum of calcium ascorbate.

C. Dilute 1 ml of solution S (see Tests) to 10 ml with *water R*. To 2 ml of the solution add 0.2 ml of a 100 g/l solution of *ferrous sulphate R*. A deep violet colour develops.

D. To 1 ml of solution S add 0.2 ml of *dilute nitric acid R* and 0.2 ml of *silver nitrate solution R2*. A grey precipitate is formed.

E. The substance gives reaction (b) of calcium (*2.3.1*).

**TESTS**

**Solution S**

Dissolve 5.00 g in *carbon dioxide-free water R* and dilute to 50.0 ml with the same solvent.

**Appearance of solution**

Solution S is clear (*2.2.1*) and not more intensely coloured than reference solution $Y_6$ (*2.2.2, Method II*). Examine the colour of the solution immediately after preparation of the solution.

**pH** (*2.2.3*)

6.8 to 7.4 for solution S.

**Specific optical rotation** (*2.2.7*)

+ 95 to + 97 (dried substance), determined using freshly prepared solution S.

**Related substances**

The thresholds indicated under Related substances (Table 2034.-1) in the general monograph *Substances for pharmaceutical use (2034)* do not apply.

**Fluorides:**

Maximum 10.0 ppm.

Potentiometry (*2.2.36, Method I*).

*Test solution* In a 50 ml volumetric flask, dissolve 1.000 g in a 10.3 g/l solution of *hydrochloric acid R*, add 5.0 ml of *fluoride standard solution (1 ppm F) R* and dilute to 50.0 ml with a 10.3 g/l solution of *hydrochloric acid R*. To 20.0 ml of the solution add 20.0 ml of *total-ionic-strength-adjustment buffer R* and 3 ml of an 82 g/l solution of *anhydrous sodium acetate R*. Adjust to pH 5.2 with *ammonia R* and dilute to 50.0 ml with *distilled water R*.

*Reference solutions* To 0.25 ml, 0.5 ml, 1.0 ml, 2.0 ml and 5.0 ml of *fluoride standard solution (10 ppm F) R* add 20.0 ml of *total-ionic-strength-adjustment buffer R* and dilute to 50.0 ml with *distilled water R*.

*Indicator electrode* Fluoride selective.

*Reference electrode* Silver-silver chloride.

Take into account the addition of fluoride to the test solution for the calculation.

**Copper**

Maximum 5.0 ppm.

Atomic absorption spectrometry (*2.2.23, Method I*).

*Test solution* Dissolve 2.0 g in a 9.7 g/l solution of *nitric acid R* and dilute to 25.0 ml with the same acid solution.

*Reference solutions* Prepare the reference solutions using *copper standard solution (10 ppm Cu) R*, diluting with a 9.7 g/l solution of *nitric acid R*.

*Source* Copper hollow-cathode lamp.

*Wavelength* 324.8 nm.

*Atomisation device* Air-acetylene flame.

**Iron**

Maximum 2.0 ppm.

Atomic absorption spectrometry (*2.2.23, Method I*).

*Test solution* Dissolve 5.0 g in a 9.7 g/l solution of *nitric acid R* and dilute to 25.0 ml with the same acid solution.

*Reference solutions* Prepare the reference solutions using *iron standard solution (10 ppm Fe) R*, diluting with a 9.7 g/l solution of *nitric acid R*.

*Source* Iron hollow-cathode lamp.

*Wavelength* 248.3 nm.

*Atomisation device* Air-acetylene flame.

**Heavy metals** (*2.4.8*)

Maximum 10 ppm.

2.0 g complies with test D. Prepare the reference solution using 2.0 ml of *lead standard solution (10 ppm Pb) R*.

**Loss on drying** (*2.2.32*)

Maximum 0.1 per cent, determined on 1.000 g by drying in an oven at 105 °C for 2 h.

**ASSAY**

Dissolve 80.0 mg in a mixture of 10 ml of *dilute sulphuric acid R* and 80 ml of *carbon dioxide-free water R*. Add 1 ml of *starch solution R*. Titrate with 0.05 M iodine until a persistent violet-blue colour is obtained.

1 ml of 0.05 M iodine is equivalent to 10.66 mg of $C_{12}H_{14}CaO_{12},2H_2O$.

**STORAGE**

In a non-metallic container, protected from light.

_____ *Ph Eur*

# Calcium Carbonate

(*Ph Eur monograph 0014*)

CaCO₃        100.1        471-34-1

**Action and use**

Antacid.

**Preparations**

Calcium Carbonate Chewable Tablets

Calcium and Colecalciferol Tablets

_____ *Ph Eur*

**DEFINITION**

**Content**

98.5 per cent to 100.5 per cent (dried substance).

**CHARACTERS**

**Appearance**

White or almost white powder.

**Solubility**

Practically insoluble in water.

**IDENTIFICATION**

A. It gives the reaction of carbonates (*2.3.1*).

B. 0.2 ml of solution S (see Tests) gives the reactions of calcium (*2.3.1*).

**TESTS**

**Solution S**

Dissolve 5.0 g in 80 ml of *dilute acetic acid R*. When the effervescence ceases, boil for 2 min. Allow to cool, dilute to 100 ml with *dilute acetic acid R* and filter, if necessary, through a sintered-glass filter (*2.1.2*).

**Substances insoluble in acetic acid**

Maximum 0.2 per cent.

Wash any residue obtained during the preparation of solution S with 4 quantities, each of 5 ml, of hot *water R* and dry at 100-105 °C for 1 h. The residue weighs a maximum of 10 mg.

**Chlorides** (*2.4.4*)

Maximum 330 ppm.

Dilute 3 ml of solution S to 15 ml with *water R*.

**Sulphates** (*2.4.13*)

Maximum 0.25 per cent.

Dilute 1.2 ml of solution S to 15 ml with *distilled water R*.

**Arsenic** (*2.4.2, Method A*)

Maximum 4 ppm, determined on 5 ml of solution S.

**Barium**

To 10 ml of solution S add 10 ml of *calcium sulphate solution R*. After at least 15 min, any opalescence in the solution is not more intense than that in a mixture of 10 ml of solution S and 10 ml of *distilled water R*.

**Iron** (*2.4.9*)

Maximum 200 ppm.

Dissolve 50 mg in 5 ml of *dilute hydrochloric acid R* and dilute to 10 ml with *water R*.

**Magnesium and alkali metals**

Maximum 1.5 per cent.

Dissolve 1.0 g in 12 ml of *dilute hydrochloric acid R*. Boil the solution for about 2 min and add 20 ml of *water R*, 1 g of *ammonium chloride R* and 0.1 ml of *methyl red solution R*. Add *dilute ammonia R1* until the colour of the indicator changes and then add 2 ml in excess. Heat to boiling and add 50 ml of hot *ammonium oxalate solution R*. Allow to stand for 4 h, dilute to 100 ml with *water R* and filter through a suitable filter. To 50 ml of the filtrate add 0.25 ml of *sulphuric acid R*. Evaporate to dryness on a water-bath and ignite to constant mass at 600 ± 50 °C. The residue weighs a maximum of 7.5 mg.

**Heavy metals** (*2.4.8*)
Maximum 20 ppm.

12 ml of solution S complies with test A. Prepare the reference solution using *lead standard solution (1 ppm Pb) R*.

**Loss on drying** (*2.2.32*)
Maximum 2.0 per cent, determined on 1.000 g by drying in an oven at 200 ± 10 °C.

**ASSAY**
Dissolve 0.150 g in a mixture of 3 ml of *dilute hydrochloric acid R* and 20 ml of *water R*. Boil for 2 min, allow to cool and dilute to 50 ml with *water R*. Carry out the complexometric titration of calcium (*2.5.11*).

1 ml of *0.1 M sodium edetate* is equivalent to 10.01 mg of $CaCO_3$.

**FUNCTIONALITY-RELATED CHARACTERISTICS**
*This section provides information on characteristics that are recognised as being relevant control parameters for one or more functions of the substance when used as an excipient (see chapter 5.15). This section is a non-mandatory part of the monograph and it is not necessary to verify the characteristics to demonstrate compliance. Control of these characteristics can however contribute to the quality of a medicinal product by improving the consistency of the manufacturing process and the performance of the medicinal product during use. Where control methods are cited, they are recognised as being suitable for the purpose, but other methods can also be used. Wherever results for a particular characteristic are reported, the control method must be indicated. The following characteristics may be relevant for calcium carbonate used as filler in tablets and capsules.*

**Particle-size distribution** (*2.9.31 or 2.9.38*).

**Powder flow** (*2.9.36*).

*_____ Ph Eur*

# Calcium Chloride Dihydrate

(*Ph Eur monograph 0015*)

CaCl₂,2H₂O        147.0        10035-04-8

**Preparations**
Calcium Chloride Injection
Compound Sodium Lactate Intravenous Infusion

*Ph Eur _____*

**DEFINITION**
**Content**
97.0 per cent to 103.0 per cent of CaCl₂,2H₂O.

**CHARACTERS**
**Appearance**
White or almost white, crystalline powder, hygroscopic.

**Solubility**
Freely soluble in water, soluble in ethanol (96 per cent).

**IDENTIFICATION**
A. Solution S (see Tests) gives reaction (a) of chlorides (*2.3.1*).

B. It gives the reactions of calcium (*2.3.1*).

C. It complies with the limits of the assay.

**TESTS**
**Solution S**
Dissolve 10.0 g in *carbon dioxide-free water R* prepared from *distilled water R* and dilute to 100 ml with the same solvent.

**Appearance of solution**
Solution S is clear (*2.2.1*) and not more intensely coloured than reference solution Y₆ (*2.2.2, Method II*).

**Acidity or alkalinity**
To 10 ml of freshly prepared solution S add 0.1 ml of *phenolphthalein solution R*. If the solution is red, not more than 0.2 ml of *0.01 M hydrochloric acid* is required to discharge the colour and if the solution is colourless, not more than 0.2 ml of *0.01 M sodium hydroxide* is required to turn it red.

**Sulphates** (*2.4.13*)
Maximum 300 ppm.

Dilute 5 ml of solution S to 15 ml with *distilled water R*.

**Aluminium**
To 10 ml of solution S add 2 ml of *ammonium chloride solution R* and 1 ml of *dilute ammonia R1* and boil the solution. No turbidity or precipitate is formed.

If intended for use in the manufacture of dialysis solutions, the above test is replaced by the following test for aluminium (*2.4.17*): maximum 1 ppm.

*Prescribed solution* Dissolve 4 g in 100 ml of *water R* and add 10 ml of *acetate buffer solution pH 6.0 R*.

*Reference solution* Mix 2 ml of *aluminium standard solution (2 ppm Al) R*, 10 ml of *acetate buffer solution pH 6.0 R* and 98 ml of *water R*.

*Blank solution* Mix 10 ml of *acetate buffer solution pH 6.0 R* and 100 ml of *water R*.

**Barium**
To 10 ml of solution S add 1 ml of *calcium sulphate solution R*. After at least 15 min, any opalescence in the solution is not more intense than that in a mixture of 1 ml of *distilled water R* and 10 ml of solution S.

**Iron** (*2.4.9*)
Maximum 10 ppm, determined on solution S.

**Magnesium and alkali metals**
Maximum 0.5 per cent.

To a mixture of 20 ml of solution S and 80 ml of *water R* add 2 g of *ammonium chloride R* and 2 ml of *dilute ammonia R1*, heat to boiling and pour into the boiling solution a hot solution of 5 g of *ammonium oxalate R* in 75 ml of *water R*. Allow to stand for 4 h, dilute to 200 ml with *water R* and filter through a suitable filter. To 100 ml of the filtrate add 0.5 ml of *sulphuric acid R*. Evaporate to dryness on a water-bath and ignite to constant mass at 600 ± 50 °C. The residue weighs a maximum of 5 mg.

**Heavy metals** (*2.4.8*)
Maximum 20 ppm.

12 ml of solution S complies with test A. Prepare the reference solution using *lead standard solution (2 ppm Pb) R*.

**ASSAY**
Dissolve 0.280 g in 100 ml of *water R* and carry out the complexometric titration of calcium (*2.5.11*).

1 ml of *0.1 M sodium edetate* is equivalent to 14.70 mg of CaCl₂,2H₂O.

**LABELLING**
The label states, where applicable, that the substance is suitable for use in the manufacture of dialysis solutions.

STORAGE
In an airtight container.

_____ Ph Eur

# Calcium Chloride Hexahydrate

(Ph Eur monograph 0707)

CaCl₂,6H₂O          219.1          7774-34-7

Ph Eur _____

## DEFINITION
**Content**
97.0 per cent to 103.0 per cent of CaCl₂,6H₂O.

## CHARACTERS
**Appearance**
White or almost white, crystalline mass or colourless crystals.

**Solubility**
Very soluble in water, freely soluble in ethanol (96 per cent).
It solidifies at about 29 °C.

## IDENTIFICATION
A. Solution S (see Tests) gives reaction (a) of chlorides
(2.3.1).

B. It gives the reactions of calcium (2.3.1).

C. It complies with the limits of the assay.

## TESTS
**Solution S**
Dissolve 15.0 g in *carbon dioxide-free water R* prepared from
*distilled water R* and dilute to 100 ml with the same solvent.

**Appearance of solution**
Solution S is clear (2.2.1) and not more intensely coloured
than reference solution Y₆ (2.2.2, Method II).

**Acidity or alkalinity**
To 10 ml of freshly prepared solution S add 0.1 ml of
*phenolphthalein solution R*. If the solution is red, not more
than 0.2 ml of *0.01 M hydrochloric acid* is required to
discharge the colour and if the solution is colourless, not
more than 0.2 ml of *0.01 M sodium hydroxide* is required to
turn it red.

**Sulphates** (2.4.13)
Maximum 200 ppm.

Dilute 5 ml of solution S to 15 ml with *distilled water R*.

**Aluminium**
To 10 ml of solution S add 2 ml of *ammonium chloride
solution R* and 1 ml of *dilute ammonia R1*. Heat to boiling.
No turbidity or precipitate is formed.

If intended for use in the manufacture of dialysis solutions,
the above test is replaced by the following test for aluminium
(2.4.17): maximum 1 ppm.

*Prescribed solution*   Dissolve 6 g in 100 ml of *water R* and add
10 ml of *acetate buffer solution pH 6.0 R*.

*Reference solution*   Mix 2 ml of *aluminium standard solution
(2 ppm Al) R*, 10 ml of *acetate buffer solution pH 6.0 R* and
98 ml of *water R*.

*Blank solution*   Mix 10 ml of *acetate buffer solution pH 6.0 R*
and 100 ml of *water R*.

**Barium**
To 10 ml of solution S add 1 ml of *calcium sulphate
solution R*. After at least 15 min, any opalescence in the

solution is not more intense than that in a mixture of 1 ml of
*distilled water R* and 10 ml of solution S.

**Iron** (2.4.9)
Maximum 7 ppm, determined on solution S.

**Magnesium and alkali metals**
Maximum 0.3 per cent.

To a mixture of 20 ml of solution S and 80 ml of *water R*
add 2 g of *ammonium chloride R* and 2 ml of *dilute
ammonia R1*, heat to boiling and pour into the boiling
solution a hot solution of 5 g of *ammonium oxalate R* in
75 ml of *water R*. Allow to stand for 4 h, dilute to 200 ml
with *water R* and filter through a suitable filter. To 100 ml of
the filtrate add 0.5 ml of *sulphuric acid R*. Evaporate to
dryness on a water-bath and ignite to constant mass at 600
± 50 °C. The residue weighs a maximum of 5 mg.

**Heavy metals** (2.4.8)
Maximum 15 ppm.

12 ml of solution S complies with test A. Prepare the
reference solution using *lead standard solution (2 ppm Pb) R*.

## ASSAY
Dissolve 0.200 g in 100 ml of *water R*. Carry out the
complexometric titration of calcium (2.5.11).

1 ml of *0.1 M sodium edetate* is equivalent to 21.91 mg of
CaCl₂,6H₂O.

## LABELLING
The label states, where applicable, that the substance is
suitable for use in the manufacture of dialysis solutions.

_____ Ph Eur

# Calcium Dobesilate Monohydrate

(Ph Eur monograph 1183)

$$Ca^{2+} \left[ \begin{array}{c} HO\text{-}\bigcirc\text{-}SO_3^- \\ OH \end{array} \right]_2 , H_2O$$

C₁₂H₁₀CaO₁₀S₂,H₂O          436.4          20123-80-2

(anhydrous)

Ph Eur _____

## DEFINITION
Calcium di(2,5-dihydroxybenzenesulphonate) monohydrate.

**Content**
99.0 per cent to 101.0 per cent (anhydrous substance).

## CHARACTERS
**Appearance**
White or almost white, hygroscopic powder.

**Solubility**
Very soluble in water, freely soluble in anhydrous ethanol,
very slightly soluble in 2-propanol, practically insoluble in
methylene chloride.

## IDENTIFICATION
A. Ultraviolet and visible absorption spectrophotometry
(2.2.25).

*Test solution*   Dissolve 0.100 g in *water R* and dilute to
200.0 ml with the same solvent. Dilute 5.0 ml of this
solution to 100.0 ml with *water R*.

*Spectral range* 210-350 nm.

*Absorption maxima* At 221 nm and 301 nm.

*Specific absorbance at the absorption maximum at 301 nm* 174 to 181.

B. Mix 1 ml of *ferric chloride solution R2*, 1 ml of a freshly prepared 10 g/l solution of *potassium ferricyanide R* and 0.1 ml of *nitric acid R*. To this mixture add 5 ml of freshly prepared solution S (see Tests): a blue colour and a precipitate are immediately produced.

C. 2 ml of freshly prepared solution S gives reaction (b) of calcium (*2.3.1*).

## TESTS
### Solution S
Dissolve 10.0 g in *carbon dioxide-free water R* and dilute to 100 ml with the same solvent.

### Appearance of solution
Solution S, when freshly prepared, is clear (*2.2.1*) and colourless (*2.2.2, Method II*).

### pH (*2.2.3*)
4.5 to 6.0 for solution S.

### Related substances
Liquid chromatography (*2.2.29*). *Keep all solutions at 2-8 °C.*

*Buffer solution* Dissolve 1.2 g of *anhydrous sodium dihydrogen phosphate R* in 900 ml of *water for chromatography R*, adjust to pH 6.5 with *disodium hydrogen phosphate solution R* and dilute to 1000 ml with *water for chromatography R*.

*Test solution* Dissolve 0.100 g of the substance to be examined in *water R* and dilute to 10.0 ml with the same solvent.

*Reference solution (a)* Dilute 1.0 ml of the test solution to 100.0 ml with *water R*. Dilute 1.0 ml of this solution to 10.0 ml with *water R*.

*Reference solution (b)* Dissolve 10 mg of the substance to be examined and 10 mg of *hydroquinone R* (impurity A) in *water R* and dilute to 10 ml with the same solvent. Dilute 1 ml of this solution to 100 ml with *water R*.

*Column:*
— *size: l* = 0.25 m, Ø = 4.6 mm;
— *stationary phase*: spherical *end-capped octadecylsilyl silica gel for chromatography R* (5 µm).

*Mobile phase* *acetonitrile R1*, buffer solution (10:90 *V/V*).

*Flow rate* 0.8 ml/min.

*Detection* Spectrophotometer at 220 nm.

*Injection* 10 µl.

*Run time* 2.5 times the retention time of dobesilate.

*Relative retention* With reference to dobesilate (retention time = about 6 min): impurity A = about 1.7.

*System suitability* Reference solution (b):
— *resolution*: minimum 8.0 between the peaks due to dobesilate and impurity A.

*Limits:*
— *correction factor*: for the calculation of content, multiply the peak area of impurity A by 0.6;
— *impurity A*: not more than the area of the principal peak in the chromatogram obtained with reference solution (a) (0.1 per cent);
— *unspecified impurities*: for each impurity, not more than the area of the principal peak in the chromatogram obtained with reference solution (a) (0.10 per cent);
— *total*: not more than twice the area of the principal peak in the chromatogram obtained with reference solution (a) (0.2 per cent);

— *disregard limit*: 0.5 times the area of the principal peak in the chromatogram obtained with reference solution (a) (0.05 per cent).

### Heavy metals (*2.4.8*)
Maximum 15 ppm.

1.0 g complies with test C. Prepare the reference solution using 1.5 ml of *lead standard solution (10 ppm Pb) R*.

### Iron (*2.4.9*)
Maximum 10 ppm, determined on 10 ml of solution S.

### Water (*2.5.12*)
4.0 per cent to 6.0 per cent, determined on 0.500 g.

### ASSAY
Dissolve 0.200 g in a mixture of 10 ml of *water R* and 40 ml of *dilute sulphuric acid R*. Titrate with *0.1 M cerium sulphate*, determining the end-point potentiometrically (*2.2.20*).

1 ml of *0.1 M cerium sulphate* is equivalent to 10.45 mg of $C_{12}H_{10}CaO_{10}S_2$.

### STORAGE
In an airtight container, protected from light.

### IMPURITIES
*Specified impurities* A.

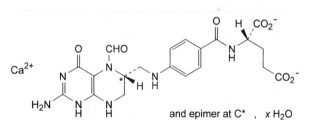

A. benzene-1,4-diol (hydroquinone).

_____ *Ph Eur*

# Calcium Folinate

(*Ph Eur monograph 0978*)

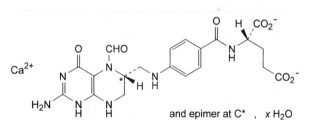

and epimer at C* , x H₂O

$C_{20}H_{21}CaN_7O_7,xH_2O$     511.5     *1492-18-8*
                                (anhydrous)          (anhydrous)

### Action and use
Antidote to folic acid antagonists.

### Preparations
Calcium Folinate Injection

Calcium Folinate Tablets

*Ph Eur* _____

### DEFINITION
Calcium (2*S*)-2-[[4-[[[(6*RS*)-2-amino-5-formyl-4-oxo-1,4,5,6,7,8-hexahydropteridin-6-yl]methyl]amino]benzoyl]amino]pentanedioate.

### Content
— *calcium folinate* ($C_{20}H_{21}CaN_7O_7$): 97.0 per cent to 102.0 per cent (anhydrous substance);

— *calcium* (Ca; $A_r$ 40.08): 7.54 per cent to 8.14 per cent (anhydrous substance).

It contains a variable amount of water.

## CHARACTERS

### Appearance

White or light yellow, amorphous or crystalline, hygroscopic powder.

### Solubility

Sparingly soluble in water, practically insoluble in acetone and in ethanol (96 per cent).

The amorphous form may produce supersaturated solutions in water.

## IDENTIFICATION

*First identification*  A, B, D.

*Second identification*  A, C, D.

A. Specific optical rotation (see Tests).

B. Infrared absorption spectrophotometry (*2.2.24*).

*Preparation*  Discs.

*Comparison*  calcium folinate CRS.

If the spectra obtained show differences, dissolve the substance to be examined and the reference substance separately in the minimum volume of *water R* and add dropwise sufficient *acetone R* to produce a precipitate. Allow to stand for 15 min, collect the precipitate by centrifugation, wash the precipitate with 2 small quantities of *acetone R* and dry. Record new spectra using the residues.

C. Thin-layer chromatography (*2.2.27*).

*Test solution*  Dissolve 15 mg of the substance to be examined in a 3 per cent *V/V* solution of *ammonia R* and dilute to 5 ml with the same solvent.

*Reference solution*  Dissolve 15 mg of *calcium folinate CRS* in a 3 per cent *V/V* solution of *ammonia R* and dilute to 5 ml with the same solvent.

*Plate*  Cellulose for chromatography $F_{254}$ R as the coating substance.

*Mobile phase*  The lower layer of a mixture of 1 volume of *isoamyl alcohol R* and 10 volumes of a 50 g/l solution of *citric acid R* previously adjusted to pH 8 with *ammonia R*.

*Application*  5 µl.

*Development*  Over a path of 15 cm.

*Drying*  In air.

*Detection*  Examine in ultraviolet light at 254 nm.

*Results*  The principal spot in the chromatogram obtained with the test solution is similar in position and size to the principal spot in the chromatogram obtained with the reference solution.

D. It gives reaction (b) of calcium (*2.3.1*).

*Carry out the tests and the assay as rapidly as possible, protected from actinic light.*

## TESTS

### Solution S

Dissolve 1.25 g in *carbon dioxide-free water R*, heating at 40 °C if necessary, and dilute to 50.0 ml with the same solvent.

### Appearance of solution

Solution S is clear (*2.2.1*) and its absorbance (*2.2.25*) at 420 nm is not greater than 0.60. Use *water R* as the compensation liquid.

### pH (*2.2.3*)

6.8 to 8.0 for solution S.

### Specific optical rotation (*2.2.7*)

+ 14.4 to + 18.0 (anhydrous substance), determined on solution S.

### Acetone, ethanol and methanol

Head-space gas chromatography (*2.2.28*): use the standard additions method.

*Test solution*  Dissolve 0.25 g of the substance to be examined in *water R* and dilute to 10.0 ml with the same solvent.

*Reference solution*  Dilute 0.125 g of *acetone R*, 0.750 g of *anhydrous ethanol R* and 0.125 g of *methanol R* in *water R* and dilute to 1000.0 ml with *water R*.

*Column:*
— *material*: fused silica;
— *size*: l = 10 m, Ø = 0.32 mm;
— *stationary phase*: styrene-divinylbenzene copolymer R.

*Carrier gas*  nitrogen for chromatography R.

*Flow rate*  4 ml/min.

*Static head-space conditions that may be used:*
— *equilibration temperature*: 80 °C;
— *equilibration time*: 20 min;
— *pressurisation time*: 30 s.

*Temperature:*

| | Time (min) | Temperature (°C) |
|---|---|---|
| Column | 0 - 6 | 125 → 185 |
| | 6 - 15 | 185 |
| Injection port | | 250 |
| Detector | | 250 |

*Detection*  Flame ionisation.

*Injection*  At least 3 times.

*Limits:*
— *acetone*: maximum 0.5 per cent;
— *ethanol*: maximum 3.0 per cent;
— *methanol*: maximum 0.5 per cent.

### Related substances

Liquid chromatography (*2.2.29*).

*Test solution*  Dissolve 10.0 mg of the substance to be examined in *water R* and dilute to 10.0 ml with the same solvent.

*Reference solution (a)*  Dissolve 10.0 mg of *calcium folinate CRS* in *water R* and dilute to 10.0 ml with the same solvent.

*Reference solution (b)*  Dilute 1.0 ml of reference solution (a) to 100.0 ml with *water R*.

*Reference solution (c)*  Dissolve 10.0 mg of *formylfolic acid CRS* (impurity D) in the mobile phase and dilute to 100.0 ml with the mobile phase. Dilute 1.0 ml of this solution to 10.0 ml with *water R*.

*Reference solution (d)*  Dilute 1.0 ml of reference solution (b) to 10.0 ml with *water R*.

*Reference solution (e)*  Dilute 5.0 ml of reference solution (c) to 10.0 ml with reference solution (b).

*Column:*
— *size*: l = 0.25 m, Ø = 4 mm;
— *stationary phase*: octadecylsilyl silica gel for chromatography R (5 µm);
— *temperature*: 40 °C.

*Mobile phase*  Mix 220 ml of *methanol R* and 780 ml of a solution containing 2.0 ml of *tetrabutylammonium hydroxide* solution (400 g/l) R and 2.2 g of *disodium hydrogen phosphate R*, previously adjusted to pH 7.8 with *phosphoric acid R*.

*Flow rate*   1 ml/min.

*Detection*   Spectrophotometer at 280 nm.

*Injection*   10 μl of the test solution and reference solutions (b), (c), (d) and (e).

*Run time*   2.5 times the retention time of folinate.

*System suitability*   Reference solution (e):
— *resolution*: minimum 2.2 between the peaks due to folinate and impurity D.

*Limits:*
— *impurity D*: not more than the area of the principal peak in the chromatogram obtained with reference solution (c) (1 per cent);
— *impurities A, B, C, E, F, G*: for each impurity, not more than the area of the principal peak in the chromatogram obtained with reference solution (b) (1 per cent);
— *sum of impurities other than D*: not more than 2.5 times the area of the principal peak in the chromatogram obtained with reference solution (b) (2.5 per cent);
— *disregard limit*: the area of the principal peak in the chromatogram obtained with reference solution (d) (0.1 per cent).

**Chlorides**
Maximum 0.5 per cent.

Dissolve 0.300 g in 50 ml of *water R* heating at 40 °C if necessary. Add 10 ml of *2M nitric acid* and titrate with *0.005 M silver nitrate* determining the end-point potentiometrically (*2.2.20*).

1 ml of *0.005 M silver nitrate* is equivalent to 0.177 mg of Cl.

**Heavy metals** (*2.4.8*)
Maximum 50 ppm.

1.0 g complies with test F. Prepare the reference solution using 5 ml of *lead standard solution (10 ppm Pb) R*.

**Platinum**
Maximum 20.0 ppm.

Atomic absorption spectrometry (*2.2.23, Method II*).

*Test solution*   Dissolve 1.00 g in *water R* and dilute to 100.0 ml with the same solvent.

*Reference solutions*   Prepare the reference solutions using *platinum standard solution (30 ppm Pt) R*, diluted as necessary with a mixture of 1 volume of *nitric acid R* and 99 volumes of *water R*.

*Source*   Platinum hollow-cathode lamp.

*Wavelength*   265.9 nm.

**Water** (*2.5.12*)
Maximum 17.0 per cent.

Dissolve 0.100 g in a mixture of 50 ml of the titration solvent and 15 ml of *formamide R*. Stir for about 6 min before titrating and use a suitable titrant that does not contain pyridine.

**Bacterial endotoxins** (*2.6.14*)
Less than 0.5 IU/mg, if intended for use in the manufacture of parenteral dosage forms without a further appropriate procedure for the removal of bacterial endotoxins.

## ASSAY

**Calcium**
Dissolve 0.400 g in 150 ml of *water R* and dilute to 300 ml with the same solvent. Carry out the complexometric titration of calcium (*2.5.11*).

1 ml of *0.1 M sodium edetate* is equivalent to 4.008 mg of Ca.

**Calcium folinate**
Liquid chromatography (*2.2.29*) as described in the test for related substances with the following modifications.

*Injection*   Test solution and reference solution (a).

*System suitability:*
— *repeatability*: maximum relative standard deviation of 2.0 per cent after 6 injections of reference solution (a).

Calculate the percentage content of $C_{20}H_{21}CaN_7O_7$ from the declared content of *calcium folinate CRS*.

## STORAGE

In an airtight container, protected from light. If the substance is sterile, store in a sterile, airtight, tamper-proof container.

## IMPURITIES

*Specified impurities*   A, B, C, D, E, F, G.

A. (2S)-2[(4-aminobenzoyl)amino]pentanedioic acid,

and epimer at C*

B. (2S)-2-[[4-[[[(6RS)-2-amino-5-formyl-4-oxo-1,4,5,6,7,8-hexahydropteridin-6-yl]methyl]formylamino]benzoyl]amino]pentanedioic acid (5,10-diformyltetrahydrofolic acid),

C. folic acid,

D. (2S)-2-[[4-[[[(2-amino-4-oxo-1,4-dihydropteridin-6-yl)methyl]formylamino]benzoyl]amino]pentanedioic acid (10-formylfolic acid),

and enantiomer

E. 4-[[[[(6RS)-2-amino-5-formyl-4-oxo-1,4,5,6,7,8-hexahydropteridin-6-yl]methyl]amino]benzoic acid (5-formyltetrahydropteroic acid),

F. R = CHO: (2S)-2-[[4-[[(2-amino-4-oxo-1,4,7,8-tetrahydropteridin-6-yl)methyl]formylamino]benzoyl]amino]pentanedioic acid (10-formyldihydrofolic acid),

G. R = H: (2S)-2-[[4-[[(2-amino-4-oxo-1,4,7,8-tetrahydropteridin-6-yl)methyl]amino]benzoyl]amino]pentanedioic acid (dihydrofolic acid).

_____ _Ph Eur_

# Calcium Glucoheptonate

(_Ph Eur monograph 1399_)

C$_{14}$H$_{26}$CaO$_{16}$          490.4          _29039-00-7_

## Action and use
Used in treatment of calcium deficiency.

_Ph Eur_ _____

## DEFINITION
Mixture in variable proportions, of calcium di(D-_glycero_-D-_gulo_-heptonate) and calcium di(D-_glycero_-D-_ido_-heptonate).

## Content
98.0 per cent to 102.0 per cent of calcium 2,3,4,5,6,7-hexahydroxyheptanoate (dried substance).

## CHARACTERS
### Appearance
White or very slightly yellow, amorphous powder, hygroscopic.

### Solubility
Very soluble in water, practically insoluble in acetone and in ethanol (96 per cent).

## IDENTIFICATION
A. Thin-layer chromatography (2.2.27).

_Test solution_   Dissolve 20 mg of the substance to be examined in 1 ml of _water R_.

_Reference solution (a)_   Dissolve 20 mg of _calcium glucoheptonate CRS_ in 1 ml of _water R_.

_Reference solution (b)_   Dissolve 10 mg of _calcium gluconate CRS_ in 0.5 ml of the test solution and dilute to 1 ml with _water R_.

_Plate_   _cellulose for chromatography R1_ as the coating substance.

_Mobile phase_   A freshly prepared mixture of 20 volumes of _anhydrous formic acid R_, 20 volumes of _water R_, 30 volumes of _acetone R_ and 30 volumes of _butanol R_.

_Application_   10 μl as bands of 20 mm by 2 mm.

_Development_   In a tank previously allowed to saturate for 10 min, over a path of 12 cm.

_Drying_   In air.

_Detection_   Spray with _0.02 M potassium permanganate_.

_System suitability_   Reference solution (b):
— the chromatogram shows 2 clearly separated spots.

_Results_   The principal spot in the chromatogram obtained with the test solution is similar in position and size to the principal spot in the chromatogram obtained with reference solution (a).

B. 0.2 ml of (see Tests) gives reaction (b) of calcium (2.3.1).

## TESTS
### Solution S
Dissolve 10.0 g in _carbon dioxide-free water R_ prepared from _distilled water R_ and dilute to 100 ml with the same solvent.

### Appearance of solution.
Solution S is clear (2.2.1) and not more intensely coloured than reference solution Y$_6$ (2.2.2, _Method II_).

### pH (2.2.3)
6.0 to 8.0 for solution S.

### Reducing sugars
Maximum 1 per cent, expressed as glucose.

Dissolve 1.0 g in 5 ml of _water R_ with the aid of gentle heat. Cool and add 20 ml of _cupri-citric solution R_ and a few glass beads. Heat so that boiling begins after 4 min and maintain boiling for 3 min. Cool rapidly and add 100 ml of a 2.4 per cent _V/V_ solution of _glacial acetic acid R_ and 20.0 ml of _0.025 M iodine_. With continuous shaking, add 25 ml of a mixture of 6 volumes of _hydrochloric acid R_ and 94 volumes of _water R_ until the precipitate dissolves, titrate the excess of iodine with _0.05 M sodium thiosulphate_ using _1 ml of starch solution R_ added towards the end of the titration, as indicator. Not less than 12.6 ml of _0.05 M sodium thiosulphate_ is required.

### Cyanide
Dissolve 5.0 g in 50 ml of _water R_ and add 2.0 g of _tartaric acid R_. Place this solution in a distillation apparatus (2.2.11). The plain bend adapter attached to the end of the condenser has a vertical part that is long enough to extend to 1 cm from the bottom of a 50 ml test-tube used as a receiver. Place 10 ml of _water R_ and 2 ml of _0.1 M sodium hydroxide_ into the receiver. Distil, collect 25 ml of distillate and dilute to 50 ml with _water R_. To 25 ml of this solution add 25 mg of _ferrous sulphate R_ and boil for a short time. After cooling to about 70 °C add 10 ml of _hydrochloric acid R1_. After 30 min, filter the solution and wash the filter. A yellow spot appears on the filter; there is no blue or green spot.

### Chlorides (2.4.4)
Maximum 100 ppm.

To 5 ml of solution S, add 10 ml of _water R_.

### Sulphates (2.4.13)
Maximum 100 ppm, determined on solution S.

### Iron (2.4.9)
Maximum 40 ppm.

Dilute 2.5 ml of to 10 ml with _water R_.

### Heavy metals (2.4.8)
Maximum 10 ppm.

Dissolve 2.0 g in 10 ml of _buffer solution pH 3.5 R_ and dilute to 20 ml with _water R_. 12 ml of the solution complies with test A. Prepare the reference solution using _lead standard solution (1 ppm Pb) R_.

**Loss on drying** (*2.2.32*)

Maximum 5.0 per cent, determined on 1.000 g by drying in an oven at 105 °C for 3 h.

**Bacterial endotoxins** (*2.6.14*)

Less than 167 IU/g, if intended for use in the manufacture of parenteral dosage forms without a further appropriate procedure for the removal of bacterial endotoxins.

## ASSAY

Dissolve 0.800 g in a mixture of 150 ml of *water R* and 2 ml of *3 M hydrochloric acid R*. While stirring, add 12.5 ml of *0.1 M sodium edetate*, 15 ml of *1 M sodium hydroxide* and 0.3 g of *hydroxynaphthol blue, sodium salt R*. Titrate with *0.1 M sodium edetate* until the colour changes from violet to pure blue.

1 ml of *0.1 M sodium edetate* is equivalent to 49.04 mg of $C_{14}H_{26}CaO_{16}$.

## STORAGE

In an airtight container. If the substance is sterile, store in a sterile, airtight, tamper-proof container.

*Ph Eur*

# Calcium Gluconate

(*Ph Eur monograph 0172*)

$C_{12}H_{22}CaO_{14},H_2O$      448.4      *18016-24-5*

**Action and use**

Used in treatment of calcium deficiency.

**Preparations**

Calcium Gluconate Tablets

Effervescent Calcium Gluconate Tablets

*Ph Eur*

## DEFINITION

Calcium D-gluconate monohydrate.

## Content

98.5 per cent to 102.0 per cent of $C_{12}H_{22}CaO_{14},H_2O$.

## CHARACTERS

**Appearance**

White or almost white, crystalline or granular powder.

**Solubility**

Sparingly soluble in water, freely soluble in boiling water.

## IDENTIFICATION

A. Thin-layer chromatography (*2.2.27*).

*Test solution*  Dissolve 20 mg of the substance to be examined in 1 ml of *water R*, heating if necessary in a water-bath at 60 °C.

*Reference solution*  Dissolve 20 mg of *calcium gluconate CRS* in 1 ml of *water R*, heating if necessary in a water-bath at 60 °C.

*Plate*  TLC silica gel G plate R.

*Mobile phase*  concentrated ammonia R, ethyl acetate R, water R, ethanol (96 per cent) R (10:10:30:50 V/V/V/V).

*Application*  5 µl.

*Development*  Over a path of 10 cm.

*Drying*  At 100 °C for 20 min. Allow to cool.

*Detection*  Spray with a 50 g/l solution of *potassium dichromate R* in a 40 per cent m/m solution of *sulphuric acid R*.

*Results*  After 5 min, the principal spot in the chromatogram obtained with the test solution is similar in position, colour and size to the principal spot in the chromatogram obtained with the reference solution.

B. Solution S (see Tests) gives the reactions of calcium (*2.3.1*).

## TESTS

**Solution S**

Dissolve 1.0 g in *water R* heated to 60 °C and dilute to 50 ml with the same solvent.

**Appearance of solution**

At 60 °C, solution S is not more intensely coloured than reference solution $Y_6$ (*2.2.2, Method II*). After cooling, it is not more opalescent than reference suspension II (*2.2.1*).

**Organic impurities and boric acid**

Introduce 0.5 g into a porcelain dish previously rinsed with *sulphuric acid R* and placed in a bath of iced water. Add 2 ml of cooled *sulphuric acid R* and mix. No yellow or brown colour develops. Add 1 ml of *chromotrope II B solution R*. A violet colour develops and does not become dark blue. The solution is not more intensely coloured than that of a mixture of 1 ml of *chromotrope II B solution R* and 2 ml of cooled *sulphuric acid R*.

**Sucrose and reducing sugars**

Dissolve 0.5 g in a mixture of 2 ml of *hydrochloric acid R1* and 10 ml of *water R*. Boil for 5 min, allow to cool, add 10 ml of *sodium carbonate solution R* and allow to stand. Dilute to 25 ml with *water R* and filter. To 5 ml of the filtrate add 2 ml of *cupri-tartaric solution R* and boil for 1 min. Allow to stand for 2 min. No red precipitate is formed.

**Chlorides** (*2.4.4*)

Maximum 200 ppm.

Dilute 12.5 ml of solution S to 15 ml with *water R*.

**Sulphates** (*2.4.13*)

Maximum 100 ppm.

Dissolve 10.0 g with heating in a mixture of 10 ml of *acetic acid R* and 90 ml of *distilled water R*.

**Magnesium and alkali metals**

Maximum 0.4 per cent.

Dissolve 1.00 g in 100 ml of boiling *water R*, add 10 ml of *ammonium chloride solution R*, 1 ml of *ammonia R* and, dropwise, 50 ml of hot *ammonium oxalate solution R*. Allow to stand for 4 h, dilute to 200 ml with *water R* and filter. Evaporate 100 ml of the filtrate to dryness and ignite. The residue weighs a maximum of 2 mg.

**Heavy metals** (*2.4.8*)

Maximum 10 ppm.

2.0 g complies with test D. Heat the substance to be examined gradually and with care until it is almost completely transformed into a white mass and then ignite. Prepare the reference solution using 2 ml of *lead standard solution (10 ppm Pb) R*.

**Microbial contamination**
TAMC: acceptance criterion $10^3$ CFU/g (*2.6.12*).
TYMC: acceptance criterion $10^2$ CFU/g (*2.6.12*).

**ASSAY**
Dissolve 0.8000 g in 20 ml of hot *water R*, allow to cool and dilute to 300 ml with *water R*. Carry out the complexometric titration of calcium (*2.5.11*).

1 ml of *0.1 M sodium edetate* is equivalent to 44.84 mg of $C_{12}H_{22}CaO_{14},H_2O$.

*Ph Eur*

# Anhydrous Calcium Gluconate

(*Ph Eur monograph 2364*)

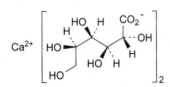

$C_{12}H_{22}CaO_{14}$          430.4          18016-24-5

(*monohydrate*)

**Action and use**
Used in treatment of calcium deficiency.

*Ph Eur*

**DEFINITION**
Anhydrous calcium D-gluconate.

**Content**
98.0 per cent to 102.0 per cent (dried substance).

**CHARACTERS**
**Appearance**
White or almost white, crystalline or granular powder.

**Solubility**
Sparingly soluble in water, freely soluble in boiling water.

**IDENTIFICATION**
A. Thin-layer chromatography (*2.2.27*).

*Test solution*   Dissolve 20 mg of the substance to be examined in 1 ml of *water R*, heating if necessary in a water-bath at 60 °C.

*Reference solution*   Dissolve 20 mg of *calcium gluconate CRS* in 1 ml of *water R*, heating if necessary in a water-bath at 60 °C.

*Plate*   *TLC silica gel plate R* (5-40 μm) [or *TLC silica gel plate R* (2-10 μm)].

*Mobile phase*   *concentrated ammonia R, ethyl acetate R, water R, ethanol (96 per cent) R* (10:10:30:50 *V/V/V/V*).

*Application*   1 μl.

*Development*   Over 2/3 of the plate.

*Drying*   At 100 °C for 20 min, then allow to cool.

*Detection*   Spray with a solution containing 25 g/l of *ammonium molybdate R* and 10 g/l of *cerium sulphate R* in *dilute sulphuric acid R*, and heat at 100-105 °C for about 10 min.

*Results*   The principal spot in the chromatogram obtained with the test solution is similar in position, colour and size to the principal spot in the chromatogram obtained with the reference solution.

B. Solution S (see Tests) gives the reactions of calcium (*2.3.1*).

C. Loss on drying (see Tests).

**TESTS**
**Solution S**
Dissolve 1.0 g in *water R* heated to 60 °C and dilute to 50 ml with the same solvent.

**Appearance of solution**
At 60 °C, solution S is not more intensely coloured than reference solution $Y_6$ (*2.2.2, Method II*). After cooling, it is not more opalescent than reference suspension II (*2.2.1*).

**Organic impurities and boric acid**
Place 0.5 g in a porcelain dish previously rinsed with *sulphuric acid R* and placed in a bath of iced water. Add 2 ml of cooled *sulphuric acid R* and mix. No yellow or brown colour develops. Add 1 ml of *chromotrope II B solution R*. A violet colour develops and does not become dark blue. Compare the colour obtained with that of a mixture of 1 ml of *chromotrope II B solution R* and 2 ml of cooled *sulphuric acid R*.

**Sucrose and reducing sugars**
Dissolve 0.5 g in a mixture of 2 ml of *hydrochloric acid R1* and 10 ml of *water R*. Boil for 5 min, allow to cool, add 10 ml of *sodium carbonate solution R* and allow to stand for 10 min. Dilute to 25 ml with *water R* and filter. To 5 ml of the filtrate add 2 ml of *cupri-tartaric solution R* and boil for 1 min. Allow to stand for 2 min. No red precipitate is formed.

**Chlorides** (*2.4.4*)
Maximum 200 ppm.

Dilute 12.5 ml of solution S to 15 ml with *water R*.

**Sulphates** (*2.4.13*)
Maximum 100 ppm.

Dissolve 10.0 g with heating in a mixture of 10 ml of *acetic acid R* and 90 ml of *distilled water R*.

**Magnesium and alkali metals**
Maximum 0.4 per cent (expressed as MgO).

Dissolve 1.00 g in 100 ml of boiling *water R*, add 10 ml of *ammonium chloride solution R*, 1 ml of *ammonia R* and, dropwise, 50 ml of hot *ammonium oxalate solution R*. Allow to stand for 4 h, dilute to 200 ml with *water R* and filter. Evaporate 100 ml of the filtrate to dryness and ignite. The residue weighs a maximum of 2 mg.

**Heavy metals** (*2.4.8*)
Maximum 10 ppm.

2.0 g complies with test D. Heat the substance to be examined gradually and with care until it is almost completely transformed into a white mass, and then ignite. Prepare the reference solution using 2 ml of *lead standard solution (10 ppm Pb) R*.

**Loss on drying** (*2.2.32*)
Maximum 2.0 per cent, determined on 1.000 g by drying in an oven at 105 °C for 16 h.

**Microbial contamination**
TAMC: acceptance criterion $10^3$ CFU/g (*2.6.12*).
TYMC: acceptance criterion $10^2$ CFU/g (*2.6.12*).

## ASSAY

Dissolve 0.350 g in 20 ml of hot *water R*, allow to cool and dilute to 300 ml with *water R*. Carry out the complexometric titration of calcium (*2.5.11*).

1 ml of *0.1 M sodium edetate* is equivalent to 43.04 mg of $C_{12}H_{22}CaO_{14}$.

*Ph Eur*

---

# Calcium Gluconate for Injection

(*Ph Eur monograph 0979*)

$C_{12}H_{22}CaO_{14},H_2O$          448.4          *18016-24-5*

### Action and use
Used in treatment of calcium deficiency.

### Preparation
Calcium Gluconate Injection

*Ph Eur*

---

## DEFINITION
Calcium D-gluconate monohydrate.

## Content
99.0 per cent to 101.0 per cent of $C_{12}H_{22}CaO_{14},H_2O$.

## CHARACTERS
### Appearance
White or almost white, crystalline or granular powder.

### Solubility
Sparingly soluble in water, freely soluble in boiling water.

## IDENTIFICATION
A. Thin-layer chromatography (*2.2.27*).

*Test solution*   Dissolve 20 mg of the substance to be examined in 1 ml of *water R*, heating if necessary in a water-bath at 60 °C.

*Reference solution*   Dissolve 20 mg of *calcium gluconate CRS* in 1 ml of *water R*, heating if necessary in a water-bath at 60 °C.

*Plate*   *TLC silica gel G plate R*.

*Mobile phase*   *concentrated ammonia R, ethyl acetate R, water R, ethanol (96 per cent) R* (10:10:30:50 *V/V/V/V*).

*Application*   5 µl.

*Development*   Over a path of 10 cm.

*Drying*   At 100 °C for 20 min and allow to cool.

*Detection*   Spray with a 50 g/l solution of *potassium dichromate R* in a 40 per cent m/m solution of *sulphuric acid R*.

*Results*   After 5 min, the principal spot in the chromatogram obtained with the test solution is similar in position, colour and size to the principal spot in the chromatogram obtained with the reference solution.

B. About 20 mg gives reaction (b) of calcium (*2.3.1*).

## TESTS
### Solution S
To 10.0 g add 90 ml of boiling distilled *water R* and boil with stirring, for not more than 10 s, until completely dissolved, then dilute to 100.0 ml with the same solvent.

### Appearance of solution
At 60 °C, solution S is not more intensely coloured than reference solution $B_7$ (*2.2.2, Method II*). After cooling to 20 °C, it is not more opalescent than reference suspension II (*2.2.1*).

### pH (*2.2.3*)
6.4 to 8.3.

Dissolve 1.0 g in 20 ml of *carbon dioxide-free water R*, heating on a water-bath.

### Organic impurities and boric acid
Introduce 0.5 g into a porcelain dish previously rinsed with *sulphuric acid R* and placed in a bath of iced water. Add 2 ml of cooled *sulphuric acid R* and mix. No yellow or brown colour develops. Add 1 ml of *chromotrope II B solution R*. A violet colour develops and does not become dark blue. The solution is not more intensely coloured than that of a mixture of 1 ml of *chromotrope II B solution R* and 2 ml of cooled *sulphuric acid R*.

### Oxalates
Liquid chromatography (*2.2.29*).

*Test solution*   Dissolve 1.00 g of the substance to be examined in *water for chromatography R* and dilute to 100.0 ml with the same solvent.

*Reference solution*   Dissolve 1.00 g of the substance to be examined in *water for chromatography R*, add 0.5 ml of a 0.152 g/l solution of *sodium oxalate R* in *water for chromatography R* and dilute to 100.0 ml with the same solvent.

*Guard column:*
— *size: l* = 30 mm, Ø = 4 mm;
— *stationary phase*: suitable strong anion exchange resin (30-50 µm).

*Columns 1 and 2:*
— *size: l* = 0.25 m, Ø = 4 mm;
— *stationary phase*: suitable strong anion exchange resin (30-50 µm).

*Anion-suppresser column*   Connected in series with the guard and analytical columns and equipped with a micromembrane that separates the mobile phase from the suppressor regeneration solution, flowing countercurrent to the mobile phase.

*Mobile phase*   Dissolve 0.212 g of *anhydrous sodium carbonate R* and 63 mg of *sodium hydrogen carbonate R* in *water for chromatography R* and dilute to 1000.0 ml with the same solvent.

*Flow rate of the mobile phase*   2 ml/min.

*Suppressor regeneration solution*   1.23 g/l solution of *sulphuric acid R* in *water for chromatography R*.

*Flow rate of the suppressor regeneration solution*   4 ml/min.

*Detection*   Conductance.

*Injection*   50 µl.

*System suitability*   Reference solution:
— *repeatability*: maximum relative standard deviation of the area of the peak due to oxalate of 2.0 per cent after 5 injections.

Inject 50 µl of each solution 3 times. Calculate the content of oxalates in parts per million using the following expression:

$$\frac{S_T \times 50}{S_R - S_T}$$

$S_T$ = area of the peak due to oxalate in the chromatogram obtained with the test solution;

$S_R$ = area of the peak due to oxalate in the chromatogram obtained with the reference solution.

*Limit:*
— *oxalates:* maximum $1.00 \times 10^2$ ppm.

**Sucrose and reducing sugars**
Dissolve 0.5 g in a mixture of 2 ml of *hydrochloric acid R1* and 10 ml of *water R.* Boil for 5 min, allow to cool, add 10 ml of *sodium carbonate solution R* and allow to stand for 10 min. Dilute to 25 ml with *water R* and filter. To 5 ml of the filtrate add 2 ml of *cupri-tartaric solution R* and boil for 1 min. Allow to stand for 2 min. No red precipitate is formed.

**Chlorides** *(2.4.4)*
Maximum 50 ppm.

To 10 ml of previously filtered solution S add 5 ml of *water R.*

**Phosphates** *(2.4.11)*
Maximum 100 ppm.

Dilute 1 ml of solution S to 100 ml with *water R.*

**Sulphates** *(2.4.13)*
Maximum 50 ppm, determined on previously filtered solution S.

Prepare the standard using a mixture of 7.5 ml of *sulphate standard solution (10 ppm SO₄) R* and 7.5 ml of *distilled water R.*

**Iron**
Maximum 5.0 ppm.

Atomic absorption spectrometry *(2.2.23, Method I).*

*Test solution* Introduce 2.0 g into a 100 ml polytetrafluoroethylene beaker and add 5 ml of *nitric acid R.* Boil, evaporating almost to dryness. Add 1 ml of *strong hydrogen peroxide solution R* and evaporate again almost to dryness. Repeat the hydrogen peroxide treatment until a clear solution is obtained. Using 2 ml of *nitric acid R,* transfer the solution into a 25 ml volumetric flask. Dilute to 25.0 ml with *dilute hydrochloric acid R.* In the same manner, prepare a compensation solution using 0.65 g of *calcium chloride R1* instead of the substance to be examined.

*Reference solutions* Prepare the reference solutions from *iron solution (20 ppm Fe) R* diluted with *dilute hydrochloric acid R.*

*Source* Iron hollow-cathode lamp.

*Wavelength* 248.3 nm.

*Atomisation device* Air-acetylene flame.

Carry out a basic correction using a deuterium lamp.

**Magnesium and alkali metals**
Maximum 0.4 per cent.

To 0.50 g add a mixture of 1.0 ml of *dilute acetic acid R* and 10.0 ml of *water R* and rapidly boil, whilst shaking, until completely dissolved. To the boiling solution add 5.0 ml of *ammonium oxalate solution R* and allow to stand for at least 6 h. Filter through a sintered-glass filter (1.6) *(2.1.2)* into a porcelain crucible. Carefully evaporate the filtrate to dryness and ignite. The residue weighs not more than 2 mg.

**Heavy metals** *(2.4.8)*
Maximum 10 ppm.

12 ml of solution S complies with test A. Prepare the reference solution using *lead standard solution (1 ppm Pb) R.*

**Bacterial endotoxins** *(2.6.14)*
Less than 167 IU/g.

**Microbial contamination**
TAMC: acceptance criterion $10^2$ CFU/g *(2.6.12).*

**ASSAY**
Dissolve 0.350 g in 20 ml of hot *water R,* allow to cool and dilute to 300 ml with *water R.* Carry out the complexometric titration of calcium *(2.5.11).* Use 50 mg of *calconecarboxylic acid triturate R.*

1 ml of *0.1 M sodium edetate* is equivalent to 44.84 mg of $C_{12}H_{22}CaO_{14},H_2O.$

*Ph Eur*

# Calcium Glycerophosphate

*(Ph Eur monograph 0980)*

$C_3H_7CaO_6P$       210.1       27214-00-2

**Action and use**
Excipient.

*Ph Eur*

**DEFINITION**
Mixture in variable proportions of the calcium salt of *(RS)*-2,3-dihydroxypropyl phosphate and of 2-hydroxy-1-(hydroxymethyl)ethyl phosphate which may be hydrated.

**Content**
18.6 per cent to 19.4 per cent of Ca (dried substance).

**CHARACTERS**
**Appearance**
White or almost white powder, hygroscopic.

**Solubility**
Sparingly soluble in water, practically insoluble in ethanol (96 per cent).

**IDENTIFICATION**
A. Mix 1 g with *1 g of potassium hydrogen sulphate R* in a test tube fitted with a glass tube. Heat strongly and direct the white vapour towards a piece of filter paper impregnated with a freshly prepared 10 g/l solution of *sodium nitroprusside R.* The filter paper develops a blue colour in contact with *piperidine R.*

B. Ignite 0.1 g in a crucible. Take up the residue with 5 ml of *nitric acid R* and heat on a water-bath for 1 min. Filter. The filtrate gives reaction (b) of phosphates *(2.3.1).*

C. It gives reaction (b) of calcium *(2.3.1).*

**TESTS**
**Solution S**
Dissolve 1.5 g at room temperature in *carbon dioxide-free water R* prepared from *distilled water R* and dilute to 150 ml with the same solvent.

**Appearance of solution**
Solution S is not more opalescent than reference suspension III *(2.2.1).*

**Acidity or alkalinity**
To 100 ml of solution S add *0.1 ml of phenolphthalein solution R.* Not more than 1.5 ml of *0.1 M hydrochloric acid* or 0.5 ml *of 0.1 M sodium hydroxide* is required to change the colour of the indicator.

**Citric acid**

Shake 5.0 g with 20 ml of *carbon dioxide-free water R* and filter. To the filtrate add 0.15 ml of *sulphuric acid R* and filter again. To the filtrate add 5 ml of *mercuric sulphate solution R* and heat to boiling. Add 0.5 ml of a 3.2 g/l solution of *potassium permanganate R* and again heat to boiling. No precipitate is formed.

**Glycerol and ethanol (96 per cent)-soluble substances**

Maximum 0.5 per cent.

Shake 1.000 g with 25 ml of *ethanol (96 per cent) R* for 1 min. Filter. Evaporate the filtrate on a water-bath and dry the residue at 70 °C for 1 h. The residue weighs a maximum of 5 mg.

**Chlorides** (*2.4.4*)

Maximum 500 ppm.

Dissolve 0.1 g in a mixture of 2 ml of *acetic acid R* and 8 ml of *water R* and dilute to 15 ml with *water R*.

**Phosphates** (*2.4.11*)

Maximum 400 ppm.

Dilute 2.5 ml of solution S to 100 ml with *water R*.

**Sulphates** (*2.4.13*)

Maximum 0.1 per cent, determined on solution S.

**Arsenic** (*2.4.2, Method A*)

Maximum 3 ppm.

Dissolve 0.33 g in *water R* and dilute to 25 ml with the same solvent.

**Iron** (*2.4.9*)

Maximum 50 ppm, detemined on 0.20 g.

**Heavy metals** (*2.4.8*)

Maximum 20 ppm.

Dissolve 2.0 g in 10 ml of *buffer solution pH 3.5 R* and dilute to 20 ml with *water R*. 12 ml of the solution complies with test A. Prepare the reference solution using *lead standard solution (2 ppm Pb) R*.

**Loss on drying** (*2.2.32*)

Maximum 12.0 per cent, determined on 1.000 g by drying in an oven at 150 °C for 4 h.

**ASSAY**

Dissolve 0.200 g in *water R*. Carry out the complexometric titration of calcium (*2.5.11*).

1 ml of *0.1 M sodium edetate* is equivalent to 4.008 mg of Ca.

*Ph Eur*

# Calcium Hydrogen Phosphate

Dibasic Calcium Phosphate

(*Calcium Hydrogen Phosphate Dihydrate, Ph Eur monograph 0116*)

$CaHPO_4,2H_2O$         172.1         7789-77-7

*Ph Eur*

## DEFINITION

**Content**

98.0 per cent to 105.0 per cent.

## CHARACTERS

**Appearance**

White or almost white, crystalline powder.

**Solubility**

Practically insoluble in water and in ethanol (96 per cent). It dissolves in dilute hydrochloric acid and in dilute nitric acid.

## IDENTIFICATION

A. Dissolve with heating 0.1 g in 10 ml of *dilute hydrochloric acid R*. Add 2.5 ml of *dilute ammonia R1*, shake and add 5 ml of a 35 g/l solution of *ammonium oxalate R*. A white precipitate is produced.

B. Dissolve 0.1 g in 5 ml of *dilute nitric acid R*, add 2 ml of *ammonium molybdate solution R* and heat at 70 °C for 2 min. A yellow precipitate is produced.

C. It complies with the limits of the assay.

## TESTS

**Solution S**

Dissolve 2.5 g in 20 ml of *dilute hydrochloric acid R*, filter if necessary and add *dilute ammonia R1* until a precipitate is formed. Add just sufficient *dilute hydrochloric acid R* to dissolve the precipitate and dilute to 50 ml with *distilled water R*.

**Acid-insoluble substances**

Maximum 0.2 per cent.

Dissolve 5.0 g in 40 ml of *water R*, add 10 ml of *hydrochloric acid R* and heat to boiling for 5 min. Cool, then collect the insoluble substances using ashless filter paper. Wash with *water R* until turbidity is no longer produced when *silver nitrate solution R2* is added to the filtrate. Ignite at 600 ± 50 °C. The residue weighs not more than 10 mg.

**Carbonates**

Shake 0.5 g with 5 ml of *carbon dioxide-free water R* and add 1 ml of *hydrochloric acid R*. No effervescence is produced.

**Chlorides**

Maximum 0.25 per cent.

*Test solution* Dissolve 0.20 g in a mixture of 20 ml of *water R* and 13 ml of *dilute nitric acid R*, dilute to 100 ml with *water R* and filter if necessary. Use 50 ml of this solution.

*Reference solution* To 0.70 ml of *0.01 M hydrochloric acid*, add 6 ml of *dilute nitric acid R* and dilute to 50 ml with *water R*.

Add 1 ml of *silver nitrate solution R2* to the test solution and to the reference solution and mix. After standing for 5 min protected from light, any opalescence in the test solution is not more intense than that in the reference solution.

**Fluorides**

Maximum 100 ppm.

Potentiometry (*2.2.36, Method II*).

*Chelating solution* Dissolve 45 g of *cyclohexylenedinitrilotetra-acetic acid R* in 75 ml of *sodium hydroxide solution R* and dilute to 250 ml with *water R*.

*Test solution* Dissolve 1.000 g in 4 ml of *hydrochloric acid R1*, add 20 ml of chelating solution, 2.7 ml of *glacial acetic acid R* and 2.8 g of *sodium chloride R*, adjust to pH 5-6 with *sodium hydroxide solution R* and dilute to 50.0 ml with *water R*.

*Reference solution* Dissolve 4.42 g of *sodium fluoride R*, previously dried at 300 °C for 12 h, in *water R* and dilute to 1000.0 ml with the same solvent. Dilute 50.0 ml of this solution to 500.0 ml with *total-ionic-strength-adjustment buffer R* (200 ppm F).

*Indicator electrode* Fluoride-selective.

*Reference electrode* Silver-silver chloride.

Carry out the measurement on 20.0 ml of the test solution. Add at least 3 times 0.10 ml of the reference solution and carry out the measurement after each addition. Calculate the concentration of fluorides using the calibration curve.

**Sulphates**

Maximum 0.5 per cent.

*Test solution* Dissolve 0.5 g in a mixture of 5 ml of *water R* and 5 ml of *dilute hydrochloric acid R* and dilute to 100 ml with *water R*. Filter if necessary. To 20 ml of this solution, add 1 ml of *dilute hydrochloric acid R* and dilute to 50 ml with *water R*.

*Reference solution* To 1.0 ml of *0.005 M sulphuric acid*, add 1 ml of *dilute hydrochloric acid R* and dilute to 50 ml with *water R*. Filter if necessary.

To the test solution and to the reference solution, add 2 ml of a 120 g/l solution of *barium chloride R* and allow to stand for 10 min. Any opalescence in the test solution is not more intense than that in the reference solution.

**Arsenic** (*2.4.2, Method A*)

Maximum 10 ppm, determined on 2 ml of solution S.

**Barium**

To 0.5 g, add 10 ml of *water R* and heat to boiling. While stirring, add 1 ml of *hydrochloric acid R* dropwise. Allow to cool and filter if necessary. Add 2 ml of a 10 g/l solution of *dipotassium sulphate R* and allow to stand for 10 min. No turbidity is produced.

**Iron** (*2.4.9*)

Maximum 400 ppm.

Dilute 0.5 ml of solution S to 10 ml with *water R*.

**Heavy metals** (*2.4.8*)

Maximum 40 ppm.

Dilute 10 ml of solution S to 20 ml with *water R*. 12 ml of the solution complies with test A. Prepare the reference solution using *lead standard solution (1 ppm Pb) R*.

**Loss on ignition**

24.5 per cent to 26.5 per cent, determined on 1.000 g by ignition to constant mass at 800-825 °C.

**ASSAY**

Dissolve 0.4 g in 12 ml of *dilute hydrochloric acid R* and dilute to 200 ml with *water R*. To 20.0 ml of this solution add 25.0 ml of *0.02 M sodium edetate*, 50 ml of *water R*, 5 ml of *ammonium chloride buffer solution pH 10.7 R* and about 25 mg of *mordant black 11 triturate R*. Titrate the excess of sodium edetate with *0.02 M zinc sulphate*. Carry out a blank titration.

1 ml of *0.02 M sodium edetate* is equivalent to 3.44 mg of $CaHPO_4,2H_2O$.

**FUNCTIONALITY-RELATED CHARACTERISTICS**

*This section provides information on characteristics that are recognised as being relevant control parameters for one or more functions of the substance when used as an excipient (see chapter 5.15). This section is a non-mandatory part of the monograph and it is not necessary to verify the characteristics to demonstrate compliance. Control of these characteristics can however contribute to the quality of a medicinal product by improving the consistency of the manufacturing process and the performance of the medicinal product during use. Where control methods are cited, they are recognised as being suitable for the purpose, but other methods can also be used. Wherever results for a particular characteristic are reported, the control method must be indicated.*

*The following characteristics may be relevant for calcium hydrogen phosphate dihydrate used as filler in tablets and capsules.*

**Particle-size distribution** (*2.9.31 or 2.9.38*).

**Bulk and tapped density** (*2.9.34*).

**Powder flow** (*2.9.36*).

_____ Ph Eur

# Anhydrous Calcium Hydrogen Phosphate

(*Ph Eur monograph 0981*)

$CaHPO_4$         136.1         7757-93-9

Ph Eur

**DEFINITION**

**Content**

98.0 per cent to 103.0 per cent.

**CHARACTERS**

**Appearance**

White or almost white, crystalline powder, or colourless crystals.

**Solubility**

Practically insoluble in water and in ethanol (96 per cent). It dissolves in dilute hydrochloric acid and in dilute nitric acid.

**IDENTIFICATION**

A. Dissolve with heating 0.1 g in 10 ml of *dilute hydrochloric acid R*. Add 2.5 ml of *dilute ammonia R1*, shake, and add 5 ml of a 35 g/l solution of *ammonium oxalate R*. A white precipitate is produced.

B. Dissolve 0.1 g in 5 ml of *dilute nitric acid R*, add 2 ml of *ammonium molybdate solution R* and heat at 70 °C for 2 min. A yellow precipitate is produced.

C. It complies with the limits of the assay.

**TESTS**

**Solution S**

Dissolve 2.5 g in 20 ml of *dilute hydrochloric acid R*, filter if necessary and add *dilute ammonia R1* until a precipitate is formed. Add just sufficient *dilute hydrochloric acid R* to dissolve the precipitate and dilute to 50 ml with *distilled water R*.

**Acid-insoluble substances**

Maximum 0.2 per cent.

Dissolve 5.0 g in 40 ml of *water R*, add 10 ml of *hydrochloric acid R* and heat to boiling for 5 min. Cool, then collect the insoluble substances using ashless filter paper. Wash with *water R* until turbidity is no longer produced when *silver nitrate solution R2* is added. Ignite at 600 ± 50 °C. The residue weighs not more than 10 mg.

**Carbonates**

Shake 0.5 g with 5 ml of *carbon dioxide-free water R* and add 1 ml of *hydrochloric acid R*. No effervescence is produced.

**Chlorides**

Maximum 0.25 per cent.

*Test solution* Dissolve 0.20 g in a mixture of 20 ml of *water R* and 13 ml of *dilute nitric acid R*, dilute to 100 ml with *water R* and filter if necessary. Use 50 ml of this solution.

*Reference solution* To 0.70 ml of *0.01 M hydrochloric acid*, add 6 ml of *dilute nitric acid R* and dilute to 50 ml with *water R*.

Add 1 ml of *silver nitrate solution R2* to the test solution and to the reference solution and mix. After standing for 5 min protected from light, any opalescence in the test solution is not more intense than that in the reference solution.

**Fluorides**

Maximum 100 ppm.

Potentiometry (*2.2.36, Method II*).

*Chelating solution* Dissolve 45 g of *cyclohexylenedinitrilotetra-acetic acid R* in 75 ml of *sodium hydroxide solution R* and dilute to 250 ml with *water R*.

*Test solution* Dissolve 1.000 g in 4 ml of *hydrochloric acid R1*, add 20 ml of chelating solution, 2.7 ml of *glacial acetic acid R* and 2.8 g of *sodium chloride R*, adjust to pH 5-6 with *sodium hydroxide solution R* and dilute to 50.0 ml with *water R*.

*Reference solution* Dissolve 4.42 g of *sodium fluoride R*, previously dried at 300 °C for 12 h, in *water R* and dilute to 1000.0 ml with the same solvent. Dilute 50.0 ml of this solution to 500.0 ml with *total-ionic-strength-adjustment buffer R* (200 ppm F).

*Indicator electrode* Fluoride-selective.

*Reference electrode* Silver-silver chloride.

Carry out the measurement on 20.0 ml of the test solution. Add at least 3 times 0.10 ml of the reference solution and carry out the measurement after each addition. Calculate the concentration of fluorides using the calibration curve.

### Sulphates
Maximum 0.5 per cent.

*Test solution* Dissolve 0.5 g in a mixture of 5 ml of *water R* and 5 ml of *dilute hydrochloric acid R* and dilute to 100 ml with *water R*. Filter if necessary. To 20 ml of this solution, add 1 ml of *dilute hydrochloric acid R* and dilute to 50 ml with *water R*.

*Reference solution* To 1.0 ml of *0.005 M sulphuric acid*, add 1 ml of *dilute hydrochloric acid R* and dilute to 50 ml with *water R*. Filter if necessary.

To the test solution and to the reference solution, add 2 ml of a 120 g/l solution of *barium chloride R* and allow to stand for 10 min. Any opalescence in the test solution is not more intense than that in the reference solution.

### Arsenic (*2.4.2, Method A*)
Maximum 10 ppm, determined on 2 ml of solution S.

### Barium
To 0.5 g, add 10 ml of *water R* and heat to boiling. While stirring, add 1 ml of *hydrochloric acid R* dropwise. Allow to cool and filter if necessary. Add 2 ml of a 10 g/l solution of *dipotassium sulphate R* and allow to stand for 10 min. No turbidity is produced.

### Iron (*2.4.9*)
Maximum 400 ppm.

Dilute 0.5 ml of solution S to 10 ml with *water R*.

### Heavy metals (*2.4.8*)
Maximum 40 ppm.

Dilute 10 ml of solution S to 20 ml with *water R*. 12 ml of the solution complies with test A. Prepare the reference solution using *lead standard solution (1 ppm Pb) R*.

### Loss on ignition
6.6 per cent to 8.5 per cent, determined on 1.000 g to constant mass at 800-825 °C.

### ASSAY
Dissolve 0.4 g in 12 ml of *dilute hydrochloric acid R* and dilute to 200 ml with *water R*. To 20.0 ml of this solution add 25.0 ml of *0.02 M sodium edetate*, 50 ml of *water R*, 5 ml of *ammonium chloride buffer solution pH 10.7 R* and about 25 mg of *mordant black 11 triturate R*. Titrate the excess of sodium edetate with *0.02 M zinc sulphate*. Carry out a blank titration.

1 ml of *0.02 M sodium edetate* is equivalent to 2.72 mg of $CaHPO_4$.

### FUNCTIONALITY-RELATED CHARACTERISTICS
*This section provides information on characteristics that are recognised as being relevant control parameters for one or more functions of the substance when used as an excipient (see chapter 5.15). This section is a non-mandatory part of the monograph and it is not necessary to verify the characteristics to demonstrate compliance. Control of these characteristics can however contribute to the quality of a medicinal product by improving the consistency of the manufacturing process and the performance of the medicinal product during use. Where control methods are cited, they are recognised as being suitable for the purpose, but other methods can also be used. Wherever results for a particular characteristic are reported, the control method must be indicated.*

*The following characteristics may be relevant for anhydrous calcium hydrogen phosphate used as filler in tablets and capsules.*

**Particle-size distribution** (*2.9.31* or *2.9.38*).

**Bulk and tapped density** (*2.9.34*).

**Powder flow** (*2.9.36*).

*Ph Eur*

# Calcium Hydroxide

(*Ph Eur monograph 1078*)

$Ca(OH)_2$      74.1      *1305-62-0*

**Preparation**
Calcium Hydroxide Solution

*Ph Eur*

### DEFINITION
**Content**
95.0 per cent to 100.5 per cent.

### CHARACTERS
**Appearance**
White or almost white, fine powder.

**Solubility**
Practically insoluble in water.

### IDENTIFICATION
A. To 0.80 g in a mortar, add 10 ml of *water R* and 0.5 ml of *phenolphthalein solution R* and mix. The suspension turns red. On addition of 17.5 ml of *1 M hydrochloric acid*, the suspension becomes colourless without effervescing. The red colour occurs again when the mixture is triturated for 1 min. On addition of a further 6 ml of *1 M hydrochloric acid* and triturating, the solution becomes colourless.

B. Dissolve about 0.1 g in *dilute hydrochloric acid R* and dilute to 10 ml with *water R*. 5 ml of the solution give reaction (b) of calcium (*2.3.1*).

### TESTS
**Matter insoluble in hydrochloric acid**
Maximum 0.5 per cent.

Dissolve 2.0 g in 30 ml of *hydrochloric acid R*. Boil the solution and filter. Wash the residue with hot *water R*. The residue weighs a maximum of 10 mg.

**Carbonates**
Maximum 5.0 per cent of $CaCO_3$.

Add 5.0 ml of *1 M hydrochloric acid* to the titrated solution obtained under Assay and titrate with *1 M sodium hydroxide* using 0.5 ml of *methyl orange solution R* as indicator.

1 ml of *1 M hydrochloric acid* is equivalent to 50.05 mg of $CaCO_3$.

**Chlorides** (*2.4.4*)

Maximum 330 ppm.

Dissolve 0.30 g in a mixture of 2 ml of *nitric acid R* and 10 ml of *water R* and dilute to 30 ml with *water R*.

**Sulphates** (*2.4.13*)

Maximum 0.4 per cent.

Dissolve 0.15 g in a mixture of 5 ml of *dilute hydrochloric acid R* and 10 ml of *distilled water R* and dilute to 60 ml with *distilled water R*.

**Arsenic** (*2.4.2, Method A*)

Maximum 4 ppm.

Dissolve 0.50 g in 5 ml of *brominated hydrochloric acid R* and dilute to 50 ml with *water R*. Use 25 ml of this solution.

**Magnesium and alkali metals**

Maximum 4.0 per cent calculated as sulphates.

Dissolve 1.0 g in a mixture of 10 ml of *hydrochloric acid R* and 40 ml of *water R*. Boil and add 50 ml of a 63 g/l solution of *oxalic acid R*. Neutralise with *ammonia R* and dilute to 200 ml with *water R*. Allow to stand for 1 h and filter through a suitable filter. To 100 ml of the filtrate, add 0.5 ml of *sulphuric acid R*. Cautiously evaporate to dryness and ignite. The residue weighs a maximum of 20 mg.

**Heavy metals** (*2.4.8*)

Maximum 20 ppm.

Dissolve 1.0 g in 10 ml of *hydrochloric acid R1* and evaporate to dryness on a water-bath. Dissolve the residue in 20 ml of *water R* and filter. 12 ml of the filtrate complies with test A. Prepare the reference solution using *lead standard solution (1 ppm Pb) R*.

**ASSAY**

To 1.500 g in a mortar, add 20-30 ml of *water R* and 0.5 ml of *phenolphthalein solution R*. Titrate with *1 M hydrochloric acid* by triturating the substance until the red colour disappears. The final solution is used in the tests for carbonates.

1 ml of *1 M hydrochloric acid* is equivalent to 37.05 mg of $Ca(OH)_2$.

_____ *Ph Eur*

# Anhydrous Calcium Lactate

(*Ph Eur monograph 2118*)

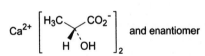

$C_6H_{10}CaO_6$         218.2         *814-80-2*

**Action and use**

Used in treatment of calcium deficiency.

*Ph Eur* _____

## DEFINITION

Calcium bis(2-hydroxypropanoate) or mixture of calcium (2*R*)-, (2*S*)- and (2*RS*)-2-hydroxypropanoates.

## Content

98.0 per cent to 102.0 per cent (dried substance).

## CHARACTERS

**Appearance:**

White or almost white, crystalline or granular powder.

**Solubility**

Soluble in water, freely soluble in boiling water, very slightly soluble in ethanol (96 per cent).

## IDENTIFICATION

A. It complies with the test for loss on drying (see Tests).

B. It gives the reaction of lactates (*2.3.1*).

C. It gives reaction (b) of calcium (*2.3.1*).

## TESTS

**Solution S**

Dissolve 5.0 g with heating in *carbon dioxide-free water R* prepared from *distilled water R*, allow to cool and dilute to 100 ml with the same solvent.

**Appearance of solution**

Solution S is not more opalescent than reference suspension II (*2.2.1*) and not more intensely coloured than reference solution $BY_6$ (*2.2.2, Method II*).

**Acidity or alkalinity**

To 10 ml of solution S add 0.1 ml of *phenolphthalein solution R* and 0.5 ml of *0.01 M hydrochloric acid*. The solution is colourless. Not more than 2.0 ml of *0.01 M sodium hydroxide* is required to change the colour of the indicator to pink.

**Chlorides** (*2.4.4*)

Maximum 200 ppm.

Dilute 5 ml of solution S to 15 ml with *water R*.

**Sulphates** (*2.4.13*)

Maximum 400 ppm.

Dilute 7.5 ml of solution S to 15 ml with *distilled water R*.

**Barium**

To 10 ml of solution S add 1 ml of *calcium sulphate solution R*. Allow to stand for 15 min. Any opalescence in the solution is not more intense than that in a mixture of 1 ml of *distilled water R* and 10 ml of solution S.

**Iron** (*2.4.9*)

Maximum 50 ppm.

Dilute 4 ml of solution S to 10 ml with *water R*.

**Magnesium and alkali salts**

Maximum 1 per cent.

To 20 ml of solution S add 20 ml of *water R*, 2 g of *ammonium chloride R* and 2 ml of *dilute ammonia R1*. Heat to boiling and rapidly add 40 ml of hot *ammonium oxalate solution R*. Allow to stand for 4 h, dilute to 100.0 ml with *water R* and filter. To 50.0 ml of the filtrate add 0.5 ml of *sulphuric acid R*. Evaporate to dryness and ignite the residue to constant mass at 600 ± 50 °C. The residue weighs a maximum of 5 mg.

**Heavy metals** (*2.4.8*)

Maximum 10 ppm.

Dissolve 2.0 g in *water R* and dilute to 20 ml with the same solvent. 12 ml of the solution complies with test A. Prepare the reference solution using *lead standard solution (1 ppm Pb) R*.

**Loss on drying** (*2.2.32*)

Maximum 3.0 per cent, determined on 0.500 g by drying in an oven at 125 °C.

## ASSAY

Dissolve 0.200 g in *water R* and dilute to 300 ml with the same solvent. Carry out the complexometric titration of calcium (*2.5.11*).

1 ml of *0.1 M sodium edetate* is equivalent to 21.82 mg of $C_6H_{10}CaO_6$.

*Ph Eur*

# Calcium Lactate Monohydrate

(*Ph Eur monograph 2117*)

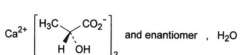

$C_6H_{10}CaO_6,H_2O$      236.0      *41372-22-9*

## Action and use
Used in treatment of calcium deficiency.

*Ph Eur*

## DEFINITION
Calcium bis(2-hydroxypropanoate) or mixture of calcium (2*R*)-, (2*S*)- and (2*RS*)-2-hydroxypropanoates monohydrates.

## Content
98.0 per cent to 102.0 per cent (dried substance).

## CHARACTERS
### Appearance
White or almost white, crystalline or granular powder.

### Solubility
Soluble in water, freely soluble in boiling water, very slightly soluble in ethanol (96 per cent).

## IDENTIFICATION
A. It complies with the test for loss on drying (see Tests).

B. It gives the reaction of lactates (2.3.1).

C. It gives reaction (b) of calcium (2.3.1).

## TESTS
### Solution S
Dissolve 5.4 g (equivalent to 5.0 g of the dried substance) with heating in *carbon dioxide-free water R* prepared from *distilled water R*, allow to cool and dilute to 100 ml with the same solvent.

### Appearance of solution
Solution S is not more opalescent than reference suspension II (2.2.1) and not more intensely coloured than reference solution BY$_6$ (2.2.2, *Method II*).

### Acidity or alkalinity
To 10 ml of solution S add 0.1 ml of *phenolphthalein solution R* and 0.5 ml of *0.01 M hydrochloric acid*. The solution is colourless. Not more than 2.0 ml of *0.01 M sodium hydroxide* is required to change the colour of the indicator to pink.

### Chlorides (2.4.4)
Maximum 200 ppm.

Dilute 5 ml of solution S to 15 ml with *water R*.

### Sulphates (2.4.13)
Maximum 400 ppm.

Dilute 7.5 ml of solution S to 15 ml with *distilled water R*.

### Barium
To 10 ml of solution S add 1 ml of *calcium sulphate solution R*. Allow to stand for 15 min. Any opalescence in the solution is not more intense than that in a mixture of 1 ml of *distilled water R* and 10 ml of solution S.

### Iron (2.4.9)
Maximum 50 ppm.

Dilute 4 ml of solution S to 10 ml with *water R*.

### Magnesium and alkali salts
Maximum 1 per cent.

To 20 ml of solution S add 20 ml of *water R*, 2 g of *ammonium chloride R* and 2 ml of *dilute ammonia R1*. Heat to boiling and rapidly add 40 ml of hot *ammonium oxalate solution R*. Allow to stand for 4 h, dilute to 100.0 ml with *water R* and filter. To 50.0 ml of the filtrate add 0.5 ml of *sulphuric acid R*. Evaporate to dryness and ignite the residue to constant mass at 600 $\pm$ 50 °C. The residue weighs a maximum of 5 mg.

### Heavy metals (2.4.8)
Maximum 10 ppm.

Dissolve a quantity equivalent to 2.0 g of the dried substance in *water R* and dilute to 20 ml with the same solvent. 12 ml of the solution complies with test A. Prepare the reference solution using *lead standard solution (1 ppm Pb) R*.

### Loss on drying (2.2.32)
5.0 per cent to 8.0 per cent, determined on 0.500 g by drying in an oven at 125 °C.

## ASSAY
Dissolve a quantity equivalent to 0.200 g of the dried substance in *water R* and dilute to 300 ml with the same solvent. Carry out the complexometric titration of calcium (2.5.11).

1 ml of *0.1 M sodium edetate* is equivalent to 21.82 mg of $C_6H_{10}CaO_6$.

*Ph Eur*

# Calcium Lactate Pentahydrate

Calcium Lactate

(*Ph Eur monograph 0468*)

$C_6H_{10}CaO_6,5H_2O$      218.2      *814-80-2*

(*approx.*)      (anhydrous)      (*anhydrous*)

## Action and use
Used in treatment of calcium deficiency.

## Preparations
Calcium and Ergocalciferol Tablets

Calcium Lactate Tablets

*Ph Eur*

## DEFINITION
Calcium bis(2-hydroxypropanoate) or mixture of calcium (2*R*)-, (2*S*)- and (2*RS*)-2-hydroxypropanoates pentahydrates.

## Content
98.0 per cent to 102.0 per cent (dried substance).

## CHARACTERS
### Appearance
White or almost white, crystalline or granular powder, slightly efflorescent.

## Solubility

Soluble in water, freely soluble in boiling water, very slightly soluble in ethanol (96 per cent).

## IDENTIFICATION

A. It complies with the test for loss on drying (see Tests).

B. It gives the reaction of lactates (*2.3.1*).

C. It gives reaction (b) of calcium (*2.3.1*).

## TESTS

### Solution S

Dissolve 7.1 g (equivalent to 5.0 g of the dried substance) with heating in *carbon dioxide-free water R* prepared from *distilled water R*, allow to cool and dilute to 100 ml with the same solvent.

### Appearance of solution

Solution S is not more opalescent than reference suspension II (*2.2.1*) and not more intensely coloured than reference solution $BY_6$ (*2.2.2, Method II*).

### Acidity or alkalinity

To 10 ml of solution S add 0.1 ml of *phenolphthalein solution R* and 0.5 ml of *0.01 M hydrochloric acid*. The solution is colourless. Not more than 2.0 ml of *0.01 M sodium hydroxide* is required to change the colour of the indicator to pink.

### Chlorides (*2.4.4*)

Maximum 200 ppm.

Dilute 5 ml of solution S to 15 ml with *water R*.

### Sulphates (*2.4.13*)

Maximum 400 ppm.

Dilute 7.5 ml of solution S to 15 ml with *distilled water R*.

### Barium

To 10 ml of solution S add 1 ml of *calcium sulphate solution R*. Allow to stand for 15 min. Any opalescence in the solution is not more intense than that in a mixture of 1 ml of *distilled water R* and 10 ml of solution S.

### Iron (*2.4.9*)

Mmaximum 50 ppm.

Dilute 4 ml of solution S to 10 ml with *water R*.

### Magnesium and alkali salts

Maximum 1 per cent.

To 20 ml of solution S add 20 ml of *water R*, 2 g of *ammonium chloride R* and 2 ml of *dilute ammonia R1*. Heat to boiling and rapidly add 40 ml of hot *ammonium oxalate solution R*. Allow to stand for 4 h, dilute to 100.0 ml with *water R* and filter. To 50.0 ml of the filtrate add 0.5 ml of *sulphuric acid R*. Evaporate to dryness and ignite the residue to constant mass at $600 \pm 50 \,°C$. The residue weighs a maximum of 5 mg.

### Heavy metals (*2.4.8*)

Maximum 10 ppm.

Dissolve a quantity equivalent to 2.0 g of the dried substance in *water R* and dilute to 20 ml with the same solvent. 12 ml of the solution complies with test A. Prepare the reference solution using *lead standard solution (1 ppm Pb) R*.

### Loss on drying (*2.2.32*)

22.0 per cent to 27.0 per cent, determined on 0.500 g by drying in an oven at 125 °C.

## ASSAY

Dissolve a quantity equivalent to 0.200 g of the dried substance in *water R* and dilute to 300 ml with the same solvent. Carry out the complexometric titration of calcium (*2.5.11*).

1 ml of *0.1 M sodium edetate* is equivalent to 21.82 mg of $C_6H_{10}CaO_6$.

*Ph Eur*

# Calcium Lactate Trihydrate

(*Ph Eur monograph 0469*)

$$Ca^{2+} \left[ \begin{array}{c} H_3C \diagdown \diagup CO_2^- \\ H \quad OH \end{array} \right]_2 \text{ and enantiomer , } 3\,H_2O$$

| $C_6H_{10}CaO_6,3H_2O$ | 218.2 | 814-80-2 |
|---|---|---|
| (*approx.*) | (anhydrous) | (anhydrous) |

### Action and use

Used in treatment of calcium deficiency.

### Preparation

Calcium Lactate Tablets

*Ph Eur*

## DEFINITION

Calcium bis(2-hydroxypropanoate) or mixture of calcium (2*R*)-, (2*S*)- and (2*RS*)-2-hydroxypropanoates trihydrates.

### Content

98.0 per cent to 102.0 per cent (dried substance).

## CHARACTERS

### Appearance

White or almost white, crystalline or granular powder.

### Solubility

Soluble in water, freely soluble in boiling water, very slightly soluble in ethanol (96 per cent).

## IDENTIFICATION

A. It complies with the test for loss on drying (see Tests).

B. It gives the reaction of lactates (*2.3.1*).

C. It gives reaction (b) of calcium (*2.3.1*).

## TESTS

### Solution S

Dissolve 6.2 g (equivalent to 5.0 g of the dried substance) with heating in *carbon dioxide-free water R* prepared from *distilled water R*, allow to cool and dilute to 100 ml with the same solvent.

### Appearance of solution

Solution S is not more opalescent than reference suspension II (*2.2.1*) and not more intensely coloured than reference solution $BY_6$ (*2.2.2, Method II*).

### Acidity or alkalinity

To 10 ml of solution S add 0.1 ml of *phenolphthalein solution R* and 0.5 ml of *0.01 M hydrochloric acid*. The solution is colourless. Not more than 2.0 ml of *0.01 M sodium hydroxide* is required to change the colour of the indicator to pink.

### Chlorides (*2.4.4*)

Maximum 200 ppm.

Dilute 5 ml of solution S to 15 ml with *water R*.

### Sulphates (*2.4.13*)

Maximum 400 ppm.

Dilute 7.5 ml of solution S to 15 ml with *distilled water R*.

**Barium**

To 10 ml of solution S add 1 ml of *calcium sulphate solution R*. Allow to stand for 15 min. Any opalescence in the solution is not more intense than that in a mixture of 1 ml of *distilled water R* and 10 ml of solution S.

**Iron** *(2.4.9)*

Maximum 50 ppm.

Dilute 4 ml of solution S to 10 ml with *water R*.

**Magnesium and alkali salts**

Maximum 1 per cent.

To 20 ml of solution S add 20 ml of *water R*, 2 g of *ammonium chloride R* and 2 ml of *dilute ammonia R1*. Heat to boiling and rapidly add 40 ml of hot *ammonium oxalate solution R*. Allow to stand for 4 h, dilute to 100.0 ml with *water R* and filter. To 50.0 ml of the filtrate add *0.5 ml of sulphuric acid R*. Evaporate to dryness and ignite the residue to constant mass at $600 \pm 50\ °C$. The residue weighs a maximum of 5 mg.

**Heavy metals** *(2.4.8)*

Maximum 10 ppm.

Dissolve a quantity equivalent to 2.0 g of the dried substance in *water R* and dilute to 20 ml with the same solvent. 12 ml of the solution complies with test A. Prepare the reference solution using *lead standard solution (1 ppm Pb) R*.

**Loss on drying** *(2.2.32)*

15.0 per cent to 20.0 per cent, determined on 0.500 g by drying in an oven at 125 °C.

**ASSAY**

Dissolve a quantity equivalent to 0.200 g of the dried substance in *water R* and dilute to 300 ml with the same solvent. Carry out the complexometric titration of calcium *(2.5.11)*.

1 ml of *0.1 M sodium edetate* is equivalent to 21.82 mg of $C_6H_{10}CaO_6$.

*Ph Eur*

# Calcium Levofolinate Pentahydrate

*(Ph Eur monograph 1606)*

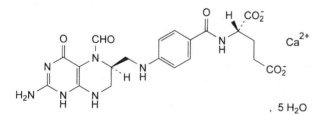

$C_{20}H_{21}CaN_7O_7,5H_2O$      511.5      *80433-71-2*

           (anhydrous)

**Action and use**

Antidote to folic acid antagonists.

*Ph Eur*

## DEFINITION

Calcium (2S)-2-[[4-[[[(6S)-2-amino-5-formyl-4-oxo-1,4,5,6,7,8-hexahydropteridin-6-yl]methyl]amino]benzoyl]amino]pentanedioate pentahydrate.

**Content:**

— *calcium levofolinate* ($C_{20}H_{21}CaN_7O_7$; $M_r$ 511.5):
  97.0 per cent to 102.0 per cent (anhydrous substance);

— *calcium* (Ca; $A_r$ 40.08): 7.54 per cent to 8.14 per cent (anhydrous substance).

## CHARACTERS

**Appearance**

White or light yellow, amorphous or crystalline powder, hygroscopic.

**Solubility**

Slightly soluble in water, practically insoluble in acetone and in ethanol (96 per cent).

## IDENTIFICATION

*First identification*  A, B, D.

*Second identification*  A, C, D.

A. Specific optical rotation (see Tests).

B. Infrared absorption spectrophotometry *(2.2.24)*.

*Preparation*  Discs.

*Comparison*  calcium folinate CRS.

If the spectra obtained show differences, dissolve the substance to be examined and the reference substance separately in the minimum quantity of *water R* and add dropwise sufficient *acetone R* to produce a precipitate. Allow to stand for 15 min, collect the precipitate by centrifugation, wash the precipitate twice with a minimum quantity of *acetone R* and dry. Record new spectra using the residues.

C. Thin-layer chromatography *(2.2.27)*.

*Test solution*  Dissolve 15 mg of the substance to be examined in a 3 per cent *V/V* solution of *ammonia R* and dilute to 5 ml with the same solvent.

*Reference solution*  Dissolve 15 mg of *calcium folinate CRS* in a 3 per cent *V/V* solution of *ammonia R* and dilute to 5 ml with the same solvent.

*Plate*  cellulose for chromatography $F_{254}$ R as the coating substance.

*Mobile phase*  the lower layer of a mixture of 1 volume of *isoamyl alcohol R* and 10 volumes of a 50 g/l solution of *citric acid R* previously adjusted to pH 8 with *ammonia R*.

*Application*  5 μl.

*Development*  Over a path of 15 cm.

*Drying*  In air.

*Detection*  Examine in ultraviolet light at 254 nm.

*Results*  The principal spot in the chromatogram obtained with the test solution is similar in position and size to the principal spot in the chromatogram obtained with the reference solution.

D. It gives reaction (b) of calcium *(2.3.1)*.

*Carry out the tests and the assay as rapidly as possible, protected from bright light.*

## TESTS

**Solution S**

Dissolve 0.40 g in *carbon dioxide-free water R*, heating at 40 °C if necessary, and dilute to 50.0 ml with the same solvent.

**Appearance of solution**

Solution S is clear *(2.2.1)* and its absorbance *(2.2.25)* at 420 nm has a maximum of 0.25.

**pH** *(2.2.3)*

7.5 to 8.5 for solution S.

**Specific optical rotation** (2.2.7)

− 10 to − 15 (anhydrous substance), measured at 25 °C.

Dissolve 0.200 g in *tris(hydroxymethyl)aminomethane solution R* previously adjusted to pH 8.1 with *sodium hydroxide solution R* or *hydrochloric acid R1* and dilute to 20.0 ml with the same solvent.

**Acetone and ethanol**

Head-space gas chromatography (2.2.28): use the standard additions method.

*Test solution* Dissolve 0.25 g of the substance to be examined in *water R* and dilute to 10.0 ml with the same solvent.

*Reference solution* Dissolve 0.125 g of *acetone R* and 0.750 g of *anhydrous ethanol R* in *water R* and dilute to 1000.0 ml with *water R*.

*Column:*
— *material:* fused silica;
— *size: l* = 10 m, Ø = 0.32 mm;
— *stationary phase: styrene-divinylbenzene copolymer R.*

*Carrier gas* *nitrogen for chromatography R.*

*Flow rate* 4 ml/min.

*Static head-space conditions which may be used:*
— *equilibration temperature:* 80 °C;
— *equilibration time:* 20 min;
— *pressurisation time:* 30 s.

*Temperature:*

|  | Time (min) | Temperature (°C) |
|---|---|---|
| Column | 0 - 14 | 80 → 220 |
| Injection port |  | 110 |
| Detector |  | 270 |

*Detection* Flame ionisation.

*Injection* At least 3 times.

*Limits:*
— *acetone:* maximum 0.5 per cent,
— *ethanol:* maximum 3.0 per cent.

**Related substances**

Liquid chromatography (2.2.29).

*Test solution* Dissolve 10.0 mg of the substance to be examined in *water R* and dilute to 10.0 ml with the same solvent.

*Reference solution (a)* Dissolve 10.0 mg of *calcium folinate CRS* in *water R* and dilute to 10.0 ml with the same solvent.

*Reference solution (b)* Dilute 1.0 ml of reference solution (a) to 100.0 ml with *water R*.

*Reference solution (c)* Dissolve 10.0 mg of *formylfolic acid CRS* in the mobile phase and dilute to 100.0 ml with the mobile phase. Dilute 1.0 ml of this solution to 10.0 ml with *water R*.

*Reference solution (d)* Dilute 1.0 ml of reference solution (b) to 20.0 ml with *water R*.

*Reference solution (e)* Dilute 5.0 ml of reference solution (c) to 10.0 ml with reference solution (b).

*Column:*
— *size: l* = 0.25 m, Ø = 4 mm;
— *stationary phase: octadecylsilyl silica gel for chromatography R* (5 µm);
— *temperature:* 40 °C.

*Mobile phase* Mix 220 ml of *methanol R* and 780 ml of a solution containing 2.0 ml of *tetrabutylammonium hydroxide solution (400 g/l) R* and 2.2 g of *disodium hydrogen phosphate R* previously adjusted to pH 7.8 with *phosphoric acid R*. If necessary adjust the concentration of *methanol R* to achieve the prescribed resolution.

*Flow rate* 1 ml/min.

*Detection* Spectrophotometer at 280 nm.

*Injection* 10 µl.

*Run time* 2.5 times the retention time of the principal peak in the chromatogram obtained with the test solution.

*System suitability* Reference solution (e):
— *resolution:* minimum of 2.2 between the peaks due to folinate and to impurity D.

*Limits:*
— *impurity D:* not more than 0.8 times the area of the principal peak in the chromatogram obtained with reference solution (c) (0.8 per cent);
— *any other impurity:* not more than 0.8 times the area of the principal peak in the chromatogram obtained with reference solution (b) (0.8 per cent);
— *sum of other impurities:* not more than twice the area of the principal peak in the chromatogram obtained with reference solution (b) (2.0 per cent);
— *disregard limit:* area of the principal peak in the chromatogram obtained with reference solution (d) (0.05 per cent).

**Impurity H**

Liquid chromatography (2.2.29): use the normalisation procedure.

*Test solution* Dissolve 50.0 mg of the substance to be examined in *water R* and dilute to 100.0 ml with the same solvent.

*Reference solution (a)* Dissolve 10.0 mg of *calcium folinate CRS* in *water R* and dilute to 20.0 ml with the same solvent.

*Reference solution (b)* Dilute 1.0 ml of reference solution (a) to 100.0 ml with *water R*.

*Column:*
— *size: l* = 0.15 m, Ø = 4 mm;
— *stationary phase: human albumin coated silica gel for chromatography R* (5 µm);
— *temperature:* 40 °C.

*Mobile phase* Dissolve 9.72 g of *sodium dihydrogen phosphate R* in 890 ml of *water R* and adjust to pH 5.0 with *sodium hydroxide solution R*; add 100 ml of *2-propanol R* and 10 ml of *acetonitrile R*.

*Flow rate* 1 ml/min.

*Detection* Spectrophotometer at 286 nm.

*Injection* 10 µl.

*Retention times* Levofolinate = about 9 min; impurity H = about 19 min.

*System suitability:*
— *resolution:* minimum of 5.0 between the peaks due to levofolinate and to impurity H in the chromatogram obtained with reference solution (a). The sum of the areas of the 2 peaks is 100 per cent. The peak area of impurity H is 48 per cent to 52 per cent. In the chromatogram obtained with reference solution (b) 2 clearly visible peaks are obtained.

*Limit:*
— *impurity H:* maximum 0.5 per cent.

**Chlorides**

Maximum 0.5 per cent.

Dissolve 0.300 g in 50 ml of *water R* heating at 40 °C if necessary. Add 10 ml of *2 M nitric acid* and titrate with *0.005 M silver nitrate* determining the end-point potentiometrically (*2.2.20*).

1 ml of *0.005 M silver nitrate* is equivalent to 0.177 mg of Cl.

**Platinum**

Maximum 10.0 ppm.

Atomic absorption spectrometry (*2.2.23, Method II*).

*Test solution*   Dissolve 1.0 g in *water R* and dilute to 100.0 ml with the same solvent.

*Reference solutions*   Prepare the reference solutions using *platinum standard solution (30 ppm Pt) R*, diluted as necessary with a mixture of 1 volume of *nitric acid R* and 99 volumes of *water R*.

*Source*   Platinum hollow-cathode lamp.

*Wavelength*   265.9 nm.

**Heavy metals** (*2.4.8*)

Maximum 50 ppm.

1.0 g complies with test F. Prepare the reference solution using 5 ml of *lead standard solution (10 ppm Pb) R*.

**Water** (*2.5.12*)

10.0 per cent to 17.0 per cent, determined on 0.200 g (ground to a very fine powder). Stir the substance to be examined in the titration solvent for about 15 min before titrating and use *iodosulphurous reagent R* as titrant.

**Bacterial endotoxins** (*2.6.14*)

Less than 0.5 IU/mg, if intended for use in the manufacture of parenteral dosage forms without a further appropriate procedure for the removal of bacterial endotoxins.

**ASSAY**

**Calcium**

Dissolve 0.400 g in 150 ml of *water R* and dilute to 300 ml with the same solvent. Carry out the complexometric titration of calcium (*2.5.11*).

1 ml of *0.1 M sodium edetate* is equivalent to 4.008 mg of Ca.

**Calcium folinate**

Liquid chromatography (*2.2.29*) as described in the test for related substances.

Calculate the percentage content of $C_{20}H21CaN_7O_7$ from the areas of the peaks in the chromatograms obtained with the test solution and reference solution (a) and the declared content of *calcium folinate CRS*.

**STORAGE**

In an airtight container, protected from light. If the substance is sterile, store in a sterile, airtight, tamper-proof container.

**IMPURITIES**

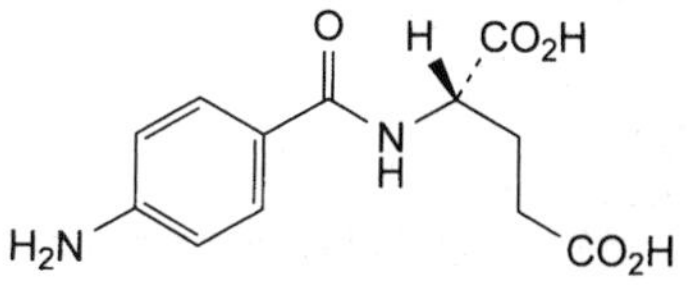

A. (2S)-2-[(4-aminobenzoyl)amino]pentanedioic acid,

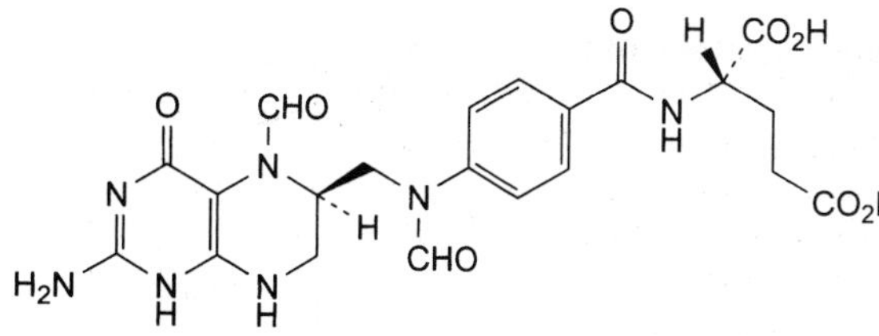

B. (2S)-2-[[4-[[[(6R)-2-amino-5-formyl-4-oxo-1,4,5,6,7,8-hexahydropteridin-6-yl]methyl]formylamino]benzoyl]amino]pentanedioic acid (5,10-diformyltetrahydrofolic acid),

C. folic acid,

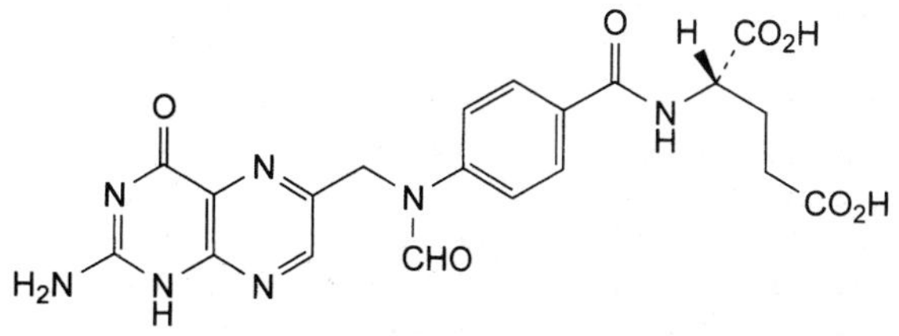

D. (2S)-2-[[4-[[(2-amino-4-oxo-1,4-dihydropteridin-6-yl)methyl]formylamino]benzoyl]amino]pentanedioic acid (10-formylfolic acid),

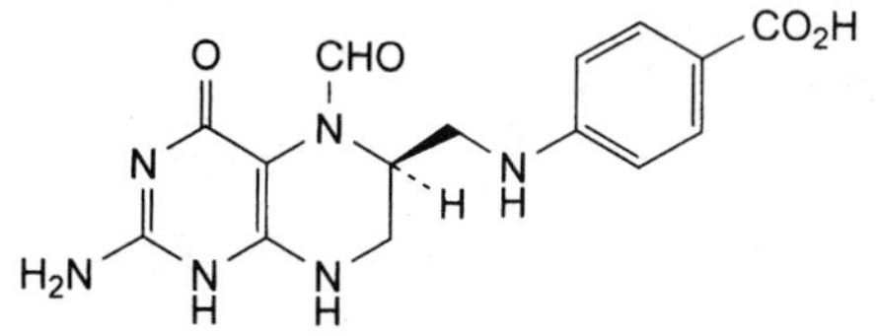

E. 4-[[[(6S)-2-amino-5-formyl-4-oxo-1,4,5,6,7,8-hexahydropteridin-6-yl]methyl]amino]benzoic acid (5-formyltetrahydropteroic acid),

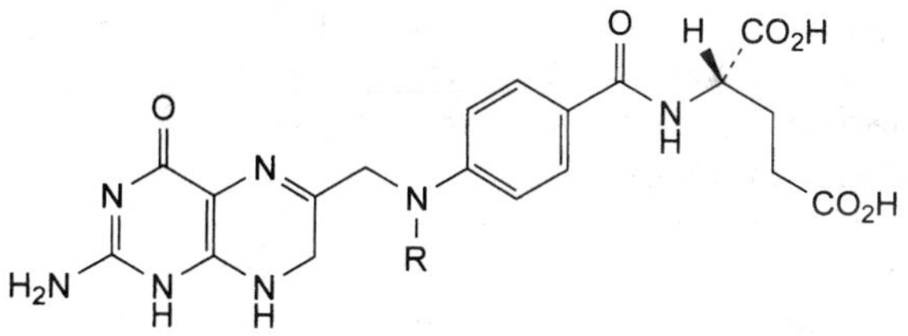

F. R = CHO: (2S)-2-[[4-[[(2-amino-4-oxo-1,4,7,8-tetrahydropteridin-6-yl)methyl]formylamino]benzoyl]amino]pentanedioic acid (10-formyldihydrofolic acid),

G. R = H: (2S)-2-[[4-[[(2-amino-4-oxo-1,4,7,8-tetrahydropteridin-6-yl)methyl]amino]benzoyl]amino]pentanedioic acid (dihydrofolic acid),

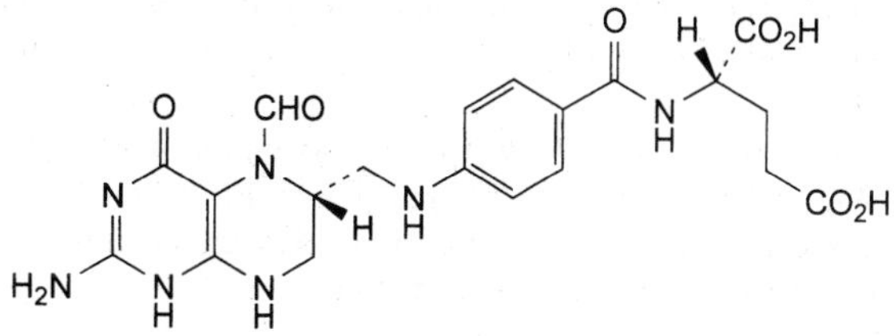

H. (2S)-2-[[4-[[[(6R)-2-amino-5-formyl-4-oxo-1,4,5,6,7,8-hexahydropteridin-6-yl]methyl]amino]benzoyl]amino]pentanedioic acid

# Calcium Levulinate Dihydrate

*(Ph Eur monograph 1296)*

$$Ca^{2+} \left[ H_3C \underset{O}{\overset{}{\diagup\diagdown}} CO_2^- \right]_2 , \; 2 H_2O$$

C$_{10}$H$_{14}$CaO$_6$,2H$_2$O        306.3        *5743-49-7*

## Action and use
Source of calcium.

*Ph Eur* _____

## DEFINITION
Calcium di(4-oxopentanoate) dihydrate.

## Content
98.0 per cent to 101.0 per cent (dried substance).

## CHARACTERS
### Appearance
White or almost white, crystalline powder.

### Solubility
Freely soluble in water, very slightly soluble in ethanol (96 per cent), practically insoluble in methylene chloride.

## IDENTIFICATION
*First identification   A, D, E.*

*Second identification   B, C, D, E.*

A. Infrared absorption spectrophotometry (*2.2.24*).

*Comparison   calcium levulinate dihydrate CRS.*

B. Thin-layer chromatography (*2.2.27*).

*Test solution*   Dissolve 60 mg of the substance to be examined in *water R* and dilute to 1 ml with the same solvent.

*Reference solution*   Dissolve 60 mg of *calcium levulinate dihydrate CRS* in *water R* and dilute to 1 ml with the same solvent.

*Plate   TLC silica gel plate R.*

*Mobile phase   concentrated ammonia R, ethyl acetate R, water R, ethanol (96 per cent) R (10:10:30:50 V/V/V/V).*

*Application   10 µl.*

*Development   Over a path of 10 cm.*

*Drying   At 100-105 °C for 20 min and allow to cool.*

*Detection*   Spray with a 30 g/l solution of *potassium permanganate R*. Dry in a current of warm air for about 5 min or until the spots become yellow. Examine in daylight.

*Results*   The principal spot in the chromatogram obtained with the test solution is similar in position, colour and size to the principal spot in the chromatogram obtained with the reference solution.

C. To 1 ml of solution S (see Tests), add 20 ml of a 2.5 g/l solution of *dinitrophenylhydrazine R* in *dilute hydrochloric acid R*. Allow to stand for 15 min. Filter, wash the precipitate with *water R*. Dry the precipitate in an oven at 100-105 °C. The melting point (*2.2.14*) is 203 °C to 210 °C.

D. It gives reaction (b) of calcium (*2.3.1*).

E. Loss on drying (see Tests).

## TESTS
### Solution S
Dissolve 10.0 g in *carbon dioxide-free water R* prepared from *distilled water R* and dilute to 100.0 ml with the same solvent.

### Appearance of solution
Solution S is clear (*2.2.1*) and not more intensely coloured than reference solution Y$_6$ (*2.2.2, Method II*).

### pH (*2.2.3*)
6.8 to 7.8 for solution S.

### Oxidisable substances
To 1 ml of solution S, add 10 ml of *water R*, 1 ml of *dilute sulphuric acid R* and 0.25 ml of a 3.0 g/l solution of *potassium permanganate R*. Mix. After 5 min, the violet colour of the mixture is still visible.

### Sucrose and reducing sugars
To 5 ml of solution S add 2 ml of *hydrochloric acid R1* and dilute to 10 ml with *water R*. Heat to boiling for 5 min and allow to cool. Add 10 ml of *sodium carbonate solution R*. Allow to stand for 5 min, dilute to 25 ml with *water R* and filter. To 5 ml of the filtrate add 2 ml of *cupri-tartaric solution R* and heat to boiling for 1 min. No red precipitate is formed.

### Chlorides (*2.4.4*)
Maximum 50 ppm.

Dilute 10 ml of solution S to 15 ml with *water R*.

### Sulphates (*2.4.13*)
Maximum 200 ppm.

Dilute 7.5 ml of solution S to 15 ml with *distilled water R*.

### Magnesium and alkali metals
Maximum 1.0 per cent.

To 10 ml of solution S, add 80 ml of *water R*, 10 ml of *ammonium chloride solution R* and 1 ml of *ammonia R*. Heat to boiling. To the boiling solution, add dropwise 50 ml of warm *ammonium oxalate solution R*. Allow to stand for 4 h, then dilute to 200 ml with *water R* and filter. To 100 ml of the filtrate, add 0.5 ml of *sulphuric acid R*. Evaporate to dryness on a water-bath and ignite to constant mass at 600 ± 50 °C. The residue weighs a maximum of 5.0 mg.

### Heavy metals (*2.4.8*)
Maximum 10 ppm.

12 ml of solution S complies with test A. Prepare the reference solution using *lead standard solution (1 ppm Pb) R*.

### Loss on drying (*2.2.32*)
11.0 per cent to 12.5 per cent, determined on 0.200 g by drying at 105 °C.

### Pyrogens (*2.6.8*)
If intended for use in the manufacture of parenteral dosage forms without a further appropriate procedure for the removal of pyrogens, it complies with the test for pyrogens. Inject per kilogram of the rabbit's mass 4 ml of a solution containing per millilitre 50 mg of the substance to be examined.

## ASSAY
Dissolve 0.240 g in 50 ml of *water R*. Carry out the complexometric titration of calcium (*2.5.11*).

1 ml of *0.1 M sodium edetate* is equivalent to 27.03 mg of C$_{10}$H$_{14}$CaO$_6$.

## STORAGE
Protected from light.

_____ *Ph Eur*

# Calcium Pantothenate

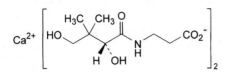

*(Ph Eur monograph 0470)*

$C_{18}H_{32}CaN_2O_{10}$      476.5      *137-08-6*

**Action and use**
Component of vitamin B.

*Ph Eur* _____

## DEFINITION
Calcium pantothenate contains not less than 98.0 per cent and not more than the equivalent of 101.0 per cent of calcium bis[3-[[(2R)-2,4-dihydroxy-3,3-dimethylbutanoyl]amino]propanoate], calculated with reference to the dried substance.

## CHARACTERS
A. white or almost white powder, slightly hygroscopic, freely soluble in water, slightly soluble in alcohol.

## IDENTIFICATION
A. It complies with the test for specific optical rotation (see Tests).

B. Examine the chromatograms obtained in the test for 3-aminopropionic acid. The principal spot in the chromatogram obtained with test solution (b) is similar in position, colour and size to the principal spot in the chromatogram obtained with reference solution (a).

C. To 1 ml of solution S (see Tests) add 1 ml of *dilute sodium hydroxide solution R* and 0.1 ml of *copper sulphate solution R*. A blue colour develops.

D. It gives reaction (a) of calcium *(2.3.1)*.

## TESTS
**Solution S**
Dissolve 2.50 g in *carbon dioxide-free water R* and dilute to 50.0 ml with the same solvent.

**Appearance of solution**
Solution S is clear *(2.2.1)* and colourless *(2.2.2, Method II)*.

**pH** *(2.2.3)*
The pH of solution S is 6.8 to 8.0.

**Specific optical rotation** *(2.2.7)*
+ 25.5 to + 27.5, determined on solution S and calculated with reference to the dried substance.

**3-Aminopropionic acid**
Examine by thin-layer chromatography *(2.2.27)*, using *silica gel G R* as the coating substance.

*Test solution (a)* Dissolve 0.2 g of the substance to be examined in *water R* and dilute to 5 ml with the same solvent.

*Test solution (b)* Dilute 1 ml of test solution (a) to 10 ml with *water R*.

*Reference solution (a)* Dissolve 20 mg of *calcium pantothenate CRS* in *water R* and dilute to 5 ml with the same solvent.

*Reference solution (b)* Dissolve 10 mg of *3-aminopropionic acid R* in *water R* and dilute to 50 ml with the same solvent.

Apply separately to the plate 5 µl of each solution. Develop over a path of 12 cm using a mixture of 35 volumes of *water R* and 65 volumes of *ethanol R*. Dry the plate in a current of air and spray with *ninhydrin solution R1*. Heat at 110 °C for 10 min. Any spot corresponding to 3-aminopropionic acid in the chromatogram obtained with test solution (a) is not more intense than the spot in the chromatogram obtained with reference solution (b) (0.5 per cent).

**Chlorides** *(2.4.4)*
5 ml of solution S diluted to 15 ml with *water R* complies with the limit test for chlorides (200 ppm).

**Heavy metals** *(2.4.8)*
12 ml of solution S complies with limit test A for heavy metals (20 ppm). Prepare the standard using *lead standard solution (1 ppm Pb) R*.

**Loss on drying** *(2.2.32)*
Not more than 3.0 per cent, determined on 1.000 g by drying in an oven at 105 °C.

## ASSAY
Dissolve 0.180 g in 50 ml of *anhydrous acetic acid R*. Titrate with *0.1 M perchloric acid* determining the end-point potentiometrically *(2.2.20)*.

1 ml of *0.1 M perchloric acid* is equivalent to 23.83 mg of $C_{18}H_{32}CaN_2O_{10}$.

## STORAGE
Store in an airtight container.

_____ *Ph Eur*

# Calcium Phosphate

Tribasic Calcium Phosphate
*(Ph Eur monograph 1052)*

**Action and use**
Excipient.

**Preparation**
Calcium and Ergocalciferol Tablets
Calcium Phosphate for Homoeopathic Preparations

*Ph Eur* _____

## DEFINITION
Mixture of calcium phosphates.

**Content**
35.0 per cent to 40.0 per cent of Ca ($A_r$ 40.08).

## CHARACTERS
**Appearance**
White or almost white powder.

**Solubility**
Practically insoluble in water. It dissolves in dilute hydrochloric acid and in dilute nitric acid.

## IDENTIFICATION
A. Dissolve 0.1 g in 5 ml of a 25 per cent *V/V* solution of *nitric acid R*. The solution gives reaction (b) of phosphates *(2.3.1)*.

B. It gives reaction (b) of calcium *(2.3.1)*. Filter before adding *potassium ferrocyanide solution R*.

C. It complies with the limits of the assay.

## TESTS
### Solution S
Dissolve 2.50 g in 20 ml of *dilute hydrochloric acid R*. If the solution is not clear, filter it. Add *dilute ammonia R1* dropwise until a precipitate is formed. Dissolve the precipitate by adding *dilute hydrochloric acid R* and dilute to 50 ml with *distilled water R*.

### Chlorides (*2.4.4*)
Maximum 0.15 per cent.

Dissolve 0.22 g in a mixture of 1 ml of *nitric acid R* and 10 ml of *water R* and dilute to 100 ml with *water R*.

### Fluorides
Maximum 75 ppm.

Potentiometry (*2.2.36, Method II*).

*Test solution*   Dissolve 0.250 g in *0.1 M hydrochloric acid*, add 5.0 ml of *fluoride standard solution (1 ppm F) R* and dilute to 50.0 ml with *0.1 M hydrochloric acid*. To 20.0 ml of this solution add 20.0 ml of *total-ionic-strength-adjustment buffer R* and 3 ml of an 82 g/l solution of *anhydrous sodium acetate R*. Adjust to pH 5.2 with *ammonia R* and dilute to 50.0 ml with *distilled water R*.

*Reference solution*   Fluoride standard solution (10 ppm F) R.

*Indicator electrode*   Fluoride-selective.

*Reference electrode*   Silver-silver chloride.

Carry out the measurements on the test solution, then add at least 3 quantities, each of 0.5 ml, of the reference solution, carrying out a measurement after each addition. Calculate the concentration of fluorides using the calibration curve, taking into account the addition of fluoride to the test solution.

### Sulphates (*2.4.13*)
Maximum 0.5 per cent.

Dilute 1 ml of solution S to 25 ml with *distilled water R*.

### Arsenic (*2.4.2, Method A*)
Maximum 4 ppm, determined on 5 ml of solution S.

### Iron (*2.4.9*)
Maximum 400 ppm.

Dilute 0.5 ml of solution S to 10 ml with *water R*.

### Heavy metals (*2.4.8*)
Maximum 30 ppm.

Dilute 13 ml of solution S to 20 ml with *water R*. 12 ml of the solution complies with test A. Prepare the reference solution using *lead standard solution (1 ppm Pb) R*.

### Acid-insoluble matter
Maximum 0.2 per cent.

Dissolve 5.0 g in a mixture of 10 ml of *hydrochloric acid R* and 30 ml of *water R*. Filter, wash the residue with *water R* and dry to constant mass at 100-105 °C. The residue weighs a maximum of 10 mg.

### Loss on ignition
Maximum 8.0 per cent, determined on 1.000 g by ignition at 800 ± 50 °C for 30 min.

## ASSAY
Dissolve 0.200 g in a mixture of 1 ml of *hydrochloric acid R1* and 5 ml of *water R*. Add 25.0 ml of *0.1 M sodium edetate* and dilute to 200 ml with *water R*. Adjust to about pH 10 with *concentrated ammonia R*. Add 10 ml of *ammonium chloride buffer solution pH 10.0 R* and a few milligrams of *mordant black 11 triturate R*. Titrate the excess sodium edetate with *0.1 M zinc sulphate* until the colour changes from blue to violet.

1 ml of *0.1 M sodium edetate* is equivalent to 4.008 mg of Ca.

## FUNCTIONALITY-RELATED CHARACTERISTICS
*This section provides information on characteristics that are recognised as being relevant control parameters for one or more functions of the substance when used as an excipient (see chapter 5.15). This section is a non-mandatory part of the monograph and it is not necessary to verify the characteristics to demonstrate compliance. Control of these characteristics can however contribute to the quality of a medicinal product by improving the consistency of the manufacturing process and the performance of the medicinal product during use. Where control methods are cited, they are recognised as being suitable for the purpose, but other methods can also be used. Wherever results for a particular characteristic are reported, the control method must be indicated.*

*The following characteristics may be relevant for calcium phosphate is used as a filler in tablets and capsules.*

**Particle-size distribution** (*2.9.31* or *2.9.38*).

**Bulk and tapped density** (*2.9.34*).

**Powder flow** (*2.9.36*).

_____ *Ph Eur*

# Calcium Polystyrene Sulphonate

### Action and use
Used in the treatment of hyperkalaemia.

## DEFINITION
Calcium Polystyrene Sulphonate is a cation-exchange resin prepared in the calcium form containing not less than 6.5% w/w and not more than 9.5% w/w of calcium, calculated with reference to the dried substance. Each g exchanges not less than 1.3 mEq and not more than 2.0 mEq of potassium, calculated with reference to the dried substance.

## CHARACTERISTICS
A cream to light brown, fine powder.

Practically insoluble in *water* and in *ethanol (96%)*.

## IDENTIFICATION
A. The *infrared absorption spectrum*, Appendix II A, is concordant with the *reference spectrum* of calcium polystyrene sulphonate *(RS 037)*.

B. Yields reaction C characteristic of *calcium salts*, Appendix VI.

## TESTS
### Particle size
Not more than 1% w/w is retained on a 150-μm sieve, Appendix XVII B. Use 20 g and sieve for 5 minutes.

### Potassium
Not more than 0.1% of K when determined by *atomic emission spectrophotometry*, Appendix II D, measuring at 766.5 nm and using a solution prepared in the following manner. To 1.1 g of the substance being examined add 5 ml of *hydrochloric acid*, heat to boiling, cool and add 10 ml of *water*. Filter, wash the filter and residue with *water* and dilute the filtrate and washings to 25 ml with *water*. Use *potassium standard solution (100 ppm K)*, suitably diluted with *water*, to prepare the standard solutions.

### Sodium
Not more than 0.1% of Na when determined by *atomic emission spectrophotometry*, Appendix II D, measuring at 589.0 nm and using a solution prepared in the following manner. To 1.1 g of the substance being examined add 5 ml

of *hydrochloric acid*, heat to boiling, cool and add 10 ml of *water*. Filter, wash the filter and residue with *water* and dilute the filtrate and washings to 25 ml with *water*. Use *sodium solution (200 ppm Na)*, suitably diluted with *water*, to prepare the standard solutions.

### Arsenic

1 g complies with the *limit test for arsenic*, Appendix VII (1 ppm).

### Heavy metals

Heat 4 g until charred, cool, add 4 ml of *lead-free nitric acid* and 0.5 ml of *sulphuric acid* drop wise and heat cautiously until white fumes are no longer evolved. Ignite in a muffle furnace at 500° to 600° until a white residue is obtained. Cool, add 4 ml of *hydrochloric acid* and dilute to 20 ml. The resulting solution complies with *limit test A for heavy metals*, Appendix VII. Use 2 ml of *lead standard solution (10 ppm Pb)* to prepare the standard (10 ppm).

### Styrene

Carry out the method for *liquid chromatography*, Appendix III D, using the following solutions. For solution (1) shake 10 g of the substance being examined with 10 ml of *acetone* for 30 minutes, centrifuge and use the supernatant liquid. Solution (2) contains 0.0001% w/v of *styrene* in *acetone*.

The chromatographic procedure may be carried out using (a) a stainless steel column (30 cm × 4 mm) packed with *octadecylsilyl silica gel for chromatography* (μBondapak C18 is suitable), (b) a mixture of equal volumes of *acetonitrile* and *water* as the mobile phase with a flow rate of 2 ml per minute and (c) a detection wavelength of 254 nm.

Inject separately 20 μl of each solution. The area of the peak corresponding to styrene in the chromatogram obtained with solution (1) is not greater than the area of the principal peak in the chromatogram obtained with solution (2) (1 ppm).

### Potassium exchange capacity

To 3 g of the substance being examined in a dry 250 ml glass-stoppered flask add 100 ml of a solution containing 0.7455% w/v of *potassium chloride* and 0.4401% w/v of *potassium hydrogen carbonate* in *water* (solution A), stopper and shake for 15 minutes. Filter and dilute 2 ml of the filtrate to 1000 ml with *water*. Determine the concentration of unbound potassium in this solution by *atomic emission spectrophotometry*, Appendix II D, measuring at 766.5 nm and using solution A suitably diluted with *water*, to prepare the standard solutions. Calculate the potassium exchange capacity of the substance being examined in milliequivalents taking the concentration of potassium in solution A as 144 milliequivalents of K per litre.

### Loss on drying

When dried at 70° at a pressure not exceeding 0.7 kPa for 16 hours, loses not more than 8.0% of its weight. Use 2 g.

### Microbial contamination

Carry out a quantitative evaluation for Enterobacteria and certain other Gram-negative bacteria, Appendix XVI B1. 0.01 g of the substance being examined gives a negative result, Table I (most probable number of bacteria per gram fewer than $10^2$).

### ASSAY

#### For calcium

Carefully heat 1 g in a platinum crucible until a white ash is obtained and dissolve in 10 ml of *2M hydrochloric acid* with the aid of heat. Transfer the resulting solution to a conical flask using 20 ml of *water*. Add 50 ml of *0.05M disodium edetate VS*, 20 ml of *ammonia buffer pH 10.9* and titrate the

excess of disodium edetate with *0.02M zinc sulphate VS*, using a 0.5% w/v solution of *mordant black 11* in *ethanol (96%)* as indicator to a red purple end point. Each ml of *0.05M disodium edetate VS* is equivalent to 2.004 mg of Ca.

### STORAGE

Calcium Polystyrene Sulphonate should be kept in an airtight container.

# Calcium Stearate

*(Ph Eur monograph 0882)*

1592-23-0

### Action and use

Excipient.

*Ph Eur*

### DEFINITION

Mixture of calcium salts of different fatty acids consisting mainly of stearic (octadecanoic) acid [$(C_{17}H_{35}COO)_2Ca$; $M_r$ 607] and palmitic (hexadecanoic) acid [$(C_{15}H_{31}COO)_2Ca$; $M_r$ 550.9] with minor proportions of other fatty acids.

*Content:*
— *calcium*: 6.4 per cent to 7.4 per cent ($A_r$ 40.08) (dried substance);
— *stearic acid in the fatty acid fraction*: minimum 40.0 per cent;
— *sum of stearic acid and palmitic acid in the fatty acid fraction*: minimum 90.0 per cent.

### CHARACTERS

#### Appearance

Fine, white or almost white, crystalline powder.

#### Solubility

Practically insoluble in water and in ethanol (96 per cent).

### IDENTIFICATION

*First identification C, D.*

*Second identification A, B, D.*

A. Freezing point (*2.2.18*): minimum 53 °C, for the residue obtained in the preparation of solution S (see Tests).

B. Acid value (*2.5.1*): 195 to 210.

Dissolve 0.200 g of the residue obtained in the preparation of solution S in 25 ml of the prescribed mixture of solvents.

C. Examine the chromatograms obtained in the test for fatty acid composition.

*Results* The retention times of the principal peaks in the chromatogram obtained with the test solution are approximately the same as those of the principal peaks in the chromatogram obtained with the reference solution.

D. Neutralise 5 ml of solution S to *red litmus paper R* using *strong sodium hydroxide solution R*. The solution gives reaction (b) of calcium (*2.3.1*).

### TESTS

#### Solution S

To 5.0 g add 50 ml of *peroxide-free ether R*, 20 ml of *dilute nitric acid R* and 20 ml of *distilled water R*. Boil under a reflux condenser until dissolution is complete. Allow to cool. In a separating funnel, separate the aqueous layer and shake the ether layer with 2 quantities, each of 5 ml, of *distilled water R*. Combine the aqueous layers, wash with 15 ml of *peroxide-free ether R* and dilute the aqueous layer to 50 ml with *distilled* water R (solution S). Evaporate the ether layer to dryness and dry the residue at 100-105 °C. Keep the residue for identification tests A and B.

## Acidity or alkalinity

To 1.0 g add 20 ml of *carbon dioxide-free water R* and boil for 1 min with continuous shaking. Cool and filter. To 10 ml of the filtrate add 0.05 ml of *bromothymol blue solution R1*. Not more than 0.5 ml of *0.01 M hydrochloric acid* or *0.01 M sodium hydroxide* is required to change the colour of the indicator.

## Chlorides (2.4.4)

Maximum 0.1 per cent.

Dilute 0.5 ml of solution S to 15 ml with *water R*.

## Sulphates (2.4.13)

Maximum 0.3 per cent.

Dilute 0.5 ml of solution S to 15 ml with *distilled water R*.

## Cadmium

Maximum 3.0 ppm.

Atomic absorption spectrometry (2.2.23, Method II).

*Test solution*  Place 50.0 mg in a polytetrafluoroethylene digestion bomb and add 0.5 ml of a mixture of 1 volume of *hydrochloric acid R* and 5 volumes of *cadmium- and lead-free nitric acid R*. Allow to digest at 170 °C for 5 h. Allow to cool. Dissolve the residue in *water R* and dilute to 5.0 ml with the same solvent.

*Reference solutions*  Prepare the reference solutions using *cadmium standard solution (10 ppm Cd) R*, diluted if necessary with a 1 per cent V/V solution of *hydrochloric acid R*.

*Source*  Cadmium hollow-cathode lamp.

*Wavelength*  228.8 nm.

*Atomisation device*  Graphite furnace.

## Lead

Maximum 10.0 ppm.

Atomic absorption spectrometry (2.2.23, Method II).

*Test solution*  Use the solution described in the test for cadmium.

*Reference solutions*  Prepare the reference solutions using *lead standard solution (10 ppm Pb) R*, diluted if necessary with *water R*.

*Source*  Lead hollow-cathode lamp.

*Wavelength*  283.3 nm; 217.0 nm may be used depending on the apparatus.

*Atomisation device*  Graphite furnace.

## Nickel

Maximum 5.0 ppm.

Atomic absorption spectrometry (2.2.23, Method II).

*Test solution*  Use the solution described in the test for cadmium.

*Reference solutions*  Prepare the reference solutions using *nickel standard solution (10 ppm Ni) R*, diluted if necessary with *water R*.

*Source*  Nickel hollow-cathode lamp.

*Wavelength*  232.0 nm.

*Atomisation device*  Graphite furnace.

## Loss on drying (2.2.32)

Maximum 6.0 per cent, determined on 1.000 g by drying in an oven at 105 °C.

## Microbial contamination

TAMC: acceptance criterion $10^3$ CFU/g (2.6.12).

TYMC: acceptance criterion $10^2$ CFU/g (2.6.12).

Absence of *Escherichia coli* (2.6.13).

Absence of *Salmonella* (2.6.13).

## ASSAY

### Calcium

To 0.500 g in a 250 ml conical flask add 50 ml of a mixture of equal volumes of *anhydrous ethanol R* and *butanol R*, 5 ml of *concentrated ammonia R*, 3 ml of *ammonium chloride buffer solution pH 10.0 R*, 30.0 ml of *0.1 M sodium edetate* and 15 mg of *mordant black 11 triturate R*. Heat to 45-50 °C until the solution is clear. Cool and titrate with *0.1 M zinc sulphate* until the colour changes from blue to violet. Carry out a blank titration.

1 ml of *0.1 M sodium edetate* is equivalent to 4.008 mg of Ca.

### Composition of fatty acids

Gas chromatography (2.2.28): use the normalisation procedure.

*Test solution*  In a conical flask fitted with a reflux condenser, dissolve 0.10 g of the substance to be examined in 5 ml of *boron trifluoride-methanol solution R*. Boil under a reflux condenser for 10 min. Add 4 ml of *heptane R* through the condenser. Boil under a reflux condenser for 10 min. Allow to cool. Add 20 ml of a *saturated sodium chloride solution R*. Shake and allow the layers to separate. Remove about 2 ml of the organic layer and dry over 0.2 g of *anhydrous sodium sulphate R*. Dilute 1.0 ml of the solution to 10.0 ml with *heptane R*.

*Reference solution*  Prepare the reference solution in the same manner as the test solution using 50.0 mg of *palmitic acid CRS* and 50.0 mg of *stearic acid CRS* instead of calcium stearate.

*Column*:
— *material*: fused silica;
— *size*: l = 30 m, Ø = 0.32 mm;
— *stationary phase*: macrogol 20 000 R (film thickness 0.5 µm).

*Carrier gas*  helium for chromatography R.

*Flow rate*  2.4 ml/min.

*Temperature*:

|  | Time (min) | Temperature (°C) |
|---|---|---|
| Column | 0 - 2 | 70 |
|  | 2 - 36 | 70 → 240 |
|  | 36 - 41 | 240 |
| Injection port |  | 220 |
| Detector |  | 260 |

*Detection*  Flame ionisation.

*Injection*  1 µl.

*Relative retention*  With reference to methyl stearate: methyl palmitate = about 0.88.

*System suitability*  Reference solution:
— *resolution*: minimum 5.0 between the peaks due to methyl palmitate and methyl stearate.

Calculate the content of palmitic acid and stearic acid. Disregard the peak due to the solvent.

*Ph Eur*

# Dried Calcium Sulphate

Exsiccated Calcium Sulphate; Plaster of Paris

$CaSO_4,\frac{1}{2}H_2O$          145.1          *26499-65-0*

## DEFINITION

Dried Calcium Sulphate is prepared by heating powdered gypsum, $CaSO_4,2H_2O$, at about 150° in a controlled manner such that it is substantially converted into the hemihydrate, $CaSO_4,\frac{1}{2}H_2O$, with minimum production of the anhydrous phases of calcium sulphate. It may contain suitable setting accelerators or decelerators.

## CHARACTERISTICS

A white or almost white powder; hygroscopic.

Slightly soluble in *water*, more soluble in dilute mineral acids; practically insoluble in *ethanol (96%)*.

## IDENTIFICATION

Yields the reactions characteristic of *calcium salts* and of *sulphates*, Appendix VI.

## TESTS

### Setting properties

20 g mixed with 10 ml of *water* at 15° to 20° in a cylindrical mould about 2.4 cm in diameter sets in 4 to 11 minutes. The mass thus produced, after standing for 3 hours, possesses sufficient hardness to resist pressure of the fingers at the edges, which retain their sharpness of outline and do not crumble.

### Loss on ignition

When ignited to constant weight at red heat, loses 4.5% to 8.0% of its weight. Use 1 g.

# Calcium Sulphate Dihydrate

(*Ph Eur monograph 0982*)

$CaSO_4,2H_2O$          172.2          *10101-41-4*

### Action and use

Excipient.

*Ph Eur* _____

## DEFINITION

### Content

98.0 per cent to 102.0 per cent of $CaSO_4,2H_2O$.

## CHARACTERS

### Appearance

White or almost white fine powder.

### Solubility

Very slightly soluble in water, practically insoluble in ethanol (96 per cent).

## IDENTIFICATION

A. Loss on ignition (see Tests).

B. Solution S (see Tests) gives reaction (a) of sulphates (2.3.1).

C. Solution S gives reaction (a) of calcium (2.3.1).

## TESTS

### Solution S

Dissolve 1.0 g in 50 ml of a 10 per cent *V/V* solution of *hydrochloric acid R* by heating at 50 °C for 5 min. Allow to cool.

### Acidity or alkalinity

Shake 1.5 g with 15 ml of *carbon dioxide-free water R* for 5 min. Allow to stand for 5 min and filter. To 10 ml of the filtrate add 0.1 ml of *phenolphthalein solution R* and 0.25 ml of *0.01 M sodium hydroxide*. The solution is red. Add 0.30 ml of *0.01 M hydrochloric acid*. The solution is colourless. Add 0.2 ml of *methyl red solution R*. The solution is reddish-orange.

### Chlorides (2.4.4)

Maximum 300 ppm.

Shake 0.5 g with 15 ml of *water R* for 5 min. Allow to stand for 15 min and filter. Dilute 5 ml of the filtrate to 15 ml with *water R*.

### Arsenic (2.4.2, Method A)

Maximum 10 ppm, determined on 5 ml of solution S.

### Iron (2.4.9)

Maximum 100 ppm.

To 0.25 g add a mixture of 5 ml of *hydrochloric acid R* and 20 ml of *water R*. Heat to boiling, cool and filter.

### Heavy metals (2.4.8)

Maximum 20 ppm.

To 2.5 g add a mixture of 2 ml of *hydrochloric acid R* and 15 ml of *water R*. Heat to boiling. Cool and then add 0.5 ml of *phenolphthalein solution R*. Cautiously add *concentrated ammonia R* until the colour changes to pink. Add 0.5 ml of *glacial acetic acid R* and dilute to 25 ml with *water R*. Filter. 12 ml of the filtrate complies with test A. Prepare the reference solution using *lead standard solution (2 ppm Pb) R*.

### Loss on ignition

18.0 per cent to 22.0 per cent, determined on 1.000 g by ignition to constant mass at 800 ± 50 °C.

## ASSAY

Dissolve 0.150 g in 120 ml of *water R*. Carry out the complexometric titration of calcium (2.5.11).

1 ml of *0.1 M sodium edetate* is equivalent to 17.22 mg of $CaSO_4,2H_2O$.

## FUNCTIONALITY-RELATED CHARACTERISTICS

*This section provides information on characteristics that are recognised as being relevant control parameters for one or more functions of the substance when used as an excipient (see chapter 5.15). This section is a non-mandatory part of the monograph and it is not necessary to verify the characteristics to demonstrate compliance. Control of these characteristics can however contribute to the quality of a medicinal product by improving the consistency of the manufacturing process and the performance of the medicinal product during use. Where control methods are cited, they are recognised as being suitable for the purpose, but other methods can also be used. Wherever results for a particular characteristic are reported, the control method must be indicated.*

*The following characteristics may be relevant for calcium sulphate dihydrate used as filler in tablets and capsules.*

**Particle-size distribution** (2.9.31 or 2.9.38).

**Bulk and tapped density** (2.9.34).

**Powder flow** (2.9.36).

_____ *Ph Eur*

# Natural Camphor

(D-Camphor, Ph Eur monograph 1400)

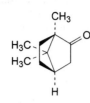

C₁₀H₁₆O        152.2        464-49-3

*Ph Eur* ___

## DEFINITION

(1R,4R)-1,7,7-Trimethylbicyclo[2.2.1]heptan-2-one.

## CHARACTERS

### Appearance

White or almost white, crystalline powder or friable, crystalline masses.

Highly volatile even at room temperature.

### Solubility

Slightly soluble in water, very soluble in alcohol and in light petroleum, freely soluble in fatty oils, very slightly soluble in glycerol.

## IDENTIFICATION

*First identification*   A, C.

*Second identification*   A, B, D.

A. Specific optical rotation (see Tests).

B. Melting point (*2.2.14*): 175 °C to 179 °C.

C. Infrared absorption spectrophotometry (*2.2.24*).

*Comparison*   racemic camphor CRS.

D. Dissolve 1.0 g in 30 ml of *methanol R*. Add 1.0 g of *hydroxylamine hydrochloride R* and 1.0 g of *anhydrous sodium acetate R*. Boil under a reflux condenser for 2 h. Allow to cool and add 100 ml of *water R*. Filter, wash the precipitate obtained with 10 ml of *water R* and recrystallise from 10 ml of a mixture of 4 volumes of *alcohol R* and 6 volumes of *water R*. The crystals, dried *in vacuo*, melt (*2.2.14*) at 118 °C to 121 °C.

## TESTS

*Carry out the weighings and dissolution rapidly.*

### Solution S

Dissolve 2.50 g in 10 ml of *alcohol R* and dilute to 25.0 ml with the same solvent.

### Appearance of solution

Solution S is clear (*2.2.1*) and colourless (*2.2.2, Method II*).

### Acidity or alkalinity

To 10 ml of solution S add 0.1 ml of *phenolphthalein solution R1*. The solution is colourless. Not more than 0.2 ml of *0.1 M sodium hydroxide* is required to change the colour of the indicator.

### Specific optical rotation (*2.2.7*)

+ 40.0 to + 43.0, determined on solution S.

### Related substances

Gas chromatography (*2.2.28*).

*Test solution*   Dissolve 2.50 g of the substance to be examined in *heptane R* and dilute to 25.0 ml with the same solvent.

*Reference solution (a)*   Dilute 1.0 ml of the test solution to 100.0 ml with *heptane R*.

*Reference solution (b)*   Dilute 10.0 ml of reference solution (a) to 20.0 ml with *heptane R*.

*Reference solution (c)*   Dissolve 0.50 g of *borneol R* in *heptane R* and dilute to 25.0 ml with the same solvent. Dilute 5.0 ml of the solution to 50.0 ml with *heptane R*.

*Reference solution (d)*   Dissolve 50 mg of *linalol R* and 50 mg of *bornyl acetate R* in *heptane R* and dilute to 100.0 ml with the same solvent.

*Column:*
— *size: l* = 30 m, Ø = 0.25 mm,
— *stationary phase: macrogol 20 000 R* (0.25 µm).

*Carrier gas*   helium for chromatography R.

*Split ratio*   1:70.

*Flow rate*   45 cm/s.

*Temperature:*

| | Time (min) | Temperature (°C) |
|---|---|---|
| Column | 0 - 10 | 50 |
| | 10 - 35 | 50 → 100 |
| | 35 - 45 | 100 → 200 |
| | 45 - 55 | 200 |
| Injection port | | 220 |
| Detector | | 250 |

*Detection*   Flame ionisation.

*Injection*   1 µl.

*System suitability*   Reference solution (d):
— *resolution*: minimum 3.0 between the peaks due to bornyl acetate and to linalol.

*Limits:*
— *borneol*: not more than the area of the principal peak in the chromatogram obtained with reference solution (c) (2.0 per cent).
— *any other impurity*: not more than half of the area of the principal peak in the chromatogram obtained with reference solution (a) (0.5 per cent),
— *total* of other impurities: not more than 4 times the area of the principal peak in the chromatogram obtained with reference solution (a) (4.0 per cent),
— *disregard limit*: 0.1 times the area of the principal peak in the chromatogram obtained with reference solution (b) (0.05 per cent).

### Halogens

Maximum 100 ppm.

Dissolve 1.0 g in 10 ml of *2-propanol R* in a distillation flask. Add 1.5 ml of *dilute sodium hydroxide solution R* and 50 mg of *nickel-aluminium alloy R*. Heat on a water-bath until the *2-propanol R* has evaporated. Allow to cool and add 5 ml of *water R*. Mix and filter through a wet filter previously washed with *water R* until free from chlorides. Dilute the filtrate to 10.0 ml with *water R*. To 5.0 ml of the solution, add *nitric acid R* dropwise until the precipitate which forms is redissolved and dilute to 15 ml with *water R*. The solution complies with the limit test for chlorides (*2.4.4*).

### Residue on evaporation (*2.8.9*)

Maximum 0.05 per cent.

Evaporate 2.0 g on a water-bath and dry in an oven at 100-105 °C for 1 h. The residue weighs a maximum of 1 mg.

**Water**
Dissolve 1 g in 10 ml of *light petroleum R*. The solution is clear (*2.2.1*).

**IMPURITIES**

and enantiomer

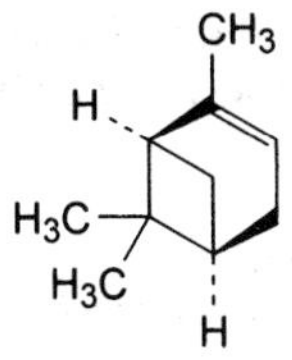

A. 2,6,6-trimethylbicyclo[3.1.1]hept-2-ene (α-pinene),

and enantiomer

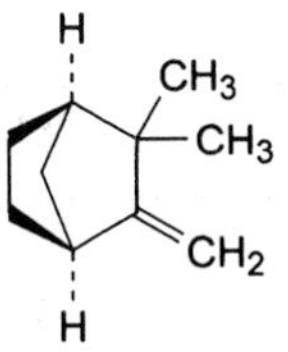

B. 2,2-dimethyl-3-methylenebicyclo[2.2.1]heptane (camphene),

and enantiomer

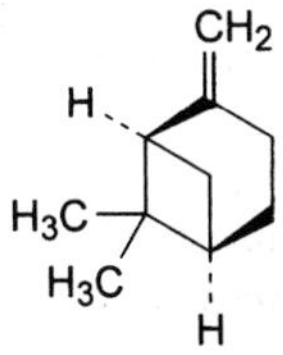

C. 6,6-dimethyl-2-methylenebicyclo[3.1.1]heptane (β-pinene),

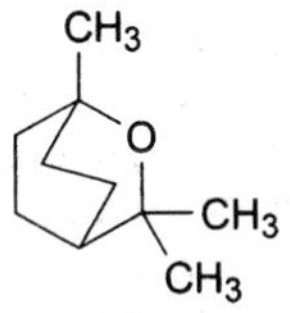

D. 3,3-dimethyl-2-oxabicyclo[2.2.2]octane (cineole),

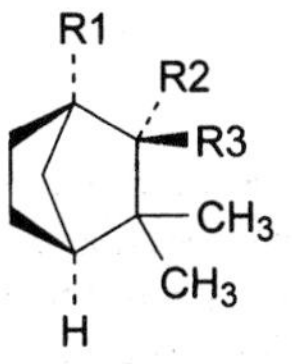

and enantiomer

E. R1 = $CH_3$, R2 + R3 = O:
1,3,3-trimethylbicyclo[2.2.1]heptan-2-one (fenchone),

F. R1 = $CH_3$, R2 = OH, R3 = H:
*exo*-1,3,3-trimethylbicyclo[2.2.1]heptan-2-ol (fenchol),

G. R1 = H, R2 = OH, R3 = $CH_3$:
*exo*-2,3,3-trimethylbicyclo[2.2.1]heptan-2-ol (camphene hydrate),

H. R1 = H, R2 = $CH_3$, R3 = OH:
*endo*-2,3,3-trimethylbicyclo[2.2.1]heptan-2-ol (methylcamphenilol),

and enantiomer

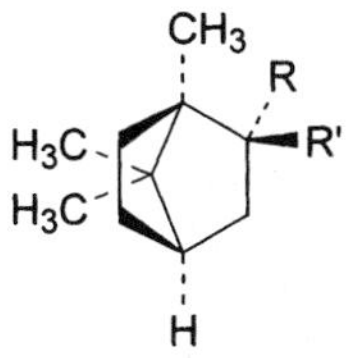

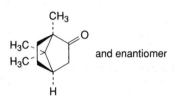

I. R = OH, R′ = H:
*exo*-1,7,7-trimethylbicyclo[2.2.1]heptan-2-ol (*exo*-borneol),

J. R = H, R′ = OH:
*endo*-1,7,7-trimethylbicyclo[2.2.1]heptan-2-ol (*endo*-borneol).

*Ph Eur*

# Racemic Camphor

(*Ph Eur monograph 0655*)

and enantiomer

$C_{10}H_{16}O$ 152.2 *76-22-2*

**Action and use**
Counter-irritant.

**Preparations**
Camphorated Opium Tincture
Concentrated Camphorated Opium Tincture
Concentrated Camphor Water

*Ph Eur*

**DEFINITION**
(1*RS*,4*RS*)-1,7,7-Trimethylbicyclo[2.2.1]heptan-2-one.

**CHARACTERS**

**Appearance**
White or almost white, crystalline powder or friable, crystalline masses, highly volatile even at room temperature.

**Solubility**
Slightly soluble in water, very soluble in ethanol (96 per cent) and in light petroleum, freely soluble in fatty oils, very slightly soluble in glycerol.

**IDENTIFICATION**
*First identification A, C.*
*Second identification A, B, D.*

A. Optical rotation (see Tests).

B. Melting point (*2.2.14*): 172 °C to 180 °C.

C. Infrared absorption spectrophotometry (*2.2.24*).
*Preparation* Mulls in *liquid paraffin R*.
*Comparison* *racemic camphor CRS*.

D. Dissolve 1.0 g in 30 ml of *methanol R*. Add 1.0 g of *hydroxylamine hydrochloride R* and 1.0 g of *anhydrous sodium acetate R*. Boil under a reflux condenser for 2 h. Allow to cool and add 100 ml of *water R*. A precipitate is formed. Filter, wash with 10 ml of *water R* and recrystallize from 10 ml of a mixture of 4 volumes of *ethanol (96 per cent) R* and 6 volumes of *water R*. The crystals, dried *in vacuo*, melt (*2.2.14*) at 118 °C to 121 °C.

## TESTS

*Carry out the weighings rapidly.*

### Solution S

Dissolve 2.50 g in 10 ml of *ethanol (96 per cent) R* and dilute to 25.0 ml with the same solvent.

### Appearance of solution

Solution S is clear (*2.2.1*) and colourless (*2.2.2, Method II*).

### Acidity or alkalinity

Dissolve 1.0 g in 10 ml of *ethanol (96 per cent) R* and add 0.1 ml of *phenolphthalein solution R1*. The solution is colourless. Not more than 0.2 ml of *0.1 M sodium hydroxide* is required to change the colour of the indicator.

### Optical rotation (*2.2.7*)

− 0.15° to + 0.15°, determined on solution S.

### Related substances

Gas chromatography (*2.2.28*).

*Test solution* Dissolve 50 mg of the substance to be examined in *hexane R* and dilute to 50.0 ml with the same solvent.

*Reference solution (a)* Dissolve 50 mg of the substance to be examined and 50 mg of *bornyl acetate R* in *hexane R* and dilute to 50.0 ml with the same solvent.

*Reference solution (b)* Dilute 1.0 ml of the test solution to 200.0 ml with *hexane R*.

*Column:*
— *size*: $l$ = 2 m, Ø = 2 mm;
— *stationary phase: diatomaceous earth for gas chromatography* R impregnated with 10 per cent m/m of *macrogol 20 000 R*.

*Carrier gas* *nitrogen for chromatography R*.

*Flow rate* 30 ml/min.

*Temperature:*
— *column*: 130 °C;
— *injection port and detector*: 200 °C.

*Detection* Flame ionisation.

*Injection* 1 μl.

*Run time* 3 times the retention time of camphor.

*System suitability:*
— *resolution*: minimum 1.5 between the peaks due to camphor and bornyl acetate in the chromatogram obtained with reference solution (a);
— *signal-to-noise ratio*: minimum 5 for the principal peak in the chromatogram obtained with reference solution (b).

*Limits:*
— *any impurity*: for each impurity, not more than 2 per cent of the area of the principal peak;
— *total*: not more than 4 per cent of the area of the principal peak;
— *disregard limit*: the area of the principal peak in the chromatogram obtained with reference solution (b).

### Halogens

Maximum 100 ppm.

Dissolve 1.0 g in 10 ml of *2-propanol R* in a distillation flask. Add 1.5 ml of *dilute sodium hydroxide solution R* and 50 mg of *nickel-aluminium alloy R*. Heat on a water-bath until the *2-propanol R* has evaporated. Allow to cool and add 5 ml of *water R*. Mix and filter through a wet filter previously washed with *water R* until free from chlorides. Dilute the filtrate to 10.0 ml with *water R*. To 5.0 ml of this solution, add *nitric acid R* dropwise until the precipitate which forms is redissolved and dilute to 15 ml with *water R*. The solution complies with the limit test for chlorides (*2.4.4*).

### Water

Dissolve 1 g in 10 ml of *light petroleum R*. The solution is clear (*2.2.1*).

### Residue on evaporation

Maximum 0.05 per cent.

Evaporate 2.0 g on a water-bath and dry at 100-105 °C for 1 h. The residue weighs not more than 1 mg.

*Ph Eur*

---

# Caprylocaproyl Macrogolglycerides

(*Ph Eur monograph 1184*)

### Action and use

Excipient.

*Ph Eur*

## DEFINITION

Mixtures of monoesters, diesters and triesters of glycerol and monoesters and diesters of macrogols with a mean relative molecular mass between 200 and 400.

They are obtained by partial alcoholysis of medium-chain triglycerides using macrogol or by esterification of glycerol and macrogol with caprylic (octanoic) acid and capric (decanoic) acid or a mixture of glycerol esters and condensates of ethylene oxide with caprylic acid and capric acid. They may contain free macrogols.

## CHARACTERS

### Appearance

Pale-yellow, oily liquid.

### Solubility

Dispersible in hot water, freely soluble in methylene chloride.

### Density

About 1.0 at 20 °C.

### Refractive index

About 1.4 at 20 °C.

## IDENTIFICATION

A. Thin-layer chromatography (*2.2.27*).

*Test solution* Dissolve 1.0 g of the substance to be examined in *methylene chloride R* and dilute to 20 ml with the same solvent.

*Plate* *TLC silica gel plate R*.

*Mobile phase* *hexane R, ether R* (30:70 *V/V*).

*Application* 50 μl.

*Development* Over a path of 15 cm.

*Drying* In air.

*Detection* Spray with a 0.1 g/l solution of *rhodamine B R* in *ethanol (96 per cent) R* and examine in ultraviolet light at 365 nm.

*Results* The chromatogram shows a spot due to triglycerides with an $R_F$ value of about 0.9 ($R_{st}$ 1) and spots due to 1,3-diglycerides ($R_{st}$ 0.7), to 1,2-diglycerides ($R_{st}$ 0.6), to monoglycerides ($R_{st}$ 0.1) and to esters of macrogol ($R_{st}$ 0).

B. Hydroxyl value (see Tests).

C. Saponification value (see Tests).

D. Composition of fatty acids (see Tests).

# TESTS

**Viscosity** (*2.2.9*)

Carry out the determination at 20 ± 0.5 °C.

| Ethylene oxide units per molecule (nominal value) | Type of macrogol | Viscosity (mPa·s) |
|---|---|---|
| 4 | 200 | 30 to 50 |
| 6 | 300 | 60 to 80 |
| 8 | 400 | 80 to 110 |

**Acid value** (*2.5.1*)

Maximum 2.0, determined on 2.0 g.

**Hydroxyl value** (*2.5.3, Method A*)

Use 1.0 g.

| Ethylene oxide units per molecule (nominal value) | Type of macrogol | Hydroxyl value |
|---|---|---|
| 4 | 200 | 80 to 120 |
| 6 | 300 | 140 to 180 |
| 8 | 400 | 170 to 205 |

**Peroxide value** (*2.5.5, Method A*)

Maximum 6.0, determined on 2.0 g.

**Saponification value** (*2.5.6*)

Use 2.0 g.

| Ethylene oxide units per molecule (nominal value) | Type of macrogol | Saponification value |
|---|---|---|
| 4 | 200 | 265 to 285 |
| 6 | 300 | 170 to 190 |
| 8 | 400 | 85 to 105 |

## Alkaline impurities

Introduce 5.0 g into a test-tube and carefully add a mixture, neutralised if necessary with *0.01 M hydrochloric acid* or with *0.01 M sodium hydroxide*, of 0.05 ml of a 0.4 g/l solution of *bromophenol blue R* in *ethanol (96 per cent) R*, 0.3 ml of *water R* and 10 ml of *ethanol (96 per cent) R*. Shake and allow to stand. Not more than 1.0 ml of *0.01 M hydrochloric acid* is required to change the colour of the upper layer to yellow.

## Free glycerol

Maximum 5.0 per cent.

Dissolve 1.20 g in 25.0 ml of *methylene chloride R*. Heat if necessary. After cooling, add 100 ml of *water R*. Shake and add 25.0 ml of *periodic acetic acid solution R*. Shake and allow to stand for 30 min. Add 40 ml of a 75 g/l solution of *potassium iodide R*. Allow to stand for 1 min. Add 1 ml of *starch solution R*. Titrate the iodine with *0.1 M sodium thiosulphate*. Carry out a blank titration.

1 ml of *0.1 M sodium thiosulphate* is equivalent to 2.3 mg of glycerol.

## Composition of fatty acids (*2.4.22, Method A*).

*Composition of the fatty-acid fraction of the substance:*
— *caproic acid*: maximum 2.0 per cent;
— *caprylic acid*: 50.0 per cent to 80.0 per cent;
— *capric acid*: 20.0 per cent to 50.0 per cent;
— *lauric acid*: maximum 3.0 per cent;
— *myristic acid*: maximum 1.0 per cent.

**Ethylene oxide and dioxan** (*2.4.25*)

Maximum 1 ppm of ethylene oxide and maximum 10 ppm of dioxan.

**Heavy metals** (*2.4.8*)

Maximum 10 ppm.

2.0 g complies with test C. Prepare the reference solution using 2 ml of *lead standard solution (10 ppm Pb) R*.

**Water** (*2.5.12*)

Maximum 1.0 per cent, determined on 1.0 g. Use a mixture of 30 volumes of *anhydrous methanol R* and 70 volumes of *methylene chloride R* as solvent.

**Total ash** (*2.4.16*)

Maximum 0.1 per cent.

## LABELLING

The label states the type of macrogol used (mean relative molecular mass) or the number of ethylene oxide units per molecule (nominal value).

*_____ Ph Eur*

# Captopril

(*Ph Eur monograph 1079*)

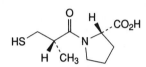

| $C_9H_{15}NO_3S$ | 217.3 | *62571-86-2* |
|---|---|---|

## Action and use

Angiotensin converting enzyme inhibitor.

## Preparations

Captopril Oral Solution

Captopril Tablets

*Ph Eur _____*

## DEFINITION

(2S)-1-[(2S)-2-Methyl-3-sulphanylpropanoyl]pyrrolidine-2-carboxylic acid.

## Content

98.0 per cent to 101.5 per cent (dried substance).

## CHARACTERS

**Appearance**

White or almost white, crystalline powder.

**Solubility**

Freely soluble in water, in methylene chloride and in methanol. It dissolves in dilute solutions of alkali hydroxides.

## IDENTIFICATION

Infrared absorption spectrophotometry (*2.2.24*).

*Comparison*   captopril CRS.

## TESTS

**Solution S**

Dissolve 0.5 g in *carbon dioxide-free water R* and dilute to 25.0 ml with the same solvent.

**Appearance of solution**

Solution S is clear (*2.2.1*) and colourless (*2.2.2, Method II*).

**pH** (*2.2.3*)

2.0 to 2.6 for solution S.

**Specific optical rotation** (*2.2.7*)
− 127 to − 132 (dried substance).
Dissolve 0.250 g in *anhydrous ethanol R* and dilute to 25.0 ml with the same solvent.

**Related substances**
Liquid chromatography (*2.2.29*).

*Test solution*  Dissolve 50 mg of the substance to be examined in the mobile phase and dilute to 100.0 ml with the mobile phase.

*Reference solution (a)*  Dilute 2.0 ml of the test solution to 100.0 ml with the mobile phase.

*Reference solution (b)*  Dissolve 10 mg of the substance to be examined in the mobile phase, add 0.25 ml of *0.05 M iodine* and dilute to 100.0 ml with the mobile phase. Dilute 10.0 ml of the solution to 100.0 ml with the mobile phase.

*Column:*
— *size: l* = 0.125 m, Ø = 4 mm,
— *stationary phase: octylsilyl silica gel for chromatography R* (5 μm).

*Mobile phase*  *phosphoric acid R, methanol R, water R* (0.05:50:50 *V/V/V*).

*Flow rate*  1 ml/min.

*Detection*  Spectrophotometer at 220 nm.

*Injection*  20 μl.

*Run time*  3 times the retention time of captopril.

*System suitability*  Reference solution (b):
— the chromatogram shows 3 peaks,
— *resolution*: minimum 2.0 between the last 2 eluting principal peaks.

*Limits:*
— *any impurity*: for each impurity, not more than 0.5 times the area of the principal peak in the chromatogram obtained with reference solution (a) (1.0 per cent),
— *total*: not more than the area of the principal peak in the chromatogram obtained with reference solution (a) (2.0 per cent),
— *disregard limit*: 0.1 times the area of the principal peak in the chromatogram obtained with reference solution (a) (0.2 per cent). Disregard any peak with a retention time less than 1.4 min.

**Heavy metals** (*2.4.8*)
Maximum 20 ppm.
1.0 g complies with limit test C. Prepare the reference solution using 2 ml of *lead standard solution (10 ppm Pb) R*.

**Loss on drying** (*2.2.32*)
Maximum 1.0 per cent, determined on 1.000 g by drying under high vacuum at 60 °C for 3 h.

**Sulphated ash** (*2.4.14*)
Maximum 0.2 per cent, determined on 1.0 g.

**ASSAY**
Dissolve 0.150 g in 30 ml of *water R*. Titrate with *0.05 M iodine*, determining the end-point potentiometrically (*2.2.20*). Use a combined platinum electrode.
1 ml of *0.05 M iodine* is equivalent to 21.73 mg of $C_9H_{15}NO_3S$.

**STORAGE**
In an airtight container.

**IMPURITIES**

A. (2S,2'S)-1,1'-[disulphanediylbis[(2S)-2-methyl-1-oxopropane-3,1-diyl]-bis[pyrrolidine-2-carboxylic] acid (captopril-disulphide).

*Ph Eur*

# Carbachol

(*Ph Eur monograph 1971*)

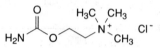

$C_6H_{15}ClN_2O_2$ 182.7 51-83-2

**Action and use**
Cholinoceptor agonist.

*Ph Eur*

**DEFINITION**
2-(Carbamoyloxy)-*N,N,N*-trimethylethanaminium chloride.

**Content**
99.0 per cent to 101.5 per cent (dried substance).

**CHARACTERS**

**Appearance**
White or almost white, crystalline, hygroscopic powder.

**Solubility**
Very soluble in water, sparingly soluble in alcohol, practically insoluble in acetone.

**IDENTIFICATION**

*First identification*  A, C.

*Second identification*  B, C.

A. Infrared absorption spectrophotometry (*2.2.24*).

*Comparison*  carbachol CRS.

B. Examine the chromatograms obtained in the test for related substances.

*Results*  The principal spot in the chromatogram obtained with test solution (b) is similar in position, colour and size to the principal spot in the chromatogram obtained with reference solution (a).

C. 0.5 ml of solution S (see Tests) gives reaction (a) of chlorides (*2.3.1*).

**TESTS**

**Solution S**
Dissolve 2.5 g in *carbon dioxide-free water R* and dilute to 25 ml with the same solvent.

**Appearance of solution**
Solution S is clear (*2.2.1*) and colourless (*2.2.2, Method II*).

**Acidity or alkalinity**
To 2.0 ml of solution S, add 0.05 ml of *methyl red mixed solution R*. Not more than 0.2 ml of *0.01 M hydrochloric acid* or *0.01 M sodium hydroxide* is required to change the colour of the indicator.

## Related substances

Thin-layer chromatography (*2.2.27*).

*Prepare the solutions immediately before use.*

*Test solution (a)* Dissolve 0.20 g of the substance to be examined in *methanol R* and dilute to 5.0 ml with the same solvent.

*Test solution (b)* Dilute 2.0 ml of test solution (a) to 20.0 ml with *methanol R*.

*Reference solution (a)* Dissolve 20 mg of *carbachol CRS* in *methanol R* and dilute to 5.0 ml with the same solvent.

*Reference solution (b)* Dissolve 8 mg of *choline chloride R* and 8 mg of *acetylcholine chloride CRS* in *methanol R* and dilute to 10.0 ml with the same solvent. Dilute 5.0 ml to 10.0 ml with *methanol R*.

*Plate* *cellulose for chromatography R* as the coating substance.

*Mobile phase* *water R, methanol R* (10:90 *V/V*).

*Application* 10 µl.

*Development* Over 2/3 of the plate.

*Detection* Spray with *potassium iodobismuthate solution R3*.

*System suitability* The chromatogram obtained with reference solution (b) shows 2 clearly separated spots.

*Limits* In the chromatogram obtained with test solution (a):
— *any impurity*: any spot, apart from the principal spot, is not more intense than one or other of the 2 principal spots in the chromatogram obtained with reference solution (b) (1 per cent). Compare the spots with the spot of the most appropriate colour in the chromatogram obtained with reference solution (b).

## Heavy metals (*2.4.8*)

Maximum 20 ppm.

12 ml of solution S complies with limit test A. Prepare the standard using *lead standard solution (2 ppm Pb) R*.

## Loss on drying (*2.2.32*)

Maximum 1.0 per cent, determined on 1.000 g by drying in an oven at 105 °C for 2 h.

## Sulphated ash (*2.4.14*)

Maximum 0.1 per cent, determined on 1.0 g of the residue obtained in the test for loss on drying.

## ASSAY

Dissolve 0.150 g in a mixture of 10 ml of *anhydrous acetic acid R* and 40 ml of *acetic anhydride R*. Titrate with *0.1 M perchloric acid*. Determine the end-point potentiometrically (*2.2.20*).

1 ml of *0.1 M perchloric acid* is equivalent to 18.27 mg of $C_6H_{15}ClN_2O_2$.

## STORAGE

In an airtight container, protected from light.

## IMPURITIES

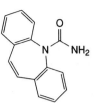

A. 2-hydroxy-*N,N,N*-trimethylethanaminium chloride (choline chloride).

——————————————— *Ph Eur*

# Carbamazepine

(*Ph Eur monograph 0543*)

$C_{15}H_{12}N_2O$      236.3      *298-46-4*

## Action and use

Antiepileptic.

## Preparation

Carbamazepine Tablets

*Ph Eur* ———————————————————————

## DEFINITION

5*H*-Dibenzo[*b,f*]azepine-5-carboxamide.

## Content

98.0 per cent to 102.0 per cent (dried substance).

## CHARACTERS

### Appearance

White or almost white, crystalline powder.

### Solubility

Very slightly soluble in water, freely soluble in methylene chloride, sparingly soluble in acetone and in ethanol (96 per cent).

It shows polymorphism (*5.9*). The acceptable crystalline form corresponds to *carbamazepine CRS*.

## IDENTIFICATION

A. Melting point (*2.2.14*): 189 °C to 193 °C.

B. Infrared absorption spectrophotometry (*2.2.24*).

*Comparison* *carbamazepine CRS*.

*Preparation* Examine the substances as discs without prior treatment.

## TESTS

### Acidity or alkalinity

To 1.0 g add 20 ml of *carbon dioxide-free water R*, shake for 15 min and filter. To 10 ml of the filtrate add 0.05 ml of *phenolphthalein solution R1* and 0.5 ml of *0.01 M sodium hydroxide*; the solution is red. Add 1.0 ml of *0.01 M hydrochloric acid*; the solution is colourless. Add 0.15 ml of *methyl red solution R*; the solution is red.

### Related substances

Liquid chromatography (*2.2.29*).

*Test solution (a)* Dissolve 60.0 mg of the substance to be examined in *methanol R2* and dilute to 20.0 ml with the same solvent. Sonicate. Dilute 10.0 ml of this solution to 20.0 ml with *water R*.

*Test solution (b)* Dilute 10.0 ml of test solution (a) to 50.0 ml with a mixture of equal volumes of *methanol R2* and *water R*.

*Reference solution (a)* Dissolve 7.5 mg of *carbamazepine CRS*, 7.5 mg of *carbamazepine impurity A CRS* and 7.5 mg of *iminodibenzyl R* (impurity E) in *methanol R2* and dilute to 100.0 ml with the same solvent. Dilute 1.0 ml of this solution to 50.0 ml with a mixture of equal volumes of *methanol R2* and *water R*.

*Reference solution (b)*   Dissolve 60.0 mg of carbamazepine CRS in *methanol R2* and dilute to 20.0 ml with the same solvent. Sonicate. Dilute 5.0 ml of this solution to 50.0 ml with a mixture of equal volumes of *methanol R2* and *water R*.

*Column:*
— *size*: $l = 0.25$ m, Ø = 4.6 mm;
— *stationary phase*: nitrile silica gel for *chromatography R1* (10 μm).

*Mobile phase*   tetrahydrofuran R, methanol R2, water R (3:12:85 *V/V/V*); to 1000 ml of this solution add 0.2 ml of *anhydrous formic acid R* and 0.5 ml of *triethylamine R*.

*Flow rate*   2.0 ml/min.

*Detection*   A spectrophotometer at 230 nm.

*Injection*   20 μl of test solution (a) and reference solution (a).

*Run time*   6 times the retention time of carbamazepine.

*Relative retention*   With reference to carbamazepine (retention time = about 10 min): impurity A = about 0.9; impurity E = about 5.1.

*System suitability:*
— *resolution*: minimum 1.7 between the peaks due to carbamazepine and impurity A in the chromatogram obtained with reference solution (a).

*Limits:*
— *impurities A, E*: for each impurity, not more than the area of the corresponding peak in the chromatogram obtained with reference solution (a) (0.1 per cent);
— *unspecified impurities*: not more than the area of the peak due to carbamazepine in the chromatogram obtained with reference solution (a) (0.10 per cent);
— *total*: not more than 5 times the area of the peak due to carbamazepine in the chromatogram obtained with reference solution (a) (0.5 per cent);
— *disregard limit*: 0.5 times the area of the peak due to carbamazepine in the chromatogram obtained with reference solution (a) (0.05 per cent).

**Chlorides** *(2.4.4)*
Maximum 140 ppm.

Suspend 0.715 g in 20 ml of *water R* and boil for 10 min. Cool and dilute to 20 ml with *water R*. Filter through a membrane filter (nominal pore size: 0.8 μm). Dilute 10 ml of the filtrate to 15 ml with *water R*. This solution complies with the limit test for chlorides.

**Heavy metals** *(2.4.8)*
Maximum 20 ppm.

1.0 g complies with test C. Prepare the reference solution using 2 ml of *lead standard solution (10 ppm Pb) R*.

**Loss on drying** *(2.2.32)*
Maximum 0.5 per cent, determined on 1.000 g by drying in an oven at 105 °C for 2h.

**Sulphated ash** *(2.4.14)*
Maximum 0.1 per cent, determined on 1.0 g.

**ASSAY**
Liquid chromatography (2.2.29) as described in the test for related substances.

*Injection*   Test solution (b) and reference solution (b).
*System suitability:*
— *repeatability*: reference solution (b).

Calculate the percentage content *m/m* of dried substance.

**STORAGE**
In an airtight container.

**IMPURITIES**
*Specified impurities*   A, E.

*Other detectable impurities* (the following substances would, if present at a sufficient level, be detected by one or other of the tests in the monograph. They are limited by the general acceptance criterion for other/unspecified impurities and/or by the general monograph *Substances for pharmaceutical use (2034)*. It is therefore not necessary to identify these impurities for demonstration of compliance. See also *5.10. Control of impurities in substances for pharmaceutical use*) : B, C, D, F.

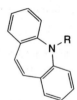

A. R = CO-NH$_2$: 10,11-dihydro-5*H*-dibenzo[*b,f*]azepine-5-carboxamide (10,11-dihydrocarbamazepine),
E. R = H: 10,11-dihydro-5*H*-dibenzo[*b,f*]azepine (iminodibenzyl),

B. 9-methylacridine,

C. R = CO-NH-CO-NH$_2$: (5*H*-dibenzo[*b,f*]azepin-5-ylcarbonyl)urea (*N*-carbamoylcarbamazepine),
D. R = H: 5*H*-dibenzo[*b,f*]azepine (iminostilbene),
F. R = CO-Cl: 5*H*-dibenzo[*b,f*]azepine-5-carbonyl chloride (5-chlorocarbonyliminostilbene).

*Ph Eur*

# Carbaryl

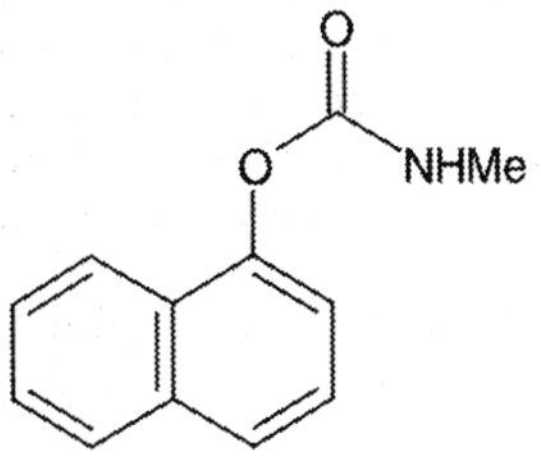

$C_{12}H_{11}NO_2$      201.2      63-25-2

**Action and use**
Insecticide.

**Preparation**
Carbaryl Lotion

## DEFINITION
Carbaryl is 1-naphthyl methylcarbamate. It contains not less than 98.0% and not more than 102.0% of $C_{12}H_{11}NO_2$, calculated with reference to the dried substance.

## CHARACTERISTICS
A white to off-white or light grey powder, which darkens on exposure to light. It melts at about 142°.

Very slightly soluble in *water*; soluble in *acetone* and in *ethanol (96%)*.

## IDENTIFICATION
The *infrared absorption spectrum*, Appendix II A, is concordant with the *reference spectrum* of carbaryl *(RS 039)*.

## TESTS
**1-Naphthol**
Carry out the method for *liquid chromatography*, Appendix III D, using the following solutions.

(1) 0.1% w/v of the substance being examined in *acetonitrile*.

(2) 0.005% w/v of *carbaryl BPCRS* in *methanol*.

(3) 0.005% w/v of the substance being examined and 0.005% w/v of *1-naphthol* in the mobile phase.

CHROMATOGRAPHIC CONDITIONS

The chromatographic conditions described under Assay may be used.

SYSTEM SUITABILITY

The test is not valid unless, in the chromatogram obtained with solution (3), the *resolution factor* between the two principal peaks is at least 2.0.

LIMITS

In the chromatogram obtained with solution (1):

the area of any peak corresponding to 1-naphthol is not greater than the area of the principal peak in the chromatogram obtained with solution (2) (1%).

**Loss on drying**
When dried to constant weight over *phosphorus pentoxide* at a pressure not exceeding 0.7 kPa, loses not more than 0.5% of its weight. Use 1 g.

## ASSAY
Carry out the method for *liquid chromatography*, Appendix III D, using the following solutions.

(1) 0.005% w/v of the substance being examined in *methanol*.

(2) 0.005% w/v of *carbaryl BPCRS* in *methanol*.

(3) 0.005% w/v of the substance being examined and 0.005% w/v of *1-naphthol* in the mobile phase.

CHROMATOGRAPHIC CONDITIONS

(a) Use a stainless steel column (10 cm × 4.6 mm) packed with *end-capped octadecylsilyl silica gel for chromatography* (5 μm) (Spherisorb ODS 2 is suitable).

(b) Use isocratic elution and the mobile phase described below.

(c) Use a flow rate of 2.5 ml per minute.

(d) Use ambient column temperature.

(e) Use a detection wavelength of 280 nm.

(f) Inject 20 μl of each solution.

*MOBILE PHASE*

1 volume of *glacial acetic acid*, 25 volumes of *acetonitrile* and 75 volumes of *water*.

SYSTEM SUITABILITY

The test is not valid unless in the chromatogram obtained with solution (3) the *resolution factor* between the two principal peaks is at least 2.0.

DETERMINATION OF CONTENT

Calculate the content of $C_{12}H_{11}NO_2$ using the declared content of $C_{12}H_{11}NO_2$ in *carbaryl BPCRS*.

## STORAGE
Carbaryl should be protected from light.

## IMPURITIES

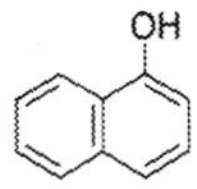

A. 1-naphthol

# Carbasalate Calcium

*(Ph Eur monograph 1185)*

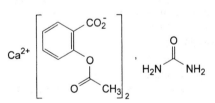

$C_{19}H_{18}CaN_2O_9$      458.4      5749-67-7

**Action and use**
Salicylate; non-selective cyclo-oxygenase inhibitor; antipyretic; analgesic; anti-inflammatory.

*Ph Eur*

## DEFINITION
Equimolecular compound of calcium di[2-(acetyloxy)benzoate] and urea.

**Content**
99.0 per cent to 101.0 per cent (anhydrous substance).

## CHARACTERS
**Appearance**
White or almost white, crystalline powder.

## Solubility

Freely soluble in water and in dimethylformamide, practically insoluble in acetone and in anhydrous methanol.

*Protect the substance from moisture during handling. Examination in aqueous solutions has to be performed immediately after preparation.*

## IDENTIFICATION

*First identification* B, E.

*Second identification* A, C, D, E.

A. Ultraviolet and visible absorption spectrophotometry (2.2.25).

*Test solution* Dissolve 0.250 g in *water R* and dilute to 100.0 ml with the same solvent. To 1.0 ml of the solution add 75 ml of *water R* and 5 ml of *dilute hydrochloric acid R*, mix and dilute to 100.0 ml with *water R*. Examine immediately.

*Spectral range* 220-350 nm.

*Absorption maxima* At 228 nm and 276 nm.

*Specific absorbances at the absorption maxima:*
— at 228 nm: 363 to 379,
— at 276 nm: 49 to 53.

B. Infrared absorption spectrophotometry (2.2.24).

*Comparison* Ph. Eur. reference spectrum of carbasalate calcium.

C. Dissolve 0.1 g in 10 ml of *water R*, boil for 2 min and cool. The solution gives reaction (a) of salicylates (2.3.1).

D. Heat 0.2 g with 0.2 g of *sodium hydroxide R*; a yellow or yellowish-brown colour is produced and the vapour turns *red litmus paper* R blue.

E. It gives reaction (a) of calcium (2.3.1).

## TESTS

### Appearance of solution

The solution is not more opalescent than reference suspension II (2.2.1) and is colourless (2.2.2, Method II).

Dissolve 2.5 g in 50 ml of *water R*.

### Related substances

Maximum 0.1 per cent, expressed as acetylsalicylsalicylic acid.

In a 100 ml volumetric flask, dissolve 0.150 g in 10 ml of *0.1 M tetrabutylammonium hydroxide in 2-propanol*. Allow to stand for 10 min shaking occasionally. Add 8.0 ml of *0.1 M hydrochloric acid* and 20.0 ml of a 19 g/l solution of *disodium tetraborate R* and mix. While swirling continuously, add 2.0 ml of a 10 g/l solution of *aminopyrazolone R* and 2.0 ml of a 10 g/l solution of *potassium ferricyanide R*. Allow to stand for 2 min, dilute to 100.0 ml with *water R*, mix and allow to stand for 20 min. Measure the absorbance (2.2.25) of the solution at the absorption maximum at 505 nm using *water R* as the compensation liquid. The absorbance is not greater than 0.125.

### Impurity C

Maximum 0.5 per cent.

In a 100 ml volumetric flask, dissolve 0.200 g in 80 ml of *water R* and add 10 ml of a 10 g/l solution of *ferric nitrate R* in a 80 g/l solution of *dilute nitric acid R*. Dilute to 100.0 ml with *water R*. Immediately after preparation, measure the absorbance (2.2.25) of the solution at the absorption maximum of 525 nm using *water R* as the compensation liquid. The absorbance is not greater than 0.115.

### Sodium

Maximum 0.10 per cent.

Atomic emission spectrometry (2.2.22, Method I).

*Test solution* Dissolve 1.0 g in 500.0 ml of *water R*.

### Heavy metals (2.4.8)

Maximum 10 ppm.

Dissolve 2.0 g in 8 ml of *water R* with heating, cool and add 12 ml of *acetone R*. 12 ml of the solution complies with test B. Prepare the reference solution using 10 ml of *lead standard solution (1 ppm Pb) R*.

### Water (2.5.12)

Maximum 0.1 per cent, determined on 1.000 g. Use a mixture of 15 ml of *anhydrous methanol R* and 15 ml of *dimethylformamide R* as the solvent.

## ASSAY

In a flask with a ground-glass stopper, dissolve 0.400 g in 25 ml of *water R*. Add 25.0 ml of *0.1 M sodium hydroxide*. Close the flask and allow to stand for 2 h. Titrate the excess of alkali with *0.1 M hydrochloric acid*, using 0.2 ml of *phenolphthalein solution R*. Carry out a blank titration.

1 ml of *0.1 M sodium hydroxide* is equivalent to 22.92 mg of $C_{19}H_{18}CaN_2O_9$.

## STORAGE

In an airtight container.

## IMPURITIES

*Specified impurities* A, B, C.

A. 2-(acetyloxy)benzoic anhydride,

B. 2-[[2-(acetyloxy)benzoyl]oxy]benzoic acid (acetylsalicylsalicylic acid),

C. 2-hydroxybenzoic acid (salicylic acid).

_____ *Ph Eur*

# Carbenoxolone Sodium

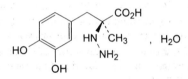

C$_{34}$H$_{48}$Na$_2$O$_7$    614.7    *7421-40-1*

## Action and use
Treatment of peptic ulcer.

## DEFINITION
Carbenoxolone Sodium is disodium 3β-(3-carboxylatopropionyloxy)-11-oxo-olean-12-en-30-oate. It contains not less than 97.0% and not more than 103.0% of C$_{34}$H$_{48}$Na$_2$O$_7$, calculated with reference to the anhydrous substance.

## CHARACTERISTICS
A white or pale cream powder; hygroscopic.

Freely soluble in *water*; sparingly soluble in *ethanol (96%)*; practically insoluble in *ether*.

## IDENTIFICATION
A. Dissolve 0.1 g in 5 ml of *water* and make just acid with *2M hydrochloric acid*, stir well and filter. Wash the residue with *water* until the washings are no longer acidic and dry to constant weight at 105°. The *infrared absorption spectrum* of the residue, Appendix II A, is concordant with the *reference spectrum* of carbenoxolone *(RS 041)*.

B. Yields the reactions characteristic of *sodium salts*, Appendix VI.

## TESTS
### Alkalinity
pH of a 10% w/v solution, 8.0 to 9.2, Appendix V L.

### Specific optical rotation
In a 1% w/v solution in a mixture of equal volumes of *methanol* and *0.02M sodium carbonate*, +132 to +140, calculated with reference to the anhydrous substance, Appendix V F.

### Related substances
Carry out the method for *thin-layer chromatography*, Appendix III A, using a silica gel F$_{254}$ precoated plate (Merck silica gel 60 F$_{254}$ plates are suitable) and a mixture of 60 volumes of *ethyl acetate*, 20 volumes of *methanol*, 11 volumes of *water* and 1 volume of *13.5M ammonia* as the mobile phase. Apply separately to the plate 5 µl of each of two solutions of the substance being examined in *methanol* containing (1) 1.50% w/v and (2) 0.030% w/v. After removal of the plate, allow it to dry in air and examine under *ultraviolet light (254 nm)*. Spray with a 1.5% w/v solution of *vanillin* in *sulphuric acid (60%)* and heat at 105° for 10 to 15 minutes. By each method of visualisation, any *secondary spot* in the chromatogram obtained with solution (1) is not more intense than the spot in the chromatogram obtained with solution (2) (2%).

### Water
Not more than 4.0% w/w, Appendix IX C. Use 0.6 g.

## ASSAY
Dissolve 1 g in 30 ml of *water*, add 30 ml of *chloroform* and 15 ml of a mixture of 1 volume of *2M hydrochloric acid* and 9 volumes of *water*, shake and allow to separate. Add the chloroform layer to 40 ml of a 20% w/v solution of *sodium chloride*, shake and allow to separate. Repeat the extraction with four 15 ml quantities of *chloroform*, combine the chloroform extracts and add sufficient *chloroform* to produce 100 ml. Evaporate 25 ml, dry the residue at 100° at a pressure of 2 kPa, dissolve in 10 ml of *dimethylformamide* and carry out Method II for *non-aqueous titration*, Appendix VIII A, using 0.1M *tetrabutylammonium hydroxide VS* as titrant and *thymol blue solution* as indicator. Each ml of 0.1M *tetrabutylammonium hydroxide VS* is equivalent to 30.73 mg of C$_{34}$H$_{48}$Na$_2$O$_7$.

# Carbidopa

*(Ph Eur monograph 0755)*

C$_{10}$H$_{14}$N$_2$O$_4$,H$_2$O    244.2    *38821-49-7*

## Action and use
Dopa decarboxylase inhibitor.

## Preparation
Co-careldopa Tablets

*Ph Eur*

## DEFINITION
(2S)-3-(3,4-Dihydroxyphenyl)-2-hydrazino-2-methylpropanoic acid monohydrate.

## Content
98.5 per cent to 101.0 per cent (dried substance).

## CHARACTERS
### Appearance
White or yellowish-white powder.

### Solubility
Slightly soluble in water, very slightly soluble in ethanol (96 per cent), practically insoluble in methylene chloride. It dissolves in dilute solutions of mineral acids.

## IDENTIFICATION
*First identification* A, C.

*Second identification* A, B, D, E.

A. Specific optical rotation (see Tests).

B. Ultraviolet and visible absorption spectrophotometry (2.2.25).

*Test solution* Dissolve 50.0 mg in a 8.5 g/l solution of *hydrochloric acid R* in *methanol R* and dilute to 100.0 ml with the same solution. Dilute 10.0 ml of this solution to 100.0 ml with a 8.5 g/l solution of *hydrochloric acid R* in *methanol R*.

*Spectral range* 230-350 nm.

*Absorption maximum* At 283 nm.

*Specific absorbance at the absorption maximum* 135 to 150 (dried substance).

C. Infrared absorption spectrophotometry (*2.2.24*).

*Preparation* Discs.

*Comparison* carbidopa CRS.

D. Shake vigorously about 5 mg with 10 ml of *water R* for 1 min and add 0.3 ml of *ferric chloride solution R2*. An intense green colour is produced, which quickly turns to reddish-brown.

E. Suspend about 20 mg in 5 ml of *water R* and add 5 ml of *cupri-tartaric solution R*. On heating, the colour of the solution changes to dark brown and a red precipitate is formed.

## TESTS

### Appearance of solution
The solution is clear (*2.2.1*) and not more intensely coloured than reference solution $BY_6$ or $B_6$ (*2.2.2, Method II*).

Dissolve 0.25 g in 25 ml of *1 M hydrochloric acid*.

### Specific optical rotation (*2.2.7*)
− 22.5 to − 26.5 (dried substance).

With the aid of an ultrasonic bath, dissolve completely 0.250 g in *aluminium chloride solution R* and dilute to 25.0 ml with the same solution.

### Hydrazine
Thin-layer chromatography (*2.2.27*).

*Test solution (a)* Dissolve 0.50 g in *dilute hydrochloric acid R* and dilute to 2.0 ml with the same acid.

*Test solution (b)* Place 25 g of *strongly basic anion exchange resin R* into each of 2 conical flasks with ground-glass stoppers. To each, add 150 ml of *carbon dioxide-free water R* and shake from time to time during 30 min. Decant the liquid from both flasks and repeat the process with further quantities, each of 150 ml, of *carbon dioxide-free water R*.

Take two 100 ml measuring cylinders 3.5-4.5 cm in internal diameter and label these A and B. Into cylinder A, transfer as completely as possible the resin from 1 conical flask using 60 ml of *carbon dioxide-free water R*; into cylinder B, transfer the 2$^{nd}$ quantity of resin, this time using 20 ml of *carbon dioxide-free water R*.

Into each cylinder, insert a gas-inlet tube, the end of which has an internal diameter of 2-3 mm and which reaches almost to the bottom of the cylinder. Pass a rapid stream of *nitrogen for chromatography R* through each mixture so that homogeneous suspensions are formed. After 30 min, without interrupting the gas flow, add 1.0 ml of test solution (a) to cylinder A; after 1 min stop the gas flow into cylinder A and transfer the contents, through a moistened filter paper, into cylinder B. After 1 min, stop the gas flow to cylinder B and pour the solution immediately through a moistened filter paper into a freshly prepared mixture of 1 ml of a 200 g/l solution of *salicylaldehyde R* in *methanol R* and 20 ml of *phosphate buffer solution pH 5.5 R* in a conical flask; shake thoroughly for 1 min and heat in a water-bath at 60 °C for 15 min. The liquid becomes clear. Allow to cool, add 2.0 ml of *toluene R* and shake vigorously for 2 min. Transfer the mixture into a centrifuge tube and centrifuge.

Separate the toluene layer in a 100 ml separating funnel and shake vigorously with 2 quantities, each of 20 ml, of a 200 g/l solution of *sodium metabisulphite R* and finally with 2 quantities, each of 50 ml, of *water R*. Separate the toluene layer.

*Reference solution (a)* Dissolve 10 mg of *hydrazine sulphate R* in *dilute hydrochloric acid* R and dilute to 50 ml with the same acid. Dilute 1.0 ml of this solution to 10.0 ml with *dilute hydrochloric acid R*.

*Reference solution (b)* Prepare the solution at the same time and in the same manner as described for test solution (b) using 1.0 ml of reference solution (a) instead of 1.0 ml of test solution (a).

*Plate* TLC silanised silica gel plate R.

*Mobile phase* water R, methanol R (10:20 *V/V*).

*Application* 10 μl of test solution (b) and reference solution (b).

*Development* Over a path of 10 cm.

*Drying* In air.

*Detection* Examine in ultraviolet light at 365 nm.

*Limit:*
— *hydrazine*: any spot showing a yellow fluorescence is not more intense than the corresponding spot in the chromatogram obtained with reference solution (b) (20 ppm).

### Methyldopa and methylcarbidopa
Liquid chromatography (*2.2.29*).

*Test solution* Dissolve 0.100 g of the substance to be examined in *0.1 M hydrochloric acid* and dilute to 10.0 ml with the same acid.

*Reference solution (a)* Dissolve the contents of a vial of *methylcarbidopa CRS* in *0.1 M hydrochloric acid*, add 1 mg of *methyldopa CRS* and dilute to 20.0 ml with the same acid.

*Reference solution (b)* Dissolve 5 mg of *carbidopa CRS* and 5 mg of *methyldopa CRS* in *0.1 M hydrochloric acid* and dilute to 10.0 ml with the same acid.

*Column:*
— *size: l = 0.25 m, Ø = 4.6 mm;*
— *stationary phase: octylsilyl silica gel for chromatography R* (5 μm).

*Mobile phase* methanol R, 14 g/l solution of *potassium dihydrogen phosphate R* (2:98 *V/V*).

*Flow rate* 1 ml/min.

*Detection* Spectrophotometer at 282 nm.

*Injection* 20 μl.

*System suitability* Reference solution (b):
— *resolution*: minimum 4.0 between the peaks due to methyldopa and carbidopa.

*Limits:*
— *methyldopa and methylcarbidopa*: for each impurity, not more than the area of the corresponding peak in the chromatogram obtained with reference solution (a) (0.5 per cent).

### Heavy metals (*2.4.8*)
Maximum 20 ppm.

1.0 g complies with test C. Prepare the reference solution using 2 ml of *lead standard solution (10 ppm Pb) R*.

### Loss on drying (*2.2.32*)
6.9 per cent to 7.9 per cent, determined on 1.000 g by drying in an oven at 105 °C.

### Sulphated ash (*2.4.14*)
Maximum 0.1 per cent, determined on 1.0 g.

## ASSAY

Dissolve 0.150 g with gentle heating in 75 ml of *anhydrous acetic acid R*. Titrate with *0.1 M perchloric acid*, determining the end-point potentiometrically (*2.2.20*).

1 ml of *0.1 M perchloric acid* is equivalent to 22.62 mg of $C_{10}H_{14}N_2O_4$.

**STORAGE**

Protected from light.

_____ *Ph Eur*

# Carbimazole

(*Ph Eur monograph 0884*)

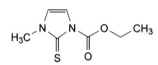

C₇H₁₀N₂O₂S          186.2          *22232-54-8*

**Action and use**

Thionamide antithyroid drug.

**Preparation**

Carbimazole Tablets

*Ph Eur* _____

## DEFINITION

Ethyl 3-methyl-2-thioxo-2,3-dihydro-1*H*-imidazole-1-carboxylate.

## Content

98.0 per cent to 102.0 per cent (dried substance).

## CHARACTERS

**Appearance**

White or yellowish-white, crystalline powder.

**Solubility**

Slightly soluble in water, soluble in acetone and in alcohol.

## IDENTIFICATION

*First identification* B.

*Second identification* A, C, D.

A. Melting point (*2.2.14*): 122 °C to 125 °C.

B. Infrared absorption spectrophotometry (*2.2.24*).

*Preparation* Discs.

*Comparison* carbimazole CRS.

C. Thin-layer chromatography (*2.2.27*).

*Test solution* Dissolve 10 mg of the substance to be examined in *methylene chloride R* and dilute to 10 ml with the same solvent.

*Reference solution* Dissolve 10 mg of *carbimazole CRS* in *methylene chloride R* and dilute to 10 ml with the same solvent.

*Plate* TLC silica gel GF₂₅₄ plate R.

*Mobile phase* acetone R, methylene chloride R (20:80 V/V).

*Application* 10 μl.

*Development* Over a path of 15 cm.

*Drying* In air for 30 min.

*Detection* Examine in ultraviolet light at 254 nm.

*Results* The principal spot in the chromatogram obtained with the test solution is similar in position and size to the principal spot in the chromatogram obtained with the reference solution.

D. Dissolve about 10 mg in a mixture of 50 ml of *water R* and 0.05 ml of *dilute hydrochloric acid R*. Add 1 ml of *potassium iodobismuthate solution R*. A red precipitate is formed.

## TESTS

**Impurity A and other related substances**

Liquid chromatography (*2.2.29*).

*Test solution* Dissolve 5.0 mg of the substance to be examined in 10.0 ml of a mixture of 20 volumes of *acetonitrile R* and 80 volumes of *water R*. Use this solution within 5 min of preparation.

*Reference solution (a)* Dissolve 5 mg of *thiamazole R* and 0.10 g of *carbimazole CRS* in a mixture of 20 volumes of *acetonitrile R* and 80 volumes of *water R* and dilute to 100.0 ml with the same mixture of solvents. Dilute 1.0 ml of this solution to 10.0 ml with a mixture of 20 volumes of *acetonitrile R* and 80 volumes of *water R*.

*Reference solution (b)* Dissolve 5.0 mg of *thiamazole R* in a mixture of 20 volumes of *acetonitrile R* and 80 volumes of *water R* and dilute to 10.0 ml with the same mixture of solvents. Dilute 1.0 ml of this solution to 100.0 ml with a mixture of 20 volumes of *acetonitrile R* and 80 volumes of *water R*.

*Column:*

— *size*: *l* = 0.15 m, Ø = 3.9 mm,

— *stationary phase*: octadecylsilyl silica gel for chromatography R (5 μm).

*Mobile phase* acetonitrile R, water R (10:90 *V/V*).

*Flow rate* 1 ml/min.

*Detection* Spectrophotometer at 254 nm.

*Injection* 10 μl.

*Run time* 1.5 times the retention time of carbimazole.

*Retention time* Carbimazole = about 6 min.

*System suitability* Reference solution (a):

— *resolution*: minimum 5.0 between the peaks due to impurity A and carbimazole.

*Limits:*

— *impurity A*: not more than half the area of the principal peak in the chromatogram obtained with reference solution (b) (0.5 per cent),

— *any other impurity*: not more than 0.1 times the area of the principal peak in the chromatogram obtained with reference solution (b) (0.1 per cent).

**Loss on drying** (*2.2.32*)

Maximum 0.5 per cent, determined on 1.000 g by drying in a desiccator over *diphosphorus pentoxide R* at a pressure not exceeding 0.7 kPa for 24 h.

**Sulphated ash** (*2.4.14*)

Maximum 0.1 per cent, determined on 1.0 g.

## ASSAY

Dissolve 50.0 mg in *water R* and dilute to 500.0 ml with the same solvent. To 10.0 ml add 10 ml of *dilute hydrochloric acid R* and dilute to 100.0 ml with *water R*. Measure the absorbance (*2.2.25*) at the maximum at 291 nm. Calculate the content of C₇H₁₀N₂O₂S taking the specific absorbance to be 557.

## IMPURITIES

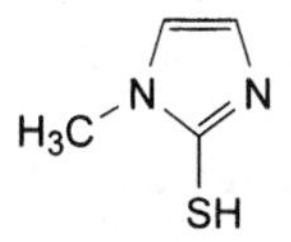

A. 1-methyl-1*H*-imidazole-2-thiol (thiamazole).

_____ *Ph Eur*

# Carbocisteine

(*Ph Eur monograph 0885*)

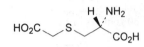

C₅H₉NO₄S        179.2        638-23-3

## Action and use
Mucolytic.

*Ph Eur*

## DEFINITION
Carbocisteine contains not less than 98.5 per cent and not more than the equivalent of 101.0 per cent of (2R)-2-amino-3-[(carboxymethyl)sulphanyl]propanoic acid, calculated with reference to the dried substance.

## CHARACTERS
A white or almost white crystalline powder, practically insoluble in water and in alcohol. It dissolves in dilute mineral acids and in dilute solutions of alkali hydroxides.

## IDENTIFICATION
*First identification*   A, B.

*Second identification*   A, C, D.

A. It complies with the test for specific optical rotation (see Tests).

B. Examine by infrared absorption spectrophotometry (*2.2.24*), comparing with the spectrum obtained with *carbocisteine CRS*. Examine the substances prepared as discs.

C. Examine the chromatograms obtained in the test for ninhydrin-positive substances. The principal spot in the chromatogram obtained with test solution (b) is similar in position, colour and size to the principal spot in the chromatogram obtained with reference solution (a).

D. Dissolve 0.1 g in 4.5 ml of *dilute sodium hydroxide solution R*. Heat on a water-bath for 10 min. Cool and add 1 ml of a 25 g/l solution of *sodium nitroprusside R*. A dark red colour is produced, which changes to brown and then to yellow within a few minutes.

## TESTS
### Solution S
Disperse 5.00 g in 20 ml of *water R* and add dropwise with shaking 2.5 ml of *strong sodium hydroxide solution R*. Adjust to pH 6.3 with *1 M sodium hydroxide* and dilute to 50.0 ml with *water R*.

### Appearance of solution
Solution S is clear (*2.2.1*) and colourless (*2.2.2, Method II*).

### pH (*2.2.3*)
Shake 0.2 g with 20 ml of *carbon dioxide-free water R*. The pH of the suspension is 2.8 to 3.0.

### Specific optical rotation (*2.2.7*)
− 32.5 to − 35.5, determined on solution S and calculated with reference to the dried substance.

### Ninhydrin-positive substances
Examine by thin-layer chromatography (*2.2.27*), using a suitable silica gel as the coating substance.

*Test solution (a)*   Dissolve 0.10 g of the substance to be examined in *dilute ammonia R2* and dilute to 10 ml with the same solvent.

*Test solution (b)*   Dilute 1 ml of test solution (a) to 50 ml with *water R*.

*Reference solution (a)*   Dissolve 10 mg of *carbocisteine CRS* in *dilute ammonia R2* and dilute to 50 ml with the same solvent.

*Reference solution (b)*   Dilute 5 ml of test solution (b) to 20 ml with *water R*.

*Reference solution (c)*   Dissolve 10 mg of *carbocisteine CRS* and 10 mg of *arginine hydrochloride CRS* in 5 ml of *dilute ammonia R2* and dilute to 25 ml with *water R*.

Apply separately to the plate 5 μl of each solution. Allow the plate to dry in air. Develop over a path of 15 cm using a mixture of 20 volumes of *glacial acetic acid R*, 20 volumes of *water R* and 60 volumes of *butanol R*. Dry the plate in a current of warm air. Spray with *ninhydrin solution R* and heat at 100 °C to 105 °C for 15 min. Any spot in the chromatogram obtained with test solution (a), apart from the principal spot, is not more intense than the spot in the chromatogram obtained with reference solution (b) (0.5 per cent). The test is not valid unless the chromatogram obtained with reference solution (c) shows two clearly separated principal spots.

### Chlorides (*2.4.4*)
Dissolve 33 mg in 5 ml of *dilute nitric acid R* and dilute to 15 ml with *water R*. The solution, without further addition of nitric acid, complies with the limit test for chlorides (0.15 per cent).

### Sulphates (*2.4.13*)
Dissolve 0.5 g in 5 ml of *dilute hydrochloric acid R* and dilute to 15 ml with *distilled water R*. The solution complies with the limit test for sulphates (300 ppm).

### Heavy metals (*2.4.8*)
2.0 g complies with limit test D for heavy metals (10 ppm). Prepare the standard using 2 ml of *lead standard solution (10 ppm Pb) R*.

### Loss on drying (*2.2.32*)
Not more than 0.5 per cent, determined on 1.000 g by drying in an oven at 105 °C for 2 h.

### Sulphated ash (*2.4.14*)
Not more than 0.3 per cent, determined on 1.0 g.

## ASSAY
Dissolve 0.150 g in 10 ml of *anhydrous formic acid R* with slight heating and shake until dissolution is complete. Add 50 ml of *anhydrous acetic acid R*. Titrate with *0.1 M perchloric acid*, determining the end-point potentiometrically (*2.2.20*).

1 ml of *0.1 M perchloric acid* is equivalent to 17.92 mg of C₅H₉NO₄S.

## STORAGE
Store protected from light.

*Ph Eur*

# Carbomers

*(Ph Eur monograph 1299)*

★ ★ ★
★   ★
★   ★
★ ★ ★

**Action and use**
Stabilizer in pharmaceutical products.

**Preparation**
Carbomer Eye Drops

*Ph Eur* _____

## DEFINITION

High-molecular-mass polymers of acrylic acid cross-linked with alkenyl ethers of sugars or polyalcohols.

## Content

56.0 per cent to 68.0 per cent of carboxylic acid (-CO$_2$H) groups (dried substance).

## CHARACTERS

**Appearance**
White or almost white, fluffy, hygroscopic powder.

**Solubility**
Swells in water and in other polar solvents after dispersion and neutralisation with sodium hydroxide solution.

## IDENTIFICATION

*First identification   A.*

*Second identification   B, C, D.*

A. Infrared absorption spectrophotometry *(2.2.24)*.

*Main bands*   At 1710 ± 5 cm$^{-1}$, 1454 ± 5 cm$^{-1}$, 1414 ± 5 cm$^{-1}$, 1245 ± 5 cm$^{-1}$, 1172 ± 5 cm$^{-1}$, 1115 ± 5 cm$^{-1}$ and 801 ± 5 cm$^{-1}$, with the strongest band at 1710 ± 5 cm$^{-1}$.

B. Adjust a 10 g/l dispersion to about pH 7.5 with *1 M sodium hydroxide*. A highly viscous gel is formed.

C. Add 2 ml of a 100 g/l solution of *calcium chloride R*, with continuous stirring, to 10 ml of the gel from identification test B. A white precipitate is immediately produced.

D. Add 0.5 ml of *thymol blue solution R* to 10 ml of a 10 g/l dispersion. An orange colour is produced. Add 0.5 ml of *cresol red solution R* to 10 ml of a 10 g/l dispersion. A yellow colour is produced.

## TESTS

**Free acrylic acid**
Liquid chromatography *(2.2.29)*.

*Test solution*   Mix 0.125 g of the substance to be examined with a 25 g/l solution of *aluminium potassium sulphate R* and dilute to 25.0 ml with the same solution. Heat the suspension at 50 °C for 20 min with shaking, then shake the suspension at room temperature for 60 min. Centrifuge and use the clear supernatant solution as the test solution.

*Reference solution*   Dissolve 62.5 mg of *acrylic acid R* in a 25 g/l solution of *aluminium potassium sulphate R* and dilute to 100.0 ml with the same solution. Dilute 1.0 ml of this solution to 50.0 ml with a 25 g/l solution of *aluminium potassium sulphate R*.

*Column:*
— *size: l* = 0.12 m, Ø = 4.6 mm;
— *stationary phase:* octadecylsilyl silica gel for chromatography R (5 μm).

*Mobile phase:*
— *mobile phase A*: 1.361 g/l solution of *potassium dihydrogen phosphate R*, adjusted to pH 2.5 using *dilute phosphoric acid R*;

— *mobile phase B*: mixture of equal volumes of a 1.361 g/l solution of *potassium dihydrogen phosphate R* and *acetonitrile for chromatography R*;

| Time (min) | Mobile phase A (per cent *V/V*) | Mobile phase B (per cent *V/V*) |
|---|---|---|
| 0 - 8 | 100 | 0 |
| 8 - 9 | 100 → 0 | 0 → 100 |
| 9 - 20 | 0 | 100 |

*Flow rate*   1 ml/min.

*Detection*   Spectrophotometer at 205 nm.

*Injection*   20 μl.

*Retention time*   Acrylic acid = about 6.0 min.

*Limit:*
— *acrylic acid*: not more than the area of the corresponding peak in the chromatogram obtained with the reference solution (0.25 per cent).

**Benzene**
Gas chromatography *(2.4.24, System A)*.

*Solution A*   Dissolve 0.100 g of *benzene R* in *dimethyl sulphoxide R* and dilute to 100.0 ml with the same solvent. Dilute 1.0 ml of the solution to 100.0 ml with *water R*. Dilute 1.0 ml of this solution to 100.0 ml with *water R*.

*Test solution*   Weigh 50.0 mg of the substance to be examined into an injection vial and add 5.0 ml of *water R* and 1.0 ml of *dimethyl sulphoxide R*.

*Reference solution*   Weigh 50.0 mg of the substance to be examined into an injection vial and add 4.0 ml of *water R*, 1.0 ml of *dimethyl sulphoxide R* and 1.0 ml of solution A.

*Close the vials with a tight rubber membrane stopper coated with polytetrafluoroethylene and secure with an aluminium crimped cap. Shake to obtain a homogeneous dispersion.*

*Static head-space conditions that may be used:*
— *equilibration temperature*: 80 °C;
— *equilibration time*: 60 min;
— *transfer-line temperature*: 90 °C.

*Injection*   1 ml of the gaseous phase of the test solution and 1 ml of the gaseous phase of the reference solution; repeat these injections twice more.

*System suitability:*
— *repeatability*: maximum relative standard deviation of the differences in area between the analyte peaks obtained from the 3 replicate pair injections of the reference solution and the test solution is 15 per cent.

*Limit:*
— *benzene*: the mean area of the peak due to benzene in the chromatograms obtained with the test solution is not greater than 0.5 times the mean area of the peak due to benzene in the chromatograms obtained with the reference solution (2 ppm).

**Heavy metals** *(2.4.8)*
Maximum 20 ppm.

1.0 g complies with test C. Prepare the reference solution using 2 ml of *lead standard solution (10 ppm Pb) R*.

**Loss on drying** *(2.2.32)*
Maximum 3.0 per cent, determined on 1.000 g by drying *in vacuo* at 80 °C for 60 min.

**Sulphated ash** *(2.4.14)*
Maximum 4.0 per cent, determined on 1.0 g.

## ASSAY

Slowly add 50 ml of *water R* to 0.120 g whilst stirring and heating at 60 °C for 15 min. Stop heating, add 150 ml of *water R* and continue stirring for 30 min. Add 2 g of *potassium chloride R* and titrate with *0.2 M sodium hydroxide*, determining the end-point potentiometrically (*2.2.20*).

1 ml of *0.2 M sodium hydroxide* is equivalent to 9.0 mg of carboxylic acid (-CO$_2$H) groups.

## STORAGE

In an airtight container.

## FUNCTIONALITY-RELATED CHARACTERISTICS

*This section provides information on characteristics that are recognised as being relevant control parameters for one or more functions of the substance when used as an excipient (see chapter 5.15). This section is a non-mandatory part of the monograph and it is not necessary to verify the characteristics to demonstrate compliance. Control of these characteristics can however contribute to the quality of a medicinal product by improving the consistency of the manufacturing process and the performance of the medicinal product during use. Where control methods are cited, they are recognised as being suitable for the purpose, but other methods can also be used. Wherever results for a particular characteristic are reported, the control method must be indicated.*

*The following characteristics may be relevant for carbomers used as viscosity-increasing agents and gelling agents.*

### Apparent viscosity (*2.2.10*)

The nominal apparent viscosity is typically between 300 mPa·s and 115 000 mPa·s. For a product with a nominal apparent viscosity of 20 000 mPa·s or greater, the apparent viscosity is typically 70.0 per cent to 130.0 per cent of the nominal value; for a product with a nominal apparent viscosity of less than 20 000 mPa·s, the apparent viscosity is typically 50.0 per cent to 150.0 per cent of the nominal value.

Dry the substance to be examined *in vacuo* at 80 °C for 1 h. Carefully add 2.50 g of the previously dried substance to be examined to 500 ml of *water R* in a 1000 ml beaker while stirring continuously at 1000 ± 50 r/min, with the stirrer shaft set at an angle of 60° to one side of the beaker. Add the previously dried substance over a period of 45-90 s, at a uniform rate, ensuring that loose agglomerates of powder are broken up, and continue stirring at 1000 ± 50 r/min for 15 min. Remove the stirrer and place the beaker containing the dispersion in a water-bath at 25 ± 1 °C for 30 min. Insert the stirrer to a depth necessary to ensure that air is not drawn into the dispersion and, while stirring at 300 ± 25 r/min, titrate with a glass-calomel electrode system to pH 7.3-7.8 by adding a 180 g/l solution of *sodium hydroxide R* below the surface, determining the end-point potentiometrically (*2.2.20*). The total volume of the 180 g/l solution of *sodium hydroxide R* used is about 6.2 ml. Allow 2-3 min before the final pH determination. If the final pH exceeds 7.8, discard the preparation and prepare another using a smaller amount of sodium hydroxide for titration. Return the neutralised preparation to the water-bath at 25 °C for 1 h, then perform the viscosity determination without delay to avoid slight viscosity changes that occur 75 min after neutralisation. Determine the viscosity using a rotating viscometer with a spindle rotating at 20 r/min, using a spindle suitable for the expected apparent viscosity.

### Carboxylic acid groups

See Assay.

*Ph Eur*

# Carbon Dioxide

★★★
★ ★
★ ★
★ ★
★★★

(*Ph Eur monograph 0375*)

CO$_2$                    44.01                    *124-38-9*

Carbon Dioxide should be kept in approved metal cylinders which are painted grey and carry a label stating 'Carbon Dioxide'. In addition, 'Carbon Dioxide' or the symbol 'CO$_2$' should be stencilled in paint on the shoulder of the cylinder.

*Ph Eur*

## DEFINITION

### Content

Minimum 99.5 per cent *V/V* of CO$_2$ in the gaseous phase.

This monograph applies to carbon dioxide for medicinal use.

## CHARACTERS

### Appearance

Colourless gas.

### Solubility

At 20 °C and at a pressure of 101 kPa, 1 volume dissolves in about 1 volume of water.

## PRODUCTION

*Examine the gaseous phase.*

*If the test is performed on a cylinder of gas, keep the cylinder of the substance to be examined at room temperature for not less than 6 h before carrying out the tests. Keep the cylinder in the vertical position with the outlet valve uppermost.*

### Carbon monoxide

Gas chromatography (*2.2.28*).

*Gas to be examined*   The substance to be examined.

*Reference gas*   A mixture containing 5 ppm *V/V* of *carbon monoxide R* in *nitrogen R1*.

*Column:*
— *material*: stainless steel,
— *size*: *l* = 2 m, Ø = 4 mm,
— *stationary phase*: an appropriate molecular sieve for chromatography (0.5 nm).

*Carrier gas*   *helium for chromatography R.*

*Flow rate*   60 ml/min.

*Temperature:*
— *column*: 50 °C,
— *injection port and detector*: 130 °C.

*Detection*   Flame ionisation with methaniser.

*Injection*   Loop injector.

Adjust the injected volumes and the operating conditions so that the height of the peak due to carbon monoxide in the chromatogram obtained with the reference gas is at least 35 per cent of the full scale of the recorder.

*Limit:*
— *carbon monoxide*: not more than the area of the corresponding peak in the chromatogram obtained with the reference gas (5 ppm *V/V*).

### Nitrogen monoxide and nitrogen dioxide

Maximum 2 ppm *V/V* in total, determined using a chemiluminescence analyser (*2.5.26*).

*Gas to be examined*   The substance to be examined.

*Reference gas (a)*   *Carbon dioxide R1.*

*Reference gas (b)*   A mixture containing 2 ppm *V/V* of *nitrogen monoxide R* in *carbon dioxide R1* or in *nitrogen R1*.

Calibrate the apparatus and set the sensitivity using reference gases (a) and (b). Measure the content of nitrogen monoxide and nitrogen dioxide in the gas to be examined.

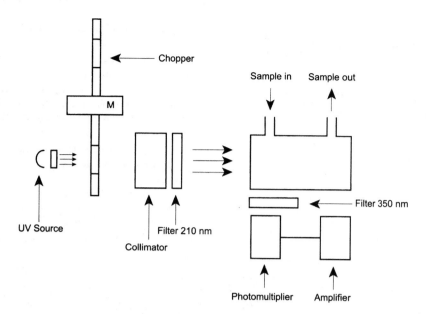

Figure 0375.-1.– *UV Fluorescence Analyser*

If nitrogen is used instead of carbon dioxide in reference gas (b), multiply the result obtained by the quenching correction factor in order to correct the quenching effect on the analyser response caused by the carbon dioxide matrix effect.

The quenching correction factor is determined by applying a known reference mixture of nitrogen monoxide in carbon dioxide and comparing the actual content with the content indicated by the analyser which has been calibrated with a NO/N₂ reference mixture.

$$\text{Quenching correction factor} = \frac{\text{actual nitrogen monoxide content}}{\text{indicated nitrogen monoxide content}}$$

**Total sulphur**
Maximum 1 ppm *V/V*, determined using an ultraviolet fluorescence analyser after oxidation of the sulphur compounds by heating at 1000 °C (Figure 0375.-1).
The apparatus consists of the following:
— a system generating ultraviolet radiation with a wavelength of 210 nm, made up of an ultraviolet lamp, a collimator, and a selective filter; the beam is blocked periodically by a chopper rotating at high speed,
— a reaction chamber through which flows the previously filtered gas to be examined,
— a system that detects radiation emitted at a wavelength of 350 nm, made up of a selective filter, a photomultiplier tube and an amplifier.

*Gas to be examined*   The substance to be examined.
*Reference gas (a)   Carbon dioxide R1.*
*Reference gas (b)*   A mixture containing between 0.5 ppm *V/V* and 2 ppm *V/V* of *hydrogen sulphide R1* in *carbon dioxide R1*.

Calibrate the apparatus and set the sensitivity using reference gases (a) and (b). Pass the gas to be examined through a quartz oven heated to 1000 °C. *Oxygen R* is circulated in the oven at a tenth of the flow rate of the gas to be examined. Measure the sulphur dioxide content in the gaseous mixture leaving the oven.

**Water**
Maximum 67 ppm *V/V*, determined using an electrolytic hygrometer (*2.5.28*).

**ASSAY**
Infrared analyser (*2.5.24*).

*Gas to be examined*   The substance to be examined. It must be filtered to avoid stray light phenomena.
*Reference gas (a)   Carbon dioxide R1.*
*Reference gas (b)*   A mixture containing 95.0 per cent *V/V* of *carbon dioxide R1* and 5.0 per cent *V/V* of *nitrogen R1*.

Calibrate the apparatus and set the sensitivity using reference gases (a) and (b). Measure the content of carbon dioxide in the gas to be examined.

**IDENTIFICATION**
*First identification   A.*
*Second identification   B, C.*

A. Infrared absorption spectrophotometry (*2.2.24*).
*Comparison   Ph. Eur. reference spectrum of carbon dioxide.*

B. Place a glowing splinter of wood in an atmosphere of the substance to be examined. It is extinguished.

C. Pass a stream of the substance to be examined through *barium hydroxide solution R*. A white precipitate is formed which dissolves with effervescence in *dilute acetic acid R*.

**TESTS**
*Examine the gaseous phase.*

*If the test is performed on a cylinder of gas, keep the cylinder of the substance to be examined at room temperature for not less than 6 h before carrying out the tests. Keep the cylinder in the vertical position with the outlet valve uppermost.*

**Carbon monoxide**
Maximum 5 ppm *V/V*, determined using a carbon monoxide detector tube (*2.1.6*).

**Hydrogen sulphide**
Maximum 1 ppm *V/V*, determined using a hydrogen sulphide detector tube (*2.1.6*).

**Nitrogen monoxide and nitrogen dioxide**
Maximum 2 ppm *V/V* in total, determined using a nitrogen monoxide and nitrogen dioxide detector tube (*2.1.6*).

**Sulphur dioxide**
Maximum 2 ppm *V/V*, determined using a sulphur dioxide detector tube (*2.1.6*).

### Water vapour

Maximum 67 ppm *V/V*, determined using a water vapour detector tube (*2.1.6*).

### STORAGE

Store liquefied under pressure in suitable containers complying with the legal regulations.

### IMPURITIES

A. nitrogen monoxide,

B. nitrogen dioxide,

C. carbon monoxide,

D. total sulphur,

E. water.

_____ *Ph Eur*

# Carboplatin

(*Ph Eur monograph 1081*)

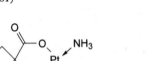

$C_6H_{12}N_2O_4Pt$          371.3          41575-94-4

### Action and use

Platinum-containing cytotoxic.

### Preparation

Carboplatin Injection

*Ph Eur* _____

### DEFINITION

(*SP*-4-2)-Diammine[cyclobutan-1,1-dicarboxylato(2-)-*O*,*O'*]platin.

### Content

98.0 per cent to 102.0 per cent (dried substance).

### CHARACTERS

### Appearance

Colourless, crystalline powder.

### Solubility

Sparingly soluble in water, very slightly soluble in acetone and in ethanol (96 per cent).

### mp

About 200 °C, with decomposition.

### IDENTIFICATION

Infrared absorption spectrophotometry (*2.2.24*).

*Comparison*   Ph. Eur. reference spectrum of carboplatin.

### TESTS

### Solution S

Dissolve 0.25 g in *carbon dioxide-free water R* and dilute to 25 ml with the same solvent.

### Appearance of solution

Solution S is clear (*2.2.1*) and colourless (*2.2.2, Method II*).

### Impurity B and acidity

Maximum 0.5 per cent, calculated as impurity B.

To 10 ml of solution S add 0.1 ml of *phenolphthalein solution R1*. The solution is colourless. Not more than 0.7 ml of *0.01 M sodium hydroxide* is required to change the colour of the indicator to pink.

### Related substances

Liquid chromatography (*2.2.29*).

*Test solution*   Dissolve 20.0 mg of the substance to be examined in a mixture of equal volumes of *acetonitrile R* and *water R* and dilute to 20.0 ml with the same mixture of solvents.

*Reference solution*   Dilute 0.5 ml of the test solution to 200.0 ml with the mobile phase.

*Column:*
— *size: l* = 0.25 m, Ø = 4.6 mm;
— *stationary phase*: aminopropylsilyl silica gel for chromatography *R* (5 μm).

*Mobile phase*   water *R*, acetonitrile *R* (13:87 *V/V*).

*Flow rate*   2 ml/min.

*Detection*   Spectrophotometer at 230 nm.

*Injection*   10 μl.

*Run time*   2.5 times the retention time of carboplatin.

*System suitability*   Test solution:
— *number of theoretical plates*: minimum 5000; if necessary, adjust the concentration of acetonitrile in the mobile phase;
— *mass distribution ratio*: minimum 4.0; if necessary, adjust the concentration of acetonitrile in the mobile phase;
— *symmetry factor*: maximum 2.0; if necessary, adjust the concentration of acetonitrile in the mobile phase.

*Limits:*
— *impurity A*: not more than the area of the principal peak in the chromatogram obtained with the reference solution (0.25 per cent);
— *total*: not more than twice the area of the principal peak in the chromatogram obtained with the reference solution (0.5 per cent);
— *disregard limit*: 0.2 times the area of the principal peak in the chromatogram obtained with the reference solution (0.05 per cent).

### Chlorides (*2.4.4*)

Maximum 100 ppm.

Dissolve 0.5 g in *water R*, heating slightly if necessary, and dilute to 20 ml with the same solvent. Filter if necessary. Dilute 10 ml of this solution to 15 ml with *water R*. Prepare the standard using 5 ml of *chloride standard solution (5 ppm Cl) R*.

### Ammonium (*2.4.1, Method B*)

Maximum 100 ppm, determined on 0.20 g.

Prepare the standard using 0.2 ml of *ammonium standard solution (100 ppm NH₄) R*.

### Silver

Maximum 10.0 ppm.

Atomic emission spectrometry (*2.2.22, Method I*).

*Test solution*   Dissolve 0.50 g in a 1 per cent *V/V* solution of *nitric acid R* and dilute to 50.0 ml with the same solution.

*Reference solutions*   Prepare the reference solutions using *silver standard solution (5 ppm Ag) R*, diluting with a 1 per cent *V/V* solution of *nitric acid R*.

*Wavelength*   328.1 nm.

### Soluble barium

Maximum 10.0 ppm.

Atomic emission spectrometry (*2.2.22, Method I*).

*Test solution*   Use the solution described in the test for silver.

*Reference solutions* Prepare the reference solutions using *barium standard solution (50 ppm Ba) R*, diluting with a 1 per cent *V/V* solution of *nitric acid R*.

*Wavelength* 455.4 nm.

**Loss on drying** (2.2.32)
Maximum 0.5 per cent, determined on 1.000 g by drying in an oven at 105 °C.

## ASSAY
Use the residue obtained in the test for loss on drying. Ignite 0.200 g of the residue to constant mass at 800 ± 50 °C.

1 mg of the residue is equivalent to 1.903 mg of $C_6H_{12}N_2O_4Pt$.

## STORAGE
Protected from light.

## IMPURITIES
*Specified impurities* A, B.

A. cisplatin,

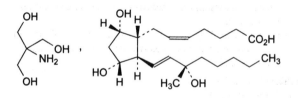

B. cyclobutane-1,1-dicarboxylic acid.

*Ph Eur*

# Carboprost Trometamol

(*Ph Eur monograph 1712*)

$C_{25}H_{47}NO_8$      489.7      *58551-69-2*

## Action and use
Prostaglandin (PGF$_{2\alpha}$) analogue.

*Ph Eur*

## DEFINITION
2-Amino-2-(hydroxymethyl)propane-1,3-diol (5Z)-7-[(1R,2R,3R,5S)-3,5-dihydroxy-2-[(1E,3S)-3-hydroxy-3-methyloct-1-enyl]cyclopentyl]hept-5-enoate ((15S)-15-methyl-PGF$_2$).

## Content
94.0 per cent to 102.0 per cent (anhydrous substance).

## CHARACTERS
**Appearance**
White or almost white powder.

**Solubility**
Soluble in water.

## IDENTIFICATION
A. Specific optical rotation (see Tests).

B. Infrared absorption spectrophotometry (2.2.24).

*Comparison* Ph. Eur. reference spectrum of carboprost trometamol.

## TESTS
**Specific optical rotation** (2.2.7)
+ 18 to + 24 (anhydrous substance).

Dissolve 0.100 g in *ethanol (96 per cent) R* and dilute to 10.0 ml with the same solvent.

**Related substances**
Liquid chromatography (2.2.29).

*Test solution* Dissolve 15.0 mg of the substance to be examined in a mixture of 23 volumes of *acetonitrile R* and 77 volumes of *water for chromatography R* and dilute to 10.0 ml with the same mixture of solvents.

*Reference solution (a)* Dissolve 15.0 mg of *carboprost trometamol CRS* (containing impurity A) in a mixture of 23 volumes of *acetonitrile R* and 77 volumes of *water for chromatography R* and dilute to 10.0 ml with the same mixture of solvents.

*Reference solution (b)* Dilute 1.0 ml of reference solution (a) and 0.15 ml of *(15R)-15-methylprostaglandin F$_{2\alpha}$ R* (impurity B) to 100.0 ml with a mixture of 23 volumes of *acetonitrile R* and 77 volumes of *water for chromatography R*.

*Reference solution (c)* Dilute 2.0 ml of the test solution to 20.0 ml with a mixture of 23 volumes of *acetonitrile R* and 77 volumes of *water for chromatography R*. Dilute 2.0 ml of this solution to 20.0 ml with a mixture of 23 volumes of *acetonitrile R* and 77 volumes of *water for chromatography R*.

*Column:*
— *size: l* = 0.15 m, Ø = 4.6 mm,
— *stationary phase: octadecylsilyl silica gel for chromatography R1* (5 μm) with a pore size of 8-10 nm and a carbon loading of 12-19 per cent.

*Mobile phase* Mix 23 volumes of *acetonitrile R1* and 77 volumes of a 2.44 g/l solution of *sodium dihydrogen phosphate R* in *water for chromatography R* previously adjusted to pH 2.5 with *phosphoric acid R*.

*Flow rate* 1.0 ml/min.

*Detection* Spectrophotometer at 200 nm.

*Injection* 20 μl.

*Run time* 1.3 times the retention time of carboprost.

*Relative retention* With reference to carboprost (retention time = about 80 min): impurity B = about 0.85; impurity A = about 0.9.

*Identification of impurities* Use the chromatogram obtained with reference solution (a) and the chromatogram supplied with *carboprost trometamol CRS* to identify the peak due to impurity A.

*System suitability:*
— *resolution:* minimum 3.4 between the peaks due to impurity B and carboprost in the chromatogram obtained with reference solution (b);
— *peak-to-valley ratio:* minimum 3.0, where $H_p$ = height above the baseline of the peak due to impurity A and $H_v$ = height above the baseline of the lowest point of the curve separating this peak from the peak due to impurity B in the chromatogram obtained with reference solution (a).

*Limits:*
— *impurity A:* not more than 3 times the area of the principal peak in the chromatogram obtained with reference solution (c) (3.0 per cent),
— *impurity B:* not more than the area of the principal peak in the chromatogram obtained with reference solution (c) (1.0 per cent),

— *any other impurity*: for each impurity, not more than 0.1 times the area of the principal peak in the chromatogram obtained with reference solution (c) (0.1 per cent),

— *total*: not more than 4 times the area of the principal peak in the chromatogram obtained with reference solution (c) (4.0 per cent),

— *disregard limit*: 0.05 times the area of the principal peak in the chromatogram obtained with reference solution (c) (0.05 per cent).

**Water** (*2.5.32*)
Maximum 0.5 per cent, determined on 50 mg.

**ASSAY**
Liquid chromatography (*2.2.29*) as described in the test for related substances with the following modifications.

*Mobile phase*   Mix 27 volumes of *acetonitrile R1* and 73 volumes of a 2.44 g/l solution of *sodium dihydrogen phosphate R* in *water for chromatography R* previously adjusted to pH 2.5 with *phosphoric acid R*.

*Injection*   Test solution and reference solution (a).

*Run time*   1.2 times the retention time of carboprost.

*Retention time*   Carboprost = about 29 min.

Calculate the percentage content of $C_{25}H_{47}NO_8$ using the declared content of *carboprost trometamol CRS*.

**STORAGE**
At a temperature below − 15 °C.

**IMPURITIES**
*Specified impurities*   A, B.

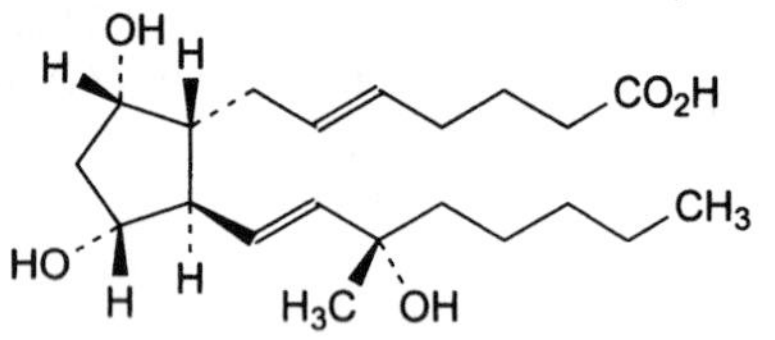

A. (5E)-7-[(1R,2R,3R,5S)-3,5-dihydroxy-2-[(1E,3S)-3-hydroxy-3-methyloct-1-enyl]cyclopentyl]hept-5-enoic acid,

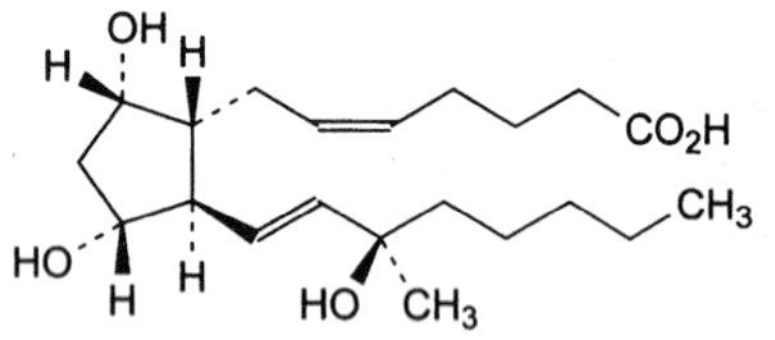

B. (5Z)-7-[(1R,2R,3R,5S)-3,5-dihydroxy-2-[(1E,3R)-3-hydroxy-3-methyloct-1-enyl]cyclopentyl]hept-5-enoic acid.

*Ph Eur*

# Carisoprodol

(*Ph Eur monograph 1689*)

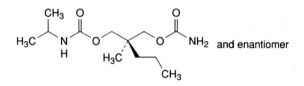

$C_{12}H_{24}N_2O_4$          260.3          78-44-4

**Action and use**
Skeletal muscle relaxant.

*Ph Eur*

**DEFINITION**
(2RS)-2-[(Carbamoyloxy)methyl]-2-methylpentyl (1-methylethyl)carbamate.

**Content**
98.0 per cent to 102.0 per cent (dried substance).

**CHARACTERS**
**Appearance**
White or almost white, fine powder.

**Solubility**
Very slightly soluble in water, freely soluble in acetone, in alcohol and in methylene chloride.

**IDENTIFICATION**
*First identification*   A, B.
*Second identification*   A, C, D.

A. Melting point (*2.2.14*): 92 °C to 95 °C.

B. Infrared absorption spectrophotometry (*2.2.24*).

*Comparison*   carisoprodol CRS.

C. Examine the chromatograms obtained in the test for related substances.

*Results:*   The principal spot in the chromatogram obtained with test solution (b) is similar in position, colour and size to the principal spot in the chromatogram obtained with reference solution (d).

D. Dissolve 0.2 g in 15 ml of a 28 g/l solution of *potassium hydroxide R* in *alcohol R* and boil under a reflux condenser for 15 min. Add 0.5 ml *of glacial acetic acid R* and 1 ml of a 50 g/l solution of *cobalt nitrate R in ethanol R*. An intense blue colour develops.

**TESTS**
**Optical rotation** (*2.2.7*)
− 0.10° to + 0.10°.

Dissolve 2.5 g in *alcohol R* and dilute to 25.0 ml with the same solvent.

**Related substances**
Thin-layer chromatography (*2.2.27*).

*Test solution (a)*   Dissolve 0.20 g of the substance to be examined in *methylene chloride R* and dilute to 10 ml with the same solvent.

*Test solution (b)*   Dilute 1 ml of test solution (a) to 10 ml with *methylene chloride R*.

*Reference solution (a)*   Dissolve 5.0 mg *of meprobamate CRS* in *methylene chloride R* and dilute to 50 ml with the same solvent.

*Reference solution (b)*   Dilute 1 ml of test solution (b) to 50 ml with *methylene chloride R*.

*Reference solution (c)*  Dilute 5 ml of reference solution (b) to 10 ml with *methylene chloride R*.

*Reference solution (d)*  Dissolve 20 mg of *carisoprodol CRS* in *methylene chloride R* and dilute to 10 ml with the same solvent.

*Reference solution (e)*  Dissolve 10 mg of *carisoprodol impurity A CRS* in 5 ml of reference solution (d) and dilute to 50 ml with *methylene chloride R*.

*Plate*  TLC silica gel plate *R*.

*Mobile phase*  acetone *R*, methylene chloride *R* (20:80 *V/V*).

*Application*  5 µl.

*Development*  Over a path of 15 cm.

*Drying*  In air for 15 min.

*Detection*  Spray with a solution prepared as follows: dissolve 5 g of *phosphomolybdic acid R* in a mixture of 50 ml of *glacial acetic acid R* and 10 ml of *sulphuric acid R*, and dilute to 100 ml with *glacial acetic acid R*. Heat the plate at 100-105 °C for 30 min.

*System suitability:*
— the chromatogram obtained with reference solution (c) shows 1 clearly visible spot,
— the chromatogram obtained with reference solution (e) shows 2 clearly separated spots.

*Limits*  In the chromatogram obtained with test solution (a):
— *impurity D*: any spot due to impurity D is not more intense than the spot in the chromatogram obtained with reference solution (a) (0.5 per cent),
— *any other impurity*: any spot, apart from the principal spot and any spot due to impurity D, is not more intense than the spot in the chromatogram obtained with reference solution (b) (0.2 per cent).

**Heavy metals** *(2.4.8)*
Maximum 10 ppm.

2.0 g complies with limit test C. Prepare the standard using 2 ml of *lead standard solution (10 ppm Pb) R*.

**Loss on drying** *(2.2.32)*
Maximum 0.5 per cent, determined on 1.000 g *in vacuo* at 60 °C for 3 h.

**Sulphated ash** *(2.4.14)*
Maximum 0.1 per cent, determined on 1.0 g.

## ASSAY

Dissolve 0.100 g in 15 ml of a 25 per cent *V/V* solution of *sulphuric acid R* and boil under a reflux condenser for 3 h. Cool, dissolve by cautiously adding 30 ml of *water R*, cool again and place in a steam-distillation apparatus. Add 40 ml of *strong sodium hydroxide solution R* and distil immediately by passing steam through the mixture. Collect the distillate into 40 ml of a 40 g/l solution of *boric acid R* until the total volume in the receiver reaches about 200 ml. Add 0.25 ml of *methyl red mixed solution R*. Titrate with *0.1 M hydrochloric acid*, until the colour changes from green to violet. Carry out a blank titration.

1 ml of *0.1 M hydrochloric acid* is equivalent to 13.02 mg of $C_{12}H_{24}N_2O_4$.

## IMPURITIES

A. (2*RS*)-2-(hydroxymethyl)-2-methylpentyl (1-methylethyl)carbamate,

B. 5-methyl-5-propyl-1,3-dioxan-2-one,

C. 2-methyl-2-propylpropane-1,3-diol,

D. meprobamate.

*Ph Eur*

# Carmellose Calcium

*(Ph Eur monograph 0886)*

9050-04-8

## Action and use
Excipient in pharmaceutical products; bulk laxative.

*Ph Eur*

## DEFINITION
Calcium salt of a partly *O*-carboxymethylated cellulose.

## CHARACTERS
**Appearance**
White or yellowish-white powder, hygroscopic after drying.

**Solubility**
Practically insoluble in acetone, in alcohol and in toluene. It swells with water to form a suspension.

## IDENTIFICATION
A. Shake 0.1 g thoroughly with 10 ml of *water R*. Add 2 ml of *dilute sodium hydroxide solution R* and allow to stand for 10 min (solution A). Dilute 1 ml of solution A to 5 ml with *water R*. To 0.05 ml add 0.5 ml of a 0.5 g/l solution of *chromotropic acid, sodium salt R* in a 75 per cent *m/m* solution of *sulphuric acid R* and heat on a water-bath for 10 min. A reddish-violet colour develops.

B. Shake 5 ml of solution A obtained in identification test A with 10 ml of *acetone R*. A white, flocculent precipitate is produced.

C. Shake 5 ml of solution A obtained in identification test A with 1 ml of *ferric chloride solution R1*. A brown, flocculent precipitate is formed.

D. Ignite 1 g and dissolve the residue in a mixture of 5 ml of *acetic acid R* and 10 ml of *water R*. Filter if necessary and boil the filtrate for a few minutes. Cool and neutralise with *dilute ammonia R1*. The solution gives reaction (a) of calcium (2.3.1).

## TESTS

### Solution S
Shake 1.0 g with 50 ml of *distilled water R*, add 5 ml of *dilute sodium hydroxide solution R* and dilute to 100 ml with *distilled water R*.

### Alkalinity
Shake 1.0 g thoroughly with 50 ml of *carbon dioxide-free water R* and add 0.05 ml of *phenolphthalein solution R*. No red colour develops.

### Chlorides (2.4.4)
Maximum 0.36 per cent.

Heat 28 ml of solution S with 10 ml of *dilute nitric acid R* on a water-bath until a flocculent precipitate is produced. Cool, centrifuge and separate the supernatant liquid. Wash the precipitate with 3 quantities, each of 10 ml, of *water R*, centrifuging each time. Combine the supernatant liquid and the washings and dilute to 100 ml with *water R*. To 25 ml add 6 ml of *dilute nitric acid R* and dilute to 50 ml with *water R*. Dilute 10 ml of the solution to 15 ml with *water R*.

### Sulphates (2.4.13)
Maximum 1 per cent.

Heat 20 ml of solution S with 1 ml of *hydrochloric acid R* on a water-bath until a flocculent precipitate is produced. Cool, centrifuge and separate the supernatant liquid. Wash the precipitate with 3 quantities, each of 10 ml, of *distilled water R*, centrifuging each time. Combine the supernatant liquid and the washings and dilute to 100 ml with *distilled water R*. To 25 ml add 1 ml of *dilute hydrochloric acid R* and dilute to 50 ml with *distilled water R*.

### Heavy metals (2.4.8)
Maximum 20 ppm.

1.0 g complies with limit test D. Prepare the standard using 2 ml of *lead standard solution (10 ppm Pb) R*.

### Loss on drying (2.2.32)
Maximum 10.0 per cent, determined on 1.000 g by drying in an oven at 105 °C for 4 h.

### Sulphated ash (2.4.14)
10.0 per cent to 20.0 per cent, determined on 1.0 g in a platinum crucible.

## STORAGE
In an airtight container.

———————————————— Ph Eur

# Carmellose Sodium

(*Ph Eur monograph 0472*)

9004-32-4

## Action and use
Excipient; bulk laxative.

## Preparation
Carmellose Sodium Eye Drops

Ph Eur

## DEFINITION
Carmellose sodium (carboxymethylcellulose sodium) is the sodium salt of a partly *O*-carboxymethylated cellulose. It contains not less than 6.5 per cent and not more than 10.8 per cent of sodium (Na), calculated with reference to the dried substance.

## CHARACTERS
A white or almost white, granular powder, hygroscopic after drying, practically insoluble in acetone, in ethanol and in toluene. It is easily dispersed in water giving colloidal solutions.

## IDENTIFICATION
A. To 10 ml of solution S (see Tests) add 1 ml of *copper sulphate solution R*. A blue, cotton-like precipitate is formed.

B. Boil 5 ml of solution S for a few minutes. No precipitate is formed.

C. The solution prepared from the sulphated ash in the test for heavy metals gives the reactions of sodium (2.3.1).

## TESTS

### Solution S
Sprinkle a quantity of the substance to be examined equivalent to 1.0 g of the dried substance onto 90 ml of *carbon dioxide-free water R* at 40 °C to 50 °C stirring vigorously. Continue stirring until a colloidal solution is obtained, cool and dilute to 100 ml with *carbon dioxide-free water R*.

### Appearance of solution
Solution S is not more opalescent than reference suspension III (2.2.1) and not more intensely coloured than reference solution $Y_6$ (2.2.2, Method II).

### pH (2.2.3)
The pH of solution S is 6.0 to 8.0.

### Apparent viscosity
While stirring, introduce a quantity of the substance to be examined equivalent to 2.00 g of the dried substance into 50 ml of *water R* heated to 90 °C. For a product of low viscosity, use if necessary, the quantity required to give the concentration indicated on the label. Allow to cool, dilute to 100.0 ml with *water R* and stir until dissolution is complete. Determine the viscosity (2.2.10) using a rotating viscometer at 20 °C and a shear rate of 10 $s^{-1}$. If it is impossible to obtain a shear rate of exactly 10 $s^{-1}$, use a shear rate slightly higher and a rate slightly lower and interpolate. The apparent viscosity is not less than 75 per cent and not more than 140 per cent of the value stated on the label.

### Sodium glycollate
Place a quantity of the substance to be examined equivalent to 0.500 g of dried substance in a beaker. Add 5 ml of *acetic acid R* and 5 ml of *water R*. Stir until dissolution is complete (about 30 min). Add 80 ml of *acetone R* and 2 g of *sodium chloride R*. Filter through a fast filter paper impregnated with *acetone R* into a volumetric flask, rinse the beaker and filter

with *acetone R* and dilute the filtrate to 100.0 ml with the same solvent. Allow to stand for 24 h without shaking. Use the clear supernatant liquid to prepare the test solution.

In a volumetric flask, dissolve 0.310 g of *glycollic acid R*, previously dried *in vacuo* over *diphosphorus pentoxide R*, in *water R* and dilute to 1000.0 ml with the same solvent. Place 5.0 ml of this solution in a volumetric flask, add 5 ml of *acetic acid R* and allow to stand for about 30 min. Add 80 ml of *acetone R* and 2 g of *sodium chloride R* and dilute to 100.0 ml with *acetone R*. Use this solution to prepare the reference solution.

Place 2.0 ml of each solution in a separate 25 ml volumetric flask. Heat on a water-bath to eliminate acetone. Cool to room temperature and add 5.0 ml of *2,7-dihydroxynaphthalene solution R* to each flask. Shake and add 15.0 ml of *2,7-dihydroxynaphthalene solution R*. Close the flasks with aluminium foil and heat on a water-bath for 20 min. Cool under running water and dilute to 25.0 ml with *sulphuric acid R*. Within 10 min, transfer 10.0 ml of each solution to a flat-bottomed tube. Examine the solutions viewing vertically. The test solution is not more intensely coloured than the reference solution (0.4 per cent).

### Chlorides (2.4.4)
Dilute 2 ml of solution S to 15 ml with *water R*. The solution complies with the limit test for chlorides (0.25 per cent).

### Heavy metals (2.4.8)
To the residue obtained in the determination of the sulphated ash, add 1 ml of *hydrochloric acid R* and evaporate on a water-bath. Take up the residue in 20 ml of *water R*. 12 ml of the solution complies with limit test A for heavy metals (20 ppm). Prepare the standard using *lead standard solution (1 ppm Pb) R*.

### Loss on drying (2.2.32)
Not more than 10.0 per cent, determined on 1.000 g by drying in an oven at 105 °C.

### Sulphated ash (2.4.14)
20.0 per cent to 33.3 per cent, determined on 1.0 g using a mixture of equal volumes of *sulphuric acid R* and *water R* and calculated with reference to the dried substance. These limits correspond to a content of 6.5 per cent to 10.8 per cent of sodium (Na).

### LABELLING
The label states the apparent viscosity in millipascal seconds for a 20 g/l solution; for a product of low viscosity, the label states the concentration of the solution to be used and the apparent viscosity in millipascal seconds.

_____ Ph Eur

# Low-substituted Carmellose Sodium

(*Ph Eur monograph 1186*)

9050-32-4

### Action and use
Excipient in pharmaceutical products; bulk laxative.

Ph Eur _____

### DEFINITION
Low-substituted sodium carboxymethylcellulose. Sodium salt of a partly *O*-(carboxymethylated) cellulose.

### Content
2.0 per cent to 4.5 per cent of sodium (Na) (dried substance).

### CHARACTERS
**Appearance**
White or almost white powder or short fibres.

**Solubility**
Practically insoluble in acetone, in anhydrous ethanol and in toluene. It swells in water to form a gel.

### IDENTIFICATION
A. Shake 1 g with 100 ml of a 100 g/l solution of *sodium hydroxide R*. A suspension is produced.

B. Shake 1 g with 50 ml of *water R*. Transfer 1 ml of the mixture to a test tube, add 1 ml of *water R* and 0.05 ml of a freshly prepared 40 g/l solution of α-*naphthol R* in *methanol R*. Incline the test tube and add carefully 2 ml of *sulphuric acid R* down the side so that it forms a lower layer. A reddish-purple colour develops at the interface.

C. Sulphated ash (*2.4.14*) (see Tests).

D. The solution prepared for the test for heavy metals gives reaction (a) of sodium (*2.3.1*).

### TESTS
**pH** (*2.2.3*)
6.0 to 8.5.

Shake 1 g with 100 ml of *carbon dioxide-free water R* for 5 min. Centrifuge.

### Sodium chloride and sodium glycollate
Maximum 0.5 per cent (dried substance) for the sum of the percentage contents.

*Sodium chloride*   Place 5.00 g in a 250 ml conical flask, add 50 ml of *water R* and 5 ml of *strong hydrogen peroxide solution R* and heat on a water bath for 20 min, stirring occasionally to ensure total hydration. Cool, add 100 ml of *water R* and 10 ml of *nitric acid R*. Titrate with *0.05 M silver nitrate* determining the end-point potentiometrically (*2.2.20*) using a silver-based indicator electrode and a double-junction reference electrode containing a 100 g/l solution of *potassium nitrate R* in the outer jacket and a standard filling solution in the inner jacket.

1 ml of *0.05 M silver nitrate* is equivalent to 2.922 mg of NaCl.

*Sodium glycollate*   Place a quantity of the substance to be examined equivalent to 0.500 g of the dried substance in a beaker. Add 5 ml of *glacial acetic acid R* and 5 ml of *water R* and stir to ensure total hydration (about 30 min). Add 80 ml of *acetone R* and 2 g of *sodium chloride R*. Stir for several minutes to ensure complete precipitation of the carboxymethylcellulose. Filter through a fast filter paper impregnated with *acetone R* into a volumetric flask, rinse the beaker and filter with *acetone R* and dilute the filtrate to 100.0 ml with the same solvent. Allow to stand for 24 h without shaking. Use the clear supernatant as the test solution.

Prepare the reference solutions as follows: in a 100 ml volumetric flask, dissolve 0.100 g of *glycollic acid R*, previously dried *in vacuo* over *diphosphorus pentoxide R*, in *water R* and dilute to 100.0 ml with the same solvent. Transfer 0.5 ml, 1.0 ml, 1.5 ml and 2.0 ml of the solution to separate volumetric flasks; dilute the contents of each flask to 5.0 ml with *water R*, add 5 ml of *glacial acetic acid R*, dilute to 100.0 ml with *acetone R* and mix.

Transfer 2.0 ml of the test solution and 2.0 ml of each of the reference solutions to separate 25 ml volumetric flasks. Heat the uncovered flasks in a water-bath to eliminate the acetone. Allow to cool and add 5.0 ml of *2,7-dihydroxynaphthalene solution R* to each flask. Mix, add a further 15.0 ml of *2,7-dihydroxynaphthalene solution R* and mix again. Close the flasks with aluminium foil and heat in a water-bath for 20 min. Cool and dilute to 25.0 ml with *sulphuric acid R*.

Measure the absorbance (*2.2.25*) of each solution at 540 nm. Prepare a blank using 2.0 ml of a solution containing 5 per cent *V/V* each of *glacial acetic acid R* and *water R* in *acetone R*. Prepare a standard curve using the absorbances obtained with the reference solutions. From the standard curve and the absorbance of the test solution, determine the mass a, in milligrams, of glycollic acid in the substance to be examined and calculate the content of sodium glycollate from the following expression:

$$\frac{10 \times 1.29 \times a}{(100 - b)\, m}$$

1.29 = the factor converting glycollic acid to sodium glycollate
*b* = the loss on drying as a percentage
*m* = the mass of the substance to be examined, in grams

### Water-soluble substances
Maximum 70.0 per cent.

Disperse 5.00 g in 400.0 ml of *water R* and stir for 1 min every 10 min during the first 30 min. Allow to stand for 1 h and centrifuge, if necessary. Decant 100.0 ml of the supernatant liquid onto a fast filter paper in a vacuum filtration funnel, apply vacuum and collect 75.0 ml of the filtrate. Evaporate to dryness and dry the residue at 100-105 °C for 4 h.

### Heavy metals (*2.4.8*)
Maximum 20 ppm.

To the residue obtained in the determination of the sulphated ash add 1 ml of *hydrochloric acid R* and evaporate on a water-bath. Take up the residue in 20 ml of *water R* (this solution is used for identification test D). 12 ml of the solution complies with test A. Prepare the reference solution using *lead standard solution (1 ppm Pb) R*.

### Loss on drying (*2.2.32*)
Maximum 10.0 per cent, determined on 1.000 g by drying in an oven at 105 °C.

### Sulphated ash (*2.4.14*)
6.5 per cent to 13.5 per cent (dried substance), corresponding to a content of 2.0 per cent to 4.5 per cent of Na.

Use 1.0 g with a mixture of equal volumes of *sulphuric acid R* and *water R*.

### FUNCTIONALITY-RELATED CHARCTERISTICS

*This section provides information on characteristics that are recognised as being relevant control parameters for one or more functions of the substance when used as an excipient. This section is a non-mandatory part of the monograph and it is not necessary to verify the characteristics to demonstrate compliance. Control of these characteristics can however contribute to the quality of a medicinal product by improving the consistency of the manufacturing process and the performance of the medicinal product during use. Where control methods are cited, they are recognised as being suitable for the purpose, but other methods can also be used. Wherever results for a particular characteristic are reported, the control method must be indicated.*

*The following characteristic may be relevant for low-substituted carmellose sodium used as disintegrant.*

### Settling volume
15.0 ml to 35.0 ml.

In a 100 ml graduated cylinder, place 20 ml of *2-propanol R*, add 5.0 g of the substance to be examined and shake vigorously. Dilute to 30 ml with *2-propanol R* then to 50 ml with *water R* and shake vigorously. Within 15 min, repeat the shaking 3 times. Allow to stand for 4 h and determine the volume of the settled mass.

*Ph Eur*

# Carmustine

(*Ph Eur monograph 1187*)

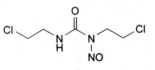

C₅H₉Cl₂N₃O₂      214.1      *154-93-8*

### Action and use
Cytotoxic alkylating agent.

*Ph Eur*

### DEFINITION
Carmustine contains not less than 98.0 per cent and not more than the equivalent of 102.0 per cent of 1,3-bis(2-chloroethyl)-1-nitrosourea, calculated with reference to the anhydrous substance.

### CHARACTERS
A yellowish, granular powder, very slightly soluble in water, very soluble in methylene chloride, freely soluble in ethanol.

It melts at about 31 °C with decomposition.

### IDENTIFICATION
Examine by infrared absorption spectrophotometry(*2.2.24*), comparing with the *Ph. Eur. reference spectrum of carmustine*. Examine the melted substances prepared as films.

### TESTS

**1,3-bis(2-chloroethyl)urea (impurity A)**
Examine by thin-layer chromatography (*2.2.27*), using a suitable silica gel as the coating substance.

*Test solution*    Dissolve 0.10 g of the substance to be examined in *methylene chloride R* and dilute to 5 ml with the same solvent.

*Reference solution (a)*    Dissolve 2 mg of *carmustine impurity A CRS* in *methylene chloride R* and dilute to 10 ml with the same solvent.

*Reference solution (b)*    Dilute 1 ml of the test solution to 10 ml with *methylene chloride R*. To 5 ml of this solution, add 5 ml of reference solution (a).

Apply separately to the plate 2 μl of each solution. Develop over a path of 10 cm using a mixture of 10 volumes of *methanol R* and 90 volumes of *methylene chloride R*. Allow the plate to dry in air. Spray with *diethylamine R* and heat at 125 °C for 10 min. Allow to cool and spray with *silver nitrate solution R2*. Expose to ultraviolet light at 365 nm until brown to black spots appear. Any spot corresponding to carmustine impurity A in the chromatogram obtained with the test solution is not more intense than the spot in the chromatogram obtained with reference solution (a) (1 per cent). The test is not valid unless the chromatogram obtained with reference solution (b) shows two clearly separated spots.

## Water (2.5.12)

Not more than 1.0 per cent, determined on 0.50 g by the semi-micro determination of water.

## ASSAY

Dissolve 0.100 g in 30 ml of *ethanol R* and dilute to 100.0 ml with *water R*. Dilute 3.0 ml of the solution to 100.0 ml with *water R*. Measure the absorbance (2.2.25) at the maximum at 230 nm.

Calculate the content of $C_5H_9C_{12}N_3O_2$ taking the specific absorbance to be 270.

## STORAGE

Store in an airtight container, protected from light, at a temperature of 2 °C to 8 °C.

## IMPURITIES

A. 1,3-bis(2-chloroethyl)urea.

*Ph Eur*

# Carnauba Wax

*(Ph Eur monograph 0597)*

**Action and use**
Excipient.

*Ph Eur*

## DEFINITION

Purified wax obtained from the leaves of *Copernicia cerifera* Mart.

## CHARACTERS

**Appearance**
Pale yellow or yellow powder, flakes or hard masses.

**Solubility**
Practically insoluble in water, soluble on heating in ethyl acetate and in xylene, practically insoluble in alcohol.

**Relative density**
About 0.97.

## IDENTIFICATION

Thin-layer chromatography (2.2.27).

*Test solution*   Dissolve 0.10 g of the substance to be examined with heating in 5 ml of *chloroform R*. Use the warm solution.

*Reference solution*   Dissolve 5 mg of *menthol R*, 5 μl of *menthyl acetate R* and 5 mg of *thymol R* in 10 ml of *toluene R*.

*Plate*   TLC silica gel plate R.

*Mobile phase*   ethyl acetate R, chloroform R (2:98 V/V).

*Application*   30 μl of the test solution and 10 μl of the reference solution as bands 20 mm by 3 mm.

*Development*   Over half of the plate.

*Drying*   In air.

*Detection*   Spray with a freshly prepared 200 g/l solution of *phosphomolybdic acid R* in *alcohol R* (about 10 ml for a 20 cm plate). Heat at 100-105 °C for 10-15 min.

*Results*   The chromatogram obtained with the reference solution shows in the lower part a dark blue zone (menthol), above this zone a reddish zone (thymol) and in the upper part a dark blue zone (menthyl acetate). The chromatogram obtained with the test solution shows a large blue zone (triacontanol = melissyl alcohol) at a level between the thymol and menthol zones in the chromatogram obtained with the reference solution. Further blue zones are visible in the upper part of the chromatogram obtained with the test solution, at levels between those of the menthyl acetate and thymol zones in the chromatogram obtained with the reference solution; above these zones further zones are visible in the chromatogram obtained with the test solution; the zone with the highest $R_F$ value is very pronounced.
A number of faint zones are visible below the triacontanol zone and the starting point is coloured blue.

## TESTS

**Appearance of solution**
The solution is clear (2.2.1) and not more intensely coloured than a 50 mg/l solution of *potassium dichromate R* (2.2.2, Method II).

Dissolve 0.10 g with heating in *chloroform R* and dilute to 10 ml with the same solvent.

**Melting point** (2.2.15)
80 °C to 88 °C.

Melt the substance to be examined carefully on a water-bath before introduction into the capillary tubes. Allow the tubes to stand in the refrigerator for 24 h or at 0 °C for 2 h.

**Acid value**
2 to 7.

To 2.000 g (m g) in a 250 ml conical flask fitted with a reflux condenser add 40 ml of *xylene R* and a few glass beads. Heat with stirring until the substance is completely dissolved. Add 20 ml of *alcohol R* and 1 ml of *bromothymol blue solution R3* and titrate the hot solution with 0.5 M alcoholic potassium hydroxide until a green colour persisting for at least 10 s is obtained ($n_1$ ml). Carry out a blank test ($n_2$ ml). Calculate the acid value from the expression:

$$\frac{28.05\,(n_1 - n_2)}{m}$$

**Saponification value**
78 to 95.

To 2.000 g (m g) in a 250 ml conical flask fitted with a reflux condenser add 40 ml of *xylene R* and a few glass beads. Heat with stirring until the substance is completely dissolved. Add 20 ml of *alcohol R* and 20.0 ml of *0.5 M alcoholic potassium hydroxide*. Boil under a reflux condenser for 3 h. Add 1 ml of *phenolphthalein solution R1* and titrate the hot solution immediately with *0.5 M hydrochloric acid* until the red colour disappears. Repeat the heating and titration until the colour no longer reappears on heating ($n_3$ ml). Carry out a blank test ($n_4$ ml). Calculate the saponification value from the expression:

$$\frac{28.05\,(n_4 - n_3)}{m}$$

**Total ash** (*2.4.16*)
Maximum 0.25 per cent, determined on 2.0 g.

**STORAGE**
Protected from light.

*Ph Eur*

# Carteolol Hydrochloride

(*Ph Eur monograph 1972*)

C₁₅H₂₅N₂O₃,HCl      328.8      *51781-21-6*

$C_{15}H_{25}N_2O_3,HCl$      328.8      *51781-21-6*

**Action and use**
Beta-adrenoceptor antagonist.

**Preparation**
Carteolol Eye Drops

*Ph Eur*

**DEFINITION**
5-[(2*RS*)-3-[(1,1-Dimethylethyl)amino]-2-hydroxypropoxy]-3,4-dihydroquinolin-2(1*H*)-one hydrochloride.

**Content**
99.0 per cent to 101.0 per cent (dried substance).

**CHARACTERS**

**Appearance**
White or almost white crystals or crystalline powder.

**Solubility**
Soluble in water, sparingly soluble in methanol, slightly soluble in alcohol, practically insoluble in methylene chloride.

**IDENTIFICATION**
A. Infrared absorption spectrophotometry (*2.2.24*).

*Comparison* Ph. Eur. reference spectrum of carteolol hydrochloride.

B. It gives reaction (a) of chlorides (*2.3.1*).

**TESTS**

**Appearance of solution**
The solution is clear (*2.2.1*) and colourless (*2.2.2*, *Method II*).

Dissolve 0.300 g in *water R* and dilute to 10 ml with the same solvent.

**pH** (*2.2.3*)
5.0 to 6.0.

Dissolve 0.250 g in *carbon dioxide-free water R* and dilute to 25 ml with the same solvent.

**Related substances**
Liquid chromatography (*2.2.29*).

*Test solution* Dissolve 20.0 mg of the substance to be examined in the mobile phase and dilute to 10.0 ml with the mobile phase.

*Reference solution (a)* Dilute 1.0 ml of the test solution to 100.0 ml with the mobile phase.

*Reference solution (b)* Dilute 1.0 ml of reference solution (a) to 10.0 ml with the mobile phase.

*Reference solution (c)* Dissolve 10 mg of *carteolol for system suitability CRS* in the mobile phase and dilute to 5 ml with the mobile phase.

*Reference solution (d)* Dilute 5.0 ml of reference solution (b) to 10.0 ml with the mobile phase.

*Column:*
— *size*: *l* = 0.25 m, Ø = 4.6 mm,
— *stationary phase*: octadecylsilyl silica gel for chromatography R (5 μm).

*Mobile phase* Mix 1 volume of *methanol R2*, 20 volumes of *acetonitrile R* and 79 volumes of a 2.82 g/l solution of *sodium hexanesulphonate R*.

*Flow rate* 1 ml/min.

*Detection* Spectrophotometer at 252 nm.

*Injection* 20 μl.

*System suitability:*
— the chromatogram obtained with reference solution (c) is similar to the chromatogram provided with *carteolol for system suitability CRS*; the peaks due to impurity H and carteolol show base-line separation,
— *signal-to-noise ratio*: minimum 10 for the principal peak in the chromatogram obtained with reference solution (d),
— *number of theoretical plates*: minimum 6000, calculated for the principal peak in the chromatogram obtained with reference solution (a).

*Limits* Locate impurity H by comparison with the chromatogram provided with *carteolol for system suitability CRS*,
— *impurity H*: not more than twice the area of the principal peak in the chromatogram obtained with reference solution (b) (0.2 per cent),
— *any other impurity*: not more than the area of the principal peak in the chromatogram obtained with reference solution (b) (0.1 per cent),
— *total*: not more than half the area of the principal peak in the chromatogram obtained with reference solution (a) (0.5 per cent),
— *disregard limit*: 0.2 times the area of the principal peak in the chromatogram obtained with reference solution (b) (0.02 per cent).

**Loss on drying** (*2.2.32*)
Maximum 0.5 per cent, determined on 1.000 g by drying in an oven at 105 °C for 3 h.

**Sulphated ash** (*2.4.14*)
Maximum 0.1 per cent, determined on 1.0 g.

**ASSAY**
Dissolve 0.250 g in 60 ml of *alcohol R*. Add 5.0 ml of *0.01 M hydrochloric acid*. Carry out a potentiometric titration (*2.2.20*), using *0.1 M sodium hydroxide*. Read the volume added between the 2 points of inflexion.

1 ml of *0.1 M sodium hydroxide* is equivalent to 32.88 mg of C₁₆H₂₅N₂O₃Cl.

**STORAGE**
In an airtight container.

**IMPURITIES**

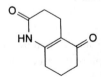

A. 4,6,7,8-tetrahydroquinoline-2,5(1*H*,3*H*)-dione,

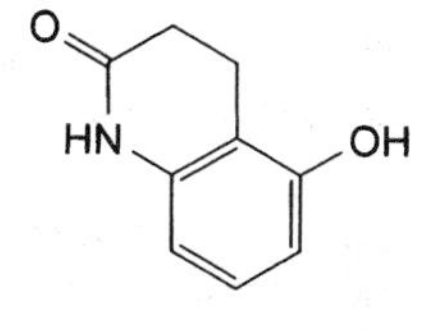

B. 5-hydroxy-3,4-dihydroquinolin-2(1*H*)-one,

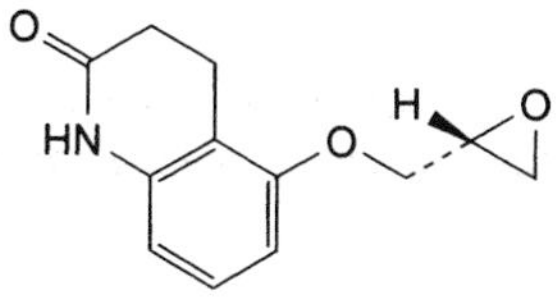

C. 5-[[(2*RS*)-oxiran-2-yl]methoxy]-3,4-dihydroquinolin-2(1*H*)-one,

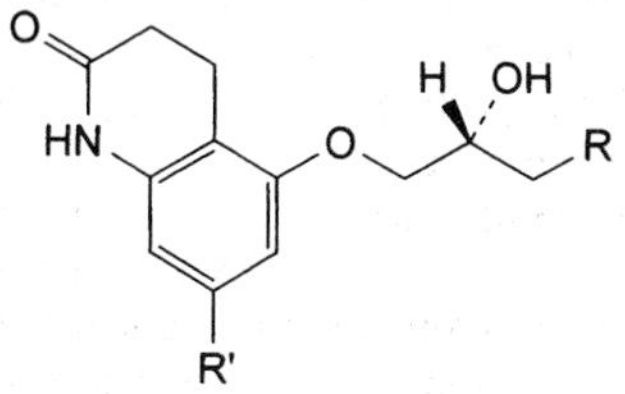

D. R = Cl, R′ = H: 5-[(2*RS*)-3-chloro-2-hydroxypropoxy]-3,4-dihydroquinolin-2(1*H*)-one,

F. R = OCH₃, R′ = H: 5-[(2*RS*)-2-hydroxy-3-methoxypropoxy]-3,4-dihydroquinolin-2(1*H*)-one,

G. R = OH, R′ = H: 5-[(2*RS*)-2,3-dihydroxypropoxy]-3,4-dihydroquinolin-2(1*H*)-one,

I. R = NH-C(CH₃)₃, R′ = Br: 7-bromo-5-[(2*RS*)-3-[(1,1-(dimethylethyl)amino]-2-hydroxypropoxy]-3,4-dihydroquinolin-2(1*H*)-one,

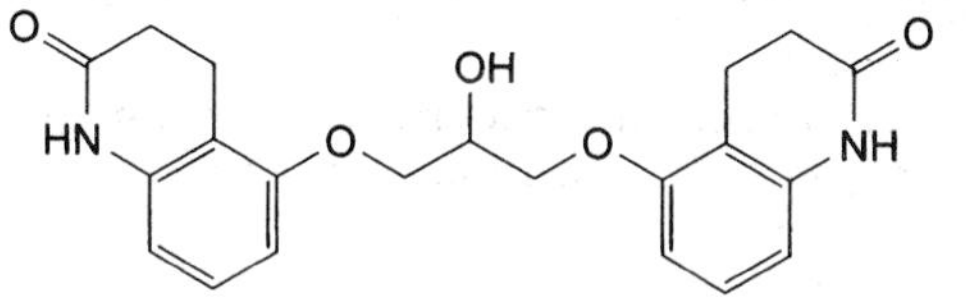

E. 5,5′-[(2-hydroxypropan-1,3-diyl)bis(oxy)]bis(3,4-dihydroquinolin-2(1*H*)-one),

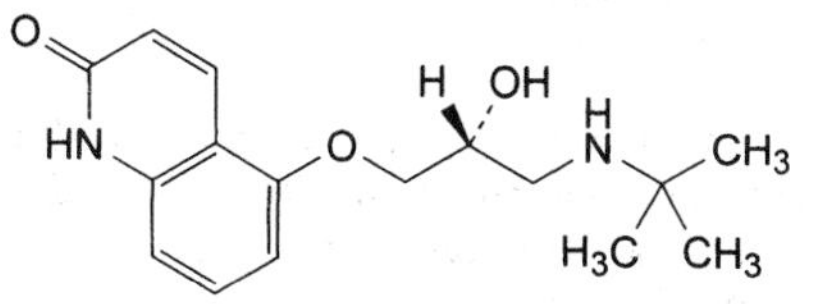

H. 5-[(2*RS*)-3-[(1,1-dimethylethyl)amino]-2-hydroxypropoxy]quinolin-2(1*H*)-one.

_____ *Ph Eur*

# Carvedilol

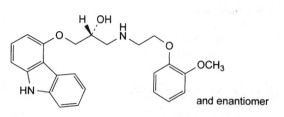

(*Ph Eur monograph 1745*)

$C_{24}H_{26}N_2O_4$        406.5        72956-09-3

**Action and use**

Beta-adrenoceptor antagonist; arteriolar vasodilator.

*Ph Eur* _____

## DEFINITION

(2*RS*)-1-(9*H*-Carbazol-4-yloxy)-3-[[2-(2-methoxyphenoxy)ethyl]amino]propan-2-ol.

**Content**

99.0 per cent to 101.0 per cent (dried substance).

## CHARACTERS

**Appearance**

White or almost white, crystalline powder.

**Solubility**

Practically insoluble in water, slightly soluble in alcohol, practically insoluble in dilute acids.

It shows polymorphism (*5.9*).

## IDENTIFICATION

Infrared absorption spectrophotometry (*2.2.24*).

*Comparison*   *Ph. Eur. reference spectrum of carvedilol.*

If the spectrum obtained shows differences, dissolve the substance to be examined in *2-propanol R*, evaporate to dryness and record a new spectrum using the residue.

## TESTS

**Related substances**

Liquid chromatography (*2.2.29*).

*Test solution*   Dissolve 25.0 mg of the substance to be examined in the mobile phase and dilute to 25.0 ml with the mobile phase.

*Reference solution (a)*   Dilute 1.0 ml of the test solution to 100.0 ml with the mobile phase. Dilute 1.0 ml of this solution to 10.0 ml with the mobile phase.

*Reference solution (b)*   Dissolve 5.0 mg of *carvedilol impurity C CRS* in 5.0 ml of the test solution and dilute to 100.0 ml with the mobile phase.

*Reference solution (c)*   Dilute 1.0 ml of reference solution (b) to 100.0 ml with the mobile phase. Dilute 2.0 ml of this solution to 10.0 ml with the mobile phase.

*Column:*

— *size: l* = 0.125 m, Ø = 4.6 mm,

— *stationary phase: octylsilyl silica gel for chromatography R* (5 μm),

— *temperature*: 55 °C.

*Mobile phase*   Dissolve 1.77 g of *potassium dihydrogen phosphate R* in *water R* and dilute to 650 ml with the same solvent; adjust to pH 2.0 with *phosphoric acid R* and add 350 ml of *acetonitrile R*.

*Flow rate*   1.0 ml/min.

*Detection*   Spectrophotometer at 240 nm.

*Injection* 20 µl.

*Run time* 8 times the retention time of carvedilol.

*Relative retention* With reference to carvedilol (retention time = about 4 min): impurity A = about 0.6; impurity C = about 3.5; impurity B = about 6.7.

*System suitability* Reference solution (b):
— *resolution*: minimum 17 between the peaks due to carvedilol and to impurity C.

*Limits*:
— *correction factor*: for the calculation of content, multiply the peak area of impurity A by 2,
— *impurity A*: not more than twice the area of the principal peak in the chromatogram obtained with reference solution (a) (0.2 per cent),
— *impurity C*: not more than twice the area of the corresponding peak in the chromatogram obtained with reference solution (c) (0.02 per cent),
— *any other impurity*: not more than the area of the principal peak in the chromatogram obtained with reference solution (a) (0.1 per cent),
— *total*: not more than 5 times the area of the principal peak in the chromatogram obtained with reference solution (a) (0.5 per cent),
— *disregard limit*: the area of the principal peak in the chromatogram obtained with reference solution (c) (0.01 per cent).

**Heavy metals** (*2.4.8*)
Maximum 10 ppm.

2.0 g complies with limit test C. Prepare the standard using 2.0 ml of *lead standard solution (10 ppm Pb) R*.

**Loss on drying** (*2.2.32*)
Maximum 0.5 per cent, determined on 1.000 g by drying in an oven at 105 °C.

**Sulphated ash** (*2.4.14*)
Maximum 0.1 per cent, determined on 1.0 g.

**ASSAY**
Dissolve 0.350 g in 60 ml of *anhydrous acetic acid R*. Titrate with *0.1 M perchloric acid*, determining the end-point potentiometrically (*2.2.20*).

1 ml of *0.1 M perchloric acid* is equivalent to 40.65 mg of $C_{24}H_{26}N_2O_4$.

**IMPURITIES**

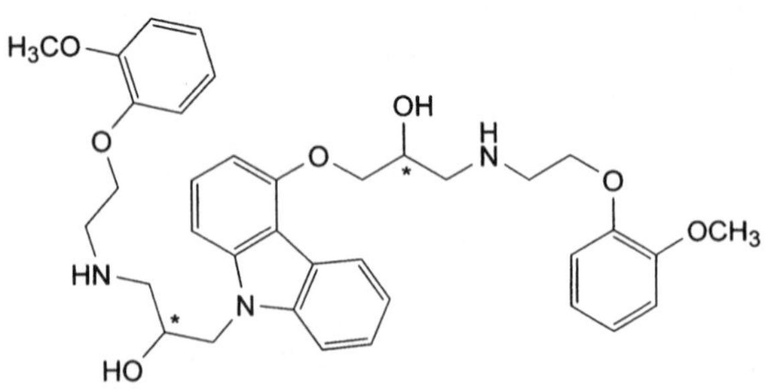

A. 1-[[9-[2-hydroxy-3-[[2-(2-methoxyphenoxy)ethyl]amino]propyl]-9*H*-carbazol-4-yl]oxy]-3-[[2-(2-methoxyphenoxy)ethyl]amino]propan-2-ol,

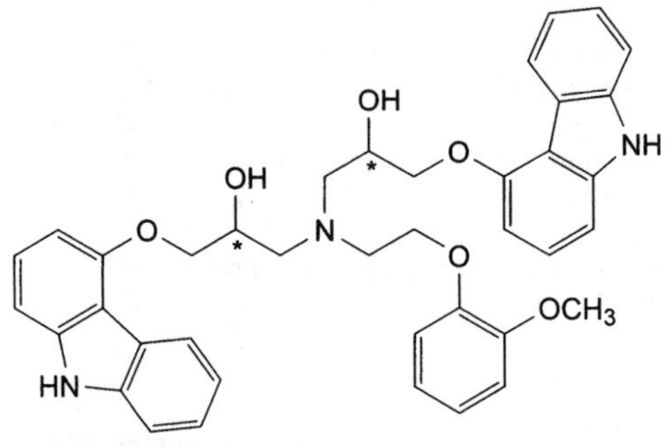

B. 1,1'-[[2-(2-methoxyphenoxy)ethyl]nitrilo]bis[3-(9*H*-carbazol-4-yloxy)propan-2-ol],

and enantiomer

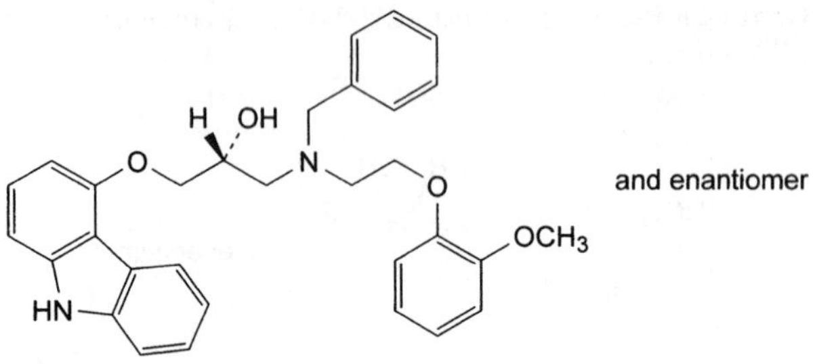

C. (2*RS*)-1-[benzyl[2-(2-methoxyphenoxy)ethyl]amino]-3-(9*H*-carbazol-4-yloxy)propan-2-ol.

*Ph Eur*

# Hydrogenated Castor Oil

(*Ph Eur monograph 1497*)

**Action and use**
Excipient.

*Ph Eur*

**DEFINITION**
Fatty oil obtained by hydrogenation of *Virgin Castor oil (0051)*. It consists mainly of the triglyceride of 12-hydroxystearic (12-hydroxyoctadecanoic) acid.

**CHARACTERS**
**Appearance**
Fine, almost white or pale yellow powder or almost white or pale yellow masses or flakes.

**Solubility**
Practically insoluble in water, slightly soluble in methylene chloride, very slightly soluble in anhydrous ethanol, practically insoluble in light petroleum.

**IDENTIFICATION**
A. Melting point (*2.2.14*): 83 °C to 88 °C.

B. Hydroxyl value (see Tests).

C. Composition of fatty acids (see Tests).

**TESTS**
**Acid value** (*2.5.1*)
Maximum 4.0, determined on 10.0 g dissolved in 75 ml of hot *ethanol (96) per cent R*.

**Hydroxyl value** (*2.5.3, Method A*)
145 to 165, determined on a warm solution.

**Iodine value** (*2.5.4, Method A*)
Maximum 5.0.

**Alkaline impurities**

Dissolve 1.0 g by gentle heating in a mixture of 1.5 ml of *ethanol (96) per cent R* and 3 ml of *toluene R*. Add 0.05 ml of a 0.4 g/l solution of *bromophenol blue R* in *ethanol (96) per cent R*. Not more than 0.2 ml of *0.01 M hydrochloric acid* is required to change the colour of the indicator to yellow.

**Composition of fatty acids** (*2.4.22*)

Use the mixture of calibrating substances in Table 2.4.22.-3.

*Test solution* Introduce 75 mg of the substance to be examined into a 10 ml centrifuge tube with a screw cap. Dissolve in 2 ml of *1,1-dimethylethyl methyl ether R1* by shaking and heat gently (50-60 °C). Add, when still warm, 1 ml of a 12 g/l solution of *sodium R* in *anhydrous methanol R*, prepared with the necessary precautions, and mix vigorously for at least 5 min. Add 5 ml of *distilled water R* and mix vigorously for about 30 s. Centrifuge for 15 min at 1500 g. Use the upper layer.

*Reference solution* Dissolve 50 mg of *methyl 12-hydroxystearate CRS* and 50 mg of *methyl stearate CRS* in 10.0 ml of *1,1-dimethylethyl methyl ether R1*.

*Column:*
— *material*: fused silica;
— *size*: l = 30 m; Ø = 0.25 mm;
— *stationary phase*: macrogol 20 000 R (film thickness 0.25 μm).

*Carrier gas* helium for chromatography R.

*Flow rate* 0.9 ml/min.

*Split ratio* 1:100.

*Temperature*:

|  | Time (min) | Temperature (°C) |
|---|---|---|
| Column | 0 - 55 | 215 |
| Injection port |  | 250 |
| Detector |  | 250 |

*Detection* Flame ionisation.

*Injection* 1 μl.

Calculate the fraction of each fatty-acid using the following expression:

$$A_{x,s,c} / \sum A_{x,s,c} \times 100 \text{ per cent } m/m$$

$A_{x,s,c}$ = corrected peak area of the fatty acid in the test solution

$$A_{x,s,c} = A_{x,s} \times R_c$$

$R_c$ = relative correction factor for the peak due to methyl 12-hydroxystearate

$$R_c = \frac{m_{1,r} \times A_{2,r}}{A_{1,r} \times m_{2,r}}$$

$R_c$ = 1 for peaks corresponding to each of the other specified fatty acids or any unspecified fatty acid

$m_{1,r}$ = mass of methyl 12-hydroxystearate in the reference solution

$m_{2,r}$ = mass of methyl stearate in the reference solution

$A_{1,r}$ = area of any peak due to methyl 12-hydroxystearate in the chromatogram obtained with the reference solution

$A_{2,r}$ = area of any peak due to methyl stearate in the chromatogram obtained with the reference solution

$A_{x,s}$ = area of the peaks due to any specified or unspecified fatty acid methyl esters

*Composition of the fatty acid fraction of the oil:*
— *palmitic acid*: not more than 2.0 per cent;
— *stearic acid*: 7.0 per cent to 14.0 per cent;
— *arachidic acid*: not more than 1.0 per cent;
— *12-oxostearic acid*: not more than 5.0 per cent;
— *12-hydroxystearic acid*: 78.0 per cent to 91.0 per cent;
— *any other fatty acid*: not more than 3.0 per cent.

**Nickel** (*2.4.31*):
Maximum 1 ppm.

**STORAGE**

In a well-filled container.

**IMPURITIES**

A. 12-oxostearic acid.

———————— Ph Eur

# Polyoxyl Castor Oil

(*Macrogolglycerol Ricinoleate*, *Ph Eur monograph 1082*)

**Action and use**

Excipient.

Ph Eur

**DEFINITION**

Contains mainly ricinoleyl glycerol ethoxylated with 30-50 molecules of ethylene oxide (nominal value), with small amounts of macrogol ricinoleate and of the corresponding free glycols. It results from the reaction of castor oil with ethylene oxide.

**CHARACTERS**

**Appearance**

Clear, yellow viscous liquid or semi-solid.

**Solubility**

Freely soluble in water, very soluble in methylene chloride, freely soluble in ethanol (96 per cent).

**Relative density**

About 1.05.

**Viscosity**

500 mPa·s to 800 mPa·s at 25 °C.

**IDENTIFICATION**

A. Iodine value (see Tests).

B. Saponification value (see Tests).

C. Thin-layer chromatography (*2.2.27*).

*Test solution* To 1 g of the substance to be examined add 100 ml of a 100 g/l solution of *potassium hydroxide R* and boil under a reflux condenser for 30 min. Allow to cool. Acidify the solution with 20 ml of *hydrochloric acid R*. Shake the mixture with 50 ml of *ether R* and allow to stand until separation of the layers is obtained. Transfer the clear upper layer to a suitable tube, add 5 g of *anhydrous sodium sulphate R*, close the tube and allow to stand for 30 min.

Filter and evaporate the filtrate to dryness on a water-bath. Dissolve 50 mg of the residue in 25 ml of *ether R*.

*Reference solution* Dissolve 50 mg of *ricinoleic acid R* in *methylene chloride R* and dilute to 25 ml with the same solvent.

*Plate* TLC *octadecylsilyl silica gel plate R*.

*Mobile phase* *methylene chloride R, glacial acetic acid R, acetone R* (10:40:50 *V/V/V*).

*Application* 2 μl.

*Development* Over a path of 8 cm.

*Drying* In a current of cold air.

*Detection* Spray with an 80 g/l solution of *phosphomolybdic acid R* in *2-propanol R* and heat at 120 °C for 1-2 min.

*Results* The principal spot in the chromatogram obtained with the test solution is similar in position and colour to the principal spot in the chromatogram obtained with the reference solution.

D. Place about 2 g of the substance to be examined in a test-tube and add 0.2 ml of *sulphuric acid R*. Close the tube using a stopper fitted with a glass tube bent twice at right angles. Heat the tube until white fumes appear. Collect the fumes in 1 ml of *mercuric chloride solution R*. A white precipitate is formed and the fumes turn a filter paper impregnated with *alkaline potassium tetraiodomercurate solution R* black.

## TESTS
### Solution S
Dissolve 5.0 g in *carbon dioxide-free water R* and dilute to 50 ml with the same solvent.

### Appearance of solution
Solution S is not more opalescent than reference suspension III (*2.2.1*) and not more intensely coloured than reference solution $BY_5$ (*2.2.2, Method II*). If intended for use in the manufacture of parenteral dosage forms, solution S is not more intensely coloured than reference solution $BY_6$ (*2.2.2, Method II*).

### Alkalinity
Dissolve 2.0 g in a hot mixture of 10 ml of *water R* and 10 ml of *ethanol (96 per cent) R*. Add *0.1 ml of bromothymol blue solution R1*. Not more than 0.5 ml of *0.1 M hydrochloric acid* is required to change the colour of the indicator to yellow.

### Acid value (*2.5.1*)
Maximum 2.0, determined on 5.0 g.

### Hydroxyl value (*2.5.3, Method A*)

### Iodine value (*2.5.4*)
25 to 35.

### Saponification value (*2.5.6*).
See table 1082.-1.

Table 1082.-1

| Ethylene oxide units per molecule (nominal value) | Hydroxyl value | Saponification value |
|---|---|---|
| 30 - 35 | 65 - 82 | 60 - 75 |
| 50 | 48 - 68 | 38 - 52 |

### Residual ethylene oxide and dioxan (*2.4.25*)
Maximum 1 ppm of residual ethylene oxide and 10 ppm of residual dioxan.

### Heavy metals (*2.4.8*)
Maximum 10 ppm.

12 ml of solution S, filtered if necessary, complies with test A. Prepare the reference solution using *lead standard solution (1 ppm Pb) R*.

### Water (*2.5.12*)
Maximum 3.0 per cent, determined on 2.000 g.

### Total ash (*2.4.16*)
Maximum 0.3 per cent, determined on 2.0 g.

## STORAGE
Protected from light.

## LABELLING
The label states:
— the amount of ethylene oxide reacted with castor oil (nominal value),
— where applicable, that the substance is suitable for use in the manufacture of parenteral dosage forms.

_____ Ph Eur

# Hydrogenated Polyoxyl Castor Oil

(*Macrogolglycerol Hydroxystearate,*
*Ph Eur monograph 1083*)

**Action and use**
Excipient.

Ph Eur

## DEFINITION
Contains mainly trihydroxystearyl glycerol ethoxylated with 7 to 60 molecules of ethylene oxide (nominal value), with small amounts of macrogol hydroxystearate and of the corresponding free glycols. It results from the reaction of hydrogenated castor oil with ethylene oxide.

## CHARACTERS
**Appearance:**
— if less than 10 units of ethylene oxide per molecule: yellowish, turbid, viscous liquid;
— if more than 20 units of ethylene oxide per molecule: white or yellowish semi-liquid or pasty mass.

**Solubility:**
— if less than 10 units of ethylene oxide per molecule: practically insoluble in water, soluble in acetone, dispersible in ethanol (96 per cent);
— if more than 20 units of ethylene oxide per molecule: freely soluble in water, in acetone and in ethanol (96 per cent), practically insoluble in light petroleum.

## IDENTIFICATION
A. It complies with the test for iodine value (see Tests).

B. It complies with the test for saponification value (see Tests).

C. Thin-layer chromatography (*2.2.27*).

*Test solution* To 1 g of the substance to be examined, add 100 ml of a 100 g/l solution of *potassium hydroxide R* and boil under a reflux condenser for 30 min. Allow to cool. Acidify the solution with 20 ml of *hydrochloric acid R*. Shake the mixture with 50 ml of *ether R* and allow to stand until separation of the layers is obtained. Transfer the clear upper layer to a suitable tube, add 5 g of *anhydrous sodium sulphate R*, close the tube and allow to stand for 30 min. Filter and evaporate the filtrate to dryness on a water-bath. Dissolve 50 mg of the residue in 25 ml of *ether R*.

*Reference solution* Dissolve 50 mg of *12-hydroxystearic acid R* in *methylene chloride R* and dilute to 25 ml with the same solvent.

*Plate* TLC octadecylsilyl silica gel plate R.

*Mobile phase* methylene chloride R, glacial acetic acid R, acetone R (10:40:50 *V/V/V*).

*Application* 2 μl.

*Development* Over a path of 8 cm.

*Drying* In a current of cold air.

*Detection* Spray with a 80 g/l solution of *phosphomolybdic acid R* in *2-propanol R* and heat at 120 °C for about 1-2 min.

*Results* The principal spot in the chromatogram obtained with the test solution is similar in position and colour to the principal spot in the chromatogram obtained with the reference solution.

D. Place about 2 g in a test-tube and add 0.2 ml of *sulphuric acid R*. Close the tube using a stopper fitted with a glass tube bent twice at right angles. Heat the tube until white fumes appear. Collect the fumes in 1 ml of *mercuric chloride solution R*. A white precipitate is formed and the fumes turn a filter paper impregnated with alkaline *potassium tetraiodomercurate solution R* black.

## TESTS

### Solution S
Dissolve 5.0 g of macrogolglycerol hydroxystearate with less than 40 units of ethylene oxide per molecule in a mixture of 50 volumes of *acetone R* and 50 volumes of *anhydrous ethanol R* and dilute to 50 ml with the same mixture of solvents.

Dissolve 5.0 g of macrogolglycerol hydroxystearate with 40 units or more of ethylene oxide per molecule in *carbon dioxide-free water R* and dilute to 50 ml with the same solvent.

### Appearance of solution
Solution S is not more opalescent than reference suspension III (*2.2.1*) and not more intensely coloured than reference solution $BY_6$ (*2.2.2, Method II*).

### Alkalinity
To 2 ml of solution S add 0.5 ml of *bromothymol blue solution R1*. The solution is not blue.

### Acid value (*2.5.1*)
Maximum 2.0, determined on 5.0 g.

### Hydroxyl value (*2.5.3, Method A*)
See Table 1083.-1.

### Iodine value (*2.5.4*)
Maximum 5.0.

### Saponification value (*2.5.6*)
See Table 1083.-1.

### Table 1083.-1

| Ethylene oxide units per molecule (nominal value) | Hydroxyl value | Saponification value |
|---|---|---|
| 7 | 115 - 135 | 125 - 140 |
| 25 | 70 - 90 | 70 - 90 |
| 40 | 60 - 80 | 45 - 69 |
| 60 | 45 - 67 | 40 - 51 |

### Residual ethylene oxide and dioxan (*2.4.25*)
Maximum 1 ppm of residual ethylene oxide and 10 ppm of residual dioxan.

### Heavy metals (*2.4.8*).
*Substances soluble in acetone/anhydrous ethanol* Maximum 10 ppm.

12 ml of solution S complies with limit test B. Prepare the reference solution using lead standard solution (1 ppm Pb) obtained by diluting *lead standard solution (100 ppm Pb) R* with a mixture of equal volumes of *acetone R* and *anhydrous ethanol R*.

*Substances soluble in water* Maximum 10 ppm.

12 ml of solution S complies with limit test A. Prepare the reference solution using *lead standard solution (1 ppm Pb) R*.

### Water (*2.5.12*)
Maximum 3.0 per cent, determined on 2.000 g.

### Total ash (*2.4.16*)
Maximum 0.3 per cent, determined on 2.0 g.

## LABELLING
The label states the number of ethylene oxide units per molecule (nominal value).

*Ph Eur*

# Refined Castor Oil

(*Ph Eur monograph 2367*)

*Ph Eur*

## DEFINITION
Fatty oil obtained from the seeds of *Ricinus communis* L. by cold expression. It is then refined. A suitable antioxidant may be added.

## PRODUCTION
During the expression step, the temperature of the oil must not exceed 50 °C.

## CHARACTERS

### Appearance
Clear, almost colourless or slightly yellow, viscous, hygroscopic liquid.

### Solubility
Slightly soluble in light petroleum, miscible with ethanol (96 per cent) and with glacial acetic acid.

### Relative density
About 0.958.

### Refractive index
About 1.479.

### Viscosity
About 1000 mPa·s.

## IDENTIFICATION
*First identification* B.

*Second identification* A.

A. A mixture of 2 ml of the substance to be examined and 8 ml of *ethanol (96 per cent) R* is clear (*2.2.1*).

B. Composition of fatty acids (see Tests).

## TESTS

### Appearance
The substance to be examined is clear (*2.2.1*) and not more intensely coloured (*2.2.2, Method II*) than 20 ml of a mixture of 0.25 ml of blue primary solution, 0.25 ml of red primary solution, 0.8 ml of yellow primary solution, and 18.7 ml of a solution prepared by diluting 4.0 ml of *hydrochloric acid R1* to 100.0 ml with *water R*.

### Optical rotation (*2.2.7*)
+ 3.5° to + 6.0°.

**Specific absorbance** (*2.2.25*)
Maximum 1.5, determined in *ethanol (96 per cent) R* at the absorption maximum between 268 nm and 270 nm.

**Acid value** (*2.5.1*)
Maximum 0.8.

Dissolve 5.00 g in 25 ml of the prescribed mixture of solvents.

**Hydroxyl value** (*2.5.3, Method A*)
Minimum 150.

**Peroxide value** (*2.5.5, Method A*)
Maximum 5.0.

**Unsaponifiable matter** (*2.5.7*)
Maximum 0.8 per cent, determined on 5.0 g.

**Oil obtained by extraction and adulteration.**
In a ground-glass-stoppered tube about 125 mm long and 18 mm in internal diameter, thoroughly mix 3 ml of the substance to be examined with 3 ml of *carbon disulphide R*. Shake for 3 min with 1 ml of *sulphuric acid R*. The mixture is less intensely coloured than a freshly prepared mixture of 3.2 ml of *ferric chloride solution R1*, 2.3 ml of *water R* and 0.5 ml of *dilute ammonia R1*.

**Composition of fatty acids**
Gas chromatography (*2.4.22*) with the following modifications.

Use the mixture of calibrating substances in Table 2.4.22.-3.

*Test solution* Introduce 75 mg of the substance to be examined into a 10 ml centrifuge tube with a screw cap. Dissolve in 2 ml of *1,1-dimethylethyl methyl ether R1* with shaking and heat gently (50-60 °C). To the still-warm solution, add 1 ml of a 12 g/l solution of *sodium R* in *anhydrous methanol R*, prepared with the necessary precautions, and shake vigorously for at least 5 min. Add 5 ml of *distilled water R* and shake vigorously for about 30 s. Centrifuge for 15 min at 1500 *g*. Use the upper layer.

*Reference solution* Dissolve 50 mg of *methyl ricinoleate CRS* and 50 mg of *methyl stearate CRS* in 10.0 ml of *1,1-dimethylethyl methyl ether R1*.

*Column:*
— *material*: fused silica;
— *size: l* = 30 m, Ø = 0.25 mm;
— *stationary phase: macrogol 20 000 R* (film thickness 0.25 μm).

*Carrier gas*   *helium for chromatography R*.

*Flow rate*   0.9 ml/min.

*Split ratio*   1:100.

*Temperature:*

|  | Time (min) | Temperature (°C) |
|---|---|---|
| Column | 0 - 55 | 215 |
| Injection port |  | 250 |
| Detector |  | 250 |

*Detection*   Flame ionisation.

*Injection*   1 μl.

Calculate the percentage content of each fatty acid by the normalisation procedure.

Correct the area of the peak due to methyl ricinoleate, multiplying by a factor (*R*) calculated using the following expression:

$$\frac{m_1 \times A_2}{A_1 \times m_2}$$

$m_1$ = mass of methyl ricinoleate in the reference solution;
$m_2$ = mass of methyl stearate in the reference solution;
$A_1$ = area of the peak due to methyl ricinoleate in the chromatogram obtained with the reference solution;
$A_2$ = area of the peak due to methyl stearate in the chromatogram obtained with the reference solution

*Composition of the fatty-acid fraction of the oil:*
— *palmitic acid*: maximum 2.0 per cent;
— *stearic acid*: maximum 2.5 per cent;
— *oleic acid and isomers*: 2.5 per cent to 6.0 per cent;
— *linoleic acid*: 2.5 per cent to 7.0 per cent;
— *linolenic acid*: maximum 1.0 per cent;
— *eicosenoic acid*: maximum 1.0 per cent;
— *ricinoleic acid*: 85.0 per cent to 92.0 per cent;
— *any other fatty acid*: maximum 1.0 per cent.

**Water** (*2.5.32*)
Maximum 0.2 per cent, determined on 5.00 g, if intended for use in the manufacture of parenteral dosage forms.

**STORAGE**
In an airtight, well-filled container, protected from light.

**LABELLING**
The label states, where applicable, that the substance is suitable for use in the manufacture of parenteral dosage forms.

_____ *Ph Eur*

# Virgin Castor Oil

Castor Oil
(*Ph Eur monograph 0051*)

**Action and use**
Stimulant laxative; emollient.

**Preparation**
Zinc and Castor Oil Ointment

*Ph Eur* _____

**DEFINITION**
Fatty oil obtained by cold expression from the seeds of *Ricinus communis L*. A suitable antioxidant may be added.

**CHARACTERS**
**Appearance**
Clear, almost colourless or slightly yellow, viscous, hygroscopic liquid.

**Solubility**
Slightly soluble in light petroleum, miscible with alcohol and with glacial acetic acid.

**Relative density**
About 0.958.

**Refractive index**
About 1.479.

**IDENTIFICATION**
*First identification   D.*
*Second identification   A, B, C.*

A. It complies with the test for optical rotation (see Tests).

B. It complies with the test for hydroxyl value (see Tests).

C. Iodine value (*2.5.4*): 82 to 90.

D. It complies with the test for composition of fatty acids (see Tests).

## TESTS

**Optical rotation** (*2.2.7*)
+ 3.5° to + 6.0°.

**Specific absorbance** (*2.2.25*)
Maximum 1.0, determined at the absorption maximum at 269 nm ± 1 nm.

To 1.0 g add *alcohol R* and dilute to 100.0 ml with the same solvent.

**Acid value** (*2.5.1*)
Maximum 2.0.

Dissolve 5.0 g in 25 ml of the prescribed mixture of solvents.

**Hydroxyl value** (*2.5.3, Method A*)
Minimum 150.

**Peroxide value** (*2.5.5*)
Maximum 10.0.

**Unsaponifiable matter** (*2.5.7*)
Maximum 0.8 per cent, determined on 5.0 g.

**Composition of fatty acids**
Gas chromatography (*2.4.22*) with the following modifications.

Use the mixture of calibrating substances in Table 2.4.22.-3.

*Test solution* Introduce 75 mg of the substance to be examined into a 10 ml centrifuge tube with a screw cap. Dissolve in 2 ml of *1,1-dimethylethyl methyl ether R1* with shaking and heat gently (50-60 °C). Add, when still warm, 1 ml of a 12 g/l solution of *sodium R* in *anhydrous methanol R*, prepared with the necessary precautions, and mix vigorously for at least 5 min. Add 5 ml of *distilled water R* and mix vigorously for about 30 s. Centrifuge for 15 min at 1500 *g*. Use the upper layer.

*Reference solution* Dissolve 50 mg of *methyl ricinoleate CRS* and 50 mg of *methyl stearate CRS* in 10.0 ml of *1,1-dimethylethyl methyl ether R1*.

*Column:*
— *material*: fused silica,
— *size*: *l* = 30 m, Ø = 0.25 mm,
— *stationary phase*: macrogol 20 000 R (film thickness 0.25 µm).

*Carrier gas*   helium for chromatography R.

*Flow rate*   0.9 ml/min.

*Split ratio*   1:100.

*Temperature:*

|  | Time (min) | Temperature (°C) |
|---|---|---|
| Column | 0 - 55 | 215 |
| Injection port |  | 250 |
| Detector |  | 250 |

*Detection*   Flame ionisation.

*Injection*   1 µl.

Calculate the percentage content of each fatty acid by normalisation.

Correct the area of the peak due to methyl ricinoleate, multiplying by a factor *R* calculated using the following expression:

$$R = \frac{m_1 \times A_2}{A_1 \times m_2}$$

$m_1$ = mass of methyl ricinoleate in the reference solution
$m_2$ = mass of methyl stearate in the reference solution
$A_1$ = area of the peak due to methyl ricinoleate in the chromatogram obtained with the reference solution
$A_2$ = area of the peak due to methyl stearate in the chromatogram obtained with the reference solution

*Composition of the fatty-acid fraction of the oil:*
— *palmitic acid*: maximum 2.0 per cent,
— *stearic acid*: maximum 2.5 per cent,
— *oleic acid and isomers* (C18:1 equivalent chain length on macrogol 20 000: 18.3): 2.5 per cent to 6.0 per cent,
— *linoleic acid* (C18:2 equivalent chain length on macrogol 20 000: 18.8): 2.5 per cent to 7.0 per cent,
— *linolenic acid* (C18:3 equivalent chain length on macrogol 20 000: 19.2): maximum 1.0 per cent,
— *eicosenoic acid* (C20:1 equivalent chain length on macrogol 20 000: 20.2): maximum 1.0 per cent,
— *ricinoleic acid* (equivalent chain length on macrogol 20 000: 23.9): 85.0 per cent to 92.0 per cent,
— *any other fatty acid*: maximum 1.0 per cent.

**Water** (*2.5.12*)
Maximum 0.3 per cent, determined on 5.0 g.

## STORAGE
In an airtight, well-filled container, protected from light.

*_____ Ph Eur*

# Cefaclor

(*Ph Eur monograph 0986*)

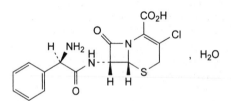

C$_{15}$H$_{14}$ClN$_3$O$_4$S,H$_2$O        385.8        *70356-03-5*

**Action and use**
Cephalosporin antibacterial.

**Preparations**
Cefaclor Capsules
Cefaclor Oral Suspension
Prolonged-release Cefaclor Tablets

*Ph Eur* _____

## DEFINITION
(6R,7R)-7-[[(2R)-2-Amino-2-phenylacetyl]amino]-3-chloro-8-oxo-5-thia-1-azabicyclo[4.2.0]oct-2-ene-2-carboxylic acid monohydrate.

Semi-synthetic product derived from a fermentation product.

**Content**
96.0 per cent to 102.0 per cent of C$_{15}$H$_{14}$ClN$_3$O$_4$S (anhydrous substance).

## CHARACTERS
**Appearance**
White or slightly yellow powder.

## Solubility

Slightly soluble in water, practically insoluble in methanol and in methylene chloride.

## IDENTIFICATION

Infrared absorption spectrophotometry (2.2.24).

*Comparison* *cefaclor CRS*.

## TESTS

**pH** (2.2.3)

3.0 to 4.5.

Suspend 0.250 g in *carbon dioxide-free water R* and dilute to 10 ml with the same solvent.

**Specific optical rotation** (2.2.7)

+ 101 to + 111 (anhydrous substance).

Dissolve 0.250 g in a 10 g/l solution of *hydrochloric acid R* and dilute to 25.0 ml with the same solution.

**Related substances**

Liquid chromatography (2.2.29).

*Test solution* Dissolve 50.0 mg of the substance to be examined in 10.0 ml of a 2.7 g/l solution of *sodium dihydrogen phosphate R* adjusted to pH 2.5 with *phosphoric acid R*.

*Reference solution (a)* Dissolve 2.5 mg of *cefaclor CRS* and 5.0 mg of *delta-3-cefaclor CRS* (impurity D) in 100.0 ml of a 2.7 g/l solution of *sodium dihydrogen phosphate R* adjusted to pH 2.5 with *phosphoric acid R*.

*Reference solution (b)* Dilute 1.0 ml of the test solution to 100.0 ml with a 2.7 g/l solution of *sodium dihydrogen phosphate R* adjusted to pH 2.5 with *phosphoric acid R*.

*Column:*
— *size:* $l = 0.25$ m, $\emptyset = 4.6$ mm;
— *stationary phase:* end-capped octadecylsilyl silica gel for chromatography R (5 μm).

*Mobile phase:*
— *mobile phase A:* 7.8 g/l solution of *sodium dihydrogen phosphate R* adjusted to pH 4.0 with *phosphoric acid R*;
— *mobile phase B:* mix 450 ml of *acetonitrile R* with 550 ml of mobile phase A;

| Time (min) | Mobile phase A (per cent *V/V*) | Mobile phase B (per cent *V/V*) |
|---|---|---|
| 0 - 30 | 95 → 75 | 5 → 25 |
| 30 - 45 | 75 → 0 | 25 → 100 |
| 45 - 55 | 0 | 100 |

*Flow rate* 1.0 ml/min.

*Detection* Spectrophotometer at 220 nm.

*Injection* 20 μl.

*System suitability* Reference solution (a):
— *resolution:* minimum 2 between the peaks due to cefaclor and impurity D; if necessary, adjust the acetonitrile content in the mobile phase;
— *symmetry factor:* maximum 1.2 for the peak due to cefaclor; if necessary, adjust the acetonitrile content in the mobile phase.

*Limits:*
— *any impurity:* for each impurity, not more than 0.5 times the area of the principal peak in the chromatogram obtained with reference solution (b) (0.5 per cent);
— *total:* not more than twice the area of the principal peak in the chromatogram obtained with reference solution (b) (2 per cent);
— *disregard limit:* 0.1 times the area of the principal peak in the chromatogram obtained with reference solution (b) (0.1 per cent).

## Heavy metals (2.4.8)

Maximum 30 ppm.

1.0 g complies with test C. Prepare the reference solution using 3 ml of *lead standard solution (10 ppm Pb) R*.

**Water** (2.5.12)

3.0 per cent to 6.5 per cent, determined on 0.200 g.

## ASSAY

Liquid chromatography (2.2.29).

*Test solution* Dissolve 15.0 mg of the substance to be examined in the mobile phase and dilute to 50.0 ml with the mobile phase.

*Reference solution (a)* Dissolve 15.0 mg of *cefaclor CRS* in the mobile phase and dilute to 50.0 ml with the mobile phase.

*Reference solution (b)* Dissolve 3.0 mg of *cefaclor CRS* and 3.0 mg of *delta-3-cefaclor CRS* (impurity D) in the mobile phase and dilute to 10.0 ml with the mobile phase.

*Column:*
— *size:* $l = 0.25$ m, $\emptyset = 4.6$ mm;
— *stationary phase:* octadecylsilyl silica gel for chromatography R (5 μm).

*Mobile phase* Add 220 ml of *methanol R* to a mixture of 780 ml of *water R*, 10 ml of *triethylamine R* and 1 g of *sodium pentanesulphonate R*, then adjust to pH 2.5 with *phosphoric acid R*.

*Flow rate* 1.5 ml/min.

*Detection* Spectrophotometer at 265 nm.

*Injection* 20 μl.

*System suitability:*
— *resolution:* minimum 2.5 between the peaks due to cefaclor and impurity D in the chromatogram obtained with reference solution (b); if necessary, adjust the concentration of methanol in the mobile phase;
— *symmetry factor:* maximum 1.5 for the peak due to cefaclor in the chromatogram obtained with reference solution (b);
— *repeatability:* maximum relative standard deviation of 1.0 per cent after 6 injections of reference solution (a).

## IMPURITIES

A. (2R)-2-amino-2-phenylacetic acid (phenylglycine),

B. (6R,7R)-7-amino-3-chloro-8-oxo-5-thia-1-azabicyclo[4.2.0]oct-2-ene-2-carboxylic acid,

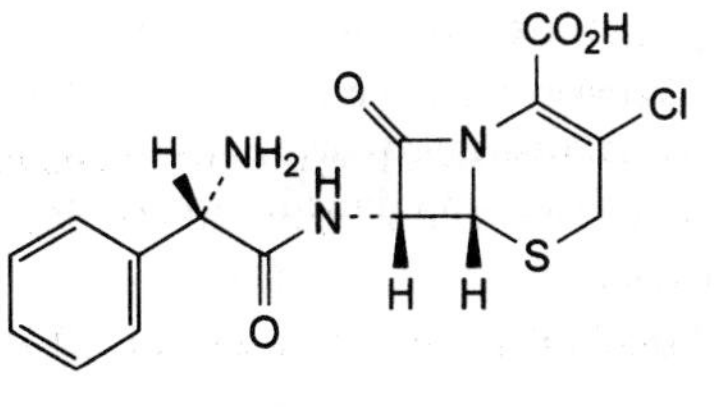

C. (6R,7R)-7-[[(2S)-2-amino-2-phenylacetyl]amino]-3-chloro-8-oxo-5-thia-1-azabicyclo[4.2.0]oct-2-ene-2-carboxylic acid,

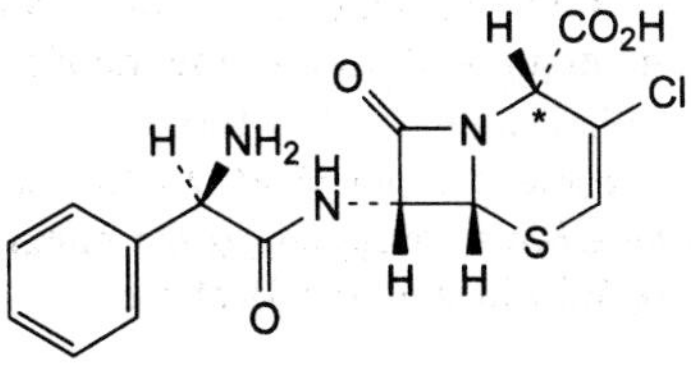

D. (2R,6R,7R)- and (2S,6R,7R)-7-[[(2R)-2-amino-2-phenylacetyl]amino]-3-chloro-8-oxo-5-thia-1-azabicyclo[4.2.0]oct-3-ene-2-carboxylic acid (delta-3-cefaclor),

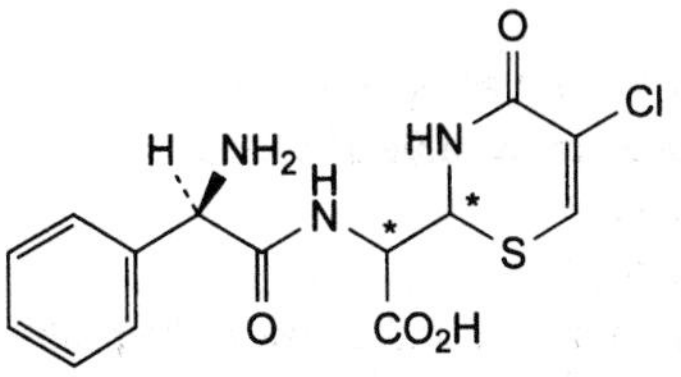

and epimer at C*

E. 2-[[(2R)-2-amino-2-phenylacetyl]amino]-2-(5-chloro-4-oxo-3,4-dihydro-2H-1,3-thiazin-2-yl)acetic acid,

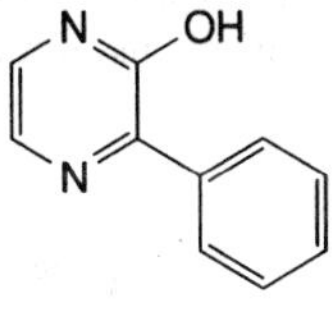

F. 3-phenylpyrazin-2-ol,

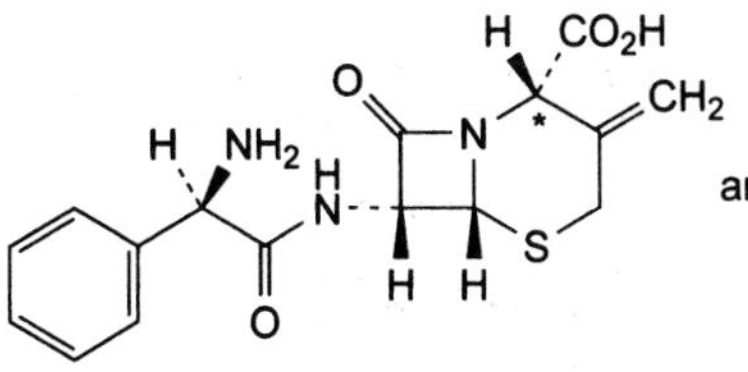

G. (2R,6R,7R)- and (2S,6R,7R)-7-[[(2R)-2-amino-2-phenylacetyl]amino]-3-methylene-8-oxo-5-thia-1-azabicyclo[4.2.0]octane-2-carboxylic acid (isocefalexine),

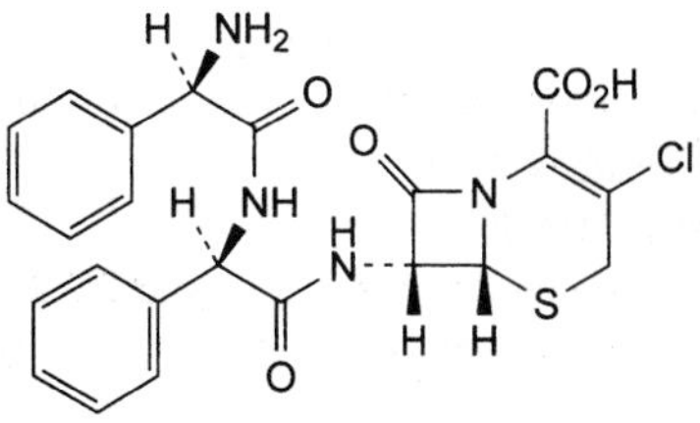

and epimer at C*

H. (6R,7R)-7-[[(2R)-2-[[(2R)-2-amino-2-phenylacetyl]amino]-2-phenylacetyl]amino]-3-chloro-8-oxo-5-thia-1-azabicyclo[4.2.0]oct-2-ene-2-carboxylic acid (N-phenylglycyl cefaclor).

_____ *Ph Eur*

# Cefadroxil Monohydrate

(*Ph Eur monograph 0813*)

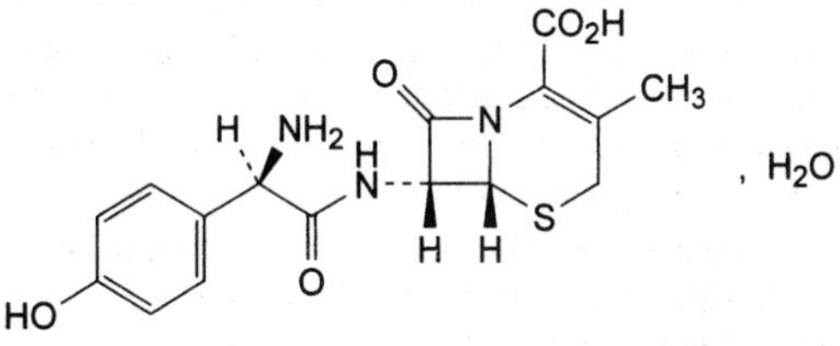

$C_{16}H_{17}N_3O_5S,H_2O$    381.4    *66592-87-8*

**Action and use**
Cephalosporin antibacterial.

**Preparations**
Cefadroxil Capsules
Cefadroxil Oral Suspension

*Ph Eur* _____

## DEFINITION
(6R,7R)-7-[[(2R)-2-Amino-2-(4-hydroxyphenyl)acetyl]amino]-3-methyl-8-oxo-5-thia-1-azabicyclo[4.2.0]oct-2-ene-2-carboxylic acid monohydrate.

Semi-synthetic product derived from a fermentation product.

**Content**
95.0 per cent to 102.0 per cent (anhydrous substance).

## CHARACTERS
**Appearance**
White or almost white powder.

**Solubility**
Slightly soluble in water, very slightly soluble in ethanol (96 per cent).

## IDENTIFICATION
Infrared absorption spectrophotometry (*2.2.24*).

*Comparison   cefadroxil CRS.*

## TESTS
**pH** (*2.2.3*)
4.0 to 6.0.

Suspend 1.0 g in *carbon dioxide-free water R* and dilute to 20 ml with the same solvent.

**Specific optical rotation** (*2.2.7*)
+ 165 to + 178 (anhydrous substance).

Dissolve 0.500 g in *water R* and dilute to 50.0 ml with the same solvent.

**Related substances**
Liquid chromatography (*2.2.29*).

*Test solution* Dissolve 50.0 mg of the substance to be examined in mobile phase A and dilute to 50.0 ml with mobile phase A.

*Reference solution (a)* Dissolve 10.0 mg of D-α-*(4-hydroxyphenyl)glycine CRS* (impurity A) in mobile phase A and dilute to 10.0 ml with mobile phase A.

*Reference solution (b)* Dissolve 10.0 mg of *7-aminodesacetoxycephalosporanic acid CRS* (impurity B) in *phosphate buffer solution pH 7.0 R5* and dilute to 10.0 ml with the same buffer solution.

*Reference solution (c)* Dilute 1.0 ml of reference solution (a) and 1.0 ml of reference solution (b) to 100.0 ml with mobile phase A.

*Reference solution (d)* Dissolve 10 mg of *dimethylformamide R* and 10 mg of *dimethylacetamide R* in mobile phase A and dilute to 10.0 ml with mobile phase A. Dilute 1.0 ml of this solution to 100.0 ml with mobile phase A.

*Reference solution (e)* Dilute 1.0 ml of reference solution (c) to 25.0 ml with mobile phase A.

*Column:*
— *size: l* = 0.10 m, Ø = 4.6 mm,
— *stationary phase*: spherical *octadecylsilyl silica gel for chromatography R* (5 μm).

*Mobile phase:*
— *mobile phase A*: phosphate buffer solution pH 5.0 R,
— *mobile phase B*: methanol R2,

| Time (min) | Mobile phase A (per cent *V/V*) | Mobile phase B (per cent *V/V*) |
|---|---|---|
| 0 - 1 | 98 | 2 |
| 1 - 20 | 98 → 70 | 2 → 30 |
| 20 - 23 | 70 → 98 | 30 → 2 |
| 23 - 30 | 98 | 2 |

*Flow rate* 1.5 ml/min.

*Detection* Spectrophotometer at 220 nm.

*Injection* 20 μl of the test solution and reference solutions (c), (d) and (e).

*Relative retention* With reference to cefadroxil (retention time = about 6 min):
dimethylformamide = about 0.4;
dimethylacetamide = about 0.75.

*System suitability:*
— *resolution*: minimum 5.0 between the peaks due to impurities A and B in the chromatogram obtained with reference solution (c),
— *signal-to-noise ratio*: minimum 10 for the 2<sup>nd</sup> peak in the chromatogram obtained with reference solution (e).

*Limits:*
— *impurity A*: not more than the area of the 1<sup>st</sup> peak in the chromatogram obtained with reference solution (c) (1.0 per cent),
— *any other impurity*: for each impurity, not more than the area of the 2<sup>nd</sup> peak in the chromatogram obtained with reference solution (c) (1.0 per cent),
— *total*: not more than 3 times the area of the 2<sup>nd</sup> peak in the chromatogram obtained with reference solution (c) (3.0 per cent),

— *disregard limit*: 0.05 times the area of the 2<sup>nd</sup> peak in the chromatogram obtained with reference solution (c) (0.05 per cent); disregard the peaks due to dimethylformamide and dimethylacetamide.

**N,N-Dimethylaniline** (*2.4.26, Method B*)
Maximum 20 ppm.

**Water** (*2.5.12*)
4.0 per cent to 6.0 per cent, determined on 0.200 g.

**Sulphated ash** (*2.4.14*)
Maximum 0.5 per cent, determined on 1.0 g.

**ASSAY**
Liquid chromatography (*2.2.29*).

*Test solution* Dissolve 50.0 mg of the substance to be examined in the mobile phase and dilute to 100.0 ml with the mobile phase.

*Reference solution (a)* Dissolve 50.0 mg of *cefadroxil CRS* in the mobile phase and dilute to 100.0 ml with the mobile phase.

*Reference solution (b)* Dissolve 5 mg of *cefadroxil CRS* and 50 mg of *amoxicillin trihydrate CRS* in the mobile phase and dilute to 100 ml with the mobile phase.

*Column:*
— *size: l* = 0.25 m, Ø = 4.6 mm,
— *stationary phase*: octadecylsilyl silica gel for chromatography R (5 μm).

*Mobile phase* acetonitrile R, a 2.72 g/l solution of *potassium dihydrogen phosphate R* (4:96 *V/V*).

*Flow rate* 1 ml/min.

*Detection* Spectrophotometer at 254 nm.

*Injection* 20 μl.

*System suitability* Reference solution (b):
— *resolution*: minimum 5.0 between the peaks due to cefadroxil and to amoxicillin.

Calculate the percentage content of cefadroxil.

**STORAGE**
Protected from light.

**IMPURITIES**

A. (2R)-2-amino-2-(4-hydroxyphenyl)acetic acid,

B. (6R,7R)-7-amino-3-methyl-8-oxo-5-thia-1-azabicyclo[4.2.0]oct-2-ene-2-carboxylic acid (7-ADCA),

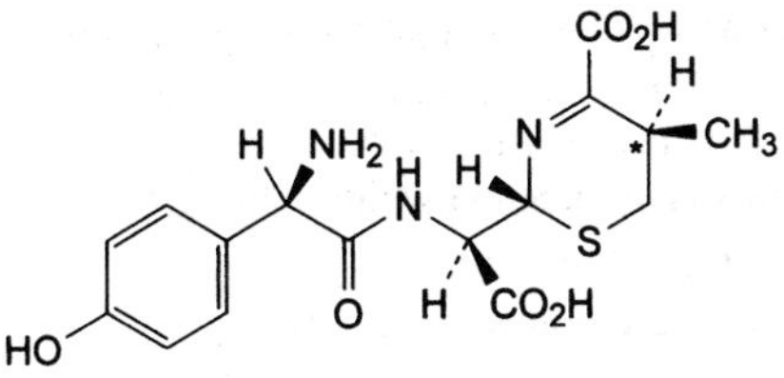

and epimer at C*

C. (2*R*,5*RS*)-2-[(*R*)-[[(2*R*)-2-amino-2-(4-hydroxyphenyl)acetyl]amino]carboxymethyl]-5-methyl-5,6-dihydro-2*H*-1,3-thiazine-4-carboxylic acid,

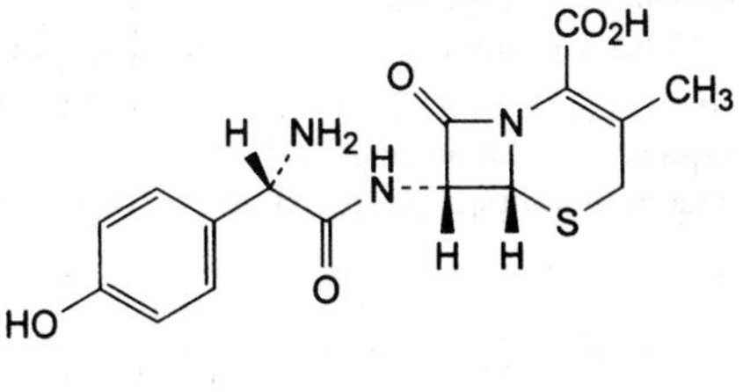

D. (6*R*,7*R*)-7-[[(2*S*)-2-amino-2-(4-hydroxyphenyl)acetyl]amino]-3-methyl-8-oxo-5-thia-1-azabicyclo[4.2.0]oct-2-ene-2-carboxylic acid (L-cefadroxil),

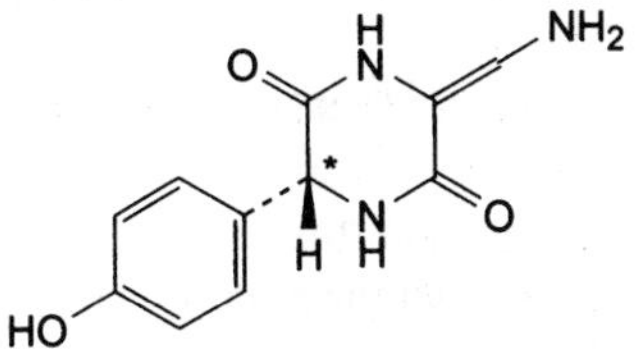

and epimer at C*

E. (6*RS*)-3-(aminomethylene)-6-(4-hydroxyphenyl)piperazine-2,5-dione,

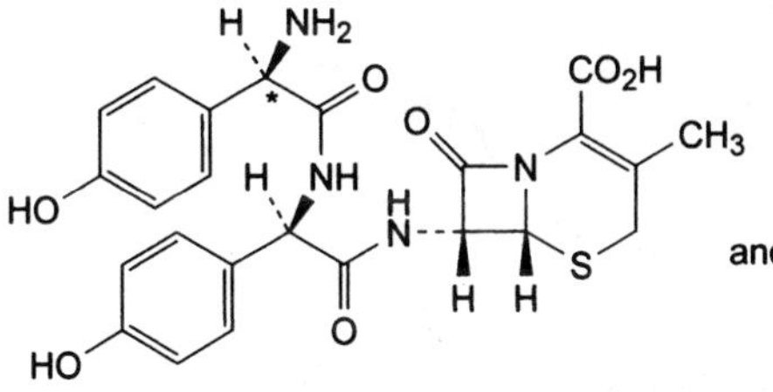

and epimer at C*

F. (6*R*,7*R*)-7-[[(2*R*)-2-[[(2*RS*)-2-amino-2-(4-hydroxyphenyl)acetyl]amino]-2-(4-hydroxyphenyl)acetyl]amino]-3-methyl-8-oxo-5-thia-1-azabicyclo[4.2.0]oct-2-ene-2-carboxylic acid,

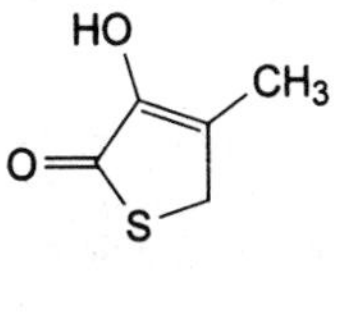

G. 3-hydroxy-4-methylthiophen-2(5*H*)-one,

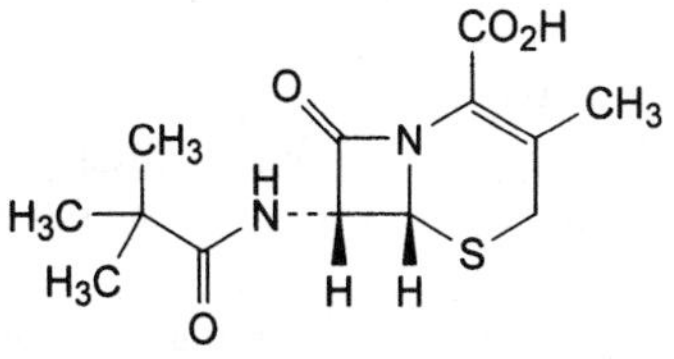

H. (6*R*,7*R*)-7-[(2,2-dimethylpropanoyl)amino]-3-methyl-8-oxo-5-thia-1-azabicyclo[4.2.0]oct-2-ene-2-carboxylic acid (7-ADCA pivalamide).

*Ph Eur*

# Cefalexin Monohydrate

(*Ph Eur monograph 0708*)

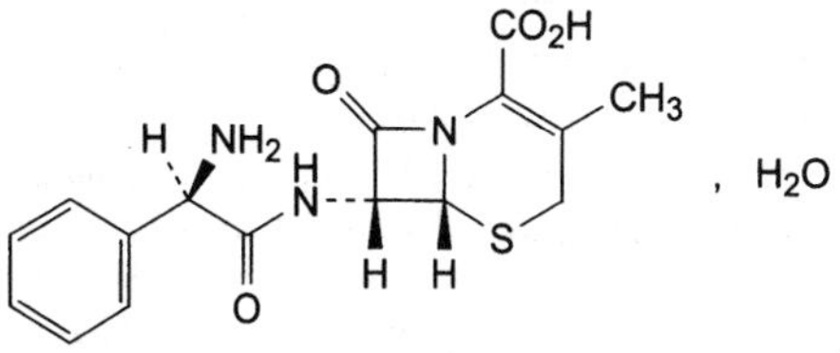

$C_{16}H_{17}N_3O_4S,H_2O$ 365.4 *23325-78-2*

**Action and use**

Cephalosporin antibacterial.

**Preparations**

Cefalexin Capsules

Cefalexin Oral Suspension

Cefalexin Tablets

*Ph Eur*

## DEFINITION

(6*R*,7*R*)-7-[[(2*R*)-2-Amino-2-phenylacetyl]amino]-3-methyl-8-oxo-5-thia-1-azabicyclo[4.2.0]oct-2-ene-2-carboxylic acid monohydrate.

Semi-synthetic product derived from a fermentation product.

**Content**

95.0 per cent to 102.0 per cent (anhydrous substance).

## CHARACTERS

**Appearance**

White or almost white, crystalline powder.

**Solubility**

Sparingly soluble in water, practically insoluble in ethanol (96 per cent).

## IDENTIFICATION

Infrared absorption spectrophotometry (*2.2.24*).

*Comparison* *cefalexin monohydrate CRS.*

## TESTS

**pH** (*2.2.3*)

4.0 to 5.5.

Dissolve 50 mg in *carbon dioxide-free water R* and dilute to 10 ml with the same solvent.

**Specific optical rotation** (*2.2.7*)

+ 149 to + 158 (anhydrous substance).

Dissolve 0.125 g in *phthalate buffer solution pH 4.4 R* and dilute to 25.0 ml with the same solvent.

**Related substances**

Liquid chromatography (*2.2.29*).

*Test solution*　Dissolve 50.0 mg of the substance to be examined in mobile phase A and dilute to 50.0 ml with mobile phase A.

*Reference solution (a)*　Dissolve 10.0 mg of D-*phenylglycine R* in mobile phase A and dilute to 10.0 ml with mobile phase A.

*Reference solution (b)*　Dissolve 10.0 mg of 7-aminodesacetoxycephalosporanic acid CRS in *phosphate buffer solution pH 7.0 R5* and dilute to 10.0 ml with mobile phase A.

*Reference solution (c)*　Dilute 1.0 ml of reference solution (a) and 1.0 ml of reference solution (b) to 100.0 ml with mobile phase A.

*Reference solution (d)*　Dissolve 10 mg of *dimethylformamide R* and 10 mg of *dimethylacetamide R* in mobile phase A and dilute to 10.0 ml with mobile phase A. Dilute 1.0 ml of this solution to 100.0 ml with mobile phase A.

*Reference solution (e)*　Dilute 1.0 ml of reference solution (c) to 20.0 ml with mobile phase A.

*Reference solution (f)*　Dissolve 10 mg of *cefotaxime sodium CRS* in mobile phase A and dilute to 10.0 ml with mobile phase A. To 1.0 ml of this solution add 1.0 ml of the test solution and dilute to 100 ml with mobile phase A.

*Column:*
— *size*: $l = 0.10$ m, $\emptyset = 4.6$ mm;
— *stationary phase*: spherical *octadecylsilyl silica gel for chromatography R* (5 μm).

*Mobile phase:*
— *mobile phase A*: *phosphate buffer solution pH 5.0 R*;
— *mobile phase B*: *methanol R2*;

| Time (min) | Mobile phase A (per cent *V/V*) | Mobile phase B (per cent *V/V*) |
|---|---|---|
| 0 - 1 | 98 | 2 |
| 1 - 20 | 98 → 70 | 2 → 30 |
| 20 - 23 | 70 → 98 | 30 → 2 |
| 23 - 30 | 98 | 2 |

*Flow rate*　1.5 ml/min.

*Detection*　Spectrophotometer at 220 nm.

*Injection*　20 μl of the test solution and reference solutions (c), (d), (e) and (f).

*System suitability:*
— *resolution*: minimum 2.0 between the peaks due to impurities A and B in the chromatogram obtained with reference solution (c) and minimum 1.5 between the peaks due to cefalexin and cefotaxime in the chromatogram obtained with reference solution (f).

*Limits:*
— *impurity B*: not more than the area of the $2^{nd}$ peak in the chromatogram obtained with reference solution (c) (1.0 per cent);
— *any other impurity*: not more than the area of the $1^{st}$ peak in the chromatogram obtained with reference solution (c) (1.0 per cent);
— *total*: not more than 3 times the area of the $1^{st}$ peak in the chromatogram obtained with reference solution (c) (3.0 per cent);
— *disregard limit*: the area of the $2^{nd}$ peak in the chromatogram obtained with reference solution (e) (0.05 per cent); disregard any peaks due to dimethylformamide or dimethylacetamide.

***N,N*-Dimethylaniline** (*2.4.26, Method B*)
Maximum 20 ppm.

**Water** (*2.5.12*)
4.0 per cent to 8.0 per cent, determined on 0.300 g.

**Sulphated ash** (*2.4.14*)
Maximum 0.2 per cent, determined on 1.0 g.

**ASSAY**

Liquid chromatography (*2.2.29*).

*Test solution*　Dissolve 50.0 mg of the substance to be examined in *water R* and dilute to 100.0 ml with the same solvent.

*Reference solution (a)*　Dissolve 50.0 mg of *cefalexin monohydrate CRS* in *water R* and dilute to 100.0 ml with the same solvent.

*Reference solution (b)*　Dissolve 10 mg of *cefradine CRS* in 20 ml of reference solution (a) and dilute to 100 ml with *water R*.

*Column:*
— *size*: $l = 0.25$ m, $\emptyset = 4.6$ mm;
— *stationary phase*: octadecylsilyl silica gel for chromatography R (5 μm).

*Mobile phase*　methanol R, acetonitrile R, 13.6 g/l solution of potassium dihydrogen phosphate R, water R (2:5:10:83 *V/V/V/V*).

*Flow rate*　1.5 ml/min.

*Detection*　Spectrophotometer at 254 nm.

*Injection*　20 μl.

*System suitability*　Reference solution (b):
— *resolution*: minimum 4.0 between the peaks due to cefalexin and cefradine.

Calculate the percentage content of cefalexin monohydrate.

**STORAGE**

Protected from light.

**IMPURITIES**

A. (2R)-2-amino-2-phenylacetic acid (D-phenylglycine),

B. (6R,7R)-7-amino-3-methyl-8-oxo-5-thia-1-azabicyclo[4.2.0]oct-2-ene-2-carboxylic acid (7-aminodesacetoxycephalosporanic acid, 7-ADCA),

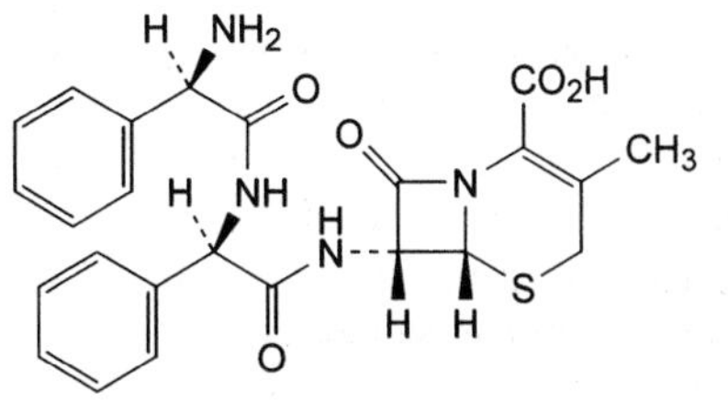

C. (6R,7R)-7-[[(2R)-2-[[(2R)-2-amino-2-phenylacetyl]amino]-2-phenylacetyl]amino]-3-methyl-8-oxo-5-thia-1-azabicyclo[4.2.0]oct-2-ene-2-carboxylic acid,

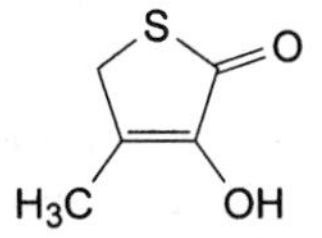

D. 3-hydroxy-4-methylthiophen-2(5H)-one,

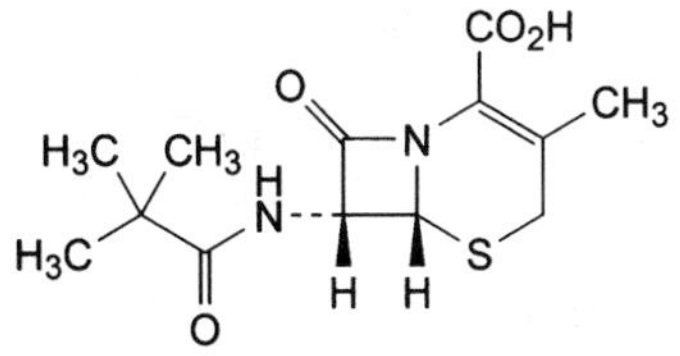

E. (6R,7R)-7-[(2,2-dimethylpropanoyl)amino]-3-methyl-8-oxo-5-thia-1-azabicyclo[4.2.0]oct-2-ene-2-carboxylic acid (7-ADCA pivalamide),

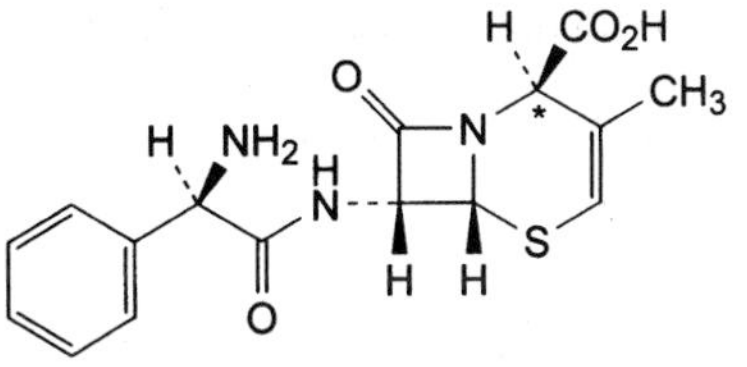

and epimer at C*

F. (2RS,6R,7R)-7-[[(2R)-2-amino-2-phenylacetyl]amino]-3-methyl-8-oxo-5-thia-1-azabicyclo[4.2.0]oct-3-ene-2-carboxylic acid (delta-2-cefalexin).

_____ Ph Eur

# Cefalotin Sodium

*(Ph Eur monograph 0987)*

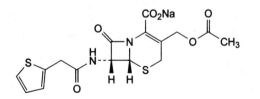

$C_{16}H_{15}N_2NaO_6S_2$      418.4      *58-71-9*

**Action and use**
Cephalosporin antibacterial.

Ph Eur

## DEFINITION
Sodium (6R,7R)-3-[(acetyloxy)methyl]-8-oxo-7-[(thiophen-2-ylacetyl)amino]-5-thia-1-azabicyclo[4.2.0]oct-2-ene-2-carboxylate.

Semi-synthetic product derived from a fermentation product.

**Content**
96.0 per cent to 102.0 per cent (anhydrous substance).

## CHARACTERS
**Appearance**
White or almost white powder.

**Solubility**
Freely soluble in water, slightly soluble in anhydrous ethanol.

## IDENTIFICATION
A. Infrared absorption spectrophotometry (2.2.24).

*Comparison* cefalotin sodium CRS.

B. It gives reaction (a) of sodium (2.3.1).

## TESTS
**Solution S**
Dissolve 2.50 g in *carbon dioxide-free water R* and dilute to 25.0 ml with the same solvent.

**Appearance of solution**
Solution S is clear (2.2.1) and its absorbance (2.2.25) at 450 nm is not greater than 0.20.

**pH** (2.2.3)
4.5 to 7.0 for solution S.

**Specific optical rotation** (2.2.7)
+ 124 to + 134 (anhydrous substance).

Dissolve 1.25 g in *water R* and dilute to 25.0 ml with the same solvent.

**Related substances**
Liquid chromatography (2.2.29)

*Prepare the solutions immediately before use.*

*Test solution (a)* Dissolve 75.0 mg of the substance to be examined in *water R* and dilute to 25.0 ml with the same solvent.

*Test solution (b)* Dilute 5.0 ml of test solution (a) to 50.0 ml with *water R*.

*Reference solution (a)* Dissolve 75.0 mg of *cefalotin sodium CRS* in *water R* and dilute to 25.0 ml with the same solvent. Dilute 5.0 ml of this solution to 50.0 ml with *water R*.

*Reference solution (b)* Dilute 1.0 ml of test solution (a) to 100.0 ml with *water R*.

*Reference solution (c)* Mix 1 ml of test solution (a), 1 ml of *hydrochloric acid R1* and 8 ml of *water R*. Heat at 60 °C for 12 min and cool to room temperature in iced water. Inject immediately.

*Reference solution (d)* Dissolve 5 mg of *cefalotin for impurity B identification CRS* in *water R* and dilute to 5 ml with the same solvent.

*Column:*
— *size:* l = 0.25 m, Ø = 4.6 mm;
— *stationary phase:* end-capped octadecylsilyl silica gel for chromatography R (5 μm);
— *temperature:* 40 °C.

*Mobile phase:*
— *mobile phase A:* mix 3 volumes of *acetonitrile R1* and 97 volumes of a 1.742 g/l solution of *dipotassium hydrogen*

*phosphate R* previously adjusted to pH 2.5 with *phosphoric acid R*;

— *mobile phase B:* mix 40 volumes of *acetonitrile R1* and 60 volumes of a 1.742 g/l solution of *dipotassium hydrogen phosphate R* previously adjusted to pH 2.5 with *phosphoric acid R*;

| Time (min) | Mobile phase A (per cent V/V) | Mobile phase B (per cent V/V) |
|---|---|---|
| 0 - 30 | 100 → 0 | 0 → 100 |
| 30 - 35 | 0 | 100 |
| 35 - 36 | 0 → 100 | 100 → 0 |
| 36 - 41 | 100 | 0 |

*Flow rate* 1.0 ml/min.

*Detection* Spectrophotometer at 220 nm.

*Injection* 20 µl of test solution (a) and reference solutions (b), (c) and (d).

*Relative retention* With reference to cefalotin (retention time = about 26 min): impurity C = about 0.2; impurity B = about 0.7; impurity A = about 0.8; impurity D = about 0.9.

*System suitability* Reference solution (c):
— *resolution*: minimum 7.0 between the peaks due to impurity D and cefalotin.

*Limits:*
— *impurity B*: not more than the area of the principal peak in the chromatogram obtained with reference solution (b) (1.0 per cent);
— *impurity D:* not more than 0.5 times the area of the principal peak in the chromatogram obtained with reference solution (b) (0.5 per cent);
— *any other impurity*: for each impurity, not more than 0.25 times the area of the principal peak in the chromatogram obtained with reference solution (b) (0.25 per cent);
— *total*: not more than 3 times the area of the principal peak in the chromatogram obtained with reference solution (b) (3.0 per cent);
— *disregard limit*: 0.05 times the area of the principal peak in the chromatogram obtained with reference solution (b) (0.05 per cent).

**N,N-Dimethylaniline** (*2.4.26, Method B*)
Maximum 20 ppm.

**2-Ethylhexanoic acid** (*2.4.28*)
Maximum 0.5 per cent.

**Water** (*2.5.12*)
Maximum 1.5 per cent, determined on 0.500 g.

**Bacterial endotoxins** (*2.6.14*)
Less than 0.13 IU/mg, if intended for use in the manufacture of parenteral dosage forms without a further appropriate procedure for the removal of bacterial endotoxins.

**ASSAY**
Liquid chromatography (*2.2.29*) as described in the test for related substances with the following modifications.

*Mobile phase* Mix 14 volumes of *acetonitrile R* and 86 volumes of a 6.967 g/l solution of *dipotassium hydrogen phosphate R* previously adjusted to pH 6.0 with *phosphoric acid R*.

*Detection* Spectrophotometer at 260 nm.

*Injection* 5 µl of test solution (b) and reference solution (a).

*Run time* 1.5 times the retention time of cefalotin (retention time = about 10 min).

Calculate the percentage content of $C_{16}H_{15}N_2NaO_6S_2$ using the chromatogram obtained with reference solution (a) and the declared content of *cefalotin sodium CRS*.

**STORAGE**
Protected from light. If the substance is sterile, store in a sterile, airtight, tamper-proof container.

**IMPURITIES**
*Specified impurities* B, D.

*Other detectable impurities* (the following substances would, if present at a sufficient level, be detected by one or other of the tests in the monograph. They are limited by the general acceptance criterion for other/unspecified impurities and/or by the general monograph *Substances for pharmaceutical use (2034)*. It is therefore not necessary to identify these impurities for demonstration of compliance. See also *5.10*.
*Control of impurities in substances for pharmaceutical use*) : A, C.

A. R = H: (6R,7R)-3-methyl-8-oxo-7-[(thiophen-2-ylacetyl)amino]-5-thia-1-azabicyclo[4.2.0]oct-2-ene-2-carboxylic acid (deacetoxycefalotin),

B. R = OH: (6R,7R)-3-(hydroxymethyl)-8-oxo-7-[(thiophen-2-ylacetyl)amino]-5-thia-1-azabicyclo[4.2.0]oct-2-ene-2-carboxylic acid (deacetylcefalotin),

C. (6R,7R)-3-[(acetyloxy)methyl]-7-amino-8-oxo-5-thia-1-azabicyclo[4.2.0]oct-2-ene-2-carboxylic acid (7-ACA),

D. (5aR,6R)-6-[(thiophen-2-ylacetyl)amino]-5a,6-dihydro-3H,7H-azeto[2,1-b]furo[3,4-d][1,3]thiazine-1,7(4H)-dione (cefalotin lactone).

Ph Eur

# Cefamandole Nafate

(*Ph Eur monograph 1402*)

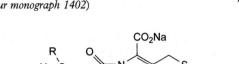

| Compound | R | Molecular Formula | $M_r$ |
|---|---|---|---|
| Cefamandole nafate | CHO | $C_{19}H_{17}N_6NaO_6S_2$ | 512.5 |
| Cefamandole sodium | H | $C_{18}H_{17}N_6NaO_5S_2$ | 484.5 |

$C_{19}H_{17}N_6NaO_6S_2$     512.5        *42540-40-9*

## Action and use
Cephalosporin antibacterial.

*Ph Eur*

## DEFINITION
Mixture of sodium (6*R*,7*R*)-7-[[(2*R*)-2-(formyloxy)-2-phenylacetyl]amino]-3-[[(1-methyl-1*H*-tetrazol-5-yl)sulphanyl]methyl]-8-oxo-5-thia-1-azabicyclo[4.2.0]oct-2-ene-2-carboxylate and sodium (6*R*,7*R*)-7-[[(2*R*)-2-hydroxy-2-phenylacetyl]amino]-3-[[(1-methyl-1*H*-tetrazol-5-yl)sulphanyl]methyl]-8-oxo-5-thia-1-azabicyclo[4.2.0]oct-2-ene-2-carboxylate (cefamandole sodium), with sodium carbonate.

Semi-synthetic product derived from a fermentation product.

**Content:**
— *cefamandole nafate* ($C_{19}H_{17}N_6NaO_6S_2$): 93.0 per cent to 102.0 per cent (anhydrous and sodium carbonate-free substance), for the sum of the content of cefamandole nafate and cefamandole sodium expressed as cefamandole nafate;
— *cefamandole sodium* ($C_{18}H_{17}N_6NaO_5S_2$): maximum 10.0 per cent (anhydrous and sodium carbonate-free substance);
— *sodium carbonate* ($Na_2CO_3$): 4.8 per cent to 6.4 per cent.

## CHARACTERS
**Appearance**
White or almost white powder.

**Solubility**
Freely soluble in water, sparingly soluble in methanol.

## IDENTIFICATION
A. Infrared absorption spectrophotometry (*2.2.24*).

*Comparison* cefamandole nafate CRS.

B. It gives reaction (a) of sodium (*2.3.1*).

## TESTS
**Solution S**
Dissolve 2.5 g in *carbon dioxide-free water R* and dilute to 25 ml with the same solvent.

**Appearance of solution**
Solution S is clear (*2.2.1*) and its absorbance (*2.2.25*) at 475 nm is not greater than 0.03.

**pH**
6.0 to 8.0 for solution S, measured after 30 min.

**Specific optical rotation** (*2.2.7*)
− 35.0 to − 45.0 (anhydrous and sodium carbonate-free substance).

Dissolve 1.00 g in *acetate buffer solution pH 4.7 R* and dilute to 10.0 ml with the same solvent.

**Related substances**
Liquid chromatography (*2.2.29*).

*Prepare the solutions immediately before use.*

*Solvent mixture* Mix 18 volumes of *acetonitrile R* and 75 volumes of a 10 per cent *V/V* solution of *triethylamine R* previously adjusted to pH 2.5 with *phosphoric acid R*.

*Test solution* Dissolve 0.100 g of the substance to be examined in the solvent mixture and dilute to 10.0 ml with the solvent mixture.

*Reference solution (a)* Dilute 1 ml of the test solution to 10 ml with the solvent mixture, then heat at 60 °C for 30 min.

*Reference solution (b)* Dilute 1.0 ml of the test solution to 100.0 ml with the solvent mixture.

*Column:*
— *size: l = 0.25 m, Ø = 4.6 mm;*
— *stationary phase: octadecylsilyl silica gel for chromatography R* (5 μm).

*Mobile phase:*
— *triethylamine phosphate solution:* dissolve 2.0 g of *sodium pentanesulphonate R* in 350 ml of *water R*, add 40 ml of *triethylamine R*, adjust to pH 2.5 with *phosphoric acid R* and dilute to 700 ml with *water R;*
— *mobile phase A:* mix 1 volume of the triethylamine phosphate solution and 2 volumes of *water R;*
— *mobile phase B:* mix equal volumes of the triethylamine phosphate solution, *methanol R* and *acetonitrile R;*

| Time (min) | Mobile phase A (per cent *V/V*) | Mobile phase B (per cent *V/V*) |
|---|---|---|
| 0 - 1 | 100 | 0 |
| 1 - 35 | 100 → 0 | 0 → 100 |
| 35 - 45 | 0 | 100 |
| 45 - 50 | 0 → 100 | 100 → 0 |

*Flow rate* 1.5 ml/min.

*Detection* Spectrophotometer at 254 nm.

*Injection* 20 μl loop injector.

*Relative retention* With reference to cefamandole nafate (retention time = about 24 min): cefamandole = about 0.8.

*System suitability* Reference solution (a):
— *resolution:* minimum 5.0 between the peaks due to cefamandole and cefamandole nafate.

*Limits:*
— *any impurity:* for each impurity, not more than the area of the principal peak in the chromatogram obtained with reference solution (b) (1.0 per cent);
— *total:* not more than 5 times the area of the principal peak in the chromatogram obtained with reference solution (b) (5.0 per cent);
— *disregard limit:* 0.1 times the area of the principal peak in the chromatogram obtained with reference solution (b) (0.1 per cent).

**2-Ethylhexanoic acid** (*2.4.28*)
Maximum 0.3 per cent *m/m*.

**Heavy metals** (*2.4.8*)
Maximum 20 ppm.

1.0 g complies with test C. Prepare the reference solution using 2 ml of *lead standard solution (10 ppm Pb) R.*

**Water** (*2.5.12*)
Maximum 2.0 per cent, determined on 0.500 g.

**Bacterial endotoxins** (*2.6.14*)
Less than 0.15 IU/mg, if intended for use in the manufacture of parenteral dosage forms without a further appropriate procedure for the removal of bacterial endotoxins.

## ASSAY

### Cefamandole nafate
Liquid chromatography (*2.2.29*).

*Prepare the solutions immediately before use.*

*Test solution*   Dissolve 50.0 mg of the substance to be examined in the mobile phase and dilute to 100.0 ml with the mobile phase.

*Reference solution (a)*   Dissolve 50.0 mg of *cefamandole nafate CRS* in the mobile phase and dilute to 100.0 ml with the mobile phase.

*Reference solution (b)*   Dilute 1 ml of the test solution to 10 ml with the mobile phase, then heat at 60 °C for 30 min.

*Column:*
— *size: l* = 0.25 m, Ø = 4.6 mm;
— *stationary phase: octadecylsilyl silica gel for chromatography R* (5 μm).

*Mobile phase*   Mix 25 volumes of *acetonitrile R* and 75 volumes of a 10 per cent *V/V* solution of *triethylamine R* previously adjusted to pH 2.5 with *phosphoric acid R.*

*Flow rate*   1.0 ml/min.

*Detection*   Spectrophotometer at 254 nm.

*Injection*   20 μl loop injector.

*System suitability:*
— *resolution*: minimum 7.0 between the 2 principal peaks in the chromatogram obtained with reference solution (b);
— *repeatability*: maximum relative standard deviation of 0.8 per cent after a series of single injections of not less than 3 freshly prepared reference solutions (a).

Calculate the percentage content of cefamandole nafate ($C_{19}H_{17}N_6NaO_6S_2$) from the sum of the contents of cefamandole nafate and cefamandole sodium expressed as cefamandole nafate, using the declared content of *cefamandole nafate CRS.*

1 mg of cefamandole sodium is equivalent to 1.0578 mg of cefamandole nafate.

### Sodium carbonate
Dissolve 0.500 g in 50 ml of *water R*. Titrate with *0.1 M hydrochloric acid*, determining the end-point potentiometrically (*2.2.20*).

1 ml of *0.1 M hydrochloric acid* is equivalent to 5.3 mg of $Na_2CO_3$.

## STORAGE
In an airtight container, protected from light. If the substance is sterile, store in a sterile, airtight, tamper-proof container.

## LABELLING
The label states that the substance contains sodium carbonate.

## IMPURITIES

A. (6*R*,7*R*)-7-[[(2*R*)-2-(formyloxy)-2-phenylacetyl]amino]-3-methyl-8-oxo-5-thia-1-azabicyclo[4.2.0]oct-2-ene-2-carboxylic acid (formylmandeloyl-7-amino-desacetoxy-cephalosporanic acid),

C. (6*R*,7*R*)-7-[[(2*R*)-2-(acetyloxy)-2-phenylacetyl]amino]-3-[[(1-methyl-1*H*-tetrazol-5-yl)sulphanyl]methyl]-8-oxo-5-thia-1-azabicyclo[4.2.0]oct-2-ene-2-carboxylic acid (*O*-acetylcefamandole),

D. 1-methyl-1*H*-tetrazole-5-thiol,

E. (6*R*,7*R*)-7-[[(2*R*)-2-(formyloxy)-2-phenylacetyl]amino]-3-[(acetyloxy)methyl]-8-oxo-5-thia-1-azabicyclo[4.2.0]oct-2-ene-2-carboxylic acid (formylmandeloyl-7-ACA).

_____ *Ph Eur*

# Cefapirin Sodium

(*Ph Eur monograph 1650*)

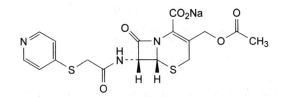

C₁₇H₁₆N₃NaO₆S₂     445.5     *24356-60-3*

**Action and use**
Cephalosporin antibacterial.

*Ph Eur* ___

## DEFINITION
Sodium (6*R*,7*R*)-3-[(acetyloxy)methyl]-8-oxo-7-[[[(pyridin-4-yl)sulphanyl]acetyl]amino]-5-thia-1-azabicyclo[4.2.0]oct-2-ene-2-carboxylate.

Semi-synthetic product derived from a fermentation product.

**Content**
96.0 per cent to 102.0 per cent (anhydrous substance).

## CHARACTERS
**Appearance**
White or pale yellow powder.

**Solubility**
Soluble in water, practically insoluble in methylene chloride.

## IDENTIFICATION
A. Infrared absorption spectrophotometry (*2.2.24*).

*Comparison*    cefapirin sodium CRS.

B. It gives reaction (a) of sodium (*2.3.1*).

## TESTS
**Appearance of solution**
Dissolve 2.0 g in *water R* and dilute to 10.0 ml with the same solvent. The solution is clear (*2.2.1*). Dilute 5.0 ml to 10.0 ml with *water R*. The absorbance (*2.2.25*) of this solution at 450 nm is not greater than 0.25.

**pH** (*2.2.3*)
6.5 to 8.5.

Dissolve 0.100 g in *carbon dioxide-free water R* and dilute to 10.0 ml with the same solvent.

**Specific optical rotation** (*2.2.7*)
+ 150 to + 165 (anhydrous substance).

Dissolve 0.500 g in *water R* and dilute to 25.0 ml with the same solvent.

**Related substances**
Liquid chromatography (*2.2.29*).

*Prepare the solutions immediately before use.*

*Test solution*    Dissolve 42 mg of the substance to be examined in the mobile phase and dilute to 200.0 ml with the mobile phase.

*Reference solution (a)*    Dissolve 42 mg of *cefapirin sodium CRS* in the mobile phase and dilute to 200.0 ml with the mobile phase.

*Reference solution (b)*    Dilute 1.0 ml of the test solution to 100.0 ml with the mobile phase.

*Reference solution (c)*    Dilute 1.0 ml of reference solution (b) to 20.0 ml with the mobile phase.

*Reference solution (d)*    Mix 1 ml of the test solution, 8 ml of the mobile phase and 1 ml of *hydrochloric acid R1*. Heat at 60 °C for 10 min.

*Column:*
— *size: l* = 0.30 m, Ø = 4 mm,
— *stationary phase: octadecylsilyl silica gel for chromatography R* (10 μm).

*Mobile phase*    Mix 80 ml of *dimethylformamide R*, 4.0 ml of *glacial acetic acid R* and 20 ml of a 4.5 per cent (m/m) solution of *potassium hydroxide R*. Dilute to 2 litres with *water R*.

*Flow rate*    2.0 ml/min.

*Detection*    Spectrophotometer at 254 nm.

*Injection*    20 μl of the test solution and reference solutions (b), (c) and (d).

*Run time*    Twice the retention time of cefapirin.

*Relative retention*    With reference to cefapirin (retention time = about 13 min): impurity B = about 0.3; impurity C = about 0.5; impurity A = about 0.75.

*System suitability*    Reference solution (d):
— *resolution*: minimum 2.0 between the peaks due to cefapirin and impurity A.

*Limits:*
— *any impurity*: for each impurity, not more than the area of the principal peak in the chromatogram obtained with reference solution (b) (1.0 per cent), and not more than 1 such peak has an area greater than 0.3 times the area of the principal peak in the chromatogram obtained with reference solution (b) (0.3 per cent),
— *total*: not more than twice the area of the principal peak in the chromatogram obtained with reference solution (b) (2.0 per cent),
— *disregard limit*: area of the principal peak in the chromatogram obtained with reference solution (c) (0.05 per cent).

**N,N-Dimethylaniline** (*2.4.26, Method B*)
Maximum 20 ppm.

**2-Ethylhexanoic acid** (*2.4.28*)
Maximum 0.5 per cent.

**Water** (*2.5.12*)
Maximum 2.0 per cent, determined on 0.300 g.

**Bacterial endotoxins** (*2.6.14*)
Less than 0.17 IU/mg, if intended for use in the manufacture of parenteral dosage forms without a further appropriate procedure for the removal of bacterial endotoxins.

## ASSAY
Liquid chromatography (*2.2.29*) as described in the test for related substances with the following modification.

*Injection*    Test solution and reference solution (a).

Calculate the percentage content of C₁₇H₁₆N₃NaO₆S₂.

## STORAGE
Protected from light. If the substance is sterile, store in a sterile, tamper-proof container.

## IMPURITIES

*Specified impurities   A, B, C.*

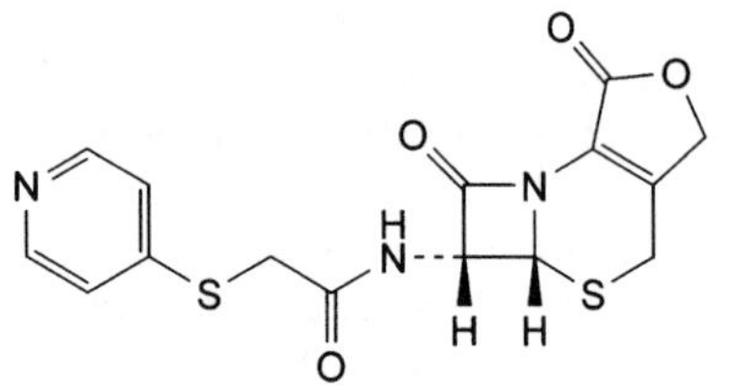

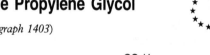

A. (5a*R*,6*R*)-6-[[[(pyridin-4-yl)sulphanyl]acetyl]amino]-5a,6-
dihydro-3*H*,7*H*-azeto[2,1-*b*]furo[3,4-*d*][1,3]thiazine-1,7(4*H*)-
dione (deacetylcefapirin lactone),

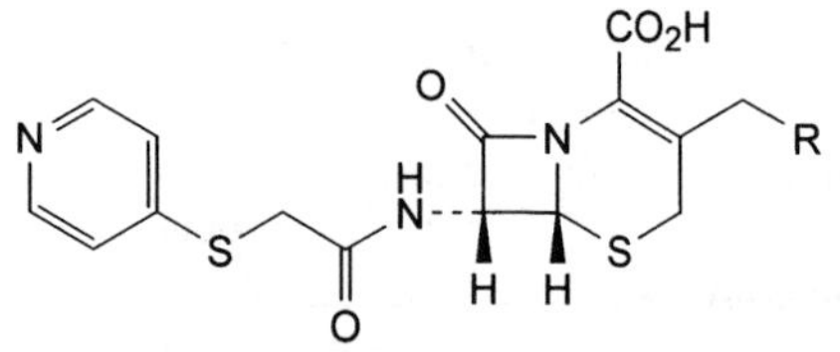

B. R = OH: (6*R*,7*R*)-3-(hydroxymethyl)-8-oxo-7-[[[(pyridin-
4-yl)sulphanyl]acetyl]amino]-5-thia-1-azabicyclo[4.2.0]oct-2-
ene-2-carboxylic acid (deacetylcefapirin),

C. R = H: (6*R*,7*R*)-3-methyl-8-oxo-7-[[[(pyridin-4-
yl)sulphanyl]acetyl]amino]-5-thia-1-azabicyclo[4.2.0]oct-2-
ene-2-carboxylic acid (deacetoxycefapirin).

_____ *Ph Eur*

# Cefatrizine Propylene Glycol

(*Ph Eur monograph 1403*)

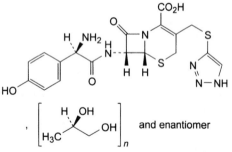

and enantiomer

$C_{18}H_{18}N_6O_5S_2,(C_3H_8O_2)_n$   462.5         *64217-62-5*

(cefatrizine)

## Action and use

Cephalosporin antibacterial.

*Ph Eur* _____

## DEFINITION

Mixture of (6*R*,7*R*)-7-[[(2*R*)-2-amino-2-
(4-hydroxyphenyl)acetyl]amino]-8-oxo-3-[[(1*H*-1,2,3-triazol-
4-yl)sulphanyl]methyl]-5-thia-1-azabicyclo[4.2.0]oct-2-ene-2-
carboxylic acid and propane-1,2-diol in molecular
proportions of about 1:1.

## Content

95.0 per cent to 102.0 per cent of $C_{18}H_{18}N_6O_5S_2$
(anhydrous substance).

## CHARACTERS

### Appearance

White or almost white powder.

### Solubility

Slightly soluble in water, practically insoluble in ethanol
(96 per cent) and in methylene chloride.

## IDENTIFICATION

A. Infrared absorption spectrophotometry (*2.2.24*).

*Comparison   cefatrizine propylene glycol CRS.*

B. Examine the chromatograms obtained in the test for
propylene glycol.

*Results*   The principal peak in the chromatogram obtained
with the test solution is similar in retention time and size to
the principal peak in the chromatogram obtained with
reference solution (b).

## TESTS

### Specific optical rotation (*2.2.7*)

+ 63 to + 69 (anhydrous substance).

Dissolve 0.400 g in *1 M hydrochloric acid* and dilute to
20.0 ml with the same acid.

### Propylene glycol

Gas chromatography (*2.2.28*).

### Solvent mixture

*acetone R, water R* (20:80 *V/V*).

*Internal standard solution*   Dissolve 1.0 g of
*dimethylacetamide R* in the solvent mixture and dilute to
50.0 ml with the solvent mixture.

*Test solution*   Introduce 0.40 g of the substance to be
examined into a ground-glass-stoppered test-tube. Add
3.0 ml of the internal standard solution, 1.0 ml of the solvent
mixture and 2.0 ml of *hydrochloric acid R*. Seal the test-tube
and shake.

*Reference solution (a)*   Dissolve 2.0 g of *propylene glycol R* in
the solvent mixture and dilute to 100.0 ml with the solvent
mixture.

*Reference solution (b)*   Introduce into a ground-glass-
stoppered test-tube 1.0 ml of reference solution (a) and
1.0 ml of the internal standard solution.

*Column:*
— *material*: stainless steel;
— *size*: *l* = 2 m, Ø = 2 mm;
— *stationary phase: ethylvinylbenzene-divinylbenzene
copolymer R* (150-180 µm).

*Carrier gas   nitrogen for chromatography R.*

*Flow rate*   30 ml/min.

*Temperature:*
— *column*: 200 °C;
— *injection port and detector*: 250 °C.

*Detection*   Flame ionisation.

*Injection*   1 µl of the test solution and reference solution (b).

*Limit:*
— *propylene glycol:* 13.0 per cent to 18.0 per cent.

### Related substances

Liquid chromatography (*2.2.29*).

*Test solution*   Dissolve 60.0 mg of the substance to be
examined in the mobile phase and dilute to 100.0 ml with
the mobile phase.

*Reference solution (a)*   Dissolve 60.0 mg of *cefatrizine
propylene glycol CRS* in the mobile phase and dilute to
100.0 ml with the mobile phase.

*Reference solution (b)*    Dissolve 30.0 mg of *cefatrizine impurity A CRS* in *buffer solution pH 7.0 R* and dilute to 100.0 ml with the same buffer solution.

*Reference solution (c)*    Dilute 0.6 ml of reference solution (a) to 100.0 ml with the mobile phase.

*Reference solution (d)*    Dilute 1.0 ml of reference solution (b) to 100.0 ml with *buffer solution pH 7.0 R.*

*Reference solution (e)*    To 1.0 ml of reference solution (a) add 1.0 ml of reference solution (b) and dilute to 10.0 ml with the mobile phase.

*Column:*
— *size: l* = 0.25 m, Ø = 4 mm;
— *stationary phase: octadecylsilyl silica gel for chromatography R* (5 μm).

*Mobile phase*    Mix 5 volumes of *acetonitrile R* and 95 volumes of a 2.72 g/l solution of *potassium dihydrogen phosphate R* in *water R.*

*Flow rate*    2 ml/min.

*Detection*    Spectrophotometer at 272 nm.

*Injection*    20 μl of the test solution and reference solutions (c), (d) and (e).

*Run time*    At least twice the retention time of cefatrizine.

*System suitability*    Reference solution (e):
— *resolution*: minimum 5.0 between the peaks due to cefatrizine and impurity A.

*Limits:*
— *impurity A*: not more than the area of the corresponding peak in the chromatogram obtained with reference solution (d) (0.5 per cent);
— *any other impurity*: for each impurity, not more than the area of the principal peak in the chromatogram obtained with reference solution (c) (0.6 per cent);
— *sum of impurities* other than A: not more than 3.5 times the area of the principal peak in the chromatogram obtained with reference solution (c) (2.1 per cent);
— *disregard limit*: 0.05 times the area of the principal peak in the chromatogram obtained with reference solution (c) (0.03 per cent).

**Water** (*2.5.12*)
Maximum 1.5 per cent, determined on 0.500 g.

**Sulphated ash** (*2.4.14*)
Maximum 0.1 per cent, determined on 1.0 g.

**ASSAY**
Liquid chromatography (*2.2.29*) as described in the test for related substances with the following modifications.

*Injection*    Test solution and reference solution (a).

*System suitability*    Reference solution (a):
— *repeatability*: maximum relative standard deviation of 1.0 per cent after 6 injections.

Calculate the percentage content of $C_{18}H_{18}N_6O_5S_2$ from the declared content of $C_{18}H_{18}N_6O_5S_2$ in *cefatrizine propylene glycol CRS.*

**IMPURITIES**
*Specified impurities    A*

A. (6*R*,7*R*)-7-amino-8-oxo-3-[[(1*H*-1,2,3-triazol-4-yl)sulphanyl]methyl]-5-thia-1-azabicyclo[4.2.0]oct-2-ene-2-carboxylic acid (7-ACA triazole).

_____ *Ph Eur*

# Cefazolin Sodium

(*Ph Eur monograph 0988*)

$C_{14}H_{13}N_8NaO_4S_3$         476.5         *27164-46-1*

**Action and use**
Cephalosporin antibacterial.

**Preparation**
Cefazolin Injection

*Ph Eur* _____

**DEFINITION**
Sodium (6*R*,7*R*)-3-[[(5-methyl-1,3,4-thiadiazol-2-yl)sulphanyl]methyl]-8-oxo-7-[(1*H*-tetrazol-1-ylacetyl)amino]-5-thia-1-azabicyclo[4.2.0]oct-2-ene-2-carboxylate.

Semi-synthetic product derived from a fermentation product.

**Content**
95.0 per cent to 102.0 per cent (anhydrous substance).

**CHARACTERS**
**Appearance**
White or almost white powder, very hygroscopic.

**Solubility**
Freely soluble in water, very slightly soluble in ethanol (96 per cent).

It shows polymorphism (*5.9*).

**IDENTIFICATION**
A. Infrared absorption spectrophotometry (*2.2.24*).

*Preparation*    Dissolve 0.150 g in 5 ml of *water R*, add 0.5 ml of *dilute acetic acid R*, swirl and allow to stand for 10 min in iced water. Filter the precipitate and rinse with 1-2 ml of *water R*. Dissolve in a mixture of 1 volume of *water R* and 9 volumes of *acetone R*. Evaporate the solvent almost to dryness, then dry in an oven at 60 °C for 30 min.

*Comparison    cefazolin CRS.*

B. It gives reaction (a) of sodium (*2.3.1*).

## TESTS

### Solution S

Dissolve 2.50 g in *carbon dioxide-free water R* and dilute to 25.0 ml with the same solvent.

### Appearance of solution

Solution S is clear (*2.2.1*) and its absorbance (*2.2.25*) at 430 nm is not greater than 0.15.

### pH (*2.2.3*)

4.0 to 6.0 for solution S.

### Specific optical rotation (*2.2.7*)

− 15 to − 24 (anhydrous substance).

Dissolve 1.25 g in *water R* and dilute to 25.0 ml with the same solvent.

### Absorbance (*2.2.25*)

Dissolve 0.100 g in *water R* and dilute to 100.0 ml with the same solvent. Dilute 2.0 ml of the solution to 100.0 ml with *sodium hydrogen carbonate solution R*. Examined between 220 nm and 350 nm, the solution shows an absorption maximum at 272 nm. The specific absorbance at the maximum is 260 to 300 (anhydrous substance).

### Related substances

Liquid chromatography (*2.2.29*).

*Test solution* Dissolve 50.0 mg of the substance to be examined in mobile phase A and dilute to 20.0 ml with the same mobile phase.

*Reference solution (a)* Dilute 1.0 ml of the test solution to 100.0 ml with mobile phase A.

*Reference solution (b)* Dissolve 20 mg of the substance to be examined in 10 ml of a 2 g/l solution of *sodium hydroxide R*. Allow to stand for 15-30 min. Dilute 1.0 ml of the solution to 20 ml with mobile phase A.

*Column:*
— *size*: *l* = 0.125 m, Ø = 4.0 mm;
— *stationary phase*: *octadecylsilyl silica gel for chromatography* R (3 µm);
— *temperature*: 45 °C.

*Mobile phase:*
— *mobile phase A:* solution containing 14.54 g/l of *disodium hydrogen phosphate R* and 3.53 g/l of *potassium dihydrogen phosphate R;*
— *mobile phase B: acetonitrile for chromatography R;*

| Time (min) | Mobile phase A (per cent V/V) | Mobile phase B (per cent V/V) |
|---|---|---|
| 0 - 2 | 98 | 2 |
| 2 - 4 | 98 → 85 | 2 → 15 |
| 4 - 10 | 85 → 60 | 15 → 40 |
| 10 - 11.5 | 60 → 35 | 40 → 65 |
| 11.5 - 12 | 35 | 65 |
| 12 - 15 | 35 → 98 | 65 → 2 |
| 15 - 21 | 98 | 2 |

*Flow rate* 1.2 ml/min.

*Detection* Spectrophotometer at 254 nm.

*Injection* 5 µl.

*System suitability* Reference solution (b):
— *resolution*: minimum 2.0 between the peaks due to cefazolin and impurity L (see Figure 0988.-1).

*Limits:*
— *any impurity*: for each impurity, not more than the area of the principal peak in the chromatogram obtained with reference solution (a) (1.0 per cent);
— *total*: not more than 3.5 times the area of the principal peak in the chromatogram obtained with reference solution (a) (3.5 per cent);
— *disregard limit*: 0.05 times the area of the principal peak in the chromatogram obtained with reference solution (a) (0.05 per cent).

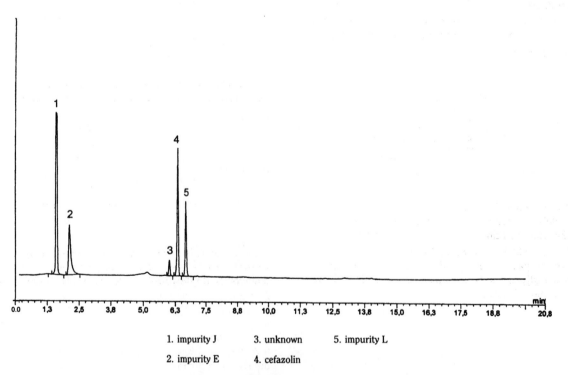

1. impurity J    3. unknown    5. impurity L
2. impurity E    4. cefazolin

Figure 0988.-1. − *Chromatogram for the test for related substances of cefazolin sodium: reference solution (b) (in situ degradation)*

**N,N-Dimethylaniline** (*2.4.26, Method B*)
Maximum 20 ppm.

**Water** (*2.5.12*)
Maximum 6.0 per cent, determined on 0.300 g.

**Bacterial endotoxins** (*2.6.14*)
less than 0.15 IU/mg, if intended for use in the manufacture
of parenteral dosage forms without a further appropriate
procedure for the removal of bacterial endotoxins.

## ASSAY

Liquid chromatography (*2.2.29*).

*Test solution* Dissolve 50.0 mg of the substance to be
examined in the mobile phase and dilute to 50.0 ml with the
mobile phase.

*Reference solution (a)* Dissolve 50.0 mg of *cefazolin CRS* in
the mobile phase and dilute to 50.0 ml with the mobile
phase.

*Reference solution (b)* Dissolve 5.0 mg of *cefuroxime
sodium CRS* in 10.0 ml of reference solution (a) and dilute to
100.0 ml with the mobile phase.

*Column:*
— *size*: l = 0.25 m, Ø = 4.6 mm;
— *stationary phase: octadecylsilyl silica gel for chromatography R*
 (5 µm).

*Mobile phase* Mix 10 volumes of *acetonitrile R* and
90 volumes of a solution containing 2.77 g/l of *disodium
hydrogen phosphate R* and 1.86 g/l of *citric acid R*.

*Flow rate* 1.0 ml/min.

*Detection* Spectrophotometer at 270 nm.

*Injection* 20 µl.

*System suitability* Reference solution (b):
— *resolution*: minimum 2.0 between the peaks due to
 cefazolin and cefuroxime.

Calculate the percentage content of cefazolin sodium by
multiplying the percentage content of cefazolin by 1.048.

## STORAGE

In an airtight container, protected from light. If the substance
is sterile, store in a sterile, airtight, tamper-proof container.

## IMPURITIES

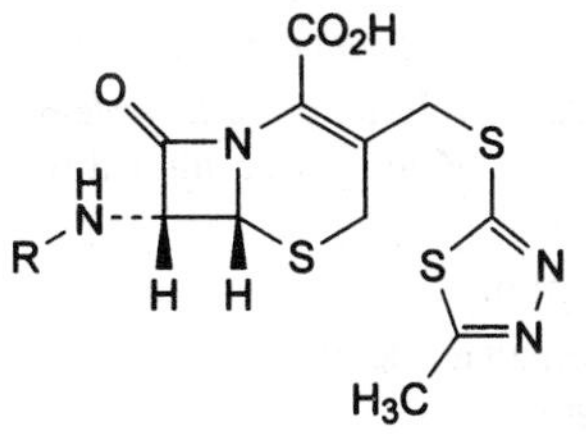

A. R = H: (6R,7R)-7-amino-3-[[(5-methyl-1,3,4-thiadiazol-
2-yl)sulphanyl]methyl]-8-oxo-5-thia-1-azabicyclo[4.2.0]oct-2-
ene-2-carboxylic acid,

B. R = CO-C(CH₃)₃: (6R,7R)-7-[(2,2-
dimethylpropanoyl)amino]-3-[[(5-methyl-1,3,4-thiadiazol-2-
yl)sulphanyl]methyl]-8-oxo-5-thia-1-azabicyclo[4.2.0]oct-2-
ene-2-carboxylic acid,

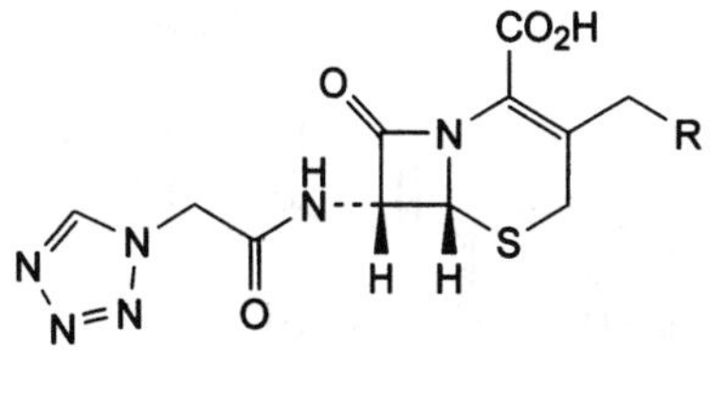

C. R = H: (6R,7R)-3-methyl-8-oxo-7-[(1H-tetrazol-1-
ylacetyl)amino]-5-thia-1-azabicyclo[4.2.0]oct-2-ene-2-
carboxylic acid,

D. R = O-CO-CH₃: (6R,7R)-3-[(acetyloxy)methyl]-8-oxo-7-
[(1H-tetrazol-1-ylacetyl)amino]-5-thia-1-azabicyclo[4.2.0]oct-
2-ene-2-carboxylic acid,

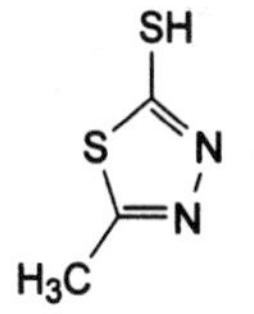

E. 5-methyl-1,3,4-thiadiazol-2-thiol (MMTD),

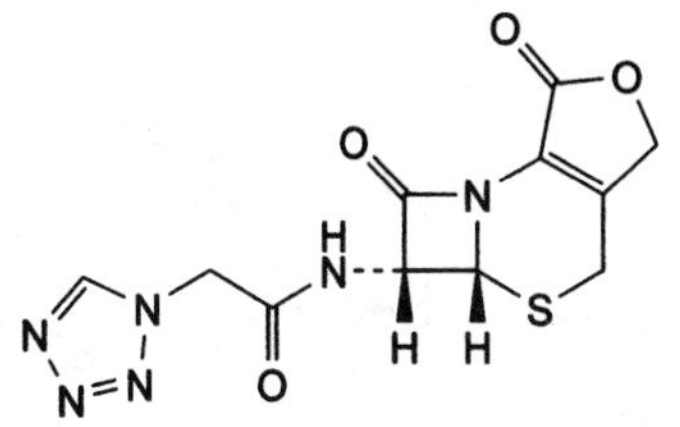

G. (5aR,6R)-6-[(1H-tetrazol-1-ylacetyl)amino]-5a,6-dihydro-
3H,7H-azeto[2,1-b]furo[3,4-d][1,3]thiazine-1,7(4H)-dione,

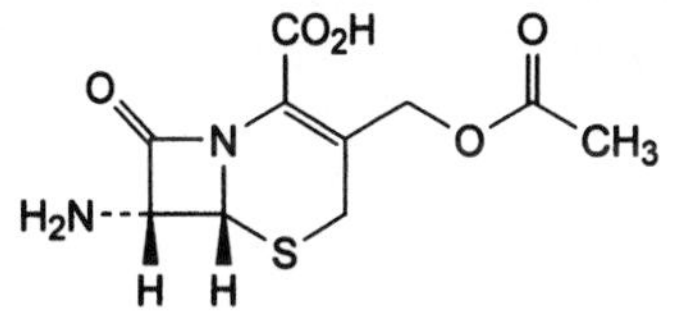

H. (6R,7R)-3-[(acetyloxy)methyl]-7-amino-8-oxo-5-thia-1-
azabicyclo[4.2.0]oct-2-ene-2-carboxylic acid (7-ACA),

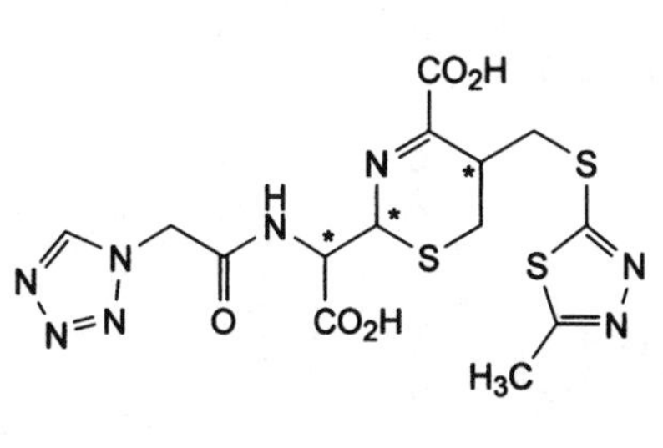

I. 2-[carboxy[(1H-tetrazol-1-ylacetyl)amino]methyl]-5-
[[(5-methyl-1,3,4-thiadiazol-2-yl)sulphanyl]methyl]-5,6-
dihydro-2H-1,3-thiazine-4-carboxylic acid (cefazoloic acid),

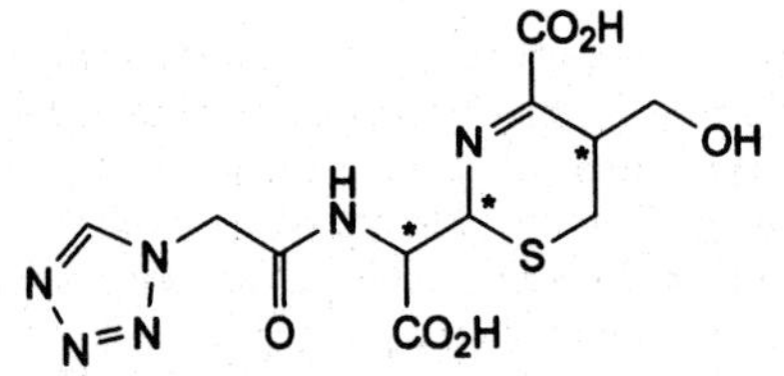

J. 2-[carboxy[(1*H*-tetrazol-1-ylacetyl)amino]methyl]-5-(hydroxymethyl)-5,6-dihydro-2*H*-1,3-thiazine-4-carboxylic acid (hydrolysed cefazoloic acid),

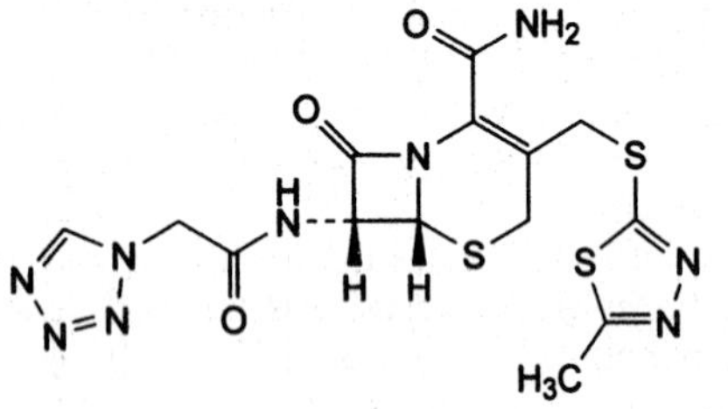

K. (6*R*,7*R*)-3-[[(5-methyl-1,3,4-thiadiazol-2-yl)sulphanyl]methyl]-8-oxo-7-[(1*H*-tetrazol-1-ylacetyl)amino]-5-thia-1-azabicyclo[4.2.0]oct-2-ene-2-carboxamide (cefazolinamide),

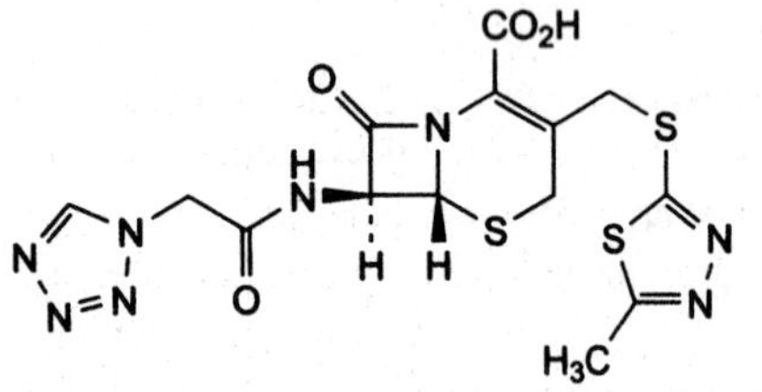

L. (6*R*,7*S*)-3-[[(5-methyl-1,3,4-thiadiazol-2-yl)sulphanyl]methyl]-8-oxo-7-[(1*H*-tetrazol-1-ylacetyl)amino]-5-thia-1-azabicyclo[4.2.0]oct-2-ene-2-carboxylic acid.

*————————————————— Ph Eur*

# Cefepime Hydrochloride Monohydrate

*(Cefepime Dihydrochloride Monohydrate, Ph Eur monograph 2126)*

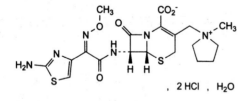

, 2 HCl , H$_2$O

C$_{19}$H$_{24}$N$_6$O$_5$S$_2$,2HCl,H$_2$O    571.5    *123171-59-5*

**Action and use**

Cephalosporin antibacterial.

*Ph Eur* _____

**DEFINITION**

(6*R*,7*R*)-7-[[(2*Z*)-(2-Aminothiazol-4-yl)(methoxyimino)acetyl]amino]-3-[(1-methylpyrrolidinio)methyl]-8-oxo-5-thia-1-azabicyclo[4.2.0]oct-2-ene-2-carboxylate dihydrochloride

monohydrate. Semi-synthetic product derived from a fermentation product.

**Content**

97.0 per cent to 102.0 per cent (anhydrous substance).

**CHARACTERS**

**Appearance**

White or almost white, crystalline powder.

**Solubility**

Freely soluble in water and in methanol, practically insoluble in methylene chloride.

**IDENTIFICATION**

A. Infrared absorption spectrophotometry (*2.2.24*).

*Comparison   cefepime dihydrochloride monohydrate CRS* .

B. It gives reaction (a) of chlorides (*2.3.1*).

**TESTS**

**Appearance of solution**

The solution is clear (*2.2.1*) and not more intensely coloured than reference solution Y$_3$ (*2.2.2, Method II*).

Dissolve 2.0 g in *water R* and dilute to 20 ml with the same solvent.

**Specific optical rotation** (*2.2.7*)

+ 40 to + 45 (anhydrous substance).

Dissolve 0.250 g in *water R* and dilute to 25.0 ml with the same solvent.

**Impurity G**

Liquid chromatography (*2.2.29*). *Prepare the solutions immediately before use.*

*Test solution*   Dissolve 0.100 g of the substance to be examined in *0.01 M nitric acid* and dilute to 10.0 ml with the same acid.

*Reference solution (a)*   Dilute 0.250 g of *N-methylpyrrolidine R* (impurity G) to 100.0 ml with *water R*. Dilute 2.0 ml of this solution to 100.0 ml with *0.01 M nitric acid*.

*Reference solution (b)*   Dilute 0.250 g of *pyrrolidine R* to 100 ml with *0.01 M nitric acid*. Dilute 2 ml of the solution to 100 ml with *0.01 M nitric acid*. Mix 5 ml of this solution with 5 ml of reference solution (a).

*Column:*

— size: *l* = 0.05 m, Ø = 4.6 mm;

— stationary phase: *strong cation-exchange resin R* (5 μm).

*Mobile phase*   Mix 1 volume of *acetonitrile R* and 100 volumes of *0.01 M nitric acid*; filter through a 0.2 μm filter.

*Flow rate*   1 ml/min.

*Detection*   Conductivity detector.

*Injection*   100 μl.

*Run time*   1.1 times the retention time of cefepime (retention time = about 50 min, eluting as a broadened peak).

*System suitability:*

— symmetry factor: maximum 2.5 for the peak due to impurity G in the chromatogram obtained with reference solution (a);

— repeatability: maximum relative standard deviation of 5.0 per cent after 6 injections of reference solution (a);

— peak-to-valley ratio: minimum 3 between the peaks due to pyrrolidine and impurity G in the chromatogram obtained with reference solution (b).

Calculate the percentage content of impurity G in the test solution using reference solution (a).

*Limit:*
— *impurity G*: maximum 0.5 per cent.

**Related substances**

Liquid chromatography (2.2.29). *Prepare the solutions immediately before use or keep refrigerated at 4-8 °C for not more than 12 h.*

*Test solution* Dissolve 70.0 mg of the substance to be examined in mobile phase A and dilute to 50.0 ml with mobile phase A. Sonicate for 30 s and stir for about 5 min.

*Reference solution (a)* Dissolve 70.0 mg of *cefepime dihydrochloride monohydrate CRS* in mobile phase A and dilute to 50.0 ml with mobile phase A. Sonicate for 30 s and stir for about 5 min.

*Reference solution (b)* Dilute 1.0 ml of the test solution to 10.0 ml with mobile phase A. Dilute 2.0 ml of this solution to 100.0 ml with mobile phase A.

*Reference solution (c)* Dissolve 7 mg of *cefepime dihydrochloride monohydrate for system suitability CRS* (containing impurities A, B, E and F) in mobile phase A and dilute to 5 ml with mobile phase A.

*Column:*
— *size: l* = 0.25 m, Ø = 4.6 mm;
— *stationary phase:* end-capped octadecylsilyl silica gel for chromatography R (5 μm).

*Mobile phase:*
— *mobile phase A*: mix 10 volumes of *acetonitrile R* and 90 volumes of a 0.68 g/l solution of *potassium dihydrogen phosphate R* previously adjusted to pH 5.0 with *0.5 M potassium hydroxide*;
— *mobile phase B*: mix equal volumes of *acetonitrile R* and a 0.68 g/l solution of *potassium dihydrogen phosphate R* previously adjusted to pH 5.0 with *0.5 M potassium hydroxide*;

| Time (min) | Mobile phase A (per cent V/V) | Mobile phase B (per cent V/V) |
|---|---|---|
| 0 - 10 | 100 | 0 |
| 10 - 30 | 100 → 50 | 0 → 50 |
| 30 - 35 | 50 | 50 |
| 35 - 36 | 50 → 100 | 50 → 0 |
| 36 - 45 | 100 | 0 |

*Flow rate* 1 ml/min.

*Detection* Spectrophotometer at 254 nm.

*Injection* 10 μl of the test solution and reference solutions (b) and (c).

*Identification of impurities* Use the chromatogram supplied with *cefepime dihydrochloride monohydrate for system suitability CRS* and the chromatogram obtained with reference solution (c) to identify the peaks due to impurities A, B, E and F.

*Relative retention* With reference to cefepime (retention time = about 7 min): impurity E = about 0.4; impurity F = about 0.8; impurity A = about 2.5; impurity B = about 4.1.

*System suitability* Reference solution (c):
— *resolution*: minimum 1.5 between the peaks due to impurity F and cefepime.

*Limits:*
— *correction factors*: for the calculation of content, multiply the peak areas of the following impurities by the corresponding correction factor: impurity A = 1.4; impurity B = 1.4; impurity E = 1.8;

— *impurity A*: not more than 1.5 times the area of the principal peak in the chromatogram obtained with reference solution (b) (0.3 per cent);
— *impurities B, F*: for each impurity, not more than the area of the principal peak in the chromatogram obtained with reference solution (b) (0.2 per cent);
— *impurity E*: not more than 0.5 times the area of the principal peak in the chromatogram obtained with reference solution (b) (0.1 per cent);
— *unspecified impurities*: for each impurity, not more than 0.5 times the area of the principal peak in the chromatogram obtained with reference solution (b) (0.10 per cent);
— *total*: not more than 5 times the area of the principal peak in the chromatogram obtained with reference solution (b) (1.0 per cent);
— *disregard limit*: 0.25 times the area of the principal peak in the chromatogram obtained with reference solution (b) (0.05 per cent).

**Water** (2.5.12)
3.0 per cent to 4.5 per cent, determined on 0.400 g.

**Bacterial endotoxins** (2.6.14)
Less than 0.04 IU/mg, if intended for use in the manufacture of parenteral dosage forms without a further appropriate procedure for the removal of bacterial endotoxins.

## ASSAY

Liquid chromatography (2.2.29) as described in the test for related substances with the following modifications.

*Mobile phase* Mobile phase A.

*Injection* Test solution and reference solution (a).

*Run time* 1.4 times the retention time of cefepime.

Calculate the percentage content of $C_{19}H_{26}Cl_2N_6O_5S_2$ from the declared content of *cefepime dihydrochloride monohydrate CRS* .

## STORAGE

Protected from light. If the substance is sterile, store in a sterile, airtight, tamper-proof container.

## IMPURITIES

*Specified impurities* A, B, E, F, G.

*Other detectable impurities* (the following substances would, if present at a sufficient level, be detected by one or other of the tests in the monograph. They are limited by the general acceptance criterion for other/unspecified impurities and/or by the general monograph *Substances for pharmaceutical use (2034)*. It is therefore not necessary to identify these impurities for demonstration of compliance. See also *5.10. Control of impurities in substances for pharmaceutical use): C, D.*

A. (6R,7R)-7-[[(2E)-(2-aminothiazol-4-yl)(methoxyimino)acetyl]amino]-3-[(1-methylpyrrolidinio)methyl]-8-oxo-5-thia-1-azabicyclo[4.2.0]oct-2-ene-2-carboxylate (*anti*-cefepime),

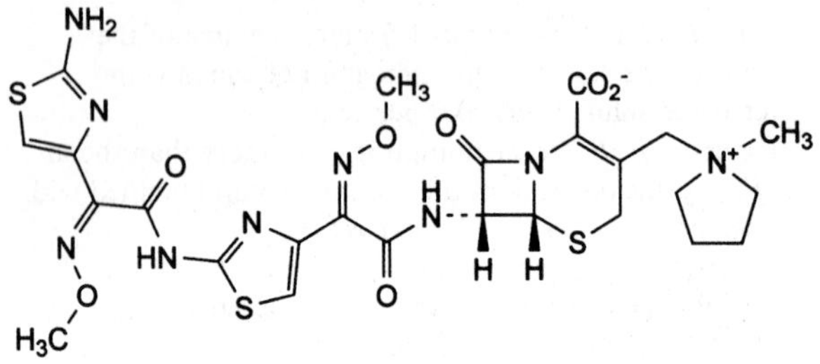

B. (6R,7R)-7-[[(2Z)-2-[[(2Z)-(2-aminothiazol-4-yl)(methoxyimino)acetyl]amino]thiazol-4-yl](methoxyimino)acetyl]amino]-3-[(1-methylpyrrolidinio)methyl]-8-oxo-5-thia-1-azabicyclo[4.2.0]oct-2-ene-2-carboxylate,

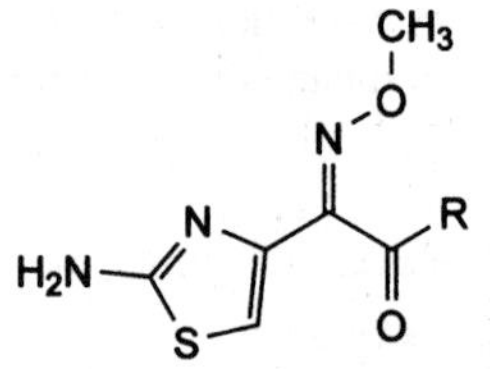

C. R = NH-CH₂-CHO: (2Z)-2-(2-aminothiazol-4-yl)-N-(formylmethyl)-2-(methoxyimino)acetamide,

D. R = OH: (2Z)-2-(2-aminothiazol-4-yl)(methoxyimino) acetic acid,

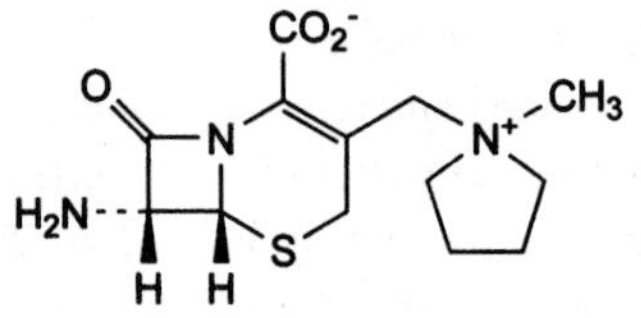

E. (6R,7R)-7-amino-3-[(1-methylpyrrolidinio)methyl]-8-oxo-5-thia-1-azabicyclo[4.2.0]oct-2-ene-2-carboxylate,

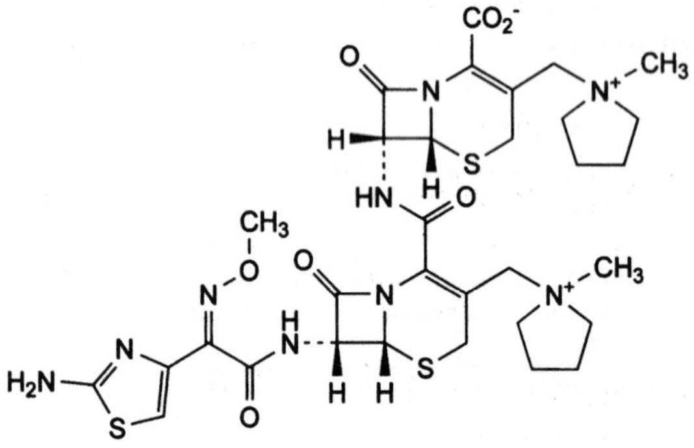

F. (6R,7R)-7-[[[(6R,7R)-7-[[(2Z)-(2-aminothiazol-4-yl)(methoxyimino)acetyl]amino]-3-[(1-methylpyrrolidinio)methyl]-8-oxo-5-thia-1-azabicyclo[4.2.0]oct-2-en-2-yl]carbonyl]amino]-3-[(1-methylpyrrolidinio)methyl]-8-oxo-5-thia-1-azabicyclo[4.2.0]oct-2-ene-2-carboxylate,

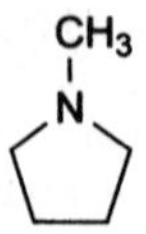

G. N-methylpyrrolidine.

_____ Ph Eur

# Cefixime

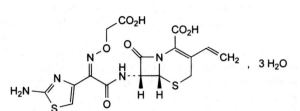

(*Ph Eur monograph 1188*

$C_{16}H_{15}N_5O_7S_2,3H_2O$     507.5     *79350-37-1*

**Action and use**
Cephalosporin antibacterial.

*Ph Eur* _____

## DEFINITION
(6R,7R)-7-[[(Z)-2-(2-Aminothiazol-4-yl)-2-[(carboxymethoxy)imino]acetyl]amino]-3-ethenyl-8-oxo-5-thia-1-azabicyclo[4.2.0]oct-2-ene-2-carboxylic acid trihydrate.

Semi-synthetic product derived from a fermentation product.

**Content**
95.0 per cent to 102.0 per cent (anhydrous substance).

## CHARACTERS
**Appearance**
White or almost white, slightly hygroscopic powder.

**Solubility**
Slightly soluble in water, soluble in methanol, sparingly soluble in anhydrous ethanol, practically insoluble in ethyl acetate.

## IDENTIFICATION
Infrared absorption spectrophotometry (*2.2.24*).

*Comparison*   cefixime CRS.

If the spectra obtained show differences, dissolve the substance to be examined and the reference substance separately in *methanol R*, evaporate to dryness and record new spectra using the residues.

## TESTS
**pH** (*2.2.3*)
2.6 to 4.1.

Suspend 0.5 g in *carbon dioxide-free water R* and dilute to 10 ml with the same solvent.

**Related substances**
Liquid chromatography (*2.2.29*).

*Test solution*   Dissolve 25.0 mg of the substance to be examined in the mobile phase and dilute to 25.0 ml with the mobile phase.

*Reference solution (a)*   Dissolve 25.0 mg of *cefixime CRS* in the mobile phase and dilute to 25.0 ml with the mobile phase.

*Reference solution (b)*   Dilute 1.0 ml of reference solution (a) to 100.0 ml with the mobile phase.

*Reference solution (c)*   Dissolve 10 mg of *cefixime CRS* in 10 ml of *water R*. Heat on a water-bath for 45 min and cool (in situ preparation of impurity D). Inject immediately.

*Column:*
— *size*: l = 0.125 m, Ø = 4 mm;
— *stationary phase: octadecylsilyl silica gel for chromatography R* (5 μm);
— *temperature*: 40 °C.

*Mobile phase* Mix 250 volumes of *acetonitrile R* and 750 volumes of a tetrabutylammonium hydroxide solution prepared as follows: dissolve 8.2 g of *tetrabutylammonium hydroxide R* in *water R* and dilute to 800 ml with the same solvent; adjust to pH 6.5 with *dilute phosphoric acid R* and dilute to 1000 ml with *water R*.

*Flow rate* 1.0 ml/min.

*Detection* Spectrophotometer at 254 nm.

*Injection* 10 μl of the test solution and reference solutions (b) and (c).

*Run time* 3 times the retention time of cefixime.

*System suitability* Reference solution (c):
— *resolution*: minimum 2.0 between the peaks due to cefixime and impurity D; if necessary, adjust the concentration of acetonitrile in the mobile phase.

*Limits:*
— *any impurity*: for each impurity, not more than 0.5 times the area of the principal peak in the chromatogram obtained with reference solution (b) (0.5 per cent);
— *total*: not more than 3 times the area of the principal peak in the chromatogram obtained with reference solution (b) (3 per cent);
— *disregard limit*: 0.1 times the area of the principal peak in the chromatogram obtained with reference solution (b) (0.1 per cent).

**Ethanol** (2.4.24)
Head-space gas chromatography (2.2.28): use the standard additions method.

*Sample solution* Dissolve 0.250 g of the substance to be examined in a mixture of 1 volume of *dimethylacetamide R* and 4 volumes of *water R* and dilute to 25.0 ml with the same mixture of solvents.

*Limit:*
— *ethanol*: maximum 1.0 per cent *m/m*.

**Water** (2.5.12)
9.0 per cent to 12.0 per cent, determined on 0.200 g.

**Sulphated ash** (2.4.14)
Maximum 0.2 per cent, determined on 1.0 g.

**ASSAY**
Liquid chromatography (2.2.29) as described in the test for related substances with the following modifications.

*Injection* The test solution and reference solution (a).

*System suitability* Reference solution (a):
— *repeatability*: maximum relative standard deviation of 1.0 per cent after 6 injections.

Calculate the percentage content of $C_{16}H_{15}N_5O_7S_2$ from the declared content of *cefixime CRS*.

**STORAGE**
In an airtight container, protected from light.

**IMPURITIES**

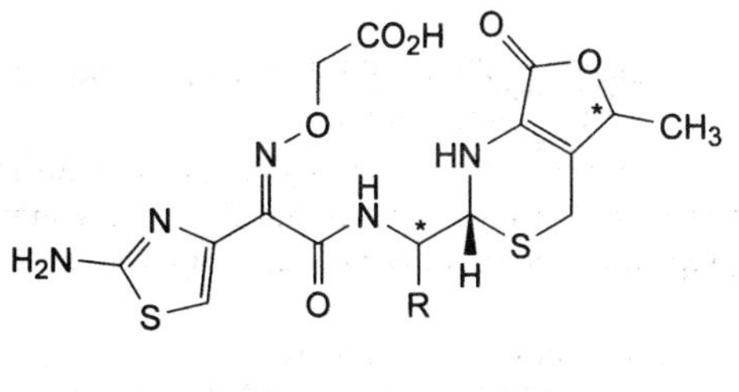

A. R = $CO_2$H: 2-[[(Z)-2-(2-aminothiazol-4-yl)-2-[(carboxymethoxy)imino]acetyl]amino]-2-[(2R)-5-methyl-7-oxo-1,2,5,7-tetrahydro-4*H*-furo[3,4-*d*][1,3]thiazin-2-yl]acetic acid,

B. R = H: 2-[[[(Z)-1-(2-aminothiazol-4-yl)-2-[[[(2R,5RS)-5-methyl-7-oxo-1,2,5,7-tetrahydro-4*H*-furo[3,4-*d*][1,3]thiazin-2-yl]methyl]amino]-2-oxoethylidene]amino]oxy]acetic acid,

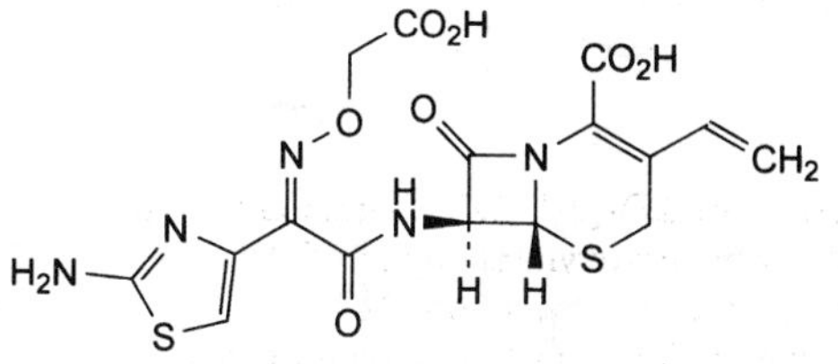

C. (6R,7S)-7-[[(Z)-2-(2-aminothiazol-4-yl)-2-[(carboxymethoxy)imino]acetyl]amino]-3-ethenyl-8-oxo-5-thia-1-azabicyclo[4.2.0]oct-2-ene-2-carboxylic acid (cefixime 7-epimer),

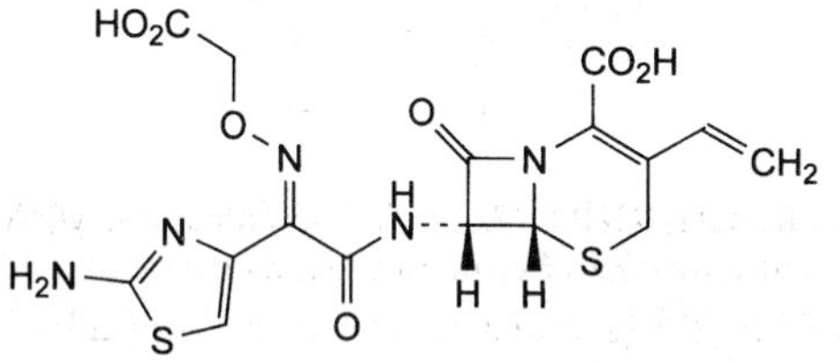

D. (6R,7R)-7-[[(E)-2-(2-aminothiazol-4-yl)-2-[(carboxymethoxy)imino]acetyl]amino]-3-ethenyl-8-oxo-5-thia-1-azabicyclo[4.2.0]oct-2-ene-2-carboxylic acid (cefixime *E*-isomer),

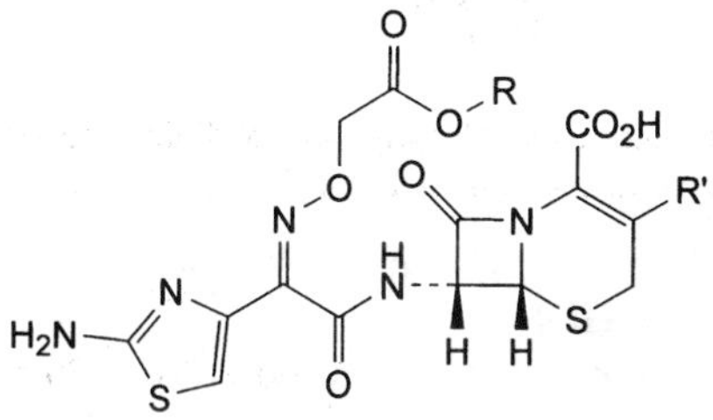

E. R = H, R' = $CH_3$: (6R,7R)-7-[[(Z)-2-(2-aminothiazol-4-yl)-2-[(carboxymethoxy)imino]acetyl]amino]-3-methyl-8-oxo-5-thia-1-azabicyclo[4.2.0]oct-2-ene-2-carboxylic acid,

F. R = $C_2H_5$, R' = CH=$CH_2$: (6R,7R)-7-[[(Z)-2-(2-aminothiazol-4-yl)-2-[(2-ethoxy-2-oxoethoxy)imino]acetyl]amino]-3-ethenyl-8-oxo-5-thia-1-azabicyclo[4.2.0]oct-2-ene-2-carboxylic acid.

*Ph Eur*

# Cefoperazone Sodium

(Ph Eur monograph 1404)

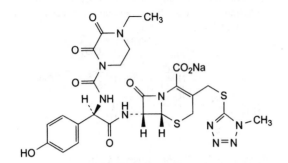

$C_{25}H_{26}N_9NaO_8S_2$     668     62893-20-3

**Action and use**
Cephalosporin antibacterial.

*Ph Eur*

## DEFINITION

Sodium (6R,7R)-7-[[(2R)-2-[[(4-ethyl-2,3-dioxopiperazin-1-yl)carbonyl]amino]-2-(4-hydroxyphenyl)acetyl]amino]-3-[[(1-methyl-1H-tetrazol-5-yl)sulphanyl]methyl]-8-oxo-5-thia-1-azabicyclo[4.2.0]oct-2-ene-2-carboxylate.

Semi-synthetic product derived from a fermentation product.

**Content**
95.0 per cent to 102.0 per cent (anhydrous substance).

## CHARACTERS

**Appearance**
White or slightly yellow, hygroscopic powder.

**Solubility**
Freely soluble in water, soluble in methanol, slightly soluble in ethanol (96 per cent).

If crystalline, it shows polymorphism (5.9).

## IDENTIFICATION

A. Infrared absorption spectrophotometry (2.2.24).

*Preparation* Dissolve the substance to be examined in *methanol R* and evaporate to dryness; examine the residue.

*Comparison* Ph. Eur. reference spectrum of cefoperazone sodium.

B. Examine the chromatograms obtained in the assay.

*Results* The principal peak in the chromatogram obtained with test solution (a) is similar in retention time and size to the principal peak in the chromatogram obtained with reference solution (a).

C. It gives reaction (a) of sodium (2.3.1).

## TESTS

**Appearance of solution**
The solution is clear (2.2.1) and its absorbance (2.2.25) at 430 nm is not greater than 0.15.

Dissolve 2.5 g in *water R* and dilute to 25.0 ml with the same solvent.

**pH** (2.2.3)
4.5 to 6.5.

Dissolve 2.5 g in *carbon dioxide-free water R* and dilute to 10 ml with the same solvent.

**Related substances**
Liquid chromatography (2.2.29). *Prepare the solutions immediately before use.*

*Test solution (a)* Dissolve 25.0 mg of the substance to be examined in the mobile phase and dilute to 250.0 ml with the mobile phase.

*Test solution (b)* Dissolve 25.0 mg of the substance to be examined in the mobile phase and dilute to 50.0 ml with the mobile phase.

*Reference solution (a)* Dissolve 25.0 mg of *cefoperazone dihydrate CRS* in the mobile phase and dilute to 250.0 ml with the mobile phase.

*Reference solution (b)* Dilute 5.0 ml of reference solution (a) to 100.0 ml with the mobile phase.

*Column:*
— size: $l$ = 0.15 m, Ø = 4.6 mm;
— stationary phase: end-capped octadecylsilyl silica gel for chromatography R (5 μm).

*Mobile phase* Mix 884 volumes of *water R*, 110 volumes of *acetonitrile R*, 3.5 volumes of a 60 g/l solution of *acetic acid R* and 2.5 volumes of a triethylammonium acetate solution prepared as follows: dilute 14 ml of *triethylamine R* and 5.7 ml of *glacial acetic acid R* to 100 ml with *water R*.

*Flow rate* 1 ml/min.

*Detection* Spectrophotometer at 254 nm.

*Injection* 20 μl of test solution (b) and reference solutions (a) and (b).

*Run time* 2.5 times the retention time of cefoperazone.

*Retention time* Cefoperazone = about 15 min.

*System suitability* Reference solution (a):
— number of theoretical plates: minimum 5000, calculated for the principal peak; if necessary, adjust the content of *acetonitrile R* in the mobile phase;
— symmetry factor: maximum 1.6 for the principal peak; if necessary, adjust the content of *acetonitrile R* in the mobile phase.

*Limits:*
— any impurity: for each impurity, not more than 1.5 times the area of the principal peak in the chromatogram obtained with reference solution (b) (1.5 per cent);
— total: not more than 4.5 times the area of the principal peak in the chromatogram obtained with reference solution (b) (4.5 per cent);
— disregard limit: 0.1 times the area of the principal peak in the chromatogram obtained with reference solution (b) (0.1 per cent).

**Acetone** (2.4.24, System B)
Maximum 2.0 per cent.

*Sample solution* Dissolve 0.500 g of the substance to be examined in *water R* and dilute to 10.0 ml with the same solvent.

*Solvent solution* Dissolve 0.350 g of *acetone R* in *water R* and dilute to 100.0 ml with the same solvent. Dilute 10.0 ml of this solution to 100.0 ml with *water R*.

Prepare each of 4 injection vials as shown in the table below:

| Vial No. | Sample solution (ml) | Solvent solution (ml) | Water R (ml) |
|---|---|---|---|
| 1 | 1.0 | 0 | 4.0 |
| 2 | 1.0 | 1.0 | 3.0 |
| 3 | 1.0 | 2.0 | 2.0 |
| 4 | 1.0 | 3.0 | 1.0 |

*Static head-space conditions that may be used:*
— *equilibration time*: 15 min;
— *transfer-line temperature*: 110 °C.
*Temperature:*
— *Column*: 40 °C for 10 min.

**Heavy metals** (*2.4.8*)
Maximum 5 ppm.

2.0 g complies with test C. Prepare the reference solution using 1 ml of *lead standard solution (10 ppm Pb) R*.

**Water** (*2.5.12*)
Maximum 5.0 per cent, determined on 0.200 g.

**Bacterial endotoxins** (*2.6.14*)
Less than 0.20 IU/mg, if intended for use in the manufacture of parenteral preparations without a further appropriate procedure for the removal of bacterial endotoxins.

**ASSAY**

Liquid chromatography (*2.2.29*) as described in the test for related substances with the following modifications.

*Injection*  Test solution (a) and reference solution (a).

*System suitability*  Reference solution (a):
— *repeatability*: maximum relative standard deviation of 1.0 per cent after 6 injections.

Calculate the percentage content of cefoperazone sodium by multiplying the percentage content of cefoperazone by 1.034.

**STORAGE**

In an airtight container, protected from light, at a temperature of 2 °C to 8 °C. If the substance is sterile, store in a sterile, airtight, tamper-proof container.

**IMPURITIES**

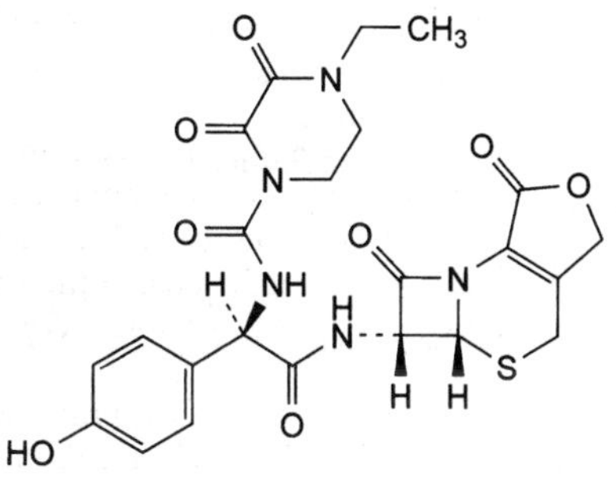

A. (5a*R*,6*R*)-6-[[(2*R*)-2-[[(4-ethyl-2,3-dioxopiperazin-1-yl)carbonyl]amino]-2-(4-hydroxyphenyl)acetyl]amino]-5a,6-dihydro-3*H*,7*H*-azeto[2,1-*b*]furo[3,4-*d*][1,3]thiazine-1,7(4*H*)-dione,

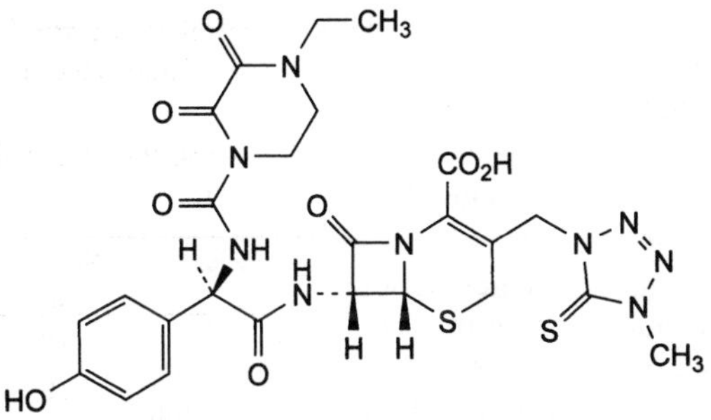

B. (6*R*,7*R*)-7-[[(2*R*)-2-[[(4-ethyl-2,3-dioxopiperazin-1-yl)carbonyl]amino]-2-(4-hydroxyphenyl)acetyl]amino]-3-[[(4-methyl-5-thioxo-4,5-dihydro-1*H*-tetrazol-1-yl)methyl]-8-oxo-5-thia-1-azabicyclo[4.2.0]oct-2-ene-2-carboxylic acid,

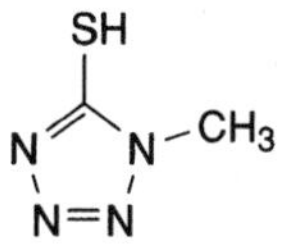

C. 1-methyl-1*H*-tetrazole-5-thiol,

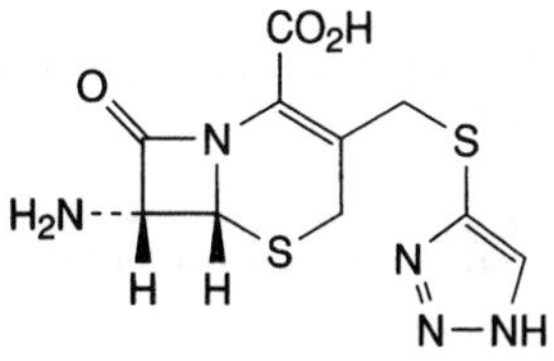

D. (6*R*,7*R*)-7-amino-8-oxo-3-[[(1*H*-1,2,3-triazol-4-ylsulphanyl)methyl]-5-thia-1-azabicyclo[4.2.0]oct-2-ene-2-carboxylic acid (7-TACA),

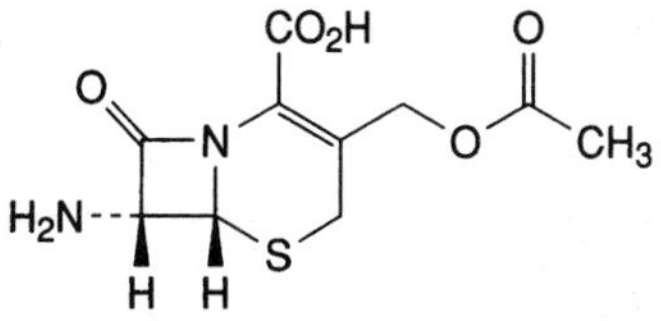

E. (6*R*,7*R*)-3-[(acetyloxy)methyl]-7-amino-8-oxo-5-thia-1-azabicyclo[4.2.0]oct-2-ene-2-carboxylic acid (7-ACA),

F. (6*R*,7*S*)-7-[[(2*R*)-2-[[(4-ethyl-2,3-dioxopiperazine-1-yl)carbonyl]amino]-2-(4-hydroxyphenyl)acetyl]amino]-3-[[[(1-methyl-1*H*-tetrazol-5-yl)sulphanyl]methyl]-8-oxo-5-thia-1-azabicyclo[4.2.0]oct-2-ene-2-carboxylic acid.

_____ *Ph Eur*

# Cefotaxime Sodium

(*Ph Eur monograph 0989*)

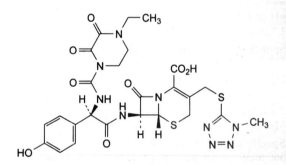

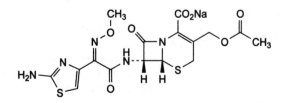

$C_{16}H_{16}N_5NaO_7S_2$     477.4     *64485-93-4*

**Action and use**
Cephalosporin antibacterial.

**Preparation**
Cefotaxime Injection

*Ph Eur*

## DEFINITION

Sodium (6*R*,7*R*)-3-[(acetyloxy)methyl]-7-[[(2*Z*)-2-(2-aminothiazol-4-yl)-2-(methoxyimino)acetyl]amino]-8-oxo-5-thia-1-azabicyclo[4.2.0]oct-2-ene-2-carboxylate.

Semi-synthetic product derived from a fermentation product.

## Content

96.0 per cent to 102.0 per cent (anhydrous substance).

## CHARACTERS

### Appearance

White or slightly yellow powder, hygroscopic.

### Solubility

Freely soluble in water, sparingly soluble in methanol.

## IDENTIFICATION

A. Infrared absorption spectrophotometry (*2.2.24*).

*Comparison*   cefotaxime sodium CRS.

B. It gives reaction (a) of sodium (*2.3.1*).

## TESTS

### Solution S

Dissolve 2.5 g in *carbon dioxide-free water R* and dilute to 25.0 ml with the same solvent.

### Appearance of solution

Solution S is clear (*2.2.1*). Add 1 ml of *glacial acetic acid R* to 10 ml of solution S. The solution, examined immediately, is clear.

### pH (*2.2.3*)

4.5 to 6.5 for solution S.

### Specific optical rotation (*2.2.7*)

+ 58.0 to + 64.0 (anhydrous substance).

Dissolve 0.100 g in *water R* and dilute to 10.0 ml with the same solvent.

### Absorbance (*2.2.25*)

Maximum 0.40 at 430 nm for solution S.

### Specific absorbance (*2.2.25*)

360 to 390, determined at the absorption maximum at 235 nm (anhydrous substance).

Dissolve 20.0 mg in *water R* and dilute to 100.0 ml with the same solvent. Dilute 10.0 ml of the solution to 100.0 ml with *water R*.

### Related substances

Liquid chromatography (*2.2.29*)

*Prepare the solutions immediately before use.*

*Solution A*   Mobile phase B, mobile phase A (14:86 *V/V*).

*Test solution*   Dissolve 40.0 mg of the substance to be examined in solution A and dilute to 50.0 ml with the same solution.

*Reference solution (a)*   Dissolve 8.0 mg of *cefotaxime acid CRS* in solution A and dilute to 10.0 ml with the same solution.

*Reference solution (b)*   Dilute 1.0 ml of the test solution to 100.0 ml with solution A.

*Reference solution (c)*   Add 1.0 ml of *dilute hydrochloric acid R* to 4.0 ml of the test solution. Heat the solution at 40 °C for 2 h. Add 5.0 ml of *buffer solution pH 6.6 R* and 1.0 ml of *dilute sodium hydroxide solution R*.

*Reference solution (d)*   Dissolve 4 mg of *cefotaxime for peak identification CRS* (containing impurities A, B, C, E and F) in 5 ml of solution A.

*Column:*
— *size*: *l* = 0.15 m, Ø = 3.9 mm,

— *stationary phase*: octadecylsilyl silica gel for chromatography R (5 µm),
— *temperature*: 30 °C.

*Mobile phase:*
— *mobile phase A*: 7.1 g/l solution of *disodium hydrogen phosphate R* adjusted to pH 6.25 using *phosphoric acid R;*
— *mobile phase B*: methanol R;

| Time (min) | Mobile phase A (per cent *V/V*) | Mobile phase B (per cent *V/V*) |
|---|---|---|
| 0 - 7 | 86 | 14 |
| 7 - 9 | 86 → 82 | 14 → 18 |
| 9 - 16 | 82 | 18 |
| 16 - 45 | 82 → 60 | 18 → 40 |
| 45 - 50 | 60 | 40 |
| 50 - 55 | 60 → 86 | 40 → 14 |
| 55 - 60 | 86 | 14 |

*Flow rate*   1.0 ml/min.

*Detection*   Spectrophotometer at 235 nm.

*Injection*   10 µl of the test solution and reference solutions (b), (c) and (d).

*Identification of impurities*   Use the chromatogram supplied with *cefotaxime for peak identification CRS* and the chromatogram obtained with reference solution (d) to identify the peaks due to impurities A, B, C, E and F.

*Relative retention*   With reference to cefotaxime (retention time = about 13 min): impurity B = about 0.3; impurity A = about 0.5; impurity E = about 0.6; impurity C = about 1.9; impurity D = about 2.3; impurity F = about 2.4; impurity G = about 3.1.

*System suitability*   Reference solution (c):
— *resolution*: minimum 3.5 between the peaks due to impurity E and cefotaxime;
— *symmetry factor*: maximum 2.0 for the peak due to cefotaxime.

*Limits:*
— *impurities A, B, C, D, E, F*: for each impurity, not more than the area of the principal peak in the chromatogram obtained with reference solution (b) (1.0 per cent);
— *any other impurity*: for each impurity, not more than 0.2 times the area of the principal peak in the chromatogram obtained with reference solution (b) (0.2 per cent);
— *total*: not more than 3 times the area of the principal peak in the chromatogram obtained with reference solution (b) (3.0 per cent);
— *disregard limit*: 0.05 times the area of the principal peak in the chromatogram obtained with reference solution (b) (0.05 per cent).

### Ethanol (*2.4.24, System A*)

Maximum 1.0 per cent.

### N,N-Dimethylaniline (*2.4.26, Method B*)

Maximum 20 ppm.

### 2-Ethylhexanoic acid (*2.4.28*)

Maximum 0.5 per cent *m/m*.

### Water (*2.5.12*)

Maximum 3.0 per cent, determined on 0.300 g.

### Bacterial endotoxins (*2.6.14*)

Less than 0.05 IU/mg, if intended for use in the manufacture of parenteral dosage forms without a further appropriate procedure for the removal of bacterial endotoxins.

## ASSAY

Liquid chromatography (*2.2.29*) as described in the test for related substances with the following modification.

*Injection*  Test solution and reference solution (a).

Calculate the percentage content of $C_{16}H_{16}N_5NaO_7S_2$ by multiplying the percentage content of cefotaxime by 1.048.

## STORAGE

In an airtight container, protected from light. If the substance is sterile, store in a sterile, airtight, tamper-proof container.

## IMPURITIES

*Specified impurities*  *A, B, C, D, E, F.*

*Other detectable impurities* (the following substances would, if present at a sufficient level, be detected by one or other of the tests in the monograph. They are limited by the general acceptance criterion for other/unspecified impurities and/or by the general monograph *Substances for pharmaceutical use (2034)*. It is therefore not necessary to identify these impurities for demonstration of compliance. See also *5.10. Control of impurities in substances for pharmaceutical use*): *G.*

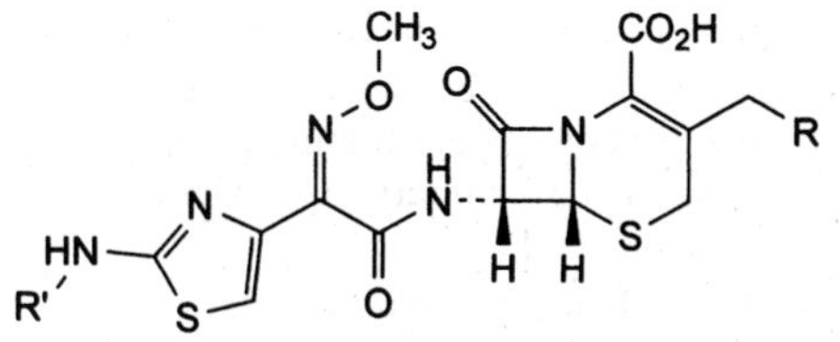

A. R = R′ = H: (6*R*,7*R*)-7-[[(2*Z*)-2-(2-aminothiazol-4-yl)-2-(methoxyimino)acetyl]amino]-3-methyl-8-oxo-5-thia-1-azabicyclo[4.2.0]oct-2-ene-2-carboxylic acid
(deacetoxycefotaxime),

B. R = OH, R′ = H: (6*R*,7*R*)-7-[[(2*Z*)-2-(2-aminothiazol-4-yl)-2-(methoxyimino)acetyl]amino]-3-(hydroxymethyl)-8-oxo-5-thia-1-azabicyclo[4.2.0]oct-2-ene-2-carboxylic acid
(deacetylcefotaxime),

C. R = O-CO-CH₃, R′ = CHO: (6*R*,7*R*)-3-[(acetyloxy)methyl]-7-[[(2*Z*)-2-[2-(formylamino)thiazol-4-yl]-2-(methoxyimino)acetyl]amino]-8-oxo-5-thia-1-azabicyclo[4.2.0]oct-2-ene-2-carboxylic acid
(*N*-formylcefotaxime),

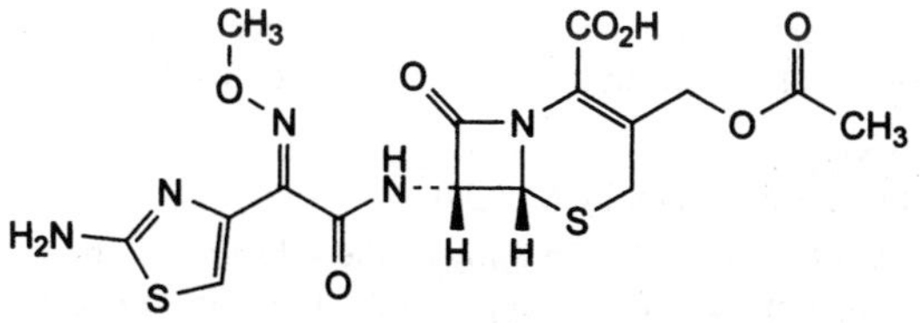

D. (6*R*,7*R*)-3-[(acetyloxy)methyl]-7-[[(2*E*)-2-(2-aminothiazol-4-yl)-2-(methoxyimino)acetyl]amino]-8-oxo-5-thia-1-azabicyclo[4.2.0]oct-2-ene-2-carboxylic acid
(*E*-cefotaxime),

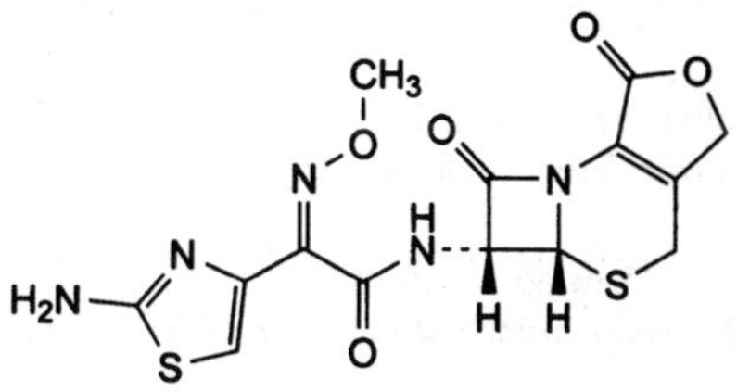

E. (5a*R*,6*R*)-6-[[(2*Z*)-2-(2-aminothiazol-4-yl)-2-(methoxyimino)acetyl]amino]-5a,6-dihydro-3*H*,7*H*-azeto[2,1-*b*]furo[3,4-*d*][1,3]thiazine-1,7(4*H*)-dione
(deacetylcefotaxime lactone),

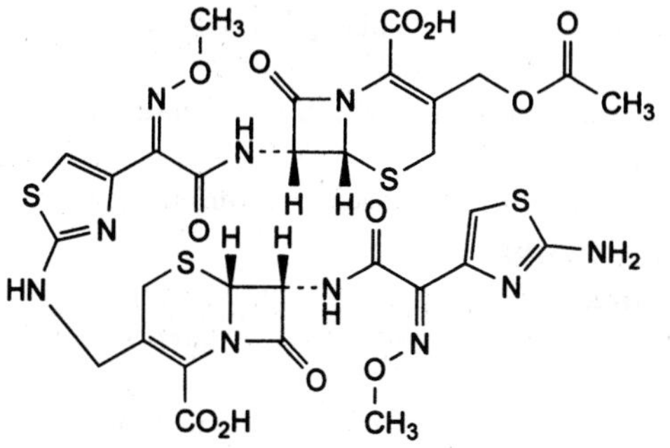

F. (6*R*,7*R*)-3-[(acetyloxy)methyl]-7-[[(2*Z*)-2-[2-[[[(6*R*,7*R*)-7-[[(2*Z*)-2-(2-aminothiazol-4-yl)-2-(methoxyimino)acetyl]amino]-2-carboxy-8-oxo-5-thia-1-azabicyclo[4.2.0]oct-2-en-2-yl]methyl]amino]thiazol-4-yl]-2-(methoxyimino)acetyl]amino]-8-oxo-5-thia-1-azabicyclo[4.2.0]oct-2-ene-2-carboxylic acid
(cefotaxime dimer),

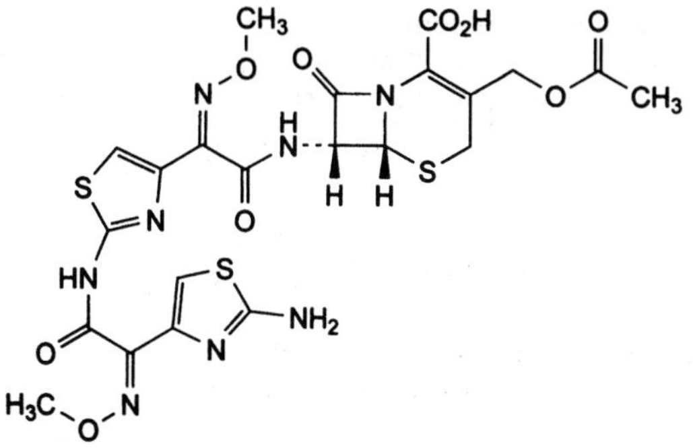

G. (6*R*,7*R*)-3-[(acetyloxy)methyl]-7-[[(2*Z*)-2-[2-[[(2*Z*)-2-(2-aminothiazol-4-yl)-2-(methoxyimino)acetyl]amino]thiazol-4-yl]-2-(methoxyimino)acetyl]amino]-8-oxo-5-thia-1-azabicyclo[4.2.0]oct-2-ene-2-carboxylic acid
(ATA cefotaxime).

*————————————————————————— Ph Eur*

# Cefoxitin Sodium

(*Ph Eur monograph 0990*)

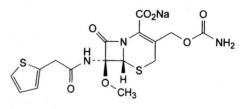

$C_{16}H_{16}N_3NaO_7S_2$        449.4        *33564-30-6*

## Action and use

Cephalosporin antibacterial.

## Preparation

Cefoxitin Injection

*Ph Eur*

## DEFINITION

Sodium (6R,7S)-3-[(carbamoyloxy)methyl]-7-methoxy-8-oxo-7-[[(thiophen-2-yl)acetyl]amino]-5-thia-1-azabicyclo[4.2.0]oct-2-ene-2-carboxylate.

Semi-synthetic product derived from a fermentation product.

## Content

95.0 per cent to 102.0 per cent (anhydrous substance).

## CHARACTERS

### Appearance

White or almost white powder, very hygroscopic.

### Solubility

Very soluble in water, sparingly soluble in alcohol.

## IDENTIFICATION

A. Infrared absorption spectrophotometry (2.2.24).

*Comparison* cefoxitin sodium CRS.

B. It gives reaction (a) of sodium (2.3.1).

## TESTS

### Solution S

Dissolve 2.50 g in *carbon dioxide-free water R* and dilute to 25 ml with the same solvent.

### Appearance of solution

Solution S is clear (2.2.1) and not more intensely coloured than intensity 5 of the range of reference solutions of the most appropriate colour (2.2.2, Method II).

### pH (2.2.3)

4.2 to 7.0.

Dilute 2 ml of solution S to 20 ml with *carbon dioxide-free water R*.

### Specific optical rotation (2.2.7)

+ 206 to + 214 (anhydrous substance).

Dissolve 0.250 g in *methanol R* and dilute to 25.0 ml with the same solvent.

### Absorbance (2.2.25)

Dissolve 0.100 g in *water R* and dilute to 100.0 ml with the same solvent. Dilute 2.0 ml of the solution to 100.0 ml with *sodium hydrogen carbonate solution R*. Examined between 220 nm and 350 nm, the solution shows an absorption maximum at 236 nm and a broad absorption maximum at about 262 nm. The specific absorbance at this broad maximum is 190 to 210 (anhydrous substance).

### Related substances

Liquid chromatography (2.2.29). *Prepare the solutions immediately before use.*

*Solution A* Dilute 20 ml of a 34.8 g/l solution of *dipotassium hydrogen phosphate R* adjusted to pH 6.8 with *phosphoric acid R* to 1000 ml with *water R*.

*Test solution* Dissolve 50.0 mg of the substance to be examined in solution A and dilute to 10.0 ml with the same solution.

*Reference solution (a)* Dilute 1.0 ml of the test solution to 100.0 ml with solution A.

*Reference solution (b)* To 1.0 ml of the test solution add 7.0 ml of *water R* and 2.0 ml of *methanol R*. Add 25 mg of *sodium carbonate R*, stir for 10 min at room temperature, then heat in a water-bath at 70 °C for 30 min. Allow to cool. Add 3 drops of *glacial acetic acid R* and 1 ml of the test solution and mix.

*Column:*
— *size*: l = 0.25 m, Ø = 4.6 mm,

— *stationary phase: phenylsilyl silica gel for chromatography R* (5 μm) with a specific surface area of 300 m²/g and a pore size of 7 nm.

*Mobile phase:*
— *mobile phase A: water R* adjusted to pH 2.7 with *anhydrous formic acid R*,
— *mobile phase B: acetonitrile R*,

| Time (min) | Mobile phase A (per cent V/V) | Mobile phase B (per cent V/V) |
|---|---|---|
| 0 - 12 | 90 | 10 |
| 12 - 37 | 90 → 80 | 10 → 20 |
| 37 - 50 | 80 → 60 | 20 → 40 |
| 50 - 55 | 60 → 20 | 40 → 80 |
| 55 - 60 | 20 | 80 |
| 60 - 62 | 20 → 90 | 80 → 10 |
| 62 - 70 | 90 | 10 |

*Flow rate* 1 ml/min.

*Detection* Spectrophotometer at 235 nm.

*Injection* 50 μl.

*Relative retentions* With reference to cefoxitin (retention time = about 34 min): impurity A = about 0.82; impurity B = about 1.16; impurity C = about 1.27; impurity D = about 1.31.

*System suitability* Reference solution (b):
— *resolution*: minimum 5.0 between the 2 principal peaks.

*Limits:*
— *any impurity*: not more than half the area of the principal peak in the chromatogram obtained with reference solution (a) (0.5 per cent),
— *total*: not more than 4 times the area of the principal peak in the chromatogram obtained with reference solution (a) (4.0 per cent),
— *disregard limit*: 0.05 times the area of the principal peak in the chromatogram obtained with reference solution (a) (0.05 per cent).

### Water (2.5.12)

Maximum 1.0 per cent, determined on 0.500 g.

### Bacterial endotoxins (2.6.14)

Less than 0.13 IU/mg, if intended for use in the manufacture of parenteral dosage forms without a further appropriate procedure for the removal of bacterial endotoxins.

## ASSAY

Liquid chromatography (2.2.29).

*Test solution* Dissolve 25.0 mg of the substance to be examined in *water R* and dilute to 25.0 ml with the same solvent.

*Reference solution (a)* Dissolve 25.0 mg of *cefoxitin sodium CRS* in *water R* and dilute to 25.0 ml with the same solvent.

*Reference solution (b)* Dissolve 20.0 mg of *2-(2-thienyl)acetic acid R* in *water R* and dilute to 25.0 ml with the same solvent.

*Reference solution (c)* Mix 1.0 ml of reference solution (a) and 5.0 ml of reference solution (b).

*Column:*
— *size*: l = 0.25 m, Ø = 4.6 mm,
— *stationary phase: octadecylsilyl silica gel for chromatography R* (5 μm).

*Mobile phase* acetic acid R, acetonitrile R, water R (1:19:81 V/V/V).

Flow rate 1 ml/min.

Detection Spectrophotometer at 254 nm.

Injection 20 µl; inject the test solution and reference solutions (a) and (c).

System suitability Reference solution (c):
— resolution: minimum 3.5 between the 2 principal peaks.

Calculate the percentage content of cefoxitin sodium.

## STORAGE

In an airtight container. If the substance is sterile, store in a sterile, airtight, tamper-proof container.

## IMPURITIES

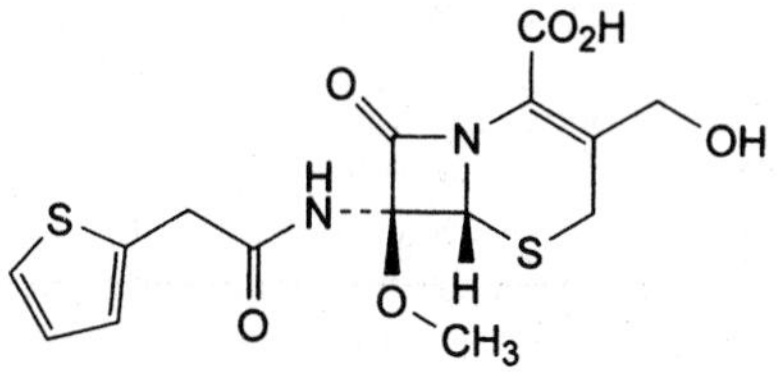

A. (6R,7S)-3-(hydroxymethyl)-7-methoxy-8-oxo-7-[[(thiophen-2-yl)acetyl]amino]-5-thia-1-azabicyclo[4.2.0]oct-2-ene-2-carboxylic acid (decarbamoylcefoxitin),

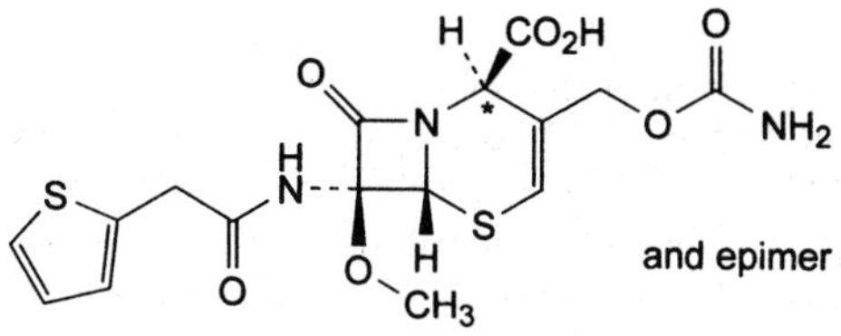

and epimer at C*

B. (2RS,6R,7S)-3-[(carbamoyloxy)methyl]-7-methoxy-8-oxo-7-[[(thiophen-2-yl)acetyl]amino]-5-thia-1-azabicyclo[4.2.0]oct-3-ene-2-carboxylic acid (delta-3-cefoxitin),

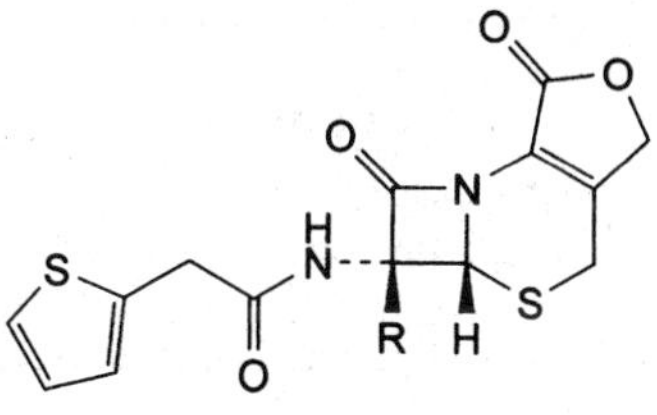

C. R = H: (5aR,6R)-6-[[(thiophen-2-yl)acetyl]amino]-5a,6-dihydro-3H,7H-azeto[2,1-b]furo[3,4-d][1,3]thiazine-1,7(4H)-dione (cefalotin lactone),

D. R = OCH₃: (5aR,6S)-6-methoxy-6-[[(thiophen-2-yl)acetyl]amino]-5a,6-dihydro-3H,7H-azeto[2,1-b]furo[3,4-d][1,3]thiazine-1,7(4H)-dione (cefoxitin lactone).

_____ Ph Eur

# Cefradine

(Ph Eur monograph 0814)

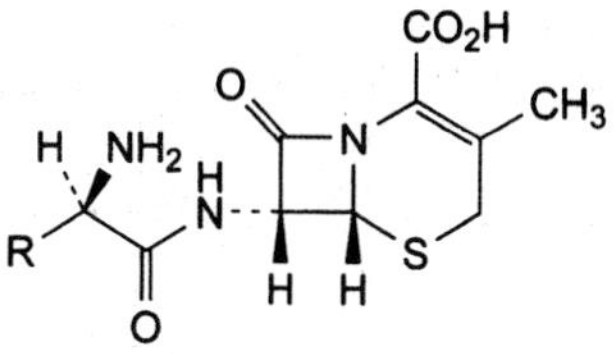

| Compound | R⁄ | Mol. Formula | $M_r$ |
|---|---|---|---|
| cefradine | 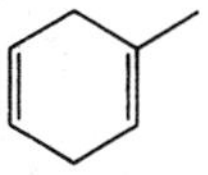  | $C_{16}H_{19}N_3O_4S$ | 349.4 |
| cefalexin | 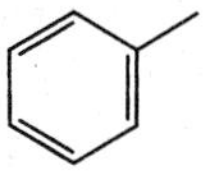  | $C_{16}H_{17}N_3O_4S$ | 347.4 |
| 4',5'-dihydrocefradine | 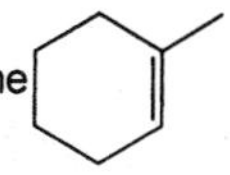  | $C_{16}H_{21}N_3O_4S$ | 351.4 |

## Action and use
Cephalosporin antibacterial.

## Preparations
Cefradine Capsules

Cefradine Oral Suspension

_Ph Eur_ _____

## DEFINITION

### Main component

(6R,7R)-7-[[(2R)-amino(cyclohexa-1,4-dienyl)acetyl]amino]-3-methyl-8-oxo-5-thia-1-azabicyclo[4.2.0]oct-2-ene-2-carboxylic acid (cefradine).

Semi-synthetic product derived from a fermentation product.

### Content:
— cefradine: minimum 90.0 per cent (anhydrous substance),
— cefalexin: maximum 5.0 per cent (anhydrous substance),
— 4',5'-dihydrocefradine: maximum 2.0 per cent (anhydrous substance).
— sum of the percentage contents of cefradine, cefalexin and 4',5'-dihydrocefradine: 96.0 per cent to 102.0 per cent (anhydrous substance).

## CHARACTERS

### Appearance
White or slightly yellow, hygroscopic powder.

### Solubility
Sparingly soluble in water, practically insoluble in ethanol 96 per cent and in hexane.

## IDENTIFICATION

Infrared absorption spectrophotometry (2.2.24).

_Comparison_ cefradine CRS.

If the spectra obtained in the solid state show differences, dissolve 30 mg of the substance to be examined and of the reference substance separately in 10 ml of _methanol R_, evaporate to dryness at 40 °C at a pressure less than 2 kPa and record new spectra using the residues.

## TESTS

### Solution S
Dissolve 2.50 g in *sodium carbonate solution R* and dilute to 25.0 ml with the same solvent.

### Appearance of solution
Solution S is not more opalescent than reference suspension II (*2.2.1*). Allow solution S to stand for 5 min. The absorbance of solution S measured at 450 nm (*2.2.25*) is not greater than 0.60.

### pH (*2.2.3*)
3.5 to 6.0.

Dissolve 0.100 g in *carbon dioxide-free water R* and dilute to 10 ml with the same solvent.

### Specific optical rotation (*2.2.7*)
+ 80.0 to + 90.0 (anhydrous substance).

Dissolve 0.250 g in *acetate buffer solution pH 4.6 R* and dilute to 25.0 ml with the same solvent.

### Related substances
Liquid chromatography (*2.2.29*).

*Test solution*   Dissolve 0.300 g of the substance to be examined in mobile phase A and dilute to 50.0 ml with mobile phase A.

*Reference solution (a)*   Dissolve 3.0 mg of *cyclohexa-1,4-dienylglycine CRS* (impurity B) in mobile phase A and dilute to 100.0 ml with mobile phase A.

*Reference solution (b)*   Dissolve 3 mg of the substance to be examined and 3 mg of *cefalexin CRS* in mobile phase A and dilute to 25 ml with mobile phase A.

*Reference solution (c)*   Dilute 1.0 ml of test solution to 100.0 ml with mobile phase A.

*Reference solution (d)*   Dissolve the contents of a vial of *cefradine for peak identification CRS* (containing impurities A, C, D, E and G) in 1 ml of *water for chromatography R*.

*Column:*
— *size*: $l = 0.15$ m, $\varnothing = 4.6$ mm,
— *stationary phase: octadecylsilyl silica gel for chromatography R* (5 μm),
— *temperature*: 30 °C.

*Mobile phase:*
— *mobile phase A*: 2.72 g/l solution of *potassium dihydrogen phosphate R* adjusted to pH 3.0 with *dilute phosphoric acid R;*
— *mobile phase B: methanol R2;*

| Time (min) | Mobile phase A (per cent V/V) | Mobile phase B (per cent V/V) |
|---|---|---|
| 0 - 2.5 | 99.5 → 97 | 0.5 → 3 |
| 2.5 - 11 | 97 → 75 | 3 → 25 |
| 11 - 13 | 75 → 60 | 25 → 40 |
| 13 - 16 | 60 | 40 |
| 16 - 19 | 60 → 20 | 40 → 80 |
| 19 - 19.1 | 20 → 99.5 | 80 → 0.5 |
| 19.1 - 25 | 99.5 | 0.5 |

*Flow rate*   1.0 ml/min.

*Detection*   Spectrophotometer at 220 nm.

*Injection*   25 μl.

*Identification of impurities*   Use the chromatogram obtained with reference solution (d) and the chromatogram supplied with *cefradine for peak identification CRS* to identify the peaks due to impurities A, C, D, E and G.

*Relative retention*   With reference to cefradine (retention time = about 15 min): impurity A = about 0.27; impurity B = about 0.32; impurity C = about 0.53; impurity D = about 0.63; impurity E = about 0.80; impurity F = about 0.92; cefalexin = about 0.95; 4′,5′-dihydrocefradine = about 1.06; impurity G = about 1.32.

*System suitability*   Reference solution (b):
— *resolution*: minimum 4.0 between the peaks due to cefalexin and cefradine.

*Limits:*
— *impurity B*: not more than 0.5 times the area of the principal peak in the chromatogram obtained with reference solution (a) (0.25 per cent);
— *impurities A, C, D, E, F, G*: for each impurity, not more than 0.25 times the area of the principal peak in the chromatogram obtained with reference solution (c) (0.25 per cent);
— *any other impurity*: for each impurity, not more than 0.25 times the area of the principal peak in the chromatogram obtained with reference solution (c) (0.25 per cent);
— *total*: not more than twice the area of the principal peak in the chromatogram obtained with reference solution (c) (2.0 per cent);
— *disregard limit*: 0.05 times the area of the principal peak in the chromatogram obtained with reference solution (c) (0.05 per cent); disregard the peaks due to cefalexin and 4′,5′-dihydrocefradine.

### N,N-Dimethylaniline (*2.4.26, Method B*)
Maximum 20 ppm.

### Water (*2.5.12*)
Maximum 6.0 per cent, determined on 0.300 g.

### Sulphated ash (*2.4.14*)
Maximum 0.2 per cent, determined on 1.0 g.

## ASSAY
Liquid chromatography (*2.2.29*).

*Test solution*   Dissolve 50.0 mg of the substance to be examined in *phosphate buffer solution pH 5.0 R* and dilute to 100.0 ml with the same solution.

*Reference solution (a)*   Dissolve 50.0 mg of *cefradine CRS* (containing 4′,5′-dihydrocefradine) in *phosphate buffer solution pH 5.0 R* and dilute to 100.0 ml with the same solution.

*Reference solution (b)*   Dissolve 5.0 mg of *cefalexin CRS* in *phosphate buffer solution pH 5.0 R* and dilute to 100.0 ml with the same solution.

*Reference solution (c)*   Dilute 1 ml of reference solution (a) to 10 ml with *phosphate buffer solution pH 5.0 R*. Mix 5 ml of this solution with 5 ml of reference solution (b).

*Column:*
— *size*: $l = 0.10$ m, $\varnothing = 4.6$ mm,
— *stationary phase: octadecylsilyl silica gel for chromatography R* (5 μm).

*Mobile phase*   methanol R, phosphate buffer solution pH 5.0 R (25:75 V/V).

*Flow rate*   1.5 ml/min.

*Detection*   Spectrophotometer at 254 nm.

*Injection*   5 μl.

*Run time*   Twice the retention time of cefradine.

*Relative retention*   With reference to cefradine (retention time = about 3 min): cefalexin = about 0.7; 4′,5′-dihydrocefradine = about 1.5.

*System suitability*   Reference solution (c):

— *resolution*: minimum 4.0 between the peaks due to cefalexin and cefradine.

Calculate the percentage content of cefradine using the chromatogram obtained with reference solution (a) and the declared content of *cefradine CRS*. Calculate the percentage content of cefalexin using the chromatogram obtained with reference solution (b) and the declared content of *cefalexin CRS*. Calculate the percentage content of 4',5'-dihydrocefradine using the chromatogram obtained with reference solution (b) and multiplying the area of the peak due to 4',5'-dihydrocefradine by a correction factor of 1.6.

## STORAGE

In an airtight container, protected from light, at a temperature of 2 °C to 8 °C.

## IMPURITIES

*Specified impurities   A, B, C, D, E, F, G.*

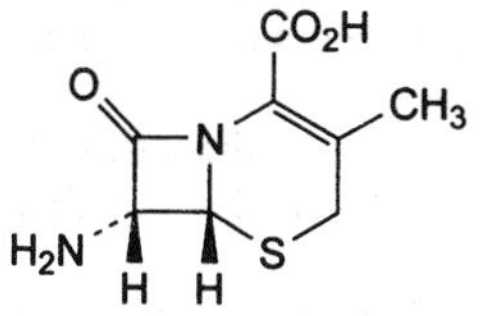

A. (6R,7R)-7-amino-3-methyl-8-oxo-5-thia-1-azabicyclo[4.2.0]oct-2-ene-2-carboxylic acid (7-aminodeacetoxycephalosporanic acid, 7-ADCA),

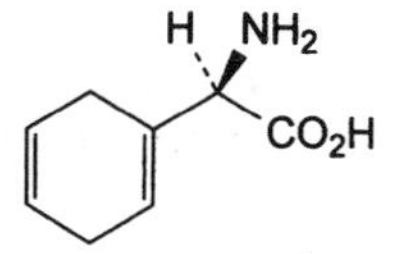

B. (2R)-amino(cyclohexa-1,4-dienyl)acetic acid (D-dihydrophenylglycine),

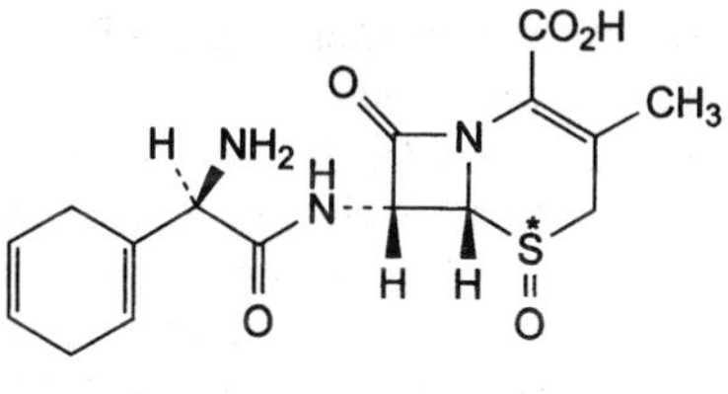

C. (6R,7R)-7-[[(2R)-amino(cyclohexa-1,4-dienyl)acetyl]amino]-3-methyl-8-oxo-5-thia-1-azabicyclo[4.2.0]oct-2-ene-2-carboxylic acid 5-oxide (isomer 1),

D. (6R,7R)-7-[[(2R)-amino(cyclohexa-1,4-dienyl)acetyl]amino]-3-methyl-8-oxo-5-thia-1-azabicyclo[4.2.0]oct-2-ene-2-carboxylic acid 5-oxide (isomer 2),

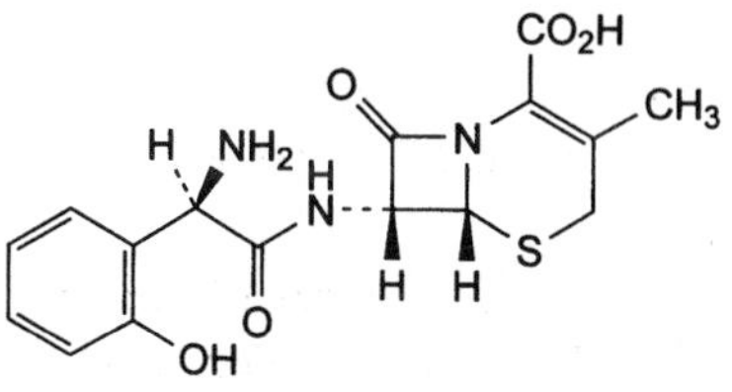

E. ((6R,7R)-7-[[(2R)-amino(2-hydroxyphenyl)acetyl]amino]-3-methyl-8-oxo-5-thia-1-azabicyclo[4.2.0]oct-2-ene-2-carboxylic acid,

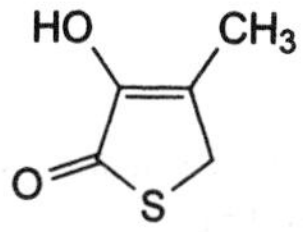

F. 3-hydroxy-4-methylthiophen-2(5H)-one,

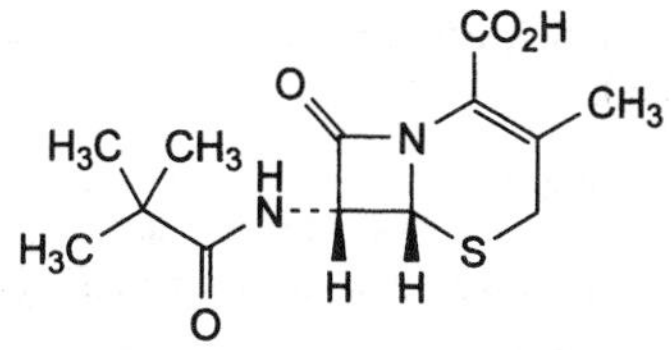

G. (6R,7R)-7-[(2,2-dimethylpropanoyl)amino]-3-methyl-8-oxo-5-thia-1-azabicyclo[4.2.0]oct-2-ene-2-carboxylic acid (7-ADCA pivalamide).

*Ph Eur*

# Ceftazidime Pentahydrate

Ceftazidime

(*Ph Eur monograph 1405*)

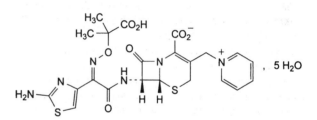

$C_{22}H_{22}N_6O_7S_2,5H_2O$          637          78439-06-2

**Action and use**
Cephalosporin antibacterial.

**Preparation**
Ceftazidime Injection

*Ph Eur*

## DEFINITION

(6R,7R)-7-[[(2Z)-2-(2-Aminothiazol-4-yl)-2-[(1-carboxy-1-methylethoxy)imino]acetyl]amino]-8-oxo-3-[(1-pyridinio)methyl]-5-thia-1-azabicyclo[4.2.0]oct-2-ene-2-carboxylate pentahydrate.

Semi-synthetic product derived from a fermentation product.

**Content**
95.0 per cent to 102.0 per cent (anhydrous substance).

## CHARACTERS

**Appearance**
White or almost white, crystalline powder.

**Solubility**
Slightly soluble in water and in methanol, practically insoluble in acetone and in ethanol (96 per cent). It dissolves in acid and alkali solutions.

## IDENTIFICATION

Infrared absorption spectrophotometry (*2.2.24*).

*Comparison   ceftazidime CRS.*

## TESTS

### Solution S

Dissolve 0.25 g in *carbon dioxide-free water R* and dilute to 50 ml with the same solvent.

### Appearance of solution

Solution S is clear (*2.2.1*) and colourless (*2.2.2, Method II*).

### pH (*2.2.3*)

3.0 to 4.0 for solution S.

### Related substances

Liquid chromatography (*2.2.29*).

*Test solution*   Suspend 0.150 g of the substance to be examined in 5 ml of *acetonitrile R*, dissolve by adding *water R* and dilute to 100 ml with the same solvent.

*Reference solution (a)*   To 1.0 ml of the test solution add 5.0 ml of *acetonitrile R* and dilute to 100.0 ml with *water R*. Dilute 1.0 ml of this solution to 5.0 ml with *water R*.

*Reference solution (b)*   Suspend 3 mg of *ceftazidime impurity A CRS* and 3 mg of *ceftazidime CRS* in 5 ml of *acetonitrile R*, dissolve by adding *water R* and dilute to 20 ml with the same solvent. Dilute 1 ml of this solution to 20 ml with *water R*.

*Reference solution (c)*   Suspend 3 mg of *ceftazidime for peak identification CRS* (containing impurities A, B and G) in 0.5 ml of *acetonitrile R*, dissolve by adding *water R* and dilute to 2 ml with the same solvent.

*Column:*
— *size:* $l$ = 0.25 m, Ø = 4.6 mm;
— *stationary phase:* octadecylsilyl silica gel for chromatography R (5 μm);
— *temperature:* 40 °C.

*Mobile phase:*
— *mobile phase A:* solution containing 3.6 g of *disodium hydrogen phosphate R* and 1.4 g of *potassium dihydrogen phosphate R* in 1 litre of *water R*, adjusted to pH 3.4 with a 10 per cent *V/V* solution of *phosphoric acid R*;
— *mobile phase B:* acetonitrile for chromatography R;

| Time (min) | Mobile phase A (per cent *V/V*) | Mobile phase B (per cent *V/V*) |
|---|---|---|
| 0 - 4 | 96 → 89 | 4 → 11 |
| 4 - 5 | 89 | 11 |
| 5 - 8 | 89 → 84 | 11 → 16 |
| 8 - 11 | 84 → 80 | 16 → 20 |
| 11 - 15 | 80 → 50 | 20 → 50 |
| 15 - 18 | 50 → 20 | 50 → 80 |
| 18 - 22 | 20 | 80 |

*Flow rate*   1.3 ml/min.

*Detection*   Spectrophotometer at 254 nm.

*Injection*   10 μl.

*Relative retention*   With reference to ceftazidime (retention time = about 8 min): impurity F = about 0.4; impurity G = about 0.8; impurity A = about 0.9; impurity B = about 1.4.

*Identification of impurities*   Use the chromatogram supplied with *ceftazidime for peak identification CRS* and the chromatogram obtained with reference solution (c) to identify the peaks due to impurities A, B and G.

*System suitability*   Reference solution (b):
— *resolution:* minimum 4.0 between the peaks due to impurity A and ceftazidime.

*Limits:*
— *correction factor:* for the calculation of content, multiply the peak area of impurity G by 3.0;
— *impurities A, B, G:* for each impurity, not more than the area of the principal peak in the chromatogram obtained with reference solution (a) (0.2 per cent);
— *unspecified impurities:* for each impurity, not more than 0.5 times the area of the principal peak in the chromatogram obtained with reference solution (a) (0.10 per cent);
— *total:* not more than 5 times the area of the principal peak in the chromatogram obtained with reference solution (a) (1.0 per cent);
— *disregard limit:* 0.25 times the area of the principal peak in the chromatogram obtained with reference solution (a) (0.05 per cent); disregard the peak due to impurity F.

### Impurity F

Liquid chromatography (*2.2.29*). *Prepare the solutions immediately before use.*

*Test solution*   Dissolve 0.500 g of the substance to be examined in a 10 per cent *V/V* solution of *phosphate buffer solution pH 7.0 R4* and dilute to 100.0 ml with the same solvent.

*Reference solution (a)*   Dissolve 1.00 g of *pyridine R* in *water R* and dilute to 100.0 ml with the same solvent. Dilute 5.0 ml of this solution to 200.0 ml with *water R*. To 1.0 ml of this solution, add 10 ml of *phosphate buffer solution pH 7.0 R4* and dilute to 100.0 ml with *water R*.

*Reference solution (b)*   Dilute 1 ml of the test solution to 200 ml with a 10 per cent *V/V* solution of *phosphate buffer solution pH 7.0 R4*. To 1 ml of this solution add 20 ml of reference solution (a) and dilute to 200 ml with a 10 per cent *V/V* solution of *phosphate buffer solution pH 7.0 R4*.

*Column:*
— *size:* $l$ = 0.25 m, Ø = 4.6 mm;
— *stationary phase:* octadecylsilyl silica gel for chromatography R (5 μm).

*Mobile phase*   Mix 8 volumes of a 28.8 g/l solution of *ammonium dihydrogen phosphate R* previously adjusted to pH 7.0 with *ammonia R*, 24 volumes of *acetonitrile R* and 68 volumes of *water R*.

*Flow rate*   1.0 ml/min.

*Detection*   Spectrophotometer at 255 nm.

*Injection*   20 μl.

*Run time*   10 min.

*System suitability*   Reference solution (b):
— *resolution:* minimum 7.0 between the peaks due to ceftazidime and impurity F.

*Limit:*
— *impurity F:* not more than the area of the principal peak in the chromatogram obtained with reference solution (a) (500 ppm).

### Heavy metals (*2.4.8*)

Maximum 20 ppm.

1.0 g complies with test F. Prepare the reference solution using 2.0 ml of *lead standard solution (10 ppm Pb) R*.

### Water (*2.5.12*)

13.0 per cent to 15.0 per cent, determined on 0.100 g.

### Bacterial endotoxins (*2.6.14*)

Less than 0.10 IU/mg, if intended for use in the manufacture of parenteral preparations without a further appropriate procedure for the removal of bacterial endotoxins.

## ASSAY

Liquid chromatography (2.2.29).

*Test solution*   Dissolve 25.0 mg of the substance to be examined in the mobile phase and dilute to 25.0 ml with the mobile phase.

*Reference solution (a)*   Dissolve 25.0 mg of *ceftazidime CRS* in the mobile phase and dilute to 25.0 ml with the mobile phase.

*Reference solution (b)*   Dissolve 5.0 mg of *ceftazidime impurity A CRS* in 5.0 ml of reference solution (a).

*Column:*
— *size: l* = 0.15 m, Ø = 4.6 mm;
— *stationary phase: hexylsilyl silica gel for chromatography R* (5 μm).

*Mobile phase*   Dissolve 4.3 g of *disodium hydrogen phosphate R* and 2.7 g of *potassium dihydrogen phosphate R* in 980 ml of *water R*, then add 20 ml of *acetonitrile R*.

*Flow rate*   2 ml/min.

*Detection*   Spectrophotometer at 245 nm.

*Injection*   20 μl.

*Run time*   6 min.

*Relative retention*   With reference to ceftazidime (retention time = about 4.5 min): impurity A = about 0.7.

*System suitability*   Reference solution (b):
— *resolution*: minimum 1.5 between the peaks due to impurity A and ceftazidime.

Calculate the content of ceftazidime ($C_{22}H_{22}N_6O_7S_2$) from the declared content of $C_{22}H_{22}N_6O_7S_2$ in *ceftazidime CRS*.

## STORAGE

In an airtight container. If the substance is sterile, store in a sterile, airtight, tamper-proof container.

## IMPURITIES

*Specified impurities*   A, B, F, G.

*Other detectable impurities*   (The following substances would, if present at a sufficient level, be detected by one or other of the tests in the monograph. They are limited by the general acceptance criterion for other/unspecified impurities and/or by the general monograph *Substances for pharmaceutical use (2034)*. It is therefore not necessary to identify these impurities for demonstration of compliance. See also *5.10. Control of impurities in substances for pharmaceutical use*):
C, E, H.

A. (2RS,6R,7R)-7-[[(2Z)-2-(2-aminothiazol-4-yl)-2-[(1-carboxy-1-methylethoxy)imino]acetyl]amino]-8-oxo-3-[(1-pyridinio)methyl]-5-thia-1-azabicyclo[4.2.0]oct-3-ene-2-carboxylate (Δ-2-ceftazidime),

B. (6R,7R)-7-[[(2E)-2-(2-aminothiazol-4-yl)-2-[(1-carboxy-1-methylethoxy)imino]acetyl]amino]-8-oxo-3-[(1-pyridinio)methyl]-5-thia-1-azabicyclo[4.2.0]oct-2-ene-2-carboxylate,

C. (6R,7R)-7-amino-8-oxo-3-[(1-pyridinio)methyl]-5-thia-1-azabicyclo[4.2.0]oct-2-ene-2-carboxylate,

E. (6R,7R)-7-[[(2Z)-2-(2-aminothiazol-4-yl)-2-[[2-(1,1-dimethylethoxy)-1,1-dimethyl-2-oxoethoxy]imino]acetyl]amino]-8-oxo-3-[(1-pyridinio)methyl]-5-thia-1-azabicyclo[4.2.0]oct-2-ene-2-carboxylate,

F. pyridine,

G. 2-[[[(1Z)-1-(2-aminothiazol-4-yl)-2-[(oxoethyl)amino]-2-oxoethylidene]amino]oxy]-2-methylpropanoic acid,

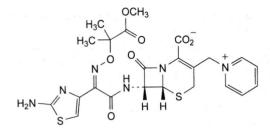

H. (6R,7R)-7-[[(2Z)-2-(2-aminothiazol-4-yl)-2-[(2-methoxy-1,1-dimethyl-2-oxoethoxy)imino]acetyl]amino]-8-oxo-3-[(1-pyridinio)methyl]-5-thia-1-azabicyclo[4.2.0]oct-2-ene-2-carboxylate.

_____ Ph Eur

# Ceftazidime Pentahydrate with Sodium Carbonate for Injection

(Ph Eur monograph 2344)

**Action and use**
Cephalosporin antibacterial.

**Preparation**
Ceftazidime Injection

Ph Eur _____

## DEFINITION

Sterile mixture of *Ceftazidime pentahydrate (1405)* and *Anhydrous sodium carbonate (0773)*.

Ceftazidime pentahydrate is a semi-synthetic product derived from a fermentation product.

**Content**
— *ceftazidime*: 93.0 per cent to 105.0 per cent (dried and carbonate-free substance);
— *sodium carbonate*: 8.0 per cent to 10.0 per cent.

## CHARACTERS

**Appearance**
White or pale yellow powder.

**Solubility**
Freely soluble in water and in methanol, practically insoluble in acetone.

## IDENTIFICATION

A. Examine the chromatograms obtained in the assay.

*Results* The principal peak in the chromatogram obtained with the test solution is similar in retention time to the principal peak in the chromatogram obtained with reference solution (a).

B. It gives the reaction of carbonates (2.3.1).

## TESTS

**Solution S**
Dissolve 2.60 g in *carbon dioxide-free water R* and dilute to 20.0 ml with the same solvent.

**Appearance of solution**
Solution S is clear (2.2.1) and its absorbance (2.2.25) at 425 nm is not greater than 0.50.

**pH** (2.2.3)
5.0 to 7.5 for solution S.

**Related substances**
Liquid chromatography (2.2.29).

*Test solution* Suspend 0.150 g of the substance to be examined in 5 ml of *acetonitrile R*, dissolve by adding *water R* and dilute to 100 ml with the same solvent.

*Reference solution (a)* To 1.0 ml of the test solution add 5.0 ml of *acetonitrile R* and dilute to 100.0 ml with *water R*. Dilute 1.0 ml of this solution to 5.0 ml with *water R*.

*Reference solution (b)* Suspend 3 mg of *ceftazidime CRS* and 3 mg of *ceftazidime impurity A CRS* in 5 ml of *acetonitrile R*, dissolve by adding *water R* and dilute to 20 ml with the same solvent. Dilute 1 ml of this solution to 20 ml with *water R*.

*Reference solution (c)* Suspend 3 mg of *ceftazidime for peak identification CRS* (containing impurities A, B and G) in 0.5 ml of *acetonitrile R*, dissolve by adding *water R* and dilute to 2 ml with the same solvent.

*Column:*
— *size*: l = 0.25 m, Ø = 4.6 mm;
— *stationary phase*: octadecylsilyl silica gel for chromatography R (5 μm);
— *temperature*: 40 °C.

*Mobile phase:*
— *mobile phase A*: solution containing 3.6 g of *disodium hydrogen phosphate R* and 1.4 g of *potassium dihydrogen phosphate R* in 1 litre of *water R*, adjusted to pH 3.4 with a 10 per cent V/V solution of *phosphoric acid R*;
— *mobile phase B*: acetonitrile for chromatography R;

| Time (min) | Mobile phase A (per cent V/V) | Mobile phase B (per cent V/V) |
|---|---|---|
| 0 - 4 | 96 → 89 | 4 → 11 |
| 4 - 5 | 89 | 11 |
| 5 - 8 | 89 → 84 | 11 → 16 |
| 8 - 11 | 84 → 80 | 16 → 20 |
| 11 - 15 | 80 → 50 | 20 → 50 |
| 15 - 18 | 50 → 20 | 50 → 80 |
| 18 - 22 | 20 | 80 |

*Flow rate* 1.3 ml/min.

*Detection* Spectrophotometer at 254 nm.

*Injection* 10 μl.

*Relative retention* With reference to ceftazidime (retention time = about 8 min): impurity F = about 0.4; impurity G = about 0.8; impurity A = about 0.9; impurity B = about 1.4.

*Identification of impurities* Use the chromatogram supplied with *ceftazidime for peak identification CRS* and the chromatogram obtained with reference solution (c) to identify the peaks due to impurities A, B and G.

*System suitability* Reference solution (b):
— *resolution*: minimum 4.0 between the peaks due to impurity A and ceftazidime.

*Limits:*
— *correction factor*: for the calculation of content, multiply the peak area of impurity G by 3.0;
— *impurities A, B, G*: for each impurity, not more than the area of the principal peak in the chromatogram obtained with reference solution (a) (0.2 per cent);
— *unspecified impurities*: for each impurity, not more than 0.5 times the area of the principal peak in the chromatogram obtained with reference solution (a) (0.10 per cent);
— *total*: not more than 5 times the area of the principal peak in the chromatogram obtained with reference solution (a) (1.0 per cent);

— *disregard limit*: 0.25 times the area of the principal peak in the chromatogram obtained with reference solution (a) (0.05 per cent); disregard the peak due to impurity F.

**Impurity F**
Liquid chromatography (*2.2.29*). *Prepare the solutions immediately before use.*

*Test solution* Dissolve 0.500 g of the substance to be examined in a 10 per cent *V/V phosphate buffer solution pH 7.0 R4* and dilute to 100.0 ml with the same buffer solution.

*Reference solution (a)* Dissolve 1.00 g of *pyridine R* in *water R* and dilute to 100.0 ml with the same solvent. Dilute 5.0 ml of this solution to 200.0 ml with *water R*. To 1.0 ml of this solution add 10.0 ml of *phosphate buffer solution pH 7.0 R4* and dilute to 100.0 ml with *water R*.

*Reference solution (b)* Dilute 1.0 ml of the test solution to 200.0 ml with a 10 per cent *V/V phosphate buffer solution pH 7.0 R4*. To 1.0 ml of this solution add 20.0 ml of reference solution (a) and dilute to 200.0 ml with a 10 per cent *V/V phosphate buffer solution pH 7.0 R4*.

*Column:*
— *size: l* = 0.25 m, Ø = 4.6 mm;
— *stationary phase: octadecylsilyl silica gel for chromatography R* (5 μm).

*Mobile phase* Mix 8 volumes of a 28.8 g/l solution of *ammonium dihydrogen phosphate R* previously adjusted to pH 7.0 with *ammonia R*, 24 volumes of *acetonitrile R* and 68 volumes of *water R*.

*Flow rate* 1.0 ml/min.

*Detection* Spectrophotometer at 255 nm.

*Injection* 20 μl.

*Run time* 10 min.

*System suitability* Reference solution (b):
— *resolution*: minimum 7.0 between the peaks due to ceftazidime and impurity F.

*Limit:*
— *impurity F*: not more than 6 times the area of the principal peak in the chromatogram obtained with reference solution (a) (0.3 per cent).

**Loss on drying** (*2.2.32*)
Maximum 13.5 per cent, determined on 0.300 g. Dry *in vacuo* at 25 °C at a pressure not exceeding 0.67 kPa for 4 h then heat the residue *in vacuo* at 100 °C at a pressure not exceeding 0.67 kPa for 3 h.

**Bacterial endotoxins** (*2.6.14*)
Less than 0.10 IU/mg, if intended for use in the manufacture of parenteral preparations without a further appropriate procedure for the removal of bacterial endotoxins.

**ASSAY**
**Ceftazidime**
Liquid chromatography (*2.2.29*).

*Test solution* Dissolve 25.0 mg of the substance to be examined in the mobile phase and dilute to 25.0 ml with the mobile phase.

*Reference solution (a)* Dissolve 25.0 mg of *ceftazidime CRS* in the mobile phase and dilute to 25.0 ml with the mobile phase.

*Reference solution (b)* Dissolve 5.0 mg of *ceftazidime impurity A CRS* in 5.0 ml of reference solution (a).

*Column:*
— *size: l* = 0.15 m, Ø = 4.6 mm;

— *stationary phase: hexylsilyl silica gel for chromatography R* (5 μm).

*Mobile phase* Dissolve 4.3 g of *disodium hydrogen phosphate R* and 2.7 g of *potassium dihydrogen phosphate R* in 980 ml of *water R*, then add 20 ml of *acetonitrile R*.

*Flow rate* 2 ml/min.

*Detection* Spectrophotometer at 245 nm.

*Injection* 20 μl.

*Run time* 6 min.

*Relative retention* With reference to ceftazidime (retention time = about 4.5 min): impurity A = about 0.7.

*System suitability* Reference solution (b):
— *resolution*: minimum 1.5 between the peaks due to impurity A and ceftazidime.

Calculate the content of ceftazidime ($C_{22}H_{22}N_6O_7S_2$) from the declared content of $C_{22}H_{22}N_6O_7S_2$ in *ceftazidime CRS*.

**Sodium carbonate**
Atomic absorption spectrometry (*2.2.23, Method I*).

*Caesium chloride buffer solution* To 12.7 g of *caesium chloride R* add 500 ml of *water R* and 86 ml of *hydrochloric acid R* and dilute to 1000.0 ml with *water R*.

*Sodium standard solution (1000 mg/l)* Dissolve 3.70 g of *sodium nitrate R* in *water R* and dilute to 500 ml with the same solvent, add 48.5 g of *nitric acid R* and dilute to 1000 ml with *water R*.

*Test solution* Dissolve 650.0 mg of the substance to be examined in *water R* and dilute to 100.0 ml with the same solvent. To 10.0 ml of this solution add 5.0 ml of caesium chloride buffer solution and dilute to 50.0 ml with *water R*.

*Reference solution* Into 4 identical flasks, each containing 20.0 ml of caesium chloride buffer solution, introduce respectively 0 ml, 5.00 ml, 10.00 ml and 15.00 ml of sodium standard solution (1000 mg/l) and dilute to 200.0 ml with *water R*.

*Source* Sodium hollow-cathode lamp.

*Wavelength* 330.2 nm to 330.3 nm.

*Atomisation device* Air-acetylene flame.

Calculate the percentage content of sodium carbonate.

**STORAGE**
In a sterile, airtight, tamper-proof container, protected from light and humidity.

**LABELLING**
The label states the percentage content m/m of ceftazidime.

**IMPURITIES**
*Specified impurities* *A, B, F, G.*

*Other detectable impurities* (The following substances would, if present at a sufficient level, be detected by one or other of the tests in the monograph. They are limited by the general acceptance criterion for other/unspecified impurities and/or by the general monograph *Substances for pharmaceutical use (2034)*. It is therefore not necessary to identify these impurities for demonstration of compliance. See also *5.10*. Control of impurities in substances for pharmaceutical use): *C, E, H.*

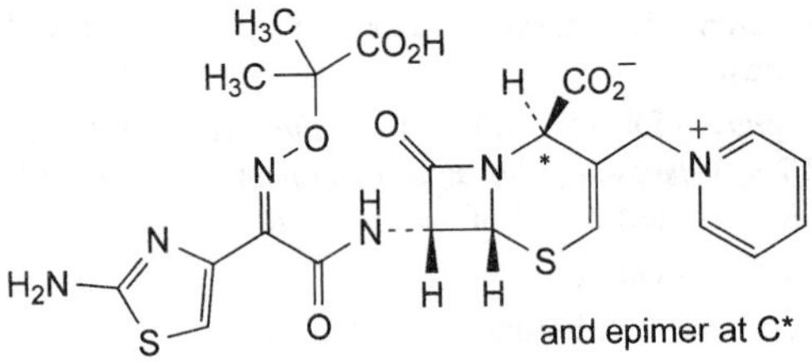

A. (2RS,6R,7R)-7-[[(2Z)-2-(2-aminothiazol-4-yl)-2-[(1-carboxy-1-methylethoxy)imino]acetyl]amino]-8-oxo-3-[(1-pyridinio)methyl]-5-thia-1-azabicyclo[4.2.0]oct-3-ene-2-carboxylate (Δ-2-ceftazidime),

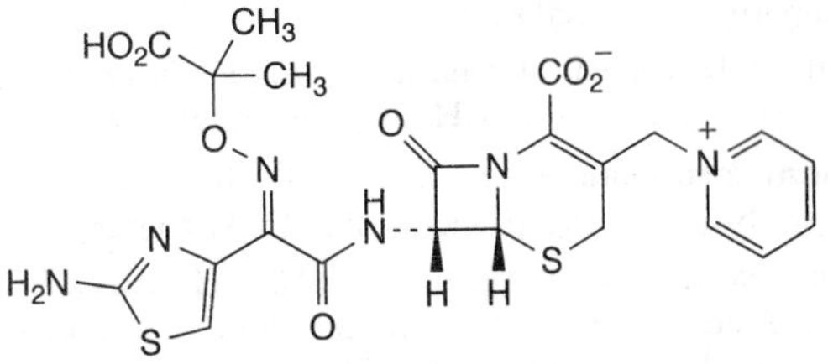

B. (6R,7R)-7-[[(2E)-2-(2-aminothiazol-4-yl)-2-[(1-carboxy-1-methylethoxy)imino]acetyl]amino]-8-oxo-3-[(1-pyridinio)methyl]-5-thia-1-azabicyclo[4.2.0]oct-2-ene-2-carboxylate,

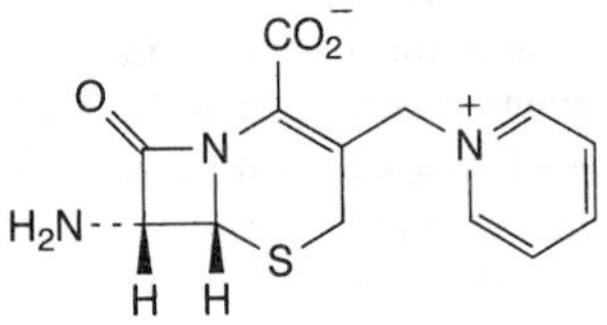

C. (6R,7R)-7-amino-8-oxo-3-[(1-pyridinio)methyl]-5-thia-1-azabicyclo[4.2.0]oct-2-ene-2-carboxylate,

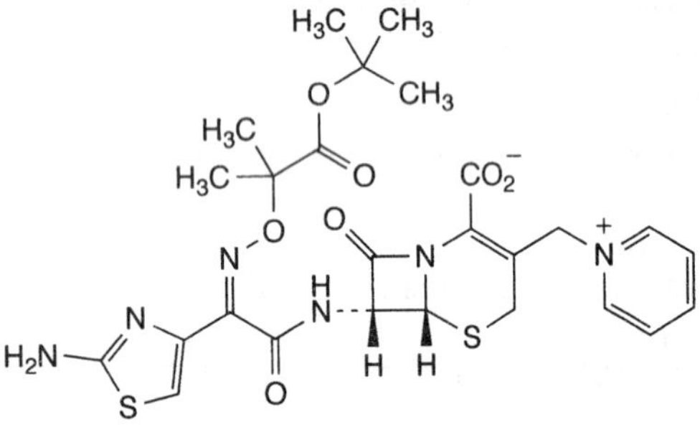

E. (6R,7R)-7-[[(2Z)-2-(2-aminothiazol-4-yl)-2-[[2-(1,1-dimethylethoxy)-1,1-dimethyl-2-oxoethoxy]imino]acetyl]amino]-8-oxo-3-[(1-pyridinio)methyl]-5-thia-1-azabicyclo[4.2.0]oct-2-ene-2-carboxylate,

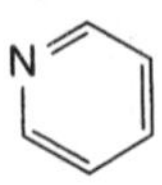

F. pyridine,

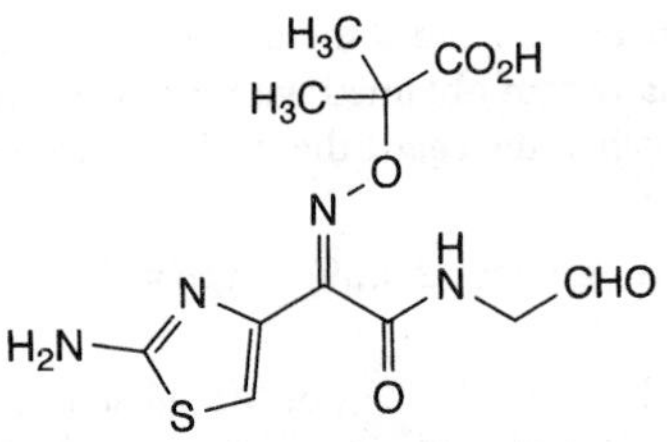

G. 2-[[[(1Z)-1-(2-aminothiazol-4-yl)-2-[(oxoethyl)amino]-2-oxoethylidene]amino]oxy]-2-methylpropanoic acid,

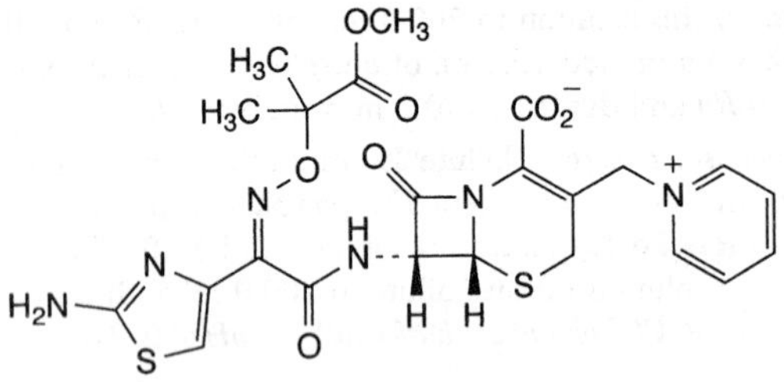

H. (6R,7R)-7-[[(2Z)-2-(2-aminothiazol-4-yl)-2-[(2-methoxy-1,1-dimethyl-2-oxoethoxy)imino]acetyl]amino]-8-oxo-3-[(1-pyridinio)methyl]-5-thia-1-azabicyclo[4.2.0]oct-2-ene-2-carboxylate.

*Ph Eur*

# Ceftriaxone Sodium

(*Ph Eur monograph 0991*)

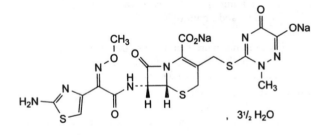

$C_{18}H_{16}N_8Na_2O_7S_3,3\frac{1}{2}H_2O$    662    *104376-79-6*

## Action and use
Cephalosporin antibacterial.

## Preparation
Ceftriaxone Injection

*Ph Eur*

## DEFINITION
Disodium (6R,7R)-7-[[(2Z)-(2-aminothiazol-4-yl)(methoxyimino)acetyl]amino]-3-[[(2-methyl-6-oxido-5-oxo-2,5-dihydro-1,2,4-triazin-3-yl)sulphanyl]methyl]-8-oxo-5-thia-1-azabicyclo[4.2.0]oct-2-ene-2-carboxylate 3.5 hydrate.

Semi-synthetic product derived from a fermentation product.

## Content
96.0 per cent to 102.0 per cent (anhydrous substance).

## CHARACTERS
### Appearance
Almost white or yellowish, slightly hygroscopic, crystalline powder.

## Solubility

Freely soluble in water, sparingly soluble in methanol, very slightly soluble in anhydrous ethanol.

## IDENTIFICATION

A. Infrared absorption spectrophotometry (*2.2.24*).

*Comparison* ceftriaxone sodium CRS.

B. It gives reaction (a) of sodium (*2.3.1*).

## TESTS

### Solution S

Dissolve 2.40 g in *carbon dioxide-free water R* and dilute to 20.0 ml with the same solvent.

### Appearance of solution

The solution is clear (*2.2.1*) and not more intensely coloured than reference solution $Y_5$ or $BY_5$ (*2.2.2*).

Dilute 2 ml of solution S to 20 ml with *water R*.

### pH (*2.2.3*)

6.0 to 8.0 for solution S.

### Specific optical rotation (*2.2.7*)

− 155 to − 170 (anhydrous substance).

Dissolve 0.250 g in *water R* and dilute to 25.0 ml with the same solvent.

### Related substances

Liquid chromatography (*2.2.29*).

*Test solution* Dissolve 30.0 mg of the substance to be examined in the mobile phase and dilute to 100.0 ml with the mobile phase.

*Reference solution (a)* Dissolve 30.0 mg of *ceftriaxone sodium CRS* in the mobile phase and dilute to 100.0 ml with the mobile phase.

*Reference solution (b)* Dissolve 5.0 mg of *ceftriaxone sodium CRS* and 5.0 mg of *ceftriaxone impurity A CRS* in the mobile phase and dilute to 100.0 ml with the mobile phase.

*Reference solution (c)* Dilute 1.0 ml of the test solution to 100.0 ml with the mobile phase.

*Column:*
— *size*: $l$ = 0.25 m, Ø = 4.6 mm;
— *stationary phase*: octadecylsilyl silica gel for chromatography R (5 µm).

*Mobile phase* Dissolve 2.0 g of *tetradecylammonium bromide R* and 2.0 g of *tetraheptylammonium bromide R* in a mixture of 440 ml of *water R*, 55 ml of *0.067 M phosphate buffer solution pH 7.0 R*, 5.0 ml of citrate buffer solution pH 5.0 prepared by dissolving 20.17 g of *citric acid R* in 800 ml of *water R*, adjusting to pH 5.0 with *strong sodium hydroxide solution R* and diluting to 1000.0 ml with *water R*, and 500 ml of *acetonitrile R*.

*Flow rate* 1.5 ml/min.

*Detection* Spectrophotometer at 254 nm.

*Injection* 20 µl of the test solution and reference solutions (b) and (c).

*Run time* Twice the retention time of ceftriaxone.

*System suitability* Reference solution (b):
— *resolution*: minimum 3.0 between the peaks due to ceftriaxone and impurity A.

*Limits:*
— *any impurity*: not more than the area of the principal peak in the chromatogram obtained with reference solution (c) (1.0 per cent);
— *total*: not more than 4 times the area of the principal peak in the chromatogram obtained with reference solution (c) (4.0 per cent);

— *disregard limit*: 0.1 times the area of the principal peak in the chromatogram obtained with reference solution (c) (0.1 per cent).

### N,N-Dimethylaniline (*2.4.26, Method B*)

Maximum 20 ppm.

### 2-Ethylhexanoic acid (*2.4.28*)

Maximum 0.8 per cent m/m.

### Water (*2.5.12*)

8.0 per cent to 11.0 per cent, determined on 0.100 g.

### Bacterial endotoxins (*2.6.14*)

Less than 0.08 IU/mg, if intended for use in the manufacture of parenteral dosage forms without a further appropriate procedure for the removal of bacterial endotoxins.

## ASSAY

Liquid chromatography (*2.2.29*) as described in the test for related substances with the following modification.

*Injection* Test solution and reference solution (a).

Calculate the percentage content of $C_{18}H_{16}N_8Na_2O_7S_3$ from the declared content of *ceftriaxone sodium CRS*.

## STORAGE

In an airtight container protected from light. If the substance is sterile, store in a sterile, airtight, tamper-proof container.

## IMPURITIES

A. (6R,7R)-7-[[(2E)-(2-aminothiazol-4-yl)(methoxyimino)acetyl]amino]-3-[[(2-methyl-5,6-dioxo-1,2,5,6-tetrahydro-1,2,4-triazin-3-yl)sulphanyl]methyl]-8-oxo-5-thia-1-azabicyclo[4.2.0]oct-2-ene-2-carboxylic acid ((E)-isomer),

B. (5aR,6R)-6-[[(2Z)-(2-aminothiazol-4-yl)(methoxyimino)acetyl]amino]-5a,6-dihydro-3H,7H-azeto[2,1-b]furo[3,4-d][1,3]thiazine-1,7(4H)-dione,

C. 2-methyl-3-sulphanyl-1,2-dihydro-1,2,4-triazine-5,6-dione,

D. *S*-benzothiazol-2-yl (2*Z*)-(2-aminothiazol-4-yl)(methoxyimino)thioacetate,

E. (6*R*,7*R*)-7-amino-3-[[(2-methyl-5,6-dioxo-1,2,5,6-tetrahydro-1,2,4-triazin-3-yl)sulphanyl]methyl]-8-oxo-5-thia-1-azabicyclo[4.2.0]oct-2-ene-2-carboxylic acid.

*Ph Eur*

# Cefuroxime Axetil

(*Ph Eur monograph 1300*)

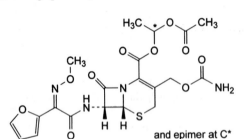

and epimer at C*

$C_{20}H_{22}N_4O_{10}S$          510.5          *64544-07-6*

**Action and use**
Cephalosporin antibacterial.

**Preparation**
Cefuroxime Axetil Tablets

*Ph Eur*

## DEFINITION
Mixture of the 2 diastereoisomers of (1*RS*)-1-(acetyloxy)ethyl (6*R*,7*R*)-3-[(carbamoyloxy)methyl]-7-[[(*Z*)-2-(furan-2-yl)-2-(methoxyimino)acetyl]amino]-8-oxo-5-thia-1-azabicyclo[4.2.0]oct-2-ene-2-carboxylate.

Semi-synthetic product derived from a fermentation product.

**Content**
96.0 per cent to 102.0 per cent (anhydrous substance).

## CHARACTERS
**Appearance**
White or almost white powder.

**Solubility**
Slightly soluble in water, soluble in acetone, in ethyl acetate and in methanol, slightly soluble in ethanol (96 per cent).

## IDENTIFICATION
A. Infrared absorption spectrophotometry (*2.2.24*).
*Comparison   cefuroxime axetil CRS.*
B. Examine the chromatograms obtained in the assay.
*Results*   The principal peaks in the chromatogram obtained with the test solution are similar in retention time and size to the peaks due to cefuroxime axetil diastereoisomers A and B in the chromatogram obtained with reference solution (d).

## TESTS
### Related substances
Liquid chromatography (*2.2.29*): use the normalisation procedure. *Prepare the test solution and reference solution (d) immediately before use.*

*Test solution*   Dissolve 10.0 mg of the substance to be examined in the mobile phase and dilute to 50.0 ml with the mobile phase.

*Reference solution (a)*   Dilute 1.0 ml of the test solution to 100.0 ml with the mobile phase.

*Reference solution (b)*   In order to prepare *in situ* impurity A, heat 5 ml of the test solution at 60 °C for 1 h.

*Reference solution (c)*   In order to prepare *in situ* impurity B, expose 5 ml of the test solution to ultraviolet light at 254 nm for 24 h.

*Reference solution (d)*   Dissolve 10.0 mg of *cefuroxime axetil CRS* in the mobile phase and dilute to 50.0 ml with the mobile phase.

*Column:*
— *size*: *l* = 0.25 m, Ø = 4.6 mm;
— *stationary phase: trimethylsilyl silica gel for chromatography R* (5 μm).

*Mobile phase   methanol R, 23 g/l solution of ammonium dihydrogen phosphate R (38:62 V/V).*

*Flow rate*   1.0 ml/min.

*Detection*   Spectrophotometer at 278 nm.

*Injection*   20 μl of the test solution and reference solutions (a), (b) and (c).

*Identification of impurities*   Use the chromatogram obtained with reference solution (b) to identify the pair of peaks due to impurity A and use the chromatogram obtained with reference solution (c) to identify the pair of peaks due to impurity B.

*Relative retention*   With reference to cefuroxime axetil diastereoisomer A: cefuroxime axetil diastereoisomer B = about 0.9, impurity A = about 1.2; impurity B = 1.7 and 2.1.

*System suitability*   Reference solution (b):
— *resolution*: minimum 1.5 between the peaks due to cefuroxime axetil diastereoisomer A and impurity A.

*Limits:*
— *impurity A*: maximum 1.5 per cent for the sum of the pair of peaks;
— *impurity B*: maximum 1.0 per cent for the sum of the pair of peaks;
— *impurity E*: maximum 0.5 per cent;
— *any other impurity*: for each impurity, maximum 0.5 per cent;
— *total*: maximum 3.0 per cent;
— *disregard limit*: 0.05 times the area of the 2 principal peaks in the chromatogram obtained with reference solution (a) (0.05 per cent).

## Diastereoisomer ratio

Liquid chromatography (*2.2.29*) as described in the test for related substances.

*Limit* Test solution:
— the ratio of the area of the peak due to cefuroxime axetil diastereoisomer A to the sum of the areas of the peaks due to cefuroxime axetil diastereoisomers A and B is between 0.48 and 0.55.

### Acetone (*2.4.24*)
Maximum 1.1 per cent.

### Water (*2.5.12*)
Maximum 1.5 per cent, determined on 0.400 g.

## ASSAY

Liquid chromatography (*2.2.29*) as described in the test for related substances with the following modifications.

*Injection* Test solution and reference solution (d).

*System suitability* Reference solution (d):
— *resolution*: minimum 1.5 between the peaks due to cefuroxime axetil diastereoisomers A and B;
— *repeatability*: maximum relative standard deviation of 2.0 per cent for the sum of the peaks due to cefuroxime axetil diastereoisomers A and B after 6 injections.

Calculate the percentage content of $C_{20}H_{22}N_4O_{10}S$ from the sum of the areas of the 2 diastereoisomer peaks and the declared content of $C_{20}H_{22}N_4O_{10}S$ in *cefuroxime axetil CRS*.

## STORAGE
In an airtight container, protected from light.

## IMPURITIES

*Specified impurities A, B, E.*

*Other detectable impurities* (the following substances would, if present at a sufficient level, be detected by one or other of the tests in the monograph. They are limited by the general acceptance criterion for other/unspecified impurities and/or by the general monograph *Substances for pharmaceutical use (2034)*. It is therefore not necessary to identify these impurities for demonstration of compliance. See also *5.10. Control of impurities in substances for pharmaceutical use*) : C, D.

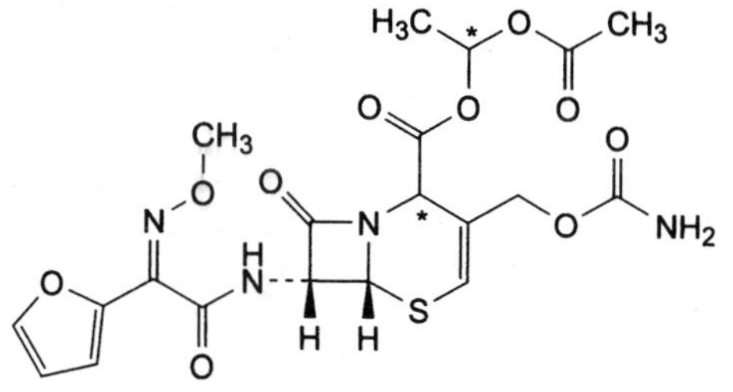

A. 1-(acetyloxy)ethyl (6R,7R)-3-[(carbamoyloxy)methyl]-7-[[(Z)-2-(furan-2-yl)-2-(methoxyimino)acetyl]amino]-8-oxo-5-thia-1-azabicyclo[4.2.0]oct-3-ene-2-carboxylate ($\Delta^3$-isomers),

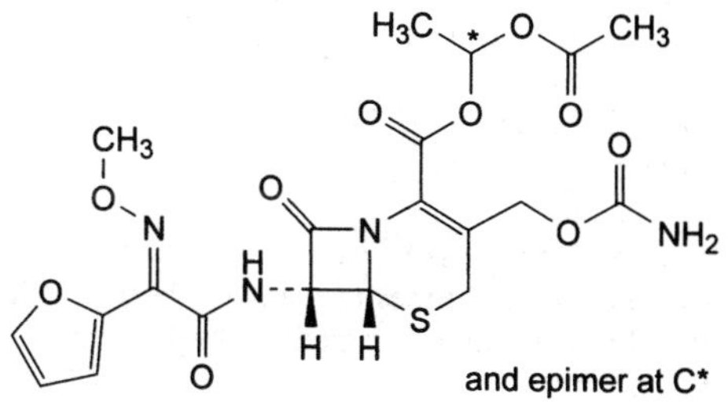

**and epimer at C\***

B. (1RS)-1-(acetyloxy)ethyl (6R,7R)-3-[(carbamoyloxy)methyl]-7-[[(E)-2-(furan-2-yl)-2-

(methoxyimino)acetyl]amino]-8-oxo-5-thia-1-azabicyclo[4.2.0]oct-2-ene-2-carboxylate ((E)-isomers),

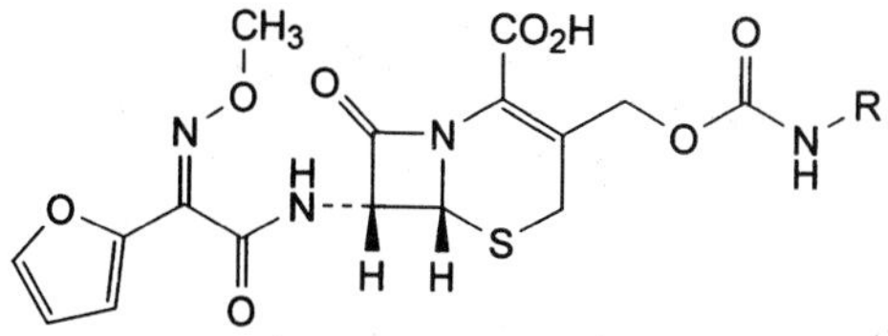

C. R = CO-CCl₃: (6R,7R)-7-[[(Z)-2-(furan-2-yl)-2-(methoxyimino)acetyl]amino]-8-oxo-3-[[[(trichloroacetyl)carbamoyl]oxy]methyl]-5-thia-1-azabicyclo[4.2.0]oct-2-ene-2-carboxylic acid,

D. R = H: cefuroxime.

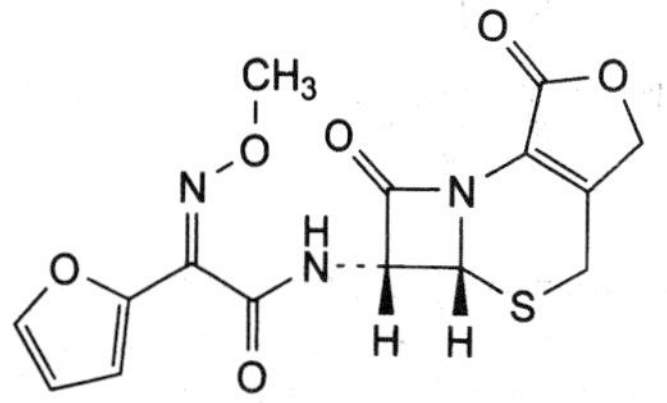

E. (5aR,6R)-6-[[(2Z)-2-(furan-2-yl)-2-(methoxyimino)acetyl]amino]-5a,6-dihydro-3H,7H-azeto[2,1-b]furo[3,4-d][1,3]thiazine-1,7(4H)-dione (descarbamoylcefuroxime lactone).

*Ph Eur*

# Cefuroxime Sodium

(*Ph Eur monograph 0992*)

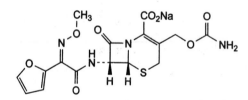

$C_{16}H_{15}N_4NaO_8S$      446.4      *56238-63-2*

## Action and use
Cephalosporin antibacterial.

## Preparation
Cefuroxime Injection

*Ph Eur*

## DEFINITION
Sodium (6R,7R)-3-[(carbamoyloxy)methyl]-7-[[(Z)-(furan-2-yl)(methoxyimino)acetyl]amino]-8-oxo-5-thia-1-azabicyclo[4.2.0]oct-2-ene-2-carboxylate.

Semi-synthetic product derived from a fermentation product.

## Content
96.0 per cent to 102.0 per cent (anhydrous substance).

## CHARACTERS
### Appearance
White or almost white, slightly hygroscopic powder.

### Solubility
Freely soluble in water, very slightly soluble in ethanol (96 per cent).

## IDENTIFICATION

A. Infrared absorption spectrophotometry (2.2.24).

*Comparison* cefuroxime sodium CRS.

B. It gives reaction (a) of sodium (2.3.1).

## TESTS

### Solution S

Dissolve 2.0 g in *carbon dioxide-free water R* and dilute to 20.0 ml with the same solvent.

### Appearance of solution

Solution S is not more opalescent than reference suspension II (2.2.1). The absorbance (2.2.25) of solution S measured at 450 nm is not greater than 0.25.

### pH (2.2.3)

5.5 to 8.5.

Dilute 2 ml of solution S to 20 ml with *carbon dioxide-free water R*.

### Specific optical rotation (2.2.7)

+ 59 to + 66 (anhydrous substance).

Dissolve 0.500 g in *acetate buffer solution pH 4.6 R* and dilute to 25.0 ml with the same buffer solution.

### Related substances

Liquid chromatography (2.2.29). *Prepare the solutions immediately before use or keep at 2-8 °C.*

*Test solution (a)* Dissolve 25.0 mg of the substance to be examined in *water R* and dilute to 25.0 ml with the same solvent.

*Test solution (b)* Dilute 5.0 ml of test solution (a) to 50.0 ml with *water R*.

*Reference solution (a)* Dissolve 25.0 mg of *cefuroxime sodium CRS* in *water R* and dilute to 25.0 ml with the same solvent. Dilute 5.0 ml to 50.0 ml with *water R*.

*Reference solution (b)* Place 20 ml of reference solution (a) in a water-bath at 80 °C for 15 min. Cool and inject immediately.

*Reference solution (c)* Dilute 1.0 ml of test solution (a) to 100.0 ml with *water R*.

*Column:*
— size: $l = 0.125$ m, $\varnothing = 4.6$ mm;
— stationary phase: *hexylsilyl silica gel for chromatography R* (5 µm).

*Mobile phase* Mix 1 volume of *acetonitrile R* and 99 volumes of an acetate buffer solution pH 3.4, prepared by dissolving 6.01 g of *glacial acetic acid R* and 0.68 g of *sodium acetate R* in *water R* and diluting to 1000 ml with the same solvent.

*Flow rate* 1.5 ml/min.

*Detection* Spectrophotometer at 273 nm.

*Injection* 20 µl loop injector; inject test solution (a) and reference solutions (b) and (c).

*Run time* 4 times the retention time of cefuroxime.

*System suitability* Reference solution (b):
— resolution: minimum 2.0 between the peaks due to cefuroxime and impurity A.

*Limits:*
— impurity A: not more than the area of the principal peak in the chromatogram obtained with reference solution (c) (1.0 per cent);
— any other impurity: not more than the area of the principal peak in the chromatogram obtained with reference solution (c) (1.0 per cent);

— total: not more than 3 times the area of the principal peak in the chromatogram obtained with reference solution (c) (3.0 per cent);
— disregard limit: 0.05 times the area of the principal peak in the chromatogram obtained with reference solution (c) (0.05 per cent).

### N,N-Dimethylaniline (2.4.26, Method B)

Maximum 20 ppm.

### 2-Ethylhexanoic acid (2.4.28)

Maximum 0.5 per cent *m/m*.

### Water (2.5.12)

Maximum 3.5 per cent, determined on 0.400 g.

### Bacterial endotoxins (2.6.14)

Less than 0.10 IU/mg, if intended for use in the manufacture of parenteral dosage forms without a further appropriate procedure for the removal of bacterial endotoxins.

## ASSAY

Liquid chromatography (2.2.29) as described in the test for related substances with the following modification.

*Injection* Test solution (b) and reference solution (a).

Calculate the percentage content of cefuroxime sodium.

## STORAGE

In an airtight container. If the substance is sterile, store in a sterile, airtight, tamper-proof container.

## IMPURITIES

A. R = OH: (6R,7R)-7-[[(Z)-(furan-2-yl)(methoxyimino)acetyl]amino]-3-(hydroxymethyl)-8-oxo-5-thia-1-azabicyclo[4.2.0]oct-2-ene-2-carboxylic acid (descarbamoylcefuroxime),

B. R = O-CO-CH₃: (6R,7R)-3-[(acetyloxy)methyl]-7-[[(Z)-(furan-2-yl)(methoxyimino)acetyl]amino]-8-oxo-5-thia-1-azabicyclo[4.2.0]oct-2-ene-2-carboxylic acid,

C. R = H: (6R,7R)-7-[[(Z)-(furan-2-yl)(methoxyimino)acetyl]amino]-3-methyl-8-oxo-5-thia-1-azabicyclo[4.2.0]oct-2-ene-2-carboxylic acid,

D. R = O-CO-NH-CO-CCl₃: (6R,7R)-7-[[(Z)-(furan-2-yl)(methoxyimino)acetyl]amino]-8-oxo-3-[[[[(trichloroacetyl)carbamoyl]oxy]methyl]-5-thia-1-azabicyclo[4.2.0]oct-2-ene-2-carboxylic acid,

E. R = O-CO-NH₂: (6R,7R)-3-[(carbamoyloxy)methyl]-7-[[(E)-(furan-2-yl)(methoxyimino)acetyl]amino]-8-oxo-5-thia-1-azabicyclo[4.2.0]oct-2-ene-2-carboxylic acid (*trans*-cefuroxime),

F. R = OH: (6R,7R)-7-[[(E)-(furan-2-yl)(methoxyimino)acetyl]amino]-3-(hydroxymethyl)-8-oxo-5-thia-1-azabicyclo[4.2.0]oct-2-ene-2-carboxylic acid,

G. R = O-CO-CH$_3$: (6R,7R)-3-[(acetyloxy)methyl]-7-[[(E)-(furan-2-yl)(methoxyimino)acetyl]amino]-8-oxo-5-thia-1-azabicyclo[4.2.0]oct-2-ene-2-carboxylic acid,

H. (5aR,6R)-6-[[(Z)-(furan-2-yl)(methoxyimino)acetyl]amino]-5a,6-dihydro-3H,7H-azeto[2,1-b]furo[3,4-d][1,3]thiazine-1,7(4H)-dione,

I. (Z)-(furan-2-yl)(methoxyimino)acetic acid.

*Ph Eur*

# Celiprolol Hydrochloride

*(Ph Eur monograph 1632)*

and enantiomer

C$_{20}$H$_{33}$N$_3$O$_4$,HCl          416.0          *57470-78-7*

## Action and use
Beta-adrenoceptor antagonist.

## Preparation
Celiprolol Hydrochloride Tablets

*Ph Eur*

## DEFINITION
3-[3-Acetyl-4-[(2RS)-3-[(1,1-dimethylethyl)amino]-2-hydroxypropoxy]phenyl]-1,1-diethylurea hydrochloride.

## Content
99.0 per cent to 101.0 per cent (dried substance).

## CHARACTERS
### Appearance
White or very slightly yellow, crystalline powder.

### Solubility
Freely soluble in water and in methanol, soluble in ethanol (96 per cent), very slightly soluble in methylene chloride.

It shows polymorphism *(5.9)*.

## IDENTIFICATION
A. Infrared absorption spectrophotometry *(2.2.24)*.

*Comparison    celiprolol hydrochloride CRS.*

If the spectra obtained in the solid state show differences, dissolve the substance to be examined and the reference substance separately in *methanol R*, evaporate to dryness and record new spectra using the residues.

B. It gives reaction (a) of chlorides *(2.3.1)*.

## TESTS
### Optical rotation *(2.2.7)*
− 0.10° to + 0.10°.

Dissolve 1.0 g in *water R* and dilute to 10.0 ml with the same solvent.

### Related substances
Liquid chromatography *(2.2.29)*. *Prepare the solutions immediately before use.*

*Test solution    Dissolve 0.100 g of the substance to be examined in mobile phase A and dilute to 20.0 ml with mobile phase A.*

*Reference solution (a)    Dissolve 2 mg of the substance to be examined and 2 mg of acebutolol hydrochloride R in mobile phase A and dilute to 50.0 ml with mobile phase A.*

*Reference solution (b)    Dissolve 10 mg of the substance to be examined in 2 ml of mobile phase A and allow to stand for 24 h (for identification of impurity A).*

*Reference solution (c)    Dilute 1.0 ml of the test solution to 100.0 ml with mobile phase A. Dilute 1.0 ml of this solution to 10.0 ml with mobile phase A.*

*Reference solution (d)    Dissolve 10 mg of celiprolol for peak identification CRS in mobile phase A and dilute to 2 ml with mobile phase A.*

*Reference solution (e)    This solution is only prepared if required (see below) and is used to determine the identity of impurity I which co-elutes with impurity H (the 2 impurities originate from different routes of synthesis). Dissolve the contents of a vial of celiprolol impurity I CRS in mobile phase A and dilute to 2.0 ml with mobile phase A.*

*Column:*
— *size: l = 0.15 m, Ø = 4.6 mm,*
— *stationary phase: octylsilyl silica gel for chromatography R (5 µm),*
— *temperature: 30 °C.*

*Mobile phase:*
— *mobile phase A: mix 91 ml of tetrahydrofuran R, 63 ml of acetonitrile R1, 0.6 ml of pentafluoropropanoic acid R and 0.2 ml of trifluoroacetic acid R; dilute to 1000 ml with water R;*
— *mobile phase B: acetonitrile R1;*

| Time (min) | Mobile phase A (per cent *V/V*) | Mobile phase B (per cent *V/V*) |
|---|---|---|
| 0 - 50 | 100 → 80 | 0 → 20 |
| 50 - 51 | 80 → 100 | 20 → 0 |
| 51 - 65 | 100 | 0 |

*Flow rate    1.4 ml/min.*

*Detection    Spectrophotometer at 232 nm.*

*Injection    10 µl.*

*Identification of impurities    Use the chromatogram supplied with celiprolol for peak identification CRS and the chromatogram obtained with reference solution (d) to identify the peaks due to impurities B, E and F.*

*Relative retention    With reference to celiprolol (retention time = about 10 min): impurity A = about 0.3; impurity D = about 0.7; impurity G = about 1.2; impurity B = about 1.4; impurity F = about 1.6;*

impurity C = about 2.2; impurity H or I = about 2.5; impurity E = about 3.9.

*System suitability*  Reference solution (a):
— *resolution*: minimum 4.0 between the peaks due to celiprolol and acebutolol.

*Limits:*
— *correction factors*: for the calculation of content, multiply the peak areas of the following impurities by the corresponding correction factor: impurity A = 4.0; impurity B = 1.5; impurity E = 2.3; impurity F = 0.5; impurity I = 1.7;
— *any impurity*: for each impurity, not more than twice the area of the principal peak in the chromatogram obtained with reference solution (c) (0.2 per cent), and not more than 1 such peak has an area greater than the area of the principal peak in the chromatogram obtained with reference solution (c) (0.1 per cent);
— *total*: not more than 5 times the area of the principal peak in the chromatogram obtained with reference solution (c) (0.5 per cent);
— if any of the above limits are exceeded and if a peak occurs with a relative retention of about 2.5 (impurity H or I), the identity of this peak has to be clarified by use of a UV spectrum recorded with a diode array detector; if this spectrum is different from the one obtained with reference solution (e), no correction factor is applied;
— *disregard limit*: 0.5 times the area of the principal peak in the chromatogram obtained with reference solution (c) (0.05 per cent).

**Loss on drying** (2.2.32)
Maximum 0.5 per cent, determined on 1.000 g by drying in an oven at 105 °C for 3 h.

**ASSAY**
Dissolve 0.350 g under an atmosphere of nitrogen in 50 ml of *ethanol (96 per cent) R* and add 1.0 ml of *0.1 M hydrochloric acid*. Carry out a potentiometric titration (2.2.20), using *0.1 M sodium hydroxide*. Read the volume added between the 2 points of inflexion.

1 ml of *0.1 M sodium hydroxide* is equivalent to 41.60 mg of $C_{20}H_{34}ClN_3O_4$.

**STORAGE**
Protected from light.

**IMPURITIES**
*Specified impurities*  *A, B, C, D, E, F, G, H, I.*

A. R1 = H, R2 = NH-C(CH$_3$)$_3$: 1-[5-amino-2-[(2*RS*)-3-[(1,1-dimethylethyl)amino]-2-hydroxypropoxy]phenyl]ethanone,

C. R1 = CO-NH-C(CH$_3$)$_3$, R2 = NH-C(CH$_3$)$_3$: 1-[3-acetyl-4-[(2*RS*)-3-[(1,1-dimethylethyl)amino]-2-hydroxypropoxy]phenyl]-3-(1,1-dimethylethyl)urea,

D. R1 = CO-N(C$_2$H$_5$)$_2$, R2 = N(C$_2$H$_5$)2: 3-[3-acetyl-4-[(2*RS*)-3-(diethylamino)-2-hydroxypropoxy]phenyl]-1,1-diethylurea,

H. R1 = CO-N(C$_2$H$_5$)2, R2 = Br: 3-[3-acetyl-4-[(2*RS*)-3-bromo-2-hydroxypropoxy]phenyl]-1,1-diethylurea (bromhydrin compound),

B. 1,3-bis[3-acetyl-4-[3-[(1,1-dimethylethyl)amino]-2-hydroxypropoxy]phenyl]urea,

E. 1,1'-[[(1,1-dimethylethyl)imino]bis[[(2-hydroxypropane-1,3-diyl)oxy(3-acetyl-1,4-phenylene)]]bis(3,3-diethylurea),

F. R1 = R3 = H, R2 = CO-CH$_3$: 3-(3-acetyl-4-hydroxyphenyl)-1,1-diethylurea,

I. R1 = CO-CH$_3$, R2 = H, R3 = C$_2$H$_5$: 1-acetyl-1-(4-ethoxyphenyl)-3,3-diethylurea,

G. 3-[3-acetyl-4-[[(*RS*)-oxiranyl]methoxy]phenyl]-1,1-diethylurea.

*Ph Eur*

# Cellacefate

(*Cellulose Acetate Phthalate, Ph Eur monograph 0314*)

9004-38-0

## Action and use
Enteric coating in pharmaceutical products.

*Ph Eur* _____

## DEFINITION
Partly *O*-acetylated and *O*-phthalylated cellulose.

## CHARACTERS
### Appearance
White or almost white, free-flowing powder or colourless flakes, hygroscopic.

### Solubility
Practically insoluble in water, freely soluble in acetone, soluble in diethylene glycol, practically insoluble in ethanol (96 per cent) and in methylene chloride. It dissolves in dilute solutions of alkali hydroxides.

## IDENTIFICATION
Infrared absorption spectrophotometry (*2.2.24*).

*Comparison   cellulose acetate phthalate CRS.*

## TESTS
### Free acid
Maximum 3.0 per cent, calculated as phthalic acid (anhydrous substance).

Shake 3.0 g for 2 h with 100 ml of a 50 per cent *V/V* solution of *methanol R* and filter. Wash the flask and the filter with 2 quantities, each of 10 ml, of a 50 per cent *V/V* solution of *methanol R*. Combine the filtrate and washings, add *phenolphthalein solution R* and titrate with *0.1 M sodium hydroxide* until a faint pink colour is obtained. Carry out a blank titration on 120 ml of a 50 per cent *V/V* solution of *methanol R*.

1 ml of *0.1 M sodium hydroxide* is equivalent to 8.3 mg of free acid, calculated as phthalic acid.

### Heavy metals (*2.4.8*)
Maximum 10 ppm.

2.0 g complies with test C. Prepare the reference solution using 2 ml of *lead standard solution (10 ppm Pb) R*.

### Water (*2.5.12*)
Maximum 5.0 per cent, determined on 0.500 g.

Carry out the test using a mixture of 2 volumes of *methylene chloride R* and 3 volumes of *anhydrous ethanol R*.

### Sulphated ash (*2.4.14*)
Maximum 0.1 per cent, determined on 1.0 g.

## STORAGE
In an airtight container.

## FUNCTIONALITY RELATED-CHARACTERISTICS
*This section provides information on characteristics that are recognised as being relevant control parameters for one or more functions of the substance when used as an excipient (see chapter 5.15). This section is a non-mandatory part of the monograph and it is not necessary to verify the characteristics to demonstrate compliance. Control of these characteristics can however contribute to the quality of a medicinal product by improving the consistency of the manufacturing process and the performance of the medicinal product during use. Where control methods are cited, they are recognised as being suitable for the purpose, but other methods can also be used. Wherever results for a particular characteristic are reported, the control method must be indicated.*

*The following characteristics may be relevant for cellulose acetate phthalate used as film former in gastro-resistant tablets and capsules.*

### Apparent viscosity (*2.2.9*)
Typically 45 mPa·s to 90 mPa·s, determined at 25 °C.

Dissolve 15 g, calculated with reference to the anhydrous substance, in 85 g of a mixture of 1 part of *water R* and 249 parts of *acetone R*.

### Solubility of a film
Dissolve about 0.15 g in 1 ml of *acetone R* and pour onto a clear glass plate. A film is formed. Take a piece of the film and place it in a flask containing *0.1 M hydrochloric acid*. It does not dissolve. Then place the piece of film in a flask containing *phosphate buffer solution pH 6.8 R*. It dissolves.

### Phthaloyl groups ($C_8H_5O_3$; $M_r$ 149.1)
Typically 30.0 per cent to 36.0 per cent (anhydrous and acid-free substance). Dissolve 1.000 g in 50 ml of a mixture of 2 volumes of *acetone R* and 3 volumes of *ethanol (96 per cent) R*. Add 0.1 ml of *phenolphthalein solution R* and titrate with *0.1 M sodium hydroxide*. Carry out a blank titration.

Calculate the percentage content of phthaloyl groups (*P*) using the following expression:

$$\frac{14\,910n}{(100-a)(100-S)m} - \frac{179.5S}{(100-S)}$$

$a$ = percentage content of water;
$m$ = mass of the substance to be examined, in grams;
$n$ = volume of *0.1 M sodium hydroxide* used, in millilitres;
$S$ = percentage content of free acid (see Tests).

### Acetyl groups ($C_2H_3O$; $M_r$ 43.05)
Typically 21.5 per cent to 26.0 per cent (anhydrous and acid free substance). To 0.100 g add 25.0 ml of *0.1 M sodium hydroxide* and heat on a water-bath under a reflux condenser for 30 min. Cool, add 0.1 ml of *phenolphthalein solution R* and titrate with *0.1 M hydrochloric acid*. Carry out a blank titration.

Calculate the percentage content of acetyl groups using the following expression:

$$\left[\frac{4305(n_2 - n_1)}{(100-a)(100-S)m} - \frac{51.8S}{(100-S)}\right] - 0.578P$$

$a$ = percentage content of water;
$m$ = mass of the substance to be examined, in grams;
$n_1$ = volume of *0.1 M hydrochloric acid* used in the test, in millilitres;
$n_2$ = volume of *0.1 M hydrochloric acid* used in the blank titration, in millilitres;
$P$ = percentage content of phthaloyl groups;
$S$ = percentage content of free acid (see Tests).

_____ *Ph Eur*

# Dispersible Cellulose

## Action and use
Pharmaceutical excipient.

## DEFINITION
Dispersible Cellulose is a colloid-forming, attrited mixture of Microcrystalline Cellulose and Carmellose Sodium.

## Content of carmellose sodium
75.0 to 125.0% w/w of the stated amount.

## CHARACTERISTICS
A white or off-white, coarse or fine powder.

Disperses in *water* producing a white, opaque dispersion or gel; practically insoluble in organic solvents and in dilute acids.

## IDENTIFICATION
A. Mix 6 g with 300 ml of *water* stirring at 18,000 revolutions per minute for 5 minutes. A white, opaque dispersion is obtained which does not produce a supernatant liquid.

B. Add several drops of the dispersion obtained in test A to a 10% w/v solution of *aluminium chloride*. Each drop forms a white, opaque globule which does not disperse on standing.

C. Add 2 ml of *iodinated potassium iodide solution* to the dispersion obtained in test A. No blue or purplish colour is produced.

D. The solution obtained in the test for Heavy metals yields the reactions characteristic of *sodium salts*, Appendix VI, except that in test A the white precipitate produced may not be dense.

## TESTS
### Acidity or alkalinity
pH of the dispersion obtained in the test for Apparent viscosity, 6.0 to 8.0, Appendix V L.

### Solubility
Add 50 mg to 10 ml of *ammoniacal solution of copper tetrammine* and shake. It dissolves completely leaving no residue.

### Apparent viscosity
60 to 140% of the declared value when determined by the following method. Calculate the quantity ($x$ g) needed to prepare exactly 600 g of a dispersion of the stated percentage w/w, with reference to the dried substance. To (600-$x$) g of *water* at 23° to 25° contained in a 1000 ml high-speed blender bowl add $x$ g of the substance being examined, stirring at reduced speed, taking care to avoid contacting the sides of the bowl with the powder. Continue stirring at low speed for 15 seconds after the addition and then stir at 18,000 revolutions per minute for exactly 2 minutes. Immerse the appropriate spindle of a rotational viscometer, switch on after 30 seconds and after a further 30 seconds determine the *viscosity*, Appendix V H, Method III, using a speed of 20 revolutions per minute (2.09 radians per second).

### Heavy metals
To the residue obtained in the test for Sulphated ash add 1 ml of *hydrochloric acid*, evaporate to dryness on a water bath and dissolve the residue in 20 ml of *water*. 12 ml of the resulting solution complies with *limit test A for heavy metals*, Appendix VII. Use *lead standard solution (1 ppm) Pb* to prepare the standard (10 ppm).

### Loss on drying
When dried to constant weight at 105°, loses not more than 8.0% of its weight. Use 1 g.

### Sulphated ash
Not more than 5.0%, Appendix IX A. Use 2 g.

## ASSAY
Heat 2 g with 75 ml of *anhydrous acetic acid* under a reflux condenser for 2 hours, cool and carry out Method I for *non-aqueous titration*, Appendix VIII A, determining the end point potentiometrically. Each ml of 0.1M *perchloric acid VS* is equivalent to 29.6 mg of carmellose sodium.

## STORAGE
Dispersible Cellulose should be stored at a temperature of 8° to 15°.

## LABELLING
The label states (1) the percentage w/w of Carmellose Sodium; (2) the viscosity of a dispersion in water of a stated percentage w/w of Carmellose Sodium.

# Microcrystalline Cellulose

*(Ph Eur monograph 0316)*

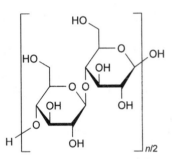

$C_{6n}H_{10n+2}O_{5n+1}$          9004-34-6

## Action and use
Excipient.

*Ph Eur*

## DEFINITION
Purified, partly depolymerised cellulose prepared by treating alpha-cellulose, obtained as a pulp from fibrous plant material, with mineral acids.

## CHARACTERS
### Appearance
White or almost white, fine or granular powder.

### Solubility
Practically insoluble in water, in acetone, in anhydrous ethanol, in toluene, in dilute acids and in a 50 g/l solution of sodium hydroxide.

## IDENTIFICATION
A. Place about 10 mg on a watch-glass and disperse in 2 ml of *iodinated zinc chloride solution R*. The substance becomes violet-blue.

B. The degree of polymerisation is not more than 350.

Transfer 1.300 g to a 125 ml conical flask. Add 25.0 ml of *water R* and 25.0 ml of *cupriethylenediamine hydroxide solution R*. Immediately purge the solution with *nitrogen R*, insert the stopper and shake until completely dissolved. Transfer an appropriate volume of the solution to a suitable capillary viscometer (*2.2.9*). Equilibrate the solution at $25 \pm 0.1$ °C for at least 5 min. Record the flow time ($t_1$) in seconds between the 2 marks on the viscometer. Calculate the kinematic viscosity ($v_1$) of the solution using the following expression:

$$t_1 \, (k_1)$$

where $k_1$ is the viscometer constant.

Dilute a suitable volume of *cupriethylenediamine hydroxide solution R* with an equal volume of *water R* and measure the flow time ($t_2$) using a suitable capillary viscometer. Calculate the kinematic viscosity ($v_2$) of the solvent using the following expression:

$$t_2 \, (k_2)$$

where $k_2$ is the viscometer constant.

Determine the relative viscosity ($\eta_{rel}$) of the substance to be examined using the following expression:

$$\nu_1 / \nu_2$$

Determine the intrinsic viscosity ($[\eta]_c$) by interpolation, using the intrinsic viscosity table (Table 0316.-1).

Calculate the degree of polymerisation (*P*) using the following expression:

$$\frac{95 \, [\eta]_c}{m \left[ (100 - b) / 100 \right]}$$

where *m* is the mass in grams of the substance to be examined and *b* is the loss on drying as a percentage.

## TESTS

### Solubility

Dissolve 50 mg in 10 ml of *ammoniacal solution of copper tetrammine R*. It dissolves completely, leaving no residue.

### pH (*2.2.3*)

5.0 to 7.5 for the supernatant liquid.

Shake 5 g with 40 ml of *carbon dioxide-free water R* for 20 min and centrifuge.

### Conductivity (*2.2.38*)

The conductivity of the test solution does not exceed the conductivity of the water by more than 75 $\mu$S·cm$^{-1}$.

Use as test solution the supernatant liquid obtained in the test for pH. Measure the conductivity of the supernatant liquid after a stable reading has been obtained and measure the conductivity of the water used to prepare the test solution.

### Ether-soluble substances

Maximum 0.05 per cent (5 mg) for the difference between the weight of the residue and the weight obtained from a blank determination.

Place 10.0 g in a chromatography column about 20 mm in internal diameter and pass 50 ml of *peroxide-free ether R* through the column. Evaporate the eluate to dryness. Dry the residue at 105 °C for 30 min, allow to cool in a dessicator and weigh. Carry out a blank determination.

### Water-soluble substances

Maximum 0.25 per cent (12.5 mg) for the difference between the mass of the residue and the mass obtained from a blank determination.

Shake 5.0 g with 80 ml of *water R* for 10 min. Filter through a filter paper with the aid of vacuum into a tared flask. Evaporate to dryness on a water-bath avoiding charring. Dry at 105 °C for 1 h and weigh. Carry out a blank determination.

### Heavy metals (*2.4.8*)

Maximum 10 ppm.

2.0 g complies with test C. Prepare the reference solution using 2 ml of *lead standard solution (10 ppm Pb) R*.

### Loss on drying (*2.2.32*)

Maximum 7.0 per cent, determined on 1.000 g by drying in an oven at 105 °C for 3 h.

### Sulphated ash (*2.4.14*)

Maximum 0.1 per cent, determined on 1.0 g.

### Microbial contamination

TAMC: acceptance criterion $10^3$ CFU/g (*2.6.12*).

TYMC: acceptance criterion $10^2$ CFU/g (*2.6.12*).

Absence of *Escherichia coli* (*2.6.13*).

Absence of *Pseudomonas aeruginosa* (*2.6.13*).

Absence of *Staphylococcus aureus* (*2.6.13*).

Absence of *Salmonella* (*2.6.13*).

## FUNCTIONALITY-RELATED CHARACTERISTICS

*This section provides information on characteristics that are recognised as being relevant control parameters for one or more functions of the substance when used as an excipient (see chapter 5.15). This section is a non-mandatory part of the monograph and it is not necessary to verify the characteristics to demonstrate compliance. Control of these characteristics can however contribute to the quality of a medicinal product by improving the consistency of the manufacturing process and the performance of the medicinal product during use. Where control methods are cited, they are recognised as being suitable for the purpose, but other methods can also be used. Wherever results for a particular characteristic are reported, the control method must be indicated.*

*The following characteristics may be relevant for microcrystalline cellulose used as binder, diluent or disintegrant.*

**Particle-size distribution** (*2.9.31* or *2.9.38*).

**Powder flow** (*2.9.36*).

## Table 0316.-1. — *Intrinsic viscosity table*

Intrinsic viscosity $[\eta]_c$ at different values of relative viscosity $\eta_{rel}$

| $\eta_{rel}$ | 0.00 | 0.01 | 0.02 | 0.03 | 0.04 | 0.05 | 0.06 | 0.07 | 0.08 | 0.09 |
|---|---|---|---|---|---|---|---|---|---|---|
| | | | | | $[\eta]_c$ | | | | | |
| 1.1 | 0.098 | 0.106 | 0.115 | 0.125 | 0.134 | 0.143 | 0.152 | 0.161 | 0.170 | 0.180 |
| 1.2 | 0.189 | 0.198 | 0.207 | 0.216 | 0.225 | 0.233 | 0.242 | 0.250 | 0.259 | 0.268 |
| 1.3 | 0.276 | 0.285 | 0.293 | 0.302 | 0.310 | 0.318 | 0.326 | 0.334 | 0.342 | 0.350 |
| 1.4 | 0.358 | 0.367 | 0.375 | 0.383 | 0.391 | 0.399 | 0.407 | 0.414 | 0.422 | 0.430 |
| 1.5 | 0.437 | 0.445 | 0.453 | 0.460 | 0.468 | 0.476 | 0.484 | 0.491 | 0.499 | 0.507 |
| 1.6 | 0.515 | 0.522 | 0.529 | 0.536 | 0.544 | 0.551 | 0.558 | 0.566 | 0.573 | 0.580 |
| 1.7 | 0.587 | 0.595 | 0.602 | 0.608 | 0.615 | 0.622 | 0.629 | 0.636 | 0.642 | 0.649 |
| 1.8 | 0.656 | 0.663 | 0.670 | 0.677 | 0.683 | 0.690 | 0.697 | 0.704 | 0.710 | 0.717 |
| 1.9 | 0.723 | 0.730 | 0.736 | 0.743 | 0.749 | 0.756 | 0.762 | 0.769 | 0.775 | 0.782 |
| 2.0 | 0.788 | 0.795 | 0.802 | 0.809 | 0.815 | 0.821 | 0.827 | 0.833 | 0.840 | 0.846 |
| 2.1 | 0.852 | 0.858 | 0.864 | 0.870 | 0.876 | 0.882 | 0.888 | 0.894 | 0.900 | 0.906 |
| 2.2 | 0.912 | 0.918 | 0.924 | 0.929 | 0.935 | 0.941 | 0.948 | 0.953 | 0.959 | 0.965 |
| 2.3 | 0.971 | 0.976 | 0.983 | 0.988 | 0.994 | 1.000 | 1.006 | 1.011 | 1.017 | 1.022 |
| 2.4 | 1.028 | 1.033 | 1.039 | 1.044 | 1.050 | 1.056 | 1.061 | 1.067 | 1.072 | 1.078 |
| 2.5 | 1.083 | 1.089 | 1.094 | 1.100 | 1.105 | 1.111 | 1.116 | 1.121 | 1.126 | 1.131 |
| 2.6 | 1.137 | 1.142 | 1.147 | 1.153 | 1.158 | 1.163 | 1.169 | 1.174 | 1.179 | 1.184 |
| 2.7 | 1.190 | 1.195 | 1.200 | 1.205 | 1.210 | 1.215 | 1.220 | 1.225 | 1.230 | 1.235 |
| 2.8 | 1.240 | 1.245 | 1.250 | 1.255 | 1.260 | 1.265 | 1.270 | 1.275 | 1.280 | 1.285 |
| 2.9 | 1.290 | 1.295 | 1.300 | 1.305 | 1.310 | 1.314 | 1.319 | 1.324 | 1.329 | 1.333 |
| 3.0 | 1.338 | 1.343 | 1.348 | 1.352 | 1.357 | 1.362 | 1.367 | 1.371 | 1.376 | 1.381 |
| 3.1 | 1.386 | 1.390 | 1.395 | 1.400 | 1.405 | 1.409 | 1.414 | 1.418 | 1.423 | 1.427 |
| 3.2 | 1.432 | 1.436 | 1.441 | 1.446 | 1.450 | 1.455 | 1.459 | 1.464 | 1.468 | 1.473 |
| 3.3 | 1.477 | 1.482 | 1.486 | 1.491 | 1.496 | 1.500 | 1.504 | 1.508 | 1.513 | 1.517 |
| 3.4 | 1.521 | 1.525 | 1.529 | 1.533 | 1.537 | 1.542 | 1.546 | 1.550 | 1.554 | 1.558 |
| 3.5 | 1.562 | 1.566 | 1.570 | 1.575 | 1.579 | 1.583 | 1.587 | 1.591 | 1.595 | 1.600 |
| 3.6 | 1.604 | 1.608 | 1.612 | 1.617 | 1.621 | 1.625 | 1.629 | 1.633 | 1.637 | 1.642 |
| 3.7 | 1.646 | 1.650 | 1.654 | 1.658 | 1.662 | 1.666 | 1.671 | 1.675 | 1.679 | 1.683 |
| 3.8 | 1.687 | 1.691 | 1.695 | 1.700 | 1.704 | 1.708 | 1.712 | 1.715 | 1.719 | 1.723 |
| 3.9 | 1.727 | 1.731 | 1.735 | 1.739 | 1.742 | 1.746 | 1.750 | 1.754 | 1.758 | 1.762 |
| 4.0 | 1.765 | 1.769 | 1.773 | 1.777 | 1.781 | 1.785 | 1.789 | 1.792 | 1.796 | 1.800 |
| 4.1 | 1.804 | 1.808 | 1.811 | 1.815 | 1.819 | 1.822 | 1.826 | 1.830 | 1.833 | 1.837 |
| 4.2 | 1.841 | 1.845 | 1.848 | 1.852 | 1.856 | 1.859 | 1.863 | 1.867 | 1.870 | 1.874 |
| 4.3 | 1.878 | 1.882 | 1.885 | 1.889 | 1.893 | 1.896 | 1.900 | 1.904 | 1.907 | 1.911 |
| 4.4 | 1.914 | 1.918 | 1.921 | 1.925 | 1.929 | 1.932 | 1.936 | 1.939 | 1.943 | 1.946 |
| 4.5 | 1.950 | 1.954 | 1.957 | 1.961 | 1.964 | 1.968 | 1.971 | 1.975 | 1.979 | 1.982 |
| 4.6 | 1.986 | 1.989 | 1.993 | 1.996 | 2.000 | 2.003 | 2.007 | 2.010 | 2.013 | 2.017 |
| 4.7 | 2.020 | 2.023 | 2.027 | 2.030 | 2.033 | 2.037 | 2.040 | 2.043 | 2.047 | 2.050 |
| 4.8 | 2.053 | 2.057 | 2.060 | 2.063 | 2.067 | 2.070 | 2.073 | 2.077 | 2.080 | 2.083 |
| 4.9 | 2.087 | 2.090 | 2.093 | 2.097 | 2.100 | 2.103 | 2.107 | 2.110 | 2.113 | 2.116 |
| 5.0 | 2.119 | 2.122 | 2.125 | 2.129 | 2.132 | 2.135 | 2.139 | 2.142 | 2.145 | 2.148 |
| 5.1 | 2.151 | 2.154 | 2.158 | 2.160 | 2.164 | 2.167 | 2.170 | 2.173 | 2.176 | 2.180 |
| 5.2 | 2.183 | 2.186 | 2.190 | 2.192 | 2.195 | 2.197 | 2.200 | 2.203 | 2.206 | 2.209 |

Intrinsic viscosity $[\eta]_c$ at different values of relative viscosity $\eta_{rel}$

| $\eta_{rel}$ | 0.00 | 0.01 | 0.02 | 0.03 | $[\eta]_c$ 0.04 | 0.05 | 0.06 | 0.07 | 0.08 | 0.09 |
|---|---|---|---|---|---|---|---|---|---|---|
| 5.3 | 2.212 | 2.215 | 2.218 | 2.221 | 2.224 | 2.227 | 2.230 | 2.233 | 2.236 | 2.240 |
| 5.4 | 2.243 | 2.246 | 2.249 | 2.252 | 2.255 | 2.258 | 2.261 | 2.264 | 2.267 | 2.270 |
| 5.5 | 2.273 | 2.276 | 2.279 | 2.282 | 2.285 | 2.288 | 2.291 | 2.294 | 2.297 | 2.300 |
| 5.6 | 2.303 | 2.306 | 2.309 | 2.312 | 2.315 | 2.318 | 2.320 | 2.324 | 2.326 | 2.329 |
| 5.7 | 2.332 | 2.335 | 2.338 | 2.341 | 2.344 | 2.347 | 2.350 | 2.353 | 2.355 | 2.358 |
| 5.8 | 2.361 | 2.364 | 2.367 | 2.370 | 2.373 | 2.376 | 2.379 | 2.382 | 2.384 | 2.387 |
| 5.9 | 2.390 | 2.393 | 2.396 | 2.400 | 2.403 | 2.405 | 2.408 | 2.411 | 2.414 | 2.417 |
| 6.0 | 2.419 | 2.422 | 2.425 | 2.428 | 2.431 | 2.433 | 2.436 | 2.439 | 2.442 | 2.444 |
| 6.1 | 2.447 | 2.450 | 2.453 | 2.456 | 2.458 | 2.461 | 2.464 | 2.467 | 2.470 | 2.472 |
| 6.2 | 2.475 | 2.478 | 2.481 | 2.483 | 2.486 | 2.489 | 2.492 | 2.494 | 2.497 | 2.500 |
| 6.3 | 2.503 | 2.505 | 2.508 | 2.511 | 2.513 | 2.516 | 2.518 | 2.521 | 2.524 | 2.526 |
| 6.4 | 2.529 | 2.532 | 2.534 | 2.537 | 2.540 | 2.542 | 2.545 | 2.547 | 2.550 | 2.553 |
| 6.5 | 2.555 | 2.558 | 2.561 | 2.563 | 2.566 | 2.568 | 2.571 | 2.574 | 2.576 | 2.579 |
| 6.6 | 2.581 | 2.584 | 2.587 | 2.590 | 2.592 | 2.595 | 2.597 | 2.600 | 2.603 | 2.605 |
| 6.7 | 2.608 | 2.610 | 2.613 | 2.615 | 2.618 | 2.620 | 2.623 | 2.625 | 2.627 | 2.630 |
| 6.8 | 2.633 | 2.635 | 2.637 | 2.640 | 2.643 | 2.645 | 2.648 | 2.650 | 2.653 | 2.655 |
| 6.9 | 2.658 | 2.660 | 2.663 | 2.665 | 2.668 | 2.670 | 2.673 | 2.675 | 2.678 | 2.680 |
| 7.0 | 2.683 | 2.685 | 2.687 | 2.690 | 2.693 | 2.695 | 2.698 | 2.700 | 2.702 | 2.705 |
| 7.1 | 2.707 | 2.710 | 2.712 | 2.714 | 2.717 | 2.719 | 2.721 | 2.724 | 2.726 | 2.729 |
| 7.2 | 2.731 | 2.733 | 2.736 | 2.738 | 2.740 | 2.743 | 2.745 | 2.748 | 2.750 | 2.752 |
| 7.3 | 2.755 | 2.757 | 2.760 | 2.762 | 2.764 | 2.767 | 2.769 | 2.771 | 2.774 | 2.776 |
| 7.4 | 2.779 | 2.781 | 2.783 | 2.786 | 2.788 | 2.790 | 2.793 | 2.795 | 2.798 | 2.800 |
| 7.5 | 2.802 | 2.805 | 2.807 | 2.809 | 2.812 | 2.814 | 2.816 | 2.819 | 2.821 | 2.823 |
| 7.6 | 2.826 | 2.828 | 2.830 | 2.833 | 2.835 | 2.837 | 2.840 | 2.842 | 2.844 | 2.847 |
| 7.7 | 2.849 | 2.851 | 2.854 | 2.856 | 2.858 | 2.860 | 2.863 | 2.865 | 2.868 | 2.870 |
| 7.8 | 2.873 | 2.875 | 2.877 | 2.879 | 2.881 | 2.884 | 2.887 | 2.889 | 2.891 | 2.893 |
| 7.9 | 2.895 | 2.898 | 2.900 | 2.902 | 2.905 | 2.907 | 2.909 | 2.911 | 2.913 | 2.915 |
| 8.0 | 2.918 | 2.920 | 2.922 | 2.924 | 2.926 | 2.928 | 2.931 | 2.933 | 2.935 | 2.937 |
| 8.1 | 2.939 | 2.942 | 2.944 | 2.946 | 2.948 | 2.950 | 2.952 | 2.955 | 2.957 | 2.959 |
| 8.2 | 2.961 | 2.963 | 2.966 | 2.968 | 2.970 | 2.972 | 2.974 | 2.976 | 2.979 | 2.981 |
| 8.3 | 2.983 | 2.985 | 2.987 | 2.990 | 2.992 | 2.994 | 2.996 | 2.998 | 3.000 | 3.002 |
| 8.4 | 3.004 | 3.006 | 3.008 | 3.010 | 3.012 | 3.015 | 3.017 | 3.019 | 3.021 | 3.023 |
| 8.5 | 3.025 | 3.027 | 3.029 | 3.031 | 3.033 | 3.035 | 3.037 | 3.040 | 3.042 | 3.044 |
| 8.6 | 3.046 | 3.048 | 3.050 | 3.052 | 3.054 | 3.056 | 3.058 | 3.060 | 3.062 | 3.064 |
| 8.7 | 3.067 | 3.069 | 3.071 | 3.073 | 3.075 | 3.077 | 3.079 | 3.081 | 3.083 | 3.085 |
| 8.8 | 3.087 | 3.089 | 3.092 | 3.094 | 3.096 | 3.098 | 3.100 | 3.102 | 3.104 | 3.106 |
| 8.9 | 3.108 | 3.110 | 3.112 | 3.114 | 3.116 | 3.118 | 3.120 | 3.122 | 3.124 | 3.126 |
| 9.0 | 3.128 | 3.130 | 3.132 | 3.134 | 3.136 | 3.138 | 3.140 | 3.142 | 3.144 | 3.146 |
| 9.1 | 3.148 | 3.150 | 3.152 | 3.154 | 3.156 | 3.158 | 3.160 | 3.162 | 3.164 | 3.166 |
| 9.2 | 3.168 | 3.170 | 3.172 | 3.174 | 3.176 | 3.178 | 3.180 | 3.182 | 3.184 | 3.186 |
| 9.3 | 3.188 | 3.190 | 3.192 | 3.194 | 3.196 | 3.198 | 3.200 | 3.202 | 3.204 | 3.206 |

| $\eta_{rel}$ | Intrinsic viscosity $[\eta]_c$ at different values of relative viscosity $\eta_{rel}$ | | | | | | | | | |
|---|---|---|---|---|---|---|---|---|---|---|
| | $[\eta]_c$ | | | | | | | | | |
| | 0.00 | 0.01 | 0.02 | 0.03 | 0.04 | 0.05 | 0.06 | 0.07 | 0.08 | 0.09 |
| 9.4 | 3.208 | 3.210 | 3.212 | 3.214 | 3.215 | 3.217 | 3.219 | 3.221 | 3.223 | 3.225 |
| 9.5 | 3.227 | 3.229 | 3.231 | 3.233 | 3.235 | 3.237 | 3.239 | 3.241 | 3.242 | 3.244 |
| 9.6 | 3.246 | 3.248 | 3.250 | 3.252 | 3.254 | 3.256 | 3.258 | 3.260 | 3.262 | 3.264 |
| 9.7 | 3.266 | 3.268 | 3.269 | 3.271 | 3.273 | 3.275 | 3.277 | 3.279 | 3.281 | 3.283 |
| 9.8 | 3.285 | 3.287 | 3.289 | 3.291 | 3.293 | 3.295 | 3.297 | 3.298 | 3.300 | 3.302 |
| 9.9 | 3.304 | 3.305 | 3.307 | 3.309 | 3.311 | 3.313 | 3.316 | 3.318 | 3.320 | 3.321 |

| $\eta_{rel}$ | Intrinsic viscosity $[\eta]_c$ at different values of relative viscosity $\eta_{rel}$ | | | | | | | | | |
|---|---|---|---|---|---|---|---|---|---|---|
| | $[\eta]_c$ | | | | | | | | | |
| | 0.0 | 0.1 | 0.2 | 0.3 | 0.4 | 0.5 | 0.6 | 0.7 | 0.8 | 0.9 |
| 10 | 3.32 | 3.34 | 3.36 | 3.37 | 3.39 | 3.41 | 3.43 | 3.45 | 3.46 | 3.48 |
| 11 | 3.50 | 3.52 | 3.53 | 3.55 | 3.56 | 3.58 | 3.60 | 3.61 | 3.63 | 3.64 |
| 12 | 3.66 | 3.68 | 3.69 | 3.71 | 3.72 | 3.74 | 3.76 | 3.77 | 3.79 | 3.80 |
| 13 | 3.80 | 3.83 | 3.85 | 3.86 | 3.88 | 3.89 | 3.90 | 3.92 | 3.93 | 3.95 |
| 14 | 3.96 | 3.97 | 3.99 | 4.00 | 4.02 | 4.03 | 4.04 | 4.06 | 4.07 | 4.09 |
| 15 | 4.10 | 4.11 | 4.13 | 4.14 | 4.15 | 4.17 | 4.18 | 4.19 | 4.20 | 4.22 |
| 16 | 4.23 | 4.24 | 4.25 | 4.27 | 4.28 | 4.29 | 4.30 | 4.31 | 4.33 | 4.34 |
| 17 | 4.35 | 4.36 | 4.37 | 4.38 | 4.39 | 4.41 | 4.42 | 4.43 | 4.44 | 4.45 |
| 18 | 4.46 | 4.47 | 4.48 | 4.49 | 4.50 | 4.52 | 4.53 | 4.54 | 4.55 | 4.56 |
| 19 | 4.57 | 4.58 | 4.59 | 4.60 | 4.61 | 4.62 | 4.63 | 4.64 | 4.65 | 4.66 |

# Microcrystalline Cellulose and Carmellose Sodium

(*Ph Eur monograph 2050*)

## Action and use
Excipient.

*Ph Eur* ___

## DEFINITION
Colloid-forming, powdered mixture of *Microcrystalline Cellulose (0316)* with 5 per cent to 22 per cent of *Carmellose sodium (0472)*.

## Content
75.0 per cent to 125.0 per cent of the nominal amount of carmellose sodium (dried substance).

## CHARACTERS
### Appearance
White or off-white, coarse or fine powder.

### Solubility
Dispersible in water producing a white, opaque colloidal dispersion; practically insoluble in organic solvents and in dilute acids.

## IDENTIFICATION
A. Mix 6 g with 300 ml of *water R* and stir at 18 000 r/min for 5 min. A white opaque dispersion is obtained which does not produce a supernatant liquid.

B. Add several drops of the dispersion obtained in identification A to a 10 per cent *V/V* solution of *aluminium chloride R*. Each drop forms a white, opaque globule which does not disperse on standing.

C. Add 2 ml of *iodinated potassium iodide solution R* to the dispersion obtained in test A. No blue or purplish colour is produced.

D. It complies with the limits of the assay.

## TESTS
### Solubility
Add 50 mg to 10 ml of *ammoniacal solution of copper tetrammine R* and shake. It dissolves completely leaving no residue.

### pH (*2.2.3*)
6.0 to 8.0 for the dispersion obtained in identification A.

### Loss on drying (*2.2.32*)
Maximum 8.0 per cent, determined on 1.000 g by drying in an oven at 105 °C.

### Sulphated ash (*2.4.14*)
Maximum 7.4 per cent, determined on 2.0 g.

### ASSAY
Heat 2.00 g with 75 ml of *anhydrous acetic acid R* under a reflux condenser for 2 h, cool and titrate with *0.1 M perchloric acid*, determining the end point potentiometrically (*2.2.20*).

1 ml of *0.1 M perchloric acid* is equivalent to 29.6 mg of carmellose sodium.

## LABELLING
The label states the nominal percentage *m/m* of carmellose sodium.

## FUNCTIONALITY-RELATED CHARACTERISTICS
*This section provides information on characteristics that are recognised as being relevant control parameters for one or more functions of the substance when used as an excipient. This section*

*is a non-mandatory part of the monograph and it is not necessary to verify the characteristics to demonstrate compliance. Control of these characteristics can however contribute to the quality of a medicinal product by improving the consistency of the manufacturing process. Where control methods are cited, they are recognised as being suitable for the purpose, but other methods can also be used. Wherever results for a particular characteristic are reported, the control method must be indicated.*

*The following characteristics may be relevant for microcrystalline cellulose and carmellose sodium used as a suspending agent.*

**Apparent viscosity** (*2.2.10*)

60 per cent to 140 per cent of the nominal value.

Calculate the quantity (*x* g) needed to prepare exactly 600 g of a dispersion of the stated percentage *m/m* (dried substance). To (600 - *x*) g of *water R* at 23-25 °C contained in a 1000 ml high-speed blender bowl add *x* g of the substance to be examined and stir at reduced speed, taking care to avoid contacting the sides of the bowl with the powder. Continue stirring at low speed for 15 s after the addition of the powder and then stir at 18 000 r/min for exactly 2 min.

Determine the viscosity with a suitable relative rotational viscometer under the following conditions:
— spindle: as appropriate;
— speed: 20 r/min.

Immerse the spindle into the suspension immediately after preparation, switch on the rotation spindle after 30 s, after a further 30 s take scale readings and calculate the viscosity according to the viscometer manual.

*Ph Eur*

# Powdered Cellulose

(*Ph Eur monograph 0315*)

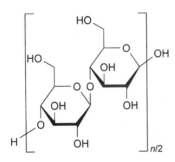

$C_{6n}H_{10n+2}O_{5n+1}$

**Action and use**

Excipient.

*Ph Eur*

## DEFINITION

Purified, mechanically disintegrated cellulose prepared by processing alpha-cellulose obtained as a pulp from fibrous plant material.

## CHARACTERS

**Appearance**

White or almost white, fine or granular powder.

**Solubility**

Practically insoluble in water, slightly soluble in a 50 g/l solution of sodium hydroxide, practically insoluble in

acetone, in anhydrous ethanol, in toluene, in dilute acids and in most organic solvents.

## IDENTIFICATION

A. Place about 10 mg on a watch-glass and disperse in 2 ml of *iodinated zinc chloride solution R*. The substance becomes violet-blue.

B. The degree of polymerisation is greater than 440.

Transfer 0.250 g to a 125 ml conical flask. Add 25.0 ml of *water R* and 25.0 ml of *cupriethylenediamine hydroxide solution R*. Immediately purge the solution with *nitrogen R*, insert the stopper and shake until completely dissolved. Transfer an appropriate volume of the solution to a suitable capillary viscometer (*2.2.9*). Equilibrate the solution at 25 ± 0.1 °C for at least 5 min. Record the flow time (*t₁*) in seconds between the 2 marks on the viscometer. Calculate the kinematic viscosity (*v₁*) of the solution using the following expression:

$$t_1 (k_1)$$

where $k_1$ is the viscometer constant.

Dilute a suitable volume of *cupriethylenediamine hydroxide solution R* with an equal volume of *water R* and measure the flow time (*t₂*) using a suitable capillary viscometer. Calculate the kinematic viscosity (*v₂*) of the solvent using the following expression:

$$t_2 (k_2)$$

where $k_2$ is the viscometer constant.

Determine the relative viscosity ($\eta_{rel}$) of the substance to be examined using the following expression:

$$\nu_1/\nu_2$$

Determine the intrinsic viscosity ($[\eta]_c$) by interpolation, using the intrinsic viscosity table (Table 0315.-1).

Calculate the degree of polymerisation (*P*) using the following expression:

$$\frac{95 [\eta]_c}{m [(100 - b)/100]}$$

where *m* is the mass in grams of the substance to be examined and *b* is the loss on drying as a percentage.

## TESTS

**Solubility**

Dissolve 50 mg in 10 ml of *ammoniacal solution of copper tetrammine R*. It dissolves completely, leaving no residue.

**pH** (*2.2.3*)

5.0 to 7.5 for the supernatant liquid.

Mix 10 g with 90 ml of *carbon dioxide-free water R* and allow to stand with occasional stirring for 1 h.

**Ether-soluble substances**

Maximum 0.15 per cent (15 mg) for the difference between the mass of the residue and the mass obtained from a blank determination.

Place 10.0 g in a chromatography column about 20 mm in internal diameter and pass 50 ml of *peroxide-free ether R* through the column. Evaporate the eluate to dryness in a previously dried and tared evaporating dish, with the aid of a current of air in a fume hood. After all the ether has evaporated, dry the residue at 105 °C for 30 min, allow to cool in a dessiccator and weigh. Carry out a blank determination.

**Water-soluble substances**

Maximum 1.5 per cent (15.0 mg) for the difference between the mass of the residue and the mass obtained from a blank determination.

Shake 6.0 g with 90 ml of *carbon dioxide-free water R* for 10 min. Filter with the aid of vacuum into a tared flask. Discard the first 10 ml of the filtrate and pass the filtrate through the same filter a second time, if necessary, to obtain a clear filtrate. Evaporate a 15.0 ml portion of the filtrate to dryness in a tared evaporating dish without charring. Dry at 105 °C for 1 h, allow to cool in a desiccator and weigh. Carry out a blank determination.

**Heavy metals** (*2.4.8*)

Maximum 10 ppm.

2.0 g complies with test C. Prepare the reference solution using 2 ml of *lead standard solution (10 ppm Pb) R*.

**Loss on drying** (*2.2.32*)

Maximum 6.5 per cent, determined on 1.000 g by drying in an oven at 105 °C for 3 h.

**Sulphated ash** (*2.4.14*)

Maximum 0.3 per cent, determined on 1.0 g (dried substance).

**Microbial contamination**

TAMC: acceptance criterion $10^3$ CFU/g (*2.6.12*).

TYMC: acceptance criterion $10^2$ CFU/g (*2.6.12*).

Absence of *Escherichia coli* (*2.6.13*).

Absence of *Pseudomonas aeruginosa* (*2.6.13*).

Absence of *Staphylococcus aureus* (*2.6.13*).

Absence of *Salmonella* (*2.6.13*).

**FUNCTIONALITY-RELATED CHARACTERISTICS**

*This section provides information on characteristics that are recognised as being relevant control parameters for one or more functions of the substance when used as an excipient (see chapter 5.15). This section is a non-mandatory part of the monograph and it is not necessary to verify the characteristics to demonstrate compliance. Control of these characteristics can however contribute to the quality of a medicinal product by improving the consistency of the manufacturing process and the performance of the medicinal product during use. Where control methods are cited they are recognised as being suitable for the purpose but other methods can also be used. Wherever results for a particular characteristic are reported, the control method must be indicated.*

*The following characteristics may be relevant for powdered cellulose used as diluent or disintegrant.*

**Particle-size distribution** (*2.9.31* or *2.9.38*).

**Powder flow** (*2.9.36*).

*_____ Ph Eur*

Table 0315.-1. – *Intrinsic viscosity table*

| $\eta_{rel}$ | Intrinsic viscosity $[\eta]_c$ at different values of relative viscosity $\eta_{rel}$ | | | | | | | | | |
|---|---|---|---|---|---|---|---|---|---|---|
| | $[\eta]_c$ | | | | | | | | | |
| | 0.00 | 0.01 | 0.02 | 0.03 | 0.04 | 0.05 | 0.06 | 0.07 | 0.08 | 0.09 |
| 1.1 | 0.098 | 0.106 | 0.115 | 0.125 | 0.134 | 0.143 | 0.152 | 0.161 | 0.170 | 0.180 |
| 1.2 | 0.189 | 0.198 | 0.207 | 0.216 | 0.225 | 0.233 | 0.242 | 0.250 | 0.259 | 0.268 |
| 1.3 | 0.276 | 0.285 | 0.293 | 0.302 | 0.310 | 0.318 | 0.326 | 0.334 | 0.342 | 0.350 |
| 1.4 | 0.358 | 0.367 | 0.375 | 0.383 | 0.391 | 0.399 | 0.407 | 0.414 | 0.422 | 0.430 |
| 1.5 | 0.437 | 0.445 | 0.453 | 0.460 | 0.468 | 0.476 | 0.484 | 0.491 | 0.499 | 0.507 |
| 1.6 | 0.515 | 0.522 | 0.529 | 0.536 | 0.544 | 0.551 | 0.558 | 0.566 | 0.573 | 0.580 |
| 1.7 | 0.587 | 0.595 | 0.602 | 0.608 | 0.615 | 0.622 | 0.629 | 0.636 | 0.642 | 0.649 |
| 1.8 | 0.656 | 0.663 | 0.670 | 0.677 | 0.683 | 0.690 | 0.697 | 0.704 | 0.710 | 0.717 |
| 1.9 | 0.723 | 0.730 | 0.736 | 0.743 | 0.749 | 0.756 | 0.762 | 0.769 | 0.775 | 0.782 |
| 2.0 | 0.788 | 0.795 | 0.802 | 0.809 | 0.815 | 0.821 | 0.827 | 0.833 | 0.840 | 0.846 |
| 2.1 | 0.852 | 0.858 | 0.864 | 0.870 | 0.876 | 0.882 | 0.888 | 0.894 | 0.900 | 0.906 |
| 2.2 | 0.912 | 0.918 | 0.924 | 0.929 | 0.935 | 0.941 | 0.948 | 0.953 | 0.959 | 0.965 |
| 2.3 | 0.971 | 0.976 | 0.983 | 0.988 | 0.994 | 1.000 | 1.006 | 1.011 | 1.017 | 1.022 |
| 2.4 | 1.028 | 1.033 | 1.039 | 1.044 | 1.050 | 1.056 | 1.061 | 1.067 | 1.072 | 1.078 |
| 2.5 | 1.083 | 1.089 | 1.094 | 1.100 | 1.105 | 1.111 | 1.116 | 1.121 | 1.126 | 1.131 |
| 2.6 | 1.137 | 1.142 | 1.147 | 1.153 | 1.158 | 1.163 | 1.169 | 1.174 | 1.179 | 1.184 |
| 2.7 | 1.190 | 1.195 | 1.200 | 1.205 | 1.210 | 1.215 | 1.220 | 1.225 | 1.230 | 1.235 |
| 2.8 | 1.240 | 1.245 | 1.250 | 1.255 | 1.260 | 1.265 | 1.270 | 1.275 | 1.280 | 1.285 |

Intrinsic viscosity $[\eta]_c$ at different values of relative viscosity $\eta_{rel}$

| $\eta_{rel}$ | $[\eta]_c$ | | | | | | | | | |
|---|---|---|---|---|---|---|---|---|---|---|
| | 0.00 | 0.01 | 0.02 | 0.03 | 0.04 | 0.05 | 0.06 | 0.07 | 0.08 | 0.09 |
| 2.9 | 1.290 | 1.295 | 1.300 | 1.305 | 1.310 | 1.314 | 1.319 | 1.324 | 1.329 | 1.333 |
| 3.0 | 1.338 | 1.343 | 1.348 | 1.352 | 1.357 | 1.362 | 1.367 | 1.371 | 1.376 | 1.381 |
| 3.1 | 1.386 | 1.390 | 1.395 | 1.400 | 1.405 | 1.409 | 1.414 | 1.418 | 1.423 | 1.427 |
| 3.2 | 1.432 | 1.436 | 1.441 | 1.446 | 1.450 | 1.455 | 1.459 | 1.464 | 1.468 | 1.473 |
| 3.3 | 1.477 | 1.482 | 1.486 | 1.491 | 1.496 | 1.500 | 1.504 | 1.508 | 1.513 | 1.517 |
| 3.4 | 1.521 | 1.525 | 1.529 | 1.533 | 1.537 | 1.542 | 1.546 | 1.550 | 1.554 | 1.558 |
| 3.5 | 1.562 | 1.566 | 1.570 | 1.575 | 1.579 | 1.583 | 1.587 | 1.591 | 1.595 | 1.600 |
| 3.6 | 1.604 | 1.608 | 1.612 | 1.617 | 1.621 | 1.625 | 1.629 | 1.633 | 1.637 | 1.642 |
| 3.7 | 1.646 | 1.650 | 1.654 | 1.658 | 1.662 | 1.666 | 1.671 | 1.675 | 1.679 | 1.683 |
| 3.8 | 1.687 | 1.691 | 1.695 | 1.700 | 1.704 | 1.708 | 1.712 | 1.715 | 1.719 | 1.723 |
| 3.9 | 1.727 | 1.731 | 1.735 | 1.739 | 1.742 | 1.746 | 1.750 | 1.754 | 1.758 | 1.762 |
| 4.0 | 1.765 | 1.769 | 1.773 | 1.777 | 1.781 | 1.785 | 1.789 | 1.792 | 1.796 | 1.800 |
| 4.1 | 1.804 | 1.808 | 1.811 | 1.815 | 1.819 | 1.822 | 1.826 | 1.830 | 1.833 | 1.837 |
| 4.2 | 1.841 | 1.845 | 1.848 | 1.852 | 1.856 | 1.859 | 1.863 | 1.867 | 1.870 | 1.874 |
| 4.3 | 1.878 | 1.882 | 1.885 | 1.889 | 1.893 | 1.896 | 1.900 | 1.904 | 1.907 | 1.911 |
| 4.4 | 1.914 | 1.918 | 1.921 | 1.925 | 1.929 | 1.932 | 1.936 | 1.939 | 1.943 | 1.946 |
| 4.5 | 1.950 | 1.954 | 1.957 | 1.961 | 1.964 | 1.968 | 1.971 | 1.975 | 1.979 | 1.982 |
| 4.6 | 1.986 | 1.989 | 1.993 | 1.996 | 2.000 | 2.003 | 2.007 | 2.010 | 2.013 | 2.017 |
| 4.7 | 2.020 | 2.023 | 2.027 | 2.030 | 2.033 | 2.037 | 2.040 | 2.043 | 2.047 | 2.050 |
| 4.8 | 2.053 | 2.057 | 2.060 | 2.063 | 2.067 | 2.070 | 2.073 | 2.077 | 2.080 | 2.083 |
| 4.9 | 2.087 | 2.090 | 2.093 | 2.097 | 2.100 | 2.103 | 2.107 | 2.110 | 2.113 | 2.116 |
| 5.0 | 2.119 | 2.122 | 2.125 | 2.129 | 2.132 | 2.135 | 2.139 | 2.142 | 2.145 | 2.148 |
| 5.1 | 2.151 | 2.154 | 2.158 | 2.160 | 2.164 | 2.167 | 2.170 | 2.173 | 2.176 | 2.180 |
| 5.2 | 2.183 | 2.186 | 2.190 | 2.192 | 2.195 | 2.197 | 2.200 | 2.203 | 2.206 | 2.209 |
| 5.3 | 2.212 | 2.215 | 2.218 | 2.221 | 2.224 | 2.227 | 2.230 | 2.233 | 2.236 | 2.240 |
| 5.4 | 2.243 | 2.246 | 2.249 | 2.252 | 2.255 | 2.258 | 2.261 | 2.264 | 2.267 | 2.270 |
| 5.5 | 2.273 | 2.276 | 2.279 | 2.282 | 2.285 | 2.288 | 2.291 | 2.294 | 2.297 | 2.300 |
| 5.6 | 2.303 | 2.306 | 2.309 | 2.312 | 2.315 | 2.318 | 2.320 | 2.324 | 2.326 | 2.329 |
| 5.7 | 2.332 | 2.335 | 2.338 | 2.341 | 2.344 | 2.347 | 2.350 | 2.353 | 2.355 | 2.358 |
| 5.8 | 2.361 | 2.364 | 2.367 | 2.370 | 2.373 | 2.376 | 2.379 | 2.382 | 2.384 | 2.387 |
| 5.9 | 2.390 | 2.393 | 2.396 | 2.400 | 2.403 | 2.405 | 2.408 | 2.411 | 2.414 | 2.417 |
| 6.0 | 2.419 | 2.422 | 2.425 | 2.428 | 2.431 | 2.433 | 2.436 | 2.439 | 2.442 | 2.444 |
| 6.1 | 2.447 | 2.450 | 2.453 | 2.456 | 2.458 | 2.461 | 2.464 | 2.467 | 2.470 | 2.472 |
| 6.2 | 2.475 | 2.478 | 2.481 | 2.483 | 2.486 | 2.489 | 2.492 | 2.494 | 2.497 | 2.500 |
| 6.3 | 2.503 | 2.505 | 2.508 | 2.511 | 2.513 | 2.516 | 2.518 | 2.521 | 2.524 | 2.526 |
| 6.4 | 2.529 | 2.532 | 2.534 | 2.537 | 2.540 | 2.542 | 2.545 | 2.547 | 2.550 | 2.553 |
| 6.5 | 2.555 | 2.558 | 2.561 | 2.563 | 2.566 | 2.568 | 2.571 | 2.574 | 2.576 | 2.579 |
| 6.6 | 2.581 | 2.584 | 2.587 | 2.590 | 2.592 | 2.595 | 2.597 | 2.600 | 2.603 | 2.605 |
| 6.7 | 2.608 | 2.610 | 2.613 | 2.615 | 2.618 | 2.620 | 2.623 | 2.625 | 2.627 | 2.630 |
| 6.8 | 2.633 | 2.635 | 2.637 | 2.640 | 2.643 | 2.645 | 2.648 | 2.650 | 2.653 | 2.655 |
| 6.9 | 2.658 | 2.660 | 2.663 | 2.665 | 2.668 | 2.670 | 2.673 | 2.675 | 2.678 | 2.680 |

| | | | | | $[\eta]_c$ | | | | | |
|---|---|---|---|---|---|---|---|---|---|---|
| | Intrinsic viscosity $[\eta]_c$ at different values of relative viscosity $\eta_{rel}$ | | | | | | | | | |
| $\eta_{rel}$ | 0.00 | 0.01 | 0.02 | 0.03 | 0.04 | 0.05 | 0.06 | 0.07 | 0.08 | 0.09 |
| 7.0 | 2.683 | 2.685 | 2.687 | 2.690 | 2.693 | 2.695 | 2.698 | 2.700 | 2.702 | 2.705 |
| 7.1 | 2.707 | 2.710 | 2.712 | 2.714 | 2.717 | 2.719 | 2.721 | 2.724 | 2.726 | 2.729 |
| 7.2 | 2.731 | 2.733 | 2.736 | 2.738 | 2.740 | 2.743 | 2.745 | 2.748 | 2.750 | 2.752 |
| 7.3 | 2.755 | 2.757 | 2.760 | 2.762 | 2.764 | 2.767 | 2.769 | 2.771 | 2.774 | 2.776 |
| 7.4 | 2.779 | 2.781 | 2.783 | 2.786 | 2.788 | 2.790 | 2.793 | 2.795 | 2.798 | 2.800 |
| 7.5 | 2.802 | 2.805 | 2.807 | 2.809 | 2.812 | 2.814 | 2.816 | 2.819 | 2.821 | 2.823 |
| 7.6 | 2.826 | 2.828 | 2.830 | 2.833 | 2.835 | 2.837 | 2.840 | 2.842 | 2.844 | 2.847 |
| 7.7 | 2.849 | 2.851 | 2.854 | 2.856 | 2.858 | 2.860 | 2.863 | 2.865 | 2.868 | 2.870 |
| 7.8 | 2.873 | 2.875 | 2.877 | 2.879 | 2.881 | 2.884 | 2.887 | 2.889 | 2.891 | 2.893 |
| 7.9 | 2.895 | 2.898 | 2.900 | 2.902 | 2.905 | 2.907 | 2.909 | 2.911 | 2.913 | 2.915 |
| 8.0 | 2.918 | 2.920 | 2.922 | 2.924 | 2.926 | 2.928 | 2.931 | 2.933 | 2.935 | 2.937 |
| 8.1 | 2.939 | 2.942 | 2.944 | 2.946 | 2.948 | 2.950 | 2.952 | 2.955 | 2.957 | 2.959 |
| 8.2 | 2.961 | 2.963 | 2.966 | 2.968 | 2.970 | 2.972 | 2.974 | 2.976 | 2.979 | 2.981 |
| 8.3 | 2.983 | 2.985 | 2.987 | 2.990 | 2.992 | 2.994 | 2.996 | 2.998 | 3.000 | 3.002 |
| 8.4 | 3.004 | 3.006 | 3.008 | 3.010 | 3.012 | 3.015 | 3.017 | 3.019 | 3.021 | 3.023 |
| 8.5 | 3.025 | 3.027 | 3.029 | 3.031 | 3.033 | 3.035 | 3.037 | 3.040 | 3.042 | 3.044 |
| 8.6 | 3.046 | 3.048 | 3.050 | 3.052 | 3.054 | 3.056 | 3.058 | 3.060 | 3.062 | 3.064 |
| 8.7 | 3.067 | 3.069 | 3.071 | 3.073 | 3.075 | 3.077 | 3.079 | 3.081 | 3.083 | 3.085 |
| 8.8 | 3.087 | 3.089 | 3.092 | 3.094 | 3.096 | 3.098 | 3.100 | 3.102 | 3.104 | 3.106 |
| 8.9 | 3.108 | 3.110 | 3.112 | 3.114 | 3.116 | 3.118 | 3.120 | 3.122 | 3.124 | 3.126 |
| 9.0 | 3.128 | 3.130 | 3.132 | 3.134 | 3.136 | 3.138 | 3.140 | 3.142 | 3.144 | 3.146 |
| 9.1 | 3.148 | 3.150 | 3.152 | 3.154 | 3.156 | 3.158 | 3.160 | 3.162 | 3.164 | 3.166 |
| 9.2 | 3.168 | 3.170 | 3.172 | 3.174 | 3.176 | 3.178 | 3.180 | 3.182 | 3.184 | 3.186 |
| 9.3 | 3.188 | 3.190 | 3.192 | 3.194 | 3.196 | 3.198 | 3.200 | 3.202 | 3.204 | 3.206 |
| 9.4 | 3.208 | 3.210 | 3.212 | 3.214 | 3.215 | 3.217 | 3.219 | 3.221 | 3.223 | 3.225 |
| 9.5 | 3.227 | 3.229 | 3.231 | 3.233 | 3.235 | 3.237 | 3.239 | 3.241 | 3.242 | 3.244 |
| 9.6 | 3.246 | 3.248 | 3.250 | 3.252 | 3.254 | 3.256 | 3.258 | 3.260 | 3.262 | 3.264 |
| 9.7 | 3.266 | 3.268 | 3.269 | 3.271 | 3.273 | 3.275 | 3.277 | 3.279 | 3.281 | 3.283 |
| 9.8 | 3.285 | 3.287 | 3.289 | 3.291 | 3.293 | 3.295 | 3.297 | 3.298 | 3.300 | 3.302 |
| 9.9 | 3.304 | 3.305 | 3.307 | 3.309 | 3.311 | 3.313 | 3.316 | 3.318 | 3.320 | 3.321 |

Intrinsic viscosity $[\eta]_c$ at different values of relative viscosity $\eta_{rel}$

| | | | | | $[\eta]_c$ | | | | | |
|---|---|---|---|---|---|---|---|---|---|---|
| $\eta_{rel}$ | 0.0 | 0.1 | 0.2 | 0.3 | 0.4 | 0.5 | 0.6 | 0.7 | 0.8 | 0.9 |
| 10 | 3.32 | 3.34 | 3.36 | 3.37 | 3.39 | 3.41 | 3.43 | 3.45 | 3.46 | 3.48 |
| 11 | 3.50 | 3.52 | 3.53 | 3.55 | 3.56 | 3.58 | 3.60 | 3.61 | 3.63 | 3.64 |
| 12 | 3.66 | 3.68 | 3.69 | 3.71 | 3.72 | 3.74 | 3.76 | 3.77 | 3.79 | 3.80 |
| 13 | 3.80 | 3.83 | 3.85 | 3.86 | 3.88 | 3.89 | 3.90 | 3.92 | 3.93 | 3.95 |
| 14 | 3.96 | 3.97 | 3.99 | 4.00 | 4.02 | 4.03 | 4.04 | 4.06 | 4.07 | 4.09 |
| 15 | 4.10 | 4.11 | 4.13 | 4.14 | 4.15 | 4.17 | 4.18 | 4.19 | 4.20 | 4.22 |
| 16 | 4.23 | 4.24 | 4.25 | 4.27 | 4.28 | 4.29 | 4.30 | 4.31 | 4.33 | 4.34 |

| $\eta_{rel}$ | 0.0 | 0.1 | 0.2 | 0.3 | 0.4 | 0.5 | 0.6 | 0.7 | 0.8 | 0.9 |
|---|---|---|---|---|---|---|---|---|---|---|
| | | | | | $[\eta]_c$ | | | | | |
| 17 | 4.35 | 4.36 | 4.37 | 4.38 | 4.39 | 4.41 | 4.42 | 4.43 | 4.44 | 4.45 |
| 18 | 4.46 | 4.47 | 4.48 | 4.49 | 4.50 | 4.52 | 4.53 | 4.54 | 4.55 | 4.56 |
| 19 | 4.57 | 4.58 | 4.59 | 4.60 | 4.61 | 4.62 | 4.63 | 4.64 | 4.65 | 4.66 |

Intrinsic viscosity $[\eta]_c$ at different values of relative viscosity $\eta_{rel}$

# Cellulose Acetate

(Ph Eur monograph 0887)

**Action and use**
Excipient.

*Ph Eur*

## DEFINITION

Partly or completely O-acetylated cellulose.

## CHARACTERS

**Appearance**
White, yellowish-white or greyish-white, hygroscopic powder or granules.

**Solubility**
Practically insoluble in water, soluble in acetone, in formic acid and in a mixture of equal volumes of methanol and methylene chloride, practically insoluble in ethanol (96 per cent).

## IDENTIFICATION

Infrared absorption spectrophotometry (2.2.24).

*Comparison* cellulose acetate CRS.

*Preparation* Prepare a 100 g/l solution of cellulose acetate, previously dried, in *dioxane R*, and spread 1 drop of the solution between 2 sodium chloride plates; separate the plates, heat them both at 105 °C for 1 h, and reassemble the dried plates.

## TESTS

**Free acid**
Maximum 0.1 per cent, calculated as acetic acid (dried substance).

To 5.00 g in a 250 ml conical flask, add 150 ml of *carbon dioxide-free water R*, insert the stopper, swirl the suspension gently and allow to stand for 3 h. Filter, then wash the flask and the filter with *carbon dioxide-free water R*, adding these washings to the filtrate. Add 0.1 ml of *phenolphthalein solution R1* and titrate the combined filtrate and washings with *0.01 M sodium hydroxide* until a pale pink colour is obtained.

1 ml of *0.01 M sodium hydroxide* is equivalent to 0.6005 mg of free acid, calculated as acetic acid.

**Heavy metals** (2.4.8)
Maximum 10 ppm.

2.0 g complies with test D. Prepare the reference solution using 2 ml of *lead standard solution (10 ppm Pb) R*.

**Loss on drying** (2.2.32)
Maximum 5.0 per cent, determined on 1.000 g by drying in an oven at 105 °C for 3 h.

**Sulphated ash** (2.4.14)
Maximum 0.1 per cent, determined on 1.0 g.

**Microbial contamination**
TAMC: acceptance criterion $10^3$ CFU/g (2.6.12).

TYMC: acceptance criterion $10^2$ CFU/g (2.6.12).

Absence of *Escherichia coli* (2.6.13).

Absence of *Salmonella* (2.6.13).

## STORAGE

In an airtight container.

## FUNCTIONALITY-RELATED CHARACTERISTICS

*This section provides information on characteristics that are recognised as being relevant control parameters for one or more functions of the substance when used as an excipient (see chapter 5.15). This section is a non-mandatory part of the monograph and it is not necessary to verify the characteristics to demonstrate compliance. Control of these characteristics can however contribute to the quality of a medicinal product by improving the consistency of the manufacturing process and the performance of the medicinal product during use. Where control methods are cited, they are recognised as being suitable for the purpose, but other methods can also be used. Wherever results for a particular characteristic are reported, the control method must be indicated.*

*The following characteristics may be relevant for cellulose acetate used as film former.*

**Apparent viscosity**
Dissolve 10 g in a mixture of 50 ml of *methanol R* and 50 ml of *methylene chloride R* by shaking. Determine the viscosity of this solution at 20 ± 0.1 °C using a rotating viscometer (2.2.10).

**Acetyl groups ($C_2H_3O$)**
Typically 29.0 per cent to 44.8 per cent of acetyl groups (dried substance) and typically 90.0 per cent to 110.0 per cent of the nominal acetyl content (dried substance).

A. Cellulose acetate containing not more than 42.0 per cent of acetyl groups

To 2.000 g in a 500 ml conical flask, add 100 ml of *acetone R* and 10 ml of *water R*. Close the flask and stir with a magnetic stirrer until dissolution is complete. Add 30.0 ml of *1 M sodium hydroxide* with constant stirring. A finely divided precipitate of regenerated cellulose, free from lumps, is obtained. Close the flask and stir with a magnetic stirrer for 30 min. Add 100 ml of *water R* at 80 °C, washing down the sides of the flask, stir for 2 min and cool to room temperature. Titrate with *0.5 M sulphuric acid*, using 0.1 ml of *phenolphthalein solution R* as indicator. Carry out a blank titration.

Calculate the percentage content of acetyl groups using the following expression:

$$\frac{4.305\,(n_2 - n_1)}{(100 - d) \times m} \times 100$$

$d$ = loss on drying as a percentage;

$m$ = mass of the substance to be examined, in grams;

$n_1$ = number of millilitres of *0.5 M sulphuric acid* used in the test;

$n_2$ = number of millilitres of *0.5 M sulphuric acid* used in the blank titration.

B. Cellulose acetate containing more than 42.0 per cent of acetyl groups

To 2.000 g in a 500 ml conical flask, add 30 ml of *dimethyl sulphoxide R* and 100 ml of *acetone R*. Close the flask and stir with a magnetic stirrer for 16 h. Add 30.0 ml of *1 M sodium hydroxide* with constant stirring. Close the flask and stir with a magnetic stirrer for 6 min. Allow to stand without stirring for 60 min. Resume stirring and add 100 ml of *water R* at 80 °C, washing down the sides of the flask, stir for 2 min and cool to room temperature. Titrate with *0.5 M hydrochloric acid*, using 0.1 ml of *phenolphthalein solution R* as indicator. Add 0.5 ml of *0.5 M hydrochloric acid* in excess, stir for 5 min and allow to stand for 30 min. Titrate with *0.5 M sodium hydroxide*, until a persistent pink colour is obtained, stirring with a magnetic stirrer. Calculate the net number of millimoles of *0.5 M sodium hydroxide* consumed, taking the mean of 2 blank titrations into consideration.

Calculate the percentage content of acetyl groups using the following expression:

$$\frac{4.305 \times n}{(100 - d) \times m} \times 100$$

$d$ = loss on drying as a percentage;
$m$ = mass of the substance to be examined, in grams;
$n$ = net number of millimoles of *0.5 M sodium hydroxide* consumed.

*The following characteristics may be relevant for cellulose acetate used as matrix former in prolonged-release tablets.*

**Apparent viscosity**
See test above.

**Acetyl groups**
See test above.

**Molecular mass distribution** (*2.2.30*).

**Particle-size distribution** (*2.9.31*).

**Powder flow** (*2.9.36*).

_____ *Ph Eur*

# Cellulose Acetate Butyrate

(*Ph Eur monograph 1406*)

**Action and use**
Excipient.

*Ph Eur* _____

## DEFINITION
Partly or completely *O*-acetylated and *O*-butyrated cellulose.
*Content:*
— *acetyl groups* ($C_2H_3O$): 2.0 per cent to 30.0 per cent (dried substance); 90.0 per cent to 110.0 per cent of that stated on the label (dried substance);
— *butyryl groups* ($C_4H_7O$): 16.0 per cent to 53.0 per cent (dried substance); 90.0 per cent to 110.0 per cent of that stated on the label (dried substance).

## CHARACTERS
**Appearance**
White, yellowish-white or greyish-white powder or granules, slightly hygroscopic.

**Solubility**
Practically insoluble in water, soluble in acetone, in formic acid and in a mixture of equal volumes of methanol and methylene chloride, practically insoluble in ethanol (96 per cent).

## IDENTIFICATION
A. Infrared absorption spectrophotometry (*2.2.24*).

*Comparison Ph. Eur. reference spectrum of cellulose acetate butyrate.*

The intensity of the bands may vary according to the degree of substitution.

B. It complies with the limits of the assay.

## TESTS
**Acidity**
To 5.00 g in a 250 ml conical flask, add 150 ml of *carbon dioxide-free water R*, insert the stopper, swirl the suspension gently and allow to stand for 3 h. Filter, wash the flask and the filter with *carbon dioxide-free water R*. Combine the filtrate and washings. Add 0.1 ml of *phenolphthalein solution R1*. Not more than 3.0 ml of *0.01 M sodium hydroxide* is required to change the colour of the indicator.

**Heavy metals** (*2.4.8*)
Maximum 20 ppm.

1.0 g complies with test F. Prepare the reference solution using 2 ml of *lead standard solution (10 ppm Pb) R*.

**Loss on drying** (*2.2.32*)
Maximum 2.0 per cent, determined on 1.000 g by drying in an oven at 105 °C for 3 h.

**Total ash** (*2.4.16*)
Maximum 0.1 per cent.

## ASSAY
Liquid chromatography (*2.2.29*).

*Test solution* To 1.000 g of the substance to be examined in a 500 ml conical flask, add 100 ml of *acetone R* and 10 ml of *water R*. Close the flask and stir with a magnetic stirrer until dissolution is complete. Add 30.0 ml of *1 M sodium hydroxide* with constant stirring. Close the flask and stir with a magnetic stirrer for 30 min. Add 100 ml of hot *water R* at 80 °C, washing down the sides of the flask and stir for 2 min. Cool, centrifuge or filter the suspension and wash the residue with *water R*. Combine the filtrate and washings, adjust to pH 3 (*2.2.3*) with *dilute phosphoric acid R* and dilute to 500.0 ml with *water R*.

*Reference solution* Dissolve 0.200 g of *glacial acetic acid R* and 0.400 g of *butyric acid R* in *water R*, adjust to pH 3 (*2.2.3*) with *dilute phosphoric acid R* and dilute to 500.0 ml with *water R*.

*Column:*
— *dimensions: l* = 0.25 m, Ø = 4.6 mm;
— *stationary phase: octadecylsilyl silica gel for chromatography R* (5 μm).

*Mobile phase:*
— *mobile phase A: methanol R*;
— *mobile phase B: phosphate buffer solution pH 3.0 R1*;

| Time (min) | Mobile phase A (per cent *V/V*) | Mobile phase B (per cent *V/V*) |
|---|---|---|
| 0 - 30 | 5 | 95 |
| 30 - 35 | 5 → 20 | 95 → 80 |
| 35 - 60 | 20 | 80 |
| 60 - 61 | 5 | 95 |

*Flow rate* 1.2 ml/min.

*Detection* Spectrophotometer at 210 nm.

*Injection* 20 μl.

Calculate the percentage content of acetic acid and butyric acid using the chromatograms obtained with the 2 solutions.

To calculate the percentage content of acetyl ($C_2H_3O$) and of butyryl ($C_4H_7O$) groups, multiply the percentage content of acetic acid and butyric acid by 0.717 and 0.807, respectively.

## STORAGE
In an airtight container.

## LABELLING
The label states the nominal percentage content of acetyl and butyryl groups.

*Ph Eur*

# Cetirizine Hydrochloride

*(Cetirizine Dihydrochloride, Ph Eur monograph 1084)*

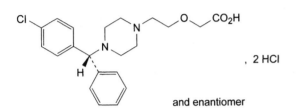

, 2 HCl

and enantiomer

$C_{21}H_{25}ClN_2O_3$,2HCl       461.8       *83881-52-1*

## Action and use
Histamine $H_1$ receptor antagonist; antihistamine.

*Ph Eur*

## DEFINITION
(*RS*)-2-[2-[4-[(4-Chlorophenyl)phenylmethyl]piperazin-1-yl]ethoxy]acetic acid dihydrochloride.

## Content
99.0 per cent to 100.5 per cent (dried substance).

## CHARACTERS
### Appearance
White or almost white powder.

### Solubility
Freely soluble in water, practically insoluble in acetone and in methylene chloride.

## IDENTIFICATION
*First identification   B, D.*

*Second identification   A, C, D.*

A. Ultraviolet and visible absorption spectrophotometry (*2.2.25*).

*Test solution*   Dissolve 20.0 mg in 50 ml of a 10.3 g/l solution of *hydrochloric acid R* and dilute to 100.0 ml with the same acid. Dilute 10.0 ml of this solution to 100.0 ml with a 10.3 g/l solution of *hydrochloric acid R*.

*Spectral range*   210-350 nm.

*Absorption maximum*   At 231 nm.

*Specific absorbance at the absorption maximum*   359 to 381.

B. Infrared absorption spectrophotometry (*2.2.24*).

*Comparison   cetirizine dihydrochloride CRS.*

C. Thin-layer chromatography (*2.2.27*).

*Test solution*   Dissolve 10 mg of the substance to be examined in *water R* and dilute to 5 ml with the same solvent.

*Reference solution (a)*   Dissolve 10 mg of *cetirizine dihydrochloride CRS* in *water R* and dilute to 5 ml with the same solvent.

*Reference solution (b)*   Dissolve 10 mg of *chlorphenamine maleate CRS* in *water R* and dilute to 5 ml with the same solvent. To 1 ml of the solution add 1 ml of reference solution (a).

*Plate   TLC silica gel GF$_{254}$ plate R.*

*Mobile phase   ammonia R, methanol R, methylene chloride R* (1:10:90 *V/V/V*).

*Application*   5 µl.

*Development*   Over 2/3 of the plate.

*Drying*   In a current of cold air.

*Detection*   Examine in ultraviolet light at 254 nm.

*System suitability*   Reference solution (b):
— the chromatogram obtained shows 2 clearly separated spots.

*Results*   The principal spot in the chromatogram obtained with the test solution is similar in position and size to the principal spot in the chromatogram obtained with reference solution (a).

D. It gives reaction (a) of chlorides (*2.3.1*).

## TESTS
### Solution S
Dissolve 1.0 g in *carbon dioxide-free water R* and dilute to 20 ml with the same solvent.

### Appearance of solution
Solution S is clear (*2.2.1*) and not more intensely coloured than reference solution BY$_7$ (*2.2.2, Method II*).

### pH (*2.2.3*)
1.2 to 1.8 for solution S.

### Related substances
Liquid chromatography (*2.2.29*).

*Test solution*   Dissolve 20.0 mg of the substance to be examined in the mobile phase and dilute to 100.0 ml with the mobile phase.

*Reference solution (a)*   Dissolve 2 mg of *cetirizine dihydrochloride CRS* and 2 mg of *cetirizine impurity A CRS* in the mobile phase and dilute to 10.0 ml with the mobile phase. Dilute 1.0 ml of the solution to 100.0 ml with the mobile phase.

*Reference solution (b)*   Dilute 2.0 ml of the test solution to 50.0 ml with the mobile phase. Dilute 5.0 ml of this solution to 100.0 ml with the mobile phase.

*Column:*
— *size: l* = 0.25 m, Ø = 4.6 mm;
— *stationary phase: silica gel for chromatography R* (5 µm).

*Mobile phase   dilute sulphuric acid R, water R, acetonitrile R* (0.4:6.6:93 *V/V/V*).

*Flow rate*   1 ml/min.

*Detection*   Spectrophotometer at 230 nm.

*Injection*   20 µl.

*Run time*   3 times the retention time of cetirizine.

*System suitability*   Reference solution (a):
— *resolution*: minimum 3 between the peaks due to cetirizine and impurity A;
— *symmetry factors*: maximum 2.0.

*Limits:*
— *impurities A, B, C, D, E, F*: for each impurity, not more than 0.5 times the area of the principal peak in the

chromatogram obtained with reference solution (b) (0.1 per cent);

— *unspecified impurities*: for each impurity, not more than 0.5 times the area of the principal peak in the chromatogram obtained with reference solution (b) (0.1 per cent);

— *total*: not more than 1.5 times the area of the principal peak in the chromatogram obtained with reference solution (b) (0.3 per cent);

— *disregard limit*: 0.1 times the area of the principal peak in the chromatogram obtained with reference solution (b) (0.02 per cent).

**Loss on drying** *(2.2.32)*
Maximum 0.5 per cent, determined on 1.000 g by drying in an oven at 105 °C.

**Sulphated ash** *(2.4.14)*
Maximum 0.2 per cent, determined on 1.0 g.

**ASSAY**
Dissolve 0.100 g in 70 ml of a mixture of 30 volumes of *water R* and 70 volumes of *acetone R*. Titrate with *0.1 M sodium hydroxide* to the 2$^{nd}$ point of inflexion. Determine the end-point potentiometrically *(2.2.20)*. Carry out a blank titration.

1 ml of *0.1 M sodium hydroxide* is equivalent to 15.39 mg of $C_{21}H_{27}Cl_3N_2O_3$.

**STORAGE**
Protected from light.

**IMPURITIES**
*Specified impurities   A, B, C, D, E, F.*

*Other detectable impurities* (the following substances would, if present at a sufficient level, be detected by one or other of the tests in the monograph. They are limited by the general acceptance criterion for other/unspecified impurities and/or by the general monograph *Substances for pharmaceutical use (2034)*. It is therefore not necessary to identify these impurities for demonstration of compliance. See also *5.10. Control of impurities in substances for pharmaceutical use): G.*

R3—⟨⟩—CH(N-piperazine-N—R1)—phenyl, R2, H

and enantiomer

A. R1 = R2 = H, R3 = Cl: (*RS*)-1-[(4-chlorophenyl)phenylmethyl]piperazine,

B. R1 = CH$_2$-CO$_2$H, R2 = H, R3 = Cl: (*RS*)-2-[4-[(4-chlorophenyl)phenylmethyl]piperazin-1-yl]acetic acid,

C. R1 = CH$_2$-CH$_2$-O-CH$_2$-CO$_2$H, R2 = Cl, R3 = H: (*RS*)-2-[2-[4-[(2-chlorophenyl)phenylmethyl]piperazin-1-yl]ethoxy]acetic acid,

E. R1 = CH$_2$-[CH$_2$-O-CH$_2$]$_2$-CO$_2$H, R2 = H, R3 = Cl: (*RS*)-2-[2-[2-[4-[(4-chlorophenyl)phenylmethyl]piperazin-1-yl]ethoxy]ethoxy]acetic acid (ethoxycetirizine),

F. R1 = CH$_2$-CH$_2$-O-CH$_2$-CO$_2$H, R2 = R3 = H: [2-[4-(diphenylmethyl)piperazin-1-yl]ethoxy]acetic acid,

G. R1 = CH$_2$-CH$_2$-OH, R2 = H, R3 = Cl: 2-[4-[(*RS*)-(4-chlorophenyl)phenylmethyl]piperazin-1-yl]ethanol,

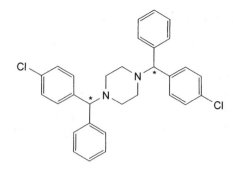

D. 1,4-bis[(4-chlorophenyl)phenylmethyl]piperazine.

*Ph Eur*

---

# Cetostearyl Alcohol

*(Ph Eur monograph 0702)*

**Action and use**
Excipient.

*Ph Eur*

**DEFINITION**
Mixture of solid aliphatic alcohols, mainly octadecan-1-ol (stearyl alcohol; $C_{18}H_{38}O$; $M_r$ 270.5) and hexadecan-1-ol (cetyl alcohol; $C_{16}H_{34}O$; $M_r$ 242.4), of animal or vegetable origin.

**Content:**
— *stearyl alcohol*: minimum 40.0 per cent,
— *sum of the contents of stearyl alcohol and cetyl alcohol*: minimum 90.0 per cent.

**CHARACTERS**
**Appearance**
White or pale yellow, wax-like mass, plates, flakes or granules.

**Solubility**
Practically insoluble in water, soluble in ethanol (96 per cent) and in light petroleum. When melted, it is miscible with fatty oils, with liquid paraffin and with melted wool fat.

**IDENTIFICATION**
Examine the chromatograms obtained in the assay.

*Results*   The 2 principal peaks in the chromatogram obtained with the test solution are similar in retention time to the principal peaks in the chromatogram obtained with the reference solution.

**TESTS**
**Appearance of solution**
The solution is clear *(2.2.1)* and not more intensely coloured than reference solution B$_6$ *(2.2.2, Method II)*.

Dissolve 0.50 g in 20 ml of boiling *ethanol (96 per cent) R*. Allow to cool.

**Melting point** *(2.2.14)*
49 °C to 56 °C.

**Acid value** *(2.5.1)*
Maximum 1.0.

**Hydroxyl value** *(2.5.3, Method A)*
208 to 228.

**Iodine value** *(2.5.4, Method A)*
Maximum 2.0.

Dissolve 2.00 g in *methylene chloride R* and dilute to 25 ml with the same solvent.

**Saponification value** (*2.5.6*)

Maximum 2.0.

## ASSAY

Gas chromatography (*2.2.28*): use the normalisation procedure.

*Test solution*   Dissolve 0.100 g of the substance to be examined in *ethanol (96 per cent) R* and dilute to 10.0 ml with the same solvent.

*Reference solution*   Dissolve 60 mg of *cetyl alcohol CRS* and 40 mg of *stearyl alcohol CRS* in *ethanol (96 per cent) R* and dilute to 10 ml with the same solvent. Dilute 1 ml of this solution to 10 ml with *ethanol (96 per cent) R*.

*Column*:
— *size*: *l* = 30 m, Ø = 0.32 mm,
— *stationary phase*: *poly(dimethyl)siloxane R* (1 μm).

*Carrier gas*   *helium for chromatography R.*

*Flow rate*   1 ml/min.

*Split ratio*   1:100.

*Temperature*:

|  | Time (min) | Temperature (°C) |
|---|---|---|
| Column | 0 - 20 | 150 → 250 |
|  | 20 - 40 | 250 |
| Injection port |  | 250 |
| Detector |  | 250 |

*Detection*   Flame ionisation.

*Injection*   1 μl.

*System suitability*   Reference solution:
— *resolution*: minimum 5.0 between the peaks due to cetyl alcohol and stearyl alcohol.

Calculate the percentage contents of $C_{16}H_{34}O$ and $C_{18}H_{38}O$.

*Ph Eur*

# Emulsifying Cetostearyl Alcohol (Type A)

(*Ph Eur monograph 0801*)

**Action and use**

Excipient.

*Ph Eur*

## DEFINITION

Mixture of cetostearyl alcohol and sodium cetostearyl sulphate. A suitable buffer may be added.

**Content**:
— *cetostearyl alcohol*: minimum 80.0 per cent (anhydrous substance);
— *sodium cetostearyl sulphate*: minimum 7.0 per cent (anhydrous substance).

## CHARACTERS

**Appearance**

White or pale yellow, waxy mass, plates, flakes or granules.

**Solubility**

Soluble in hot water giving an opalescent solution, practically insoluble in cold water, slightly soluble in ethanol (96 per cent).

## IDENTIFICATION

*First identification*   *B, C, D.*

*Second identification*   *A, C.*

A. Thin-layer chromatography (*2.2.27*).

*Test solution (a)*   Dissolve 0.1 g of the substance to be examined in 10 ml of *trimethylpentane R*, heating on a water-bath. Shake with 2 ml of *ethanol (70 per cent V/V) R* and allow to separate. Use the lower layer as test solution (b). Dilute 1 ml of the upper layer to 8 ml with *trimethylpentane R*.

*Test solution (b)*   Use the lower layer obtained in the preparation of test solution (a).

*Reference solution (a)*   Dissolve 24 mg of *cetyl alcohol CRS* and 16 mg of *stearyl alcohol CRS* in 10 ml of *trimethylpentane R*.

*Reference solution (b)*   Dissolve 20 mg of *sodium cetostearyl sulphate R* in 10 ml of *ethanol (70 per cent V/V) R*, heating on a water-bath.

*Plate*   *TLC silanised silica gel plate R.*

*Mobile phase*   *water R, acetone R, methanol R* (20:40:40 *V/V/V*).

*Application*   2 μl.

*Development*   Over a path of 12 cm.

*Drying*   In air.

*Detection*   Spray with a 50 g/l solution of *phosphomolybdic acid R* in *ethanol (96 per cent) R*; heat at 120 °C until spots appear (about 3 h).

*Results*:
— the 2 principal spots in the chromatogram obtained with test solution (a) are similar in position and colour to the principal spots in the chromatogram obtained with reference solution (a);
— 2 of the spots in the chromatogram obtained with test solution (b) are similar in position and colour to the principal spots in the chromatogram obtained with reference solution (b).

B. Examine the chromatograms obtained in the assay.

*Results*   The 2 principal peaks in the chromatogram obtained with test solution (b) are similar in retention time to the 2 principal peaks in the chromatogram obtained with the reference solution.

C. It gives a yellow colour to a non-luminous flame.

D. To 0.3 g add 20 ml of *anhydrous ethanol R* and heat to boiling on a water-bath with shaking. Filter the mixture immediately, evaporate to dryness and take up the residue in 7 ml of *water R*. To 1 ml of the solution add 0.1 ml of a 1 g/l solution of *methylene blue R*, 2 ml of *dilute sulphuric acid R* and 2 ml of *methylene chloride R* and shake. A blue colour develops in the lower layer.

## TESTS

**Acid value** (*2.5.1*)

Maximum 2.0.

**Iodine value** (*2.5.4, Method A*)

Maximum 3.0.

Dissolve 2.00 g in 25 ml of *methylene chloride R*.

**Saponification value** (*2.5.6*)

Maximum 2.0.

**Water** *(2.5.12)*
Maximum 3.0 per cent, determined on 2.50 g.

## ASSAY

### Cetostearyl alcohol

Gas chromatography *(2.2.28)*.

*Internal standard solution*   Dissolve 0.60 g of *heptadecanol CRS* in *anhydrous ethanol R* and dilute to 150 ml with the same solvent.

*Test solution (a)*   Dissolve 0.300 g of the substance to be examined in 50 ml of the internal standard solution, add 50 ml of *water R* and shake with 4 quantities, each of 25 ml, of *pentane R*, adding *sodium chloride R*, if necessary, to facilitate the separation of the layers. Combine the organic layers. Wash with 2 quantities, each of 30 ml, of *water R*, dry over *anhydrous sodium sulphate R* and filter.

*Test solution (b)*   Dissolve 0.300 g of the substance to be examined in 50 ml of *anhydrous ethanol R*, add 50 ml of *water R* and shake with 4 quantities, each of 25 ml, of *pentane R*, adding *sodium chloride R*, if necessary, to facilitate the separation of the layers. Combine the organic layers. Wash with 2 quantities, each of 30 ml, of *water R*, dry over *anhydrous sodium sulphate R* and filter.

*Reference solution*   Dissolve 50 mg of *cetyl alcohol CRS* and 50 mg of *stearyl alcohol CRS* in *anhydrous ethanol R* and dilute to 10 ml with the same solvent.

*Column:*
— *material*: fused silica;
— *size*: $l = 25$ m, $\varnothing = 0.25$ mm;
— *stationary phase*: poly(dimethyl)siloxane R.

*Carrier gas*   nitrogen for chromatography R.

*Flow rate*   1 ml/min.

*Split ratio*   1:100.

*Temperature:*

|  | Time (min) | Temperature (°C) |
|---|---|---|
| Column | 0 - 20 | 150 → 250 |
| Injection port |  | 250 |
| Detector |  | 250 |

*Detection*   Flame ionisation.

*Elution order*   Cetyl alcohol, heptadecanol, stearyl alcohol.

Inject 1 µl of test solution (a) and 1 µl of test solution (b). If the chromatogram obtained with test solution (b) shows a peak with the same retention time as the peak due to the internal standard in the chromatogram obtained with test solution (a), calculate the ratio *r* using the following expression:

$$\frac{S_{ci}}{S_i}$$

$S_{ci}$   = area of the peak due to cetyl alcohol in the chromatogram obtained with test solution (b);
$S_i$   = area of the peak with the same retention time as the peak due to the internal standard in the chromatogram obtained with test solution (a).

If *r* is less than 300, calculate the corrected area $S_{Ha(corr)}$ of the peak due to the internal standard in the chromatogram obtained with test solution (a) using the following expression:

$$S'_{Ha} - \frac{S_i \times S_c}{S_{ci}}$$

$S'_{Ha} =$   area of the peak due to the internal standard in the chromatogram obtained with test solution (a);
$S_c$   =   area of the peak due to cetyl alcohol in the chromatogram obtained with test solution (a).

Inject, under the same conditions, equal volumes of the reference solution and of test solution (a). Identify the peaks in the chromatogram obtained with test solution (a) by comparing their retention times with those of the peaks in the chromatogram obtained with the reference solution and determine the area of each peak.

Calculate the percentage content of cetyl alcohol using the following expression:

$$S_A \frac{100 \times m_H}{S_{Ha(corr)} \times m}$$

$S_A$   =   area of the peak due to cetyl alcohol in the chromatogram obtained with test solution (a);
$m_H$   =   mass of the internal standard in test solution (a), in milligrams;
$S_{Ha(corr)} =$   corrected area of the peak due to the internal standard in the chromatogram obtained with test solution (a);
$m$   =   mass of the substance to be examined in test solution (a), in milligrams.

Calculate the percentage content of stearyl alcohol using the following expression:

$$S_B \frac{100 \times m_H}{S_{Ha(corr)} \times m}$$

$S_B$   =   area of the peak due to stearyl alcohol in the chromatogram obtained with test solution (a).

The percentage content of cetostearyl alcohol corresponds to the sum of the percentage content of cetyl alcohol and of stearyl alcohol.

### Sodium cetostearyl sulphate

Disperse 0.300 g in 25 ml of *methylene chloride R*. Add 50 ml of *water R* and 10 ml of *dimidium bromide-sulphan blue mixed solution R*. Titrate with *0.004 M benzethonium chloride*, using sonication, heating and allowing the layers to separate before each addition, until the colour of the lower layer changes from pink to grey.

1 ml of *0.004 M benzethonium chloride* is equivalent to 1.434 mg of sodium cetostearyl sulphate.

## LABELLING

The label states, where applicable, the name and concentration of any added buffer.

*Ph Eur*

# Emulsifying Cetostearyl Alcohol (Type B)

(*Ph Eur monograph 0802*)

**Action and use**
Excipient.

*Ph Eur* _____

## DEFINITION

Mixture of cetostearyl alcohol and sodium laurilsulfate. A suitable buffer may be added.

**Content:**
— *cetostearyl alcohol*: minimum 80.0 per cent (anhydrous substance);
— *sodium laurilsulfate*: minimum 7.0 per cent (anhydrous substance).

## CHARACTERS

**Appearance**
White or pale yellow, waxy mass, plates, flakes or granules.

**Solubility**
Soluble in hot water giving an opalescent solution, practically insoluble in cold water, slightly soluble in ethanol (96 per cent).

## IDENTIFICATION

*First identification* B, C, D.

*Second identification* A, C.

A. Thin-layer chromatography (2.2.27).

*Test solution (a)* Dissolve 0.1 g of the substance to be examined in 10 ml of *trimethylpentane R*, heating on a water-bath. Shake with 2 ml of *ethanol (70 per cent V/V) R* and allow to separate. Use the lower layer as test solution (b). Dilute 1 ml of the upper layer to 8 ml with *trimethylpentane R*.

*Test solution (b)* Use the lower layer obtained in the preparation of test solution (a).

*Reference solution (a)* Dissolve 24 mg of *cetyl alcohol CRS* and 16 mg of *stearyl alcohol CRS* in 10 ml of *trimethylpentane R*.

*Reference solution (b)* Dissolve 20 mg of *sodium laurilsulfate CRS* in 10 ml of *ethanol (70 per cent V/V) R*, heating on a water-bath.

*Plate* TLC silanised silica gel plate R.

*Mobile phase* water R, acetone R, methanol R (20:40:40 V/V/V).

*Application* 2 μl.

*Development* Over a path of 12 cm.

*Drying* In air.

*Detection* Spray with a 50 g/l solution of *phosphomolybdic acid R* in *ethanol (96 per cent) R*; heat at 120 °C until spots appear (about 3 h).

*Results:*
— the 2 principal spots in the chromatogram obtained with test solution (a) are similar in position and colour to the principal spots in the chromatogram obtained with reference solution (a);
— 1 of the spots in the chromatogram obtained with test solution (b) is similar in position and colour to the principal spot in the chromatogram obtained with reference solution (b).

B. Examine the chromatograms obtained in the assay.

*Results* The 2 principal peaks in the chromatogram obtained with test solution (b) are similar in retention time to the 2 principal peaks in the chromatogram obtained with the reference solution.

C. It gives a yellow colour to a non-luminous flame.

D. To 0.3 g add 20 ml of *anhydrous ethanol R* and heat to boiling on a water-bath with shaking. Filter the mixture immediately, evaporate to dryness and take up the residue in 7 ml of *water R*. To 1 ml of the solution add 0.1 ml of a 1 g/l solution of *methylene blue R*, 2 ml of *dilute sulphuric acid R* and 2 ml of *methylene chloride R* and shake. A blue colour develops in the lower layer.

## TESTS

**Acid value** (2.5.1)
Maximum 2.0.

**Iodine value** (2.5.4, Method A)
Maximum 3.0.

Dissolve 2.00 g in 25 ml of *methylene chloride R*.

**Saponification value** (2.5.6)
Maximum 2.0.

**Water** (2.5.12)
Maximum 3.0 per cent, determined on 2.50 g.

## ASSAY

**Cetostearyl alcohol**
Gas chromatography (2.2.28).

*Internal standard solution* Dissolve 0.60 g of *heptadecanol CRS* in *anhydrous ethanol R* and dilute to 150 ml with the same solvent.

*Test solution (a)* Dissolve 0.300 g of the substance to be examined in 50 ml of the internal standard solution, add 50 ml of *water R* and shake with 4 quantities, each of 25 ml, of *pentane R*, adding *sodium chloride R*, if necessary, to facilitate the separation of the layers. Combine the organic layers. Wash with 2 quantities, each of 30 ml, of *water R*, dry over *anhydrous sodium sulphate R* and filter.

*Test solution (b)* Dissolve 0.300 g of the substance to be examined in 50 ml of *anhydrous ethanol R*, add 50 ml of *water R* and shake with 4 quantities, each of 25 ml, of *pentane R*, adding *sodium chloride R*, if necessary, to facilitate the separation of the layers. Combine the organic layers. Wash with 2 quantities, each of 30 ml, of *water R*, dry over *anhydrous sodium sulphate R* and filter.

*Reference solution* Dissolve 50 mg of *cetyl alcohol CRS* and 50 mg of *stearyl alcohol CRS* in *anhydrous ethanol R* and dilute to 10 ml with the same solvent.

*Column:*
— *material*: fused silica;
— *size*: l = 25 m, Ø = 0.25 mm;
— *stationary phase*: poly(dimethyl)siloxane R.

*Carrier gas* nitrogen for chromatography R.

*Flow rate* 1 ml/min.

*Split ratio* 1:100.

*Temperature:*

|  | Time (min) | Temperature (°C) |
|---|---|---|
| Column | 0 - 20 | 150 → 250 |
| Injection port |  | 250 |
| Detector |  | 250 |

*Detection* Flame ionisation.

*Elution order* Cetyl alcohol, heptadecanol, stearyl alcohol.

Inject 1 µl of test solution (a) and 1 µl of test solution (b). If the chromatogram obtained with test solution (b) shows a peak with the same retention time as the peak due to the internal standard in the chromatogram obtained with test solution (a), calculate the ratio $r$ using the following expression:

$$\frac{S_{ci}}{S_i}$$

$S_{ci}$ = area of the peak due to cetyl alcohol in the chromatogram obtained with test solution (b);

$S_i$ = area of the peak with the same retention time as the peak due to the internal standard in the chromatogram obtained with test solution (a).

If $r$ is less than 300, calculate the corrected area $S_{Ha(corr)}$ of the peak due to the internal standard in the chromatogram obtained with test solution (a) using the following expression:

$$S'_{Ha} - \frac{S_i \times S_c}{S_{ci}}$$

$S'_{Ha}$ = area of the peak due to the internal standard in the chromatogram obtained with test solution (a);

$S_c$ = area of the peak due to cetyl alcohol in the chromatogram obtained with test solution (a).

Inject, under the same conditions, equal volumes of the reference solution and of test solution (a). Identify the peaks in the chromatogram obtained with test solution (a) by comparing their retention times with those of the peaks in the chromatogram obtained with the reference solution and determine the area of each peak.

Calculate the percentage content of cetyl alcohol using the following expression:

$$S_A \frac{100 \times m_H}{S_{Ha(corr)} \times m}$$

$S_A$ = area of the peak due to cetyl alcohol in the chromatogram obtained with test solution (a);

$m_H$ = mass of the internal standard in test solution (a), in milligrams;

$S_{Ha(corr)}$ = corrected area of the peak due to the internal standard in the chromatogram obtained with test solution (a);

$m$ = mass of the substance to be examined in test solution (a), in milligrams.

Calculate the percentage content of stearyl alcohol using the following expression:

$$S_B \frac{100 \times m_H}{S_{Ha(corr)} \times m}$$

$S_B$ = area of the peak due to stearyl alcohol in the chromatogram obtained with test solution (a).

The percentage content of cetostearyl alcohol corresponds to the sum of the percentage content of cetyl alcohol and of stearyl alcohol.

## Sodium laurilsulfate

Disperse 0.300 g in 25 ml of *methylene chloride R*. Add 50 ml of *water R* and 10 ml of *dimidium bromide-sulphan blue mixed solution R*. Titrate with *0.004 M benzethonium chloride*, using sonication, heating, and allowing the layers to separate before each addition, until the colour of the lower layer changes from pink to grey.

1 ml of *0.004 M benzethonium chloride* is equivalent to 1.154 mg of sodium laurilsulfate.

## LABELLING

The label states, where applicable, the name and concentration of any added buffer.

———————— *Ph Eur*

# Cetostearyl Isononanoate

(*Ph Eur monograph 1085*)

## Action and use

Excipient.

*Ph Eur*

## DEFINITION

Mixture of esters of cetostearyl alcohol with isononanoic acid, mainly 3,5,5-trimethylhexanoic acid.

## CHARACTERS

### Appearance

Clear, colourless or slightly yellowish liquid.

### Solubility

Practically insoluble in water, soluble in ethanol (96 per cent) and in light petroleum, miscible with fatty oils and with liquid paraffins.

### Viscosity

15 mPa·s to 30 mPa·s.

### Relative density

0.85 to 0.86.

### Refractive index

1.44 to 1.45.

## IDENTIFICATION

A. On cooling, turbidity occurs below 15 °C.

B. Saponification value (see Tests).

C. Infrared absorption spectrophotometry (*2.2.24*).

*Comparison   Ph. Eur. reference spectrum of cetostearyl isononanoate.*

## TESTS

### Appearance

The substance to be examined is clear (*2.2.1*) and not more intensely coloured than reference solution $Y_6$ (*2.2.2, Method I*).

**Acid value** (*2.5.1*)

Maximum 1.0, determined on 5.0 g.

**Hydroxyl value** (*2.5.3, Method A*)

Maximum 5.0.

**Iodine value** (*2.5.4, Method A*)

Maximum 1.0.

**Saponification value** (*2.5.6*)

135 to 148, determined on 1.0 g.

**Heavy metals** (*2.4.8*)

Maximum 10 ppm.

2.0 g complies with test D. Prepare the reference solution using 2 ml of *lead standard solution (10 ppm Pb) R*.

**Water** (*2.5.12*)

Maximum 0.2 per cent, determined on 10.0 g.

**Total ash** (*2.4.16*)
Maximum 0.2 per cent, determined on 2.0 g.

*Ph Eur*

# Cetrimide

(*Ph Eur monograph 0378*)

**Action and use**
Antiseptic.

**Preparations**
Cetrimide Cream
Cetrimide Emulsifying Ointment

*Ph Eur*

## DEFINITION
Cetrimide consists of trimethyltetradecylammonium bromide and may contain smaller amounts of dodecyl- and hexadecyl-trimethylammonium bromides.

## Content
96.0 per cent to 101.0 per cent of alkyltrimethylammonium bromides, calculated as $C_{17}H_{38}BrN$ ($M_r$ 336.4) (dried substance).

## CHARACTERS
**Appearance**
White or almost white, voluminous, free-flowing powder.

**Solubility**
Freely soluble in water and in alcohol.

## IDENTIFICATION
A. Dissolve 0.25 g in *alcohol R* and dilute to 25.0 ml with the same solvent. At wavelengths from 260 nm to 280 nm, the absorbance (*2.2.25*) of the solution has a maximum of 0.05.

B. Dissolve about 5 mg in 5 ml of *buffer solution pH 8.0 R*. Add about 10 mg of *potassium ferricyanide R*. A yellow precipitate is formed. Prepare a blank in the same manner but omitting the substance to be examined: a yellow solution is observed but no precipitate is formed.

C. Solution S (see Tests) froths copiously when shaken.

D. Thin-layer chromatography (*2.2.27*).

*Test solution* Dissolve 0.10 g of the substance to be examined in *water R* and dilute to 5 ml with the same solvent.

*Reference solution* Dissolve 0.10 g of *trimethyltetradecylammonium bromide CRS* in *water R* and dilute to 5 ml with the same solvent.

*Plate* TLC silica gel $F_{254}$ *silanised plate R*.

*Mobile phase* acetone R, 270 g/l solution of *sodium acetate R, methanol R* (20:35:45 *V/V/V*).

*Application* 1 µl.

*Development* Over a path of 12 cm.

*Drying* In a current of hot air.

*Detection* Allow to cool; expose the plate to iodine vapour and examine in daylight.

*Result* The principal spot in the chromatogram obtained with the test solution is similar in position, colour and size to the principal spot in the chromatogram obtained with the reference solution.

E. It gives reaction (a) of bromides (*2.3.1*).

## TESTS
**Solution S**
Dissolve 2.0 g in *carbon dioxide-free water R* and dilute to 100 ml with the same solvent.

**Appearance of solution**
Solution S is clear (*2.2.1*) and colourless (*2.2.2, Method II*).

**Acidity or alkalinity**
To 50 ml of solution S add 0.1 ml of *bromocresol purple solution R*. Not more than 0.1 ml of *0.1 M hydrochloric acid* or *0.1 M sodium hydroxide* is required to change the colour of the indicator.

**Amines and amine salts**
Dissolve 5.0 g in 30 ml of a mixture of 1 volume of *1 M hydrochloric acid* and 99 volumes of *methanol R* and add 100 ml of *2-propanol R*. Pass a stream of *nitrogen R* slowly through the solution. Gradually add 15.0 ml of *0.1 M tetrabutylammonium hydroxide* and record the potentiometric titration curve (*2.2.20*). If the curve shows 2 points of inflexion, the volume of titrant added between the 2 points is not greater than 2.0 ml.

**Loss on drying** (*2.2.32*)
Maximum 2.0 per cent, determined on 1.000 g by drying in an oven at 105 °C for 2 h.

**Sulphated ash** (*2.4.14*)
Maximum 0.5 per cent, determined on 1.0 g.

## ASSAY
Dissolve 2.000 g in *water R* and dilute to 100.0 ml with the same solvent. Transfer 25.0 ml of the solution to a separating funnel, add 25 ml of *chloroform R*, 10 ml of *0.1 M sodium hydroxide* and 10.0 ml of a freshly prepared 50 g/l solution of *potassium iodide R*. Shake, allow to separate and discard the chloroform layer. Shake the aqueous layer with 3 quantities, each of 10 ml, of *chloroform R* and discard the chloroform layers. Add 40 ml of *hydrochloric acid R*, allow to cool and titrate with *0.05 M potassium iodate* until the deep brown colour is almost discharged. Add 2 ml of *chloroform R* and continue the titration, shaking vigorously, until the colour of the chloroform layer no longer changes. Carry out a blank titration on a mixture of 10.0 ml of the freshly prepared 50 g/l solution of *potassium iodide R*, 20 ml of *water R* and 40 ml of *hydrochloric acid R*.

1 ml of *0.05 M potassium iodate* is equivalent to 33.64 mg of $C_{17}H_{38}B_rN$.

*Ph Eur*

# Strong Cetrimide Solution

**Action and use**
Antiseptic.

**Preparation**
Cetrimide Solution

## DEFINITION
Strong Cetrimide Solution is an aqueous solution of cetrimide. It contains 20 to 40% w/v of cetrimide, calculated as $C_{17}H_{38}BrN$. It contains Ethanol (96 per cent) or Isopropyl Alcohol or both. It may be perfumed and may contain colouring matter.

## PRODUCTION

In making Strong Cetrimide Solution, Ethanol (96 per cent) may be replaced by Industrial Methylated Spirit, provided that the law and the statutory regulations governing the use of Industrial Methylated Spirit are observed.

### Content of cetrimide C₁₇H₃₈BrN

Content of cetrimide $C_{17}H_{38}BrN$
95.0 to 105.0% of the stated amount.

## IDENTIFICATION

A. Dilute a volume of the solution containing 0.1 g of cetrimide to 5 ml with *water* and add 2 ml of a 5% w/v solution of *potassium hexacyanoferrate(III)*. A yellow precipitate is produced.

B. Shake together 5 ml of *water*, 1 ml of 2M *sulphuric acid*, 2 ml of *chloroform* and 0.05 ml of *methyl orange solution*; the chloroform layer is colourless. Add 0.1 ml of the solution being examined and shake; a yellow colour is produced slowly in the chloroform layer.

C. Yields reaction A characteristic of *bromides*, Appendix VI.

## TESTS

### Acidity or alkalinity

Dilute a volume of the solution containing 10 g of cetrimide to 100 ml and add 0.1 ml of *bromocresol purple solution*. Not more than 1.0 ml of either 0.1M *hydrochloric acid VS* or 0.1M *sodium hydroxide VS* is required to change the colour of the solution.

### Miscibility with ethanol

Mix a volume of the solution containing 1.6 g of cetrimide with a mixture of 2 ml of *water* and 16 ml of *ethanol (96%)*. The solution remains *clear*, Appendix IV A.

### Neutral substances

To a volume of the solution containing 10 g of cetrimide add 25 ml of *ethanol (50%)*, acidify to *bromophenol blue solution* by the drop wise addition of *hydrochloric acid* and add 0.05 ml in excess. Transfer quantitatively to the extraction compartment of an apparatus designed for continuous liquid-liquid extraction by fluids of a lesser density than water, washing out the beaker with 10 ml *ethanol (50%)* and adding the washings to the bulk of the solution in the extractor. Add sufficient *ethanol (50%)*, if necessary, to half-fill the extraction chamber to the level of the overflow limb. Add sufficient *purified hexane* to fill the extraction chamber, secure an overflow volume of about 30 ml in the ebullition flask and heat using an electrically heated mantle. Ensure that a continuous flow of hexane through the aqueous ethanol layer is observed and continue the extraction for 16 hours.
Transfer the hexane extract to a separating funnel, washing out the flask with 10 ml of *purified hexane*. Shake the combined extract and washings with 25 ml of *ethanol (50%)* and discard the aqueous ethanol layer. Filter the hexane layer through a dry filter paper (Whatman No. 1 is suitable) into a tared flask and remove the solvent using a rotary evaporator at 40° and then at room temperature at a pressure not exceeding 0.7 kPa for 2 hours. The residue weighs not more than 0.4 g.

### Non-quaternised amines

To a volume of the solution containing 10 g of cetrimide add a mixture of 100 ml of *propan-2-ol*, 0.1 ml of *hydrochloric acid* and 20 ml of *methanol*. Titrate with 0.1M *tetrabutylammonium hydroxide VS* passing a slow current of *nitrogen* through the solution and determining the end point potentiometrically using a platinum-glass electrode system. Inflections in the titration curve indicate (A) neutralisation of excess hydrochloric acid and (B) neutralisation of non-quaternised amine salts. The difference between the volumes

corresponding to A and B is not more than 10 ml (2.4%, calculated as $C_{16}H_{35}N$).

### Ethanol; Isopropyl alcohol

Carry out one or both of the following methods according to the declared alcohol content of the solution being examined.

*Ethanol*   Not more than 10.0% v/v, by the method for the *determination of ethanol*, Appendix VIII F. Use on-column injection and do not heat the injection port.

*Isopropyl alcohol*   Not more than 10.0% v/v, by the method for the *determination of ethanol*, Appendix VIII F, with the following modifications. For solution (1) use a solution containing 5.0% v/v of *propan-2-ol* and 5.0% v/v of *propan-1-ol* (internal standard). For solution (2) use the solution being examined, diluted with *water*, if necessary, to contain about 5.0% v/v of isopropyl alcohol. Maintain the column temperature at 170°, use on-column injection and do not heat the injection port.

## ASSAY

Dilute a volume containing 4 g of cetrimide with sufficient *water* to produce 100 ml. Transfer 25 ml of the solution to a separating funnel and add 25 ml of *chloroform*, 10 ml of 0.1M *sodium hydroxide* and 10 ml of a freshly prepared 8.0% w/v solution of *potassium iodide*. Shake well, allow to separate and discard the chloroform layer. Wash the aqueous layer with three 10 ml quantities of *chloroform* and discard the washings. Add 40 ml of *hydrochloric acid*, cool and titrate with 0.05M *potassium iodate VS* until the deep brown colour is almost discharged. Add 2 ml of *chloroform* and continue the titration, with shaking, until the chloroform layer becomes colourless. Carry out a blank titration on a mixture of 10 ml of the freshly prepared potassium iodide solution, 20 ml of *water* and 40 ml of *hydrochloric acid*. The difference between the titrations represents the amount of potassium iodate required. Each ml of 0.05M *potassium iodate VS* is equivalent to 33.64 mg of $C_{17}H_{38}BrN$.

## STORAGE

Strong Cetrimide Solution should be stored at a temperature above 15°.

## LABELLING

The label states whether Ethanol, Isopropyl Alcohol or both are present and the percentage of cetrimide, weight in volume.

# Cetyl Alcohol

*(Ph Eur monograph 0540)*

36653-82-4

**Action and use**
Excipient.

*Ph Eur* _____

## DEFINITION

Mixture of solid alcohols, mainly hexadecan-1-ol ($C_{16}H_{34}O$; $M_r$ 242.4), of animal or vegetable origin.

### Content

Minimum 95.0 per cent of $C_{16}H_{34}O$.

## CHARACTERS

### Appearance

White or almost white, unctuous mass, powder, flakes or granules.

## Solubility

Practically insoluble in water, freely soluble or sparingly soluble in *ethanol (96 per cent)*. When melted, it is miscible with vegetable and animal oils, with liquid paraffin and with melted wool fat.

## IDENTIFICATION

Examine the chromatograms obtained in the assay.

*Results*  The principal peak in the chromatogram obtained with the test solution is similar in retention time to the principal peak in the chromatogram obtained with reference solution (a).

## TESTS

### Appearance of solution

The solution is clear (*2.2.1*) and not more intensely coloured than reference solution $B_6$ (*2.2.2, Method II*).

Dissolve 0.50 g in 20 ml of boiling *ethanol (96 per cent) R*. Allow to cool.

### Melting point (*2.2.14*)

46 °C to 52 °C.

### Acid value (*2.5.1*)

Maximum 1.0.

### Hydroxyl value (*2.5.3, Method A*)

218 to 238.

### Iodine value (*2.5.4, Method A*)

Maximum 2.0.

Dissolve 2.00 g in *methylene chloride R* and dilute to 25 ml with the same solvent.

### Saponification value (*2.5.6*)

Maximum 2.0.

## ASSAY

Gas chromatography (*2.2.28*): use the normalisation procedure.

*Test solution*  Dissolve 0.100 g of the substance to be examined in *ethanol (96 per cent) R* and dilute to 10.0 ml with the same solvent.

*Reference solution (a)*  Dissolve 50 mg of *cetyl alcohol CRS* in *ethanol (96 per cent) R* and dilute to 5 ml with the same solvent.

*Reference solution (b)*  Dissolve 50 mg of *stearyl alcohol R* in *ethanol (96 per cent) R* and dilute to 10 ml with the same solvent.

*Reference solution (c)*  Mix 1 ml of reference solution (a) and 1 ml of reference solution (b) and dilute to 10 ml with *ethanol (96 per cent) R*.

*Column:*
— *size*: $l$ = 30 m, Ø = 0.32 mm,
— *stationary phase*: *poly(dimethyl)siloxane R* (1 μm).

*Carrier gas*  helium for chromatography *R*.

*Flow rate*  1 ml/min.

*Split ratio*  1:100.

*Temperature:*

|  | Time (min) | Temperature (°C) |
|---|---|---|
| Column | 0 - 20 | 150 → 250 |
|  | 20 - 40 | 250 |
| Injection port |  | 250 |
| Detector |  | 250 |

*Detection*  Flame ionisation.

*Injection*  1 μl of the test solution and reference solutions (a) and (c).

*System suitability*  Reference solution (c):
— *resolution*: minimum 5.0 between the peaks due to cetyl alcohol and stearyl alcohol.

Calculate the percentage content of $C_{16}H_{34}O$.

*Ph Eur*

# Cetyl Palmitate

(*Ph Eur monograph 1906*)

## Action and use

Excipient.

*Ph Eur*

## DEFINITION

Mixture of $C_{14}$-$C_{18}$ esters of lauric (dodecanoic), myristic (tetradecanoic), palmitic (hexadecanoic) and stearic (octadecanoic) acids ('Cetyl esters wax').

### Content (expressed as hexadecyl hexadecanoate)

10.0 per cent to 20.0 per cent for Cetyl palmitate 15, 60.0 per cent to 70.0 per cent for Cetyl palmitate 65 and minimum 90.0 per cent for Cetyl palmitate 95.

## CHARACTERS

### Appearance

White or almost white, waxy plates, flakes or powder.

### Solubility

Practically insoluble in water, soluble in boiling anhydrous ethanol and in methylene chloride, slightly soluble in light petroleum, practically insoluble in anhydrous ethanol.

### mp

About 45 °C for Cetyl palmitate 15 and Cetyl palmitate 65 and about 52 °C for Cetyl palmitate 95.

## IDENTIFICATION

A. It complies with the limits of the assay and the chromatogram obtained with the test solution shows the typical main peak(s).

B. Saponification value (see Tests).

## TESTS

### Appearance of solution

The solution is not more intensely coloured than reference solution $Y_6$ (*2.2.2, Method II*).

Dissolve 4.0 g in *methylene chloride R* and dilute to 20 ml with the same solvent.

### Acid value (*2.5.1*)

Maximum 4.0.

Dissolve 10.0 g in 50 ml of the solvent mixture described by heating under reflux on a water-bath for 5 min.

### Hydroxyl value (*2.5.3, Method A*)

Maximum 20.0.

### Iodine value (*2.5.4, Method A*):

Maximum 2.0.

### Saponification value (*2.5.6*)

105 to 120.

Heat under reflux for 2 h.

### Alkaline impurities

Dissolve 2.0 g 'with gentle heating' in a mixture of 1.5 ml of *ethanol (96 per cent) R* and 3 ml of *toluene R*. Add 0.05 ml of a 0.4 g/l solution of *bromophenol blue R* in *ethanol (96 per cent) R*. Not more than 0.4 ml of *0.01 M hydrochloric acid* is required to change the colour of the solution to yellow.

**Nickel** (*2.4.31*)

Maximum 1 ppm.

**Water** (*2.5.12*)

Maximum 0.3 per cent, determined on 1.0 g using a mixture of equal volumes of *anhydrous methanol R* and *methylene chloride R* as solvent.

**Total ash** (*2.4.16*)

Maximum 0.2 per cent, determined on 1.0 g.

## ASSAY

Gas chromatography (*2.2.28*): use the normalisation procedure.

*Test solution*   Dissolve 20.0 mg of the substance to be examined in *hexane R* and dilute to 20.0 ml with the same solvent.

*Reference solution (a)*   Dissolve 20.0 mg of *cetyl palmitate 95 CRS* in *hexane R* and dilute to 20.0 ml with the same solvent.

*Reference solution (b)*   Dissolve 20.0 mg of *cetyl palmitate 15 CRS* in *hexane R* and dilute to 20.0 ml with the same solvent.

*Column:*
— *material*: stainless steel;
— *size*: $l = 10$ m, $\emptyset = 0.53$ mm;
— *stationary phase*: *poly(dimethyl)siloxane R* (film thickness 2.65 μm).

*Carrier gas*   helium for chromatography R.

*Flow rate*   6.5 ml/min.

*Split ratio*   1:10.

*Temperature:*

|  | Time (min) | Temperature (°C) |
|---|---|---|
| Column | 0 - 10 | 100 → 300 |
|  | 10 - 15 | 300 |
| Injection port |  | 350 |
| Detector |  | 350 |

*Detection*   Flame ionisation.

*Injection*   1 μl.

*Relative retention*   With reference to cetyl palmitate (retention time = about 9 min): cetyl alcohol = about 0.3; palmitic acid = about 0.4; lauric ester = about 0.8; myristic ester = about 0.9; stearic ester = about 1.1.

*System suitability*   Reference solution (b):
— *resolution*: minimum of 1.5 between the peaks due to cetyl palmitate and cetyl stearate.

## STORAGE

At a temperature not exceeding 25 °C.

## LABELLING

The label states the type of cetyl palmitate.

_____ *Ph Eur*

# Cetylpyridinium Chloride

(*Ph Eur monograph 0379*)

$C_{21}H_{38}ClN,H_2O$          358.0          *6004-24-6*

**Action and use**

Antiseptic.

*Ph Eur* _____

## DEFINITION

Cetylpyridinium chloride contains not less than 96.0 per cent and not more than the equivalent of 101.0 per cent of 1-hexadecylpyridinium chloride, calculated with reference to the anhydrous substance.

## CHARACTERS

A white or almost white powder, slightly soapy to the touch, soluble in water and in alcohol. An aqueous solution froths copiously when shaken.

## IDENTIFICATION

*First identification*   B, D.

*Second identification*   A, C, D.

A. Dissolve 0.10 g in *water R* and dilute to 100.0 ml with the same solvent. Dilute 5.0 ml of this solution to 100.0 ml with *water R*. Examined between 240 nm and 300 nm (*2.2.25*), the solution shows an absorption maximum at 259 nm and 2 shoulders at about 254 nm and at about 265 nm. The specific absorbance at the maximum is 126 to 134, calculated with reference to the anhydrous substance.

B. Examine by infrared absorption spectrophotometry (*2.2.24*), comparing with the spectrum obtained with *cetylpyridinium chloride CRS*. Examine the substances in the solid state.

C. To 5 ml of *dilute sodium hydroxide solution R* add 0.1 ml of *bromophenol blue solution R1* and 5 ml of *chloroform R* and shake. The chloroform layer is colourless. Add 0.1 ml of solution S (see Tests) and shake. The chloroform layer becomes blue.

D. Solution S gives reaction (a) of chlorides (*2.3.1*).

## TESTS

### Solution S

Dissolve 1.0 g in *carbon dioxide-free water R* and dilute to 100 ml with the same solvent.

### Appearance of solution

Solution S is not more opalescent than reference suspension II (*2.2.1*) and is colourless (*2.2.2, Method II*).

### Acidity

To 50 ml of solution S add 0.1 ml of *phenolphthalein solution R*. Not more than 2.5 ml of *0.02 M sodium hydroxide* is required to change the colour of the indicator.

### Amines and amine salts

Dissolve 5.0 g with heating in 20 ml of a mixture of 3 volumes of *1 M hydrochloric acid* and 97 volumes of *methanol R* and add 100 ml of *2-propanol R*. Pass a stream of *nitrogen R* slowly through the solution. Gradually add 12.0 ml of *0.1 M tetrabutylammonium hydroxide* and record the potentiometric titration curve (*2.2.20*). If the curve shows 2 points of inflexion, the volume of titrant added between the two points is not greater than 5.0 ml. If the curve shows no point of inflexion, the substance to be examined does not comply with the test. If the curve shows one point of inflexion, repeat the test but add 3.0 ml of a 25.0 g/l solution of *dimethyldecylamine R* in *2-propanol R* before the titration. If the titration curve after the addition of 12.0 ml of the titrant shows only one point of inflexion, the substance to be examined does not comply with the test.

**Water** (*2.5.12*)

4.5 per cent to 5.5 per cent, determined on 0.300 g by the semi-micro determination of water.

**Sulphated ash** (*2.4.14*)

Not more than 0.2 per cent, determined on 1.0 g.

## ASSAY

Dissolve 2.00 g in *water R* and dilute to 100.0 ml with the same solvent. Transfer 25.0 ml of the solution to a separating funnel, add 25 ml of *chloroform R*, 10 ml of *0.1 M sodium hydroxide* and 10.0 ml of a freshly prepared 50 g/l solution of *potassium iodide R*. Shake well, allow to separate and discard the chloroform layer. Shake the aqueous layer with three quantities, each of 10 ml, of *chloroform R* and discard the chloroform layers. To the aqueous layer add 40 ml of *hydrochloric acid R*, allow to cool and titrate with *0.05 M potassium iodate* until the deep-brown colour is almost discharged. Add 2 ml of *chloroform R* and continue the titration, shaking vigorously, until the chloroform layer no longer changes colour. Carry out a blank titration on a mixture of 10.0 ml of the freshly prepared 50 g/l solution of *potassium iodide R*, 20 ml of *water R* and 40 ml of *hydrochloric acid R*.

1 ml of *0.05 M potassium iodate* is equivalent to 34.0 mg of $C_{21}H_{38}ClN$.

*———— Ph Eur*

# Chalk

Prepared Chalk

$CaCO_3$           100.1

**Action and use**

Antacid.

## DEFINITION

Chalk is a native form of calcium carbonate freed from most of its impurities by elutriation and dried. It contains not less than 97.0% and not more than 100.5% of $CaCO_3$, calculated with reference to the dried substance.

## CHARACTERISTICS

Chalk absorbs water readily.

Practically insoluble in *water*; slightly soluble in *water* containing carbon dioxide.

*Macroscopical* White or greyish white, small friable masses, usually conical in form, or in powder; amorphous; earthy; soft to the touch.

*Microscopical* Consists of the calcareous shells and detritus of various foraminifera; the calcareous shells vary from about 35 to 100 µm in breadth and from about 50 to 180 µm in length; among the detritus are numerous small rings and discs about 5 to 10 µm in diameter.

## IDENTIFICATION

A. A solution in 6M *acetic acid* yields reaction C characteristic of *calcium salts*, Appendix VI.

B. Yields reaction A characteristic of *carbonates*, Appendix VI.

## TESTS

**Acidity or alkalinity**

1 g, boiled with 50 ml of *water* and filtered, yields a filtrate which is neutral to *bromothymol blue solution R3* or requires not more than 0.05 ml of 0.1M *hydrochloric acid VS* to make it so.

**Aluminium, iron, phosphate and matter insoluble in hydrochloric acid**

Dissolve 2 g in a mixture of 5 ml of *hydrochloric acid* and 75 ml of *water*, boil to remove carbon dioxide and make alkaline with 5M *ammonia* using *methyl red solution* as indicator. Boil for 1 minute, filter and wash the precipitate with a hot 2% w/v solution of *ammonium chloride*. Dissolve the precipitate as completely as possible by passing 20 ml of hot 2M *hydrochloric acid* through the filter and wash the filter with sufficient hot *water* to adjust the volume of the solution to 50 ml. Boil the solution and make alkaline with 5M *ammonia* using *methyl red solution* as indicator. Boil for 1 minute, filter through the same filter, wash the precipitate with a hot 2% w/v solution of *ammonium nitrate*, dry and ignite at a temperature not lower than 1000°. The residue weighs not more than 40 mg.

**Arsenic**

Dissolve 0.5 g in 5 ml of *brominated hydrochloric acid* and dilute to 50 ml with *water*. 25 ml of the resulting solution complies with the *limit test for arsenic*, Appendix VII (4 ppm).

**Heavy metals**

Dissolve 1.0 g in 10 ml of 2M *hydrochloric acid*, add 0.1 ml of *nitric acid* and boil to remove carbon dioxide. Cool, make alkaline with 5M *ammonia*, filter and wash the precipitate with *water*. Pass 5 ml of hot 2M *hydrochloric acid* through the filter, cool the filtrate, add 0.5 g of *ammonium thiocyanate* and extract with two 5 ml quantities of a mixture of equal volumes of *isoamyl alcohol* and *ether*. To the aqueous layer add 0.5 g of *citric acid* and dilute to 20 ml with *water*. 12 ml of the resulting solution complies with *limit test A for heavy metals*, Appendix VII. Use *lead standard solution (2 ppm Pb)* to prepare the standard (40 ppm).

**Chloride**

Dissolve 0.3 g in 2 ml of *nitric acid* and 10 ml of *water*, filter and dilute the filtrate to 30 ml with *water*. 15 ml of the resulting solution complies with the *limit test for chlorides*, Appendix VII (330 ppm).

**Sulphate**

Dissolve 0.25 g in 5.5 ml of 2M *hydrochloric acid*, dilute to 30 ml with *water* and filter. 15 ml of the resulting solution complies with the *limit test for sulphates*, Appendix VII (0.12%).

**Loss on drying**

When dried to constant weight at 105°, loses not more than 1.0% of its weight. Use 1 g.

## ASSAY

To 2 g in 100 ml of *water* add 50 ml of 1M *hydrochloric acid VS*, boil to remove carbon dioxide, cool and titrate the excess of acid with 1M *sodium hydroxide VS* using *methyl orange solution* as indicator. Each ml of 1M *hydrochloric acid VS* is equivalent to 50.04 mg of $CaCO_3$.

# Activated Charcoal

Decolourising Charcoal

(*Ph Eur monograph 0313*)

*Ph Eur* _____

## Action and use
Adsorbent.

## DEFINITION
Obtained from vegetable matter by suitable carbonisation processes intended to confer a high adsorption power.

## CHARACTERS
### Appearance
Black, light powder free from grittiness.

### Solubility
Practically insoluble in all usual solvents.

## IDENTIFICATION
A. When heated to redness it burns slowly without a flame.

B. Adsorption power (see Tests).

## TESTS
### Solution S
To 2.0 g in a conical flask with a ground-glass neck add 50 ml of *dilute hydrochloric acid R*. Boil gently under a reflux condenser for 1 h, filter and wash the filter with *dilute hydrochloric acid R*. Evaporate the combined filtrate and washings to dryness on a water-bath, dissolve the residue in *0.1 M hydrochloric acid* and dilute to 50.0 ml with the same acid.

### Acidity or alkalinity
To 2.0 g add 40 ml of *water R* and boil for 5 min. Cool, restore to the original mass with *carbon dioxide-free water R* and filter. Reject the first 20 ml of the filtrate. To 10 ml of the filtrate add 0.25 ml of *bromothymol blue solution R1* and 0.25 ml of *0.02 M sodium hydroxide*. The solution is blue. Not more than 0.75 ml of *0.02 M hydrochloric acid* is required to change the colour of the indicator to yellow.

### Acid-soluble substances
Maximum 3 per cent.

To 1.0 g add 25 ml of *dilute nitric acid R* and boil for 5 min. Filter whilst hot through a sintered-glass filter (10) (*2.1.2*) and wash with 10 ml of hot *water R*. Evaporate the combined filtrate and washings to dryness on a water-bath, add to the residue 1 ml of *hydrochloric acid R*, evaporate to dryness again and dry the residue to constant mass at 100-105 °C. The residue weighs a maximum of 30 mg.

### Alkali-soluble coloured substances
To 0.25 g add 10 ml of *dilute sodium hydroxide solution R* and boil for 1 min. Cool, filter and dilute the filtrate to 10 ml with *water R*. The solution is not more intensely coloured than reference solution $GY_4$ (*2.2.2, Method II*).

### Ethanol (96 per cent) soluble substances
Maximum 0.5 per cent.

To 2.0 g add 50 ml of *ethanol (96 per cent) R* and boil under a reflux condenser for 10 min. Filter immediately, cool, and dilute to 50 ml with *ethanol (96 per cent) R*. The filtrate is not more intensely coloured than reference solution $Y_6$ or $BY_6$ (*2.2.2, Method II*). Evaporate 40 ml of the filtrate to dryness and dry to constant mass at 100-105 °C. The residue weighs a maximum of 8 mg.

### Fluorescent substances
In an intermittent-extraction apparatus, treat 10.0 g with 100 ml of *cyclohexane R1* for 2 h. Collect the liquid and dilute to 100 ml with *cyclohexane R1*. Examine in ultraviolet light at 365 nm. The fluorescence of the solution is not more intense than that of a solution of 83 µg of *quinine R* in 1000 ml of *0.005 M sulphuric acid* examined under the same conditions.

### Sulphides
To 1.0 g in a conical flask add 5 ml of *hydrochloric acid R1* and 20 ml of *water R*. Heat to boiling. The fumes released do not turn *lead acetate paper R* brown.

### Copper
Maximum 25.0 ppm.

Atomic absorption spectrometry (*2.2.23, Method I*).

*Test solution*  Use solution S.

*Reference solutions*  Prepare the reference solutions using *copper standard solution (0.1 per cent Cu) R* and diluting with *0.1 M hydrochloric acid*.

*Source*  Copper hollow-cathode lamp.

*Wavelength*  325.0 nm.

*Atomisation device*  Air-acetylene flame.

### Lead
Maximum 10.0 ppm.

Atomic absorption spectrometry (*2.2.23, Method I*).

*Test solution*  Use solution S.

*Reference solutions*  Prepare the reference solutions using *lead standard solution (100 ppm Pb) R* and diluting with *0.1 M hydrochloric acid*.

*Source*  Lead hollow-cathode lamp.

*Wavelength*  283.3 nm; 217.0 nm may be used depending on the apparatus.

*Atomisation device*  Air-acetylene flame.

### Zinc
Maximum 25.0 ppm.

Atomic absorption spectrometry (*2.2.23, Method I*).

*Test solution*  Use solution S.

*Reference solutions*  Prepare the reference solutions using *zinc standard solution (100 ppm Zn) R* and diluting with *0.1 M hydrochloric acid*.

*Source*  Zinc hollow-cathode lamp.

*Wavelength*  214.0 nm.

*Atomisation device*  Air-acetylene flame.

### Loss on drying (*2.2.32*)
Maximum 15 per cent, determined on 1.00 g by drying in an oven at 120 °C for 4 h.

### Sulphated ash (*2.4.14*)
Maximum 5.0 per cent, determined on 1.0 g.

### Adsorption power
To 0.300 g in a 100 ml ground-glass-stoppered conical flask add 25.0 ml of a freshly prepared solution of 0.5 g of *phenazone R* in 50 ml of *water R*. Shake thoroughly for 15 min. Filter and reject the first 5 ml of filtrate. To 10.0 ml of the filtrate add 1.0 g of *potassium bromide R* and 20 ml of *dilute hydrochloric acid R*. Using 0.1 ml of *methyl red solution R* as indicator, titrate with *0.0167 M potassium bromate* until the red colour is discharged. Titrate slowly (1 drop every 15 s) towards the end of the titration. Carry out a blank titration using 10.0 ml of the phenazone solution.

Calculate the quantity of phenazone adsorbed per 100 g of activated charcoal from the following expression:

$$\frac{2.353\,(a - b)}{m}$$

$a$ = number of millilitres of *0.0167 M potassium bromate* used for the blank;

$b$ = number of millilitres of *0.0167 M potassium bromate* used for the test;

$m$ = mass in grams of the substance to be examined.

Minimum 40 g of phenazone is adsorbed per 100 g of activated charcoal, calculated with reference to the dried substance.

### Microbial contamination
TAMC: acceptance criterion $10^3$ CFU/g (*2.6.12*).

TYMC: acceptance criterion $10^2$ CFU/g (*2.6.12*).

### STORAGE
In an airtight container.

_____ *Ph Eur*

# Chenodeoxycholic Acid

(*Ph Eur monograph 1189*)

$C_{24}H_{40}O_4$        392.6        474-25-9

**Action and use**
Bile acid; treatment of gallstones.

*Ph Eur* _____

### DEFINITION
Chenodeoxycholic acid contains not less than 99.0 per cent and not more than the equivalent of 101.0 per cent of $3\alpha,7\alpha$-dihydroxy-$5\beta$-cholan-24-oic acid, calculated with reference to the dried substance.

### CHARACTERS
A white or almost white powder, very slightly soluble in water, freely soluble in alcohol, soluble in acetone, slightly soluble in methylene chloride.

### IDENTIFICATION
*First identification*   A.

*Second identification*   B, C.

A. Examine by infrared absorption spectrophotometry (*2.2.24*), comparing with the spectrum obtained with *chenodeoxycholic acid CRS*. Examine the substances prepared as discs using *potassium bromide R*.

B. Examine the chromatograms obtained in the test for related substances. The principal spot in the chromatogram obtained with test solution (b) is similar in position, colour and size to the principal spot in the chromatogram obtained with reference solution (a).

C. Dissolve about 10 mg in 1 ml of *sulphuric acid R*. Add 0.1 ml of *formaldehyde solution R* and allow to stand for 5 min. Add 5 ml of *water R*. The suspension obtained is greenish-blue.

### TESTS
**Specific optical rotation** (*2.2.7*)
Dissolve 0.500 g in *methanol R* and dilute to 25.0 ml with the same solvent. The specific optical rotation is + 11.0 to + 13.0, calculated with reference to the dried substance.

**Related substances**
Examine by thin-layer chromatography (*2.2.27*), using a suitable silica gel as the coating substance.

*Test solution (a)*   Dissolve 0.40 g of the substance to be examined in a mixture of 1 volume of *water R* and 9 volumes of *acetone R* and dilute to 10 ml with the same mixture of solvents.

*Test solution (b)*   Dilute 1 ml of test solution (a) to 10 ml with a mixture of 1 volume of *water R* and 9 volumes of *acetone R*.

*Reference solution (a)*   Dissolve 40 mg of *chenodeoxycholic acid CRS* in a mixture of 1 volume of *water R* and 9 volumes of *acetone R* and dilute to 10 ml with the same mixture of solvents.

*Reference solution (b)*   Dissolve 20 mg of *lithocholic acid CRS* in a mixture of 1 volume of *water R* and 9 volumes of *acetone R* and dilute to 10 ml with the same mixture of solvents. Dilute 2 ml of the solution to 100 ml with a mixture of 1 volume of *water R* and 9 volumes of *acetone R*.

*Reference solution (c)*   Dissolve 20 mg of *ursodeoxycholic acid CRS* in a mixture of 1 volume of *water R* and 9 volumes of *acetone R* and dilute to 50 ml with the same mixture of solvents.

*Reference solution (d)*   Dissolve 20 mg of *cholic acid CRS* in a mixture of 1 volume of *water R* and 9 volumes of *acetone R* and dilute to 100 ml with the same mixture of solvents.

*Reference solution (e)*   Dilute 0.5 ml of test solution (a) to 20 ml with a mixture of 1 volume of *water R* and 9 volumes of *acetone R*. Dilute 1 ml of the solution to 10 ml with a mixture of 1 volume of *water R* and 9 volumes of *acetone R*.

*Reference solution (f)*   Dissolve 10 mg of *chenodeoxycholic acid CRS* in reference solution (c) and dilute to 25 ml with the same solution.

Apply separately to the plate 5 μl of each solution. Develop in an unsaturated tank over a path of 15 cm using a mixture of 1 volume of *glacial acetic acid R*, 30 volumes of *acetone R* and 60 volumes of *methylene chloride R*. Dry the plate at 120 °C for 10 min. Spray the plate immediately with a 47.6 g/l solution of *phosphomolybdic acid R* in a mixture of 1 volume of *sulphuric acid R* and 20 volumes of *glacial acetic acid R* and heat again at 120 °C until blue spots appear on a lighter background. In the chromatogram obtained with test solution (a): any spot corresponding to lithocholic acid is not more intense than the principal spot in the chromatogram obtained with reference solution (b) (0.1 per cent); any spot corresponding to ursodeoxycholic acid is not more intense than the principal spot in the chromatogram obtained with reference solution (c) (1 per cent); any spot corresponding to cholic acid is not more intense than the principal spot in the chromatogram obtained with reference solution (d) (0.5 per cent); any spot apart from the principal spot and any spots corresponding to lithocholic acid, ursodeoxycholic acid and cholic acid, is not more intense than the principal spot in the chromatogram obtained with reference solution (e) (0.25 per cent). The test is not valid unless the chromatogram obtained with reference solution (f) shows two clearly separated principal spots.

**Heavy metals** (*2.4.8*)

1.0 g complies with limit test C for heavy metals (20 ppm). Prepare the standard using 2 ml of *lead standard solution (10 ppm Pb) R*.

**Loss on drying** (*2.2.32*)

Not more than 1.5 per cent, determined on 1.000 g by drying in an oven at 105 °C.

**Sulphated ash** (*2.4.14*)

Not more than 0.1 per cent, determined on 1.0 g.

## ASSAY

Dissolve 0.350 g in 50 ml of *alcohol R*, previously neutralised to 0.2 ml of *phenolphthalein solution R*. Add 50 ml of *water R* and titrate with *0.1 M sodium hydroxide* until a pink colour is obtained.

1 ml of *0.1 M sodium hydroxide* is equivalent to 39.26 mg of $C_{24}H_{40}O_4$.

## IMPURITIES

A. R = H, R1 = OH, R2 = H, R3 = H: ursodeoxycholic acid,

B. R = H, R1 = H, R2 = OH, R3 = OH: 3α,7α,12α-trihydroxy-5β-cholan-24-oic acid (cholic acid),

C. R = H, R1 = H, R2 = H, R3 = H: 3α-hydroxy-5β-cholan-24-oic acid (lithocholic acid),

D. R = H, R1 = OH, R2 = H, R3 = OH: 3α,7β,12α-trihydroxy-5β-cholan-24-oic acid (ursocholic acid),

E. R = H, R1 = H, R2 = H, R3 = OH: 3α,12α-dihydroxy-5β-cholan-24-oic acid (deoxycholic acid),

F. R = H, R1+R2 = = O, R3 = H: 3α-hydroxy-7-oxo-5β-cholan-24-oic acid,

G. R = CH₃, R1 = OH, R2 = H, R3 = H: methyl 3α,7β-dihydroxy-5β-cholan-24-oate.

*Ph Eur*

# Chitosan Hydrochloride

(*Ph Eur monograph 1774*)

*Ph Eur*

## DEFINITION

Chitosan hydrochloride is the chloride salt of an unbranched binary heteropolysaccharide consisting of the two units *N*-acetyl-D-glucosamine and D-glucosamine, obtained by partial deacetylation of chitin normally leading to a degree of deacetylation of 70.0 per cent to 95.0 per cent. Chitin is extracted from the shells of shrimp and crab.

## PRODUCTION

The animals from which chitosan hydrochloride is derived must fulfil the requirements for the health of animals suitable for human consumption to the satisfaction of the competent authority. It must have been shown to what extent the method of production allows inactivation or removal of any contamination by viruses or other infectious agents.

## CHARACTERS

**Appearance**

White or almost white, fine powder.

**Solubility**

Sparingly soluble in water, practically insoluble in anhydrous ethanol.

## IDENTIFICATION

A. Infrared absorption spectrophotometry (*2.2.24*).

*Preparation*  Discs.

*Comparison*  chitosan hydrochloride CRS.

B. It gives reaction (a) of chlorides (*2.3.1*).

C. Dilute 50 ml of solution S (see Tests) to 250 ml with a 25 per cent *V/V* solution of *ammonia R*. A voluminous gelatinous mass is formed.

D. To 10 ml of solution S add 90 ml of *acetone R*. A voluminous gelatinous mass is formed.

## TESTS

**Solution S**

Dissolve 1.0 g in 100 ml of *water R* and stir vigorously for 20 min with a mechanical stirrer.

**Appearance of solution**

Solution S is not more opalescent than reference suspension II (*2.2.1*) and not more intensely coloured than reference solution $BY_5$ (*2.2.2, Method II*).

**Matter insoluble in water**

Maximum 0.5 per cent.

Add 2.00 g to 400.0 ml of *water R* while stirring until no further dissolution takes place. Transfer the solution to a 2 litre beaker, and add 200 ml of *water R*. Boil the solution gently for 2 h, covering the beaker during the operation. Filter through a sintered-glass filter (40) (*2.1.2*), wash the residue with water and dry to constant weight in an oven at 100-105 °C. The residue weighs a maximum of 10 mg.

**pH** (*2.2.3*)

4.0 to 6.0 for solution S.

**Viscosity** (*2.2.10*)

80 per cent to 120 per cent of the value stated on the label, determined on solution S.

Determine the viscosity using a rotating viscometer at 20 °C with a spindle rotating at 20 r/min, using a suitable spindle for the range of the expected viscosity.

**Degree of deacetylation**

*Test solution*  Dissolve 0.250 g in *water R* and dilute to 50.0 ml with the same solvent, stirring vigorously. Dilute 1.0 ml of this solution to 100.0 ml with *water R*. Measure the absorbance (*2.2.25*) from 200 nm to 205 nm as the first derivative of the absorbance curve. Determine the pH of the solution.

*Reference solutions*  Prepare solutions of 1.0 μg/ml, 5.0 μg/ml, 15.0 μg/ml and 35.0 μg/ml of *N-acetylglucosamine R* in *water R*. Measure the absorbance (*2.2.25*) from 200 nm to 205 nm of each solution as the first derivative of the absorption curve. Make a standard curve by plotting the first derivative at 202 nm as a function of the concentration of *N*-acetylglucosamine, and calculate the slope of the curve by least squares linear regression. Use the standard curve to determine the equivalent amount of *N*-acetylglucosamine for the substance to be examined.

Calculate the degree of deacetylation (molar) using the following expression:

$$\frac{100 \times M_1 \times (C_1 - C_2)}{(M_1 \times C_1) - [(M_1 - M_3) \times C_2]}$$

$C_1$ = concentration of chitosan hydrochloride in the test solution in micrograms per millilitre;

$C_2$ = concentration of N-acetylglucosamine in the test solution, as determined from the standard curve prepared using the reference solution in micrograms per millilitre;

$M_1$ = 203 (relative molecular mass of N-acetylglucosamine unit ($C_8H_{13}NO_5$) in polymer);

$M_3$ = relative molecular mass of chitosan hydrochloride.

$M_3$ is calculated from the pH in solution, assuming a pKa value of 6.8, using the following equations:

$$M_3 = f \times M_2 + (1 - f) \times (M_2 + 36.5)$$

$$f = \frac{p}{1 + p}$$

$$p = 10^{(\mathrm{pH} - \mathrm{pKa})}$$

$M_2$ = 161 (relative molecular mass of deacetylated unit (glucosamine) ($C_6H_{11}NO_4$) in polymer).

**Chlorides**

10.0 per cent to 20.0 per cent.

Introduce 0.200 g into a 250 ml borosilicate flask fitted with a reflux condenser. Add 40 ml of a mixture of 1 volume of *nitric acid R* and 2 volumes of *water R*. Boil gently under a reflux condenser for 5 min. Cool and add 25 ml of *water R* through the condenser. Add 16.0 ml of *0.1 M silver nitrate*, shake vigorously and titrate with *0.1 M ammonium thiocyanate*, using 1 ml of *ferric ammonium sulphate solution R2* as indicator, and shaking vigorously towards the end-point. Carry out a blank titration.

1 ml of *0.1 M silver nitrate* is equivalent to 3.55 mg of Cl.

**Heavy metals** (*2.4.8*)

Maximum 40 ppm.

1.0 g complies with test F. Prepare the reference solution using 4 ml of *lead standard solution (10 ppm Pb) R*.

**Loss on drying** (*2.2.32*)

Maximum 10 per cent, determined on 1.000 g by drying in an oven at 105 °C.

**Sulphated ash** (*2.4.14*)

Maximum 1.0 per cent, determined on 1.0 g.

**STORAGE**

At a temperature of 2-8 °C, protected from moisture and light.

**LABELLING**

The label states the nominal viscosity in millipascal seconds for a 10 g/l solution in *water R*.

# Chloral Hydrate

(*Ph Eur monograph 0265*)

| $C_2H_3Cl_3O_2$ | 165.4 | *302-17-0* |
|---|---|---|

**Action and use**

Hypnotic.

**Preparation**

Chloral Hydrate Oral Solution

*Ph Eur*

**DEFINITION**

2,2,2-Trichloroethane-1,1-diol.

**Content**

98.5 per cent to 101.0 per cent.

**CHARACTERS**

**Appearance**

Colourless, transparent crystals.

**Solubility**

Very soluble in water, freely soluble in ethanol (96 per cent).

**IDENTIFICATION**

A. To 10 ml of solution S (see Tests) add 2 ml of *dilute sodium hydroxide solution R*. The mixture becomes cloudy and, when heated, gives off an odour of chloroform.

B. To 1 ml of solution S add 2 ml of *sodium sulphide solution R*. A yellow colour develops which quickly becomes reddish-brown. On standing for a short time, a red precipitate may be formed.

**TESTS**

**Solution S**

Dissolve 3.0 g in *carbon dioxide-free water R* and dilute to 30 ml with the same solvent.

**Appearance of solution**

Solution S is clear (*2.2.1*) and colourless (*2.2.2, Method II*).

**pH** (*2.2.3*)

3.5 to 5.5 for solution S.

**Chloral alcoholate**

Warm 1.0 g with 10 ml of *dilute sodium hydroxide solution R*, filter the supernatant solution and add *0.05 M iodine* dropwise until a yellow colour is obtained. Allow to stand for 1 h. No precipitate is formed.

**Chlorides** (*2.4.4*)

Maximum 100 ppm.

Dilute 5 ml of solution S to 15 ml with *water R*.

**Heavy metals** (*2.4.8*)

Maximum 20 ppm.

10 ml of solution S diluted to 20 ml with *water R* complies with test A. Prepare the reference solution using *lead standard solution (1 ppm Pb) R*.

**Non-volatile residue**

Maximum 0.1 per cent.

Evaporate 2.000 g on a water-bath. The residue weighs a maximum of 2 mg.

**ASSAY**

Dissolve 4.000 g in 10 ml of *water R* and add 40.0 ml of *1 M sodium hydroxide*. Allow to stand for exactly 2 min and titrate with *0.5 M sulphuric acid*, using 0.1 ml of *phenolphthalein solution R* as indicator. Titrate the neutralised solution with *0.1 M silver nitrate*, using 0.2 ml of *potassium chromate solution R* as indicator. Calculate the number of millilitres of *1 M sodium hydroxide* used by deducting from the volume of *1 M sodium hydroxide*, added at the beginning of the titration, the volume *of 0.5 M sulphuric acid* used in the 1$^{st}$ titration and two-fifteenths of the volume *of 0.1 M silver nitrate* used in the 2$^{nd}$ titration.

1 ml of *1 M sodium hydroxide* is equivalent to 0.1654 g of $C_2H_3Cl_3O_2$.

**STORAGE**

In an airtight container.

_____ *Ph Eur*

# Chlorambucil

(*Ph Eur monograph 0137*)

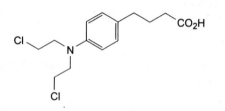

$C_{14}H_{19}Cl_2NO_2$          304.2          *305-03-3*

**Action and use**

Cytotoxic alkylating agent.

**Preparation**

Chlorambucil Tablets

*Ph Eur* _____

**DEFINITION**

Chlorambucil contains not less than 98.5 per cent and not more than the equivalent of 101.0 per cent of 4-4-[di(2-chloroethyl)amino]phenylbutyric acid, calculated with reference to the anhydrous substance.

**CHARACTERS**

A white or almost white, crystalline powder, practically insoluble in water, freely soluble in acetone and in alcohol.

**IDENTIFICATION**

*First identification*  A, B.

*Second identification*  A, C, D.

A. Melting point (*2.2.14*): 64 °C to 67 °C.

B. Examine by infrared absorption spectrophotometry (*2.2.24*), comparing with the spectrum obtained with *chlorambucil CRS*.

C. To 0.4 g add 10 ml of *dilute hydrochloric acid R*, mix and allow to stand for 30 min, shaking from time to time. Filter and wash the precipitate with 2 quantities, each of 10 ml, of *water R*. To 10 ml of the combined filtrate and washings add 0.5 ml of *potassium tetraiodomercurate solution R*. A pale-brown precipitate is formed. To another 10 ml of the combined filtrate and washings add 0.2 ml of *potassium permanganate solution R*. The colour of the latter is discharged immediately.

D. Dissolve 50 mg in 5 ml of *acetone R* and dilute to 10 ml with *water R*. Add 0.05 ml of *dilute nitric acid R* and 0.2 ml of *silver nitrate solution R2*. No opalescence is produced

immediately. Heat the solution on a water-bath; an opalescence develops.

**TESTS**

**Related substances**

Examine by thin-layer chromatography (*2.2.27*), using *silica gel GF$_{254}$ R* as the coating substance. *Carry out all operations as rapidly as possible protected from light. Prepare the solutions immediately before use.*

*Test solution*  Dissolve 0.2 g of the substance to be examined in *acetone R* and dilute to 10 ml with the same solvent.

*Reference solution (a)*  Dilute 1 ml of the test solution to 50 ml with *acetone R*.

*Reference solution (b)*  Dilute 25 ml of reference solution (a) to 100 ml with *acetone R*.

Apply separately to the plate 5 µl of each solution. Develop over a path of 10 cm using a mixture of 20 volumes of *methyl ethyl ketone R*, 20 volumes of *heptane R*, 25 volumes of *methanol R* and 40 volumes of *toluene R*. Examine in ultraviolet light at 254 nm. Any spot in the chromatogram obtained with the test solution, apart from the principal spot, is not more intense than the spot in the chromatogram obtained with reference solution (a) (2.0 per cent) and at most 1 such spot is more intense than the spot in the chromatogram obtained with reference solution (b) (0.5 per cent).

**Water** (*2.5.12*)

Not more than 0.5 per cent, determined on 1.000 g by the semi-micro determination of water.

**Sulphated ash** (*2.4.14*)

Not more than 0.1 per cent, determined on 1.0 g.

**ASSAY**

Dissolve 0.200 g in 10 ml of *acetone R* and add 10 ml of *water R*. Titrate with *0.1 M sodium hydroxide*, using 0.1 ml of *phenolphthalein solution R* as indicator.

1 ml of *0.1 M sodium hydroxide* is equivalent to 30.42 mg of $C_{14}H_{19}Cl_2NO_2$.

**STORAGE**

Store protected from light.

_____ *Ph Eur*

# Chloramphenicol

(*Ph Eur monograph 0071*)

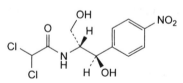

$C_{11}H_{12}Cl_2N_2O_5$          323.1          *56-75-7*

**Action and use**

Antibacterial.

**Preparations**

Chloramphenicol Capsules

Chloramphenicol Ear Drops

Chloramphenicol Eye Drops

Chloramphenicol Eye Ointment

Ph Eur

## DEFINITION

Chloramphenicol is 2,2-dichloro-N-[(1R,2R)-2-hydroxy-1-(hydroxymethyl)-2-(4-nitrophenyl)ethyl]acetamide, produced by the growth of certain strains of *Streptomyces venezuelae* in a suitable medium. It is normally prepared by synthesis. It contains not less than 98.0 per cent and not more than the equivalent of 102.0 per cent of $C_{11}H_{12}Cl_2N_2O_5$, calculated with reference to the dried substance.

## CHARACTERS

A white, greyish-white or yellowish-white, fine, crystalline powder or fine crystals, needles or elongated plates, slightly soluble in water, freely soluble in alcohol and in propylene glycol.

A solution in ethanol is dextrorotatory and a solution in ethyl acetate is laevorotatory.

## IDENTIFICATION

*First identification* A, B.

*Second identification* A, C, D, E.

A. Melting point (2.2.14): 149 °C to 153 °C.

B. Examine by infrared absorption spectrophotometry (2.2.24), comparing with the spectrum obtained with *chloramphenicol CRS*.

C. Examine the chromatograms obtained in the test for related substances. The principal spot in the chromatogram obtained with 1 µl of the test solution is similar in position and size to the principal spot in the chromatogram obtained with reference solution (a).

D. Dissolve about 10 mg in 1 ml of *alcohol (50 per cent V/V) R*, add 3 ml of a 10 g/l solution of *calcium chloride R* and 50 mg of *zinc powder R and* heat on a water-bath for 10 min. Filter the hot solution and allow to cool. Add 0.1 ml of *benzoyl chloride R* and shake for 1 min. Add 0.5 ml of *ferric chloride solution R1* and 2 ml of *chloroform R* and shake. The aqueous layer is coloured light violet-red to purple.

E. To 50 mg in a porcelain crucible add 0.5 g of *anhydrous sodium carbonate R*. Heat over an open flame for 10 min. Allow to cool. Take up the residue with 5 ml of *dilute nitric acid R* and filter. To 1 ml of the filtrate add 1 ml of *water R*. The solution gives reaction (a) of chlorides (2.3.1).

## TESTS

### Acidity or alkalinity

To 0.1 g add 20 ml of *carbon dioxide-free water R*, shake and add 0.1 ml of *bromothymol blue solution R1*. Not more than 0.1 ml of *0.02 M hydrochloric acid* or *0.02 M sodium hydroxide* is required to change the colour of the indicator.

### Specific optical rotation (2.2.7)

Dissolve 1.50 g in *ethanol R* and dilute to 25.0 ml with the same solvent. The specific optical rotation is + 18.5 to + 20.5.

### Related substances

Examine by thin-layer chromatography (2.2.27), using *silica gel GF254 R* as the coating substance.

*Test solution* Dissolve 0.10 g of the substance to be examined in *acetone R* and dilute to 10 ml with the same solvent.

*Reference solution (a)* Dissolve 0.10 g of *chloramphenicol CRS* in *acetone R* and dilute to 10 ml with the same solvent.

*Reference solution (b)* Dilute 0.5 ml of reference solution (a) to 100 ml with *acetone R*.

Apply separately to the plate 1 µl and 20 µl of the test solution, 1 µl of reference solution (a) and 20 µl of reference

solution (b). Develop over a path of 15 cm using a mixture of 1 volume of *water R*, 10 volumes of *methanol R* and 90 volumes of *chloroform R*. Allow the plate to dry in air and examine in ultraviolet light at 254 nm. Any spot in the chromatogram obtained with 20 µl of the test solution, apart from the principal spot, is not more intense than the spot in the chromatogram obtained with reference solution (b) (0.5 per cent).

### Chlorides (2.4.4)

To 1.00 g add 20 ml of *water R* and 10 ml of *nitric acid R* and shake for 5 min. Filter through a filter paper previously washed by filtering 5 ml portions of *water R* until 5 ml of filtrate no longer becomes opalescent on addition of 0.1 ml of *nitric acid R* and 0.1 ml of *silver nitrate solution R1*. 15 ml of the filtrate complies with the limit test for chlorides (100 ppm).

### Loss on drying (2.2.32)

Not more than 0.5 per cent, determined on 1.000 g by drying in an oven at 105 °C.

### Sulphated ash (2.4.14)

Not more than 0.1 per cent, determined on 2.0 g.

### Pyrogens (2.6.8)

If intended for use in the manufacture of a parenteral dosage form without a further appropriate procedure for the removal of pyrogens, it complies with the test for pyrogens. Inject per kilogram of the rabbit's mass 2.5 ml of a solution containing per millilitre 2 mg of the substance to be examined.

## ASSAY

Dissolve 0.100 g in *water R* and dilute to 500.0 ml with the same solvent. Dilute 10.0 ml of this solution to 100.0 ml with *water R*. Measure the absorbance (2.2.25) at the maximum at 278 nm.

Calculate the content of $C_{11}H_{12}Cl_2N_2O_5$ taking the specific absorbance to be 297.

## STORAGE

Store protected from light. If the substance is sterile, store in a sterile, airtight, tamper-proof container.

Ph Eur

# Chloramphenicol Palmitate

(*Ph Eur monograph 0473*)

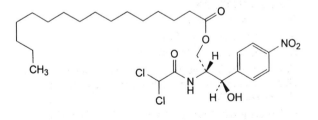

$C_{27}H_{42}Cl_2N_2O_6$      561.6      *530-43-8*

### Action and use

Antibacterial.

Ph Eur

## DEFINITION

Chloramphenicol palmitate contains not less than 98.0 per cent and not more than the equivalent of 102.0 per cent of (2R,3R)-2-[(dichloroacetyl)amino]-3-

hydroxy-3-(4-nitrophenyl)propyl hexadecanoate, calculated with reference to the dried substance.

Semi-synthetic product derived from a fermentation product.

## CHARACTERS

A white or almost white, fine, unctuous powder, practically insoluble in water, freely soluble in acetone, sparingly soluble in ethanol (96 per cent), very slightly soluble in hexane.

It melts at 87 °C to 95 °C.

It shows polymorphism (5.9). The thermodynamically stable form has low bioavailability following oral administration.

## IDENTIFICATION

A. Examine by thin-layer chromatography (2.2.27), using TLC silanised silica gel plate R.

*Test solution*   Dissolve 50 mg of the substance to be examined in a mixture of 1 ml of *1 M sodium hydroxide* and 5 ml of *acetone R* and allow to stand for 30 min. Add 1.1 ml of *1 M hydrochloric acid* and 3 ml of *acetone R*.

*Reference solution (a)*   Dissolve 10 mg of *chloramphenicol CRS* in *acetone R* and dilute to 5 ml with the same solvent.

*Reference solution (b)*   Dissolve 10 mg of *palmitic acid R* in *acetone R* and dilute to 5 ml with the same solvent.

*Reference solution (c)*   Dissolve 10 mg of the substance to be examined in *acetone R* and dilute to 5 ml with the same solvent.

Apply to the plate 4 µl of each solution. Develop over a path of 15 cm using a mixture of 30 volumes of a 100 g/l solution of *ammonium acetate R* and 70 volumes of *ethanol (96 per cent) R*. Allow the plate to dry in air and spray with a solution containing 0.2 g/l of *dichlorofluorescein R* and 0.1 g/l of *rhodamine B R* in *ethanol (96 per cent) R*. Allow the plate to dry in air and examine in ultraviolet light at 254 nm. The chromatogram obtained with the test solution shows 3 spots corresponding in position to the principal spots in the chromatograms obtained with reference solutions (a), (b) and (c).

B. Dissolve 0.2 g in 2 ml of *pyridine R*, add 2 ml of a 100 g/l solution of *potassium hydroxide R* and heat on a water-bath. A red colour is produced.

C. Dissolve about 10 mg in 5 ml of *ethanol (96 per cent) R* and add 4.5 ml of *dilute sulphuric acid R* and 50 mg of *zinc powder R*. Allow to stand for 10 min and if necessary decant the supernatant liquid or filter. Cool the solution in iced water and add 0.5 ml of *sodium nitrite solution R*. Allow to stand for 2 min and add 1 g of *urea R*, 2 ml of *strong sodium hydroxide solution R* and 1 ml of *β-naphthol solution R*. A red colour develops.

## TESTS

### Acidity

Dissolve 1.0 g in 5 ml of a mixture of equal volumes of *ethanol (96 per cent) R* and *ether R*, warming to 35 °C. Add 0.2 ml of *phenolphthalein solution R*. Not more than 0.4 ml of *0.1 M sodium hydroxide* is required to produce a pink colour persisting for 30 s.

### Specific optical rotation (2.2.7)

Dissolve 1.25 g in *anhydrous ethanol R* and dilute to 25.0 ml with the same solvent. The specific optical rotation is + 22.5 to + 25.5.

### Free chloramphenicol

Maximum 450 ppm. Dissolve 1.0 g, with gentle heating, in 80 ml of *xylene R*. Cool and shake with 3 quantities, each of 15 ml, of *water R*. Dilute the combined aqueous extracts to 50 ml with *water R* and shake with 10 ml of *toluene R*. Allow

to separate and discard the toluene layer. Centrifuge a portion of the aqueous layer and measure the absorbance (A) (2.2.25) at the maximum at 278 nm using as the compensation liquid a blank solution having an absorbance not greater than 0.05.

Calculate the content of free chloramphenicol in parts per million from the expression:

$$\frac{A \times 10^4}{5.96}$$

### Related substances

Examine by thin-layer chromatography (2.2.27), using *silica gel GF$_{254}$ R* as the coating substance.

*Test solution*   Dissolve 0.1 g of the substance to be examined in *acetone R* and dilute to 10 ml with the same solvent.

*Reference solution (a)*   Dissolve 20 mg of *chloramphenicol palmitate isomer CRS* in *acetone R* and dilute to 10 ml with the same solvent. Dilute 1 ml of this solution to 10 ml with *acetone R*.

*Reference solution (b)*   Dissolve 20 mg of *chloramphenicol dipalmitate CRS* in *acetone R* and dilute to 10 ml with the same solvent. Dilute 1 ml of this solution to 10 ml with *acetone R*.

*Reference solution (c)*   Dissolve 5 mg of *chloramphenicol CRS* in *acetone R* and dilute to 10 ml with the same solvent. Dilute 1 ml of this solution to 10 ml with *acetone R*.

Apply to the plate 10 µl of each solution. Develop over a path of 15 cm using a mixture of 10 volumes of *methanol R*, 40 volumes of *chloroform R* and 50 volumes of *cyclohexane R*. Allow the plate to dry in air and examine in ultraviolet light at 254 nm. In the chromatogram obtained with the test solution, any spots due to chloramphenicol palmitate isomer and chloramphenicol dipalmitate are not more intense than the corresponding spots in the chromatograms obtained with reference solutions (a) and (b) respectively (2.0 per cent) and any spot, apart from the principal spot and the spots due to chloramphenicol palmitate isomer and chloramphenicol dipalmitate, is not more intense than the principal spot in the chromatogram obtained with reference solution (c) (0.5 per cent).

### Loss on drying (2.2.32)

Maximum 0.5 per cent, determined on 1.000 g by heating at 80 °C over *diphosphorus pentoxide R* at a pressure not exceeding 0.1 kPa for 3 h.

### Sulphated ash (2.4.14)

Maximum 0.1 per cent, determined on 1.0 g.

## ASSAY

Dissolve 90.0 mg in *ethanol (96 per cent) R* and dilute to 100.0 ml with the same solvent. Dilute 10.0 ml of this solution to 250.0 ml with *ethanol (96 per cent) R*. Measure the absorbance (2.2.25) of the solution at the maximum at 271 nm.

Calculate the content of $C_{27}H_{42}Cl_2N_2O_6$ taking the specific absorbance to be 178.

## STORAGE

Protected from light.

## IMPURITIES

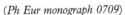

A. (1R,2R)-2-[(dichloroacetyl)amino]-3-hydroxy-1-(4-nitrophenyl)propyl hexadecanoate (chloramphenicol palmitate isomer),

B. (1R,2R)-2-[(dichloroacetyl)amino]-1-(4-nitrophenyl)propane-1,3-diyl bishexadecanoate (chloramphenicol dipalmitate).

*Ph Eur*

# Chloramphenicol Sodium Succinate

(*Ph Eur monograph 0709*)

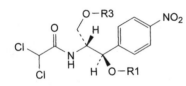

1 isomer : R1 = CO-CH₂-CH₂-CO₂Na, R3 = H
3 isomer : R1 = H, R3 = CO-CH₂-CH₂-CO₂Na

$C_{15}H_{15}Cl_2N_2NaO_8$     445.2     982-57-0

### Action and use
Antibacterial.

### Preparation
Chloramphenicol Sodium Succinate Injection

*Ph Eur*

## DEFINITION
Mixture in variable proportions of sodium (2R,3R)-2-[(dichloroacetyl)amino]-3-hydroxy-3-(4-nitrophenyl)propyl butanedioate (3 isomer) and of sodium (1R,2R)-2-[(dichloroacetyl)amino]-3-hydroxy-1-(4-nitrophenyl)propyl butanedioate (1 isomer).

Semi-synthetic product derived from a fermentation product.

### Content
98.0 per cent to 102.0 per cent (anhydrous substance).

## CHARACTERS
### Appearance
White or yellowish-white powder, hygroscopic.

### Solubility
Very soluble in water, freely soluble in ethanol (96 per cent).

## IDENTIFICATION
A. Thin-layer chromatography (*2.2.27*).

*Test solution*   Dissolve 20 mg of the substance to be examined in 2 ml of *acetone R*.

*Reference solution (a)*   Dissolve 20 mg of *chloramphenicol sodium succinate CRS* in 2 ml of *acetone R*.

*Reference solution (b)*   Dissolve 20 mg of *chloramphenicol CRS* in 2 ml of *acetone R*.

*Plate*   TLC silica gel GF₂₅₄ plate R.

*Mobile phase*   dilute acetic acid R, methanol R, chloroform R (1:14:85 *V/V/V*).

*Application*   2 µl.

*Development*   Over a path of 15 cm.

*Drying*   In air.

*Detection*   Examine in ultraviolet light at 254 nm.

*Results*   The 2 principal spots in the chromatogram obtained with the test solution are similar in position and size to the 2 principal spots in the chromatogram obtained with reference solution (a); their positions are different from that of the principal spot in the chromatogram obtained with reference solution (b).

B. Dissolve about 10 mg in 1 ml of *ethanol (50 per cent V/V) R*, add 3 ml of a 10 g/l solution of *calcium chloride R* and 50 mg of *zinc powder R* and heat on a water-bath for 10 min. Filter the hot solution and allow to cool. Add 0.1 ml of *benzoyl chloride R* and shake for 1 min. Add 0.5 ml of *ferric chloride solution R1* and 2 ml of *chloroform R* and shake. The upper layer is light violet-red or purple.

C. Dissolve 50 mg in 1 ml of *pyridine R*. Add 0.5 ml of *dilute sodium hydroxide solution R* and 1.5 ml of *water R*. Heat in a water-bath for 3 min. A red colour develops. Add 2 ml of *nitric acid R* and cool under running water. Add 1 ml of *0.1 M silver nitrate*. A white precipitate is formed slowly.

D. It gives reaction (a) of sodium (*2.3.1*).

## TESTS
**pH** (*2.2.3*)
6.4 to 7.0.

Dissolve 2.50 g in *carbon dioxide-free water R* and dilute to 10 ml with the same solvent.

**Specific optical rotation** (*2.2.7*)
+ 5.0 to + 8.0 (anhydrous substance).

Dissolve 0.50 g in *water R* and dilute to 10.0 ml with the same solvent.

**Chloramphenicol and chloramphenicol disodium disuccinate**
Liquid chromatography (*2.2.29*).

*Test solution*   Dissolve 25.0 mg of the substance to be examined in the mobile phase and dilute to 100.0 ml with the mobile phase.

*Reference solution (a)*   Dissolve 10.0 mg of *chloramphenicol CRS* in the mobile phase and dilute to 100.0 ml with the mobile phase (solution A). Dilute 5.0 ml of this solution to 100.0 ml with the mobile phase.

*Reference solution (b)*   Dissolve 10.0 mg of *chloramphenicol disodium disuccinate CRS* in the mobile phase and dilute to 100.0 ml with the mobile phase (solution B). Dilute 5.0 ml of this solution to 100.0 ml with the mobile phase.

*Reference solution (c)*   Dissolve 25 mg of the substance to be examined in the mobile phase, add 5 ml of solution A and

5 ml of solution B and dilute to 100 ml with the mobile phase.

*Column:*
— *size:* $l = 0.25$ m, Ø = 4.6 mm;
— *stationary phase: octadecylsilyl silica gel for chromatography R* (5 µm).

*Mobile phase* 20 g/l solution of *phosphoric acid R, methanol R, water R* (5:40:55 *V/V/V*).

*Flow rate* 1.0 ml/min.

*Detection* Spectrophotometer at 275 nm.

*Injection* 20 µl.

*System suitability* Reference solution (c):
— the 2 peaks corresponding to those in the chromatograms obtained with reference solutions (a) and (b) are clearly separated from the peaks corresponding to the 2 principal peaks in the chromatogram obtained with the test solution; if necessary, adjust the methanol content of the mobile phase.

*Limits:*
— *chloramphenicol:* not more than the area of the principal peak in the chromatogram obtained with reference solution (a) (2.0 per cent);
— *chloramphenicol disodium disuccinate:* not more than the area of the principal peak in the chromatogram obtained with reference solution (b) (2.0 per cent).

**Water** (*2.5.12*)
Maximum 2.0 per cent, determined on 0.500 g.

**Pyrogens** (*2.6.8*)
If intended for use in the manufacture of a parenteral dosage form without a further appropriate procedure for removal of pyrogens, it complies with the test for pyrogens. Inject per kilogram of the rabbit's mass 2.5 ml of a solution in *water for injections R* containing 2 mg of the substance to be examined per millilitre.

**ASSAY**
Dissolve 0.200 g in *water R* and dilute to 500.0 ml with the same solvent. Dilute 5.0 ml of this solution to 100.0 ml with *water R*. Measure the absorbance (*2.2.25*) at the absorption maximum at 276 nm.

Calculate the content of $C_{15}H_{15}Cl_2N_2NaO_8$, taking the specific absorbance to be 220.

**STORAGE**
In an airtight container, protected from light. If the substance is sterile, store in a sterile, airtight, tamper-proof container, protected from light.

———————————————————— *Ph Eur*

# Chlorcyclizine Hydrochloride

(*Ph Eur monograph 1086*)

and enantiomer , HCl

$C_{18}H_{21}ClN_2,HCl$          337.3          1620-21-9

**Action and use**
Histamine $H_1$ receptor antagonist; antihistamine.

*Ph Eur* ————————————————————

**DEFINITION**
Chlorcyclizine hydrochloride contains not less than 99.0 per cent and not more than the equivalent of 101.0 per cent of (*RS*)-1-[(4-chlorophenyl)phenylmethyl]-4-methylpiperazine hydrochloride, calculated with reference to the dried substance.

**CHARACTERS**
A. white or almost white, crystalline powder, freely soluble in water and in methylene chloride, soluble in alcohol.

**IDENTIFICATION**
*First identification* B, D.
*Second identification* A, C, D.

A. Dissolve 10.0 mg in a 5 g/l solution of *sulphuric acid R* and dilute to 100.0 ml with the same acid. Dilute 10.0 ml of the solution to 100.0 ml with a 5 g/l solution of *sulphuric acid R*. Examined between 215 nm and 300 nm (*2.2.25*), the solution shows an absorption maximum at 231 nm. The specific absorbance at the maximum is 475 to 525, calculated with reference to the dried substance.

B. Examine by infrared absorption spectrophotometry (*2.2.24*), comparing with the spectrum obtained with *chlorcyclizine hydrochloride CRS*. Examine the substances prepared as discs.

C. Examine the chromatograms obtained in the test for related substances (see Tests). The principal spot in the chromatogram obtained with test solution (b) is similar in position and size to the principal spot in the chromatogram obtained with reference solution (a).

D. It gives reaction (a) of chlorides (*2.3.1*).

**TESTS**
**Appearance of solution**
Dissolve 0.5 g in *water R* and dilute to 10 ml with the same solvent. The solution is clear (*2.2.1*) and colourless (*2.2.2, Method II*).

**pH** (*2.2.3*)
Dissolve 0.10 g in *carbon dioxide-free water R* and dilute to 10 ml with the same solvent. The pH of the solution is 5.0 to 6.0.

**Related substances**
Examine by thin-layer chromatography (*2.2.27*), using a plate coated with a suitable silica gel.

*Test solution (a)* Dissolve 0.20 g of the substance to be examined in *methanol R* and dilute to 10 ml with the same solvent.

*Test solution (b)* Dilute 5 ml of test solution (a) to 100 ml with *methanol R*.

*Reference solution (a)* Dissolve 10 mg of *chlorcyclizine hydrochloride CRS* in *methanol R* and dilute to 10 ml with the same solvent.

*Reference solution (b)* Dissolve 5 mg of *methylpiperazine R* in *methanol R* and dilute to 50 ml with the same solvent.

*Reference solution (c)* Dilute 1 ml of test solution (b) to 25 ml with *methanol R*.

*Reference solution (d)* Dissolve 10 mg of *hydroxyzine hydrochloride CRS* and 10 mg of *chlorcyclizine hydrochloride CRS* in *methanol R* and dilute to 10 ml with the same solvent.

Apply separately to the plate 10 µl of each solution and develop over a path of 15 cm using a mixture of 2 volumes of *concentrated ammonia R*, 13 volumes of *methanol R* and 85 volumes of *methylene chloride R*. Allow the plate to dry in air and expose it to iodine vapour for 10 min. In the chromatogram obtained with test solution (a): any spot corresponding to methylpiperazine is not more intense than the spot in the chromatogram obtained with reference solution (b) (0.5 per cent); any spot, apart from the principal spot and any spot corresponding to methylpiperazine, is not more intense than the spot in the chromatogram obtained with reference solution (c) (0.2 per cent). The test is not valid unless the chromatogram obtained with reference solution (d) shows two clearly separated spots.

**Loss on drying** (*2.2.32*)
Not more than 1.0 per cent, determined on 1.000 g by drying in an oven at 130 °C.

**Sulphated ash** (*2.4.14*)
Not more than 0.1 per cent, determined on 1.0 g.

**ASSAY**
Dissolve 0.200 g in a mixture of 1 ml of *0.1 M hydrochloric acid* and 50 ml of *methanol R*. Carry out a potentiometric titration (*2.2.20*), using *0.1 M sodium hydroxide*. Read the volume added between the two points of inflexion.

1 ml of *0.1 M sodium hydroxide* is equivalent to 33.73 mg of $C_{18}H_{22}Cl_2N_2$.

**STORAGE**
Store protected from light.

**IMPURITIES**

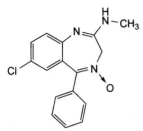

A. *N*-methylpiperazine.

*Ph Eur*

# Chlordiazepoxide

*(Ph Eur monograph 0656)*

$C_{16}H_{14}ClN_3O$        299.8        58-25-3

**Action and use**
Benzodiazepine.

*Ph Eur*

**DEFINITION**
7-Chloro-*N*-methyl-5-phenyl-3*H*-1,4-benzodiazepin-2-amine 4-oxide.

**Content**
99.0 per cent to 101.0 per cent (dried substance).

**CHARACTERS**
**Appearance**
Almost white or light yellow, crystalline powder.

**Solubility**
Practically insoluble in water, sparingly soluble in ethanol (96 per cent).

It shows polymorphism (*5.9*).

**IDENTIFICATION**
Infrared absorption spectrophotometry (*2.2.24*).

*Comparison* chlordiazepoxide CRS.

If the spectra obtained in the solid state show differences, dissolve the substance to be examined and the reference substance separately in *methylene chloride R*, evaporate to dryness and record new spectra using the residues.

**TESTS**
**Related substances**
Liquid chromatography (*2.2.29*). *Carry out the test protected from bright light and prepare the solutions immediately before use.*

*Test solution* Dissolve 20.0 mg of the substance to be examined in the mobile phase and dilute to 100.0 ml with the mobile phase.

*Reference solution (a)* Dilute 1.0 ml of the test solution to 100.0 ml with the mobile phase. Dilute 2.0 ml of this solution to 10.0 ml with the mobile phase.

*Reference solution (b)* Dissolve 5 mg of *chlordiazepoxide impurity A CRS* in the mobile phase, add 25.0 ml of the test solution and dilute to 100.0 ml with the mobile phase. Dilute 2.0 ml of this solution to 50.0 ml with the mobile phase.

*Reference solution (c)* Dissolve 4.0 mg of *aminochlorobenzophenone R* in the mobile phase and dilute to 100.0 ml with the mobile phase. Dilute 1.0 ml of this solution to 100.0 ml with the mobile phase.

*Column:*
— size: *l* = 0.15 m, Ø = 4.6 mm,
— stationary phase: *octadecylsilyl silica gel for chromatography R* (5 µm).

*Mobile phase* *acetonitrile R*, *water R* (50:50 *V/V*).

*Flow rate*  1.0 ml/min.

*Detection*  Spectrophotometer at 254 nm.

*Injection*  10 µl.

*Run time*  6 times the retention time of chlordiazepoxide.

*Relative retention*  With reference to chlordiazepoxide (retention time = about 3.6 min): impurity A = about 0.7; impurity B = about 2.3; impurity C = about 3.9.

*System suitability*  Reference solution (b):
— *resolution*: minimum 5.0 between the peaks due to impurity A and chlordiazepoxide.

*Limits:*
— *impurities A, B*: for each impurity, not more than the area of the principal peak in the chromatogram obtained with reference solution (a) (0.2 per cent),
— *impurity C*: not more than the area of the principal peak in the chromatogram obtained with reference solution (c) (0.2 per cent),
— *any other impurity*: for each impurity, not more than 0.5 times the area of the principal peak in the chromatogram obtained with reference solution (a) (0.1 per cent),
— *total*: not more than 2.5 times the area of the principal peak in the chromatogram obtained with reference solution (a) (0.5 per cent),
— *disregard limit*: 0.25 times the area of the principal peak in the chromatogram obtained with reference solution (a) (0.05 per cent).

**Loss on drying** (2.2.32)
Maximum 0.5 per cent, determined on 1.000 g by drying in an oven at 105 °C.

**Sulphated ash** (2.4.14)
Maximum 0.1 per cent, determined on 1.0 g.

**ASSAY**
Dissolve 0.250 g, with heating if necessary, in 80 ml of *anhydrous acetic acid R*. Titrate with *0.1 M perchloric acid* determining the end-point potentiometrically (2.2.20).

1 ml of *0.1 M perchloric acid* is equivalent to 29.98 mg of $C_{16}H_{14}ClN_3O$.

**STORAGE**
Protected from light.

**IMPURITIES**
*Specified impurities*  A, B, C.

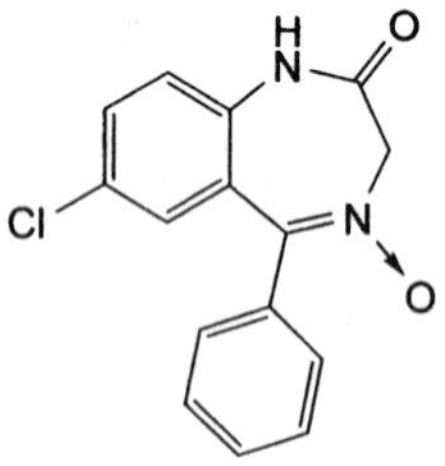

A. 7-chloro-5-phenyl-1,3-dihydro-2H-1,4-benzodiazepin-2-one 4-oxide,

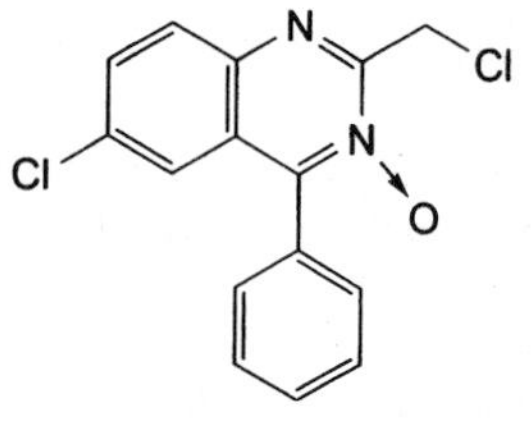

B. 6-chloro-2-(chloromethyl)-4-phenylquinazoline 3-oxide,

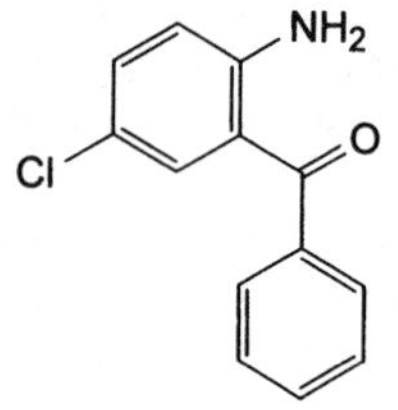

C. (2-amino-5-chlorophenyl)phenylmethanone (aminochlorobenzophenone).

*Ph Eur*

# Chlordiazepoxide Hydrochloride

*(Ph Eur monograph 0474)*

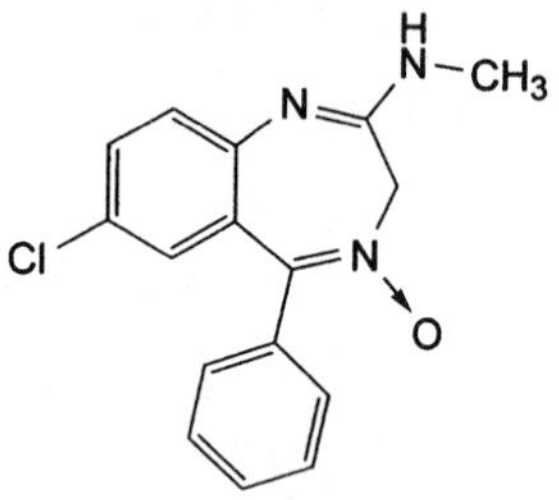

$C_{16}H_{14}ClN_3O,HCl$          336.2          *438-41-5*

**Action and use**
Benzodiazepine.

*Ph Eur*

**DEFINITION**
7-Chloro-N-methyl-5-phenyl-3H-1,4-benzodiazepin-2-amine 4-oxide hydrochloride.

**Content**
99.0 per cent to 101.0 per cent (dried substance).

**CHARACTERS**
**Appearance**
White or slightly yellow, crystalline powder.

**Solubility**
Soluble in water, sparingly soluble in ethanol (96 per cent).
It shows polymorphism (5.9).

**IDENTIFICATION**
A. Infrared absorption spectrophotometry (2.2.24).

*Comparison*  chlordiazepoxide hydrochloride CRS.

If the spectra obtained in the solid state show differences, dissolve 100 mg in 9 ml of *water R* and add 1 ml of *dilute sodium hydroxide solution R*. Extract with 10 ml of *methylene chloride R* in a separating funnel. Evaporate the organic layer and dry the residue obtained at 100-105 °C. Proceed in the same way with the reference substance. Record new spectra using the residues.

B. Dissolve 50 mg in 5 ml of *water R*, add 1 ml of *dilute ammonia R1*, mix, allow to stand for 5 min and filter. Acidify the filtrate with *dilute nitric acid R*. The solution gives reaction (a) of chlorides (*2.3.1*).

## TESTS

### Appearance of solution

The solution is clear (*2.2.1*) and not more intensely coloured than reference solution $GY_6$ (*2.2.2, Method II*).

Dissolve 2.5 g in *water R* and dilute to 25 ml with the same solvent.

### Related substances

Liquid chromatography (*2.2.29*). *Carry out the following operations protected from bright light and prepare the solutions immediately before use.*

*Test solution*  Dissolve 20.0 mg of the substance to be examined in the mobile phase and dilute to 100.0 ml with the mobile phase.

*Reference solution (a)*  Dilute 1.0 ml of the test solution to 100.0 ml with the mobile phase. Dilute 2.0 ml of this solution to 10.0 ml with the mobile phase.

*Reference solution (b)*  Dissolve 5 mg of *chlordiazepoxide impurity A CRS* in the mobile phase, add 25.0 ml of the test solution and dilute to 100.0 ml with the mobile phase. Dilute 2.0 ml of this solution to 50.0 ml with the mobile phase.

*Reference solution (c)*  Dissolve 4.0 mg of *aminochlorobenzophenone R* in the mobile phase and dilute to 100.0 ml with the mobile phase. Dilute 1.0 ml of this solution to 100.0 ml with the mobile phase.

*Column:*
— *size*: $l = 0.15$ m, Ø = 4.6 mm,
— *stationary phase: octadecylsilyl silica gel for chromatography R* (5 μm).

*Mobile phase*  *acetonitrile R, water R* (50:50 *V/V*).

*Flow rate*  1.0 ml/min.

*Detection*  Spectrophotometer at 254 nm.

*Injection*  10 μl.

*Run time*  6 times the retention time of chlordiazepoxide.

*Relative retention*  With reference to chlordiazepoxide (retention time = about 3.6 min): impurity A = about 0.7; impurity B = about 2.3; impurity C = about 3.9.

*System suitability*  Reference solution (b):
— *resolution*: minimum 5.0 between the peaks due to impurity A and chlordiazepoxide.

*Limits:*
— *impurities A, B*: for each impurity, not more than the area of the principal peak in the chromatogram obtained with reference solution (a) (0.2 per cent),
— *impurity C*: not more than the area of the principal peak in the chromatogram obtained with reference solution (c) (0.2 per cent),
— *any other impurity*: for each impurity, not more than 0.5 times the area of the principal peak in the chromatogram obtained with reference solution (a) (0.1 per cent),
— *total*: not more than 2.5 times the area of the principal peak in the chromatogram obtained with reference solution (a) (0.5 per cent),
— *disregard limit*: 0.25 times the area of the principal peak in the chromatogram obtained with reference solution (a) (0.05 per cent).

**Loss on drying** (*2.2.32*)
Maximum 0.5 per cent, determined on 1.000 g by drying *in vacuo* at 60 °C for 4 h.

**Sulphated ash** (*2.4.14*)
Maximum 0.1 per cent, determined on 1.0 g.

## ASSAY
Dissolve 0.250 g in 50 ml of *water R*. Titrate with *0.1 M silver nitrate*, determining the end-point potentiometrically (*2.2.20*).

1 ml of *0.1 M silver nitrate* is equivalent to 33.62 mg of $C_{16}H_{15}Cl_2N_3O$.

## STORAGE
Protected from light.

## IMPURITIES
*Specified impurities*  *A, B, C.*

A. 7-chloro-5-phenyl-1,3-dihydro-2*H*-1,4-benzodiazepin-2-one 4-oxide,

B. 6-chloro-2-(chloromethyl)-4-phenylquinazoline 3-oxide,

C. (2-amino-5-chlorophenyl)phenylmethanone (aminochlorobenzophenone).

_____ *Ph Eur*

# Chlorhexidine Acetate

(*Chlorhexidine Diacetate, Ph Eur monograph 0657*)

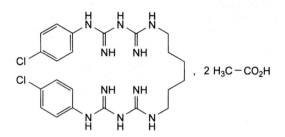

, 2 H₃C — CO₂H

$C_{22}H_{30}Cl_2N_{10},2C_2H_4O_2$     625.6          *56-95-1*

## Action and use
Antiseptic.

## Preparation
Chlorhexidine Irrigation Solution

*Ph Eur* _____

## DEFINITION
1,1'-(Hexane-1,6-diyl)bis[5-(4-chlorophenyl)biguanide] diacetate.

## Content
98.0 per cent to 101.0 per cent (dried substance).

## CHARACTERS
### Appearance
White or almost white, microcrystalline powder.

### Solubility
Sparingly soluble in water, soluble in ethanol (96 per cent), slightly soluble in glycerol and in propylene glycol.

## IDENTIFICATION
*First identification*   A.

*Second identification*   B, C, D.

A. Infrared absorption spectrophotometry (*2.2.24*).

*Comparison*   chlorhexidine diacetate CRS.

B. Dissolve about 5 mg in 5 ml of a warm 10 g/l solution of *cetrimide R* and add 1 ml of *strong sodium hydroxide solution R* and 1 ml of *bromine water R*. A deep red colour is produced.

C. Dissolve 0.3 g in 10 ml of a mixture of equal volumes of *hydrochloric acid R* and *water R*. Add 40 ml of *water R*, filter if necessary and cool in iced water. Make alkaline to *titan yellow paper R* by adding dropwise, and with stirring, *strong sodium hydroxide solution R* and add 1 ml in excess. Filter, wash the precipitate with *water R* until the washings are free from alkali and recrystallise from *ethanol (70 per cent V/V) R*. Dry at 100-105 °C. The residue melts (*2.2.14*) at 132 °C to 136 °C.

D. It gives reaction (a) of acetates (*2.3.1*).

## TESTS
### Chloroaniline
Maximum 500 ppm.

Dissolve 0.20 g in 25 ml of *water R* with shaking if necessary. Add 1 ml of *hydrochloric acid R* and dilute to 30 ml with *water R*. Add rapidly and with thorough mixing after each addition: 2.5 ml of *dilute hydrochloric acid R*, 0.35 ml of *sodium nitrite solution R*, 2 ml of a 50 g/l solution of *ammonium sulphamate R*, 5 ml of a 1.0 g/l solution of *naphthylethylenediamine dihydrochloride R* and 1 ml of *ethanol (96 per cent) R*, dilute to 50.0 ml with *water R* and allow to stand for 30 min. Any reddish-blue colour in the solution is

not more intense than that in a standard prepared at the same time and in the same manner, using a mixture of 10.0 ml of a 0.010 g/l solution of *chloroaniline R* in *dilute hydrochloric acid R* and 20 ml of *dilute hydrochloric acid R* instead of the solution of the substance to be examined.

### Related substances
Liquid chromatography (*2.2.29*).

*Test solution*   Dissolve 0.200 g of the substance to be examined in the mobile phase and dilute to 100 ml with the mobile phase.

*Reference solution (a)*   Dissolve 15 mg of *chlorhexidine for performance test CRS* in the mobile phase and dilute to 10.0 ml with the mobile phase.

*Reference solution (b)*   Dilute 2.5 ml of the test solution to 100 ml with the mobile phase.

*Reference solution (c)*   Dilute 2.0 ml of reference solution (b) to 10 ml with the mobile phase. Dilute 1.0 ml of this solution to 10 ml with the mobile phase.

*Column:*
— *size*: $l = 0.2$ m, Ø = 4 mm;
— *stationary phase*: octadecylsilyl silica gel for chromatography R (5 μm).

*Mobile phase*   Solution of 2.0 g of sodium *octanesulphonate R* in a mixture of 120 ml of *glacial acetic acid R*, 270 ml of *water R* and 730 ml of *methanol R*.

*Flow rate*   1.0 ml/min.

*Detection*   Spectrophotometer at 254 nm.

*Equilibration*   With the mobile phase for at least 1 h.

*Injection*   10 μl.

*Run time*   6 times the retention time of chlorhexidine.

*System suitability*   Reference solution (a):
— the chromatogram obtained is similar to the chromatogram supplied with *chlorhexidine for performance test CRS* in that the peaks due to impurity A and impurity B precede that due to chlorhexidine; if necessary, adjust the concentration of acetic acid in the mobile phase (increasing the concentration decreases the retention times).

*Limits:*
— *total*: not more than the area of the principal peak in the chromatogram obtained with reference solution (b) (2.5 per cent);
— *disregard limit*: the area of the principal peak in the chromatogram obtained with reference solution (c) (0.05 per cent); disregard any peak with a relative retention time with reference to chlorhexidine of 0.25 or less.

## Loss on drying (*2.2.32*)
Maximum 3.5 per cent, determined on 1.000 g by drying in an oven at 105 °C.

## Sulphated ash (*2.4.14*)
Maximum 0.15 per cent, determined on 1.0 g.

## ASSAY
Dissolve 0.140 g in 100 ml of *anhydrous acetic acid R* and titrate with *0.1 M perchloric acid*. Determine the end-point potentiometrically (*2.2.20*).

1 ml of *0.1 M perchloric acid* is equivalent to 15.64 mg of $C_{26}H_{38}Cl_2N_{10}O_4$.

**IMPURITIES**

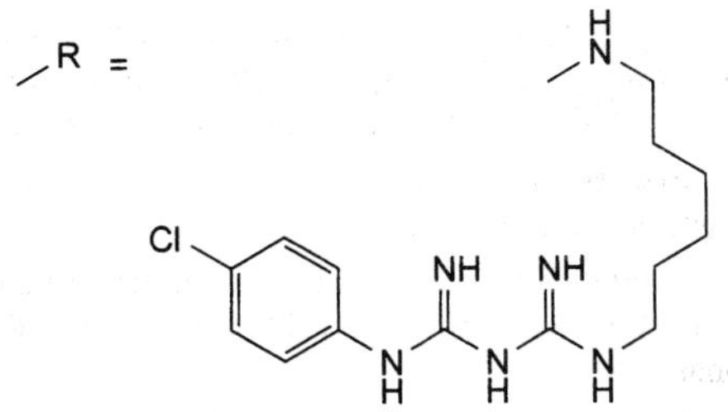

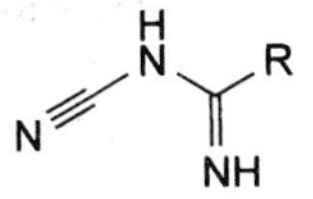

R =

A. 1-(4-chlorophenyl)-5-[6-
(3-cyanoguanidino)hexyl]biguanide,

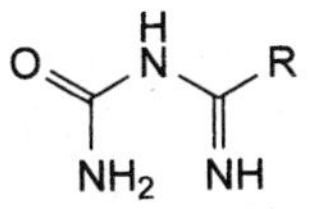

B. [[[6-[5-(4-chlorophenyl)guanidino]hexyl]amino]
iminomethyl]urea,

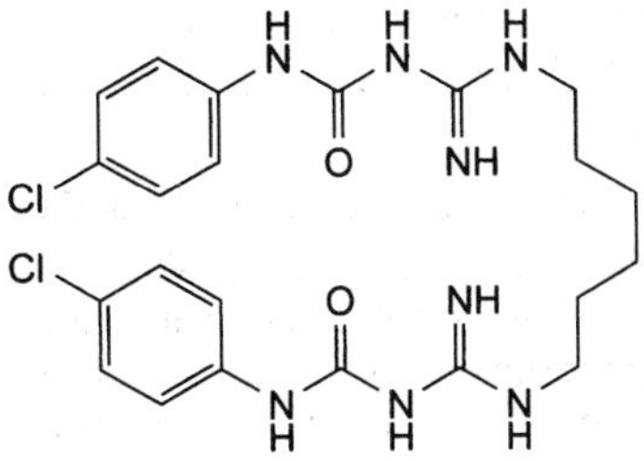

C. 1,1'-[hexane-1,6-diylbis[imino(iminocarbonyl)]]bis[3-
(4-chlorophenyl)urea],

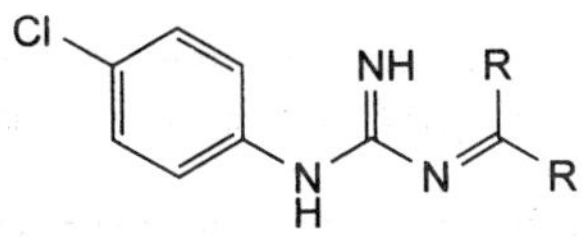

D. 1,1'-[[[[[(4-chlorophenyl)amino]iminomethyl]imino]
methylene]bis[imino(hexane-1,6-diyl)]]bis[5-
(4-chlorophenyl)biguanide].

— *Ph Eur*

# Chlorhexidine Gluconate Solution

(*Chlorhexidine Digluconate Solution,
Ph Eur monograph 0658*)

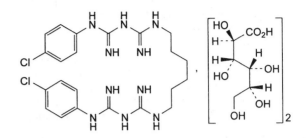

$C_{22}H_{30}Cl_2N_{10},2C_6H_{12}O_7$    898    *18472-51-0*

## Action and use
Antiseptic.

## Preparations
Chlorhexidine Gluconate Gel

Chlorhexidine Irrigation Solution

Chlorhexidine Mouthwash

Lidocaine and Chlorhexidine Gel

*Ph Eur*

## DEFINITION
Aqueous solution of 1,1'-(hexane-1,6-diyl)bis[5-
(4-chlorophenyl)biguanide] di-D-gluconate.

## Content
190 g/l to 210 g/l.

## CHARACTERS
### Appearance
Almost colourless or pale-yellowish liquid.

### Solubility
Miscible with water, with not more than 3 parts of acetone
and with not more than 5 parts of ethanol (96 per cent).

## IDENTIFICATION
*First identification*   A, B.

*Second identification*   B, C, D.

A. Infrared absorption spectrophotometry (*2.2.24*).

*Preparation*   To 1 ml add 40 ml of *water R*, cool in iced
water, make alkaline to *titan yellow paper R* by adding
dropwise, and with stirring, *strong sodium hydroxide solution R*
and add 1 ml in excess. Filter, wash the precipitate with
*water R* until the washings are free from alkali and
recrystallise from *ethanol (70 per cent V/V) R*. Dry at
100-105 °C. Examine the residue.

*Comparison*   chlorhexidine CRS.

B. Thin-layer chromatography (*2.2.27*).

*Test solution*   Dilute 10.0 ml of the preparation to be
examined to 50 ml with *water R*.

*Reference solution*   Dissolve 25 mg of *calcium gluconate CRS*
in 1 ml of *water R*.

*Plate*   TLC silica gel G plate R.

*Mobile phase*   concentrated ammonia R, ethyl acetate R,
water R, ethanol (96 per cent) R (10:10:30:50 V/V/V/V).

*Application*   5 µl.

*Development*   Over a path of 10 cm.

*Drying*   At 100 °C for 20 min and allow to cool.

*Detection* Spray with a 50 g/l solution of *potassium dichromate R* in a 40 per cent *m/m* solution of *sulphuric acid R*.

*Results* After 5 min, the principal spot in the chromatogram obtained with the test solution is similar in position, colour and size to the principal spot in the chromatogram obtained with the reference solution.

C. To 1 ml add 40 ml of *water R*, cool in iced water, make alkaline to *titan yellow paper R* by adding dropwise, and with stirring, *strong sodium hydroxide solution R* and add 1 ml in excess. Filter, wash the precipitate with *water R* until the washings are free from alkali and recrystallise from *ethanol (70 per cent V/V) R*. Dry at 100-105 °C. The residue melts (*2.2.14*) at 132 °C to 136 °C.

D. To 0.05 ml add 5 ml of a 10 g/l solution of *cetrimide R*, 1 ml of *strong sodium hydroxide solution R* and 1 ml of *bromine water R*; a deep red colour is produced.

## TESTS

**Relative density** (*2.2.5*)
1.06 to 1.07.

**pH** (*2.2.3*)
5.5 to 7.0.

Dilute 5.0 ml to 100 ml with *carbon dioxide-free water R*.

**Chloroaniline**
Maximum 0.25 per cent, calculated with reference to chlorhexidine digluconate at a nominal concentration of 200 g/l.

Dilute 2.0 ml to 100 ml with *water R*. To 10 ml of this solution add 2.5 ml of *dilute hydrochloric acid R* and dilute to 20 ml with *water R*. Add rapidly and with thorough mixing after each addition: 0.35 ml of *sodium nitrite solution R*, 2 ml of a 50 g/l solution of *ammonium sulphamate R*, 5 ml of a 1 g/l solution of *naphthyle thylenediamine dihydrochloride R*, 1 ml of *ethanol (96 per cent) R*; dilute to 50.0 ml with *water R* and allow to stand for 30 min. Any reddish-blue colour in the solution is not more intense than that in a standard prepared at the same time and in the same manner using a mixture of 10.0 ml of a 0.010 g/l solution of *chloroaniline R* in *dilute hydrochloric acid R* and 10 ml of *water R* instead of the dilution of the preparation to be examined.

**Related substances**
Liquid chromatography (*2.2.29*).

*Test solution* Dilute 5.0 ml of the preparation to be examined to 50.0 ml with the mobile phase. Dilute 5.0 ml of this solution to 50.0 ml with the mobile phase.

*Reference solution (a)* Dissolve 15 mg of *chlorhexidine for performance test CRS* in the mobile phase and dilute to 10.0 ml with the mobile phase.

*Reference solution (b)* Dilute 3.0 ml of the test solution to 100 ml with the mobile phase.

*Reference solution (c)* Dilute 1.0 ml of reference solution (b) to 50 ml with the mobile phase.

*Column:*
— size: *l* = 0.2 m, Ø = 4 mm;
— stationary phase: *octadecylsilyl silica gel for chromatography R* (5 µm).

*Mobile phase* solution of 2.0 g of *sodium octanesulphonate R* in a mixture of 120 ml of *glacial acetic acid R*, 270 ml of *water R* and 730 ml of *methanol R*.

*Flow rate* 1.0 ml/min.

*Detection* Spectrophotometer at 254 nm.

*Equilibration* With the mobile phase for at least 1 hour.

*Injection* 10 µl.

*Run time* 6 times the retention time of chlorhexidine.

*System suitability* Reference solution (a):
— the chromatogram obtained is similar to the chromatogram supplied with *chlorhexidine for performance test CRS* in that the peaks due to impurity A and impurity B precede that due to chlorhexidine; if necessary, adjust the concentration of acetic acid in the mobile phase (increasing the concentration decreases the retention times).

*Limits:*
— *total*: not more than the area of the principal peak in the chromatogram obtained with reference solution (b) (3.0 per cent);
— *disregard limit*: the area of the principal peak in the chromatogram obtained with reference solution (c) (0.06 per cent); disregard any peak with a relative retention time with reference to the principal peak of 0.25 or less.

## ASSAY
Determine the density (*2.2.5*) of the preparation to be examined. Transfer 1.00 g to a 250 ml beaker and add 50 ml of *anhydrous acetic acid R*. Titrate with *0.1 M perchloric acid*. Determine the end-point potentiometrically (*2.2.20*).

1 ml of *0.1 M perchloric acid* is equivalent to 22.44 mg of $C_{34}H_{54}Cl_2N_{10}O_{14}$.

## STORAGE
Protected from light.

## IMPURITIES

A. 1-(4-chlorophenyl)-5-[6-(3-cyanoguanidino)hexyl]biguanide,

B. [[[6-[5-(4-chlorophenyl)guanidino]hexyl]amino]iminomethyl]urea,

C. 1,1'-[hexane-1,6-diylbis[imino(iminocarbonyl)]]bis[3-(4-chlorophenyl)urea],

D. 1,1'-[[[[[(4-chlorophenyl)amino]iminomethyl]imino]methylene]bis[imino(hexane-1,6-diyl)]]bis[5-(4-chlorophenyl)biguanide].

_____ *Ph Eur*

# Chlorhexidine Hydrochloride

(*Chlorhexidine Dihydrochloride,*
*Ph Eur monograph 0659*)

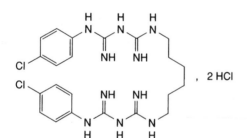

C22H30Cl2N10,2HCl          578.4          *3697-42-5*

**Action and use**
Antiseptic.

*Ph Eur* _____

## DEFINITION
1,1'-(Hexane-1,6-diyl)bis[5-(4-chlorophenyl)biguanide] dihydrochloride.

## Content
98.0 per cent to 101.0 per cent (dried substance).

## CHARACTERS
**Appearance**
White or almost white, crystalline powder.

**Solubility**
Sparingly soluble in water and in propylene glycol, very slightly soluble in ethanol (96 per cent).

## IDENTIFICATION
*First identification* A, D.

*Second identification* B, C, D.

A. Infrared absorption spectrophotometry (*2.2.24*).

*Comparison* chlorhexidine dihydrochloride CRS.

B. Dissolve about 5 mg in 5 ml of a warm 10 g/l solution of *cetrimide R* and add 1 ml of *strong sodium hydroxide solution R* and 1 ml of *bromine water R*. A dark red colour is produced.

C. Dissolve 0.3 g in 10 ml of a mixture of equal volumes of *hydrochloric acid R* and *water R*. Add 40 ml of *water R*, filter if necessary and cool in iced water. Make alkaline to *titan yellow paper R* by adding dropwise, and with stirring, *strong sodium hydroxide solution R* and add 1 ml in excess. Filter, wash the precipitate with *water R* until the washings are free from alkali and recrystallise from *ethanol (70 per cent V/V) R*. Dry at 100-105 °C. The residue melts (*2.2.14*) at 132 °C to 136 °C.

D. It gives reaction (a) of chlorides (*2.3.1*).

## TESTS
**Chloroaniline**
Maximum 500 ppm.

To 0.20 g add 1 ml of *hydrochloric acid R*, shake for about 30 s, dilute to 30 ml with *water R* and shake until a clear solution is obtained. Add rapidly and with thorough mixing after each addition: 2.5 ml of *dilute hydrochloric acid R*, 0.35 ml of *sodium nitrite solution R*, 2 ml of a 50 g/l solution of *ammonium sulphamate R*, 5 ml of a 1.0 g/l solution of *naphthylethylenediamine dihydrochloride R* and 1 ml of *ethanol (96 per cent) R;* dilute to 50.0 ml with *water R* and allow to stand for 30 min. Any reddish-blue colour in the solution is not more intense than that in a standard prepared at the same time and in the same manner using a mixture of 10.0 ml of a 0.010 g/l solution of *chloroaniline R* in *dilute hydrochloric acid R* and 20 ml of *dilute hydrochloric acid R* instead of the solution of the substance to be examined.

**Related substances**
Liquid chromatography (*2.2.29*).

*Test solution* Dissolve 0.200 g of the substance to be examined in the mobile phase and dilute to 100 ml with the mobile phase.

*Reference solution (a)* Dissolve 15 mg of *chlorhexidine for performance test CRS* in the mobile phase and dilute to 10.0 ml with the mobile phase.

*Reference solution (b)* Dilute 2.5 ml of the test solution to 100 ml with the mobile phase.

*Reference solution (c)* Dilute 2.0 ml of reference solution (b) to 10 ml with the mobile phase. Dilute 1.0 ml of this solution to 10 ml with the mobile phase.

*Column:*
— size: $l$ = 0.2 m, Ø = 4 mm;
— stationary phase: octadecylsilyl silica gel for chromatography R (5 μm).

*Mobile phase* Solution of 2.0 g of *sodium octanesulphonate R* in a mixture of 120 ml of *glacial acetic acid R*, 270 ml of *water R* and 730 ml of *methanol R*.

*Flow rate* 1.0 ml/min.

*Detection* Spectrophotometer at 254 nm.

*Equilibration* With the mobile phase for at least 1 h.

*Injection* 10 μl.

*Run time* 6 times the retention time of chlorhexidine.

*System suitability* Reference solution (a):
— the chromatogram obtained is similar to the chromatogram supplied with *chlorhexidine for performance test CRS* in that the peaks due to impurity A and impurity B precede that due to chlorhexidine; if necessary, adjust the concentration of acetic acid in the mobile phase (increasing the concentration decreases the retention times).

*Limits:*
— *total*: not more than the area of the principal peak in the chromatogram obtained with reference solution (b) (2.5 per cent);
— *disregard limit*: the area of the principal peak in the chromatogram obtained with reference solution (c) (0.05 per cent); disregard any peak with a relative retention time with reference to chlorhexidine of 0.25 or less.

**Loss on drying** (2.2.32)
Maximum 1.0 per cent, determined on 1.000 g by drying in an oven at 105 °C.

**Sulphated ash** (2.4.14)
Maximum 0.1 per cent, determined on 1.0 g.

**ASSAY**
Dissolve 100.0 mg in 5 ml of *anhydrous formic acid R* and add 70 ml of *acetic anhydride R*. Titrate with *0.1 M perchloric acid*, determining the end-point potentiometrically (2.2.20).
1 ml of *0.1 M perchloric acid* is equivalent to 14.46 mg of $C_{22}H_{32}Cl_4N_{10}$.

**IMPURITIES**

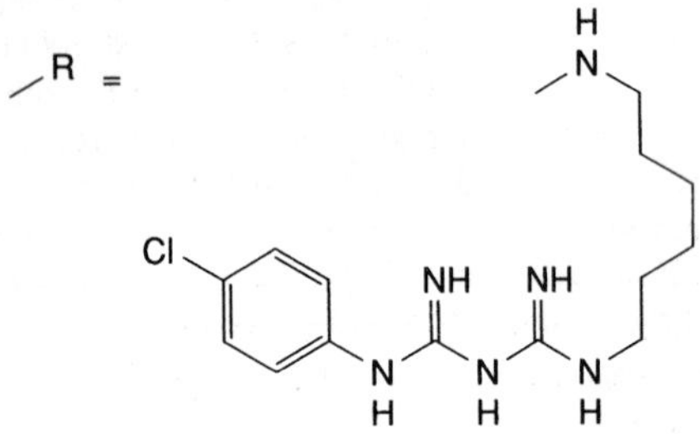

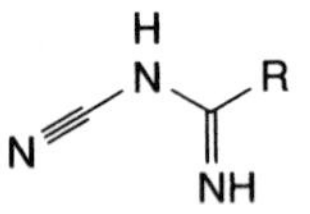

A. 1-(4-chlorophenyl)-5-[6-(3-cyanoguanidino)hexyl]biguanide,

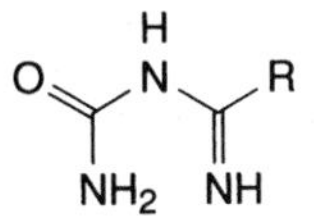

B. [[[6-[5-(4-chlorophenyl)guanidino]hexyl]amino]iminomethyl]urea,

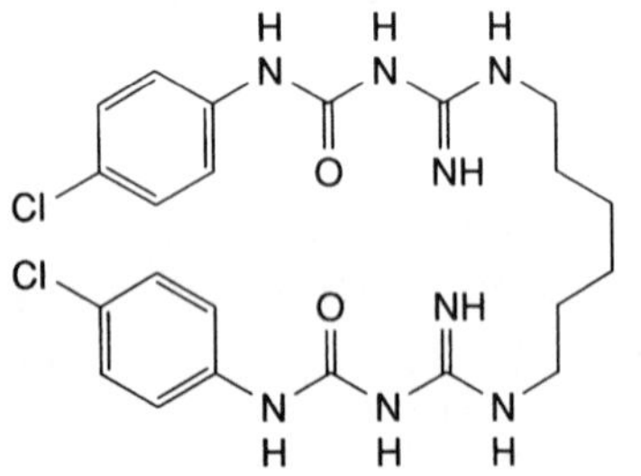

C. 1,1′-[hexane-1,6-diylbis[imino(iminocarbonyl)]]bis[3-(4-chlorophenyl)urea],

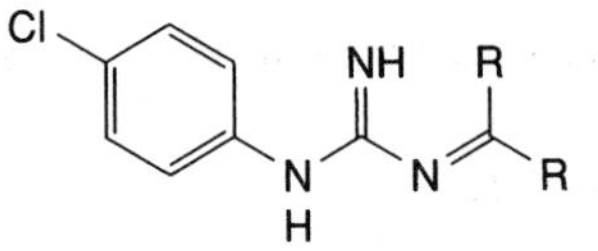

D. 1,1′-[[[[[(4-chlorophenyl)amino]iminomethyl]imino]methylene]bis[imino(hexane-1,6-diyl)]]bis[5-(4-chlorophenyl)biguanide].

*Ph Eur*

# Chlorinated Lime

**Action and use**
Disinfectant.

**DEFINITION**
Chlorinated Lime contains not less than 30.0% w/w of available chlorine, Cl.

**CHARACTERISTICS**
A dull white powder.
Partly soluble in *water* and in *ethanol (96%)*.

**IDENTIFICATION**
A. Evolves chlorine copiously on the addition of 2M *hydrochloric acid*.

B. When shaken with *water* and filtered, the filtrate yields reaction C characteristic of *calcium salts* and reaction A characteristic of *chlorides*, Appendix VI.

**ASSAY**
Triturate 4 g with successive small quantities of *water*, dilute to 1000 ml with *water* and shake thoroughly. Mix 100 ml of the resulting suspension with a solution containing 3 g of *potassium iodide* in 100 ml of *water*, acidify with 5 ml of 6M *acetic acid* and titrate the liberated iodine with 0.1M *sodium thiosulphate VS*. Each ml of 0.1M *sodium thiosulphate VS* is equivalent to 3.545 mg of available chlorine, Cl.

**STORAGE**
On exposure to air Chlorinated Lime becomes moist and gradually decomposes, carbon dioxide being absorbed and chlorine evolved.

# Chlormethine Hydrochloride

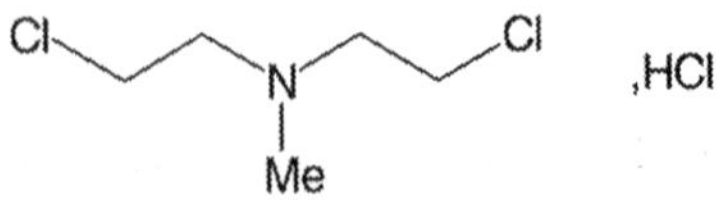

$C_5H_{11}Cl_2N,HCl$      192.5      55-86-7

**Action and use**
Cytotoxic alkylating agent.

**Preparation**
Chlormethine Injection

**DEFINITION**
Chlormethine Hydrochloride is bis(2-chloroethyl)methylamine hydrochloride. It contains not

less than 98.0% and not more than 101.0% of
C<sub>5</sub>H<sub>11</sub>Cl<sub>2</sub>N,HCl.

## CHARACTERISTICS

A white or almost white crystalline powder or mass;
hygroscopic; vesicant.

Very soluble in *water*.

## IDENTIFICATION

A. Dissolve 50 mg in 5 ml of *water* and add 1 ml of
5M *sodium hydroxide*. Oily globules are produced which
dissolve on warming.

B. Dissolve 50 mg in 5 ml of *water* and add 0.02 ml of
*potassium tetraiodomercurate solution*. A cream precipitate is
produced.

C. *Melting point*, about 108°, Appendix V A.

## ASSAY

To 0.2 g add 15 ml of 1M *ethanolic potassium hydroxide* and
15 ml of *water* and boil under a reflux condenser for 2 hours.
Evaporate the solution to half its volume on a water bath,
dilute to 150 ml with *water*, add 3 ml of *nitric acid* and 50 ml
of 0.1M *silver nitrate VS*, shake vigorously and filter. Wash the
residue with *water* and titrate the excess of silver nitrate in
the combined filtrate and washings with 0.1M *ammonium
thiocyanate VS* using 1 ml of *ammonium iron(III) sulphate
solution R2* as indicator. Each ml of 0.1M *silver nitrate VS* is
equivalent to 6.418 mg of C<sub>5</sub>H<sub>11</sub>Cl<sub>2</sub>N,HCl.

## STORAGE

Chlormethine Hydrochloride should be stored at a
temperature of 8° to 15°.

## LABELLING

The label states that the contents of the container are
strongly vesicant.

# Chlorobutanol

(*Chlorobutanol Hemihydrate,
Ph Eur monograph 0383*)

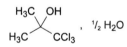

C<sub>4</sub>H<sub>7</sub>Cl<sub>3</sub>O,½H<sub>2</sub>O        186.5        *6001-64-5*

## Action and use

Disinfectant preservative.

*Ph Eur* _____

## DEFINITION

1,1,1-Trichloro-2-methylpropan-2-ol hemihydrate.

## Content

98.0 per cent to 101.0 per cent (anhydrous substance).

## CHARACTERS

### Appearance

White or almost white crystalline powder or colourless
crystals, sublimes readily.

### Solubility

Slightly soluble in water, very soluble in ethanol
(96 per cent), soluble in glycerol (85 per cent).

mp: about 78 °C (without previous drying).

## IDENTIFICATION

A. Add about 20 mg to a mixture of 1 ml of *pyridine R* and
2 ml of *strong sodium hydroxide solution R*. Heat in a water-
bath and shake. Allow to stand. The pyridine layer becomes
red.

B. Add about 20 mg to 5 ml of *ammoniacal silver nitrate
solution R* and warm slightly. A black precipitate is formed.

C. To about 20 mg add 3 ml of *1 M sodium hydroxide* and
shake to dissolve. Add 5 ml of *water R* and then, slowly, 2 ml
of *iodinated potassium iodide solution R*. A yellowish precipitate
is formed.

D. Water (see Tests).

## TESTS

### Solution S

Dissolve 5 g in *ethanol (96 per cent) R* and dilute to 10 ml
with the same solvent.

### Appearance of solution

Solution S is not more opalescent than reference suspension
II (*2.2.1*) and not more intensely coloured than reference
solution BY<sub>5</sub> (*2.2.2, Method II*).

### Acidity

To 4 ml of solution S add 15 ml of *ethanol (96 per cent) R*
and 0.1 ml of *bromothymol blue solution R1*. Not more than
1.0 ml of *0.01 M sodium hydroxide* is required to change the
colour of the indicator to blue.

### Chlorides (*2.4.4*)

Maximum 100 ppm.

To 1 ml of solution S add 4 ml of *ethanol (96 per cent) R* and
dilute to 15 ml with *water R*. When preparing the standard,
replace the 5 ml of *water R* by 5 ml of *ethanol (96 per cent) R*.

### Water (*2.5.12*)

4.5 per cent to 5.5 per cent, determined on 0.300 g.

### Sulphated ash (*2.4.14*)

Maximum 0.1 per cent, determined on 1.0 g.

## ASSAY

Dissolve 0.100 g in 20 ml of *ethanol (96 per cent) R*. Add
10 ml of *dilute sodium hydroxide solution R*, heat in a water-
bath for 5 min and cool. Add 20 ml of *dilute nitric acid R*,
25.0 ml of *0.1 M silver nitrate* and 2 ml of *dibutyl phthalate R*
and shake vigorously. Add 2 ml of *ferric ammonium sulphate
solution R2* and titrate with *0.1 M ammonium thiocyanate* until
an orange colour is obtained.

1 ml of *0.1 M silver nitrate* is equivalent to 5.92 mg of
C<sub>4</sub>H<sub>7</sub>Cl<sub>3</sub>O.

## STORAGE

In an airtight container.

_____ *Ph Eur*

# Anhydrous Chlorobutanol

(*Ph Eur monograph 0382*)

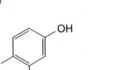

C₄H₇Cl₃O          177.5          57-15-8

**Action and use**
Disinfectant preservative.

*Ph Eur* _____

## DEFINITION
1,1,1-Trichloro-2-methylpropan-2-ol.

**Content**
98.0 per cent to 101.0 per cent (anhydrous substance).

## CHARACTERS
**Appearance**
White or almost white crystalline powder or colourless crystals, sublimes readily.

**Solubility**
Slightly soluble in water, very soluble in ethanol (96 per cent), soluble in glycerol (85 per cent).

mp: about 95 °C (without previous drying).

## IDENTIFICATION
A. Add about 20 mg to a mixture of 1 ml of *pyridine R* and 2 ml of *strong sodium hydroxide solution R*. Heat in a water-bath and shake. Allow to stand. The pyridine layer becomes red.

B. Add about 20 mg to 5 ml of *ammoniacal silver nitrate solution R* and warm slightly. A black precipitate is formed.

C. To about 20 mg add 3 ml of *1 M sodium hydroxide* and shake to dissolve. Add 5 ml of *water R* and then, slowly, 2 ml of *iodinated potassium iodide solution R*. A yellowish precipitate is formed.

D. Water (see Tests).

## TESTS
**Solution S**
Dissolve 5 g in *ethanol (96 per cent) R* and dilute to 10 ml with the same solvent.

**Appearance of solution**
Solution S is not more opalescent than reference suspension II (*2.2.1*) and not more intensely coloured than reference solution BY₅ (*2.2.2, Method II*).

**Acidity**
To 4 ml of solution S add 15 ml of *ethanol (96 per cent) R* and 0.1 ml of *bromothymol blue solution R1*. Not more than 1.0 ml of *0.01 M sodium hydroxide* is required to change the colour of the indicator to blue.

**Chlorides** (*2.4.4*)
Maximum 300 ppm.

Dissolve 0.17 g in 5 ml of *ethanol (96 per cent) R* and dilute to 15 ml with *water R*. When preparing the standard, replace the 5 ml of *water R* by 5 ml of *ethanol (96 per cent) R*.

**Water** (*2.5.12*)
Maximum 1.0 per cent, determined on 2.00 g.

**Sulphated ash** (*2.4.14*)
Maximum 0.1 per cent, determined on 1.0 g.

## ASSAY
Dissolve 0.100 g in 20 ml of *ethanol (96 per cent) R*. Add 10 ml of *dilute sodium hydroxide solution R*, heat in a water-bath for 5 min and cool. Add 20 ml of *dilute nitric acid R*, 25.0 ml of *0.1 M silver nitrate* and 2 ml of *dibutyl phthalate R* and shake vigorously. Add 2 ml of *ferric ammonium sulphate solution R2* and titrate with *0.1 M ammonium thiocyanate* until an orange colour is obtained.

1 ml of *0.1 M silver nitrate* is equivalent to 5.92 mg of C₄H₇Cl₃O.

## STORAGE
In an airtight container.

_____ *Ph Eur*

# Chlorocresol

(*Ph Eur monograph 0384*)

C₇H₇ClO          142.6          59-50-7

**Action and use**
Antiseptic; antimicrobial preservative.

*Ph Eur* _____

## DEFINITION
4-Chloro-3-methylphenol.

**Content**
98.0 per cent to 101.0 per cent.

## CHARACTERS
**Appearance**
White or almost white, crystalline powder or compacted crystalline masses supplied as pellets or colourless or white crystals.

**Solubility**
Slightly soluble in water, very soluble in ethanol (96 per cent), freely soluble in fatty oils. It dissolves in solutions of alkali hydroxides.

## IDENTIFICATION
A. Melting point (*2.2.14*): 64 °C to 67 °C.

B. To 0.1 g add 0.2 ml of *benzoyl chloride R* and 0.5 ml of *dilute sodium hydroxide solution R*. Shake vigorously until a white, crystalline precipitate is formed. Add 5 ml of *water R* and filter. The precipitate, recrystallised from 5 ml of *methanol R* and dried at 70 °C, melts (*2.2.14*) at 85 °C to 88 °C.

C. To 5 ml of solution S (see Tests) add 0.1 ml of *ferric chloride solution R1*. A bluish colour is produced.

## TESTS
**Solution S**
To 3.0 g, finely powdered, add 60 ml of *carbon dioxide-free water R*, shake for 2 min and filter.

**Appearance of solution**
The solution is clear (*2.2.1*) and not more intensely coloured than reference solution BY₆ (*2.2.2, Method II*).

Dissolve 1.25 g in *ethanol (96 per cent) R* and dilute to 25 ml with the same solvent.

## Acidity

To 10 ml of solution S add 0.1 ml of *methyl red solution R*. The solution is orange or red. Not more than 0.2 ml of *0.01 M sodium hydroxide* is required to produce a pure yellow colour.

## Related substances

Gas chromatography (*2.2.28*): use the normalisation procedure.

*Test solution* Dissolve 1.0 g of the substance to be examined in *acetone R* and dilute to 100 ml with the same solvent.

*Column:*
— *material*: glass;
— *size*: $l = 1.80$ m, Ø = 3-4 mm;
— *stationary phase*: *silanised diatomaceous earth for gas chromatography R* impregnated with 3-5 per cent *m/m* of *polymethylphenylsiloxane R*.

*Carrier gas* *nitrogen for chromatography R.*

*Flow rate* 30 ml/min.

*Temperature:*
— *column*: 125 °C;
— *injection port*: 210 °C;
— *detector*: 230 °C.

*Detection* Flame ionisation.

*Run time* 3 times the retention time of chlorocresol.

*Retention time* Chlorocresol = about 8 min.

*Limits:*
— *total*: maximum 1 per cent;
— *disregard limit*: disregard the peak due to the solvent.

## Non-volatile matter

Maximum 0.1 per cent.

Evaporate 2.0 g to dryness on a water-bath and dry the residue at 100-105 °C. The residue weighs not more than 2 mg.

## ASSAY

In a ground-glass-stoppered flask, dissolve 70.0 mg in 30 ml of *glacial acetic acid R*. Add 25.0 ml of *0.0167 M potassium bromate*, 20 ml of a 150 g/l solution of *potassium bromide R* and 10 ml of *hydrochloric acid R*. Allow to stand protected from light for 15 min. Add 1 g of *potassium iodide R* and 100 ml of *water R*. Titrate with *0.1 M sodium thiosulphate*, shaking vigorously and using *1 ml of starch solution R*, added towards the end of the titration, as indicator. Carry out a blank titration.

1 ml of *0.0167 M potassium bromate* is equivalent to 3.565 mg of $C_7H_7ClO$.

## STORAGE

Protected from light.

*Ph Eur*

# Chloroform

CHCl₃          119.4          67-66-3

## Action and use

General anaesthetic; antimicrobial preservative.

## Preparations

Chloroform Spirit

Double-strength Chloroform Water

## DEFINITION

Chloroform is trichloromethane to which either 1.0 to 2.0% of ethanol or 50 mg per litre of amylene has been added.

## CHARACTERISTICS

A colourless, volatile liquid.

Slightly soluble in *water*; miscible with *absolute ethanol*, with *ether*, with fixed and volatile oils and with most organic solvents.

## IDENTIFICATION

The *infrared absorption spectrum*, Appendix II A, of the substance being examined after washing with *water* and drying with *anhydrous sodium sulphate* is concordant with the *reference spectrum* of chloroform (*RS 053*).

## TESTS

### Distillation range

Not more than 5.0% v/v distils below 60° and the remainder distils at 60° to 62°, Appendix V C.

### Weight per ml

1.474 to 1.479 g, Appendix V G.

### Acidity or alkalinity

Shake 10 ml with 20 ml of freshly boiled and cooled *water* for 3 minutes and allow to separate. To 5 ml of the aqueous layer add 0.1 ml of neutral *litmus solution*. The colour produced is the same as that produced on adding 0.1 ml of the neutral litmus solution to 5 ml of freshly boiled and cooled *water*.

### Chloride

To 5 ml of the aqueous layer obtained in the test for Acidity or alkalinity add 5 ml of *water* and 0.2 ml of *silver nitrate solution*. The solution is *clear*, Appendix IV A.

### Free chlorine

To 10 ml of the aqueous layer obtained in the test for Acidity or alkalinity add 1 ml of a 5.0% w/v solution of *zinc iodide* and 0.1 ml of *starch mucilage*. No blue colour is produced.

### Aldehyde

Shake 5 ml with 5 ml of *water* and 0.2 ml of *alkaline potassium tetraiodomercurate solution* in a glass-stoppered flask and allow to stand in the dark for 15 minutes. Not more than a pale yellow colour is produced.

### Foreign chlorine compounds

Shake 20 ml for 5 minutes with 10 ml of *sulphuric acid* in a glass-stoppered flask previously rinsed with *sulphuric acid*, allow to stand in the dark for 30 minutes and discard the acid layer. Shake 15 ml of the chloroform layer with 30 ml of *water* in a glass-stoppered flask for 3 minutes and allow to separate. To the aqueous layer add 0.2 ml of *silver nitrate solution* and allow to stand in the dark for 5 minutes. No opalescence is produced.

### Related substances

Carry out the method for *gas chromatography*, Appendix III B, injecting 0.1 μl of each of the following solutions. Solution (1) contains 0.2% v/v of *carbon tetrachloride*, 0.2% v/v of *1,1,1-trichloroethane* (internal standard), 0.2% v/v of *dichloromethane*, 0.2% v/v of *ethanol*, 0.5% v/v of *bromochloromethane* and 0.2% v/v of the substance being examined in *propan-1-ol*. Solution (2) is the substance being examined. Solution (3) contains 0.2% v/v of the internal standard in the substance being examined. Solution (4) is *propan-1-ol*.

The chromatographic procedure may be carried out using a glass column (4 m × 3.0 mm) packed with *acid-washed kieselguhr* (60 to 100 mesh) coated with 15% w/w of *di-2-cyanoethyl ether* and maintained at 40° with both the inlet port and the detector at 100° and a flow rate of 30 ml per minute for the carrier gas.

The test is not valid unless the *column efficiency*, determined using the chloroform peak in the chromatogram obtained with solution (1), is greater than 700 plates per metre and the total number of plates is greater than 2,500.

In the chromatogram obtained with solution (1) the peaks, in order of emergence, are due to carbon tetrachloride, 1,1,1-trichloroethane, dichloromethane, chloroform, ethanol, bromochloromethane and propan-1-ol (solvent).

Using the chromatogram obtained with solution (4), make any corrections due to the contribution of *secondary peaks* from the solvent to the peaks in the chromatogram obtained with solution (1).

In the chromatogram obtained with solution (3), the ratio of the areas of any peaks due to carbon tetrachloride, dichloromethane and bromochloromethane to the area of the peak due to the internal standard is not greater than the corresponding ratios in the chromatogram obtained with solution (1) and the ratio of the area of any other *secondary peak* that elutes prior to the solvent peak, except for the peak corresponding to ethanol, to the area of the peak due to the internal standard is not greater than the ratio of the area of the peak due to chloroform to the area of the peak due to the internal standard in the chromatogram obtained with solution (1).

Calculate the percentage content of each of the specified impurities and also calculate the percentage content of each of any other impurities assuming the same response per unit volume as for chloroform. The total content of all impurities is not more than 1.0% v/v.

**Ethanol**

Carry out the following test for Chloroform that contains ethanol. Carry out the method for *gas chromatography*, Appendix III B, injecting 0.1 µl of each of the following solutions. Solution (1) contains 1.0% v/v of *absolute ethanol* and 1.0% v/v of *propan-1-ol* (internal standard) in *water*. Solution (2) is the substance being examined. Solution (3) contains 1.0% v/v of the internal standard in the substance being examined.

The chromatographic procedure described under Related substances may be used.

The test is not valid unless the height of the trough separating the ethanol peak from the chloroform peak in the chromatogram obtained with solution (2) is less than 15% of the height of the ethanol peak.

Calculate the percentage content of ethanol from the areas of the peaks due to ethanol and the internal standard in the chromatograms obtained with solutions (1) and (3).

**Non-volatile matter**

25 ml, when evaporated to dryness and dried at 105°, leaves not more than 1 mg of residue.

**STORAGE**

Chloroform should be kept in a well-closed container with a glass stopper or other suitable closure and protected from light.

**LABELLING**

The label states whether it contains ethanol or amylene.

**IMPURITIES**

A. carbon tetrachloride,

B. dichloromethane,

C. bromochloromethane

# Chloroquine Phosphate

*(Ph Eur monograph 0544)*

and enantiomer

, 2 H₃PO₄

$C_{18}H_{26}ClN_3,2H_3PO_4$     515.9     50-63-5

**Action and use**

Antiprotozoal (malaria).

**Preparation**

Chloroquine Phosphate Tablets

*Ph Eur*

**DEFINITION**

Chloroquine phosphate contains not less than 98.5 per cent and not more than the equivalent of 101.0 per cent of $N^4$-(7-chloroquinolin-4-yl)-$N^1$,$N^1$-diethylpentane-1,4-diamine bis(dihydrogen phosphate), calculated with reference to the dried substance.

**CHARACTERS**

A white or almost white, crystalline powder, hygroscopic, freely soluble in water, very slightly soluble in alcohol and in methanol.

It exists in 2 forms, one of which melts at about 195 °C and the other at about 218 °C.

**IDENTIFICATION**

*First identification   B, D.*

*Second identification   A, C, D.*

A. Dissolve 0.100 g in *water R* and dilute to 100.0 ml with the same solvent. Dilute 1.0 ml of this solution to 100.0 ml with *water R*. Examined between 210 nm and 370 nm (*2.2.25*), the solution shows absorption maxima at 220 nm, 235 nm, 256 nm, 329 nm and 342 nm. The specific absorbances at the maxima are respectively 600 to 660, 350 to 390, 300 to 330, 325 to 355 and 360 to 390.

B. Examine by infrared absorption spectrophotometry (*2.2.24*), comparing with the spectrum obtained with the base isolated from *chloroquine sulphate CRS*. Record the spectra using solutions prepared as follows: dissolve separately 0.1 g of the substance to be examined and 80 mg of the reference substance in 10 ml of *water R*, add 2 ml of *dilute sodium hydroxide solution R* and shake with 2 quantities, each of 20 ml, of *methylene chloride R*; combine the organic layers, wash with *water R*, dry over *anhydrous sodium sulphate R*, evaporate to dryness and dissolve the residues separately, each in 2 ml of *methylene chloride R*.

C. Dissolve 25 mg in 20 ml of *water R* and add 8 ml of *picric acid solution R1*. The precipitate, washed with *water R*, with *alcohol R* and finally with *methylene chloride R*, melts (*2.2.14*) at 206-209 °C.

D. Dissolve 0.1 g in 10 ml of *water R*, add 2 ml of *dilute sodium hydroxide solution R* and shake with 2 quantities, each of 20 ml, of *methylene chloride R*. The aqueous layer, acidified by the addition of *nitric acid R*, gives reaction (b) of phosphates (*2.3.1*).

## TESTS
### Solution S
Dissolve 2.5 g in *carbon dioxide-free water R* and dilute to 25 ml with the same solvent.

### Appearance of solution
Solution S is clear (*2.2.1*) and not more intensely coloured than reference solution $BY_5$ or $GY_5$ (*2.2.2, Method II*).

### pH (*2.2.3*)
The pH of solution S is 3.8 to 4.3.

### Related substances
Examine by thin-layer chromatography (*2.2.27*), using silica gel $GF_{254}$ R as the coating substance.

*Test solution*   Dissolve 0.50 g of the substance to be examined in *water R* and dilute to 10 ml with the same solvent.

*Reference solution (a)*   Dilute 1 ml of the test solution to 100 ml with *water R*.

*Reference solution (b)*   Dilute 5 ml of reference solution (a) to 10 ml with *water R*.

Apply to the plate 2 µl of each solution. Develop over a path of 12 cm using a mixture of 10 volumes of *diethylamine R*, 40 volumes of *cyclohexane R* and 50 volumes of *chloroform R*. Allow the plate to dry in air. Examine in ultraviolet light at 254 nm. Any spot in the chromatogram obtained with the test solution, apart from the principal spot, is not more intense than the spot in the chromatogram obtained with reference solution (a) (1.0 per cent) and not more than one such spot is more intense than the spot in the chromatogram obtained with reference solution (b) (0.5 per cent).

### Heavy metals (*2.4.8*)
Dissolve 2.0 g in 10 ml of *water R*. Add 5 ml of *concentrated ammonia R* and shake with 40 ml of *methylene chloride R*. Filter the aqueous layer and neutralise the filtrate with *glacial acetic acid R*. Heat on a water-bath to eliminate methylene chloride, allow to cool and dilute to 20.0 ml with *water R*. 12 ml of this solution complies with limit test A for heavy metals (20 ppm). Prepare the standard using *lead standard solution (2 ppm Pb) R*.

### Loss on drying (*2.2.32*)
Maximum 2.0 per cent, determined on 1.000 g by drying in an oven at 105 °C.

## ASSAY
Dissolve 0.200 g in 50 ml of *anhydrous acetic acid R*. Titrate with *0.1 M perchloric acid* determining the end-point potentiometrically (*2.2.20*).

1 ml of *0.1 M perchloric acid* is equivalent to 25.79 mg of $C_{18}H_{32}ClN_3O_8P_2$.

## STORAGE
In an airtight container, protected from light.

_____ *Ph Eur*

# Chloroquine Sulphate

(*Ph Eur monograph 0545*)

and enantiomer

, $H_2SO_4$ , $H_2O$

$C_{18}H_{26}ClN_3,H_2SO_4,H_2O$    436.0    *132-73-0*

### Action and use
Antiprotozoal (malaria).

### Preparations
Chloroquine Sulphate Injection
Chloroquine Sulphate Tablets

*Ph Eur* _____

## DEFINITION
Chloroquine sulphate contains not less than 98.5 per cent and not more than the equivalent of 101.0 per cent of $N^4$-(7-chloroquinolin-4-yl)-$N^1$,$N^1$-diethylpentane-1,4-diamine sulphate, calculated with reference to the anhydrous substance.

## CHARACTERS
A white or almost white, crystalline powder, freely soluble in water and in methanol, very slightly soluble in ethanol (96 per cent).

It melts at about 208 °C (instantaneous method).

## IDENTIFICATION
*First identification   B, D.*

*Second identification   A, C, D.*

A. Dissolve 0.100 g in *water R* and dilute to 100.0 ml with the same solvent. Dilute 1.0 ml of this solution to 100.0 ml with *water R*. Examined between 210 nm and 370 nm (*2.2.25*), the solution shows absorption maxima at 220 nm, 235 nm, 256 nm, 329 nm and 342 nm. The specific absorbances at the maxima are respectively 730 to 810, 430 to 470, 370 to 410, 400 to 440 and 430 to 470.

B. Examine by infrared absorption spectrophotometry (*2.2.24*), comparing with the spectrum obtained with the base isolated from *chloroquine sulphate CRS*. Record the spectra using solutions prepared as follows: dissolve separately 0.1 g of the substance to be examined and of the reference substance in 10 ml of *water R*, add 2 ml of *dilute sodium hydroxide solution R* and shake with 2 quantities, each of 20 ml, of *methylene chloride R;* combine the organic layers, wash with *water R*, dry over *anhydrous sodium sulphate R*, evaporate to dryness and dissolve the residues separately each in 2 ml of *methylene chloride R*.

C. Dissolve 25 mg in 20 ml of *water R* and add 8 ml of *picric acid solution R1*. The precipitate, washed with *water R*, with *ethanol (96 per cent) R* and finally with *ether R*, melts (*2.2.14*) at 206 °C to 209 °C.

D. It gives reaction (a) of sulphates (*2.3.1*).

## TESTS
### Solution S
Dissolve 2.0 g in *carbon dioxide-free water R* and dilute to 25 ml with the same solvent.

**Appearance of solution**

Solution S is clear (2.2.1) and not more intensely coloured than reference solution $BY_5$ or $GY_5$ (2.2.2, Method II).

**pH** (2.2.3)

The pH of solution S is 4.0 to 5.0.

**Related substances**

Examine by thin-layer chromatography (2.2.27), using *silica gel GF*$_{254}$ *R* as the coating substance.

*Test solution* Dissolve 0.50 g of the substance to be examined in *water R* and dilute to 10 ml with the same solvent.

*Reference solution (a)* Dilute 1 ml of the test solution to 100 ml with *water R*.

*Reference solution (b)* Dilute 5 ml of reference solution (a) to 10 ml with *water R*.

Apply separately to the plate 2 µl of each solution. Develop over a path of 12 cm using a mixture of 10 volumes of *diethylamine R*, 40 volumes of *cyclohexane R* and 50 volumes of *methylene chloride R*. Allow the plate to dry in air. Examine in ultraviolet light at 254 nm. Any spot in the chromatogram obtained with the test solution, apart from the principal spot, is not more intense than the spot in the chromatogram obtained with reference solution (a) (1.0 per cent) and not more than one such spot is more intense than the spot in the chromatogram obtained with reference solution (b) (0.5 per cent).

**Heavy metals** (2.4.8)

Dissolve 2.0 g in 10 ml of *water R*. Add 5 ml of *concentrated ammonia R* and shake with 40 ml of *ether R*. Filter the aqueous layer and neutralise the filtrate with *glacial acetic acid R*. Heat on a water-bath to eliminate ether, allow to cool and dilute to 20.0 ml with *water R*. 12 ml of this solution complies with test A (20 ppm). Prepare the reference solution using *lead standard solution (2 ppm Pb) R*.

**Water** (2.5.12)

3.0 per cent to 5.0 per cent, determined on 0.500 g.

**Sulphated ash** (2.4.14)

Not more than 0.1 per cent, determined on 1.0 g.

**ASSAY**

Dissolve 0.400 g in 50 ml of *anhydrous acetic acid R*. Titrate with *0.1 M perchloric acid* determining the end-point potentiometrically (2.2.20).

1 ml of *0.1 M perchloric acid* is equivalent to 41.8 mg of $C_{18}H_{28}ClN_3O_4S$.

**STORAGE**

Store in an airtight container, protected from light.

_____ *Ph Eur*

# Chlorothiazide

(*Ph Eur monograph 0385*)

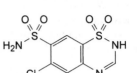

$C_7H_6ClN_3O_4S_2$     295.7     58-94-6

**Action and use**

Diuretic.

*Ph Eur* _____

**DEFINITION**

Chlorothiazide contains not less than 98.0 per cent and not more than the equivalent of 102.0 per cent of 6-chloro-2*H*-1,2,4-benzothiadiazine-7-sulphonamide 1,1-dioxide, calculated with reference to the dried substance.

**CHARACTERS**

A white or almost white, crystalline powder, very slightly soluble in water, sparingly soluble in acetone, slightly soluble in alcohol. It dissolves in dilute solutions of alkali hydroxides.

**IDENTIFICATION**

*First identification* B, C.

*Second identification* A, C, D.

A. Dissolve 80.0 mg in 100 ml of *0.1 M sodium hydroxide* and dilute to 1000.0 ml with *water R*. Dilute 10.0 ml of the solution to 100.0 ml with *0.01 M sodium hydroxide*. Examined between 220 nm and 320 nm (2.2.25), the solution shows 2 absorption maxima, at 225 nm and 292 nm, and a shoulder at about 310 nm. The specific absorbances at the maxima are 725 to 800 and 425 to 455, respectively.

B. Examine by infrared absorption spectrophotometry (2.2.24), comparing with the spectrum obtained with *chlorothiazide CRS*.

C. Examine by thin-layer chromatography (2.2.27), using *silica gel GF*$_{254}$ *R* as the coating substance.

*Test solution* Dissolve 25 mg of the substance to be examined in *acetone R* and dilute to 5 ml with the same solvent.

*Reference solution* Dissolve 25 mg of *chlorothiazide CRS* in *acetone R* and dilute to 5 ml with the same solvent.

Apply to the plate 2 µl of each solution. Develop over a path of 10 cm using *ethyl acetate R*. Dry the plate in a current of air and examine in ultraviolet light at 254 nm. The principal spot in the chromatogram obtained with the test solution is similar in position and size to the principal spot in the chromatogram obtained with the reference solution.

D. To 0.1 g add a pellet of *sodium hydroxide R* and heat strongly. Gas is evolved which turns *red litmus paper R* blue. After cooling, take up the residue with 10 ml of *dilute hydrochloric acid R*. Gas is evolved which turns lead *acetate paper R* black.

**TESTS**

**Solution S**

To 1.0 g of the powdered substance to be examined add 50 ml of *water R*, shake for 2 min and filter.

**Acidity or alkalinity**

To 10 ml of solution S add 0.2 ml of *0.01 M sodium hydroxide* and 0.15 ml of *methyl red solution R*. The solution is yellow. Not more than 0.4 ml of *0.01 M hydrochloric acid* is required to change the colour of the indicator to red.

**Related substances**

Examine by thin-layer chromatography (*2.2.27*), using *silica gel G R* as the coating substance.

*Test solution*  Dissolve 25 mg of the substance to be examined in *acetone R* and dilute to 5 ml with the same solvent.

*Reference solution*  Dilute 1 ml of the test solution to 100 ml with *acetone R*.

Apply to the plate 5 µl of each solution. Develop over a path of 15 cm using a mixture of 15 volumes of *2-propanol R* and 85 volumes of *ethyl acetate R*. Dry the plate in a current of air until the solvents have evaporated (about 10 min) and spray with a mixture of equal volumes of *alcoholic solution of sulphuric acid R* and *alcohol R*; use about 10 ml for a plate 200 mm square and spray in small portions, allowing the solvent to evaporate each time to avoid excessive wetting. Heat at 100-105 °C for 30 min and immediately place the plate above, but not in contact with, 10 ml of a saturated solution of *sodium nitrite R* in a glass tank. Carefully add 0.5 ml of *sulphuric acid R* to the sodium nitrite solution, close the tank, and allow to stand for 15 min. Remove the plate, heat in a ventilated oven at 40 °C for 15 min and spray with 3 quantities, each of 5 ml, of a freshly prepared 5 g/l solution of *naphthylethylenediamine dihydrochloride R* in *alcohol R*. Examine the plate by transmitted light. Any spot in the chromatogram obtained with the test solution, apart from the principal spot, is not more intense than the spot in the chromatogram obtained with the reference solution (1.0 per cent).

**Chlorides** (*2.4.4*)

15 ml of solution S complies with the limit test for chlorides (160 ppm).

**Heavy metals** (*2.4.8*)

1.0 g complies with limit test C for heavy metals (20 ppm). Prepare the standard using 2 ml of *lead standard solution (10 ppm Pb) R*.

**Loss on drying** (*2.2.32*)

Not more than 1.0 per cent, determined on 1.000 g by drying in an oven at 105 °C.

**Sulphated ash** (*2.4.14*)

Not more than 0.1 per cent, determined on 1.0 g.

**ASSAY**

Dissolve 0.250 g in 50 ml of *dimethylformamide R*. Titrate with *0.1 M tetrabutylammonium hydroxide* in 2-propanol determining the end-point potentiometrically (*2.2.20*) at the first point of inflexion. Carry out a blank titration.

1 ml of *0.1 M tetrabutylammonium hydroxide* in 2-propanol is equivalent to 29.57 mg of $C_7H_6ClN_3O_4S_2$.

_____ *Ph Eur*

# Chloroxylenol

$C_8H_9ClO$       156.6       *88-04-0*

**Action and use**

Antiseptic.

**Preparation**

Chloroxylenol Solution

## DEFINITION

Chloroxylenol is 4-chloro-3,5-xylenol. It contains not less than 98.0% and not more than 103.0% of $C_8H_9ClO$.

## CHARACTERISTICS

White or cream crystals or crystalline powder. It is volatile in steam.

Very slightly soluble in *water*, freely soluble in *ethanol (96%)*; soluble in *ether*, in terpenes and in fixed oils. It dissolves in solutions of the alkali hydroxides.

## IDENTIFICATION

A. The *infrared absorption spectrum*, Appendix II A, is concordant with the *reference spectrum* of chloroxylenol (*RS 055*).

B. Dissolve 0.1 g in 5 ml of *chloroform* and add 0.5 ml of a filtered 1% w/v solution of *anhydrous iron(III) chloride* in *chloroform* and 0.1 ml of *pyridine*. A blue colour is produced.

C. To 5 ml of a saturated solution in *water* add 0.5 ml of *iron(III) chloride solution R1*. No blue colour is produced.

D. Mix 50 mg with 0.5 g of *anhydrous sodium carbonate* and ignite strongly, cool, boil the residue with 5 ml of *water*, acidify with *nitric acid*, filter and add *silver nitrate solution*. A white precipitate is produced.

## TESTS

**Melting point**

114° to 116°, Appendix V A.

**Related substances**

Carry out the method for *gas chromatography*, Appendix III B, using solutions in *chloroform* containing (1) 2.0% w/v of the substance being examined and (2) 2.0% w/v of the substance being examined and 0.040% w/v of *4-chloro-o-cresol* (internal standard).

The chromatographic procedure may be carried out using a glass column (1.5 m × 4 mm) packed with *acid-washed diatomaceous support* (80 to 100 mesh) coated with 3% w/w of polyethylene glycol (Carbowax 20M is suitable) and maintained at 160°.

In the chromatogram obtained with solution (2) the sum of the areas of any *secondary peaks* is not greater than the area of the peak due to the internal standard.

## ASSAY

Dissolve 70 mg in 30 ml of *glacial acetic acid*, add 25 ml of 0.0167M *potassium bromate VS*, 20 ml of a 15% w/v solution of *potassium bromide* and 10 ml of *hydrochloric acid*, stopper the flask and allow to stand protected from light for 15 minutes. Add 1 g of *potassium iodide* and 100 ml of *water* and titrate with 0.1M *sodium thiosulphate VS*, shaking vigorously and using 1 ml of *starch solution*, added towards the end of the titration, as indicator. Repeat the operation without the substance being examined. The difference between the titrations represents the amount of potassium bromate required. Each ml of 0.0167M *potassium bromate VS* is equivalent to 3.915 mg of $C_8H_9ClO$.

# Chlorphenamine Maleate

*(Ph Eur monograph 0386)*

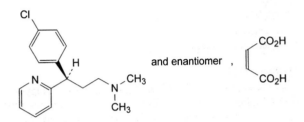

$C_{16}H_{19}ClN_2,C_4H_4O_4$    390.9    *113-92-8*

## Action and use
Histamine $H_1$ receptor antagonist; antihistamine.

## Preparations
Chlorphenamine Injection

Chlorphenamine Oral Solution

Chlorphenamine Tablets

*Ph Eur* _____

## DEFINITION
(3*RS*)-3-(4-Chlorophenyl)-*N*,*N*-dimethyl-3-(pyridin-2-yl)propan-1-amine hydrogen (*Z*)-butenedioate.

## Content
98.0 per cent to 101.0 per cent (dried substance).

## CHARACTERS
### Appearance
White or almost white, crystalline powder.

### Solubility
Freely soluble in water, soluble in ethanol (96 per cent).

## IDENTIFICATION
A. Melting point (*2.2.14*): 130 °C to 135 °C.

B. Infrared absorption spectrophotometry (*2.2.24*).

*Comparison*   chlorphenamine maleate CRS.

C. Optical rotation (see Tests).

## TESTS
### Solution S
Dissolve 2.0 g in *water R* and dilute to 20.0 ml with the same solvent.

### Appearance of solution
Solution S is clear (*2.2.1*) and not more intensely coloured than reference solution $BY_6$ (*2.2.2, Method II*).

### Optical rotation (2.2.7)
− 0.10° to + 0.10°, determined on solution S.

### Related substances
Liquid chromatography (*2.2.29*).

*Test solution*   Dissolve 0.100 g of the substance to be examined in the mobile phase and dilute to 100.0 ml with the mobile phase.

*Reference solution (a)*   Dilute 0.5 ml of the test solution to 100.0 ml with the mobile phase.

*Reference solution (b)*   Dilute 1.0 ml of reference solution (a) to 10.0 ml with the mobile phase.

*Reference solution (c)*   Dissolve 5 mg of *chlorphenamine impurity C CRS* in 5 ml of the test solution and dilute to 50.0 ml with the mobile phase. Dilute 2 ml of this solution to 20 ml with the mobile phase.

*Reference solution (d)*   Dissolve 5 mg of *2,2'-dipyridylamine R* (impurity B) in the mobile phase and dilute to 100 ml with the mobile phase.

*Reference solution (e)*   Dissolve the contents of a vial of *chlorphenamine impurity A CRS* in 2 ml of the test solution. Sonicate for 5 min.

*Column:*
— *size: l* = 0.30 m, Ø = 3.9 mm;
— *stationary phase: octadecylsilyl silica gel for chromatography R* (10 µm).

*Mobile phase*   Mix 20 volumes of *acetonitrile R* and 80 volumes of a 8.57 g/l solution of *ammonium dihydrogen phosphate R* previously adjusted to pH 3.0 with *phosphoric acid R*.

*Flow rate*   1.2 ml/min.

*Detection*   Spectrophotometer at 225 nm.

*Injection*   20 µl.

*Run time*   3.5 times the retention time of chlorphenamine.

*Relative retention*   With reference to chlorphenamine (retention time = about 11 min): maleic acid = about 0.2; impurity A = about 0.3; impurity B = about 0.4; impurity C = about 0.9; impurity D = about 3.0.

*System suitability*   Reference solution (c):
— *resolution*: minimum 1.5 between the peaks due to impurity C and chlorphenamine.

*Limits:*
— *correction factors*: for the calculation of contents, multiply the peak areas of the following impurities by the corresponding correction factor: impurity A = 1.5; impurity B = 1.4;
— *impurity A*: not more than 0.4 times the area of the principal peak in the chromatogram obtained with reference solution (a) (0.2 per cent);
— *impurities B, C, D*: for each impurity, not more than 0.2 times the area of the principal peak in the chromatogram obtained with reference solution (a) (0.1 per cent);
— *unspecified impurities*: for each impurity, not more than 0.2 times the area of the principal peak in the chromatogram obtained with reference solution (a) (0.10 per cent);
— *total*: not more than the area of the principal peak in the chromatogram obtained with reference solution (a) (0.5 per cent);
— *disregard limit*: the area of the principal peak in the chromatogram obtained with reference solution (b) (0.05 per cent); disregard the peaks due to the blank and maleic acid.

### Heavy metals (2.4.8)
Maximum 20 ppm.

1.0 g complies with test C. Prepare the reference solution using 2 ml *of lead standard solution (10 ppm Pb) R*.

### Loss on drying (2.2.32)
Maximum 0.5 per cent, determined on 1.000 g by drying in an oven at 105 °C for 4 h.

**Sulphated ash** (*2.4.14*)

Maximum 0.1 per cent, determined on 1.0 g.

**ASSAY**

Dissolve 0.150 g in 25 ml of *anhydrous acetic acid R*. Titrate with *0.1 M perchloric acid*, determining the end-point potentiometrically (*2.2.20*).

1 ml of *0.1 M perchloric acid* is equivalent to 19.54 mg of $C_{20}H_{23}ClN_2O_4$.

**STORAGE**

Protected from light.

**IMPURITIES**

*Specified impurities   A, B, C, D.*

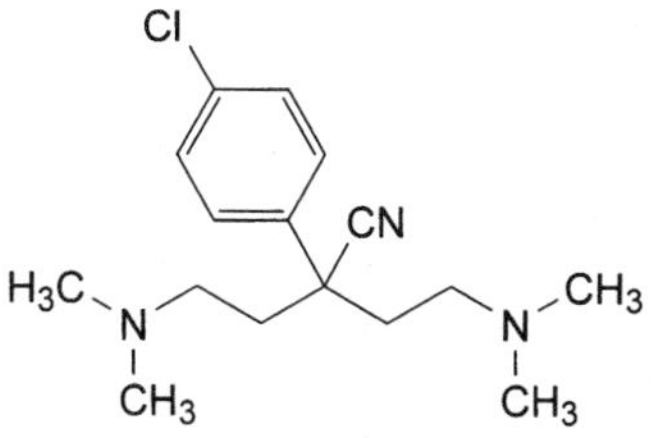

A. 2-(4-chlorophenyl)-4-(dimethylamino)-2-[2-(dimethylamino)ethyl]butanenitrile,

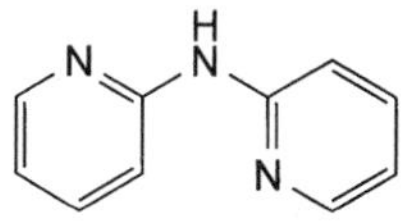

B. *N*-(pyridin-2-yl)pyridin-2-amine (2,2′-dipyridylamine),

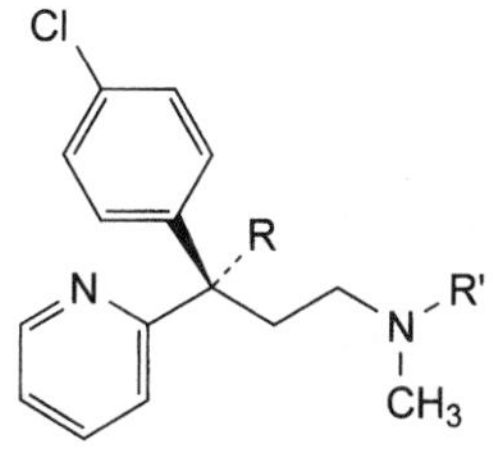

and enantiomer

C. R = R′ = H: (3*RS*)-3-(4-chlorophenyl)-*N*-methyl-3-(pyridin-2-yl)propan-1-amine,

D. R = CN, R′ = CH₃: (2*RS*)-2-(4-chlorophenyl)-4-(dimethylamino)-2-(pyridin-2-yl)butanenitrile.

_____ *Ph Eur*

# Chlorpromazine

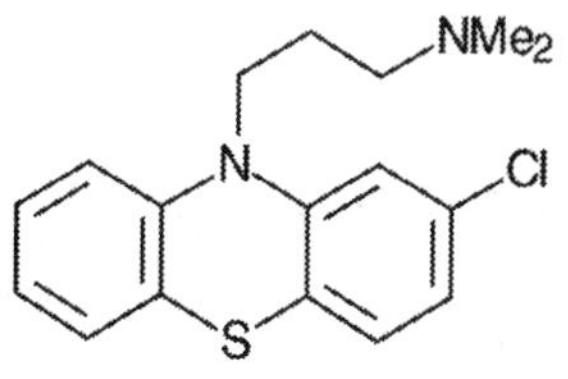

$C_{17}H_{19}ClN_2S$        318.9        50-53-3

**Action and use**

Dopamine receptor antagonist; neuroleptic.

**Preparation**

Chlorpromazine Suppositories

**DEFINITION**

Chlorpromazine is [3-(2-chlorophenothiazin-10-yl)propyl]-dimethylamine. It contains not less than 99.0% and not more than 101.0% of $C_{17}H_{19}ClN_2S$, calculated with reference to the dried substance.

**CHARACTERISTICS**

A white or creamy white powder or waxy solid.

Practically insoluble in *water*; freely soluble in *ethanol (96%)* and in *ether*.

**IDENTIFICATION**

A. The *infrared absorption spectrum*, Appendix II A, is concordant with the *reference spectrum* of chlorpromazine (*RS 056*).

B. Complies with the test for *identification of phenothiazines*, Appendix III A, using *chlorpromazine hydrochloride EPCRS* to prepare solution (2).

**TESTS**

**Melting point**

56° to 58°, Appendix V A.

**Related substances**

Complies with the test for *related substances in phenothiazines*, Appendix III A, using *mobile phase A*.

**Loss on drying**

When dried to constant weight over *phosphorus pentoxide* at a pressure not exceeding 0.7 kPa, loses not more than 0.5% of its weight. Use 1 g.

**Sulphated ash**

Not more than 0.1%, Appendix IX A.

**ASSAY**

Dissolve 0.8 g in 300 ml of *acetone* and carry out Method I for *non-aqueous titration*, Appendix VIII A, using 3 ml of a saturated solution of *methyl orange* in *acetone* as indicator. Each ml of 0.1M *perchloric acid VS* is equivalent to 31.89 mg of $C_{17}H_{19}ClN_2S$.

**STORAGE**

Chlorpromazine should be protected from light.

# Chlorpromazine Hydrochloride

(*Ph Eur monograph 0475*)

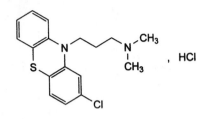

C$_{17}$H$_{19}$ClN$_2$S,HCl      355.3      69-09-0

## Action and use
Dopamine receptor antagonist; neuroleptic.

## Preparations
Chlorpromazine Injection

Chlorpromazine Oral Solution

Chlorpromazine Tablets

*Ph Eur* _____

## DEFINITION
3-(2-Chloro-10*H*-phenothiazin-10-yl)-*N*,*N*-dimethylpropan-1-amine hydrochloride.

## Content
99.0 per cent to 101.0 per cent (dried substance).

## CHARACTERS

### Appearance
White or almost white, crystalline powder.

### Solubility
Very soluble in water, freely soluble in ethanol (96 per cent).

It decomposes on exposure to air and light.

### mp
About 196 °C.

## IDENTIFICATION
*First identification   B, D.*

*Second identification   A, C, D.*

A. Ultraviolet and visible absorption spectrophotometry (*2.2.25*). *Prepare the solutions protected from bright light and measure the absorbances immediately.*

*Test solution*   Dissolve 50.0 mg in a 10.3 g/l solution of *hydrochloric acid R* and dilute to 500.0 ml with the same solution. Dilute 5.0 ml of the solution to 100.0 ml with a 10.3 g/l solution of *hydrochloric acid R*.

*Spectral range*   230-340 nm.

*Absorption maximum*   At 254 nm and 306 nm.

*Specific absorbance at the absorption maximum*
— at 254 nm: 890 to 960.

B. Infrared absorption spectrophotometry (*2.2.24*).

*Comparison   chlorpromazine hydrochloride CRS.*

C. Identification test for phenothiazines by thin-layer chromatography (*2.3.3*): use *chlorpromazine hydrochloride CRS* to prepare the reference solution.

D. It gives reaction (b) of chlorides (*2.3.1*).

## TESTS
**pH** (*2.2.3*)

3.5 to 4.5. Carry out the test protected from light and use freshly prepared solutions.

Dissolve 1.0 g in *carbon dioxide-free water R* and dilute to 10 ml with the same solvent.

### Related substances
Liquid chromatography (*2.2.29*). *Carry out the test protected from light and use freshly prepared solutions.*

*Test solution*   Dissolve 40 mg of the substance to be examined in the mobile phase and dilute to 100.0 ml with the mobile phase.

*Reference solution (a)*   Dissolve 4 mg of *chlorpromazine impurity D CRS* in the mobile phase and dilute to 10.0 ml with the mobile phase. To 1 ml of this solution add 1 ml of the test solution and dilute to 100.0 ml with the mobile phase.

*Reference solution (b)*   Dilute 1.0 ml of the test solution to 20.0 ml with the mobile phase. Dilute 1.0 ml of this solution to 10.0 ml with the mobile phase.

*Reference solution (c)*   Dissolve 4.0 mg of *chlorpromazine impurity A CRS* in the mobile phase and dilute to 100.0 ml with the mobile phase. Dilute 1.0 ml of this solution to 100.0 ml with the mobile phase.

*Reference solution (d)*   Dissolve 4 mg of *promazine hydrochloride CRS* (impurity C) and 4.0 mg of *chlorpromazine impurity E CRS* in the mobile phase and dilute to 100.0 ml with the mobile phase. Dilute 1.0 ml of this solution to 100.0 ml with the mobile phase.

*Column:*
— *size: l* = 0.25 m, Ø = 4.0 mm,
— *stationary phase: base-deactivated octylsilyl silica gel for chromatography R* (5 µm).

*Mobile phase*   Mix 0.2 volumes of *thiodiethylene glycol R* with 50 volumes of *acetonitrile R* and 50 volumes of a 0.5 per cent *V/V* solution of *trifluoroacetic acid R* previously adjusted to pH 5.3 with *tetramethylethylenediamine R*.

*Flow rate*   1.0 ml/min.

*Detection*   Spectrophotometer at 254 nm.

*Injection*   10 µl.

*Run time*   4 times the retention time of chlorpromazine.

*Relative retention*

With reference to chlorpromazine (retention time = about 8 min): impurity A = about 0.4; impurity B = about 0.5; impurity C = about 0.7; impurity D = about 0.9; impurity E = about 3.4.

*System suitability*   Reference solution (a):
— *resolution*: minimum 2.0 between the peaks due to impurity D and chlorpromazine.

*Limits:*
— *impurity A*: not more than the area of the corresponding peak in the chromatogram obtained with reference solution (c) (0.1 per cent);
— *impurities B, C, D*: for each impurity, not more than 0.6 times the area of the principal peak in the chromatogram obtained with reference solution (b) (0.3 per cent);
— *impurity E*: not more than the area of the corresponding peak in the chromatogram obtained with reference solution (d) (0.1 per cent);
— *any other impurity*: for each impurity, not more than 0.2 times the area of the principal peak in the chromatogram obtained with reference solution (b) (0.1 per cent);
— *total*: not more than twice the area of the principal peak in the chromatogram obtained with reference solution (b) (1.0 per cent);

— *disregard limit*: 0.1 times the area of the principal peak in the chromatogram obtained with reference solution (b) (0.05 per cent).

**Heavy metals** (*2.4.8*)

Maximum 10 ppm.1.0 g complies with test C. Prepare the reference solution using 1 ml of *lead standard solution (10 ppm Pb) R*.

**Loss on drying** (*2.2.32*)

Maximum 0.5 per cent, determined on 1.000 g by drying in an oven at 105 °C.

**Sulphated ash** (*2.4.14*)

Maximum 0.1 per cent, determined on 1.0 g.

## ASSAY

Dissolve 0.250 g in a mixture of 5.0 ml of *0.1 M hydrochloric acid* and 50 ml of *ethanol (96 per cent) R*. Carry out a potentiometric titration (*2.2.20*), using *0.1 M sodium hydroxide*. Read the volume added between the 2 points of inflexion.

1 ml of *0.1 M sodium hydroxide* is equivalent to 35.53 mg of $C_{17}H_{20}Cl_2N_2S$.

## STORAGE

In an airtight container, protected from light.

## IMPURITIES

*Specified impurities*   *A, B, C, D, E.*

A. 3-(2-chloro-10*H*-phenothiazin-10-yl)-*N,N*-dimethylpropan-1-amine *S*-oxide (chlorpromazine sulphoxide),

B. R1 = [CH₂]₃-N(CH₃)₂, R2 = Cl: *N*-[3-(2-chloro-10*H*-phenothiazin-10-yl)propyl]-*N,N',N'*-trimethylpropane-1,2-diamine,

C. R1 = CH₃, R2 = H: promazine,

D. R1 = H, R2 = Cl: 3-(2-chloro-10*H*-phenothiazin-10-yl)-*N*-methylpropan-1-amine (desmethylchlorpromazine),

E. 2-chloro-10*H*-phenothiazine.

# Chlorpropamide

*(Ph Eur monograph 1087)*

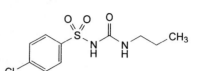

$C_{10}H_{13}ClN_2O_3S$      276.7      94-20-2

**Action and use**

Inhibition of ATP-dependent potassium channels (sulfonylurea); treatment of diabetes mellitus.

**Preparation**

Chlorpropamide Tablets

*Ph Eur*

## DEFINITION

Chlorpropamide contains not less than 99.0 per cent and not more than the equivalent of 101.0 per cent of 1-[(4-chlorophenyl)sulphonyl]-3-propylurea, calculated with reference to the dried substance.

## CHARACTERS

A white or almost white, crystalline powder, practically insoluble in water, freely soluble in acetone and in methylene chloride, soluble in alcohol. It dissolves in dilute solutions of alkali hydroxides.

It shows polymorphism (*5.9*).

## IDENTIFICATION

*First identification*   C, D.

*Second identification*   A, B, D.

A. Melting point (*2.2.14*): 126 °C to 130 °C.

B. Dissolve 0.10 g in *methanol R* and dilute to 50.0 ml with the same solvent. Dilute 5.0 ml of the solution to 100.0 ml with *0.01 M hydrochloric acid*. Dilute 10.0 ml of the solution to 100.0 ml with *0.01 M hydrochloric acid*. Examined between 220 nm and 350 nm (*2.2.25*), the solution shows an absorption maximum at 232 nm. The specific absorption at the maximum is 570 to 630.

C. Examine by infrared absorption spectrophotometry (*2.2.24*), comparing with the spectrum obtained with *chlorpropamide CRS*. Examine the substances prepared as discs. If the spectra obtained show differences, dissolve the substance to be examined and the reference substance in *methylene chloride R*, evaporate to dryness and record the new spectra using the residues.

D. Heat 0.1 g with 2 g of *anhydrous sodium carbonate R* until a dull red colour appears for 10 min. Allow to cool, extract the residue with about 5 ml of *water R*, dilute to 10 ml with *water R* and filter. The solution gives the reaction (a) of chloride (*2.3.1*).

## TESTS

**Related substances**

Examine by thin-layer chromatography (*2.2.27*), using a suitable *silica gel* as the coating substance.

*Test solution*   Dissolve 0.50 g of the substance to be examined in *acetone R* and dilute to 10 ml with the same solvent.

*Reference solution (a)*   Dissolve 15 mg of *4-chlorobenzenesulphonamide R* (chlorpropamide impurity A) in *acetone R* and dilute to 100 ml with the same solvent.

*Reference solution (b)* Dissolve 15 mg of *chlorpropamide impurity B CRS* in *acetone R* and dilute to 100 ml with the same solvent.

*Reference solution (c)* Dilute 0.3 ml of the test solution to 100 ml with *acetone R*.

*Reference solution (d)* Dilute 5 ml of reference solution (c) to 15 ml with *acetone R*.

*Reference solution (e)* Dissolve 0.10 g of the substance to be examined, 5 mg of *4-chlorobenzenesulphonamide R* and 5 mg of *chlorpropamide impurity B CRS* in *acetone R* and dilute to 10 ml with the same solvent.

Apply to the plate 5 µl of each solution. Develop over a path of 15 cm using a mixture of 11.5 volumes of *concentrated ammonia R*, 30 volumes of *cyclohexane R*, 50 volumes of *methanol R* and 100 volumes of *methylene chloride R*. Allow the plate to dry in a current of cold air, heat at 110 °C for 10 min. At the bottom of a chromatographic tank, place an evaporating dish containing a mixture of 1 volume of *hydrochloric acid R*, 1 volume of *water R* and 2 volumes of a 50 g/l solution of *potassium permanganate R*, close the tank and allow to stand for 15 min. Place the dried hot plate in the tank and close the tank. Leave the plate in contact with the chlorine vapour for 2 min. Withdraw the plate and place it in a current of cold air until the excess of chlorine is removed and an area of coating below the points of application does not give a blue colour with a drop of *potassium iodide* and *starch solution R*. Spray with *potassium iodide* and *starch solution R*. In the chromatogram obtained with the test solution: any spot corresponding to impurity A is not more intense than the spot in the chromatogram obtained with reference solution (a) (0.3 per cent); any spot corresponding to impurity B is not more intense than the spot in the chromatogram obtained with reference solution (b) (0.3 per cent); any spot, apart from the principal spot and any spot corresponding to impurity A and B, is not more intense than the spot in the chromatogram obtained with reference solution (c) (0.3 per cent); not more than two such spots are more intense than the spot in the chromatogram obtained with reference solution (d) (0.1 per cent). The test is not valid unless the chromatogram obtained with reference solution (e) shows three clearly separated spots with approximate $R_F$ values of 0.4, 0.6 and 0.9 corresponding to chlorpropamide, impurity A and impurity B respectively.

**Heavy metals** *(2.4.8)*
Dissolve 2.0 g in a mixture of 15 volumes of *water R* and 85 volumes of *acetone R* and dilute to 20 ml with the same mixture of solvents. 12 ml of solution complies with limit test B for heavy metals (20 ppm). Prepare the standard using lead standard solution (2 ppm Pb) prepared by diluting *lead standard solution (100 ppm Pb) R* with a mixture of 15 volumes of *water R* and 85 volumes of *acetone R*.

**Loss on drying** *(2.2.32)*
Not more than 0.5 per cent, determined on 1.000 g by drying in an oven at 100 °C to 105 °C.

**Sulphated ash** *(2.4.14)*
Not more than 0.1 per cent, determined on 1.0 g.

**ASSAY**
Dissolve 0.250 g in 50 ml of *alcohol R* previously neutralised using *phenolphthalein solution R1* as indicator and add 25 ml of *water R*. Titrate with *0.1 M sodium hydroxide* until a pink colour is obtained.

1 ml of *0.1 M sodium hydroxide* is equivalent to 27.67 mg of $C_{10}H_{13}ClN_2O_3S$.

**STORAGE**
Store protected from light.

**IMPURITIES**

A. R = H: 4-chlorobenzenesulphonamide,

C. R = CO-NH₂: [(4-chlorophenyl)sulphonyl]urea.

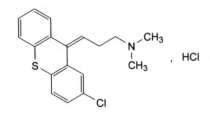

B. 1,3-dipropylurea,

*———————————————————— Ph Eur*

# Chlorprothixene Hydrochloride

*(Ph Eur monograph 0815)*

C₁₈H₁₈ClNS,HCl                 352.3                 6469-93-8

**Action and use**
Dopamine receptor antagonist; neuroleptic.

*Ph Eur ——————————————————————————*

**DEFINITION**
(Z)-3-(2-Chloro-9H-thioxanthen-9-ylidene)-N,N-dimethylpropan-1-amine hydrochloride.

**Content**
99.0 per cent to 101.0 per cent (dried substance).

**CHARACTERS**

**Appearance**
White or almost white, crystalline powder.

**Solubility**
Soluble in water and in alcohol, slightly soluble in methylene chloride.

**mp**
About 220 °C.

**IDENTIFICATION**

*First identification A, E.*

*Second identification B, C, D, E.*

A. Infrared absorption spectrophotometry *(2.2.24)*.

*Preparation* Dissolve 0.25 g in 10 ml of *water R*. Add 1 ml of *dilute sodium hydroxide solution R*. Shake with 20 ml of *methylene chloride R*. Separate the organic layer and wash with 5 ml of *water R*. Evaporate the organic layer to dryness and dry the residue at 40-50 °C. Examine the residues prepared as discs.

*Comparison*   chlorprothixene hydrochloride CRS.

B. Dissolve 0.2 g in a mixture of 5 ml of *dioxan R* and 5 ml of a 1.5 g/l solution of *sodium nitrite R*. Add 0.8 ml of *nitric acid R*. After 10 min add the solution to 20 ml of *water R*. 1 h later filter the precipate formed. The filtrate is used immediately for identification test C. Dissolve the precipitate by warming in about 15 ml of *alcohol R* and add the solution to 10 ml of *water R*. Filter and dry the precipitate at 100-105 °C for 2 h. The melting point (*2.2.14*) is 152 °C to 154 °C.

C. To 1 ml of the filtrate obtained in identification test B, add 0.2 ml of a suspension of 50 mg of *fast red B salt R* in 1 ml of *alcohol R*. Add 1 ml of *0.5 M alcoholic potassium hydroxide*. A dark red colour is produced. Carry out a blank test.

D. Dissolve about 20 mg in 2 ml of *nitric acid R*. A red colour is produced. Add 5 ml of *water R* and examine in ultraviolet light at 365 nm. The solution shows green fluorescence.

E. It gives reaction (a) of chlorides (*2.3.1*).

**TESTS**
**Solution S**
Dissolve 0.25 g in *carbon dioxide-free water R* and dilute to 25 ml with the same solvent.

**Appearance of solution**
Solution S is clear (*2.2.1*) and colourless (*2.2.2, Method II*).

**pH** (*2.2.3*)
4.4 to 5.2 for solution S.

**Related substances**
Liquid chromatography (*2.2.29*). *Carry out the test protected from bright light.*

*Test solution*   Dissolve 20.0 mg of the substance to be examined in the mobile phase and dilute to 20.0 ml with the mobile phase.

*Reference solution (a)*   Dissolve 20.0 mg of *chlorprothixene hydrochloride CRS* (with a defined content of *E*-isomer) in the mobile phase and dilute to 20.0 ml with the mobile phase.

*Reference solution (b)*   Dilute 2.0 ml of the test solution to 100.0 ml with the mobile phase. Dilute 3.0 ml of this solution to 20.0 ml with the mobile phase.

*Column:*
— *size*: $l$ = 0.12 m, Ø = 4.0 mm,
— *stationary phase*: base-deactivated *octadecylsilyl silica gel for chromatography R* (3 µm or 5 µm).

*Mobile phase*   Solution containing 6.0 g/l of *potassium dihydrogen phosphate R*, 2.9 g/l of *sodium laurilsulfate R* and 9 g/l of *tetrabutylammonium bromide R* in a mixture of 50 volumes of *methanol R*, 400 volumes of *acetonitrile R* and 550 volumes of *distilled water R*.

*Flow rate*   1.5 ml/min.

*Detection*   Spectrophotometer at 254 nm.

*Equilibration*   For about 30 min with the mobile phase.

*Injection*   20 µl.

*Run time*   Twice the retention time of chlorprothixene.

*Relative retention*   With reference to chlorprothixene: impurity E = about 1.55.

*System suitability*   Reference solution (a):
— *retention time*: chlorprothixene = about 10 min,
— *relative retention* with reference to chlorprothixene: *E*-isomer = about 1.35.

*Limits:*
— *E-isomer*: not more than 2.0 per cent, calculated from the area of the corresponding peak in the chromatogram obtained with reference solution (a) and taking into account the assigned content of this isomer in *chlorprothixene hydrochloride CRS*,
— *impurity E*: not more than 3 times the area of the principal peak in the chromatogram obtained with reference solution (b) (0.3 per cent taking into account a response factor of 3),
— *any other impurity*: not more than the area of the principal peak in the chromatogram obtained with reference solution (b) (0.3 per cent),
— *total* of any other impurity: not more than 2.33 times the area of the principal peak in the chromatogram obtained with reference solution (b) (0.7 per cent),
— *disregard limit*: 0.1 times the area of the principal peak in the chromatogram obtained with reference solution (b) (0.03 per cent).

**Heavy metals** (*2.4.8*)
Maximum 20 ppm.

1.0 g complies with limit test F. Prepare the standard using 2 ml *of lead standard solution (10 ppm Pb) R*.

**Loss on drying** (*2.2.32*)
Maximum 0.5 per cent, determined on 1.000 g by drying *in vacuo* at 60 °C for 3 h.

**Sulphated ash** (*2.4.14*)
Maximum 0.1 per cent, determined on 1.0 g.

**ASSAY**
Dissolve 0.300 g in a mixture of 5.0 ml of *0.01 M hydrochloric acid* and 50 ml of *alcohol R*. Carry out a potentiometric titration (*2.2.20*), using *0.1 M sodium hydroxide*. Read the volume added between the 2 points of inflexion.

1 ml of *0.1 M sodium hydroxide* is equivalent to 35.23 mg of $C_{18}H_{19}Cl_2NS$.

**STORAGE**
Protected from light.

**IMPURITIES**
*Specified impurities*   A, B, C, D, E, F.

A. (*RS*)-2-chloro-9-[3-(dimethylamino)propyl]-9*H*-thioxanthen-9-ol,

B. R1 = H, R2 = CH-CH₂-CH₂-N(CH₃)₂, R3 = H:
*N,N*-dimethyl-3-(9*H*-thioxanthen-9-ylidene)propan-1-amine,

C R1 = Cl, R2 = CH-CH₂-CH₂-NH-CH₃, R3 = H: (Z)-3-(2-chloro-9H-thioxanthen-9-ylidene)-N-methylpropan-1-amine,

D. R1 = H, R2 = CH-CH₂-CH₂-N(CH₃)₂, R3 = Cl: (Z)-3-(4-chloro-9H-thioxanthen-9-ylidene)-N,N-dimethylpropan-1-amine,

E. R1 = Cl, R2 = O, R3 = H: 2-chloro-9H-thioxanthen-9-one,

F. (E)-3-(2-chloro-9H-thioxanthen-9-ylidene)-N,N-dimethylpropan-1-amine (E-isomer).

*Ph Eur*

# Chlortalidone

(*Ph Eur monograph 0546*)

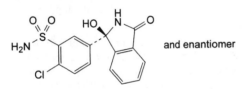

and enantiomer

C₁₄H₁₁ClN₂O₄S          338.8          77-36-1

**Action and use**
Thiazide-like diuretic.

**Preparations**
Chlortalidone Tablets
Co-tenidone Tablets

*Ph Eur*

## DEFINITION
2-Chloro-5-[(1RS)-1-hydroxy-3-oxo-2,3-dihydro-1H-isoindol-1-yl]benzenesulphonamide.

## Content
97.0 per cent to 102.0 per cent (dried substance).

## CHARACTERS
**Appearance**
White or yellowish-white powder.

**Solubility**
Very slightly soluble in water, soluble in acetone and in methanol, practically insoluble in methylene chloride.
It dissolves in dilute solutions of alkali hydroxides.

It shows polymorphism (5.9)

## IDENTIFICATION
Infrared absorption spectrophotometry (2.2.24).

*Comparison* chlortalidone CRS.

If the spectra obtained in the solid state show differences, dissolve the substance to be examined and the reference substance separately in *methanol R*, evaporate to dryness and record new spectra using the residues.

## TESTS
**Acidity**
Dissolve 1.0 g with heating in a mixture of 25 ml of *acetone R* and 25 ml of *carbon dioxide-free water R*. Cool. Titrate with *0.1 M sodium hydroxide*, determining the end-point potentiometrically (2.2.20). Not more than 0.75 ml of *0.1 M sodium hydroxide* is required.

**Related substances**
Liquid chromatography (2.2.29).

*Solvent mixture* Mix 2 volumes of a 2 g/l solution of *sodium hydroxyde R*, 48 volumes of mobile phase B and 50 volumes of mobile phase A.

*Test solution (a)* Dissolve 50.0 mg of the substance to be examined in the solvent mixture and dilute to 50.0 ml with the solvent mixture.

*Test solution (b)* Dilute 10.0 ml of test solution (a) to 100.0 ml with the solvent mixture.

*Reference solution (a)* Dilute 1.0 ml of test solution (a) to 100.0 ml with the solvent mixture. Dilute 1.0 ml of this solution to 10.0 ml with the solvent mixture.

*Reference solution (b)* Dissolve the contents of a vial of *chlortalidone for peak identification CRS* (containing impurities B, G and J) in 1 ml of the solvent mixture.

*Reference solution (c)* Dissolve 50.0 mg of *chlortalidone CRS* in the solvent mixture and dilute to 50.0 ml with the solvent mixture. Dilute 10.0 ml of this solution to 100.0 ml with the solvent mixture.

*Column:*
— size: l = 0.25 m, Ø = 4.6 mm;
— stationary phase: octylsilyl silica gel for chromatography R (5 µm);
— temperature: 40 °C.

*Mobile phase:*
— mobile phase A: dissolve 1.32 g of *ammonium phosphate R* in about 900 ml of *water R* and adjust to pH 5.5 with *dilute phosphoric acid R*; dilute to 1000 ml with *water R*;
— mobile phase B: *methanol R2*;

| Time (min) | Mobile phase A (per cent V/V) | Mobile phase B (per cent V/V) |
|---|---|---|
| 0 - 16 | 65 | 35 |
| 16 - 21 | 65 → 50 | 35 → 50 |
| 21 - 35 | 50 | 50 |
| 35 - 45 | 50 → 65 | 50 → 35 |

*Flow rate* 1.4 ml/min.

*Detection* Spectrophotometer at 220 nm.

*Injection* 20 µl of test solution (a) and reference solutions (a) and (b).

*Identification of impurities* Use the chromatogram obtained with reference solution (b) and the chromatogram supplied with *chlortalidone for peak identification CRS* to identify the peaks due to impurities B, G and J.

*Relative retention* With reference to chlortalidone (retention time = about 7 min): impurity B = about 0.7; impurity J = about 0.9; impurity G = about 6.

*System suitability* Reference solution (b):
— resolution: minimum 1.5 between the peaks due to impurity J and chlortalidone.

*Limits:*
— impurity B: not more than 7 times the area of the principal peak in the chromatogram obtained with reference solution (a) (0.7 per cent);

— *impurity J*: not more than 3 times the area of the principal peak in the chromatogram obtained with reference solution (a) (0.3 per cent);

— impurity G: not more than 2 times the area of the principal peak in the chromatogram obtained with reference solution (a) (0.2 per cent);

— *unspecified impurities*: for each impurity, not more than the area of the principal peak in the chromatogram obtained with reference solution (a) (0.10 per cent);

— *total*: not more than 12 times the area of the principal peak in the chromatogram obtained with reference solution (a) (1.2 per cent);

— *disregard limit*: 0.5 times the area of the principal peak in the chromatogram obtained with reference solution (a) (0.05 per cent).

**Chlorides** (*2.4.4*)

Maximum 350 ppm.

Triturate 0.3 g finely, add 30 ml of *water R*, shake for 5 min and filter. 15 ml of the filtrate complies with the test. Prepare the standard using 10 ml of *chloride standard solution (5 ppm Cl) R*.

**Loss on drying** (*2.2.32*)

Maximum 0.5 per cent, determined on 1.000 g by drying in an oven at 105 °C.

**Sulphated ash** (*2.4.14*)

Maximum 0.1 per cent, determined on 1.0 g.

**ASSAY**

Liquid chromatography (*2.2.29*) as described in the test for related substances with the following modification.

*Injection*   20 µl of test solution (b) and reference solution (c).

Calculate the percentage content of $C_{14}H_{11}ClN_2O_4S$ from the declared content of *chlortalidone CRS*.

**IMPURITIES**

*Specified impurities   B, G, J.*

*Other detectable impurities* (the following substances would, if present at a sufficient level, be detected by one or other of the tests in the monograph. They are limited by the general acceptance criterion for other/unspecified impurities and/or by the general monograph *Substances for pharmaceutical use (2034)*. It is therefore not necessary to identify these impurities for demonstration of compliance. See also *5.10. Control of impurities in substances for pharmaceutical use)*: *A, C, D, E, F, H, I.*

A. R = H, R′ = OH:
2-(4-chloro-3-sulphobenzoyl)benzoic acid,

B. R = H, R′ = NH₂:
2-(4-chloro-3-sulphamoylbenzoyl)benzoic acid,

C. R = C₂H₅, R′ = NH₂:
ethyl 2-(4-chloro-3-sulphamoylbenzoyl)benzoate,

I. R = CH(CH₃)₂, R′ = NH₂:
1-methylethyl 2-(4-chloro-3-sulphamoylbenzoyl)benzoate,

D. R = OC₂H₅, R′ = SO₂-NH₂: 2-chloro-5-[(1*RS*)-1-ethoxy-3-oxo-2,3-dihydro-1*H*-isoindol-1-yl]benzenesulphonamide,

E. R = H, R′ = SO₂-NH₂: 2-chloro-5-[(1*RS*)-3-oxo-2,3-dihydro-1*H*-isoindol-1-yl]benzenesulphonamide,

G. R = OH, R′ = Cl: (3*RS*)-3-(3,4-dichlorophenyl)-3-hydroxy-2,3-dihydro-1*H*-isoindol-1-one,

H. R = OCH(CH₃)₂, R′ = SO₂-NH₂: 2-chloro-5-[(1*RS*)-1-(1-methylethoxy)-3-oxo-2,3-dihydro-1*H*-isoindol-1-yl]benzenesulphonamide,

F. bis[2-chloro-5-(1-hydroxy-3-oxo-2,3-dihydro-1*H*-isoindol-1-yl)benzenesulphonyl]amine,

J. impurity of unknown structure with a relative retention of about 0.9.

*Ph Eur*

# Chlortetracycline Hydrochloride

(*Ph Eur monograph 0173*)

| Compound | R | Molecular formula | $M_r$ |
|---|---|---|---|
| Chlortetracycline hydrochloride | Cl | $C_{22}H_{24}Cl_2N_2O_8$ | 515.3 |
| Tetracycline hydrochloride | H | $C_{22}H_{25}ClN_2O_8$ | 480.9 |

**Action and use**

Tetracycline antibacterial.

*Ph Eur*

**DEFINITION**

Mixture of antibiotics, the main component being the hydrochloride of (4*S*,4a*S*,5a*S*,6*S*,12a*S*)-7-chloro-4-(dimethylamino)-3,6,10,12,12a-pentahydroxy-6-methyl-1,11-dioxo-1,4,4a,5,5a,6,11,12a-octahydrotetracene-2-carboxamide (chlortetracycline hydrochloride), a substance produced by the growth of certain strains of *Streptomyces aureofaciens* or obtained by any other means.

*Content:*

— $C_{22}H_{24}Cl_2N_2O_8$: minimum 89.5 per cent (anhydrous substance),

— $C_{22}H_{25}ClN_2O_8$: maximum 8.0 per cent (anhydrous substance),

— 94.5 per cent to 102.0 per cent for the sum of the contents of chlortetracycline hydrochloride and tetracycline hydrochloride (anhydrous substance).

## CHARACTERS

**Appearance**

Yellow powder.

**Solubility**

Slightly soluble in water and in alcohol. It dissolves in solutions of alkali hydroxides and carbonates.

## IDENTIFICATION

A. Thin-layer chromatography (2.2.27).

*Test solution*   Dissolve 5 mg of the substance to be examined in *methanol R* and dilute to 10 ml with the same solvent.

*Reference solution (a)*   Dissolve 5 mg of *chlortetracycline hydrochloride CRS* in *methanol R* and dilute to 10 ml with the same solvent.

*Reference solution (b)*   Dissolve 5 mg of *chlortetracycline hydrochloride CRS*, 5 mg of *doxycycline R* and 5 mg of *demeclocycline hydrochloride R* in *methanol R* and dilute to 10 ml with the same solvent.

*Plate*   TLC octadecylsilyl silica gel $F_{254}$ plate R.

*Mobile phase*   Mix 20 volumes of *acetonitrile R*, 20 volumes of *methanol R* and 60 volumes of a 63 g/l solution of *oxalic acid R* previously adjusted to pH 2 with *concentrated ammonia R*.

*Application*   1 µl.

*Development*   Over 3/4 of the plate.

*Drying*   In air.

*Detection*   Examine in ultraviolet light at 254 nm.

*System suitability*   The chromatogram obtained with reference solution (b) shows 3 clearly separated spots.

*Results*   The principal spot in the chromatogram obtained with the test solution is similar in position and size to the principal spot in the chromatogram obtained with reference solution (a).

B. To about 2 mg add 5 ml of *sulphuric acid R*. A deep blue colour develops which becomes bluish-green. Add the solution to 2.5 ml of *water R*. The colour becomes brownish.

C. It gives reaction (a) of chlorides (2.3.1).

## TESTS

**pH** (2.2.3)

2.3 to 3.3.

Dissolve 0.1 g in 10 ml of *carbon dioxide-free water R*, heating slightly.

**Specific optical rotation** (2.2.7)

− 235 to − 250 (anhydrous substance).

Dissolve 0.125 g in *water R* and dilute to 50.0 ml with the same solvent.

**Absorbance** (2.2.25)

Maximum 0.40 at 460 nm.

Dissolve 0.125 g in *water R* and dilute to 25.0 ml with the same solvent.

**Related substances**

Liquid chromatography (2.2.29). *Prepare the solutions immediately before use.*

*Test solution*   Dissolve 25.0 mg of the substance to be examined in *0.01 M hydrochloric acid* and dilute to 25.0 ml with the same acid.

*Reference solution (a)*   Dissolve 25.0 mg of *chlortetracycline hydrochloride CRS* in *0.01 M hydrochloric acid* and dilute to 25.0 ml with the same acid.

*Reference solution (b)*   Dissolve 10.0 mg of *4-epichlortetracycline hydrochloride CRS* in *0.01 M hydrochloric acid* and dilute to 25.0 ml with the same acid.

*Reference solution (c)*   Dissolve 20.0 mg of *tetracycline hydrochloride CRS* in *0.01 M hydrochloric acid* and dilute to 25.0 ml with the same acid.

*Reference solution (d)*   Mix 5.0 ml of reference solution (a) and 10.0 ml of reference solution (b) and dilute to 25.0 ml with *0.01 M hydrochloric acid*.

*Reference solution (e)*   Mix 5.0 ml of reference solution (b) and 5.0 ml of reference solution (c) and dilute to 50.0 ml with *0.01 M hydrochloric acid*.

*Reference solution (f)*   Dilute 1.0 ml of reference solution (c) to 20.0 ml with *0.01 M hydrochloric acid*. Dilute 5.0 ml of this solution to 200.0 ml with *0.01 M hydrochloric acid*.

*Column:*

— *size*: $l$ = 0.25 m, Ø = 4.6 mm,

— *stationary phase*: octylsilyl silica gel for chromatography R (5 µm),

— *temperature*: 35 °C.

*Mobile phase*   To 500 ml of *water R*, add 50 ml of *perchloric acid solution R*, shake and add 450 ml of *dimethyl sulphoxide R*,

*Flow rate*   1 ml/min.

*Detection*   Spectrophotometer at 280 nm.

*Injection*   20 µl; inject the test solution and reference solutions (d), (e) and (f).

*System suitability*   Reference solution (d):

— *resolution*: minimum 2.0 between the peaks due to impurity A and to chlortetracycline; if necessary, adjust the dimethyl sulphoxide content in the mobile phase,

— *symmetry factor*: maximum 1.3 for the peak due to chlortetracycline.

*Limits:*

— *impurity A*: not more than the area of the corresponding peak in the chromatogram obtained with reference solution (e) (4.0 per cent),

— *total of other impurities eluting between the solvent peak and the peak corresponding to chlortetracycline*: not more than 0.25 times the area of the peak due to impurity A in the chromatogram obtained with reference solution (e) (1.0 per cent),

— *disregard limit*: area of the principal peak in the chromatogram obtained with reference solution (f) (0.1 per cent).

**Heavy metals** (2.4.8)

Maximum 50 ppm.

0.5 g complies with limit test C. Prepare the standard using 2.5 ml of *lead standard solution (10 ppm Pb) R*.

**Water** (2.5.12)

Maximum 2.0 per cent, determined on 0.300 g.

**Sulphated ash** (2.4.14)

Maximum 0.5 per cent, determined on 1.0 g.

**Bacterial endotoxins** (2.6.14)

Less than 1 IU/mg, if intended for use in the manufacture of parenteral dosage forms without a further appropriate procedure for the removal of bacterial endotoxins.

## ASSAY

Liquid chromatography (*2.2.29*) as described in the test for related substances with the following modification.

*Injection*   Test solution and reference solutions (a) and (e).

Calculate the percentage content of $C_{22}H_{24}Cl_2N_2O_8$ using the chromatogram obtained with reference solution (a). Calculate the percentage content of $C_{22}H_{25}ClN_2O_8$ using the chromatogram obtained with reference solution (e).

## STORAGE

Protected from light. If the substance is sterile, store in a sterile, airtight, tamper-proof container.

## IMPURITIES

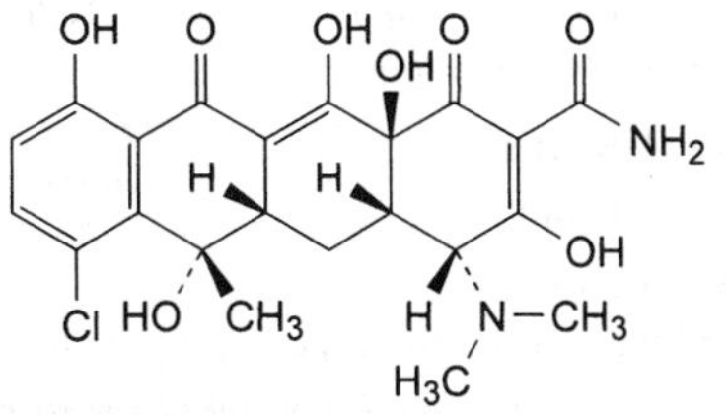

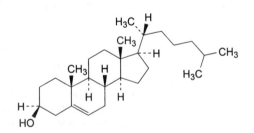

A. (4*R*,4a*S*,5a*S*,6*S*,12a*S*)-7-chloro-4-(dimethylamino)-3,6,10,12,12a-pentahydroxy-6-methyl-1,11-dioxo-1,4,4a,5,5a,6,11,12a-octahydrotetracene-2-carboxamide (4-epichlortetracycline),

B. demeclocycline.

*Ph Eur*

# Cholesterol

(*Ph Eur monograph 0993*)

$C_{27}H_{46}O$       386.7       57-88-5

## Action and use

Excipient.

*Ph Eur*

## DEFINITION

Cholest-5-en-3β-ol.

## Content:

— *cholesterol*: minimum 95.0 per cent (dried substance);
— *total sterols*: 97.0 per cent to 103.0 per cent (dried substance).

## CHARACTERS

### Appearance

White or almost white, crystalline powder.

### Solubility

Practically insoluble in water, sparingly soluble in acetone and in ethanol (96 per cent).

It is sensitive to light.

## IDENTIFICATION

A. Melting point (*2.2.14*): 147 °C to 150 °C.

B. Thin-layer chromatography (*2.2.27*). *Prepare the solutions immediately before use.*

*Test solution*   Dissolve 10 mg of the substance to be examined in ethylene chloride R and dilute to 5 ml with the same solvent.

*Reference solution*   Dissolve 10 mg of *cholesterol CRS* in ethylene chloride R and dilute to 5 ml with the same solvent.

*Plate*   TLC silica gel G plate R.

*Mobile phase*   ethyl acetate R, toluene R (33:66 *V/V*).

*Application*   20 µl.

*Development*   Immediately, protected from light, over a path of 15 cm.

*Drying*   In air.

*Detection*   Spray 3 times with *antimony trichloride solution R*; examine within 3-4 min.

*Results*   The principal spot in the chromatogram obtained with the test solution is similar in position, colour and size to the principal spot in the chromatogram obtained with the reference solution.

C. Dissolve about 5 mg in 2 ml of *methylene chloride R*. Add 1 ml of *acetic anhydride R*, 0.01 ml of *sulphuric acid R* and shake. A pink colour is produced which rapidly changes to red, then to blue and finally to brilliant green.

## TESTS

### Solubility in ethanol (96 per cent)

In a stoppered flask, dissolve 0.5 g in 50 ml of *ethanol (96 per cent) R* at 50 °C. Allow to stand for 2 h. No deposit or turbidity is formed.

### Acidity

Dissolve 1.0 g in 10 ml of *ether R*, add 10.0 ml of *0.1 M sodium hydroxide* and shake for about 1 min. Heat gently to eliminate ether and then boil for 5 min. Cool, add 10 ml of *water R* and *0.1 ml of phenolphthalein solution R* as indicator and titrate with *0.1 M hydrochloric acid* until the pink colour just disappears, stirring the solution vigorously throughout the titration. Carry out a blank titration. The difference between the volumes of *0.1 M hydrochloric acid* required to change the colour of the indicator in the blank and in the test is not more than 0.3 ml.

### Loss on drying (*2.2.32*)

Maximum 0.3 per cent, determined on 1.000 g by drying *in vacuo* at 60 °C for 4 h.

### Sulphated ash (*2.4.14*)

Maximum 0.1 per cent, determined on 1.0 g.

## ASSAY

Gas chromatography (*2.2.28*).

*Internal standard solution*   Dissolve 0.100 g of *pregnenolone isobutyrate CRS* in *heptane R* and dilute to 100.0 ml with the same solvent.

*Test solution*   Dissolve 25.0 mg of the substance to be examined in the internal standard solution and dilute to 25.0 ml with the same solution.

*Reference solution*   Dissolve 25.0 mg of *cholesterol CRS* in the internal standard solution and dilute to 25.0 ml with the same solution.

*Column:*

— *material*: fused silica;
— *size*: l = 30 m, Ø = 0.25 mm;
— *stationary phase*: poly(dimethyl)siloxane R (film thickness 0.25 µm).

*Carrier gas*   *helium for chromatography R.*

*Flow rate*   2 ml/min.

*Split ratio*   1:25.

*Temperature:*
— column: 275 °C;
— injection port: 285 °C;
— detector: 300 °C.

*Detection*   Flame ionisation.

*Injection*   1.0 μl.

*System suitability*   Reference solution:
— *resolution*: minimum 10.0 between the peaks due to pregnenolone isobutyrate and cholesterol.

Calculate the percentage content of cholesterol from the declared content in *cholesterol CRS*. Calculate the percentage content of total sterols by adding together the contents of cholesterol and other substances with a retention time less than or equal to 1.5 times the retention time of cholesterol. Disregard the peaks due to the internal standard and the solvent.

## STORAGE

Protected from light.

## LABELLING

The label states the source material for the production of cholesterol (for example bovine brain and spinal cord, wool fat or chicken eggs).

## IMPURITIES

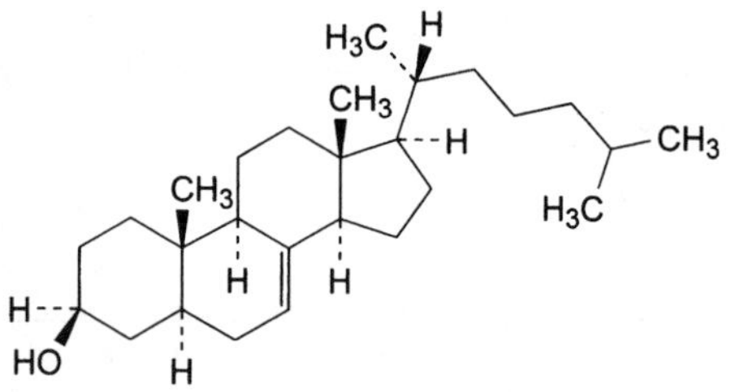

A. 5α-cholest-7-en-3β-ol (lathosterol),

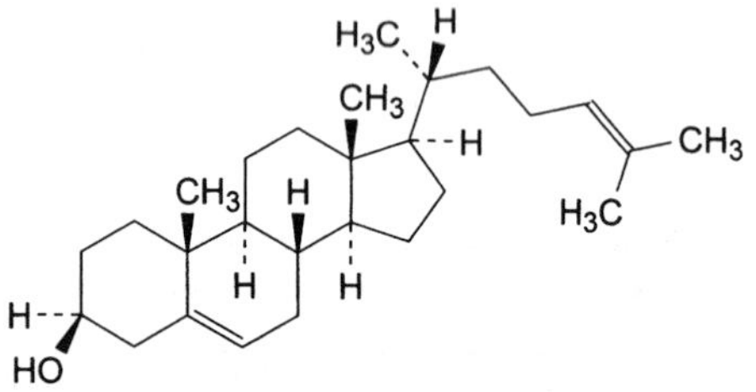

B. cholesta-5,24-dien-3β-ol (desmosterol),

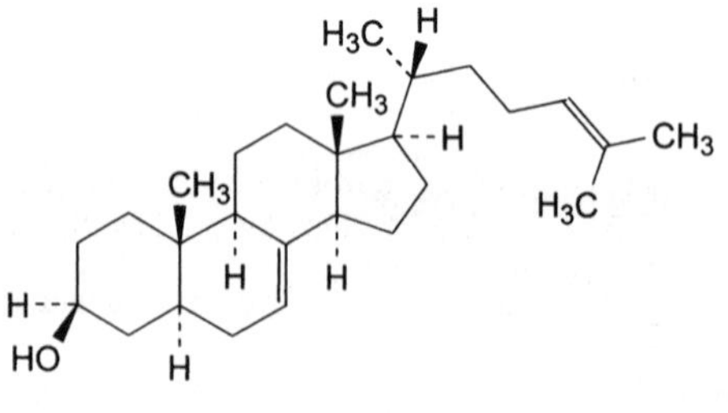

C. 5α-cholesta-7,24-dien-3β-ol.

_____ *Ph Eur*

# Choline Salicylate Solution

## Action and use

Salicylate; non-selective cyclo-oxygenase inhibitor; analgesic; anti-inflammatory.

## Preparations

Choline Salicylate Ear Drops

Choline Salicylate Oromucosal Gel

*Ph Eur* _____

## DEFINITION

Choline Salicylate Solution is an aqueous solution of choline salicylate. It contains not less than 47.5% w/v and not more than 52.5% w/v of choline salicylate, $C_{12}H_{19}NO_4$. It may contain a suitable antimicrobial preservative.

## CHARACTERISTICS

A clear, colourless liquid.

## IDENTIFICATION

A. Mix 0.5 ml with 10 ml of *methanol*, dry with *anhydrous sodium sulphate*, filter and evaporate the *methanol* to dryness. The *infrared absorption spectrum* of the residue, Appendix II A, is concordant with the *reference spectrum* of choline salicylate *(RS 059)*.

B. Dilute 5 ml to 25 ml with *water*. The resulting solution yields the reactions characteristic of *salicylates*, Appendix VI.

## TESTS

### Acidity

Dilute 4 ml to 20 ml with *water* and add 0.1 ml of *phenol red solution*. The solution is yellow and not more than 0.4 ml of 0.1M *sodium hydroxide VS* is required to change the colour of the solution to reddish violet.

### Clarity and colour of solution

Dilute 1 volume of the solution to 5 volumes with *water*. The resulting solution is *clear*, Appendix IV A, and *colourless*, Appendix IV B, Method II.

### Weight per ml

1.070 to 1.110 g, Appendix V G.

### Chloride

Mix 0.2 ml with 10 ml of *water* and add carefully, with mixing, 0.1 ml of a mixture of 10 volumes of *silver nitrate solution* and 1 volume of *nitric acid*. The resulting solution is not more opalescent than a standard prepared by treating 10 ml of a 0.00164% w/v solution of *sodium chloride* in the same manner beginning at the words 'add carefully ...' (0.1%).

## ASSAY

To 1 g add 50 ml of *1,4-dioxan* and 5 ml of *acetic anhydride* and carry out Method I for *non-aqueous titration*, Appendix VIII A, using 0.25 ml of *methyl orange-xylene cyanol FF solution* as indicator. Each ml of 0.1M *perchloric acid VS* is equivalent to 24.13 mg of $C_{12}H_{19}NO_4$. Use the *weight per ml* to calculate the percentage of $C_{12}H_{19}NO_4$, weight in volume.

_____ *Ph Eur*

# Choline Theophyllinate

$C_{12}H_{21}N_5O_3$      283.3      *4499-40-5*

### Action and use
Non-selective phosphodiesterase inhibitor (xanthine);
treatment of reversible airways obstruction.

### Preparation
Choline Theophyllinate Tablets

### DEFINITION
Choline Theophyllinate is choline 1,2,3,6-tetrahydro-1,3-
dimethyl-2,6-dioxo-7*H*-purin-7-ide. It contains not less than
41.9% and not more than 43.6% of choline, $C_5H_{15}NO_2$, and
not less than 61.7% and not more than 65.5% of
theophylline, $C_7H_9N_4O_2$, each calculated with reference to
the dried substance.

### CHARACTERISTICS
A white, crystalline powder. It melts between 187° and 192°,
Appendix V A.

Very soluble in *water*; soluble in *ethanol (96%)*; very slightly
soluble in *ether*.

### IDENTIFICATION
A. The *light absorption*, Appendix II B, in the range 230 to
350 nm of a 0.002% w/v solution in 0.01M *sodium hydroxide*
exhibits a maximum only at 275 nm. The *absorbance* at
275 nm is about 0.83.

B. The *infrared absorption spectrum*, Appendix II A, is
concordant with the *reference spectrum* of choline
theophyllinate *(RS 060)*.

### TESTS
**Clarity and colour of solution**
50 ml of a 10% w/v solution is *clear*, Appendix IV A, and
not more intensely coloured than *reference solution GY₄*,
Appendix IV B, Method I.

**Related substances**
Carry out the method for *thin-layer chromatography*,
Appendix III A, using *silica gel HF₂₅₄* as the coating
substance and a mixture of 95 volumes of *chloroform* and
5 volumes of *ethanol (96%)* as the mobile phase. Apply
separately to the plate 5 µl of each of two solutions of the
substance being examined in *ethanol (96%)* containing (1)
1.0% w/v and (2) 0.010% w/v. After removal of the plate,
allow it to dry in air and examine under *ultraviolet light*
(254 nm). Any *secondary spot* in the chromatogram obtained
with solution (1) is not more intense than the spot in the
chromatogram obtained with solution (2) (1%).

**Loss on drying**
When dried to constant weight at 105°, loses not more than
0.5% of its weight. Use 1 g.

**Sulphated ash**
Not more than 0.1%, Appendix IX A.

### ASSAY
*For choline*
Dissolve 0.6 g in 50 ml of *water* and titrate with
0.05M *sulphuric acid VS*, using *methyl red mixed solution* as
indicator, until a violet end point is obtained. Each ml of
0.05M *sulphuric acid VS* is equivalent to 12.12 mg of choline,
$C_5H_{15}NO_2$.

*For theophylline*
To the solution obtained in the Assay for choline, add 25 ml
of 0.1M *silver nitrate VS* and warm on a water bath for
15 minutes. Cool in ice for 30 minutes, filter and wash the
residue with three 10 ml quantities of *water*. Titrate the
combined filtrate and washings with 0.1M *sodium hydroxide
VS*. Each ml of 0.1M *sodium hydroxide VS* is equivalent to
18.02 mg of theophylline, $C_7H_8N_4O_2$.

### STORAGE
Choline Theophyllinate should be protected from light.

# Chondroitin Sulphate Sodium

*(Ph Eur monograph 2064)*

R = SO₃Na and R' = H
or
R = H and R' = SO₃Na

$H_2O(C_{14}H_{19}NNa_2O_{14}S)_x$      *9082-07-9*

### Action and use
Acid mucopolysaccharide; treatment of osteoarthritis.

*Ph Eur*

### DEFINITION
Natural copolymer based mainly on the 2 disaccharides: [4)-
(β-D-glucopyranosyluronic acid)-(1→3)-[2-(acetylamino)-2-
deoxy-β-D-galactopyranosyl 4-sulphate]-(1→] and [4)-(β-D-
glucopyranosyluronic acid)-(1→3)-[2-(acetylamino)-2-deoxy-
β-D-galactopyranosyl 6-sulphate]-(1→], sodium salt. On
complete hydrolysis it liberates D-galactosamine, D-glucuronic
acid, acetic acid and sulphuric acid. It is obtained from
cartilage of both terrestrial and marine origins. Depending on
the animal species of origin, it shows different proportions of
4-sulphate and 6-sulphate groups.

### Content
95 per cent to 105 per cent (dried substance).

### PRODUCTION
The animals from which chondroitin sulphate sodium is
derived must fulfil the requirements for the health of animals
suitable for human consumption.

### CHARACTERS
**Appearance**
White or almost white, hygroscopic powder.

**Solubility**
Freely soluble in water, practically insoluble in acetone and
in ethanol (96 per cent).

## IDENTIFICATION

A. Infrared absorption spectrophotometry (*2.2.24*).

*Preparation*    Discs of *potassium bromide R*.

*Comparison*    For chondroitin sulphate sodium of terrestrial origin use *chondroitin sulphate sodium CRS* and for chondroitin sulphate sodium of marine origine use *chondroitin sulphate sodium (marine) CRS*.

B. Solution S1 (see Tests) gives reaction (b) of sodium (*2.3.1*).

C. Examine the electropherograms obtained in the test for related substances.

*Results*    The principal band in the electropherogram obtained with the test solution is similar in position to the principal band in the electropherogram obtained with reference solution (a).

## TESTS

### Solution S1
Dissolve 2.500 g in 50.0 ml of *carbon dioxide-free water R*.

### Solution S2
Dilute 1.0 ml of solution S1 to 10.0 ml with *water R*.

### pH (*2.2.3*)
5.5 to 7.5 for solution S1.

### Specific optical rotation (*2.2.7*)
− 20 to − 30 (terrestrial origin) or − 12 to − 19 (marine origin) (dried substance), determined on solution S1.

### Intrinsic viscosity
0.01 $m^3$/kg to 0.15 $m^3$/kg.

*Test solution (a)*    Weigh 5.000 g ($m_{0p}$) of the substance to be examined and add about 80 ml of an 11.7 g/l solution of *sodium chloride R* at room temperature. Dissolve by shaking at room temperature for 30 min. Dilute to 100.0 ml with an 11.7 g/l solution of *sodium chloride R*. Filter through a 0.45 µm filter membrane and discard the first 10 ml. The concentration of test solution (a) is only indicative and must be adjusted after an initial measurement of the viscosity of test solution (a).

*Test solution (b)*    To 15.0 ml of test solution (a) add 5.0 ml of an 11.7 g/l solution of *sodium chloride R*.

*Test solution (c)*    To 10.0 ml of test solution (a) add 10.0 ml of an 11.7 g/l solution of *sodium chloride R*.

*Test solution (d)*    To 5.0 ml of test solution (a) add 15.0 ml of an 11.7 g/l solution of *sodium chloride R*.

Determine the flow-time (*2.2.9*) for an 11.7 g/l solution of *sodium chloride R* ($t_0$) and the flow times for the 4 test solutions ($t_1$, $t_2$, $t_3$ and $t_4$), at 25.00 ± 0.03 °C. Use an appropriate suspended level viscometer (specifications: viscometer constant = about 0.005 $mm^2/s^2$, kinematic viscosity range = 1-5 $mm^2$/s, internal diameter of tube R = 0.53 mm, volume of bulb C = 5.6 ml, internal diameter of tube N = 2.8-3.2 mm) with a funnel-shaped lower capillary end. Use the same viscometer for all measurements; measure all outflow times in triplicate. The test is not valid unless the results do not differ by more than 0.35 per cent from the mean and if the flow time $t_1$ is not less than 1.6 × $t_0$ and not more than 1.8 × $t_0$. If this is not the case, adjust the concentration of test solution (a) and repeat the procedure.

*Calculation of the relative viscosities*    Since the densities of the chondroitin sulphate solutions and of the solvent are almost equal, the relative viscosities $\eta_{ri}$ (being $\eta_{r1}$, $\eta_{r2}$, $\eta_{r3}$, $\eta_{r4}$) can be calculated from the ratio of the flow times for the respective solutions $t_i$ (being $t_1$, $t_2$, $t_3$ and $t_4$) to the flow time

of the solvent $t_0$, but taking into account the kinetic energy correction factor for the capillary (B = 30 800 $s^3$), as shown below:

$$\frac{t_i - \dfrac{B}{t_i^2}}{t_0 - \dfrac{B}{t_0^2}}$$

*Calculation of the concentrations*    Calculate the concentration $c_1$ (expressed in kg/$m^3$) of chondroitin sulphate sodium in test solution (a) using the following expression:

$$m_{0p} \times \frac{x}{100} \times \frac{100 - h}{100} \times 10$$

$x$ = percentage content of chondroitin sulphate sodium as determined in the assay;

$h$ = loss on drying as a percentage

Calculate the concentration $c_2$ (expressed in kg/$m^3$) of chondroitin sulphate sodium in test solution (b) using the following expression:

$$c_1 \times 0.75$$

Calculate the concentration $c_3$ (expressed in kg/$m^3$) of chondroitin sulphate sodium in test solution (c) using the following expression:

$$c_1 \times 0.50$$

Calculate the concentration $c_4$ (expressed in kg/$m^3$) of chondroitin sulphate sodium in test solution (d) using the following expression:

$$c_1 \times 0.25$$

*Calculation of the intrinsic viscosity*    The specific viscosity $\eta_{si}$ of the test solution (being $\eta_{s1}$, $\eta_{s2}$, $\eta_{s3}$ and $\eta_{s4}$) is calculated from the relative viscosities $\eta_{ri}$ (being $\eta_{r1}$, $\eta_{r2}$, $\eta_{r3}$ and $\eta_{r4}$) according to the following expression:

$$\eta_{ri} - 1$$

The intrinsic viscosity [$\eta$], defined as

$$[\eta] = \lim_{c \to 0} \left( \frac{\eta_s}{c} \right)$$

is calculated by linear least-squares regression analysis using the following equation:

$$\frac{\eta_{si}}{c_i} = c_i \times k_H + [\eta]$$

$c_i$ = concentration of the substance to be examined expressed in kg/$m^3$;

$k_H$ = Huggins' constant.

### Related substances
Electrophoresis (*2.2.31*).

*Buffer solution A (0.1 M barium acetate pH 5.0)*    Dissolve 25.54 g of *barium acetate R* in 900 ml of *water R*. Adjust to pH 5.0 with *glacial acetic acid R* and dilute to 1000.0 ml with *water R*.

*Buffer solution B* (1 M barium acetate pH 5.0)   Dissolve 255.43 g of *barium acetate R* in 900 ml of *water R*. Adjust to pH 5.0 with *glacial acetic acid R* and dilute to 1000.0 ml with *water R*.

*Staining solution*   Dissolve 1.0 g of *toluidine blue R* and 2.0 g of *sodium chloride R* in 1000 ml of *0.01 M hydrochloric acid*. Filter.

*Test solution*   Prepare a 30 mg/ml solution of the substance to be examined in *water R*.

*Reference solution (a)*   Prepare a 30 mg/ml solution of *chondroitin sulphate sodium CRS* in *water R*.

*Reference solution (b)*   Dilute 2.0 ml of reference solution (a) to 100.0 ml with *water R*.

*Reference solution (c)*   Mix equal volumes of reference solution (b) and *water R*.

*Procedure*   Allow the electrophoresis support to cool the plate to 10 °C. Pre-equilibrate the agarose gel for 1 min in buffer solution A. Remove excess liquid by careful decanting. Dry the gel for approximately 5 min. Place 400 ml of buffer solution B into each of the containers of the electrophoresis equipment. Transfer 1 μl of each solution to the slots of the agarose gel. Pipette a few millilitres of a 50 per cent *V/V* solution of *glycerol R* onto the cooled plate of the electrophoresis equipment and place the gel in the middle of the ceramic plate. Place a wick, saturated with buffer solution B, at the positive and negative sides of the agarose gel. Ensure that there is good contact between the electrophoresis buffer and the agarose gel. Perform the electrophoresis under the following conditions: 75 mA/gel, resulting in a voltage of 100-150 V (maximum 300-400 V) for a gel of about 12 cm × 10 cm. Carry out the electrophoresis for 12 min. Place the gel in a mixture consisting of 10 volumes of *anhydrous ethanol R* and 90 volumes of buffer solution A for 2 min. Carry out the electrophoresis for 20 min. Place the gel in a mixture consisting of 30 volumes of *anhydrous ethanol R* and 70 volumes of buffer solution A for 2 min. Carry out the electrophoresis for 20 min. Stain the gel in the staining solution for 10 min. Destain the gel for 15 min under running tap water followed by 10-15 min with *water R* until the band in the electropherogram obtained with reference solution (c) is visible. Allow the gel to dry.

*System suitability:*
— the electropherogram obtained with reference solution (c) shows a visible band;
— the band in the electropherogram obtained with reference solution (b) is clearly visible and similar in position to the band in the electropherogram obtained with reference solution (a).

*Results*   Any secondary band in the electropherogram obtained with the test solution is not more intense than the band in the electropherogram obtained with reference solution (b) (2 per cent).

**Protein** (*2.5.33, Method 2*)
Maximum 3.0 per cent (dried substance).

*Test solution*   Dilute 1.0 ml of solution S1 to 50.0 ml with *0.1 M sodium hydroxide*.

*Reference solutions*   Dissolve about 0.100 g of *bovine albumin R*, accurately weighed, in *0.1 M sodium hydroxide* and dilute to 50.0 ml with the same solvent. Carry out all additional dilutions using *0.1 M sodium hydroxide*.

**Chlorides** (*2.4.4*)
Maximum 0.5 per cent.

Dilute 1 ml of solution S2 to 15 ml with *water R*. Do not add diluted nitric acid. Prepare the standard using 5 ml of *chloride standard solution (5 ppm Cl)* and 10 ml of *water R*.

**Heavy metals** (*2.4.8*)
Maximum 20 ppm.

1.0 g complies with test C. Prepare the reference solution using 2 ml of *lead standard solution (10 ppm Pb) R*.

**Loss on drying** (*2.2.32*)
Maximum 12.0 per cent, determined on 1.000 g by drying in an oven at 105 °C for 4 h.

**Microbial contamination**
TAMC: acceptance criterion $10^3$ CFU/g (*2.6.12*).
TYMC: acceptance criterion $10^2$ CFU/g (*2.6.12*).
Absence of *Staphylococcus aureus* (*2.6.13*).
Absence of *Pseudomonas aeruginosa* (*2.6.13*).
Absence of *Escherichia coli* (*2.6.13*).
Absence of *Salmonella* (*2.6.13*).
Absence of bile-tolerant gram-negative bacteria (*2.6.13*).

**ASSAY**
*Test solution (a)*   Weigh 0.100 g ($m_1$) of the substance to be examined, dissolve in *water R* and dilute to 100.0 ml with the same solvent.

*Test solution (b)*   Dilute 5.0 ml of test solution (a) to 50.0 ml with *water R*.

*Reference solution (a)*   Weigh 0.100 g ($m_0$) of *chondroitin sulphate sodium CRS*, previously dried as described in the test for loss on drying, dissolve in *water R* and dilute to 100.0 ml with the same solvent.

*Reference solution (b)*   Dilute 5.0 ml of reference solution (a) to 50.0 ml with *water R*.

*Titrant solution (a)*   Weigh 4.000 g of *cetylpyridinium chloride monohydrate R* and dilute to 1000 ml with *water R*.

*Titrant solution (b)*   Weigh 1.000 g of *cetylpyridinium chloride monohydrate R* and dilute to 1000 ml with *water R*.

Perform either visual or photometric titration as follows:

*Visual titration*   Titrate 40.0 ml of reference solution (a) and 40.0 ml of test solution (a) with titrant solution (a). The solution becomes turbid. At the end point, the liquid appears clear, with an almost-white precipitate in suspension. The precipitate is more apparent if 0.1 ml of a 1 per cent solution of *methylene blue R* is added before starting the titration. The precipitated particles are more apparent against the blue background.

*Photometric titration*   Titrate 50.0 ml of reference solution (b) and 50.0 ml of test solution (b) with titrant solution (b). To determine the end point, use a suitable autotitrator equipped with a phototrode at a suitable wavelength (none is critical) in the visible range.

Calculate the percentage content of chondroitin sulphate sodium using the following expression:

$$\frac{v_1 \times m_0}{v_0 \times m_1} \times \frac{100}{100 - h} \times Z$$

$v_0$ = volume of appropriate titrant solution when titrating the appropriate reference solution, in millilitres;

$v_1$ = volume of appropriate titrant solution when titrating the appropriate test solution, in millilitres;

$h$ = loss on drying of the substance to be examined, as a percentage;

$Z$ = percentage content of $H_2O(C_{14}H_{19}NNa_2O_{14}S)_x$ in *chondroitin sulphate sodium CRS*.

**STORAGE**

In an airtight container, protected from light.

**LABELLING**

The label states the origin of the substance (marine or terrestrial).

_____ *Ph Eur*

# Chorionic Gonadotrophin

(*Ph Eur monograph 0498*)

**Action and use**
Gonadotrophic hormone.

**Preparation**
Chorionic Gonadotrophin Injection

*Ph Eur* _____

**DEFINITION**

Chorionic gonadotrophin is a dry preparation of placental glycoproteins which have luteinising activity. The potency is not less than 2500 IU/mg.

**PRODUCTION**

Chorionic gonadotrophin is extracted from the urine of pregnant women using a suitable fractionation procedure. It is either dried under reduced pressure or freeze-dried.

**CHARACTERS**

**Appearance**
White to yellowish-white, amorphous powder.

**Solubility**
Soluble in water.

**IDENTIFICATION**

When administered to immature rats as prescribed in the assay, it causes an increase in the mass of the seminal vesicles and of the prostate gland.

**TESTS**

**Water** (*2.5.32*)
Maximum 5.0 per cent.

**Bacterial endotoxins** (*2.6.14*)
Less than 0.02 IU per IU of chorionic gonadotrophin, if intended for use in the manufacture of parenteral dosage forms without a further appropriate procedure for the removal of bacterial endotoxins.

**ASSAY**

The potency of chorionic gonadotrophin is estimated by comparing under given conditions its effect of increasing the mass of the seminal vesicles (or the prostate gland) of immature rats with the same effect of the International Standard of chorionic gonadotrophin or of a reference preparation calibrated in International Units.

The International Unit is the activity contained in a stated amount of the International Standard, which consists of a mixture of a freeze-dried extract of chorionic gonadotrophin from the urine of pregnant women with lactose. The equivalence in International Units of the International Standard is stated by the World Health Organisation.

Use immature male rats of the same strain, 19 to 28 days old, differing in age by not more than 3 days and having body masses such that the difference between the heaviest and the lightest rat is not more than 10 g. Assign the rats at random to 6 equal groups of at least 5 animals. If sets of 6 litter mates are available, assign one litter mate from each set to each group and mark according to litter.

Choose 3 doses of the reference preparation and 3 doses of the preparation to be examined such that the smallest dose is sufficient to produce a positive response in some of the rats and the largest dose does not produce a maximal response in all the rats. Use doses in geometric progression and as an initial approximation total doses of 4 IU, 8 IU and 16 IU may be tried although the dose will depend on the sensitivity of the animals used, which may vary widely.

Dissolve separately the total quantities of the preparation to be examined and of the reference preparation corresponding to the daily doses to be used in sufficient *phosphate-albumin buffered saline pH 7.2 R* such that the daily dose is administered in a volume of about 0.5 ml. Add a suitable antimicrobial preservative such as 4 g/l of phenol or 0.02 g/l of thiomersal. Store the solutions at $5 \pm 3$ °C.

Inject subcutaneously into each rat the daily dose allocated to its group, on 4 consecutive days at the same time each day. On the fifth day, about 24 h after the last injection, euthanise the rats and remove the seminal vesicles. Remove any extraneous fluid and tissue and weigh the vesicles immediately. Calculate the results by the usual statistical methods, using the mass of the vesicles as the response. (The precision of the assay may be improved by a suitable correction of the organ mass with reference to the body mass of the animal from which it was taken; an analysis of covariance may be used).

The estimated potency is not less than 80 per cent and not more than 125 per cent of the stated potency. The confidence limits ($P = 0.95$) of the estimated potency are not less than 64 per cent and not more than 156 per cent of the stated potency.

**STORAGE**

In an airtight, tamper-proof container, protected from light at a temperature of 2 °C to 8 °C. If the substance is sterile, store in a sterile, airtight, tamper-proof container.

**LABELLING**

The label states:
— the number of International Units per container,
— the potency in International Units per milligram.

_____ *Ph Eur*

# Chymotrypsin

(*Ph Eur monograph 0476*)

**Action and use**
Proteolytic enzyme.

*Ph Eur* _____

**DEFINITION**

Chymotrypsin is a proteolytic enzyme obtained by the activation of chymotrypsinogen extracted from the pancreas of beef (*Bos taurus* L.). It has an activity of not less than 5.0 microkatals per milligram. In solution it has maximal enzymic activity at about pH 8; the activity is reversibly inhibited at pH 3, at which pH it is most stable.

## PRODUCTION

The animals from which chymotrypsin is derived must fulfil the requirements for the health of animals suitable for human consumption. Furthermore, the tissues used shall not include any specified risk material as defined by any relevant international or, where appropriate, national legislation.

The method of manufacture is validated to demonstrate that the product, if tested, would comply with the following test.

### Histamine (2.6.10)

Not more than 1 µg (calculated as histamine base) per 5 microkatals of chymotrypsin activity. Before carrying out the test, heat the solution of the substance to be examined on a water-bath for 30 min.

## CHARACTERS

A white or almost white, crystalline or amorphous powder, sparingly soluble in water. The amorphous form is hygroscopic.

## IDENTIFICATION

A. Dilute 1 ml of solution S (see Tests) to 10 ml with *water R*. In a depression in a white spot plate, mix 0.05 ml of this solution with 0.2 ml of substrate solution. A purple colour develops.

*Substrate solution* To 24.0 mg of *acetyltyrosine ethyl ester R* add 0.2 ml of *ethanol (96 per cent) R*, and swirl until solution is effected. Add 2.0 ml of *0.067 M phosphate buffer solution pH 7.0 R* and 1 ml of *methyl red mixed solution R* and dilute to 10.0 ml with *water R*.

B. Dilute 0.5 ml of solution S to 5 ml with *water R*. Add 0.10 ml of a 20 g/l solution of *tosylphenylalanylchloromethane R* in *ethanol (96 per cent) R*. Adjust to pH 7.0 and shake for 2 h. In a depression in a white spot plate, mix 0.05 ml of this solution with 0.2 ml of the substrate solution (see Identification test A). No colour develops within 3 min of mixing.

## TESTS

### Solution S

Dissolve 0.10 g in *carbon dioxide-free water R* and dilute to 10.0 ml with the same solvent.

### Appearance of solution

Solution S is not more opalescent than reference suspension II (2.2.1).

### pH (2.2.3)

The pH of solution S is 3.0 to 5.0.

### Absorbance (2.2.25)

Dissolve 30.0 mg in *0.001 M hydrochloric acid* and dilute to 100.0 ml with the same acid. The solution shows an absorption maximum at 281 nm and a minimum at 250 nm. The specific absorbance at the absorption maximum is 18.5 to 22.5 and at the absorption minimum is not greater than 8.

### Trypsin

Transfer to a depression in a white spot plate 0.05 ml of *tris(hydroxymethyl)aminomethane buffer solution pH 8.1 R* and 0.1 ml of solution S. Add 0.2 ml of substrate solution (test solution). At the same time and in the same manner, prepare a reference solution using the substance to be examined to which not more than 1 per cent *m/m* of *trypsin BRP* has been added. Start a timer. No colour appears in the test solution within 3-5 min after the addition of the substrate solution. A purple colour is produced in the control solution.

*Substrate solution* To 98.5 mg of *tosylarginine methyl ester hydrochloride R*, suitable for assaying trypsin, add 5 ml of *tris(hydroxymethyl)aminomethane buffer solution pH 8.1 R* and

swirl to dissolve. Add 2.5 ml of *methyl red mixed solution R* and dilute to 25.0 ml with *water R*.

### Loss on drying (2.2.32)

Not more than 5.0 per cent, determined on 0.100 g by drying at 60 °C at a pressure not exceeding 0.7 kPa for 2 h.

## ASSAY

The activity of chymotrypsin is determined by comparing the rate at which it hydrolyses *acetyltyrosine ethyl ester R* with the rate at which *chymotrypsin BRP* hydrolyses the same substrate under the same conditions.

*Apparatus* Use a reaction vessel of about 30 ml capacity provided with:
— a device that will maintain a temperature of 25.0 ± 0.1 °C;
— a stirring device, for example a magnetic stirrer;
— a lid with holes for the insertion of electrodes, the tip of a burette, a tube for the admission of nitrogen and the introduction of reagents.

An automatic or manual titration apparatus may be used. For the latter the burette is graduated in 0.005 ml and the pH meter is provided with a wide scale and glass-calomel or glass-silver-silver chloride electrodes.

*Test solution* Dissolve 25.0 mg of the substance to be examined in *0.001 M hydrochloric acid* and dilute to 250.0 ml with the same acid.

*Reference solution* Dissolve 25.0 mg of *chymotrypsin BRP* in *0.001 M hydrochloric acid* and dilute to 250.0 ml with the same acid.

Store the solutions at 0-5 °C. Warm 1 ml of each solution to about 25 °C over 15 min and use 50 µl of each solution (corresponding to about 25 nanokatals) for each titration. Carry out the titration in an atmosphere of nitrogen. Transfer 10.0 ml of *0.01 M calcium chloride solution R* to the reaction vessel and, while stirring, add 0.35 ml of *0.2 M acetyltyrosine ethyl ester solution R*. When the temperature is steady at 25.0 ± 0.1 °C (after about 5 min) adjust the pH to exactly 8.0 with *0.02 M sodium hydroxide*. Add 50 µl of the test solution (equivalent to about 5 µg of the substance to be examined) and start a timer. Maintain the pH at 8.0 by the addition of *0.02 M sodium hydroxide*, noting the volume added every 30 s. Calculate the volume of *0.02 M sodium hydroxide* used per second between 30 s and 210 s. Carry out a titration in the same manner using the reference solution and calculate the volume of *0.02 M sodium hydroxide* used per second.

Calculate the activity in microkatals per milligram using the following expression:

$$\frac{m' \times V}{m \times V'} \times A$$

$m$ = mass of the substance to be examined, in milligrams,
$m'$ = mass of *chymotrypsin BRP*, in milligrams,
$V$ = volume of *0.02 M sodium hydroxide* used per second by the test solution,
$V'$ = volume of *0.02 M sodium hydroxide* used per second by the reference solution,
$A$ = activity of *chymotrypsin BRP*, in microkatals per milligram.

## STORAGE

In an airtight container at 2 °C to 8 °C, protected from light.

## LABELLING

The label states:
— the quantity of chymotrypsin and the total activity in microkatals per container;
— for the amorphous substance, that it is hygroscopic.

*———————————————————— Ph Eur*

# Ciclopirox

*(Ph Eur monograph 1407)*

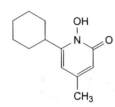

C₁₂H₁₇NO₂      207.3      *29342-05-0*

## Action and use

Antifungal.

*Ph Eur* _____

## DEFINITION

6-Cyclohexyl-1-hydroxy-4-methylpyridin-2(1*H*)-one.

## Content

98.0 per cent to 101.0 per cent (dried substance).

## CHARACTERS

### Appearance

White or yellowish-white, crystalline powder.

### Solubility

Slightly soluble in water, freely soluble in anhydrous ethanol and in methylene chloride.

## IDENTIFICATION

*First identification  B.*

*Second identification  A, C.*

A. Melting point (*2.2.14*): 140 °C to 145 °C.

B. Infrared absorption spectrophotometry (*2.2.24*).

*Comparison  ciclopirox CRS.*

C. Thin-layer chromatography (*2.2.27*).

*Test solution*  Dissolve 20 mg of the substance to be examined in *methanol R* and dilute to 10 ml with the same solvent.

*Reference solution*  Dissolve 20 mg of *ciclopirox CRS* in *methanol R* and dilute to 10 ml with the same solvent.

*Plate*  TLC silica gel F₂₅₄ plate R.

*Pretreatment*  Before use predevelop with the mobile phase until the solvent front has migrated to the top of the plate. Allow to dry in air for 5 min.

*Mobile phase*  concentrated ammonia R, water R, ethanol (96 per cent) R (10:15:75 *V/V/V*).

*Application*  10 μl.

*Development*  Over a path of 15 cm.

*Drying*  In air for 10 min.

*Detection A*  Examine in ultraviolet light at 254 nm.

*Results A*  The principal spot in the chromatogram obtained with the test solution is similar in position and size to the principal spot in the chromatogram obtained with the reference solution.

*Detection B*  Spray with a 20 g/l solution of *ferric chloride R* in *anhydrous ethanol R*.

*Results B*  The principal spot in the chromatogram obtained with the test solution is similar in position, colour and size to the principal spot in the chromatogram obtained with the reference solution.

## TESTS

### Appearance of solution

The solution is clear (*2.2.1*) and not more intensely coloured than reference solution Y₅ (*2.2.2, Method II*).

Dissolve 2.0 g in *methanol R* and dilute to 10 ml with the same solvent.

### Related substances

Liquid chromatography (*2.2.29*). *Carry out the operations avoiding exposure to actinic light. All materials which are in direct contact with the substance to be examined like column materials, reagents, solvents and others should contain only very low amounts of extractable metal cations.*

*Solvent mixture*  acetonitrile R, mobile phase (1:9 *V/V*).

*Test solution*  Dissolve 30.0 mg of the substance to be examined in 15 ml of the solvent mixture. If necessary, use an ultrasonic bath. Dilute to 20.0 ml with the solvent mixture.

*Reference solution (a)*  Dissolve 15.0 mg of *ciclopirox impurity A CRS* and 15.0 mg of *ciclopirox impurity B CRS* in the solvent mixture and dilute to 10.0 ml with the solvent mixture.

*Reference solution (b)*  Dilute 1.0 ml of reference solution (a) to 200.0 ml with the solvent mixture.

*Reference solution (c)*  Dilute 2.0 ml of reference solution (b) to 10.0 ml with the solvent mixture.

*Reference solution (d)*  Mix 5 ml of reference solution (a) with 5 ml of the test solution.

*Column:*
— *size: l = 0.08 m, Ø = 4 mm;*
— *stationary phase: nitrile silica gel for chromatography R2 (5 μm).*

In order to ensure desorption of disruptive metal ions, every new column is to be rinsed with the rinsing solution over a period of not less than 15 h and then with the mobile phase for not less than 5 h at a flow rate of 0.2 ml/min.

*Rinsing solution*  glacial acetic acid R, acetylacetone R, acetonitrile R, water R (1:1:500:500 *V/V/V/V*).

*Mobile phase*  Mix 0.1 ml of *glacial acetic acid R*, 230 ml of *acetonitrile R* and 770 ml of a 0.96 g/l solution of *sodium edetate R*.

*Flow rate*  0.7 ml/min.

*Detection*  Spectrophotometer at 220 nm and at 298 nm.

*Injection*  10 μl of the test solution and reference solutions (b), (c) and (d); inject the solvent mixture as a blank.

*Run time*  2.5 times the retention time of ciclopirox.

*Retention time*  Ciclopirox = 8 min to 11 min; if necessary adjust the ratio of the 0.96 g/l solution of sodium edetate to acetonitrile in the mobile phase.

*Relative retention*  With reference to ciclopirox: impurity A = about 0.5; impurity C = about 0.9; impurity B = about 1.3.

*System suitability:*
— *resolution*: minimum 2.0 between the peaks due to ciclopirox and impurity B in the chromatogram obtained with reference solution (d);
— *signal-to-noise ratio*: minimum 3 for the peak due to impurity B in the chromatogram obtained with reference solution (c) at 298 nm;
— *symmetry factor*: 0.8 to 2.0 for the principal peak in the chromatogram obtained with the test solution.

*Limits:*
— *impurity A at 220 nm*: not more than the area of the corresponding peak in the chromatogram obtained with reference solution (b) (0.5 per cent);
— *impurities B, C at 298 nm*: for each impurity, not more than the area of the peak due to impurity B in the chromatogram obtained with reference solution (b) (0.5 per cent);
— *sum of impurities other than B at 298 nm*: not more than the area of the peak due to impurity B in the chromatogram obtained with reference solution (b) (0.5 per cent);
— *disregard limit at 298 nm*: 0.5 times the area of the peak due to impurity B in the chromatogram obtained with reference solution (c) (0.05 per cent).

**Heavy metals** (*2.4.8*)
Maximum 10 ppm.

2.0 g complies with test C. Prepare the reference solution using 2 ml of *lead standard solution (10 ppm Pb) R*.

**Loss on drying** (*2.2.32*)
Maximum 1.5 per cent, determined on 1.000 g by drying *in vacuo* at 60 °C over *diphosphorus pentoxide R*.

**Sulphated ash** (*2.4.14*)
Maximum 0.1 per cent, determined on 1.0 g.

**ASSAY**
Dissolve 0.150 g in 20 ml of *methanol R*. Add 20 ml of *water R* and titrate with *0.1 M sodium hydroxide*, determining the end-point potentiometrically (*2.2.20*). Carry out a blank titration.

1 ml of *0.1 M sodium hydroxide* is equivalent to 20.73 mg of $C_{12}H_{17}NO_2$.

**STORAGE**
Protected from light.

**IMPURITIES**
*Specified impurities   A, B, C.*

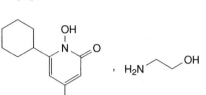

and enantiomer

A. (*RS*)-2-(3-cyclohexyl-5-methyl-4,5-dihydroisoxazol-5-yl)acetic acid,

B. X = O: 6-cyclohexyl-4-methyl-2*H*-pyran-2-one,

C. X = NH: 6-cyclohexyl-4-methylpyridin-2(1*H*)-one.

_____ *Ph Eur*

# Ciclopirox Olamine

(*Ph Eur monograph 1302*)

$C_{12}H_{17}NO_2.C_2H_7NO$      268.4      *41621-49-2*

**Action and use**
Antifungal.

*Ph Eur* _____

**DEFINITION**
6-Cyclohexyl-1-hydroxy-4-methylpyridin-2(1*H*)-one and 2-aminoethanol.

*Content:*
— ciclopirox ($C_{12}H_{17}NO_2$; $M_r$ 207.3): 76.0 per cent to 78.5 per cent (dried substance),
— 2-aminoethanol ($C_2H_7NO$; $M_r$ 61.1): 22.2 per cent to 23.3 per cent (dried substance).

**CHARACTERS**
**Appearance**
White or pale yellow, crystalline powder.

**Solubility**
Sparingly soluble in water, very soluble in alcohol and in methylene chloride, slightly soluble in ethyl acetate, practically insoluble in cyclohexane.

It shows polymorphism (*5.9*).

**IDENTIFICATION**
*First identification   A.*
*Second identification   B.*

A. Infrared absorption spectrophotometry (*2.2.24*).

*Comparison   ciclopirox olamine CRS.*

If the spectra obtained in the solid state show differences, dissolve the substance to be examined and the reference substance separately in the minimum volume of *ethyl acetate R*, evaporate to dryness on a water-bath and record new spectra using the residues.

B. Thin-layer chromatography (*2.2.27*).

*Test solution   Dissolve 25 mg of the substance to be examined in *methanol* R and dilute to 10 ml with the same solvent.

*Reference solution   Dissolve 25 mg of *ciclopirox olamine CRS* in *methanol R* and dilute to 10 ml with the same solvent.

*Plate   TLC silica gel $F_{254}$ plate R.*

Before use wash 2 plates by allowing a mixture of 10 volumes of *concentrated ammonia R*, 15 volumes of *water R* and 75 volumes of *ethanol R* to migrate until the solvent front has reached the top of the plate. Allow the plates to dry in air for 5 min.

*Mobile phase   concentrated ammonia R, water R, ethanol R (10:15:75 V/V/V).*

*Application   10 μl.*

*Development   Over a path of 15 cm.*

*Drying   In air for 10 min.*

*Detection A   Examine in ultraviolet light at 254 nm.*

*Results A* The principal spot in the chromatogram obtained with the test solution is similar in position and size to the principal spot in the chromatogram obtained with the reference solution.

*Detection B* Spray one plate with *ferric chloride solution R3.*

*Results B* The principal spot in the chromatogram obtained with the test solution is similar in position, colour and size to the principal spot in the chromatogram obtained with the reference solution.

*Detection C* Spray the second plate with *ninhydrin solution R.* Heat at 110 °C until the spots appear.

*Results C* The principal spot in the chromatogram obtained with the test solution is similar in position, colour and size to the principal spot in the chromatogram obtained with the reference solution.

## TESTS

### Appearance of solution

The solution is clear (*2.2.1*) and not more intensely coloured than reference solution $BY_7$ (*2.2.2, Method II*).

Dissolve 2.0 g in *methanol R* and dilute to 20 ml with the same solvent.

### pH (*2.2.3*)

8.0 to 9.0.

Dissolve 1.0 g in *carbon dioxide-free water R* and dilute to 100 ml with the same solvent.

### Related substances

Liquid chromatography (*2.2.29*). *Carry out the operations avoiding exposure to actinic light. All materials which are in direct contact with the substance to be examined, such as column materials, reagents, solvents, etc. should contain only small amounts of extractable metal cations.*

*Test solution* Dissolve 40.0 mg of the substance to be examined (corresponding to about 30 mg of ciclopirox) in a mixture of 20 µl of *anhydrous acetic acid R*, 2 ml of *acetonitrile R*, and 15 ml of the mobile phase. If necessary, use an ultrasonic bath. Dilute to 20.0 ml with the mobile phase.

*Reference solution (a)* Dissolve 15.0 mg of *ciclopirox impurity A CRS* and 15.0 mg of *ciclopirox impurity B CRS* in a mixture of 1 ml of *acetonitrile R* and 7 ml of the mobile phase. Dilute to 10.0 ml with the mobile phase.

*Reference solution (b)* Dilute 1.0 ml of reference solution (a) to 200.0 ml with a mixture of 1 volume of *acetonitrile R* and 9 volumes of the mobile phase.

*Reference solution (c)* Dilute 2.0 ml of reference solution (b) to 10.0 ml with a mixture of 1 volume of *acetonitrile R* and 9 volumes of the mobile phase.

*Reference solution (d)* Mix 5 ml of reference solution (a) with 5 ml of the test solution.

*Column:*
— *size:* $l = 80$ mm, $\emptyset = 4$ mm,
— *stationary phase: nitrile silica gel for chromatography R* (5 µm).

In order to ensure desorption of interfering metal ions, a new column is to be rinsed with the rinsing solution over a period of at least 15 h and then with the mobile phase for at least 5 h at a flow rate of 0.2 ml/min.

*Rinsing solution* A mixture of 1 volume of *anhydrous acetic acid R*, 1 volume of *acetylacetone R*, 500 volumes of *acetonitrile R* and 500 volumes of *water R.*

*Mobile phase* A mixture of 0.1 volumes of *anhydrous acetic acid R*, 230 volumes of *acetonitrile R* and 770 volumes of a 0.96 g/l solution of *sodium edetate R*. If the retention time of the principal peak in the chromatogram obtained with the test solution is not between 8 min and 11 min adjust the ratio of the 0.96 g/l solution of sodium edetate to acetonitrile accordingly.

*Flow rate* 0.7 ml/min.

*Detection* Variable wavelength spectrophotometer capable of operating at 220 nm and 298 nm.

*Injection* 10 µl; inject the test solution and reference solutions (b), (c) and (d).

*Run time* 2.5 times the retention time of ciclopirox.

*Relative retention* With reference to ciclopirox: impurity A = about 0.5; impurity C = about 0.9; impurity B = about 1.3.

*System suitability:*
— *resolution*: minimum of 2.0 between the peaks corresponding to impurity B and ciclopirox in the chromatogram obtained with reference solution (d),
— *signal-to-noise ratio*: minimum of 10 for the peak corresponding to impurity B in the chromatogram obtained with reference solution (c) at 298 nm,
— *symmetry factor*: 0.8 to 2.0 for the principal peak in the chromatogram obtained with the test solution.

*Limits:*
— *impurity A at 220 nm*: not more than the area of the corresponding peak in the chromatogram obtained with reference solution (b) at the same wavelength (0.5 per cent),
— *any impurity at 298 nm*: not more than the area of the peak due to impurity B in the chromatogram obtained with reference solution (b) at the same wavelength (0.5 per cent),
— *total at 298 nm apart from impurity B*: not more than the area of the peak due to impurity B in the chromatogram obtained with reference solution (b) (0.5 per cent),
— *disregard limit at 298 nm*: area of the peak due to impurity B in the chromatogram obtained with reference solution (c) at the same wavelength (0.1 per cent).

### Heavy metals (*2.4.8*)

Maximum 20 ppm.

1.0 g complies with limit test C. Prepare the standard using 2 ml of *lead standard solution (10 ppm Pb) R.*

### Loss on drying (*2.2.32*)

Maximum 1.5 per cent, determined on 1.000 g by drying under high vacuum.

### Sulphated ash (*2.4.14*)

Maximum 0.1 per cent, determined on 1.0 g.

### ASSAY

#### 2-Aminoethanol

Dissolve 0.250 g in 25 ml of *anhydrous acetic acid R*. Titrate with *0.1 M perchloric acid*, determining the end-point potentiometrically (*2.2.20*).

1 ml of *0.1 M perchloric acid* is equivalent to 6.108 mg of $C_2H_7NO$.

#### Ciclopirox

Dissolve 0.200 g in 2 ml of *methanol R*. Add 38 ml of *water R*, swirl and titrate immediately with *0.1 M sodium hydroxide*, determining the end-point potentiometrically (*2.2.20*). Carry out a blank titration.

Use *0.1 M sodium hydroxide*, the titre of which has been determined under the conditions prescribed above using 0.100 g of *benzoic acid RV.*

1 ml of *0.1 M sodium hydroxide* is equivalent to 20.73 mg of $C_{12}H_{17}NO_2$.

## STORAGE
Protected from light.

## IMPURITIES

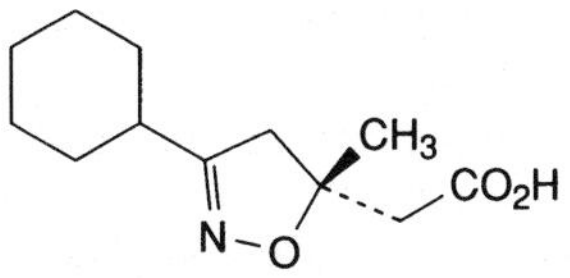

A. (*RS*)-2-(3-cyclohexyl-5-methyl-4,5-dihydroisoxazol-5-yl)acetic acid,

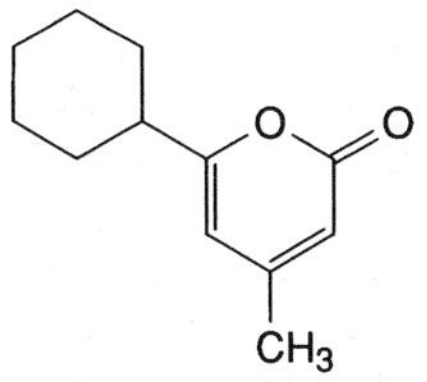

B. 6-cyclohexyl-4-methyl-2*H*-pyran-2-one,

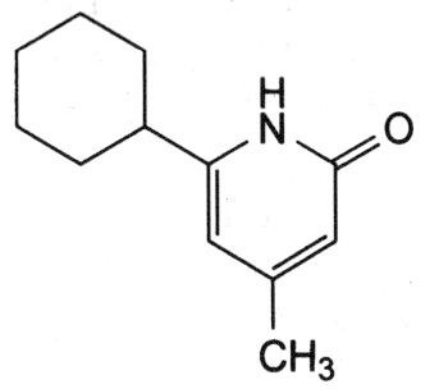

C. 6-cyclohexyl-4-methylpyridin-2(1*H*)-one.

*——————————————— Ph Eur*

# Ciclosporin

*(Ph Eur monograph 0994)*

$C_{62}H_{111}N_{11}O_{12}$      1203      59865-13-3

### Action and use
Calcineurin inhibitor; immunosuppressant.

*Ph Eur* _____

## DEFINITION
Cyclo[[(2*S*,3*R*,4*R*,6*E*)-3-hydroxy-4-methyl-2-(methylamino)oct-6-enoyl]-L-2-aminobutanoyl-*N*-methylglycyl-*N*-methyl-L-leucyl-L-valyl-*N*-methyl-L-leucyl-L-alanyl-D-alanyl-*N*-methyl-L-leucyl-*N*-methyl-L-leucyl-*N*-methyl-L-valyl].

Substance produced by *Beauveria nivea* (*Tolypocladium inflatum Gams*) or obtained by any other means.

## Content
98.5 per cent to 102.0 per cent (dried substance).

## CHARACTERS
### Appearance
White or almost white powder.

### Solubility
Practically insoluble in water, freely soluble in anhydrous ethanol and in methylene chloride.

## IDENTIFICATION
A. Infrared absorption spectrophotometry (*2.2.24*).

*Comparison* ciclosporin CRS.

B. Examine the chromatograms obtained in the assay.

*Results* The principal peak in the chromatogram obtained with the test solution is similar in retention time to the principal peak in the chromatogram obtained with reference solution (a).

## TESTS
### Appearance of solution
The solution is clear (*2.2.1*) and not more intensely coloured than reference solution $Y_5$, $BY_5$ or $R_7$ (*2.2.2, Method II*).

Dissolve 1.5 g in *anhydrous ethanol R* and dilute to 15 ml with the same solvent.

### Specific optical rotation (*2.2.7*)
− 185 to − 193 (dried substance).

Dissolve 0.125 g in *methanol R* and dilute to 25.0 ml with the same solvent.

### Related substances
Liquid chromatography (*2.2.29*).

*Solvent mixture* acetonitrile R, water R (50:50 *V/V*).

*Test solution* Dissolve 30.0 mg of the substance to be examined in the solvent mixture and dilute to 25.0 ml with the solvent mixture.

*Reference solution (a)* Dissolve 30.0 mg of *ciclosporin CRS* in the solvent mixture and dilute to 25.0 ml with the solvent mixture.

*Reference solution (b)* Dilute 2.0 ml of reference solution (a) to 200.0 ml with the solvent mixture.

*Reference solution (c)* Dissolve the contents of a vial of *ciclosporin for system suitability CRS* in 5.0 ml of the mobile phase.

*Column:*
— *size:* $l = 0.25$ m, $\varnothing = 4$ mm;
— *stationary phase:* octadecylsilyl silica gel for chromatography R (3-5 µm);
— *temperature:* 80 °C.

The column is connected to the injection port by a steel capillary tube about 1 m long, having an internal diameter of 0.25 mm and maintained at 80 °C.

*Mobile phase* phosphoric acid R, 1,1-dimethylethyl methyl ether R, acetonitrile R, water R (1:50:430:520 *V/V/V/V*).

*Flow rate* 1.5 ml/min.

*Detection* Spectrophotometer at 210 nm.

*Injection* 20 µl of the test solution and reference solutions (b) and (c).

*Run time* 1.7 times the retention time of ciclosporin.

*System suitability* Reference solution (c):
— *retention time:* ciclosporin = 25 min to 30 min; if necessary, adjust the ratio of acetonitrile to water in the mobile phase;
— *peak-to-valley ratio:* minimum 1.4, where $H_p$ = height above the baseline of the peak due to ciclosporin U and

$H_v$ = height above the baseline of the lowest point of the curve separating this peak from the peak due to ciclosporin; if necessary, adjust the ratio of 1,1-dimethylethyl methyl ether to acetonitrile in the mobile phase.

*Limits:*

— *any impurity*: for each impurity, not more than 0.7 times the area of the principal peak in the chromatogram obtained with reference solution (b) (0.7 per cent);

— *total*: not more than 1.5 times the area of the principal peak in the chromatogram obtained with reference solution (b) (1.5 per cent);

— *disregard limit*: 0.05 times the area of the principal peak in the chromatogram obtained with reference solution (b) (0.05 per cent).

**Heavy metals** *(2.4.8)*
Maximum 20 ppm.
The residue obtained in the test for loss on drying complies with test C. Prepare the reference solution using 2 ml of *lead standard solution (10 ppm Pb) R.*

**Loss on drying** *(2.2.32)*
Maximum 2.0 per cent, determined on 1.000 g at 60 °C at a pressure not exceeding 15 Pa for 3 h.

**Bacterial endotoxins** *(2.6.14)*
Less than 0.84 IU/mg, if intended for use in the manufacture of parenteral dosage forms without a further appropriate procedure for the removal of bacterial endotoxins. Dissolve 50 mg of the substance to be examined in a mixture of 280 mg of *ethanol (96 per cent) R* and 650 mg of *polyoxyethylated castor oil R* and dilute to the required concentration using water for BET.

**ASSAY**
Liquid chromatography *(2.2.29)* as described in the test for related substances with the following modifications.

*Injection*  Test solution and reference solution (a).

*System suitability*  Reference solutions (a):

— *repeatability*: maximum relative standard deviation of 1.0 per cent after 6 injections.

Calculate the percentage content of $C_{62}H_{111}N_{11}O_{12}$ from the declared content of *ciclosporin CRS.*

**STORAGE**
In an airtight container, protected from light. If the substance is sterile, store in a sterile, airtight, tamper-proof container.

**IMPURITIES**

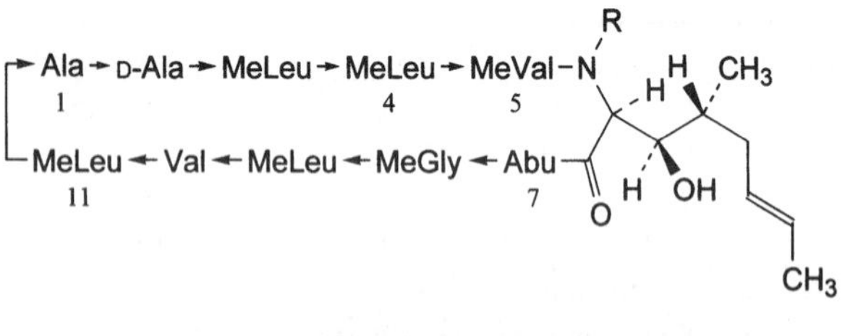

Ala → D-Ala → MeLeu → MeLeu → MeVal → N
   1                    4          5
MeLeu ← Val ← MeLeu ← MeGly ← Abu
  11                              7

A. different ciclosporins [difference with ciclosporin (R = CH$_3$: ciclosporin A)]: ciclosporin B [7-L-Ala]; ciclosporin C [7-L-Thr]; ciclosporin D [7-L-Val]; ciclosporin E [5-L-Val]; ciclosporin G [7-(L-2-aminopentanoyl)]; ciclosporin H [5-D-MeVal]; ciclosporin L [R = H]; ciclosporin T [4-L-Leu]; ciclosporin U [11-L-Leu]; ciclosporin V [1-L-Abu],

Ala → D-Ala → MeLeu → MeLeu → MeVal → N
MeLeu ← Val ← MeLeu ← MeGly ← Abu

B. [6-[(2S,3R,4R)-3-hydroxy-4-methyl-2-(methylamino)octanoic acid]]ciclosporin A,

C. isociclosporin A.

*Ph Eur*

# Cilastatin Sodium

*(Ph Eur monograph 1408)*

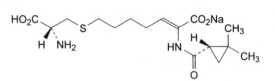

$C_{16}H_{25}N_2NaO_5S$       380.4       *81129-83-1*

**Action and use**
Dehydropeptidase-I inhibitor; inhibition of the renal metabolism of imipenem.

*Ph Eur*

**DEFINITION**
Sodium (Z)-7-[[(R)-2-amino-2-carboxyethyl]sulphanyl]-2-[[[(1S)-2,2-dimethylcyclopropyl]carbonyl]amino]hept-2-enoate.

**Content**
98.0 per cent to 101.5 per cent (anhydrous substance).

**CHARACTERS**

**Appearance**
White or light yellow amorphous, hygroscopic powder.

**Solubility**
Very soluble in water and in methanol, slightly soluble in anhydrous ethanol, very slightly soluble in dimethyl sulphoxide, practically insoluble in acetone and in methylene chloride.

**IDENTIFICATION**
A. Specific optical rotation (see Tests).

B. Infrared absorption spectrophotometry *(2.2.24)*.

*Comparison*  cilastatin sodium CRS.

C. It gives reaction (a) of sodium *(2.3.1)*.

**TESTS**
Solution S. Dissolve 1.0 g in *carbon dioxide-free water R* and dilute to 100 ml with the same solvent.

**Appearance of solution**
Solution S is clear *(2.2.1)* and not more intensely coloured than reference solution $Y_6$ *(2.2.2, Method II)*.

**pH** *(2.2.3)*
6.5 to 7.5 for solution S.

**Specific optical rotation** *(2.2.7)*
+ 41.5 to + 44.5 (anhydrous substance).

Dissolve 0.250 g in a mixture of 1 volume of *hydrochloric acid R* and 120 volumes of *methanol R*, then dilute to 25.0 ml with the same mixture of solvents.

### Related substances

Liquid chromatography (*2.2.29*).

*Test solution* Dissolve 32.0 mg of the substance to be examined in *water R* and dilute to 20.0 ml with the same solvent.

*Reference solution (a)* Dilute 2.0 ml of the test solution to 100.0 ml with *water R*. Dilute 5.0 ml of this solution to 100.0 ml with *water R*.

*Reference solution (b)* Dilute 5.0 ml of the test solution to 100.0 ml with *water R*. Dilute 2.0 ml of this solution to 20.0 ml with *water R*.

*Reference solution (c)* Dissolve 16 mg of the substance to be examined in *dilute hydrogen peroxide solution R* and dilute to 10.0 ml with the same solution. Allow to stand for 30 min. Dilute 1 ml of this solution to 100 ml with *water R*.

*Reference solution (d)* Dissolve 32 mg of *mesityl oxide R* (impurity D) in 100 ml of *water R*. Dilute 1 ml of this solution to 50 ml with *water R*.

*Column:*
— *size:* $l$ = 0.25 m, Ø = 4.6 mm;
— *stationary phase:* octadecylsilyl silica gel for chromatography R (5 µm);
— *temperature:* 50 °C.

*Mobile phase:*
— *mobile phase A:* mix 300 volumes of *acetonitrile R1* and 700 volumes of a 0.1 per cent *V/V* solution of *phosphoric acid R* in *water R;*
— *mobile phase B:* 0.1 per cent *V/V* solution of *phosphoric acid R* in *water R;*

| Time (min) | Mobile phase A (per cent *V/V*) | Mobile phase B (per cent *V/V*) |
|---|---|---|
| 0 - 30 | 15 → 100 | 85 → 0 |
| 30 - 46 | 100 | 0 |
| 46 - 56 | 100 → 15 | 0 → 85 |

*Flow rate* 2.0 ml/min.

*Detection* Spectrophotometer at 210 nm.

*Injection* 20 µl.

*System suitability:*
— the chromatogram obtained with reference solution (c) shows 3 principal peaks: the first 2 peaks (impurity A) may elute without being completely resolved;
— *mass distribution ratio:* minimum 10 for the peak due to cilastatin (3$^{rd}$ peak) in the chromatogram obtained with reference solution (c);
— *signal-to-noise ratio:* minimum 5.0 for the principal peak in the chromatogram obtained with reference solution (a).

*Limits:*
— *impurities A, B, C:* for each impurity, not more than the area of the principal peak in the chromatogram obtained with reference solution (b) (0.5 per cent);
— *total:* not more than twice the area of the principal peak in the chromatogram obtained with reference solution (b) (1 per cent);
— *disregard limit:* the area of the principal peak in the chromatogram obtained with reference solution (a) (0.1 per cent); disregard any peak corresponding to the peak due to impurity D in the chromatogram obtained with reference solution (d).

### Impurity D, acetone and methanol

Gas chromatography (*2.2.28*).

*Internal standard solution* Dissolve 0.5 ml of *propanol R* in *water R* and dilute to 1000 ml with the same solvent.

*Test solution* Dissolve 0.200 g of the substance to be examined in *water R*, add 2.0 ml of the internal standard solution and dilute to 10.0 ml with *water R*.

*Reference solution* Dissolve 2.0 ml of *acetone R*, 0.5 ml of *methanol R* and 0.5 ml of *mesityl oxide R* (impurity D) in *water R* and dilute to 1000 ml with the same solvent. To 2.0 ml of this solution add 2.0 ml of the internal standard solution and dilute to 10.0 ml with *water R*. This solution contains 316 µg of acetone, 79 µg of methanol and 86 µg of impurity D per millilitre.

*Column:*
— *material:* fused silica;
— *size:* $l$ = 30 m, Ø = 0.53 mm;
— *stationary phase:* macrogol 20 000 R (film thickness 1.0 µm).

*Carrier gas* helium for chromatography R.

*Flow rate* 9 ml/min.

*Temperature:*

| | Time (min) | Temperature (°C) |
|---|---|---|
| Column | 0 - 2.5 | 50 |
| | 2.5 - 5 | 50 → 70 |
| | 5 - 5.5 | 70 |
| Injection port | | 160 |
| Detector | | 220 |

*Detection* Flame ionisation.

*Injection* 1 µl.

Calculate the percentage contents of acetone, methanol and impurity D using the following expression:

$$\left(\frac{C}{W}\right) \times \left(\frac{R_u}{R_s}\right)$$

$C$ = concentration of the solvent in the reference solution, in µg/ml
$W$ = quantity of cilastatin sodium in the test solution, in milligrams
$R_u$ = ratio of the area of the solvent peak to the area of the propanol peak in the chromatogram obtained with the test solution
$R_s$ = ratio of the area of the solvent peak to the area of the propanol peak in the chromatogram obtained with the reference solution.

*Limits:*
— *acetone:* maximum 1.0 per cent *m/m*;
— *methanol:* maximum 0.5 per cent *m/m*;
— *impurity D:* maximum 0.4 per cent *m/m*.

### Heavy metals (*2.4.8*)

Maximum 20 ppm.

1.0 g complies with test C. Prepare the reference solution using 2.0 ml of *lead standard solution (10 ppm Pb) R*.

### Water (*2.5.12*)

Maximum 2.0 per cent, determined on 0.50 g.

**Bacterial endotoxins** (2.6.14)
Less than 0.17 IU/mg, if intended for use in the manufacture of parenteral dosage forms without a further appropriate procedure for the removal of bacterial endotoxins.

## ASSAY
Dissolve 0.300 g in 30 ml of *methanol R* and add 5 ml of *water R*. Add *0.1 M hydrochloric acid* to a pH of about 3.0. Carry out a potentiometric titration (2.2.20), using *0.1 M sodium hydroxide*. 3 jumps of potential are observed. Titrate to the 3rd equivalence point.

1 ml of *0.1 M sodium hydroxide* is equivalent to 19.02 mg of $C_{16}H_{25}N_2NaO_5S$.

## STORAGE
In an airtight container, at a temperature not exceeding 8 °C. If the substance is sterile, store in a sterile, airtight, tamper-proof container.

## IMPURITIES
*Specified impurities*   *A, B, C, D.*

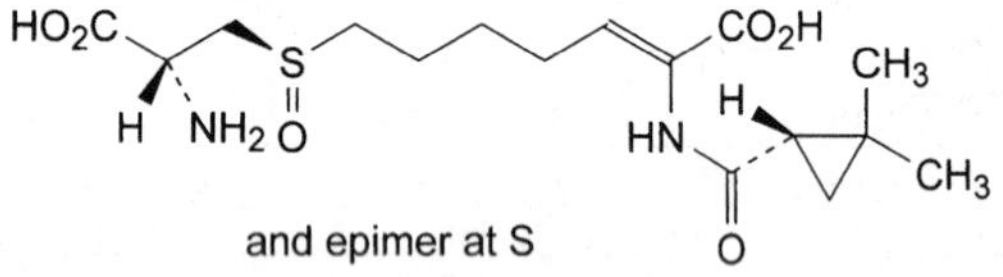

A. (Z)-7-[(RS)-[(R)-2-amino-2-carboxyethyl]sulphinyl]-2-[[[(1S)-2,2-dimethylcyclopropyl]carbonyl]amino]hept-2-enoic acid,

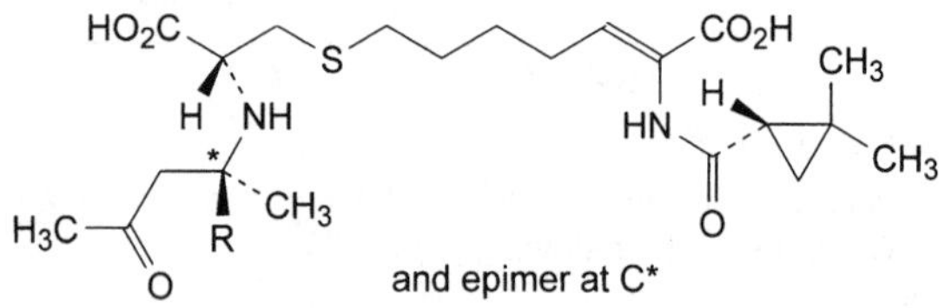

B. R = H: (Z)-7-[[(R)-2-[[(1RS)-1-methyl-3-oxobutyl]amino]2-carboxyethyl]sulphanyl]-2-[[[(1S)-2,2-dimethylcyclopropyl]carbonyl]amino]hept-2-enoic acid,
C. R = CH₃: (Z)-7-[[(R)-2-[(1,1-dimethyl-3-oxobutyl)amino]2-carboxyethyl]sulphanyl]-2-[[[(1S)-2,2-dimethylcyclopropyl]carbonyl]amino]hept-2-enoic acid,

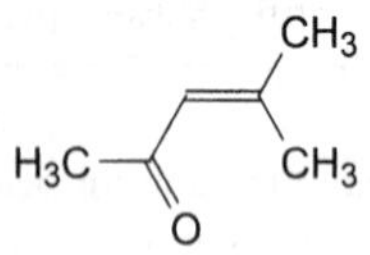

D. 4-methylpent-3-en-2-one (mesityl oxide).

*———————————————— Ph Eur*

# Cilazapril

*(Ph Eur monograph 1499)*

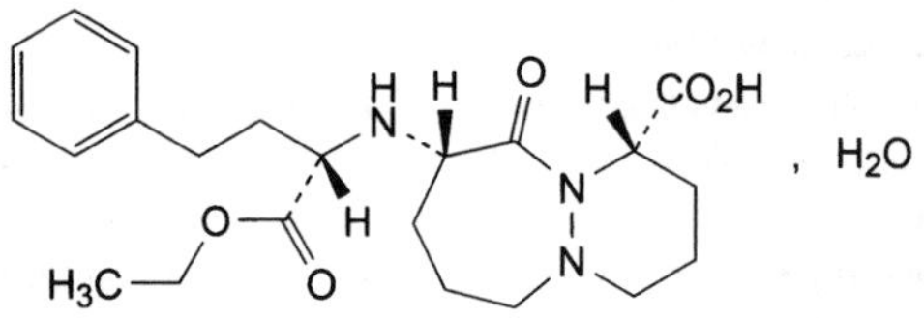

$C_{22}H_{31}N_3O_5,H_2O$          435.5          *92077-78-6*

## Action and use
Angiotensin converting enzyme inhibitor.

*Ph Eur* ———————————————————————

## DEFINITION
(1S,9S)-9-[[(1S)-1-(Ethoxycarbonyl)-3-phenylpropyl]amino]-10-oxooctahydro-6H-pyridazino[1,2-a][1,2]diazepine-1-carboxylic acid monohydrate.

## Content
98.5 per cent to 101.5 per cent (anhydrous substance).

## CHARACTERS
**Appearance**
White or almost white, crystalline powder.

**Solubility**
Slightly soluble in water, freely soluble in methanol and in methylene chloride.

## IDENTIFICATION
A. Infrared absorption spectrophotometry (2.2.24).
*Comparison*   cilazapril CRS.
B. Specific optical rotation (see Tests).

## TESTS
**Specific optical rotation** (2.2.7)
− 383 to − 399 (anhydrous substance).

Dissolve 0.200 g in *0.067 M phosphate buffer solution pH 7.0 R*, with the aid of ultrasound if necessary, and dilute to 50.0 ml with the same buffer solution. Carry out the determination at 365 nm.

**Impurity A**
Thin-layer chromatography (2.2.27).

*Test solution*   Dissolve 0.20 g of the substance to be examined in *methanol R* and dilute to 5.0 ml with the same solvent.

*Reference solution (a)*   Dissolve 2 mg of *cilazapril impurity A CRS* in *methanol R* and dilute to 50.0 ml with the same solvent.

*Reference solution (b)*   Dissolve 5 mg of *cilazapril impurity A CRS* and 5 mg of the substance to be examined in *methanol R* and dilute to 10.0 ml with the same solvent.

*Plate*   TLC silica gel plate R.

*Mobile phase*   glacial acetic acid R, water R, hexane R, methanol R, ethyl acetate R (5:5:15:15:60 V/V/V/V/V).

*Application*   5 µl.

*Development*   Over a path of 10 cm.

*Drying*   In a current of cold air for 10 min.

*Detection*   Spray with a freshly prepared mixture of 1 volume of *potassium iodobismuthate solution R* and 10 volumes of *dilute acetic acid R* and then with *dilute hydrogen peroxide solution R*.

*System suitability*   Reference solution (b):
— the chromatogram shows 2 clearly separated spots.

*Limit:*
— *impurity A*: any spot due to impurity A is not more intense than the corresponding spot in the chromatogram obtained with reference solution (a) (0.1 per cent).

**Related substances**

Liquid chromatography (*2.2.29*).

*Test solution* Dissolve 25.0 mg of the substance to be examined in the mobile phase and dilute to 50.0 ml with the mobile phase.

*Reference solution (a)* Dilute 1.0 ml of the test solution to 50.0 ml with the mobile phase. Dilute 5.0 ml of this solution to 20.0 ml with the mobile phase.

*Reference solution (b)* Dissolve 5.0 mg of *cilazapril impurity D CRS* in the test solution and dilute to 10.0 ml with the test solution.

*Column:*
— *size*: $l$ = 0.25 m, Ø = 4.6 mm;
— *stationary phase*: octadecylsilyl silica gel for chromatography R (5 μm).

*Mobile phase* Mix 10 volumes of *triethylamine R* and 750 volumes of *water R*, adjust to pH 2.30 with *phosphoric acid R*, and add 200 volumes of *tetrahydrofuran R*.

*Flow rate* 1.0 ml/min.

*Detection* Spectrophotometer at 214 nm.

*Injection* 20 μl.

*Run time* Twice the retention time of cilazapril; when impurity A is present, it may be necessary to continue the chromatography until it is eluted.

*Relative retention* With reference to cilazapril: impurity B = about 0.6; impurity D = about 0.9; impurity C = about 1.6; impurity A = 4 to 5.

*System suitability* Reference solution (b):
— *resolution*: minimum 2.5 between the peaks due to impurity D and cilazapril;
— *symmetry factor*: maximum 3.0 for the peak due to cilazapril.

*Limits:*
— *impurity B*: not more than the area of the principal peak in the chromatogram obtained with reference solution (a) (0.5 per cent);
— *impurity D*: not more than 0.4 times the area of the principal peak in the chromatogram obtained with reference solution (a) (0.2 per cent);
— *impurity C*: not more than 0.2 times the area of the principal peak in the chromatogram obtained with reference solution (a) (0.1 per cent);
— *unspecified impurities*: for each impurity, not more than 0.2 times the area of the principal peak in the chromatogram obtained with reference solution (a) (0.10 per cent);
— *total*: not more than twice the area of the principal peak in the chromatogram obtained with reference solution (a) (1 per cent);
— *disregard limit*: 0.1 times the area of the principal peak in the chromatogram obtained with reference solution (a) (0.05 per cent); disregard any peak due to impurity A.

**Water** (*2.5.12*)

3.5 per cent to 5.0 per cent, determined on 0.300 g.

**Sulphated ash** (*2.4.14*)

Maximum 0.1 per cent, determined on 1.0 g.

**ASSAY**

Dissolve 0.300 g in 10 ml of *anhydrous ethanol R* and add 50 ml of *water R*. Titrate with *0.1 M sodium hydroxide*,

determining the end-point potentiometrically (*2.2.20*). Carry out a blank titration.

1 ml of *0.1 M sodium hydroxide* is equivalent to 41.75 mg of $C_{22}H_{31}N_3O_5$.

**STORAGE**

Protected from light.

**IMPURITIES**

*Specified impurities* A, B, C, D.

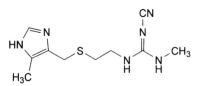

A. R = $C(CH_3)_3$, R′ = $C_2H_5$: 1,1-dimethylethyl (1*S*,9*S*)-9-[[(*S*)-1-(ethoxycarbonyl)-3-phenylpropyl]amino]-10-oxooctahydro-6*H*-pyridazino[1,2-*a*][1,2]diazepine-1-carboxylate,

B. R = R′ = H: (1*S*,9*S*)-9-[[(*S*)-1-carboxy-3-phenylpropyl]amino]-10-oxooctahydro-6*H*-pyridazino[1,2-*a*][1,2]diazepine-1-carboxylic acid,

C. R = R′ = $C_2H_5$: ethyl (1*S*,9*S*)-9-[[(*S*)-1-(ethoxycarbonyl)-3-phenylpropyl]amino]-10-oxooctahydro-6*H*-pyridazino[1,2-*a*][1,2]diazepine-1-carboxylate,

D (1*S*,9*S*)-9-[[(*R*)-1-(ethoxycarbonyl)-3-phenylpropyl]amino]-10-oxooctahydro-6*H*-pyridazino-[1,2-*a*][1,2]diazepine-1-carboxylic acid.

*Ph Eur*

# Cimetidine

(*Ph Eur monograph 0756*)

$C_{10}H_{16}N_6S$ 252.3 *51481-61-9*

**Action and use**

Histamine $H_2$ receptor antagonist; treatment of peptic ulceration.

**Preparations**

Cimetidine Injection

Cimetidine Oral Solution

Cimetidine Oral Suspension

Cimetidine Tablets

*Ph Eur*

## DEFINITION

Cimetidine contains not less than 98.5 per cent and not more than the equivalent of 101.5 per cent of 2-cyano-1-methyl-3-[2-[[(5-methyl-1*H*-imidazol-4-yl)methyl]sulphanyl]ethyl]guanidine, calculated with reference to the dried substance.

## CHARACTERS

A white or almost white powder, slightly soluble in water, soluble in alcohol, practically insoluble in methylene chloride. It dissolves in dilute mineral acids.

It shows polymorphism (*5.9*).

## IDENTIFICATION

*First identification  B.*

*Second identification  A, C, D.*

A. Melting point (*2.2.14*): 139 °C to 144 °C. If necessary, dissolve the substance to be examined in *2-propanol R*, evaporate to dryness and determine the melting point again.

B. Examine by infrared absorption spectrophotometry (*2.2.24*), comparing with the spectrum obtained with *cimetidine CRS*. If the spectra obtained in the solid state show differences, dissolve the substance to be examined and the reference substance separately in *2-propanol R*, evaporate to dryness and record the spectra again.

C. Examine the chromatograms obtained in the test for related substances. The principal spot in the chromatogram obtained with test solution (b) is similar in position, colour and size to the principal spot in the chromatogram obtained with reference solution (d).

D. Dissolve about 1 mg in a mixture of 1 ml of *ethanol R* and 5 ml of a freshly prepared 20 g/l solution of *citric acid R* in *acetic anhydride R*. Heat in a water-bath for 10 min to 15 min. A reddish-violet colour develops.

## TESTS

**Appearance of solution**

Dissolve 3.0 g in 12 ml of *1 M hydrochloric acid* and dilute to 20 ml with *water R*. The solution is clear (*2.2.1*) and not more intensely coloured than reference solution $Y_5$ (*2.2.2, Method II*).

**Related substances**

Examine by thin-layer chromatography (*2.2.27*), using *silica gel GF$_{254}$ R* as the coating substance.

*Test solution (a)*  Dissolve 0.50 g of the substance to be examined in *methanol R* and dilute to 10 ml with the same solvent.

*Test solution (b)*  Dilute 1 ml of test solution (a) to 10 ml with *methanol R*.

*Reference solution (a)*  Dilute 1 ml of test solution (a) to 100 ml with *methanol R*. Dilute 20 ml of this solution to 100 ml with *methanol R*.

*Reference solution (b)*  Dilute 5 ml of reference solution (a) to 10 ml with *methanol R*.

*Reference solution (c)*  Dilute 5 ml of reference solution (b) to 10 ml with *methanol R*.

*Reference solution (d)*  Dissolve 10 mg of *cimetidine CRS* in 2 ml of *methanol R*.

A. Apply separately to the plate 4 µl of each solution. Allow the plate to stand for 15 min in the chromatographic tank saturated with vapour from the mobile phase which consists of a mixture of 15 volumes of *concentrated ammonia R*, 20 volumes of *methanol R* and 65 volumes of *ethyl acetate R* and develop immediately over a path of 15 cm using the same mixture of solvents. Dry the plate in a stream of cold air, expose to iodine vapour until maximum contrast of the spots has been obtained and examine in ultraviolet light at 254 nm. Any spot in the chromatogram obtained with test solution (a), apart from the principal spot, is not more intense than the principal spot in the chromatogram obtained with reference solution (a) (0.2 per cent) and not more than two such spots are more intense than the principal spot in the chromatogram obtained with reference solution (b) (0.1 per cent). The test is not valid unless the chromatogram obtained with reference solution (c) shows a clearly visible spot.

B. Apply separately to the plate 4 µl of each solution. Develop over a path of 15 cm using a mixture of 8 volumes of *concentrated ammonia R*, 8 volumes of *methanol R* and 84 volumes of *ethyl acetate R*. Dry the plate in a stream of cold air, expose to iodine vapour until maximum contrast of the spots has been obtained and examine in ultraviolet light at 254 nm. Any spot in the chromatogram obtained with the test solution (a), apart from the principal spot, is not more intense than the principal spot in the chromatogram obtained with reference solution (a) (0.2 per cent) and not more than two such spots are more intense than the principal spot in the chromatogram obtained with reference solution (b) (0.1 per cent). The test is not valid unless the chromatogram obtained with reference solution (c) shows a clearly visible spot.

**Heavy metals** (*2.4.8*)

1.0 g complies with limit test C for heavy metals (20 ppm). Prepare the standard using 2 ml of *lead standard solution (10 ppm Pb) R*.

**Loss on drying** (*2.2.32*)

Not more than 0.5 per cent, determined on 1.000 g by drying in an oven at 105 °C.

**Sulphated ash** (*2.4.14*)

Not more than 0.2 per cent, determined on 1.0 g.

## ASSAY

Dissolve 0.200 g in 60 ml of *anhydrous acetic acid R*. Titrate with *0.1 M perchloric acid* determining the end-point potentiometrically (*2.2.20*).

1 ml of *0.1 M perchloric acid* is equivalent to 25.23 mg of $C_{10}H_{16}N_6S$.

## STORAGE

Store in an airtight container, protected from light.

*Ph Eur*

# Cimetidine Hydrochloride

(*Ph Eur monograph 1500*)

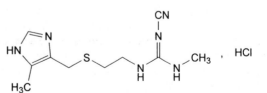

$C_{10}H_{16}N_6S,HCl$        288.8        70059-30-2

**Action and use**

Histamine $H_2$ receptor antagonist; treatment of peptic ulceration.

*Ph Eur*

## DEFINITION
Cimetidine hydrochloride contains not less than 98.5 per cent and not more than the equivalent of 101.5 per cent of 2-cyano-1-methyl-3-[2-[[(5-methyl-1*H*-imidazol-4-yl)methyl]sulphanyl]ethyl]guanidine hydrochloride, calculated with reference to the dried substance.

## CHARACTERS
A white or almost white, crystalline powder, freely soluble in water, sparingly soluble in ethanol.

## IDENTIFICATION
*First identification   B, E.*

*Second identification   A, C, D, E.*

A. Dissolve 70 mg in *0.2 M sulphuric acid* and dilute to 100.0 ml with the same acid. Dilute 2.0 ml of the solution to 100.0 ml with *0.2 M sulphuric acid*. Measure the absorbance (*2.2.25*) at the absorption maximum at 218 nm. The specific absorbance at the maximum is 650 to 705.

B. Examine by infrared absorption spectrophotometry (*2.2.24*), comparing with the spectrum obtained with *cimetidine hydrochloride CRS*.

C. Examine the chromatograms obtained in the test for related substances. The principal spot in the chromatogram obtained with test solution (b) is similar in position, colour and size to the principal spot in the chromatogram obtained with reference solution (d).

D. Dissolve about 1 mg in a mixture of 1 ml of *ethanol R* and 5 ml of a freshly prepared 20 g/l solution of *citric acid R* in *acetic anhydride R*. Heat on a water-bath for 10 min to 15 min. A reddish-violet colour develops.

E. It gives reaction (a) of chlorides (*2.3.1*).

## TESTS
### Appearance of solution
Dissolve 3.0 g in 12 ml of *1 M hydrochloric acid* and dilute to 20 ml with *water R*. The solution is clear (*2.2.1*) and not more intensely coloured than reference solution $Y_5$ (*2.2.2*, *Method II*).

### pH (*2.2.3*)
Dissolve 100 mg in *carbon dioxide-free water R* and dilute to 10.0 ml with the same solvent. The pH of the solution is 4.0 to 5.0.

### Related substances
Examine by thin-layer chromatography (*2.2.27*), using a TLC *silica gel GF$_{254}$ plate R*.

*Test solution (a)*   Dissolve 0.50 g of the substance to be examined in *methanol R* and dilute to 10 ml with the same solvent.

*Test solution (b)*   Dilute 1 ml of test solution (a) to 10 ml with *methanol R*.

*Reference solution (a)*   Dilute 2 ml of test solution (b) to 100 ml with *methanol R*.

*Reference solution (b)*   Dilute 5 ml of reference solution (a) to 10 ml with *methanol R*.

*Reference solution (c)*   Dilute 5 ml of reference solution (b) to 10 ml with *methanol R*.

*Reference solution (d)*   Dissolve 10 mg of *cimetidine hydrochloride CRS* in 2 ml of *methanol R*.

A. Apply to the plate 4 µl of each solution. Allow the plate to stand for 15 min in a chromatographic tank saturated with vapour from the mobile phase, which consists of a mixture of 15 volumes of *concentrated ammonia R*, 20 volumes of *methanol R* and 65 volumes of *ethyl acetate R*, and develop immediately over a path of 15 cm using the same mixture of solvents. Dry the plate in a stream of cold air, expose to iodine vapour until maximum contrast of the spots has been obtained and examine in ultraviolet light at 254 nm. Any spot in the chromatogram obtained with test solution (a), apart from the principal spot, is not more intense than the principal spot in the chromatogram obtained with reference solution (a) (0.2 per cent) and at most two such spots are more intense than the principal spot in the chromatogram obtained with reference solution (b) (0.1 per cent). The test is not valid unless the chromatogram obtained with reference solution (c) shows a clearly visible spot.

B. Apply to the plate 4 µl of each solution. Develop over a path of 15 cm using a mixture of 8 volumes of *concentrated ammonia R*, 8 volumes of *methanol R* and 84 volumes of *ethyl acetate R*. Dry the plate in a stream of cold air, expose to iodine vapour until maximum contrast of the spots has been obtained and examine in ultraviolet light at 254 nm. Any spot in the chromatogram obtained with test solution (a), apart from the principal spot, is not more intense than the principal spot in the chromatogram obtained with reference solution (a) (0.2 per cent) and at most two such spots are more intense than the principal spot in the chromatogram obtained with reference solution (b) (0.1 per cent). The test is not valid unless the chromatogram obtained with reference solution (c) shows a clearly visible spot.

### Heavy metals (*2.4.8*)
1.0 g complies with limit test C for heavy metals (20 ppm). Prepare the standard using 2 ml of *lead standard solution (10 ppm Pb) R*.

### Loss on drying (*2.2.32*)
Not more than 1.0 per cent, determined on 1.000 g by drying in an oven at 105 °C.

### Sulphated ash (*2.4.14*)
Not more than 0.2 per cent, determined on 1.0 g.

## ASSAY
Dissolve 0.200 g of the substance to be examined in a mixture of 5 ml of *0.01 M hydrochloric acid* and 50 ml of *alcohol R*. Carry out a potentiometric titration (*2.2.20*), using *0.1 M sodium hydroxide*. Read the volume added between the two points of inflexion.

1 ml of *0.1 M sodium hydroxide* is equivalent to 28.88 mg of $C_{10}H_{17}ClN_6S$.

## STORAGE
Store in an airtight container, protected from light.

## IMPURITIES

A. R1 = CN, R2 = SCH$_3$:
3-cyano-2-methyl-1-[2-[[(5-methyl-1*H*-imidazol-4-yl)methyl]sulphanyl]ethyl]isothiourea,

B. R1 = CN, R2 = OCH$_3$: 3-cyano-2-methyl-1-[2-[[(5-methyl-1*H*-imidazol-4-yl)methyl]sulphanyl]ethyl]isourea,

C. R1 = CONH$_2$, R2 = NHCH$_3$:
1-[(methylamino)[[2-[[(5-methyl-1*H*-imidazol-4-yl)methyl]sulphanyl]ethyl]amino]methylene]urea,

D. R1 = H, R2 = NHCH₃: 1-methyl-3-[2-[[(5-methyl-1*H*-imidazol-4-yl)methyl]sulphanyl]ethyl]guanidine,

E. 2-cyano-1-methyl-3-[2-[[(5-methyl-1*H*-imidazol-4-yl)methyl]sulphinyl]ethyl]guanidine,

F. 2-cyano-1,3-bis[2-[[(5-methyl-1*H*-imidazol-4-yl)methyl]sulphanyl]ethyl]guanidine.

*Ph Eur*

# Cinchocaine Hydrochloride

*(Ph Eur monograph 1088)*

C₂₀H₂₉N₃O₂, HCl      379.9      *61-12-1*

**Action and use**
Local anaesthetic.

*Ph Eur*

## DEFINITION
Cinchocaine hydrochloride contains not less than
98.5 per cent and not more than the equivalent of
101.0 per cent of 2-butoxy-*N*-[2-(diethylamino)ethyl]
quinoline-4-carboxamide hydrochloride, calculated with
reference to the dried substance.

## CHARACTERS
A white or almost white, crystalline powder or colourless
crystals, hygroscopic, very soluble in water, freely soluble in
acetone, in alcohol and in methylene chloride. It
agglomerates very easily.

## IDENTIFICATION
*First identification   B, E.*
*Second identification   A, C, D, E.*

A. Dissolve 60.0 mg in *1 M hydrochloric acid* and dilute to
100 ml with the same acid. Dilute 2 ml of the solution to
100 ml with *1 M hydrochloric a*cid. Examined between
220 nm and 350 nm (*2.2.25*), the solution shows two
absorption maxima, at 246 nm and 319 nm. The ratio of the
absorbance measured at 246 nm to that measured at 319 nm
is 2.7 to 3.0.

B. Examine by infrared absorption spectrophotometry
(*2.2.24*), comparing with the spectrum obtained with
*cinchocaine hydrochloride CRS*. Examine the substances
prepared as discs using *potassium chloride R*.

C. Examine the chromatograms obtained in the test for
related substances. The principal spot in the chromatogram
obtained with test solution (b) is similar in position and size
to the principal spot in the chromatogram obtained with
reference solution (a).

D. Dissolve 0.5 g in 5 ml of *water R*. Add 1 ml of *dilute
ammonia R2*. A white precipitate is formed. Filter, wash the
precipitate with five quantities, each of 10 ml, of *water R* and
dry in a desiccator. It melts at 64 °C to 66 °C (*2.2.14*).

E. It gives reaction (a) of chlorides (*2.3.1*).

## TESTS
### Solution S
Dissolve 5.0 g in *carbon dioxide-free water R* prepared from
*distilled water R*, and dilute to 50 ml with the same solvent.

### Appearance of solution
Solution S is clear (*2.2.1*) and not more intensely coloured
than reference solution Y₆ (*2.2.2, Method II*).

### pH (*2.2.3*)
Dilute 10 ml of solution S to 50 ml with *carbon dioxide-free
water R*. The pH of the solution is 5.0 to 6.0.

### Related substances
Examine by thin-layer chromatography (*2.2.27*), using as the
coating substance a suitable silica gel with a fluorescent
indicator having an optimal intensity at 254 nm.

*Test solution (a)*   Dissolve 0.20 g of the substance to be
examined in *methanol R* and dilute to 5 ml with the same
solvent.

*Test solution (b)*   Dilute 1 ml of test solution (a) to 10 ml
with *methanol R*.

*Reference solution (a)*   Dissolve 20 mg of *cinchocaine
hydrochloride CRS* in *methanol R* and dilute to 5 ml with the
same solvent.

*Reference solution (b)*   Dilute 1 ml of test solution (b) to
20 ml with *methanol R*.

*Reference solution (c)*   Dilute 1 ml of test solution (b) to
50 ml with *methanol R*.

*Reference solution (d)*   Dissolve 20 mg of *benzocaine CRS* in
*methanol R* and dilute to 5 ml with the same solvent. Dilute
1 ml of the solution and 1 ml of reference solution (a) to
20 ml with *methanol R*.

Apply separately to the plate 5 µl of each solution. Develop
over a path of 15 cm using a mixture of 1 volume of
*ammonia R*, 5 volumes of *methanol R*, 30 volumes of
*acetone R* and 50 volumes of *toluene R*. Dry the plate in a
current of warm air for 15 min. Examine in ultraviolet light
at 254 nm. Any spot in the chromatogram obtained with test
solution (a), apart from the principal spot, is not more
intense than the principal spot in the chromatogram obtained
with reference solution (b) (0.5 per cent) and at most one
such spot is more intense than the spot in the chromatogram
obtained with reference solution (c) (0.2 per cent). The test
is not valid unless the chromatogram obtained with reference
solution (d) shows two clearly separated spots.

### Heavy metals (*2.4.8*)
12 ml of solution S complies with limit test A for heavy
metals (20 ppm). Prepare the standard using *lead standard
solution (2 ppm Pb) R*.

**Loss on drying** (2.2.32)

Not more than 2.0 per cent, determined on 0.500 g by drying in vacuo at 60 °C.

**Sulphated ash** (2.4.14)

Not more than 0.1 per cent, determined on 1.0 g.

## ASSAY

Dissolve 0.300 g in a mixture of 15.0 ml of *0.01 M hydrochloric acid* and 50 ml of *alcohol R*. Carry out a potentiometric titration (2.2.20), using *0.1 M sodium hydroxide*. Read the volume added between the two points of inflexion.

1 ml of *0.1 M sodium hydroxide* is equivalent to 37.99 mg of $C_{20}H_{30}ClN_3O_2$.

## STORAGE

Store in an airtight container, protected from light.

## IMPURITIES

A R1 = Cl, R2 = NH-[CH₂]₂-N(C₂H₅)₂: 2-chloro-*N*-[2-(diethylamino)ethyl]quinoline-4-carboxamide,

B. R1 = R2 = OH: 2-hydroxyquinoline-4-carboxylic acid,

C. R1 = OH, R2 = NH-[CH₂]₂-N(C₂H₅)₂: *N*-[2-(diethylamino)ethyl]-2-hydroxyquinoline-4-carboxamide,

D. R1 = O-[CH₂]₃-CH₃, R2 = OH: 2-butoxyquinoline-4-carboxylic acid.

_____ *Ph Eur*

# Cineole

★★★
★ ★
★ ★
★ ★
★★★

(*Ph Eur monograph 1973*)

$C_{10}H_{18}O$        154.3        470-82-6

*Ph Eur* _____

## DEFINITION

1,3,3-Trimethyl-2-oxabicyclo[2.2.2]octane.

## CHARACTERS

**Appearance**

Clear colourless liquid.

**Solubility**

Practically insoluble in water, miscible with alcohol and with methylene chloride.

It solidifies at about 0.5 °C.

## IDENTIFICATION

A. It complies with the test for refractive index (see Tests).

B. Thin-layer chromatography (2.2.27).

*Test solution*   Dilute 1 ml of solution S (see Tests) to 25 ml with *alcohol R*.

*Reference solution*   Mix 80 mg of *cineole CRS* with *alcohol R* and dilute to 10 ml with the same solvent.

*Plate*   TLC silica gel plate R.

*Mobile phase*   ethyl acetate R, toluene R (10:90 V/V).

*Application*   2 μl.

*Development*   Over 2/3 of the plate.

*Drying*   In a current of cold air.

*Detection*   Spray with *anisaldehyde solution R*, heat at 100-105 °C for 5 min.

*Results*   The principal spot in the chromatogram obtained with the test solution is similar in position, colour and size to the principal spot in the chromatogram obtained with the reference solution.

C. To 0.1 ml add 4 ml of *sulphuric acid R*. An orange-red colour develops. Add 0.2 ml of *formaldehyde solution R*. The colour changes to deep brown.

## TESTS

**Solution S**

Dilute 2.00 g to 10.0 ml with *alcohol R*.

**Appearance of solution**

Solution S is clear (2.2.1) and colourless (2.2.2, *Method I*).

**Chiral impurities**

The optical rotation (2.2.7) of solution S is − 0.10° to + 0.10°.

**Refractive index** (2.2.6)

1.456 to 1.460.

**Related substances**

Gas chromatography (2.2.28).

*Internal standard solution*   Dissolve 1.0 g of *camphor R* in *heptane R* and dilute to 200 ml with the same solvent.

*Test solution (a)*   Dissolve 2.5 g of the substance to be examined in *heptane R* and dilute to 25.0 ml with the same solvent.

*Test solution (b)*   Dissolve 2.5 g of the substance to be examined in *heptane R*, add 5.0 ml of the internal standard solution and dilute to 25.0 ml with *heptane R*.

*Reference solution (a)*   To 2.0 ml of test solution (a) add 20.0 ml of the internal standard solution and dilute to 100.0 ml with *heptane R*.

*Reference solution (b)*   Dissolve 50 mg of *1,4-cineole R* and 50 mg of the substance to be examined in *heptane R* and dilute to 50.0 ml with the same solvent.

*Column:*
— size: l = 30 m, Ø = 0.25 mm,
— stationary phase: macrogol 20 000 R (film thickness 0.25 μm).

*Carrier gas*   helium for chromatography R.

*Linear velocity*   45 cm/s.

*Split-ratio*   1:70.

*Temperature:*

|  | Time (min) | Temperature (°C) |
|---|---|---|
| Column | 0 - 10 | 50 |
|  | 10 - 35 | 50 → 100 |
|  | 35 - 45 | 100 → 200 |
|  | 45 - 55 | 200 |
| Injection port |  | 220 |
| Detector |  | 250 |

*Detection*  Flame ionisation.

*Injection*  1 µl.

*System suitability*  Reference solution (b):
— *resolution*: minimum 10 between the peaks due to impurity A and to cineole.

*Limits*:
— *total*: calculate the ratio (R) of the area of the peak due to cineole to the area of the peak due to the internal standard from the chromatogram obtained with reference solution (a); from the chromatogram obtained with test solution (b), calculate the ratio of the sum of the areas of any peaks, apart from the principal peak and the peak due to the internal standard, to the area of the peak due to internal standard: this ratio is not greater than R (2 per cent),
— *disregard limit*: 0.025 times the area of the principal peak in the chromatogram obtained with reference solution (a) (0.05 per cent).

**Residue on evaporation**

Maximum 0.1 per cent.

To 2.0 g add 5 ml of *water R*, evaporate to dryness on a water-bath and dry at 100-105 °C for 1 h. The residue weighs a maximum of 2 mg.

**STORAGE**

In an airtight container, protected from light.

**IMPURITIES**

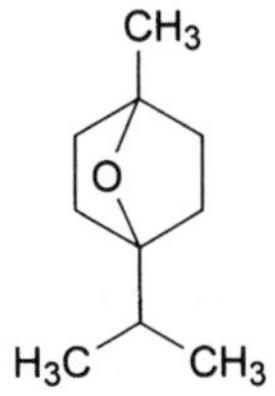

A. 1-methyl-4-(1-methylethyl)-7-oxabicyclo[2.2.1]heptane (1,4-cineole).

*Ph Eur*

# Cinnamic Acid

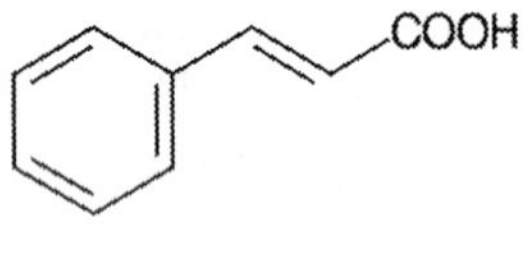

$C_9H_8O_2$          148.2          *621-82-9*

**Action and use**

Antimicrobial preservative; excipient.

**DEFINITION**

Cinnamic Acid is (E)-3-phenylprop-2-enoic acid. It contains not less than 99.0% and not more than 100.5% of $C_9H_8O_2$, calculated with reference to the dried substance.

**CHARACTERISTICS**

Colourless crystals.

Very slightly soluble in *water*; freely soluble in *ethanol (96%)*; soluble in *ether*.

**IDENTIFICATION**

A. The *infrared absorption spectrum*, Appendix II A, is concordant with the *reference spectrum* of cinnamic acid (RS 062).

B. The *light absorption*, Appendix II B, in the range 230 to 350 nm of a 0.0010% w/v solution in 0.1M *sodium hydroxide* exhibits a maximum only at 267 nm. The *absorbance* at 267 nm is about 1.4.

**TESTS**

**Melting point**

132° to 134°, Appendix V A.

**Ethanol-insoluble matter**

A 10% w/v solution in *ethanol (96%)* is *clear*, Appendix IV A.

**Related substances**

Carry out the method for *thin-layer chromatography*, Appendix III A, using the following solutions in *methanol*.

(1) 5.0% w/v of the substance being examined.

(2) 0.025% w/v of the substance being examined.

CHROMATOGRAPHIC CONDITIONS

(a) Use as the coating *silica gel GF_254*.

(b) Use the mobile phase as described below.

(c) Apply 5 µl of each solution.

(d) Develop the plate to 15 cm.

(e) After removal of the plate, dry in air and examine under *ultraviolet light (254 nm)*.

MOBILE PHASE

10 volumes of *glacial acetic acid* and 90 volumes of *toluene*.

LIMITS

Any *secondary spot* in the chromatogram obtained with solution (1) is not more intense than the spot in the chromatogram obtained with solution (2).

**Loss on drying**

When dried to constant weight at 60° at a pressure not exceeding 0.7 kPa, loses not more than 1.0% of its weight. Use 1 g.

**Sulphated ash**

Not more than 0.1%, Appendix IX A.

**ASSAY**

Dissolve 0.5 g in 15 ml of *ethanol (96%)* previously neutralised to *phenol red solution* and titrate with 0.1M *sodium hydroxide VS* using *phenol red solution* as indicator. Each ml of 0.1M *sodium hydroxide VS* is equivalent to 14.82 mg of $C_9H_8O_2$.

# Cinnarizine

*(Ph Eur monograph 0816)*

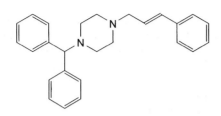

C₂₆H₂₈N₂      368.5      298-57-7

$C_{26}H_{28}N_2$    368.5    298-57-7

## Action and use

Histamine H₁ receptor antagonist; antihistamine.

*Ph Eur*

## DEFINITION

(*E*)-1-(Diphenylmethyl)-4-(3-phenylprop-2-enyl)piperazine.

## Content

99.0 per cent to 101.0 per cent (dried substance).

## CHARACTERS

### Appearance

White or almost white powder.

### Solubility

Practically insoluble in water, freely soluble in methylene chloride, soluble in acetone, slightly soluble in ethanol (96 per cent) and in methanol.

## IDENTIFICATION

*First identification*   A, B.

*Second identification*   A, C, D.

A. Melting point (*2.2.14*)

118 °C to 122 °C.

B. Infrared absorption spectrophotometry (*2.2.24*).

*Preparation*   Discs.

*Comparison*   cinnarizine CRS.

C. Thin-layer chromatography (*2.2.27*).

*Test solution*   Dissolve 10 mg of the substance to be examined in *methanol R* and dilute to 20 ml with the same solvent.

*Reference solution (a)*   Dissolve 10 mg of *cinnarizine CRS* in *methanol R* and dilute to 20 ml with the same solvent.

*Reference solution (b)*   Dissolve 10 mg of *cinnarizine CRS* and 10 mg of *flunarizine dihydrochloride CRS* in *methanol R* and dilute to 20 ml with the same solvent.

*Plate*   TLC octadecylsilyl silica gel F₂₅₄ plate R.

*Mobile phase*   1 M sodium chloride, methanol R, acetone R (20:30:50 *V/V/V*).

*Application*   5 μl.

*Development*   In an unsaturated tank, over a path of 15 cm.

*Drying*   In air.

*Detection*   Examine in ultraviolet light at 254 nm.

*System suitability*   Reference solution (b):
— the chromatogram shows 2 clearly separated spots.

*Results*   The principal spot in the chromatogram obtained with the test solution is similar in position and size to the principal spot in the chromatogram obtained with reference solution (a).

D. Dissolve 0.2 g of *anhydrous citric acid R* in 10 ml of *acetic anhydride R* in a water-bath at 80 °C and maintain the temperature of the water-bath at 80 °C for 10 min. Add about 20 mg of the substance to be examined. A purple colour develops.

## TESTS

### Appearance of solution

The solution is clear (*2.2.1*) and not more intensely coloured than reference solution BY₇ (*2.2.2, Method II*).

Dissolve 0.5 g in *methylene chloride R* and dilute to 20 ml with the same solvent.

### Acidity or alkalinity

Suspend 0.5 g in 15 ml of *water R*. Boil for 2 min. Cool and filter. Dilute the filtrate to 20 ml with *carbon dioxide-free water R*. To 10 ml of this solution add 0.1 ml of *phenolphthalein solution R* and 0.25 ml of *0.01 M sodium hydroxide*. The solution is pink. To 10 ml of the solution add 0.1 ml of *methyl red solution R* and 0.25 ml of *0.01 M hydrochloric acid*. The solution is red.

### Related substances

Liquid chromatography (*2.2.29*).

*Test solution*   Dissolve 25.0 mg of the substance to be examined in *methanol R* and dilute to 10.0 ml with the same solvent.

*Reference solution (a)*   Dissolve 12.5 mg of *cinnarizine CRS* and 15.0 mg of *flunarizine dihydrochloride CRS* in *methanol R* and dilute to 100.0 ml with the same solvent. Dilute 1.0 ml of this solution to 20.0 ml with *methanol R*.

*Reference solution (b)*   Dilute 1.0 ml of the test solution to 100.0 ml with *methanol R*. Dilute 5.0 ml of this solution to 20.0 ml with *methanol R*.

*Column:*
— size: l = 0.1 m, Ø = 4.0 mm;
— stationary phase: *base-deactivated octadecylsilyl silica gel for chromatography R* (3 μm).

*Mobile phase:*
— mobile phase A: 10 g/l solution of *ammonium acetate R*;
— mobile phase B: 0.2 per cent *V/V* solution of *glacial acetic acid R* in *acetonitrile R1*;

| Time (min) | Mobile phase A (per cent *V/V*) | Mobile phase B (per cent *V/V*) |
|---|---|---|
| 0 - 20 | 75 → 10 | 25 → 90 |
| 20 - 25 | 10 | 90 |

If necessary, adjust the concentration of glacial acetic acid in mobile phase B to obtain a horizontal baseline in the chromatogram.

*Flow rate*   1.5 ml/min.

*Detection*   Spectrophotometer at 230 nm.

*Equilibration*   With the mobile phase at the initial composition for at least 30 min.

*Injection*   10 μl; inject *methanol R* as a blank.

*Retention time*   Cinnarizine = about 11 min; flunarizine = about 11.5 min.

*System suitability*   Reference solution (a):
— resolution: minimum 5.0 between the peaks due to cinnarizine and flunarizine; if necessary, adjust the time programme for the gradient elution.

*Limits:*
— impurities A, B, C, D, E: for each impurity, not more than the area of the principal peak in the chromatogram obtained with reference solution (b) (0.25 per cent);

— *total:* not more than twice the area of the principal peak in the chromatogram obtained with reference solution (b) (0.5 per cent);

— *disregard limit:* 0.2 times the area of the principal peak in the chromatogram obtained with reference solution (b) (0.05 per cent); disregard any peak due to the blank.

### Heavy metals (2.4.8)
Maximum 20 ppm.

Dissolve 1.0 g in a mixture of 15 volumes of *water R* and 85 volumes of *acetone R.* Add *dilute hydrochloric acid R* until dissolution is complete. Dilute to 20 ml with a mixture of 15 volumes of *water R* and 85 volumes of *acetone R.* 12 ml of the solution complies with test B. Prepare the reference solution using 10 ml of *lead standard solution (1 ppm Pb)* obtained by diluting *lead standard solution (100 ppm Pb) R* with a mixture of 15 volumes of *water R* and 85 volumes of *acetone R.*

### Loss on drying (2.2.32)
Maximum 0.5 per cent, determined on 1.000 g by drying in an oven *in vacuo* at 60 °C for 4 h.

### Sulphated ash (2.4.14)
Maximum 0.1 per cent, determined on 1.0 g.

### ASSAY
Dissolve 0.150 g in 50 ml of a mixture of 1 volume of *anhydrous acetic acid R* and 7 volumes of *ethyl methyl ketone R.* Titrate with *0.1 M perchloric acid,* using 0.2 ml of *naphtholbenzein solution R* as indicator.

1 ml of *0.1 M perchloric acid* is equivalent to 18.43 mg of $C_{26}H_{28}N_2$.

### STORAGE
Protected from light.

### IMPURITIES
*Specified impurities   A, B, C, D, E.*

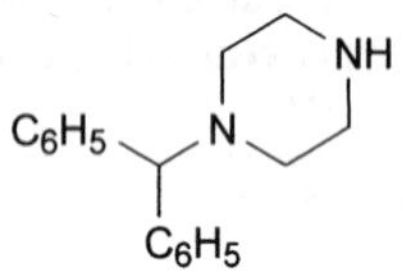

A. 1-(diphenylmethyl)piperazine,

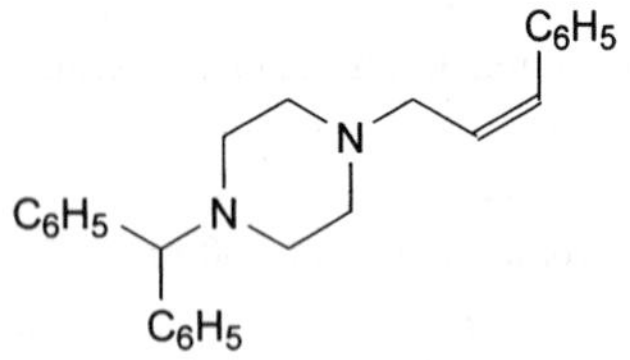

B. (Z)-1-(diphenylmethyl)-4-(3-phenylprop-2-enyl)piperazine,

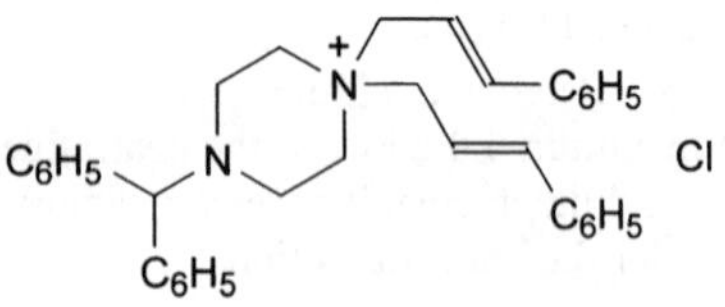

C. (4-(diphenylmethyl)-1,1-bis[(E)-3-phenylprop-2-enyl]piperazinium chloride,

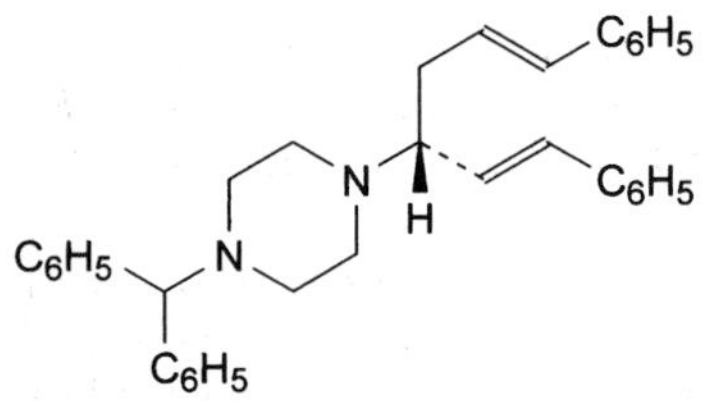

D. 1-(diphenylmethyl)-4-[(1RS,3E)-4-phenyl-1-[(E)-2-phenylethenyl]but-3-enyl]piperazine,

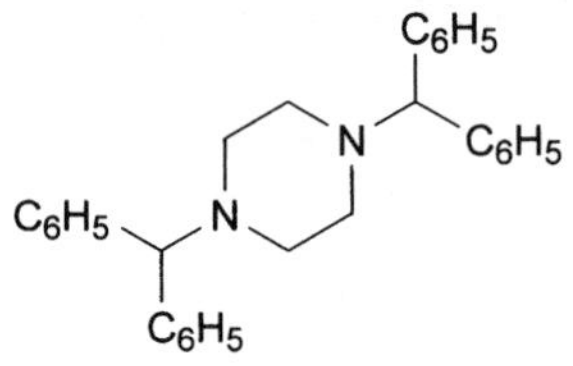

E. 1,4-bis(diphenylmethyl)piperazine.

*Ph Eur*

## Ciprofibrate

*(Ph Eur monograph 2013)*

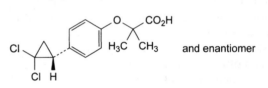

$C_{13}H_{14}Cl_2O_3$          289.2          52214-84-3

### Action and use
Fibrate; lipid-regulating drug.

*Ph Eur*

### DEFINITION
2-[4-[(1RS)-2,2-Dichlorocyclopropyl]phenoxy]-2-methylpropanoic acid.

### Content
99.0 per cent to 101.0 per cent (anhydrous substance).

### CHARACTERS
**Appearance**
White or slightly yellow, crystalline powder.

**Solubility**
Practically insoluble in water, freely soluble in anhydrous ethanol, soluble in toluene.

**mp**
About 115 °C.

### IDENTIFICATION
Infrared absorption spectrophotometry (2.2.24).

*Comparison   ciprofibrate CRS.*

### TESTS
**Appearance of solution**
The solution is clear (2.2.1) and not more intensely coloured than reference solution $BY_4$ (2.2.2, Method II).

Dissolve 1.0 g in *anhydrous ethanol R* and dilute to 10.0 ml with the same solvent.

**Related substances**
Liquid chromatography (2.2.29).

*Test solution* Dissolve 0.125 g of the substance to be examined in a mixture of equal volumes of *acetonitrile R* and *water R* and dilute to 50 ml with the same mixture of solvents.

*Reference solution (a)* Dilute 1.0 ml of the test solution to 100.0 ml with a mixture of equal volumes of *acetonitrile R* and *water R*. Dilute 1.0 ml of this solution to 10.0 ml with a mixture of equal volumes of *acetonitrile R* and *water R*.

*Reference solution (b)* Dissolve the contents of a vial of *ciprofibrate for system suitability CRS* in 2.0 ml of a mixture of equal volumes of *acetonitrile R* and *water R*.

*Column:*
— *size:* $l$ = 0.15 m, Ø = 4.6 mm,
— *stationary phase:* octylsilyl silica gel for chromatography R (5 μm).

*Mobile phase:*
— *mobile phase A*: 1.36 g/l solution of *potassium dihydrogen phosphate R* adjusted to pH 2.2 with *phosphoric acid R*,
— *mobile phase B*: acetonitrile R,

| Time (min) | Mobile phase A (per cent *V/V*) | Mobile phase B (per cent *V/V*) |
|---|---|---|
| 0 - 30 | 75 → 30 | 25 → 70 |
| 30 - 40 | 30 | 70 |
| 40 - 42 | 30 → 75 | 70 → 25 |

*Flow rate* 1.5 ml/min.

*Detection* Spectrophotometer at 230 nm.

*Injection* 10 μl.

*Identification of impurities* Use the chromatogram supplied with *ciprofibrate for system suitability CRS* to identify the peaks due to impurities A, B, C, D and E.

*Relative retention* With reference to ciprofibrate (retention time = about 18 min): impurity A = about 0.7; impurity B = about 0.8; impurity C = about 0.95; impurity D = about 1.3; impurity E = about 1.5.

*System suitability* Reference solution (b):
— *resolution*: baseline separation between the peaks due to impurity C and ciprofibrate.

*Limits:*
— *correction factor*: for the calculation of content, multiply the peak area of impurity A by 2.3,
— *impurities A, C, D*: for each impurity, not more than the area of the principal peak in the chromatogram obtained with reference solution (a) (0.1 per cent),
— *impurity B*: not more than twice the area of the principal peak in the chromatogram obtained with reference solution (a) (0.2 per cent),
— *impurity E*: not more than 8 times the area of the principal peak in the chromatogram obtained with reference solution (a) (0.8 per cent),
— *any other impurity*: for each impurity, not more than the area of the principal peak in the chromatogram obtained with reference solution (a) (0.1 per cent),
— *total of other impurities*: not more than 5 times the area of the principal peak in the chromatogram obtained with reference solution (a) (0.5 per cent),
— *disregard limit*: 0.5 times the area of the principal peak in the chromatogram obtained with reference solution (a) (0.05 per cent).

**Chlorides** (*2.4.4*)
Maximum 350 ppm.

To 0.190 g add 20 ml of *water R* and treat in an ultrasonic bath for 8 min. Filter. 15 ml of the filtrate complies with the test.

**Water** (*2.5.12*)
Maximum 0.5 per cent, determined on 1.000 g.

**Sulphated ash** (*2.4.14*)
Maximum 0.1 per cent, determined on 1.0 g.

**ASSAY**

Dissolve 0.250 g in a mixture of 20 ml of *water R* and 40 ml of *anhydrous ethanol R*. Titrate with *0.1 M sodium hydroxide*, determining the end-point potentiometrically (*2.2.20*).

1 ml of *0.1 M sodium hydroxide* is equivalent to 28.92 mg of $C_{13}H_{14}Cl_2O_3$.

**STORAGE**

In an airtight container, protected from light.

**IMPURITIES**

*Specified impurities* A, B, C, D, E.

A. 2-(4-ethenylphenoxy)-2-methylpropanoic acid,

B. 4-[(1*RS*)-2,2-dichlorocyclopropyl]phenol,

C. R = $CH_2OH$: 2-[4-[(1*RS*)-2,2-dichlorocyclopropyl]phenoxy]-2-methylpropan-1-ol,
D. R = $CO-OCH_3$: methyl 2-[4-[(1*RS*)-2,2-dichlorocyclopropyl]phenoxy]-2-methylpropanoate,
E. R = $CO-OC_2H_5$: ethyl 2-[4-[(1*RS*)-2,2-dichlorocyclopropyl]phenoxy]-2-methylpropanoate.

*Ph Eur*

# Ciprofloxacin

(*Ph Eur monograph 1089*)

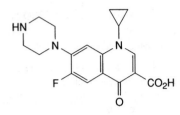

$C_{17}H_{18}FN_3O_3$      331.4      *85721-33-1*

## Action and use
Fluoroquinolone antibacterial.

## Preparation
Ciprofloxacin Intravenous Infusion

*Ph Eur* _____

## DEFINITION
1-Cyclopropyl-6-fluoro-4-oxo-7-(piperazin-1-yl)-1,4-dihydroquinoline-3-carboxylic acid.

## Content
99.0 per cent to 101.0 per cent (dried substance).

## CHARACTERS
### Appearance
Almost white or pale yellow, crystalline powder, slightly hygroscopic.

### Solubility
Practically insoluble in water, very slightly soluble in ethanol and in methylene chloride.

## IDENTIFICATION
Infrared absorption spectrophotometry (*2.2.24*).

*Comparison*   *ciprofloxacin CRS.*

## TESTS
### Appearance of solution
The solution is clear (*2.2.1*) and not more intensely coloured than reference solution $GY_5$ (*2.2.2, Method II*).

Dissolve 0.25 g in *0.1 M hydrochloric acid* and dilute to 20 ml with the same solvent.

### Impurity A
Thin-layer chromatography (*2.2.27*).

*Test solution*   Dissolve 50 mg of the substance to be examined in *dilute ammonia R1* and dilute to 5 ml with the same solvent.

*Reference solution*   Dissolve 10 mg of *ciprofloxacin impurity A CRS* in a mixture of 0.1 ml of *dilute ammonia R1* and 90 ml of *water R* and dilute to 100 ml with *water R*. Dilute 2 ml of the solution to 10 ml with *water R*.

*Plate*   TLC silica gel $F_{254}$ plate R.

*Application*   5 μl.

At the bottom of a chromatographic tank, place an evaporating dish containing 50 ml of *concentrated ammonia R*. Expose the plate to the ammonia vapour for 15 min in the closed tank. Withdraw the plate, transfer to a second chromatographic tank and proceed with development.

*Mobile phase*   *acetonitrile R, concentrated ammonia R, methanol R, methylene chloride R* (10:20:40:40 *V/V/V/V*).

*Development*   Over 3/4 of the plate.

*Drying*   In air.

*Detection*   Examine in ultraviolet light at 254 nm.

*Limit:*
— *impurity A*: any spot corresponding to impurity A is not more intense than the principal spot in the chromatogram obtained with the reference solution (0.2 per cent).

### Related substances
Liquid chromatography (*2.2.29*).

*Test solution*   To 25.0 mg of the substance to be examined add 0.2 ml of *dilute phosphoric acid R* and dilute to 50.0 ml with the mobile phase and treat in an ultrasonic bath until a clear solution is obtained.

*Reference solution (a)*   Dilute 1.0 ml of the test solution to 100.0 ml with the mobile phase. Dilute 1.0 ml of this solution to 5.0 ml with the mobile phase.

*Reference solution (b)*   Dissolve 5 mg of *ciprofloxacin hydrochloride for peak identification CRS* in the mobile phase and dilute to 10.0 ml with the mobile phase.

*Column:*
— *size*: l = 0.25 m, Ø = 4.6 mm;
— *stationary phase*: base-deactivated octadecylsilyl silica gel for chromatography R (5 μm);
— *temperature*: 40 °C.

*Mobile phase*   Mix 13 volumes of *acetonitrile R* and 87 volumes of a 2.45 g/l solution of *phosphoric acid R*, previously adjusted to pH 3.0 with *triethylamine R*.

*Flow rate*   1.5 ml/min.

*Detection*   Spectrophotometer at 278 nm.

*Injection*   50 μl.

*Run time*   Twice the retention time of ciprofloxacin.

*Relative retention*   With reference to ciprofloxacin (retention time = about 9 min): impurity E = about 0.4; impurity F = about 0.5; impurity B = about 0.6; impurity C = about 0.7; impurity D = about 1.2.

*System suitability*   Reference solution (b):
— *resolution*: minimum 1.3 between the peaks due to impurity B and impurity C.

*Limits:*
— *correction factors*: for the calculation of contents, multiply the peak areas of the following impurities by the corresponding correction factor: impurity B = 0.7; impurity C = 0.6; impurity D = 1.4; impurity E = 6.7; use the chromatogram obtained with reference solution (b) and the type chromatogram supplied with the CRS to identify the corresponding peaks;
— *impurities B, C, D, E*: for each impurity, not more than the area of the principal peak in the chromatogram obtained with reference solution (a) (0.2 per cent);
— *any other impurity*: not more than half the area of the principal peak in the chromatogram obtained with reference solution (a) (0.1 per cent);
— *total*: not more than 2.5 times the area of the principal peak in the chromatogram obtained with reference solution (a) (0.5 per cent);
— *disregard limit*: 0.25 times the area of the principal peak in the chromatogram obtained with reference solution (a) (0.05 per cent).

### Heavy metals (*2.4.8*)
Maximum 20 ppm.

Dissolve 0.5 g in *dilute acetic acid R* and dilute to 30 ml with the same solvent. Add 2 ml of *water R* instead of 2 ml of *buffer solution pH 3.5 R*. The filtrate complies with limit test E. Prepare the standard using 10 ml of *lead standard solution (1 ppm Pb) R*.

**Loss on drying** (2.2.32)

Maximum 1.0 per cent, determined on 1.000 g by drying under vacuum at 120 °C.

**Sulphated ash** (2.4.14)

Maximum 0.1 per cent, determined on 1.0 g in a platinum crucible.

## ASSAY

Dissolve 0.300 g in 80 ml of *glacial acetic acid R*. Titrate with *0.1 M perchloric acid*, determining the end-point potentiometrically (2.2.20).

1 ml of *0.1 M perchloric acid* is equivalent to 33.14 mg of $C_{17}H_{18}FN_3O_3$.

## STORAGE

In an airtight container, protected from light.

## IMPURITIES

*Specified impurities    A, B, C, D, E.*

*Other detectable impurities* (the following substances would, if present at a sufficient level, be detected by one or other of the tests in the monograph. They are limited by the general acceptance criterion for other/unspecified impurities and/or by the general monograph *Substances for pharmaceutical use (2034)*. It is therefore not necessary to identify these impurities for demonstration of compliance. See also 5.10. *Control of impurities in substances for pharmaceutical use*) : *F*.

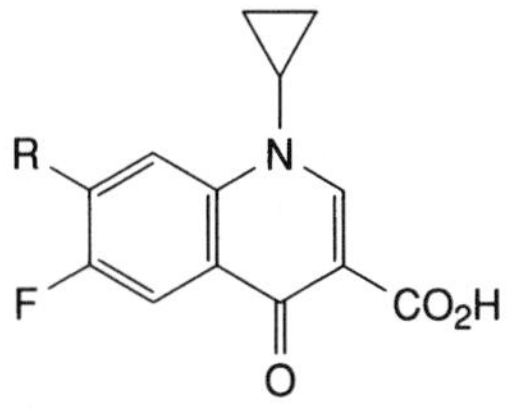

A. R = Cl: 7-chloro-1-cyclopropyl-6-fluoro-4-oxo-1,4-dihydroquinoline-3-carboxylic acid (fluoroquinolonic acid),

C. R = NH-[CH$_2$]$_2$-NH$_2$: 7-[(2-aminoethyl)amino]-1-cyclopropyl-6-fluoro-4-oxo-1,4-dihydroquinoline-3-carboxylic acid (ethylenediamine compound),

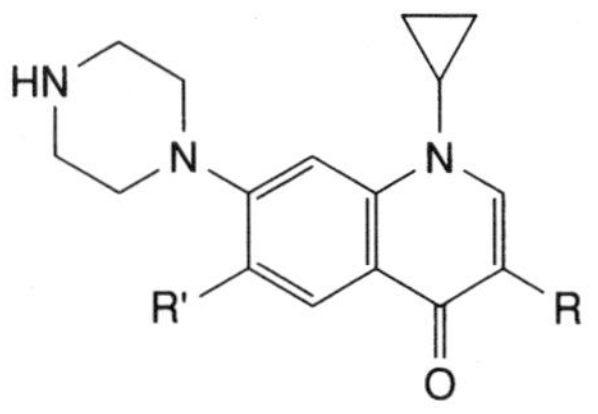

B  R = CO$_2$H, R' = H: 1-cyclopropyl-4-oxo-7-(piperazin-1-yl)-1,4-dihydroquinoline-3-carboxylic acid (desfluoro compound),

E  R = H, R' = F: 1-cyclopropyl-6-fluoro-7-(piperazin-1-yl)quinolin-4(1*H*)-one (decarboxylated compound),

F. R = CO$_2$H, R' = OH: 1-cyclopropyl-6-hydroxy-4-oxo-7-(piperazin-1-yl)-1,4-dihydroquinoline-3-carboxylic acid,

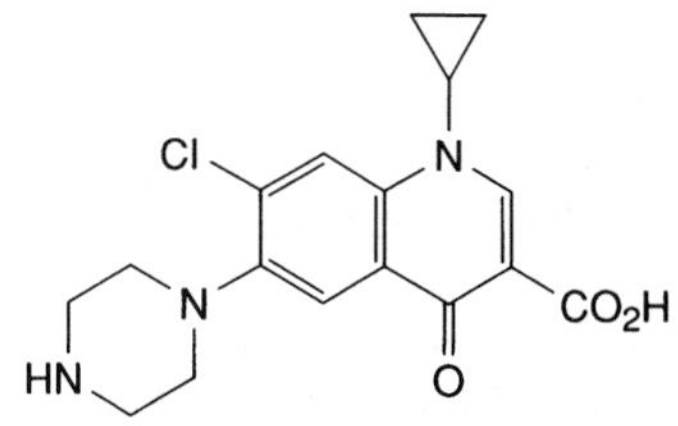

D. 7-chloro-1-cyclopropyl-4-oxo-6-(piperazin-1-yl)-1,4-dihydroquinoline-3-carboxylic acid.

*——————————————————— Ph Eur*

# Ciprofloxacin Hydrochloride

(*Ph Eur monograph 0888*)

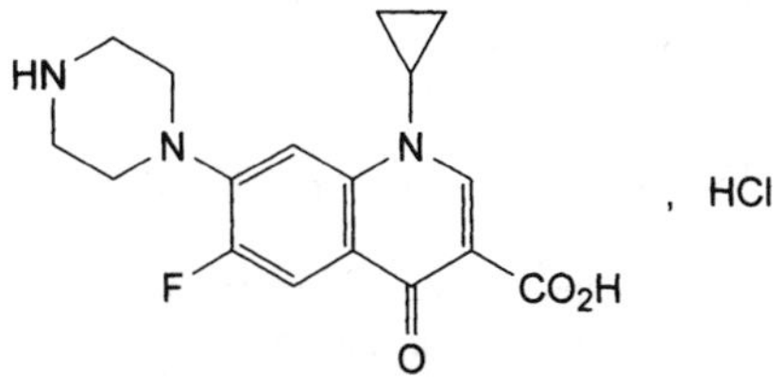

$C_{17}H_{18}FN_3O_3,HCl$          367.8          *86393-32-0*

**Action and use**

Fluoroquinolone antibacterial.

**Preparation**

Ciprofloxacin Tablets

*Ph Eur* _____

## DEFINITION

1-Cyclopropyl-6-fluoro-4-oxo-7-(piperazin-1-yl)-1,4-dihydroquinoline-3-carboxylic acid hydrochloride.

**Content**

98.0 per cent to 102.0 per cent (anhydrous substance).

## CHARACTERS

**Appearance**

Pale yellow, crystalline powder, slightly hygroscopic.

**Solubility**

Soluble in water, slightly soluble in methanol, very slightly soluble in ethanol, practically insoluble in acetone, in ethyl acetate and in methylene chloride.

## IDENTIFICATION

A. Infrared absorption spectrophotometry (2.2.24).

*Preparation*  Discs.

*Comparison*   *ciprofloxacin hydrochloride CRS*.

B. 0.1 g gives reaction (b) of chlorides (2.3.1).

## TESTS

**Solution S**

Dissolve 0.5 g in *carbon dioxide-free water R* and dilute to 20 ml with the same solvent.

**Appearance of solution**

The solution is clear (2.2.1) and not more intensely coloured than reference solution GY$_5$ (2.2.2, *Method II*).

Dilute 10 ml of solution S to 20 ml with *carbon dioxide-free water R*.

**pH** (2.2.3)

3.5 to 4.5 for solution S.

**Impurity A**

Thin-layer chromatography (*2.2.27*).

*Test solution*   Dissolve 50 mg of the substance to be examined in *water R* and dilute to 5 ml with the same solvent.

*Reference solution*   Dissolve 10 mg of *ciprofloxacin impurity A CRS* in a mixture of 0.1 ml of *dilute ammonia R1* and 90 ml of *water R* and dilute to 100 ml with *water R*. Dilute 2 ml of the solution to 10 ml with *water R*.

*Plate*   TLC silica gel $F_{254}$ plate R.

*Application*   5 µl.

At the bottom of a chromatographic tank, place an evaporating dish containing 50 ml of *concentrated ammonia R*. Expose the plate to the ammonia vapour for 15 min in the closed tank. Withdraw the plate, transfer to a second chromatographic tank and proceed with development.

*Mobile phase*   acetonitrile R, concentrated ammonia R, methanol R, methylene chloride R (10:20:40:40 *V/V/V/V*).

*Development*   Over 3/4 of the plate.

*Drying*   In air.

*Detection*   Examine in ultraviolet light at 254 nm.

*Limit:*
— *impurity A*: any spot corresponding to impurity A is not more intense than the principal spot in the chromatogram obtained with the reference solution (0.2 per cent).

**Related substances**

Liquid chromatography (*2.2.29*).

*Test solution*   Dissolve 25.0 mg of the substance to be examined in the mobile phase and dilute to 50.0 ml with the mobile phase.

*Reference solution (a)*   Dissolve 25.0 mg of *ciprofloxacin hydrochloride CRS* in the mobile phase and dilute to 50.0 ml with the mobile phase.

*Reference solution (b)*   Dissolve 5 mg of *ciprofloxacin hydrochloride for peak identification CRS* in the mobile phase and dilute to 10.0 ml with the mobile phase.

*Reference solution (c)*   Dilute 1.0 ml of the test solution to 50.0 ml with the mobile phase. Dilute 1.0 ml of this solution to 10.0 ml with the mobile phase.

*Column:*
— *size: l* = 0.25 m, Ø = 4.6 mm;
— *stationary phase*: base-deactivated octadecylsilyl silica gel for chromatography R (5 µm);
— *temperature*: 40 °C.

*Mobile phase*   Mix 13 volumes of *acetonitrile R* and 87 volumes of a 2.45 g/l solution of *phosphoric acid R*, previously adjusted to pH 3.0 with *triethylamine R*.

*Flow rate*   1.5 ml/min.

*Detection*   Spectrophotometer at 278 nm.

*Injection*   50 µl.

*Run time*   Twice the retention time of ciprofloxacin.

*Relative retention*   With reference to ciprofloxacin (retention time = about 9 min): impurity E = about 0.4; impurity F = about 0.5; impurity B = about 0.6; impurity C = about 0.7; impurity D = about 1.2.

*System suitability*   Reference solution (b):
— *resolution*: minimum 1.3 between the peaks due to impurity B and impurity C.

*Limits:*
— *correction factors*: for the calculation of contents, multiply the peak areas of the following impurities by the corresponding correction factor: impurity B = 0.7;

impurity C = 0.6; impurity D = 1.4; impurity E = 6.7; use the chromatogram obtained with reference solution (b) and the type chromatogram supplied with the CRS to identify the corresponding peaks;
— *impurities B, C, D, E*: for each impurity, not more than the area of the principal peak in the chromatogram obtained with reference solution (c) (0.2 per cent);
— *any other impurity*: not more than half the area of the principal peak in the chromatogram obtained with reference solution (c) (0.1 per cent);
— *total*: not more than 2.5 times the area of the principal peak in the chromatogram obtained with reference solution (c) (0.5 per cent);
— *disregard limit*: 0.25 times the area of the principal peak in the chromatogram obtained with reference solution (c) (0.05 per cent).

**Heavy metals** (*2.4.8*)

Maximum 20 ppm.

Dissolve 0.25 g in *water R* and dilute to 30 ml with the same solvent. Carry out the prefiltration. The filtrate complies with limit test E. Prepare the standard using 5 ml of *lead standard solution (1 ppm Pb) R*.

**Water** (*2.5.12*)

Maximum 6.7 per cent, determined on 0.200 g.

**Sulphated ash** (*2.4.14*)

Maximum 0.1 per cent, determined on 1.0 g in a platinum crucible.

**ASSAY**

Liquid chromatography (*2.2.29*) as described in the test for related substances with the following modifications.

*Injection*   10 µl; inject the test solution and reference solution (a).

Calculate the percentage content of $C_{17}H_{19}ClFN_3O_3$.

**STORAGE**

In an airtight container, protected from light.

**IMPURITIES**

*Specified impurities*   A, B, C, D, E.

*Other detectable impurities* (the following substances would, if present at a sufficient level, be detected by one or other of the tests in the monograph. They are limited by the general acceptance criterion for other/unspecified impurities and/or by the general monograph *Substances for pharmaceutical use* (2034). It is therefore not necessary to identify these impurities for demonstration of compliance. See also 5.10. *Control of impurities in substances for pharmaceutical use*) : F.

A. R = Cl: 7-chloro-1-cyclopropyl-6-fluoro-4-oxo-1,4-dihydroquinoline-3-carboxylic acid (fluoroquinolonic acid),

C. R = NH-[CH₂]₂-NH₂: 7-[(2-aminoethyl)amino]-1-cyclopropyl-6-fluoro-4-oxo-1,4-dihydroquinoline-3-carboxylic acid (ethylenediamine compound),

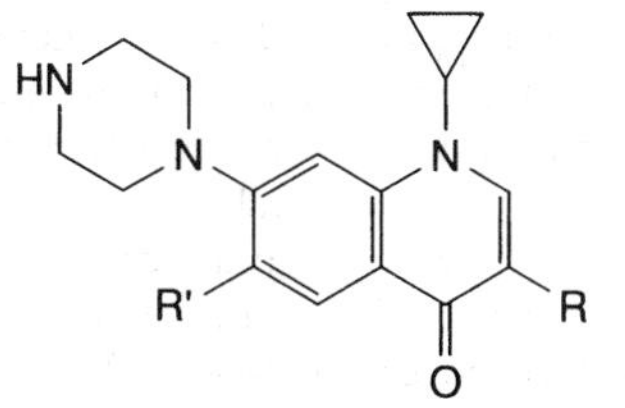

B. R = CO$_2$H, R′ = H: 1-cyclopropyl-4-oxo-7-(piperazin-1-yl)-1,4-dihydroquinoline-3-carboxylic acid (desfluoro compound),

E. R = H, R′ = F: 1-cyclopropyl-6-fluoro-7-(piperazin-1-yl)quinolin-4(1H)-one (decarboxylated compound),

F. R = CO$_2$H, R′ = OH: 1-cyclopropyl-6-hydroxy-4-oxo-7-(piperazin-1-yl)-1,4-dihydroquinoline-3-carboxylic acid,

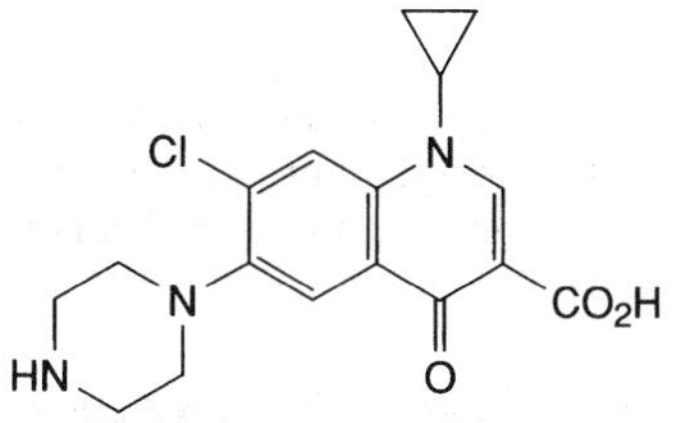

D. 7-chloro-1-cyclopropyl-4-oxo-6-(piperazin-1-yl)-1,4-dihydroquinoline-3-carboxylic acid.

*Ph Eur*

# Cisapride

(*Cisapride Monohydrate, Ph Eur monograph 0995*)

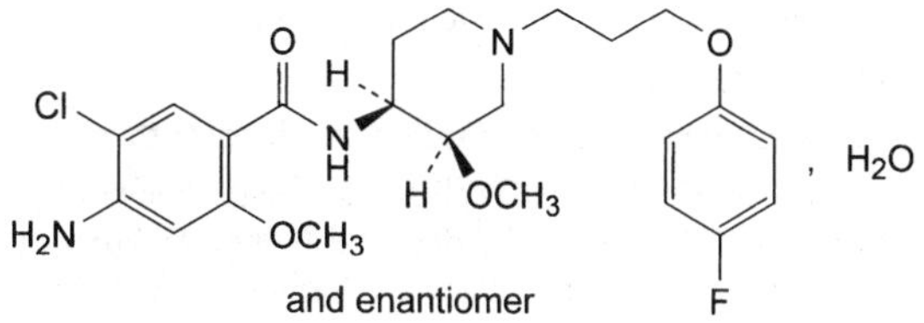

, H$_2$O

and enantiomer

C$_{23}$H$_{29}$ClFN$_3$O$_4$, H$_2$O        484.0        *81098-60-4*

*(anhydrous)*

## Action and use
Enterokinetic agent.

*Ph Eur*

## DEFINITION
4-Amino-5-chloro-N-[(3RS,4SR)-1-[3-(4-fluorophenoxy)propyl]-3-methoxypiperidin-4-yl]-2-methoxybenzamide monohydrate.

## Content
99.0 per cent to 101.0 per cent (anhydrous substance).

## CHARACTERS
### Appearance
White or almost white powder.

### Solubility
Practically insoluble in water, freely soluble in dimethylformamide, soluble in methylene chloride, sparingly soluble in methanol.

It shows polymorphism (*5.9*).

## IDENTIFICATION
Infrared absorption spectrophotometry (*2.2.24*).

*Preparation*   Discs.

*Comparison*   *cisapride monohydrate CRS.*

If the spectra obtained show differences, dissolve the substance to be examined and the reference substance separately in the minimum volume of *methanol R*, evaporate to dryness in a current of air and record new spectra using the residues.

## TESTS
### Solution S
Dissolve 0.20 g in *methylene chloride R* and dilute to 20.0 ml with the same solvent.

### Appearance of solution
Solution S is clear (*2.2.1*) and not more intensely coloured than reference solution BY$_6$ (*2.2.2, Method II*).

### Optical rotation (*2.2.7*)
− 0.1° to + 0.1°, determined on solution S.

### Related substances
Liquid chromatography (*2.2.29*).

*Test solution*   Dissolve 0.100 g of the substance to be examined in *methanol R* and dilute to 10.0 ml with the same solvent.

*Reference solution (a)*   Dissolve 5.0 mg of *cisapride monohydrate CRS* and 40.0 mg of *haloperidol CRS* in *methanol R* and dilute to 100.0 ml with the same solvent.

*Reference solution (b)*   Dilute 5.0 ml of the test solution to 100.0 ml with *methanol R*. Dilute 1.0 ml of this solution to 10.0 ml with *methanol R*.

*Column:*
— size: l = 0.1 m, Ø = 4.0 mm;
— stationary phase: *base-deactivated octadecylsilyl silica gel for chromatography R* (3 µm).

*Mobile phase:*
— mobile phase A: 20 g/l solution *of tetrabutylammonium hydrogen sulphate R*;
— mobile phase B: *methanol R*;

| Time (min) | Mobile phase A (per cent V/V) | Mobile phase B (per cent V/V) |
|---|---|---|
| 0 - 20 | 80 → 55 | 20 → 45 |
| 20 - 21 | 55 → 5 | 45 → 95 |
| 21 - 25 | 5 | 95 |

*Flow rate*   1.2 ml/min.

*Detection*   Spectrophotometer at 275 nm.

*Injection*   10 µl; inject *methanol R* as a blank.

*Retention time*   cisapride = about 15 min; haloperidol = about 16 min.

*System suitability*   Reference solution (a):
— resolution: minimum 2.5 between the peaks due to cisapride and haloperidol; if necessary, adjust the concentration of methanol in the mobile phase or adjust the time programme for the linear gradient.

*Limits:*
— impurities A, B, C, E: for each impurity, not more than the area of the principal peak in the chromatogram obtained with reference solution (b) (0.5 per cent);
— total: not more than twice the area of the principal peak in the chromatogram obtained with reference solution (b) (1 per cent);

— *disregard limit*: 0.1 times the area of the principal peak in the chromatogram obtained with reference solution (b) (0.05 per cent).

**Water** (*2.5.12*)
3.4 per cent to 4.0 per cent, determined on 0.500 g.

**Sulphated ash** (*2.4.14*)
Maximum 0.1 per cent, determined on 1.0 g in a platinum crucible.

**ASSAY**
Dissolve 0.350 g in 70 ml of a mixture of 1 volume of *anhydrous acetic acid R* and 7 volumes of *methyl ethyl ketone R* and titrate with *0.1 M perchloric acid*. Determine the end-point potentiometrically (*2.2.20*).

1 ml of *0.1 M perchloric acid* is equivalent to 46.60 mg of $C_{23}H_{29}ClFN_3O_4$.

**STORAGE**
Protected from light.

**IMPURITIES**
*Specified impurities   A, B, C, E.*

*Other detectable impurities* (the following substances would, if present at a sufficient level, be detected by one or other of the tests in the monograph. They are limited by the general acceptance criterion for other/unspecified impurities and/or by the general monograph *Substances for pharmaceutical use (2034)*. It is therefore not necessary to identify these impurities for demonstration of compliance. See also *5.10. Control of impurities in substances for pharmaceutical use*) : D.

A. R1 = R3 = H, R2 = OCH₃: 4-amino-5-chloro-2-methoxy-*N*-[(3*RS*,4*SR*)-3-methoxy-1-(3-phenoxypropyl)piperidin-4-yl]benzamide,

B. R1 = F, R2 = R3 = H: 4-amino-5-chloro-*N*-[1-[3-(4-fluorophenoxy)propyl]piperidin-4-yl]-2-methoxybenzamide,

C. R1 = F, R2 = H, R3 = OCH₃: 4-amino-5-chloro-*N*-[(3*RS*,4*RS*)-1-[3-(4-fluorophenoxy)propyl]-3-methoxypiperidin-4-yl-2-methoxybenzamide,

E. R1 = F, R2 = OH, R3 = H: 4-amino-5-chloro-*N*-[(3*RS*,4*SR*)-1-[3-(4-fluorophenoxy)propyl]-3-hydroxypiperidin-4-yl]-2-methoxybenzamide,

D. 4-[(4-amino-5-chloro-2-methoxybenzoyl)amino]-5-chloro-*N*-[(3*RS*,4*SR*)-1-[3-(4-fluorophenoxy)propyl]-3-methoxypiperidin-4-yl]-2-methoxybenzamide.

——————————————————————— *Ph Eur*

# Cisapride Tartrate

(*Ph Eur monograph 1503*)

$C_{23}H_{29}ClFN_3O_6,C_4H_6O_6$     616.0

**Action and use**
Enterokinetic agent.

*Ph Eur* ————————————————————

**DEFINITION**
4-Amino-5-chloro-*N*-[(3*RS*,4*SR*)-1-[3-(4-fluorophenoxy)propyl]-3-methoxypiperidin-4-yl]-2-methoxybenzamide (2*R*,3*R*)-2,3-dihydroxybutanedioate.

**Content**
99.0 per cent to 101.0 per cent (dried substance).

**CHARACTERS**
**Appearance**
White or almost white powder.

**Solubility**
Slightly soluble in water, freely soluble in dimethylformamide, slightly soluble in methanol, very slightly soluble in ethanol (96 per cent).

It shows polymorphism (*5.9*).

**IDENTIFICATION**
A. Infrared absorption spectrophotometry (*2.2.24*).

*Preparation*   Discs.

*Comparison   cisapride tartrate CRS.*

If the spectra obtained show differences, dissolve the substance to be examined and the reference substance separately in the minimum volume of *ethanol (96 per cent) R*, evaporate to dryness in a current of air and record new spectra using the residues.

B. Specific optical rotation (see Tests).

**TESTS**
**Specific optical rotation** (*2.2.7*)
+ 5.0 to + 10.0 (dried substance).

Dissolve 0.100 g in *methanol R* and dilute to 25.0 ml with the same solvent.

**Related substances**
Liquid chromatography (*2.2.29*).

*Solvent mixture   water R, methanol R* (10:90 *V/V*).

*Test solution*   Dissolve 0.100 g of the substance to be examined in the solvent mixture, with gentle warming if necessary, and dilute to 10.0 ml with the solvent mixture.

*Reference solution (a)*   Dissolve 5.0 mg of *cisapride tartrate CRS* and 30.0 mg of *haloperidol CRS* in the solvent mixture and dilute to 100.0 ml with the solvent mixture.

*Reference solution (b)*   Dilute 1.0 ml of the test solution to 100.0 ml with the solvent mixture. Dilute 5.0 ml of this solution to 20.0 ml with the solvent mixture.

*Column:*
— *size: l* = 0.1 m, Ø = 4.0 mm;

— *stationary phase: base-deactivated octadecylsilyl silica gel for chromatography R* (3 μm).

*Mobile phase:*
— *mobile phase A*: 20 g/l solution of *tetrabutylammonium hydrogen sulphate R;*
— *mobile phase B: methanol R;*

| Time (min) | Mobile phase A (per cent *V/V*) | Mobile phase B (per cent *V/V*) |
|---|---|---|
| 0 - 20 | 80 → 55 | 20 → 45 |
| 20 - 21 | 55 → 5 | 45 → 95 |
| 21 - 25 | 5 | 95 |

*Flow rate*   1.2 ml/min.

*Detection*   Spectrophotometer at 275 nm.

*Injection*   10 μl; inject the solvent mixture as a blank.

*Retention time*   Cisapride = about 15 min; haloperidol = about 16 min.

*System suitability*   Reference solution (a):
— *resolution*: minimum 2.5 between the peaks due to cisapride and haloperidol; if necessary, adjust the concentration of methanol in the mobile phase or adjust the time programme for the linear gradient.

*Limits:*
— *impurities A, C*: for each impurity, not more than the area of the principal peak in the chromatogram obtained with reference solution (b) (0.25 per cent);
— *total*: not more than twice the area of the principal peak in the chromatogram obtained with reference solution (b) (0.5 per cent);
— *disregard limit*: 0.2 times the area of the principal peak in the chromatogram obtained with reference solution (b) (0.05 per cent); disregard any peak due to the blank.

**Loss on drying** (*2.2.32*)
Maximum 0.5 per cent, determined on 1.000 g by drying in an oven at 105 °C.

**Sulphated ash** (*2.4.14*)
Maximum 0.1 per cent, determined on 1.0 g in a platinum crucible.

**ASSAY**
Dissolve 0.500 g in 70 ml of *anhydrous acetic acid R* and titrate with *0.1 M perchloric acid*. Determine the end-point potentiometrically (*2.2.20*).

1 ml of *0.1 M perchloric acid* is equivalent to 61.60 mg of $C_{27}H_{35}ClFN_3O_{10}$.

**STORAGE**
Protected from light.

**IMPURITIES**
*Specified impurities   A, C.*

*Other detectable impurities* (the following substances would, if present at a sufficient level, be detected by one or other of the tests in the monograph. They are limited by the general acceptance criterion for other/unspecified impurities and/or by the general monograph *Substances for pharmaceutical use* (*2034*). It is therefore not necessary to identify these impurities for demonstration of compliance. See also *5.10*. *Control of impurities in substances for pharmaceutical use* : *B, D, E.*

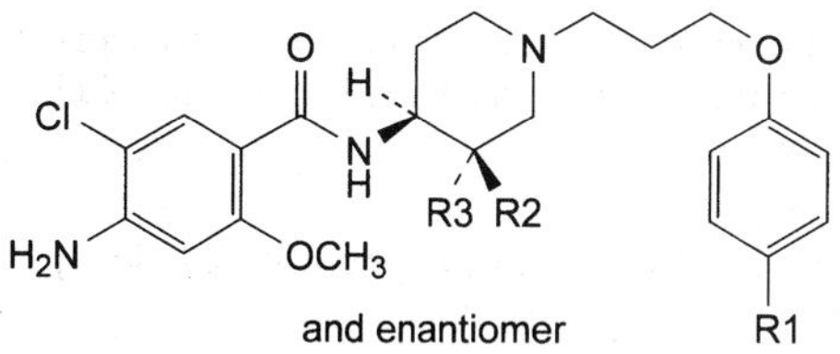

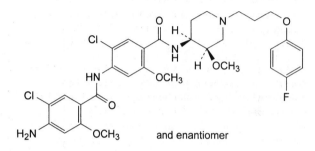

and enantiomer

A. R1 = R3 = H, R2 = OCH₃: 4-amino-5-chloro-2-methoxy-*N*-[(3*RS*,4*SR*)-3-methoxy-1-(3-phenoxypropyl)piperidin-4-yl]benzamide,

B. R1 = F, R2 = R3 = H: 4-amino-5-chloro-*N*-[1-[3-(4-fluorophenoxy)propyl]piperidin-4-yl]-2-methoxybenzamide,

C. R1 = F, R2 = H, R3 = OCH₃: 4-amino-5-chloro-*N*-[(3*RS*,4*RS*)-1-[3-(4-fluorophenoxy)propyl]-3-methoxypiperidin-4-yl]-2-methoxybenzamide,

E. R1 = F, R2 = OH, R3 = H: 4-amino-5-chloro-*N*-[(3*RS*,4*SR*)-1-[3-(4-fluorophenoxy)propyl]-3-hydroxypiperidin-4-yl]-2-methoxybenzamide,

and enantiomer

D. 4-[(4-amino-5-chloro-2-methoxybenzoyl)amino]-5-chloro-*N*-[(3*RS*,4*SR*)-1-[3-(4-fluorophenoxy)propyl]-3-methoxypiperidin-4-yl]-2-methoxybenzamide.

*Ph Eur*

# Cisplatin

(*Ph Eur monograph 0599*)

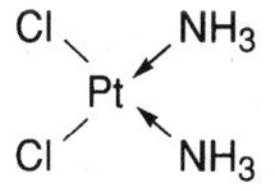

| $H_6Cl_2N_2Pt$ | 300.0 | *15663-27-1* |
|---|---|---|

**Action and use**
Platinum-containing cytotoxic.

**Preparation**
Cisplatin Injection

*Ph Eur*

**DEFINITION**
*cis*-Diamminedichloroplatinum(II).

**Content**
97.0 per cent to 102.0 per cent.

**CHARACTERS**
**Appearance**
Yellow powder, or yellow or orange-yellow crystals.

## Solubility

Slightly soluble in water, sparingly soluble in dimethylformamide, practically insoluble in ethanol (96 per cent).

*Carry out identification test B, the tests (except that for silver) and the assay protected from light.*

## IDENTIFICATION

*First identification   A, B.*

*Second identification   B, C.*

A. Infrared absorption spectrophotometry (*2.2.24*).

*Comparison   cisplatin CRS.*

B. Thin-layer chromatography (*2.2.27*).

*Test solution*   Dilute 1 ml of solution S2 (see Tests) to 10 ml with *dimethylformamide R*.

*Reference solution*   Dissolve 10 mg of *cisplatin CRS* in 5 ml of *dimethylformamide R*.

*Plate*   *cellulose for chromatography R1* as the coating substance.

*Pretreatment*   Activate the plate by heating at 150 °C for 1 h.

*Mobile phase*   *acetone R, dimethylformamide R* (10:90 *V/V*).

*Application*   2 μl.

*Development*   Over 2/3 of the plate.

*Drying*   In air.

*Detection*   Spray with a 50 g/l solution of *stannous chloride R* in a mixture of equal volumes of *dilute hydrochloric acid R* and *water R*. Examine after 1 h.

*Results*   The principal spot in the chromatogram obtained with the test solution is similar in position, colour and size to the principal spot in the chromatogram obtained with the reference solution.

C. Add 50 mg to 2 ml of *dilute sodium hydroxide solution R* in a glass dish. Evaporate to dryness. Dissolve the residue in a mixture of 0.5 ml of *nitric acid R* and 1.5 ml of *hydrochloric acid R*. Evaporate to dryness. The residue is orange. Dissolve the residue in 0.5 ml of *water R* and add 0.5 ml of *ammonium chloride solution R*. A yellow, crystalline precipitate is formed.

## TESTS

### Solution S1

Dissolve 25 mg in a 9 g/l solution of *sodium chloride R* in *carbon dioxide-free water R* and dilute to 25 ml with the same solvent.

### Solution S2

Dissolve 0.20 g in *dimethylformamide R* and dilute to 10 ml with the same solvent.

### Appearance of solution S1

Solution S1 is clear (*2.2.1*) and not more intensely coloured than reference solution GY$_5$ (*2.2.2, Method II*).

### Appearance of solution S2

Solution S2 is clear (*2.2.1*).

### pH (*2.2.3*)

4.5 to 6.0 for solution S1, measured immediately after preparation.

### Related substances

Liquid chromatography (*2.2.29*). *Carry out the test protected from light. Do not heat or sonicate any platinum-containing solution. All solutions are to be used within 4 h.*

*Test solution*   Dissolve 25.0 mg of the substance to be examined in a 9.0 g/l solution of *sodium chloride R* and dilute to 25.0 ml with the same solution.

*Reference solution (a)*   Dissolve 25.0 mg of *cisplatin CRS* in a 9.0 g/l solution of *sodium chloride R* and dilute to 25.0 ml with the same solution.

*Reference solution (b)*   Dissolve 5.0 mg of *cisplatin impurity A CRS* in a 9.0 g/l solution of *sodium chloride R* and dilute to 50.0 ml with the same solution.

*Reference solution (c)*   Dissolve 5.6 mg of *cisplatin impurity B CRS* in a 9.0 g/l solution of *sodium chloride R* and dilute to 100.0 ml with the same solution.

*Reference solution (d)*   Mix 0.05 ml of the test solution with 5.0 ml of reference solution (b) and 5.0 ml of reference solution (c) and dilute to 25.0 ml with a 9.0 g/l solution of *sodium chloride R*.

*Reference solution (e)*   Dilute 5.0 ml of reference solution (d) to 20.0 ml with a 9.0 g/l solution of *sodium chloride R*.

*Blank solution*   9.0 g/l solution of *sodium chloride R*.

*Column:*
— *size*: l = 0.25 m, Ø = 4.0 mm;
— *stationary phase*: base-deactivated octylsilyl silica gel for chromatography R (4 μm);
— *temperature*: 30 °C.

*Mobile phase*   Dissolve 1.08 g of *sodium octanesulphonate R*, 1.70 g of *tetrabutylammonium hydrogen sulphate R* and 2.72 g of *potassium dihydrogen phosphate R* in *water for chromatography R* and dilute to 950 ml with the same solvent. Adjust to pH 5.9 with *1 M sodium hydroxide* and dilute to 1000 ml with *water for chromatography R*.

*Flow rate*   1.0 ml/min.

*Detection*   Spectrophotometer at 210 nm.

*Injection*   20 μl of the test solution, reference solutions (d) and (e), and the blank solution.

*Run time*   3 times the retention time of cisplatin.

The displacement peak is the latest eluting peak of the group of injection peaks in the chromatogram obtained with the blank solution.

*Identification of cisplatin aquo complex*   Use the chromatogram supplied with *cisplatin CRS* and the chromatogram obtained with reference solution (a) to identify the peak due to cisplatin aquo complex.

*Relative retention*   With reference to cisplatin (retention time = about 3.8 min):
displacement peak = about 0.5; impurity A = about 0.6; impurity B = about 0.7; cisplatin aquo complex = about 1.2.

*System suitability*   Reference solution (d):
— *resolution*: minimum 2.5 between the peaks due to impurities A and B, the displacement peak and the peak due to impurity A are well separated.

*Limits:*
— *impurity A*: not more than the area of the corresponding peak in the chromatogram obtained with reference solution (d) (2.0 per cent);
— *impurity B*: not more than the area of the corresponding peak in the chromatogram obtained with reference solution (d) (1.0 per cent);
— *unspecified impurities*: for each impurity, not more than 0.5 times the area of the peak due to cisplatin in the chromatogram obtained with reference solution (d) (0.10 per cent);
— *sum of impurities other than A and B*: not more than 2.5 times the area of the peak due to cisplatin in the chromatogram obtained with reference solution (d) (0.5 per cent);

— *disregard limit*: the area of the peak due to cisplatin in the chromatogram obtained with reference solution (e) (0.05 per cent). Disregard any peak due to the cisplatin aquo complex.

**Silver**

Maximum $2.50 \times 10^{2}$ ppm.

Atomic absorption spectrometry (*2.2.23, Method I*).

*Test solution*   Dissolve 0.100 g in 15 ml of *nitric acid R*, heating to 80 °C. Cool and dilute to 25.0 ml with *water R*.

*Reference solutions*   To suitable volumes (10 ml to 30 ml) of *silver standard solution (5 ppm Ag) R* add 50 ml of *nitric acid R* and dilute to 100.0 ml with *water R*.

*Source*   Silver hollow-cathode lamp, preferably using a transmission band of 0.5 nm.

*Wavelenth*   328 nm.

*Atomisation device*   Fuel-lean air-acetylene flame.

Carry out a blank determination.

**ASSAY**

Liquid chromatography (*2.2.29*) as described in the test for related substances with the following modification.

*Injection*   10 μl of the test solution and reference solution (a).

Calculate the percentage content of $PtCl_2(NH_3)_2$ from the sum of the areas of the peaks due to cisplatin and cisplatin aquo complex and from the declared content of *cisplatin CRS*.

**STORAGE**

In an airtight container, protected from light.

**IMPURITIES**

*Specified impurities*   A, B.

*Other detectable impurities*   (The following substances would, if present at a sufficient level, be detected by one or other of the tests in the monograph. They are limited by the general acceptance criterion for other/unspecified impurities and/or by the general monograph *Substances for pharmaceutical use (2034)*. It is therefore not necessary to identify these impurities for demonstration of compliance. See also *5.10. Control of impurities in substances for pharmaceutical use*): C.

A. *trans*-diamminedichloroplatinum(II) (transplatin),

B. amminetrichloroplatinate(−),

C. tetrachloroplatinate(2−).

*Ph Eur*

# Citalopram Hydrobromide

(*Ph Eur monograph 2288*)

and enantiomer , HBr

$C_{20}H_{22}BrFN_2O$          405.3          59729-32-7

**Action and use**

Selective serotonin reuptake inhibitor; antidepressant.

*Ph Eur*

**DEFINITION**

(1*RS*)-1-[3-(Dimethylamino)propyl]-1-(4-fluorophenyl)-1,3-dihydroisobenzofuran-5-carbonitrile hydrobromide.

**Content**

99.0 per cent to 101.5 per cent (dried substance).

**CHARACTERS**

**Appearance**

White or almost white, crystalline powder.

**Solubility**

Sparingly soluble in water and in anhydrous ethanol.

**IDENTIFICATION**

A. Optical rotation (see Tests).

B. Infrared absorption spectrophotometry (*2.2.24*).

*Comparison*   citalopram hydrobromide CRS.

C. It gives reaction (a) of bromides (*2.3.1*).

**TESTS**

**Optical rotation** (*2.2.7*)

− 0.10° to + 0.10°.

Dissolve 1.0 g in *methanol R* and dilute to 20 ml with the same solvent.

**Related substances**

Liquid chromatography (*2.2.29*).

*Test solution*   Dissolve 50 mg of the substance to be examined in mobile phase A and dilute to 100.0 ml with mobile phase A.

*Reference solution (a)*   Dilute 1.0 ml of the test solution to 100.0 ml with mobile phase A (solution A). Dilute 1.0 ml of solution A to 10.0 ml with mobile phase A.

*Reference solution (b)*   Dissolve the contents of a vial of *citalopram for system suitability CRS* (impurities B, D, F and G) in 1.0 ml of solution A.

*Column:*
— *size: l* = 0.25 m, Ø = 4.6 mm;
— *stationary phase: end-capped octadecylsilyl silica gel for chromatography R* (4 μm);
— *temperature*: 40 °C.

*Mobile phase:*
— *mobile phase A*: dissolve 1.58 g of *ammonium formate R* in 500 ml of a mixture of 4 volumes of *acetonitrile R*, 32 volumes of *methanol R* and 64 volumes of *water R*;
— *mobile phase B*: dissolve 1.58 g of *ammonium formate R* in 500 ml of a mixture of 32 volumes of *water R* and 68 volumes of *acetonitrile R*;

| Time (min) | Mobile phase A (per cent V/V) | Mobile phase B (per cent V/V) |
|---|---|---|
| 0 - 2 | 100 | 0 |
| 2 - 25 | 100 → 40 | 0 → 60 |
| 25 - 30 | 40 | 60 |

*Flow rate*   1.0 ml/min.

*Detection*   Spectrophotometer at 230 nm and at 254 nm.

*Injection*   40 µl.

*Identification of impurities*   Use the chromatogram supplied with *citalopram for system suitability CRS* and the chromatogram obtained with reference solution (b) to identify the peaks due to impurities B, D, F and G.

*Relative retention*   With reference to citalopram (retention time = about 19 min): impurity G = about 0.5; impurity B = about 0.7; impurity D = about 0.9; impurity F = about 1.6.

*System suitability*   Reference solution (b):
— *resolution*: minimum 1.5 between the peaks due to impurity D and citalopram at 230 nm.

*Limits*:
— *correction factors*: for the calculation of content, multiply the peak area of the following impurities by the corresponding correction factor: impurity F = 1.4; impurity G = 0.6;
— *impurity D at 230 nm*: not more than twice the area of the principal peak in the chromatogram obtained with reference solution (a) (0.2 per cent);
— *impurities B, F at 230 nm*: for each impurity, not more than 1.5 times the area of the principal peak in the chromatogram obtained with reference solution (a) (0.15 per cent);
— *impurity G at 254 nm*: not more than 1.5 times the area of the principal peak in the chromatogram obtained with reference solution (a) (0.15 per cent);
— *unspecified impurities at 230 nm and 254 nm*: for each impurity, not more than the area of the principal peak in the chromatogram obtained with reference solution (a) (0.10 per cent);
— *sum of impurities at 230 nm*: not more than 5 times the area of the principal peak in the chromatogram obtained with reference solution (a) (0.5 per cent);
— *disregard limit at 230 nm*: 0.5 times the area of the principal peak in the chromatogram obtained with reference solution (a) (0.05 per cent).

**Heavy metals** (*2.4.8*)
Maximum 20 ppm.

Dissolve 0.5 g in *ethanol (96 per cent) R* and dilute to 20 ml with the same solvent. 12 ml of the solution complies with test B. Prepare the reference solution using lead standard solution (0.5 ppm Pb) obtained by diluting *lead standard solution (100 ppm Pb) R* with *ethanol (96 per cent) R*. Filter the solutions through a membrane filter (nominal pore size 0.45 µm).

**Loss on drying** (*2.2.32*)
Maximum 0.5 per cent, determined on 1.000 g by drying in an oven at 105 °C for 4 h.

**Sulphated ash** (*2.4.14*)
Maximum 0.1 per cent, determined on 1.0 g in a platinum crucible.

**ASSAY**

Dissolve 0.300 g in 50 ml of *ethanol (96 per cent) R* and add 0.5 ml of *0.1 M hydrochloric acid*. Carry out a potentiometric titration (*2.2.20*), using *0.1 M sodium hydroxide*. Read the volume added between the 2 points of inflexion.

1 ml of *0.1 M sodium hydroxide* is equivalent to 40.53 mg of $C_{20}H_{22}BrFN_2O$.

**IMPURITIES**

*Specified impurities*   B, D, F, G.

*Other detectable impurities*   (The following substances would, if present at a sufficient level, be detected by one or other of the tests in the monograph. They are limited by the general acceptance criterion for other/unspecified impurities and/or by the general monograph *Substances for pharmaceutical use (2034)*. It is therefore not necessary to identify these impurities for demonstration of compliance. See also *5.10*. Control of impurities in substances for pharmaceutical use): A, C, E.

and enantiomer

A. R = CO-NH$_2$, X = H$_2$: (1*RS*)-1-[3-(dimethylamino)propyl]-1-(4-fluorophenyl)-1,3-dihydroisobenzofuran-5-carboxamide,

C. R = CN, X = O: (3*RS*)-6-cyano-3-[3-(dimethylamino)propyl]-3-(4-fluorophenyl)isobenzofuran-1(3*H*)-one,

E. R = Cl, X = H$_2$: 3-[(1*RS*)-5-chloro-1-(4-fluorophenyl)-1,3-dihydroisobenzofuran-1-yl]-*N*,*N*-dimethylpropan-1-amine,

its epimer at C*
and their enantiomers

B. 1-[3-(dimethylamino)propyl]-1-(4-fluorophenyl)-3-hydroxy-1,3-dihydroisobenzofuran-5-carbonitrile,

and enantiomer

D. R1 = CN, R2 = H: (1*RS*)-1-(4-fluorophenyl)-1-[3-(methylamino)propyl]-1,3-dihydroisobenzofuran-5-carbonitrile,

F. R1 = Br, R2 = CH$_3$: 3-[(1*RS*)-5-bromo-1-(4-fluorophenyl)-1,3-dihydroisobenzofuran-1-yl]-*N*,*N*-dimethylpropan-1-amine,

G. R1 = CO-[CH$_2$]$_3$-N(CH$_3$)$_2$, R2 = CH$_3$:
4-(dimethylamino)-1-[(1*RS*)-1-[3-(dimethylamino)propyl]-1-(4-fluorophenyl)-1,3-dihydroisobenzofuran-5-yl]butan-1-one.

*Ph Eur*

# Citalopram Hydrochloride

(*Ph Eur monograph 2203*)

C$_{20}$H$_{22}$ClFN$_2$O        360.9        85118-27-0

**Action and use**

Selective serotonin reuptake inhibitor; antidepressant.

*Ph Eur*

## DEFINITION

(1*RS*)-1-[3-(Dimethylamino)propyl]-1-(4-fluorophenyl)-1,3-dihydroisobenzofuran-5-carbonitrile hydrochloride.

**Content**

99.0 per cent to 101.5 per cent (dried substance).

## CHARACTERS

**Appearance**

White or almost white, crystalline powder.

**Solubility**

Very soluble in water, freely soluble in anhydrous ethanol.

## IDENTIFICATION

A. Optical rotation (see Tests).

B. Infrared absorption spectrophotometry (*2.2.24*).

*Comparison*    citalopram hydrochloride CRS.

C. It gives reaction (a) of chlorides (*2.3.1*).

## TESTS

**Solution S**

Dissolve 1.0 g in *methanol R* and dilute to 20 ml with the same solvent.

**Appearance of solution**

Solution S, examined immediately after preparation, is clear (*2.2.1*) and not more intensely coloured than reference solution Y$_6$ (*2.2.2, Method II*).

**Optical rotation** (*2.2.7*)

− 0.10° to + 0.10°, determined on solution S.

**Related substances**

Liquid chromatography (*2.2.29*).

*Test solution*    Dissolve 50 mg of the substance to be examined in mobile phase A and dilute to 100.0 ml with mobile phase A.

*Reference solution (a)*    Dilute 1.0 ml of the test solution to 100.0 ml with mobile phase A (solution A). Dilute 1.0 ml of solution A to 10.0 ml with mobile phase A.

*Reference solution (b)*    Dissolve the contents of a vial of citalopram for system suitability CRS (impurities B and D) in 1.0 ml of solution A.

*Column:*
— *size: l* =  0.25 m, Ø = 4.6 mm;
— *stationary phase: end-capped octadecylsilyl silica gel for chromatography R* (4 µm);
— *temperature*: 40 °C.

*Mobile phase:*
— *mobile phase A*: dissolve 1.58 g of *ammonium formate R* in 500 ml of a mixture of 4 volumes of *acetonitrile R*, 32 volumes of *methanol R* and 64 volumes of *water R*;
— *mobile phase B*: dissolve 1.58 g of *ammonium formate R* in 500 ml of a mixture of 32 volumes of *water R* and 68 volumes of *acetonitrile R*;

| Time (min) | Mobile phase A (per cent *V/V*) | Mobile phase B (per cent *V/V*) |
|---|---|---|
| 0 - 2 | 100 | 0 |
| 2 - 25 | 100 → 40 | 0 → 60 |
| 25 - 30 | 40 | 60 |

*Flow rate*    1.0 ml/min.

*Detection*    Spectrophotometer at 230 nm.

*Injection*    40 µl.

*Identification of impurities*    Use the chromatogram supplied with *citalopram for system suitability CRS* and the chromatogram obtained with reference solution (b) to identify the peaks due to impurities B and D.

*Relative retention*    With reference to citalopram (retention time = about 19 min): impurity B = about 0.7; impurity D = about 0.9.

*System suitability*    Reference solution (b):
— *resolution*: minimum 1.5 between the peaks due to impurity D and citalopram.

*Limits:*
— *impurity B*: not more than 1.5 times the area of the principal peak in the chromatogram obtained with reference solution (a) (0.15 per cent);
— *unspecified impurities*: for each impurity, not more than the area of the principal peak in the chromatogram obtained with reference solution (a) (0.10 per cent);
— *total*: not more than twice the area of the principal peak in the chromatogram obtained with reference solution (a) (0.2 per cent);
— *disregard limit*: 0.5 times the area of the principal peak in the chromatogram obtained with reference solution (a) (0.05 per cent).

**Heavy metals** (*2.4.8*)

Maximum 20 ppm.

Dissolve 1.0 g in 20 ml of *water R*. 12 ml of the solution complies with test A. Prepare the reference solution using *lead standard solution (1 ppm Pb) R*.

**Loss on drying** (*2.2.32*)

Maximum 0.5 per cent, determined on 1.000 g by drying in an oven at 105 °C for 4 h.

**Sulphated ash** (*2.4.14*)

Maximum 0.1 per cent, determined on 1.0 g in a platinum crucible.

## ASSAY

Dissolve 0.250 g in 50 ml of *ethanol (96 per cent) R* and add 0.5 ml of *0.1 M hydrochloric acid*. Carry out a potentiometric titration (*2.2.20*), using *0.1 M sodium hydroxide*. Read the volume added between the 2 points of inflexion.

1 ml of *0.1 M sodium hydroxide* is equivalent to 36.09 mg of C$_{20}$H$_{22}$ClFN$_2$O.

## IMPURITIES

*Specified impurities*    B.

*Other detectable impurities*    (The following substances would, if present at a sufficient level, be detected by one or other of the tests in the monograph. They are limited by the general acceptance criterion for other/unspecified impurities and/or by the general monograph *Substances for pharmaceutical use (2034)*. It is therefore not necessary to identify these impurities for demonstration of compliance. See also *5.10. Control of impurities in substances for pharmaceutical use*): A, C, D, E, F.

and enantiomer

A. R1 = CO-NH$_2$, R2 = CH$_3$, X = H$_2$: (1RS)-1-[3-(dimethylamino)propyl]-1-(4-fluorophenyl)-1,3-dihydroisobenzofuran-5-carboxamide,

C. R1 = CN, R2 = CH$_3$, X = O: (3RS)-6-cyano-3-[3-(dimethylamino)propyl]-3-(4-fluorophenyl)isobenzofuran-1(3H)-one,

D. R1 = CN, R2 = H, X = H$_2$: (1RS)-1-(4-fluorophenyl)-1-[3-(methylamino)propyl]-1,3-dihydroisobenzofuran-5-carbonitrile,

E. R1 = Cl, R2 = CH$_3$, X = H$_2$: 3-[(1RS)-5-chloro-1-(4-fluorophenyl)-1,3-dihydroisobenzofuran-1-yl]-N,N-dimethylpropan-1-amine,

F. R1 = Br, R2 = CH$_3$, X = H$_2$: 3-[(1RS)-5-bromo-1-(4-fluorophenyl)-1,3-dihydroisobenzofuran-1-yl]-N,N-dimethylpropan-1-amine,

its epimer at C*
and their enantiomers

B. 1-[3-(dimethylamino)propyl]-1-(4-fluorophenyl)-3-hydroxy-1,3-dihydroisobenzofuran-5-carbonitrile.

_____ *Ph Eur*

# Anhydrous Citric Acid

Citric Acid

*(Ph Eur monograph 0455)*

$C_6H_8O_7$                    192.1                    77-92-9

*Ph Eur* _____

## DEFINITION
2-Hydroxypropane-1,2,3-tricarboxylic acid.

**Content**
99.5 per cent to 100.5 per cent (anhydrous substance).

## CHARACTERS
**Appearance**
White or almost white, crystalline powder, colourless crystals or granules.

**Solubility**
Very soluble in water, freely soluble in ethanol (96 per cent).

mp: about 153 °C, with decomposition.

## IDENTIFICATION
*First identification*    B, E.

*Second identification*    A, C, D, E.

A. Dissolve 1 g in 10 ml of *water R*. The solution is strongly acidic (*2.2.4*).

B. Infrared absorption spectrophotometry (*2.2.24*).

*Preparation*    Dry the substance to be examined and the reference substance at 100-105 °C for 2 h.

*Comparison*    anhydrous citric acid CRS.

C. Add about 5 mg to a mixture of 1 ml of *acetic anhydride R* and 3 ml of *pyridine R*. A red colour develops.

D. Dissolve 0.5 g in 5 ml of *water R*, neutralise using *1 M sodium hydroxide* (about 7 ml), add 10 ml of *calcium chloride solution R* and heat to boiling. A white precipitate is formed.

E. Water (see Tests).

## TESTS
**Appearance of solution**
The solution is clear (*2.2.1*) and not more intensely coloured than reference solution Y$_7$, BY$_7$ or GY$_7$ (*2.2.2, Method II*).

Dissolve 2.0 g in *water R* and dilute to 10 ml with the same solvent.

**Readily carbonisable substances**
To 1.0 g in a cleaned test tube add 10 ml of *sulphuric acid R* and immediately heat the mixture in a water-bath at 90 ± 1 °C for 60 min. Cool rapidly immediately afterwards. The solution is not more intensely coloured than a mixture of 1 ml of red primary solution and 9 ml of yellow primary solution (*2.2.2, Method I*).

**Oxalic acid**
Maximum 360 ppm, calculated as anhydrous oxalic acid.

Dissolve 0.80 g in 4 ml of *water R*. Add 3 ml of *hydrochloric acid R* and 1 g of *zinc R* in granules. Boil for 1 min. Allow to stand for 2 min. Transfer the supernatant liquid to a test-tube containing 0.25 ml of a 10 g/l solution of *phenylhydrazine hydrochloride R* and heat to boiling. Cool rapidly, transfer to a graduated cylinder and add an equal volume of *hydrochloric acid R* and 0.25 ml of a 50 g/l solution of *potassium ferricyanide R*. Shake and allow to stand for 30 min. Any pink colour in the solution is not more intense than that in a standard prepared at the same time in the same manner using 4 ml of a 0.1 g/l solution of *oxalic acid R*.

**Sulphates** (*2.4.13*)

Maximum 150 ppm.

Dissolve 2.0 g in *distilled water R* and dilute to 30 ml with the same solvent.

**Aluminium** (*2.4.17*)

Maximum 0.2 ppm, if intended for use in the manufacture of dialysis solutions.

*Prescribed solution*   Dissolve 20 g in 100 ml of *water R* and add 10 ml of *acetate buffer solution pH 6.0 R*.

*Reference solution*   Mix 2 ml of *aluminium standard solution (2 ppm Al) R*, 10 ml of *acetate buffer solution pH 6.0 R* and 98 ml of *water R*.

*Blank solution*   Mix 10 ml of *acetate buffer solution pH 6.0 R* and 100 ml of *water R*.

**Heavy metals** (*2.4.8*)

Maximum 10 ppm.

Dissolve 5.0 g in several portions in 39 ml of *dilute sodium hydroxide solution R* and dilute to 50 ml with *distilled water R*. 12 ml of the solution complies with test A. Prepare the reference solution using *lead standard solution (1 ppm Pb) R*.

**Water** (*2.5.12*)

Maximum 1.0 per cent, determined on 2.000 g.

**Sulphated ash** (*2.4.14*)

Maximum 0.1 per cent, determined on 1.0 g.

**Bacterial endotoxins** (*2.6.14*)

Less than 0.5 IU/mg, if intended for use in the manufacture of parenteral dosage forms without a further appropriate procedure for the removal of bacterial endotoxins.

**ASSAY**

Dissolve 0.550 g in 50 ml of *water R*. Titrate with *1 M sodium hydroxide*, using 0.5 ml of *phenolphthalein solution R* as indicator.

1 ml of *1 M sodium hydroxide* is equivalent to 64.03 mg of $C_6H_8O_7$.

**LABELLING**

The label states, where applicable, that the substance is intended for use in the manufacture of dialysis solutions.

*Ph Eur*

# Citric Acid Monohydrate

(*Ph Eur monograph 0456*)

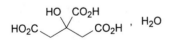

| | | |
|---|---|---|
| $C_6H_8O_7,H_2O$ | 210.1 | *5949-29-1* |

*Ph Eur*

**DEFINITION**

2-Hydroxypropane-1,2,3-tricarboxylic acid monohydrate.

**Content**

99.5 per cent to 100.5 per cent (anhydrous substance).

**CHARACTERS**

**Appearance**

White or almost white, crystalline powder, colourless crystals or granules, efflorescent.

**Solubility**

Very soluble in water, freely soluble in ethanol (96 per cent).

**IDENTIFICATION**

*First identification*   B, E.

*Second identification*   A, C, D, E.

A. Dissolve 1 g in 10 ml of *water R*. The solution is strongly acidic (*2.2.4*).

B. Infrared absorption spectrophotometry (*2.2.24*).

*Preparation*   Dry the substance to be examined and the reference substance at 100-105 °C for 2 h.

*Comparison*   *citric acid monohydrate CRS*.

C. Add about 5 mg to a mixture of 1 ml of *acetic anhydride R* and 3 ml of *pyridine R*. A red colour develops.

D. Dissolve 0.5 g in 5 ml of *water R*, neutralise using *1 M sodium hydroxide* (about 7 ml), add 10 ml of *calcium chloride solution R* and heat to boiling. A white precipitate is formed.

E. Water (see Tests).

**TESTS**

**Appearance of solution**

The solution is clear (*2.2.1*) and not more intensely coloured than reference solution $Y_7$, $BY_7$ or $GY_7$ (*2.2.2, Method II*).

Dissolve 2.0 g in *water R* and dilute to 10 ml with the same solvent.

**Readily carbonisable substances**

To 1.0 g in a cleaned test tube add 10 ml of *sulphuric acid R* and immediately heat the mixture in a water-bath at 90 ± 1 °C for 60 min. Cool rapidly immediately afterwards. The solution is not more intensely coloured than a mixture of 1 ml of red primary solution and 9 ml of yellow primary solution (*2.2.2, Method I*).

**Oxalic acid**

Maximum 360 ppm, calculated as anhydrous oxalic acid.

Dissolve 0.80 g in 4 ml of *water R*. Add 3 ml of *hydrochloric acid R* and 1 g of *zinc R* in granules. Boil for 1 min. Allow to stand for 2 min. Transfer the supernatant liquid to a test-tube containing 0.25 ml of a 10 g/l solution of *phenylhydrazine hydrochloride R* and heat to boiling. Cool rapidly, transfer to a graduated cylinder and add an equal volume of *hydrochloric acid R* and 0.25 ml of a 50 g/l solution of *potassium ferricyanide R*. Shake and allow to stand for 30 min. Any pink colour in the solution is not more intense than that in a standard prepared at the same time in the same manner using 4 ml of a 0.1 g/l solution of *oxalic acid R*.

**Sulphates** (*2.4.13*)

Maximum 150 ppm.

Dissolve 2.0 g in distilled *water R* and dilute to 30 ml with the same solvent.

**Aluminium** (*2.4.17*)

Maximum 0.2 ppm, if intended for use in the manufacture of dialysis solutions.

*Prescribed solution*   Dissolve 20 g in 100 ml of *water R* and add 10 ml of *acetate buffer solution pH 6.0 R*.

*Reference solution*   Mix 2 ml of *aluminium standard solution (2 ppm Al) R*, 10 ml of *acetate buffer solution pH 6.0 R* and 98 ml of *water R*.

*Blank solution*   Mix 10 ml of *acetate buffer solution pH 6.0 R* and 100 ml of *water R*.

**Heavy metals** (*2.4.8*)

Maximum 10 ppm.

Dissolve 5.0 g in several portions in 39 ml of *dilute sodium hydroxide solution R* and dilute to 50 ml with *distilled water R*.

12 ml of the solution complies with test A. Prepare the reference solution using *lead standard solution (1 ppm Pb) R*.

**Water** (*2.5.12*)
7.5 per cent to 9.0 per cent, determined on 0.500 g.

**Sulphated ash** (*2.4.14*)
Maximum 0.1 per cent, determined on 1.0 g.

**Bacterial endotoxins** (*2.6.14*)
Less than 0.5 IU/mg, if intended for use in the manufacture of parenteral dosage forms without a further appropriate procedure for the removal of bacterial endotoxins.

**ASSAY**
Dissolve 0.550 g in 50 ml of *water R*. Titrate with *1 M sodium hydroxide*, using 0.5 ml of *phenolphthalein solution R* as indicator.

1 ml of *1 M sodium hydroxide* is equivalent to 64.03 mg of $C_6H_8O_7$.

**STORAGE**
In an airtight container.

**LABELLING**
The label states, where applicable, that the substance is intended for use in the manufacture of dialysis solutions.

*—————————————————— Ph Eur*

# Cladribine

(*Ph Eur monograph 2174*)

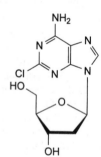

$C_{10}H_{12}ClN_5O_3$      285.7      *4291-63-8*

**Action and use**
Purine analogue; cytostatic.

*Ph Eur* _____

**DEFINITION**
2-Chloro-9-(2-deoxy-β-D-*erythro*-pentofuranosyl)-9*H*-purin-6-amine.

**Content**
97.0 per cent to 102.0 per cent (anhydrous substance).

**CHARACTERS**

**Appearance**
White or almost white, crystalline powder.

**Solubility**
Slightly soluble in water, soluble in dimethyl sulphoxide, slightly soluble in methanol, practically insoluble in acetonitrile.

It shows polymorphism (*5.9*).

**IDENTIFICATION**
A. Specific optical rotation (see Tests).

B. Infrared absorption spectrophotometry (*2.2.24*).
*Comparison* cladribine CRS.

If the spectra obtained in the solid state show differences, dissolve the substance to be examined in the minimum volume of *methanol R* and evaporate to dryness. Dry the precipitate at 100 °C for 2 h and record a new spectrum using the residue.

**TESTS**

**Solution S**
Disperse 0.15 g in *carbon dioxide-free water R*, dilute to 50 ml with the same solvent and sonicate until dissolution is complete.

**Appearance of solution**
Solution S is clear (*2.2.1*) and colourless (*2.2.2, Method II*).

**pH** (*2.2.3*)
7.0 to 8.1 for solution S.

**Specific optical rotation** (*2.2.7*)
− 21.0 to − 27.0 (anhydrous substance).

Dissolve 0.25 g in *dimethyl sulphoxide R* and dilute to 25.0 ml with the same solvent.

**Impurity E**
Thin-layer chromatography (*2.2.27*).

*Test solution* Dissolve 40.0 mg of the substance to be examined in *dimethylformamide R* and dilute to 2.0 ml with the same solvent.

*Reference solution (a)* Dissolve 5.0 mg of *2-deoxy-D-ribose R* (impurity E) in *dimethylformamide R* and dilute to 25.0 ml with the same solvent. Dilute 3.0 ml of this solution to 10.0 ml with *dimethylformamide R*.

*Reference solution (b)* Dissolve 10.0 mg of *2-deoxy-D-ribose R* (impurity E) in *dimethylformamide R* and dilute to 5.0 ml with the same solvent. Mix 9 volumes of this solution with 1 volume of the test solution.

*Plate* TLC silica gel $F_{254}$ plate R.

*Mobile phase* Concentrated ammonia R, ethanol (96 per cent) R, ethyl acetate R (20:40:40 *V/V/V*).

*Application* 5 µl as bands of 10 mm; thoroughly dry the starting points in a current of warm air.

*Development* Over 2/3 of the plate.

*Drying* In air, then heat at 45 °C for 10 min.

*Detection* Spray with a solution containing 0.5 g of *thymol R* in a mixture of 5 ml of *sulphuric acid R* and 95 ml of *ethanol (96 per cent) R*; heat at 110 °C for 20 min or until the spots appear.

*System suitability* Reference solution (b):
— the chromatogram shows 2 clearly separated spots.
*Limit:*
— *impurity E*: any spot due to impurity E is not more intense than the spot in the chromatogram obtained with reference solution (a) (0.3 per cent).

**Related substances**
Liquid chromatography (*2.2.29*).

*Solvent mixture* acetonitrile R, water R (10:90 *V/V*).

*Test solution (a)* Dissolve 25.0 mg of the substance to be examined in the solvent mixture and dilute to 5.0 ml with the solvent mixture.

*Test solution (b)* Dissolve 20.0 mg of the substance to be examined in the solvent mixture and dilute to 100.0 ml with the solvent mixture.

*Reference solution (a)* Dissolve 20.0 mg of *cladribine CRS* in the solvent mixture and dilute to 100.0 ml with the solvent mixture.

*Reference solution (b)* Dilute 1.0 ml of test solution (a) to 100.0 ml with the solvent mixture.

*Reference solution (c)* Dilute 1.0 ml of reference solution (b) to 10.0 ml with the solvent mixture.

*Reference solution (d)* Dissolve 1.0 mg of *cladribine impurity C CRS* in reference solution (b) and dilute to 25.0 ml with the same solution.

*Reference solution (e)* Dilute 5.0 ml of reference solution (c) to 10.0 ml with the solvent mixture.

*Reference solution (f)* Dissolve 3 mg of *cladribine for peak identification CRS* (containing impurities A, B, C and D) in 2 ml of the solvent mixture.

*Column:*
— size: $l$ = 0.25 m, Ø = 4.6 mm;
— stationary phase: base-deactivated octylsilyl silica gel for chromatography R (5 μm).

*Mobile phase:*
— mobile phase A: *water for chromatography R*;
— mobile phase B: *acetonitrile for chromatography R*;
— mobile phase C: 50 g/l solution of *phosphoric acid R* in *water for chromatography R*;

| Time (min) | Mobile phase A (per cent *V/V*) | Mobile phase B (per cent *V/V*) | Mobile phase C (per cent *V/V*) |
|---|---|---|---|
| 0 - 10 | 80 → 70 | 10 → 20 | 10 |
| 10 - 25 | 70 → 20 | 20 → 70 | 10 |
| 25 - 30 | 20 | 70 | 10 |
| 30 - 31 | 20 → 80 | 70 → 10 | 10 |
| 31 - 39 | 80 | 10 | 10 |

*Flow rate* 0.8 ml/min.

*Detection* Spectrophotometer at 252 nm.

*Injection* 20 μl of test solution (a) and reference solutions (c), (d), (e) and (f).

*Identification of impurities* Use the chromatogram supplied with *cladribine for peak identification CRS* to identify the peaks due to impurities A, B, C and D.

*Relative retention* With reference to cladribine (retention time = about 10 min): impurity A = about 0.33; impurity B = about 0.44; impurity C = about 0.73; impurity D = about 0.92.

*System suitability* Reference solution (d):
— resolution: minimum 4.5 between the peaks due to impurity C and cladribine.

*Limits:*
— correction factors: for the calculation of content, multiply the peak areas of the following impurities by the corresponding correction factor: impurity B = 1.7; impurity C = 0.8;
— impurities A, C: for each impurity, not more than 3 times the area of the principal peak in the chromatogram obtained with reference solution (c) (0.3 per cent);
— impurities B, D: for each impurity, not more than twice the area of the principal peak in the chromatogram obtained with reference solution (c) (0.2 per cent);
— unspecified impurities: for each impurity, not more than the area of the principal peak in the chromatogram obtained with reference solution (c) (0.10 per cent);

— total: not more than 10 times the area of the principal peak in the chromatogram obtained with reference solution (c) (1.0 per cent);
— disregard limit: the area of the principal peak in the chromatogram obtained with reference solution (e) (0.05 per cent).

**Water** (*2.5.32*)
Maximum 0.5 per cent, determined on 0.100 g.

**Bacterial endotoxins** (*2.6.14*)
Less than 3 IU/mg, if intended for use in the manufacture of parenteral dosage forms without a further appropriate procedure for the removal of bacterial endotoxins.

**ASSAY**
Liquid chromatography (*2.2.29*) as described in the test for related substances with the following modification.

*Injection* Test solution (b) and reference solution (a).

Calculate the percentage content of $C_{10}H_{12}ClN_5O_3$ from the declared content of *cladribine CRS*.

**STORAGE**
Protected from light, at a temperature of 2 °C to 8 °C. If the substance is sterile, store in a sterile, airtight, tamper-proof container.

**IMPURITIES**
*Specified impurities* A, B, C, D, E.

*Other detectable impurities* (the following substances would, if present at a sufficient level, be detected by one or other of the tests in the monograph. They are limited by the general acceptance criterion for other/unspecified impurities and/or by the general monograph *Substances for pharmaceutical use (2034)*. It is therefore not necessary to identify these impurities for demonstration of compliance. See also *5.10. Control of impurities in substances for pharmaceutical use*) : F, G.

A. R = $NH_2$: 9-(2-deoxy-β-D-*erythro*-pentofuranosyl)-9*H*-purin-2,6-diamine,

B. R = $OCH_3$: 9-(2-deoxy-β-D-*erythro*-pentofuranosyl)-2-methoxy-9*H*-purin-6-amine,

C. 2-chloro-7*H*-purin-6-amine (2-chloroadenine),

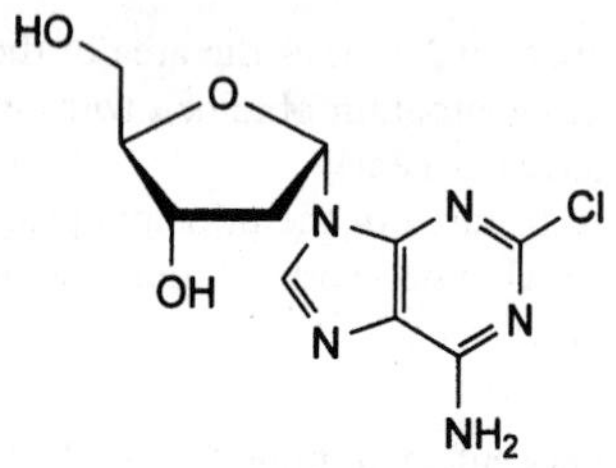

D. 2-chloro-9-(2-deoxy-α-D-*erythro*-pentofuranosyl)-9*H*-purin-6-amine,

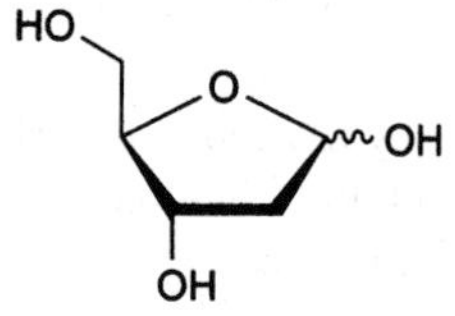

E. 2-deoxy-D-*erythro*-pentofuranose (2-deoxy-D-ribose),

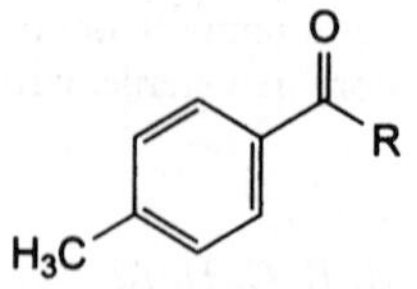

F. R = NH₂: 4-methylbenzamide,
G. R = OCH₃: methyl 4-methylbenzoate.

*Ph Eur*

# Clarithromycin

(*Ph Eur monograph 1651*)

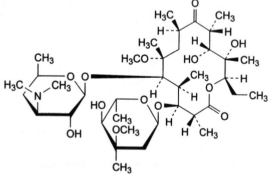

C₃₈H₆₉NO₁₃     748     *81103-11-9*

**Action and use**
Macrolide antibacterial.

**Preparations**
Clarithromycin Tablets
Prolonged-release Clarithromycin Tablets

*Ph Eur*

**DEFINITION**
(3*R*,4*S*,5*S*,6*R*,7*R*,9*R*,11*R*,12*R*,13*S*,14*R*)-4-[(2,6-Dideoxy-3-*C*-methyl-3-*O*-methyl-α-L-*ribo*-hexopyranosyl)oxy]-14-ethyl-12,13-dihydroxy-7-methoxy-3,5,7,9,11,13-hexamethyl-6-[[3,4,6-trideoxy-3-(dimethylamino)-β-D-*xylo*-

hexopyranosyl]oxy]oxacyclotetradecane-2,10-dione (6-*O*-methylerythromycin A).

Semi-synthetic product derived from a fermentation product.

**Content**
96.0 per cent to 102.0 per cent (anhydrous substance).

**CHARACTERS**

**Appearance**
White or almost white, crystalline powder.

**Solubility**
Practically insoluble in water, soluble in acetone and in methylene chloride, slightly soluble in methanol.

**IDENTIFICATION**
Infrared absorption spectrophotometry (*2.2.24*).

*Comparison*   clarithromycin CRS.

**TESTS**
**Solution S**
Dissolve 0.500 g in *methylene chloride R* and dilute to 50.0 ml with the same solvent.

**Appearance of solution**
Solution S is clear or not more opalescent than reference suspension II (*2.2.1*) and not more intensely coloured than reference solution Y₇ (*2.2.2, Method II*).

**Specific optical rotation** (*2.2.7*)
− 94 to − 102 (anhydrous substance), determined on solution S.

**Related substances**
Liquid chromatography (*2.2.29*).

*Test solution*   Dissolve 75.0 mg of the substance to be examined in 25 ml of *acetonitrile R1* and dilute to 50.0 ml with *water R*.

*Reference solution (a)*   Dissolve 75.0 mg of clarithromycin CRS in 25 ml of *acetonitrile R1* and dilute to 50.0 ml with *water R*.

*Reference solution (b)*   Dilute 5.0 ml of reference solution (a) to 100.0 ml with a mixture of equal volumes of *acetonitrile R1* and *water R*.

*Reference solution (c)*   Dilute 1.0 ml of reference solution (b) to 10.0 ml with a mixture of equal volumes of *acetonitrile R1* and *water R*.

*Reference solution (d)*   Dissolve 15.0 mg of *clarithromycin for peak identification CRS* in 5.0 ml of *acetonitrile R1* and dilute to 10.0 ml with *water R*.

*Blank solution*   Dilute 25.0 ml of *acetonitrile R1* to 50.0 ml with *water R* and mix.

*Column:*
— *size:* l = 0.10 m, Ø = 4.6 mm,
— *stationary phase: octadecylsilyl silica gel for chromatography R* (3.5 μm),
— *temperature:* 40 °C.

*Mobile phase:*
— *mobile phase A:* a 4.76 g/l solution of *potassium dihydrogen phosphate R* adjusted to pH 4.4 with *dilute phosphoric acid R* or a 45 g/l solution of *potassium hydroxide R*, filtered through a C18 filtration kit,
— *mobile phase B: acetonitrile R1*,

| Time (min) | Mobile phase A (per cent V/V) | Mobile phase B (per cent V/V) |
|---|---|---|
| 0 - 32 | 75 → 40 | 25 → 60 |
| 32 - 34 | 40 | 60 |
| 34 - 36 | 40 → 75 | 60 → 25 |
| 36 - 42 | 75 | 25 |

*Flow rate*  1.1 ml/min.

*Detection*  Spectrophotometer at 205 nm.

*Injection*  10 μl of the blank solution, the test solution and reference solutions (b), (c) and (d).

*Relative retention r* (not $r_G$) with reference to clarithromycin (retention time = about 11 min): impurity I = about 0.38; impurity A = about 0.42; impurity J = about 0.63; impurity L = about 0.74; impurity B = about 0.79; impurity M = about 0.81; impurity C = about 0.89; impurity D = about 0.96; impurity N = about 1.15; impurity E = about 1.27; impurity F = about 1.33; impurity P = about 1.35; impurity O = about 1.41; impurity K = about 1.59; impurity G = about 1.72; impurity H = about 1.82.

*System suitability:*
— *symmetry factor*: maximum 1.7 for the peak due to clarithromycin in the chromatogram obtained with reference solution (b),
— *peak-to-valley ratio*: minimum 3.0, where $H_p$ = height above the baseline of the peak due to impurity D and $H_v$ = height above the baseline of the lowest point of the curve separating this peak from the peak due to clarithromycin in the chromatogram obtained with reference solution (d).

*Limits:*
— *correction factors*: for the calculation of contents, multiply the peak areas of the following impurities by the corresponding correction factor: impurity G = 0.27; impurity H = 0.15; use the chromatogram supplied with *clarithromycin for peak identification CRS* to identify the peaks;
— *any impurity*: not more than twice the area of the principal peak in the chromatogram obtained with reference solution (c) (1.0 per cent), and not more than 4 such peaks have an area greater than 0.8 times the area of the principal peak in the chromatogram obtained with reference solution (c) (0.4 per cent);
— *total*: not more than 7 times the area of the principal peak in the chromatogram obtained with reference solution (c) (3.5 per cent);
— *disregard limit*: 0.2 times the area of the principal peak in the chromatogram obtained with reference solution (c) (0.1 per cent); disregard the peaks eluting before impurity I and after impurity H.

**Heavy metals** (*2.4.8*)
Maximum 20 ppm.

Dissolve 1.0 g in a mixture of 15 volumes of *water R* and 85 volumes of *dioxan R* and dilute to 20 ml with the same mixture of solvents. 12 ml of the solution complies with limit test B. Prepare the reference solution using lead standard solution (1 ppm Pb) obtained by diluting *lead standard solution (100 ppm Pb) R* with a mixture of 15 volumes of *water R* and 85 volumes of *dioxan R*.

**Water** (*2.5.12*)
Maximum 2.0 per cent, determined on 0.500 g.

**Sulphated ash** (*2.4.14*)
Maximum 0.2 per cent, determined on 0.5 g.

**ASSAY**
Liquid chromatography (*2.2.29*) as described in the test for related substances with the following modifications.

*Injection*  Test solution and reference solution (a).

Calculate the percentage content of $C_{38}H_{69}NO_{13}$.

**IMPURITIES**
*Specified impurities*  A, B, C, D, E, F, G, H, I, J, K, L, M, N, O, P.

A. R1 = CH₃, R2 = OH, R3 = H:
2-demethyl-2-(hydroxymethyl)-6-O-methylerythromycin A (clarithromycin F),

B. R1 = R2 = R3 = H: 6-O-methyl-15-norerythromycin A,

P. R1 = R3 = CH₃, R2 = H:
4′,6-di-O-methylerythromycin A,

C. R1 = R2 = CH₃, R3 = H:
6-O-methylerythromycin A (E)-9-oxime,

G. R1 = R2 = R3 = CH₃:
6-O-methylerythromycin A (E)-9-(O-methyloxime),

J. R1 = CH₃, R2 = R3 = H: erythromycin A (E)-9-oxime,

M. R1 = R3 = H, R2 = CH₃:
3″-N-demethyl-6-O-methylerythromycin A (E)-9-oxime,

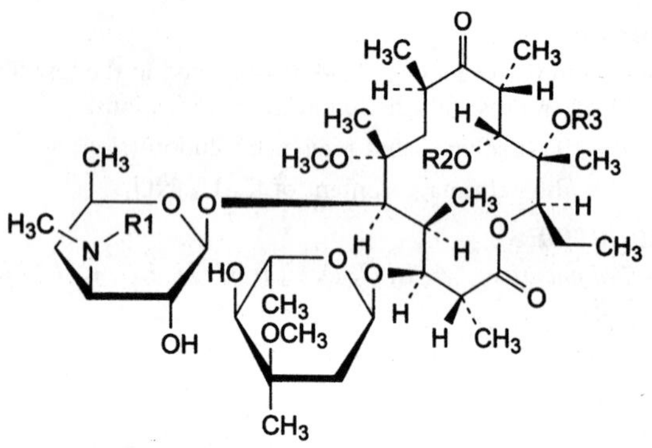

D. R1 = R2 = R3 = H:
3″-*N*-demethyl-6-*O*-methylerythromycin A,

E. R1 = R2 = CH₃, R3 = H:
6,11-di-*O*-methylerythromycin A,

F. R1 = R3 = CH₃, R2 = H:
6,12-di-*O*-methylerythromycin A,

H. R1 = CHO, R2 = R3 = H:
3″-*N*-demethyl-3′-*N*-formyl-6-*O*-methylerythromycin A,

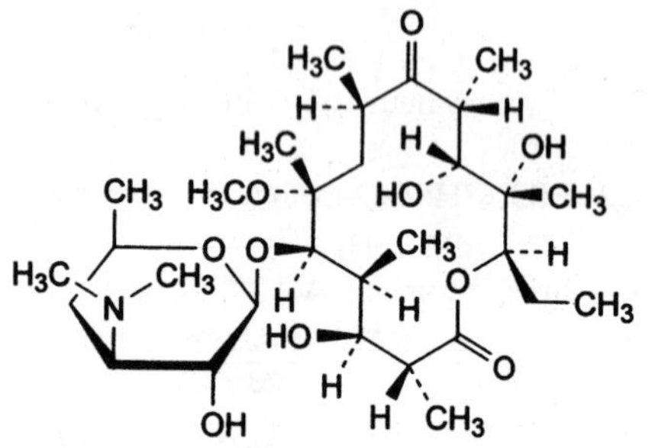

I. 3-*O*-decladinosyl-6-*O*-methylerythromycin A,

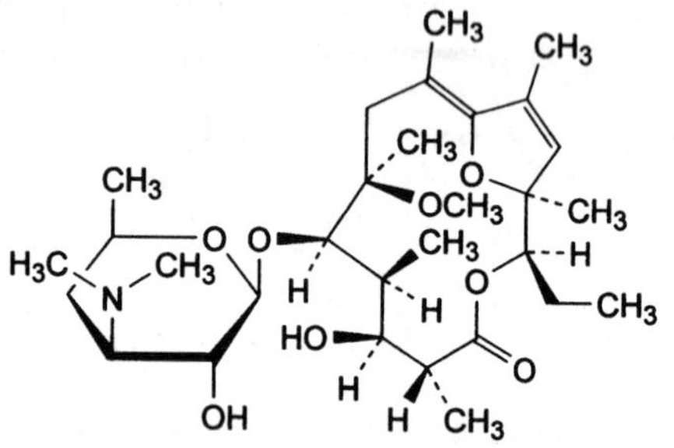

K. (1*S*,2*R*,5*R*,6*S*,7*S*,8*R*,9*R*,11*Z*)-2-ethyl-6-hydroxy-9-methoxy-1,5,7,9,11,13-hexamethyl-8-[[3,4,6-trideoxy-3-(dimethylamino)-β-D-*xylo*-hexopyranosyl]oxy]-3,15-dioxabicyclo[10.2.1]pentadeca-11,13-dien-4-one (3-*O*-decladinosyl-8,9:10,11-dianhydro-6-*O*-methylerythromycin A-9,12-hemiketal,

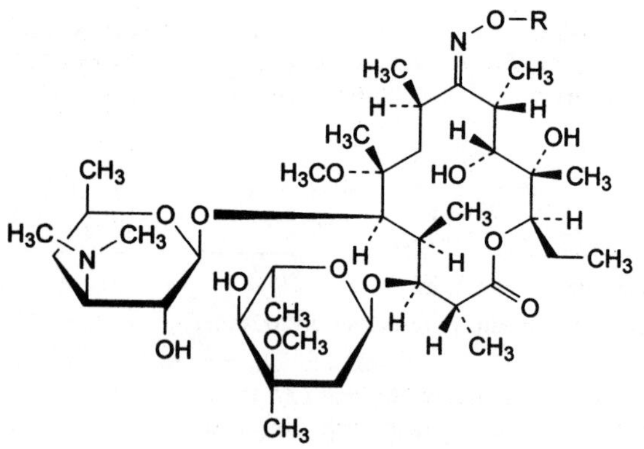

L. R = H: 6-*O*-methylerythromycin A (*Z*)-9-oxime,

O. R = CH₃:
6-*O*-methylerythromycin A (*Z*)-9-(*O*-methyloxime),

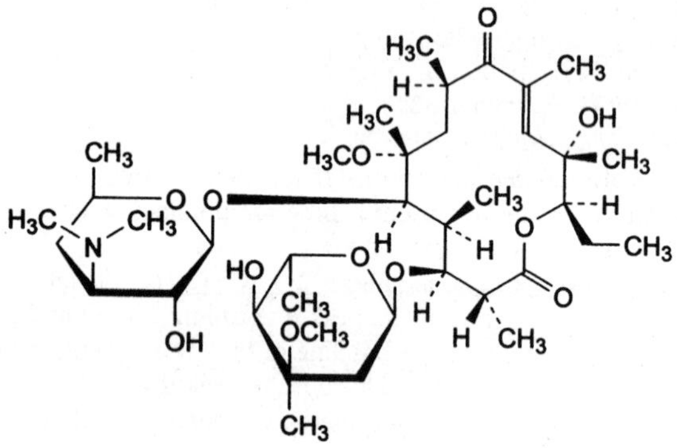

N. (10*E*)-10,11-didehydro-11-deoxy-6-*O*-methylerythromycin A.

*Ph Eur*

# Clebopride Malate

(*Ph Eur monograph 1303*)

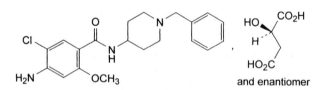

$C_{20}H_{24}ClN_3O_2,C_4H_6O_5$    508.0    *57645-91-7*

**Action and use**
Dopamine receptor antagonist; antiprotozoal (veterinary).

*Ph Eur*

## DEFINITION
4-Amino-*N*-(1-benzylpiperidin-4-yl)-5-chloro-2-methoxybenzamide acid (*RS*)-2-hydroxybutanedioate.

## Content
98.5 per cent to 101.0 per cent (dried substance).

## CHARACTERS
### Appearance
White or almost white, crystalline powder.

**Solubility**

Sparingly soluble in water and in methanol, slightly soluble in anhydrous ethanol, practically insoluble in methylene chloride.

mp: about 164 °C, with decomposition.

## IDENTIFICATION

*First identification*  B, C.

*Second identification*  A, C, D.

A. Ultraviolet and visible absorption spectrophotometry (*2.2.25*).

*Test solution*  Dissolve 20.0 mg in *water R* and dilute to 100.0 ml with the same solvent. Dilute 10.0 ml of this solution to 100.0 ml with *water R*.

*Spectral range*  230-350 nm.

*Absorption maxima*  At 270 nm and 307 nm.

*Specific absorbances at the absorption maxima:*
— at 270 nm: 252 to 278;
— at 307 nm: 204 to 226.

B. Infrared absorption spectrophotometry (*2.2.24*).

*Preparation*  Discs.

*Comparison*  *clebopride malate CRS*.

C. Dissolve 20 mg in 1 ml of *sulphuric acid R*, add 1 ml of β-naphthol solution R1 and mix. The solution examined in daylight is yellow with blue fluorescence.

D. Thin-layer chromatography (*2.2.27*).

*Test solution*  Dissolve 5 mg of the substance to be examined in *anhydrous ethanol R* and dilute to 10 ml with the same solvent.

*Reference solution (a)*  Dissolve 5 mg of *clebopride malate CRS* in *anhydrous ethanol R* and dilute to 10 ml with the same solvent.

*Reference solution (b)*  Dissolve 5 mg of *clebopride malate CRS* and 5 mg of *metoclopramide hydrochloride CRS* in *anhydrous ethanol R* and dilute to 10 ml with the same solvent.

*Plate*  *TLC silica gel F$_{254}$ plate R*.

*Mobile phase*  concentrated ammonia R, acetone R, methanol R, toluene R (2:14:14:70 *V/V/V/V*).

*Application*  5 µl, as bands of 10 mm by 3 mm.

*Development*  Over a path of 15 cm.

*Drying*  In air.

*Detection*  Examine in ultraviolet light at 254 nm.

*System suitability*  Reference solution (b):
— the chromatogram shows 2 clearly separated bands.

*Results*  The principal band in the chromatogram obtained with the test solution is similar in position and size to the principal band in the chromatogram obtained with reference solution (a).

## TESTS

### Solution S

Dissolve 1.0 g in *carbon dioxide-free water R* and dilute to 100.0 ml with the same solvent.

### Appearance of solution

Solution S, examined immediately after preparation, is clear (*2.2.1*) and colourless (*2.2.2, Method I*).

### pH (*2.2.3*)

3.8 to 4.2 for solution S.

### Related substances

Liquid chromatography (*2.2.29*).

*Test solution*  Dissolve 0.10 g of the substance to be examined in the mobile phase and dilute to 100.0 ml with the mobile phase.

*Reference solution (a)*  Dilute 1.0 ml of the test solution to 100.0 ml with the mobile phase. Dilute 1.0 ml of this solution to 10.0 ml with the mobile phase.

*Reference solution (b)*  Dissolve 10.0 mg of *clebopride malate CRS* and 10.0 mg of *metoclopramide hydrochloride CRS* in the mobile phase and dilute to 100.0 ml with the mobile phase. Dilute 1.0 ml of this solution to 10.0 ml with the mobile phase.

*Column:*
— *size*: l = 0.12 m, Ø = 4.0 mm;
— *stationary phase*: octadecylsilyl silica gel for chromatography R (5 µm).

*Mobile phase*  Mix 20 volumes of *acetonitrile R1* and 80 volumes of a 1 g/l solution of *sodium heptanesulphonate R* adjusted to pH 2.5 with *phosphoric acid R*.

*Flow rate*  1 ml/min.

*Detection*  Spectrophotometer at 215 nm.

*Equilibration*  With the mobile phase for 30 min.

*Injection*  20 µl.

*Run time*  Twice the retention time of clebopride.

*System suitability*  Reference solution (b):
— *retention time*: clebopride (2$^{nd}$ peak) = about 15 min;
— *relative retention* with reference to clebopride: metoclopramide (1$^{st}$ peak) = about 0.45.

*Limits:*
— *any impurity*: for each impurity, not more than the area of the principal peak in the chromatogram obtained with reference solution (a) (0.1 per cent);
— *total*: not more than 3 times the area of the principal peak in the chromatogram obtained with reference solution (a) (0.3 per cent);
— *disregard limit*: 0.25 times the area of the principal peak in the chromatogram obtained with reference solution (a) (0.025 per cent); disregard the 2 peaks eluting within the first 2 min.

### Chlorides

Maximum 100 ppm.

*Prepare the solutions at the same time.*

*Test solution*  Dissolve 0.530 g in 20.0 ml of *anhydrous acetic acid R*, add 6 ml of *dilute nitric acid R* and dilute to 50.0 ml with *water R*.

*Reference solution*  To 1.5 ml of *0.001 M hydrochloric acid*, add 20.0 ml of *anhydrous acetic acid R* and 6 ml of *dilute nitric acid R* and dilute to 50.0 ml with *water R*.

Transfer both recently prepared solutions to separate test-tubes. Add to each tube 1 ml of *silver nitrate solution R2*. Allow to stand for 5 min protected from light. Examine the tubes laterally against a black background. Any opalescence in the test solution is not more intense than that in the reference solution.

### Sulphates

Maximum 100 ppm.

*Prepare the solutions at the same time.*

*Test solution*  Dissolve 3.00 g in 20.0 ml of *glacial acetic acid R*, heating gently if necessary. Allow to cool and dilute to 50.0 ml with *water R*.

*Reference solution*  To 9 ml of *sulphate standard solution (10 ppm SO$_4$) R1*, add 6 ml of *glacial acetic acid R*.

Into 2 test tubes introduce 1.5 ml of *sulphate standard solution (10 ppm SO₄) R1* and add 1 ml of a 250 g/l solution of *barium chloride R*. Shake and allow to stand for 1 min. To one of the tubes add 15 ml of the test solution and to the other add 15 ml of the reference solution. After 5 min, any opalescence in the tube containing the test solution is not more intense than that in the tube containing the reference solution.

**Heavy metals** *(2.4.8)*
Maximum 20 ppm.

1.0 g complies with test D. Prepare the reference solution using 2 ml of *lead standard solution (10 ppm Pb) R*.

**Loss on drying** *(2.2.32)*
Maximum 0.5 per cent, determined on 1.000 g by drying in an oven at 105 °C.

**Sulphated ash** *(2.4.14)*
Maximum 0.1 per cent, determined on 1.0 g.

**ASSAY**
Dissolve 0.400 g in 50 ml of *anhydrous acetic acid R*. Titrate with *0.1 M perchloric acid*, determining the end-point potentiometrically *(2.2.20)*.

1 ml of *0.1 M perchloric acid* is equivalent to 50.80 mg of $C_{24}H_{30}ClN_3O_7$.

**STORAGE**
Protected from light.

**IMPURITIES**

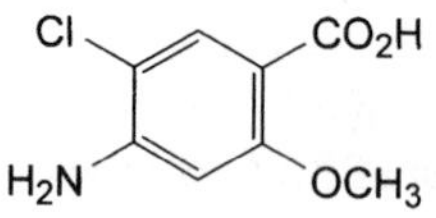

A. 4-amino-5-chloro-2-methoxybenzoic acid,

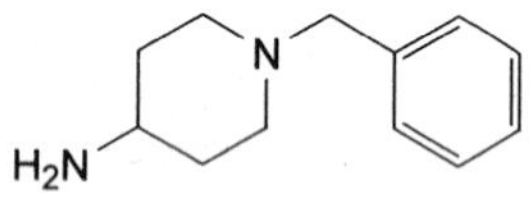

B. 1-benzylpiperidin-4-amine,

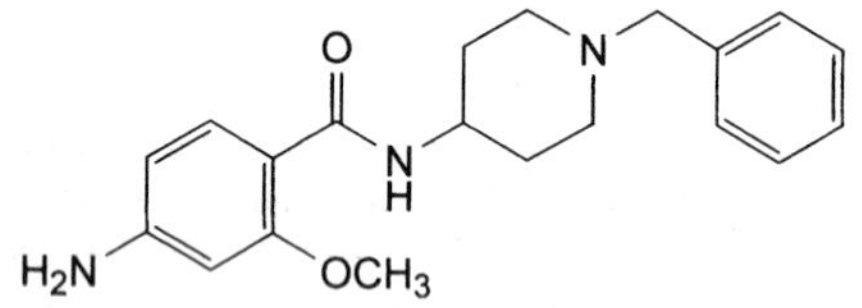

C. 4-amino-*N*-(1-benzylpiperidin-4-yl)-2-methoxybenzamide.

*———— Ph Eur*

# Clemastine Fumarate

Clemastine Hydrogen Fumarate
*(Ph Eur monograph 1190)*

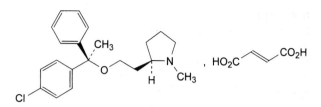

$C_{21}H_{26}ClNO,C_4H_4O_4$        460.0        *14976-57-9*

**Action and use**
Histamine $H_1$ receptor antagonist; antihistamine.

**Preparations**
Clemastine Oral Solution
Clemastine Tablets

*Ph Eur* ————

**DEFINITION**
(2R)-2-[2-[(R)-1-(4-Chlorophenyl)-1-phenylethoxy]ethyl]-1-methylpyrrolidine (*E*)-butenedioate.

**Content**
98.5 per cent to 101.0 per cent (dried substance).

**CHARACTERS**
**Appearance**
White or almost white, crystalline powder.

**Solubility**
Very slightly soluble in water, sparingly soluble in ethanol (70 per cent *V/V*), slightly soluble in ethanol (50 per cent *V/V*) and in methanol.

**IDENTIFICATION**
*First identification   A, B.*

*Second identification   A, C, D.*

A. Specific optical rotation (see Tests).

B. Infrared absorption spectrophotometry *(2.2.24)*.

*Comparison   clemastine fumarate CRS.*

C. Examine the chromatograms obtained in the test for related substances.

*Results*   The principal spot in the chromatogram obtained with test solution (b) is similar in position, colour and size to the principal spot in the chromatogram obtained with reference solution (a).

D. Thin-layer chromatography *(2.2.27)*.

*Test solution*   Dissolve 40 mg of the substance to be examined in *methanol R* and dilute to 2 ml with the same solvent.

*Reference solution*   Dissolve 50 mg of *fumaric acid CRS* in ethanol (96 per cent) R and dilute to 10 ml with the same solvent.

*Plate*   TLC silica gel G plate R.

*Mobile phase*   water R, anhydrous formic acid R, di-isopropyl ether R (5:25:70 *V/V/V*).

*Application*   5 μl.

*Development*   Over a path of 15 cm.

*Drying*   At 100-105 °C for 30 min and allow to cool.

*Detection*   Spray with a 16 g/l solution of *potassium permanganate R* and examine in daylight.

*Results*   The spot with the highest $R_F$ value in the chromatogram obtained with the test solution is similar in position, colour and size to the principal spot in the chromatogram obtained with the reference solution.

## TESTS

### Solution S
Dissolve 0.500 g in *methanol R* and dilute to 50.0 ml with the same solvent.

### Appearance of solution
Solution S is clear (*2.2.1*) and not more intensely coloured than reference solution $BY_7$ (*2.2.2, Method II*).

### pH (*2.2.3*)
3.2 to 4.2.

Suspend 1.0 g in 10 ml of *carbon dioxide-free water R*.

### Specific optical rotation (*2.2.7*)
+ 15.0 to + 18.0 (dried substance), determined on solution S.

### Related substances
Thin-layer chromatography (*2.2.27*).

*Test solution (a)*   Dissolve 0.100 g of the substance to be examined in *methanol R* and dilute to 5.0 ml with the same solvent.

*Test solution (b)*   Dilute 1.0 ml of test solution (a) to 10.0 ml with *methanol R*.

*Reference solution (a)*   Dissolve 20.0 mg of *clemastine fumarate CRS* in *methanol R* and dilute to 10.0 ml with the same solvent.

*Reference solution (b)*   Dilute 1.5 ml of test solution (b) to 50.0 ml with *methanol R*.

*Reference solution (c)*   Dilute 0.5 ml of test solution (b) to 50.0 ml with *methanol R*.

*Reference solution (d)*   Dissolve 10.0 mg of *diphenhydramine hydrochloride CRS* in 5.0 ml of reference solution (a).

*Plate*   TLC silica gel G plate R.

*Mobile phase*   concentrated ammonia R, methanol R, tetrahydrofuran R (1:20:80 V/V/V).

*Application*   5 µl.

*Development*   Over a path of 15 cm.

*Drying*   In a current of cold air for 5 min.

*Detection*   Spray with a freshly prepared mixture of 1 volume of *potassium iodobismuthate solution R* and 10 volumes of *dilute acetic acid R* and then with *dilute hydrogen peroxide solution R;* cover the plate immediately with a glass plate of the same size and examine the chromatograms after 2 min.

*System suitability*   Reference solution (d):
— the chromatogram shows 2 clearly separated spots.

*Limits*   Test solution (a):
— *any impurity:* any spot, apart from the principal spot, is not more intense than the principal spot in the chromatogram obtained with reference solution (b) (0.3 per cent) and at most 4 such spots are more intense than the principal spot in the chromatogram obtained with reference solution (c) (0.1 per cent);
— *disregard limit:* disregard any spot remaining at the starting point (fumaric acid).

### Impurity C
Liquid chromatography (*2.2.29*).

*Solvent mixture*   acetonitrile R1, 10 g/l solution of *ammonium dihydrogen phosphate R* (25:75 V/V).

*Test solution*   Dissolve 20 mg of the substance to be examined in the solvent mixture and dilute to 100 ml with the solvent mixture.

*Reference solution (a)*   Dissolve 6 mg of *1-(4-chlorophenyl)-1-phenylethanol CRS* (impurity C) in the solvent mixture and dilute to 100 ml with the solvent mixture.

*Reference solution (b)*   Dilute 1 ml of reference solution (a) to 100 ml with the solvent mixture.

*Reference solution (c)*   Dissolve 10 mg of the substance to be examined in the solvent mixture and dilute to 100 ml with the solvent mixture. To 1 ml of this solution add 1 ml of reference solution (a) and dilute to 100 ml with the solvent mixture.

*Column:*
— size: $l = 0.1$ m, $\varnothing = 4.6$ mm;
— stationary phase: octadecylsilyl silica gel for chromatography R (5 µm).

*Mobile phase*   phosphoric acid R, acetonitrile R1, 10 g/l solution of *ammonium dihydrogen phosphate R* (0.1:45:55 V/V/V).

*Flow rate*   1 ml/min.

*Detection*   Spectrophotometer at 220 nm.

*Injection*   100 µl.

*System suitability*   Reference solution (c):
— resolution: minimum 2.2 between the peaks due to clemastine and impurity C.

*Limit:*
— impurity C: not more than the area of the principal peak in the chromatogram obtained with reference solution (b) (0.3 per cent).

### Loss on drying (*2.2.32*)
Maximum 0.5 per cent, determined on 1.000 g by drying in an oven at 105 °C for 6 h.

### Sulphated ash (*2.4.14*)
Maximum 0.1 per cent, determined on 1.0 g.

## ASSAY
Dissolve 0.350 g in 60 ml of *anhydrous acetic acid R*. Titrate with *0.1 M perchloric acid*, determining the end-point potentiometrically (*2.2.20*).

1 ml of *0.1 M perchloric acid* is equivalent to 46.00 mg of $C_{25}H_{30}ClNO_5$.

## IMPURITIES

*Specified impurities*   A, B, C.

*Other detectable impurities*   (The following substances would, if present at a sufficient level, be detected by one or other of the tests in the monograph. They are limited by the general acceptance criterion for other/unspecified impurities and/or by the general monograph *Substances for pharmaceutical use (2034)*. It is therefore not necessary to identify these impurities for demonstration of compliance. See also *5.10. Control of impurities in substances for pharmaceutical use*): D.

and epimer at N

A. (1RS,2R)-2-[2-[(R)-1-(4-chlorophenyl)-1-phenylethoxy]ethyl]-1-methylpyrrolidine 1-oxide,

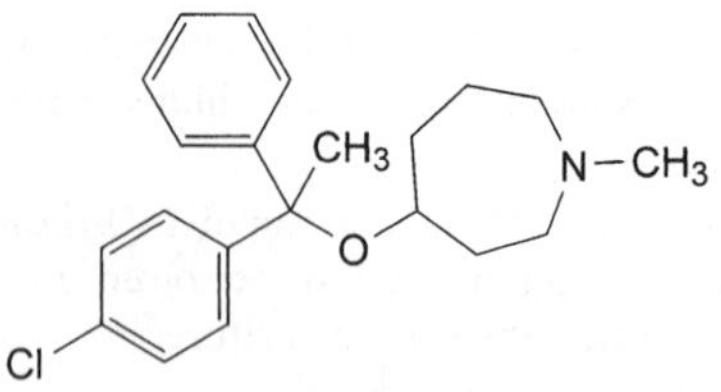

B. 4-[1-(4-chlorophenyl)-1-phenylethoxy]-1-methylazepane,

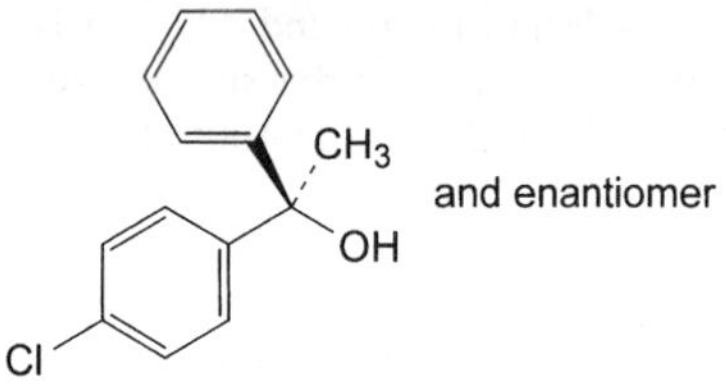

C. (RS)-1-(4-chlorophenyl)-1-phenylethanol,

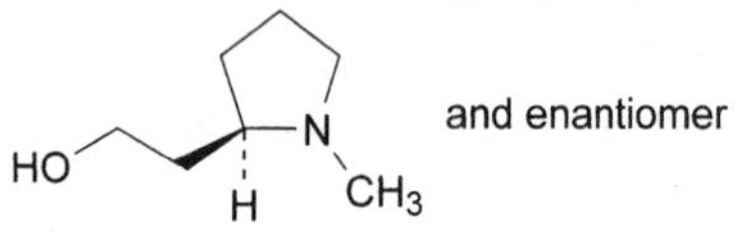

and enantiomer

D. 2-[(2RS)-1-methylpyrrolidin-2-yl]ethanol.

_____ Ph Eur

# Clenbuterol Hydrochloride

(Ph Eur monograph 1409)

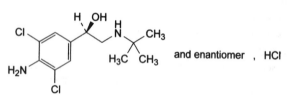

and enantiomer , HCl

$C_{12}H_{18}Cl_2N_2O,HCl$     313.7     21898-19-1

## Action and use
Beta$_2$-adrenoceptor agonist; bronchodilator.

Ph Eur _____

## DEFINITION
(1RS)-1-(4-Amino-3,5-dichlorophenyl)-2-[(1,1-dimethylethyl)amino]ethanol hydrochloride.

## Content
99.0 per cent to 101.0 per cent (anhydrous substance).

## CHARACTERS
### Appearance
White or almost white, crystalline powder.

### Solubility
Soluble in water and in ethanol (96 per cent), slightly soluble in acetone.

### mp
About 173 °C, with decomposition.

## IDENTIFICATION
*First identification*   A, C.

*Second identification*   B, C.

A. Infrared absorption spectrophotometry (2.2.24).

*Comparison*   clenbuterol hydrochloride CRS.

B. Thin-layer chromatography (2.2.27).

*Test solution*   Dissolve 10 mg of the substance to be examined in 10 ml of *methanol R*.

*Reference solution*   Dissolve 10 mg of *clenbuterol hydrochloride CRS* in 10 ml of *methanol R*.

*Plate*   TLC silica gel F$_{254}$ plate R.

*Mobile phase*   ammonia R, anhydrous ethanol R, toluene R (0.15:10:15 V/V/V).

*Application*   10 µl.

*Development*   Over a path of 10 cm.

*Drying*   In air.

*Detection*   Spray with a 10 g/l solution of *sodium nitrite R* in 1 M hydrochloric acid and dip after 10 min in a 4 g/l solution of *naphthylethylenediamine dihydrochloride R* in *methanol R*. Allow to dry in air.

*Results*   The principal spot in the chromatogram obtained with the test solution is similar in position, colour and size to the principal spot in the chromatogram obtained with the reference solution.

C. It gives reaction (a) of chlorides (2.3.1).

## TESTS
### Solution S
Dissolve 0.5 g in 10 ml of *carbon dioxide-free water R*.

### Appearance of solution
Solution S is not more opalescent than reference suspension II (2.2.1) and not more intensely coloured than reference solution Y$_6$ (2.2.2, Method II).

### pH (2.2.3)
5.0 to 7.0 for solution S.

### Optical rotation (2.2.7)
− 0.10° to + 0.10°.

Dissolve 0.30 g in *water R* and dilute to 10.0 ml with the same solvent. Filter if necessary.

### Related substances
Liquid chromatography (2.2.29).

*Test solution*   Disperse 100.0 mg of the substance to be examined in the mobile phase and dilute to 50.0 ml with the mobile phase.

*Reference solution (a)*   Dilute 0.1 ml of the test solution to 100.0 ml with *water R*.

*Reference solution (b)*   Dissolve 5 mg of *clenbuterol impurity B CRS* in 10 ml of the mobile phase, add 2.5 ml of the test solution and dilute to 25.0 ml with the mobile phase.

*Column:*
— *size: l = 0.125 m, Ø = 4 mm,*
— *stationary phase: end-capped octadecylsilyl silica gel for chromatography R (5 µm),*
— *temperature: 40 °C.*

*Mobile phase*   Mix 200 volumes of *acetonitrile R*, 200 volumes of *methanol R* and 600 volumes of a solution prepared as follows: dissolve 3.0 g of *sodium decanesulphonate R* and 5.0 g of *potassium dihydrogen phosphate R* in 900 ml of *water R*, adjust to pH 3.0 with *dilute phosphoric acid R* and dilute to 1000 ml with *water R*.

*Flow rate*   0.5 ml/min.

*Detection*   Spectrophotometer at 215 nm.

*Injection*   5 µl.

*Run time*   1.5 times the retention time of clenbuterol .

*Retention time*   Clenbuterol = about 29 min.

*System suitability*   Reference solution (b):
— *resolution*: minimum 4.0 between the peaks due to impurity B and clenbuterol.

*Limits:*
— *impurities A, B, C, D, E, F*: for each impurity, not more than the area of the principal peak in the chromatogram obtained with reference solution (a) (0.1 per cent),
— *any other impurity*: for each impurity, not more than the area of the principal peak in the chromatogram obtained with reference solution (a) (0.1 per cent),
— *total*: not more than twice the area of the principal peak in the chromatogram obtained with reference solution (a) (0.2 per cent),
— *disregard limit*: 0.5 times the area of the principal peak in the chromatogram obtained with reference solution (a) (0.05 per cent).

**Water** (*2.5.12*)
Maximum 1.0 per cent, determined on 0.500 g.

**Sulphated ash** (*2.4.14*)
Maximum 0.1 per cent, determined on 1.0 g.

## ASSAY
Dissolve 0.250 g in 50 ml of *ethanol (96 per cent) R* and add 5.0 ml of *0.01 M hydrochloric acid*. Titrate with *0.1 M sodium hydroxide*, determining the end-point potentiometrically (*2.2.20*). Read the volume added between the 2 points of inflexion.

1 ml of *0.1 M sodium hydroxide* is equivalent to 31.37 mg of $C_{12}H_{19}C_{13}N_2O$.

## IMPURITIES
*Specified impurities*   *A, B, C, D, E, F.*

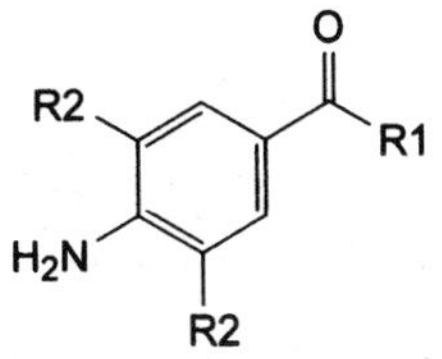

A. R1 = H, R2 = Cl: 4-amino-3,5-dichlorobenzaldehyde,

B. R1 = CH$_2$-NH-C(CH$_3$)$_3$, R2 = Cl: 1-(4-amino-3,5-dichlorophenyl)-2-[(1,1-dimethylethyl)amino]ethanone,

C. R1 = CH$_3$, R2 = Cl:
1-(4-amino-3,5-dichlorophenyl)ethanone,

D. R1 = CH$_3$, R2 = H: 1-(4-aminophenyl)ethanone,

E. R1 = CH$_2$Br, R2 = Cl:
1-(4-amino-3,5-dichlorophenyl)-2-bromoethanone,

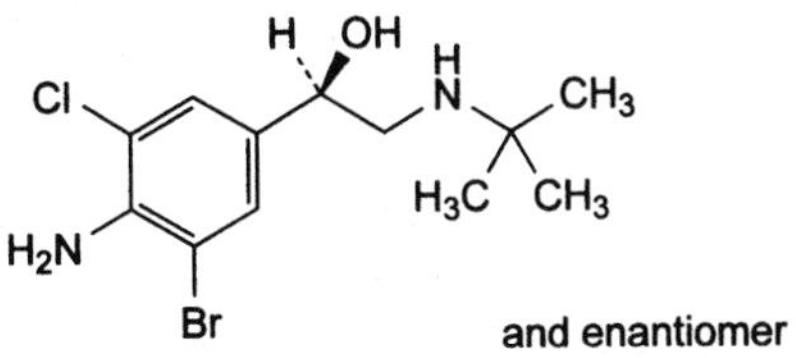

**and enantiomer**

F. (1RS)-1-(4-amino-3-bromo-5-chlorophenyl)-2-[(1,1-dimethylethyl)amino]ethanol.

*Ph Eur*

# Clindamycin Hydrochloride

(*Ph Eur monograph 0582*)

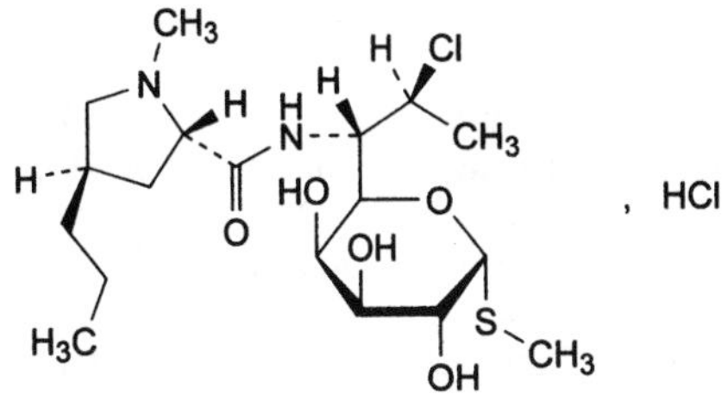

$C_{18}H_{33}ClN_2O_5S$,HCl     461.5     *21462-39-5*

**Action and use**
Lincosamide antibacterial.

**Preparation**
Clindamycin Capsules

*Ph Eur*

## DEFINITION
Methyl 7-chloro-6,7,8-trideoxy-6-[[[(2S,4R)-1-methyl-4-propylpyrrolidin-2-yl]carbonyl]amino]-1-thio-L-*threo*-α-D-*galacto*-octopyranoside hydrochloride. It contains a variable quantity of water.

Semi-synthetic product derived from a fermentation product.

**Content**
91.0 per cent to 102.0 per cent (anhydrous substance).

## CHARACTERS
**Appearance**
White or almost white, crystalline powder.

**Solubility**
Very soluble in water, slightly soluble in ethanol (96 per cent).

## IDENTIFICATION
*First identification*   *A, D.*

*Second identification*   *B, C, D.*

A. Infrared absorption spectrophotometry (*2.2.24*).

*Comparison*   *clindamycin hydrochloride CRS.*

B. Thin-layer chromatography (*2.2.27*).

*Test solution*   Dissolve 10 mg of the substance to be examined in *methanol R* and dilute to 10 ml with the same solvent.

*Reference solution (a)*   Dissolve 10 mg of *clindamycin hydrochloride CRS* in *methanol R* and dilute to 10 ml with the same solvent.

*Reference solution (b)*   Dissolve 10 mg of *clindamycin hydrochloride CRS* and 10 mg of *lincomycin hydrochloride CRS* in *methanol R* and dilute to 10 ml with the same solvent.

*Plate*   *TLC silica gel G plate R.*

*Mobile phase*   Mix 19 volumes of *2-propanol R*, 38 volumes of a 150 g/l solution of *ammonium acetate R* adjusted to pH 9.6 with *ammonia R*, and 43 volumes of *ethyl acetate R*.

*Application*   5 µl.

*Development*   Over a path of 15 cm using the upper layer of the mobile phase.

*Drying*   In air.

*Detection*   Spray with a 1 g/l solution of *potassium permanganate R*.

*System suitability* The chromatogram obtained with reference solution (b) shows 2 clearly separated spots.

*Results* The principal spot in the chromatogram obtained with the test solution is similar in position, colour and size to the principal spot in the chromatogram obtained with reference solution (a).

C. Dissolve about 10 mg in 2 ml of *dilute hydrochloric acid R* and heat on a water-bath for 3 min. Add 3 ml of *sodium carbonate solution R* and 1 ml of a 20 g/l solution of *sodium nitroprusside R*. A violet-red colour develops.

D. Dissolve 0.1 g in *water R* and dilute to 10 ml with the same solvent. The solution gives reaction (a) of chlorides (*2.3.1*).

## TESTS

**pH** (*2.2.3*)

3.0 to 5.0.

Dissolve 1.0 g in *carbon dioxide-free water R* and dilute to 10 ml with the same solvent.

**Specific optical rotation** (*2.2.7*)

+ 135 to + 150 (anhydrous substance).

Dissolve 1.000 g in *water R* and dilute to 25.0 ml with the same solvent.

**Related substances**

Liquid chromatography (*2.2.29*).

*Test solution* Dissolve 50.0 mg of the substance to be examined in the mobile phase and dilute to 50.0 ml with the mobile phase.

*Reference solution (a)* Dissolve 50.0 mg of *clindamycin hydrochloride CRS* in the mobile phase and dilute to 50.0 ml with the mobile phase.

*Reference solution (b)* Dilute 2.0 ml of the test solution to 100.0 ml with the mobile phase.

*Column:*
— *size*: l = 0.25 m, Ø = 4.6 mm,
— *stationary phase*: octadecylsilyl silica gel for chromatography R (5 μm).

*Mobile phase* Mix 45 volumes of *acetonitrile R* and 55 volumes of a 6.8 g/l solution of *potassium dihydrogen phosphate R* adjusted to pH 7.5 with a 250 g/l solution of *potassium hydroxide R*.

*Flow rate* 1 ml/min.

*Detection* Spectrophotometer at 210 nm.

*Injection* 20 μl.

*Run time* Twice the retention time of clindamycin.

*System suitability* Reference solution (a):
— *Relative retention* with reference to clindamycin (retention time = about 10 min): impurity A = about 0.4; impurity B = about 0.65; impurity C = about 0.8.

*Limits:*
— *impurity B*: not more than the area of the principal peak in the chromatogram obtained with reference solution (b) (2.0 per cent),
— *impurity C*: not more than twice the area of the principal peak in the chromatogram obtained with reference solution (b) (4.0 per cent),
— *any other impurity*: not more than 0.5 times the area of the principal peak in the chromatogram obtained with reference solution (b) (1.0 per cent),
— *total*: not more than 3 times the area of the principal peak in the chromatogram obtained with reference solution (b) (6.0 per cent),

— *disregard limit*: 0.025 times the area of the principal peak in the chromatogram obtained with reference solution (b) (0.05 per cent).

**Water** (*2.5.12*)

3.0 per cent to 6.0 per cent, determined on 0.500 g.

**Sulphated ash** (*2.4.14*)

Maximum 0.5 per cent, determined on 1.0 g.

## ASSAY

Liquid chromatography (*2.2.29*) as described in the test for related substances with the following modifications.

*Injection* 20 μl of the test solution and reference solution (a).

*System suitability:*
— *repeatability*: maximum relative standard deviation of 0.85 per cent after 6 injections of reference solution (a).

## STORAGE

In an airtight container.

## IMPURITIES

A. R1 = CH$_2$-CH$_2$-CH$_3$, R2 = OH, R3 = H: methyl 6,8-dideoxy-6-[[[(2S,4R)-1-methyl-4-propylpyrrolidin-2-yl]carbonyl]amino]-1-thio-D-*erythro*-α-D-*galacto*-octopyranoside (lincomycin),

B. R1 = C$_2$H$_5$, R2 = H, R3 = Cl: methyl 7-chloro-6,7,8-trideoxy-6-[[[(2S,4R)-4-ethyl-1-methylpyrrolidin-2-yl]carbonyl]amino]-1-thio-L-*threo*-α-D-*galacto*-octopyranoside (clindamycin B),

C. R1 = CH$_2$-CH$_2$-CH$_3$, R2 = Cl, R3 = H: methyl 7-chloro-6,7,8-trideoxy-6-[[[(2S,4R)-1-methyl-4-propylpyrrolidin-2-yl]carbonyl]amino]-1-thio-D-*erythro*-α-D-*galacto*-octopyranoside (7-epiclindamycin).

*Ph Eur*

# Clindamycin Phosphate

(Ph Eur monograph 0996)

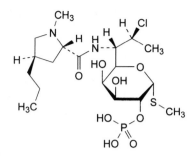

C₁₈H₃₄ClN₂O₈PS $\quad$ 505.0 $\quad$ 24729-96-2

**Action and use**

Lincosamide antibacterial.

**Preparation**

Clindamycin Injection

*Ph Eur* _____

## DEFINITION

Methyl 7-chloro-6,7,8-trideoxy-6-[[[(2S,4R)-1-methyl-4-propylpyrrolidin-2-yl]carbonyl]amino]-1-thio-L-*threo*-α-D-*galacto*-octopyranoside 2-(dihydrogen phosphate).

Semi-synthetic product derived from a fermentation product.

## Content

95.0 per cent to 102.0 per cent (anhydrous substance).

## CHARACTERS

**Appearance**

White or almost white, slightly hygroscopic powder.

**Solubility**

Freely soluble in water, very slightly soluble in ethanol (96 per cent), practically insoluble in methylene chloride.

It shows polymorphism (5.9).

## IDENTIFICATION

*First identification* A, D.

*Second identification* B, C, D.

A. Infrared absorption spectrophotometry (2.2.24).

*Preparation* Discs of *potassium bromide R*.

In 2 separate tubes place 50 mg of the substance to be examined and 50 mg of *clindamycin phosphate CRS*. Add 0.2 ml of *water R* and heat until completely dissolved. Evaporate to dryness under reduced pressure and dry the residues at 100-105 °C for 2 h.

*Comparison* *clindamycin phosphate CRS*.

B. Thin-layer chromatography (2.2.27).

*Test solution* Dissolve 20 mg of the substance to be examined in *methanol R* and dilute to 10 ml with the same solvent.

*Reference solution (a)* Dissolve 20 mg of *clindamycin phosphate CRS* in *methanol R* and dilute to 10 ml with the same solvent.

*Reference solution (b)* Dissolve 10 mg of *lincomycin hydrochloride CRS* in 5 ml of reference solution (a).

*Plate* TLC silica gel plate R.

*Mobile phase* glacial acetic acid R, water R, butanol R (20:20:60 *V/V/V*).

*Application* 5 μl.

*Development* Over a path of 12 cm.

*Drying* At 100-105 °C for 30 min.

*Detection* Spray with a 1 g/l solution of *potassium permanganate R*.

*System suitability* Reference solution (b):
— the chromatogram shows 2 principal spots.

*Results* The principal spot in the chromatogram obtained with the test solution is similar in position, colour and size to the principal spot in the chromatogram obtained with reference solution (a).

C. Dissolve about 10 mg in 2 ml of *dilute hydrochloric acid R* and heat in a water-bath for 3 min. Add 4 ml of *sodium carbonate solution R* and 1 ml of a 20 g/l solution of *sodium nitroprusside R*. Prepare a standard in the same manner using *clindamycin phosphate CRS*. The colour of the test solution corresponds to that of the standard.

D. Boil 0.1 g under a reflux condenser with a mixture of 5 ml of *strong sodium hydroxide solution R* and 5 ml of *water R* for 90 min. Cool and add 5 ml of *nitric acid R*. Extract with 3 quantities, each of 15 ml, of *methylene chloride R* and discard the extracts. Filter the upper layer through a paper filter. The filtrate gives reaction (b) of phosphates (2.3.1).

## TESTS

**Solution S**

Dissolve 1.00 g in *carbon dioxide-free water R*. Heat gently if necessary. Cool and dilute to 25.0 ml with *carbon dioxide-free water R*.

**Appearance of the solution**

Solution S is clear (2.2.1) and colourless (2.2.2, Method II).

**pH** (2.2.3)

3.5 to 4.5.

Dilute 5.0 ml of solution S to 20 ml with *carbon dioxide-free water R*.

**Specific optical rotation** (2.2.7)

+ 115 to + 130 (anhydrous substance).

Dissolve 0.250 g in *water R* and dilute to 25.0 ml with the same solvent.

**Related substances**

Liquid chromatography (2.2.29).

*Test solution* Dissolve 75.0 mg of the substance to be examined in the mobile phase and dilute to 25.0 ml with the mobile phase.

*Reference solution (a)* Dissolve 75.0 mg of *clindamycin phosphate CRS* in the mobile phase and dilute to 25.0 ml with the mobile phase.

*Reference solution (b)* Dissolve 5.0 mg of *lincomycin hydrochloride CRS* (impurity A) and 15.0 mg of *clindamycin hydrochloride CRS* (impurity E) in 5.0 ml of reference solution (a), then dilute to 100.0 ml with the mobile phase.

*Reference solution (c)* Dilute 1.0 ml of reference solution (a) to 100.0 ml with the mobile phase.

*Column:*
— size: l = 0.25 m, Ø = 4.6 mm;
— stationary phase: octylsilyl silica gel for chromatography R (5-10 μm).

*Mobile phase* Mix 200 ml of *acetonitrile R1* and 800 ml of a 13.6 g/l solution of *potassium dihydrogen phosphate R* previously adjusted to pH 2.5 with *phosphoric acid R*.

*Flow rate* 1.0 ml/min.

*Detection* Spectrophotometer at 210 nm.

*Injection* 20 μl of the test solution and reference solutions (b) and (c).

*Run time* The retention time of impurity E.

*System suitability* Reference solution (b):
— *resolution*: minimum 6.0 between the peaks due to clindamycin phosphate (2$^{nd}$ peak) and impurity E (3$^{rd}$ peak); if necessary, adjust the concentration of acetonitrile in the mobile phase;
— *symmetry factor*: maximum 1.5 for the peak due to clindamycin phosphate;
— the peak due to impurity A (1$^{st}$ peak) is clearly separated from the peak due to the solvent.

*Limits:*
— *any impurity*: for each impurity, not more than 2.5 times the area of the peak due to clindamycin phosphate in the chromatogram obtained with reference solution (c) (2.5 per cent);
— *total*: not more than 4 times the area of the peak due to clindamycin phosphate in the chromatogram obtained with reference solution (c) (4.0 per cent);
— *disregard limit*: 0.1 times the area of the principal peak in the chromatogram obtained with reference solution (c) (0.1 per cent).

**Water** (*2.5.12*)
Maximum 6.0 per cent, determined on 0.250 g.

**Bacterial endotoxins** (*2.6.14*)
Less than 0.6 IU/mg, if intended for use in the manufacture of parenteral dosage forms without a further appropriate procedure for removal of bacterial endotoxins.

**ASSAY**
Liquid chromatography (*2.2.29*) as described in the test for related substances with the following modifications.

*Injection* The test solution and reference solution (a).

*System suitability* Reference solution (a):
— *repeatability*: maximum relative standard deviation of 1.0 per cent after 6 injections; if necessary, adjust the integrator parameters.

Calculate the percentage content of $C_{18}H_{34}ClN_2O_8PS$ from the declared content of *clindamycin phosphate CRS*.

**STORAGE**
In an airtight container, at a temperature not exceeding 30 °C. If the substance is sterile, store in a sterile, airtight, tamper-proof container.

**IMPURITIES**
A. lincomycin,

B. R1 = PO$_3$H$_2$, R2 = R3 = H, R4 = C$_2$H$_5$: clindamycin B 2-(dihydrogen phosphate),

C. R1 = R3 = H, R2 = PO$_3$H$_2$, R4 = C$_3$H$_7$: clindamycin 3-(dihydrogen phosphate),

D. R1 = R2 = H, R3 = PO$_3$H$_2$, R4 = C$_3$H$_7$: clindamycin 4-(dihydrogen phosphate),

E. R1 = R2 = R3 = H, R4 = C$_3$H$_7$: clindamycin.

_____ *Ph Eur*

# Clioquinol

(*Ph Eur monograph 2111*)

C$_9$H$_5$ClINO        305.5        130-26-7

**Action and use**
Antibacterial; antiprotozoal.

**Preparations**
Betamethasone and Clioquinol Cream
Betamethasone and Clioquinol Ointment
Hydrocortisone and Clioquinol Cream
Hydrocortisone and Clioquinol Ointment

*Ph Eur* _____

**DEFINITION**
5-Chloro-7-iodoquinolin-8-ol.

**Content**
98.0 per cent to 102.0 per cent (dried substance).

**CHARACTERS**
**Appearance**
Almost white, light yellow, brownish-yellow or yellowish-grey powder.

**Solubility**
Practically insoluble in water, sparingly soluble in methylene chloride, very slightly soluble or slightly soluble in ethanol (96 per cent).

**IDENTIFICATION**
*First identification* B.

*Second identification* A, C, D.

A. Dissolve 40.0 mg in *methanol R* and dilute to 100.0 ml with the same solvent. Dilute 10.0 ml to 100.0 ml with *methanol R* (solution A). Examined between 280 nm and 350 nm (*2.2.25*), solution A shows an absorption maximum at 321 nm. Dilute 10.0 ml of solution A to 100.0 ml with *methanol R* (solution B). Examined between 230 nm and 280 nm, solution B shows an absorption maximum at 255 nm. The specific absorbance at this absorption maximum is 1530 to 1660.

B. Infrared absorption spectrophotometry (*2.2.24*).

*Preparation* Discs of *potassium bromide R*.

*Comparison* clioquinol CRS.

C. When heated, violet fumes are produced.

D. Dissolve about 1 mg in 5 ml of *ethanol (96 per cent) R*. Add 0.05 ml of *ferric chloride solution R1*. A dark green colour develops.

**TESTS**
**Acidity or alkalinity**
Shake 0.5 g with 10 ml of *carbon dioxide-free water R* and filter. To the filtrate add 0.2 ml of *phenolphthalein solution R*. The solution is colourless. Not more than 0.5 ml of *0.01 M sodium hydroxide* is required to change the colour of the indicator to pink.

**Related substances**

Liquid chromatography (2.2.29).

*Test solution* Dissolve 50.0 mg of the substance to be examined in *methanol R* and dilute to 50.0 ml with the same solvent, heating gently if necessary. Dilute 10.0 ml of the solution to 25.0 ml with the mobile phase.

*Reference solution (a)* Dissolve 20.0 mg of *5-chloroquinolin-8-ol R*, 10.0 mg of *5,7-dichloroquinolin-8-ol R*, 5 mg of the substance to be examined and 10.0 mg of *5,7-diiodoquinolin-8-ol R* in *methanol R*, heating gently if necessary and dilute to 20.0 ml with the same solvent. Dilute 4.0 ml of the solution to 50.0 ml with the mobile phase.

*Reference solution (b)* Dilute 1.0 ml of reference solution (a) to 10.0 ml with the mobile phase.

*Reference solution (c)* Dilute 1.0 ml of the test solution to 100.0 ml with the mobile phase. Dilute 1.0 ml of this solution to 20.0 ml with the mobile phase.

*Column:*
— *size*: $l = 0.15$ m, $\varnothing = 3.9$ mm,
— *stationary phase*: octylsilyl silica gel for chromatography R (5 μm).

*Mobile phase* Dissolve 0.50 g of *sodium edetate R* in 350 ml of *water R*, add 4.0 ml of *hexylamine R* and mix. Adjust to pH 3.0 with *phosphoric acid R*. Add 600 ml of *methanol R* and dilute to 1000 ml with *water R*.

*Flow rate* 1.3 ml/min.

*Detection* Spectrophotometer at 254 nm.

*Injection* 20 μl.

*Run time* 4 times the retention time of clioquinol.

*Relative retention* With reference to clioquinol (retention time = about 10 min): impurity A = about 0.4; impurity B = about 0.7; impurity C = about 1.3.

*System suitability* Reference solution (a):
— *resolution*: minimum 3.0 between the peaks due to clioquinol and impurity C.

*Limits:*
— *impurity A*: not more than the area of the corresponding peak in the chromatogram obtained with reference solution (b) (2.0 per cent),
— *impurity B*: not more than the area of the corresponding peak in the chromatogram obtained with reference solution (b) (1.0 per cent),
— *impurity C*: not more than the area of the corresponding peak in the chromatogram obtained with reference solution (b) (1.0 per cent),
— *any other impurity*: for each impurity, not more than twice the area of the principal peak in the chromatogram obtained with reference solution (c) (0.1 per cent),
— *total of the nominal contents of impurities A, B, C and any other impurities*: maximum 3.0 per cent,
— *disregard limit*: the area of the principal peak in the chromatogram obtained with reference solution (c) (0.05 per cent).

**Halides**

Maximum 140 ppm, expressed as chlorides.

Shake 0.5 g with 25 ml of *water R* for 1 min and filter. To the filtrate add 0.5 ml of *dilute nitric acid R* and 0.5 ml of *silver nitrate solution R2*. Allow to stand for 5 min. Any opalescence is not more intense than that in a standard prepared at the same time by adding 0.5 ml of *silver nitrate solution R2* to 25 ml of *water R* containing 0.2 ml of *0.01 M hydrochloric acid* and 0.5 ml of *dilute nitric acid R*.

**Loss on drying** (2.2.32)

Maximum 0.5 per cent, determined on 1.000 g by drying over *diphosphorus pentoxide R* at a pressure not exceeding 0.7 kPa for 24 h.

**Sulphated ash** (2.4.14)

Maximum 0.1 per cent, determined on 1.0 g.

**ASSAY**

Dissolve 0.200 g in 20 ml of *acetic anhydride R* and add 30 ml of *glacial acetic acid R*. Titrate with *0.1 M perchloric acid*, determining the end-point potentiometrically (2.2.20). 1 ml of *0.1 M perchloric acid* is equivalent to 30.55 mg of total quinolines, calculated as clioquinol.

**STORAGE**

Protected from light.

**IMPURITIES**

*Specified impurities   A, B, C.*

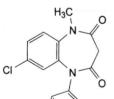

A. R1 = Cl, R2 = H: 5-chloroquinolin-8-ol,
B. R1 = R2 = Cl: 5,7-dichloroquinolin-8-ol,
C. R1 = R2 = I: 5,7-diiodoquinolin-8-ol.

_____ *Ph Eur*

# Clobazam

(*Ph Eur monograph 1974*)

$C_{16}H_{13}ClN_2O_2$      300.7      *22316-47-8*

**Action and use**

Benzodiazepine.

**Preparation**

Clobazam Capsules

*Ph Eur* _____

**DEFINITION**

7-Chloro-1-methyl-5-phenyl-1,5-dihydro-3*H*-1,5-benzodiazepine-2,4-dione.

**Content**

97.0 per cent to 103.0 per cent (dried substance).

**CHARACTERS**

**Appearance**

White or almost white, crystalline powder.

**Solubility**

Slightly soluble in water, freely soluble in methylene chloride, sparingly soluble in alcohol.

## IDENTIFICATION

Infrared absorption spectrophotometry (2.2.24).

*Comparison   Ph. Eur. reference spectrum of clobazam.*

## TESTS

**Related substances**

Liquid chromatography (2.2.29).

*Test solution*   Dissolve 10.0 mg of the substance to be examined in the mobile phase and dilute to 50.0 ml with the mobile phase.

*Reference solution (a)*   Dissolve 5.0 mg of *clobazam impurity A CRS* in the mobile phase and dilute to 50.0 ml with the mobile phase. Dilute 1.0 ml of the solution to 100.0 ml with the mobile phase.

*Reference solution (b)*   Dissolve 5 mg of *chlordiazepoxide CRS* and 5 mg of *clonazepam CRS* in the mobile phase and dilute to 50 ml with the mobile phase. Dilute 1 ml of the solution to 100 ml with the mobile phase.

*Reference solution (c)*   Dilute 1.0 ml of the test solution to 200.0 ml with the mobile phase.

*Column:*
— *size*: $l$ = 0.25 m, Ø = 4.6 mm,
— *stationary phase*: octadecylsilyl silica gel for chromatography R (5 μm).

*Mobile phase   acetonitrile R, water R (40:60 V/V).*

*Flow rate   1 ml/min.*

*Detection   Spectrophotometer at 230 nm.*

*Injection   20 μl.*

*Run time   5 times the retention time of clobazam.*

*Retention time   clobazam = about 15 min.*

*System suitability   Reference solution (b):*
— *resolution*: minimum 1.3 between the peaks due to chlordiazepoxide and clonazepam.

*Limits:*
— *impurity A*: not more than the area of the principal peak in the chromatogram obtained with reference solution (a) (0.5 per cent),
— *any other impurity*: not more than 0.4 times the area of the principal peak in the chromatogram obtained with reference solution (c) (0.2 per cent),
— *total of other impurities*: not more than twice the area of the principal peak in the chromatogram obtained with reference solution (c) (1.0 per cent),
— *disregard limit*: 0.1 times the area of the principal peak in the chromatogram obtained with reference solution (c) (0.05 per cent).

**Loss on drying** (2.2.32)

Maximum 0.5 per cent, determined on 1.000 g by drying in an oven at 105 °C.

**Sulphated ash** (2.4.14)

Maximum 0.1 per cent, determined on the residue obtained in the test for loss on drying.

## ASSAY

Dissolve 50.0 mg in *alcohol R* and dilute to 100.0 ml with the same solvent. Dilute 2.0 ml of the solution to 250.0 ml with *alcohol R*. Measure the absorbance (2.2.25) at the maximum at 232 nm.

Calculate the content of $C_{16}H_{13}ClN_2O_2$ taking the specific absorbance to be 1380.

## IMPURITIES

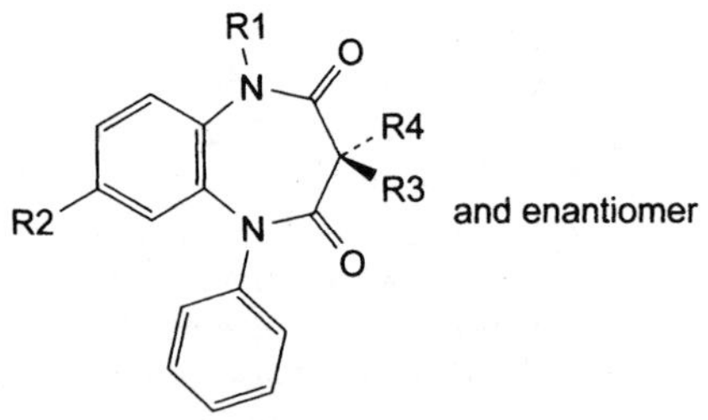

A. R1 = R3 = R4 = H, R2 = Cl: 7-chloro-5-phenyl-1,5-dihydro-3H-1,5-benzodiazepine-2,4-dione,

B. R1 = CH₃, R2 = R3 = R4 = H: 1-methyl-5-phenyl-1,5-dihydro-3H-1,5-benzodiazepine-2,4-dione,

C. R1 = R3 = CH₃, R2 = Cl, R4 = H: (3RS)-7-chloro-1,3-dimethyl-5-phenyl-1,5-dihydro-3H-1,5-benzodiazepine-2,4-dione,

D. R1 = R3 = R4 = CH₃, R2 = Cl: 7-chloro-1,3,3-trimethyl-5-phenyl-1,5-dihydro-3H-1,5-benzodiazepine-2,4-dione,

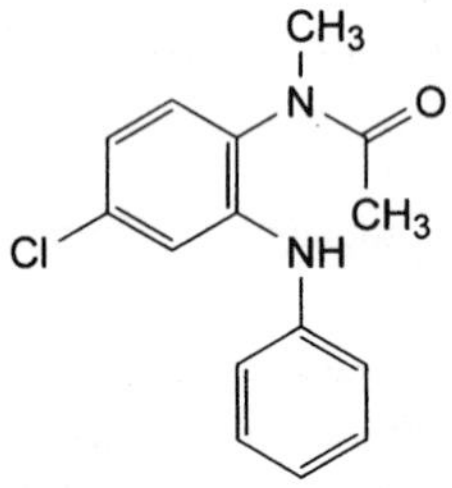

E. *N*-[4-chloro-2-(phenylamino)phenyl]-*N*-methylacetamide,

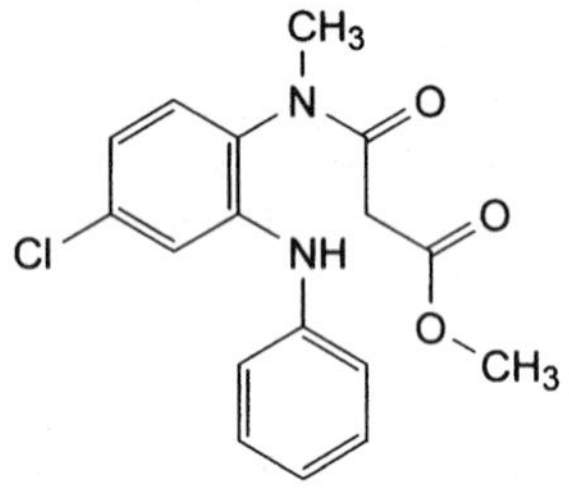

F. methyl 3-[[4-chloro-2-(phenylamino)phenyl]methylamino]-3-oxopropanoate.

# Clobetasol Propionate

*(Ph Eur monograph 2127)*

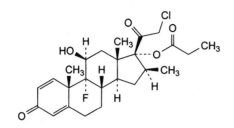

C₂₅H₃₂ClFO₅      467.0      25122-46-7

**Action and use**

Glucocorticoid.

*Ph Eur*

## DEFINITION

21-Chloro-9-fluoro-11β-hydroxy-16β-methyl-3,20-dioxopregna-1,4-dien-17-yl propanoate.

**Content**

97.0 per cent to 102.0 per cent (dried substance).

## CHARACTERS

**Appearance**

White or almost white, crystalline powder.

**Solubility**

Practically insoluble in water, freely soluble in acetone, sparingly soluble in ethanol (96 per cent).

## IDENTIFICATION

Infrared absorption spectrophotometry *(2.2.24)*.

*Comparison* clobetasol propionate CRS.

## TESTS

**Specific optical rotation** *(2.2.7)*

+ 112 to + 118 (dried substance).

Dissolve 0.500 g in *acetone R* and dilute to 50.0 ml with the same solvent.

**Related substances**

Liquid chromatography *(2.2.29)*.

*Test solution (a)* Dissolve 20.0 mg of the substance to be examined in the mobile phase and dilute to 20.0 ml with the mobile phase.

*Test solution (b)* Dissolve 20.0 mg of the substance to be examined in the mobile phase and dilute to 100.0 ml with the mobile phase.

*Reference solution (a)* Dissolve 20.0 mg of *clobetasol propionate CRS* in the mobile phase and dilute to 100.0 ml with the mobile phase.

*Reference solution (b)* Dissolve the contents of a vial of *clobetasol impurity J CRS* in 2.0 ml of the mobile phase. To 0.5 ml of this solution add 0.5 ml of test solution (b) and dilute to 20.0 ml with the mobile phase.

*Reference solution (c)* Dissolve the contents of a vial of *clobetasol for peak identification CRS* (containing impurities A, B, C, D, E, L and M) in 2 ml of the mobile phase.

*Reference solution (d)* Dilute 1.0 ml of test solution (a) to 50.0 ml with the mobile phase. Dilute 5.0 ml of this solution to 20.0 ml with the mobile phase.

*Column:*

— *size:* l = 0.15 m, Ø = 4.6 mm;

— *stationary phase:* spherical octadecylsilyl silica gel for chromatography R (5 µm);

— *temperature:* 30 °C.

*Mobile phase* Mix 10 volumes of *methanol R*, 42.5 volumes of a 7.85 g/l solution of *sodium dihydrogen phosphate monohydrate R* adjusted to pH 5.5 with a 100 g/l solution of *sodium hydroxide R* and 47.5 volumes of *acetonitrile R*.

*Flow rate* 1.0 ml/min.

*Detection* Spectrophotometer at 240 nm.

*Injection* 10 µl of test solution (a) and reference solutions (b), (c) and (d).

*Run time* 3 times the retention time of clobetasol propionate.

*Identification of impurities* Use the chromatogram supplied with *clobetasol for peak identification CRS* and the chromatogram obtained with reference solution (c) to identify the peaks due to impurities A, B, C, D, E, L and M.

*Relative retention* With reference to clobetasol propionate (retention time = about 10 min): impurity A = about 0.4; impurity B = about 0.6; impurity C = about 0.9; impurity J = about 1.1; impurity D = about 1.2; impurity L = about 1.3; impurity M = about 1.6; impurity E = about 2.1.

*System suitability:*

— *resolution:* minimum 2.0 between the peaks due to clobetasol propionate and impurity J in the chromatogram obtained with reference solution (b);

— the chromatogram obtained with reference solution (c) is similar to the chromatogram supplied with *clobetasol for peak identification CRS*.

*Limits:*

— *correction factors:* for the calculation of content, multiply the peak areas of the following impurities by the corresponding correction factor: impurity B = 0.6; impurity C = 1.5;

— *impurity E:* not more than 1.4 times the area of the principal peak in the chromatogram obtained with reference solution (d) (0.7 per cent);

— *impurity D:* not more than the area of the principal peak in the chromatogram obtained with reference solution (d) (0.5 per cent);

— *impurities B, C:* for each impurity, not more than 0.6 times the area of the principal peak in the chromatogram obtained with reference solution (d) (0.3 per cent);

— *impurities A, L, M:* for each impurity, not more than 0.4 times the area of the principal peak in the chromatogram obtained with reference solution (d) (0.2 per cent);

— *unspecified impurities:* for each impurity, not more than 0.2 times the area of the principal peak in the chromatogram obtained with reference solution (d) (0.10 per cent);

— *total:* not more than 4 times the area of the principal peak in the chromatogram obtained with reference solution (d) (2.0 per cent);

— *disregard limit:* 0.1 times the area of the principal peak in the chromatogram obtained with reference solution (d) (0.05 per cent).

**Loss on drying** *(2.2.32)*

Maximum 0.5 per cent, determined on 1.000 g by drying in an oven at 105 °C for 3 h.

**Sulphated ash** *(2.4.14)*

Maximum 0.1 per cent, determined on 1.0 g.

## ASSAY

Liquid chromatography (*2.2.29*) as described in the test for related substances with the following modification.

*Injection* Test solution (b) and reference solution (a).

Calculate the percentage content of $C_{25}H_{32}ClFO_5$ using the chromatogram obtained with reference solution (a) and the declared content of *clobetasol propionate CRS*.

## STORAGE

Protected from light.

## IMPURITIES

*Specified impurities* A, B, C, D, E, L, M.

*Other detectable impurities* (the following substances would, if present at a sufficient level, be detected by one or other of the tests in the monograph. They are limited by the general acceptance criterion for other/unspecified impurities and/or by the general monograph *Substances for pharmaceutical use (2034)*. It is therefore not necessary to identify these impurities for demonstration of compliance. See also *5.10. Control of impurities in substances for pharmaceutical use*): F, G, H, I, J, K.

A. R1 = CO-C$_2$H$_5$, R2 = OH: 9-fluoro-11β,21-dihydroxy-16β-methyl-3,20-dioxopregna-1,4-dien-17-yl propanoate (betamethasone 17-propionate),

G. R1 = H, R2 = Cl: 21-chloro-9-fluoro-11β,17-dihydroxy-16β-methylpregna-1,4-diene-3,20-dione (clobetasol),

H. R1 = CO-C$_2$H$_5$, R2 = H: 9-fluoro-11β-hydroxy-16β-methyl-3,20-dioxopregna-1,4-dien-17-yl propanoate,

I. R1 = CO-C$_2$H$_5$, R2 = O-SO$_2$-CH$_3$: 9-fluoro-11β-hydroxy-16β-methyl-21-[(methylsulphonyl)oxy]-3,20-dioxopregna-1,4-dien-17-yl propanoate,

K. R1 = H, R2 = O-CO-C$_2$H$_5$: 9-fluoro-11β,17-dihydroxy-16β-methyl-3,20-dioxopregna-1,4-dien-21-yl propanoate (betamethasone 21-propionate),

B. 21-chloro-9-fluoro-11β-hydroxy-16-methylpregna-1,4,16-triene-3,20-dione,

C. q21-chloro-9-fluoro-11β-hydroxy-16α-methyl-3,20-dioxopregna-1,4-dien-17-yl propanoate,

D. 21-chloro-9-fluoro-11β-hydroxy-16β-methyl-3,20-dioxopregn-4-en-17-yl propanoate (1,2-dihydroclobetasol 17-propionate),

E. 21-chloro-16β-methyl-3,20-dioxopregna-1,4-dien-17-yl propanoate,

F. 9-fluoro-11β-hydroxy-16β-methyl-3-oxopregna-1,4,17(20)-trien-21-oic acid,

J. (17R)-4′-chloro-5′-ethyl-9-fluoro-11β-hydroxy-16β-methylspiro[androsta-1,4-diene-17,2′(3′H)-furan]-3,3′-dione (17α-spiro compound),

L. unknown structure,

M. unknown structure.

# Clobetasone Butyrate

*(Ph Eur monograph 1090)*

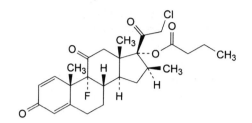

C₂₆H₃₂ClFO₅      479.0      *25122-57-0*

**Action and use**

Glucocorticoid.

**Preparations**

Clobetasone Cream

Clobetasone Ointment

*Ph Eur* _____

## DEFINITION

Clobetasone butyrate contains not less than 97.0 per cent and not more than the equivalent of 102.0 per cent of 21-chloro-9-fluoro-16β-methyl-3,11,20-trioxopregna-1,4-dien-17-yl butanoate, calculated with reference to the dried substance.

## CHARACTERS

A white or almost white powder, practically insoluble in water, freely soluble in acetone and in methylene chloride, slightly soluble in alcohol.

It melts at about 178 °C.

## IDENTIFICATION

A. Examine by infrared absorption spectrophotometry *(2.2.24)*, comparing with the spectrum obtained with *clobetasone butyrate CRS*. Examine the substances prepared as discs.

B. Examine by thin-layer chromatography *(2.2.27)*, using as the coating substance a suitable silica gel with a fluorescent indicator having an optimal intensity at 254 nm.

*Test solution* Dissolve 10 mg of the substance to be examined in a mixture of equal volumes of *methanol R* and *methylene chloride R* and dilute to 10 ml with the same mixture of solvents.

*Reference solution (a)* Dissolve 10 mg of *clobetasone butyrate CRS* in a mixture of equal volumes of *methanol R* and *methylene chloride R* and dilute to 10 ml with the same mixture of solvents.

*Reference solution (b)* Dissolve 10 mg of *clobetasol propionate R* in a mixture of equal volumes of *methanol R* and *methylene chloride R* and dilute to 10 ml with the same mixture of solvents. Dilute 5 ml of this solution to 10 ml with reference solution (a).

Apply separately to the plate 5 µl of each solution. Develop over a path of 15 cm using a mixture of equal volumes of *cyclohexane R* and *methyl acetate R*. Allow the plate to dry in air and examine in ultraviolet light at 254 nm. The principal spot in the chromatogram obtained with the test solution is similar in position and size to the principal spot in the chromatogram obtained with reference solution (a). The test is not valid unless the chromatogram obtained with reference solution (b) shows two clearly separated spots.

C. Mix about 5 mg with 45 mg of *heavy magnesium oxide R* and ignite in a crucible until an almost white residue is obtained (usually less than 5 min). Allow to cool, add 1 ml of *water R*, 0.05 ml of *phenolphthalein solution R1* and about 1 ml of *dilute hydrochloric acid R* to render the solution colourless. Filter. To a freshly prepared mixture of 0.1 ml *alizarin S solution R* and 0.1 ml of *zirconyl nitrate solution R*, add 1.0 ml of the filtrate. Mix, allow to stand for 5 min and compare the colour of the solution with that of a blank prepared in the same manner. The colour of the test solution is yellow and that of the blank is red.

## TESTS

**Specific optical rotation** *(2.2.7)*

Dissolve 0.250 g in *dioxan R* and dilute to 25.0 ml with the same solvent. The specific optical rotation is + 127 to + 133, calculated with reference to the dried substance.

**Related substances**

*Prepare the solutions immediately before use.*

Examine by liquid chromatography *(2.2.29)*.

*Test solution* Dissolve 50.0 mg of the substance to be examined in 5.0 ml of *ethanol R* and dilute to 50.0 ml with the mobile phase.

*Reference solution (a)* Dissolve 2 mg of *clobetasone butyrate CRS* and 1.5 mg of *clobetasol propionate R* in 5 ml of *ethanol R* and dilute to 100 ml with the mobile phase.

*Reference solution (b)* Dilute 1.0 ml of the test solution to 100.0 ml with the mobile phase.

The chromatographic procedure may be carried out using:
— a stainless steel column 0.20 m long and 4.6 mm in internal diameter, packed with *octadecylsilyl silica gel for chromatography R* (5 µm),
— as mobile phase at a flow rate of 1 ml/min a mixture of 45 volumes of *ethanol R* and 55 volumes of *water R*,
— as detector a spectrophotometer set at 241 nm,

Maintaining the temperature of the column at 60 °C. Inject 20 µl of reference solution (a). When using a recorder, adjust the sensitivity of the system so that the height of the two principal peaks are at least 50 per cent of the full scale of the recorder. The test is not valid unless the resolution between the first peak (clobetasol propionate) and the second peak (clobetasone butyrate) is at least five.

Inject 20 µl of the test solution and 20 µl of reference solution (b). Continue the chromatography for 2.5 times the retention time of the principal peak. In the chromatogram obtained with the test solution: the area of any peak, apart from the principal peak, is not greater than the area of the principal peak in the chromatogram obtained with reference solution (b) (1.0 per cent) and not more than one such peak has an area greater than half the area of the principal peak in the chromatogram obtained with reference solution (b) (0.5 per cent); the sum of the areas of all the peaks, apart from the principal peak, is not greater than 1.5 times the area of the principal peak in the chromatogram obtained with reference solution (b) (1.5 per cent). Disregard any peak with an area less than 0.05 times the area of the principal peak in the chromatogram obtained with reference solution (b).

**Loss on drying** *(2.2.32)*

Not more than 0.5 per cent, determined on 1.000 g by drying in an oven at 105 °C.

## ASSAY

Dissolve 20.0 mg in *alcohol R* and dilute to 100.0 ml with the same solvent. Dilute 5.0 ml of the solution to 50.0 ml with alcohol R. Measure the absorbance (2.2.25) at the maximum at 235 nm.

Calculate the content of $C_{26}H_{32}ClFO_5$, taking the specific absorbance to be 327.

## STORAGE

Store protected from light.

## IMPURITIES

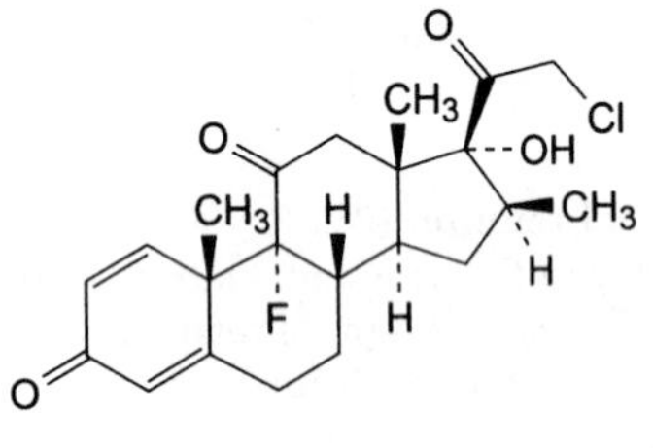

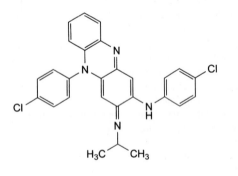

A. clobetasone,

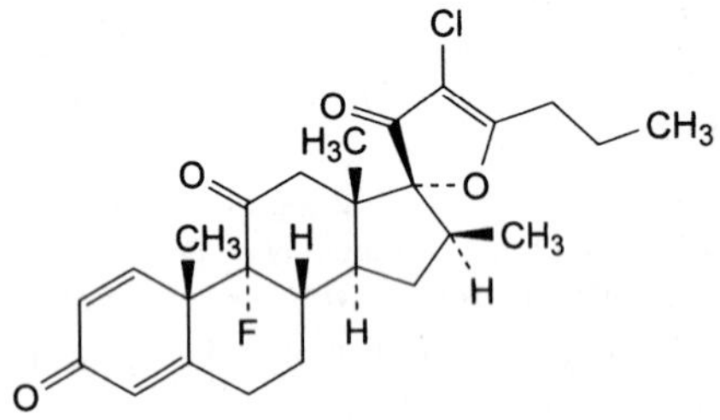

B. (17R)-4'-chloro-9-fluoro-16β-methyl-5'-propylspiro[androsta-1,4-diene-17,2'(3'H)furan]-3,3',11-trione.

*Ph Eur*

# Clofazimine

(*Ph Eur monograph 2054*)

$C_{27}H_{22}Cl_2N_4$      473.4      2030-63-9

## Action and use

Antileprosy drug.

## Preparation

Clofazimine Capsules

*Ph Eur*

## DEFINITION

N,5-Bis(4-chlorophenyl)-3-[(1-methylethyl)imino]-3,5-dihydrophenazin-2-amine.

## Content

99.0 per cent to 101.0 per cent (dried substance).

## CHARACTERS

### Appearance

Reddish-brown, fine powder.

### Solubility

Practically insoluble in water, soluble in methylene chloride, very slightly soluble in ethanol (96 per cent).

It shows polymorphism (5.9).

## IDENTIFICATION

*First identification* A.

*Second identification* B, C.

A. Infrared absorption spectrophotometry (2.2.24).

*Comparison* clofazimine CRS.

If the spectra obtained in the solid state show differences, dissolve the substance to be examined and the reference substance separately in *methylene chloride R*, evaporate to dryness and record new spectra using the residues.

B. Thin-layer chromatography (2.2.27).

*Test solution* Dissolve 10 mg of the substance to be examined in *methylene chloride R* and dilute to 10 ml with the same solvent.

*Reference solution* Dissolve 10 mg of *clofazimine CRS* in *methylene chloride R* and dilute to 10 ml with the same solvent.

*Plate* TLC silica gel GF$_{254}$ plate R.

*Mobile phase* propanol R, methylene chloride R (6:85 V/V).

*Application* 5 µl.

*First development* Over 2/3 of the plate.

*Drying* Horizontally in air for 5 min.

*Second development* Over 2/3 of the plate.

*Drying* In air for 5 min.

*Detection* Examine in ultraviolet light at 254 nm.

*Results* The principal spot in the chromatogram obtained with the test solution is similar in position and size to the principal spot in the chromatogram obtained with the reference solution.

C. Dissolve 2 mg in 3 ml of *acetone R* and add 0.1 ml of *hydrochloric acid R*. An intense violet colour is produced. Add 0.5 ml of a 200 g/l solution of *sodium hydroxide R*; the colour changes to orange-red.

## TESTS

### Related substances

Liquid chromatography (2.2.29). *Prepare the solutions immediately before use.*

*Test solution* Dissolve 50 mg of the substance to be examined in the mobile phase and dilute to 100 ml with the mobile phase.

*Reference solution (a)* Dilute 1.0 ml of the test solution to 100.0 ml with the mobile phase. Dilute 1.0 ml of this solution to 10.0 ml with the mobile phase.

*Reference solution (b)* Dissolve 5.0 mg of *clofazimine for system suitability CRS* in the mobile phase and dilute to 10.0 ml with the mobile phase.

*Column:*
— *size: l = 0.25 m, Ø = 4.6 mm,*
— *stationary phase: octylsilyl silica gel for chromatography R* (5 µm).

*Mobile phase* Dissolve 2.25 g of *sodium laurilsulfate R*, 0.85 g of *tetrabutylammonium hydrogen sulphate* R and 0.885 g of *disodium hydrogen phosphate R* in *water R*. Adjust to pH 3.0 with *dilute phosphoric acid R* and dilute to 500 ml with water *R*. Mix 35 volumes of this solution and 65 volumes of *acetonitrile R*.

*Flow rate*   1 ml/min.

*Detection*   Spectrophotometer at 280 nm.

*Injection*   20 μl.

*Run time*   3 times the retention time of clofazimine.

*Identification of impurities*   Use the chromatogram supplied with *clofazimine for system suitability CRS* to identify the peak due to impurity B.

*Relative retention*   With reference to clofazimine (retention time = about 15 min): impurity A = about 0.7; impurity B = about 0.8.

*System suitability*   Reference solution (b):
— *resolution*: baseline separation between the peaks due to impurity B and clofazimine.

*Limits*:
— *impurity A*: not more than the area of the principal peak in the chromatogram obtained with reference solution (a) (0.1 per cent),
— *impurity B*: not more than 3 times the area of the principal peak in the chromatogram obtained with reference solution (a) (0.3 per cent),
— *any other impurity*: for each impurity, not more than the area of the principal peak in the chromatogram obtained with reference solution (a) (0.1 per cent),
— *total*: not more than 5 times the area of the principal peak in the chromatogram obtained with reference solution (a) (0.5 per cent),
— *disregard limit*: 0.5 times the area of the principal peak in the chromatogram obtained with reference solution (a) (0.05 per cent).

**Heavy metals** *(2.4.8)*
Maximum 10 ppm.

2.0 g complies with limit test C. Prepare the reference solution using 2 ml of *lead standard solution (10 ppm Pb) R*.

**Loss on drying** *(2.2.32)*
Maximum 0.5 per cent, determined on 1.000 g by drying in an oven at 105 °C.

**Sulphated ash** *(2.4.14)*
Maximum 0.1 per cent, determined on 1.0 g.

**ASSAY**
Dissolve 0.400 g in 5 ml of *methylene chloride R* and add 20 ml of *acetone R* and 5 ml of *anhydrous acetic acid R*. Titrate with *0.1 M perchloric acid*, determining the end-point potentiometrically *(2.2.20)*.

1 ml of *0.1 M perchloric acid* is equivalent to 47.34 mg of $C_{27}H_{22}Cl_2N_4$.

**IMPURITIES**
*Specified impurities*   *A, B*.

A. R1 = Cl, R2 = H: *N*,5-bis(4-chlorophenyl)-3-imino-3,5-dihydrophenazin-2-amine,

B. R1 = H, R2 = CH(CH₃)₂:
5-(4-chlorophenyl)-3-[(1-methylethyl)imino]-*N*-phenyl-3,5-dihydrophenazin-2-amine.

*Ph Eur*

# Clofibrate

*(Ph Eur monograph 0318)*

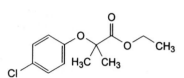

$C_{12}H_{15}ClO_3$          242.7          637-07-0

**Action and use**
Fibrate; lipid-regulating drug.

**Preparation**
Clofibrate Capsules

*Ph Eur*

**DEFINITION**
Ethyl 2-(4-chlorophenoxy)-2-methylpropionate.

**CHARACTERS**

**Appearance**
Clear, almost colourless liquid.

**Solubility**
Very slightly soluble in water, miscible with ethanol (96 per cent).

**IDENTIFICATION**
A. Infrared absorption spectrophotometry *(2.2.24)*.

*Comparison*   clofibrate CRS.

B. Ultraviolet and visible absorption spectrophotometry *(2.2.25)*.

*Test solution (a)*   Dissolve 0.10 g in *methanol R* and dilute to 100.0 ml with the same solvent. Dilute 10.0 ml of this solution to 100.0 ml with *methanol R*.

*Test solution (b)*   Dilute 10.0 ml of test solution (a) to 100.0 ml with *methanol R*.

*Spectral range*   250-350 nm for test solution (a); 220-250 nm for test solution (b).

*Absorption maxima*   At 280 nm and 288 nm for test solution (a); at 226 nm for test solution (b).

*Specific absorbances at the absorption maxima:*
— at 226 nm: about 460 for test solution (b);
— at 280 nm: about 44 for test solution (a);
— at 288 nm: about 31 for test solution (a).

**TESTS**
**Relative density** *(2.2.5)*
1.138 to 1.147.

**Refractive index** *(2.2.6)*
1.500 to 1.505.

**Acidity**
To 1.0 g add 10 ml of *anhydrous ethanol R* and 0.1 ml of *phenol red solution R*. Not more than 1.0 ml of *0.01 M sodium hydroxide* is required to change the colour of the indicator.

**Volatile related substances**
Gas chromatography *(2.2.28)*.

*Test solution* To 10.0 g of the substance to be examined add a mixture of 10 ml of *dilute sodium hydroxide solution R* and 10 ml of *water R*. Shake, separate the lower (organic) layer, wash with 5 ml of *water R* and add the washings to the aqueous layer. Dry the organic layer with *anhydrous sodium sulphate R* and use as the test solution. Reserve the aqueous layer for the test for 4-chlorophenol.

*Reference solution (a)* Dissolve 0.12 g of the substance to be examined in *chloroform R* and dilute to 100.0 ml with the same solvent. Dilute 1.0 ml of this solution to 10.0 ml with *chloroform R*.

*Reference solution (b)* Dissolve 0.12 g of *methyl 2-(4-chlorophenoxy)-2-methylpropionate CRS* in the substance to be examined and dilute to 10.0 ml with the same solvent. Dilute 1.0 ml of the solution to 10.0 ml with the substance to be examined. Dilute 1.0 ml of this solution to 10.0 ml with the substance to be examined.

*Column:*
— *size*: $l = 1.5$ m, $\emptyset = 4$ mm;
— *stationary phase: silanised diatomaceous earth for gas chromatography R* (250-420 μm) impregnated with 30 per cent *m/m* of *poly(dimethyl)siloxane R*; or *silanised diatomaceous earth for gas chromatography R* (150-180 μm) impregnated with 10 per cent *m/m* of *poly(dimethyl)siloxane R*;
— *temperature*: 185 °C.

*Carrier gas nitrogen for chromatography R.*

*Detection* Flame ionisation.

*Injection* 2 μl.

*System suitability* Reference solution (b):
— *peak-to-valley ratio*: minimum 4, where $H_p$ = height above the baseline of the peak due to methyl 2-(4-chlorophenoxy)-2-methylpropionate and $H_v$ = height above the baseline of the lowest point of the curve separating this peak from the peak due to clofibrate.

*Limit:*
— *total*: not more than 10 times the area of the peak due to clofibrate in the chromatogram obtained with reference solution (a) (0.1 per cent).

### 4-Chlorophenol

Gas chromatography (*2.2.28*) as described in the test for volatile related substances with the following modifications.

*Test solution* Shake the aqueous layer reserved in the test for volatile related substances with 2 quantities, each of 5 ml, of *chloroform R* and discard the organic layers. Acidify the aqueous layer by the dropwise addition of *hydrochloric acid R*. Shake with 3 quantities, each of 3 ml, of *chloroform R*. Combine the organic layers and dilute to 10.0 ml with *chloroform R*.

*Reference solution* Dissolve 0.25 g of *chlorophenol R* in *chloroform R* and dilute to 100.0 ml with the same solvent. Dilute 1.0 ml of this solution to 100.0 ml with *chloroform R*.

*Limit:*
— 4-chlorophenol: not more than the area of the peak due to 4-chlorophenol in the chromatogram obtained with the reference solution (25 ppm).

*Ph Eur*

# Clomethiazole

C₆H₈ClNS      161.6      533-45-9

**Action and use**
Hypnotic.

**Preparation**
Clomethiazole Capsules

## DEFINITION

Clomethiazole is 5-(2-chloroethyl)-4-methyl-thiazole. It contains not less than 98.0% and not more than 101.0% of C₆H₈ClNS.

## CHARACTERISTICS

A colourless to slightly yellowish brown liquid.

Slightly soluble in *water*; miscible with *ethanol (96%)* and with *ether*.

## IDENTIFICATION

A. The *light absorption*, Appendix II B, in the range 230 to 350 nm of a 0.004% w/v solution in 0.1M *hydrochloric acid* exhibits a maximum only at 257 nm. The *absorbance* at the maximum is about 1.1.

B. The *infrared absorption spectrum*, Appendix II A, is concordant with the *reference spectrum* of clomethiazole *(RS 051)*.

C. Mix 0.1 g with 0.2 g of powdered *sodium hydroxide*, heat to fusion and continue heating for a further few seconds. Cool, add 0.5 ml of *water* and a slight excess of 2M *hydrochloric acid* and warm. Any fumes evolved do not turn moistened *starch iodate paper* blue (distinction from clomethiazole edisilate).

## TESTS

**Acidity or alkalinity**
pH of a 0.5% w/v solution, 5.5 to 7.0, Appendix V L.

**Heavy metals**
Moisten the residue obtained in the test for Sulphated ash with 2 ml of *hydrochloric acid* and evaporate to dryness. Dissolve the residue in *water* and add sufficient *water* to produce 20 ml. 12 ml of the resulting solution complies with *limit test A for heavy metals*, Appendix VII. Use *lead standard solution (1 ppm Pb)* to prepare the standard (20 ppm).

**Related substances**
Carry out the method for *liquid chromatography*, Appendix III D, using the following solutions. Solution (1) contains 0.20% w/v of the substance being examined in the mobile phase. For solution (2) dilute 1 volume of solution (1) to 1000 volumes with the mobile phase. For solution (3) dilute 1 volume of a 0.030% w/v solution of *4-methyl-5-vinylthiazole edisilate BPCRS* in *methanol* (solution A) to 50 volumes with the mobile phase. For solution (4) dilute 1 volume of a 0.020% w/v solution of *5-(2-chloroethyl)-4-methyl-3-[2-(4-methylthiazol-5-yl)ethyl]-thiazolium chloride BPCRS* (quaternary dimer) in *methanol* (solution B) to 50 volumes with the mobile phase. For solution (5) dilute 1 volume of a 0.020% w/v solution of *4-methyl-5-(2-hydroxyethyl)thiazole BPCRS* in *methanol* (solution C) to

50 volumes with the mobile phase. For solution (6) add 1 ml each of solutions A, B and C to 0.10 g of the substance being examined and dilute to 50 ml with the mobile phase.

The chromatographic procedure may be carried out using (a) a stainless steel column (20 cm × 4 mm) packed with *octadecylsilyl silica gel for chromatography* (10 µm) (Lichrosorb RP18 is suitable), (b) as the mobile phase with a flow rate of 1 ml per minute, a mixture of 70 volumes of a solution containing 0.13% w/v of *sodium hexanesulphonate* and 2.7% w/v of *tetramethylammonium hydrogen sulphate*, adjusted to pH 2.0 with 5M *sodium hydroxide*, and 30 volumes of *methanol* and (c) a detection wavelength of 257 nm.

The test is not valid unless in the chromatogram obtained with solution (6) baseline separation is achieved between the peaks due to the three specified impurities and also between the principal peak and the two adjacent specified impurity peaks.

Calculate the content of each of the three specified impurities in the substance being examined expressing the content of 4-methyl-5-vinylthiazole as the base (1 mg of 4-methyl-5-vinylthiazole edisilate is equivalent to 0.568 mg of base). The total content of the three specified impurities is not greater than 0.5%. In the chromatogram obtained with solution (1) the area of any other *secondary peak* is not greater than the area of the peak in the chromatogram obtained with solution (2).

### Sulphated ash
Not more than 0.1%, Appendix IX A. Use 1 g.

### ASSAY
Carry out Method I for *non-aqueous titration*, Appendix VIII A, using 0.3 g and determining the end point potentiometrically. Each ml of 0.1M *perchloric acid VS* is equivalent to 16.16 mg of $C_6H_8ClNS$.

### STORAGE
Clomethiazole should be stored at a temperature of 2° to 8°.

# Clomethiazole Edisilate

$(C_6H_8ClNS)_2,C_2H_6O_6S_2$     513.5          *1867-58-9*

### Action and use
Hypnotic.

### Preparations
Clomethiazole Intravenous Infusion

Clomethiazole Oral Solution

### DEFINITION
Clomethiazole Edisilate is 5-(2-chloroethyl)-4-methylthiazole ethanedisulphonate. It contains not less than 99.0% and not more than 101.0% of $(C_6H_8ClNS)_2,C_2H_6O_6S_2$, calculated with reference to the dried substance.

### CHARACTERISTICS
A white, crystalline powder.

Freely soluble in *water*; soluble in *ethanol (96%)*; practically insoluble in *ether*.

### IDENTIFICATION
A. *Melting point*, about 128°, Appendix V A.

B. The *light absorption*, Appendix II B, in the range 230 to 350 nm of a 0.005% w/v solution in 0.1M *hydrochloric acid* exhibits a maximum only at 257 nm. The *absorbance* at the maximum is about 0.92.

C. The *infrared absorption spectrum*, Appendix II A, is concordant with the *reference spectrum* of clomethiazole edisilate *(RS 052)*.

D. Mix 0.1 g with 0.2 g of powdered *sodium hydroxide*, heat to fusion and continue heating for a further few seconds. Cool, add 0.5 ml of *water* and a slight excess of 2M *hydrochloric acid* and warm. Fumes are evolved which turn moistened *starch iodate paper* blue (distinction from clomethiazole).

### TESTS
#### Calcium
10 ml of a 10.0% w/v solution diluted to 15 ml with *water* complies with the *limit test for calcium*, Appendix VII (100 ppm).

#### Heavy metals
Moisten the residue obtained in the test for Sulphated ash with 2 ml of *hydrochloric acid* and evaporate to dryness. Dissolve the residue in *water* and add sufficient *water* to produce 20 ml. 12 ml of the resulting solution complies with *limit test A for heavy metals*, Appendix VII. Use *lead standard solution (1 ppm Pb)* to prepare the standard (20 ppm).

#### Chloride
10 ml of a 10% w/v solution diluted to 15 ml with *water* complies with the *limit test for chlorides*, Appendix VII (50 ppm).

#### Sulphate
10 ml of a 1.0% w/v solution diluted to 15 ml with *distilled water* complies with the *limit test for sulphates*, Appendix VII (0.15%).

#### Related substances
Carry out the method for *liquid chromatography*, Appendix III D, using the following solutions. Solution (1) contains 0.30% w/v of the substance being examined in the mobile phase. For solution (2) dilute 1 volume of solution (1) to 1000 volumes with the mobile phase. For solution (3) dilute 1 volume of a 0.030% w/v solution of *4-methyl-5-vinylthiazole edisilate BPCRS* in *methanol* (solution A) to 50 volumes with the mobile phase. For solution (4) dilute 1 volume of a 0.020% w/v solution of *5-(2-chloroethyl)-4-methyl-3-[2-(4-methylthiazol-5-yl)ethyl]-thiazolium chloride BPCRS* (quaternary dimer) in *methanol* (solution B) to 50 volumes with the mobile phase. For solution (5) dilute 1 volume of a 0.020% w/v solution of *4-methyl-5-(2-hydroxyethyl)thiazole BPCRS* in *methanol* (solution C) to 50 volumes with the mobile phase. For solution (6) add 1 ml each of solutions A, B and C to 0.15 g of the substance being examined and dilute to 50 ml with the mobile phase.

The chromatographic procedure may be carried out using (a) a stainless steel column (20 cm × 4 mm) packed with *octadecylsilyl silica gel for chromatography* (10 µm) (Lichrosorb RP18 is suitable), (b) as the mobile phase with a flow rate of 1 ml per minute, a mixture of 70 volumes of a solution containing 0.13% w/v of *sodium hexanesulphonate* and

University College Library Cork

2.7% w/v of *tetramethylammonium hydrogen sulphate*, adjusted to pH 2.0 with 5M *sodium hydroxide*, and 30 volumes of *methanol* and (c) a detection wavelength of 257 nm.

The test is not valid unless in the chromatogram obtained with solution (6) baseline separation is achieved between the peaks due to the three specified impurities and also between the principal peak and the two adjacent specified impurity peaks.

Calculate the content of each of the three specified impurities in the substance being examined with reference to clomethiazole base (1 mg of clomethiazole edisilate is equivalent to 0.629 mg of base) expressing the content of 4-methyl-5-vinylthiazole as the base (1 mg of 4-methyl-5-vinylthiazole edisilate is equivalent to 0.568 mg of base). The total content of the three specified impurities is not greater than 0.5%. In the chromatogram obtained with solution (1) the area of any other *secondary peak* is not greater than the area of the peak in the chromatogram obtained with solution (2).

### Loss on drying
When dried at 50° at a pressure not exceeding 0.7 kPa for 6 hours, loses not more than 0.5% of its weight. Use 1 g.

### Sulphated ash
Not more than 0.3%, Appendix IX A. Use 1 g.

### ASSAY
Dissolve 0.4 g in 50 ml of *water* and titrate with 0.1M *sodium hydroxide VS* using *phenolphthalein solution R1* as indicator. Each ml of 0.1M *sodium hydroxide VS* is equivalent to 25.67 mg of $(C_6H_8ClNS)_2,C_2H_6O_6S_2$.

# Clomifene Citrate

*(Ph Eur monograph 0997)*

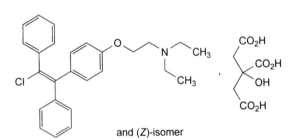

and (Z)-isomer

$C_{26}H_{28}ClNO,C_6H_8O_7$ 598.1 *50-41-9*

### Action and use
Estrogen receptor modulator.

### Preparation
Clomifene Tablets

*Ph Eur*

### DEFINITION
Mixture of the (*E*)- and (*Z*)-isomers of 2-[4-(2-chloro-1,2diphenylethenyl)phenoxy]-*N,N*-diethylethanamine dihydrogen citrate.

### Content
98.0 per cent to 101.0 per cent (anhydrous substance).

### CHARACTERS
### Appearance
White or pale yellow, crystalline powder.

### Solubility
Slightly soluble in water, sparingly soluble in ethanol (96 per cent).

### IDENTIFICATION
A. Infrared absorption spectrophotometry (2.2.24).

*Preparation*   Discs of *potassium bromide R*.

*Comparison*   clomifene citrate CRS.

B. Dissolve about 5 mg in 5 ml of a mixture of 1 volume of *acetic anhydride R* and 5 volumes of *pyridine R*, then heat in a water-bath. A deep red colour is produced.

### TESTS
*Prepare the solutions protected from light in brown-glass vessels. Ensure minimum exposure of the solutions to daylight until they are required for chromatography.*

### Related substances
Liquid chromatography (2.2.29).

*Test solution*   Dissolve 12.5 mg of the substance to be examined in the mobile phase and dilute to 10.0 ml with the mobile phase.

*Reference solution (a)*   Dissolve 12.5 mg of *clomifene citrate for performance test CRS* in the mobile phase and dilute to 10.0 ml with the mobile phase.

*Reference solution (b)*   Dilute 1.0 ml of the test solution to 50.0 ml with the mobile phase.

*Column:*
— *size*: $l = 0.25$ m, $\varnothing = 4.6$ mm;
— *stationary phase*: butylsilyl silica gel for chromatography R (5 μm).

*Mobile phase*   Mix 400 ml of *acetonitrile R* with 600 ml of *water R* and add 8.0 ml of *diethylamine R*; adjust to pH 6.2 with about 1-2 ml of *phosphoric acid R*, taking care to reduce progressively the volume of each addition as the required pH is approached.

*Flow rate*   1.2 ml/min.

*Detection*   Spectrophotometer at 233 nm.

*Equilibration*   With the mobile phase for about 1 h.

*Injection*   10 μl.

*Run time*   4 times the retention time of clomifene.

*System suitability*   Reference solution (a):
— *peak-to-valley ratio*: minimum 15, where $H_p$ = height above the baseline of the peak due to impurity A and $H_v$ = height above the baseline of the lowest point of the curve separating this peak from the peak due to clomifene; if necessary, adjust the concentration of acetonitrile in the mobile phase;
— the chromatogram obtained is similar to the chromatogram supplied with *clomifene citrate for performance test CRS*.

*Limits:*
— *impurity A*: not more than the area of the principal peak in the chromatogram obtained with reference solution (b) (2.0 per cent);
— *impurities B, C, D, E, F, G, H*: for each impurity, not more than 0.5 times the area of the principal peak in the chromatogram obtained with reference solution (b) (1.0 per cent);
— *total*: not more than 1.25 times the area of the principal peak in the chromatogram obtained with reference solution (b) (2.5 per cent);
— *disregard limit*: 0.025 times the area of the principal peak in the chromatogram obtained with reference solution (b)

(0.05 per cent); disregard any peak with a retention time relative to the clomifene peak of 0.2 or less.

## (Z)-isomer

Liquid chromatography (2.2.29).

*Test solution* Dissolve 25 mg of the substance to be examined in 25 ml of *0.1 M hydrochloric acid*, add 5 ml of *1 M sodium hydroxide* and shake with 3 quantities, each of 25 ml, of *ethanol-free chloroform R*. Wash the combined extracts with 10 ml of *water R*, dry over *anhydrous sodium sulphate R* and dilute to 100 ml with *ethanol-free chloroform R*. To 20 ml of this solution add 0.1 ml of *triethylamine R* and dilute to 100 ml with *hexane R*.

*Reference solution* Dissolve 25 mg of *clomifene citrate CRS* in 25 ml of *0.1 M hydrochloric acid*, add 5 ml of *1 M sodium hydroxide* and shake with 3 quantities, each of 25 ml, of *ethanol-free chloroform R*. Wash the combined extracts with 10 ml of *water R*, dry over *anhydrous sodium sulphate R* and dilute to 100 ml with *ethanol-free chloroform R*. To 20 ml of this solution add 0.1 ml of *triethylamine R* and dilute to 100 ml with *hexane R*.

*Column:*
— *size: l* = 0.3 m, Ø = 4 mm;
— *stationary phase: silica gel for chromatography R* (10 μm).

*Mobile phase* *triethylamine R, ethanol-free chloroform R, hexane R* (1:200:800 *V/V/V*).

*Flow rate* 2 ml/min.

*Detection* Spectrophotometer at 302 nm.

*Equilibration* With the mobile phase for about 2 h.

*Injection* 50 μl.

*Identification of peaks* The chromatogram obtained with the reference solution shows a peak due to the (E)-isomer just before a peak due to the (Z)-isomer.

*System suitability* Reference solution:
— *resolution*: minimum 1.0 between the peaks due to the (E)- and (Z)-isomers; if necessary, adjust the relative proportions of ethanol-free chloroform and hexane in the mobile phase.

Measure the area of the peak due to the (Z)-isomer in the chromatograms obtained with the test solution and the reference solution. Calculate the content of the (Z)-isomer, as a percentage of the total clomifene citrate present, from the declared content of *clomifene citrate CRS*.

*Limit:*
— *(Z)-isomer*: 30.0 per cent to 50.0 per cent.

## Water (2.5.12)

Maximum 1.0 per cent, determined on 1.000 g.

## ASSAY

Dissolve 0.500 g in 50 ml of *anhydrous acetic acid R*. Titrate with *0.1 M perchloric acid*, determining the end-point potentiometrically (2.2.20).

1 ml of *0.1 M perchloric acid* is equivalent to 59.81 mg of $C_{32}H_{36}ClNO_8$.

## STORAGE

Protected from light.

## IMPURITIES

*Specified impurities* *A, B, C, D, E, F, G, H.*

A. 2-[4-(1,2-diphenylethenyl)phenoxy]-*N,N*-diethylethanamine,

B. [4-[2-(diethylamino)ethoxy]phenyl]phenylmethanone,

C. (2RS)-2-[4-[2-(diethylamino)ethoxy]phenyl]-1,2-diphenylethanone,

D. 2,2-bis[4-[2-(diethylamino)ethoxy]phenyl]-1,2-diphenylethanone,

E. 2-[4-[1,2-bis(4-chlorophenyl)ethenyl]phenoxy]-*N,N*-diethylethanamine,

F. 2-[4-[2-chloro-2-(4-chlorophenyl)-1-phenylethenyl]phenoxy]-*N,N*-diethylethanamine,

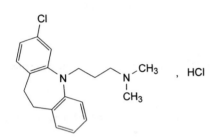

GH. 2-[2-chloro-4-(2-chloro-1,2-diphenylethenyl)phenoxy]-
*N,N*-diethylethanamine (G. higher-melting-point isomer; *H.*
lower-melting-point isomer).

_____ *Ph Eur*

# Clomipramine Hydrochloride

(*Ph Eur monograph 0889*)

$C_{19}H_{23}ClN_2,HCl$          351.3          *17321-77-6*

**Action and use**
Monoamine reuptake inhibitor; tricyclic antidepressant.

**Preparation**
Clomipramine Capsules

*Ph Eur* _____

## DEFINITION
3-(3-Chloro-10,11-dihydro-5*H*-dibenzo[*b,f*]azepin-5-yl)-
*N,N*-dimethylpropan-1-amine hydrochloride.

## Content
99.0 per cent to 101.0 per cent (dried substance).

## CHARACTERS
**Appearance**
White or slightly yellow, crystalline powder, slightly
hygroscopic.

**Solubility**
Freely soluble in water and in methylene chloride, soluble
in alcohol.

It shows polymorphism (*5.9*).

## IDENTIFICATION
*First identification* B, E.

*Second identification* A, C, D, E.

A. Melting point (*2.2.14*): 191 °C to 195 °C.

B. Infrared absorption spectrophotometry (*2.2.24*).

*Preparation* Discs of *potassium bromide R*. The transmittance
at about 2000 cm$^{-1}$ (5 µm) is at least 65 per cent without
compensation.

*Comparison* clomipramine hydrochloride CRS.

C. Thin-layer chromatography (*2.2.27*). *Prepare the solutions
immediately before use and protected from light.*

*Test solution* Dissolve 20 mg of the substance to be
examined in *methanol R* and dilute to 10 ml with the same
solvent.

*Reference solution* Dissolve 20 mg of *clomipramine
hydrochloride CRS* in *methanol R* and dilute to 10 ml with the
same solvent.

*Plate* TLC silica gel G plate R.

*Mobile phase* concentrated ammonia R, acetone R, ethyl
acetate R (5:25:75 *V/V/V*).

*Application* 5 µl.

*Development* Over a path of 15 cm.

*Drying* In air.

*Detection* Spray with a 5 g/l solution of *potassium
dichromate R* in a 20 per cent *V/V* solution of *sulphuric acid R.*
Examine immediately.

*Results* The principal spot in the chromatogram obtained
with the test solution is similar in position, colour and size to
the principal spot in the chromatogram obtained with the
reference solution.

D. Dissolve about 5 mg in 2 ml of *nitric acid R*. An intense
blue colour develops.

E. Dissolve about 50 mg in 5 ml of *water R* and add 1 ml of
*dilute ammonia R1*. Mix, allow to stand for 5 min and filter.
Acidify the filtrate with *dilute nitric acid R*. The solution gives
reaction (a) of chlorides (*2.3.1*).

## TESTS
**Solution S**
Dissolve 2.0 g in *carbon dioxide-free water R* and dilute to
20 ml with the same solvent.

**Appearance of solution**
Solution S is clear (*2.2.1*) and not more intensely coloured
than reference solution Y$_5$ (*2.2.2, Method I*).

**pH** (*2.2.3*)
3.5 to 5.0 for solution S.

**Related substances**
Liquid chromatography (*2.2.29*). *Prepare the solutions
immediately before use and protected from light.*

*Test solution* Dissolve 20.0 mg of the substance to be
examined in a mixture of 25 volumes of mobile phase B and
75 volumes of mobile phase A and dilute to 10.0 ml with the
same mixture of mobile phases.

*Reference solution (a)* Dissolve 22.6 mg of *imipramine
hydrochloride CRS*, 4.0 mg of *clomipramine impurity C CRS*,
4.0 mg of *clomipramine impurity D CRS* and 2.0 mg of
*clomipramine impurity F CRS* in a mixture of 25 volumes of
mobile phase B and 75 volumes of mobile phase A and
dilute to 100.0 ml with the same mixture of mobile phases.
Dilute 1.0 ml of this solution to 10.0 ml with a mixture of
25 volumes of mobile phase B and 75 volumes of mobile
phase A.

*Reference solution (b)* Dilute 1.0 ml of the test solution to
100.0 ml with a mixture of 25 volumes of mobile phase B
and 75 volumes of mobile phase A.

*Reference solution (c)* Dissolve 10.0 mg of *clomipramine
hydrochloride CRS* and 3.0 mg of *clomipramine impurity C CRS*
in a mixture of 25 volumes of mobile phase B and
75 volumes of mobile phase A and dilute to 20.0 ml with the
same mixture of mobile phases. Dilute 1.0 ml of this solution
to 10.0 ml with a mixture of 25 volumes of mobile phase B
and 75 volumes of mobile phase A.

*Column:*
— *size: l* = 0.25 m, Ø = 4.6 mm,
— *stationary phase:* cyanopropylsilyl silica gel for
  chromatography R (5 µm),
— *temperature*: 30 °C.

*Mobile phase:*
— *mobile phase A*: dissolve 1.2 g of *sodium dihydrogen phosphate R* in *water R*, add 1.1 ml of *nonylamine R*, adjust to pH 3.0 with *phosphoric acid R* and dilute to 1000 ml with *water R*,
— *mobile phase B*: acetonitrile R.

| Time (min) | Mobile phase A (per cent *V/V*) | Mobile phase B (per cent *V/V*) |
|---|---|---|
| 0 - 10 | 75 | 25 |
| 10 - 20 | 75 → 65 | 25 → 35 |
| 20 - 32 | 65 | 35 |
| 32 - 34 | 65 → 75 | 35 → 25 |
| 34 - 44 | 75 | 25 |

*Flow rate*   1.5 ml/min.

*Detection*   Spectrophotometer at 254 nm.

*Injection*   20 µl.

*Relative retentions*   With reference to clomipramine (retention time = about 8 min): impurity A = about 0.5; impurity B = about 0.7; impurity C = about 0.9; impurity D = about 1.7; impurity E = about 2.5; impurity F = about 3.4; impurity G = about 4.3.

*System suitability*   Reference solution (c):
— *resolution*: minimum 3.0 between the peaks due to clomipramine and to impurity C.

*Limits:*
— *impurity B*: not more than the area of the corresponding peak in the chromatogram obtained with reference solution (a) (1.0 per cent),
— *impurity C, D*: for each impurity, not more than the area of the corresponding peak in the chromatogram obtained with reference solution (a) (0.2 per cent),
— *impurity F*: not more than the area of the corresponding peak in the chromatogram obtained with reference solution (a) (0.1 per cent),
— *any other impurity*: not more than 0.1 times the area of the principal peak in the chromatogram obtained with reference solution (b) (0.1 per cent),
— *total of other impurities*: not more than 0.2 times the area of the principal peak in the chromatogram obtained with reference solution (b) (0.2 per cent),
— *total*: not more than the area of the principal peak in the chromatogram obtained with reference solution (b) (1.0 per cent),
— *disregard limit*: 0.01 times the area of the principal peak in the chromatogram obtained with reference solution (b) (0.01 per cent).

**Heavy metals** (*2.4.8*)
Maximum 20 ppm.

2.0 g complies with limit test C. Prepare the standard using 4 ml of *lead standard solution (10 ppm Pb) R*.

**Loss on drying** (*2.2.32*)
Maximum 0.5 per cent, determined on 1.000 g by drying in an oven at 105 °C.

**Sulphated ash** (*2.4.14*)
Maximum 0.1 per cent, determined on 1.0 g.

**ASSAY**

Dissolve 0.250 g in 50 ml of *alcohol R* and add 5.0 ml of *0.01 M hydrochloric acid*. Carry out a potentiometric titration (*2.2.20*), using *0.1 M sodium hydroxide*. Read the volume added between the 2 points of inflexion.

1 ml of *0.1 M sodium hydroxide* is equivalent to 35.13 mg of $C_{19}H_{24}Cl_2N_2$.

**STORAGE**

In an airtight container, protected from light.

**IMPURITIES**

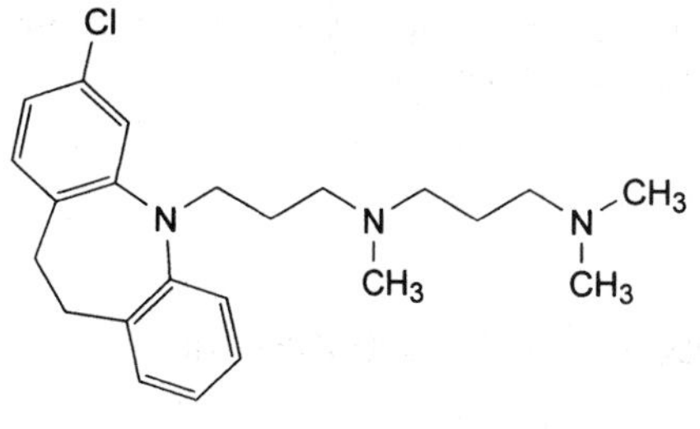

A. *N*-[3-(3-chloro-10,11-dihydro-5*H*-dibenzo[*b,f*]azepin-5-yl)propyl]-*N*,*N'*,*N'*-trimethylpropane-1,3-diamine,
B. imipramine,

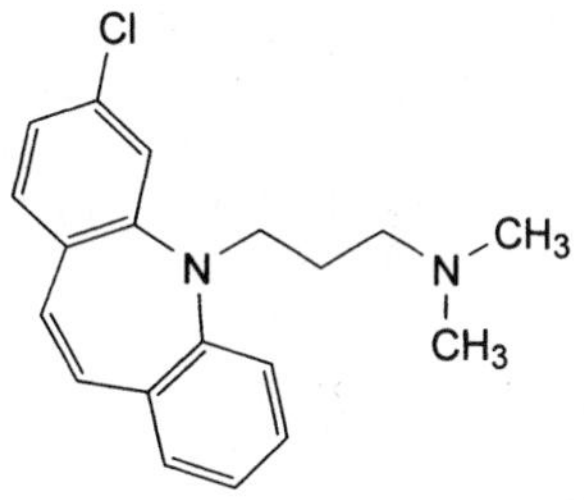

C. 3-(3-chloro-5*H*-dibenzo[*b,f*]azepin-5-yl)-*N*,*N*-dimethylpropan-1-amine,

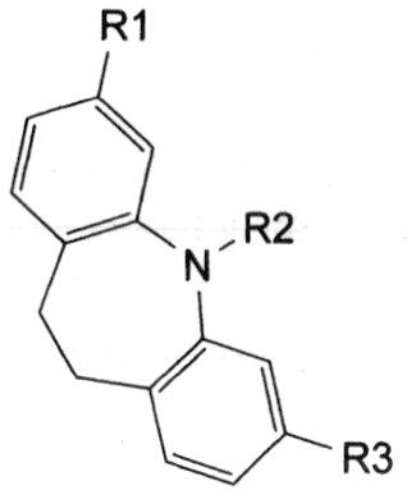

D. R1 = R3 = Cl, R2 = CH₂-CH₂-CH₂-N(CH₃)₂: 3-(3,7-dichloro-10,11-dihydro-5*H*-dibenzo[*b,f*]azepin-5-yl)-*N*,*N*-dimethylpropan-1-amine,
E. R1 = R2 = R3 = H: 10,11-dihydro-5*H*-dibenzo[*b,f*]azepine (iminodibenzyl),
F. R1 = Cl, R2 = R3 = H: 3-chloro-10,11-dihydro-5*H*-dibenzo[*b,f*]azepine,
G. R1 = Cl, R2 = CH₂-CH=CH₂, R3 = H: 3-chloro-5-(prop-2-enyl)-10,11-dihydro-5*H*-dibenzo[*b,f*]azepine.

_____ *Ph Eur*

# Clonazepam

*(Ph Eur monograph 0890)*

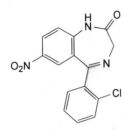

$C_{15}H_{10}ClN_3O_3$     315.7     *1622-61-3*

## Action and use
Benzodiazepine.

## Preparation
Clonazepam Injection

Clonazepam Tablets

*Ph Eur*

## DEFINITION
5-(2-Chlorophenyl)-7-nitro-1,3-dihydro-2*H*-1,4-benzodiazepin-2-one.

## Content
99.0 per cent to 101.0 per cent (dried substance).

## CHARACTERS
### Appearance
Slightly yellowish, crystalline powder.

### Solubility
Practically insoluble in water, slightly soluble in alcohol and in methanol.

### mp
About 239 °C.

## IDENTIFICATION
Infrared absorption spectrophotometry (2.2.24).

*Comparison*   Ph. Eur. reference spectrum of clonazepam.

## TESTS
### Related substances
Liquid chromatography (2.2.29). *Carry out the test protected from light and prepare the solutions immediately before use.*

*Solvent mixture*   tetrahydrofuran R, methanol R, water R (10:42:48 *V/V/V*).

*Test solution*   Dissolve 0.100 g of the substance to be examined in *methanol R* and dilute to 20.0 ml with the same solvent. Dilute 1.0 ml to 10.0 ml with the solvent mixture.

*Reference solution (a)*   Dilute 1.0 ml of the test solution to 100.0 ml with the solvent mixture. Dilute 1.0 ml of the solution to 10.0 ml with the solvent mixture.

*Reference solution (b)*   Dissolve 5 mg of the substance to be examined and 5 mg of *flunitrazepam R* in the solvent mixture and dilute to 100.0 ml with the solvent mixture.

*Reference solution (c)*   Dissolve 1.0 mg of *clonazepam impurity B CRS* in the solvent mixture and dilute to 20.0 ml with the solvent mixture. Dilute 1.0 ml of the solution to 100.0 ml with the solvent mixture.

*Column:*
— *size*: *l* = 0.15 m, Ø = 4.6 mm,
— *stationary phase: end-capped octylsilyl silica gel for chromatography R* (5 μm).

*Mobile phase*   Mix 10 volumes of *tetrahydrofuran R*, 42 volumes of *methanol R* and 48 volumes of a 6.6 g/l solution of *ammonium phosphate R* previously adjusted to pH 8.0 with a 40 g/l solution of *sodium hydroxide R* or *dilute phosphoric acid R*.

*Flow rate*   1.0 ml/min.

*Detection*   Spectrophotometer at 254 nm.

*Injection*   10 μl.

*Run time*   3 times the retention time of clonazepam.

*Relative retention*   With reference to clonazepam (retention time = about 7 min): impurity B = about 2.1; impurity A = about 2.4.

*System suitability*   Reference solution (b):
— *resolution*: minimum 1.8 between the peaks due to flunitrazepam and to clonazepam.

*Limits:*
— *impurity A*: not more than the area of the principal peak in the chromatogram obtained with reference solution (a) (0.1 per cent),
— *impurity B*: not more than the area of the principal peak in the chromatogram obtained with reference solution (c) (0.1 per cent)
— *any other impurity*: for each impurity, not more than the area of the principal peak in the chromatogram obtained with reference solution (a) (0.1 per cent),
— *total*: not more than twice the area of the principal peak in the chromatogram obtained with reference solution (a) (0.2 per cent),
— *disregard limit*: 0.5 times the area of the principal peak in the chromatogram obtained with reference solution (a) (0.05 per cent).

**Loss on drying** (2.2.32)
Maximum 0.5 per cent, determined on 1.000 g by drying in an oven at 105 °C for 4 h.

**Sulphated ash** (2.4.14)
Maximum 0.1 per cent, determined on 1.0 g.

## ASSAY
Dissolve 0.275 g in 50 ml of *acetic anhydride R*. Titrate with *0.1 M perchloric acid*, determining the end-point potentiometrically (2.2.20).

1 ml of *0.1 M perchloric acid* is equivalent to 31.57 mg of $C_{15}H_{10}ClN_3O_3$.

## STORAGE
Protected from light.

## IMPURITIES
*Specified impurities*   A, B.

A. (2-amino-5-nitrophenyl)(2-chlorophenyl)methanone,

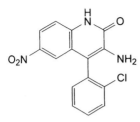

B. 3-amino-4-(2-chlorophenyl)-6-nitroquinolin-2(1*H*)-one.

_____ *Ph Eur*

# Clonidine Hydrochloride

★ ★ ★
★    ★
★    ★
★ ★ ★

*(Ph Eur monograph 0477)*

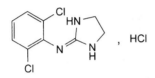

$C_9H_9Cl_2N_3,HCl$      266.6      *4205-91-8*

## Action and use

Alpha₂-adrenoceptor agonist; treatment of hypertension.

## Preparations

Clonidine Injection

Clonidine Tablets

*Ph Eur* _____

## DEFINITION

2,6-Dichloro-*N*-(imidazolidin-2-ylidene)aniline hydrochloride.

## Content

98.5 per cent to 101.0 per cent (dried substance).

## CHARACTERS

### Appearance

White or almost white, crystalline powder.

### Solubility

Soluble in water and in anhydrous ethanol.

## IDENTIFICATION

*First identification*   B, D.

*Second identification*   A, C, D.

A. Ultraviolet and visible absorption spectrophotometry *(2.2.25)*.

*Test solution*   Dissolve 30.0 mg in *0.01 M hydrochloric acid* and dilute to 100.0 ml with the same acid.

*Spectral range*   245-350 nm.

*Absorption maxima*   At 272 nm and 279 nm.

*Point of inflexion*   At 265 nm.

*Specific absorbance at the absorption maxima:*

— at 272 nm: about 18;

— at 279 nm: about 16.

B. Infrared absorption spectrophotometry *(2.2.24)*.

*Comparison*   *clonidine hydrochloride CRS*.

C. Thin-layer chromatography *(2.2.27)*.

*Test solution*   Dissolve 5 mg of the substance to be examined in *methanol R* and dilute to 5 ml with the same solvent.

*Reference solution*   Dissolve 5 mg of *clonidine hydrochloride CRS* in *methanol R* and dilute to 5 ml with the same solvent.

*Plate*   *TLC silica gel G plate R*.

*Mobile phase*   *glacial acetic acid R, butanol R, water R* (10:40:50 *V/V/V*); allow to separate, filter the upper layer and use the filtrate.

*Application*   10 µl.

*Development*   Over 2/3 of the plate.

*Drying*   In air.

*Detection*   Spray with *potassium iodobismuthate solution R2*. Allow to dry in air for 1 h. Spray again with *potassium iodobismuthate solution R2* and then immediately spray with a 50 g/l solution of *sodium nitrite R*.

*Results*   The principal spot in the chromatogram obtained with the test solution is similar in position, colour and size to the principal spot in the chromatogram obtained with the reference solution.

D. It gives reaction (a) of chlorides *(2.3.1)*.

## TESTS

### Solution S

Dissolve 1.25 g in *carbon dioxide-free water R* and dilute to 25 ml with the same solvent.

### Appearance of solution

Solution S is clear *(2.2.1)* and not more intensely coloured than reference solution Y₇ *(2.2.2, Method II)*.

### pH *(2.2.3)*

4.0 to 5.0 for solution S.

### Related substances

Liquid chromatography *(2.2.29)*.

*Test solution*   Dissolve 50 mg of the substance to be examined in mobile phase A and dilute to 50 ml with mobile phase A.

*Reference solution (a)*   Dilute 1.0 ml of the test solution to 100.0 ml with mobile phase A. Dilute 1.0 ml of this solution to 10.0 ml with mobile phase A.

*Reference solution (b)*   Dissolve 5 mg of *clonidine impurity B CRS* in 2 ml of *acetonitrile R* and dilute to 5 ml with mobile phase A. To 1 ml of this solution, add 1 ml of the test solution and dilute to 10 ml with mobile phase A.

*Column:*

— *size: l* = 0.15 m, Ø = 3.0 mm;

— *stationary phase: propylsilyl silica gel for chromatography R* (5 µm);

— *temperature*: 40 °C.

*Mobile phase:*

— *mobile phase A*: dissolve 4 g of *potassium dihydrogen phosphate R* in 1000 ml of water R, and adjust to pH 4.0 with *phosphoric acid R*;

— *mobile phase B*: mobile phase A, *acetonitrile R1* (25:75 *V/V*);

| Time (min) | Mobile phase A (per cent *V/V*) | Mobile phase B (per cent *V/V*) |
|---|---|---|
| 0 | 90 | 10 |
| 0 - 15 | 90 → 30 | 10 → 70 |
| 15 - 15.1 | 30 → 90 | 70 → 10 |
| 15.1 - 20 | 90 | 10 |

*Flow rate*   1.5 ml/min.

*Detection*   Spectrophotometer at 210 nm.

*Injection*   5 µl.

*System suitability* Reference solution (b):
— *resolution*: minimum 5 between the peaks due to clonidine and impurity B.

*Limits*:
— *unspecified impurities*: for each impurity, not more than the area of the principal peak in the chromatogram obtained with reference solution (a) (0.10 per cent);
— *total*: not more than twice the area of the principal peak in the chromatogram obtained with reference solution (a) (0.2 per cent);
— *disregard limit*: 0.5 times the area of the principal peak in the chromatogram obtained with reference solution (a) (0.05 per cent).

**Loss on drying** (*2.2.32*)
Maximum 0.5 per cent, determined on 1.000 g by drying in an oven at 105 °C.

**Sulphated ash** (*2.4.14*)
Maximum 0.1 per cent, determined on 1.0 g.

## ASSAY
Dissolve 0.200 g in 70 ml of *ethanol (96 per cent) R*. Titrate with *0.1 M ethanolic sodium hydroxide* determining the end-point potentiometrically (*2.2.20*).

1 ml of *0.1 M sodium hydroxide* is equivalent to 26.66 mg of $C_9H_{10}Cl_3N_3$.

## IMPURITIES
*Other detectable impurities* (The following substances would, if present at a sufficient level, be detected by one or other of the tests in the monograph. They are limited by the general acceptance criterion for other/unspecified impurities and/or by the general monograph *Substances for pharmaceutical use* (*2034*). It is therefore not necessary to identify these impurities for demonstration of compliance. See also *5.10. Control of impurities in substances for pharmaceutical use*): *A, B, C*.

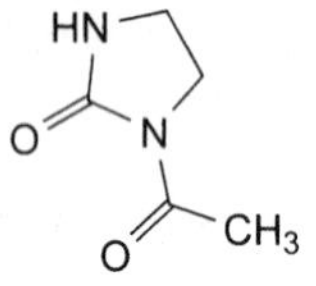

A. 1-acetylimidazolidin-2-one,

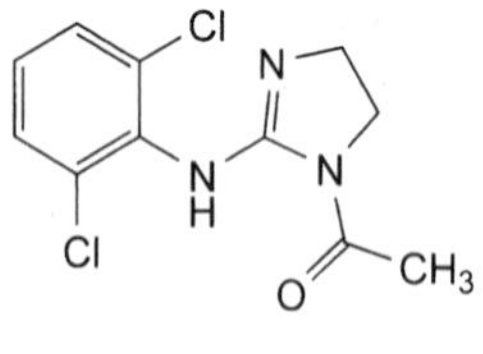

B. 1-acetyl-2-[(2,6-dichlorophenyl)amino]-4,5-dihydro-1*H*-imidazole,

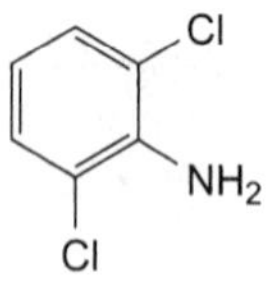

C. 2,6-dichloroaniline.

*Ph Eur*

# Clopamide

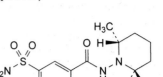

(*Ph Eur monograph 1747*)

$C_{14}H_{20}ClN_3O_3S$      345.8      *636-54-4*

## Action and use
Thiazide-like diuretic.

*Ph Eur*

## DEFINITION
4-Chloro-*N*-[(2*RS*,6*SR*)-2,6-dimethylpiperidin-1-yl]-3-sulfamoylbenzamide.

### Content
99.0 per cent to 101.0 per cent (dried substance).

## PRODUCTION
The production method is evaluated to determine the potential for formation of an *N*-nitroso compound (*cis*-2,6-dimethyl-1-nitrosopiperidine). Where necessary, the production method is validated to demonstrate that the *N*-nitroso compound is absent in the final product.

## CHARACTERS
### Appearance
White or almost white, hygroscopic, crystalline powder.

### Solubility
Slightly soluble in water and in anhydrous ethanol, sparingly soluble in methanol.

It shows polymorphism (*5.9*).

## IDENTIFICATION
Infrared absorption spectrophotometry (*2.2.24*).

*Comparison* clopamide CRS.

If the spectra obtained in the solid state show differences, dissolve the substance to be examined and the reference substance separately in the minimum volume of *methanol R*, evaporate to dryness on a water-bath and record new spectra using the residues.

## TESTS
### Related substances
Liquid chromatography (*2.2.29*).

*Test solution* Dissolve 100 mg of the substance to be examined in *methanol R* and dilute to 10.0 ml with the same solvent.

*Reference solution (a)* Dissolve 10 mg of *clopamide for system suitability CRS* (containing impurities B, C and H) in 1.0 ml of *methanol R*.

*Reference solution (b)* Dilute 2.0 ml of the test solution to 100.0 ml with *methanol R*. Dilute 2.0 ml of this solution to 40.0 ml with *methanol R*.

*Column*:
— *size*: *l* = 0.15 m, Ø = 4.6 mm;
— *stationary phase*: end-capped octylsilyl silica gel for chromatography R (5 µm);

*Mobile phase:*
— *mobile phase A*: dissolve 1.0 g of *ammonium acetate R* in 950 ml of *water R*, adjust to pH 2.0 with *phosphoric acid R* and dilute to 1000 ml with *water R;*
— *mobile phase B*: *acetonitrile R;*
— *mobile phase C*: *water R, tetrahydrofuran for chromatography R* (20:80 *V/V*); this mobile phase allows adequate rinsing of the system;

| Time (min) | Mobile phase A (per cent *V/V*) | Mobile phase B (per cent *V/V*) | Mobile phase C (per cent *V/V*) |
|---|---|---|---|
| 0 - 35 | 95 → 75 | 5 → 25 | 0 |
| 35 - 45 | 75 → 35 | 25 → 65 | 0 |
| 45 - 50 | 35 → 30 | 65 → 0 | 0 → 70 |
| 50 - 60 | 30 | 0 | 70 |
| 60 - 63 | 30 → 95 | 0 → 5 | 70 → 0 |
| 63 - 73 | 95 | 5 | 0 |

*Flow rate*   0.4 ml/min.

*Detection*   Spectrophotometer at 235 nm.

*Injection*   10 μl.

*Identification of impurities*   Use the chromatogram supplied with *clopamide for system suitability CRS* and the chromatogram obtained with reference solution (a) to identify the peaks due to impurities B, C and H.

*Relative retention*   With reference to clopamide (retention time = about 33 min): impurity C = about 0.8; impurity H = about 1.2; impurity B = about 1.4.

*System suitability*   Reference solution (a):
— *resolution*: minimum 3 between the peaks due to impurity C and clopamide.

*Limits:*
— *correction factors*: for the calculation of content, multiply the peak areas of the following impurities by the corresponding correction factor: impurity B = 0.5; impurity H = 0.4;
— *impurities B, C, H*: for each impurity, not more than twice the area of the principal peak in the chromatogram obtained with reference solution (b) (0.2 per cent);
— *unspecified impurities*: for each impurity, not more than the area of the principal peak in the chromatogram obtained with reference solution (b) (0.10 per cent);
— *total*: not more than 10 times the area of the principal peak in the chromatogram obtained with reference solution (b) (1.0 per cent);
— *disregard limit*: 0.5 times the area of the principal peak in the chromatogram obtained with reference solution (b) (0.05 per cent).

**Heavy metals** (*2.4.8*)
Maximum 20 ppm.

Dissolve 0.25 g in a mixture of 20 volumes of *acetone R* and 85 volumes of *methanol R* and dilute to 20 ml with the same mixture of solvents. 20 ml of the solution complies with modified test B. Prepare the reference solution by diluting 0.5 ml of *lead standard solution (10 ppm Pb) R* to 20 ml with a mixture of 20 volumes of *acetone R* and 85 volumes of *methanol R*. Prepare the blank solution by using 20 ml of a mixture of 20 volumes of *acetone R* and 85 volumes of *methanol R*.

Filter the solutions through a membrane filter (0.45 μm) to evaluate the result.

**Loss on drying** (*2.2.32*)
Maximum 2.5 per cent, determined on 1.000 g by drying in an oven at 105 °C.

**Sulphated ash** (*2.4.14*)
Maximum 0.1 per cent, determined on 1.0 g.

**ASSAY**

Dissolve 0.280 g in 70 ml of *anhydrous acetic acid R*. Titrate with *0.1 M perchloric acid*, determining the end-point potentiometrically (*2.2.20*).

1 ml of *0.1 M perchloric acid* is equivalent to 34.58 mg of $C_{14}H_{20}ClN_3O_3S$.

**STORAGE**

In an airtight container, protected from light.

**IMPURITIES**

*Specified impurities   B, C, H.*

*Other detectable impurities*   (The following substances would, if present at a sufficient level, be detected by one or other of the tests in the monograph. They are limited by the general acceptance criterion for other/unspecified impurities and/or by the general monograph *Substances for pharmaceutical use (2034)*. It is therefore not necessary to identify these impurities for demonstration of compliance. See also *5.10. Control of impurities in substances for pharmaceutical use*):
*A, G.*

A. R = CH₃: 4-chloro-N-[(2RS,6RS)-2,6-dimethylpiperidin-1-yl]-3-sulfamoylbenzamide (*trans*-clopamide),
G. R = H: 4-chloro-N-[(2RS)-2-methylpiperidin-1-yl]-3-sulfamoylbenzamide,

B. R = H: 4-chlorobenzoic acid,
C. R = SO₂-NH₂: 4-chloro-3-sulfamoylbenzoic acid,

H. 4-chloro-3-[(E)-[(dimethylamino)methylene]sulfamoyl]-N-[(2RS,6SR)-2,6-dimethylpiperidin-1-yl]benzamide.

*Ph Eur*

# Clotrimazole

*(Ph Eur monograph 0757)*

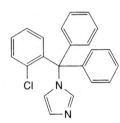

$C_{22}H_{17}ClN_2$      344.8      23593-75-1

## Action and use
Antifungal.

## Preparations
Clotrimazole Cream

Clotrimazole Pessaries

*Ph Eur* _____

## DEFINITION
1-[(2-Chlorophenyl)diphenylmethyl]-1*H*-imidazole.

## Content
98.5 per cent to 100.5 per cent (dried substance).

## CHARACTERS
### Appearance
White or pale yellow, crystalline powder.

### Solubility
Practically insoluble in water, soluble in ethanol (96 per cent) and in methylene chloride.

## IDENTIFICATION
*First identification*  B.

*Second identification*  A, C.

A. Melting point (*2.2.14*): 141 °C to 145 °C.

B. Infrared absorption spectrophotometry (*2.2.24*).

*Comparison*  clotrimazole CRS.

C. Thin-layer chromatography (*2.2.27*).

*Test solution*  Dissolve 50 mg of the substance to be examined in *ethanol (96 per cent) R* and dilute to 5 ml with the same solvent.

*Reference solution*  Dissolve 50 mg of *clotrimazole CRS* in *ethanol (96 per cent) R* and dilute to 5 ml with the same solvent.

*Plate*  TLC silica gel $F_{254}$ plate R.

*Mobile phase*  concentrated ammonia R1, propanol R, toluene R (0.5:10:90 *V/V/V*).

*Application*  10 µl.

*Development*  Over 2/3 of the plate.

*Drying*  In air.

*Detection*  Examine in ultraviolet light at 254 nm.

*Results*  The principal spot in the chromatogram obtained with the test solution is similar in position and size to the principal spot in the chromatogram obtained with the reference solution.

## TESTS
### Related substances
Liquid chromatography (*2.2.29*).

*Test solution*  Dissolve 50.0 mg of the substance to be examined in *acetonitrile R1* and dilute to 50.0 ml with the same solvent.

*Reference solution (a)*  Dilute 1.0 ml of the test solution to 100.0 ml with *acetonitrile R1*. Dilute 1.0 ml of this solution to 10.0 ml with *acetonitrile R1*.

*Reference solution (b)*  Dissolve the contents of a vial of *clotrimazole for peak identification CRS* (containing impurities A, B and F) in 1.0 ml of *acetonitrile R1*.

*Reference solution (c)*  Dissolve 5.0 mg of *imidazole CRS* (impurity D) and 5.0 mg of *clotrimazole impurity E CRS* in *acetonitrile R1* and dilute to 100.0 ml with the same solvent. Dilute 1.0 ml of this solution to 25.0 ml with *acetonitrile R1*.

*Column:*
— *size*: $l$ = 0.15 m, Ø = 4.6 mm;
— *stationary phase*: spherical *end-capped octylsilyl silica gel for chromatography R* (5 µm);
— *temperature*: 40 °C.

*Mobile phase:*
— *mobile phase A*: dissolve 1.0 g of *potassium dihydrogen phosphate R* and 0.5 g of *tetrabutylammonium hydrogen sulphate R1* in *water R* and dilute to 1000 ml with the same solvent;
— *mobile phase B*: acetonitrile R1;

| Time (min) | Mobile phase A (per cent *V/V*) | Mobile phase B (per cent *V/V*) |
|---|---|---|
| 0 - 3 | 75 | 25 |
| 3 - 25 | 75 → 20 | 25 → 80 |
| 25 - 30 | 20 | 80 |

*Flow rate*  1.0 ml/min.

*Detection*  Spectrophotometer at 210 nm.

*Injection*  10 µl.

*Relative retention*  With reference to clotrimazole (retention time = about 12 min): impurity D = about 0.1; impurity F = about 0.9; impurity B = about 1.1; impurity E = about 1.5; impurity A = about 1.8.

*System suitability*  Reference solution (b):
— *resolution*: minimum 1.5 between the peaks due to impurity F and clotrimazole;
— the chromatogram obtained is similar to the chromatogram supplied with *clotrimazole for peak identification CRS*.

*Limits:*
— *impurities A, B*: for each impurity, not more than twice the area of the principal peak in the chromatogram obtained with reference solution (a) (0.2 per cent);
— *impurities D, E*: for each impurity, not more than the area of the corresponding peak in the chromatogram obtained with reference solution (c) (0.2 per cent);
— *impurity F*: not more than the area of the principal peak in the chromatogram obtained with reference solution (a) (0.1 per cent);
— *unspecified impurities*: for each impurity, not more than the area of the principal peak in the chromatogram obtained with reference solution (a) (0.10 per cent);
— *total*: not more than 5 times the area of the principal peak in the chromatogram obtained with reference solution (a) (0.5 per cent);
— *disregard limit*: 0.5 times the area of the principal peak in the chromatogram obtained with reference solution (a) (0.05 per cent).

**Loss on drying** (*2.2.32*)
Maximum 0.5 per cent, determined on 1.000 g by drying in an oven at 105 °C.

**Sulphated ash** (*2.4.14*)
Maximum 0.1 per cent, determined on 1.0 g.

## ASSAY
Dissolve 0.300 g in 80 ml of *anhydrous acetic acid R*. Using 0.3 ml of *naphtholbenzein solution R* as indicator, titrate with *0.1 M perchloric acid* until the colour changes from brownish-yellow to green.

1 ml of *0.1 M perchloric acid* is equivalent to 34.48 mg of $C_{22}H_{17}ClN_2$.

## STORAGE
Protected from light.

## IMPURITIES
*Specified impurities* A, B, D, E, F.

*Other detectable impurities* (The following substances would, if present at a sufficient level, be detected by one or other of the tests in the monograph. They are limited by the general acceptance criterion for other/unspecified impurities and/or by the general monograph *Substances for pharmaceutical use (2034)*. It is therefore not necessary to identify these impurities for demonstration of compliance. See also *5.10. Control of impurities in substances for pharmaceutical use*): C.

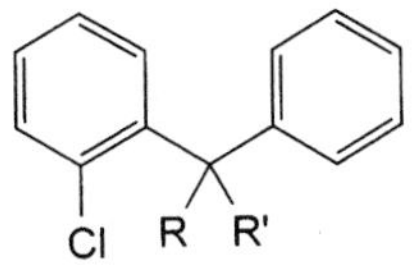

A. R = OH, R′ = $C_6H_5$: (2-chlorophenyl)diphenylmethanol,

C. R = Cl, R′ = $C_6H_5$:
1-chloro-2-(chlorodiphenylmethyl)benzene,

E. R + R′ = O: (2-chlorophenyl)phenylmethanone
(2-chlorobenzophenone),

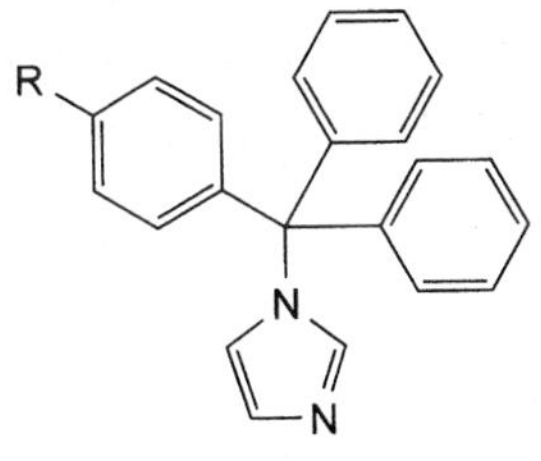

B. R = Cl:
1-[(4-chlorophenyl)diphenylmethyl]-1*H*-imidazole,

F. R = H: 1-(triphenylmethyl)-1*H*-imidazole
(deschloroclotrimazole),

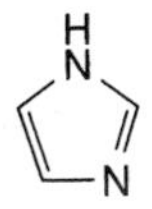

D. imidazole.

*Ph Eur*

# Cloxacillin Sodium

(*Ph Eur monograph 0661*)

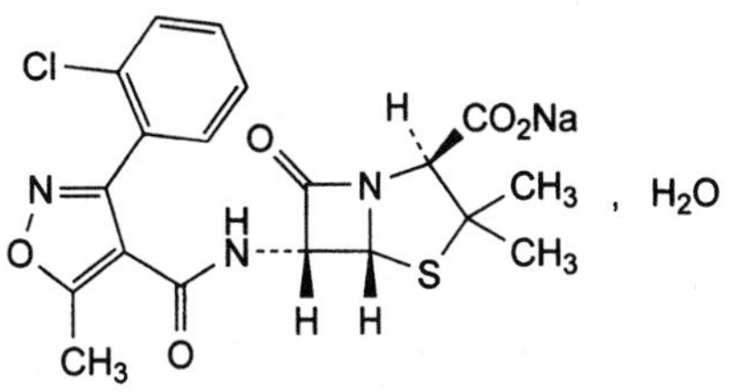

$C_{19}H_{17}ClN_3NaO_5S,H_2O$    475.9    *7081-44-9*

**Action and use**
Penicillin antibacterial.

*Ph Eur*

## DEFINITION
Sodium (2*S*,5*R*,6*R*)-6-[[[3-(2-chlorophenyl)-5-methylisoxazol-4-yl]carbonyl]amino]-3,3-dimethyl-7-oxo-4-thia-1-azabicyclo[3.2.0]heptane-2-carboxylate monohydrate.

Semi-synthetic product derived from a fermentation product.

## Content
95.0 per cent to 102.0 per cent (anhydrous substance).

## CHARACTERS
**Appearance**
White or almost white, hygroscopic, crystalline powder.

**Solubility**
Freely soluble in water and in methanol, soluble in ethanol (96 per cent).

## IDENTIFICATION
*First identification* A, D.

*Second identification* B, C, D.

A. Infrared absorption spectrophotometry (*2.2.24*).

*Preparation* Discs.

*Comparison* cloxacillin sodium CRS.

B. Thin-layer chromatography (*2.2.27*).

*Test solution* Dissolve 25 mg of the substance to be examined in 5 ml of *water R*.

*Reference solution (a)* Dissolve 25 mg of *cloxacillin sodium CRS* in 5 ml of *water R*.

*Reference solution (b)* Dissolve 25 mg of *cloxacillin sodium CRS*, 25 mg of *dicloxacillin sodium CRS* and 25 mg of *flucloxacillin sodium CRS* in 5 ml of *water R*.

*Plate* TLC silanised silica gel plate R.

*Mobile phase* Mix 30 volumes of *acetone R* and 70 volumes of a 154 g/l solution of *ammonium acetate R*, then adjust to pH 5.0 with *glacial acetic acid R*.

*Application* 1 µl.

*Development* Over a path of 15 cm.

*Drying* In air.

*Detection* Expose to iodine vapour until the spots appear; examine in daylight.

*System suitability* Reference solution (b):
— the chromatogram shows 3 clearly separated spots.

*Results* The principal spot in the chromatogram obtained with the test solution is similar in position, colour and size to the principal spot in the chromatogram obtained with reference solution (a).

C. Place about 2 mg in a test-tube about 150 mm long and 15 mm in diameter. Moisten with 0.05 ml of *water R* and add 2 ml of *sulphuric acid-formaldehyde reagent R*. Mix the contents of the tube by swirling; the solution is slightly greenish-yellow. Place the test-tube in a water-bath for 1 min; the solution becomes yellow.

D. It gives reaction (a) of sodium (2.3.1).

## TESTS

### Solution S
Dissolve 2.50 g in *carbon dioxide-free water R* and dilute to 25.0 ml with the same solvent.

### Appearance of solution
Solution S is clear (2.2.1) and its absorbance (2.2.25) at 430 nm is not greater than 0.04.

### pH (2.2.3)
5.0 to 7.0 for solution S.

### Specific optical rotation (2.2.7)
+ 160 to + 169 (anhydrous substance).

Dissolve 0.250 g in *water R* and dilute to 25.0 ml with the same solvent.

### Related substances
Liquid chromatography (2.2.29).

*Test solution (a)* Dissolve 50.0 mg of the substance to be examined in the mobile phase and dilute to 50.0 ml with the mobile phase.

*Test solution (b)* Dilute 5.0 ml of test solution (a) to 50.0 ml with the mobile phase.

*Reference solution (a)* Dissolve 50.0 mg of *cloxacillin sodium CRS* in the mobile phase and dilute to 50.0 ml with the mobile phase. Dilute 5.0 ml of this solution to 50.0 ml with the mobile phase.

*Reference solution (b)* Dilute 5.0 ml of test solution (b) to 50.0 ml with the mobile phase.

*Reference solution (c)* Dissolve 5 mg of *flucloxacillin sodium CRS* and 5 mg of *cloxacillin sodium CRS* in the mobile phase and dilute to 50.0 ml with the mobile phase.

*Column:*
— *size*: l = 0.25 m, Ø = 4 mm;
— *stationary phase: octadecylsilyl silica gel for chromatography R* (5 μm).

*Mobile phase* Mix 25 volumes of *acetonitrile R* and 75 volumes of a 2.7 g/l solution of *potassium dihydrogen phosphate R* adjusted to pH 5.0 with *dilute sodium hydroxide solution R*.

*Flow rate* 1.0 ml/min.

*Detection* Spectrophotometer at 225 nm.

*Injection* 20 μl of test solution (a) and reference solutions (b) and (c).

*Run time* 5 times the retention time of cloxacillin.

*System suitability* Reference solution (c):
— *resolution*: minimum 2.5 between the peaks due to cloxacillin (1st peak) and flucloxacillin (2nd peak).

*Limits:*
— *any impurity*: not more than the area of the principal peak in the chromatogram obtained with reference solution (b) (1.0 per cent);
— *total*: not more than 5 times the area of the principal peak in the chromatogram obtained with reference solution (b) (5.0 per cent);
— *disregard limit*: 0.05 times the area of the principal peak in the chromatogram obtained with reference solution (b) (0.05 per cent).

**N,N-Dimethylaniline** (2.4.26, *Method B*)
Maximum 20 ppm.

**2-Ethylhexanoic acid** (2.4.28)
Maximum 0.8 per cent m/m.

**Water** (2.5.12)
3.0 per cent to 4.5 per cent, determined on 0.300 g.

**Bacterial endotoxins** (2.6.14)
Less than 0.20 IU/mg, if intended for use in the manufacture of parenteral dosage forms without a further appropriate procedure for the removal of bacterial endotoxins.

## ASSAY
Liquid chromatography (2.2.29) as described in the test for related substances with the following modifications.

*Injection* Test solution (b) and reference solution (a).

*System suitability:*
— *repeatability*: maximum relative standard deviation of 1.0 per cent after 6 injections of reference solution (a).

Calculate the percentage content of $C_{19}H_{17}ClN_3NaO_5S$ from the declared content of *cloxacillin sodium CRS*.

## STORAGE
In an airtight container, at a temperature not exceeding 25 °C. If the substance is sterile, store in a sterile, airtight, tamper-proof container.

## IMPURITIES

A. R = $CO_2H$: (4S)-2-[carboxy[[[3-(2-chlorophenyl)-5-methylisoxazol-4-yl]carbonyl]amino]methyl]-5,5-dimethylthiazolidine-4-carboxylic acid (penicilloic acid of cloxacillin),

B. R = H: (2RS,4S)-2-[[[[3-(2-chlorophenyl)-5-methylisoxazol-4-yl]carbonyl]amino]methyl]-5,5-dimethylthiazolidine-4-carboxylic acid (penilloic acid of cloxacillin),

C. (2S,5R,6R)-6-amino-3,3-dimethyl-7-oxo-4-thia-1-azabicyclo[3.2.0]heptane-2-carboxylic acid (6-aminopenicillanic acid),

D. 3-(2-chlorophenyl)-5-methylisoxazole-4-carboxylic acid,

E. (2S,5R,6R)-6-[[[(2S,5R,6R)-6-[[[3-(2-chlorophenyl)-5-methylisoxazol-4-yl]carbonyl]amino]-3,3-dimethyl-7-oxo-4-thia-1-azabicyclo[3.2.0]hept-2-yl]carbonyl]amino]-3,3-dimethyl-7-oxo-4-thia-1-azabicyclo[3.2.0]heptane-2-carboxylic acid (6-APA cloxacillin amide).

*Ph Eur*

# Clozapine

*(Ph Eur monograph 1191)*

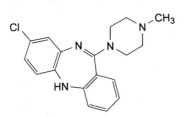

C$_{18}$H$_{19}$ClN$_4$      326.8      *5786-21-0*

## Action and use
Dopamine D$_4$ receptor antagonist; neuroleptic.

*Ph Eur*

## DEFINITION
8-Chloro-11-(4-methylpiperazin-1-yl)-5H-dibenzo[b,e][1,4]diazepine.

## Content
99.0 per cent to 101.0 per cent (dried substance).

## CHARACTERS
### Appearance
Yellow, crystalline powder.

### Solubility
Practically insoluble in water, freely soluble in methylene chloride, soluble in ethanol (96 per cent). It dissolves in dilute acetic acid.

## IDENTIFICATION
A. Melting point (*2.2.14*). 182 °C to 186 °C.

B. Infrared absorption spectrophotometry (*2.2.24*).

*Comparison*   clozapine CRS.

## TESTS
### Related substances
Liquid chromatography (*2.2.29*).

*Solvent mixture*   water R, methanol R2 (20:80 V/V).

*Solution A*   Dissolve 2.04 g of *potassium dihydrogen phosphate R* in 1000 ml of *water R* and adjust to pH 2.4 ± 0.05 with *dilute phosphoric acid R*.

*Test solution*   Dissolve 75 mg of the substance to be examined in 80 ml of *methanol R2* and dilute to 100 ml with *water R*.

*Reference solution (a)*   Dilute 1.0 ml of the test solution to 10.0 ml with the solvent mixture. Dilute 1.0 ml of this solution to 100.0 ml with the solvent mixture.

*Reference solution (b)*   Dissolve the contents of a vial of *clozapine for peak identification CRS* (containing impurities A, B, C and D) in 1.0 ml of the solvent mixture.

*Column:*
— *size:* l = 0.125 m, Ø = 4.6 mm;
— *stationary phase:* end-capped octadecylsilyl silica gel for chromatography R (5 µm).

*Mobile phase:*
— *mobile phase A:* acetonitrile for chromatography R, methanol R2, solution A (1:1:8 V/V/V);
— *mobile phase B:* acetonitrile for chromatography R, methanol R2, solution A (4:4:2 V/V/V);

| Time (min) | Mobile phase A (per cent V/V) | Mobile phase B (per cent V/V) |
|---|---|---|
| 0 - 4 | 100 | 0 |
| 4 - 24 | 100 → 0 | 0 → 100 |
| 24 - 29 | 0 | 100 |

*Flow rate*   1.2 ml/min.

*Detection*   Spectrophotometer at 257 nm.

*Injection*   20 µl.

*Identification of impurities*   Use the chromatogram supplied with *clozapine for peak identification CRS* and the chromatogram obtained with reference solution (b) to identify the peaks due to impurities A, B, C and D.

*Relative retention*   With reference to clozapine (retention time = about 11 min): impurity C = about 0.9; impurity D = about 1.1; impurity A = about 1.6; impurity B = about 1.7.

*System suitability*   Reference solution (b):
— *resolution:* minimum 2.5 between the peaks due to impurity C and clozapine;
— the chromatogram obtained with reference solution (b) is similar to the chromatogram supplied with *clozapine for peak identification CRS*.

*Limits:*
— *correction factor:* for the calculation of content, multiply the peak area of impurity D by 2.7;
— *impurity A:* not more than the area of the principal peak in the chromatogram obtained with reference solution (a) (0.1 per cent);
— *impurities B, D:* for each impurity, not more than twice the area of the principal peak in the chromatogram obtained with reference solution (a) (0.2 per cent);
— *impurity C:* not more than 3 times the area of the principal peak in the chromatogram obtained with reference solution (a) (0.3 per cent);
— *unspecified impurities:* for each impurity, not more than the area of the principal peak in the chromatogram obtained with reference solution (a) (0.10 per cent);
— *total:* not more than 6 times the area of the principal peak in the chromatogram obtained with reference solution (a) (0.6 per cent);
— *disregard limit:* 0.5 times the area of the principal peak in the chromatogram obtained with reference solution (a) (0.05 per cent).

**Heavy metals** (2.4.8)

Maximum 20 ppm.

1.0 g complies with test C. Prepare the reference solution using 2 ml of *lead standard solution (10 ppm Pb) R*.

**Loss on drying** (2.2.32)

Maximum 0.5 per cent, determined on 1.000 g by drying in an oven at 105 °C.

**Sulphated ash** (2.4.14)

Maximum 0.1 per cent, determined on 1.0 g.

**ASSAY**

Dissolve 0.100 g in 50 ml of *anhydrous acetic acid R*. Titrate with *0.1 M perchloric acid*, determining the end-point potentiometrically (2.2.20).

1 ml of *0.1 M perchloric acid* is equivalent to 16.34 mg of $C_{18}H_{19}ClN_4$.

**IMPURITIES**

*Specified impurities   A, B, C, D.*

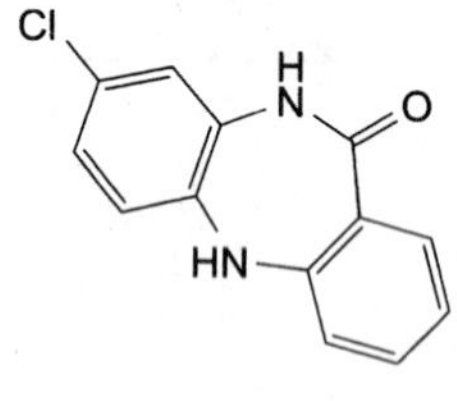

A. 8-chloro-5,10-dihydro-11*H*-dibenzo[*b,e*][1,4]diazepin-11-one,

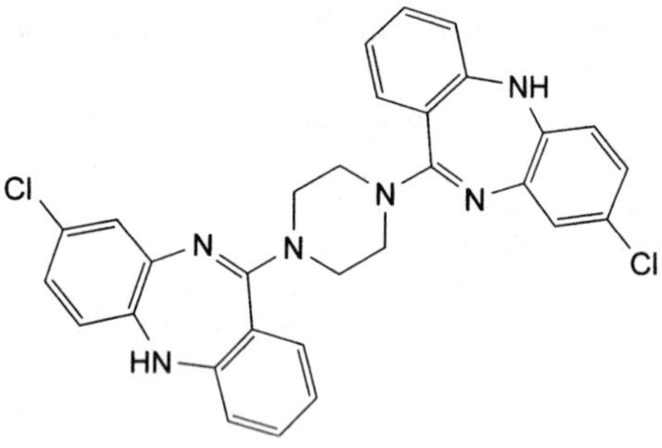

B. 11,11′-(piperazine-1,4-diyl)bis(8-chloro-5*H*-dibenzo[*b,e*][1,4]diazepine),

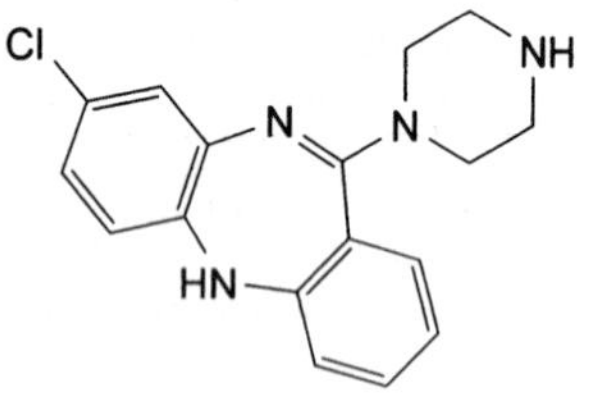

C 8-chloro-11-(piperazin-1-yl)-5*H*-dibenzo[*b,e*][1,4]diazepine,

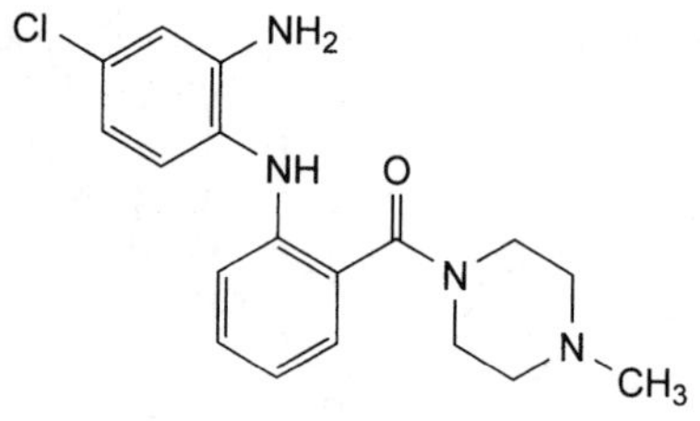

D. 1-[2-[[(2-amino-4-chlorophenyl)amino]benzoyl]-4-methylpiperazine.

_____ *Ph Eur*

# Cocaine

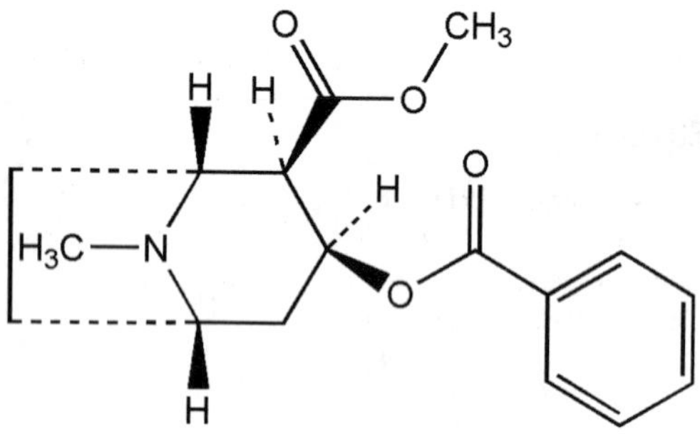

$C_{17}H_{21}NO_4$          303.4          *50-36-2*

**Action and use**

Local anaesthetic.

**DEFINITION**

Cocaine is methyl (1*R*,2*R*,3*S*,5*S*)-3-(benzoyloxy)-8-methyl-8-azabicyclo[3.2.1]octane-2-carboxylate and may be obtained from the leaves of *Erythroxylum coca* Lam. and other species of *Erythroxylum* or by synthesis. It contains not less than 98.0% and not more than 101.0% of $C_{17}H_{21}NO_4$, calculated with reference to the dried substance.

**CHARACTERISTICS**

Colourless crystals or a white, crystalline powder. Slightly volatile.

Practically insoluble in *water*; freely soluble in *ethanol (96%)* and in *ether*; soluble in arachis oil; slightly soluble in *liquid paraffin*.

**IDENTIFICATION**

The *infrared absorption spectrum*, Appendix II A, is concordant with the *reference spectrum* of cocaine *(RS 071)*.

**TESTS**

**Melting point**

96° to 98°, Appendix V A.

**Specific optical rotation**

In a 2.4 % w/v solution in 0.1M *hydrochloric acid*, −79 to −81, calculated with reference to the dried substance, Appendix V F.

**Related substances**

Carry out the method for *liquid chromatography*, Appendix III D, using the following solutions.

(1) 0.05% w/v of the substance being examined in the mobile phase

(2) Dilute 1 volume of solution (1) to 50 volumes with the mobile phase, dilute 5.0 ml of this solution to 100.0 ml with the mobile phase.

(3) Dissolve 25 mg of the substance being examined in 0.01M *sodium hydroxide* and dilute to 100.0 ml with the same solvent. Allow the solution to stand for 15 minutes.

CHROMATOGRAPHIC CONDITIONS

(a) Use a stainless steel column (15 cm × 4.6 mm) packed with *base-deactivated octadecylsilyl silica gel for chromatography* (5 μm) (Waters Symmetry is suitable).

(b) Use isocratic elution and the mobile phase described below.

(c) Use a flow rate of 1 ml per minute.

(d) Use a column temperature of 35°.

(e) Use a detection wavelength of 216 nm.

(f) Inject 20 μl of each solution.

*MOBILE PHASE*

1 volume of *triethylamine*, 200 volumes of *tetrahydrofuran*, 860 volumes of *acetonitrile* and 959 volumes of *water*.

SYSTEM SUITABILITY

The test is not valid unless, in the chromatogram obtained with solution (3), the *resolution factor* between the peaks due to cocaine (retention time, about 7 minutes) and the degradation product is at least 5.0.

LIMITS

In the chromatogram obtained with solution (1):

the area of any peak eluting after the principal peak is not greater than the area of the peak in the chromatogram obtained with solution (2) (0.1%);

the sum of the areas of any *secondary peaks* is not greater than 5 times the area of the principal peak in the chromatogram obtained with solution (2) (0.5%).

Disregard any peak with an area less than 0.5 times the area of the principal peak in the chromatogram obtained with solution (2) (0.05 %).

**Loss on drying**

When dried to constant weight at 80°, loses not more than 0.5% of its weight, Appendix IX D. Use 1 g.

**Sulphated ash**

Not more than 0.1%, Appendix IX A.

**ASSAY**

Carry out Method I for *non-aqueous titration*, Appendix VIII A, using 0.7 g dissolved in 50 ml of *1,4-dioxan* and *crystal violet solution* as indicator. Each ml of 0.1M *perchloric acid VS* is equivalent to 30.34 mg of $C_{17}H_{21}NO_4$.

**STORAGE**

Cocaine should be stored protected from light.

IMPURITIES

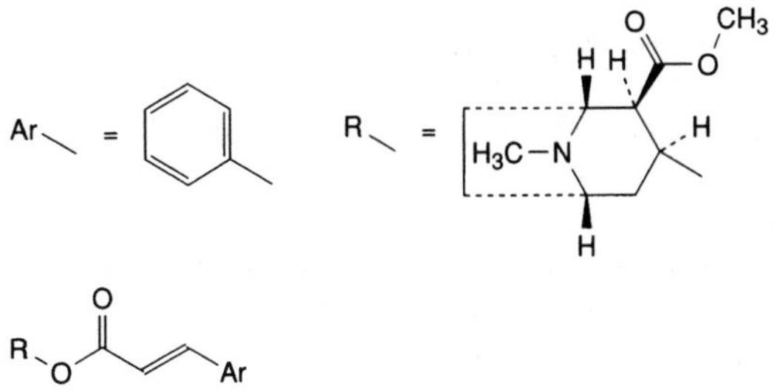

A. methyl (1R,2R,3S,5S)-8-methyl-3-[[(E)-3-phenylpropenoyl]oxy]-8-azabicyclo[3.2.1]octane-2-carboxylate (cinnamoylcocaine),

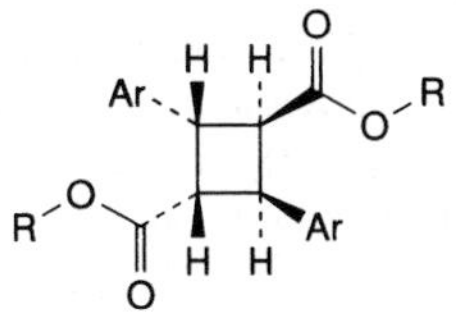

B. bis[(1R,2R,3S,5S)-2-(methoxycarbonyl)-8-methyl-8-azabicyclo[3.2.1]oct-3-yl] (1r,2c,3t,4t)-2,4-diphenylcyclobutane-1,3-dicarboxylate (α-truxilline),

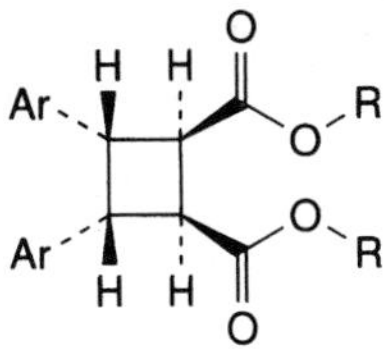

C. bis[(1R,2R,3S,5S)-2-(methoxycarbonyl)-8-methyl-8-azabicyclo[3.2.1]oct-3-yl] (1r,2c,3t,4t)-3,4-diphenylcyclobutane-1,2-dicarboxylate (β-truxilline).

# Cocaine Hydrochloride

*(Ph Eur monograph 0073)*

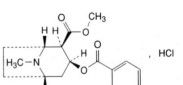

C$_{17}$H$_{21}$NO$_4$,HCl          339.8          *53-21-4*

**Action and use**

Local anaesthetic.

**Preparations**

Adrenaline and Cocaine Intranasal Solution

Cocaine Eye Drops

Cocaine Paste

*Ph Eur*

**DEFINITION**

Methyl (1R,2R,3S,5S)-3-(benzoyloxy)-8-methyl-8-azabicyclo[3.2.1]octane-2-carboxylate hydrochloride.

**Content**

98.5 per cent to 101.0 per cent (dried substance).

## CHARACTERS

**Appearance**

White or almost white, crystalline powder or colourless crystals.

**Solubility**

Very soluble in water, freely soluble in alcohol, slightly soluble in methylene chloride.

**mp**

About 197 °C, with decomposition.

## IDENTIFICATION

*First identification*   B, D.

*Second identification*   A, C, D, E.

A. Dissolve 20.0 mg in *0.01 M hydrochloric acid* and dilute to 100.0 ml with the same acid. Dilute 5.0 ml of the solution to 50.0 ml with *0.01 M hydrochloric acid*. Examined between 220 nm and 350 nm (*2.2.25*), the solution shows 2 absorption maxima, at 233 nm and 273 nm. The specific absorbance at 233 nm is 378 to 402.

B. Infrared absorption spectrophotometry (*2.2.24*).

*Comparison*   Ph. Eur. reference spectrum of cocaine hydrochloride.

C. Dissolve 0.1 g in 5 ml of *water R* and add 1 ml of *dilute ammonia R2*. A white precipitate is formed. Initiate crystallisation by scratching the wall of the tube with a glass rod. The crystals, washed with *water R* and dried *in vacuo*, melt (*2.2.14*) at 96 °C to 99 °C.

D. It gives reaction (a) of chlorides (*2.3.1*).

E. It gives the reaction of alkaloids (*2.3.1*).

## TESTS

**Solution S**

Dissolve 0.5 g in *water R* and dilute to 25 ml with the same solvent.

**Appearance of solution**

Solution S is clear (*2.2.1*) and colourless (*2.2.2, Method II*).

**Acidity**

To 10 ml of solution S add 0.05 ml of *methyl red solution R*. Not more than 0.2 ml of *0.02 M sodium hydroxide* is required to change the colour of the indicator.

**Specific optical rotation** (*2.2.7*)

− 70 to − 73 (dried substance).

Dissolve 0.50 g in *water R* and dilute to 20.0 ml with the same solvent.

**Readily carbonisable substances**

To 0.2 g add 2 ml of *sulphuric acid R*. After 15 min, the solution is not more intensely coloured than reference solution $BY_5$ (*2.2.2, Method I*).

**Related substances**

Examine by liquid chromatography (*2.2.29*).

*Test solution*   Dissolve 25.0 mg of the substance to be examined in the mobile phase and dilute to 50.0 ml with the mobile phase.

*Reference solution (a)*   Dilute 1.0 ml of the test solution to 50.0 ml with the mobile phase. Dilute 5.0 ml of this solution to 100.0 ml with the mobile phase.

*Reference solution (b)*   Dissolve 25 mg of the substance to be examined in *0.01 M sodium hydroxide* and dilute to 10.0 ml with the same solvent. Dilute 1.0 ml of the solution to 10.0 ml with *0.01 M sodium hydroxide*. Allow the solution to stand for 15 min.

*Column:*

— *size: l = 0.15 m, Ø = 4.6 mm,*

— *stationary phase: end-capped octadecylsilyl silica gel for chromatography R (5 μm) with a specific surface area of 335 m²/g, a pore size of 10 nm and a carbon loading of 19.1 per cent,*

— *temperature: 35 °C.*

*Mobile phase*   *triethylamine R, tetrahydrofuran R, acetonitrile R, water R (0.5:100:430:479.5 V/V/V/V).*

*Flow rate*   1 ml/min.

*Detection*   Spectrophotometer at 216 nm.

*Injection*   20 μl.

*Relative retention*   With reference to cocaine (retention time = about 7.4 min): degradation product = about 0.7.

*System suitability*   Reference solution (b):

— *resolution*: minimum of 5 between the peaks due to cocaine and to the degradation product.

*Limits:*

— *any impurity eluting after the principal peak*: not more than the area of the principal peak in the chromatogram obtained with reference solution (a) (0.1 per cent),

— *total*: not more than 5 times the area of the principal peak in the chromatogram obtained with reference solution (a) (0.5 per cent),

— *disregard limit*: 0.5 times the area of the principal peak in the chromatogram obtained with reference solution (a) (0.05 per cent).

**Loss on drying** (*2.2.32*)

Maximum 0.5 per cent, determined on 1.000 g by drying in an oven at 105 °C.

**Sulphated ash** (*2.4.14*)

Maximum 0.1 per cent, determined on the residue from the test for loss on drying.

## ASSAY

Dissolve 0.250 g in a mixture of 5.0 ml of *0.01 M hydrochloric acid* and 50 ml of *alcohol R*. Carry out a potentiometric titration (*2.2.20*), using *0.1 M sodium hydroxide*. Read the volume added between the 2 points of inflexion.

1 ml of *0.1 M sodium hydroxide* is equivalent to 33.98 mg of $C_{17}H_{22}ClNO_4$.

## STORAGE

Protected from light.

## IMPURITIES

A. methyl (1R,2R,3S,5S)-8-methyl-3-[[(E)-3-phenylpropenoyl]oxy]-8-azabicyclo[3.2.1]octane-2-carboxylate (cinnamoylcocaine),

B. bis[(1*R*,2*R*,3*S*,5*S*)-2-(methoxycarbonyl)-8-methyl-8-azabicyclo[3.2.1]oct-3-yl] (1*r*,2*c*,3*t*,4*t*)-2,4-diphenylcyclobutane-1,3-dicarboxylate (α-truxilline),

C. bis[(1*R*,2*R*,3*S*,5*S*)-2-(methoxycarbonyl)-8-methyl-8-azabicyclo[3.2.1]oct-3-yl] (1*r*,2*c*,3*t*,4*t*)-3,4-diphenylcyclobutane-1,2-dicarboxylate (β-truxilline).

*Ph Eur*

# Cochineal

## DEFINITION
Cochineal is the dried female insect, *Dactylopius coccus* Costa, containing eggs and larvae.

## CHARACTERISTICS
Odour, characteristic.

*Macroscopical* Purplish black or purplish grey; about 3.5 to 5.5 mm long and 3 to 4.5 mm wide, plano-convex and somewhat oval in outline; the convex dorsal surface is transversely wrinkled and shows about 11 segments; the flat or slightly concave ventral surface carries upon the anterior part two seven-jointed straight antennae, three pairs of short legs, each terminating in a single claw, and a mouth from which projects the remains of a long filiform proboscis; these appendages are frequently more or less broken. Easily reduced to powder, which is dark red or puce.

*Microscopical* Scattered irregularly over the whole dermis are numerous solitary and grouped, short, tubular wax glands; within each insect are found numerous larvae, which are characterised by their proboscides appearing as two circular coils.

## TESTS
### Colour value
To 0.5 g in *moderately fine powder* add 60 ml of *phosphate buffer pH 8.0* and heat on a water bath for 30 minutes. Cool, add sufficient *phosphate buffer pH 8.0* to produce 100 ml and filter. Dilute 5 ml of the filtrate to 100 ml with *phosphate buffer pH 8.0*. The *absorbance* of the resulting solution at the maximum at 530 nm is not less than 0.25, Appendix II B.

### Foreign matter
Complies with the test for *foreign matter*, Appendix XI D.

### Water-insoluble matter
When the insects are placed in *water*, no insoluble powder separates.

### Ash
Not more than 7.0%, Appendix XI J.

### Microbial contamination
1 g is free from *Escherichia coli*; 10 g is free from Salmonella, Appendix XVI B1.

# Coconut Oil

(*Refined Coconut Oil, Ph Eur monograph 1410*)

*8001-31-8*

## Action and use
Excipient.

*Ph Eur*

## DEFINITION
Fatty oil obtained from the dried, solid part of the endosperm of *Cocos nucifera* L., then refined.

## CHARACTERS
### Appearance
White or almost white, unctuous mass.

### Solubility
Practically insoluble in water, freely soluble in methylene chloride and in light petroleum (bp: 65-70 °C), very slightly soluble in ethanol (96 per cent).

### Refractive index
About 1.449, determined at 40 °C.

## IDENTIFICATION
A. Melting point (see Tests).

B. Composition of fatty acids (see Tests).

## TESTS
### Melting point (*2.2.14*)
23 °C to 26 °C.

### Acid value (*2.5.1*)
Maximum 0.5, determined on 20.0 g.

### Peroxide value (*2.5.5, Method A*)
Maximum 5.0.

### Unsaponifiable matter (*2.5.7*)
Maximum 1.0 per cent, determined on 5.0 g.

### Alkaline impurities in fatty oils (*2.4.19*)
It complies with the test.

### Composition of fatty acids (*2.4.22, Method B*)
Refined coconut oil is melted under gentle heating to a homogeneous liquid prior to sampling.

*Reference solution* Dissolve 15.0 mg of *tricaproin CRS*, 80.0 mg of *tristearin CRS*, 0.150 g of *tricaprin CRS*, 0.200 g of *tricaprylin CRS*, 0.450 g of *trimyristin CRS* and 1.25 g of *trilaurin CRS* in a mixture of 2 volumes of *methylene chloride R* and 8 volumes of *heptane R*, then dilute to 50 ml with the same mixture of solvents heating at 45-50 °C. Transfer 2 ml of this mixture to a 10 ml centrifuge tube with a screw cap and evaporate the solvent in a current of *nitrogen R*. Dissolve with 1 ml of *heptane R* and 1 ml of *dimethyl carbonate R* and mix vigorously under gentle heating (50-60 °C). Add, while still warm, 1 ml of a 12 g/l solution of *sodium R* in *anhydrous methanol R*, prepared with the necessary precautions, and mix vigorously for about 5 min. Add 3 ml of *distilled water R* and mix vigorously for about 30 s. Centrifuge for 15 min at 1500 *g*. Inject 1 μl of the organic phase.

Calculate the percentage content of each fatty acid using the following expression:

$$\frac{A_{x,s,c}}{\sum A_{x,s,c}} \times 100 \text{ per cent } m/m$$

$A_{x,s,c}$ is the corrected peak area of each fatty acid in the test solution:

$$A_{x,s,c} = A_{x,s} \times R_c$$

$R_c$ is the relative correction factor:

$$R_c = \frac{m_{x,r} \times A_{1,r}}{A_{x,r} \times m_{1,r}}$$

for the peaks due to caproic, caprylic, capric, lauric and myristic acid methyl esters.

$m_{x,r}$ = mass of tricaproin, tricaprylin, tricaprin, trilaurin or trimyristin in the reference solution, in milligrams;

$m_{1,r}$ = mass of tristearin in the reference solution, in milligrams:

$A_{x,r}$ = area of the peaks due to caproic, caprylic, capric, lauric and myristic acid methyl esters in the reference solution;

$A_{1,r}$ = area of the peak due to stearic acid methyl ester in the reference solution;

$A_{x,s}$ = area of the peaks due to any specified or unspecified fatty acid methyl esters;

$R_c$ = 1 for the peaks due to each of the remaining specified fatty acid methyl esters or any unspecified fatty acid methyl ester.

*Composition of the fatty-acid fraction of the oil:*
— *caproic acid ($R_{Rt}$ 0.11)*: maximum 1.5 per cent;
— *caprylic acid ($R_{Rt}$ 0.23)*: 5.0 per cent to 11.0 per cent;
— *capric acid ($R_{Rt}$ 0.56)*: 4.0 per cent to 9.0 per cent;
— *lauric acid ($R_{Rt}$ 0.75)*: 40.0 per cent to 50.0 per cent;
— *myristic acid ($R_{Rt}$ 0.85)*: 15.0 per cent to 20.0 per cent;
— *palmitic acid ($R_{Rt}$ 0.93)*: 7.0 per cent to 12.0 per cent;
— *stearic acid ($R_{Rt}$ 1.00)*: 1.5 per cent to 5.0 per cent;
— *oleic acid and isomers ($R_{Rt}$ 1.01)*: 4.0 per cent to 10.0 per cent;
— *linoleic acid ($R_{Rt}$ 1.03)*: 1.0 per cent to 3.0 per cent;
— *linolenic acid ($R_{Rt}$ 1.06)*: maximum 0.2 per cent;
— *arachidic acid ($R_{Rt}$ 1.10)*: maximum 0.2 per cent;
— *eicosenoic acid ($R_{Rt}$ 1.11)*: maximum 0.2 per cent.

## STORAGE
In a well-filled container, protected from light.

*Ph Eur*

# Cocoyl Caprylocaprate

*(Ph Eur monograph 1411)*

**Action and use**
Excipient.

*Ph Eur*

## DEFINITION
Mixture of esters of saturated $C_{12}$ - $C_{18}$ alcohols with caprylic (octanoic) and capric (decanoic) acids obtained by the reaction of these acids with vegetable saturated fatty alcohols.

## CHARACTERS
**Appearance**
Slightly yellowish liquid.

**Solubility**
Practically insoluble in water, miscible with ethanol (96 per cent) and with liquid paraffin.

**Relative density**
About 0.86.

**Refractive index**
About 1.445.

**Viscosity**
About 11 mPa·s.

## IDENTIFICATION
A. Freezing point (*2.2.18*): Maximum 15 °C.

B. Infrared absorption spectrophotometry (*2.2.24*).

*Comparison   cocoyl caprylocaprate CRS.*

C. Composition of fatty acids and fatty alcohols (see Tests).

## TESTS
**Appearance**
The substance to be examined is not more intensely coloured than reference solution $Y_5$ (*2.2.2, Method I*).

**Acid value** (*2.5.1*)
Maximum 0.5, determined on 5.00 g.

**Hydroxyl value** (*2.5.3, Method A*)
Maximum 5.0.

**Iodine value** (*2.5.4, Method A*)
Maximum 1.0.

**Saponification value** (*2.5.6*)
160 to 173.

**Composition of fatty acids and fatty alcohols** (*2.4.22, Method C*)
Use the chromatogram obtained with the following reference solution for identification of the peaks due to the fatty alcohols.

*Reference solution*   Dissolve the amounts of the substances listed in the following table in 10 ml of *heptane R*.

| Substance | Amount (mg) |
|---|---|
| *Methyl caproate R* | 10 |
| *Methyl caprylate R* | 90 |
| *Methyl caprate R* | 50 |
| *Methyl laurate R* | 20 |
| *Methyl myristate R* | 10 |
| *Methyl palmitate R* | 10 |
| *Methyl stearate R* | 10 |
| *Capric alcohol R* | 10 |
| *Lauryl alcohol R* | 100 |
| *Myristyl alcohol R* | 40 |
| *Cetyl alcohol CRS* | 30 |
| *Stearyl alcohol CRS* | 20 |

Consider the sum of the areas of the peaks due to the fatty acids listed below to be equal to 100 and the sum of the areas of the peaks due to the fatty alcohols listed below to be equal to 100.

Composition of the fatty acid fraction of the substance:
— *caproic acid*: maximum 2.0 per cent,
— *caprylic acid*: 50.0 per cent to 80.0 per cent,
— *capric acid*: 20.0 per cent to 50.0 per cent,
— *lauric acid*: maximum 3.0 per cent,
— *myristic acid*: maximum 2.0 per cent.

Composition of the fatty alcohol fraction of the substance:
— *capric alcohol*: maximum 3.0 per cent,
— *lauryl alcohol*: 48.0 per cent to 63.0 per cent,
— *myristyl alcohol*: 18.0 per cent to 27.0 per cent,
— *cetyl alcohol*: 6.0 per cent to 13.0 per cent,

— *stearyl alcohol*: 9.0 per cent to 16.0 per cent.

**Water** (*2.5.12*)

Maximum 0.1 per cent, determined on 5.00 g.

**Total ash** (*2.4.16*)

Maximum 0.1 per cent, determined on 1.0 g.

_____ *Ph Eur*

# Codeine

(*Ph Eur monograph 0076*)

$C_{18}H_{21}NO_3,H_2O$          317.4          76-57-3

**Action and use**

Opioid receptor agonist; analgesic.

*Ph Eur* _____

**DEFINITION**

7,8-Didehydro-4,5α-epoxy-3-methoxy-17-methylmorphinan-6α-ol.

**Content**

99.0 per cent to 101.0 per cent (dried substance).

**CHARACTERS**

**Appearance**

White or almost white, crystalline powder or colourless crystals.

**Solubility**

Soluble in boiling water, freely soluble in ethanol (96 per cent).

**IDENTIFICATION**

*First identification   A, C.*

*Second identification   A, B, D, E.*

A. Melting point (*2.2.14*): 155 °C to 159 °C.

B. To 2.0 ml of solution S (see Tests) add 50 ml of *water R* then 10 ml of *1 M sodium hydroxide* and dilute to 100.0 ml with *water R*. Examined between 250 nm and 350 nm (*2.2.25*), the solution shows only 1 absorption maximum, at 284 nm. The specific absorbance at the absorption maximum is about 50 (dried substance).

C. Infrared absorption spectrophotometry (*2.2.24*).

*Preparation*   Dried substance prepared as a disc of *potassium bromide R*.

*Comparison*   codeine CRS.

D. To about 10 mg add 1 ml of *sulphuric acid R* and 0.05 ml of *ferric chloride solution R2* and heat on a water-bath. A blue colour develops. Add 0.05 ml of *nitric acid R*. The colour changes to red.

E. It gives the reaction of alkaloids (*2.3.1*).

**TESTS**

**Solution S**

Dissolve 50 mg in *carbon dioxide-free water R* and dilute to 10.0 ml with the same solvent.

**Appearance of solution**

Solution S is clear (*2.2.1*) and colourless (*2.2.2, Method II*).

**Specific optical rotation** (*2.2.7*)

− 142 to − 146 (dried substance).

Dissolve 0.50 g in *ethanol (96 per cent) R* and dilute to 25.0 ml with the same solvent.

**Related substances**

Liquid chromatography (*2.2.29*).

*Test solution*   Dissolve 0.100 g of the substance to be examined and 0.100 g of *sodium octanesulphonate R* in the mobile phase and dilute to 10.0 ml with the mobile phase.

*Reference solution (a)*   Dissolve 5.0 mg of *codeine impurity A CRS* in the mobile phase and dilute to 5.0 ml with the mobile phase.

*Reference solution (b)*   Dilute 1.0 ml of reference solution (a) to 20.0 ml with the mobile phase.

*Reference solution (c)*   Dilute 1.0 ml of the test solution to 50.0 ml with the mobile phase. Dilute 5.0 ml of this solution to 100.0 ml with the mobile phase.

*Reference solution (d)*   To 0.25 ml of the test solution, add 2.5 ml of reference solution (a).

*Column:*

— *size: l* = 0.25 m, Ø = 4.6 mm;

— *stationary phase*: end-capped octylsilyl silica gel for chromatography R (5 μm).

*Mobile phase*   Dissolve 1.08 g of *sodium octanesulphonate R* in a mixture of 20 ml of *glacial acetic acid R* and 250 ml of *acetonitrile R* and dilute to 1000 ml with *water R*.

*Flow rate*   2 ml/min.

*Detection*   Spectrophotometer at 245 nm.

*Injection*   10 μl.

*Run time*   10 times the retention time of codeine.

*Relative retention*   With reference to codeine (retention time = about 6 min): impurity B = about 0.6; impurity E = about 0.7; impurity A = about 2.0; impurity C = about 2.3; impurity D = about 3.6.

*System suitability*   Reference solution (d):

— *resolution*: minimum 3 between the peaks due to codeine and impurity A.

*Limits:*

— *correction factor*: for the calculation of content, multiply the peak area of impurity C by 0.25;

— *impurity A*: not more than twice the area of the principal peak in the chromatogram obtained with reference solution (b) (1.0 per cent);

— *impurities B, C, D, E*: for each impurity, not more than twice the area of the principal peak in the chromatogram obtained with reference solution (c) (0.2 per cent);

— *any other impurity*: for each impurity, not more than the area of the principal peak in the chromatogram obtained with reference solution (c) (0.1 per cent);

— *sum of impurities other than A*: not more than 10 times the area of the principal peak in the chromatogram obtained with reference solution (c) (1.0 per cent);

— *disregard limit*: 0.5 times the area of the principal peak in the chromatogram obtained with reference solution (c) (0.05 per cent).

**Loss on drying** (*2.2.32*)

4.0 per cent to 6.0 per cent, determined on 1.000 g by drying in an oven at 105 °C.

**Sulphated ash** (*2.4.14*)

Maximum 0.1 per cent, determined on 1.0 g.

## ASSAY

Dissolve 0.250 g in 10 ml of *anhydrous acetic acid R*. Add 20 ml of *dioxan R*. Titrate with *0.1 M perchloric acid*, using 0.05 ml of *crystal violet solution R* as indicator.

1 ml of *0.1 M perchloric acid* is equivalent to 29.94 mg of $C_{18}H_{21}NO_3$.

## STORAGE

Protected from light.

## IMPURITIES

*Specified impurities*   A, B, C, D, E.

*Other detectable impurities*   (The following substances would, if present at a sufficient level, be detected by one or other of the tests in the monograph. They are limited by the general acceptance criterion for other/unspecified impurities and/or by the general monograph *Substances for pharmaceutical use (2034)*. It is therefore not necessary to identify these impurities for demonstration of compliance. See also *5.10*. *Control of impurities in substances for pharmaceutical use*): F, G.

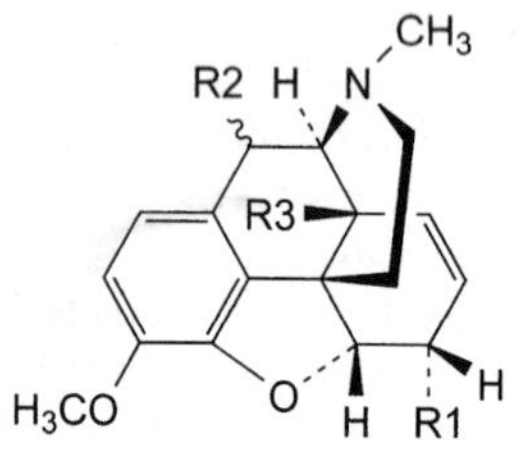

A. R1 = OCH₃, R2 = R3 = H: 7,8-didehydro-4,5α-epoxy-3,6α-dimethoxy-17-methylmorphinan (methylcodeine),

E. R1 = R2 = OH, R3 = H: 7,8-didehydro-4,5α-epoxy-3-methoxy-17-methylmorphinan-6α,10-diol,

F. R1 = R3 = OH, R2 = H: 7,8-didehydro-4,5α-epoxy-3-methoxy-17-methylmorphinan-6α,14-diol,

B. morphine,

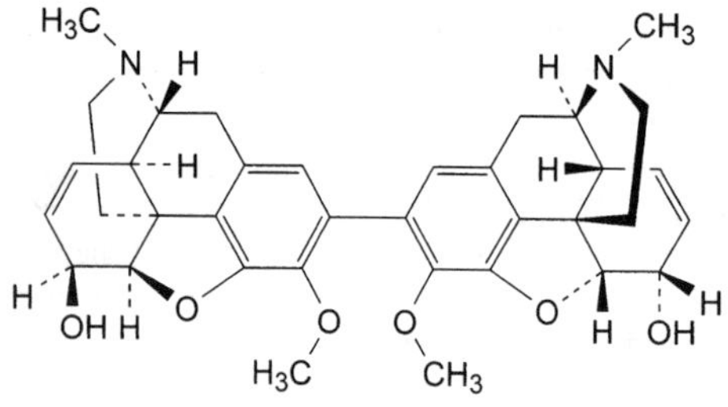

C. 7,7′,8,8′-tetradehydro-4,5α:4′,5′α-diepoxy-3,3′-dimethoxy-17,17′-dimethyl-2,2′-bimorphinanyl-6α,6′α-diol (codeine dimer),

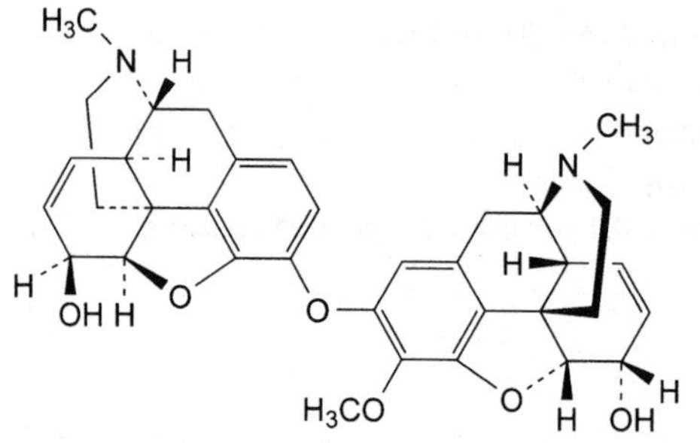

D. 7,8-didehydro-2-[(7,8-didehydro-4,5α-epoxy-6α-hydroxy-17-methylmorphinan-3-yl)oxy]-4,5α-epoxy-3-methoxy-17-methylmorphinan-6α-ol (3-*O*-(codein-2-yl)morphine),

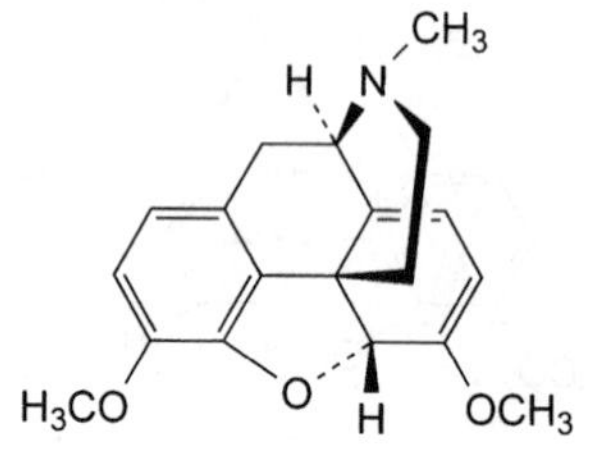

G. 6,7,8,14-tetradehydro-4,5α-epoxy-3,6-dimethoxy-17-methylmorphinan (thebaine).

*—————————— Ph Eur*

# Codeine Hydrochloride

(*Codeine Hydrochloride Dihydrate, Ph Eur monograph 1412*)

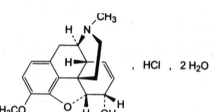

$C_{18}H_{21}NO_3,HCl,2H_2O$      371.9      *1422-07-7*

**Action and use**

Opioid receptor agonist; analgesic.

*Ph Eur _____*

## DEFINITION

7,8-Didehydro-4,5α-epoxy-3-methoxy-17-methylmorphinan-6α-ol hydrochloride dihydrate.

**Content**

99.0 per cent to 101.0 per cent (anhydrous substance).

## CHARACTERS

**Appearance**

White or almost white, crystalline powder or small, colourless crystals.

**Solubility**

Soluble in water, slightly soluble in ethanol (96 per cent), practically insoluble in cyclohexane.

## IDENTIFICATION

*First identification*   A, D.

*Second identification*   B, C, D, E.

A. Infrared absorption spectrophotometry (*2.2.24*).

*Comparison   Ph. Eur. reference spectrum of codeine hydrochloride dihydrate.*

B. To 5 ml of solution S (see Tests) add 1 ml of a mixture of equal volumes of *strong sodium hydroxide solution R* and *water R* and initiate crystallisation, if necessary, by scratching the wall of the tube with a glass rod and cooling in iced water. Wash the precipitate with *water R* and dry at 100-105 °C.It melts (*2.2.15*) at 155 °C to 159 °C.

C. To about 10 mg add 1 ml of *sulphuric acid R* and 0.05 ml of *ferric chloride solution R2* and heat on a water-bath. A blue colour develops. Add 0.05 ml of *nitric acid R*. The colour changes to red.

D. Solution S gives reaction (a) of chlorides (*2.3.1*).

E. It gives the reaction of alkaloids (*2.3.1*).

## TESTS

### Solution S
Dissolve 2.00 g in *carbon dioxide-free water R* prepared from *distilled water R* and dilute to 50.0 ml with the same solvent.

### Appearance of solution
Solution S is clear (*2.2.1*) and not more intensely coloured than reference solution $Y_6$ (*2.2.2, Method II*).

### Acidity or alkalinity
To 5 ml of solution S add 5 ml of *carbon dioxide-free water R*. Add 0.05 ml of *methyl red solution R* and 0.2 ml of *0.02 M hydrochloric acid*; the solution is red. Add 0.4 ml of *0.02 M sodium hydroxide*; the solution becomes yellow.

### Specific optical rotation (*2.2.7*)
– 117 to – 121 (anhydrous substance).

Dilute 5.0 ml of solution S to 10.0 ml with *water R*.

### Related substances
Liquid chromatography (*2.2.29*).

*Test solution*   Dissolve 0.100 g of the substance to be examined and 0.100 g of *sodium octanesulphonate R* in the mobile phase and dilute to 10.0 ml with the mobile phase.

*Reference solution (a)*   Dissolve 5.0 mg of *codeine impurity A CRS* in the mobile phase and dilute to 5.0 ml with the mobile phase.

*Reference solution (b)*   Dilute 1.0 ml of reference solution (a) to 20.0 ml with the mobile phase.

*Reference solution (c)*   Dilute 1.0 ml of the test solution to 50.0 ml with the mobile phase. Dilute 5.0 ml of this solution to 100.0 ml with the mobile phase.

*Reference solution (d)*   To 0.25 ml of the test solution add 2.5 ml of reference solution (a).

*Column:*
— *size: l* = 0.25 m, Ø = 4.6 mm,
— *stationary phase: end-capped octylsilyl silica gel for chromatography R* (5 μm).

*Mobile phase*   Dissolve 1.08 g of *sodium octanesulphonate R* in a mixture of 20 ml of *glacial acetic acid R* and 250 ml of *acetonitrile R* and dilute to 1000 ml with *water R*.

*Flow rate*   2 ml/min.

*Detection*   Spectrophotometer at 245 nm.

*Injection*   10 μl.

*Run time*   10 times the retention time of codeine.

*Relative retention*   With reference to codeine (retention time = about 6 min): impurity B = about 0.6; impurity E = about 0.7; impurity A = about 2.0; impurity C = about 2.3; impurity D = about 3.6.

*System suitability*   Reference solution (d):

— *resolution*: minimum 3 between the peaks due to codeine and impurity A.

*Limits:*
— *correction factor*: for the calculation of content, multiply the peak area of impurity C by 0.25,
— *impurity A*: not more than twice the area of the principal peak in the chromatogram obtained with reference solution (b) (1.0 per cent),
— *impurities B, C, D, E*: for each impurity, not more than twice the area of the principal peak in the chromatogram obtained with reference solution (c) (0.2 per cent),
— *any other impurity*: for each impurity, not more than the area of the principal peak in the chromatogram obtained with reference solution (c) (0.1 per cent),
— *sum of impurities other than A*: not more than 10 times the area of the principal peak in the chromatogram obtained with reference solution (c) (1.0 per cent),
— *disregard limit*: 0.5 times the area of the principal peak in the chromatogram obtained with reference solution (c) (0.05 per cent).

### Sulphates (*2.4.13*)
Maximum 0.1 per cent.

Dilute 5 ml of solution S to 20 ml with *distilled water R*. 15 ml of the solution complies with the limit test for sulphates.

### Water (*2.5.12*)
8.0 per cent to 10.5 per cent, determined on 0.250 g.

## ASSAY
Dissolve 0.300 g in a mixture of 5 ml of *0.01 M hydrochloric acid R* and 30 ml of *ethanol (96 per cent) R*. Carry out a potentiometric titration (*2.2.20*), using *0.1 M sodium hydroxide*. Read the volume added between the 2 points of inflexion.

1 ml of *0.1 M sodium hydroxide* is equivalent to 33.59 mg of $C_{18}H_{22}ClNO_3$.

## STORAGE
Protected from light.

## IMPURITIES
*Specified impurities   A, B, C, D, E.*

*Other detectable impurities (the following substances would, if present at a sufficient level, be detected by one or other of the tests in the monograph. They are limited by the general acceptance criterion for other/unspecified impurities and/or by the general monograph Substances for pharmaceutical use (2034). It is therefore not necessary to identify these impurities for demonstration of compliance. See also 5.10. Control of impurities in substances for pharmaceutical use) : F, G.*

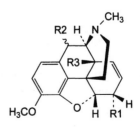

A. R1 = OCH₃, R2 = R3 = H: 7,8-didehydro-4,5α-epoxy-3,6α-dimethoxy-17-methylmorphinan (methylcodeine),

E. R1 = R2 = OH, R3 = H: 7,8-didehydro-4,5α-epoxy-3-methoxy-17-methylmorphinan-6α,10-diol,

F. R1 = R3 = OH, R2 = H: 7,8-didehydro-4,5α-epoxy-3-methoxy-17-methylmorphinan-6α,14-diol,

B. morphine,

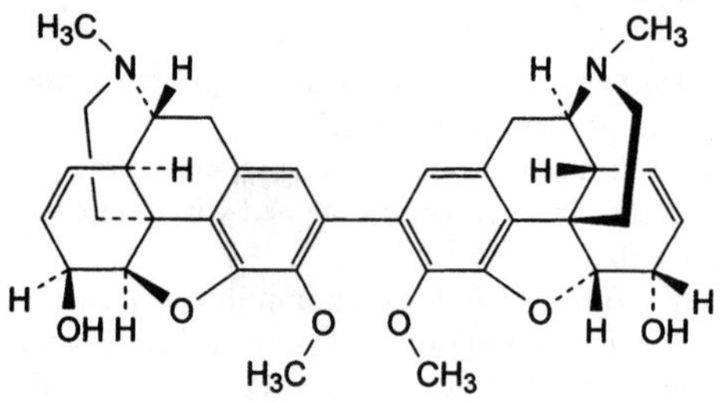

C. 7,7',8,8'-tetrahydro-4,5α:4',5'α-diepoxy-3,3'-dimethoxy-17,17'-dimethyl-2,2'-bimorphinanyl-6α,6'α-diol (codeine dimer),

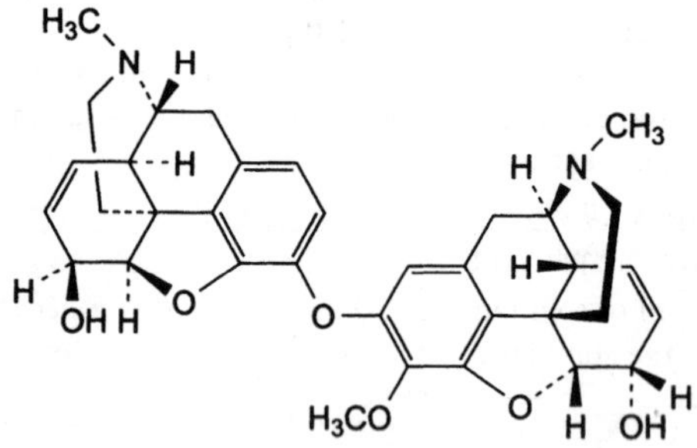

D. 7,8-didehydro-2-[(7,8-didehydro-4,5α-epoxy-6α-hydroxy-17-methylmorphinan-3-yl)oxy]-4,5α-epoxy-3-methoxy-17-methylmorphinan-6α-ol (3-O-(codein-2-yl)morphine),

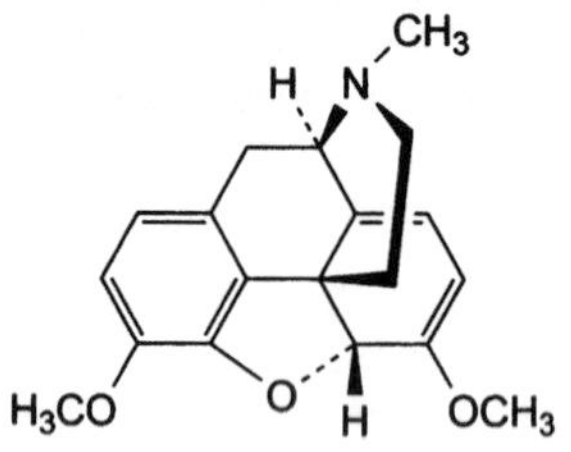

G. 6,7,8,14-tetrahydro-4,5α-epoxy-3,6-dimethoxy-17-methylmorphinan (thebaine).

*Ph Eur*

# Codeine Phosphate

(*Codeine Phosphate Hemihydrate,*
*Ph Eur monograph 0074*)

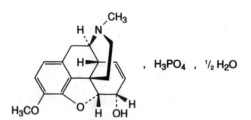

, H₃PO₄ , ½ H₂O

$C_{18}H_{21}NO_3,H_3PO_4,\frac{1}{2}H_2O$   406.4          41444-62-6

## Action and use
Opioid receptor agonist; analgesic.

## Preparations
Co-codamol Capsules

Co-codamol Tablets
Effervescent Co-codamol Tablets
Co-codaprin Tablets
Dispersible Co-codaprin Tablets
Codeine Linctus
Paediatric Codeine Linctus
Codeine Phosphate Injection
Codeine Phosphate Oral Solution
Codeine Phosphate Tablets
Paracetamol, Codeine Phosphate and Caffeine Capsules
Paracetamol, Codeine Phosphate and Caffeine Tablets

*Ph Eur*

## DEFINITION
7,8-Didehydro-4,5α-epoxy-3-methoxy-17-methylmorphinan-6α-ol phosphate hemihydrate.

## Content
98.5 per cent to 101.0 per cent (dried substance).

## CHARACTERS
### Appearance
White or almost white, crystalline powder or small, colourless crystals.

### Solubility
Freely soluble in water, slightly soluble or very slightly soluble in ethanol (96 per cent).

## IDENTIFICATION
*First identification*   B, E, F.

*Second identification*   A, C, D, E, F, G.

A. Dilute 1.0 ml of solution S (see Tests) to 100.0 ml with *water R*. To 25.0 ml of this solution add 25 ml of *water R* then 10 ml of *1 M sodium hydroxide* and dilute to 100.0 ml with *water R*. Examined between 250 nm and 350 nm (*2.2.25*), the solution shows only 1 absorption maximum, at 284 nm. The specific absorbance at the absorption maximum is about 38 (dried substance).

B. Infrared absorption spectrophotometry (*2.2.24*).

*Preparation*   Dissolve 0.20 g in 4 ml of *water R*. Add 1 ml of a mixture of equal volumes of *strong sodium hydroxide solution R* and *water R* and initiate crystallisation, if necessary, by scratching the wall of the tube with a glass rod and cooling in iced water. Wash the precipitate with *water R* and dry at 100-105 °C. Examine the dried precipitate prepared as discs using *potassium bromide R*.

*Comparison*   Ph. Eur. reference spectrum of codeine.

C. Dissolve 0.20 g in 4 ml of *water R*. Add 1 ml of a mixture of equal volumes of *strong sodium hydroxide solution R* and *water R* and initiate crystallisation, if necessary, by scratching the wall of the tube with a glass rod and cooling in iced water. The precipitate, washed with *water R* and dried at 100-105 °C, melts (*2.2.14*) at 155 °C to 159 °C.

D. To about 10 mg add 1 ml of *sulphuric acid R* and 0.05 ml of *ferric chloride solution R2* and heat on a water-bath. A blue colour develops. Add 0.05 ml of *nitric acid R*. The colour changes to red.

E. It complies with the test for loss on drying (see Tests).

F. Solution S gives reaction (a) of phosphates (*2.3.1*).

G. It gives the reaction of alkaloids (*2.3.1*).

## TESTS

### Solution S

Dissolve 1.00 g in *carbon dioxide-free water R* prepared from *distilled water R* and dilute to 25.0 ml with the same solvent.

### pH (*2.2.3*)

4.0 to 5.0 for solution S.

### Specific optical rotation (*2.2.7*)

− 98 to − 102 (dried substance).

Dilute 5.0 ml of solution S to 10.0 ml with *water R*.

### Related substances

Liquid chromatography (*2.2.29*).

*Test solution* Dissolve 0.100 g of the substance to be examined and 0.100 g of *sodium octanesulphonate R* in the mobile phase and dilute to 10.0 ml with the mobile phase.

*Reference solution (a)* Dissolve 5.0 mg of *codeine impurity A CRS* in the mobile phase and dilute to 5.0 ml with the mobile phase.

*Reference solution (b)* Dilute 1.0 ml of reference solution (a) to 20.0 ml with the mobile phase.

*Reference solution (c)* Dilute 1.0 ml of the test solution to 50.0 ml with the mobile phase. Dilute 5.0 ml of this solution to 100.0 ml with the mobile phase.

*Reference solution (d)* To 0.25 ml of the test solution add 2.5 ml of reference solution (a).

*Column:*
— *size*: $l$ = 0.25 m, Ø = 4.6 mm,
— *stationary phase*: end-capped octylsilyl silica gel for chromatography R (5 μm).

*Mobile phase* Dissolve 1.08 g of *sodium octanesulphonate R* in a mixture of 20 ml of *glacial acetic acid R* and 250 ml of *acetonitrile R* and dilute to 1000 ml with *water R*.

*Flow rate* 2 ml/min.

*Detection* Spectrophotometer at 245 nm.

*Injection* 10 μl.

*Run time* 10 times the retention time of codeine.

*Relative retention* With reference to codeine (retention time = about 6 min): impurity B = about 0.6; impurity E = about 0.7; impurity A = about 2.0; impurity C = about 2.3; impurity D = about 3.6.

*System suitability* Reference solution (d):
— *resolution*: minimum 3 between the peaks due to codeine and impurity A.

*Limits:*
— *correction factor*: for the calculation of content, multiply the peak area of impurity C by 0.25,
— *impurity A*: not more than twice the area of the principal peak in the chromatogram obtained with reference solution (b) (1.0 per cent),
— *impurities B, C, D, E*: for each impurity, not more than twice the area of the principal peak in the chromatogram obtained with reference solution (c) (0.2 per cent),
— *any other impurity*: for each impurity, not more than the area of the principal peak in the chromatogram obtained with reference solution (c) (0.1 per cent),
— *sum of impurities other than A*: not more than 10 times the area of the principal peak in the chromatogram obtained with reference solution (c) (1.0 per cent),
— *disregard limit*: 0.5 times the area of the principal peak in the chromatogram obtained with reference solution (c) (0.05 per cent).

### Sulphates (*2.4.13*)

Maximum 0.1 per cent.

Dilute 5 ml of solution S to 20 ml with *distilled water R*. 15 ml of the solution complies with the limit test for sulphates.

### Loss on drying (*2.2.32*)

1.5 per cent to 3.0 per cent, determined on 1.000 g by drying in an oven at 105 °C.

## ASSAY

Dissolve 0.350 g in a mixture of 10 ml of *anhydrous acetic acid R* and 20 ml of *dioxan R*. Titrate with *0.1 M perchloric acid* using 0.05 ml of *crystal violet solution R* as indicator.

1 ml of *0.1 M perchloric acid* is equivalent to 39.74 mg of $C_{18}H_{24}NO_7P$.

## STORAGE

Protected from light.

## IMPURITIES

*Specified impurities A, B, C, D, E.*

*Other detectable impurities* (the following substances would, if present at a sufficient level, be detected by one or other of the tests in the monograph. They are limited by the general acceptance criterion for other/unspecified impurities and/or by the general monograph *Substances for pharmaceutical use (2034)*. It is therefore not necessary to identify these impurities for demonstration of compliance. See also *5.10*. *Control of impurities in substances for pharmaceutical use*) : *F, G*.

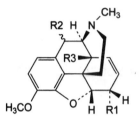

A. R1 = OCH₃, R2 = R3 = H: 7,8-didehydro-4,5α-epoxy-3,6α-dimethoxy-17-methylmorphinan (methylcodeine),

E. R1 = R2 = OH, R3 = H: 7,8-didehydro-4,5α-epoxy-3-methoxy-17-methylmorphinan-6α,10-diol,

F. R1 = R3 = OH, R2 = H: 7,8-didehydro-4,5α-epoxy-3-methoxy-17-methylmorphinan-6α,14-diol,

B. morphine,

C. 7,7′,8,8′-tetradehydro-4,5α:4′,5′α-diepoxy-3,3′-dimethoxy-17,17′-dimethyl-2,2′-bimorphinanyl-6α,6′α-diol (codeine dimer),

D. 7,8-didehydro-2-[(7,8-didehydro-4,5α-epoxy-6α-hydroxy-17-methylmorphinan-3-yl)oxy]-4,5α-epoxy-3-methoxy-17-methylmorphinan-6α-ol (3-*O*-(codein-2-yl)morphine),

G. 6,7,8,14-tetradehydro-4,5α-epoxy-3,6-dimethoxy-17-methylmorphinan (thebaine).

*Ph Eur*

# Codeine Phosphate Sesquihydrate

*(Ph Eur monograph 0075)*

, H₃PO₄ , 1½ H₂O

$C_{18}H_{21}NO_3,H_3PO_4,1\frac{1}{2}H_2O$    424.4    *5913-76-8*

**Action and use**
Opioid receptor agonist; analgesic.

**Preparations**
Codeine Linctus
Paediatric Codeine Linctus
Codeine Phosphate Oral Solution
Codeine Phosphate Tablets

*Ph Eur*

## DEFINITION
7,8-Didehydro-4,5α-epoxy-3-methoxy-17-methylmorphinan-6α-ol phosphate sesquihydrate.

**Content**
98.5 per cent to 101.0 per cent (dried substance).

## CHARACTERS
**Appearance**
White or almost white, crystalline powder or small, colourless crystals.

**Solubility**
Freely soluble in water, slightly soluble in ethanol (96 per cent).

## IDENTIFICATION
*First identification*    B, E, F.

*Second identification*    A, C, D, E, F, G.

A. Dilute 1.0 ml of solution S (see Tests) to 100.0 ml with *water R*. To 25.0 ml of this solution add 25 ml of *water R* then 10 ml of *1 M sodium hydroxide* and dilute to 100.0 ml with *water R*. Examined between 250 nm and 350 nm (*2.2.25*), the solution shows only 1 absorption maximum, at 284 nm. The specific absorbance at the absorption maximum is about 38 (dried substance).

B. Infrared absorption spectrophotometry (*2.2.24*).

*Preparation*    Dissolve 0.20 g in 4 ml of *water R*. Add 1 ml of a mixture of equal volumes of *strong sodium hydroxide solution R* and *water R* and initiate crystallisation, if necessary, by scratching the wall of the tube with a glass rod and cooling in iced water. Wash the precipitate with *water R* and dry at 100-105 °C. Examine the dried precipitate prepared as discs using *potassium bromide R*.

*Comparison*    Ph. Eur. reference spectrum of codeine.

C. Dissolve 0.20 g in 4 ml of *water R*. Add 1 ml of a mixture of equal volumes of *strong sodium hydroxide solution R* and *water R* and initiate crystallisation, if necessary, by scratching the wall of the tube with a glass rod and cooling in iced water. The precipitate, washed with *water R* and dried at 100-105 °C, melts (*2.2.14*) at 155 °C to 159 °C.

D. To about 10 mg add 1 ml of *sulphuric acid R* and 0.05 ml of *ferric chloride solution R2* and heat on a water-bath. A blue colour develops. Add 0.05 ml of *nitric acid R*. The colour changes to red.

E. It complies with the test for loss on drying (see Tests).

F. Solution S gives reaction (a) of phosphates (*2.3.1*).

G. It gives the reaction of alkaloids (*2.3.1*).

## TESTS
**Solution S**
Dissolve 1.00 g in *carbon dioxide-free water R* prepared from *distilled water R* and dilute to 25.0 ml with the same solvent.

**pH** (*2.2.3*)
4.0 to 5.0 for solution S.

**Specific optical rotation** (*2.2.7*)
− 98 to − 102 (dried substance).

Dilute 5.0 ml of solution S to 10.0 ml with *water R*.

**Related substances**
Liquid chromatography (*2.2.29*).

*Test solution*    Dissolve 0.100 g of the substance to be examined and 0.100 g of *sodium octanesulphonate R* in the mobile phase and dilute to 10.0 ml with the mobile phase.

*Reference solution (a)*    Dissolve 5.0 mg of *codeine impurity A CRS* in the mobile phase and dilute to 5.0 ml with the mobile phase.

*Reference solution (b)*    Dilute 1.0 ml of reference solution (a) to 20.0 ml with the mobile phase.

*Reference solution (c)*    Dilute 1.0 ml of the test solution to 50.0 ml with the mobile phase. Dilute 5.0 ml of this solution to 100.0 ml with the mobile phase.

*Reference solution (d)*    To 0.25 ml of the test solution add 2.5 ml of reference solution (a).

*Column:*
— *size*: *l* = 0.25 m, Ø = 4.6 mm,

— *stationary phase: end-capped octylsilyl silica gel for chromatography R* (5 μm).

*Mobile phase*   Dissolve 1.08 g of *sodium octanesulphonate R* in a mixture of 20 ml of *glacial acetic acid R* and 250 ml of *acetonitrile R* and dilute to 1000 ml with *water R*.

*Flow rate*   2 ml/min.

*Detection*   Spectrophotometer at 245 nm.

*Injection*   10 μl.

*Run time*   10 times the retention time of codeine.

*Relative retention*   With reference to codeine (retention time = about 6 min): impurity B = about 0.6; impurity E = about 0.7; impurity A = about 2.0; impurity C = about 2.3; impurity D = about 3.6.

*System suitability*   Reference solution (d):
— *resolution*: minimum 3 between the peaks due to codeine and impurity A.

*Limits:*
— *correction factor*: for the calculation of content, multiply the peak area of impurity C by 0.25,
— *impurity A*: not more than twice the area of the principal peak in the chromatogram obtained with reference solution (b) (1.0 per cent),
— *impurities B, C, D, E*: for each impurity, not more than twice the area of the principal peak in the chromatogram obtained with reference solution (c) (0.2 per cent),
— *any other impurity*: for each impurity, not more than the area of the principal peak in the chromatogram obtained with reference solution (c) (0.1 per cent),
— *sum of impurities other than A*: not more than 10 times the area of the principal peak in the chromatogram obtained with reference solution (c) (1.0 per cent),
— *disregard limit*: 0.5 times the area of the principal peak in the chromatogram obtained with reference solution (c) (0.05 per cent).

**Sulphates** (*2.4.13*)
Maximum 0.1 per cent.

Dilute 5 ml of solution S to 20 ml with *distilled water R*. 15 ml of the solution complies with the limit test for sulphates.

**Loss on drying** (*2.2.32*)
5.0 per cent to 7.5 per cent, determined on 0.500 g by drying in an oven at 105 °C.

**ASSAY**

Dissolve 0.350 g in a mixture of 10 ml of *anhydrous acetic acid R* and 20 ml of *dioxan R*. Titrate with *0.1 M perchloric acid* using 0.05 ml of *crystal violet solution R* as indicator.

1 ml of *0.1 M perchloric acid* is equivalent to 39.74 mg of $C_{18}H_{24}NO_7P$.

**STORAGE**

Protected from light.

**IMPURITIES**

*Specified impurities   A, B, C, D, E.*

*Other detectable impurities* (the following substances would, if present at a sufficient level, be detected by one or other of the tests in the monograph. They are limited by the general acceptance criterion for other/unspecified impurities and/or by the general monograph *Substances for pharmaceutical use (2034)*. It is therefore not necessary to identify these impurities for demonstration of compliance. See also *5.10*. *Control of impurities in substances for pharmaceutical use) : F, G.*

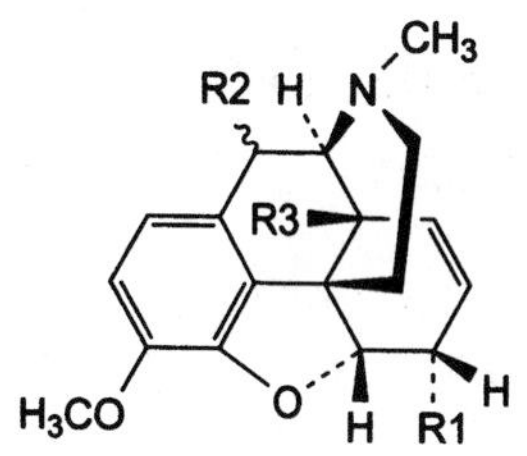

A. R1 = OCH₃, R2 = R3 = H: 7,8-didehydro-4,5α-epoxy-3,6α-dimethoxy-17-methylmorphinan (methylcodeine),

E. R1 = R2 = OH, R3 = H: 7,8-didehydro-4,5α-epoxy-3-methoxy-17-methylmorphinan-6α,10-diol,

F. R1 = R3 = OH, R2 = H: 7,8-didehydro-4,5α-epoxy-3-methoxy-17-methylmorphinan-6α,14-diol,

B. morphine,

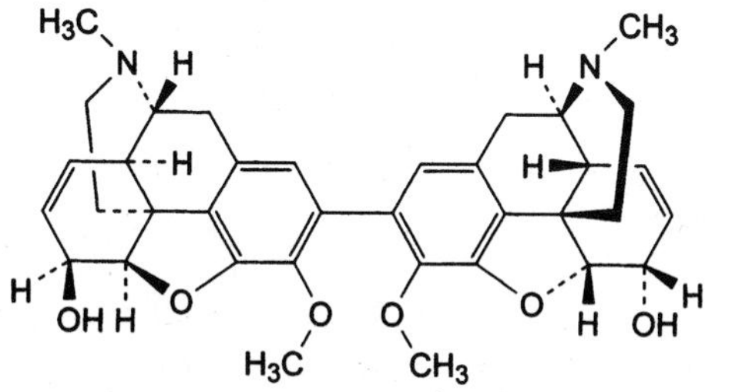

C. 7,7′,8,8′-tetradehydro-4,5α:4′,5′α-diepoxy-3,3′-dimethoxy-17,17′-dimethyl-2,2′-bimorphinanyl-6α,6′α-diol (codeine dimer),

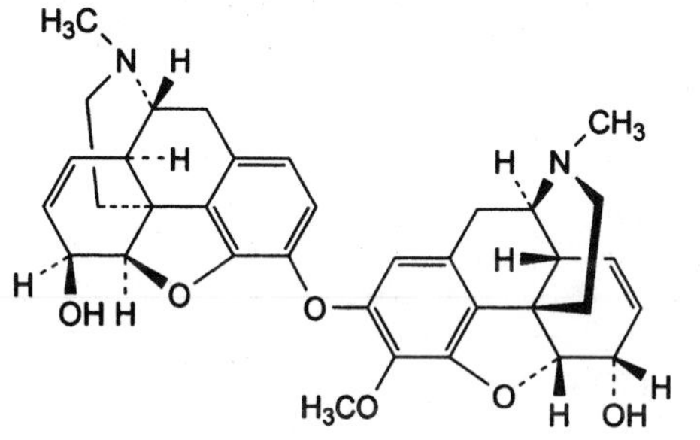

D. 7,8-didehydro-2-[(7,8-didehydro-4,5α-epoxy-6α-hydroxy-17-methylmorphinan-3-yl)oxy]-4,5α-epoxy-3-methoxy-17-methylmorphinan-6α-ol (3-O-(codein-2-yl)morphine),

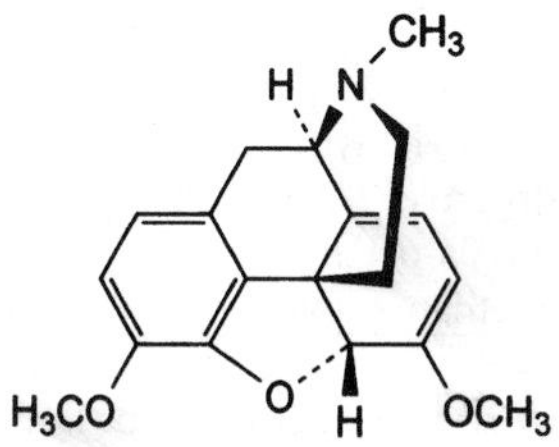

G. 6,7,8,14-tetradehydro-4,5α-epoxy-3,6-dimethoxy-17-methylmorphinan (thebaine).

# Codergocrine Mesilate

*(Ph Eur monograph 2060)*

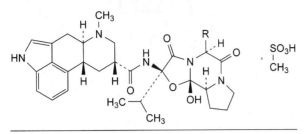

| Name | Mol. Formula | $M_r$ | R |
|------|-------------|-------|---|
| dihydroergocornine mesilate | $C_{32}H_{45}N_5O_8S$ | 660 | H₃C–CH(CH₃)– |
| dihydroergocristine mesilate | $C_{36}H_{45}N_5O_8S$ | 708 | –CH₂–C₆H₅ |
| α-dihydroergocryptine mesilate | $C_{33}H_{47}N_5O_8S$ | 674 | –CH₂–CH(CH₃)₂ |
| β-dihydroergocryptine mesilate | $C_{33}H_{47}N_5O_8S$ | 674 | H₃C–CH–CH₂–CH₃ |

## Action and use
Vasodilator.

## Preparation
Codergocrine Tablets

*Ph Eur*

## DEFINITION
A mixture of:
— (6aR,9R,10aR)-N-[(2R,5S,10aS,10bS)-10b-hydroxy-2,5-bis(1-methylethyl)-3,6-dioxooctahydro-8H-oxazolo[3,2-a]pyrrolo[2,1-c]pyrazin-2-yl]-7-methyl-4,6,6a,7,8,9,10,10a-octahydroindolo[4,3-fg]quinoline-9-carboxamide methanesulphonate (dihydroergocornine mesilate);
— (6aR,9R,10aR)-N-[(2R,5S,10aS,10bS)-5-benzyl-10b-hydroxy-2-(1-methylethyl)-3,6-dioxooctahydro-8H-oxazolo[3,2-a]pyrrolo[2,1-c]pyrazin-2-yl]-7-methyl-4,6,6a,7,8,9,10,10a-octahydroindolo[4,3-fg]quinoline-9-carboxamide methanesulphonate (dihydroergocristine mesilate);
— (6aR,9R,10aR)-N-[(2R,5S,10aS,10bS)-10b-hydroxy-2-(1-methylethyl)-5-(2-methylpropyl)-3,6-dioxooctahydro-8H-oxazolo[3,2-a]pyrrolo[2,1-c]pyrazin-2-yl]-7-methyl-4,6,6a,7,8,9,10,10a-octahydroindolo[4,3-fg]quinoline-9-carboxamide methanesulphonate (α-dihydroergocryptine mesilate);
— (6aR,9R,10aR)-N-[(2R,5S,10aS,10bS)-10b-hydroxy-2-(1-methylethyl)-5-[(1RS)-1-methylpropyl]-3,6-dioxooctahydro-8H-oxazolo[3,2-a]pyrrolo[2,1-c]pyrazin-2-yl]-7-methyl-4,6,6a,7,8,9,10,10a-octahydroindolo[4,3-fg]quinoline-9-carboxamide methanesulphonate (β-dihydroergocryptine mesilate or epicriptine mesilate).

## Content
98.0 per cent to 102.0 per cent (dried substance).

## PRODUCTION
The production method must be evaluated to determine the potential for formation of alkyl mesilates, which is particularly likely to occur if the reaction medium contains lower alcohols. Where necessary, the production method is validated to demonstrate that alkyl mesilates are not detectable in the final product.

## CHARACTERS
### Appearance
White or yellowish powder.

### Solubility
Sparingly soluble in water, sparingly soluble to soluble in ethanol (96 per cent), slightly soluble in methylene chloride.

## IDENTIFICATION
A. Thin-layer chromatography (2.2.27).

*Test solution*   Dissolve 0.20 g of the substance to be examined in a mixture of 1 volume of *methanol R* and 9 volumes of *methylene chloride R* and dilute to 5 ml with the same mixture of solvents.

*Reference solution*   Dissolve 0.20 g of *methanesulphonic acid R* in a mixture of 1 volume of *methanol R* and 9 volumes of *methylene chloride R* and dilute to 5 ml with the same mixture of solvents.

*Plate*   TLC silica gel plate R.

*Mobile phase*   water R, concentrated ammonia R, butanol R, acetone R (5:10:20:65 V/V/V/V).

*Application*   10 µl.

*Development*   Over 2/3 of the plate.

*Drying*   In a current of cold air for not more than 1 min.

*Detection*   Spray with a 1 g/l solution of *bromocresol purple R* in *methanol R*, adjusted to a violet-red colour with 0.05 ml of *dilute ammonia R1*.

*Drying*   In a current of hot air at 100 °C.

*Results*   The principal spot in the chromatogram obtained with the test solution is similar in position and colour to the principal spot in the chromatogram obtained with the reference solution.

B. Examine the chromatograms obtained in the test for composition.

*Results*   The 4 principal peaks in the chromatogram obtained with the test solution are similar in retention time to the 4 principal peaks in the chromatogram obtained with the reference solution.

## TESTS
**pH** (2.2.3)
4.2 to 5.2.

Dissolve 0.10 g in *carbon dioxide-free water R* and dilute to 20 ml with the same solvent.

### Composition
Liquid chromatography (2.2.29): use the normalisation procedure.

*Test solution*   Dissolve 20 mg of the substance to be examined in a mixture of 1 volume of *anhydrous ethanol R* and 2 volumes of a 10 g/l solution of *tartaric acid R* and dilute to 10 ml with the same mixture of solvents.

*Reference solution*   Dissolve 20 mg of *codergocrine mesilate CRS* in a mixture of 1 volume of *anhydrous ethanol R* and 2 volumes of a 10 g/l solution of *tartaric acid R* and dilute to 10 ml with the same mixture of solvents.

*Column:*
— *size: l* = 0.15 m, Ø = 4.6 mm;
— *stationary phase*: octadecylsilyl silica gel for chromatography R (5 μm).

*Mobile phase*   triethylamine R, acetonitrile R, water R (2.5:25:75 *V/V/V*).

*Flow rate*   1.5 ml/min.

*Detection*   Spectrophotometer at 280 nm.

*Injection*   20 μl.

*Run time*   20 min.

*Elution order*   Dihydroergocornine, α-dihydroergocryptine, dihydroergocristine, β-dihydroergocryptine.

*System suitability*   Test solution:
— *resolution*: minimum 3 between any 2 consecutive principal peaks.

*Composition:*
— *dihydroergocornine*: 30.0 per cent to 35.0 per cent;
— *α-dihydroergocryptine*: 20.0 per cent to 25.0 per cent;
— *dihydroergocristine*: 30.0 per cent to 35.0 per cent;
— *β-dihydroergocryptine*: 10.0 per cent to 13.0 per cent;
— *disregard limit*: 1.0 per cent.

### Related substances

Thin-layer chromatography (2.2.27). *Perform the test as rapidly as possible and protected from direct light. Prepare the test solution last and immediately before application on the plate.*

*Test solution*   Dissolve 0.40 g of the substance to be examined in a mixture of 1 volume of *methanol R* and 9 volumes of *methylene chloride R* and dilute to 5.0 ml with the same mixture of solvents.

*Reference solution (a)*   Dissolve 40 mg of *dihydroergocristine mesilate CRS* in a mixture of 1 volume of *methanol R* and 9 volumes of *methylene chloride R* and dilute to 10.0 ml with the same mixture of solvents. Dilute 3.0 ml of the solution to 50.0 ml with a mixture of 1 volume of *methanol R* and 9 volumes of *methylene chloride R*.

*Reference solution (b)*   To 2.0 ml of reference solution (a), add 1.0 ml of a mixture of 1 volume of *methanol R* and 9 volumes of *methylene chloride R*.

*Reference solution (c)*   To 1.0 ml of reference solution (a), add 2.0 ml of a mixture of 1 volume of *methanol R* and 9 volumes of *methylene chloride R*.

*Reference solution (d)*   To 1.0 ml of reference solution (a), add 5.0 ml of a mixture of 1 volume of *methanol R* and 9 volumes of *methylene chloride R*.

*Plate*   TLC silica gel plate R.

*Mobile phase*   concentrated ammonia R, methanol R, ethyl acetate R, methylene chloride R (1:3:50:50 *V/V/V/V*).

*Application*   10 μl.

*Drying*   In the dark for 2 min after the application of the last solution.

*First development*   In an unsaturated tank, over 2/3 of the plate.

*Drying*   In a current of cold air for not more than 1 min.

*Second development*   In an unsaturated tank, over 2/3 of the plate; use freshly prepared mobile phase.

*Drying*   In a current of cold air for not more than 1 min.

*Detection*   Spray thoroughly with *dimethylaminobenzaldehyde solution R7* and dry in a current of hot air until the spot in the chromatogram obtained with reference solution (d) is clearly visible.

*System suitability*   Test solution:

— the chromatogram shows at least 3 separated secondary spots.

*Limits:*
— *any impurity*: any spots, apart from the principal spot, are not more intense than the spot in the chromatogram obtained with reference solution (a) (0.3 per cent); not more than 4 such spots are more intense than the spot in the chromatogram obtained with reference solution (c) (0.1 per cent) and 2 of these may be more intense than the spot in the chromatogram obtained with reference solution (b) (0.2 per cent).

### Loss on drying (2.2.32)

Maximum 5.0 per cent, determined on 0.500 g by drying at 120 °C under high vacuum.

### ASSAY

Dissolve 0.500 g in 60 ml of *pyridine R*. Pass a stream of *nitrogen R* over the surface of the solution and titrate with *0.1 M tetrabutylammonium hydroxide*, determining the end-point potentiometrically (2.2.20).

1 ml of *0.1 M tetrabutylammonium hydroxide* is equivalent to 68.04 mg of codergocrine mesilate (average $M_r$ = 680).

### STORAGE

Protected from light.

_____ *Ph Eur*

# Cod-Liver Oil Farmed

(*Ph Eur monograph 2398*)

### Action and use
Source of vitamins A and D.

*Ph Eur* _____

### DEFINITION

Purified fatty oil obtained from the fresh livers of farmed cod, *Gadus morhua* L., solid substances being removed by cooling and filtering.

*Content:*
— *sum of the contents of EPA and DHA (expressed as triglycerides)*: 10.0 per cent to 28.0 per cent;
— *vitamin A*: 50 IU (15 μg) to 500 IU (150 μg) per gram;
— *vitamin D₃*: maximum 50 IU (1.3 μg) per gram.

Authorised antioxidants in concentrations not exceeding the levels specified by the competent authority may be added.

### PRODUCTION

The fish shall only be given feed with a composition that is in accordance with the relevant EU or other applicable regulations.

### CHARACTERS
**Appearance**
Clear, pale yellowish liquid.

**Solubility**
Practically insoluble in water, slightly soluble in alcohol (96 per cent), miscible with light petroleum.

### IDENTIFICATION

A. Examine the $^{13}$C NMR spectra obtained in the test for positional distribution (β(2)-acyl) of fatty acids (see Tests). The spectra contain peaks between 172 ppm and 173 ppm with shifts similar to those in the spectrum shown in Figure 2398-1.

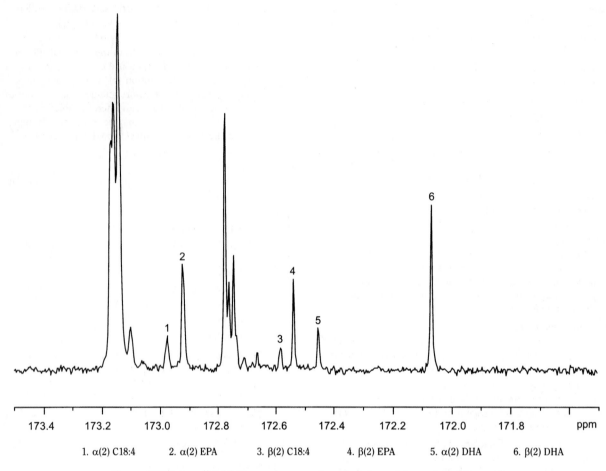

1. α(2) C18:4    2. α(2) EPA    3. β(2) C18:4    4. β(2) EPA    5. α(2) DHA    6. β(2) DHA

*Figure 2398.-1. – $^{13}C$ NMR spectrum carbonyl region of farmed cod-liver oil*

The positional distribution (β(2)-acyl) for cervonic (docosahexaenoic) acid (C22:6 n-3; DHA), timnodonic (eicosapentaenoic) acid (C20:5 n-3; EPA) and moroctic acid (C18:4 n-3) complies with the limits.

B. Linoleic acid (see Tests).

## TESTS

**Acid value** (*2.5.1*)
Maximum 2.0.

**Anisidine value** (*2.5.36*)
Maximum 10.0.

**Peroxide value** (*2.5.5, Method B*)
Maximum 5.0.

**Unsaponifiable matter** (*2.5.7*)
Maximum 1.5 per cent, determined on 2.0 g, and extracting with 3 quantities, each of 50 ml, of *peroxide-free ether R*.

**Stearin**

Heat at least 10 ml to 60-90 °C then allow to cool for 3 h in a bath of iced water or a thermostatically controlled bath at 0 ± 0.5 °C. If necessary, to eliminate insoluble matter, filter the sample after heating. The sample remains clear.

**Positional distribution (β(2)-acyl) of fatty acids**
Nuclear magnetic resonance spectrometry (*2.2.33*).

*Test solution* Dissolve 190-210 mg of the substance to be examined in 500 μl of *deuterated chloroform R*. Prepare at least 3 samples and examine within 3 days.

*Apparatus* High resolution FT-NMR spectrometer operating at minimum 300 MHz.

*Acquisition of $^{13}C$ NMR spectra* The following parameters may be used:
— *sweep width*: 200 ppm (− 5 ppm to 195 ppm);
— *irradiation frequency offset*: 95 ppm;
— *time domain*: 64 K;
— *pulse delay*: 2 s;
— *pulse program*: zgig 30 (inverse gated, 30° excitation pulse);
— *dummy scans*: 4;
— *number of scans*: 4096.

*Processing and plotting* The following parameters may be used:
— *size*: 64 K (zero-filling);
— *window multiplication*: exponential;
— *Lorentzian broadening factor*: 0.2 Hz.

Use the $CDCl_3$ signal for shift referencing. The shift of the central peak of the 1:1:1 triplet is set to 77.16 ppm.

Plot the spectral region δ 171.5-173.5 ppm. Compare the spectrum with the spectrum shown in Figure 2398.-1. The shift values lie within the ranges given in Table 2398.-1.

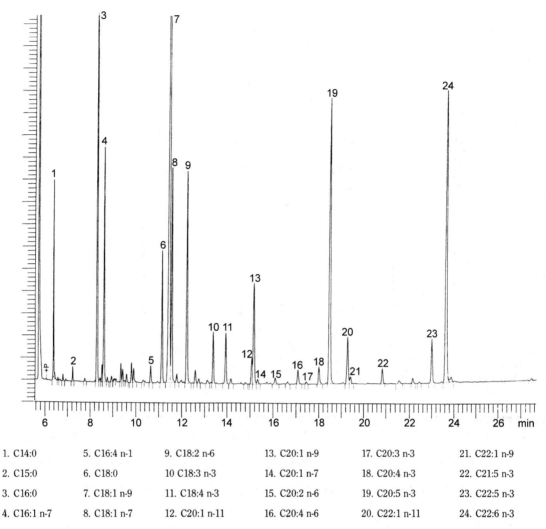

Figure 2398.-2. – *Chromatogram for the test for composition of fatty acids of farmed cod-liver oil*

| | | | | | |
|---|---|---|---|---|---|
| 1. C14:0 | 5. C16:4 n-1 | 9. C18:2 n-6 | 13. C20:1 n-9 | 17. C20:3 n-3 | 21. C22:1 n-9 |
| 2. C15:0 | 6. C18:0 | 10 C18:3 n-3 | 14. C20:1 n-7 | 18. C20:4 n-3 | 22. C21:5 n-3 |
| 3. C16:0 | 7. C18:1 n-9 | 11. C18:4 n-3 | 15. C20:2 n-6 | 19. C20:5 n-3 | 23. C22:5 n-3 |
| 4. C16:1 n-7 | 8. C18:1 n-7 | 12. C20:1 n-11 | 16. C20:4 n-6 | 20. C22:1 n-11 | 24. C22:6 n-3 |

Table 2398.-1. – *Shift values*

| Signal | Shift range (ppm) |
|---|---|
| β(2) DHA | 172.05 - 172.09 |
| α(2) DHA | 172.43 - 172.47 |
| β(2) EPA | 172.52 - 172.56 |
| α(2) EPA | 172.90 - 172.94 |
| β(2) C18:4 | 172.56 - 172.60 |
| α(2) C18:4 | 172.95 - 172.99 |

*System suitability:*

— *signal-to-noise ratio*: minimum 5 for the smallest relevant peak corresponding to α(2) C18:4 signal (in the range δ 172.95-172.99 ppm);

— *peak width at half-height*: maximum 0.02 ppm for the central CDCl$_3$ signal (at δ 77.16 ppm).

*Calculation of positional distribution (β(2)-acyl)* Use the following expression:

$$\frac{100 \times \beta(2)}{\alpha(2) + \beta(2)}$$

α(2) = peak area of the corresponding α(2)-carbonyl peak;

β(2) = peak area of β(2)-carbonyl peak from C22:6 n-3, C20:5 n-3 or C18:4 n-3, respectively.

*Limits:*

The positional distribution (β(2)-acyl) is 71 per cent to 81 per cent for cervonic (docosahexaenoic) acid (C22:6 n-3; DHA), 32 per cent to 40 per cent for timnodonic (eicosapentaenoic) acid (C20:5 n-3; EPA) and 28 per cent to 38 per cent for moroctic acid (C18:4 n-3).

**Composition of fatty acids** (*2.4.29*)

For identification of the peaks, see the chromatogram shown in Figure 2398.-2.

The 24 largest peaks of the methyl esters account for more than 90 per cent of the total area (these correspond to, in common elution order: 14:0, 15:0, 16:0, 16:1 n-7, 16:4 n-1, 18:0, 18:1 n-9, 18:1 n-7, 18:2 n-6, 18:3 n-3, 18:4 n-3, 20:1 n-11, 20:1 n-9, 20:1 n-7, 20:2 n-6, 20:4 n-6, 20:3 n-3, 20:4 n-3, 20:5 n-3, 22:1 n-11, 22:1 n-9, 21:5 n-3, 22:5 n-3, 22:6 n-3).

**Linoleic acid** (*2.4.29*)

3.0 per cent to 11.0 per cent.

**ASSAY**

**EPA and DHA** (*2.4.29*)

See the chromatogram shown in Figure 2398.-2.

**Vitamin A**

*Carry out the test as rapidly as possible, avoiding exposure to actinic light and air, oxidising agents, oxidation catalysts (for example, copper and iron) and acids.*

Use method A. If method A is found not to be valid, use method B.

**Method A**

Ultraviolet absorption spectrophotometry (*2.2.25*).

*Test solution* To 1.00 g in a round-bottomed flask, add 3 ml of a freshly prepared 50 per cent *m/m* solution of *potassium hydroxide R* and 30 ml of *anhydrous ethanol R*. Boil under reflux in a current of *nitrogen R* for 30 min. Cool rapidly and add 30 ml of *water R*. Extract with 50 ml of *ether R*. Repeat the extraction 3 times and discard the lower layer after complete separation. Wash the combined upper layers with 4 quantities, each of 50 ml, of *water R*, and evaporate to dryness under a gentle current of *nitrogen R* at a temperature not exceeding 30 °C or in a rotary evaporator at a temperature not exceeding 30 °C under reduced pressure (water ejector). Dissolve the residue in sufficient *2-propanol R1* to give an expected concentration of vitamin A equivalent to 10-15 IU/ml.

Measure the absorbances of the solution at 300 nm, 310 nm, 325 nm and 334 nm and at the wavelength of maximum absorption with a suitable spectrophotometer in 1 cm specially matched cells, using *2-propanol R1* as the compensation liquid.

Calculate the content of vitamin A, as all-*trans*-retinol, in International Units per gram, using the following expression:

$$A_{325} \times \frac{1821}{100m} \times V$$

$A_{325}$ = absorbance at 325 nm;
$m$ = mass of the substance to be examined, in grams;
$V$ = total volume of solution containing 10-15 IU of vitamin A per millilitre;
1821 = conversion factor for the specific absorbance of all-*trans*-retinol, in International Units.

The above expression can be used only if $A_{325}$ has a value of not greater than $A_{325,\text{corr}}/0.970$, where $A_{325,\text{corr}}$ is the corrected absorbance at 325 nm and is given by the following equation:

$$A_{325,\,\text{corr}} = 6.815A_{325} - 2.555A_{310} - 4.260A_{334}$$

A designates the absorbance at the wavelength indicated by the subscript.

If $A_{325}$ has a value greater than $A_{325,\text{corr}}/0.970$, calculate the content of vitamin A using the following expression:

$$A_{325,\,\text{corr}} \times \frac{1821}{100m} \times V$$

The assay is not valid unless:
— the wavelength of maximum absorption lies between 323 nm and 327 nm;
— the absorbance at 300 nm relative to that at 325 nm is at most 0.73.

**Method B**

Liquid chromatography (*2.2.29*).

*Test solution* Prepare duplicates. To 2.00 g in a round-bottomed flask, add 5 ml of a freshly prepared 100 g/l solution of *ascorbic acid R*, 10 ml of a freshly prepared 800 g/l

solution of *potassium hydroxide R* and 100 ml of *anhydrous ethanol R*. Boil under a reflux condenser on a water-bath for 15 min. Add 100 ml of a 10 g/l solution of *sodium chloride R* and cool. Transfer the solution to a 500 ml separating funnel, rinsing the round-bottomed flask with about 75 ml of a 10 g/l solution of *sodium chloride R* and then with 150 ml of a mixture of equal volumes of light *petroleum R1* and *ether R*. Shake for 1 min. When the layers have separated completely, discard the lower layer and wash the upper layer, first with 50 ml of a 30 g/l solution of *potassium hydroxide R* in a 10 per cent *V/V* solution of *anhydrous ethanol R* and then with 3 quantities, each of 50 ml, of a 10 g/l solution of *sodium chloride R*. Filter the upper layer through 5 g of *anhydrous sodium sulphate R* on a fast filter paper into a 250 ml flask suitable for a rotary evaporator. Wash the funnel with 10 ml of fresh extraction mixture, filter and combine the upper layers. Distil them at a temperature not exceeding 30 °C under reduced pressure (water ejector) and fill with *nitrogen R* when evaporation is completed. Alternatively, evaporate the solvent under a gentle current of *nitrogen R* at a temperature not exceeding 30 °C. Dissolve the residue in *2-propanol R*, transfer to a 25 ml volumetric flask and dilute to 25 ml with *2-propanol R*. Gentle heating in an ultrasonic bath may be required. A large fraction of the white residue is cholesterol, constituting approximately 50 per cent *m/m* of the unsaponifiable matter of cod-liver oil.

*Reference solution (a)* Prepare a solution of *retinol acetate CRS* in *2-propanol R1* so that 1 ml contains about 1000 IU of all-*trans*-retinol.

The exact concentration of reference solution (a) is assessed by ultraviolet absorption spectrophotometry (*2.2.25*). Dilute reference solution (a) with *2-propanol R1* to a presumed concentration of 10-15 IU/ml and measure the absorbance at 326 nm in matched 1 cm cells using *2-propanol R1* as the compensation liquid.

Calculate the content of vitamin A in International Units per millilitre of reference solution (a) using the following expression, taking into account the assigned content of *retinol acetate CRS*:

$$A_{326} \times \frac{1900 \times V_2}{100 \times V_1}$$

$A_{326}$ = absorbance at 326 nm;
$V_1$ = volume of reference solution (a) used;
$V_2$ = volume of the diluted solution;
1900 = conversion factor for the specific absorbance of *retinol acetate CRS*, in International Units.

*Reference solution (b)* Proceed as described for the test solution but using 2.00 ml of reference solution (a) in place of the substance to be examined.

The exact concentration of reference solution (b) is assessed by ultraviolet absorption spectrophotometry (*2.2.25*). Dilute reference solution (b) with *2-propanol R1* to a presumed all-*trans*-retinol concentration of 10-15 IU/ml and measure the absorbance at 325 nm in matched 1 cm cells using *2-propanol R1* as the compensation liquid.

Calculate the content of all-*trans*-retinol in International Units per millilitre of reference solution (b), using the following expression:

$$A_{325} \times \frac{1821 \times V_3}{100 \times V_4}$$

$A_{325}$ = absorbance at 325 nm;
$V_3$ = volume of the diluted solution;
$V_4$ = volume of reference solution (b) used;
1821 = conversion factor for the specific absorbance of all-*trans*-retinol, in International Units.

*Column:*
— *size: l* = 0.25 m, Ø = 4.6 mm;
— *stationary phase: octadecylsilyl silica gel for chromatography R* (5-10 µm).

*Mobile phase   water R, methanol R* (3:97 *V/V*).

*Flow rate*   1 ml/min.

*Detection*   Spectrophotometer at 325 nm.

*Injection*   10 µl; inject in triplicate the test solution and reference solution (b).

*Retention time*   all-*trans*-retinol = 5 ± 1 min.

*System suitability:*
— the chromatogram obtained with the test solution shows a peak that corresponds to the peak due to all-*trans*-retinol in the chromatogram obtained with reference solution (b);
— the results obtained with the duplicate test solutions do not differ by more than 5 per cent;
— the recovery of all-*trans*-retinol in reference solution (b) as assessed by direct absorption spectrophotometry is greater than 95 per cent.

Calculate the content of vitamin A using the following expression:

$$A_1 \times \frac{C \times V}{A_2} \times \frac{1}{m}$$

$A_1$ = area of the peak due to all-*trans*-retinol in the chromatogram obtained with the test solution;
$A_2$ = area of the peak due to all-*trans*-retinol in the chromatogram obtained with reference solution (b);
$C$ = concentration of *retinol acetate CRS* in reference solution (a) as assessed prior to the saponification, in International Units per millilitre (= 1000 IU/ml);
$V$ = volume of reference solution (a) treated (2.00 ml);
$m$ = mass of the substance to be examined in the test solution (2.00 g).

**Vitamin D$_3$**

Liquid chromatography (*2.2.29*). *Carry out the assay as rapidly as possible, avoiding exposure to actinic light and air.*

*Internal standard solution*   Dissolve 0.50 mg of *ergocalciferol CRS* in 100 ml of *anhydrous ethanol R*.

*Test solution (a)*   To 4.00 g in a round-bottomed flask, add 5 ml of a freshly prepared 100 g/l solution of *ascorbic acid R*, 10 ml of a freshly prepared 800 g/l solution of *potassium hydroxide R* and 100 ml of *anhydrous ethanol R*. Boil under a reflux condenser on a water-bath for 30 min. Add 100 ml of a 10 g/l solution of *sodium chloride R* and cool the solution to room temperature. Transfer the solution to a 500 ml separating funnel, rinsing the round-bottomed flask with about 75 ml of a 10 g/l solution of *sodium chloride R* and then with 150 ml of a mixture of equal volumes of *light petroleum R1* and *ether R*. Shake for 1 min. When the layers have separated completely, discard the lower layer and wash the upper layer, first with 50 ml of a 30 g/l solution of *potassium hydroxide R* in a 10 per cent *V/V* solution of *anhydrous ethanol R*, and then with 3 quantities, each of 50 ml, of a 10 g/l solution of *sodium chloride R*. Filter the

upper layer through 5 g of *anhydrous sodium sulphate R* on a fast filter paper into a 250 ml flask suitable for a rotary evaporator. Wash the funnel with 10 ml of fresh extraction mixture, filter and combine the upper layers. Distil them at a temperature not exceeding 30 °C under reduced pressure (water ejector) and fill with *nitrogen R* when evaporation is completed. Alternatively, evaporate the solvent under a gentle current of nitrogen R at a temperature not exceeding 30 °C. Dissolve the residue in 1.5 ml of the mobile phase described under Purification. Gentle heating in an ultrasonic bath may be required. *A large fraction of the white residue is cholesterol, constituting approximately 50 per cent m/m of the unsaponifiable matter of cod-liver oil.*

*Test solution (b)*   Prepare duplicates. To 4.00 g add 2.0 ml of the internal standard solution and proceed as described for test solution (a).

*Reference solution (a)*   Dissolve 0.50 mg of *cholecalciferol CRS* in 100.0 ml of anhydrous ethanol R.

*Reference solution (b)*   In a round-bottomed flask, add 2.0 ml of reference solution (a) and 2.0 ml of the internal standard solution and proceed as described for test solution (a).

**Purification**
*Column:*
— *size: l* = 0.25 m, Ø = 4.6 mm;
— *stationary phase: nitrile silica gel for chromatography R* (10 µm).

*Mobile phase   isoamyl alcohol R, hexane R* (1.6:98.4 *V/V*).

*Flow rate*   1.1 ml/min.

*Detection*   Spectrophotometer at 265 nm.

Inject 350 µl of reference solution (b). Collect the eluate from 2 min before until 2 min after the retention time of cholecalciferol, in a ground-glass-stoppered tube containing 1 ml of a 1 g/l solution of *butylhydroxytoluene R* in *hexane R*. Repeat the procedure with test solutions (a) and (b). Evaporate the eluates obtained from reference solution (b) and from test solutions (a) and (b), separately, to dryness at a temperature not exceeding 30 °C under a gentle current of *nitrogen R*. Dissolve each residue in 1.5 ml of *acetonitrile R*.

**Determination**
*Column:*
— *size: l* = 0.15 m, Ø = 4.6 mm;
— *stationary phase: octadecylsilyl silica gel for chromatography R* (5 µm).

*Mobile phase   phosphoric acid R*, 96 per cent *V/V* solution of *acetonitrile R* (0.2:99.8 *V/V*).

*Flow rate*   1.0 ml/min.

*Detection*   Spectrophotometer at 265 nm.

*Injection*   2 quantities not exceeding 200 µl of each of the 3 solutions obtained under Purification.

*System suitability:*
— *resolution*: minimum 1.4 between the peaks due to ergocalciferol and cholecalciferol in the chromatogram obtained with reference solution (b);
— the results obtained with the test solution (b) duplicates do not differ by more than 5 per cent.

Calculate the content of vitamin D$_3$ in International Units per gram using the following expression, taking into account the assigned content of *cholecalciferol CRS*:

$$\frac{A_2}{A_6} \times \frac{A_3}{A_4 - \left[\dfrac{A_5}{A_1}\right] \times A_2} \times \frac{m_2}{m_1} \times \frac{V_2}{V_1} \times 40$$

$m_1$ = mass of the sample in test solution (b), in grams;

$m_2$ = total mass of *cholecalciferol CRS* used for the preparation of reference solution (a), in micrograms (500 µg);

$A_1$ = area (or height) of the peak due to cholecalciferol in the chromatogram obtained with test solution (a);

$A_2$ = area (or height) of the peak due to cholecalciferol in the chromatogram obtained with test solution (b);

$A_3$ = area (or height) of the peak due to ergocalciferol in the chromatogram obtained with reference solution (b);

$A_4$ = area (or height) of the peak due to ergocalciferol in the chromatogram obtained with test solution (b);

$A_5$ = area (or height) of a possible peak in the chromatogram obtained with test solution (a) with the same retention time as the peak co-eluting with ergocalciferol in test solution (b);

$A_6$ = area (or height) of the peak due to cholecalciferol in the chromatogram obtained with reference solution (b);

$V_1$ = total volume of reference solution (a) (100 ml);

$V_2$ = volume of reference solution (a) used for preparing reference solution (b) (2.0 ml).

## STORAGE

In an airtight and well-filled container, protected from light. If no antioxidant is added, store under an inert gas.

Once the container has been opened, its contents are used as soon as possible and any part of the contents not used at once is protected by an atmosphere of inert gas.

## LABELLING

The label states:
— the concentration of EPA and DHA as a sum;
— the number of International Units of vitamin A per gram;
— the number of International Units of vitamin $D_3$ per gram.

*Ph Eur*

# Cod-liver Oil (Type A)

*(Ph Eur monograph 1192)*

## Action and use

Source of vitamins A and D.

Each IU of vitamin $D_3$ is equivalent to 0.025 µg of colecalciferol.

*Ph Eur* _____

## DEFINITION

Purified fatty oil obtained from the fresh livers of wild cod, *Gadus morhua* L. and other species of *Gadidae*, solid substances being removed by cooling and filtering. A suitable antioxidant may be added.

## Content

600 IU (180 µg) to 2500 IU (750 µg) of vitamin A per gram and 60 IU (1.5 µg) to 250 IU (6.25 µg) of vitamin $D_3$ per gram.

## CHARACTERS

### Appearance

Clear, yellowish, liquid.

### Solubility

Practically insoluble in water, slightly soluble in ethanol (96 per cent), miscible with light petroleum.

## IDENTIFICATION

*First identification* A, B, C.

*Second identification* C, D.

A. In the assay for vitamin A using method A, the test solution shows an absorption maximum *(2.2.25)* at 325 ± 2 nm. In the assay for vitamin A using method B, the chromatogram obtained with the test solution shows a peak corresponding to the peak of all-*trans*-retinol in the chromatogram obtained with the reference solution.

B. In the assay for vitamin $D_3$, the chromatogram obtained with test solution (a) shows a peak corresponding to the peak of cholecalciferol in the chromatogram obtained with reference solution (b).

C. Composition of fatty acids (see Tests).

D. To 0.1 g add 0.5 ml of *methylene chloride R* and 1 ml of *antimony trichloride solution R*. Mix. A deep blue colour develops in about 10 s.

## TESTS

### Colour

Not more intensely coloured than a reference solution prepared as follows: to 3.0 ml of red primary solution add 25.0 ml of yellow primary solution and dilute to 50.0 ml with a 10 g/l solution of *hydrochloric acid R* *(2.2.2, Method II)*.

### Relative density *(2.2.5)*

0.917 to 0.930.

### Refractive index *(2.2.6)*

1.477 to 1.484.

### Acid value *(2.5.1)*

Maximum 2.0.

### Anisidine value *(2.5.36)*

Maximum 30.0.

### Iodine value *(2.5.4, Method B)*

150 to 180.

Use *starch solution R2*.

### Peroxide value *(2.5.5, Method B)*

Maximum 10.0.

### Unsaponifiable matter *(2.5.7)*

Maximum 1.5 per cent, determined on 2.0 g, and extracting with 3 quantities, each of 50 ml, of *peroxide-free ether R*.

### Stearin

Heat at least 10 ml to 60-90 °C then allow to cool for 3 h in a bath of iced water or a thermostatically-controlled bath at 0 ± 0.5 °C. If necessary, to eliminate insoluble matter, filter the sample after heating. The sample remains clear.

### Composition of fatty acids

Gas chromatography *(2.2.28)*.

*Test solution* Introduce about 0.45 g of the substance to be examined into a 10 ml volumetric flask, dissolve in *hexane R* containing 50 mg of *butylhydroxytoluene R* per litre and dilute to 10.0 ml with the same solvent. Transfer 2.0 ml of this solution into a quartz tube and evaporate the solvent with a gentle current of *nitrogen R*. Add 1.5 ml of a 20 g/l solution of *sodium hydroxide R* in *methanol R*, cover with *nitrogen R*, cap tightly with a polytetrafluoroethylene-lined cap, mix and heat in a water-bath for 7 min. Cool, add 2 ml of *boron trichloride-methanol solution R*, cover with *nitrogen R*, cap tightly, mix and heat in a water-bath for 30 min. Cool to 40-50 °C, add 1 ml of *trimethylpentane R*, cap and vortex or shake vigorously for at least 30 s. Immediately add 5 ml of *saturated sodium chloride solution R*, cover with *nitrogen R*, cap and vortex or shake vigorously for at least 15 s. Allow the upper layer to become clear and transfer it to a separate

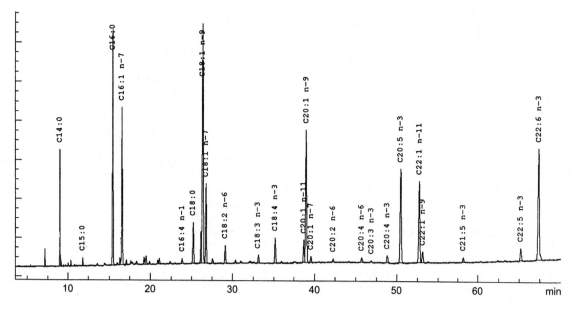

Figure 1192.-1. – *Chromatogram for the test for composition of fatty acids of cod-liver oil (type A)*

| Trivial name of fatty acid | Nomenclature | Lower limit area (per cent) | Upper limit area (per cent) |
|---|---|---|---|
| *Saturated fatty acids:* | | | |
| Myristic acid | 14:0 | 2.0 | 6.0 |
| Palmitic acid | 16:0 | 7.0 | 14.0 |
| Stearic acid | 18:0 | 1.0 | 4.0 |
| *Mono-unsaturated fatty acids:* | | | |
| Palmitoleic acid | 16:1 n-7 | 4.5 | 11.5 |
| *cis*-Vaccenic acid | 18:1 n-7 | 2.0 | 7.0 |
| Oleic acid | 18:1 n-9 | 12.0 | 21.0 |
| Gadoleic acid | 20:1 n-11 | 1.0 | 5.5 |
| Gondoic acid | 20:1 n-9 | 5.0 | 17.0 |
| Erucic acid | 22:1 n-9 | 0 | 1.5 |
| Cetoleic acid (22:1 n-11) | 22:1 n-11+13 | 5.0 | 12.0 |
| *Poly-unsaturated fatty acids:* | | | |
| Linoleic acid | 18:2 n-6 | 0.5 | 3.0 |
| α-Linolenic acid | 18:3 n-3 | 0 | 2.0 |
| Moroctic acid | 18:4 n-3 | 0.5 | 4.5 |
| Timnodonic (eicosapentaenoic) acid (EPA) | 20:5 n-3 | 7.0 | 16.0 |
| Cervonic (docosahexaenoic) acid (DHA) | 22:6 n-3 | 6.0 | 18.0 |

tube. Shake the methanol layer once more with 1 ml of *trimethylpentane R* and combine the trimethylpentane extracts. Wash the combined extracts with 2 quantities, each of 1 ml, of *water R* and dry over *anhydrous sodium sulphate R*. Prepare 2 solutions for each sample.

*Column:*
— *material*: fused silica;
— *size: l* = 30 m, Ø = 0.25 mm;
— *stationary phase: macrogol 20 000 R* (film thickness 0.25 µm).

*Carrier gas*   hydrogen for chromatography *R* or *helium for chromatography R*, where oxygen scrubber is applied.

*Split ratio*   1:200.

*Temperature:*

| | Time (min) | Temperature (°C) |
|---|---|---|
| Column | 0 - 55 | 170 → 225 |
| | 55 - 75 | 225 |
| Injection port | | 250 |
| Detector | | 280 |

*Detection*   Flame ionisation.

*Injection*   1 µl, twice.

*System suitability:*
— the 15 fatty acids to be tested are satisfactorily identified from the chromatogram shown in Figure 1192.-1;
— injection of a mixture of equal amounts of *methyl palmitate R, methyl stearate R, methyl arachidate R* and *methyl behenate R* gives area percentages of 24.4, 24.8, 25.2 and 25.6 (± 0.5 per cent), respectively;
— *resolution*: minimum 1.3 between the peaks due to methyl oleate and methyl *cis*-vaccenate; the resolution between the pair due to methyl gadoleate and methyl gondoate is sufficient for purposes of identification and area measurement.

Calculate the area per cent for each fatty acid methyl ester using the following expression:

$$\frac{A_x}{A_t} \times 100$$

$A_x$ =   peak area of fatty acid $x$;
$A_t$ =   sum of the peak areas (up to C22:6 n-3).

The calculation is not valid unless:
— the total area is based only on peaks due solely to fatty acid methyl esters;
— the number of fatty acid methyl ester peaks exceeding 0.05 per cent of the total area is at least 24;
— the 24 largest peaks of the methyl esters account for more than 90 per cent of the total area. (These correspond to, in common elution order: 14:0, 15:0, 16:0, 16:1 n-7, 16:4 n-1, 18:0, 18:1 n-9, 18:1 n-7, 18:2 n-6, 18:3 n-3,

18:4 n-3, 20:1 n-11, 20:1 n-9, 20:1 n-7, 20:2 n-6, 20:4 n-6, 20:3 n-3, 20:4 n-3, 20:5 n-3, 22:1 n-11, 22:1 n-9, 21:5 n-3, 22:5 n-3, 22:6 n-3).

## ASSAY

### Vitamin A

*Carry out the test as rapidly as possible, avoiding exposure to actinic light and air, oxidising agents, oxidation catalysts (for example, copper and iron) and acids.*

Use method A. If method A is found not to be valid, use method B.

### Method A

Ultraviolet absorption spectrophotometry (*2.2.25*).

*Test solution*   To 1.00 g in a round-bottomed flask, add 3 ml of a freshly prepared 50 per cent *m/m* solution of *potassium hydroxide R* and 30 ml of *anhydrous ethanol R*. Boil under reflux in a current of *nitrogen R* for 30 min. Cool rapidly and add 30 ml of *water R*. Extract with 50 ml of *ether R*. Repeat the extraction 3 times and discard the lower layer after complete separation. Wash the combined upper layers with 4 quantities, each of 50 ml, of *water R*, and evaporate to dryness under a gentle current of *nitrogen R* at a temperature not exceeding 30 °C or in a rotary evaporator at a temperature not exceeding 30 °C under reduced pressure (water ejector). Dissolve the residue in sufficient *2-propanol R1* to give an expected concentration of vitamin A equivalent to 10-15 IU/ml.

Measure the absorbances of the solution at 300 nm, 310 nm, 325 nm and 334 nm and at the wavelength of maximum absorption with a suitable spectrophotometer in 1 cm specially matched cells, using *2-propanol R1* as the compensation liquid.

Calculate the content of vitamin A, as all-*trans*-retinol, in International Units per gram, using the following expression:

$$A_{325} \times \frac{1821}{100m} \times V$$

$A_{325}$ = absorbance at 325 nm;
$m$ = mass of the substance to be examined, in grams;
$V$ = total volume of solution containing 10-15 IU of vitamin A per millilitre;
1821 = conversion factor for the specific absorbance of all-*trans*-retinol, in International Units.

The above expression can be used only if $A_{325}$ has a value of not greater than $A_{325,\text{corr}}/0.970$, where $A_{325,\text{corr}}$ is the corrected absorbance at 325 nm and is given by the following equation:

$$A_{325,\text{corr}} = 6.815A_{325} - 2.555A_{310} - 4.260A_{334}$$

A designates the absorbance at the wavelength indicated by the subscript.

If $A_{325}$ has a value greater than $A_{325,\text{corr}}/0.970$, calculate the content of vitamin A using the following expression:

$$A_{325,\text{corr}} \times \frac{1821}{100m} \times V$$

The assay is not valid unless:
— the wavelength of the maximum absorption lies between 323 nm and 327 nm;
— the absorbance at 300 nm relative to that at 325 nm is at most 0.73.

### Method B

Liquid chromatography (*2.2.29*).

*Test solution*   Prepare duplicates. To 2.00 g in a round-bottomed flask, add 5 ml of a freshly prepared 100 g/l solution of *ascorbic acid R*, 10 ml of a freshly prepared 800 g/l solution of *potassium hydroxide R* and 100 ml of *anhydrous ethanol R*. Boil under a reflux condenser on a water-bath for 15 min. Add 100 ml of a 10 g/l solution of *sodium chloride R* and cool. Transfer the solution to a 500 ml separating funnel, rinsing the round-bottomed flask with about 75 ml of a 10 g/l solution of *sodium chloride R* and then with 150 ml of a mixture of equal volumes of *light petroleum R1* and *ether R*. Shake for 1 min. When the layers have separated completely, discard the lower layer and wash the upper layer, first with 50 ml of a 30 g/l solution of *potassium hydroxide R* in a 10 per cent *V/V* solution of *anhydrous ethanol R* and then with 3 quantities, each of 50 ml, of a 10 g/l solution of *sodium chloride R*. Filter the upper layer through 5 g of *anhydrous sodium sulphate R* on a fast filter paper into a 250 ml flask suitable for a rotary evaporator. Wash the funnel with 10 ml of fresh extraction mixture, filter and combine the upper layers. Distil them at a temperature not exceeding 30 °C under reduced pressure (water ejector) and fill with *nitrogen R* when evaporation is completed. Alternatively, evaporate the solvent under a gentle current of *nitrogen R* at a temperature not exceeding 30 °C. Dissolve the residue in *2-propanol R*, transfer to a 25 ml volumetric flask and dilute to 25 ml with *2-propanol R*. Gentle heating in an ultrasonic bath may be required. A large fraction of the white residue is cholesterol, constituting approximately 50 per cent *m/m* of the unsaponifiable matter of cod-liver oil.

*Reference solution (a)*   Prepare a solution of *retinol acetate CRS* in *2-propanol R1* so that 1 ml contains about 1000 IU of all-*trans*-retinol.

The exact concentration of reference solution (a) is assessed by ultraviolet absorption spectrophotometry (*2.2.25*). Dilute reference solution (a) with *2-propanol R1* to a presumed concentration of 10-15 IU/ml and measure the absorbance at 326 nm in matched 1 cm cells using *2-propanol R1* as the compensation liquid.

Calculate the content of vitamin A in International Units per millilitre of reference solution (a) using the following expression, taking into account the assigned content of *retinol acetate CRS*:

$$A_{326} \times \frac{1900 \times V_2}{100 \times V_1}$$

$A_{326}$ = absorbance at 326 nm;
$V_1$ = volume of reference solution (a) used;
$V_2$ = volume of the diluted solution;
1900 = conversion factor for the specific absorbance of *retinol acetate CRS*, in International Units.

*Reference solution (b)*   Proceed as described for the test solution but using 2.00 ml of reference solution (a) in place of the substance to be examined.

The exact concentration of reference solution (b) is assessed by ultraviolet absorption spectrophotometry (*2.2.25*). Dilute reference solution (b) with *2-propanol R1* to a presumed all-*trans*-retinol concentration of 10-15 IU/ml and measure the absorbance at 325 nm in matched 1 cm cells using *2-propanol R1* as the compensation liquid.

Calculate the content of all-*trans*-retinol in International Units per millilitre of reference solution (b), using the following expression:

$$A_{325} \times \frac{1821 \times V_3}{100 \times V_4}$$

$A_{325}$ = absorbance at 325 nm;

$V_3$ = volume of the diluted solution;

$V_4$ = volume of reference solution (b) used;

1821 = conversion factor for the specific absorbance of all-*trans*-retinol, in International Units.

*Column:*
— *size:* $l = 0.25$ m, $\varnothing = 4.6$ mm;
— *stationary phase: octadecylsilyl silica gel for chromatography R* (5-10 μm).

*Mobile phase    water R, methanol R* (3:97 *V/V*).

*Flow rate    1 ml/min.*

*Detection    Spectrophotometer at 325 nm.*

*Injection    10 μl; inject in triplicate the test solution and reference solution (b).*

*Retention time    all-*trans*-retinol = 5 ± 1 min.*

*System suitability:*
— the chromatogram obtained with the test solution shows a peak that corresponds to the peak due to all-*trans*-retinol in the chromatogram obtained with reference solution (b);
— the results obtained with the duplicate test solutions do not differ by more than 5 per cent;
— the recovery of all-*trans*-retinol in reference solution (b) as assessed by direct absorption spectrophotometry is greater than 95 per cent.

Calculate the content of vitamin A using the following expression:

$$A_1 \times \frac{C \times V}{A_2} \times \frac{1}{m}$$

$A_1$ = area of the peak due to all-*trans*-retinol in the chromatogram obtained with the test solution;

$A_2$ = area of the peak due to all-*trans*-retinol in the chromatogram obtained with reference solution (b);

$C$ = concentration of *retinol acetate CRS* in reference solution (a) as assessed prior to the saponification, in International Units per millilitre (= 1000 IU/ml);

$V$ = volume of reference solution (a) treated (2.00 ml);

$m$ = mass of the substance to be examined in the test solution (2.00 g).

## Vitamin D₃

Liquid chromatography (*2.2.29*). *Carry out the assay as rapidly as possible, avoiding exposure to actinic light and air.*

*Internal standard solution    Dissolve 0.50 mg of ergocalciferol CRS* in 100 ml of *anhydrous ethanol R*.

*Test solution (a)    To 4.00 g in a round-bottomed flask, add 5 ml of a freshly prepared 100 g/l solution of *ascorbic acid R*, 10 ml of a freshly prepared 800 g/l solution of *potassium hydroxide R* and 100 ml of *anhydrous ethanol R*. Boil under a reflux condenser on a water-bath for 30 min. Add 100 ml of a 10 g/l solution of *sodium chloride R* and cool the solution to room temperature. Transfer the solution to a 500 ml separating funnel, rinsing the round-bottomed flask with about 75 ml of a 10 g/l solution of *sodium chloride R* and then with 150 ml of a mixture of equal volumes of *light petroleum R1* and *ether R*. Shake for 1 min. When the layers have separated completely, discard the lower layer and wash the upper layer, first with 50 ml of a 30 g/l solution of *potassium hydroxide R* in a 10 per cent *V/V* solution of *anhydrous ethanol R*, and then with 3 quantities, each of 50 ml, of a 10 g/l solution of *sodium chloride R*. Filter the upper layer through 5 g of *anhydrous sodium sulphate R* on a fast filter paper into a 250 ml flask suitable for a rotary evaporator. Wash the funnel with 10 ml of fresh extraction mixture, filter and combine the upper layers. Distil them at a temperature not exceeding 30 °C under reduced pressure (water ejector) and fill with *nitrogen R* when evaporation is completed. Alternatively, evaporate the solvent under a gentle current of *nitrogen R* at a temperature not exceeding 30 °C. Dissolve the residue in 1.5 ml of the mobile phase described under Purification. Gentle heating in an ultrasonic bath may be required. *A large fraction of the white residue is cholesterol, constituting approximately 50 per cent m/m of the unsaponifiable matter of cod-liver oil.*

*Test solution (b)    Prepare duplicates. To 4.00 g add 2.0 ml of the internal standard solution and proceed as described for test solution (a).*

*Reference solution (a)    Dissolve 0.50 mg of *cholecalciferol CRS* in 100.0 ml of *anhydrous ethanol R*.

*Reference solution (b)    Into a round-bottomed flask, add 2.0 ml of reference solution (a) and 2.0 ml of the internal standard solution and proceed as described for test solution (a).

**Purification**

*Column:*
— *size:* $l = 0.25$ m, $\varnothing = 4.6$ mm;
— *stationary phase: nitrile silica gel for chromatography R* (10 μm).

*Mobile phase    isoamyl alcohol R, hexane R* (1.6:98.4 *V/V*).

*Flow rate    1.1 ml/min.*

*Detection    Spectrophotometer at 265 nm.*

Inject 350 μl of reference solution (b). Collect the eluate from 2 min before until 2 min after the retention time of cholecalciferol, in a ground-glass-stoppered tube containing 1 ml of a 1 g/l solution of *butylhydroxytoluene R* in *hexane R*. Repeat the procedure with test solutions (a) and (b). Evaporate the eluates obtained from reference solution (b) and from test solutions (a) and (b), separately, to dryness at a temperature not exceeding 30 °C under a gentle current of *nitrogen R*. Dissolve each residue in 1.5 ml of *acetonitrile R*.

**Determination**

*Column:*
— *size:* $l = 0.15$ m, $\varnothing = 4.6$ mm;
— *stationary phase: octadecylsilyl silica gel for chromatography R* (5 μm).

*Mobile phase    phosphoric acid R, 96 per cent V/V solution of acetonitrile R* (0.2:99.8 *V/V*).

*Flow rate    1.0 ml/min.*

*Detection    Spectrophotometer at 265 nm.*

*Injection    2 quantities not exceeding 200 μl of each of the 3 solutions obtained under Purification.*

*System suitability:*
— *resolution:* minimum 1.4 between the peaks due to ergocalciferol and cholecalciferol in the chromatogram obtained with reference solution (b);
— the results obtained with test solution (b) duplicates do not differ by more than 5 per cent.

Calculate the content of vitamin $D_3$ in International Units per gram using the following expression, taking into account the assigned content of *cholecalciferol CRS*:

$$\frac{A_2}{A_6} \times \frac{A_3}{A_4 - \left[\dfrac{A_5}{A_1}\right] \times A_2} \times \frac{m_2}{m_1} \times \frac{V_2}{V_1} \times 40$$

$m_1 =$ mass of the sample in test solution (b), in grams;

$m_2 =$ total mass of *cholecalciferol CRS* used for the preparation of reference solution (a), in micrograms (500 μg);

$A_1 =$ area (or height) of the peak due to cholecalciferol in the chromatogram obtained with test solution (a);

$A_2 =$ area (or height) of the peak due to cholecalciferol in the chromatogram obtained with test solution (b);

$A_3 =$ area (or height) of the peak due to ergocalciferol in the chromatogram obtained with reference solution (b);

$A_4 =$ area (or height) of the peak due to ergocalciferol in the chromatogram obtained with test solution (b);

$A_5 =$ area (or height) of a possible peak in the chromatogram obtained with test solution (a) with the same retention time as the peak co-eluting with ergocalciferol in test solution (b);

$A_6 =$ area (or height) of the peak due to cholecalciferol in the chromatogram obtained with reference solution (b);

$V_1 =$ total volume of reference solution (a) (100 ml);

$V_2 =$ volume of reference solution (a) used for preparing reference solution (b) (2.0 ml).

## STORAGE
In an airtight and well-filled container, protected from light. If no antioxidant is added, store under an inert gas.

Once the container has been opened, its contents are used as soon as possible and any part of the contents not used at once is protected by an atmosphere of inert gas.

## LABELLING
The label states:
— the number of International Units of vitamin A per gram;
— the number of International Units of vitamin $D_3$ per gram.

*Ph Eur*

# Cod-liver Oil (Type B)

(*Ph Eur monograph 1193*)

## Action and use
Source of vitamins A and D.

Each IU of vitamin $D_3$ is equivalent to 0.025 μg of colecalciferol.

*Ph Eur*

## DEFINITION
Purified fatty oil obtained from the fresh livers of wild cod, *Gadus morhua* L. and other species of *Gadidae*, solid substances being removed by cooling and filtering. A suitable antioxidant may be added.

## Content
600 IU (180 μg) to 2500 IU (750 μg) of vitamin A per gram and 60 IU (1.5 μg) to 250 IU (6.25 μg) of vitamin $D_3$ per gram.

## CHARACTERS
### Appearance
Clear, yellowish liquid.

### Solubility
Practically insoluble in water, slightly soluble in alcohol, miscible with light petroleum.

## IDENTIFICATION
*First identification   A, B, C.*

*Second identification   C, D.*

A. In the assay for vitamin A using method A, the test solution shows an absorption maximum (*2.2.25*) at $325 \pm 2$ nm. In the assay for vitamin A using method B, the chromatogram obtained with the test solution shows a peak corresponding to the peak of all-*trans*-retinol in the chromatogram obtained with the reference solution.

B. In the assay for vitamin $D_3$, the chromatogram obtained with test solution (a) shows a peak corresponding to the peak of cholecalciferol in the chromatogram obtained with reference solution (b).

C. It complies with the test for composition of fatty acids (see Tests).

D. To 0.1 g add 0.5 ml of *methylene chloride R* and 1 ml of *antimony trichloride solution R*. Mix. A deep blue colour develops in about 10 s.

## TESTS
### Colour
Not more intensely coloured than a reference solution prepared as follows: to 3.0 ml of red primary solution add 25.0 ml of yellow primary solution and dilute to 50.0 ml with a 10 g/l solution of *hydrochloric acid R* (*2.2.2, Method II*).

### Relative density (*2.2.5*)
0.917 to 0.930.

### Refractive index (*2.2.6*)
1.477 to 1.484.

### Acid value (*2.5.1*)
Maximum 2.0.

### Iodine value (*2.5.4, Method B*)
150 to 180.

Use *starch solution R2*.

### Peroxide value (*2.5.5, Method B*)
Maximum 10.0.

### Unsaponifiable matter (*2.5.7*)
Maximum 1.5 per cent, determined on 2.0 g and extracting with 3 quantities, each of 50 ml, of *peroxide-free ether R*.

### Stearin
Heat at least 10 ml to 60-90 °C then allow to cool for 3 h in a bath of iced water or a thermostatically-controlled bath at $0 \pm 0.5$ °C. If necessary, to eliminate insoluble matter, filter the sample after heating. The sample remains clear.

### Composition of fatty acids
Gas chromatography (*2.2.28*).

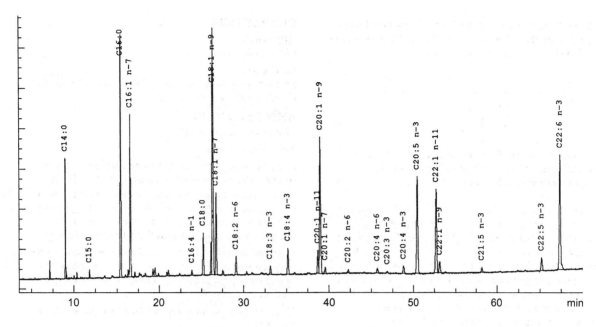

Figure 1193.-1. – *Chromatogram for the test for composition of fatty acids of cod-liver oil (type B)*

| Trivial name of fatty acid | Nomenclature | Lower limit area (per cent) | Upper limit area (per cent) |
|---|---|---|---|
| *Saturated fatty acids:* | | | |
| Myristic acid | 14:0 | 2.0 | 6.0 |
| Palmitic acid | 16:0 | 7.0 | 14.0 |
| Stearic acid | 18:0 | 1.0 | 4.0 |
| *Mono-unsaturated fatty acids:* | | | |
| Palmitoleic acid | 16:1 n-7 | 4.5 | 11.5 |
| *cis*-Vaccenic acid | 18:1 n-7 | 2.0 | 7.0 |
| Oleic acid | 18:1 n-9 | 12.0 | 21.0 |
| Gadoleic acid | 20:1 n-11 | 1.0 | 5.5 |
| Gondoic acid | 20:1 n-9 | 5.0 | 17.0 |
| Erucic acid | 22:1 n-9 | 0 | 1.5 |
| Cetoleic acid (22:1 n-11) | 22:1 n-11+13 | 5.0 | 12.0 |
| *Poly-unsaturated fatty acids:* | | | |
| Linoleic acid | 18:2 n-6 | 0.5 | 3.0 |
| α-Linolenic acid | 18:3 n-3 | 0 | 2.0 |
| Moroctic acid | 18:4 n-3 | 0.5 | 4.5 |
| Timnodonic (eicosapentaenoic) acid (EPA) | 20:5 n-3 | 7.0 | 16.0 |
| Cervonic (docosahexaenoic) acid (DHA) | 22:6 n-3 | 6.0 | 18.0 |

*Test solution*  Introduce about 0.45 g of the substance to be examined into a 10 ml volumetric flask, dissolve in *hexane R* containing 50 mg of *butylhydroxytoluene R* per litre and dilute to 10.0 ml with the same solvent. Transfer 2.0 ml of the solution into a quartz tube and evaporate the solvent with a gentle current of *nitrogen R*. Add 1.5 ml of a 20 g/l solution of *sodium hydroxide R* in *methanol R*, cover with *nitrogen R*, cap tightly with a polytetrafluoroethylene lined cap, mix and heat in a water-bath for 7 min. Cool, add 2 ml of *boron trichloride-methanol solution R*, cover with *nitrogen R*, cap tightly, mix and heat in a water-bath for 30 min. Cool to 40-50 °C, add 1 ml of *trimethylpentane R*, cap and vortex or shake vigorously for at least 30 s. Immediately add 5 ml of *saturated sodium chloride solution R*, cover with *nitrogen R*, cap

and vortex or shake thoroughly for at least 15 s. Allow the upper layer to become clear and transfer to a separate tube. Shake the methanol layer once more with 1 ml of *trimethylpentane R* and combine the trimethylpentane extracts. Wash the combined extracts with 2 quantities, each of 1 ml, of *water R* and dry over *anhydrous sodium sulphate R*. Prepare 2 solutions for each sample.

*Column:*
— *material*: fused silica;
— *size*: $l$ = 30 m, Ø = 0.25 mm;
— *stationary phase*: *macrogol 20 000 R* (film thickness 0.25 μm).

*Carrier gas*  *hydrogen for chromatography R* or *helium for chromatography R*, where oxygen scrubber is applied.

*Split ratio*  1:200.

*Temperature:*

| | Time (min) | Temperature (°C) |
|---|---|---|
| Column | 0 - 55 | 170 → 225 |
| | 55 - 75 | 225 |
| Injection port | | 250 |
| Detector | | 280 |

*Detection*  Flame ionisation.

*Injection*  1 μl, twice.

*System suitability:*
— the 15 fatty acids to be tested are satisfactorily identified from the chromatogram shown in Figure 1193.-1;
— injection of a mixture of equal amounts of *methyl palmitate R*, *methyl stearate R*, *methyl arachidate R*, and *methyl behenate R* give area percentages of 24.4, 24.8, 25.2 and 25.6 (± 0.5 per cent), respectively;
— *resolution*: minimum of 1.3 between the peaks due to methyl oleate and methyl *cis*-vaccenate; the resolution between the pair due to methyl gadoleate and methyl gondoate is sufficient for purposes of identification and area measurement.

Calculate the area per cent for each fatty acid methyl ester from the expression:

$$\frac{A_x}{A_t} \times 100$$

$A_x$ = peak area of fatty acid $x$;
$A_t$ = sum of the peak areas (up to C22:6 n-3).

The calculation is not valid unless:
— the total area is based only on peaks due to solely fatty acids methyl esters;
— the number of fatty acid methyl ester peaks exceeding 0.05 per cent of the total area is at least 24;
— the 24 largest peaks of the methyl esters account for more than 90 per cent of the total area. (These correspond to, in common elution order: 14:0, 15:0, 16:0, 16:1 n-7, 16:4 n-1, 18:0, 18:1 n-9, 18:1 n-7, 18:2 n-6, 18:3 n-3, 18:4 n-3, 20:1 n-11, 20:1 n-9, 20:1 n-7, 20:2 n-6, 20:4 n-6, 20:3 n-3, 20:4 n-3, 20:5 n-3, 22:1 n-11, 22:1 n-9, 21:5 n-3, 22:5 n-3, 22:6 n-3).

## ASSAY
### Vitamin A
*Carry out the test as rapidly as possible, avoiding exposure to actinic light and air, oxidising agents, oxidation catalysts (for example, copper and iron) and acids.*

Use method A. If method A is found not to be valid, use method B.

### Method A
Ultraviolet absorption spectrophotometry (*2.2.25*).

*Test solution*   To 1.00 g in a round-bottomed flask, add 3 ml of a freshly prepared 50 per cent *m/m* solution of *potassium hydroxide R* and 30 ml of *ethanol R*. Boil under reflux in a current of *nitrogen R* for 30 min. Cool rapidly and add 30 ml of *water R*. Extract with 50 ml of *ether R*. Repeat the extraction 3 times and discard the lower layer after complete separation. Wash the combined upper layers with 4 quantities, each of 50 ml, of *water R* and evaporate to dryness under a gentle current of *nitrogen R* at a temperature not exceeding 30 °C or in a rotary evaporator at a temperature not exceeding 30 °C under reduced pressure (water ejector). Dissolve the residue in sufficient *2-propanol R1* to give an expected concentration of vitamin A equivalent to 10-15 IU/ml.

Measure the absorbances of the solution at 300 nm, 310 nm, 325 nm and 334 nm and at the wavelength of maximum absorption with a suitable spectrophotometer in 1 cm specially matched cells, using *2-propanol R1* as the compensation liquid.

Calculate the content of vitamin A, as all-*trans*-retinol, in International Units per gram from the expression:

$$A_{325} \times \frac{1821}{100m} \times V$$

$A_{325}$ = absorbance at 325 nm;
$m$ = mass of the substance to be examined, in grams;
$V$ = total volume of solution containing 10-15 IU of vitamin A per millilitre;
1821 = conversion factor for the specific absorbance of all-*trans*-retinol, in International Units.

The above expression can be used only if $A_{325}$ has a value of not greater than $A_{325,\text{corr}}/0.970$ where $A_{325,\text{corr}}$ is the corrected absorbance at 325 nm and is given by the equation:

$$A_{325,\text{corr}} = 6.815A_{325} - 2.555A_{310} - 4.260A_{334}$$

A designates the absorbance at the wavelength indicated by the subscript.

If $A_{325}$ has a value greater than $A_{325,\text{corr}}/0.970$, calculate the content of vitamin A from the expression:

$$A_{325,\text{corr}} \times \frac{1821}{100m} \times V$$

The assay is not valid unless:
— the wavelength of maximum absorption lies between 323 nm and 327 nm;
— the absorbance at 300 nm relative to that at 325 nm is at most 0.73.

### Method B
Liquid chromatography (*2.2.29*).

*Test solution*   Prepare duplicates. To 2.00 g in a round-bottomed flask, add 5 ml of a freshly prepared 100 g/l solution of *ascorbic acid R* and 10 ml of a freshly prepared 800 g/l solution of *potassium hydroxide R* and 100 ml of *ethanol R*. Boil under a reflux condenser on a water-bath for 15 min. Add 100 ml of a 10 g/l solution of *sodium chloride R* and cool. Transfer the solution to a 500 ml separating funnel rinsing the round-bottomed flask with about 75 ml of a 10 g/l solution of *sodium chloride R* and then with 150 ml of a mixture of equal volumes of *light petroleum R1* and *ether R*. Shake for 1 min. When the layers have separated completely, discard the lower layer and wash the upper layer, first with 50 ml of a 30 g/l solution of *potassium hydroxide R* in a 10 per cent *V/V* solution of *ethanol R* and then with 3 quantities, each of 50 ml, of a 10 g/l solution of *sodium chloride R*. Filter the upper layer through 5 g of *anhydrous sodium sulphate R* on a fast filter paper into a 250 ml flask suitable for a rotary evaporator. Wash the funnel with 10 ml of fresh extraction mixture, filter and combine the upper layers. Distil them at a temperature not exceeding 30 °C under reduced pressure (water ejector) and fill with *nitrogen R* when evaporation is completed. Alternatively evaporate the solvent under a gentle current of *nitrogen R* at a temperature not exceeding 30 °C. Dissolve the residue in *2-propanol R*, transfer to a 25 ml volumetric flask and dilute to 25 ml with *2-propanol R*. Gentle heating in an ultrasonic bath may be required. (A large fraction of the white residue is cholesterol, constituting approximately 50 per cent of the unsaponifiable matter of cod-liver oil).

*Reference solution (a)*   Prepare a solution of *retinol acetate CRS* in *2-propanol R1* so that 1 ml contains about 1000 IU of all-*trans*-retinol.

The exact concentration of reference solution (a) is assessed by ultraviolet absorption spectrophotometry (*2.2.25*). Dilute reference solution (a) with *2-propanol R1* to a presumed concentration of 10-15 IU/ml and measure the absorbance at 326 nm in matched 1 cm cells using *2-propanol R1* as the compensation liquid.

Calculate the content of vitamin A in International Units per millilitre of reference solution (a) using the following expression, taking into account the assigned content of *retinol acetate CRS*:

$$A_{326} \times \frac{1900 \times V_2}{100 \times V_1}$$

$A_{326}$ = absorbance at 326 nm;

$V_1$ = volume of reference solution (a) used;

$V_2$ = volume of the diluted solution;

1900 = conversion factor for the specific absorbance of retinol acetate CRS, in International Units.

*Reference solution (b)* Proceed as described for the test solution but using 2.00 ml of reference solution (a) in place of the substance to be examined.

The exact concentration of reference solution (b) is assessed by ultraviolet absorption spectrophotometry (2.2.25). Dilute reference solution (b) with *2-propanol R1* to a presumed concentration of 10-15 IU/ml of all-*trans*-retinol and measure the absorbance at 325 nm in matched 1 cm cells using *2-propanol R1* as the compensation liquid.

Calculate the content of all-*trans*-retinol in International Units per millilitre of reference solution (b) from the expression:

$$A_{325} \times \frac{1821 \times V_3}{100 \times V_4}$$

$A_{325}$ = absorbance at 325 nm;

$V_3$ = volume of the diluted solution;

$V_4$ = volume of reference solution (b) used;

1821 = conversion factor for the specific absorbance of all-*trans*-retinol, in International Units.

*Column:*
— size: $l = 0.25$ m, $\varnothing = 4.6$ mm;
— stationary phase: *octadecylsilyl silica gel for chromatography R* (5-10 µm).

*Mobile phase* water R, methanol R (3:97 *V/V*).

*Flow rate* 1 ml/min.

*Detection* Spectrophotometer at 325 nm.

*Injection* 10 µl; inject in triplicate the test solution and reference solution (b).

*Retention time* all-*trans*-retinol = 5 ± 1 min.

*System suitability:*
— the chromatogram obtained with the test solution shows a peak due to that of all-*trans*-retinol in the chromatogram obtained with reference solution (b);
— the results obtained with the duplicate test solutions do not differ by more than 5 per cent;
— the recovery of all-*trans*-retinol in reference solution (b) as assessed by direct absorption spectrophotometry is greater than 95 per cent.

Calculate the content of vitamin A using the following expression:

$$A_1 \times \frac{C \times V}{A_2} \times \frac{1}{m}$$

$A_1$ = area of the peak due to all-*trans*-retinol in the chromatogram obtained with the test solution;

$A_2$ = area of the peak due to all-*trans*-retinol in the chromatogram obtained with reference solution (b);

$C$ = concentration of *retinol acetate CRS* in reference solution (a) as assessed prior to the saponification, in International Units per millilitre (= 1000 IU/ml);

$V$ = volume of reference solution (a) treated (2.00 ml);

$m$ = mass of the substance to be examined in the test solution (2.00 g).

## Vitamin D$_3$

Liquid chromatography (2.2.29). *Carry out the assay as rapidly as possible, avoiding exposure to actinic light and air.*

Internal standard solution

Dissolve 0.50 mg of *ergocalciferol CRS* in 100 ml of *ethanol R*.

*Test solution (a)* To 4.00 g in a round-bottomed flask, add 5 ml of a freshly prepared 100 g/l solution of *ascorbic acid R*, 10 ml of a freshly prepared 800 g/l solution of *potassium hydroxide R* and 100 ml of *ethanol R*. Boil under a reflux condenser on a water-bath for 30 min. Add 100 ml of a 10 g/l solution of *sodium chloride R* and cool the solution to room temperature. Transfer the solution to a 500 ml separating funnel rinsing the round-bottomed flask with about 75 ml of a 10 g/l solution of *sodium chloride R* and then with 150 ml of a mixture of equal volumes of *light petroleum R1* and *ether R*. Shake for 1 min. When the layers have separated completely, discard the lower layer and wash the upper layer, first with 50 ml of a 30 g/l solution of *potassium hydroxide R* in a 10 per cent *V/V* solution of *ethanol R*, and then with 3 quantities, each of 50 ml, of a 10 g/l solution of *sodium chloride R*. Filter the upper layer through 5 g of *anhydrous sodium sulphate R* on a fast filter paper into a 250 ml flask suitable for a rotary evaporator. Wash the funnel with 10 ml of fresh extraction mixture, filter and combine the upper layers. Distil them at a temperature not exceeding 30 °C under reduced pressure (water ejector) and fill with *nitrogen R* when evaporation is completed. Alternatively evaporate the solvent under a gentle current of *nitrogen R* at a temperature not exceeding 30 °C. Dissolve the residue in 1.5 ml of the mobile phase described under Purification. Gentle heating in an ultrasonic bath may be required. (A large fraction of the white residue is cholesterol, constituting approximately 50 per cent *m/m* of the unsaponifiable matter of cod-liver oil).

*Test solution (b)* Prepare duplicates. To 4.00 g add 2.0 ml of the internal standard solution and proceed as described for test solution (a).

*Reference solution (a)* Dissolve 0.50 mg of *cholecalciferol CRS* in 100.0 ml of *ethanol R*.

*Reference solution (b)* In a round-bottomed flask, add 2.0 ml of reference solution (a) and 2.0 ml of the internal standard solution and proceed as described for test solution (a).

### Purification

*Column:*
— size: $l = 0.25$ m, $\varnothing = 4.6$ mm;
— stationary phase: *nitrile silica gel for chromatography R* (10 µm).

*Mobile phase* isoamyl alcohol R, hexane R (1.6:98.4 *V/V*).

*Flow rate* 1.1 ml/min.

*Detection* Spectrophotometer at 265 nm.

Inject 350 µl of reference solution (b). Collect the eluate from 2 min before until 2 min after the retention time of cholecalciferol, in a ground-glass-stoppered tube containing 1 ml of a 1 g/l solution of *butylhydroxytoluene R* in *hexane R*. Repeat the procedure with test solutions (a) and (b). Evaporate the eluates obtained from reference solution (b) and from test solutions (a) and (b), separately, to dryness at a temperature not exceeding 30 °C under a gentle current of *nitrogen R*. Dissolve each residue in 1.5 ml of *acetonitrile R*.

## Determination

*Column:*
— *size:* $l = 0.15$ m, $\emptyset = 4.6$ mm;
— *stationary phase:* octadecylsilyl silica gel for chromatography R (5 µm).

*Mobile phase* phosphoric acid R, a 96 per cent $V/V$ solution of acetonitrile R (0.2:99.8 $V/V$).

*Flow rate* 1.0 ml/min.

*Detection* Spectrophotometer at 265 nm.

*Injection* 2 quantities not exceeding 200 µl of each of the 3 solutions obtained under Purification.

*System suitability:*
— *resolution:* minimum 1.4 between the peaks due to ergocalciferol and cholecalciferol in the chromatogram obtained with reference solution (b);
— the results obtained with the test solution (b) duplicates do not differ by more than 5 per cent.

Calculate the content of vitamin $D_3$ in International Units per gram using the following expression, taking into account the assigned content of *cholecalciferol CRS*:

$$\frac{A_2}{A_6} \times \frac{A_3}{A_4 - \left[\dfrac{A_5}{A_1}\right] \times A_2} \times \frac{m_2}{m_1} \times \frac{V_2}{V_1} \times 40$$

$m_1 =$ mass of the sample in test solution (b) in grams;

$m_2 =$ total mass of *cholecalciferol CRS* used for the preparation of reference solution (a) in micrograms (500 µg);

$A_1 =$ area (or height) of the peak due to cholecalciferol in the chromatogram obtained with test solution (a);

$A_2 =$ area (or height) of the peak due to cholecalciferol in the chromatogram obtained with test solution (b);

$A_3 =$ area (or height) of the peak due to ergocalciferol in the chromatogram obtained with reference solution (b);

$A_4 =$ area (or height) of the peak due to ergocalciferol in the chromatogram obtained with test solution (b);

$A_5 =$ area (or height) of a possible peak in the chromatogram obtained with test solution (a) with the same retention time as the peak co-eluting with ergocalciferol in test solution (b);

$A_6 =$ area (or height) of the peak due to cholecalciferol in the chromatogram obtained with reference solution (b);

$V_1 =$ total volume of reference solution (a) (100 ml);

$V_2 =$ volume of reference solution (a) used for preparing reference solution (b) (2.0 ml).

## STORAGE

In an airtight and well-filled container, protected from light. If no antioxidant is added, store under an inert gas.

Once the container has been opened, its contents are used as soon as possible and any part of the contents not used at once is protected by an atmosphere of inert gas.

## LABELLING

The label states:
— the number of International Units of vitamin A, per gram;
— the number of International Units of vitamin $D_3$, per gram.

*Ph Eur*

# Colchicine

(*Ph Eur monograph 0758*)

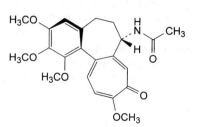

$C_{22}H_{25}NO_6$      399.4      64-86-8

**Action and use**
Used in treatment of gout.

**Preparation**
Colchicine Tablets

*Ph Eur*

## DEFINITION

(-)-*N*-[(7S,12aS)-1,2,3,10-Tetramethoxy-9-oxo-5,6,7,9-tetrahydrobenzo[*a*]heptalen-7-yl]acetamide.

**Content**
97.0 per cent to 102.0 per cent (anhydrous substance).

## CHARACTERS

**Appearance**
Yellowish-white, amorphous or crystalline powder.

**Solubility**
Very soluble in water, rapidly recrystallising from concentrated solutions as the sesquihydrate, freely soluble in alcohol, practically insoluble in cyclohexane.

## IDENTIFICATION

*First identification* B.

*Second identification* A, C, D.

A. Dissolve 5 mg in *alcohol R* and dilute to 100.0 ml with the same solvent. Dilute 5.0 ml of the solution to 25.0 ml with *alcohol R*. Examined between 230 nm and 400 nm (*2.2.25*), the solution shows 2 absorption maxima, at 243 nm and 350 nm. The ratio of the absorbance measured at 243 nm to that measured at 350 nm is 1.7 to 1.9.

B. Infrared absorption spectrophotometry (*2.2.24*).

*Preparation* Discs of *potassium bromide R*.

*Comparison* colchicine CRS.

C. To 0.5 ml of solution S (see Tests) add 0.5 ml of *dilute hydrochloric acid R* and 0.15 ml of *ferric chloride solution R1*. The solution is yellow and becomes dark green on boiling for 30 s. Cool, add 2 ml of *methylene chloride R* and shake. The organic layer is greenish-yellow.

D. Dissolve about 30 mg in 1 ml of *alcohol R* and add 0.15 ml of *ferric chloride solution R1*. A brownish-red colour develops.

## TESTS

**Solution S**
Dissolve 0.10 g in *water R* and dilute to 20 ml with the same solvent.

**Appearance of solution**
Solution S is clear (*2.2.1*) and not more intensely coloured than reference solution $GY_3$ (*2.2.2, Method II*).

## Acidity or alkalinity

To 10 ml of solution S add 0.1 ml of *bromothymol blue solution R1*. Either the solution does not change colour or it becomes green. Not more than 0.1 ml of *0.01 M sodium hydroxide* is required to change the colour of the indicator to blue.

## Specific optical rotation (*2.2.7*)

− 235 to − 250 (anhydrous substance).

Dissolve 50.0 mg in *alcohol R* and dilute to 10.0 ml with the same solvent.

## Related substances

Liquid chromatography (*2.2.29*).

*Test solution*  Dissolve 20.0 mg of the substance to be examined in a mixture of equal volumes of *methanol R* and water R and dilute to 20.0 ml with the same mixture of solvents.

*Reference solution (a)*  Dissolve 20.0 mg of *colchicine for system suitability CRS* in a mixture of equal volumes of *methanol R* and *water R* and dilute to 20.0 ml with the same mixture of solvents.

*Reference solution (b)*  Dilute 1.0 ml of the test solution to 100.0 ml with a mixture of equal volumes of *methanol R* and *water R*.

*Reference solution (c)*  Dilute 1 ml of reference solution (b) to 20.0 ml with a mixture of equal volumes of *methanol R* and *water R*.

*Column:*
— *size*: $l$ = 0.25 m, Ø = 4.6 mm;
— *stationary phase: octylsilyl silica gel for chromatography R1* (5 µm).

*Mobile phase*  Mix 450 volumes of a 6.8 g/l solution of *potassium dihydrogen phosphate R* and 530 volumes of *methanol R*. After cooling to room temperature, adjust the volume to 1000 ml with *methanol R*. Adjust the apparent pH to 5.5 with *dilute phosphoric acid R*.

*Flow rate*  1 ml/min.

*Detection*  Spectrophotometer at 254 nm.

*Injection*  20 µl.

*Run time*  3 times the retention time of colchicine.

*Relative retention*  With reference to colchicine (retention time = about 7 min): impurity D = about 0.4; impurity E = about 0.7; impurity B = about 0.8; impurity A = about 0.94; impurity C = about 1.2.

*System suitability*  Reference solution (a):

*Peak-to-valley ratio*  Minimum 2, where $H_P$ = height above the baseline of the peak due to impurity A and $H_V$ = height above the baseline of the lowest point of the curve separating this peak from the peak due to colchicine.

*Limits:*
— *impurity A*: not more than 3.5 times the area of the principal peak in the chromatogram obtained with reference solution (b) (3.5 per cent);
— *any other impurity*: not more than the area of the principal peak in the chromatogram obtained with reference solution (b) (1 per cent);
— *total*: not more than 5 times the area of the principal peak in the chromatogram obtained with reference solution (b) (5 per cent);
— *disregard limit*: area of the principal peak in the chromatogram obtained with reference solution (c) (0.05 per cent).

## Colchiceine

Maximum 0.2 per cent.

Dissolve 50 mg in *water R* and dilute to 5 ml with the same solvent. Add 0.1 ml of *ferric chloride solution R1*. The solution is not more intensely coloured than a mixture of 1 ml of red primary solution, 2 ml of yellow primary solution and 2 ml of blue primary solution (*2.2.2, Method II*).

## Chloroform (*2.4.24*)

Maximum 500 ppm.

## Ethyl acetate (*2.4.24*)

Maximum 6.0 per cent *m/m*.

## Water (*2.5.12*)

Maximum 2.0 per cent, determined on 0.500 g.

## Sulphated ash (*2.4.14*)

Maximum 0.1 per cent, determined on 0.5 g.

## ASSAY

Dissolve 0.250 g with gentle heating in a mixture of 10 ml of *acetic anhydride R* and 20 ml of *toluene R*. Titrate with *0.1 M perchloric acid*, determining the end-point potentiometrically (*2.2.20*).

1 ml of *0.1 M perchloric acid* is equivalent to 39.94 mg of $C_{22}H_{25}NO_6$.

## STORAGE

Protected from light.

## IMPURITIES

A. R1 = R3 = $CH_3$, R2 = H: *N*-[(7*S*,12a*S*)-1,2,3,10-tetramethoxy-9-oxo-5,6,7,9-tetrahydrobenzo[*a*]heptalen-7-yl]formamide (*N*-deacetyl-*N*-formylcolchicine),

E. R1 = H, R2 = R3 = $CH_3$: *N*-[(7*S*,12a*S*)-3-hydroxy-1,2,10-trimethoxy-9-oxo-5,6,7,9-tetrahydrobenzo[*a*]heptalen-7-yl]acetamide (3-*O*-demethylcolchicine),

F. R1 = R2 = $CH_3$, R3 = H: *N*-[(7*S*,12a*S*)-10-hydroxy-1,2,3-trimethoxy-9-oxo-5,6,7,9-tetrahydrobenzo[*a*]heptalen-7-yl]acetamide (colchiceine),

B. (-)-*N*-[(7*S*,12a*R*)-1,2,3,10-tetramethoxy-9-oxo-5,6,7,9-tetrahydrobenzo[*a*]heptalen-7-yl]acetamide (conformational isomer),

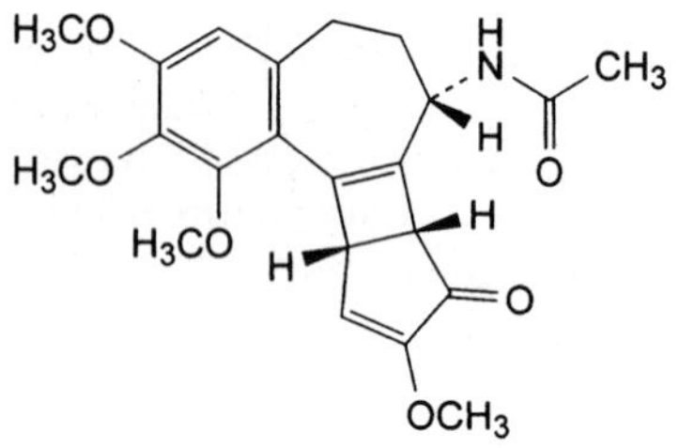

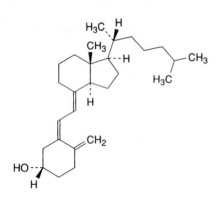

C. N-[(7S,7bR,10aS)-1,2,3,9-tetramethoxy-8-oxo-5,6,7,7b,8,10a-hexahydrobenzo[a]cyclopenta[3,4]cyclobuta[1,2-c]cyclohepten-7-yl]acetamide (β-lumicolchicine),

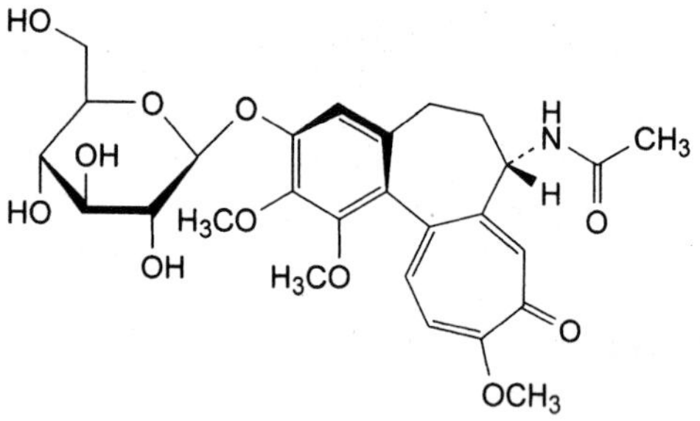

D. N-[(7S,12aS)-3-(β-D-glucopyranosyloxy)-1,2,10-trimethoxy-9-oxo-5,6,7,9-tetrahydrobenzo[a]heptalen-7-yl]acetamide (colchicoside).

_____ Ph Eur

# Colecalciferol

(*Cholecalciferol, Ph Eur monograph 0072*)

C27H44O          384.6          67-97-0

**Action and use**

Vitamin D3 analogue.

**Preparations**

Calcium and Colecalciferol Tablets

Colecalciferol Injection

Colecalciferol Tablets

Paediatric Vitamins A, C and D Oral Drops

When cholecalciferol or vitamin D3 is prescribed or demanded, Colecalciferol shall be dispensed or supplied. When calciferol or vitamin D is prescribed or demanded, Colecalciferol or Ergocalciferol shall be dispensed or supplied.

Ph Eur

**DEFINITION**

(5Z,7E)-9,10-Secocholesta-5,7,10(19)-trien-3β-ol.

**Content**

97.0 per cent to 102.0 per cent.

1 mg of cholecalciferol is equivalent to 40 000 IU of antirachitic activity (vitamin D) in rats.

**CHARACTERS**

**Appearance**

White or almost white crystals.

**Solubility**

Practically insoluble in water, freely soluble in ethanol (96 per cent), soluble in trimethylpentane and in fatty oils.

It is sensitive to air, heat and light. Solutions in solvents without an antioxidant are unstable and are to be used immediately.

A reversible isomerisation to pre-cholecalciferol takes place in solution, depending on temperature and time. The activity is due to both compounds.

**IDENTIFICATION**

Infrared absorption spectrophotometry (2.2.24).

*Comparison*   cholecalciferol CRS.

**TESTS**

**Specific optical rotation** (2.2.7)

+ 105 to + 112, determined within 30 min of preparing the solution.

Dissolve 0.200 g rapidly in *aldehyde-free alcohol R* without heating and dilute to 25.0 ml with the same solvent.

**Related substances**

Liquid chromatography (2.2.29)

*Prepare the solutions immediately before use, avoiding exposure to actinic light and air.*

*Test solution*   Dissolve 10.0 mg of the substance to be examined in *trimethylpentane R* without heating and dilute to 10.0 ml with the same solvent.

*Reference solution (a)*   Dissolve 10.0 mg of *cholecalciferol CRS* in *trimethylpentane R* without heating and dilute to 10.0 ml with the same solvent.

*Reference solution (b)*   Dilute 1.0 ml of *cholecalciferol for system suitability CRS* (containing impurity A) to 5.0 ml with the mobile phase. Heat in a water-bath at 90 °C under a reflux condenser for 45 min and cool (formation of pre-cholecalciferol).

*Reference solution (c)*   Dilute 10.0 ml of reference solution (a) to 100.0 ml with the mobile phase. Dilute 1.0 ml of this solution to 100.0 ml with the mobile phase.

*Column:*

— *size: l* = 0.25 m, Ø = 4.6 mm;

— *stationary phase: silica gel for chromatography R* (5 μm).

*Mobile phase*   pentanol R, hexane R (3:997 V/V).

*Flow rate*   2 ml/min.

*Detection*   Spectrophotometer at 265 nm.

*Injection*   5 μl of the test solution and reference solutions (b) and (c).

*Run time*   Twice the retention time of cholecalciferol.

*Relative retention*   With reference to cholecalciferol (retention time = about 19 min):

pre-cholecalciferol = about 0.5; impurity A = about 0.6.

*System suitability*   Reference solution (b):

— *resolution*: minimum 1.5 between the peaks due to pre-cholecalciferol and impurity A.

*Limits*:
— *impurity A*: not more than the area of the principal peak in the chromatogram obtained with reference solution (c) (0.1 per cent);
— *unspecified impurities*: for each impurity, not more than the area of the principal peak in the chromatogram obtained with reference solution (c) (0.10 per cent);
— *total*: not more than 10 times the area of the principal peak in the chromatogram obtained with reference solution (c) (1.0 per cent);
— *disregard limit*: 0.5 times the area of the principal peak in the chromatogram obtained with reference solution (c) (0.05 per cent); disregard the peak due to pre-cholecalciferol.

## ASSAY

Liquid chromatography (*2.2.29*) as described in the test for related substances, with the following modification.

*Injection* Test solution and reference solution (a).

Calculate the percentage content of cholecalciferol ($C_{27}H_{44}O$) from the declared content of *cholecalciferol CRS*.

## STORAGE

In an airtight container, under nitrogen, protected from light, at a temperature of 2 °C to 8 °C.

The contents of an opened container are to be used immediately.

## IMPURITIES

*Specified impurities* A.

*Other detectable impurities* (the following substances would, if present at a sufficient level, be detected by one or other of the tests in the monograph. They are limited by the general acceptance criterion for other/unspecified impurities and/or by the general monograph *Substances for pharmaceutical use (2034)*. It is therefore not necessary to identify these impurities for demonstration of compliance. See also *5.10. Control of impurities in substances for pharmaceutical use*): B, C, D, E.

A. (5E,7E)-9,10-secocholesta-5,7,10(19)-trien-3β-ol (*trans*-cholecalciferol, *trans*-vitamin D$_3$),

B. cholesta-5,7-dien-3β-ol (7,8-didehydrocholesterol, provitamin D$_3$),

C. 9β,10α-cholesta-5,7-dien-3β-ol (lumisterol$_3$),

D. (6E)-9,10-secocholesta-5(10),6,8(14)-trien-3β-ol (iso-tachysterol$_3$),

E. (6E)-9,10-secocholesta-5(10),6,8-trien-3β-ol (tachysterol$_3$).

# Colecalciferol Concentrate (Oily Form)

(*Cholecalciferol Concentrate (Oily Form)*, Ph Eur monograph 0575)

**Action and use**

Vitamin D analogue (Vitamin D$_3$).

*Ph Eur* _____

## DEFINITION

Solution of *Cholecalciferol (0072)* in a suitable vegetable fatty oil, authorised by the competent authority.

## Content

90.0 per cent to 110.0 per cent of the cholecalciferol content stated on the label, which is not less than 500 000 IU/g.

It may contain suitable stabilisers such as antioxidants.

## CHARACTERS

**Appearance**

Clear, yellow liquid.

**Solubility**

Practically insoluble in water, slightly soluble in anhydrous ethanol, miscible with solvents of fats.

Partial solidification may occur, depending on the temperature.

## IDENTIFICATION

*First identification*   A, C.

*Second identification*   A, B.

A. Thin-layer chromatography (*2.2.27*). *Prepare the solutions immediately before use.*

*Test solution*   Dissolve an amount of the preparation to be examined corresponding to 400 000 IU in *ethylene chloride R* containing 10 g/l of *squalane R* and 0.1 g/l of *butylhydroxytoluene R* and dilute to 4 ml with the same solution.

*Reference solution (a)*   Dissolve 10 mg of *cholecalciferol CRS* in *ethylene chloride R* containing 10 g/l of *squalane R* and 0.1 g/l of *butylhydroxytoluene R* and dilute to 4 ml with the same solution.

*Reference solution (b)*   Dissolve 10 mg of *ergocalciferol CRS* in *ethylene chloride R* containing 10 g/l of *squalane R* and 0.1 g/l of *butylhydroxytoluene R* and dilute to 4 ml with the same solution.

*Plate*   TLC silica gel G plate R.

*Mobile phase*   A 0.1 g/l solution of *butylhydroxytoluene R* in a mixture of equal volumes of *cyclohexane R* and *peroxide-free ether R*.

*Application*   20 μl.

*Development*   Immediately, protected from light, over a path of 15 cm.

*Drying*   In air.

*Detection*   Spray with *sulphuric acid R*.

*Results*   The chromatogram obtained with the test solution shows immediately a bright yellow principal spot which rapidly becomes orange-brown, then gradually greenish-grey, remaining so for 10 min. This spot is similar in position, colour and size to the spot in the chromatogram obtained with reference solution (a). The chromatogram obtained with reference solution (b) shows immediately at the same level an orange principal spot which gradually becomes reddish-brown and remains so for 10 min.

B. Ultraviolet and visible absorption spectrophotometry (*2.2.25*).

*Test solution*   Prepare a solution in *cyclohexane R* containing the equivalent of about 400 IU/ml.

*Spectral range*   250-300 nm.

*Absorption maximum*   At 267 nm.

C. Examine the chromatograms obtained in the assay.

*Results*   The principal peak in the chromatogram obtained with the test solution is similar in retention time to the principal peak in the chromatogram obtained with reference solution (a).

## TESTS

**Acid value** (*2.5.1*)

Maximum 2.0.

Dissolve 5.0 g in 25 ml of the prescribed mixture of solvents.

**Peroxide value** (*2.5.5, Method A*)

Maximum 20.

**Related substances**

The thresholds indicated under Related substances (Table 2034.-1) in the general monograph *Substances for pharmaceutical use (2034)* do not apply.

## ASSAY

*Carry out the assay as rapidly as possible, avoiding exposure to actinic light and air.*

Liquid chromatography (*2.2.29*).

*Test solution*   Dissolve a quantity of the preparation to be examined, weighed with an accuracy of 0.1 per cent, equivalent to about 400 000 IU, in 10.0 ml of *toluene R* and dilute to 100.0 ml with the mobile phase.

*Reference solution (a)*   Dissolve 10.0 mg of *cholecalciferol CRS* without heating in 10.0 ml of *toluene R* and dilute to 100.0 ml with the mobile phase.

*Reference solution (b)*   Dilute 1.0 ml of *cholecalciferol for system suitability CRS* to 5.0 ml with the mobile phase. Heat in a water-bath at 90 °C under a reflux condenser for 45 min and cool.

*Reference solution (c)*   Dissolve 0.10 g of *cholecalciferol CRS* without heating in *toluene R* and dilute to 100.0 ml with the same solvent.

*Reference solution (d)*   Dilute 5.0 ml of reference solution (c) to 50.0 ml with the mobile phase. Keep the solution in iced water.

*Reference solution (e)*   Place 5.0 ml of reference solution (c) in a volumetric flask, add about 10 mg of *butylhydroxytoluene R* and displace air from the flask with *nitrogen R*. Heat in a water-bath at 90 °C under a reflux condenser protected from light and under *nitrogen R* for 45 min. Cool and dilute to 50.0 ml with the mobile phase.

*Column:*
— *size: l* = 0.25 m, Ø = 4.6 mm;
— *stationary phase*: silica gel for chromatography R (5 μm).

*Mobile phase*   pentanol R, hexane R (3:997 *V/V*).

*Flow rate*   2 ml/min.

*Detection*   Spectrophotometer at 254 nm.

*Injection*   The chosen volume of each solution (the same volume for reference solution (a) and for the test solution); automatic injection device or sample loop recommended.

*Relative retention*   With reference to cholecalciferol:
pre-cholecalciferol = about 0.4;
*trans*-cholecalciferol = about 0.5.

*System suitability*   Reference solution (b):

— *resolution*: minimum 1.0 between the peaks due to pre-cholecalciferol and *trans*-cholecalciferol; if necessary adjust the proportions of the constituents and the flow rate of the mobile phase to obtain this resolution;

— *repeatability*: maximum relative standard deviation of 1.0 per cent for the peak due to cholecalciferol after 6 injections.

Calculate the conversion factor (*f*) using the following expression:

$$\frac{K - L}{M}$$

$K$ = area (or height) of the peak due to cholecalciferol in the chromatogram obtained with reference solution (d);

$L$ = area (or height) of the peak due to cholecalciferol in the chromatogram obtained with reference solution (e);

$M$ = area (or height) of the peak due to pre-cholecalciferol in the chromatogram obtained with reference solution (e).

The value of *f* determined in duplicate on different days may be used during the entire procedure.

Calculate the content of cholecalciferol in International Units per gram using the following expression:

$$\frac{m'}{V'} \times \frac{V}{m} \times \frac{S_D + (f \times S_p)}{S'_D} \times 40\,000 \times 1000$$

$m$ = mass of the preparation to be examined in the test solution, in milligrams;

$m'$ = mass of *cholecalciferol CRS* in reference solution (a), in milligrams;

$V$ = volume of the test solution (100 ml);

$V'$ = volume of reference solution (a) (100 ml);

$S_D$ = area (or height) of the peak due to cholecalciferol in the chromatogram obtained with the test solution;

$S'_D$ = area (or height) of the peak due to cholecalciferol in the chromatogram obtained with reference solution (a);

$S_p$ = area (or height) of the peak due to pre-cholecalciferol in the chromatogram obtained with the test solution;

$f$ = conversion factor.

## STORAGE

In an airtight, well-filled container, protected from light. The contents of an opened container are to be used as soon as possible; any unused part is to be protected by an atmosphere of nitrogen.

## LABELLING

The label states:
— the number of International Units per gram;
— the method of restoring the solution if partial solidification occurs.

*Ph Eur*

# Colecalciferol Concentrate (Powder Form)

*(Cholecalciferol Concentrate (Powder Form), Ph Eur monograph 0574)*

## Action and use
Vitamin D analogue (Vitamin D$_3$).

*Ph Eur*

## DEFINITION
Powder concentrate obtained by dispersing an oily solution of *Cholecalciferol (0072)* in an appropriate matrix, which is usually based on a combination of gelatin and carbohydrates of suitable quality, authorised by the competent authority.

## Content
90.0 per cent to 110.0 per cent of the cholecalciferol content stated on the label, which is not less than 100 000 IU/g.

It may contain suitable stabilisers such as antioxidants.

## CHARACTERS
### Appearance
White or yellowish-white, small particles.

### Solubility
Practically insoluble, swells, or forms a dispersion in water, depending on the formulation.

## IDENTIFICATION
*First identification* A, C.

*Second identification* A, B.

A. Thin-layer chromatography (2.2.27). *Prepare the solutions immediately before use.*

*Test solution* Place 10.0 ml of the test solution prepared for the assay in a suitable flask and evaporate to dryness under reduced pressure by swirling in a water-bath at 40 °C. Cool under running water and restore atmospheric pressure with *nitrogen R*. Dissolve the residue immediately in 0.4 ml of *ethylene chloride R* containing 10 g/l of *squalane R* and 0.1 g/l of *butylhydroxytoluene R*.

*Reference solution (a)* Dissolve 10 mg of *cholecalciferol CRS* in *ethylene chloride R* containing 10 g/l of *squalane R* and 0.1 g/l of *butylhydroxytoluene R* and dilute to 4 ml with the same solution.

*Reference solution (b)* Dissolve 10 mg of *ergocalciferol CRS* in *ethylene chloride R* containing 10 g/l of *squalane R* and 0.1 g/l of *butylhydroxytoluene R* and dilute to 4 ml with the same solution.

*Plate* TLC silica gel G plate R.

*Mobile phase* A 0.1 g/l solution of *butylhydroxytoluene R* in a mixture of equal volumes of *cyclohexane R* and *peroxide-free ether R*.

*Application* 20 μl.

*Development* Immediately, protected from light, over a path of 15 cm.

*Drying* In air.

*Detection* Spray with *sulphuric acid R*.

*Results* The chromatogram obtained with the test solution shows immediately a bright yellow principal spot, which rapidly becomes orange-brown, then gradually greenish-grey, remaining so for 10 min. This spot is similar in position, colour and size to the spot in the chromatogram obtained with reference solution (a). The chromatogram obtained with reference solution (b) shows immediately at the same level an orange principal spot, which gradually becomes reddish-brown and remains so for 10 min.

B. Ultraviolet and visible absorption spectrophotometry (2.2.25).

*Test solution*   Place 5.0 ml of the test solution prepared for the assay in a suitable flask and evaporate to dryness under reduced pressure by swirling in a water-bath at 40 °C. Cool under running water and restore atmospheric pressure with *nitrogen R*. Dissolve the residue immediately in 50.0 ml of *cyclohexane R*.

*Spectral range*   250-300 nm.

*Absorption maximum*   At 265 nm.

C. Examine the chromatograms obtained in the assay.

*Results*   The principal peak in the chromatogram obtained with the test solution is similar in retention time to the principal peak in the chromatogram obtained with reference solution (a).

## TESTS

### Related substances

The thresholds indicated under Related substances (Table 2034.-1) in the general monograph *Substances for pharmaceutical use (2034)* do not apply.

## ASSAY

*Carry out the assay as rapidly as possible, avoiding exposure to actinic light and air.*

Liquid chromatography (2.2.29).

*Test solution*   Introduce into a saponification flask a quantity of the preparation to be examined, weighed with an accuracy of 0.1 per cent, equivalent to about 100 000 IU. Add 5 ml of *water R*, 20 ml of *anhydrous ethanol R*, 1 ml of *sodium ascorbate solution R* and 3 ml of a freshly prepared 50 per cent *m/m* solution of *potassium hydroxide R*. Heat in a water-bath under a reflux condenser for 30 min. Cool rapidly under running water. Transfer the liquid to a separating funnel with the aid of 2 quantities, each of 15 ml, of *water R*, 1 quantity of 10 ml of *ethanol (96 per cent) R* and 2 quantities, each of 50 ml, of *pentane R*. Shake vigorously for 30 s. Allow to stand until the 2 layers are clear. Transfer the lower aqueous-alcoholic layer to a 2$^{nd}$ separating funnel and shake with a mixture of 10 ml of *ethanol (96 per cent) R* and 50 ml of *pentane R*. After separation, transfer the aqueous-alcoholic layer to a 3$^{rd}$ separating funnel and the pentane layer to the 1$^{st}$ separating funnel, washing the 2$^{nd}$ separating funnel with 2 quantities, each of 10 ml, of *pentane R* and adding the washings to the 1$^{st}$ separating funnel. Shake the aqueous-alcoholic layer with 50 ml of *pentane R* and add the pentane layer to the 1$^{st}$ funnel. Wash the pentane layer with 2 quantities, each of 50 ml, of a freshly prepared 30 g/l solution of *potassium hydroxide R* in *ethanol (10 per cent V/V) R*, shaking vigorously, then wash with successive quantities, each of 50 ml, of *water R* until the washings are neutral to phenolphthalein. Transfer the washed pentane extract to a ground-glass-stoppered flask. Evaporate the contents of the flask to dryness under reduced pressure by swirling in a water-bath at 40 °C. Cool under running water and restore atmospheric pressure with *nitrogen R*. Dissolve the residue immediately in 5.0 ml of *toluene R* and add 20.0 ml of the mobile phase to obtain a solution containing about 4000 IU/ml.

*Reference solution (a)*   Dissolve 10.0 mg of *cholecalciferol CRS*, without heating, in 10.0 ml of *toluene R* and dilute to 100.0 ml with the mobile phase.

*Reference solution (b)*   Dilute 1.0 ml of *cholecalciferol for system suitability CRS* to 5.0 ml with the mobile phase. Heat in a water-bath at 90 °C under a reflux condenser for 45 min and cool.

*Reference solution (c)*   Dissolve 0.10 g of *cholecalciferol CRS*, without heating, in *toluene R* and dilute to 100.0 ml with the same solvent.

*Reference solution (d)*   Dilute 5.0 ml of reference solution (c) to 50.0 ml with the mobile phase. Keep the solution in iced water.

*Reference solution (e)*   Place 5.0 ml of reference solution (c) in a volumetric flask, add about 10 mg of *butylhydroxytoluene R* and displace the air from the flask with *nitrogen R*. Heat in a water-bath at 90 °C under a reflux condenser, protected from light and under *nitrogen R*, for 45 min. Cool and dilute to 50.0 ml with the mobile phase.

*Column:*
— *size*: $l = 0.25$ m, $\emptyset = 4.6$ mm;
— *stationary phase*: *silica gel for chromatography R* (5 μm).

*Mobile phase*   pentanol R, hexane R (3:997 *V/V*).

*Flow rate*   2 ml/min.

*Detection*   Spectrophotometer at 254 nm.

*Injection*   The chosen volume of each solution (the same volume for reference solution (a) and for the test solution); automatic injection device or sample loop recommended.

*Relative retention*   With reference to cholecalciferol:
pre-cholecalciferol = about 0.4;
*trans*-cholecalciferol = about 0.5.

*System suitability*   Reference solution (b):
— *resolution*: minimum 1.0 between the peaks due to pre-cholecalciferol and *trans*-cholecalciferol; if necessary, adjust the proportions of the constituents and the flow rate of the mobile phase to obtain this resolution;
— *repeatability*: maximum relative standard deviation of 1.0 per cent for the peak due to cholecalciferol after 6 injections.

Calculate the conversion factor (*f*) using the following expression:

$$\frac{K - L}{M}$$

$K$ =   area (or height) of the peak due to cholecalciferol in the chromatogram obtained with reference solution (d);
$L$ =   area (or height) of the peak due to cholecalciferol in the chromatogram obtained with reference solution (e);
$M$ =   area (or height) of the peak due to pre-cholecalciferol in the chromatogram obtained with reference solution (e).

The value of *f* determined in duplicate on different days may be used during the entire procedure.

Calculate the content of cholecalciferol in International Units per gram using the following expression:

$$\frac{m'}{V'} \times \frac{V}{m} \times \frac{S_D + (f \times S_p)}{S'_D} \times 40\,000 \times 1000$$

$m$ =   mass of the preparation to be examined in the test solution, in milligrams;
$m'$ =   mass of *cholecalciferol CRS* in reference solution (a), in milligrams;

$V$ = volume of the test solution (25 ml);

$V'$ = volume of reference solution (a) (100 ml);

$S_D$ = area (or height) of the peak due to cholecalciferol in the chromatogram obtained with the test solution;

$S'_D$ = area (or height) of the peak due to cholecalciferol in the chromatogram obtained with reference solution (a);

$S_p$ = area (or height) of the peak due to pre-cholecalciferol in the chromatogram obtained with the test solution;

$f$ = conversion factor.

## STORAGE

In an airtight, well-filled container, protected from light. The contents of an opened container are to be used as soon as possible; any unused part is to be protected by an atmosphere of nitrogen.

## LABELLING

The label states the number of International Units per gram.

_____ *Ph Eur*

# Colecalciferol Concentrate (Water-dispersible Form)

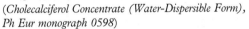

*(Cholecalciferol Concentrate (Water-Dispersible Form), Ph Eur monograph 0598)*

## Action and use
Vitamin D analogue (Vitamin $D_3$).

*Ph Eur* _____

## DEFINITION
Solution of *Cholecalciferol (0072)* in a suitable vegetable fatty oil, authorised by the competent authority, to which suitable solubilisers have been added.

## Content
90.0 per cent to 115.0 per cent of the cholecalciferol content stated on the label, which is not less than 100 000 IU/g.

It may contain suitable stabilisers such as antioxidants.

## CHARACTERS
### Appearance
Slightly yellowish liquid of variable opalescence and viscosity.

Highly concentrated solutions may become cloudy at low temperatures or form a gel at room temperature.

## IDENTIFICATION
*First identification* A, C, D.

*Second identification* A, B, D.

A. Thin-layer chromatography (*2.2.27*). *Prepare the solutions immediately before use.*

*Test solution* Place 10.0 ml of the test solution prepared for the assay in a suitable flask and evaporate to dryness under reduced pressure by swirling in a water-bath at 40 °C. Cool under running water and restore atmospheric pressure with *nitrogen R*. Dissolve the residue immediately in 0.4 ml of *ethylene chloride R* containing 10 g/l of *squalane R* and 0.1 g/l of *butylhydroxytoluene R*.

*Reference solution (a)* Dissolve 10 mg of *cholecalciferol CRS* in *ethylene chloride R* containing 10 g/l of *squalane R* and 0.1 g/l of *butylhydroxytoluene R* and dilute to 4 ml with the same solution.

*Reference solution (b)* Dissolve 10 mg of *ergocalciferol CRS* in *ethylene chloride R* containing 10 g/l of *squalane R* and 0.1 g/l of *butylhydroxytoluene R* and dilute to 4 ml with the same solution.

*Plate* TLC silica gel G plate R.

*Mobile phase* A 0.1 g/l solution of *butylhydroxytoluene R* in a mixture of equal volumes of *cyclohexane R* and *peroxide-free ether R*.

*Application* 20 µl.

*Development* Immediately, protected from light, over a path of 15 cm.

*Drying* In air.

*Detection* Spray with *sulphuric acid R*.

*Results* The chromatogram obtained with the test solution shows immediately a bright yellow principal spot, which rapidly becomes orange-brown, then gradually greenish-grey, remaining so for 10 min. This spot is similar in position, colour and size to the principal spot in the chromatogram obtained with reference solution (a). The chromatogram obtained with reference solution (b) shows immediately at the same level an orange principal spot, which gradually becomes reddish-brown and remains so for 10 min.

B. Ultraviolet and visible absorption spectrophotometry (*2.2.25*).

*Test solution* Place 5.0 ml of the test solution prepared for the assay in a suitable flask and evaporate to dryness under reduced pressure by swirling in a water-bath at 40 °C. Cool under running water and restore atmospheric pressure with *nitrogen R*. Dissolve the residue immediately in 50.0 ml of *cyclohexane R*.

*Spectral range* 250-300 nm.

*Absorption maximum* At 265 nm.

C. Examine the chromatograms obtained in the assay.

*Results* The principal peak in the chromatogram obtained with the test solution is similar in retention time to the principal peak in the chromatogram obtained with reference solution (a).

D. Mix about 1 g with 10 ml of *water R* previously warmed to 50 °C, and cool to 20 °C. Immediately after cooling, a uniform, slightly opalescent and slightly yellow dispersion is obtained.

## TESTS
### Related substances
The thresholds indicated under Related substances (Table 2034.-1) in the general monograph *Substances for pharmaceutical use (2034)* do not apply.

## ASSAY
*Carry out the assay as rapidly as possible, avoiding exposure to actinic light and air.*

Liquid chromatography (*2.2.29*).

*Test solution* Introduce into a saponification flask a quantity of the preparation to be examined, weighed with an accuracy of 0.1 per cent, equivalent to about 100 000 IU. Add 5 ml of *water R*, 20 ml of *anhydrous ethanol R*, 1 ml of *sodium ascorbate solution R* and 3 ml of a freshly prepared 50 per cent m/m solution of *potassium hydroxide R*. Heat in a water-bath under a reflux condenser for 30 min. Cool rapidly under running water. Transfer the liquid to a separating funnel with the aid of 2 quantities, each of 15 ml, of *water R*, 1 quantity of 10 ml of *ethanol (96 per cent) R* and 2 quantities, each of 50 ml, of *pentane R*. Shake vigorously for 30 s. Allow to stand until the 2 layers are clear. Transfer the aqueous-alcoholic layer to a 2nd separating funnel and shake with a mixture of 10 ml of *ethanol (96 per cent) R* and 50 ml of *pentane R*. After separation, transfer the aqueous-alcoholic layer to a 3$^{rd}$ separating funnel and the pentane layer to the 1$^{st}$ separating funnel, washing the 2$^{nd}$ separating funnel with 2 quantities, each of 10 ml, of *pentane R* and adding the washings to the 1$^{st}$ separating funnel. Shake the aqueous-alcoholic layer with 50 ml of *pentane R* and add the pentane layer to the 1$^{st}$ funnel. Wash the pentane layer with 2 quantities, each of 50 ml, of a freshly prepared 30 g/l solution of *potassium hydroxide R* in *ethanol (10 per cent V/V) R*, shaking vigorously, and then wash with successive quantities, each of 50 ml, of *water R* until the washings are neutral to phenolphthalein. Transfer the washed pentane extract to a ground-glass-stoppered flask. Evaporate the contents of the flask to dryness under reduced pressure by swirling in a water-bath at 40 °C. Cool under running water and restore atmospheric pressure with *nitrogen R*. Dissolve the residue immediately in 5.0 ml of *toluene R* and add 20.0 ml of the mobile phase to obtain a solution containing about 4000 IU/ml.

*Reference solution (a)*   Dissolve 10.0 mg of *cholecalciferol CRS*, without heating, in 10.0 ml of *toluene R* and dilute to 100.0 ml with the mobile phase.

*Reference solution (b)*   Dilute 1.0 ml of *cholecalciferol for system suitability CRS* to 5.0 ml with the mobile phase. Heat in a water-bath at 90 °C under a reflux condenser for 45 min and cool.

*Reference solution (c)*   Dissolve 0.10 g of *cholecalciferol CRS*, without heating, in *toluene R* and dilute to 100.0 ml with the same solvent.

*Reference solution (d)*   Dilute 5.0 ml of reference solution (c) to 50.0 ml with the mobile phase. Keep the solution in iced water.

*Reference solution (e)*   Place 5.0 ml of reference solution (c) in a volumetric flask, add about 10 mg of *butylhydroxytoluene R* and displace the air from the flask with *nitrogen R*. Heat in a water-bath at 90 °C under a reflux condenser, protected from light and under *nitrogen R*, for 45 min. Cool and dilute to 50.0 ml with the mobile phase.

*Column:*
— *size: l* = 0.25 m, Ø = 4.6 mm;
— *stationary phase: silica gel for chromatography R* (5 µm).

*Mobile phase*   *pentanol R, hexane R* (3:997 *V/V*).

*Flow rate*   2 ml/min.

*Detection*   Spectrophotometer at 254 nm.

*Injection*   The chosen volume of each solution (the same volume for reference solution (a) and for the test solution); automatic injection device or sample loop recommended.

*Relative retention*   With reference to cholecalciferol:
pre-cholecalciferol = about 0.4;
*trans*-cholecalciferol = about 0.5.

*System suitability*   Reference solution (b):
— *resolution*: minimum 1.0 between the peaks due to pre-cholecalciferol and *trans*-cholecalciferol; if necessary, adjust the proportions of the constituents and the flow rate of the mobile phase to obtain this resolution;
— *repeatability*: maximum relative standard deviation of 1.0 per cent for the peak due to cholecalciferol after 6 injections.

Calculate the conversion factor (*f*) using the following expression:

$$\frac{K - L}{M}$$

*K* = area (or height) of the peak due to cholecalciferol in the chromatogram obtained with reference solution (d);
*L* = area (or height) of the peak due to cholecalciferol in the chromatogram obtained with reference solution (e);
*M* = area (or height) of the peak due to pre-cholecalciferol in the chromatogram obtained with reference solution (e).

The value of *f* determined in duplicate on different days may be used during the entire procedure.

Calculate the content of cholecalciferol in International Units per gram using the following expression:

$$\frac{m'}{V'} \times \frac{V}{m} \times \frac{S_D + (f \times S_p)}{S'_D} \times 40\,000 \times 1000$$

*m* = mass of the preparation to be examined in the test solution, in milligrams;
*m'* = mass of *cholecalciferol CRS* in reference solution (a), in milligrams;
*V* = volume of the test solution (25 ml);
*V'* = volume of reference solution (a) (100 ml);
$S_D$ = area (or height) of the peak due to cholecalciferol in the chromatogram obtained with the test solution;
$S'_D$ = area (or height) of the peak due to cholecalciferol in the chromatogram obtained with reference solution (a);
$S_p$ = area (or height) of the peak due to pre-cholecalciferol in the chromatogram obtained with the test solution;
*f* = conversion factor.

**STORAGE**

In an airtight, well-filled container, protected from light, at the temperature stated on the label.

The contents of an opened container are to be used as soon as possible; any unused part is to be protected by an atmosphere of inert gas.

**LABELLING**

The label states:
— the number of International Units per gram;
— the storage temperature.

_____ *Ph Eur*

# Colestipol Hydrochloride

*37296-80-3*

**Action and use**
Lipid-regulating drug.

**Preparation**
Colestipol Granules

**DEFINITION**
Colestipol Hydrochloride is a co-polymer of diethylenetriamine and 1-chloro-2,3-epoxypropane. Each g binds not less than 1.1 mEq and not more than 1.7 mEq of sodium cholate, determined in the test for Cholate binding capacity and calculated with reference to the dried material.

**CHARACTERISTICS**
Yellow to orange beads; hygroscopic.

Practically insoluble in *ethanol (96%)* and in *dichloromethane*; swells but does not dissolve in *water* and dilute aqueous solutions of acids and alkalis.

## IDENTIFICATION

Carry out the method for *gas chromatography*, Appendix III B, using a suitable gas chromatograph fitted with a pyrolysis unit. Operate the unit in accordance with the manufacturer's instructions to obtain a pyrogram for *colestipol hydrochloride BPCRS* that is similar to that supplied with the reference material.

(1) To prepare the sample, mix 1 part of n-*eicosane* and 4 parts of the substance being examined and grind the mixture in a mortar with *chloroform* until the substance being examined is uniformly coated with the *n*-eicosane.

(2) Prepare the standard in the same manner but adding 4 parts of *colestipol hydrochloride BPCRS* in place of the substance being examined.

CHROMATOGRAPHIC CONDITIONS

(a) Use a a glass column (1.8 m × 3 mm) packed with *acid-washed, silanised diatomaceous support* (80 to 100 mesh) (Chromosorb W is suitable) coated with 0.25% w/w of *potassium hydroxide* and 5% w/w of *polyethylene glycol 20,000* (Carbowax 20M is suitable).

(b) Use *helium* as the carrier gas at 60 ml per minute.

(c) Use isothermal conditions maintained at 85°.

(d) Use a pyrolysis unit capable of attaining a temperature of about 1000° when fitted with a platinum ribbon probe.

(e) Use a detector at a temperature of 270°.

(f) Load the sample and the standard separately into the pyrolysis unit.

CONFIRMATION

The pyrogram obtained with the substance being examined is concordant with that obtained with *colestipol hydrochloride BPCRS*.

## TESTS

### Acidity or alkalinity

Shake a 10% w/w suspension in a stoppered vial at approximately 10-minute intervals for 1 hour and centrifuge. Transfer a portion of the clear supernatant liquid to a suitable container and record the pH as soon as the reading has stabilised. The pH is 6.0 to 7.5, Appendix V L.

### Water-soluble substances

Place 5 g in a glass-stoppered, 125 ml conical flask, add 80 ml of *water*, close the flask and shake in a water bath at 36° to 38° for 72 hours. Filter the contents of the flask through a fine-porosity, sintered glass funnel or woven glass-fibre filter, collecting the filtrate in a tared 125 ml conical flask. Rinse any residual contents in the flask with two 5 ml quantities of *water*, filter the washings and combine the filtrates from the washings with the filtrate obtained previously. Evaporate the filtrate to dryness, using filtered air or nitrogen, if necessary, to aid in the evaporation. Dry the residue at 75° at a pressure of not more than 2 kPa for 1 hour, allow to cool in a desiccator and weigh. Repeat the procedure at the same time without the substance being examined beginning at the words 'add 80 ml of *water* ...'. The difference in the weights of the residues is not more than 25 mg (0.5%).

### Heavy metals

Transfer 1.0 g to a suitable crucible, wet with *sulphuric acid* and carefully ignite at a low temperature until thoroughly charred. To the carbonised substance add 2 ml of *nitric acid* and 0.25 ml of *sulphuric acid* and heat cautiously until white fumes are no longer evolved. Ignite, preferably in a muffle furnace, at 500° to 600°, until the carbon is completely removed and cool. Add 4 ml of 6M *hydrochloric acid*, cover, heat on a water bath for 15 minutes, uncover and slowly evaporate to dryness. Dissolve the residue using two 5 ml quantities of 2M *hydrochloric acid*. Add 0.1 ml of *phenolphthalein solution* and 13.5M *ammonia* drop wise until a pink colour is produced. Cool, add *glacial acetic acid* until the solution is decolourised and add a further 0.5 ml. Filter if necessary and dilute the solution to 20 ml with *water*. 12 ml of the resulting solution complies with *limit test A for heavy metals*, Appendix VII (20 ppm). Prepare the standard using a mixture of 2 ml of the test solution obtained above and 10 ml of *lead standard solution (2 ppm Pb)*.

### Loss on drying

When dried at 75° at a pressure of not more than 2 kPa for 16 hours, loses not more than 1.0% of its weight.

### Sulphated ash

Not more than 0.3%, Appendix IX A.

### Chloride content

Not less than 6.5% and not more than 9.0% calculated with reference to the dried substance. Burn 20 mg by the method for *oxygen-flask combustion*, Appendix VIII C, using 10 ml of 0.05M *sodium hydroxide* as the absorbing liquid. When the process is complete shake the flask vigorously, allow to stand with frequent shaking for about 40 minutes or until no cloudiness is observed; add 20 ml of *ethanol (96%)* and 0.2 ml of *nitric acid*. Titrate the resulting solution with 0.05M *silver nitrate VS*, determining the end point potentiometrically using a silver-silver chloride electrode and a glass reference electrode ($V$ ml). Repeat the procedure without the substance being examined adding 10 ml of 0.0075M *sodium chloride* to the solution in the flask ($V_1$ ml). Add 10 ml of 0.0075M *sodium chloride* to a flask containing a mixture of 10 ml of *water* and 20 ml of *ethanol (96%)*, add 0.2 ml of *nitric acid* and titrate with 0.05M *silver nitrate VS*, determining the end point potentiometrically using a silver-silver chloride electrode and a glass reference electrode ($V_2$ ml). Determine the volume of 0.05M *silver nitrate VS* required by the substance being examined using the following expression:

$$V-(V_1-V_2)$$

Each ml of 0.05M *silver nitrate VS* is equivalent to 1.773 mg of Cl.

### Water absorption capacity

Each g of Colestipol Hydrochloride absorbs not less than 3.3 g and not more than 5.3 g of *water* when determined in the following manner. Transfer 5 g to a dry, plastic container and add 80 g of *water*. Cover the container and allow the resulting suspension to equilibrate for 72 hours. Filter the resulting slurry through a medium-porosity fritted-glass funnel (KIMAX 60 ml-40M is suitable) at a pressure of 2kPa; collect the filtrate in a tared, plastic container, disconnecting the vacuum 2 minutes after collection of the last portion of the filtrate. Immediately weigh the container and the filtrate and determine the weight, in g, of the filtrate. Calculate the weight of water absorbed per g from the difference between the weight of the filtrate and the original weight of *water* used in the test.

### Cholate binding capacity

Prepare a solution containing 1.0% w/v of *sodium cholate* and 0.9% w/v of *sodium chloride* and adjust to pH 6.4 by the drop wise addition of *hydrochloric acid* (solution A). Transfer 1 g (*m* g) of the substance being examined to a ground-glass-stoppered flask, add 100 ml of freshly prepared solution A and shake vigorously for 90 minutes with the flask positioned horizontally. Remove the flask from the shaker and allow the contents to settle for 5 minutes. Adjust the pH of a 20 ml aliquot of the supernatant liquid to 10.5 by the drop wise addition of 1M *sodium hydroxide* and titrate potentiometrically with 0.1M *hydrochloric acid* VS to the second inflection point of the pH curve. Determine the volume of titrant added between the inflection points. Carry out a blank titration on 20 ml of freshly prepared solution A. The difference between the titrations represents the amount of hydrochloric acid required (*V* ml). Calculate the cholate binding capacity of the substance being examined in milliequivalents from the expression 0.5*V*/*m*.

### Colestipol exchange capacity limit

Not less than 9.0 mEq per g and not more than 11.0 mEq per g determined in the following manner. Transfer not less than 2 g and 100 ml of 1M *sodium hydroxide* to a stoppered flask and shake for 4 hours. Filter the suspension through a coarse-porosity sintered-glass funnel and wash the resin with 500 ml of *water*. Transfer the resin to a 1000 ml beaker, add 200 ml of *water* and allow to stand for 10 minutes. Filter the suspension, check the pH of the filtrate and repeat the washing procedure with 200 ml quantities of *water* until the pH of the filtrate is less than 8 [5 litres may be required]. Dry the resin and funnel at 60° at a pressure of 2 kPa for at least 16 hours, breaking up any aggregates with a spatula and store in a dessicator.

Place 1 g (*w* g) of the free base resin prepared above and add 100 ml of 0.2M *hydrochloric acid* VS in a stoppered flask and shake for not less than 2.5 hours. Filter a portion of the suspension through glass wool. Titrate 8 ml of the filtrate with 0.2M *sodium hydroxide* VS, determining the end point potentiometrically (*a* ml). Carry out a blank titration on 5 ml of the 0.2M *hydrochloric acid* VS used to equilibrate the free-base resin diluted with 5 ml of *water* (*b* ml). Calculate the exchange capacity in milliequivalents per g from the expression:

$$(20/w)(b/5 - a/8)$$

### STORAGE

Colestipol Hydrochloride should be kept in an airtight container.

# Colestyramine

(*Ph Eur* monograph 1775)

11041-12-6

### Action and use
Lipid-regulating drug.

### Preparation
Colestyramine Oral Powder

Ph Eur

## DEFINITION

Strongly basic anion-exchange resin in chloride form, consisting of styrene-divinylbenzene copolymer with quaternary ammonium groups.

### Nominal exchange capacity

1.8 g to 2.2 g of sodium glycocholate per gram (dried substance).

## CHARACTERS

### Appearance
White or almost white, fine powder, hygroscopic.

### Solubility
Insoluble in water, in methylene chloride and in ethanol (96 per cent).

## IDENTIFICATION

A. Infrared absorption spectrophotometry (*2.2.24*).

*Comparison*   colestyramine CRS.

B. Chloride (see Tests).

## TESTS

**pH** (*2.2.3*)

4.0 to 6.0.

Suspend 0.100 g in 10 ml of *water R* and allow to stand for 10 min.

### Dialysable quaternary amines

Maximum 500 ppm, expressed as benzyltrimethylammonium chloride.

*Test solution*   Place a 25 cm piece of cellulose dialysis tubing having a molecular weight cut-off of 12 000-14 000 and an inflated diameter of 3-6 cm (flat width of 5-9 cm) in *water R* to hydrate until pliable, appropriately sealing one end. Introduce 2.0 g of the substance to be examined into the tube and add 10 ml of *water R*. Seal the tube and completely immerse it in 100 ml of *water R* in a suitable vessel and stir the liquid for 16 h to effect dialysis. Use the dialysate as test solution.

*Reference solution*   Prepare the reference solution in a similar manner but using 10 ml of a freshly prepared 0.1 g/l solution of *benzyltrimethylammonium chloride R* instead of the substance to be examined.

Transfer 5.0 ml of the test solution to a separating funnel and add 5 ml of a 3.8 g/l solution of *disodium tetraborate R*, 1 ml of a solution containing 1.5 g/l of *bromothymol blue R* and 4.05 g/l of *sodium carbonate R* and 10 ml of *chloroform R*. Shake the mixture vigorously for 1 min, allow the phases to separate and transfer the clear organic layer to a 25 ml volumetric flask. Repeat the extraction with a further 10 ml of *chloroform R*, combine the organic layers and dilute to 25 ml with *chloroform R*. Measure the absorbance (*2.2.25*) of the solution at the absorption maximum at 420 nm, using as compensation liquid a solution prepared in the same manner but using 5.0 ml of *water R* instead of the test solution.

Repeat the operation using 5.0 ml of the reference solution.

The absorbance obtained with the test solution is not greater than that obtained with the reference solution.

### Impurity A

Liquid chromatography (*2.2.29*).

*Test solution*   Shake 5.0 g with 10 ml of *acetone R* for 30 min. Centrifuge and use the supernatant liquid.

*Reference solution (a)*   Dissolve 5 mg of *styrene R* in *acetone R* and dilute to 100.0 ml with the same solvent. Dilute 1.0 ml of the solution to 100.0 ml with *acetone R*.

*Reference solution (b)*   Dissolve 0.35 ml of *styrene R* in *acetone R* and dilute to 100.0 ml with the same solvent. Dilute 1.0 ml of the solution to 100.0 ml with *acetone R*.

*Reference solution (c)*   Dissolve 0.35 ml of *toluene R* in *acetone R* and dilute to 100.0 ml with the same solvent.

*Reference solution (d)*   Mix 1.0 ml of reference solution (b) and 1.0 ml of reference solution (c) with *acetone R* and dilute to 100.0 ml with the same solvent.

Column:
— size: l = 0.30 m, Ø = 3.9 mm,
— stationary phase: octadecylsilyl silica gel for chromatography R (10 μm) with a specific surface area of 330 m2/g and a pore size of 12.5 nm.

Mobile phase   acetonitrile R, water R (50:50 V/V).

Flow rate   2.0 ml/min.

Detection   Spectrophotometer at 254 nm.

Injection   20 μl of test solution and reference solutions (a) and (d).

System suitability   Reference solution (d):
— resolution: minimum 1.5 between the peaks due to impurity A and toluene.

Limit:
— impurity A: not more than the area of the principal peak in the chromatogram obtained with reference solution (a) (1 ppm).

**Chloride**
13.0 per cent to 17.0 per cent (dried substance).

To 0.2 g add 100 ml of water R and 50 mg of potassium nitrate R. Add, with stirring, 2 ml of nitric acid R and titrate with 0.1 M silver nitrate, determining the end-point potentiometrically (2.2.20).

1 ml of 0.1 M silver nitrate is equivalent to 3.55 mg of Cl.

**Heavy metals** (2.4.8)
Maximum 20 ppm.

1.0 g complies with test F. Prepare the reference solution using 2 ml of lead standard solution (10 ppm Pb) R.

**Loss on drying** (2.2.32)
Maximum 12 per cent, determined on 1.000 g by drying in an oven at 70 °C over diphosphorus pentoxide R at a pressure not exceeding 7 kPa for 16 h.

**Sulphated ash** (2.4.14)
Maximum 0.1 per cent, determined on 1.0 g.

**ASSAY**
**Exchange capacity**
Liquid chromatography (2.2.29).

Solution A   Dissolve 1.500 g of sodium glycocholate R in a solution containing 4 g/l of potassium dihydrogen phosphate R and 12 g/l of dipotassium hydrogen phosphate R and dilute to 100.0 ml with the same solution.

Test solution   Add 20.0 ml of solution A to a quantity of the substance to be examined equivalent to about 0.100 g of the dried substance. Shake mechanically for 2 h and centrifuge for 15 min. Dilute 5.0 ml of the supernatant liquid to 50.0 ml with water R.

Reference solution (a)   Dilute 4.0 ml of solution A to 100.0 ml with water R.

Reference solution (b)   Dissolve 60 mg of sodium glycocholate R and 30 mg of sodium taurodeoxycholate R in water R and dilute to 100 ml with the same solvent. Dilute 1 ml of the solution to 10 ml with water R.

Column:
— size: l = 0.25 m, Ø = 4.6 mm;
— stationary phase: octadecylsilyl silica gel for chromatography R (5 μm).

Mobile phase   Mix 35 volumes of acetonitrile R and 65 volumes of a 10.9 g/l solution of potassium dihydrogen phosphate R adjusted to pH 3.0 with phosphoric acid R.

Flow rate   1.5 ml/min.

Detection   Spectrophotometer at 214 nm.

Injection   50 μl.

Run time   Twice the retention time of glycocholate.

System suitability   Reference solution (b):
— resolution: minimum 1.5 between the peaks due to glycocholate and taurodeoxycholate.

Calculate the nominal exchange capacity using the following expression:

$$\frac{(2.5\,A_1 - A_2) \times m_1 \times 1.2}{12.5 \times A_1 \times m_2}$$

$A_1$ = area of the peak due to glycocholate in the chromatogram obtained with reference solution (a),
$A_2$ = area of the peak due to glycocholate in the chromatogram obtained with the test solution,
$m_1$ = mass, in milligrams, of sodium glycocholate R used in the preparation of solution A,
$m_2$ = mass, in milligrams, of the dried substance to be examined used in the preparation of the test solution,
1.2 = correction factor to convert the true exchange capacity to the conventionally used nominal exchange capacity.

**STORAGE**
In an airtight container.

**IMPURITIES**
Specified impurities   A.

A. styrene.

_____ Ph Eur

# Colistimethate Sodium

(Ph Eur monograph 0319)

Ph Eur _____

**Action and use**
Antibacterial.

**Preparation**
Colistimethate Injection

**DEFINITION**
Colistimethate sodium is prepared from colistin by the action of formaldehyde and sodium hydrogen sulphite.

Semi-synthetic product derived from a fermentation product.

**Content**
Minimum 11 500 IU/mg (dried substance).

**CHARACTERS**
**Appearance**
White or almost white, hygroscopic powder.

**Solubility**
Very soluble in water, slightly soluble in ethanol (96 per cent), practically insoluble in acetone.

**IDENTIFICATION**
A. Thin-layer chromatography (2.2.27).

Test solution   Dissolve 5 mg of the substance to be examined in 1 ml of a mixture of equal volumes of hydrochloric acid R and water R. Heat at 135 °C in a sealed tube for 5 h. Evaporate to dryness on a water-bath and continue the heating until the hydrochloric acid has evaporated. Dissolve the residue in 0.5 ml of water R.

Reference solution (a)   Dissolve 20 mg of leucine R in water R and dilute to 10 ml with the same solvent.

*Reference solution (b)* Dissolve 20 mg of *threonine R* in *water R* and dilute to 10 ml with the same solvent.

*Reference solution (c)* Dissolve 20 mg of *phenylalanine R* in *water R* and dilute to 10 ml with the same solvent.

*Reference solution (d)* Dissolve 20 mg of *serine R* in *water R* and dilute to 10 ml with the same solvent.

*Plate* TLC silica gel G plate R.

*Carry out the following procedures protected from light.*

*Mobile phase* water R, phenol R (25:75 V/V).

*Application* 5 µl as bands of 10 mm, then place the plate in the chromatographic tank so that it is not in contact with the mobile phase, and allow it to become impregnated with the vapour of the mobile phase for at least 12 h.

*Development* Over a path of 12 cm using the same mobile phase.

*Drying* At 100-105 °C.

*Detection* Spray with *ninhydrin solution R1* and heat at 110 °C for 5 min.

*Results* The chromatogram obtained with the test solution shows zones corresponding to those in the chromatograms obtained with reference solutions (a) and (b), but shows no zones corresponding to those in the chromatograms obtained with reference solutions (c) and (d); the chromatogram obtained with the test solution also shows a zone with a very low $R_F$ value (2,4-diaminobutyric acid).

B. Dissolve about 5 mg in 3 ml of *water R*. Add 3 ml of *dilute sodium hydroxide solution R*. Shake and add 0.5 ml of a 10 g/l solution of *copper sulphate R*. A violet colour is produced.

C. Dissolve about 50 mg in 1 ml of *1 M hydrochloric acid* and add 0.5 ml of *0.01 M iodine*. The solution is decolourised and gives reaction (a) of sulphates (*2.3.1*).

D. It gives reaction (b) of sodium (*2.3.1*).

## TESTS

### Appearance of solution

The solution is clear (*2.2.1*).

Dissolve 0.16 g in 10 ml of *water R*.

### pH (*2.2.3*)

6.5 to 8.5.

Dissolve 0.1 g in *carbon dioxide-free water R* and dilute to 10 ml with the same solvent. Measure after 30 min.

### Specific optical rotation (*2.2.7*)

− 46 to − 51 (dried substance).

Dissolve 1.25 g in *water R* and dilute to 25.0 ml with the same solvent.

### Free colistin

Dissolve 80 mg in 3 ml of *water R*. Add 0.1 ml of a 100 g/l solution of *silicotungstic acid R*; 10-20 s after addition of the reagent, the solution is not more opalescent than reference suspension II (*2.2.1*).

### Total sulphite

*Work in a fume cupboard.* Dissolve 0.100 g in 50 ml of *water R* and add 5 ml of a 100 g/l solution of *sodium hydroxide R* and 0.3 g of *potassium cyanide R*. Boil gently for 3 min and then cool. Neutralise with *0.5 M sulphuric acid* using 0.2 ml of *methyl orange solution R* as indicator. Add an excess of *0.5 ml of the acid* and 0.2 g of *potassium iodide R*. Titrate with *0.05 M iodine* using 1 ml of *starch solution R* as indicator. The volume of *0.05 M iodine* used in the titration is 5.5 ml to 7.0 ml.

### Loss on drying (*2.2.32*)

Maximum 5.0 per cent, determined on 1.000 g by drying at 60 °C over *diphosphorus pentoxide R* at a pressure not exceeding 670 Pa for 3 h.

### Sulphated ash (*2.4.14*)

16 per cent to 21 per cent, determined on 0.50 g.

### Pyrogens (*2.6.8*)

If intended for use in the manufacture of parenteral dosage forms without a further appropriate procedure for removal of pyrogens, it complies with the test. Inject, per kilogram of the rabbit's mass, 1 ml of a solution in *water for injections R* containing 2.5 mg of the substance to be examined per millilitre.

## ASSAY

Carry out the microbiological assay of antibiotics (*2.7.2*).

## STORAGE

In an airtight container, protected from light. If the substance is sterile, store in a sterile, airtight, tamper-proof container.

_____ *Ph Eur*

# Colistin Sulphate

(*Ph Eur monograph 0320*)

| polymyxin | X | R1 | R2 | R3 | Mol. Formula | $M_r$ |
|---|---|---|---|---|---|---|
| E1 | D-Leu | $CH_3$ | $CH_3$ | H | $C_{53}H_{100}N_{16}O_{13}$ | 1170 |
| E2 | D-Leu | $CH_3$ | H | H | $C_{52}H_{98}N_{16}O_{13}$ | 1155 |
| E3 | D-Leu | H | $CH_3$ | H | $C_{52}H_{98}N_{16}O_{13}$ | 1155 |
| E1-I | D-Ile | $CH_3$ | $CH_3$ | H | $C_{53}H_{100}N_{16}O_{13}$ | 1170 |
| E1-7MOA | D-Leu | H | $CH_3$ | $CH_3$ | $C_{53}H_{100}N_{16}O_{13}$ | 1170 |

DAB = 2,4-diaminobutanoic acid

*1264-72-8*

### Action and use

Antibacterial.

### Preparation

Colistin Tablets

*Ph Eur* _____

## DEFINITION

A mixture of the sulphates of polypeptides produced by certain strains of *Bacillus polymyxa* var. *colistinus* or obtained by any other means.

*Content:*

— *sum of polymyxins E1, E2, E3, E1-I and E1-7MOA*: minimum 77.0 per cent (dried substance);

— *polymyxin E1-I*: maximum 10.0 per cent (dried substance);

— *polymyxin E1-7MOA*: maximum 10.0 per cent (dried substance);

— *polymyxin E3*: maximum 10.0 per cent (dried substance).

## CHARACTERS

**Appearance**

White or almost white, hygroscopic powder.

**Solubility**

Freely soluble in water, slightly soluble in ethanol
(96 per cent), practically insoluble in acetone.

## IDENTIFICATION

*First identification  B, E.*

*Second identification   A, C, D, E.*

A. Thin-layer chromatography (*2.2.27*).

*Test solution*   Dissolve 5 mg of the substance to be examined
in 1 ml of a mixture of equal volumes of *hydrochloric acid R*
and *water R*. Heat at 135 °C in a sealed tube for 5 h.
Evaporate to dryness on a water-bath and continue the
heating until moistened *blue litmus paper R* does not turn red.
Dissolve the residue in 0.5 ml of *water R*.

*Reference solution (a)*   Dissolve 20 mg of *leucine R* in *water R*
and dilute to 10 ml with the same solvent.

*Reference solution (b)*   Dissolve 20 mg of *threonine* R in
*water R* and dilute to 10 ml with the same solvent.

*Reference solution (c)*   Dissolve 20 mg of *phenylalanine R* in
*water R* and dilute to 10 ml with the same solvent.

*Reference solution (d)*   Dissolve 20 mg of *serine R* in *water R*
and dilute to 10 ml with the same solvent.

*Plate*   *TLC silica gel G plate R*.

*Carry out the following procedures protected from light.*

*Mobile phase*   *water R, phenol R* (25:75 *V/V*).

*Application*   5 µl as 10 mm bands, then place the plate in
the chromatographic tank so that it is not in contact with the
mobile phase, and allow it to become impregnated with the
vapour of the mobile phase for at least 12 h.

*Development*   Over a path of 12 cm.

*Drying*   At 100-105 °C.

*Detection*   Spray with *ninhydrin solution R1* and heat at
110 °C for 5 min.

*Results*   The chromatogram obtained with the test solution
shows zones corresponding to those in the chromatograms
obtained with reference solutions (a) and (b), but shows no
zones corresponding to those in the chromatograms obtained
with reference solutions (c) and (d); the chromatogram
obtained with the test solution also shows a zone with a very
low $R_F$ value (2,4-diaminobutyric acid).

B. Examine the chromatograms obtained in the assay.

*Results*   The peaks due to polymyxin E1 and polymyxin E2
in the chromatogram obtained with the test solution are
similar in retention time to the corresponding peaks in the
chromatogram obtained with reference solution (a).

C. Dissolve about 5 mg in 3 ml of *water R*. Add 3 ml of
*dilute sodium hydroxide solution R*. Shake and add 0.5 ml of a
10 g/l solution of *copper sulphate R*. A violet colour is
produced.

D. Dissolve about 50 mg in 1 ml of *1 M hydrochloric acid* and
add 0.5 ml of *0.01 M iodine*. The solution remains coloured.

E. It gives reaction (a) of sulphates (*2.3.1*).

## TESTS

**pH** (*2.2.3*)

4.0 to 6.0.

Dissolve 0.1 g in *carbon dioxide-free water R* and dilute to
10 ml with the same solvent.

**Specific optical rotation** (*2.2.7*)

− 63 to − 73 (dried substance).

Dissolve 1.25 g in *water R* and dilute to 25.0 ml with the
same solvent.

**Related substances**

Liquid chromatography (*2.2.29*); use the normalisation
procedure.

*Test solution*   Dissolve 25.0 mg of the substance to be
examined in 40 ml of *water R* and dilute to 50.0 ml with
*acetonitrile R*.

*Reference solution (a)*   Dissolve 25.0 mg of *colistin
sulphate CRS* in 40 ml of *water R* and dilute to 50.0 ml with
*acetonitrile R*.

*Reference solution (b)*   Dilute 1.0 ml of reference solution (a)
to 100.0 ml with a mixture of 20 volumes of *acetonitrile R*
and 80 volumes of *water R*.

*Column:*
— *size: l* = 0.15 m, Ø = 4.6 mm;
— *stationary phase:* end-capped octadecylsilyl silica gel for
    chromatography R (3.5 µm);
— *temperature:* 30 °C.

*Mobile phase*   Mix 22 volumes of *acetonitrile R* and
78 volumes of a solution prepared as follows: dissolve 4.46 g
of *anhydrous sodium sulphate R* in 900 ml of *water R*, adjust to
pH 2.4 with *dilute phosphoric acid R* and dilute to 1000 ml
with *water R*.

*Flow rate*   1.0 ml/min.

*Detection*   Spectrophotometer at 215 nm.

*Injection*   20 µl.

*Run time*   1.5 times the retention time of polymyxin E1.

*Relative retention*   With reference to polymyxin E1
(retention time = about 16 min):
polymyxin E2 = about 0.45; polymyxin E3 = about 0.5;
polymyxin E1-I = about 0.8;
polymyxin E1-7MOA = about 1.1.

*System suitability*   Reference solution (a):
— *resolution:* minimum 8.0 between the peaks due to
    polymyxin E2 and polymyxin E1, minimum 6.0 between
    the peaks due to polymyxin E2 and polymyxin E1-I,
    minimum 2.5 between the peaks due to polymyxin E1-I
    and polymyxin E1, minimum 1.5 between the peaks due
    to polymyxin E1 and polymyxin E1-7MOA;
— the chromatogram obtained is similar to the
    chromatogram supplied with *colistin sulphate CRS*.

*Limits:*
— *any impurity:* maximum 4.0 per cent;
— *total:* maximum 23.0 per cent;
— *disregard limit:* the area of the peak due to polymyxin E1
    in the chromatogram obtained with reference solution (b);
    disregard the peaks due to polymyxins E2, E3, E1-I, E1
    and E1-7MOA.

**Sulphate**

16.0 per cent to 18.0 per cent (dried substance).

Dissolve 0.250 g in 100 ml of *water R* and adjust to pH 11
with *concentrated ammonia R*. Add 10.0 ml of *0.1 M barium
chloride* and about 0.5 mg of *phthalein purple R*. Titrate with
*0.1 M sodium edetate*, adding 50 ml of *ethanol (96 per cent) R*
when the colour of the solution begins to change and
continuing the titration until the violet-blue colour
disappears.

1 ml of *0.1 M barium chloride* is equivalent to 9.606 mg of
SO4.

**Loss on drying** (*2.2.32*)

Maximum 3.5 per cent, determined on 1.000 g by drying at 60 °C over *diphosphorus pentoxide R* at a pressure not exceeding 670 Pa for 3 h.

**Sulphated ash** (*2.4.14*)

Maximum 1.0 per cent, determined on 1.0 g.

## ASSAY

Liquid chromatography (*2.2.29*) as described in the test for related substances with the following modification.

*Injection* Test solution and reference solution (a).

Calculate the percentage content of polymyxin E3, of polymyxin E1-I, of polymyxin E1-7MOA, and of the sum of polymyxins E1, E2, E3, E1-I and E1-7MOA, using the following expression:

$$C_{\mathrm{E}i} = \frac{A_{\mathrm{E}i} \times m_2 \times D_{\mathrm{E}i}}{m_1 \times B_{\mathrm{E}i}}$$

$C_{Ei}$ = percentage content of polymyxin E$i$,

$A_{Ei}$ = area of the peak due to polymyxin E$i$ in the chromatogram obtained with the test solution,

$m_1$ = mass in milligrams of the substance to be examined (dried substance) in the test solution,

$B_{Ei}$ = area of the peak due to polymyxin E$i$ in the chromatogram obtained with reference solution (a),

$m_2$ = mass in milligrams of *colistin sulphate CRS* in reference solution (a),

$D_{Ei}$ = declared percentage content for polymyxin E$i$ in *colistin sulphate CRS*.

## STORAGE

In an airtight container, protected from light.

——————————————————————— *Ph Eur*

# Copovidone

★ ★ ★
★    ★
★    ★
★    ★
★ ★ ★

(*Ph Eur monograph 0891*)

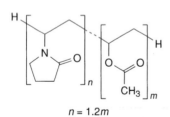

$n = 1.2m$

$(C_6H_9NO)_n + (C_4H_6O_2)_m$     $(111.1)_n + (86.1)_m$

**Action and use**

Excipient in pharmaceutical products.

*Ph Eur* _____

## DEFINITION

Copovidone is a copolymer of 1-ethenylpyrrolidin-2-one and ethenyl acetate in the mass proportion 3:2.

**Content:**

— nitrogen (N; $A_r$ 14.01): 7.0 per cent to 8.0 per cent (dried substance);

— ethenyl acetate $C_4H_6O_2$; $M_r$ 86.10): 35.3 per cent to 42.0 per cent (dried substance).

## K-value

90.0 per cent to 110.0 per cent of the value stated on the label.

## CHARACTERS

**Aspect**

White or yellowish-white powder or flakes, hygroscopic.

**Solubility**

Freely soluble in water, in alcohol and in methylene chloride.

## IDENTIFICATION

*First identification* A.

*Second identification* B, C.

A. Infrared absorption spectrophotometry (*2.2.24*).

*Comparison* Ph. Eur. reference spectrum of copovidone.

B. To 1 ml of solution S (see Tests) add 5 ml of *water R* and 0.2 ml of *0.05 M iodine*. A red colour appears.

C. Dissolve 0.7 g of *hydroxylamine hydrochloride R* in 10 ml of *methanol R*, add 20 ml of a 40 g/l solution of *sodium hydroxide R* and filter if necessary. To 5 ml of the solution add 0.1 g of the substance to be examined and boil for 2 min. Transfer 50 μl to a filter paper and add 0.1 ml of a mixture of equal volumes of *ferric chloride solution R1* and *hydrochloric acid R*. A violet colour appears.

## TESTS

**Solution S**

Dissolve 10 g in *water R* and dilute to 100 ml with the same solvent. Add the substance to be examined to the *water R* in small portions with constant stirring.

**Appearance of solution**

Solution S is not more opalescent than reference suspension III (*2.2.1*) and not more intensely coloured than reference solution $B_5$, $R_5$ or $BY_5$ (*2.2.2, Method II*).

**Aldehydes**

Maximum 500 ppm, expressed as acetaldehyde.

*Test solution* Dissolve 1.0 g of the substance to be examined in *phosphate buffer solution pH 9.0 R* and dilute to 100.0 ml with the same solvent. Stopper the flask and heat at 60 °C for 1 h. Allow to cool.

*Reference solution* Dissolve 0.140 g of *acetaldehyde ammonia trimer trihydrate R* in *water R* and dilute to 200.0 ml with the same solvent. Dilute 1.0 ml of this solution to 100.0 ml with *phosphate buffer solution pH 9.0 R*.

Into 3 identical spectrophotometric cells with a path length of 1 cm, introduce separately 0.5 ml of the test solution, 0.5 ml of the reference solution and 0.5 ml of *water R* (blank). To each cell, add 2.5 ml of *phosphate buffer solution pH 9.0 R* and 0.2 ml of *nicotinamide-adenine dinucleotide solution R*. Mix and stopper tightly. Allow to stand at 22 ± 2 °C for 2-3 min and measure the absorbance (*2.2.25*) of each solution at 340 nm, using *water R* as the compensation liquid. To each cell, add 0.05 ml of *aldehyde dehydrogenase solution R*, mix and stopper tightly. Allow to stand at 22 ± 2 °C for 5 min. Measure the absorbance of each solution at 340 nm using *water R* as compensation liquid. Determine the content of aldehydes using the expression:

$$\frac{(A_{t2} - A_{t1}) - (A_{b2} - A_{b1})}{(A_{s2} - A_{s1}) - (A_{b2} - A_{b1})} \times \frac{100\,000 \times C}{m}$$

$A_{t1}$ = absorbance of the test solution before the addition of aldehyde dehydrogenase,

$A_{t2}$ = absorbance of the test solution after the addition of aldehyde dehydrogenase,

$A_{s1}$ = absorbance of the reference solution before the addition of aldehyde dehydrogenase,

$A_{s2}$ = absorbance of the reference solution after the addition of aldehyde dehydrogenase,

$A_{b1}$ = absorbance of the blank before the addition of aldehyde dehydrogenase,

$A_{b2}$ = absorbance of the blank after the addition of aldehyde dehydrogenase,

$m$ = mass of povidone, in grams, calculated with reference to the dried substance,

$C$ = concentration (mg/ml), of acetaldehyde in the reference solution, calculated from the weight of the acetaldehyde ammonia trimer trihydrate with the factor 0.72.

**Peroxides**

Maximum 400 ppm, expressed as $H_2O_2$.

Dilute 10 ml of solution S to 25 ml with *water R*. Add 2 ml of *titanium trichloride-sulphuric acid reagent R* and allow to stand for 30 min. The absorbance (*2.2.25*) of the solution, measured at 405 nm using a mixture of 25 ml of a 40 g/l solution of the substance to be examined and 2 ml of a 13 per cent *V/V* solution of *sulphuric acid R* as the compensation liquid, is not greater than 0.35.

**Hydrazine**

Thin-layer chromatography (*2.2.27*). Use *freshly prepared solutions*.

*Test solution*   To 25 ml of solution S add 0.5 ml of a 50 g/l solution of *salicylaldehyde R* in *methanol R*, mix and heat in a water-bath at 60 °C for 15 min. Allow to cool, add 2.0 ml of *xylene R*, shake for 2 min and centrifuge. Use the clear supernatant layer.

*Reference solution*   Dissolve 9 mg of *salicylaldehyde azine R* in *xylene R* and dilute to 100 ml with the same solvent. Dilute 1 ml of this solution to 10 ml with *xylene R*.

*Plate*   TLC silanised silica gel plate R.

*Mobile phase*   water R, methanol R (20:80 *V/V*).

*Application*   10 µl.

*Development*   Over a path of 15 cm.

*Drying*   In air.

*Detection*   Examine in ultraviolet light at 365 nm.

*Limit:*

— hydrazine: any spot corresponding to salicylaldehyde azine in the chromatogram obtained with the test solution is not more intense than the spot in the chromatogram obtained with the reference solution (1 ppm).

**Monomers**

Maximum 0.1 per cent.

Dissolve 10.0 g in 30 ml of *methanol R* and add slowly 20.0 ml of *iodine bromide solution R*. Allow to stand for 30 min protected from light with repeated shaking. Add 10 ml of a 100 g/l solution of *potassium iodide R* and titrate with *0.1 M sodium thiosulphate* until a yellow colour is obtained. Continue titration dropwise until the solution becomes colourless. Carry out a blank titration. Not more than 1.8 ml of *0.1 M sodium thiosulphate* is used.

**Impurity A**

Liquid chromatography (*2.2.29*).

*Test solution*   Dissolve 100 mg of the substance to be examined in *water R* and dilute to 50.0 ml with the same solvent.

*Reference solution*   Dissolve 100 mg of *2-pyrrolidone R* in *water R* and dilute to 100 ml with the same solvent. Dilute 1.0 ml to 100.0 ml with *water R*.

*Precolumn:*

— size: $l$ = 0.025 m, Ø = 4 mm;

— stationary phase: end-capped octadecylsilyl silica gel for chromatography R (5 µm).

*Column:*

— size: $l$ = 0.25 m, Ø = 4 mm;

— stationary phase: spherical aminohexadecylsilyl silica gel for chromatography R (5 µm);

— temperature: 30 °C.

*Mobile phase*   water R, adjusted to pH 2.4 with *phosphoric acid R*.

*Flow rate*   1 ml/min.

*Detection*   Spectrophotometer at 205 nm. A detector is placed between the precolumn and the analytical column. A second detector is placed after the analytical column.

*Injection*   10 µl. When impurity A has left the precolumn (after about 1.2 min) switch the flow directly from the pump to the analytical column. Before the next chromatogram is run, wash the precolumn by reversed flow.

*Limit:*

— impurity A: not more than the area of the principal peak obtained with the reference solution (0.5 per cent).

**Heavy metals** (*2.4.8*)

Maximum 20 ppm.

12 ml of solution S complies with limit test A. Prepare the standard using *lead standard solution (2 ppm Pb) R*.

**Loss on drying** (*2.2.32*)

Maximum 5.0 per cent, determined on 0.500 g by drying in an oven at 105 °C.

**Sulphated ash** (*2.4.14*)

Maximum 0.1 per cent, determined on 1.0 g.

**Viscosity, expressed as *K*-value**

Dilute 5.0 ml of solution S to 50.0 ml with *water R*. Allow to stand for 1 h and determine the viscosity (*2.2.9*) of the solution at 25 ± 0.1 °C using viscometer No. 1 with a minimum flow time of 100 s. Calculate the *K*-value from the expression:

$$\frac{1.5 \log \eta - 1}{0.15 + 0.003c} + \frac{\sqrt{300c \log \eta + (c + 1.5c \log \eta)^2}}{0.15c + 0.003c^2}$$

$c$ = percentage concentration (g/100 ml) of the substance to be examined, calculated with reference to the dried substance,

$\eta$ = viscosity of the solution relative to that of water.

**ASSAY**

**Ethenyl acetate**

Determine the saponification value (*2.5.6*) on 2.00 g of the substance to be examined. Multiply the result obtained by 0.1534 to obtain the percentage content of the ethenyl acetate component.

**Nitrogen**

Carry out the determination of nitrogen (*2.5.9*) using 30.0 mg of the substance to be examined and 1 g of a mixture of 3 parts of *copper sulphate R* and 997 parts of *dipotassium sulphate R*, heating until a clear, light green solution is obtained and then for a further 45 min.

**STORAGE**

In an airtight container.

## LABELLING

The label states the K-value.

## IMPURITIES

A. pyrrolidin-2-one (2-pyrrolidone).

_____ *Ph Eur*

# Anhydrous Copper Sulphate

(*Ph Eur monograph 0893*)

CuSO₄      159.6      7758-98-7

**Action and use**
Used in treatment of copper deficiency.

*Ph Eur* _____

## DEFINITION

**Content**
99.0 per cent to 101.0 per cent (dried substance).

## CHARACTERS

**Appearance**
Greenish-grey powder, very hygroscopic.

**Solubility**
Freely soluble in water, slightly soluble in methanol, practically insoluble in ethanol (96 per cent).

## IDENTIFICATION

A. Add several drops of *dilute ammonia R2* to 1 ml of solution S (see Tests). A blue precipitate is formed. On further addition of *dilute ammonia R2* the precipitate dissolves and a dark blue colour is produced.

B. Loss on drying (see Tests).

C. Dilute 1 ml of solution S to 5 ml with *water R*. The solution gives reaction (a) of sulphates (*2.3.1*).

## TESTS

**Solution S**
Dissolve 1.6 g in *water R* and dilute to 50 ml with the same solvent.

**Appearance of solution**
Solution S is clear (*2.2.1*).

**Chlorides** (*2.4.4*)
Maximum 150 ppm.
Dilute 10 ml of solution S to 15 ml with *water R*.

**Iron**
Maximum $1.50 \times 10^2$ ppm.
Atomic absorption spectrometry (*2.2.23, Method I*).

*Test solution*    Dissolve 0.32 g in 10 ml of *water R*, add 2.5 ml of *lead-free nitric acid R* and dilute to 25.0 ml with *water R*.

*Reference solutions*    Prepare the reference solutions using *iron standard solution (20 ppm Fe) R*, adding 2.5 ml of *lead-free nitric acid R* and diluting to 25.0 ml with *water R*.

*Source*    Iron hollow-cathode lamp.

*Wavelength*    248.3 nm.

*Atomisation device*    Air-acetylene flame.

*Copper may form explosive acetylides with acetylene. Therefore, clean the burner thoroughly before any residues become dry.*

**Lead**
Maximum 80.0 ppm.
Atomic absorption spectrometry (*2.2.23, Method I*).

*Test solution*    Dissolve 1.6 g in 10 ml of *water R*, add 2.5 ml of *lead-free nitric acid R* and dilute to 25.0 ml with *water R*.

*Reference solutions*    Prepare the reference solutions using *lead standard solution (100 ppm Pb) R*, adding 2.5 ml of *lead-free nitric acid R* and diluting to 25.0 ml with *water R*.

*Source*    Lead hollow-cathode lamp.

*Wavelength*    217.0 nm.

*Atomisation device*    Air-acetylene flame.

*Copper may form explosive acetylides with acetylene. Therefore, clean the burner thoroughly before any residues become dry.*

**Loss on drying** (*2.2.32*)
Maximum 1.0 per cent, determined on 0.500 g by drying in an oven at 250 ± 10 °C.

## ASSAY

Dissolve 0.125 g in 50 ml of *water R*. Add 2 ml of *sulphuric acid R* and 3 g of *potassium iodide R*. Titrate with *0.1 M sodium thiosulphate*, using 1 ml of *starch solution R*, added towards the end of the titration.

1 ml of *0.1 M sodium thiosulphate* is equivalent to 15.96 mg of CuSO₄.

## STORAGE

In an airtight container.

_____ *Ph Eur*

# Copper Sulphate Pentahydrate

Copper Sulphate
(*Ph Eur monograph 0894*)

CuSO₄,5H₂O      249.7      7758-99-8

**Action and use**
Used in treatment of copper deficiency.

*Ph Eur* _____

## DEFINITION

**Content**
99.0 per cent to 101.0 per cent.

## CHARACTERS

**Appearance**
Blue, crystalline powder or transparent, blue crystals.

**Solubility**
Freely soluble in water, soluble in methanol, practically insoluble in ethanol (96 per cent).

## IDENTIFICATION

A. Add several drops of *dilute ammonia R2* to 1 ml of solution S (see Tests). A blue precipitate is formed. On further addition of *dilute ammonia R2* the precipitate dissolves and a dark blue colour is produced.

B. Loss on drying (see Tests).

C. Dilute 1 ml of solution S to 5 ml with *water R*. The solution gives reaction (a) of sulphates (*2.3.1*).

# TESTS

## Solution S
Dissolve 5 g in *water R* and dilute to 100 ml with the same solvent.

## Appearance of solution
Solution S is clear (*2.2.1*).

## Chlorides (*2.4.4*)
Maximum 100 ppm.

Dilute 10 ml of solution S to 15 ml with *water R*.

## Iron
Maximum $1.00 \times 10^2$ ppm.

Atomic absorption spectrometry (*2.2.23, Method I*).

*Test solution*   Dissolve 0.5 g in 10 ml of *water R*, add 2.5 ml of *lead-free nitric acid R* and dilute to 25.0 ml with *water R*.

*Reference solutions*   Prepare the reference solutions using *iron standard solution (20 ppm Fe) R*, adding 2.5 ml of *lead-free nitric acid R* and diluting to 25.0 ml with *water R*.

*Source*   Iron hollow-cathode lamp.

*Wavelength*   248.3 nm.

*Atomisation device*   Air-acetylene flame.

*Copper may form explosive acetylides with acetylene. Therefore, clean the burner thoroughly before any residues become dry.*

## Lead
Maximum 50.0 ppm.

Atomic absorption spectrometry (*2.2.23, Method I*).

*Test solution*   Dissolve 2.5 g in 10 ml of *water R*, add 2.5 ml of *lead-free nitric acid R* and dilute to 25.0 ml with *water R*.

*Reference solutions*   Prepare the reference solutions using *lead standard solution (100 ppm Pb) R*, adding 2.5 ml of *lead-free nitric acid R* and diluting to 25.0 ml with *water R*.

*Source*   Lead hollow-cathode lamp.

*Wavelength*   217.0 nm.

*Atomisation device*   Air-acetylene flame.

*Copper may form explosive acetylides with acetylene. Therefore, clean the burner thoroughly before any residues become dry.*

## Loss on drying (*2.2.32*)
35.0 per cent to 36.5 per cent, determined on 0.500 g by drying in an oven at $250 \pm 10$ °C.

# ASSAY
Dissolve 0.200 g in 50 ml of *water R*. Add 2 ml of *sulphuric acid R* and 3 g of *potassium iodide R*. Titrate with *0.1 M sodium thiosulphate*, adding 1 ml of *starch solution R* towards the end of the titration.

1 ml *0.1 M sodium thiosulphate* is equivalent to 24.97 mg of $CuSO_4,5H_2O$.

# Cortisone Acetate

(*Ph Eur monograph 0321*)

$C_{23}H_{30}O_6$        402.5        50-04-4

**Action and use**
Corticosteroid.

**Preparation**
Cortisone Tablets

*Ph Eur* _____

# DEFINITION
17-Hydroxy-3,11,20-trioxopregn-4-en-21-yl acetate.

**Content**
97.0 per cent to 103.0 per cent (dried substance).

# CHARACTERS

## Appearance
White or almost white, crystalline powder.

## Solubility
Practically insoluble in water, freely soluble in methylene chloride, soluble in dioxan, sparingly soluble in acetone, slightly soluble in ethanol (96 per cent) and in methanol.

It shows polymorphism (*5.9*).

# IDENTIFICATION
*First identification*   A, B.

*Second identification*   C, D, E.

A. Infrared absorption spectrophotometry (*2.2.24*).

*Comparison*   cortisone acetate CRS.

If the spectra obtained in the solid state show differences, record new spectra using 50 g/l solutions in *methylene chloride R* in a 0.2 mm cell.

B. Thin-layer chromatography (*2.2.27*).

*Solvent mixture*   methanol R, methylene chloride R (1:9 *V/V*).

*Test solution*   Dissolve 10 mg of the substance to be examined in the solvent mixture and dilute to 10 ml with the solvent mixture.

*Reference solution (a)*   Dissolve 20 mg of *cortisone acetate CRS* in the solvent mixture and dilute to 20 ml with the solvent mixture.

*Reference solution (b)*   Dissolve 10 mg of *hydrocortisone acetate R* in reference solution (a) and dilute to 10 ml with reference solution (a).

*Plate*   TLC silica gel $F_{254}$ plate R.

*Mobile phase*   Add a mixture of 1.2 volumes of *water R* and 8 volumes of *methanol R* to a mixture of 15 volumes of *ether R* and 77 volumes of *methylene chloride R*.

*Application*   5 µl.

*Development*   Over a path of 15 cm.

*Drying*   In air.

*Detection A*   Examine in ultraviolet light at 254 nm.

*Results A* The principal spot in the chromatogram obtained with the test solution is similar in position and size to the principal spot in the chromatogram obtained with reference solution (a).

*Detection B* Spray with *alcoholic solution of sulphuric acid R*. Heat at 120 °C for 10 min or until the spots appear. Allow to cool. Examine in daylight and in ultraviolet light at 365 nm.

*Results B* The principal spot in the chromatogram obtained with the test solution is similar in position, colour in daylight, fluorescence in ultraviolet light at 365 nm and size to the principal spot in the chromatogram obtained with reference solution (a).

*System suitability* Reference solution (b):
— the chromatogram shows 2 clearly separated spots.

C. Thin-layer chromatography (*2.2.27*).

*Test solution (a)* Dissolve 25 mg of the substance to be examined in *methanol R* with gentle heating and dilute to 5 ml with the same solvent (solution A). Dilute 2 ml of this solution to 10 ml with *methylene chloride R*.

*Test solution (b)* Transfer 2 ml of solution A to a 15 ml glass tube with a ground-glass stopper or a polytetrafluoroethylene cap. Add 10 ml of *saturated methanolic potassium hydrogen carbonate solution R* and immediately pass a stream of *nitrogen R* briskly through the solution for 5 min. Stopper the tube. Heat in a water-bath at 45 °C protected from light for 2.5 h. Allow to cool.

*Reference solution (a)* Dissolve 25 mg of *cortisone acetate CRS* in *methanol R* with gentle heating and dilute to 5 ml with the same solvent (solution B). Dilute 2 ml of this solution to 10 ml with *methylene chloride R*.

*Reference solution (b)* Transfer 2 ml of solution B to a 15 ml glass tube with a ground-glass stopper or a polytetrafluoroethylene cap. Add 10 ml of *saturated methanolic potassium hydrogen carbonate solution R* and immediately pass a stream of *nitrogen R* briskly through the solution for 5 min. Stopper the tube. Heat in a water-bath at 45 °C protected from light for 2.5 h. Allow to cool.

*Plate* *TLC silica gel F254 plate R*.

*Mobile phase* Add a mixture of 1.2 volumes of *water R* and 8 volumes of *methanol R* to a mixture of 15 volumes of *ether R* and 77 volumes of *methylene chloride R*.

*Application* 5 µl.

*Development* Over a path of 15 cm.

*Drying* In air.

*Detection A* Examine in ultraviolet light at 254 nm.

*Results A* The principal spot in each of the chromatograms obtained with the test solutions is similar in position and size to the principal spot in the chromatogram obtained with the corresponding reference solution.

*Detection B* Spray with *alcoholic solution of sulphuric acid R* and heat at 120 °C for 10 min or until the spots appear. Allow to cool. Examine in daylight and in ultraviolet light at 365 nm.

*Results B* The principal spot in each of the chromatograms obtained with the test solutions is similar in position, colour in daylight, fluorescence in ultraviolet light at 365 nm and size to the principal spot in the chromatogram obtained with the corresponding reference solution. The principal spots in the chromatograms obtained with test solution (b) and reference solution (b) have an $R_F$ value distinctly lower than that of the principal spots in the chromatograms obtained with test solution (a) and reference solution (a).

D. Add about 2 mg to 2 ml of *sulphuric acid R* and shake to dissolve. Within 5 min, a faint yellow colour develops. Add this solution to 10 ml of *water R* and mix. The colour is discharged and a clear solution remains.

E. About 10 mg gives the reaction of acetyl (*2.3.1*).

## TESTS

**Specific optical rotation** (*2.2.7*)
+ 211 to + 220 (dried substance).

Dissolve 0.250 g in *dioxan R* and dilute to 25.0 ml with the same solvent.

**Related substances**

Liquid chromatography (*2.2.29*). *Prepare the solutions immediately before use.*

*Test solution* Dissolve 25.0 mg of the substance to be examined in *acetonitrile R* and dilute to 10.0 ml with the same solvent.

*Reference solution (a)* Dissolve 2 mg of *cortisone acetate CRS* and 2 mg of *hydrocortisone acetate CRS* (impurity A) in *acetonitrile R* and dilute to 100.0 ml with the same solvent.

*Reference solution (b)* Dilute 1.0 ml of the test solution to 100.0 ml with *acetonitrile R*.

*Column:*
— *size*: $l = 0.25$ m, Ø = 4.6 mm;
— *stationary phase*: *octadecylsilyl silica gel for chromatography R* (5 µm).

*Mobile phase* In a 1000 ml volumetric flask mix 400 ml of *acetonitrile R* with 550 ml of *water R* and allow to equilibrate; dilute to 1000 ml with *water R* and mix again.

*Flow rate* 1 ml/min.

*Detection* Spectrophotometer at 254 nm.

*Equilibration* With the mobile phase for about 30 min.

*Injection* 20 µl; inject *acetonitrile R* as a blank.

*Run time* Twice the retention time of cortisone acetate.

*Retention time* Impurity A = about 10 min; cortisone acetate = about 12 min.

*System suitability* Reference solution (a):
— *resolution*: minimum 4.2 between the peaks due to impurity A and cortisone acetate; if necessary, adjust the concentration of acetonitrile in the mobile phase.

*Limits:*
— *impurity A*: not more than 0.5 times the area of the principal peak in the chromatogram obtained with reference solution (b) (0.5 per cent);
— *total*: not more than 1.5 times the area of the principal peak in the chromatogram obtained with reference solution (b) (1.5 per cent);
— *disregard limit*: 0.05 times the area of the principal peak in the chromatogram obtained with reference solution (b) (0.05 per cent).

**Loss on drying** (*2.2.32*)
Maximum 0.5 per cent, determined on 0.500 g by drying in an oven at 105 °C.

## ASSAY

Dissolve 0.100 g in *ethanol (96 per cent) R* and dilute to 100.0 ml with the same solvent. Dilute 2.0 ml of this solution to 100.0 ml with *ethanol (96 per cent) R*. Measure the absorbance (*2.2.25*) at the absorption maximum at 237 nm.

Calculate the content of $C_{23}H_{30}O_6$ taking the specific absorbance to be 395.

**STORAGE**

Protected from light.

**IMPURITIES**

*Specified impurities  A.*

A. hydrocortisone acetate.

_____ *Ph Eur*

# Cresol

**Action and use**

Antiseptic; antimicrobial preservative.

**DEFINITION**

Cresol is a mixture of cresols and other phenols obtained from coal tar.

**CHARACTERISTICS**

An almost colourless to pale brownish yellow liquid.

Almost completely soluble in 50 volumes of *water*; freely soluble in *ethanol (96%)*, in *ether* and in fixed and volatile oils.

**IDENTIFICATION**

Shake 0.5 ml with 300 ml of *water* and filter. The filtrate complies with the following tests.

A. Add *iron(III) chloride solution R1*. A transient blue colour is produced.

B. Add *bromine water*. A pale yellow flocculent precipitate is produced.

**TESTS**

**Acidity**

A 2.0% w/v solution is neutral to *bromocresol purple solution*.

**Distillation range**

Not more than 2% v/v distils below 188° and not less than 80% v/v distils between 195° and 205°, Appendix V C.

**Weight per ml**

1.029 to 1.044 g, Appendix V G.

**Hydrocarbons**

Place 50 ml in a 500 ml round-bottomed flask, add 150 ml of 5M *sodium hydroxide* and 30 ml of *water* and mix thoroughly. Connect the flask to a splash-bulb and air-condenser about 60 cm long, with the end of the air-condenser fitting closely into the neck of a 250 ml pear-shaped separating funnel and passing well into the separating funnel, which has a cylindrical graduated portion above the stopcock. Fill the graduated portion of the separating funnel with *water*. Distil rapidly until 75 ml of distillate has been collected, cooling the separating funnel in running water if necessary. Allow the separating funnel to stand in a vertical position until separation is complete and draw off the aqueous liquid into a titration flask for use in the test for Volatile bases.

Allow the separating funnel to stand for a few minutes, measure the volume of hydrocarbon oil in the graduated portion and warm, if necessary, to keep the oil in the liquid state. Subtract the volume of volatile bases in the hydrocarbon oil, as determined in the following test. Not more than 0.15% v/v of hydrocarbon oil is present.

**Volatile bases**

To the aqueous liquid reserved in the test for Hydrocarbons add any aqueous liquid still remaining in the separating funnel and neutralise, if necessary, with 0.1M *hydrochloric acid*

using *phenolphthalein solution R1* as indicator. Titrate with 1M *hydrochloric acid VS* using *methyl orange solution* as indicator. Wash the oil from the separating funnel into the titration flask with *water* and again titrate with 1M *hydrochloric acid VS*. From the volume of additional 1M *hydrochloric acid VS*, calculate the proportion of volatile bases in the hydrocarbon oil. From the total volume of 1M *hydrochloric acid VS* used in both titrations calculate the volume of volatile bases in the substance being examined. Each ml of 1M *hydrochloric acid VS* is equivalent to 0.080 ml of volatile bases. Not more than 0.15% v/v of volatile bases is present.

**Hydrocarbons and volatile bases**

The sum of the contents of hydrocarbon oil and volatile bases, as determined in the tests for Hydrocarbons and for Volatile bases, does not exceed 0.25% v/v.

**Sulphur compounds**

Place 20 ml in a small conical flask and over the mouth of the flask fix a piece of filter paper moistened with a 10% w/v solution of *lead(II) acetate*. Heat the flask on a water bath for 5 minutes. Not more than a light yellow colour is produced on the filter paper.

**Non-volatile matter**

When evaporated on a water bath and dried at 105°, leaves not more than 0.1% w/v of residue.

**STORAGE**

Cresol should be protected from light. It darkens with age or on exposure to light.

# Crude Cresol

(*Ph Eur monograph 1628*)

C₇H₈O                    108.1

$C_7H_8O$                    108.1

**Action and use**

Antiseptic.

*Ph Eur* _____

**DEFINITION**

Mixture of 2-, 3- and 4-methylphenol.

**CHARACTERS**

**Appearance**

Colourless or pale brown liquid.

**Solubility**

Sparingly soluble in water, miscible with alcohol and with methylene chloride.

**IDENTIFICATION**

A. To 0.5 ml add 300 ml of *water R*, mix and filter. To 10 ml of the filtrate add 1 ml of *ferric chloride solution R1*. A blue colour is produced.

B. To 10 ml of the filtrate obtained in identification test A, add 1 ml of *bromine water R*. A pale yellow flocculent precipitate is produced.

C. It complies with the test for relative density (see Tests).

## TESTS

### Solution S

To 2.5 g of the substance to be examined add 50 ml of *water R*, shake for 1 min and filter through a moistened filter.

### Acidity or alkalinity

To 10 ml of solution S add 0.1 ml of *methyl red solution R* and 0.2 ml of *0.01 M sodium hydroxide*. The solution is yellow. Add 0.3 ml of *0.01 M hydrochloric acid*. The solution is red.

### Relative density (*2.2.5*)

1.029 to 1.044.

### Distillation range (*2.2.11*)

A maximum of 2.0 per cent *V/V* distils below 188 °C and a minimum of 80 per cent *V/V* distils between 195 °C and 205 °C.

### Sulphur compounds

Place 20 ml in a small conical flask. Over the mouth of the flask fix a piece of filter paper moistened with *lead acetate solution R*. Heat on a water-bath for 5 min. Not more than a light yellow colour is produced on the filter paper.

### Residue on evaporation

Maximum 0.1 per cent.

Evaporate 2.0 g to dryness on a water-bath and dry at 100-105 °C for 1 h. The residue weighs not more than 2 mg.

### STORAGE

Protected from light.

_____ *Ph Eur*


# Croscarmellose Sodium

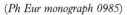

(*Ph Eur monograph 0985*)

### Action and use

Excipient.

*Ph Eur* _____

### DEFINITION

Cross-linked sodium carboxymethylcellulose.

Sodium salt of a cross-linked, partly *O*-carboxymethylated cellulose.

### CHARACTERS

#### Appeareance

White or greyish-white powder.

#### Solubility

Practically insoluble in acetone, in anhydrous ethanol and in toluene.

### IDENTIFICATION

A. Mix 1 g with 100 ml of a solution containing 4 ppm of *methylene blue R*, stir the mixture and allow it to settle. The substance to be examined absorbs the methylene blue and settles as a blue, fibrous mass.

B. Mix 1 g with 50 ml of *water R*. Transfer 1 ml of the mixture to a small test-tube and add 1 ml of *water R* and 0.05 ml of a freshly prepared 40 g/l solution of α-*naphthol R* in *methanol R*. Incline the test-tube and carefully add 2 ml of *sulphuric acid R* down the side so that it forms a lower layer. A reddish-violet colour develops at the interface.

C. The solution prepared from the sulphated ash in the test for heavy metals (see Tests) gives reaction (a) of sodium (*2.3.1*).

## TESTS

### pH (*2.2.3*)

5.0 to 7.0 for the suspension.

Shake 1 g with 100 ml of *carbon dioxide-free water R* for 5 min.

### Sodium chloride and sodium glycollate

Maximum 0.5 per cent (dried substance) for the sum of the percentage contents of sodium chloride and sodium glycollate.

*Sodium chloride*   Place 5.00 g in a 250 ml conical flask, add 50 ml of *water R* and 5 ml of *strong hydrogen peroxide solution R* and heat on a water-bath for 20 min, stirring occasionally to ensure total hydration. Cool, add 100 ml of *water R* and 10 ml of *nitric acid R*. Titrate with *0.05 M silver nitrate*, determining the end-point potentiometrically (*2.2.20*) using a silver indicator electrode and a double-junction reference electrode containing a 100 g/l solution of *potassium nitrate R* in the outer jacket and a standard filling solution in the inner jacket, and stirring constantly.

1 ml of *0.05 M silver nitrate* is equivalent to 2.922 mg of NaCl.

*Sodium glycollate*   Place a quantity of the substance to be examined equivalent to 0.500 g of the dried substance in a 100 ml beaker. Add 5 ml of *glacial acetic acid R* and 5 ml of *water R* and stir to ensure total hydration (about 15 min). Add 50 ml of *acetone R* and 1 g of *sodium chloride R*. Stir for several minutes to ensure complete precipitation of the carboxymethylcellulose. Filter through a fast filter paper impregnated with *acetone R* into a volumetric flask, rinse the beaker and the filter with 30 ml of *acetone R* and dilute the filtrate to 100.0 ml with the same solvent. Allow to stand for 24 h without shaking. Use the clear supernatant to prepare the test solution.

Prepare the reference solutions as follows: in a 100 ml volumetric flask, dissolve 0.100 g of *glycollic acid R*, previously dried *in vacuo* over *diphosphorus pentoxide R* at room temperature overnight, in *water R* and dilute to 100.0 ml with the same solvent; use the solution within 30 days; transfer 1.0 ml, 2.0 ml, 3.0 ml and 4.0 ml of the solution to separate volumetric flasks, dilute the contents of each flask to 5.0 ml with *water R*, add 5 ml of *glacial acetic acid R*, dilute to 100.0 ml with *acetone R* and mix.

Transfer 2.0 ml of the test solution and 2.0 ml of each of the reference solutions to separate 25 ml volumetric flasks. Heat the uncovered flasks for 20 min on a water-bath to eliminate acetone. Allow to cool and add 5.0 ml of *2,7-dihydroxynaphthalene solution R* to each flask. Mix, add a further 15.0 ml of *2,7-dihydroxynaphthalene solution R* and mix again. Close the flasks with aluminium foil and heat on a water-bath for 20 min. Cool and dilute to 25.0 ml with *sulphuric acid R*.

Measure the absorbance (*2.2.25*) of each solution at 540 nm. Prepare a blank using 2.0 ml of a solution containing 5 per cent *V/V* each of *glacial acetic acid R* and *water R* in *acetone R*. Prepare a standard curve using the absorbances obtained with the reference solutions. From the standard curve and the absorbance of the test solution, determine the mass (*a*) of glycollic acid in the substance to be examined, in milligrams, and calculate the content of sodium glycollate using the following expression:

$$\frac{10 \times 1.29 \times a}{(100 - b)\,m}$$

1.29 = the factor converting glycollic acid to sodium glycollate;

*b* = loss on drying as a percentage;

*m* = mass of the substance to be examined, in grams.

## Water-soluble substances

Maximum 10.0 per cent.

Disperse 10.00 g in 800.0 ml of *water R* and stir for 1 min every 10 min during the first 30 min. Allow to stand for 1 h and centrifuge if necessary. Decant 200.0 ml of the supernatant liquid onto a fast filter paper in a vacuum filtration funnel, apply vacuum and collect 150.0 ml of the filtrate. Evaporate to dryness and dry the residue at 100-105 °C for 4 h.

## Heavy metals (*2.4.8*)

Maximum 20 ppm.

To the residue obtained in the determination of the sulphated ash add 1 ml of *hydrochloric acid R* and evaporate on a water-bath. Take up the residue in 20 ml of *water R*. 12 ml of the solution complies with test A. Prepare the reference solution using *lead standard solution (1 ppm Pb) R*.

## Loss on drying (*2.2.32*)

Maximum 10.0 per cent, determined on 1.000 g by drying in an oven at 105 °C for 6 h.

## Sulphated ash(*2.4.14*)

14.0 per cent to 28.0 per cent (dried substance), determined on 1.0 g, using a mixture of equal volumes of *sulphuric acid R* and *water R*.

## Microbial contamination

TAMC: acceptance criterion $10^3$ CFU/g (*2.6.12*).

TYMC: acceptance criterion $10^2$ CFU/g (*2.6.12*).

Absence of *Escherichia coli* (*2.6.13*).

## FUNCTIONALITY-RELATED CHARACTERISTICS

*This section provides information on characteristics that are recognised as being relevant control parameters for one or more functions of the substance when used as an excipient (see chapter 5.15). This section is a non-mandatory part of the monograph and it is not necessary to verify the characteristics to demonstrate compliance. Control of these characteristics can however contribute to the quality of a medicinal product by improving the consistency of the manufacturing process and the performance of the medicinal product during use. Where control methods are cited, they are recognised as being suitable for the purpose, but other methods can also be used. Wherever results for a particular characteristic are reported, the control method must be indicated.*

*The following characteristics may be relevant for croscarmellose sodium used as disintegrant.*

## Settling volume

Place 75 ml of *water R* in a 100 ml graduated cylinder and add 1.5 g of the substance to be examined in 0.5 g portions, shaking vigorously after each addition. Dilute to 100.0 ml with *water R* and shake again until the substance is homogeneously distributed. Allow to stand for 4 h. The settling volume is between 10.0 ml and 30.0 ml.

## Degree of substitution

0.60 to 0.85 (dried substance).

Place 1.000 g in a 500 ml conical flask, add 300 ml of a 100 g/l solution of *sodium chloride R* and 25.0 ml of *0.1 M sodium hydroxide*, stopper the flask and allow to stand for 5 min, shaking occasionally. Add 0.05 ml of *m-cresol purple solution R* and about 15 ml of *0.1 M hydrochloric acid* from a burette. Insert the stopper and shake. If the solution is violet, add *0.1 M hydrochloric acid* in 1 ml portions until the solution

becomes yellow, shaking after each addition. Titrate with *0.1 M sodium hydroxide* until the colour turns to violet. Calculate the number of milliequivalents (*M*) of base required to neutralise the equivalent of 1 g of dried substance.

Calculate the degree of acid carboxymethyl substitution (*A*) using the following expression:

$$\frac{1150M}{(7102 - 412M - 80C)}$$

*C* = sulphated ash as a percentage.

Calculate the degree of sodium carboxymethyl substitution (*S*) using the following expression:

$$\frac{(162 + 58A)\,C}{(7102 - 80C)}$$

The degree of substitution is the sum of *A* and *S*.

**Particle size distribution** (*2.9.31* or *2.9.38*).

**Hausner ratio** (*2.9.36*).

*Ph Eur*

# Crospovidone

(*Ph Eur monograph 0892*)

$(C_6H_9NO)_n$ $(111.1)_n$ 9003-39-8

## Action and use

Excipient in pharmaceutical products.

*Ph Eur*

## DEFINITION

Cross-linked homopolymer of 1-ethenylpyrrolidin-2-one.

## Content

11.0 per cent to 12.8 per cent of N ($A_r$ 14.01) (dried substance).

## CHARACTERS

### Appearance

Hygroscopic, white or yellowish-white powder or flakes.

2 types of crospovidone are available, depending on the particle size: type A and type B.

### Solubility

Practically insoluble in water, in ethanol 96 per cent and in methylene chloride.

## IDENTIFICATION

A. Infrared absorption spectrophotometry (*2.2.24*).

*Comparison    crospovidone CRS.*

B. Suspend 1 g in 10 ml of *water R*, add 0.1 ml of *0.05 M iodine* and shake for 30 s. Add 1 ml of *starch solution R* and shake. No blue colour develops within 30 s.

C. To 10 ml of *water R*, add 0.1 g and shake. A suspension is formed and no clear solution is obtained within 15 min.

D. The analytical screens must be clean and dry. For this purpose the screens are washed in hot water and allowed to dry overnight in a drying cabinet at 105 °C.

Place 20 g in a 1000 ml conical flask, add 500 ml of *water R* and shake the suspension for 30 min. Pour the suspension through a 63 μm analytical screen, previously tared, and rinse the screen with *water R* until the filtrate is clear. Dry the screen and sample residue at 105 °C for 5 h in a drying cabinet without circulating air. Cool in a desiccator for 30 min and weigh.

Calculate the percentage screening residue (fraction of sample particles having a diameter of more than 63 μm), using the following expression:

$$\frac{m_1 - m_3}{m_2} \times 100$$

$m_1$ = mass of the screen and sample residue, after drying for 5 h, in grams;
$m_2$ = mass of the sample, in grams;
$m_3$ = mass of the screen, in grams.

If the screening residue fraction is more than 15 per cent, the substance is classified as type A; if the screening residue fraction is less than or equal to 15 per cent, the substance is classified as type B.

## TESTS

### Peroxides
Type A: maximum 400 ppm expressed as $H_2O_2$; type B: maximum 1000 ppm expressed as $H_2O_2$.

Suspend 2.0 g in 50 ml of *water R*. To 25 ml of this suspension add 2 ml of *titanium trichloride-sulphuric acid reagent R*. Allow to stand for 30 min and filter. The absorbance (*2.2.25*) of the filtrate, measured at 405 nm using a mixture of 25 ml of a filtered 40 g/l suspension of the substance to be examined and 2 ml of a 13 per cent *V/V* solution of *sulphuric acid R* as the compensation liquid, has a maximum of 0.35.

For type B use 10 ml of the suspension and dilute to 25 ml with *water R* for the test.

### Water-soluble substances
Maximum 1.0 per cent.

Place 25.0 g in a 400 ml beaker, add 200 ml of *water R* and stir for 1 h using a magnetic stirrer. Transfer the suspension to a 250.0 ml volumetric flask, rinsing with *water R*, and dilute to volume with the same solvent. Allow the bulk of the solids to settle. Filter about 100 ml of the almost clear supernatant liquid through a membrane filter (nominal pore size 0.45 μm), protected by superimposing a membrane filter (nominal pore size 3 μm). While filtering, stir the liquid above the membrane filter manually or by means of a mechanical stirrer, taking care not to damage the membrane filter. Transfer 50.0 ml of the clear filtrate to a tared 100 ml beaker, evaporate to dryness and dry at 105-110 °C for 3 h. The residue weighs a maximum of 50 mg.

### Impurity A
Liquid chromatography (*2.2.29*).

*Test solution* Suspend 1.250 g in 50.0 ml of *methanol R* and shake for 60 min. Leave the bulk to settle and filter through a filter membrane (nominal pore size 0.2 μm).

*Reference solution (a)* Dissolve 50 mg of *1-vinylpyrrolidin-2-one R* (impurity A) in *methanol R* and dilute to 100.0 ml with the same solvent. Dilute 1.0 ml of this solution to 100.0 ml with *methanol R*. Dilute 5.0 ml of this solution to 100.0 ml with the mobile phase.

*Reference solution (b)* Dissolve 10 mg of *1-vinylpyrrolidin-2-one R* (impurity A) and 0.50 g of *vinyl acetate R* in *methanol R* and dilute to 100 ml with the same solvent. Dilute 1.0 ml of this solution to 100.0 ml with the mobile phase.

*Precolumn:*
— *size: l = 0.025 m, Ø = 4 mm;*
— *stationary phase: octadecylsilyl silica gel for chromatography R* (5 μm).

*Column:*
— *size: l = 0.25 m, Ø = 4 mm;*
— *stationary phase: octadecylsilyl silica gel for chromatography R* (5 μm);
— *temperature*: 40 °C.

*Mobile phase* acetonitrile R, water R (10:90 *V/V*).

*Flow rate* Adjusted so that the retention time of the peak due to impurity A is about 10 min.

*Detection* Spectrophotometer at 235 nm.

*Injection* 50 μl. After each injection of the test solution, wash the precolumn by passing the mobile phase backwards, at the same flow rate as applied in the test, for 30 min.

*System suitability:*
— *resolution*: minimum 2.0 between the peaks due to impurity A and vinyl acetate in the chromatogram obtained with reference solution (b);
— *repeatability*: maximum relative standard deviation of 2.0 per cent after 5 injections of reference solution (a).

*Limits:*
— *impurity A*: not more than the area of the principal peak in the chromatogram obtained with reference solution (a) (10 ppm).

### Heavy metals (*2.4.8*)
Maximum 10 ppm.

2.0 g complies with test D. Prepare the reference solution using 2 ml of *lead standard solution (10 ppm Pb) R*.

### Loss on drying (*2.2.32*)
Maximum 5.0 per cent, determined on 0.500 g by drying in an oven at 105 °C.

### Sulphated ash (*2.4.14*)
Maximum 0.1 per cent, determined on 1.0 g.

### ASSAY
Place 100.0 mg of the substance to be examined (*m* mg) in a combustion flask and add 5 g of a mixture of 1 g of *copper sulphate R*, 1 g of *titanium dioxide R* and 33 g of *dipotassium sulphate R*, and 3 glass beads. Wash any adhering particles from the neck into the flask with a small quantity of *water R*. Add 7 ml of *sulphuric acid R*, allowing it to run down the insides of the flask, and mix the contents by rotation. Close the mouth of the flask loosely, for example by means of a glass bulb with a short stem, to avoid excessive loss of sulphuric acid. Heat gradually at first, then increase the temperature until there is vigorous boiling with condensation of sulphuric acid in the neck of the flask; precautions are to be taken to prevent the upper part of the flask from becoming overheated. Continue the heating for 45 min. Cool, dissolve the solid material by cautiously adding 20 ml of *water R* to the mixture, cool again and place in a steam-distillation apparatus. Add 30 ml of *strong sodium hydroxide solution R* through the funnel, rinse the funnel cautiously with 10 ml of *water R* and distil immediately by

passing steam through the mixture. Collect 80-100 ml of distillate in a mixture of 30 ml of a 40 g/l solution of *boric acid R* and 0.05 ml of *bromocresol green-methyl red solution R* and enough *water R* to cover the tip of the condenser. Towards the end of the distillation lower the receiver so that the tip of the condenser is above the surface of the acid solution and rinse the end part of the condenser with a small quantity of *water R*. Titrate the distillate with *0.025 M sulphuric acid* until the colour of the solution changes from green through pale greyish-blue to pale greyish-red-purple ($n_1$ ml of *0.025 M sulphuric acid*).

Repeat the test using about 100 mg of *glucose R* in place of the substance to be examined ($n_2$ ml of *0.025 M sulphuric acid*).

Percentage content of nitrogen:

$$\frac{0.7004\,(n_1 - n_2)}{m} \times 100$$

## STORAGE

In an airtight container.

## LABELLING

The label states the type (type A or type B).

## IMPURITIES

A. 1-ethenylpyrrolidin-2-one (1-vinylpyrrolidin-2-one).

## FUNCTIONALITY-RELATED CHARACTERISTICS

*This section provides information on characteristics that are recognised as being relevant control parameters for one or more functions of the substance when used as an excipient (see chapter 5.15). This section is a non-mandatory part of the monograph and it is not necessary to verify the characteristics to demonstrate compliance. Control of these characteristics can however contribute to the quality of a medicinal product by improving the consistency of the manufacturing process and the performance of the medicinal product during use. Where control methods are cited, they are recognised as being suitable for the purpose, but other methods can also be used. Wherever results for a particular characteristic are reported, the control method must be indicated.*

*The following characteristics may be relevant for crospovidone used as disintegrant.*

### Hydration capacity

Introduce 2.0 g into a 100 ml centrifuge tube and add 40 ml of *water R*. Shake vigorously until a suspension is obtained. Shake again 5 min and 10 min later, then centrifuge for 15 min at 750 *g*. Decant the supernatant liquid and weigh the residue. The hydration capacity is the ratio of the mass of the residue to the initial mass of the sample. It is typically 3 to 9.

### Particle-size distribution *(2.9.31)*.

### Powder flow *(2.9.36)*.

*The following characteristic may be relevant for crospovidone used as suspension stabiliser.*

### Settling volume

Introduce 10 g into a 100 ml graduated cylinder and add 90 ml of *water R*. Shake vigorously. Dilute to 100 ml with *water R*, washing the powder residues from the walls of the

cylinder. Allow to stand for 24 h, then read the volume of the sediment. It is typically greater than 60 ml.

————————————————————— *Ph Eur*

# Crotamiton

*(Ph Eur monograph 1194)*

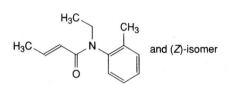

C₁₃H₁₇NO        203.3        483-63-6

**Action and use**
Acaricide.

**Preparations**
Crotamiton Cream
Crotamiton Lotion

*Ph Eur*

## DEFINITION

*N*-Ethyl-*N*-(2-methylphenyl)but-2-enamide.

*Content:*
— *sum of the E- and Z-isomers*: 96.0 per cent to 102.0 per cent;
— *Z-isomer*: maximum 15.0 per cent.

## CHARACTERS

### Appearance

Colourless or pale yellow, oily liquid.

### Solubility

Slightly soluble in water, miscible with ethanol (96 per cent).

At low temperatures it may partly or completely solidify.

## IDENTIFICATION

*First identification* B.

*Second identification* A, C, D.

A. Ultraviolet and visible absorption spectrophotometry *(2.2.25)*.

*Test solution* Dissolve 25.0 mg in *cyclohexane R* and dilute to 100.0 ml with the same solvent. Dilute 1.0 ml of this solution to 10.0 ml with *cyclohexane R*.

*Spectral range* 220-300 nm.

*Absorption maximum* At 242 nm.

*Specific absorbance at the absorption maximum* 300 to 330.

B. Infrared absorption spectrophotometry *(2.2.24)*.

*Comparison* crotamiton CRS.

C. Thin-layer chromatography *(2.2.27)*.

*Test solution.*

Dissolve 25 mg of the substance to be examined in *anhydrous ethanol R* and dilute to 10 ml with the same solvent.

*Reference solution* Dissolve 25 mg of *crotamiton CRS* in *anhydrous ethanol R* and dilute to 10 ml with the same solvent.

*Plate* TLC silica gel F₂₅₄ plate R.

*Mobile phase* Shake 98 volumes of *methylene chloride R* with 2 volumes of *concentrated ammonia R*, dry over *anhydrous* sodium sulphate R, filter and mix 97 volumes of the filtrate with 3 volumes of 2-propanol R.

*Application* 5 μl.

*Development* Over a path of 15 cm.

*Drying* In air.

*Detection* Examine in ultraviolet light at 254 nm.

*Results* The principal spot in the chromatogram obtained with the test solution is similar in position and size to the principal spot in the chromatogram obtained with the reference solution.

D. To 10 ml of a saturated solution add a few drops of a 3 g/l solution of *potassium permanganate R*. A brown colour is produced and a brown precipitate is formed on standing.

## TESTS

**Relative density** (*2.2.5*)
1.006 to 1.011.

**Refractive index** (*2.2.6*)
1.540 to 1.542.

**Free amines**
Maximum 500 ppm, expressed as ethylaminotoluene.

Dissolve 5.00 g in 16 ml of *methylene chloride R* and add 4.0 ml of *glacial acetic acid R*. Add 0.1 ml of *metanil yellow solution R* and 1.0 ml of *0.02 M perchloric acid*. The solution is red-violet.

**Chlorides**
Maximum 100 ppm.

Boil 5.0 g under a reflux condenser for 1 h with 25 ml of *ethanol (96 per cent) R* and 5 ml of a 200 g/l solution of *sodium hydroxide R*. Cool, add 5 ml of *water R* and shake with 25 ml of *ether R*. Dilute the lower layer to 20 ml with *water R*; add 5 ml of *nitric acid R*, dilute to 50 ml with *water R* and add 1 ml of a freshly prepared 50 g/l solution of *silver nitrate R*. Any opalescence in the solution is not more intense than that in a mixture of 1 ml of a freshly prepared 50 g/l solution of *silver nitrate R* and a solution prepared by diluting 5 ml of a 200 g/l solution of *sodium hydroxide R* to 20 ml with *water R* and adding 1.5 ml of *0.01 M hydrochloric acid*, 5 ml of *nitric acid R* and diluting to 50 ml with water R.

**Related substances**
Liquid chromatography (*2.2.29*).

*Test solution (a)* Dissolve 50.0 mg of the substance to be examined in the mobile phase and dilute to 100.0 ml with the mobile phase.

*Test solution (b)* Dilute 1.0 ml of test solution (a) to 20.0 ml with the mobile phase.

*Reference solution (a)* Dissolve 50.0 mg of *crotamiton CRS* in the mobile phase and dilute to 100.0 ml with the mobile phase. Dilute 1.0 ml of this solution to 20.0 ml with the mobile phase.

*Reference solution (b)* Dissolve 15.0 mg of *crotamiton impurity A CRS* in the mobile phase and dilute to 20.0 ml with the mobile phase. Dilute 1.0 ml of this solution to 50.0 ml with the mobile phase.

*Reference solution (c)* Dilute 1.0 ml of test solution (a) to 100.0 ml with the mobile phase.

*Reference solution (d)* Dissolve 15 mg of *crotamiton impurity A CRS* in the mobile phase and dilute to 100 ml with the mobile phase. Dilute 1 ml of this solution to 10 ml with test solution (a).

*Column:*
— *size*: $l$ = 0.25 m, Ø = 4 mm;
— *stationary phase*: silica gel for *chromatography R* (5 μm).

*Mobile phase* tetrahydrofuran R, cyclohexane R (8:92 V/V).

*Flow rate* 1.0 ml/min.

*Detection* Spectrophotometer at 242 nm.

*Injection* 20 μl of test solution (a) and reference solutions (b), (c) and (d).

*Run time* 2.5 times the retention time of the E-isomer.

*Relative retention* With reference to the E-isomer: Z-isomer = about 0.5; impurity A = about 0.8.

*System suitability* Reference solution (d):
— *resolution*: minimum 4.5 between the peaks due to impurity A and the E-isomer.

*Limits:*
— *impurity A*: not more than the area of the corresponding peak in the chromatogram obtained with reference solution (b) (3 per cent);
— *sum of impurities other than A*: not more than the sum of the areas of the peaks due to the Z- and E-isomers in the chromatogram obtained with reference solution (c) (1 per cent);
— *disregard limit*: 0.02 times the area of the principal peak in the chromatogram obtained with reference solution (c); disregard any peak due to the Z-isomer.

**Sulphated ash** (*2.4.14*)
Maximum 0.1 per cent, determined on 1.0 g.

## ASSAY

Liquid chromatography (*2.2.29*) as described in the test for related substances with the following modification.

*Injection* Test solution (b) and reference solution (a).

Calculate the percentage content of $C_{13}H_{17}NO$ from the sum of the areas of the peaks due to the Z- and E-isomers in the chromatograms obtained. Calculate the content of the Z-isomer, as a percentage of the total content of the E- and Z-isomers, from the chromatogram obtained with test solution (b).

## STORAGE

Protected from light.

## IMPURITIES

*Specified impurities* A.

N-ethyl-N-(2-methylphenyl)but-3-enamide.

Ph Eur

# Cyanocobalamin

*(Ph Eur monograph 0547)*

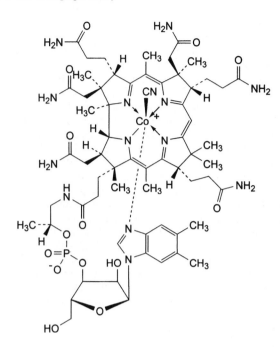

C$_{63}$H$_{88}$CoN$_{14}$O$_{14}$P        1355        68-19-9

**Action and use**

Vitamin B$_{12}$ analogue.

**Preparation**

Cyanocobalamin Tablets

*Ph Eur*

## DEFINITION

α-(5,6-Dimethylbenzimidazol-1-yl)cobamide cyanide.

**Content**

96.0 per cent to 102.0 per cent (dried substance).

This monograph applies to cyanocobalamin produced by fermentation.

## CHARACTERS

**Appearance**

Dark red, crystalline powder or dark red crystals.

**Solubility**

Sparingly soluble in water and in ethanol (96 per cent), practically insoluble in acetone.

The anhydrous substance is very hygroscopic.

## IDENTIFICATION

A. Ultraviolet and visible absorption spectrophotometry *(2.2.25)*.

*Test solution* Dissolve 2.5 mg in *water R* and dilute to 100.0 ml with the same solvent.

*Spectral range* 260-610 nm.

*Absorption maxima* At 278 nm, 361 nm and from 547 nm to 559 nm.

*Absorbance ratio*

— $A_{361} / A_{547-559}$ = 3.15 to 3.45;

— $A_{361} / A_{278}$ = 1.70 to 1.90.

B. Thin-layer chromatography *(2.2.27)*. *Carry out the test protected from light.*

*Test solution* Dissolve 2 mg of the substance to be examined in 1 ml of a mixture of equal volumes of *ethanol (96 per cent) R* and *water R*.

*Reference solution* Dissolve 2 mg of *cyanocobalamin CRS* in 1 ml of a mixture of equal volumes of *ethanol (96 per cent) R* and *water R*.

*Plate* TLC silica gel G plate R.

*Mobile phase* *dilute ammonia R1, methanol R, methylene chloride R* (9:30:45 *V/V/V*).

*Application* 10 μl.

*Development* In an unsaturated tank, over a path of 12 cm.

*Drying* In air.

*Detection* Examine in daylight.

*Results* The principal spot in the chromatogram obtained with the test solution is similar in position, colour and size to the principal spot in the chromatogram obtained with the reference solution.

## TESTS

**Related substances**

Liquid chromatography *(2.2.29)*.

*Test solution* Dissolve 10.0 mg of the substance to be examined in the mobile phase and dilute to 10.0 ml with the mobile phase. *Use within 1 h.*

*Reference solution (a)* Dilute 3.0 ml of the test solution to 100.0 ml with the mobile phase. *Use within 1 h.*

*Reference solution (b)* Dilute 5.0 ml of the test solution to 50.0 ml with the mobile phase. Dilute 1.0 ml of this solution to 100.0 ml with the mobile phase. *Use within 1 h.*

*Reference solution (c)* Dissolve 25 mg of the substance to be examined in 10 ml of *water R*, warming if necessary. Allow to cool and add 5 ml of a 1.0 g/l solution of *chloramine R* and 0.5 ml of *0.05 M hydrochloric acid*, then dilute to 25 ml with *water R*. Shake and allow to stand for 5 min. Dilute 1 ml of this solution to 10 ml with the mobile phase and inject immediately.

*Column:*

— *size:* $l$ = 0.25 m, Ø = 4 mm;

— *stationary phase:* octylsilyl silica gel for chromatography R (5 μm).

*Mobile phase* Mix 26.5 volumes of *methanol R* and 73.5 volumes of a 10 g/l solution of *disodium hydrogen phosphate R* adjusted to pH 3.5 with *phosphoric acid R* and use within 2 days.

*Flow rate* 0.8 ml/min.

*Detection* Spectrophotometer at 361 nm.

*Injection* 20 μl.

*Run time* 3 times the retention time of cyanocobalamin.

*System suitability:*

— the chromatogram obtained with reference solution (c) shows 2 principal peaks;

— *resolution:* minimum 2.5 between the 2 principal peaks in the chromatogram obtained with reference solution (c);

— *signal-to-noise ratio:* minimum 5 for the principal peak in the chromatogram obtained with reference solution (b).

*Limits:*

— *total:* not more than the area of the principal peak in the chromatogram obtained with reference solution (a) (3 per cent);

— *disregard limit:* the area of the principal peak in the chromatogram obtained with reference solution (b) (0.1 per cent).

**Loss on drying** (*2.2.32*)

Maximum 12.0 per cent, determined on 20.00 mg by drying *in vacuo* at 105 °C for 2 h.

**ASSAY**

Dissolve 25.00 mg in *water R* and dilute to 1000.0 ml with the same solvent. Measure the absorbance (*2.2.25*) at the absorption maximum at 361 nm.

Calculate the content of $C_{63}H_{88}CoN_{14}O_{14}P$ taking the specific absorbance to be 207.

**STORAGE**

In an airtight container, protected from light.

*———————————————————————— Ph Eur*

# Cyclizine

$C_{18}H_{22}N_2$ 266.4 *82-92-8*

**Action and use**

Histamine $H_1$ receptor antagonist; antihistamine.

**Preparation**

Cyclizine Injection

**DEFINITION**

Cyclizine is 1-benzhydryl-4-methylpiperazine. It contains not less than 98.5% and not more than 101.0% of $C_{18}H_{22}N_2$, calculated with reference to the dried substance.

**CHARACTERISTICS**

A white or creamy white, crystalline powder.

Practically insoluble in *water*. It dissolves in most organic solvents and in dilute acids.

**IDENTIFICATION**

A. The *infrared absorption spectrum*, Appendix II A, is concordant with the *reference spectrum* of cyclizine *(RS 075)*.

B. The *light absorption*, Appendix II B, in the range 220 to 350 nm of a freshly prepared 0.002% w/v solution in 0.05M *sulphuric acid* exhibits a maximum at 227 nm with a series of ill-defined maxima between 258 and 272 nm. The *absorbance* at 227 nm is about 0.87.

C. *Melting point*, about 107°, Appendix V A.

**TESTS**

**Alkalinity**

Shake 1 g with 25 ml of *carbon dioxide-free water* for 5 minutes and filter. The pH of the filtrate is 7.6 to 8.6, Appendix V L.

**Clarity of solution**

A 1.0% w/v solution in *ether* and a 1.0% w/v solution in 2M *hydrochloric acid* are clear, Appendix IV A.

**Chloride**

Dissolve 0.20 g in 2 ml of *methanol* and dilute to 30 ml with 2M *nitric acid*. 15 ml of the resulting solution complies with the *limit test for chlorides*, Appendix VII (500 ppm).

**Related substances**

Carry out the method for *thin-layer chromatography*, Appendix III A, using *silica gel G* as the coating substance and as the mobile phase the lower layer obtained after shaking together a mixture of 2 volumes of 13.5M *ammonia*, 8 volumes of *methanol* and 90 volumes of *dichloromethane* and allowing the layers to separate. Apply separately to the plate 20 µl of each of four freshly prepared solutions in *methanol* containing (1) 2.0% w/v of the substance being examined, (2) 0.010% w/v of the substance being examined, (3) 0.010% w/v of N-*methylpiperazine* and (4) 0.10% w/v of each of the substance being examined and *hydroxyzine hydrochloride BPCRS*. After removal of the plate, allow it to dry in air and expose to iodine vapour for 10 minutes. Any spot corresponding to N-*methylpiperazine* in the chromatogram obtained with solution (1) is not more intense than the spot in the chromatogram obtained with solution (3) (0.5%). Any other *secondary spot* in the chromatogram obtained with solution (1) is not more intense than the spot in the chromatogram obtained with solution (2) (0.5%). The test is not valid unless the chromatogram obtained with solution (4) shows two clearly separated spots.

**Loss on drying**

When dried to constant weight at 80°, loses not more than 1.0% of its weight. Use 1 g.

**Sulphated ash**

Not more than 0.1%, Appendix IX A.

**ASSAY**

Carry out Method I for *non-aqueous titration*, Appendix VIII A, using 0.1 g and determining the end point potentiometrically. Each ml of 0.1M *perchloric acid VS* is equivalent to 13.32 mg of $C_{18}H_{22}N_2$.

# Cyclizine Hydrochloride

(*Ph Eur monograph 1092*)

$C_{18}H_{22}N_2,HCl$ 302.8 *305-25-3*

**Action and use**

Histamine $H_1$ receptor antagonist; antihistamine.

**Preparations**

Cyclizine Injection

Cyclizine Tablets

Dipipanone and Cyclizine Tablets

*Ph Eur ———————————————————————————*

**DEFINITION**

1-(Diphenylmethyl)-4-methylpiperazine hydrochloride.

**Content**

98.5 per cent to 101.0 per cent (dried substance).

## CHARACTERS

**Appearance**

White or almost white, crystalline powder.

**Solubility**

Slightly soluble in water and in ethanol (96 per cent).

## IDENTIFICATION

*First identification* B, E.

*Second identification* A, C, D, E.

A. Ultraviolet and visible absorption spectrophotometry
(*2.2.25*).

*Test solution (a)* Dissolve 20.0 mg in a 5 g/l solution of
*sulphuric acid R* and dilute to 100.0 ml with the same acid
solution.

*Test solution (b)* Dilute 10.0 ml of test solution (a) to
100.0 ml with a 5 g/l solution of *sulphuric acid R*.

*Spectral range* 240-350 nm for test solution (a); 210-240 nm
for test solution (b).

*Resolution (2.2.25)* Minimum 1.7.

*Absorption maxima* At 258 nm and 262 nm for test solution
(a); at 225 nm for test solution (b).

*Absorbance ratio* $A_{262}/A_{258}$ = 1.0 to 1.1.

*Specific absorbance at the absorption maximum at
225 nm* 370 to 410 for test solution (b).

B. Infrared absorption spectrophotometry (*2.2.24*).

*Comparison* cyclizine hydrochloride CRS.

C. Thin-layer chromatography (*2.2.27*).

*Test solution* Dissolve 10 mg of the substance to be
examined in *methanol R* and dilute to 10 ml with the same
solvent.

*Reference solution* Dissolve 10 mg of *cyclizine
hydrochloride CRS* in *methanol R* and dilute to 10 ml with the
same solvent.

*Plate* TLC silica gel $GF_{254}$ plate R.

*Mobile phase* concentrated ammonia R, methanol R, methylene
chloride R (2:13:85 *V/V/V*).

*Application* 20 μl.

*Development* Over 2/3 of the plate.

*Drying* In air for 30 min.

*Detection* Expose to iodine vapour for 10 min.

*Results* The principal spot in the chromatogram obtained
with the test solution is similar in position, colour and size to
the principal spot in the chromatogram obtained with the
reference solution.

D. Dissolve 0.5 g in 10 ml of *ethanol (60 per cent) R*, heating
if necessary. Cool in iced water. Add 1 ml of *dilute sodium
hydroxide solution R* and 10 ml of *water R*. Filter, wash the
precipitate with *water R* and dry at 60 °C at a pressure not
exceeding 0.7 kPa for 2 h. The melting point (*2.2.14*) is
105 °C to 108 °C.

E. It gives reaction (a) of chlorides (*2.3.1*).

## TESTS

**pH** (*2.2.3*)

4.5 to 5.5.

Dissolve 0.5 g in a mixture of 40 volumes of *ethanol
(96 per cent) R* and 60 volumes of *carbon dioxide-free water R*
and dilute to 25 ml with the same mixture of solvents.

**Related substances**

Gas chromatography (*2.2.28*). *Prepare the solutions immediately
before use.*

*Test solution* Dissolve 0.250 g of the substance to be
examined in 4.0 ml of *methanol R* and dilute to 5.0 ml with
*1 M sodium hydroxide*.

*Reference solution (a)* Dissolve 25 mg of the substance to be
examined in 10.0 ml of *methanol R*. Dilute 1.0 ml of this
solution to 50.0 ml with *methanol R*.

*Reference solution (b)* Dissolve 5 mg of the substance to be
examined, 5.0 mg of *cyclizine impurity A CRS* and 5.0 mg of
*cyclizine impurity B CRS* in *methanol R* and dilute to 20.0 ml
with the same solvent.

*Column:*

— *material*: fused silica;

— *size*: $l$ = 25 m, Ø = 0.33 mm;

— *stationary phase*: poly(dimethyl)(diphenyl)siloxane R (film
thickness 0.50 μm).

*Carrier gas* helium for chromatography R.

*Flow rate* 1.0 ml/min.

*Split ratio* 1:25.

*Temperature:*

|  | Time (min) | Temperature (°C) |
|---|---|---|
| Column | 0 - 14 | 100 → 240 |
|  | 14 - 16 | 240 → 270 |
|  | 16 - 30 | 270 |
| Injection port |  | 250 |
| Detector |  | 290 |

*Detection* Flame ionisation.

*Injection* 1 μl.

*Relative retention* With reference to cyclizine
(retention time = about 15 min): impurity A = about 0.2;
impurity B = about 0.7.

*System suitability* Reference solution (b):

— *peak-to-valley ratio*: minimum 50, where $H_p$ = height
above the baseline of the peak due to impurity A and
$H_v$ = height above the baseline of the lowest point of the
curve separating this peak from the peak due to methanol.

*Limits:*

— *impurities A, B*: for each impurity, not more than the area
of the corresponding peak in the chromatogram obtained
with reference solution (b) (0.5 per cent);

— *unspecified impurities*: for each impurity, not more than the
area of the principal peak in the chromatogram obtained
with reference solution (a) (0.10 per cent);

— *total*: not more than 10 times the area of the principal
peak in the chromatogram obtained with reference
solution (a) (1.0 per cent);

— *disregard limit*: 0.5 times the area of the principal peak in
the chromatogram obtained with reference solution (a)
(0.05 per cent).

**Loss on drying** (*2.2.32*)

Maximum 1.0 per cent, determined on 1.000 g by drying in
an oven at 130 °C.

**Sulphated ash** (*2.4.14*)

Maximum 0.1 per cent, determined on 1.0 g.

## ASSAY

*In order to avoid overheating in the reaction medium, mix thoroughly throughout and stop the titration immediately after the end-point has been reached.*

Dissolve 0.120 g in 15 ml of *anhydrous formic acid R* and add 40 ml of *acetic anhydride R*. Titrate with *0.1 M perchloric acid*, determining the end-point potentiometrically *(2.2.20)*.

1 ml of *0.1 M perchloric acid* is equivalent to 15.14 mg of $C_{18}H_{23}ClN_2$.

## STORAGE

Protected from light.

## IMPURITIES

*Specified impurities   A, B.*

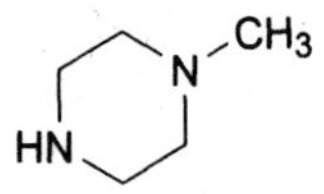

A. 1-methylpiperazine,

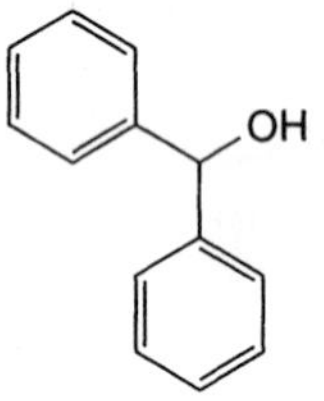

B. diphenylmethanol (benzhydrol).

*Ph Eur*

# Cyclopenthiazide

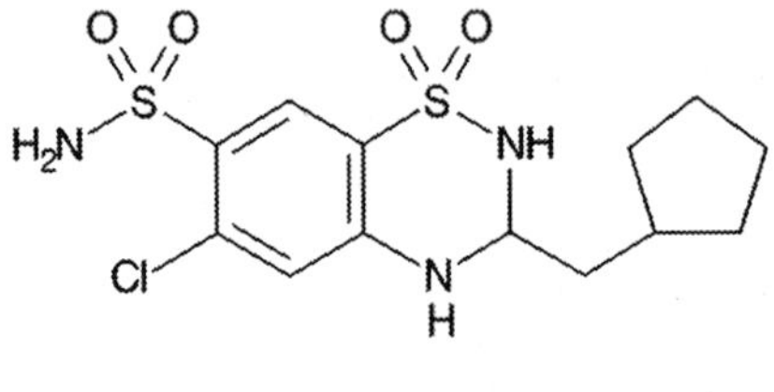

$C_{13}H_{18}ClN_3O_4S_2$ · · · · · 379.9 · · · · · *742-20-1*

## Action and use

Thiazide-diuretic.

## Preparation

Cyclopenthiazide Tablets

## DEFINITION

Cyclopenthiazide is 6-chloro-3-cyclopentylmethyl-3,4-dihydro-1,2,4-benzothiadiazine-7-sulphonamide 1,1-dioxide. It contains not less than 98.0% and not more than 102.0% of $C_{13}H_{18}ClN_3O_4S_2$, calculated with reference to the dried substance.

## CHARACTERISTICS

A white powder.

Practically insoluble in *water*; soluble in *acetone* and in *ethanol (96%)*; very slightly soluble in *ether*.

## IDENTIFICATION

A. The *infrared absorption spectrum*, Appendix II A, is concordant with the *reference spectrum* of cyclopenthiazide *(RS 077)*.

B. The *light absorption*, Appendix II B, in the range 230 to 350 nm of a 0.002% w/v solution in 0.01M *sodium hydroxide* exhibits two maxima, at 273 nm and 320 nm. The *absorbance* at 273 nm is about 0.88 and at 320 nm is about 0.12.

C. Carry out the method for *thin-layer chromatography*, Appendix III A, using *silica gel GF*$_{254}$ as the coating substance and *ethyl acetate* as the mobile phase. Apply separately to the plate 5 µl of each of two solutions in *acetone* containing (1) 0.1% w/v of the substance being examined and (2) 0.1% w/v of *cyclopenthiazide BPCRS*. After removal of the plate, dry it in a current of air, examine under *ultraviolet light (254 nm)* and then reveal the spots by *Method I*. By each method of visualisation the principal spot in the chromatogram obtained with solution (1) corresponds in colour and intensity to that in the chromatogram obtained with solution (2).

## TESTS

### Related substances

Carry out the method for *thin-layer chromatography*, Appendix III A, using *silica gel G* as the coating substance and *ethyl acetate* as the mobile phase. Apply separately to the plate 5 µl of each of two solutions of the substance being examined in *acetone* containing (1) 0.50% w/v and (2) 0.0050% w/v. After removal of the plate, dry it in a current of air and reveal the spots by *Method I*. Any *secondary spot* in the chromatogram obtained with solution (1) is not more intense than the spot in the chromatogram obtained with solution (2).

### Loss on drying

When dried to constant weight at 105°, loses not more than 0.5% of its weight. Use 1 g.

### Sulphated ash

Not more than 0.1%, Appendix IX A.

## ASSAY

Dissolve 0.5 g in 50 ml of *butylamine* and carry out Method II for *non-aqueous titration*, Appendix VIII A, using 0.1M *tetrabutylammonium hydroxide VS* as titrant and *magneson solution* as indicator; titrate to a pure blue end point. Each ml of 0.1M *tetrabutylammonium hydroxide VS* is equivalent to 18.99 mg of $C_{13}H_{18}ClN_3O_4S_2$.

# Cyclopentolate Hydrochloride

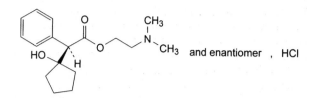

*(Ph Eur monograph 1093)*

and enantiomer , HCl

C₁₇H₂₅NO₃,HCl          327.8          *5870-29-1*

$C_{17}H_{25}NO_3$,HCl          327.8          *5870-29-1*

## Action and use
Anticholinergic.

## Preparation
Cyclopentolate Eye Drops

*Ph Eur* _____

## DEFINITION
2-(Dimethylamino)ethyl (2RS)-
(1-hydroxycyclopentyl)(phenyl)acetate hydrochloride.

## Content
98.5 per cent to 101.5 per cent (dried substance).

## CHARACTERS
### Appearance
White or almost white, crystalline powder.

### Solubility
Very soluble in water, freely soluble in ethanol (96 per cent).
It shows polymorphism (*5.9*).

## IDENTIFICATION
*First identification*   B, D.

*Second identification*   A, C, D.

A. Melting point (*2.2.14*): 135 °C to 141 °C.

B. Infrared absorption spectrophotometry (*2.2.24*).

*Preparation*   Discs of potassium chloride R.

*Comparison*   cyclopentolate hydrochloride CRS.

If the spectra obtained show differences, dissolve the
substance to be examined and the reference substance
separately in *ethanol (96 per cent) R*, evaporate to dryness and
record new spectra using the residues.

C. Thin-layer chromatography (*2.2.27*).

*Test solution*   Dissolve 10 mg of the substance to be
examined in 5 ml of *ethanol (96 per cent) R*.

*Reference solution*   Dissolve 10 mg of *cyclopentolate
hydrochloride CRS* in *ethanol (96 per cent) R* and dilute to
5 ml with the same solvent.

*Plate*   *TLC silica gel plate R*.

*Mobile phase*   concentrated ammonia R, water R, butyl
acetate R, 2-propanol R (5:15:30:50 *V/V/V/V*).

*Application*   10 μl.

*Development*   Over 2/3 of the plate.

*Drying*   In air.

*Detection*   Spray with alcoholic solution of *sulphuric acid R*
and heat at 120 °C for 30 min; examine in ultraviolet light at
365 nm.

*Result*   The principal spot in the chromatogram obtained
with the test solution is similar in position, fluorescence and
size to the principal spot in the chromatogram obtained with
the reference solution.

D. It gives reaction (a) of chlorides (*2.3.1*).

## TESTS
**pH** (*2.2.3*)
4.5 to 5.5.

Dissolve 0.2 g in *carbon dioxide-free water R* and dilute to
20 ml with the same solvent.

**Related substances**
Liquid chromatography (*2.2.29*). *Prepare the solutions
immediately before use.*

*Test solution*   Dissolve 20 mg of the substance to be
examined in *water R* and dilute to 20.0 ml with the same
solvent.

*Reference solution (a)*   Dilute 1.0 ml of the test solution to
100.0 ml with *water R*. Dilute 5.0 ml of this solution to
10.0 ml with *water R*.

*Reference solution (b)*   Dissolve 10 mg of *cyclopentolate for
system suitability CRS* (containing impurity C) in *water R* and
dilute to 10.0 ml with the same solvent.

*Column:*
— *size: l* = 0.125 m, Ø = 4.0 mm;
— *stationary phase: spherical end-capped hexylsilyl silica gel for
   chromatography R* (5 μm).

*Mobile phase*   Dissolve 0.66 g of *ammonium phosphate R* in
*water R*, adjust to pH 3.0 with *phosphoric acid R* and dilute to
1000 ml with *water R*; mix and filter; mix 55 volumes of this
solution and 45 volumes of *acetonitrile R1*.

*Flow rate*   1.0 ml/min.

*Detection*   Spectrophotometer at 220 nm.

*Injection*   20 μl.

*Run time*   2.5 times the retention time of cyclopentolate.

*Identification of impurities*   Use the chromatogram supplied
with *cyclopentolate for system suitability CRS* and the
chromatogram obtained with reference solution (b) to
identify the peak due to impurity C.

*Relative retention*   With reference to cyclopentolate
(retention time = about 4 min): impurity C = about 0.9.

*System suitability*   Reference solution (b):
— *peak-to-valley ratio*: minimum 6, where $H_p$ = height above
   the baseline of the peak due to impurity C and
   $H_v$ = height above the baseline of the lowest point of the
   curve separating this peak from the peak due to
   cyclopentolate.

*Limits:*
— *correction factor*: for the calculation of content, multiply the
   peak area of impurity C by 2.0;
— *impurity C*: not more than the area of the principal peak
   in the chromatogram obtained with reference solution (a)
   (0.5 per cent);
— *unspecified impurities*: for each impurity, not more than
   0.2 times the area of the principal peak in the
   chromatogram obtained with reference solution (a)
   (0.10 per cent);
— *total*: not more than twice the area of the principal peak in
   the chromatogram obtained with reference solution (a)
   (1.0 per cent);
— *disregard limit*: 0.1 times the area of the principal peak in
   the chromatogram obtained with reference solution (a)
   (0.05 per cent).

**Loss on drying** (*2.2.32*)
Maximum 0.5 per cent, determined on 1.000 g by drying in
an oven at 105 °C for 4 h.

**Sulphated ash** *(2.4.14)*

Maximum 0.1 per cent, determined on 1.0 g.

## ASSAY

Dissolve 0.250 g in a mixture of 1.0 ml of *0.1 M hydrochloric acid* and 50 ml of *ethanol (96 per cent) R*. Carry out a potentiometric titration *(2.2.20)*, using *0.1 M sodium hydroxide*. Read the volume added between the 2 points of inflexion.

1 ml of *0.1 M sodium hydroxide* is equivalent to 32.79 mg of $C_{17}H_{26}ClNO_3$.

## IMPURITIES

*Specified impurities   C.*

*Other detectable impurities*   (The following substances would, if present at a sufficient level, be detected by one or other of the tests in the monograph. They are limited by the general acceptance criterion for other/unspecified impurities and/or by the general monograph *Substances for pharmaceutical use (2034)*. It is therefore not necessary to identify these impurities for demonstration of compliance. See also *5.10. Control of impurities in substances for pharmaceutical use*): A, B.

and enantiomer

A. (2RS)-(1-hydroxycyclopentyl)(phenyl)acetic acid,

B. phenylacetic acid,

C. 2-(dimethylamino)ethyl phenylacetate.

*Ph Eur*

# Cyclophosphamide

*(Ph Eur monograph 0711)*

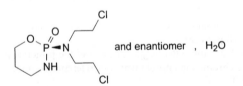

and enantiomer , $H_2O$

$C_7H_{15}Cl_2N_2O_2P,H_2O$          279.1          6055-19-2

## Action and use

Cytotoxic alkylating agent.

## Preparations

Cyclophosphamide Injection

Cyclophosphamide Tablets

*Ph Eur*

## DEFINITION

Cyclophosphamide contains not less than 98.0 per cent and not more than the equivalent of 102.0 per cent of (2RS)-N,N-bis(2-chloroethyl)tetrahydro-2H-1,3,2-oxazaphosphorin-2-amine 2-oxide, calculated with reference to the anhydrous substance.

## CHARACTERS

A white or almost white, crystalline powder, soluble in water, freely soluble in alcohol.

## IDENTIFICATION

*First identification   B.*

*Second identification   A, C, D.*

A. Determine the melting point *(2.2.14)* of the substance to be examined. Mix equal parts of the substance to be examined and *cyclophosphamide CRS* and determine the melting point of the mixture. The difference between the melting points (which are about 51 °C) is not greater than 2 °C.

B. Examine by infrared absorption spectrophotometry *(2.2.24)*, comparing with the spectrum obtained with *cyclophosphamide CRS*.

C. Examine the chromatograms obtained in the test for related substances. The principal spot in the chromatogram obtained with test solution (b) is similar in position, colour and size to the principal spot in the chromatogram obtained with reference solution (a).

D. Dissolve 0.1 g in 10 ml of *water R* and add 5 ml of *silver nitrate solution R1*; the solution remains clear. Boil, a white precipitate is formed which dissolves in *concentrated ammonia R* and is reprecipitated on the addition of *dilute nitric acid R*.

## TESTS

**Solution S**

Dissolve 0.50 g in *carbon dioxide-free water R* and dilute to 25.0 ml with the same solvent.

**Appearance of solution**

Solution S is clear *(2.2.1)* and not more intensely coloured than reference solution $Y_6$ *(2.2.2, Method II)*.

**pH** *(2.2.3)*

The pH of solution S is 4.0 to 6.0, determined immediately after preparation of the solution.

**Related substances**

Examine by thin-layer chromatography *(2.2.27)*, using *silica gel G R* as the coating substance.

*Test solution (a)*   Dissolve 0.10 g of the substance to be examined in *alcohol R* and dilute to 5 ml with the same solvent.

*Test solution (b)*   Dilute 1 ml of test solution (a) to 10 ml with *alcohol R*.

*Reference solution (a)*   Dissolve 10 mg of *cyclophosphamide CRS* in *alcohol R* and dilute to 5 ml with the same solvent.

*Reference solution (b)*   Dilute 0.1 ml of test solution (a) to 10 ml with *alcohol R*.

Apply separately to the plate 10 µl of each solution. Develop over a path of 15 cm using a mixture of 2 volumes of *anhydrous formic acid R*, 4 volumes of *acetone R*, 12 volumes of *water R* and 80 volumes of *methyl ethyl ketone R*. Dry the plate in a current of warm air and heat at 110 °C for 10 min. At the bottom of a chromatography tank, place an evaporating dish containing a 50 g/l solution of *potassium permanganate R* and add an equal volume of *hydrochloric acid R*. Place the plate whilst still hot in the tank and close the tank. Leave the plate in contact with the chlorine gas for 2 min. Withdraw the plate and place it in a current of cold air until the excess of chlorine is removed and an area of coating below the points of application gives at most a very faint blue colour with a drop of *potassium iodide and starch solution R*. Avoid prolonged exposure to cold air. Spray with *potassium iodide and starch solution R* and allow to stand for 5 min. Any spot in the chromatogram obtained with test solution (a), apart from the principal spot, is not more intense than the spot in the chromatogram obtained with reference solution (b) (1.0 per cent). Disregard any spot remaining at the starting-point.

**Chlorides** *(2.4.4)*

Dissolve 0.15 g in *water R* and dilute to 15 ml with the same solvent. The freshly prepared solution complies with the limit test for chlorides (330 ppm).

**Phosphates** *(2.4.11)*

Dissolve 0.10 g in *water R* and dilute to 100 ml with the same solvent. The solution complies with the limit test for phosphates (100 ppm).

**Heavy metals** *(2.4.8)*

1.0 g complies with limit test C for heavy metals (20 ppm). Prepare the standard using 2 ml of *lead standard solution (10 ppm Pb) R*.

**Water** *(2.5.12)*

6.0 per cent to 7.0 per cent, determined on 0.300 g by the semi-micro determination of water.

**ASSAY**

Dissolve 0.100 g in 50 ml of a 1 g/l solution of *sodium hydroxide R* in *ethylene glycol R* and boil under a reflux condenser for 30 min. Allow to cool and rinse the condenser with 25 ml of *water R*. Add 75 ml of *2-propanol R*, 15 ml of *dilute nitric acid R*, 10.0 ml of *0.1 M silver nitrate* and 2.0 ml of *ferric ammonium sulfate solution R2* and titrate with *0.1 M ammonium thiocyanate*.

1 ml of *0.1 M silver nitrate* is equivalent to 13.05 mg of $C_7H_{15}Cl_2N_2O_2P$.

*Ph Eur*

# Cyproheptadine Hydrochloride

*(Ph Eur monograph 0817)*

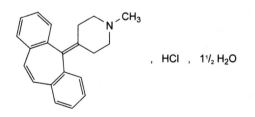

, HCl , $1\frac{1}{2}$ $H_2O$

$C_{21}H_{21}N,HCl,1\frac{1}{2}H_2O$     350.9     *41354-29-4*

**Action and use**

Histamine $H_1$ receptor antagonist; antihistamine.

**Preparation**

Cyproheptadine Tablets

*Ph Eur*

**DEFINITION**

4-(5*H*-Dibenzo[*a,d*][7]annulen-5-ylidene)-1-methylpiperidine hydrochloride sesquihydrate.

**Content**

98.5 per cent to 101.0 per cent (anhydrous substance).

**CHARACTERS**

**Appearance**

White or slightly yellow, crystalline powder.

**Solubility**

Slightly soluble in water, freely soluble in methanol, sparingly soluble in ethanol (96 per cent).

**IDENTIFICATION**

A. Infrared absorption spectrophotometry *(2.2.24)*.

*Comparison  cyproheptadine hydrochloride CRS.*

B. A saturated solution gives reaction (b) of chlorides *(2.3.1)*.

**TESTS**

**Acidity**

Dissolve 0.10 g in *water R* and dilute to 25 ml with the same solvent. Add 0.1 ml of *methyl red solution R*. Not more than 0.15 ml of *0.01 M sodium hydroxide* is required to change the colour of the indicator.

**Related substances**

Liquid chromatography *(2.2.29)*.

*Test solution*  Dissolve 40.0 mg of the substance to be examined in mobile phase A and dilute to 20.0 ml with mobile phase A.

*Reference solution (a)*  Dilute 1.0 ml of the test solution to 100.0 ml with mobile phase A. Dilute 1.0 ml of this solution to 10.0 ml with mobile phase A.

*Reference solution (b)*  Dissolve 2.0 mg of *dibenzocycloheptene CRS* (impurity A), 2.0 mg of *dibenzosuberone CRS* (impurity B) and 2.0 mg of *cyproheptadine impurity C CRS* in mobile phase A, add 1.0 ml of the test solution and dilute to 100.0 ml with mobile phase A.

*Reference solution (c)*  Dilute 1.0 ml of reference solution (b) to 10.0 ml with mobile phase A.

*Column:*
— *size: l* = 0.25 m, Ø = 4.6 mm;
— *stationary phase: octylsilyl silica gel for chromatography R* (5 μm).

*Mobile phase:*
— *mobile phase A*: dissolve 6.12 g of *potassium dihydrogen phosphate R* in 900 ml of *water R*, adjust to pH 4.5 with *phosphoric acid R* and dilute to 1000 ml with *water R*; mix 60 volumes of this solution and 40 volumes of *acetonitrile for chromatography R*;
— *mobile phase B*: dissolve 6.12 g of *potassium dihydrogen phosphate R* in 900 ml of *water R*, adjust to pH 4.5 with *phosphoric acid R* and dilute to 1000 ml with *water R*; mix 40 volumes of this solution and 60 volumes of *acetonitrile for chromatography R*;

| Time (min) | Mobile phase A (per cent V/V) | Mobile phase B (per cent V/V) |
|---|---|---|
| 0 - 10.0 | 100 | 0 |
| 10.0 - 10.1 | 100 → 0 | 0 → 100 |
| 10.1 - 35 | 0 | 100 |

*Flow rate*  1.0 ml/min.

*Detection*  Spectrophotometer at 230 nm.

*Injection*   10 µl.

*Relative retention*   With reference to cyproheptadine (retention time = about 8 min): impurity C = about 0.7; impurity B = about 2.6; impurity A = about 3.9.

*System suitability*   Reference solution (b):
— *resolution*: minimum 7.0 between the peaks due to impurity C and cyproheptadine.

*Limits:*
— *impurities A, B, C*: for each impurity, not more than 1.5 times the area of the corresponding peak in the chromatogram obtained with reference solution (c) (0.15 per cent);
— *unspecified impurities*: for each impurity, not more than the area of the principal peak in the chromatogram obtained with reference solution (a) (0.10 per cent);
— *total*: not more than 5 times the area of the principal peak in the chromatogram obtained with reference solution (a) (0.5 per cent);
— *disregard limit*: 0.5 times the area of the principal peak in the chromatogram obtained with reference solution (a) (0.05 per cent).

**Water** (*2.5.12*)
7.0 per cent to 9.0 per cent, determined on 0.200 g.

**Sulphated ash** (*2.4.14*)
Maximum 0.1 per cent, determined on 1.0 g.

**ASSAY**
Dissolve 0.250 g in a mixture of 5.0 ml of *0.01 M hydrochloric acid* and 50 ml of *ethanol (96 per cent) R*. Carry out a potentiometric titration (*2.2.20*), using *0.1 M sodium hydroxide*. Read the volume added between the 2 points of inflexion.

1 ml of *0.1 M sodium hydroxide* is equivalent to 32.39 mg of $C_{21}H_{22}ClN$.

**STORAGE**
Protected from light.

**IMPURITIES**
*Specified impurities   A, B, C.*

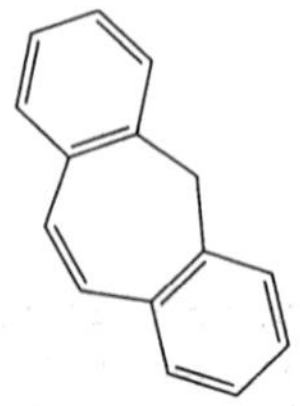

A. 5*H*-dibenzo[*a,d*][7]annulene (dibenzocycloheptene),

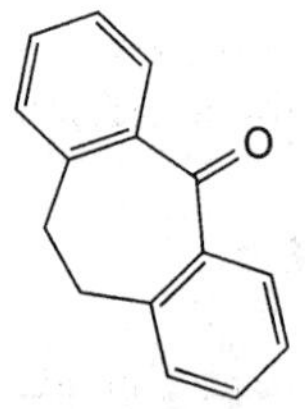

B. 10,11-dihydro-5*H*-dibenzo[*a,d*][7]annulen-5-one (dibenzosuberone),

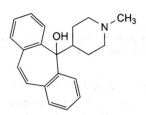

C. 5-(1-methylpiperidin-4-yl)-5*H*-dibenzo[*a,d*][7]annulen-5-ol.

*Ph Eur*

# Cyproterone Acetate

(*Ph Eur monograph 1094*)

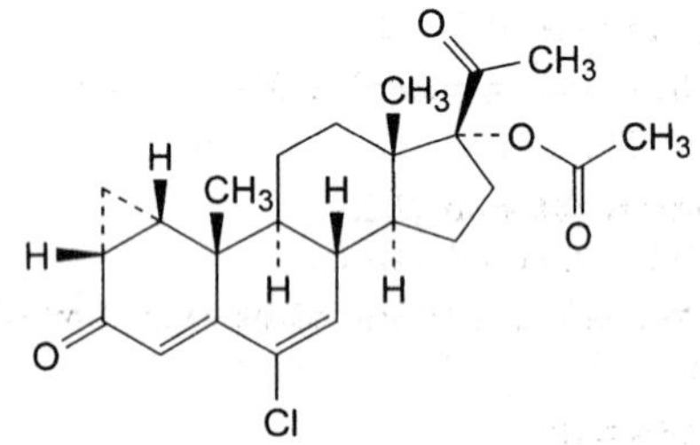

$C_{24}H_{29}ClO_4$          416.9          427-51-0

**Action and use**
Anti-estrogen.

**Preparation**
Cyproterone Tablets

*Ph Eur*

**DEFINITION**
6-Chloro-3,20-dioxo-1β,2β-dihydro-3′*H*-cyclopropa[1,2]pregna-1,4,6-trien-17-yl acetate.

**Content**
97.0 per cent to 103.0 per cent (dried substance).

**CHARACTERS**
**Appearance**
White or almost white, crystalline powder.

**Solubility**
Practically insoluble in water, very soluble in methylene chloride, freely soluble in acetone, soluble in methanol, sparingly soluble in anhydrous ethanol.

mp: about 210 °C.

**IDENTIFICATION**
*First identification   A.*

*Second identification   B, C, D, E.*

A. Infrared absorption spectrophotometry (*2.2.24*).

*Comparison   cyproterone acetate CRS.*

B. Thin-layer chromatography (*2.2.27*).

*Test solution*   Dissolve 20 mg of the substance to be examined in *methylene chloride R* and dilute to 10 ml with the same solvent.

*Reference solution*   Dissolve 10 mg of *cyproterone acetate CRS* in *methylene chloride R* and dilute to 5 ml with the same solvent.

*Plate   TLC silica gel F₂₅₄ plate R.*

*Mobile phase   cyclohexane R, ethyl acetate R* (50:50 *V/V*).

*Application* 5 µl.

*Development* Twice over a path of 15 cm; dry the plate in air between the 2 developments.

*Drying* In air.

*Detection* Examine in ultraviolet light at 254 nm.

*Results* The principal spot in the chromatogram obtained with the test solution is similar in position and size to the principal spot in the chromatogram obtained with the reference solution.

C. To about 1 mg add 2 ml of *sulphuric acid R* and heat on a water-bath for 2 min. A red colour develops. Cool. Add this solution cautiously to 4 ml of *water R* and shake. The solution becomes violet.

D. Incinerate about 30 mg with 0.3 g of *anhydrous sodium carbonate R* over a naked flame for about 10 min. Cool and dissolve the residue in 5 ml of *dilute nitric acid R*. Filter. To 1 ml of the filtrate add 1 ml of *water R*. The solution gives reaction (a) of chlorides (*2.3.1*).

E. It gives the reaction of acetyl (*2.3.1*).

## TESTS

**Specific optical rotation** (*2.2.7*)
+ 152 to + 157 (dried substance).

Dissolve 0.25 g in *acetone R* and dilute to 25.0 ml with the same solvent.

**Related substances**
Liquid chromatography (*2.2.29*).

*Test solution* Dissolve 10.0 mg of the substance to be examined in *acetonitrile R* and dilute to 10.0 ml with the same solvent.

*Reference solution (a)* Dilute 1.0 ml of the test solution to 100.0 ml with *acetonitrile R*.

*Reference solution (b)* Dissolve 5 mg of *medroxyprogesterone acetate CRS* in *acetonitrile R* and dilute to 50.0 ml with the same solvent. Dilute 1.0 ml of this solution to 10.0 ml with reference solution (a).

*Column:*
— *size: l* = 0.125 m, Ø = 4.6 mm;
— *stationary phase: octadecylsilyl silica gel for chromatography R* (3 µm).

*Mobile phase* acetonitrile R, water R (40:60 V/V).

*Flow rate* 1.5 ml/min.

*Detection* Spectrophotometer at 254 nm.

*Injection* 20 µl.

*Run time* Twice the retention time of cyproterone acetate.

*System suitability* Reference solution (b):
— *resolution*: minimum 3.0 between the peaks due to cyproterone acetate and medroxyprogesterone acetate.

*Limits:*
— *total*: not more than 0.5 times the area of the principal peak in the chromatogram obtained with reference solution (a) (0.5 per cent);
— *disregard limit*: 0.05 times the area of the principal peak in the chromatogram obtained with reference solution (a) (0.05 per cent).

**Loss on drying** (*2.2.32*)
Maximum 0.5 per cent, determined on 1.000 g by drying at 80 °C at a pressure not exceeding 0.7 kPa.

**Sulphated ash** (*2.4.14*)
Maximum 0.1 per cent, determined on 1.0 g.

## ASSAY

Dissolve 50.0 mg in *methanol R* and dilute to 50.0 ml with the same solvent. Dilute 1.0 ml of this solution to 100.0 ml with *methanol R*. Measure the absorbance (*2.2.25*) at the absorption maximum at 282 nm.

Calculate the content of $C_{24}H_{29}ClO_4$ taking the specific absorbance to be 414.

## STORAGE
Protected from light.

## IMPURITIES

A. R = H: 3,20-dioxo-1β,2β-dihydro-3′*H*-cyclopropa[1,2]pregna-1,4,6-trien-17-yl acetate,

B. R = OCH₃: 6-methoxy-3,20-dioxo-1β,2β-dihydro-3′*H*-cyclopropa[1,2]pregna-1,4,6-trien-17-yl acetate.

*Ph Eur*

# Cysteine Hydrochloride

(*Cysteine Hydrochloride Monohydrate,
Ph Eur monograph 0895*)

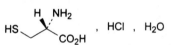

$C_3H_7NO_2S,HCl,H_2O$     175.6     7048-04-6

**Action and use**
Amino acid.

*Ph Eur*

## DEFINITION
Cysteine hydrochloride monohydrate contains not less than 98.5 per cent and not more than the equivalent of 101.0 per cent of (2R)-2-amino-3-sulfanylpropanoic acid hydrochloride, calculated with reference to the dried substance.

## CHARACTERS
A white or almost white, crystalline powder or colourless crystals, freely soluble in water, slightly soluble in alcohol.

## IDENTIFICATION
*First identification* A, B, E.
*Second identification* A, C, D, E.

A. It complies with the test for specific optical rotation (see Tests).

B. Examine by infrared absorption spectrophotometry (*2.2.24*), comparing with the spectrum obtained with *cysteine hydrochloride monohydrate CRS*. Examine the substances prepared as discs.

C. Examine the chromatograms obtained in the test for ninhydrin-positive substances. The principal spot in the chromatogram obtained with test solution (b) is similar in position, colour, and size to the principal spot in the chromatogram obtained with reference solution (b).

D. Dissolve about 5 mg in 1 ml of *dilute sodium hydroxide solution R*. Add 1 ml of a 30 g/l solution of *sodium nitroprusside R*. An intense violet colour develops which becomes brownish-red and then orange. Add 1 ml of *hydrochloric acid R*. The solution becomes green.

E. It gives reaction (a) of chlorides (*2.3.1*).

## TESTS

### Solution S
Dissolve 2.5 g in *distilled water R* and dilute to 50 ml with the same solvent.

### Appearance of solution
Dilute 10 ml of solution S to 20 ml with *water R*. The solution is clear (*2.2.1*) and not more intensely coloured than reference solution $BY_6$ (*2.2.2, Method II*).

### Specific optical rotation (*2.2.7*)
Dissolve 2.00 g in *hydrochloric acid R1* and dilute to 25.0 ml with the same acid. The specific optical rotation is + 5.5 to + 7.0, calculated with reference to the dried substance.

### Ninhydrin-positive substances
Examine by thin-layer chromatography (*2.2.27*), using a *TLC silica gel plate R*.

*Test solution (a)*   Dissolve 0.20 g of the substance to be examined in *water R* and dilute to 10 ml with the same solvent. To 5 ml of the solution add 5 ml of a 40 g/l solution of *N-ethylmaleimide R* in *alcohol R*. Allow to stand for 5 min.

*Test solution (b)*   Dilute 1 ml of test solution (a) to 50 ml with *water R*.

*Reference solution (a)*   Dissolve 20 mg of *cysteine hydrochloride monohydrate CRS* in *water R* and dilute to 10 ml with the same solvent. Add 10 ml of a 40 g/l solution of *N-ethylmaleimide R* in *alcohol R*. Allow to stand for 5 min.

*Reference solution (b)*   Dilute 2 ml of reference solution (a) to 10 ml with *water R*.

*Reference solution (c)*   Dilute 5 ml of test solution (b) to 20 ml with *water R*.

*Reference solution (d)*   Dissolve 10 mg of *tyrosine CRS* in 10 ml of reference solution (a) and dilute to 25 ml with *water R*.

Apply separately to the plate 5 μl of each test solution and reference solutions (b), (c), and (d). Develop over a path of 15 cm using a mixture of 20 volumes of *glacial acetic acid R*, 20 volumes of *water R* and 60 volumes of *butanol R*. Dry the plate at 80 °C for 30 min. Spray with *ninhydrin solution R* and heat at 100 °C to 105 °C for 15 min. Any spot in the chromatogram obtained with test solution (a), apart from the principal spot, is not more intense than the spot in the chromatogram obtained with reference solution (c) (0.5 per cent). The test is not valid unless the chromatogram obtained with reference solution (d) shows 2 clearly separated principal spots.

### Sulphates (*2.4.13*)
Dilute 10 ml of solution S to 15 ml with *distilled water R*. The solution complies with the limit test for sulphates (300 ppm).

### Ammonium (*2.4.1*)
50 mg complies with limit test B for ammonium (200 ppm). Prepare the standard using 0.1 ml of *ammonium standard solution (100 ppm NH₄) R*.

### Iron (*2.4.9*)
In a separating funnel, dissolve 0.50 g in 10 ml of *dilute hydrochloric acid R*. Shake with 3 quantities, each of 10 ml, of *methyl isobutyl ketone R1*, shaking for 3 min each time. To the combined organic layers add 10 ml of *water R* and shake for 3 min. The aqueous layer complies with the limit test for iron (20 ppm).

### Heavy metals (*2.4.8*)
Dissolve 2.0 g in *water R*. Adjust to pH 3 to 4 with *concentrated ammonia R* and dilute to 20 ml with *water R*. 12 ml of the solution complies with limit test A for heavy metals (10 ppm). Prepare the standard using *lead standard solution (1 ppm Pb) R*.

### Loss on drying (*2.2.32*)
8.0 per cent to 12.0 per cent, determined on 1.000 g by drying at a pressure not exceeding 0.7 kPa for 24 h.

### Sulphated ash (*2.4.14*)
Not more than 0.1 per cent, determined on 1.0 g.

## ASSAY
In a ground-glass stoppered flask dissolve 0.300 g of the substance to be examined and 4 g of *potassium iodide R* in 20 ml of *water R*. Cool the solution in iced water and add 3 ml of *hydrochloric acid R1* and 25.0 ml of *0.05 M iodine*. Stopper the flask and allow to stand in the dark for 20 min. Titrate with *0.1 M sodium thiosulphate* using 3 ml of *starch solution R*, added towards the end of the titration, as indicator. Carry out a blank titration.

1 ml of *0.05 M iodine* is equivalent to 15.76 mg of $C_3H_8ClNO_2S$.

## STORAGE
Store protected from light.

*Ph Eur*

# Cystine

(*Ph Eur monograph 0998*)

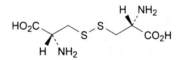

$C_6H_{12}N_2O_4S_2$                     240.3                     56-89-3

### Action and use
Amino acid.

*Ph Eur*

## DEFINITION
Cystine contains not less than 98.5 per cent and not more than the equivalent of 101.0 per cent of 3,3′-disulfanediylbis[(2R)-2-aminopropanoic acid], calculated with reference to the dried substance.

## CHARACTERS
A white or almost white, crystalline powder, practically insoluble in water and in alcohol. It dissolves in dilute solutions of alkali hydroxides.

## IDENTIFICATION
*First identification   A, B.*

*Second identification   A, C, D.*

A. It complies with the test for specific optical rotation (see Tests).

B. Examine by infrared absorption spectrophotometry (2.2.24), comparing with the spectrum obtained with *cystine CRS*. Examine the substances prepared as discs.

C. Examine the chromatograms obtained in the test for ninhydrin-positive substances. The principal spot in the chromatogram obtained with test solution (b) is similar in position, colour and size to the principal spot in the chromatogram obtained with reference solution (a).

D. To 0.1 g carefully add 1 ml of *strong hydrogen peroxide solution R* and 0.1 ml of *ferric chloride solution R1*. Allow to cool. Add 1 ml of *dilute hydrochloric acid R* and 5 ml of *water R*. Add 1 ml of *barium chloride solution R1*. Turbidity or a white precipitate develops within 3 min.

## TESTS

### Appearance of solution
Dissolve 1.0 g in *dilute hydrochloric acid R* and dilute to 10 ml with the same acid. The solution is clear (2.2.1) and not more intensely coloured than reference solution $Y_7$ (2.2.2, Method II).

### Specific optical rotation (2.2.7)
Dissolve 0.50 g in *1 M hydrochloric acid* and dilute to 25.0 ml with the same acid. The specific optical rotation is − 218 to − 224, calculated with reference to the dried substance.

### Ninhydrin-positive substances
Examine by thin-layer chromatography (2.2.27), using a *TLC silica gel plate R*.

*Test solution (a)*   Dissolve 0.10 g of the substance to be examined in *1 M hydrochloric acid* and dilute to 10 ml with the same acid.

*Test solution (b)*   Dilute 1 ml of test solution (a) to 50 ml with *water R*.

*Reference solution (a)*   Dissolve 10 mg of *cystine CRS* in 1 ml of *1 M hydrochloric acid* and dilute to 50 ml with *water R*.

*Reference solution (b)*   Dilute 2 ml of test solution (b) to 20 ml with *water R*.

*Reference solution (c)*   Dissolve 10 mg of *cystine CRS* and 10 mg of *arginine hydrochloride CRS* in 1 ml of *1 M hydrochloric acid* and dilute to 25 ml with *water R*.

Apply separately to the plate 5 µl of each solution. Develop over a path of 15 cm using a mixture of 30 volumes of *concentrated ammonia R* and 70 volumes of *2-propanol R*. Allow the plate to dry in air. Spray with *ninhydrin solution R* and heat at 100 °C to 105 °C for 15 min. Any spot in the chromatogram obtained with test solution (a), apart from the principal spot, is not more intense than the spot in the chromatogram obtained with reference solution (b) (0.2 per cent). The test is not valid unless the chromatogram obtained with reference solution (c) shows two clearly separated spots.

### Chlorides (2.4.4)
Dissolve 0.25 g in 5 ml of *dilute nitric acid R* and dilute to 15 ml with *water R*. The solution, without further addition of nitric acid, complies with the limit test for chlorides (200 ppm).

### Sulphates (2.4.13)
Dissolve 0.5 g in 5 ml of *dilute hydrochloric acid R* and dilute to 15 ml with *distilled water R*. The solution complies with the limit test for sulphates (300 ppm).

### Ammonium (2.4.1)
0.10 g complies with limit test B for ammonium (200 ppm). Prepare the standard using 0.2 ml of *ammonium standard solution (100 ppm NH4) R*.

### Iron (2.4.9)
In a separating funnel, dissolve 1.0 g in 10 ml of *dilute hydrochloric acid R*. Shake with three quantities, each of 10 ml, of *methyl isobutyl ketone R1*, shaking for 3 min each time. To the combined organic layers add 10 ml of *water R* and shake for 3 min. The aqueous layer complies with the limit test for iron (10 ppm).

### Heavy metals (2.4.8)
2.0 g complies with limit test D for heavy metals (10 ppm). Prepare the standard using 2 ml of *lead standard solution (10 ppm Pb) R*.

### Loss on drying (2.2.32)
Not more than 0.5 per cent, determined on 1.000 g by drying in an oven at 105 °C.

### Sulphated ash (2.4.14)
Not more than 0.1 per cent, determined on 1.0 g.

## ASSAY
In a flask with a ground-glass stopper, dissolve 0.100 g in a mixture of 2 ml of *dilute sodium hydroxide solution R* and 10 ml of *water R*. Add 10 ml of a 200 g/l solution of *potassium bromide R*, 50.0 ml of *0.0167 M potassium bromate* and 15 ml of *dilute hydrochloric acid R*. Stopper the flask and cool in iced water. Allow to stand in the dark for 10 min. Add 1.5 g of *potassium iodide R*. After 1 min, titrate with *0.1 M sodium thiosulphate*, using 2 ml of *starch solution R*, added towards the end-point, as indicator. Carry out a blank titration.

1 ml of *0.0167 M potassium bromate* is equivalent to 2.403 mg of $C_6H_{12}N_2O_4S_2$.

## STORAGE
Store protected from light.

_____ *Ph Eur*

# Cytarabine

*(Ph Eur monograph 0760)*

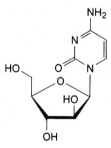

$C_9H_{13}N_3O_5$                 243.2                 *147-94-4*

### Action and use
Pyrimidine analogue, cytotoxic.

### Preparation
Cytarabine Injection

*Ph Eur*

## DEFINITION

Cytarabine contains not less than 99.0 per cent and not more than the equivalent of 100.5 per cent of 4-amino-1-β-D-arabinofuranosylpyrimidin-2(1H)-one, calculated with reference to the dried substance.

## CHARACTERS

A white or almost white, crystalline powder, freely soluble in water, very slightly soluble in alcohol and in methylene chloride.

It melts at about 215 °C.

## IDENTIFICATION

A. Dissolve 20.0 mg in *0.1 M hydrochloric acid* and dilute to 100.0 ml with the same acid. Dilute 5.0 ml of the solution to 100.0 ml with *0.1 M hydrochloric acid*. Examined between 230 nm and 350 nm (*2.2.25*), the solution shows an absorption maximum at 281 nm. The specific absorbance at the maximum is 540 to 570.

B. Examine by infrared absorption spectrophotometry (*2.2.24*), comparing with the spectrum obtained with *cytarabine CRS*. Examine the substances prepared as discs.

C. Examine the chromatograms obtained in the test for related substances in ultraviolet light at 254 nm. The principal spot in the chromatogram obtained with test solution (b) is similar in position and size to the principal spot in the chromatogram obtained with reference solution (a).

## TESTS

### Appearance of solution

Dissolve 1.0 g in *water R* and dilute to 10 ml with the same solvent. The solution is clear (*2.2.1*) and not more intensely coloured than reference solution $Y_5$ (*2.2.2, Method II*).

### Specific optical rotation (*2.2.7*)

Dissolve 0.250 g in *water R* and dilute to 25.0 ml with the same solvent. The specific optical rotation is + 154 to + 160, calculated with reference to the dried substance.

### Related substances

Examine by thin-layer chromatography (*2.2.27*), using *silica gel GF$_{254}$ R* as the coating substance.

*Test solution (a)*  Dissolve 0.25 g of the substance to be examined in *water R* and dilute to 5 ml with the same solvent.

*Test solution (b)*  Dilute 2 ml of test solution (a) to 50 ml with *water R*.

*Reference solution (a)*  Dissolve 10 mg of *cytarabine CRS* in *water R* and dilute to 5 ml with the same solvent.

*Reference solution (b)*  Dilute 0.5 ml of test solution (a) to 100 ml with *water R*.

*Reference solution (c)*  Dissolve 20 mg of *uridine R* and 20 mg of *uracil arabinoside CRS* in *methanol R* and dilute to 10 ml with the same solvent.

Apply separately to the plate 5 μl of each solution. Develop over a path of 15 cm using a mixture of 15 volumes of *water R*, 20 volumes of *acetone R* and 65 volumes of *methyl ethyl ketone R*. Allow the plate to dry in air and examine in ultraviolet light at 254 nm. Any spot in the chromatogram obtained with test solution (a), apart from the principal spot, is not more intense than the spot in the chromatogram obtained with reference solution (b) (0.5 per cent). The test is not valid unless the chromatogram obtained with reference solution (c) shows two clearly separated spots.

### Loss on drying (*2.2.32*)

Not more than 1.0 per cent, determined on 0.250 g by drying over *diphosphorus pentoxide R* at 60 °C at a pressure of 0.2 kPa to 0.7 kPa for 3 h.

### Sulphated ash (*2.4.14*)

Not more than 0.5 per cent, determined on 1.0 g.

## ASSAY

Dissolve 0.200 g in 60 ml of *anhydrous acetic acid R*, warming if necessary. Titrate with *0.1 M perchloric acid* determining the end-point potentiometrically (*2.2.20*).

1 ml of *0.1 M perchloric acid* is equivalent to 24.32 mg of $C_9H_{13}N_3O_5$.

## STORAGE

Store in an airtight container, protected from light.

## IMPURITIES

A. R = OH, R′ = H: 1-β-D-arabinofuranosylpyrimidine-2,4(1H,3H)-dione (uracil arabonoside),

B. R = H, R′ = OH: 1-β-D-ribofuranosylpyrimidine-2,4(1H,3H)-dione (uridine).

*Ph Eur*

# Dacarbazine

(*Ph Eur monograph 1691*)

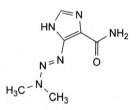

$C_6H_{10}N_6O$      182.2      *4342-03-4*

## Action and use

Cytotoxic alkylating agent

*Ph Eur*

## DEFINITION

5-[(1E)-3,3-Dimethyltriaz-1-enyl]-1H-imidazole-4-carboxamide.

## Content

98.5 per cent to 101.0 per cent (anhydrous substance).

## CHARACTERS

### Appearance

White or slightly yellowish, crystalline powder.

**Solubility**

Slightly soluble in water and in anhydrous ethanol, practically insoluble in methylene chloride.

## IDENTIFICATION

*First identification*  B.

*Second identification*  A, C.

A. Ultraviolet and visible absorption spectrophotometry (*2.2.25*).

*Test solution*  Dissolve 15.0 mg in 100.0 ml of *0.1 M hydrochloric acid*. Dilute 5.0 ml of this solution to 100.0 ml with *0.1 M hydrochloric acid*.

*Spectral range*  200-400 nm.

*Absorption maximum*  At 323 nm.

*Shoulder*  At 275 nm.

*Specific absorbance at the absorption maximum*  1024 to 1131.

B. Infrared absorption spectrophotometry (*2.2.24*).

*Comparison*  dacarbazine CRS.

C. Thin-layer chromatography (*2.2.27*).

*Test solution*  Dissolve 2.0 mg of the substance to be examined in *methanol R* and dilute to 5.0 ml with the same solvent.

*Reference solution*  Dissolve 2.0 mg of *dacarbazine CRS* in *methanol R* and dilute to 5.0 ml with the same solvent.

*Plate*  TLC silica gel $F_{254}$ plate R.

*Mobile phase*  glacial acetic acid R, water R, butanol R (1:2:5 *V/V/V*).

*Application*  10 µl.

*Development*  Over 2/3 of the plate.

*Drying*  In air.

*Detection*  Examine in ultraviolet light at 254 nm.

*Results*  The principal spot in the chromatogram obtained with the test solution is similar in position and size to the principal spot in the chromatogram obtained with the reference solution.

## TESTS

**Appearance of solution**

The solution is clear (*2.2.1*) and not more intensely coloured than reference solution $BY_6$ (*2.2.2, Method II*).

Dissolve 0.25 g in a 210 g/l solution of *citric acid R* and dilute to 25.0 ml with the same solution.

**Related substances**

A. Liquid chromatography (*2.2.29*). Use freshly prepared solutions and protect them from light.

*Test solution*  Dissolve 50.0 mg of the substance to be examined and 75 mg of *citric acid R* in *distilled water R* and dilute to 5.0 ml with the same solvent.

*Reference solution (a)*  Dissolve 5.0 mg of *dacarbazine impurity A CRS* in *distilled water R* and dilute to 50.0 ml with the same solvent. Dilute 5.0 ml of this solution to 25.0 ml with *distilled water R*.

*Reference solution (b)*  Dissolve 5.0 mg of *dacarbazine impurity B CRS* in *distilled water R*, add 0.5 ml of the test solution and dilute to 10.0 ml with *distilled water R*. Dilute 1.0 ml of this solution to 50.0 ml with *distilled water R*.

*Column*:
— *size*: $l$ = 0.25 m, Ø = 4.5 mm;
— *stationary phase*: octadecylsilyl silica gel for chromatography R (5 µm).

*Mobile phase*  15.63 g/l solution of *glacial acetic acid R* containing 2.33 g/l of *sodium dioctyl sulfosuccinate R*. As the

mobile phase contains sodium dioctyl sulfosuccinate, it must be freshly prepared every day, and the column must be flushed with a mixture of equal volumes of *methanol R* and *water R*, after all tests have been completed or at the end of the day, for at least 2 h.

*Flow rate*  1.2 ml/min.

*Detection*  Spectrophotometer at 254 nm.

*Injection*  25 µl of the test solution and reference solution (a).

*Run time*  3 times the retention time of impurity A.

*Retention time*  Impurity A = about 3 min.

*Limits*:
— *impurity A*: not more than the area of the corresponding peak in the chromatogram obtained with reference solution (a) (0.2 per cent);
— *unspecified impurities eluting after impurity A*: for each impurity, not more than 0.5 times the area of the principal peak in the chromatogram obtained with reference solution (a) (0.10 per cent).

B. Liquid chromatography (*2.2.29*) as described in related substances test A with the following modifications.

*Mobile phase*  Mix 45 volumes of a 15.63 g/l solution of *glacial acetic acid R* containing 2.33 g/l of *sodium dioctyl sulfosuccinate R* with 55 volumes of *methanol R*.

*Injection*  10 µl of the test solution and reference solution (b).

*Run time*  Twice the retention time of dacarbazine.

*Relative retention*  With reference to dacarbazine (retention time = about 12 min): impurity B = about 0.7.

*System suitability*  Reference solution (b):
— *resolution*: minimum 1.5 between the peaks due to impurity B and dacarbazine.

*Limits*:
— *impurity B*: not more than the area of the corresponding peak in the chromatogram obtained with reference solution (b) (0.1 per cent);
— *unspecified impurities*: for each impurity, not more than the area of the peak due to dacarbazine in the chromatogram obtained with reference solution (b) (0.10 per cent);
— *total*: not more than 5 times the area of the peak due to dacarbazine in the chromatogram obtained with reference solution (b) (0.5 per cent);
— *disregard limit*: 0.5 times the area of the peak due to dacarbazine in the chromatogram obtained with reference solution (b) (0.05 per cent).

**Impurity D**

Head-space gas chromatography (*2.2.28*).

*Test solution*  Introduce 0.200 g of the substance to be examined into a 20 ml vial and firmly attach the septum and cap. Using a 10 µl syringe, inject 5 µl of *water R* into the vial.

*Reference solution (a)*  Dilute 2.5 ml of *dimethylamine solution R* (impurity D) to 100.0 ml with *water R* (solution A). Firmly attach the septum and cap to a 20 ml vial. Using a 10 µl syringe, inject 10 µl of solution A into the vial.

*Reference solution (b)*  Firmly attach the septum and cap to a 20 ml vial. Using a 10 µl syringe, inject 10 µl of solution A and 10 µl of a 10 g/l solution of *triethylamine R* into the vial.

*Column*:
— *material*: fused silica;
— *size*: $l$ = 30.0 m, Ø = 0.53 mm;
— *stationary phase*: base-deactivated polyethyleneglycol R (film thickness 1.0 µm).

*Carrier gas*  helium for chromatography R.

*Flow rate*   13 ml/min.

*Split ratio*   1:1.

*Static head-space conditions that may be used:*
— *equilibration temperature*: 60 °C;
— *equilibration time*: 10 min;
— *transfer-line temperature*: 90 °C;
— *pressurisation time*: 30 s.

*Temperature:*

|  | Time (min) | Temperature (°C) |
|---|---|---|
| Column | 0 - 3 | 35 |
|  | 3 - 11 | 35 → 165 |
| Injection port |  | 180 |
| Detector |  | 220 |

*Detection*   Flame ionisation.

*Injection*   1 ml.

*System suitability*   Reference solution (b):
— *resolution*: minimum 2.5 between the peaks due to impurity D and triethylamine.

*Limit:*
— *impurity D*: not more than the area of the corresponding peak in the chromatogram obtained with reference solution (a) (0.05 per cent).

**Water** (*2.5.12*)

Maximum 0.5 per cent, determined on 1.00 g.

**Sulphated ash** (*2.4.14*)

Maximum 0.1 per cent, determined on 1.0 g.

**ASSAY**

Dissolve 0.150 g in 30 ml of *anhydrous acetic acid R*. Titrate with *0.1 M perchloric acid*, determining the end-point potentiometrically (*2.2.20*).

1 ml of *0.1 M perchloric acid* is equivalent to 18.22 mg of $C_6H_{10}N_6O$.

**STORAGE**

At a temperature of 2 °C to 8 °C, protected from light.

**IMPURITIES**

*Specified impurities*   A, B, D.

*Other detectable impurities*   (The following substances would, if present at a sufficient level, be detected by one or other of the tests in the monograph. They are limited by the general acceptance criterion for other/unspecified impurities and/or by the general monograph *Substances for pharmaceutical use (2034)*. It is therefore not necessary to identify these impurities for demonstration of compliance. See also *5.10. Control of impurities in substances for pharmaceutical use)*: C.

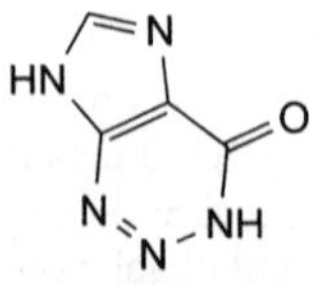

A. 3,7-dihydro-4*H*-imidazo[4,5-*d*]-1,2,3-triazin-4-one (2-azahypoxanthine),

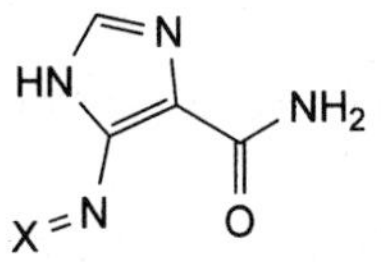

B. X = H₂: 5-amino-1*H*-imidazole-4-carboxamide,

C. X = NH: 5-diazenyl-1*H*-imidazole-4-carboxamide,

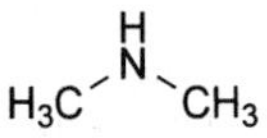

D. *N*-methylmethanamine.

*———————————————————————— Ph Eur*

# Dalteparin Sodium

(*Ph Eur monograph 1195*)

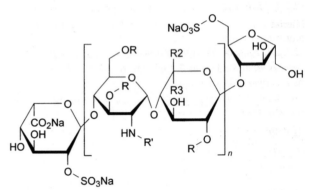

**Action and use**

Low molecular weight heparin.

*Ph Eur* _____

**DEFINITION**

Dalteparin sodium is the sodium salt of a low-molecular-mass heparin that is obtained by nitrous acid depolymerisation of heparin from porcine intestinal mucosa. The majority of the components have a 2-*O*-sulpho-α-L-idopyranosuronic acid structure at the non-reducing end and a 6-*O*-sulpho-2,5-anhydro-D-mannitol structure at the reducing end of their chain.

*Dalteparin sodium complies with the monograph Low-molecular-mass heparins (0828) with the modifications and additional requirements below.*

The mass-average relative molecular mass ranges between 5600 and 6400, with a characteristic value of about 6000.

The degree of sulphatation is 2.0 to 2.5 per disaccharide unit.

The potency is not less than 110 IU and not more than 210 IU of anti-factor Xa activity per milligram, calculated with reference to the dried substance. The anti-factor IIa activity is not less than 35 IU/mg and not more than 100 IU/mg, calculated with reference to the dried substance. The ratio of anti-factor Xa activity to anti-factor IIa activity is between 1.9 and 3.2.

**PRODUCTION**

Dalteparin sodium is produced by a validated manufacturing and purification procedure under conditions designed to minimise the presence of N-NO groups.

The manufacturing procedure must have been shown to reduce any contamination by N-NO groups to approved limits using an appropriate, validated quantification method.

## IDENTIFICATION

Carry out identification test A as described in the monograph *Low-molecular-mass heparins (0828)* using *dalteparin sodium CRS*.

Carry out identification test C as described in the monograph *Low-molecular-mass heparins (0828)*. The following requirements apply.

The mass-average relative molecular mass ranges between 5600 and 6400. The mass percentage of chains lower than 3000 is not more than 13.0 per cent. The mass percentage of chains higher than 8000 ranges between 15.0 per cent and 25.0 per cent.

## TESTS

### Appearance of solution

Dissolve 1 g in 10 ml of *water R*. The solution is clear (*2.2.1*) and not more intensely coloured than intensity 5 of the range of reference solutions of the most appropriate colour (*2.2.2, Method II*).

### Nitrite

Not more than 5 ppm. Examine by liquid chromatography (*2.2.29*). *Rinse all volumetric flasks at least three times with water R before the preparation of the solutions.*

*Test solution*   Dissolve 80.0 mg of the substance to be examined in *water R* and dilute to 10.0 ml with the same solvent. Allow to stand for at least 30 min.

*Reference solution (a)*   Dissolve 60.0 mg of *sodium nitrite R* in *water R* and dilute to 1000.0 ml with the same solvent.

*For the preparation of reference solution (b), use a pipette previously rinsed with reference solution (a).*

*Reference solution (b)*   Dilute 1.00 ml of reference solution (a) to 50.0 ml with *water R*.

*Before preparing reference solutions (c), (d) and (e), rinse all pipettes with reference solution (b).*

*Reference solution (c)*   Dilute 1.00 ml of reference solution (b) to 100.0 ml with *water R* (corresponding to 1 ppm of nitrite in the test sample).

*Reference solution (d)*   Dilute 3.00 ml of reference solution (b) to 100.0 ml with *water R* (corresponding to 3 ppm of nitrite in the test sample).

*Reference solution (e)*   Dilute 5.00 ml of reference solution (b) to 100.0 ml with *water R* (corresponding to 5 ppm of nitrite in the test sample).

The chromatographic procedure may be carried out using:
— a column 0.125 m long and 4.3 mm in internal diameter packed with a strong anion-exchange resin;
— as mobile phase at a flow rate of 1.0 ml/min a solution consisting of 13.61 g of *sodium acetate R* dissolved in *water R*, adjusted to pH 4.3 with *phosphoric acid R* and diluted to 1000 ml with *water R*;
— as detector an appropriate electrochemical device with the following characteristics and settings: a suitable working electrode, a detector potential of + 1.00 V versus Ag/AgCl reference electrode and a detector sensitivity of 0.1 µA full scale.

Inject 100 µl of reference solution (d). When the chromatograms are recorded in the prescribed conditions, the retention time for nitrite is 3.3 to 4.0 min. The test is not valid unless:
— the number of theoretical plates calculated for the nitrite peak is at least 7000 per metre per column (dalteparin

sodium will block the binding sites of the stationary phase, which will cause shorter retention times and lower separation efficiency for the analyte; the initial performance of the column may be partially restored using a 58 g/l solution of *sodium chloride R* at a flow rate of 1.0 ml/min for 1 h; after regeneration the column is rinsed with 200 ml to 400 ml of *water R*);
— the symmetry factor for the nitrite peak is less than 3;
— the relative standard deviation of the peak area for nitrite obtained from 6 injections is less than 3.0 per cent.

Inject 100 µl each of reference solutions (c) and (e). The test is not valid unless:
— the correlation factor for a linear relationship between concentration and response for reference solutions (c), (d) and (e) is at least 0.995;
— the signal-to-noise ratio for reference solution (c) is not less than 5 (if the noise level is too high, electrode recalibration is recommended);
— a blank injection of *water R* does not give rise to spurious peaks.

Inject 100 µl of the test solution. Calculate the content of nitrite from the peak areas in the chromatogram obtained with reference solutions (c), (d) and (e).

### Boron

Not more than 1 ppm, determined by inductively coupled plasma atomic emission spectroscopy.

Boron is determined by measurement of the emission from an inductively coupled plasma (ICP) at a wavelength specific to boron. The emission line at 249.733 nm is used. Use an appropriate apparatus, whose settings have been optimised as directed by the manufacturer.

*Test solution*   Dissolve 0.2500 g of the substance to be examined in about 2 ml of *water for chromatography R*, add 100 µl of *nitric acid R* and dilute to 10.00 ml with the same solvent.

*Reference solution (a)*   Prepare a 1 per cent V/V solution of *nitric acid R* in *water for chromatography R* (blank).

*Reference solution (b)*   Prepare a 11.4 µg/ml solution of *boric acid R* in a 1 per cent V/V solution of *nitric acid R* in *water for chromatography R* ($STD_{cal}$).

*Reference solution (c)*   Dissolve 0.2500 g of a reference dalteparin sodium with no detectable boron in about 2 ml of *water for chromatography R*, add 100 µl of *nitric acid R* and dilute to 10.00 ml with the same solvent ($STD_0$).

*Reference solution (d)*   Dissolve 0.2500 g of a reference dalteparin sodium with no boron detected in about 2 ml of a 1 per cent V/V solution of *nitric acid R* in *water for chromatography R*, add 10 µl of a 5.7 mg/ml solution of *boric acid R* and dilute to 10.00 ml with the same solvent ($STD_1$). This solution contains 1 µg/ml of boron.

Calculate the content of boron in the substance to be examined, using the following correction factor:

$$f = \frac{(STD_1 - STD_0) \times 2}{(STD_{cal} - \text{blank})}$$

### Loss on drying (*2.2.32*)

Not more than 5.0 per cent, determined on 1.000 g by drying in an oven at 60 °C over *diphosphorus pentoxide R* at a pressure not exceeding 670 Pa for 3 h.

# Danaparoid Sodium

(*Ph Eur monograph 2090*)

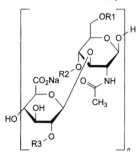

Chondroitin sulfate family | Heparan sulfate family

| ΔDi | R1 | R2 | R3 |
|---|---|---|---|
| -OS | H | H | H |
| -6S | SO₃Na | H | H |
| -4S | H | SO₃Na | H |
| -US | H | H | SO₃Na |
| -(U,6)S | SO₃Na | H | SO₃Na |
| -(U,4)S | H | SO₃Na | SO₃Na |
| -(4,6)S | SO₃Na | SO₃Na | H |
| -(U,4,6)S | SO₃Na | SO₃Na | SO₃Na |

| ΔDiHS | R1 | R2 | R3 |
|---|---|---|---|
| -OS | H | Ac | H |
| -6S | SO₃Na | Ac | H |
| -NS | H | SO₃Na | H |
| -US | H | Ac | SO₃Na |
| -(U,N)S | H | SO₃Na | SO₃Na |
| -(6,N)S | SO₃Na | SO₃Na | H |
| -(U,N,6)S | SO₃Na | SO₃Na | SO₃Na |

*83513-48-8*

## Action and use

Heparinoid; prevention of deep vein thrombosis.

*Ph Eur* _____

## DEFINITION

Preparation containing the sodium salts of a mixture of sulphated glycosaminoglycans present in porcine tissues. Its major constituents are heparan sulphate and dermatan sulphate. On complete hydrolysis it liberates D-glucosamine, D-galactosamine, D-glucuronic acid, L-iduronic acid, acetic acid and sulphuric acid. It has the characteristic property of enhancing the inactivation of activated factor X (factor Xa) by antithrombin. It has a negligible effect on the inactivation rate of thrombin by antithrombin.

### Potency

11.0 to 17.0 anti-factor Xa units per milligram (dried substance).

## PRODUCTION

Danaparoid sodium is prepared from the intestinal mucosa of pigs. It is prepared using a process that ensures that the relative proportion of active sulphated glycosaminoglycans is consistent. It is produced by methods of manufacturing designed to minimise or eliminate endotoxins and hypotensive substances.

## CHARACTERS

### Appearance

White or almost white, hygroscopic powder.

### Solubility

Freely soluble in water.

## IDENTIFICATION

A. The ratio of anti-factor Xa activity to anti-factor IIa activity, determined as described under Assay and Tests respectively, is not less than 22.

B. It complies with the test for molecular mass distribution (see Tests): the mass-average relative molecular mass ranges between 4000 and 7000.

## TESTS

### pH (*2.2.3*)

5.5 to 7.0.

Dissolve 0.5 g of the dried substance to be examined in *carbon dioxide-free water R* and dilute to 50 ml with the same solvent.

### Anti-factor IIa activity

Maximum 0.5 units per milligram (dried substance).

*Test solutions*   Prepare 2 independent series of dilutions in geometric progression of the substance to be examined in *phosphate buffer solution pH 6.5 R* and in the concentration range of 0.0005 to 0.005 units of anti-factor IIa activity per millilitre.

*Reference solutions*   Prepare 2 independent series of dilutions in geometric progression of *danaparoid sodium CRS* in *phosphate buffer solution pH 6.5 R* and in the concentration range of 0.0005 to 0.005 units of anti-factor IIa activity per millilitre.

Transfer 50 µl of each solution into the wells of a 96-well microtitre plate. To each well add 50 µl of *antithrombin III solution R3* and 50 µl of *human thrombin solution R1*. Shake the microtitre plate but do not allow bubbles to form. Incubate for 75 min. To each well add 50 µl of *chromogenic substrate R4*. Shake the microtitre plate. Measure the absorbances at 405 nm (*2.2.25*) using a suitable reading device, exactly 4 min after the addition of the chromogenic substrate. The reaction may be stopped using 75 µl of a 20 per cent *V/V* solution of *glacial acetic acid R*. Determine the blank amidolytic activity in a similar manner, using *phosphate buffer solution pH 6.5 R* as the blank solution (minimum 10 blanks per microtitre plate). Calculate the activity of the substance to be examined in units of anti-factor IIa activity per milligram using a suitable statistical method, for example the parallel-line assay.

### Chondroitin sulphate and dermatan sulphate

Chondroitin sulphate: maximum 8.5 per cent (dried substance); dermatan sulphate: 8.0 per cent to 16.0 per cent (dried substance).

Determine by selective enzymatic degradation.

*Test solutions*   Dry the substance to be examined at 60 °C over *diphosphorus pentoxide R* at a pressure of about 670 Pa for 3 h. Dissolve 0.200 g of the dried substance in 10.0 ml of *water R*. Dilute this solution as necessary to obtain 3 test solutions containing 20 mg/ml, 10 mg/ml and 5 mg/ml of the dried substance to be examined in *water R*.

*Chondroitin sulphate reference solutions*   Dry *chondroitin sulphate CRS* over *diphosphorus pentoxide R* at room temperature at a pressure of about 670 Pa for 16 h. Prepare solutions containing 1 mg/ml, 2 mg/ml and 3 mg/ml of dried *chondroitin sulphate CRS* in *water R*.

*Dermatan sulphate reference solutions*   Dry *dermatan sulphate CRS* over *diphosphorus pentoxide R* at room temperature at a pressure of about 670 Pa for 16 h. Prepare solutions containing 1 mg/ml, 2 mg/ml and 3 mg/ml of dried *dermatan sulphate CRS* in *water R*.

*Chondroitinase ABC solution*   Dissolve *chondroitinase ABC R* in *tris-sodium acetate-sodium chloride buffer solution pH 8.0 R* to obtain an activity of 0.5-1.0 units per millilitre.

*Chondroitinase AC solution*   Dissolve *chondroitinase AC R* in *tris-sodium acetate-sodium chloride buffer solution pH 7.4 R* to obtain an activity of 1.0-2.0 units per millilitre.

*Procedure:*

— *Degradation with chondroitinase ABC*: label 2 sets of 10 tubes in triplicate: T1, T2 and T3 for the test solutions;

SD1, SD2 and SD3 for the dermatan sulphate reference solutions; SC1, SC2 and SC3 for the chondroitin sulphate reference solutions; and B for the blank (*water R*). To each tube add 1.25 ml of *tris-sodium acetate buffer solution pH 8.0 R* and 150 μl of the test solutions, dermatan sulphate reference solutions, chondroitin sulphate reference solutions or *water R*. To each tube in 1 set of tubes add 75 μl of chondroitinase ABC solution. To determine the blank response level, add 75 μl *of tris-sodium acetate-sodium chloride buffer solution pH 8.0 R* to each tube in the other set of tubes. Mix the contents of the tubes using a vortex mixer, cover with appropriate stoppers and incubate at 37 °C for at least 24 h.

— *Degradation with chondroitinase AC*: label 7 tubes in triplicate: T1, T2 and T3 for the test solutions; SC1, SC2 and SC3 for the chondroitin sulphate reference solutions; and B for the blank (*water R*). To each tube add 1.25 ml of *tris-sodium acetate buffer solution pH 7.4 R* and 150 μl of the test solutions, chondroitin sulphate reference solutions or *water R*. Add 75 μl of chondroitinase AC solution to each tube. Mix the contents of the tubes using a vortex mixer, cover with appropriate stoppers and incubate at 37 °C for at least 24 h. After the incubation period mix the contents of the tubes using a vortex mixer and dilute to 12 times with *water R*. Measure the absorbances (*2.2.25*) of the diluted solutions at 234 nm against *water R* using a suitable spectrophotometer.

*Calculation*    Calculate the mean blank absorbance of each reference solution, i.e. the mean of the absorbances of the reference solutions to which no chondroitinase ABC has been added. Subtract the mean blank absorbance value from the individual absorbance of each reference solution. Calculate linear regression curves for the 2 chondroitin sulphate reference and the dermatan sulphate reference by plotting the blank-corrected absorbances against the concentrations.

Calculate the average percentage content of dermatan sulphate in the test solutions of all tested concentrations using the following expression:

$$\frac{A_2 - A_1 - \dfrac{(A_3 - A_1 - I_1) \times B_2}{B_1} - I_2 - I_3}{B_3 \times C} \times 100$$

$A_1$ = blank absorbance of the test solution;

$A_2$ = absorbance of the test solution with chondroitinase ABC;

$A_3$ = absorbance of the test solution with chondroitinase AC;

$B_1$ = gradient of the curve obtained with the chondroitin sulphate reference solutions with chondroitinase AC;

$B_2$ = gradient of the curve obtained with the chondroitin sulphate reference solutions with chondroitinase ABC;

$B_3$ = gradient of the curve obtained with the dermatan sulphate reference solutions with chondroitinase ABC;

$C$ = concentration of the test solution, in milligrams per millilitre;

$I_1$ = y-intercept of the curve obtained with the chondroitin sulphate reference solutions with chondroitinase AC;

$I_2$ = y-intercept of the curve obtained with the chondroitin sulphate reference solutions with chondroitinase ABC;

$I_3$ = y-intercept of the curve obtained with the dermatan sulphate reference solutions with chondroitinase ABC.

Calculate the average percentage content of chondroitin sulphate in the test solutions for all tested concentrations using the following expression:

$$\frac{(A_3 - A_1 - I_1) \times 100}{B_1 \times C}$$

## Molecular mass distribution

Size-exclusion chromatography (*2.2.30*).

*Test solution*    Dissolve 10 mg of the substance to be examined in 2 ml of the mobile phase.

*Reference solution*    Dissolve 10 mg of *danaparoid sodium CRS* in 2 ml of the mobile phase.

*Column:*
— *size: l* = 0.60 m, Ø = 7.5 mm;
— *stationary phase*: *hydrophilic silica gel for chromatography R* (10 μm) with a fractionation range for proteins with a relative molecular mass of approximately 5000-100 000;
— *temperature*: 30 °C.

*Mobile phase*    28.4 g/l solution of *anhydrous sodium sulphate R* adjusted to pH 5.0 with *dilute sulphuric acid R*.

*Flow rate*    0.9 ml/min ± 2 per cent.

*Detection*    Spectrophotometer at 210 nm.

*Injection*    100 μl.

*Run time*    For a period of time ensuring complete elution of sample and solvent peaks (about 40 min).

*System suitability*    Inject the reference solution twice.

The difference between the retention times corresponding to the maxima of the peaks is not more than 5 s.

*Calibration*    Calibration is achieved by taking the relevant part of the chromatogram obtained with the reference solution, i.e. excluding the sharp peak at the end of the chromatogram, and matching the chromatogram obtained with the test solution with the calibration table obtained with the reference solution. From the calibration curve obtained, determine the molecular mass distribution of the sample. A calibration table is supplied with *danaparoid sodium CRS*.

*Limits:*
— *chains with a relative molecular mass less than 2000*: maximum 13 per cent;
— *chains with a relative molecular mass less than 4000*: maximum 39 per cent;
— *chains with a relative molecular mass between 4000 and 8000*: minimum 50 per cent;
— *chains with a relative molecular mass higher than 8000*: maximum 19 per cent;
— *chains with a relative molecular mass higher than 10 000*: maximum 11 per cent.

## Nitrogen (*2.5.9*)
2.4 per cent to 3.0 per cent (dried substance).

## Nucleic acids
Maximum 0.5 per cent (dried substance).

*Test solution*    Weigh about 50 mg of the dried substance to be examined into a centrifuge tube and dissolve in 200 μl of *water R*.

*Reference solution* Dissolve about 50 mg of *ribonucleic acid CRS* in 5 ml of *0.1 M sodium hydroxide* and dilute to 20.0 ml with *water R*. Transfer 200 µl of the solution into a centrifuge tube.

Add 4.0 ml of a 50 g/l solution of *trichloroacetic acid R* to each tube and mix. Place all tubes in boiling water for 30 min. Allow to cool to room temperature. Add again 4.0 ml of a 50 g/l solution of *trichloroacetic acid R* to each tube and mix. If any of the test solutions is not clear, sonicate all the tubes in an ultrasonic bath for 10 min and centrifuge at 1500 g for 15 min. Dilute 1.0 ml of the clear supernatant to 4.0 ml with *water R*. Measure the absorbances of the diluted reference and test solutions at 265 nm (*2.2.25*) against a blank solution prepared in the same manner, and calculate the percentage nucleic acid content of the sample.

**Total protein** (*2.5.33, Method 2*)
Maximum 0.5 per cent.
Dissolve the substance to be examined in *water R*. Use *bovine albumin R* as the reference substance.

**Sodium**
9.0 per cent to 11.0 per cent (dried substance).
Atomic absorption spectrometry (*2.2.23, Method I*).

*Test solution* Dissolve 0.125 g of the substance to be examined in 100.0 ml of a 1.27 mg/ml solution of *caesium chloride R* in *0.1 M hydrochloric acid*.

*Reference solutions*
Prepare reference solutions containing 50 ppm, 100 ppm and 150 ppm of Na by diluting *sodium standard solution (1000 ppm Na) R* with a 1.27 mg/ml solution of *caesium chloride R* in *0.1 M hydrochloric acid*.

*Source* Sodium hollow-cathode lamp.

*Wavelength* 330.3 nm.

*Atomisation device* Air-acetylene flame.

**Loss on drying** (*2.2.32*)
Maximum 5.0 per cent, determined on 0.500 g by drying in an oven at 60 °C over *diphosphorus pentoxide R* at a pressure of 670 Pa for 3 h.

**Bacterial endotoxins** (*2.6.14*)
Less than 0.02 IU per unit of anti-factor Xa activity, if intended for use in the manufacture of parenteral dosage forms without a further appropriate procedure for the removal of bacterial endotoxins.

**ASSAY**
The anticoagulant activity of danaparoid sodium is determined *in vitro* by an assay which determines its ability to accelerate the inhibition of factor Xa by antithrombin III (anti-factor Xa assay).

*Test solutions* Prepare 2 independent series of dilutions in geometric progression of the substance to be examined in *tris(hydroxymethyl)aminomethane EDTA buffer solution pH 8.4 R* and in the concentration range of 0.1 to 0.32 units of anti-factor Xa activity per millilitre.

*Reference solutions* Prepare 2 independent series of dilutions in geometric progression of *danaparoid sodium CRS* in *tris(hydroxymethyl)aminomethane EDTA buffer solution pH 8.4 R* and in the concentration range of 0.08 to 0.35 units of anti-factor Xa activity per millilitre.

Transfer 40 µl of each solution into the wells of a 96-well microtitre plate. Add 40 µl of *antithrombin III solution R4* to each well and shake the microtitre plate but do not allow bubbles to form. Add 40 µl of *bovine factor Xa solution R1* to each well. Exactly 2 min after the addition of the factor Xa

solution, add 80 µl of *chromogenic substrate R5*. Measure the absorbance at 405 nm (*2.2.25*) using a suitable reading device, exactly 4 min after the addition of the factor Xa solution. The reaction may be stopped using 75 µl of a 20 per cent *V/V* solution of *glacial acetic acid R*. Determine the blank amidolytic activity in the same manner, using *tris(hydroxymethyl)aminomethane EDTA buffer solution pH 8.4 R* as the blank (minimum 8 blanks per microtitre plate). Calculate the potency of the substance to be examined in units of anti-factor Xa activity per milligram using a suitable statistical method, for example the parallel-line assay.

**STORAGE**
In an airtight container. If the substance is sterile, store in a sterile, airtight, tamper-proof container.

**LABELLING**
The label states the number of units of anti-factor Xa activity per milligram.

_____ *Ph Eur*

# Dantrolene Sodium

$C_{14}H_9N_4NaO_5,3\frac{1}{2}H_2O$      399.3      24868-20-0

**Action and use**
Skeletal muscle relaxant.

**Preparation**
Dantrolene Oral Suspension

**DEFINITION**
Dantrolene Sodium is 1-(5-*p*-nitrophenylfurfurylideneamino)hydantoin sodium. It contains not less than 98.0% and not more than 102.0% of $C_{14}H_9N_4NaO_5$, calculated with reference to the anhydrous substance.

**CHARACTERISTICS**
A yellowish-orange to orange crystalline powder.

Very slightly soluble in *water*; slightly soluble in *ethanol (96%)*; sparingly soluble in *methanol*; practically insoluble in *acetone*.

**IDENTIFICATION**
A. The *infrared absorption spectrum*, Appendix II A, is concordant with the *reference spectrum* of dantrolene sodium (*RS 422*).

B. In the Assay, the chromatogram obtained with solution (1) shows a peak with the same retention time as the principal peak in the chromatogram obtained with solution (2).

C. To 0.1 g of the substance being examined add 20 ml of *water* and 2 drops of *acetic acid*, shake well and filter. The filtrate yields the reactions characteristic of *sodium salts*, Appendix VI.

## TESTS

**Alkalinity**

Shake 0.7 g in 10 ml of *water* for 5 minutes and centrifuge. To 5 ml of the supernatant add 45 ml of *water* and 3 drops of *phenolphthalein solution R1* and 0.1 ml of 0.1M *hydrochloric acid VS*. A red colour is not produced.

**Related substances**

Carry out the method for *liquid chromatography*, Appendix III D, using the following solutions.

(1) Dissolve 50 mg of the substance being examined in 20 ml of *tetrahydrofuran* and 2 ml of *glacial acetic acid* and dilute with sufficient *absolute ethanol* to produce 100 ml.

(2) Dilute 1 ml of solution (1) to 100 ml with *absolute ethanol*.

(3) Dissolve 5 mg of *dantrolene sodium BPCRS* and 0.1 g of *theophylline BPCRS* in 20 ml of *tetrahydrofuran* and 2 ml of *glacial acetic acid* and dilute with sufficient *absolute ethanol* to produce 100 ml. Further dilute 10 ml of this solution to 100 ml with *absolute ethanol*.

CHROMATOGRAPHIC CONDITIONS

(a) Use a stainless steel column (15 cm × 4.6 mm) packed with *silica gel for chromatography* (5 μm) (Zorbax Sil is suitable).

(b) Use isocratic elution and the mobile phase described below.

(c) Adjust the flow rate of the mobile phase so that the retention time of the peak corresponding to Dantrolene Sodium is about 8 minutes.

(d) Use a column temperature of 30°.

(e) Use a detection wavelength of 300 nm.

(f) Inject 10 μl of each solution.

(g) For solution (1) allow the chromatography to proceed for at least twice the retention time of the principal peak.

MOBILE PHASE

9 volumes of *absolute ethanol*, 10 volumes of *glacial acetic acid* and 90 volumes of *hexane*.

SYSTEM SUITABILITY

The test is not valid unless, in the chromatogram obtained with solution (3), the *resolution factor* between the peaks corresponding to theophylline and dantrolene is at least 6.

LIMITS

In the chromatogram obtained with solution (1):

the total area of all the *secondary peaks* is not greater than the area of the principal peak in the chromatogram obtained with solution (2) (1%).

**Heavy metals**

1.0 g complies with *limit test C for heavy metals*, Appendix VII. Use 2 ml of *lead standard solution (10 ppm Pb)* to prepare the standard (20 ppm).

**Water**

14.5 to 17.0% w/w, Appendix IX C. Use 0.2 g

## ASSAY

Carry out the method for *liquid chromatography*, Appendix III D, using the following solutions.

(1) Dissolve 60 mg of the substance being examined in 50 ml of *dimethylformamide* and dilute 1 volume of the resulting solution to 100 volumes with the mobile phase.

(2) Dilute 1 volume of a 0.12% w/v solution of *dantrolene sodium BPCRS* in *dimethylformamide* to 100 volumes with the mobile phase.

CHROMATOGRAPHIC CONDITIONS

(a) Use a stainless steel column (15 cm × 4.6 mm) packed with spherical particles of silica, 5 μm in diameter, the surface of which has been modified with chemically-bonded nitrile groups (Spherisorb CN is suitable).

(b) Use isocratic elution and the mobile phase described below.

(c) Use a flow rate of 1 ml per minute.

(d) Use an ambient column temperature.

(e) Use a detection wavelength of 262 nm.

(f) Inject 20 μl of each solution.

MOBILE PHASE

15 volumes of *acetonitrile* and 85 volumes of a phosphate buffer pH 6.8 prepared by dissolving 11.88 g of *disodium hydrogen orthophosphate* and 9.08 g of *potassium dihydrogen orthophosphate* in 1000 ml of *water*.

DETERMINATION OF CONTENT

Calculate the content of $C_{14}H_9N_4NaO_5$ in the substance being examined using the declared content of $C_{14}H_9N_4NaO_5$ in *dantrolene sodium BPCRS*.

# Dantron

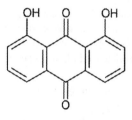

| $C_{14}H_8O_4$ | 240.2 | *117-10-2* |

**Action and use**

Anthraquinone stimulant laxative.

**Preparation**

Co-danthrusate Capsules

## DEFINITION

Dantron is mainly 1,8-dihydroxyanthraquinone. It contains not less than 98.0% and not more than 102.0% of total phenols, calculated as $C_{14}H_8O_4$ and with reference to the dried substance.

## CHARACTERISTICS

An orange, crystalline powder.

Practically insoluble in *water*, slightly soluble in *ether*, very slightly soluble in *ethanol (96%)*. It dissolves in solutions of alkali hydroxides.

## IDENTIFICATION

A. The *infrared absorption spectrum*, Appendix II A, is concordant with the *reference spectrum* of dantron *(RS 083)*.

B. The *light absorption*, Appendix II B, in the range 230 to 350 nm of a 0.001% w/v solution in *dichloromethane* exhibits maxima at 255 nm and 285 nm and a less well-defined maximum at 275 nm. The *absorbance* at the maximum at 255 nm is about 0.82 and at the maximum at 285 nm is about 0.48, each calculated with reference to the dried substance.

C. Dissolve 5 mg in 5 ml of 1M *sodium hydroxide*. A clear red solution is produced immediately.

## TESTS

### Mercury

To 0.50 g in a Kjeldahl flask add 2.5 ml of *nitric acid* and allow to stand until the initial vigorous reaction has subsided. Add 2.5 ml of *sulphuric acid* and heat until dense white fumes are evolved. Cool, add 2.5 ml of *nitric acid* and heat until fumes are again evolved. Repeat the procedure with a further 2.5 ml of *nitric acid*, cool, add 50 ml of *water*, boil the solution until the volume has been reduced to about 25 ml and cool. Transfer to a separating funnel using *water*, dilute to about 50 ml with *water* and add 50 ml of 0.5M *sulphuric acid*. Add 100 ml of *water*, 2 g of *hydroxylamine hydrochloride*, 1 ml of 0.05M *disodium edetate*, 1 ml of *glacial acetic acid* and 5 ml of *dichloromethane*, shake, allow to separate and discard the dichloromethane layer. Titrate the aqueous layer with a 0.0008% w/v solution of *dithizone* in *dichloromethane*, shaking vigorously after each addition, allowing the layers to separate and discarding the dichloromethane layer, until the dichloromethane layer remains green. Repeat the operation using a solution prepared by diluting 1 ml of *mercury standard solution (5 ppm Hg)* to 100 ml with 0.5M *sulphuric acid* and beginning at the words 'Add 100 ml of *water* ...'. The volume of the dithizone solution required by the substance being examined does not exceed that required by the mercury standard solution.

### Related substances

Carry out the method for *liquid chromatography*, Appendix III D, using the following solutions.

(1) Dissolve 50 mg of the substance being examined in 20 ml of *tetrahydrofuran* and dilute to 100 ml with the mobile phase.

(2) Dilute 1 volume of solution (1) to 50 volumes with the mobile phase.

(3) Dissolve 50 mg of *dantron impurity standard BPCRS* in 20 ml of *tetrahydrofuran* and dilute to 100 ml with the mobile phase.

CHROMATOGRAPHIC CONDITIONS

(a) Use a stainless steel column (25 cm x 4.6 mm) packed with *octadecylsilyl silica gel for chromatography* (5 μm) (Nucleosil C18 is suitable).

(b) Use an isocratic system using the mobile phase described below.

(c) Use a flow rate of 1 ml per minute.

(d) Use an ambient column temperature.

(e) Use a detection wavelength of 254 nm.

(f) Inject 20 μl of each solution.

(g) Allow the chromatography to proceed for 1.5 times the retention time of the principal peak.

MOBILE PHASE

A mixture of 2.5 volumes of *glacial acetic acid*, 40 volumes of *tetrahydrofuran* and 60 volumes of *water*.

SYSTEM SUITABILITY

The test is not valid unless, in the chromatogram obtained with solution (3):

— a peak due to 1-hydroxyanthraquinone appears immediately before the principal peak, as indicated in the reference chromatogram supplied with *dantron impurity standard BPCRS*;

— the height of the trough separating the two peaks is not greater than one third of the height of the peak due to 1-hydroxyanthraquinone.

LIMITS

In the chromatogram obtained with solution (1):

— the area of any peak corresponding to 1-hydroxyanthraquinone is not greater than 2.5 times the area of the principal peak in the chromatogram obtained with solution (2) (3.3% taking into account the correction factor of the impurity);

— the sum of the areas of any other *secondary peaks* is not greater than the area of the principal peak in the chromatogram obtained with solution (2) (2%);

— disregard any peak with a retention time less than one third of that of the principal peak.

### Loss on drying

When dried to constant weight at 105°, loses not more than 0.5% of its weight. Use 1 g.

## ASSAY

Dissolve 0.2 g in 50 ml of *anhydrous pyridine* and carry out Method II for *non-aqueous titration*, Appendix VIII A, using 0.1M *tetrabutylammonium hydroxide VS* as titrant and determining the end point potentiometrically. Each ml of 0.1M *tetrabutylammonium hydroxide VS* is equivalent to 24.02 mg of total phenols, calculated as $C_{14}H_8O_4$.

# Dapsone

*(Ph Eur monograph 0077)*

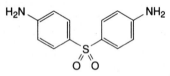

| $C_{12}H_{12}N_2O_2S$ | 248.3 | *80-08-0* |
|---|---|---|

### Action and use

Folic acid synthesis inhibitor; treatment of leprosy.

### Preparation

Dapsone Tablets

*Ph Eur*

### DEFINITION

Dapsone contains not less than 99.0 per cent and not more than the equivalent of 101.0 per cent of 4,4'-sulphonyldianiline, calculated with reference to the dried substance.

### CHARACTERS

A white or slightly yellowish-white, crystalline powder, very slightly soluble in water, freely soluble in acetone, sparingly soluble in alcohol. It dissolves freely in dilute mineral acids.

### IDENTIFICATION

A. Melting point (*2.2.14*): 175 °C to 181 °C.

B. Dissolve 50.0 mg in *methanol R* and dilute to 100.0 ml with the same solvent. Dilute 1.0 ml of this solution to 100.0 ml with *methanol R*. Examined between 230 nm and 350 nm (*2.2.25*), the solution shows 2 absorption maxima, at 260 nm and 295 nm. The specific absorbances at these maxima are 700 to 760 and 1150 to 1250, respectively.

C. Examine the chromatograms obtained in the test for related substances. The principal spot in the chromatogram obtained with test solution (b) is similar in position, colour and size to the principal spot in the chromatogram obtained with reference solution (a).

## TESTS

### Related substances
Examine by thin-layer chromatography (2.2.27), using *silica gel G R* as the coating substance.

*Test solution (a)*    Dissolve 0.10 g of the substance to be examined in *methanol R* and dilute to 10 ml with the same solvent.

*Test solution (b)*    Dilute 1 ml of test solution (a) to 10 ml with *methanol R*.

*Reference solution (a)*    Dissolve 10 mg of *dapsone CRS* in *methanol R* and dilute to 10 ml with the same solvent.

*Reference solution (b)*    Dilute 1 ml of test solution (b) to 10 ml with *methanol R*.

*Reference solution (c)*    Dilute 2 ml of reference solution (b) to 10 ml with *methanol R*.

Apply separately to the plate 1 μl of test solution (b), 1 μl of reference solution (a), 10 μl of test solution (a), 10 μl of reference solution (b) and 10 μl of reference solution (c). Develop in an unsaturated tank over a path of 15 cm using a mixture of 1 volume of *concentrated ammonia R*, 6 volumes of *methanol R*, 20 volumes of *ethyl acetate R* and 20 volumes of *heptane R*. Allow the plate to dry in air. Spray the plate with a 1 g/l solution of *4-dimethylaminocinnamaldehyde R* in a mixture of 1 volume of *hydrochloric acid R* and 99 volumes of *alcohol R*. Examine in daylight. Any spot in the chromatogram obtained with test solution (a), apart from the principal spot, is not more intense than the spot in the chromatogram obtained with reference solution (b) (1.0 per cent) and not more than 2 such spots are more intense than the spot in the chromatogram obtained with reference solution (c) (0.2 per cent).

### Loss on drying (2.2.32)
Not more than 1.5 per cent, determined on 1.000 g by drying in an oven at 105 °C.

### Sulphated ash (2.4.14)
Not more than 0.1 per cent, determined on 1.0 g.

## ASSAY
Dissolve 0.100 g in 50 ml of *dilute hydrochloric acid R*. Carry out the determination of primary aromatic amino-nitrogen (2.5.8).

1 ml of *0.1 M sodium nitrite* is equivalent to 12.42 mg of $C_{12}H_{12}N_2O_2S$.

## STORAGE
Store protected from light.

———————————————————————— *Ph Eur*

# Daunorubicin Hydrochloride

*(Ph Eur monograph 0662)*

$C_{27}H_{30}ClNO_{10}$          564.0          23541-50-6

## Action and use
Cytostatic; anthracycline antibacterial.

*Ph Eur* ————————————————————————

## DEFINITION
(8*S*,10*S*)-8-Acetyl-10-[(3-amino-2,3,6-trideoxy-α-L-*lyxo*-hexopyranosyl)oxy]-6,8,11-trihydroxy-1-methoxy-7,8,9,10-tetrahydrotetracene-5,12-dione hydrochloride.

Substance produced by certain strains of *Streptomyces coeruleorubidus* or of *Streptomyces peucetius* or obtained by any other means.

## Content
95.0 per cent to 102.0 per cent (anhydrous substance).

## PRODUCTION
It is produced by methods of manufacture designed to eliminate or minimise the presence of histamine.

## CHARACTERS

### Appearance
Crystalline, orange-red powder, hygroscopic.

### Solubility
Freely soluble in water and in methanol, slightly soluble in alcohol, practically insoluble in acetone.

## IDENTIFICATION
A. Infrared absorption spectrophotometry (2.2.24).

*Comparison    daunorubicin hydrochloride CRS.*

B. Dissolve about 10 mg in 0.5 ml of *nitric acid R*, add 0.5 ml of *water R* and heat over a flame for 2 min. Allow to cool and add 0.5 ml of *silver nitrate solution R1*. A white precipitate is formed.

## TESTS

### pH (2.2.3)
4.5 to 6.5.

Dissolve 50 mg in *carbon dioxide-free water R* and dilute to 10 ml with the same solvent.

### Related substances
Liquid chromatography (2.2.29). *Prepare the solutions immediately before use.*

*Test solution*    Dissolve 50.0 mg of the substance to be examined in the mobile phase and dilute to 50.0 ml with the mobile phase.

*Reference solution (a)*    Dissolve 50.0 mg of *daunorubicin hydrochloride CRS* in the mobile phase and dilute to 50.0 ml with the mobile phase.

*Reference solution (b)*    Dissolve 10 mg of *doxorubicin hydrochloride CRS* and 10 mg of *epirubicin hydrochloride CRS* in the mobile phase and dilute to 100.0 ml with the mobile phase. Dilute 1.0 ml of the solution to 10.0 ml with the mobile phase.

*Reference solution (c)*   Dissolve 5.0 mg of *daunorubicinone CRS* and 5.0 mg of *doxorubicin hydrochloride CRS* in the mobile phase and dilute to 100.0 ml with the mobile phase. Dilute 1.0 ml of the solution to 10.0 ml with the mobile phase.

*Reference solution (d)*   Dilute 1.0 ml of reference solution (a) to 200.0 ml with the mobile phase.

*Column:*
— *size:* $l = 0.25$ m, $\emptyset = 4.0$ mm,
— *stationary phase:* end-capped octadecylsilyl silica gel for chromatography R (5 μm).

*Mobile phase*   Mixture of equal volumes of *acetonitrile R* and a solution containing 2.88 g/l of *sodium laurilsulfate R* and 2.25 g/l of *phosphoric acid R*.

*Flow rate*   1 ml/min.

*Detection*   Spectrophotometer at 254 nm.

*Injection*   5 μl; inject the test solution and reference solutions (b), (c) and (d).

*Run time*   Twice the retention time of daunorubicin.

*Relative retention*   With reference to daunorubicin (retention time = about 15 min): impurity A = about 0.4; impurity D = about 0.5; epirubicin = about 0.6; impurity B = about 0.7.

*System suitability*   Reference solution (b):
— *resolution:* minimum of 2.0 between the peaks due to impurity D and epirubicin.

*Limits:*
— *impurity A:* not more than the area of the corresponding peak in the chromatogram obtained with reference solution (c) (0.5 per cent),
— *impurity B:* not more than 3 times the area of the principal peak in the chromatogram obtained with reference solution (d) (1.5 per cent),
— *impurity D:* not more than the area of the corresponding peak in the chromatogram obtained with reference solution (c) (0.5 per cent),
— *any other impurity:* not more than the area of the principal peak in the chromatogram obtained with reference solution (d) (0.5 per cent),
— *total of other impurities:* not more than 5 times the area of the principal peak in the chromatogram obtained with reference solution (d) (2.5 per cent),
— *disregard limit:* 0.1 times the area of the principal peak in the chromatogram obtained with reference solution (d) (0.05 per cent).

**Butanol** *(2.4.24, System B)*
Maximum 1.0 per cent.

**Water** *(2.5.12)*
Maximum 3.0 per cent, determined on 0.100 g.

**Bacterial endotoxins** *(2.6.14)*
Less than 4.3 IU/mg, if intended for use in the manufacture of parenteral dosage forms without a further appropriate procedure for the removal of bacterial endotoxins.

## ASSAY
Liquid chromatography *(2.2.29)* as described in the test for related substances.

*Injection*   Test solution and reference solution (a).

Calculate the percentage content of $C_{27}H_{30}ClNO_{10}$.

## STORAGE
In an airtight container, protected from light. If the substance is sterile, store in a sterile, airtight, tamper-proof container.

## IMPURITIES

A. R = CO-CH$_3$: (8*S*,10*S*)-8-acetyl-6,8,10,11-tetrahydroxy-1-methoxy-7,8,9,10-tetrahydrotetracene-5,12-dione (daunorubicin aglycone, daunorubicinone),

E. R = CHOH-CH$_3$: (8*S*,10*S*)-6,8,10,11-tetrahydroxy-8-[(1*RS*)-1-hydroxyethyl]-1-methoxy-7,8,9,10-tetrahydrotetracene-5,12-dione (13-dihydrodaunorubicinone),

B. R = CHOH-CH$_3$: (8*S*,10*S*)-10-[(3-amino-2,3,6-trideoxy-α-L-*lyxo*-hexopyranosyl)oxy]-6,8,11-trihydroxy-8-[(1*RS*)-1-hydroxyethyl]-1-methoxy-7,8,9,10-tetrahydrotetracene-5,12-dione (daunorubicinol),

C. R = CH$_2$-CO-CH$_3$: (8*S*,10*S*)-10-[(3-amino-2,3,6-trideoxy-α-L-*lyxo*-hexopyranosyl)oxy]-6,8,11-trihydroxy-1-methoxy-8-(2-oxopropyl)-7,8,9,10-tetrahydrotetracene-5,12-dione (feudomycin B),

D. R = CO-CH$_2$-OH: doxorubicin,

F. R = CO-CH$_2$-CH$_3$: (8*S*,10*S*)-10-[(3-amino-2,3,6-trideoxy-α-L-*lyxo*-hexopyranosyl)oxy]-6,8,11-trihydroxy-1-methoxy-8-propanoyl-7,8,9,10-tetrahydrotetracene-5,12-dione (8-ethyldaunorubicin).

*Ph Eur*

# Debrisoquine Sulphate

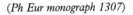

$(C_{10}H_{13}N_3)_2,H_2SO_4$      448.5      *581-88-4*

## Action and use
Adrenergic neuron blocker.

## DEFINITION
Debrisoquine Sulphate is 1,2,3,4-tetrahydroisoquinoline-2-carboxamidine sulphate. It contains not less than 99.0% and not more than 101.0% of $(C_{10}H_{13}N_3)_2,H_2SO_4$, calculated with reference to the dried substance.

## CHARACTERISTICS
A white, crystalline powder.

Sparingly soluble in *water*; very slightly soluble in *ethanol (96%)*; practically insoluble in *ether*.

## IDENTIFICATION
A. The *light absorption*, Appendix II B, in the range 230 to 350 nm of a 0.05% w/v solution in 0.05M *sulphuric acid* exhibits two maxima, at 262 nm and 270 nm. The *absorbance* at the maximum at 262 nm is about 0.69 and at the maximum at 270 nm is about 0.51.

B. Carry out the method for *thin-layer chromatography*, Appendix III A, using the following solutions in *water*.

(1) 0.25% w/v of the substance being examined.

(2) 0.25% w/v of *debrisoquine sulphate BPCRS*.

(3) A mixture of equal volumes of solutions (1) and (2).

CHROMATOGRAPHIC CONDITIONS

(a) Use as the coating *silica gel G*.

(b) Use the mobile phase as described below.

(c) Apply 10 μl of each solution.

(d) Develop the plate to 15 cm.

(e) After removal of the plate, dry in air and spray with a solution prepared by adding 1 ml of *sulphuric acid* to 40 ml of a freshly prepared mixture of equal volumes of a 0.135% w/v solution of *chloroplatinic(IV) acid* and a 1.1% w/v solution of *potassium iodide*.

*MOBILE PHASE*

15 volumes of *glacial acetic acid*, 25 volumes of *water* and 60 volumes of *butan-1-ol*.

CONFIRMATION

The principal spot in the chromatogram obtained with solution (1) corresponds to that in the chromatogram obtained with solution (2). The principal spot in the chromatogram obtained with solution (3) appears as a single compact spot.

C. Yields the reactions characteristic of *sulphates*, Appendix VI.

## TESTS
### Acidity
pH of a 3% w/v solution, 5.3 to 6.8, Appendix V L.

## Related substances
Carry out the method for *thin-layer chromatography*, Appendix III A, using the following solutions in *water*.

(1) 2.0% w/v of the substance being examined.

(2) 0.010% w/v of *debrisoquine sulphate BPCRS*.

CHROMATOGRAPHIC CONDITIONS

(a) Use as the coating *silica gel G*.

(b) Use the mobile phase as described below.

(c) Apply 10 μl of each solution.

(d) Develop the plate to 15 cm.

(e) After removal of the plate, dry in air and spray with a solution prepared by adding 1 ml of *sulphuric acid* to 40 ml of a freshly prepared mixture of equal volumes of a 0.135% w/v solution of *chloroplatinic(IV) acid* and a 1.1% w/v solution of *potassium iodide*.

*MOBILE PHASE*

15 volumes of *glacial acetic acid*, 25 volumes of *water* and 60 volumes of *butan-1-ol*.

LIMITS

Any *secondary spot* in the chromatogram obtained with solution (1) is not more intense than the spot in the chromatogram obtained with solution (2).

### Loss on drying
When dried to constant weight at 105°, loses not more than 0.5% of its weight. Use 1 g.

### Sulphated ash
Not more than 0.1%, Appendix IX A.

## ASSAY
Carry out Method I for *non-aqueous titration*, Appendix VIII A, using 1 g and determining the end point potentiometrically. Each ml of 0.1M *perchloric acid VS* is equivalent to 44.85 mg of $(C_{10}H_{13}N_3)_2,H_2SO_4$.

## STORAGE
Debrisoquine Sulphate should be protected from light.

# Decyl Oleate

*(Ph Eur monograph 1307)*

## Action and use
Excipient.

*Ph Eur*

## DEFINITION
Mixture consisting of decyl esters of fatty acids, mainly oleic (*cis*-9-octadecenoic) acid.

A suitable antioxidant may be added.

## CHARACTERS
### Appearance
Clear, pale yellow or colourless liquid.

### Solubility
Practically insoluble in water, miscible with ethanol (96 per cent), with methylene chloride and with light petroleum (40-60 °C).

## IDENTIFICATION
A. Relative density (see Tests).

B. Saponification value (see Tests).

C. Oleic acid (see Tests).

## TESTS

**Relative density** (*2.2.5*)
0.860 to 0.870.

**Acid value** (*2.5.1*)
Maximum 1.0, determined on 10.0 g.

**Iodine value** (*2.5.4, Method A*)
55 to 70.

**Peroxide value** (*2.5.5, Method A*)
Maximum 10.0.

**Saponification value** (*2.5.6*)
130 to 140, determined on 2.0 g.

**Oleic acid** (*2.4.22, Method A*)
Minimum 60.0 per cent in the fatty acid fraction of the substance.

**Water** (*2.5.12*)
Maximum 1.0 per cent, determined on 1.00 g.

**Total ash** (*2.4.16*)
Maximum 0.1 per cent, determined on 2.0 g.

## STORAGE
Protected from light.

_____ *Ph Eur*

# Demeclocycline Hydrochloride

(*Ph Eur monograph 0176*)

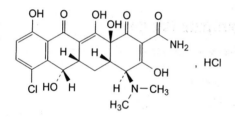

C₂₁H₂₁ClN₂O₈,HCl        501.3            *64-73-3*

$C_{21}H_{21}ClN_2O_8,HCl$        501.3            *64-73-3*

**Action and use**
Tetracycline antibacterial.

**Preparation**
Demeclocycline Capsules

*Ph Eur* _____

## DEFINITION
(4*S*,4a*S*,5a*S*,6*S*,12a*S*)-7-Chloro-4-(dimethylamino)-
3,6,10,12,12a-pentahydroxy-1,11-dioxo-1,4,4a,5,5a,6,11,
12a-octahydrotetracene-2-carboxamide hydrochloride.

Substance produced by certain strains of *Streptomyces aureofaciens* or obtained by any other means.

**Content**
89.5 per cent to 102.0 per cent (anhydrous substance).

## CHARACTERS
**Appearance**
Yellow powder.

**Solubility**
Soluble or sparingly soluble in water, slightly soluble in alcohol, very slightly soluble in acetone. It dissolves in solutions of alkali hydroxides and carbonates.

## IDENTIFICATION
A. Thin-layer chromatography (*2.2.27*).

*Test solution*   Dissolve 5 mg of the substance to be examined in *methanol R* and dilute to 10 ml with the same solvent.

*Reference solution (a)*   Dissolve 5 mg of *demeclocycline hydrochloride CRS* in *methanol R* and dilute to 10 ml with the same solvent.

*Reference solution (b)*   Dissolve 5 mg of *demeclocycline hydrochloride CRS*, 5 mg of *chlortetracycline hydrochloride R* and 5 mg of *tetracycline hydrochloride R* in *methanol R* and dilute to 10 ml with the same solvent.

*Plate*   TLC octadecylsilyl silica gel F₂₅₄ plate R.

*Mobile phase*   Mix 20 volumes of *acetonitrile R*, 20 volumes of *methanol R* and 60 volumes of a 63 g/l solution of *oxalic acid R* previously adjusted to pH 2 with *concentrated ammonia R*.

*Application*   1 µl.

*Development*   Over 3/4 of the plate.

*Drying*   In air.

*Detection*   Examine in ultraviolet light at 254 nm.

*System suitability*   The chromatogram obtained with reference solution (b) shows 3 clearly separated spots.

*Results*   The principal spot in the chromatogram obtained with the test solution is similar in position and size to the principal spot in the chromatogram obtained with reference solution (a).

B. To about 2 mg add 5 ml of *sulphuric acid R*. A violet colour develops. Add the solution to 2.5 ml of *water R*. The colour becomes yellow.

C. It gives reaction (a) of chlorides (*2.3.1*).

## TESTS
**pH** (*2.2.3*)
2.0 to 3.0.
Dissolve 0.1 g in *carbon dioxide-free water R* and dilute to 10 ml with the same solvent.

**Specific optical rotation** (*2.2.7*)
− 248 to − 263 (anhydrous substance).
Dissolve 0.250 g in *0.1 M hydrochloric acid* and dilute to 25.0 ml with the same acid.

**Specific absorbance** (*2.2.25*)
340 to 370 determined at the maximum at 385 nm (anhydrous substance).
Dissolve 10.0 mg in *0.01 M hydrochloric acid* and dilute to 100.0 ml with the same acid. To 10.0 ml of the solution add 12 ml of *dilute sodium hydroxide solution R* and dilute to 100.0 ml with *water R*.

**Related substances**
Liquid chromatography (*2.2.29*). *Prepare the solutions immediately before use.*

*Test solution*   Dissolve 25.0 mg of the substance to be examined in *0.01 M hydrochloric acid* and dilute to 25.0 ml with the same acid.

*Reference solution (a)*   Dissolve 25.0 mg of *demeclocycline hydrochloride CRS* in *0.01 M hydrochloric acid* and dilute to 25.0 ml with the same acid.

*Reference solution (b)*   Dissolve 5.0 mg of *4-epidemeclocycline hydrochloride CRS* in *0.01 M hydrochloric acid* and dilute to 25.0 ml with the same acid.

*Reference solution (c)*   Mix 1.0 ml of reference solution (a) and 5.0 ml of reference solution (b) and dilute to 25.0 ml with *0.01 M hydrochloric acid*.

*Reference solution (d)*   Dilute 5.0 ml of reference solution (a) to 100.0 ml with *0.01 M hydrochloric acid*.

*Column:*
— *size: l* = 0.25 m, Ø = 4.6 mm,
— *stationary phase:* styrene-divinylbenzene copolymer R (8 μm),
— *temperature:* 60 °C,

*Mobile phase* Weigh 80.0 g of *2-methyl-2-propanol R* and transfer to a 1000 ml volumetric flask with the aid of 200 ml of *water R*; add 100 ml of a 35 g/l solution *of dipotassium hydrogen phosphate R* adjusted to pH 9.0 with *dilute phosphoric acid R*, 150 ml of a 10 g/l solution of *tetrabutylammonium hydrogen sulphate R* adjusted to pH 9.0 with *dilute sodium hydroxide solution R* and 10 ml of a 40 g/l solution of *sodium edetate R* adjusted to pH 9.0 with *dilute sodium hydroxide solution R*; dilute to 1000 ml with *water R*.

*Flow rate* 1 ml/min.

*Detection* Spectrophotometer at 254 nm.

*Injection* 20 μl; inject the test solution and reference solutions (c) and (d).

*System suitability* Reference solution (c):
— *resolution:* minimum of 2.8 between the peaks due to impurity B (1st peak) and demeclocycline (2nd peak); if necessary, adjust the 2-methyl-2-propanol content of the mobile phase or lower the pH of the mobile phase,
— *symmetry factor:* maximum 1.25 for the peak due to demeclocycline.

*Limits:*
— *any impurity:* not more than the area of the principal peak in the chromatogram obtained with reference solution (d) (5.0 per cent), and not more than 1 such peak has an area greater than 0.8 times the area of the principal peak in the chromatogram obtained with reference solution (d) (4.0 per cent),
— *total:* not more than twice the area of the principal peak in the chromatogram obtained with reference solution (d) (10.0 per cent),
— *disregard limit:* 0.02 times the area of the principal peak in the chromatogram obtained with reference solution (d) (0.1 per cent).

**Heavy metals** (*2.4.8*)
Maximum 50 ppm.

0.5 g complies with limit test C. Prepare the standard using 2.5 ml of *lead standard solution (10 ppm Pb) R*.

**Water** (*2.5.12*)
Maximum 3.0 per cent, determined on 1.000 g.

**Sulphated ash** (*2.4.14*)
Maximum 0.5 per cent, determined on 1.0 g.

**ASSAY**
Liquid chromatography (*2.2.29*) as described in the test for related substances with the following modification.

*Injection* Test solution and reference solution (a).

Calculate the percentage content of $C_{21}H_{22}Cl_2N_2O_8$.

**STORAGE**
Protected from light.

**IMPURITIES**

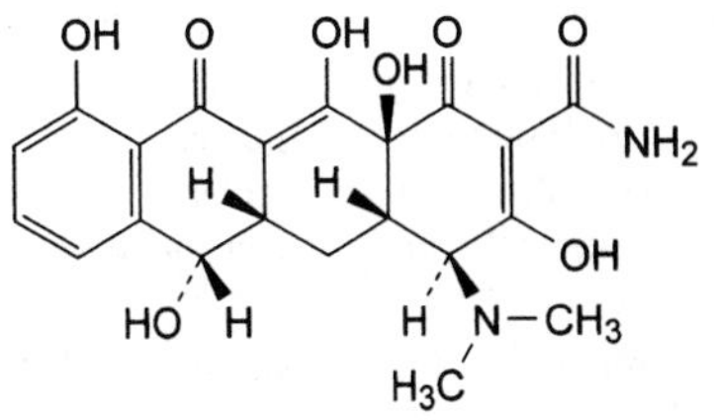

A. (4S,4aS,5aS,6S,12aS)-4-(dimethylamino)-3,6,10,12,12a-pentahydroxy-1,11-dioxo-1,4,4a,5,5a,6,11,12a-octahydrotetracene-2-carboxamide (demethyltetracycline),

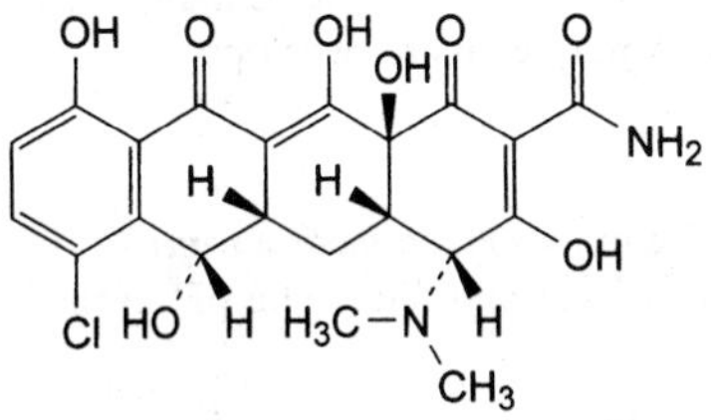

B. (4R,4aS,5aS,6S,12aS)-7-chloro-4-(dimethylamino)-3,6,10,12,12a-pentahydroxy-1,11-dioxo-1,4,4a,5,5a,6,11,12a-octahydrotetracene-2-carboxamide (4-epidemeclocycline).

*——————— Ph Eur*

# Deptropine Citrate

*(Ph Eur monograph 1308)*

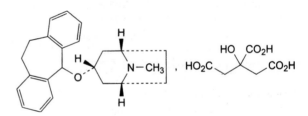

$C_{23}H_{27}NO,C_6H_8O_7$          525.6          2169-75-7

**Action and use**
Histamine $H_1$ receptor antagonist; anticholinergic.

*Ph Eur* _____

**DEFINITION**
Deptropine citrate contains not less than 98.0 per cent and not more than the equivalent of 101.0 per cent of (1R,3r,5S)-3-(10,11-dihydro-5H-dibenzo[a,d][7]annulen-5-yloxy)-8-methyl-8-azabicyclo[3.2.1]octane dihydrogen citrate, calculated with reference to the dried substance.

**CHARACTERS**
A white or almost white, microcrystalline powder, very slightly soluble in water and in ethanol, practically insoluble in methylene chloride.

It melts at about 170 °C, with decomposition.

**IDENTIFICATION**
*First identification* A.
*Second identification* B, C, D, E.

A. Examine by infrared absorption spectrophotometry (*2.2.24*), comparing with the spectrum obtained with *deptropine citrate CRS*.

B. Examine the chromatograms obtained in the test for related substances. The principal spot in the chromatogram obtained with test solution (b) is similar in position, colour and size to the principal spot in the chromatogram obtained with reference solution (b).

C. To about 1 mg add 0.5 ml of *sulphuric acid R*. A stable red-orange colour develops.

D. Dissolve about 1 mg in 0.25 ml of *perchloric acid R* and warm gently until the solution becomes turbid. Add 5 ml of *glacial acetic acid R*; a pink colour with an intense green fluorescence appears.

E. To about 5 mg add 1 ml of *acetic anhydride R* and 5 ml of *pyridine R*. A purple colour develops.

## TESTS

**pH** (*2.2.3*).

Suspend 0.25 g in *carbon dioxide-free water R*, dilute to 25 ml with the same solvent and filter. The pH of the solution is 3.7 to 4.5.

### Related substances

Examine by thin-layer chromatography (*2.2.27*), using as the coating substance a suitable silica gel with a fluorescent indicator having an optimal intensity at 254 nm.

*Test solution (a)* Dissolve 0.10 g of the substance to be examined in *methanol R* and dilute to 10 ml with the same solvent.

*Test solution (b)* Dilute 1 ml of test solution (a) to 10 ml with *methanol R*.

*Reference solution (a)* Dilute 1.0 ml of test solution (a) to 100.0 ml with *methanol R*.

*Reference solution (b)* Dissolve 20 mg of *deptropine citrate CRS* in *methanol R* and dilute to 2 ml with the same solvent. Dilute 1 ml of the solution to 10 ml with *methanol R*.

*Reference solution (c)* Dissolve 5 mg of *tropine CRS* in *methanol R* and dilute to 100.0 ml with the same solvent.

*Reference solution (d)* Dissolve 10 mg of *deptropine citrate CRS* and 10 mg of *tropine CRS* in *methanol R* and dilute to 25 ml with the same solvent.

Apply to the plate 40 μl of each solution. Develop over a path of 10 cm using a mixture of 8 volumes of *concentrated ammonia R* and 92 volumes of *butanol R*. Dry the plate at 100 °C to 105 °C until the ammonia has completely evaporated. Examine in ultraviolet light at 254 nm. Any spot in the chromatogram obtained with test solution (a), apart from the principal spot, is not more intense than the spot in the chromatogram obtained with reference solution (a) (1 per cent). Spray with *dilute potassium iodobismuthate solution R* and then with a 10 g/l solution of *sodium nitrite R*. Expose the plate to iodine vapours. Examine in daylight and in ultraviolet light at 254 nm. In the chromatogram obtained with test solution (a): any spot corresponding to tropine is not more intense than the spot in the chromatogram obtained with reference solution (c) (0.5 per cent); any spot, apart from the principal spot and any spot corresponding to tropine, is not more intense than the spot in the chromatogram obtained with reference solution (a) (1 per cent). The test is not valid unless the chromatogram obtained with reference solution (d) shows two clearly separated spots.

**Heavy metals** (*2.4.8*)

1.0 g complies with limit test C for heavy metals (20 ppm). Prepare the standard using 2 ml of *lead standard solution (10 ppm Pb) R*.

**Loss on drying** (*2.2.32*)

Not more than 2.0 per cent, determined on 1.000 g by drying in an oven at 105 °C for 4 h.

**Sulphated ash** (*2.4.14*)

Not more than 0.1 per cent, determined on 1.0 g.

### ASSAY

Dissolve 0.400 g in 50 ml of *anhydrous acetic acid R*. Titrate with *0.1 M perchloric acid*, determining the end-point potentiometrically (*2.2.20*).

1 ml of *0.1 M perchloric acid* is equivalent to 52.56 mg of $C_{29}H_{35}NO_8$.

### STORAGE

Store protected from light.

### IMPURITIES

A. (1R,3r,5S)-8-methyl-8-azabicyclo[3.2.1]octan-3-ol (tropine),

B. (1R,3s,5S)-3-(10,11-dihydro-5H-dibenzo[a,d][7]annulen-5-yloxy)-8-methyl-8-azabicyclo[3.2.1]octane (pseudodeptropine),

C. 10,11-dihydro-5H-dibenzo[a,d][7]annulen-5-ol (dibenzocycloheptadienol),

D. (1R,3r,5S)-3-(10,11-dihydro-5H-dibenzo[a,d][7]annulen-5-yloxy)-8-azabicyclo[3.2.1]octane (demethyldeptropine).

# Dequalinium Chloride

(*Ph Eur monograph 1413*)

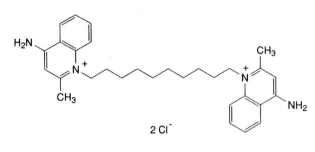

C$_{30}$H$_{40}$Cl$_2$N$_4$      527.6      *522-51-0*

## Action and use
Antiseptic.

*Ph Eur* _____

## DEFINITION
Dequalinium chloride contains not less than 95.0 per cent and not more than the equivalent of 101.0 per cent of 1,1'-(decane-1,10-diyl)bis(4-amino-2-methylquinolinium) dichloride, calculated with reference to the dried substance.

## CHARACTERS
A white or yellowish-white powder, hygroscopic, slightly soluble in water and in alcohol.

## IDENTIFICATION
*First identification*   B, E.

*Second identification*    A, C, D, E.

A. Dissolve about 10 mg in *water R* and dilute to 100 ml with the same solvent. Dilute 10 ml of the solution to 100 ml with *water R*. Examined between 230 nm and 350 nm (*2.2.25*), the solution shows 2 absorption maxima, at 240 nm and 326 nm and a shoulder at 336 nm. The ratio of the absorbance measured at the maximum at 240 nm to that measured at the maximum at 326 nm is 1.56 to 1.80 and the ratio of the absorbance measured at the maximum at 326 nm to that measured at the shoulder at 336 nm is 1.12 to 1.30.

B. Examine by infrared absorption spectrophotometry between 600 cm$^{-1}$ and 2000 cm$^{-1}$ (*2.2.24*), comparing with the spectrum obtained with *dequalinium chloride CRS*.

C. To 5 ml of solution S (see Tests) add 5 ml of *potassium ferricyanide solution R*. A yellow precipitate is formed.

D. To 10 ml of solution S add 1 ml of *dilute nitric acid R*. A white precipitate is formed. Filter and reserve the filtrate for identification test E.

E. The filtrate from identification test D gives reaction (a) of chlorides (*2.3.1*).

## TESTS
### Solution S
Dissolve 0.2 g in 90 ml of *carbon dioxide-free water R*, heating if necessary, and dilute to 100 ml with the same solvent.

### Appearance of solution
Solution S is clear (*2.2.1*) and colourless (*2.2.2, Method II*).

### Acidity or alkalinity
To 5 ml of solution S add 0.1 ml of *bromothymol blue solution R1*. Not more than 0.2 ml of *0.01 M hydrochloric acid* or *0.01 M sodium hydroxide* is required to change the colour of the indicator.

### Related substances
Examine by liquid chromatography (*2.2.29*).

*Test solution*   Dissolve 10.0 mg of the substance to be examined in the mobile phase and dilute to 10.0 ml with the mobile phase.

*Reference solution (a)*   Dissolve 10.0 mg of *dequalinium chloride for performance test CRS* in the mobile phase and dilute to 10.0 ml with the mobile phase.

*Reference solution (b)*   Dissolve 10.0 mg of *dequalinium chloride CRS* in the mobile phase and dilute to 10.0 ml with the mobile phase. Dilute 1.0 ml to 50.0 ml with the mobile phase.

The chromatographic procedure may be carried out using:
— a stainless steel column 0.25 m long and 4.6 mm in internal diameter packed with an *end-capped octadecylsilyl silica gel for chromatography R*,
— as mobile phase at a flow rate of 1.5 ml/min the following solution: dissolve 2 g of *sodium hexanesulphonate R* in 300 ml of *water R*. Adjust to pH 4.0 with *acetic acid R* and add 700 ml of *methanol R*,
— as detector a spectrophotometer set at 240 nm.

Adjust the sensitivity of the system so that the height of the peak due to impurity B in the chromatogram obtained with 10 µl of reference solution (a) is at least 25 per cent of the full scale of the recorder. Measure the height *(A)* above the baseline of the peak due to impurity B and the height *(B)* above the baseline at the lowest point of the curve separating this peak from the peak due to dequalinium chloride. The test is not valid unless *A* is greater than twice *B*. If necessary, adjust the concentration of methanol in the mobile phase.

Inject 10 µl of the test solution and 10 µl of reference solution (b). Continue the chromatography of the test solution for 5 times the retention time of the peak due to dequalinium chloride. In the chromatogram obtained with the test solution: the area of any peak due to impurity A is not greater than half the area of the principal peak in the chromatogram obtained with reference solution (b) (1 per cent); and the sum of the areas of all the peaks, apart from the principal peak, is not greater than 5 times the area of the principal peak in the chromatogram obtained with reference solution (b) (10 per cent). Disregard any peak with an area less than 0.025 times the area of the principal peak in the chromatogram obtained with reference solution (b).

### Readily carbonisable substances
Dissolve 20 mg in 2 ml of *sulphuric acid R*. After 5 min the solution is not more intensely coloured than reference solution BY$_4$ (*2.2.2, Method I*).

### Loss on drying (*2.2.32*)
Not more than 7.0 per cent, determined on 1.000 g by drying at 105 °C at a pressure not exceeding 0.7 kPa.

### Sulphated ash (*2.4.14*)
Not more than 0.1 per cent, determined on 1.0 g.

## ASSAY
*In order to avoid overheating in the reaction medium, mix thoroughly throughout and stop the titration immediately after the end-point has been reached.*

Dissolve 0.200 g in 5 ml of *anhydrous formic acid R* and add 50 ml of *acetic anhydride R*. Titrate with *0.1 M perchloric acid*, determining the end-point potentiometrically (*2.2.20*).

1 ml of *0.1 M perchloric acid* is equivalent to 26.38 mg of C$_{30}$H$_{40}$Cl$_2$N$_4$.

## STORAGE
In an airtight container.

## IMPURITIES

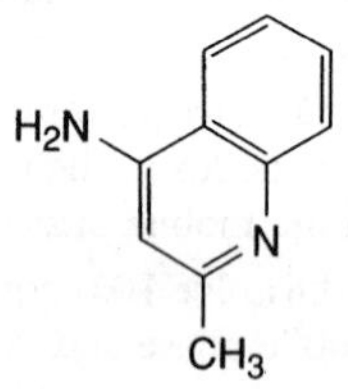

A. 2-methylquinolin-4-amine,

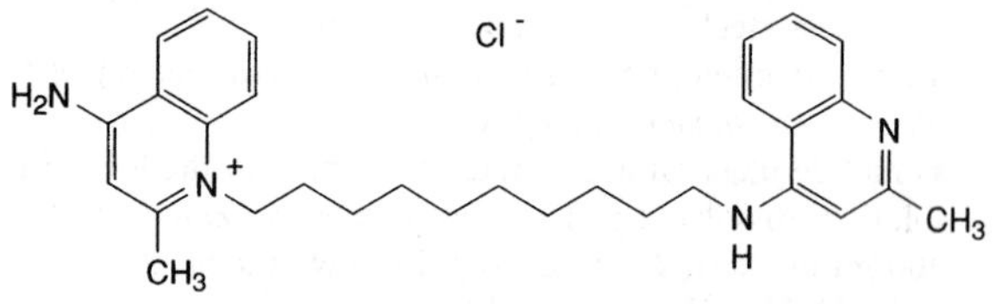

B. 4-amino-1-[10-[(2-methylquinolin-4-yl)amino]decyl]-2-methylquinolinium chloride,

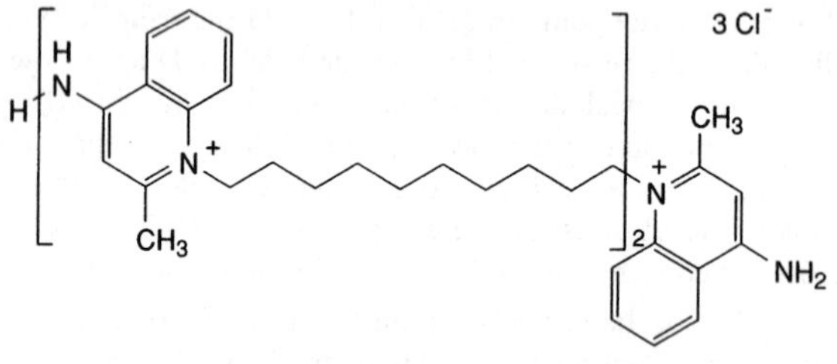

C. 1-[10-(4-amino-2-methylquinolinio)decyl]-4-[[10-(4-amino-2-methylquinolinio)decyl]amino]-2-methylquinolinium trichloride.

*Ph Eur*

# Desferrioxamine Mesilate

*(Deferoxamine Mesilate, Ph Eur monograph 0896)*

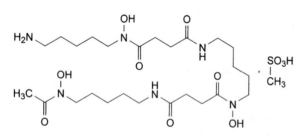

C₂₅H₄₈N₆O₈,CH₄SO₃        657        *138-14-7*

$C_{25}H_{48}N_6O_8,CH_4SO_3$        657        *138-14-7*

### Action and use
Chelating agent (iron).

### Preparation
Desferrioxamine Injection

*Ph Eur*

## DEFINITION

*N'*-[5-[[4-[[5-(Acetylhydroxyamino)pentyl]amino]-4-oxobutanoyl]hydroxyamino]pentyl]-*N*-(5-aminopentyl)-*N*-hydroxybutanediamide methanesulfonate.

### Content
98.0 per cent to 102.0 per cent (anhydrous substance).

## PRODUCTION

The production method must be evaluated to determine the potential for formation of alkyl mesilates, which is particularly likely to occur if the reaction medium contains lower alcohols. Where necessary, the production method is validated to demonstrate that alkyl mesilates are not detectable in the final product.

## CHARACTERS

### Appearance
White or almost white powder.

### Solubility
Freely soluble in water, slightly soluble in methanol, very slightly soluble in ethanol (96 per cent).

## IDENTIFICATION

*First identification   A, D.*

*Second identification   B, C, D.*

A. Infrared absorption spectrophotometry (*2.2.24*).

*Preparation*   Discs.

*Comparison   deferoxamine mesilate CRS.*

If the spectra obtained show differences, dissolve the substance to be examined and the reference substance separately in *ethanol (96 per cent) R*, evaporate to dryness and record new spectra using the residues.

B. Dissolve about 5 mg in 5 ml of *water R*. Add 2 ml of a 5 g/l solution of *trisodium phosphate dodecahydrate R* and 0.5 ml of a 25 g/l solution of *sodium naphthoquinonesulphonate R*. A brownish-black colour develops.

C. Solution A obtained in the Assay is brownish-red. To 10 ml of solution A add 3 ml of *ether R* and shake. The organic layer is colourless. To 10 ml of solution A add 3 ml of *benzyl alcohol R* and shake. The organic layer is brownish-red.

D. Dissolve 0.1 g in 5 ml of *dilute hydrochloric acid R*. Add 1 ml of *barium chloride solution R2*. The solution is clear. In a porcelain crucible, mix 0.1 g with 1 g of *anhydrous sodium carbonate R*, heat and ignite over a naked flame. Allow to cool. Dissolve the residue in 10 ml of *water R*, heating if necessary, and filter. The filtrate gives reaction (a) of sulphates (*2.3.1*).

## TESTS

### Solution S
Dissolve 2.5 g in *carbon dioxide-free water R* prepared from *distilled water R* and dilute to 25 ml with the same solvent.

### Appearance of solution
Solution S is clear (*2.2.1*) and not more intensely coloured than reference solution Y₅ (*2.2.2, Method II*).

### pH (*2.2.3*)
3.7 to 5.5 for freshly prepared solution S.

### Related substances
Liquid chromatography (*2.2.29*). *Prepare the solutions immediately before use, protected from light.*

*Test solution*   Dissolve 50.0 mg of the substance to be examined in the mobile phase and dilute to 50.0 ml with the mobile phase.

*Reference solution (a)*   Dissolve 10.0 mg of *deferoxamine mesilate CRS* in the mobile phase and dilute to 10.0 ml with the mobile phase.

*Reference solution (b)*   Dilute 1.0 ml of the test solution to 25.0 ml with the mobile phase.

*Column:*
— *size:* $l = 0.25$ m, $\varnothing = 4.6$ mm;
— *stationary phase:* octadecylsilyl silica gel for chromatography R (10 μm).

*Mobile phase* Dissolve 1.32 g of *ammonium phosphate R* and 0.37 g of *sodium edetate R* in 950 ml of *water R*; adjust to pH 2.8 with *phosphoric acid R* (about 3-4 ml) and add 55 ml of *tetrahydrofuran R*.

*Flow rate* 2 ml/min.

*Detection* Spectrophotometer at 220 nm.

*Injection* 20 μl.

*Run time* 3 times the retention time of deferoxamine.

*System suitability* Reference solution (a):
— *resolution:* minimum 1.0 between the peak with a relative retention time of about 0.8 and the principal peak.

*Limits:*
— *impurity A:* not more than the area of the principal peak in the chromatogram obtained with reference solution (b) (4.0 per cent);
— *total:* not more than 1.75 times the area of the principal peak in the chromatogram obtained with reference solution (b) (7.0 per cent);
— *disregard limit:* 0.02 times the area of the principal peak in the chromatogram obtained with reference solution (b) (0.08 per cent).

**Chlorides** *(2.4.4)*
Maximum 330 ppm.

Dilute 2 ml of solution S to 20 ml with *water R*.

**Sulphates** *(2.4.13)*
Maximum 400 ppm.

Dilute 5 ml of solution S to 20 ml with *distilled water R*.

**Heavy metals** *(2.4.8)*
Maximum 10 ppm.

2.0 g complies with test C. Prepare the reference solution using 2 ml of *lead standard solution (10 ppm Pb) R*.

**Water** *(2.5.12)*
Maximum 2.0 per cent, determined on 1.000 g.

**Sulphated ash** *(2.4.14)*
Maximum 0.1 per cent, determined on 1.0 g.

**Bacterial endotoxins** *(2.6.14)*
Less than 0.025 IU/mg, if intended for use in the manufacture of parenteral dosage forms without a further appropriate procedure for the removal of bacterial endotoxins.

**ASSAY**
Dissolve 0.500 g in 25 ml of *water R*. Add 4 ml of *0.05 M sulphuric acid*. Titrate with *0.1 M ferric ammonium sulphate*. Towards the end of the titration, titrate uniformly and at a rate of about 0.2 ml/min. Determine the end-point potentiometrically *(2.2.20)* using a platinum indicator electrode and a calomel reference electrode. Retain the titrated solution (solution A) for identification test C.

1 ml of *0.1 M ferric ammonium sulphate* is equivalent to 65.68 mg of $C_{26}H_{52}N_6O_{11}S$.

**STORAGE**
Protected from light, at a temperature of 2 °C to 8 °C. If the substance is sterile, store in a sterile, airtight, tamper-proof container.

**IMPURITIES**
*Specified impurities A.*

*Other detectable impurities* (the following substances would, if present at a sufficient level, be detected by one or other of the tests in the monograph. They are limited by the general acceptance criterion for other/unspecified impurities and/or by the general monograph *Substances for pharmaceutical use (2034)*. It is therefore not necessary to identify these impurities for demonstration of compliance. See also *5.10*. *Control of impurities in substances for pharmaceutical use*): *B*.

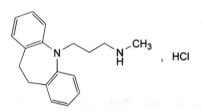

A. *N′*-[5-[[4-[[4-(acetylhydroxyamino)butyl]amino]-4-oxobutanoyl]hydroxyamino]pentyl]-*N*-(5-aminopentyl)-*N*-hydroxybutanediamide (desferrioxamine $A_1$),

B. other desferrioxamines.

——————————————————— *Ph Eur*

# Desipramine Hydrochloride

*(Ph Eur monograph 0481)*

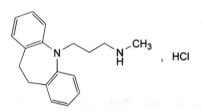

$C_{18}H_{22}N_2,HCl$          302.8          58-28-6

**Action and use**
Monoamine reuptake inhibitor; tricyclic antidepressant.

**Preparation**
Desipramine Tablets

*Ph Eur* ——————————————————————

**DEFINITION**
Desipramine hydrochloride contains not less than 99.0 per cent and not more than the equivalent of 101.0 per cent of 3-(10,11-dihydro-5*H*-dibenzo[*b,f*]azepin-5-yl)-*N*-methylpropan-1-amine hydrochloride, calculated with reference to the dried substance.

**CHARACTERS**
A white or almost white, crystalline powder, soluble in water and in alcohol.

It melts at about 214 °C.

**IDENTIFICATION**
*First identification B, E.*

*Second identification A, C, D, E.*

A. Dissolve 40.0 mg in *0.01 M hydrochloric acid* and dilute to 100.0 ml with the same acid. Dilute 5.0 ml of the solution to 100.0 ml with *0.01 M hydrochloric acid*. Examined between

230 nm and 350 nm (*2.2.25*), the solution shows an absorption maximum at 251 nm and a shoulder at 270 nm. The specific absorbance at the maximum is 255 to 285.

B. Examine by infrared absorption spectrophotometry (*2.2.24*), comparing with the spectrum obtained with *desipramine hydrochloride CRS*.

C. Examine the chromatograms obtained in the test for related substances. The principal spot in the chromatogram obtained with test solution (b) is similar in position, colour and size to the principal spot in the chromatogram obtained with reference solution (a).

D. Dissolve about 50 mg in 3 ml of *water R* and add 0.05 ml of a 25 g/l solution of *quinhydrone R* in *methanol R*. An intense pink colour develops within about 15 min.

E. To 0.5 ml of solution S (see Tests) add 1.5 ml of *water R*. The solution gives reaction (a) of chlorides (*2.3.1*).

## TESTS

### Solution S
Dissolve 1.25 g in *carbon dioxide-free water R*, warming to not more than 30 °C if necessary, and dilute to 25 ml with the same solvent.

### Appearance of solution
Solution S, examined immediately after preparation, is not more intensely coloured than reference solution BY$_6$ (*2.2.2, Method II*).

### Acidity or alkalinity
To 10 ml of solution S add 0.1 ml of *methyl red solution R* and 0.3 ml of *0.01 M sodium hydroxide*. The solution is yellow. Not more than 0.5 ml of *0.01 M hydrochloric acid* is required to change the colour of the indicator to red.

### Related substances
*Carry out the test protected from bright light.* Examine by thin-layer chromatography (*2.2.27*), using a *TLC silica gel plate R*.

*Test solution (a)*   Dissolve 0.10 g of the substance to be examined in a mixture of equal volumes of *ethanol R* and *methylene chloride R* and dilute to 10 ml with the same mixture of solvents. *Prepare immediately before use.*

*Test solution (b)*   Dilute 1 ml of test solution (a) to 10 ml with a mixture of equal volumes of *ethanol R* and *methylene chloride R*.

*Reference solution (a)*   Dissolve 25 mg of *desipramine hydrochloride CRS* in a mixture of equal volumes of *ethanol R* and *methylene chloride R* and dilute to 25 ml with the same mixture of solvents. *Prepare immediately before use.*

*Reference solution (b)*   Dilute 1 ml of reference solution (a) to 50 ml with a mixture of equal volumes of *ethanol R* and *methylene chloride R*.

Apply to the plate 5 μl of each solution. Develop over a path of 7 cm using a mixture of 1 volume of *water R*, 10 volumes of *anhydrous acetic acid R* and 10 volumes of *toluene R*. Dry the plate in a current of air for 10 min, spray with a 5 g/l solution of *potassium dichromate R* in a mixture of 1 volume of *sulphuric acid R* and 4 volumes of *water R* and examine immediately. Any spot in the chromatogram obtained with test solution (a), apart from the principal spot, is not more intense than the spot in the chromatogram obtained with reference solution (b) (0.2 per cent).

### Heavy metals (*2.4.8*)
2.0 g complies with limit test C for heavy metals (20 ppm). Prepare the standard using 4 ml of *lead standard solution (10 ppm Pb) R*.

### Loss on drying (*2.2.32*)
Not more than 0.5 per cent, determined on 1.000 g by drying in an oven at 105 °C.

### Sulphated ash (*2.4.14*)
Not more than 0.1 per cent, determined on 1.0 g.

## ASSAY
Dissolve 0.2500 g in a mixture of 5 ml of *0.01 M hydrochloric acid* and 50 ml of *alcohol R*. Carry out a potentiometric titration (*2.2.20*), using *0.1 M sodium hydroxide*. Read the volume added between the two points of inflexion.

1 ml of *0.1 M sodium hydroxide* is equivalent to 30.28 mg of $C_{18}H_{23}ClN_2$.

## STORAGE
Store protected from light.

_____ Ph Eur

# Desflurane

(*Ph Eur monograph 1666*)

$C_3H_2F_6O$          168.0          57041-67-5

Ph Eur _____

## DEFINITION
(2RS)-2-(Difluoromethoxy)-1,1,1,2-tetrafluoroethane.

## CHARACTERS

### Appearance
Clear, colourless, mobile, heavy liquid.

### Solubility
Practically insoluble in water, miscible with anhydrous ethanol.

### Relative density
1.47, determined at 15 °C.

### bp
About 22 °C.

## IDENTIFICATION
Infrared absorption spectrophotometry (*2.2.24*).

*Preparation*   Examine the substance in the gaseous state.

*Comparison*   *Ph. Eur. reference spectrum of desflurane.*

## TESTS
The substance to be examined must be cooled to a temperature below 10 °C and the tests must be carried out at a temperature below 20 °C.

### Acidity or alkalinity
To 20 ml add 20 ml of *carbon dioxide-free water R*, shake for 3 min and allow to stand. Collect the upper layer and add 0.2 ml of *bromocresol purple solution R*. Not more than 0.1 ml of *0.01 M sodium hydroxide* or 0.6 ml of *0.01 M hydrochloric acid* is required to change the colour of the indicator.

### Related substances
Gas chromatography (*2.2.28*).

*Test solution*   The substance to be examined.

*Reference solution (a)*   Introduce 25 ml of the substance to be examined into a 50 ml flask fitted with a septum, and add 0.50 ml of *desflurane impurity A CRS* and 1.0 ml of *isoflurane CRS* (impurity B). Add 50 µl of *acetone R* (impurity H), 10 µl of *chloroform R* (impurity F) and 50 µl of *methylene chloride R* (impurity E) to the solution, using an airtight syringe, and dilute to 50.0 ml with the substance to be examined. Dilute 5.0 ml of this solution to 50.0 ml with the substance to be examined. Store at a temperature below 10 °C.

*Reference solution (b)*  Dilute 5.0 ml of reference solution (a) to 50.0 ml with the substance to be examined. Store at a temperature below 10 °C.

*Reference solution (c)*  Dilute 5.0 ml of reference solution (b) to 25.0 ml with the substance to be examined. Store at a temperature below 10 °C.

*Column:*
— *material:* fused silica;
— *size:* $l = 105$ m, $\emptyset = 0.32$ mm;
— *stationary phase:*
  *poly[methyl(trifluoropropylmethyl)siloxane] R* (film thickness 1.5 µm).

*Carrier gas*  *helium for chromatography R.*

*Flow rate*  2.0 ml/min.

*Split ratio*  1:25.

*Temperature:*
— *column:* 30 °C;
— *injection port:* 150 °C;
— *detector:* 200 °C.

*Detection*  Flame ionisation.

*Injection*  2.0 µl.

*Run time*  35 min.

*Relative retention*  With reference to desflurane (retention time = about 11.5 min): impurity C = about 1.06; impurity D = about 1.09; impurity A = about 1.14; impurity G = about 1.39; impurity E = about 1.5; impurity B = about 1.7; impurity F = about 2.2; impurity H = about 2.6.

*System suitability*  Reference solution (a):
— *number of theoretical plates:* minimum 20 000, calculated for the peak due to impurity A;
— *symmetry factor:* maximum 2.0 for the peak due to impurity B.

*Limits:*
— *impurity B:* not more than the difference between the area of the corresponding peak in the chromatogram obtained with reference solution (a) and the area of the corresponding peak in the chromatogram obtained with the test solution (0.2 per cent *V/V*);
— *impurity A:* not more than the difference between the area of the corresponding peak in the chromatogram obtained with reference solution (a) and the area of the corresponding peak in the chromatogram obtained with the test solution (0.1 per cent *V/V*);
— *impurities C, D, G:* for each impurity, not more than the difference between the area of the peak due to impurity A in the chromatogram obtained with reference solution (b) and the area of the peak due to impurity A in the chromatogram obtained with the test solution (0.01 per cent *V/V*);
— *impurities E, H:* for each impurity, not more than the difference between the area of the corresponding peak in the chromatogram obtained with reference solution (a) and the area of the corresponding peak in the chromatogram obtained with the test solution (0.01 per cent *V/V*);

— *impurity F:* not more than the difference between the area of the corresponding peak in the chromatogram obtained with reference solution (a) and the area of the corresponding peak in the chromatogram obtained with the test solution (0.002 per cent *V/V*);
— *unspecified impurities:* for each impurity, not more than 0.5 times the difference between the area of the peak due to impurity A in the chromatogram obtained with reference solution (b) and the area of the peak due to impurity A in the chromatogram obtained with the test solution (0.005 per cent *V/V*);
— *sum of impurities other than A, B, C, D, E, F, G and H:* not more than the difference between the area of the peak due to impurity A in the chromatogram obtained with reference solution (b) and the area of the peak due to impurity A in the chromatogram obtained with the test solution (0.01 per cent *V/V*);
— *disregard limit:* the difference between the area of the peak due to impurity A in the chromatogram obtained with reference solution (c) and the area of the peak due to impurity A in the chromatogram obtained with the test solution (0.002 per cent *V/V*).

**Fluorides**
Maximum 10.0 ppm.

Potentiometry (2.2.36, Method I).

*Test solution*  To 10.0 ml in a separating funnel, add 10 ml of a mixture of 30.0 ml of *dilute ammonia R2* and 70.0 ml of *distilled water R*. Shake for 1 min and collect the upper layer. Repeat this extraction procedure twice, collecting the upper layer each time. Adjust the combined upper layers to pH 5.2 with *dilute hydrochloric acid R*. Add 5.0 ml of *fluoride standard solution (1 ppm F) R* and dilute to 50.0 ml with *distilled water R*. To 20.0 ml of this solution add 20.0 ml of *total-ionic-strength-adjustment buffer R* and dilute to 50.0 ml with *distilled water R*.

*Reference solutions*  To each of 1.0 ml, 2.0 ml, 3.0 ml, 4.0 ml and 5.0 ml of *fluoride standard solution (10 ppm F) R* add 20.0 ml of *total-ionic-strength-adjustment buffer R* and dilute to 50.0 ml with *distilled water R*.

*Indicator electrode*  Fluoride selective.

*Reference electrode*  Silver-silver chloride.

Carry out the measurements on 20 ml of each solution. Calculate the concentration of fluorides using the calibration curve, taking into account the addition of fluoride to the test solution.

**Antimony**
Maximum 3.0 ppm.

Atomic absorption spectrometry (2.2.23, Method I).

*Solvent mixture*  hydrochloric acid R, nitric acid R (50:50 *V/V*).

*Test solution*  Transfer 10 g, cooled to below 10 °C, to a tared flask containing 20 ml of *water R* cooled to below 5 °C. Add 1 ml of the solvent mixture and leave at room temperature until the desflurane has evaporated completely. Subsequently, reduce the volume to about 8 ml on a hot plate. Cool to room temperature and transfer to a volumetric flask. Add 1 ml of the solvent mixture and adjust to 10.0 ml with *water R*.

*Reference solutions*  To each of 1.0 ml, 2.0 ml, 3.0 ml, 4.0 ml and 5.0 ml of *antimony standard solution (100 ppm Sb) R* add 20 ml of the solvent mixture and dilute to 100.0 ml with *water R*.

*Source*  Antimony hollow-cathode lamp using a transmission band of 0.2 nm and a 75 per cent lamp current.

*Wavelength*   217.6 nm.

*Atomisation device*   Air-acetylene flame.

**Non-volatile matter**

Maximum 100 mg/l.

Evaporate 20.0 ml to dryness with the aid of a stream of *nitrogen R*. The residue weighs not more than 2.0 mg.

**STORAGE**

In a glass bottle fitted with a polyethylene-lined cap. Before opening the bottle, cool the contents to below 10 °C.

**IMPURITIES**

*Specified impurities*   A, B, C, D, E, F, G, H.

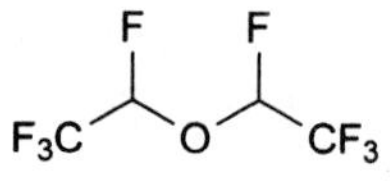

A. 1,1′-oxybis(1,2,2-tetrafluoroethane),

B. isoflurane,

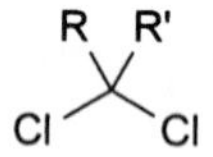

C. R = H, R′ = F: dichlorofluoromethane,

D. R = Cl, R′ = F: trichlorofluoromethane,

E. R = R′ = H: dichloromethane (methylene chloride),

F. R = H, R′ = Cl: trichloromethane (chloroform),

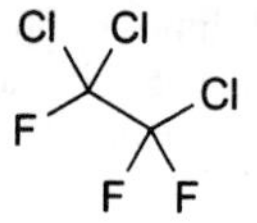

G. 1,1,2-trichloro-1,2,2-trifluoroethane,

H. acetone.

*Ph Eur*

# Deslanoside

(*Ph Eur monograph 0482*)

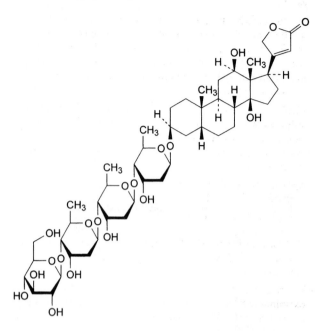

$C_{47}H_{74}O_{19}$                 943.1                 *17598-65-1*

**Action and use**

Na / K-ATPase inhibitor; cardiac glycoside.

*Ph Eur*

**DEFINITION**

Deslanoside contains not less than 95.0 per cent and not more than the equivalent of 105.0 per cent of 3β-[(*O*-β-D-glucopyranosyl-(1→4)-*O*-2,6-dideoxy-β-D-*ribo*-hexopyranosyl-(1→4)-*O*-2,6-dideoxy-β-D-*ribo*-hexopyranosyl-(1→4)-2,6-dideoxy-β-D-*ribo*-hexopyranosyl)oxy]-12β,14-dihydroxy-5β,14β-card-20(22)-enolide, calculated with reference to the dried substance.

**CHARACTERS**

A white or almost white, crystalline or finely crystalline powder, hygroscopic, practically insoluble in water, very slightly soluble in alcohol. In an atmosphere of low relative humidity, it loses water.

**IDENTIFICATION**

*First identification*   A.

*Second identification*   B, C, D.

A. Examine by infrared absorption spectrophotometry (*2.2.24*), comparing with the spectrum obtained with *deslanoside CRS*. When comparing the spectra, special attention is given to the absence of a distinct absorption maximum at about 1260 cm⁻¹ and to the intensity of the absorption maximum at about 1740 cm⁻¹. Examine the substances in discs prepared by dissolving 1 mg of the substance to be examined or 1 mg of the reference substance in 0.3 ml of *methanol R* and triturating with about 0.4 g of dry, finely powdered *potassium bromide R* until the mixture is uniform and completely dry.

B. Examine the chromatograms obtained in the test for related substances. The principal band in the chromatogram obtained with test solution (b) is similar in position, colour and size to the principal band in the chromatogram obtained with reference solution (a).

C. Suspend about 0.5 mg in 0.2 ml of *alcohol (60 per cent V/V) R*. Add 0.1 ml of *dinitrobenzoic acid solution R* and 0.1 ml of *dilute sodium hydroxide solution R*. A violet colour develops.

D. Dissolve about 5 mg in 5 ml of *glacial acetic acid R* and add 0.05 ml of *ferric chloride solution R1*. Cautiously add 2 ml of *sulphuric acid R*, avoiding mixing the two liquids. Allow to stand; a brown but not reddish ring develops at the interface and a greenish-yellow, then bluish-green colour diffuses from it to the upper layer.

## TESTS

### Solution S
Dissolve 0.20 g in a mixture of equal volumes of *chloroform R* and *methanol R* and dilute to 10 ml with the same mixture of solvents.

### Appearance of solution
Solution S is clear (*2.2.1*) and colourless (*2.2.2, Method II*).

### Specific optical rotation (*2.2.7*)
Dissolve 0.200 g in *anhydrous pyridine R* and dilute to 10.0 ml with the same solvent. The specific optical rotation is + 6.5 to + 8.5, calculated with reference to the dried substance.

### Related substances
Examine by thin-layer chromatography (*2.2.27*), using *silica gel G R* as the coating substance.

*Test solution (a)*  Use solution S.

*Test solution (b)*  Dilute 1 ml of test solution (a) to 10 ml with a mixture of equal volumes of *chloroform R* and *methanol R*.

*Reference solution (a)*  Dissolve 20 mg of *deslanoside CRS* in a mixture of equal volumes of *chloroform R* and *methanol R* and dilute to 10 ml with the same mixture of solvents.

*Reference solution (b)*  Dilute 2.5 ml of reference solution (a) to 10 ml with a mixture of equal volumes of *chloroform R* and *methanol R*.

*Reference solution (c)*  Dilute 1 ml of reference solution (a) to 10 ml with a mixture of equal volumes of *chloroform R* and *methanol R*.

Apply separately to the plate as 10 mm bands 5 μl of each solution. Develop immediately over a path of 15 cm using a mixture of 3 volumes of *water R*, 36 volumes of *methanol R* and 130 volumes of *methylene chloride R*. Dry the plate in a current of warm air, spray with a mixture of 5 volumes of *sulphuric acid R* and 95 volumes of *alcohol R* and heat at 140 °C for 15 min. Examine in daylight. In the chromatogram obtained with test solution (a), any band, apart from the principal band, is not more intense than the band in the chromatogram obtained with reference solution (b) (2.5 per cent) and at most two such bands are more intense than the band in the chromatogram obtained with reference solution (c) (1.0 per cent).

### Loss on drying (*2.2.32*)
Not more than 5.0 per cent, determined on 0.500 g by drying *in vacuo* at 105 °C.

### Sulphated ash (*2.4.14*)
Not more than 0.1 per cent, determined on the residue obtained in the test for loss on drying.

## ASSAY
Dissolve 50.0 mg in *alcohol R* and dilute to 50.0 ml with the same solvent. Dilute 5.0 ml of this solution to 100.0 ml with *alcohol R*. Prepare a reference solution in the same manner, using 50.0 mg of *deslanoside CRS* (undried). To 5.0 ml of each solution add 3.0 ml of *alkaline sodium picrate solution R*

and allow to stand protected from bright light in a water-bath at 20 ± 1 °C for 40 min. Measure the absorbance (*2.2.25*) of each solution at the maximum at 484 nm, using as the compensation liquid a mixture of 3.0 ml of *alkaline sodium picrate solution R* and 5.0 ml of *alcohol R* prepared at the same time.

Calculate the content of $C_{47}H_{74}O_{19}$ from the absorbances measured and the concentrations of the solutions.

## STORAGE
Store in an airtight, glass container, protected from light, at a temperature below 10 °C.

*Ph Eur*

# Desmopressin

*(Ph Eur monograph 0712)*

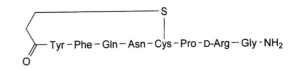

$C_{46}H_{64}N_{14}O_{12}S_2$      1069      *16679-58-6*

### Action and use
Vasopressin analogue; treatment of diabetes insipidus; nocturnal enuresis; haemophilia; von Willebrand's disease.

### Preparations
Desmopressin Tablets

Desmopressin Injection

Desmopressin Intranasal Solution

*Ph Eur*

## DEFINITION
(3-Sulphanylpropanoyl)-L-tyrosyl-L-phenylalanyl-L-glutaminyl-L-asparaginyl-L-cysteinyl-L-prolyl-D-arginylglycinamide cyclic (1→6)-disulfide.

Synthetic cyclic nonapeptide, available as an acetate.

### Content
95.0 per cent to 105.0 per cent
(anhydrous and acetic acid-free substance).

## CHARACTERS

### Appearance
White or almost white, fluffy powder.

### Solubility
Soluble in water, in ethanol (96 per cent) and in glacial acetic acid.

## IDENTIFICATION
A. Examine the chromatograms obtained in the assay.

*Results*  The retention time and size of the principal peak in the chromatogram obtained with the test solution are approximately the same as those of the principal peak in the chromatogram obtained with the reference solution.

B. Amino acid analysis (*2.2.56*). For hydrolysis use Method 1 and for analysis use Method 1.

Express the content of each amino acid in moles. Calculate the relative proportions of the amino acids, taking 1/6 of the sum of the number of moles of aspartic acid, glutamic acid, proline, glycine, arginine and phenylalanine as equal to 1. The values fall within the following limits: aspartic acid:

0.90 to 1.10; glutamic acid: 0.90 to 1.10; proline: 0.90 to 1.10; glycine: 0.90 to 1.10; arginine: 0.90 to 1.10; phenylalanine: 0.90 to 1.10; tyrosine: 0.70 to 1.05; half-cystine: 0.30 to 1.05. Lysine, isoleucine and leucine are absent; not more than traces of other amino acids are present.

## TESTS

**Specific optical rotation** (2.2.7)

– 72 to – 82 (anhydrous and acetic acid-free substance).

Dissolve 10.0 mg in a 1 per cent $V/V$ solution of *glacial acetic acid R* and dilute to 5.0 ml with the same acid.

**Related substances**

Liquid chromatography (2.2.29): use the normalisation procedure.

*Test solution*   Dissolve 1.0 mg of the substance to be examined in 2.0 ml of *water R*.

*Resolution solution*   Dissolve the contents of a vial of *oxytocin/desmopressin validation mixture CRS* in 500 µl of *water R*.

*Column:*
— *size: l* = 0.12 m, Ø = 4.0 mm;
— *stationary phase: octadecylsilyl silica gel for chromatography R* (5 µm).

*Mobile phase:*
— *mobile phase A*: 0.067 M *phosphate buffer solution pH 7.0 R*; filter and degas;
— *mobile phase B: acetonitrile for chromatography R*, mobile phase A (50:50 $V/V$); filter and degas.

| Time (min) | Mobile phase A (per cent $V/V$) | Mobile phase B (per cent $V/V$) |
|---|---|---|
| 0 - 4 | 76 | 24 |
| 4 - 18 | 76 → 58 | 24 → 42 |
| 18 - 35 | 58 → 48 | 42 → 52 |
| 35 - 40 | 48 → 76 | 52 → 24 |
| 40 - 50 | 76 | 24 |

*Flow rate*   1.5 ml/min.

*Detection*   Spectrophotometer at 220 nm.

*Injection*   50 µl.

*Retention time*   Desmopressin = about 16 min; oxytocin = about 17 min.

*System suitability*   Resolution solution:
— *resolution*: minimum 1.5 between the peaks due to desmopressin and oxytoxin.

*Limits:*
— *unspecified impurities*: for each impurity, maximum 0.5 per cent;
— *total*: maximum 1.5 per cent;
— *disregard limit*: 0.05 per cent.

**Acetic acid** (2.5.34)

3.0 per cent to 8.0 per cent.

*Test solution*   Dissolve 20.0 mg of the substance to be examined in a mixture of 5 volumes of mobile phase B and 95 volumes of mobile phase A and dilute to 10.0 ml with the same mixture of mobile phases.

**Water** (2.5.32)

Maximum 6.0 per cent, determined on 20.0 mg.

**Bacterial endotoxins** (2.6.14)

Less than 500 IU/mg, if intended for use in the manufacture of parenteral preparations without a further appropriate procedure for the removal of bacterial endotoxins.

## ASSAY

Liquid chromatography (2.2.29) as described in the test for related substances with the following modifications.

*Reference solution*   Dissolve the contents of a vial of *desmopressin CRS* in *water R* to obtain a concentration of 0.5 mg/ml.

*Mobile phase*   Mobile phase B, mobile phase A (40:60 $V/V$).

*Flow rate*   2.0 ml/min.

*Retention time*   Desmopressin = about 5 min.

Calculate the content of desmopressin ($C_{46}H_{64}N_{14}O_{12}S_2$) from the declared content of $C_{46}H_{64}N_{14}O_{12}S_2$ in *desmopressin CRS*.

## STORAGE

In an airtight container, protected from light, at a temperature of 2 °C to 8 °C. If the substance is sterile, store in a sterile, airtight, tamper-proof container.

## LABELLING

The label states:
— the mass of peptide per container;
— where applicable, that the substance is suitable for use in the manufacture of parenteral preparations.

## IMPURITIES

*Other detectable impurities*   (The following substances would, if present at a sufficient level, be detected by one or other of the tests in the monograph. They are limited by the general acceptance criterion for other/unspecified impurities and/or by the general monograph *Substances for pharmaceutical use (2034)*. It is therefore not necessary to identify these impurities for demonstration of compliance. See also *5.10. Control of impurities in substances for pharmaceutical use*): A, B, C, D, E, F, G.

A. X = Gln, Y = Asp, Z = D-Arg: [5-L-aspartic acid]desmopressin,

B. X = Glu, Y = Asn, Z = D-Arg: [4-L-glutamic acid]desmopressin,

D. X = Gln, Y = Asn, Z = L-Arg: [8-L-arginine]desmopressin,

C. R = OH, R4 = R5 = H: [9-glycine]desmopressin,

E. R = NH$_2$, R4 = CH$_2$-NH-CO-CH$_3$, R5 = H: $N^{5.4}$-[(acetylamino)methyl]desmopressin,

F. R = NH$_2$, R4 = H, R5 = CH$_2$-NH-CO-CH$_3$: $N^{4.5}$-[(acetylamino)methyl]desmopressin,

G. R = N(CH$_3$)$_2$, R4 = R5 = H: $N^{1.9}$,$N^{1.9}$-dimethyldesmopressin.

# Desogestrel

(*Ph Eur monograph 1717*)

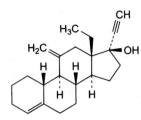

C$_{22}$H$_{30}$O       310.5       54024-22-5

**Action and use**
Progestogen.

**Preparation**
Desogestrel Tablets

*Ph Eur*

## DEFINITION
13-Ethyl-11-methylidene-18,19-dinor-17α-pregn-4-en-20-yn-17-ol.

**Content**
98.0 per cent to 102.0 per cent (dried substance).

## CHARACTERS
**Appearance**
White or almost white, crystalline powder.

**Solubility**
Practically insoluble in water, very soluble in methanol, freely soluble in anhydrous ethanol and in methylene chloride.

## IDENTIFICATION
A. Infrared absorption spectrophotometry (*2.2.24*).

*Comparison* desogestrel CRS.

B. Specific optical rotation (see Tests).

## TESTS
**Specific optical rotation** (*2.2.7*)
+ 53 to + 57 (dried substance).

Dissolve 0.250 g in *anhydrous ethanol R* and dilute to 25.0 ml with the same solvent.

**Related substances**
Liquid chromatography (*2.2.29*).

*Test solution* Dissolve 20.0 mg of the substance to be examined in 25 ml of *acetonitrile R1* and dilute to 50.0 ml with *water R*.

*Reference solution (a)* Dissolve 4 mg of *desogestrel for system suitability CRS* (containing impurities A, B, C and D) in 5 ml of *acetonitrile R1* and dilute to 10.0 ml with *water R*.

*Reference solution (b)* Dilute 1.0 ml of the test solution to 100.0 ml with a mixture of equal volumes of *acetonitrile R1* and *water R*.

*Reference solution (c)* Dilute 1.0 ml of reference solution (b) to 10.0 ml with a mixture of equal volumes of *acetonitrile R1* and *water R*.

*Reference solution (d)* Dissolve 20.0 mg of *desogestrel CRS* in 25 ml of *acetonitrile R1* and dilute to 50.0 ml with *water R*.

*Column:*
— *size:* l = 0.25 m, Ø = 4.6 mm,
— *stationary phase:* sterically protected *octadecylsilyl silica gel for chromatography R* (5 μm),
— *temperature:* 50 °C.

*Mobile phase* Water R, acetonitrile R1 (27:73 *V/V*).

*Flow rate* 1.0 ml/min.

*Detection* Spectrophotometer at 205 nm.

*Injection* 15 μl of the test solution and reference solutions (a), (b) and (c).

*Run time* 2.5 times the retention time of desogestrel.

*Identification of impurities* Use the chromatogram supplied with *desogestrel for system suitability CRS* and the chromatogram obtained with reference solution (a) to identify the peaks due to impurities A, B, C and D.

*Relative retention* With reference to desogestrel (retention time = about 22 min): impurity E = about 0.2; impurity D = about 0.25; impurity B = about 0.7; impurity A = about 0.95; impurity C = about 1.05.

*System suitability* Reference solution (a):
— *peak-to-valley ratio:* minimum 2.0, where $H_p$ = height above the baseline of the peak due to impurity C and $H_v$ = height above the baseline of the lowest point of the curve separating this peak from the peak due to desogestrel.

*Limits:*
— *correction factors:* for the calculation of content, multiply the peak area of the following impurities by the corresponding correction factor: impurity A = 1.8, impurity D = 1.5;
— *impurities A, B, C:* for each impurity, not more than twice the area of the principal peak in the chromatogram obtained with reference solution (c) (0.2 per cent);
— *impurity D:* not more than the area of the principal peak in the chromatogram obtained with reference solution (c) (0.1 per cent);
— *unspecified impurities:* for each impurity, not more than the area of the principal peak in the chromatogram obtained with reference solution (c) (0.10 per cent);
— *total:* not more than 0.5 times the area of the principal peak in the chromatogram obtained with reference solution (b) (0.5 per cent);
— *disregard limit:* 0.5 times the area of the principal peak in the chromatogram obtained with reference solution (c) (0.05 per cent).

**Loss on drying** (*2.2.32*)
Maximum 0.5 per cent, determined on 1.000 g by drying *in vacuo* at a pressure not exceeding 2 kPa.

**Sulphated ash** (*2.4.14*)
Maximum 0.1 per cent, determined on 1.0 g.

## ASSAY
Liquid chromatography (*2.2.29*) as described in the test for related substances with the following modification.

*Injection* Test solution and reference solution (d).

Calculate the percentage content of C$_{22}$H$_{30}$O from the areas of the peaks and the declared content of *desogestrel CRS*.

## IMPURITIES

*Specified impurities   A, B, C, D.*

*Other detectable impurities*   (The following substances would, if present at a sufficient level, be detected by one or other of the tests in the monograph. They are limited by the general acceptance criterion for other/unspecified impurities and/or by the general monograph *Substances for pharmaceutical use (2034)*. It is therefore not necessary to identify these impurities for demonstration of compliance. See *also 5.10. Control of impurities in substances for pharmaceutical use*): E.

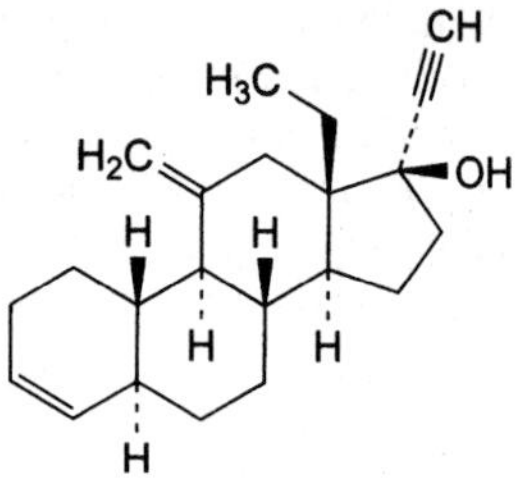

A. 13-ethyl-11-methylidene-18,19-dinor-5α,17α-pregn-3-en-20-yn-17-ol (desogestrel Δ³-isomer),

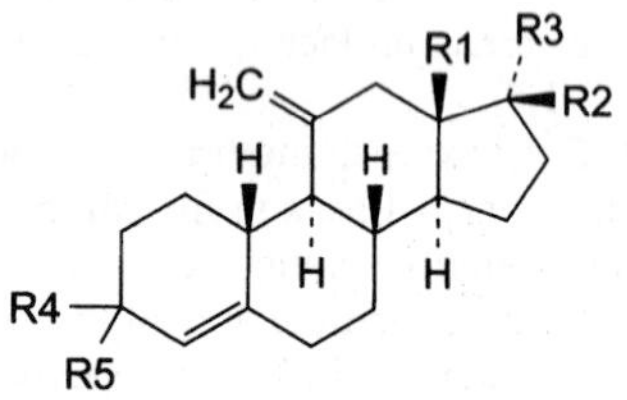

B. R1 = CH₃, R2 = OH, R3 = C≡CH, R4 = R5 = H:
11-methylidene-19-nor-17α-pregn-4-en-20-yn-17-ol,

C. R1 = C₂H₅, R2 + R3 = O, R4 = R5 = H:
13-ethyl-11-methylidenegon-4-en-17-one,

D. R1 = C₂H₅, R2 = OH, R3 = C≡CH, R4 + R5 = O:
13-ethyl-17-hydroxy-11-methylidene-18,19-dinor-17α-pregn-4-en-20-yn-3-one,

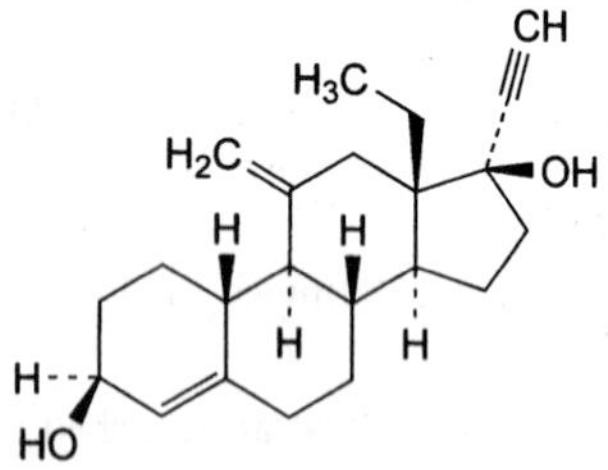

E. 13-ethyl-11-methylidene-18,19-dinor-17α-pregn-4-en-20-yne-3β,17-diol.

_____ *Ph Eur*

# Desoxycortone Acetate

(*Ph Eur monograph 0322*)

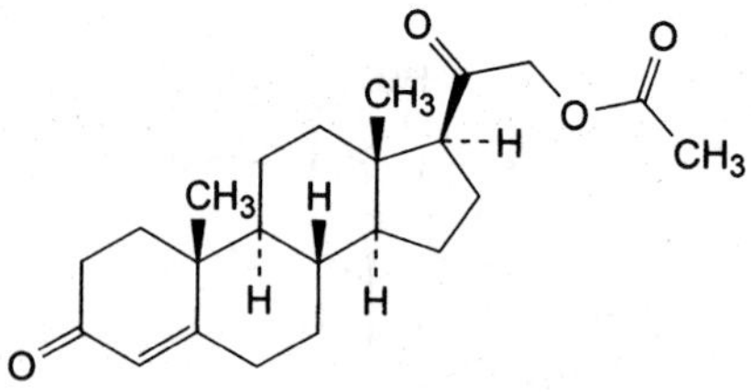

C₂₃H₃₂O₄          372.5          56-47-3

**Action and use**
Mineralocorticoid.

*Ph Eur* _____

## DEFINITION
3,20-Dioxopregn-4-en-21-yl acetate.

**Content**
97.0 per cent to 103.0 per cent (dried substance).

## CHARACTERS
**Appearance**
White or almost white, crystalline powder or colourless crystals.

**Solubility**
Practically insoluble in water, freely soluble in methylene chloride, soluble in acetone, sparingly soluble in ethanol (96 per cent), slightly soluble in propylene glycol and in fatty oils.

## IDENTIFICATION
*First identification   B, C.*

*Second identification   A, C, D, E.*

A. Melting point (*2.2.14*): 157 °C to 161 °C.

B. Infrared absorption spectrophotometry (*2.2.24*).

*Comparison   sesoxycortone acetate CRS.*

C. Thin-layer chromatography (*2.2.27*).

*Solvent mixture   methanol R, methylene chloride R (1:9 V/V).*

*Test solution*   Dissolve 10 mg of the substance to be examined in the solvent mixture and dilute to 10 ml with the solvent mixture.

*Reference solution (a)*   Dissolve 20 mg of *desoxycortone acetate CRS* in the solvent mixture and dilute to 20 ml with the solvent mixture.

*Reference solution (b)*   Dissolve 10 mg of *cortisone acetate R* in reference solution (a) and dilute to 10 ml with reference solution (a).

*Plate   TLC silica gel F₂₅₄ plate R.*

*Mobile phase*   Add a mixture of 1.2 volumes of *water R* and 8 volumes of *methanol R* to a mixture of 15 volumes of *ether R* and 77 volumes of *methylene chloride R*.

*Application*   5 µl.

*Development*   Over a path of 15 cm.

*Drying*   In air.

*Detection A*   Examine in ultraviolet light at 254 nm.

*Results A*   The principal spot in the chromatogram obtained with the test solution is similar in position and size to the principal spot in the chromatogram obtained with reference solution (a).

*Detection B* Spray with *alcoholic solution of sulphuric acid R*, heat at 120 °C for 10 min or until the spots appear, and allow to cool; examine in daylight and in ultraviolet light at 365 nm.

*Results B* The principal spot in the chromatogram obtained with the test solution is similar in position, colour in daylight, fluorescence in ultraviolet light at 365 nm and size to the principal spot in the chromatogram obtained with reference solution (a).

*System suitability* Reference solution (b):
— The chromatogram shows 2 clearly separated spots.

D. Add about 2 mg to 2 ml of *sulphuric acid R* and shake to dissolve. Within 5 min, a yellow colour develops. Add this solution to 2 ml of *water R* and mix. The resulting solution is dichroic, showing an intense blue colour by transparency, and red fluorescence that is particularly intense in ultraviolet light at 365 nm.

E. About 10 mg gives the reaction of acetyl (*2.3.1*).

## TESTS

**Specific optical rotation** (*2.2.7*)
+ 171 to + 179 (dried substance).

Dissolve 0.250 g in *dioxan R* and dilute to 25.0 ml with the same solvent.

**Related substances**
Liquid chromatography (*2.2.29*).

*Test solution* Dissolve 25.0 mg of the substance to be examined in the mobile phase and dilute to 10.0 ml with the mobile phase.

*Reference solution (a)* Dissolve 2 mg of *desoxycortone acetate CRS* and 2 mg of *betamethasone 17-valerate CRS* in the mobile phase and dilute to 200.0 ml with the mobile phase.

*Reference solution (b)* Dilute 1.0 ml of the test solution to 200.0 ml with the mobile phase.

*Column:*
— size: *l* = 0.25 m, Ø = 4.6 mm;
— stationary phase: *octadecylsilyl silica gel for chromatography R* (5 µm).

*Mobile phase* In a 1000 ml volumetric flask mix 350 ml of *water R* with 600 ml of *acetonitrile R* and allow to equilibrate; dilute to 1000 ml with *water R* and mix again.

*Flow rate* 1 ml/min.

*Detection* Spectrophotometer at 254 nm.

*Equilibration* With the mobile phase for about 30 min.

*Injection* 20 µl.

*Run time* 3 times the retention time of desoxycortone acetate.

*Retention time* Betamethasone 17-valerate = about 7.5 min; desoxycortone acetate = about 9.5 min.

*System suitability* Reference solution (a):
— resolution: minimum 4.5 between the peaks due to betamethasone 17-valerate and desoxycortone acetate; if necessary, adjust the concentration of acetonitrile in the mobile phase.

*Limits:*
— total: not more than the area of the principal peak in the chromatogram obtained with reference solution (b) (0.5 per cent);
— disregard limit: 0.1 times the area of the principal peak in the chromatogram obtained with reference solution (b) (0.05 per cent).

**Loss on drying** (*2.2.32*)
Maximum 0.5 per cent, determined on 0.500 g by drying in an oven at 105 °C.

## ASSAY
Dissolve 0.100 g in *ethanol (96 per cent) R* and dilute to 100.0 ml with the same solvent. Dilute 2.0 ml of this solution to 100.0 ml with *ethanol (96 per cent) R*. Measure the absorbance (*2.2.25*) at the absorption maximum at 240 nm.

Calculate the content of $C_{23}H_{32}O_4$ taking the specific absorbance to be 450.

## STORAGE
Protected from light.

*Ph Eur*

# Dexamethasone

(*Ph Eur monograph 0388*)

$C_{22}H_{29}FO_5$        392.5        50-02-2

**Action and use**
Glucocorticoid.

**Preparations**
Dexamethasone Eye Drops, Suspension
Dexamethasone and Neomycin Ear Spray
Dexamethasone Tablets

*Ph Eur*

## DEFINITION
9-Fluoro-11β,17,21-trihydroxy-16α-methylpregna-1,4-diene-3,20-dione.

**Content**
97.0 per cent to 103.0 per cent (dried substance).

## CHARACTERS
**Appearance**
White or almost white, crystalline powder.

**Solubility**
Practically insoluble in water, sparingly soluble in anhydrous ethanol, slightly soluble in methylene chloride.

## IDENTIFICATION
*First identification* B, C.

*Second identification* A, C, D, E.

A. Dissolve 10.0 mg in *anhydrous ethanol R* and dilute to 100.0 ml with the same solvent. Place 2.0 ml of this solution in a stoppered test tube, add 10.0 ml of *phenylhydrazine-sulphuric acid solution R*, mix and heat in a water-bath at 60 °C for 20 min. Cool immediately. The absorbance (*2.2.25*) measured at the absorption maximum at 419 nm is not less than 0.4.

B. Infrared absorption spectrophotometry (*2.2.24*).

*Comparison* dexamethasone CRS.

C. Thin-layer chromatography (2.2.27).

*Solvent mixture* methanol R, methylene chloride R (1:9 V/V).

*Test solution* Dissolve 10 mg of the substance to be examined in the solvent mixture and dilute to 10 ml with the solvent mixture.

*Reference solution (a)* Dissolve 20 mg of *dexamethasone CRS* in the solvent mixture and dilute to 20 ml with the solvent mixture.

*Reference solution (b)* Dissolve 10 mg of *betamethasone CRS* in reference solution (a) and dilute to 10 ml with reference solution (a).

*Plate* TLC silica gel $F_{254}$ plate R.

*Mobile phase* Butanol R saturated with water R, toluene R, ether R (5:10:85 V/V/V).

*Application* 5 μl.

*Development* Over a path of 15 cm.

*Drying* In air.

*Detection A* Examine in ultraviolet light at 254 nm.

*Results A* The principal spot in the chromatogram obtained with the test solution is similar in position and size to the principal spot in the chromatogram obtained with reference solution (a).

*Detection B* Spray with *alcoholic solution of sulphuric acid R*. Heat at 120 °C for 10 min or until the spots appear. Allow to cool. Examine in daylight and in ultraviolet light at 365 nm.

*Results B* The principal spot in the chromatogram obtained with the test solution is similar in position, colour in daylight, fluorescence in ultraviolet light at 365 nm and size to the principal spot in the chromatogram obtained with reference solution (a).

*System suitability* Reference solution (b):
— the chromatogram shows 2 spots which may, however, not be completely separated.

D. Add about 2 mg to 2 ml of *sulphuric acid R* and shake to dissolve. Within 5 min, a faint reddish-brown colour develops. Add this solution to 10 ml of *water R* and mix. The colour is discharged.

E. Mix about 5 mg with 45 mg of *heavy magnesium oxide R* and ignite in a crucible until an almost white residue is obtained (usually less than 5 min). Allow to cool, add 1 ml of *water R*, 0.05 ml of *phenolphthalein solution R1* and about 1 ml of *dilute hydrochloric acid R* to render the solution colourless. Filter. To a freshly prepared mixture of 0.1 ml of *alizarin S solution R* and 0.1 ml of *zirconyl nitrate solution R*, add 1.0 ml of the filtrate. Mix, allow to stand for 5 min and compare the colour of the solution with that of a blank prepared in the same manner. The test solution is yellow and the blank is red.

## TESTS

**Specific optical rotation** (2.2.7)
+ 75 to + 80 (dried substance).
Dissolve 0.250 g in *dioxan R* and dilute to 25.0 ml with the same solvent.

**Related substances**
Liquid chromatography (2.2.29).

*Test solution* Place 25.0 mg of the substance to be examined in a 10.0 ml volumetric flask, add 1.5 ml of *acetonitrile R* and then 5 ml of mobile phase A. Mix with the aid of an ultrasonic bath until complete dissolution, and dilute to 10.0 ml with mobile phase A.

*Reference solution (a)* Dissolve 2 mg of *dexamethasone CRS* and 2 mg of *methylprednisolone CRS* in mobile phase A, then dilute to 100.0 ml with mobile phase A.

*Reference solution (b)* Dilute 1.0 ml of the test solution to 100.0 ml with mobile phase A.

*Column:*
— size: $l$ = 0.25 m, Ø = 4.6 mm;
— stationary phase: octadecylsilyl silica gel for chromatography R (5 μm);
— temperature: 45 °C.

*Mobile phase:*
— mobile phase A: in a 1000 ml volumetric flask, mix 250 ml of *acetonitrile R* with 700 ml of *water R* and allow to equilibrate; dilute to 1000 ml with *water R* and mix again;
— mobile phase B: acetonitrile R;

| Time (min) | Mobile phase A (per cent V/V) | Mobile phase B (per cent V/V) |
|---|---|---|
| 0 - 15 | 100 | 0 |
| 15 - 40 | 100 → 0 | 0 → 100 |
| 40 - 41 | 0 → 100 | 100 → 0 |
| 41 - 46 | 100 | 0 |

*Flow rate* 2.5 ml/min.

*Detection* Spectrophotometer at 254 nm.

*Equilibration* With mobile phase B for at least 30 min and then with mobile phase A for 5 min; for subsequent chromatograms, use the conditions described from 40.0 min to 46.0 min.

*Injection* 20 μl; inject mobile phase A as a blank.

*Retention time* Methylprednisolone = about 11.5 min; dexamethasone = about 13 min.

*System suitability* Reference solution (a):
— resolution: minimum 2.8 between the peaks due to methylprednisolone and dexamethasone; if necessary, adjust the concentration of acetonitrile in mobile phase A.

*Limits:*
— any impurity: for each impurity, not more than 0.5 times the area of the principal peak in the chromatogram obtained with reference solution (b) (0.5 per cent);
— total: not more than the area of the principal peak in the chromatogram obtained with reference solution (b) (1 per cent);
— disregard limit: 0.05 times the area of the principal peak in the chromatogram obtained with reference solution (b) (0.05 per cent).

**Loss on drying** (2.2.32)
Maximum 0.5 per cent, determined on 0.500 g by drying in an oven at 105 °C.

## ASSAY

Dissolve 0.100 g in *ethanol (96 per cent) R* and dilute to 100.0 ml with the same solvent. Dilute 2.0 ml of this solution to 100.0 ml with *ethanol (96 per cent) R*. Measure the absorbance (2.2.25) at the absorption maximum at 238.5 nm.

Calculate the content of $C_{22}H_{29}FO_5$ taking the specific absorbance to be 394.

## STORAGE

Protected from light.

# Dexamethasone Acetate

(*Ph Eur monograph 0548*)

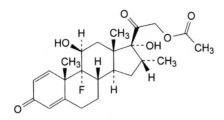

$C_{24}H_{31}FO_6$      434.5      *55812-90-3*

**Action and use**

Glucocorticoid.

*Ph Eur* _____

## DEFINITION

9-Fluoro-11β,17-dihydroxy-16α-methyl-3,20-dioxopregna-1,4-dien-21-yl acetate.

## Content

97.0 per cent to 103.0 per cent (dried substance).

## CHARACTERS

**Appearance**

White or almost white, crystalline powder.

**Solubility**

Practically insoluble in water, freely soluble in acetone and in ethanol (96 per cent), slightly soluble in methylene chloride.

It shows polymorphism (*5.9*).

## IDENTIFICATION

*First identification*  B, C.

*Second identification*  A, C, D, E, F.

A. Dissolve 10.0 mg in *anhydrous ethanol R* and dilute to 100.0 ml with the same solvent. Place 2.0 ml of this solution in a ground-glass-stoppered tube, add 10.0 ml of *phenylhydrazine-sulphuric acid solution R*, mix and heat in a water-bath at 60 °C for 20 min. Cool immediately. The absorbance (*2.2.25*) measured at the absorption maximum at 419 nm is not less than 0.35.

B. Infrared absorption spectrophotometry (*2.2.24*).

*Comparison*  dexamethasone acetate CRS.

If the spectra obtained in the solid state show differences, record new spectra using saturated solutions (about 30 g/l) in *chloroform R* in a 0.2 mm cell.

C. Thin-layer chromatography (*2.2.27*).

*Solvent mixture*  methanol R, methylene chloride R (1:9 *V/V*).

*Test solution*  Dissolve 10 mg of the substance to be examined in the solvent mixture and dilute to 10 ml with the solvent mixture.

*Reference solution (a)*  Dissolve 20 mg of *dexamethasone acetate CRS* in the solvent and dilute to 20 ml with the solvent mixture.

*Reference solution (b)*  Dissolve 10 mg of *cortisone acetate R* in reference solution (a) and dilute to 10 ml with reference solution (a).

*Plate*  TLC silica gel $F_{254}$ plate R.

*Mobile phase*  Add a mixture of 1.2 volumes of *water R* and 8 volumes of *methanol R* to a mixture of 15 volumes of *ether R* and 77 volumes of *methylene chloride R*.

*Application*  5 µl.

*Development*  Over a path of 15 cm.

*Drying*  In air.

*Detection A*  Examine in ultraviolet light at 254 nm.

*Results A*  The principal spot in the chromatogram obtained with the test solution is similar in position and size to the principal spot in the chromatogram obtained with reference solution (a).

*Detection B*  Spray with alcoholic solution of *sulphuric acid R*. Heat at 120 °C for 10 min or until the spots appear. Allow to cool. Examine in daylight and in ultraviolet light at 365 nm.

*Results B*  The principal spot in the chromatogram obtained with the test solution is similar in position, colour in daylight, fluorescence in ultraviolet light at 365 nm and size to the principal spot in the chromatogram obtained with reference solution (a).

*System suitability*  Reference solution (b):

— the chromatogram shows 2 clearly separated spots.

D. Add about 2 mg to 2 ml of *sulphuric acid R* and shake to dissolve. Within 5 min, a faint reddish-brown colour develops. Add this solution to 10 ml of *water R* and mix. The colour is discharged and a clear solution remains.

E. Mix about 5 mg with 45 mg of *heavy magnesium oxide R* and ignite in a crucible until an almost white residue is obtained (usually less than 5 min). Allow to cool, add 1 ml of *water R*, 0.05 ml of *phenolphthalein solution R1* and about 1 ml of *dilute hydrochloric acid R* to render the solution colourless. Filter. To a freshly prepared mixture of 0.1 ml of *alizarin S solution R* and 0.1 ml of *zirconyl nitrate solution R*, add 1.0 ml of the filtrate. Mix, allow to stand for 5 min and compare the colour of the solution with that of a blank prepared in the same manner. The test solution is yellow and the blank is red.

F. About 10 mg gives the reaction of acetyl (*2.3.1*).

## TESTS

**Specific optical rotation** (*2.2.7*)

+ 84 to + 90 (dried substance).

Dissolve 0.250 g in *dioxan R* and dilute to 25.0 ml with the same solvent.

**Related substances**

Liquid chromatography (*2.2.29*).

*Test solution*  Dissolve 25.0 mg of the substance to be examined in about 4 ml of *acetonitrile R* and dilute to 10.0 ml with *water R*.

*Reference solution (a)*  Dissolve 2 mg of *dexamethasone acetate CRS* and 2 mg of *betamethasone acetate CRS* in the mobile phase and dilute to 100.0 ml with the mobile phase.

*Reference solution (b)*  Dilute 1.0 ml of the test solution to 100.0 ml with the mobile phase.

*Column:*

— *size: l* = 0.25 m, Ø = 4.6 mm;

— *stationary phase: octadecylsilyl silica gel for chromatography R* (5 µm).

*Mobile phase*  In a 1000 ml volumetric flask mix 380 ml of *acetonitrile R* with 550 ml of *water R* and allow to equilibrate; dilute to 1000 ml with *water R* and mix again.

*Flow rate*  1 ml/min.

*Detection*  Spectrophotometer at 254 nm.

*Equilibration*  With the mobile phase for about 30 min.

*Injection*  20 µl.

*Run time*  1.5 times the retention time of dexamethasone acetate.

*Retention time* Betamethasone acetate = about 19 min; dexamethasone acetate = about 22 min.

*System suitability* Reference solution (a):
— *resolution*: minimum 3.3 between the peaks due to betamethasone acetate and dexamethasone acetate; if necessary, adjust the concentration of acetonitrile in the mobile phase.

*Limits:*
— *any impurity*: for each impurity, not more than 0.5 times the area of the principal in the chromatogram obtained with reference solution (b) (0.5 per cent);
— *total*: not more than the area of the principal in the chromatogram obtained with reference solution (b) (1.0 per cent);
— *disregard limit*: 0.05 times the area of the principal peak in the chromatogram obtained with reference solution (b) (0.05 per cent).

### Loss on drying (2.2.32)
Maximum 0.5 per cent, determined on 0.500 g by drying *in vacuo* in an oven at 105 °C.

### ASSAY
Dissolve 0.100 g in *ethanol (96 per cent) R* and dilute to 100.0 ml with the same solvent. Dilute 2.0 ml of this solution to 100.0 ml with *ethanol (96 per cent) R*. Measure the absorbance (*2.2.25*) at the absorption maximum at 238.5 nm.

Calculate the content of $C_{24}H_{31}FO_6$ taking the specific absorbance to be 357.

### STORAGE
Protected from light.

_____ *Ph Eur*

# Dexamethasone Isonicotinate

(*Ph Eur monograph 2237*)

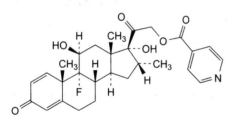

$C_{28}H_{32}FNO_6$          497.6          2265-67-7

### Action and use
Glucocorticoid.

*Ph Eur* _____

### DEFINITION
9-Fluoro-11β,17-dihydroxy-16α-methyl-3,20-dioxopregna-1,4-dien-21-yl pyridine-4-carboxylate.

### Content
99.0 per cent to 101.0 per cent (dried substance).

### CHARACTERS
**Appearance**
White or almost white crystalline powder.

**Solubility**
Practically insoluble in water, slightly soluble in anhydrous ethanol and in acetone.

### IDENTIFICATION
Infrared absorption spectrophotometry (*2.2.24*).

*Comparison* dexamethasone isonicotinate CRS.

### TESTS
**Specific optical rotation** (*2.2.7*)
+ 142 to + 146 (dried substance).

Suspend 0.200 g in 4.0 ml of *ethyl acetate R* and dilute to 20.0 ml with *ethanol (96 per cent) R*. Treat in an ultrasonic bath until a clear solution is obtained.

**Related substances**
Liquid chromatography (*2.2.29*). *Prepare solutions immediately before use.*

*Test solution* Suspend 50.0 mg in 7 ml of *acetonitrile R* and dilute to 10.0 ml with *water R*. Treat in an ultrasonic bath until a clear solution is obtained.

*Reference solution (a)* Suspend 5.0 mg of *dexamethasone CRS* and 5.0 mg of *dexamethasone acetate CRS* in 70 ml of *acetonitrile R*, add 1.0 ml of the test solution and dilute to 100.0 ml with *water R*. Treat in an ultrasonic bath until a clear solution is obtained.

*Reference solution (b)* Dilute 1.0 ml of reference solution (a) to 10.0 ml with *water R*.

*Reference solution (c)* Suspend 5 mg of *dexamethasone isonicotinate for impurity C identification CRS* in 0.7 ml of *acetonitrile R* and dilute to 1 ml with *water R*. Treat in an ultrasonic bath until a clear solution is obtained.

*Column:*
— *size: l* = 0.125 m, Ø = 4.0 mm,
— *stationary phase: octadecylsilyl silica gel for chromatography R* (5 μm).

*Mobile phase:*
— *mobile phase A: water R,*
— *mobile phase B: acetonitrile R,*

| Time (min) | Mobile phase A (per cent V/V) | Mobile phase B (per cent V/V) |
|---|---|---|
| 0 - 2 | 68 | 32 |
| 2 - 20 | 68 → 50 | 32 → 50 |
| 20 - 25 | 50 → 68 | 50 → 32 |
| 25 - 35 | 68 | 32 |

*Flow rate* 1.2 ml/min.

*Detection* Spectrophotometer at 240 nm.

*Injection* 10 μl.

*Identification of impurities* Use the chromatogram supplied with *dexamethasone isonicotinate for impurity C identification CRS* and the chromatogram obtained with reference solution (c) to identify the peak due to impurity C.

*Relative retention* With reference to dexamethasone isonicotinate (retention time = about 12 min):
impurity A = about 0.4; impurity C = about 0.6; impurity B = about 0.8.

*System suitability* Reference solution (a):
— *resolution*: minimum 5.0 between the peaks due to impurity B and dexamethasone isonicotinate.

*Limits:*
— *impurity A*: not more than 5 times the area of the corresponding peak in the chromatogram obtained with reference solution (b) (0.5 per cent),
— *impurity B*: not more than 3 times the area of the corresponding peak in the chromatogram obtained with reference solution (b) (0.3 per cent),

— *impurity C*: not more than 3 times the area of the peak
due to dexamethasone isonicotinate in the chromatogram
obtained with reference solution (b) (0.3 per cent),

— *unspecified impurities*: for each impurity, not more than the
area of the peak due to dexamethasone isonicotinate in
the chromatogram obtained with reference solution (b)
(0.1 per cent),

— *total*: not more than 8 times the area of the peak due to
dexamethasone isonicotinate in the chromatogram
obtained with reference solution (b) (0.8 per cent),

— *disregard limit*: 0.5 times the area of the peak due to
dexamethasone isonicotinate in the chromatogram
obtained with reference solution (b) (0.05 per cent).

### Loss on drying (*2.2.32*)

Maximum 1.0 per cent, determined on 1.000 g by drying in
an oven at 102 °C under high vacuum for 4 h.

### ASSAY

Dissolve 0.400 g in a mixture of 5 ml of *anhydrous formic
acid R* and 50 ml of *glacial acetic acid R*. Titrate with *0.1 M
perchloric acid*, determining the end-point potentiometrically
(*2.2.20*).

1 ml of *0.1 M perchloric acid* is equivalent to 49.76 mg of
$C_{28}H_{32}FNO_6$.

### IMPURITIES

*Specified impurities   A, B, C.*

A. dexamethasone,

B. dexamethasone acetate,

C. 9-fluoro-11,17-dihydroxy-16-methylpregna-1,4-diene-
3,20-dione (21-deoxydexamethasone).

_____ *Ph Eur*

# Dexamethasone Sodium Phosphate

(*Ph Eur monograph 0549*)

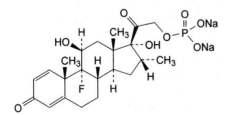

$C_{22}H_{28}FNa_2O_8P$          516.4          *2392-39-4*

### Action and use

Glucocorticoid.

### Preparation

Dexamethasone Sodium Phosphate Eye Drops, Solution

*Ph Eur*

### DEFINITION

9-Fluoro-11β,17-dihydroxy-16α-methyl-3,20-dioxopregna-
1,4-dien-21-yl disodium phosphate.

### Content

97.0 per cent to 103.0 per cent (anhydrous substance).

### CHARACTERS

#### Appearance

White or almost white, very hygroscopic powder.

#### Solubility

Freely soluble in water, slightly soluble in ethanol
(96 per cent), practically insoluble in methylene chloride.

It shows polymorphism (*5.9*).

### IDENTIFICATION

*First identification   B, C.*

*Second identification   A, C, D, E, F.*

A. Dissolve 10.0 mg in 5 ml of *water R* and dilute to
100.0 ml with *anhydrous ethanol R*. Place 2.0 ml of this
solution in a ground-glass-stoppered tube, add 10.0 ml of
*phenylhydrazine-sulphuric acid solution R*, mix and heat in a
water-bath at 60 °C for 20 min. Cool immediately. The
absorbance (*2.2.25*) measured at the absorption maximum
at 419 nm is at least 0.20.

B. Infrared absorption spectrophotometry (*2.2.24*).

*Comparison   dexamethasone sodium phosphate CRS.*

If the spectra obtained in the solid state show differences,
dissolve the substance to be examined and the reference
substance separately in the minimum volume of *ethanol
(96 per cent) R*, evaporate to dryness on a water-bath and
record new spectra using the residues.

C. Thin-layer chromatography (*2.2.27*).

*Test solution   Dissolve 10 mg of the substance to be
examined in methanol R and dilute to 10 ml with the same
solvent.*

*Reference solution (a)   Dissolve 20 mg of dexamethasone
sodium phosphate CRS in methanol R and dilute to 20 ml with
the same solvent.*

*Reference solution (b)   Dissolve 10 mg of prednisolone sodium
phosphate CRS in reference solution (a) and dilute to 10 ml
with reference solution (a).*

*Plate   TLC silica gel F_{254} plate R.*

*Mobile phase   Glacial acetic acid R, water R, butanol R
(20:20:60 V/V/V).*

*Application   5 μl.*

*Development   Over a path of 15 cm.*

*Drying   In air.*

*Detection A   Examine in ultraviolet light at 254 nm.*

*Results A   The principal spot in the chromatogram obtained
with the test solution is similar in position and size to the
principal spot in the chromatogram obtained with reference
solution (a).*

*Detection B   Spray with alcoholic solution of sulphuric acid R.
Heat at 120 °C for 10 min or until the spots appear. Allow
to cool. Examine in daylight and in ultraviolet light at
365 nm.*

*Results B   The principal spot in the chromatogram obtained
with the test solution is similar in position, colour in daylight,
fluorescence in ultraviolet light at 365 nm and size to the
principal spot in the chromatogram obtained with reference
solution (a).*

*System suitability*  Reference solution (b):
— the chromatogram shows 2 spots which may, however, not be completely separated.

D. Add about 2 mg to 2 ml of *sulphuric acid R* and shake to dissolve. Within 5 min, a faint yellowish-brown colour develops. Add this solution to 10 ml of *water R* and mix. The colour fades and a clear solution remains.

E. Mix about 5 mg with 45 mg of *heavy magnesium oxide R* and ignite in a crucible until an almost white residue is obtained (usually less than 5 min). Allow to cool, add 1 ml of *water R*, 0.05 ml of *phenolphthalein solution R1* and about 1 ml of *dilute hydrochloric acid R* to render the solution colourless. Filter. To a freshly prepared mixture of 0.1 ml of *alizarin S solution R* and 0.1 ml of *zirconyl nitrate solution R*, add 1.0 ml of the filtrate. Mix, allow to stand for 5 min and compare the colour of the solution with that of a blank prepared in the same manner. The test solution is yellow and the blank is red.

F. To 40 mg add 2 ml of *sulphuric acid R* and heat gently until white fumes are evolved, add *nitric acid R* dropwise, continue the heating until the solution is almost colourless and cool. Add 2 ml of *water R*, heat until white fumes are again evolved, cool, add 10 ml of *water R* and neutralise to *red litmus paper R* with *dilute ammonia R1*. The solution gives reaction (a) of sodium (*2.3.1*) and reaction (b) of phosphates (*2.3.1*).

## TESTS

### Solution S
Dissolve 1.0 g in *carbon dioxide-free water R* and dilute to 20 ml with the same solvent.

### Appearance of solution
Solution S is clear (*2.2.1*) and not more intensely coloured than reference solution $B_7$ (*2.2.2, Method II*).

### pH (*2.2.3*)
7.5 to 9.5.

Dilute 1 ml of solution S to 5 ml with *carbon dioxide-free water R*.

### Specific optical rotation (*2.2.7*)
+ 75 to + 83 (anhydrous substance).

Dissolve 0.250 g in *water R* and dilute to 25.0 ml with the same solvent.

### Related substances
Liquid chromatography (*2.2.29*).

*Test solution*  Dissolve 25.0 mg of the substance to be examined in the mobile phase and dilute to 10.0 ml with the mobile phase.

*Reference solution (a)*  Dissolve 2 mg of *dexamethasone sodium phosphate CRS* and 2 mg of *betamethasone sodium phosphate CRS* in the mobile phase, then dilute to 100.0 ml with the mobile phase.

*Reference solution (b)*  Dilute 1.0 ml of the test solution to 100.0 ml with the mobile phase.

*Column:*
— *size: l* = 0.25 m, Ø = 4.6 mm;
— *stationary phase: octadecylsilyl silica gel for chromatography R* (5 μm).

*Mobile phase*  In a 250 ml conical flask, weigh 1.360 g of *potassium dihydrogen phosphate R* and 0.600 g of *hexylamine R*, mix and allow to stand for 10 min and then dissolve in 182.5 ml of *water R*; add 67.5 ml of *acetonitrile R*, mix and filter (0.45 μm).

*Flow rate*  1 ml/min.

*Detection*  Spectrophotometer at 254 nm.

*Equilibration*  With the mobile phase for about 45 min.

*Injection*  20 μl.

*Run time*  Twice the retention time of dexamethasone sodium phosphate.

*Retention time*  impurity B = about 12.5 min; dexamethasone sodium phosphate = about 14 min.

*System suitability*  Reference solution (a):
— *resolution*: minimum 2.2 between the peaks due to impurity B and dexamethasone sodium phosphate; if necessary, adjust slightly the concentration of acetonitrile or increase the concentration of water in the mobile phase.

*Limits:*
— *impurities A, B*: for each impurity, not more than 0.5 times the area of the principal peak in the chromatogram obtained with reference solution (b) (0.5 per cent);
— *total*: not more than the area of the principal peak in the chromatogram obtained with reference solution (b) (1 per cent);
— *disregard limit*: 0.05 times the area of the principal peak in the chromatogram obtained with reference solution (b) (0.05 per cent).

### Inorganic phosphates
Maximum 1 per cent.

Dissolve 50 mg in *water R* and dilute to 100 ml with the same solvent. To 10 ml of this solution add 5 ml of *molybdovanadic reagent R*, mix and allow to stand for 5 min. Any yellow colour in the solution is not more intense than that in a standard prepared at the same time in the same manner using 10 ml of *phosphate standard solution (5 ppm $PO_4$) R*.

### Ethanol
Gas chromatography (*2.2.28*).

*Internal standard solution*  Dilute 1.0 ml of *propanol R* to 100.0 ml with *water R*.

*Test solution*  Dissolve 0.50 g of the substance to be examined in 5.0 ml of the internal standard solution and dilute to 10.0 ml with *water R*.

*Reference solution*  Dilute 1.0 g of *anhydrous ethanol R* to 100.0 ml with *water R*. To 2.0 ml of this solution add 5.0 ml of the internal standard solution and dilute to 10.0 ml with *water R*.

*Column:*
— *size: l* = 1 m, Ø = 3.2 mm;
— *stationary phase: ethylvinylbenzene-divinylbenzene copolymer R1* (150-180 μm).

*Carrier gas*  *Nitrogen for chromatography R.*

*Flow rate*  30 ml/min.

*Temperature:*
— *column*: 150 °C;
— *injection port*: 250 °C;
— *detector*: 280 °C.

*Detection*  Flame ionisation.

*Injection*  2 μl.

*Limit:*
— *ethanol*: maximum 3.0 per cent *m/m*.

### Ethanol and water
Maximum 13.0 per cent *m/m* for the sum of the percentage contents.

Determine the water content using 0.200 g (2.5.12). Add the percentage content of water and the percentage content of ethanol obtained in the test for ethanol.

**ASSAY**

Dissolve 0.100 g in *water R* and dilute to 100.0 ml with the same solvent. Dilute 10.0 ml of this solution to 500.0 ml with *water R*. Measure the absorbance (2.2.25) at the absorption maximum at 241.5 nm.

Calculate the content of $C_{22}H_{28}FNa_2O_8P$ taking the specific absorbance to be 303.

**STORAGE**

In an airtight container, protected from light.

**IMPURITIES**

*Specified impurities   A, B.*

A. dexamethasone,

B. betamethasone sodium phosphate.

_____ *Ph Eur*

# Dexamfetamine Sulphate

$(C_9H_{13}N)_2,H_2SO_4$         368.5         *51-63-8*

**Action and use**

Amfetamine.

**Preparation**

Dexamfetamine Tablets

**DEFINITION**

Dexamfetamine Sulphate is (S)-α-methylphenethylamine sulphate. It contains not less than 99.0% and not more than 100.5% of $(C_9H_{13}N)_2,H_2SO_4$, calculated with reference to the dried substance.

**CHARACTERISTICS**

A white or almost white, crystalline powder.

Freely soluble in *water*; slightly soluble in *ethanol (96%)*; practically insoluble in *ether*.

**IDENTIFICATION**

A. Dissolve 1 g in 50 ml of *water*, add 10 ml of 5M *sodium hydroxide* and 0.5 ml of *benzoyl chloride* and shake. Repeat the addition of *benzoyl chloride* in 0.5 ml quantities until no further precipitate is produced. The *melting point* of the precipitate, after recrystallising twice from *ethanol (50%)*, is about 157°, Appendix V A.

B. Dissolve 2 mg in 4 ml of *water*, add 1 ml of 1M *hydrochloric acid*, 2 ml of *diazotised nitroaniline solution*, 4 ml of 1M *sodium hydroxide* and 2 ml of *butan-1-ol*, shake and allow to separate. A red colour is produced in the butanol layer (distinction from methylamfetamine).

C. Yields the reactions characteristic of *sulphates*, Appendix VI.

**TESTS**

**Acidity or alkalinity**

Dissolve 0.5 g in 10 ml of *water* and titrate with 0.01M *hydrochloric acid VS* or 0.01M *sodium hydroxide VS*

using *methyl red solution* as indicator. Not more than 0.1 ml of 0.01M *hydrochloric acid VS* or 0.01M *sodium hydroxide VS* is required to change the colour of the solution.

**Specific optical rotation**

In an 8.0% w/v solution, +19.5 to +22.0, calculated with reference to the dried substance, Appendix V F.

**Loss on drying**

When dried to constant weight at 105°, loses not more than 1.0% of its weight. Use 1 g.

**Sulphated ash**

Not more than 0.1%, Appendix IX A.

**ASSAY**

Dissolve 0.4 g in 120 ml of *water*, add 2 ml of 5M *sodium hydroxide* and distil into 50 ml of 0.1M *hydrochloric acid VS*, continuing the distillation until only 5 ml of liquid is left in the distillation flask. Titrate the excess of acid with 0.1M *sodium hydroxide VS* using *methyl red solution* as indicator. Each ml of 0.1M *hydrochloric acid VS* is equivalent to 18.42 mg of $(C_9H_{13}N)_2,H_2SO_4$.

# Dexchlorpheniramine Maleate

*(Ph Eur monograph 1196)*

$C_{16}H_{19}ClN_2,C_4H_4O_4$         390.9         *2438-32-6*

**Action and use**

Histamine $H_1$ receptor antagonist; antihistamine.

*Ph Eur* _____

**DEFINITION**

(3S)-3-(4-Chlorophenyl)-*N,N*-dimethyl-3-(pyridin-2-yl)propan-1-amine (Z)-butenedioate.

**Content**

98.0 per cent to 100.5 per cent (dried substance).

**CHARACTERS**

**Appearance**

White or almost white, crystalline powder.

**Solubility**

Very soluble in water, freely soluble in ethanol (96 per cent), in methanol and in methylene chloride.

**IDENTIFICATION**

*First identification:   A, C, E.*

*Second identification   A, B, D, E.*

A. Specific optical rotation (see Tests).

B. Melting point (2.2.14): 110 °C to 115 °C.

C. Infrared absorption spectrophotometry (2.2.24).

*Preparation*   Discs of *potassium bromide R*.

*Comparison*   dexchlorpheniramine maleate CRS.

D. Thin-layer chromatography (2.2.27).

*Test solution* Dissolve 0.10 g of the substance to be examined in *methanol R* and dilute to 5.0 ml with the same solvent.

*Reference solution* Dissolve 56 mg of *maleic acid R* in *methanol R* and dilute to 10 ml with the same solvent.

*Plate* *TLC silica gel F$_{254}$ plate R*.

*Mobile phase* *water R, anhydrous formic acid R, methanol R, di-isopropyl ether R* (3:7:20:70 *V/V/V/V*).

*Application* 5 μl.

*Development* Over a path of 12 cm.

*Drying* In a current of air for a few minutes.

*Detection* Examine in ultraviolet light at 254 nm.

*Results* The chromatogram obtained with the test solution shows 2 clearly separated spots. The upper spot is similar in position and size to the spot in the chromatogram obtained with the reference solution.

E. To 0.15 g in a porcelain crucible add 0.5 g of *anhydrous sodium carbonate R*. Heat over an open flame for 10 min. Allow to cool. Take up the residue with 10 ml of *dilute nitric acid R* and filter. To 1 ml of the filtrate add 1 ml of *water R*. The solution gives reaction (a) of chlorides (*2.3.1*).

## TESTS
### Solution S
Dissolve 2.0 g in *water R* and dilute to 20.0 ml with the same solvent.

### Appearance of solution
Solution S is clear (*2.2.1*) and not more intensely coloured than reference solution BY$_6$ (*2.2.2, Method II*).

### pH (*2.2.3*)
4.5 to 5.5.

Dissolve 0.20 g in 20 ml of *water R*.

### Specific optical rotation (*2.2.7*)
+ 22 to + 23 (dried substance), determined on solution S.

### Related substances
Gas chromatography (*2.2.28*).

*Test solution* Dissolve 10.0 mg of the substance to be examined in 1.0 ml of *methylene chloride R*.

*Reference solution* Dissolve 5.0 mg of *brompheniramine maleate CRS* in 0.5 ml of *methylene chloride R* and add 0.5 ml of the test solution. Dilute 0.5 ml of this solution to 50.0 ml with *methylene chloride R*.

*Column:*
— *material*: glass;
— *size*: $l = 2.3$ m, Ø = 2 mm;
— *stationary phase*: acid- and base- washed *silanised diatomaceous earth for gas chromatography R* (135-175 μm) impregnated with 3 per cent *m/m* of a mixture of 50 per cent of poly(dimethyl)siloxane and 50 per cent of poly(diphenyl)siloxane.

*Carrier gas* *Nitrogen for chromatography R*.

*Flow rate* 20 ml/min.

*Temperature:*
— *column*: 205 °C;
— *injection port and detector*: 250 °C.

*Detection* Flame ionisation.

*Injection* 1 μl.

*Run time* 2.5 times the retention time of dexchlorpheniramine.

*System suitability* Reference solution:
— *resolution*: minimum 1.5 between the peaks due to dexchlorpheniramine and brompheniramine.

*Limits:*
— *impurities A, B*: for each impurity, not more than 0.8 times the area of the peak due to dexchlorpheniramine in the chromatogram obtained with the reference solution (0.4 per cent);
— *total*: not more than twice the area of the peak due to dexchlorpheniramine in the chromatogram obtained with the reference solution (1 per cent).

### Enantiomeric purity
Liquid chromatography (*2.2.29*).

*Test solution* Dissolve 10.0 mg of the substance to be examined in 3 ml of *water R*. Add a few drops of *concentrated ammonia R* until an alkaline reaction is produced. Shake with 5 ml of *methylene chloride R*. Separate the layers. Evaporate the lower, methylene chloride layer to an oily residue on a water-bath. Dissolve the oily residue in *2-propanol R* and dilute to 10.0 ml with the same solvent.

*Reference solution (a)* Dissolve 10.0 mg of *dexchlorpheniramine maleate CRS* in 3 ml of *water R*. Add a few drops of *concentrated ammonia R* until an alkaline reaction is produced. Shake with 5 ml of *methylene chloride R*. Separate the layers. Evaporate the lower, methylene chloride layer to an oily residue on a water-bath. Dissolve the oily residue in *2-propanol R* and dilute to 10.0 ml with the same solvent.

*Reference solution (b)* Dissolve 10.0 mg of *chlorphenamine maleate CRS* in 3 ml of *water R*. Add a few drops of *concentrated ammonia R* until an alkaline reaction is produced. Shake with 5 ml of *methylene chloride R*. Separate the layers. Evaporate the lower, methylene chloride layer to an oily residue on a water-bath. Dissolve the oily residue in *2-propanol R* and dilute to 10.0 ml with the same solvent.

*Reference solution (c)* Dilute 1.0 ml of the test solution to 50 ml with *2-propanol R*.

*Column:*
— *size*: $l = 0.25$ m, Ø = 4.6 mm;
— *stationary phase*: amylose derivative of silica gel for chromatography R.

*Mobile phase* *diethylamine R, 2-propanol R, hexane R* (3:20:980 *V/V/V*).

*Flow rate* 1 ml/min.

*Detection* Spectrophotometer at 254 nm.

*Injection* 10 μl.

Under these conditions the peak of the (*S*)-isomer appears first.

*System suitability:*
— *resolution*: minimum 1.5 between the peaks due to the (*R*)-enantiomer and to the (*S*)-enantiomer in the chromatogram obtained with reference solution (b);
— the retention times of the principal peaks in the chromatograms obtained with the test solution and reference solution (a) are identical ((*S*)-enantiomer).

*Limits:*
— *(R)-enantiomer*: not more than the area of the principal peak in the chromatogram obtained with reference solution (c) (2 per cent);
— *any other impurity*: for each impurity, not more than 0.25 times the area of the principal peak in the chromatogram obtained with reference solution (c) (0.5 per cent).

### Heavy metals (*2.4.8*)
Maximum 20 ppm.

1.0 g complies with test C. Prepare the reference solution using 2 ml of *lead standard solution (10 ppm Pb) R.*

**Loss on drying** (*2.2.32*)
Maximum 0.5 per cent, determined on 1.000 g by drying in an oven at 65 °C for 4 h.

**Sulphated ash** (*2.4.14*)
Maximum 0.1 per cent, determined on 1.0 g.

**ASSAY**
Dissolve 0.150 g in 25 ml of *anhydrous acetic acid R.* Titrate with *0.1 M perchloric acid*, determining the end-point potentiometrically (*2.2.20*).

1 ml of *0.1 M perchloric acid* is equivalent to 19.54 mg of $C_{20}H_{23}ClN_2O_4$.

**STORAGE**
Protected from light.

**IMPURITIES**
*Specified impurities A, B.*

A. (3*RS*)-*N*,*N*-dimethyl-3-phenyl-3-(pyridin-2-yl)propan-1-amine,

B. (3*R*)-3-(4-chlorophenyl)-*N*,*N*-dimethyl-3-(pyridin-2-yl)propan-1-amine.

*Ph Eur*

# Dexpanthenol

(*Ph Eur monograph 0761*)

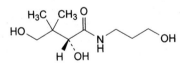

$C_9H_{19}NO_4$       205.3       *81-13-0*

**Action and use**
Vitamin B₅ analogue.

*Ph Eur*

**DEFINITION**
Dexpanthenol contains not less than 98.0 per cent and not more than the equivalent of 101.0 per cent of (2*R*)-2,4-dihydroxy-*N*-(3-hydroxypropyl)-3,3-dimethylbutanamide, calculated with reference to the anhydrous substance.

**CHARACTERS**
A colourless or slightly yellowish, viscous hygroscopic liquid, or a white or almost white, crystalline powder, very soluble in water, freely soluble in ethanol (96 per cent).

**IDENTIFICATION**
*First identification   A, B.*

*Second identification   A, C, D.*

A. It complies with the test for specific optical rotation (see Tests).

B. Examine by infrared absorption spectrophotometry (*2.2.24*), comparing with the spectrum obtained with *dexpanthenol CRS.* Examine the substances using discs prepared as follows: dissolve the substance to be examined and the reference substance separately in 1.0 ml of *anhydrous ethanol R* to obtain a concentration of 5 mg/ml. Place dropwise 0.5 ml of this solution on a disc of *potassium bromide R.* Dry the disc at 100-105 °C for 15 min.

C. Examine the chromatograms obtained in the test for 3-aminopropanol. The principal spot in the chromatogram obtained with test solution (b) is similar in position, colour and size to the principal spot in the chromatogram obtained with reference solution (a).

D. To 1 ml of solution S (see Tests) add 1 ml of *dilute sodium hydroxide solution R* and 0.1 ml of *copper sulphate solution R.* A blue colour develops.

**TESTS**
**Solution S**
Dissolve 2.500 g in *carbon dioxide-free water R* and dilute to 50.0 ml with the same solvent.

**Appearance of solution**
Solution S is clear (*2.2.1*) and not more intensely coloured than reference solution B₆ (*2.2.2, Method II*).

**pH** (*2.2.3*)
The pH of solution S is not greater than 10.5.

**Specific optical rotation** (*2.2.7*)
The specific optical rotation is + 29.0 to + 32.0, determined on solution S and calculated with reference to the anhydrous substance.

**3-Aminopropanol**
Examine by thin-layer chromatography (*2.2.27*), using *silica gel G R* as the coating substance.

*Test solution (a)*   Dissolve 0.25 g of the substance to be examined in *anhydrous ethanol R* and dilute to 5 ml with the same solvent.

*Test solution (b)*   Dilute 1 ml of test solution (a) to 10 ml with *anhydrous ethanol R.*

*Reference solution (a)*   Dissolve the contents of a vial of *dexpanthenol CRS* in 1.0 ml of *anhydrous ethanol R* to obtain a concentration of 5 mg/ml.

*Reference solution (b)*   Dissolve 25 mg of *3-aminopropanol R* in *anhydrous ethanol R* and dilute to 100 ml with the same solvent.

Apply separately to the plate 10 µl of each solution. Develop over a path of 15 cm using a mixture of 20 volumes of *concentrated ammonia R*, 25 volumes of *methanol R* and 55 volumes of *butanol R.* Allow the plate to dry in air, spray with a 100 g/l solution of *trichloroacetic acid R* in *methanol R* and heat at 150 °C for 10 min. Spray with a 1 g/l solution of *ninhydrin R* in *methanol R* and heat at 120 °C until a colour appears. Any spot due to 3-aminopropanol in the chromatogram obtained with test solution (a) is not more intense than the spot in the chromatogram obtained with reference solution (b) (0.5 per cent).

**Heavy metals** (*2.4.8*)

12 ml of solution S complies with limit test A for heavy metals (20 ppm). Prepare the reference solution using *lead standard solution (1 ppm Pb) R*.

**Water** (*2.5.12*)

Not more than 1.0 per cent, determined on 1.000 g.

**Sulphated ash** (*2.4.14*)

Not more than 0.1 per cent, determined on 1.0 g.

**ASSAY**

To 0.400 g add 50.0 ml of *0.1 M perchloric acid*. Boil under a reflux condenser for 5 h protected from humidity. Allow to cool. Add 50 ml of *dioxan R* by rinsing the condenser, protected from humidity. Add 0.2 ml of *naphtholbenzein solution R* and titrate with *0.1 M potassium hydrogen phthalate* until the colour changes from green to yellow. Carry out a blank titration.

1 ml of *0.1 M perchloric acid* is equivalent to 20.53 mg of $C_9H_{19}NO_4$.

**STORAGE**

In an airtight container.

_____ *Ph Eur*

# Dextran 1 for Injection

★ ★ ★
★ ★
★ ★
★ ★ ★

(*Ph Eur monograph 1506*)

**Action and use**

Plasma substitute.

*Ph Eur* _____

**DEFINITION**

Low-molecular-weight fraction of dextran, consisting of a mixture of isomaltooligosaccharides.

*Average relative molecular mass*: about 1000.

**PRODUCTION**

It is obtained by hydrolysis and fractionation of dextrans produced by fermentation of sucrose using *Leuconostoc mesenteroides* strain NRRL B-512 = CIP 78 59 or substrains thereof (for example *L. mesenteroides* B-512 F = NCTC 10817).

It is prepared in conditions designed to minimise the risk of microbial contamination.

**CHARACTERS**

**Appearance**

White or almost white hygroscopic powder.

**Solubility**

Very soluble in water, very slightly soluble in ethanol (96 per cent).

**IDENTIFICATION**

A. Dissolve 3.000 g in *water R*, heat on a water-bath and dilute to 100.0 ml with the same solvent. The specific optical rotation (*2.2.7*) is + 148 to + 164, calculated with reference to the dried substance. Dry an aliquot of the solution first on a water-bath and then to constant weight *in vacuo* at 70 °C. Calculate the dextran content after correction for the content of sodium chloride.

B. Infrared absorption spectrophotometry (*2.2.24*).

*Preparation* To 1-2 mg add 1 or a few drops of *water R*. Grind in an agate mortar for 1-2 min. Add about 300 mg of *potassium bromide R* and mix to a slurry but do not grind. Dry *in vacuo* at 40 °C for 15 min. Crush the residue. If it is not dry, dry for another 15 min. Prepare a disc using *potassium bromide R*.

*Comparison* Repeat the operations using *dextran 1 CRS*.

*Blank* Run the infrared spectrum with a blank disc using *potassium bromide R* in the reference beam.

C. Molecular-mass distribution (see Tests).

**TESTS**

**Solution S**

Dissolve 7.5 g in *carbon dioxide-free water R*, heat on a water-bath and dilute to 50 ml with the same solvent.

**Absorbance** (*2.2.25*)

Maximum 0.12, determined at 375 nm on solution S.

**Acidity or alkalinity**

To 10 ml of solution S add 0.1 ml of *phenolphthalein solution R*. The solution is colourless. Add 0.2 ml of *0.01 M sodium hydroxide*. The solution is pink. Add 0.4 ml of *0.01 M hydrochloric acid*. The solution is colourless. Add 0.1 ml of *methyl red solution R*. The solution is red or orange.

**Nitrogen-containing substances**

Maximum 110 ppm of N.

Carry out the determination of nitrogen by sulphuric acid digestion (*2.5.9*), using 0.200 g and heating for 2 h. Collect the distillate in a mixture of 0.5 ml of *bromocresol green solution R*, 0.5 ml of *methyl red solution R* and 20 ml of *water R*. Titrate with *0.01 M hydrochloric acid*. Not more than 0.15 ml of *0.01 M hydrochloric acid* is required to change the colour of the indicator.

**Sodium chloride**

Maximum 1.5 per cent.

Accurately weigh 3-5 g and dissolve in 100 ml of *water R*. Add 0.3 ml of *potassium chromate solution R* and titrate with *0.1 M silver nitrate* until the yellowish-white colour changes to reddish-brown.

1 ml of *0.1 M silver nitrate* is equivalent to 5.844 mg of NaCl.

**Molecular-mass distribution**

Size-exclusion chromatography (*2.2.30*).

*Test solution* Dissolve 6.0-6.5 mg of the substance to be examined in 1.0 ml of the mobile phase.

*Reference solution (a)* Dissolve 6.0-6.5 mg of *dextran 1 CRS* in 1.0 ml of the mobile phase.

*Reference solution (b)* Dissolve the content of an ampoule of *isomaltooligosaccharide CRS* in 1 ml of the mobile phase, and mix. This corresponds to approximately 45 μg of isomaltotriose (3 glucose units), approximately 45 μg of isomaltononaose (9 glucose units), and approximately 60 μg of sodium chloride per 100 μl.

*Column* 2 columns coupled in series:
— *size: l* = 0.30 m, Ø = 10 mm;
— *stationary phase*: dextran covalently bound to highly cross-linked porous agarose beads, allowing resolution of oligosaccharides in the molecular mass range of 180 to 3000;
— *temperature*: 20-25 °C.

*Mobile phase* 2.92 g/l solution of *sodium chloride R*.

*Flow rate* 0.07-0.08 ml/min maintained constant to ± 1 per cent.

*Detection* Differential refractometer.

*Injection*   100 µl.

*Identification of peaks*   Use the chromatogram obtained with reference solution (b) to identify the peaks due to isomaltotriose, isomaltononaose and sodium chloride.

Determine the peak areas. Disregard any peak due to sodium chloride. Calculate the average relative molecular mass $M_w$ and the amount of the fraction with less than 3 and more than 9 glucose units, of *dextran 1 CRS* and of the substance to be examined, using the following expression:

$$M_w = \sum w_i \times m_i$$

$M_w$ = average molecular mass of the dextran;
$m_i$ = molecular mass of oligosaccharide $i$;
$w_i$ = weight proportion of oligosaccharide $i$.

Use the following $m_i$ values for the calculation:

| Oligosaccharide *i* | $m_i$ |
| --- | --- |
| glucose | 180 |
| isomaltose | 342 |
| isomaltotriose | 504 |
| isomaltotetraose | 666 |
| isomaltopentaose | 828 |
| isomaltohexaose | 990 |
| isomaltoheptaose | 1152 |
| isomaltooctaose | 1314 |
| isomaltononaose | 1476 |
| isomaltodecaose | 1638 |
| isomaltoundecaose | 1800 |
| isomaltododecaose | 1962 |
| isomaltotridecaose | 2124 |
| isomaltotetradecaose | 2286 |
| isomaltopentadecaose | 2448 |
| isomaltohexadecaose | 2610 |
| isomaltoheptadecaose | 2772 |
| isomaltooctadecaose | 2934 |
| isomaltononadecaose | 3096 |

*System suitability*   The values obtained for *dextran 1 CRS* are within the values stated on the label.

*Limits:*
— *average molecular mass ($M_w$)*: 850 to 1150;
— *fraction with less than 3 glucose units*: less than 15 per cent;
— *fraction with more than 9 glucose units*: less than 20 per cent

**Heavy metals** *(2.4.8)*
Maximum 10 ppm.

Dilute 20 ml of solution S to 30 ml with *water R*. 12 ml of solution complies with test A. Prepare the reference solution using *lead standard solution (1 ppm Pb) R*.

**Loss on drying** *(2.2.32)*
Maximum 5.0 per cent, determined on 5.000 g by drying in an oven at 105 °C for 5 h.

**Bacterial endotoxins** *(2.6.14)*
Less than 25 IU/g.

**Microbial contamination**
TAMC: acceptance criterion $10^2$ CFU/g *(2.6.12)*.

*Ph Eur*

# Dextran 40 for Injection

*(Ph Eur monograph 0999)*

**Action and use**
Plasma substitute.

**Preparation**
Dextran 40 Intravenous Infusion

*Ph Eur*

**DEFINITION**
Mixture of polysaccharides, principally of the α-1,6-glucan type.
*Average relative molecular mass*: about 40 000.

**PRODUCTION**
It is obtained by hydrolysis and fractionation of dextrans produced by fermentation of sucrose using *Leuconostoc mesenteroides* strain NRRL B-512 = CIP 78.59 or substrains thereof (for example *L. mesenteroides* B-512F = NCTC 10817).

It is prepared in conditions designed to minimise the risk of microbial contamination.

**CHARACTERS**
**Appearance**
White or almost white powder.

**Solubility**
Very soluble in water, very slightly soluble in ethanol (96 per cent).

**IDENTIFICATION**
A. Specific optical rotation *(2.2.7)*: + 195 to + 201 (dried substance).

Dissolve 1.0 g in *water R*, heating on a water-bath, and dilute to 50.0 ml with the same solvent.

B. Infrared absorption spectrophotometry *(2.2.24)*.

*Comparison*   dextran CRS.

C. Molecular-mass distribution (see Tests).

**TESTS**
**Solution S**
Dissolve 5.0 g in *distilled water R*, heating on a water-bath, and dilute to 50 ml with the same solvent.

**Appearance of solution**
Solution S is clear *(2.2.1)* and colourless *(2.2.2, Method II)*.

**Acidity or alkalinity**
To 10 ml of solution S add 0.1 ml of *phenolphthalein solution R*. The solution remains colourless. Add 0.2 ml of *0.01 M sodium hydroxide*. The solution is red. Add 0.4 ml of *0.01 M hydrochloric acid*. The solution is colourless. Add 0.1 ml of *methyl red solution R*. The solution is red or orange.

**Nitrogen-containing substances**
Maximum 110 ppm N.

Carry out the determination of nitrogen by sulphuric acid digestion *(2.5.9)*, using 0.200 g and heating for 2 h. Collect the distillate in a mixture of 0.5 ml of *bromocresol green solution R*, 0.5 ml of *methyl red solution R* and 20 ml of *water R*. Titrate with *0.01 M hydrochloric acid*. Not more than

0.15 ml of *0.01 M hydrochloric acid* is required to change the colour of the indicator.

**Residual solvents**

Gas chromatography (*2.2.28*).

*Internal standard   propanol R.*

*Test solution*   Dissolve 5 g of the substance to be examined in 100 ml of *water R* and distil. Collect the first 45 ml of the distillate, add 1 ml of a 25 g/l solution of *propanol R* and dilute to 50 ml with *water R*.

*Reference solution*   Mix 0.5 ml of a 25 g/l solution of *anhydrous ethanol R*, 0.5 ml of a 25 g/l solution of *propanol R* and 0.5 ml of a 2.5 g/l solution of *methanol R* and dilute to 25.0 ml with *water R*.

*Column:*
— *material*: stainless steel;
— *size*: l = 1.8 m, Ø = 2 mm;
— *stationary phase*: *ethylvinylbenzene-divinylbenzene copolymer R* (125-150 μm).

*Carrier gas   nitrogen for chromatography R.*

*Flow rate   25 ml/min.*

*Temperature:*
— *column*: 190 °C;
— *injection port*: 240 °C;
— *detector*: 210 °C.

*Detection   Flame ionisation.*

*Injection   The chosen volume of each solution.*

*Limits:*
— *ethanol*: not more than the area of the corresponding peak in the chromatogram obtained with the reference solution (0.5 per cent);
— *methanol*: not more than the area of the corresponding peak in the chromatogram obtained with the reference solution (0.05 per cent);
— *sum of solvents other than ethanol, methanol and propanol*: not more than the area of the peak due to the internal standard (0.5 per cent, calculated as propanol).

**Molecular-mass distribution** (*2.2.39*)

The average molecular mass ($M_w$) is 35 000 to 45 000. The average molecular mass of the 10 per cent high fraction is not greater than 110 000. The average molecular mass of the 10 per cent low fraction is not less than 7000.

**Heavy metals** (*2.4.8*)

Maximum 10 ppm.

12 ml of solution S complies with test A. Prepare the reference solution using *lead standard solution (1 ppm Pb) R*.

**Loss on drying** (*2.2.32*)

Maximum 7.0 per cent, determined on 0.200 g by heating in an oven at 105 ± 2 °C for 5 h.

**Sulphated ash** (*2.4.14*)

Maximum 0.3 per cent, determined on 0.50 g.

**Bacterial endotoxins** (*2.6.14*)

Less than 10 IU/g.

**Microbial contamination**

TAMC: acceptance criterion $10^2$ CFU/g (*2.6.12*).

_____ *Ph Eur*

# Dextran 60 for Injection

(*Ph Eur monograph 1000*)

**Action and use**

Plasma substitute.

*Ph Eur* _____

## DEFINITION

Mixture of polysaccharides, principally of the α-1,6-glucan type.

*Average relative molecular mass*: about 60 000.

## PRODUCTION

It is obtained by hydrolysis and fractionation of dextrans produced by fermentation of sucrose using *Leuconostoc mesenteroides* strain NRRL B-512 = CIP 78.59 or substrains thereof (for example *L. mesenteroides* B-512F = NCTC 10817).

It is prepared in conditions designed to minimise the risk of microbial contamination.

## CHARACTERS

**Appearance**

White or almost white powder.

**Solubility**

Very soluble in water, very slightly soluble in ethanol (96 per cent).

## IDENTIFICATION

A. Specific optical rotation (*2.2.7*): + 195 to + 201 (dried substance).

Dissolve 1.0 g in *water R*, heating on a water-bath, and dilute to 50.0 ml with the same solvent.

B. Infrared absorption spectrophotometry (*2.2.24*).

*Comparison   dextran CRS.*

C. Molecular-mass distribution (see Tests).

## TESTS

**Solution S**

Dissolve 5.0 g in *distilled water R*, heating on a water-bath, and dilute to 50 ml with the same solvent.

**Appearance of solution**

Solution S is clear (*2.2.1*) and colourless (*2.2.2, Method II*).

**Acidity or alkalinity**

To 10 ml of solution S add 0.1 ml of *phenolphthalein solution R*. The solution remains colourless. Add 0.2 ml of *0.01 M sodium hydroxide*. The solution is red. Add 0.4 ml of *0.01 M hydrochloric acid*. The solution is colourless. Add 0.1 ml of *methyl red solution R*. The solution is red or orange.

**Nitrogen-containing substances**

Maximum 110 ppm of N.

Carry out the determination of nitrogen by sulphuric acid digestion (*2.5.9*), using 0.200 g and heating for 2 h. Collect the distillate in a mixture of 0.5 ml of *bromocresol green solution R*, 0.5 ml of *methyl red solution R* and 20 ml of *water R*. Titrate with *0.01 M hydrochloric acid*. Not more than 0.15 ml of *0.01 M hydrochloric acid* is required to change the colour of the indicator.

**Residual solvents**

Gas chromatography (*2.2.28*).

*Internal standard   propanol R.*

*Test solution*   Dissolve 5 g of the substance to be examined in 100 ml of *water R* and distil. Collect the first 45 ml of the distillate, add 1 ml of a 25 g/l solution of *propanol R* and dilute to 50 ml with *water R*.

*Reference solution* Mix 0.5 ml of a 25 g/l solution of *anhydrous ethanol R*, 0.5 ml of a 25 g/l solution of *propanol R* and 0.5 ml of a 2.5 g/l solution of *methanol R* and dilute to 25.0 ml with *water R*.

*Column:*
— *material*: stainless steel;
— *size*: $l = 1.8$ m, $\emptyset = 2$ mm;
— *stationary phase*: ethylvinylbenzene-divinylbenzene copolymer R (125-150 µm).

*Carrier gas* nitrogen for chromatography R.

*Flow rate* 25 ml/min.

*Temperature:*
— *column*: 190 °C;
— *injection port*: 240 °C;
— *detector*: 210 °C.

*Detection* Flame ionisation.

*Injection* The chosen volume of each solution.

*Limits:*
— *ethanol*: not more than the area of the corresponding peak in the chromatogram obtained with the reference solution (0.5 per cent);
— *methanol*: not more than the area of the corresponding peak in the chromatogram obtained with the reference solution (0.05 per cent);
— *sum of solvents other than ethanol, methanol and propanol*: not more than the area of the peak due to the internal standard (0.5 per cent, calculated as propanol).

**Molecular-mass distribution** (2.2.39)
The average molecular mass ($M_w$) is 54 000 to 66 000. The average molecular mass of the 10 per cent high fraction is not greater than 180 000. The average molecular mass of the 10 per cent low fraction is not less than 14 000.

**Heavy metals** (2.4.8)
Maximum 10 ppm.

12 ml of solution S complies with test A. Prepare the reference solution using *lead standard solution (1 ppm Pb) R*.

**Loss on drying** (2.2.32)
Maximum 7.0 per cent, determined on 0.200 g by heating in an oven at 105 ± 2 °C for 5 h.

**Sulphated ash** (2.4.14)
Maximum 0.3 per cent, determined on 0.50 g.

**Bacterial endotoxins** (2.6.14)
Less than 16 IU/g.

**Microbial contamination**
TAMC: acceptance criterion $10^2$ CFU/g (2.6.12).

_____ *Ph Eur*

# Dextran 70 for Injection

*(Ph Eur monograph 1001)*

**Action and use**
Plasma substitute.

**Preparation**
Dextran 70 Intravenous Infusion

*Ph Eur* _____

## DEFINITION
Mixture of polysaccharides, principally of the α-1,6-glucan type.
*Average relative molecular mass*: about 70 000.

## PRODUCTION
It is obtained by hydrolysis and fractionation of dextrans produced by fermentation of sucrose using *Leuconostoc mesenteroides* strain NRRL B-512 = CIP 78.59 or substrains thereof (for example *L. mesenteroides* B-512F = NCTC 10817).

It is prepared in conditions designed to minimise the risk of microbial contamination.

## CHARACTERS
**Appearance**
White or almost white powder.

**Solubility**
Very soluble in water, very slightly soluble in ethanol (96 per cent).

## IDENTIFICATION
A. Specific optical rotation (2.2.7): + 195 to + 201 (dried substance).

Dissolve 1.0 g in *water R*, heating on a water-bath, and dilute to 50.0 ml with the same solvent.

B. Infrared absorption spectrophotometry (2.2.24).

*Comparison* dextran CRS.

C. Molecular-mass distribution (see Tests).

## TESTS
**Solution S**
Dissolve 5.0 g in *distilled water R*, heating on a water-bath, and dilute to 50 ml with the same solvent.

**Appearance of solution**
Solution S is clear (2.2.1) and colourless (2.2.2, Method II).

**Acidity or alkalinity**
To 10 ml of solution S add 0.1 ml of *phenolphthalein solution R*. The solution remains colourless. Add 0.2 ml of *0.01 M sodium hydroxide*. The solution is red. Add 0.4 ml of *0.01 M hydrochloric acid*. The solution is colourless. Add 0.1 ml of *methyl red solution R*. The solution is red or orange.

**Nitrogen-containing substances**
Maximum 110 ppm of N.

Carry out the determination of nitrogen by sulphuric acid digestion (2.5.9), using 0.200 g and heating for 2 h. Collect the distillate in a mixture of 0.5 ml of *bromocresol green solution R*, 0.5 ml of *methyl red solution R* and 20 ml of *water R*. Titrate with *0.01 M hydrochloric acid*. Not more than 0.15 ml of *0.01 M hydrochloric acid* is required to change the colour of the indicator.

**Residual solvents**
Gas chromatography (2.2.28).

*Internal standard* propanol R.

*Test solution*   Dissolve 5 g of the substance to be examined in 100 ml of *water R* and distil. Collect the first 45 ml of the distillate, add 1 ml of a 25 g/l solution of *propanol R* and dilute to 50 ml with *water R*.

*Reference solution*   Mix 0.5 ml of a 25 g/l solution of *anhydrous ethanol R*, 0.5 ml of a 25 g/l solution of *propanol R* and 0.5 ml of a 2.5 g/l solution of *methanol R* and dilute to 25.0 ml with *water R*.

*Column:*
— *material*: stainless steel;
— *size*: $l$ = 1.8 m, Ø = 2 mm;
— *stationary phase*: ethylvinylbenzene-divinylbenzene copolymer R (125-150 μm).

*Carrier gas*   nitrogen for chromatography R.

*Flow rate*   25 ml/min.

*Temperature:*
— column: 190 °C;
— injection port: 240 °C;
— detector: 210 °C.

*Detection*   Flame ionisation.

*Injection*   The chosen volume of each solution.

*Limits:*
— *ethanol*: not more than the area of the corresponding peak in the chromatogram obtained with the reference solution (0.5 per cent);
— *methanol*: not more than the area of the corresponding peak in the chromatogram obtained with the reference solution (0.05 per cent);
— *sum of solvents other than ethanol, methanol and propanol*: not more than the area of the peak due to the internal standard (0.5 per cent, calculated as propanol).

**Molecular-mass distribution** (*2.2.39*)
The average molecular mass ($M_w$) is 64 000 to 76 000. The average molecular mass of the 10 per cent high fraction is not greater than 185 000. The average molecular mass of the 10 per cent low fraction is not less than 15 000.

**Heavy metals** (*2.4.8*)
Maximum 10 ppm.

12 ml of solution S complies with test A. Prepare the reference solution using *lead standard solution (1 ppm Pb) R*.

**Loss on drying** (*2.2.32*)
Maximum 7.0 per cent, determined on 0.200 g by heating in an oven at 105 ± 2 °C for 5 h.

**Sulphated ash** (*2.4.14*)
Maximum 0.3 per cent, determined on 0.50 g.

**Bacterial endotoxins** (*2.6.14*)
Less than 16 IU/g.

**Microbial contamination**
TAMC: acceptance criterion $10^2$ CFU/g (*2.6.12*).

*Ph Eur*

# Dextranomer

(*Ph Eur monograph 2238*)

56087-11-7

**Action and use**
Fluid absorber; treatment of burns, wounds and skin ulcers; preparation for skin grafting.

*Ph Eur*

**DEFINITION**
Three-dimensional network made of dextran chains $O,O'$-cross-linked with 2-hydroxypropane-1,3-diyl bridges and $O$-substituted with 2,3-dihydroxypropyl and 2-hydroxy-1-(hydroxymethyl)ethyl groups.

**CHARACTERS**
**Appearance**
White or almost white, spherical beads.

**Solubility**
Practically insoluble in water. It swells in water and electrolyte solutions.

**PRODUCTION**
The absorption capacity is determined using a 9.0 g/l solution of *sodium chloride R* containing 20 μl/l of *polysorbate 20 R* or another suitable solution, with a suitable, validated method.

The particle size is controlled to a minimum of 80 per cent of the number of dry beads within 100 μm to 300 μm and a maximum of 7 per cent of their number below 100 μm using a suitable, validated method.

**IDENTIFICATION**
A. The substance to be examined is practically insoluble in *water R*. It swells in *water R*.

B. Infrared absorption spectrophotometry (*2.2.24*).

*Preparation*   Grind the substance to be examined in *acetone R*. Evaporate the solvent at room temperature and use the residue.

*Comparison*   dextranomer CRS.

**TESTS**
**pH** (*2.2.3*)
5.3 to 7.5.

Introduce 0.50 g to 30 ml of a freshly prepared 74.6 g/l solution of *potassium chloride R*. Allow to stand for 2 min. Determine the pH on the mucilage obtained.

**Boron**
Maximum 30 ppm.

Inductively coupled plasma-atomic emission spectroscopy (ICP-AES) (*2.2.57*).

*Test solution*   Introduce 3.0 g into a platinum dish, moisten with 5 ml of a 32.1 g/l solution of *magnesium nitrate R* in a mixture of equal volumes of *ethanol (96 per cent) R* and *distilled water R*. Evaporate to dryness on a water-bath. Ignite at 550 °C for 5 h. Take up the residue with 5 ml of *6 M hydrochloric acid R* and transfer to a 50 ml volumetric flask. Add about 20 ml of *distilled water R* and allow to digest for 1 h on a water-bath. Allow to cool and dilute to 50.0 ml with *distilled water R*.

*Standard solutions*   Prepare the standard solutions using a solution of *boric acid R* containing 10 ppm of boron. Proceed as described for the test solution.

*Wavelength*   249.773 nm.

**Heavy metals** (2.4.8)

Maximum 30 ppm.

1.0 g complies with test F. Prepare the reference solution using 3 ml of *lead standard solution (10 ppm Pb) R*.

**Loss on drying** (2.2.32)

Maximum 10.0 per cent.

To 1.000 g, add *distilled water R* dropwise until the sample has completely swollen. Dry in an oven at 105 °C.

**Sulphated ash** (2.4.14)

Maximum 0.4 per cent, determined on 1.0 g.

**Microbial contamination**

Total aerobic microbial count (TAMC) (2.6.12) not more than $10^2$ CFU per gram, determined using the pour-plate method.

_____ *Ph Eur*

# Dextrin

(*Ph Eur monograph 1507*)

**Action and use**

Excipient.

*Ph Eur* _____

## DEFINITION

Maize, potato or cassava starch partly hydrolysed and modified by heating with or without the presence of acids, alkalis or pH-control agents.

## CHARACTERS

**Appearance**

White or almost white, free-flowing powder.

**Solubility**

Very soluble in boiling water forming a mucilaginous solution, slowly soluble in cold water, practically insoluble in ethanol (96 per cent).

## IDENTIFICATION

A. Suspend 1 g in 50 ml of *water R*, boil for 1 min and cool. To 1 ml of the solution add 0.05 ml of *iodine solution R1*. A dark blue or reddish-brown colour is produced, which disappears on heating.

B. Centrifuge 5 ml of the mucilage obtained in identification test A. To the upper layer add 2 ml of *dilute sodium hydroxide solution R* and, dropwise with shaking, 0.5 ml of *copper sulphate solution R* and boil. A red precipitate is produced.

C. It is very soluble in boiling *water R*, forming a mucilaginous solution.

## TESTS

**pH** (2.2.3)

2.0 to 8.0.

Disperse 5.0 g in 100 ml of *carbon dioxide-free water R*.

**Chlorides**

Maximum 0.2 per cent.

Dissolve 2.5 g in 50 ml of boiling *water R*, dilute to 100 ml with *water R* and filter. Dilute 1 ml of the filtrate to 15 ml, add 1 ml of *dilute nitric acid R*, pour the mixture as a single addition into 1 ml of *silver nitrate solution R2* and allow to stand for 5 min protected from light. When viewed transversely against a black background any opalescence produced is not more intense than that obtained by treating a mixture of 10 ml of *chloride standard solution (5 ppm Cl) R* and 5 ml of *water R*, prepared in the same manner.

**Reducing sugars**

Maximum 10 per cent, calculated as glucose $C_6H_{12}O_6$.

To a quantity of dextrin equivalent to 2.0 g (dried substance) add 100 ml of *water R*, shake for 30 min, dilute to 200.0 ml with *water R* and filter. To 10.0 ml of *alkaline cupri-tartaric solution R* add 20.0 ml of the filtrate, mix, and heat on a hot plate adjusted to bring the solution to boil within 3 min. Boil for 2 min, and cool immediately. Add 5 ml of a 300 g/l solution of *potassium iodide R* and 10 ml of *1 M sulphuric acid*, mix, and titrate immediately with *0.1 M sodium thiosulphate*, using *starch solution R*, added towards the end of the titration, as indicator. Repeat the procedure beginning with "To 10.0 ml of...", using, in place of the filtrate, 20.0 ml of a 1 g/l solution of *glucose R*, accurately prepared. Perform a blank titration. $(V_B - V_U)$ is not greater than $(V_B - V_S)$, in which $V_B$, $V_U$ and $V_S$ are the number of millilitres of *0.1 M sodium thiosulphate* consumed in the titrations of the blank, the dextrin and the glucose, respectively.

**Heavy metals** (2.4.8)

Maximum 20 ppm.

1.0 g complies with test C. Prepare the reference solution using 2 ml of *lead standard solution (10 ppm Pb) R*.

**Loss on drying** (2.2.32)

Maximum 13.0 per cent, determined on 1.000 g by drying at 130-135 °C for 90 min.

**Sulphated ash** (2.4.14)

Maximum 0.5 per cent, determined on 1.0 g.

## FUNCTIONALITY-RELATED CHARACTERISTICS

*This section provides information on characteristics that are recognised as being relevant control parameters for one or more functions of the substance when used as an excipient (see chapter 5.15). This section is a non-mandatory part of the monograph and it is not necessary to verify the characteristics to demonstrate compliance. Control of these characteristics can however contribute to the quality of a medicinal product by improving the consistency of the manufacturing process and the performance of the medicinal product during use. Where control methods are cited, they are recognised as being suitable for the purpose, but other methods can also be used. Wherever results for a particular characteristic are reported, the control method must be indicated.*

*The following characteristics may be relevant for dextrin used as filler and binder, in tablets and capsules.*

**Particle-size distribution** (2.9.31 or 2.9.38).

**Powder flow** (2.9.36).

*The following characteristic may be relevant for dextrin used as viscosity-increasing agent.*

**Apparent viscosity** (2.2.10)

Typically 100 mPa·s to 350 mPa·s (dried substance), depending on the grade of dextrin.

In a beaker, prepare a 10-50 per cent slurry so that the viscosity value ranges from 100 mPa·s to 350 mPa·s. The total mass of the sample plus water must be 600 g. Mix with a plastic rod to obtain a homogeneous slurry. Place the beaker in a water-bath at 100 ± 1 °C. Introduce the paddle of a stirrer into the beaker and close the beaker with a lid. Start agitation at 250 rpm as rapidly as possible and carry on for exactly 30 min. Transfer the paste immediately to the beaker to be used for viscosity measurement, placed in a water-bath at 40 ± 1 °C. Stir until the temperature in the beaker is 40 ± 1 °C then measure the apparent viscosity using spindle no. 2 and a rotation speed of 100 rpm.

_____ *Ph Eur*

# Dextromethorphan Hydrobromide

*(Ph Eur monograph 0020)*

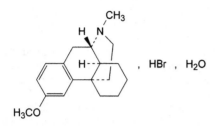

$C_{18}H_{26}BrNO,H_2O$     370.3     *6700-34-1*

## Action and use
Opioid receptor agonist; cough suppressant.

*Ph Eur* _____

## DEFINITION
*ent*-3-Methoxy-17-methylmorphinan hydrobromide monohydrate.

## Content
99.0 per cent to 101.0 per cent (anhydrous substance).

## CHARACTERS
### Appearance
Almost white, crystalline powder.

### Solubility
Sparingly soluble in water, freely soluble in alcohol.

### mp
About 125 °C, with decomposition.

## IDENTIFICATION
*First identification* A, B, D.

*Second identification* A, C, D.

A. It complies with the test for specific optical rotation (see Tests).

B. Infrared absorption spectrophotometry (*2.2.24*).

*Preparation* Discs.

*Comparison* dextromethorphan hydrobromide CRS.

C. Thin-layer chromatography (*2.2.27*).

*Test solution* Dissolve 25 mg of the substance to be examined in *methanol R* and dilute to 10 ml with the same solvent.

*Reference solution* Dissolve 25 mg of *dextromethorphan hydrobromide CRS* in *methanol R* and dilute to 10 ml with the same solvent.

*Plate* TLC silica gel G plate R.

*Mobile phase* concentrated ammonia R, methylene chloride R, methanol R, ethyl acetate R, toluene R (2:10:13:20:55 *V/V/V/V/V*).

*Application* 5 µl.

*Development* Over 2/3 of the plate.

*Drying* In air.

*Detection* Spray with *potassium iodobismuthate solution R2*.

*Results* The principal spot in the chromatogram obtained with the test solution is similar in position and size to the principal spot in the chromatogram obtained with the reference solution.

D. It gives reaction (a) of bromides (*2.3.1*).

## TESTS
### Solution S
Dissolve 1.0 g in *alcohol R* and dilute to 20 ml with the same solvent.

### Appearance of solution
Solution S is clear (*2.2.1*) and colourless (*2.2.2, Method II*).

### Acidity or alkalinity
Dissolve 0.4 g in *carbon dioxide-free water R* with gentle heating, cool and dilute to 20 ml with the same solvent. Add 0.1 ml of *methyl red solution R* and 0.2 ml of *0.01 M sodium hydroxide*. The solution is yellow. Not more than 0.4 ml of *0.01 M hydrochloric acid* is required to change the colour of the indicator to red.

### Specific optical rotation (*2.2.7*)
+ 28 to + 30 ( anhydrous substance).

Dissolve 0.200 g in *0.1 M hydrochloric acid* and dilute to 10.0 ml with the same acid.

### Related substances
Liquid chromatography (*2.2.29*).

*Test solution* Dissolve 10.0 mg of the substance to be examined in the mobile phase and dilute to 10.0 ml with the mobile phase.

*Reference solution (a)* Dissolve 2 mg of *dextromethorphan impurity A CRS* in 2 ml of the test solution and dilute to 25.0 ml with the mobile phase.

*Reference solution (b)* Dilute 1.0 ml of the test solution to 200.0 ml with the mobile phase.

*Column:*
— size: $l$ = 0.25 m, Ø = 4.6 mm,
— stationary phase: octadecylsilyl silica gel for chromatography R (5 µm).

*Mobile phase* Dissolve 3.11 g of *docusate sodium R* in a mixture of 400 ml of *water R* and 600 ml of *acetonitrile R*. Add 0.56 g of *ammonium nitrate R*. Adjust to apparent pH 2.0 with *glacial acetic acid R*.

*Flow rate* 1.0 ml/min.

*Detection* Spectrophotometer at 280 nm.

*Injection* 20 µl.

*Run time* Twice the retention time of dextromethorphan.

*Relative retention* With reference to dextromethorphan (retention time = about 21.9 min): impurity B = about 0.44; impurity C = about 0.85; impurity D = about 0.90; impurity A = about 1.13.

*System suitability* Reference solution (a):
— resolution: minimum 1.5 between the peaks due to impurity A and dextromethorphan.

*Limits:*
— correction factor: for the calculation of content, multiply the peak area of impurity C by 0.2,
— any impurity: not more than the area of the principal peak in the chromatogram obtained with reference solution (b) (0.5 per cent), and not more than 1 such peak has an area greater than half the area of the principal peak in the chromatogram obtained with reference solution (b) (0.25 per cent),

— *total*: not more than twice the area of the principal peak in the chromatogram obtained with reference solution (b) (1 per cent),

— *disregard limit*: 0.1 times the area of the principal peak in the chromatogram obtained with reference solution (b) (0.05 per cent).

### *N,N*-Dimethylaniline
Maximum 10 ppm.

Dissolve 0.5 g with heating in 20 ml of *water R*. Allow to cool, add 2 ml of *dilute acetic acid R* and 1 ml of a 10 g/l solution of *sodium nitrite R* and dilute to 25 ml with *water R*. The solution is not more intensely coloured than a reference solution prepared at the same time in the same manner using 20 ml of a 0.25 mg/l solution of *dimethylaniline R*.

### Water (*2.5.12*)
4.0 per cent to 5.5 per cent, determined on 0.200 g.

### Sulphated ash (*2.4.14*)
Maximum 0.1 per cent, determined on 1.0 g.

### ASSAY
Dissolve 0.300 g in a mixture of 5.0 ml of *0.01 M hydrochloric acid* and 20 ml of *alcohol R*. Titrate with *0.1 M sodium hydroxide*, determining the end-point potentiometrically (*2.2.20*). Read the volume added between the 2 points of inflexion.

1 ml of *0.1 M sodium hydroxide* is equivalent to 35.23 mg of $C_{18}H_{26}BrNO$.

### STORAGE
Protected from light.

### IMPURITIES

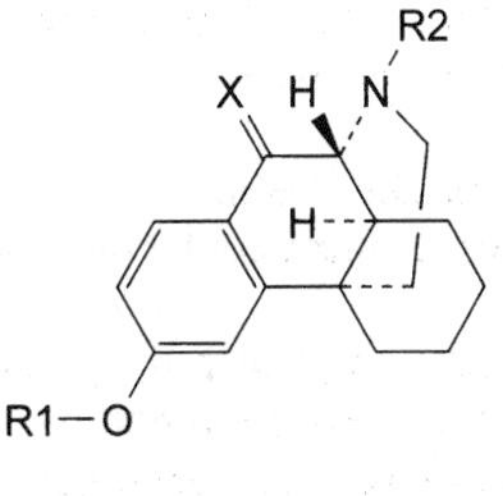

A. R1 = $CH_3$, R2 = H, X = $H_2$: *ent*-3-methoxymorphinan,

B. R1 = H, R2 = $CH_3$, X = $H_2$: *ent*-17-methylmorphinan-3-ol,

C. R1 = R2 = $CH_3$, X = O: *ent*-3-methoxy-17-methylmorphinan-10-one,

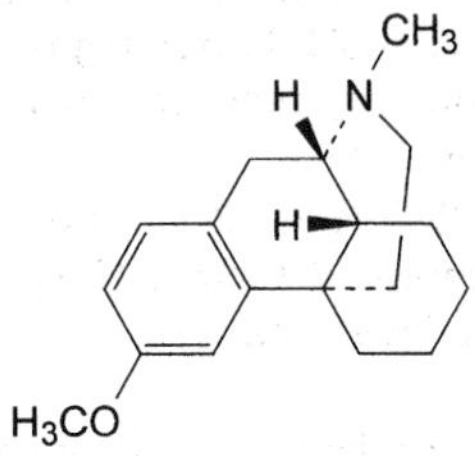

D. *ent*-(14*S*)-3-methoxy-17-methylmorphinan.

*Ph Eur*

# Dextromoramide Tartrate

(*Ph Eur monograph 0021*)

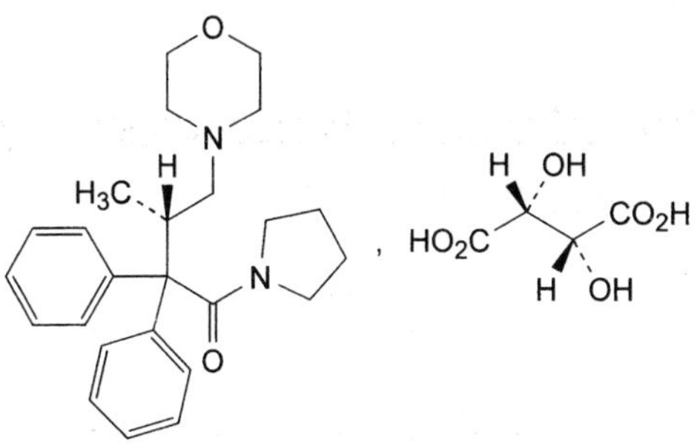

$C_{25}H_{32}N_2O_2,C_4H_6O_6$     542.6     *2922-44-3*

### Action and use
Opioid receptor agonist; analgesic.

### Preparation
Dextromoramide Tablets

*Ph Eur*

### DEFINITION
Dextromoramide tartrate contains not less than 98.0 per cent and not more than the equivalent of 101.0 per cent of 1-[(3*S*)-3-methyl-4-(morpholin-4-yl)-2,2-diphenylbutanoyl]pyrrolidine hydrogen (2*R*,3*R*)-2,3-dihydroxybutanedioate, calculated with reference to the dried substance.

### CHARACTERS
A white or almost white, amorphous or crystalline powder, soluble in water, sparingly soluble in alcohol.

It melts at about 190 °C, with slight decomposition.

### IDENTIFICATION
A. Dissolve 75 mg in *1 M hydrochloric* acid and dilute to 100.0 ml with the same acid. Examined between 230 nm and 350 nm (*2.2.25*), the solution shows 3 absorption maxima, at 254 nm, 259 nm and 264 nm. The specific absorbances at the maxima are about 6.9, 7.7 and 6.5, respectively.

B. Dissolve about 50 mg in *water R* and dilute to 10 ml with the same solvent. To 2 ml of the solution add 3 ml of *ammoniacal silver nitrate solution R* and heat on a water-bath. A grey or black precipitate is formed.

C. It gives reaction (b) of tartrates (*2.3.1*).

### TESTS
**pH** (*2.2.3*)
Dissolve 0.2 g in *carbon dioxide-free water R* and dilute to 20 ml with the same solvent. The pH of the solution is 3.0 to 4.0.

**Specific optical rotation** (*2.2.7*)
Dissolve 0.50 g in *0.1 M hydrochloric acid* and dilute to 10.0 ml with the same acid. The specific optical rotation is + 21 to + 23.

**Related substances**
Examine by thin-layer chromatography (*2.2.27*), using *silica gel G R* as the coating substance.

*Test solution*   Dissolve 0.2 g of the substance to be examined in *methanol R* and dilute to 10 ml with the same solvent.

*Reference solution*   Dilute 1 ml of the test solution to 100 ml with *methanol R*.

Apply separately to the plate 10 µl of each solution. Develop over a path of 15 cm using *methanol R*. Allow the plate to dry in air and spray with *dilute potassium iodobismuthate solution R*. Any spot in the chromatogram obtained with the test solution, apart from the principal spot, is not more intense than the spot in the chromatogram obtained with the reference solution (1.0 per cent).

**Loss on drying** (*2.2.32*)
Not more than 0.5 per cent, determined on 1.00 g by drying in an oven at 105 °C.

**Sulphated ash** (*2.4.14*)
Not more than 0.1 per cent, determined on 1.0 g.

**ASSAY**
Dissolve 0.250 g in 30 ml of *anhydrous acetic acid R*. Titrate with *0.05 M perchloric acid* using 0.15 ml of *naphtholbenzein solution R* as indicator.

1 ml of *0.05 M perchloric acid* is equivalent to 27.13 mg of $C_{29}H_{38}N_2O_8$.

*Ph Eur*

# Dextropropoxyphene Hydrochloride

(*Ph Eur monograph 0713*)

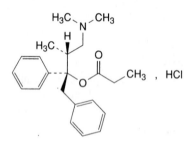

$C_{22}H_{29}NO_2,HCl$     375.9     *1639-60-7*

**Action and use**
Opioid receptor agonist; analgesic.

**Preparation**
Co-proxamol Tablets

*Ph Eur*

## DEFINITION
Dextropropoxyphene hydrochloride contains not less than 98.5 per cent and not more than the equivalent of 101.0 per cent of (1*S*,2*R*)-1-benzyl-3-(dimethylamino)-2-methyl-1-phenylpropyl propanoate hydrochloride, calculated with reference to the dried substance.

## CHARACTERS
A white or almost white, crystalline powder, very soluble in water, freely soluble in alcohol.

It melts at about 165 °C.

## IDENTIFICATION
*First identification* A, C, D.

*Second identification* A, B, D.

A. It complies with the test for specific optical rotation (see Tests).

B. Dissolve 50.0 mg in *0.01 M hydrochloric acid* and dilute to 100.0 ml with the same acid. Examined between 220 nm and 360 nm (*2.2.25*), the solution shows 3 absorption

maxima, at 252 nm, 257 nm and 263 nm and 2 shoulders, at 240 nm and 246 nm. The ratio of the absorbance at the maximum at 257 nm to that at the maximum at 252 nm is 1.22 to 1.28. The ratio of the absorbance at the maximum at 257 nm to that at the maximum at 263 nm is 1.29 to 1.35. The test is not valid unless, in the test for resolution (*2.2.25*), the ratio of the absorbances is at least 1.5.

C. Examine by infrared absorption spectrophotometry (*2.2.24*), comparing with the *Ph. Eur. reference spectrum of dextropropoxyphene hydrochloride*.

D. Solution S (see Tests) gives reaction (a) of chlorides (*2.3.1*).

## TESTS
**Solution S**
Dissolve 1.5 g in *carbon dioxide-free water R* and dilute to 30 ml with the same solvent.

**Appearance of solution**
Solution S is clear (*2.2.1*) and colourless (*2.2.2, Method II*).

**Acidity or alkalinity**
Dilute 10 ml of solution S to 25 ml with *carbon dioxide-free water R*. To 10 ml of this solution, add 0.1 ml of *methyl red solution R* and 0.2 ml *of 0.01 M sodium hydroxide*. The solution is yellow. Add 0.4 ml of *0.01 M hydrochloric acid*. The solution is red.

**Specific optical rotation** (*2.2.7*)
Dissolve 0.100 g in *water R* and dilute to 10.0 ml with the same solvent. The specific optical rotation is + 52 to + 57.

**Related substances**
Examine by liquid chromatography (*2.2.29*).

*Test solution* Dissolve 50.0 mg of the substance to be examined in the mobile phase and dilute to 10.0 ml with the mobile phase.

*Reference solution (a)* Dilute 0.50 ml of the test solution to 100.0 ml with the mobile phase.

*Reference solution (b)* Dissolve 50.0 mg of the substance to be examined in 2.5 ml of *2 M alcoholic potassium hydroxide*. Add 2.5 ml of *water R* and boil under a reflux condenser for 30 min. Add 2.5 ml of *dilute hydrochloric acid R* and dilute to 50 ml with the mobile phase.

The chromatographic procedure may be carried out using:
— a column 0.125 m long and 4.6 mm in internal diameter packed with *silica gel for chromatography R* (5 µm),
— a guard column packed with a suitable silica gel, equilibrated with the mobile phase and placed between the column and the injection device,
— as mobile phase at a flow rate of 1.0 ml/min a mixture of 50 volumes of *0.2 M phosphate buffer solution pH 7.5 R*, 84 volumes of *tetrahydrofuran R*, 350 volumes of *methanol R* and 516 volumes of *water R*, containing 0.9 g/l of *cetyltrimethylammonium bromide R*,
— as detector a spectrophotometer set at 220 nm,
— a loop injector.

Equilibrate the chromatographic system by passage of the mobile phase for 16 h (the mobile phase may be recirculated after 6 h).

Inject 20 µl of each solution and record the chromatograms for twice the retention time of the principal peak. The test is not valid unless:
— the chromatogram obtained with reference solution (a) shows a peak with a signal-to-noise ratio of at least 5,
— the chromatogram obtained with reference solution (b) shows 2 peaks with a resolution of not less than 2.0.

In the chromatogram obtained with the test solution, the area of any peak, apart from the principal peak, is not greater than the area of the principal peak in the chromatogram obtained with reference solution (a) (0.5 per cent).

**Heavy metals** (*2.4.8*)
12 ml of solution S complies with limit test A (20 ppm). Prepare the standard using *lead standard solution (1 ppm Pb) R*.

**Loss on drying** (*2.2.32*)
Not more than 1.0 per cent, determined on 1.000 g by drying in an oven at 105 °C.

**Sulphated ash** (*2.4.14*)
Not more than 0.1 per cent, determined on 1.0 g.

**ASSAY**
Dissolve 0.270 g in 60 ml of *acetic anhydride R*. Titrate with *0.1 M perchloric acid*, determining the end-point potentiometrically (*2.2.20*).

1 ml of *0.1 M perchloric acid* is equivalent to 37.59 mg of $C_{22}H_{30}ClNO_2$.

**STORAGE**
Protected from light.

**IMPURITIES**

A. R = H: (2*S*,3*R*)-4-(dimethylamino)-1,2-diphenyl-3-methyl-butan-2-ol,

B. R = CO-CH₃: (1*S*,2*R*)-1-benzyl-3-(dimethylamino)-2-methyl-1-phenylpropyl acetate.

_____ *Ph Eur*


# Dextropropoxyphene Napsilate

$C_{22}H_{29}NO_2,C_{10}H_8O_3S,H_2O$    565.8         *26570-10-5*

**Action and use**
Opioid receptor agonist; analgesic.

**Preparation**
Dextropropoxyphene Capsules

**DEFINITION**
Dextropropoxyphene Napsilate is (1*S*,2*R*)-1-benzyl-3-dimethylamino-2-methyl-1phenylpropyl propionate naphthalene-2-sulphonate monohydrate. It contains not less than 98.0% and not more than 101.0% of

$C_{22}H_{29}NO_2,C_{10}H_8O_3S$, calculated with reference to the anhydrous substance.

**CHARACTERISTICS**
A white powder. It exhibits polymorphism.

Practically insoluble in *water*; soluble in *ethanol (96%)*.

**IDENTIFICATION**
A. The *infrared absorption spectrum*, Appendix II A, is concordant with the *reference spectrum* of dextropropoxyphene napsilate *(RS 092)*. If the spectra are not concordant, dissolve a sufficient quantity in the minimum volume of *dichloromethane IR*, evaporate to dryness, dry the residue at 105° for 1 hour and prepare a new spectrum.

B. Dissolve 25 mg in 5 ml of *dichloromethane*, evaporate 0.05 ml of the solution in a porcelain dish and streak the spot with *sulphuric acid* containing 5% v/v of *formaldehyde solution*. A purple colour is produced.

C. Burn 20 mg by the method for *oxygen-flask combustion*, Appendix VIII C, using 5 ml of 1.25M *sodium hydroxide* as the absorbing liquid. When the process is complete, dilute the liquid to 25 ml with *water*. To 5 ml of the solution so obtained add 1 ml of *hydrogen peroxide solution (100 vol)* and 1 ml of 1M *hydrochloric acid*, mix and add 0.05 ml of *barium chloride solution*. The solution becomes turbid.

**TESTS**
**Specific optical rotation**
In a 5% w/v solution in *ethanol (96%)*, +26 to +31, calculated with reference to the anhydrous substance, Appendix V F.

**Related substances**
Carry out the method for *gas chromatography*, Appendix III B. Dissolve 10 mg of *triphenylamine* (internal standard) in sufficient *dichloromethane* to produce 50 ml (solution A).

(1) Dissolve 0.3 g of the substance being examined in 5 ml of *dichloromethane*, add 10 ml of *water*, 2 ml of 1.25M *sodium hydroxide* and 15 ml of *dichloromethane* and shake. Extract the aqueous layer with two 20-ml quantities of *dichloromethane*. Shake the combined dichloromethane extracts with 5 g of *anhydrous sodium sulphate*, filter and evaporate to dryness at a temperature not exceeding 40° using a rotary evaporator. Dissolve the residue in 10 ml of *dichloromethane*.

(2) Prepare solution (2) in the same manner as solution (1) but add 5 ml of solution A to the initial solution of the substance being examined.

(3) Add 5 ml of solution A, 10 ml of *water*, 2 ml of 1.25M *sodium hydroxide* and 15 ml of *dichloromethane* to 5 ml of a solution in *dichloromethane* containing 0.022% w/v of *(1S,2R)-1-benzyl-3-dimethylamino-2-methyl-1-phenylpropyl acetate BPCRS* and 0.020% w/v of *4-dimethylamino-3-methyl-1,2-diphenylbutan-2-ol hydrochloride BPCRS* and shake. Extract the aqueous layer with two 20-ml quantities of *dichloromethane*. Shake the combined dichloromethane extracts with 5 g of *anhydrous sodium sulphate*, filter and evaporate to dryness at a temperature not exceeding 40° using a rotary evaporator. Dissolve the residue in 10 ml of *dichloromethane*.

CHROMATOGRAPHIC CONDITIONS

(a) Use a glass column (60 cm × 3 mm) packed with *acid-washed, silanised diatomaceous support* (100 to 120 mesh) coated with 3% w/w of dimethyl silicone fluid (OV-101 is suitable).

(b) Use *helium* as the carrier gas at 60 ml per minute.

(c) Use isothermal conditions maintained at 160°.

(d) Use an inlet temperature of 150°.

(e) Use a flame ionisation detector.

SYSTEM SUITABILITY

The peaks, other than the solvent peak, in the chromatogram obtained with solution (3) are due, in order of emergence, to (a) the internal standard, (b) (1*S*,2*R*)-1-benzyl-3-dimethylamino-2-methyl-1-phenylpropyl acetate and (c) 4-dimethylamino-3-methyl-1,2-diphenylbutan-2-ol hydrochloride.

LIMITS

In the chromatogram obtained with solution (2):

the ratio of the area of any peak corresponding to (b) to that of the peak due to (a) and the ratio of the area of any peak corresponding to (c) to that of the peak due to (a) are not greater than the corresponding ratios in the chromatogram obtained with solution (3) (0.67% each).

**Sulphated ash**

Not more than 0.1%, Appendix IX A.

**Water**

3.0 to 5.0% w/w, Appendix IX C. Use 0.5 g.

**ASSAY**

To 0.75 g add 50 ml of *water*, swirl to disperse, add 5 ml of 5M *sodium hydroxide* and extract with five 25-ml quantities of *dichloromethane*, washing each extract with the same 20 ml of *water*. Dry the combined extracts with *anhydrous sodium sulphate*, evaporate to about 3 ml on a water bath in a current of air and allow to evaporate to dryness at room temperature. Carry out Method I for *non-aqueous titration* on the residue, Appendix VIII A, using *1-naphtholbenzein solution* as indicator. Each ml of 0.1M *perchloric acid VS* is equivalent to 54.78 mg of $C_{22}H_{29}NO_2,C_{10}H_8O_3S$.

# Diamorphine Hydrochloride

$C_{21}H_{23}NO_5,HCl,H_2O$     423.9     *1502-95-0*

**Action and use**

Opioid receptor agonist; analgesic.

**Preparation**

Diamorphine Injection

## DEFINITION

Diamorphine Hydrochloride is 4,5-epoxy-17-methylmorphinan-3,6-diyl diacetate hydrochloride monohydrate. It contains not less than 98.0% and not more than 102.0% of $C_{21}H_{23}NO_5,HCl$, calculated with reference to the dried substance.

## CHARACTERISTICS

A white or almost white, crystalline powder.

Freely soluble in *water*; soluble in *ethanol (96%)*; practically insoluble in *ether*.

## IDENTIFICATION

A. Dissolve a sufficient quantity in the minimum volume of *dichloromethane* and evaporate to dryness. The *infrared absorption spectrum* of the residue, Appendix II A, is concordant with the *reference spectrum* of diamorphine hydrochloride *(RS 093)*.

B. Yields reaction A characteristic of *chlorides*, Appendix VI.

## TESTS

**Acidity**

Dissolve 0.2 g in 10 ml of *carbon dioxide-free water* and titrate with 0.02M *sodium hydroxide VS* using *methyl red solution* as indicator. Not more than 0.2 ml of 0.02M *sodium hydroxide VS* is required.

**Related substances**

Carry out the method for *liquid chromatography*, Appendix III D, using the following solutions. Solution (1) contains 0.5% w/v of the substance being examined in *water*. For solution (2) dilute 1 volume of solution (1) to 50 volumes with *water*. For solution (3) use a freshly prepared solution containing 0.1% w/v of the substance being examined in 0.01M *sodium hydroxide*. For solution (1) allow the chromatography to proceed for twice the retention time of the principal peak.

The chromatographic procedure may be carried out using (a) a stainless steel column (12.5 cm × 4.6 mm) packed with *base-deactivated octylsilyl silica gel for chromatography*, (5 μm) (Lichrospher RP-select B is suitable), (b) as the mobile phase with a flow rate of 1 ml per minute a solution containing 0.11 % w/v of *sodium octanesulphonate* in 10 volumes of *glacial acetic acid*, 10 volumes of *methanol*, 115 volumes of *acetonitrile* and 365 volumes of *water* and (c) a detection wavelength of 283 nm.

The chromatogram obtained with solution (3) exhibits two *secondary peaks* with retention times relative to the principal peak of about 0.23 (morphine) and 0.43 (6-*O*-acetyl-morphine). The test is not valid unless the *resolution factor* between the peaks due to morphine and 6-*O*-acetyl-morphine is at least 2.

In the chromatogram obtained with solution (1) the area of any peak corresponding to 6-*O*-acetylmorphine is not greater than the area of the peak in the chromatogram obtained with solution (2) (2%) and the sum of the areas of any other *secondary peaks* is not greater than 0.25 times the area of the peak in the chromatogram obtained with solution (2) (0.5%). Disregard any peak with an area less than 0.05 times the area of the peak in the chromatogram obtained with solution (2) (0.1%).

**Loss on drying**

When dried to constant weight at 105°, loses 3.0 to 4.5% of its weight. Use 1 g.

**Sulphated ash**

Not more than 0.1%, Appendix IX A.

## ASSAY

Dissolve 0.40 g in 50 ml of *ethanol (96%)* and add 5.0 ml of 0.01M *hydrochloric acid VS*. Titrate with 0.1M *sodium hydroxide VS*, determining the end point potentiometrically. Measure the volume of titrant required between the two points of inflection. Each ml of 0.1M *sodium hydroxide VS* is equivalent to 40.59 mg of $C_{21}H_{23}NO_5,HCl$.

## STORAGE

Diamorphine Hydrochloride should be protected from light.

## IMPURITIES

The impurities listed by the requirements of this monograph include:

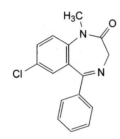

A. 6-*O*-acetylmorphine.

# Diazepam

(*Ph Eur monograph 0022*)

$C_{16}H_{13}ClN_2O$      284.7      *439-14-5*

**Action and use**
Benzodiazepine.

**Preparations**
Diazepam Injection
Diazepam Oral Solution
Diazepam Rectal Solution
Diazepam Tablets

*Ph Eur* _____

## DEFINITION
7-Chloro-1-methyl-5-phenyl-1,3-dihydro-2*H*-1,4-benzodiazepin-2-one.

**Content**
99.0 per cent to 101.0 per cent (dried substance).

## CHARACTERS
**Appearance**
White or almost white, crystalline powder.

**Solubility**
Very slightly soluble in water, soluble in ethanol (96 per cent).

## IDENTIFICATION
Infrared absorption spectrophotometry (*2.2.24*).

*Comparison*  diazepam CRS.

## TESTS
**Related substances**
Liquid chromatography (*2.2.29*). *Prepare the solutions protected from bright light.*

*Test solution*  Dissolve 25.0 mg of the substance to be examined in 0.5 ml of *acetonitrile R* and dilute to 50.0 ml with the mobile phase.

*Reference solution (a)*  Dilute 1.0 ml of the test solution to 100.0 ml with the mobile phase. Dilute 1.0 ml of this solution to 10.0 ml with the mobile phase.

*Reference solution (b)*  Dissolve the contents of a vial of *diazepam for system suitability CRS* (containing impurities A, B and E) in 1.0 ml of the mobile phase.

*Column:*
— *size: l* = 0.15 m, Ø = 4.6 mm;
— *stationary phase*: spherical *end-capped octylsilyl silica gel for chromatography R* (5 μm);
— *temperature*: 30 °C.

*Mobile phase*  Mix 22 volumes of *acetonitrile R*, 34 volumes of *methanol R* and 44 volumes of a 3.4 g/l solution of *potassium dihydrogen phosphate R* previously adjusted to pH 5.0 with *dilute sodium hydroxide solution R*.

*Flow rate*  1.0 ml/min.

*Detection*  Spectrophotometer at 254 nm.

*Injection*  20 μl.

*Run time*  About 4 times the retention time of diazepam.

*Identification of impurities*  Use the chromatogram supplied with *diazepam for system suitability CRS* and the chromatogram obtained with reference solution (b) to identify the peaks due to impurities A, B and E.

*Relative retention*  With reference to diazepam (retention time = about 9 min): impurity E = about 0.7; impurity A = about 0.8; impurity B = about 1.3.

*System suitability*  Reference solution (b):
— *resolution*: minimum 2.5 between the peaks due to impurities E and A and minimum 6.0 between the peaks due to impurity A and diazepam.

*Limits:*
— *correction factors*: for the calculation of content, multiply the peak areas of the following impurities by the corresponding correction factor: impurity B = 1.3; impurity E = 1.3;
— *impurities A, B, E*: for each impurity, not more than the area of the principal peak in the chromatogram obtained with reference solution (a) (0.1 per cent);
— *unspecified impurities*: for each impurity, not more than the area of the principal peak in the chromatogram obtained with reference solution (a) (0.10 per cent);
— *total*: not more than twice the area of the principal peak in the chromatogram obtained with reference solution (a) (0.2 per cent);
— *disregard limit*: 0.5 times the area of the principal peak in the chromatogram obtained with reference solution (a) (0.05 per cent).

**Heavy metals** (*2.4.8*)
Maximum 20 ppm.

2.0 g complies with test C. Prepare the reference solution using 4 ml of *lead standard solution (10 ppm Pb) R*.

**Loss on drying** (*2.2.32*)
Maximum 0.5 per cent, determined on 1.000 g by drying *in vacuo* at 60 °C for 4 h.

**Sulphated ash** (*2.4.14*)
Maximum 0.1 per cent, determined on 1.0 g.

## ASSAY
Dissolve 0.200 g in 50 ml of *acetic anhydride R*. Titrate with *0.1 M perchloric acid*, determining the end-point potentiometrically (*2.2.20*).

1 ml of *0.1 M perchloric acid* is equivalent to 28.47 mg of $C_{16}H_{13}ClN_2O$.

## STORAGE
Protected from light.

## IMPURITIES
*Specified impurities* A, B, E.

*Other detectable impurities* (the following substances would, if present at a sufficient level, be detected by one or other of the tests in the monograph. They are limited by the general acceptance criterion for other/unspecified impurities and/or by the general monograph *Substances for pharmaceutical use (2034)*. It is therefore not necessary to identify these impurities for demonstration of compliance. See also *5.10. Control of impurities in substances for pharmaceutical use)*: C, D, F.

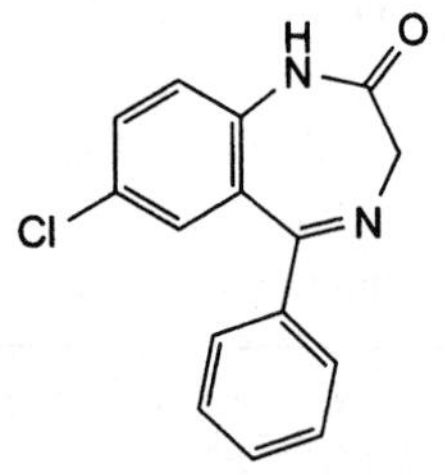

A. 7-chloro-5-phenyl-1,3-dihydro-2H-1,4-benzodiazepin-2-one (nordazepam),

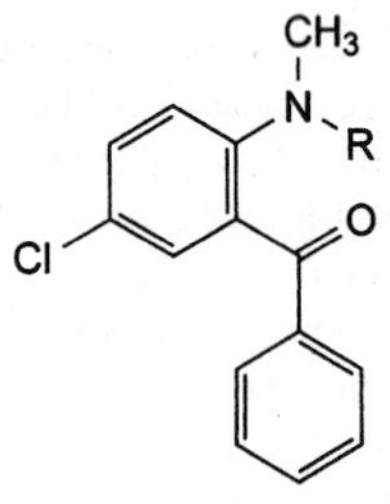

B. R = CO-CH₂-Cl:
2-chloro-N-(4-chloro-2-benzoylphenyl)-N-methylacetamide,
D. R = H:
[5-chloro-2-(methylamino)phenyl]phenylmethanone,

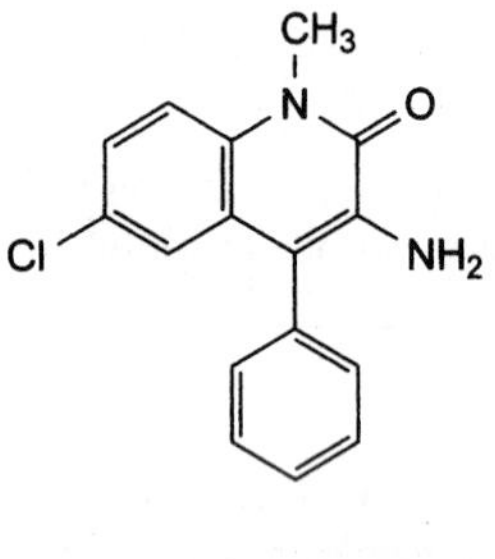

C. 3-amino-6-chloro-1-methyl-4-phenylquinolin-2(1H)-one,

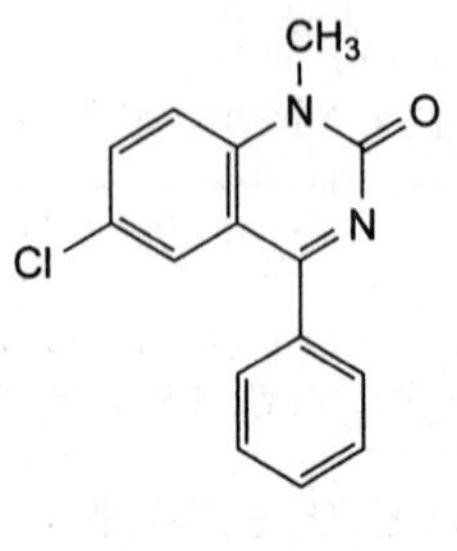

E. 6-chloro-1-methyl-4-phenylquinazolin-2(1H)-one,

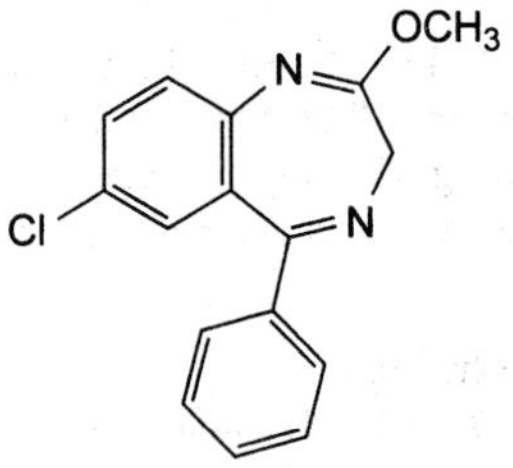

F. 7-chloro-2-methoxy-5-phenyl-3H-1,4-benzodiazepine.

*Ph Eur*

# Diazoxide

*(Ph Eur monograph 0550)*

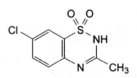

C₈H₇ClN₂O₂S            230.7            *364-98-7*

## Action and use
Vasodilator; Treatment of hypertension.

## Preparations
Diazoxide Injection
Diazoxide Tablets

*Ph Eur*

## DEFINITION
Diazoxide contains not less than 98.0 per cent and not more than the equivalent of 101.0 per cent of 7-chloro-3-methyl-2H-1,2,4-benzothiadiazine 1,1-dioxide, calculated with reference to the dried substance.

## CHARACTERS
A white or almost white, fine or crystalline powder, practically insoluble in water, freely soluble in dimethylformamide, slightly soluble in alcohol. It is very soluble in dilute solutions of the alkali hydroxides.

## IDENTIFICATION
*First identification* B.
*Second identification* A, C, D.

A. Dissolve 50.0 mg in 5 ml of *1 M sodium hydroxide* and dilute to 50.0 ml with *water R*. Dilute 1.0 ml of this solution to 100.0 ml with *0.1 M sodium hydroxide*. Examined between 230 nm and 350 nm (*2.2.25*), the solution shows an absorption maximum at 280 nm and a shoulder at 304 nm. The specific absorbance at the maximum is 570 to 610.

B. Examine by infrared absorption spectrophotometry (*2.2.24*), comparing with the spectrum obtained with *diazoxide CRS*. Examine the substances prepared as discs using *potassium bromide R*.

C. Examine the chromatograms obtained in the test for related substances in ultraviolet light at 254 nm. The principal spot in the chromatogram obtained with test solution (b) is similar in position and size to the principal spot in the chromatogram obtained with reference solution (b).

D. Dissolve about 20 mg in a mixture of 5 ml of *hydrochloric acid R* and 10 ml of *water R*. Add 0.1 g of *zinc powder R*. Boil for 5 min, cool and filter. To the filtrate add 2 ml of a 1 g/l solution of *sodium nitrite R* and mix. Allow to stand for 1 min and add 1 ml of a 5 g/l solution of *naphthylethylenediamine dihydrochloride R*. A red or violet-red colour develops.

## TESTS

### Appearance of solution

Dissolve 0.4 g in 2 ml of *1 M sodium hydroxide* and dilute to 20 ml with *water R*. The solution is clear (*2.2.1*) and not more intensely coloured than reference solution $Y_7$ (*2.2.2, Method II*).

### Acidity or alkalinity

To 0.5 g of the powdered substance to be examined add 30 ml of *carbon dioxide-free water R*, shake for 2 min and filter. To 10 ml of the filtrate add 0.2 ml of *0.01 M sodium hydroxide* and 0.15 ml of *methyl red solution R*. The solution is yellow. Not more than 0.4 ml of *0.01 M hydrochloric acid* is required to change the colour of the indicator to red.

### Related substances

Examine by thin-layer chromatography (*2.2.27*), using *silica gel GF$_{254}$ R* as the coating substance.

*Test solution (a)* Dissolve 0.1 g of the substance to be examined in a mixture of 0.5 ml of *1 M sodium hydroxide* and 1 ml of *methanol R* and dilute to 5 ml with *methanol R*.

*Test solution (b)* Dilute 1 ml of test solution (a) to 5 ml with a mixture of 1 volume of *1 M sodium hydroxide* and 9 volumes of *methanol R*.

*Reference solution (a)* Dilute 0.5 ml of test solution (a) to 100 ml with a mixture of 1 volume of *1 M sodium hydroxide* and 9 volumes of *methanol R*.

*Reference solution (b)* Dissolve 20 mg of *diazoxide CRS* in a mixture of 0.5 ml of *1 M sodium hydroxide* and 1 ml of *methanol R* and dilute to 5 ml with *methanol R*.

Apply separately to the plate 5 μl of each solution. Develop over a path of 15 cm using a mixture of 7 volumes of *concentrated ammonia R*, 25 volumes of *methanol R* and 68 volumes of *chloroform R*. Allow the plate to dry in air and examine in ultraviolet light at 254 nm. Any spot in the chromatogram obtained with test solution (a), apart from the principal spot, is not more intense than the spot in the chromatogram obtained with reference solution (a) (0.5 per cent).

### Loss on drying (*2.2.32*)

Not more than 0.5 per cent, determined on 1.000 g by drying in an oven at 105 °C for 2 h.

### Sulphated ash (*2.4.14*)

Not more than 0.1 per cent, determined on 1.0 g.

## ASSAY

Dissolve 0.200 g with gentle heating in 50 ml of a mixture of 1 volume of *water R* and 2 volumes of *dimethylformamide R*. Titrate with *0.1 M sodium hydroxide*, determining the end-point potentiometrically (*2.2.20*). Carry out a blank titration.

1 ml of *0.1 M sodium hydroxide* is equivalent to 23.07 mg of $C_8H_7ClN_2O_2S$.

*Ph Eur*

# Dibrompropamidine Isetionate

(*Dibrompropamidine Diisetionate, Ph Eur monograph 2300*)

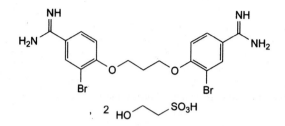

$C_{17}H_{18}Br_2N_4O_2,2C_2H_6O_4S$    722    614-87-9

### Action and use

Antiseptic.

*Ph Eur*

## DEFINITION

3,3′-Dibromo-4,4′-(propane-1,3-diylbisoxy)dibenzimidamide bis(2-hydroxyethanesulphonate).

## Content

99.0 per cent to 101.0 per cent (dried substance).

## PRODUCTION

The production method must be evaluated to determine the potential for formation of alkyl 2-hydroxyethanesulphonates, which is particularly likely to occur if the reaction medium contains lower alcohols. Where necessary, the production method is validated to demonstrate that alkyl 2-hydroxyethanesulphonates are not detectable in the final product.

## CHARACTERS

### Appearance

White or almost white, crystalline powder.

### Solubility

Freely soluble or soluble in water, slightly soluble in ethanol (96 per cent), practically insoluble in methylene chloride.

## IDENTIFICATION

A. Infrared absorption spectrophotometry (*2.2.24*).

*Comparison   dibrompropamidine diisetionate CRS.*

B. Mix 0.1 g with 0.5 g of *anhydrous sodium carbonate R*, ignite and take up the residue with 20 ml of *water R*. Filter and neutralise the filtrate to *blue litmus paper R* with *nitric acid R*. The filtrate gives reaction (a) of bromides (*2.3.1*).

## TESTS

### pH (*2.2.3*)

5.0 to 6.0.

Dissolve 0.50 g in *carbon dioxide-free water R* and dilute to 10 ml with the same solvent.

### Related substances

Liquid chromatography (*2.2.29*).

*Solvent mixture   anhydrous formic acid R, methanol R, ethyl acetate R* (0.01:8:12 *V/V/V*).

*Test solution* To 8 ml of *methanol R* add 20.0 mg of the substance to be examined and dissolve with the aid of an ultrasonic bath. Add 11 ml of *ethyl acetate R* then 10 μl of *anhydrous formic acid R* and mix. Dilute to 20.0 ml with *ethyl acetate R*.

*Reference solution (a)* Dilute 1.0 ml of the test solution to 100.0 ml with the solvent mixture. Dilute 1.0 ml of this solution to 10.0 ml with the solvent mixture.

*Reference solution (b)* Dissolve 10 mg of *dibrompropamidine for system suitability CRS* (containing impurities A and B) in 4 ml of *methanol R* using an ultrasonic bath. Add 5 ml of *ethyl acetate R* then 5 µl of *anhydrous formic acid R* and mix. Dilute to 10.0 ml with *ethyl acetate R*.

*Column:*
— *size: l* = 0.25 m, Ø = 4.6 mm,
— *stationary phase: strong cation-exchange silica gel for chromatography R* (5 µm).

*Mobile phase* Mix 4 volumes of a 25 g/l solution of *ammonium formate R* in *methanol R* and 6 volumes of *ethyl acetate R*.

*Flow rate* 1 ml/min.

*Detection* Spectrophotometer at 254 nm.

*Injection* 40 µl.

*Run time* 1.5 times the retention time of dibrompropamidine.

*Identification of impurities* Use the chromatogram supplied with *dibrompropamidine for system suitability CRS* and the chromatogram obtained with reference solution (b) to identify the peaks due to impurities A and B.

*Relative retention* With reference to dibrompropamidine (retention time = about 20 min): impurity A = about 0.4; impurity B = about 1.1.

*System suitability* Reference solution (b):
— *peak-to-valley* ratio: minimum 1.5, where $H_p$ = height above the baseline of the peak due to impurity B and $H_v$ = height above the baseline of the lowest point of the curve separating this peak from the peak due to dibrompropamidine.

*Limits:*
— *impurity A*: not more than 3 times the area of the principal peak in the chromatogram obtained with reference solution (a) (0.3 per cent);
— *impurity B*: not more than 5 times the area of the principal peak in the chromatogram obtained with reference solution (a) (0.5 per cent);
— *unspecified impurities*: for each impurity, not more than the area of the principal peak in the chromatogram obtained with reference solution (a) (0.1 per cent);
— *total*: not more than 10 times the area of the principal peak in the chromatogram obtained with reference solution (a) (1.0 per cent);
— *disregard limit*: 0.5 times the area of the principal peak in the chromatogram obtained with reference solution (a) (0.05 per cent).

**Loss on drying** (*2.2.32*)
Maximum 2.0 per cent, determined on 1.000 g by drying in an oven at 105 °C.

**Sulphated ash** (*2.4.14*)
Maximum 0.1 per cent, determined on 1.0 g.

**ASSAY**
Dissolve 0.250 g in 50 ml of *dimethylformamide R*. Titrate with *0.1 M tetrabutylammonium hydroxide* under a current of *nitrogen R*, determining the end-point potentiometrically (*2.2.20*).

1 ml of *0.1 M tetrabutylammonium hydroxide* is equivalent to 36.12 mg of $C_{21}H_{30}Br_2N_4O_{10}S_2$.

**IMPURITIES**
*Specified impurities* A, B.

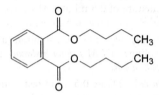

A. R = Br, X = O: 3-bromo-4-[3-(2-bromo-4-carbamimidoylphenoxy)propoxy]benzamide,

B. R = H, X = NH: 3-bromo-4-[3-(4-carbamimidoylphenoxy)propoxy]benzimidamide.

_____ *Ph Eur*

# Dibutyl Phthalate

*(Ph Eur monograph 0762)*

$C_{16}H_{22}O_4$          278.3          84-74-2

**Action and use**
Insect repellent.

*Ph Eur* _____

**DEFINITION**
Dibutyl benzene-1,2-dicarboxylate.

**Content**
99.0 per cent *m/m* to 101.0 per cent *m/m*.

**CHARACTERS**
**Appearance**
Clear, oily liquid, colourless or very slightly yellow.

**Solubility**
Practically insoluble in water, miscible with ethanol (96 per cent).

**IDENTIFICATION**
*First identification* B, C.

*Second identification* A, D, E.

A. Relative density (*2.2.5*): 1.043 to 1.048.

B. Refractive index (*2.2.6*): 1.490 to 1.495.

C. Infrared absorption spectrophotometry (*2.2.24*).

*Comparison* dibutyl phthalate CRS.

D. Thin-layer chromatography (*2.2.27*).

*Test solution* Dissolve 50 mg of the substance to be examined in *ether R* and dilute to 10 ml with the same solvent.

*Reference solution* Dissolve 50 mg of *dibutyl phthalate CRS* in *ether R* and dilute to 10 ml with the same solvent.

*Plate* TLC silica gel GF$_{254}$ plate R.

*Mobile phase* heptane R, ether R (30:70 *V/V*).

*Application* 10 µl.

*Development* Over a path of 15 cm.

*Drying* In air.

*Detection* Examine in ultraviolet light at 254 nm.

*Results* The principal spot in the chromatogram obtained with the test solution is similar in position and size to the principal spot in the chromatogram obtained with the reference solution.

E. To about 0.1 ml add 0.25 ml of *sulphuric acid R* and 50 mg of *resorcinol R*. Heat in a water-bath for 5 min. Allow to cool. Add 10 ml of *water R* and 1 ml of *strong sodium hydroxide solution R*. The solution becomes yellow or brownish-yellow and shows a green fluorescence.

## TESTS

### Appearance

The substance to be examined is clear (*2.2.1*) and not more intensely coloured than reference solution $Y_6$ (*2.2.2*, *Method II*).

### Acidity

Dissolve 20.0 g in 50 ml of *ethanol (96 per cent) R* previously neutralised to *phenolphthalein solution R1*. Add 0.2 ml of *phenolphthalein solution R1*. Not more than 0.50 ml of *0.1 M sodium hydroxide* is required to change the colour of the indicator.

### Related substances

Gas chromatography (*2.2.28*).

*Internal standard solution* Dissolve 60 mg of *bibenzyl R* in *methylene chloride R* and dilute to 20 ml with the same solvent.

*Test solution (a)* Dissolve 1.0 g of the substance to be examined in *methylene chloride R* and dilute to 20.0 ml with the same solvent.

*Test solution (b)* Dissolve 1.0 g of the substance to be examined in *methylene chloride R*, add 2.0 ml of the internal standard solution and dilute to 20.0 ml with *methylene chloride R*.

*Reference solution* To 1.0 ml of test solution (a) add 10.0 ml of the internal standard solution and dilute to 100.0 ml with *methylene chloride R*.

*Column:*
— *material*: glass;
— *size*: $l$ = 1.5 m, Ø = 4 mm;
— *stationary phase: silanised diatomaceous earth for gas chromatography R* (150-180 µm) impregnated with 3 per cent m/m of *polymethylphenylsiloxane R*.

*Carrier gas nitrogen for chromatography R*.

*Flow rate* 30 ml/min.

*Temperature:*
— *column*: 190 °C;
— *injection port and detector*: 225 °C.

*Detection* Flame ionisation.

*Injection* 1 µl.

*Run time* 3 times the retention time of dibutyl phthalate.

*Elution order* Bibenzyl, dibutyl phthalate.

*Retention time* Dibutyl phthalate = about 12 min.

*System suitability:*
— *resolution*: minimum 12 between the peaks due to bibenzyl and dibutyl phthalate in the chromatogram obtained with the reference solution;
— in the chromatogram obtained with test solution (a), there is no peak with the same retention time as the internal standard.

*Limit:*
— *total*: calculate the ratio ($R$) of the area of the peak due to dibutyl phthalate to the area of the peak due to the internal standard from the chromatogram obtained with the reference solution; from the chromatogram obtained with test solution (b), calculate the ratio of the sum of the areas of any peaks, apart from the principal peak and the peak due to the internal standard, to the area of the peak due to the internal standard: this ratio is not greater than $R$ (1.0 per cent).

**Water** (*2.5.12*)
Maximum 0.2 per cent, determined on 10.00 g.

**Sulphated ash** (*2.4.14*)
Maximum 0.1 per cent, determined on 1.0 g.

## ASSAY

Introduce 0.750 g into a 250 ml borosilicate glass flask. Add 25.0 ml of *0.5 M alcoholic potassium hydroxide* and a few glass beads. Heat in a water-bath under a reflux condenser for 1 h. Add 1 ml of *phenolphthalein solution R1* and titrate immediately with *0.5 M hydrochloric acid* until the colour changes from red to colourless. Carry out a blank titration. Calculate the volume of potassium hydroxide used in the saponification.

1 ml of *0.5 M alcoholic potassium hydroxide* is equivalent to 69.59 mg of $C_{16}H_{22}O_4$.

## STORAGE

In an airtight container.

_____ *Ph Eur*

# Dichloromethane

(*Methylene Chloride, Ph Eur monograph 0932*)

| CH₂Cl₂ | 84.9 | 75-09-02 |

**Action and use**
Excipient.

*Ph Eur* _____

## DEFINITION

Dichloromethane.

It may contain maximum 2.0 per cent *V/V* of ethanol and/or maximum 0.03 per cent *V/V* of 2-methylbut-2-ene as stabiliser.

## CHARACTERS

### Appearance

Clear, colourless, volatile liquid.

### Solubility

Sparingly soluble in water, miscible with ethanol (96 per cent).

## IDENTIFICATION

*First identification* B, C.

*Second identification* A, D, E.

A. Relative density (see Tests).

B. Refractive index (see Tests).

C. Examine the chromatograms obtained in the test for related substances.

*Results* The principal peak in the chromatogram obtained with test solution (b) is similar in retention time and size to the principal peak in the chromatogram obtained with reference solution (a).

D. Heat 2 ml with 2 g of *potassium hydroxide R* and 20 ml of *ethanol (96 per cent) R* under a reflux condenser for 30 min. Allow to cool. Add 15 ml of *dilute sulphuric acid R* and filter. To 1 ml of the filtrate add 1 ml of a 15 g/l solution of *chromotropic acid, sodium salt R*, 2 ml of *water R* and 8 ml of *sulphuric acid R*. A violet colour is produced.

E. 2 ml of the filtrate obtained in identification test D gives reaction (a) of chlorides (*2.3.1*).

## TESTS

### Appearance

It is clear (*2.2.1*) and colourless (*2.2.2, Method II*).

### Acidity

To 50 ml of *methanol R* previously neutralised to 0.1 ml of *bromothymol blue solution R1*, add 50 g of the substance to be examined. Not more than 0.15 ml of *0.1 M sodium hydroxide* is required to change the colour of the indicator to blue.

### Relative density (*2.2.5*)

1.320 to 1.332.

### Refractive index (*2.2.6*)

1.423 to 1.425.

### Related substances

Gas chromatography (*2.2.28*).

*Test solution (a)*  The substance to be examined.

*Test solution (b)*  Dilute 0.5 ml of test solution (a) to 100.0 ml with *water R*.

*Reference solution (a)*  Dilute 0.5 ml of *methylene chloride CRS* to 100.0 ml with *water R*.

*Reference solution (b)*  Dilute 2.0 ml of test solution (b) to 10.0 ml with *water R*.

*Reference solution (c)*  To 20.0 ml of *anhydrous ethanol R* (impurity C), add 0.3 ml of *2-methylbut-2-ene R* (impurity E) and dilute to 100.0 ml with test solution (a). Dilute 1.0 ml of this solution to 10.0 ml with test solution (a).

*Reference solution (d)*  Dilute 0.1 ml of *methanol R* (impurity D) and 0.1 ml of *methylene chloride CRS* to 100.0 ml with *water R*.

*Column:*
— *material*: glass;
— *size: l = 2 m, Ø = 2 mm*;
— *stationary phase*: *ethylvinylbenzene-divinylbenzene copolymer R* (136-173 µm).

*Carrier gas*  *nitrogen for chromatography R*.

*Flow rate*  30 ml/min.

*Temperature:*

|  | Time (min) | Temperature (°C) |
|---|---|---|
| Column |  | 90 |
|  | 0 - 25 | 90 → 190 |
|  | 25 - 40 | 190 |
| Injection port |  | 240 |
| Detector |  | 240 |

*Detection*  Flame ionisation.

*Injection*  1 µl of reference solution (d) and 2 µl of the test solution and reference solutions (a), (b) and (c).

*System suitability:*
— *resolution*: minimum 3.0 between the peaks due to impurity D and methylene chloride in the chromatogram obtained with reference solution (d);
— inject twice 2 µl of reference solution (c), if the peaks obtained show an area difference greater than

1.0 per cent, verify the repeatability by making 4 separate injections of reference solution (c); the test is not valid unless the maximum relative standard deviation of the peak area is 5.0 per cent.

*Limits*  Test solution (a):
— *impurity C*: not more than the difference between the area of the peak due to impurity C in the chromatogram obtained with reference solution (c) and that of the peak due to impurity C in the chromatogram obtained with test solution (a) (2.0 per cent);
— *impurity E*: not more than the difference between the area of the peak due to impurity E in the chromatogram obtained with reference solution (c) and that of the peak due to impurity E in the chromatogram obtained with test solution (a) (0.03 per cent);
— *sum of impurities other than C and E*: not more than the area of the principal peak in the chromatogram obtained with reference solution (b) (0.1 per cent).

### Free chlorine

Place 5 ml in a ground-glass-stoppered tube. Add 5 ml of a 100 g/l solution of *potassium iodide R* and 0.2 g of *soluble starch R*. Shake for 30 s and allow to stand for 5 min. No blue colour develops.

### Heavy metals (*2.4.8*)

Maximum 1 ppm.

Evaporate 25.0 g to dryness on a water-bath. Allow to cool. Add 1 ml of *hydrochloric acid R* and evaporate again. Dissolve the residue in 1 ml of *acetic acid R* and dilute to 25 ml with *water R*. 12 ml of the solution complies with test A. Prepare the reference solution using 10 ml of *lead standard solution (1 ppm Pb) R*.

### Residue on evaporation

Maximum 20 ppm.

Evaporate 50.0 g to dryness on a water-bath and dry at 100-105 °C for 30 min. The residue weighs a maximum of 1 mg.

### Water (*2.5.12*)

Maximum 0.05 per cent *m/m*, determined on 10.00 g.

## STORAGE

In an airtight container, protected from light.

## IMPURITIES

*Specified impurities*  C, E.

*Other detectable impurities* (the following substances would, if present at a sufficient level, be detected by one or other of the tests in the monograph. They are limited by the general acceptance criterion for other/unspecified impurities and/or by the general monograph *Substances for pharmaceutical use (2034)*. It is therefore not necessary to identify these impurities for demonstration of compliance. See also *5.10. Control of impurities in substances for pharmaceutical use*): A, B, D.

A. carbon tetrachloride,

B. chloroform,

C. ethanol,

D. methanol,

E. 2-methylbut-2-ene.

# Dichlorophen

$C_{13}H_{10}Cl_2O_2$      269.1      97-23-4

**Action and use**
Antihelminthic.

**Preparation**
Dichlorophen Tablets

## DEFINITION

Dichlorophen is 4,4'-dichloro-2,2'-methylenediphenol. It contains not less than 97.0% and not more than 101.0% of $C_{13}H_{10}Cl_2O_2$, calculated with reference to the dried substance.

## CHARACTERISTICS

A white or not more than slightly cream powder.

Practically insoluble in *water*; very soluble in *ether*; freely soluble in *ethanol (96%)*.

## IDENTIFICATION

A. The *light absorption*, Appendix II B, in the range 220 to 350 nm of a 0.002% w/v solution in 0.1M *sodium hydroxide* exhibits two maxima, at 245 nm and 304 nm. The *absorbances* at the maxima are about 1.3 and about 0.54, respectively.

B. Dissolve 0.2 g in a mixture of 5 ml of *water* and 5 ml of 5M *sodium hydroxide*, cool in ice and add a solution prepared by mixing 1 ml of *sodium nitrite solution* with a cold solution containing 0.15 ml of *aniline* in a mixture of 4 ml of *water* and 1 ml of *hydrochloric acid*. A reddish brown precipitate is produced.

C. Fuse 0.5 g with 2 g of *anhydrous sodium carbonate*, cool, extract the residue with *water* and filter. The filtrate yields reaction A characteristic of *chlorides*, Appendix VI.

D. *Melting point*, about 175°, Appendix V A.

## TESTS

### Chloride

Dissolve 1.0 g in 2 ml of *ethanol (96%)*, dilute to 100 ml with *water*, allow to stand for 5 minutes and filter through a slow filter paper (Whatman No. 42 is suitable). 15 ml of the filtrate complies with the *limit test for chlorides*, Appendix VII (350 ppm).

### Sulphate

Shake 0.8 g with 16 ml of *water* for 2 minutes, filter and dilute 5 ml of the filtrate to 15 ml with *water*. The solution complies with the *limit test for sulphates*, Appendix VII (600 ppm).

### Related substances

Carry out the method for *liquid chromatography*, Appendix III D, using three solutions in the mobile phase containing (1) 1.0% w/v of *dichlorophen impurity standard BPCRS*, (2) 1.0% w/v of the substance being examined and (3) 0.0010% w/v of *4-chlorophenol*.

The chromatographic procedure may be carried out using (a) a stainless steel column (20 cm × 5 mm) packed with *octadecylsilyl silica gel for chromatography* (10 μm) (Spherisorb ODS 1 is suitable), (b) as the mobile phase with a flow rate of 1.5 ml per minute a mixture of 25 volumes of *water* and 1 volume of *glacial acetic acid* and sufficient *methanol* to produce a chromatogram with solution (1) closely resembling the reference chromatogram supplied with the impurity standard (75 volumes of *methanol* is usually suitable) and (c) a detection wavelength of 280 nm. Record the chromatograms until all of the peaks named on the reference chromatogram have emerged.

In the chromatogram obtained with solution (2) the area of any peak corresponding to 4-chlorophenol is not greater than the area of the principal peak in the chromatogram obtained with solution (3) (0.1%). The content of 4,4'-dichloro-2,2'-(2-hydroxy-4-chloro-*m*-xylene-α,α'-diyl)diphenol in the substance being examined does not exceed 8.0% w/w and the sum of the contents of any other impurities, excluding 4-chlorophenol, is not greater than 2.0% w/w calculated using the declared content of 4,4'-dichloro-2,2'-(2-hydroxy-4-chloro-*m*-xylene-α,α'-diyl)diphenol in *dichlorophen impurity standard BPCRS*.

### Loss on drying

When dried to constant weight at 105°, loses not more than 1.0% of its weight. Use 1 g.

### Sulphated ash

Not more than 0.1%, Appendix IX A.

## ASSAY

Dissolve 0.5 g in 20 ml of *propan-2-ol* and carry out Method II for *non-aqueous titration*, Appendix VIII A, using 0.1M *tetrabutylammonium hydroxide VS* as titrant and determining the end point potentiometrically. Each ml of 0.1M *tetrabutylammonium hydroxide VS* is equivalent to 26.91 mg of $C_{13}H_{10}Cl_2O_2$.

# Diclofenac Diethylamine

$C_{18}H_{22}Cl_2N_2O_2$      369.29      78213-16-8

**Action and use**
Cyclo-oxygenase inhibitor; analgesic; anti-inflammatory.

**Preparation**
Diclofenac Gel

## DEFINITION

Diclofenac Diethylamine is diethylammonium 2-[(2,6-dichloroanilino)phenyl]acetate. It contains not less than 99.0% and not more than 101.0% of $C_{18}H_{22}Cl_2N_2O_2$, calculated with reference to the dried substance.

## CHARACTERISTICS

A white to light beige, crystalline powder.

Sparingly soluble in *water* and in *acetone*; freely soluble in *ethanol (96%)* and in *methanol*; practically insoluble in 1M *sodium hydroxide*.

It melts at about 154°, with decomposition.

## IDENTIFICATION

A. The *infrared absorption spectrum*, Appendix II A, is concordant with the *reference spectrum* of diclofenac diethylamine *(RS 371)*.

B. Carry out the method for *thin-layer chromatography*, Appendix III A, using the following solutions in *methanol*.

(1) 5.0% w/v of the substance being examined.

(2) 5.0% w/v of *diclofenac diethylamine BPCRS*.

CHROMATOGRAPHIC CONDITIONS

(a) Use a silica gel precoated plate (Macherey Nagel SIL G-25 HR or silica gel $60F_{254}$ HPTLC plates are suitable).

(b) Use the mobile phase as described below.

(c) Apply 2 µl of each solution.

(d) Develop the plate to 15 cm.

(e) After removal of the plate, dry it in a stream of warm air for 10 minutes. Spray with *ninhydrin solution* and heat at 110° for 15 minutes.

MOBILE PHASE

1 volume of *hydrochloric acid*, 1 volume of *water*, 6 volumes of *glacial acetic acid* and 11 volumes of *ethyl acetate*.

SYSTEM SUITABILITY

The test is not valid unless the chromatogram obtained with solution (2) shows two clearly separated spots.

CONFIRMATION

The two principal spots in the chromatogram obtained with solution (1) are similar in position, colour and size to the corresponding spots in the chromatogram obtained with solution (2).

## TESTS

### Acidity or alkalinity
pH of a 1% w/v solution in *ethanol (10%)*, 6.4 to 8.4, Appendix V L.

### Clarity and colour of solution
A 5% w/v solution in *methanol* is *clear*, Appendix IV A. The *absorbance* of the solution measured at 440 nm is not greater than 0.05, Appendix II B.

### Heavy metals
2 g complies with *limit test C for heavy metals*, Appendix VII. Use 2 ml of *lead standard solution (10 ppm Pb)* to prepare the standard (10 ppm).

### Related substances
Carry out the method for *liquid chromatography*, Appendix III D, using the following solutions in the mobile phase.

(1) 0.10% w/v of the substance being examined.

(2) Dilute 2 volumes of solution (1) to 100 volumes and dilute 1 volume of this solution to 10 volumes.

(3) Dissolve 1 mg of *diclofenac impurity A BPCRS* add 1 ml of solution (1) and dilute to 200 ml.

CHROMATOGRAPHIC CONDITIONS

(a) Use a stainless steel column (25 cm × 4.6 mm) packed with *end-capped octylsilyl silica gel for chromatography* (5 µm) (end-capped Zorbax C8 is suitable).

(b) Use isocratic elution and the mobile phase described below.

(c) Use a flow rate of 1 ml per minute.

(d) Use an ambient column temperature.

(e) Use a detection wavelength of 254 nm.

(f) Inject 20 µl of each solution.

(g) Allow the chromatography to proceed for 1.5 times the retention time of diclofenac.

Inject 20 µl of solution (3). When the chromatograms are recorded under the prescribed conditions, the retention times are about 25 minutes for diclofenac and about 12 minutes for diclofenac impurity A.

MOBILE PHASE

34 volumes of a mixture of equal volumes of a 0.1% w/v solution of *orthophosphoric acid* and a 0.16% w/v solution of *sodium dihydrogen orthophosphate* adjusted to pH 2.5 and 66 volumes of *methanol*.

SYSTEM SUITABILITY

The test is not valid unless, in the chromatogram obtained with solution (3), the *resolution factor* between the peaks corresponding to diclofenac and diclofenac impurity A is at least 6.5.

LIMITS

In the chromatogram obtained with solution (1):

the area of any *secondary peak* is not greater than the area of the principal peak in the chromatogram obtained with solution (2) (0.2%);

the sum of the areas of any *secondary peaks* is not greater than 2.5 times the area of the principal peak in the chromatogram obtained with solution (2) (0.5%).

Disregard any peak with an area less than 0.25 times the area of the principal peak in the chromatogram obtained with solution (2) (0.05%).

### Loss on drying
When dried at a pressure not exceeding 1 kPa for 24 hours, loses not more than 0.5% of its weight. Use 1 g.

### Sulphated ash
Not more than 0.1%, Appendix IX A, Method II. Use 1 g.

## ASSAY
Dissolve 0.5 g in 30 ml of *anhydrous acetic acid* and carry out Method I for *non-aqueous titration*, Appendix VIII A, determining the end point potentiometrically. Each ml of 0.1M *perchloric acid VS* is equivalent to 36.93 mg of $C_{18}H_{22}Cl_2N_2O_2$.

## STORAGE
Diclofenac Diethylamine should be kept in an airtight container and protected from light.

## IMPURITIES
The impurities limited by the requirements of this monograph include those listed under Diclofenac Sodium.

# Diclofenac Potassium

*(Ph Eur monograph 1508)*

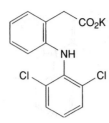

$C_{14}H_{10}Cl_2KNO_2$     334.2     *15307-81-0*

### Action and use
Cyclo-oxygenase inhibitor; analgesic; anti-inflammatory.

*Ph Eur* _____

## DEFINITION
Potassium [2-[(2,6-dichlorophenyl)amino]phenyl]acetate.

## Content
99.0 per cent to 101.0 per cent (dried substance).

## CHARACTERS
### Appearance
White or slightly yellowish, slightly hygroscopic, crystalline powder.

### Solubility
Sparingly soluble in water, freely soluble in methanol, soluble in ethanol (96 per cent), slightly soluble in acetone.

## IDENTIFICATION
*First identification*   A, D.

*Second identification*   B, C, D.

A. Infrared absorption spectrophotometry (2.2.24).

*Preparation*   Discs.

*Comparison*   diclofenac potassium CRS.

B. Thin-layer chromatography (2.2.27).

*Test solution*   Dissolve 25 mg of the substance to be examined in *methanol R* and dilute to 5 ml with the same solvent.

*Reference solution (a)*   Dissolve 25 mg of *diclofenac potassium CRS* in *methanol R* and dilute to 5 ml with the same solvent.

*Reference solution (b)*   Dissolve 10 mg of *indometacin R* in reference solution (a) and dilute to 2 ml with the same solution.

*Plate*   TLC silica gel GF$_{254}$ plate R.

*Mobile phase*   concentrated ammonia R, methanol R, ethyl acetate R (10:10:80 V/V/V).

*Application*   5 μl.

*Development*   Over a path of 10 cm.

*Drying*   In air.

*Detection*   Examine in ultraviolet light at 254 nm.

*System suitability*   Reference solution (b):
— the chromatogram shows 2 clearly separated spots.

*Results*   The principal spot in the chromatogram obtained with the test solution is similar in position and size to the principal spot in the chromatogram obtained with reference solution (a).

C. Dissolve about 10 mg in 10 ml of *ethanol (96 per cent) R*. To 1 ml of this solution add 0.2 ml of a mixture, prepared immediately before use, of equal volumes of a 6 g/l solution of *potassium ferricyanide R* and a 9 g/l solution of *ferric chloride R*. Allow to stand protected from light for 5 min. Add 3 ml of a 10 g/l solution of *hydrochloric acid R*. Allow to stand protected from light for 15 min. A blue colour develops and a precipitate is formed.

D. Suspend 0.5 g in 10 ml of *water R*. Stir and add *water R* until the substance is dissolved. Add 2 ml of *hydrochloric acid R1*, stir for 1 h and filter with the aid of vacuum. Neutralise with *sodium hydroxide solution R*. The solution gives reaction (b) of potassium (2.3.1).

## TESTS
### Appearance of solution
The solution is clear (2.2.1) and its absorbance (2.2.25) at 440 nm is not greater than 0.05.

Dissolve 1.25 g in *methanol R* and dilute to 25.0 ml with the same solvent.

### Related substances
Liquid chromatography (2.2.29).

*Test solution*   Dissolve 50.0 mg of the substance to be examined in *methanol R* and dilute to 50.0 ml with the same solvent.

*Reference solution (a)*   Dilute 2.0 ml of the test solution to 100.0 ml with *methanol R*. Dilute 1.0 ml of this solution to 10.0 ml with *methanol R*.

*Reference solution (b)*   Dilute 1.0 ml of the test solution to 200.0 ml with *methanol R*. In 1.0 ml of this solution dissolve the contents of a vial of *diclofenac impurity A CRS*.

*Column:*
— *size:* $l$ = 0.25 m, Ø = 4.6 mm;
— *stationary phase:* end-capped octylsilyl silica gel for chromatography R (5 μm).

*Mobile phase*   Mix 34 volumes of a solution containing 0.5 g/l of *phosphoric acid R* and 0.8 g/l of *sodium dihydrogen phosphate R*, adjusted to pH 2.5 with *phosphoric acid R*, and 66 volumes of *methanol R*.

*Flow rate*   1 ml/min.

*Detection*   Spectrophotometer at 254 nm.

*Injection*   20 μl.

*Run time*   1.5 times the retention time of diclofenac.

*Retention time*   Impurity A = about 12 min; diclofenac = about 25 min.

*System suitability*   Reference solution (b):
— *resolution:* minimum 6.5 between the peaks due to impurity A and diclofenac.

*Limits:*
— *impurities A, B, C, D, E:* for each impurity, not more than the area of the principal peak in the chromatogram obtained with reference solution (a) (0.2 per cent);
— *total:* not more than 2.5 times the area of the principal peak in the chromatogram obtained with reference solution (a) (0.5 per cent);
— *disregard limit:* 0.25 times the area of the principal peak in the chromatogram obtained with reference solution (a) (0.05 per cent).

### Heavy metals (2.4.8)
Maximum 10 ppm.

2.0 g complies with test C. Use a quartz crucible. Prepare the reference solution using 2 ml of *lead standard solution (10 ppm Pb) R*.

**Loss on drying** (2.2.32)

Maximum 0.5 per cent, determined on 1.000 g by drying in an oven at 105 °C for 3 h.

## ASSAY

Dissolve 0.250 g in 30 ml of *anhydrous acetic acid R*. Titrate with *0.1 M perchloric acid*, determining the end-point potentiometrically (2.2.20).

1 ml of *0.1 M perchloric acid* is equivalent to 33.42 mg of $C_{14}H_{10}Cl_2KNO_2$.

## STORAGE

In an airtight container, protected from light.

## IMPURITIES

*Specified impurities*   *A, B, C, D, E.*

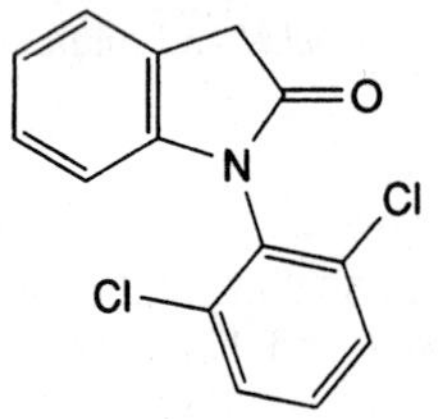

A. 1-(2,6-dichlorophenyl)-1,3-dihydro-2*H*-indol-2-one,

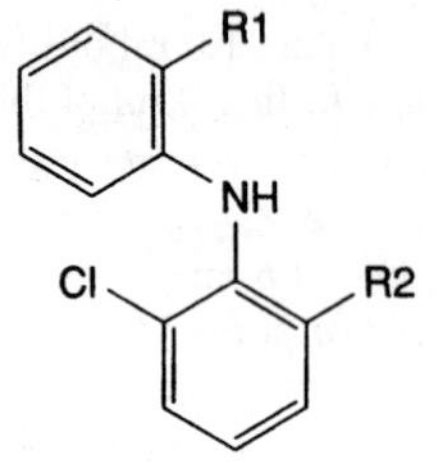

B. R1 = CHO, R2 = Cl:
2-[(2,6-dichlorophenyl)amino]benzaldehyde,

C. R1 = CH2OH, R2 = Cl:
[2-[(2,6-dichlorophenyl)amino]phenyl]methanol,

D. R1 = CH2-CO2H, R2 = Br:
2-[2-[(2-bromo-6-chlorophenyl)amino]phenyl]acetic acid,

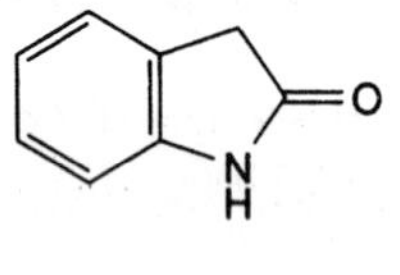

E. 1,3-dihydro-2*H*-indol-2-one.

*Ph Eur*

# Diclofenac Sodium

(*Ph Eur monograph 1002*)

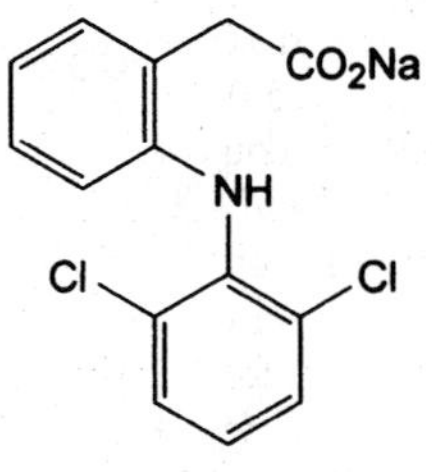

$C_{14}H_{10}Cl_2NNaO_2$        318.1        *15307-79-6*

### Action and use
Cyclo-oxygenase inhibitor; analgesic; anti-inflammatory.

### Preparations
Prolonged-release Diclofenac Capsules

Gastro-resistant Diclofenac Tablets

Prolonged-release Diclofenac Tablets

*Ph Eur*

## DEFINITION

Sodium 2-[(2,6-dichlorophenyl)amino]phenyl]acetate.

**Content**

99.0 per cent to 101.0 per cent (dried substance).

## CHARACTERS

**Appearance**

White or slightly yellowish, slightly hygroscopic, crystalline powder.

**Solubility**

Sparingly soluble in water, freely soluble in methanol, soluble in ethanol (96 per cent), slightly soluble in acetone.

mp: about 280 °C, with decomposition.

## IDENTIFICATION

*First identification   A, D.*

*Second identification   B, C, D.*

A. Infrared absorption spectrophotometry (2.2.24).

*Preparation*   Discs.

*Comparison*   diclofenac sodium CRS.

B. Thin-layer chromatography (2.2.27).

*Test solution*   Dissolve 25 mg of the substance to be examined in *methanol R* and dilute to 5 ml with the same solvent.

*Reference solution (a)*   Dissolve 25 mg of *diclofenac sodium CRS* in *methanol R* and dilute to 5 ml with the same solvent.

*Reference solution (b)*   Dissolve 10 mg of *indometacin R* in reference solution (a) and dilute to 2 ml with the same solution.

*Plate*   TLC silica gel GF254 plate R.

*Mobile phase*   concentrated ammonia R, methanol R, ethyl acetate R (10:10:80 V/V/V).

*Application*   5 µl.

*Development*   Over a path of 10 cm.

*Drying*   In air.

*Detection*   Examine in ultraviolet light at 254 nm.

*System suitability*   Reference solution (b):

— the chromatogram shows 2 clearly separated spots.

*Results* The principal spot in the chromatogram obtained with the test solution is similar in position and size to the principal spot in the chromatogram obtained with reference solution (a).

C. Dissolve about 10 mg in 10 ml of *ethanol (96 per cent) R*. To 1 ml of this solution add 0.2 ml of a mixture, prepared immediately before use, of equal volumes of a 6 g/l solution of *potassium ferricyanide R* and a 9 g/l solution of *ferric chloride R*. Allow to stand protected from light for 5 min. Add 3 ml of a 10 g/l solution of *hydrochloric acid R*. Allow to stand, protected from light, for 15 min. A blue colour develops and a precipitate is formed.

D. Dissolve 60 mg in 0.5 ml of *methanol R* and add 0.5 ml of *water R*. The solution gives reaction (b) of sodium (*2.3.1*).

## TESTS

### Appearance of solution
The solution is clear (*2.2.1*) and its absorbance (*2.2.25*) at 440 nm is not greater than 0.05.

Dissolve 1.25 g in *methanol R* and dilute to 25.0 ml with the same solvent.

### Related substances
Liquid chromatography (*2.2.29*).

*Test solution* Dissolve 50.0 mg of the substance to be examined in *methanol R* and dilute to 50.0 ml with the same solvent.

*Reference solution (a)* Dilute 2.0 ml of the test solution to 100.0 ml with *methanol R*. Dilute 1.0 ml of this solution to 10.0 ml with *methanol R*.

*Reference solution (b)* Dilute 1.0 ml of the test solution to 200.0 ml with *methanol R*. In 1.0 ml of this solution dissolve the contenst of a vial of *diclofenac impurity A CRS*.

*Column:*
— *size: l* = 0.25 m, Ø = 4.6 mm;
— *stationary phase: end-capped octylsilyl silica gel for chromatography R* (5 µm).

*Mobile phase* Mix 34 volumes of a solution containing 0.5 g/l of *phosphoric acid R* and 0.8 g/l of *sodium dihydrogen phosphate R*, adjusted to pH 2.5 with *phosphoric acid R*, and 66 volumes of *methanol R*.

*Flow rate* 1 ml/min.

*Detection* Spectrophotometer at 254 nm.

*Injection* 20 µl.

*Run time* 1.5 times the retention time of diclofenac.

*Retention times* impurity A = about 12 min; diclofenac = about 25 min.

*System suitability* Reference solution (b):
— *resolution*: minimum 6.5 between the peaks due to impurity A and diclofenac.

*Limits:*
— *impurities A, B, C, D, E*: for each impurity, not more than the area of the principal peak in the chromatogram obtained with reference solution (a) (0.2 per cent);
— *total*: not more than 2.5 times the area of the principal peak in the chromatogram obtained with reference solution (a) (0.5 per cent);
— *disregard limit*: 0.25 times the area of the principal peak in the chromatogram obtained with reference solution (a) (0.05 per cent).

### Heavy metals (*2.4.8*)
Maximum 10 ppm.

2.0 g complies with test C. Use a quartz crucible. Prepare the reference solution using 2 ml of *lead standard solution (10 ppm Pb) R*.

**Loss on drying** (*2.2.32*)
Maximum 0.5 per cent, determined on 1.000 g by drying in an oven at 105 °C for 3 h.

## ASSAY
Dissolve 0.250 g in 30 ml of *anhydrous acetic acid R*. Titrate with *0.1 M perchloric acid*, determining the end-point potentiometrically (*2.2.20*).

1 ml of *0.1 M perchloric acid* is equivalent to 31.81 mg of $C_{14}H_{10}Cl_2NNaO_2$.

## STORAGE
In an airtight container, protected from light.

## IMPURITIES
*Specified impurities*   *A, B, C, D, E.*

A. 1-(2,6-dichlorophenyl)-1,3-dihydro-2*H*-indol-2-one,

B. R1 = CHO, R2 = Cl:
2-[(2,6-dichlorophenyl)amino]benzaldehyde,

C. R1 = CH$_2$OH, R2 = Cl:
[2-[(2,6-dichlorophenyl)amino]phenyl]methanol,

D. R1 = CH$_2$-CO$_2$H, R2 = Br:
2-[2-[(2-bromo-6-chlorophenyl)amino]phenyl]acetic acid,

E. 1,3-dihydro-2*H*-indol-2-one.

*Ph Eur*

# Dicloxacillin Sodium

(*Ph Eur monograph 0663*)

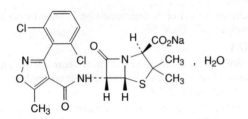

$C_{19}H_{16}Cl_2N_3NaO_5S,H_2O$    510.3    *13412-64-1*

**Action and use**

Penicillin antibacterial.

*Ph Eur* ___

## DEFINITION

Sodium (2S,5R,6R)-6-[[[3-(2,6-dichlorophenyl)-5-methylisoxazol-4-yl]carbonyl]amino]-3,3-dimethyl-7-oxo-4-thia-1-azabicyclo[3.2.0]heptane-2-carboxylate monohydrate.

Semi-synthetic product derived from a fermentation product.

## Content

95.0 per cent to 102.0 per cent (anhydrous substance).

## CHARACTERS

**Appearance**

White or almost white, hygroscopic, crystalline powder.

**Solubility**

Freely soluble in water, soluble in ethanol (96 per cent) and in methanol.

## IDENTIFICATION

*First identification*  A, D.

*Second identification*  B, C, D.

A. Infrared absorption spectrophotometry (2.2.24).

*Preparation*  Discs.

*Comparison*  dicloxacillin sodium CRS.

B. Thin-layer chromatography (2.2.27).

*Test solution*  Dissolve 25 mg of the substance to be examined in 5 ml of *water R*.

*Reference solution (a)*  Dissolve 25 mg of *dicloxacillin sodium CRS* in 5 ml of *water R*.

*Reference solution (b)*  Dissolve 25 mg of *cloxacillin sodium CRS*, 25 mg of *dicloxacillin sodium CRS* and 25 mg of *flucloxacillin sodium CRS* in 5 ml of *water R*.

*Plate*  TLC silanised silica gel plate R.

*Mobile phase*  Mix 30 volumes of *acetone R* and 70 volumes of a 154 g/l solution of *ammonium acetate* R adjusted to pH 5.0 with *glacial acetic acid R*.

*Application*  1 µl.

*Development*  Over a path of 15 cm.

*Drying*  In air.

*Detection*  Expose to iodine vapour until the spots appear and examine in daylight.

*System suitability*  Reference solution (b):
— the chromatogram shows 3 clearly separated spots.

*Results*  The principal spot in the chromatogram obtained with the test solution is similar in position, colour and size to the principal spot in the chromatogram obtained with reference solution (a).

C. Place about 2 mg in a test-tube about 150 mm long and about 15 mm in diameter. Moisten with 0.05 ml of *water R* and add 2 ml of *sulphuric acid-formaldehyde reagent R*. Mix the contents of the tube by swirling; the solution is slightly greenish-yellow. Place the test-tube in a water-bath for 1 min; a yellow colour develops.

D. It gives reaction (a) of sodium (2.3.1).

## TESTS

**Solution S**

Dissolve 2.50 g in *carbon dioxide-free water R* and dilute to 25.0 ml with the same solvent.

**Appearance of solution**

Solution S is clear (2.2.1) and its absorbance (2.2.25) at 430 nm is not greater than 0.04.

**pH** (2.2.3)

5.0 to 7.0 for solution S.

**Specific optical rotation** (2.2.7)

+ 128 to + 143 (anhydrous substance).

Dissolve 0.250 g in *water R* and dilute to 25.0 ml with the same solvent.

**Related substances**

Liquid chromatography (2.2.29).

*Test solution (a)*  Dissolve 50.0 mg of the substance to be examined in the mobile phase and dilute to 50.0 ml with the mobile phase.

*Test solution (b)*  Dilute 5.0 ml of test solution (a) to 50.0 ml with the mobile phase.

*Reference solution (a)*  Dissolve 50.0 mg of *dicloxacillin sodium CRS* in the mobile phase and dilute to 50.0 ml with the mobile phase. Dilute 5.0 ml of this solution to 50.0 ml with the mobile phase.

*Reference solution (b)*  Dilute 5.0 ml of test solution (b) to 50.0 ml with the mobile phase.

*Reference solution (c)*  Dissolve 5 mg of *flucloxacillin sodium CRS* and 5 mg of *dicloxacillin sodium CRS* in the mobile phase, then dilute to 50.0 ml with the mobile phase.

*Column:*
— *size: l = 0.25 m, Ø = 4 mm;*
— *stationary phase: octadecylsilyl silica gel for chromatography R* (5 µm).

*Mobile phase*  Mix 25 volumes of *acetonitrile R* and 75 volumes of a 2.7 g/l solution of *potassium dihydrogen phosphate R* adjusted to pH 5.0 with *dilute sodium hydroxide solution R*.

*Flow rate*  1.0 ml/min.

*Detection*  Spectrophotometer at 225 nm.

*Injection*  20 µl of test solution (a) and reference solutions (b) and (c).

*Run time*  5 times the retention time of dicloxacillin.

*Retention time*  Dicloxacillin = about 10 min.

*System suitability*  Reference solution (c):
— *resolution:* minimum 2.5 between the peaks due to flucloxacillin (1st peak) and dicloxacillin (2nd peak).

*Limits:*
— *any impurity:* for each impurity, not more than the area of the principal peak in the chromatogram obtained with reference solution (b) (1 per cent);
— *total:* not more than 5 times the area of the principal peak in the chromatogram obtained with reference solution (b) (5 per cent);

— *disregard limit:* 0.05 times the area of the principal peak in the chromatogram obtained with reference solution (b) (0.05 per cent).

**N,N-Dimethylaniline** (*2.4.26, Method B*)
Maximum 20 ppm.

**2-Ethylhexanoic acid** (*2.4.28*)
Maximum 0.8 per cent *m/m*.

**Water** (*2.5.12*)
3.0 per cent to 4.5 per cent, determined on 0.300 g.

**Pyrogens** (*2.6.8*)
If intended for use in the manufacture of parenteral dosage forms without a further appropriate procedure for the removal of pyrogens, it complies with the test for pyrogens. Inject per kilogram of the rabbit's mass 1 ml of a solution in *water for injections R* containing 20 mg of the substance to be examined per millilitre.

## ASSAY
Liquid chromatography (*2.2.29*) as described in the test for related substances with the following modifications.

*Injection*  Test solution (b) and reference solution (a).

*System suitability*  Reference solution (a):
— *repeatability*: maximum relative standard deviation of 1.0 per cent after 6 injections.

## STORAGE
In an airtight container, at a temperature not exceeding 25 °C. If the substance is sterile, store in a sterile, airtight, tamper-proof container.

## IMPURITIES

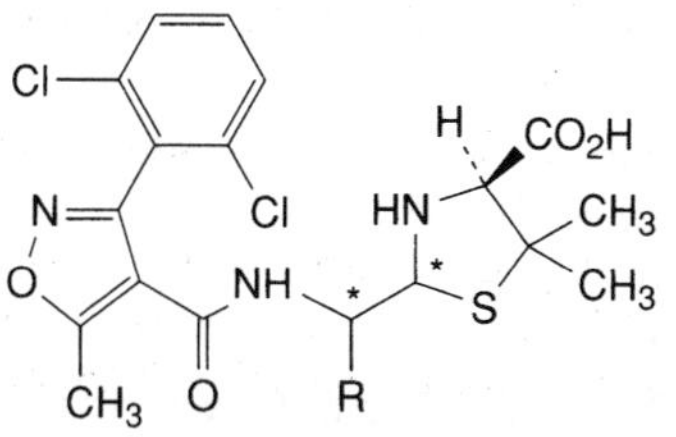

A. R = CO₂H: $(4S)$-2-[carboxy[[[3-(2,6-dichlorophenyl)-5-methylisoxazol-4-yl]carbonyl]amino]methyl]-5,5-dimethylthiazolidine-4-carboxylic acid (penicilloic acids of dicloxacillin),

B. R = H: $(2RS,4S)$-2-[[[[3-(2,6-dichlorophenyl)-5-methylisoxazol-4-yl]carbonyl]amino]methyl]-5,5-dimethylthiazolidine-4-carboxylic acid (penilloic acids of dicloxacillin),

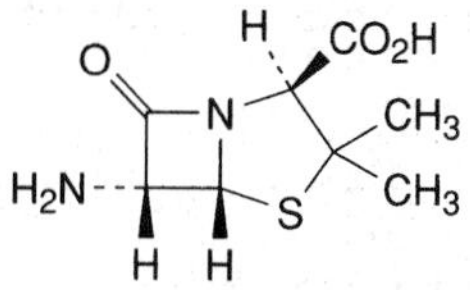

C. $(2S,5R,6R)$-6-amino-3,3-dimethyl-7-oxo-4-thia-1-azabicyclo[3.2.0]heptane-2-carboxylic acid (6-aminopenicillanic acid),

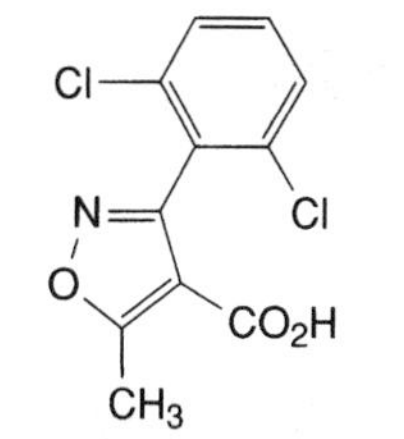

D. 3-(2,6-dichlorophenyl)-5-methylisoxazole-4-carboxylic acid.

*Ph Eur*

# Dicycloverine Hydrochloride

(*Ph Eur monograph 1197*)

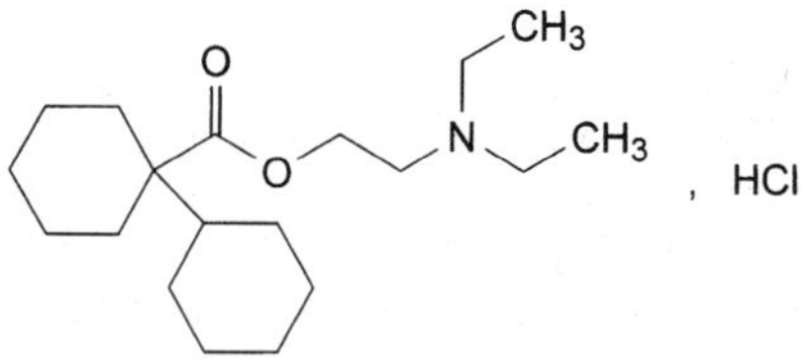

$C_{19}H_{35}NO_2,HCl$         346.0         67-92-5

**Action and use**
Anticholinergic.

**Preparations**
Dicycloverine Oral Solution
Dicycloverine Tablets

*Ph Eur*

## DEFINITION
Dicycloverine hydrochloride contains not less than 99.0 per cent and not more than the equivalent of 101.0 per cent of 2-(diethylamino)ethyl bicyclohexyl-1-carboxylate hydrochloride, calculated with reference to the dried substance.

## CHARACTERS
A white or almost white, crystalline powder, soluble in water, freely soluble in alcohol and in methylene chloride.

It shows polymorphism (*5.9*).

## IDENTIFICATION
*First identification*  A, D.

*Second identification*  B, C, D.

A. Examine by infrared absorption spectrophotometry (*2.2.24*), comparing with the spectrum obtained with *dicycloverine hydrochloride CRS*. Examine the substances prepared as discs using *potassium chloride R*. If the spectra obtained show differences, dissolve the substance to be examined and the reference substance separately in *acetone R*, evaporate to dryness and record new spectra using the residues.

B. Examine the chromatograms obtained in the test for related substances. The principal spot in the chromatogram obtained with test solution (b) is similar in position, colour and size to the principal spot in the chromatogram obtained with reference solution (b).

C. To 3 ml of a 1.0 g/l solution of *sodium laurilsulfate R* add 5 ml of *methylene chloride R* and 0.05 ml of a 2.5 g/l solution of *methylene blue R*, mix gently and allow to stand; the lower layer is blue. Add 2 ml of a 20 g/l solution of the substance to be examined, mix gently and allow to stand; the upper layer is blue and the lower layer is colourless.

D. It gives reaction (a) of chlorides (*2.3.1*).

## TESTS

### pH (*2.2.3*)
Dissolve 0.5 g in *water R* and dilute to 50 ml with the same solvent. The pH of the solution is 5.0 to 5.5.

### Related substances
Examine by thin-layer chromatography (*2.2.27*), using a suitable silica gel as the coating substance.

*Test solution (a)*   Dissolve 0.25 g to the substance to be examined in *methanol R* and dilute to 5 ml with the same solvent.

*Test solution (b)*   Dilute 1 ml of test solution (a) to 50 ml with *methanol R*.

*Reference solution (a)*   Dilute 1 ml of test solution (b) to 10 ml with *methanol R*.

*Reference solution (b)*   Dissolve 10 mg of *dicycloverine hydrochloride CRS* in *methanol R* and dilute to 10 ml with the same solvent.

*Reference solution (c)*   Dissolve 5 mg of *tropicamide CRS* in reference solution (b) and dilute to 5 ml with the same solution.

Apply separately to the plate 10 μl of each solution. Develop over a path of 15 cm using a mixture of 5 volumes of *concentrated ammonia R*, 10 volumes of *ethyl acetate R*, 10 volumes of water R and 75 volumes of *propanol R*. Dry the plate in a current of warm air. Spray with *dilute potassium iodobismuthate solution R*. Any spot in the chromatogram obtained with test solution (a), apart from the principal spot, is not more intense than the spot in the chromatogram obtained with reference solution (a) (0.2 per cent). The test is not valid unless the chromatogram obtained with reference solution (c) shows two clearly separated spots.

### Loss on drying (*2.2.32*)
Not more than 1.0 per cent, determined on 1.000 g by drying in an oven at 105 °C.

### Sulphated ash (*2.4.14*)
Not more than 0.1 per cent, determined on 1.0 g.

## ASSAY
Dissolve 0.300 g in a mixture of 5.0 ml of *0.01 M hydrochloric acid* and 50 ml of *alcohol R*. Carry out a potentiometric titration (*2.2.20*), using *0.1 M sodium hydroxide*. Read the volume added between the two points of inflexion.

1 ml of *0.1 M sodium hydroxide* is equivalent to 34.60 mg of $C_{19}H_{36}ClNO_2$.

## IMPURITIES

A. bicyclohexyl-1-carboxylic acid.

*Ph Eur*

# Didanosine

(*Ph Eur monograph 2200*)

$C_{10}H_{12}N_4O_3$          236.2          69655-05-6

## Action and use
Nucleoside reverse transcriptase inhibitor; antiviral (HIV).

*Ph Eur*

## DEFINITION
9-(2,3-Dideoxy-β-D-*glycero*-pentofuranosyl)-1,9-dihydro-6*H*-purin-6-one (2′,3′-dideoxyinosine).

## Content
98.5 per cent to 101.0 per cent (anhydrous substance).

## CHARACTERS

### Appearance
White or almost white, crystalline powder.

### Solubility
Sparingly soluble in water, freely soluble in dimethyl sulfoxide, slightly soluble in methanol and in ethanol (96 per cent).

## IDENTIFICATION
A. Infrared absorption spectrophotometry (*2.2.24*).

*Comparison*   didanosine CRS.

B. Specific optical rotation (*2.2.7*): − 24.2 to − 28.2 (anhydrous substance).

Dissolve 0.100 g in *water R* and dilute to 10.0 ml with the same solvent.

## TESTS

### Related substances
Liquid chromatography (*2.2.29*). *Prepare the solutions immediately before use.*

*Solvent mixture*   Mix 8 volumes of mobile phase B and 92 volumes of mobile phase A.

*Test solution*   Dissolve 25.0 mg of the substance to be examined in 50.0 ml of the solvent mixture.

*Reference solution (a)*   Dilute 1.0 ml of the test solution to 100.0 ml with the solvent mixture. Dilute 1.0 ml of this solution to 10.0 ml with the solvent mixture.

*Reference solution (b)*   Dissolve 5.0 mg of *didanosine impurity A CRS* in the solvent mixture and dilute to 100.0 ml with the solvent mixture. Dilute 1.0 ml to 20.0 ml with the solvent mixture.

*Reference solution (c)*   Dissolve 5 mg of *didanosine for system suitability CRS* (containing impurities A to F) in the solvent mixture and dilute to 10 ml with the solvent mixture.

*Reference solution (d)*   Dissolve 5 mg of *didanosine impurity G CRS* in the solvent mixture and dilute to 100 ml with the solvent mixture. Dilute 1 ml to 20 ml with the solvent mixture.

*Column:*
— size: *l* = .25 m, Ø = 4.6 mm,

— *stationary phase*: *base-deactivated octadecylsilyl silica gel for chromatography R* (5 μm).

*Mobile phase:*

— *mobile phase A*: mix 8 volumes of *methanol R* and 92 volumes of a 3.86 g/l solution of *ammonium acetate R* adjusted to pH 8.0 with *concentrated ammonia R*,

— *mobile phase B*: mix 30 volumes of *methanol R* and 70 volumes of a 3.86 g/l solution of *ammonium acetate R* adjusted to pH 8.0 with *concentrated ammonia R*,

| Time (min) | Mobile phase A (per cent *V/V*) | Mobile phase B (per cent *V/V*) |
|---|---|---|
| 0 - 18 | 100 | 0 |
| 18 - 25 | 100 → 0 | 0 → 100 |
| 25 - 45 | 0 | 100 |
| 45 - 50 | 0 → 100 | 100 → 0 |
| 50 - 60 | 100 | 0 |

*Flow rate*   1.0 ml/min.

*Detection*   Spectrophotometer at 254 nm.

*Injection*   20 μl.

*Identification of impurities*   Use the chromatogram supplied with *didanosine for system suitability CRS* and the chromatogram obtained with reference solution (c) to identify the peaks due to impurities A to F and use the chromatogram obtained with reference solution (d) to identify the peak due to impurity G.

*Relative retention*   With reference to didanosine (retention time = about 13-15 min): impurity A = about 0.3; impurity B = about 0.4; impurity C = about 0.44; impurity D = about 0.48; impurity E = about 0.5; impurity F = about 0.8; impurity I = about 1.4; impurity G = about 1.6; impurity H = about 2.0.

*System suitability*   Reference solution (c):

— *resolution*: minimum 2.5 between the peaks due to impurity C and impurity D.

*Limits:*

— *impurity A*: not more than the area of the principal peak in the chromatogram obtained with reference solution (b) (0.5 per cent),

— *impurities B, C, D, E, F, G*: for each impurity, not more than twice the area of the principal peak in the chromatogram obtained with reference solution (a) (0.2 per cent),

— *any other impurity*: for each impurity, not more than the area of the principal peak in the chromatogram obtained with reference solution (a) (0.1 per cent),

— *total*: not more than 10 times the area of the principal peak in the chromatogram obtained with reference solution (a) (1.0 per cent),

— *disregard limit*: 0.5 times the area of the principal peak in the chromatogram obtained with reference solution (a) (0.05 per cent).

**Heavy metals** (*2.4.8*)

Maximum 20 ppm.

1.0 g complies with limit test F. Prepare the reference solution using 2 ml of *lead standard solution (10 ppm Pb) R*.

**Water** (*2.5.12*)

Maximum 2.0 per cent, determined on 0.500 g.

**Sulphated ash** (*2.4.14*)

Maximum 0.1 per cent, determined on 1.0 g.

**ASSAY**

Dissolve 0.200 g in 50 ml of *glacial acetic acid R*. Titrate with *0.1 M perchloric acid*, determining the end-point potentiometrically (*2.2.20*).

1 ml of *0.1 M perchloric acid* is equivalent to 23.62 mg of $C_{10}H_{12}N_4O_3$.

**IMPURITIES**

*Specified impurities   A, B, C, D, E, F, G.*

*Other detectable impurities* (the following substances would, if present at a sufficient level, be detected by one or other of the tests in the monograph. They are limited by the general acceptance criterion for other/unspecified impurities and/or by the general monograph *Substances for pharmaceutical use (2034)*. It is therefore not necessary to identify these impurities for demonstration of compliance. See also *5.10. Control of impurities in substances for pharmaceutical use): H, I.*

A. 1,7-dihydro-6*H*-purin-6-one (hypoxanthine),

B. R = R′ = OH: 9-β-D-ribofuranosyl-1,9-dihydro-6*H*-purin-6-one (inosine),

C. R = H, R′ = OH: 9-(2-deoxy-β-D-*erythro*-pentofuranosyl)-1,9dihydro-6*H*-purin-6-one (2′-deoxyinosine),

D. R = OH, R′ = H: 9-(3-deoxy-β-D-*erythro*-pentofuranosyl)-1,9dihydro-6*H*-purin-6-one (3′-deoxyinosine),

E. R + R′ = O: 9-(2,3-anhydro-β-D-ribofuranosyl)-1,9-dihydro-6*H*-purin-6-one (2′,3′-anhydroinosine),

F. 9-(2,3-dideoxy-β-D-*glycero*-pent-2-enofuranosyl)-1,9-dihydro-6*H*-purin-6-one (2′,3′-dideoxy-2′,3′-didehydroinosine),

G. R = OH: 9-(2,3-dideoxy-β-D-*glycero*-pentofuranosyl)-9*H*-purin-6-amine (2′,3′-dideoxyadenosine),

H. R = H: 9-(2,3,5-trideoxy-β-D-*glycero*-pentofuranosyl)-9*H*-purin-6-amine (2′,3′,5′-trideoxyadenosine),

I. 9-(2,3-dideoxy-β-D-*glycero*-pent-2-enofuranosyl)-9*H*-purin-6-amine (2′,3′-dideoxy-2′,3′-didehydroadenosine).

*Ph Eur*

# Dienestrol

*(Ph Eur monograph 0483)*

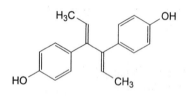

C₁₈H₁₈O₂      266.3      *84-17-3*

**Action and use**
Estrogen.

*Ph Eur*

## DEFINITION

Dienestrol contains not less than 98.5 per cent and not more than the equivalent of 101.5 per cent of (*E,E*)-4,4′-(1,2-diethylidene-ethylene)diphenol, calculated with reference to the dried substance.

## CHARACTERS

A white or almost white, crystalline powder, practically insoluble in water, freely soluble in acetone and in alcohol. It dissolves in dilute solutions of the alkali hydroxides.

## IDENTIFICATION

*First identification*   A, D.

*Second identification*   B, C, D.

A. Examine by infrared absorption spectrophotometry (*2.2.24*), comparing with the spectrum obtained with *dienestrol CRS*. Examine the substances prepared as discs.

B. Examine the chromatograms obtained in the test for related substances. The principal spot in the chromatogram obtained with test solution (b) is similar in position, colour and size to the spot in the chromatogram obtained with reference solution (a).

C. Dissolve about 1 mg in 5 ml of *glacial acetic acid R*, add 1 ml of a 1 per cent *V/V* solution of *bromine R* in *glacial acetic acid R* and heat in a water-bath for 2 min. Place 0.5 ml of this solution in a dry test-tube, add 0.5 ml of *ethanol R*, mix and add 10 ml of *water R*. A reddish-violet colour is produced. Add 5 ml of *chloroform R*, shake vigorously and allow to separate. The chloroform layer is red and the aqueous layer is almost colourless.

D. Dissolve about 0.5 mg in 0.2 ml of *glacial acetic acid R*, add 1 ml of *phosphoric acid R* and heat on a water-bath for 3 min. A reddish-violet colour is produced.

## TESTS

**Melting range**
Determined by the capillary method (*2.2.14*), the melting point is 227 °C to 234 °C. The temperature interval between the formation of a definite meniscus in the melt and the disappearance of the last particle does not exceed 3 °C.

**Related substances**
Examine by thin-layer chromatography (*2.2.27*), using *silica gel G R* as the coating substance.

*Test solution (a)*   Dissolve 0.2 g of the substance to be examined in 2 ml of *alcohol R*.

*Test solution (b)*   Dilute 1 ml of test solution (a) to 20 ml with *alcohol R*.

*Reference solution (a)*   Dissolve 25 mg of *dienestrol CRS* in *alcohol R* and dilute to 5 ml with the same solvent.

*Reference solution (b)*   Dilute 1 ml of reference solution (a) to 10 ml with *alcohol R*.

*Reference solution (c)*   Dissolve 10 mg of *diethylstilbestrol CRS* in 2 ml of *alcohol R*. To 1 ml of this solution add 1 ml of reference solution (a).

Apply separately to the plate 1 μl of each solution. Develop over a path of 15 cm using a mixture of 10 volumes of *diethylamine R* and 90 volumes of *toluene R*. Allow the plate to dry in air, spray with *alcoholic solution of sulphuric acid R* and heat at 120 °C for 10 min. Any spot in the chromatogram obtained with test solution (a), apart from the principal spot, is not more intense than the spot in the chromatogram obtained with reference solution (b) (0.5 per cent). The test is not valid unless the chromatogram obtained with reference solution (c) shows at least two clearly separated spots having approximately the same intensity.

**Loss on drying** (*2.2.32*)
Not more than 0.5 per cent, determined on 1.000 g by drying in an oven at 105 °C.

**Sulphated ash** (*2.4.14*)
Not more than 0.1 per cent, determined on 1.0 g.

## ASSAY

Dissolve 25.0 mg in *ethanol R* and dilute to 100.0 ml with the same solvent. To 5.0 ml of this solution add 10 ml of *ethanol R* and dilute to 250.0 ml with *0.1 M sodium hydroxide*. Prepare a reference solution in the same manner using 25.0 mg of *dienestrol CRS*. Measure the absorbance (*2.2.25*) of the solutions at the maximum at 245 nm.

Calculate the content of C₁₈H₁₈O₂ from the measured absorbances and the concentrations of the solutions.

## STORAGE

Store protected from light.

*Ph Eur*

# Diethyl Phthalate

*(Ph Eur monograph 0897)*

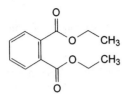

C₁₂H₁₄O₄      222.2      84-66-2

$C_{12}H_{14}O_4$    222.2    84-66-2

## Action and use
Excipient.

*Ph Eur*

## DEFINITION
Diethyl benzene-1,2-dicarboxylate.

## Content
99.0 per cent *m/m* to 101.0 per cent *m/m*.

## CHARACTERS

### Appearance
Clear, colourless or very slightly yellow, oily liquid.

### Solubility
Practically insoluble in water, miscible with ethanol
(96 per cent).

## IDENTIFICATION
*First identification*  B, C.

*Second identification*  A, D, E.

A. Relative density (*2.2.5*): 1.117 to 1.121.

B. Refractive index (*2.2.6*): 1.500 to 1.505.

C. Infrared absorption spectrophotometry (*2.2.24*).

*Preparation*  Thin films.

*Comparison*  diethyl phthalate CRS.

D. Thin-layer chromatography (*2.2.27*).

*Test solution*  Dissolve 50 mg of the substance to be
examined in *ether R* and dilute to 10 ml with the same
solvent.

*Reference solution*  Dissolve 50 mg of *diethyl phthalate CRS*
in *ether R* and dilute to 10 ml with the same solvent.

*Plate*  TLC silica gel GF₂₅₄ plate R.

*Mobile phase*  heptane R, ether R (30:70 *V/V*).

*Application*  10 µl.

*Development*  Over 2/3 of the plate.

*Drying*  In air.

*Detection*  Examine in ultraviolet light at 254 nm.

*Results*  The principal spot in the chromatogram obtained
with the test solution is similar in position and size to the
principal spot in the chromatogram obtained with the
reference solution.

E. To about 0.1 ml add 0.25 ml of *sulphuric acid R* and
50 mg of *resorcinol R*. Heat on a water-bath for 5 min. Allow
to cool. Add 10 ml of *water R* and 1 ml of *strong sodium
hydroxide solution R*. The solution becomes yellow or
brownish-yellow and shows green fluorescence.

## TESTS

### Appearance
The substance to be examined is clear (*2.2.1*) and not more
intensely coloured than reference solution Y₆ (*2.2.2,
Method II*).

### Acidity
Dissolve 20.0 g in 50 ml of *ethanol (96 per cent) R* previously
neutralised to *phenolphthalein solution R1*. Add 0.2 ml of
*phenolphthalein solution R1*. Not more than 0.1 ml of *0.1 M
sodium hydroxide* is required to change the colour of the
indicator to pink.

### Related substances
Gas chromatography (*2.2.28*).

*Internal standard solution*  Dissolve 60 mg of *naphthalene R* in
*methylene chloride R* and dilute to 20 ml with the same
solvent.

*Test solution (a)*  Dissolve 1.0 g of the substance to be
examined in *methylene chloride R* and dilute to 20.0 ml with
the same solvent.

*Test solution (b)*  Dissolve 1.0 g of the substance to be
examined in *methylene chloride R*, add 2.0 ml of the internal
standard solution and dilute to 20.0 ml with *methylene
chloride R*.

*Reference solution*  To 1.0 ml of test solution (a) add 10.0 ml
of the internal standard solution and dilute to 100.0 ml with
*methylene chloride R*.

*Column:*
— *material*: glass;
— *size*: *l* = 2 m, Ø = 2 mm;
— *stationary phase*: *silanised diatomaceous earth for gas
  chromatography R* (150-180 µm) impregnated with
  3 per cent *m/m* of *polymethylphenylsiloxane R*.

*Carrier gas*  *nitrogen for chromatography R*.

*Flow rate*  30 ml/min.

*Temperature:*
— *column*: 150 °C;
— *injection port and detector*: 225 °C.

*Detection*  Flame ionisation.

*Injection*  1 µl.

*Run time*  3 times the retention time of diethyl phthalate.

*Elution order*  Naphthalene, diethyl phtalate.

*System suitability:*
— *resolution*: minimum 10 between the peaks due to
  naphthalene and diethyl phthalate in the chromatogram
  obtained with the reference solution;
— in the chromatogram obtained with test solution (a), there
  is no peak with the same retention time as the internal
  standard.

*Limit:*
— *total*: calculate the ratio (*R*) of the area of the peak due to
  diethyl phthalate to the area of the peak due to the
  internal standard from the chromatogram obtained with
  the reference solution; from the chromatogram obtained
  with test solution (b), calculate the ratio of the sum of the
  areas of any peaks, apart from the principal peak and the
  peak due to the internal standard, to the area of the peak
  due to the internal standard: this ratio is not greater than
  *R* (1.0 per cent).

### Water (*2.5.12*)
Maximum 0.2 per cent, determined on 10.0 g.

### Sulphated ash (*2.4.14*)
Maximum 0.1 per cent, determined on 1.0 g.

## ASSAY

Introduce 0.750 g into a 250 ml borosilicate glass flask. Add 25.0 ml of *0.5 M alcoholic potassium hydroxide* and a few glass beads. Boil in a water-bath under a reflux condenser for 1 h. Add 1 ml of *phenolphthalein solution R1* and titrate immediately with *0.5 M hydrochloric acid*. Carry out a blank titration. Calculate the volume of *0.5 M alcoholic potassium hydroxide* used in the saponification.

1 ml of *0.5 M alcoholic potassium hydroxide* is equivalent to 55.56 mg of $C_{12}H_{14}O_4$.

## STORAGE

In an airtight container.

*———————————————————— Ph Eur*

# Diethylamine Salicylate

$C_{11}H_{17}NO_3$ 211.3 *4419-92-5*

## Action and use
Counter-irritant.

## Preparation
Diethylamine Salicylate Cream

## DEFINITION

Diethylamine Salicylate contains not less than 99.0% and not more than 101.0% of $C_{11}H_{17}NO_3$.

## CHARACTERISTICS

White or almost white crystals.

Very soluble in *water*; freely soluble in *ethanol (96%)*.

## IDENTIFICATION

A. The *infrared absorption spectrum*, Appendix II A, is concordant with the *reference spectrum* of diethylamine salicylate *(RS 099)*.

B. To 0.2 g add 5 ml of 1M *sodium hydroxide*, heat to boiling point, cool and acidify with 2M *hydrochloric acid*; a white precipitate is produced. The *melting point* of the precipitate, after recrystallisation from *water* and drying at 105°, is about 160°, Appendix V A.

## TESTS

### Acidity

Dissolve 2 g in 25 ml of *water* and titrate with 0.1M *sodium hydroxide VS* using *phenol red solution* as indicator. Not more than 0.2 ml of 0.1M *sodium hydroxide VS* is required to change the colour of the solution.

### Clarity and colour of solution

A 50% w/v solution is *clear*, Appendix IV A, and not more intensely coloured than *reference solution BY$_5$*, Appendix IV B, Method II.

### Melting point

100° to 102°, Appendix V A.

## Heavy metals

12 ml of a 10.0% w/v solution complies with *limit test A for heavy metals*, Appendix VII. Use *lead standard solution (1 ppm Pb)* to prepare the standard (10 ppm).

## Sulphate

0.6 g complies with the *limit test for sulphates*, Appendix VII (250 ppm).

## Loss on drying

When dried at 60° for 3 hours, loses not more than 0.1% of its weight. Use 1 g.

## ASSAY

Carry out Method I for *non-aqueous titration*, Appendix VIII A, using 0.4 g and *1-naphtholbenzein solution* as indicator. Each ml of 0.1M *perchloric acid VS* is equivalent to 21.13 mg of $C_{11}H_{17}NO_3$.

## STORAGE

Diethylamine Salicylate should be protected from light. It should not be allowed to come into contact with iron or iron salts.

# Diethylcarbamazine Citrate

*(Ph Eur monograph 0271)*

$C_{10}H_{21}N_3O,C_6H_8O_7$ 391.4 *1642-54-2*

## Action and use
Antihelminthic.

## Preparation
Diethylcarbamazine Tablets

*Ph Eur ————————————————————*

## DEFINITION

*N,N*-Diethyl-4-methylpiperazine-1-carboxamide dihydrogen 2-hydroxypropane-1,2,3-tricarboxylate.

## Content
98.0 per cent to 102.0 per cent (dried substance).

## CHARACTERS

### Appearance
White or almost white, crystalline powder, slightly hygroscopic.

### Solubility
Very soluble in water, soluble in ethanol (96 per cent), practically insoluble in acetone.

mp: about 138 °C, with decomposition.

## IDENTIFICATION

*First identification* A, C.

*Second identification* B, C.

A. Infrared absorption spectrophotometry *(2.2.24)*.

*Comparison* diethylcarbamazine citrate CRS.

B. Examine the chromatograms obtained in the test for impurities A and B.

*Results* The principal spot in the chromatogram obtained with the test solution is similar in position, colour and size to the principal spot in the chromatogram obtained with reference solution (a).

C. Dissolve 0.1 g in 5 ml of *water R*. The solution gives the reaction of citrates (*2.3.1*).

## TESTS

### Solution S

Shake 2.5 g with *water R* until dissolved and dilute to 25 ml with the same solvent.

### Appearance of solution

Solution S is not more opalescent than reference suspension II (*2.2.1*) and not more intensely coloured than reference solution $BY_6$ (*2.2.2, Method II*).

### Impurities A and B

Thin-layer chromatography (*2.2.27*).

*Test solution*  Dissolve 0.5 g of the substance to be examined in *methanol R* and dilute to 10 ml with the same solvent.

*Reference solution (a)*  Dissolve 0.1 g of *diethylcarbamazine citrate CRS* in *methanol R* and dilute to 2.0 ml with the same solvent.

*Reference solution (b)*  Dissolve 10 mg of *methylpiperazine R* (impurity A) in *methanol R* and dilute to 100 ml with the same solvent.

*Reference solution (c)*  Dissolve 10 mg of *dimethylpiperazine R* (impurity B) in *methanol R* and dilute to 100 ml with the same solvent.

*Plate*  *TLC silica gel plate R.*

*Mobile phase*  concentrated ammonia R, methyl ethyl ketone R, methanol R (5:30:65 *V/V/V*).

*Application*  10 µl.

*Development*  Over 2/3 of the plate.

*Drying*  At 100-105 °C.

*Detection*  Expose to iodine vapour for 30 min.

*Retardation factors*  Impurity A = about 0.2; impurity B = about 0.5.

*Limits:*
— *impurity A:* any spot due to impurity A is not more intense than the corresponding spot in the chromatogram obtained with reference solution (b) (0.2 per cent);
— *impurity B:* any spot due to impurity B is not more intense than the corresponding spot in the chromatogram obtained with reference solution (c) (0.2 per cent).

### Related substances

Liquid chromatography (*2.2.29*).

*Solution A*  Dissolve 31.2 g of *potassium dihydrogen phosphate R* in *water R* and dilute to 1000 ml with the same solvent.

*Test solution (a)*  Suspend 0.30 g of the substance to be examined in solution A and dilute to 100 ml with solution A. Filter or centrifuge and use the clear filtrate or supernatant.

*Test solution (b)*  Dissolve 10.0 mg of the substance to be examined in solution A and dilute to 100.0 ml with solution A.

*Reference solution (a)*  Dilute 1.0 ml of test solution (a) to 100.0 ml with solution A. Dilute 1.0 ml of this solution to 10.0 ml with solution A.

*Reference solution (b)*  Dissolve 10 mg of *citric acid R* in solution A and dilute to 10 ml with solution A.

*Reference solution (c)*  To 3 ml of test solution (a) add 0.5 ml of *strong hydrogen peroxide solution R* and maintain at 80 °C for 3 h. Dilute to 100 ml with solution A.

*Reference solution (d)*  Dissolve 5.0 mg of *diethylcarbamazine citrate CRS* in solution A and dilute to 50.0 ml with solution A.

*Column:*
— *size: l* = 0.15 m, Ø = 3.9 mm;
— *stationary phase:* end-*capped octadecylsilyl silica gel for chromatography R* (5 µm).

*Mobile phase*  Mix 100 volumes of *methanol R2* and 900 volumes of a 10 g/l solution of *potassium dihydrogen phosphate R*.

*Flow rate*  0.8 ml/min.

*Detection*  Spectrophotometer at 220 nm.

*Injection*  20 µl of test solution (a) and reference solutions (a), (b) and (c).

*Run time*  Twice the retention time of diethylcarbamazine.

*Identification of impurities*  Use the chromatogram obtained with reference solution (b) to identify the peak due to the citrate.

*Relative retention*  With reference to diethylcarbamazine (retention time = about 7 min): citrate = about 0.2; degradation product = about 1.6.

*System suitability*  Reference solution (c):
— *resolution:* minimum 5 between the peaks due to diethylcarbamazine and the degradation product.

*Limits:*
— *unspecified impurities:* for each impurity, not more than the area of the principal peak in the chromatogram obtained with reference solution (a) (0.10 per cent);
— *total:* not more than 5 times the area of the principal peak in the chromatogram obtained with reference solution (a) (0.5 per cent);
— *disregard limit:* 0.5 times the area of the principal peak in the chromatogram obtained with reference solution (a) (0.05 per cent); disregard the peak due to the citrate.

### Heavy metals (*2.4.8*)

Maximum 20 ppm.

12 ml of solution S complies with test A. Prepare the reference solution using 10 ml *of lead standard solution (2 ppm Pb) R.*

### Loss on drying (*2.2.32*)

Maximum 0.5 per cent, determined on 1.000 g by drying *in vacuo* at 60 °C for 4 h.

### Sulphated ash (*2.4.14*)

Maximum 0.1 per cent, determined on 1.0 g.

## ASSAY

Liquid chromatography (*2.2.29*) as described in the test for related substances with the following modification.

*Injection*  20 µl of test solution (b) and reference solution (d).

Calculate the percentage content of $C_{16}H_{29}N_3O_8$ from the declared content of *diethylcarbamazine citrate CRS.*

## STORAGE

In an airtight container.

## IMPURITIES

*Specified impurities*  *A, B.*

A. R = H: 1-methylpiperazine,

B. R = $CH_3$: 1,4-dimethylpiperazine.

*Ph Eur*

# Diethylene Glycol Monoethyl Ether

*(Ph Eur monograph 1198)*

H3C~O~~O~~OH

C₆H₁₄O₃      134.2      *111-90-0*

$C_6H_{14}O_3$    134.2     *111-90-0*

**Action and use**
Excipient.

*Ph Eur* _____

## DEFINITION
2-(2-Ethoxyethoxy)ethanol, produced by condensation of
ethylene oxide and alcohol, followed by distillation.

## CHARACTERS
**Appearance**
Clear, colourless, hygroscopic liquid.

**Solubility**
Miscible with water, with acetone and with alcohol, miscible
in certain proportions with vegetable oils, not miscible with
mineral oils.

**Relative density**
About 0.991.

## IDENTIFICATION
A. Refractive index (*2.2.6*): 1.426 to 1.428.

B. Infrared absorption spectrophotometry (*2.2.24*).

*Comparison*  Ph. Eur. reference spectrum of diethylene glycol
monoethyl ether.

## TESTS
**Acid value** (*2.5.1*)
Maximum 0.1.

Mix 30.0 ml with 30 ml of *alcohol R* previously neutralised
with *0.1 M potassium hydroxide* using *phenolphthalein
solution R* as indicator. Titrate with *0.01 M alcoholic potassium
hydroxide.*

**Peroxide value** (*2.5.5*)
Maximum 8.0, determined on 2.00 g.

**Related substances**
Gas chromatography (*2.2.28*).

*Internal standard solution*  Dilute 1.00 g of *decane R* to
100.0 ml with *methanol R.*

*Test solution*  To 5.00 g of the substance to be examined,
add 0.1 ml of the internal standard solution and dilute to
10.0 ml with *methanol R.*

*Reference solution (a)*  Dilute 25.0 mg *of ethylene glycol
monomethyl ether R*, 80.0 mg of *ethylene glycol monoethyl
ether R*, 0.310 g of *ethylene glycol R* and 0.125 g of *diethylene
glycol R* to 100.0 ml with *methanol R.* To 1.0 ml of this
solution add 0.1 ml of the internal standard solution and
dilute to 10.0 ml with *methanol R.*

*Reference solution (b)*  Dilute 25.0 mg of *ethylene glycol
monomethyl ether R* and 25.0 mg of *ethylene glycol R* to 100.0 ml
with *methanol R.* Dilute 1.0 ml of this solution to 5.0 ml with
*methanol R.*

*Reference solution (c)*  Dilute 1.00 g of the substance to be
examined to 100.0 ml with *methanol R.* To 1.0 ml of this
solution add 0.1 ml of the internal standard solution and
dilute to 10.0 ml with *methanol R.*

*Column:*
— *material*: fused silica,

— *size: l* = 30 m, Ø = 0.32 mm,
— *stationary phase:*
   poly(cyanopropyl) (7) (phenyl) (7) methyl (86) siloxane R (film
   thickness 1 μm).

*Carrier gas   nitrogen for chromatography R* or *helium for
chromatography R.*

*Flow rate*  2.0 ml/min.

*Split ratio*  1:80.

*Temperature:*

|  | Time (min) | Temperature (°C) |
|---|---|---|
| Column | 0 - 1 | 120 |
|  | 1 - 10 | 120 → 225 |
|  | 10 - 12 | 225 |
| Injection port |  | 275 |
| Detector |  | 250 |

*Detection*  Flame ionisation.

*Injection*  0.5 μl.

*Relative retentions*  With reference to diethylene glycol
monoethyl ether (retention time = about 4 min):
ethylene glycol monomethyl ether = about 0.4;
ethylene glycol monoethyl ether = about 0.5;
ethylene glycol = about 0.55; diethylene glycol = about 1.1.

*System suitability:*
— *resolution*: minimum 3.0 between the peaks due to
   ethylene glycol monoethyl ether and to ethylene glycol in
   the chromatogram obtained with reference solution (b),
— *signal-to-noise ratio*: minimum 3.0 for the peak due to
   ethylene glycol monomethyl ether in the chromatogram
   obtained with reference solution (a),

*Limits*   (take into account the impurity/internal standard
peak area ratio):
— *ethylene glycol monomethyl ether*: not more than the area of
   the corresponding peak in the chromatogram obtained
   with reference solution (a) (50 ppm),
— *ethylene glycol monoethyl ether*: not more than the area of
   the corresponding peak in the chromatogram obtained
   with reference solution (a) (160 ppm),
— *ethylene glycol*: not more than the area of the
   corresponding peak in the chromatogram obtained with
   reference solution (a) (620 ppm),
— *diethylene glycol*: not more than the area of the
   corresponding peak in the chromatogram obtained with
   reference solution (a) (250 ppm),
— *total*: not more than the area of the principal peak in the
   chromatogram obtained with reference solution (c)
   (0.2 per cent).

**Ethylene oxide**
Head-space gas chromatography (*2.2.28*).

*Test solution*  To 1.00 g of the substance to be examined in a
vial, add 50 μl of *water R.*

*Reference solution*  To 1.00 g of the substance to be examined
in a vial, add 50 μl of *ethylene oxide solution R4* and close
tightly.

*Column:*
— *material*: fused silica,
— *size: l* = 30 m, Ø = 0.32 mm,
— *stationary phase:*
   poly(cyanopropyl) (7) (phenyl) (7) methyl (86) siloxane R (film
   thickness 1 μm).

*Carrier gas   helium for chromatography R.*

*Flow rate*  1.1 ml/min.

*Static head-space conditions which may be used:*
— *equilibration temperature*: 80 °C,
— *equilibration time*: 45 min,
— *transfer line temperature*: 110 °C,
— *pressurisation time*: 2 min,
— *injection time*: 12 s.

*Temperature:*

| | Time (min) | Temperature (°C) |
|---|---|---|
| Column | 0 - 5 | 40 |
| | 5 - 18 | 40 → 200 |
| Injection port | | 150 |
| Detector | | 250 |

*Detection*  Flame ionisation.

*Injection*  1.0 ml.

The peak due to ethylene oxide is identified by injecting solutions of ethylene oxide of increasing concentration.

Determine the content of ethylene oxide (ppm) in the substance to be examined using the following expression:

$$\frac{S_T \times C}{(S_S \times M_T) - (S_T \times M_S)}$$

$S_T$ = area of the peak corresponding to ethylene oxide in the chromatogram obtained with the test solution,

$S_S$ = area of the peak corresponding to ethylene oxide in the chromatogram obtained with the reference solution,

$M_T$ = mass of the substance to be examined in the test solution, in grams,

$M_S$ = mass of the substance to be examined in the reference solution, in grams,

$C$ = mass of added ethylene oxide in the reference solution, in micrograms.

*Limit:*
— *ethylene oxide*: maximum 1 ppm.

**Water** (*2.5.12*)
Maximum 0.1 per cent, determined on 10.0 g.

**STORAGE**
Under an inert gas, in an airtight container.

**LABELLING**
The label states that the substance is stored under an inert gas.

*Ph Eur*

---

# Diethylene Glycol Palmitostearate

(*Ph Eur monograph 1415*)

**Action and use**
Excipient.

*Ph Eur* _____

**DEFINITION**
Mixture of diethylene glycol mono- and diesters of stearic (octadecanoic) and palmitic (hexadecanoic) acids.

It is produced by esterification of diethylene glycol and stearic acid 50 (see *Stearic acid (1474)*) of vegetable or animal origin.

**Content:**
— *monoesters*: 45.0 per cent to 60.0 per cent;
— *diesters*: 35.0 per cent to 55.0 per cent.

**CHARACTERS**
**Appearance**
White or almost white, waxy solid.

**Solubility**
Practically insoluble in water, soluble in acetone and in hot ethanol (96 per cent).

**IDENTIFICATION**
A. Melting point (see Tests).
B. Composition of fatty acids (see Tests).
C. It complies with the limit of the assay (monoesters content).

**TESTS**
**Melting point** (*2.2.15*)
43 °C to 50 °C.

**Acid value** (*2.5.1*)
Maximum 4.0.

**Iodine value** (*2.5.4, Method A*)
Maximum 3.0.

**Saponification value** (*2.5.6*)
155 to 180, determined on 2.0 g.

**Composition of fatty acids** (*2.4.22, Method A*)
Use the mixture of calibrating substances in Table 2.4.22.-1.
*Composition of the fatty acid fraction of the substance:*
— *stearic acid*: 40.0 per cent to 60.0 per cent;
— *sum of contents of palmitic acid and stearic acid*: minimum 90.0 per cent.

**Free diethylene glycol**
Maximum 2.5 per cent, determined as described in the assay.

**Total ash** (*2.4.16*)
Maximum 0.1 per cent.

**ASSAY**
Size-exclusion chromatography (*2.2.30*).

*Test solution*  Into a 15 ml flask, weigh 0.200 g (m). Add 5.0 ml of *tetrahydrofuran R* and shake to dissolve. Heat gently, if necessary. Reweigh the flask and calculate the total mass of solvent and substance (*M*).

*Reference solutions*  Into four 15 ml flasks, weigh, 2.5 mg, 5.0 mg, 10.0 mg and 20.0 mg respectively of *diethylene glycol R*. Add 5.0 ml of *tetrahydrofuran R*. Weigh the flasks again and calculate the concentration of diethylene glycol in milligrams per gram for each reference solution.

*Column:*
— *size*: *l* = 0.6 m, Ø = 7 mm,
— *stationary phase*: styrene-divinylbenzene copolymer R (5 μm) with a pore size of 10 nm.

*Mobile phase*  tetrahydrofuran R.

*Flow rate*  1 ml/min.

*Detection*  Differential refractometer.

*Injection*  40 μl.

*Relative retention*  With reference to diethylene glycol: diesters = about 0.78; monoesters = about 0.84.

*Calculations:*
— *free diethylene glycol*: from the calibration curve obtained with the reference solutions, determine the concentration (*C*) of diethylene glycol in milligrams per gram in the test solution and calculate the percentage content of free

diethylene glycol in the substance to be examined using the following expression:

$$\frac{C \times M}{m \times 10}$$

— *monoesters*: calculate the percentage content of monoesters using the following expression:

$$\frac{A}{A + B} \times (100 - D)$$

$A$ = area of the peak due to the monoesters,
$B$ = area of the peak due to the diesters,
$D$ = percentage content of free diethylene glycol + percentage content of free fatty acids.

Calculate the percentage content of free fatty acids using the following expression:

$$\frac{I_A \times 270}{561.1}$$

$I_A$ = acid value.

— *diesters*: calculate the percentage content of diesters using the following expression:

$$\frac{B}{A + B} \times (100 - D)$$

## STORAGE

Protected from light.

_____ *Ph Eur*

# Diethylstilbestrol

*(Ph Eur monograph 0484)*

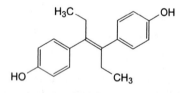

C$_{18}$H$_{20}$O$_2$     268.4     *56-53-1*

## Action and use

Estrogen.

## Preparations

Diethylstilbestrol Pessaries

Diethylstilbestrol Tablets

*Ph Eur* _____

## DEFINITION

Diethylstilbestrol contains not less than 97.0 per cent and not more than the equivalent of 101.0 per cent of (E)-4,4′-(1,2-diethylethene-1,2-diyl)diphenol, calculated with reference to the dried substance.

## CHARACTERS

A white or almost white, crystalline powder, practically insoluble in water, freely soluble in alcohol. It dissolves in solutions of the alkali hydroxides.

It melts at about 172 °C.

## IDENTIFICATION

*First identification*  B, D.

*Second identification*  A, C, D.

A. Examined between 230 nm and 450 nm (*2.2.25*), the irradiated solution of the substance to be examined prepared as prescribed in the assay shows two absorption maxima, at 292 nm and 418 nm.

B. Examine by infrared absorption spectrophotometry (*2.2.24*), comparing with the spectrum obtained with *diethylstilbestrol CRS*. Examine the substances prepared as discs.

C. Examine the chromatograms obtained in the test for mono-and dimethyl ethers. The principal spot in the chromatogram obtained with test solution (b) is similar in position, colour and size to the principal spot in the chromatogram obtained with reference solution (a).

D. Dissolve about 0.5 mg in 0.2 ml of *glacial acetic acid R*, add 1 ml of *phosphoric acid R* and heat on a water-bath for 3 min. A deep-yellow colour develops.

## TESTS

### 4,4′-Dihydroxystilbene and related ethers

Dissolve 0.100 g in *ethanol R* and dilute to 10.0 ml with the same solvent. The absorbance (*2.2.25*) of the solution measured at 325 nm is not greater than 0.50.

### Mono- and dimethyl ethers

Examine by thin-layer chromatography (*2.2.27*), using *silica gel G R* as the coating substance.

*Test solution (a)*  Dissolve 0.2 g of the substance to be examined in 2 ml of *alcohol R*.

*Test solution (b)*  Dilute 1 ml of test solution (a) to 20 ml with *alcohol R*.

*Reference solution (a)*  Dissolve 10 mg of *diethylstilbestrol CRS* in 2 ml of *alcohol R*.

*Reference solution (b)*  Dissolve 5 mg of *diethylstilbestrol monomethyl ether CRS* in *alcohol R* and dilute to 10 ml with the same solvent.

*Reference solution (c)*  Dissolve 5 mg of *diethylstilbestrol dimethyl ether CRS* in *alcohol R* and dilute to 10 ml with the same solvent.

*Reference solution (d)*  Dissolve 10 mg of *dienestrol CRS* in 2 ml of *alcohol R*. To 1 ml of this solution add 1 ml of reference solution (a).

Apply to the plate 1 µl of each solution. Develop over a path of 15 cm using a mixture of 10 volumes of *diethylamine R* and 90 volumes of *toluene R*. Allow the plate to dry in air, spray with *alcoholic solution of sulphuric acid R* and heat at 120 °C for 10 min. In the chromatogram obtained with test solution (a), any spots corresponding to diethylstilbestrol monomethyl ether and diethylstilbestrol dimethyl ether are not more intense than the spots in the chromatograms obtained with reference solutions (b) and (c) respectively (0.5 per cent). Diethylstilbestrol gives one or sometimes two spots. The test is not valid unless the chromatogram obtained with reference solution (d) shows at least two clearly separated spots having approximately the same intensity.

### Loss on drying (*2.2.32*)

Not more than 0.5 per cent, determined on 1.000 g by drying in an oven at 105 °C.

### Sulphated ash (*2.4.14*)

Not more than 0.1 per cent, determined on 1.0 g.

## ASSAY

Dissolve 20.0 mg in *ethanol R* and dilute to 100.0 ml with the same solvent. Dilute 10.0 ml of the solution to 100.0 ml with *ethanol R*. To 25.0 ml of the resulting solution add 25.0 ml of a solution of 1 g of *dipotassium hydrogen phosphate R* in 55 ml of *water R*. Prepare in the same manner a reference solution using 20.0 mg of *diethylstilbestrol CRS*. Transfer an equal volume of each solution to separate 1 cm quartz cells and close the cells; place the two cells about 5 cm from a low-pressure, short-wave 2 W to 20 W mercury lamp and irradiate for about 5 min. Measure the absorbance (*2.2.25*) of the irradiated solutions at the maximum at 418 nm, using *water R* as the compensation liquid. Continue the irradiation for successive periods of 3 min to 15 min, depending on the power of the lamp, and repeat the measurement of the absorbances at 418 nm until the maximum absorbance (about 0.7) is obtained. If necessary, adjust the geometry of the irradiation apparatus to obtain a maximum, reproducible absorbance at 418 nm.

Calculate the content of $C_{18}H_{20}O_2$ from the measured absorbances and the concentrations of the solutions.

## STORAGE

Store protected from light.

*_____ Ph Eur*

# Diflucortolone Valerate

$C_{27}H_{36}F_2O_5$      478.6      *59198-70-8*

### Action and use
Glucocorticoid.

### Preparations
Diflucortolone Cream

Diflucortolone Oily Cream

Diflucortolone Ointment

## DEFINITION

Diflucortolone Valerate is 6α,9α-difluoro-3,20-dioxo-11β-hydroxy-16α-methylpregna-1,4-dien-21-yl valerate. It contains not less than 97.0% and not more than 102.0% of $C_{27}H_{36}F_2O_5$, calculated with reference to the dried substance.

## CHARACTERISTICS

A white to creamy white, crystalline powder.

Practically insoluble in *water*; freely soluble in *dichloromethane* and in *1,4-dioxan*; slightly soluble in *methanol*; sparingly soluble in *ether*.

## IDENTIFICATION

A. The *light absorption*, Appendix II B, in the range 210 to 350 nm of a 0.002% w/v solution in *methanol* exhibits a maximum only at 238 nm. The *absorbance* at the maximum at 238 nm is about 0.69.

B. The *infrared absorption spectrum*, Appendix II A, is concordant with the *reference spectrum* of diflucortolone valerate *(RS 100)*.

## TESTS

### Specific optical rotation
In a *1% w/v* solution in *1,4-dioxan*, +98 to +103, Appendix V F, calculated with reference to the dried substance.

### Related substances
Carry out the method for *liquid chromatography*, Appendix III D, injecting 20 µl of each of the following solutions in a mixture of 25 volumes of *water* and 75 volumes of *acetonitrile*. Solution (1) contains 0.060% w/v of the substance being examined. For solution (2) dilute 1 volume of solution (1) to 100 volumes. Solution (3) contains 0.060% w/v of *diflucortolone valerate impurity standard BPCRS*.

The chromatographic procedure may be carried out using (a) a stainless steel column (10 cm × 4.6 mm) packed with *end-capped octadecylsilyl silica gel for chromatography* (3 µm) (Spherisorb ODS 2 is suitable), (b) a mixture of equal volumes of *acetonitrile* and *water* as the mobile phase with a flow rate of 2 ml per minute and (c) a detection wavelength of 238 nm. If necessary the composition of the mobile phase may be altered so that the chromatogram obtained with solution (3) shows similar resolution to the reference chromatogram supplied with *diflucortolone valerate impurity standard BPCRS*.

Continue the chromatography for twice the retention time of the principal peak. In the chromatogram obtained with solution (1) the area of any *secondary peak* is not greater than the area of the principal peak in the chromatogram obtained with solution (2) (1%) and the sum of the areas of any *secondary peaks* is not greater than twice the area of the principal peak in the chromatogram obtained with solution (2) (2%).

### Loss on drying
When dried to constant weight at 105°, loses not more than 0.5% of its weight. Use 1 g.

## ASSAY

Carry out the method for *liquid chromatography*, Appendix III D, using the following three solutions in a mixture of 25 volumes of *water* and 75 volumes of *acetonitrile* containing (1) 0.03% w/v of the substance being examined, (2) 0.03% w/v of *diflucortolone valerate BPCRS* and (3) 0.03% w/v of *diflucortolone valerate impurity standard BPCRS*.

The chromatographic procedure described under Related substances may be used.

Calculate the content of $C_{27}H_{36}F_2O_5$ from the declared content of $C_{27}H_{36}F_2O_5$ in *diflucortolone valerate BPCRS*.

## STORAGE

Diflucortolone Valerate should be protected from light.

## IMPURITIES

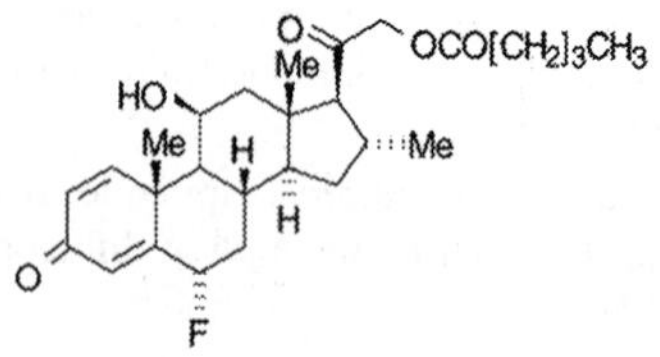

A. 6α-fluoro-3,20-dioxo-11β-hydroxy-16α-methylpregna-1,4-dien-21-yl valerate

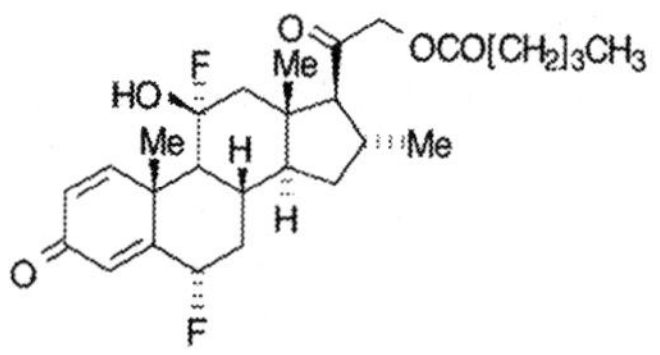

B. 6α,12α-difluoro-3,20-dioxo-11β-hydroxy-16α-methylpregna-1,4-dien-21-yl valerate

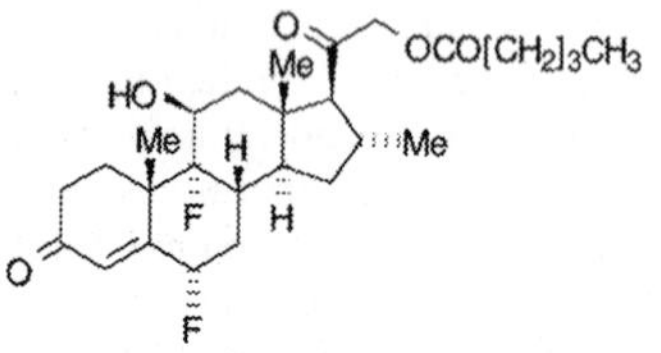

C. 6α,9α-difluoro-3,20-dioxo-11β-hydroxy-16α-methylpregna-1,4-dien-21-yl valerate

# Diflunisal

*(Ph Eur monograph 0818)*

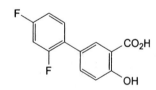

$C_{13}H_8F_2O_3$          250.2          22494-42-4

## Action and use
Salicylate; non-selective cyclo-oxygenase inhibitor; antipyretic; analgesic; anti-inflammatory.

## Preparation
Diflunisal Tablets

*Ph Eur*

## DEFINITION
2′,4′-Difluoro-4-hydroxybiphenyl-3-carboxylic acid.

## Content
99.0 per cent to 101.0 per cent (dried substance).

## CHARACTERS
### Appearance
White or almost white, crystalline powder.

### Solubility
Practically insoluble in water, soluble in ethanol (96 per cent). It dissolves in dilute solutions of alkali hydroxides.

It shows polymorphism (*5.9*).

## IDENTIFICATION
*First identification   B.*

*Second identification   A, C, D.*

A. Ultraviolet and visible absorption spectrophotometry (*2.2.25*).

*Test solution   Dissolve 10 mg in a 0.3 per cent V/V solution of hydrochloric acid R in methanol R and dilute to 100.0 ml with the same solution. Dilute 2.0 ml of this solution to 10.0 ml with a 0.3 per cent V/V solution of hydrochloric acid R in methanol R.*

*Spectral range   230-350 nm.*

*Absorption maxima   At 251 nm and 315 nm.*

*Absorbance ratio   $A_{251} / A_{315}$ = 4.2 to 4.6.*

B. Infrared absorption spectrophotometry (*2.2.24*).

*Comparison   diflunisal CRS.*

If the spectra obtained show differences, dissolve the substance to be examined and the reference substance separately in *ethanol (96 per cent) R*, evaporate to dryness and record new spectra using the residues.

C. Dissolve about 2 mg in 10 ml of *ethanol (96 per cent) R* and add 0.1 ml of *ferric chloride solution R1*. A violet-red colour is produced.

D. Mix about 5 mg with 45 mg of *heavy magnesium oxide R* and ignite in a crucible until an almost white residue is obtained (usually less than 5 min). Allow to cool, add 1 ml of *water R*, 0.05 ml of *phenolphthalein solution R1* and about 1 ml of *dilute hydrochloric acid R* to render the solution colourless. Filter. Add 1.0 ml of the filtrate to a freshly prepared mixture of 0.1 ml of *alizarin S solution R* and 0.1 ml of *zirconyl nitrate solution R*. Mix, allow to stand for 5 min and compare the colour of the solution with that of a blank prepared in the same manner. The test solution is yellow and the blank is red.

## TESTS
### Appearance of solution
The solution is clear (*2.2.1*) and not more intensely coloured than reference solution $Y_7$ (*2.2.2, Method II*).

Dissolve 0.5 g in *ethanol (96 per cent) R* and dilute to 50 ml with the same solvent.

### Related substances
A. Thin-layer chromatography (*2.2.27*).

*Test solution   Dissolve 0.20 g of the substance to be examined in methanol R and dilute to 10 ml with the same solvent.*

*Reference solution (a)   Dissolve 30 mg of biphenyl-4-ol R (impurity A) in methanol R and dilute to 100 ml with the same solvent. Dilute 1 ml of this solution to 10 ml with methanol R.*

*Reference solution (b)   Dissolve 20 mg of biphenyl-4-ol R (impurity A) in methanol R, add 1 ml of the test solution and dilute to 10 ml with methanol R.*

*Plate   TLC silica gel GF$_{254}$ plate R.*

*Mobile phase   glacial acetic acid R, acetone R, methylene chloride R (10:20:70 V/V/V).*

*Application   10 μl.*

*Development   Over a path of 15 cm.*

*Drying* In a current of warm air.

*Detection* Examine in ultraviolet light at 254 nm.

*System suitability* Reference solution (b):
— the chromatogram shows 2 clearly separated principal spots.

*Limit:*
— *any impurity*: any spot, apart from the principal spot, is not more intense than the principal spot in the chromatogram obtained with reference solution (a) (0.15 per cent).

B. Liquid chromatography (*2.2.29*).

*Test solution* Dissolve 50.0 mg of the substance to be examined in the reference solution and dilute to 10.0 ml with the reference solution.

*Reference solution* Dissolve 55.0 mg of *fluoranthene R* in a mixture of 1 volume of *water R* and 4 volumes of *acetonitrile R* and dilute to 100.0 ml with the same mixture of solvents. Dilute 1.0 ml of this solution to 100.0 ml with a mixture of 1 volume of *water R* and 4 volumes of *acetonitrile R*.

*Column:*
— *size*: l = 0.25 m, Ø = 4 mm;
— *stationary phase*: octadecylsilyl silica gel for chromatography R (10 µm).

*Mobile phase* glacial acetic acid R, methanol R, water R, acetonitrile R (2:25:55:70 V/V/V/V).

*Flow rate* 2 ml/min.

*Detection* Spectrophotometer at 254 nm.

*Injection* 20 µl.

*Run time* 3 times the retention time of fluoranthene.

*Limits:*
— *sum of the impurities with a retention time greater than that of fluoroanthene*: not more than the area of the principal peak in the chromatogram obtained with the reference solution (0.1 per cent);
— *disregard limit*: 0.05 times the area of the principal peak in the chromatogram obtained with the reference solution (0.005 per cent).

**Heavy metals** (*2.4.8*)
Maximum 10 ppm.

2.0 g complies with test C. Use a platinum crucible. Prepare the reference solution using 2 ml of *lead standard solution (10 ppm Pb) R*.

**Loss on drying** (*2.2.32*)
Maximum 0.3 per cent, determined on 1.000 g by drying at 60 °C at a pressure not exceeding 0.7 kPa for 2 h.

**Sulphated ash** (*2.4.14*)
Maximum 0.1 per cent, determined on 1.0 g in a platinum crucible.

**ASSAY**
Dissolve 0.200 g in 40 ml of *methanol R*. Add 5 ml of *water R* and 0.2 ml of *phenol red solution R*. Titrate with *0.1 M sodium hydroxide* until the colour changes from yellow to reddish-violet.

1 ml of *0.1 M sodium hydroxide* is equivalent to 25.02 mg of $C_{13}H_8F_2O_3$.

**STORAGE**
Protected from light.

**IMPURITIES**

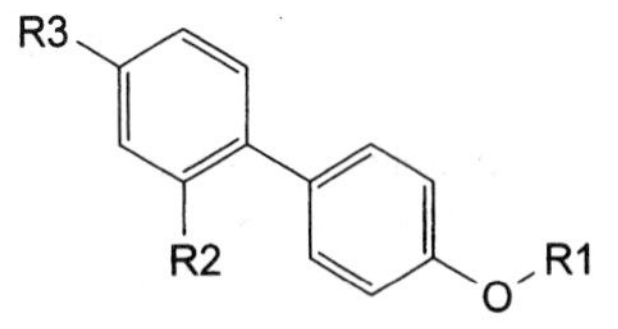

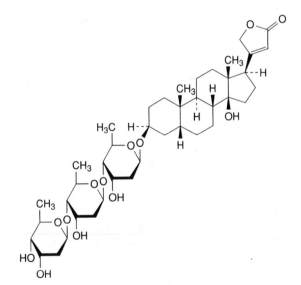

A. R1 = R2 = R3 = H: biphenyl-4-ol,
B. R1 = H, R2 = R3 = F: 2',4'-difluorobiphenyl-4-ol,
C. R1 = CO-CH₃, R2 = R3 = F: 2',4'-difluorobiphenyl-4-yl acetate,
D. condensation products.

*Ph Eur*

# Digitoxin

(*Ph Eur monograph 0078*)

$C_{41}H_{64}O_{13}$     765     71-63-6

**Action and use**
Na/K-ATPase inhibitor; cardiac glycoside.

**Preparation**
Digitoxin Tablets

*Ph Eur*

**DEFINITION**
Digitoxin contains not less than 95.0 per cent and not more than the equivalent of 103.0 per cent of 3β-[(O-2,6-dideoxy-β-D-*ribo*-hexopyranosyl-(1→4)-O-2,6-dideoxy-β-D-*ribo*-hexopyranosyl-(1→4)-2,6-dideoxy-β-D-*ribo*-hexopyranosyl)oxy]-14-hydroxy-5β,14β-card-20(22)-enolide, calculated with reference to the dried substance.

**CHARACTERS**
A white or almost white powder, practically insoluble in water, freely soluble in a mixture of equal volumes of methanol and methylene chloride, slightly soluble in alcohol and in methanol.

**IDENTIFICATION**
*First identification A.*

*Second identification* B, C, D.

A. Examine by infrared absorption spectrophotometry (*2.2.24*), comparing with the spectrum obtained with *digitoxin CRS*.

B. Examine the chromatograms obtained in the test for related substances. The principal spot in the chromatogram obtained with the test solution is similar in position, colour and size to the principal spot in the chromatogram obtained with reference solution (a).

C. Suspend about 0.5 mg in 0.2 ml of *alcohol (60 per cent V/V) R*. Add 0.1 ml of *dinitrobenzoic acid solution R* and 0.1 ml of *dilute sodium hydroxide solution R*. A violet colour develops.

D. Dissolve about 0.5 mg in 1 ml of *glacial acetic acid R*, heating gently, allow to cool and add 0.05 ml of *ferric chloride solution R1*. Cautiously add 1 ml of *sulphuric acid R*, avoiding mixing the two liquids. A brown ring develops at the interface and on standing a green, then blue colour passes to the upper layer.

## TESTS

### Appearance of solution

Dissolve 50 mg in a mixture of equal volumes of *methanol R* and *methylene chloride R* and dilute to 10 ml with the same mixture of solvents. The solution is clear (*2.2.1*) and colourless (*2.2.2, Method I*).

### Specific optical rotation (*2.2.7*)

Dissolve 0.25 g in *chloroform R* and dilute to 10.0 ml with the same solvent. The specific optical rotation is + 16.0 to + 18.5.

### Related substances

Examine by thin-layer chromatography (*2.2.27*), using a *TLC silica gel G plate R*.

*Test solution* Dissolve 20 mg of the substance to be examined in a mixture of equal volumes of *methanol R* and *methylene chloride R* and dilute to 2 ml with the same mixture of solvents.

*Reference solution (a)* Dissolve 20 mg of *digitoxin CRS* in a mixture of equal volumes of *methanol R* and *methylene chloride R* and dilute to 2 ml with the same mixture of solvents.

*Reference solution (b)* Dilute 0.5 ml of reference solution (a) to 50 ml with a mixture of equal volumes of *methanol R* and *methylene chloride R*.

*Reference solution (c)* Dissolve 10 mg of *gitoxin CRS* with stirring in a mixture of equal volumes of *methanol R* and *methylene chloride R* and dilute to 50 ml with the same mixture of solvents.

*Reference solution (d)* Dilute 1 ml of reference solution (b) to 2 ml with a mixture of equal volumes of *methanol R* and *methylene chloride R*.

*Reference solution (e)* Mix 1 ml of reference solution (a) and 1 ml of reference solution (c).

Apply to the plate 5 µl of each solution. Develop immediately over a path of 15 cm using a mixture of 15 volumes of *methanol R*, 40 volumes of *cyclohexane R* and 90 volumes of *methylene chloride R*. Dry the plate in a stream of cold air for 5 min. Repeat the development and dry the plate in a stream of cold air for 5 min. Spray with a mixture of 1 volume of *sulphuric acid R* and 9 volumes of *alcohol R* and heat at 130 °C for 15 min. Examine in daylight.

*Gitoxin* Any spot corresponding to gitoxin in the chromatogram obtained with the test solution is not more intense than the spot in the chromatogram obtained with reference solution (c) (2.0 per cent).

*Other glycosides* Any spot in the chromatogram obtained with the test solution, apart from the principal spot and the spot corresponding to gitoxin, is not more intense than the spot in the chromatogram obtained with reference solution (b) (1.0 per cent). The test is not valid unless the chromatogram obtained with reference solution (e) shows clearly separated spots corresponding to digitoxin, gitoxin and other glycosides and the spot in the chromatogram obtained with reference solution (d) is clearly visible.

### Loss on drying (*2.2.32*)

Not more than 1.5 per cent, determined on 0.500 g by drying in an oven at 105 °C for 2 h.

### Sulphated ash (*2.4.14*)

Not more than 0.1 per cent, determined on the residue from the test for loss on drying.

## ASSAY

Dissolve 40.0 mg in *alcohol R* and dilute to 50.0 ml with the same solvent. Dilute 5.0 ml of the solution to 100.0 ml with *alcohol R*. Prepare a reference solution in the same manner, using 40.0 mg of *digitoxin CRS*. To 5.0 ml of each solution add 3.0 ml of *alkaline sodium picrate solution R*, allow to stand protected from bright light for 30 min and measure the absorbance (*2.2.25*) of each solution at the maximum at 495 nm, using as the compensation liquid a mixture of 5.0 ml of *alcohol R* and 3.0 ml of *alkaline sodium picrate solution R* prepared at the same time.

Calculate the content of $C_{41}H_{64}O_{13}$ from the absorbances measured and the concentrations of the solutions.

## STORAGE

Store protected from light.

*Ph Eur*

# Digoxin

*(Ph Eur monograph 0079)*

C$_{41}$H$_{64}$O$_{14}$ 781 20830-75-5

### Action and use
Na/K-ATPase inhibitor; cardiac glycoside.

### Preparations
Digoxin Injection

Paediatric Digoxin Injection

Paediatric Digoxin Oral Solution

Digoxin Tablets

*Ph Eur*

### DEFINITION
3β-[(2,6-Dideoxy-β-D-*ribo*-hexopyranosyl-(1→4)-2,6-dideoxy-β-D-*ribo*-hexopyranosyl-(1→4)-2,6-dideoxy-β-D-*ribo*-hexopyranosyl)oxy]-12β,14-dihydroxy-5β-card-20(22)-enolide.

### Content
96.0 per cent to 102.0 per cent (dried substance).

### CHARACTERS

#### Appearance
White or almost white powder, or colourless crystals.

#### Solubility
Practically insoluble in water, freely soluble in a mixture of equal volumes of methanol and methylene chloride, slightly soluble in ethanol (96 per cent).

### IDENTIFICATION
Infrared absorption spectrophotometry (*2.2.24*).

*Comparison* digoxin CRS.

### TESTS

#### Appearance of solution
The solution is clear (*2.2.1*) and colourless (*2.2.2, Method I*).

Dissolve 50 mg in a mixture of equal volumes of *methanol R* and *methylene chloride R* and dilute to 10 ml with the same mixture of solvents.

#### Specific optical rotation (*2.2.7*)
+ 13.9 to + 15.9 (dried substance).

Dissolve 0.50 g in a mixture of equal volumes of *methanol R* and *methylene chloride R* and dilute to 25.0 ml with the same mixture of solvents.

#### Related substances
Liquid chromatography (*2.2.29*).

*Test solution* Dissolve 50.0 mg of the substance to be examined in 100.0 ml of *methanol R*.

*Reference solution (a)* Dissolve 10.0 mg of *digoxin CRS* in *methanol R* and dilute to 20.0 ml with the same solvent.

*Reference solution (b)* Dilute 1.0 ml of the test solution to 100.0 ml with *methanol R*.

*Reference solution (c)* Dissolve 2.5 mg of *digoxigenin CRS* (impurity C) in *methanol R* and dilute to 5.0 ml with the same solvent. Dilute 1.0 ml of the solution to 50.0 ml with *methanol R*. Dilute 1.0 ml of this solution to 10.0 ml with *methanol R*.

*Reference solution (d)* Dissolve 50.0 mg of *lanatoside C R* (impurity H) in *methanol R* and dilute to 100.0 ml with the same solvent. To 1.0 ml of this solution, add 1.0 ml of the test solution and dilute to 20.0 ml with *methanol R*.

*Reference solution (e)* Dissolve 5.0 mg of *digoxin for peak identification CRS* in *methanol R* and dilute to 10.0 ml with the same solvent.

*Column:*
— *size: l* = 15 m, Ø = 3.9 mm;
— *stationary phase: octadecylsilyl silica gel for chromatography R* (5 µm).

*Mobile phase:*
— *mobile phase A: acetonitrile R, water R* (10:90 *V/V*);
— *mobile phase B: water R, acetonitrile R* (10:90 *V/V*);

| Time (min) | Mobile phase A (per cent *V/V*) | Mobile phase B (per cent *V/V*) |
|---|---|---|
| 0 - 5 | 78 | 22 |
| 5 - 15 | 78 → 30 | 22 → 70 |
| 15 - 16 | 30 → 78 | 70 → 22 |
| 16 - 30 | 78 | 22 |

*Flow rate* 1.5 ml/min.

*Detection* Spectrophotometer at 220 nm.

*Injection* 10 µl of the test solution and reference solutions (b), (c), (d) and (e).

*Identification of impurities* Use the chromatogram supplied with *digoxin for peak identification CRS* and the chromatogram obtained with reference solution (e) to identify the peaks due to impurities A, B, C, E, F, G, K.

*Relative retention* With reference to digoxin (retention time = about 4.3 min): impurity C = about 0.3; impurity E = about 0.5; impurity F = about 0.6; impurity G = about 0.8; impurity L = about 1.4; impurity K = about 1.6; impurity B = about 2.2; impurity A = about 2.6.

*System suitability* Reference solution (d):
— *resolution*: minimum 1.5 between the peaks due to impurity H and digoxin.

*Limits:*
— *impurities E, K*: for each impurity, not more than the area of the principal peak in the chromatogram obtained with reference solution (b) (1.0 per cent);
— *impurity L*: not more than 0.3 times the area of the principal peak in the chromatogram obtained with reference solution (b) (0.3 per cent);

— *impurity G*: not more than 0.8 times the area of the principal peak in the chromatogram obtained with reference solution (b) (0.8 per cent);

— *impurities A, B*: for each impurity, not more than 0.5 times the area of the principal peak in the chromatogram obtained with reference solution (b) (0.5 per cent);

— *impurity F*: not more than 2.5 times the area of the principal peak in the chromatogram obtained with reference solution (b) (2.5 per cent);

— *impurity C*: not more than 5 times the area of the corresponding peak in the chromatogram obtained with reference solution (c) (1.0 per cent);

— *any other impurity*: for each impurity, not more than 0.2 times the area of the principal peak in the chromatogram obtained with reference solution (b) (0.2 per cent);

— *sum of impurities other than A, B, C, E, F, G, K, L*: not more than 0.7 times the area of the principal peak in the chromatogram obtained with reference solution (b) (0.7 per cent);

— *total*: not more than 3.5 times the area of the principal peak in the chromatogram obtained with reference solution (b) (3.5 per cent);

— *disregard limit*: 0.05 times the area of the principal peak in the chromatogram obtained with reference solution (b) (0.05 per cent).

The thresholds indicated under Related Substances (Table 2034.-1) in the general monograph *Substances for pharmaceutical use (2034)* do not apply.

**Loss on drying** (*2.2.32*)
Maximum 1.0 per cent, determined on 0.500 g by drying in an oven *in vacuo*.

**Sulphated ash** (*2.4.14*)
Maximum 0.1 per cent, determined on the residue obtained in the test for loss on drying.

**ASSAY**
Liquid chromatography (*2.2.29*) as described in the test for related substances with the following modification.

*Injection*   Test solution and reference solution (a).

Calculate the percentage content of $C_{41}H_{64}O_{14}$ from the declared content of *digoxin CRS*.

**STORAGE**
Protected from light.

**IMPURITIES**
Specified impurities
*A, B, C, E, F, G, K, L.*

*Other detectable impurities* (the following substances would, if present at a sufficient level, be detected by one or other of the tests in the monograph. They are limited by the general acceptance criterion for other/unspecified impurities and/or by the general monograph *Substances for pharmaceutical use (2034)*. It is therefore not necessary to identify these impurities for demonstration of compliance. See also *5.10. Control of impurities in substances for pharmaceutical use*): *D, H, I, J.*

Gdd = 2,6-dideoxy-β-D-glucopyranosyl

Dig = β-D-digitoxosyl

Glu = β-D-glucopyranosyl

A. R1 = R2 = R3 = R4 = H: digitoxin,

B. R1 = R3 = R4 = H, R2 = OH: 3β-[(2,6-dideoxy-β-D-*ribo*-hexopyranosyl-(1→4)-2,6-dideoxy-β-D-*ribo*-hexopyranosyl-(1→4)-2,6-dideoxy-β-D-*ribo*-hexopyranosyl)oxy]-14,16β-dihydroxy-5β-card-20(22)-enolide (gitoxin),

E. R1 = R2 = OH, R3 = R4 = H: 3β-[(2,6-dideoxy-β-D-*ribo*-hexopyranosyl-(1→4)-2,6-dideoxy-β-D-*ribo*-hexopyranosyl-(1→4)-2,6-dideoxy-β-D-*ribo*-hexopyranosyl)oxy]- 12β,14,16β-trihydroxy-5β-card-20(22)-enolide (diginatin),

H. R1 = OH, R2 = H, R3 = CO-CH₃, R4 = Glu: 3β-[(β-D-glucopyranosyl-(1→4)-3-O-acetyl-2,6-dideoxy-β-D -*ribo*-hexopyranosyl-(1→4)-2,6-dideoxy-β-D-*ribo*-hexopyranosyl-(1→4)-2,6-dideoxy-β-D-*ribo*-hexopyranosyl)oxy]-12β,14-dihydroxy-5β-card-20(22)-enolide (lanatoside C),

I. R1 = OH, R2 = R4 = H, R3 = CO-CH₃: 3β-[(3-O-acetyl-2,6-dideoxy-β-D-*ribo*-hexopyranosyl-(1→4)-2,6-dideoxy-β-D-*ribo*-hexopyranosyl-(1→4)-2,6-dideoxy-β-D-*ribo*-hexopyranosyl)oxy]-12β,14-dihydroxy-5β-card-20(22)-enolide (α-acetyldigoxin),

J. R1 = OH, R2 = R3 = H, R4 = CO-CH₃: 3β-[(4-O-acetyl-2,6-dideoxy-β-D-*ribo*-hexopyranosyl-(1→4)-2,6-dideoxy-β-D-*ribo*-hexopyranosyl-(1→4)-2,6-dideoxy-β-D-*ribo*-hexopyranosyl)oxy]-12β,14-dihydroxy-5β-card-20(22)-enolide (β-acetyldigoxin),

K. R1 = OH, R2 = R3 = H, R4 = Dig: 3β-[(2,6-dideoxy-β-D-*ribo*-hexopyranosyl-(1→4)-2,6-dideoxy-β-D-*ribo*-hexopyranosyl-(1→4)-2,6-dideoxy-β-D-*ribo*-hexopyranosyl-(1→4)-2,6-dideoxy-β-D-*ribo*-hexopyranosyl)oxy]-12β,14-dihydroxy-5β-card-20(22)-enolide (digoxigenin tetrakisdigitoxoside),

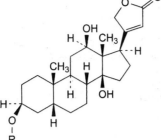

C. R = H: 3β,12β,14-trihydroxy-5β-card-20(22)-enolide (digoxigenin),

D. R = Dig: 3β-(2,6-dideoxy-β-D-*ribo*-hexopyranosyloxy)-12β,14-dihydroxy-5β-card-20(22)-enolide (digoxigenin monodigitoxoside),

F. R = Dig-(1→4)-Dig: 3β-[(2,6-dideoxy-β-D-*ribo*-hexopyranosyl-(1→4)-2,6-dideoxy-β-D-*ribo*-hexopyranosyl)oxy]-12β,14-dihydroxy-5β-card-20(22)-enolide (digoxigenin bisdigitoxoside),

G. R = Gdd-(1→4)-Dig-(1→4)-Dig: 3β-[(2,6-dideoxy-β-D-*arabino*-hexopyranosyl-(1→4)-2,6-dideoxy-β-D-*ribo*-hexopyranosyl-(1→4)-2,6-dideoxy-β-D-*ribo*-hexopyranosyl)oxy]-12β,14-dihydroxy-5β-card-20(22)-enolide (neodigoxin),

L. unknown structure.

*Ph Eur*

# Hydrated Dihydralazine Sulphate

(*Ph Eur monograph 1310*)

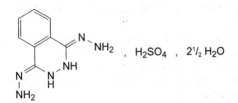

$C_8H_{10}N_6,H_2SO_4,2\frac{1}{2}H_2O$     333.3     *7327-87-9 (anhydrous)*

**Action and use**
Vasodilator.

*Ph Eur*

## DEFINITION
(Phthalazine-1,4(2*H*,3*H*)-diylidene)dihydrazine sulphate 2.5-hydrate.

### Content
98.0 per cent to 102.0 per cent (dried substance).

## CHARACTERS
### Appearance
White or slightly yellow, crystalline powder.

### Solubility
Slightly soluble in water, practically insoluble in anhydrous ethanol. It dissolves in dilute mineral acids.

## IDENTIFICATION
A. Infrared absorption spectrophotometry (*2.2.24*).

*Comparison*   Ph. Eur. reference spectrum of dihydralazine sulphate hydrated.

B. Dissolve about 50 mg in 5 ml of *dilute hydrochloric acid R*. The solution gives reaction (a) of sulphates (*2.3.1*).

## TESTS
### Appearance of solution
The solution is clear (*2.2.1*) and not more intensely coloured than reference solution $BY_6$ (*2.2.2, Method II*).

Dissolve 0.20 g in *dilute nitric acid R* and dilute to 10 ml with the same acid.

### Related substances
Liquid chromatography (*2.2.29*)

*Prepare the solutions immediately before use.*

*Test solution*   Dissolve 50.0 mg of the substance to be examined in a 6 g/l solution of *glacial acetic acid R* and dilute to 50.0 ml with the same solution.

*Reference solution (a)*   Dilute 1.0 ml of the test solution to 100.0 ml with the mobile phase containing 0.5 g/l of *sodium edetate R*. Dilute 1.0 ml of this solution to 10.0 ml with the mobile phase containing 0.5 g/l of *sodium edetate R*.

*Reference solution (b)*   Dilute 1.0 ml of the test solution to 50.0 ml with the mobile phase containing 0.5 g/l of *sodium edetate R*.

*Reference solution (c)*   Dissolve 5 mg of *dihydralazine for system suitability CRS* in a 6 g/l solution of *glacial acetic acid R* and dilute to 5.0 ml with the same solution.

*Column:*
— *size: l* = 0.25 m, Ø = 4.6 mm;
— *stationary phase: nitrile silica gel for chromatography R* (5 μm).

*Mobile phase*   Mix 22 volumes of *acetonitrile R1* and 78 volumes of a solution containing 1.44 g/l of *sodium laurilsulfate R* and 0.75 g/l of *tetrabutylammonium bromide R*, then adjust to pH 3.0 with *0.05 M sulphuric acid*.

*Flow rate*   1.5 ml/min.

*Detection*   Spectrophotometer at 230 nm.

*Injection*   20 μl.

*Run time*   Twice the retention time of dihydralazine.

*Relative retention*   With reference to dihydralazine: impurity A = about 0.8.

*System suitability*   Reference solution (c):
— the peaks due to impurity A and dihydralazine are baseline separated as in the chromatogram supplied with *dihydralazine for system suitability CRS*.

*Limits:*
— *impurity A*: not more than the area of the principal peak in the chromatogram obtained with reference solution (b) (2 per cent);
— *impurity C*: not more than the area of the principal peak in the chromatogram obtained with reference solution (a) (0.1 per cent);
— *unspecified impurities*: for each impurity, not more than the area of the principal peak in the chromatogram obtained with reference solution (a) (0.10 per cent);
— *sum of impurities other than A*: not more than 5 times the area of the principal peak in the chromatogram obtained with reference solution (a) (0.5 per cent);
— *disregard limit*: 0.1 times the area of the principal peak in the chromatogram obtained with reference solution (a) (0.01 per cent).

### Impurity B
Liquid chromatography (*2.2.29*). *Prepare the solutions immediately before use.*

*Test solution* Dissolve 40.0 mg of *hydrazine sulphate R* (impurity B) in *water R* and dilute to 100.0 ml with the same solvent. Dilute 1.0 ml of the solution to 25.0 ml with *water R*. To 0.50 ml of this solution, add 0.200 g of the substance to be examined and dissolve in 6 ml of *dilute hydrochloric acid R*, then dilute to 10.0 ml with *water R*. In a centrifuge tube with a ground-glass stopper, place immediately 0.50 ml of this solution and 2.0 ml of a 60 g/l solution of *benzaldehyde R* in a mixture of equal volumes of *methanol R* and *water R*. Shake for 90 s. Add 1.0 ml of *water R* and 5.0 ml of *heptane R*. Shake for 1 min and centrifuge. Use the upper layer.

*Reference solution* Dissolve 40.0 mg of *hydrazine sulphate R* (impurity B) in *water R* and dilute to 100.0 ml with the same solvent. Dilute 1.0 ml of the solution to 25.0 ml with *water R*. To 0.50 ml of this solution, add 6 ml of *dilute hydrochloric acid R* and dilute to 10.0 ml with *water R*. In a centrifuge tube with a ground-glass stopper, place 0.50 ml of this solution and 2.0 ml of a 60 g/l solution of *benzaldehyde R* in a mixture of equal volumes of *methanol R* and *water R*. Shake for 90 s. Add 1.0 ml of *water R* and 5.0 ml of *heptane R*. Shake for 1 min and centrifuge. Use the upper layer.

*Blank solution* Prepare in the same manner as for the reference solution but replacing the 0.50 ml of hydrazine sulphate solution by 0.50 ml of *water R*.

*Column:*
— *size: l* = 0.25 m, Ø = 4.6 mm;
— *stationary phase: octadecylsilyl silica gel for chromatography R* (5 μm).

*Mobile phase* 0.3 g/l solution of *sodium edetate R*, *acetonitrile R* (30:70 *V/V*).

*Flow rate* 1 ml/min.

*Detection* Spectrophotometer at 305 nm.

*Injection* 20 μl.

*Relative retention* With reference to benzaldehyde: benzaldehyde azine (benzalazine) corresponding to impurity B = about 1.8.

*Limit:*
— *impurity B:* the area of the peak due to benzaldehyde azine is not greater than twice the area of the corresponding peak in the chromatogram obtained with the reference solution (10 ppm).

**Iron** (*2.4.9*)
Maximum 20 ppm.

To the residue obtained in the test for sulphated ash add 0.2 ml of *sulphuric acid R* and heat carefully until the acid is almost completely eliminated. Allow to cool and dissolve the residue with heating in 5.5 ml of *hydrochloric acid R1*. Filter the hot solution through a filter previously washed 3 times with *dilute hydrochloric acid R*. Wash the crucible and the filter with 5 ml of *water R*. Combine the filtrate and the washings and neutralise with about 3.5 ml of *strong sodium hydroxide solution R*. Adjust to pH 3-4 with *acetic acid R* and dilute to 20 ml with *water R*. Prepare the standard with 5 ml of *iron standard solution (2 ppm Fe) R* and 5 ml of *water R*.

**Loss on drying** (*2.2.32*)
13.0 per cent to 15.0 per cent, determined on 1.000 g by drying in an oven at 50 °C at a pressure not exceeding 0.7 kPa for 5 h.

**Sulphated ash** (*2.4.14*)
Maximum 0.1 per cent, determined on 1.0 g.

## ASSAY

Dissolve 60.0 mg in 25 ml of *water R*. Add 35 ml of *hydrochloric acid R* and titrate slowly with *0.05 M potassium iodate*, determining the end-point potentiometrically (*2.2.20*), using a calomel reference electrode and a platinum indicator electrode.

1 ml of *0.05 M potassium iodate* is equivalent to 7.208 mg of $C_8H_{12}N_6O_4S$.

## IMPURITIES

*Specified impurities* A, B, C.

A. R = NH₂: 4-hydrazinophthalazin-1-amine,
C. R = H: (phthalazin-1-yl)hydrazine (hydralazine),
B. H₂N-NH₂: hydrazine.

*Ph Eur*

# Dihydrocodeine Tartrate

(*Dihydrocodeine Hydrogen Tartrate,
Ph Eur monograph 1776*)

$C_{18}H_{23}NO_3,C_4H_6O_6$      451.5      *5965-13-9*

**Action and use**
Opioid receptor agonist; analgesic.

**Preparations**
Co-dydramol Tablets
Dihydrocodeine Injection
Dihydrocodeine Oral Solution
Dihydrocodeine Tablets

*Ph Eur*

## DEFINITION

4,5α-Epoxy-3-methoxy-17-methylmorphinan-6α-ol hydrogen (2R,3R)-2,3-dihydroxybutanedioate.

**Content**
98.5 per cent to 101.0 per cent (anhydrous substance).

## CHARACTERS

**Appearance**
White or almost white, crystalline powder.

**Solubility**
Freely soluble in water, sparingly soluble in alcohol, practically insoluble in cyclohexane.

## IDENTIFICATION

*First identification* A.

*Second identification B, C, D.*

A. Infrared absorption spectrophotometry (*2.2.24*).

*Comparison Ph. Eur. reference spectrum of dihydrocodeine hydrogen tartrate.*

B. To about 0.1 g add 1 ml of *sulphuric acid R* and 0.05 ml of *ferric chloride solution R1* and heat on a water-bath. A brownish-yellow colour develops. Add 0.05 ml of *dilute nitric acid R*. The colour does not become red.

C. To 1 ml of solution S (see Tests) add 5 ml of *picric acid solution R*. Heat on a water-bath until a clear solution is obtained. Allow to cool. A precipitate is formed. Filter, wash with 5 ml of *water R* and dry at 100-105 °C. The crystals melt (*2.2.14*) at 220 °C to 223 °C.

D. It gives reaction (b) of tartrates (*2.3.1*).

**TESTS**

**Solution S**

Dissolve 2.50 g in *carbon dioxide-free water R* and dilute to 25.0 ml with the same solvent.

**Appearance of solution**

Solution S is clear (*2.2.1*) and not more intensely coloured than reference solution BY$_5$ (*2.2.2, Method II*).

**pH** (*2.2.3*)

3.2 to 4.2 for solution S.

**Specific optical rotation** (*2.2.7*)

− 70.5 to − 73.5 (anhydrous substance).

Dilute 10.0 ml of solution S to 20.0 ml with *water R*.

**Related substances**

Liquid chromatography (*2.2.29*).

*Test solution* Dissolve 10.0 mg of the substance to be examined in the mobile phase and dilute to 10.0 ml with the mobile phase.

*Reference solution (a)* Dissolve 2.0 mg of *codeine phosphate R* in 2.0 ml of the test solution and dilute to 25.0 ml with the mobile phase.

*Reference solution (b)* Dilute 1.0 ml of the test solution to 200 ml with the mobile phase.

*Column:*
— *size: l* = 0.25 m, Ø = 4.6 mm,
— *stationary phase: octylsilyl silica gel for chromatography R* (5 μm).

*Mobile phase* To 1.0 g of *sodium heptanesulphonate R*, add 10.0 ml of *glacial acetic acid R* and 4.0 ml of a solution of 5.0 ml of *triethylamine R* diluted to 25.0 ml with a mixture of equal volumes of *water R* and *acetonitrile R*. Add 170 ml of *acetonitrile R* and dilute to 1000 ml with *water R*.

*Flow rate* 1 ml/min.

*Detection* Spectrophotometer at 284 nm.

*Injection* 20 μl.

*Run time* 5 times the retention time of dihydrocodeine.

*Retention time* Dihydrocodeine = about 14 min.

*System suitability*

Reference solution (a):
— *resolution*: minimum of 2 between the peaks due to dihydrocodeine and to impurity A.

*Limits:*
— *impurity A*: not more than the area of the principal peak in the chromatogram obtained with reference solution (b) (0.5 per cent),
— *any other peak*: not more than 0.6 times the area of the principal peak in the chromatogram obtained with reference solution (b) (0.3 per cent),

— *total*: not more than twice the area of the principal peak in the chromatogram obtained with reference solution (b) (1 per cent); disregard any peak due to tartaric acid (relative retention with reference to dihydrocodeine = about 0.25),
— *disregard limit*: 0.1 times the area of the principal peak in the chromatogram obtained with reference solution (b) (0.05 per cent).

**Water** (*2.5.12*)

Maximum 0.7 per cent, determined on 1.00 g.

**Sulphated ash** (*2.4.14*)

Maximum 0.1 per cent, determined on 1.0 g.

**ASSAY**

Dissolve 0.350 g in 60 ml of *anhydrous acetic acid R*. Titrate with *0.1 M perchloric acid* determining the end-point potentiometrically (*2.2.20*).

1 ml of *0.1 M perchloric acid* is equivalent to 45.15 mg of $C_{22}H_{29}NO_9$.

**STORAGE**

Protected from light.

**IMPURITIES**

A. codeine,

B. morphine,

C. 4,5α-epoxy-3-methoxy-17-methylmorphinan-6-one (hydrocodone),

D. 4,5α-epoxy-3,6α-dimethoxy-17-methylmorphinan (tetrahydrothebaine).

*Ph Eur*

# Dihydroergocristine Mesilate

(*Ph Eur monograph 1416*)

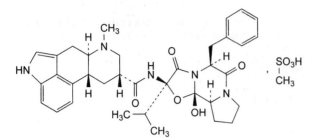

C₃₆H₄₅N₅O₈S      708      24730-10-7

**Action and use**

Vasodilator.

*Ph Eur*

## DEFINITION

(6a*R*,9*R*,10a*R*)-*N*-[(2*R*,5*S*,10a*S*,10b*S*)-5-Benzyl-10b-hydroxy-2-(1-methylethyl)-3,6-dioxo-octahydro-8*H*-oxazolo[3,2-*a*]pyrrolo[2,1-*c*]pyrazin-2-yl]-7-methyl-4,6,6a,7,8,9,10,10a-octahydroindolo[4,3-*fg*]quinoline-9-carboxamide methanesulphonate.

## Content

98.0 per cent to 102.0 per cent (dried substance).

## PRODUCTION

The production method must be evaluated to determine the potential for formation of alkyl mesilates, which is particularly likely to occur if the reaction medium contains lower alcohols. Where necessary, the production method is validated to demonstrate that alkyl mesilates are not detectable in the final product.

## CHARACTERS

### Appearance

White or almost white, fine crystalline powder.

### Solubility

Slightly soluble in water, soluble in methanol.

## IDENTIFICATION

A. Infrared absorption spectrophotometry (*2.2.24*).

*Preparation* Discs.

*Comparison* dihydroergocristine mesilate CRS.

B. Thin-layer chromatography (*2.2.27*).

*Test solution* Dissolve 0.10 g of the substance to be examined in a mixture of 1 volume of *methanol R* and 9 volumes of *methylene chloride R* and dilute to 5 ml with the same mixture of solvents.

*Reference solution* Dissolve 0.10 g of *dihydroergocristine mesilate CRS* in a mixture of 1 volume of *methanol R* and 9 volumes of *methylene chloride R* and dilute to 5 ml with the same mixture of solvents.

*Plate* TLC silica gel F₂₅₄ plate R.

*Mobile phase* concentrated ammonia R, dimethylformamide R, ether R (2:15:85 *V/V/V*).

*Application* 5 μl.

*Development* Over 2/3 of the plate protected from light.

*Drying* In a current of cold air for 5 min.

*Detection* Spray with *dimethylaminobenzaldehyde solution R7* and dry in a current of hot air for 2 min.

*Results* The principal spot in the chromatogram obtained with the test solution is similar in position, colour and size to the principal spot in the chromatogram obtained with the reference solution.

C. Thin-layer chromatography (*2.2.27*).

*Test solution* Dissolve 0.20 g of the substance to be examined in a mixture of 1 volume of *methanol R* and 9 volumes of *methylene chloride R* and dilute to 5 ml with the same mixture of solvents.

*Reference solution* Dissolve 0.20 g of *methanesulphonic acid R* in a mixture of 1 volume of *methanol R* and 9 volumes of *methylene chloride R* and dilute to 5 ml with the same mixture of solvents. Dilute 1 ml of the solution to 10 ml with a mixture of 1 volume of *methanol* R and 9 volumes of *methylene chloride R*.

*Plate* TLC silica gel F₂₅₄ plate R.

*Mobile phase* water R, concentrated ammonia R, butanol R, acetone R (5:10:20:65 *V/V/V/V*).

*Application* 10 μl.

*Development* Over a path of 10 cm protected from light.

*Drying* In a current of cold air for not more than 1 min.

*Detection* Spray with a 1 g/l solution of *bromocresol purple R* in *methanol R*, adjusting the colour to violet-red with one drop of *dilute ammonia R1* and dry the plate in a current of hot air at 100 °C.

*Results* The principal spot in the chromatogram obtained with the test solution is similar in position, colour and size to the principal spot in the chromatogram obtained with the reference solution.

## TESTS

### Appearance of solution

The solution is clear (*2.2.1*) and not more intensely coloured than reference solution B₇ (*2.2.2, Method II*).

Dissolve 0.50 g in *methanol R* and dilute to 25.0 ml with the same solvent.

### pH (*2.2.3*)

4.0 to 5.0.

Dissolve 0.10 g in *carbon dioxide-free water R* and dilute to 20 ml with the same solvent.

### Specific optical rotation (*2.2.7*)

− 37 to − 43 (dried substance).

Dissolve 0.250 g in *anhydrous pyridine R* and dilute to 25.0 ml with the same solvent.

### Related substances

Liquid chromatography (*2.2.29*). *Carry out the test and preparation of the solutions protected from bright light.*

*Test solution* Dissolve 75.0 mg of the substance to be examined in 10 ml of *acetonitrile R*. Add 10 ml of a 1.0 g/l solution of *phosphoric acid R* and dilute to 50.0 ml with *water R*.

*Reference solution* Dissolve 20.0 mg of *codergocrine mesilate CRS* in 10 ml of *acetonitrile R*. Add 10 ml of a 1.0 g/l solution of *phosphoric acid R* and dilute to 50.0 ml with *water R*. Dilute 6.0 ml of the solution to 50.0 ml with a mixture of 20 volumes of *acetonitrile R*, 20 volumes of a 1.0 g/l solution of *phosphoric acid R* and 60 volumes of *water R*.

*Column:*

— size: *l* = 0.25 m, Ø = 4.6 mm,
— stationary phase: *octadecylsilyl silica gel for chromatography R* (5 μm) with a pore size of 10 nm and a carbon loading of 19 per cent.

*Mobile phase:*
— *mobile phase A*: mix 100 volumes of *acetonitrile R* with 900 volumes of *water R* and add 10 volumes of *triethylamine R*,
— *mobile phase B*: mix 100 volumes of *water R* with 900 volumes of *acetonitrile R* and add 10 volumes of *triethylamine R*.

| Time (min) | Mobile phase A (per cent *V/V*) | Mobile phase B (per cent *V/V*) |
| --- | --- | --- |
| 0 - 5 | 75 | 25 |
| 5 - 20 | 75 → 25 | 25 → 75 |
| 20 - 22 | 25 → 75 | 75 → 25 |
| 22 - 30 | 75 | 25 |

*Flow rate*   1.2 ml/min.

*Detection*   Spectrophotometer at 280 nm.

*Injection*   10 μl.

*Relative retention*   With reference to dihydroergocristine (retention time = 13.7 min): impurity F = about 0.8; impurity H = about 0.9; impurity I = about 1.02.

*System suitability*   Reference solution:
— the chromatogram shows 4 peaks,
— *resolution*: minimum 1 between the peaks corresponding to dihydroergocristine and impurity I.

*Limits:*
— *any impurity*: not more than the area of the peak corresponding to dihydroergocristine in the chromatogram obtained with the reference solution (1 per cent),
— *total*: not more than twice the area of the peak corresponding to dihydroergocristine in the chromatogram obtained with the reference solution (2 per cent),
— *disregard limit*: 0.1 times the area of the peak corresponding to dihydroergocristine in the chromatogram obtained with the reference solution (0.1 per cent).

**Loss on drying** (*2.2.32*)
Maximum 3.0 per cent, determined on 0.500 g by drying under high vacuum at 80 °C.

**ASSAY**
Dissolve 0.300 g in 60 ml of *pyridine R*. Pass a stream of *nitrogen R* over the surface of the solution and titrate with *0.1 M tetrabutylammonium hydroxide*, determining the end-point potentiometrically (*2.2.20*). Note the volume used at the second point of inflexion.

1 ml of *0.1 M tetrabutylammonium hydroxide* is equivalent to 35.39 mg of $C_{36}H_{45}N_5O_8S$.

**STORAGE**
Store protected from light.

**IMPURITIES**

A. (6a*R*,9*R*,10a*R*)-7-methyl-4,6,6a,7,8,9,10,10a-octahydroindolo[4,3-*fg*]quinoline-9-carboxamide (6-methylergoline-8β-carboxamide),

B. (6a*R*,9*S*,10a*S*)-7-methyl-4,6,6a,7,8,9,10,10a-octahydroindolo[4,3-*fg*]quinoline-9-carboxamide (6-methylisoergoline-8α-carboxamide),

C. (6a*R*,9*R*,10a*R*)-N-[(2*S*,5*S*,10a*S*,10b*S*)-5-benzyl-10b-hydroxy-2-(1-methylethyl)-3,6-dioxooctahydro-8*H*-oxazolo[3,2-a]pyrrolo[2,1-c]pyrazin-2-yl]-7-methyl-4,6,6a,7,8,9,10,10a-octahydroindolo[4,3-*fg*]quinoline-9-carboxamide (2′-epidihydroergocristine),

D. R1 = CH(CH$_3$)$_2$, R2 = CH$_3$: (6a*R*,9*R*,10a*R*)-N-[(2*R*,5*S*,10a*S*,10b*S*)-10b-hydroxy-2-methyl-5-(1-methylethyl)-3,6-dioxooctahydro-8*H*-oxazolo[3,2-a]pyrrolo[2,1-c]pyrazin-2-yl]-7-methyl-4,6,6a,7,8,9,10,10a-octahydroindolo[4,3-*fg*]quinoline-9-carboxamide (dihydroergosine),

E. R1 = CH$_2$-C$_6$H$_5$, R2 = CH$_3$: (6a*R*,9*R*,10a*R*)-N-[(2*R*,5*S*,10a*S*,10b*S*)-5-benzyl-10b-hydroxy-2-methyl-3,6-dioxooctahydro-8*H*-oxazolo[3,2-a]pyrrolo[2,1-c]pyrazin-2-yl]-7-methyl-4,6,6a,7,8,9,10,10a-octahydroindolo[4,3-*fg*]quinoline- 9-carboxamide (dihydroergotamine),

F. R1 = R2 = CH(CH$_3$)$_2$: (6a*R*,9*R*,10a*R*)-N-[(2*R*,5*S*,10a*S*,10b*S*)10b-hydroxy-2,5-bis(1-methylethyl)-3,6-dioxooctahydro-8*H*-oxazolo[3,2-a]pyrrolo[2,1-c]pyrazin-2-yl]-7-methyl-4,6,6a,7,8,9,10,10a-octahydroindolo[4,3-*fg*]quinoline-9-carboxamide (dihydroergocornine),

G. R1 = CH$_2$-C$_6$H$_5$, R2 = CH$_2$-CH$_3$: (6a*R*,9*R*,10a*R*)-N-[(2*R*,5*S*,10a*S*,10b*S*)-5-benzyl-2-ethyl-10b-hydroxy-3,6-dioxooctahydro-8*H*-oxazolo[3,2-a]pyrrolo[2,1-c]pyrazin-2-yl]-7-methyl-4,6,6a,7,8,9,10,10a-octahydroindolo[4,3-*fg*]quinoline-9-carboxamide (dihydroergostine),

H. R1 = CH$_2$-CH(CH$_3$)$_2$, R2 = CH(CH$_3$)$_2$: (6a*R*,9*R*,10a*R*)-N-[(2*R*,5*S*,10a*S*,10b*S*)-10b-hydroxy-2-(1-methylethyl)-5-(2-methylpropyl)-3,6-dioxooctahydro-8*H*-oxazolo[3,2-a]pyrrolo[2,1-c]pyrazin-2-yl]-7-methyl-4,6,6a,7,8,9,10,10a-octahydroindolo[4,3-*fg*]quinoline-9-carboxamide (α-dihydroergocryptine),

I. R1 = C*H(CH$_3$)-CH$_2$-CH$_3$, R2 = CH(CH$_3$)$_2$: (6a*R*,9*R*,10a*R*)-N-[(2*R*,5*S*,10a*S*,10b*S*)-10b-hydroxy-2-

(1-methylethyl)-5-[(1RS-1-methylpropyl]-3,6-
dioxooctahydro-8H-oxazolo[3,2-a]pyrrolo[2,1-c]pyrazin-2-yl]-
7-methyl-4,6,6a,7,8,9,10,10a-octahydroindolo[4,3-
fg]quinoline-9-carboxamide (β-dihydroergocryptine or
epicriptine),

J. R1 = CH₂-C₆H₅, R2 = C*H(CH₃)-CH₂-CH₃:
(6aR,9R,10aR)-N-[(2R,5S,10aS,10bS)-5-benzyl-10b-
hydroxy-2-[(1RS)-1-methylpropyl]-3,6-dioxooctahydro-8H-
oxazolo[3,2-a]pyrrolo[2,1-c]pyrazin-2-yl]-7-methyl-
4,6,6a,7,8,9,10,10a-octahydroindolo[4,3-fg]quinoline-9-
carboxamide (dihydroergosedmine),

K. (6aR,9R,10aR)-N-[(2R,5S,10aS,10bS)-5-benzyl-10b-
hydroxy-2-(1-methylethyl)-3,6-dioxooctahydro-8H-
oxazolo[3,2-a]pyrrolo[2,1-c]pyrazin-2-yl]-7-methyl-
4,6,6a,7,8,9-hexahydroindolo[4,3-fg]quinoline-9-carboxamide
(ergocristine),

L. (6aR,7RS,9R,10aR)-N-[(2R,5S,10aS,10bS)-5-benzyl-10b-
hydroxy-2-(1-methylethyl)-3,6-dioxooctahydro-8H-
oxazolo[3,2-a]pyrrolo[2,1-c]pyrazin-2-yl]-7-methyl-
4,6,6a,7,8,9,10,10a-octahydroindolo[4,3-fg]quinoline-9-
carboxamide 7-oxide (dihydroergocristine 6-oxide).

_____ Ph Eur

# Dihydroergotamine Mesilate

(Ph Eur monograph 0551)

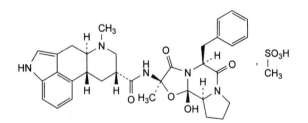

C₃₃H₃₇N₅O₅,CH₄SO₃          680          6190-39-2

## Action and use
Vasodilator.

Ph Eur

## DEFINITION
(6aR,9R,10aR)-N-[(2R,5S,10aS,10bS)-5-Benzyl-10b-
hydroxy-2-methyl-3,6-dioxooctahydro-8H-oxazolo[3,2-
a]pyrrolo[2,1-c]pyrazin-2-yl]-7-methyl-4,6,6a,7,8,9,10,10a-
octahydroindolo[4,3-fg]quinoline-9-carboxamide
methanesulphonate.

## Content
98.0 per cent to 101.0 per cent (dried substance).

## PRODUCTION
The production method must be evaluated to determine the
potential for formation of alkyl mesilates, which is particularly
likely to occur if the reaction medium contains lower
alcohols. Where necessary, the production method is
validated to demonstrate that alkyl mesilates are not
detectable in the final product.

## CHARACTERS
### Appearance
White or almost white, crystalline powder or colourless
crystals.

### Solubility
Slightly soluble in water, sparingly soluble in methanol,
slightly soluble in ethanol (96 per cent).

## IDENTIFICATION
*First identification*   B, C.

*Second identification*   A, C, D.

A. Ultraviolet and visible absorption spectrophotometry
(2.2.25).

*Test solution*   Dissolve 5.0 mg in *methanol R* and dilute to
100.0 ml with the same solvent.

*Spectral range*   250-350 nm.

*Absorption maxima*   At 281 nm and 291 nm.

*Shoulder*   At 275 nm.

*Absorbance*   Negligible above 320 nm.

*Specific absorbance at the absorption maximum at
281 nm*   95 to 105 (dried substance).

B. Infrared absorption spectrophotometry (2.2.24).

*Comparison*   dihydroergotamine mesilate CRS.

C. Thin-layer chromatography (2.2.27). Prepare the reference
solution and the test solution immediately before use.

*Solvent mixture*   methanol R, methylene chloride R (10:90 V/V).

*Test solution*   Dissolve 5 mg of the substance to be examined
in the solvent mixture and dilute to 2.5 ml with the solvent
mixture.

*Reference solution*   Dissolve 5 mg of *dihydroergotamine
mesilate CRS* in the solvent mixture and dilute to 2.5 ml with
the solvent mixture.

*Plate*   TLC silica gel G plate R.

*Mobile phase*   concentrated ammonia R, methanol R, ethyl
acetate R, methylene chloride R (1:6:50:50 V/V/V/V).

*Application*   5 µl.

*Development*   Protected from light, over a path of 15 cm; dry
in a current of cold air for not longer than 1 min and repeat
the development protected from light over a path of 15 cm
using a freshly prepared amount of the mobile phase.

*Drying*   In a current of cold air.

*Detection*   Spray abundantly with *dimethylaminobenzaldehyde
solution R7* and dry in a current of hot air for about 2 min.

*Results*   The principal spot in the chromatogram obtained
with the test solution is similar in position, colour and size to

the principal spot in the chromatogram obtained with the reference solution.

D. To 0.1 g of the substance to be examined, add 5 ml of *dilute hydrochloric acid R* and shake for about 5 min. Filter, then add 1 ml of *barium chloride solution R1*. The filtrate remains clear. Mix 0.1 g of the substance to be examined with 0.4 g of powdered *sodium hydroxide R*, heat to fusion and continue to heat for 1 min. Cool, add 5 ml of *water R*, boil and filter. Acidify the filtrate with *hydrochloric acid R1* and filter again. The filtrate gives reaction (a) of sulphates (*2.3.1*).

## TESTS

### Appearance of solution
The solution is clear (*2.2.1*) and not more intensely coloured than reference solution $Y_7$ or $BY_7$ (*2.2.2, Method II*).

Dissolve 0.10 g in a mixture of 0.1 ml of a 70 g/l solution of *methanesulphonic acid R* and 50 ml of *water R*.

### pH (*2.2.3*)
4.4 to 5.4.

Dissolve 0.10 g in *carbon dioxide-free water R* and dilute to 100 ml with the same solvent.

### Specific optical rotation (*2.2.7*)
− 42 to − 47 (dried substance).

Dissolve 0.250 g in *anhydrous pyridine R* and dilute to 25.0 ml with the same solvent.

### Related substances
Liquid chromatography (*2.2.29*). *Carry out the test protected from light.*

*Solvent mixture* acetonitrile R, water R (50:50 *V/V*).

*Test solution* Dissolve 70 mg of the substance to be examined in the solvent mixture and dilute to 100.0 ml with the solvent mixture.

*Reference solution (a)* Dilute 1.0 ml of the test solution to 10.0 ml with the solvent mixture. Dilute 1.0 ml of this solution to 100.0 ml with the solvent mixture.

*Reference solution (b)* Dissolve 7 mg of the substance to be examined and 6.8 mg of *ergotamine tartrate CRS* (impurity A) (equivalent to 7 mg of ergotamine mesilate) in the solvent mixture and dilute to 100 ml with the solvent mixture. Dilute 5 ml of this solution to 10 ml with the solvent mixture.

*Reference solution (c)* Dissolve 5 mg of *dihydroergotamine for peak identification CRS* (containing impurities A, B, C, D and E) in the solvent mixture, add 100 µl of *dilute sulphuric acid R* and dilute to 5 ml with the solvent mixture.

*Column:*
— *size: l* = 0.15 m, Ø = 4.6 mm;
— *stationary phase: spherical end-capped octadecylsilyl silica gel for chromatography R* (3 µm);
— *temperature:* 25 °C.

*Mobile phase:*
— *mobile phase A*: 3 g/l solution of *sodium heptanesulphonate monohydrate R* adjusted to pH 2.0 with *phosphoric acid R*;
— *mobile phase B*: mobile phase A, *acetonitrile for chromatography R* (20:80 *V/V*);

| Time (min) | Mobile phase A (per cent *V/V*) | Mobile phase B (per cent *V/V*) |
|---|---|---|
| 0 - 15 | 58 → 40 | 42 → 60 |

*Flow rate* 1.5 ml/min.

*Detection* Spectrophotometer at 220 nm.

*Injection* 5 µl.

*Identification of impurities* Use the chromatogram supplied with *dihydroergotamine for peak identification CRS* and the chromatogram obtained with reference solution (c) to identify the peaks due to impurities A, B, C, D and E.

*Relative retention* With reference to dihydroergotamine (retention time = about 6.5 min): impurity D = about 0.7; impurity C = about 0.86; impurity A = about 0.95; impurity B = about 1.2; impurity E = about 1.4.

*System suitability* Reference solution (b):
— *resolution*: minimum 1.5 between the peaks due to impurity A and dihydroergotamine.

*Limits:*
— *correction factors*: for the calculation of content, multiply the peak areas of the following impurities by the corresponding correction factor: impurity A = 1.3; impurity C = 1.3;
— *impurities B, E*: for each impurity, not more than 5 times the area of the principal peak in the chromatogram obtained with reference solution (a) (0.5 per cent);
— *impurity C*: not more than 3 times the area of the principal peak in the chromatogram obtained with reference solution (a) (0.3 per cent);
— *impurities A, D*: for each impurity, not more than 1.5 times the area of the principal peak in the chromatogram obtained with reference solution (a) (0.15 per cent);
— *unspecified impurities*: for each impurity, not more than the area of the principal peak in the chromatogram obtained with reference solution (a) (0.10 per cent);
— *total*: not more than 10 times the area of the principal peak in the chromatogram obtained with reference solution (a) (1.0 per cent);
— *disregard limit*: 0.5 times the area of the principal peak in the chromatogram obtained with reference solution (a) (0.05 per cent).

### Loss on drying (*2.2.32*)
Maximum 4.0 per cent, determined on 0.500 g by drying at 105 °C at a pressure not exceeding 0.1 kPa for 5 h.

## ASSAY
Dissolve 0.500 g in a mixture of 10 ml of *anhydrous acetic acid R* and 70 ml of *acetic anhydride R*. Titrate with *0.1 M perchloric acid*, determining the end-point potentiometrically (*2.2.20*).

1 ml of *0.1 M perchloric acid* is equivalent to 68.00 mg of $C_{34}H_{41}N_5O_8S$.

## STORAGE
Protected from light.

## IMPURITIES
*Specified impurities* A, B, C, D, E.

A. (6a*R*,9*R*)-*N*-[(2*R*,5*S*,10a*S*,10b*S*)-5-benzyl-10b-hydroxy-2-methyl-3,6-dioxooctahydro-8*H*-oxazolo[3,2-*a*]pyrrolo[2,1-*c*]pyrazin-2-yl]-7-methyl-4,6,6a,7,8,9-hexahydroindolo[4,3-*fg*]quinoline-9-carboxamide (ergotamine),

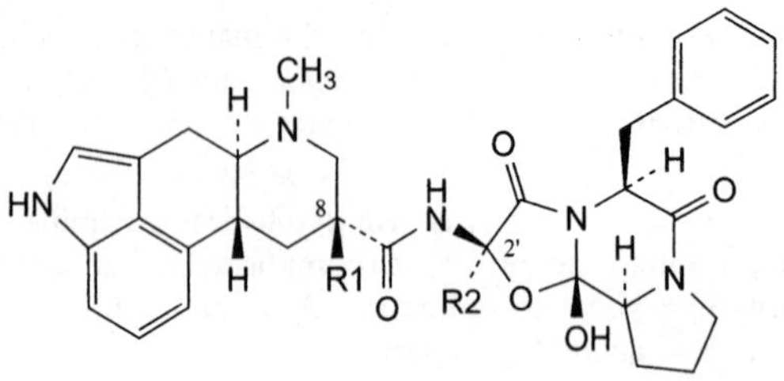

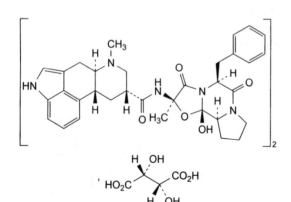

**B.** R1 = H, R2 = C₂H₅: (6aR,9R,10aR)-N-[(2R,5S,10aS,10bS)-5-benzyl-2-ethyl-10b-hydroxy-3,6-dioxooctahydro-8H-oxazolo[3,2-a]pyrrolo[2,1-c]pyrazin-2-yl]-7-methyl-4,6,6a,7,8,9,10,10a-octahydroindolo[4,3-fg]quinoline-9-carboxamide (9,10-dihydroergostine),

**C.** R1 = OH, R2 = CH₃: (6aR,9S,10aR)-N-[(2R,5S,10aS,10bS)-5-benzyl-10b-hydroxy-2-methyl-3,6-dioxooctahydro-8H-oxazolo[3,2-a]pyrrolo[2,1-c]pyrazin-2-yl]-9-hydroxy-7-methyl-4,6,6a,7,8,9,10,10a-octahydroindolo[4,3-fg]quinoline-9-carboxamide (8-hydroxy-9,10-dihydroergotamine),

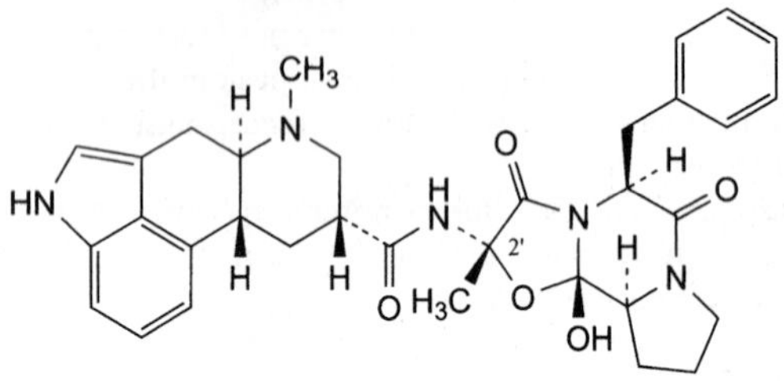

**D.** (6aR,9R,10aR)-N-[(2S,5S,10aS,10bS)-5-benzyl-10b-hydroxy-2-methyl-3,6-dioxooctahydro-8H-oxazolo[3,2-a]pyrrolo[2,1-c]pyrazin-2-yl]-7-methyl-4,6,6a,7,8,9,10,10a-octahydroindolo[4,3-fg]quinoline-9-carboxamide (2′-epi-9,10-dihydroergotamine),

**E.** dihydroergocristine.

_____ _Ph Eur_

# Dihydroergotamine Tartrate

(*Ph Eur monograph 0600*)

(C₃₃H₃₇N₅O₅)₂,C₄H₆O₆        1317                    5989-77-5

**Action and use**
Vasodilator.

_Ph Eur_ _____

**DEFINITION**
Bis[(6aR,9R,10aR)-N-[(2R,5S,10aS,10bS)-5-benzyl-10b-hydroxy-2-methyl-3,6-dioxooctahydro-8H-oxazolo[3,2-a]pyrrolo[2,1-c]pyrazin-2-yl]-7-methyl-4,6,6a,7,8,9,10,10a-octahydroindolo[4,3-fg]quinoline-9-carboxamide] (2R,3R)-2,3-dihydroxybutanedioate.

**Content**
98.0 per cent to 101.0 per cent (dried substance).

**CHARACTERS**
**Appearance**
White or almost white, crystalline powder or colourless crystals.

**Solubility**
Very slightly soluble in water, sparingly soluble in alcohol.

**IDENTIFICATION**
*First identification   B, C.*

*Second identification   A, C, D.*

A. Dissolve 5.0 mg in *methanol R* and dilute to 100.0 ml with the same solvent. Examined between 250 nm and 350 nm (*2.2.25*), the solution shows 2 absorption maxima, at 281 nm and 291 nm, and a shoulder at 275 nm. Above 320 nm the absorbance is negligible. The specific absorbance at the maximum at 281 nm is 95 to 115 (dried substance).

B. Infrared absorption spectrophotometry (*2.2.24*).

*Preparation   Discs.*

*Comparison   dihydroergotamine tartrate CRS.*

C. Examine the chromatograms obtained in the test for related substances.

*Results   The principal spot in the chromatogram obtained with test solution (b) is similar in position, colour and size to the principal spot in the chromatogram obtained with reference solution (a).

D. Suspend about 15 mg in 1 ml of *water R*. 0.1 ml of the suspension gives reaction (b) of tartrates (*2.3.1*).

**TESTS**
**Appearance of solution**
The solution is clear (*2.2.1*) and not more intensely coloured than reference solution Y₇ or BY₇ (*2.2.2, Method II*).

Dissolve 0.1 g in *alcohol (85 per cent V/V) R* warming carefully in a water-bath at 40 °C and dilute to 50 ml with the same solvent.

**pH** (*2.2.3*)
4.0 to 5.5 for the clear supernatant.

Suspend 50 mg in 50 ml of *carbon dioxide-free water R* and shake for 10 min. Allow to stand.

**Specific optical rotation** (*2.2.7*)
− 52 to − 57 (dried substance).

Dissolve 0.250 g in *anhydrous pyridine R* and dilute to 25.0 ml with the same solvent.

**Related substances**
Thin-layer chromatography (*2.2.27*). *Prepare the reference solutions and the test solutions immediately before use and in the order indicated.*

*Reference solution (a)   Dissolve 20 mg of *dihydroergotamine tartrate CRS* in a mixture of 1 volume of *methanol R* and 9 volumes of *chloroform R* and dilute to 10 ml with the same mixture of solvents.

*Reference solution (b)*  Dilute 2.5 ml of reference solution (a) to 50 ml with a mixture of 1 volume of *methanol R* and 9 volumes of *chloroform R*.

*Reference solution (c)*  Dilute 2 ml of reference solution (b) to 5 ml with a mixture of 1 volume of *methanol R* and 9 volumes of *chloroform R*.

*Test solution (a)*  Dissolve 0.10 g of the substance to be examined in a mixture of 1 volume of *methanol R* and 9 volumes of *chloroform R* and dilute to 5 ml with the same mixture of solvents.

*Test solution (b)*  Dilute 1 ml of test solution (a) to 10 ml with a mixture of 1 volume of *methanol R* and 9 volumes of *chloroform R*.

*Plate*  TLC silica gel G plate R.

*Mobile phase*  concentrated ammonia R, methanol R, ethyl acetate R, methylene chloride R (1:6:50:50 V/V/V/V).

*Application*  5 µl.

*Development*  Protected from light over a path of 15 cm. Dry the plate in a current of cold air for not longer than 1 min. Repeat the development protected from light over a path of 15 cm using a freshly prepared amount of the mobile phase.

*Drying*  In a current of cold air.

*Detection*  Spray the plate abundantly with *dimethylaminobenzaldehyde solution R7* and dry in a current of hot air for about 2 min.

*Limits*  In the chromatogram obtained with test solution (a):
— *any impurity*: any spot, apart from the principal spot, is not more intense than the principal spot in the chromatogram obtained with reference solution (b) (0.5 per cent) and not more than 2 such spots are more intense than the principal spot in the chromatogram obtained with reference solution (c) (0.2 per cent).

**Loss on drying** (*2.2.32*)
Maximum 5.0 per cent, determined on 0.200 g by drying in an oven at 105 °C.

## ASSAY
Dissolve 0.250 g in 50 ml of *anhydrous acetic acid R*. Titrate with *0.05 M perchloric acid*, determining the end-point potentiometrically (*2.2.20*).

1 ml of *0.05 M perchloric acid* is equivalent to 32.93 mg of $C_{70}H_{80}N_{10}O_{16}$.

## STORAGE
Protected from light.

*Ph Eur*

# Dihydrotachysterol
*(Ph Eur monograph 2014)*

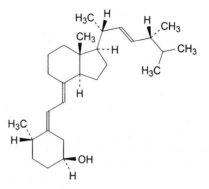

$C_{28}H_{46}O$        398.7        *67-96-9*

**Action and use**
Vitamin D analogue.

*Ph Eur*

## DEFINITION
(5E,7E,22E)-9,10-Seco-10α-ergosta-5,7,22-trien-3β-ol.

**Content**
97.0 per cent to 102.0 per cent.

## CHARACTERS
**Appearance**
Colourless crystals or white or almost white crystalline powder.

**Solubility**
Practically insoluble in water, freely soluble in acetone and hexane, sparingly soluble in ethanol (96 per cent).

It shows polymorphism (*5.9*).

## IDENTIFICATION
Infrared absorption spectrophotometry (*2.2.24*).

*Comparison*  dihydrotachysterol CRS.

If the spectra obtained in the solid state show differences, record new spectra using the residues after recrystallisation from *methanol R*.

## TESTS
**Specific optical rotation** (*2.2.7*)
+ 99 to + 103.

Dissolve 0.500 g in *ethanol (96 per cent) R* and dilute to 25.0 ml with the same solvent.

**Related substances**
Liquid chromatography (*2.2.29*).

*Test solution*  Dissolve 10.00 mg of the substance to be examined in *acetonitrile R* and dilute to 50.0 ml with the same solvent.

*Reference solution (a)*  Dissolve 1.0 mg of *dihydrotachysterol for system suitability CRS* (containing impurities A, B and C) in *acetonitrile R* and dilute to 5.0 ml with the same solvent.

*Reference solution (b)*  Dissolve 10.00 mg of *dihydrotachysterol CRS* in *acetonitrile R* and dilute to 50.0 ml with the same solvent.

*Reference solution (c)*  Dilute 5.0 ml of the test solution to 100.0 ml with *acetonitrile R*. Dilute 5.0 ml of this solution to 50.0 ml with *acetonitrile R*.

*Column:*
— size: $l$ = 0.25 m, Ø = 3.0 mm,
— *stationary phase*: spherical trifunctional *end-capped octadecylsilyl silica gel for chromatography R* (4 μm),
— *temperature*: 40 °C.

*Mobile phase*  *decanol R, water for chromatography R, acetonitrile for chromatography R* (1:25:1000 *V/V/V*).

*Flow rate*  0.5 ml/min.

*Detection*  Variable-wavelength spectrophotometer capable of operating at 251 nm and at 203 nm.

*Injection*  5 μl of the test solution and reference solutions (a) and (c).

*Run time*  Twice the retention time of dihydrotachysterol.

*Identification of impurities*  Reference solution (a):
— use the chromatogram obtained at 203 nm and the chromatogram obtained at 203 nm supplied with *dihydrotachysterol for system suitability CRS* to identify the peak due to impurity A,
— use the chromatogram obtained at 251 nm and the chromatogram obtained at 251 nm supplied with *dihydrotachysterol for system suitability CRS* to identify the peak due to impurities B and C.

*Relative retention*  With reference to dihydrotachysterol (retention time = about 15 min); impurity B = about 0.9; impurity C = about 1.2; impurity A (not visible at 251 nm, detected at 203 nm) = about 1.2.

*System suitability*  Reference solution (a):
— *peak-to-valley ratio*: minimum of 4, where $H_p$ = height above the baseline of the peak due to impurity B, and $H_v$ = height above the baseline of the lowest point of the curve separating this peak from the peak due to dihydrotachysterol in the chromatogram obtained at 251 nm.

Examine the chromatogram obtained at 203 nm for impurity A and the chromatogram obtained at 251 nm for the impurities other than A.

*Limits:*
— *impurity A*: not more than the area of the principal peak in the chromatogram obtained with reference solution (c) (0.5 per cent),
— *impurities B, C*: for each impurity, not more than the area of the principal peak in the chromatogram obtained with reference solution (c) (0.5 per cent),
— *any other impurity*: for each impurity, not more than 0.2 times the area of the principal peak in the chromatogram obtained with reference solution (c) (0.1 per cent),
— *total (including A)*: not more than twice the area of the principal peak in the chromatogram obtained with reference solution (c) at 251 nm (1.0 per cent),
— *disregard limit*: 0.1 times the area of the principal peak in the chromatogram obtained with reference solution (c) (0.05 per cent).

**Water** (*2.5.32*)
Maximum 0.1 per cent, determined on 40.0 mg.

**ASSAY**
Liquid chromatography (*2.2.29*) as described in the test for related substances with the following modifications.

*Detection*  Spectrophotometer at 251 nm.

*Injection*  Test solution and reference solution (b).

Calculate the percentage content of $C_{28}H_{46}O$ using the chromatograms obtained with the test solution and reference solution (b) and the declared content of *dihydrotachysterol CRS*.

**STORAGE**
Under an inert gas, in an airtight container, at a temperature of 2 °C to 8 °C.

The contents of an opened container are to be used immediately.

**IMPURITIES**
*Specified impurities*  *A, B, C.*

A. (7*E*,22*E*)-9,10-secoergosta-5(10),7,22-trien-3β-ol (dihydrovitamin D$_2$-I),

B. (5*E*,7*E*,22*E*)-9,10-secoergosta-5,7,22-trien-3β-ol (dihydrovitamin D$_2$-IV),

C. (5*E*,7*E*)-9,10-seco-10α-ergosta-5,7-dien-3β-ol (dihydrotachysterol$_4$).

# Diloxanide Furoate

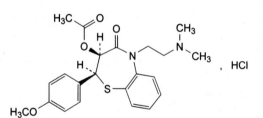

C₁₄H₁₁Cl₂NO₄     328.2     *3736-81-0*

$C_{14}H_{11}Cl_2NO_4$     328.2     *3736-81-0*

## Action and use
Antiprotozoal.

## Preparation
Diloxanide Tablets

## DEFINITION
Diloxanide Furoate is 4-(*N*-methyl-2,2-dichloroacetamido)phenyl 2-furoate. It contains not less than 98.0% and not more than 102.0% of $C_{14}H_{11}Cl_2NO_4$, calculated with reference to the dried substance.

## CHARACTERISTICS
A white or almost white, crystalline powder.

Very slightly soluble in *water*; slightly soluble in *ethanol (96%)* and in *ether*.

## IDENTIFICATION
A. The *infrared absorption spectrum*, Appendix II A, is concordant with the *reference spectrum* of diloxanide furoate *(RS 103)*.

B. The *light absorption*, Appendix II B, in the range 240 to 350 nm of a 0.0014% w/v solution in *ethanol (96%)* exhibits a maximum only at 258 nm. The *absorbance* at the maximum is about 0.98.

C. Burn 20 mg by the method for *oxygen-flask combustion*, Appendix VIII C, using 10 ml of 1M *sodium hydroxide* as the absorbing liquid. When the process is complete, acidify the liquid with *nitric acid* and add *silver nitrate solution*. A white precipitate is produced.

## TESTS
### Melting point
114° to 116°, Appendix V A.

### Free acidity
Shake 3 g with 50 ml of *water*, filter and wash the residue with three 20 ml quantities of *water*. Titrate the combined filtrate and washings with 0.1M *sodium hydroxide VS* using *phenolphthalein solution R1* as indicator. Not more than 1.3 ml is required.

### Related substances
Carry out the method for *thin-layer chromatography*, Appendix III A, using *silica gel HF₂₅₄* as the coating substance and a mixture of 96 volumes of *dichloromethane* and 4 volumes of *methanol* as the mobile phase. Apply separately to the plate 5 μl of each of two solutions of the substance being examined in *dichloromethane* containing (1) 10.0% w/v and (2) 0.025% w/v. After removal of the plate, allow it to dry in air and examine under *ultraviolet light (254 nm)*. Any *secondary spot* in the chromatogram obtained with solution (1) is not more intense than the spot in the chromatogram obtained with solution (2).

## Loss on drying
When dried to constant weight at 105°, loses not more than 0.5% of its weight. Use 1 g.

## Sulphated ash
Not more than 0.1%, Appendix IX A.

## ASSAY
Dissolve 0.3 g in 50 ml of *anhydrous pyridine* and carry out Method II for *non-aqueous titration*, Appendix VIII A, using 0.1M *tetrabutylammonium hydroxide VS* as titrant and determining the end point potentiometrically. Each ml of 0.1M *tetrabutylammonium hydroxide VS* is equivalent to 32.82 mg of $C_{14}H_{11}Cl_2NO_4$.

## STORAGE
Diloxanide Furoate should be protected from light.

# Diltiazem Hydrochloride

*(Ph Eur monograph 1004)*

C₂₂H₂₆N₂O₄S,HCl     451.0     *33286-22-5*

$C_{22}H_{26}N_2O_4S,HCl$     451.0     *33286-22-5*

## Action and use
Calcium channel blocker.

*Ph Eur*

## DEFINITION
Hydrochloride of (2S,3S)-5-[2-(dimethylamino)ethyl]-2-(4-methoxyphenyl)-4-oxo-2,3,4,5-tetrahydro-1,5-benzothiazepin-3-yl acetate.

## Content
98.5 per cent to 101.0 per cent (dried substance).

## CHARACTERS
### Appearance
White or almost white, crystalline powder.

### Solubility
Freely soluble in water, in methanol and in methylene chloride, slightly soluble in anhydrous ethanol.

### mp
About 213 °C, with decomposition.

## IDENTIFICATION
*First identification A, D.*

*Second identification B, C, D.*

A. Infrared absorption spectrophotometry (2.2.24).

*Comparison diltiazem hydrochloride CRS.*

B. Thin-layer chromatography (2.2.27).

*Test solution* Dissolve 0.10 g of the substance to be examined in *methylene chloride R* and dilute to 10 ml with the same solvent.

*Reference solution* Dissolve 0.10 g of *diltiazem hydrochloride CRS* in *methylene chloride R* and dilute to 10 ml with the same solvent.

*Plate*   TLC silica gel $F_{254}$ plate R.

*Mobile phase*   acetic acid R, water R, methylene chloride R, anhydrous ethanol R (1:3:10:12 V/V/V/V).

*Application*   10 μl.

*Development*   Over 2/3 of the plate.

*Drying*   In air.

*Detection*   Examine in ultraviolet light at 254 nm.

*Results*   The principal spot in the chromatogram obtained with the test solution is similar in position and size to the principal spot in the chromatogram obtained with the reference solution.

C. Dissolve 50 mg in 5 ml of *water R*. Add 1 ml of *ammonium reineckate solution R*. A pink precipitate is produced.

D. It gives reaction (a) of chlorides (*2.3.1*).

## TESTS

### Solution S

Dissolve 1.00 g in *carbon-dioxide free water R* and dilute to 20.0 ml with the same solvent.

### Appearance of solution

Solution S is clear (*2.2.1*) and colourless (*2.2.2, Method II*).

### pH (*2.2.3*)

4.3 to 5.3.

Dilute 2.0 ml of solution S to 10.0 ml with *carbon dioxide-free water R*.

### Specific optical rotation (*2.2.7*)

+ 115 to + 120 (dried substance).

Dilute 5.0 ml of solution S to 25.0 ml with *water R*.

### Related substances

Liquid chromatography (*2.2.29*).

*Test solution*   Dissolve 50.0 mg of the substance to be examined in the mobile phase and dilute to 200.0 ml with the mobile phase.

*Reference solution (a)*   Dissolve 50.0 mg of *diltiazem hydrochloride CRS* in the mobile phase and dilute to 200.0 ml with the mobile phase. Dilute 1.2 ml of this solution to 100.0 ml with the mobile phase.

*Reference solution (b)*   Dissolve the contents of a vial of *diltiazem impurity A CRS* in 1.0 ml of reference solution (a).

*Reference solution (c)*   Dilute 0.3 ml of the test solution to 100.0 ml with the mobile phase.

*Column:*
— *size: l* = 0.10 m, Ø = 4.6 mm;
— *stationary phase: octadecylsilyl silica gel for chromatography R* (3 μm).

*Mobile phase*   Mix 5 volumes of *anhydrous ethanol R*, 25 volumes of *acetonitrile R* and 70 volumes of a solution containing 6.8 g/l of *potassium dihydrogen phosphate R* and 0.1 ml/l of *N,N-dimethyloctylamine R*, adjusted to pH 4.5 with *dilute phosphoric acid R*.

*Flow rate*   1.5 ml/min.

*Detection*   Spectrophotometer at 240 nm.

*Injection*   20 μl.

*Run time*   5 times the retention time of diltiazem.

*System suitability*   Reference solution (b):
— *resolution*: minimum 4.0 between the peaks due to impurity A and diltiazem; if necessary, adjust the concentration of *N,N-dimethyloctylamine* in the mobile phase;
— *symmetry factor*: maximum 2.0 for the peaks due to impurity A and diltiazem; if necessary, adjust the concentration of *N,N-dimethyloctylamine* in the mobile phase.

*Limits:*
— *total*: not more than the area of the principal peak in the chromatogram obtained with reference solution (c) (0.3 per cent);
— *disregard limit*: 0.025 times the area of the principal peak in the chromatogram obtained with reference solution (c).

### Heavy metals (*2.4.8*)

Maximum 10 ppm.

Dissolve 2.0 g in *water R* and dilute to 20.0 ml with the same solvent. 12 ml of the solution complies with test A. Prepare the reference solution using *lead standard solution (1 ppm Pb) R*.

### Loss on drying (*2.2.32*)

Maximum 0.5 per cent, determined on 1.000 g by drying in an oven at 105 °C for 2 h.

### Sulphated ash (*2.4.14*)

Maximum 0.1 per cent, determined on 1.0 g.

## ASSAY

Dissolve 0.400 g in a mixture of 2 ml of *anhydrous formic acid R* and 60 ml of *acetic anhydride R* and titrate with *0.1 M perchloric acid*, determining the end-point potentiometrically (*2.2.20*).

1 ml of *0.1 M perchloric acid* is equivalent to 45.1 mg of $C_{22}H_{27}ClN_2O_4S$.

## STORAGE

In an airtight container, protected from light.

## IMPURITIES

A. (2R,3S)-5-[2-(dimethylamino)ethyl]-2-(4-methoxyphenyl)-4-oxo-2,3,4,5-tetrahydro-1,5-benzothiazepin-3-yl acetate,

B. R1 = CO-CH₃, R2 = H, R3 = OCH₃:
(2S,3S)-2-(4-methoxyphenyl)-4-oxo-2,3,4,5-tetrahydro-1,5-benzothiazepin-3-yl acetate,

C. R1 = CO-CH₃, R2 = CH₂-CH₂-N(CH₃)₂, R3 = OH:
(2S,3S)-5-[2-(dimethylamino)ethyl]-2-(4-hydroxyphenyl)-4-oxo-2,3,4,5-tetrahydro-1,5-benzothiazepin-3-yl acetate,

D. R1 = CO-CH₃, R2 = CH₂-CH₂-NH-CH₃, R3 = OCH₃:
(2S,3S)-2-(4-methoxyphenyl)-5-[2-(methylamino)ethyl]-4-oxo-2,3,4,5-tetrahydro-1,5-benzothiazepin-3-yl acetate,

E. R1 = R2 = H, R3 = OCH₃:
(2S,3S)-3-hydroxy-2-(4-methoxyphenyl)-2,3-dihydro-1,5-benzothiazepin-4(5H)-one,

F. R1 = H, R2 = CH₂-CH₂-N(CH₃)₂, R3 = OCH₃: (2*S*,3*S*)-5-[2-(dimethylamino)ethyl]-3-hydroxy-2-(4-methoxyphenyl)-2,3-dihydro-1,5-benzothiazepin-4(5*H*)-one.

*Ph Eur*

# Dimenhydrinate

(*Ph Eur monograph 0601*)

C₁₇H₂₁NO,C₇H₇ClN₄O₂     470.0     *523-87-5*

## Action and use
Histamine H₁ receptor antagonist; antihistamine.

## Preparation
Dimenhydrinate Tablets

*Ph Eur*

## DEFINITION
Diphenhydramine [2-(diphenylmethoxy)-*N*,*N*-dimethylethanamine] 8-chlorotheophylline (8-chloro-1,3-dimethyl-3,7-dihydro-1*H*-purine-2,6-dione).

*Content:*
— diphenhydramine (C₁₇H₂₁NO; *M*$_r$ 255.4): 53.0 per cent to 55.5 per cent (dried substance);
— 8-chlorotheophylline (C₇H₇ClN₄O₂; *M*$_r$ 214.6): 44.0 per cent to 46.5 per cent (dried substance).

## CHARACTERS
### Appearance
White or almost white, crystalline powder or colourless crystals.

### Solubility
Slightly soluble in water, freely soluble in ethanol (96 per cent).

## IDENTIFICATION
*First identification   C.*

*Second identification   A, B, D.*

A. Melting point (*2.2.14*): 102 °C to 106 °C.

B. Dissolve 0.1 g in a mixture of 3 ml of *water R* and 3 ml of *ethanol (96 per cent) R*, add 6 ml of *water R* and 1 ml of *dilute hydrochloric acid R* and cool in iced water for 30 min, scratching the wall of the tube with a glass rod if necessary to initiate crystallisation. Dissolve about 10 mg of the precipitate obtained in 1 ml of *hydrochloric acid R*, add 0.1 g of *potassium chlorate R* and evaporate to dryness in a porcelain dish. A reddish residue is obtained that becomes violet-red when exposed to ammonia vapour.

C. Infrared absorption spectrophotometry (*2.2.24*).

*Comparison   dimenhydrinate CRS.*

D. Dissolve 0.2 g in 10 ml of *ethanol (96 per cent) R*. Add 10 ml of *picric acid solution R* and initiate crystallisation by scratching the wall of the tube with a glass rod. The

precipitate, washed with *water R* and dried at 100-105 °C, melts (*2.2.14*) at 130 °C to 134 °C.

## TESTS
### Appearance of solution
The solution is clear (*2.2.1*) and colourless (*2.2.2*, *Method II*).

Dissolve 1.0 g in *ethanol (96 per cent) R* and dilute to 20 ml with the same solvent.

### pH (*2.2.3*)
7.1 to 7.6 for the filtrate.

To 0.4 g add 20 ml of *carbon dioxide-free water R*, shake for 2 min and filter.

### Related substances
Liquid chromatography (*2.2.29*).

*Solvent mixture   acetonitrile R, water R* (18:82 *V/V*).

*Test solution   Dissolve 0.100 g of the substance to be examined in the solvent mixture and dilute to 100.0 ml with the solvent mixture.*

*Reference solution (a)   Dissolve 57 mg of diphenhydramine hydrochloride CRS in the solvent mixture and dilute to 50.0 ml with the solvent mixture.*

*Reference solution (b)   Dilute 1.0 ml of reference solution (a) to 100.0 ml with the solvent mixture. Dilute 2.0 ml of this solution to 10.0 ml with the solvent mixture.*

*Reference solution (c)   Dissolve 5.0 mg of diphenhydramine impurity A CRS (impurity F) in 5.0 ml of reference solution (a) and dilute to 50.0 ml with the solvent mixture.*

*Reference solution (d)   Dissolve the contents of a vial of dimenhydrinate for peak identification CRS (containing impurities A and E) in 1.0 ml of the solvent mixture.*

*Column:*
— *size: l = 0.25 m, Ø = 4.6 mm;*
— *stationary phase: end-capped octadecylsilyl silica gel for chromatography R (5 μm);*
— *temperature: 30 °C.*

*Mobile phase:*
— *mobile phase A: dissolve 10.0 g of triethylamine R2 in 950 ml of water R, adjust to pH 2.5 with phosphoric acid R and dilute to 1000 ml with water R;*
— *mobile phase B: acetonitrile R1;*

| Time (min) | Mobile phase A (per cent *V/V*) | Mobile phase B (per cent *V/V*) | Flow rate (ml/min) |
|---|---|---|---|
| 0 - 2 | 82 | 18 | 1.2 |
| 2 - 15 | 82 → 50 | 18 → 50 | 1.2 |
| 15 - 20 | 50 → 20 | 50 → 80 | 1.2 → 2.0 |
| 20 - 30 | 20 | 80 | 2.0 |

*Detection   Spectrophotometer at 225 nm.*

*Injection   10 μl.*

*Identification of impurities   Use the chromatogram supplied with dimenhydrinate for peak identification CRS and the chromatogram obtained with reference solution (d) to identify the peaks due to impurities A and E; use the chromatogram obtained with reference solution (c) to identify impurity F.*

*Relative retention   With reference to diphenhydramine (retention time = about 13 min): impurity A = about 0.3; impurity E = about 0.7; impurity F = about 0.95.*

*System suitability   Reference solution (c):*
— *resolution: minimum 1.5 between the peaks due to impurity F and diphenhydramine.*

*Limits:*
— *impurities A, F*: for each impurity, not more than the area of the principal peak in the chromatogram obtained with reference solution (b) (0.2 per cent);
— *impurity E*: not more than 0.75 times the area of the principal peak in the chromatogram obtained with reference solution (b) (0.15 per cent);
— *unspecified impurities*: for each impurity, not more than 0.5 times the area of the principal peak in the chromatogram obtained with reference solution (b) (0.10 per cent);
— *total*: not more than 2.5 times the area of the principal peak in the chromatogram obtained with reference solution (b) (0.5 per cent);
— *disregard limit*: 0.25 times the area of the principal peak in the chromatogram obtained with reference solution (b) (0.05 per cent).

**Loss on drying** (*2.2.32*)
Maximum 0.5 per cent, determined on 1.000 g by drying *in vacuo.*

**Sulphated ash** (*2.4.14*)
Maximum 0.2 per cent, determined on 1.0 g.

## ASSAY
**Diphenhydramine**
Dissolve 0.200 g in 60 ml of *anhydrous acetic acid R*. Titrate with *0.1 M perchloric acid*, determining the end-point potentiometrically (*2.2.20*).

1 ml of *0.1 M perchloric acid* is equivalent to 25.54 mg of $C_{17}H_{21}NO$.

**8-Chlorotheophylline**
To 0.800 g add 50 ml of *water R*, 3 ml of *dilute ammonia R1* and 0.6 g of *ammonium nitrate R* and heat on a water-bath for 5 min. Add 25.0 ml of *0.1 M silver nitrate* and continue heating on a water-bath for 15 min with frequent swirling. Cool, add 25 ml of *dilute nitric acid R* and dilute to 250.0 ml with *water R*. Filter and discard the first 25 ml of the filtrate. Using 5 ml of *ferric ammonium sulphate solution R2* as indicator, titrate 100.0 ml of the filtrate with *0.1 M ammonium thiocyanate* until a yellowish-brown colour is obtained.

1 ml of *0.1 M silver nitrate* is equivalent to 21.46 mg of $C_7H_7ClN_4O_2$.

## IMPURITIES
*Specified impurities   A, E, F.*

*Other detectable impurities*   (The following substances would, if present at a sufficient level, be detected by one or other of the tests in the monograph. They are limited by the general acceptance criterion for other/unspecified impurities and/or by the general monograph *Substances for pharmaceutical use (2034)*. It is therefore not necessary to identify these impurities for demonstration of compliance. See also *5.10. Control of impurities in substances for pharmaceutical use*): *C, D, G, H, I, J, K.*

A. theophylline,
C. caffeine,

D. R1 = CH$_2$-N(CH$_3$)$_2$, R2 = H:
*N*-[2-(diphenylmethoxy)ethyl]-*N*,*N'*,*N'*-trimethylethane-1,2-diamine,
G. R1 = H, R2 = CH$_3$: *N*,*N*-dimethyl-2-[(*RS*)-(4-methylphenyl)(phenyl)methoxy]ethanamine (4-methyldiphenhydramine),
H. R1 = H, R2 = Br: 2-[(*RS*)-(4-bromophenyl)-(phenyl)methoxy]-*N*,*N*-dimethylethanamine (4-bromodiphenhydramine),

E. 8-chloro-1,3,7-trimethyl-3,7-dihydro-1*H*-purine-2,6-dione (8-chlorocaffeine),

F. 2-(diphenylmethoxy)-*N*-methylethanamine (diphenhydramine impurity A),

I. R = H: diphenylmethanol (benzhydrol),
K. R = CH(C$_6$H$_5$)$_2$: [oxybis(methanetriyl)]tetrabenzene,

J. diphenylmethanone(benzophenone).

# Dimercaprol

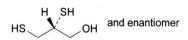

(*Ph Eur monograph 0389*)

$C_3H_8OS_2$            124.2            59-52-9

### Action and use
Chelating agent for use in heavy metal poisoning.

### Preparation
Dimercaprol Injection

When B.A.L. is prescribed or demanded, Dimercaprol shall be dispensed or supplied.

*Ph Eur* _____

### DEFINITION
(2*RS*)-2,3-Disulfanylpropan-1-ol.

### Content
98.5 per cent to 101.5 per cent.

### CHARACTERS
**Appearance**
Clear, colourless or slightly yellow liquid.

**Solubility**
Soluble in water and in arachis oil, miscible with ethanol (96 per cent) and with benzyl benzoate.

### IDENTIFICATION
A. Dissolve 0.05 ml in 2 ml of *water R*. Add 1 ml of *0.05 M iodine*. The colour of the iodine is discharged immediately.

B. Dissolve 0.1 ml in 5 ml of *water R* and add 2 ml of *copper sulphate solution R*. A bluish-black precipitate is formed which quickly becomes dark grey.

C. In a ground-glass-stoppered tube, suspend 0.6 g of *sodium bismuthate R*, previously heated to 200 °C for 2 h, in a mixture of 2.8 ml of *dilute phosphoric acid R* and 6 ml of *water R*. Add 0.2 ml of the substance to be examined, mix and allow to stand for 10 min with frequent shaking. To 1 ml of the supernatant liquid add 5 ml of a 4 g/l solution of *chromotropic acid, sodium salt R* in *sulphuric acid R* and mix. Heat in a water-bath for 15 min. A violet-red colour develops.

### TESTS
**Appearance**
It is clear (*2.2.1*) and not more intensely coloured than reference solution B₆ or BY₆ (*2.2.2, Method II*).

**Acidity or alkalinity**
Dissolve 0.2 g in *carbon dioxide-free water R* and dilute to 10 ml with the same solvent. Add 0.25 ml of *bromocresol green solution R* and 0.3 ml of *0.01 M hydrochloric acid*. The solution is yellow. Not more than 0.5 ml of *0.01 M sodium hydroxide* is required to change the colour of the indicator to blue.

**Refractive index** (*2.2.6*)
1.568 to 1.574.

**Halides**
To 2.0 g add 25 ml of *alcoholic potassium hydroxide solution R* and boil under a reflux condenser for 2 h. Eliminate the ethanol by evaporation in a stream of hot air. Add 20 ml of *water R* and cool. Add 40 ml of *water R* and 10 ml of *strong hydrogen peroxide solution R*, boil gently for 10 min, cool and filter rapidly. Add 10 ml of *dilute nitric acid R* and 5.0 ml of

*0.1 M silver nitrate*. Using 2 ml of *ferric ammonium sulphate solution R2* as indicator, titrate with *0.1 M ammonium thiocyanate* until a reddish-yellow colour is obtained. Carry out a blank titration. The difference between the titration volumes is not greater than 1.0 ml.

### ASSAY
Dissolve 0.100 g in 40 ml of *methanol R*. Add 20 ml of *0.1 M hydrochloric acid* and 50.0 ml of *0.05 M iodine*. Allow to stand for 10 min and titrate with *0.1 M sodium thiosulphate*. Carry out a blank titration.

1 ml of *0.05 M iodine* is equivalent to 6.21 mg of $C_3H_8OS_2$.

### STORAGE
In a well-filled, airtight container, protected from light, at a temperature of 2 °C to 8 °C.

_____ *Ph Eur*

# Dimethylacetamide

(*Ph Eur monograph 1667*)

$C_4H_9NO$            87.1            127-19-5

### Action and use
Excipient.

*Ph Eur* _____

### DEFINITION
*N,N*-Dimethylacetamide.

### CHARACTERS
**Appearance**
Clear, colourless, slightly hygroscopic liquid.

**Solubility**
Miscible with water, with ethanol (96 per cent), and with most common organic solvents.

bp: about 165 °C.

### IDENTIFICATION
*First identification   C.*

*Second identification   A, B, D.*

A. Relative density (*2.2.5*): 0.941 to 0.944.

B. Refractive index (*2.2.6*): 1.435 to 1.439.

C. Infrared absorption spectrophotometry (*2.2.24*).

*Preparation   Films.*

*Comparison   Ph. Eur. reference spectrum of dimethylacetamide.*

D. Dilute 50 mg with 1 ml of *methanol R*. Add 1 ml of a 15 g/l solution of *hydroxylamine hydrochloride R* and mix. Add 1 ml of *dilute sodium hydroxide solution R*, mix and allow to stand for 30 min. Add 1 ml of *dilute hydrochloric acid R* and add 1 ml of a 100 g/l solution of *ferric chloride R* in *0.1 M hydrochloric acid*. A reddish-brown colour develops, reaching a maximum intensity after about 5 min.

## TESTS

### Appearance
The substance to be examined is clear (2.2.1) and not more intensely coloured than reference solution $Y_7$ (2.2.2, Method II).

### Acidity
Dilute 50 ml with 50 ml of *water R* previously adjusted with *0.02 M potassium hydroxide* or *0.02 M hydrochloric acid* to a bluish-green colour, using 0.5 ml of *bromothymol blue solution R1* as indicator. Not more than 5.0 ml of *0.02 M potassium hydroxide* is required to restore the initial (bluish-green) colour.

### Alkalinity
To 50 ml add 50 ml of *water R* previously adjusted with *0.02 M potassium hydroxide* or *0.02 M hydrochloric acid* to a yellow colour, using 0.5 ml of *bromothymol blue solution R1* as indicator. Not more than 0.5 ml of *0.02 M hydrochloric acid* is required to restore the initial (yellow) colour.

### Related substances
Gas chromatography (2.2.28): use the normalisation procedure.

*Test solution*   The substance to be examined.

*Reference solution (a)*   Dilute a mixture of 1 ml of the substance to be examined and 1 ml of *dimethylformamide R* to 20 ml with *methylene chloride R*.

*Reference solution (b)*   Dilute 1 ml of the substance to be examined to 20.0 ml with *methylene chloride R*. Dilute 0.1 ml of the solution to 10.0 ml with *methylene chloride R*.

*Column:*
— *material*: fused silica,
— *size*: $l = 30$ m, $\emptyset = 0.32$ mm,
— *stationary phase*: macrogol 20 000 R (film thickness 1 µm).

*Carrier gas*   nitrogen for chromatography R.

*Linear velocity*   30 cm/s.

*Split ratio*   1:20.

*Temperature:*

|  | Time (min) | Temperature (°C) |
|---|---|---|
| Column | 0 - 15 | 80 → 200 |
| Injection port |  | 250 |
| Detector |  | 250 |

*Detection*   Flame ionisation.

*Injection*   0.5 µl.

*System suitability:*
— *resolution*: minimum 5.0 between the peaks due to dimethylacetamide and impurity B in the chromatogram obtained with reference solution (a),
— *signal-to-noise ratio*: minimum 10 for the principal peak in the chromatogram obtained with reference solution (b).

*Limits:*
— *any impurity*: maximum 0.1 per cent,
— *total*: maximum 0.3 per cent,
— *disregard limit*: the area of the peak in the chromatogram obtained with reference solution (b) (0.05 per cent).

### Heavy metals (2.4.8)
Maximum 10 ppm.

Dilute 4.0 g to 20.0 ml with *water R*. 12 ml of the solution complies with limit test A. Prepare the reference solution using *lead standard solution (2 ppm Pb) R*.

### Non-volatile matter
Maximum 20 ppm.

Evaporate 50 g to dryness using a rotary evaporator at a pressure not exceeding 1 kPa and on a water-bath. Dry the residue in an oven at 170-175 °C. The residue weighs not more than 1 mg.

### Water (2.5.32)
Maximum 0.1 per cent, determined on 0.100 g.

## STORAGE
In an airtight container, protected from light.

## IMPURITIES
A. acetic acid,

B. R = H: *N,N*-dimethylformamide,
C. R = $C_2H_5$: *N,N*-dimethylpropanamide,
D. R = $CH_2$-$CH_2$-$CH_3$: *N,N*-dimethylbutanamide.

_____ *Ph Eur*


# Dimethyl Phthalate

| $C_{10}H_{10}O_4$ | 194.2 | *131-11-3* |
|---|---|---|

### Action and use
Insect repellent.

### DEFINITION
Dimethyl Phthalate contains not less than 99.0% and not more than 100.5% w/w of $C_{10}H_{10}O_4$.

### CHARACTERISTICS
A colourless or faintly coloured liquid.

Slightly soluble in *water*; miscible with *ethanol (96%)*, with *ether* and with most organic solvents.

### IDENTIFICATION
A. The *infrared absorption spectrum*, Appendix II A, is concordant with the *reference spectrum* of dimethyl phthalate (RS 105).

B. Gently boil 1 g with 5 ml of 2M *methanolic potassium hydroxide* for 10 minutes, add 5 ml of *water*, evaporate the mixture to half its volume and cool. Add 1 ml of *hydrochloric acid*, filter, melt the dried precipitate in a small tube, add 0.5 g of *resorcinol* and 0.05 ml of *chloroform* and heat to about 180° for 3 minutes. Cool, add 1 ml of 5M *sodium hydroxide* and pour into *water*. An intense yellowish green fluorescence is produced.

### TESTS

#### Acidity
Mix 20 ml with 50 ml of *ethanol (96%)* previously neutralised to *phenolphthalein solution R1*. Not more than 0.1 ml of 0.1M *sodium hydroxide VS* is required to neutralise the solution using *phenolphthalein solution R1* as indicator.

**Refractive index**

1.515 to 1.517, Appendix V E.

**Weight per ml**

1.186 to 1.192 g, Appendix V G.

**Related substances**

Prepare a 0.075% w/v solution of *phenyl benzoate* (internal standard) in *chloroform* (solution A). Carry out the method for *gas chromatography*, Appendix III B, using solutions of the substance being examined containing (1) 0.10% w/v in solution A, (2) 5.0% w/v in *chloroform* and (3) 5.0% w/v in solution A.

The chromatographic procedure may be carried out using a glass column (1.5 m × 4 mm) packed with *acid-washed, silanised diatomaceous support* (80 to 100 mesh) coated with 3% w/w of phenyl methyl silicone fluid (50% phenyl) (OV-17 is suitable) and maintained at 145°.

In the chromatogram obtained with solution (3) the ratio of the sum of the areas of any *secondary peaks* to the area of the peak due to the internal standard is not greater than the ratio of the area of the peak due to dimethyl phthalate to the area of the peak due to the internal standard in the chromatogram obtained with solution (1).

**Sulphated ash**

Not more than 0.1% w/w, Appendix IX A.

**Water**

Not more than 0.1% w/w, Appendix IX C. Use 20 g.

**ASSAY**

In a borosilicate glass flask dissolve 1.5 g of the substance being examined in 5 ml of carbon dioxide-free ethanol prepared by boiling *ethanol (96%)* thoroughly and neutralising to *phenolphthalein solution R1*. Neutralise the free acid in the solution with 0.1M *ethanolic potassium hydroxide VS* using 0.2 ml of *phenolphthalein solution R1* as indicator. Add 50 ml of 0.5M *ethanolic potassium hydroxide VS* and boil under a reflux condenser on a water bath for 1 hour. Add 20 ml of *water* and titrate the excess of alkali with 0.5M *hydrochloric acid VS* using a further 0.2 ml of *phenolphthalein solution R1* as indicator. Repeat the operation without the substance being examined. The difference between the titrations represents the alkali required to saponify the esters. Each ml of 0.5M *ethanolic potassium hydroxide VS* is equivalent to 48.55 mg of $C_{10}H_{10}O_4$.

# Dimethyl Sulfoxide

(*Ph Eur monograph 0763*)

$C_2H_6OS$       78.1       67-68-5

**Action and use**

Pharmaceutical solvent; excipient.

When dimethyl sulphoxide is demanded, Dimethyl Sulfoxide shall be supplied.

*Ph Eur*

**DEFINITION**

Sulphinylbismethane.

**CHARACTERS**

**Appearance**

Colourless liquid or colourless crystals, hygroscopic.

**Solubility**

Miscible with water and with ethanol (96 per cent).

**IDENTIFICATION**

*First identification C.*

*Second identification A, B, D.*

A. Relative density (see Tests).

B. Refractive index (see Tests).

C. Infrared absorption spectrophotometry (*2.2.24*).

*Comparison* dimethyl sulfoxide CRS.

D. Dissolve 50 mg of *nickel chloride R* in 5 ml of the substance to be examined. The solution is greenish-yellow. Heat in a water-bath at 50 °C. The colour changes to green or bluish-green. Cool. The colour changes to greenish-yellow.

**TESTS**

**Acidity**

Dissolve 50.0 g in 100 ml of *carbon dioxide-free water R*. Add 0.1 ml of *phenolphthalein solution R1*. Not more than 5.0 ml of *0.01 M sodium hydroxide* is required to produce a pink colour.

**Relative density** (*2.2.5*)

1.100 to 1.104.

**Refractive index** (*2.2.6*)

1.478 to 1.479.

**Freezing point** (*2.2.18*)

Minimum 18.3 °C.

**Absorbance** (*2.2.25*)

Purge with *nitrogen R* for 15 min. The absorbance, measured using *water R* as the compensation liquid, is not more than 0.30 at 275 nm and not more than 0.20 at both 285 nm and 295 nm. Examined between 270 nm and 350 nm, the substance to be examined shows no absorption maximum.

**Related substances**

Gas chromatography (*2.2.28*).

*Internal standard solution* Dissolve 0.125 g of *bibenzyl R* in *acetone R* and dilute to 50 ml with the same solvent.

*Test solution (a)* Dissolve 5.0 g of the substance to be examined in *acetone R* and dilute to 10.0 ml with the same solvent.

*Test solution (b)* Dissolve 5.0 g of the substance to be examined in *acetone R*, add 1.0 ml of the internal standard solution and dilute to 10.0 ml with *acetone R*.

*Reference solution* Dissolve 50.0 mg of the substance to be examined and 50 mg of *dimethyl sulphone R* in *acetone R*, add 10.0 ml of the internal standard solution and dilute to 100.0 ml with *acetone R*.

*Column:*

— *material*: glass;

— *size*: *l* = 1.5 m, Ø = 4 mm;

— *stationary phase*: *diatomaceous earth for gas chromatography R* (125-180 µm) impregnated with 10 per cent m/m of *polyethyleneglycol adipate R*.

*Carrier gas* nitrogen for chromatography R.

*Flow rate* 30 ml/min.

*Temperature:*

— *column*: 165 °C;

— *injection port and detector*: 190 °C.

*Detection* Flame ionisation.

*Injection* 1 µl.

*Run time*   4 times the retention time of dimethyl sulfoxide.

*Elution order*   Dimethyl sulfoxide, dimethyl sulphone, bibenzyl.

*Retention time*   Dimethyl sulfoxide = about 5 min.

*System suitability:*
— *resolution*: minimum 3 between the peaks due to dimethyl sulfoxide and dimethyl sulphone in the chromatogram obtained with the reference solution;
— in the chromatogram obtained with test solution (a) there is no peak with the same retention time as the internal standard.

*Limit:*
— *total*: calculate the ratio R of the area of the peak due to dimethyl sulfoxide to the area of the peak due to the internal standard from the chromatogram obtained with the reference solution; from the chromatogram obtained with test solution (b), calculate the ratio of the sum of the areas of any peaks, apart from the principal peak and the peak due to the internal standard to the area of the peak due to the internal standard: this ratio is not greater than R (0.1 per cent).

**Water** *(2.5.12)*

Maximum 0.2 per cent, determined on 10.0 g.

**STORAGE**

In an airtight, glass container, protected from light.

_____ *Ph Eur*

# Dimeticone

*(Ph Eur monograph 0138)*

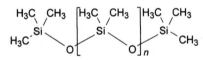

9006-75-9

**Action and use**

Antifoaming agent; water repellent.

When dimethicone is demanded, Dimeticone shall be supplied.

*Ph Eur* _____

## DEFINITION

Poly(dimethylsiloxane) obtained by hydrolysis and polycondensation of dichlorodimethylsilane and chlorotrimethylsilane. Different grades of dimeticone exist which are distinguished by a number indicating the nominal kinematic viscosity placed after the name.

Their degree of polymerisation ($n = 20$ to $400$) is such that their kinematic viscosities are nominally between $20 \text{ mm}^2 \cdot \text{s}^{-1}$ and $1300 \text{ mm}^2 \cdot \text{s}^{-1}$.

*Dimeticones with a nominal viscosity of $50 \text{ mm}^2 \cdot \text{s}^{-1}$ or lower are intended for external use only.*

## CHARACTERS

**Appearance**

Clear, colourless liquid of various viscosities.

**Solubility**

Practically insoluble in water, very slightly soluble or practically insoluble in anhydrous ethanol, miscible with ethyl acetate, with methyl ethyl ketone and with toluene.

## IDENTIFICATION

A. It is identified by its kinematic viscosity at 25 °C (see Tests).

B. Infrared absorption spectrophotometry *(2.2.24)*.

*Comparison*   dimeticone CRS.

The region of the spectrum from 850 cm⁻¹ to 750 cm⁻¹ is not taken into account.

C. Heat 0.5 g in a test-tube over a small flame until white fumes begin to appear. Invert the tube over a 2ⁿᵈ tube containing 1 ml of a 1 g/l solution of *chromotropic acid, sodium salt R* in *sulphuric acid R* so that the fumes reach the solution. Shake the 2ⁿᵈ tube for about 10 s and heat on a water-bath for 5 min. The solution is violet.

D. In a platinum crucible, prepare the sulphated ash *(2.4.14)* using 50 mg. The residue is a white powder that gives the reaction of silicates *(2.3.1)*.

## TESTS

**Acidity**

To 2.0 g add 25 ml of a mixture of equal volumes of *anhydrous ethanol R* and *ether R*, previously neutralised to 0.2 ml of *bromothymol blue solution R1* and shake. Not more than 0.15 ml of *0.01 M sodium hydroxide* is required to change the colour of the solution to blue.

**Viscosity** *(2.2.9)*

90 per cent to 110 per cent of the nominal kinematic viscosity stated on the label, determined at 25 °C.

**Mineral oils**

Place 2 g in a test-tube and examine in ultraviolet light at 365 nm. The fluorescence is not more intense than that of a solution containing 0.1 ppm of *quinine sulphate R* in *0.005 M sulphuric acid* examined in the same conditions.

**Phenylated compounds**

Dissolve 5.0 g with shaking in 10 ml of *cyclohexane R*. At wavelengths from 250 nm to 270 nm, the absorbance *(2.2.25)* of the solution is not greater than 0.2.

**Heavy metals**

Maximum 5 ppm.

Mix 1.0 g with *methylene chloride R* and dilute to 20 ml with the same solvent. Add 1.0 ml of a freshly prepared 0.02 g/l solution of *dithizone R* in *methylene chloride R*, 0.5 ml of *water R* and 0.5 ml of a mixture of 1 volume of *dilute ammonia R2* and 9 volumes of a 2 g/l solution of *hydroxylamine hydrochloride R*. At the same time, prepare a reference solution as follows: to 20 ml of *methylene chloride R* add 1.0 ml of a freshly prepared 0.02 g/l solution of *dithizone R* in *methylene chloride R*, 0.5 ml of *lead standard solution (10 ppm Pb) R* and 0.5 ml of a mixture of 1 volume of *dilute ammonia R2* and 9 volumes of a 2 g/l solution of *hydroxylamine hydrochloride R*. Immediately shake each solution vigorously for 1 min. Any red colour in the test solution is not more intense than that in the reference solution.

**Volatile matter**

Maximum 0.3 per cent, for dimeticones with a nominal viscosity greater than 50 mm²·s⁻¹, determined on 1.00 g by heating in an oven at 150 °C for 2 h. Carry out the test using a dish 60 mm in diameter and 10 mm deep.

## LABELLING

The label states:
— the nominal kinematic viscosity by a number placed after the name of the product,

— where applicable, that the product is intended for external use.

*Ph Eur*

# Dimetindene Maleate

(*Ph Eur monograph 1417*)

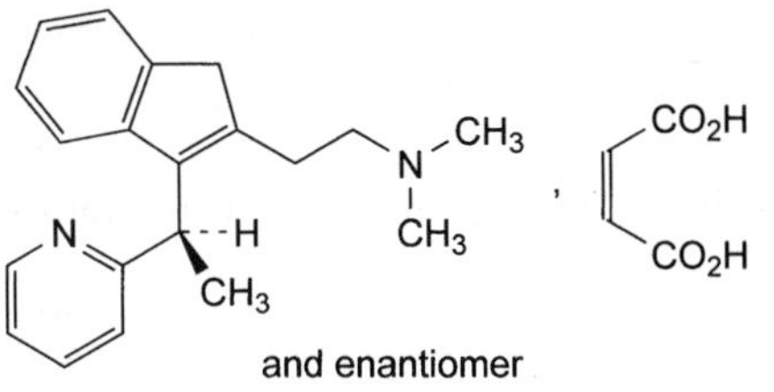

C$_{24}$H$_{28}$N$_2$O$_4$      408.5      *3614-69-5*

**Action and use**

Histamine H$_1$ receptor antagonist; antihistamine.

*Ph Eur*

## DEFINITION

*N,N*-Dimethyl-2-[3-[(*RS*)-1-(pyridin-2-yl)ethyl]-1*H*-inden-2-yl]ethanamine (*Z*)-butenedioate.

## Content

99.0 per cent to 101.0 per cent (dried substance).

## CHARACTERS

**Appearance**

White or almost white, crystalline powder.

**Solubility**

Slightly soluble in water, soluble in methanol.

## IDENTIFICATION

Infrared absorption spectrophotometry (*2.2.24*).

*Preparation*   Discs.

*Comparison*   dimetindene maleate CRS.

## TESTS

**Solution S**

Dissolve 0.20 g in *methanol R* and dilute to 20.0 ml with the same solvent.

**Appearance of solution**

Solution S is clear (*2.2.1*) and not more intensely coloured than Y$_6$ (*2.2.2, Method II*).

**Optical rotation** (*2.2.7*):

− 0.10° to + 0.10°, determined on solution S.

**Related substances**

Gas chromatography (*2.2.28*).

*Solvent mixture*   acetone R, methylene chloride R (50:50 *V/V*).

*Test solution*   Dissolve 50.0 mg of the substance to be examined in the solvent mixture and dilute to 5.0 ml with the solvent mixture.

*Reference solution (a)*   Dilute 1 ml of the test solution to 100.0 ml with the solvent mixture.

*Reference solution (b)*   Dissolve 5.0 mg of *2-ethylpyridine R* (impurity A) in the solvent mixture and dilute to 50.0 ml with the solvent mixture. Dilute 10.0 ml of this solution to 100.0 ml with the solvent mixture.

*Column:*

— *material*: fused silica;

— *size*: *l* = 30 m, Ø = 0.32 mm;

— *stationary phase*: *polymethylphenylsiloxane R* (film thickness 0.25 μm).

*Carrier gas*   helium for chromatography R.

*Linear velocity*   About 30 cm/s.

*Temperature:*

| | Time (min) | Temperature (°C) |
|---|---|---|
| Column | 0 - 1 | 60 |
| | 1 - 34.3 | 60 → 260 |
| | 34.3 - 46.3 | 260 |
| Injection port | | 240 |
| Detector | | 260 |

*Detection*   Flame ionisation.

*Injection*   2 μl; inject via a split injector with a split flow of 30 ml/min.

*Run time*   1.3 times the retention time of dimetindene.

*Elution order*   Impurity A and maleic acid appear during the first 8 min.

*System suitability*   Reference solution (a):

— *symmetry factor*: maximum 1.3 for the principal peak.

*Limits:*

— *impurity A*: not more than the area of the corresponding peak in the chromatogram obtained with reference solution (b) (0.1 per cent);

— *impurities B, C, D, E, F, G, H, I*: for each impurity, not more than 0.2 times the area of the principal peak in the chromatogram obtained with reference solution (a) (0.2 per cent);

— *sum of impurities other than A*: not more than 0.5 times the area of the principal peak in the chromatogram obtained with reference solution (a) (0.5 per cent);

— *disregard limit*: 0.05 times the area of the principal peak in the chromatogram obtained with reference solution (a) (0.05 per cent); disregard the peak due to maleic acid.

**Loss on drying** (*2.2.32*)

Maximum 0.1 per cent, determined on 1.000 g by drying in an oven at 105 °C for 2 h.

**Sulphated ash** (*2.4.14*)

Maximum 0.1 per cent, determined on 1.0 g.

## ASSAY

Dissolve 0.150 g in 80 ml of *anhydrous acetic acid R*. Titrate with *0.1 M perchloric acid*, determining the end-point potentiometrically (*2.2.20*).

1 ml of *0.1 M perchloric acid* is equivalent to 20.43 mg of C$_{24}$H$_{28}$N$_2$O$_4$.

## STORAGE

Protected from light.

## IMPURITIES

*Specified impurities*   *A, B, C, D, E, F, G, H, I.*

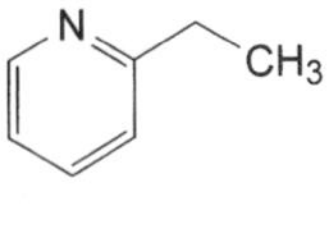

A. 2-ethylpyridine,

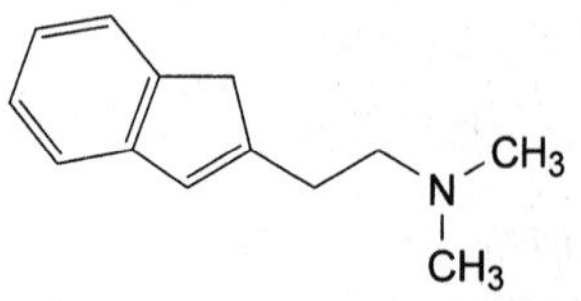

B. 2-(1H-inden-2-yl)-N,N-dimethylethanamine,

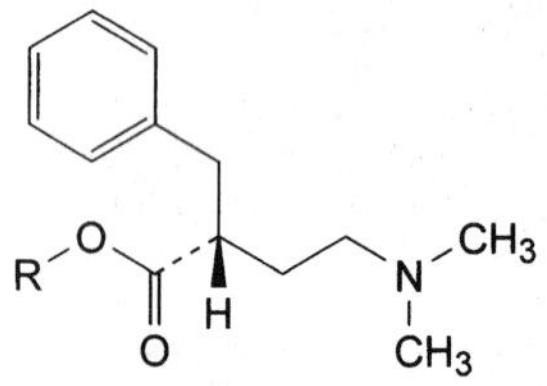

and enantiomer

C. R = C₂H₅:
ethyl (2RS)-2-benzyl-4-(dimethylamino)butanoate,

D. R = H: (2RS)-2-benzyl-4-(dimethylamino)butanoic acid,

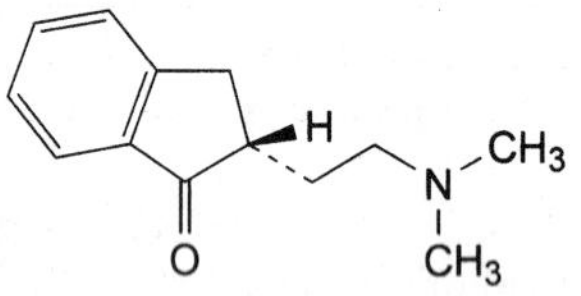

and enantiomer

E. (2RS)-2-[2-(dimethylamino)ethyl]indan-1-one,

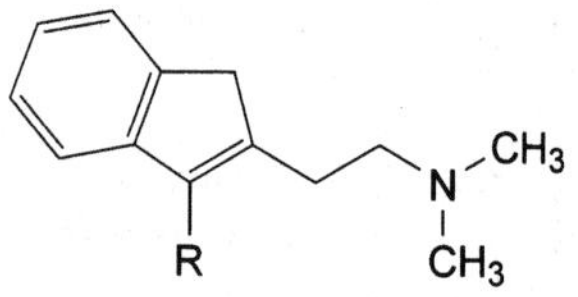

F. R = [CH₂]₃-CH₃:
2-(3-butyl-1H-inden-2-yl)-N,N-dimethylethanamine,

G. R = C₆H₅:
N,N-dimethyl-2-(3-phenyl-1H-inden-2-yl)ethanamine,

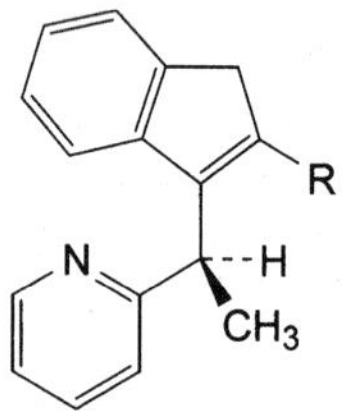

and enantiomer

H. R = CH = CH₂:
2-[(1RS)-1-(2-ethenyl-1H-inden-3-yl)ethyl]pyridine,

I. R = CH₂-CH₂-NH-CH₃: N-methyl-2-[3-[(1RS)-1-(pyridin-2-yl)ethyl]-1H-inden-2-yl]ethanamine.

_____ Ph Eur

# Dinoprost Trometamol

(*Ph Eur monograph 1312*)

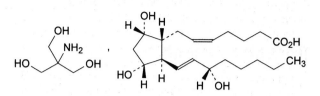

C₂₀H₃₄O₅,C₄H₁₁NO₃     475.6     38562-01-5

## Action and use
Prostaglandin F₂α(PGF₂α); inducer of uterine muscle contraction.

*Ph Eur* _____

## DEFINITION
Trometamol (Z)-7-[(1R,2R,3R,5S)-3,5-dihydroxy-2-[(E)-(3S)-3-hydroxyoct-1-enyl]cyclopentyl]hept-5-enoate (PGF₂α).

## Content
96.0 per cent to 102.0 per cent (anhydrous substance).

## CHARACTERS
### Appearance
White or almost white powder.

### Solubility
Very soluble in water, freely soluble in ethanol (96 per cent), practically insoluble in acetonitrile.

## IDENTIFICATION
A. Specific optical rotation (*2.2.7*): + 19 to + 26 (anhydrous substance).

Dissolve 0.100 g in *ethanol (96 per cent) R* and dilute to 10.0 ml with the same solvent.

B. Infrared absorption spectrophotometry (*2.2.24*).

*Comparison* dinoprost trometamol CRS.

## TESTS
### Related substances
Liquid chromatography (*2.2.29*).

*Solvent mixture* acetonitrile R, water R (23:77 V/V).

*Test solution* Dissolve 10.0 mg of the substance to be examined in the solvent mixture and dilute to 10.0 ml with the solvent mixture.

*Reference solution (a)* *Degradation of dinoprost trometamol to impurity B*. Dissolve 1 mg of the substance to be examined in 1 ml of the mobile phase and heat the solution on a water-bath at 85 °C for 5 min and cool.

*Reference solution (b)* Dilute 2.0 ml of the test solution to 20.0 ml with the solvent mixture. Dilute 2.0 ml of this solution to 20.0 ml with the solvent mixture.

*Column:*
— *size: l* = 0.15 m, Ø = 3.9 mm;
— *stationary phase*: octadecylsilyl silica gel for chromatography R1 (5 µm) with a pore size of 10 nm and a carbon loading of 19 per cent.

*Mobile phase* Dissolve 2.44 g of *sodium dihydrogen phosphate R* in *water R* and dilute to 1000 ml with *water R*; adjust to pH 2.5 with *phosphoric acid R* (about 0.6 ml); mix 770 ml of this solution with 230 ml of *acetonitrile R1*.

*Flow rate* 1 ml/min.

*Detection* Spectrophotometer at 200 nm.

*Injection* 20 µl.

*Run time* 2.5 times the retention time of the principal peak (to elute degradation products formed during heating) for reference solution (a) and 10 min after the elution of dinoprost for the test solution and reference solution (b).

*Retention time* Impurity B = about 55 min; impurity A = about 60 min; dinoprost = about 66 min.

*System suitability* Reference solution (a):
— *resolution*: minimum 1.5 between the peaks due to impurities B and A and minimum 2.0 between the peaks due to impurity A and dinoprost; if necessary, adjust the composition of the mobile phase by increasing the concentration of acetonitrile to decrease the retention times;
— *symmetry factor*: maximum 1.2 for the peaks due to impurities A and B.

*Limits*:
— *impurity A*: not more than twice the area of the principal peak obtained with reference solution (b) (2 per cent);
— *impurities B, C, D*: for each impurity, not more than 1.5 times the area of the principal peak obtained with reference solution (b) (1.5 per cent) and not more than one such peak has an area greater than 0.5 times the area of the principal peak obtained with reference solution (b) (0.5 per cent);
— *sum of impurities other than A*: not more than twice the area of the principal peak obtained with reference solution (b) (2 per cent);
— *disregard limit*: 0.05 times the area of the principal peak obtained with reference solution (b) (0.05 per cent); disregard any peak due to trometamol (retention time = about 1.5 min).

**Water** (*2.5.12*)
Maximum 1.0 per cent, determined on 0.500 g.

**ASSAY**
Liquid chromatography (*2.2.29*).

*Solvent mixture* acetonitrile R, water R (23:77 *V/V*).

*Test solution* Dissolve 10.0 mg of the substance to be examined in the solvent mixture and dilute to 10.0 ml with the solvent mixture.

*Reference solution* Dissolve 10.0 mg of *dinoprost trometamol CRS* in the solvent mixture and dilute to 10.0 ml with the solvent mixture.

*Column*:
— *size: l* = 0.15 m, Ø = 3.9 mm;
— *stationary phase*: octadecylsilyl *silica gel for chromatography R1* (5 μm) with a pore size of 10 nm and a carbon loading of 19 per cent.

*Mobile phase* Dissolve 2.44 g of *sodium dihydrogen phosphate R* in *water R* and dilute to 1000 ml with *water R*; adjust to pH 2.5 with *phosphoric acid R* (about 0.6 ml); mix 730 ml of this solution with 270 ml of *acetonitrile R1*.

*Flow rate* 1 ml/min.

*Detection* Spectrophotometer at 200 nm.

*Injection* 20 μl.

*Retention time* Dinoprost = about 23 min.

*System suitability* Reference solution:
— *repeatability*: maximum relative standard deviation of 2.0 per cent for the peak due to dinoprost after 6 injections.

Calculate the percentage of dinoprost trometamol from the declared content of *dinoprost trometamol CRS*.

**IMPURITIES**
*Specified impurities* A, B, C, D.

A. (*E*)-7-[(1*R*,2*R*,3*R*,5*S*)-3,5-dihydroxy-2-[(*E*)-(3*S*)-3-hydroxyoct-1-enyl]cyclopentyl]hept-5-enoic acid ((5*E*)-PGF$_{2\alpha}$; 5,6-*trans*-PGF$_{2\alpha}$),

B. (*Z*)-7-[(1*R*,2*R*,3*R*,5*S*)-3,5-dihydroxy-2-[(*E*)-(3*R*)-3-hydroxyoct-1-enyl]cyclopentyl]hept-5-enoic acid ((15*R*)-PGF$_{2\alpha}$;15-epiPGF$_{2\alpha}$),

C. (*Z*)-7-[(1*S*,2*R*,3*R*,5*S*)-3,5-dihydroxy-2-[(*E*)-(3*S*)-3-hydroxyoct-1-enyl]cyclopentyl]hept-5-enoic acid ((8*S*)-PGF$_{2\alpha}$; 8-epiPGF$_{2\alpha}$),

D. (*Z*)-7-[(1*R*,2*R*,3*S*,5*S*)-3,5-dihydroxy-2-[(*E*)-(3*S*)-3-hydroxyoct-1-enyl]cyclopentyl]hept-5-enoic acid (11β-PGF$_{2\alpha}$; 11-epiPGF$_{2\alpha}$).

*_____ Ph Eur*

# Dinoprostone

(*Ph Eur monograph 1311*)

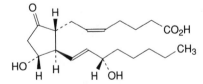

C$_{20}$H$_{32}$O$_5$          352.5          363-24-6

**Action and use**
Prostaglandin E$_2$(PGE$_2$); inducer of uterine muscle contraction.

*Ph Eur*

## DEFINITION

(Z)-7-[(1R,2R,3R)-3-hydroxy-2-[(E)-(3S)-3-hydroxyoct-1-enyl]-5-oxocyclopentyl]hept-5-enoic acid (PGE₂).

## Content

95.0 per cent to 102.0 per cent (anhydrous substance).

## CHARACTERS

### Appearance

White or almost white, crystalline powder or colourless crystals.

### Solubility

Practically insoluble in water, very soluble in methanol, freely soluble in alcohol.

The substance degrades at room temperature.

## IDENTIFICATION

A. Specific optical rotation (2.2.7): − 82 to − 90 (anhydrous substance).

Immediately before use, dissolve 50.0 mg in *alcohol R* and dilute to 10.0 ml with the same solvent.

B. Infrared absorption spectrophotometry (2.2.24).

*Comparison* dinoprostone CRS.

## TESTS

*Prepare the solutions immediately before use.*

### Related substances

Liquid chromatography (2.2.29).

*Test solution (a)* Dissolve 10.0 mg of the substance to be examined in a 58 per cent V/V solution of *methanol R2* and dilute to 2.0 ml with the same solvent.

*Test solution (b)* Dissolve 20.0 mg of the substance to be examined in a 58 per cent V/V solution of *methanol R2* and dilute to 20.0 ml with the same solvent.

*Reference solution (a)* Dissolve 1 mg of *dinoprostone CRS* and 1 mg of *dinoprostone impurity C CRS* in a 58 per cent V/V solution of *methanol R2* and dilute to 10.0 ml with the same solvent. Dilute 4.0 ml of the solution to 10.0 ml with a 58 per cent V/V solution of *methanol R2*.

*Reference solution (b)* Dilute 0.5 ml of test solution (a) to 10.0 ml with a 58 per cent V/V solution of *methanol R2*. Dilute 1.0 ml of the solution to 10.0 ml with a 58 per cent V/V solution of *methanol R2*.

*Reference solution (c)* In order to prepare *in situ* the degradation compounds (impurity D and impurity E), dissolve 1 mg of the substance to be examined in 100 μl of *1 M sodium hydroxide* (the solution becomes brownish-red), wait 4 min, add 150 μl of *1 M acetic acid* (yellowish-white opalescent solution) and dilute to 5.0 ml with a 58 per cent V/V solution of *methanol R2*.

*Reference solution (d)* Dissolve 20 mg of *dinoprostone CRS* in a 58 per cent V/V solution of *methanol R2* and dilute to 20.0 ml with the same solvent.

*Column:*
— *size:* l = 0.25 m, Ø = 4.6 mm,
— *stationary phase: end-capped octadecylsilyl silica gel for chromatography R,*
— *temperature:* 30 °C.

*Mobile phase* Mix 42 volumes of a 0.2 per cent V/V solution of *acetic acid R* and 58 volumes of *methanol R2*.

*Flow rate* 1.0 ml/min.

*Detection* Spectrophotometer at 210 nm.

*Injection* 20 μl; inject test solution (a) and reference solutions (a), (b) and (c).

*Relative retention* With reference to dinoprostone (retention time = about 18 min): impurity C = about 1.2; impurity D = about 1.8; impurity E = about 2.0.

*System suitability* Reference solution (a):
— *resolution:* minimum of 3.8 between the peaks due to dinoprostone and to impurity C. If necessary adjust the concentration of the acetic acid solution and/or methanol (increase the concentration of the acetic acid solution to increase the retention time for dinoprostone and impurity C and increase the concentration of methanol to decrease the retention time for both compounds).

*Limits:*
— *correction factors:* for the calculation of contents, multiply the peak areas of the following impurities by the corresponding correction factor: impurity D = 0.2; impurity E = 0.7,
— *impurity C:* not more than 3 times the area of the principal peak in the chromatogram obtained with reference solution (b) (1.5 per cent),
— *impurity D:* not more than twice the area of the principal peak in the chromatogram obtained with reference solution (b) (1 per cent),
— *impurity E:* not more than the area of the principal peak in the chromatogram obtained with reference solution (b) (0.5 per cent),
— *any other impurity:* not more than the area of the principal peak in the chromatogram obtained with reference solution (b) (0.5 per cent),
— *total of other impurities:* not more than twice the area of the principal peak in the chromatogram obtained with reference solution (b) (1 per cent),
— *disregard limit:* 0.1 times the area of the principal peak in the chromatogram obtained with reference solution (b) (0.05 per cent).

If any peak with a relative retention to dinoprostone of about 0.8 is greater than 0.5 per cent or if the total of other impurities is greater than 1.0 per cent, record the chromatogram of test solution (a) with a detector set at 230 nm. If the area of the peak at 230 nm is twice the area of the peak at 210 nm, multiply the area at 210 nm by 0.2 (correction factor for impurity F).

### Water (2.5.12)

Maximum 0.5 per cent, determined on 0.50 g.

## ASSAY

*Prepare the solutions immediately before use.*

Liquid chromatography (2.2.29) as described in the test for related substances.

*Injection* Test solution (b) and reference solution (d).

Calculate the percentage content of $C_{20}H_{32}O_5$.

## STORAGE

At a temperature not exceeding - 15 °C.

## IMPURITIES

A. (Z)-7-[(1R,2R,3R)-3-hydroxy-2-[(E)-(3R)-3-hydroxyoct-1-enyl]-5-oxocyclopentyl]hept-5-enoic acid (15-epiPGE₂; (15R)-PGE₂),

B. (Z)-7-[(1S,2R,3R)-3-hydroxy-2-[(E)-(3S)-3-hydroxyoct-1-enyl]-5-oxocyclopentyl]hept-5-enoic acid (8-epiPGE₂; (8S)-PGE₂),

C. (E)-7-[(1R,2R,3R)-3-hydroxy-2-[(E)-(3S)-3-hydroxyoct-1-enyl]-5-oxocyclopentyl]hept-5-enoic acid (5-trans-PGE₂; (5E)-PGE₂),

D. (Z)-7-[(1R,2S)-2-[(E)-(3S)-3-hydroxyoct-1-enyl]-5-oxocyclopent-3-enyl]hept-5-enoic acid (PGA₂),

E. (Z)-7-[2-[(E)-(3S)-3-hydroxyoct-1-enyl]-5-oxocyclopent-1-enyl]hept-5-enoic acid (PGB₂),

F. (Z)-7-[(1R,2R,3R)-3-hydroxy-2-[(E)-3-oxo-oct-1-enyl]-5-oxocyclopentyl]hept-5-enoic acid (15-oxo-PGE₂; 15-keto-PGE₂).

_____ Ph Eur

# Diosmin

(Ph Eur monograph 1611)

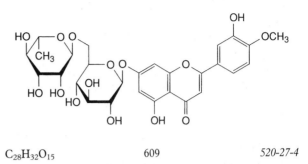

$C_{28}H_{32}O_{15}$     609     520-27-4

**Action and use**
Chronic venous insufficiency (flavonoid).

Ph Eur _____

## DEFINITION
7-[[6-O-(6-Deoxy-α-L-mannopyranosyl)-β-D-glucopyranosyl]oxy]-5-hydroxy-2-(3-hydroxy-4-methoxyphenyl)-4H-1-benzopyran-4-one.

Substance obtained through iodine-assisted oxidation of (2S)-7-[[6-O-(6-deoxy-α-L-mannopyranosyl)-β-D-glucopyranosyl]oxy]-5-hydroxy-2-(3-hydroxy-4-methoxyphenyl)-2,3-dihydro-4H-1-benzopyran-4-one (hesperidin) of natural origin.

**Content**
90.0 per cent to 102.0 per cent (anhydrous substance).

## CHARACTERS
**Appearance**
Greyish-yellow or light yellow hygroscopic powder.

**Solubility**
Practically insoluble in water, soluble in dimethyl sulphoxide, practically insoluble in alcohol. It dissolves in dilute solutions of alkali hydroxides.

## IDENTIFICATION
A. Infrared absorption spectrophotometry (2.2.24).

Comparison diosmin CRS.

B. Examine the chromatograms obtained in the assay.

Results The principal peak in the chromatogram obtained with the test solution is similar in retention time and size to the principal peak in the chromatogram obtained with reference solution (a).

## TESTS
**Iodine**
Maximum 0.1 per cent.

Determine the total content of iodine by potentiometry, using an iodide-selective electrode (2.2.36), after oxygen combustion (2.5.10).

Test solution Wrap 0.100 g of the substance to be examined in a piece of filter paper and place it in a sample carrier. Introduce into the flask 50 ml of a 0.2 g/l solution of hydrazine R. Flush the flask with oxygen for 10 min. Ignite the filter paper. Stir the contents of the flask immediately after the end of the combustion to dissolve completely the combustion products. Continue stirring for 1 h.

Reference solution Dilute 2.0 ml of a 16.6 g/l solution of potassium iodide R to 100.0 ml with water R. Dilute 10.0 ml of the solution to 100.0 ml with water R.

Introduce into a beaker 30 ml of a 200 g/l solution of *potassium nitrate R* in *0.1 M nitric acid*. Immerse the electrodes and stir for 10 min. The potential of the solution ($nT_1$) must remain stable. Add 1 ml of the test solution and measure the potential ($nT_2$).

Introduce into a beaker 30 ml of a 200 g/l solution of *potassium nitrate R* in *0.1 M nitric acid*. Immerse the electrodes and stir for 10 min. The potential of the solution must remain stable ($nR_1$). Add 80 µl of the reference solution and measure the potential ($nR_2$).

The absolute value $|nT_2 - nT_1|$ is not higher than the absolute value $|nR_2 - nR_1|$.

**Related substances**

Liquid chromatography (2.2.29).

*Test solution*   Dissolve 25.0 mg of the substance to be examined in *dimethyl sulphoxide R* and dilute to 25.0 ml with the same solvent.

*Reference solution (a)*   Dissolve 25.0 mg of *diosmin CRS* in *dimethyl sulphoxide R* and dilute to 25.0 ml with the same solvent.

*Reference solution (b)*   Dilute 5.0 ml of reference solution (a) to 100.0 ml with *dimethyl sulphoxide R*.

*Reference solution (c)*   Dissolve 5.0 mg of *diosmin for system suitability CRS* in *dimethyl sulphoxide R* and dilute to 5.0 ml with the same solvent.

*Column:*
— *size: l* = 0.10 m, Ø = 4.6 mm,
— *stationary phase: octadecylsilyl silica gel for chromatography R* (3 µm),
— *temperature:* 40 °C.

*Mobile phase*   acetonitrile R, glacial acetic acid R, methanol R, water R (2:6:28:66 *V/V/V/V*).

*Flow rate*   1.5 ml/min.

*Detection*   Spectrophotometer at 275 nm.

*Injection*   10 µl loop injector; inject the test solution and reference solutions (b) and (c).

*Run time*   6 times the retention time of diosmin.

*Relative retention*   With reference to diosmin (retention time = about 4.6 min): impurity A = about 0.5, impurity B = about 0.6, impurity C = about 0.8, impurity D = about 2.2, impurity E = about 2.6, impurity F = about 4.5.

*System suitability*   Reference solution (c):
— *resolution*: minimum of 2.5 between the peaks due to impurities B and C.

*Limits:*
— *correction factors*: for the calculation of contents, multiply the peak areas of the following impurities by the corresponding correction factor: impurity A = 0.38; impurity F = 0.61,
— *impurity A*: not more than 0.2 times the area of the principal peak in the chromatogram obtained with reference solution (b) (1 per cent),
— *impurity B*: not more than the area of the principal peak in the chromatogram obtained with reference solution (b) (5 per cent),
— *impurity C*: not more than 0.6 times the area of the principal peak in the chromatogram obtained with reference solution (b) (3 per cent),
— *impurity E*: not more than 0.6 times the area of the principal peak in the chromatogram obtained with reference solution (b) (3 per cent),

— *impurity F*: not more than 0.6 times the area of the principal peak in the chromatogram obtained with reference solution (b) (3 per cent),
— *any other impurity*: not more than 0.2 times the area of the principal peak in the chromatogram obtained with reference solution (b) (1 per cent),
— *total of other impurities and impurity A*: not more than 0.2 times the area of the principal peak in the chromatogram obtained with reference solution (b) (1 per cent),
— *total*: not more than twice the area of the principal peak in the chromatogram obtained with reference solution (b) (10 per cent),
— *disregard limit*: 0.02 times the area of the principal peak in the chromatogram obtained with reference solution (b) (0.1 per cent).

**Heavy metals** (2.4.8)
Maximum 20 ppm.

2.0 g complies with limit test C. Prepare the standard using 4.0 ml of *lead standard solution (10 ppm Pb) R*.

**Water** (2.5.12)
Maximum 6.0 per cent, determined on 0.300 g.

**Sulphated ash** (2.4.14)
Maximum 0.2 per cent, determined on 1.0 g.

**ASSAY**
Liquid chromatography (2.2.29), as described in the test for related substances.

*Injection*   Test solution and reference solution (a).

**STORAGE**
In an airtight container.

**IMPURITIES**

A. 1-(3-hydroxy-4-methoxyphenyl)ethanone (acetoisovanillone),

B. (2*S*)-7-[[6-*O*-(6-deoxy-α-ʟ-mannopyranosyl)-β-ᴅ-glucopyranosyl]oxy]-5-hydroxy-2-(3-hydroxy-4-methoxyphenyl)-2,3-dihydro-4*H*-1-benzopyran-4-one (hesperidin),

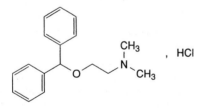

C. R1 = R3 = H, R2 = OH: 7-[[6-O-(6-deoxy-α-L-mannopyranosyl)-β-D-glucopyranosyl]oxy]-5-hydroxy-2-(4-hydroxyphenyl)-4*H*-1-benzopyran-4-one (isorhoifolin),

D. R1 = OH, R2 = OCH₃, R3 = I: 7-[[6-*O*-(6-deoxy-α-L-mannopyranosyl)-β-D-glucopyranosyl]oxy]-5-hydroxy-2-(3-hydroxy-4-methoxyphenyl)-6-iodo-4*H*-1-benzopyran-4-one (6-iododiosmin),

E. R1 = R3 = H, R2 = OCH₃: 7-[[6-*O*-(6-deoxy-α-L-mannopyranosyl)-β-D-glucopyranosyl]oxy]-5-hydroxy-2-(4-methoxyphenyl)-4*H*-1-benzopyran-4-one (linarin),

F. 5,7-dihydroxy-2-(3-hydroxy-4-methoxyphenyl)-4*H*-1-benzopyran-4-one (diosmetin).

*———— Ph Eur*

# Diphenhydramine Hydrochloride

*(Ph Eur monograph 0023)*

C₁₇H₂₁NO,HCl        291.8        *147-24-0*

## Action and use
Histamine H₁ receptor antagonist; antihistamine.

## Preparation
Diphenhydramine Oral Solution

*Ph Eur* ————

## DEFINITION
2-(Diphenylmethoxy)-*N*,*N*-dimethylethanamine hydrochloride.

## Content
99.0 per cent to 101.0 per cent (dried substance).

## CHARACTERS
### Appearance
White or almost white, crystalline powder.

## Solubility
Very soluble in water, freely soluble in alcohol.

## IDENTIFICATION
*First identification   C, D.*

*Second identification   A, B, D.*

A. Melting point (*2.2.14*): 168 °C to 172 °C.

B. Dissolve 50 mg in *alcohol R* and dilute to 100.0 ml with the same solvent. Examined between 230 nm and 350 nm, the solution shows 3 absorption maxima (*2.2.25*), at 253 nm, 258 nm and 264 nm. The ratio of the absorbance measured at the maximum at 258 nm to that measured at the maximum at 253 nm is 1.1 to 1.3. The ratio of the absorbance measured at the maximum at 258 nm to that measured at the maximum at 264 nm is 1.2 to 1.4.

C. Infrared absorption spectrophotometry (*2.2.24*).

*Preparation   Discs.*

*Comparison   diphenhydramine hydrochloride CRS.*

D. It gives the reactions of chlorides (*2.3.1*).

## TESTS
### Solution S
Dissolve 1.0 g in *carbon dioxide-free water R* and dilute to 20 ml with the same solvent.

### Appearance of solution
Solution S and a fivefold dilution of solution S are clear (*2.2.1*). Solution S is not more intensely coloured than reference solution BY₆ (*2.2.2, Method II*).

### Acidity or alkalinity
To 10 ml of solution S add 0.15 ml of *methyl red solution R* and 0.25 ml of *0.01 M hydrochloric acid*. The solution is pink. Not more than 0.5 ml of *0.01 M sodium hydroxide* is required to change the colour of the indicator to yellow.

### Related substances
Liquid chromatography (*2.2.29*).

*Test solution   Dissolve 70 mg of the substance to be examined in the mobile phase and dilute to 20.0 ml with the mobile phase. Dilute 2.0 ml of the solution to 10.0 ml with the mobile phase.*

*Reference solution (a)   Dilute 1.0 ml of the test solution to 10.0 ml with the mobile phase. Dilute 1.0 ml of this solution to 20.0 ml with the mobile phase.*

*Reference solution (b)   Dissolve 5 mg of diphenhydramine impurity A CRS and 5 mg of diphenylmethanol R in the mobile phase and dilute to 10.0 ml with the mobile phase. To 2.0 ml of this solution add 1.5 ml of the test solution and dilute to 10.0 ml with the mobile phase.*

*Column:*
— *size: l = 0.25 m, Ø = 4.6 mm,*
— *stationary phase: base-deactivated octylsilyl silica gel for chromatography R (5 µm).*

*Mobile phase   Mix 35 volumes of acetonitrile R and 65 volumes of a 5.4 g/l solution of potassium dihydrogen phosphate R adjusted to pH 3.0 using phosphoric acid R.*

*Flow rate   1.2 ml/min.*

*Detection   Spectrophotometer at 220 nm.*

*Injection   10 µl.*

*Run time   7 times the retention time of diphenhydramine.*

*Relative retention   With reference to diphenhydramine (retention time = about 6 min): impurity A = about 0.9; impurity B = about 1.5; impurity C = about 1.8; impurity D = about 2.6; impurity E = about 5.1.*

*System suitability   Reference solution (b):*

— *resolution*: minimum 2.0 between the peaks due to diphenhydramine and to impurity A.

*Limits:*

— *correction factor*: for the calculation of content, multiply the peak area of impurity D by 0.7,

— *impurity A*: not more than the area of the principal peak in the chromatogram obtained with reference solution (a) (0.5 per cent),

— *any other impurity*: not more than 0.6 times the area of the principal peak in the chromatogram obtained with reference solution (a) (0.3 per cent),

— *total*: not more than twice the area of the principal peak in the chromatogram obtained with reference solution (a) (1.0 per cent),

— *disregard limit*: 0.1 times the area of the principal peak in the chromatogram obtained with reference solution (a) (0.05 per cent).

**Loss on drying** (*2.2.32*)

Maximum 0.5 per cent, determined on 1.000 g by drying in an oven at 105 °C.

**Sulphated ash** (*2.4.14*)

Maximum 0.1 per cent, determined on 1.0 g.

**ASSAY**

Dissolve 0.250 g in 50 ml of *alcohol R* and add 5.0 ml of *0.01 M hydrochloric acid*. Carry out a potentiometric titration (*2.2.20*), using *0.1 M sodium hydroxide*. Read the volume added between the 2 points of inflexion.

1 ml of *0.1 M sodium hydroxide* is equivalent to 29.18 mg of $C_{17}H_{22}ClNO$.

**STORAGE**

Protected from light.

**IMPURITIES**

*Specified impurities   A, B, C, D, E.*

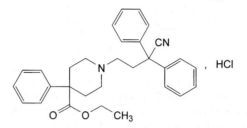

A. R = R′ = H: 2-(diphenylmethoxy)-*N*-methylethanamine,

B. R = R′ = CH₃: 2-[(*RS*)-(4-methylphenyl)phenylmethoxy]-*N,N*-dimethylethanamine,

C. R = Br, R′ = CH₃: 2-[(*RS*)-(4-bromophenyl)phenylmethoxy]-*N,N*-dimethylethanamine,

D. R = OH, R′ = H: diphenylmethanol (benzhydrol),

E. R + R′ = O: diphenylmethanone (benzophenone).

_____ *Ph Eur*

# Diphenoxylate Hydrochloride

(*Ph Eur monograph 0819*)

$C_{30}H_{32}N_2O_2$,HCl          489.1          *3810-80-8*

**Action and use**

Opioid receptor agonist; treatment of diarrhoea.

*Ph Eur* _____

**DEFINITION**

Diphenoxylate hydrochloride contains not less than 98.0 per cent and not more than the equivalent of 102.0 per cent of ethyl 1-(3-cyano-3,3-diphenylpropyl)-4-phenylpiperidine-4-carboxylate hydrochloride, calculated with reference to the dried substance.

**CHARACTERS**

A white or almost white, crystalline powder, very slightly soluble in water, freely soluble in methylene chloride, sparingly soluble in alcohol.

It melts at about 220 °C, with decomposition.

**IDENTIFICATION**

A. Examine by infrared absorption spectrophotometry (*2.2.24*), comparing with the *Ph. Eur. reference spectrum of diphenoxylate hydrochloride*.

B. Dissolve about 30 mg in 5 ml of *methanol R*. Add 0.25 ml of *nitric acid R* and 0.4 ml of *silver nitrate solution R1*. Shake and allow to stand. A curdled precipitate is formed. Centrifuge and rinse the precipitate with three quantities, each of 2 ml, of *methanol R*. Carry out this operation rapidly and protected from bright light. Suspend the precipitate in 2 ml of *water R* and add 1.5 ml of *ammonia R*. The precipitate dissolves easily.

**TESTS**

**Appearance of solution**

Dissolve 1.0 g in *methylene chloride R* and dilute to 10 ml with the same solvent. The solution is clear (*2.2.1*) and not more intensely coloured than reference solution Y₆ (*2.2.2, Method II*).

**Related substances**

Examine by thin-layer chromatography (*2.2.27*), using a plate coated with a suitable octadecylsilyl silica gel (5 μm) with a fluorescent indicator having an optimal intensity at 254 nm.

*Test solution*   Dissolve 1.0 g in a mixture of 1 volume of *methanol R* and 2 volumes of *methylene chloride R* and dilute to 20 ml with the same mixture of solvents.

*Reference solution (a)*   Dilute 0.5 ml of the test solution to 100 ml with a mixture of 1 volume of *methanol R* and 2 volumes of *methylene chloride R*.

*Reference solution (b)*   Dissolve 0.50 g of the substance to be examined in 25 ml of a 15 g/l solution of *potassium hydroxide R* in *methanol R* and add 1 ml of *water R*. Heat on a water-bath under a reflux condenser for 4 h. Cool and add 25 ml of 0.5 M *hydrochloric acid*. Shake with 100 ml of *methylene chloride R*. Evaporate the lower layer to dryness on a water-bath. Dissolve the residue in 10 ml of a mixture of 1 volume of *methanol R* and 2 volumes of *methylene chloride R*, add 10 ml of the test solution and dilute to 25 ml with a mixture of 1 volume of *methanol R* and 2 volumes of *methylene chloride R*.

Apply separately to a plate (100 mm square) 1 µl of each solution. Develop in an unsaturated tank over a path of 7 cm using a mixture of 10 volumes of *methanol R*, 30 volumes of a 59 g/l solution of *sodium chloride R* and 60 volumes of *dioxan R*. Allow the plate to dry in an oven at 160 °C for 15 min and place the hot plate in a closed tank containing about 20 ml of *fuming nitric acid R* for 30 min. Remove the plate and heat it again at 160 °C for 15 min. Allow to cool and examine immediately in ultraviolet light at 254 nm. Any spot in the chromatogram obtained with the test solution, apart from the principal spot, is not more intense than the spot in the chromatogram obtained with reference solution (a) (0.5 per cent). The test is not valid unless the chromatogram obtained with reference solution (b) shows two clearly separated principal spots.

**Loss on drying** *(2.2.32)*

Not more than 0.5 per cent, determined on 1.000 g by drying in an oven at 105 °C.

**Sulphated ash** *(2.4.14)*

Not more than 0.1 per cent, determined on 1.0 g.

## ASSAY

Dissolve 0.400 g in 40 ml of *alcohol R* and add 5.0 ml of *0.01 M hydrochloric acid*. Carry out a potentiometric titration *(2.2.20)*, using *0.1 M ethanolic sodium hydroxide*. Read the volume added between the two points of inflexion.

1 ml of *0.1 M ethanolic sodium hydroxide* is equivalent to 48.91 mg of $C_{30}H_{33}ClN_2O_2$.

## STORAGE

Store protected from light.

*Ph Eur*

# Diphenylpyraline Hydrochloride

$C_{19}H_{23}NO,HCl$          317.9          *132-18-3*

**Action and use**

Histamine $H_1$ receptor antagonist; antihistamine.

## DEFINITION

Diphenylpyraline Hydrochloride is 4-benzhydryloxy-1-methylpiperidine hydrochloride. It contains not less than 98.0% and not more than 101.0% of $C_{19}H_{23}NO,HCl$, calculated with reference to the dried substance.

## CHARACTERISTICS

A white or almost white powder; odourless or almost odourless.

Freely soluble in *water* and in *ethanol (96%)*; practically insoluble in *ether*.

## IDENTIFICATION

A. The *infrared absorption spectrum*, Appendix II A, is concordant with the *reference spectrum* of diphenylpyraline hydrochloride *(RS 106)*.

B. Yields the reactions characteristic of *chlorides*, Appendix VI.

## TESTS

**Related substances**

Carry out the method for *gas chromatography*, Appendix III B, using the following solutions.

(1) Dissolve 45 mg of *bibenzyl* (internal standard) in sufficient *dichloromethane* to produce 100 ml.

(2) Dissolve 0.20 g of the substance being examined in 20 ml of *water*, make the solution alkaline with 5M *ammonia* and extract with three 25-ml quantities of *dichloromethane*. Shake the combined extracts with 10 g of *anhydrous sodium sulphate*, filter, evaporate the filtrate to dryness at about 30° and dissolve the residue in 2 ml of *dichloromethane*.

(3) Prepare solution (3) in the same manner as solution (2) but dissolve the residue in 2 ml of solution (1).

CHROMATOGRAPHIC CONDITIONS

(a) Use a glass column (1.5 m × 4 mm) packed with *silanised diatomaceous support* (80 to 100 mesh) coated with 3% w/w of phenyl methyl silicone fluid (50% phenyl) (OV-17 is suitable).

(b) Use *nitrogen* as the carrier gas.

(c) Use an oven temperature of 165°. Allow the chromatography to proceed for 3 times the retention time of bibenzyl.

(d) Increase the oven temperature to 240° to elute the diphenylpyraline from the column.

LIMITS

In the chromatogram obtained with solution (3):

the sum of the areas of any *secondary peaks* is not greater than the area of the peak due to the internal standard.

**Loss on drying**

When dried to constant weight at 105°, loses not more than 1.0% of its weight. Use 1 g.

**Sulphated ash**

Not more than 0.1%, Appendix IX A.

## ASSAY

Carry out Method I for *non-aqueous titration*, Appendix VIII A, using 0.2 g, adding 5 ml of *mercury(II) acetate solution* and determining the end-point potentiometrically. Each ml of 0.1M *perchloric acid VS* is equivalent to 31.79 mg of $C_{19}H_{23}NO,HCl$.

# Dipipanone Hydrochloride

C₂₄H₃₁NO,HCl,H₂O     404.0        *856-87-1*

$C_{24}H_{31}NO,HCl,H_2O$    404.0      *856-87-1*

**Action and use**
Opioid receptor agonist.

**Preparation**
Dipipanone and Cyclizine Tablets

## DEFINITION

Dipipanone Hydrochloride is (*RS*)-4,4-diphenyl-6-piperidinoheptan-3-one hydrochloride monohydrate. It contains not less than 99.0% and not more than 101.0% of $C_{24}H_{31}NO,HCl$, calculated with reference to the anhydrous substance.

## CHARACTERISTICS

A white, crystalline powder; odourless or almost odourless.

Sparingly soluble in *water*; freely soluble in *acetone* and in *ethanol (96%)*; practically insoluble in *ether*.

## IDENTIFICATION

A. Dissolve 20 mg in 5 ml of *water* and make alkaline to *litmus paper* with 2M *sodium hydroxide*. Extract with two 10 ml quantities of *chloroform*, evaporate the chloroform extracts and dry at 50° at a pressure not exceeding 0.7 kPa for 2 hours. The *infrared absorption spectrum* of a thin film of the oily residue, Appendix II A, is concordant with the *reference spectrum* of dipipanone (*RS 107*).

B. Yields the reactions characteristic of *chlorides*, Appendix VI.

## TESTS

**Acidity**
pH of a 2.5% w/v solution, 4.0 to 6.0, Appendix V L.

**Melting point**
124° to 127°, determined on the undried substance, Appendix V A.

**Related substances**
Carry out the method for *thin-layer chromatography*, Appendix III A, using a silica gel precoated plate (Merck silica gel 60 plates are suitable) and *methanol* as the mobile phase. Apply separately to the plate 5 μl of each of two solutions freshly prepared in *methanol* containing (1) 2.0% w/v of the substance being examined and (2) 0.020% w/v of *3-methyl-2,2-diphenyl-4-piperidinobutyronitrile BPCRS*. After removal of the plate, allow it to dry in air and expose to iodine vapour for 10 minutes. Any *secondary spot* in the chromatogram obtained with solution (1) is not more intense than the spot in the chromatogram obtained with solution (2).

**Sulphated ash**
Not more than 0.1%, Appendix IX A.

**Water**
4.0 to 5.0% w/w, Appendix IX C. Use 0.5 g.

## ASSAY

Carry out Method I for *non-aqueous titration*, Appendix VIII A, using 0.8 g and determining the end point potentiometrically. Each ml of 0.1M *perchloric acid VS* is equivalent to 38.60 mg of $C_{24}H_{31}NO,HCl$.

# Dipivefrine Hydrochloride

(*Ph Eur monograph 1719*)

$C_{19}H_{29}NO_5,HCl$     387.9        *64019-93-8*

**Action and use**
Adrenaline prodrug; treatment of glaucoma.

**Preparation**
Dipivefrine Eye Drops

*Ph Eur*

## DEFINITION

Hydrochloride of 4-[(1*RS*)-1-hydroxy-2-(methylamino)ethyl]-1,2-phenylene bis(2,2-dimethylpropanoate).

**Content**
97.5 per cent to 102.0 per cent (dried substance).

## CHARACTERS

**Appearance**
White or almost white, crystalline powder.

**Solubility**
Freely soluble in water, very soluble in methanol, freely soluble in ethanol (96 per cent) and in methylene chloride.

**mp**
About 160 °C.

## IDENTIFICATION

A. Infrared absorption spectrophotometry (*2.2.24*).

*Preparation* Discs.

*Comparison* dipivefrine hydrochloride CRS.

B. It gives reaction (a) of chlorides (*2.3.1*).

## TESTS

**Impurities A and B**
Liquid chromatography (*2.2.29*).

*Test solution* Dissolve 0.100 g of the substance to be examined in *0.01 M hydrochloric acid* and dilute to 10.0 ml with the same acid.

*Reference solution* Dissolve 10.0 mg of *adrenaline R* and 10.0 mg of *adrenalone hydrochloride R* in *0.01 M hydrochloric acid* and dilute to 100.0 ml with the same acid. Dilute 1.0 ml of this solution to 10.0 ml with *0.01 M hydrochloric acid*. *Protect this solution from light.*

*Column:*
— *size: l* = 0.15 m, Ø = 4.6 mm;

— *stationary phase*: end-capped polar-embedded octadecylsilyl amorphous organosilica polymer R (5 μm).

*Mobile phase:*
— *mobile phase A*: 0.1 per cent *V/V* solution of *anhydrous formic acid R*;
— *mobile phase B*: *methanol R2, acetonitrile R* (40:60 *V/V*);

| Time (min) | Mobile phase A (per cent *V/V*) | Mobile phase B (per cent *V/V*) |
|---|---|---|
| 0 - 3 | 100 | 0 |
| 3 - 5 | 100 → 40 | 0 → 60 |
| 5 - 10 | 40 | 60 |
| 10 - 11 | 40 → 100 | 60 → 0 |
| 11 - 25 | 100 | 0 |

*Flow rate*   1 ml/min.

*Detection*   Spectrophotometer at 260 nm.

*Injection*   10 μl.

*Retention times*   Impurity A = about 2.2 min; impurity B = about 3.2 min.

*System suitability*   Reference solution:
— *resolution*: minimum 2.0 between the peaks due to impurity A and impurity B.

*Limits:*
— *impurities A, B*: for each impurity, not more than the area of the corresponding peak in the chromatogram obtained with the reference solution (0.1 per cent).

**Related substances**

Liquid chromatography (*2.2.29*).

*Solvent mixture*   Mix 40 volumes of *methanol R2* and 60 volumes of *acetonitrile R*. Mix 55 volumes of this mixture and 45 volumes of *0.01 M hydrochloric acid*.

*Test solution*   Dissolve 50.0 mg of the substance to be examined in the solvent mixture and dilute to 5.0 ml with the solvent mixture.

*Reference solution (a)*   Dilute 1.0 ml of the test solution to 100.0 ml with the solvent mixture.

*Reference solution (b)*   Dissolve 5 mg of *dipivefrine for system suitability CRS* (containing impurities C, D and E) in the solvent mixture and dilute to 2.0 ml with the solvent mixture.

*Reference solution (c)*   Dissolve 5.0 mg of *dipivefrine hydrochloride CRS* in the solvent mixture and dilute to 2.0 ml with the solvent mixture. Dilute 1.0 ml of this solution to 25.0 ml with the solvent mixture.

*Column:*
— *size: l* = 0.15 m, Ø = 4.6 mm;
— *stationary phase*: end-capped polar-embedded octadecylsilyl amorphous organosilica polymer R (5 μm).

*Mobile phase*   Mix 45 volumes of a 2.7 g/l solution of *concentrated ammonia R* adjusted to pH 10.0 with *dilute acetic acid R* and 55 volumes of a mixture of 40 volumes of *methanol R2* and 60 volumes of *acetonitrile R*.

*Flow rate*   1 ml/min.

*Detection*   Spectrophotometer at 260 nm.

*Injection*   10 μl.

*Run time*   2.5 times the retention time of dipivefrine.

*Relative retention*   With reference to dipivefrine (retention time = about 7 min):
impurities C and D = about 0.4; impurity E = about 1.3; impurity F = about 2.0.

*System suitability*   Reference solution (b):

— *resolution*: minimum 3.0 between the peaks due to dipivefrine and impurity E.

*Limits:*
— *correction factors*: for the calculation of content, multiply the peak areas of the following impurities by the corresponding correction factor:
impurities C and D = 0.5; impurity E = 0.06;
— *sum of impurities C and D*: not more than 0.3 times the area of the principal peak in the chromatogram obtained with reference solution (a) (0.3 per cent);
— *impurities E, F*: for each impurity, not more than 0.1 times the area of the principal peak in the chromatogram obtained with reference solution (a) (0.1 per cent);
— *unspecified impurities*: for each impurity, not more than 0.1 times the area of the principal peak in the chromatogram obtained with reference solution (a) (0.10 per cent);
— *total*: not more than 0.5 times the area of the principal peak in the chromatogram obtained with reference solution (a) (0.5 per cent);
— *disregard limit*: 0.05 times the area of the principal peak in the chromatogram obtained with reference solution (a) (0.05 per cent); disregard any peak with a mass distribution ratio less than 0.5.

**Loss on drying** (*2.2.32*)

Maximum 1.0 per cent, determined on 1.000 g by drying *in vacuo* at 60 °C for 6 h.

**Sulphated ash** (*2.4.14*)

Maximum 0.1 per cent, determined on 1.0 g.

**ASSAY**

Liquid chromatography (*2.2.29*) as described in the test for related substances with the following modification.

*Injection*   20 μl of reference solutions (a) and (c).

*System suitability*   Reference solution (c):
— *symmetry factor*: maximum 2.0 for the peak due to dipivefrine.

Calculate the percentage content of $C_{19}H_{30}ClNO_5$ using the chromatograms obtained with reference solutions (a) and (c) and the declared content of *dipivefrine hydrochloride CRS*.

**IMPURITIES**

*Specified impurities*   *A, B, C, D, E, F.*

A. R1 = R2 = R3 = H: 4-[(1*RS*)-1-hydroxy-2-(methylamino)ethyl]benzene-1,2-diol ((±)-adrenaline),

C. R1 = R3 = H, R2 = CO-C(CH₃)₃: 2-hydroxy-5-[(1*RS*)-1-hydroxy-2-(methylamino)ethyl]phenyl 2,2-dimethylpropanoate,

D. R1 = CO-C(CH₃)₃, R2 = R3 = H: 2-hydroxy-4-[(1*RS*)-1-hydroxy-2-(methylamino)ethyl]phenyl 2,2-dimethylpropanoate,

F. R1 = R2 = CO-C(CH₃)₃, R3 = C₂H₅: 4-[(1*RS*)-2-(ethylmethylamino)-1-hydroxyethyl]-1,2-phenylene bis(2,2-dimethylpropanoate),

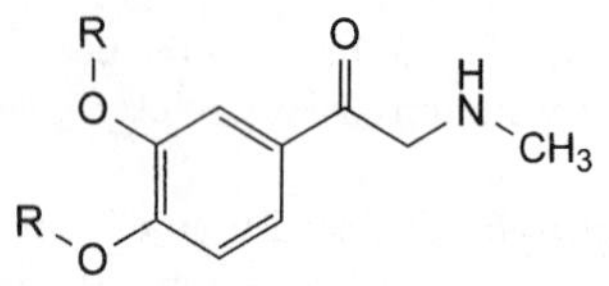

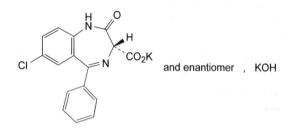

B. R = H: 1-(3,4-dihydroxyphenyl)-2-(methylamino)ethanone (adrenalone),

E. R = CO-C(CH₃)₃: 4-[(methylamino)acetyl]-1,2-phenylene bis(2,2-dimethylpropanoate) (adrenalone dipivalate ester).

*Ph Eur*

# Dipotassium Clorazepate

Potassium Clorazepate

(*Ph Eur monograph 0898*)

and enantiomer , KOH

$C_{16}H_{11}ClK_2N_2O_4$     408.9     *57109-90-7*

**Action and use**

Hypnotic; anxiolytic.

*Ph Eur*

## DEFINITION

Potassium (3*RS*)-7-chloro-2-oxo-5-phenyl-2,3-dihydro-1*H*-1,4-benzodiazepine-3-carboxylate compound with potassium hydroxide (1:1).

### Content

99.0 per cent to 101.0 per cent (dried substance).

## CHARACTERS

### Appearance

White or light yellow, crystalline powder.

### Solubility

Freely soluble to very soluble in water, very slightly soluble in alcohol, practically insoluble in methylene chloride.

Solutions in water and in alcohol are unstable and are to be used immediately.

## IDENTIFICATION

*First identification  B, E.*

*Second identification  A, C, D, E.*

A. Dissolve 10.0 mg in a 0.3 g/l solution of *potassium carbonate R* and dilute to 100.0 ml with the same solution (solution A). Dilute 10.0 ml of solution A to 100.0 ml with a 0.3 g/l solution of *potassium carbonate R* (solution B). Examined between 280 nm and 350 nm (*2.2.25*), solution A shows a broad absorption maximum at about 315 nm. The specific absorbance at the absorption maximum at 315 nm is 49 to 56. Examined between 220 nm and 280 nm (*2.2.25*), solution B shows an absorption maximum at 230 nm. The specific absorbance at the absorption maximum at 230 nm is 800 to 870.

B. Infrared absorption spectrophotometry (*2.2.24*).

Preparation  Discs.

*Comparison  Ph. Eur. reference spectrum of dipotassium clorazepate.*

C. Dissolve about 20 mg in 2 ml of *sulphuric acid R*. Observed in ultraviolet light at 365 nm, the solution shows yellow fluorescence.

D. Dissolve 0.5 g in 5 ml of *water R*. Add 0.1 ml of *thymol blue solution R*. The solution is violet-blue.

E. Place 1.0 g in a crucible and add 2 ml of *dilute sulphuric acid R*. Heat at first on a water-bath, then ignite until all black particles have disappeared. Allow to cool. Take up the residue with *water R* and dilute to 20 ml with the same solvent. The solution gives reaction (b) of potassium (*2.3.1*).

## TESTS

### Appearance of solution

The solution is clear (*2.2.1*) and not more intensely coloured than reference solution GY₅ (*2.2.2, Method II*).

Rapidly dissolve 2.0 g with shaking in *water R* and dilute to 20.0 ml with the same solvent. Observe immediately.

### Related substances

Thin-layer chromatography (*2.2.27*). *Prepare the solutions immediately before use and carry out the test protected from light.*

*Test solution*  Dissolve 0.20 g of the substance to be examined in *water R* and dilute to 5.0 ml with the same solvent. Shake immediately with 2 quantities, each of 5.0 ml, of *methylene chloride R*. Combine the organic layers and dilute to 10.0 ml with *methylene chloride R*.

*Reference solution (a)*  Dissolve 10 mg of *aminochlorobenzophenone R* in *methylene chloride R* and dilute to 100.0 ml with the same solvent. Dilute 5.0 ml of the solution to 25.0 ml with *methylene chloride R*.

*Reference solution (b)*  Dissolve 5 mg of *nordazepam CRS* in *methylene chloride R* and dilute to 25.0 ml with the same solvent. Dilute 5.0 ml of the solution to 25.0 ml with *methylene chloride R*.

*Reference solution (c)*  Dilute 10.0 ml of reference solution (b) to 20.0 ml with *methylene chloride R*.

*Reference solution (d)*  Dissolve 5 mg of *nordazepam CRS* and 5 mg of *nitrazepam CRS* in *methylene chloride R* and dilute to 25 ml with the same solvent.

*Plate  TLC silica gel F₂₅₄ plate R.*

*Mobile phase  acetone R, methylene chloride R (15:85 V/V).*

*Application  5 μl.*

*Development  Over 2/3 of the plate.*

*Drying  In air.*

*Detection A  Examine in ultraviolet light at 254 nm.*

*System suitability*  The chromatogram obtained with reference solution (d) shows 2 clearly separated spots.

*Limits A:*

— *impurity B*: any spot due to impurity B is not more intense than the spot in the chromatogram obtained with reference solution (b) (0.2 per cent),

— *any other impurity*: any spot, apart from any spot due to impurity B, is not more intense than the spot in the chromatogram obtained with reference solution (c) (0.1 per cent).

*Detection B*  Spray with a freshly prepared 10 g/l solution of *sodium nitrite R* in *dilute hydrochloric acid R*. Dry in a current of warm air and spray with a 4 g/l solution of *naphthylethylenediamine dihydrochloride R* in *alcohol R*.

*Limits B:*
— *impurity A*: any spot due to impurity A is not more intense than the spot in the chromatogram obtained with reference solution (a) (0.1 per cent).

## Loss on drying (2.2.32)
Maximum 0.5 per cent, determined on 1.000 g by drying *in vacuo* at 60 °C for 4 h.

## ASSAY
Dissolve 0.130 g in 10 ml of *anhydrous acetic acid R*. Add 30 ml of *methylene chloride R*. Titrate with *0.1 M perchloric acid*, determining the 2 points of inflexion by potentiometry (2.2.20).

At the 2$^{nd}$ point of inflexion, 1 ml of *0.1 M perchloric acid* is equivalent to 13.63 mg of $C_{16}H_{11}ClK_2N_2O_4$.

## STORAGE
In an airtight container, protected from light.

## IMPURITIES
*Specified impurities    A, B.*

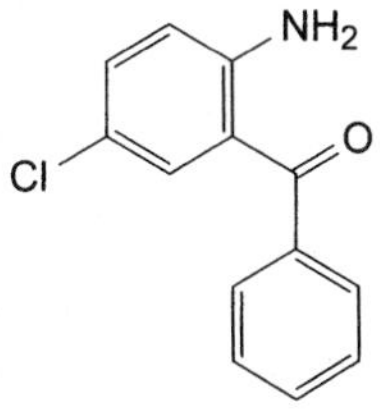

A. (2-amino-5-chlorophenyl)phenylmethanone (aminochlorobenzophenone),

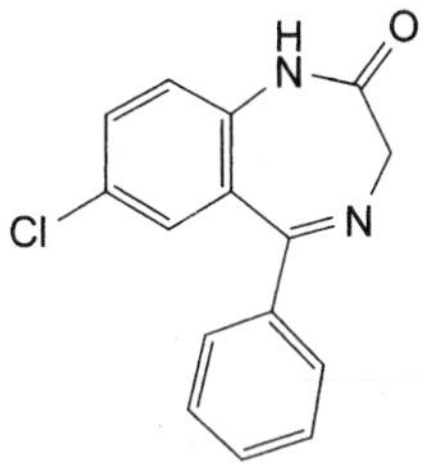

B. 7-chloro-5-phenyl-1,3-dihydro-2$H$-1,4-benzodiazepin-2-one (nordazepam).

_____ *Ph Eur*

# Dipotassium Hydrogen Phosphate

(*Dipotassium Phosphate, Ph Eur monograph 1003*)

| $K_2HPO_4$ | 174.2 | 7758-11-4 |
|---|---|---|

## Action and use
Excipient.

## Preparation
Dipotassium Hydrogen Phosphate Injection

*Ph Eur* _____

## DEFINITION
### Content
98.0 per cent to 101.0 per cent (dried substance).

## CHARACTERS
### Appearance
White or almost white powder or colourless crystals, very hygroscopic.

### Solubility
Very soluble in water, very slightly soluble in ethanol (96 per cent).

## IDENTIFICATION
A. Solution S (see Tests) is slightly alkaline (2.2.4).

B. Solution S gives reaction (b) of phosphates (2.3.1).

C. Solution S gives reaction (a) of potassium (2.3.1).

## TESTS
### Solution S
Dissolve 5.0 g in *distilled water R* and dilute to 50 ml with the same solvent.

### Appearance of solution
Solution S is clear (2.2.1) and colourless (2.2.2, *Method II*).

### Reducing substances
To 5 ml of solution S add 5 ml of *dilute sulphuric acid R* and 0.25 ml of *0.02 M potassium permanganate* and heat on a water-bath for 5 min. The solution remains faintly pink.

### Monopotassium phosphate
Maximum 2.5 per cent.

From the volume of *1 M hydrochloric acid* (10.0 ml) and of *1 M sodium hydroxide* ($n_1$ ml and $n_2$ ml) used in the assay, calculate the following ratio:

$$\frac{n_2 - 10}{10 - n_1}$$

This ratio is not greater than 0.025.

### Chlorides (2.4.4)
Maximum 200 ppm.

To 2.5 ml of solution S add 10 ml of *dilute nitric acid R* and dilute to 15 ml with *water R*.

### Sulphates (2.4.13)
Maximum 0.1 per cent.

To 1.5 ml of solution S add 2 ml of *dilute hydrochloric acid R* and dilute to 15 ml with *distilled water R*.

### Arsenic (2.4.2, *Method A*)
Maximum 2 ppm, determined on 5 ml of solution S.

### Iron (2.4.9)
Maximum 10 ppm, determined on solution S.

### Heavy metals (2.4.8)
Maximum 10 ppm.

Dissolve 2.0 g in 8 ml of *water R*. Acidify with about 6 ml of *dilute hydrochloric acid R* (pH 3-4) and dilute to 20 ml with *water R*. 12 ml of this solution complies with test A. Prepare the reference solution using *lead standard solution (1 ppm Pb) R*.

### Sodium
Maximum 0.10 per cent, if intended for use in the manufacture of parenteral dosage forms.

Atomic emission spectrometry (2.2.22, *Method I*).

*Test solution*   Dissolve 1.00 g in *water R* and dilute to 100.0 ml with the same solvent.

*Reference solutions*   Prepare the reference solutions using *sodium standard solution (200 ppm Na) R*, diluted as necessary with *water R*.

*Wavelength*   589 nm.

### Loss on drying (2.2.32)
Maximum 2.0 per cent, determined on 1.000 g by drying in an oven at 125-130 °C.

**Bacterial endotoxins** (*2.6.14*)

Less than 1.1 IU/mg, if intended for use in the manufacture of parenteral dosage forms without a further appropriate procedure for the removal of bacterial endotoxins.

## ASSAY

Dissolve 0.800 g (m) in 40 ml of *carbon dioxide-free water R* and add 10.0 ml of *1 M hydrochloric acid*. Carry out a potentiometric titration (*2.2.20*) using *1 M sodium hydroxide*. Read the volume added at the $1^{st}$ inflexion point ($n_1$ ml). Continue the titration to the $2^{nd}$ inflexion point (total volume of *1 M sodium hydroxide* required, $n_2$ ml).

Calculate the percentage content of $K_2HPO_4$ from the following expression:

$$\frac{1742\,(10 - n_1)}{m\,(100 - d)}$$

$d$ = percentage loss on drying.

## STORAGE

In an airtight container.

## LABELLING

The label states, where applicable, that the substance is suitable for use in the manufacture of parenteral dosage forms.

*———————————————————— Ph Eur*

# Diprophylline

(*Ph Eur monograph 0486*)

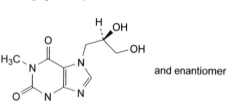

and enantiomer

$C_{10}H_{14}N_4O_4$       254.2       *479-18-5*

## Action and use

Non-selective phosphodiesterase inhibitor (xanthine); treatment of reversible airways obstruction.

*Ph Eur _____*

## DEFINITION

Diprophylline contains not less than 98.5 per cent and not more than the equivalent of 101.0 per cent of 7-[(2*RS*)-2,3-dihydroxypropyl]-1,3-dimethyl-3,7-dihydro-1*H*-purine-2,6-dione, calculated with reference to the dried substance.

## CHARACTERS

A white or almost white, crystalline powder, freely soluble in water, slightly soluble in alcohol.

## IDENTIFICATION

*First identification*  B, C.

*Second identification*  A, C, D.

A. Melting point (*2.2.14*): 160 °C to 165 °C.

B. Examine by infrared absorption spectrophotometry (*2.2.24*), comparing with the spectrum obtained with *diprophylline CRS*. Examine the substances as discs prepared

using 0.5 mg to 1 mg of the substance to be examined in 0.3 g of *potassium bromide R*.

C. Dissolve 1 g in 5 ml of *acetic anhydride R* and boil under a reflux condenser for 15 min. Allow to cool and add 100 ml of a mixture of 20 volumes of *ether R* and 80 volumes of *light petroleum R*. Cool in iced water for at least 20 min, shaking from time to time. Filter, wash the precipitate with a mixture of 20 volumes of *ether R* and 80 volumes of *light petroleum R*, recrystallise from *alcohol R* and dry *in vacuo*. The crystals melt (*2.2.14*) at 142 °C to 148 °C.

D. It gives the reaction of xanthines (*2.3.1*).

## TESTS

### Solution S

Dissolve 2.5 g in *carbon dioxide-free water R* and dilute to 50 ml with the same solvent.

### Appearance of solution

Solution S is clear (*2.2.1*) and colourless (*2.2.2, Method II*).

### Acidity or alkalinity

To 10 ml of solution S add 0.25 ml of *bromothymol blue solution R1*. The solution is yellow or green. Not more than 0.4 ml of *0.01 M sodium hydroxide* is required to change the colour of the indicator to blue.

### Related substances

Examine by thin-layer chromatography (*2.2.27*), using *silica gel HF$_{254}$ R* as the coating substance.

*Test solution*  Dissolve 0.3 g of the substance to be examined in a mixture of 20 volumes of *water R* and 30 volumes of *methanol R* and dilute to 10 ml with the same mixture of solvents. *Prepare immediately before use.*

*Reference solution (a)*  Dilute 1 ml of the test solution to 100 ml with *methanol R*.

*Reference solution (b)*  Dilute 0.2 ml of the test solution to 100 ml with *methanol R*.

*Reference solution (c)*  Dissolve 10 mg of *theophylline R* in *methanol R*, add 0.3 ml of the test solution and dilute to 10 ml with *methanol R*.

Apply to the plate 10 μl of each solution. Develop over a path of 15 cm using a mixture of 1 volume of *concentrated ammonia R*, 10 volumes of *ethanol R* and 90 volumes of *chloroform R*. Allow the plate to dry in air and examine in ultraviolet light at 254 nm. Any spot in the chromatogram obtained with the test solution, apart from the principal spot, is not more intense than the spot in the chromatogram obtained with reference solution (a) (1 per cent) and at most one such spot is more intense than the spot in the chromatogram obtained with reference solution (b) (0.2 per cent). The test is not valid unless the chromatogram obtained with reference solution (c) shows two clearly separated spots.

### Chlorides (*2.4.4*)

Dilute 2.5 ml of solution S to 15 ml with *water R*. The solution complies with the limit test for chlorides (400 ppm).

### Heavy metals (*2.4.8*)

12 ml of solution S complies with limit test A for heavy metals (20 ppm). Prepare the standard using *lead standard solution (1 ppm Pb) R*.

### Loss on drying (*2.2.32*)

Not more than 0.5 per cent, determined on 1.000 g by drying in an oven at 105 °C.

### Sulphated ash (*2.4.14*)

Not more than 0.1 per cent, determined on 1.0 g.

## ASSAY

*In order to avoid overheating in the reaction medium, mix thoroughly throughout and stop the titration immediately after the end-point has been reached.*

Dissolve 0.200 g in 3.0 ml of *anhydrous formic acid R* and add 50.0 ml of *acetic anhydride R*. Titrate with *0.1 M perchloric acid*, determining the end-point potentiometrically (*2.2.20*).

1 ml of *0.1 M perchloric acid* is equivalent to 25.42 mg of $C_{10}H_{14}N_4O_4$.

## STORAGE

Store protected from light.

*_____ Ph Eur*

# Dipyridamole

*(Ph Eur monograph 1199)*

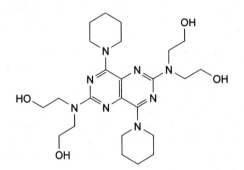

$C_{24}H_{40}N_8O_4$         504.6         58-32-2

## Action and use

Adenosine reuptake inhibitor; inhibitor of platelet aggregation.

## Preparation

Dipyridamole Tablets

*Ph Eur _____*

## DEFINITION

2,2',2'',2'''-[[4,8-Di(piperidin-1-yl)pyrimido[5,4-d]pyrimidine-2,6-diyl]dinitrilo]tetraethanol.

## Content

98.5 per cent to 101.5 per cent (dried substance).

## CHARACTERS

### Appearance

Bright yellow, crystalline powder.

### Solubility

Practically insoluble in water, freely soluble in acetone, soluble in anhydrous ethanol. It dissolves in dilute mineral acids.

## IDENTIFICATION

Infrared absorption spectrophotometry (*2.2.24*).

*Preparation*   Discs of *potassium bromide R*.

*Comparison*   *dipyridamole CRS*.

## TESTS

### Related substances

Liquid chromatography (*2.2.29*)

*Prepare the solutions immediately before use.*

*Test solution*   Dissolve 0.100 g of the substance to be examined in *methanol R* and dilute to 50 ml with the same solvent.

*Reference solution (a)*   Dilute 1.0 ml of the test solution to 100.0 ml with *methanol R*. Dilute 1.0 ml of this solution to 10.0 ml with *methanol R*.

*Reference solution (b)*   Dissolve the contents of a vial of *dipyridamole for peak identification CRS* (containing impurities A, B, C, D, E and F) in 1 ml of *methanol R*.

*Column:*
— *size:* $l = 0.10$ m, Ø = 4.0 mm;
— *stationary phase:* spherical *end-capped octadecylsilyl silica gel for chromatography R* (5 μm);
— *temperature:* 45 °C.

*Mobile phase:*
— *mobile phase A:* dissolve 1.0 g of *potassium dihydrogen phosphate R* in 900 ml of *water R*, adjust to pH 7.0 with *0.5 M sodium hydroxide* and dilute to 1000 ml with *water R*;
— *mobile phase B: methanol R*;

| Time (min) | Mobile phase A (per cent V/V) | Mobile phase B (per cent V/V) |
|---|---|---|
| 0 - 5 | 40 | 60 |
| 5 - 19 | 40 → 5 | 60 → 95 |
| 19 - 24 | 5 → 40 | 95 → 60 |
| 24 - 29 | 40 | 60 |

*Flow rate*   1.2 ml/min.

*Detection*   Spectrophotometer at 295 nm.

*Injection*   5 μl.

*Identification of impurities*   Use the chromatogram supplied with *dipyridamole for peak identification CRS* and the chromatogram obtained with reference solution (b) to identify the peaks due to impurities A, B, C, D, E and F.

*Relative retention*   With reference to dipyridamole (retention time = about 8 min): impurity B = about 0.2; impurity F = about 0.3; impurity D = about 0.9; impurity E = about 1.3; impurity C = about 1.6; impurity A = about 2.2.

*System suitability*   Reference solution (b):
— *resolution:* minimum 2.0 between the peaks due to impurity D and dipyridamole;
— *peak-to-valley ratio:* minimum 4, where $H_p$ = height above the baseline of the peak due to impurity B and $H_v$ = height above the baseline of the lowest point of the curve separating this peak from the peak due to impurity F.

*Limits:*
— *correction factor:* for the calculation of content, multiply the peak area of impurity B by 1.7;
— *impurities A, B, C:* for each impurity, not more than 5 times the area of the principal peak in the chromatogram obtained with reference solution (a) (0.5 per cent);
— *impurities D, E:* for each impurity, not more than twice the area of the principal peak in the chromatogram obtained with reference solution (a) (0.2 per cent);
— *unspecified impurities:* for each impurity, not more than the area of the principal peak in the chromatogram obtained with reference solution (a) (0.10 per cent);
— *total:* not more than 10 times the area of the principal peak in the chromatogram obtained with reference solution (a) (1.0 per cent);

— *disregard limit*: 0.5 times the area of the principal peak in the chromatogram obtained with reference solution (a) (0.05 per cent).

**Chlorides** (*2.4.4*)

Maximum 200 ppm.

To 0.250 g add 10 ml of *water R* and shake vigorously. Filter, rinse the filter with 5 ml of *water R* and dilute to 15 ml with *water R*.

**Loss on drying** (*2.2.32*)

Maximum 0.5 per cent, determined on 1.000 g by drying in an oven at 105 °C.

**Sulphated ash** (*2.4.14*)

Maximum 0.1 per cent, determined on 1.0 g.

**ASSAY**

Dissolve 0.400 g in 70 ml of *methanol R*. Titrate with *0.1 M perchloric acid*, determining the end-point potentiometrically (*2.2.20*).

1 ml of *0.1 M perchloric acid* is equivalent to 50.46 mg of $C_{24}H_{40}N_8O_4$.

**STORAGE**

Protected from light.

**IMPURITIES**

*Specified impurities   A, B, C, D, E.*

*Other detectable impurities* (the following substances would, if present at a sufficient level, be detected by one or other of the tests in the monograph. They are limited by the general acceptance criterion for other/unspecified impurities and/or by the general monograph *Substances for pharmaceutical use (2034)*. It is therefore not necessary to identify these impurities for demonstration of compliance. See also *5.10. Control of impurities in substances for pharmaceutical use): F, G.*

A. R1 = N(CH$_2$-CH$_2$-OH)$_2$, R2 = R3 = NC$_5$H$_{10}$: 2,2′-[[4,6,8-tri(piperidin-1-yl)pyrimido[5,4-*d*]pyrimidin-2-yl]nitrilo]diethanol,

B. R1 = R2 = R3 = N(CH$_2$-CH$_2$-OH)$_2$: 2,2′,2″,2‴,2⁗,2⁗′[[8-(piperidin-1-yl)pyrimido[5,4-*d*]pyrimidine-2,4,6-triyl]trinitrilo]hexaethanol,

C. R1 = N(CH$_2$-CH$_2$-OH)$_2$, R2 = NC$_5$H$_{10}$, R3 = Cl: 2,2′-[[6-chloro-4,8-di(piperidin-1-yl)pyrimido[5,4-*d*]pyrimidin-2-yl]nitrilo]diethanol,

D. R1 = N(CH$_2$-CH$_2$-OH)$_2$, R2 = NC$_5$H$_{10}$, R3 = NH-CH$_2$-CH$_2$-OH: 2,2′-[[6-[(2-hydroxyethyl)amino]-4,8-di(piperidin-1-yl)pyrimido[5,4-*d*]pyrimidin-2-yl]nitrilo]diethanol,

E. R1 = R2 = N(CH$_2$-CH$_2$-OH)$_2$, R3 = NC$_5$H$_{10}$: 2,2′,2″,2‴-[[6,8-di(piperidin-1-yl)pyrimido[5,4-*d*]pyrimidine-2,4-diyl]dinitrilo]tetraethanol,

F. R1 = R3 = N(CH$_2$-CH$_2$-OH)$_2$, R2 = NH-CH$_2$-CH$_2$-OH: 2,2′,2″,2‴-[[4-[(2-hydroxyethyl)amino]-8-(piperidin-1-yl)pyrimido[5,4-*d*]pyrimidine-2,6-diyl]dinitrilo]tetraethanol,

G. R1 = R3 = Cl, R2 = NC$_5$H$_{10}$: 2,6-dichloro-4,8-di(piperidin-1-yl)pyrimido[5,4-*d*]pyrimidine.

*Ph Eur*

# Dipyrone

(*Metamizole Sodium, Ph Eur monograph 1346*)

$C_{13}H_{16}N_3NaO_4S,H_2O$          351.4          5907-38-0

**Action and use**

Analgesic.

*Ph Eur*

**DEFINITION**

Sodium [(1,5-dimethyl-3-oxo-2-phenyl-2,3-dihydro-1*H*-pyrazol-4-yl)-*N*-methylamino]methanesulphonate monohydrate.

**Content**

99.0 per cent to 101.0 per cent (dried substance).

**CHARACTERS**

**Appearance**

White or almost white, crystalline powder.

**Solubility**

Very soluble in water, soluble in ethanol (96 per cent).

**IDENTIFICATION**

*First identification   A, D.*

*Second identification   B, C, D.*

A. Infrared absorption spectrophotometry (*2.2.24*).

*Comparison   metamizole sodium CRS.*

B. Dissolve 50 mg in 1 ml of *strong hydrogen peroxide solution R*. A blue colour is produced which fades rapidly and turns to intense red in a few minutes.

C. Place 0.10 g in a test tube, add some glass beads and dissolve the substance in 1.5 ml of *water R*. Add 1.5 ml of *dilute hydrochloric acid R* and place a filter paper wetted with a solution of 20 mg of *potassium iodate R* in 2 ml of *starch solution R* at the open end of the test tube. Heat gently, the evolving vapour of sulphur dioxide colours the filter paper blue. After heating gently for 1 min take a glass rod with a drop of a 10 g/l solution of *chromotropic acid, sodium salt R* in *sulphuric acid R* and place in the opening of the tube. Within 10 min, a blue-violet colour develops in the drop of the reagent.

D. 0.5 ml of solution S (see Tests) gives reaction (a) of sodium (*2.3.1*).

**TESTS**

**Solution S**

Dissolve 2.0 g in *carbon dioxide-free water R* and dilute to 40 ml with the same solvent.

**Appearance of solution**

Solution S is clear (*2.2.1*) and immediately after preparation, not more intensely coloured than reference solution BY$_6$ (*2.2.2, Method I*).

**Acidity or alkalinity**

To 5 ml of solution S, add 0.1 ml of *phenolphthalein solution R1*. The solution is colourless. Not more than 0.1 ml of *0.02 M sodium hydroxide* is required to change the colour of the indicator to pink.

**Related substances**

Liquid chromatography (*2.2.29*). *Prepare the solutions immediately before use.*

*Test solution* Dissolve 50.0 mg of the substance to be examined in *methanol R* and dilute to 10.0 ml with the same solvent.

*Reference solution (a)* Dissolve 10.0 mg of *metamizole impurity A CRS* in *methanol R* and dilute to 20.0 ml with the same solvent.

*Reference solution (b)* Dilute 1.0 ml of reference solution (a) to 20.0 ml with *methanol R*.

*Reference solution (c)* Dissolve 40 mg of *metamizole sodium CRS* in *methanol* R and dilute to 20.0 ml with the same solvent.

*Reference solution (d)* In order to prepare impurity C *in situ*, boil 10 ml of reference solution (c) under reflux for 10 min. Allow to cool to room temperature and dilute to 20.0 ml with *methanol R*.

*Reference solution (e)* To 6 ml of reference solution (a) add 1 ml of reference solution (c).

*Column:*
— *size: l* = 0.25 m, Ø = 4.6 mm;
— *stationary phase: base-deactivated octadecylsilyl silica gel for chromatography R* (5 μm).

*Mobile phase* Mix 28 volumes of *methanol R* and 72 volumes of a buffer solution prepared as follows : mix 1000 volumes of a 6.0 g/l solution of *sodium dihydrogen phosphate R* and 1 volume of *triethylamine R*, then adjust to pH 7.0 with *strong sodium hydroxide solution R*.

*Flow rate* 1.0 ml/min.

*Detection* Spectrophotometer at 254 nm.

*Injection* 10 μl of the test solution and reference solutions (b), (d) and (e).

*Run time* 3.5 times the retention time of metamizole.

*Elution order* Impurity A, metamizole, impurity B, impurity C, impurity D.

*System suitability* Reference solution (e):
— *resolution*: minimum 2.5 between the peaks due to impurity A and metamizole.

*Limits:*
— *impurity C*: not more than the area of the principal peak in the chromatogram obtained with reference solution (b) (0.5 per cent);
— *impurities A, B, D*: for each impurity, not more 0.4 times the area of the principal peak in the chromatogram obtained with reference solution (b) (0.2 per cent);
— *total*: not more than the area of the principal peak in the chromatogram obtained with reference solution (b) (0.5 per cent);
— *disregard limit*: 0.05 times the area of the principal peak in the chromatogram obtained with the reference solution (b) (0.025 per cent).

**Sulphates** (*2.4.13*)

Maximum 0.1 per cent.

Dissolve 0.150 g in *distilled water R* and dilute to 15 ml with the same solvent.

**Heavy metals** (*2.4.8*)

Maximum 20 ppm.

Dissolve 2.0 g in *water R* and dilute to 20 ml with the same solvent. 12 ml of the freshly prepared solution complies with test A. Prepare the reference solution using *lead standard solution (2 ppm Pb) R*.

**Loss on drying** (*2.2.32*)

4.9 per cent to 5.3 per cent, determined on 1.000 g by drying in an oven at 105 °C.

**ASSAY**

Dissolve 0.200 g in 10 ml of *0.01 M hydrochloric acid* previously cooled in iced water and titrate immediately, dropwise, with *0.05 M iodine*. Before each addition of *0.05 M iodine* dissolve the precipitate by swirling. At the end of the titration add 2 ml of *starch solution R* and titrate until the blue colour of the solution persists for at least 2 min. The temperature of the solution during the titration must not exceed 10 °C.

1 ml of *0.05 M iodine* is equivalent to 16.67 mg of $C_{13}H_{16}N_3NaO_4S$.

**STORAGE**

Protected from light.

**IMPURITIES**

*Specified impurities   A, B, C, D.*

A. R = NHCHO: 4-formylamino-1,5-dimethyl-2-phenyl-1,2-dihydro-3*H*-pyrazol-3-one,

B. R = NH₂: 4-amino-1,5-dimethyl-2-phenyl-1,2-dihydro-3*H*-pyrazol-3-one,

C. R = NHCH₃: 4-methylamino-1,5-dimethyl-2-phenyl-1,2-dihydro-3H-pyrazol-3-one,

D. R = N(CH₃)₂: 4-dimethylamino-1,5-dimethyl-2-phenyl-1,2-dihydro-3*H*-pyrazol-3-one.

_____ *Ph Eur*

# Dirithromycin

(*Ph Eur monograph 1313*)

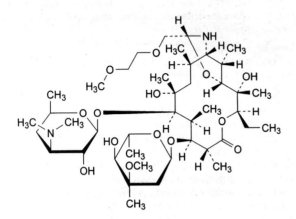

$C_{42}H_{78}N_2O_{14}$　　　835　　　62013-04-1

## Action and use
Macrolide antibacterial.

*Ph Eur*

## DEFINITION
(1*R*,2*S*,3*R*,6*R*,7*S*,8*S*,9*R*,10*R*,12*R*,13*S*,15*R*,17*S*)-9-[[3-
(Dimethylamino)-3,4,6-trideoxy-β-D-*xylo*-hexopyranosyl]oxy]-
3-ethyl-2,10-dihydroxy-15-[(2-methoxyethoxy)methyl]-
2,6,8,10,12,17-hexamethyl-7-[(3-*C*-methyl-3-*O*-methyl-
2,6dideoxy-α-L-*ribo*-hexopyranosyl)oxy]-4,16-dioxa-
14azabicyclo[11.3.1]heptadecan-5-one (or (9*S*)-9,11-
[imino[(1*R*)-2-(2-methoxyethoxy)ethylidene]oxy]-9-deoxo-
11-deoxyerythromycin).

Semi-synthetic product derived from a fermentation product.

## Content
96.0 per cent to 102.0 per cent for the sum of the percentage
contents of $C_{42}H_{78}N_2O_{14}$ and dirithromycin 15*S*-epimer
(anhydrous substance).

## CHARACTERS
### Appearance
White or almost white powder.

### Solubility
Very slightly soluble in water, very soluble in methanol and
in methylene chloride.

It shows polymorphism (*5.9*).

## IDENTIFICATION
A. Infrared absorption spectrophotometry (*2.2.24*).

Comparison

*dirithromycin CRS.*

B. Examine the chromatograms obtained in the assay.

*Results* The principal peak in the chromatogram obtained
with test solution (a) is similar in retention time and size to
the principal peak in the chromatogram obtained with
reference solution (a).

## TESTS
### Related substances
Liquid chromatography (*2.2.29*).

*Solvent mixture* methanol *R*, acetonitrile *R1* (30:70 *V/V*).

*Test solution (a)* Dissolve 20.0 mg of the substance to be
examined in the solvent mixture and dilute to 10.0 ml with
the solvent mixture.

*Test solution (b)* Dissolve 0.10 g of the substance to be
examined in the solvent mixture and dilute to 10.0 ml with
the solvent mixture.

*Reference solution (a)* Dissolve 20.0 mg of *dirithromycin CRS*
in the solvent mixture and dilute to 10.0 ml with the solvent
mixture.

*Reference solution (b)* Dilute 5.0 ml of reference solution (a)
to 50.0 ml with the solvent mixture.

*Reference solution (c)* Dissolve 20 mg of *dirithromycin CRS* in
the mobile phase and dilute to 10 ml with the mobile phase.
Allow to stand for 24 h before use.

*Column:*
— *size: l* = 0.25 m, Ø = 4.6 mm;
— *stationary phase: octadecylsilyl silica gel for chromatography R*
　(5 μm);
— *temperature*: 40 °C.

*Mobile phase* Mix 9 volumes of *water R*, 19 volumes of
*methanol R*, 28 volumes of a solution containing 1.9 g/l of
*potassium dihydrogen phosphate R* and 9.1 g/l of *dipotassium
hydrogen phosphate R* adjusted to pH 7.5 if necessary with a
100 g/l solution of *potassium hydroxide R*, and 44 volumes of
*acetonitrile R1.*

*Flow rate* 2.0 ml/min.

*Detection* Spectrophotometer at 205 nm.

*Injection* 10 μl of test solution (b) and reference solutions
(b) and (c).

*Run time* 3 times the retention time of dirithromycin.

*Relative retention* With reference to dirithromycin:
impurity A = about 0.7; 15*S*-epimer = about 1.1.

*System suitability* Reference solution (c):
— *resolution*: minimum 2.0 between the peaks due to
　dirithromycin and its 15*S*-epimer; if necessary, adjust the
　concentration of the organic modifiers in the mobile
　phase.

*Limits:*
— *impurity A*: not more than 0.75 times the area of the
　principal peak in the chromatogram obtained with
　reference solution (b) (1.5 per cent);
— *any other impurity*: for each impurity, not more than
　0.5 times the area of the principal peak in the
　chromatogram obtained with reference solution (b)
　(1 per cent);
— *disregard limit*: disregard the peak due to the 15*S*-epimer.

### Dirithromycin 15*S*-epimer
Liquid chromatography (*2.2.29*) as described in the test for
related substances with the following modifications.

*Injection* Test solution (b) and reference solution (b).

*System suitability* Reference solution (b):
— *repeatability*: maximum relative standard deviation of
　5.0 per cent after 6 injections.

*Limit:*
— *15S-epimer*: maximum 1.5 per cent.

### Acetonitrile (*2.4.24, System A*)
Maximum 0.1 per cent.

Prepare the solutions using *dimethylformamide R* instead of
*water R.*

*Sample solution* Dissolve 0.200 g of the substance to be
examined in *dimethylformamide R* and dilute to 20.0 ml with
the same solvent.

*Static head-space injection conditions that may be used:*
— *equilibration temperature*: 120 °C;
— *equilibration time*: 60 min;

— *transfer-line temperature*: 125 °C.

**Heavy metals** (*2.4.8*)

Maximum 20 ppm.

Dissolve 1.0 g in 20 ml of a mixture of equal volumes of *methanol R* and *water R*. 12 ml of the solution complies with test B. Prepare the reference solution using lead standard solution (1 ppm Pb) obtained by diluting *lead standard solution (100 ppm Pb) R* with a mixture of equal volumes of *methanol R* and *water R*.

**Water** (*2.5.12*)

Maximum 1.0 per cent, determined on 1.00 g.

**Sulphated ash** (*2.4.14*)

Maximum 0.1 per cent, determined on 1.0 g.

**ASSAY**

Liquid chromatography (*2.2.29*) as described in the test for related substances with the following modifications.

*Injection* Test solution (a) and reference solution (a).

*System suitability* Reference solution (a):
— *repeatability*: maximum relative standard deviation of 1.0 per cent after 6 injections.

**IMPURITIES**

*Specified impurities* A.

*Other detectable impurities* (The following substances would, if present at a sufficient level, be detected by one or other of the tests in the monograph. They are limited by the general acceptance criterion for other/unspecified impurities and/or by the general monograph *Substances for pharmaceutical use (2034)*. It is therefore not necessary to identify these impurities for demonstration of compliance. See also *5.10. Control of impurities in substances for pharmaceutical use*): B, C, D, E.

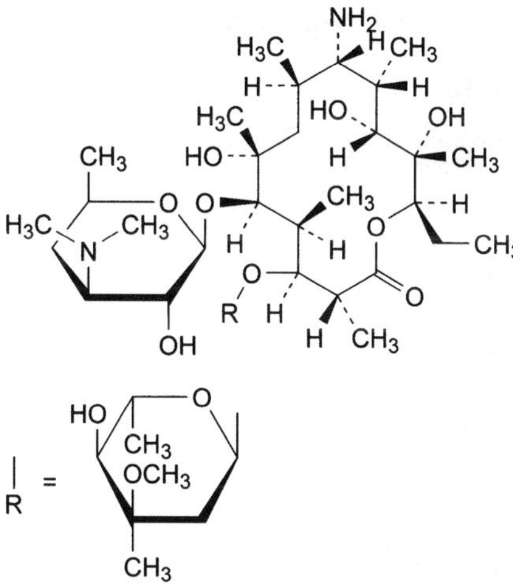

A. (9*S*)-9-amino-9-deoxoerythromycin,

B. R = H: (9*S*)-9-amino-3-de(2,6-dideoxy-3-*C*-methyl-3-*O*-methyl-α-L-*ribo*-hexopyranosyl)-9-deoxoerythromycin,

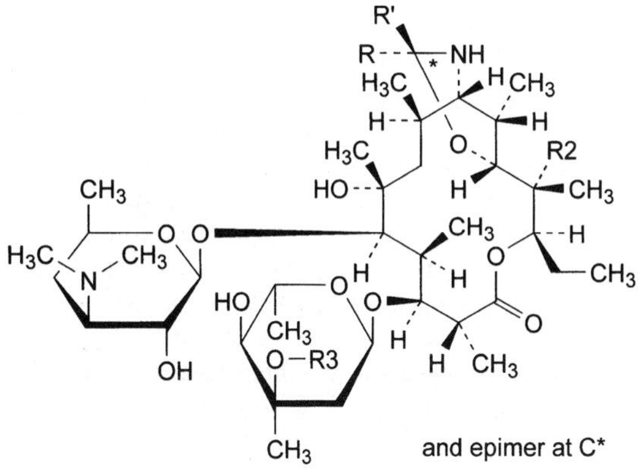

C. R = CH$_2$-*O*-CH$_2$-CH$_2$-*O*-CH$_3$, R′ = H, R2 = H, R3 = CH$_3$: (9*S*)-9,11-[imino[(1*RS*)-2-(2-methoxyethoxy)ethylidene]oxy]-9-deoxo-11,12-dideoxyerythromycin (dirithromycin B),

D. R = CH$_2$-*O*-CH$_2$-CH$_2$-*O*-CH$_3$, R′ = H, R2 = OH, R3 = H: (9*S*)-9,11-[imino[(1*RS*)-2-(2-methoxyethoxy)ethylidene]oxy]-3′-*O*-demethyl-9-deoxo-11-deoxyerythromycin (dirithromycin C),

E. R = CH$_3$, R′ = CH$_3$, R2 = OH, R3 = CH$_3$: 9,11-[imino(1-methylethylidene)oxy]-9-deoxo-11-deoxyerythromycin.

*Ph Eur*

# Disodium Edetate

(*Ph Eur monograph 0232*)

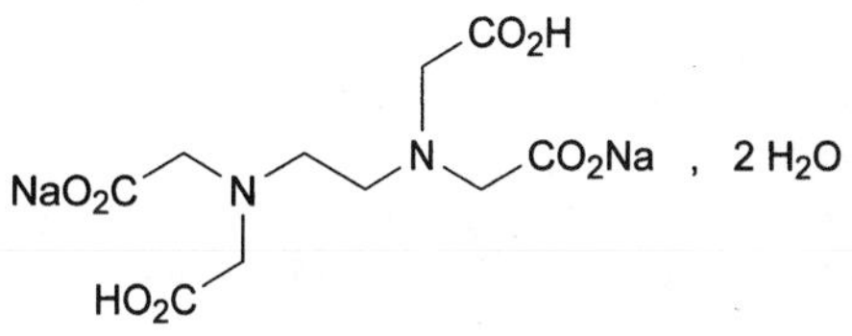

C$_{10}$H$_{14}$N$_2$Na$_2$O$_8$,2H$_2$O        372.2        *6381-92-6*

**Action and use**

Chelating agent.

**Preparation**

Trisodium Edetate Intravenous Infusion

*Ph Eur*

**DEFINITION**

Disodium dihydrogen (ethylenedinitrilo)tetraacetate dihydrate.

**Content**

98.5 per cent to 101.0 per cent.

**CHARACTERS**

**Appearance**

White or almost white, crystalline powder.

**Solubility**

Soluble in water, practically insoluble in ethanol (96 per cent).

**IDENTIFICATION**

*First identification* A, B, D.

*Second identification* B, C, D.

A. Infrared absorption spectrophotometry (*2.2.24*).

*Preparation*   Discs.

*Comparison   disodium edetate CRS.*

B. Dissolve 2 g in 25 ml of *water R*, add 6 ml of *lead nitrate solution R*, shake and add 3 ml of *potassium iodide solution R*. No yellow precipitate is formed. Make alkaline to *red litmus paper R* by the addition of *dilute ammonia R2*. Add 3 ml of *ammonium oxalate solution R*. No precipitate is formed.

C. Dissolve 0.5 g in 10 ml of *water R* and add 0.5 ml of *calcium chloride solution R*. Make alkaline to *red litmus paper R* by the addition of *dilute ammonia R2* and add 3 ml of *ammonium oxalate solution R*. No precipitate is formed.

D. It gives the reactions of sodium (*2.3.1*).

## TESTS

### Solution S
Dissolve 5.0 g in *carbon dioxide-free water R* and dilute to 100 ml with the same solvent.

### Appearance of solution
Solution S is clear (*2.2.1*) and colourless (*2.2.2, Method II*).

### pH (*2.2.3*)
4.0 to 5.5 for solution S.

### Impurity A
Liquid chromatography (*2.2.29*). *Carry out the test protected from light.*

*Solvent mixture*   Dissolve 10.0 g of *ferric sulphate pentahydrate R* in 20 ml of *0.5 M sulphuric acid* and add 780 ml of *water R*. Adjust to pH 2.0 with *1 M sodium hydroxide* and dilute to 1000 ml with *water R*.

*Test solution*   Dissolve 0.100 g of the substance to be examined in the solvent mixture and dilute to 25.0 ml with the solvent mixture.

*Reference solution*   Dissolve 40.0 mg of *nitrilotriacetic acid R* in the solvent mixture and dilute to 100.0 ml with the solvent mixture. To 1.0 ml of the solution add 0.1 ml of the test solution and dilute to 100.0 ml with the solvent mixture.

*Column:*
— *size: l* = 0.10 m, Ø = 4.6 mm,
— *stationary phase*: spherical graphitised carbon for chromatography R1 (5 µm) with a specific surface area of 120 m²/g and a pore size of 25 nm.

*Mobile phase*   Dissolve 50.0 mg of *ferric sulphate pentahydrate R* in 50 ml of *0.5 M sulphuric acid* and add 750 ml of *water R*. Adjust to pH 1.5 with *0.5 M sulphuric acid* or *1 M sodium hydroxide*, add 20 ml of *ethylene glycol R* and dilute to 1000 ml with *water R*.

*Flow rate*   1 ml/min.

*Detection*   Spectrophotometer at 273 nm.

*Injection*   20 µl; filter the solutions and inject immediately.

*Run time*   4 times the retention time of the iron complex of impurity A.

*Retention times*   Iron complex of impurity A = about 5 min; iron complex of edetic acid = about 10 min.

*System suitability*   Reference solution:
— *resolution*: minimum 7 between the peaks due to the iron complex of impurity A and the iron complex of edetic acid,
— *signal-to-noise ratio*: minimum 50 for the peak due to impurity A.

*Limit:*
— *impurity A*: not more than the area of the corresponding peak in the chromatogram obtained with the reference solution (0.1 per cent).

### Iron (*2.4.9*)
Maximum 80 ppm.

Dilute 2.5 ml of solution S to 10 ml with *water R*. Add 0.25 g of *calcium chloride R* to the test solution and the standard before the addition of the *thioglycollic acid R*.

### Heavy metals (*2.4.8*)
Maximum 20 ppm.

1.0 g complies with test F. Prepare the reference solution using 2 ml of *lead standard solution (10 ppm Pb) R*.

## ASSAY
Dissolve 0.300 g in *water R* and dilute to 300 ml with the same solvent. Add 2 g of *hexamethylenetetramine R* and 2 ml of *dilute hydrochloric acid R*. Titrate with *0.1 M lead nitrate*, using about 50 mg of *xylenol orange triturate R* as indicator.

1 ml of *0.1 M lead nitrate* is equivalent to 37.22 mg of $C_{10}H_{14}N_2Na_2O_8,2H_2O$.

## STORAGE
Protected from light.

## IMPURITIES
*Specified impurities   A.*

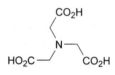

A. nitrilotriacetic acid.

*Ph Eur*

# Anhydrous Disodium Hydrogen Phosphate

(*Anhydrous Disodium Phosphate, Ph Eur monograph 1509*)

$Na_2HPO_4$                142.0                7558-79-4

**Action and use**
Excipient.

**Preparation**
Phosphates Enema

*Ph Eur*

## DEFINITION
### Content
98.0 per cent to 101.0 per cent (dried substance).

## CHARACTERS
### Appearance
White or almost white powder, hygroscopic.

### Solubility
Soluble in water, practically insoluble in ethanol (96 per cent).

## IDENTIFICATION
A. Solution S (see Tests) is slightly alkaline (*2.2.4*).

B. Loss on drying (see Tests).

C. Solution S gives reaction (b) of phosphates (*2.3.1*).

D. Solution S gives reaction (a) of sodium (*2.3.1*).

**TESTS**

**Solution S**

Dissolve 5.0 g in *distilled water R* and dilute to 100.0 ml with the same solvent.

**Appearance of solution**

Solution S is clear (*2.2.1*) and colourless (*2.2.2, Method II*).

**Reducing substances**

To 10 ml of solution S add 5 ml of *dilute sulphuric acid R* and 0.25 ml of *0.02 M potassium permanganate* and heat on a water-bath for 5 min. The solution retains a slight red colour.

**Monosodium phosphate**

Maximum 2.5 per cent.

From the volume of *1 M hydrochloric acid* (25 ml) and of *1 M sodium hydroxide* ($n_1$ ml and $n_2$ ml) used in the assay, calculate the following ratio:

$$\frac{n_2 - 25}{25 - n_1}$$

This ratio is not greater than 0.025.

**Chlorides** (*2.4.4*)

Maximum 200 ppm.

Dilute 5 ml of solution S to 15 ml with *dilute nitric acid R*.

**Sulphates** (*2.4.13*)

Maximum 500 ppm.

To 6 ml of solution S add 2 ml of *dilute hydrochloric acid R* and dilute to 15 ml with *distilled water R*.

**Arsenic** (*2.4.2, Method A*)

Maximum 2 ppm, determined on 10 ml of solution S.

**Iron** (*2.4.9*)

Maximum 20 ppm, determined on solution S.

**Heavy metals** (*2.4.8*)

Maximum 10 ppm.

12 ml of solution S complies with test A. Prepare the reference solution using 5 ml of *lead standard solution (1 ppm Pb) R* and 5 ml of *water R*.

**Loss on drying** (*2.2.32*)

Maximum 1.0 per cent, determined on 1.000 g by drying in an oven at 105 °C for 4 h.

**ASSAY**

Dissolve 1.600 g (m) in 25.0 ml of *carbon dioxide-free water R* and add 25.0 ml of *1 M hydrochloric acid*. Carry out a potentiometric titration (*2.2.20*) using *1 M sodium hydroxide*. Read the volume added at the 1$^{st}$ inflexion point ($n_1$ ml). Continue the titration to the 2$^{nd}$ inflexion point (total volume of *1 M sodium hydroxide* required, $n_2$ ml).

Calculate the percentage content of $Na_2HPO_4$ from the following expression:

$$\frac{1420\,(25 - n_1)}{m\,(100 - d)}$$

$d$ = percentage loss on drying.

**STORAGE**

In an airtight container.

*Ph Eur*

# Disodium Hydrogen Phosphate Dihydrate

Sodium Phosphate Dihydrate

(*Disodium Phosphate Dihydrate, Ph Eur monograph 0602*)

$Na_2HPO_4,2H_2O$      178.0      *10028-24-7*

**Action and use**

Excipient.

**Preparations**

Phosphates Enema

Phosphate Oral Solution

*Ph Eur*

**DEFINITION**

**Content**

98.0 per cent to 101.0 per cent (dried substance).

**CHARACTERS**

**Appearance**

White or almost white powder or colourless crystals.

**Solubility**

Soluble in water, practically insoluble in ethanol (96 per cent).

**IDENTIFICATION**

A. Solution S (see Tests) is slightly alkaline (*2.2.4*).

B. Loss on drying (see Tests).

C. Solution S gives reaction (b) of phosphates (*2.3.1*).

D. Solution S gives reaction (a) of sodium (*2.3.1*).

**TESTS**

**Solution S**

Dissolve 5.0 g in *distilled water R* and dilute to 100 ml with the same solvent.

**Appearance of solution**

Solution S is clear (*2.2.1*) and colourless (*2.2.2, Method II*).

**Reducing substances**

To 5 ml of solution S add 5 ml of *dilute sulphuric acid R* and 0.25 ml of *0.02 M potassium permanganate* and heat on a water-bath for 5 min. The solution retains a slight red colour.

**Monosodium phosphate**

Maximum 2.5 per cent.

From the volume of *1 M hydrochloric acid* (25 ml) and of *1 M sodium hydroxide* ($n_1$ ml and $n_2$ ml) used in the assay, calculate the following ratio:

$$\frac{n_2 - 25}{25 - n_1}$$

This ratio is not greater than 0.025.

**Chlorides** (*2.4.4*)

Maximum 400 ppm.

To 2.5 ml of solution S add 10 ml of *dilute nitric acid R* and dilute to 15 ml with *water R*.

**Sulphates** (*2.4.13*)

Maximum 0.1 per cent.

To 3 ml of solution S add 2 ml of *dilute hydrochloric acid R* and dilute to 15 ml with *distilled water R*.

**Arsenic** (*2.4.2, Method A*)

Maximum 4 ppm, determined on 5 ml of solution S.

**Iron** (*2.4.9*)

Maximum 40 ppm

Dilute 5 ml of solution S to 10 ml with *water R*.

**Heavy metals** (*2.4.8*)
Maximum 20 ppm.

12 ml of solution S complies with test A. Prepare the reference solution using *lead standard solution (1 ppm Pb) R*.

**Loss on drying** (*2.2.32*)
19.5 per cent to 21.0 per cent, determined on 1.000 g by drying in an oven at 130 °C.

**ASSAY**
Dissolve 2.000 g (*m*) in 50 ml of *water R* and add 25.0 ml of *1 M hydrochloric acid*. Carry out a potentiometric titration (*2.2.20*) using *1 M sodium hydroxide*. Read the volume added at the 1$^{st}$ inflexion point ($n_1$ ml). Continue the titration to the 2$^{nd}$ inflexion point (total volume of *1 M sodium hydroxide required*, $n_2$ ml).

Calculate the percentage content of $Na_2HPO_4$ from the following expression:

$$\frac{1420\,(25 - n_1)}{m\,(100 - d)}$$

$d$ = percentage loss on drying.

*Ph Eur*

# Disodium Hydrogen Phosphate Dodecahydrate

★★★
★     ★
★     ★
★★★

Disodium Hydrogen Phosphate, Sodium Phosphate
(*Disodium Phosphate Dodecahydrate, Ph Eur monograph 0118*)

$Na_2HPO_4,12H_2O$          358.1          *10039-32-4*

**Preparation**
Phosphates Enema

*Ph Eur*

**DEFINITION**
**Content**
98.5 per cent to 102.5 per cent.

**CHARACTERS**
**Appearance**
Colourless, transparent crystals, very efflorescent.

**Solubility**
Very soluble in water, practically insoluble in ethanol (96 per cent).

**IDENTIFICATION**
A. Solution S (see Tests) is slightly alkaline (*2.2.4*).

B. Water (see Tests).

C. Solution S gives reaction (b) of phosphates (*2.3.1*).

D. Solution S gives reaction (a) of sodium (*2.3.1*).

**TESTS**
**Solution S**
Dissolve 5.0 g in *distilled water R* and dilute to 50 ml with the same solvent.

**Appearance of solution**
Solution S is clear (*2.2.1*) and colourless (*2.2.2, Method II*).

**Reducing substances**
To 5 ml of solution S add 5 ml of *dilute sulphuric acid R* and 0.25 ml of *0.02 M potassium permanganate* and heat on a water-bath for 5 min. The solution retains a slight red colour.

**Monosodium phosphate**
Maximum 2.5 per cent.

From the volume of *1 M hydrochloric acid* (25 ml) and of *1 M sodium hydroxide* ($n_1$ ml and $n_2$ ml) used in the assay, calculate the following ratio:

$$\frac{n_2 - 25}{25 - n_1}$$

This ratio is not greater than 0.025.

**Chlorides** (*2.4.4*)
Maximum 200 ppm.

To 2.5 ml of solution S add 10 ml of *dilute nitric acid R* and dilute to 15 ml with *water R*.

**Sulphates** (*2.4.13*)
Maximum 500 ppm.

To 3 ml of solution S add 2 ml of *dilute hydrochloric acid R* and dilute to 15 ml with *distilled water R*.

**Arsenic** (*2.4.2, Method A*)
Maximum 2 ppm, determined on 5 ml of solution S.

**Iron** (*2.4.9*)
Maximum 20 ppm.

Dilute 5 ml of solution S to 10 ml with *water R*.

**Heavy metals** (*2.4.8*)
Maximum 10 ppm.

12 ml of solution S complies with test A. Prepare the reference solution using *lead standard solution (1 ppm Pb) R*.

**Water** (*2.5.12*)
57.0 per cent to 61.0 per cent, determined on 50.0 mg. Use a mixture of 10 volumes of *anhydrous methanol R* and 40 volumes of *formamide R1* as solvent.

**ASSAY**
Dissolve 4.00 g (*m*) in 25 ml of *water R* and add 25.0 ml of *1 M hydrochloric acid*. Carry out a potentiometric titration (*2.2.20*) using *1 M sodium hydroxide*. Read the volume added at the 1$^{st}$ inflexion point ($n_1$ ml). Continue the titration to the 2$^{nd}$ inflexion point (total volume of *1 M sodium hydroxide required*, $n_2$ ml).

Calculate the percentage content of $Na_2HPO_4,12H_2O$ from the following expression:

$$\frac{3581\,(25 - n_1)}{m \times 100}$$

*Ph Eur*

# Disopyramide

*(Ph Eur monograph 1006)*

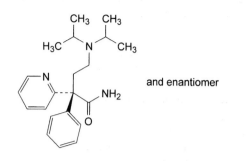

and enantiomer

$C_{21}H_{29}N_3O$      339.5      *3737-09-5*

### Action and use
Class I antiarrhythmic.

### Preparation
Disopyramide Capsules

*Ph Eur*

## DEFINITION
Disopyramide contains not less than 98.5 per cent and not more than the equivalent of 101.5 per cent of (2RS)-4-[bis(1-methylethyl)amino]-2-phenyl-2-(pyridin-2-yl)butanamide, calculated with reference to the dried substance.

## CHARACTERS
A white or almost white powder, slightly soluble in water, freely soluble in methylene chloride, soluble in alcohol.

## IDENTIFICATION
*First identification  B.*

*Second identification  A, C.*

A. Dissolve 40.0 mg in a 5 g/l solution of *sulphuric acid R* in *methanol R* and dilute to 100.0 ml with the same solution. Dilute 5.0 ml of this solution to 50.0 ml with a 5 g/l solution of *sulphuric acid R* in *methanol R*. Examined between 240 nm and 350 nm *(2.2.25)*, the solution shows an absorption maximum at 269 nm and a shoulder at 263 nm. The specific absorbance at the maximum is 190 to 210.

B. Examine by infrared absorption spectrophotometry *(2.2.24)*, comparing with the spectrum obtained with *disopyramide CRS*. Examine the substances as discs prepared by placing 50 µl of a 50 g/l solution in *methylene chloride R* on a disc of *potassium bromide R*. Dry the discs at 60 °C for 1 h before use.

C. Examine the chromatograms obtained in the test for related substances in ultraviolet light at 254 nm. The principal spot in the chromatogram obtained with test solution (b) is similar in position and size to the principal spot in the chromatogram obtained with reference solution (a). Spray with *dilute potassium iodobismuthate solution R*. Examine in daylight. The principal spot in the chromatogram obtained with test solution (b) is similar in position, colour and size to the principal spot in the chromatogram obtained with reference solution (a).

## TESTS
### Related substances
Examine by thin-layer chromatography *(2.2.27)*, using *silica gel GF254 R* as the coating substance.

*Test solution (a)*  Dissolve 0.20 g of the substance to be examined in *methanol R* and dilute to 10 ml with the same solvent.

*Test solution (b)*  Dilute 1 ml of test solution (a) to 10 ml with *methanol R*.

*Reference solution (a)*  Dissolve 20 mg of *disopyramide CRS* in *methanol R* and dilute to 10 ml with the same solvent.

*Reference solution (b)*  Dilute 0.5 ml of test solution (b) to 20 ml with *methanol R*.

Apply to the plate 10 µl of each solution. Develop over a path of 15 cm using a mixture of 1 volume of *concentrated ammonia R*, 30 volumes of *acetone R* and 30 volumes of *cyclohexane R*. Dry the plate in a current of warm air and examine in ultraviolet light at 254 nm. Any spot in the chromatogram obtained with test solution (a), apart from the principal spot, is not more intense than the spot in the chromatogram obtained with reference solution (b) (0.25 per cent).

### Heavy metals *(2.4.8)*
2.0 g complies with limit test C for heavy metals (10 ppm). Prepare the standard using 2 ml of *lead standard solution (10 ppm Pb) R*.

### Loss on drying *(2.2.32)*
Not more than 0.5 per cent, determined on 1.000 g by drying at 80 °C over *diphosphorus pentoxide R* at a pressure not exceeding 0.7 kPa for 2 h.

### Sulphated ash *(2.4.14)*
Not more than 0.2 per cent, determined on 1.0 g.

## ASSAY
Dissolve 0.130 g in 30 ml of *anhydrous acetic acid R*. Add 0.2 ml of *naphtholbenzein solution R*. Titrate with *0.1 M perchloric acid* until the colour changes from yellow to green.

1 ml of *0.1 M perchloric acid* is equivalent to 16.97 mg of $C_{21}H_{29}N_3O$.

## STORAGE
Store protected from light.

## IMPURITIES

and enantiomer

A. R = CN, R′ = CH(CH₃)₂:
(2RS)-4-[bis(1-methylethyl)amino]-2-phenyl-2-(pyridin-2-yl)butanenitrile (di-isopyronitrile),

B. R = H, R′ = CH(CH₃)₂: (3RS)-N,N-bis(1-methylethyl)-3-phenyl-3-(pyridin-2-yl)propan-1-amine,

C. R = CO-NH₂, R′ = H: (2RS)-4-[(1-methylethyl)amino]-2-phenyl-2-(pyridin-2-yl)butanamide,

and enantiomer

D. (RS)-phenyl(pyridin-2-yl)acetonitrile (pyronitrile).

*Ph Eur*

# Disopyramide Phosphate

(*Ph Eur monograph 1005*)

and enantiomer , $H_3PO_4$

$C_{21}H_{29}N_3O,H_3PO_4$ 437.5 22059-60-5

**Action and use**
Antiarrhythmic.

**Preparation**
Disopyramide Phosphate Capsules

*Ph Eur*

## DEFINITION

Disopyramide phosphate contains not less than 98.0 per cent and not more than the equivalent of 102.0 per cent of (2RS)-4-[bis(1-methylethyl)amino]-2-phenyl-2-(pyridin-2-yl)butanamide dihydrogen phosphate, calculated with reference to the dried substance.

## CHARACTERS

A white or almost white powder, soluble in water, sparingly soluble in alcohol, practically insoluble in methylene chloride.

## IDENTIFICATION

*First identification B.*

*Second identification A, C, D.*

A. Dissolve 50.0 mg in a 5 g/l solution of *sulphuric acid R* in *methanol R* and dilute to 100.0 ml with the same solution. Dilute 5.0 ml of this solution to 50.0 ml with a 5 g/l solution of *sulphuric acid R* in *methanol R*. Examined between 240 nm and 350 nm (*2.2.25*), the solution shows an absorption maximum at 269 nm and a shoulder at 263 nm. The specific absorbance at the maximum is 147 to 163.

B. Examine by infrared absorption spectrophotometry (*2.2.24*), comparing with the spectrum obtained with *disopyramide phosphate CRS*. Examine the substances prepared as discs.

C. Examine the chromatograms obtained in the test for related substances in ultraviolet light at 254 nm. The principal spot in the chromatogram obtained with test solution (b) is similar in position and size to the principal spot in the chromatogram obtained with reference solution

(a). Spray with *dilute potassium iodobismuthate solution R*. Examine in daylight. The principal spot in the chromatogram obtained with test solution (b) is similar in position, colour and size to the principal spot in the chromatogram obtained with reference solution (a).

D. Solution S (see Tests) gives reaction (a) of phosphates (*2.3.1*).

## TESTS

**Solution S**

Dissolve 1.0 g in *carbon dioxide-free water R* and dilute to 20 ml with the same solvent.

**Appearance of solution**

Solution S is clear (*2.2.1*) and colourless (*2.2.2, Method II*).

**pH** (*2.2.3*)

The pH of solution S is 4.0 to 5.0.

**Related substances**

Examine by thin-layer chromatography (*2.2.27*), using *silica gel GF$_{254}$ R* as the coating substance.

*Test solution (a)* Dissolve 0.25 g of the substance to be examined in *methanol R* and dilute to 10 ml with the same solvent.

*Test solution (b)* Dilute 1 ml of test solution (a) to 10 ml with *methanol R*.

*Reference solution (a)* Dissolve 25 mg of *disopyramide phosphate CRS* in *methanol R* and dilute to 10 ml with the same solvent.

*Reference solution (b)* Dilute 1 ml of test solution (b) to 20 ml with *methanol R*.

Apply to the plate 10 µl of each solution. Develop over a path of 15 cm using a mixture of 1 volume of *concentrated ammonia R*, 30 volumes of *acetone R* and 30 volumes of *cyclohexane R*. Dry the plate in a current of warm air and examine in ultraviolet light at 254 nm. Any spot in the chromatogram obtained with test solution (a), apart from the principal spot, is not more intense than the spot in the chromatogram obtained with reference solution (b) (0.5 per cent).

**Heavy metals** (*2.4.8*)

2.0 g complies with limit test C for heavy metals (10 ppm). Prepare the standard using 2 ml of *lead standard solution (10 ppm Pb) R*.

**Loss on drying** (*2.2.32*)

Not more than 0.5 per cent, determined on 1.000 g by drying in an oven at 105 °C.

## ASSAY

Dissolve 0.180 g in 30 ml of *anhydrous acetic acid R*. Add 0.2 ml of *naphtholbenzein solution R*. Titrate with *0.1 M perchloric acid* until the colour changes from yellow to green.

1 ml of *0.1 M perchloric acid* is equivalent to 21.88 mg of $C_{21}H_{32}N_3O_5P$.

## STORAGE

Store protected from light.

## IMPURITIES

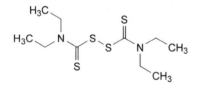

A. R = CN, R' = CH(CH$_3$)$_2$:
(2RS)-4-[bis(1-methylethyl)amino]-2-phenyl-2-(pyridin-2-yl)butanenitrile (di-isopyronitrile),

B. R = H, R' = CH(CH$_3$)$_2$: (3RS)-N,N-bis(1-methylethyl)-3-phenyl-3-(pyridin-2-yl)propan-1-amine,

C. R = CO-NH$_2$, R' = H: (2RS)-4-[(1-methylethyl)amino]-2-phenyl-2-(pyridin-2-yl)butanamide,

D. (RS)-phenyl(pyridin-2-yl)acetonitrile (pyronitrile).

*Ph Eur*

# Disulfiram

*(Ph Eur monograph 0603)*

C$_{10}$H$_{20}$N$_2$S$_4$      296.5      *97-77-8*

### Action and use
Aldehyde dehyrogenase inhibitor; treatment of alcoholism.

### Preparation
Disulfiram Tablets

*Ph Eur*

## DEFINITION
Disulfiram contains not less than 98.5 per cent and not more than the equivalent of 101.0 per cent of tetraethyldisulfanedicarbothioamide, calculated with reference to the dried substance.

## CHARACTERS
A white or almost white, crystalline powder, practically insoluble in water, freely soluble in methylene chloride, sparingly soluble in alcohol.

## IDENTIFICATION
*First identification*   A, B.

*Second identification*   A, C, D.

A. Melting point (*2.2.14*) 70 °C to 73 °C.

B. Examine by infrared absorption spectrophotometry (*2.2.24*), comparing with the spectrum obtained with *disulfiram CRS*. Examine the substances prepared as discs.

C. Examine the chromatograms obtained in the test for related substances. The principal spot in the chromatogram obtained with test solution (b) is similar in position and size to the principal spot in the chromatogram obtained with reference solution (a).

D. Dissolve about 10 mg in 10 ml of *methanol R*. Add 2 ml of a 0.5 g/l solution of *cupric chloride R* in *methanol R*. A yellow colour develops which becomes greenish-yellow.

## TESTS
### Related substances
Examine by thin-layer chromatography (*2.2.27*), using as the coating substance a suitable silica gel with a fluorescent indicator having an optimal intensity at 254 nm.

*Test solution (a)*   Dissolve 0.20 g of the substance to be examined in *ethyl acetate R* and dilute to 10 ml with the same solvent.

*Test solution (b)*   Dilute 1 ml of test solution (a) to 10 ml with *ethyl acetate R*.

*Reference solution (a)*   Dissolve 10 mg of *disulfiram CRS* in *ethyl acetate R* and dilute to 5 ml with the same solvent.

*Reference solution (b)*   Dilute 1 ml of test solution (b) to 20 ml with *ethyl acetate R*.

Apply to the plate 10 µl of each solution. Develop over a path of 15 cm using a mixture of 30 volumes of *butyl acetate R* and 70 volumes of *hexane R*. Allow the plate to dry in air and examine in ultraviolet light at 254 nm. Any spot in the chromatogram obtained with test solution (a), apart from the principal spot, is not more intense than the spot in the chromatogram obtained with reference solution (b) (0.5 per cent).

### Diethyldithiocarbamate
Dissolve 0.20 g in 10 ml of *peroxide-free ether R*, add 5 ml of *buffer solution pH 8.0 R* and shake vigorously. Discard the upper layer and wash the lower layer with 10 ml of *peroxide-free ether R*. Add to the lower layer 0.2 ml of a 4 g/l solution of *copper sulphate R* and 5 ml of *cyclohexane R*. Shake. Any yellow colour in the upper layer is not more intense than that of a standard prepared at the same time using 0.2 ml of a freshly prepared 0.15 g/l solution of *sodium diethyldithiocarbamate R* (150 ppm).

### Heavy metals (*2.4.8*)
1.0 g complies with limit test C for heavy metals (20 ppm). Prepare the standard using 2 ml of *lead standard solution (10 ppm Pb) R*.

### Loss on drying (*2.2.32*)
Not more than 0.5 per cent, determined on 1.000 g by drying *in vacuo* at 50 °C.

### Sulphated ash (*2.4.14*)
Not more than 0.1 per cent, determined on 1.0 g.

## ASSAY
Dissolve 0.450 g in 80 ml of *acetone R* and add 20 ml of a 20 g/l solution of *potassium nitrate R*. Titrate with *0.1 M silver nitrate*. Determine the end-point potentiometrically (*2.2.20*), using a silver electrode and a silver-silver chloride double-junction electrode saturated with potassium nitrate.

1 ml of *0.1 M silver nitrate* is equivalent to 59.30 mg of C$_{10}$H$_{20}$N$_2$S$_4$.

## STORAGE

Store protected from light.

## IMPURITIES

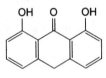

A. diethylthiocarbamic thioanhydride (sulfiram),

B. diethyldithiocarbamate.

_____ *Ph Eur*

# Dithranol

*(Ph Eur monograph 1007)*

$C_{14}H_{10}O_3$         226.2         *1143-38-0*

## Action and use

Coal tar extract; treatment of psoriasis.

## Preparations

Dithranol Cream

Dithranol Ointment

Dithranol Paste

_____

*Ph Eur*

## DEFINITION

1,8-Dihydroxyanthracen-9(10*H*)-one.

## Content

98.5 per cent to 101.0 per cent (dried substance).

## CHARACTERS

### Appearance

Yellow or brownish-yellow, crystalline powder.

### Solubility

Practically insoluble in water, soluble in methylene chloride, sparingly soluble in acetone, slightly soluble in ethanol (96 per cent). It dissolves in dilute solutions of alkali hydroxides.

*Carry out all tests protected from bright light and use freshly prepared solutions.*

## IDENTIFICATION

*First identification   A, B.*

*Second identification   A, C, D.*

A. Melting point (*2.2.14*): 178 °C to 182 °C.

B. Infrared absorption spectrophotometry (*2.2.24*).

*Comparison   dithranol CRS.*

C. Thin-layer chromatography (*2.2.27*).

*Test solution*   Dissolve 10 mg of the substance to be examined in *methylene chloride R* and dilute to 10 ml with the same solvent.

*Reference solution (a)*   Dissolve 10 mg of *dithranol CRS* in *methylene chloride R* and dilute to 10 ml with the same solvent.

*Reference solution (b)*   Dissolve about 5 mg of *dantron R* in 5 ml of reference solution (a).

*Plate   TLC silica gel plate R.*

*Mobile phase   hexane R, methylene chloride R (50:50 V/V).*

*Application   10 μl.*

*Development   Over a path of 12 cm.*

*Drying   In air.*

*Detection*   Place the plate in a tank saturated with ammonia vapour until the spots appear. Examine in daylight.

*System suitability*   Reference solution (b):
— the chromatogram shows 2 clearly separated spots.

*Results*   The principal spot in the chromatogram obtained with the test solution is similar in position, colour and size to the principal spot in the chromatogram obtained with reference solution (a).

D. To 5 mg add 0.1 g of *anhydrous sodium acetate R* and 1 ml of *acetic anhydride R*. Boil for 30 s. Add 20 ml of *ethanol (96 per cent) R*. Examined in ultraviolet light at 365 nm, the solution shows a blue fluorescence.

## TESTS

### Related substances

A. Liquid chromatography (*2.2.29*).

*Test solution*   Dissolve 0.200 g of the substance to be examined in 20 ml of *methylene chloride R*, add 1.0 ml of *glacial acetic acid R* and dilute to 100.0 ml with *hexane R*.

*Reference solution*   Dissolve 5.0 mg of *anthrone R* (impurity A), 5.0 mg of *dantron R* (impurity B), 5.0 mg of *dithranol impurity C CRS* and 5.0 mg of *dithranol CRS* in *methylene chloride R* and dilute to 5.0 ml with the same solvent. To 1.0 ml of this solution, add 19.0 ml of *methylene chloride R* and 1.0 ml of *glacial acetic acid R*, and dilute to 50.0 ml with *hexane R*.

*Column:*
— *size: l = 0.25 m, Ø = 4.6 mm;*
— *stationary phase: silica gel for chromatography R (5 μm).*

*Mobile phase   glacial acetic acid R, methylene chloride R, hexane R (1:5:82 V/V/V).*

*Flow rate   2 ml/min.*

*Detection   Spectrophotometer at 260 nm.*

*Injection   20 μl.*

*Run time   1.5 times the retention time of impurity C.*

*Elution order   dithranol, impurity B, impurity A, impurity C.*

*System suitability*   Reference solution:
— *resolution*: minimum 2.0 between the peaks due to dithranol and impurity B.

*Limits:*
— *impurities A, B, C*: for each impurity, not more than the area of the corresponding peak in the chromatogram obtained with the reference solution (1 per cent).

B. Liquid chromatography (*2.2.29*).

*Test solution*   Dissolve 25.0 mg of the substance to be examined in 5 ml of *tetrahydrofuran R* and dilute to 25.0 ml with the mobile phase.

*Reference solution* Dissolve 5.0 mg of *dithranol impurity D CRS* and 5.0 mg of *dithranol CRS* in 5 ml of *tetrahydrofuran R* and dilute to 10.0 ml with the mobile phase. Dilute 1.0 ml of this solution to 20.0 ml with the mobile phase.

*Column:*
— *size: l* = 0.20 m, Ø = 4.6 mm;
— *stationary phase: octadecylsilyl silica gel for chromatography R* (5 μm).

*Mobile phase* glacial acetic acid R, tetrahydrofuran R, water R (2.5:40:60 *V/V/V*).

*Flow rate* 0.9 ml/min.

*Detection* Spectrophotometer at 254 nm.

*Injection* 20 μl.

*Run time* 3 times the retention time of dithranol.

*System suitability* Reference solution:
— *resolution*: minimum 2.5 between the peaks due to impurity D and dithranol.

*Limit:*
— *impurity D*: not more than the area of the corresponding peak in the chromatogram obtained with the reference solution (2.5 per cent).

*Total (tests A + B)* Maximum 3.0 per cent for the sum of the contents of all impurities.

**Chlorides** (*2.4.4*)
Maximum 100 ppm.

Shake 1.0 g with 20 ml of *water R* for 1 min and filter. Dilute 10 ml of the filtrate to 15 ml with *water R*.

**Loss on drying** (*2.2.32*)
Maximum 0.5 per cent, determined on 1.000 g by drying in an oven at 105 °C.

**Sulphated ash** (*2.4.14*)
Maximum 0.1 per cent, determined on 1.0 g.

**ASSAY**
Dissolve 0.200 g in 50 ml of *anhydrous pyridine R*. Titrate with *0.1 M tetrabutylammonium hydroxide* under *nitrogen R*. Determine the end-point potentiometrically (*2.2.20*), using a glass indicator electrode and a calomel reference electrode containing, as the electrolyte, a saturated solution of *potassium chloride R* in *methanol R*.

1 ml of *0.1 M tetrabutylammonium hydroxide* is equivalent to 22.62 mg of $C_{14}H_{10}O_3$.

**STORAGE**
Protected from light.

**IMPURITIES**
*Specified impurities* A, B, C, D.

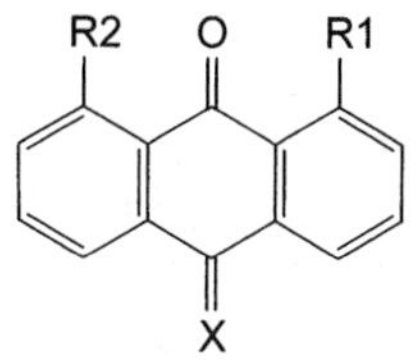

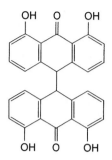

A. R1 = R2 = H, X = $H_2$: anthracen-9(10*H*)-one (anthrone),

B. R1 = R2 = OH, X = O: 1,8-dihydroxyanthracene-9,10-dione (dantron),

D. R1 = OH, R2 = H, X = $H_2$: 1-hydroxyanthracen-9(10*H*)-one,

C. 4,4′,5,5′-tetrahydroxy-9,9′-bianthracenyl-10,10′(9*H*,9′*H*)-dione.

*———————————————————————————— Ph Eur*

# Dobutamine Hydrochloride

(*Ph Eur monograph 1200*)

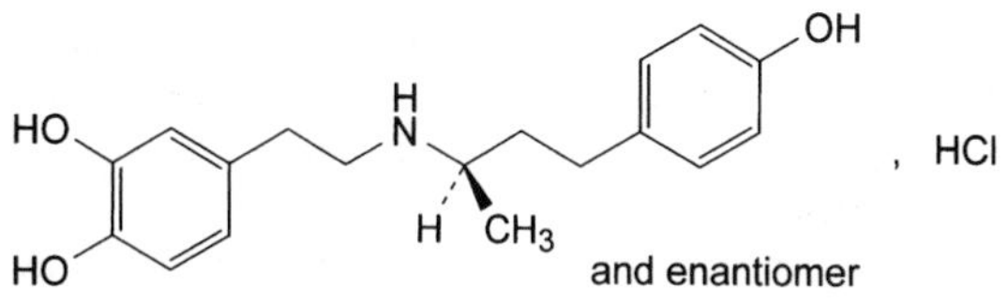

$C_{18}H_{23}NO_3$,HCl          337.9          *49745-95-1*

**Action and use**
Beta₁-adrenoceptor agonist.

**Preparation**
Dobutamine Intravenous Infusion

*Ph Eur* ———————————————————

**DEFINITION**
(*RS*)-4-[2-[[3-(4-Hydroxyphenyl)-1-methylpropyl]amino]ethyl]benzene-1,2-diol hydrochloride.

**Content**
98.5 per cent to 101.0 per cent (dried substance).

**CHARACTERS**
**Appearance**
White or almost white, crystalline powder.

**Solubility**
Sparingly soluble in water, soluble in methanol, sparingly soluble in ethanol (96 per cent).

**IDENTIFICATION**
*First identification* C, E.

*Second identification* A, B, D, E.

A. Melting point (*2.2.14*) 189 °C to 192 °C.

B. Ultraviolet and visible absorption spectrophotometry (*2.2.25*).

*Test solution* Dissolve 20.0 mg in *methanol R* and dilute to 100.0 ml with the same solvent. Dilute 10.0 ml of this solution to 100.0 ml with *methanol R*.

*Spectral range* 220-300 nm.

*Absorption maxima* At 223 nm and 281 nm.

*Absorbance ratio* $A_{281} / A_{223}$ = 0.34 to 0.36.

C. Infrared absorption spectrophotometry (*2.2.24*).

*Preparation* Discs.

*Comparison* dobutamine hydrochloride CRS.

D. Thin-layer chromatography (2.2.27).

*Solvent mixture* glacial acetic acid R, methanol R (50:50 V/V).

*Test solution* Dissolve 10 mg of the substance to be examined in the solvent mixture and dilute to 10 ml with the solvent mixture.

*Reference solution (a)* Dissolve 10.0 mg of *dobutamine hydrochloride CRS* in the solvent mixture and dilute to 10 ml with the solvent mixture.

*Reference solution (b)* Dissolve 5.0 mg of *dopamine hydrochloride CRS* in 5 ml of the test solution.

*Plate* TLC silica gel G plate R.

*Mobile phase* water R, glacial acetic acid R, ether R, butanol R (5:15:30:45 V/V/V/V).

*Application* 10 µl.

*Development* Over a path of 15 cm.

*Drying* In air.

*Detection* Spray with a 1 g/l solution of *potassium permanganate R*.

*System suitability* Reference solution (b):
— the chromatogram shows 2 clearly separated spots.

*Results* The principal spot in the chromatogram obtained with the test solution is similar in position, colour and size to the principal spot in the chromatogram obtained with reference solution (a).

E. It gives reaction (a) of chlorides (2.3.1) using a mixture of equal volumes of *methanol R* and *water R*.

## TESTS

### Acidity or alkalinity

Dissolve 0.1 g in *water R* with gentle heating and dilute to 10 ml with the same solvent. Add 0.1 ml of *methyl red solution R* and 0.2 ml of *0.01 M sodium hydroxide*. The solution is yellow. Add 0.4 ml of *0.01 M hydrochloric acid*. The solution is red.

### Optical rotation (2.2.7)

− 0.05° to + 0.05°.

Dissolve 0.50 g in *methanol R* and dilute to 10.0 ml with the same solvent.

### Absorbance (2.2.25)

Maximum 0.04 at 480 nm.

Dissolve 0.5 g in a mixture of equal volumes of *methanol R* and of *water R* with heating, if necessary, at 30-35 °C and dilute to 25 ml with the same mixture of solvents. Cool quickly. Examine immediately.

### Related substances

Liquid chromatography (2.2.29).

*Solvent mixture* mobile phase B, mobile phase A (35:65 V/V).

*Test solution* Dissolve 0.10 g of the substance to be examined in the solvent mixture and dilute to 20.0 ml with the solvent mixture.

*Reference solution (a)* Dilute 4.0 ml of the test solution to 100.0 ml with a 0.05 g/l solution of *anisaldehyde R* in the solvent mixture. Dilute 1.0 ml of this solution to 10.0 ml with the solvent mixture.

*Reference solution (b)* Dilute 5.0 ml of the test solution to 100.0 ml with the solvent mixture. Dilute 1.0 ml of this solution to 10.0 ml with the solvent mixture.

*Column:*
— *size:* l = 0.15 m, Ø = 4.6 mm;
— *stationary phase:* octadecylsilyl silica gel for chromatography R (5 µm).

*Mobile phase:*
— *mobile phase A:* dissolve 2.60 g of *sodium octanesulphonate R* in 1000 ml of *water R*, add 3 ml of *triethylamine R* and adjust to pH 2.5 with *phosphoric acid R*;
— *mobile phase B:* acetonitrile R, methanol R (18:82 V/V);

| Time (min) | Mobile phase A (per cent V/V) | Mobile phase B (per cent V/V) |
|---|---|---|
| 0 - 5 | 65 | 35 |
| 5 - 20 | 65 → 20 | 35 → 80 |
| 20 - 25 | 20 | 80 |

*Flow rate* 1 ml/min.

*Detection* Spectrophotometer at 280 nm.

*Injection* 20 µl.

*System suitability* Reference solution (a):
— *resolution:* minimum 4.0 between the peaks due to dobutamine and anisaldehyde.

*Limits:*
— *impurities A, B, C:* for each impurity, not more than the area of the principal peak in the chromatogram obtained with reference solution (b) (0.5 per cent);
— *total:* not more than twice the area of the principal peak in the chromatogram obtained with the reference solution (b) (1 per cent);
— *disregard limit:* 0.1 times the area of the principal peak in the chromatogram obtained with reference solution (b) (0.05 per cent).

### Heavy metals (2.4.8)

Maximum 10 ppm.

2.0 g complies with test C. Prepare the reference solution using 2 ml of *lead standard solution (10 ppm Pb) R*.

### Loss on drying (2.2.32)

Mximum 0.5 per cent, determined on 1.000 g by drying in an oven at 105 °C.

### Sulphated ash (2.4.14)

Maximum 0.1 per cent, determined on 1.0 g.

## ASSAY

*In order to avoid overheating in the reaction medium, mix thoroughly throughout and stop the titration immediately after the end-point has been reached.*

Dissolve 0.250 g in 10 ml of *anhydrous formic acid R*. Add 50 ml of *acetic anhydride R*. Titrate with *0.1 M perchloric acid*, determining the end-point potentiometrically (2.2.20).

1 ml of *0.1 M perchloric acid* is equivalent to 33.79 mg of $C_{18}H_{24}ClNO_3$.

## STORAGE

Protected from light.

## IMPURITIES

*Specified impurities* A, B, C.

A. dopamine,

B. 4-(4-hydroxyphenyl)butan-2-one,

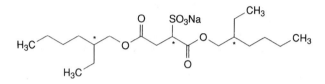

C. (2RS)-N-[2-(3,4-dimethoxyphenyl)ethyl]-4-(4-methoxyphenyl)butan-2-amine.

*Ph Eur*

# Docusate Sodium

Dioctyl Sodium Sulphosuccinate

(*Ph Eur monograph 1418*)

$C_{20}H_{37}NaO_7S$      444.6      *577-11-7*

**Action and use**

Stimulant laxative; faecal softener.

**Preparations**

Co-danthrusate Capsules

Docusate Capsules

Compound Docusate Enema

Docusate Oral Solution

Paediatric Docusate Oral Solution

*Ph Eur*

## DEFINITION

Sodium 1,4-bis[(2-ethylhexyl)oxy]-1,4-dioxobutane-2-sulphonate.

**Content**

98.0 to 101.0 per cent (anhydrous substance).

## CHARACTERS

**Appearance**

White or almost white, waxy masses or flakes, hygroscopic.

**Solubility**

Sparingly soluble in water, freely soluble in ethanol (96 per cent) and in methylene chloride.

## IDENTIFICATION

A. Infrared absorption spectrophotometry (*2.2.24*).

*Preparation* Place about 3 mg of the substance to be examined on a sodium chloride plate, add 0.05 ml of *acetone R* and immediately cover with another sodium chloride plate. Rub the plates together to dissolve the substance to be examined, slide the plates apart and allow the acetone to evaporate.

*Comparison* Ph. Eur. reference spectrum of docusate sodium.

B. In a crucible, ignite 0.75 g in the presence of *dilute sulphuric acid R*, until an almost white residue is obtained. Allow to cool and take up the residue with 5 ml of *water R*. Filter. 2 ml of the filtrate gives reaction (a) of sodium (*2.3.1*).

## TESTS

**Alkalinity**

Dissolve 1.0 g in 100 ml of a mixture of equal volumes of *methanol R* and *water R*, previously neutralised to *methyl red solution R*. Add 0.1 ml of *methyl red solution R*. Not more than 0.2 ml of *0.1 M hydrochloric acid* is required to change the colour of the indicator to red.

**Related non-ionic substances**

Gas chromatography (*2.2.28*).

*Internal standard solution* Dissolve 10 mg of *methyl behenate R* in *hexane R* and dilute to 50 ml with the same solvent.

*Test solution (a)* Dissolve 0.10 g of the substance to be examined in 2.0 ml of the internal standard solution and dilute to 5.0 ml with *hexane R*. Pass the solution, at a rate of about 1.5 ml/min, through a column 10 mm in internal diameter, packed with 5 g of *basic aluminium oxide R* and previously washed with 25 ml of *hexane R*. Elute with 5 ml of *hexane R* and discard the eluate. Elute with 20 ml of a mixture of equal volumes of *ether R* and *hexane R*. Evaporate the eluate to dryness and dissolve the residue in 2.0 ml of *hexane R*.

*Test solution (b)* Prepare as described for test solution (a) but dissolving 0.10 g of the substance to be examined in *hexane R*, diluting to 5.0 ml with the same solvent, and using a new column.

*Reference solution* Dilute 2.0 ml of the internal standard solution to 5.0 ml with *hexane R*.

*Column*:

— *material*: glass,

— *size*: $l$ = 2 m, Ø = 2 mm,

— *stationary phase*: silanised *diatomaceous earth for gas chromatography R* impregnated with 3 per cent m/m of *polymethylphenylsiloxane R*.

*Carrier gas* *nitrogen for chromatography R*.

*Flow rate* 30 ml/min.

*Temperature*:

— *column*: 230 °C,

— *injection port and detector*: 280 °C.

*Detection* Flame ionisation.

*Injection* 1 µl.

*Run time* 2.5 times the retention time of the internal standard.

*System suitability* There is no peak with the same retention time as the internal standard in the chromatogram obtained with test solution (b).

*Limits* Test solution (a):

— *any impurity*: for each impurity, not more than the area of the peak due to the internal standard (0.4 per cent).

**Chlorides**

Maximum 350 ppm.

Dissolve 5.0 g in 50 ml of *ethanol (50 per cent V/V) R* and add 0.1 ml of *potassium dichromate solution R*. Not more than 0.5 ml of *0.1 M silver nitrate* is required to change the colour of the indicator from yellow to orange.

**Sodium sulphate**

Maximum 2 per cent.

Dissolve 0.25 g in 40 ml of a mixture of 20 volumes of *water R* and 80 volumes of *2-propanol R*. Adjust to pH between 2.5 and 4.0 using *perchloric acid solution R*. Add 0.4 ml of *naphtharson solution R* and 0.1 ml of a 0.125 g/l solution of *methylene blue R*. Not more than 1.5 ml of

*0.025 M barium perchlorate* is required to change the colour of the indicator from yellowish-green to yellowish-pink.

### Heavy metals (2.4.8)

Maximum 10 ppm.

Dissolve 4.0 g in *ethanol (80 per cent V/V) R* and dilute to 20 ml with the same solvent. 12 ml of the solution complies with test B. Prepare the reference solution using lead standard solution (2 ppm Pb) obtained by diluting *lead standard solution (100 ppm Pb) R* with *ethanol (80 per cent V/V) R*.

### Water (2.5.12)

Maximum 3.0 per cent, determined on 0.250 g.

### ASSAY

To 1.000 g in a 250 ml conical flask fitted with a reflux condenser add 25.0 ml of *0.5 M alcoholic potassium hydroxide* and heat on a water-bath under reflux for 45 min. Allow to cool. Add 0.25 ml of *phenolphthalein solution R1* and titrate with *0.5 M hydrochloric acid* until the red colour disappears. Carry out a blank titration.

1 ml of *0.5 M alcoholic potassium hydroxide* is equivalent to 0.1112 g of $C_{20}H_{37}NaO_7S$.

### STORAGE

In an airtight container.

_____ *Ph Eur*

# Dodecyl Gallate

(*Ph Eur monograph 2078*)

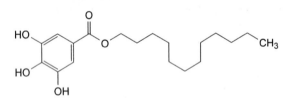

$C_{19}H_{30}O_5$        338.4        1166-52-5

### Action and use

Antioxidant.

*Ph Eur* _____

### DEFINITION

Dodecyl 3,4,5-trihydroxybenzoate.

### Content

97.0 per cent to 103.0 per cent (dried substance).

### CHARACTERS

### Appearance

White or almost white, crystalline powder.

### Solubility

Very slightly soluble or practically insoluble in water, freely soluble in ethanol (96 per cent), slightly soluble in methylene chloride.

### IDENTIFICATION

A. Melting point (2.2.14).

Determine the melting point of the substance to be examined. Mix equal parts of the substance to be examined and *dodecyl gallate CRS* and determine the melting point of the mixture. The difference between the melting points (which are about 96 °C) is not greater than 2 °C.

B. Examine the chromatograms obtained in the test for impurity A.

*Results* The principal spot in the chromatogram obtained with test solution (b) is similar in position, colour and size to the principal spot in the chromatogram obtained with reference solution (a).

### TESTS

### Impurity A

Thin-layer chromatography (2.2.27).

*Test solution (a)* Dissolve 0.20 g of the substance to be examined in *acetone R* and dilute to 10 ml with the same solvent.

*Test solution (b)* Dilute 1.0 ml of test solution (a) to 20 ml with *acetone R*.

*Reference solution (a)* Dissolve 10 mg of *dodecyl gallate CRS* in *acetone R* and dilute to 10 ml with the same solvent.

*Reference solution (b)* Dissolve 20 mg of *gallic acid R* in *acetone R* and dilute to 20 ml with the same solvent.

*Reference solution (c)* Dilute 1.0 ml of reference solution (b) to 10 ml with *acetone R*.

*Reference solution (d)* Dilute 1.0 ml of reference solution (b) to 5 ml with test solution (a).

*Plate* TLC silica gel plate R.

*Mobile phase* anhydrous formic acid R, ethyl formate R, toluene R (10:40:50 V/V/V).

*Application* 5 µl of test solutions (a) and (b) and reference solutions (a), (c) and (d).

*Development* Over 2/3 of the plate.

*Drying* In air for 10 min.

*Detection* Spray with a mixture of 1 volume of *ferric chloride solution R1* and 9 volumes of *ethanol (96 per cent) R*.

*System suitability* Reference solution (d):
— the chromatogram shows 2 clearly separated principal spots.

*Limit* Test solution (a):
— *impurity A*: any spot due to impurity A is not more intense than the spot in the chromatogram obtained with reference solution (c) (0.5 per cent).

### Chlorides (2.4.4)

Maximum 100 ppm.

To 1.65 g add 50 ml of *water R*. Shake for 5 min. Filter. 15 ml of the filtrate complies with the test.

### Heavy metals (2.4.8)

Maximum 10 ppm.

2.0 g complies with limit test C. Prepare the reference solution using 2 ml of *lead standard solution (10 ppm Pb) R*.

### Loss on drying (2.2.32)

Maximum 0.5 per cent, determined on 1.000 g by drying in an oven at 70 °C.

### Sulphated ash (2.4.14)

Maximum 0.1 per cent, determined on 1.0 g.

### ASSAY

Dissolve 0.100 g in *methanol R* and dilute to 250.0 ml with the same solvent. Dilute 5.0 ml of the solution to 200.0 ml with *methanol R*. Measure the absorbance (2.2.25) at the absorption maximum at 275 nm.

Calculate the content of $C_{19}H_{30}O_5$ taking the specific absorbance to be 321.

### STORAGE

In a non-metallic container, protected from light.

## IMPURITIES

*Specified impurities A.*

HO—, HO—, —CO₂H, —OH structure

A. 3,4,5-trihydroxybenzoic acid (gallic acid).

*Ph Eur*

# Domiphen Bromide

structure

$C_{22}H_{40}BrNO$     414.5     *538-71-6*

## Action and use
Antiseptic.

## DEFINITION
Domiphen Bromide consists chiefly of dodecyldimethyl-2-phenoxyethylammonium bromide. It contains not less than 97.0% and not more than 100.5% of $C_{22}H_{40}BrNO$, calculated with reference to the dried substance.

## CHARACTERISTICS
Colourless or faintly yellow, crystalline flakes.

Freely soluble in *water* and in *ethanol (96%)*; soluble in *acetone*.

## IDENTIFICATION
A. The *infrared absorption spectrum*, Appendix II A, is concordant with the *reference spectrum* of domiphen bromide (*RS 383*).

B. Dissolve 10 mg in 10 ml of *water* and add 0.1 ml of a 0.5% w/v solution of *eosin* and 100 ml of *water*. An intense pink colour is produced.

C. Yields the reactions characteristic of *bromides*, Appendix VI.

*Melting point*, 106° to 116°, Appendix V A.

## TESTS
### Acidity or alkalinity
Add 0.5 ml of *bromothymol blue solution R3* to each of 10 ml of *phosphate buffer pH 6.4* (solution A) and 10 ml of *phosphate buffer pH 7.6* (solution B). Dissolve 0.10 g in 10 ml of *carbon dioxide-free water* and add 0.5 ml of *bromothymol blue solution R3*. The resulting solution is not more yellow than solution A and not more blue than solution B.

### Clarity and colour of solution
Dissolve 1.0 g in 10 ml of *carbon dioxide-free water*. The solution is not more opalescent than *reference suspension II*, Appendix IV A, and not more intensely coloured than *reference solution Y₇*, Appendix IV B, Method I.

### Non-quaternary amines
Carry out the Assay described below using a further 25 ml of the original solution and 10 ml of 0.1M *hydrochloric acid* in place of the 0.1M *sodium hydroxide*. The difference between

the volume of 0.05M *potassium iodate VS* required in this titration and that required in the Assay is not more than 0.5 ml for each g of substance taken.

### Loss on drying
When dried to constant weight at 70° at a pressure not exceeding 0.7 kPa, loses not more than 1.0% of its weight. Use 1 g.

### Sulphated ash
Not more than 0.1%, Appendix IX A.

## ASSAY
Dissolve 2 g in sufficient *water* to produce 100 ml. Transfer 25 ml to a separating funnel and add 25 ml of *chloroform*, 10 ml of 0.1M *sodium hydroxide* and 10 ml of a freshly prepared 5% w/v solution of *potassium iodide*. Shake well, allow to separate and discard the chloroform layer. Wash the aqueous layer with three 10 ml quantities of *chloroform* and discard the chloroform solutions. Add 40 ml of *hydrochloric acid*, allow to cool and titrate with 0.05M *potassium iodate VS* until the deep brown colour is discharged. Add 2 ml of *chloroform* and continue the titration, shaking vigorously, until the chloroform layer no longer changes colour. Carry out a blank titration on a mixture of 10 ml of the freshly prepared potassium iodide solution, 20 ml of *water* and 40 ml of *hydrochloric acid*. The difference between the titrations represents the amount of potassium iodate required. Each ml of 0.05M *potassium iodate VS* is equivalent to 41.45 mg of $C_{22}H_{40}BrNO$.

# Domperidone

(*Ph Eur monograph 1009*)

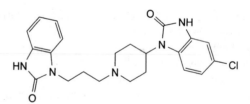

$C_{22}H_{24}ClN_5O_2$     425.9     *57808-66-9*

## Action and use
Peripheral dopamine receptor antagonist; antiemetic.

*Ph Eur*

## DEFINITION
5-Chloro-1-[1-[3-(2-oxo-2,3-dihydro-1*H*-benzimidazol-1-yl)propyl]piperidin-4-yl]-1,3-dihydro-2H-benzimidazol-2-one.

### Content
99.0 per cent to 101.0 per cent (dried substance).

## CHARACTERS
### Appearance
White or almost white powder.

### Solubility
Practically insoluble in water, soluble in dimethylformamide, slightly soluble in ethanol (96 per cent) and in methanol.

## IDENTIFICATION
*First identification A, B.*

*Second identification A, C, D.*

A. Melting point (*2.2.14*): 244 °C to 248 °C.

B. Infrared absorption spectrophotometry (*2.2.24*).

*Preparation*  Discs.

*Comparison*  domperidone CRS.

C. Thin-layer chromatography (*2.2.27*).

*Test solution*  Dissolve 20 mg of the substance to be examined in *methanol R* and dilute to 10 ml with the same solvent.

*Reference solution (a)*  Dissolve 20 mg of *domperidone CRS* in *methanol R* and dilute to 10 ml with the same solvent.

*Reference solution (b)*  Dissolve 20 mg of *domperidone CRS* and 20 mg of *droperidol CRS* in *methanol R* and dilute to 10 ml with the same solvent.

*Plate*  TLC octadecylsilyl silica gel plate R.

*Mobile phase*  ammonium acetate solution R, dioxan R, methanol R (20:40:40 *V/V/V*).

*Application*  5 µl.

*Development*  Over a path of 15 cm.

*Drying*  In a current of warm air for 15 min.

*Detection*  Expose to iodine vapour until the spots appear. Examine in daylight.

*System suitability*  Reference solution (b):
— the chromatogram shows 2 clearly separated spots.

*Results*  The principal spot in the chromatogram obtained with the test solution is similar in position and size to the principal spot in the chromatogram obtained with reference solution (a).

D. It gives the reaction of non-nitrogen substituted barbiturates (*2.3.1*).

## TESTS

### Appearance of solution

The solution is clear (*2.2.1*) and not more intensely coloured than reference solution $Y_6$ (*2.2.2, Method II*).

Dissolve 0.20 g in *dimethylformamide R* and dilute to 20.0 ml with the same solvent.

### Related substances

Liquid chromatography (*2.2.29*)

*Prepare the solutions immediately before use.*

*Test solution*  Dissolve 0.10 g of the substance to be examined in *dimethylformamide R* and dilute to 10.0 ml with the same solvent.

*Reference solution (a)*  Dissolve 10.0 mg of *domperidone CRS* and 15.0 mg of *droperidol CRS* in *dimethylformamide R* and dilute to 100.0 ml with the same solvent.

*Reference solution (b)*  Dilute 1.0 ml of the test solution to 100.0 ml with *dimethylformamide R*. Dilute 5.0 ml of this solution to 20.0 ml with *dimethylformamide R*.

*Column:*
— *size: l* = 0.1 m, Ø = 4.6 mm;
— *stationary phase: base-deactivated octadecylsilyl silica gel for chromatography R* (3 µm).

*Mobile phase:*
— *mobile phase A*: 5 g/l solution of *ammonium acetate R*;
— *mobile phase B: methanol R*;

| Time (min) | Mobile phase A (per cent *V/V*) | Mobile phase B (per cent *V/V*) |
|---|---|---|
| 0 - 10 | 70 → 0 | 30 → 100 |
| 10 - 12 | 0 | 100 |

*Flow rate*  1.5 ml/min.

*Detection*  Spectrophotometer at 280 nm.

*Equilibration*  With *methanol R* for at least 30 min and then with the mobile phase at the initial composition for at least 5 min.

*Injection*  10 µl; inject *dimethylformamide R* as a blank.

*Retention time*  Domperidone = about 6.5 min; droperidol = about 7 min.

*System suitability*  Reference solution (a):
— *resolution: minimum 2.0 between the peaks due to domperidone and droperidol; if necessary, adjust the concentration of methanol in the mobile phase or adjust the time programme for the linear gradient.*

*Limits:*
— *impurities A, B, C, D, E, F*: for each impurity, not more than the area of the principal peak in the chromatogram obtained with reference solution (b) (0.25 per cent);
— *total*: not more than twice the area of the principal peak in the chromatogram obtained with reference solution (b) (0.5 per cent);
— *disregard limit*: 0.2 times the area of the principal peak in the chromatogram obtained with reference solution (b) (0.05 per cent); disregard any peak due to the blank.

### Heavy metals (*2.4.8*)
Maximum 20 ppm.

1.0 g complies with test D. Prepare the reference solution using 2 ml of *lead standard solution (10 ppm Pb) R*.

### Loss on drying (*2.2.32*)
Maximum 0.5 per cent, determined on 1.000 g by drying in an oven at 105 °C.

### Sulphated ash (*2.4.14*)
Maximum 0.1 per cent, determined on 1.0 g.

## ASSAY

Dissolve 0.300 g in 50 ml of a mixture of 1 volume of *anhydrous acetic acid R* and 7 volumes of *methyl ethyl ketone R*. Titrate with *0.1 M perchloric acid* until the colour changes from orange-yellow to green using 0.2 ml of *naphtholbenzein solution R* as indicator.

1 ml of *0.1 M perchloric acid* is equivalent to 42.59 mg of $C_{22}H_{24}ClN_5O_2$.

## STORAGE
Protected from light.

## IMPURITIES

*Specified impurities*  A, B, C, D, E, F.

A. 5-chloro-1-(piperidin-4-yl)-1,3-dihydro-2*H*-benzimidazol-2-one,

B. 4-(5-chloro-2-oxo-2,3-dihydro-1*H*-benzimidazol-1-yl)-1-formylpiperidine,

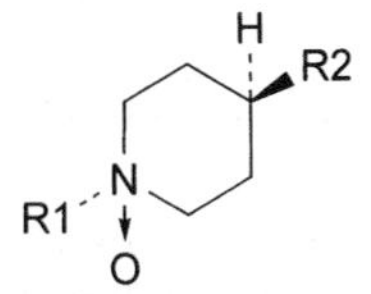

C. *cis*-4-(5-chloro-2-oxo-2,3-dihydro-1*H*-benzimidazol-1-yl)-1-[3-(2-oxo-2,3-dihydro-1*H*-benzimidazol-1-yl)propyl]piperidine 1-oxide,

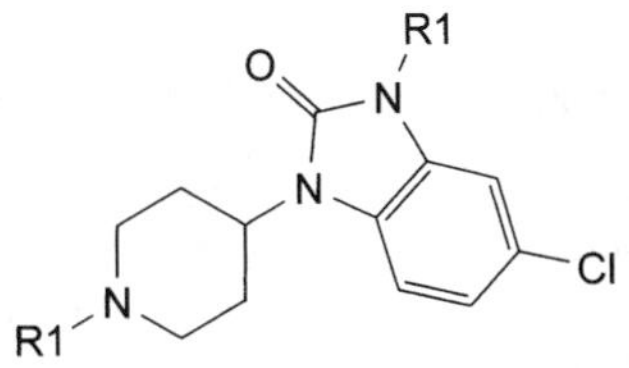

D. 5-chloro-3-[3-(2-oxo-2,3-dihydro-1*H*-benzimidazol-1-yl)propyl]-1-[1-[3-(2-oxo-2,3-dihydro-1*H*-benzimidazol-1-yl)propyl]piperidin-4-yl]-1,3-dihydro-2*H*-benzimidazol-2-one,

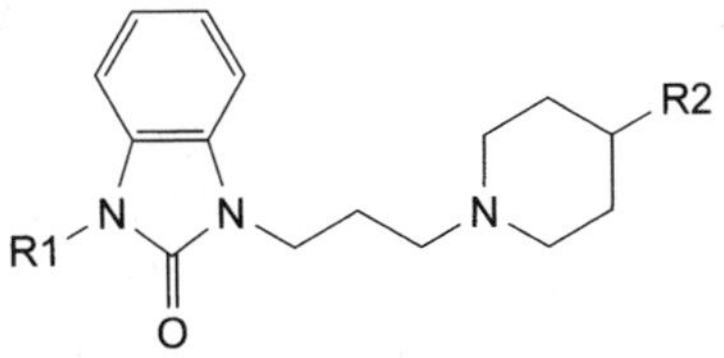

E. 1-[3-[4-(5-chloro-2-oxo-2,3-dihydro-1*H*-benzimidazol-1-yl)piperidin-1-yl]propyl]-3-[3-(2-oxo-2,3-dihydro-1*H*-benzimidazol-1-yl)propyl]-1,3-dihydro-2*H*-benzimidazol-2-one,

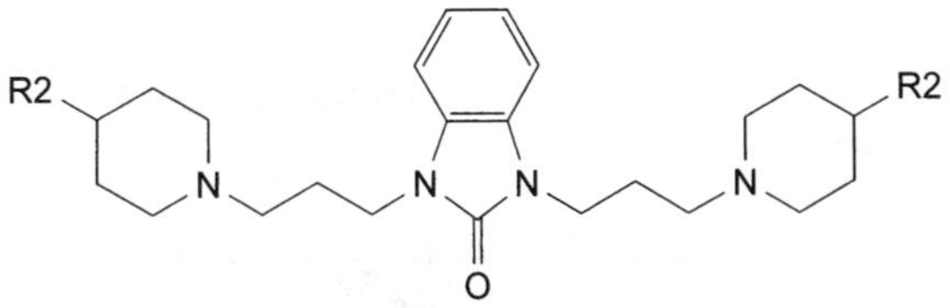

F. 1,3-bis[3-[4-(5-chloro-2-oxo-2,3-dihydro-1*H*-benzimidazol-1-yl)piperidin-1-yl]propyl]-1,3-dihydro-2*H*-benzimidazol-2-one.

_____ *Ph Eur*

# Domperidone Maleate

(*Ph Eur monograph 1008*)

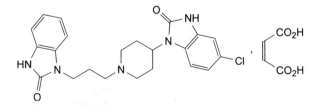

$C_{22}H_{24}ClN_5O_2,C_4H_4O_4$     542.0     *99497-03-7*

### Action and use
Peripheral dopamine receptor antagonist; antiemetic.

### Preparation
Domperidone Tablets

*Ph Eur*

## DEFINITION
5-Chloro-1-[1-[3-(2-oxo-2,3-dihydro-1*H*-benzimidazol-1-yl)propyl]piperidin-4-yl]-1,3-dihydro-2H-benzimidazol-2-one hydrogen (*Z*)-butenedioate.

### Content
99.0 per cent to 101.0 per cent (dried substance).

## CHARACTERS
### Appearance
White or almost white powder.

### Solubility
Very slightly soluble in water, sparingly soluble in dimethylformamide, slightly soluble in methanol, very slightly soluble in ethanol (96 per cent).

It shows polymorphism (*5.9*).

## IDENTIFICATION
*First identification*   A.

*Second identification*   B, C.

A. Infrared absorption spectrophotometry (*2.2.24*).

*Preparation*   Discs.

*Comparison*   domperidone maleate CRS.

If the spectra obtained show differences, dissolve the substance to be examined and the reference substance separately in the minimum volume of *2-propanol R*, evaporate to dryness on a water-bath and record new spectra using the residues.

B. Thin-layer chromatography (*2.2.27*).

*Test solution*   Dissolve 20 mg of the substance to be examined in *methanol R* and dilute to 10 ml with the same solvent.

*Reference solution (a)*   Dissolve 20 mg of *domperidone maleate CRS* in *methanol R* and dilute to 10 ml with the same solvent.

*Reference solution (b)*   Dissolve 20 mg of *domperidone maleate CRS* and 20 mg of *droperidol CRS* in *methanol R* and dilute to 10 ml with the same solvent.

*Plate*   TLC *octadecylsilyl silica gel plate R*.

*Mobile phase*   ammonium acetate solution R, dioxan R, methanol R (20:40:40 *V/V/V*).

*Application*   5 μl.

*Development*   Over a path of 15 cm.

*Drying*   In a current of warm air for 15 min.

*Detection*   Expose to iodine vapour until the spots appear. Examine in daylight.

*System suitability*   Reference solution (b):
— the chromatogram shows 2 clearly separated spots.

*Results*   The principal spot in the chromatogram obtained with the test solution is similar in position and size to the principal spot in the chromatogram obtained with reference solution (a).

C. Triturate 0.1 g with a mixture of 1 ml of *strong sodium hydroxide solution R* and 3 ml of *water R*. Shake with 3 quantities, each of 5 ml, of *ether R*. To 0.1 ml of the aqueous layer add a solution of 10 mg of *resorcinol R* in 3 ml of *sulphuric acid R*. Heat on a water-bath for 15 min. No colour develops. To the remainder of the aqueous layer add 2 ml of *bromine solution R*. Heat on a water-bath for 15 min and then heat to boiling. Cool. To 0.1 ml of this solution add a solution of 10 mg of *resorcinol R* in 3 ml of *sulphuric acid R*. Heat on a water-bath for 15 min. A violet colour develops.

## TESTS

### Appearance of solution
The solution is clear (2.2.1) and not more intensely coloured than reference solution $Y_6$ (2.2.2, Method II).

Dissolve 0.20 g in dimethylformamide R and dilute to 20.0 ml with the same solvent.

### Related substances
Liquid chromatography (2.2.29)

*Prepare the solutions immediately before use.*

*Test solution* Dissolve 0.10 g of the substance to be examined in dimethylformamide R and dilute to 10.0 ml with the same solvent.

*Reference solution (a)* Dissolve 10.0 mg of domperidone maleate CRS and 15.0 mg of droperidol CRS in dimethylformamide R and dilute to 100.0 ml with the same solvent.

*Reference solution (b)* Dilute 1.0 ml of the test solution to 100.0 ml with dimethylformamide R. Dilute 5.0 ml of this solution to 20.0 ml with dimethylformamide R.

*Column:*
— size: $l$ = 0.1 m, Ø = 4.6 mm;
— stationary phase: base-deactivated octadecylsilyl silica gel for chromatography R (3 μm).

*Mobile phase:*
— mobile phase A: 5 g/l solution of ammonium acetate R;
— mobile phase B: methanol R;

| Time (min) | Mobile phase A (per cent V/V) | Mobile phase B (per cent V/V) |
|---|---|---|
| 0 - 10 | 70 → 0 | 30 → 100 |
| 10 - 12 | 0 | 100 |

*Flow rate* 1.5 ml/min.

*Detection* Spectrophotometer at 280 nm.

*Equilibration* With methanol R for at least 30 min and then with the mobile phase at the initial composition for at least 5 min.

*Injection* 10 μl; inject dimethylformamide R as a blank.

*Retention time* Domperidone = about 6.5 min; droperidol = about 7 min.

*System suitability* Reference solution (a):
— resolution: minimum 2.0 between the peaks due to domperidone and droperidol; if necessary, adjust the concentration of methanol in the mobile phase or adjust the time programme for the linear gradient.

*Limits:*
— impurities A, B, C, D, E, F: for each impurity, not more than the area of the principal peak in the chromatogram obtained with reference solution (b) (0.25 per cent);
— total: not more than twice the area of the principal peak in the chromatogram obtained with reference solution (b) (0.5 per cent);
— disregard limit: 0.2 times the area of the principal peak in the chromatogram obtained with reference solution (b) (0.05 per cent); disregard any peak due to the blank.

### Heavy metals (2.4.8)
Maximum 20 ppm.

1.0 g complies with test D. Prepare the reference solution using 2 ml of lead standard solution (10 ppm Pb) R.

### Loss on drying (2.2.32)
Maximum 0.5 per cent, determined on 1.000 g by drying in an oven at 105 °C.

### Sulphated ash (2.4.14)
Maximum 0.1 per cent, determined on 1.0 g.

### ASSAY
Dissolve 0.400 g in 50 ml of anhydrous acetic acid R. Using 0.2 ml of naphtholbenzein solution R as indicator, titrate with 0.1 M perchloric acid until the colour changes from orange-yellow to green.

1 ml of 0.1 M perchloric acid is equivalent to 54.20 mg of $C_{26}H_{28}ClN_5O_2$.

### STORAGE
Protected from light.

### IMPURITIES
*Specified impurities* A, B, C, D, E, F.

A. 5-chloro-1-(piperidin-4-yl)-1,3-dihydro-2H-benzimidazol-2-one,

B. 4-(5-chloro-2-oxo-2,3-dihydro-1H-benzimidazol-1-yl)-1-formylpiperidine,

C. cis-4-(5-chloro-2-oxo-2,3-dihydro-1H-benzimidazol-1-yl)-1-[3-(2-oxo-2,3-dihydro-1H-benzimidazol-1-yl)propyl]piperidine 1-oxide,

D. 5-chloro-3-[3-(2-oxo-2,3-dihydro-1H-benzimidazol-1-yl)propyl]-1-[1-[3-(2-oxo-2,3-dihydro-1H-benzimidazol-1-yl)propyl]piperidin-4-yl]-1,3-dihydro-2H-benzimidazol-2-one,

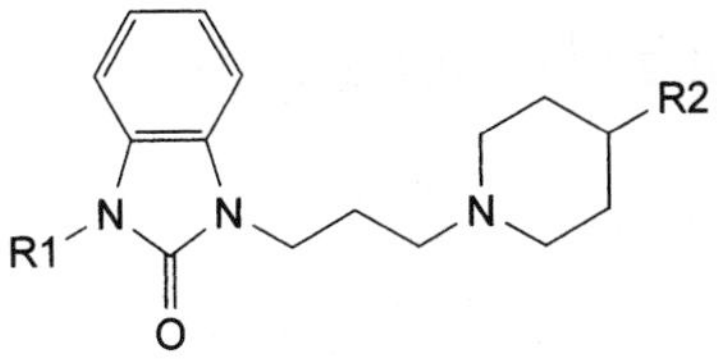

E. 1-[3-[4-(5-chloro-2-oxo-2,3-dihydro-1*H*-benzimidazol-1-yl)piperidin-1-yl]propyl]-3-[3-(2-oxo-2,3-dihydro-1*H*-benzimidazol-1-yl)propyl]-1,3-dihydro-2*H*-benzimidazol-2-one,

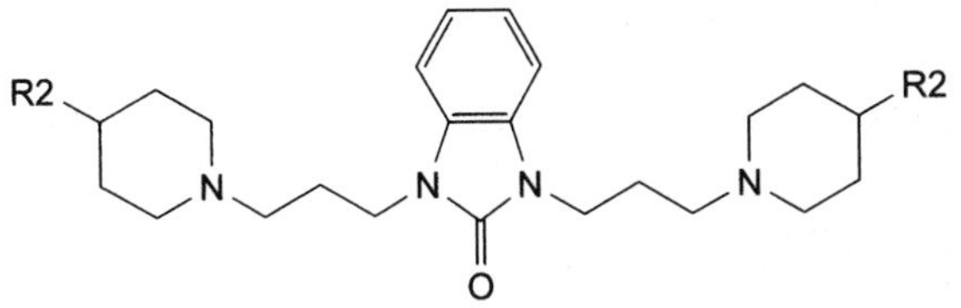

F. 1,3-bis[3-[4-(5-chloro-2-oxo-2,3-dihydro-1*H*-benzimidazol-1-yl)piperidin-1-yl]propyl]-1,3-dihydro-2*H*-benzimidazol-2-one.

*Ph Eur*

# Dopamine Hydrochloride

*(Ph Eur monograph 0664)*

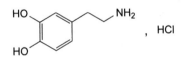

C$_8$H$_{11}$NO$_2$,HCl         189.6         62-31-7

**Action and use**

Dopamine receptor antagonist; beta$_1$-adrenoceptor agonist; alpha-adrenoceptor agonist.

**Preparation**

Dopamine Intravenous Infusion

*Ph Eur* _____

**DEFINITION**

4-(2-Aminoethyl)benzene-1,2-diol hydrochloride.

**Content**

99.0 per cent to 101.0 per cent (dried substance).

**CHARACTERS**

**Appearance**

White or almost white, crystalline powder.

**Solubility**

Freely soluble in water, soluble in ethanol (96 per cent), sparingly soluble in acetone and in methylene chloride.

**IDENTIFICATION**

*First identification*  B, E.

*Second identification*  A, C, D, E.

A. Ultraviolet and visible absorption spectrophotometry (*2.2.25*).

*Test solution*  Dissolve 40.0 mg in *0.1 M hydrochloric acid* and dilute to 100.0 ml with the same acid. Dilute 10.0 ml of this solution to 100.0 ml with *0.1 M hydrochloric acid*.

*Spectral range*  230-350 nm.

*Absorption maximum*  At 280 nm.

*Specific absorbance at the absorption maximum*  136 to 150.

B. Infrared absorption spectrophotometry (*2.2.24*).

*Comparison*  dopamine hydrochloride CRS.

C. Dissolve about 5 mg in a mixture of 5 ml of *1 M hydrochloric acid* and 5 ml of *water R*. Add 0.1 ml of *sodium nitrite solution R* containing 100 g/l of *ammonium molybdate R*. A yellow colour develops which becomes red on the addition of *strong sodium hydroxide solution R*.

D. Dissolve about 2 mg in 2 ml of *water R* and add 0.2 ml of *ferric chloride solution R2*. A green colour develops which changes to bluish-violet on the addition of 0.1 g of *hexamethylenetetramine R*.

E. It gives reaction (a) of chlorides (*2.3.1*).

**TESTS**

**Appearance of solution**

The solution is clear (*2.2.1*) and not more intensely coloured than reference solution B$_6$ or Y$_6$ (*2.2.2, Method II*).

Dissolve 0.4 g in *water R* and dilute to 10 ml with the same solvent.

**Acidity or alkalinity**

Dissolve 0.5 g in *carbon dioxide-free water R* and dilute to 10 ml with the same solvent. Add 0.1 ml of *methyl red solution R* and 0.75 ml of *0.01 M sodium hydroxide*. The solution is yellow. Add 1.5 ml of *0.01 M hydrochloric acid*. The solution is red.

**Related substances**

Liquid chromatography (*2.2.29*). *Protect the solutions from light.*

*Buffer solution*  Dissolve 21 g of *citric acid R* in 200 ml of *1 M sodium hydroxide* and dilute to 1000 ml with *water R*. To 600 ml of this solution add 400 ml of *0.1 M hydrochloric acid*.

*Test solution*  Dissolve 50 mg of the substance to be examined in mobile phase A and dilute to 25 ml with mobile phase A.

*Reference solution (a)*  Dilute 1.0 ml of the test solution to 100.0 ml with mobile phase A. Dilute 1.0 ml of this solution to 10.0 ml with mobile phase A.

*Reference solution (b)*  Dissolve 10 mg of *3-O-methyldopamine hydrochloride R* (impurity B) and 10 mg of *4-O-methyldopamine hydrochloride R* (impurity A) in mobile phase A and dilute to 100 ml with mobile phase A. Dilute 6 ml of this solution to 25 ml with mobile phase A.

*Column:*

— *size: l* = 0.15 m, Ø = 3.9 mm;

— *stationary phase: spherical end-capped octadecylsilyl silica gel for chromatography R* (4 µm).

*Mobile phase:*

— *mobile phase A*: dissolve 1.08 g of *sodium octanesulphonate R* in 880 ml of the buffer solution and add 50 ml of *methanol R* and 70 ml of *acetonitrile R*;

— *mobile phase B*: dissolve 1.08 g of *sodium octanesulphonate R* in 700 ml of the buffer solution and add 100 ml of *methanol R* and 200 ml of *acetonitrile R*;

| Time (min) | Mobile phase A (per cent *V/V*) | Mobile phase B (per cent *V/V*) |
|---|---|---|
| 0 - 5 | 90 | 10 |
| 5 - 20 | 90 → 40 | 10 → 60 |
| 20 - 25 | 40 | 60 |

*Flow rate*  1.0 ml/min.

*Detection*  Spectrophotometer at 280 nm.

*Injection* 10 μl.

*Retention time* Dopamine = about 5 min.

*System suitability* Reference solution (b):
— *resolution*: minimum 5.0 between the peaks due to impurities B and A.

*Limits:*
— *unspecificied impurities*: for each impurity, not more than the area of the principal peak in the chromatogram obtained with reference solution (a) (0.10 per cent);
— *total*: not more than twice the area of the principal peak in the chromatogram obtained with reference solution (a) (0.2 per cent);
— *disregard limit*: 0.5 times the area of the principal peak in the chromatogram obtained with reference solution (a) (0.05 per cent).

**Heavy metals** (*2.4.8*)
Maximum 20 ppm.

1.0 g complies with test C. Prepare the reference solution using 2 ml of *lead standard solution (10 ppm Pb) R*.

**Loss on drying** (*2.2.32*)
Maximum 0.5 per cent, determined on 1.000 g by drying in an oven at 105 °C for 2 h.

**Sulphated ash** (*2.4.14*)
Maximum 0.1 per cent, determined on 1.0 g.

## ASSAY

*In order to avoid overheating in the reaction medium, mix thoroughly throughout the titration and stop the titration immediately after the end-point has been reached.*

Dissolve 0.150 g in 10 ml of *anhydrous formic acid R*. Add 50 ml of *acetic anhydride R*. Titrate with *0.1 M perchloric acid*, determining the end-point potentiometrically (*2.2.20*).

1 ml of *0.1 M perchloric acid* is equivalent to 18.96 mg of $C_8H_{12}ClNO_2$.

## STORAGE

In an airtight container, under nitrogen, protected from light.

## IMPURITIES

*Other detectable impurities (the following substances would, if present at a sufficient level, be detected by one or other of the tests in the monograph. They are limited by the general acceptance criterion for other/unspecified impurities and/or by the general monograph Substances for pharmaceutical use (2034). It is therefore not necessary to identify these impurities for demonstration of compliance. See also 5.10. Control of impurities in substances for pharmaceutical use)*
*A, B, C.*

A. R = CH₃, R′ = H: 5-(2-aminoethyl)-2-methoxyphenol (4-*O*-methyldopamine),

B. R = H, R′ = CH₃: 4-(2-aminoethyl)-2-methoxyphenol (3-*O*-methyldopamine),

C. R = R′ = CH₃: 2-(3,4-dimethoxyphenyl)ethanamine.

*Ph Eur*

# Dopexamine Hydrochloride

*(Dopexamine Dihydrochloride,
Ph Eur monograph 1748)*

$C_{22}H_{32}N_2O_2,2HCl$    429.4    *86484-91-5*

*Ph Eur*

## DEFINITION

4-[2-[[6-[(2-Phenylethyl)amino]hexyl]amino]ethyl]benzene1,2-diol dihydrochloride.

### Content

98.5 per cent to 101.0 per cent (anhydrous substance).

## CHARACTERS

### Appearance

White or almost white, crystalline powder.

### Solubility

Soluble in water, sparingly soluble in ethanol (96 per cent) and in methanol, practically insoluble in acetone.

## IDENTIFICATION

A. Infrared absorption spectrophotometry (*2.2.24*).

*Comparison* dopexamine dihydrochloride CRS.

B. It gives reaction (a) of chlorides (*2.3.1*).

## TESTS

### Appearance of solution

The solution is clear (*2.2.1*) and not more intensely coloured than reference solution BY₇ (*2.2.2*, *Method II*).

Dissolve 0.10 g in *0.1 M hydrochloric acid* and dilute to 10 ml with the same acid.

### pH (*2.2.3*)
3.7 to 5.7.

Dissolve 0.20 g in *carbon dioxide-free water R* and dilute to 20 ml with the same solvent.

### Related substances
Liquid chromatography (*2.2.29*).

*Test solution* Dissolve 0.100 g of the substance to be examined in mobile phase A and dilute to 10.0 ml with mobile phase A.

*Reference solution (a)* Dilute 1.0 ml of the test solution to 100.0 ml with mobile phase A. Dilute 1.0 ml of this solution to 10.0 ml with mobile phase A.

*Reference solution (b)* Dissolve 5 mg of the substance to be examined and 5 mg of *dopexamine impurity B CRS* in mobile phase A and dilute to 10.0 ml with mobile phase A.

*Reference solution (c)* Dissolve 5 mg of *dopexamine impurity F CRS* in mobile phase A and dilute to 100 ml with mobile phase A.

*Column:*
— *size*: $l$ = 0.15 m, Ø = 4.6 mm;
— *stationary phase*: octadecylsilyl silica gel for chromatography R (5 μm);
— *temperature*: 45 °C.

*Mobile phase:*
— *mobile phase A*: mix 5 volumes of *buffer solution pH 2.5 R* and 95 volumes of *water R*;
— *mobile phase B*: mix 5 volumes of *buffer solution pH 2.5 R* and 95 volumes of a 60 per cent *V/V* solution of *acetonitrile R*;

| Time (min) | Mobile phase A (per cent *V/V*) | Mobile phase B (per cent *V/V*) |
|---|---|---|
| 0 - 10 | 81 → 77 | 19 → 23 |
| 10 - 25 | 77 → 50 | 23 → 50 |
| 25 - 30 | 50 | 50 |
| 30 - 31 | 50 → 81 | 50 → 19 |
| 31 - 39 | 81 | 19 |

*Flow rate*    1 ml/min.

*Detection*    Spectrophotometer at 280 nm.

*Preconditioning of the column*    Rinse for 5 min with a mixture of 19 volumes of mobile phase B and 81 volumes of mobile phase A.

*Injection*    20 µl.

*Relative retention*    With reference to dopexamine (retention time = about 5 min): impurity A = about 0.5; impurity B = about 2.0; impurity C = about 2.3; impurity D = about 2.8; impurity E = about 2.9; impurity F = about 3.0; impurity I = about 3.6; impurity J = about 5.0; impurity K = about 5.9.

*System suitability*    Reference solution (b):
— *resolution*: minimum 2 between the peaks due to dopexamine and impurity B.

*Limits:*
— *correction factors*: for the calculation of content, multiply the peak areas of the following impurities by the corresponding correction factor: impurity A = 1.4; impurity F = 0.7;
— *impurities A, B, C, D, E, F, I, K*: for each impurity, not more than the area of the principal peak in the chromatogram obtained with reference solution (a) (0.1 per cent);
— *unspecified impurities*: for each impurity, not more than the area of the principal peak in the chromatogram obtained with reference solution (a) (0.10 per cent);
— *total*: not more than 5 times the area of the principal peak in the chromatogram obtained with reference solution (a) (0.5 per cent);
— *disregard limit*: 0.5 times the area of the principal peak in the chromatogram obtained with reference solution (a) (0.05 per cent).

**Impurity J**

Liquid chromatography (*2.2.29*) as described in the test for related substances with the following modification.

*Detection*    Spectrophotometer at 210 nm.

*Limit:*
— *impurity J*: not more than the area of the principal peak in the chromatogram obtained with reference solution (a) (0.1 per cent).

**Heavy metals** (*2.4.8*

Maximum 10 ppm.

Dissolve 0.50 g in *water R* and dilute to 20 ml with the same solvent. 12 ml of the solution complies with test A. Prepare the reference solution using *lead standard solution (0.25 ppm Pb) R*. For the evaluation of the results, filter the solutions through a membrane filter (0.45 µm).

**Water** (*2.5.12*)

Maximum 0.5 per cent, determined on 1.00 g.

**Sulphated ash** (*2.4.14*)

Maximum 0.1 per cent, determined on 1.0 g.

**Bacterial endotoxins** (*2.6.14*)

Less than 10 IU/mg.

**ASSAY**

*Carry out the titration immediately after preparation of the test solution. In order to avoid overheating in the reaction medium, mix thoroughly throughout and stop the titration immediately after the end-point has been reached.*

Dissolve 0.150 g in 10 ml of *anhydrous formic acid R*. Add 50 ml of *acetic anhydride R*. Titrate with *0.1 M perchloric acid*, determining the end-point potentiometrically (*2.2.20*).

1 ml of *0.1 M perchloric acid* is equivalent to 21.47 mg of $C_{22}H_{34}Cl_2N_2O_2$.

**STORAGE**

Protected from light.

**IMPURITIES**

*Specified impurities*    A, B, C, D, E, F, I, J, K.

*Other detectable impurities (the following substances would, if present at a sufficient level, be detected by one or other of the tests in the monograph. They are limited by the general acceptance criterion for other/unspecified impurities and/or by the general monograph Substances for pharmaceutical use (2034). It is therefore not necessary to identify these impurities for demonstration of compliance. See also 5.10. Control of impurities in substances for pharmaceutical use)*: G, H.

A. 4,4'-[hexane-1,6-diylbis(iminoethylene)]dibenzene-1,2-diol,

B. R1 = OH, R2 = OCH₃, R3 = H: 2-methoxy-4-[2-[[6-[(2-phenylethyl)amino]hexyl]amino]ethyl]phenol,

C. R1 = OCH₃, R2 = OH, R3 = H: 2-methoxy-5-[2-[[6-[(2-phenylethyl)amino]hexyl]amino]ethyl]phenol,

F. R1 = R2 = OH, R3 = Cl: 4-chloro-5-[2-[[6-[(2-phenylethyl)amino]hexyl]amino]ethyl]benzene-1,2-diol,

H. R1 = R2 = OCH₃, R3 = H: N-[2-(3,4-dimethoxyphenyl)ethyl]-N'-(2-phenylethyl)hexane-1,6-diamine,

J. R1 = R2 = R3 = H: N,N'-bis(2-phenylethyl)hexane-1,6-diamine,

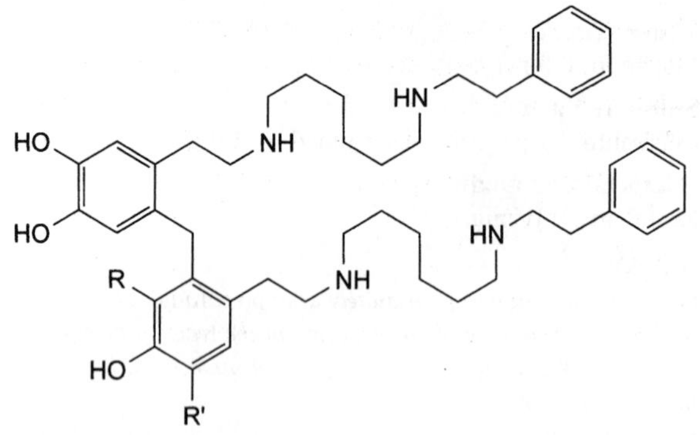

D. R = H, R' = OH: 4,4'-methylenebis[5-[2-[[6-[(2-phenylethyl)amino]hexyl]amino]ethyl]benzene-1,2-diol],

E. R = OH, R' = H: 3-[4,5-dihydroxy-2-[2-[[6-[(2-phenylethyl)amino]hexyl]amino]ethyl]benzyl]-4-[2-[[6-[(2-phenylethyl)amino]hexyl]amino]ethyl]benzene-1,2-diol,

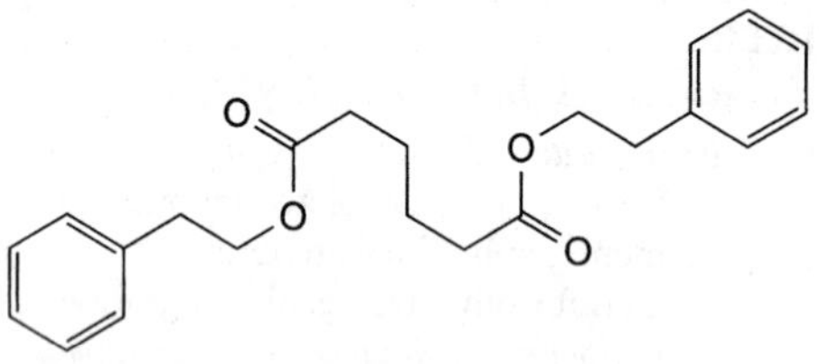

G. bis(2-phenylethyl) hexanedioate,

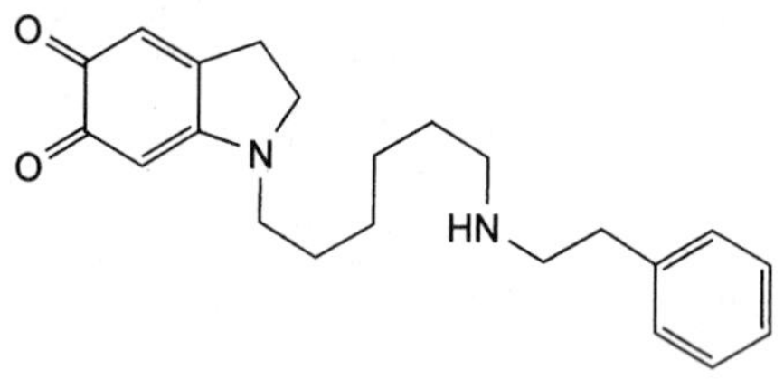

I. 1-[6-[(2-phenylethyl)amino]hexyl]-2,3-dihydro-1*H*-indole5,6-dione (dopexamine aminochrome),

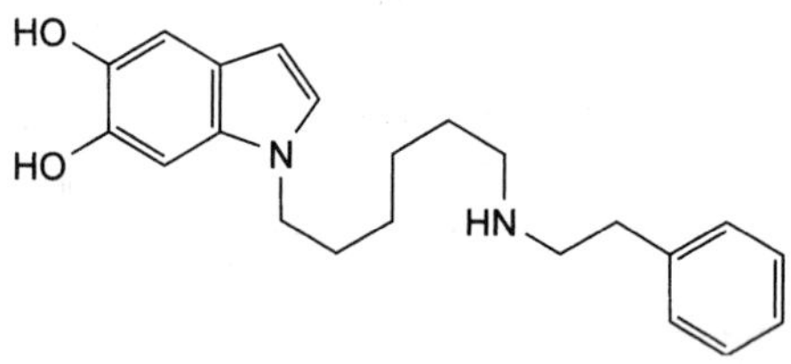

K. 1-[6-[(2-phenylethyl)amino]hexyl]-1*H*-indole-5,6-diol.

*— Ph Eur*

# Dorzolamide Hydrochloride

(*Ph Eur monograph 2359*)

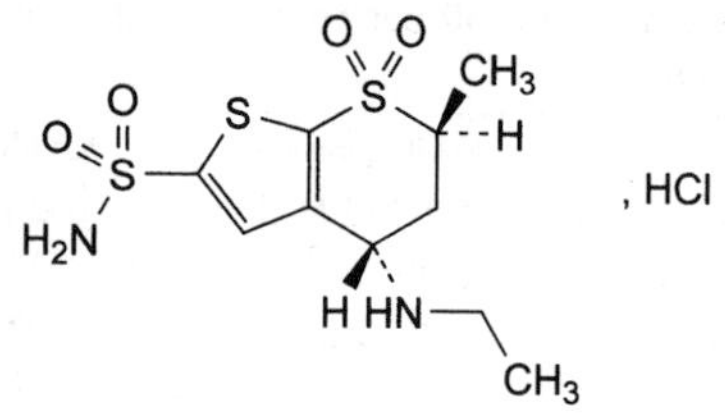

$C_{10}H_{16}N_2O_4S_3,HCl$     360.9     *130693-82-2*

**Action and use**

Carbonic anhydrase inhibitor; treatment of glaucoma and ocular hypertension.

*Ph Eur* _____

## DEFINITION

(4*S*,6*S*)-4-(Ethylamino)-6-methyl-5,6-dihydro-4*H*-thieno[2,3-*b*]thiopyran-2-sulphonamide 7,7-dioxide hydrochloride.

**Content**

99.0 per cent to 101.0 per cent (dried substance).

## CHARACTERS

**Appearance**

White or almost white, crystalline powder.

**Solubility**

Soluble in water, slightly soluble in methanol, very slightly soluble in anhydrous ethanol.

It shows polymorphism (*5.9*).

## IDENTIFICATION

A. Infrared absorption spectrophotometry (*2.2.24*).

*Comparison* dorzolamide hydrochloride CRS.

If the spectra obtained in the solid state show differences, dissolve the substance to be examined and the reference substance separately in *methanol R*, evaporate to dryness and record new spectra using the residues.

B. It complies with the test for impurity A (see Tests).

C. It gives reaction (a) of chlorides (*2.3.1*).

## TESTS

**Impurity A**

Liquid chromatography (*2.2.29*).

*Solvent mixture* acetonitrile R, glacial acetic acid R, 1,1-dimethylethyl methyl ether R (3:10:87 *V/V/V*).

*Test solution* In a centrifuge tube, dissolve 20.0 mg of the substance to be examined in 4 ml of *dilute ammonia R4*, add 4 ml of *ethyl acetate R*, and mix. Separate the organic layer and transfer it to a separate centrifuge tube. Add 4 ml of *ethyl acetate R* to the aqueous layer, mix, separate the organic layer, and combine it with the 1st extract. Evaporate the combined organic layers to dryness in a water-bath at 50 °C under a stream of *nitrogen R*. Dissolve the residue in 3 ml of *acetonitrile R*, add 0.06 ml of *(S)-(−)-α-methylbenzyl isocyanate R*, and heat in a water-bath at 50 °C for 5 min. Evaporate to dryness in a water-bath at 50 °C under a stream of *nitrogen R*. Dissolve the residue in 10 ml of the solvent mixture.

*Reference solution* In a centrifuge tube, dissolve 18.0 mg of *dorzolamide hydrochloride CRS* and 2.0 mg of *dorzolamide impurity A CRS* in 4 ml of *dilute ammonia R4*, and proceed as indicated for the test solution beginning with "add 4 ml of *ethyl acetate R*, and mix".

*Column:*
— *size:* l = 0.25 m, Ø = 4.6 mm;
— *stationary phase: silica gel for chromatography R (5 μm).*

*Mobile phase* *water R, acetonitrile R, heptane R, 1,1-dimethylethyl methyl ether R (0.2:2:35:63 V/V/V/V).*

*Flow rate* 2 ml/min.

*Detection* Spectrophotometer at 254 nm.

*Injection* 10 μl.

*Run time* 3 times the retention time of dorzolamide.

*Relative retention* With reference to dorzolamide (retention time = about 10 min): impurity A = about 1.4.

*System suitability* Reference solution:
— *resolution:* minimum 4.0 between the peaks due to dorzolamide and impurity A.

Calculate the percentage content of impurity A using the following expression:

$$\frac{A}{A + B} \times 100$$

A = area of the peak due to impurity A in the chromatogram obtained with the test solution;
B = area of the peak due to dorzolamide in the chromatogram obtained with the test solution.

*Limit:*
— *impurity A:* maximum 0.5 per cent.

**Related substances**
Liquid chromatography (2.2.29).

*Test solution* Dissolve 30.0 mg of the substance to be examined in mobile phase A and dilute to 50.0 ml with mobile phase A.

*Reference solution (a)* Dissolve 1.0 ml of the test solution to 100.0 ml with mobile phase A. Dilute 1.0 ml of this solution to 10.0 ml with mobile phase A.

*Reference solution (b)* Dissolve 2 mg of *dorzolamide for system suitability CRS* (containing impurity C) in 2 ml of mobile phase A.

*Column:*
— *size:* l = 0.25 m, Ø = 4.6 mm;
— *stationary phase: end-capped octadecylsilyl silica gel for chromatography R (5 μm);*
— *temperature:* 35 °C.

*Mobile phase:*
— mobile phase A: mix 65 ml of *acetonitrile R* and 935 ml of a 3.7 g/l solution of *potassium dihydrogen phosphate R;*
— *mobile phase B: acetonitrile R;*

| Time (min) | Mobile phase A (per cent V/V) | Mobile phase B (per cent V/V) |
|---|---|---|
| 0 - 15 | 100 | 0 |
| 15 - 30 | 100 → 50 | 0 → 50 |
| 30 - 37 | 50 → 100 | 50 → 0 |
| 37 - 44 | 100 | 0 |

*Flow rate* 1.5 ml/min.

*Detection* Spectrophotometer at 254 nm.

*Injection* 10 μl.

*Identification of impurities* Use the chromatogram supplied with *dorzolamide for system suitability CRS* and the

chromatogram obtained with reference solution (b) to identify the peak due to impurity C.

*Relative retention* With reference to dorzolamide (retention time = about 11 min): Impurity C = about 0.9.

*System suitability* Reference solution (b):
— *resolution:* minimum 2.0 between the peaks due to impurity C and dorzolamide.

*Limits:*
— *impurity C:* not more than 1.5 times the area of the principal peak in the chromatogram obtained with reference solution (a) (0.15 per cent);
— *unspecified impurities:* for each impurity, not more than the area of the principal peak in the chromatogram obtained with reference solution (a) (0.10 per cent);
— *total:* not more than 3 times the area of the principal peak in the chromatogram obtained with reference solution (a) (0.3 per cent);
— *disregard limit:* 0.5 times the area of the principal peak in the chromatogram obtained with reference solution (a) (0.05 per cent).

**Loss on drying** (2.2.32)
Maximum 0.5 per cent, determined on 1.000 g by drying in an oven at 105 °C.

**Sulphated ash** (2.4.14)
Maximum 0.1 per cent, determined on 1.0 g.

**ASSAY**
Dissolve 0.150 g in a mixture of 5.0 ml of *0.01 M hydrochloric acid* and 50 ml of *ethanol (96 per cent) R*, using sonication if necessary. Carry out a potentiometric titration (2.2.20), using *0.1 M sodium hydroxide*. Read the volume added between the 1st and the 3rd points of inflexion.

1 ml of *0.1 M sodium hydroxide* is equivalent to 18.05 mg of $C_{10}H_{17}N_2O_4S_3Cl$.

**IMPURITIES**
*Specified impurities* A, C.

*Other detectable impurities* (The following substances would, if present at a sufficient level, be detected by one or other of the tests in the monograph. They are limited by the general acceptance criterion for other/unspecified impurities and/or by the general monograph *Substances for pharmaceutical use (2034)*. It is therefore not necessary to identify these impurities for demonstration of compliance. See also 5.10. *Control of impurities in substances for pharmaceutical use)*: B, D.

A. (4R,6R)-4-(ethylamino)-6-methyl-5,6-dihydro-4H-thieno[2,3-b]thiopyran-2-sulphonamide 7,7-dioxide,

B. (4RS,6SR)-4-(ethylamino)-6-methyl-5,6-dihydro-4H-thieno[2,3-b]thiopyran-2-sulphonamide 7,7-dioxide,

C. R = CH₂-CH₂-B(OH)₂: [2-[[(4S,6S)-6-methyl-7,7-dioxo-2-sulphamoyl-4,5,6,7-tetrahydro-7λ⁶-thieno[2,3-b]thiopyran-4-yl]amino]ethyl]boronic acid,

D. R = H: (4S,6S)-4-amino-6-methyl-5,6-dihydro-4H-thieno[2,3-b]thiopyran-2-sulphonamide 7,7-dioxide.

*_____ Ph Eur*

# Dosulepin Hydrochloride

(Ph Eur monograph 1314)

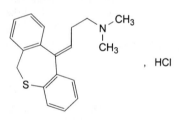

C₁₉H₂₁NS,HCl        331.9        *1897-15-4*

**Action and use**
Monoamine reuptake inhibitor; tricyclic antidepressant.

**Preparations**
Dosulepin Capsules
Dosulepin Tablets

*Ph Eur* _____

## DEFINITION
(E)-3-(Dibenzo[b,e]thiepin-11(6H)-ylidene)-N,N-dimethylpropan-1-amine hydrochloride.

## Content
98.0 per cent to 101.0 per cent (dried substance).

## CHARACTERS
**Appearance**
White or faintly yellow, crystalline powder.

**Solubility**
Freely soluble in water, in alcohol and in methylene chloride.

## IDENTIFICATION
*First identification*  B, D.

*Second identification*  A, C, D.

A. Dissolve 25.0 mg in a 1 g/l solution of *hydrochloric acid R* in *methanol R* and dilute to 100.0 ml with the same solution. Dilute 2.0 ml to 50.0 ml with a 1 g/l solution of *hydrochloric*

*acid R* in *methanol R*. Examined between 220 nm and 350 nm (*2.2.25*), the solution shows 2 absorption maxima at 231 nm and 306 nm and a shoulder at about 260 nm. The specific absorbance at the maximum at 231 nm is 660 to 730.

B. Infrared absorption spectrophotometry (*2.2.24*).

*Preparation*  Discs.

*Comparison*  dosulepin hydrochloride CRS.

C. Dissolve about 1 mg in 5 ml of *sulphuric acid R*. A dark red colour is produced.

D. It gives reaction (b) of chlorides (*2.3.1*).

## TESTS
**Appearance of solution**
The solution is clear (*2.2.1*) and not more intensely coloured than reference solution Y₅ (*2.2.2, Method II*).

Dissolve 1 g in *water R* and dilute to 20 ml with the same solvent.

**pH** (*2.2.3*)
4.2 to 5.2.

Dissolve 1 g in *carbon dioxide-free water R* and dilute to 10 ml with the same solvent.

**Impurity E and related substances**
Liquid chromatography (*2.2.29*). *Prepare the solutions immediately before use and protect from light.*

*Test solution*  Dissolve 50.0 mg of the substance to be examined in 5 ml of *methanol R* and dilute to 100.0 ml with the mobile phase.

*Reference solution (a)*  Dissolve 12.5 mg of *dosulepin impurity A CRS* in 5 ml of *methanol R* and dilute to 50.0 ml with the mobile phase. Dilute 0.5 ml to 100.0 ml with the mobile phase.

*Reference solution (b)*  Dissolve 10.0 mg of *dosulepin hydrochloride CRS* in 5 ml of *methanol R* and dilute to 20.0 ml with the mobile phase.

*Column:*
— *size: l* = 0.25 m, Ø = 4.6 mm;
— *stationary phase: nitrile silica gel for chromatography R1* (5 μm);
— *temperature*: 35 °C.

*Mobile phase*  0.83 per cent *V/V* solution of *perchloric acid R*, *propanol R*, *methanol R*, *water R* (1:10:30:60 *V/V/V/V*).

*Flow rate*  1 ml/min.

*Detection*  Spectrophotometer at 229 nm.

*Injection*  5 μl.

*Run time*  2.5 times the retention time of dosulepin (E-isomer).

*Relative retention*  With reference to dosulepin (E-isomer; retention time = about 25 min): impurity E = about 0.9.

*System suitability*  Reference solution (b):
— *peak-to-valley ratio*: minimum 4, where $H_p$ = height above the baseline of the peak due to impurity E and $H_v$ = height above the baseline of the lowest point of the curve separating this peak from the peak due to dosulepin (E-isomer).

*Limits:*
— *impurity E*: not more than 5 per cent of the sum of the areas of the peak due to impurity E and the principal peak in the chromatogram obtained with the test solution;
— *impurity A*: not more than the area of the principal peak in the chromatogram obtained with reference solution (a) (0.25 per cent);

— *any other impurity*: not more than 0.4 times the area of the principal peak in the chromatogram obtained with reference solution (a) (0.1 per cent);

— *total of other impurities and impurity A*: not more than twice the area of the principal peak in the chromatogram obtained with reference solution (a) (0.5 per cent);

— *disregard limit*: 0.2 times the area of the principal peak in the chromatogram obtained with reference solution (a) (0.05 per cent).

**Heavy metals** (*2.4.8*)

Maximum 20 ppm.

1.0 g complies with limit test C. Prepare the standard using 2 ml of *lead standard solution (10 ppm Pb) R*.

**Loss on drying** (*2.2.32*)

Maximum 0.5 per cent, determined on 1.000 g by drying in an oven at 105 °C.

**Sulphated ash** (*2.4.14*)

Maximum 0.1 per cent, determined on 1.0 g.

**ASSAY**

Dissolve 0.250 g in a mixture of 5 ml of *anhydrous acetic acid R* and 35 ml of *acetic anhydride R*. Titrate with *0.1 M perchloric acid*, determining the end-point potentiometrically (*2.2.20*).

1 ml of *0.1 M perchloric acid* is equivalent to 33.19 mg of $C_{19}H_{22}ClNS$.

**STORAGE**

Protected from light.

**IMPURITIES**

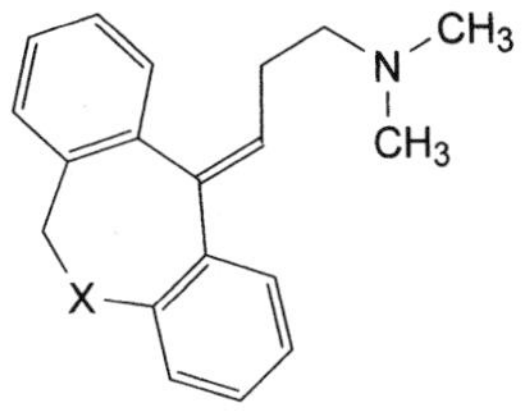

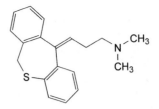

A. X = SO: (*E*)-3-(5-oxo-5$\lambda^4$-dibenzo[*b,e*]thiepin-11(6*H*)-ylidene)-*N,N*-dimethylpropan-1-amine,

D. X = SO$_2$: (*E*)-3-(5,5-dioxo-5$\lambda^6$-dibenzo[*b,e*]thiepin-11(6*H*)-ylidene)-*N,N*-dimethylpropan-1-amine,

and enantiomer

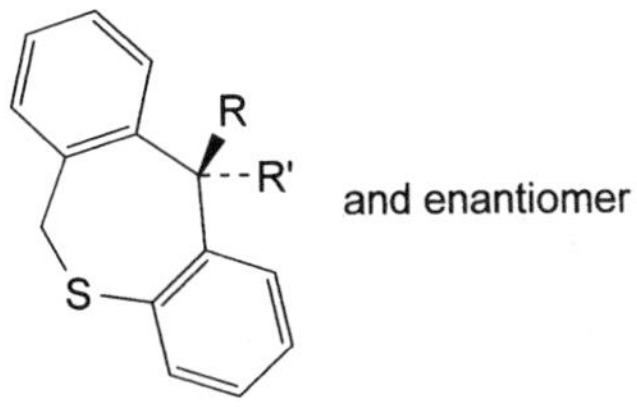

B. R + R′ = O: dibenzo[*b,e*]thiepin-11(6*H*)-one,

C. R = OH, R′ = [CH$_2$]$_3$-N(CH$_3$)$_2$: (11*RS*)-11-[3-(dimethylamino)propyl]-6,11-dihydrodibenzo[*b,e*]thiepin-11-ol,

E. (*Z*)-3-(dibenzo[*b,e*]thiepin-11(6*H*)-ylidene)-*N,N*-dimethylpropan-1-amine.

_____ *Ph Eur*

# Doxapram Hydrochloride

(*Ph Eur monograph 1201*)

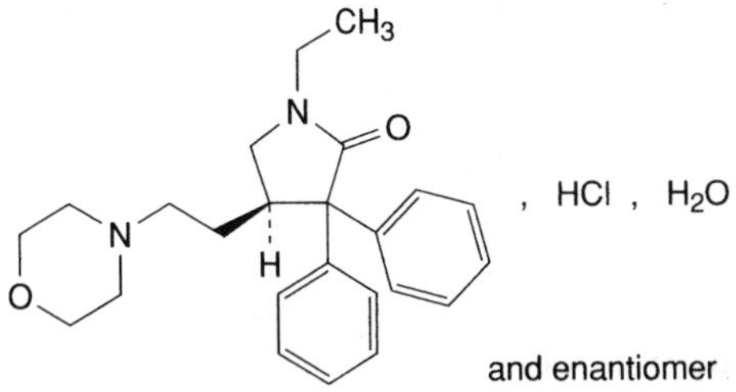

$C_{24}H_{30}N_2O_2,HCl,H_2O$     433.0          *7081-53-0*

**Action and use**

Respiratory stimulant.

**Preparation**

Doxapram Injection

*Ph Eur* _____

**DEFINITION**

(4*RS*)-1-Ethyl-4-[2-(morpholin-4-yl)ethyl]-3,3-diphenylpyrrolidin-2-one hydrochloride.

**Content**

98.0 per cent to 100.5 per cent (dried substance).

**CHARACTERS**

**Appearance**

White or almost white, crystalline powder.

**Solubility**

Soluble in water, in alcohol and in methylene chloride.

**IDENTIFICATION**

*First identification* A, C.

*Second identification* B, C.

A. Infrared absorption spectrophotometry (*2.2.24*).

*Preparation* Discs.

*Comparison* doxapram hydrochloride CRS.

B. Thin-layer chromatography (*2.2.27*).

*Test solution* Dissolve 10 mg of the substance to be examined in *methanol R* and dilute to 10 ml with the same solvent.

*Reference solution* Dissolve 10 mg of *doxapram hydrochloride CRS* in *methanol R* and dilute to 10 ml with the same solvent.

*Plate* TLC silica gel plate R.

*Mobile phase* Solution of *ammonia R* containing 17 g/l of NH$_3$, 2-*propanol R*, 2-*methylpropanol R* (10:10:80 *V/V/V*).

*Application* 10 µl.

*Development*   Over a path of 15 cm.

*Drying*   In air.

*Detection*   Spray with *dilute potassium iodobismuthate solution R* and examine immediately.

*Results*   The principal spot in the chromatogram obtained with the test solution is similar in position, colour and size to the principal spot in the chromatogram obtained with the reference solution.

C. It gives reaction (a) of chlorides (*2.3.1*).

## TESTS

### Solution S

Dissolve 2.500 g in *carbon dioxide-free water R* and dilute to 50.0 ml with the same solvent.

### Appearance of solution

The solution is clear (*2.2.1*) and colourless (*2.2.2, Method II*).

Dilute 10 ml of solution S to 25 ml with *water R*.

### pH (*2.2.3*)

3.5 to 5.0.

Dilute 5 ml of solution S to 25 ml with *carbon dioxide-free water R*.

### Optical rotation (*2.2.7*)

− 0.10° to + 0.10°, determined on solution S.

### Related substances

Liquid chromatography (*2.2.29*). *Prepare the solutions immediately before use.*

*Test solution*   Dissolve 10.0 mg of the substance to be examined in the mobile phase and dilute to 10.0 ml with the mobile phase.

*Reference solution (a)*   Dilute 1.0 ml of the test solution to 100.0 ml with the mobile phase.

*Reference solution (b)*   Dilute 1.0 ml of reference solution (a) to 5.0 ml with the mobile phase.

*Reference solution (c)*   Dissolve 5 mg of *doxapram impurity B CRS* in the mobile phase and dilute to 5.0 ml with the mobile phase. To 1.0 ml of the solution, add 1.0 ml of the test solution and dilute to 100.0 ml with the mobile phase.

*Column:*
— *size: l* = 0.25 m, Ø = 4.6 mm;
— *stationary phase:* spherical *end-capped octadecylsilyl silica gel for chromatography R* (5 μm) with a carbon loading of 14 per cent, a specific surface area of 350 m₂/g and a pore size of 10 nm.

*Mobile phase*   Mix 50 volumes of *acetonitrile R* and 50 volumes of a 0.82 g/l solution of *sodium acetate R* adjusted to pH 4.5 with *glacial acetic acid R*.

*Flow rate*   1.5 ml/min.

*Detection*   Spectrophotometer at 214 nm.

*Injection*   20 μl.

*Run time*   4 times the retention time of doxapram.

*Retention time*   Doxapram = about 6 min.

*System suitability*   Reference solution (c):
— *resolution:* minimum of 3.0 between the peaks corresponding to doxapram and to impurity B.

*Limits:*
— *any impurity:* not more than the area of the principal peak in the chromatogram obtained with reference solution (b) (0.2 per cent);

— *total:* not more than the area of the principal peak in the chromatogram obtained with reference solution (a) (1.0 per cent);
— *disregard limit:* 0.05 times the area of the principal peak in the chromatogram obtained with reference solution (a) (0.05 per cent).

### Heavy metals (*2.4.8*)

Maximum 20 ppm.

Dissolve 2.0 g in a mixture of 15 volumes of *water R* and 85 volumes of *methanol R* and dilute to 20 ml with the same mixture of solvents. 12 ml of the solution complies with limit test B. Prepare the standard using lead standard solution (2 ppm Pb) obtained by diluting *lead standard solution (100 ppm Pb) R* with a mixture of 15 volumes of *water R* and 85 volumes of *methanol R*.

### Loss on drying (*2.2.32*)

3.0 per cent to 4.5 per cent, determined on 1.000 g by drying in an oven at 105 °C.

### Sulphated ash (*2.4.14*)

Maximum 0.1 per cent, determined on 1.0 g.

## ASSAY

Dissolve 0.300 g in a mixture of 10 ml of *0.01 M hydrochloric acid* and 50 ml of *alcohol R*. Carry out a potentiometric titration (*2.2.20*) using *0.1 M sodium hydroxide*. Read the volume added between the 2 points of inflexion.

1 ml of *0.1 M sodium hydroxide* is equivalent to 41.50 mg of $C_{24}H_{31}ClN_2O_2$.

## IMPURITIES

A. R = Cl: (4*RS*)-4-(2-chloroethyl)-1-ethyl-3,3-diphenylpyrrolidin-2-one,

B. R = NH-CH₂-CH₂-OH: (4*RS*)-1-ethyl-4-[2-[(2-hydroxyethyl)amino]ethyl]-3,3-diphenylpyrrolidin-2-one.

*Ph Eur*

# Doxazosin Mesilate

(*Ph Eur monograph 2125*)

$C_{23}H_{25}N_5O_5,CH_3SO_3H$     547.6     *77883-43-3*

## Action and use

Alpha₁-adrenoceptor antagonist.

*Ph Eur*

# DEFINITION

1-(4-Amino-6,7-dimethoxyquinazolin-2-yl)-4-[(2*RS*)-2,3-dihydro-1,4-benzodioxin-2-ylcarbonyl]piperazine methanesulphonate.

## Content

98.0 per cent to 102.0 per cent (anhydrous substance).

# PRODUCTION

The production method must be evaluated to determine the potential for formation of alkyl mesilates, which is particularly likely to occur if the reaction medium contains lower alcohols. Where necessary, the production method is validated to demonstrate that alkyl mesilates are not detectable in the final product.

# CHARACTERS

## Appearance

White or almost white crystalline powder.

## Solubility

Slightly soluble in water, soluble in a mixture of 15 volumes of water and 35 volumes of tetrahydrofuran, slightly soluble in methanol, practically insoluble in acetone.

It shows polymorphism (*5.9*), some forms may be hygroscopic.

# IDENTIFICATION

Infrared absorption spectrophotometry (*2.2.24*).

*Comparison   doxazosin mesilate CRS.*

If the spectra obtained in the solid state show differences, mix 1 part of the substance to be examined and 1 part of the reference substance separately with 10 parts of *anhydrous ethanol R* and heat to boiling. Continue heating the suspension under a reflux condenser for about 3 h. Cool and filter. Record new spectra using the previously dried residues on the filters.

# TESTS

## Appearance of solution

The solution is clear (*2.2.1*) and not more intensely coloured than reference solution BY$_6$ (*2.2.2, Method II*).

Dissolve 1.0 g in a mixture of 15 ml of *water R* and 35 ml of *tetrahydrofuran R*.

## Related substances

Liquid chromatography (*2.2.29*).

*Test solution*   Dissolve 25.0 mg of the substance to be examined in 5 ml of mobile phase B, adding *water R*, and dilute to 50.0 ml with *water R*.

*Reference solution (a)*   Dilute 5.0 ml of the test solution to 100.0 ml with *water R*. Dilute 2.0 ml of this solution to 100.0 ml with *water R*.

*Reference solution (b)*   Dissolve 5 mg of *doxazosin impurity D CRS* and 5 mg of *doxazosin impurity F CRS* in 5 ml of mobile phase B, adding *water R*, and dilute to 50.0 ml with *water R*. Dilute 10.0 ml of this solution to 50.0 ml with *water R*.

*Reference solution (c)*   Dilute 5.0 ml of reference solution (a) to 10.0 ml with *water R*.

*Reference solution (d)*   Dissolve 25.0 mg of *doxazosin mesilate CRS* in 5 ml of mobile phase B, adding *water R*, and dilute to 50.0 ml with *water R*.

*Column:*
— *size: l* = 0.25 m, Ø = 4.0 mm;
— *stationary phase: base-deactivated octylsilyl silica gel for chromatography R* (5 μm);

— *temperature*: 35 °C.

*Mobile phase:*
— *mobile phase A*: 10 g/l solution of *phosphoric acid R*;
— *mobile phase B*: 10 g/l solution of *phosphoric acid R* in *acetonitrile R1*;

| Time (min) | Mobile phase A (per cent *V/V*) | Mobile phase B (per cent *V/V*) |
|---|---|---|
| 0 - 5 | 90 | 10 |
| 5 - 40 | 90 → 50 | 10 → 50 |
| 40 - 45 | 50 | 50 |
| 45 - 46 | 50 → 90 | 50 → 10 |
| 46 - 50 | 90 | 10 |

*Flow rate*   0.8 ml/min.

*Detection*   Spectrophotometer at 210 nm.

*Injection*   10 μl of the test solution and reference solutions (a), (b) and (c).

*Relative retention*   With reference to doxazosin (retention time = about 30 min): impurity D = about 0.5; impurity F = about 0.6.

*System suitability*   Reference solution (b):
— *resolution*: minimum 4.5 between the peaks due to impurities D and F.

*Limits:*
— *unspecified impurities*: for each impurity, not more than the area of the principal peak in the chromatogram obtained with reference solution (a) (0.10 per cent);
— *total*: not more than 3 times the area of the principal peak in the chromatogram obtained with reference solution (a) (0.3 per cent);
— *disregard limit*: the area of the principal peak in the chromatogram obtained with reference solution (c) (0.05 per cent).

**Water** (*2.5.12*)
Maximum 1.5 per cent, determined on 0.500 g.

**Sulphated ash** (*2.4.14*)
Maximum 0.1 per cent, determined on 1.0 g.

# ASSAY

Liquid chromatography (*2.2.29*) as described in the test for related substances with the following modification.

*Injection*   Test solution and reference solution (d).

Calculate the percentage content of $C_{24}H_{29}N_5O_8S$ using the chromatogram obtained with reference solution (d) and the declared content of *doxazosin mesilate CRS*.

# STORAGE

In an airtight container.

# IMPURITIES

*Other detectable impurities* (the following substances would, if present at a sufficient level, be detected by one or other of the tests in the monograph. They are limited by the general acceptance criterion for other/unspecified impurities and/or by the general monograph *Substances for pharmaceutical use* (2034). It is therefore not necessary to identify these impurities for demonstration of compliance. See also *5.10*.
*Control of impurities in substances for pharmaceutical use)*

*A, B, C, D, E, F, G, H.*

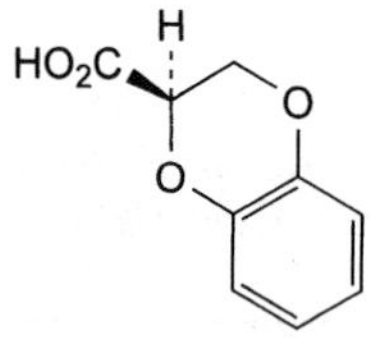

A. (2RS)-2,3-dihydro-1,4-benzodioxine-2-carboxylic acid,

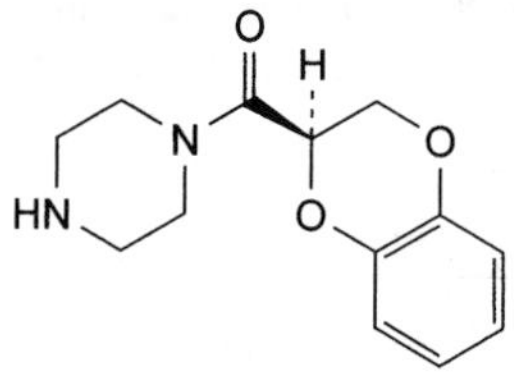

B. 1-[(2RS)-2,3-dihydro-1,4-benzodioxin-2-ylcarbonyl]piperazine,

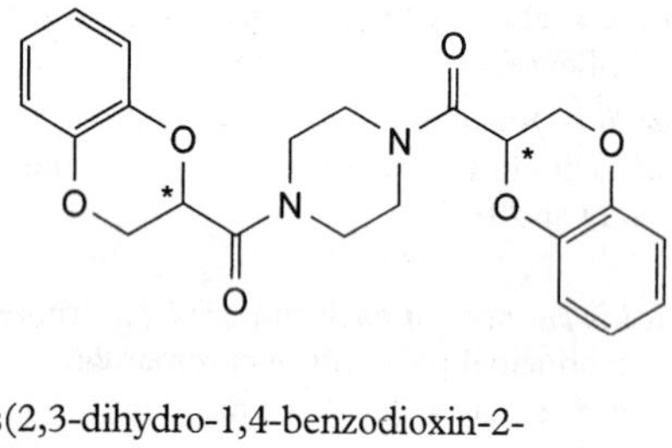

C. 1,4-bis(2,3-dihydro-1,4-benzodioxin-2-ylcarbonyl)piperazine,

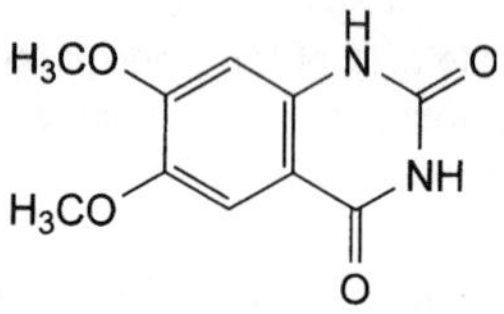

D. 6,7-dimethoxyquinazoline-2,4(1H,3H)-dione,

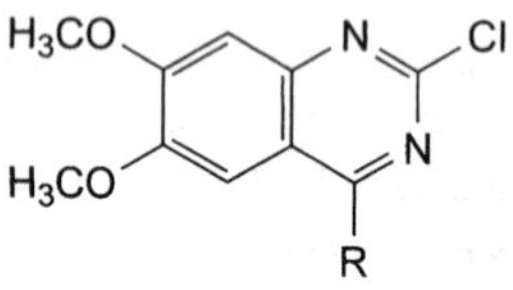

E. R = Cl: 2,4-dichloro-6,7-dimethoxyquinazoline,
F. R = NH₂: 2-chloro-6,7-dimethoxyquinazolin-4-amine,

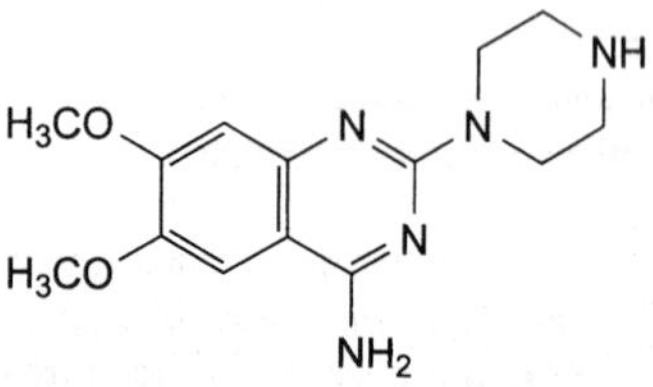

G. 6,7-dimethoxy-2-(piperazin-1-yl)quinazolin-4-amine,

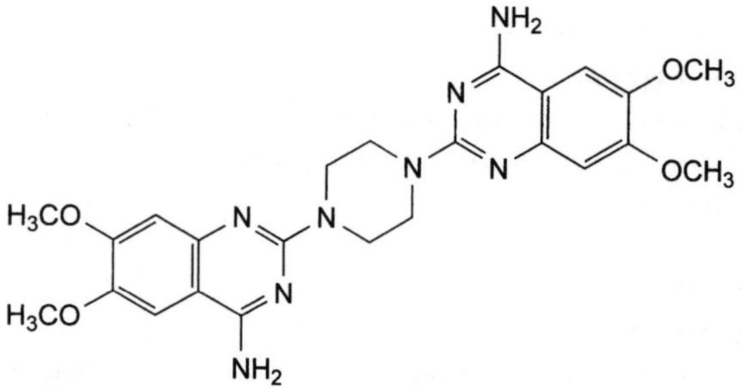

H. 2,2′-(piperazine-1,4-diyl)bis(6,7-dimethoxyquinazolin-4-amine).

*_____ Ph Eur*

# Doxepin Hydrochloride

(*Ph Eur monograph 1096*)

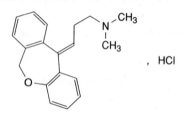

, HCl

$C_{19}H_{21}NO,HCl$      315.8      *1229-29-4*

### Action and use
Monoamine reuptake inhibitor; tricyclic antidepressant.

### Preparation
Doxepin Capsules

*Ph Eur* _____

### DEFINITION
(*E*)-3-(Dibenzo[*b,e*]oxepin-11(6*H*)-ylidene)-*N,N*-dimethylpropan-1-amine hydrochloride.

### Content
98.0 per cent to 101.0 per cent of $C_{19}H_{22}ClNO$ (dried substance).

### CHARACTERS
#### Appearance
White or almost white, crystalline powder.

#### Solubility
Freely soluble in water, in ethanol (96 per cent) and in methylene chloride.

### IDENTIFICATION
*First identification*    C, E.

*Second identification*    A, B, D, E.

A. Melting point (*2.2.14*): 185 °C to 191 °C.

B. Ultraviolet and visible absorption spectrophotometry (*2.2.25*).

*Test solution*    Dissolve 50.0 mg in a 1 g/l solution of *hydrochloric acid R* in *methanol R* and dilute to 100.0 ml with the same acid solution. Dilute 5.0 ml to 50.0 ml with a 1 g/l solution of *hydrochloric acid R* in *methanol R*.

*Spectral range*    230-350 nm.

*Absorption maximum*    At 297 nm.

*Specific absorbance at the absorption maximum*    128 to 142.

C. Infrared absorption spectrophotometry (2.2.24).

*Comparison   doxepin hydrochloride CRS.*

D. Dissolve about 5 mg in 2 ml of *sulphuric acid R*. A dark red colour is produced.

E. Solution S (see Tests) gives reaction (a) of chlorides (2.3.1).

## TESTS
### Solution S
Dissolve 1.5 g in *carbon dioxide-free water R* and dilute to 30 ml with the same solvent.

### Appearance of solution
Dilute 10 ml of solution S to 25 ml with *water R*. The solution is clear (2.2.1) and colourless (2.2.2, Method II).

### Acidity
To 10 ml of solution S add 0.1 ml of *methyl red solution R*. Not more than 0.1 ml of *0.1 M sodium hydroxide* is required to change the colour of the indicator to yellow.

### Related substances
Liquid chromatography (2.2.29). *Prepare the solutions immediately before use and protect them from light.*

*Phosphate buffer solution*   Dissolve 1.42 g of *anhydrous disodium hydrogen phosphate R* in *water R*, adjust to pH 7.7 with *dilute phosphoric acid R* and dilute to 1000 ml with *water R*.

*Solvent mixture*   Mix 1 volume of *1 M sodium hydroxide* and 250 volumes of the mobile phase.

*Test solution*   Dissolve 50 mg of the substance to be examined in the solvent mixture and dilute to 50.0 ml with the solvent mixture.

*Reference solution (a)*   Dilute 1.0 ml of the test solution to 100.0 ml with the solvent mixture. Dilute 1.0 ml of this solution to 10.0 ml with the solvent mixture.

*Reference solution (b)*   Dissolve the contents of a vial of *doxepin for system suitability CRS* (containing impurities A, B and C) in 1.0 ml of mobile phase.

*Column:*
— *size: l = 0.25 m, Ø = 4.6 mm;*
— *stationary phase: end-capped octadecylsilyl silica gel for chromatography R (5 μm);*
— *temperature: 30 °C.*

*Mobile phase   acetonitrile R1*, phosphate buffer solution, *methanol R1* (20:30:50 *V/V/V*).

*Flow rate*   1.0 ml/min.

*Detection*   Spectrophotometer at 215 nm.

*Injection*   20 μl.

*Run time*   1.5 times the retention time of doxepin.

*Identification of impurities*   Use the chromatogram supplied with *doxepin for system suitability CRS* and the chromatogram obtained with reference solution (b) to identify the peaks due to impurities A, B and C.

*Relative retention*   With reference to doxepin (retention time = about 18 min): impurity A = about 0.5; impurity C = about 0.6; impurity B = about 0.7; the peak due to doxepin might show a shoulder caused by the (Z)-isomer (impurity D).

*System suitability*   Reference solution (b):
— *resolution*: minimum 1.5 between the peaks due to impurities A and C, and minimum 1.5 between the peaks due to impurities C and B;
— the chromatogram obtained is similar to the chromatogram supplied with *doxepin for system suitability CRS*.

*Limits:*
— *correction factor*: for the calculation of content, multiply the peak area of impurity B by 1.7;
— *impurities A, B*: for each impurity, not more than the area of the principal peak in the chromatogram obtained with reference solution (a) (0.1 per cent);
— *impurity C*: not more than twice the area of the principal peak in the chromatogram obtained with reference solution (a) (0.2 per cent);
— *unspecified impurities*: for each impurity, not more than the area of the principal peak in the chromatogram obtained with reference solution (a) (0.10 per cent);
— *total*: not more than 3 times the area of the principal peak in the chromatogram obtained with reference solution (a) (0.3 per cent);
— *disregard limit*: 0.5 times the area of the principal peak in the chromatogram obtained with reference solution (a) (0.05 per cent).

### (Z)-Isomer
Liquid chromatography (2.2.29).

*Test solution*   Dissolve 20.0 mg of the substance to be examined in the mobile phase and dilute to 20.0 ml with the mobile phase. Dilute 1.0 ml of this solution to 10.0 ml with the mobile phase.

*Column:*
— *size: l = 0.12 m, Ø = 4 mm;*
— *stationary phase: spherical octylsilyl silica gel for chromatography R (5 μm)* with a specific surface area of 220 m²/g and a pore size of 80 nm;
— *temperature*: 50 °C.

*Mobile phase*   Mix 30 volumes of *methanol R* and 70 volumes of a 30 g/l solution of *sodium dihydrogen phosphate R* previously adjusted to pH 2.5 with *phosphoric acid R*.

*Flow rate*   1 ml/min.

*Detection*   Spectrophotometer at 254 nm.

*Injection*   20 μl.

*System suitability:*
— *resolution*: minimum 1.5 between the peaks due to the (E)-isomer (1st peak) and to the (Z)-isomer (2nd peak).

*Results:*
— calculate the ratio of the area of the peak due to the (E)-isomer to the area of the peak due to the (Z)-isomer: this ratio is 4.4 to 6.7 (13.0 per cent to 18.5 per cent of the (Z)-isomer).

### Heavy metals (2.4.8)
Maximum 20 ppm.

Dissolve 2.0 g in *water R* and dilute to 20 ml with the same solvent. 12 ml of the solution complies with test A. Prepare the reference solution using *lead standard solution (2 ppm Pb) R*.

### Loss on drying (2.2.32)
Maximum 0.5 per cent, determined on 1.000 g by drying in an oven at 105 °C.

### Sulphated ash (2.4.14)
Maximum 0.1 per cent, determined on 1.0 g.

## ASSAY
Dissolve 0.250 g in a mixture of 5 ml of *anhydrous acetic acid R* and 35 ml of *acetic anhydride R*. Using 0.2 ml of *crystal violet solution R* as indicator, titrate with *0.1 M perchloric acid* until the colour changes from blue to green.

1 ml of *0.1 M perchloric acid* is equivalent to 31.58 mg of $C_{19}H_{22}ClNO$.

## STORAGE
Protected from light.

## IMPURITIES
*Specified impurities*    *A, B, C, D.*

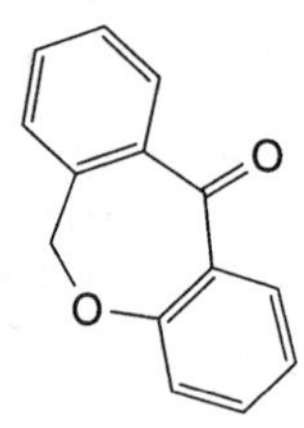

A. dibenzo[*b*,*e*]oxepin-11(6*H*)-one (doxepinone),

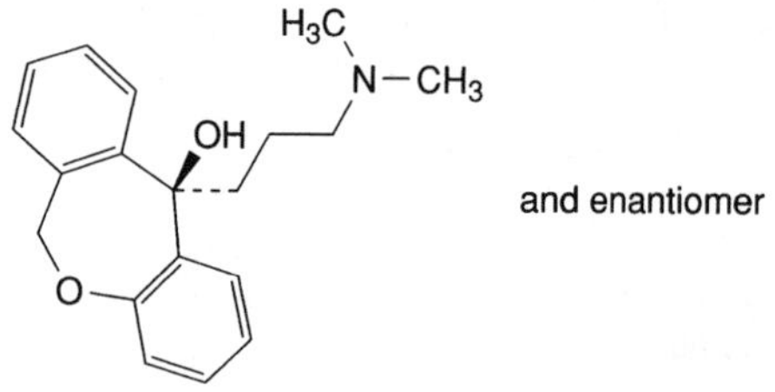

and enantiomer

B. (11*RS*)-11-[3-(dimethylamino)propyl]-6,11-dihydrodibenzo[*b*,*e*]oxepin-11-ol (doxepinol),

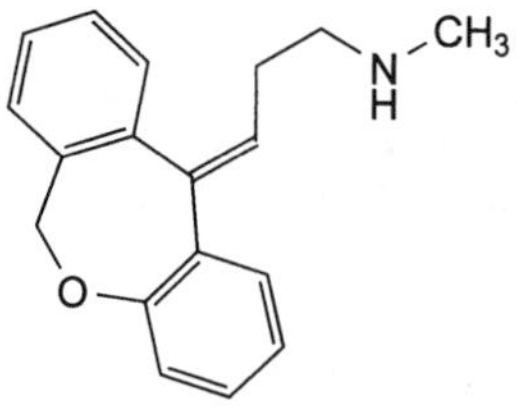

C. (*E*)-3-(dibenzo[*b*,*e*]oxepin-11(6*H*)-ylidene)-*N*-methylpropan-1-amine (desmethyldoxepin),

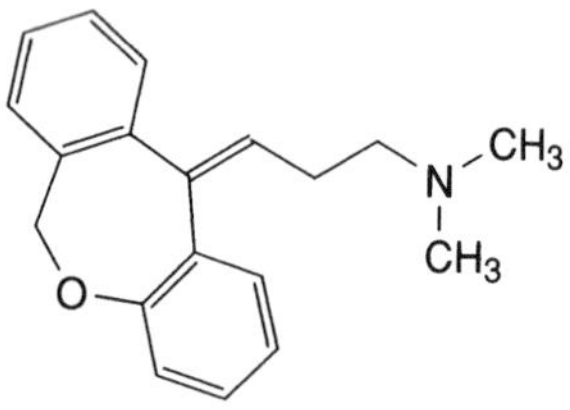

D. (*Z*)-3-(dibenzo[*b*,*e*]oxepin-11(6*H*)-ylidene)-*N*,*N*-dimethylpropan-1-amine.

— *Ph Eur*

# Doxorubicin Hydrochloride

(*Ph Eur monograph 0714*)

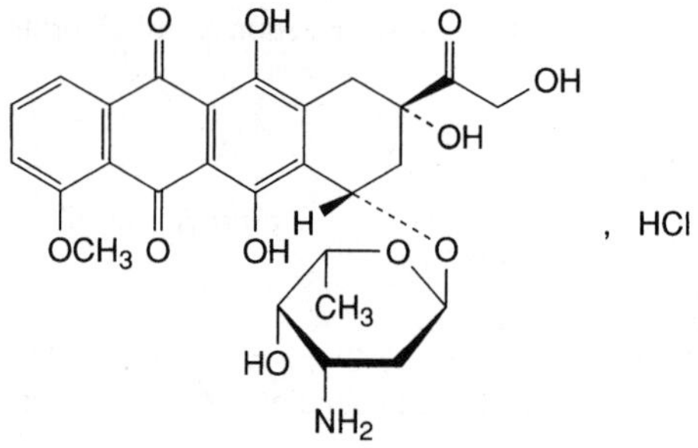

, HCl

$C_{27}H_{29}NO_{11},HCl$        580.0        *25316-40-9*

## Action and use
Anthracycline antibiotic; cytotoxic.

## Preparation
Doxorubicin Injection

*Ph Eur* _____

## DEFINITION
(8*S*,10*S*)-10-[(3-Amino-2,3,6-trideoxy-α-L-*lyxo*-hexopyranosyl)oxy]-6,8,11-trihydroxy-8-(hydroxyacetyl)-1-methoxy-7,8,9,10-tetrahydrotetracene-5,12-dione hydrochloride.

Substance produced by certain strains of *Streptomyces coeruleorubidus* or *Streptomyces peucetius* or obtained by any other means.

## Content
98.0 per cent to 102.0 per cent (anhydrous substance).

## CHARACTERS
### Appearance
Orange-red, crystalline powder, hygroscopic.

## SOLUBILITY
Soluble in water, slightly soluble in methanol.

## IDENTIFICATION
A. Infrared absorption spectrophotometry (*2.2.24*).

*Comparison*    doxorubicin hydrochloride CRS.

B. Dissolve about 10 mg in 0.5 ml of *nitric acid R*, add 0.5 ml of *water R* and heat over a flame for 2 min. Allow to cool and add 0.5 ml of *silver nitrate solution R1*. A white precipitate is formed.

## TESTS
**pH** (*2.2.3*)
4.0 to 5.5.

Dissolve 50 mg in *carbon dioxide-free water R* and dilute to 10 ml with the same solvent.

### Related substances
Liquid chromatography (*2.2.29*). *Prepare the solutions immediately before use.*

*Test solution (a)*    Dissolve 50.0 mg of the substance to be examined in the mobile phase and dilute to 50.0 ml with the mobile phase.

*Test solution (b)*    Dilute 10.0 ml of test solution (a) to 100.0 ml with the mobile phase.

*Reference solution (a)*    Dissolve 10.0 mg of *doxorubicin hydrochloride CRS* and 10 mg of *epirubicin hydrochloride CRS* in the mobile phase and dilute to 50.0 ml with the mobile phase. Dilute 10.0 ml of the solution to 100.0 ml with the mobile phase.

*Reference solution (b)* Dilute 5.0 ml of reference solution (a) to 20.0 ml with the mobile phase.

*Reference solution (c)* Dissolve 50.0 mg of *doxorubicin hydrochloride CRS* in the mobile phase and dilute to 50.0 ml with the mobile phase. Dilute 10.0 ml of the solution to 100.0 ml with the mobile phase.

*Column:*
— *size: l = 0.25 m, Ø = 4.0 mm,*
— *stationary phase: end-capped octadecylsilyl silica gel for chromatography R (5 μm).*

*Mobile phase* Mix equal volumes of *acetonitrile R* and a solution containing 2.88 g/l of *sodium laurilsulfate R* and 2.25 g/l of *phosphoric acid R.*

*Flow rate* 1 ml/min.

*Detection* Spectrophotometer at 254 nm.

*Injection* 5 μl; inject test solution (a) and reference solutions (a) and (b).

*Run time* 3.5 times the retention time of doxorubicin.

*Retention time* Doxorubicin = about 8 min.

*System suitability* Reference solution (a):
— *resolution*: minimum of 2.0 between the peaks due to doxorubicin and to epirubicin.

*Limits:*
— *any impurity*: not more than the area of the peak corresponding to doxorubicin in the chromatogram obtained with reference solution (b) (0.5 per cent),
— *disregard limit*: 0.1 times the area of the peak corresponding to doxorubicin in the chromatogram obtained with reference solution (b) (0.05 per cent).

**Ethanol** (*2.4.24, System B*)
Maximum 1.0 per cent.

**Water** (*2.5.12*)
Maximum 4.0 per cent, determined on 0.100 g.

**Bacterial endotoxins** (*2.6.14*)
Less than 2.2 IU/mg, if intended for use in the manufacture of parenteral dosage forms without a further appropriate procedure for the removal of bacterial endotoxins.

## ASSAY
Liquid chromatography (*2.2.29*) as described in the test for related substances.

*Injection* Test solution (b) and reference solution (c).

Calculate the percentage content of $C_{27}H_{30}ClNO_{11}$.

## STORAGE
In an airtight container. If the substance is sterile, store in a sterile, airtight, tamper-proof container.

## IMPURITIES
A. daunorubicin,

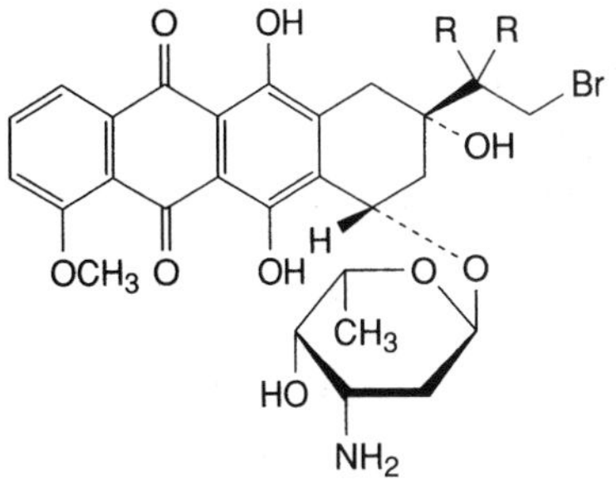

B. R = OCH₃: (8*S*,10*S*)-10[(3-amino-2,3,6-trideoxy-α-L-*lyxo*-hexopyranosyl)oxy]-8-(2-bromo-1,1-dimethoxyethyl)-6,8,11-trihydroxy-1-methoxy-7,8,9,10-tetrahydrotetracene-5,12-dione,

C. R + R = O: (8*S*,10*S*)-10[(3-amino-2,3,6-trideoxy-α-L-*lyxo*-hexopyranosyl)oxy]-8-(bromoacetyl)-6,8,11-trihydroxy-1-methoxy-7,8,9,10-tetrahydrotetracene-5,12-dione,

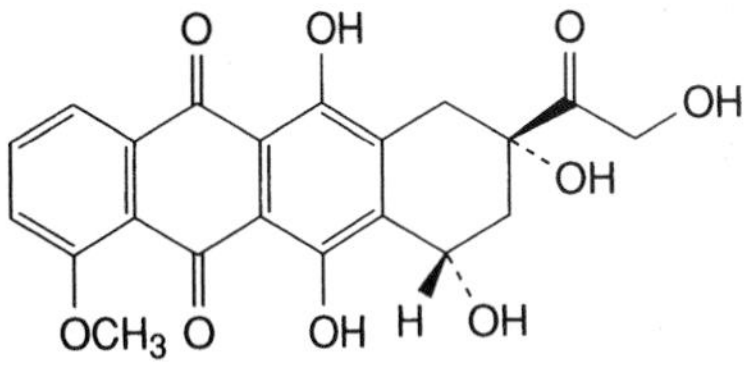

D. (8*S*,10*S*)-6,8,10,11-tetrahydroxy-8-(hydroxyacetyl)-1-methoxy-7,8,9,10-tetrahydrotetracene-5,12-dione (doxorubicin aglycone, doxorubicinone).

*Ph Eur*

# Doxycycline Hyclate

(*Ph Eur monograph 0272*)

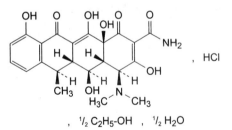

$C_{22}H_{24}N_2O_8,HCl,\frac{1}{2}C_2H_6O,\frac{1}{2}H_2O$   512.9   *24390-14-5*

**Action and use**
Tetracycline antibacterial.

**Preparation**
Doxycycline Capsules

*Ph Eur*

## DEFINITION
Hydrochloride hemiethanol hemihydrate of (4*S*,4a*R*,5*S*,5a*R*,6*R*,12a*S*)-4-(dimethylamino)-3,5,10,12,12a-pentahydroxy-6-methyl-1,11-dioxo-1,4,4a,5,5a,6,11,12a-octahydrotetracene-2-carboxamide.

Substance obtained from oxytetracycline or metacycline or by any other means.

Semi-synthetic product derived from a fermentation product.

## Content
95.0 per cent to 102.0 per cent of $C_{22}H_{25}ClN_2O_8$ (anhydrous substance).

## CHARACTERS

### Appearance
Yellow, crystalline powder, hygroscopic.

### Solubility
Freely soluble in water and in methanol, sparingly soluble in ethanol (96 per cent). It dissolves in solutions of alkali hydroxides and carbonates.

## IDENTIFICATION
A. Examine the chromatograms obtained in the assay.

*Results* The principal peak in the chromatogram obtained with the test solution is similar in retention time and size to the principal peak in the chromatogram obtained with reference solution (a).

B. To about 2 mg add 5 ml of *sulphuric acid R*. A yellow colour develops.

C. It gives reaction (a) of chlorides (*2.3.1*).

## TESTS

### pH (*2.2.3*)
2.0 to 3.0.

Dissolve 0.1 g in *carbon dioxide-free water R* and dilute to 10 ml with the same solvent.

### Specific optical rotation (*2.2.7*)
− 105 to − 120 (anhydrous substance).

Dissolve 0.250 g in a mixture of 1 volume of *1 M hydrochloric acid* and 99 volumes of *methanol R* and dilute to 25.0 ml with the same mixture of solvents. Carry out the measurement within 5 min of preparing the solution.

### Specific absorbance (*2.2.25*)
300 to 335, determined at the absorption maximum at 349 nm (anhydrous substance).

Dissolve 25.0 mg in a mixture of 1 volume of *1 M hydrochloric acid* and 99 volumes of *methanol R* and dilute to 25.0 ml with the same mixture of solvents. Dilute 1.0 ml of the solution to 100.0 ml with a mixture of 1 volume of *1 M hydrochloric acid* and 99 volumes of *methanol R*. Carry out the measurement within 1 h of preparing the solution.

### Light-absorbing impurities
The absorbance (*2.2.25*), determined at 490 nm is not greater than 0.07 (anhydrous and ethanol-free substance).

Dissolve 0.10 g in a mixture of 1 volume of *1 M hydrochloric acid* and 99 volumes of *methanol R* and dilute to 10.0 ml with the same mixture of solvents. Carry out the measurement within 1 h of preparing the solution.

### Related substances
Liquid chromatography (*2.2.29*). *Prepare the solutions immediately before use.*

*Test solution* Dissolve 20.0 mg of the substance to be examined in *0.01 M hydrochloric acid* and dilute to 25.0 ml with the same acid.

*Reference solution (a)* Dissolve 20.0 mg of *doxycycline hyclate CRS* in *0.01 M hydrochloric acid* and dilute to 25.0 ml with the same acid.

*Reference solution (b)* Dissolve 20.0 mg of *6-epidoxycycline hydrochloride CRS* in *0.01 M hydrochloric acid* and dilute to 25.0 ml with the same acid.

*Reference solution (c)* Dissolve 20.0 mg of *metacycline hydrochloride CRS* in *0.01 M hydrochloric acid* and dilute to 25.0 ml with the same acid.

*Reference solution (d)* Mix 4.0 ml of reference solution (a), 1.5 ml of reference solution (b) and 1.0 ml of reference solution (c) and dilute to 25.0 ml with *0.01 M hydrochloric acid*.

*Reference solution (e)* Mix 2.0 ml of reference solution (b) and 2.0 ml of reference solution (c) and dilute to 100.0 ml with *0.01 M hydrochloric acid*.

*Column:*
— *size*: $l$ = 0.25 m, Ø = 4.6 mm,
— *stationary phase*: styrene-divinylbenzene copolymer R (8 µm),
— *temperature*: 60 °C.

*Mobile phase* Weigh 60.0 g of *2-methyl-2-propanol R* and transfer to a 1000 ml volumetric flask with the aid of 200 ml of *water R*; add 400 ml of *buffer solution pH 8.0 R*, 50 ml of a 10 g/l solution of *tetrabutylammonium hydrogen sulphate R* adjusted to pH 8.0 with *dilute sodium hydroxide solution R* and 10 ml of a 40 g/l solution of *sodium edetate R* adjusted to pH 8.0 with *dilute sodium hydroxide solution R*; dilute to 1000.0 ml with *water R*.

*Flow rate* 1.0 ml/min.

*Detection* Spectrophotometer at 254 nm.

*Injection* 20 µl of the test solution and reference solutions (d) and (e).

*Relative retention* With reference to doxycycline: impurity E = about 0.2; impurity D = about 0.3; impurity C = about 0.5; impurity F = about 1.2.

*System suitability* Reference solution (d):
— *resolution*: minimum 1.25 between the peaks due to impurity B (1st peak) and impurity A (2nd peak) and minimum 2.0 between the peaks due to impurity A and doxycycline (3rd peak); if necessary, adjust the 2-methyl-2-propanol content in the mobile phase;
— *symmetry factor*: maximum 1.25 for the peak due to doxycycline.

*Limits:*
— *impurity A*: not more than the area of the corresponding peak in the chromatogram obtained with reference solution (e) (2.0 per cent),
— *impurity B*: not more than the area of the corresponding peak in the chromatogram obtained with reference solution (e) (2.0 per cent),
— *impurities C, D, E, F*: for each impurity, not more than 0.25 times the area of the peak due to impurity A in the chromatogram obtained with reference solution (e) (0.5 per cent),
— *any other impurity*: for each impurity, not more than 0.25 times the area of the peak due to impurity A in the chromatogram obtained with reference solution (e) (0.5 per cent),
— *disregard limit*: 0.05 times the area of the peak due to impurity A in the chromatogram obtained with reference solution (e) (0.1 per cent).

### Ethanol
Gas chromatography (*2.2.28*).

*Internal standard solution* Dilute 0.50 ml of *propanol R* to 1000.0 ml with *water R*.

*Test solution (a)* Dissolve 0.10 g of the substance to be examined in *water R* and dilute to 10.0 ml with the same solvent.

*Test solution (b)* Dissolve 0.10 g of the substance to be examined in the internal standard solution and dilute to 10.0 ml with the same solution.

*Reference solution* Dilute 0.50 ml of *ethanol R* to 100.0 ml with the internal standard solution. Dilute 1.0 ml of this solution to 10.0 ml with the internal standard solution.

*Column:*
— *size: l* = 1.5 m, Ø = 4.0 mm,
— *stationary phas*e: ethylvinylbenzene-divinylbenzene *copolymer R* (150-180 μm).

*Carrier gas nitrogen for chromatography R.*

*Temperature:*
— *column*: 135 °C,
— *injection port and detector*: 150 °C.

*Detection* Flame ionisation.

Calculate the content of ethanol taking the density (*2.2.5*) at 20 °C to be 0.790 g/ml.

*Limit:*
— *ethanol*: 4.3 per cent to 6.0 per cent.

**Heavy metals** (*2.4.8*)
Maximum 50 ppm.

0.5 g complies with limit test C. Prepare the reference solution using 2.5 ml of *lead standard solution (10 ppm Pb) R.*

**Water** (*2.5.12*)
1.4 per cent to 2.8 per cent, determined on 1.20 g.

**Sulphated ash** (*2.4.14*)
Maximum 0.4 per cent, determined on 1.0 g.

**Bacterial endotoxins** (*2.6.14*)
Less than 1.14 IU/mg, if intended for use in the manufacture of parenteral dosage forms without a further appropriate procedure for the removal of bacterial endotoxins.

**ASSAY**
Liquid chromatography (*2.2.29*) as described in the test for related substances with the following modification.

*Injection* Test solution and reference solution (a).

Calculate the percentage content of $C_{22}H_{25}ClN_2O_8$ ($M_r$ = 480.9).

**STORAGE**
In an airtight container, protected from light. If the substance is sterile, store in a sterile, airtight, tamper-proof container.

**IMPURITIES**
*Specified impurities* A, B, C, D, E, F.

A. R1 = $NH_2$, R2 = R5 = H, R3 = $N(CH_3)_2$, R4 = $CH_3$: (4S,4aR,5S,5aR,6S,12aS)-4-(dimethylamino)-3,5,10,12,12a-pentahydroxy-6-methyl-1,11-dioxo-1,4,4a,5,5a,6,11,12a-octahydrotetracene-2-carboxamide (6-epidoxycycline),

B. R1 = $NH_2$, R2 = H, R3 = $N(CH_3)_2$, R4 + R5 = $CH_2$: (4S,4aR,5S,5aR,12aS)-4-(dimethylamino)-3,5,10,12,12a-pentahydroxy-6-methylene-1,11-dioxo-1,4,4a,5,5a,6,11,12a-octahydrotetracene-2-carboxamide (metacycline),

C. R1 = $NH_2$, R2 = $N(CH_3)_2$, R3 = R4 = H, R5 = $CH_3$: (4R,4aR,5S,5aR,6R,12aS)-4-(dimethylamino)-3,5,10,12,12a-pentahydroxy-6-methyl-1,11-dioxo-1,4,4a,5,5a,6,11,12a-octahydrotetracene-2-carboxamide (4-epidoxycycline),

D. R1 = $NH_2$, R2 = $N(CH_3)_2$, R3 = R5 = H, R4 = $CH_3$: (4R,4aR,5S,5aR,6S,12aS)-4-(dimethylamino)-3,5,10,12,12a-

pentahydroxy-6-methyl-1,11-dioxo-1,4,4a,5,5a,6,11,12a-octahydrotetracene-2-carboxamide (4-epi-6-epidoxycycline),

E. R1 = $NH_2$, R2 = H, R3 = $N(CH_3)_2$, R4 = OH, R5 = $CH_3$: oxytetracycline,

F. R1 = $CH_3$, R2 = R4 = H, R3 = $N(CH_3)_2$, R5 = $CH_3$: (4S,4aR,5S,5aR,6R,12aS)-2-acetyl-4-(dimethylamino)-3,5,10,12,12a-pentahydroxy-6-methyl-4a,5a,6,12a-tetrahydrotetracene-1,11(4H,5H)-dione (2-acetyl-2-decarbamoyldoxycycline).

*—————————————————————————— Ph Eur*

# Doxycycline Monohydrate

(*Ph Eur monograph 0820*)

$C_{22}H_{24}N_2O_8,H_2O$ \qquad 462.5 \qquad *17086-28-1*

**Action and use**
Tetracycline antibacterial.

**Preparation**
Dispersible Doxycycline Tablets

*Ph Eur* _____

**DEFINITION**
(4S,4aR,5S,5aR,6R,12aS)-4-(Dimethylamino)-3,5,10,12,12a-pentahydroxy-6-methyl-1,11-dioxo-1,4,4a,5,5a,6,11,12a-octahydrotetracene-2-carboxamide monohydrate.

Substance obtained from oxytetracycline or metacycline or by any other means.

Semi-synthetic product derived from a fermentation product.

**Content**
95.0 per cent to 102.0 per cent (anhydrous substance).

**CHARACTERS**

**Appearance**
Yellow, crystalline powder.

**Solubility**
Very slightly soluble in water and in alcohol. It dissolves in dilute solutions of mineral acids and in solutions of alkali hydroxides and carbonates.

**IDENTIFICATION**

A. Examine the chromatograms obtained in the assay.

*Results* The principal peak in the chromatogram obtained with the test solution is similar in retention time and size to the principal peak in the chromatogram obtained with reference solution (a).

B. To about 2 mg add 5 ml of *sulphuric acid R*. A yellow colour develops.

C. Dissolve 25 mg in a mixture of 0.2 ml of *dilute nitric acid R* and 1.8 ml of *water R*. The solution does not give reaction (a) of chlorides (*2.3.1*).

## TESTS

**pH** (*2.2.3*)

5.0 to 6.5.

Suspend 0.1 g in *carbon dioxide-free water R* and dilute to 10 ml with the same solvent.

**Specific optical rotation** (*2.2.7*)

− 113 to − 130 (anhydrous substance).

Dissolve 0.250 g in a mixture of 0.5 volumes of *hydrochloric acid R* and 99.5 volumes of *methanol R* and dilute to 25.0 ml with the same mixture of solvents. Carry out the measurement within 5 min of preparing the solution.

**Specific absorbance** (*2.2.25*)

325 to 363 determined at the maximum at 349 nm (anhydrous substance).

Dissolve 25.0 mg in a mixture of 0.5 volumes of *hydrochloric acid R* and 99.5 volumes of *methanol R* and dilute to 50.0 ml with the same mixture of solvents. Dilute 2.0 ml of the solution to 100.0 ml with a mixture of 0.5 volumes of *1 M hydrochloric acid* and 99.5 volumes of *methanol R*. Carry out the measurement within 1 h of preparing the solution.

**Light-absorbing impurities**

The absorbance (*2.2.25*) determined at 490 nm has a maximum of 0.07 (anhydrous substance).

Dissolve 0.10 g in a mixture of 0.5 volumes of *hydrochloric acid R* and 99.5 volumes of *methanol R* and dilute to 10.0 ml with the same mixture of solvents. Carry out the measurement within 1 h of preparing the solution.

**Related substances**

Liquid chromatography (*2.2.29*). *Prepare the solutions immediately before use.*

*Test solution*   Dissolve 20.0 mg of the substance to be examined in *0.01 M hydrochloric acid* and dilute to 25.0 ml with the same acid.

*Reference solution (a)*   Dissolve 20.0 mg of *doxycycline hyclate CRS* in *0.01 M hydrochloric acid* and dilute to 25.0 ml with the same acid.

*Reference solution (b)*   Dissolve 20.0 mg of *6-epidoxycycline hydrochloride CRS* in *0.01 M hydrochloric acid* and dilute to 25.0 ml with the same acid.

*Reference solution (c)*   Dissolve 20.0 mg of *metacycline hydrochloride CRS* in *0.01 M hydrochloric acid* and dilute to 25.0 ml with the same acid.

*Reference solution (d)*   Mix 4.0 ml of reference solution (a), 1.5 ml of reference solution (b) and 1.0 ml of reference solution (c) and dilute to 25.0 ml with *0.01 M hydrochloric acid*.

*Reference solution (e)*   Mix 2.0 ml of reference solution (b) and 2.0 ml of reference solution (c) and dilute to 100.0 ml with *0.01 M hydrochloric acid*.

*Column:*

— *size: l* = 0.25 m, Ø = 4.6 mm,
— *stationary phase: styrene-divinylbenzene copolymer R* (8 μm),
— *temperature*: 60 °C.

*Mobile phase*   Weigh 60.0 g of *2-methyl-2-propanol R* and transfer into a 1000 ml volumetric flask with the aid of 200 ml of *water R*; add 400 ml of *buffer solution pH 8.0 R*, 50 ml of a 10 g/l solution of *tetrabutylammonium hydrogen sulphate R* adjusted to pH 8.0 with *dilute sodium hydroxide solution R* and 10 ml of a 40 g/l solution of *sodium edetate R* adjusted to pH 8.0 with *dilute sodium hydroxide solution R*; dilute to 1000.0 ml with *water R*.

*Flow rate*   1.0 ml/min.

*Detection*   Spectrophotometer at 254 nm.

*Injection*   20 μl; inject the test solution and reference solutions (d) and (e).

*Relative retention*   With reference to doxycycline: impurity E = about 0.2; impurity D = about 0.3; impurity C = about 0.5; impurity F = about 1.2.

*System suitability*   Reference solution (d):

— *resolution*: minimum 1.25 between the peaks due to impurity B (1st peak) and impurity A (2nd peak) and minimum 2.0 between the peaks due to impurity A and doxycycline (3rd peak); if necessary, adjust the 2-methyl-2-propanol content in the mobile phase,
— *symmetry factor*: maximum 1.25 for the peak due to doxycycline.

*Limits:*

— *impurity A*: not more than the area of the corresponding peak in the chromatogram obtained with reference solution (e) (2.0 per cent),
— *impurity B*: not more than the area of the corresponding peak in the chromatogram obtained with reference solution (e) (2.0 per cent),
— *any other impurity*: not more than 0.25 times the area of the peak due to impurity A in the chromatogram obtained with reference solution (e) (0.5 per cent),
— *disregard limit*: 0.05 times the area of the peak due to impurity A in the chromatogram obtained with reference solution (e) (0.1 per cent).

**Heavy metals** (*2.4.8*)

Maximum 50 ppm.

0.5 g complies with limit test C. Prepare the standard using 2.5 ml of *lead standard solution (10 ppm Pb) R*.

**Water** (*2.5.12*)

3.6 per cent to 4.6 per cent, determined on 0.200 g.

**Sulphated ash** (*2.4.14*)

Maximum 0.4 per cent, determined on 1.0 g.

## ASSAY

Liquid chromatography (*2.2.29*) as described in the test for related substances with the following modification.

*Injection*   Test solution and reference solution (a).

Calculate the percentage content of $C_{22}H_{24}N_2O_8$.

## STORAGE

Protected from light.

## IMPURITIES

A. R1 = NH$_2$, R2 = R5 = H, R3 = N(CH$_3$)$_2$, R4 = CH$_3$: (4*S*,4a*R*,5*S*,5a*R*,6*S*,12a*S*)-4-(dimethylamino)-3,5,10,12,12a-pentahydroxy-6-methyl-1,11-dioxo-1,4,4a,5,5a,6,11,12a-octahydrotetracene-2-carboxamide (6-epidoxycycline),

B. R1 = NH$_2$, R2 = H, R3 = N(CH$_3$)$_2$, R4 + R5 = CH$_2$: (4*S*,4a*R*,5*S*,5a*R*,12a*S*)-4-(dimethylamino)-3,5,10,12,12a-pentahydroxy-6-methylene-1,11-dioxo-1,4,4a,5,5a,6,11,12a-octahydrotetracene-2-carboxamide (metacycline),

C. R1 = NH$_2$, R2 = N(CH$_3$)$_2$, R3 = R4 = H, R5 = CH$_3$: (4*R*,4a*R*,5*S*,5a*R*,6*R*,12a*S*)-4-(dimethylamino)-3,5,10,12,12a-pentahydroxy-6-methyl-1,11-dioxo-1,4,4a,5,5a,6,11,12a-octahydrotetracene-2-carboxamide (4-epidoxycycline),

D. R1 = NH$_2$, R2 = N(CH$_3$)$_2$, R3 = R5 = H, R4 = CH$_3$: (4R,4aR,5S,5aR,6S,12aS)-4-(dimethylamino)-3,5,10,12,12a-pentahydroxy-6-methyl-1,11-dioxo-1,4,4a,5,5a,6,11,12a-octahydrotetracene-2-carboxamide (4-epi-6-epidoxycycline),

E. R1 = NH$_2$, R2 = H, R3 = N(CH$_3$)$_2$, R4 = OH, R5 = CH$_3$: oxytetracycline,

F. R1 = CH$_3$, R2 = R4 = H, R3 = N(CH$_3$)$_2$, R5 = CH$_3$: (4S,4aR,5S,5aR,6R,12aS)-2-acetyl-4-(dimethylamino)-3,5,10,12,12a-pentahydroxy-6-methyl-4a,5a,6,12a-tetrahydrotetracene-1,11(4H,5H)-dione (2-acetyl-2-decarbamoyldoxycycline).

_____ Ph Eur

# Doxylamine Succinate

(*Doxylamine Hydrogen Succinate,*
*Ph Eur monograph 1589*)

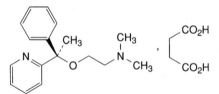

and enantiomer

C$_{17}$H$_{22}$N$_2$O,C$_4$H$_6$O$_4$          388.5          562-10-7

**Action and use**

Histamine H$_1$ receptor antagonist; antihistamine.

_Ph Eur_ _____

## DEFINITION

N,N-dimethyl-2-[(1RS)-1-phenyl-1-(pyridin-2-yl)ethoxy(ethanamine hydrogen butanedioate.

## Content

99.0 per cent to 101.0 per cent (anhydrous substance).

## CHARACTERS

**Appearance**

A white or almost white powder.

**Solubility**

Very soluble in water, freely soluble in ethanol (96 per cent).

## IDENTIFICATION

*First identification   C.*

*Second identification   A, B.*

A. Melting point (*2.2.14*): 103 °C to 108 °C.

B. Dissolve 0.200 g in *0.1 M hydrochloric acid* and dilute to 100.0 ml with the same solvent. Dilute 1.0 ml of this solution to 100.0 ml with *0.1 M hydrochloric acid*. Examined between 230 nm and 350 nm (*2.2.25*), the solution shows an absorption maximum at 262 nm. The specific absorbance at the maximum is 229 to 243 (anhydrous substance).

C. Infrared absorption spectrophotometry (*2.2.24*).

*Comparison   Ph. Eur. reference spectrum of doxylamine hydrogen succinate.*

## TESTS

### Appearance of solution

The solution is clear (*2.2.1*) and colourless (*2.2.2, Method II*).

Dissolve 0.4 g of the substance to be examined in *water R* and dilute to 20 ml with the same solvent.

**Optical rotation** (*2.2.7*)

- 0.10° to + 0.10°.

Dissolve 2.50 g of the substance to be examined in *water R* and dilute to 25.0 ml with the same solvent.

### Related substances

Gas chromatography (*2.2.28*).

*Test solution*   Dissolve 0.650 g of the substance to be examined in 20 ml of *0.1 M hydrochloric acid*. Add 3 ml of a 100 g/l solution of *sodium hydroxide R* and extract with 3 quantities, each of 25 ml, of *methylene chloride R*. Combine the methylene chloride extracts and filter using hydrophobic phase-separation filter paper. Rinse the filter with 10 ml of *methylene chloride R* and combine the rinsings with the methylene chloride extracts. Evaporate the solvent under reduced pressure at a temperature not exceeding 40 °C. Dissolve the residue in 20.0 ml of *anhydrous ethanol R*.

*Reference solution (a)*   Dilute 1.0 ml of the test solution to 200.0 ml with *anhydrous ethanol R*.

*Reference solution (b)*   Dissolve 4 mg of *doxylamine impurity A CRS* and 4 mg of *2-benzoylpyridine R* in *anhydrous ethanol R* and dilute to 40 ml with the same solvent.

*Column:*
— *material:* fused silica;
— *size: l* = 30 m, Ø = 0.53 mm;
— *stationary phase: poly(dimethyl)(diphenyl)siloxane R* (film thickness 1.5 µm).

*Carrier gas   helium for chromatography R.*

*Flow rate   7 ml/min.*

*Temperature:*

|  | Time (min) | Temperature (°C) |
|---|---|---|
| Column | 0 - 12 | 160 → 220 |
|  | 12 - 27 | 220 |
| Injection port |  | 250 |
| Detector |  | 250 |

*Detection   Flame ionisation.*

*Injection   1 µl.*

*System suitability*   Reference solution (b):
— *resolution*: minimum 1.5 between the peaks due to impurities A and D.

*Limits:*
— *any impurity*: not more than the area of the principal peak in the chromatogram obtained with reference solution (a) (0.5 per cent);
— *total*: not more than twice the area of the principal peak in the chromatogram obtained with reference solution (a) (1 per cent);
— *disregard limit*: 0.1 times the area of the principal peak in the chromatogram obtained with reference solution (a) (0.05 per cent).

**Water** (*2.5.12*)

Maximum 0.5 per cent, determined on 2.00 g.

**Sulphated ash** (*2.4.14*)

Maximum 0.1 per cent, determined on 1.0 g.

## ASSAY

Dissolve 0.150 g in 50 ml of *anhydrous acetic acid R*. Titrate with *0.1 M perchloric acid*, determining the end-point potentiometrically (*2.2.20*).

1 ml of *0.1 M perchloric acid* is equivalent to 19.43 mg of $C_{21}H_{28}N_2O_5$.

## IMPURITIES

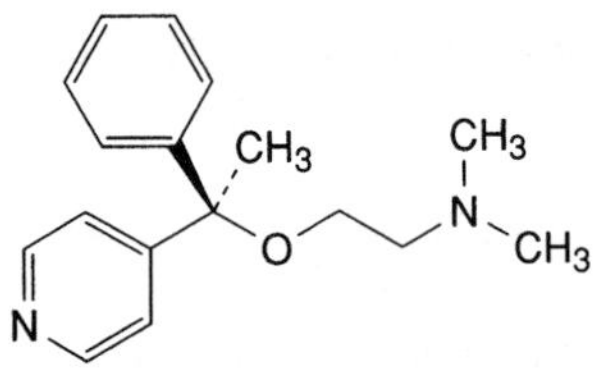

A. *N,N*-dimethyl-2-[1(*RS*)-1-phenyl-1-(pyridin-4-yl)ethoxy]ethanamine,

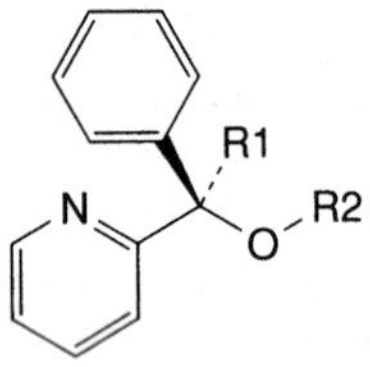

B. R1 = CH$_3$, R2 = H: (1*RS*)-1-phenyl-1-(pyridin-2-yl)ethanol,

C. R1 = H, R2 = CH$_2$-CH$_2$-N(CH$_3$)$_2$: *N,N*-dimethyl-2-[(*RS*)-1-phenyl(pyridin-2-yl)methoxy]ethanamine,

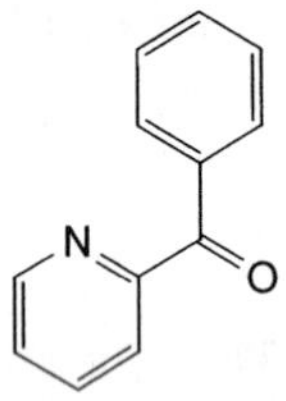

D. phenyl(pyridin-2-yl)methanone (2-benzoylpyridine).

*Ph Eur*

# Droperidol

(*Ph Eur monograph 1010*)

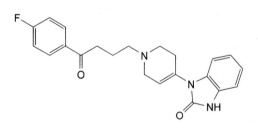

$C_{22}H_{22}FN_3O_2$        379.4        548-73-2

## Action and use

Dopamine receptor antagonist; beta$_1$-adrenoceptor agonist; alpha-adrenoceptor agonist; neuroleptic.

## Preparations

Droperidol Injection

Droperidol Tablets

*Ph Eur*

## DEFINITION

1-[1-[4-(4-Fluorophenyl)-4-oxobutyl]-1,2,3,6-tetrahydropyridin-4-yl]-1,3-dihydro-2*H*-benzimidazol-2-one.

## Content

99.0 per cent to 101.0 per cent (dried substance).

## CHARACTERS

### Appearance

White or almost white powder.

### Solubility

Practically insoluble in water, freely soluble in dimethylformamide and in methylene chloride, sparingly soluble in ethanol (96 per cent).

It shows polymorphism (*5.9*).

## IDENTIFICATION

*First identification*   A.

*Second identification*   B, C, D.

A. Infrared absorption spectrophotometry (*2.2.24*).

*Preparation*   Discs.

*Comparison*   droperidol CRS.

If the spectra obtained show differences, dissolve the substance to be examined and the reference substance separately in the minimum volume of *acetone R*, evaporate to dryness on a water-bath and record new spectra using the residues.

B. Thin-layer chromatography (*2.2.27*).

*Test solution*   Dissolve 30 mg of the substance to be examined in the mobile phase and dilute to 10 ml with the mobile phase.

*Reference solution (a)*   Dissolve 30 mg of *droperidol CRS* in the mobile phase and dilute to 10 ml with the mobile phase.

*Reference solution (b)*   Dissolve 30 mg of *droperidol CRS* and 30 mg of *benperidol CRS* in the mobile phase, then dilute to 10 ml with the mobile phase.

*Plate*   TLC silica gel GF$_{254}$ plate R.

*Mobile phase*   acetone R, methanol R (1:9 *V/V*).

*Application*   10 μl.

*Development*   Over a path of 15 cm.

*Drying*   In air.

*Detection*   Examine in ultraviolet light at 254 nm.

*System suitability*   Reference solution (b):
— the chromatogram shows 2 clearly separated spots.

*Results*   The principal spot in the chromatogram obtained with the test solution is similar in position and size to the principal spot in the chromatogram obtained with reference solution (a).

C. Dissolve about 10 mg in 5 ml of *anhydrous ethanol R*. Add 0.5 ml of *dinitrobenzene solution R* and 0.5 ml of *2 M alcoholic potassium hydroxide R*. A violet colour is produced and becomes brownish-red after 20 min.

D. Mix about 5 mg with 45 mg of *heavy magnesium oxide R* and ignite in a crucible until an almost white residue is obtained (usually less than 5 min). Allow to cool, add 1 ml of *water R*, 0.05 ml of *phenolphthalein solution R1* and about 1 ml of *dilute hydrochloric acid R* to render the solution colourless. Filter. To a freshly prepared mixture of 0.1 ml of *alizarin S solution R* and 0.1 ml of *zirconyl nitrate solution R*, add 1.0 ml of the filtrate. Mix, allow to stand for 5 min and compare the colour of the solution with that of a blank prepared in the same manner. The test solution is yellow and the blank is red.

## TESTS

### Appearance of solution

The solution is clear (2.2.1) and not more intensely coloured than reference solution $BY_5$ (2.2.2, Method II).

Dissolve 0.20 g in *methylene chloride R* and dilute to 20.0 ml with the same solvent.

### Related substances

Liquid chromatography (2.2.29). *Prepare the solutions immediately before use.*

*Test solution* Dissolve 0.10 g of the substance to be examined in *dimethylformamide R* and dilute to 10.0 ml with the same solvent.

*Reference solution (a)* Dissolve 2.5 mg of *droperidol CRS* and 2.5 mg of *benperidol CRS* in *dimethylformamide R*, then dilute to 100.0 ml with the same solvent.

*Reference solution (b)* Dilute 1.0 ml of the test solution to 100.0 ml with *dimethylformamide R*. Dilute 5.0 ml of this solution to 20.0 ml with *dimethylformamide R*.

*Column:*
— *size: l* = 0.10 m, Ø = 4.6 mm;
— *stationary phase: base-deactivated octadecylsilyl silica gel for chromatography R* (3 µm).

*Mobile phase:*
— *mobile phase A: acetonitrile R*;
— *mobile phase B:* 10 g/l solution of *tetrabutylammonium hydrogen sulphate R1*;

| Time (min) | Mobile phase A (per cent *V/V*) | Mobile phase B (per cent *V/V*) |
|---|---|---|
| 0 - 15 | 0 → 40 | 100 → 60 |
| 15 - 20 | 40 | 60 |
| 20 - 25 | 40 → 0 | 60 → 100 |

*Flow rate* 1.5 ml/min.

*Detection* Spectrophotometer at 275 nm.

*Injection* 10 µl; inject *dimethylformamide R* as a blank.

*Retention time* Benperidol = about 6.5 min; droperidol = about 7 min.

*System suitability* Reference solution (a):
— *resolution:* minimum 2.0 between the peaks due to benperidol and droperidol; if necessary, adjust the final concentration of acetonitrile in the mobile phase or adjust the time programme for the linear gradient.

*Limits:*
— *impurities A, B, C, D, E:* for each impurity, not more than the area of the principal peak in the chromatogram obtained with reference solution (b) (0.25 per cent);
— *total:* not more than twice the area of the principal peak in the chromatogram obtained with reference solution (b) (0.5 per cent);
— *disregard limit:* 0.2 times the area of the principal peak in the chromatogram obtained with reference solution (b) (0.05 per cent).

### Heavy metals (2.4.8)

Maximum 20 ppm.

1.0 g complies with test D. Prepare the reference solution using 2 ml of *lead standard solution (10 ppm Pb) R*.

### Loss on drying (2.2.32)

Maximum 0.5 per cent, determined on 1.000 g by drying in an oven at 105 °C

### Sulphated ash (2.4.14)

Maximum 0.1 per cent, determined on 1.0 g.

### ASSAY

Dissolve 0.300 g in 50 ml of a mixture of 1 volume of *anhydrous acetic acid R* and 7 volumes of *methyl ethyl ketone R*. Using 0.2 ml of *naphtholbenzein solution R*, titrate with *0.1 M perchloric acid* until the colour changes from orange-yellow to green.

1 ml of *0.1 M perchloric acid* is equivalent to 37.94 mg of $C_{22}H_{22}FN_3O_2$.

### STORAGE

Protected from light.

### IMPURITIES

*Specified impurities    A, B, C, D, E.*

A. 1-(1,2,3,6-tetrahydropyridin-4-yl)-1,3-dihydro-2*H*-benzimidazol-2-one,

B. 1-[1-[4-(2-fluorophenyl)-4-oxobutyl]-1,2,3,6-tetrahydropyridin-4-yl]-1,3-dihydro-2*H*-benzimidazol-2-one,

C. 1-[4-(4-fluorophenyl)-4-oxobutyl]-4-(2-oxo-2,3-dihydro-1*H*-benzimidazol-1-yl)pyridinium chloride,

and enantiomer

D. (1*RS*)-1-[4-(4-fluorophenyl)-4-oxobutyl]-4-(2-oxo-2,3-dihydro-1*H*-benzimidazol-1-yl)-1,2,3,6-tetrahydropyridine 1-oxide,

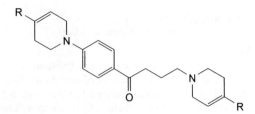

E. 1-[1-[4-[4-[4-(2-oxo-2,3-dihydro-1*H*-benzimidazol-1-yl)-3,6-dihydropyridin-1(2*H*)-yl]-1-oxobutyl]phenyl]-1,2,3,6-tetrahydropyridin-4-yl]-1,3-dihydro-2*H*-benzimidazol-2-one.

_____ *Ph Eur*

# Drospirenone

*(Ph Eur monograph 2404)*

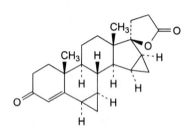

C₂₄H₃₀O₃        366.5        *67392-87-4*

**Action and use**

Aldosterone receptor antagonist.

*Ph Eur* _____

## DEFINITION

3-Oxo-6α,7α,15α,16α-tetrahydro-3'*H*,3''*H*-dicyclopropa[6,7:15,16]-17α-pregn-4-en-21,17-carbolactone.

## Content

98.0 per cent to 102.0 per cent (dried substance).

## CHARACTERS

### Appearance

White or almost white powder.

### Solubility

Practically insoluble in water, freely soluble in methylene chloride, soluble in methanol, sparingly soluble in ethanol (96 per cent).

## IDENTIFICATION

A. Specific optical rotation (see Tests).

B. Infrared absorption spectrophotometry (*2.2.24*).

*Comparison*    drospirenone CRS.

## TESTS

### Specific optical rotation (*2.2.7*)

− 187 to − 193 (dried substance).

Dissolve 0.100 g in *methanol R* and dilute to 10.0 ml with the same solvent.

### Related substances

Liquid chromatography (*2.2.29*).

*Solvent mixture*    acetonitrile R, water R (50:50 *V/V*).

*Test solution*    Dissolve 30.0 mg of the substance to be examined in the solvent mixture and dilute to 50.0 ml with the solvent mixture.

*Reference solution (a)*    Dilute 1.0 ml of the test solution to 10.0 ml with the solvent mixture. Use 1.0 ml of this solution to dissolve the contents of a vial of *drospirenone impurity E CRS*.

*Reference solution (b)*    Dilute 1.0 ml of the test solution to 100.0 ml with the solvent mixture. Dilute 1.0 ml of this solution to 10.0 ml with the solvent mixture.

*Reference solution (c)*    Dissolve 30.0 mg of *drospirenone CRS* in the solvent mixture and dilute to 50.0 ml with the solvent mixture.

*Column:*

— *size*: *l* = 0.25 m, Ø = 4.6 mm;

— *stationary phase*: spherical *end-capped octadecylsilyl silica gel for chromatography R* (3 μm);

— *temperature*: 35 °C.

*Mobile phase:*

— *mobile phase A*: *water R*;

— *mobile phase B*: *acetonitrile R*;

| Time (min) | Mobile phase A (per cent *V/V*) | Mobile phase B (per cent *V/V*) |
|---|---|---|
| 0 - 2 | 63 | 37 |
| 2 - 16 | 63 → 52 | 37 → 48 |
| 16 - 23 | 52 | 48 |
| 23 - 31 | 52 → 20 | 48 → 80 |
| 31 - 39 | 20 | 80 |

*Flow rate*    1.0 ml/min.

*Detection*    Spectrophotometer at 245 nm.

*Injection*    10 μl of the test solution and reference solutions (a) and (b).

*Relative retention*    With reference to drospirenone (retention time = about 22 min): impurity E = about 1.1.

*System suitability*    Reference solution (a):

— *resolution*: minimum 5.0 between the peaks due to drospirenone and impurity E.

*Limits:*

— *unspecified impurities*: for each impurity, not more than the area of the principal peak in the chromatogram obtained with reference solution (b) (0.10 per cent);

— *total*: not more than 3 times the area of the principal peak in the chromatogram obtained with reference solution (b) (0.3 per cent);

— *disregard limit*: 0.5 times the area of the principal peak in the chromatogram obtained with reference solution (b) (0.05 per cent).

**Loss on drying** (*2.2.32*)

Maximum 0.5 per cent, determined on 1.000 g by drying in an oven at 105 °C for 3 h.

## ASSAY

Liquid chromatography (*2.2.29*) as described in the test for related substances with the following modification.

*Injection*    10 μl of the test solution and reference solution (c).

Calculate the percentage content of C₂₄H₃₀O₃ from the declared content of *drospirenone CRS*.

## IMPURITIES

*Other detectable impurities* (The following substances would, if present at a sufficient level, be detected by one or other of the tests in the monograph. They are limited by the general acceptance criterion for other/unspecified impurities and/or by the general monograph *Substances for pharmaceutical use (2034)*. It is therefore not necessary to identify these impurities for demonstration of compliance. See also *5.10. Control of impurities in substances for pharmaceutical use)*: A, B, C, D, E, F, G, H, I, K.

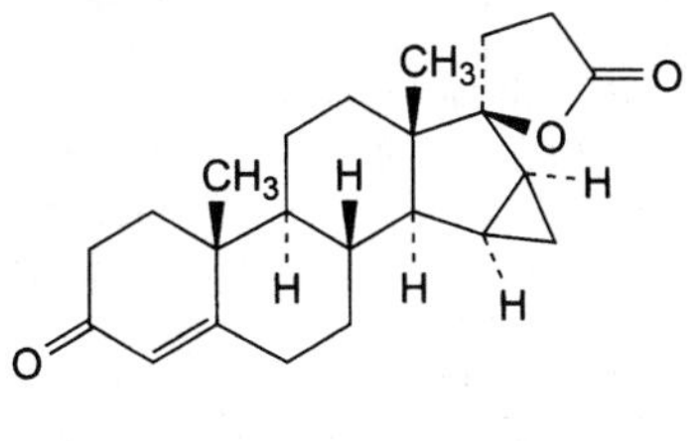

A. 3-oxo-15α,16α-dihydro-3′H-cyclopropa[15,16]-17α-pregn-4-ene-21,17-carbolactone (6,7-desmethylenedrospirenone),

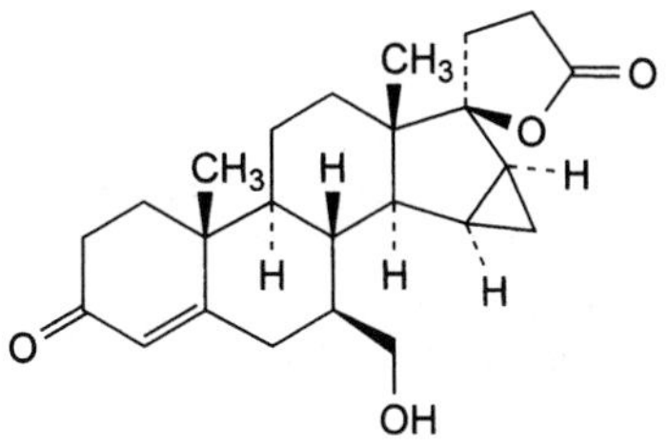

B. 7β-(hydroxymethyl)-3-oxo-15α,16α-dihydro-3′H-cyclopropa[15,16]-17α-pregn-4-ene-21,17-carbolactone (7β-hydroxymethyl derivative),

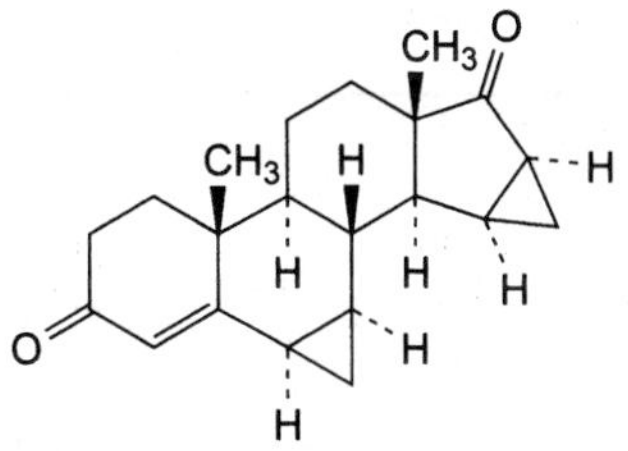

C. 6α,7α,15α,16α-tetrahydro-3′H,3″H -dicyclopropa[6,7:15,16]androst-4-ene-3,17-dione (17-keto derivative),

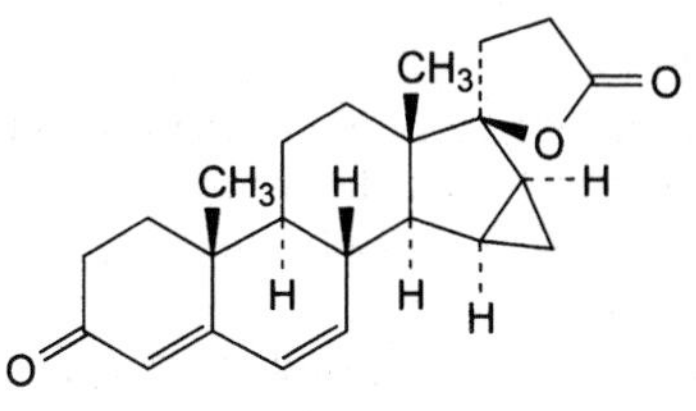

D. 3-oxo-15α,16α-dihydro-3′H-cyclopropa[15,16]-17α-pregna-4,6-diene-21,17-carbolactone (Δ6-drospirenone),

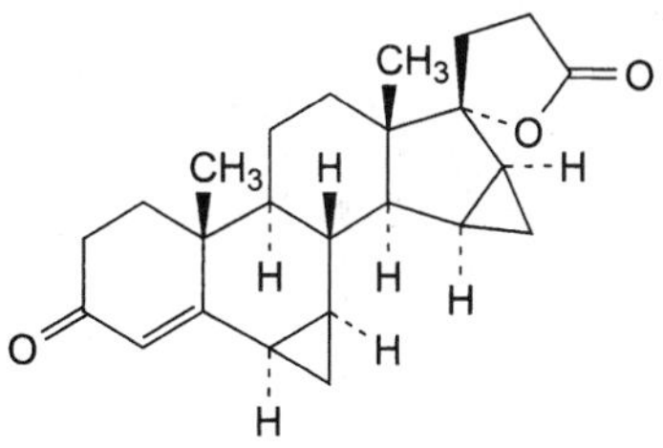

E. 3-oxo-6α,7α,15α,16α-tetrahydro-3′H,3″H dicyclopropa[6,7:15,16]pregn-4-ene-21,17-carbolactone (17-epidrospirenone),

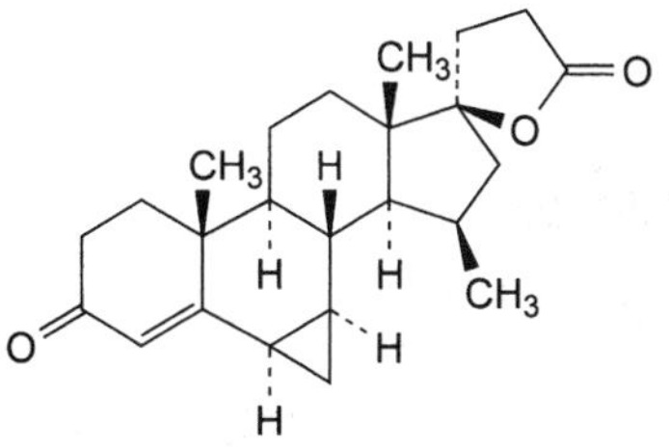

F. 15β-methyl-3-oxo-6α,7α-dihydro-3′H-cyclopropa[6,7]-17α-pregn-4-ene-21,17-carbolactone (3″-16-secodrospirenone),

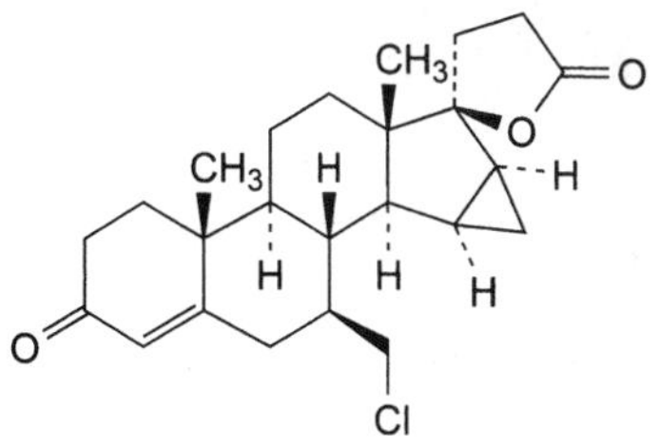

G. 7β-(chloromethyl)-3-oxo-15α,16α-dihydro-3′H-cyclopropa[15,16]-17α-pregn-4-ene-21,17-carbolactone (3′-chloro-3′,6-secodrospirenone),

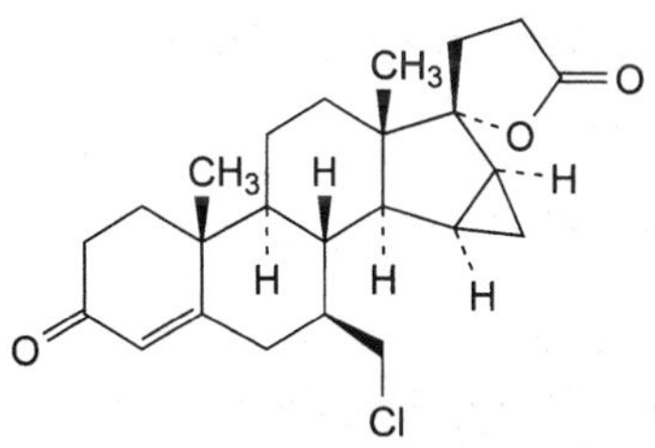

H. 7β-(chloromethyl)-3-oxo-15α,16α-dihydro-3′H-cyclopropa[15,16]pregn-4-ene-21,17-carbolactone (3′-chloro-3′,6-seco-17-epidrospirenone),

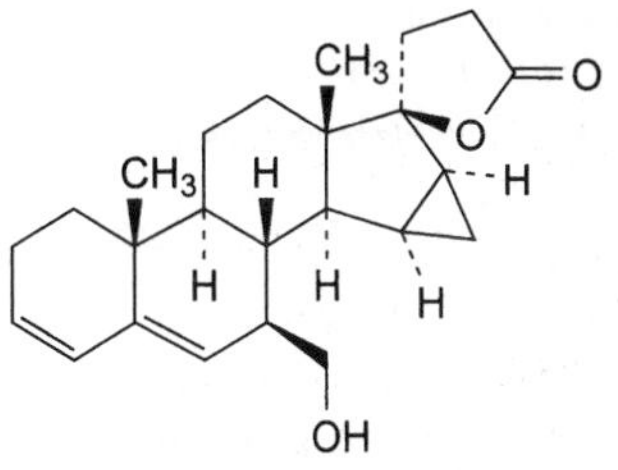

I. 7β-(hydroxymethyl)-15α,16α-dihydro-3′H-cyclopropa[15,16]-17α-pregna-3,5-diene-21,17-carbolactone (7β-hydroxymethyldiene derivative),

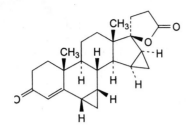

K. 3-oxo-6β,7β,15α,16α-tetrahydro-3'H,3"H-dicyclopropa[6,7:15,16]-17α-pregn-4-ene-21,17-carbolactone (6α,7α-drospirenone).

Ph Eur

# Dydrogesterone

(*Ph Eur monograph 2357*)

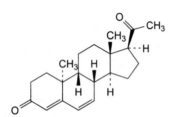

C₂₁H₂₈O₂ $C_{21}H_{28}O_2$      312.5      *152-62-5*

**Action and use**
Progestogen.

**Preparation**
Dydrogesterone Tablets.

Ph Eur

**DEFINITION**
9β,10α-Pregna-4,6-diene-3,20-dione.

**Content**
98.0 per cent to 102.0 per cent (dried substance).

**CHARACTERS**

**Appearance**
White or almost white, crystalline powder.

**Solubility**
Practically insoluble in water, soluble in acetone, sparingly soluble in ethanol (96 per cent).

**IDENTIFICATION**
Infrared absorption spectrophotometry (*2.2.24*).

*Comparison* dydrogesterone CRS.

**TESTS**

**Specific optical rotation** (*2.2.7*)
− 469 to − 485 (dried substance), measured at 25 °C.

Dissolve 0.100 g in *methylene chloride R* and dilute to 20.0 ml with the same solvent.

**Related substances**
Liquid chromatography (*2.2.29*).

*Test solution (a)* Dissolve 50.0 mg of the substance to be examined in the mobile phase and dilute to 100.0 ml with the mobile phase.

*Test solution (b)* Dissolve 20.0 mg of the substance to be examined in the mobile phase and dilute to 100.0 ml with the mobile phase.

*Reference solution (a)* Dissolve 3.0 mg of *dydrogesterone impurity A CRS* in the mobile phase and dilute to 20.0 ml with the mobile phase. Dilute 1.0 ml of this solution to 100.0 ml with the mobile phase.

*Reference solution (b)* Dilute 1.0 ml of test solution (a) to 100.0 ml with the mobile phase. Dilute 1.0 ml of this solution to 10.0 ml with the mobile phase.

*Reference solution (c)* Dissolve 10 mg of the substance to be examined in 10 ml of reference solution (a).

*Reference solution (d)* Dissolve 10 mg of the substance to be examined in 30 ml of *ethanol (96 per cent) R*. Add 1 ml of a 8.4 g/l solution of *sodium hydroxide R* and heat at 85 °C for 10 min. Cool to room temperature, add 1 ml of a 20.6 g/l solution of *hydrochloric acid R*, add 20 ml of *acetonitrile R*, 2 mg of *dydrogesterone impurity B CRS*, dilute to 100 ml with *water R* and mix. This solution contains dydrogesterone and impurities B and C.

*Reference solution (e)* Dissolve 20.0 mg of *dydrogesterone CRS* in the mobile phase and dilute to 100.0 ml with the mobile phase.

*Column:*
— *size: l = 0.15 m, Ø = 4.6 mm;*
— *stationary phase: spherical end-capped octadecylsilyl silica gel for chromatography R (3 μm);*
— *temperature: 40 °C.*

*Mobile phase* acetonitrile R, ethanol (96 per cent) R, water R (21:25:54 *V/V/V*).

*Flow rate* 1.0 ml/min.

*Detection* Spectrophotometer at 280 nm and at 385 nm.

*Injection* 10 μl of test solution (a) and reference solutions (a), (b), (c) and (d).

*Run time* Twice the retention time of dydrogesterone.

*Relative retention* At 385 nm with reference to dydrogesterone (retention time = about 13 min): impurity A = about 0.9.

*Relative retention* At 280 nm with reference to dydrogesterone (retention time = about 13 min): impurity B = about 1.1; impurity C = about 1.2.

*System suitability:*
— *resolution at 385 nm*: minimum 1.1 between the peaks due to impurity A and dydrogesterone in the chromatogram obtained with reference solution (c);
— *resolution at 280 nm*: minimum 4.5 between the peaks due to dydrogesterone and impurity B and minimum 1.5 between the peaks due to impurity B and impurity C in the chromatogram obtained with reference solution (d).

*Limits:*
— *impurity A at 385 nm*: not more than the area of the corresponding peak in the chromatogram obtained with reference solution (a) (0.3 per cent);
— *impurity B at 280 nm*: not more than 1.5 times the area of the principal peak in the chromatogram obtained with reference solution (b) (0.15 per cent);
— *impurity C at 280 nm*: not more than 3 times the area of the principal peak in the chromatogram obtained with reference solution (b) (0.3 per cent);
— *unspecified impurities at 280 nm*: for each impurity, not more than the area of the principal peak in the chromatogram obtained with reference solution (b) (0.10 per cent);
— *total at 280 nm*: not more than 5 times the area of the principal peak in the chromatogram obtained with reference solution (b) (0.5 per cent);

— *disregard limit at 280 nm*: 0.5 times the area of the principal peak in the chromatogram obtained with reference solution (b) (0.05 per cent).

**Loss on drying** (*2.2.32*)
Maximum 0.5 per cent, determined on 1.000 g by drying in an oven at 105 °C for 3 h.

**Sulphated ash** (*2.4.14*)
Maximum 0.1 per cent, determined on 1.0 g.

## ASSAY
Liquid chromatography (*2.2.29*) as described in the test for related substances with the following modifications.

*Detection* Spectrophotometer at 280 nm.

*Injection* Test solution (b) and reference solution (e).

Calculate the percentage content of $C_{21}H_{28}O_2$ from the declared content of *dydrogesterone CRS*.

## IMPURITIES
*Specified impurities* A, B, C.

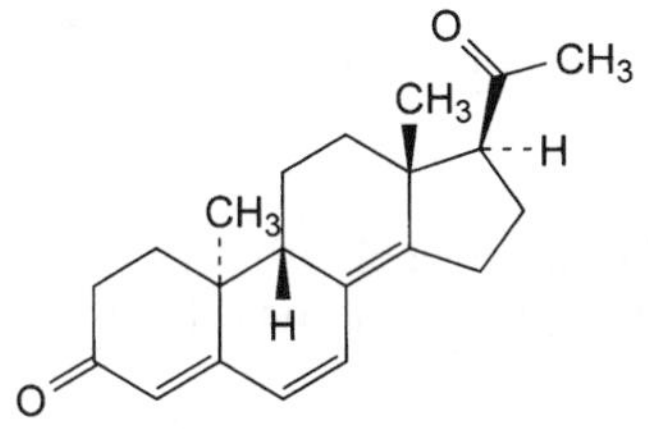

A. 9β,10α-pregna-4,6,8(14)-triene-3,20-dione,

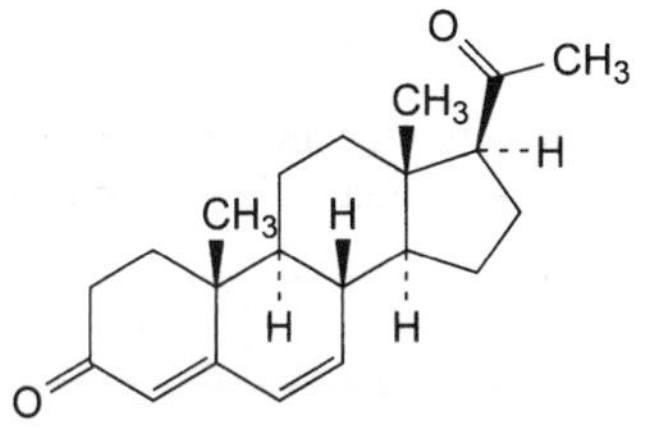

B. pregna-4,6-diene-3,20-dione,

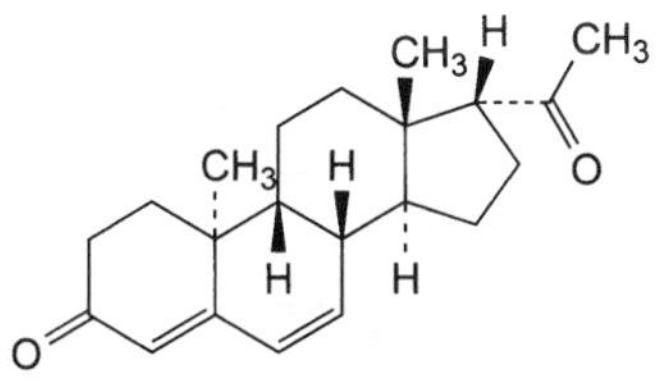

C. 9β,10α,17α-pregna-4,6-diene-3,20-dione.

*Ph Eur*

# Ebastine

(*Ph Eur monograph 2015*)

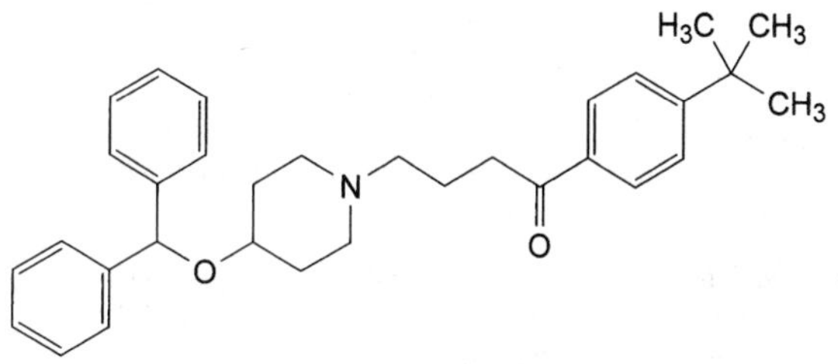

$C_{32}H_{39}NO_2$    469.7    *90729-43-4*

## Action and use
Histamine $H_1$ receptor antagonist; antihistamine.

*Ph Eur*

## DEFINITION
1-[4-(1,1-Dimethylethyl)phenyl]-4-[4-(diphenylmethoxy)piperidin-1-yl]butan-1-one.

**Content**
99.0 per cent to 101.0 per cent (anhydrous substance).

## CHARACTERS
**Appearance**
White or almost white, crystalline powder.

**Solubility**
Practically insoluble in water, very soluble in methylene chloride, sparingly soluble in methanol.

**mp**
About 86 °C.

## IDENTIFICATION
Infrared absorption spectrophotometry (*2.2.24*).

*Comparison* Ph. Eur. reference spectrum of ebastine.

## TESTS
**Related substances**
Liquid chromatography (*2.2.29*). *Keep the solutions protected from light.*

*Solution A.* Mix 65 volumes of *acetonitrile R* and 35 volumes of a 1.1 g/l solution of *phosphoric acid R* adjusted to pH 5.0 with a 40 g/l solution of *sodium hydroxide R*.

*Test solution* Dissolve 0.125 g of the substance to be examined in solution A and dilute to 50.0 ml with the same solution.

*Reference solution (a)* Dissolve 5.0 mg of *ebastine impurity C CRS* and 5.0 mg of *ebastine impurity D CRS* in solution A and dilute to 20.0 ml with the same solution. Dilute 1.0 ml of the solution to 100.0 ml with solution A.

*Reference solution (b)* Dilute 1.0 ml of the test solution to 100.0 ml with solution A. Dilute 1.0 ml of this solution to 10.0 ml with solution A.

*Column:*
— *size*: $l$ = 0.25 m, Ø = 4.6 mm,
— *stationary phase*: *nitrile silica gel for chromatography R* (5 μm).

*Mobile phase* Mix 35 volumes of *acetonitrile R* and 65 volumes of a 1.1 g/l solution of *phosphoric acid R* adjusted to pH 5.0 with a 40 g/l solution of *sodium hydroxide R*. Adjust the percentage of acetonitrile to between 30 per cent *V/V* and 40 per cent *V/V* so that the retention time of ebastine is about 110 min.

*Flow rate*   1 ml/min.

*Detection*   Spectrophotometer at 210 nm.

*Injection*   10 µl.

*Run time*   1.4 times the retention time of ebastine.

*Relative retention*   With reference to ebastine:
impurity A = about 0.04; impurity B = about 0.05;
impurity D = about 0.20; impurity C = about 0.22;
impurity F = about 0.42; impurity G = about 0.57;
impurity E = about 1.14.

*System suitability*   Reference solution (a):
— *resolution*: minimum 2.0 between the peaks due to
  impurity D and impurity C.

*Limits:*
— *impurities A, B, C, D, E, F, G*: for each impurity, not
  more than the area of the principal peak in the
  chromatogram obtained with reference solution (b)
  (0.1 per cent),
— *any other impurity*: for each impurity, not more than the
  area of the principal peak in the chromatogram obtained
  with reference solution (b) (0.1 per cent),
— *total*: not more than 4 times the area of the principal peak
  in the chromatogram obtained with reference solution (b)
  (0.4 per cent),
— *disregard limit*: 0.5 times the area of the principal peak in
  the chromatogram obtained with reference solution (b)
  (0.05 per cent).

**Sulphates** (*2.4.13*)
Maximum 100 ppm.

Suspend 2.5 g in 25 ml of *dilute nitric acid R*. Boil under a
reflux condenser for 10 min. Cool and filter. 15 ml of the
filtrate complies with the limit test for sulphates.

**Water** (*2.5.12*)
Maximum 0.5 per cent, determined on 0.500 g.

**Sulphated ash** (*2.4.14*)
Maximum 0.1 per cent, determined on 1.0 g.

**ASSAY**
Dissolve 0.350 g in 50 ml of *anhydrous acetic acid R*. Titrate
with *0.1 M perchloric acid*, determining the end-point
potentiometrically (*2.2.20*).

1 ml of *0.1 M perchloric acid* is equivalent to 46.97 mg of
$C_{32}H_{39}NO_2$.

**STORAGE**
Protected from light.

**IMPURITIES**

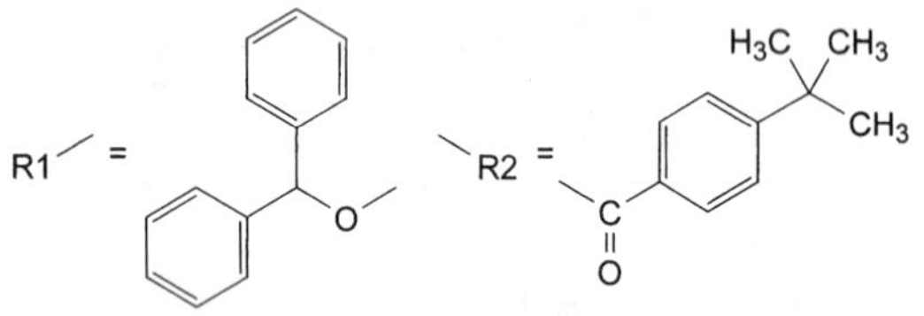

A. R1–H: diphenylmethanol (benzhydrol),

B. R2–CH₃: 1-[4-(1,1-dimethylethyl)phenyl]ethanone,

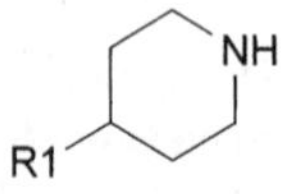

C. 4-(diphenylmethoxy)piperidine,

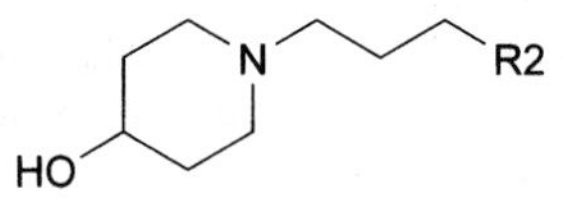

D. 1-[4-(1,1-dimethylethyl)phenyl]-4-(4-hydroxypiperidin-1-
yl)butan-1-one,

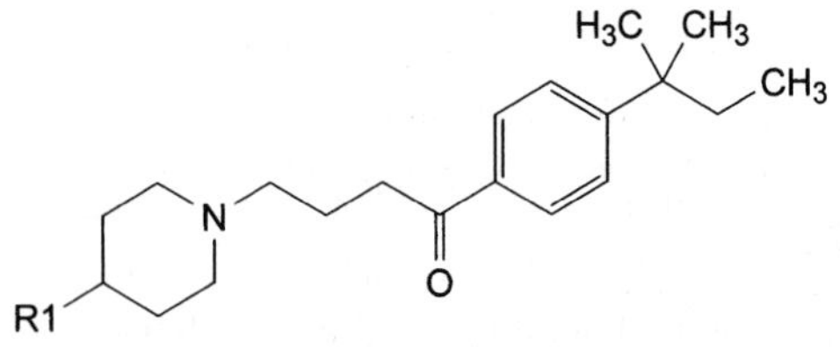

E. 1-[4-(1,1-dimethylpropyl)phenyl]-4-[4-
(diphenylmethoxy)piperidin-1-yl]butan-1-one,

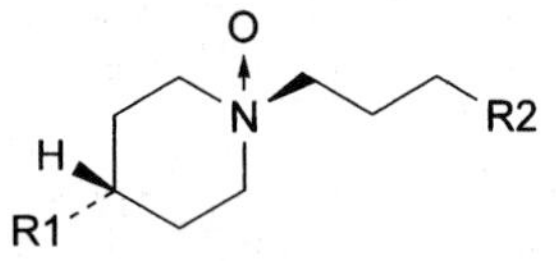

F. 1-[4-(1,1-dimethylethyl)phenyl]-4-[*cis*-4-
(diphenylmethoxy)-1-oxidopiperidin-1-yl]butan-1-one,

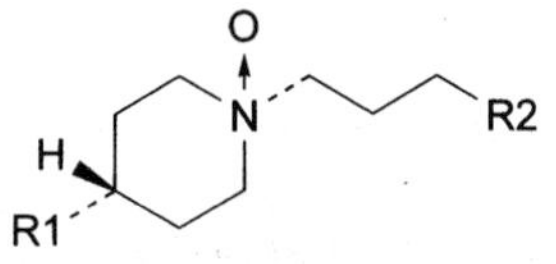

G. 1-[4-(1,1-dimethylethyl)phenyl]-4-[*trans*-4-
(diphenylmethoxy)-1-oxidopiperidin-1-yl]butan-1-one.

_____ *Ph Eur*

# Econazole

(*Ph Eur monograph 2049*)

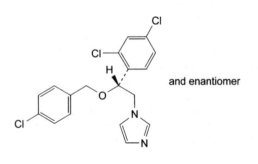

and enantiomer

$C_{18}H_{15}Cl_3N_2O$          381.7          27220-47-9

**Action and use**
Antifungal.

*Ph Eur* _____

**DEFINITION**
1-[(2*RS*)-2-[(4-Chlorobenzyl)oxy]-2-(2,4-
dichlorophenyl)ethyl]-1*H*-imidazole.

**Content**
99.0 per cent to 101.0 per cent (dried substance).

## CHARACTERS

**Appearance**

White or almost white powder.

**Solubility**

Practically insoluble in water, very soluble in alcohol and in methylene chloride.

## IDENTIFICATION

A. Melting point (*2.2.14*): 88 °C to 92 °C.

B. Infrared absorption spectrophotometry (*2.2.24*).

*Comparison  Ph. Eur. reference spectrum of econazole.*

## TESTS

**Related substances**

Liquid chromatography (*2.2.29*).

*Test solution*  Dissolve 0.100 g of the substance to be examined in *methanol R* and dilute to 10.0 ml with the same solvent.

*Reference solution (a)*  Dissolve 10 mg of *econazole for system suitability CRS* in *methanol R* and dilute to 1.0 ml with the same solvent.

*Reference solution (b)*  Dilute 1.0 ml of the test solution to 20.0 ml with *methanol R*. Dilute 1.0 ml of this solution to 25.0 ml with *methanol R*.

*Column:*
— *size*: $l$ = 0.10 m, $\varnothing$ = 4.6 mm,
— *stationary phase*: *base-deactivated octadecylsilyl silica gel for chromatography R* (3 µm),
— *temperature*: 35 °C.

*Mobile phase:*
— *mobile phase A*: mix 20 volumes of *methanol R* and 80 volumes of a 0.77 g/l solution of *ammonium acetate R*,
— *mobile phase B*: *methanol R, acetonitrile R* (40:60 *V/V*),

| Time (min) | Mobile phase A (per cent *V/V*) | Mobile phase B (per cent *V/V*) |
|---|---|---|
| 0 - 25 | 60 → 10 | 40 → 90 |
| 25 - 27 | 10 | 90 |
| 27 - 28 | 10 → 60 | 90 → 40 |
| 28 - 33 | 60 | 40 |

*Flow rate*  1.5 ml/min.

*Detection*  Spectrophotometer at 225 nm.

*Injection*  10 µl.

*Relative retention*  With reference to econazole (retention time = about 15 min): impurity A = about 0.2; impurity B = about 0.6; impurity C = about 1.1.

*System suitability*  Reference solution (a):
— *peak-to-valley ratio*: minimum 1.5, where $H_p$ = height above the baseline of the peak due to impurity C and $H_v$ = height above the baseline of the lowest point of the curve separating this peak from the peak due to econazole.

*Limits:*
— *correction factor*: for the calculation of content, multiply the peak area of impurity A by 1.4,
— *impurities A, B, C*: for each impurity, not more than the area of the principal peak in the chromatogram obtained with reference solution (b) (0.2 per cent),
— *total*: not more than 1.5 times the area of the principal peak in the chromatogram obtained with reference solution (b) (0.3 per cent),
— *disregard limit*: 0.25 times the area of the principal peak in the chromatogram obtained with reference solution (b) (0.05 per cent).

**Loss on drying** (*2.2.32*)

Maximum 0.5 per cent, determined on 1.000 g by drying *in vacuo* at 60 °C for 4 h.

**Sulphated ash** (*2.4.14*)

Maximum 0.1 per cent, determined on 1.0 g.

## ASSAY

Dissolve 0.300 g in 75 ml of *anhydrous acetic acid R*. Titrate with *0.1 M perchloric acid*, determining the end-point potentiometrically (*2.2.20*). Carry out a blank titration.

1 ml of *0.1 M perchloric acid* is equivalent to 38.17 mg of $C_{18}H_{15}Cl_3N_2O$.

## STORAGE

Protected from light.

## IMPURITIES

*Specified impurities*

*A, B, C.*

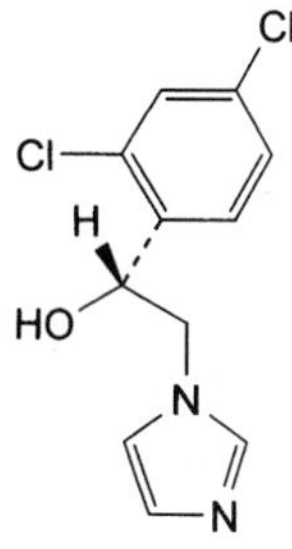

and enantiomer

A. (1*RS*)-1-(2,4-dichlorophenyl)-2-(1*H*-imidazol-1-yl)ethanol,

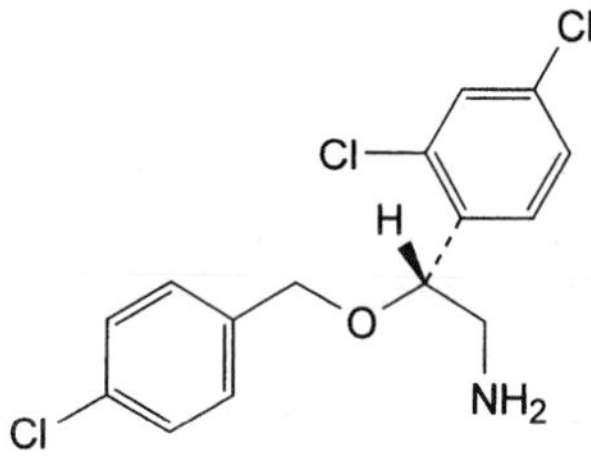

and enantiomer

B. (2*RS*)-2-[(4-chlorobenzyl)oxy]-2-(2,4-dichlorophenyl)ethanamine,

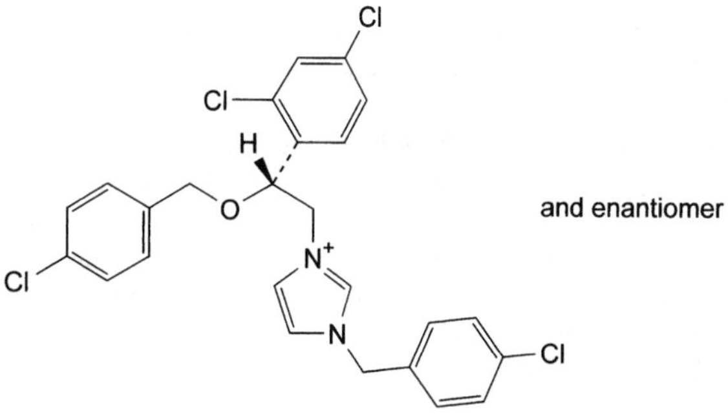

and enantiomer

C. 1-(4-chlorobenzyl)-3-[(2*RS*)-2-[(4-chlorobenzyl)oxy]-2-(2,4-dichlorophenyl)ethyl]imidazolium.

# Econazole Nitrate

*(Ph Eur monograph 0665)*

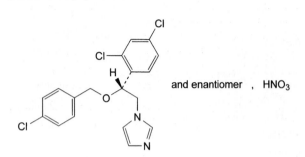

and enantiomer , HNO$_3$

$C_{18}H_{15}Cl_3N_2O,HNO_3$     444.7         *68797-31-9*

**Action and use**
Antifungal.

**Preparations**
Econazole Cream
Econazole Pessaries

*Ph Eur* _____

## DEFINITION

1-[(2RS)-2-[(4-Chlorobenzyl)oxy]-2-(2,4-dichlorophenyl)ethyl]-1H-imidazole nitrate.

**Content**
99.0 per cent to 101.0 per cent (dried substance).

## CHARACTERS

**Appearance**
White or almost white crystalline powder.

**Solubility**
Very slightly soluble in water, soluble in methanol, sparingly soluble in methylene chloride, slightly soluble in alcohol.

**mp**
About 165 °C, with decomposition.

## IDENTIFICATION

Infrared absorption spectrophotometry (*2.2.24*).

*Comparison* Ph. Eur. reference spectrum of econazole nitrate.

## TESTS

**Related substances**
Liquid chromatography (*2.2.29*).

*Test solution* Dissolve 0.100 g of the substance to be examined in *methanol R* and dilute to 10.0 ml with the same solvent.

*Reference solution (a)* Dissolve 10 mg of *econazole for system suitability CRS* in *methanol R* and dilute to 1.0 ml with the same solvent.

*Reference solution (b)* Dilute 1.0 ml of the test solution to 20.0 ml with *methanol R*. Dilute 1.0 ml of the solution to 25.0 ml with *methanol R*.

*Column:*
— *size*: *l* = 0.10 m, Ø = 4.6 mm,
— *stationary phase*: base-deactivated octadecylsilyl silica gel for chromatography R (3 μm),
— *temperature*: 35 °C.

*Mobile phase:*
— *mobile phase A*: mix 20 volumes of *methanol R* and 80 volumes of a 0.77 g/l solution of *ammonium acetate R*,
— *mobile phase B*: methanol R, acetonitrile R (40:60 *V/V*),

| Time (min) | Mobile phase A (per cent *V/V*) | Mobile phase B (per cent *V/V*) |
|---|---|---|
| 0 - 25 | 60 → 10 | 40 → 90 |
| 25 - 27 | 10 | 90 |
| 27 - 28 | 10 → 60 | 90 → 40 |
| 28 - 33 | 60 | 40 |

*Flow rate* 1.5 ml/min.

*Detection* Spectrophotometer at 225 nm.

*Injection* 10 μl.

*Relative retention* With reference to econazole (retention time = about 15 min): impurity A = about 0.2; impurity B = about 0.6; impurity C = about 1.1.

*System suitability* Reference solution (a):
— *peak-to-valley ratio*: minimum of 1.5, where $H_p$ = height above the baseline of the peak due to impurity C, and $H_v$ = height above the baseline of the lowest point of the curve separating this peak from the peak due to econazole.

*Limits:*
— *correction factor*: for the calculation of content, multiply the peak area of impurity A by 1.4,
— *impurities A, B, C*: for each impurity, not more than the area of the principal peak in the chromatogram obtained with reference solution (b) (0.2 per cent),
— *total*: not more than 1.5 times the area of the principal peak in the chromatogram obtained with reference solution (b) (0.3 per cent),
— *disregard limit*: 0.25 times the area of the principal peak in the chromatogram obtained with reference solution (b) (0.05 per cent); disregard the peak due to the nitrate ion at the beginning of the chromatogram.

**Loss on drying** (*2.2.32*)
Maximum 0.5 per cent, determined on 1.000 g by drying in an oven at 105 °C for 4 h.

**Sulphated ash** (*2.4.14*)
Maximum 0.1 per cent, determined on 1.0 g.

## ASSAY

Dissolve 0.400 g in 50 ml of *anhydrous acetic acid R*. Titrate with *0.1 M perchloric acid*, determining the end-point potentiometrically (*2.2.20*). Carry out a blank titration.

1 ml of *0.1 M perchloric acid* is equivalent to 44.47 mg of $C_{18}H_{16}Cl_3N_3O_4$.

## STORAGE

Protected from light.

## IMPURITIES

*Specified impurities* A, B, C.

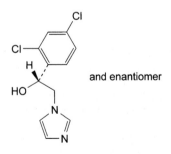

A. (1RS)-1-(2,4-dichlorophenyl)-2-(1H-imidazol-1-yl)ethanol,

B. (2RS)-2-[(4-chlorobenzyl)oxy]-2-(2,4-dichlorophenyl)ethanamine,

C. 1-(4-chlorobenzyl)-3-[(2RS)-2-[(4-chlorobenzyl)oxy]-2-(2,4-dichlorophenyl)ethyl]imidazolium.

_____ *Ph Eur*

# Edetic Acid

*(Ph Eur monograph 1612)*

$C_{10}H_{16}N_2O_8$          292.2          60-00-4

**Action and use**
Chelating agent.

*Ph Eur* _____

## DEFINITION
(Ethylenedinitrilo)tetraacetic acid.

## Content
98.0 per cent to 101.0 per cent.

## CHARACTERS
**Appearance**
White or almost white, crystalline powder or colourless crystals.

**Solubility**
Practically insoluble in water and in ethanol (96 per cent). It dissolves in dilute solutions of alkali hydroxides.

## IDENTIFICATION
*First identification*   A.

*Second identification*   B, C.

A. Infrared absorption spectrophotometry (*2.2.24*).

*Preparation*   Discs, after drying the substance to be examined in an oven at 100-105 °C for 2 h.

*Comparison   sodium edetate R*, treated as follows: dissolve 0.25 g of *sodium edetate R* in 5 ml of *water R*, add 1.0 ml of *dilute hydrochloric acid R*. Filter, wash the residue with 2 quantities, each of 5 ml, of *water R* and dry the residue in an oven at 100-105 °C for 2 h.

B. To 5 ml of *water R* add 0.1 ml of *ammonium thiocyanate solution R* and 0.1 ml of *ferric chloride solution R1* and mix. The solution is red. Add 0.5 ml of solution S (see Tests). The solution becomes yellowish.

C. To 10 ml of solution S add 0.5 ml of *calcium chloride solution R*. Make alkaline to *red litmus paper R* by the addition of *dilute ammonia R2* and add 3 ml of *ammonium oxalate solution R*. No precipitate is formed.

## TESTS
**Solution S**
Dissolve 5.0 g in 20 ml of *dilute sodium hydroxide solution R* and dilute to 100 ml with *water R*.

**Appearance of solution**
Solution S is clear (*2.2.1*) and colourless (*2.2.2, Method II*).

**Impurity A**
Liquid chromatography (*2.2.29*). *Carry out the test protected from light.*

*Solvent mixture*   Dissolve 10.0 g of *ferric sulphate pentahydrate R* in 20 ml of *0.5 M sulphuric acid* and add 780 ml of *water R*. Adjust to pH 2.0 with *1 M sodium hydroxide* and dilute to 1000 ml with *water R*.

*Test solution*   Dissolve 0.100 g of the substance to be examined in 1.0 ml of *1 M sodium hydroxide* and dilute to 25.0 ml with the solvent mixture.

*Reference solution*   Dissolve 40.0 mg of *nitrilotriacetic acid R* in the solvent mixture and dilute to 100.0 ml with the solvent mixture. To 1.0 ml of the solution add 0.1 ml of the test solution and dilute to 100.0 ml with the solvent mixture.

*Column:*
— *size*: $l$ = 0.10 m, Ø = 4.6 mm,
— *stationary phase*: spherical *graphitised carbon for chromatography R1* (5 μm) with a specific surface area of 120 $m^2$/g and a pore size of 25 nm.

*Mobile phase*   Dissolve 50.0 mg of *ferric sulphate pentahydrate R* in 50 ml of *0.5 M sulphuric acid* and add 750 ml of *water R*. Adjust to pH 1.5 with *0.5 M sulphuric acid* or *1 M sodium hydroxide*, add 20 ml of *ethylene glycol R* and dilute to 1000 ml with *water R*.

*Flow rate*   1 ml/min.

*Detection*   Spectrophotometer at 273 nm.

*Injection*   20 μl; filter the solutions and inject immediately.

*Run time*   4 times the retention time of the iron complex of impurity A.

*Retention time*   Iron complex of impurity A = about 5 min; iron complex of edetic acid = about 10 min.

*System suitability*   Reference solution:
— *resolution*: minimum 7 between the peaks due to the iron complex of impurity A and the iron complex of edetic acid,
— *signal-to-noise ratio*: minimum 50 for the peak due to impurity A.

*Limit:*
— *impurity A*: not more than the area of the corresponding peak in the chromatogram obtained with the reference solution (0.1 per cent).

**Chlorides** (*2.4.4*)
Maximum 200 ppm.

To 10 ml of solution S add 8 ml of *nitric acid R* and stir for 10 min. A precipitate is formed. Filter and wash the filter with *water R*. Collect the filtrate and the washings and dilute to 20 ml with *water R*. Dilute 10 ml of this solution to 15 ml with *water R*.

**Iron** *(2.4.9)*

Maximum 80 ppm.

Dilute 2.5 ml of solution S to 10 ml with *water R* and add 0.25 g of *calcium chloride R* before adding the *thioglycollic acid R*. Allow to stand for 5 min. Also add 0.25 g of *calcium chloride* R to the standard.

**Heavy metals** *(2.4.8)*

Maximum 20 ppm.

1.0 g complies with test F. Prepare the reference solution using 2 ml of *lead standard solution (10 ppm Pb) R*.

**Sulphated ash** *(2.4.14)*

Maximum 0.2 per cent, determined on 1.0 g.

**ASSAY**

Dissolve 0.250 g in 2.0 ml of *dilute sodium hydroxide solution R* and dilute to 300 ml with water R. Add 2 g of *hexamethylenetetramine R* and 2 ml of *dilute hydrochloric acid R*. Titrate with *0.1 M zinc sulphate* using about 50 mg of *xylenol orange triturate R* as indicator.

1 ml of *0.1 M zinc sulphate* corresponds to 29.22 mg of $C_{10}H_{16}N_2O_8$.

**STORAGE**

Protected from light.

**IMPURITIES**

*Specified impurities A.*

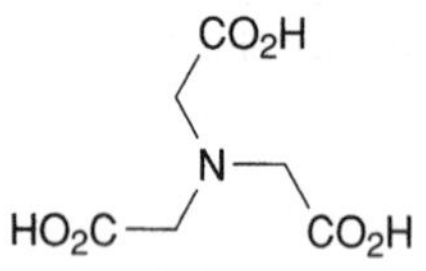

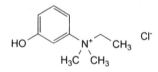

A. nitrilotriacetic acid.

——————————————————————— *Ph Eur*

# Edrophonium Chloride

*(Ph Eur monograph 2106)*

$C_{10}H_{16}ClNO$      201.71      *16-38-1*

**Action and use**

Cholinesterase inhibitor.

**Preparation**

Edrophonium Injection

*Ph Eur* ——————————————————————

**DEFINITION**

*N*-Ethyl-3-hydroxy-*N*,*N*-dimethylanilinium chloride.

**Content**

99.0 per cent to 101.0 per cent (dried substance).

**CHARACTERS**

**Appearance**

White or almost white, crystalline powder.

**Solubility**

Very soluble in water, freely soluble in ethanol (96 per cent), practically insoluble in methylene chloride.

**IDENTIFICATION**

A. Infrared absorption spectrophotometry *(2.2.24)*.

*Comparison edrophonium chloride CRS.*

B. It gives reaction (a) of chlorides *(2.3.1)*.

**TESTS**

**Appearance of solution**

The solution is clear *(2.2.1)* and colourless *(2.2.2, Method II)*.

Dissolve 0.5 g in *water R* and dilute to 25 ml with the same solvent.

**pH** *(2.2.3)*

4.0 to 5.0.

Dissolve 1.0 g in *carbon dioxide-free water R* and dilute to 10.0 ml with the same solvent.

**Related substances**

Liquid chromatography *(2.2.29)*.

*Test solution*    Dissolve 50.0 mg in *water R* and dilute to 50.0 ml with the same solvent.

*Reference solution (a)*    Dissolve 10.0 mg of *3-dimethylaminophenol R* in *acetonitrile R* and dilute to 10.0 ml with the same solvent.

*Reference solution (b)*    Mix 1.0 ml of the test solution and 1.0 ml of reference solution (a) and dilute to 100.0 ml with *water R*. Dilute 10.0 ml of this solution to 100.0 ml with *water R*.

*Column:*

— *size: l* = 0.25 m, Ø = 4.6 mm,
— *stationary phase: styrene-divinylbenzene copolymer R* (8-10 μm).

*Mobile phase*    Mix 10 volumes of *acetonitrile R* and 90 volumes of a 7.7 g/l solution of *tetramethylammonium bromide R* previously adjusted to pH 3.0 with *phosphoric acid R*.

*Flow rate*    1 ml/min.

*Detection*    Spectrophotometer at 281 nm.

*Injection*    20 μl.

*Run time*    Twice the retention time of edrophonium.

*Relative retention*    With reference to edrophonium (retention time = about 3.8 min): impurity A = about 1.3.

*System suitability*    Reference solution (b):
— *resolution*: minimum 2.0 between the peaks due to edrophonium and impurity A.

*Limits:*

— *impurity A*: not more than the area of the corresponding peak in the chromatogram obtained with reference solution (b) (0.1 per cent),
— *any other impurity*: for each impurity, not more than the area of the peak due to edrophonium in the chromatogram obtained with reference solution (b) (0.1 per cent),
— *total*: not more than 5 times the area of the peak due to edrophonium in the chromatogram obtained with reference solution (b) (0.5 per cent),

— *disregard limit*: 0.5 times the area of the peak due to edrophonium in the chromatogram obtained with reference solution (b) (0.05 per cent).

**Loss on drying** (*2.2.32*)
Maximum 0.5 per cent, determined on 1.000 g by drying in a desiccator over *diphosphorus pentoxide R* at a pressure not exceeding 0.7 kPa for 24 h.

**Sulphated ash** (*2.4.14*)
Maximum 0.1 per cent, determined on 1.0 g.

**Bacterial endotoxins** (*2.6.14*)
Less than 8.3 IU/mg.

**ASSAY**
Dissolve 0.150 g in 60 ml of a mixture of equal volumes of *acetic anhydride R* and *anhydrous acetic acid R*. Titrate with *0.1 M perchloric acid*, determining the end-point potentiometrically (*2.2.20*).

1 ml of *0.1 M perchloric acid* is equivalent to 20.17 mg of $C_{10}H_{16}ClNO$.

**STORAGE**
Protected from light.

**IMPURITIES**
*Specified impurities   A.*

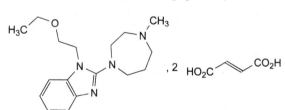

A. 3-(dimethylamino)phenol.

_____ *Ph Eur*

# Emedastine Fumarate

(*Emedastine Difumarate, Ph Eur monograph 2242*)

$C_{25}H_{34}N_4O_9$        534.6        *87233-62-3*

**Action and use**
Histamine $H_1$ receptor antagonist; antihistamine.

*Ph Eur* _____

**DEFINITION**
1-(2-Ethoxyethyl)-2-(4-methylhexahydro-1*H*-1,4-diazepin-1-yl)-1*H*-benzimidazole bis[hydrogen (2*E*)-butenedioate].

**Content**
99.0 per cent to 101.0 per cent (dried substance).

**CHARACTERS**

**Appearance**
White or yellowish powder.

**Solubility**
Soluble in water, sparingly soluble in anhydrous ethanol, very slightly soluble in acetone.

It shows polymorphism (*5.9*).

**IDENTIFICATION**
Infrared absorption spectrophotometry (*2.2.24*).

*Comparison   emedastine difumarate CRS.*

If the spectra obtained in the solid state show differences, dissolve the substance to be examined and the reference substance separately in *anhydrous ethanol R*, evaporate to dryness and record new spectra using the residues.

**TESTS**

**Appearance of solution**
The solution is clear (*2.2.1*) and not more intensely coloured than reference solution $Y_5$ (*2.2.2, Method II*).

Dissolve 2.50 g in *water R* and dilute to 50 ml with the same solvent.

**pH** (*2.2.3*)
3.0 to 4.5.

Dissolve 0.20 g in 100 ml of *carbon dioxide-free water R*.

**Related substances**
Liquid chromatography (*2.2.29*).

*Test solution*   Dissolve 10 mg of the substance to be examined in the mobile phase and dilute to 10 ml with the mobile phase.

*Reference solution (a)*   Dissolve 5 mg of *emedastine impurity E CRS* in the mobile phase and dilute to 25 ml with the mobile phase.

*Reference solution (b)*   Dissolve 10 mg of the substance to be examined in the mobile phase. Add 0.5 ml of reference solution (a) and dilute to 10 ml with the mobile phase.

*Reference solution (c)*   Dilute 5.0 ml of the test solution to 50.0 ml with the mobile phase. Dilute 1.0 ml of this solution to 100.0 ml with the mobile phase.

*Column*:
— *size*: $l$ = 0.15 m, Ø = 4.6 mm,
— *stationary phase*: octadecylsilyl silica gel for chromatography *R* (5 μm).

*Mobile phase*   Dissolve 3.9 g of *disodium hydrogen phosphate R* and 2.5 g of *sodium dodecyl sulphate R* in *water R* and dilute to 1000.0 ml with the same solvent. Adjust to pH 2.4 with *phosphoric acid R*. Mix 550 volumes of this solution with 450 volumes of *acetonitrile R*.

*Flow rate*   1.0 ml/min.

*Detection*   Spectrophotometer at 280 nm.

*Injection*   10 μl of the test solution and reference solutions (b) and (c).

*Run time*   Twice the retention time of emedastine.

*Relative retention*   With reference to emedastine (retention time = about 18 min): fumaric acid = about 0.1; impurity A = about 0.2; impurity B = about 0.3; impurity C = about 0.5; impurity D = about 0.7; impurity E = about 0.9; impurity F = about 1.4.

*System suitability*   Reference solution (b):
— *peak-to-valley ratio*: minimum 4, where $H_p$ = height above the baseline of the peak due to impurity E and $H_v$ = height above the baseline of the lowest point of the curve separating this peak from the peak due to emedastine.

*Limits*:
— *impurities A, B, C, D, E, F*: for each impurity, not more than the area of the principal peak in the chromatogram obtained with reference solution (c) (0.1 per cent);

— *unspecified impurities*: for each impurity, not more than the area of the principal peak in the chromatogram obtained with reference solution (c) (0.1 per cent);

— *total*: not more than twice the area of the principal peak in the chromatogram obtained with reference solution (c) (0.2 per cent);

— *disregard limit*: 0.5 times the area of the principal peak in the chromatogram obtained with reference solution (c) (0.05 per cent); disregard the peak due to fumaric acid.

**Loss on drying** (*2.2.32*)
Maximum 0.5 per cent, determined on 1.000 g by drying in an oven at 105 °C for 3 h.

**Sulphated ash** (*2.4.14*)
Maximum 0.1 per cent, determined on 1.0 g.

**ASSAY**
Dissolve 0.200 g in 50 ml of *glacial acetic acid R*. Titrate with *0.1 M perchloric acid*, determining the end-point potentiometrically (*2.2.20*).

1 ml of *0.1 M perchloric acid* is equivalent to 26.73 mg of $C_{25}H_{34}N_4O_9$.

**STORAGE**
Protected from light.

**IMPURITIES**
*Specified impurities   A, B, C, D, E, F.*

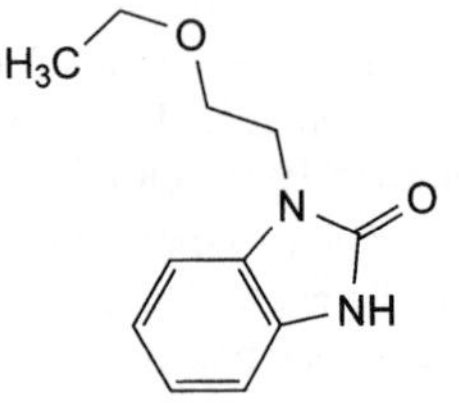

A. 1-(2-ethoxyethyl)-1,3-dihydro-2*H*-benzimidazol-2-one,

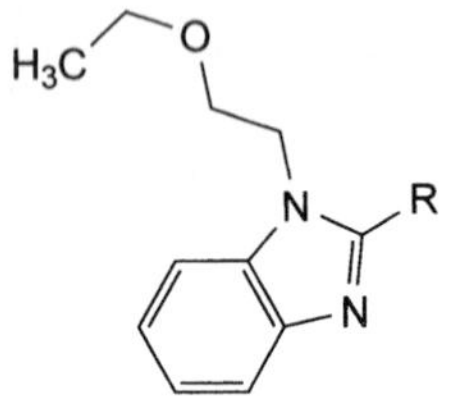

B. R = Cl: 2-chloro-1-(2-ethoxyethyl)-1*H*-benzimidazole,

F. R = NH-[CH$_2$]$_3$-NH-CH$_3$: *N*-[1-(2-ethoxyethyl)-1*H*-benzimidazol-2-yl]-*N'*-methylpropane-1,3-diamine,

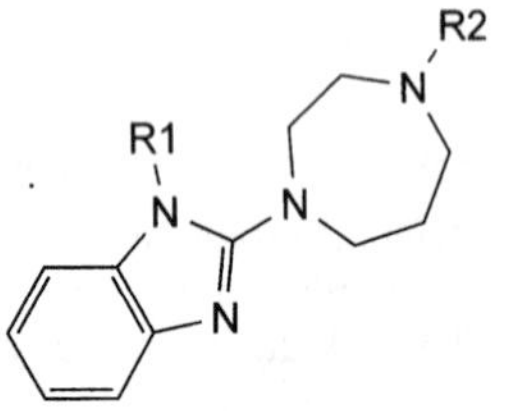

C. R1 = CH$_2$-CH$_2$OH, R2 = CH$_3$:
2-[2-(4-methylhexahydro-1*H*-1,4-diazepin-1-yl)-1*H*-benzimidazol-1-yl]ethanol,

D. R1 = CH=CH$_2$, R2 = CH$_3$:
1-ethenyl-2-(4-methylhexahydro-1*H*-1,4-diazepin-1-yl)-1*H*-benzimidazole,

E. R1 = CH$_2$-CH$_2$-O-C$_2$H$_5$, R2 = H: 1-(2-ethoxyethyl)-2-(hexahydro-1*H*-1,4-diazepin-1-yl)-1*H*-benzimidazole.

*Ph Eur*

# Emetine Hydrochloride

(*Emetine Hydrochloride Heptahydrate,*
*Ph Eur monograph 0080*)

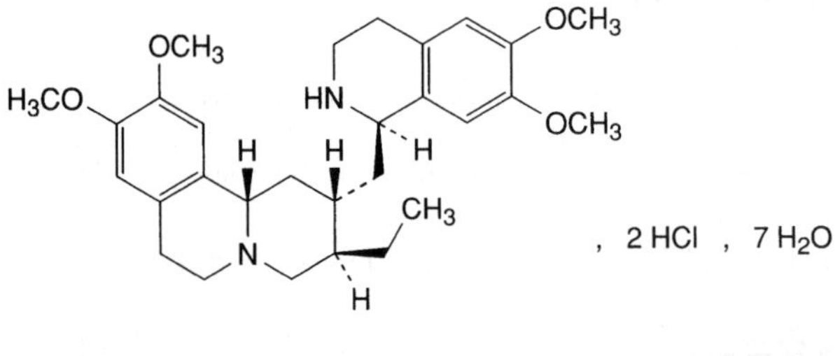

$C_{29}H_{40}N_2O_4,2HCl,7H_2O$     679.7            *316-42-7*
                                            *(anhydrous)*

**Action and use**
Antiprotozoal.

*Ph Eur*

**DEFINITION**
Emetine hydrochloride heptahydrate contains not less than 98.0 per cent and not more than the equivalent of 102.0 per cent of (2*S*,3*R*,11b*S*)-2-[[(1*R*)-6,7-dimethoxy-1,2,3,4-tetrahydroisoquinolin-1-yl]methyl]-3-ethyl-9,10-dimethoxy-1,3,4,6,7,11b-hexahydro-2*H*-benzo[*a*]quinolizine dihydrochloride, calculated with reference to the dried substance.

**CHARACTERS**
A white or slightly yellowish, crystalline powder, freely soluble in water and in alcohol.

**IDENTIFICATION**
*First identification   A, E.*
*Second identification   B, C, D, E.*

A. Examine by infrared absorption spectrophotometry (*2.2.24*), comparing with the spectrum obtained with *emetine hydrochloride CRS*.

B. Examine the chromatograms obtained in the test for related substances in ultraviolet light at 365 nm. The principal spot in the chromatogram obtained with the test solution is similar in position, fluorescence and size to the spot in the chromatogram obtained with reference solution (a).

C. Dissolve about 10 mg in 2 ml of *dilute hydrogen peroxide solution R*, add 1 ml of *hydrochloric acid R* and heat. An orange colour develops.

D. Sprinkle about 5 mg on the surface of 1 ml of *sulphomolybdic reagent R2*. A bright-green colour develops.

E. It gives reaction (a) of chlorides (*2.3.1*).

**TESTS**
**Solution S**
Dissolve 1.25 g in *carbon dioxide-free water R* and dilute to 25 ml with the same solvent.

**Appearance of solution**
Solution S is clear (*2.2.1*) and not more intensely coloured than reference solution Y$_5$ or BY$_5$ (*2.2.2, Method II*).

## pH (2.2.3)

Dilute 4 ml of solution S to 10 ml with *carbon dioxide-free water R*. The pH of the solution is 4.0 to 6.0.

## Specific optical rotation (2.2.7)

Dissolve in *water R* a quantity of the substance to be examined corresponding to 1.250 g of dried substance and dilute to 25.0 ml with the same solvent. The specific optical rotation is + 16 to + 19, calculated with reference to the dried substance.

## Related substances

Examine by thin-layer chromatography (2.2.27), using a *TLC silica gel G plate R. Prepare the solutions immediately before use.*

*Test solution*   Dissolve 50 mg of the substance to be examined in *methanol R* containing 1 per cent *V/V* of *dilute ammonia R2* and dilute to 100 ml with the same solvent.

*Reference solution (a)*   Dissolve 50 mg of *emetine hydrochloride CRS* in *methanol R* containing 1 per cent *V/V* of *dilute ammonia R2* and dilute to 100 ml with the same solvent.

*Reference solution (b)*   Dissolve 10 mg of *isoemetine hydrobromide CRS* in *methanol R* containing 1 per cent *V/V* of *dilute ammonia R2* and dilute to 100 ml with the same solvent. Dilute 5 ml of this solution to 50 ml with *methanol R* containing 1 per cent *V/V* of *dilute ammonia R2*.

*Reference solution (c)*   Dissolve 10 mg of *cephaeline hydrochloride CRS* in *methanol R* containing 1 per cent *V/V* of *dilute ammonia R2* and dilute to 100 ml with the same solvent. Dilute 5 ml of this solution to 50 ml with *methanol R* containing 1 per cent *V/V* of *dilute ammonia R2*.

*Reference solution (d)*   Dilute 1 ml of reference solution (a) to 100 ml with *methanol R* containing 1 per cent *V/V* of *dilute ammonia R2*.

*Reference solution (e)*   To 1 ml of reference solution (a) add 1 ml of reference solution (b) and 1 ml of reference solution (c).

Apply to the plate 10 µl of the test solution and each of reference solutions (a), (b), (c) and (d) and 30 µl of reference solution (e). Develop over a path of 15 cm using a mixture of 0.5 volumes of *diethylamine R*, 2 volumes of *water R*, 5 volumes of *methanol R*, 20 volumes of *ethylene glycol monomethyl ether R* and 100 volumes of *chloroform R*. Allow the plate to dry in air until the solvent has evaporated. Spray in a well ventilated fume-cupboard with *chloroformic solution of iodine R* and heat at 60 °C for 15 min. Examine in ultraviolet light at 365 nm. In the chromatogram obtained with the test solution, any spots corresponding to isoemetine and cephaeline are not more intense than the spots in the chromatograms obtained with reference solutions (b) and (c) respectively (2.0 per cent); any spot, apart from the principal spot and the spots corresponding to isoemetine and cephaeline, is not more intense than the spot in the chromatogram obtained with reference solution (d) (1.0 per cent). The test is not valid unless the chromatogram obtained with reference solution (e) shows three clearly separated spots.

## Loss on drying (2.2.32)

15.0 per cent to 19.0 per cent, determined on 1.00 g by drying in an oven at 105 °C for 3 h.

## Sulphated ash (2.4.14)

Not more than 0.1 per cent, determined on 1.0 g.

## ASSAY

Dissolve 0.200 g in a mixture of 5.0 ml of *0.01 M hydrochloric acid* and 50 ml of *alcohol R*. Carry out a potentiometric titration (2.2.20), using *0.1 M sodium hydroxide*. Read the volume added between the 2 points of inflexion.

1 ml of *0.1 M sodium hydroxide* is equivalent to 27.68 mg of $C_{29}H_{42}Cl_2N_2O_4$.

## STORAGE

Store protected from light.

*Ph Eur*

# Emetine Hydrochloride Pentahydrate

*(Ph Eur monograph 0081)*

$C_{29}H_{40}N_2O_4,2HCl,5H_2O$     643.6     *316-42-7 (anhydrous)*

## Action and use

Antiprotozoal.

*Ph Eur*

## DEFINITION

Emetine hydrochloride pentahydrate contains not less than 98.0 per cent and not more than the equivalent of 102.0 per cent of (2S,3R,11bS)-2-[[(1R)-6,7-dimethoxy-1,2,3,4-tetrahydroisoquinolin-1-yl]methyl]-3-ethyl-9,10-dimethoxy-1,3,4,6,7,11b-hexahydro-2H-benzo[a]quinolizine dihydrochloride, calculated with reference to the dried substance.

## CHARACTERS

A white or slightly yellowish, crystalline powder, freely soluble in water and in alcohol.

## IDENTIFICATION

*First identification   A, E.*

*Second identification   B, C, D, E.*

A. Examine by infrared absorption spectrophotometry (2.2.24), comparing with the spectrum obtained with *emetine hydrochloride CRS*.

B. Examine the chromatograms obtained in the test for related substances in ultraviolet light at 365 nm. The principal spot in the chromatogram obtained with the test solution is similar in position, fluorescence and size to the spot in the chromatogram obtained with reference solution (a).

C. Dissolve about 10 mg in 2 ml of *dilute hydrogen peroxide solution R*, add 1 ml of *hydrochloric acid R* and heat. An orange colour develops.

D. Sprinkle about 5 mg on the surface of 1 ml of *sulphomolybdic reagent R2*. A bright-green colour develops.

E. It gives reaction (a) of chlorides (2.3.1).

## TESTS

### Solution S
Dissolve 1.25 g in *carbon dioxide-free water R* and dilute to 25 ml with the same solvent.

### Appearance of solution
Solution S is clear (2.2.1) and not more intensely coloured than reference solution $Y_5$ or $BY_5$ (2.2.2, *Method II*).

### pH (2.2.3)
Dilute 4 ml of solution S to 10 ml with *carbon dioxide-free water R*. The pH of the solution is 4.0 to 6.0.

### Specific optical rotation (2.2.7)
Dissolve in *water R* a quantity of the substance to be examined corresponding to 1.250 g of dried substance and dilute to 25.0 ml with the same solvent. The specific optical rotation is + 16 to + 19, calculated with reference to the dried substance.

### Related substances
Examine by thin-layer chromatography (2.2.27), using a *TLC silica gel G plate R. Prepare the solutions immediately before use.*

*Test solution* Dissolve 50 mg of the substance to be examined in *methanol R* containing 1 per cent *V/V* of *dilute ammonia R2* and dilute to 100 ml with the same solvent.

*Reference solution (a)* Dissolve 50 mg of *emetine hydrochloride CRS* in *methanol R* containing 1 per cent *V/V* of *dilute ammonia R2* and dilute to 100 ml with the same solvent.

*Reference solution (b)* Dissolve 10 mg of *isoemetine hydrobromide CRS* in *methanol R* containing 1 per cent *V/V* of *dilute ammonia R2* and dilute to 100 ml with the same solvent. Dilute 5 ml of this solution to 50 ml with *methanol R* containing 1 per cent *V/V* of *dilute ammonia R2*.

*Reference solution (c)* Dissolve 10 mg of *cephaeline hydrochloride CRS* in *methanol R* containing 1 per cent *V/V* of *dilute ammonia R2* and dilute to 100 ml with the same solvent. Dilute 5 ml of this solution to 50 ml with *methanol R* containing 1 per cent *V/V* of *dilute ammonia R2*.

*Reference solution (d)* Dilute 1 ml of reference solution (a) to 100 ml with *methanol R* containing 1 per cent *V/V* of *dilute ammonia R2*.

*Reference solution (e)* To 1 ml of reference solution (a) add 1 ml of reference solution (b) and 1 ml of reference solution (c).

Apply to the plate 10 μl of the test solution and each of reference solutions (a), (b), (c) and (d) and 30 μl of reference solution (e). Develop over a path of 15 cm using a mixture of 0.5 volumes of *diethylamine R*, 2 volumes of *water R*, 5 volumes of *methanol R*, 20 volumes of *ethylene glycol monomethyl ether R* and 100 volumes of *chloroform R*. Allow the plate to dry in air until the solvent has evaporated. Spray in a well ventilated fume-cupboard with *chloroformic solution of iodine R* and heat at 60 °C for 15 min. Examine in ultraviolet light at 365 nm. In the chromatogram obtained with the test solution, any spots corresponding to isoemetine and cephaeline are not more intense than the spots in the chromatograms obtained with reference solutions (b) and (c) respectively (2.0 per cent); any spot, apart from the principal spot and the spots corresponding to isoemetine and cephaeline, is not more intense than the spot in the chromatogram obtained with reference solution (d) (1.0 per cent). The test is not valid unless the chromatogram

obtained with reference solution (e) shows three clearly separated spots.

### Loss on drying (2.2.32)
11.0 per cent to 15.0 per cent, determined on 1.00 g by drying in an oven at 105 °C for 3 h.

### Sulphated ash (2.4.14)
Not more than 0.1 per cent, determined on 1.0 g.

## ASSAY
Dissolve 0.200 g in a mixture of 5.0 ml of *0.01 M hydrochloric acid* and 50 ml of *alcohol R*. Carry out a potentiometric titration (2.2.20), using *0.1 M sodium hydroxide*. Read the volume added between the two points of inflexion.

1 ml of *0.1 M sodium hydroxide* is equivalent to 27.68 mg of $C_{29}H_{42}Cl_2N_2O_4$.

## STORAGE
Store protected from light.

*Ph Eur*

---

# Enalapril Maleate

*(Ph Eur monograph 1420)*

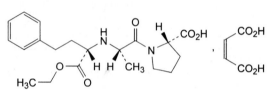

$C_{20}H_{28}N_2O_5,C_4H_4O_4$    492.5    76095-16-4

### Action and use
Angiotensin converting enzyme inhibitor.

*Ph Eur*

## DEFINITION
(2*S*)-1-[(2*S*)-2-[[(1*S*)-1-(Ethoxycarbonyl)-3-phenylpropyl]amino]propanoyl]pyrrolidine-2-carboxylic acid (*Z*)-butenedioate.

### Content
98.5 per cent to 101.5 per cent (dried substance).

## CHARACTERS

### Appearance
White or almost white, crystalline powder.

### Solubility
Sparingly soluble in water, freely soluble in methanol, practically insoluble in methylene chloride. It dissolves in dilute solutions of alkali hydroxides.

### mp
About 144 °C.

## IDENTIFICATION
Infrared absorption spectrophotometry (2.2.24).

*Comparison   enalapril maleate CRS.*

## TESTS

### Solution S
Dissolve 0.25 g in *carbon dioxide-free water R* and dilute to 25.0 ml with the same solvent.

### Appearance of solution
Solution S is clear (2.2.1) and colourless (2.2.2, *Method II*).

**pH** *(2.2.3)*

2.4 to 2.9 for solution S.

**Specific optical rotation** *(2.2.7)*

− 48 to − 51 (dried substance), determined on solution S.

**Related substances**

Liquid chromatography *(2.2.29)*.

*Buffer solution A*   Dissolve 2.8 g of *sodium dihydrogen phosphate monohydrate R* in 950 ml of *water R*. Adjust to pH 2.5 with *phosphoric acid R* and dilute to 1000 ml with *water R*.

*Buffer solution B*   Dissolve 2.8 g of *sodium dihydrogen phosphate monohydrate R* in 950 ml of *water R*. Adjust to pH 6.8 with *strong sodium hydroxide solution R* and dilute to 1000 ml with *water R*.

*Dissolution mixture*   Mix 50 ml of *acetonitrile R1* and 950 ml of buffer solution A.

*Test solution*   Dissolve 30.0 mg of the substance to be examined in the dissolution mixture and dilute to 100.0 ml with the dissolution mixture.

*Reference solution (a)*   Dilute 1.0 ml of the test solution to 100.0 ml with the dissolution mixture.

*Reference solution (b)*   Dissolve 3.0 mg of *enalapril for system suitability CRS* in the dissolution mixture and dilute to 10.0 ml with the dissolution mixture.

*Column:*
— *size: l* = 0.15 m, Ø = 4.1 mm;
— *stationary phase:* styrene-divinylbenzene copolymer *R* (5 μm);
— *temperature:* 70 °C.

*Mobile phase:*
— *mobile phase A:* mix 50 ml of *acetonitrile R1* and 950 ml of buffer solution B;
— *mobile phase B:* mix 340 ml of buffer solution B and 660 ml of *acetonitrile R1*;

| Time (min) | Mobile phase A (per cent *V/V*) | Mobile phase B (per cent *V/V*) |
|---|---|---|
| 0 - 20 | 95 → 40 | 5 → 60 |
| 20 - 25 | 40 | 60 |
| 25 - 26 | 40 → 95 | 60 → 5 |
| 26 - 30 | 95 | 5 |

*Flow rate*   1.4 ml/min.

*Detection*   Spectrophotometer at 215 nm.

*Injection*   50 μl.

*Retention time*   Enalapril = about 11 min; impurity A = about 12 min.

*System suitability*   Reference solution (b):
— *peak-to-valley ratio:* minimum 10, where $H_p$ = height above the baseline of the peak due to impurity A and $H_v$ = height above the baseline of the lowest point of the curve separating this peak from the peak due to enalapril.

*Limits:*
— *impurity A:* not more than the area of the principal peak in the chromatogram obtained with reference solution (a) (1.0 per cent);
— *impurities B, C, D, E, H:* for each impurity, not more than 0.3 times the area of the principal peak in the chromatogram obtained with reference solution (a) (0.3 per cent);
— *sum of impurities other than A:* not more than the area of the principal peak in the chromatogram obtained with reference solution (a) (1.0 per cent);

— *disregard limit:* 0.05 times the area of the principal peak in the chromatogram obtained with reference solution (a) (0.05 per cent); disregard the peak due to maleic acid.

**Heavy metals** *(2.4.8)*

Maximum 10 ppm.

2.0 g complies with test C. Prepare the reference solution using 2 ml of *lead standard solution (10 ppm Pb) R*.

**Loss on drying** *(2.2.32)*

Maximum 1.0 per cent, determined on 1.000 g by drying in an oven at 105 °C for 3 h.

**Sulphated ash** *(2.4.14*

Maximum 0.1 per cent, determined on 1.0 g.

**ASSAY**

Dissolve 0.100 g in *carbon dioxide-free water R* and dilute to 30 ml with the same solvent. Titrate with *0.1 M sodium hydroxide* determining the end-point potentiometrically *(2.2.20)*. Titrate to the 2$^{nd}$ point of inflexion.

1 ml of *0.1 M sodium hydroxide* is equivalent to 16.42 mg of $C_{24}H_{32}N_2O_9$.

**STORAGE**

Protected from light.

**IMPURITIES**

*Specified impurities   A, B, C, D, E, H.*

*Other detectable impurities* (The following substances would, if present at a sufficient level, be detected by one or other of the tests in the monograph. They are limited by the general acceptance criterion for other/unspecified impurities and/or by the general monograph Substances for pharmaceutical use (2034). It is therefore not necessary to identify these impurities for demonstration of compliance. See also 5.10. Control of impurities in substances for pharmaceutical use)

*F, G, I.*

A. (2*S*)-1-[(2*S*)-2-[[(1*R*)-1-(ethoxycarbonyl)-3-phenylpropyl]amino]propanoyl]pyrrolidine-2-carboxylic acid,

B. (2*S*)-2-[[(1*S*)-1-(ethoxycarbonyl)-3-phenylpropyl]amino]propanoic acid,

C. R = H: (2*S*)-1-[(2*S*)-2-[[(1*S*)-1-carboxy-3-phenylpropyl]amino]propanoyl]pyrrolidine-2-carboxylic acid,

E. R = CH₂-CH₂-C₆H₅: (2*S*)-1-[(2*S*)-2-[[(1*S*)-3-phenyl-1-[(2phenylethoxy)carbonyl]propyl]amino]propanoyl] pyrrolidine-2-carboxylic acid,

F. R = C₄H₉: (2S)-1-[(2S)-2-[[(1S)-1-(butoxycarbonyl)-3-phenylpropyl]amino]propanoyl]pyrrolidine-2-carboxylic acid,

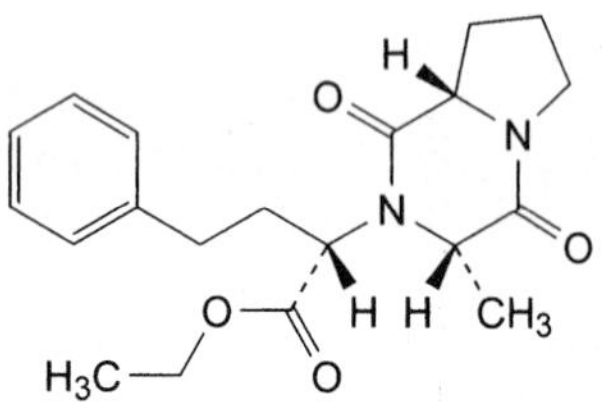

D. ethyl (2S)-2-[(3S,8aS)-3-methyl-1,4-dioxo-octahydropyrrolo[1,2-a]pyrazin-2-yl]-4-phenylbutanoate,

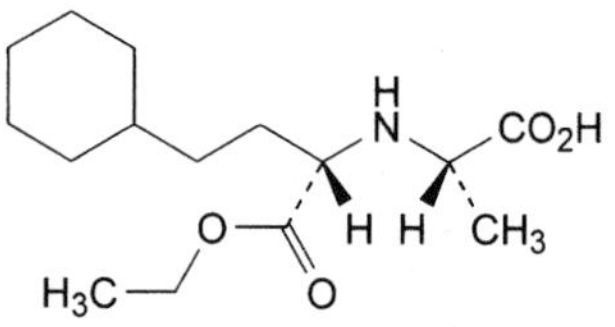

G (2S)-2-[[(1S)-3-cyclohexyl-1-(ethoxycarbonyl)propyl]amino]propanoic acid,

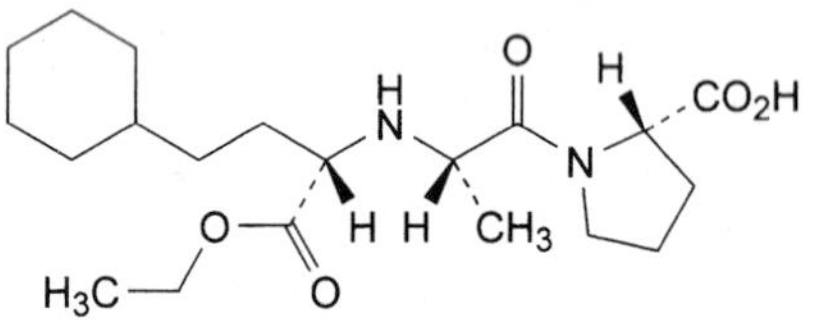

H. (2S)-1-[(2S)-2-[[(1S)-3-cyclohexyl-1-(ethoxycarbonyl)propyl]amino]propanoyl]pyrrolidine-2-carboxylic acid,

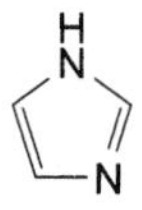

I. 1H-imidazole.

*Ph Eur*

# Enalaprilat Dihydrate

(*Ph Eur monograph 1749*)

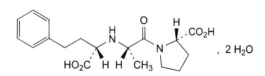

C₁₈H₂₄N₂O₅,2H₂O        384.4        76420-72-9

(*anhydrous*)

## Action and use

Angiotensin converting enzyme inhibitor.

*Ph Eur*

## DEFINITION

(2S)-1-[(2S)-2-[[(1S)-1-Carboxy-3-phenylpropyl]amino]propanoyl)pyrrolidine-2-carboxylic acid dihydrate.

## Content

98.5 per cent to 101.5 per cent (anhydrous substance).

## CHARACTERS

### Appearance

White or almost white, hygroscopic, crystalline powder.

### Solubility

Very slightly soluble or slightly soluble in water, sparingly soluble in methanol, practically insoluble in acetonitrile.

It shows pseudopolymorphism (*5.9*).

## IDENTIFICATION

A. Specific optical rotation (see Tests).

B. Infrared absorption spectrophotometry (*2.2.24*).

*Preparation* Mulls in *liquid paraffin R*.

*Comparison* enalaprilat dihydrate CRS.

If the spectra obtained show differences, expose the substance to be examined and the reference substance to a 98 per cent relative humidity for 3 days using a chamber conditioned with a saturated solution of *calcium sulphate R*. Record new spectra.

## TESTS

### Appearance of solution

The solution is clear (*2.2.1*) and colourless (*2.2.2*, *Method II*).

Dissolve 0.10 g in *water R* and dilute to 100.0 ml with the same solvent.

### Specific optical rotation (*2.2.7*)

− 53.0 to − 56.0 (anhydrous substance).

Dissolve 0.200 g in *methanol R* and dilute to 20.0 ml with the same solvent.

### Related substances

Liquid chromatography (*2.2.29*). *Use freshly prepared solutions.*

*Buffer solution* Dissolve 1.36 g of *potassium dihydrogen phosphate R* in 950 ml of *water R*. Adjust to pH 3.0 with *phosphoric acid R* and dilute to 1000 ml with *water R*.

*Solvent mixture* Buffer solution, *acetonitrile R1*, *methanol R1* (1:2:2 *V/V/V*).

*Dissolution mixture* Solvent mixture, buffer solution (8:92 *V/V*).

*Test solution* Dissolve 25.0 mg of the substance to be examined in 2.5 ml of *methanol R1* and dilute to 25.0 ml with the dissolution mixture.

*Reference solution (a)* Dilute 1.0 ml of the test solution to 100.0 ml with the dissolution mixture. Dilute 5.0 ml of this solution to 10.0 ml with the dissolution mixture.

*Reference solution (b)* Dissolve 5 mg of *enalaprilat for system suitability CRS* (containing impurity C) in 0.5 ml of *methanol R1* and dilute to 5 ml with the dissolution mixture.

*Reference solution (c)* Dissolve the contents of a vial of *enalaprilat impurity G CRS* in 1 ml of the test solution.

*Column:*

— *size: l* = 0.25 m, Ø = 4.6 mm;

— *stationary phase*: end-*capped octadecylsilyl silica gel for chromatography R* (5 μm);

— *temperature*: 70 °C.

*Mobile phase:*
— *mobile phase A*: solvent mixture, buffer solution (10:90 *V/V*);
— *mobile phase B*: acetonitrile R1;

| Time (min) | Mobile phase A (per cent *V/V*) | Mobile phase B (per cent *V/V*) |
|---|---|---|
| 0 - 25 | 100 | 0 |
| 25 - 50 | 100 → 90 | 0 → 10 |
| 50 - 80 | 90 | 10 |
| 80 - 81 | 90 → 100 | 10 → 0 |
| 81 - 85 | 100 | 0 |

*Flow rate* 2.0 ml/min.

*Detection* Spectrophotometer at 210 nm.

*Injection* 20 µl.

*Identification of impurities* Use the chromatogram supplied with *enalaprilat for system suitability CRS* and the chromatogram obtained with reference solution (b) to identify the peak due to impurity C; use the chromatogram obtained with reference solution (c) to identify the peak due to impurity G.

*Relative retention* With reference to enalaprilat (retention time = about 21 min): impurity C = about 1.2; impurity G = about 2.9.

*System suitability* Reference solution (b):
— *peak-to-valley ratio*: minimum 2.0, where $H_p$ = height above the baseline of the peak due to impurity C and $H_v$ = height above the baseline of the lowest point of the curve separating this peak from the peak due to enalaprilat.

*Limits:*
— *impurities C, G*: for each impurity, not more than the area of the principal peak in the chromatogram obtained with reference solution (a) (0.5 per cent);
— *unspecified impurities*: for each impurity, not more than 0.2 times the area of the principal peak in the chromatogram obtained with reference solution (a) (0.10 per cent);
— *total*: not more than twice the area of the principal peak in the chromatogram obtained with reference solution (a) (1.0 per cent);
— *disregard limit*: 0.1 times the area of the principal peak in the chromatogram obtained with reference solution (a) (0.05 per cent).

**Heavy metals** (*2.4.8*)
Maximum 10 ppm.

2.0 g complies with test G. Prepare the reference solution using 2 ml of *lead standard solution (10 ppm Pb) R*.

**Water** (*2.5.12*)
7.0 per cent to 11.0 per cent, determined on 0.100 g.

**Sulphated ash** (*2.4.14*)
Maximum 0.1 per cent, determined on 1.0 g.

**Bacterial endotoxins** (*2.6.14*)
Less than 0.1 IU/mg.

**ASSAY**
Dissolve 0.300 g in *glacial acetic acid R* and dilute to 50 ml with the same solvent. Titrate with *0.1 M perchloric acid*, determining the end point potentiometrically (*2.2.20*).

1 ml of *0.1 M perchloric acid* is equivalent to 34.84 mg of $C_{18}H_{24}N_2O_5$.

**STORAGE**
In an airtight container.

**IMPURITIES**
*Specified impurities C, G.*

*Other detectable impurities* (the following substances would, if present at a sufficient level, be detected by one or other of the tests in the monograph. They are limited by the general acceptance criterion for other/unspecified impurities and/or by the general monograph *Substances for pharmaceutical use (2034)*. It is therefore not necessary to identify these impurities for demonstration of compliance. See also *5.10. Control of impurities in substances for pharmaceutical use)*
*A, B, D, E, F.*

and enantiomer

A. R = H: (2*SR*)-2-[[(1*SR*)-1-carboxyethyl]amino]-4-phenylbutanoic acid,
F. R = $C_2H_5$: (2*SR*)-2-[[(1*SR*)-1-(ethoxycarbonyl)-3-phenylpropyl]amino]propanoic acid,

and enantiomer

B. R1 = R4 = H, R2 = $CO_2H$, R3 = $CH_3$:
(2*SR*)-1-[(2*RS*)-2-[[(1*RS*)-1-carboxy-3-phenylpropyl]amino]propanoyl]pyrrolidine-2-carboxylic acid,
C. R1 = R3 = H, R2 = $CO_2H$, R4 = $CH_3$:
(2*SR*)-1-[(2*SR*)-2-[[(1*RS*)-1-carboxy-3-phenylpropyl]amino]propanoyl]pyrrolidine-2-carboxylic acid,
D. R1 = $CO_2H$, R2 = R4 = H, R3 = $CH_3$:
(2*SR*)-1-[(2*RS*)-2-[[(1*SR*)-1-carboxy-3-phenylpropyl]amino]propanoyl]pyrrolidine-2-carboxylic acid,

and enantiomer

E. (2*SR*)-1-[[(2*SR*)-1-[(2*SR*)-2-[[(1*SR*)-1-carboxy-3-phenylpropyl]amino]propanoyl]pyrrolidin-2-yl]carbonyl]pyrrolidine-2-carboxylic acid,

and enantiomer

G. (2*SR*)-2-[(3*SR*,8a*RS*)-3-methyl-1,4-dioxohexahydropyrrolo[1,2-*a*]pyrazin-2(1*H*)-yl]-4-phenylbutanoic acid.

# Enoxaparin Sodium

*(Ph Eur monograph 1097)*

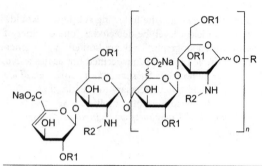

|  | Structure at the 'reducing end' | |
|---|---|---|
|  | 1,6-anhydro | non 1,6-anhydro |
| *n* | 0 to 20 | 1 to 21 |

R1 = H or SO₃Na     R2 = SO₃Na or CO-CH₃

R1 = H or $SO_3Na$     R2 = $SO_3Na$ or $CO\text{-}CH_3$

## Action and use

Low molecular weight heparin.

*Ph Eur* ___

## DEFINITION

Enoxaparin sodium is the sodium salt of a low-molecular-mass heparin that is obtained by alkaline depolymerisation of the benzyl ester derivative of heparin from porcine intestinal mucosa. Enoxaparin consists of a complex set of oligosaccharides that have not yet been completely characterised. Based on current knowledge, the majority of the components have a 4-enopyranose uronate structure at the non-reducing end of their chain. 15 per cent to 25 per cent of the components have a 1,6-anhydro structure at the reducing end of their chain.

*Enoxaparin sodium complies with the monograph Low-molecular-mass heparins (0828) with the modifications and additional requirements below.*

The mass-average relative molecular mass ranges between 3800 and 5000, with a characteristic value of about 4500.

The degree of sulphatation is about 2 per disaccharide unit.

The potency is not less than 90 IU and not more than 125 IU of anti-factor Xa activity per milligram, calculated with reference to the dried substance. The anti-factor IIa activity is not less than 20.0 IU and not more than 35.0 IU per milligram, calculated with reference to the dried substance. The ratio of anti-factor Xa activity to anti-factor IIa activity is between 3.3 and 5.3.

## PRODUCTION

Enoxaparin is produced by alkaline depolymerisation of benzyl ester derivatives of heparin from porcine intestinal mucosa under conditions that yield a product complying with the structural requirements stated under Definition.

## IDENTIFICATION

Carry out identification test A as described in the monograph *Low-molecular-mass heparins (0828)* using *enoxaparin sodium CRS*.

Carry out identification test C as described in the monograph *Low-molecular-mass heparins (0828)*. The following requirements apply.

The mass-average relative molecular mass ranges between 3800 and 5000. The mass percentage of chains lower than 2000 ranges between 12.0 per cent and 20.0 per cent. The mass percentage of chains between 2000 and 8000 ranges between 68.0 per cent and 82.0 per cent.

## TESTS

### Appearance of solution

The solution is clear (*2.2.1*) and not more intensely coloured than intensity 6 of the range of reference solutions of the most appropriate colour (*2.2.2, Method II*).

Dissolve 1.0 g in 10 ml of *water R*.

### pH (*2.2.3*)

6.2 to 7.7.

Dissolve 1.0 g in *carbon dioxide-free water R* and dilute to 10.0 ml with the same solvent.

### Specific absorbance (*2.2.25*)

14.0 to 20.0 (dried substance), determined at 231 nm.

Dissolve 50.0 mg in 100 ml of *0.01 M hydrochloric acid*.

### Benzyl alcohol

Liquid chromatography (*2.2.29*).

*Internal standard solution*   1 g/l solution of *3,4-dimethylphenol R* in *methanol R*.

*Test solution*   Dissolve about 0.500 g of the substance to be examined in 5.0 ml of *1 M sodium hydroxide*. Allow to stand for 1 h. Add 1.0 ml of *glacial acetic acid R* and 1.0 ml of the internal standard solution and dilute to 10.0 ml with *water R*.

*Reference solution*   Prepare a 0.25 g/l solution of *benzyl alcohol R* in *water R*. Mix 0.50 ml of this solution with 1.0 ml of the internal standard solution and dilute to 10.0 ml with *water R*.

*Precolumn:*
— *size: l* = 0.02 m, Ø = 4.6 mm;
— *stationary phase: octylsilyl silica gel for chromatography R* (5 μm).

*Column:*
— *size: l* = 0.15 m, Ø = 4.6 mm;
— *stationary phase: octylsilyl silica gel for chromatography R* (5 μm).

*Mobile phase*   methanol R, acetonitrile R, water R (5:15:80 *V/V/V*).

*Flow rate*   1 ml/min.

*Detection*   Spectrophotometer at 256 nm.

From the chromatogram obtained with the reference solution, calculate the ratio ($R_1$) of the height of the peak due to benzyl alcohol to the height of the peak due to the internal standard. From the chromatogram obtained with the test solution, calculate the ratio ($R_2$) of the height of the peak due to benzyl alcohol to the height of the peak due to the internal standard.

Calculate the percentage content (*m/m*) of benzyl alcohol using the following expression:

$$\frac{0.0125 \times R_2}{m \times R_1}$$

m = mass of the substance to be examined, in grams.

*Limit:*
— *benzyl alcohol*: maximum 0.1 per cent *m/m*.

**Sodium** (*2.2.23, Method I*)
11.3 per cent to 13.5 per cent (dried substance).

_____ *Ph Eur*

# Enoxolone

*(Ph Eur monograph 1511)*

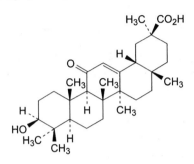

$C_{30}H_{46}O_4$          470.7          *471-53-4*

**Action and use**
Treatment of benign peptic ulcer disease.

*Ph Eur* _____

## DEFINITION
(20β)-3β-Hydroxy-11-oxo-olean-12-en-29-oic acid.

## Content
98.0 per cent to 101.0 per cent (dried substance).

## CHARACTERS
**Appearance**
White or almost white crystalline powder.

**Solubility**
Practically insoluble in water, soluble in ethanol, sparingly soluble in methylene chloride.

It shows polymorphism (*5.9*).

## IDENTIFICATION
*First identification    A.*

*Second identification    B, C.*

A. Examine by infrared absorption spectrophotometry (*2.2.24*).

*Comparison    enoxolone CRS.*

If the spectra obtained in the solid state show differences, dissolve 0.2 g of the substance to be examined and 0.2 g of the reference substance separately in 6 ml of *ethanol R*. Boil under a reflux condenser for 1 h and add 6 ml of *water R*. A precipitate is formed. Cool to about 10 °C and filter with the aid of vacuum. Wash the precipitate with 10 ml of *alcohol R*, dry in an oven at 80 °C and record new spectra.

B. Thin-layer chromatography (*2.2.27*).

*Test solution*    Dissolve 10 mg of the substance to be examined in *methylene chloride R* and dilute to 10 ml with the same solvent.

*Reference solution*    Dissolve 10 mg of *enoxolone CRS* in *methylene chloride R* and dilute to 10 ml with the same solvent.

*Plate    TLC silica gel plate R.*

*Mobile phase    glacial acetic acid R, acetone R, methylene chloride R (5:10:90 V/V/V).*

*Application    5 μl.*

*Development    Over 2/3 of the plate.*

*Drying    In air for 5 min.*

*Detection    Spray with anisaldehyde solution R and heat at 100-105 °C for 10 min.*

*Results    The principal spot in the chromatogram obtained with the test solution is similar in position, colour and size to the principal spot in the chromatogram obtained with the reference solution.

C. Dissolve 50 mg in 10 ml of *methylene chloride R*. To 2 ml of this solution, add 1 ml of *acetic anhydride R* and 0.3 ml of *sulphuric acid R*. A pink colour is produced.

## TESTS
**Appearance of solution**
The solution is clear (*2.2.1*) and not more intensely coloured than reference solution $Y_6$ (*2.2.2, Method II*).

Dissolve 0.1 g in *ethanol R* and dilute to 10 ml with the same solvent.

**Specific optical rotation** (*2.2.7*)
+ 145 to + 154 (dried substance).

Dissolve 0.50 g in *dioxan R* and dilute to 50.0 ml with the same solvent.

**Related substances**
Liquid chromatography (*2.2.29*).

*Test solution*    Dissolve 0.10 g of the substance to be examined in the mobile phaseand dilute to 100.0 ml with the mobile phase.

*Reference solution (a)*    Dilute 2.0 ml of the test solution to 100.0 ml with the mobile phase.

*Reference solution (b)*    Dilute 5.0 ml of reference solution (a) to 100.0 ml with the mobile phase.

*Reference solution (c)*    Dissolve 0.1 g of *18α-glycyrrhetinic acid R* in *tetrahydrofuran R* and dilute to 100.0 ml with the same solvent. To 2.0 ml of the solution, add 2.0 ml of the test solution and dilute to 100.0 ml with the mobile phase.

*Column:*
— *size: l = 0.25 m, Ø = 4.6 mm,*
— *stationary phase: octadecylsilyl silica gel for chromatography R (5 μm),*
— *temperature: 30 °C.*

*Mobile phase    Mix 430 volumes of tetrahydrofuran R and 570 volumes of a 1.36 g/l solution of sodium acetate R adjusted to pH 4.8 with glacial acetic acid R.*

*Flow rate    0.8 ml/min.*

*Detection    Spectrophotometer at 250 nm.*

*Injection    20 μl loop injector; inject the test solution and the reference solutions.*

*Run time    4 times the retention time of enoxolone.*

*System suitability:*
— *resolution*: minimum of 2.0 between the peaks due to enoxolone and to 18α-glycyrrhetinic acid in the chromatogram obtained with reference solution (c).

*Limits:*
— *any impurity*: not more than 7 times the area of the principal peak in the chromatogram obtained with reference solution (b) (0.7 per cent),
— *total*: not more than the area of the principal peak in the chromatogram obtained with reference solution (a) (2.0 per cent),

— *disregard limit*: 0.5 times the area of the principal peak in the chromatogram obtained with reference solution (b) (0.05 per cent).

**Heavy metals** (*2.4.8*)

Maximum 20 ppm.

1.0 g complies with limit test F. Prepare the standard using 2 ml of *lead standard solution (10 ppm Pb) R*.

**Loss on drying** (*2.2.32*)

Maximum 0.5 per cent, determined on 1.000 g by drying in an oven at 105 °C for 4 h.

**Sulphated ash** (*2.4.14*)

Maximum 0.2 per cent, determined on 1.0 g.

**ASSAY**

Dissolve 0.330 g in 40 ml of *dimethylformamide R*. Titrate with *0.1 M tetrabutylammonium hydroxide*, determining the end-point potentiometrically (*2.2.20*). Carry out a blank titration.

1 ml of *0.1 M tetrabutylammonium hydroxide* is equivalent to 47.07 mg of $C_{30}H_{46}O_4$.

**STORAGE**

Protected from light.

**IMPURITIES**

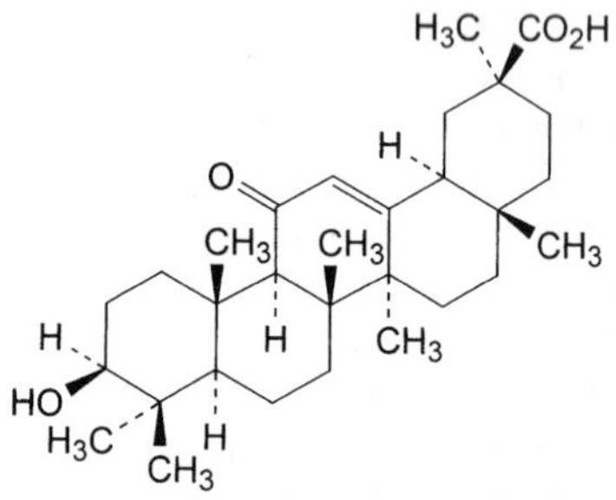

A. (20β)-3β-hydroxy-11-oxo-18α-olean-12-en-29-oic acid,

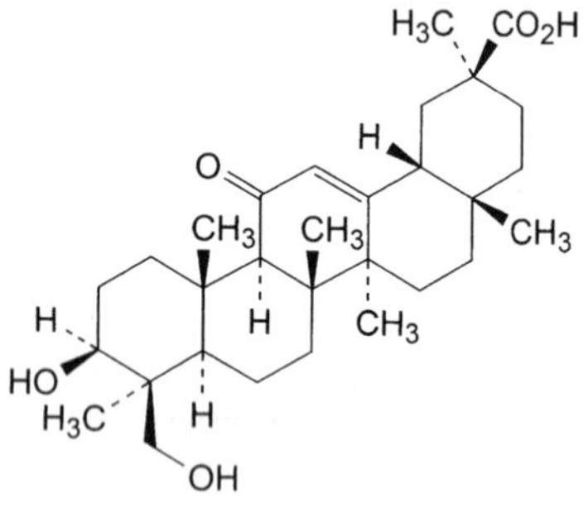

B. (4β,20β)-3β,23-dihydroxy-11-oxo-olean-12-en-29-oic acid.

*Ph Eur*

# Ephedrine

(*Ephedrine Hemihydrate, Ph Eur monograph 0489*)

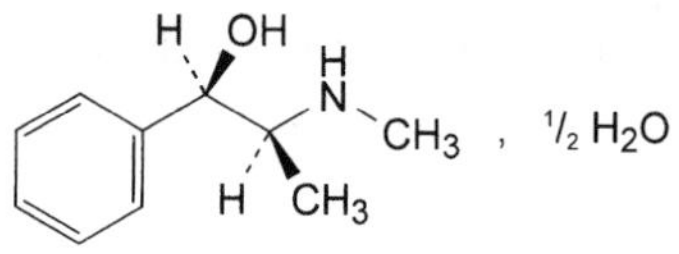

$C_{10}H_{15}NO,\frac{1}{2}H_2O$      174.2      *50906-05-3*

**Action and use**

Adrenoceptor agonist.

*Ph Eur*

**DEFINITION**

Ephedrine hemihydrate contains not less than 99.0 per cent and not more than the equivalent of 101.0 per cent of (1*R*,2*S*)-2-(methylamino)-1-phenylpropan-1-ol, calculated with reference to the anhydrous substance.

**CHARACTERS**

A white or almost white, crystalline powder or colourless crystals, soluble in water, very soluble in alcohol.

It melts at about 42 °C, determined without previous drying.

**IDENTIFICATION**

*First identification*   B, D.

*Second identification*   A, C, D, E.

A. It complies with the test for specific optical rotation (see Tests).

B. Examine by infrared absorption spectrophotometry (*2.2.24*), comparing with the spectrum obtained with the base isolated from *ephedrine hydrochloride CRS*. Examine the substances in discs prepared as follows: dissolve 40 mg of the substance to be examined in 1 ml of *water R*, add 1 ml of *dilute sodium hydroxide solution R* and 4 ml of *chloroform R* and shake; dry the organic layer over 0.2 g of *anhydrous sodium sulphate R*; prepare a blank disc using about 0.3 g of *potassium bromide R*; apply dropwise to the disc 0.1 ml of the organic layer, allowing the solvent to evaporate between applications; dry the disc at 50 °C for 2 min. Repeat the operations using 50 mg of *ephedrine hydrochloride CRS*.

C. Examine the chromatograms obtained in the test for related substances. The principal spot in the chromatogram obtained with test solution (b) is similar in position, colour and size to the principal spot in the chromatogram obtained with reference solution (a).

D. Dissolve about 10 mg in 1 ml of *water R*. Add 0.2 ml of *strong sodium hydroxide solution R* and 0.2 ml of *copper sulphate solution R*. A violet colour is produced. Add 2 ml of *ether R* and shake. The ether layer is purple and the aqueous layer blue.

E. It complies with the test for water (see Tests).

**TESTS**

**Appearance of solution**

Dissolve 0.25 g in *water R* and dilute to 10 ml with the same solvent. The solution is clear (*2.2.1*) and colourless (*2.2.2, Method II*).

**Specific optical rotation** (*2.2.7*)

Dissolve 2.25 g in 15 ml of *dilute hydrochloric acid R* and dilute to 50.0 ml with *water R*. The specific optical rotation is − 41 to − 43, calculated with reference to the anhydrous substance.

## Related substances

Examine by thin-layer chromatography (2.2.27), using *silica gel G R* as the coating substance.

*Test solution (a)*  Dissolve 0.2 g of the substance to be examined in *methanol R* and dilute to 10 ml with the same solvent.

*Test solution (b)*  Dilute 1 ml of test solution (a) to 10 ml with *methanol R*.

*Reference solution (a)*  Dissolve 25 mg of *ephedrine hydrochloride CRS* in *methanol R* and dilute to 10 ml with the same solvent.

*Reference solution (b)*  Dilute 1.0 ml of test solution (a) to 200 ml with *methanol R*.

Apply separately to the plate 10 μl of each solution. Develop over a path of 15 cm using a mixture of 5 volumes of *chloroform R*, 15 volumes of *concentrated ammonia R* and 80 volumes of *2-propanol R*. Allow the plate to dry in air and spray with *ninhydrin solution R*. Heat at 110 °C for 5 min. Any spot in the chromatogram obtained with test solution (a), apart from the principal spot, is not more intense than the spot in the chromatogram obtained with reference solution (b) (0.5 per cent). Disregard any spot of lighter colour than the background.

## Chlorides

Dissolve 0.18 g in 10 ml of *water R*. Add 5 ml of *dilute nitric acid R* and 0.5 ml of *silver nitrate solution R1*. Allow to stand for 2 min, protected from bright light. Any opalescence in the solution is not more intense than that in a standard prepared at the same time and in the same manner using 10 ml of *chloride standard solution (5 ppm Cl) R*, 5 ml of *dilute nitric acid R* and 0.5 ml of *silver nitrate solution R1* (280 ppm).

## Water (2.5.12)

4.5 per cent to 5.5 per cent, determined on 0.300 g by the semi-micro determination of water.

## Sulphated ash (2.4.14)

Not more than 0.1 per cent, determined on 1.0 g.

## ASSAY

Dissolve 0.200 g in 5 ml of *alcohol R* and add 20.0 ml of *0.1 M hydrochloric acid*. Using 0.05 ml of *methyl red solution R* as indicator, titrate with *0.1 M sodium hydroxide* until a yellow colour is obtained.

1 ml of *0.1 M hydrochloric acid* is equivalent to 16.52 mg of $C_{10}H_{15}NO$.

## STORAGE

Store protected from light.

Ph Eur

# Anhydrous Ephedrine

(*Ephedrine, Anhydrous, Ph Eur monograph 0488*)

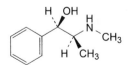

| $C_{10}H_{15}NO$ | 165.2 | 299-42-3 |

## Action and use

Adrenoceptor agonist.

Ph Eur

## DEFINITION

Anhydrous ephedrine contains not less than 99.0 per cent and not more than the equivalent of 101.0 per cent of (1R,2S)-2-methylamino-1-phenylpropan-1-ol, calculated with reference to the anhydrous substance.

## CHARACTERS

A white or almost white, crystalline powder or colourless crystals, soluble in water, very soluble in alcohol.

It melts at about 36 °C.

## IDENTIFICATION

*First identification*  B, D.

*Second identification*  A, C, D, E.

A. It complies with the test for specific optical rotation (see Tests).

B. Examine by infrared absorption spectrophotometry (2.2.24), comparing with the spectrum obtained with the base isolated from *ephedrine hydrochloride CRS*. Examine the substances in discs prepared as follows: dissolve 40 mg of the substance to be examined in 1 ml of *water R*, add 1 ml of *dilute sodium hydroxide solution R* and 4 ml of *chloroform R* and shake; dry the organic layer over 0.2 g of *anhydrous sodium sulphate R*; prepare a blank disc using about 0.3 g of *potassium bromide R*; apply dropwise to the disc 0.1 ml of the organic layer, allowing the solvent to evaporate between applications; dry the disc at 50 °C for 2 min. Repeat the operations using 50 mg of *ephedrine hydrochloride CRS*.

C. Examine the chromatograms obtained in the test for related substances. The principal spot in the chromatogram obtained with test solution (b) is similar in position, colour and size to the principal spot in the chromatogram obtained with reference solution (a).

D. Dissolve about 10 mg in 1 ml of *water R*. Add 0.2 ml of *strong sodium hydroxide solution R* and 0.2 ml of *copper sulphate solution R*. A violet colour is produced. Add 2 ml of *ether R* and shake. The ether layer is purple and the aqueous layer blue.

E. It complies with the test for water (see Tests).

## TESTS

### Appearance of solution

Dissolve 0.25 g in *water R* and dilute to 10 ml with the same solvent. The solution is clear (2.2.1) and colourless (2.2.2, Method II).

### Specific optical rotation (2.2.7)

Dissolve 2.25 g in 15 ml of *dilute hydrochloric acid R* and dilute to 50.0 ml with *water R*. The specific optical rotation is − 41 to − 43, calculated with reference to the anhydrous substance.

### Related substances

Examine by thin-layer chromatography (2.2.27), using *silica gel G R* as the coating substance.

*Test solution (a)*  Dissolve 0.2 g of the substance to be examined in *methanol R* and dilute to 10 ml with the same solvent.

*Test solution (b)*  Dilute 1 ml of test solution (a) to 10 ml with *methanol R*.

*Reference solution (a)*  Dissolve 25 mg of *ephedrine hydrochloride CRS* in *methanol R* and dilute to 10 ml with the same solvent.

*Reference solution (b)*  Dilute 1.0 ml of test solution (a) to 200 ml with *methanol R*.

Apply separately to the plate 10 µl of each solution. Develop over a path of 15 cm using a mixture of 5 volumes of *chloroform R*, 15 volumes of *concentrated ammonia R* and 80 volumes of *2-propanol R*. Allow the plate to dry in air and spray with *ninhydrin solution R*. Heat at 110 °C for 5 min. Any spot in the chromatogram obtained with test solution (a), apart from the principal spot, is not more intense than the spot in the chromatogram obtained with reference solution (b) (0.5 per cent). Disregard any spot of lighter colour than the background.

### Chlorides

Dissolve 0.17 g in 10 ml of *water R*. Add 5 ml of *dilute nitric acid R* and 0.5 ml of *silver nitrate solution R1*. Allow to stand for 2 min, protected from bright light. Any opalescence in the solution is not more intense than that in a standard prepared at the same time and in the same manner using 10 ml of *chloride standard solution (5 ppm Cl) R*, 5 ml of *dilute nitric acid R* and 0.5 ml of *silver nitrate solution R1* (290 ppm).

### Water (2.5.12)

Not more than 0.5 per cent, determined on 2.000 g by the semi-micro determination of water.

### Sulphated ash (2.4.14)

Not more than 0.1 per cent, determined on 1.0 g.

### ASSAY

Dissolve 0.200 g in 5 ml of *alcohol R* and add 20.0 ml of *0.1 M hydrochloric acid*. Using 0.05 ml of *methyl red solution R* as indicator, titrate with *0.1 M sodium hydroxide* until a yellow colour is obtained.

1 ml of *0.1 M hydrochloric acid* is equivalent to 16.52 mg of $C_{10}H_{15}NO$.

### STORAGE

Store protected from light.

_____ *Ph Eur*

# Ephedrine Hydrochloride

(*Ph Eur monograph 0487*)

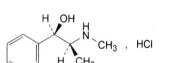

$C_{10}H_{15}NO,HCl$       201.7       *50-98-6*

### Action and use

Adrenoceptor agonist.

### Preparations

Ephedrine Elixir

Ephedrine Nasal Drops

Ephedrine Hydrochloride Tablets

Ephedrine Injection

*Ph Eur* _____

### DEFINITION

(1*R*,2*S*)-2-(Methylamino)-1-phenylpropan-1-ol hydrochloride.

### Content

99.0 per cent to 101.0 per cent (dried substance).

## CHARACTERS

### Appearance

White or almost white, crystalline powder or colourless crystals.

### Solubility

Freely soluble in water, soluble in ethanol (96 per cent).

### mp

About 219 °C.

### IDENTIFICATION

*First identification*    B, E.

*Second identification*    A, C, D, E.

A. Specific optical rotation (see Tests).

B. Infrared absorption spectrophotometry (2.2.24).

*Comparison*    ephedrine hydrochloride CRS.

C. Thin-layer chromatography (2.2.27).

*Test solution*    Dissolve 20 mg of the substance to be examined in *methanol R* and dilute to 10 ml with the same solvent.

*Reference solution*    Dissolve 10 mg of *ephedrine hydrochloride CRS* in *methanol R* and dilute to 5 ml with the same solvent.

*Plate*    TLC silica gel plate R.

*Mobile phase*    methylene chloride R, concentrated ammonia R, 2-propanol R (5:15:80 V/V/V).

*Application*    10 µl.

*Development*    Over 2/3 of the plate.

*Drying*    In air.

*Detection*    Spray with *ninhydrin solution R*; heat at 110 °C for 5 min.

*Results*    The principal spot in the chromatogram obtained with the test solution is similar in position, colour and size to the principal spot in the chromatogram obtained with the reference solution.

D. To 0.1 ml of solution S (see Tests) add 1 ml of *water R*, 0.2 ml of *copper sulphate solution R* and 1 ml of *strong sodium hydroxide solution R*. A violet colour is produced. Add 2 ml of *methylene chloride R* and shake. The lower (organic) layer is dark grey and the upper (aqueous) layer is blue.

E. To 5 ml of solution S (see Tests) add 5 ml of *water R*. The solution gives reaction (a) of chlorides (2.3.1).

### TESTS

### Solution S

Dissolve 5.00 g in distilled *water R* and dilute to 50.0 ml with the same solvent.

### Appearance of solution

Solution S is clear (2.2.1) and colourless (2.2.2, Method II).

### Acidity or alkalinity

To 10 ml of solution S add 0.1 ml of *methyl red solution R* and 0.2 ml of *0.01 M sodium hydroxide*. The solution is yellow. Add 0.4 ml of *0.01 M hydrochloric acid*. The solution is red.

### Specific optical rotation (2.2.7)

− 33.5 to − 35.5 (dried substance).

Dilute 12.5 ml of solution S to 25.0 ml with *water R*.

### Related substances

Liquid chromatography (2.2.29).

*Test solution*    Dissolve 75 mg of the substance to be examined in the mobile phase and dilute to 10 ml with the mobile phase.

*Reference solution (a)* Dilute 2.0 ml of the test solution to 100.0 ml with the mobile phase. Dilute 1.0 ml of this solution to 10.0 ml with the mobile phase.

*Reference solution (b)* Dissolve 5 mg of the substance to be examined and 5 mg of *pseudoephedrine hydrochloride CRS* in the mobile phase and dilute to 50 ml with the mobile phase.

*Column:*
— *size:* $l$ = 0.15 m, Ø = 4.6 mm,
— *stationary phase:* spherical *phenylsilyl silica gel for chromatography R* (3 µm).

*Mobile phase* Mix 6 volumes of *methanol R* and 94 volumes of a 11.6 g/l solution of *ammonium acetate R* adjusted to pH 4.0 with *glacial acetic acid R.*

*Flow rate* 1.0 ml/min.

*Detection* Spectrophotometer at 257 nm.

*Injection* 20 µl.

*Run time* 2.5 times the retention time of ephedrine.

*Relative retention* With reference to ephedrine (retention time = about 8 min): impurity B = about 1.1; impurity A = about 1.4.

*System suitability* Reference solution (b):
— *resolution:* minimum 2.0 between the peaks due to ephedrine and impurity B.

*Limits:*
— *correction factor:* for the calculation of content, multiply the peak area of impurity A by 0.4,
— *impurity A:* not more than the area of the principal peak in the chromatogram obtained with reference solution (a) (0.2 per cent),
— *unspecified impurities:* for each impurity, not more than 0.5 times the area of the principal peak in the chromatogram obtained with reference solution (a) (0.1 per cent),
— *sum of impurities other than A:* not more than 2.5 times the area of the principal peak in the chromatogram obtained with reference solution (a) (0.5 per cent),
— *disregard limit:* 0.25 times the area of the principal peak in the chromatogram obtained with reference solution (a) (0.05 per cent).

**Sulphates** *(2.4.13)*
Maximum 100 ppm, determined on solution S.

**Loss on drying** *(2.2.32)*
Maximum 0.5 per cent, determined on 1.000 g by drying in an oven at 105 °C.

**Sulphated ash** *(2.4.14)*
Maximum 0.1 per cent, determined on 1.0 g.

**ASSAY**
Dissolve 0.150 g in 50 ml of *ethanol (96 per cent) R* and add 5.0 ml of *0.01 M hydrochloric acid.* Carry out a potentiometric titration *(2.2.20)*, using *0.1 M sodium hydroxide.* Read the volume added between the 2 points of inflexion.

1 ml of *0.1 M sodium hydroxide* is equivalent to 20.17 mg of $C_{10}H_{16}ClNO.$

**STORAGE**
Protected from light.

**IMPURITIES**
*Specified impurities   A.*

*Other detectable impurities* (the following substances would, if present at a sufficient level, be detected by one or other of the tests in the monograph. They are limited by the general acceptance criterion for other/unspecified impurities and/or by the general monograph *Substances for pharmaceutical use*

*(2034).* It is therefore not necessary to identify these impurities for demonstration of compliance. See also *5.10. Control of impurities in substances for pharmaceutical use: B.*

A. (−)-(1*R*)-1-hydroxy-1-phenylpropan-2-one,

B. pseudoephedrine.

*_____ Ph Eur*

# Epirubicin Hydrochloride

*(Ph Eur monograph 1590)*

$C_{27}H_{29}NO_{11},HCl$       580       *56390-09-1*

**Action and use**
Cytotoxic.

*Ph Eur* _____

**DEFINITION**
(8*S*,10*S*)-10-[(3-Amino-2,3,6-trideoxy-α-L-arabino-hexopyranosyl)oxy]-6,8,11-trihydroxy-8-(hydroxyacetyl)-1-methoxy-7,8,9,10-tetrahydrotetracene-5,12-dione hydrochloride.

Substance obtained by chemical transformation of a substance produced by certain strains of *Streptomyces peucetius.*

**Content**
97.0 per cent to 102.0 per cent (anhydrous substance).

**CHARACTERS**
**Appearance**
Orange-red powder.

**Solubility**
Soluble in water and in methanol, slightly soluble in anhydrous ethanol, practically insoluble in acetone.

**IDENTIFICATION**
A. Infrared absorption spectrophotometry *(2.2.24)*.
*Comparison   epirubicin hydrochloride CRS.*

B. Examine the chromatograms obtained in the assay.

*Results* The principal peak in the chromatogram obtained with the test solution is similar in retention time to the principal peak in the chromatogram obtained with reference solution (a).

C. Dissolve about 10 mg in 0.5 ml of *nitric acid R*, add 0.5 ml of *water R* and heat over a flame for 2 min. Allow to cool and add 0.5 ml of *silver nitrate solution R1*. A white precipitate is formed.

## TESTS

**pH** *(2.2.3)*

4.0 to 5.5.

Dissolve 50 mg in *carbon dioxide-free water R* and dilute to 10 ml with the same solvent.

**Related substances**

Liquid chromatography *(2.2.29)*. *Allow the solutions to stand for 3 h before use.*

*Test solution* Dissolve 25.0 mg of the substance to be examined in the mobile phase and dilute to 25.0 ml with the mobile phase.

*Reference solution (a)* Dissolve 25.0 mg of *epirubicin hydrochloride CRS* in the mobile phase and dilute to 25.0 ml with the mobile phase.

*Reference solution (b)* Dissolve 10 mg of *epirubicin hydrochloride CRS* and 10 mg of *doxorubicin hydrochloride CRS* in the mobile phase and dilute to 100 ml with the mobile phase.

*Reference solution (c)* Dissolve 10 mg of *doxorubicin hydrochloride CRS* in a mixture of 5 ml of *water R* and 5 ml of *phosphoric acid R*. Allow to stand for 30 min. Adjust to pH 2.6 with an 80 g/l solution of *sodium hydroxide R*. Add 15 ml of *acetonitrile R* and 10 ml of *methanol R*. Mix.

*Reference solution (d)* Dilute 1.0 ml of the test solution to 100.0 ml with the mobile phase.

*Column:*
— *size:* $l = 0.25$ m, $\emptyset = 4.6$ mm;
— *stationary phase: trimethylsilyl silica gel for chromatography R* (6 µm);
— *temperature:* 35 °C.

*Mobile phase* Mix 17 volumes of *methanol R*, 29 volumes of *acetonitrile R* and 54 volumes of a solution containing 3.7 g/l of *sodium laurilsulfate R* and 2.8 per cent *V/V* of *dilute phosphoric acid R*.

*Flow rate* 2.5 ml/min.

*Detection* Spectrophotometer at 254 nm.

*Injection* 10 µl of the test solution and reference solutions (b), (c) and (d).

*Run time* 3.5 times the retention time of epirubicin.

*Identification of impurities* Use the 2nd most abundant peak present in the chromatogram obtained with reference solution (c) to identify impurity A.

*Relative retention* With reference to epirubicin (retention time = about 9.5 min): impurity A = about 0.3; impurity B = about 0.4; impurity C = about 0.8; impurity E = about 1.1; impurity D = about 1.5; impurity F = about 1.7; impurity G = about 2.1.

*System suitability* Reference solution (b):
— *resolution:* minimum 2.0 between the peaks due to impurity C and epirubicin.

*Limits:*
— *correction factor:* for the calculation of content, multiply the peak area of impurity A by 0.7;
— *impurity A:* not more than the area of the principal peak in the chromatogram obtained with reference solution (d) (1.0 per cent);
— *impurity C:* not more than the area of the principal peak in the chromatogram obtained with reference solution (d) (1.0 per cent);
— *any other impurity:* for each impurity, not more than 0.5 times the area of the principal peak in the

chromatogram obtained with reference solution (d) (0.5 per cent);
— *total:* not more than twice the area of the principal peak in the chromatogram obtained with reference solution (d) (2.0 per cent);
— *disregard limit:* 0.05 times the area of the principal peak in the chromatogram obtained with reference solution (d) (0.05 per cent).

**Acetone** *(2.4.24)*

Maximum 1.5 per cent.

**Water** *(2.5.12)*

Maximum 4.0 per cent, determined on 0.100 g.

**Bacterial endotoxins** *(2.6.14)*

Less than 1.1 IU/mg, if intended for use in the manufacture of parenteral dosage forms without a further appropriate procedure for removal of bacterial endotoxins.

## ASSAY

Liquid chromatography *(2.2.29)* as described in the test for related substances with the following modification.

*Injection* Test solution and reference solution (a).

Calculate the percentage content of $C_{27}H_{30}ClNO_{11}$.

## STORAGE

In an airtight container, protected from light, at a temperature of 2 °C to 8 °C. If the substance is sterile, store in a sterile, airtight, tamper-proof container.

## IMPURITIES

A. R = OH: (8*S*,10*S*)-6,8,10,11-tetrahydroxy-8-(hydroxyacetyl)-1-methoxy-7,8,9,10-tetrahydrotetracene-5,12-dione (doxorubicinone),

B. R = H: (8*S*,10*S*)-8-acetyl-6,8,10,11-tetrahydroxy-1-methoxy-7,8,9,10-tetrahydrotetracene-5,12-dione (daunorubicinone),

C. doxorubicin,

D. daunorubicin,

and epimer at C*

E. (8*S*,10*S*)-10-[(3-amino-2,3,6-trideoxy-α-L-*lyxo*-hexopyranosyl)oxy]-6,8,11-trihydroxy-8-[(1*RS*)-1-hydroxyethyl]-1-methoxy-7,8,9,10-tetrahydrotetracene-5,12-dione (dihydrodaunorubicin),

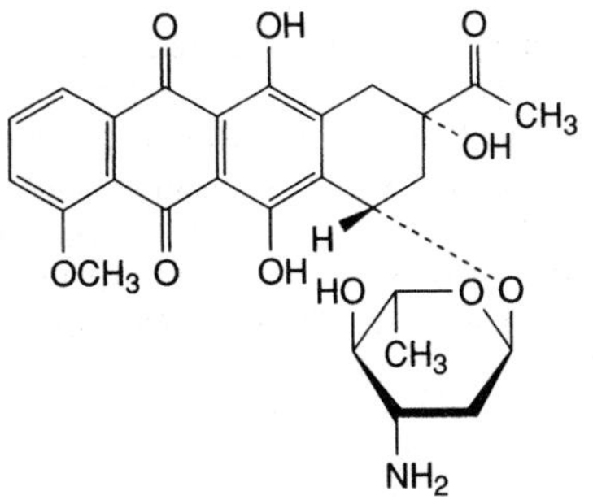

F. (8*S*,10*S*)-8-acetyl-10-[(3-amino-2,3,6-trideoxy-α-L-*arabino*-hexopyranosyl)oxy]-6,8,11-trihydroxy-1-methoxy-7,8,9,10-tetrahydrotetracene-5,12-dione (epi-daunorubicin),

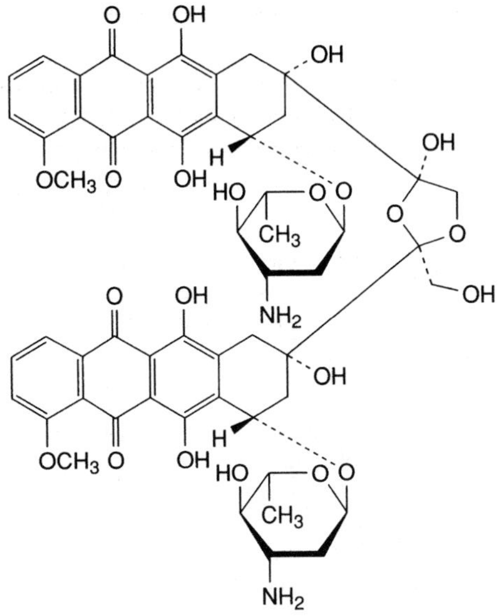

G. 8,8′-[(2*R*,4*R*)-4-hydroxy-2-(hydroxymethyl)-1,3-dioxolan-2,4-diyl]bis[(8*S*,10*S*)-10-[(3-amino-2,3,6-trideoxy-α-L-*arabino*-hexopyranosyl)oxy]-6,8,11-trihydroxy-1-methoxy-7,8,9,10-tetrahydrotetracene-5,12-dione] (epirubicin dimer).

*Ph Eur*

# Ergocalciferol

(*Ph Eur monograph 0082*)

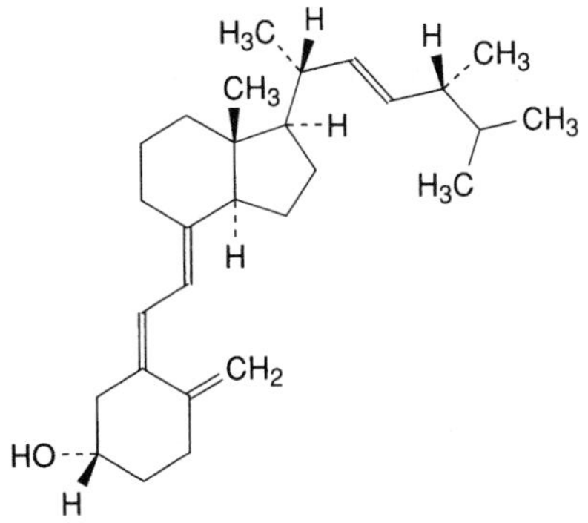

$C_{28}H_{44}O$        396.7        *50-14-6*

## Action and use
Vitamin D analogue (Vitamin $D_2$).

## Preparations
Calcium and Ergocalciferol Tablets

Ergocalciferol Injection

Ergocalciferol Tablets

When vitamin $D_2$ is prescribed or demanded, Ergocalciferol shall be dispensed or supplied. When calciferol or vitamin D is prescribed or demanded, Ergocalciferol or Colecalciferol shall be dispensed or supplied.

*Ph Eur*

## DEFINITION
Ergocalciferol contains not less than 97.0 per cent and not more than the equivalent of 103.0 per cent of (5*Z*,7*E*,22*E*)-9,10-secoergosta-5,7,10(19),22-tetraen-3β-ol.

1 mg of ergocalciferol is equivalent to 40 000 IU of antirachitic activity (vitamin D) in rats.

## CHARACTERS
A white or slightly yellowish, crystalline powder or white or almost white crystals, practically insoluble in water, freely soluble in alcohol, soluble in fatty oils. It is sensitive to air, heat and light. Solutions in volatile solvents are unstable and are to be used immediately.

A reversible isomerisation to pre-ergocalciferol takes place in solution, depending on temperature and time. The activity is due to both compounds.

## IDENTIFICATION
Examine by infrared absorption spectrophotometry (*2.2.24*), comparing with the spectrum obtained with *ergocalciferol CRS*. Examine the substances prepared as discs.

## TESTS
### Specific optical rotation (*2.2.7*)
Dissolve 0.200 g rapidly and without heating in *aldehyde-free alcohol R* and dilute to 25.0 ml with the same solvent. The specific optical rotation, determined within 30 min of preparing the solution, is + 103 to + 107.

### Reducing substances
Dissolve 0.1 g in *aldehyde-free alcohol R* and dilute to 10.0 ml with the same solvent. Add 0.5 ml of a 5 g/l solution of *tetrazolium blue R* in *aldehyde-free alcohol R* and 0.5 ml of *dilute tetramethylammonium hydroxide solution R*. Allow to stand for exactly 5 min and add 1.0 ml of *glacial acetic*

*acid R*. Prepare a reference solution at the same time and in the same manner using 10.0 ml of a solution containing 0.2 µg/ml of *hydroquinone R* in *aldehyde-free alcohol R*. Measure the absorbance (*2.2.25*) of the two solutions at 525 nm using as the compensation liquid 10.0 ml of *aldehyde-free alcohol R* treated in the same manner. The absorbance of the test solution is not greater than that of the reference solution (20 ppm).

**Ergosterol**

Examine by thin-layer chromatography (*2.2.27*), using a *TLC silica gel G plate R*.

*Test solution*  Dissolve 0.25 g of the substance to be examined in *ethylene chloride R* containing 10 g/l of *squalane R* and 0.1 g/l of *butylhydroxytoluene R* and dilute to 5 ml with the same solvent. Prepare immediately before use.

*Reference solution (a)*  Dissolve 0.10 g of *ergocalciferol CRS* in *ethylene chloride R* containing 10 g/l of *squalane R* and 0.1 g/l of *butylhydroxytoluene R* and dilute to 2 ml with the same solvent. Prepare immediately before use.

*Reference solution (b)*  Dissolve 5 mg of *ergosterol CRS* in *ethylene chloride R* containing 10 g/l of *squalane R* and 0.1 g/l of *butylhydroxytoluene R* and dilute to 50 ml with the same solvent. Prepare immediately before use.

*Reference solution (c)*  Mix equal volumes of reference solution (a) and reference solution (b). Prepare immediately before use.

Apply to the plate 10 µl of the test solution, 10 µl of reference solution (a), 10 µl of reference solution (b) and 20 µl of reference solution (c). Develop immediately, protected from light, over a path of 15 cm using a mixture of equal volumes of *cyclohexane R* and *peroxide-free ether R*, the mixture containing 0.1 g/l of *butylhydroxytoluene R*. Allow the plate to dry in air and spray three times with *antimony trichloride solution R1*. Examine the chromatograms for 3 min to 4 min after spraying. The principal spot in the chromatogram obtained with the test solution is initially orange-yellow and then becomes brown. In the chromatogram obtained with the test solution, any slowly appearing violet spot (corresponding to ergosterol) immediately below the principal spot is not more intense than the spot in the chromatogram obtained with reference solution (b) (0.2 per cent). There is no spot in the chromatogram obtained with the test solution that does not correspond to one of the spots in the chromatograms obtained with reference solutions (a) and (b). The test is not valid unless the chromatogram obtained with reference solution (c) shows two clearly separated spots.

**ASSAY**

*Carry out the operations as rapidly as possible, avoiding exposure to actinic light and air.*

Examine by liquid chromatography (*2.2.29*).

*Test solution*  Dissolve 10.0 mg of the substance to be examined without heating in 10.0 ml of *toluene R* and dilute to 100.0 ml with the mobile phase.

*Reference solution (a)*  Dissolve 10.0 mg of *ergocalciferol CRS* without heating in 10.0 ml of *toluene R* and dilute to 100.0 ml with the mobile phase.

*Reference solution (b)*  Dilute 1.0 ml of *cholecalciferol for system suitability CRS* to 5.0 ml with the mobile phase. Heat in a water-bath at 90 °C under a reflux condenser for 45 min and cool.

The chromatographic procedure may be carried out using:
— a stainless steel column 0.25 m long and 4.6 mm in internal diameter packed with a suitable silica gel (5 µm),

— as mobile phase at a flow rate of 2 ml/min a mixture of 3 volumes of *pentanol R* and 997 volumes of *hexane R*,
— as detector a spectrophotometer set at 254 nm.

An automatic injection device or a sample loop is recommended. Inject a suitable volume of reference solution (b). Adjust the sensitivity of the system so that the height of the principal peak is at least 50 per cent of the full scale of the recorder. Inject reference solution (b) 6 times. When the chromatograms are recorded in the prescribed conditions, the approximate relative retention times with reference to cholecalciferol are 0.4 for pre-cholecalciferol and 0.5 for *trans*-cholecalciferol. The relative standard deviation of the response for cholecalciferol is not greater than 1 per cent and the resolution between the peaks corresponding to pre-cholecalciferol and *trans*-cholecalciferol is not less than 1.0. If necessary adjust the proportions of the constituents and the flow rate of the mobile phase to obtain this resolution.

Inject a suitable volume of reference solution (a). Adjust the sensitivity of the system so that the height of the principal peak is at least 50 per cent of the full scale of the recorder. Inject the same volume of the test solution and record the chromatogram in the same manner.

Calculate the percentage content of ergocalciferol from the expression:

$$\frac{m'}{m} \times \frac{S_D}{S'_D} \times 100$$

$m$ = mass of the substance to be examined in the test solution, in milligrams;

$m'$ = mass of *ergocalciferol CRS* in reference solution (a), in milligrams;

$S_D$ = area (or height) of the peak due to ergocalciferol in the chromatogram obtained with the test solution;

$S'_D$ = area (or height) of the peak due to ergocalciferol in the chromatogram obtained with reference solution (a).

**STORAGE**

Store in an airtight container, under nitrogen, protected from light, at a temperature between 2 °C and 8 °C.

The contents of an opened container are to be used immediately.

**IMPURITIES**

A. (5E,7E,22E)-9,10-secoergosta-5,7,10(19),22-tetraen-3β-ol (*trans*-vitamin D₂),

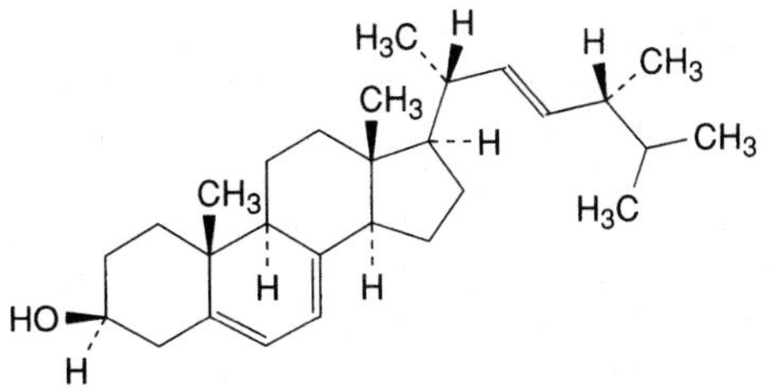

B. (22E)-ergosta-5,7,22-trien-3β-ol (ergosterol),

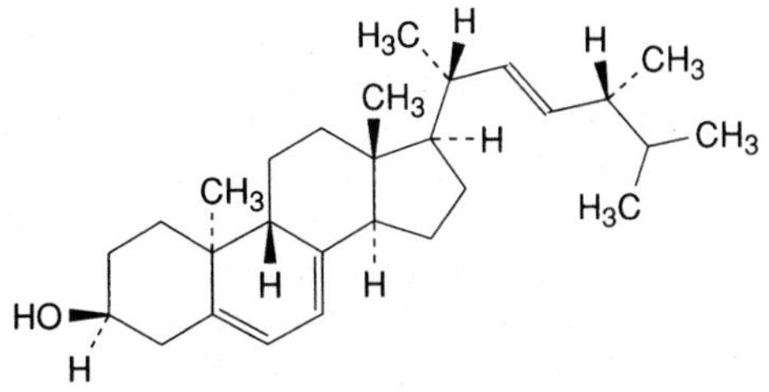

C. (9β,10α,22E)-ergosta-5,7,22-trien-3β-ol (lumisterol₂),

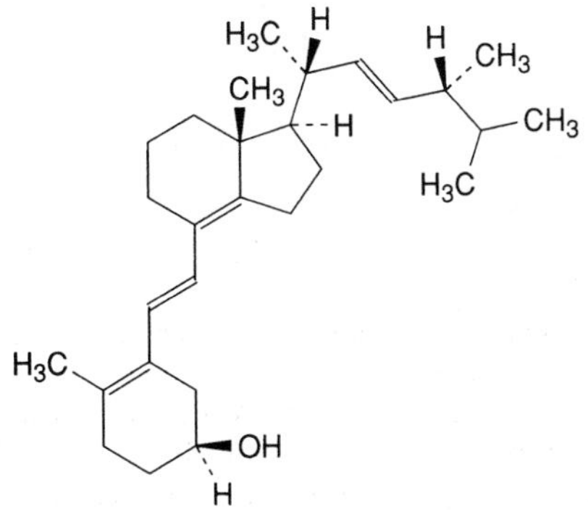

D. (6E,22E)-9,10-secoergosta-5(10),6,8(14),22-tetraen-3β-ol (iso-tachysterol₂),

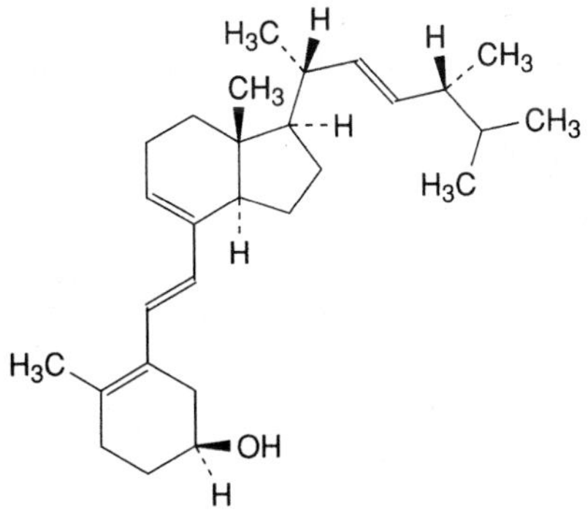

E. (6E,22E)-9,10-secoergosta-5(10),6,8,22-tetraen-3β-ol (tachysterol₂).

*Ph Eur*

# Ergometrine Maleate

(*Ph Eur monograph 0223*)

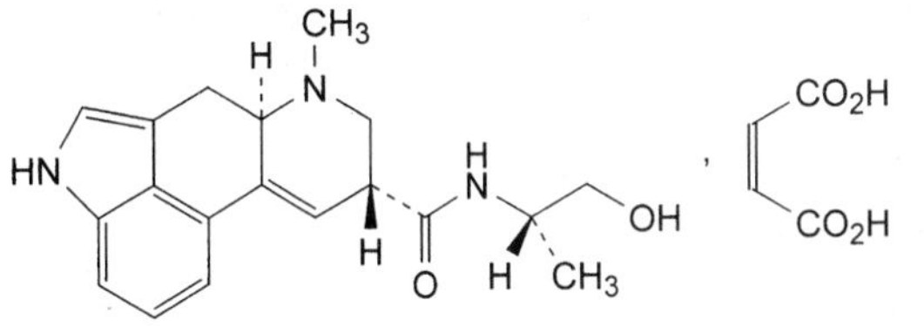

$C_{19}H_{23}N_3O_2,C_4H_4O_4$    441.5    *129-51-1*

**Action and use**

Oxytocic.

**Preparations**

Ergometrine Injection

Ergometrine and Oxytocin Injection

Ergometrine Tablets

*Ph Eur*

## DEFINITION

Ergometrine maleate contains not less than 98.0 per cent and not more than the equivalent of 101.0 per cent of (6aR,9R)-N-[(S)-2-hydroxy-1-methylethyl]-7-methyl-4,6,6a,7,8,9-hexahydro-indolo[4,3-*fg*]quinoline-9-carboxamide (Z)-butenedioate, calculated with reference to the dried substance.

## CHARACTERS

A white or almost white or slightly coloured, crystalline powder, sparingly soluble in water, slightly soluble in alcohol.

## IDENTIFICATION

*First identification   B, C.*

*Second identification   A, C, D, E.*

A. Dissolve 30 mg in *0.01 M hydrochloric acid* and dilute to 100.0 ml with the same acid. Dilute 10.0 ml of the solution to 100.0 ml with *0.01 M hydrochloric acid*. Examined between 250 nm and 360 nm (*2.2.25*), the solution shows an absorption maximum at 311 nm and a minimum at 265 nm to 272 nm. The specific absorbance at the maximum is 175 to 195.

B. Examine by infrared absorption spectrophotometry (*2.2.24*), comparing with the spectrum obtained with *ergometrine maleate CRS*. Examine the substances prepared as discs.

C. Examine the chromatograms obtained in the test for related substances. The principal spot in the chromatogram obtained with test solution (b) is similar in position, colour and size to the principal spot in the chromatogram obtained with reference solution (a).

D. To 0.1 ml of solution S (see Tests) add 1 ml of *glacial acetic acid R*, 0.05 ml of *ferric chloride solution R1* and 1 ml of *phosphoric acid R* and heat in a water-bath at 80 °C. After about 10 min, a blue or violet colour develops which becomes more intense on standing.

E. Dissolve 0.1 g in a mixture of 0.5 ml of *dilute sulphuric acid R* and 2.5 ml of *water R*. Add 5 ml of *ether R* and 1 ml of *strong sodium hydroxide solution R* and shake. Separate the aqueous layer and shake with two quantities, each of 5 ml, of *ether R*. To 0.1 ml of the aqueous layer add a solution of 10 mg of *resorcinol R* in 3 ml of *sulphuric acid R*. Heat on a water-bath for 15 min. No colour develops. To the rest of the aqueous layer add 1 ml of *bromine water R*. Heat on a water-bath for 10 min, then heat to boiling and cool. To 0.2 ml of this solution add a solution of 10 mg of *resorcinol R* in 3 ml of *sulphuric acid R*. Heat on a water-bath for 15 min. A pinkish-violet colour develops.

## TESTS

### Solution S
Dissolve 0.100 g, without heating and protected from light, in 9 ml of *carbon dioxide-free water R* and dilute to 10.0 ml with the same solvent.

### Appearance of solution
Solution S is clear (*2.2.1*) and not more intensely coloured than reference solution $Y_5$ or $BY_5$ (*2.2.2, Method II*).

### pH (*2.2.3*)
The pH of solution S is 3.6 to 4.4.

### Specific optical rotation (*2.2.7*)
+ 50 to + 56, determined on solution S and calculated with reference to the dried substance.

### Related substances
Examine by thin-layer chromatography (*2.2.27*), using *silica gel G R* as the coating substance. *Carry out all operations as rapidly as possible, protected from light. Prepare the test and reference solutions immediately before use.*

*Test solution (a)* Dissolve 50 mg of the substance to be examined in a mixture of 1 volume of *concentrated ammonia R* and 9 volumes of *alcohol (80 per cent V/V) R* and dilute to 5.0 ml with the same mixture of solvents.

*Test solution (b)* Dilute 1.0 ml of test solution (a) to 10.0 ml with a mixture of 1 volume of *concentrated ammonia R* and 9 volumes of *alcohol (80 per cent V/V) R*.

*Reference solution (a)* Dissolve 10 mg of *ergometrine maleate CRS* in a mixture of 1 volume of *concentrated ammonia R* and 9 volumes of *alcohol (80 per cent V/V) R* and dilute to 10.0 ml with the same mixture of solvents.

*Reference solution (b)* Dilute 5.0 ml of reference solution (a) to 50.0 ml with a mixture of 1 volume of *concentrated ammonia R* and 9 volumes of *alcohol (80 per cent V/V) R*.

*Reference solution (c)* To 2.0 ml of reference solution (b) add 2.0 ml of a mixture of 1 volume of *concentrated ammonia R* and 9 volumes of *alcohol (80 per cent V/V) R*.

Apply separately to the plate 5 µl of each solution. Develop immediately over a path of 14 cm using a mixture of 3 volumes of *water R*, 25 volumes of *methanol R* and 75 volumes of *chloroform R*. Dry the plate in a current of cold air and spray with *dimethylaminobenzaldehyde solution R7*. Dry the plate in a current of warm air for about 2 min. Any spot in the chromatogram obtained with test solution (a), apart from the principal spot, is not more intense than the principal spot in the chromatogram obtained with reference solution (b) (1.0 per cent) and at most one such spot is more intense than the principal spot in the chromatogram obtained with reference solution (c) (0.5 per cent).

### Loss on drying (*2.2.32*)
Not more than 2.0 per cent, determined on 0.20 g by drying over *diphosphorus pentoxide R* at 80 °C at a pressure not exceeding 2.7 kPa for 2 h.

### ASSAY
Dissolve 0.150 g in 40 ml of *anhydrous acetic acid R*. Titrate with *0.05 M perchloric acid*, determining the end-point potentiometrically (*2.2.20*).

1 ml of *0.05 M perchloric acid* is equivalent to 22.07 mg of $C_{23}H_{27}N_3O_6$.

## STORAGE
Store in an airtight, glass container, protected from light, at a temperature of 2 °C to 8 °C.

*Ph Eur*

# Ergotamine Tartrate

(*Ph Eur monograph 0224*)

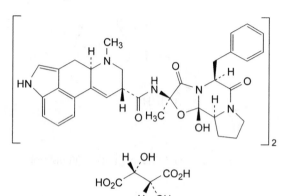

$(C_{33}H_{35}N_5O_5)_2,C_4H_6O_6$     1313     *379-79-3*

### Action and use
Oxytocic.

### Preparation
Ergotamine Sublingual Tablets

*Ph Eur*

## DEFINITION
Ergotamine tartrate contains not less than 98.0 per cent and not more than the equivalent of 101.0 per cent of bis[(6a*R*,9*R*)-*N*-[(2*R*,5*S*,10a*S*,10b*S*)-5-benzyl-10b-hydroxy-2-methyl-3,6-dioxo-octahydro-8*H*-oxazolo[3,2-*a*]pyrrolo[2,1-*c*]pyrazin-2-yl]-7-methyl-4,6,6a,7,8,9-hexahydroindolo[4,3-*fg*]quinoline-9-carboxamide] tartrate, calculated with reference to the dried substance. It may contain two molecules of methanol of crystallisation.

## CHARACTERS
A white or almost white, crystalline powder or colourless crystals, slightly hygroscopic, slightly soluble in alcohol. Aqueous solutions slowly become cloudy owing to hydrolysis; this may be prevented by the addition of tartaric acid.

## IDENTIFICATION
*First identification* B, C.

*Second identification* A, C, D, E.

A. Dissolve 50 mg in *0.01 M hydrochloric acid* and dilute to 100.0 ml with the same acid. Dilute 10.0 ml of the solution to 100.0 ml with *0.01 M hydrochloric acid*. Examined between 250 nm and 360 nm (*2.2.25*), the solution shows an absorption maximum at 311 nm to 321 nm and a minimum at 265 nm to 275 nm. The specific absorbance at the maximum is 118 to 128, calculated with reference to the dried substance.

B. Examine by infrared absorption spectrophotometry (*2.2.24*), comparing with the spectrum obtained with *ergotamine tartrate CRS*. Examine the substances as discs prepared as follows: triturate the substance to be examined and the reference substance separately with 0.2 ml of methanol R and then with *potassium bromide R* as prescribed in the general method.

C. Examine for not more than 1 min in ultraviolet light at 365 nm the chromatograms obtained in the test for related substances. The principal spot in the chromatogram obtained with test solution (b) is similar in position and fluorescence to the principal spot in the chromatogram obtained with reference solution (a). After spraying with *dimethylaminobenzaldehyde solution R7*, examine in daylight. The principal spot in the chromatogram obtained with test solution (b) is similar in position, colour and size to the principal spot in the chromatogram obtained with reference solution (a).

D. To 0.1 ml of solution S (see Tests) add 1 ml of *glacial acetic acid R*, 0.05 ml of *ferric chloride solution R1* and 1 ml of *phosphoric acid R* and heat in a water-bath at 80 °C. After about 10 min, a blue or violet colour develops which becomes more intense on standing.

E. Dissolve about 10 mg in 1.0 ml of *0.1 M sodium hydroxide*. Transfer to a separating funnel and shake with 5 ml of *methylene chloride R*. Discard the organic layer. Neutralise the aqueous layer with a few drops of *dilute hydrochloric acid R*. 0.1 ml of this solution gives reaction (b) of tartrates (*2.3.1*). Pour the reaction mixture into 1 ml of *water R* to observe the colour change to red or brownish-red.

## TESTS

*Carry out all operations as rapidly as possible, protected from light.*

### Solution S

Triturate 30 mg finely with about 15 mg of *tartaric acid R* and dissolve with shaking in 6 ml of *water R*.

### Appearance of solution

Solution S is clear (*2.2.1*) and not more intensely coloured than reference solution $Y_6$ (*2.2.2, Method II*).

### pH (*2.2.3*)

Shake 10 mg, finely powdered, with 4 ml of *carbon dioxide-free water R*. The pH of the suspension is 4.0 to 5.5.

### Specific optical rotation (*2.2.7*)

Dissolve 0.40 g in 40 ml of a 10 g/l solution of *tartaric acid R*. Add 0.5 g of *sodium hydrogen carbonate R* cautiously in several portions and mix thoroughly. Shake with four quantities, each of 10 ml, of *chloroform R* previously washed with five quantities of *water R*, each of 50 ml per 100 ml of *chloroform R*. Combine the organic layers. Filter through a small filter moistened with *chloroform R* previously washed as described above. Dilute the filtrate to 50.0 ml with *chloroform R* previously washed as described above. Measure the angle of rotation.

Determine the amount of ergotamine base in the chloroformic solution as follows: to 25.0 ml of the solution add 50 ml of *anhydrous acetic acid R* and titrate with *0.05 M perchloric acid*, determining the end-point potentiometrically (*2.2.20*).

1 ml of *0.05 M perchloric acid* is equivalent to 29.08 mg of $C_{33}H_{35}N_5O_5$.

The specific optical rotation is − 154 to − 165, calculated from the angle of rotation and the concentration of ergotamine base.

### Related substances

Examine by thin-layer chromatography (*2.2.27*), using a *TLC silica gel G plate R*. Prepare the reference solutions and the test solutions immediately before use and in the order indicated below.

*Reference solution (a)* Dissolve 10 mg of *ergotamine tartrate CRS* in a mixture of 1 volume of *methanol R* and 9 volumes of *methylene chloride R* and dilute to 10.0 ml with the same mixture of solvents.

*Reference solution (b)* Dilute 7.5 ml of reference solution (a) to 50.0 ml with a mixture of 1 volume of *methanol R* and 9 volumes of *methylene chloride R*.

*Reference solution (c)* To 2.0 ml of reference solution (b) add 4.0 ml of a mixture of 1 volume of *methanol R* and 9 volumes of *methylene chloride R*.

*Test solution (a)* Dissolve 50 mg of the substance to be examined in a mixture of 1 volume of *methanol R* and 9 volumes of *methylene chloride R* and dilute to 5.0 ml with the same mixture of solvents.

*Test solution (b)* Dilute 1.0 ml of test solution (a) to 10.0 ml with a mixture of 1 volume of *methanol R* and 9 volumes of *methylene chloride R*.

Apply immediately to the plate 5 µl of each reference solution and then 5 µl of each test solution. Expose the starting points immediately to ammonia vapour and for exactly 20 s by moving the starting line from side to side above a beaker 55 mm high and 45 mm in diameter containing about 20 ml of *concentrated ammonia R*. Dry the starting line in a current of cold air for exactly 20 s. Develop immediately over a path of 17 cm using a mixture of 5 volumes of *ethanol R*, 10 volumes of *methylene chloride R*, 15 volumes of *dimethylformamide R* and 70 volumes of *ether R*. Dry the plate in a current of cold air for about 2 min. Examine for not more than 1 min in ultraviolet light at 365 nm for the identification. Spray the plate abundantly with *dimethylaminobenzaldehyde solution R7* and dry in a current of warm air for about 2 min. Any spot in the chromatogram obtained with test solution (a), apart from the principal spot, is not more intense than the principal spot in the chromatogram obtained with reference solution (b) (1.5 per cent) and at most one such spot is more intense than the principal spot in the chromatogram obtained with reference solution (c) (0.5 per cent).

### Loss on drying (*2.2.32*)

Not more than 6.0 per cent, determined on 0.100 g by drying *in vacuo* at 95 °C for 6 h.

## ASSAY

Dissolve 0.200 g in 40 ml of *anhydrous acetic acid R*. Titrate with *0.05 M perchloric acid*, determining the end-point potentiometrically (*2.2.20*).

1 ml of *0.05 M perchloric acid* is equivalent to 32.84 mg of $C_{70}H_{76}N_{10}O_{16}$.

## STORAGE

Store in an airtight, glass container, protected from light, at a temperature of 2 °C to 8 °C.

_____ *Ph Eur*

# Erythritol

*(Ph Eur monograph 1803)*

C$_4$H$_{10}$O$_4$      122.1      *149-32-6*

*Ph Eur*

## DEFINITION
(2*R*,3*S*)-Butane1,2,3,4-tetrol (*meso*-erythritol).

## Content
96.0 per cent to 102.0 per cent (anhydrous substance).

## CHARACTERS
### Appearance
White or almost white, crystalline powder or free-flowing granules.

### Solubility
Freely soluble in water, very slightly soluble in ethanol (96 per cent).

## IDENTIFICATION
A. Melting point (*2.2.14*): 119 °C to 122 °C.

B. Infrared absorption spectrophotometry (*2.2.24*).

*Comparison*    *erythritol CRS.*

## TESTS
### Appearance of solution
The solution is clear (*2.2.1*) and colourless (*2.2.2, Method II*).

Dissolve 5.0 g in *water R* and dilute to 50 ml with the same solvent.

### Conductivity (*2.2.38*)
Maximum 20 μS·cm$^{-1}$.

Dissolve 20.0 g in *carbon dioxide-free water R* prepared from *distilled water R* and dilute to 100.0 ml with the same solvent. Measure the conductivity of the solution, while gently stirring with a magnetic stirrer.

### Related substances
Liquid chromatography (*2.2.29*).

*Test solution*    Dissolve 0.50 g of the substance to be examined in *water R* and dilute to 10.0 ml with the same solvent.

*Reference solution (a)*    Dissolve 0.50 g of *erythritol CRS* in *water R* and dilute to 10.0 ml with the same solvent.

*Reference solution (b)*    Dilute 2.0 ml of the test solution to 100.0 ml with *water R*.

*Reference solution (c)*    Dilute 5.0 ml of reference solution (b) to 100.0 ml with *water R*.

*Reference solution (d)*    Dissolve 1.0 g of *erythritol R* and 1.0 g of *glycerol R* in *water R* and dilute to 20.0 ml with the same solvent.

*Column:*
— *size: l* = 0.3 m, Ø = 7.8 mm;
— *stationary phase: cation-exchange resin R* (9 μm);
— *temperature*: 70 °C.

*Mobile phase*    0.01 per cent *V/V* solution of *sulphuric acid R*.

*Flow rate*    0.8 ml/min.

*Detection*    Refractometer maintained at a constant temperature.

*Injection*    20 μl; inject the test solution and reference solutions (b), (c) and (d).

*Run time*    3 times the retention time of erythritol.

*Relative retention*    With reference to erythritol (retention time = about 11 min): impurity A = about 0.77; impurity B = about 0.90; impurity C = about 0.94; impurity D = about 1.10.

*System suitability*    Reference solution (d):
— *resolution*: minimum 2 between the peaks due to erythritol and impurity D.

*Limits:*
— *any impurity*: not more than the area of the principal peak in the chromatogram obtained with reference solution (b) (2.0 per cent);
— *total*: not more than the area of the principal peak in the chromatogram obtained with reference solution (b) (2.0 per cent);
— *disregard limit*: area of the principal peak in the chromatogram obtained with reference solution (c) (0.1 per cent).

### Lead (*2.4.10*)
Maximum 0.5 ppm.

### Water (*2.5.12*)
Maximum 0.5 per cent, determined on 1.00 g.

### Microbial contamination
If intended for use in the manufacture of parenteral preparations:
— TAMC: acceptance criterion 10$^2$ CFU/g (*2.6.12*).

If not intended for use in the manufacture of parenteral preparations:
— TAMC: acceptance criterion 10$^3$ CFU/g (*2.6.12*);
— TYMC: acceptance criterion 10$^2$ CFU/g (*2.6.12*);
— absence of *Escherichia coli* (*2.6.13*);
— absence of *Salmonella* (*2.6.13*).

### Bacterial endotoxins (*2.6.14*)
If intended for use in the manufacture of parenteral preparations without a further appropriate procedure for the removal of bacterial endotoxins:
— less than 4 IU/g for parenteral preparations having a concentration of 100 g/l or less of erythritol;
— less than 2.5 IU/g for parenteral preparations having a concentration of more than 100 g/l of erythritol.

## ASSAY
Liquid chromatography (*2.2.29*) as described in the test for related substances with the following modification.

*Injection*    Test solution and reference solution (a).

Calculate the percentage content of erythritol using the chromatogram obtained with reference solution (a) and the declared content of *erythritol CRS*.

## LABELLING
The label states where applicable, that the substance is suitable for use in the manufacture of parenteral preparations.

## IMPURITIES
A. maltitol,

B. sorbitol,

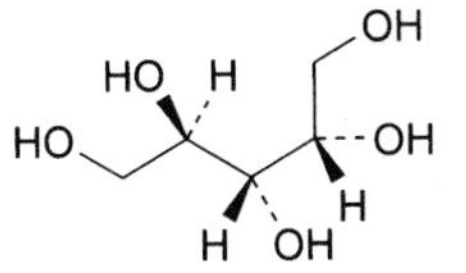

C. (2R,3s,4S)-pentane-1,2,3,4,5-pentol (*meso*-ribitol),

D. glycerol.

*Ph Eur*

# Erythromycin

(*Ph Eur monograph 0179*)

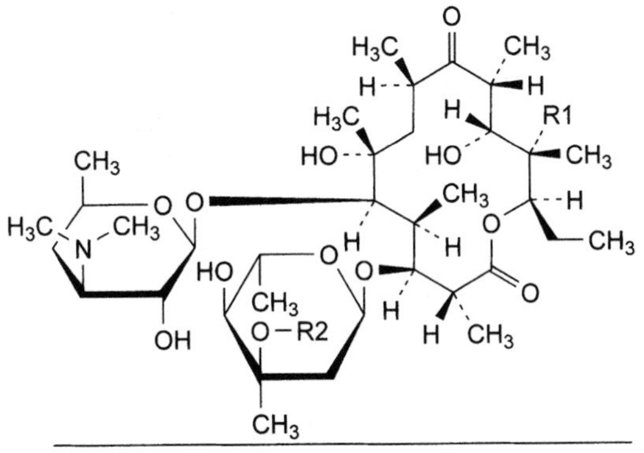

| Erythromycin | Mol. Formula | M_r | R1 | R2 |
|---|---|---|---|---|
| A | $C_{37}H_{67}NO_{13}$ | 734 | OH | CH_3 |
| B | $C_{37}H_{67}NO_{12}$ | 718 | H | CH_3 |
| C | $C_{36}H_{65}NO_{13}$ | 720 | OH | H |

*114-07-8*

## Action and use

Macrolide antibacterial.

## Preparations

Gastro-resistant Erythromycin Capsules

Gastro-resistant Erythromycin Tablets

Erythromycin and Zinc Acetate Lotion

*Ph Eur*

## DEFINITION

Mixture of macrolide antibiotics produced by a strain of *Streptomyces erythreus*, the main component being (3R,4S,5S,6R,7R,9R,11R,12R,13S,14R)-4-[(2,6-dideoxy-3-C-methyl-3-O-methyl-α-L-*ribo*-hexopyranosyl)oxy]-14-ethyl-7,12,13-trihydroxy-3,5,7,9,11,13-hexamethyl-6-[(3,4,6-trideoxy-3-dimethylamino-β-D-*xylo*-hexopyranosyl)-oxy]oxacyclotetradecane-2,10-dione (erythromycin A).

## Content:

— sum of the contents of erythromycin A, erythromycin B and erythromycin C: 93.0 per cent to 102.0 per cent (anhydrous substance),

— erythromycin B: maximum 5.0 per cent,

— erythromycin C: maximum 5.0 per cent.

## CHARACTERS

### Appearance

White or slightly yellow powder or colourless or slightly yellow crystals, slightly hygroscopic.

### Solubility

Slightly soluble in water (the solubility decreases as the temperature rises), freely soluble in alcohol, soluble in methanol.

## IDENTIFICATION

*First identification* A.

*Second identification* B, C, D.

A. Infrared absorption spectrophotometry (*2.2.24*).

*Comparison* erythromycin A CRS.

Disregard any band in the region from 1980 cm$^{-1}$ to 2050 cm$^{-1}$.

If the spectra obtained show differences, dissolve 50 mg of the substance to be examined and of the reference substance separately in 1.0 ml of *methylene chloride R*, dry at 60 °C at a pressure not exceeding 670 Pa for 3 h and record new spectra using the residues.

B. Thin-layer chromatography (*2.2.27*).

*Test solution* Dissolve 10 mg of the substance to be examined in *methanol R* and dilute to 10 ml with the same solvent.

*Reference solution (a)* Dissolve 10 mg of *erythromycin A CRS* in *methanol R* and dilute to 10 ml with the same solvent.

*Reference solution (b)* Dissolve 20 mg of *spiramycin CRS* in *methanol R* and dilute to 10 ml with the same solvent.

*Plate* TLC silica gel G plate R.

*Mobile phase* Mix 4 volumes of *2-propanol R*, 8 volumes of a 150 g/l solution of *ammonium acetate R* previously adjusted to pH 9.6 with *ammonia R* and 9 volumes of *ethyl acetate R*. Allow to settle and use the upper layer.

*Application* 10 µl.

*Development* Over 2/3 of the plate.

*Drying* In air.

*Detection* Spray with *anisaldehyde solution R1* and heat at 110 °C for 5 min.

*Results* The principal spot in the chromatogram obtained with the test solution is similar in position, colour and size to the principal spot in the chromatogram obtained with reference solution (a) and its position and colour are different from those of the spots in the chromatogram obtained with reference solution (b).

C. To about 5 mg add 5 ml of a 0.2 g/l solution of *xanthydrol R* in a mixture of 1 volume of *hydrochloric acid R* and 99 volumes of *acetic acid R* and heat on a water-bath. A red colour develops.

D. Dissolve about 10 mg in 5 ml of *hydrochloric acid R1* and allow to stand for 10-20 min. A yellow colour develops.

## TESTS

### Specific optical rotation (*2.2.7*)

− 71 to − 78 (anhydrous substance).

Dissolve 1.00 g in *ethanol R* and dilute to 50.0 ml with the same solvent. The specific optical rotation is determined at least 30 min after preparing the solution.

### Related substances

Liquid chromatography (*2.2.29*).

*Test solution* Dissolve 40.0 mg of the substance to be examined in a mixture of 1 volume of *methanol R* and 3 volumes of *phosphate buffer solution pH 7.0 R1* and dilute to 10.0 ml with the same mixture of solvents.

*Reference solution (a)* Dissolve 40.0 mg of *erythromycin A CRS* in a mixture of 1 volume of *methanol R* and

3 volumes of *phosphate buffer solution pH 7.0 R1* and dilute to 10.0 ml with the same mixture of solvents.

*Reference solution (b)* Dissolve 10.0 mg of *erythromycin B CRS* and 10.0 mg of *erythromycin C CRS* in a mixture of 1 volume of *methanol R* and 3 volumes of *phosphate buffer solution pH 7.0 R1* and dilute to 50.0 ml with the same mixture of solvents.

*Reference solution (c)* Dissolve 5 mg of *N-demethylerythromycin A CRS* in reference solution (b). Add 1.0 ml of reference solution (a) and dilute to 25 ml with reference solution (b).

*Reference solution (d)* Dilute 3.0 ml of reference solution (a) to 100.0 ml with a mixture of 1 volume of *methanol R* and 3 volumes of *phosphate buffer solution pH 7.0 R1*.

*Reference solution (e)* Transfer 40 mg of *erythromycin A CRS* to a glass vial and spread evenly such that it forms a layer not more than about 1 mm thick. Heat at 130 °C for 4 h. Allow to cool and dissolve in a mixture of 1 volume of *methanol R* and 3 volumes of *phosphate buffer solution pH 7.0 R1* and dilute to 10 ml with the same mixture of solvents.

*Column:*
— *size: l* = 0.25 m, Ø = 4.6 mm,
— *stationary phase: styrene-divinylbenzene copolymer R* (8 μm) with a pore size of 100 nm,
— *temperature*: 70 °C using a water-bath for the column and at least one-third of the tubing preceding the column.

*Mobile phase* To 50 ml of a 35 g/l solution of *dipotassium hydrogen phosphate R* adjusted to pH 9.0 ± 0.05 with *dilute phosphoric acid R*, add 400 ml of *water R*, 165 ml of *2-methyl-2-propanol R* and 30 ml of *acetonitrile R*, and dilute to 1000 ml with *water R*.

*Flow rate* 2.0 ml/min.

*Detection* Spectrophotometer at 215 nm.

*Injection* 100 μl; inject the test solution and reference solutions (c), (d) and (e).

*Run time* 5 times the retention time of erythromycin A.

*Relative retention* With reference to erythromycin A (retention time = about 15 min): impurity A = about 0.3; impurity B = about 0.45; erythromycin C = about 0.5; impurity C = about 0.9; impurity D = about 1.4; impurity F = about 1.5; erythromycin B = about 1.8; impurity E = about 4.3.

*System suitability* Reference solution (c):
— *resolution*: minimum 0.8 between the peaks due to impurity B and erythromycin C and minimum 5.5 between the peaks due to impurity B and erythromycin A. If necessary, adjust the concentration of 2-methyl-2-propanol in the mobile phase or reduce the flow rate to 1.5 ml or 1.0 ml/min.

*Limits:*
— *correction factors*: for the calculation of contents, multiply the peak areas of the following impurities (use the chromatogram obtained with reference solution (e) to identify them) by the corresponding correction factor: impurity E = 0.09; impurity F = 0.15,
— *any impurity*: not more than the area of the principal peak in the chromatogram obtained with reference solution (d) (3.0 per cent),
— *total*: not more than 2.3 times the area of the principal peak in the chromatogram obtained with reference solution (d) (7.0 per cent),
— *disregard limit*: 0.02 times the area of the principal peak in the chromatogram obtained with reference solution (d)

(0.06 per cent); disregard the peaks due to erythromycin B and erythromycin C.

**Thiocyanate**
Maximum 0.3 per cent.

*Prepare the solutions immediately before use and protect from actinic light.*

*Compensation liquid* Dilute 1.0 ml of a 90 g/l solution of *ferric chloride R* to 50.0 ml with *methanol R*.

*Test solution* Dissolve 0.100 g (m g) of the substance to be examined in 20 ml of *methanol R*, add 1.0 ml of a 90 g/l solution of *ferric chloride R* and dilute to 50.0 ml with *methanol R*.

*Prepare 2 independent reference solutions.*

*Reference solution* Dissolve 0.100 g of *potassium thiocyanate R*, previously dried at 105 °C for 1 h, in *methanol R* and dilute to 50.0 ml with the same solvent. Dilute 5.0 ml to 50.0 ml with *methanol R*. To 5.0 ml of this solution, add 1.0 ml of a 90 g/l solution of *ferric chloride R* and dilute to 50.0 ml with *methanol R*.

Measure the absorbances (*2.2.25*) of each reference solution ($A_1$, $A_2$) and of the test solution ($A$) at the maximum (about 492 nm).

*Suitability value:*

$$S = \frac{m_2 \times A_1}{m_1 \times A_2}$$

$m_1$, $m_2$ = mass of the potassium thiocyanate used to prepare the respective reference solutions, in grams.

The test is not valid unless $S$ is not less than 0.985 and not more than 1.015.

Calculate the percentage content of thiocyanate from the expression:

$$\frac{A \times 58.08 \times 0.5}{m \times 97.18} \times \left( \frac{m_1}{A_1} + \frac{m_2}{A_2} \right)$$

58.08 = relative molecular mass of the thiocyanate moiety,
97.18 = relative molecular mass of potassium thiocyanate.

**Water** (*2.5.12*)
Maximum 6.5 per cent, determined on 0.200 g.

Use a 100 g/l solution of *imidazole R* in *anhydrous methanol R* as the solvent.

**Sulphated ash** (*2.4.14*)
Maximum 0.2 per cent, determined on 1.0 g.

**ASSAY**
Liquid chromatography (*2.2.29*) as described in the test for related substances with the following modifications.

*Injection* Test solution and reference solutions (a) and (b).

*System suitability* Reference solution (a):
— *repeatability*: maximum relative standard deviation of 1.2 per cent for 6 replicate injections.

Calculate the percentage content of erythromycin A using the chromatogram obtained with reference solution (a). Calculate the percentage contents of erythromycin B and erythromycin C using the chromatogram obtained with reference solution (b).

**STORAGE**
Protected from light.

**IMPURITIES**

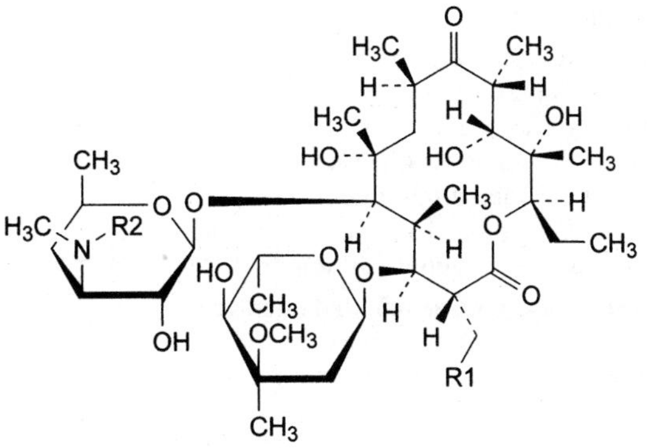

A. R1 = OH, R2 = CH₃: erythromycin F,

A. $R1 = OH$, $R2 = CH_3$: erythromycin F,
B. $R1 = R2 = H$: *N*-demethylerythromycin A,

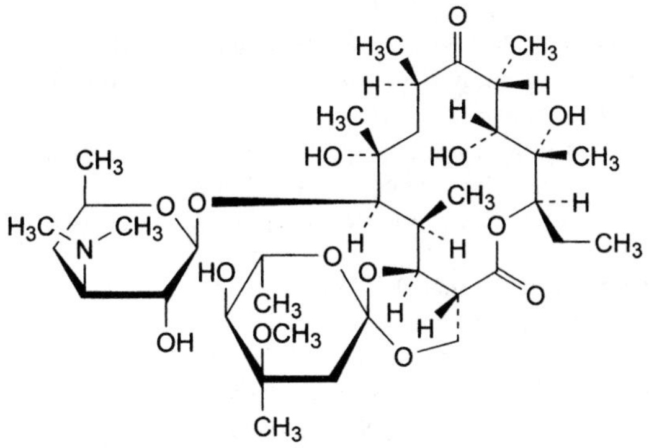

C. erythromycin E,

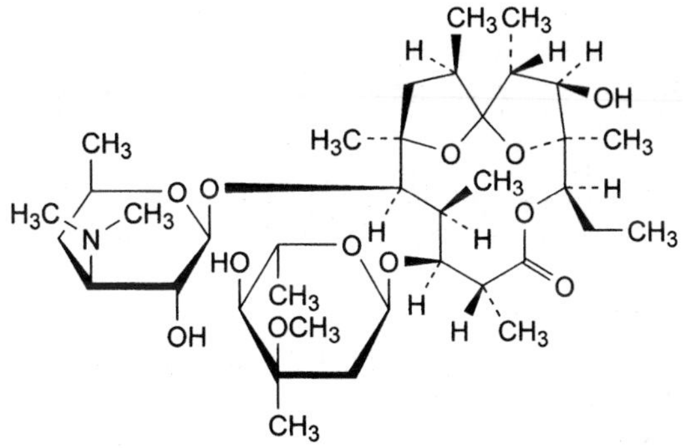

D. anhydroerythromycin A,

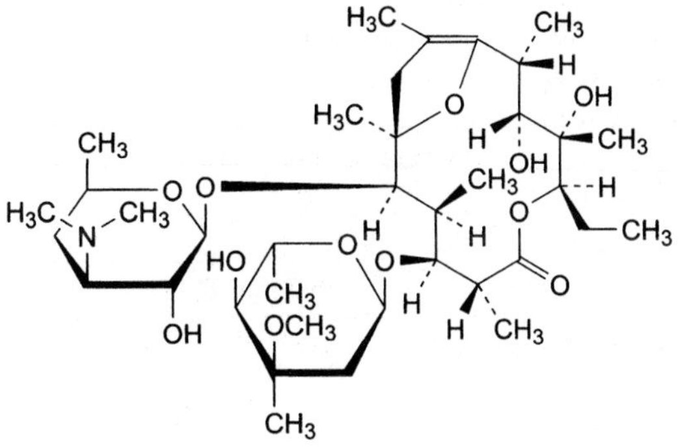

E. erythromycin A enol ether,

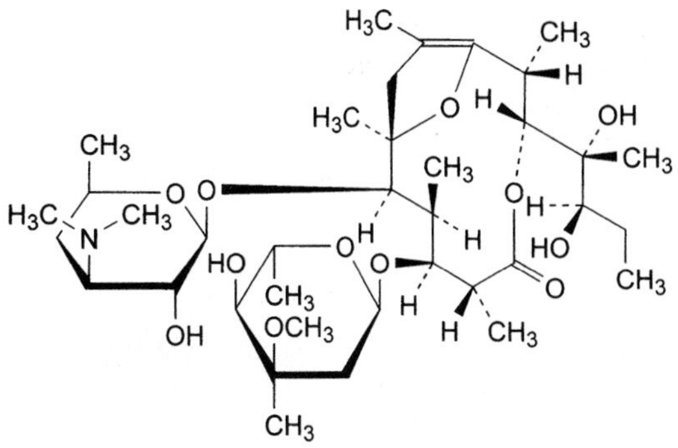

F. pseudoerythromycin A enol ether.

*Ph Eur*

# Erythromycin Estolate

(*Ph Eur monograph 0552*)

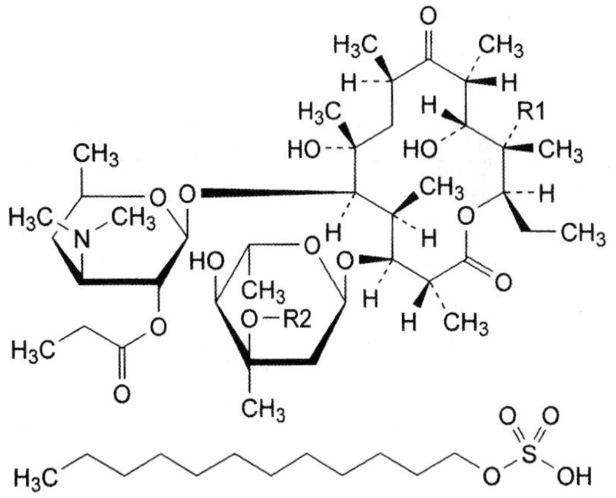

| Erythromycin (estolate) | Mol. Formula | $M_r$ | R1 | R2 |
|---|---|---|---|---|
| A | $C_{52}H_{97}NO_{18}S$ | 1056 | OH | CH₃ |
| B | $C_{52}H_{97}NO_{17}S$ | 1040 | H | CH₃ |
| C | $C_{51}H_{95}NO_{18}S$ | 1042 | OH | H |

$C_{40}H_{71}NO_{14},C_{12}H_{26}O_4S$    1056    *3521-62-8*

## Action and use
Macrolide antibacterial.

## Preparation
Erythromycin Estolate Capsules

*Ph Eur*

## DEFINITION
### Main component
(3R,4S,5S,6R,7R,9R,11R,12R,13S,14R)-4-[(2,6-Dideoxy-3-
*C*-methyl-3-O-methyl-α-L-*ribo*-hexopyranosyl)oxy]-14-ethyl-
7,12,13-trihydroxy-3,5,7,9,11,13-hexamethyl-6-[[3,4,6-
trideoxy-3-(dimethylamino)-2-O-propionyl-β-D-*xylo*-
hexopyranosyl]oxy]oxacyclotetradecane-2,10-dione dodecyl
sulphate (erythromycin A 2″-propionate dodecyl sulphate).

Semi-synthetic product derived from a fermentation product.

### Content:
— *erythromycin estolate*: 86.0 per cent to 102.0 per cent
(anhydrous substance),

— *erythromycin B*: maximum 5.0 per cent (anhydrous substance),
— *erythromycin C*: maximum 5.0 per cent (anhydrous substance).

## CHARACTERS

### Appearance
White or almost white, crystalline powder.

### Solubility
Practically insoluble in water, freely soluble in ethanol (96 per cent), soluble in acetone. It is practically insoluble in dilute hydrochloric acid.

## IDENTIFICATION
Infrared absorption spectrophotometry (*2.2.24*).

*Comparison* erythromycin estolate CRS.

## TESTS

### Related substances
Liquid chromatography (*2.2.29*).

*Hydrolysis solution* A 20 g/l solution of *dipotassium hydrogen phosphate R* adjusted to pH 8.0 with *phosphoric acid R*.

*Test solution* Dissolve 0.150 g of the substance to be examined in 25 ml of *methanol R*. Add 20 ml of the hydrolysis solution, mix and allow to stand at room temperature for at least 12 h. Dilute to 50.0 ml with the hydrolysis solution.

*Reference solution (a)* Dissolve 40.0 mg of *erythromycin A CRS* in 10 ml of *methanol R* and dilute to 20.0 ml with the hydrolysis solution.

*Reference solution (b)* Dissolve 10.0 mg of *erythromycin B CRS* and 10.0 mg of *erythromycin C CRS* in 50.0 ml of *methanol R*. Add 5.0 ml of reference solution (a) and dilute to 100.0 ml with the hydrolysis solution.

*Reference solution (c)* Dissolve 2 mg of *N-demethylerythromycin A CRS* in 20 ml of reference solution (b).

*Reference solution (d)* Dilute 3.0 ml of reference solution (a) to 100.0 ml with a mixture of equal volumes of *methanol R* and the hydrolysis solution.

*Reference solution (e)* Dissolve 40 mg of *erythromycin A CRS*, previously heated at 130 °C for 3 h, in 10 ml of *methanol R* and dilute to 20 ml with the hydrolysis solution (in situ preparation of impurities E and F).

*Reference solution (f)* Dissolve 2 mg of *erythromycin A CRS* in 10 ml of *0.01 M hydrochloric acid*. Allow to stand at room temperature for 30 min. Dilute to 20 ml with the hydrolysis solution (*in situ* preparation of impurity D).

*Column:*
— *size: l* = 0.25 m, Ø = 4.6 mm,
— *stationary phase*: styrene-divinylbenzene copolymer R (8 µm) with a pore size of 100 nm,
— *temperature*: 70 °C using a water-bath for the column and at least one third of the tubing preceding the column.

*Mobile phase* To 50 ml of a 35 g/l solution of *dipotassium hydrogen phosphate R* adjusted to pH 8.0 with *dilute phosphoric acid R*, add 400 ml of *water R*, 165 ml of *2-methyl-2-propanol R* and 30 ml of *acetonitrile R*, and dilute to 1000 ml with *water R*.

*Flow rate* 2.0 ml/min.

*Detection* Spectrophotometer at 215 nm.

*Injection* 200 µl of the test solution and reference solutions (c), (d), (e) and (f).

*Run time* 5 times the retention time of erythromycin A; begin integration after the hydrolysis peak.

*Identification of impurities* Use the chromatogram obtained with reference solution (e) to identify the peaks due to impurities E and F.

*Relative retention* With reference to erythromycin A (retention time = about 15 min):
hydrolysis peak = less than 0.3; impurity A = about 0.3; impurity B = about 0.45; erythromycin C = about 0.5; impurity C = about 0.9; impurity G = about 1.3; impurity D = about 1.4; impurity F = about 1.5; erythromycin B = about 1.8; impurity E = about 4.3.

*System suitability* Reference solution (c):
— *resolution*: minimum 0.8 between the peaks due to impurity B and erythromycin C and minimum 5.5 between the peaks due to impurity B and erythromycin A.

*Limits:*
— *correction factors*: for the calculation of content, multiply the peak areas of the following impurities by the corresponding correction factor: impurity E = 0.09; impurity F = 0.15; impurity G = 0.14;
— *impurities A, B, C, D, E, F, G*: for each impurity, not more than the area of the principal peak in the chromatogram obtained with reference solution (d) (3.0 per cent);
— *any other impurity*: for each impurity, not more than 0.067 times the area of the principal peak in the chromatogram obtained with reference solution (d) (0.2 per cent);
— *total*: not more than 1.67 times the area of the principal peak in the chromatogram obtained with reference solution (d) (5.0 per cent);
— *disregard limit*: 0.02 times the area of the principal peak in the chromatogram obtained with reference solution (d) (0.06 per cent).

### Free erythromycin
Liquid chromatography (*2.2.29*). *Prepare the solutions immediately before use.*

*Test solution* Dissolve 0.250 g of the substance to be examined in the mobile phase and dilute to 50.0 ml with the mobile phase.

*Reference solution* Dissolve 75.0 mg of *erythromycin A CRS* in the mobile phase and dilute to 50.0 ml with the mobile phase. Dilute 5.0 ml of the solution to 25.0 ml with *acetonitrile R*.

*Column:*
— *size: l* = 0.25 m, Ø = 4.6 mm,
— *stationary phase*: octylsilyl silica gel for chromatography R (5 µm),
— *temperature*: 30 °C.

*Mobile phase* Mix 35 volumes of *acetonitrile R1* and 65 volumes of a solution containing 3.4 g/l of *potassium dihydrogen phosphate R* and 2.75 ml/l *of triethylamine R*, adjusted to pH 3.0 with *dilute phosphoric acid R*.

*Flow rate* 1 ml/min.

*Detection* Spectrophotometer at 195 nm.

*Injection* 20 µl.

*Run time* Twice the retention time of erythromycin A for the reference solution and 4.5 times the retention time of the 1st peak of erythromycin propionate for the test solution.

*Retention time* Erythromycin A = about 5 min; 1st peak of erythromycin propionate = about 10 min.

*Limit:*
— *free erythromycin*: not more than the area of the principal peak in the chromatogram obtained with the reference solution (6.0 per cent).

**Dodecyl sulphate**

23.0 per cent to 25.5 per cent of $C_{12}H_{26}O_4S$ (anhydrous substance).

Dissolve 0.500 g in 25 ml of *dimethylformamide R*. Titrate with *0.1 M sodium methoxide* using 0.05 ml of a 3 g/l solution of *thymol blue R* in *methanol R* as indicator.

1 ml of *0.1 M sodium methoxide* is equivalent to 26.64 mg of $C_{12}H_{26}O_4S$.

**Water** (*2.5.12*)

Maximum 4.0 per cent, determined on 0.300 g.

Use a 100 g/l solution of *imidazole R* in *anhydrous methanol R* as the solvent.

**Sulphated ash** (*2.4.14*)

Maximum 0.5 per cent, determined on 0.5 g.

**ASSAY**

Liquid chromatography (*2.2.29*) as described in the test for related substances with the following modifications.

*Injection*

Test solution and reference solutions (a) and (b).

*System suitability:*

— *repeatability*: maximum relative standard deviation of 1.2 per cent after 6 injections of reference solution (a).

Calculate the percentage content of erythromycin A using the chromatogram obtained with reference solution (a). Express the result as erythromycin A estolate by multiplying the percentage content of erythromycin A by 1.4387.

Calculate the percentage contents of erythromycin B and erythromycin C using the chromatogram obtained with reference solution (b). Express the result as erythromycin B estolate and as erythromycin C estolate by multiplying by 1.4387.

For the calculation of content of erythromycin estolate use the sum of erythromycins A, B and C expressed as estolate as described above.

**STORAGE**

Protected from light.

**IMPURITIES**

*Specified impurities   A, B, C, D, E, F, G.*

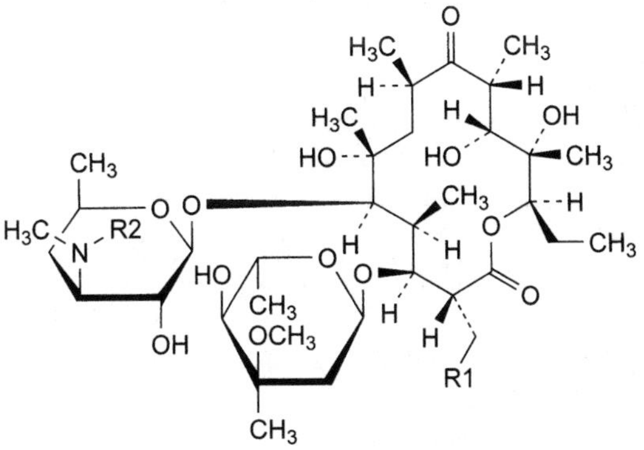

A. R1 = OH, R2 = CH₃: erythromycin F,

B. R1 = R2 = H: *N*-demethylerythromycin A,

G. R1 = H, R2 = CO-C₂H₅:
*N*-demethyl-*N*-propanoylerythromycin A,

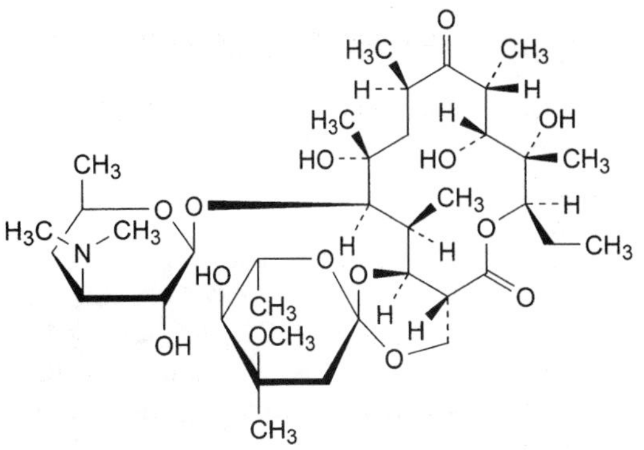

C. erythromycin E,

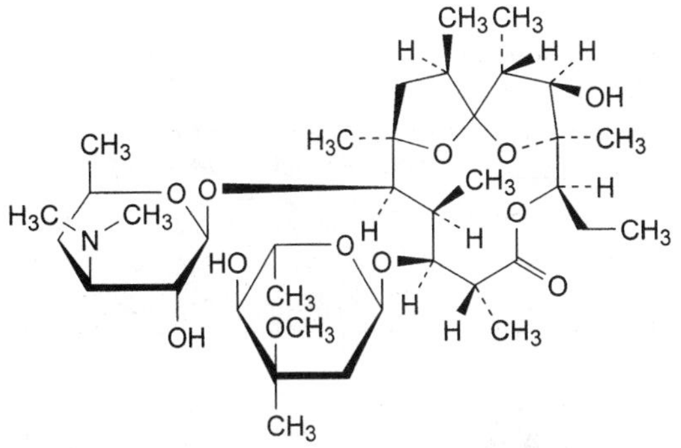

D. anhydroerythromycin A,

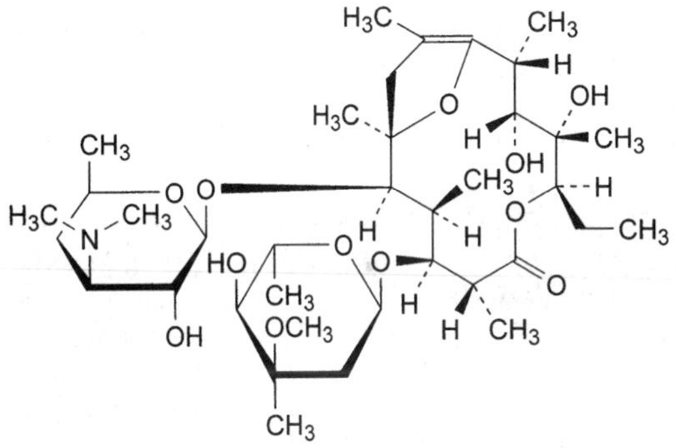

E. erythromycin A enol ether,

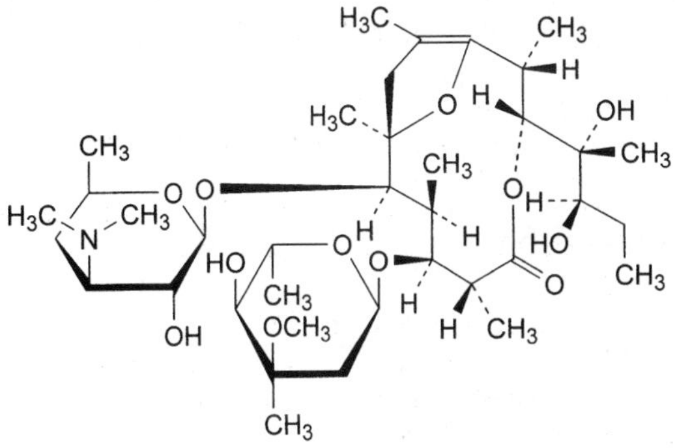

F. pseudoerythromycin A enol ether.

# Erythromycin Ethyl Succinate

*(Erythromycin Ethylsuccinate,*
*Ph Eur monograph 0274)*

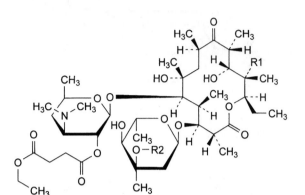

| Ethylsuccinate compound | Mol. Formula | $M_r$ | R1 | R2 |
|---|---|---|---|---|
| Erythromycin A | $C_{43}H_{75}NO_{16}$ | 862 | OH | $CH_3$ |
| Erythromycin B | $C_{43}H_{75}NO_{15}$ | 846 | H | $CH_3$ |
| Erythromycin C | $C_{42}H_{73}NO_{16}$ | 848 | OH | H |

*41342-53-4*

## Action and use
Macrolide antibacterial.

## Preparations
Erythromycin Ethyl Succinate Oral Suspension
Erythromycin Ethyl Succinate Tablets

*Ph Eur*

## DEFINITION
### Main component
(3R,4S,5S,6R,7R,9R,11R,12R,13S,14R)-4-[(2,6-dideoxy-3-
C-methyl-3-O-methyl-α-L-*ribo*-hexopyranosyl)oxy]-14-ethyl-
7,12,13-trihydroxy-3,5,7,9,11,13-hexamethyl-6-[[3,4,6-
trideoxy-3-(dimethylamino)-2-O-(4-ethoxy-4-oxobutanoyl)-β-
D-*xylo*-hexopyranosyl]oxy]oxacyclotetradecane-2,10-dione
(erythromycin A ethylsuccinate).

Semi-synthetic product derived from a fermentation product.

### Content:
— sum of erythromycin A, erythromycin B and erythromycin
  C: minimum 78.0 per cent (anhydrous substance),
— erythromycin B: maximum 5.0 per cent (anhydrous
  substance),
— erythromycin C: maximum 5.0 per cent (anhydrous
  substance).

## CHARACTERS
### Appearance
White or almost white, crystalline powder, hygroscopic.

### Solubility
Practically insoluble in water, freely soluble in acetone,
in ethanol and in methanol.

## IDENTIFICATION
Infrared absorption spectrophotometry *(2.2.24)*.

*Comparison   erythromycin ethylsuccinate CRS.*

## TESTS
### Specific optical rotation *(2.2.7)*
− 70 to − 82 (anhydrous substance).

Dissolve 0.100 g in *acetone R* and dilute to 10.0 ml with the
same solvent. Measure the angle of rotation at least 30 min
after preparing the solution.

### Related substances
Liquid chromatography *(2.2.29)*.

*Hydrolysis solution*   A 20 g/l solution of *dipotassium hydrogen
phosphate R* adjusted to pH 8.0 with *phosphoric acid R*.

*Test solution*   Dissolve 0.115 g of the substance to be
examined in 25 ml of *methanol R*. Add 20 ml of the
hydrolysis solution, mix and allow to stand at room
temperature for at least 12 h. Dilute to 50.0 ml with the
hydrolysis solution.

*Reference solution (a)*   Dissolve 40.0 mg of *erythromycin
A CRS* in 10 ml of *methanol R* and dilute to 20.0 ml with
the hydrolysis solution.

*Reference solution (b)*   Dissolve 10.0 mg of *erythromycin
B CRS* and 10.0 mg of *erythromycin C CRS* in 50 ml of
*methanol R*. Add 5.0 ml of reference solution (a) and dilute
to 100.0 ml with the hydrolysis solution.

*Reference solution (c)*   Dissolve 2 mg of *N-
demethylerythromycin A CRS* in 20 ml of reference solution
(b).

*Reference solution (d)*   Dilute 3.0 ml of reference solution (a)
to 100.0 ml with a mixture of equal volumes of *methanol R*
and the hydrolysis solution.

*Reference solution (e)*   Dissolve 40 mg of *erythromycin A CRS*,
previously heated at 130 °C for 3 h, in 10 ml of *methanol R*
and dilute to 20 ml with the hydrolysis solution.

*Column:*
— *size: l* = 0.25 m, Ø = 4.6 mm,
— *stationary phase*: styrene-*divinylbenzene copolymer R* (8 μm)
  with a pore size of 100 nm,
— *temperature*: 70 °C using a water-bath for the column and
  at least one third of the tubing preceding the column.

*Mobile phase*   To 50 ml of a 35 g/l solution of *dipotassium
hydrogen phosphate R* adjusted to pH 8.0 with *dilute
phosphoric acid R*, add 400 ml of *water R*, 165 ml of
*2-methyl-2-propanol R* and 30 ml of *acetonitrile R*,
and dilute to 1000 ml with *water R*.

*Flow rate*   2.0 ml/min.

*Detection*   Spectrophotometer at 215 nm.

*Injection*   200 μl; inject the test solution and reference
solutions (a), (c), (d) and (e).

*Run time*   5 times the retention time of erythromycin A;
begin integration after the hydrolysis peak.

*Relative retention*   With reference to erythromycin A
(retention time = about 15 min):
hydrolysis peak = less than 0.3; impurity B = about 0.45;
erythromycin C = about 0.5; impurity C = about 0.9;
impurity G = about 1.3; impurity D = about 1.4;
impurity F = about 1.5; erythromycin B = about 1.8;
impurity E = about 4.3.

*System suitability*   Reference solution (c):
— resolution: minimum 0.8 between the peaks due to
  impurity B and to erythromycin C and minimum 5.5
  between the peaks due to impurity B and to
  erythromycin A.

*Limits:*
— correction factors: for the calculation of contents, multiply
  the peak areas of the following impurities by the
  corresponding correction factor: impurity E = 0.09;
  impurity F = 0.15; impurity G = 0.14; use the

chromatogram obtained with reference solution (e) to identify the peaks due to impurities E and F.

— *any impurity*: not more than the area of the principal peak in the chromatogram obtained with reference solution (d) (3.0 per cent).

— *total*: not more than 1.67 times the area of the principal peak in the chromatogram obtained with reference solution (d) (5.0 per cent).

— *disregard limit*: 0.02 times the area of the principal peak in the chromatogram obtained with reference solution (d) (0.06 per cent).

**Free erythromycin**

Liquid chromatography (*2.2.29*).

*Test solution*    Dissolve 0.250 g of the substance to be examined in *acetonitrile R* and dilute to 50.0 ml with the same solvent.

*Reference solution*    Dissolve 75.0 mg of *erythromycin A CRS* in *acetonitrile R* and dilute to 50.0 ml with the same solvent. Dilute 5.0 ml of the solution to 25.0 ml with *acetonitrile R*.

*Column:*

— *size: l* = 0.25 m, Ø = 4.6 mm,

— *stationary phase*: octylsilyl silica gel for chromatography R (5 μm).

*Mobile phase*    Mix 35 volumes of *acetonitrile R* and 65 volumes of a solution containing 3.4 g/l of *potassium dihydrogen phosphate R* and 2.0 g/l of *triethylamine R*, adjusted to pH 3.0 with *dilute phosphoric acid R*.

*Flow rate*    1 ml/min.

*Detection*    Spectrophotometer at 195 nm.

*Injection*    20 μl.

*Run time*    Twice the retention time of erythromycin A (retention time = about 8 min) for the reference solution and twice the retention time of erythromycin ethylsuccinate (retention time = about 24 min) for the test solution.

*Limit:*

— *free erythromycin*: not more than the area of the principal peak in the chromatogram obtained with the reference solution (6.0 per cent).

**Water** (*2.5.12*)

Maximum 3.0 per cent, determined on 0.30 g.

Use a 100 g/l solution of *imidazole R* in *anhydrous methanol R* as the solvent.

**Sulphated ash** (*2.4.14*)

Maximum 0.3 per cent, determined on 1.0 g.

**ASSAY**

Liquid chromatography (*2.2.29*) as described in the test for related substances.

*Injection*    Inject the test solution and reference solutions (a) and (b).

*System suitability*    Reference solution (a):

— *relative standard deviation*: maximum 1.2 per cent for 6 replicate injections.

Calculate the percentage content of erythromycin A using the chromatogram obtained with reference solution (a). Calculate the percentage contents of erythromycin B and erythromycin C using the chromatogram obtained with reference solution (b).

**STORAGE**

In an airtight container, protected from light.

**IMPURITIES**

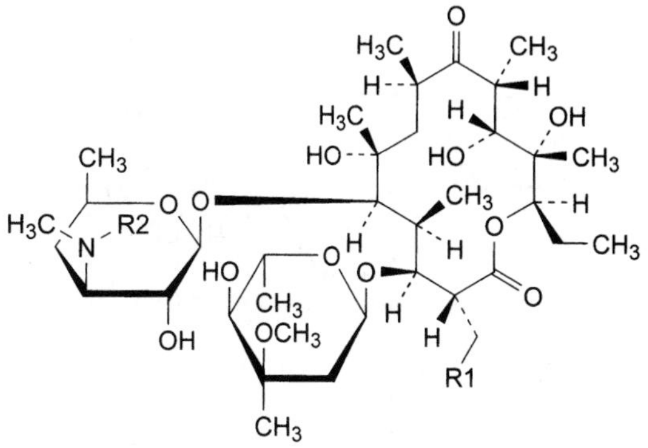

A. R1 = OH, R2 = CH₃: erythromycin F,
B. R1 = R2 = H: *N*-demethylerythromycin A,

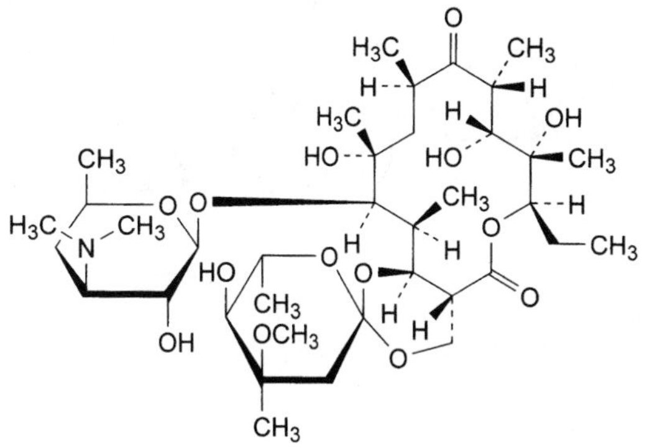

C. erythromycin E,

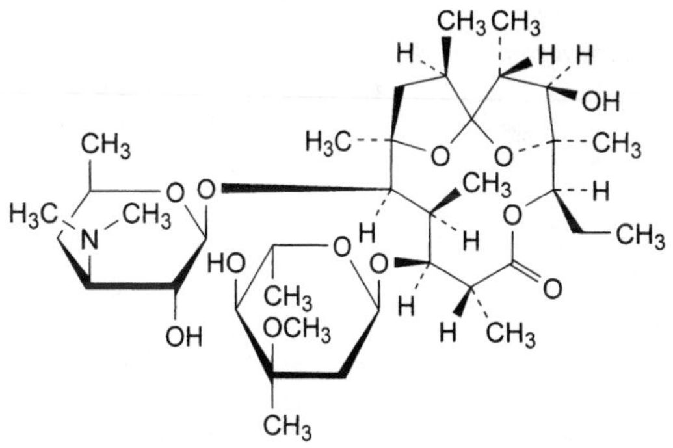

D. anhydroerythomycin A,

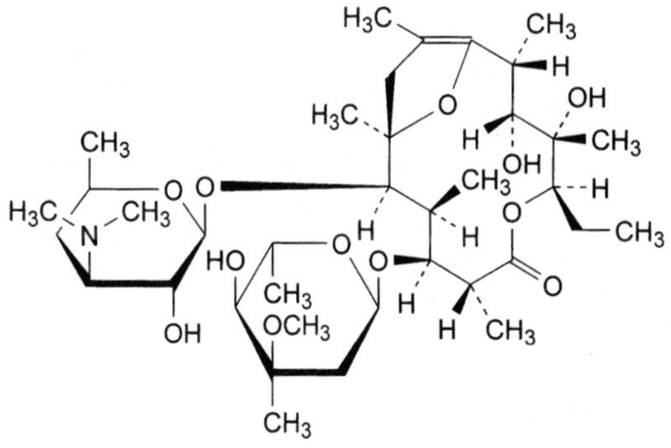

E. erythromycin A enol ether,

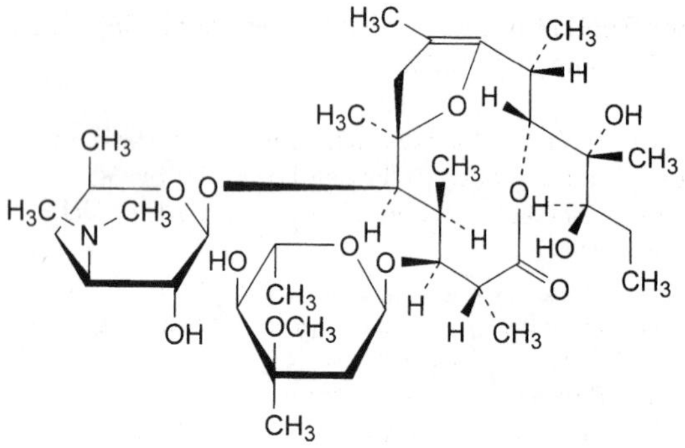

F. pseudoerythromycin A enol ether,

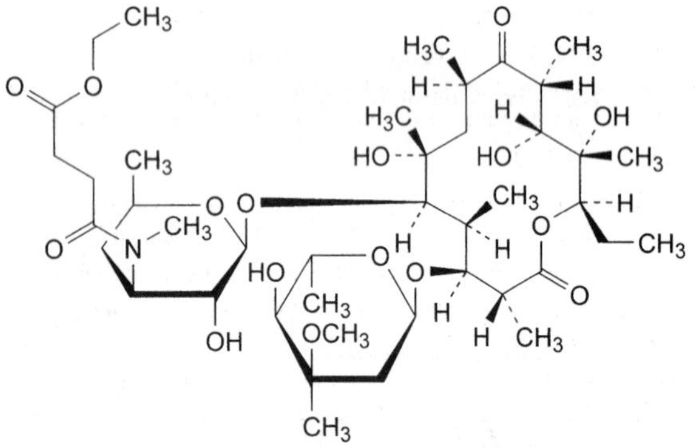

G. erythromycin *N*-ethylsuccinate.

_____ *Ph Eur*

# Erythromycin Lactobionate

(*Ph Eur monograph 1098*)

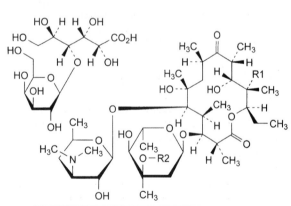

| Erythromycin (lactobionate) | Mol. Formula | $M_r$ | R1 | R2 |
|---|---|---|---|---|
| A | $C_{49}H_{89}NO_{25}$ | 1092 | OH | CH₃ |
| B | $C_{49}H_{89}NO_{24}$ | 1076 | H | CH₃ |
| C | $C_{48}H_{87}NO_{25}$ | 1078 | OH | H |

3847-29-8

## Action and use
Macrolide antibacterial.

## Preparation
Erythromycin Lactobionate Intravenous Infusion

*Ph Eur*

## DEFINITION
### Main component
(3*R*,4*S*,5*S*,6*R*,7*R*,9*R*,11*R*,12*R*,13*S*,14*R*)-4-[(2,6-dideoxy-3-*C*-methyl-3-*O*-methyl-α-L-*ribo*-hexopyranosyl)oxy]-14-ethyl-7,12,13-trihydroxy-3,5,7,9,11,13-hexamethyl-6-[[3,4,6-trideoxy-3-(dimethylamino)-β-D-*xylo*-hexopyranosyl]oxy]oxacyclotetradecane-2,10-dione 4-*O*-β-D-galactopyranosyl-D-gluconate (erythromycin A lactobionate).

Salt of a product obtained by fermentation using a strain of *Streptomyces erythreus*.

### Content:
— *sum of erythromycin A lactobionate, erythromycin B lactobionate and erythromycin C lactobionate*: 93.0 per cent to 102.0 per cent (anhydrous substance);
— *erythromycin B lactobionate*: maximum 5.0 per cent (anhydrous substance);
— *erythromycin C lactobionate*: maximum 5.0 per cent (anhydrous substance).

## CHARACTERS
### Appearance
White or slightly yellow hygroscopic, powder.

### Solubility
Soluble in water, freely soluble in anhydrous ethanol and in methanol, very slightly soluble in acetone and in methylene chloride.

## IDENTIFICATION
A. Thin-layer chromatography (*2.2.27*).

*Test solution*   Dissolve 30 mg of the substance to be examined in *methanol R* and dilute to 10 ml with the same solvent.

*Reference solution (a)*   Dissolve 20 mg of *erythromycin A CRS* in *methanol R* and dilute to 10 ml with the same solvent.

*Reference solution (b)*   Dissolve 10 mg of *lactobionic acid R* in *water R* and dilute to 10 ml with the same solvent.

*Plate*   TLC silica gel plate R.

*Mobile phase*   glacial acetic acid R, water R, methanol R (3:10:90 *V/V/V*).

*Application*   5 µl.

*Development*   Over 3/4 of the plate.

*Drying*   In air.

*Detection*   Spray with a 5 g/l solution of *potassium permanganate R* in *1 M sodium hydroxide* and heat at 110 °C for 5 min.

*Results*   The 2 spots in the chromatogram obtained with the test solution are similar in position, colour and size, one to the principal spot in the chromatogram obtained with reference solution (a) and the other to the principal spot in the chromatogram obtained with reference solution (b).

B. To about 5 mg add 5 ml of a 0.2 g/l solution of *xanthydrol R* in a mixture of 1 volume of *hydrochloric acid R* and 99 volumes of *acetic acid R*. A red colour develops.

C. Dissolve about 10 mg in 5 ml of *hydrochloric acid R1*. A yellowish-green colour develops.

## TESTS
### Appearance of solution
The solution is clear (*2.2.1*) and colourless (*2.2.2, Method II*).

Dissolve 1.0 g in 20 ml of *water R*.

### pH (*2.2.3*)
6.5 to 7.5.

Dissolve 0.50 g in *carbon dioxide-free water R* and dilute to 25 ml with the same solvent.

**Related substances**

Liquid chromatography (*2.2.29*)

*The test solution and the reference solutions can be used within 24 h if stored at 2-8 °C.*

*Solvent mixture* methanol R, phosphate buffer solution *pH 7.0 R (25:75 V/V).*

*Test solution* Dissolve 60.0 mg of the substance to be examined in the solvent mixture and dilute to 10.0 ml with the solvent mixture.

*Reference solution (a)* Dissolve 40.0 mg of *erythromycin A CRS* in the solvent mixture and dilute to 10.0 ml with the solvent mixture.

*Reference solution (b)* Dissolve 10.0 mg of *erythromycin B CRS* and 10.0 mg of *erythromycin C CRS* in the solvent mixture and dilute to 50.0 ml with the solvent mixture.

*Reference solution (c)* Dissolve 5 mg of *N-demethylerythromycin A CRS* (impurity B) in reference solution (b). Add 1.0 ml of reference solution (a) and dilute to 25 ml with reference solution (b).

*Reference solution (d)* Dilute 3.0 ml of reference solution (a) to 100.0 ml with the solvent mixture.

*Reference solution (e)* Dissolve 40 mg of *erythromycin A CRS*, previously heated at 130 °C for 4 h, in the solvent mixture and dilute to 10 ml with the solvent mixture (in situ preparation of impurities E and F).

*Reference solution (f)* Dissolve 2 mg of *erythromycin A CRS* in 5 ml of *0.01 M hydrochloric acid*. Allow to stand at room temperature for 30 min. Dilute to 10 ml with the solvent mixture (in situ preparation of impurity D).

*Column:*
— *size: l* = 0.25 m, Ø = 4.6 mm;
— *stationary phase:* styrene-divinylbenzene copolymer R (8 µm) with a pore size of 100 nm;
— *temperature:* 70 °C using a water-bath for the column and at least 1/3 of the tubing preceding the column.

*Mobile phase* To 50 ml of a 35 g/l solution of *dipotassium hydrogen phosphate R* adjusted to pH 9.0 with *dilute phosphoric acid R*, add 400 ml of *water R*, 165 ml of *2-methyl-2-propanol R* and 30 ml of *acetonitrile R1*, and dilute to 1000 ml with *water R*.

*Flow rate* 2.0 ml/min.

*Detection* Spectrophotometer at 215 nm.

*Injection* 100 µl of the test solution and reference solutions (a), (c), (d), (e) and (f).

*Run time* 5 times the retention time of erythromycin A.

*Identification of impurities* Use the chromatogram obtained with reference solution (c) to identify the peak due to impurity B, with reference solution (e) to identify the peaks due to impurities E and F, and with reference solution (f) to identify the peak due to impurity D.

*Relative retention* With reference to erythromycin A (retention time = about 15 min): impurity A = about 0.3; impurity B = about 0.45; erythromycin C = about 0.5; impurity C = about 0.9; impurity D = about 1.4; impurity F = about 1.5; erythromycin B = about 1.8; impurity E = about 4.3.

*System suitability* Reference solution (c):
— *resolution:* minimum 0.8 between the peaks due to impurity B and erythromycin C and minimum 5.5 between the peaks due to impurity B and erythromycin A. If necessary adjust the concentration of 2-methyl-2-

propanol in the mobile phase or reduce the flow rate to 1.5 ml/min or 1.0 ml/min.

*Limits:*
— *correction factors:* for the calculation of content, multiply the peak areas of the following impurities by the corresponding correction factor: impurity E = 0.09; impurity F = 0.15;
— *impurities A, B, C, D, E, F:* for each impurity, not more than the area of the principal peak in the chromatogram obtained with reference solution (d) (3.0 per cent);
— *any other impurity:* for each impurity, not more than 0.067 times the area of the principal peak in the chromatogram obtained with reference solution (d) (0.2 per cent);
— *total:* not more than twice the area of the principal peak in the chromatogram obtained with reference solution (d) (6.0 per cent);
— *disregard limit:* 0.02 times the area of the principal peak in the chromatogram obtained with reference solution (d) (0.06 per cent).

**Free lactobionic acid**

Mximum 1.0 per cent of $C_{12}H_{22}O_{12}$ (anhydrous substance).

Dissolve 0.400 g in 50 ml of *water R*. Titrate with *0.1 M sodium hydroxide*, determining the end-point potentiometrically (*2.2.20*). Calculate the volume of *0.1 M sodium hydroxide* required per gram of the substance to be examined ($n_1$ ml). Dissolve 0.500 g in 40 ml of *anhydrous acetic acid R* and titrate with *0.1 M perchloric acid*, determining the end-point potentiometrically (*2.2.20*). Calculate the volume of *0.1 M perchloric acid* required per gram of the substance to be examined ($n_2$ ml).

Calculate the percentage content of $C_{12}H_{22}O_{12}$ using the following expression:

$$3.580\,(n_1 - n_2)$$

**Water** (*2.5.12*)

Maximum 5.0 per cent, determined on 0.200 g.

Use a 100 g/l solution of *imidazole R* in *anhydrous methanol R* as the solvent.

**Sulphated ash** (*2.4.14*)

Maximum 0.5 per cent, determined on 1.0 g.

**Bacterial endotoxins** (*2.6.14*)

Less than 0.35 IU/mg of erythromycin, if intended for use in the manufacture of parenteral dosage forms without a further appropriate procedure for the removal of bacterial endotoxins.

**ASSAY**

Liquid chromatography (*2.2.29*) as described in the test for related substances with the following modifications.

*Injection* Test solution and reference solutions (a) and (b).

*System suitability:*
— *repeatability:* maximum relative standard deviation of 2.0 per cent after 6 injections of reference solution (a).

Calculate the percentage content of erythromycin A using the chromatogram obtained with reference solution (a). Express the result as erythromycin A lactobionate by multiplying the percentage content of erythromycin A by 1.4877. Calculate the percentage contents of erythromycin B and erythromycin C using the chromatogram obtained with reference solution (b). Express the result as erythromycin B lactobionate and as erythromycin C lactobionate by multiplying by 1.4877.

## STORAGE

In an airtight container. If the substance is sterile, store in a sterile, airtight, tamper-proof container.

## IMPURITIES

*Specified impurities*   *A, B, C, D, E, F.*

A. R1 = OH, R2 = CH₃: erythromycin F,

B. R1 = R2 = H: *N*-demethylerythromycin A,

C. erythromycin E,

D. anhydroerythromycin A,

E. erythromycin A enol ether,

F pseudoerythromycin A enol ether.

*Ph Eur*

## Erythromycin Stearate

(*Ph Eur monograph 0490*)

| Erythromycin | Mol. Formula | R1 | R2 |
|---|---|---|---|
| A | C₅₅H₁₀₃NO₁₅ | OH | CH₃ |
| B | C₅₅H₁₀₃NO₁₄ | H | CH₃ |
| C | C₅₄H₁₀₁NO₁₅ | OH | H |

1018                                    1643-22-1

## Action and use

Macrolide antibacterial.

## Preparation

Erythromycin Stearate Tablets

*Ph Eur*

## DEFINITION

A mixture of the stearates of erythromycin and stearic acid. The main component is the octadecanoate of (3*R*,4*S*,5*S*,6*R*,7*R*,9*R*,11*R*,12*R*,13*S*,14*R*)-4-[(2,6-dideoxy-3-*C*-methyl-3-*O*-methyl-α-L-*ribo*-hexopyranosyl)oxy]-14-ethyl-7,12,13-trihydroxy-3,5,7,9,11,13-hexamethyl-6-[[3,4,6-trideoxy-3-(dimethylamino)-β-D-*xylo*-hexopyranosyl]oxy]oxacyclotetradecane-2,10-dione (erythromycin A stearate).

Fermentation product.

### Content:

— sum of the contents of erythromycin A, erythromycin B and erythromycin C: minimum 60.5 per cent (anhydrous substance),
— erythromycin B: maximum 5.0 per cent,
— erythromycin C: maximum 5.0 per cent.

## CHARACTERS

### Appearance

White or almost white, crystalline powder.

### Solubility

Practically insoluble in water, soluble in acetone and in methanol.

Solutions may be opalescent.

## IDENTIFICATION

A. Infrared absorption spectrophotometry (*2.2.24*).

*Comparison*   erythromycin stearate CRS.

B. Thin-layer chromatography (*2.2.27*).

*Test solution*   Dissolve 28 mg of the substance to be examined in *methanol R* and dilute to 10 ml with the same solvent.

*Reference solution (a)*   Dissolve 20 mg of *erythromycin A CRS* in *methanol R* and dilute to 10 ml with the same solvent.

*Reference solution (b)*   Dissolve 10 mg of *stearic acid R* in *methanol R* and dilute to 10 ml with the same solvent.

*Plate*   *TLC silica gel G plate R*.

*Mobile phase*   Mix 4 volumes of *2-propanol R*, 8 volumes of a 150 g/l solution of *ammonium acetate R* previously adjusted to pH 9.6 with *ammonia R* and 9 volumes of *ethyl acetate R*. Allow to settle and use the upper layer.

*Application*   5 μl.

*Development*   Over 2/3 of the plate.

*Drying*   In air.

*Detection A*   Spray with a solution containing 0.2 g/l of *dichlorofluorescein* R and 0.1 g/l of *rhodamine B R* in *alcohol R*. Maintain the plate for a few seconds in the vapour above a water-bath. Examine in ultraviolet light at 365 nm.

*Results A*   The chromatogram obtained with the test solution shows 2 spots, one of which corresponds in position to the principal spot in the chromatogram obtained with reference solution (a) and the other to the principal spot in the chromatogram obtained with reference solution (b).

*Detection B*   Spray the plate with *anisaldehyde solution R1*. Heat at 110 °C for 5 min and examine in daylight.

*Results B*   The spot in the chromatogram obtained with the test solution corresponds in position, colour and size to the principal spot in the chromatogram obtained with reference solution (a).

## TESTS

### Free stearic acid

Maximum 14.0 per cent (anhydrous substance) of $C_{18}H_{36}O_2$.

Dissolve 0.400 g in 50 ml of *methanol R*. Titrate with *0.1 M sodium hydroxide*, determining the end-point potentiometrically (*2.2.20*). Calculate the volume of *0.1 M sodium hydroxide* required per gram of the substance to be examined ($n_1$ ml). Dissolve 0.500 g in 30 ml of *methylene chloride R*. If the solution is opalescent, filter and shake the residue with 3 quantities, each of 25 ml, of *methylene chloride R*. Filter, if necessary, and rinse the filter with *methylene chloride R*. Reduce the volume of the combined filtrate and rinsings to 30 ml by evaporation on a water-bath. Add 50 ml of *glacial acetic acid R* and titrate with *0.1 M perchloric acid*, determining the end-point potentiometrically (*2.2.20*). Calculate the volume of *0.1 M perchloric acid* required per gram of the substance to be examined ($n_2$ ml).

Calculate the percentage content of $C_{18}H_{36}O_2$ from the expression:

$$2.845\,(n_1 - n_2) \times \frac{100}{100 - h}$$

$h$ = percentage water content.

### Related substances

Liquid chromatography (*2.2.29*).

*Test solution*   Dissolve 55.0 mg of the substance to be examined in 5.0 ml of *methanol R* and dilute to 10.0 ml with *buffer solution pH 8.0 R1*. Centrifuge and use the clear solution.

*Reference solution (a)*   Dissolve 40.0 mg of *erythromycin A CRS* in 5.0 ml of *methanol R* and dilute to 10.0 ml with *buffer solution pH 8.0 R1*.

*Reference solution (b)*   Dissolve 10.0 mg of *erythromycin B CRS* and 10.0 mg of *erythromycin C CRS* in 25.0 ml of *methanol R* and dilute to 50.0 ml with *buffer solution pH 8.0 R1*.

*Reference solution (c)*   Dissolve 5 mg of *N-demethylerythromycin A CRS* in reference solution (b). Add 1.0 ml of reference solution (a) and dilute to 25 ml with reference solution (b).

*Reference solution (d)*   Dilute 3.0 ml of reference solution (a) to 100.0 ml with a mixture of equal volumes of *methanol R* and *buffer solution pH 8.0 R1*.

*Reference solution (e)*   Transfer 40 mg of *erythromycin A CRS* to a glass vial and spread evenly such that it forms a layer not more than about 1 mm thick. Heat at 130 °C for 4 h. Allow to cool and dissolve in a mixture of 1 volume of *methanol R* and 3 volumes of *buffer solution pH 8.0 R1* and dilute to 10 ml with the same mixture of solvents.

*Column:*

— *size: l* = 0.25 m, Ø = 4.6 mm,
— *stationary phase: styrene-divinylbenzene copolymer R* (8 μm) with a pore size of 100 nm,
— *temperature*: 70 °C using a water-bath for the column and at least one third of the tubing preceding the column.

*Mobile phase*   To 50 ml of a 35 g/l solution of *dipotassium hydrogen phosphate R* adjusted to pH 9.0 ± 0.05 with *dilute phosphoric* acid R, add 400 ml of *water R*, 165 ml of *2-methyl-2-propanol R* and 30 ml of *acetonitrile R*, and dilute to 1000 ml with *water R*.

*Flow rate*   2.0 ml/min.

*Detection*   Spectrophotometer at 215 nm.

*Injection*   100 µl; inject the test solution and reference solutions (c), (d) and (e).

*Run time*   5 times the retention time of erythromycin A.

*Relative retention*   With reference to erythromycin A (retention time = about 15 min): impurity A = about 0.3; impurity B = about 0.45; erythromycin C = about 0.5; impurity C = about 0.9; impurity D = about 1.4; impurity F = about 1.5; erythromycin B = about 1.8; impurity E = about 4.3.

*System suitability*   Reference solution (c):
— *resolution*: minimum 0.8 between the peaks due to impurity B and to erythromycin C and minimum 5.5 between the peaks due to impurity B and to erythromycin A. If necessary, adjust the concentration of 2-methyl-2-propanol in the mobile phase or reduce the flow rate to 1.5 ml/min or 1.0 ml/min.

*Limits*:
— *correction factors*: for the calculation of contents, multiply the peak areas of the following impurities (use the chromatogram obtained with reference solution (e) to identify them) by the corresponding correction factor: impurity E = 0.09; impurity F = 0.15,
— *any impurity*: not more than the area of the principal peak in the chromatogram obtained with reference solution (d) (3 per cent),
— *total*: not more than twice the area of the principal peak in the chromatogram obtained with reference solution (d) (6 per cent),
— *disregard limit*: 0.02 times the area of the principal peak in the chromatogram obtained with reference solution (d) (0.06 per cent); disregard the peaks due to erythromycin B and to erythromycin C.

**Water** (*2.5.12*)

Maximum 4.0 per cent, determined on 0.300 g.

Use a 100 g/l solution of *imidazole R* in *anhydrous methanol R* as the solvent.

**Sulphated ash** (*2.4.14*)

Maximum 0.5 per cent, determined on 1.0 g.

**ASSAY**

Liquid chromatography (*2.2.29*) as described in the test for related substances with the following modifications.

*Injection*   Test solution and reference solutions (a) and (b).

*System suitability*   Reference solution (a):
— *repeatability*: maximum relative standard deviation of 1.2 per cent for 6 replicate injections.

Calculate the percentage content of erythromycin A using the chromatogram obtained with reference solution (a). Calculate the percentage contents of erythromycin B and erythromycin C using the chromatogram obtained with reference solution (b).

**IMPURITIES**

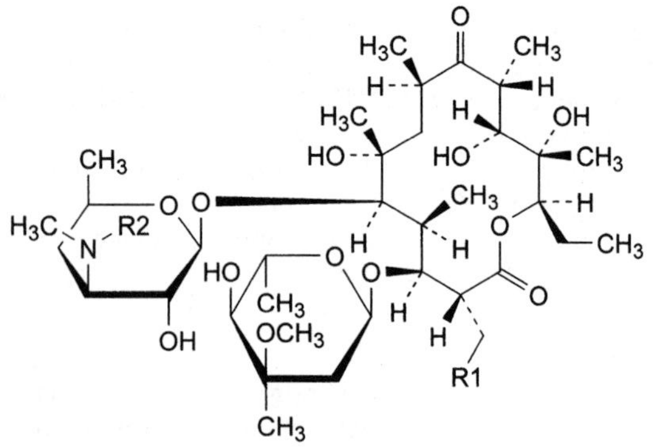

A. R1 = OH, R2 = CH₃: erythromycin F,

B. R1 = R2 = H: *N*-demethylerythromycin A,

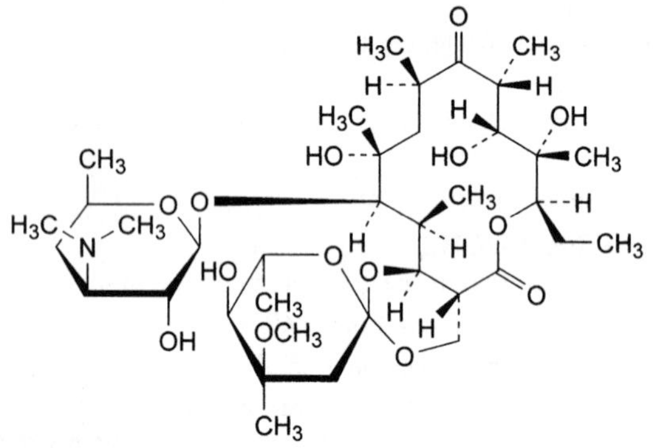

C. erythromycin E,

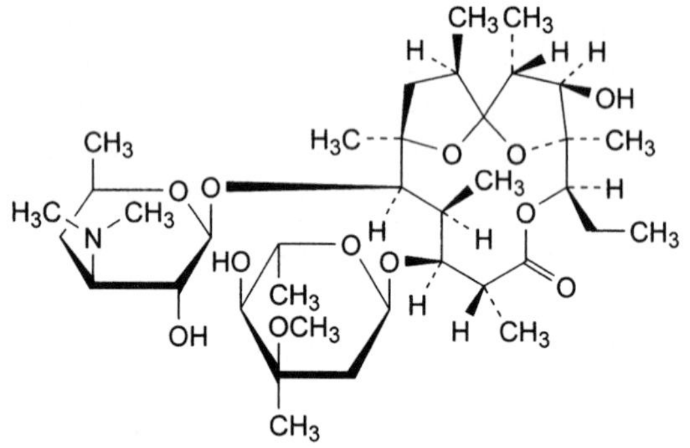

D. anhydroerythromycin A,

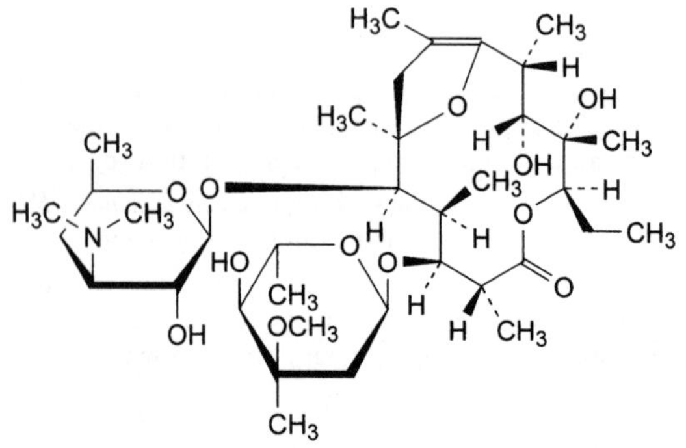

E. erythromycin A enol ether,

F. pseudoerythromycin A enol ether.

_____ Ph Eur

# Erythropoietin Concentrated Solution

(*Ph Eur monograph 1316*)

```
APPRLICDSR    VLERYLLEAK    EAENITTGCA

EHCSLNENIT    VPDTKVNFYA    WKRMEVGQQA

VEVWQGLALL    SEAVLRGGQAL   LVNSSQPWEP

LQLHVDKAVS    GLRSLTTLLR    ALGAQKEAIS

PPDAASAAPL    RTITADTFRK    LFRVYSNFLR

GKLKLYTGEA    CRTGD
```

Molecular weight 30,600 (approx)

The label states (1) the type of erythropoeitin using the appropriate International Nonproprietary Name (Epoetin Alfa, Epoetin Beta, etc) and (2) the approved code in lower case letters indicative of the method of production.

### Action and use
Erythropoietin analogue.

### Preparation
Erythropoietin Injection

 *Ph Eur* _____

## DEFINITION
Erythropoietin concentrated solution is a solution containing a family of closely-related glycoproteins which are indistinguishable from the naturally occurring human erythropoietin (urinary erythropoietin) in terms of amino acid sequence (165 amino acids) and average glycosylation pattern, at a concentration of 0.5-10 mg/ml. It may also contain buffer salts and other excipients. It has a potency of not less than 100 000 IU/mg of active substance determined using the conditions described under Assay and in the test for protein.

## PRODUCTION
Erythropoietin is produced in rodent cells *in vitro* by a method based on recombinant DNA technology.

Prior to batch release, the following tests are carried out on each batch of the final product, unless exemption has been granted by the competent authority.

**Host cell-derived proteins**
The limit is approved by the competent authority.

**Host cell- and vector-derived DNA**
The limit is approved by the competent authority.

## CHARACTERS
### Appearance
Clear or slightly turbid, colourless solution.

## IDENTIFICATION
A. It gives the appropriate response when examined using the conditions described under Assay.

B. Capillary zone electrophoresis (*2.2.47*).

*Test solution* Dilute the preparation to be examined with *water R* to obtain a concentration of 1 mg/ml. Desalt 0.25 ml of the solution by passage through a micro-concentrator cartridge provided with a membrane with a molecular mass cut-off of not more than 10 000 Da. Add 0.2 ml of *water R* to the sample and desalt again. Repeat the desalting procedure once more. Dilute the sample with *water R*, determine its protein concentration as described under Tests and adjust to a concentration of approximately 1 mg/ml with *water R*.

*Reference solution* Dissolve the contents of a vial of *erythropoietin BRP* in 0.25 ml of *water R*. Proceed with desalting as described for the test solution.

*Capillary:*
— *material*: uncoated fused silica,
— *size*: effective length = about 100 cm, Ø = 50 μm,

*Temperature* 35 °C.

*CZE buffer concentrate* (*0.1 M sodium chloride, 0.1 M tricine, 0.1 M sodium acetate*). Dissolve 0.584 g of *sodium chloride R*, 1.792 g of *tricine R* and 0.820 g of *anhydrous sodium acetate R* in *water R* and dilute to 100.0 ml with the same solvent.

*1 M putrescine solution.* Dissolve 0.882 g of *putrescine R* in 10 ml of *water R*. Distribute in 0.5 ml aliquots.

*CZE buffer* (*0.01 M tricine, 0.01 M sodium chloride, 0.01 M sodium acetate, 7 M urea, 2.5 mM putrescine*). Dissolve 21.0 g of *urea R* in 25 ml of *water R* by warming in a water-bath at 30 °C. Add 5.0 ml of CZE buffer concentrate and 125 μl of 1 M putrescine solution. Dilute to 50.0 ml with *water R*. Using *dilute acetic acid R*, adjust to pH 5.55 at 30 °C and filter through a 0.45 μm membrane filter.

*Detection* Spectrophotometer at 214 nm.

*Set the autosampler to store the samples at 4 °C during analysis.*

*Preconditioning of the capillary* Rinse the capillary for 60 min with *0.1 M sodium hydroxide* filtered through a 0.45 μm membrane filter and for 60 min with CZE buffer. Apply voltage for 12 h (20 kV).

*Between-run rinsing* Rinse the capillary for 10 min with *water R*, for 5 min with *0.1 M sodium hydroxide* filtered through a 0.45 μm membrane filter and for 10 min with CZE buffer.

*Injection* Under pressure or vacuum.

*Migration* Apply a field strength of 143 V/cm (15.4 kV for capillaries of 107 cm total length) for 80 min, using CZE buffer as the electrolyte in both buffer reservoirs.

*System suitability* In the electropherogram obtained with the reference solution, a pattern of well separated peaks corresponding to the peaks in the electropherogram of erythropoietin supplied with *erythropoietin BRP* is seen, and the largest peak is at least 50 times greater than the baseline noise. If necessary, adjust the sample load to give peaks of sufficient height. Identify the peaks due to isoforms 1 to 8.

Isoform 1 may not be visible. The peak due to isoform 8 is detected and the resolution between the peaks due to isoforms 5 and 6 is not less than 1. Repeat the separation at least 3 times. The baseline is stable, showing little drift, and the distribution of peaks is qualitatively and quantitatively similar to the distribution of peaks in the electropherogram of erythropoietin supplied with *erythropoietin BRP*. The relative standard deviation of the migration time of the peak due to isoform 2 is less than 2 per cent.

*Limits*   Identify the peaks due to isoforms 1 to 8 in the electropherogram obtained with the test solution by comparison with the electropherogram obtained with the reference solution. Calculate the percentage content of each isoform from the corresponding peak area. The percentages are within the following ranges:

| Isoform | Content (per cent) |
|---------|--------------------|
| 1 | 0 - 15 |
| 2 | 0 - 15 |
| 3 | 1 - 20 |
| 4 | 10 - 35 |
| 5 | 15 - 40 |
| 6 | 10 - 35 |
| 7 | 5 - 25 |
| 8 | 0 - 15 |

C. Polyacrylamide gel electrophoresis and immunoblotting.

(a) Polyacrylamide gel electrophoresis (*2.2.31*)

*Gel dimensions*   0.75 mm thick, about 16 cm square.

*Resolving gel*   12 per cent acrylamide.

*Sample buffer*   *SDS-PAGE sample buffer (concentrated) R.*

*Test solution (a)*   Dilute the preparation to be examined in *water R* to obtain a concentration of 1.0 mg/ml. To 1 volume of this solution add 1 volume of sample buffer.

*Test solution (b)*   Dilute the preparation to be examined in *water R* to obtain a concentration of 0.1 mg/ml. To 1 volume of this solution add 1 volume of sample buffer.

*Reference solution (a)*   Dissolve the contents of a vial of *erythropoietin BRP* in 0.25 ml of *water R*. To 1 volume of this solution add 1 volume of sample buffer.

*Reference solution (b)*   Dissolve the contents of a vial of *erythropoietin BRP* in *water R* and dilute with the same solvent to obtain a concentration of 0.1 mg/ml. To 1 volume of this solution add 1 volume of sample buffer.

*Reference solution (c)*   A solution of molecular mass markers suitable for calibrating SDS-polyacrylamide gels in the range of 10-70 kDa.

*Reference solution (d)*   A solution of pre-stained molecular mass markers suitable for calibrating SDS-polyacrylamide gels in the range of 10-70 kDa and suitable for the electrotransfer to an appropriate membrane.

*Sample treatment*   Boil for 2 min.

*Application*   20 µl, in the following order: reference solution (c), reference solution (a), test solution (a), empty well, reference solution (b), test solution (b), reference solution (d).

At the end of the separation, remove the gel-cassette from the apparatus and cut the gel into 2 parts: the first part containing reference solution (c), reference solution (a) and test solution (a); the second part containing reference solution (b), test solution (b) and reference solution (d).

*Detection*   By Coomassie staining on the first part of the gel.

*System suitability*   Reference solution (c):
— the validation criteria are met.

*Results*   The electropherogram obtained with test solution (a) shows a single diffuse band corresponding in position and intensity to the single band seen in the electropherogram obtained with reference solution (a).

(b) Immunoblotting

Transfer the second part of the gel onto a membrane suitable for the immobilisation of proteins, using commercially available electrotransfer equipment and following the manufacturer's instructions. After electrotransfer, incubate the membrane in a neutral isotonic buffer containing a suitable blocking agent (for example, 50 g/l of dried milk or 10 per cent *V/V* foetal calf serum), for 1-2 h, followed by incubation for 1-14 h in the same blocking solution with a suitable dilution of either a polyclonal or monoclonal anti-erythropoietin antibody. Detect erythropoietin-bound antibody using a suitable enzyme- or radiolabelled antibody (for example, an alkaline phosphatase-conjugated second antibody). The precise details of blocking agents, concentrations and incubation times should be optimised using the principles set out in *Immunochemical methods (2.7.1)*.

*System suitability*   In the electropherogram obtained with reference solution (d), the molecular mass markers are resolved on the membrane into discrete bands, with a linear relationship between distance migrated and logarithm$_{10}$ of the molecular mass.

*Results*   The electropherogram obtained with test solution (b) shows a single broad band corresponding in position and intensity to the single band seen in the electropherogram obtained with reference solution (b).

D. Peptide mapping (*2.2.55*)

Liquid chromatography (*2.2.29*).

*Test solution*   Dilute the preparation to be examined in *tris-acetate buffer solution pH 8.5 R* to a concentration of 1.0 mg/ml. Equilibrate the solution in *tris-acetate buffer solution pH 8.5 R* using a suitable procedure (dialysis against *tris-acetate buffer solution pH 8.5 R*, or membrane filtration using the procedure described under Identification B, but reconstituting the desalted sample with *tris-acetate buffer solution pH 8.5 R*, are suitable). Transfer the dialysed solution to a polypropylene centrifuge tube. Freshly prepare a solution of *trypsin for peptide mapping R* at a concentration of 1 mg/ml in *water R*, and add 5 µl to 0.25 ml of the dialysed solution. Cap the tube and place in a water-bath at 37 °C for 18 h. Remove the sample from the water-bath and stop the reaction immediately by freezing.

*Reference solution*   Dissolve the contents of a vial of *erythropoietin BRP* in 0.25 ml of *water R*. Prepare as for the test solution, ensuring that all procedures are carried out simultaneously, and under identical conditions.

*Column:*
— *size: l* = 0.25 m, Ø = 4.6 mm,
— *stationary phase: butylsilyl silica gel for chromatography R* (5-10 µm).

*Mobile phase:*
— *mobile phase A*: 0.06 per cent *V/V* solution of *trifluoroacetic acid R*,

— *mobile phase B*: to 100 ml of *water R* add 0.6 ml of *trifluoroacetic acid R* and dilute to 1000 ml with *acetonitrile for chromatography R*,

| Time (min) | Flow rate (ml/min) | Mobile phase A (per cent *V/V*) | Mobile phase B (per cent *V/V*) |
|---|---|---|---|
| 0 - 10 | 0.75 | 100 | 0 |
| 10 - 125 | 0.75 | 100 → 39 | 0 → 61 |
| 125 - 135 | 1.25 | 39 → 17 | 61 → 83 |
| 135 - 145 | 1.25 | 17 → 0 | 83 → 100 |
| 145 - 150 | 1.25 | 100 | 0 |

*Detection*  Spectrophotometer at 214 nm.

*Equilibration*  At initial conditions for at least 15 min. Carry out a blank run using the above-mentioned gradient.

*Injection*  50 µl.

*System suitability*  The chromatograms obtained with the test solution and the reference solution are qualitatively similar to the chromatogram of erythropoietin digest supplied with *erythropoietin BRP*.

*Results*  The profile of the chromatogram obtained with the test solution corresponds to that of the chromatogram obtained with the reference solution.

E. *N*-terminal sequence analysis.

The first 15 amino acids are: Ala - Pro - Pro - Arg - Leu - Ile - (no recovered peak) - Asp - Ser - Arg - Val - Leu - Glu - Arg - Tyr.

Perform the Edman degradation using an automated solid-phase sequencer, operated in accordance with the manufacturer's instructions.

Desalt the equivalent of 50 µg of erythropoietin. For example, dilute a volume of the preparation to be examined equivalent to 50 µg of the active substance in 1 ml of a 0.1 per cent *V/V* solution of *trifluoroacetic acid R*. Pre-wash a C18 reverse-phase sample preparation cartridge according to the instructions supplied and equilibrate the cartridge in a 0.1 per cent *V/V* solution of *trifluoroacetic acid R*. Apply the sample to the cartridge, and wash successively with a 0.1 per cent *V/V* solution of *trifluoroacetic acid R* containing 0 per cent, 10 per cent and 50 per cent *V/V* of *acetonitrile R* according to the manufacturer's instructions. Lyophilise the 50 per cent *V/V* acetonitrile R eluate.

Redissolve the desalted sample in 50 µl of a 0.1 per cent *V/V* solution of *trifluoroacetic acid R* and couple to a sequencing cartridge using the protocol provided by the manufacturer. Run 15 sequencing cycles, using the reaction conditions for proline when running the 2$^{nd}$ and 3$^{rd}$ cycles.

Identify the phenylthiohydantoin (PTH)-amino acids released at each sequencing cycle by reverse-phase liquid chromatography. The procedure may be carried out using the column and reagents recommended by the manufacturer of the sequencing equipment for the separation of PTH-amino-acids.

The separation procedure is calibrated using:
— the mixture of PTH-amino acids provided by the manufacturer of the sequencer, with the gradient conditions adjusted as indicated to achieve optimum resolution of all amino acids,
— a sample obtained from a blank sequencing cycle obtained as recommended by the equipment manufacturer.

## TESTS

**Protein** (*2.5.33, Method I*)

80 per cent to 120 per cent of the stated concentration.

*Test solution*  Dilute the preparation to be examined in a 4 g/l solution of *ammonium hydrogen carbonate R*.

Record the absorbance spectrum between 250 nm and 400 nm. Measure the value at the absorbance maximum (276-280 nm), after correction for any light scattering, measured up to 400 nm. Calculate the concentration of erythropoietin taking the specific absorbance to be 7.43.

**Dimers and related substances of higher molecular mass**

Size-exclusion chromatography (*2.2.30*).

*Test solution*  Dilute the preparation to be examined in the mobile phase to obtain a concentration of 0.2 mg/ml.

*Reference solution*  To 0.02 ml of the test solution add 0.98 ml of the mobile phase.

*Column*:
— *size*: *l* = 0.6 m, Ø = 7.5 mm,
— *stationary phase*: *hydrophilic silica gel for chromatography R*, of a grade suitable for fractionation of globular proteins in the relative molecular mass range of 20 000 to 200 000.

*Mobile phase*  Dissolve 1.15 g of *anhydrous disodium hydrogen phosphate R*, 0.2 g of *potassium dihydrogen phosphate R* and 23.4 g of *sodium chloride R* in 1 litre of *water R* (1.5 mM potassium dihydrogen phosphate, 8.1 mM disodium hydrogen phosphate, 0.4 M sodium chloride, pH 7.4); adjust to pH 7.4 if necessary.

*Flow rate*  0.5 ml/min.

*Detection*  Spectrophotometer at 214 nm.

*Injection*  100 µl.

*Run time*  Minimum 1 h.

*System suitability*  The area of the principal peak in the chromatogram obtained with the reference solution is 1.5 per cent to 2.5 per cent of the area of the principal peak in the chromatogram obtained with the test solution.

*Limits*:
— *total of any peaks eluted before the principal peak*: not more than the area of the principal peak in the chromatogram obtained with the reference solution (2 per cent).

**Sialic acids**

Minimum 10 mol of sialic acids (calculated as *N*-acetylneuraminic acid) per mole of erythropoietin.

*Test solution (a)*  Dilute the preparation to be examined in the mobile phase used in the test for dimers and related substances of higher molecular mass to obtain a concentration of 0.3 mg/ml.

*Test solution (b)*  To 0.5 ml of test solution (a) add 0.5 ml of the mobile phase used in the test for dimers and related substances of higher molecular mass.

*Reference solution (a)*  Dissolve a suitable amount of *N*-acetylneuraminic acid R in *water R* to obtain a concentration of 0.1 mg/ml.

*Reference solution (b)*  To 0.8 ml of reference solution (a) add 0.2 ml of *water R*.

*Reference solution (c)*  To 0.6 ml of reference solution (a) add 0.4 ml of *water R*.

*Reference solution (d)*  To 0.4 ml of reference solution (a) add 0.6 ml of *water R*.

*Reference solution (e)*  To 0.2 ml of reference solution (a) add 0.8 ml of *water R*.

*Reference solution (f)*  Use *water R*.

Carry out the test in triplicate. Transfer 100 µl of each of the test and reference solutions to 10 ml glass test tubes.

To each tube add 1.0 ml of *resorcinol reagent R*. Stopper the tubes and incubate at 100 °C for 30 min. Cool on ice.

To each tube, add 2.0 ml of a mixture of 12 volumes of *butanol R* and 48 volumes of *butyl acetate R*. Mix vigorously, and allow the 2 phases to separate. Ensuring that the upper phase is completely clear, remove the upper phase, taking care to exclude completely any of the lower phase. Measure the absorbance (*2.2.25*) of all samples at 580 nm. Using the calibration curve generated by the reference solutions, determine the content of sialic acids in test solutions (a) and (b) and calculate the mean. Calculate the number of moles of sialic acids per mole of erythropoietin assuming that the relative molecular mass of erythropoietin is 30 600 and that the relative molecular mass of *N*-acetylneuraminic acid is 309.

*System suitability:*
— the individual replicates agree to within ± 10 per cent of each other,
— the value obtained from reference solution (a) is between 1.5 and 3.3 times that obtained with test solution (a).

**Bacterial endotoxins** (*2.6.14*)
Less than 20 IU in the volume that contains 100 000 IU of erythropoietin.

## ASSAY

The activity of the preparation is compared with that of *erythropoietin BRP* and expressed in International Units (IU).

The estimated potency is not less than 80 per cent and not more than 125 per cent of the stated potency. The confidence limits of the estimated potency ($P = 0.95$) are not less than 64 per cent and not more than 156 per cent of the stated potency.

Carry out the determination of potency by Method A or B.

### A. In polycythaemic mice

The activity of the preparation is estimated by examining, under given conditions, its effect in stimulating the incorporation of $^{59}$Fe into circulating red blood cells of mice made polycythaemic by exposure to reduced atmospheric pressure.

The following schedule, using treatment in a hypobaric chamber, has been found to be suitable.

Induce polycythaemia in female mice of the same strain, weighing 16-18 g. Place the mice in a hypoxic chamber and reduce the pressure to 0.6 atmospheres. After 3 days at 0.6 atmospheres, further reduce the pressure to 0.4-0.5 atmospheres and maintain the animals at this pressure for a further 11 days (the partial vacuum is interrupted daily for a maximum of 1 h at about 11:00 a.m., in order to clean the cages and feed the animals). At the end of the specified period, return the mice to normal atmospheric conditions. Randomly distribute the mice into cages, each containing 6 animals, and mark them.

*Test solution (a)* Dilute the substance to be examined in *phosphate-albumin buffered saline pH 7.2 R1* to obtain a concentration of 0.2 IU/ml.

*Test solution (b)* Mix equal volumes of test solution (a) and *phosphate-albumin buffered saline pH 7.2 R1*.

*Test solution (c)* Mix equal volumes of test solution (b) and *phosphate-albumin buffered saline pH 7.2 R1*.

*Reference solution (a)* Dissolve *erythropoietin BRP* in *phosphate-albumin buffered saline pH 7.2 R1* to obtain a concentration of 0.2 IU/ml.

*Reference solution (b)* Mix equal volumes of reference solution (a) and *phosphate-albumin buffered saline pH 7.2 R1*.

*Reference solution (c)* Mix equal volumes of reference solution (b) and *phosphate-albumin buffered saline pH 7.2 R1*.

*Radiolabelled ferric [$^{59}$Fe] chloride solution, concentrated* Use a commercially available solution of [$^{59}$Fe]ferric chloride (approximate specific activity: 100-1000 MBq/mg of Fe).

*Radiolabelled [$^{59}$Fe]ferric chloride solution* Dilute the concentrated radiolabelled [$^{59}$Fe]ferric chloride solution in *sodium citrate buffer solution pH 7.8 R* to obtain a solution with an activity of $3.7 \times 10^4$ Bq/ml.

The concentrations of the test solutions and reference solutions may need to be modified, based on the response range of the animals used.

3 days after returning the animals to atmospheric pressure, inject each animal subcutaneously with 0.2 ml of one of the solutions. The 6 animals in each cage must each receive one of the 6 different treatments (3 test solutions and 3 reference solutions), and the order of injection must be separately randomised for each cage. A minimum of 8 cages is recommended. 2 days after injection of the test or reference solution, inject each animal intraperitoneally with 0.2 ml of radiolabelled [$^{59}$Fe]ferric chloride solution. The order of the injections must be the same as that of the erythropoietin injections, and the time interval between administration of the erythropoietin and the radiolabelled ferric chloride solution must be the same for each animal. After a further 48 h, anaesthetise each animal by injection of a suitable anaesthetic, record body weights and withdraw blood samples (0.65 ml) into haematocrit capillaries from the bifurcation of the aorta. After determining the packed cell volume for each sample, measure the radioactivity.

Calculate the response (percentage of iron-59 in total circulating blood) for each mouse using the expression:

$$\frac{A_s \times M \times 7.5}{A_t \times V_s}$$

$A_s$ = radioactivity in the sample,
$A_t$ = total radioactivity injected,
7.5 = total blood volume as per cent body weight,
$M$ = body weight, in grams,
$V_s$ = sample volume.

Calculate the potency by the usual statistical methods for a parallel line assay. Eliminate from the calculation any animal where the packed cell volume is less than 54 per cent, or where the body weight is more than 24 g.

### B. In normocythaemic mice

The assay is based on the measurement of stimulation of reticulocyte production in normocythaemic mice.

The assay may be carried out using the following procedure:

*Test solution (a)* Dilute the preparation to be examined in *phosphate-albumin buffered saline pH 7.2 R1* to obtain a concentration of 80 IU/ml.

*Test solution (b)* Mix equal volumes of test solution (a) and *phosphate-albumin buffered saline pH 7.2 R1*.

*Test solution (c)* Mix equal volumes of test solution (b) and *phosphate-albumin buffered saline pH 7.2 R1*.

*Reference solution (a)* Dissolve *erythropoietin BRP* in *phosphate-albumin buffered saline pH 7.2 R1* to obtain a concentration of 80 IU/ml.

*Reference solution (b)* Mix equal volumes of reference solution (a) and *phosphate-albumin buffered saline pH 7.2 R1*.

*Reference solution (c)* Mix equal volumes of reference solution (b) and *phosphate-albumin buffered saline pH 7.2 R1.*

The exact concentrations of the test solutions and reference solutions may need to be modified, based on the response range of the animals used.

At the beginning of the assay procedure, randomly distribute mice of a suitable age and strain (8-week old B6D2F1 mice are suitable) into 6 cages. A minimum of 8 mice per cage is recommended. Inject each animal subcutaneously with 0.5 ml of the appropriate treatment (one solution per cage) and put the animal in a new cage. Combine the mice in such a way that each cage housing the treated mice contains one mouse out of the 6 different treatments (3 test solutions and 3 reference solutions, 6 mice per cage). 4 days after the injections, collect blood samples from the animals and determine the number of reticulocytes using a suitable procedure.

The following method may be employed:

*The volume of blood, dilution procedure and fluorescent reagent may need to be modified to ensure maximum development and stability of fluorescence.*

*Colorant solution, concentrated* Use a solution of thiazole orange suitable for the determination of reticulocytes. Prepare at a concentration twice that necessary for the analysis.

Proceed with the following dilution steps. Dilute whole blood 500-fold in the buffer used to prepare the colorant solution. Dilute this solution 2-fold in the concentrated colorant solution. After staining for 3-10 min, determine the reticulocyte count microfluorometrically in a flow cytometer. The percentage of reticulocytes is determined using a biparametric histogram: number of cells/red fluorescence (620 nm).

Calculate the potency by the usual statistical methods for a parallel line assay.

## STORAGE

In an airtight container at a temperature below − 20 °C. Avoid repeated freezing and thawing.

## LABELLING

The label states:
— the erythropoietin content in milligrams per millilitre,
— the activity in International Units per millilitre,
— the name and the concentration of any other excipients.

_____ *Ph Eur*

# Esketamine Hydrochloride

*(Ph Eur monograph 1742)*

$C_{13}H_{16}ClNO,HCl$     274.2     *33795-24-3*

**Action and use**
General anaesthetic.

*Ph Eur* _____

## DEFINITION
(2S)-2-(2-Chlorophenyl)-2-(methylamino)cyclohexanone hydrochloride.

**Content**
99.0 per cent to 101.0 per cent.

## CHARACTERS
**Appearance**
White or almost white, crystalline powder.

**Solubility**
Freely soluble in water and in methanol, soluble in alcohol.

## IDENTIFICATION
A. Specific optical rotation (2.2.7): + 85.0 to + 95.0.

Dilute 12.5 ml of solution S (see Tests) to 40.0 ml with *water R*.

B. Infrared absorption spectrophotometry (2.2.24).

*Comparison* Ph. Eur. *reference spectrum of esketamine hydrochloride.*

C. It gives reaction (a) of chlorides (2.3.1).

## TESTS
**Solution S**
Dissolve 8.0 g in *carbon dioxide-free water R* and dilute to 50.0 ml with the same solvent.

**Appearance of solution**
Solution S is clear (2.2.1) and colourless (2.2.2, *Method II*).

**pH** (2.2.3)
3.5 to 4.5.

Dilute 12.5 ml of solution S to 20 ml with *carbon dioxide-free water R*.

**Impurity D**
Liquid chromatography (2.2.29).

*Test solution* Dissolve 25.0 mg of the substance to be examined in *water R* and dilute to 100.0 ml with the same solvent.

*Reference solution (a)* Dissolve 5 mg of *esketamine impurity D CRS* in *water R*, add 20 ml of the test solution and dilute to 50 ml with *water R*. Dilute 10 ml of this solution to 100 ml with *water R*.

*Reference solution (b)* Dilute 5.0 ml of the test solution to 25.0 ml with *water R*. Dilute 5.0 ml of this solution to 50.0 ml with *water R*.

*Reference solution (c)* Dilute 2.5 ml of reference solution (b) to 10.0 ml with *water R*. Dilute 1.0 ml of this solution to 10.0 ml with *water R*.

*Precolumn:*
— size: l = 0.01 m, Ø = 3.0 mm,

— *stationary phase*: *silica gel AGP for chiral chromatography R* (5 μm),
— *temperature*: 30 °C.

*Column*:
— *size*: *l* = 0.125 m, Ø = 4.6 mm,
— *stationary phase*: *silica gel AGP for chiral chromatography R* (5 μm),
— *temperature*: 30 °C.

*Mobile phase*   Mix 16 volumes of *methanol R* and 84 volumes of a 6.8 g/l solution of *potassium dihydrogen phosphate R* previously adjusted to pH 7.0 with *potassium hydroxide R*.

*Flow rate*   0.8 ml/min.

*Detection*   Spectrophotometer at 215 nm.

*Injection*   20 μl.

*Run time*   20 min.

*Relative retention*   With reference to esketamine (retention time = about 10 min): impurity D = about 1.3.

*System suitability*:
— *resolution*: minimum 2.0 between the peaks due to esketamine and impurity D in the chromatogram obtained with reference solution (a),
— *signal-to-noise ratio*: minimum 3 for the principal peak in the chromatogram obtained with reference solution (c).

*Limit*:
— *impurity D*: not more than the area of the principal peak in the chromatogram obtained with reference solution (b) (2.0 per cent).

**Related substances**
Liquid chromatography (2.2.29).

*Test solution*   Dissolve 50.0 mg of the substance to be examined in the mobile phase and dilute to 50.0 ml with the mobile phase.

*Reference solution (a)*   Dissolve 5 mg of *ketamine impurity A CRS* in the mobile phase (using ultrasound, if necessary) and dilute to 10 ml with the mobile phase. To 1 ml of the solution add 0.5 ml of the test solution and dilute to 100 ml with the mobile phase. Prepare immediately before use.

*Reference solution (b)*   Dilute 1.0 ml of the test solution to 10.0 ml with the mobile phase. Dilute 1.0 ml of this solution to 20.0 ml with the mobile phase.

*Column*:
— *size*: *l* = 0.125 m, Ø = 4.0 mm,
— *stationary phase*: *spherical octadecylsilyl silica gel for chromatography R* (5 μm).

*Mobile phase*   Dissolve 0.95 g of *sodium hexanesulphonate R* in 1000 ml of a mixture of 25 volumes of *acetonitrile R* and 75 volumes of *water R* and add 4 ml of *acetic acid R*.

*Flow rate*   1.0 ml/min.

*Detection*   Spectrophotometer at 215 nm.

*Injection*   20 μl.

*Run time*   10 times the retention time of esketamine.

*Relative retention*   With reference to esketamine: impurity A = about 1.6; impurity B = about 3.3; impurity C = about 4.6.

*System suitability*   Reference solution (a):
— *retention time*: esketamine = 3.0 min to 4.5 min,
— *resolution*: minimum 1.5 between the peaks due to impurity A and esketamine.

*Limits*:
— *impurities A, B, C*: for each impurity, not more than 0.4 times the area of the principal peak in the chromatogram obtained with reference solution (b) (0.2 per cent),
— *any other impurity*: for each impurity, not more than 0.2 times the area of the principal peak in the chromatogram obtained with reference solution (b) (0.1 per cent),
— *total*: not more than the area of the principal peak in the chromatogram obtained with reference solution (b) (0.5 per cent),
— *disregard limit*: 0.2 times the area of the principal peak in the chromatogram obtained with reference solution (b) (0.1 per cent).

**Heavy metals** (2.4.8)
Maximum 20 ppm.

Dilute 12.5 ml of solution S to 20 ml with *water R*. 12 ml of the solution complies with limit test A. Prepare the standard using *lead standard solution (2 ppm Pb) R*.

**Sulphated ash** (2.4.14)
Maximum 0.1 per cent, determined on 1.0 g.

**ASSAY**
Dissolve 0.200 g in 50 ml of *methanol R* and add 1.0 ml of *0.1 M hydrochloric acid*. Carry out a potentiometric titration (2.2.20), using *0.1 M sodium hydroxide*. Read the volume added between the 2 points of inflexion.

1 ml of *0.1 M sodium hydroxide* is equivalent to 27.42 mg of $C_{13}H_{17}Cl_2NO$.

**STORAGE**
Protected from light.

**IMPURITIES**
*Specified impurities   A, B, C, D.*

A. X = N-CH₃:
1-[(2-chlorophenyl)(methylimino)methyl]cyclopentanol,
C. X = O:
(2-chlorophenyl)(1-hydroxycyclopentyl)methanone,

and enantiomer

B. (2*RS*)-2-(2-chlorophenyl)-2-hydroxycyclohexanone,

D. (2*R*)-2-(2-chlorophenyl)-2-(methylamino)cyclohexanone ((*R*)-ketamine).

# Esomeprazole Magnesium Trihydrate

(*Ph Eur monograph 2372*)

C$_{34}$H$_{36}$MgN$_6$O$_6$S$_2$,3H$_2$O    767.2    *217087-09-7*

## Action and use
Proton pump inhibitor; treatment of peptic ulcer disease.

*Ph Eur* _____

## DEFINITION
Magnesium bis[5-methoxy-2-[(*S*)-[(4-methoxy-3,5-dimethylpyridin-2-yl)methyl]sulphinyl]-1*H*-benzimidazol-1-ide] trihydrate.

## Content
98.0 per cent to 102.0 per cent (anhydrous substance).

## CHARACTERS
### Appearance
White or slightly coloured powder, slightly hygroscopic.

### Solubility
Slightly soluble in water, soluble in methanol, practically insoluble in heptane.

## IDENTIFICATION
Carry out either tests A, B, C or A, B, E or B, C, D or B, D, E.

A. Specific optical rotation (*2.2.7*): − 137 to − 155.

Dissolve 0.250 g in *methanol R* and dilute to 25.0 ml with the same solvent.

B. Infrared absorption spectrophotometry (*2.2.24*).

*Comparison*   esomeprazole magnesium trihydrate CRS.

C. Atomic absorption spectrometry (*2.2.23*) as described in the test for magnesium.

The test solution shows the absorption maximum at 285.2 nm.

D. Enantiomeric purity (see Tests).

E. Ignite about 0.5 g of the substance to be examined according to the procedure for the sulphated ash test (*2.4.14*). Dissolve the residue in 10 ml of *water R*. 2 ml of this solution gives the reaction of magnesium (*2.3.1*).

## TESTS
### Absorbance (*2.2.25*)
Maximum 0.20 at 440 nm.

Dissolve 0.500 g in *methanol R* and dilute to 25.0 ml with the same solvent. Filter the solution through a membrane filter (nominal pore size 0.45 μm).

### Related substances
Liquid chromatography (*2.2.29*). Use the normalisation procedure. *Use freshly prepared solutions.*

*Test solution*   Dissolve 3.5 mg of the substance to be examined in the mobile phase and dilute to 25.0 ml with the mobile phase.

*Reference solution (a)*   Dissolve 1 mg of *omeprazole CRS* and 1 mg of *omeprazole impurity D CRS* in the mobile phase and dilute to 10.0 ml with the mobile phase.

*Reference solution (b)*   Dissolve 3 mg of the *omeprazole for peak identification CRS* (containing impurity E) in the mobile phase and dilute to 20.0 ml with the mobile phase.

*Reference solution (c)*   Dilute 1.0 ml of the test solution to 100.0 ml with the mobile phase. Dilute 1.0 ml of this solution to 10.0 ml with the mobile phase.

*Column:*
— *size: l* = 0.125 m, Ø = 4.6 mm;
— *stationary phase: octylsilyl silica gel for chromatography R* (5 μm).

*Mobile phase*   Mix 27 volumes of *acetonitrile R* and 73 volumes of a 1.4 g/l solution of *disodium hydrogen phosphate R* previously adjusted to pH 7.6 with *phosphoric acid R*.

*Flow rate*   1 ml/min.

*Detection*   Spectrophotometer at 280 nm.

*Injection*   40 μl.

*Run time*   5 times the retention time of esomeprazole.

*Relative retention*   With reference to esomeprazole (retention time = about 9 min): impurity E = about 0.6; impurity D = about 0.8.

*System suitability*   Reference solution (a):
— *resolution*: minimum 3.0 between the peaks due to impurity D and omeprazole. If necessary, adjust the pH of the aqueous part of the mobile phase or its proportion of acetonitrile; an increase in the pH will improve the resolution.

*Limits:*
— *impurity D*: maximum 0.2 per cent;
— *impurity E*: maximum 0.1 per cent;
— *unspecified impurities*: for each impurity, maximum 0.10 per cent;
— *total*: maximum 0.5 per cent;
— *disregard limit*: 0.5 times the area of the principal peak in the chromatogram obtained with reference solution (c) (0.05 per cent).

### Enantiomeric purity
Liquid chromatography (*2.2.29*).

*Buffer solution pH 6.0*   Mix 70 ml of a 156.0 g/l solution of *sodium dihydrogen phosphate R* with 20 ml of a 179.1 g/l solution of *disodium hydrogen phosphate R*. Dilute to 1000 ml with *water R*, then dilute 250 ml of this solution to 1000.0 ml with *water R*.

*Buffer solution pH 11.0*   Mix 11 ml of a 95.0 g/l solution of *trisodium phosphate dodecahydrate R* with 22 ml of a 179.1 g/l solution of *disodium hydrogen phosphate R*, then dilute to 1000.0 ml with *water R*.

*Test solution*   Dissolve 40 mg of the substance to be examined in 5 ml of *methanol R* and dilute to 25 ml with buffer solution pH 11.0. Dilute 1.0 ml of this solution to 50.0 ml with buffer solution pH 11.0.

*Reference solution (a)*   Dissolve 2 mg of *omeprazole CRS* in buffer solution pH 11.0 and dilute to 10.0 ml with the same buffer solution. Dilute 1.0 ml of this solution to 50.0 ml with buffer solution pH 11.0.

*Reference solution (b)*   Dilute 1.0 ml of reference solution (a) to 50.0 ml with buffer solution pH 11.0.

*Column:*
— *size: l* = 0.1 m, Ø = 4.0 mm;

— *stationary phase: silica gel AGP for chiral chromatography R* (5 μm).

*Mobile phase*   *acetonitrile R*, buffer solution pH 6.0 (65:435 *V/V*).

*Flow rate*   0.6 ml/min.

*Detection*   Spectrophotometer at 302 nm.

*Injection*   20 μl.

*Elution order*   Impurity F, esomeprazole.

*Retention time*   Esomeprazole = about 4 min.

*System suitability:*
— *resolution*: minimum 3.0 between the peaks due to impurity F and esomeprazole in the chromatogram obtained with reference solution (a);
— *signal-to-noise ratio*: minimum 10 for the peak due to impurity F in the chromatogram obtained with reference solution (b).

Calculate the percentage content of impurity F using the following expression:

$$100 \left( \frac{r_i}{r_s} \right)$$

$r_i$ = area of the peak due to impurity F in the chromatogram obtained with the test solution;

$r_s$ = sum of the areas of the peaks due to esomeprazole and impurity F in the chromatogram obtained with the test solution.

*Limits:*
— *impurity F*: maximum 0.2 per cent.

**Magnesium**

3.30 per cent to 3.55 per cent (anhydrous substance).

Atomic absorption spectrometry (*2.2.23, Method I*).

*Test solution*   Dissolve 0.250 g in 20 ml of a 103 g/l solution of *hydrochloric acid R*, adding the acid slowly, and dilute to 100.0 ml with *water R*. Dilute 10.0 ml of this solution to 200.0 ml with *water R*. To 10.0 ml of the solution obtained add 4 ml of *lanthanum chloride solution R* and dilute to 100.0 ml with *water R*.

*Reference solutions*   Prepare the reference solutions using *magnesium standard solution (1000 ppm Mg) R*, diluted as necessary with a mixture of 1 ml of a 103 g/l solution of *hydrochloric acid R* in 1000.0 ml of *water R*.

*Wavelength*   285.2 nm.

**Water** (*2.5.12*)

6.0 per cent to 8.0 per cent, determined on 0.200 g.

**ASSAY**

Liquid chromatography (*2.2.29*).

*Buffer solution pH 11.0*   Mix 11 ml of a 95.0 g/l solution of *trisodium phosphate dodecahydrate R* with 22 ml of a 179.1 g/l solution of *disodium hydrogen phosphate R*, and dilute to 100.0 ml with *water R*.

*Test solution*   Dissolve 10.0 mg of the substance to be examined in about 10 ml of *methanol R*, add 10 ml of buffer solution pH 11.0 and dilute to 200.0 ml with *water R*.

*Reference solution*   Dissolve 10.0 mg of *omeprazole CRS* in about 10 ml of *methanol R*, add 10 ml of buffer solution pH 11.0 and dilute to 200.0 ml with *water R*.

*Column:*
— *size: l* = 0.125 m, Ø = 4 mm;
— *stationary phase: octylsilyl silica gel for chromatography R* (5 μm).

*Mobile phase*   Mix 35 volumes of *acetonitrile R* with 65 volumes of a 1.4 g/l solution of *disodium hydrogen phosphate R* previously adjusted to pH 7.6 with *phosphoric acid R*.

*Flow rate*   1 ml/min.

*Detection*   Spectrophotometer at 280 nm.

*Injection*   20 μl.

*Run time*   1.5 times the retention time of esomeprazole.

*Retention time*   Esomeprazole = about 4 min.

Calculate the percentage content of $C_{34}H_{36}MgN_6O_6S_2$ from the declared content of *omeprazole CRS*.

1 g of omeprazole is equivalent to 1.032 g of esomeprazole magnesium.

**STORAGE**

In an airtight container, protected from light.

**IMPURITIES**

*Specified impurities*   D, E, F.

*Other detectable impurities*   (The following substances would, if present at a sufficient level, be detected by one or other of the tests in the monograph. They are limited by the general acceptance criterion for other/unspecified impurities and/or by the general monograph *Substances for pharmaceutical use (2034)*. It is therefore not necessary to identify these impurities for demonstration of compliance. See also *5.10. Control of impurities in substances for pharmaceutical use*): A, B, C.

A. 5-methoxy-1*H*-benzimidazole-2-thiol,

B. R = H, X = SO: 2-[(*RS*)-[(3,5-dimethylpyridin-2-yl)methyl]sulphinyl]-5-methoxy-1*H*-benzimidazole,

C. R = OCH₃, X = S: 5-methoxy-2-[[(4-methoxy-3,5-dimethylpyridin-2-yl)methyl]sulphanyl]-1*H*-benzimidazole (ufiprazole),

D. R = OCH₃, X = SO₂: 5-methoxy-2-[[(4-methoxy-3,5-dimethylpyridin-2-yl)methyl]sulphonyl]-1*H*-benzimidazole (omeprazole sulphone),

and enantiomer

E. 4-methoxy-2-[[(*RS*)-(5-methoxy-1*H*-benzimidazol-2-yl)sulphinyl]methyl]-3,5-dimethylpyridine 1-oxide.

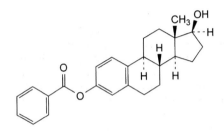

F. 5-methoxy-2-[(R)-[(4-methoxy-3,5-dimethylpyridin-2-yl)methyl]sulphinyl]-1H-benzimidazole((R)-omeprazole).

*Ph Eur*

# Estradiol Benzoate

*(Ph Eur monograph 0139)*

C₂₅H₂₈O₃ — 376.5 — 50-50-0

$C_{25}H_{28}O_3$      376.5      *50-50-0*

**Action and use**
Estrogen.

**Preparation**
Estradiol Injection

*Ph Eur* ___

## DEFINITION
17β-Hydroxyestra-1,3,5(10)-trien-3-yl benzoate.

## Content
97.0 per cent to 103.0 per cent (dried substance).

## CHARACTERS
**Appearance**
Almost white, crystalline powder or colourless crystals.

**Solubility**
Practically insoluble in water, freely soluble in methylene chloride, sparingly soluble in acetone, slightly soluble in methanol.

It shows polymorphism (*5.9*).

## IDENTIFICATION
Infrared absorption spectrophotometry (*2.2.24*).

*Comparison*   estradiol benzoate CRS.

If the spectra obtained in the solid state show differences, dissolve the substance to be examined and the reference substance separately in *acetone R*, evaporate to dryness and record new spectra using the residues.

## TESTS
**Specific optical rotation** (*2.2.7*)
+ 55.0 to + 59.0 (dried substance).

Dissolve 0.250 g in *acetone R* and dilute to 25.0 ml with the same solvent.

**Related substances**
Liquid chromatography (*2.2.29*)

*Test solution*   Dissolve 20 mg of the substance to be examined in *acetonitrile R1* and dilute to 10.0 ml with the same solvent.

*Reference solution (a)*   Dissolve 5 mg of *estradiol benzoate for system suitability CRS* (containing impurities A, B, C, E and G) in *acetonitrile R1* and dilute to 2.5 ml with the same solvent.

*Reference solution (b)*   Dilute 0.5 ml of the test solution to 100.0 ml with *acetonitrile R1*.

*Column*:
— *size*: l = 0.25 m, Ø = 4.6 mm;
— *stationary phase*: end-capped octylsilyl silica gel for chromatography R (5 μm).

*Mobile phase*:
— *mobile phase A*: water R, acetonitrile R1 (40:60 *V/V*);
— *mobile phase B*: acetonitrile R1;

| Time (min) | Mobile phase A (per cent *V/V*) | Mobile phase B (per cent *V/V*) |
|---|---|---|
| 0 - 20 | 100 | 0 |
| 20 - 21 | 100 → 10 | 0 → 90 |
| 21 - 31 | 10 | 90 |

*Flow rate*   1.0 ml/min.

*Detection*   Spectrophotometer at 230 nm.

*Injection*   10 μl.

*Identification of impurities*   Use the chromatogram supplied with *estradiol benzoate for system suitability CRS* and the chromatogram obtained with reference solution (a) to identify the peaks due to impurities A, B, C, E and G.

*Relative retention*   With reference to estradiol benzoate (retention time = about 19 min): impurity A = about 0.3; impurity E = about 1.1; impurity B = about 1.2; impurity G = about 1.3; impurity C = about 1.5.

*System suitability*   Reference solution (a):
— *peak-to-valley ratio*: minimum 2.0, where $H_p$ = height above the baseline of the peak due to impurity E and $H_v$ = height above the baseline of the lowest point of the curve separating this peak from the peak due to estradiol benzoate.

*Limits*:
— *correction factors*: for the calculation of content, multiply the peak areas of the following impurities by the corresponding correction factor: impurity A = 3.3; impurity C = 0.7;
— *impurity C*: not more than the area of the principal peak in the chromatogram obtained with reference solution (b) (0.5 per cent);
— *impurities B, E, G*: for each impurity, not more than 0.6 times the area of the principal peak in the chromatogram obtained with reference solution (b) (0.3 per cent);
— *impurity A*: not more than 0.4 times the area of the principal peak in the chromatogram obtained with reference solution (b) (0.2 per cent);
— *unspecified impurities*: for each impurity, not more than 0.2 times the area of the principal peak in the chromatogram obtained with reference solution (b) (0.10 per cent);
— *total*: not more than twice the area of the principal peak in the chromatogram obtained with reference solution (b) (1.0 per cent);
— *disregard limit*: 0.1 times the area of the principal peak in the chromatogram obtained with reference solution (b) (0.05 per cent).

## Loss on drying (2.2.32)

Maximum 0.5 per cent, determined on 1.000 g by drying in an oven at 105 °C for 3 h.

## ASSAY

Dissolve 25.0 mg in *anhydrous ethanol R* and dilute to 250.0 ml with the same solvent. Dilute 10.0 ml of this solution to 100.0 ml with *anhydrous ethanol R*. Measure the absorbance (2.2.25) at the absorption maximum at 231 nm.

Calculate the content of $C_{25}H_{28}O_3$ taking the specific absorbance to be 500.

## IMPURITIES

*Specified impurities*   *A, B, C, E, G.*

*Other detectable impurities*   (The following substances would, if present at a sufficient level, be detected by one or other of the tests in the monograph. They are limited by the general acceptance criterion for other/unspecified impurities and/or by the general monograph *Substances for pharmaceutical use (2034)*. It is therefore not necessary to identify these impurities for demonstration of compliance. See also *5.10. Control of impurities in substances for pharmaceutical use):*
*D, F, H.*

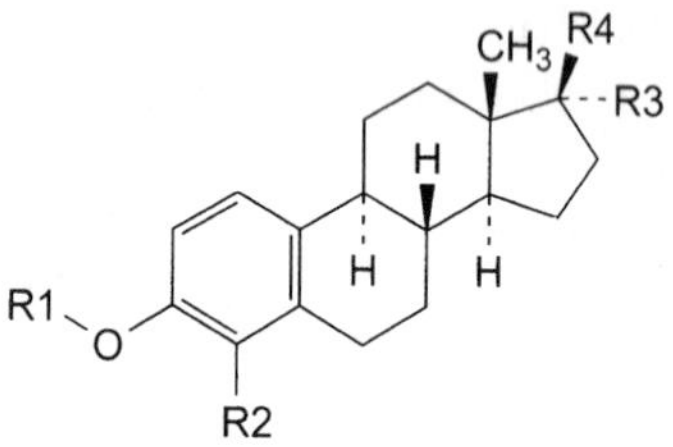

A. R1 = R2 = R3 = H, R4 = OH: estradiol,

B. R1 = CO-C₆H₅, R2 = CH₃, R3 = H, R4 = OH:
17β-hydroxy-4-methylestra-1,3,5(10)-trien-3-yl benzoate,

C. R1 = CO-C₆H₅, R2 = R3 = H, R4 = O-CO-C₆H₅:
estra-1,3,5(10)-triene-3,17β-diyl dibenzoate,

E. R1 = CO-C₆H₅, R2 = R4 = H, R3 = OH:
17α-hydroxyestra-1,3,5(10)-trien-3-yl benzoate,

G. R1 = CO-C₆H₅, R2 = H, R3 + R4 = O: 17-oxoestra-1,3,5(10)-trien-3-yl benzoate (estrone benzoate),

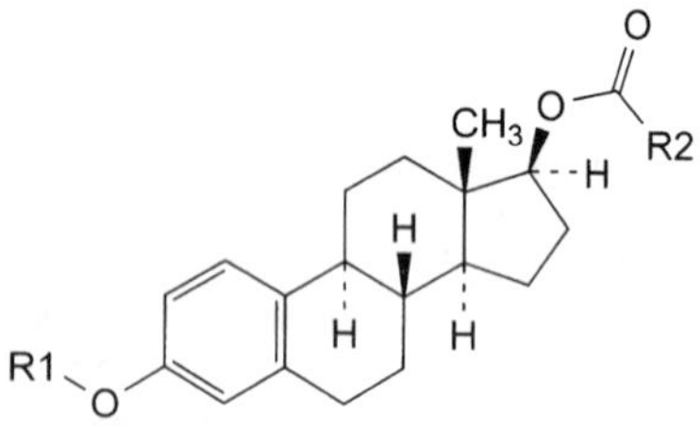

D. R1 = H, R2 = C₆H₅:
3-hydroxyestra-1,3,5(10)-trien-17β-yl benzoate,

H. R1 = CO-C₆H₅, R2 = CH₃:
estra-1,3,5(10)-triene-3,17β-diyl 17-acetate 3-benzoate,

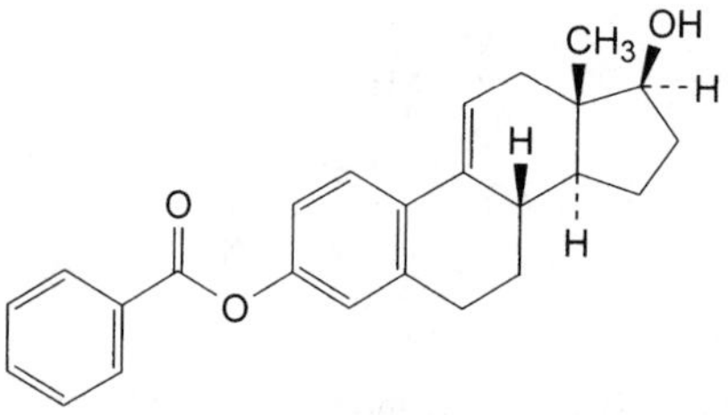

F. 17β-hydroxyestra-1,3,5(10),9(11)-tetraen-3-yl benzoate.

*Ph Eur*

# Estradiol Hemihydrate

*(Ph Eur monograph 0821)*

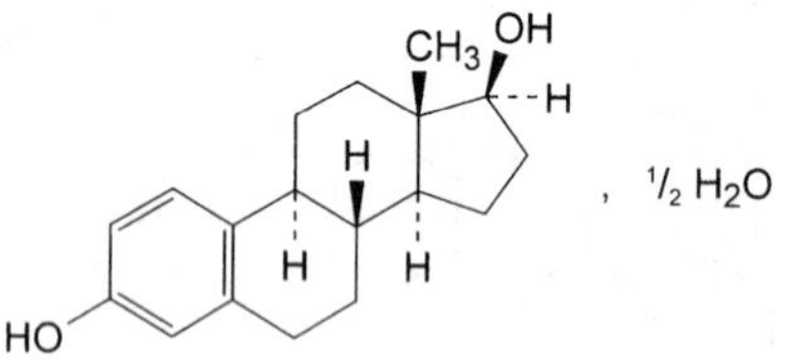

$C_{18}H_{24}O_2,\tfrac{1}{2}H_2O$        281.4        50-28-2
(anhydrous)

## Action and use
Estrogen.

## Preparation
Estradiol Transdermal Patches

Estradiol and Norethisterone Tablets

Estradiol and Norethisterone Acetate Tablets

*Ph Eur*

## DEFINITION
Estra-1,3,5(10)-triene-3,17β-diol hemihydrate.

## Content
97.0 per cent to 103.0 per cent (anhydrous substance).

## CHARACTERS

### Appearance
White or almost white, crystalline powder or colourless crystals.

### Solubility
Practically insoluble in water, soluble in acetone, sparingly soluble in alcohol, slightly soluble in methylene chloride.

## IDENTIFICATION
*First identification*   B.

*Second identification*   A, C, D, E.

A. Melting point (2.2.14): 175 °C to 180 °C.

B. Infrared absorption spectrophotometry (2.2.24).

*Comparison*   estradiol hemihydrate CRS.

C. Thin-layer chromatography (2.2.27).

*Test solution*   Dissolve 50 mg of the substance to be examined in *methanol R* and dilute to 50 ml with the same solvent.

*Reference solution (a)*   Dissolve 50 mg of *estradiol hemihydrate CRS* in *methanol R* and dilute to 50 ml with the same solvent.

*Reference solution (b)*   Dissolve 25 mg of *ethinylestradiol CRS* in reference solution (a) and dilute to 25 ml with reference solution (a).

*Plate*   *TLC silica gel plate R.*

*Mobile phase*   *alcohol R, toluene R* (20:80 *V/V*).

*Application*   5 μl.

*Development*   Over 3/4 of the plate.

*Drying*   In air until the solvent has evaporated.

*Detection*   Heat at 110 °C for 10 min. Spray the hot plate with *alcoholic solution of sulphuric acid R*. Heat again at 110 °C for 10 min. Allow to cool. Examine in daylight and in ultraviolet light at 365 nm.

*System suitability*   The chromatogram obtained with reference solution (b) shows 2 spots which may however not be completely separated.

*Results*   The principal spot in the chromatogram obtained with the test solution is similar in position, colour in daylight, fluorescence in ultraviolet light at 365 nm and size to the principal spot in the chromatogram obtained with reference solution (a).

D. To about 1 mg add 0.5 ml of freshly prepared *sulphomolybdic reagent R2*. A blue colour develops which in ultraviolet light at 365 nm has an intense green fluorescence. Add 1 ml of *sulphuric acid R* and 9 ml of *water R*. The colour becomes pink with a yellowish fluorescence.

E. It complies with the test for water (see Tests).

## TESTS

**Specific optical rotation** (*2.2.7*)
+ 76.0 to + 83.0 (anhydrous substance).

Dissolve 0.250 g in *alcohol R* and dilute to 25.0 ml with the same solvent.

**Related substances**
Liquid chromatography (*2.2.29*).

*Test solution*   Dissolve 25.0 mg of the substance to be examined in 10 ml of *acetonitrile R* and dilute to 25.0 ml with *methanol R2*.

*Reference solution (a)*   Dilute 1.0 ml of the test solution to 100.0 ml with the mobile phase. Dilute 2.0 ml of the solution to 10.0 ml with the mobile phase.

*Reference solution (b)*   Dissolve 2 mg of *17α-estradiol R* in 5.0 ml of *acetonitrile R*. Mix 2.0 ml of this solution with 1.0 ml of the test solution and dilute to 5.0 ml with the mobile phase.

*Reference solution (c)*   Mix equal volumes of a 1 mg/ml solution of the substance to be examined in *methanol R2* and of a 1 mg/ml solution of *2,3-dichloro-5,6-dicyanobenzoquinone R* in *methanol R2*. Allow to stand for 30 min before injection.

*Reference solution (d)*   Dissolve 5 mg of *estradiol for peak identification CRS* (estradiol hemihydrate spiked with impurities A, B and C at about 0.5 per cent) in 2 ml of *acetonitrile R* and dilute to 5 ml with *methanol R2*.

*Column:*
— *size: l* = 0.25 m, Ø = 4.6 mm,
— *stationary phase: end-capped octadecylsilyl silica gel for chromatography R* (5 μm).

*Mobile phase*   To 400 ml of *acetonitrile R* add 50 ml of *methanol R2* and 400 ml of *water R*; allow to stand for 10 min, dilute to 1000 ml with *water R* and mix again.

*Flow rate*   1 ml/min.

*Detection*   Spectrophotometer at 280 nm.

*Equilibration*   About 60 min.

*Injection*   20 μl.

*Run time*   Twice the retention time of the principal peak.

*Relative retention*   With reference to estradiol (retention time = about 13 min): impurity D = about 0.9; impurity B = about 1.1; impurity A = about 1.4; impurity C = about 1.9.

*System suitability*   Reference solution (b):
— *resolution*: minimum 2.5 between the peaks due to estradiol and impurity B.

*Limits:*
— *correction factor*: for the calculation of content, multiply the peak area of impurity D by 0.4 (use the chromatogram obtained with reference solution (c) to identify this peak),
— *impurities A, B, C, D*: for each impurity, not more than 1.5 times the area of the principal peak obtained with reference solution (a) (0.3 per cent),
— *any other impurity*: for each impurity, not more than 0.5 times the area of the principal peak obtained with reference solution (a) (0.1 per cent),
— *total*: not more than 2.5 times the area of the principal peak in the chromatogram obtained with reference solution (a) (0.5 per cent),
— *disregard limit*: 0.25 times the area of the principal peak in the chromatogram obtained with reference solution (a) (0.05 per cent).

**Water** (*2.5.12*)
2.9 per cent to 3.5 per cent, determined on 0.500 g.

## ASSAY

Dissolve 20.0 mg in *alcohol R* and dilute to 100.0 ml with the same solvent. Dilute 5.0 ml of the solution to 50.0 ml with *0.1 M sodium hydroxide*. Allow to cool to room temperature. Measure the absorbance (*2.2.25*) of the solution at the maximum at 238 nm.

Calculate the content of $C_{18}H_{24}O_2$ taking the specific absorbance to be 335.

## IMPURITIES

*Specified impurities*   *A, B, C, D.*

A. R1 = H, R2 + R3 = O:
3-hydroxyestra-1,3,5(10)-trien-17-one (estrone),

B. R1 = R3 = H, R2 = OH:
estra-1,3,5(10)-triene-3,17α-diol (17α-estradiol),

C. R1 = CH₃, R2 = H, R3 = OH:
4-methylestra-1,3,5(10)-triene-3,17β-diol,

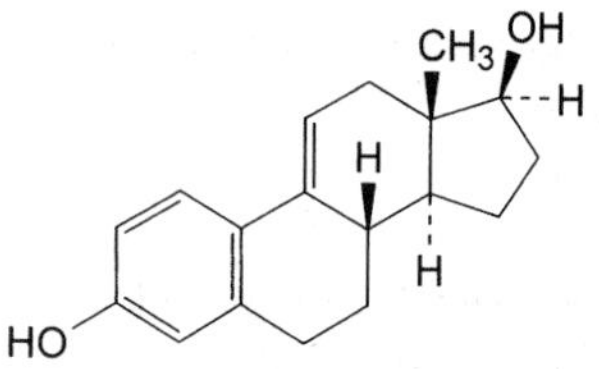

D. estra-1,3,5(10),9(11)-tetraene-3,17β-diol.

*Ph Eur*

# Estradiol Valerate

(*Ph Eur monograph 1614*)

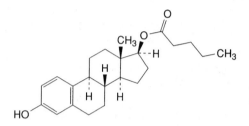

C$_{23}$H$_{32}$O$_3$    356.5    *979-32-8*

## Action and use
Estrogen.

*Ph Eur*

## DEFINITION
3-Hydroxyestra-1,3,5(10)-trien-17β-yl pentanoate.

## Content
97.0 per cent to 103.0 per cent (dried substance).

## CHARACTERS
### Appearance
White or almost white, crystalline powder or colourless crystals.

### Solubility
Practically insoluble in water, soluble in alcohol.

### mp
About 145 °C.

## IDENTIFICATION
Infrared absorption spectrophotometry (*2.2.24*).

*Comparison*   estradiol valerate CRS.

## TESTS
### Solution S
Dissolve 0.500 g in *methanol R* and dilute to 20.0 ml with the same solvent.

### Appearance of solution
Solution S is clear (*2.2.1*) and colourless (*2.2.2, Method II*).

### Specific optical rotation (*2.2.7*)
+ 41 to + 47 (dried substance), determined on solution S.

### Related substances
Liquid chromatography (*2.2.29*).

*Solvent mixture*   Mix 15 volumes of *water R* and 135 volumes of *acetonitrile R*.

*Test solution*   Dissolve 0.100 g of the substance to be examined in the solvent mixture and dilute to 10.0 ml with the solvent mixture.

*Reference solution (a)*   Dissolve 2 mg of *estradiol valerate CRS* and 2 mg of *estradiol butyrate CRS* in the solvent mixture and dilute to 10 ml with the solvent mixture.

*Reference solution (b)*   Dilute 0.5 ml of the test solution to 100.0 ml with the solvent mixture.

*Column*:
— *size*: *l* = 0.25 m, Ø = 4.6 mm,
— *stationary phase*: octadecylsilyl silica gel for chromatography R (5 µm),
— *temperature*: 40 °C.

*Mobile phase*:
— *mobile phase A*: water R,
— *mobile phase B*: acetonitrile R,

| Time (min) | Mobile phase A (per cent *V/V*) | Mobile phase B (per cent *V/V*) |
|---|---|---|
| 0 - 15 | 40 → 0 | 60 → 100 |
| 15 - 25 | 0 | 100 |
| 25 - 30 | 40 | 60 |
| 30 = 0 | 40 | 60 |

*Flow rate*   1.0 ml/min.

*Detection*   Spectrophotometer at 220 nm.

*Injection*   10 µl.

*Relative retention*   With reference to estradiol valerate (retention time = about 12 min): impurity F = about 0.9.

*System suitability*   Reference solution (a):
— *resolution*: minimum of 5.0 between the peaks due to impurity F and to estradiol valerate.

*Limits*:
— *any impurity*: not more than the area of the principal peak in the chromatogram obtained with reference solution (b) (0.5 per cent),
— *total*: not more than twice the area of the principal peak in the chromatogram obtained with reference solution (b) (1.0 per cent),
— *disregard limit*: 0.1 times the area of the principal peak in the chromatogram obtained with reference solution (b) (0.05 per cent).

## Loss on drying (*2.2.32*)
Maximum 1.0 per cent, determined on 0.500 g by drying in an oven at 105 °C for 3 h.

## ASSAY
Dissolve 25.0 mg in *alcohol R* and dilute to 250.0 ml with the same solvent. Measure the absorbance (*2.2.25*) at the maximum at 280 nm.

Calculate the content of C$_{23}$H$_{32}$O$_3$ taking the specific absorbance to be 58.0.

## STORAGE
Protected from light.

## IMPURITIES

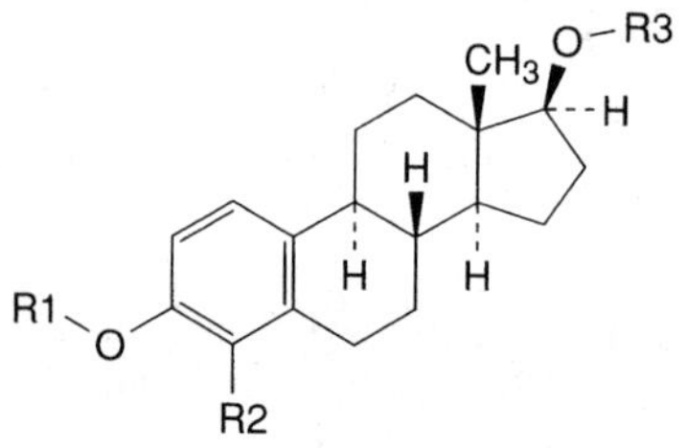

A. R1 = R2 = R3 = H: estradiol,

B. R1 = CO-[CH$_2$]$_3$-CH$_3$, R2 = R3 = H:
17β-hydroxyestra-1,3,5(10)-trien-3-yl pentanoate,

D. R1 = H,R2 = CH$_3$,R3 = CO-[CH$_2$]$_3$-CH$_3$:
3-hydroxy-4-methylestra-1,3,5(10)-trien-17β-yl pentanoate,

E. R1 = R3 = CO-[CH$_2$]$_3$-CH$_3$,R2 = H:
estra-1,3,5(10)-trien-3,17β-diyl dipentanoate,

F. R1 = R2 = H,R3 = CO-[CH$_2$]$_2$-CH$_3$: 3-hydroxyestra-1,3,5(10)-trien-17β-yl butanoate (estradiol butyrate),

C. 3-hydroxyestra-1,3,5(10),9(11)-tetraen-17β-yl pentanoate.

_____ *Ph Eur*

# Estramustine Sodium Phosphate

C$_{23}$H$_{30}$Cl$_2$NNa$_2$O$_6$P      564.4      *52205-73-9*

### Action and use
Cytotoxic alkylating agent.

### Preparation
Estramustine Phosphate Capsules

### DEFINITION
Estramustine Sodium Phosphate is disodium
3-[bis(2-chloroethyl)carbamoyloxy]estra-1,3,5(10)-trien-17β-yl orthophosphate. It contains not less than 97.0% and not more than 103.0% of C$_{23}$H$_{30}$Cl$_2$NNa$_2$O$_6$P, calculated with reference to the anhydrous substance.

### CHARACTERISTICS
A white or almost white powder.

Freely soluble in *water* and in *methanol*; very slightly soluble in *absolute ethanol*.

### IDENTIFICATION
A. The *light absorption*, Appendix II B, in the range 230 to 350 nm of a 0.05% w/v solution exhibits maxima at 267 nm and 275 nm. The *absorbance* at 267 nm is about 0.76 and at 275 nm is about 0.71.

B. The *infrared absorption spectrum*, Appendix II A, is concordant with the *reference spectrum* of estramustine sodium phosphate *(RS 128)*. In preparing the potassium bromide disc precautions should be taken to exclude moisture and avoid excessive grinding; if necessary heat the prepared disc at 90° for 2 minutes.

C. A 1% w/v solution yields the reactions characteristic of *sodium salts*, Appendix VI.

### TESTS
### Alkalinity
pH of a 0.5% w/v solution, 8.5 to 10.0, Appendix V L.

### Clarity and colour of solution
A 5.0% w/v solution is not more opalescent than *reference suspension II*, Appendix IV A, and is *colourless*, Appendix IV B, Method I.

### Specific optical rotation
In a 2% w/v solution, +11 to +13, Appendix V F, calculated with reference to the anhydrous substance.

### Ionisable chlorine
Dissolve 0.10 g in 10 ml of *water*, add carefully, with mixing, 0.1 ml of a mixture of 10 volumes of *silver nitrate solution* and 1 volume of *nitric acid* and examine immediately. Any opalescence produced is not more intense than that obtained by treating a solution containing 13.4 μg of *sodium chloride* in 10 ml in the same manner (0.1%).

### Estradiol 17β-phosphate
Dissolve 50 mg in 5 ml of 0.2M *sodium hydroxide*, add sufficient *ethanol (96%)* to produce 10 ml, mix and immediately measure the *absorbance* at the maxima at 300 nm and 350 nm, Appendix II B. The difference between the two absorbances is not more than 0.34 (1.0%).

### Inorganic phosphate
Dissolve 25 mg in 10 ml of *water*, add 4 ml of 1M *sulphuric acid*, 1 ml of a 10% w/v solution of *ammonium molybdate* and 2 ml of *methylaminophenol-sulphite reagent* and allow to stand for 15 minutes. Add sufficient *water* to produce 25 ml, allow to stand for 15 minutes and filter. The *absorbance* of the filtrate at 730 nm, Appendix II B, is not greater than the *absorbance* at 730 nm of a solution obtained by repeating the operation using 10 ml of a 0.00180% w/v solution of *potassium dihydrogen orthophosphate* and beginning at the words 'add 4 ml of 1M *sulphuric acid* . . .'.

### Volatile matter
Carry out the method for *gas chromatography*, Appendix III B, using solutions in *water* containing (1) 0.0040% v/v of *pyridine*, 0.020% v/v of *absolute ethanol* and 0.020% v/v of *butan-1-ol* (internal standard), (2) 4.0% w/v of the substance being examined and (3) 4.0% w/v of the substance being examined and 0.020% v/v of the internal standard.

The chromatographic procedure may be carried out using a glass column (1.5 m × 4 mm) packed with *acid-washed, silanised diatomaceous support* (80 to 100 mesh) coated with 20% w/w of polyethylene glycol (Carbowax 20M is suitable) and maintained at 120°.

In the chromatogram obtained with solution (1) the area of the peak due to pyridine is greater than the area of any corresponding peak in the chromatogram obtained with solution (3). In the chromatogram obtained with solution (1) the area of the peak due to ethanol is greater than the sum of the areas of any peaks with a retention time less than that of the peak due to the internal standard in the chromatogram obtained with solution (3).

### Related substances
Carry out the method for *thin-layer chromatography*, Appendix III A, using *silica gel G* as the coating substance and a mixture of equal volumes of *butan-2-one, propan-2-ol* and *triethylamine hydrogen carbonate solution* as the mobile phase. Apply separately to the plate 10 μl of each of four freshly prepared solutions in a mixture of 49 volumes of

*methanol* and 1 volume of *triethylamine* containing (1) 4.0% w/v of the substance being examined, (2) 0.020% w/v of the substance being examined, (3) 0.080% w/v of *17β,17'β-bis3-[bis(2-chloroethyl)carbamoyloxy]estra1,3,5(10)-trienyl pyrophosphate BPCRS* and (4) 0.040% of *estramustine BPCRS*. After removal of the plate, allow it to dry in air, spray with *methanolic sulphuric acid (20%)* and heat at 110° for 10 minutes. The principal spots in the chromatograms obtained with solutions (3) and (4) are more intense than any corresponding spots in the chromatogram obtained with solution (1) (2 and 1% respectively). Any other *secondary spot* in the chromatogram obtained with solution (1) is not more intense than the spot in the chromatogram obtained with solution (2) (0.5%).

## Water

Not more than 5.0% w/w, Appendix IX C. Use 0.2 g.

## ASSAY

To 0.5 g add 40 ml of 1M *sodium hydroxide* and boil under a reflux condenser for 60 minutes. Cool and transfer the mixture to a 250 ml graduated flask with the aid of *water*. Add 100 ml of 0.1M *silver nitrate VS* and 10 ml of *nitric acid*, dilute to 250 ml with *water* and mix. Filter and titrate the excess of silver nitrate in 50 ml of the filtrate with 0.1M *ammonium thiocyanate VS* using 3 ml of *ammonium iron(III) sulphate solution R2* as indicator. Each ml of 0.1M *silver nitrate VS* is equivalent to 28.22 mg of $C_{23}H_{30}Cl_2NNa_2O_6P$.

## STORAGE

Estramustine Sodium Phosphate should be protected from light.

# Estriol

(*Ph Eur monograph 1203*)

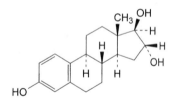

$C_{18}H_{24}O_3$       288.4       50-27-1

## Action and use

Estrogen.

## Preparation

Estriol Cream

*Ph Eur* _____

## DEFINITION

Estra-1,3,5(10)-triene-3,16α,17β-triol.

## Content

97.0 per cent to 103.0 per cent (dried substance).

## CHARACTERS

### Appearance

White or almost white, crystalline powder.

### Solubility

Practically insoluble in water, sparingly soluble in ethanol (96 per cent).

mp : about 282 °C.

## IDENTIFICATION

A. Infrared absorption spectrophotometry (*2.2.24*).

*Comparison*  estriol CRS.

B. Thin-layer chromatography (*2.2.27*).

*Test solution*  Dissolve 10 mg of the substance to be examined in *methanol R* and dilute to 10 ml with the same solvent.

*Reference solution (a)*  Dissolve 10 mg of *estriol CRS* in *methanol R* and dilute to 10 ml with the same solvent.

*Reference solution (b)*  Dissolve 5 mg of *estradiol hemihydrate CRS* in reference solution (a) and dilute to 5 ml with reference solution (a).

*Plate*  TLC silica gel plate R.

*Mobile phase*  ethanol (96 per cent) R, toluene R (20:80 V/V).

*Application*  5 µl.

*Development*  Over a path of 15 cm.

*Drying*  In air.

*Detection*  Spray with *alcoholic solution of sulphuric acid R*. Heat at 100 °C for 10 min or until the spots appear. Allow to cool. Examine in daylight and ultraviolet light at 365 nm.

*System suitability*  Reference solution (b):
— the chromatogram shows 2 clearly separated spots.

*Results*  The principal spot in the chromatogram obtained with the test solution is similar in position, colour in daylight, fluorescence in ultraviolet light at 365 nm and size to the principal spot in the chromatogram obtained with the reference solution (a).

## TESTS

**Specific optical rotation** (*2.2.7*)
+ 60 to + 65 (dried substance).

Dissolve 80 mg in *anhydrous ethanol R* and dilute to 10 ml with the same solvent.

**Related substances**
Liquid chromatography (*2.2.29*).

*Solvent mixture*  2-propanol R1, heptane R (20:80 V/V).

*Test solution*  Dissolve 20.0 mg of the substance to be examined in 5 ml of *2-propanol R1* and dilute to 20.0 ml with the solvent mixture.

*Reference solution (a)*  Dissolve 5 mg of *estriol CRS* and 2.0 mg of *estriol impurity A CRS* in 5 ml of *2-propanol R1*, then dilute to 10.0 ml with the solvent mixture. Dilute 1.0 ml of this solution to 20.0 ml with the solvent mixture.

*Reference solution (b)*  Dilute 1.0 ml of the test solution to 10.0 ml with the solvent mixture. Dilute 1.0 ml of this solution to 10.0 ml with the solvent mixture.

*Column:*
— *size: l* = 0.15 m, Ø = 4.0 mm;
— *stationary phase*: diol silica gel for chromatography R (5 µm);
— *temperature*: 40 °C.

*Mobile phase:*
— mobile phase A: heptane R;
— mobile phase B: 2-propanol R1;

| Time (min) | Mobile phase A (per cent V/V) | Mobile phase B (per cent V/V) |
|---|---|---|
| 0 - 10 | 95 → 88 | 5 → 12 |
| 10 - 20 | 88 | 12 |
| 20 - 30 | 88 → 95 | 12 → 5 |
| 30 - 35 | 95 | 5 |

*Flow rate*  1.2 ml/min.

*Detection*  Spectrophotometer at 280 nm.

*Equilibration*  With the solvent mixture until a stable baseline is obtained.

*Injection*  20 µl; inject the solvent mixture as a blank.

*Retention time*  Estriol = about 19 min;
impurity A = about 21 min; if the retention times increase, wash the column first with *acetone R* and then with *heptane R.*

*System suitability*  Reference solution (a):
— *resolution*: minimum 2.2 between the peaks due to estriol and impurity A; if the resolution decreases, wash the column first with *acetone R* and then with *heptane R.*

*Limits:*
— *impurity A*: not more than 0.5 times the area of the corresponding peak in the chromatogram obtained with reference solution (a) (0.5 per cent);
— *impurities B, C, D, E, F, G*: for each impurity, not more than 0.5 times the area of the principal peak in the chromatogram obtained with reference solution (b) (0.5 per cent);
— *sum of impurities other than A*: not more than the area of the principal peak in the chromatogram obtained with reference solution (b) (1 per cent);
— *disregard limit*: 0.05 times the area of the principal peak in the chromatogram obtained with reference solution (b) (0.05 per cent).

**Loss on drying** (2.2.32)
Maximum 0.5 per cent, determined on 1.000 g by drying in an oven at 105 °C for 3 h.

**ASSAY**
Dissolve 25.0 mg in *ethanol (96 per cent) R* and dilute to 50.0 ml with the same solvent. Dilute 10.0 ml of this solution to 50.0 ml with *ethanol (96 per cent) R*. Measure the absorbance (2.2.25) at the absorption maximum at 281 nm. Calculate the content of $C_{18}H_{24}O_3$ taking the specific absorbance to be 72.5.

**IMPURITIES**

*Specified impurities*  *A, B, C, D, E, F, G.*

*Other detectable impurities* (the following substances would, if present at a sufficient level, be detected by one or other of the tests in the monograph. They are limited by the general acceptance criterion for other/unspecified impurities and/or by the general monograph *Substances for pharmaceutical use (2034)*. It is therefore not necessary to identify these impurities for demonstration of compliance. See also *5.10*. *Control of impurities in substances for pharmaceutical use): H, I.*

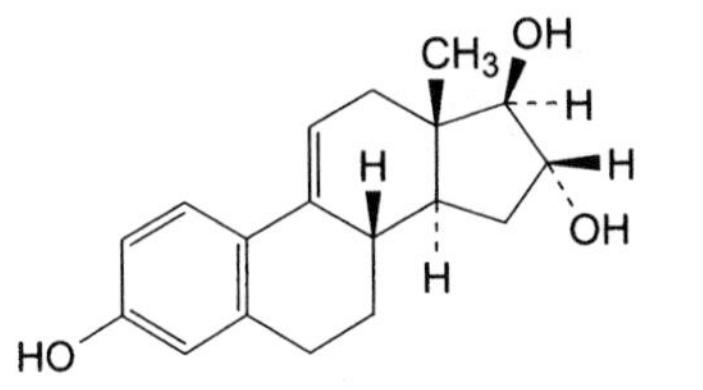

A. estra-1,3,5(10),9(11)-tetraene-3,16α,17β-triol (9,11-didehydroestriol),

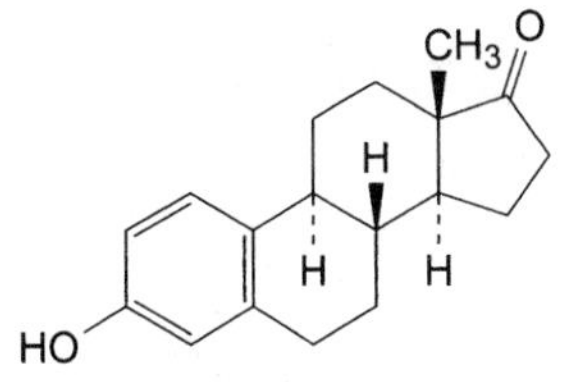

B. 3-hydroxyestra-1,3,5(10)-trien-17-one (estrone),

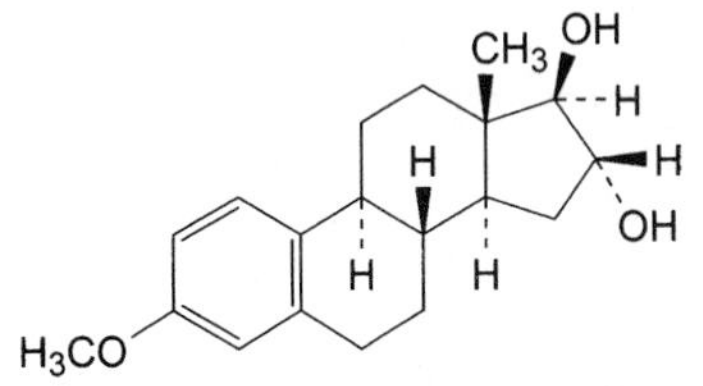

C. 3-methoxyestra-1,3,5(10)-triene-16α,17β-diol (estriol 3-methyl ether),

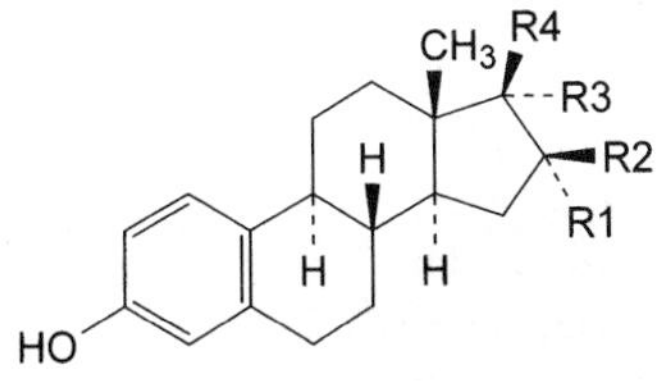

D. R1 = R2 = R3 = H, R4 = OH: estradiol,

E. R1 = R3 = OH, R2 = R4 = H: estra-1,3,5(10)-triene-3,16α,17α-triol (17-epi-estriol),

F. R1 = R3 = H, R2 = R4 = OH: estra-1,3,5(10)-triene-3,16β,17β-triol (16-epi-estriol),

G. R1 = R4 = H, R2 = R3 = OH: estra-1,3,5(10)-triene-3,16β,17α-triol (16,17-epi-estriol),

H. R1 = OH, R2 = H, R3 + R4 = O: 3,16α-dihydroxyestra-1,3,5(10)-trien-17-one,

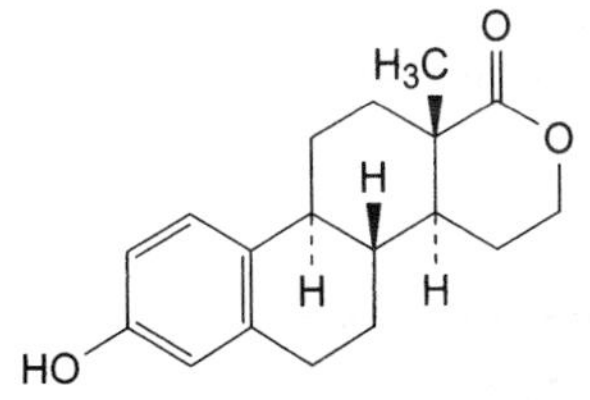

I. 3-hydroxy-17-oxa-*D*-homoestra-1,3,5(10)-trien-17a-one.

*Ph Eur*

# Conjugated Estrogens

Conjugated Oestrogens

(*Ph Eur monograph 1512*)

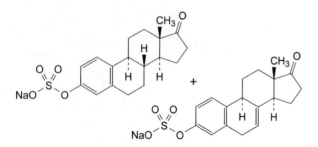

$C_{18}H_{21}O_5NaS + C_{18}H_{19}O_5NaS$  372.4+ 370.4

**Action and use**

Estrogen.

*Ph Eur*

## DEFINITION

Mixture of various conjugated forms of estrogens obtained from the urine of pregnant mares or by synthesis, dispersed in a suitable powdered diluent.

The 2 principal components are 17-oxoestra-1,3,5(10)-trien-3-yl sodium sulphate (sodium estrone sulphate) and 17-oxoestra-1,3,5(10),7-tetraen-3-yl sodium sulphate (sodium equilin sulphate). Concomitants are sodium 17α-estradiol sulphate, sodium 17α-dihydroequilin sulphate and sodium 17β-dihydroequilin sulphate.

### Content (percentages related to the labelled content)

— *sodium estrone sulphate*: 52.5 per cent to 61.5 per cent;
— *sodium equilin sulphate*: 22.5 per cent to 30.5 per cent;
— *sodium 17α-estradiol sulphate*: 2.5 per cent to 9.5 per cent;
— *sodium 17α-dihydroequilin sulphate*: 13.5 per cent to 19.5 per cent;
— *sodium 17β-dihydroequilin sulphate*: 0.5 per cent to 4.0 per cent;
— *sum of sodium estrone sulphate and sodium equilin sulphate*: 79.5 per cent to 88.0 per cent.

## CHARACTERS

**Appearance**

Almost white or brownish, amorphous powder.

## IDENTIFICATION

A. Examine the chromatograms obtained in the assay.

*Results*  The 2 principal peaks due to estrone and equilin in the chromatogram obtained with test solution (a) are similar in retention time and size to the 2 principal peaks in the chromatogram obtained with reference solution (a).

B. Examine the chromatogram obtained in the test for chromatographic profile.

*Results*  The chromatogram obtained with test solution (b) exhibits additional peaks due to 17α-estradiol, 17α-dihydroequilin and 17β-dihydroequilin, at relative retentions with reference to 3-*O*-methylestrone (internal standard) of about 0.24, 0.30 and 0.35 respectively.

## TESTS

**Chromatographic profile**

Gas chromatography (*2.2.28*).

*Internal standard solution*  Dissolve 8 mg of 3-*O*-methylestrone R in 10.0 ml of *anhydrous ethanol R*. Dilute 2.0 ml of this solution to 10.0 ml with *anhydrous ethanol R*.

*Acetate buffer solution pH 5.2*  Dissolve 10 g of *sodium acetate R* in 100 ml of *water R* and add 10 ml of *dilute acetic acid R*. Dilute to 500 ml with *water R* and adjust to pH 5.2 ± 0.1.

*Test solution (a)*  Considering the labelled content, transfer an accurately weighed quantity corresponding to about 2 mg of conjugated estrogens to a 50 ml centrifuge tube containing 15 ml of the acetate buffer solution pH 5.2 and 1 g of *barium chloride R*. Cap the tube tightly and shake for 30 min. If necessary, adjust to pH 5.0 ± 0.5 with *acetic acid R* or a 120 g/l solution of *sodium acetate R*. Sonicate for 30 s, then shake for 30 min. Add a suitable sulphatase preparation equivalent to 2500 units and shake mechanically for 10 min in a water-bath at 50 ± 1 °C. Swirl the tube by hand, then shake mechanically for 10 min in the water-bath. Allow to cool. Add 15.0 ml of *ethylene chloride R* to the mixture, immediately cap the tube tightly and shake for 15 min. Centrifuge for 10 min or until the lower layer is clear. Draw out the organic layer to a screw-cap tube, add 5 g of *anhydrous sodium sulphate R* and shake. Allow the solution to stand until clear. Protect the solution from any loss due to evaporation. Transfer 3.0 ml of the clear solution to a suitable centrifuge tube fitted with a screw cap. Add 1.0 ml of the internal standard solution. Evaporate the mixture to dryness with the aid of a stream of *nitrogen R*, maintaining the temperature below 50 °C. To the dry residue add 15 μl of *anhydrous pyridine R* and 65 μl of *N,O-bis(trimethylsilyl)trifluoroacetamide R* containing 1 per cent of *chlorotrimethylsilane R*. Immediately cap the tube tightly, mix thoroughly and allow to stand for 15 min. Add 0.5 ml of *toluene R* and mix mechanically.

*Test solution (b)*  Prepare as described in test solution (a), but do not add the sulphatase and use 6.0 ml of the upper layer instead of 3.0 ml. Prepare a blank in the same manner.

*Reference solution (a)*  Dissolve separately 8 mg of estrone CRS, 7 mg of *equilin CRS* and 5 mg of 17α-dihydroequilin CRS in 10.0 ml of *anhydrous ethanol R*. Dilute together 2.0 ml, 1.0 ml and 1.0 ml respectively of these solutions to 10.0 ml with *anhydrous ethanol R*. Transfer 1.0 ml of this solution and 1.0 ml of the internal standard solution to a centrifuge tube fitted with a screw cap. Evaporate the mixture to dryness with the aid of a stream of *nitrogen R*, maintaining the temperature below 50 °C. To the dry residue add 15 μl of *anhydrous pyridine R* and 65 μl of *N,O-bis(trimethylsilyl)trifluoroacetamide R* containing 1 per cent of *chlorotrimethylsilane R*. Immediately cap the tube tightly, mix and allow to stand for 15 min. Add 0.5 ml of *toluene R*.

*Reference solution (b)*  Prepare as described in reference solution (a), but dilute tenfold with *anhydrous ethanol R* before adding the internal standard.

*Column:*
— *material*: fused silica;
— *size*: $l$ = 15 m, Ø = 0.25 mm;
— *stationary phase*: poly[(cyanopropyl)(methyl)][(phenyl)(methyl)]siloxane R (film thickness 0.25 μm).

*Carrier gas*  hydrogen for chromatography R.

*Flow rate*  2 ml/min.

*Split ratio*  1:20 to 1:30.

*Temperature:*
— *column*: 220 °C;
— *injection port and detector*: 260 °C.

*Detection*  Flame ionisation.

Table 1512.-1

| Relative retention (to 3-*O*-methylestrone) | Analyte | Quantified with reference to CRS | Present as |
|---|---|---|---|
| 0.24 | 17α-estradiol | *17α-dihydroequilin CRS* | sodium sulphate |
| 0.29 | 17β-estradiol | *estrone CRS* | sodium sulphate |
| 0.30 | 17α-dihydroequilin | *17α-dihydroequilin CRS* | free steroid, sodium sulphate (assay) |
| 0.35 | 17β-dihydroequilin | *17α-dihydroequilin CRS* | sodium sulphate |
| 0.56 | 17α-dihydroequilenin | *estrone CRS* | sodium sulphate |
| 0.64 | 17β-dihydroequilenin | *estrone CRS* | sodium sulphate |
| 0.80 | estrone | *estrone CRS* | free steroid, sodium sulphate (assay) |
| 0.87 | equilin | *equilin CRS* | free steroid, sodium sulphate (assay) |
| 0.90 | 8,9-didehydroestrone | *estrone CRS* | sodium sulphate |
| 1 | 3-*O*-methylestrone | (internal standard) | |
| 1.3 | equilenin | *estrone CRS* | sodium sulphate |

*Injection*   1 μl.

*Relative retention*   With reference to 3-*O*-methylestrone: 17α-dihydroequilin = about 0.30; estrone = about 0.80; equilin = about 0.87.

*System suitability*   Reference solution (a):
— *resolution*: minimum 1.2 between the peaks due to estrone and equilin; if necessary, adjust the temperature and the flow rate of the carrier gas.

In the chromatogram obtained with reference solution (a), measure the areas of the peaks due to 17α-dihydroequilin, estrone and 3-*O*-methylestrone.

In the chromatogram obtained with test solution (a), locate the peaks with relative retentions with reference to 3-*O*-methylestrone of 1 and about 0.24, 0.29, 0.30, 0.35, 0.56, 0.64, 0.90 and 1.3 and measure their areas.

Calculate the percentage content of the components occurring as sodium sulphate salts using expression (1) below.

In the chromatogram obtained with reference solution (b), measure the areas of the peaks due to estrone and 3-*O*-methylestrone.

In the chromatogram obtained with test solution (b), locate the peaks with relative retentions with reference to 3-*O*-methylestrone of about 0.30, 0.80 and 0.87 and measure the sum of the areas.

Calculate the percentage content of 17α-dihydroequilin, estrone and equilin occurring as free steroids using expression (2) below.

$$\frac{S'_A \times S_I \times m_R \times 137.8 \times 1000}{S_R \times S'_I \times m \times LC}$$

$$\frac{S'_{FS} \times S_I \times m_E \times 100 \times 1000}{S_E \times S'_I \times m \times LC}$$

$S_I$ = area of the peak due to the internal standard in the chromatogram obtained with the corresponding reference solution;

$S'_I$ = area of the peak due to the internal standard in the chromatogram obtained with the corresponding test solution;

$S_R$ = area of the peak due to the reference substance (Table 1512.-1) in the chromatogram obtained with the corresponding reference solution;

$S'_A$ = area of the peak due to the analyte in the chromatogram obtained with the corresponding test solution;

$m_R$ = mass of the reference substance (Table 1512.-1) in the corresponding reference solution, in milligrams;

$m$ = mass of the substance to be examined in the corresponding test solution, in milligrams;

$S'_{FS}$ = sum of the areas of the peaks due to 17α-dihydroequilin, estrone and equilin in the chromatogram obtained with the corresponding test solution;

$S_E$ = area of the peak due to *estrone CRS* in the chromatogram obtained with the corresponding reference solution;

$m_E$ = mass of *estrone CRS* in the corresponding reference solution, in milligrams;

$L_C$ = labelled content, in milligrams per gram.

The percentages are within the following ranges:
— *sodium 17α-estradiol sulphate*: 2.5 per cent to 9.5 per cent;
— *sodium 17α-dihydroequilin sulphate*: 13.5 per cent to 19.5 per cent;
— *sodium 17β-dihydroequilin sulphate*: 0.5 per cent to 4.0 per cent;
— *sodium 17β-estradiol sulphate*: maximum 2.25 per cent;
— *sodium 17α-dihydroequilenin sulphate*: maximum 3.25 per cent;
— *sodium 17β-dihydroequilenin sulphate*: maximum 2.75 per cent;
— *sodium 8,9-didehydroestrone sulphate*: maximum 6.25 per cent;
— *sodium equilenin sulphate*: maximum 5.5 per cent;
— *sum of estrone, equilin and 17α-dihydroequilin*: maximum 1.3 per cent.

**ASSAY**

Gas chromatography (*2.2.28*) as described in the test for chromatographic profile with the following modifications.

*Injection*   Test solution (a) and reference solution (a).

*System suitability*   Reference solution (a):
— *repeatability*: maximum relative standard deviation of 2.0 per cent for the ratio of the area of the peak due to estrone to that due to the internal standard after at least 6 injections.

In the chromatogram obtained with reference solution (a), measure the areas of the peaks due to estrone or equilin and 3-O-methylestrone. In the chromatogram obtained with test solution (a), measure the areas of the peaks due to estrone, equilin and 3-O-methylestrone.

Calculate the percentage content of sodium estrone sulphate and sodium equilin sulphate using expression (1).

## LABELLING

The label states:
— the name of the substance;
— the content of the substance;
— the nature of the diluent.

## IMPURITIES AND CONCOMITANTS

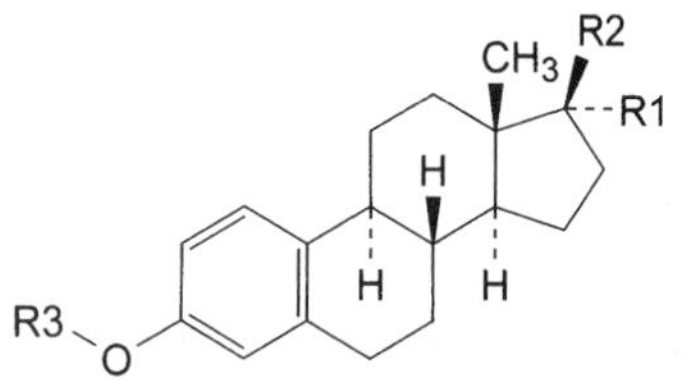

A. R1 = OH, R2 = H, R3 = SO3Na:
17α-hydroxyestra-1,3,5(10)-trien-3-yl sodium sulphate (sodium 17α-estradiol sulphate),

D. R1 = H, R2 = OH, R3 = SO3Na:
17β-hydroxyestra-1,3,5(10)-trien-3-yl sodium sulphate (sodium 17β-estradiol sulphate),

I. R1 + R2 = O, R3 = H:
3-hydroxyestra-1,3,5(10)-trien-17-one (estrone),

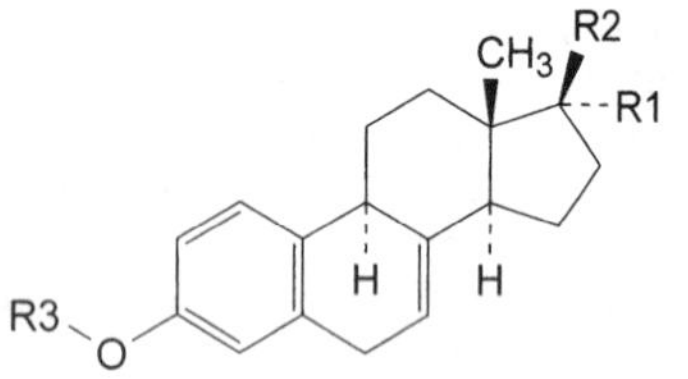

B. R1 = OH, R2 = H, R3 = SO3Na:
17α-hydroxyestra-1,3,5(10),7-tetraen-3-yl sodium sulphate (sodium 17α-dihydroequilin sulphate),

C. R1 = H, R2 = OH, R3 = SO3Na:
17β-hydroxyestra-1,3,5(10),7-tetraen-3-yl sodium sulphate (sodium 17β-dihydroequilin sulphate),

J. R1 + R2 = O, R3 = H:
3-hydroxyestra-1,3,5(10),7-tetraen-17-one (equilin),

K. R1 = OH, R2 = R3 = H:
estra-1,3,5(10),7-tetraene-3,17α-diol (17α-dihydroequilin),

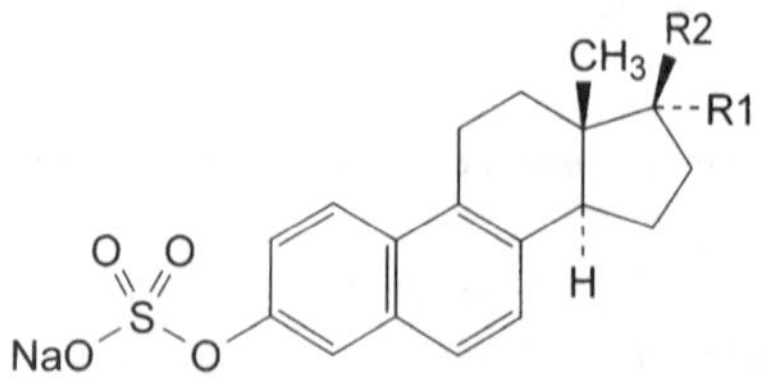

E. R1 = OH, R2 = H:
17α-hydroxyestra-1,3,5(10),6,8-pentaen-3-yl sodium sulphate (sodium 17α-dihydroequilenin sulphate),

F. R1 = H, R2 = OH:
17β-hydroxyestra-1,3,5(10),6,8-pentaen-3-yl sodium sulphate (sodium 17β-dihydroequilenin sulphate),

H. R1 + R2 = O: 17-oxoestra-1,3,5(10),6,8-pentaen-3-yl sodium sulphate (sodium equilenin sulphate),

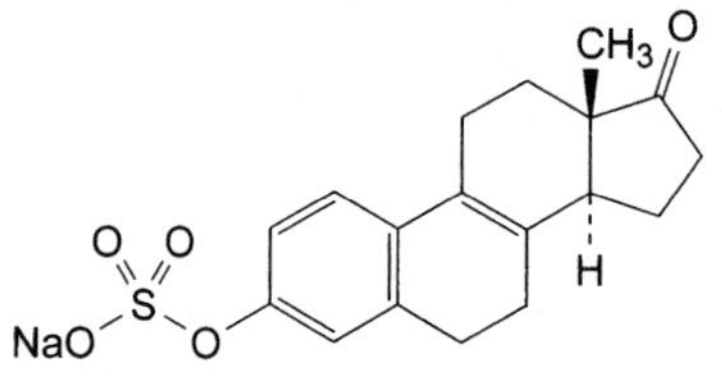

G. 17-oxoestra-1,3,5(10),8-tetraen-3-yl sodium sulphate (sodium 8,9-didehydroestrone sulphate).

_____ _Ph Eur_

# Estropipate

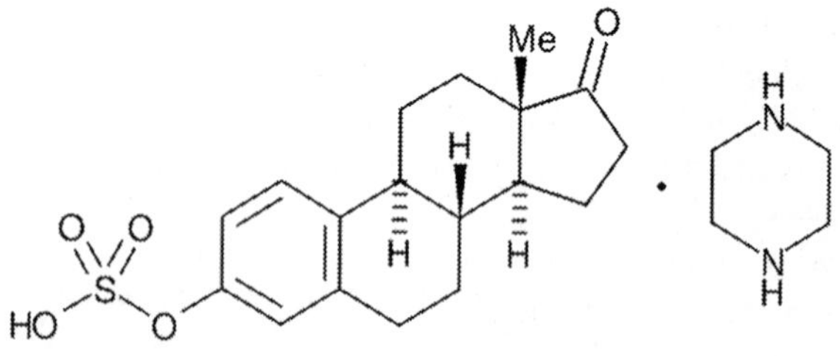

$C_{18}H_{22}O_5S,C_4H_{10}N_2$        436.6        _7280-37-7_

## Action and use
Estrogen.

## Preparation
Estropipate Tablets

## DEFINITION
Estropipate is piperazine 17-oxoestra-1,3,5-(10)-trien-3-yl hydrogen sulphate (1:1). It contains not less than 97.0% and not more than 103.0% of $C_{18}H_{22}O_5S,C_4H_{10}N_2$, calculated with reference to the dried substance.

## CHARACTERISTICS
A white or almost white, crystalline powder.

Very slightly soluble in _water_, in _ethanol (96%)_ and in _ether_.

## IDENTIFICATION
The _infrared absorption spectrum_, Appendix II A, is concordant with the _reference spectrum_ of estropipate _(RS 129)_.

## TESTS
### Free estrone
Carry out the method for _liquid chromatography_, Appendix III D, using the following solutions in _methanol_.

(1) 0.10% w/v of the substance being examined.

(2) 0.0020% w/v of _estrone BPCRS_.

CHROMATOGRAPHIC CONDITIONS

(a) Use a stainless steel column (30 cm × 3.9 mm) packed with _end-capped octadecylsilyl silica gel for chromatography_, (10 μm) (μBondapak C18 is suitable).

(b) Use isocratic elution and the mobile phase described below.

(c) Use a flow rate of 1.5 ml per minute.

(d) Use an ambient column temperature.

(e) Use a detection wavelength of 213 nm.

(f) Inject 20 μl of each solution.

MOBILE PHASE

35 volumes of *acetonitrile* and 65 volumes of 0.025M *potassium dihydrogen orthophosphate*.

The peak due to estrone has a retention time, relative to the peak due to estropipate, of about 5.

LIMITS

In the chromatogram obtained with solution (1):

the area of any peak corresponding to estrone is not greater than the area of the peak in the chromatogram obtained with solution (2) (2%).

### Loss on drying

When dried at 105° for 1 hour, loses not more than 1.0% of its weight. Use 1 g.

### Sulphated ash

Not more than 0.5%, Appendix IX A. Use 1 g.

### ASSAY

Carry out the method for *liquid chromatography*, Appendix III D, using the following solutions in *methanol*.

(1) 0.01% w/v of the substance being examined.

(2) 0.01% w/v of *estropipate BPCRS*.

CHROMATOGRAPHIC CONDITIONS

The chromatographic procedure described under Free estrone may be used.

DETERMINATION OF CONTENT

Calculate the content of $C_{18}H_{22}O_5S,C_4H_{10}N_2$ in the substance being examined using the declared content of $C_{18}H_{22}O_5S,C_4H_{10}N_2$ in *estropipate BPCRS*.

### IMPURITIES

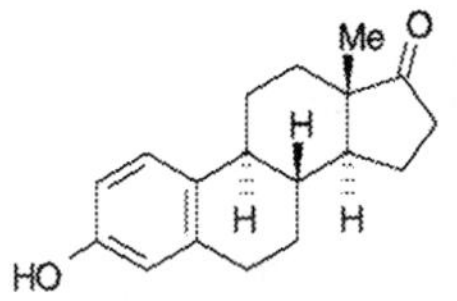

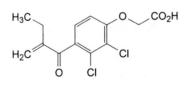

A. Estrone.

# Etacrynic Acid

(*Ph Eur monograph 0457*)

$C_{13}H_{12}Cl_2O_4$          303.1          58-54-8

### Action and use

Loop diuretic.

### Preparation

Sodium Etacrynate Injection

*Ph Eur* _____

## DEFINITION

[2,3-Dichloro-4-(2-methylenebutanoyl)phenoxy]acetic acid

### Content

98.0 per cent to 102.0 per cent (dried substance).

## CHARACTERS

### Appearance

White or almost white, crystalline powder.

### Solubility

Very slightly soluble in water, freely soluble in ethanol (96 per cent). It dissolves in ammonia and in dilute solutions of alkali hydroxides and carbonates.

## IDENTIFICATION

*First identification   C.*

*Second identification   A, B, D, E.*

A. Melting point (*2.2.14*): 121 °C to 124 °C.

B. Ultraviolet and visible absorption spectrophotometry (*2.2.25*).

*Solvent mixture*   103 g/l solution of *hydrochloric acid R*, *methanol R* (1:99 V/V).

*Test solution*   Dissolve 50.0 mg in the solvent mixture and dilute to 100.0 ml with the solvent mixture. Dilute 10.0 ml of this solution to 100.0 ml with the solvent mixture.

*Spectral range*   230-350 nm.

*Absorption maximum*   At 270 nm.

*Shoulder*   At about 285 nm.

*Specific absorbance at the absorption maximum*   110 to 120.

C. Infrared absorption spectrophotometry (*2.2.24*).

*Comparison   etacrynic acid CRS*.

D. Dissolve about 30 mg in 2 ml of *aldehyde-free alcohol R*. Dissolve 70 mg of *hydroxylamine hydrochloride R* in 0.1 ml of *water R*, add 7 ml of *alcoholic potassium hydroxide solution R* and dilute to 10 ml with *aldehyde-free alcohol R*. Allow to stand and add 1 ml of the supernatant liquid to the solution of the substance to be examined. Heat the mixture on a water-bath for 3 min. After cooling, add 3 ml of *water R* and 0.15 ml of *hydrochloric acid R*. Examined in ultraviolet light at 254 nm, the mixture shows an intense blue fluorescence.

E. Dissolve about 25 mg in 2 ml of a 42 g/l solution of *sodium hydroxide R* and heat in a water-bath for 5 min. Cool and add 0.25 ml of a mixture of equal volumes of *sulphuric acid R* and *water R*. Add 0.5 ml of a 100 g/l solution of chromotropic acid, *sodium salt R* and, carefully, 2 ml of *sulphuric acid R*. An intense violet colour is produced.

## TESTS

### Related substances

Liquid chromatography (*2.2.29*).

*Solvent mixture   acetonitrile R, water R* (40:60 V/V).

*Test solution*   Dissolve 25 mg of the substance to be examined in the solvent mixture and dilute to 25.0 ml with the solvent mixture.

*Reference solution (a)*   Dilute 1.0 ml of the test solution to 100.0 ml with the solvent mixture. Dilute 1.0 ml of this solution to 10.0 ml with the solvent mixture.

*Reference solution (b)*   Dissolve 5 mg of *etacrynic acid for system suitability CRS* (containing impurities A, B and C) in 5.0 ml of the solvent mixture.

*Column:*

— *size: l* = 0.25 m, Ø = 4.0 mm;

— *stationary phase: end-capped octadecylsilyl silica gel for chromatography R* (5 μm);

— *temperature*: 25 °C.

*Mobile phase:*
— *mobile phase A*: 1 per cent *V/V* solution of *triethylamine R* adjusted to pH 6.8 with *phosphoric acid R*;
— *mobile phase B*: *acetonitrile R*;

| Time (min) | Mobile phase A (per cent *V/V*) | Mobile phase B (per cent *V/V*) |
|---|---|---|
| 0-2.5 | 70 | 30 |
| 2.5-3 | 70→65 | 30→35 |
| 3-6 | 65 | 35 |
| 6-7 | 65→45 | 35→55 |
| 7-22 | 45 | 55 |

*Flow rate*  0.8 ml/min.

*Detection*  Spectrophotometer at 280 nm.

*Injection*  10 µl.

*Identification of impurities*  Use the chromatogram supplied with *etacrynic acid for system suitability CRS* and the chromatogram obtained with reference solution (b) to identify the peaks due to impurities A, B and C.

*Relative retention*  With reference to etacrynic acid (retention time = about 9 min): impurity A = about 0.8; impurity B = about 1.3; impurity C = about 1.7.

*System suitability*  Reference solution (b):
— *resolution*: minimum 4.0 between the peaks due to impurity A and etacrynic acid.

*Limits:*
— *correction factors*: for the calculation of contents, multiply the peak areas of the following impurities by the corresponding correction factor: impurity A = 0.6; impurity B = 0.6; impurity C = 1.3;
— *impurity C*: not more than 3 times the area of the principal peak in the chromatogram obtained with reference solution (a) (0.3 per cent);
— *impurities A, B*: for each impurity, not more than 1.5 times the area of the principal peak in the chromatogram obtained with reference solution (a) (0.15 per cent);
— *unspecified impurities*: for each impurity, not more than the area of the principal peak in the chromatogram obtained with reference solution (a) (0.10 per cent);
— *total*: not more than 8 times the area of the principal peak in the chromatogram obtained with reference solution (a) (0.8 per cent);
— *disregard limit*: 0.5 times the area of the principal peak in the chromatogram obtained with reference solution (a) (0.05 per cent).

**Heavy metals** (*2.4.8*)
Maximum 20 ppm.

1.0 g complies with test F. Prepare the reference solution using 2 ml of *lead standard solution (10 ppm Pb) R*.

**Loss on drying** (*2.2.32*)
Maximum 0.5 per cent, determined on 2.000 g by drying at 60 °C over *diphosphorus pentoxide R* at a pressure of 0.1-0.5 kPa.

**Sulphated ash** (*2.4.14*)
Maximum 0.1 per cent, determined on 1.0 g.

**ASSAY**
Dissolve 0.250 g in 100 ml of *methanol R* and add 5 ml of *water R*. Titrate with *0.1 M sodium hydroxide*, determining the end-point potentiometrically (*2.2.20*).

1 ml of *0.1 M sodium hydroxide* is equivalent to 30.31 mg of $C_{13}H_{12}Cl_2O_4$.

**IMPURITIES**
*Specified impurities*  *A, B, C.*

A. R = H: (4-butanoyl-2,3-dichlorophenoxy)acetic acid,

B. R = $CH_2Cl$: [2,3-dichloro-4-[2-(chloromethyl)butanoyl]phenoxy]acetic acid,

C. [4-[2-[4-(carboxymethoxy)-2,3-dichlorobenzoyl]-2,5-diethyl-3,4-dihydro-2*H*-pyran-6-yl]-2,3-dichlorophenoxy]acetic acid.

*————————————— Ph Eur*

# Etamsylate

(*Ph Eur monograph 1204*)

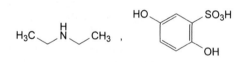

| $C_{10}H_{17}NO_5S$ | 263.3 | *2624-44-4* |

**Action and use**
Antifibrinolytic.

*Ph Eur* _____

**DEFINITION**
*N*-Ethylethanamine 2,5-dihydroxybenzenesulphonate.

**Content**
99.0 per cent to 101.0 per cent (dried substance).

**CHARACTERS**

**Appearance**
White or almost white, crystalline powder.

**Solubility**
Very soluble in water, freely soluble in methanol, soluble in anhydrous ethanol, practically insoluble in methylene chloride.

It shows polymorphism (*5.9*).

**IDENTIFICATION**
*First identification*  B.

*Second identification*  A, C, D.

A. Melting point (*2.2.14*): 127 °C to 134 °C.

B. Infrared absorption spectrophotometry (*2.2.24*).

*Comparison*  etamsylate CRS.

C. Ultraviolet and visible absorption spectrophotometry (*2.2.25*).

*Test solution*   Dissolve 0.100 g in *water R* and dilute to 200.0 ml with the same solvent. Dilute 5.0 ml of this solution to 100.0 ml with *water R*. Examine immediately.

*Spectral range*   210-350 nm.

*Absorption maxima*   At 221 nm and 301 nm.

*Specific absorbance at the absorption maximum at 301 nm*   145 to 151.

D. Into a test-tube, introduce 2 ml of freshly prepared solution S (see Tests) and 0.5 g of *sodium hydroxide R*. Warm the mixture and place a wet strip of *red litmus paper R* near the open end of the tube. The colour of the paper becomes blue.

## TESTS
### Solution S
Dissolve 10.0 g in *carbon dioxide-free water R* and dilute to 100 ml with the same solvent.

### Appearance of solution
Solution S, when freshly prepared, is clear (*2.2.1*) and colourless (*2.2.2, Method II*).

### pH (*2.2.3*)
4.5 to 5.6 for solution S.

### Related substances
Liquid chromatography (*2.2.29*). *Keep all solutions at 2-8 °C.*

*Buffer solution*   Dissolve 1.2 g of *anhydrous sodium dihydrogen phosphate R* in 900 ml of *water for chromatography R*. Adjust to pH 6.5 with *disodium hydrogen phosphate solution R* and dilute to 1000 ml with *water for chromatography R*.

*Test solution*   Dissolve 0.100 g of the substance to be examined in *water R* and dilute to 10.0 ml with the same solvent.

*Reference solution (a)*   Dilute 1.0 ml of the test solution to 100.0 ml with *water R*. Dilute 1.0 ml of this solution to 10.0 ml with *water R*.

*Reference solution (b)*   Dissolve 10 mg of the substance to be examined and 10 mg of *hydroquinone R* (impurity A) in *water R* and dilute to 10 ml with the same solvent. Dilute 1 ml of this solution to 100 ml with *water R*.

*Column:*
— *size: l* = 0.25 m, Ø = 4.6 mm;
— *stationary phase: spherical end-capped octadecylsilyl silica gel for chromatography R* (5 µm).

*Mobile phase*   *acetonitrile R1*, buffer solution (10:90 *V/V*).

*Flow rate*   0.8 ml/min.

*Detection*   Spectrophotometer at 220 nm.

*Injection*   10 µl.

*Run time*   2.5 times the retention time of etamsylate.

*Relative retention*   With reference to etamsylate (retention time = about 6 min): impurity A = about 1.7.

*System suitability*   Reference solution (b):
— *resolution*: minimum 8.0 between the peaks due to etamsylate and impurity A.

*Limits:*
— *correction factor*: for the calculation of content, multiply the peak area of impurity A by 0.5;
— *impurity A*: not more than the area of the principal peak in the chromatogram obtained with reference solution (a) (0.1 per cent);
— *unspecified impurities*: for each impurity, not more than the area of the principal peak in the chromatogram obtained with reference solution (a) (0.10 per cent);

— *total*: not more than twice the area of principal peak in the chromatogram obtained with reference solution (a) (0.2 per cent);
— *disregard limit*: 0.5 times the area of the principal peak in the chromatogram obtained with reference solution (a) (0.05 per cent).

### Iron (*2.4.9*)
Maximum 10 ppm, determined on solution S.

### Heavy metals (*2.4.8*)
Maximum 15 ppm.

1.0 g complies with test C. Prepare the reference solution using 1.5 ml of *lead standard solution (10 ppm Pb) R*.

### Loss on drying (*2.2.32*)
Maximum 0.5 per cent, determined on 1.000 g by drying *in vacuo* in an oven at 60 °C.

### Sulphated ash (*2.4.14*)
Maximum 0.1 per cent, determined on 1.0 g.

## ASSAY
Dissolve 0.200 g in a mixture of 10 ml of *water R* and 40 ml of *dilute sulphuric acid R*. Titrate with *0.1 M cerium sulphate*, determining the end-point potentiometrically (*2.2.20*).

1 ml of *0.1 M cerium sulphate* is equivalent to 13.16 mg of $C_{10}H_{17}NO_5S$.

## STORAGE
In an airtight container, protected from light.

## IMPURITIES
*Specified impurities*   A.

A. benzene-1,4-diol (hydroquinone).

_____ *Ph Eur*


# Ethacridine Lactate Monohydrate

*(Ph Eur monograph 1591)*

$C_{15}H_{15}N_3O,C_3H_6O_3,H_2O$   361.4          *6402-23-9*

### Action and use
Antiseptic.

*Ph Eur* _____

## DEFINITION
7-Ethoxyacridine-3,9-diamine (2RS)-2-hydroxypropanoate monohydrate.

### Content
99.0 per cent to 101.0 per cent (dried substance).

## CHARACTERS
### Appearance
Yellow crystalline powder.

## Solubility

Sparingly soluble in water, very slightly soluble in ethanol (96 per cent), practically insoluble in methylene chloride.

## IDENTIFICATION

*First identification   A.*

*Second identification   B, C, D.*

A. Infrared absorption spectrophotometry (*2.2.24*).

*Comparison   ethacridine lactate monohydrate CRS.*

B. Mix 0.1 ml of solution S (see Tests) and 100 ml of *water R*. The solution is greenish-yellow and shows a strong green fluorescence in ultraviolet light at 365 nm. Add 5 ml of *1 M hydrochloric acid*. The fluorescence remains.

C. To 0.5 ml of solution S add 1.0 ml of *water R*, 0.1 ml of a 10 g/l solution of *cobalt chloride R* and 0.1 ml of a 50 g/l solution of *potassium ferrocyanide R*. The solution is green.

D. To 50 ml of solution S add 10 ml of *dilute sodium hydroxide solution R*. Filter. To 5 ml of the filtrate, add 1 ml of *dilute sulphuric acid R*. 5 ml of the solution obtained gives the reaction of lactates (*2.3.1*).

## TESTS

### Solution S

Dissolve 2.0 g in *carbon dioxide-free water R* and dilute to 100.0 ml with the same solvent.

### pH (*2.2.3*)

5.5 to 7.0 for solution S.

### Related substances

Liquid chromatography (*2.2.29*).

*Test solution*   Dissolve 10.0 mg of the substance to be examined in the mobile phase and dilute to 25.0 ml with the mobile phase.

*Reference solution (a)*   Dilute 1.0 ml of test solution to 100.0 ml with the mobile phase.

*Reference solution (b)*   Dilute 1.0 ml of reference solution (a) to 10.0 ml with the mobile phase.

*Column:*
— *size*: $l$ = 0.25 m, Ø = 4.6 mm,
— *stationary phase*: octadecylsilyl silica gel for chromatography R (5 μm).

*Mobile phase*   Dissolve 1.0 g of *sodium octanesulphonate R* in a mixture of 300 ml of *acetonitrile R* and 700 ml of *phosphate buffer solution pH 2.8 R*.

*Flow rate*   1 ml/min.

*Detection*   Spectrophotometer at 268 nm.

*Injection*   10 μl.

*Run time*   3 times the retention time of ethacridine.

*Retention time*   Ethacridine = about 15 min.

*Limits:*
— *any impurity*: not more than 3 times the area of the principal peak in the chromatogram obtained with reference solution (b) (0.3 per cent),
— *total*: not more than the area of the principal peak in the chromatogram obtained with reference solution (a) (1 per cent),
— *disregard limit*: 0.5 times the area of the principal peak in the chromatogram obtained with reference solution (b) (0.05 per cent).

### Heavy metals (*2.4.8*)

Maximum 50 ppm.

1.0 g complies with test F. Prepare the reference solution using 5.0 ml of *lead standard solution (10 ppm Pb) R*.

### Loss on drying (*2.2.32*)

4.5 per cent to 5.5 per cent, determined on 1.000 g by drying in an oven *in vacuo* at 105 °C.

### Sulphated ash (*2.4.14*)

Maximum 0.1 per cent, determined on 1.0 g.

## ASSAY

Dissolve 0.270 g in 5.0 ml of *anhydrous formic acid R*. Add 60.0 ml of *acetic anhydride R* and titrate with *0.1 M perchloric acid*, determining the end-point potentiometrically (*2.2.20*).

1 ml of *0.1 M perchloric acid* is equivalent to 34.34 mg of $C_{18}H_{21}N_3O_4$.

## STORAGE

Protected from light.

## IMPURITIES

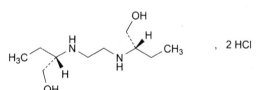

A. 6-amino-2-ethoxyacridin-9(10*H*)-one,

B. R = Cl: 6-chloro-2-ethoxyacridin-9-amine,

C. R = O-CH₂-CH₂-OH:
2-[(9-amino-7-ethoxyacridin-3-yl)oxy]ethanol.

*Ph Eur*

# Ethambutol Hydrochloride

(*Ph Eur monograph 0553*)

$C_{10}H_{26}Cl_2N_2O_2$          277.2          *1070-11-7*

## Action and use

Antituberculosis drug.

## Preparation

Ethambutol Tablets

*Ph Eur*

## DEFINITION

(2*S*,2'*S*)-2,2'-(ethylenediimino)dibutan-1-ol dihydrochloride.

## Content

99.0 per cent to 101.0 per cent (dried substance).

## CHARACTERS

### Appearance
White or almost white, crystalline powder, hygroscopic.

### Solubility
Freely soluble in water, soluble in ethanol (96 per cent).

## IDENTIFICATION
*First identification   A, D, E.*

*Second identification   B, C, D.*

A. Infrared absorption spectrophotometry (2.2.24).

*Comparison   ethambutol hydrochloride CRS.*

B. Examine the chromatograms obtained in the test for impurity A.

*Results*   The principal spot in the chromatogram obtained with test solution (b) is similar in position, colour and size to the principal spot in the chromatogram obtained with reference solution (b).

C. Dissolve 0.1 g in 10 ml of *water R*. Add 0.2 ml of *copper sulphate solution R* and 0.5 ml of *dilute sodium hydroxide solution R*; a blue colour is produced.

D. It gives reaction (a) of chlorides (2.3.1).

E. Related substances (see Tests).

## TESTS
### pH (2.2.3)
3.7 to 4.0.

Dissolve 0.2 g in 10 ml of *carbon dioxide-free water R*.

### Impurity A
Thin-layer chromatography (2.2.27).

*Test solution (a)*   Dissolve 0.50 g of the substance to be examined in *methanol R* and dilute to 10 ml with the same solvent.

*Test solution (b)*   Dilute 1 ml of test solution (a) to 10 ml with *methanol R*.

*Reference solution (a)*   Dissolve 50.0 mg of *2-aminobutanol R* (impurity A) in *methanol R* and dilute to 10.0 ml with the same solvent. Dilute 1.0 ml of this solution to 10.0 ml with *methanol R*.

*Reference solution (b)*   Dissolve 50 mg of *ethambutol hydrochloride CRS* and 5 mg of *2-aminobutanol R* in *methanol R* and dilute to 10 ml with the same solvent.

*Plate   TLC silica gel plate R.*

*Mobile phase   concentrated ammonia R, water R, methanol R* (10:15:75 *V/V/V*).

*Application   2 µl.*

*Development   Over 2/3 of the plate.*

*Drying   In air; heat at 110 °C for 10 min.*

*Detection   Cool then spray with ninhydrin solution R1*; heat at 110 °C for 5 min.

*System suitability*   Reference solution (b):
— the chromatogram shows 2 clearly separated spots.

*Limit:*
— *impurity A*: any spot due to impurity A in the chromatogram obtained with test solution (a) is not more intense than the spot in the chromatogram obtained with reference solution (a) (1.0 per cent).

### Related substances
Liquid chromatography (2.2.29). *Prepare the solutions immediately before use.*

*Test solution*   Suspend 4.0 mg of the substance to be examined in 4.0 ml of *acetonitrile R1* and add 100 µl of *triethylamine R*. Sonicate the mixture for 5 min. Add 15 µl of *(R)-(+)-α-methylbenzyl isocyanate R* and heat at 70 °C for 20 min.

*Reference solution (a)*   Dilute 0.50 ml of the test solution to 100.0 ml with *acetonitrile R1*.

*Reference solution (b)*   Treat 4.0 mg of *ethambutol for system suitability CRS* (containing impurity B) as described for the test solution.

*Column:*
— *size: l* = 0.10 m, Ø = 4.6 mm;
— *stationary phase*: end-capped octadecylsilyl silica gel for chromatography R (3 µm);
— *temperature*: 40 °C.

*Mobile phase:*
— *mobile phase A*: methanol R, water R (50:50 *V/V*);
— *mobile phase B*: methanol R;

| Time (min) | Mobile phase A (per cent *V/V*) | Mobile phase B (per cent *V/V*) |
|---|---|---|
| 0 - 30 | 71 | 29 |
| 30 - 35 | 71 → 0 | 29 → 100 |
| 35 - 37 | 0 | 100 |
| 37 - 38 | 0 → 71 | 100 → 29 |

*Flow rate   1.0 ml/min.*

*Detection   Spectrophotometer at 215 nm.*

*Injection   10 µl.*

*Relative retention*   With reference to ethambutol (retention time = about 14 min): impurity B = about 1.3.

*System suitability*   Reference solution (b):
— *resolution*: minimum 4.0 between the peaks due to ethambutol and impurity B.

*Limits:*
— *impurity B*: not more than twice the area of the principal peak in the chromatogram obtained with reference solution (a) (1.0 per cent);
— *unspecified impurities with a relative retention of 0.75 to 1.5 with reference to ethambutol*: for each impurity, not more than 0.2 times the area of the peak due to ethambutol in the chromatogram obtained with reference solution (a) (0.10 per cent);
— *total* (impurity B and unspecified impurities with a relative retention of 0.75 to 1.5 with reference to ethambutol): not more than twice the area of the principal peak in the chromatogram obtained with reference solution (a) (1.0 per cent);
— *disregard limit*: 0.1 times the area of the peak due to ethambutol in the chromatogram obtained with reference solution (a) (0.05 per cent).

### Impurity D (1,2-dichloroethane) (2.4.24)
Maximum 5 ppm.

### Heavy metals (2.4.8)
Maximum 10 ppm.

Dissolve 2.0 g in *water R* and dilute to 20 ml with the same solvent. 12 ml of the solution complies with test A. Prepare the reference solution using 10 ml of *lead standard solution (1 ppm Pb) R*.

### Loss on drying (2.2.32)
Maximum 0.5 per cent, determined on 0.500 g by drying in an oven at 105 °C for 3 h.

### Sulphated ash (2.4.14)
Maximum 0.1 per cent, determined on 1.0 g.

## ASSAY

Dissolve 0.200 g in 50 ml of *water R* and add 1.0 ml of *0.1 M hydrochloric acid*. Carry out a potentiometric titration (*2.2.20*), using *0.1 M sodium hydroxide*. Read the volume added between the 2 points of inflexion.

1 ml of *0.1 M sodium hydroxide* is equivalent to 27.72 mg of $C_{10}H_{26}Cl_2N_2O_2$.

## STORAGE

In an airtight container.

## IMPURITIES

*Specified impurities   A, B, D.*

*Other detectable impurities*   (The following substances would, if present at a sufficient level, be detected by one or other of the tests in the monograph. They are limited by the general acceptance criterion for other/unspecified impurities and/or by the general monograph *Substances for pharmaceutical use (2034)*. It is therefore not necessary to identify these impurities for demonstration of compliance. See also *5.10. Control of impurities in substances for pharmaceutical use*): *C.*

A. 2-aminobutan-1-ol,

B. R = $CH_2$-OH, R′ = H: (2R,2′S)-2,2′-(ethylenediimino)dibutan-1-ol (meso-ethambutol),

C. R = H, R′ = $CH_2$-OH: (2R,2′R)-2,2′-(ethylenediimino)dibutan-1-ol ((R,R)-ethambutol),

D. 1,2-dichloroethane (ethylene chloride).

*——————————————— Ph Eur*

# Ethanol

Absolute Alcohol; Dehydrated Alcohol

*(Anhydrous Ethanol, Ph Eur monograph 1318)*

| $C_2H_6O$ | 46.07 | *64-17-5* |

*Ph Eur ———————————————*

## DEFINITION

### Content

Not less than 99.5 per cent *V/V* of $C_2H_6O$ (99.2 per cent *m/m*), at 20 °C, calculated from the relative density using the alcoholimetric tables (*5.5*).

## CHARACTERS

### Appearance

Colourless, clear, volatile, flammable liquid, hygroscopic.

### Solubility

Miscible with water and with methylene chloride.

It burns with a blue, smokeless flame.

bp : about 78 °C.

## IDENTIFICATION

*First identification   A, B.*

*Second identification   A, C, D.*

A. It complies with the test for relative density (see Tests).

B. Infrared absorption spectrophotometry (*2.2.24*).

*Comparison   Ph. Eur. reference spectrum of anhydrous ethanol.*

C. Mix 0.1 ml with 1 ml of a 10 g/l solution of *potassium permanganate R* and 0.2 ml of *dilute sulphuric acid R* in a test-tube. Cover immediately with a filter paper moistened with a freshly prepared solution containing 0.1 g of *sodium nitroprusside R* and 0.5 g of *piperazine hydrate R* in 5 ml of *water R*. After a few minutes, an intense blue colour appears on the paper and becomes paler after 10-15 min.

D. To 0.5 ml add 5 ml of *water R*, 2 ml of *dilute sodium hydroxide solution R*, then slowly add 2 ml of *0.05 M iodine*. A yellow precipitate is formed within 30 min.

## TESTS

### Appearance

It is clear (*2.2.1*) and colourless (*2.2.2, Method II*) when compared with *water R*. Dilute 1.0 ml to 20 ml with *water R*. After standing for 5 min, the dilution remains clear (*2.2.1*) when compared with *water R*.

### Acidity or alkalinity

To 20 ml add 20 ml of *carbon dioxide-free water R* and 0.1 ml of *phenolphthalein solution R*. The solution is colourless. Add 1.0 ml of *0.01 M sodium hydroxide*. The solution is pink (30 ppm, expressed as acetic acid).

### Relative density (*2.2.5*)

0.790 to 0.793.

### Absorbance (*2.2.25*)

Maximum 0.40 at 240 nm, 0.30 between 250 nm and 260 nm, and 0.10 between 270 nm and 340 nm. The absorption curve is smooth.

Examined between 235 nm and 340 nm in a 5 cm cell using *water R* as the compensation liquid.

### Volatile impurities

Gas chromatography (*2.2.28*).

*Test solution (a)*   The substance to be examined.

*Test solution (b)*   Add 150 µl of *4-methylpentan-2-ol R* to 500.0 ml of the substance to be examined.

*Reference solution (a)*   Dilute 100 µl of *anhydrous methanol R* to 50.0 ml with the substance to be examined. Dilute 5.0 ml of the solution to 50.0 ml with the substance to be examined.

*Reference solution (b)*   Dilute 50 µl of *anhydrous methanol R* and 50 µl of *acetaldehyde R* to 50.0 ml with the substance to be examined. Dilute 100 µl of the solution to 10.0 ml with the substance to be examined.

*Reference solution (c)*   Dilute 150 µl of *acetal R* to 50.0 ml with the substance to be examined. Dilute 100 µl of the solution to 10.0 ml with the substance to be examined.

*Reference solution (d)*   Dilute 100 µl of *benzene R* to 100.0 ml with the substance to be examined. Dilute 100 µl of the solution to 50.0 ml with the substance to be examined.

*Column:*
— *material*: fused silica,
— *size:* l = 30 m, Ø = 0.32 mm,
— *stationary phase*:
poly[(cyanopropyl)(phenyl)][dimethyl]siloxane R (film thickness 1.8 μm).

*Carrier gas   helium for chromatography R.*

*Linear velocity   35 cm/s.*

*Split ratio   1:20.*

*Temperature:*

|  | Time (min) | Temperature (°C) |
|---|---|---|
| Column | 0 - 12 | 40 |
|  | 12 - 32 | 40 → 240 |
|  | 32 - 42 | 240 |
| Injection port |  | 200 |
| Detector |  | 280 |

*Detection   Flame ionisation.*

*Injection   1 μl.*

*System suitability   Reference solution (b):*
— *resolution*: minimum 1.5 between the first peak (acetaldehyde) and the second peak (methanol).

*Limits:*
— *methanol*: in the chromatogram obtained with test solution (a): not more than half the area of the corresponding peak in the chromatogram obtained with reference solution (a) (200 ppm *V/V*) .
— *acetaldehyde + acetal*: maximum of 10 ppm *V/V*, expressed as acetaldehyde.

Calculate the sum of the contents of acetaldehyde and acetal in parts per million (*V/V*) using the following expression:

$$\frac{10 \times A_E}{A_T - A_E} + \frac{30 \times C_E}{C_T - C_E}$$

$A_E$ = area of the acetaldehyde peak in the chromatogram obtained with test solution (a),
$A_T$ = area of the acetaldehyde peak in the chromatogram obtained with reference solution (b),
$C_E$ = area of the acetal peak in the chromatogram obtained with test solution (a),
$C_T$ = area of the acetal peak in the chromatogram obtained with reference solution (c).

— *benzene*: maximum 2 ppm V/V.

Calculate the content of benzene in parts per million (*V/V*) using the following expression:

$$\frac{2B_E}{B_T - B_E}$$

$B_E$ = area of the benzene peak in the chromatogram obtained with the test solution (a),
$B_T$ = area of the benzene peak in the chromatogram obtained with reference solution (d).

If necessary, the identity of benzene can be confirmed using another suitable chromatographic system (stationary phase with a different polarity).
— *total of other impurities* in the chromatogram obtained with test solution (b): not more than the area of the peak due to 4-methylpentan-2-ol in the chromatogram obtained with test solution (b) (300 ppm),

— *disregard limit*: 0.03 times the area of the peak corresponding to 4-methylpentan-2-ol in the chromatogram obtained with test solution (b) (9 ppm).

**Residue on evaporation**
Maximum 25 ppm *m/V*.

Evaporate 100 ml to dryness on a water-bath and dry at 100-105 °C for 1 h. The residue weighs a maximum of 2.5 mg.

**STORAGE**
Protected from light.

**IMPURITIES**

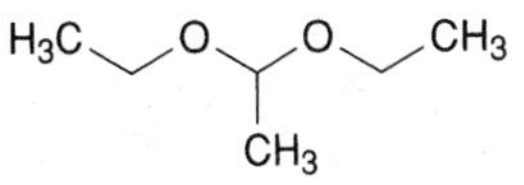

A. 1,1-diethoxyethane (acetal),

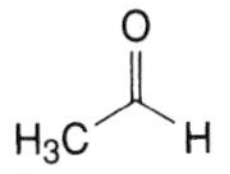

B. acetaldehyde,

C. acetone,

D. benzene,

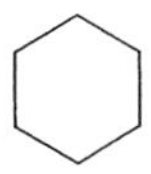

E. cyclohexane,

F. CH₃-OH: methanol,

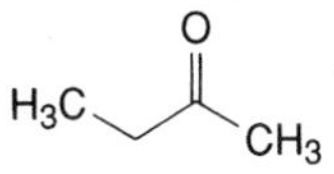

G. butan-2-one (methyl ethyl ketone),

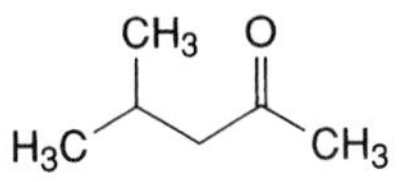

H. 4-methylpentan-2-one (methyl isobutyl ketone),

I. CH₃-(CH₂)₂-OH: propanol,

J. propan-2-ol (isopropyl alcohol),

K. CH₃-(CH₂)₃-OH: butanol,

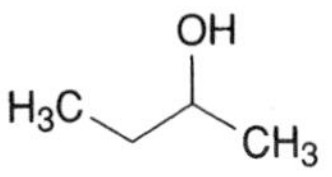

L. butan-2-ol,

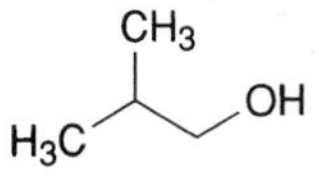

M. 2-methylpropanol (isobutanol),

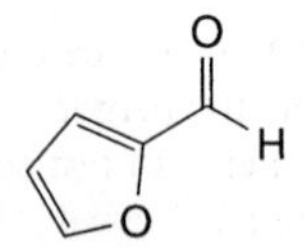

N. furane-2-carbaldehyde (furfural),

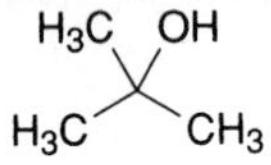

O. 2-methylpropan-2-ol (1,1-dimethylethyl alcohol),

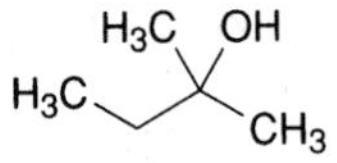

P. 2-methylbutan-2-ol,

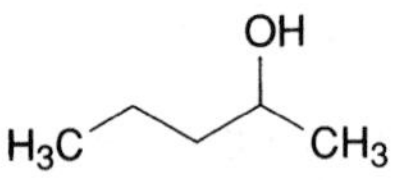

Q. pentan-2-ol,

R. $CH_3$-$(CH_2)_4$-OH: pentanol,

S. $CH_3$-$(CH_2)_5$-OH: hexanol,

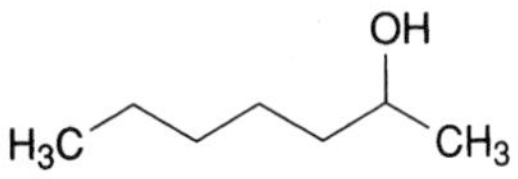

T. heptan-2-ol,

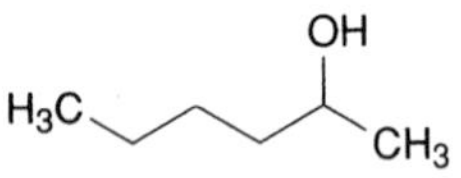

U. hexan-2-ol,

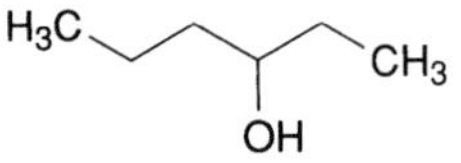

V. hexan-3-ol.

—————————————————————————————— *Ph Eur*

# Ethanol (96 per cent)

Alcohol (96 per cent)

*(Ph Eur monograph 1317)*

*Ph Eur* _____

## DEFINITION

### Content:

— ethanol ($C_2H_6O$; $M_r$ 46.07): 95.1 per cent *V/V*
 (92.6 per cent *m/m*) to 96.9 per cent *V/V* (95.2 per cent
 *m/m*) at 20 °C, calculated from the relative density using
 the alcoholimetric tables (5.5),

— water.

## CHARACTERS

### Appearance

Colourless, clear, volatile, flammable liquid, hygroscopic.

### Solubility

Miscible with water and with methylene chloride.

It burns with a blue, smokeless flame.

bp: about 78 °C.

## IDENTIFICATION

*First identification   A, B.*

*Second identification   A, C, D.*

A. It complies with the test for relative density (see Tests).

B. Infrared absorption spectrophotometry (*2.2.24*).

*Comparison   Ph. Eur. reference spectrum ethanol (96 per cent).*

C. Mix 0.1 ml with 1 ml of a 10 g/l solution of *potassium permanganate R* and 0.2 ml of *dilute sulphuric acid R* in a test-tube. Cover immediately with a filter paper moistened with a freshly prepared solution containing 0.1 g of *sodium nitroprusside R* and 0.5 g of *piperazine hydrate R* in 5 ml of *water R*. After a few minutes, an intense blue colour appears on the paper and becomes paler after 10-15 min.

D. To 0.5 ml add 5 ml of *water R*, 2 ml of *dilute sodium hydroxide solution R*, then slowly add 2 ml of *0.05 M iodine*. A yellow precipitate is formed within 30 min.

## TESTS

### Appearance

It is clear (*2.2.1*) and colourless (*2.2.2, Method II*) when compared with *water R*. Dilute 1.0 ml to 20 ml with *water R*. After standing for 5 min, the dilution remains clear (*2.2.1*) when compared with *water R*.

### Acidity or alkalinity

To 20 ml add 20 ml of *carbon dioxide-free water R* and 0.1 ml of *phenolphthalein solution R*. The solution is colourless. Add 1.0 ml of *0.01 M sodium hydroxide*. The solution is pink (30 ppm, expressed as acetic acid).

### Relative density (*2.2.5*)

0.805 to 0.812.

### Absorbance (*2.2.25*)

Maximum 0.40 at 240 nm, 0.30 between 250 nm and 260 nm and 0.10 between 270 nm and 340 nm. The absorption curve is smooth.

Examine between 235 nm and 340 nm, in a 5 cm cell using *water R* as the compensation liquid.

### Volatile impurities

Gas chromatography (*2.2.28*).

*Test solution (a)*   The substance to be examined.

*Test solution (b)*   Add 150 µl of *4-methylpentan-2-ol R* to 500.0 ml of the substance to be examined.

*Reference solution (a)*   Dilute 100 µl of *anhydrous methanol R* to 50.0 ml with the substance to be examined. Dilute 5.0 ml of the solution to 50.0 ml with the substance to be examined.

*Reference solution (b)*   Dilute 50 µl of *anhydrous methanol R* and 50 µl of *acetaldehyde R* to 50.0 ml with the substance to be examined. Dilute 100 µl of the solution to 10.0 ml with the substance to be examined.

*Reference solution (c)*   Dilute 150 µl of *acetal R* to 50.0 ml with the substance to be examined. Dilute 100 µl of the solution to 10.0 ml with the substance to be examined.

*Reference solution (d)*   Dilute 100 µl of *benzene R* to 100.0 ml with the substance to be examined. Dilute 100 µl of the solution to 50.0 ml with the substance to be examined.

*Column:*

— *material*: fused silica,

— *size*: l = 30 m, Ø = 0.32 mm,

— *stationary phase*:
*poly[(cyanopropyl)(phenyl)][dimethyl]siloxane R* (film thickness 1.8 µm).

*Carrier gas* *helium for chromatography R.*

*Linear velocity* 35 cm/s.

*Split ratio* 1:20.

*Temperature:*

|  | Time (min) | Temperature (°C) |
|---|---|---|
| Column | 0 - 12 | 40 |
|  | 12 - 32 | 40 → 240 |
|  | 32 - 42 | 240 |
| Injection port |  | 200 |
| Detector |  | 280 |

*Detection* Flame ionisation.

*Injection* 1 µl.

*System suitability* Reference solution (b):
— *resolution*: minimum 1.5 between the first peak (acetaldehyde) and the second peak (methanol).

*Limits:*
— *methanol* in the chromatogram obtained with test solution (a): not more than half the area of the corresponding peak in the chromatogram obtained with reference solution (a) (200 ppm *V/V*),
— *acetaldehyde + acetal*: maximum 10 ppm *V/V*, expressed as acetaldehyde.

Calculate the sum of the contents of acetaldehyde and acetal in parts per million (V/V) using the following expression:

$$\frac{10 \times A_E}{A_T - A_E} + \frac{30 \times C_E}{C_T - C_E}$$

$A_E$ = area of the acetaldehyde peak in the chromatogram obtained with test solution (a),

$A_T$ = area of the acetaldehyde peak in the chromatogram obtained with reference solution (b),

$C_E$ = area of the acetal peak in the chromatogram obtained with test solution (a),

$C_T$ = area of the acetal peak in the chromatogram obtained with reference solution (c).

— *benzene*: maximum 2 ppm *V/V*.

Calculate the content of benzene in parts per million (V/V) using the following expression:

$$\frac{2B_E}{B_T - B_E}$$

$B_E$ = area of the benzene peak in the chromatogram obtained with the test solution (a),

$B_T$ = area of the benzene peak in the chromatogram obtained with reference solution (d).

If necessary, the identity of benzene can be confirmed using another suitable chromatographic system (stationary phase with a different polarity).
— *total of other impurities* in the chromatogram obtained with test solution (b): not more than the area of the peak due to 4-methylpentan-2-ol in the chromatogram obtained with test solution (b) (300 ppm),
— *disregard limit*: 0.03 times the area of the peak corresponding to 4-methylpentan-2-ol in the chromatogram obtained with test solution (b) (9 ppm).

**Residue on evaporation**

Maximum 25 ppm *m/V*.

Evaporate 100 ml to dryness on a water-bath and dry at 100-105 °C for 1 h. The residue weighs a maximum of 2.5 mg.

**STORAGE**

Protected from light.

**IMPURITIES**

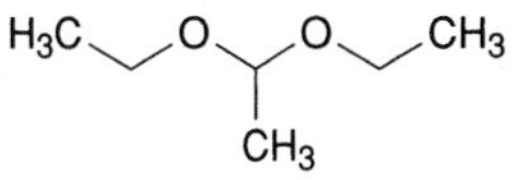

A. 1,1-diethoxyethane (acetal),

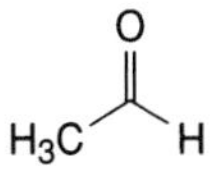

B. acetaldehyde,

C. acetone,

D. benzene,

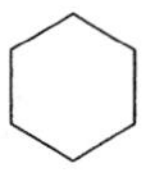

E. cyclohexane,

F. $CH_3$-OH: methanol,

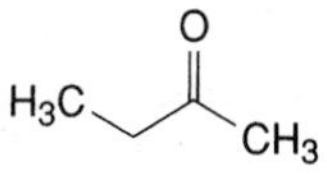

G. butan-2-one (methyl ethyl ketone),

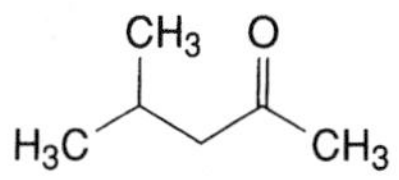

H. 4-methylpentan-2-one (methyl isobutyl ketone),

I. $CH_3$-$(CH_2)_2$-OH: propanol,

J. propan-2-ol (isopropyl alcohol),

K. $CH_3$-$(CH_2)_3$-OH: butanol,

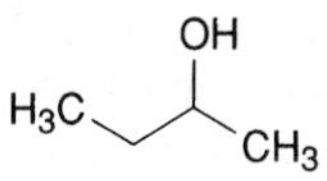

L. butan-2-ol,

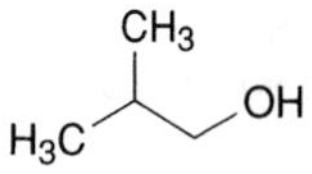

M. 2-methylpropanol (isobutanol),

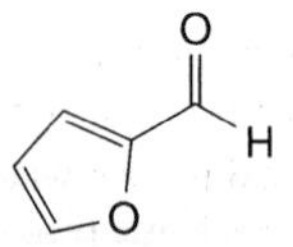

N. furane-2-carbaldehyde (furfural),

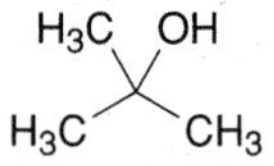

O. 2-methylpropan-2-ol (1,1-dimethylethyl alcohol),

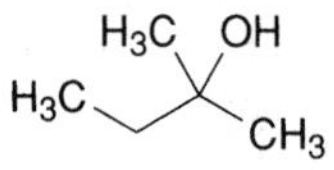

P. 2-methylbutan-2-ol,

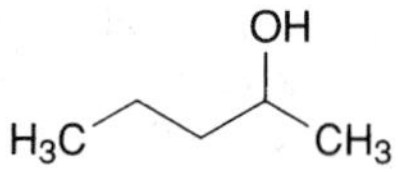

Q. pentan-2-ol,
R. $CH_3$-$(CH_2)_4$-OH: pentanol,
S. $CH_3$-$(CH_2)_5$-OH: hexanol,

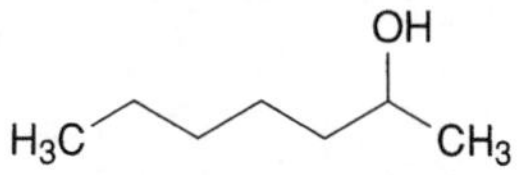

T. heptan-2-ol,

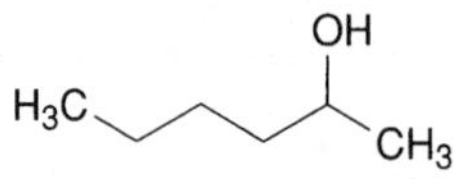

U. hexan-2-ol,

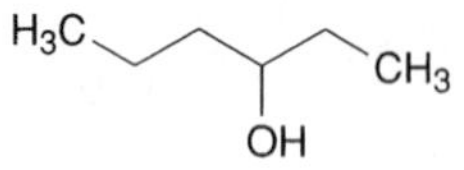

V. hexan-3-ol.

_____ _Ph Eur_

# Dilute Ethanols

## DEFINITION
The official Dilute Ethanols contain 90, 80, 70, 60, 50, 45, 25 and 20% v/v respectively of ethanol. They may be prepared as described below, the final adjustment of volume being made at the same temperature, 20°, as that at which the Ethanol (96 per cent) is measured.

NOTE _On mixing ethanol and water, contraction of volume and rise of temperature occur._

## TESTS
**Acidity or alkalinity; Appearance; Volatile impurities; Residue on evaporation**
Comply with the requirements stated under Ethanol (96 per cent).

## ETHANOL (90 PER CENT)
Alcohol (90 per cent); Rectified Spirit

Dilute 934 ml of Ethanol (96 per cent) to 1000 ml with Purified Water.

**Content of ethanol**
89.6 to 90.5% v/v.

**Apparent density**
826.4 to 829.4 kg m$^{-3}$, Appendix V G.

## ETHANOL (80 PER CENT)
Alcohol (80 per cent)

Dilute 831 ml of Ethanol (96 per cent) to 1000 ml with Purified Water.

**Content of ethanol**
79.5 to 80.3% v/v.

**Apparent density**
857.4 to 859.6 kg m$^{-3}$, Appendix V G.

## ETHANOL (70 PER CENT)
Alcohol (70 per cent)

Dilute 727 ml of Ethanol (96 per cent) to 1000 ml with Purified Water.

**Content of ethanol**
69.5 to 70.4% v/v.

**Apparent density**
883.5 to 885.8 kg m$^{-3}$, Appendix V G.

## ETHANOL (60 PER CENT)
Alcohol (60 per cent)

Dilute 623 ml of Ethanol (96 per cent) to 1000 ml with Purified Water.

**Content of ethanol**
59.7 to 60.2% v/v.

**Apparent density**
907.6 to 908.7 kg m$^{-3}$, Appendix V G.

## ETHANOL (50 PER CENT)
Alcohol (50 per cent)

Dilute 519 ml of Ethanol (96 per cent) to 1000 ml with Purified Water.

**Content of ethanol**
49.6 to 50.2% v/v.

**Apparent density**
928.6 to 929.8 kg m$^{-3}$, Appendix V G.

## ETHANOL (45 PER CENT)
Alcohol (45 per cent)

Dilute 468 ml of Ethanol (96 per cent) to 1000 ml with Purified Water.

**Content of ethanol**
44.7 to 45.3% v/v.

**Apparent density**
938.0 to 939.0 kg m$^{-3}$, Appendix V G.

## ETHANOL (25 PER CENT)
Alcohol (25 per cent)

Dilute 259 ml of Ethanol (96 per cent) to 1000 ml with Purified Water.

**Content of ethanol**
24.6 to 25.4% v/v.

**Apparent density**
966.6 to 967.5 kg m$^{-3}$, Appendix V G.

## ETHANOL (20 PER CENT)
Alcohol (20 per cent)

Dilute 207 ml of Ethanol (96 per cent) to 1000 ml with Purified Water.

**Content of ethanol**
19.5 to 20.5% v/v.

**Apparent density**
972.0 to 973.1 kg m⁻³, Appendix V G.

# Ethanolamine

Monoethanolamine

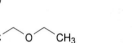

C₂H₇NO         61.08         *141-43-5*

**Action and use**
Sclerosant.

**Preparation**
Ethanolamine Oleate Injection

## DEFINITION
Ethanolamine is 2-aminoethanol. It contains not less than 98.0% and not more than 100.5% of C₂H₇NO.

## CHARACTERISTICS
A clear, colourless or pale yellow liquid.

Miscible with *water* and with *ethanol (96%)*; slightly soluble in *ether*.

## IDENTIFICATION
A. To 0.1 ml add 0.3 g of *picric acid* and 1 ml of *water* and evaporate to dryness on a water bath. The *melting point* of the residue, after recrystallisation from *ethanol (96%)* and drying at 105°, is about 160°, Appendix V A.

B. When freshly distilled the second half of the distillate freezes at about 10°.

C. It is alkaline to *litmus solution*.

## TESTS
**Refractive index**
1.453 to 1.459, Appendix V E.

**Weight per ml**
1.014 to 1.023 g, Appendix V G.

**Related substances**
Prepare a 0.1% w/v solution of *3-aminopropan-1-ol* (internal standard) in *dichloromethane* (solution A). Carry out the method for *gas chromatography*, Appendix III B, using the following solutions prepared in suitable sealed reaction vials. For solution (1) prepare a solution containing 0.05% w/v of *ethanolamine* and 0.1% w/v each of *diethanolamine* and *triethanolamine* in solution A. To 0.5 ml of this solution add 0.5 ml of *trifluoroacetic anhydride*, mix and allow to stand for 10 minutes. For solution (2) prepare a 10% w/v solution of the substance being examined in solution A. To 0.5 ml of this solution add 0.5 ml of *trifluoroacetic anhydride*, mix and allow to stand for 10 minutes.

The chromatographic procedure may be carried out using (a) a fused silica capillary column (25 m × 0.22 mm) bonded with a 0.25-μm layer of dimethylpolysiloxane, (b) *helium* as the carrier gas at a flow rate of 1.0 ml per minute with a flow rate of the make up gas of 20 ml per minute and (c) a split injection system with a split ratio of 40 to 1 maintained at 240° and a detector temperature of 250°. Maintain the temperature of the column at 80° for

2 minutes, then increase to 200° at a rate of 8° per minute and maintain this temperature for 10 minutes.

In the chromatogram obtained with solution (1) the peaks eluting after the solvent peak in order of emergence are due to (a) ethanolamine, (b) 3-aminopropan-1-ol, (c) diethanolamine and (d) triethanolamine. In the chromatogram obtained with solution (2) calculate the content of diethanolamine and triethanolamine by reference to the corresponding peaks in the chromatogram obtained with solution (1). Calculate the content of any other impurity by reference to the peak due to ethanolamine in the chromatogram obtained with solution (1). The content of diethanolamine and triethanolamine is not more than 1.0% w/w of each, the content of any other impurity is not more than 0.5% w/w and the sum of the contents of all the impurities is not more than 2.0% w/w.

## ASSAY
Dissolve 2.5 g in 50 ml of 1M *hydrochloric acid VS* and titrate the excess of acid with 1M *sodium hydroxide VS* using *methyl red solution* as indicator. Each ml of 1M *hydrochloric acid VS* is equivalent to 61.08 mg of C₂H₇NO.

# Ether

*(Ph Eur monograph 0650)*

H₃C   O   CH₃

C₄H₁₀O         74.1         *60-29-7*

*Ph Eur*

## DEFINITION
Diethyl ether.

It may contain a suitable non-volatile antioxidant at a suitable concentration.

## CHARACTERS
**Appearance**
Clear, colourless liquid, volatile.

**Solubility**
Soluble in water, miscible with ethanol (96 per cent), with methylene chloride and with fatty oils.

It is highly flammable.

## IDENTIFICATION
A. Relative density (see Tests).

B. Distillation range (see Tests).

## TESTS
**Acidity**
To 20 ml of *ethanol (96 per cent) R* add 0.25 ml of *bromothymol blue solution R1* and, dropwise, *0.02 M sodium hydroxide* until a blue colour persists for 30 s. Add 25 ml of the substance to be examined, shake and add, dropwise, *0.02 M sodium hydroxide* until the blue colour reappears and persists for 30 s. Not more than 0.4 ml of *0.02 M sodium hydroxide* is required.

**Relative density** *(2.2.5)*
0.714 to 0.716.

**Distillation range** *(2.2.11)*
*Do not distil if the substance to be examined does not comply with the test for peroxides.* It distils completely between 34.0 °C and 35.0 °C. Carry out the test using a suitable heating device

and taking care to avoid directly heating the flask above the level of the liquid.

### Aldehydes

To 10.0 ml in a ground-glass-stoppered cylinder add 1 ml of *alkaline potassium tetraiodomercurate solution R* and shake for 10 s. Allow to stand for 5 min, protected from light. The lower layer may show a yellow or reddish-brown opalescence but not a grey or black opalescence.

### Peroxides

Place 8 ml of *potassium iodide and starch solution R* in a 12 ml ground-glass-stoppered cylinder about 15 mm in diameter. Fill completely with the substance to be examined, mix and allow to stand protected from light for 5 min. No colour develops.

### Non-volatile matter

Maximum 20 mg/l.

*After ensuring that the substance to be examined complies with the test for peroxides*, evaporate 50 ml to dryness on a water-bath and dry the residue in an oven at 100-105 °C. The residue weighs a maximum of 1 mg.

### Substances with a foreign odour

Moisten a disc of filter paper 80 mm in diameter with 5 ml of the substance to be examined and allow to evaporate. No foreign odour is perceptible immediately after the evaporation.

### Water (*2.5.12*)

Maximum 2 g/l, determined on 20 ml.

### STORAGE

In an airtight container, protected from light, at a temperature of 8 °C to 15 °C.

———————————————— *Ph Eur*

# Anaesthetic Ether

*(Ph Eur monograph 0367)*

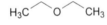

$H_3C$ — O — $CH_3$

| $C_4H_{10}O$ | 74.1 | *60-29-7* |

*Ph Eur* ————————————————

### DEFINITION

Diethyl ether.

It may contain a suitable non-volatile antioxidant at an appropriate concentration.

### CHARACTERS

**Appearance**

Clear, colourless liquid, volatile, very mobile.

**Solubility**

Soluble in 15 parts of water, miscible with ethanol (96 per cent) and with fatty oils.

It is highly flammable.

### IDENTIFICATION

A. Relative density (see Tests).

B. Distillation range (see Tests).

### TESTS

**Acidity**

To 20 ml of *ethanol (96 per cent) R* add 0.25 ml of *bromothymol blue solution R1* and, dropwise, *0.02 M sodium hydroxide* until a blue colour persists for 30 s. Add 25 ml

of the substance to be examined, shake and add, dropwise, *0.02 M sodium hydroxide* until the blue colour reappears and persists for 30 s. Not more than 0.4 ml of *0.02 M sodium hydroxide* is required.

### Relative density (*2.2.5*)

0.714 to 0.716.

### Distillation range (*2.2.11*)

*Do not distil if the substance to be examined does not comply with the test for peroxides.* It distils completely between 34.0 °C and 35.0 °C. Carry out the test using a suitable heating device and taking care to avoid directly heating the flask above the level of the liquid.

### Acetone and aldehydes

To 10.0 ml in a ground-glass-stoppered cylinder add 1 ml of *alkaline potassium tetra-iodomercurate solution R* and shake for 10 s. Allow to stand for 5 min, protected from light. The lower layer shows only a slight opalescence.

If the substance to be examined does not comply with the test, distil 40 ml, *after ensuring that the substance to be examined complies with the test for peroxides*, until only 5 ml remains. Collect the distillate in a receiver cooled in a bath of iced water and repeat the test described above using 10.0 ml of the distillate.

### Peroxides

Place 8 ml of *potassium iodide and starch solution R* in a 12 ml ground-glass-stoppered cylinder about 15 mm in diameter. Fill completely with the substance to be examined, shake vigorously and allow to stand protected from light for 30 min. No colour develops.

### Non-volatile matter

Maximum 20 mg/l.

*After ensuring that the substance to be examined complies with the test for peroxides*, evaporate 50 ml to dryness on a water-bath and dry the residue in an oven at 100-105 °C. The residue weighs a maximum of 1 mg.

### Substances with a foreign odour

Moisten a disc of filter paper 80 mm in diameter with 5 ml of the substance to be examined and allow to evaporate. No foreign odour is perceptible immediately after the evaporation.

### Water (*2.5.12*)

Maximum 2 g/l, determined on 20 ml.

### STORAGE

In an airtight container, protected from light, at a temperature of 8 °C to 15 °C. The contents of a partly filled container may deteriorate rapidly.

———————————————— *Ph Eur*

# Ethinylestradiol

*(Ph Eur monograph 0140)*

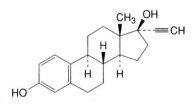

C₂₀H₂₄O₂      296.4      57-63-6

**Action and use**
Estrogen.

**Preparations**
Ethinylestradiol Tablets
Levonorgestrel and Ethinylestradiol Tablets

*Ph Eur*

## DEFINITION
19-Nor-17α-pregna-1,3,5(10)-trien-20-yne-3,17-diol.

## Content
97.0 per cent to 102.0 per cent (dried substance).

## CHARACTERS
**Appearance**
White or slightly yellowish-white, crystalline powder.

**Solubility**
Practically insoluble in water, freely soluble in alcohol. It dissolves in dilute alkaline solutions.

## IDENTIFICATION
A. Infrared absorption spectrophotometry *(2.2.24)*.

*Comparison* ethinylestradiol CRS.

If the spectra obtained in the solid state show differences, dissolve the substance to be examined and the reference substance in *methanol R*, evaporate to dryness and record new spectra using the residues.

B. Thin-layer chromatography *(2.2.27)*.

*Test solution* Dissolve 25 mg of the substance to be examined in a mixture of 1 volume of *methanol R* and 9 volumes of *methylene chloride R* and dilute to 25 ml with the same mixture of solvents.

*Reference solution* Dissolve 25 mg of *ethinylestradiol CRS* in a mixture of 1 volume of *methanol R* and 9 volumes of *methylene chloride R* and dilute to 25 ml with the same mixture of solvents.

*Plate* TLC silica gel G plate R.

*Mobile phase* alcohol R, toluene R (10:90 V/V).

*Application* 5 µl.

*Development* Over a path of 15 cm.

*Drying* In air until the solvent has evaporated.

*Detection* Heat at 110 °C for 10 min, spray the hot plate with *alcoholic solution of sulphuric acid R* and heat again at 110 °C for 10 min. Examine in daylight and in ultraviolet light at 365 nm.

*Results* The principal spot in the chromatogram obtained with the test solution is similar in position, colour, fluorescence and size to the principal spot in the chromatogram obtained with the reference solution.

## TESTS
**Specific optical rotation** *(2.2.7)*
− 27 to − 30 (dried substance).

Dissolve 1.25 g in *pyridine R* and dilute to 25.0 ml with the same solvent.

**Related substances**
Liquid chromatography *(2.2.29)*.

*Test solution* Dissolve 0.10 g of the substance to be examined in the mobile phase and dilute to 100.0 ml with the mobile phase.

*Reference solution (a)* Dissolve 10 mg of *estradiol R* in the mobile phase, add 10.0 ml of the test solution and dilute to 50.0 ml with the mobile phase. Dilute 1.0 ml of this solution to 10.0 ml with the mobile phase.

*Reference solution (b)* Dilute 10.0 ml of the test solution to 50.0 ml with the mobile phase. Dilute 1.0 ml of this solution to 20.0 ml with the mobile phase.

*Column:*
— *size: l* = 0.15 m, Ø = 4.6 mm,
— *stationary phase*: octadecylsilyl silica gel for chromatography R (5 µm).

*Mobile phase* acetonitrile R, water R (45:55 V/V).

*Flow rate* 1 ml/min.

*Detection* Spectrophotometer at 280 nm.

*Injection* 20 µl.

*Run time* 2.5 times the retention time of ethinylestradiol.

*Relative retention* With reference to ethinylestradiol (retention time = about 4.6 min): impurity D = about 0.76, impurity B = about 0.94.

*System suitability* Reference solution (a):
— *resolution*: minimum 3.5 between the peaks due to impurity D and ethinylestradiol.

*Limits:*
— *impurity B*: not more than the area of the principal peak in the chromatogram obtained with reference solution (b) (1.0 per cent),
— *any other impurity*: not more than 0.25 times the area of the principal peak in the chromatogram obtained with reference solution (b) (0.25 per cent),
— *total* of other impurities: not more than half the area of the principal peak in the chromatogram obtained with reference solution (b) (0.5 per cent)
— *disregard limit*: 0.05 times the area of the principal peak in the chromatogram obtained with reference solution (b) (0.05 per cent)

**Loss on drying** *(2.2.32)*
Maximum 1.0 per cent, determined on 0.500 g by drying in an oven at 105 °C for 3 h.

## ASSAY
Dissolve 0.200 g in 40 ml of *tetrahydrofuran R* and add 5 ml of a 100 g/l solution of *silver nitrate R*. Titrate with *0.1 M sodium hydroxide*, determining the end-point potentiometrically *(2.2.20)*. Carry out a blank titration.

1 ml of *0.1 M sodium hydroxide* is equivalent to 29.64 mg of C₂₀H₂₄O₂.

## STORAGE
Protected from light.

## IMPURITIES

A. R1 = OH, R2 = C≡CH: 19-norpregna-1,3,5(10)-trien-20-yne-3,17-diol (17β-ethinylestradiol),

C. R1 + R2 = O: 3-hydroxyestra-1,3,5(10)-trien-17-one (estrone),

D. R1 = H, R2 = OH: estradiol,

B. 19-nor-17α-pregna-1,3,5(10),9(11)-tetraen-20-yne-3,17-diol.

_____ *Ph Eur*

# Ethionamide

*(Ph Eur monograph 0141)*

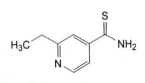

C$_8$H$_{10}$N$_2$S      166.2      *536-33-4*

## Action and use

Antituberculosis drug.

*Ph Eur* _____

## DEFINITION

Ethionamide contains not less than 98.5 per cent and not more than the equivalent of 101.0 per cent of 2-ethylpyridine-4-carbothioamide, calculated with reference to the dried substance.

## CHARACTERS

A yellow, crystalline powder or small, yellow crystals, practically insoluble in water, soluble in methanol, sparingly soluble in alcohol.

## IDENTIFICATION

*First identification*  A, C.

*Second identification*  A, B, D.

A. Melting point *(2.2.14)* 158 °C to 164 °C.

B. Dissolve 10.0 mg in *methanol R* and dilute to 100.0 ml with the same solvent. Dilute 10.0 ml of the solution to 100.0 ml with *methanol R*. Examined between 230 nm and 350 nm *(2.2.25)*, the solution shows an absorption maximum at 290 nm. The specific absorbance at the maximum is 380 to 440.

C. Examine by infrared absorption spectrophotometry *(2.2.24)*, comparing with the spectrum obtained with *ethionamide CRS*.

D. Dissolve about 10 mg in 5 ml of *methanol R*. Add 5 ml of *silver nitrate solution R2*. A dark-brown precipitate is formed.

## TESTS

### Appearance of solution

Dissolve 0.5 g in 10 ml of *methanol R*, heating to about 50 °C. Allow to cool to room temperature. The solution is not more opalescent than reference suspension II *(2.2.1)*.

### Acidity

Dissolve 2.0 g in 20 ml of *methanol R*, heating to about 50 °C, and add 20 ml of *water R*. Cool slightly while shaking until crystallisation begins and then allow to cool to room temperature. Add 60 ml of *water R* and 0.2 ml of *cresol red solution R*. Not more than 0.2 ml of *0.1 M sodium hydroxide* is required to change the colour of the indicator to red.

### Related substances

Examine by thin-layer chromatography *(2.2.27)*, using *silica gel GF$_{254}$ R* as the coating substance.

*Test solution*  Dissolve 0.2 g of the substance to be examined in *acetone R* and dilute to 10 ml with the same solvent.

*Reference solution (a)*  Dilute 0.5 ml of the test solution to 100 ml with *acetone R*.

*Reference solution (b)*  Dilute 0.2 ml of the test solution to 100 ml with *acetone R*.

Apply separately to the plate 10 μl of each solution. Develop over a path of 15 cm using a mixture of 10 volumes of *methanol R* and 90 volumes of *chloroform R*. Allow the plate to dry in air. Examine in ultraviolet light at 254 nm. Any spot in the chromatogram obtained with the test solution, apart from the principal spot, is not more intense than the spot in the chromatogram obtained with reference solution (a) (0.5 per cent) and at most 1 such spot is more intense than the spot in the chromatogram obtained with reference solution (b) (0.2 per cent).

### Heavy metals *(2.4.8)*

1.0 g complies with limit test D for heavy metals (20 ppm). Prepare the standard using 2 ml of *lead standard solution (10 ppm Pb) R*.

### Loss on drying *(2.2.32)*

Not more than 0.5 per cent, determined on 1.00 g by drying in an oven at 105 °C for 3 h.

### Sulphated ash *(2.4.14)*

Not more than 0.1 per cent, determined on 1.0 g.

## ASSAY

Dissolve 0.150 g in 50 ml of *anhydrous acetic acid R*. Titrate with *0.1 M perchloric acid*, determining the end-point potentiometrically *(2.2.20)*.

1 ml of *0.1 M perchloric acid* is equivalent to 16.62 mg of C$_8$H$_{10}$N$_2$S.

_____ *Ph Eur*

# Ethosuximide

*(Ph Eur monograph 0764)*

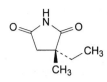

C₇H₁₁NO₂      141.2      77-67-8

$C_7H_{11}NO_2$    141.2    77-67-8

**Action and use**

Antiepileptic.

**Preparations**

Ethosuximide Capsules

Ethosuximide Oral Solution

*Ph Eur* _____

## DEFINITION

(*RS*)-3-Ethyl-3-methylpyrrolidine-2,5-dione.

**Content**

99.0 per cent to 101.0 per cent (anhydrous substance).

## CHARACTERS

**Appearance**

White or almost white, powder or waxy solid.

**Solubility**

Freely soluble in water, very soluble in ethanol (96 per cent) and in methylene chloride.

It shows polymorphism (*5.9*).

## IDENTIFICATION

*First identification* A, C.

*Second identification* A, B, D, E.

A. Melting point (*2.2.14*) 45 °C to 50 °C.

B. Dissolve 50.0 mg in *ethanol (96 per cent) R* and dilute to 50.0 ml with the same solvent. Examined between 230 nm and 300 nm (*2.2.25*), the solution shows an absorption maximum at 248 nm. The specific absorbance at the absorption maximum is 8 to 9.

C. Infrared absorption spectrophotometry (*2.2.24*).

*Preparation* Discs of *potassium bromide R*.

*Comparison* ethosuximide CRS.

If the spectra obtained in the solid state show differences, dissolve the substance to be examined and the reference substance separately in *methylene chloride R*, evaporate to dryness and record new spectra using the residues.

D. Dissolve 0.1 g in 3 ml of *methanol R*. Add 0.05 ml of a 100 g/l solution of *cobalt chloride R* and 0.05 ml of a 100 g/l solution of *calcium chloride R* and add 0.1 ml of *dilute sodium hydroxide solution R*. A purple colour develops and no precipitate is formed.

E. To about 10 mg add 10 mg of *resorcinol R* and 0.2 ml of *sulphuric acid R*. Heat at 140 °C for 5 min and cool. Add 5 ml of *water R* and 2 ml of *concentrated ammonia R1*. A brown colour is produced. Add about 100 ml of *water R*. A green fluorescence is produced.

## TESTS

**Solution S**

Dissolve 2.5 g in water R and dilute to 25 ml with the same solvent.

**Appearance of solution**

Solution S is clear (*2.2.1*) and colourless (*2.2.2, Method II*).

**Cyanide**

Liquid chromatography (*2.2.29*).

*Test solution* Dissolve 0.50 g of the substance to be examined in *water R* and dilute to 10.0 ml with the same solvent.

*Reference solution (a)* Dissolve 0.125 g of *potassium cyanide R* in *water R* and dilute to 50.0 ml with the same solvent. Dilute 1.0 ml of the solution to 100.0 ml with *water R*. Dilute 0.5 ml of this solution to 10.0 ml with *water R*.

*Reference solution (b)* Dissolve 0.50 g of the substance to be examined in *water R*, add 0.5 ml of reference solution (a) and dilute to 10.0 ml with *water R*.

*Column:*

— *size*: *l* = 0.075 m, Ø = 7.5 mm,

— *stationary phase*: *spherical weak anion exchange resin R* (10 μm).

*Mobile phase* Dissolve 2.1 g of *lithium hydroxide R* and 85 mg of *sodium edetate R* in *water for chromatography R* and dilute to 1000.0 ml with the same solvent.

*Flow rate* 2.0 ml/min.

*Detection* Electrochemical detector (direct amperometry) with a silver working electrode, a silver-silver chloride reference electrode, held at + 0.05 V oxidation potential, and a detector sensitivity of 20 nA full scale.

*Injection* 20 μl of the test solution and reference solution (b).

*System suitability* Reference solution (b):

— *peak-to-valley ratio*: minimum 3, where $H_p$ = height above the baseline of the peak due to cyanide and $H_v$ = height above the baseline of the lowest point of the curve separating this peak from the peak due to ethosuximide.

*Limit:*

— *cyanide*: not more than 0.5 times the height of the corresponding peak in the chromatogram obtained with reference solution (b) (0.5 ppm).

**Related substances**

Gas chromatography (*2.2.28*).

*Internal standard solution* Dissolve 20 mg of *myristyl alcohol R* in *anhydrous ethanol R* and dilute to 10.0 ml with the same solvent.

*Test solution* Dissolve 1.00 g of the substance to be examined in *anhydrous ethanol R* add 1.0 ml of the internal standard solution and dilute to 20.0 ml with *anhydrous ethanol R*.

*Reference solution (a)* Dissolve 10.0 mg of *ethosuximide impurity A CRS* in *anhydrous ethanol R* and dilute to 5.0 ml with the same solvent. To 0.5 ml of the solution add 1.0 ml of the internal standard solution and dilute to 20.0 ml with *anhydrous ethanol R*.

*Reference solution (b)* Dissolve 0.500 g of the substance to be examined in *anhydrous ethanol R* and dilute to 10.0 ml with the same solvent. Dilute 1.0 ml of the solution to 50.0 ml with *anhydrous ethanol R*. To 2.0 ml of this solution add 1.0 ml of the internal standard solution and dilute to 20.0 ml with *anhydrous ethanol R*.

*Column:*

— *material*: fused silica,

— *size*: *l* = 30 m, Ø = 0.25 mm,

— *stationary phase*: *poly(cyanopropyl)(phenylmethyl) siloxane R* (film thickness 0.25 μm).

*Carrier gas* helium for chromatography R.

*Flow rate* 1 ml/min.

*Split ratio* 1:67.

*Temperature:*

— *column*: 175 °C,

— *injection port and detector*: 240 °C.

*Detection* Flame ionisation.

*Injection* 1 µl.

*Run time* 1.5 times the retention time of ethosuximide.

*Relative retention* With reference to the internal standard (retention time = about 8 min): impurity A = about 0.7; ethosuximide = about 1.1.

*System suitability* Reference solution (b):

— *resolution*: minimum 5 between the peaks due to the internal standard and ethosuximide.

*Limits:*

— *impurity A*: calculate the ratio ($R$) of the area of the peak due to impurity A to the area of the peak due to the internal standard from the chromatogram obtained with reference solution (a); from the chromatogram obtained with the test solution, calculate the ratio of the area of any peak due to impurity A to the area of the peak due to the internal standard: this ratio is not greater than $R$ (0.1 per cent);

— *any other impurity*: calculate the ratio ($R$) of half the area of the peak due to ethosuximide to the area of the peak due to the internal standard from the chromatogram obtained with reference solution (b); from the chromatogram obtained with the test solution, calculate the ratio of the area of any peak, apart from the principal peak and the peaks due to impurity A and to the internal standard, to the area of the peak due to the internal standard: this ratio is not greater than $R$ (0.1 per cent);

— *total*: calculate the ratio ($R$) of the area of the peak due to ethosuximide to the area of the peak due to the internal standard from the chromatogram obtained with reference solution (b); from the chromatogram obtained with the test solution, calculate the ratio of the sum of the areas of any peaks, apart from the principal peak and the peak due to the internal standard, to the area of the peak due to the internal standard: this ratio is not greater than $R$ (0.2 per cent);

— *disregard limit*: calculate the ratio ($R$) of 0.25 times the area of the peak due to impurity A to the area of the peak due to the internal standard from the chromatogram obtained with reference solution (a); from the chromatogram obtained with the test solution, calculate the ratio of the area of any peak, apart from the principal peak and the peak due to the internal standard, to the area of the peak due to the internal standard: disregard any peak which has a ratio less than $R$ (0.025 per cent).

**Heavy metals** (*2.4.8*)

Maximum 10 ppm.

12 ml of solution S complies with test A. Prepare the reference solution using *lead standard solution (1 ppm Pb) R*.

**Water** (*2.5.12*)

Maximum 0.5 per cent, determined on 1.00 g.

**Sulphated ash** (*2.4.14*)

Maximum 0.1 per cent, determined on 1.0 g.

**ASSAY**

Dissolve 0.120 g in 20 ml of *dimethylformamide R* and carry out a potentiometric titration (*2.2.20*) using *0.1 M tetrabutylammonium hydroxide*. Protect the solution from atmospheric carbon dioxide throughout the titration. Carry out a blank titration.

1 ml of *0.1 M tetrabutylammonium hydroxide* is equivalent to 14.12 mg of $C_7H_{11}NO_2$.

**STORAGE**

Protected from light.

**IMPURITIES**

*Specified impurities* A.

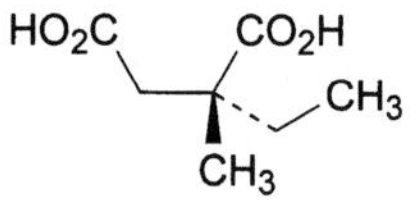

A. (2*RS*)-2-ethyl-2-methylbutanedioic acid.

_____ *Ph Eur*

# Ethyl Acetate

*(Ph Eur monograph 0899)*

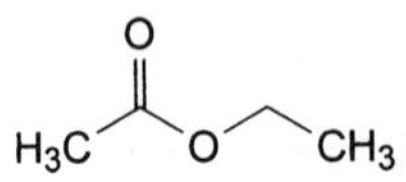

$C_4H_8O_2$        88.1        *141-78-6*

**Action and use**

Excipient.

*Ph Eur* _____

**DEFINITION**

Ethyl ethanoate.

**CHARACTERS**

**Appearance**

Clear, colourless, volatile liquid.

**Solubility**

Soluble in water, miscible with acetone, with ethanol (96 per cent) and with methylene chloride.

**IDENTIFICATION**

*First identification* B.

*Second identification* A, C, D.

A. Boiling point (*2.2.12*) 76 °C to 78 °C.

B. Infrared absorption spectrophotometry (*2.2.24*).

*Comparison* Ph. Eur. reference spectrum of ethyl acetate.

C. It gives the reaction of acetyl (*2.3.1*).

D. It gives the reaction of esters (*2.3.1*).

**TESTS**

**Appearance of solution**

The solution is clear (*2.2.1*) and colourless (*2.2.2, Method II*).

Mix 1 ml of the substance to be examined and 15 ml of *water R*.

**Acidity**

To 10 ml of *ethanol (96 per cent) R* add 0.1 ml of *phenolphthalein solution R* and *0.01 M sodium hydroxide* until the colour changes to pink. Add 5.5 ml of the substance to be examined and 0.25 ml of *0.02 M sodium hydroxide*. The solution remains pink for not less than 15 s.

**Relative density** (*2.2.5*)
0.898 to 0.902.

**Refractive index** (*2.2.6*)
1.370 to 1.373.

**Reaction with sulphuric acid**
Carefully add 2 ml to 10 ml of *sulphuric acid R*. After 15 min, the interface between the 2 liquids is not coloured.

**Related substances**
Gas chromatography (*2.2.28*).

*Test solution*   The substance to be examined.

*Column:*
— *material*: glass;
— *size*: $l$ = 2 m, Ø = 2 mm;
— *stationary phase*: ethylvinylbenzene-divinylbenzene copolymer R (136-173 µm).

*Carrier gas*   *nitrogen for chromatography R*.

*Flow rate*   30 ml/min.

*Temperature:*

|  | Time (min) | Temperature (°C) |
|---|---|---|
| Column | 0 - 18.8 | 90 → 240 |
|  | 18.8 - 26.8 | 240 |
| Injection port |  | 240 |
| Detector |  | 240 |

*Detection*   Flame ionisation.

*Injection*   1 µl.

*Limit:*
— *total*: not more than 0.2 per cent of the area of the principal peak.

**Residue on evaporation**
Maximum 30 ppm.

Evaporate 100.0 g to dryness on a water-bath and dry in an oven at 100-105 °C. The residue weighs not more than 3 mg.

**Water** (*2.5.12*)
Maximum 0.1 per cent, determined on 10.0 ml.

**STORAGE**
Protected from light, at a temperature not exceeding 30 °C.

**IMPURITIES**
A. methyl acetate,

B. ethanol,

C. methanol.

*Ph Eur*

# Ethyl Cinnamate

$C_{11}H_{12}O_2$                176.2                *103-36-6*

**DEFINITION**
Ethyl Cinnamate is predominantly ethyl (*E*)-3-phenylprop-2-enoate. It contains not less than 99.0% and not more than 100.5% of $C_{11}H_{12}O_2$, calculated with reference to the anhydrous substance.

**CHARACTERISTICS**
A clear, colourless or almost colourless liquid.

Practically insoluble in *water*; miscible with most organic solvents.

**IDENTIFICATION**
A. The *infrared absorption spectrum*, Appendix II A, is concordant with the *reference spectrum* of ethyl cinnamate (*RS 136*).

B. The *light absorption*, Appendix II B, in the range 230 to 350 nm of a 0.001% w/v solution in *ethanol (96%)* exhibits a maximum only at 276 nm. The *absorbance* at the maximum is about 1.23.

C. To 1 g add 25 ml of 1M *sodium hydroxide*, boil under a reflux condenser for 1 hour, cool and acidify with *hydrochloric acid*. The *melting point* of the resulting precipitate, after filtration, washing with *water* and drying at 60° at a pressure not exceeding 0.7 kPa, is about 133°, Appendix V A.

**TESTS**
**Acidity**
Mix 30 g with 150 ml of *ethanol (96%)* previously neutralised to *phenolphthalein solution R1*. Not more than 1.0 ml of 0.1M *sodium hydroxide VS* is required for neutralisation using *phenolphthalein solution R1* as indicator.

**Refractive index**
1.558 to 1.560, Appendix V E.

**Weight per ml**
1.048 to 1.051 g, Appendix V G.

**Related substances**
Carry out the method for *gas chromatography*, Appendix III B, using the following solutions. Solution (1) contains 1.0% w/v of the substance being examined in *chloroform*. Solution (2) is the substance being examined.

The chromatographic procedure may be carried out using a glass column (1.5 m × 4 mm) packed with *acid-washed, silanised diatomaceous support* coated with 3% w/w of cyanopropylmethyl phenyl methyl silicone fluid (OV-225 is suitable) and maintained at 150°.

In the chromatogram obtained with solution (2) the sum of the areas of any *secondary peaks* is not greater than 1% by *normalisation*.

**Sulphated ash**
Not more than 0.1%, Appendix IX A.

**Water**
Not more than 0.1% w/w, Appendix IX C. Use 5 g.

**ASSAY**
In a borosilicate glass flask dissolve 2.5 g of the substance being examined in 5 ml of carbon dioxide-free ethanol prepared by boiling *ethanol (96%)* thoroughly and neutralising to *phenolphthalein solution R1*. Neutralise the free acid in the solution with 0.1M *ethanolic potassium hydroxide VS* using 0.2 ml of *phenolphthalein solution R1* as indicator. Add 50 ml of 0.5M *ethanolic potassium hydroxide VS* and boil under a reflux condenser on a water bath for 1 hour. Add 20 ml of *water* and titrate the excess of alkali with 0.5M *hydrochloric acid VS* using a further 0.2 ml of *phenolphthalein solution R1* as indicator. Repeat the operation without the substance being examined. The difference between the titrations represents the alkali required to saponify the esters. Each ml of 0.5M *ethanolic potassium hydroxide VS* is equivalent to 88.11 mg of $C_{11}H_{12}O_2$.

# Ethyl Gallate

$C_9H_{10}O_5$        198.2        *831-61-8*

## Action and use
Antioxidant.

## DEFINITION
Ethyl Gallate is ethyl 3,4,5-trihydroxybenzoate.

## CHARACTERISTICS
A white to creamy white, crystalline powder.

Slightly soluble in *water*; freely soluble in *ethanol (96%)* and in *ether*; practically insoluble in arachis oil.

## IDENTIFICATION
A. The *light absorption*, Appendix II B, in the range 230 to 350 nm of a 0.002% w/v solution in *methanol* exhibits a maximum only at 275 nm. The *absorbance* at the maximum is about 1.08.

B. Carry out the method for *gas chromatography*, Appendix III B using the following solutions.

(1) Boil 0.5 g with 50 ml of 5M *sodium hydroxide* under a reflux condenser for 10 minutes and distil 5 ml.

(2) *Absolute ethanol.*

CHROMATOGRAPHIC CONDITIONS

(a) Use a glass column (1.5 m × 4 mm) packed with *acid-washed, silanised diatomaceous support* (80 to 100 mesh) coated with 10% w/w of free fatty acid phase (Supelco FFAP is suitable).

(b) Use *nitrogen* as the carrier gas at 40 ml per minute.

(c) Use isothermal conditions maintained at 80°.

(d) Use a flame ionisation detector.

(e) Inject 1 µl of each solution.

CONFIRMATION

The chromatogram obtained with solution (1) shows a peak with the same retention time as the peak due to absolute ethanol in the chromatogram obtained with solution (2).

C. Dissolve 5 mg in a mixture of 25 ml of *acetone* and 25 ml of *water* and add 0.05 ml of *iron(III) chloride solution*.
A purplish black colour is produced which rapidly becomes bluish black.

## TESTS
### Melting point
151° to 154°, Appendix V A.

### Acidity
Dissolve 0.4 g in 100 ml of warm *carbon dioxide-free water*, cool and titrate with 0.1M *sodium hydroxide VS* using *bromocresol green solution* as indicator. Not more than 0.1 ml of 0.1M *sodium hydroxide VS* is required.

### Chloride
Shake 0.50 g with 50 ml of *water* for 5 minutes and filter. 15 ml of the resulting solution complies with the *limit test for chlorides*, Appendix VII (330 ppm).

### Loss on drying
When dried to constant weight at 105°, loses not more than 1.0% of its weight. Use 1 g.

### Sulphated ash
Not more than 0.1%, Appendix IX A.

## STORAGE
Ethyl Gallate should be protected from light. Contact with metals should be avoided.

# Ethyl Hydroxybenzoate

Ethyl paraben

*(Ethyl Parahydroxybenzoate, Ph Eur monograph 0900)*

$C_9H_{10}O_3$        166.2        *120-47-8*

*Ph Eur*

## DEFINITION
Ethyl 4-hydroxybenzoate.

### Content
98.0 per cent to 102.0 per cent.

## CHARACTERS
### Appearance
White or almost white, crystalline powder or colourless crystals.

### Solubility
Very slightly soluble in water, freely soluble in alcohol and in methanol.

## IDENTIFICATION
*First identification*   A, B.

*Second identification*   A, C, D.

A. Melting point *(2.2.14)* 115 °C to 118 °C.

B. Infrared absorption spectrophotometry *(2.2.24)*.

*Comparison*   ethyl parahydroxybenzoate CRS.

C. Examine the chromatograms obtained in the test for related substances.

*Results*   The principal spot in the chromatogram obtained with test solution (b) is similar in position and size to the principal spot in the chromatogram obtained with reference solution (b).

D. To about 10 mg in a test-tube add 1 ml of *sodium carbonate solution R*, boil for 30 s and cool (solution A). To a further 10 mg in a similar test-tube add 1 ml of *sodium carbonate solution R*; the substance partly dissolves (solution B). Add at the same time to solution A and solution B 5 ml of *aminopyrazolone solution R* and 1 ml of *potassium ferricyanide solution R* and mix. Solution B is yellow to orange-brown. Solution A is orange to red, the colour being clearly more intense than any similar colour which may be obtained with solution B.

## TESTS
### Solution S
Dissolve 1.0 g in *alcohol R* and dilute to 10 ml with the same solvent.

## Appearance of solution
Solution S is clear (2.2.1) and not more intensely coloured than reference solution $BY_6$ (2.2.2, Method II).

## Acidity
To 2 ml of solution S add 3 ml of *alcohol R*, 5 ml of *carbon dioxide-free water R* and 0.1 ml of *bromocresol green solution R*. Not more than 0.1 ml of *0.1 M sodium hydroxide* is required to change the colour of the indicator to blue.

## Related substances
Thin-layer chromatography (2.2.27).

*Test solution (a)*  Dissolve 0.10 g of the substance to be examined in *acetone R* and dilute to 10 ml with the same solvent.

*Test solution (b)*  Dilute 1 ml of test solution (a) to 10 ml with acetone R.

*Reference solution (a)*  Dilute 0.5 ml of test solution (a) to 100 ml with *acetone R*.

*Reference solution (b)*  Dissolve 10 mg of *ethyl parahydroxybenzoate CRS* in *acetone R* and dilute to 10 ml with the same solvent.

*Reference solution (c)*  Dissolve 10 mg of *methyl parahydroxybenzoate R* in 1 ml of test solution (a) and dilute to 10 ml with *acetone R*.

*Plate*  Suitable octadecylsilyl silica gel with a fluorescent indicator having an optimal intensity at 254 nm as the coating substance.

*Mobile phase*  glacial acetic acid R, water R, methanol R (1:30:70 *V/V/V*).

*Application*  2 μl.

*Development*  Over a path of 15 cm.

*Drying*  In air.

*Detection*  Examine in ultraviolet light at 254 nm.

*System suitability*  The chromatogram obtained with reference solution (c) shows 2 clearly separated principal spots.

*Limits*:
— *any impurity*: any spot in the chromatogram obtained with test solution (a), apart from the principal spot, is not more intense than the spot in the chromatogram obtained with reference solution (a) (0.5 per cent).

## Sulphated ash (2.4.14)
Maximum 0.1 per cent, determined on 1.0 g.

## ASSAY
To 1.000 g add 20.0 ml of *1 M sodium hydroxide*. Heat at about 70 °C for 1 h. Cool rapidly in an ice bath. Prepare a blank in the same manner. Carry out the titration on the solutions at room temperature. Titrate the excess sodium hydroxide with *0.5 M sulphuric acid*, continuing the titration until the second point of inflexion and determining the end-point potentiometrically (2.2.20).

1 ml of *1 M sodium hydroxide* is equivalent to 166.2 mg of $C_9H_{10}O_3$.

## IMPURITIES

A. R = H: 4-hydroxybenzoic acid,

B. R = $CH_3$: methyl 4-hydroxybenzoate,

C. R = $CH_2$-$CH_2$-$CH_3$: propyl 4-hydroxybenzoate,

D. R = $CH_2$-$CH_2$-$CH_2$-$CH_3$: butyl 4-hydroxybenzoate.

*Ph Eur*

# Ethyl Hydroxybenzoate Sodium

Ethylparaben Sodium

(*Ethyl Parahydroxybenzoate Sodium, Ph Eur monograph 2134*)

| $C_9H_9NaO_3$ | 188.2 | 35285-68-8 |

*Ph Eur*

## DEFINITION
Sodium 4-(ethoxycarbonyl)phenolate.

## Content
99.0 per cent to 103.0 per cent (anhydrous substance).

## CHARACTERS
### Appearance
White or almost white, hygroscopic, crystalline powder.

### Solubility
Freely soluble in water, soluble in anhydrous ethanol, practically insoluble in methylene chloride.

## IDENTIFICATION
*First identification*  A, B, E.

*Second identification*  A, C, D, E.

A. Dissolve 0.5 g in 50 ml of *water R*. Immediately add 5 ml of *hydrochloric acid R1*. Filter and wash the precipitate with *water R*. Dry *in vacuo* at 80 °C for 2 h. It melts (2.2.14) at 115 °C to 118 °C.

B. Infrared absorption spectrophotometry (2.2.24).

*Preparation*  The precipitate obtained in identification A.

*Comparison*  ethyl parahydroxybenzoate CRS.

C. Examine the chromatograms obtained in the test for related substances.

*Results*  The principal spot in the chromatogram obtained with test solution (b) is similar in position and size to the principal spot in the chromatogram obtained with reference solution (c).

D. To about 10 mg in a test-tube add 1 ml of *sodium carbonate solution R*, boil for 30 s and cool. Add 5 ml of *aminopyrazolone solution R* and 1 ml of *potassium ferricyanide solution R* and mix. An orange or red colour develops.

E. To 1 ml of solution S (see Tests) add 1 ml of *water R*. The solution gives reaction (a) of sodium (2.3.1).

## TESTS
### Solution S
Dissolve 5.0 g in *carbon dioxide-free water R* prepared from *distilled water R* and dilute to 50 ml with the same solvent.

### Appearance of solution
Solution S examined immediately after preparation is clear (2.2.1) and not more intensely coloured than reference solution $BY_6$ (2.2.2, Method II).

### pH (2.2.3)
9.5 to 10.5.

Dilute 1 ml of solution S to 100 ml with *carbon dioxide-free water R*.

## Related substances

Thin-layer chromatography (2.2.27).

*Test solution (a)* Dissolve 0.100 g of the substance to be examined in 10 ml of *water R*. Immediately add 2 ml of *hydrochloric acid R* and shake with 50 ml of *methylene chloride R*. Evaporate the lower layer to dryness and take up the residue with 10 ml of *acetone R*.

*Test solution (b)* Dilute 1 ml of test solution (a) to 10 ml with *acetone R*.

*Reference solution (a)* Dissolve 34.3 mg of *4-hydroxybenzoic acid R* (impurity A) in *acetone R* and dilute to 100 ml with the same solvent.

*Reference solution (b)* Dilute 0.5 ml of test solution (a) to 100 ml with *acetone R*.

*Reference solution (c)* Dissolve 5 mg of *ethyl parahydroxybenzoate CRS* in *acetone R* and dilute to 5 ml with the same solvent.

*Reference solution (d)* Dissolve 5 mg of *methyl parahydroxybenzoate CRS* (impurity B) in 0.5 ml of test solution (a) and dilute to 5 ml with *acetone R*.

*Plate* TLC octadecylsilyl silica gel $F_{254}$ plate R.

*Mobile phase* glacial acetic acid R, water R, methanol R (1:30:70 *V/V/V*).

*Application* 5 µl.

*Development* Over 2/3 of the plate.

*Drying* In air.

*Detection* Examine in ultraviolet light at 254 nm.

*System suitability* Reference solution (d):
— the chromatogram shows 2 clearly separated principal spots.

*Limits* Test solution (a):
— *impurity A: any spot due to impurity A is not more intense than the spot in the chromatogram obtained with reference solution (a) (4 per cent);*
— *any other impurity: any spot is not more intense than the spot in the chromatogram obtained with reference solution (b) (0.5 per cent).*

## Chlorides (2.4.4)

Maximum 350 ppm.

To 10 ml of solution S add 30 ml of *water R* and 1 ml of *nitric acid R* and dilute to 50 ml with *water R*. Shake and filter. Dilute 10 ml of the filtrate to 15 ml with *water R*. The solution complies with the test. Prepare the standard using a mixture of 1 ml of *water R* and 14 ml of *chloride standard solution (5 ppm Cl) R*.

## Sulphates (2.4.13)

Maximum 300 ppm.

To 25 ml of solution S add 5 ml of *distilled water R* and 10 ml of *hydrochloric acid R* and dilute to 50 ml with *distilled water R*. Shake and filter. Dilute 10 ml of the filtrate to 15 ml with *distilled water R*.

## Heavy metals (2.4.8)

Maximum 10 ppm.

Dissolve 2.0 g in *water R* and dilute to 20.0 ml with the same solvent. 12 ml of the solution complies with test A. Prepare the reference solution using 1 ml of *lead standard solution (10 ppm Pb) R*.

After the addition of *buffer solution pH 3.5 R*, the substance precipitates. Dilute each solution to 40 ml with *anhydrous ethanol R*: the substance dissolves completely. Continue the test as described for Method A. Filter the solutions through a membrane filter (pore size 0.45 µm) to evaluate the result.

## Water (2.5.12)

Maximum 5.0 per cent, determined on 0.500 g.

## ASSAY

Dissolve 0.150 g in 50 ml of *anhydrous acetic acid R*. Titrate with *0.1 M perchloric acid*, determining the end-point potentiometrically (2.2.20).

1 ml of *0.1 M perchloric acid* is equivalent to 18.82 mg of $C_9H_9NaO_3$.

## STORAGE

In an airtight container.

## IMPURITIES

A. R = H: 4-hydroxybenzoic acid,

B. R = CH$_3$: methyl 4-hydroxybenzoate,

C. R = CH$_2$-CH$_2$-CH$_3$: propyl 4-hydroxybenzoate,

D. R = CH$_2$-CH$_2$-CH$_2$-CH$_3$: butyl 4-hydroxybenzoate.

*Ph Eur*

# Ethyl Oleate

(Ph Eur monograph 1319)

*Ph Eur*

## DEFINITION

Mixture consisting of the ethyl esters of fatty acids, mainly oleic (*cis*-9-octadecenoic) acid.

A suitable antioxidant may be added.

## CHARACTERS

**Appearance**

Clear, pale yellow or colourless liquid.

**Solubility**

Practically insoluble in water, miscible with ethanol (96 per cent), with methylene chloride and with light petroleum (40-60 °C).

## IDENTIFICATION

A. Relative density (see Tests).

B. Saponification value (see Tests).

C. Oleic acid (see Tests).

## TESTS

**Relative density (2.2.5)**

0.866 to 0.874.

**Acid value (2.5.1)**

Maximum 0.5, determined on 10.0 g.

**Iodine value (2.5.4, Method A)**

75 to 90.

**Peroxide value (2.5.5, Method A)**

Maximum 10.0.

**Saponification value (2.5.6)**

177 to 188, determined on 2.0 g.

**Oleic acid** (*2.4.22*, *Method A*)

Minimum 60.0 per cent in the fatty acid fraction of the substance to be examined.

**Water** (*2.5.12*)

Maximum 1.0 per cent, determined on 1.00 g.

**Total ash** (*2.4.16*)

Maximum 0.1 per cent, determined on 2.0 g.

## STORAGE

Protected from light.

_____ *Ph Eur*

# Ethylcellulose

(*Ph Eur monograph 0822*)

**Action and use**

Excipient.

*Ph Eur* _____

## DEFINITION

Partly *O*-ethylated cellulose.

**Content**

44.0 per cent to 51.0 per cent of ethoxy (-$OC_2H_5$) groups (dried substance).

## CHARACTERS

**Appearance**

White or yellowish-white powder or granular powder, odourless or almost odourless.

**Solubility**

Practically insoluble in water, soluble in methylene chloride and in a mixture of 20 g of ethanol (96 per cent) and 80 g of toluene, slightly soluble in ethyl acetate and in methanol, practically insoluble in glycerol (85 per cent) and in propylene glycol. The solutions may show a slight opalescence.

## IDENTIFICATION

A. Infrared absorption spectrophotometry (*2.2.24*).

*Comparison   Ph. Eur. reference spectrum of ethylcellulose.*

B. It complies with the limits of the assay.

## TESTS

**Acidity or alkalinity**

To 0.5 g add 25 ml of *carbon dioxide-free water R* and shake for 15 min. Filter through a sintered-glass filter (40) (*2.1.2*). To 10 ml of the solution add 0.1 ml of *phenolphthalein solution R* and 0.5 ml of *0.01 M sodium hydroxide*. The solution is pink. To 10 ml of the solution add *0.1 ml of methyl red solution R* and 0.5 ml of *0.01 M hydrochloric acid*. The solution is red.

**Viscosity** (*2.2.9*)

80.0 per cent to 120.0 per cent of that stated on the label for a nominal viscosity greater than 6 mPa·s; 75.0 per cent to 140.0 per cent of that stated on the label for a nominal viscosity not greater than 6 mPa·s.

Shake a quantity of the substance to be examined equivalent to 5.00 g of the dried substance with 95 g of a mixture of 20 g of *ethanol (96 per cent) R* and 80 g of *toluene R* until the substance is dissolved. Determine the viscosity in mPa·s at 25 °C using a capillary viscometer.

**Acetaldehyde**

Maximum 100 ppm.

Introduce 3.0 g into a 250 ml conical flask with a ground-glass stopper, add 10 ml of *water R* and stir mechanically for 1 h. Allow to stand for 24 h, filter and dilute the filtrate to 100.0 ml with *water R*. Transfer 5.0 ml of the filtrate to a 25 ml volumetric flask, add 5 ml of a 0.5 g/l solution of *methylbenzothiazolone hydrazone hydrochloride R* and heat in a water-bath at 60 °C for 5 min. Add 2 ml of *ferric chloride-sulphamic acid reagent R* and heat again in a water-bath at 60 °C for 5 min. Cool and dilute to 25.0 ml with *water R*. The solution is not more intensely coloured than a standard prepared at the same time and in the same manner using instead of the 5.0 ml of filtrate, 5.0 ml of a reference solution prepared by diluting 3.0 ml of *acetaldehyde standard solution (100 ppm $C_2H_4O$) R1* to 100.0 ml with *water R*.

**Chlorides** (*2.4.4*)

Maximum 0.1 per cent.

Disperse 0.250 g in 50 ml of *water R*, heat to boiling and allow to cool, shaking occasionally. Filter and discard the first 10 ml of the filtrate. Dilute 10 ml of the filtrate to 15 ml with *water R*.

**Heavy metals** (*2.4.8*)

Maximum 20 ppm.

1.0 g complies with test C. Prepare the reference solution using 2 ml of *lead standard solution (10 ppm Pb) R*.

**Loss on drying** (*2.2.32*)

Maximum 3.0 per cent, determined on 1.000 g by drying in an oven at 105 °C for 2 h.

**Sulphated ash** (*2.4.14*)

Maximum 0.5 per cent, determined on 1.0 g.

## ASSAY

Gas chromatography (*2.2.28*).

*CAUTION: hydriodic acid and its reaction by-products are highly toxic. Perform all steps for preparation of the test and reference solutions in a properly functioning hood.*

*Internal standard solution*   Dilute 120 µl of *toluene R* to 10 ml with *o-xylene R*.

*Test solution*   Transfer 50.0 mg of the substance to be examined, 50.0 mg of *adipic acid R* and 2.0 ml of the internal standard solution into a suitable 5 ml thick-walled reaction vial with a pressure-tight septum-type closure. Cautiously add 2.0 ml of *hydriodic acid R*, immediately close the vial tightly and weigh the contents and the vial accurately. Shake the vial for 30 s, heat to 125 °C for 10 min, allow to cool for 2 min, shake again for 30 s and heat to 125 °C for 10 min. Afterwards allow to cool for 2 min and repeat shaking and heating for a 3rd time. Allow the vial to cool for 45 min and reweigh. If the loss is greater than 10 mg, discard the mixture and prepare another. Use the upper layer.

*Reference solution*   Transfer 100.0 mg of *adipic acid R*, 4.0 ml of the internal standard solution and 4.0 ml of *hydriodic acid R* into a suitable 10 ml thick-walled reaction vial with a pressure-tight septum-type closure. Close the vial tightly and weigh the vial and contents accurately. Afterwards inject 50 µl of *iodoethane R* through the septum with a syringe, weigh the vial again and calculate the mass of iodoethane added, by difference. Shake well and allow the layers to separate. Use the upper layer.

*Column:*

— *material*: stainless steel,

— *size*: l = 5.0 m, Ø = 2 mm,

— *stationary phase*: *diatomaceous earth for gas chromatography R* (150-180 µm) impregnated with 3 per cent m/m of *poly(dimethyl)siloxane R*.

*Carrier gas*   *nitrogen for chromatography R.*

*Flow rate*   15 ml/min.

*Temperature:*
— *column:* 80 °C;
— *injection port and detector:* 200 °C.

*Detection*   Fame ionisation.

*Injection*   1 μl.

*Relative retention*   With reference to toluene: iodoethane = about 0.6; *o*-xylene = about 2.3.

*System suitability*   Reference solution:
— *resolution:* minimum 2.0 between the peaks due to iodoethane and toluene.

Calculate the percentage content of ethoxy groups using the following expression:

$$\frac{Q_1 \times m_2 \times 45.1 \times 100 \times 100}{2 \times Q_2 \times m_1 \times 156.0 \times (100 - d)}$$

$Q_1$ = ratio of iodoethane peak area to toluene peak area in the chromatogram obtained with the test solution,

$Q_2$ = ratio of iodoethane peak area to toluene peak area in the chromatogram obtained with the reference solution,

$m_1$ = mass of the substance to be examined used in the test solution, in milligrams,

$m_2$ = mass of iodoethane used in the reference solution, in milligrams,

$d$ = percentage loss on drying.

## LABELLING

The label states the nominal viscosity in millipascal seconds for a 5 per cent *m/m* solution.

*———————————— Ph Eur*

# Ethylene Glycol Monopalmitostearate

Ethylene Glycol Monostearate

*(Ph Eur monograph 1421)*

## Action and use
Excipient.

*Ph Eur _____*

## DEFINITION

Mixture of ethylene glycol mono- and diesters of stearic (octadecanoic) and palmitic (hexadecanoic) acids, produced from the condensation of ethylene glycol and stearic acid 50 of vegetable or animal origin (see *Stearic acid (1474)*).

## Content
Minimum of 50.0 per cent of monoesters.

## CHARACTERS

### Appearance
White or almost white, waxy solid.

### Solubility
Practically insoluble in water, soluble in acetone and in hot alcohol.

## IDENTIFICATION

A. It complies with the test for melting point (see Tests).

B. It complies with the test for composition of fatty acids (see Tests).

C. It complies with the assay (monoesters content).

## TESTS

### Melting point *(2.2.15)*
54 °C to 60 °C.

### Acid value *(2.5.1)*
Maximum 3.0, determined on 10.0 g.

### Iodine value *(2.5.4)*
Maximum 3.0.

### Saponification value *(2.5.6)*
170 to 195, determined on 2.0 g.

### Composition of fatty acids *(2.4.22, Method A)*
The fatty acid fraction has the following composition:
— *stearic acid:* 40.0 per cent to 60.0 per cent,
— *sum of contents of palmitic acid and stearic acid:* minimum 90.0 per cent.

### Free ethylene glycol
Maximum 5.0 per cent, determined as prescribed under Assay.

### Total ash *(2.4.16)*
Mximum 0.1 per cent, determined on 1.0 g.

## ASSAY

Size-exclusion chromatography *(2.2.30)*.

*Test solution*   Into a 15 ml flask, weigh about 0.2 g (*m*), to the nearest 0.1 mg. Add 5.0 ml of *tetrahydrofuran R* and shake to dissolve. Heat gently, if necessary. Reweigh the flask and calculate the total mass of solvent and substance (*M*).

*Reference solutions*   Into four 15 ml flasks, weigh, to the nearest 0.1 mg, about 2.5 mg, 5.0 mg, 10.0 mg and 20.0 mg of *ethylene glycol R*. Add 5.0 ml of *tetrahydrofuran R* and shake to dissolve. Weigh the flasks again and calculate the concentration of ethylene glycol in milligrams per gram for each reference solution.

*Column:*
— *size: l* = 0.6 m, Ø = 7 mm,
— *stationary phase: styrene-divinylbenzene copolymer R* (particle diameter 5 μm and pore size 10 nm).

*Mobile phase*   *tetrahydrofuran R.*

*Flow rate*   1 ml/min.

*Detection*   Dfferential refractometer.

*Injection*   40 μl.

*Relative retention*   With reference to ethylene glycol: diesters = about 0.76, monoesters = about 0.83.

*Limits:*
— *free ethylene glycol:* from the calibration curve obtained with the reference solutions, determine the concentration (*C*) in milligrams per gram in the test solution and calculate the percentage content in the substance to be examined using the following expression:

$$\frac{C \times M}{m \times 10}$$

— *monoesters:* calculate the percentage content of monoesters using the following expression:

$$\frac{A}{A + B} \times (100 - D)$$

$A$ = area of the peak due to the monoesters,
$B$ = area of the peak due to the diesters,

$D$ = percentage content of free ethylene glycol + percentage content of free fatty acids which may be determined using the following expression:

$$\frac{I_A \times 270}{561.1}$$

$I_A$ = acid value.

**STORAGE**

Protected from light.

_____ *Ph Eur*

# Ethylenediamine

*(Ph Eur monograph 0716)*

$C_2H_8N_2$                     60.1                     *107-15-3*

*Ph Eur* _____

**DEFINITION**

Ethane-1,2-diamine.

**Content**

98.0 per cent to 101.0 per cent.

**CHARACTERS**

**Appearance**

Clear, colourless or slightly yellow liquid, hygroscopic.

**Solubility**

Miscible with water and with anhydrous ethanol.

On exposure to air, white fumes are evolved. On heating, it evaporates completely.

**IDENTIFICATION**

A. Relative density (*2.2.5*): 0.895 to 0.905.

B. Boiling point (*2.2.12*): 116 °C to 118 °C.

C. To 0.2 ml add 0.5 ml of *acetic anhydride R*. Boil. A crystalline mass forms after cooling, which dissolves in 5 ml of *2-propanol R* with heating. Cool the solution and add 5 ml of *ether R*. If necessary, initiate crystallisation by scratching the walls of the test-tube with a glass rod. Filter through a sintered-glass filter (*2.1.2*), wash with several portions of *ether R* and dry at 100-105 °C. The residue melts (*2.2.14*) at 173 °C to 177 °C.

**TESTS**

**Solution S**

Mix 10 g with *carbon dioxide-free water R* and dilute to 100 ml with the same solvent.

**Appearance of solution**

Solution S is clear (*2.2.1*) and not more intensely coloured than the reference solution $BY_6$ (*2.2.2, Method II*).

**Carbonate**

A mixture of 4 ml of solution S and 6 ml of *calcium hydroxide solution R* is not more opalescent than reference suspension II (*2.2.1*).

**Chlorides** (*2.4.4*)

Maximum 100 ppm.

To 5 ml of solution S add 5 ml of *dilute nitric acid R* and dilute to 15 ml with *water R*.

**Ammonia and other bases**

Dissolve 1.2 g in 20 ml of *ethanol (96 per cent) R* and add, dropwise with stirring, 4.5 ml of *hydrochloric acid R*. Evaporate to dryness on a water-bath, breaking up any resulting cake with a glass rod, and dry at 100-105 °C for 1 h. 1 g of the residue is equivalent to 0.4518 g of $C_2H_8N_2$. Calculate the percentage content of $C_2H_8N_2$: it does not vary by more than 0.5 from the percentage content determined in the assay.

**Iron** (*2.4.9*)

Maximum 10 ppm, determined on solution S.

**Heavy metals** (*2.4.8*)

Maximum 10 ppm.

12 ml of solution S complies with test A. Prepare the reference solution using *lead standard solution (1 ppm Pb) R*.

**Residue on evaporation**

Maximum 0.3 per cent.

Evaporate 5.00 g to dryness on a water-bath and dry at 100-105 °C for 1 h. The residue weighs a maximum of 15 mg.

**ASSAY**

Place 25.0 ml of *1 M hydrochloric acid* and 0.2 ml of *methyl red mixed solution R* in a flask. Add 0.600 g of the substance to be examined. Titrate with *1 M sodium hydroxide* until the colour changes from violet-red to green.

1 ml of *1 M hydrochloric acid* is equivalent to 30.05 mg of $C_2H_8N_2$.

**STORAGE**

In an airtight container, protected from light.

_____ *Ph Eur*

# Ethylmorphine Hydrochloride

*(Ph Eur monograph 0491)*

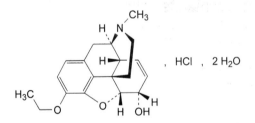

$C_{19}H_{23}NO_3,HCl,2H_2O$          385.9                    *125-30-4*

**Action and use**

Opioid receptor agonist; analgesic.

*Ph Eur* _____

**DEFINITION**

7,8-Didehydro-4,5α-epoxy-3-ethoxy-17-methylmorphinan-6α-ol hydrochloride dihydrate.

**Content**

99.0 per cent to 101.0 per cent (anhydrous substance).

**CHARACTERS**

**Appearance**

White or almost white, crystalline powder.

**Solubility**

Soluble in water and in alcohol, insoluble in cyclohexane.

## IDENTIFICATION

*First identification   A, D.*

*Second identification   B, C, D.*

A. Infrared absorption spectrophotometry (*2.2.24*).

*Comparison   Ph. Eur. reference spectrum of ethylmorphine hydrochloride .*

B. In a test-tube, dissolve 0.5 g in 6 ml of *water R* and add 15 ml of *0.1 M sodium hydroxide*. Scratch the wall of the tube with a glass rod. A white, crystalline precipitate is formed. Collect the precipitate, wash and dissolve in 20 ml of *water R* heated to 80 °C. Filter and cool in iced water. The crystals, after drying *in vacuo* for 12 h, melt (*2.2.14*) at 85 °C to 89 °C.

C. To about 10 mg add 1 ml of *sulphuric acid R* and 0.05 ml of *ferric chloride solution R2*. Heat on a water-bath. A blue colour develops. Add 0.05 ml of *nitric acid R*. The colour becomes red.

D. Solution S (see Tests) gives reaction (a) of chlorides (*2.3.1*).

## TESTS

### Solution S

Dissolve 0.500 g in *carbon dioxide-free water R* and dilute to 25.0 ml with the same solvent.

### Appearance of solution

Solution S is clear (*2.2.1*) and not more intensely coloured than reference solution $BY_6$ (*2.2.2, Method II*).

### Acidity or alkalinity

To 10 ml of solution S add 0.05 ml of *methyl red solution R* and 0.2 ml of *0.02 M hydrochloric acid*, the solution is red. Add 0.4 ml of *0.02 M sodium hydroxide*, the solution becomes yellow.

### Specific optical rotation (*2.2.7*)

− 102 to − 105 (anhydrous substance), determined on solution S.

### Related substances

Liquid chromatography (*2.2.29*).

*Test solution   Dissolve 50.0 mg of the substance to be examined in the mobile phase and dilute to 20.0 ml with the mobile phase.*

*Reference solution (a)   Dilute 1.0 ml of the test solution to 25.0 ml with the mobile phase. Dilute 1.0 ml of this solution to 20.0 ml with the mobile phase.*

*Reference solution (b)   Dissolve 12.5 mg of codeine R in the mobile phase and dilute to 5.0 ml with the mobile phase.*

*Reference solution (c)   Dilute 0.5 ml of reference solution (b) to 100.0 ml with the mobile phase.*

*Reference solution (d)   To 1.0 ml of the test solution, add 1.0 ml of reference solution (b) and dilute to 50.0 ml with the mobile phase.*

*Column:*
— *size: l = 0.25 m, Ø = 4.6 mm;*
— *stationary phase: octylsilyl silica gel for chromatography R (5 μm);*
— *temperature: 30 °C.*

*Mobile phase   Add 1.25 g of sodium heptanesulphonate R to a mixture of 12.5 ml of glacial acetic acid R and 5 ml of a 20 per cent V/V solution of triethylamine R in a mixture of equal volumes of methanol R and water R. Dilute to 1000 ml with water R. To 550 ml of this solution add 450 ml of methanol R.*

*Flow rate   1 ml/min.*

*Detection   Spectrophotometer at 230 nm.*

*Injection   10 μl.*

*Run time   4 times the retention time of ethylmorphine.*

*Relative retention   With reference to ethylmorphine (retention time = about 6.2 min): impurity B = about 0.7; impurity C = about 0.8; impurity D = about 1.3; impurity A = about 2.5.*

*System suitability   Reference solution (d):*
— *resolution: minimum 5 between the peaks due to ethylmorphine and impurity C.*

*Limits:*
— *correction factor: for the calculation of content, multiply the peak area of impurity D by 0.4;*
— *impurities A, B, D: for each impurity, not more than the area of the principal peak in the chromatogram obtained with reference solution (a) (0.2 per cent);*
— *impurity C: not more than the area of the principal peak in the chromatogram obtained with reference solution (c) (0.5 per cent);*
— *any other impurity: for each impurity, not more than 0.5 times the area of the principal peak in the chromatogram obtained with reference solution (a) (0.1 per cent);*
— *total of impurities other than C: not more than 2.5 times the area of the principal peak in the chromatogram obtained with reference solution (a) (0.5 per cent);*
— *disregard limit: 0.25 times the area of the principal peak in the chromatogram obtained with reference solution (a) (0.05 per cent).*

### Water (*2.5.12*)

8.0 per cent to 10.0 per cent, determined on 0.250 g.

### Sulphated ash (*2.4.14*)

Maximum 0.1 per cent, determined on 1.0 g.

## ASSAY

Dissolve 0.300 g in a mixture of 5 ml of *0.01 M hydrochloric acid* and 30 ml of *alcohol R*. Carry out a potentiometric titration (*2.2.20*), using *0.1 M sodium hydroxide*. Read the volume added between the 2 points of inflexion.

1 ml of *0.1 M sodium hydroxide* is equivalent to 34.99 mg of $C_{19}H_{24}ClNO_3$.

## STORAGE

Protected from light.

## IMPURITIES

*Specified impurities   A, B, C, D.*

A. R = R′ = $C_2H_5$:
7,8-didehydro-4,5α-epoxy-3,6α-diethoxy-17-methylmorphinan,

B. R = R′ = H: morphine,

C. R = $CH_3$, R′ = H: codeine,

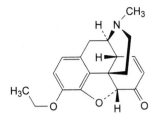

D. 7,8-didehydro-4,5α-epoxy-3-ethoxy-17-methylmorphinan-6-one (ethylmorphinone).

*Ph Eur*

# Etidronate Disodium

(*Ph Eur monograph 1778*)

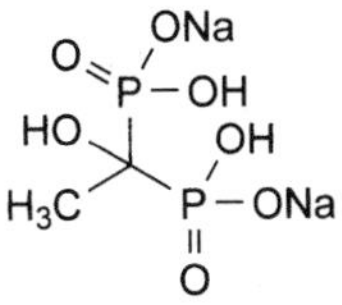

C₂H₆Na₂O₇P₂     250.0     7414-83-7

**Action and use**

Bisphosphonate; treatment of osteoporosis; Paget's disease.

*Ph Eur*

## DEFINITION

Disodium dihydrogen (1-hydroxyethylidene)bisphosphonate.

## Content

98.0 per cent to 102.0 per cent (anhydrous substance).

## CHARACTERS

**Appearance**

White or yellowish, hygroscopic powder.

**Solubility**

Freely soluble in water, practically insoluble in acetone and in ethanol (96 per cent).

## IDENTIFICATION

A. Infrared absorption spectrophotometry (*2.2.24*).

*Comparison* etidronate disodium CRS.

The transmittance at about 2000 cm⁻¹ (5 μm) is not less than 40 per cent without compensation.

B. It gives reaction (a) of sodium (*2.3.1*).

## TESTS

**pH** (*2.2.3*)

4.2 to 5.2.

Dissolve 1.0 g in *carbon dioxide-free water R* and dilute to 100 ml with the same solvent.

**Impurities A and B**

Liquid chromatography (*2.2.29*).

*Test solution* Dissolve 20.0 mg of the substance to be examined in *water R* and dilute to 10.0 ml with the same solvent.

*Reference solution* To 2.0 ml of a 0.3 g/l solution of *phosphoric acid R* add 2.0 ml of a 0.25 g/l solution of *phosphorous acid R* and dilute to 50.0 ml with *water R*.

*Column:*
— *size: l* = 0.15 m, Ø = 4.6 mm;
— *stationary phase: anion exchange resin R* (5 μm);

— *temperature*: 35 °C.

*Mobile phase* Mix 0.2 ml of *anhydrous formic acid R* and 1000 ml of *water R*; adjust to pH 3.5 with an 80 g/l solution of *sodium hydroxide R*.

*Flow rate* 1.0 ml/min.

*Detection* Differential refractometer.

*Injection* 100 μl.

*System suitability* Reference solution:
— *resolution*: minimum 2.5 between the peaks due to impurity A and impurity B.

*Limits*:
— *impurities A, B*: for each impurity, not more than the area of the corresponding peak in the chromatogram obtained with the reference solution (0.5 per cent).

**Heavy metals** (*2.4.8*)

Maximum 20 ppm.

1.0 g complies with test F. Prepare the reference solution using 2 ml of *lead standard solution (10 ppm Pb) R*.

**Water** (*2.5.32*)

Maximum 5.0 per cent.

Dissolve 50.0 mg in a mixture of equal volumes of *anhydrous acetic acid R* and *formamide R* and dilute to 5.0 ml with the same mixture of solvents. Use 1.0 ml of the solution.

## ASSAY

Dissolve 0.100 g in 2 ml of *formic acid R* and dilute to 50 ml with *glacial acetic acid R*. Titrate with *0.1 M perchloric acid*, determining the end-point potentiometrically (*2.2.20*).

1 ml of *0.1 M perchloric acid* is equivalent to 12.50 mg of C₂H₆Na₂O₇P₂.

## STORAGE

In an airtight container.

## IMPURITIES

*Specified impurities* A, B.

A. phosphoric acid,

B. phosphorous acid.

*Ph Eur*

# Etilefrine Hydrochloride

(*Ph Eur monograph 1205*)

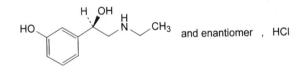

C₁₀H₁₅NO₂,HCl     217.7     943-17-9

**Action and use**

Adrenoceptor agonist.

*Ph Eur*

## DEFINITION

(1*RS*)-2-(Ethylamino)-1-(3-hydroxyphenyl)ethanol hydrochloride.

## Content

98.0 per cent to 101.0 per cent (dried substance).

## CHARACTERS

### Appearance

White or almost white, crystalline powder or colourless crystals.

### Solubility

Freely soluble in water, soluble in ethanol (96 per cent), practically insoluble in methylene chloride.

## IDENTIFICATION

*First identification   B, E.*

*Second identification   A, C, D, E.*

A. Melting point (*2.2.14*): 118 °C to 122 °C.

B. Infrared absorption spectrophotometry (*2.2.24*).

*Preparation   Discs of potassium chloride R.*

*Comparison   etilefrine hydrochloride CRS.*

C. Thin-layer chromatography (*2.2.27*).

*Prepare the solutions protected from bright light and develop the chromatograms protected from light.*

*Test solution   Dissolve 25 mg of the substance to be examined in methanol R and dilute to 5 ml with the same solvent.*

*Reference solution (a)   Dissolve 25 mg of etilefrine hydrochloride CRS in methanol R and dilute to 5 ml with the same solvent.*

*Reference solution (b)   Dissolve 10 mg of phenylephrine hydrochloride CRS in 2 ml of reference solution (a) and dilute to 10 ml with methanol R.*

*Plate   TLC silica gel plate R.*

*Mobile phase   concentrated ammonia R, methanol R, methylene chloride R (5:25:70 V/V/V).*

*Application   5 μl.*

*Development   Over a path of 15 cm.*

*Drying   In a current of warm air.*

*Detection   Spray with a 10 g/l solution of potassium permanganate R; examine in daylight after 15 min.*

*System suitability   Reference solution (b):*
— the chromatogram shows 2 clearly separated spots.

*Results   The principal spot in the chromatogram obtained with the test solution is similar in position, colour and size to the principal spot in the chromatogram obtained with reference solution (a).*

D. To 0.2 ml of solution S (see Tests), add 1 ml of *water R*, 0.1 ml of *copper sulphate solution R* and 1 ml of *strong sodium hydroxide solution R*. A blue colour is produced. Add 2 ml of *ether R* and shake. The upper layer is colourless.

E. Dilute 1 ml of solution S to 10 ml with *water R*. The solution gives reaction (a) of chlorides (*2.3.1*).

## TESTS

### Solution S

Dissolve 2.50 g in *carbon dioxide-free water R* prepared from *distilled water R* and dilute to 50.0 ml with the same solvent.

### Appearance of solution

Solution S is clear (*2.2.1*) and colourless (*2.2.2, Method II*).

### Acidity or alkalinity

Dilute 4 ml of solution S to 10 ml with *carbon dioxide-free water R*. Add 0.1 ml of *methyl red solution R* and 0.2 ml of *0.01 M sodium hydroxide*. The solution is yellow. Not more than 0.4 ml of *0.01 M hydrochloric acid* is required to change the colour of the indicator to red.

### Optical rotation (*2.2.7*)

− 0.10° to + 0.10°, determined on solution S.

## Related substances

Liquid chromatography (*2.2.29*). *Prepare the solutions immediately before use.*

*Test solution   Dissolve 50.0 mg of the substance to be examined in water R and dilute to 50.0 ml with the same solvent.*

*Reference solution (a)   Dilute 1.0 ml of the test solution to 10.0 ml with water R. Dilute 1.0 ml of this solution to 50.0 ml with water R.*

*Reference solution (b)   Dissolve 10.0 mg of etilefrine impurity A CRS in water R and dilute to 50.0 ml with the same solvent. Dilute 1.0 ml of the solution to 50.0 ml with water R.*

*Reference solution (c)   To 10.0 ml of reference solution (a) add 5.0 ml of reference solution (b) and dilute to 20.0 ml with water R.*

*Column:*
— *size: l = 0.25 m, Ø = 4.6 mm;*
— *stationary phase: octylsilyl silica gel for chromatography R (5 μm).*

*Mobile phase   Mix 35 volumes of acetonitrile R and 65 volumes of a 1.1 g/l solution of sodium laurilsulfate R adjusted to pH 2.3 with phosphoric acid R.*

*Flow rate   1 ml/min.*

*Detection   Spectrophotometer at 220 nm.*

*Injection*

20 μl.

*Run time   5 times the retention time of etilefrine.*

*Relative retention   With reference to etilefrine (retention time = about 9 min): impurity E = about 0.5; impurity C = about 0.8; impurity B = about 0.9; impurity A = about 1.2; impurity F = about 1.7; impurity D = about 4.5.*

*System suitability   Reference solution (c):*
— *resolution: minimum 2.5 between the peaks due to etilefrine and impurity A.*

*Limits:*
— *impurity A:* not more than the area of the principal peak in the chromatogram obtained with reference solution (b) (0.4 per cent);
— *impurities B, C, D, E:* for each impurity, not more than the area of the principal peak in the chromatogram obtained with reference solution (a) (0.2 per cent);
— *any other impurity:* for each impurity, not more than 0.5 times the area of the principal peak in the chromatogram obtained with reference solution (a) (0.1 per cent);
— *sum of impurities other than A:* not more than 5 times the area of the principal peak in the chromatogram obtained with reference solution (a) (1 per cent);
— *disregard limit:* 0.1 times the area of the principal peak in the chromatogram obtained with reference solution (a) (0.02 per cent); disregard any peak due to the solvent.

### Sulphates (*2.4.13*)

Maximum 200 ppm, determined on 15 ml of solution S.

### Heavy metals (*2.4.8*)

Maximum 20 ppm.

Dissolve 2.0 g in 20 ml of *water R*. 12 ml of the solution complies with limit test A. Prepare the reference solution using *lead standard solution (2 ppm Pb) R*.

### Loss on drying (*2.2.32*)

Maximum 0.5 per cent, determined on 1.000 g by drying in an oven at 105 °C.

**Sulphated ash** (*2.4.14*)
Maximum 0.1 per cent, determined on 1.0 g.

## ASSAY
Dissolve 0.150 g in a mixture of 20 ml of *anhydrous acetic acid R* and 50 ml of *acetic anhydride R*. Titrate with *0.1 M perchloric acid*, determining the end-point potentiometrically (*2.2.20*).

1 ml of *0.1 M perchloric acid* is equivalent to 21.77 mg of $C_{10}H_{16}ClNO_2$.

## STORAGE
In an airtight container, protected from light.

## IMPURITIES
*Specified impurities   A, B, C, D, E.*

*Other detectable impurities* (the following substances would, if present at a sufficient level, be detected by one or other of the tests in the monograph. They are limited by the general acceptance criterion for other/unspecified impurities and/or by the general monograph *Substances for pharmaceutical use* (*2034*). It is therefore not necessary to identify these impurities for demonstration of compliance. See also *5.10. Control of impurities in substances for pharmaceutical use*) : *F.*

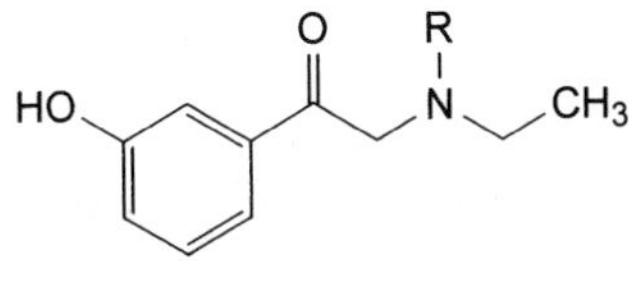

A. R = H: 2-(ethylamino)-1-(3-hydroxyphenyl)ethanone (etilefrone),

D. R = $CH_2$-$C_6H_5$: 2-(benzylethylamino)-1-(3-hydroxyphenyl)ethanone (benzyletilefrone),

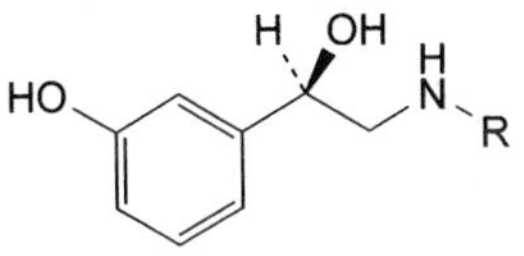

B. R = $CH_3$: (1*RS*)-1-(3-hydroxyphenyl)-2-(methylamino)ethanol (phenylephrine),

C. R = H: (1*RS*)-2-amino-1-(3-hydroxyphenyl)ethanol (norfenefrine),

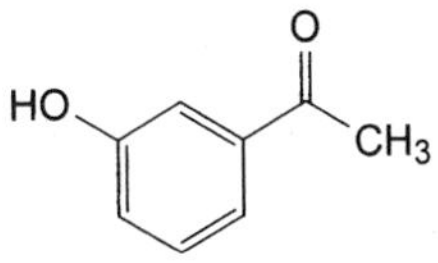

E. 1-(3-hydroxyphenyl)ethanone (3-hydroxyacetophenone),

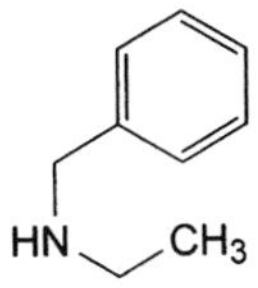

F. *N*-benzylethanamine (benzylethylamine).

_____ *Ph Eur*

# Etodolac
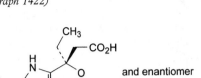

(*Ph Eur monograph 1422*)

$C_{17}H_{21}NO_3$         287.4         41340-25-4

## Action and use
Cyclo-oxygenase inhibitor; analgesic; anti-inflammatory.

## Preparations
Etodolac Capsules

Etodolac Tablets

*Ph Eur* _____

## DEFINITION
2-[(1*RS*)-1,8-Diethyl-1,3,4,9-tetrahydropyrano[3,4-*b*]indol-1-yl]acetic acid.

## Content
98.0 per cent to 102.0 per cent (anhydrous substance).

## CHARACTERS
### Appearance
White or almost white, crystalline powder.

### Solubility
Practically insoluble in water, freely soluble in acetone and in ethanol (96 per cent).

## IDENTIFICATION
*First identification   B.*

*Second identification   A, C.*

A. Melting point (*2.2.14*): 144 °C to 150 °C.

B. Infrared absorption spectrophotometry (*2.2.24*).

*Comparison   etodolac CRS.*

C. Thin-layer chromatography (*2.2.27*).

*Test solution   Dissolve 10 mg of the substance to be examined in acetone R and dilute to 10 ml with the same solvent.*

*Reference solution   Dissolve 10 mg of etodolac CRS in acetone R and dilute to 10 ml with the same solvent.*

*Plate   TLC silica gel GF$_{254}$ plate R* previously activated by heating at 105 °C for 1 h.

Place the plate in an unsaturated chamber containing a mixture of 20 volumes of a 25 g/l solution of *ascorbic acid R* and 80 volumes of *methanol R*. Allow the solution to ascend 1 cm above the line of application on the plate, remove the plate and allow it to dry for at least 30 min.

*Mobile phase   glacial acetic acid R, anhydrous ethanol R, toluene R* (0.5:30:70 *V/V/V*).

*Application   10 µl.*

*Development   2/3 of the plate.*

*Drying   In air.*

*Detection   Examine in ultraviolet light at 254 nm.*

*Results   The principal spot in the chromatogram obtained with the test solution is similar in position and size to the principal spot in the chromatogram obtained with the reference solution.*

## TESTS

### Related substances

Liquid chromatography (2.2.29).

*Test solution* Dissolve 20.0 mg of the substance to be examined in *acetonitrile R1* and dilute to 50.0 ml with the same solvent.

*Reference solution (a)* Dilute 1.0 ml of the test solution to 50.0 ml with *acetonitrile R1*. Dilute 1.0 ml of this solution to 20.0 ml with *acetonitrile R1*.

*Reference solution (b)* Dissolve 4 mg of *etodolac impurity H CRS* in the test solution and dilute to 10 ml with the same solution. Dilute 0.5 ml of this solution to 50 ml with *acetonitrile R1*.

*Reference solution (c)* Dissolve 4 mg of *etodolac for peak identification CRS* (containing impurities A, B, C, D, E, F, G, H, I and K) in 10 ml of *acetonitrile R1*.

*Column:*
— *size*: l = 0.15 m, Ø = 4.6 mm;
— *stationary phase: end-capped butylsilyl silica gel for chromatography R* (3.5 μm);
— *temperature*: 35 °C.

*Mobile phase A*  0.77g/l solution of *ammonium acetate R*;

*Mobile phase B*  mobile phase A, *acetonitrile R1* (10:90 V/V);

| Time (min) | Mobile phase A (per cent V/V) | Mobile phase B (per cent V/V) |
|---|---|---|
| 0 - 25 | 80 → 50 | 20 → 50 |
| 25 - 42 | 50 | 50 |
| 42 - 48 | 50 → 80 | 50 → 20 |

*Flow rate*  1 ml/min.

*Detection*  Spectrophotometer at 225 nm.

*Injection*  5 μl.

*Identification of impurities*  Use the chromatogram supplied with *etodolac for peak identification CRS* and the chromatogram obtained with reference solution (c) to identify the peaks due to impurities A, B, C, D, E, F, G, H, I and K.

*Relative retention*  With reference to etodolac (retention time = about 16.7 min): impurity A = about 0.68; impurity B = about 0.83; impurity C = about 0.85; impurity H = about 1.09; impurity D = about 1.17; impurity G = about 1.19; impurity E = about 1.20; impurity F = about 1.22; impurity I = about 1.50; impurity K = about 2.37.

*System suitability*  Reference solution (b):
— *resolution*: minimum 5.0 between the peaks due to etodolac and impurity H.

*Limits:*
— *impurity C*: not more than 5 times the area of the principal peak in the chromatogram obtained with reference solution (a) (0.5 per cent);
— *impurities A, B, D, E, F, G, H, I, K*: for each impurity, not more than twice the area of the principal peak in the chromatogram obtained with reference solution (a) (0.2 per cent);
— *unspecified impurities*: for each impurity, not more than the area of the principal peak in the chromatogram obtained with reference solution (a) (0.10 per cent);
— *total*: not more than 10 times the area of the principal peak in the chromatogram obtained with reference solution (a) (1.0 per cent);

— *disregard limit*: 0.5 times the area of the principal peak in the chromatogram obtained with reference solution (a) (0.05 per cent).

### Chlorides

Maximum 300 ppm.

Dissolve 1.0 g of the substance to be examined in 60 ml of *methanol R*, add 10 ml of *water R* and 20 ml of *dilute nitric acid R*. Titrate with *0.01 M silver nitrate*, determining the end-point potentiometrically (2.2.20).

1 ml of *0.01 M silver nitrate* is equivalent to 0.3545 mg of Cl.

### Heavy metals (2.4.8)

Maximum 10 ppm.

2.0 g complies with test C. Prepare the reference solution using 2 ml of *lead standard solution (10 ppm Pb) R*.

### Water (2.5.12)

Maximum 0.5 per cent, determined on 1.00 g.

### Sulphated ash (2.4.14)

Maximum 0.1 per cent, determined on 1.0 g.

## ASSAY

Dissolve 0.250 g in 60 ml of *methanol R*. Titrate with *0.1 M tetrabutylammonium hydroxide* determining the end-point potentiometrically (2.2.20). Carry out a blank titration.

1 ml of *0.1 M tetrabutylammonium hydroxide* is equivalent to 28.74 mg of $C_{17}H_{21}NO_3$.

## IMPURITIES

*Specified impurities*   A, B, C, D, E, F, G, H, I, K.

*Other detectable impurities* (the following substances would, if present at a sufficient level, be detected by one or other of the tests in the monograph. They are limited by the general acceptance criterion for other/unspecified impurities and/or by the general monograph *Substances for pharmaceutical use* (2034). It is therefore not necessary to identify these impurities for demonstration of compliance. See also 5.10. *Control of impurities in substances for pharmaceutical use): J, L.*

and enantiomer

A. R1 = H, R2 = $CH_2$-$CH_3$: 2-[(1RS)-1-ethyl-1,3,4,9-tetrahydropyrano[3,4-b]indol-1-yl]acetic acid (8-desethyl etodolac),

B. R1 = $CH_3$, R2 = $CH_2$-$CH_3$: 2-[(1RS)-1-ethyl-8-methyl-1,3,4,9-tetrahydropyrano[3,4-b]indol-1-yl]acetic acid (8-methyl etodolac),

C. R1 = $CH_2$-$CH_3$, R2 = $CH_3$: 2-[(1RS)-8-ethyl-1-methyl-1,3,4,9-tetrahydropyrano[3,4-b]indol-1-yl]acetic acid (1-methyl etodolac),

D. R1 = $CH(CH_3)_2$, R2 = $CH_2$-$CH_3$: 2-[(1RS)-1-ethyl-8-(1-methylethyl)-1,3,4,9-tetrahydropyrano[3,4-b]indol-1-yl]acetic acid (8-isopropyl etodolac),

E. R1 = $CH_2$-$CH_2$-$CH_3$, R2 = $CH_2$-$CH_3$: 2-[(1RS)-1-ethyl-8-propyl-1,3,4,9-tetrahydropyrano[3,4-b]indol-1-yl]acetic acid (8-propyl etodolac),

F. R1 = $CH_2$-$CH_3$, R2 = $CH(CH_3)_2$: 2-[(1RS)-8-ethyl-1-(1-methylethyl)-1,3,4,9-tetrahydropyrano[3,4-b]indol-1-yl]acetic acid (1-isopropyl etodolac),

G. R1 = CH₂-CH₃, R2 = CH₂-CH₂-CH₃: 2-[(1*RS*)-8-ethyl-1-propyl-1,3,4,9-tetrahydropyrano[3,4-*b*]indol-1-yl]acetic acid (1-propyl etodolac),

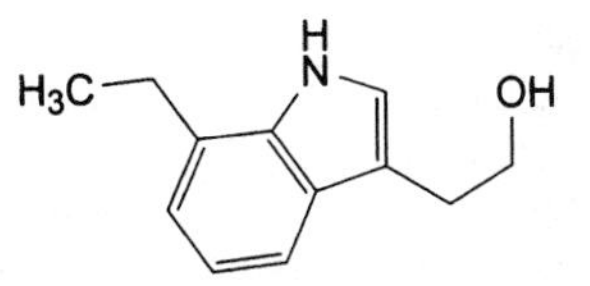

H. 2-(7-ethyl-1*H*-indol-3-yl)ethanol,

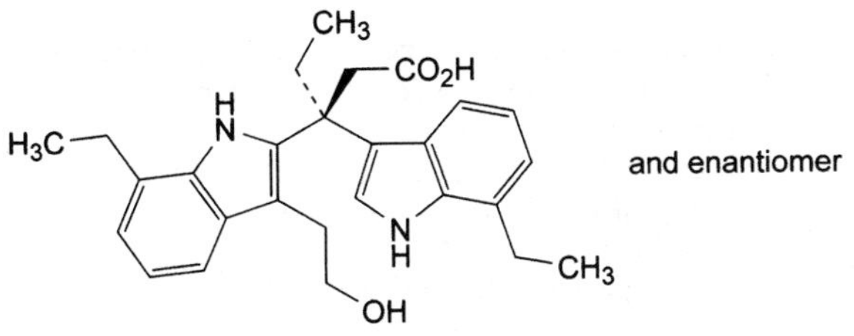

I. (3*RS*)-3-[7-ethyl-3-(2-hydroxyethyl)-1*H*-indol-2-yl]-3-(7-ethyl-1*H*-indol-3-yl)pentanoic acid (etodolac dimer),

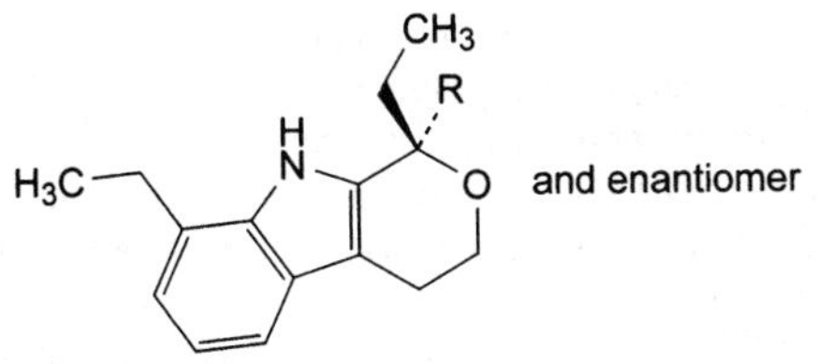

and enantiomer

J. R = CH₃: (1*RS*)-1,8-diethyl-1-methyl-1,3,4,9-tetrahydropyrano[3,4-*b*]indole (decarboxy etodolac),

K. R = CH₂-CO-O-CH₃: methyl 2-[(1*RS*)-1,8-diethyl-1,3,4,9-tetrahydropyrano[3,4-*b*]indol-1-yl]acetate (etodolac methyl ester),

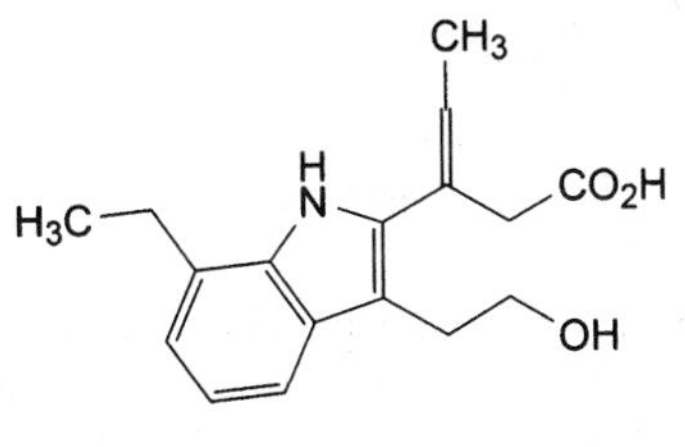

L. (*EZ*)-3-[7-ethyl-3-(2-hydroxyethyl)-1*H*-indol-2-yl]pent-3-enoic acid.

*Ph Eur*

# Etofenamate

*(Ph Eur monograph 1513)*

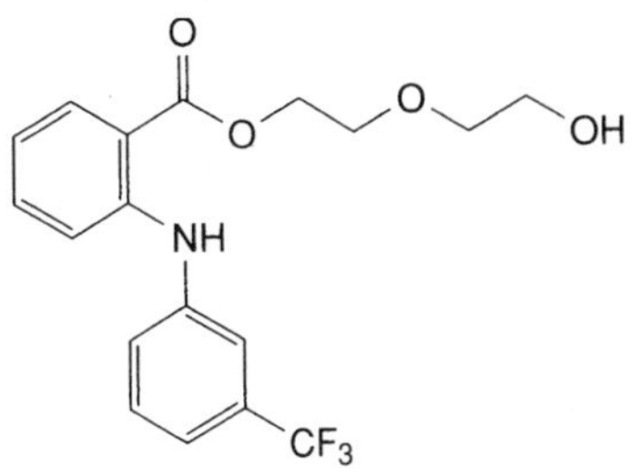

$C_{18}H_{18}F_3NO_4$          369.4          *30544-47-9*

## Action and use
Cyclo-oxygenase inhibitor; analgesic; anti-inflammatory.

*Ph Eur*

## DEFINITION
2-(2-Hydroxyethoxy)ethyl 2-[[3-(trifluoromethyl)phenyl]amino]benzoate.

## Content
98.5 per cent to 101.5 per cent (anhydrous substance).

## CHARACTERS
### Appearance
Yellowish viscous liquid.

### Solubility
Practically insoluble in water, miscible with alcohol and with ethyl acetate.

## IDENTIFICATION
Infrared absorption spectrophotometry (*2.2.24*).

*Comparison*   etofenamate CRS.

*Preparation*   Films.

## TESTS
### Appearance
The substance to be examined is clear (*2.2.1*) and not more intensely coloured than reference solution GY₁ (*2.2.2, Method II*).

### Impurity F
Gas chromatography (*2.2.28*).

*Internal standard*   tetradecane R.

*Solution A*   Dissolve 6.0 mg of *tetradecane R* in *hexane R* and dilute to 10.0 ml with the same solvent.

*Solution B*   To 6.0 mg of *diethylene glycol R* in a 10 ml volumetric flask add 3 ml of *N-methyltrimethylsilyl-trifluoroacetamide R* and heat for 30 min at 50 °C. After cooling dilute to 10.0 ml with *N-methyltrimethylsilyl-trifluoroacetamide R*.

*Test solution*   To 0.200 g of the substance to be examined add 10 µl of solution A. Add 2 ml of *N-methyltrimethylsilyl-trifluoroacetamide R* and heat for 30 min at 50 °C.

*Reference solution*   To 2.0 ml of *N-methyltrimethylsilyl-trifluoroacetamide R* add 10 µl of solution A and 10 µl of solution B.

*Column:*
— *size: l* = 25 m, Ø = 0.20 mm;
— *stationary phase: poly(dimethyl)(diphenyl)siloxane R* (film thickness 0.33 µm).

*Carrier gas*   hydrogen for chromatography R.

*Flow rate*   0.9 ml/min.

*Temperature:*

| | Time (min) | Temperature (°C) | Rate (°C/min) |
|---|---|---|---|
| Column | 0 - 13 | 60 → 150 | 7 |
| | 13 - 19 | 150 → 300 | 25 |
| | 19 - 34 | 300 | |
| Injection port | | 150 | |
| Detector | | 300 | |

*Detection*   Flame ionisation.

*Injection*   0.2 μl.

*Limit:*

— *impurity F*: maximum 0.1 per cent.

**Related substances**

Liquid chromatography (*2.2.29*).

*Test solution*   Dissolve 50.0 mg of the substance to be examined in 30 ml of *methanol R* and dilute to 50.0 ml with *water R*.

*Reference solution (a)*   Dissolve 10.0 mg of *etofenamate impurity G CRS* in *methanol R* and dilute to 20.0 ml with the same solvent. Dilute 0.2 ml of the solution to 50.0 ml with a mixture of 40 volumes of *water R* and 60 volumes of *methanol R*.

*Reference solution (b)*   Dilute 0.2 ml of the test solution to 100.0 ml with a mixture of 40 volumes of *water R* and 60 volumes of *methanol R*.

*Reference solution (c)*   To 5.0 ml of reference solution (a), add 5.0 ml of reference solution (b).

*Reference solution (d)*   Dissolve 10.0 mg of *etofenamate for peak identification CRS* (contains etofenamate spiked with about 1 per cent of impurities A, B, C, D and E) in 6.0 ml of *methanol R* and dilute to 10.0 ml with *water R*.

*Column:*

— *size: l* = 0.10 m, Ø = 4.0 mm;
— *stationary phase: octadecylsilyl silica gel for chromatography R* (3 μm);
— *temperature*: 40 °C.

*Mobile phase A*   Dissolve 1.3 g of *ammonium phosphate R* and 4.0 g of *tetrabutylammonium hydroxide R* in 900 ml of *water R*. Adjust the pH to 8.0 with *dilute phosphoric acid R* and dilute to 1000 ml with *water R,*

*Mobile phase B*   *methanol R,*

| Time | Mobile phase A (per cent *V/V*) | Mobile phase B (per cent *V/V*) |
|---|---|---|
| 0 - 13 | 40 | 60 |
| 13 - 20 | 40 → 10 | 60 → 90 |
| 20 - 25 | 10 | 90 |
| 25 - 26 | 10 → 40 | 90 → 60 |
| 26 - 31 | 40 | 60 |

*Flow rate*   1.2 ml/min.

*Detection*   Spectrophotometer at 286 nm.

*Injection*   20 μl.

*Relative retention*   With reference to etofenamate (retention time = about 13 min): impurity A = about 0.2; impurity C = about 0.7; impurity G = about 0.85; impurity E = about 1.5; impurity B = about 1.6; impurity D = about 1.7.

*System suitability*   Reference solution (c):

— *resolution*: minimum of 2.3 between the peaks due to impurity G and to etofenamate.

*Limits:*

— *correction factors*: for the calculation of contents, multiply the peak areas of the following impurities by the corresponding correction factor: impurity A = 0.62; impurity C = 0.45; impurity D = 0.77;
— *impurity A*: not more than 1.25 times the area of the principal peak in the chromatogram obtained with reference solution (b) (0.25 per cent);
— *impurity B*: not more than the area of the principal peak in the chromatogram obtained with reference solution (b) (0.2 per cent);
— *impurity C*: not more than the area of the principal peak in the chromatogram obtained with reference solution (b) (0.2 per cent);
— *impurity D*: not more than 2.5 times the area of the principal peak in the chromatogram obtained with reference solution (b) (0.5 per cent);
— *impurity E*: not more than the area of the principal peak in the chromatogram obtained with reference solution (b) (0.2 per cent);
— *impurity G*: not more than the area of the principal peak in the chromatogram obtained with reference solution (a) (0.2 per cent);
— *any other impurity*: not more than half the area of the principal peak in the chromatogram obtained with reference solution (b) (0.1 per cent);
— *total*: not more than 6 times the area of the principal peak in the chromatogram obtained with reference solution (b) (1.2 per cent);
— *disregard limit*: 0.25 times the area of the principal peak in the chromatogram obtained with reference solution (b) (0.05 per cent).

**Heavy metals** (*2.4.8*)

Maximum 10 ppm.

2.0 g complies with limit test C. Prepare the standard using 2 ml of *lead standard solution (10 ppm Pb) R*.

**Water** (*2.5.12*)

Maximum 0.5 per cent, determined on 1.00 g.

**Sulphated ash** (*2.4.14*)

Maximum 0.1 per cent, determined on 1.0 g.

**ASSAY**

To 3.000 g add 20 ml of *2-propanol R* and 20.0 ml of *1 M sodium hydroxide* and heat under reflux for 2 h. Add 0.1 ml of *bromothymol blue solution R1*. Titrate after cooling with *1 M hydrochloric acid* until the colour disappears. Carry out a blank titration.

1 ml of *1 M sodium hydroxide* is equivalent to 0.3694 g of $C_{18}H_{18}F_3NO_4$.

**IMPURITIES**

A. R = $CO_2H$: 2-[[3-(trifluoromethyl)phenyl]amino]benzoic acid (flufenamic acid),

B. R = CO-O-C₄H₉: butyl 2-[[3-(trifluoromethyl)phenyl]amino]benzoate (butyl flufenamate),

C. R = H: *N*-phenyl-3-(trifluoromethyl)aniline,

E. R = CO-[O-CH₂-CH₂]₃-CH₂-CH₃: 2-(2-butoxyethoxy)ethyl 2-[[3-(trifluoromethyl)phenyl]amino]benzoate,

G. R = CO-O-CH₂-CH₂-OH: 2-hydroxyethyl 2-[[3-(trifluoromethyl)phenyl]amino]benzoate,

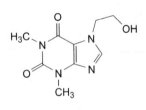

D. 2,2'-oxybis(ethylene) bis[2-[[3-(trifluoromethyl)phenyl]amino]benzoate],

F. 2,2'-oxydiethanol.

*Ph Eur*

# Etofylline

*(Ph Eur monograph 0492)*

C₉H₁₂N₄O₃          224.2          519-37-9

### Action and use

Non-selective phosphodiestarase inhibitor (xanthine); treatment of reversible airways obstruction.

*Ph Eur*

### DEFINITION

Etofylline contains not less than 98.5 per cent and not more than the equivalent of 101.0 per cent of 7-(2-hydroxyethyl)-1,3-dimethyl-3,7-dihydro-1*H*-purine-2,6-dione, calculated with reference to the dried substance.

### CHARACTERS

A white or almost white, crystalline powder, soluble in water, slightly soluble in alcohol.

### IDENTIFICATION

*First identification*    B, C.

*Second identification*    A, C, D.

A. Melting point (2.2.14): 161 °C to 166 °C.

B. Examine by infrared absorption spectrophotometry (2.2.24), comparing with the spectrum obtained with *etofylline CRS*. Examine the substances as discs prepared using 0.5 mg to 1 mg of the substance to be examined in 0.3 g of *potassium bromide R*.

C. Dissolve 1 g in 5 ml of *acetic anhydride R* and boil under a reflux condenser for 15 min. Allow to cool and add 100 ml of a mixture of 20 volumes of *ether R* and 80 volumes of *light petroleum R*. Cool in iced water for at least 20 min, shaking from time to time. Filter, wash the precipitate with a mixture of 20 volumes of *ether R* and 80 volumes of *light petroleum R*, recrystallise from *alcohol R* and dry *in vacuo*. The crystals melt (2.2.14) at 101 °C to 105 °C.

D. It gives the reaction of xanthines (2.3.1).

### TESTS
#### Solution S
Dissolve 2.5 g in *carbon dioxide-free water R* and dilute to 50 ml with the same solvent.

#### Appearance of solution
Solution S is clear (2.2.1) and colourless (2.2.2, *Method II*).

#### Acidity or alkalinity
To 10 ml of solution S add 0.25 ml of *bromothymol blue solution R1*. The solution is yellow or green. Not more than 0.4 ml of *0.01 M sodium hydroxide* is required to change the colour of the indicator to blue.

#### Related substances
Examine by thin-layer chromatography (2.2.27), using *silica gel HF₂₅₄ R* as the coating substance.

*Test solution*    Dissolve 0.3 g of the substance to be examined in a mixture of 20 volumes of *water R* and 30 volumes of *methanol R* and dilute to 10 ml with the same mixture of solvents. Prepare immediately before use.

*Reference solution (a)*    Dilute 1 ml of the test solution to 100 ml with *methanol R*.

*Reference solution (b)*    Dilute 0.2 ml of the test solution to 100 ml with *methanol R*.

*Reference solution (c)*    Dissolve 10 mg of *theophylline R* in *methanol R*, add 0.3 ml of the test solution and dilute to 10 ml with *methanol R*.

Apply to the plate 10 μl of each solution. Develop over a path of 15 cm using a mixture of 1 volume of *concentrated ammonia R*, 10 volumes of *ethanol R* and 90 volumes of *chloroform R*. Allow the plate to dry in air and examine in ultraviolet light at 254 nm. Any spot in the chromatogram obtained with the test solution, apart from the principal spot, is not more intense than the spot in the chromatogram obtained with reference solution (a) (1 per cent) and at most one such spot is more intense than the spot in the chromatogram obtained with reference solution (b) (0.2 per cent). The test is not valid unless the chromatogram obtained with reference solution (c) shows two clearly separated spots.

#### Chlorides (2.4.4)
Dilute 2.5 ml of solution S to 15 ml with *water R*. The solution complies with the limit test for chlorides (400 ppm).

#### Heavy metals (2.4.8)
12 ml of solution S complies with limit test A for heavy metals (20 ppm). Prepare the standard using *lead standard solution (1 ppm Pb) R*.

#### Loss on drying (2.2.32)
Not more than 0.5 per cent, determined on 1.000 g by drying in an oven at 105 °C.

#### Sulphated ash (2.4.14)
Not more than 0.1 per cent, determined on 1.0 g.

## ASSAY

*In order to avoid overheating in the reaction medium, mix thoroughly throughout and stop the titration immediately after the end-point has been reached.*

Dissolve 0.200 g in 3.0 ml of *anhydrous formic acid R* and add 50.0 ml of *acetic anhydride R*. Titrate with *0.1 M perchloric acid*, determining the end-point potentiometrically (*2.2.20*).

1 ml of *0.1 M perchloric acid* is equivalent to 22.42 mg of $C_9H_{12}N_4O_3$.

## STORAGE

Store protected from light.

*_____ Ph Eur*

# Etomidate

*(Ph Eur monograph 1514)*

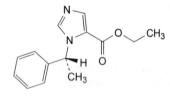

$C_{14}H_{16}N_2O_2$        244.3        *33125-97-2*

## Action and use

Intravenous general anaesthetic.

*Ph Eur _____*

## DEFINITION

Ethyl 1-[(1*R*)-1-phenylethyl]-1*H*-imidazole-5-carboxylate.

## Content

99.0 per cent to 101.0 per cent (dried substance).

## CHARACTERS

### Appearance

White or almost white powder.

### Solubility

Very slightly soluble in water, freely soluble in ethanol (96 per cent) and in methylene chloride.

mp : about 68 °C.

## IDENTIFICATION

A. Infrared absorption spectrophotometry (*2.2.24*).

*Comparison* etomidate CRS.

B. Specific optical rotation (see Tests).

## TESTS

### Solution S

Dissolve 0.25 g in *anhydrous ethanol R* and dilute to 25.0 ml with the same solvent.

### Appearance of solution

Solution S is clear (*2.2.1*) and colourless (*2.2.2, Method II*).

### Specific optical rotation (*2.2.7*)

+ 67 to + 70 (dried substance), determined on solution S.

### Related substances

Liquid chromatography (*2.2.29*).

*Solvent mixture* anhydrous ethanol R, water R (50:50 V/V).

*Test solution* Dissolve 0.100 g of the substance to be examined in the solvent mixture and dilute to 10.0 ml with the solvent mixture.

*Reference solution(a)* Dissolve 5.0 mg of *etomidate CRS* and 5.0 mg of *etomidate impurity B CRS* in the solvent mixture, then dilute to 250.0 ml with the solvent mixture.

*Reference solution(b)* Dilute 1.0 ml of the test solution to 100.0 ml with the solvent mixture. Dilute 5.0 ml of this solution to 25.0 ml with the solvent mixture.

*Column*

— *size: l* = 0.1 m, Ø = 4.6 mm;

— *stationary phase: octadecylsilyl silica gel for chromatography R* (3 µm).

*Mobile phase A* 5 g/l solution of *ammonium carbonate R*,

*Mobile phase B* acetonitrile R,

| Time (min) | Mobile phase A (per cent *V/V*) | Mobile phase B (per cent *V/V*) |
|---|---|---|
| 0 - 5 | 90 → 30 | 10 → 70 |
| 5 - 6 | 30 → 10 | 70 → 90 |
| 6 - 10 | 10 | 90 |
| 10 - 11 | 10 → 90 | 90 → 10 |
| 11 - 15 | 90 | 10 |

*Flow rate* 2.0 ml/min.

*Detection* Spectrophotometer at 235 nm.

*Equilibration* With *acetonitrile R* for at least 30 min and then with the mobile phase at the initial composition for at least 5 min.

*Injection* 10 µl.

*Retention time* Impurity B = about 4.5 min; etomidate = about 5.0 min.

*System suitability* Reference solution(a):

— *resolution*: minimum 5.0 between the peaks due to impurity B and etomidate; if necessary, adjust the concentration of ammonium carbonate in the mobile phase or the time programme of the linear gradient.

*Limits:*

— *impurities A, B, C*: for each impurity, not more than the area of the principal peak in the chromatogram obtained with reference solution (b) (0.2 per cent);

— *total*: not more than 1.5 times the area of the principal peak in the chromatogram obtained with reference solution (b) (0.3 per cent);

— *disregard limit*: 0.25 times the area of the principal peak in the chromatogram obtained with reference solution (b) (0.05 per cent).

## Loss on drying (*2.2.32*)

Maximum 0.5 per cent, determined on 1.000 g by drying *in vacuo* at 40 °C for 4 h.

## Sulphated ash (*2.4.14*)

Maximum 0.1 per cent, determined on 1.0 g.

## ASSAY

Dissolve 0.200 g in 50 ml of a mixture of 1 volume of *anhydrous acetic acid R* and 7 volumes of *methyl ethyl ketone R*. Titrate with 0.1 M perchloric acid using 0.2 ml of *naphtholbenzein solution R* as indicator.

1 ml of *0.1 M perchloric acid* is equivalent to 24.43 mg of $C_{14}H_{16}N_2O_2$.

## STORAGE

Protected from light.

## IMPURITIES
*Specified impurities   A, B, C.*

and enantiomer

A. R = H: 1-[(1*RS*)-1-phenylethyl]-1*H*-imidazole-5-carboxylic acid,

B. R = CH₃: methyl 1-[(1*RS*)-1-phenylethyl]-1*H*-imidazole-5-carboxylate (metomidate),

C. R = CH(CH₃)₂: 1-methylethyl 1-[(1*RS*)-1-phenylethyl]-1*H*-imidazole-5-carboxylate.

———————————————— *Ph Eur*

# Etoposide

*(Ph Eur monograph 0823)*

C₂₉H₃₂O₁₃          588.6          33419-42-0

## Action and use
Inhibitor of DNA topoisomerase type II; cytotoxic.

## Preparations
Etoposide Capsules

Etoposide Intravenous Infusion.

*Ph Eur* _____

## DEFINITION
(5*R*,5a*R*,8a*R*,9*S*)-9-[[4,6-O-[(*R*)-Ethylidene]-β-ᴅ-glucopyranosyl]oxy]-5-(4-hydroxy-3,5-dimethoxyphenyl)-5,8,8a,9-tetrahydroisobenzofuro[5,6-*f*][1,3]benzodioxol-6(5a*H*)-one.

## Content
98.0 per cent to 101.0 per cent (anhydrous substance).

## CHARACTERS
### Appearance
White or almost white crystalline powder.

### Solubility
Practically insoluble in water, sparingly soluble in methanol, slightly soluble in alcohol and in methylene chloride.

## IDENTIFICATION
*First identification   A, B.*

*Second identification   C, D.*

A. Specific optical rotation (see Tests).

B. Infrared absorption spectrophotometry (*2.2.24*).

*Comparison   etoposide CRS .*

C. Thin-layer chromatography (*2.2.27*).

*Test solution*   Dissolve 10 mg of the substance to be examined in a mixture of 1 volume of *methanol R* and 9 volumes of *methylene chloride R* and dilute to 2 ml with the same mixture of solvents.

*Reference solution*   Dissolve 10 mg of etoposide CRS in a mixture of 1 volume of *methanol R* and 9 volumes of *methylene chloride R* and dilute to 2 ml with the same mixture of solvents.

*Plate*   Plate with *silica gel H R* as coating substance.

*Mobile phase*   water R, glacial acetic acid R, acetone R, methylene chloride R (1.5:8:20:100 *V/V/V/V*).

*Application*   5 µl as 10 mm bands.

*Development*   Immediately, over a path of 17 cm.

*Drying*   In a current of warm air for 5 min.

*Detection*   Spray with a mixture of 1 volume of *sulphuric acid R* and 9 volumes of *alcohol R* and heat at 140 °C for 15 min. Cover the plate immediately with a glass plate of the same size. Examine in daylight.

*Results*   The principal band in the chromatogram obtained with the test solution is similar in position, colour and size to the principal band in the chromatogram obtained with the reference solution.

D. In a test-tube dissolve about 5 mg in 5 ml of *glacial acetic acid R* and add 0.05 ml of *ferric chloride solution R1*. Mix and cautiously add 2 ml of *sulphuric acid R*. Avoid mixing the 2 layers. Allow to stand for about 30 min; a pink to reddish-brown ring develops at the interface and the upper layer is yellow.

## TESTS
### Appearance of solution
The solution is clear (*2.2.1*) and not more intensely coloured than reference solution Y₆ or BY₆ (*2.2.2, Method II*).

Dissolve 0.6 g in a mixture of 1 volume of *methanol R* and 9 volumes of *methylene chloride R* and dilute to 20 ml with the same mixture of solvents.

### Specific optical rotation (*2.2.7*)
− 106 to − 114 (anhydrous substance).

Dissolve 50 mg in a mixture of 1 volume of *methanol R* and 9 volumes of *methylene chloride R* and dilute to 10.0 ml with the same mixture of solvents.

### Related substances
Liquid chromatography (*2.2.29*).

*Test solution (a)*   Dissolve 40 mg of the substance to be examined in a mixture of equal volumes of mobile phase A and mobile phase B and dilute to 10.0 ml with the same mixture of mobile phases.

*Test solution (b)*   Dissolve 50.0 mg of the substance to be examined in a mixture of equal volumes of mobile phase A and mobile phase B and dilute to 50.0 ml with the same mixture of mobile phases.

*Reference solution (a)*   Dilute 1.0 ml of test solution (a) to 10.0 ml with a mixture of equal volumes of mobile phase A and mobile phase B. Dilute 1.0 ml of this solution to 20.0 ml with a mixture of equal volumes of mobile phase A and mobile phase B.

*Reference solution (b)*   Dilute 4.0 ml of reference solution (a) to 10.0 ml with a mixture of equal volumes of mobile phase A and mobile phase B.

*Reference solution (c)*   Dissolve 50.0 mg of etoposide CRS in a mixture of equal volumes of mobile phase A and mobile

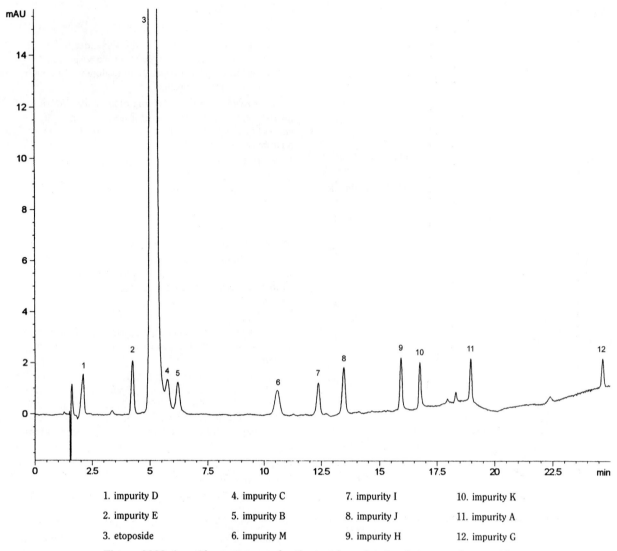

1. impurity D
2. impurity E
3. etoposide
4. impurity C
5. impurity B
6. impurity M
7. impurity I
8. impurity J
9. impurity H
10. impurity K
11. impurity A
12. impurity G

Figure 0823.-1. – *Chromatogram for the test for related substances of etoposide*

phase B and dilute to 50.0 ml with the same mixture of mobile phases.

*Reference solution (d)* To 10 ml of test solution (b), add 0.1 ml of a 4 per cent V/V solution of *glacial acetic acid R* and 0.1 ml of *phenolphthalein solution R*. Add *1 M sodium hydroxide* until the solution becomes faintly pink (about 0.15 ml). After 15 min, add 0.1 ml of a 4 per cent V/V solution of *glacial acetic acid R*.

*Column:*
— *size: l* = 0.125 m, Ø = 4.6 mm,
— *stationary phase: octadecylsilyl silica gel for chromatography R* (5 μm),
— *temperature:* 40 °C.

*Mobile phase:*
— *mobile phase A: triethylamine R, anhydrous formic acid R, water R* (1:1:998 *V/V/V*),
— *mobile phase B: triethylamine R, anhydrous formic acid R, acetonitrile R* (1:1:998 *V/V/V*),

| Time (min) | Mobile phase A (per cent *V/V*) | Mobile phase B (per cent *V/V*) |
|---|---|---|
| 0 - 7 | 75 | 25 |
| 7 - 23 | 75 → 27 | 25 → 73 |
| 23 - 25 | 27 → 75 | 73 → 25 |
| 25 - 40 | 75 | 25 |

*Flow rate* 1 ml/min.

*Detection* Spectrophotometer at 285 nm.

*Injection* 10 μl; inject test solution (a) and reference solutions (a), (b) and (d).

*Retention times* The retention times and the elution order of the peaks are similar to those shown in the chromatogram (Figure 0823.-1).

*System suitability* Reference solution (d): continue the chromatography until the peak due to phenolphtalein is eluted.
— the chromatogram shows 2 principal peaks corresponding to etoposide and to impurity B. Disregard any peak due to phenolphtalein.
— *resolution*: minimum 3.0 between the peaks due to etoposide and to impurity B.

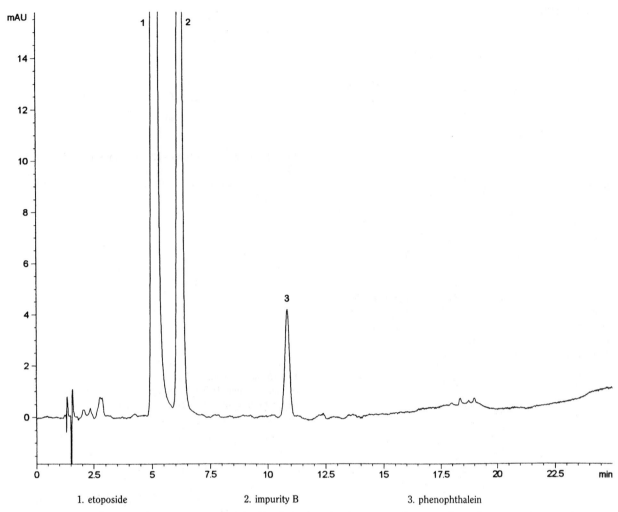

1. etoposide             2. impurity B             3. phenophthalein

Figure 0823.-2. – *Chromatogram for the test for related substances of etoposide: reference solution (d)*

If necessary, increase slightly the proportion of mobile phase A during the isocratic phase of the gradient. When the chromatograms are recorded under the prescribed conditions, the retention times of the peaks in the chromatogram obtained with reference solution (d) are similar to those shown in the chromatogram (Figure 0823.-2).

*Limits:*

— *any impurity*: not more than the area of the principal peak in the chromatogram obtained with reference solution (a) (0.5 per cent) and not more than 2 such peaks have an area greater than the area of the principal peak in the chromatogram obtained with reference solution (b) (0.2 per cent),

— *total*: not more than twice the area of the principal peak in the chromatogram obtained with reference solution (a) (1 per cent),

— *disregard limit*: 0.1 times the area of the principal peak in the chromatogram obtained with reference solution (a). Disregard any peak due to the solvent.

**Heavy metals** (*2.4.8*)

Maximum 20 ppm.

1.0 g complies with limit test C. Prepare the reference solution using 2 ml of *lead standard solution (10 ppm Pb) R.*

**Water** (*2.5.12*)

Maximum 6.0 per cent, determined on 0.250 g.

**Sulphated ash** (*2.4.14*)

Maximum 0.1 per cent, determined on 1.0 g.

**ASSAY**

Liquid chromatography (*2.2.29*) as described in the test for related substances with the following modifications.

*Injection* Test solution (b) and reference solution (c).

*System suitability:*

— *repeatability*: maximum relative standard deviation of 1.0 per cent after 6 injections of reference solution (c).

Calculate the percentage content of $C_{29}H_{32}O_{13}$ from the areas of the peaks and the declared content of *etoposide CRS*.

**STORAGE**

In an airtight container.

## IMPURITIES

A. (5R,5aR,8aR,9S)-5-[4-[[(benzyloxy)carbonyl]oxy]-3,5-dimethoxyphenyl]-9-[[4,6-O-[(R)-ethylidene]-β-D-glucopyranosyl]oxy]-5,8,8a,9-tetrahydroisobenzofuro[5,6-f][1,3]benzodioxol-6(5aH)-one (4′-carbobenzoyloxyethylidene-lignan P),

B. (5R,5aS,8aR,9S)-9-[[4,6-O-[(R)-ethylidene]-β-D-glucopyranosyl]oxy]-5-(4-hydroxy-3,5-dimethoxyphenyl)-5,8,8a,9-tetrahydroisobenzofuro[5,6-f][1,3]benzodioxol-6(5aH)-one (picroethylidene-lignan P; cis-etoposide),

C. (5R,5aR,8aR,9S)-9-[[4,6-O-[(R)-ethylidene]-α-D-glucopyranosyl]oxy]-5-(4-hydroxy-3,5-dimethoxyphenyl)-5,8,8a,9-tetrahydroisobenzofuro[5,6-f][1,3]benzodioxol-6(5aH)-one (α-etoposide),

D. (5R,5aR,8aR,9S)-9-(β-D-glucopyranosyloxy)-5-(4-hydroxy-3,5-dimethoxyphenyl)-5,8,8a,9-tetrahydroisobenzofuro[5,6-f][1,3]benzodioxol-6(5aH)-one (lignan P),

E. (5R,5aR,8aR,9S)-9-hydroxy-5-(4-hydroxy-3,5-dimethoxyphenyl)-5,8,8a,9-tetrahydroisobenzofuro[5,6-f][1,3]benzodioxol-6(5aH)-one (4′-demethylepipodophyllotoxin),

F. (5R,5aR,8aR,9S)-9-[[4,6-O-[(R)-ethylidene]-β-D-glucopyranosyl]oxy]-5-[4-[(phenoxyacetyl)oxy]-3,5-dimethoxyphenyl]-5,8,8a,9-tetrahydroisobenzofuro[5,6-f][1,3]benzodioxol-6(5aH)-one (4′-phenoxyacetyletoposide),

G. (5R,5aR,8aR,9S)-5-[4-[[(benzyloxy)carbonyl]oxy]-3,5-dimethoxyphenyl]-9-[[4,6-O-[(R)-ethylidene]-2,3-di-O-formyl-β-D-glucopyranosyl]oxy]-5,8,8a,9-tetrahydroisobenzofuro[5,6-f][1,3]benzodioxol-6(5aH)-one (4′-carbobenzoyloxydiformylethylidene-lignan P),

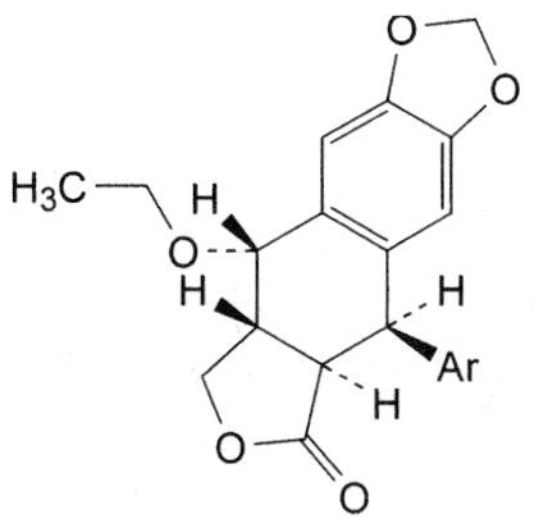

H. (5R,5aR,8aR,9S)-9-ethoxy-5-(4-hydroxy-3,5-dimethoxyphenyl)-5,8,8a,9-tetrahydroisobenzofuro[5,6-f][1,3]benzodioxol-6(5aH)-one (4'-O-demethyl-1-O-ethylepipodophyllotoxin),

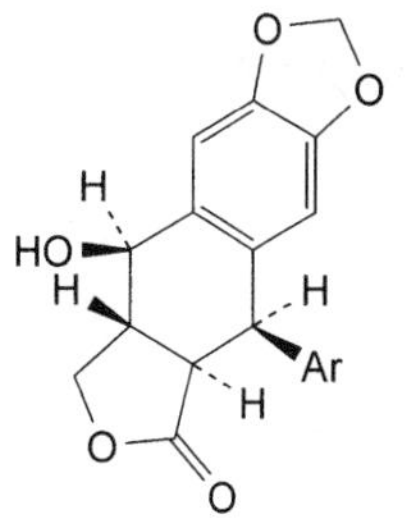

L. (5R,5aR,8aR,9R)-9-hydroxy-5-(4-hydroxy-3,5-dimethoxyphenyl)-5,8,8a,9-tetrahydroisobenzofuro[5,6-f][1,3]benzodioxol-6(5aH)-one (4'-O-demethylpodophyllotoxin),

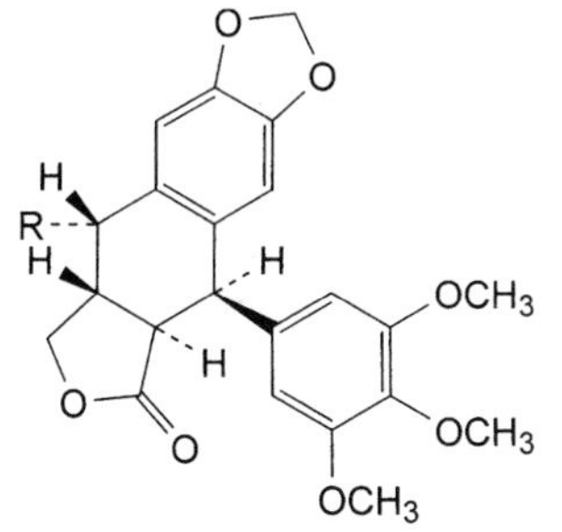

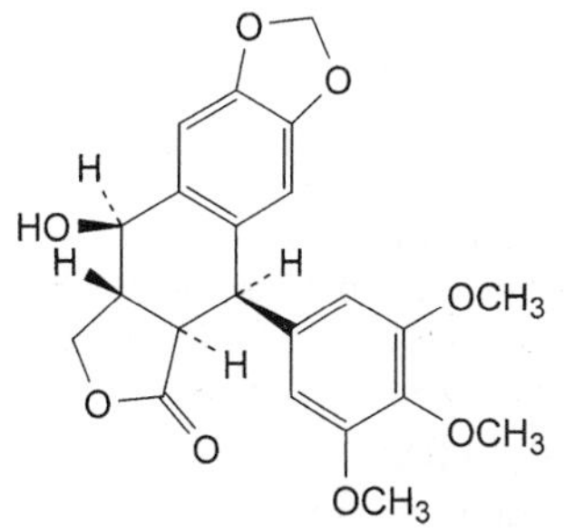

I. (5R,5aR,8aR,9S)-9-[[4,6-O-[(R)-ethylidene]-β-D-glucopyranosyl]oxy]-5-(3,4,5-trimethoxyphenyl)-5,8,8a,9-tetrahydroisobenzofuro[5,6-f][1,3]benzodioxol-6(5aH)-one (4-O-methylethylidene-lignan P),

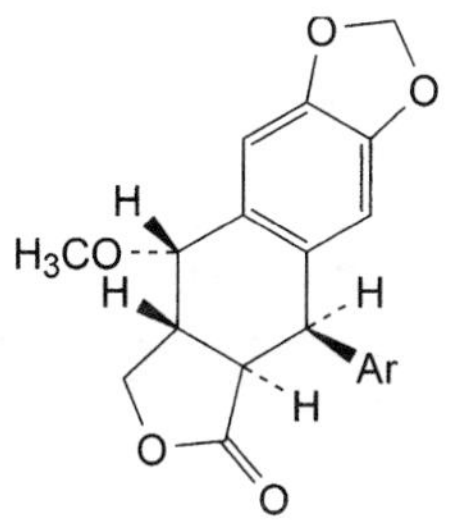

M. (5R,5aR,8aR,9R)-9-hydroxy-5-(3,4,5-trimethoxyphenyl)-5,8,8a,9-tetrahydroisobenzofuro[5,6-f][1,3]benzodioxol-6(5aH)-one (podophyllotoxin),

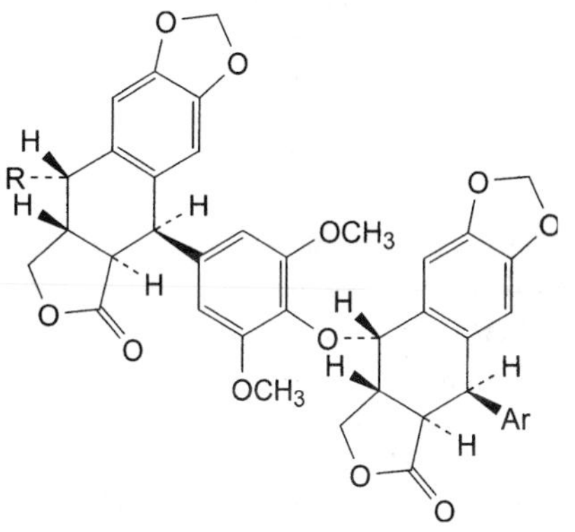

J. (5R,5aR,8aR,9S)-5-(4-hydroxy-3,5-dimethoxyphenyl)-9-methoxy-5,8,8a,9-tetrahydroisobenzofuro[5,6-f][1,3]benzodioxol-6(5aH)-one (4'-O-demethyl-1-O-methylepipodophyllotoxin),

N. (5R,5aR,8aR,9S)-9-[[4,6-O-[(R)-ethylidene]-β-D-glucopyranosyl]oxy]-5-[4-[[(5R,5aR,8aR,9S)-5-(4-hydroxy-3,5-dimethoxyphenyl)-6-oxo-5,5a,6,8,8a,9-hexahydroisobenzofuro[5,6-f][1,3]benzodioxol-9-yl]oxy]-3,5-dimethoxyphenyl]-5,8,8a,9-tetrahydroisobenzofuro[5,6-f][1,3]benzodioxol-6(5aH)-one.

*Ph Eur*

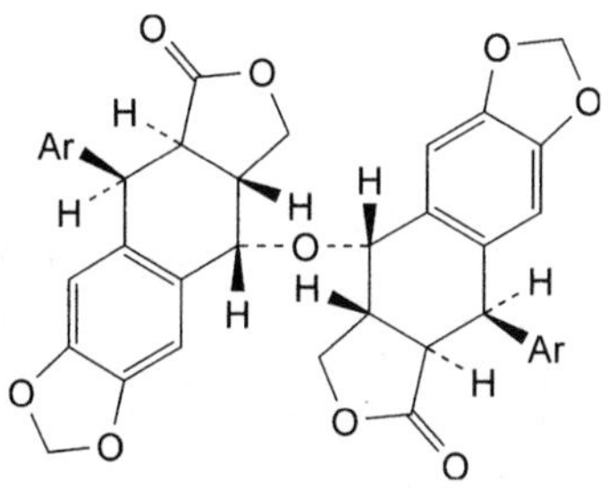

K. 9,9'-oxybis[(5R,5aR,8aR,9S)-5-(4-hydroxy-3,5-dimethoxyphenyl)-5,8,8a,9-tetrahydroisobenzofuro[5,6-f][1,3]benzodioxol-6(5aH)-one] (di-4'-O-demethylepipodophyllotoxin),

# Etynodiol Diacetate

C₂₄H₃₂O₄ 384.5 297-76-7

$C_{24}H_{32}O_4$ 384.5 *297-76-7*

### Action and use
Progestogen.

### DEFINITION
Etynodiol Diacetate is 19-nor-17α-pregn-4-en-20-yne-3β,17β-diyl diacetate. It contains not less than 97.0% and not more than 102.0% of $C_{24}H_{32}O_4$, calculated with reference to the dried substance.

### CHARACTERISTICS
A white or almost white, crystalline powder.

Very slightly soluble in *water*, freely soluble in *ether*, soluble in *ethanol (96%)*.

### IDENTIFICATION
A. The *light absorption*, Appendix II B, in the range 220 to 350 nm of the solution obtained in the test for Light absorption exhibits a maximum only at 236 nm and shoulders at 229 and 243 nm.

B. The *infrared absorption spectrum*, Appendix II A, is concordant with the *reference spectrum* of etynodiol diacetate *(RS 138)*.

C. Yields the reaction characteristic of *acetyl groups*, Appendix VI.

### TESTS
**Light absorption**
Dissolve 50 mg in sufficient *methanol* to produce 50 ml (solution A). To 10 ml of solution A add 40 ml of *methanol* and a mixture of 3 ml of *hydrochloric acid* and 2 ml of *water*, mix and boil on a water bath for exactly 10 minutes. Cool, dilute to 100 ml with *methanol* and dilute 10 ml of the solution to 100 ml with *methanol*. The *absorbance* of the resulting solution at the maximum at 236 nm, Appendix II B, is 0.47 to 0.50, calculated with reference to the dried substance, using in the reference cell a solution prepared by diluting 1 ml of solution A to 100 ml with *methanol*.

**Melting point**
126° to 131°, Appendix V A.

**Specific optical rotation**
In a 1% w/v solution in *chloroform*, –70 to –76, Appendix V F, calculated with reference to the dried substance.

**Conjugated compounds**
*Absorbance* of a 0.050% w/v solution in *methanol* at 236 nm, not more than 0.47, calculated with reference to the dried substance, Appendix II B.

**Loss on drying**
When dried to constant weight at 105°, loses not more than 0.5% of its weight. Use 1 g.

**Sulphated ash**
Not more than 0.1%, Appendix IX A.

### ASSAY
Dissolve 0.2 g in 40 ml of *tetrahydrofuran*, add 10 ml of a 10% w/v solution of *silver nitrate* and titrate with 0.1M *sodium hydroxide VS*, determining the end point potentiometrically. Each ml of 0.1M *sodium hydroxide VS* is equivalent to 38.45 mg of $C_{24}H_{32}O_4$.

### STORAGE
Etynodiol Diacetate should be protected from light.

# Eugenol

*(Ph Eur monograph 1100)*

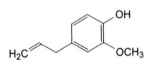

C₁₀H₁₂O₂ 164.2 97-53-0

$C_{10}H_{12}O_2$ 164.2 *97-53-0*

*Ph Eur*

### DEFINITION
2-Methoxy-4-(prop-2-enyl)phenol.

### CHARACTERS
**Appearance**
Colourless or pale yellow, clear liquid, darkening on exposure to air.

It has a strong odour of clove.

**Solubility**
Practically insoluble in water, freely soluble in ethanol (70 per cent *V/V*), practically insoluble in glycerol, miscible with ethanol (96 per cent), with glacial acetic acid, with methylene chloride and with fatty oils.

### IDENTIFICATION
*First identification* B.

*Second identification* A, C, D.

A. Refractive index (see Tests).

B. Infrared absorption spectrophotometry *(2.2.24)*.

*Comparison* eugenol CRS .

C. Thin-layer chromatography *(2.2.27)*.

*Test solution* Dissolve 50 µl of the substance to be examined in *ethanol (96 per cent) R* and dilute to 25 ml with the same solvent.

*Reference solution* Dissolve 50 µl of eugenol CRS in *ethanol (96 per cent) R* and dilute to 25 ml with the same solvent.

*Plate* TLC silica gel $F_{254}$ plate R.

*Mobile phase* ethyl acetate R, toluene R (10:90 *V/V*).

*Application* 5 µl.

*Development* Over a path of 15 cm.

*Drying* In a current of cold air.

*Detection A* Examine in ultraviolet light at 254 nm.

*Results A* The principal spot in the chromatogram obtained with the test solution is similar in position and size to the principal spot in the chromatogram obtained with the reference solution.

*Detection B* Spray with *anisaldehyde solution R* and heat at 100-105 °C for 10 min.

*Results B* The principal spot in the chromatogram obtained with the test solution is similar in position, colour and size to the principal spot in the chromatogram obtained with the reference solution.

D. Dissolve 0.05 ml in 2 ml of *ethanol (96 per cent)* R and add 0.1 ml of *ferric chloride solution R1*. A dark green colour is produced which changes to yellowish-green within 10 min.

## TESTS

**Relative density** (*2.2.5*)
1.066 to 1.070.

**Refractive index** (*2.2.6*)
1.540 to 1.542.

**Dimeric and oligomeric compounds**
Dissolve 0.150 g in *anhydrous ethanol* R and dilute to 100.0 ml with the same solvent. The absorbance (*2.2.25*) of the solution at 330 nm is not greater than 0.25.

**Related substances**
*Gas chromatography* (*2.2.28*)   Use the normalisation procedure.

*Test solution*   Dissolve 1.00 g of the substance to be examined in *anhydrous ethanol* R and dilute to 5.0 ml with the same solvent.

*Reference solution (a)*   Dilute 1.0 ml of the test solution to 100.0 ml with *anhydrous ethanol* R.

*Reference solution (b)*   Dissolve 50 mg of *vanillin* R (impurity H) in 1 ml of the test solution and dilute to 5 ml with *anhydrous ethanol* R.

*Column:*
— *material*: fused silica;
— *size: l* = 30 m, Ø = 0.25 mm;
— *stationary phase*: *polymethylphenylsiloxane* R (film thickness 0.25 μm).

*Carrier gas*   *helium for chromatography* R.

*Flow rate*   1 ml/min.

*Split ratio*   1:40.

*Temperature:*

|  | Time (min) | Temperature (°C) |
|---|---|---|
| Column | 0 - 2 | 80 |
|  | 2 - 27 | 80 → 280 |
|  | 27 - 47 | 280 |
| Injection port |  | 250 |
| Detector |  | 280 |

*Detection*   Flame ionisation.

*Injection*   1 μl.

*System suitability*   Reference solution (b):
— *relative retention* with reference to eugenol: impurity H = minimum 1.1.

*Limits:*
— *any impurity*: for each impurity, maximum 0.5 per cent;
— *sum of impurities with a relative retention greater than 2.0 with reference to eugenol* : maximum 1.0 per cent;
— *total*: maximum 3.0 per cent;
— *disregard limit*: 0.05 times the area of the principal peak in the chromatogram obtained with reference solution (a) (0.05 per cent).

**Hydrocarbons**
Dissolve 1 ml in 5 ml of *dilute sodium hydroxide solution R* and add 30 ml of *water R* in a stoppered test-tube. Examined immediately, the solution is yellow and clear (*2.2.1*).

**Sulphated ash** (*2.4.14*)
Maximum 0.1 per cent, determined on 1.0 g.

## STORAGE
In a well-filled container, protected from light.

## IMPURITIES

A. (1R,4E,9S)-4,11,11-trimethyl-8-methylenebicyclo[7.2.0]undec-4-ene (β-caryophyllene),

B. (1E,4E,8E)-2,6,6,9-tetramethylcycloundeca-1,4,8-triene (α-humulene, α-caryophyllene),

C. (1R,4R,6R,10S)-4,12,12-trimethyl-9-methylene-5-oxatricyclo[8.2.0.0$^{4,6}$]dodecane (β-caryophyllene oxide),

D. R1 = H, R2 = H, R3 = CH$_2$-CH=CH$_2$: 4-(prop-2-enyl)phenol,

E. R1 = CH$_3$, R2 = OCH$_3$, R3 = CH$_2$-CH=CH$_2$: 1,2-dimethoxy-4-(prop-2-enyl)benzene (eugenol methyl ether),

F. R1 = H, R2 = OCH$_3$, R3 = CH=CH-CH$_3$ (*cis*): 2-methoxy-4-[(Z)-prop-1-enyl]phenol (*cis*-isoeugenol),

G. R1 = H, R2 = OCH$_3$, R3 = CH=CH-CH$_3$ (*trans*): 2-methoxy-4-[(E)-prop-1-enyl]phenol (*trans*-isoeugenol),

H. R1 = H, R2 = OCH$_3$, R3 = CHO: 4-hydroxy-3-methoxybenzaldehyde (vanillin),

I. R1 = CO-CH$_3$, R2 = OCH$_3$, R3 = CH$_2$-CH=CH$_2$: 2-methoxy-4-(prop-2-enyl)phenyl acetate (acetyleugenol),

J. R1 = H, R2 = OCH$_3$, R3 = CO-CH=CH$_2$: 1-(4-hydroxy-3-methoxyphenyl)prop-2-enone,

K. R1 = H, R2 = OCH$_3$, R3 = CH=CH-CHO: (E)-3-(4-hydroxy-3-methoxyphenyl)prop-2-enal (*trans*-coniferyl aldehyde),

L. 2-methoxy-4-[3-methyl-5-(prop-2-enyl)-2,3-dihydrobenzofuran-2-yl]phenol (dehydrodi-isoeugenol),

M. 3,3′-dimethoxy-5,5′-bis(prop-2-enyl)biphenyl-2,2′-diol (dehydrodieugenol),

N. O. 2 further unknown dimeric compounds,

P. toluene.

_____ *Ph Eur*

# Famotidine

*(Ph Eur monograph 1012)*

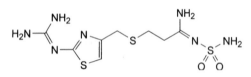

C₈H₁₅N₇O₂S₃      337.5      76824-35-6

$C_8H_{15}N_7O_2S_3$    337.5    76824-35-6

## Action and use
Histamine $H_2$ receptor antagonist; treatment of peptic ulceration.

## Preparation
Famotidine Tablets

*Ph Eur* _____

## DEFINITION
3-[[[2-[(Diaminomethylene)amino]thiazol-4-yl]methyl]sulphanyl]-*N*′-sulphamoylpropanimidamide.

## Content
98.5 per cent to 101.5 per cent (dried substance).

## CHARACTERS
### Appearance
White or yellowish-white, crystalline powder or crystals.

### Solubility
Very slightly soluble in water, freely soluble in glacial acetic acid, very slightly soluble in anhydrous ethanol, practically insoluble in ethyl acetate. It dissolves in dilute mineral acids.
It shows polymorphism (*5.9*).

## IDENTIFICATION
Infrared absorption spectrophotometry (*2.2.24*).

*Preparation*    Discs.

*Comparison*    *famotidine CRS.*

If the spectra obtained show differences, suspend 0.10 g of the substance to be examined and 0.10 g of the reference substance separately in 5 ml of *water R*. Heat to boiling and allow to cool, scratching the wall of the tube with a glass rod to initiate crystallisation. Filter, wash the crystals with 2 ml of iced *water R* and dry in an oven at 80 °C at a pressure not exceeding 670 Pa for 1 h. Record new spectra using the residues.

## TESTS
### Appearance of solution
Dissolve 0.20 g in a 50 g/l solution of *hydrochloric acid R*, heating to 40 °C if necessary, and dilute to 20 ml with the same acid. The solution is clear (*2.2.1*) and not more intensely coloured than reference solution $BY_7$ (*2.2.2, Method II*).

### Related substances
Liquid chromatography (*2.2.29*).

*Test solution*    Dissolve 12.5 mg of the substance to be examined in mobile phase A and dilute to 25.0 ml with mobile phase A.

*Reference solution (a)*    Dilute 1.0 ml of the test solution to 10.0 ml with mobile phase A. Dilute 1.0 ml of this solution to 100.0 ml with mobile phase A.

*Reference solution (b)*    Dissolve 2.5 mg of *famotidine impurity D CRS* in *methanol R* and dilute to 10.0 ml with the same solvent. To 1.0 ml of the solution add 0.50 ml of the test solution and dilute to 100.0 ml with mobile phase A.

*Reference solution (c)*    Dissolve 5.0 mg of *famotidine for system suitability CRS* (famotidine containing impurities A, B, C, D, E, F, G) in mobile phase A and dilute to 10.0 ml with mobile phase A.

*Column:*
— *size:* $l = 0.25$ m, $\varnothing = 4.6$ mm,
— *stationary phase:* end-capped octadecylsilyl silica gel for chromatography R (5 μm),
— *temperature:* 50 °C.

*Mobile phase:*
— *mobile phase A*: mix 6 volumes of *methanol R*, 94 volumes of *acetonitrile R* and 900 volumes of a 1.882 g/l solution of *sodium hexanesulphonate R* previously adjusted to pH 3.5 with *acetic acid R*,
— *mobile phase B*: *acetonitrile R*,

| Time (min) | Mobile phase A (per cent *V/V*) | Mobile phase B (per cent *V/V*) | Flow rate (ml/min) |
|---|---|---|---|
| 0 - 23 | 100 → 96 | 0 → 4 | 1 |
| 23 - 27 | 96 | 4 | 1 → 2 |
| 27 - 47 | 96 → 78 | 4 → 22 | 2 |
| 47 - 48 | 78 → 100 | 22 → 0 | 2 |
| 48 - 54 | 100 | 0 | 2 → 1 |

*Detection*    Spectrophotometer at 265 nm.

*Injection*    20 μl.

*Relative retention* with reference to famotidine (retention time = about 21 min): impurity D = about 1.1; impurity C = about 1.2; impurity G = about 1.4; impurity F = about 1.5; impurity A = about 1.6; impurity B = about 2.0; impurity E = about 2.1.

*System suitability:*
— the chromatogram obtained with reference solution (c) is similar to the chromatogram supplied with *famotidine for system suitability CRS*;
— *retention time*: famotidine = 19-23 min in all the chromatograms; impurity E = maximum 48 min in the chromatogram obtained with reference solution (c);
— *resolution*: minimum 3.5 between the peaks due to famotidine and impurity D in the chromatogram obtained with reference solution (b).

*Limits:*
— *correction factors*: for the calculation of contents, multiply the peak areas of the following impurities by the corresponding correction factor: impurity A = 1.9; impurity B = 2.5; impurity C = 1.9; impurity F = 1.7; impurity G = 1.4;
— *impurities A, G*: for each impurity, not more than twice the area of the principal peak in the chromatogram obtained with reference solution (a) (0.2 per cent);
— *impurities B, C, D, E*: for each impurity, not more than 3 times the area of the principal peak in the chromatogram obtained with reference solution (a) (0.3 per cent), and not more than 3 such peaks have an area greater than the area of the principal peak in the chromatogram obtained with reference solution (a) (0.1 per cent);
— *impurity F*: not more than the area of the principal peak in the chromatogram obtained with reference solution (a) (0.1 per cent);
— *any other impurity*: for each impurity, not more than the area of the principal peak in the chromatogram obtained with reference solution (a) for the peaks eluting by 25 min, and not more than 0.5 times the area of the principal peak in the chromatogram obtained with reference solution (a) for the peaks eluting after 25 min (0.1 per cent);
— *total*: not more than 10 times the area of the principal peak in the chromatogram obtained with reference solution (a) (1.0 per cent);
— *disregard limit*: 0.2 times the area of the principal peak in the chromatogram obtained with reference solution (a).

**Heavy metals** (*2.4.8*)
Maximum 10 ppm.

2.0 g complies with limit test D. Prepare the reference solution using 2 ml of *lead standard solution (10 ppm Pb) R*.

**Loss on drying** (*2.2.32*)
Maximum 0.5 per cent, determined on 1.000 g by drying in an oven at 80 °C at a pressure not exceeding 670 Pa for 5 h.

**Sulphated ash** (*2.4.14*)
Maximum 0.1 per cent, determined on 1.0 g.

**ASSAY**
Dissolve 0.120 g in 60 ml of *anhydrous acetic acid R*. Titrate with *0.1 M perchloric acid*, determining the end-point potentiometrically (*2.2.20*).

1 ml of *0.1 M perchloric acid* is equivalent to 16.87 mg of $C_8H_{15}N_7O_2S_3$.

**STORAGE**
Protected from light.

**IMPURITIES**
*Specified impurities*  A, B, C, D, E, F, G.

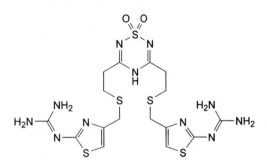

A. R = NH$_2$, X = NH:
3-[[[2-[(diaminomethylene)amino]thiazol-4-yl]methyl]sulphanyl]propanimidamide,

C. R = NH-SO$_2$-NH$_2$, X = O:
3-[[[2-[(diaminomethylene)amino]thiazol-4-yl]methyl]sulphanyl]-*N*-sulphamoylpropanamide,

D. R = NH$_2$, X = O:
3-[[[2-[(diaminomethylene)amino]thiazol-4-yl]methyl]sulphanyl]propanamide,

F. R = OH, X = O:
3-[[[2-[(diaminomethylene)amino]thiazol-4-yl]methyl]sulphanyl]propanoic acid,

G. R = NH-CN, X = NH:
*N*-cyano-3-[[[2-[(diaminomethylene)amino]thiazol-4-yl]methyl]sulphanyl]propanimidamide,

B. 3,5-bis[2-[[[2-[(diaminomethylene)amino]thiazol-4-yl]methyl]sulphanyl]ethyl]-4*H*-1,2,4,6-thiatriazine 1,1-dioxide,

E. 2,2'-[disulphanediylbis(methylenethiazole-4,2-diyl)]diguanidine.

*Ph Eur*

# Hard Fat

(*Ph Eur monograph 0462*)

*Ph Eur*

**DEFINITION**
Mixture of triglycerides, diglycerides and monoglycerides, which may be obtained either by esterification of fatty acids of natural origin with glycerol or by transesterification of natural fats.

Each type of hard fat is characterised by its melting point, its hydroxyl value and its saponification value.

It contains no added substances.

## CHARACTERS

### Appearance

White or almost white, waxy, brittle mass.

### Solubility

Practically insoluble in water, slightly soluble in anhydrous ethanol.

When heated to 50 °C, it melts giving a colourless or slightly yellowish liquid.

## IDENTIFICATION

Thin-layer chromatography (2.2.27).

*Test solution* Dissolve 1.0 g of the substance to be examined in *ethylene chloride R* and dilute to 10 ml with the same solvent.

*Plate* TLC silica gel G plate R.

*Mobile phase* ether R, ethylene chloride R (10:90 V/V).

*Application* 2 μl.

*Development* Over a path of 12 cm.

*Drying* In air.

*Detection* Expose to iodine vapour until the spots appear and examine in daylight.

*Results* The chromatogram shows a spot with an $R_F$ value of about 0.6 due to triglycerides ($R_{st}$ 1) and may show spots due to 1,3-diglycerides ($R_{st}$ 0.5), to 1,2-diglycerides ($R_{st}$ 0.3) and to 1-monoglycerides ($R_{st}$ 0.05). If spots due to partial glycerides are not detectable the tests for melting point and for hydroxyl value (see Tests) are carried out in addition to confirm identification.

## TESTS

### Alkaline impurities

Dissolve 2.00 g in a mixture of 1.5 ml of *ethanol (96 per cent) R* and 3.0 ml of *ether R*. Add 0.05 ml of *bromophenol blue solution R*. Not more than 0.15 ml of *0.01 M hydrochloric acid* is required to change the colour of the indicator to yellow.

### Melting point (2.2.15)

30 °C to 45 °C, and within 2 °C of the nominal value.

Introduce the melted substance into the capillary tube and allow to stand at a temperature below 10 °C for 24 h.

### Acid value (2.5.1)

Maximum 0.5.

Dissolve 5.0 g in 50 ml of the prescribed mixture of solvents.

### Hydroxyl value (2.5.3, Method A)

Maximum 50, and within 5 units of the nominal value; maximum 5 if the nominal value is less than 5.

### Iodine value (2.5.4, Method A)

Maximum 3.

### Peroxide value (2.5.5, Method A)

Maximum 3.

### Saponification value (2.5.6)

210 to 260, and within 5 per cent of the nominal value, determined on 2.0 g.

### Unsaponifiable matter (2.5.7)

Maximum 0.6 per cent, determined on 5.0 g.

### Heavy metals (2.4.8)

Maximum 10 ppm.

2.0 g complies with test D. Prepare the reference solution using 2 ml of *lead standard solution (10 ppm Pb) R*.

### Total ash (2.4.16)

Maximum 0.05 per cent, determined on 2.00 g.

## STORAGE

Protected from light and heat.

## LABELLING

The label states:
— the nominal melting point;
— the nominal hydroxyl value;
— the nominal saponification value.

_____ *Ph Eur*

# Felbinac

(*Ph Eur monograph 2304*)

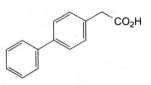

C$_{14}$H$_{12}$O$_2$         212.2         5728-52-9

### Action and use

Cyclo-oxygenase inhibitor; analgesic; anti-inflammatory.

*Ph Eur* _____

## DEFINITION

(Biphenyl-4-yl)acetic acid.

### Content

99.0 per cent to 101.0 per cent (dried substance).

## CHARACTERS

### Appearance

White or almost white, crystalline powder.

### Solubility

Practically insoluble in water, soluble in methanol, sparingly soluble in ethanol (96 per cent).

mp: about 164 °C.

## IDENTIFICATION

Infrared absorption spectrophotometry (2.2.24).

*Comparison* felbinac CRS.

## TESTS

### Related substances

Liquid chromatography (2.2.29). *Protect the solutions from light and inject within 20 min of preparation.*

*Test solution* Dissolve 0.100 g of the substance to be examined in *methanol R* and dilute to 10.0 ml with the same solvent.

*Reference solution* Dissolve 5.0 mg of *felbinac impurity A CRS* and 5.0 mg of *biphenyl R* (impurity B) in *methanol R*, add 0.5 ml of the test solution and dilute to 50.0 ml with *methanol R*. Dilute 1.0 ml of this solution to 10.0 ml with *methanol R*.

*Column:*
— *size: l* = 0.15 m, Ø = 4.6 mm;
— *stationary phase:* octadecylsilyl silica gel for chromatography R (5 μm).

*Mobile phase* Mix 45 volumes of a 0.1 per cent V/V solution of *glacial acetic acid R* and 55 volumes of *methanol R*.

*Flow rate* 2 ml/min.

*Detection* Spectrophotometer at 254 nm.

*Injection* 20 μl.

*Run time* 3.5 times the retention time of felbinac.

*Relative retention* With reference to felbinac (retention time = about 15 min): impurity A = about 1.3; impurity B = about 2.8.

*System suitability* Reference solution:
— *resolution*: minimum 3.0 between the peaks due to felbinac and impurity A.

*Limits:*
— *impurity A*: not more than the area of the corresponding peak in the chromatogram obtained with the reference solution (0.1 per cent);
— *impurity B*: not more than the area of the peak due to felbinac in the chromatogram obtained with the reference solution (0.1 per cent);
— *unspecified impurities*: for each impurity, not more than the area of the peak due to felbinac in the chromatogram obtained with the reference solution (0.10 per cent);
— *total*: not more than twice the area of the peak due to felbinac in the chromatogram obtained with the reference solution (0.2 per cent);
— *disregard limit*: 0.5 times the area of the peak due to felbinac in the chromatogram obtained with the reference solution (0.05 per cent).

**Chlorides**

Maximum 110 ppm.

Dissolve 1.0 g in 40 ml of *acetone R*, add 6 ml of a 10 per cent *V/V* solution of *nitric acid R*, dilute to 50.0 ml with *water R* and mix. Pour 15.0 ml of this solution as a single addition into 1 ml of *0.1 M silver nitrate* and allow to stand for 5 min protected from light. When viewed horizontally against a black background, any opalescence produced is not more intense than that obtained by treating in the same manner 15.0 ml of a mixture of 1.5 ml of *0.002 M hydrochloric acid*, 40 ml of *acetone R*, 6 ml of 10 per cent *V/V* solution of *nitric acid R*, diluted to 50.0 ml with *water R*.

**Sulphates**

Maximum 130 ppm.

Dissolve 1.5 g in 40 ml of *dimethylformamide R*, add 1 ml of a 10 per cent *V/V* solution of *hydrochloric acid R*, dilute to 50.0 ml with *dimethylformamide R* and mix. To 15.0 ml of this solution add 2.0 ml of a 120 g/l solution of *barium chloride R* and allow to stand for 5 min. Any opalescence produced is not more intense than that of a standard prepared in the same manner but using 2.0 ml of *0.001 M sulphuric acid* instead of the substance to be examined.

**Loss on drying** *(2.2.32)*

Maximum 0.5 per cent, determined on 1.000 g by drying in an oven at 105 °C for 3 h.

**Sulphated ash** *(2.4.14)*

Maximum 0.1 per cent, determined on 1.0 g.

**ASSAY**

Dissolve 0.160 g in 50 ml of *methanol R*. Titrate with *0.1 M alcoholic potassium hydroxide* determining the end-point potentiometrically *(2.2.20)*.

1 ml of *0.1 M alcoholic potassium hydroxide* is equivalent to 21.23 mg of $C_{14}H_{12}O_2$.

**IMPURITIES**

*Specified impurities* A, B.

A. R = CO-CH$_3$: 4-acetyl biphenyl,

B. R = H: biphenyl.

*Ph Eur*

# Felodipine

*(Ph Eur monograph 1013)*

and enantiomer

$C_{18}H_{19}Cl_2NO_4$      384.3      *72509-76-3*

**Action and use**

Calcium channel blocker.

**Preparation**

Prolonged-release Felodipine Tablets

*Ph Eur*

**DEFINITION**

Ethyl methyl (4RS)-4-(2,3-dichlorophenyl)-2,6-dimethyl-1,4-dihydropyridine-3,5-dicarboxylate.

**Content**

99.0 per cent to 101.0 per cent (dried substance).

**CHARACTERS**

**Appearance**

White or light yellow, crystalline powder.

**Solubility**

Practically insoluble in water, freely soluble in acetone, in anhydrous ethanol, in methanol and in methylene chloride.

**IDENTIFICATION**

*First identification* B.

*Second identification* A, C, D.

A. Ultraviolet and visible absorption spectrophotometry *(2.2.25)*.

*Test solution* Dissolve 50 mg in *methanol R* and dilute to 100 ml with the same solvent. Dilute 3 ml of this solution to 100 ml with *methanol R*.

*Spectral range* 220-400 nm.

*Absorption maxima* At 238 nm and 361 nm.

*Absorbance ratio* $A_{361} / A_{238} = 0.34$ to 0.36.

B. Infrared absorption spectrophotometry *(2.2.24)*.

*Preparation* Discs.

*Comparison* felodipine CRS.

C. Thin-layer chromatography (*2.2.27*).

*Test solution* Dissolve 10 mg of the substance to be examined in *methanol R* and dilute to 10 ml with the same solvent.

*Reference solution (a)* Dissolve 10 mg of *felodipine CRS* in *methanol R* and dilute to 10 ml with the same solvent.

*Reference solution (b)* Dissolve 5 mg of *nifedipine CRS* in reference solution (a) and dilute to 5 ml with reference solution (a).

*Plate* TLC silica gel $F_{254}$ *plate R*.

*Mobile phase* ethyl acetate R, cyclohexane R (40:60 *V/V*).

*Application* 5 μl.

*Development* Over a path of 15 cm.

*Drying* In air.

*Detection* Examine in ultraviolet light at 254 nm.

*System suitability* Reference solution (b):
— the chromatogram shows 2 clearly separated spots.

*Results* The principal spot in the chromatogram obtained with the test solution is similar in position, fluorescence and size to the principal spot in the chromatogram obtained with reference solution (a).

D. Ultraviolet and visible absorption spectrophotometry (*2.2.25*).

*Test solution* Dissolve 0.150 g in a mixture of 25 ml of *2-methyl-2-propanol R* and 25 ml of *perchloric acid solution R*. Add 10 ml of *0.1 M cerium sulphate*, allow to stand for 15 min, add 3.5 ml of *strong sodium hydroxide solution R* and neutralise with *dilute sodium hydroxide solution R*. Shake with 25 ml of *methylene chloride R*. Evaporate the lower layer to dryness on a water-bath under nitrogen (the residue is also used in the test for related substances). Dissolve about 20 mg of the residue in *methanol R* and dilute to 50 ml with the same solvent. Dilute 2 ml of this solution to 50 ml with *methanol R*.

*Spectral range* 220-400 nm.

*Absorption maximum* At 273 nm.

## TESTS
### Solution S
Dissolve 1.00 g in *methanol R* and dilute to 20.0 ml with the same solvent.

### Appearance of solution
Solution S is clear (*2.2.1*).

### Absorbance (*2.2.25*)
Maximum 0.10, determined at 440 nm on solution S.

### Related substances
Liquid chromatography (*2.2.29*).

*Test solution* Dissolve 25.0 mg of the substance to be examined in the mobile phase and dilute to 50.0 ml with the mobile phase.

*Reference solution (a)* Dilute 1.0 ml of the test solution to 100.0 ml with the mobile phase.

*Reference solution (b)* Dilute 1.0 ml of reference solution (a) to 10.0 ml with the mobile phase.

*Reference solution (c)* Dissolve 50.0 mg of the residue obtained in identification test D (impurity A) and 25.0 mg of *felodipine CRS* in the mobile phase, then dilute to 50.0 ml with the mobile phase. Dilute 1.0 ml of this solution to 100.0 ml with the mobile phase. Dilute 1.0 ml of the solution to 10 ml with the mobile phase.

*Column:*
— *size: l* = 0.125-0.15 m, Ø = 4 mm;

— *stationary phase*: octadecylsilyl silica gel for chromatography R (5 μm).

*Mobile phase* Mix 20 volumes of *methanol R*, 40 volumes of *acetonitrile R* and 40 volumes of a phosphate buffer solution pH 3.0 containing 0.8 g/l of *phosphoric acid R* and 8 g/l of *sodium dihydrogen phosphate R*.

*Flow rate* 1 ml/min.

*Detection* Spectrophotometer at 254 nm.

*Injection* 20 μl.

*Run time* Twice the retention time of felodipine.

*Elution order* Impurity B, impurity A, felodipine, impurity C.

*Retention time* Felodipine = about 12 min.

*System suitability* Reference solution (c):
— *resolution*: minimum 2.5 between the peaks due to impurity A and felodipine.

*Limits:*
— *sum of impurities B and C*: not more than the area of the principal peak in the chromatogram obtained with reference solution (a) (1.0 per cent);
— *unspecified impurities*: for each impurity, not more than the area of the principal peak in the chromatogram obtained with reference solution (b) (0.10 per cent);
— *sum of impurities other than B and C*: not more than 3 times the area of the principal peak in the chromatogram obtained with reference solution (b) (0.3 per cent);
— *disregard limit*: 0.2 times the area of the principal peak in the chromatogram obtained with reference solution (b) (0.02 per cent).

### Loss on drying (*2.2.32*)
Maximum 0.5 per cent, determined on 1.000 g by drying in an oven at 105 °C for 3 h.

### Sulphated ash (*2.4.14*)
Maximum 0.1 per cent, determined on 1.0 g.

## ASSAY
Dissolve 0.160 g in a mixture of 25 ml of *2-methyl-2-propanol R* and 25 ml of *perchloric acid solution R*. Add 0.05 ml of *ferroin R*. Titrate with *0.1 M cerium sulphate* until the pink colour disappears. Titrate slowly towards the end of the titration.

1 ml of *0.1 M cerium sulphate* is equivalent to 19.21 mg of $C_{18}H_{19}Cl_2NO_4$.

## STORAGE
Protected from light.

## IMPURITIES
*Specified impurities* B, C.

*Other detectable impurities* (the following substances would, if present at a sufficient level, be detected by one or other of the tests in the monograph. They are limited by the general acceptance criterion for other/unspecified impurities and/or by the general monograph *Substances for pharmaceutical use (2034)*. It is therefore not necessary to identify these impurities for demonstration of compliance. See also *5.10. Control of impurities in substances for pharmaceutical use*): A.

A. ethyl methyl 4-(2,3-dichlorophenyl)-2,6-dimethylpyridine-3,5-dicarboxylate,

B. R = CH₃: dimethyl 4-(2,3-dichlorophenyl)-2,6-dimethyl-1,4-dihydropyridine-3,5-dicarboxylate,

C. R = C₂H₅: diethyl 4-(2,3-dichlorophenyl)-2,6-dimethyl-1,4-dihydropyridine-3,5-dicarboxylate.

*Ph Eur*

# Felypressin

(*Ph Eur monograph 1634*)

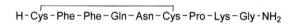

H-Cys-Phe-Phe-Gln-Asn-Cys-Pro-Lys-Gly-NH₂

$C_{46}H_{65}N_{13}O_{11}S_2$      1039      56-59-7

## Action and use
Vasopressin analogue; vasoconstrictor in local anaesthesia.

*Ph Eur*

## DEFINITION
L-Cysteinyl-L-phenylalanyl-L-phenylalanyl-L-glutaminyl-L-asparaginyl-L-cysteinyl-L-prolyl-L-lysylglycinamide cyclic (1,6)-disulphide.

Synthetic nonapeptide having a vasoconstricting activity. It is available as an acetate.

## Content
95.0 per cent to 102.0 per cent (anhydrous and acetic acid-free substance).

## CHARACTERS
### Appearance
White or almost white, powder or flakes.

### Solubility
Freely soluble in water, practically insoluble in acetone and ethanol (96 per cent). It dissolves in dilute solutions of alkali hydroxides.

## IDENTIFICATION
A. Examine the chromatograms obtained in the assay.

*Results* The principal peak in the chromatogram obtained with test solution (b) is similar in retention time and size to the principal peak in the chromatogram obtained with the reference solution.

B. Amino acid analysis (*2.2.56*). For hydrolysis use Method 1 and for analysis use Method 1.

Express the content of each amino acid in moles. Calculate the relative proportions of amino acids, taking one-seventh of the sum of the number of moles of glutamic acid, aspartic acid, proline, lysine, glycine and phenylalanine as equal to one. The values fall within the following limits: aspartic acid: 0.9 to 1.1; glutamic acid: 0.9 to 1.1; proline: 0.9 to 1.1; glycine: 0.9 to 1.1; phenylalanine: 1.8 to 2.2; half-cystine: 1.8 to 2.2; lysine: 0.9 to 1.1.

## TESTS
### Specific optical rotation (*2.2.7*)
− 35 to − 29, determined at 25 °C (anhydrous and acetic acid-free substance).

Dissolve 20.0 mg in a 1 per cent *V/V* solution of *glacial acetic acid R* and dilute to 10.0 ml with the same solution.

### Related substances
Liquid chromatography (*2.2.29*); use the normalisation procedure. *The solutions are stable for 24 h at room temperature or for 1 week at 2-8 °C.*

*Test solution (a)* Dissolve 5.0 mg of the substance to be examined in 5.0 ml of mobile phase A.

*Test solution (b)* Dilute 1.0 ml of test solution (a) to 5.0 ml with mobile phase A.

*Reference solution* Dissolve the contents of a vial of *felypressin CRS* in mobile phase A to obtain a concentration of 0.2 mg/ml.

*Column:*
— *size:* l = 0.15 m, Ø = 3.9 mm,
— *stationary phase*: octadecylsilyl silica gel for chromatography R (5 µm),
— *temperature*: 50 °C.

*Mobile phase:*
— *mobile phase A*: dissolve 3.62 g of *tetramethylammonium hydroxide R* in 900 ml *water R*; adjust to pH 2.5 with *phosphoric acid R* and dilute to 1000 ml with *water R*;
— *mobile phase B*: dissolve 1.81 g of *tetramethylammonium hydroxide R* in 450 ml of a 50 per cent *V/V* solution of *acetonitrile for chromatography R*; adjust to pH 2.5 with *phosphoric acid R* and dilute to 500 ml with a 50 per cent *V/V* solution of *acetonitrile for chromatography R*;

| Time (min) | Mobile phase A (per cent *V/V*) | Mobile phase B (per cent *V/V*) |
|---|---|---|
| 0 - 20 | 80 → 50 | 20 → 50 |
| 20 - 25 | 50 | 50 |
| 25 - 26 | 50 → 80 | 50 → 20 |
| 26 - 36 | 80 | 20 |

*Flow rate* 1.0 ml/min.

*Detection* Spectrophotometer at 210 nm.

*Injection* 10 µl of test solution (a) and 50 µl of the reference solution.

*Identification of impurities* Use the chromatogram supplied with *felypressin CRS* to identify the peaks due to impurities A to F.

*Relative retention* with reference to felypressin:
impurity A = about 0.9; impurity B = about 1.1; impurity F = about 1.2; impurity C = about 1.3; impurity D = about 1.4; impurity E = about 2.1.

*System suitability* Reference solution:

— *retention time*: felypressin = about 7.5 min;
— *resolution*: minimum 1.5 between the peaks due to impurity C and impurity D.

*Limits:*
— *impurities A, B, C, D, E, F*: for each impurity, maximum 0.5 per cent,
— *any other impurity*: for each impurity, maximum 0.1 per cent,
— *total*: maximum 3.0 per cent,
— *disregard limit*: 0.05 per cent.

**Acetic acid** (*2.5.34*)
9.0 per cent to 13.0 per cent.

*Test solution* Dissolve 10.0 mg of the substance to be examined in a mixture of 5 volumes of mobile phase B and 95 volumes of mobile phase A and dilute to 10.0 ml with the same mixture of mobile phases.

**Water** (*2.5.32*)
Maximum 7.0 per cent.

**Bacterial endotoxins** (*2.6.14*)
Less than 100 IU/mg, if intended for use in the manufacture of parenteral dosage forms without a further appropriate procedure for the removal of bacterial endotoxins.

## ASSAY
Liquid chromatography (*2.2.29*) as described in the test for related substances with the following modification.

*Injection* 10 µl of test solution (b) and of the reference solution.

Calculate the content of felypressin ($C_{46}H_{65}N_{13}O_{11}S_2$) from the areas of the peaks and the declared content of $C_{46}H_{65}N_{13}O_{11}S_2$ in *felypressin CRS*.

## STORAGE
In an airtight container, protected from light, at a temperature of 2 °C to 8 °C. If the substance is sterile, store in a sterile, airtight, tamper-proof container.

## LABELLING
The label states the mass of peptide in the container.

## IMPURITIES
*Specified impurities* A, B, C, D, E, F.

H₃C — O
NH
S|
H - Cys - Phe - Phe - Gln - Asn - Cys - Pro - Lys - Gly - NH₂

A. $S^1,S^6$-bis[(acetylamino)methyl]-(reduced felypressin),

H - Cys - Phe - Phe - Gln - Asp - Cys - Pro - Lys - Gly - NH₂

B. [5-aspartic acid]felypressin,

H - Cys - Phe - Phe - Gln - Asn - Cys - Pro - Lys - Gly - NH₂
H - Cys - Phe - Phe - Gln - Asn - Cys - Pro - Lys - Gly - NH₂

C. bis(reduced felypressin) (1,6′),(1′,6)-bis(disulfide),

H - Cys - Phe - Phe - Gln - Asn - Cys - Pro - Lys - Gly - NH₂
H - Cys - Phe - Phe - Gln - Asn - Cys - Pro - Lys - Gly - NH₂

D. bis(reduced felypressin) (1,1′),(6,6′)-bis(disulfide),

Cys - Phe - Phe - Gln - Asn - Cys - Pro - Lys - Gly - NH₂
O=
CH₃

E. $N^1$-acetylfelypressin,

H - Cys - Phe - Phe - Glu - Asn - Cys - Pro - Lys - Gly - NH₂

F. [4-glutamic acid]felypressin.

*Ph Eur*

# Fenbufen

*(Ph Eur monograph 1209)*

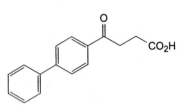

$C_{16}H_{14}O_3$     254.3     *36330-85-5*

**Action and use**
Cyclo-oxygenase inhibitor; analgesic; anti-inflammatory.

**Preparations**
Fenbufen Capsules
Fenbufen Tablets

*Ph Eur*

## DEFINITION
4-(Biphenyl-4-yl)-4-oxobutanoic acid.

**Content**
98.5 per cent to 101.0 per cent (dried substance).

## CHARACTERS
**Appearance**
White or almost white, fine, crystalline powder.

**Solubility**
Very slightly soluble in water, slightly soluble in acetone, in ethanol (96 per cent) and in methylene chloride.

## IDENTIFICATION
*First identification* B.

*Second identification* A, C.

A. Melting point (*2.2.14*): 186 °C to 189 °C.

B. Infrared absorption spectrophotometry (*2.2.24*).

*Comparison* fenbufen CRS .

C. Thin-layer chromatography (*2.2.27*).

*Test solution* Dissolve 10 mg of the substance to be examined in *methylene chloride R* and dilute to 10 ml with the same solvent.

*Reference solution (a)* Dissolve 10 mg of *fenbufen CRS* in *methylene chloride R* and dilute to 10 ml with the same solvent.

*Reference solution (b)* Dissolve 10 mg of *ketoprofen CRS* in *methylene chloride R* and dilute to 10 ml with the same solvent. To 5 ml of this solution, add 5 ml of reference solution (a).

*Plate* TLC silica gel $F_{254}$ plate R.

*Mobile phase*  anhydrous acetic acid R, ethyl acetate R, hexane R (5:25:75 V/V/V).

*Application*  10 μl.

*Development*  Over a path of 15 cm.

*Drying*  In air.

*Detection*  Examine in ultraviolet light at 254 nm.

*System suitability*  Reference solution (b):
— the chromatogram shows 2 clearly separated spots.

*Results*  The principal spot in the chromatogram obtained with the test solution is similar in position and size to the principal spot in the chromatogram obtained with reference solution (a).

## TESTS

### Related substances

Liquid chromatography (2.2.29).

*Solvent mixture*  dimethylformamide R, mobile phase A (40:60 V/V).

*Test solution*  Dissolve 50.0 mg of the substance to be examined in the solvent mixture and dilute to 10.0 ml with the solvent mixture.

*Reference solution (a)*  Dilute 0.5 ml of the test solution to 50.0 ml with the solvent mixture. Dilute 1.0 ml of this solution to 10.0 ml with the solvent mixture.

*Reference solution (b)*  Dissolve 25 mg of *fenbufen CRS* and 6 mg of *ketoprofen CRS* in the solvent mixture and dilute to 10 ml with the solvent mixture. Dilute 1 ml of this solution to 100 ml with the solvent mixture.

*Column:*
— *size*: l = 0.125 m, Ø = 4.0 mm;
— *stationary phase*: octadecylsilyl silica gel for chromatography R (5 μm).

*Mobile phase:*
— *mobile phase A*: mix 32 volumes of *acetonitrile R* and 68 volumes of a mixture of 1 volume of *glacial acetic acid R* and 55 volumes of *water R*;
— *mobile phase B*: mix 45 volumes of *acetonitrile R* and 55 volumes of a mixture of 1 volume of *glacial acetic acid R* and 55 volumes of *water R*;

| Time (min) | Mobile phase A (per cent V/V) | Mobile phase B (per cent V/V) |
|---|---|---|
| 0 – 15 | 100 | 0 |
| 15 – 20 | 100 → 0 | 0 → 100 |
| 20 – 35 | 0 | 100 |
| 35 – 40 | 0 → 100 | 100 → 0 |
| 40 - 45 | 100 | 0 |

*Flow rate*  2 ml/min.

*Detection*  Spectrophotometer at 254 nm.

*Injection*  20 μl.

*System suitability*  Reference solution (b):
— *resolution*: minimum 5.0 between the peaks due to ketoprofen and fenbufen.

*Limits:*
— *any impurity*: for each impurity, not more than the area of the principal peak in the chromatogram obtained with reference solution (a) (0.1 per cent);
— *total*: not more than 5 times the area of the principal peak in the chromatogram obtained with reference solution (a) (0.5 per cent);

— *disregard limit*: 0.2 times the area of the principal peak in the chromatogram obtained with reference solution (a) (0.02 per cent).

**Heavy metals** (2.4.8)
Maximum 20 ppm.

1.0 g complies with test C. Prepare the reference solution using 2 ml of *lead standard solution (10 ppm Pb) R*.

**Loss on drying** (2.2.32)
Maximum 0.5 per cent, determined on 1.000 g by drying in an oven at 105 °C for 3 h.

**Sulphated ash** (2.4.14)
Maximum 0.1 per cent, determined on 1.0 g.

## ASSAY

Dissolve 0.200 g in 75 ml of *acetone R* previously neutralised with *phenolphthalein solution R1* and add 50 ml of *water R*. Add 0.2 ml of *phenolphthalein solution R1* and titrate with *0.1 M sodium hydroxide*. Carry out a blank titration.

1 ml of *0.1 M sodium hydroxide* is equivalent to 25.43 mg of $C_{16}H_{14}O_3$.

## IMPURITIES

A. 3-(4-chlorophenyl)-3-oxopropanoic acid,

B. R = CO-CH=CH-$CO_2$H, R' = H: 4-(biphenyl-4-yl)-4-oxobut-2-enoic acid,

C. R = R' = H: biphenyl,

D. R = CO-$CH_2$-$CH_2$-$CO_2$H, R' = OH: 4-(4'-hydroxybiphenyl-4-yl)-4-oxobutanoic acid.

———————————————————————————— *Ph Eur*

# Fenofibrate

(*Ph Eur monograph 1322*)

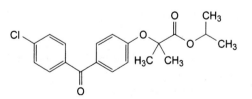

$C_{20}H_{21}ClO_4$          360.8          49562-28-9

**Action and use**
Fibrate; lipid-regulating drug.

Ph Eur

## DEFINITION

1-Methylethyl 2-[4-(4-chlorobenzoyl)phenoxy]-2-methylpropanoate.

## Content

98.0 per cent to 102.0 per cent (dried substance).

## CHARACTERS

### Appearance

White or almost white, crystalline powder.

### Solubility

Practically insoluble in water, very soluble in methylene chloride, slightly soluble in ethanol (96 per cent).

## IDENTIFICATION

A. Melting point (2.2.14): 79 °C to 82 °C.

B. Infrared absorption spectrophotometry (2.2.24).

*Preparation*   Discs.

*Comparison*   *fenofibrate CRS* .

## TESTS

### Solution S

To 5.0 g, add 25 ml of *distilled water R* and heat at 50 °C for 10 min. Cool and dilute to 50.0 ml with the same solvent. Filter. Use the filtrate as solution S.

### Appearance of solution

The solution is clear (2.2.1) and not more intensely coloured than reference solution $BY_6$ (2.2.2, Method II).

Dissolve 0.50 g in *acetone R* and dilute to 10.0 ml with the same solvent.

### Acidity

Dissolve 1.0 g in 50 ml of *ethanol (96 per cent) R* previously neutralised using 0.2 ml of *phenolphthalein solution R1*. Not more than 0.2 ml of *0.1 M sodium hydroxide* is required to change the colour of the indicator to pink.

### Related substances

Liquid chromatography (2.2.29).

*Test solution*   Dissolve 0.100 g of the substance to be examined in the mobile phase and dilute to 100.0 ml with the mobile phase.

*Reference solution (a)*   Dissolve 25.0 mg of *fenofibrate CRS* in the mobile phase and dilute to 25.0 ml with the mobile phase.

*Reference solution (b)*   Dissolve 5.0 mg of *fenofibrate CRS*, 5.0 mg of *fenofibrate impurity A CRS*, 5.0 mg of *fenofibrate impurity B CRS* and 10.0 mg of *fenofibrate impurity G CRS* in the mobile phase and dilute to 100.0 ml with the mobile phase. Dilute 1.0 ml of this solution to 50.0 ml with the mobile phase.

*Column:*
— *size:* $l = 0.25$ m, Ø = 4.0 mm;
— *stationary phase: octadecylsilyl silica gel for chromatography R* (5 μm).

*Mobile phase*   Mix 30 volumes of *water R* acidified to pH 2.5 with *phosphoric acid R* and 70 volumes of *acetonitrile R*.

*Flow rate*   1 ml/min.

*Detection*   Spectrophotometer at 286 nm.

*Injection*   20 μl of the test solution and reference solution (b).

*Run time*   Twice the retention time of fenofibrate.

*Relative retention* with reference to fenofibrate:

impurity A = about 0.34; impurity B = about 0.36; impurity C = about 0.50; impurity D = about 0.65;

impurity E = about 0.80, impurity F = about 0.85; impurity G = about 1.35.

*System suitability*   Reference solution (b):
— *resolution*: minimum 1.5 between the peaks due to impurities A and B.

*Limits:*
— *impurities A, B*: for each impurity, not more than the area of the corresponding peak in the chromatogram obtained with reference solution (b) (0.1 per cent);
— *impurity G*: not more than the area of the corresponding peak in the chromatogram obtained with reference solution (b) (0.2 per cent);
— *unspecified impurities*: for each impurity, not more than the area of the peak due to fenofibrate in the chromatogram obtained with reference solution (b) (0.10 per cent);
— *total*: not more than 5 times the area of the peak due to fenofibrate in the chromatogram obtained with reference solution (b) (0.5 per cent);
— *disregard limit*: 0.1 times the area of the peak due to fenofibrate in the chromatogram obtained with reference solution (b) (0.01 per cent).

### Halides expressed as chlorides (2.4.4)

Maximum 100 ppm.

To 5 ml of solution S add 10 ml of *distilled water R*.

### Sulphates (2.4.13)

Maximum 100 ppm, determined on solution S.

### Heavy metals (2.4.8)

Maximum 20 ppm.

1.0 g complies with test C. Prepare the reference solution using 2 ml of *lead standard solution (10 ppm Pb) R*.

### Loss on drying (2.2.32)

Maximum 0.5 per cent, determined on 1.000 g by drying *in vacuo* at 60 °C.

### Sulphated ash (2.4.14)

Maximum 0.1 per cent, determined on 1.0 g.

## ASSAY

Liquid chromatography (2.2.29) as described in the test for related substances with the following modifications.

*Injection*   5 μl of the test solution and reference solution (a).

*System suitability*   Reference solution (a):
— *repeatability*: maximum relative standard deviation of 1.0 per cent after 6 injections.

## STORAGE

Protected from light.

## IMPURITIES

*Specified impurities*   A, B, G.

*Other detectable impurities* (the following substances would, if present at a sufficient level, be detected by one or other of the tests in the monograph. They are limited by the general acceptance criterion for other/unspecified impurities and/or by the general monograph *Substances for pharmaceutical use (2034)*. It is therefore not necessary to identify these impurities for demonstration of compliance. See also 5.10. *Control of impurities in substances for pharmaceutical use*): C, D, E, F.

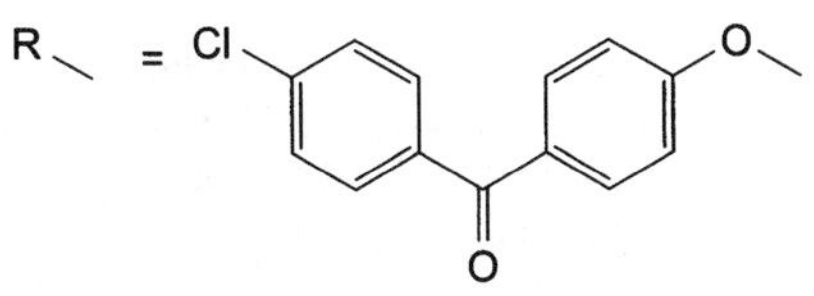

R = Cl — (structure)

A. R-H: (4-chlorophenyl)(4-hydroxyphenyl)methanone,

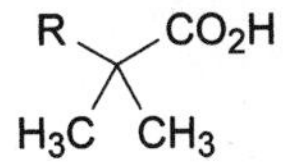

B. 2-[4-(4-chlorobenzoyl)phenoxy]-2-methylpropanoic acid (fenofibric acid),

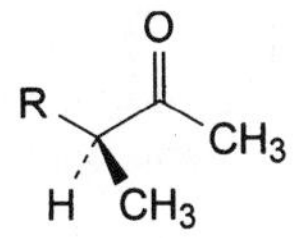

C. (3RS)-3-[4-(4-chlorobenzoyl)phenoxy]butan-2-one,

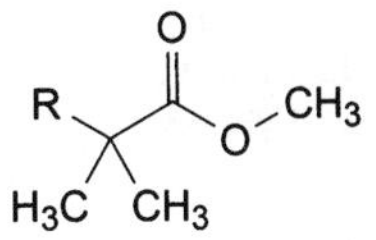

D. methyl 2-[4-(4-chlorobenzoyl)phenoxy]-2-methylpropanoate,

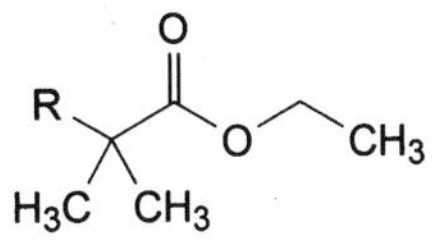

E. ethyl 2-[4-(4-chlorobenzoyl)phenoxy]-2-methylpropanoate,

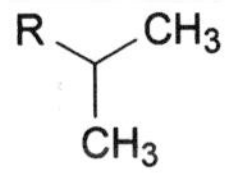

F. (4-chlorophenyl)[4-(1-methylethoxy)phenyl]methanone,

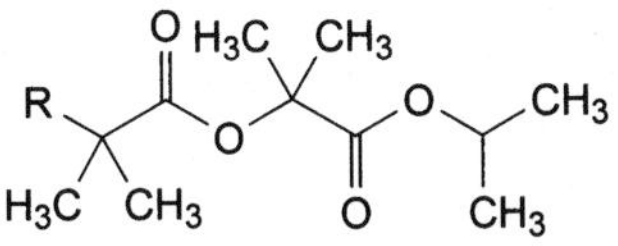

G. 1-methylethyl 2-[[2-[4-(4-chlorobenzoyl)phenoxy]-2-methylpropanoyl]oxy]-2-methylpropanoate.

*Ph Eur*

# Fenoprofen Calcium

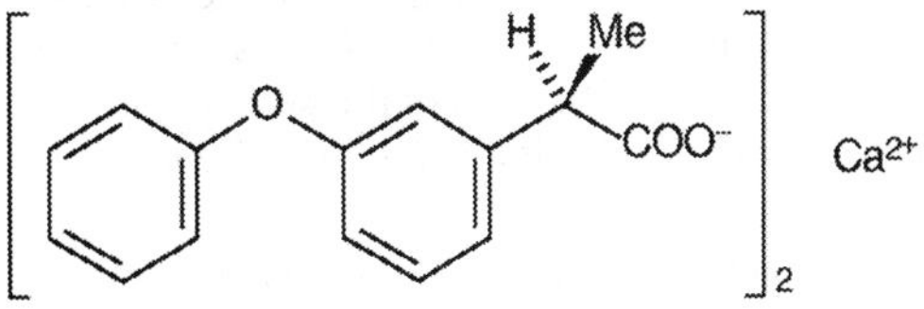

and enantiomer

$(C_{15}H_{13}O_3)_2Ca,2H_2O$        558.6        *34957-40-5*

## Action and use
Cyclo-oxygenase inhibitor; analgesic; anti-inflammatory.

## Preparation
Fenoprofen Tablets

## DEFINITION
Fenoprofen Calcium is calcium (RS)-2-(3-phenoxyphenyl) propionate dihydrate. It contains not less than 97.5% and not more than 101.0% of $(C_{15}H_{13}O_3)_2Ca$, calculated with reference to the anhydrous substance.

## CHARACTERISTICS
A white or almost white, crystalline powder.

Slightly soluble in *water*; soluble in *ethanol (96%)*.

## IDENTIFICATION
A. Dissolve 0.1 g in 5 ml of *glacial acetic acid* and add sufficient *methanol* to produce 100 ml. Dilute 5 ml of this solution to 50 ml with *methanol*. The *light absorption* of the resulting solution, Appendix II B, in the range 230 to 350 nm exhibits two maxima, at 272 nm and 278 nm, and a shoulder at 266 nm. The *absorbance* at the maximum at 272 nm is about 0.70 and at the maximum at 278 nm is about 0.65.

B. The *infrared absorption spectrum*, Appendix II A, is concordant with the *reference spectrum* of fenoprofen calcium (RS 142).

C. The residue on ignition yields the reactions characteristic of *calcium salts*, Appendix VI.

## TESTS
### Related substances
Carry out the method for *liquid chromatography*, Appendix III D, using three solutions in the mobile phase containing (1) 0.0025% w/v of the substance being examined, (2) 0.50% w/v of the substance being examined and (3) 0.04% w/v of *fenoprofen calcium* and 0.0015% w/v of *4,4'-dimethoxybenzophenone*.

The chromatographic procedure may be carried out using (a) a stainless steel column (25 cm × 4.6 mm) packed with *octadecylsilyl silica gel for chromatography* (7 to 8 µm) (Zorbax ODS is suitable), (b) a mixture of 61 volumes of *water*, 30 volumes of *acetonitrile*, 7 volumes of *tetrahydrofuran* and 2 volumes of *glacial acetic acid* as the mobile phase with a flow rate of 2 ml per minute and (c) a detection wavelength of 270 nm. For solution (2) allow the chromatography to proceed for 3 times the retention time of the peak due to fenoprofen.

The test is not valid unless the *resolution factor* between the peaks corresponding to fenoprofen and 4,4'-dimethoxybenzophenone in the chromatogram obtained with solution (3) is at least 3.0.

In the chromatogram obtained with solution (2) the area of any *secondary peak* is not greater than twice the area of the peak in the chromatogram obtained with solution (1) (1%), not more than one such peak has an area greater than the area of the peak in the chromatogram obtained with solution (1) (0.5%) and the sum of the areas of all such peaks is not greater than four times the area of the peak in the chromatogram obtained with solution (1) (2%).

**Water**

5.0 to 8.0% w/w, Appendix IX C. Use 0.2 g.

**ASSAY**

Carry out Method I for *non-aqueous titration*, Appendix VIII A, using 0.5 g and determining the end point potentiometrically. Each ml of 0.1M *perchloric acid VS* is equivalent to 26.13 mg of $(C_{15}H_{13}O_3)_2Ca$.

# Fenoterol Hydrobromide

(*Ph Eur monograph 0901*)

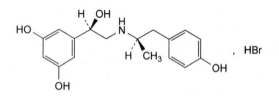

$C_{17}H_{21}NO_4,HBr$        384.3        *1944-12-3*

**Action and use**

Beta$_2$-adrenoceptor agonist; bronchodilator.

**Preparation**

Fenoterol Pressurised Inhalation

*Ph Eur*

**DEFINITION**

(1*RS*)-1-(3,5-Dihydroxyphenyl)-2-[[(1*RS*)-2-(4-hydroxyphenyl)-1-methylethyl]amino]ethanol hydrobromide.

**Content**

99.0 per cent to 101.0 per cent (dried substance).

**CHARACTERS**

**Appearance**

White or almost white, crystalline powder.

**Solubility**

Soluble in water and in ethanol (96 per cent).

**IDENTIFICATION**

*First identification*    B, E.

*Second identification*    A, C, D, E.

A. Ultraviolet and visible absorption spectrophotometry (*2.2.25*).

*Test solution*    Dissolve 50.0 mg in *dilute hydrochloric acid R1* and dilute to 50.0 ml with the same acid. Dilute 5.0 ml of this solution to 50.0 ml with *dilute hydrochloric acid R1*.

*Spectral range*    230-350 nm.

*Absorption maximum*    At 275 nm.

*Shoulder*    At about 280 nm.

*Specific absorbance at the absorption maximum*    80 to 86.

B. Infrared absorption spectrophotometry (*2.2.24*).

*Comparison*    fenoterol hydrobromide CRS .

C. Thin-layer chromatography (*2.2.27*).

*Test solution*    Dissolve 10 mg of the substance to be examined in *ethanol (96 per cent) R* and dilute to 10 ml with the same solvent.

*Reference solution*    Dissolve 10 mg of *fenoterol hydrobromide CRS* in *ethanol (96 per cent) R* and dilute to 10 ml with the same solvent.

*Plate*    TLC silica gel G plate R.

*Mobile phase*    concentrated ammonia R, water R, aldehyde-free methanol R (1.5:10:90 V/V/V).

*Application*    2 µl.

*Development*    Over a path of 15 cm.

*Drying*    In air.

*Detection*    Spray with a 10 g/l solution of *potassium permanganate R*.

*Results*    The principal spot in the chromatogram obtained with the test solution is similar in position, colour and size to the principal spot in the chromatogram obtained with the reference solution.

D. Dissolve about 10 mg in a 20 g/l solution of *disodium tetraborate R* and dilute to 50 ml with the same solution. Add 1 ml of a 10 g/l solution of *aminopyrazolone R*, 10 ml of a 2 g/l solution of *potassium ferricyanide R* and 10 ml of *methylene chloride R*. Shake and allow to separate. A reddish-brown colour develops in the lower layer.

E. It gives reaction (a) of bromides (*2.3.1*).

**TESTS**

**Solution S**

Dissolve 2.00 g in *carbon dioxide-free water R* and dilute to 50.0 ml with the same solvent.

**Appearance of solution**

Solution S is clear (*2.2.1*) and not more intensely coloured than reference solution Y$_7$ (*2.2.2, Method II*).

**pH** (*2.2.3*)

4.2 to 5.2 for solution S.

**Related substances**

Liquid chromatography (*2.2.29*). *Prepare the solutions immediately before use.*

*Test solution*    Dissolve 24.0 mg of the substance to be examined in *water R* and dilute to 20.0 ml with the same solvent.

*Reference solution (a)*    Dissolve 24.0 mg of *fenoterol hydrobromide CRS* (containing impurity A) in *water R* and dilute to 20.0 ml with the same solvent.

*Reference solution (b)*    Dissolve the contents of a vial of *fenoterol for peak identification CRS* (containing impurities B and C) in 1.0 ml of *water R*.

*Reference solution (c)*    Dilute 10.0 ml of the test solution to 50.0 ml with *water R*. Dilute 1.0 ml of this solution to 100.0 ml with *water R*.

*Column:*
— *size: l = 0.15 m, Ø = 4.6 mm;*
— *stationary phase: octadecylsilyl silica gel for chromatography R* (5 µm).

*Mobile phase*    Dissolve 24 g of *disodium hydrogen phosphate R* in 1000 ml of *water R*. Mix 69 volumes of this solution with 1 volume of a 9 g/l solution of *potassium of hydrogen phosphate R*, adjust to pH 8.5 with *phosphoric acid R* and add 35 volumes of *methanol R2*.

*Flow rate*    1 ml/min.

*Detection*    Spectrophotometer at 215 nm.

*Injection*    20 µl.

*Run time* 3 times the retention time of fenoterol.

*Relative retention* with reference to fenoterol
(retention time = about 7 min): impurity A = about 1.3;
impurity B = about 2.0; impurity C = about 2.2.

*System suitability:*
— *resolution:*
— minimum 3 between the peaks due to fenoterol and
impurity A in the chromatogram obtained with
reference solution (a);
— minimum 1.5 between the peaks due to impurities B
and C in the chromatogram obtained with reference
solution (b).

*Limits:*
— *correction factor:* for the calculation of content, multiply the
peak area of impurity B by 0.6;
— *impurity A:* maximum 4.0 per cent, calculated from the
area of the corresponding peak in the chromatogram
obtained with reference solution (a) and taking into
account the declared content of impurity A in *fenoterol
hydrobromide CRS;*
— *impurity C:* not more than 1.5 times the area of the
principal peak in the chromatogram obtained with
reference solution (c) (0.3 per cent);
— *impurity B:* not more than the area of the principal peak
in the chromatogram obtained with reference solution (c)
(0.2 per cent);
— *unspecified impurities:* for each impurity, not more than
0.5 times the area of the principal peak in the
chromatogram obtained with reference solution (c)
(0.10 per cent);
— *sum of impurities other than A:* not more than 1.5 times the
area of the principal peak in the chromatogram obtained
with reference solution (c) (0.3 per cent);
— *disregard limit:* 0.25 times the area of the principal peak in
the chromatogram obtained with reference solution (c)
(0.05 per cent).

**Iron** *(2.4.9)*
Maximum 10 ppm.
Dissolve the residue obtained in the test for sulphated ash in
2.5 ml of *dilute hydrochloric acid R* and dilute to 10 ml with
*water R.*

**Loss on drying** *(2.2.32)*
Maximum 0.5 per cent, determined on 1.000 g by drying in
an oven at 105 °C.

**Sulphated ash** *(2.4.14)*
Maximum 0.1 per cent, determined on 1.0 g.

**ASSAY**
Dissolve 0.600 g in 50 ml of *water R* and add 5 ml of *dilute
nitric acid R*, 25.0 ml of *0.1 M silver nitrate* and 2 ml of *ferric
ammonium sulphate solution R2.* Shake and titrate with *0.1 M
ammonium thiocyanate* until an orange colour is obtained.
Carry out a blank titration.

1 ml of *0.1 M silver nitrate* is equivalent to 38.43 mg of
$C_{17}H_{22}BrNO_4$.

**STORAGE**
Protected from light.

**IMPURITIES**
*Specified impurities* A, B, C.

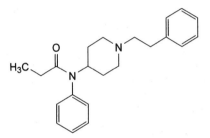

A. R1 = OH, R2 = R3 = H:
(1*RS*)-1-(3,5-dihydroxyphenyl)-2-[[(1*SR*)-2-
(4-hydroxyphenyl)-1-methylethyl]amino]ethanol,

B. R1 + R2 = O, R3 = H: 1-(3,5-dihydroxyphenyl)-2-
[[(1*RS*)-2-(4-hydroxyphenyl)-1-methylethyl]amino]ethanone,

C. R1 = H, R2 = OH, R3 = CH₃:
(1*RS*)-1-(3,5-dihydroxyphenyl)-2-[[(1*RS*)-2-(4-hydroxy-3-
methylphenyl)-1-methylethyl]amino]ethanol.

_____ *Ph Eur*

# Fentanyl

*(Ph Eur monograph 1210)*

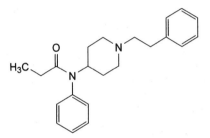

$C_{22}H_{28}N_2O$          336.5          *437-38-7*

**Action and use**
Opioid receptor agonist; analgesic.

*Ph Eur* _____

**DEFINITION**
*N*-Phenyl-*N*-[1-(2-phenylethyl)piperidin-4-yl]propanamide.

**Content**
99.0 per cent to 101.0 per cent (dried substance).

**CHARACTERS**
**Appearance**
White or almost white powder.

**Solubility**
Practically insoluble in water, freely soluble in ethanol
(96 per cent) and in methanol.

It shows polymorphism *(5.9).*

**IDENTIFICATION**
Infrared absorption spectrophotometry *(2.2.24).*

*Comparison* Ph. Eur. reference spectrum of fentanyl .

If the spectrum obtained in the solid state shows differences,
dissolve the substance to be examined in the minimum
volume of *anhydrous ethanol R*, evaporate to dryness at room
temperature under an air-stream and record the spectrum
again using the residue.

## TESTS

### Related substances

Liquid chromatography (*2.2.29*).

*Test solution*   Dissolve 0.100 g of the substance to be examined in *methanol R* and dilute to 10.0 ml with the same solvent.

*Reference solution (a)*   In order to prepare the *in situ* degradation compound (impurity D), dissolve 10 mg of the substance to be examined in 10.0 ml of *dilute hydrochloric acid R*. Heat on a water-bath under a reflux condenser for 4 h. Neutralise with 10.0 ml of *dilute sodium hydroxide solution R*. Evaporate to dryness on a water-bath. Cool and take up the residue in 10 ml of *methanol R*. Filter.

*Reference solution (b)*   Dilute 1.0 ml of the test solution to 100.0 ml with *methanol R*. Dilute 5.0 ml of this solution to 20.0 ml with *methanol R*.

*Column:*
— *size: l* = 0.1 m, Ø = 4.6 mm;
— *stationary phase: octadecylsilyl silica gel for chromatography R* (3 µm).

*Mobile phase:*
— *mobile phase A*: 5 g/l solution of *ammonium carbonate R* in a mixture of 10 volumes of *tetrahydrofuran R* and 90 volumes of *water R*;
— *mobile phase B*: *acetonitrile R1*;

| Time (min) | Mobile phase A (per cent *V/V*) | Mobile phase B (per cent *V/V*) |
|---|---|---|
| 0 - 15 | 90 → 40 | 10 → 60 |
| 15 - 20 | 40 | 60 |

*Flow rate*   1.5 ml/min.

*Detection*   Spectrophotometer at 220 nm.

*Equilibration*   With *acetonitrile R* for at least 30 min and then with the mobile phase at the initial composition for at least 5 min.

*Injection*   10 µl; inject *methanol R* as a blank.

*Retention time*   Fentanyl = about 10 min; impurity D = about 12 min.

*System suitability*   Reference solution (a):
— *resolution*: minimum 8.0 between the peaks due to fentanyl and impurity D; if necessary, adjust the concentration of acetonitrile in the mobile phase or adjust the time programme for the linear gradient elution.

*Limits:*
— *impurities A, B, C, D*: for each impurity, not more than the area of the principal peak in the chromatogram obtained with reference solution (b) (0.25 per cent);
— *total*: not more than twice the area of the principal peak in the chromatogram obtained with reference solution (b) (0.5 per cent);
— *disregard limit*: 0.2 times the area of the principal peak in the chromatogram obtained with reference solution (b) (0.05 per cent).

### Loss on drying (*2.2.32*)

Maximum 0.5 per cent, determined on 1.000 g by drying *in vacuo* at 50 °C.

## ASSAY

Dissolve 0.200 g in 50 ml of a mixture of 1 volume of *anhydrous acetic acid R* and 7 volumes of *methyl ethyl ketone R* and titrate with *0.1 M perchloric acid*, using 0.2 ml of *naphtholbenzein solution R* as indicator.

1 ml of *0.1 M perchloric acid* is equivalent to 33.65 mg of $C_{22}H_{28}N_2O$.

## STORAGE

Protected from light.

## IMPURITIES

*Specified impurities*   A, B, C, D.

*Other detectable impurities (the following substances would, if present at a sufficient level, be detected by one or other of the tests in the monograph. They are limited by the general acceptance criterion for other/unspecified impurities and/or by the general monograph Substances for pharmaceutical use (2034). It is therefore not necessary to identify these impurities for demonstration of compliance. See also 5.10. Control of impurities in substances for pharmaceutical use) :* E, F, G.

A. *N*-phenyl-*N*-[*cis*,*trans*-1-oxido-1-(2-phenylethyl)piperidin-4-yl]propanamide,

B. R = CO-C₂H₅, R′ = H:
*N*-phenyl-*N*-(piperidin-4-yl)propanamide,

C. R = CO-CH₃, R′ = CH₂-CH₂-C₆H₅:
*N*-phenyl-*N*-[1-(2-phenylethyl)piperidin-4-yl]acetamide,

D. R = H, R′ = CH₂-CH₂-C₆H₅:
*N*-phenyl-1-(2-phenylethyl)piperidin-4-amine,

E. R = CHO: benzaldehyde,

F. R = NH₂: aniline (phenylamine),

G. R = NH-CO-C₂H₅: *N*-phenylpropanamide.

*Ph Eur*

# Fentanyl Citrate

(*Ph Eur monograph 1103*)

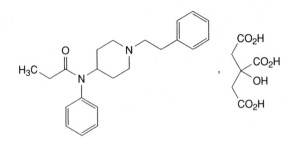

C$_{22}$H$_{28}$N$_2$O,C$_6$H$_8$O$_7$        528.6        990-73-8

## Action and use
Opioid receptor agonist; analgesic.

## Preparations
Bupivacaine and Fentanyl Injection

Fentanyl Injection

*Ph Eur* _____

## DEFINITION
*N*-Phenyl-*N*-[1-(2-phenylethyl)piperidin-4-yl]propanamide
dihydrogen 2-hydroxypropane-1,2,3-tricarboxylate.

## Content
99.0 per cent to 101.0 per cent (dried substance).

## CHARACTERS
### Appearance
White or almost white powder.

### Solubility
Soluble in water, freely soluble in methanol, sparingly soluble
in ethanol (96 per cent).

mp: about 152 °C, with decomposition.

## IDENTIFICATION
Infrared absorption spectrophotometry (*2.2.24*).

*Comparison*  *Ph. Eur. reference spectrum of fentanyl citrate.*

## TESTS
### Appearance of solution
The solution is clear (*2.2.1*) and colourless (*2.2.2,
Method II*).

Dissolve 0.2 g of the substance to be examined in *water R*
and dilute to 20 ml with the same solvent.

### Related substances
Liquid chromatography (*2.2.29*).

*Test solution*  Dissolve 0.100 g of the substance to be
examined in *methanol R* and dilute to 10.0 ml with the same
solvent.

*Reference solution (a)*  In order to prepare the *in situ*
degradation compound (impurity D), dissolve 10 mg of the
substance to be examined in 10.0 ml of *dilute hydrochloric
acid R*. Heat on a water-bath under a reflux condenser for
4 h. Neutralise with 10.0 ml of *dilute sodium hydroxide
solution R*. Evaporate to dryness on a water-bath. Cool and
take up the residue in 10 ml of *methanol R*. Filter.

*Reference solution (b)*  Dilute 1.0 ml of the test solution to
100.0 ml with *methanol R*. Dilute 5.0 ml of this solution to
20.0 ml with *methanol R*.

*Column*:
— *size*: *l* = 0.1 m, Ø = 4.6 mm;

— *stationary phase*: *octadecylsilyl silica gel for chromatography R*
(3 μm).

*Mobile phase*:
— *mobile phase A*: 5 g/l solution of *ammonium carbonate R* in
a mixture of 10 volumes of *tetrahydrofuran R* and
90 volumes of *water R*;
— *mobile phase B*: *acetonitrile R1*;

| Time (min) | Mobile phase A (per cent *V/V*) | Mobile phase B (per cent *V/V*) |
|---|---|---|
| 0 - 15 | 90 → 40 | 10 → 60 |
| 15 - 20 | 40 | 60 |

*Flow rate*  1.5 ml/min.

*Detection*  Spectrophotometer at 220 nm.

*Equilibration*  With *acetonitrile R* for at least 30 min, and then
with the mobile phase at the initial composition for at least
5 min.

*Injection*  10 μl; inject *methanol R* as a blank.

*Retention time*  Fentanyl = about 10 min;
impurity D = about 12 min.

*System suitability*  Reference solution (a):
— *resolution*: minimum 8.0 between the peaks due to
fentanyl and impurity D; if necessary, adjust the
concentration of acetonitrile in the mobile phase or adjust
the time programme for the linear gradient elution.

*Limits*:
— *impurities A, B, C, D*: for each impurity, not more than
the area of the principal peak in the chromatogram
obtained with reference solution (b) (0.25 per cent);
— *total*: not more than twice the area of the principal peak in
the chromatogram obtained with reference solution (b)
(0.5 per cent);
— *disregard limit*: 0.2 times the area of the principal peak in
the chromatogram obtained with reference solution (b)
(0.05 per cent); disregard any peak with a retention time
relative to the principal peak of 0.05 or less.

## Loss on drying (*2.2.32*)
Maximum 0.5 per cent, determined on 1.000 g by drying
*in vacuo* at 60 °C.

## ASSAY
Dissolve 0.300 g in 50 ml of a mixture of 1 volume of
*anhydrous acetic acid R* and 7 volumes of *methyl ethyl ketone R*.
Titrate with *0.1 M perchloric acid* using 0.2 ml of
*naphtholbenzein solution R* as indicator.

1 ml of *0.1 M perchloric acid* is equivalent to 52.86 mg of
C$_{28}$H$_{36}$N$_2$O$_8$.

## STORAGE
Protected from light.

## IMPURITIES
*Specified impurities*  *A, B, C, D.*

*Other detectable impurities* (the following substances would, if
present at a sufficient level, be detected by one or other of
the tests in the monograph. They are limited by the general
acceptance criterion for other/unspecified impurities and/or
by the general monograph *Substances for pharmaceutical use*
(*2034*). It is therefore not necessary to identify these
impurities for demonstration of compliance. See also *5.10.
Control of impurities in substances for pharmaceutical use*) : *E.*

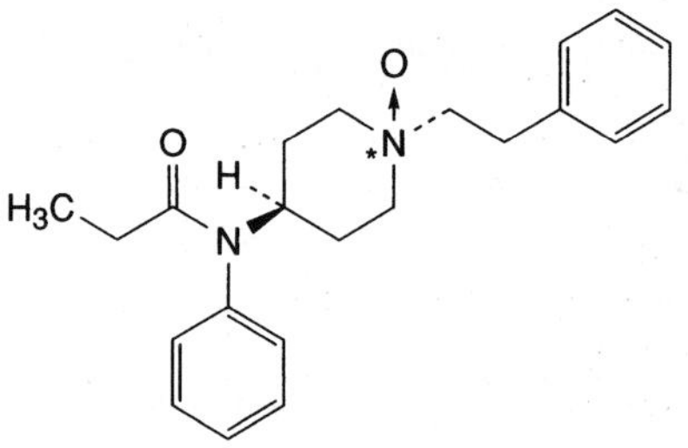

A. N-phenyl-N-[cis,trans-1-oxido-1-(2-phenylethyl)piperidin-4-yl]propanamide,

and epimer at N*

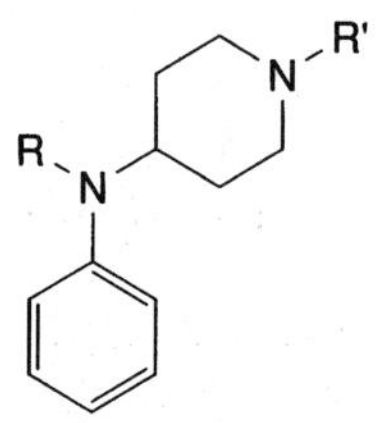

B. R = CO-C₂H₅, R′ = H:
N-phenyl-N-(piperidin-4-yl)propanamide,

C. R = CO-CH₃, R′ = CH₂-CH₂-C₆H₅:
N-phenyl-N-[1-(2-phenylethyl)piperidin-4-yl]acetamide,

D. R = H, R′ = CH₂-CH₂-C₆H₅:
N-phenyl-1-(2-phenylethyl)piperidin-4-amine,

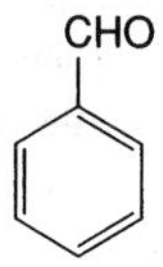

E. benzaldehyde.

*—— Ph Eur*

# Fenticonazole Nitrate

*(Ph Eur monograph 1211)*

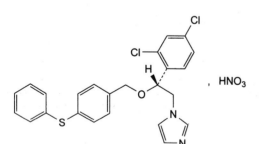

$C_{24}H_{20}Cl_2N_2OS,HNO_3$      518.4      *73151-29-8*

## Action and use
Antifungal.

*Ph Eur*

## DEFINITION
1-[(2RS)-2-(2,4-Dichlorophenyl)-2-[[4-(phenylsulphanyl)benzyl]oxy]ethyl]-1H-imidazole nitrate.

## Content
99.0 per cent to 101.0 per cent (dried substance).

## CHARACTERS
**Appearance**
White or almost white, crystalline powder.

**Solubility**
Practically insoluble in water, freely soluble in dimethylformamide and in methanol, sparingly soluble in anhydrous ethanol.

## IDENTIFICATION
*First identification   C, D.*

*Second identification   A, B, D.*

A. Melting point (*2.2.14*): 134 °C to 137 °C.

B. Ultraviolet and visible absorption spectrophotometry (*2.2.25*).

*Test solution* Dissolve 20.0 mg in *anhydrous ethanol R* and dilute to 100.0 ml with the same solvent. Dilute 1.0 ml of this solution to 10.0 ml with *anhydrous ethanol R*.

*Spectral range* 230-350 nm.

*Absorption maximum* At 252 nm.

*Shoulder* At about 270 nm.

*Absorption minimum* At 236 nm.

*Specific absorbance at the absorption maximum* 260 to 280.

C. Infrared absorption spectrophotometry (*2.2.24*).

*Comparison   fenticonazole nitrate CRS .*

D. It gives the reaction of nitrates (*2.3.1*).

## TESTS
**Optical rotation** (*2.2.7*)
− 0.10° to + 0.10°.

Dissolve 0.10 g in *methanol R* and dilute to 10.0 ml with the same solvent.

**Related substances**
Liquid chromatography (*2.2.29*).

*Test solution* Dissolve 25.0 mg of the substance to be examined in the mobile phase and dilute to 25.0 ml with the mobile phase.

*Reference solution (a)* Dilute 1.0 ml of the test solution to 200.0 ml with the mobile phase.

*Reference solution (b)* Dilute 10.0 ml of reference solution (a) to 25.0 ml with the mobile phase.

*Reference solution (c)* Dilute 1.0 ml of reference solution (a) to 10.0 ml with the mobile phase.

*Reference solution (d)* To 5 ml of the test solution add 5.0 mg of *fenticonazole impurity D CRS* , dissolve in the mobile phase and dilute to 100.0 ml with the mobile phase. Dilute 2.0 ml of this solution to 10.0 ml with the mobile phase.

*Column:*
— size: *l* = 0.25 m, Ø = 4 mm;
— stationary phase: *octadecylsilyl silica gel for chromatography R* (5-10 μm).

*Mobile phase* Mix 70 volumes of *acetonitrile R1* and 30 volumes of a phosphate buffer solution prepared by dissolving 3.4 g of *potassium dihydrogen phosphate R* in 900 ml of *water R*, adjusting to pH 3.0 with *phosphoric acid R* and diluting to 1000 ml with *water R*.

*Flow rate* 1.0 ml/min.

*Detection* Spectrophotometer at 229 nm.

*Injection* 10 μl.

*Run time* 5.5 times the retention time of fenticonazole.

*System suitability:*
— *resolution*: minimum 2.0 between the peaks due to impurity D and fenticonazole in the chromatogram obtained with reference solution (d);
— *signal-to-noise ratio*: minimum 5 for the principal peak in the chromatogram obtained with reference solution (c).

*Limits:*
— *impurities A, B, C, D, E*: for each impurity, not more than the area of the principal peak in the chromatogram obtained with reference solution (b) (0.2 per cent);
— *total*: not more than the area of the principal peak in the chromatogram obtained with reference solution (a) (0.5 per cent);
— *disregard limit*: the area of the principal peak in the chromatogram obtained with reference solution (c) (0.05 per cent); disregard the peak due to the nitric ion (which corresponds to the dead volume of the column).

**Toluene**
Head-space gas chromatography (*2.2.28*): use the standard additions method.

*Test solution* Disperse 0.2 g of the substance to be examined in a 10 ml vial with 5 ml of *water R*.

*Reference solution* Mix 4 mg of *toluene R* with *water R* and dilute to 1000 ml with the same solvent. Place 5 ml of this solution in a 10 ml vial.

*Column:*
— *size: l* = 25 m, Ø = 0.32 mm;
— *stationary phase*:
 poly(cyanopropyl) (7) (phenyl) (7) (methyl) (86) siloxane R (film thickness 1.2 μm).

*Carrier gas* *helium for chromatography R*.

*Split ratio* 1:25.

*Column head pressure* 40 kPa.

*Static head-space conditions which may be used:*
— *equilibration temperature*: 90 °C;
— *equilibration time*: 1 h.

*Temperature:*
— *column*: 80 °C;
— *injection port*: 180 °C;
— *detector*: 220 °C.

*Detection* Flame ionisation.

*Injection* 1 ml of the gaseous phase.

*Limit:*
— *toluene*: maximum 100 ppm.

**Loss on drying** (*2.2.32*)
Maximum 0.5 per cent, determined on 1.000 g by drying *in vacuo* at 60 °C.

**Sulphated ash** (*2.4.14*)
Maximum 0.1 per cent, determined on 1.0 g.

**ASSAY**
Dissolve 0.450 g in 50 ml of a mixture of equal volumes of *anhydrous acetic acid R* and *methyl ethyl ketone R*. Titrate with *0.1 M perchloric acid*, determining the end-point potentiometrically (*2.2.20*).

1 ml of *0.1 M perchloric acid* is equivalent to 51.84 mg of $C_{24}H_{21}Cl_2N_3O_4S$.

**STORAGE**
Protected from light.

**IMPURITIES**
*Specified impurities* *A, B, C, D, E.*

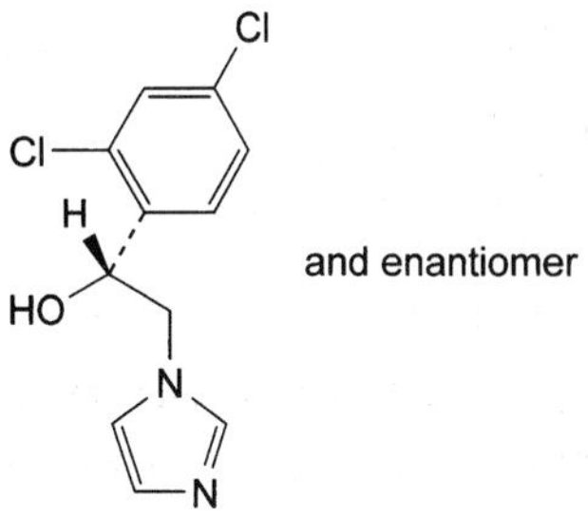

A. (*RS*)-1-(2,4-dichlorophenyl)-2-(1*H*-imidazol-1-yl)ethanol,

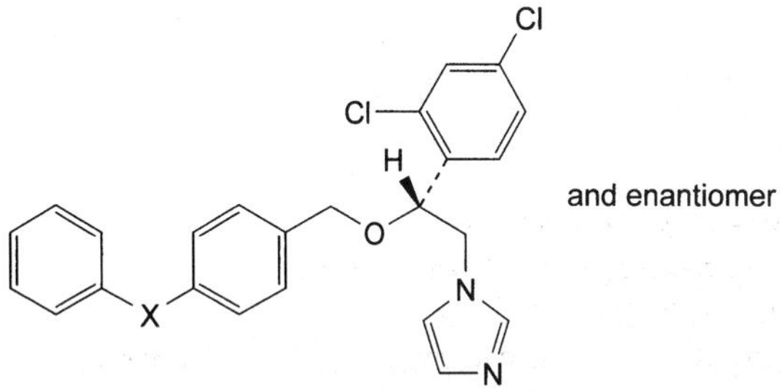

B. X = SO: 1-[(2*RS*)-2-(2,4-dichlorophenyl)-2-[[4-(phenylsulphinyl)benzyl]oxy]ethyl]-1*H*-imidazole,
C. X = SO₂: 1-[(2*RS*)-2-(2,4-dichlorophenyl)-2-[[4-(phenylsulphonyl)benzyl]oxy]ethyl]-1*H*-imidazole,

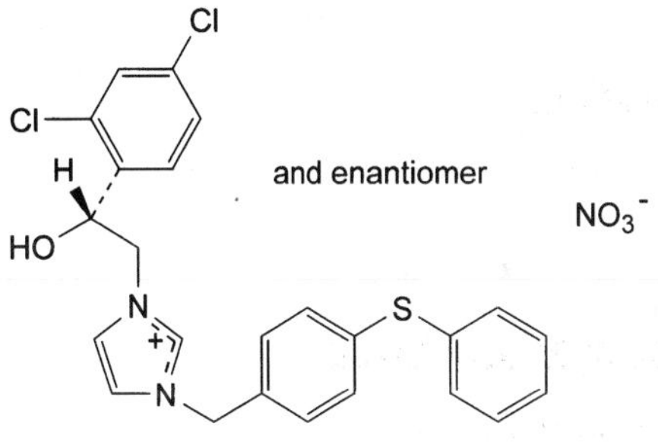

D. (*RS*)-1-[2-(2,4-dichlorophenyl)-2-hydroxyethyl]-3-[4-(phenylsulphanyl)benzyl]imidazolium nitrate,

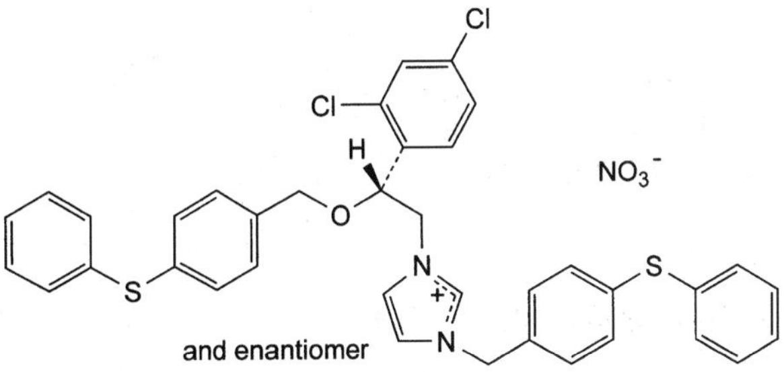

E. (*RS*)-1-[2-(2,4-dichlorophenyl)-2-[4-(phenylsulphanyl)benzyloxy]ethyl]-3-[4-(phenylsulphanyl)benzyl]imidazolium nitrate.

# Products of Fermentation

*(Ph Eur monograph 1468)*

Ph Eur _____

*This monograph applies to indirect gene products obtained by fermentation. It is not applicable to:*
— *monographs in the Pharmacopoeia concerning vaccines for human or veterinary use;*
— *products derived from continuous cell lines of human or animal origin;*
— *direct gene products that result from the transcription and translation from nucleic acid to protein, whether or not subject to post-translational modification;*
— *products obtained by semi-synthesis from a product of fermentation and those obtained by biocatalytic transformation;*
— *whole broth concentrates or raw fermentation products.*

*This monograph provides general requirements for the development and manufacture of products of fermentation. These requirements are not necessarily comprehensive in a given case and requirements complementary or additional to those prescribed in this monograph may be imposed in an individual monograph or by the competent authority.*

## DEFINITION

For the purposes of this monograph, products of fermentation are active or inactive pharmaceutical substances produced by controlled fermentation as indirect gene products. They are primary or secondary metabolites of micro-organisms such as bacteria, yeasts, fungi and micro-algae, whether or not modified by traditional procedures or recombinant DNA (rDNA) technology. Such metabolites include vitamins, amino acids, antibiotics, alkaloids and polysaccharides.

They may be obtained by batch or continuous fermentation processes followed by procedures such as extraction, concentration, purification and isolation.

## PRODUCTION

Production is based on a process that has been validated and shown to be suitable. The extent of validation depends on the critical nature of the respective process step.

## CHARACTERISATION OF THE PRODUCER MICRO-ORGANISM

The history of the micro-organism used for production is documented. The micro-organism is adequately characterised. This may include determination of the phenotype of the micro-organism, macroscopic and microscopic methods and biochemical tests and, if appropriate, determination of the genotype of the micro-organism and molecular genetic tests.

## PROCESSES USING A SEED-LOT SYSTEM

The *master cell bank* is a homogeneous suspension or lyophilisate of the original cells distributed into individual containers for storage. The viability and productivity of the cells under the selected storage conditions and their suitability for initiating a satisfactory production process after storage must be demonstrated.

Propagation of the master cell bank may take place through a seed-lot system that uses a working cell bank.

The *working cell bank* is a homogeneous suspension or lyophilisate of the cell material derived from the master cell bank, distributed in equal volumes into individual containers for storage (for example, in liquid nitrogen).

Production may take place by batch or continuous culture and may be terminated under defined conditions.

All containers in a cell bank are stored under identical conditions. Once removed from storage, the individual ampoules, vials or culture straws are not returned to the cell bank.

## PROCESSES USING STAGED GROWTH IN CULTURES

The contents of a container of the working cell bank are used, if necessary after resuspension, to prepare an inoculum in a suitable medium. After a suitable period of growth, the cultures are used to initiate the fermentation process, if necessary following preculture in a prefermentor. The conditions to be used at each stage of the process are defined and must be met with each production run.

## CHANGE CONTROL

If the production process is altered in a way that causes a significant change in the impurity profile of the product, the critical steps associated with this change in impurity profile are revalidated.

If a significant change has taken place in the micro-organism used for production that causes a significant change in the impurity profile of the product, the critical steps of the production process associated with this change, particularly the procedure for purification and isolation, are revalidated.

Revalidation includes demonstration that new impurities present in the product as a result of the change are adequately controlled by the test procedures. If necessary, additional or alternative tests must be introduced with appropriate limits. If the change in the process or in the micro-organism results in an increase in the level of an impurity already present, the acceptability of such an increase is addressed.

When a master cell bank is replaced, the critical steps of the production process must be revalidated to the extent necessary to demonstrate that no adverse change has occurred in the quality and safety of the product. Particular attention must be given to possible changes in the impurity profile of the product if a modified or new micro-organism is introduced into the process.

## RAW MATERIALS

The raw materials employed in the fermentation and/or down-stream processing are of suitable quality for the intended purpose. They are tested to ensure that they comply with written specifications.

Levels of bioburden in media or in the inlet air for aeration are reduced to an adequately low level to ensure that if microbiological contamination occurs, it does not adversely affect the quality, purity and safety of the product. Addition of components such as nutrients, precursors, and substrates during fermentation takes place aseptically.

## IN-PROCESS CONTROLS

In-process controls are in place to ensure the consistency of the conditions during fermentation and down-stream processing and of the quality of the isolated product. Particular attention must be paid to ensure that any microbial contamination that adversely affects the quality, purity and safety of the product is detected by the controls applied.

Production conditions may be monitored, as appropriate, by suitable procedures for example to control and check:
— temperature,
— pH,
— rate of aeration,
— rate of agitation,
— pressure,

and to monitor the concentration of the required product.

## DOWN-STREAM PROCESSING

At the end of fermentation, the producer micro-organism is inactivated or removed. Further processing is designed to reduce residues originating from the culture medium to an acceptable level and to ensure that the desired product is recovered with consistent quality.

Various purification processes may be used, for example, charcoal treatment, ultrafiltration and solvent extraction. It must be demonstrated that the process or processes chosen reduce to a minimum or remove:

— residues from the producer micro-organism, culture media, substrates and precursors,

— unwanted transformation products of substrates and precursors.

If necessary, suitable tests are performed either as in-process controls or on the isolated product of fermentation.

## IDENTIFICATION, TESTS AND ASSAY

The requirements with which the product must comply throughout its period of validity, as well as specific test methods, are stated in the individual monographs.

*Ph Eur*

# Ferric Chloride Hexahydrate

*(Ph Eur monograph 1515)*

FeCl₃,6H₂O        270.3        *10025-77-1*

*Ph Eur*

## DEFINITION
### Content
98.0 per cent to 102.0 per cent.

## CHARACTERS
### Appearance
Crystalline mass or orange-yellow or brownish-yellow crystals, very hygroscopic.

### Solubility
Very soluble in water and in ethanol (96 per cent), freely soluble in glycerol.

## IDENTIFICATION
A. It gives reaction (a) of chlorides (*2.3.1*).

B. It gives reaction (c) of iron (*2.3.1*).

## TESTS
### Solution S
Dissolve 10 g in *distilled water R* and dilute to 100 ml with the same solvent.

### Acidity
In a suitable polyethylene container, dissolve 3.0 g of *potassium fluoride R* in 15 ml of *water R*. Titrate with *0.1 M sodium hydroxide* using 0.1 ml of *phenolphthalein solution R* as indicator until a pink colour is obtained. Add 10 ml of solution S and allow to stand for 3 h. Filter and use 12.5 ml of the filtrate. Not more than 0.30 ml of *0.1 M sodium hydroxide* is required to change the colour of the indicator to pink.

### Free chlorine
Heat 5 ml of solution S. The vapour does not turn *starch iodide paper R* blue.

### Sulphates (*2.4.13*)
Maximum 100 ppm.

Heat 15 ml of solution S on a water-bath and add 5 ml of *strong sodium hydroxide solution R*. Allow to cool and filter. Neutralise the filtrate to *blue litmus paper R* using *hydrochloric acid R1* and evaporate to 15 ml.

### Ferrous ions
Maximum 50 ppm.

To 10 ml of solution S, add 1 ml of *water R*, and 0.05 ml of *potassium ferricyanide solution R* followed by 4 ml of *phosphoric acid R*. After 10 min, any blue colour in the solution is not more intense than that in a standard prepared at the same time and in the same manner using 10 ml of *water R* and 1 ml of a freshly prepared 0.250 g/l solution of *ferrous sulphate R*.

### Heavy metals (*2.4.8*)
Maximum 50 ppm.

Dissolve 1.0 g in 10 ml of *hydrochloric acid R1*. Add 2 ml of *strong hydrogen peroxide solution R*, then evaporate to 5 ml. Allow to cool and dilute to 20 ml with *hydrochloric acid R1* and transfer the solution to a separating funnel. Shake 3 times, for 3 min each time, with 20 ml of *methyl isobutyl ketone R1*. Separate the lower phase, reduce to half its volume by evaporation and dilute to 25 ml with *water R*. Neutralise 10 ml of the solution with *dilute ammonia R1* to *red litmus paper R* and dilute to 20 ml with *water R*. 12 ml of the solution complies with test A. Prepare the reference solution using *lead standard solution (1 ppm Pb) R*.

## ASSAY
In a conical flask with a ground-glass stopper, dissolve 0.200 g in 20 ml of *water R*. Add 10 ml of *dilute hydrochloric acid R* and 2 g of *potassium iodide R*. Allow the stoppered flask to stand for 1 h protected from light. Titrate with *0.1 M sodium thiosulphate*, adding 5 ml of *starch solution R* towards the end of the titration.

1 ml of *0.1 M sodium thiosulphate* is equivalent to 27.03 mg of FeCl₃,6H₂O.

## STORAGE
In an airtight container, protected from light.

*Ph Eur*

# Ferrous Fumarate

*(Ph Eur monograph 0902)*

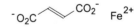

C₄H₂FeO₄        169.9        *141-01-5*

## Action and use
Used in prevention and treatment of anaemias.

## Preparations
Ferrous Fumarate Capsules

Ferrous Fumarate Oral Suspension

Ferrous Fumarate Tablets

Ferrous Fumarate and Folic Acid Tablets

Ferrous Fumarate contains in 200 mg about 65 mg of iron.

*Ph Eur*

## DEFINITION
Iron(II) (*E*)-butenedioate.

## Content
93.0 per cent to 101.0 per cent (dried substance).

## CHARACTERS
### Appearance
Fine, reddish-orange or reddish-brown powder.

### Solubility
Slightly soluble in water, very slightly soluble in ethanol (96 per cent).

## IDENTIFICATION
A. Thin-layer chromatography (2.2.27).

*Test solution* To 1.0 g add 25 ml of a mixture of equal volumes of *hydrochloric acid R* and *water R* and heat on a water-bath for 15 min. Cool and filter. Use the filtrate for identification test C. Wash the residue with 50 ml of a mixture of 1 volume of *dilute hydrochloric acid R* and 9 volumes of *water R* and discard the washings. Dry the residue at 100-105 °C. Dissolve 20 mg of the residue in *acetone R* and dilute to 10 ml with the same solvent.

*Reference solution* Dissolve 20 mg of *fumaric acid CRS* in *acetone R* and dilute to 10 ml with the same solvent.

*Plate* TLC silica gel $F_{254}$ plate R.

*Mobile phase* anhydrous formic acid R, methylene chloride R, butanol R, heptane R (12:16:32:44 V/V/V/V).

*Application* 5 µl.

*Development* In an unsaturated tank, over a path of 10 cm.

*Drying* At 105 °C for 15 min.

*Detection* Examine in ultraviolet light at 254 nm.

*Results* The principal spot in the chromatogram obtained with the test solution is similar in position and size to the principal spot in the chromatogram obtained with the reference solution.

B. Mix 0.5 g with 1 g of *resorcinol R*. To 0.5 g of the mixture in a crucible add 0.15 ml of *sulphuric acid R* and heat gently. A dark red semi-solid mass is formed. Add the mass, with care, to 100 ml of *water R*. An orange-yellow colour develops and the solution shows no fluorescence.

C. The filtrate obtained during preparation of the test solution in identification test A gives reaction (a) of iron (2.3.1).

## TESTS
### Solution S
Dissolve 2.0 g in a mixture of 10 ml of *lead-free hydrochloric acid R* and 80 ml of *water R*, heating slightly if necessary. Allow to cool, filter if necessary and dilute to 100 ml with *water R*.

### Sulphates (2.4.13)
Maximum 0.2 per cent.

Heat 0.15 g with 8 ml of *dilute hydrochloric acid R* and 20 ml of *distilled water R*. Cool in iced water, filter and dilute to 30 ml with *distilled water R*.

### Arsenic (2.4.2, Method A)
Maximum 5 ppm.

Mix 1.0 g with 15 ml of *water R* and 15 ml of *sulphuric acid R*. Warm to precipitate the fumaric acid completely. Cool and add 30 ml of *water R*. Filter. Wash the precipitate with *water R*. Dilute the combined filtrate and washings to 125 ml with *water R*. 25 ml of the solution complies with the test.

### Ferric ion
Maximum 2.0 per cent.

In a flask with a ground-glass stopper, dissolve 3.0 g in a mixture of 10 ml of *hydrochloric acid R* and 100 ml of *water R* by heating rapidly to boiling. Boil for 15 s. Cool rapidly, add 3 g of *potassium iodide R*, stopper the flask and allow to stand protected from light for 15 min. Add 2 ml of *starch solution R* as indicator. Titrate the liberated iodine with *0.1 M sodium thiosulphate*. Carry out a blank test. The difference between the volumes used in the 2 titrations corresponds to the amount of iodine liberated by ferric ion.

1 ml of *0.1 M sodium thiosulphate* is equivalent to 5.585 mg of ferric ion.

### Cadmium
Maximum 10.0 ppm.

Atomic absorption spectrometry (2.2.23, Method I).

*Test solution* Solution S.

*Reference solutions* Prepare the reference solutions using *cadmium standard solution (0.1 per cent Cd) R* and diluting with a 10 per cent V/V solution of *lead-free hydrochloric acid R*.

*Source* Cadmium hollow-cathode lamp.

*Wavelength* 228.8 nm.

*Atomisation device* Air-acetylene flame.

### Chromium
Maximum $2.00 \times 10^2$ ppm.

Atomic absorption spectrometry (2.2.23, Method I).

*Test solution* Solution S.

*Reference solutions* Prepare the reference solutions using *chromium standard solution (0.1 per cent Cr) R* and diluting with a 10 per cent V/V solution of *lead-free hydrochloric acid R*.

*Source* Chromium hollow-cathode lamp.

*Wavelength* 357.9 nm.

*Atomisation device* Air-acetylene flame.

### Lead
Maximum 20.0 ppm.

Atomic absorption spectrometry (2.2.23, Method I).

*Test solution* Solution S.

*Reference solutions* Prepare the reference solutions using *lead standard solution (10 ppm Pb) R* and diluting with a 10 per cent V/V solution of *lead-free hydrochloric acid R*.

*Source* Lead hollow-cathode lamp.

*Wavelength* 283.3 nm.

*Atomisation device* Air-acetylene flame.

### Mercury
Maximum 1.0 ppm.

Atomic absorption spectrometry (2.2.23, Method I).

*Test solution* Solution S.

*Reference solutions* Prepare the reference solutions using *mercury standard solution (10 ppm Hg) R* and diluting with a 25 per cent V/V solution of *lead-free hydrochloric acid R*.

*Source* Mercury hollow-cathode lamp.

*Wavelength* 253.7 nm.

Following the recommendations of the manufacturer, introduce 5 ml of solution S or 5 ml of the reference solutions into the reaction vessel of the cold-vapour mercury assay accessory, add 10 ml of *water R* and 1 ml of *stannous chloride solution R1*.

### Nickel
Maximum $2.00 \times 10^2$ ppm.

Atomic absorption spectrometry (2.2.23, Method I).

*Test solution*  Solution S.

*Reference solutions*  Prepare the reference solutions using *nickel standard solution (10 ppm Ni) R* and diluting with a 10 per cent *V/V* solution of *lead-free hydrochloric acid R*.

*Source*  Nickel hollow-cathode lamp.

*Wavelength*  232 nm.

*Atomisation device*  Air-acetylene flame.

### Zinc
Maximum $5.00 \times 10^2$ ppm.

Atomic absorption spectrometry (*2.2.23, Method I*).

*Test solution*  Solution S diluted to 10 volumes.

*Reference solutions*  Prepare the reference solutions using *zinc standard solution (10 ppm Zn) R* and diluting with a 1 per cent *V/V* solution of *lead-free hydrochloric acid R*.

*Source*  Zinc hollow-cathode lamp.

*Wavelength*  213.9 nm.

*Atomisation device*  Air-acetylene flame.

### Loss on drying (*2.2.32*)
Maximum 1.0 per cent, determined on 1.000 g by drying in an oven at 105 °C.

### ASSAY
Dissolve with slight heating 0.150 g in 7.5 ml of *dilute sulphuric acid R*. Cool and add 25 ml of *water R*. Add 0.1 ml of *ferroin R*. Titrate immediately with *0.1 M cerium sulphate* until the colour changes from orange to light bluish-green.

1 ml of *0.1 M cerium sulphate* is equivalent to 16.99 mg of $C_4H_2FeO_4$.

### STORAGE
In an airtight container, protected from light.

*Ph Eur*

# Ferrous Gluconate

(*Ph Eur monograph 0493*)

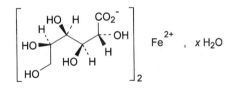

$C_{12}H_{22}FeO_{14}, xH_2O$      446.1      *299-29-6*

(anhydrous)      (anhydrous)

### Action and use
Used in prevention and treatment of iron deficiency.

### Preparation
Ferrous Gluconate Tablets

Ferrous Gluconate contains in 600 mg about 70 mg of iron.

*Ph Eur*

### DEFINITION
Iron(II) di(D-gluconate).

### Content
11.8 per cent to 12.5 per cent of iron(II) (dried substance). It contains a variable amount of water.

### CHARACTERS
### Appearance
Greenish-yellow or grey powder or granules.

### Solubility
Freely but slowly soluble in water giving a greenish-brown solution, more readily soluble in hot water, practically insoluble in ethanol (96 per cent).

### IDENTIFICATION
A. Thin-layer chromatography (*2.2.27*).

*Test solution*  Dissolve 20 mg of the substance to be examined in 2 ml of *water R*, heating if necessary in a water-bath at 60 °C.

*Reference solution*  Dissolve 20 mg of *ferrous gluconate CRS* in 2 ml of *water R*, heating if necessary in a water-bath at 60 °C.

*Plate*  *TLC silica gel G plate R*.

*Mobile phase*  *concentrated ammonia R, ethyl acetate R, water R, ethanol (96 per cent) R* (10:10:30:50 *V/V/V/V*).

*Application*  5 µl.

*Development*  Over a path of 10 cm.

*Drying*  At 100-105 °C for 20 min.

*Detection*  Allow to cool and spray with a 50 g/l solution of *potassium dichromate R* in a 40 per cent *m/m* solution of *sulphuric acid R*.

*Results*  After 5 min, the principal spot in the chromatogram obtained with the test solution is similar in position, colour and size to the principal spot in the chromatogram obtained with the reference solution.

B. 1 ml of solution S (see Tests) gives reaction (a) of iron (*2.3.1*).

### TESTS
### Solution S
Dissolve 5.0 g in *carbon dioxide-free water R* prepared from *distilled water R* and heated to about 60 °C, allow to cool and dilute to 50 ml with *carbon dioxide-free water R* prepared from *distilled water R*.

### Appearance of solution
The solution is clear (*2.2.1*).

Dilute 2 ml of solution S to 10 ml with *water R*. Examine the solution against the light.

### pH (*2.2.3*)
4.0 to 5.5 for solution S, measured 3-4 h after preparation.

### Sucrose and reducing sugars
Dissolve 0.5 g in 10 ml of warm *water R* and add 1 ml of *dilute ammonia R1*. Pass *hydrogen sulphide R* through the solution and allow to stand for 30 min. Filter and wash the precipitate with 2 quantities, each of 5 ml, of *water R*. Acidify the combined filtrate and washings to *blue litmus paper R* with *dilute hydrochloric acid R* and add 2 ml in excess. Boil until the vapour no longer darkens *lead acetate paper R* and continue boiling, if necessary, until the volume is reduced to about 10 ml. Cool, add 15 ml of *sodium carbonate solution R*, allow to stand for 5 min and filter. Dilute the filtrate to 100 ml with *water R*. To 5 ml of this solution add 2 ml of *cupri-tartaric solution R* and boil for 1 min. Allow to stand for 1 min. No red precipitate is formed.

### Chlorides (*2.4.4*)
Maximum 0.06 per cent.

Dilute 0.8 ml of solution S to 15 ml with *water R*.

### Oxalates

Dissolve 5.0 g in a mixture of 10 ml of *dilute sulphuric acid R* and 40 ml of *water R*. Shake the solution with 50 ml of *ether R* for 5 min. Separate the aqueous layer and shake it with 20 ml of *ether R* for 5 min. Combine the ether layers, evaporate to dryness and dissolve the residue in 15 ml of *water R*. Filter, boil the filtrate until the volume is reduced to 5 ml and add 1 ml of *dilute acetic acid R* and 1.5 ml of *calcium chloride solution R*. Allow to stand for 30 min. No precipitate is formed.

### Sulphates (2.4.13)

Maximum 500 ppm.

To 3.0 ml of solution S add 3 ml of *acetic acid R* and dilute to 15 ml with *distilled water R*. Examine the solutions against the light.

### Arsenic (2.4.2, Method A)

Maximum 2 ppm, determined on 0.5 g.

### Barium

Dilute 10 ml of solution S to 50 ml with *distilled water R* and add 5 ml of *dilute sulphuric acid R*. Allow to stand for 5 min. Any opalescence in the solution is not more intense than that in a mixture of 10 ml of solution S and 45 ml of *distilled water R*.

### Ferric ion

Maximum 1.0 per cent.

In a ground-glass-stoppered flask, dissolve 5.00 g in a mixture of 10 ml of *hydrochloric acid R* and 100 ml of *carbon dioxide-free water R*. Add 3 g of *potassium iodide R*, close the flask and allow to stand protected from light for 5 min. Titrate with *0.1 M sodium thiosulphate*, using 0.5 ml of *starch solution R*, added towards the end of the titration, as indicator. Carry out a blank titration. Not more than 9.0 ml of *0.1 M sodium thiosulphate* is used.

### Heavy metals (2.4.8)

Maximum 20 ppm.

Thoroughly mix 2.5 g with 0.5 g of *magnesium oxide R1* in a silica crucible. Ignite to dull redness until a homogeneous mass is obtained. Heat at $800 \pm 50$ °C for about 1 h, allow to cool and take up the residue in 20 ml of hot *hydrochloric acid R*. Allow to cool. Transfer the liquid to a separating funnel and shake for 3 min with 3 quantities, each of 20 ml, of methyl isobutyl ketone saturated with hydrochloric acid (prepared by shaking 100 ml of freshly distilled *methyl isobutyl ketone R* with 1 ml of *hydrochloric acid R*). Allow to stand, separate the aqueous layer, reduce to half its volume by boiling, allow to cool and dilute to 25 ml with *water R*. Neutralise 10 ml of this solution to *red litmus paper R* using *dilute ammonia R1* and dilute to 20 ml with *water R*. 12 ml of the solution complies with test A. Prepare the reference solution using *lead standard solution (1 ppm Pb) R*.

### Loss on drying (2.2.32)

5.0 per cent to 10.5 per cent, determined on 0.500 g by drying in an oven at 105 °C for 5 h.

### Microbial contamination

TAMC: acceptance criterion $10^3$ CFU/g (2.6.12).

TYMC: acceptance criterion $10^2$ CFU/g (2.6.12).

### ASSAY

Dissolve 0.5 g of *sodium hydrogen carbonate R* in a mixture of 30 ml of *dilute sulphuric acid R* and 70 ml of *water R*. When the effervescence stops, dissolve 1.00 g of the substance to be examined with gentle shaking. Using 0.1 ml of *ferroin R* as indicator, titrate with *0.1 M ammonium and cerium nitrate* until the red colour disappears.

1 ml of *0.1 M ammonium and cerium nitrate* is equivalent to 5.585 mg of iron(II).

### STORAGE

Protected from light.

_____ *Ph Eur*

# Dried Ferrous Sulphate

(*Ph Eur monograph 2340*)

| | | |
|---|---|---|
| $FeSO_4$ | 151.9 | *13463-43-9* |

*Ph Eur* _____

### DEFINITION

Hydrated ferrous sulphate from which part of the water of hydration has been removed by drying.

**Content**

86.0 per cent to 90.0 per cent.

### CHARACTERS

**Appearance**

Greyish-white powder.

**Solubility**

Slowly but freely soluble in water, very soluble in boiling water, practically insoluble in ethanol (96 per cent).

It is oxidised in moist air, becoming brown.

### IDENTIFICATION

A. It gives the reactions of sulphates (2.3.1).

B. It gives reaction (a) of iron (2.3.1).

C. It complies with the limits of the assay.

### TESTS

**Solution S**

Dissolve 2.00 g in a 5 per cent *V/V* solution of *lead-free nitric acid R* and dilute to 100.0 ml with the same acid.

**pH** (2.2.3)

3.0 to 4.0.

Dissolve 1.0 g in *carbon dioxide-free water R* and dilute to 20 ml with the same solvent.

**Chlorides** (2.4.4)

Maximum 300 ppm.

Dissolve 2.5 g in *water R*, add 0.5 ml of *dilute sulphuric acid R* and dilute to 50 ml with *water R*. Dilute 3.3 ml of this solution to 10 ml with *water R* and add 5 ml of *dilute nitric acid R*. Prepare the standard using a mixture of 10 ml of *chloride standard solution (5 ppm Cl) R* and 5 ml of *dilute nitric acid R*. Use 0.15 ml of *silver nitrate solution R2* in this test.

**Chromium**

Maximum $1.00 \times 10^2$ ppm.

Atomic absorption spectrometry (2.2.23, Method I).

*Test solution*    Solution S.

*Reference solutions*    Prepare the reference solutions using *chromium standard solution (100 ppm Cr) R*, diluted as necessary with a 5 per cent *V/V* solution of *lead-free nitric acid R*.

*Source*    Chromium hollow-cathode lamp using a transmission band preferably of 1 nm.

*Wavelength*    357.9 nm.

*Atomisation device*    Air-acetylene flame.

**Copper**

Maximum 50.0 ppm.

Atomic absorption spectrometry (*2.2.23, Method II*).

*Test solution*   Solution S.

*Reference solutions*   Prepare the reference solutions using *copper standard solution (0.1 per cent Cu) R*, diluted as necessary with a 5 per cent *V/V* solution of *lead-free nitric acid R*.

*Source*   Copper hollow-cathode lamp using a transmission band preferably of 1 nm.

*Wavelength*   324.7 nm.

*Atomisation device*   Air-acetylene flame.

**Ferric ions**
Maximum 0.50 per cent.

In a ground-glass-stoppered flask, dissolve 5.00 g in a mixture of 10 ml of *hydrochloric acid R* and 100 ml of *carbon dioxide-free water R*. Add 3 g of *potassium iodide R*, close the flask and allow to stand in the dark for 5 min. Titrate the liberated iodine with *0.1 M sodium thiosulphate*, using 0.5 ml of *starch solution R*, added towards the end of titration, as indicator. Carry out a blank test in the same conditions. Not more than 4.5 ml of *0.1 M sodium thiosulphate* is used.

**Manganese**
Maximum 0.10 per cent.

Atomic absorption spectrometry (*2.2.23, Method II*).

*Test solution*   Dilute 1.0 ml of solution S to 20.0 ml with a 5 per cent *V/V* solution of *lead-free nitric acid R*.

*Reference solutions*   Prepare the reference solutions using *manganese standard solution (1000 ppm Mn) R*, diluted as necessary with a 5 per cent *V/V* solution of *lead-free nitric acid R*.

*Source*   Manganese hollow-cathode lamp using a transmission band preferably of 1 nm.

*Wavelength*   279.5 nm.

*Atomisation device*   Air-acetylene flame.

**Nickel**
Maximum $1.00 \times 10^2$ ppm.

Atomic absorption spectrometry (*2.2.23, Method I*).

*Test solution*   Solution S.

*Reference solutions*   Prepare the reference solutions using *nickel standard solution (10 ppm Ni) R*, diluted as necessary with a 5 per cent *V/V* solution of *lead-free nitric acid R*.

*Source*   Nickel hollow-cathode lamp using a transmission band preferably of 1 nm.

*Wavelength*   232.0 nm.

*Atomisation device*   Air-acetylene flame.

**Zinc**
Maximum $1.00 \times 10^2$ ppm.

Atomic absorption spectrometry (*2.2.23, Method II*).

*Test solution*   Solution S.

*Reference solutions*   Prepare the reference solutions using *zinc standard solution (100 ppm Zn) R*, diluted as necessary with a 5 per cent *V/V* solution of *lead-free nitric acid R*.

*Source*   Zinc hollow-cathode lamp using a transmission band preferably of 1 nm.

*Wavelength*   213.9 nm.

*Atomisation device*   Air-acetylene flame.

**ASSAY**
Dissolve 2.5 g of *sodium hydrogen carbonate R* in a mixture of 150 ml of *water R* and 10 ml of *sulphuric acid R*. When the effervescence ceases, add to the solution 0.140 g of the substance to be examined and dissolve with gentle shaking.

Add 0.1 ml of *ferroin R* and titrate with *0.1 M ammonium and cerium nitrate* until the red colour disappears.

1 ml of *0.1 M ammonium and cerium nitrate* is equivalent to 15.19 mg of $FeSO_4$.

**STORAGE**
In an airtight container.

_____ *Ph Eur*

# Ferrous Sulphate Heptahydrate

(*Ph Eur monograph 0083*)

$FeSO_4,7H_2O$                 278.0                 7720-78-7

**Action and use**
Used in prevention and treatment of anaemias.

**Preparation**
Paediatric Ferrous Sulphate Oral Solution

Ferrous Sulphate contains in 300 mg about 60 mg of iron.

*Ph Eur* _____

**DEFINITION**
**Content**
98.0 per cent to 105.0 per cent.

**CHARACTERS**
**Appearance**
Light green, crystalline powder or bluish-green crystals, efflorescent in air.

**Solubility**
Freely soluble in water, very soluble in boiling water, practically insoluble in alcohol.

Ferrous sulphate is oxidised in moist air, becoming brown.

**IDENTIFICATION**
A. It gives the reaction of sulphates (*2.3.1*).

B. It gives reaction (a) of iron (*2.3.1*).

C. It complies with the limits of the assay.

**TESTS**
**Solution S**
Dissolve 2.5 g in *carbon dioxide-free water R*, add 0.5 ml of *dilute sulphuric acid R* and dilute to 50 ml with *water R*.

**Appearance of solution**
Solution S is not more opalescent than reference suspension II (*2.2.1*).

**pH** (*2.2.3*)
3.0 to 4.0.

Dissolve 0.5 g in *carbon dioxide-free water R* and dilute to 10 ml with the same solvent.

**Chlorides** (*2.4.4*)
Maximum 300 ppm.

Dilute 3.3 ml of solution S to 10 ml with *water R* and add 5 ml of *dilute nitric acid R*. The solution complies with the limit test for chlorides. Prepare the standard using a mixture of 10 ml of *chloride standard solution (5 ppm Cl) R* and 5 ml of *dilute nitric acid R*. Use 0.15 ml of *silver nitrate solution R2* in this test.

**Ferric ions**
Maximum 0.5 per cent.

In a ground-glass-stoppered flask, dissolve 5.00 g in a mixture of 10 ml of *hydrochloric acid R* and 100 ml of *carbon dioxide-free water R*. Add 3 g of *potassium iodide R*, close the flask and allow to stand in the dark for 5 min. Titrate the liberated iodine with *0.1 M sodium thiosulphate*, using 0.5 ml of *starch solution R*, added towards the end of the titration, as indicator. Carry out a blank test in the same conditions. Not more than 4.5 ml of *0.1 M sodium thiosulphate* is used, taking into account the blank titration.

## Manganese

Maximum 0.1 per cent.

Dissolve 1.0 g in 40 ml of *water R*, add 10 ml of *nitric acid R* and boil until red fumes are evolved. Add 0.5 g of *ammonium persulphate R* and boil for 10 min. Discharge any pink colour by adding dropwise a 50 g/l solution of *sodium sulphite R* and boil until any odour of sulphur dioxide is eliminated. Add 10 ml of *water R*, 5 ml of *phosphoric acid R* and 0.5 g of *sodium periodate R*, boil for 1 min and allow to cool. The solution is not more intensely coloured than a standard prepared at the same time in the same manner using 1.0 ml of *0.02 M potassium permanganate* and adding the same volumes of the same reagents.

## Zinc

Maximum 500 ppm.

To 5 ml of solution A obtained in the test for heavy metals add 1 ml of *potassium ferrocyanide solution R* and dilute to 13 ml with *water R*. After 5 min, any turbidity produced is not more intense than that of a standard prepared at the same time by mixing 10 ml of *zinc standard solution (10 ppm Zn) R*, 2 ml of *hydrochloric acid R1* and 1 ml of *potassium ferrocyanide solution R*.

## Heavy metals (2.4.8)

Maximum 50 ppm.

Dissolve 1.0 g in 10 ml of *hydrochloric acid R1*, add 2 ml of *strong hydrogen peroxide solution R* and boil until the volume is reduced to 5 ml. Allow to cool, dilute to 20 ml with *hydrochloric acid R1*, transfer the solution to a separating funnel and shake for 3 min with 3 quantities, each of 20 ml, of methyl isobutyl ketone saturated with hydrochloric acid (prepared by shaking 100 ml of freshly distilled *methyl isobutyl ketone R* with 1 ml of *hydrochloric acid R1*). Allow to stand, separate the aqueous layer and reduce to half its volume by boiling, allow to cool and dilute to 25 ml with *water R* (solution A). Neutralise 10 ml of solution A to *litmus paper R* using *dilute ammonia R1* and dilute to 20 ml with *water R*. 12 ml of the solution complies with limit test A. Prepare the standard using *lead standard solution (1 ppm Pb) R*.

## ASSAY

Dissolve 2.5 g of *sodium hydrogen carbonate R* in a mixture of 150 ml of *water R* and 10 ml of *sulphuric acid R*. When the effervescence ceases add to the solution 0.500 g of the substance to be examined and dissolve with gentle shaking. Add *0.1 ml of ferroin R* and titrate with *0.1 M ammonium and cerium nitrate* until the red colour disappears.

1 ml of *0.1 M ammonium and cerium nitrate* is equivalent to 27.80 mg of $FeSO_4,7H_2O$.

## STORAGE

In an airtight container.

_____ *Ph Eur*

# Fexofenadine Hydrochloride

*(Ph Eur monograph 2280)*

$C_{32}H_{39}NO_4,HCl$      538.1      *153439-40-8*

## Action and use

Histamine $H_1$ receptor antagonist; antihistamine.

*Ph Eur* _____

## DEFINITION

2-[4-[(1*RS*)-1-hydroxy-4-[4-(hydroxydiphenylmethyl)piperidin-1-yl]butyl]phenyl]-2-methylpropanoic acid hydrochloride.

## Content

98.0 per cent to 102.0 per cent (anhydrous substance).

## CHARACTERS

### Appearance

White or almost white powder.

### Solubility

Slightly soluble in water, freely soluble in methanol, very slightly soluble in acetone.

It shows polymorphism (5.9).

## IDENTIFICATION

A. Infrared absorption spectrophotometry (2.2.24).

*Comparison*  *fexofenadine hydrochloride CRS*.

If the spectra obtained in the solid state show differences, dissolve the substance to be examined and the reference substance separately in *methanol R*, evaporate to dryness and record new spectra using the residues.

B. Dissolve 30 mg of the substance to be examined in a mixture of equal volumes of *methanol R* and *water R*; sonicate if necessary and dilute to 2 ml with the same mixture of solvents. The solution gives reaction (a) of chlorides (2.3.1).

## TESTS

### Impurity B

Liquid chromatography (2.2.29).

*Test solution*  Dissolve 50.0 mg of the substance to be examined in the mobile phase and dilute to 100.0 ml with the mobile phase.

*Reference solution (a)*  Dissolve the contents of a vial of *fexofenadine impurity B CRS* in the test solution and dilute to 2.0 ml with the test solution.

*Reference solution (b)*  Dilute 1.0 ml of the test solution to 100.0 ml with the mobile phase. Dilute 1.0 ml of this solution to 10.0 ml with the mobile phase.

*Column:*
— *size: l* = 0.25 m, Ø = 4.6 mm;
— *stationary phase: silica gel BC for chiral chromatography R1* (5 μm).

*Mobile phase*  Mix 20 volumes of *acetonitrile for chromatography R* and 80 volumes of a buffer solution prepared as follows: to 1.15 ml of *glacial acetic acid R* add *water for chromatography R*, adjust to pH 4.0 ± 0.1 with *dilute ammonia R1* and dilute to 1000 ml with *water for chromatography R*.

*Flow rate*　0.5 ml/min.

*Detection*　Spectrophotometer at 220 nm.

*Injection*　20 μl.

*Run time*　1.2 times the retention time of fexofenadine.

*Relative retention*　With reference to fexofenadine (retention time = about 20 min):impurity B = about 0.7.

*System suitability*　Reference solution (a):
— *resolution*: minimum 3.0 between the peaks due to fexofenadine and impurity B.

*Limits:*
— *correction factor*: for the calculation of content, multiply the peak area of impurity B by 1.3;
— *impurity B*: not more than the area of the principal peak in the chromatogram obtained with reference solution (b) (0.1 per cent).

**Related substances**

Liquid chromatography (*2.2.29*).

*Buffer solution*　Dissolve 6.64 g of *sodium dihydrogen phosphate monohydrate R* and 0.84 g of *sodium perchlorate R* in *water for chromatography R*, adjust to pH 2.0 ± 0.1 with *phosphoric acid R* and dilute to 1000 ml with *water for chromatography R*.

*Solvent mixture*　Mix equal volumes of *acetonitrile for chromatography R* and the buffer solution.

*Test solution (a)*　Dissolve 25.0 mg of the substance to be examined in 25.0 ml of the solvent mixture.

*Test solution (b)*　Dilute 3.0 ml of test solution (a) to 50.0 ml with the mobile phase.

*Reference solution (a)*　Dissolve 25.0 mg of *fexofenadine hydrochloride CRS* in the solvent mixture and dilute to 25.0 ml with the solvent mixture. Dilute 3.0 ml of this solution to 50.0 ml with the mobile phase.

*Reference solution (b)*　Dilute 1.0 ml of test solution (a) to 100.0 ml with the mobile phase. Dilute 1.0 ml of this solution to 10.0 ml with the mobile phase.

*Reference solution (c)*　Dissolve 1 mg each of *fexofenadine impurity A CRS* and *fexofenadine impurity C CRS* in 20 ml of reference solution (a) and dilute to 200.0 ml with the mobile phase.

*Column:*
— *size: l* = 0.25 m, Ø = 4.6 mm;
— *stationary phase: phenylsilyl silica gel for chromatography R* (5 μm).

*Mobile phase*　Mix 350 volumes of *acetonitrile for chromatography R* and 650 volumes of the buffer solution; add 3 volumes of *triethylamine R* and mix.

*Flow rate*　1.5 ml/min.

*Detection*　Spectrophotometer at 220 nm.

*Injection*　20 μl of test solution (a) and reference solutions (b) and (c).

*Relative retention*　With reference to fexofenadine (retention time = about 9 min): impurity A = about 1.7; impurity D = about 2.3; impurity C = about 3.2.

*Run time*　6 times the retention time of fexofenadine for test solution (a) and reference solution (c), twice the retention time of fexofenadine for reference solution (b).

*System suitability*　Reference solution (c):
— *resolution*: minimum 10 between the peaks due to fexofenadine and impurity A.

*Limits:*
— *correction factor*: for the calculation of content, multiply the peak area of impurity A by 1.4;
— *impurities A, C, D*: not more than the area of the principal peak in the chromatogram obtained with reference solution (b) (0.1 per cent);
— *unspecified impurities*: for each impurity, not more than the area of the principal peak in the chromatogram obtained with reference solution (b) (0.10 per cent);
— *total*: not more than 3 times the area of the principal peak in the chromatogram obtained with reference solution (b) (0.3 per cent);
— *disregard limit*: 0.5 times the area of the principal peak in the chromatogram obtained with reference solution (b) (0.05 per cent).

**Heavy metals** (*2.4.8*)
Maximum 10 ppm.

Dissolve 1.0 g in a mixture of 15 volumes of *water R* and 85 volumes of *methanol R* and dilute to 20 ml with the same mixture of solvents. 12 ml of the solution complies with test B. Prepare the reference solution using 5 ml of *lead standard solution (1 ppm Pb) R*.

**Water** (*2.5.32*)
Maximum 0.5 per cent.

Dissolve 1.000 g in *anhydrous methanol R* and dilute to 5.0 ml with the same solvent. Use 1.0 ml of this solution.

**Sulphated ash** (*2.4.14*)
Maximum 0.1 per cent, determined on 1.0 g.

**ASSAY**

Liquid chromatography (*2.2.29*) as described in the test for related substances with the following modifications.

*Injection*　Test solution (b) and reference solution (a).

*Run time*　Twice the retention time of fexofenadine.

Calculate the percentage content of fexofenadine hydrochloride from the declared content of *fexofenadine hydrochloride CRS*.

**IMPURITIES**

*Specified impurities*　A, B, C, D.

*Other detectable impurities*　(The following substances would, if present at a sufficient level, be detected by one or other of the tests in the monograph. They are limited by the general acceptance criterion for other/unspecified impurities and/or by the general monograph *Substances for pharmaceutical use (2034)*. It is therefore not necessary to identify these impurities for demonstration of compliance. See also *5.10*. *Control of impurities in substances for pharmaceutical use*): E, F, G.

A. 2-[4-[4-[4-(hydroxydiphenylmethyl)piperidin-1-yl]butanoyl]phenyl]-2-methylpropanoic acid,

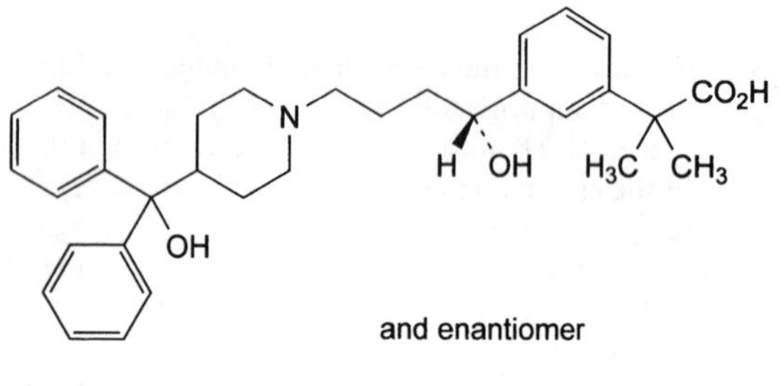

B. 2-[3-[(1RS)-1-hydroxy-4-[4-(hydroxydiphenylmethyl)piperidin-1-yl]butyl]phenyl]-2-methylpropanoic acid,

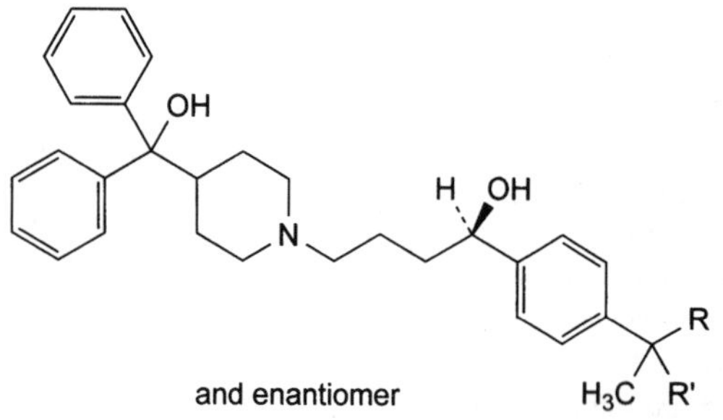

C. R = H, R′ = CH₃:
(1RS)-4-[4-(hydroxydiphenylmethyl)piperidin-1-yl]-1-[4-(1-methylethyl)phenyl]butan-1-ol,

D. R = CO-OCH₃, R′ = CH₃: methyl 2-[4-[(1RS)-1-hydroxy-4-[4-(hydroxydiphenylmethyl)piperidin-1-yl]butyl]phenyl]-2-methylpropanoate,

F. R = CO₂H, R′ = H: 2-[4-[1-hydroxy-4-[4-(hydroxydiphenylmethyl)piperidin-1-yl]butyl]phenyl]propanoic acid,

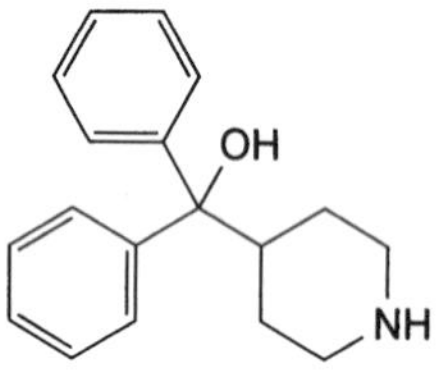

E. diphenyl(piperidin-4-yl)methanol,

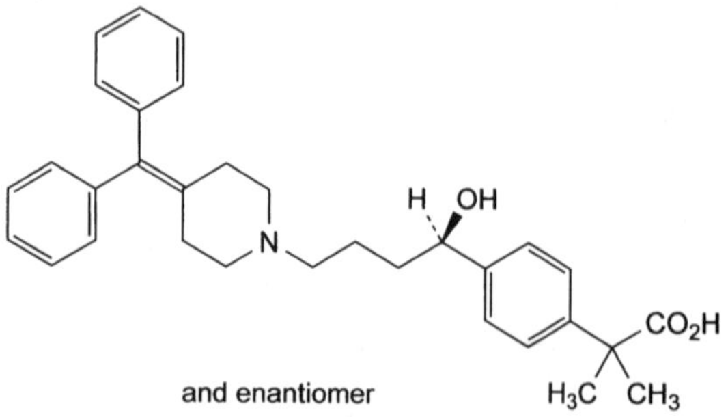

G. 2-[4-[(1RS)-4-[4-(diphenylmethylidene)piperidin-1-yl]-1-hydroxybutyl]phenyl]-2-methylpropanoic acid.

*Ph Eur*

# Filgrastim Concentrated Solution

*(Ph Eur monograph 2206)*

| | | | |
|---|---|---|---|
| MTPLGPASSL | PQSFLLKCLE | QVRKIQGDGA | ALQEKLCATY |
| KLCHPEELVL | LGHSLGIPWA | PLSSCPSQAL | QLAGCLSQLH |
| SGLFLYQGLL | QALEGISPEL | GPTLDTLQLD | VADFATTIWQ |
| QMEELGMAPA | LQPTQGAMPA | FASAFQRRAG | GVLVASHLQS |
| FLEVSYRVLR | HLAQP | | |

$C_{845}H_{1339}N_{223}O_{243}S_9$     18 799

*Ph Eur*

## DEFINITION

Solution of a protein having the primary structure of the granulocyte colony-stimulating factor plus 1 additional amino acid, an *N*-terminal methionine (r-met HU G-CSF). In contrast to its natural counterpart, the protein is not glycosylated. Human G-CSF is produced and secreted by endothelium, monocytes and other immune cells. The protein stimulates the differentiation and proliferation of leucocyte stem cells into mature granulocytes.

### Content
Minimum 0.9 mg of protein per millilitre.

### Potency
Minimum $1.0 \times 10^8$ IU per milligram of protein.

## PRODUCTION

Filgrastim concentrated solution is produced by a method based on recombinant DNA (rDNA) technology, using bacteria as host cells.

Prior to release, the following tests are carried out on each batch of the final bulk product, unless exemption has been granted by the competent authority.

### Host-cell-derived proteins
The limit is approved by the competent authority.

### Host-cell- or vector-derived DNA
The limit is approved by the competent authority.

## CHARACTERS
### Appearance
Clear, colourless or slightly yellowish liquid.

## IDENTIFICATION

A. It complies with the requirements described under Assay.

B. Examine the electropherograms obtained in the test for impurities with charges differing from that of filgrastim.

*Results* The principal band in the electropherogram obtained with the test solution is similar in position to the principal band in the electropherogram obtained with reference solution (a).

C. Examine the chromatograms obtained in the test for impurities with molecular masses higher than that of filgrastim.

*Results* The principal peak in the chromatogram obtained with the test solution is similar in retention time to the principal peak in the chromatogram obtained with the reference solution.

D. Examine the electropherograms obtained under both reducing and non-reducing conditions in the test for impurities with molecular masses differing from that of filgrastim.

*Results* The principal band in the electropherogram obtained with test solution (a) is similar in position to the principal band obtained with the reference solution.

E. Peptide mapping (*2.2.55*).

### SELECTIVE CLEAVAGE OF THE PEPTIDE BONDS

*Test solution* Introduce 50 µl of a 0.05 M sodium phosphate buffer solution pH 8.0 into a polypropylene tube and add a volume of the substance to be examined corresponding to 25 µg of protein. Add 25 µl of a 0.1 mg/ml solution of *glutamyl endopeptidase for peptide mapping R*, dilute to 1 ml with *water R*, stopper the tube and incubate at about 37 °C for 18 h. Add 125 µl of a 764 g/l (8 M) solution of *guanidine hydrochloride R* and mix well; add 10 µl of a 154.2 g/l (1 M) solution of *dithiothreitol R* and mix well. Place the capped tube in boiling water for 1 min, then allow to cool to room temperature.

*Reference solution* Prepare at the same time and in the same manner as for the test solution but using *filgrastim CRS* instead of the preparation to be examined.

### CHROMATOGRAPHIC SEPARATION

Liquid chromatography (*2.2.29*).

*Column:*
— *size: l* = 0.10 m, Ø = 2.0 mm;
— *stationary phase: octadecylsilyl silica gel for chromatography R* (5 µm) with a pore size of 20 nm;
— *temperature*: 60 °C.

*Mobile phase:*
— *mobile phase A*: dilute 0.5 ml of *trifluoroacetic acid R* in 950 ml of *water R*, add 50 ml of *acetonitrile for chromatography R* and mix;
— *mobile phase B*: dilute 0.5 ml of *trifluoroacetic acid R* in 50 ml of *water R*, add 950 ml of *acetonitrile for chromatography R* and mix;

| Time (min) | Mobile phase A (per cent *V/V*) | Mobile phase B (per cent *V/V*) |
|---|---|---|
| 0 - 8 | 97 → 94 | 3 → 6 |
| 8 - 25 | 94 → 66 | 6 → 34 |
| 25 - 40 | 66 → 10 | 34 → 90 |
| 40 - 45 | 10 | 90 |
| 45 - 46 | 10 → 97 | 90 → 3 |
| 46 - 65 | 97 | 3 |

*Flow rate* 0.2 ml/min.

*Detection* Spectrophotometer at 215 nm.

*Equilibration* At initial conditions for at least 30 min.

*Injection* 10 µl.

*System suitability* The chromatogram obtained with the reference solution is similar to the chromatogram of filgrastim digest supplied with *filgrastim CRS*.

*Results* The profile of the chromatogram obtained with the test solution corresponds to that of the chromatogram obtained with the reference solution.

## TESTS

### Impurities with molecular masses higher than that of filgrastim

Size-exclusion chromatography (*2.2.30*): use the normalisation procedure.

*Solution A* Dissolve 4.1 g of *sodium acetate R* in 400 ml of *water R*, adjust to pH 4.0 with *acetic acid R* and dilute to 500 ml with water R.

*Test solution* Dilute the preparation to be examined with solution A to obtain a concentration of 0.4 mg/ml.

*Reference solution* Dilute *filgrastim CRS* with solution A to obtain a concentration of 0.4 mg/ml.

*Resolution solution* Mix a sample of the reference solution for about 30 s using a vortex mixer.

*Column:*
— *size: l* = 0.3 m, Ø = 7.8 mm;
— *stationary phase: hydrophilic silica gel for chromatography R* (5 µm), of a grade suitable for fractionation of globular proteins in the relative molecular mass range of 10 000 to 500 000;
— *temperature*: 30 °C.

*Mobile phase* Dissolve 7.9 g of *ammonium hydrogen carbonate R* in 1000 ml of *water R* and adjust to pH 7.0 with *phosphoric acid R*; dilute to 2000 ml with *water R*.

*Flow rate* 0.5 ml/min.

*Detection* Spectrophotometer at 215 nm.

*Injection* 20 µl.

*Relative retention* With reference to the filgrastim monomer (retention time = about 19 min): aggregates = about 0.60; filgrastim oligomer 1 = about 0.75; filgrastim oligomer 2 = about 0.80; filgrastim dimmer = about 0.85.

*System suitability* Resolution solution:
— *retention time*: filgrastim monomer = 17 min to 20 min;
— *resolution*: minimum 3 between the peaks due to the filgrastim dimer and the filgrastim monomer.

Calculate the percentage content of the dimer, oligomers and aggregates.

*Limit:*
— *total of the peaks with retention times less than that of the principal peak*: maximum 2 per cent.

### Impurities with molecular masses differing from that of filgrastim

Polyacrylamide gel electrophoresis (*2.2.31*) under both reducing and non-reducing conditions.

*Gel dimensions* 1 mm thick.

*Resolving gel* 13 per cent acrylamide.

*Sample buffer (non-reducing conditions)* Mix equal volumes of *water R* and *concentrated SDS-PAGE sample buffer R*.

*Sample buffer (reducing conditions)* Mix equal volumes of *water R* and *concentrated SDS-PAGE sample buffer for reducing conditions R* containing 2-mercaptoethanol as the reducing agent.

*Test solution (a)* Dilute the preparation to be examined with sample buffer to obtain a protein concentration of 100 µg/ml.

*Test solution (b)* To 0.20 ml of test solution (a) add 0.20 ml of sample buffer.

*Test solution (c)* Dilute 0.20 ml of test solution (b) to 1 ml with sample buffer.

*Test solution (d)* Dilute 0.20 ml of test solution (c) to 1 ml with sample buffer.

*Test solution (e)* To 0.20 ml of test solution (d) add 0.20 ml of sample buffer.

*Reference solution* Solution of molecular mass markers suitable for calibrating SDS-polyacrylamide gels in the range of 14.4-94 kDa.

*Sample treatment* Boil for 5 min.

*Application* 20 µl.

*Detection* By silver staining.

*System suitability:*
— *reference solution*: the validation criteria are met;
— a band is seen in the electropherogram obtained with test solution (e);
— a gradation of intensity of staining is seen in the electropherograms obtained with test solutions (a) to (e).

*Limit* Test solution (a):
— *impurities with molecular masses lower or higher than that of filgrastim*: no band is more intense than the principal band in the electropherogram obtained with test solution (d) (2.0 per cent).

### Impurities with charges differing from that of filgrastim

Isoelectric focusing (*2.2.54*).

*Test solution* Dilute the preparation to be examined with *water R* to obtain a concentration of 0.3 mg/ml.

*Reference solution (a)* Dilute *filgrastim CRS* with *water R* to obtain a concentration of 0.3 mg/ml.

*Reference solution (b)* Dilute *filgrastim CRS* with *water R* to obtain a concentration of 0.03 mg/ml.

*Reference solution (c)* Use an isoelectric point (pI) calibration solution, in the pI range of 2.5-6.5, prepared according to the manufacturer's instructions.

*Focusing:*
— *pH gradient*: 4.5-8.0;
— *catholyte*: 1 M solution of *sodium hydroxide R*;
— *anolyte*: 0.04 M solution of *glutamic acid R* in a 0.0025 per cent *V/V* solution of *phosphoric acid R*;
— *application*: 20 µl.

*Detection* As described in *2.2.54*.

*System suitability:*
— in the electropherogram obtained with reference solution (c), the relevant isoelectric point markers are distributed along the entire length of the gel;
— in the electropherogram obtained with reference solution (a), the pI of the principal band is 5.7 to 6.3.

*Limit:*
— *any impurity*: no band is more intense than the principal band in the electropherogram obtained with reference solution (b) (10 per cent).

### Related proteins

Liquid chromatography (*2.2.29*): use the normalisation procedure.

*Solution A* A 100 mM sodium acetate buffer solution pH 4.0, containing 0.1 mg/ml of *polysorbate 80 R* and 50 mg/ml of *sorbitol CRS*.

*Test solution* Dilute the preparation to be examined with solution A to obtain a concentration of 0.3 mg/ml.

*Reference solution (a)* Dilute *filgrastim CRS* with solution A to obtain a concentration of 0.3 mg/ml.

*Reference solution (b)* To 570 µl of reference solution (a) add 6.8 µl of a 0.45 per cent *V/V* solution of hydrogen peroxide and mix; incubate at 25 °C for 1 h, then add 2.5 mg of *methionine CRS*.

*Column:*
— *size*: $l$ = 0.15 m, Ø = 4.6 mm;
— *stationary phase*: octadecylsilyl silica gel for chromatography R (3 µm) with a pore size of 20 nm;
— *temperature*: 65 °C.

*Mobile phase:*
— *mobile phase A*: mix 499 ml of *acetonitrile for chromatography R* and 500 ml of *water R* and add 1 ml of *trifluoroacetic acid R*;

— *mobile phase B*: mix 49 ml of *water R* and 950 ml of *acetonitrile for chromatography R* and add 1 ml of *trifluoroacetic acid R*;

| Time (min) | Mobile phase A (per cent V/V) | Mobile phase B (per cent V/V) |
|---|---|---|
| 0 - 4 | 92 | 8 |
| 4 - 19 | 92 → 72 | 8 → 28 |
| 19 - 19.1 | 72 → 0 | 28 → 100 |
| 19.1 - 21 | 0 | 100 |
| 21 - 21.1 | 0 → 92 | 100 → 8 |
| 21.1 - 25 | 92 | 8 |

*Flow rate* 0 ml/min.

*Detection* Spectrophotometer at 215 nm.

*Injection* 50 µl of the test solution and reference solution (b).

*Relative retention* With reference to filgrastim (retention time = about 12 min):
oxidised filgrastim 1 = about 0.90;
oxidised filgrastim 2 = about 0.95.

*System suitability* Reference solution (b):
— the chromatogram shows 2 peaks corresponding to oxidised filgrastim 1 and oxidised filgrastim 2 that elute before the principal peak, the 2nd peak not being completely separated from the principal peak.

*Limits:*
— *any impurity*: for each impurity, maximum 2.0 per cent;
— *total*: maximum 3.5 per cent.

### Bacterial endotoxins (*2.6.14*)

Less than 2 IU in the volume that contains 1.0 mg of protein.

### ASSAY

#### Protein

Liquid chromatography (*2.2.29*) as described in the test for related proteins with the following modification.

*Injection* Test solution and reference solution (a).

Calculate the content of filgrastim ($C_{845}H_{1339}N_{223}O_{243}S_9$) from the declared content of $C_{845}H_{1339}N_{223}O_{243}S_9$ in *filgrastim CRS*.

#### Potency

The potency of the preparation to be examined is determined by comparison of the dilutions of the test preparation with the dilutions of the International Standard of filgrastim or with a reference preparation calibrated in International Units.

The International Unit is the activity contained in a stated amount of the appropriate International Standard. The equivalence in International Units of the International Standard is stated by the World Health Organisation.

Carry out the assay using a suitable method such as the following, which uses the conversion of a tetrazolium salt (MTS) as a staining method. Alternative methods of quantifying cell proliferation, such as measurement of intracellular ATP by luciferase bioluminescence, have also been found suitable, and may be used as the assay readout, subject to appropriate validation. The assay conditions (for example, cell concentration, incubation time and dilution steps) are then adapted accordingly.

Use an established cell line responsive to filgrastim. NFS-60 cells (ATCC No. CRL-1838) have been found suitable. Incubate with varying dilutions of test and reference preparations of filgrastim. Then incubate with a solution of *tetrazolium salt R*. This cytochemical stain is converted by cellular dehydrogenases to a coloured formazan product. The formazan is then measured spectrophotometrically.

Add 50 μl of dilution medium to all wells of a 96-well microtitre plate. Add an additional 50 μl of this solution to the wells designed for the blanks. Add 50 μl of each solution to be tested in triplicate (test preparation and reference preparation at a concentration of about 800 IU/ml, plus a series of 10 twofold dilutions to obtain a standard curve). Prepare a suspension of NFS-60 cells containing $7 \times 10^5$ cells per millilitre. Immediately before use, add 2-mercaptoethanol to a final concentration of 0.1 mM, and add 50 μl of the prepared cell suspension to each well, maintaining the cells in a uniform suspension during addition.

Incubate the plate at 36.0-38.0 °C for 44-48 h in a humidified incubator using $6 \pm 1$ per cent $CO_2$. Add 20 μl of a 5.0 g/l sterile solution of *tetrazolium salt R* to each well and reincubate for 4 h. Estimate the quantity of formazan produced using a microtitre well plate reader at 490 nm.

Calculate the potency of the preparation to be examined using a suitable statistical method, for example the parallel line assay (*5.3*).

The estimated potency is not less than 80 per cent and not more than 125 per cent of the stated potency. The confidence limits ($P = 0.95$) are not less than 74 per cent and not more than 136 per cent of the estimated potency.

### LABELLING

The label states:
— the content, in milligrams of protein per millilitre;
— the potency, in International Units per milligram of protein.

*Ph Eur*

# Finasteride

*(Ph Eur monograph 1615)*

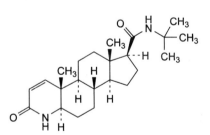

C₂₃H₃₆N₂O₂      372.6      98319-26-7

### Action and use

5-Alpha reductase inhibitor; treatment of benign prostatic hyperplasia.

### Preparation

Finasteride Tablets

*Ph Eur*

## DEFINITION

*N*-(1,1-Dimethylethyl)-3-oxo-4-aza-5α-androst-1-ene-17β-carboxamide.

### Content

98.0 per cent to 102.0 per cent (dried substance).

## CHARACTERS

### Appearance

White or almost white, crystalline powder.

### Solubility

Practically insoluble in water, freely soluble in ethanol and in methylene chloride.

It shows polymorphism (*5.9*).

## IDENTIFICATION

Infrared absorption spectrophotometry (*2.2.24*).

*Comparison   finasteride CRS.*

If the spectra obtained in the solid state show differences, dissolve the substance to be examined and the reference substance separately in *methanol R*, evaporate to dryness and record new spectra using the residues.

## TESTS

### Specific optical rotation (*2.2.7*)

+ 12.0 to + 14.0 (dried substance).

Dissolve 0.250 g in *methanol R* and dilute to 25.0 ml with the same solvent.

### Related substances

Liquid chromatography (*2.2.29*).

*Test solution (a)*   Dissolve 25.0 mg of the substance to be examined in a mixture of equal volumes of *acetonitrile R* and *water R* and dilute to 50.0 ml with the same mixture of solvents.

*Test solution (b)*   Dissolve 0.100 g of the substance to be examined in a mixture of equal volumes of *acetonitrile R* and *water R* and dilute to 10.0 ml with the same mixture of solvents.

*Reference solution (a)*   Dissolve 25.0 mg of *finasteride CRS* in a mixture of equal volumes of *acetonitrile R* and *water R* and dilute to 50.0 ml with the same mixture of solvents.

*Reference solution (b)*   Dissolve 50.0 mg of *finasteride for system suitability CRS* in a mixture of equal volumes of *acetonitrile R* and *water R* and dilute to 5.0 ml with the same mixture of solvents.

*Reference solution (c)*   Dilute 2.0 ml of test solution (b) to 100.0 ml in a mixture of equal volumes of *acetonitrile R* and *water R*. Dilute 1.0 ml of this solution to 10.0 ml with a mixture of equal volumes of *acetonitrile R* and *water R*.

*Column:*
— *size: l* = 0.25 m, Ø = 4.0 mm,
— *stationary phase: end-capped octadecylsilyl silica gel for chromatography R* (5 μm) with a ratio of specific surface area ($m^2g^{-1}$)/carbon-percentage less than 20,
— *temperature*: 60 °C.

*Mobile phase*   acetonitrile R, tetrahydrofuran R, water R (10:10:80 *V/V/V*).

*Flow rate*   1.5 ml/min.

*Detection*   Spectrophotometer at 210 nm.

*Injection*   15 μl; inject test solution (b) and reference solutions (b) and (c).

*Run time*   Twice the retention time of finasteride.

*Relative retention*   With reference to finasteride (retention time = about 28 min): impurity A = about 0.94; impurity B = about 1.22; impurity C = about 1.36.

*System suitability*   Reference solution (b):
— *peak-to-valley ratio*: minimum 2.5, where $H_p$ = height above the baseline of the peak due to impurity A, and $H_v$ = height above the baseline of the lowest point of the

curve separating this peak from the peak due to finasteride.

*Limits:*

— *impurity A*: maximum 0.3 per cent, calculated from the area of the corresponding peak in the chromatogram obtained with reference solution (b) and taking into account the assigned value of impurity A in *finasteride for system suitability CRS*;

— *impurity B*: not more than 1.5 times the area of the principal peak in the chromatogram obtained with reference solution (c) (0.3 per cent);

— *impurity C*: not more than 1.5 times the area of the principal peak in the chromatogram obtained with reference solution (c) (0.3 per cent);

— *any other impurity*: not more than half the area of the principal peak in the chromatogram obtained with reference solution (c) (0.1 per cent);

— *total*: not more than 3 times the area of the principal peak in the chromatogram obtained with reference solution (c) (0.6 per cent);

— *disregard limit*: 0.25 times the area of the principal peak in the chromatogram obtained with reference solution (c) (0.05 per cent).

**Loss on drying** (*2.2.32*)

Maximum 0.5 per cent, determined on 1.000 g by drying in an oven at 105 °C.

**ASSAY**

Liquid chromatography (*2.2.29*) as described in the test for related substances.

*Injection*   Test solution (a) and reference solution (a).

Calculate the percentage content of $C_{23}H_{36}N_2O_2$.

**STORAGE**

Protected from light.

**IMPURITIES**

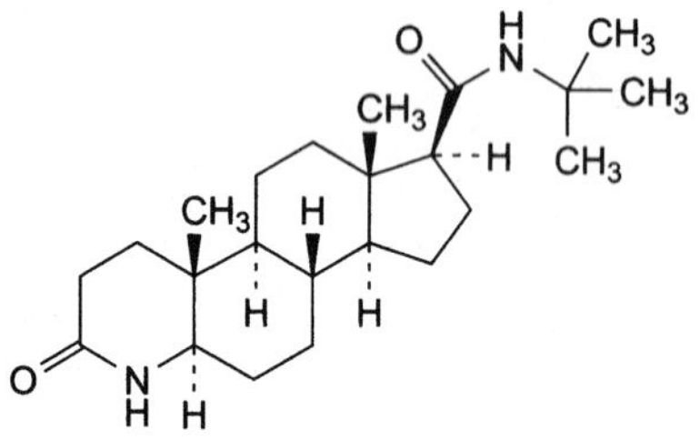

A. *N*-(1,1-dimethylethyl)-3-oxo-4-aza-5α-androstane-17β-carboxamide (dihydrofinasteride),

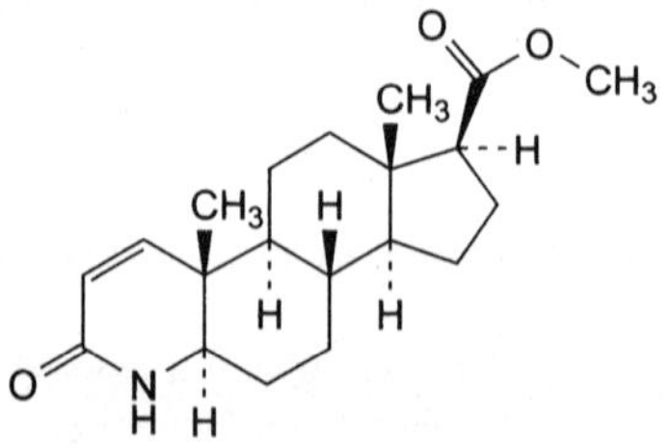

B. methyl 3-oxo-4-aza-5α-androst-1-ene-17β-carboxylate (Δ-1-aza ester),

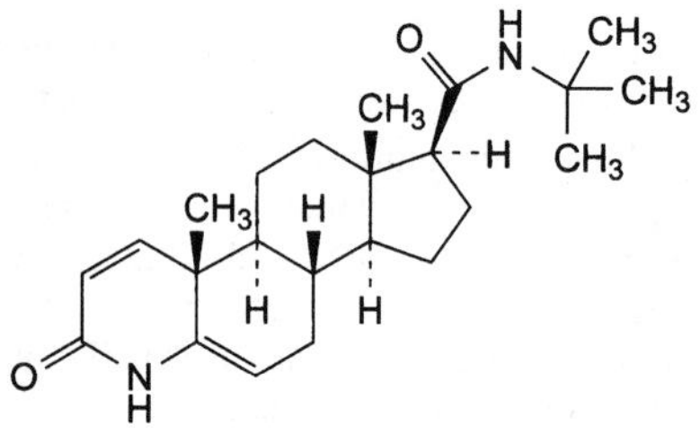

C. *N*-(1,1-dimethylethyl)-3-oxo-4-azaandrosta-1,5-diene-17β-carboxamide (Δ-1,5-aza amide).

_____ *Ph Eur*

# Fish Oil, Rich in Omega-3-Acids

(*Ph Eur monograph 1912*)

*Ph Eur* _____

**DEFINITION**

Purified, winterised and deodorised fatty oil obtained from fish of the families *Engraulidae*, *Carangidae*, *Clupeidae*, *Osmeridae*, *Scombridae* and *Ammodytidae*. The omega-3 acids are defined as the following acids: *alpha*-linolenic acid (C18:3 n-3), moroctic acid (C18:4 n-3), eicosatetraenoic acid (C20:4 n-3), timnodonic (eicosapentaenoic) acid (C20:5 n-3; EPA), heneicosapentaenoic acid (C21:5 n-3), clupanodonic acid (C22:5 n-3) and cervonic (docosahexaenoic) acid (C22:6 n-3; DHA).

**Content:**

— *EPA, expressed as triglycerides:* minimum 13.0 per cent,

— *DHA, expressed as triglycerides*: minimum 9.0 per cent,

— *total omega-3 acids, expressed as triglycerides*: minimum 28.0 per cent.

Authorised antioxidants in concentrations not exceeding the levels specified by the competent authorities may be added.

**CHARACTERS**

**Appearance**

Pale yellow liquid.

**Solubility**

Practically insoluble in water, very soluble in acetone and in heptane, slightly soluble in anhydrous ethanol.

**IDENTIFICATION**

Examine the chromatograms obtained in the assay for EPA and DHA.

*Results*   The peaks due to eicosapentaenoic acid methyl ester and to docosahexaenoic acid methyl ester in the chromatogram obtained with test solution (b) are similar in retention time to the corresponding peaks in the chromatogram obtained with reference solution (a).

**TESTS**

**Appearance**

The substance to be examined is not more intensely coloured than a reference solution prepared as follows: to 3.0 ml of red primary solution add 25.0 ml of yellow primary solution and dilute to 50.0 ml with a 10 g/l solution of *hydrochloric acid R* (*2.2.2*, *Method II*).

**Absorbance** (*2.2.25*)

Maximum 0.70 at 233 nm.

Dilute 0.300 g of the substance to be examined to 50.0 ml with *trimethylpentane R*. Dilute 2.0 ml of this solution to 50.0 ml with *trimethylpentane R*.

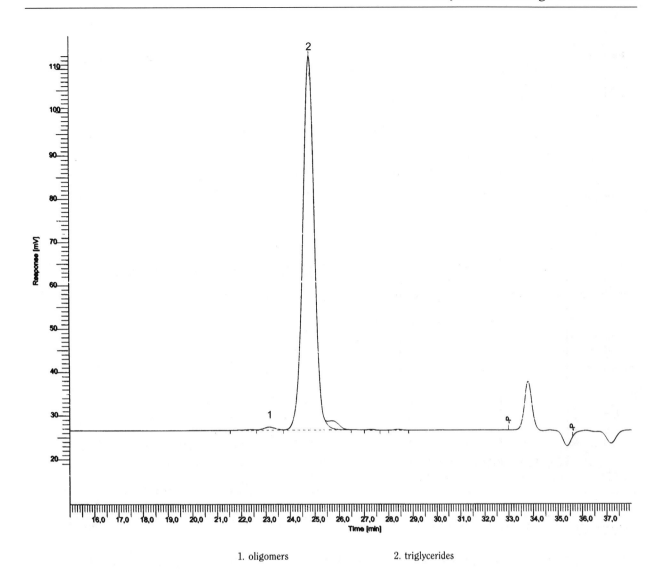

1. oligomers          2. triglycerides

Figure 1912.-1. – *Chromatogram of the test for oligomers in fish oil rich in omega-3 acids*

**Acid value** (*2.5.1*)

Maximum 0.5, determined on 20.0 g in 50 ml of the prescribed mixture of solvents.

**Anisidine value**

Maximum 30.0.

The anisidine value is defined as 100 times the absorbance measured in a 1 cm cell filled with a solution containing 1 g of the substance to be examined in 100 ml of a mixture of solvents and reagents according to the method described below.

*Carry out the operations as rapidly as possible, avoiding exposure to actinic light.*

*Test solution (a)*   Dilute 0.500 g of the substance to be examined to 25.0 ml with *trimethylpentane R*.

*Test solution (b)*   To 5.0 ml of test solution (a) add 1.0 ml of a 2.5 g/l solution of *p-anisidine R* in *glacial acetic acid R*, shake and store protected from light.

*Reference solution*   To 5.0 ml of *trimethylpentane R* add 1.0 ml of a 2.5 g/l solution of *p-anisidine R* in *glacial acetic acid R*, shake and store protected from light.

Measure the absorbance (*2.2.25*) of test solution (a) at 350 nm using *trimethylpentane R* as the compensation liquid. Measure the absorbance of test solution (b) at 350 nm

exactly 10 min after its preparation, using the reference solution as the compensation liquid.

Calculate the anisidine value from the expression:

$$\frac{25 \times (1.2\,A_s - A_b)}{m}$$

$A_s$ = absorbance of test solution (b),
$A_b$ = absorbance of test solution (a),
$m$   = mass of the substance to be examined in test solution (a), in grams.

**Peroxide value** (*2.5.5, Method A*)

Maximum 10.0.

**Unsaponifiable matter** (*2.5.7*)

Maximum 1.5 per cent, determined on 5.0 g.

**Stearin**

10 ml remains clear after cooling at 0 °C for 3 h.

**Oligomers**

Size-exclusion chromatography (*2.2.30*).

*Test solution*   Dilute 10.0 mg of the substance to be examined to 10.0 ml with *tetrahydrofuran R*.

*Reference solution*   In a 100 ml volumetric flask dissolve 50 mg of *monodocosahexaenoin R*, 30 mg of

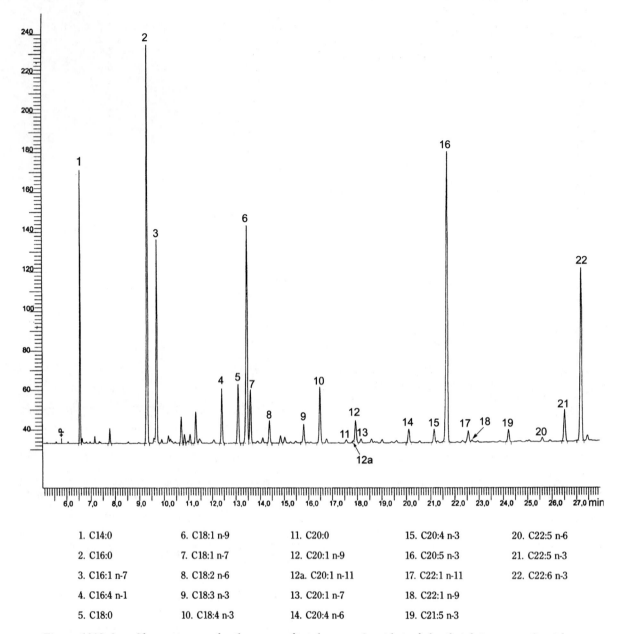

| 1. C14:0 | 6. C18:1 n-9 | 11. C20:0 | 15. C20:4 n-3 | 20. C22:5 n-6 |
| 2. C16:0 | 7. C18:1 n-7 | 12. C20:1 n-9 | 16. C20:5 n-3 | 21. C22:5 n-3 |
| 3. C16:1 n-7 | 8. C18:2 n-6 | 12a. C20:1 n-11 | 17. C22:1 n-11 | 22. C22:6 n-3 |
| 4. C16:4 n-1 | 9. C18:3 n-3 | 13. C20:1 n-7 | 18. C22:1 n-9 | |
| 5. C18:0 | 10. C18:4 n-3 | 14. C20:4 n-6 | 19. C21:5 n-3 | |

Figure 1912.-2. – *Chromatogram for the assay of total omega-3 acids in fish oil rich in omega-3 acids*

didocosahexaenoin R and 20 mg of *tridocosahexaenoin* R in *tetrahydrofuran* R and dilute to 100.0 ml with the same solvent.

*Column 1:*
— *size: l* = 0.3 m, Ø = 7.8 mm,
— *stationary phase: styrene-divinylbenzene copolymer* R (7 μm) with a pore size of 10 nm.

*Columns 2 and 3,* placed closest to the injector:
— *size: l* = 0.3 m, Ø = 7.8 mm,
— *stationary phase: styrene-divinylbenzene copolymer* R (7 μm) with a pore size of 50 nm.

*Mobile phase    tetrahydrofuran* R.

*Flow rate    0.8 ml/min.*

*Detection    Differential refractometer.*

*Injection    40 μl.*

*System suitability    Reference solution:*

— *elution order:* tridocosahexaenoin, didocosahexaenoin, monodocosahexaenoin.
— *resolution:* minimum of 2.0 between the peaks due to monodocosahexaenoin and to didocosahexaenoin and minimum of 1.0 between the peaks due to didocosahexaenoin and to tridocosahexaenoin.

Identify the peaks from the chromatogram (Figure 1912.-1). Calculate the percentage content of oligomers using the following expression:

$$\frac{B}{A} \times 100$$

$A$ = sum of the areas of all the peaks in the chromatogram,
$B$ = area of the peak with a retention time less than the retention time of the triglyceride peak.

*Limit:*
— *oligomers:* maximum 1.5 per cent.

## ASSAY

**EPA and DHA** (2.4.29)
See Figure 1912.-2.

**Total omega-3 acids** (2.4.29)
See Figure 1912.-2.

## STORAGE

In an airtight, well-filled container, protected from light, under inert gas.

## LABELLING

The label states the concentration of EPA, DHA and total omega-3 acids, expressed as triglycerides.

*Ph Eur*

# Flavoxate Hydrochloride

(*Ph Eur monograph 1692*)

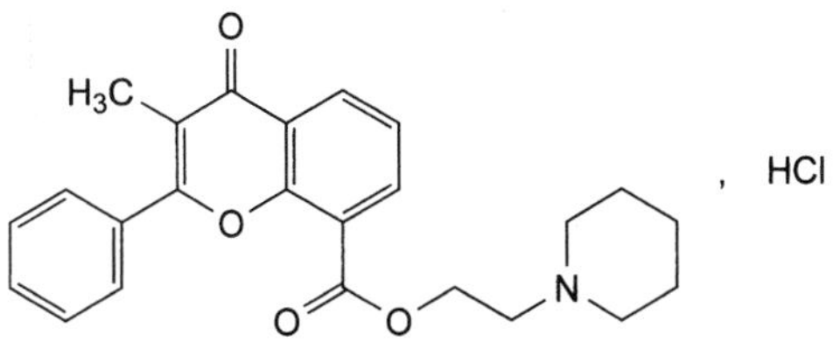

$C_{24}H_{25}NO_4,HCl$      427.9      *3717-88-2*

## Action and use

Anticholinergic.

*Ph Eur*

## DEFINITION

2-(Piperidin-1-yl)ethyl 3-methyl-4-oxo-2-phenyl-4*H*-1-benzopyran-8-carboxylate hydrochloride.

## Content

99.0 per cent to 101.0 per cent (dried substance).

## CHARACTERS

**Appearance**
White or almost white, crystalline powder.

**Solubility**
Slightly soluble in water, sparingly soluble in methylene chloride, slightly soluble in ethanol (96 per cent).

## IDENTIFICATION

A. Infrared absorption spectrophotometry (2.2.24).

*Comparison* flavoxate hydrochloride CRS.

B. It gives reaction (a) of chlorides (2.3.1).

## TESTS

**Related substances**
Liquid chromatography (2.2.29). *Use freshly prepared solutions.*

*Solvent mixture* Mix 20 volumes of a 0.4 g/l solution of *potassium dihydrogen phosphate R* adjusted to pH 3.0 with *phosphoric acid R* and 80 volumes of *acetonitrile R*.

*Test solution* Dissolve 10.0 mg of the substance to be examined in the solvent mixture and dilute to 10.0 ml with the solvent mixture.

*Reference solution (a)* Dilute 1.0 ml of the test solution to 100.0 ml with the solvent mixture.

*Reference solution (b)* Dilute 1.0 ml of reference solution (a) to 10.0 ml with the solvent mixture.

*Reference solution (c)* Dissolve 6.0 mg of *flavoxate impurity A CRS* and 3.0 mg of *flavoxate impurity B CRS* in the solvent mixture, add 2.0 ml of the test solution and dilute to 100.0 ml with the solvent mixture. Dilute 1.0 ml of this solution to 20.0 ml with the solvent mixture.

*Column:*
— *size: l* = 0.25 m, Ø = 4.6 mm;
— *stationary phase: spherical end-capped octadecylsilyl silica gel for chromatography R* (5 μm).

*Mobile phase:*
— *mobile phase A*: 0.435 g/l solution of *dipotassium hydrogen phosphate R* adjusted to pH 7.5 with *phosphoric acid R*;
— *mobile phase B*: *acetonitrile R*;

| Time (min) | Mobile phase A (per cent *V/V*) | Mobile phase B (per cent *V/V*) |
|---|---|---|
| 0 - 10 | 20 | 80 |
| 10 - 20 | 20 → 10 | 80 → 90 |
| 20 - 25 | 10 | 90 |

*Flow rate* 0.8 ml/min.

*Detection* Spectrophotometer at 254 nm.

*Injection* 10 μl.

*Relative retention* With reference to flavoxate (retention time = about 10 min): impurity A = about 0.2; impurity B = about 0.8.

*System suitability* Reference solution (c):
— *resolution*: minimum 4.0 between the peaks due to impurity B and flavoxate.

*Limits:*
— *impurity A*: not more than the area of the corresponding peak in the chromatogram obtained with reference solution (c) (0.3 per cent);
— *impurity B*: not more than the area of the corresponding peak in the chromatogram obtained with reference solution (c) (0.15 per cent);
— *unspecified impurities*: for each impurity, not more than the area of the principal peak in the chromatogram obtained with reference solution (b) (0.10 per cent);
— *total of unspecified impurities*: not more than 0.5 times the area of the principal peak in the chromatogram obtained with reference solution (a) (0.5 per cent);
— *disregard limit*: 0.5 times the area of the principal peak in the chromatogram obtained with reference solution (b) (0.05 per cent).

**Heavy metals** (2.4.8)
Maximum 10 ppm.

2.0 g complies with test F. Prepare the reference solution using 2 ml of *lead standard solution (10 ppm Pb) R*.

**Loss on drying** (2.2.32)
Maximum 0.5 per cent, determined on 1.000 g by drying in an oven at 105 °C.

**Sulphated ash** (2.4.14)
Maximum 0.1 per cent, determined on 1.0 g.

## ASSAY

*In order to avoid overheating in the reaction medium, mix thoroughly throughout and stop the titration immediately after the end-point has been reached.*

Dissolve 0.350 g in 10 ml of *anhydrous formic acid R* and add 40 ml of *acetic anhydride R*. Titrate with *0.1 M perchloric acid*, determining the end-point potentiometrically (2.2.20).

1 ml of *0.1 M perchloric acid* is equivalent to 42.79 mg of $C_{24}H_{26}ClNO_4$.

## STORAGE
Protected from light.

## IMPURITIES
*Specified impurities* A, B.

*Other detectable impurities* (The following substances would, if present at a sufficient level, be detected by one or other of the tests in the monograph. They are limited by the general acceptance criterion for other/unspecified impurities and/or by the general monograph *Substances for pharmaceutical use (2034)*. It is therefore not necessary to identify these impurities for demonstration of compliance. See also *5.10. Control of impurities in substances for pharmaceutical use*): C.

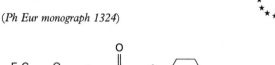

A. R = H: 3-methyl-4-oxo-2-phenyl-4*H*-1-benzopyran-8-carboxylic acid,

B. R = $C_2H_5$: ethyl 3-methyl-4-oxo-2-phenyl-4*H*-1-benzopyran-8-carboxylate,

C. R = $CH(CH_3)_2$: 1-methylethyl 3-methyl-4-oxo-2-phenyl-4*H*-1-benzopyran-8-carboxylate.

*Ph Eur*

# Flecainide Acetate

*(Ph Eur monograph 1324)*

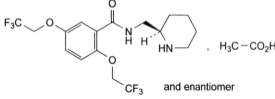

and enantiomer

$C_{17}H_{20}F_6N_2O_3,C_2H_4O_2$      474.4      *54143-56-5*

## Action and use
Class I antiarrhythmic.

## Preparations
Flecainide Injection

Flecainide Tablets

*Ph Eur*

## DEFINITION
*N*-[(*RS*)-(Piperidin-2-ylmethyl)]-2,5-bis(2,2,2-trifluoroethoxy)benzamide acetate.

## Content
98.0 per cent to 101.0 per cent (dried substance).

## CHARACTERS
### Appearance
White or almost white, very hygroscopic, crystalline powder.

### Solubility
Soluble in water and in anhydrous ethanol. It is freely soluble in dilute acetic acid and practically insoluble in dilute hydrochloric acid.

## IDENTIFICATION
*First identification* A, C.

*Second identification* A, B, D.

A. Melting point (*2.2.14*): 146 °C to 152 °C, with a melting range not greater than 3 °C.

B. Ultraviolet and visible absorption spectrophotometry (*2.2.25*).

*Test solution* Dissolve 50 mg in *ethanol (96 per cent) R* and dilute to 50.0 ml with the same solvent. Dilute 5.0 ml of this solution to 50.0 ml with *ethanol (96 per cent) R*.

*Spectral range* 230-350 nm.

*Absorption maximum* At 298 nm.

*Specific absorbance at the absorption maximum* 61 to 65.

C. Infrared absorption spectrophotometry (*2.2.24*).

*Comparison*

*flecainide acetate CRS* .

D. It gives reaction (b) of acetates (*2.3.1*).

## TESTS
### Appearance of solution.
The solution is clear (*2.2.1*) and colourless (*2.2.2*, *Method II*).

Dissolve 0.25 g in *water R*, add 0.05 ml of *glacial acetic acid R* and dilute to 10 ml with *water R*.

### pH (*2.2.3*)
6.7 to 7.1.

Dissolve 0.25 g in *carbon dioxide-free water R* and dilute to 10 ml with the same solvent.

### Impurity B
Thin-layer chromatography (*2.2.27*).

*Test solution* Dissolve 0.10 g of the substance to be examined in *methanol R* and dilute to 2 ml with the same solvent.

*Reference solution* Dissolve 10 mg of *flecainide impurity B CRS* in *methanol R* and dilute to 100 ml with the same solvent (solution A). Dissolve 0.10 g of *flecainide acetate CRS* in solution A and dilute to 2 ml with the same solution.

*Plate* TLC silica gel $F_{254}$ plate R.

*Mobile phase* Freshly prepared mixture of 5 volumes of concentrated *ammonia R* and 95 volumes of *acetone R*.

*Application* 5 µl.

*Development* Over a path of 10 cm.

*Drying* At 100-105 °C until the ammonia has evaporated.

*Detection* Examine in ultraviolet light at 254 nm to establish the position of the flecainide spot, then spray with a freshly prepared 2 g/l solution of *ninhydrin R* in *methanol R* and heat at 100-110 °C for 2-5 min; examine in daylight.

*System suitability* Reference solution:
— the chromatogram shows 2 clearly separated spots.

*Limit:*
— *impurity B*: any spot due to impurity B is not more intense than the corresponding spot in the chromatogram obtained with the reference solution (0.2 per cent).

### Related substances
Liquid chromatography (*2.2.29*).

*Test solution*   Dissolve 0.25 g of the substance to be examined in *methanol R* and dilute to 25.0 ml with the same solvent.

*Reference solution (a)*   Dilute 5.0 ml of the test solution to 100.0 ml with *methanol R*. Dilute 1.0 ml of this solution to 10.0 ml with *methanol R*.

*Reference solution (b)*   Dissolve 25 mg of *flecainide acetate CRS* and 25 mg of *flecainide impurity A CRS* in *methanol R* and dilute to 25.0 ml with the same solvent.

*Column:*
— *size: l* = 0.15 m, Ø = 4.6 mm;
— *stationary phase: octylsilyl silica gel for chromatography R* (5 μm).

*Mobile phase:*
— *mobile phase A*: mix 2 ml of *concentrated ammonia R*, 4 ml of *triethylamine R* and 985 ml of *water R*; add 6 ml of *phosphoric acid R* and adjust to pH 2.8 with concentrated ammonia *R*;
— *mobile phase B*: *acetonitrile R*;

| Time (min) | Mobile phase A (per cent *V/V*) | Mobile phase B (per cent *V/V*) |
|---|---|---|
| 0 - 12 | 90 → 30 | 10 → 70 |
| 12 - 17 | 30 | 70 |
| 17 - 19 | 30 → 90 | 70 → 10 |
| 19 - 21 | 90 | 10 |

If a suitable baseline cannot be obtained, use another grade of triethylamine.

*Flow rate*   2 ml/min.

*Detection*   Spectrophotometer at 300 nm.

*Injection*   20 μl.

*System suitability*   Reference solution (b):
— *resolution*: minimum 4 between the peaks due to flecainide and impurity A.

*Limits:*
— *impurities A, C, D, E*: for each impurity, not more than 0.4 times the area of the principal peak in the chromatogram obtained with reference solution (a) (0.2 per cent);
— *total*: not more than the area of the principal peak in the chromatogram obtained with reference solution (a) (0.5 per cent);
— *disregard limit*: 0.02 times the area of the principal peak in the chromatogram obtained with reference solution (a) (0.01 per cent).

**Heavy metals** (*2.4.8*)
Maximum 20 ppm.

1.0 g complies with test C. Prepare the reference solution using 2 ml of *lead standard solution (10 ppm Pb) R*.

**Loss on drying** (*2.2.32*)
Maximum 0.5 per cent, determined on 1.000 g by drying in an oven at 60 °C under a pressure not exceeding 0.6 kPa for 2 h.

**Sulphated ash** (*2.4.14*)
Maximum 0.1 per cent, determined on 1.0 g in a platinum crucible.

## ASSAY

Dissolve 0.400 g in 25 ml of *anhydrous acetic acid R*. Titrate with *0.1 M perchloric acid*, determining the end-point potentiometrically (*2.2.20*).

1 ml of *0.1 M perchloric acid* is equivalent to 47.44 mg of $C_{19}H_{24}F_6N_2O_5$.

## STORAGE
Protected from light.

## IMPURITIES
*Specified impurities   A, B, C, D, E.*

A. (8a*RS*)-3-[2,5-bis(2,2,2-trifluoroethoxy)phenyl]-1,5,6,7,8,8a-hexahydroimidazo[1,5-*a*]pyridine,

B. (*RS*)-(piperidin-2-yl)methanamine,

C. (*RS*)-4-hydroxy-*N*-(piperidin-2-ylmethyl)-2,5-bis(2,2,2-trifluoroethoxy)benzamide,

D. 2,5-bis(2,2,2-trifluoroethoxy)benzoic acid,

E. *N*-(pyridin-2-ylmethyl)-2,5-bis(2,2,2-trifluoroethoxy) benzamide.

*Ph Eur*

# Flubendazole

(*Ph Eur monograph 1721*)

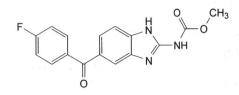

$C_{16}H_{12}FN_3O_3$    313.3    *31430-15-6*

**Action and use**

Benzimadazole antihelminthic.

*Ph Eur* _____

## DEFINITION

Methyl [5-(4-fluorobenzoyl)-1*H*-benzimidazol-2-yl]carbamate

**Content**

99.0 per cent to 101.0 per cent (dried substance).

## CHARACTERS

**Appearance**

White or almost white powder.

**Solubility**

Practically insoluble in water, in alcohol and in methylene chloride.

It shows polymorphism (*5.9*).

## IDENTIFICATION

Infrared absorption spectrophotometry (*2.2.24*), without recrystallisation.

*Comparison* flubendazole CRS .

## TESTS

**Related substances**

Liquid chromatography (*2.2.29*).

*Test solution* Dissolve 0.100 g of the substance to be examined in *dimethylformamide R* and dilute to 100.0 ml with the same solvent.

*Reference solution (a)* Dissolve 5 mg of *flubendazole for system suitability CRS* in *dimethylformamide R* and dilute to 5.0 ml with the same solvent.

*Reference solution (b)* Dilute 1.0 ml of the test solution to 100.0 ml with *dimethylformamide R*. Dilute 5.0 ml of this solution to 20.0 ml with *dimethylformamide R*.

*Column:*
— *size: l* = 0.10 m, Ø = 4.6 mm,
— *stationary phase: base-deactivated octadecylsilyl silica gel for chromatography R* (3 μm),
— *temperature*: 40 °C.

*Mobile phase:*
— *mobile phase A*: 7.5 g/l solution of ammonium *acetate R*,
— *mobile phase B*: *acetonitrile R*,

| Time (min) | Mobile phase A (per cent *V/V*) | Mobile phase B (per cent *V/V*) |
|---|---|---|
| 0 - 15 | 90 → 75 | 10 → 25 |
| 15 - 30 | 75 → 45 | 25 → 55 |
| 30 - 32 | 45 → 10 | 55 → 90 |
| 32 - 37 | 10 | 90 |
| 37 - 38 | 10 → 90 | 90 → 10 |
| 38 - 42 | 90 | 10 |

*Flow rate* 1.2 ml/min.

*Detection* Spectrophotometer at 250 nm.

*Injection* 10 μl.

*System suitability* Reference solution (a):
— the chromatogram obtained is similar to the chromatogram supplied with *flubendazole for system suitability CRS* .

*Limits:*
— *correction factors*: for the calculation of contents, multiply the peak areas of the following impurities by the corresponding correction factor: impurity A = 1.4; impurity C = 1.3; impurity D = 1.3; impurity G = 1.4,
— *impurities A, B, C, D, E, G*: for each impurity, not more than the area of the principal peak in the chromatogram obtained with reference solution (b) (0.25 per cent),
— *impurity F*: not more than twice the area of the principal peak in the chromatogram obtained with reference solution (b) (0.5 per cent),
— *any other impurity with a relative retention between 1.2 and 1.3*: not more than the area of the principal peak in the chromatogram obtained with reference solution (b) (0.25 per cent),
— *total*: not more than 6 times the area of the principal peak in the chromatogram obtained with reference solution (b) (1.5 per cent),
— *disregard limit*: 0.2 times the area of the principal peak in the chromatogram obtained with reference solution (b) (0.05 per cent).

**Loss on drying** (*2.2.32*)

Maximum 0.5 per cent, determined on 1.000 g by drying in an oven at 105 °C, for 4 h.

**Sulphated ash** (*2.4.14*)

Maximum 0.1 per cent, determined on 1.0 g.

## ASSAY

Dissolve 0.250 g in 3 ml of *anhydrous formic acid R* and add 50 ml of a mixture of 1 volume of *anhydrous acetic acid R* and 7 volumes of *methyl ethyl ketone R*. Titrate with *0.1 M perchloric acid*, determining the end-point potentiometrically (*2.2.20*).

1 ml of *0.1 M perchloric acid* is equivalent to 31.33 mg of $C_{16}H_{12}FN_3O_3$.

## STORAGE

Protected from light.

## IMPURITIES

*Specified impurities    A, B, C, D, E, F, G.*

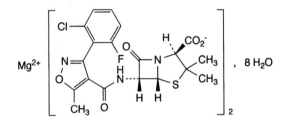

A. R1 = R2 = H, R4 = NH-CHO: methyl [5-[4-(formylamino)benzoyl]-1*H*-benzimidazol-2-yl]carbamate,

E. R1 = R4 = H, R2 = F: methyl [5-(2-fluorobenzoyl)-1*H*-benzimidazol-2-yl]carbamate,

F. R1 = CH₃, R2 = H, R4 = F:
methyl [5-(4-fluorobenzoyl)-1-methyl-1*H*-benzimidazol-2-yl]carbamate,

G. R1 = R2 = H, R4 = O-CH(CH₃)₂: methyl [5-[4-(1-methylethoxy)benzoyl]-1*H*-benzimidazol-2-yl]carbamate,

B. R = NH₂: (2-amino-1*H*-benzimidazol-5-yl)(4-fluorophenyl)methanone,

C. R = OH: (4-fluorophenyl)(2-hydroxy-1*H*-benzimidazol-5-yl)methanone,

D. R = H:
(1*H*-benzimidazol-5-yl)(4-fluorophenyl)methanone.

_____ *Ph Eur*

# Flucloxacillin Magnesium Octahydrate

Flucloxacillin Magnesium

(*Ph Eur monograph 2346*)

C₃₈H₃₂Cl₂F₂MgN₆O₁₀S₂,8H₂O    1074        *58486-36-5*

### Action and use
Penicillin antibacterial.

### Preparations
Flucloxacillin Oral Suspension

Co-fluampicil Oral Suspension

*Ph Eur* _____

## DEFINITION
Magnesium bis[(2*S*,5*R*,6*R*)-6-[[[3-(2-chloro-6-fluorophenyl)-5-methylisoxazol-4-yl]carbonyl]amino]-3,3-dimethyl-7-oxo-4-thia-1-azabicyclo[3.2.0]heptane-2-carboxylate] octahydrate.

Semi-synthetic product derived from a fermentation product.

### Content
95.0 per cent to 102.0 per cent (anhydrous substance).

## CHARACTERS
### Appearance
White or almost white, crystalline powder.

### Solubility
Slightly soluble in water, freely soluble in methanol.

## IDENTIFICATION
*First identification    A, C.*

*Second identification    B, C.*

A. Infrared absorption spectrophotometry (*2.2.24*).

*Comparison    flucloxacillin magnesium octahydrate CRS.*

B. Thin-layer chromatography (*2.2.27*).

*Test solution*    Dissolve 25 mg of the substance to be examined in 5 ml of *water R*.

*Reference solution (a)*    Dissolve 25 mg of *flucloxacillin sodium CRS* in 5 ml of *water R*.

*Reference solution (b)*    Dissolve 25 mg of *cloxacillin sodium CRS*, 25 mg of *dicloxacillin sodium CRS* and 25 mg of *flucloxacillin sodium CRS* in 5 ml of *water R*.

*Plate    TLC silanised silica gel plate R.*

*Mobile phase*    Mix 30 volumes of *acetone R* and 70 volumes of a 154 g/l solution of *ammonium acetate R* previously adjusted to pH 5.0 with *glacial acetic acid R*.

*Application*    1 µl.

*Development*    Over 2/3 of the plate.

*Drying*    In air.

*Detection*    Expose the plate to iodine vapour until the spots appear.

*System suitability*    Reference solution (b):
— the chromatogram shows 3 clearly separated spots.

*Results*    The principal spot in the chromatogram obtained with the test solution is similar in position, colour and size to the principal spot in the chromatogram obtained with reference solution (a).

C. It gives the reaction of magnesium (*2.3.1*).

## TESTS
### pH (*2.2.3*)
4.5 to 6.5.

Dissolve 0.25 g in *carbon dioxide-free water R* and dilute to 50 ml with the same solvent.

### Specific optical rotation (*2.2.7*)
+ 163 to + 175 (anhydrous substance).

Dissolve 0.250 g in *water R* and dilute to 50.0 ml with the same solvent.

### Related substances
Liquid chromatography (*2.2.29*). *Prepare the solutions immediately before use.*

*Test solution (a)*    Dissolve 50.0 mg of the substance to be examined in the mobile phase and dilute to 50.0 ml with the mobile phase.

*Test solution (b)*    Dilute 5.0 ml of test solution (a) to 50.0 ml with the mobile phase.

*Reference solution (a)*    Dissolve 50.0 mg of *flucloxacillin sodium CRS* in the mobile phase and dilute to 50.0 ml with the mobile phase. Dilute 5.0 ml of this solution to 50.0 ml with the mobile phase.

*Reference solution (b)* Dilute 5.0 ml of test solution (b) to 50.0 ml with the mobile phase.

*Reference solution (c)* In order to prepare impurity A *in situ*, add 1 ml of *sodium carbonate solution R* to 10 mg of the substance to be examined, dilute to 25 ml with *water R* and place in an oven at 70 °C for 20 min.

*Reference solution (d)* Dilute 1 ml of reference solution (c) to 10 ml with a 27 g/l solution of *dipotassium hydrogen phosphate R* previously adjusted to pH 3.5 with *dilute phosphoric acid R*.

*Reference solution (e)* In order to prepare impurity B *in situ*, add 5 ml of *dilute hydrochloric acid R* to 10 ml of reference solution (c), dilute to 25 ml with *water R* and place in an oven at 70 °C for 1 h. Dilute 1 ml of this solution to 5 ml with a 27 g/l solution of *dipotassium hydrogen phosphate R* previously adjusted to pH 7.0 with *phosphoric acid R*.

*Reference solution (f)* Dilute 2 ml of reference solution (a) to 10 ml with reference solution (e).

*Reference solution (g)* Dissolve 1.5 mg of *flucloxacillin impurity C CRS* in 1 ml of the mobile phase and dilute to 50 ml with the mobile phase.

*Reference solution (h)* Dissolve 1 mg of *flucloxacillin impurity D CRS* in 100 ml of the mobile phase.

*Reference solution (i)* Dissolve 1 mg of *flucloxacillin impurity E CRS* in 100 ml of the mobile phase.

*Column:*
— size: $l = 0.25$ m, Ø = 4 mm;
— stationary phase: *octadecylsilyl silica gel for chromatography R* (5 µm);
— temperature: 40 °C.

*Mobile phase* Mix 25 volumes of *acetonitrile R1* and 75 volumes of a 2.7 g/l solution of *potassium dihydrogen phosphate R* previously adjusted to pH 5.0 with *dilute sodium hydroxide solution R*.

*Flow rate* 1 ml/min.

*Detection* Spectrophotometer at 225 nm.

*Injection* 20 µl of test solution (a) and reference solutions (b), (d), (e), (f), (g), (h) and (i).

*Run time* 7 times the retention time of flucloxacillin.

*Identification of impurities* Use the chromatograms obtained with reference solutions (d), (e), (g), (h) and (i) to identify the peaks due to impurities A, B, C, D and E respectively.

*Relative retention* WIth reference to flucloxacillin (retention time = about 8 min):
impurity C = about 0.2; impurity A (isomer 1) = about 0.3; impurity A (isomer 2) = about 0.5; impurity D = about 0.6; impurity B (isomer 1) = about 0.8; impurity B (isomer 2) = about 0.9; impurity E = about 6.

*System suitability* Reference solution (f):
— resolution: minimum 2.0 between the 2$^{nd}$ peak due to impurity B (isomer 2) and the peak due to flucloxacillin.

*Limits:*
— correction factor: for the calculation of content, multiply the peak area of impurity C by 3.3;
— impurity A (sum of the 2 isomers): the sum of the areas of the 2 peaks is not more than twice the area of the principal peak in the chromatogram obtained with reference solution (b) (2.0 per cent);
— impurity B (sum of the 2 isomers): the sum of the areas of the 2 peaks is not more than the area of the principal peak in the chromatogram obtained with reference solution (b) (1.0 per cent);

— impurity C: not more than the area of the principal peak in the chromatogram obtained with reference solution (b) (1.0 per cent);
— impurities D, E: for each impurity, not more than 0.3 times the area of the principal peak in the chromatogram obtained with reference solution (b) (0.3 per cent);
— any other impurity: for each impurity, not more than 0.3 times the area of the principal peak in the chromatogram obtained with reference solution (b) (0.3 per cent);
— total: not more than 3 times the area of the principal peak in the chromatogram obtained with reference solution (b) (3.0 per cent);
— disregard limit: 0.05 times the area of the principal peak in the chromatogram obtained with reference solution (b) (0.05 per cent).

**2-Ethylhexanoic acid** (*2.4.28*)
Maximum 0.8 per cent m/m.

**Water** (*2.5.12*)
12.0 per cent to 15.0 per cent, determined on 0.100 g.

**ASSAY**
Liquid chromatography (*2.2.29*) as described in the test for related substances with the following modifications.

*Injection* Test solution (b) and reference solution (a).

Calculate the percentage content of $C_{38}H_{32}Cl_2F_2MgN_6O_{10}S_2$ from the declared content of *flucloxacillin sodium CRS*, multiplying by 0.9773.

**IMPURITIES**
*Specified impurities A, B, C, D, E.*

A. R = $CO_2H$: (4*S*)-2-[carboxy[[[3-(2-chloro-6-fluorophenyl)-5-methylisoxazol-4-yl]carbonyl]amino]methyl]-5,5-dimethylthiazolidine-4-carboxylic acid (penicilloic acids of flucloxacillin),

B. R = H: (2*RS*,4*S*)-2-[[[[3-(2-chloro-6-fluorophenyl)-5-methylisoxazol-4-yl]carbonyl]amino]methyl]-5,5-dimethylthiazolidine-4-carboxylic acid (penilloic acids of flucloxacillin),

C. (2*S*,5*R*,6*R*)-6-amino-3,3-dimethyl-7-oxo-4-thia-1-azabicyclo[3.2.0]heptane-2-carboxylic acid (6-aminopenicillanic acid),

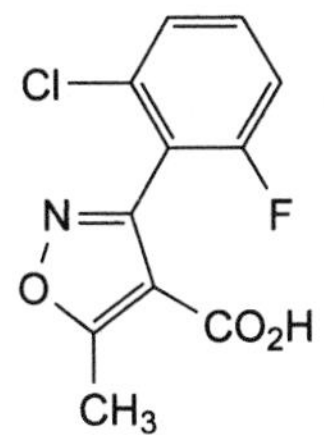

D. 3-(2-chloro-6-fluorophenyl)-5-methylisoxazole-4-
carboxylic acid,

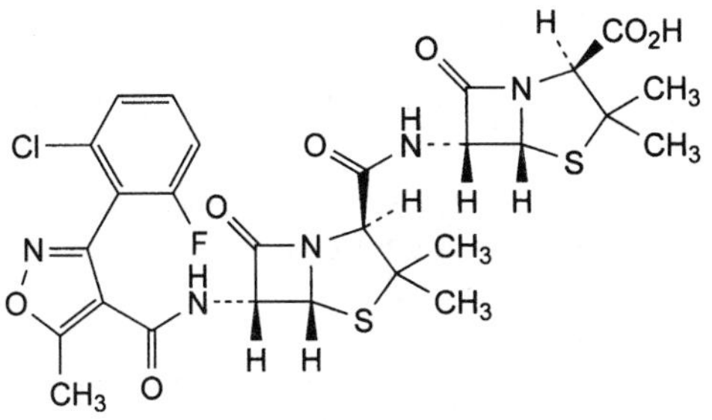

E. (2S,5R,6R)-6-[[[(2S,5R,6R)-6-[[[3-(2-chloro-6-
fluorophenyl)-5-methylisoxazol-4-yl]carbonyl]amino]-3,3-
dimethyl-7-oxo-4-thia-1-azabicyclo[3.2.0]hept-2-
yl]carbonyl]amino]-3,3-dimethyl-7-oxo-4-thia-1-
azabicyclo[3.2.0]heptane-2-carboxylic acid
(6-APA flucloxacillin amide).

*Ph Eur*

# Flucloxacillin Sodium

(*Ph Eur monograph 0668*)

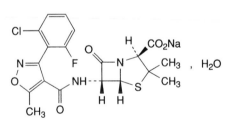

$C_{19}H_{16}ClFN_3NaO_5S,H_2O$   493.9   *1847-24-1*

## Action and use
Penicillin antibacterial.

## Preparations
Flucloxacillin Capsules

Co-fluampicil Capsules

Flucloxacillin Injection

Flucloxacillin Oral Solution

*Ph Eur*

## DEFINITION
Sodium (2S,5R,6R)-6-[[[3-(2-chloro-6-fluorophenyl)-5-
methylisoxazol-4-yl]carbonyl]amino]-3,3-dimethyl-7-oxo-4-
thia-1-azabicyclo[3.2.0]heptane-2-carboxylate monohydrate.

Semi-synthetic product derived from a fermentation product.

## Content
95.0 per cent to 102.0 per cent (anhydrous substance).

## CHARACTERS
### Appearance
White or almost white, hygroscopic, crystalline powder.

### Solubility
Freely soluble in water and in methanol, soluble in ethanol
(96 per cent).

## IDENTIFICATION
*First identification*   A, D.

*Second identification*   B, C, D.

A. Infrared absorption spectrophotometry (*2.2.24*).

*Comparison*   flucloxacillin sodium CRS .

B. Thin-layer chromatography (*2.2.27*).

*Test solution*   Dissolve 25 mg of the substance to be
examined in 5 ml of *water R*.

*Reference solution (a)*   Dissolve 25 mg of *flucloxacillin
sodium CRS* in 5 ml of *water R*.

*Reference solution (b)*   Dissolve 25 mg of *cloxacillin
sodium CRS*, 25 mg of *dicloxacillin sodium CRS* and 25 mg of
*flucloxacillin sodium CRS* in 5 ml of *water R*.

*Plate*   TLC silanised silica gel plate R.

*Mobile phase*   Mix 30 volumes of *acetone R* and 70 volumes
of a 154 g/l solution of *ammonium acetate R* adjusted to
pH 5.0 with *glacial acetic acid R*.

*Application*   1 μl.

*Development*   Over a path of 15 cm.

*Drying*   In air.

*Detection*   Expose to iodine vapour until the spots appear
and examine in daylight.

*System suitability*   Reference solution (b):
— the chromatogram shows 3 clearly separated spots.

*Results*   The principal spot in the chromatogram obtained
with the test solution is similar in position, colour and size to
the principal spot in the chromatogram obtained with
reference solution (a).

C. Place about 2 mg in a test-tube about 150 mm long and
15 mm in diameter. Moisten with 0.05 ml of *water R* and
add 2 ml of *sulphuric acid-formaldehyde reagent R*. Mix the
contents of the tube by swirling; the colour of the solution is
slightly greenish-yellow. Place the test-tube in a water-bath
for 1 min; the solution becomes yellow.

D. It gives reaction (a) of sodium (*2.3.1*).

## TESTS
### Solution S
Dissolve 2.50 g in *carbon dioxide-free water R* and dilute to
25.0 ml with the same solvent.

### Appearance of solution
Solution S is clear (*2.2.1*) and its absorbance (*2.2.25*) at
430 nm is not greater than 0.04.

### pH (*2.2.3*)
5.0 to 7.0 for solution S.

### Specific optical rotation (*2.2.7*)
+ 158 to + 168 (anhydrous substance).

Dissolve 0.250 g in *water R* and dilute to 25.0 ml with the
same solvent.

### Related substances
Liquid chromatography (*2.2.29*).

*Test solution (a)*   Dissolve 50.0 mg of the substance to be
examined in the mobile phase and dilute to 50.0 ml with the
mobile phase.

*Test solution (b)* Dilute 5.0 ml of test solution (a) to 50.0 ml with the mobile phase.

*Reference solution (a)* Dissolve 50.0 mg of *flucloxacillin sodium CRS* in the mobile phase and dilute to 50.0 ml with the mobile phase. Dilute 5.0 ml of this solution to 50.0 ml with the mobile phase.

*Reference solution (b)* Dilute 5.0 ml of reference solution (a) to 50.0 ml with the mobile phase.

*Reference solution (c)* Dissolve 5 mg of *flucloxacillin sodium CRS* and 5 mg of *cloxacillin sodium CRS* in the mobile phase, then dilute to 50.0 ml with the mobile phase.

*Column:*
— *size:* $l = 0.25$ m, $\emptyset = 4$ mm;
— *stationary phase*: octadecylsilyl *silica gel for chromatography R* (5 µm).

*Mobile phase* Mix 25 volumes of *acetonitrile R1* and 75 volumes of a 2.7 g/l solution of *potassium dihydrogen phosphate R* adjusted to pH 5.0 with *dilute sodium hydroxide solution R*.

*Flow rate* 1 ml/min.

*Detection* Spectrophotometer at 225 nm.

*Injection* 20 µl of test solution (a) and reference solutions (b) and (c).

*Run time* 6 times the retention time of flucloxacillin.

*System suitability* Reference solution (c):
— *resolution*: minimum 2.5 between the peaks due to cloxacillin (1$^{st}$ peak) and flucloxacillin (2$^{nd}$ peak).

*Limits:*
— *impurities A, B, C, D, E*: for each impurity, not more than the area of the principal peak in the chromatogram obtained with reference solution (b) (1 per cent);
— *total*: not more than 5 times the area of the principal peak in the chromatogram obtained with reference solution (b) (5 per cent);
— *disregard limit*: 0.05 times the area of the principal peak in the chromatogram obtained with reference solution (b) (0.05 per cent).

**N,N-Dimethylaniline** *(2.4.26, Method B)*
Maximum 20 ppm.

**2-Ethylhexanoic acid** *(2.4.28)*
Maximum 0.8 per cent m/m.

**Water** *(2.5.12)*
3.0 per cent to 4.5 per cent, determined on 0.300 g.

**Pyrogens** *(2.6.8)*
If intended for use in the manufacture of parenteral dosage forms without a further appropriate procedure for the removal of pyrogens, it complies with the test. Inject per kilogram of the rabbit's mass 1 ml of a solution in *water for injections R* containing 20 mg of the substance to be examined per millilitre.

**ASSAY**
Liquid chromatography *(2.2.29)* as described in the test for related substances with the following modifications.

*Injection* Test solution (b) and reference solution (a).

*System suitability* Reference solution (a):
— *repeatability*: maximum relative standard deviation of 1.0 per cent after 6 injections.

Calculate the percentage content of $C_{19}H_{16}ClFN_3NaO_5S$ from the declared content of *flucloxacillin sodium CRS*.

**STORAGE**
In an airtight container, at a temperature not exceeding 25 °C. If the substance is sterile, store in a sterile, airtight, tamper-proof container.

**IMPURITIES**
*Specified impurities A, B, C, D, E.*

A. R = $CO_2H$: (4*S*)-2-[carboxy[[[3-(2-chloro-6-fluorophenyl)-5-methylisoxazol-4-yl]carbonyl]amino]methyl]-5,5-dimethylthiazolidine-4-carboxylic acid (penicilloic acids of flucloxacillin),

B. R = H: (2*RS*,4*S*)-2-[[[[3-(2-chloro-6-fluorophenyl)-5-methylisoxazol-4-yl]carbonyl]amino]methyl]-5,5-dimethylthiazolidine-4-carboxylic acid (penilloic acids of flucloxacillin),

C. (2*S*,5*R*,6*R*)-6-amino-3,3-dimethyl-7-oxo-4-thia-1-azabicyclo[3.2.0]heptane-2-carboxylic acid (6-aminopenicillanic acid),

D. 3-(2-chloro-6-fluorophenyl)-5-methylisoxazole-4-carboxylic acid,

E. (2*S*,5*R*,6*R*)-6-[[[(2*S*,5*R*,6*R*)-6-[[[3-(2-chloro-6-fluorophenyl)-5-methylisoxazol-4-yl]carbonyl]amino]-3,3-dimethyl-7-oxo-4-thia-1-azabicyclo[3.2.0]hept-2-yl]carbonyl]amino]-3,3-dimethyl-7-oxo-4-thia-1-azabicyclo[3.2.0]heptane-2-carboxylic acid.

# Fluconazole

*(Ph Eur monograph 2287)*

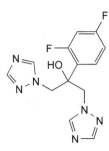

C₁₃H₁₂F₂N₆O        306.3        *86386-73-4*

**Action and use**
Antifungal.

*Ph Eur* _____

## DEFINITION
2-(2,4-Difluorophenyl)-1,3-bis(1*H*-1,2,4-triazol-1-yl)propan-2-ol.

## Content
99.0 per cent to 101.0 per cent (dried substance).

## CHARACTERS
**Appearance**
White or almost white, hygroscopic, crystalline powder.

**Solubility**
Slightly soluble in water, freely soluble in methanol, soluble in acetone.

It shows polymorphism (*5.9*).

## IDENTIFICATION
Infrared absorption spectrophotometry (*2.2.24*).

*Comparison* fluconazole CRS .

If the spectra obtained in the solid state show differences, dissolve the substance to be examined and the reference substance separately in the minimum volume of *methylene chloride R*, evaporate to dryness on a water-bath and record new spectra using the residues.

## TESTS
**Appearance of solution**
The solution is clear (*2.2.1*) and colourless (*2.2.2, Method II*).

Dissolve 1.0 g in *methanol R* and dilute to 20 ml with the same solvent.

**Related substances**
Liquid chromatography (*2.2.29*).

*Test solution* Dissolve 0.100 g of the substance to be examined in the mobile phase, sonicate if necessary, and dilute to 10.0 ml with the mobile phase.

*Reference solution (a)* Dilute 5.0 ml of the test solution to 100.0 ml with the mobile phase. Dilute 1.0 ml of this solution to 10.0 ml with the mobile phase.

*Reference solution (b)* Dissolve 5 mg of *fluconazole for peak identification CRS* (containing impurity A) in the mobile phase, sonicate if necessary, and dilute to 10 ml with the mobile phase.

*Reference solution (c)* Dissolve 3.0 mg of *fluconazole impurity B CRS* in the mobile phase, sonicate if necessary and, dilute to 100.0 ml with the mobile phase.

*Reference solution (d)* Dissolve 2.0 mg of *fluconazole impurity C CRS* in the mobile phase and dilute to 20.0 ml with the mobile phase. To 1.0 ml of this solution add 1.0 ml of the test solution and dilute to 10.0 ml with the mobile phase.

*Column:*
— *size: l* = 0.15 m, Ø = 4.6 mm;
— *stationary phase*: octadecylsilyl silica gel for chromatography R1 (5 μm);
— *temperature*: 40 °C.

*Mobile phase* acetonitrile R, 0.63 g/l solution of ammonium formate R (14:86 *V/V*).

*Flow rate* 1.0 ml/min.

*Detection* Spectrophotometer at 260 nm.

*Injection* 20 μl.

*Run time* 3.5 times the retention time of fluconazole.

*Identification of impurities* Use the chromatogram supplied with *fluconazole for peak identification CRS* and the chromatogram obtained with reference solution (b) to identify the peak due to impurity A; use the chromatogram obtained with reference solution (c) to identify the peak due to impurity B and the chromatogram obtained with reference solution (d) to identify the peak due to impurity C.

*Relative retention* With reference to fluconazole (retention time = about 11 min): impurity B = about 0.4; impurity A = about 0.5; impurity C = about 0.8.

*System suitability* Reference solution (d):
— *resolution*: minimum 3.0 between the peaks due to impurity C and fluconazole.

*Limits:*
— *impurity A*: not more than 0.8 times the area of the principal peak in the chromatogram obtained with reference solution (a) (0.4 per cent);
— *impurity B*: not more than the area of the principal peak in the chromatogram obtained with reference solution (c) (0.3 per cent);
— *impurity C*: not more than the area of the corresponding peak in the chromatogram obtained with reference solution (d) (0.1 per cent);
— *unspecified impurities*: for each impurity, not more than 0.2 times the area of the principal peak in the chromatogram obtained with reference solution (a) (0.10 per cent);
— *total*: not more than 1.2 times the area of the principal peak in the chromatogram obtained with reference solution (a) (0.6 per cent);
— *disregard limit*: 0.1 times the area of the principal peak in the chromatogram obtained with reference solution (a) (0.05 per cent);

**Heavy metals** (*2.4.8*)
Maximum 10 ppm.

Dissolve 2.0 g in a mixture of 15 volumes of *water R* and 85 volumes of *methanol R* and dilute to 20.0 ml with the same mixture of solvents. 12 ml of the solution complies with test B. Prepare the reference solution using *lead standard solution (1 ppm Pb) R*.

**Loss on drying** (*2.2.32*)
Maximum 0.5 per cent, determined on 1.000 g by drying in an oven at 105 °C.

**Sulphated ash** (*2.4.14*)
Maximum 0.1 per cent, determined on 1.0 g.

## ASSAY

Dissolve 0.125 g in 60 ml of *anhydrous acetic acid R*. Titrate with *0.1 M perchloric acid*, determining the end-point potentiometrically (2.2.20).

1 ml of *0.1 M perchloric acid* is equivalent to 15.32 mg of $C_{13}H_{12}F_2N_6O$.

## STORAGE

In an airtight container.

## IMPURITIES

*Specified impurities   A, B, C.*

*Other detectable impurities* (the following substances would, if present at a sufficient level, be detected by one or other of the tests in the monograph. They are limited by the general acceptance criterion for other/unspecified impurities and/or by the general monograph *Substances for pharmaceutical use (2034)*. It is therefore not necessary to identify these impurities for demonstration of compliance. See also 5.10. *Control of impurities in substances for pharmaceutical use) : D, E, F, G, H, I.*

A. (2RS)-2-(2,4-difluorophenyl)-1-(1H-1,2,4-triazol-1-yl)-3-(4H-1,2,4-triazol-4-yl)propan-2-ol,

B. 2-[2-fluoro-4-(1H-1,2,4-triazol-1-yl)phenyl]-1,3-bis(1H-1,2,4-triazol-1-yl)propan-2-ol,

C. 1,1′-(1,3-phenylene)di-1H-1,2,4-triazole,

D. 2-(4-fluorophenyl)-1,3-bis(1H-1,2,4-triazol-1-yl)propan-2-ol,

E. 1-[(6RS)-4,6-difluoro-6-(1H-1,2,4-triazol-1-yl)cyclohexa-1,4-dienyl]ethanone,

F. R = OH: (2RS)-2-(2,4-difluorophenyl)-3-(1H-1,2,4-triazol-1-yl)propane-1,2-diol,

H. R = Br: (2RS)-1-bromo-2-(2,4-difluorophenyl)-3-(1H-1,2,4-triazol-1-yl)propan-2-ol,

G. [3-[[(2RS)-2-(2,4-difluorophenyl)oxiran-2-yl]methyl]1H-1,2,4-triazol-1-yl]methanesulphonic acid,

I. 4-amino-1-[(2RS)-2-(2,4-difluorophenyl)-2-hydroxy-3(1H-1,2,4-triazol-1-yl)propyl]-4H-1,2,4-triazolium.

# Flucytosine

(*Ph Eur monograph 0766*)

C₄H₄FN₃O      129.1      *2022-85-7*

**Action and use**
Antifungal.

**Preparation**
Flucytosine Tablets

*Ph Eur* _____

## DEFINITION

Flucytosine contains not less than 98.5 per cent and not more than the equivalent of 101.0 per cent of 4-amino-5-fluoropyrimidin-2(1*H*)-one, calculated with reference to the dried substance.

## CHARACTERS

A white or almost white, crystalline powder, sparingly soluble in water, slightly soluble in ethanol.

## IDENTIFICATION

*First identification   A.*

*Second identification   B, C, D.*

A. Examine by infrared absorption spectrophotometry (*2.2.24*), comparing with the spectrum obtained with *flucytosine CRS*.

B. Examine the chromatograms obtained in the test for related substances. The principal spot in the chromatogram obtained with test solution (b) is similar in position and size to the principal spot in the chromatogram obtained with reference solution (a).

C. Mix about 5 mg with 45 mg of *heavy magnesium oxide R* and ignite in a crucible until an almost white residue is obtained (usually less than 5 min). Allow to cool, add 1 ml of *water R*, 0.05 of *phenolphthalein solution R*1 and about 1 ml of *dilute hydrochloric acid R* to render the solution colourless. Filter and add to the filtrate a freshly prepared mixture of 0.1 ml of *alizarin S solution R* and 0.1 ml of *zirconyl nitrate solution R*. Mix, allow to stand for 5 min and compare the colour of the solution with that of a blank prepared in the same manner. The colour of the solution changes from red to yellow.

D. To 5 ml of solution S (see Tests) add 0.15 ml of *bromine water R* and shake. The colour of the solution is discharged.

## TESTS

**Solution S**
Dissolve 0.5 g in *carbon dioxide-free water R* and dilute to 50 ml with the same solvent.

**Appearance of solution**
Solution S is clear (*2.2.1*) and not more intensely coloured than reference solution BY₇ or Y₇ (*2.2.2, Method II*).

**Related substances**
Examine by thin-layer chromatography (*2.2.27*), using a suitable silica gel as the coating substance.

*Test solution (a)*   Dissolve 50 mg of the substance to be examined in a mixture of 10 volumes of *water R* and 15 volumes of *methanol R* and dilute to 5 ml with the same mixture of solvents.

*Test solution (b)*   Dilute 1 ml of test solution (a) to 10 ml with a mixture of 10 volumes of *water R* and 15 volumes of *methanol R*.

*Reference solution (a)*   Dissolve 10 mg of *flucytosine CRS* in a mixture of 10 volumes of *water R* and 15 volumes of *methanol R* and dilute to 10 ml with the same mixture of solvents.

*Reference solution (b)*   Dilute 1 ml of test solution (b) to 100 ml with a mixture of 10 volumes of *water R* and 15 volumes of *methanol R*.

*Reference solution (c)*   Dissolve 5 mg of *fluorouracil CRS* in 5 ml of reference solution (a).

Apply separately to the plate 10 μl of each solution. Develop over a path of 12 cm in an unsaturated tank using a mixture of 1 volume of *anhydrous formic acid R*, 15 volumes of *water R*, 25 volumes of *methanol R* and 60 volumes of *ethyl acetate R*. Allow the solvents to evaporate. At the bottom of a chromatography tank place an evaporating dish containing a mixture of 2 volumes of a 15 g/l solution of *potassium permanganate R*, 1 volume of *hydrochloric acid R1* and 1 volume of *water R*, close the tank and allow to stand for 15 min. Place the dried plate in the tank and close the tank. Leave the plate in contact with the chlorine vapour for 5 min. Withdraw the plate and place it in a current of cold air until the excess of chlorine is removed and an area of the coating below the points of application does not give a blue colour with a drop of *potassium iodide and starch solution R*. Spray with *potassium iodide and starch solution R*. Examine the plate in daylight. Any spot in the chromatogram obtained with test solution (a), apart from the principal spot, is not more intense than the spot in the chromatogram obtained with reference solution (b) (0.1 per cent). The test is not valid unless the chromatogram obtained with reference solution (c) shows two clearly separated spots.

**Fluoride**
Not more than 200 ppm. Carry out a potentiometric determination of fluoride ion, using a fluoride-selective indicator electrode and a silver-silver chloride reference electrode.

*Prepare and store all solutions in plastic containers.*

*Buffer solution*   Dissolve 58 g of *sodium chloride R* in 500 ml of *water R*. Add 57 ml of *glacial acetic acid R* and 200 ml of a 100 g/l solution of *cyclohexylenedinitrilotetra-acetic acid R* in *1 M sodium hydroxide*. Adjust the pH to 5.0 to 5.5 with a 200 g/l solution of *sodium hydroxide R* and dilute to 1000.0 ml with *water R*.

*Test solution*   Dissolve 1.00 g of the substance to be examined in *water R* and dilute to 100.0 ml with the same solvent.

*Reference solutions*   Dissolve 4.42 g of *sodium fluoride R*, previously dried at 120 °C for 2 h, in 300 ml of *water R* and dilute to 1000.0 ml with the same solvent (solution (a): 1.9 g/l of fluoride). Prepare three reference solutions by dilution of solution (a) 1 in 100, 1 in 1000 and 1 in 10 000.

To 20.0 ml of each reference solution, add 10.0 ml of the buffer solution and stir with a magnetic stirrer. Introduce the electrodes into the solution and allow to stand for 5 min with constant stirring. Determine the potential difference between the electrodes. Plot on semi-logarithmic graph paper the potential difference obtained for each solution as a function of concentration of fluoride. Using exactly the same conditions, determine the potential difference obtained with the test solution and calculate the content of fluoride.

**Heavy metals** (*2.4.8*)

1.0 g complies with limit test C for heavy metals (20 ppm). *Use a platinum crucible.* Prepare the standard using 2 ml of *lead standard solution (10 ppm Pb) R*.

**Loss on drying** (*2.2.32*)

Not more than 1.0 per cent, determined on 1.000 g by drying in an oven at 105 °C.

**Sulphated ash** (*2.4.14*)

Not more than 0.1 per cent, determined on 1.0 g in a platinum crucible.

## ASSAY

Dissolve 0.100 g in 40 ml of *anhydrous acetic acid R* and add 100 ml of *acetic anhydride R*. Titrate with *0.1 M perchloric acid* determining the end-point potentiometrically (*2.2.20*).

1 ml of *0.1 M perchloric acid* is equivalent to 12.91 mg of $C_4H_4FN_3O$.

## STORAGE

Store protected from light.

*———————————————— Ph Eur*

# Fludarabine Phosphate

(*Ph Eur monograph 1781*)

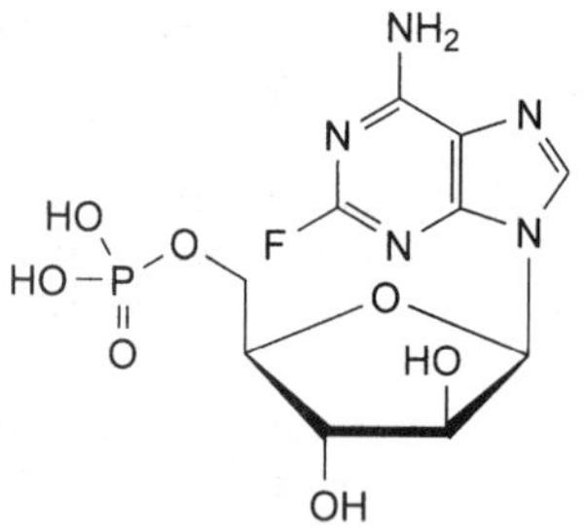

$C_{10}H_{13}FN_5O_7P$       365.2       75607-67-9

**Action and use**

Purine analogue; cytotoxic.

*Ph Eur* _____

## DEFINITION

2-Fluoro-9-(5-*O*-phosphono-β-D-arabinofuranosyl)-9*H*-purin-6-amine.

**Content**

97.0 per cent to 102.0 per cent (anhydrous substance).

## CHARACTERS

**Appearance**

White or almost white, crystalline powder, hygroscopic.

**Solubility**

Slightly soluble in water, freely soluble in dimethylformamide, very slightly soluble in anhydrous ethanol.

## IDENTIFICATION

Infrared absorption spectrophotometry (*2.2.24*).

*Comparison*  *fludarabine phosphate CRS* .

## TESTS

**Appearance of solution**

The solution is clear (*2.2.1*) and not more intensely coloured than reference solution $BY_5$ (*2.2.2, Method II*).

Dissolve 50 mg in 5.0 ml of *dimethylformamide R* with the aid of ultrasound.

**Specific optical rotation** (*2.2.7*)

+ 10.0 to + 14.0 (anhydrous substance).

Dissolve 0.100 g in *water R* and dilute to 20.0 ml with the same solvent with the aid of ultrasound.

**Related substances**

Liquid chromatography (*2.2.29*): use the normalisation procedure. *Prepare the solutions immediately before use.*

*Test solution*  With the aid of ultrasound, dissolve 20 mg of the substance to be examined in 50 ml of *water R* and dilute to 100.0 ml with the same solvent.

*Reference solution (a)*  With the aid of ultrasound, dissolve 20 mg of *fludarabine phosphate CRS* in 50 ml of *water R* and dilute to 100.0 ml with the same solvent.

*Reference solution (b)*  With the aid of ultrasound, dissolve 20 mg of the substance to be examined in 20 ml of *0.1 M hydrochloric acid*. Heat in a water-bath at 80 °C for 15 min, cool to room temperature, mix and dilute to 100.0 ml with *water R*.

*Reference solution (c)*  Dilute 1.0 ml of reference solution (a) to 100.0 ml with *water R*. Dilute 1.0 ml of this solution to 20.0 ml with *water R*.

*Blank solution*  *0.02 M hydrochloric acid.*

A. Early eluting impurities.

*Column:*

— *size: l* = 0.15 m, Ø = 4.6 mm,

— *stationary phase:* end-capped octadecylsilyl silica gel for chromatography R (5 μm).

*Mobile phase*  Mix 60 volumes of *methanol R* and 940 volumes of a 1.36 g/l solution of *potassium dihydrogen phosphate R*.

*Flow rate*  1 ml/min.

*Detection*  Spectrophotometer at 260 nm and 292 nm.

*Injection*  10 μl; inject the solutions and record the chromatograms at 260 nm.

*Run time*  4.5 times the retention time of the principal peak in the chromatogram obtained with the test solution.

*Identification of impurities*  Identify the impurity peaks in the chromatogram obtained with reference solution (a) and in the chromatogram obtained with the test solution by comparison with Figure 1781.-1. Additionally, inject the test solution and reference solution (a) and record the chromatograms at 292 nm to identify impurities A and B, the response of which is much higher than that at 260 nm.

*Relative retention*  With reference to fludarabine phosphate (retention time = about 9 min): impurity A = about 0.26; impurity B = about 0.34; impurity C = about 0.42.

*System suitability*  Reference solution (b) at 292 nm:

— *resolution*: minimum 2.0 between the peaks due to impurities A and B.

*Limits*  At 260 nm:

— *correction factors*: for the calculation of contents, multiply the peak areas of the following impurities by the corresponding correction factor: impurity A = 4.0; impurity B = 2.5; impurity C = 1.9;

— *impurity A*: maximum 0.8 per cent;

— *impurity B*: maximum 0.2 per cent;

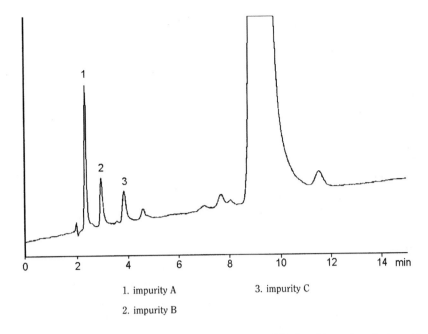

1. impurity A        3. impurity C

2. impurity B

Figure 1781.-1. – *Chromatogram for test A for related substances of fludarabine phosphate: reference solution (a) at 260 nm*

— *impurity C*: maximum 0.4 per cent;
— *any other impurity preceding fluarabine phosphate* : maximum 0.1 per cent;
— *disregard limit*: the area of the principal peak in the chromatogram obtained with reference solution (c) (0.05 per cent), and any peak eluting after fludarabine phosphate.

B. Late eluting impurities.

Conditions as described under Test A with the following modifications.

*Mobile phase*   Mix 200 volumes of *methanol R* and 800 volumes of a 1.36 g/l solution of *potassium dihydrogen phosphate R*.

*Detection*   Spectrophotometer at 260 nm.

*Injection*   10 µl.

*Run time*   8 times the retention time of the principal peak in the chromatogram obtained with the test solution.

*Identification of impurities*   Identify the impurity peaks in the chromatogram obtained with reference solution (a) and in the chromatogram obtained with the test solution by comparison with Figure 1781.-2.

*Relative retention*   With reference to fludarabine phosphate (retention time = about 2.5 min): impurity D = about 1.5; impurity E = about 1.9; impurity G = about 2.2; impurity H = about 2.4; impurity F = about 2.5.

*System suitability*   Reference solution (a):
— *peak-to-valley ratio*: minimum 2.0, where $H_p$ = height above the baseline of the peak due to impurity G and $H_v$ = height above the baseline of the lowest point of the curve separating this peak from the peak due to impurity H.

*Limits*:
— *correction factors*: for the calculation of contents, multiply the peak areas of the following impurities by the corresponding correction factor: impurity D = 0.5; impurity E = 0.6; impurity F = 1.8;
— *impurity D*: maximum 0.1 per cent;
— *impurity E*: maximum 0.2 per cent;

— *impurity F*: maximum 0.2 per cent;
— *any other impurity eluting after fludarabine phosphate* : maximum 0.1 per cent;
— *disregard limit*: the area of the principal peak in the chromatogram obtained with reference solution (c) (0.05 per cent), and any peak eluting before fludarabine phosphate.

*Total of impurities eluting before fludarabine phosphate in test A, apart from impurities A, B and C, and of impurities eluting after fludarabine phosphate in test B, apart from impurities D, E and F   Maximum 0.5 per cent.*

*Total of all impurities eluting before fludarabine phosphate in test A and after fludarabine phosphate in test B   Maximum 2.0 per cent.*

**Ethanol** (*2.4.24, System A*)
Maximum 1.0 per cent.

**Heavy metals** (*2.4.8*)
Maximum 20 ppm.

Dissolve 1.0 g by heating in 10 ml of *water R*. Allow to cool. Add *ammonia R* until the litmus paper reaction is slightly alkaline. Adjust to pH 3.0-4.0 with *dilute acetic acid R* and dilute to 20 ml with *water R*. 12 ml of the solution complies with limit test A. Prepare the reference solution using *lead standard solution (1 ppm Pb) R*.

**Water** (*2.5.12*)
Maximum 3.0 per cent, determined on 0.200 g (ground to a very fine powder). Stir the substance in 15 ml of *anhydrous methanol R* for about 15 s before titrating.

**ASSAY**
Liquid chromatography (*2.2.29*) as described in test A for related substances with the following modifications.

*Test solution*   With the aid of ultrasound, dissolve 24.0 mg of the substance to be examined in 50 ml of *water R* and dilute to 100.0 ml with the same solvent. Dilute 25.0 ml of the solution to 100.0 ml with the mobile phase.

*Reference solution*   With the aid of ultrasound, dissolve 24.0 mg of *fludarabine phosphate CRS* in 50 ml of *water R*

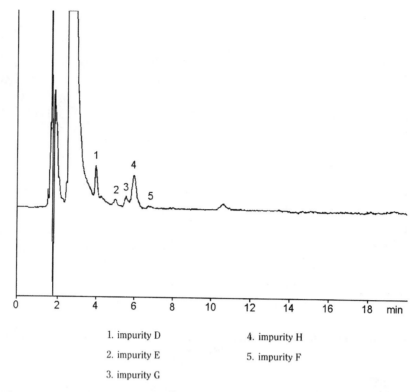

Figure 1781.-2. – *Chromatogram for test B for related substances of fludarabine phosphate: reference solution (a) at 260 nm.*

1. impurity D
2. impurity E
3. impurity G
4. impurity H
5. impurity F

and dilute to 100.0 ml with the same solvent. Dilute 25.0 ml of the solution to 100.0 ml with the mobile phase.

*Detection* Spectrophotometer at 260 nm.

*Injection* 10 µl.

Calculate the percentage content of $C_{10}H_{13}FN_5O_7P$ using the chromatograms obtained with the test solution and the reference solution, and the declared content of *fludarabine phosphate CRS.*

## STORAGE

In an airtight container, protected from light, at a temperature of 2 °C to 8 °C.

## IMPURITIES

*Specified impurities* *A, B, C, D, E, F, G.*

*Other detectable impurities* (the following substances would, if present at a sufficient level, be detected by one or other of the tests in the monograph. They are limited by the general acceptance criterion for other/unspecified impurities and/or by the general monograph *Substances for pharmaceutical use (2034)*. It is therefore not necessary to identify these impurities for demonstration of compliance. See also *5.10. Control of impurities in substances for pharmaceutical use)* : *H, I, J.*

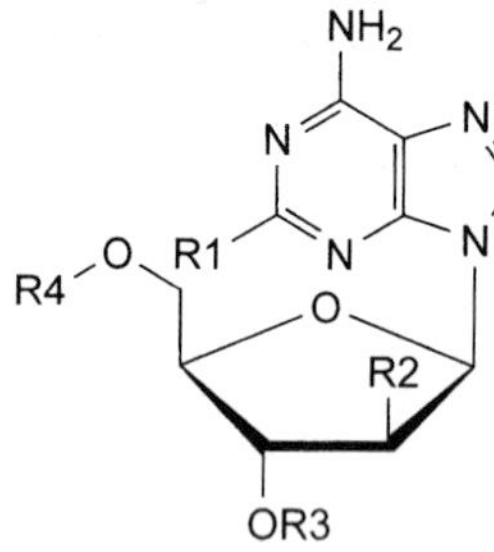

A. R1 = R2 = OH, R3 = H, R4 = PO₃H₂: 6-amino-9-(5-O-phosphono-β-D-arabinofuranosyl)-9*H*-purin-2-ol,

C. R1 = F, R2 = OH, R3 = R4 = PO₃H₂: 9-(3,5-di-O-phosphono-β-D-arabinofuranosyl)-2-fluoro-9*H*-purin-6-amine,

E. R1 = F, R2 = OH, R3 = R4 = H: 9-β-D-arabinofuranosyl-2-fluoro-9*H*-purin-6-amine,

F. R1 = O-C₂H₅, R2 = OH, R3 = H, R4 = PO₃H₂: 2-ethoxy-9-(5-O-phosphono-β-D-arabinofuranosyl)-9*H*-purin-6-amine,

G. R1 = F, R2 = Cl, R3 = H, R4 = PO₃H₂: 9-(2-chloro-2-deoxy-5-O-phosphono-β-D-arabinofuranosyl)-2-fluoro-9*H*-purin-6-amine,

I. R1 = NH₂, R2 = OH, R3 = H, R4 = PO₃H₂: 9-(5-O-phosphono-β-D-arabinofuranosyl)-9*H*-purine-2,6-diamine,

J. R1 = OCH₃, R2 = OH, R3 = H, R4 = PO₃H₂: 2-methoxy-9-(5-O-phosphono-β-D-arabinofuranosyl)-9*H*-purin-6-amine,

B. R = OH: 6-amino-7H-purin-2-ol,

D. R = F: 2-fluoro-7H-purin-6-amine,

H. 9-(2,5-anhydro-β-D-arabinofuranosyl)-2-fluoro-9H-purin-6-amine.

*—————————————————— Ph Eur*

# Fludrocortisone Acetate

*(Ph Eur monograph 0767)*

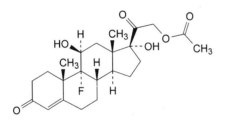

C₂₃H₃₁FO₆      422.5      *514-36-3*

$C_{23}H_{31}FO_6$     422.5     *514-36-3*

### Action and use
Mineralocorticoid.

### Preparation
Fludrocortisone Tablets

*Ph Eur* _____

## DEFINITION
9-Fluoro-11β,17-dihydroxy-3,20-dioxopregn-4-en-21-yl acetate.

### Content
97.0 per cent to 103.0 per cent (dried substance).

## CHARACTERS
### Appearance
White or almost white, crystalline powder.

### Solubility
Practically insoluble in water, sparingly soluble in anhydrous ethanol.

## IDENTIFICATION
*First identification*   *A, B.*

*Second identification*   *C, D, E.*

A. Infrared absorption spectrophotometry (2.2.24).

*Comparison*   fludrocortisone acetate CRS .

If the spectra obtained in the solid state show differences, dissolve the substance to be examined and the reference

substance separately in the minimum volume of *acetone R*, evaporate to dryness and record new spectra using the residues.

B. Thin-layer chromatography (2.2.27).

*Solvent mixture*   methanol R, methylene chloride R (1:9 V/V).

*Test solution*   Dissolve 10 mg of the substance to be examined in the solvent mixture and dilute to 10 ml with the solvent mixture.

*Reference solution (a)*   Dissolve 10 mg of *fludrocortisone acetate CRS* in the solvent mixture and dilute to 10 ml with the solvent mixture.

*Reference solution (b)*   Dissolve 5 mg of *cortisone acetate CRS* in 5 ml of reference solution (a).

*Plate*   TLC silica gel F₂₅₄ plate R.

*Mobile phase*   Add a mixture of 1.2 volumes of *water R* and 8 volumes of *methanol R* to a mixture of 15 volumes of *ether R* and 77 volumes of *methylene chloride R*.

*Application*   5 μl.

*Development*   Over a path of 15 cm.

*Drying*   In air.

*Detection A*   Examine in ultraviolet light at 254 nm.

*Results A*   The principal spot in the chromatogram obtained with the test solution is similar in position and size to the principal spot in the chromatogram obtained with reference solution (a).

*Detection B*   Spray with *alcoholic solution of sulphuric acid R*. Heat at 120 °C for 10 min or until the spots appear. Allow to cool. Examine in daylight and in ultraviolet light at 365 nm.

*Results B*   The principal spot in the chromatogram obtained with the test solution is similar in position, colour in daylight, fluorescence in ultraviolet light at 365 nm and size to the principal spot in the chromatogram obtained with reference solution (a).

*System suitability*   Reference solution (b):
— the chromatogram shows 2 clearly separated spots.

C. Thin-layer chromatography (2.2.27).

*Test solution (a)*   Dissolve 25 mg of the substance to be examined in *methanol R* and dilute to 5 ml with the same solvent (solution A). Dilute 2 ml of this solution to 10 ml with *methylene chloride R*.

*Test solution (b)*   Transfer 2 ml of solution A to a 15 ml glass tube with a ground-glass stopper or a polytetrafluoroethylene cap. Add 10 ml of *saturated methanolic potassium hydrogen carbonate solution R* and immediately pass a stream of *nitrogen R* through the solution for 5 min. Stopper the tube. Heat on a water-bath at 45 °C protected from light for 2 h 30 min. Allow to cool.

*Reference solution (a)*   Dissolve 25 mg of *fludrocortisone acetate CRS* in *methanol R* and dilute to 5 ml with the same solvent (solution B). Dilute 2 ml of this solution to 10 ml with *methylene chloride R*.

*Reference solution (b)*   Transfer 2 ml of solution B to a 15 ml glass tube with a ground-glass stopper or a polytetrafluoroethylene cap. Add 10 ml of *saturated methanolic potassium hydrogen carbonate solution R* and immediately pass a stream of *nitrogen R* through the solution for 5 min. Stopper the tube. Heat on a water bath at 45 °C protected from light for 2 h 30 min. Allow to cool.

*Plate*   TLC silica gel F₂₅₄ plate R.

*Mobile phase* Add a mixture of 1.2 volumes of *water R* and 8 volumes of *methanol R* to a mixture of 15 volumes of ether R and 77 volumes of *methylene chloride R*.

*Application* 5 µl.

*Development* Over a path of 15 cm.

*Drying* In air.

*Detection A* Examine in ultraviolet light at 254 nm.

*Results A* The principal spot in each of the chromatograms obtained with the test solutions is similar in position and size to the principal spot in the chromatogram obtained with the corresponding reference solution.

*Detection B* Spray with *alcoholic solution of sulphuric acid R*. Heat at 120 °C for 10 min or until the spots appear. Allow to cool. Examine in daylight and in ultraviolet light at 365 nm.

*Results B* The principal spot in each of the chromatograms obtained with the test solutions is similar in position, colour in daylight, fluorescence in ultraviolet light at 365 nm and size to the principal spot in the chromatogram obtained with the corresponding reference solution. The principal spots in the chromatograms obtained with test solution (b) and reference solution (b) have $R_F$ values distinctly lower than those of the principal spots in the chromatograms obtained with test solution (a) and reference solution (a).

D. Mix about 5 mg with 45 mg of *heavy magnesium oxide R* and ignite in a crucible until an almost white residue is obtained (usually less than 5 min). Allow to cool, add 1 ml of *water R*, 0.05 ml of *phenolphthalein solution R1* and about 1 ml of *dilute hydrochloric acid R* to render the solution colourless. Filter and add to the filtrate a freshly prepared mixture of 0.1 ml of *alizarin S solution R* and 0.1 ml of *zirconyl nitrate solution R*. Mix, allow to stand for 5 min and compare the colour of the solution with that of a blank prepared in the same manner. The colour of the solution to be examined changes from red to yellow.

E. About 10 mg gives the reaction of acetyl (*2.3.1*).

## TESTS

**Specific optical rotation** (*2.2.7*)
+ 148 to + 156 (dried substance).

Dissolve 0.250 g in *dioxan R* and dilute to 25.0 ml with the same solvent.

**Related substances**
Liquid chromatography (*2.2.29*).

*Test solution* Dissolve 20.0 mg of the substance to be examined in the mobile phase and dilute to 10.0 ml with the mobile phase.

*Reference solution (a)* Dissolve 2.0 mg of *fludrocortisone acetate CRS* and 2.0 mg of *hydrocortisone acetate CRS* in the mobile phase, then dilute to 50.0 ml with the mobile phase.

*Reference solution (b)* Dilute 1.0 ml of the test solution to 50.0 ml with the mobile phase.

*Column:*
— *size: l* = 0.2 m, Ø = 4.6 mm;
— *stationary phase: octadecylsilyl silica gel for chromatography R*.

*Mobile phase* tetrahydrofuran R, water R (35:65 *V/V*).

*Flow rate* 1 ml/min.

*Detection* Spectrophotometer at 254 nm.

*Equilibration* With the mobile phase for about 30 min.

*Injection* 20 µl.

*Run time* Twice the retention time of fludrocortisone acetate.

*Retention time* Hydrocortisone acetate = about 8.5 min; fludrocortisone acetate = about 10 min.

*System suitability* Reference solution (a):
— *resolution*: minimum 1.0 between the peaks due to hydrocortisone acetate and fludrocortisone acetate; if necessary, adjust slightly the concentration of tetrahydrofuran in the mobile phase (an increase in the concentration of tetrahydrofuran reduces the retention times).

*Limits:*
— *any impurity*: for each impurity, not more than 0.5 times the area of the principal peak in the chromatogram obtained with reference solution (b) (1.0 per cent);
— *total*: not more than 0.75 times the area of the principal peak in the chromatogram obtained with reference solution (b) (1.5 per cent);
— *disregard limit*: 0.025 times the area of the principal peak in the chromatogram obtained with reference solution (b) (0.05 per cent).

**Loss on drying** (*2.2.32*)
Maximum 1.0 per cent, determined on 0.500 g by drying in an oven at 105 °C.

## ASSAY

Dissolve 10.0 mg in *ethanol (96 per cent) R* and dilute to 100.0 ml with the same solvent. Dilute 5.0 ml of this solution to 50.0 ml with *ethanol (96 per cent) R*. Measure the absorbance (*2.2.25*) at the absorption maximum at 238 nm.

Calculate the content of $C_{23}H_{31}FO_6$ taking the specific absorbance to be 405.

*Ph Eur*

# Flumazenil

(*Ph Eur monograph 1326*)

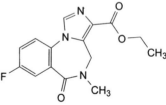

$C_{15}H_{14}FN_3O_3$        303.3        78755-81-4

**Action and use**
Benzodiazepine receptor antagonist.

*Ph Eur*

## DEFINITION

Ethyl 8-fluoro-5-methyl-6-oxo-5,6-dihydro-4*H*-imidazo[1,5-*a*][1,4]benzodiazepine-3-carboxylate.

## Content

99.0 per cent to 101.0 per cent (dried substance).

## CHARACTERS

**Appearance**
White or almost white, crystalline powder.

**Solubility**
Very slightly soluble in water, freely soluble in methylene chloride, sparingly soluble in methanol.

**mp**

198 °C to 202 °C.

## IDENTIFICATION

Infrared absorption spectrophotometry (*2.2.24*).

*Comparison* Ph. Eur. reference spectrum of flumazenil.

## TESTS

### Appearance of solution

The solution is clear (*2.2.1*) and is not more intensely coloured than reference solution $BY_7$ (*2.2.2, Method II*).

Dissolve 0.10 g in *methanol R* and dilute to 10 ml with the same solvent.

### Impurity C

Maximum 1 per cent.

Dissolve 0.10 g in 0.5 ml of *methylene chloride R* and dilute to 10 ml with *butanol R*. To 5.0 ml of this solution add 2.0 ml of *ninhydrin solution R* and heat in a water-bath at 95 °C for 15 min. Any blue-purple colour in the solution is not more intense than that in a standard prepared at the same time and in the same manner using 5.0 ml of a 0.1 g/l solution of *dimethylformamide diethylacetal R* in *butanol R*.

### Related substances

Liquid chromatography (*2.2.29*).

*Test solution* Dissolve 50.0 mg of the substance to be examined in 5 ml of *methanol R* and dilute to 25.0 ml with the mobile phase.

*Reference solution (a)* Dissolve 2.0 mg of *flumazenil impurity B CRS* and 2.0 mg of the substance to be examined in the mobile phase and dilute to 25.0 ml with the mobile phase. Dilute 2.0 ml of this solution to 25.0 ml with the mobile phase.

*Reference solution (b)* Dilute 10.0 ml of the test solution to 100.0 ml with the mobile phase. Dilute 1.0 ml of this solution to 100.0 ml with the mobile phase.

*Column:*
— *size: l* = 0.25 m, Ø = 4.6 mm,
— *stationary phase: end-capped octadecylsilyl silica gel for chromatography R* (5 µm).

*Mobile phase* To 800 ml of *water R* adjusted to pH 2.0 with *phosphoric acid R*, add 130 ml of *methanol R* and 70 ml of *tetrahydrofuran R* and mix.

*Flow rate* 1 ml/min.

*Detection* Spectrophotometer at 230 nm.

*Injection* 20 µl.

*Run time* 3 times the retention time of flumazenil.

*Relative retention* With reference to flumazenil (retention time = about 14 min): impurity A = about 0.4; impurity D = about 0.5; impurity E = about 0.6; impurity B = about 0.7; impurity F = about 2.4.

*System suitability* Reference solution (a):
— *resolution*: minimum 3.0 between the peaks due to impurity B and flumazenil.

*Limits:*
— *impurity B*: not more than twice the area of the principal peak in the chromatogram obtained with reference solution (b) (0.2 per cent),
— *any other impurity*: for each impurity, not more than the area of the principal peak in the chromatogram obtained with reference solution (b) (0.1 per cent),
— *total*: not more than twice the area of the principal peak in the chromatogram obtained with reference solution (b) (0.2 per cent),

— *disregard limit*: 0.5 times the area of the principal peak in the chromatogram obtained with reference solution (b) (0.05 per cent).

### Loss on drying (*2.2.32*)

Maximum 0.5 per cent, determined on 1.000 g by drying in an oven at 105 °C.

### Sulphated ash (*2.4.14*)

Maximum 0.1 per cent, determined on 1.0 g in a platinum crucible.

## ASSAY

Dissolve 0.250 g in 50 ml of a mixture of 2 volumes of *acetic anhydride R* and 3 volumes of *anhydrous acetic acid R*. Titrate with *0.1 M perchloric acid*, determining the end-point potentiometrically (*2.2.20*).

1 ml of *0.1 M perchloric acid* is equivalent to 30.33 mg of $C_{15}H_{14}FN_3O_3$.

## IMPURITIES

*Specified impurities* B, C.

*Other detectable impurities* (the following substances would, if present at a sufficient level, be detected by one or other of the tests in the monograph. They are limited by the general acceptance criterion for other/unspecified impurities and/or by the general monograph *Substances for pharmaceutical use* (2034). It is therefore not necessary to identify these impurities for demonstration of compliance. See also *5.10*. *Control of impurities in substances for pharmaceutical use*) : A, D, E, F.

A. R = H, R′ = F: 8-fluoro-5-methyl-6-oxo-5,6-dihydro-*4H*-imidazo[1,5-*a*][1,4]benzodiazepine-3-carboxylic acid,

B. R = $C_2$-$H_5$, R′ = OH: ethyl 8-hydroxy-5-methyl-6-oxo-5,6-dihydro-*4H*-imidazo[1,5-*a*][1,4]benzodiazepine-3-carboxylate,

E. R = $C_2H_5$, R′ = H: ethyl 5-methyl-6-oxo-5,6-dihydro-*4H*-imidazo[1,5-*a*][1,4]benzodiazepine-3-carboxylate,

F. R = $C_2H_5$, R′ = Cl: ethyl 8-chloro-5-methyl-6-oxo-5,6-dihydro-*4H*-imidazo[1,5-*a*][1,4]benzodiazepine-3-carboxylate,

C. diethoxy-*N,N*-dimethylmethanamine,

D. 7-fluoro-4-methyl-3,4-dihydro-1*H*-1,4-benzodiazepine-2,5-dione.

# Flumequine

*(Ph Eur monograph 1517)*

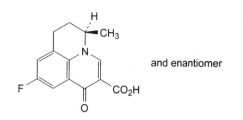

and enantiomer

C₁₄H₁₂FNO₃     261.3     42835-25-6

$C_{14}H_{12}FNO_3$     261.3     42835-25-6

## Action and use

Antibacterial.

*Ph Eur*

## DEFINITION

(*RS*)-9-Fluoro-5-methyl-1-oxo-6,7-dihydro-1*H*,5*H*-benzo[*i,j*]quinolizine-2-carboxylic acid.

## Content

99.0 per cent to 101.0 per cent (dried substance).

## CHARACTERS

### Appearance

White or almost white, microcrystalline powder.

### Solubility

Practically insoluble in water, sparingly soluble in methylene chloride, very slightly soluble in methanol. It is freely soluble in dilute solutions of alkali hydroxides.

## IDENTIFICATION

*First identification*   A, B.

*Second identification*   B, C, D.

A. Infrared absorption spectrophotometry (*2.2.24*).

*Comparison*   flumequine CRS.

B. Optical rotation (see Tests).

C. Thin-layer chromatography (*2.2.27*).

*Test solution*   Dissolve 5 mg of the substance to be examined in 10 ml of *methylene chloride R*.

*Reference solution*   Dissolve 5 mg of *flumequine CRS* in 10 ml of *methylene chloride R*.

*Plate*   TLC silica gel F₂₅₄ plate R.

*Mobile phase*   ammonia R, water R, ethanol (96 per cent) R (10:10:90 V/V/V).

*Application*   5 μl.

*Development*   Over a path of 15 cm.

*Drying*   In air.

*Detection*   Examine in ultraviolet light at 254 nm.

*Results*   The principal spot in the chromatogram obtained with the test solution is similar in position and size to the principal spot in the chromatogram obtained with the reference solution.

D. Mix about 5 mg with 45 mg of *heavy magnesium oxide R* and ignite in a crucible until an almost white residue is obtained (usually less than 5 min). Allow to cool, add 1 ml of *water R*, 0.05 ml of *phenolphthalein solution R1* and about 2 ml of *dilute hydrochloric acid R* to render the solution colourless. Filter and add to the filtrate a freshly prepared mixture of 0.1 ml of *alizarin S solution R* and 0.1 ml of *zirconyl nitrate solution R*. Mix, allow to stand for 5 min and compare the colour of the solution with that of a blank

prepared in the same manner. The test solution changes from red to yellow and the blank remains red.

## TESTS

### Solution S

Dissolve 5.00 g in *0.5 M sodium hydroxide* and dilute to 50.0 ml with the same solvent.

### Appearance of solution

Solution S is clear (*2.2.1*) and not more intensely coloured than reference solution BY₅ (*2.2.2, Method II*).

### Optical rotation (*2.2.7*)

− 0.10° to + 0.10°, determined on solution S.

### Related substances

Liquid chromatography (*2.2.29*).

*Test solution*   Dissolve 35.0 mg of the substance to be examined in *dimethylformamide R* and dilute to 100.0 ml with the same solvent.

*Reference solution (a)*   Dissolve the contents of a vial of *flumequine impurity B CRS* in 2.0 ml of a 50 μg/ml solution of *flumequine CRS* in *dimethylformamide R*.

*Reference solution (b)*   Dilute 1.0 ml of the test solution to 200.0 ml with *dimethylformamide R*.

*Column:*
— *size: l* = 0.15 m, Ø = 4.6 mm;
— *stationary phase: octadecylsilyl silica gel for chromatography R* (5 μm).

*Mobile phase*   methanol R, 1.36 g/l solution of *potassium dihydrogen phosphate R* (49:51 V/V).

*Flow rate*   0.8 ml/min.

*Detection*   Spectrophotometer at 313 nm.

*Injection*   10 μl; inject *dimethylformamide R* as a blank.

*Run time*   3 times the retention time of flumequine.

*Relative retention*   With reference to flumequine (retention time = about 13 min): impurity A = about 0.67; impurity B = about 0.85.

*System suitability:*   Reference solution (a):
— *resolution*: minimum 2.0 between the peaks due to impurity B and flumequine.

*Limits:*
— *impurities A, B*: for each impurity, not more than the area of the principal peak in the chromatogram obtained with reference solution (b) (0.5 per cent);
— *total*: not more than twice the area of the principal peak in the chromatogram obtained with reference solution (b) (1 per cent);
— *disregard limit*: 0.1 times the area of the principal peak in the chromatogram obtained with reference solution (b) (0.05 per cent).

### Heavy metals (*2.4.8*)

Maximum 10 ppm.

2.0 g complies with test C. Prepare the reference solution using 2 ml of *lead standard solution (10 ppm Pb) R*.

### Loss on drying (*2.2.32*)

Maximum 0.5 per cent, determined on 1.000 g by drying in an oven at 105 °C for 3 h.

### Sulphated ash (*2.4.14*)

Maximum 0.1 per cent, determined on 1.0 g in a platinum crucible.

## ASSAY

Dissolve 0.500 g in 50 ml of *dimethylformamide R*. Titrate with *0.1 M tetrabutylammonium hydroxide*, determining the end-point potentiometrically (*2.2.20*).

1 ml of *0.1 M tetrabutylammonium hydroxide* is equivalent to 26.13 mg of $C_{14}H_{12}FNO_3$.

## IMPURITIES

*Specified impurities   A, B.*

and enantiomer

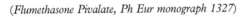

A. R = R′ = H: (*RS*)-5-methyl-1-oxo-6,7-dihydro-1*H*,5*H*-benzo[*i,j*]quinolizine-2-carboxylic acid (defluoroflumequine),

B. R = C₂H₅, R′ = F: ethyl (*RS*)-9-fluoro-5-methyl-1-oxo-6,7-dihydro-1*H*,5*H*-benzo[*i,j*]quinolizine-2-carboxylate (flumequine ethyl ester).

*Ph Eur*

# Flumetasone Pivalate

(*Flumethasone Pivalate, Ph Eur monograph 1327*)

$C_{27}H_{36}F_2O_6$          494.6          *2002-29-1*

## Action and use
Glucocorticoid.

*Ph Eur*

## DEFINITION
6α,9-Difluoro-11β,17-dihydroxy-16α-methyl-3,20-dioxopregna-1,4-dien-21-yl 2,2-dimethylpropanoate.

## Content
97.0 per cent to 103.0 per cent (dried substance).

## CHARACTERS
### Appearance
White or almost white, crystalline powder.

### Solubility
Practically insoluble in water, sparingly soluble in acetone, slightly soluble in ethanol (96 per cent) and in methylene chloride.

It shows polymorphism (*5.9*).

## IDENTIFICATION
*First identification   A, B.*

*Second identification   B, C, D.*

A. Infrared absorption spectrophotometry (*2.2.24*).

*Comparison   flumetasone pivalate CRS.*

If the spectra obtained in the solid state show differences, dissolve the substance to be examined and the reference

substance separately in *acetone R*, evaporate to dryness on a water-bath and record new spectra using the residues.

B. Thin-layer chromatography (*2.2.27*).

*Test solution*   Dissolve 10 mg of the substance to be examined in *acetone R* and dilute to 10 ml with the same solvent.

*Reference solution (a)*   Dissolve 10 mg of *flumetasone pivalate CRS* in *acetone R* and dilute to 10 ml with the same solvent.

*Reference solution (b)*   Dissolve 10 mg of *desoxycortone acetate CRS* in *acetone R* and dilute to 10 ml with the same solvent. Dilute 5 ml of this solution to 10 ml with reference solution (a).

*Plate*   *TLC silica gel F₂₅₄ plate R.*

*Mobile phase*   Add a mixture of 1.2 volumes of *water R* and 8 volumes of *methanol R* to a mixture of 15 volumes of *ether R* and 77 volumes of *methylene chloride R*.

*Application*   5 µl.

*Development*   Over a path of 15 cm.

*Drying*   In air.

*Detection A*   Examine in ultraviolet light at 254 nm.

*Results A*   The principal spot in the chromatogram obtained with the test solution is similar in position and size to the principal spot in the chromatogram obtained with reference solution (a).

*Detection B*   Spray with *alcoholic solution of sulphuric acid R*. Heat at 120 °C for 10 min or until the spots appear. Allow to cool. Examine in daylight and in ultraviolet light at 365 nm.

*Results B*   The principal spot in the chromatogram obtained with the test solution is similar in position, colour in daylight, fluorescence in ultraviolet light at 365 nm and size to the principal spot in the chromatogram obtained with reference solution (a).

*System suitability*   Reference solution (b):
— the chromatogram shows 2 clearly separated spots.

C. Add about 2 mg to 2 ml of a mixture of 0.5 ml of *water R* and 1.5 ml of *sulphuric acid R* and shake to dissolve. Within 5 min, a pink colour develops. Add this solution to 10 ml of *water R* and mix. The colour fades and a clear solution remains.

D. Mix about 5 mg with 45 mg of *heavy magnesium oxide R* and ignite in a crucible until an almost white residue is obtained (usually less than 5 min). Allow to cool, add 1 ml of *water R*, 0.05 ml of *phenolphthalein solution R1* and about 1 ml of *dilute hydrochloric acid R* to render the solution colourless. Filter. To a freshly prepared mixture of 0.1 ml of *alizarin S solution R* and 0.1 ml of *zirconyl nitrate solution R* add 1.0 ml of the filtrate. Mix, allow to stand for 5 min and compare the colour of the solution with that of a blank prepared in the same manner. The test solution is yellow and the blank is red.

## TESTS
### Solution S
Dissolve 0.50 g in *acetone R* and dilute to 25.0 ml with the same solvent.

### Appearance of solution
Solution S is clear (*2.2.1*) and not more intensely coloured than reference solution BY₆ (*2.2.2, Method II*).

### Specific optical rotation (*2.2.7*)
+ 69 to + 77 (dried substance), determined on solution S.

## Related substances

Liquid chromatography (2.2.29).

*Test solution*   Dissolve 25.0 mg of the substance to be examined in the mobile phase and dilute to 25.0 ml with the mobile phase. Dilute 5.0 ml of this solution to 50.0 ml with the mobile phase.

*Reference solution (a)*   Dissolve 10 mg of *dexamethasone pivalate CRS* in the mobile phase and dilute to 100.0 ml with the mobile phase. To 5.0 ml of this solution, add 5.0 ml of the test solution, mix and dilute to 50.0 ml with the mobile phase.

*Reference solution (b)*   Dilute 2.0 ml of the test solution to 100.0 ml with the mobile phase.

*Column:*
— *size: l* = 0.25 m, Ø = 4.6 mm;
— *stationary phase: octadecylsilyl silica gel for chromatography R* (5 μm).

*Mobile phase*   tetrahydrofuran R, acetonitrile R, water R, methanol R (5:30:30:35 *V/V/V/V*).

*Flow rate*   0.6 ml/min.

*Detection*   Spectrophotometer at 254 nm.

*Injection*   20 μl.

*Run time*   1.5 times the retention time of flumetasone pivalate.

*Relative retention*   With reference to flumetasone pivalate: impurity C = about 1.1.

*System suitability*   Reference solution (a):
— *resolution*: minimum 2.8 between the peaks due to flumetasone pivalate and impurity C; if necessary, adjust the concentration of tetrahydrofuran in the mobile phase.

*Limits:*
— *impurities A, B, C, D*: for each impurity, not more than 0.75 times the area of the principal peak in the chromatogram obtained with reference solution (b) (1.5 per cent);
— *total*: not more than the area of the principal peak in the chromatogram obtained with reference solution (b) (2 per cent);
— *disregard limit*: 0.025 times the area of the principal peak in the chromatogram obtained with reference solution (b) (0.05 per cent).

## Loss on drying (2.2.32)

Maximum 1.0 per cent, determined on 0.500 g by drying in an oven at 105 °C for 4 h.

## ASSAY

Dissolve 50.0 mg in *ethanol (96 per cent) R* and dilute to 100.0 ml with the same solvent. Dilute 2.0 ml of this solution to 100.0 ml with *ethanol (96 per cent) R*. Measure the absorbance (2.2.25) at the absorption maximum at 239 nm.

Calculate the content of $C_{27}H_{36}F_2O_6$ taking the specific absorbance to be 336.

## STORAGE

Protected from light.

## IMPURITIES

*Specified impurities    A, B, C, D.*

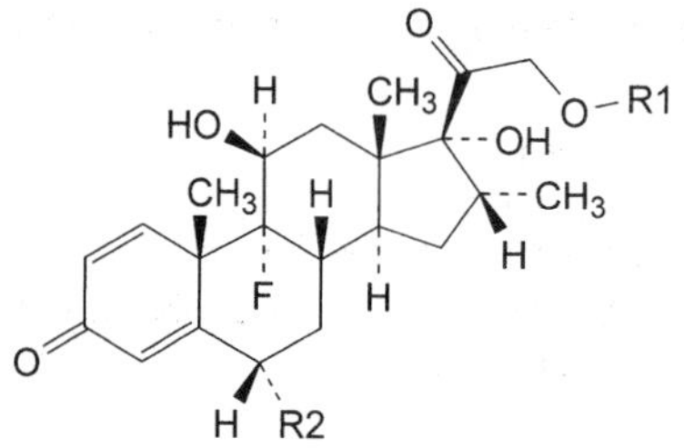

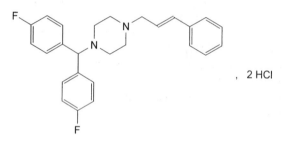

A. R1 = H, R2 = F: 6α,9-difluoro-11β,17,21-trihydroxy-16α-methylpregna-1,4-diene-3,20-dione (flumetasone),

B. R1 = CO-CH₃, R2 = F: 6α,9-difluoro-11β,17-dihydroxy-16α-methyl-3,20-dioxopregna-1,4-dien-21-yl acetate (flumetasone acetate),

C. R1 = CO-C(CH₃)₃, R2 = H: 9-fluoro-11β,17-dihydroxy-16α-methyl-3,20-dioxopregna-1,4-dien-21-yl 2,2-dimethylpropanoate (dexamethasone pivalate),

D. R1 = CO-C(CH₃)₃, R2 = Cl: 6α-chloro-9-fluoro-11β,17-dihydroxy-16α-methyl-3,20-dioxopregna-1,4-dien-21-yl 2,2-dimethylpropanoate (chlordexamethasone pivalate).

*_____ Ph Eur*

# Flunarizine Dihydrochloride

(*Ph Eur monograph 1722*)

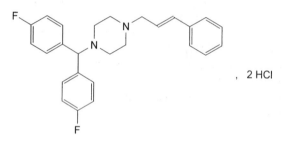

, 2 HCl

$C_{26}H_{28}Cl_2F_2N_2$          477.4          *30484-77-6*

## Action and use

Calcium channel blocker.

*Ph Eur _____*

## DEFINITION

1-[Bis(4-fluorophenyl)methyl]-4-[(2E)-3-phenylprop-2-enyl]piperazine dihydrochloride.

## Content

99.0 per cent to 101.5 per cent (dried substance).

## CHARACTERS

### Appearance

White or almost white powder, hygroscopic.

### Solubility

Slightly soluble in water, sparingly soluble in methanol, slightly soluble in alcohol and in methylene chloride.

### mp

About 208 °C, with decomposition.

## IDENTIFICATION

A. Infrared absorption spectrophotometry (2.2.24).

*Comparison* Ph. Eur. *reference spectrum of flunarizine dihydrochloride* .

B. Dissolve 25 mg in 2 ml of *methanol R* and add 0.5 ml of *water R*. The solution gives reaction (a) of chlorides (*2.3.1*).

## TESTS

### Related substances

Liquid chromatography (*2.2.29*). *Prepare the solutions immediately before use and protect from light.*

*Test solution* Dissolve 0.100 g of the substance to be examined in *methanol R* and dilute to 10.0 ml with the same solvent.

*Reference solution (a)* Dissolve 10 mg of *flunarizine dihydrochloride for system suitability CRS* in *methanol R* and dilute to 1.0 ml with the same solvent.

*Reference solution (b)* Dilute 1.0 ml of the test solution to 100.0 ml with *methanol R*. Dilute 5.0 ml of this solution to 20.0 ml with *methanol R*.

*Column:*
— *size: l* = 0.10 m, Ø = 4.6 mm,
— *stationary phase: base-deactivated octadecylsilyl silica gel for chromatography R* (3 µm).

*Mobile phase:*
— *mobile phase A*: solution containing 23.8 g/l of *tetrabutylammonium hydrogen sulphate R* and 7 g/l of *ammonium acetate R*,
— *mobile phase B*: *acetonitrile R*,

| Time (min) | Mobile phase A (per cent *V/V*) | Mobile phase B (per cent *V/V*) |
|---|---|---|
| 0 - 12 | 80 → 40 | 20 → 60 |
| 12 - 15 | 40 | 60 |
| 15 - 16 | 40 → 80 | 60 → 20 |
| 16 - 20 | 80 | 20 |

*Flow rate* 1.5 ml/min.

*Detection* Spectrophotometer at 230 nm.

*Injection* 10 µl.

*System suitability* Reference solution (a):
— *peak-to-valley ratio*: minimum 1.5, where $H_p$ = height above the baseline of the peak due to impurity C and $H_v$ = height above the baseline of the lowest point of the curve separating this peak from the peak due to flunarizine,
— the chromatogram obtained is concordant with the chromatogram supplied with *flunarizine dihydrochloride for system suitability CRS* .

*Limits:*
— *correction factor*: for the calculation of content, multiply the peak area of impurity A by 1.5,
— *impurities A, D*: for each impurity, not more than 0.4 times the area of the principal peak in the chromatogram obtained with reference solution (b) (0.1 per cent),
— *impurity B*: not more than twice the area of the principal peak in the chromatogram obtained with reference solution (b) (0.5 per cent),
— *impurity C*: not more than the area of the principal peak in the chromatogram obtained with reference solution (b) (0.25 per cent),
— *any other impurity*: for each impurity, not more than 0.4 times the area of the principal peak in the chromatogram obtained with reference solution (b) (0.1 per cent),

— *total*: not more than 4 times the area of the principal peak in the chromatogram obtained with reference solution (b) (1.0 per cent),
— *disregard limit*: 0.2 times the area of the principal peak in the chromatogram obtained with reference solution (b) (0.05 per cent).

### Loss on drying (*2.2.32*)

Maximum 5.0 per cent, determined on 1.000 g by drying in an oven at 105 °C for 4 h.

### Sulphated ash (*2.4.14*)

Maximum 0.1 per cent, determined on 1.0 g in a platinum crucible.

## ASSAY

Dissolve 0.200 g in 70 ml of *alcohol R*. Carry out a potentiometric titration (*2.2.20*), using *0.1 M sodium hydroxide*. Read the volume added at the second point of inflexion. Carry out a blank titration.

1 ml of *0.1 M sodium hydroxide* is equivalent to 23.87 mg of $C_{26}H_{28}Cl_2F_2N_2$.

## STORAGE

In an airtight container, protected from light.

## IMPURITIES

*Specified impurities* A, B, C, D.

A. 1-[bis(4-fluorophenyl)methyl]piperazine,

and enantiomer

B. R1 = R2 = R3 = H, R4 = $C_6H_5$:
1-[(*RS*)-(4-fluorophenyl)phenylmethyl]-4-[(2*E*)-3-phenylprop-2-enyl]piperazine,

C. R1 = F, R2 = R3 = H, R4 = $C_6H_5$:
1-[(*RS*)-(2-fluorophenyl)(4-fluorophenyl)methyl]-4-[(2*E*)-3-phenylprop-2-enyl]piperazine,

D. R1 = R4 = H, R2 = F, R3 = $C_6H_5$:
1-[bis(4-fluorophenyl)methyl]-4-[(2*Z*)-3-phenylprop-2-enyl]piperazine.

*Ph Eur*

# Flunitrazepam

*(Ph Eur monograph 0717)*

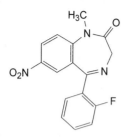

C₁₆H₁₂FN₃O₃      313.3      *1622-62-4*

**Action and use**

Benzodiazepine.

*Ph Eur* ___

## DEFINITION

5-(2-Fluorophenyl)-1-methyl-7-nitro-1,3-dihydro-2*H*-1,4-benzodiazepin-2-one.

### Content

99.0 per cent to 101.0 per cent (dried substance).

## CHARACTERS

### Appearance

White or yellowish, crystalline powder.

### Solubility

Practically insoluble in water, soluble in acetone, slightly soluble in alcohol.

## IDENTIFICATION

Infrared absorption spectrophotometry (*2.2.24*).

*Comparison* Ph. Eur. reference spectrum of flunitrazepam.

## TESTS

### Related substances

Liquid chromatography (*2.2.29*). *Prepare the solutions immediately before use.*

*Test solution* Dissolve 100.0 mg of the substance to be examined in 10 ml of *acetonitrile R* and dilute to 50.0 ml with the mobile phase.

*Reference solution (a)* Dilute 1.0 ml of the test solution to 100.0 ml with the mobile phase. Dilute 5.0 ml of this solution to 50.0 ml with the mobile phase.

*Reference solution (b)* Dissolve 4 mg of the substance to be examined and 4 mg of *nitrazepam R* in 5 ml of *acetonitrile R* and dilute to 20.0 ml with the mobile phase. Dilute 1.0 ml of the solution to 20.0 ml with the mobile phase.

*Column:*
— *size*: *l* = 0.15 m, Ø = 4.6 mm,
— *stationary phase*: octadecylsilyl silica gel for chromatography R (5 μm).

*Mobile phase* methanol R, acetonitrile R, water R (50:305:645 *V/V/V*).

*Flow rate* 1.0 ml/min.

*Detection* Spectrophotometer at 254 nm.

*Injection* 20 μl.

*Run time* 6 times the retention time of flunitrazepam.

*Relative retention* With reference to flunitrazepam (retention time = about 11 min): impurity A = about 0.2; impurity B = about 0.6; impurity C = about 2.3; impurity D = about 4.0.

*System suitability* Reference solution (b):
— *resolution*: minimum 4.0 between the peaks due to nitrazepam and flunitrazepam.

*Limits:*
— *correction factor*: for the calculation of content, multiply the peak area of impurity C by 2.44,
— *any impurity*: not more than the area of the principal peak in the chromatogram obtained with reference solution (a) (0.1 per cent),
— *total*: not more than 3 times the area of the principal peak in the chromatogram obtained with reference solution (a) (0.3 per cent),
— *disregard limit*: 0.5 times the area of the principal peak in the chromatogram obtained with reference solution (a) (0.05 per cent).

**Loss on drying** (*2.2.32*)

Maximum 0.5 per cent, determined on 1.000 g by drying in an oven at 105 °C.

**Sulphated ash** (*2.4.14*)

Maximum 0.1 per cent, determined on 1.0 g.

## ASSAY

Dissolve 0.250 g in 20 ml of *anhydrous acetic acid R* and add 50 ml of *acetic anhydride R*. Titrate with *0.1 M perchloric acid*, determining the end-point potentiometrically (*2.2.20*).

1 ml of *0.1 M perchloric acid* is equivalent to 31.33 mg of C₁₆H₁₂FN₃O₃.

## STORAGE

Protected from light.

## IMPURITIES

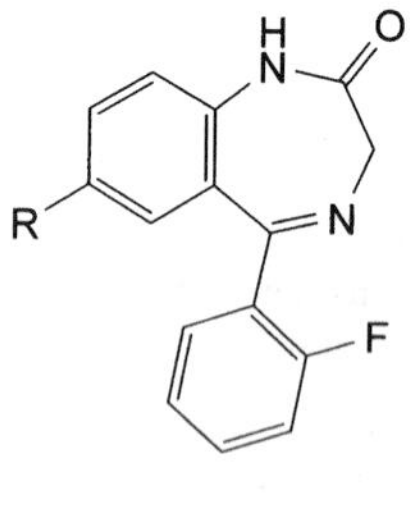

A. R = NH₂: 7-amino-5-(2-fluorophenyl)-1,3-dihydro-2*H*-1,4-benzodiazepin-2-one (7-aminodemethylflunitrazepam),

B. R = NO₂: 5-(2-fluorophenyl)-7-nitro-1,3-dihydro-2*H*-1,4-benzodiazepin-2-one (demethylflunitrazepam),

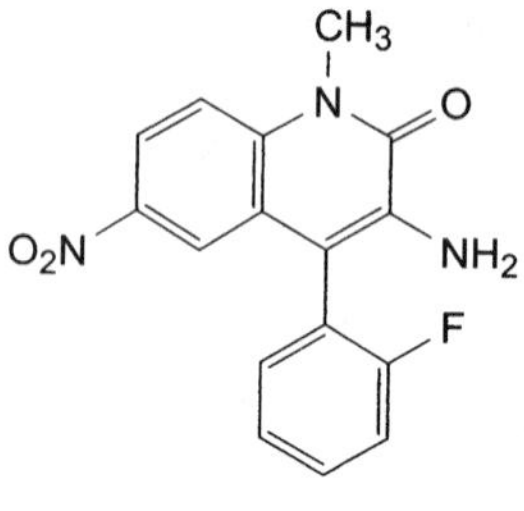

C. 3-amino-4-(2-fluorophenyl)-1-methyl-6-nitroquinolin-2(1*H*)-one,

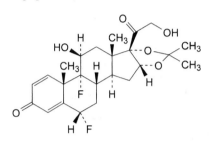

D. (2-fluorophenyl)[2-(methylamino)-5-nitrophenyl]methanone.

*Ph Eur*

# Fluocinolone Acetonide

(*Ph Eur monograph 0494*)

$C_{24}H_{30}F_2O_6$     452.5     67-73-2

### Action and use
Glucocorticoid.

### Preparations
Fluocinolone Cream

Fluocinolone Ointment

*Ph Eur*

## DEFINITION
6α,9-Difluoro-11β,21-dihydroxy-16α,17-(1-methylethylidenedioxy)pregna-1,4-diene-3,20-dione.

### Content
97.0 per cent to 103.0 per cent (dried substance).

## CHARACTERS
### Appearance
White or almost white, crystalline powder.

### Solubility
Practically insoluble in water, soluble in acetone and in ethanol.

It shows polymorphism (*5.9*).

## IDENTIFICATION
A. Infrared absorption spectrophotometry (*2.2.24*).

*Comparison* fluocinolone acetonide CRS.

If the spectra obtained in the solid state show differences, dissolve the substance to be examined and the reference substance separately in *ethanol R*, evaporate to dryness and record new spectra using the residues.

B. Examine the chromatograms obtained in the test for related substances.

*Results* The principal peak in the chromatogram obtained with the reference solution (b) is similar in retention time to the peak due to *fluocinolone acetonide CRS* in the chromatogram obtained with the reference solution (a).

## TESTS
### Specific optical rotation (*2.2.7*)
+ 100 to + 104 (dried substance).

Dissolve 0.100 g in *ethanol R* and dilute to 10.0 ml with the same solvent.

### Related substances
Liquid chromatography (*2.2.29*). *Carry out the test protected from light.*

*Test solution* Dissolve 25.0 mg of the substance to be examined in *acetonitrile R* and dilute to 10.0 ml with the same solvent.

*Reference solution (a)* Dissolve 2.5 mg of *fluocinolone acetonide CRS* and 2.5 mg of *triamcinolone acetonide R* in 45 ml of *acetonitrile R* and dilute to 100.0 ml with *water R*.

*Reference solution (b)* Dilute 1.0 ml of the test solution to 100.0 ml with *acetonitrile R*.

*Column:*
— *size: l* = 0.25 m, Ø = 4.6 mm,
— *stationary phase: base-deactivated end-capped octadecylsilyl silica gel for chromatography R* (5 μm).

*Mobile phase* Mix 450 ml of *acetonitrile R* with 500 ml of *water R* and allow to equilibrate; adjust the volume to 1000.0 ml with *water R* and mix again.

*Flow rate* 1 ml/min.

*Detection* Spectrophotometer at 238 nm.

*Injection* 20 μl.

*Run time* 4 times the retention time of fluocinolone acetonide.

*Retention times* Triamcinolone acetonide = about 8.5 min; fluocinolone acetonide = about 10 min.

*System suitability:*
— *resolution:* minimum of 3.0 between the peaks due to triamcinolone acetonide and fluocinolone acetonide in the chromatogram obtained with reference solution (a).

*Limits:*
— *any impurity:* not more than the area of the principal peak in the chromatogram obtained with reference solution (b) (1 per cent) and not more than 1 such peak has an area greater than half the area of the principal peak in the chromatogram obtained with reference solution (b) (0.5 per cent),
— *total:* not more than 2.5 times the area of the principal peak in the chromatogram obtained with reference solution (b) (2.5 per cent),
— *disregard limit:* 0.05 times the area of the principal peak in the chromatogram obtained with reference solution (b) (0.05 per cent).

### Loss on drying (*2.2.32*)
Maximum 1.0 per cent, determined on 1.000 g by drying in an oven at 105 °C for 3 h.

## ASSAY
*Protect the solutions from light throughout the assay.*

Dissolve 50.0 mg in *alcohol R* and dilute to 50.0 ml with the same solvent. Dilute 2.0 ml of this solution to 100.0 ml with *alcohol R*. Measure the absorbance (*2.2.25*) at the maximum at 238 nm.

Calculate the content of $C_{24}H_{30}F_2O_6$ taking the specific absorbance to be 355.

## STORAGE
Protected from light.

**IMPURITIES**

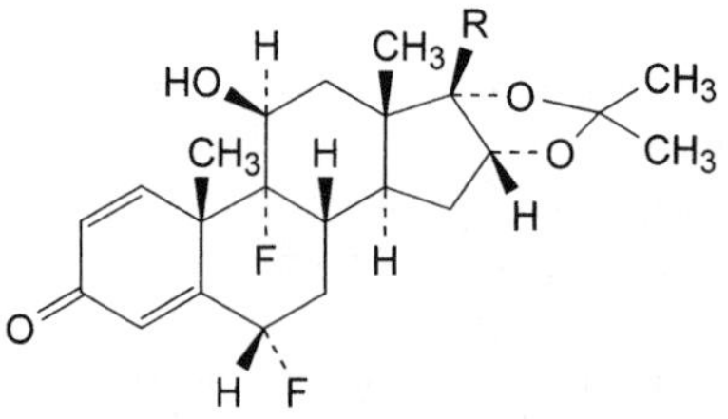

A. R = CO-CO₂H: 6α,9-difluoro-11β-hydroxy-16α,17-(1-methylethylidenedioxy)-3,20-dioxopregna-1,4-dien-21-oic acid,

B. R = CO₂H: 6α,9-difluoro-11β-hydroxy-16α,17-(1-methylethylidenedioxy)-3-oxoandrosta-1,4-diene-17β-carboxylic acid,

D. R = CO-CH=O: 6α,9-difluoro-11β-hydroxy-16α,17-(1-methylethylidenedioxy)-3,20-dioxopregna-1,4-dien-21-al,

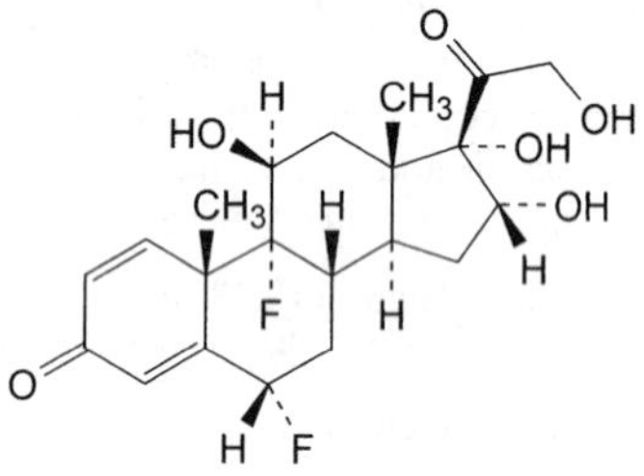

C. 6α,9-difluoro-11β,16α,17,21-tetrahydroxypregna-1,4-diene-3,20-dione (fluocinolone),

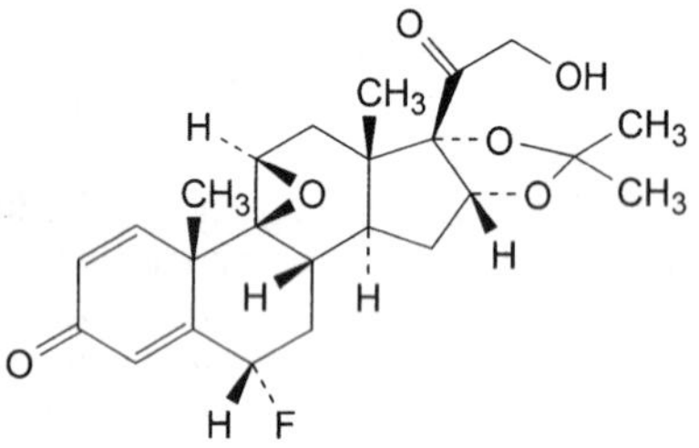

E. 9,11β-epoxy-6α-fluoro-21-hydroxy-16α,17-(1-methylethylidenedioxy)-9β-pregna-1,4-diene-3,20-dione,

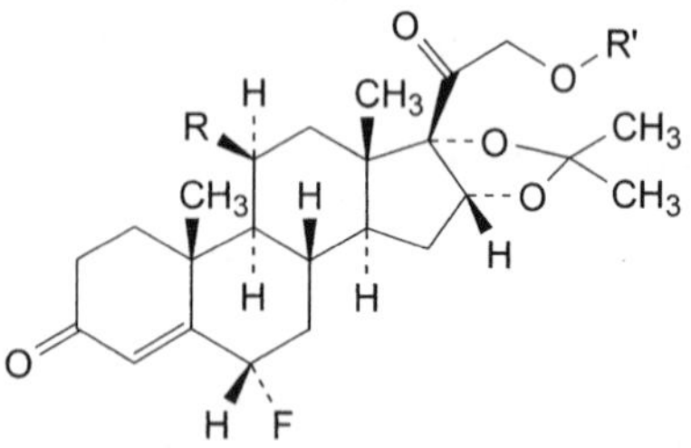

F. R = R′ = H: 6α-fluoro-21-hydroxy-16α,17-(1-methylethylidenedioxy)pregn-4-ene-3,20-dione,

G. R = OH, R′ = CO-CH₃: 6α-fluoro-11β-hydroxy-16α,17-(1-methylethylidenedioxy)-3,20-dioxopregn-4-en-21-yl acetate.

*Ph Eur*

# Fluocinolone Acetonide Dihydrate

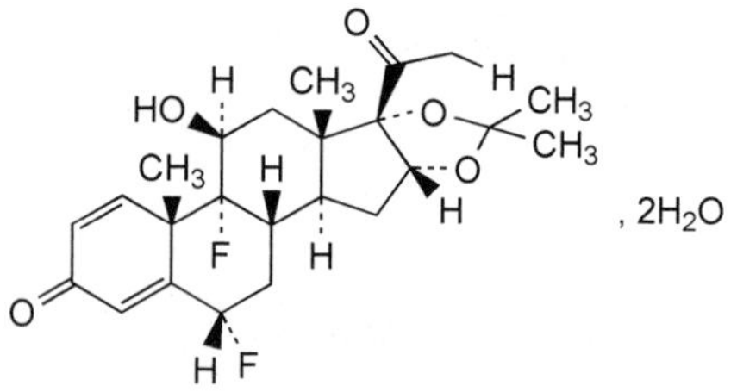

C₂₄H₃₀F₂O₆,2H₂O          488.5          67-73-2

*(anhydrous)*

**Action and use**

Glucocorticoid.

**Preparations**

Fluocinolone Cream

Fluocinolone Ointment

**DEFINITION**

Fluocinolone Acetonide Dihydrate is 6α,9α-difluoro-11β,21-dihydroxy-16α-,17α-isopropylidenedioxypregna-1,4-diene-3,20-dione dihydrate. It contains not less than 96.0% and not more than 104.0% of C₂₄H₃₀F₂O₆, calculated with reference to the anhydrous substance.

**CHARACTERISTICS**

A white or almost white, crystalline powder.

Practically insoluble in *water*; freely soluble in *acetone*; soluble in *absolute ethanol*; sparingly soluble in *dichloromethane* and in *methanol*; practically insoluble in *hexane*.

**IDENTIFICATION**

A. The *infrared absorption spectrum*, Appendix II A, is concordant with the *reference spectrum* of fluocinolone acetonide dihydrate *(RS 147)*.

B. Complies with the test for *identification of steroids*, Appendix III A, using *impregnating solvent I* and *mobile phase H*. Apply 5 μl of each of the three solutions.

C. Complies with the test for *identification of steroids*, Appendix III A, using the conditions specified in test B but using solutions prepared in the following manner. For solution (1) dissolve 10 mg in 1.5 ml of *glacial acetic acid* in a separating funnel, add 0.5 ml of a 2% w/v solution of *chromium(VI) oxide* and allow to stand for 30 minutes. Add 5 ml of *water* and 2 ml of *dichloromethane* and shake vigorously for 2 minutes. Allow to separate and use the lower layer. Prepare solution (2) in the same manner but using 10 mg of *fluocinolone acetonide EPCRS*.

**TESTS**

**Light absorption**

Dissolve 15 mg in sufficient *absolute ethanol* to produce 100 ml. Dilute 10 ml of the solution to 100 ml with *absolute ethanol*. The A(1%, 1 cm) of the resulting solution at the maximum at 239 nm is 345 to 375, calculated with reference to the anhydrous substance, Appendix II B.

**Specific optical rotation**

In a 1% w/v solution in *1,4-dioxan*, +92 to +96, calculated with reference to the anhydrous substance, Appendix V F.

**Related substances**

Carry out the method for *liquid chromatography*, Appendix III D, using the following solutions.

(1) 0.25% w/v of the substance being examined in *acetonitrile*.

(2) 0.025% w/v each of *fluocinolone acetonide BPCRS* and *triamcinolone acetonide BPCRS* in 45% w/v of *acetonitrile*.

(3) Dilute 1 volume of solution (1) to 100 volumes with *acetonitrile*.

(4) Dilute 1 volume of solution (3) to 20 volumes with *acetonitrile*.

CHROMATOGRAPHIC CONDITIONS

(a) Use a stainless steel column (25 cm × 4.6 mm) packed with *base-deactivated end-capped octadecylsilyl silica gel for chromatography* (5 μm) (Hypersil BDS is suitable).

(b) Use isocratic elution and the mobile phase described below.

(c) Use a flow rate of 1 ml per minute.

(d) Use an ambient column temperature.

(e) Use a detection wavelength of 238 nm.

(f) Inject 20 μl of each solution.

(g) Allow the chromatography to proceed for 4 times the retention time of the principal peak.

MOBILE PHASE

45 volumes of *acetonitrile* and 55 volumes of *water*.

SYSTEM SUITABILITY

The test is not valid unless:

in the chromatogram obtained with solution (2), the *resolution factor* between the peaks due to triamcinolone acetonide and fluocinolone acetonide is at least 3.0;

in the chromatogram obtained with solution (4), the *signal-to-noise ratio* of the principal peak is at least 10.

LIMITS

In the chromatogram obtained with solution (1):

the area of any *secondary peak* is not greater than the area of the principal peak in the chromatogram obtained with solution (3) (1%);

the area of not more than one *secondary peak* is greater than 0.5 times the area of the principal peak in the chromatogram obtained with solution (3) (0.5%);

the sum of the areas of any *secondary peaks* is not greater than 2.5 times the area of the principal peak in the chromatogram obtained with solution (3) (2.5%).

Disregard any peak with an area less than the area of the principal peak in the chromatogram obtained with solution (4) (0.05%).

**Water**

7.0 to 8.5% w/w, Appendix IX C. Use 0.5 g.

**ASSAY**

Carry out the *tetrazolium assay of steroids*, Appendix VIII J, and calculate the content of $C_{24}H_{30}F_2O_6$ from the *absorbance* obtained by repeating the operation using *fluocinolone acetonide EPCRS* in place of the substance being examined.

**STORAGE**

Fluocinolone Acetonide Dihydrate should be protected from light.

# Fluocinonide

$C_{26}H_{32}F_2O_7$        494.5        *356-12-7*

**Action and use**

Glucocorticoid.

**Preparations**

Fluocinonide Cream

Fluocinonide Ointment

**DEFINITION**

Fluocinonide is 6α,9α-difluoro-11β-hydroxy-16α,17α-isopropylidenedioxy-3,20-dioxopregna-1,4-dien-21-yl acetate. It contains not less than 97.0% and not more than 103.0% of $C_{26}H_{32}F_2O_7$, calculated with reference to the dried substance.

**CHARACTERISTICS**

A white or almost white, crystalline powder.

Practically insoluble in *water*; slightly soluble in *absolute ethanol*. It melts at about 220°, with decomposition.

**IDENTIFICATION**

A. The *infrared absorption spectrum*, Appendix II A, is concordant with the *reference spectrum* of fluocinonide (RS 148).

B. Carry out the method for *thin-layer chromatography*, Appendix III A, using a silica gel $F_{254}$ precoated plate (Merck silica gel 60 $F_{254}$ plates are suitable) and a mixture of 12 volumes of *water*, 80 volumes of *methanol*, 150 volumes of *ether* and 770 volumes of *dichloromethane* as the mobile phase; mix the water and the methanol before adding to the remaining components of the mobile phase. Apply separately to the plate 5 μl of each of the following solutions. For solution (1) dissolve 25 mg of the substance being examined in 5 ml of *methanol* (solution A); dilute 2 ml of solution A to 10 ml with *chloroform*. For solution (2) transfer 2 ml of solution A to a 15 ml glass tube with a ground-glass stopper, add 10 ml of *saturated methanolic potassium hydrogen carbonate solution* and immediately pass a current of *nitrogen* briskly through the solution for 2 minutes. Stopper the tube, heat in a water bath at 45° protected from light for 2.5 hours and allow to cool. For solution (3) dissolve 25 mg of *fluocinonide BPCRS* in 5 ml of *methanol* (solution B); dilute 2 ml of solution B to 10 ml with *chloroform*. Prepare solution (4) in the same manner as solution (2) but use 2 ml of solution B in place of 2 ml of solution A. After removal of the plate, allow it to dry in air and examine under *ultraviolet light (254 nm)*. The principal spots in each of the chromatograms obtained with solutions (1) and (2) are similar in position and size to those in the chromatograms obtained with solutions (3) and (4), respectively.

## TESTS

### Specific optical rotation

In a 1.0% w/v solution in *chloroform*, +81 to +89, calculated with reference to the dried substance, Appendix V F.

### Related substances

Carry out the method for *thin-layer chromatography*, Appendix III A, using the precoated plate and the mobile phase specified in test B for Identification. Apply separately to the plate 5 μl of each of four solutions in *chloroform* containing (1) 0.50% w/v of the substance being examined, (2) 0.010% w/v of the substance being examined, (3) 0.0050% w/v of the substance being examined and (4) 0.010% w/v of *fluocinolone acetonide BPCRS*. After removal of the plate, allow it to dry in air, heat the plate at 105° for 10 minutes, cool and spray with *alkaline tetrazolium blue solution*. Any *secondary spot* in the chromatogram obtained with solution (1) is not more intense than the spot in the chromatogram obtained with solution (2) (2%) and not more than one such spot is more intense than the spot in the chromatogram obtained with solution (3) (1%). The test is not valid unless the principal spot in the chromatogram obtained with solution (2) has an $R_f$ value relative to the spot in the chromatogram obtained with solution (4) of at least 1.5.

### Loss on drying

When dried at 100° to 105° for 3 hours, loses not more than 1.0% of its weight. Use 1 g.

### ASSAY

Carry out the method for *liquid chromatography*, Appendix III D, using two solutions in *methanol* containing (1) 0.012% w/v of the substance being examined and (2) 0.012% w/v of *fluocinonide BPCRS*.

The chromatographic procedure may be carried out using (a) a stainless steel column (20 cm × 4.6 mm) packed with *octadecylsilyl silica gel for chromatography* (5 μm) (Spherisorb ODS 1 is suitable), (b) as the mobile phase with a flow rate of 1 ml per minute a mixture of 1 volume of *glacial acetic acid*, 450 volumes of *acetonitrile* and 550 volumes of *water* and (c) a detection wavelength of 238 nm.

Calculate the content of $C_{26}H_{32}F_2O_7$ using the declared content of $C_{26}H_{32}F_2O_7$ in *fluocinonide BPCRS*.

### STORAGE

Fluocinonide should be protected from light.

### IMPURITIES

A. 6α,9α-difluoro-16α,17α-isopropylidene-3,11,20-trioxopregna-1,4-dien-21-yl acetate,

B. 6α,9α-difluoro-11β,21-dihydroxy-16α,17α-isopropylidenepregna-1,4-diene-3,20dione.

# Fluocortolone Hexanoate

$C_{28}H_{39}FO_5$      474.6      *303-40-2*

### Action and use

Glucocorticoid.

### Preparation

Fluocortolone Cream

### DEFINITION

Fluocortolone Hexanoate is 6α-fluoro-11β-hydroxy-16α-methyl-3,20-dioxopregna-1,4-dien-21-yl hexanoate. It contains not less than 97.0% and not more than 103.0% of $C_{28}H_{39}FO_5$, calculated with reference to the dried substance.

### CHARACTERISTICS

A white or creamy white, crystalline powder.

Practically insoluble in *water* and in *ether*; slightly soluble in *acetone* and in *1,4-dioxan*; very slightly soluble in *ethanol (96%)* and in *methanol*.

It exhibits polymorphism.

### IDENTIFICATION

The *infrared absorption spectrum*, Appendix II A, is concordant with the *reference spectrum* of fluocortolone hexanoate *(RS 149)*.

### TESTS

### Light absorption

Ratio of the *absorbance* of the solution prepared as directed in the Assay at the maximum at 242 nm to that at 263 nm, 2.15 to 2.35, Appendix II B.

### Specific optical rotation

In a 1% w/v solution in *1,4-dioxan*, prepared with the aid of heat, +97 to +103, calculated with reference to the dried substance, Appendix V F.

### Related substances

Carry out the method for *liquid chromatography*, Appendix III D, using the following solutions. Solution (1) contains 0.04% w/v of the substance being examined in a mixture of 1 volume of *water* and 9 volumes of *acetonitrile*. For solution (2) dilute 1 volume of solution (1) to 100 volumes with a mixture of 1 volume of *water* and 9 volumes of *acetonitrile*. Solution (3) contains 0.002% w/v each of *fluocortolone pivalate BPCRS* and *fluocortolone hexanoate BPCRS* in a mixture of 1 volume of *water* and 9 volumes of *acetonitrile*.

The chromatographic procedure may be carried out using (a) a stainless steel column (25 cm × 4.6 mm) packed with *octadecylsilyl silica gel for chromatography* (5 μm) (Spherisorb ODS 2 is suitable), (b) as the mobile phase with a flow rate of 1.5 ml per minute a mixture of 25 volumes of *methanol*, 32 volumes of *water* and 50 volumes of *acetonitrile* and (c) a detection wavelength of 242 nm.

Inject solution (2). Adjust the sensitivity of the system so that the height of the principal peak in the chromatogram obtained is at least 50% of the full scale of the recorder.

Inject solution (3). The test is not valid unless, in the chromatogram obtained, the *resolution factor* between the two principal peaks is at least 6.0.

Inject solution (1). Continue the chromatography for twice the retention time of fluocortolone hexanoate. In the chromatogram obtained with solution (1), the area of any *secondary peak* is not greater than the area of the principal peak in the chromatogram obtained with solution (2) (1%) and the sum of the areas of any *secondary peaks* is not greater than twice the area of the principal peak in the chromatogram obtained with solution (2) (2%). Disregard any peak due to the solvent and any peak with an area less than 0.025 times that of the principal peak in the chromatogram obtained with solution (2) (0.025%).

**Loss on drying**
When dried to constant weight at 105°, loses not more than 0.5% of its weight. Use 1 g.

**Sulphated ash**
Not more than 0.1%, Appendix IX A.

**ASSAY**
Dissolve 15 mg in sufficient *methanol* to produce 100 ml, dilute 20 ml to 100 ml with *methanol* and measure the *absorbance* of the resulting solution at the maximum at 242 nm, Appendix II B. Calculate the content of $C_{28}H_{39}FO_5$ taking 340 as the value of A(1%, 1 cm) at the maximum at 242 nm.

**STORAGE**
Fluocortolone Hexanoate should be protected from light.

**IMPURITIES**

A. 6α-fluoro-11β-hydroxy-16α-methyl-3-oxoandrosta-1,4-diene-17β-carboxylic acid,

B. 6α-fluoro-11β,21-dihydroxy-16α-methylpregna-1,4-diene-3,20-dione,

C. 6α-fluoro-11β-hydroxy-16α-methyl-3,20-dioxopregna-1,4-dien-21-yl pentanoate,

D. 6α-fluoro-16α-methyl-3,11,20-trioxopregna-1,4-dien-21-yl hexanoate,

E. 6α-fluoro-11β-hydroxy-16α-methyl-3,11-dioxopregnen-21-yl hexanoate.

# Fluocortolone Pivalate

(Ph Eur monograph 1212)

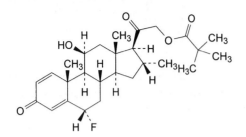

C$_{27}$H$_{37}$FO$_5$        460.6        29205-06-9

### Action and use
Glucocorticoid.

### Preparation
Fluocortolone Cream

*Ph Eur* _____

## DEFINITION
6α-Fluoro-11β-hydroxy-16α-methyl-3,20-dioxopregna-1,4-dien-21-yl 2,2-dimethylpropanoate.

### Content
97.0 per cent to 103.0 per cent (dried substance).

## CHARACTERS
### Appearance
White or almost white, crystalline powder.

### Solubility
Practically insoluble in water, freely soluble in methylene chloride and in dioxan, sparingly soluble in ethanol (96 per cent).

## IDENTIFICATION
*First identification*  A, B.

*Second identification*  B, C, D.

A. Infrared absorption spectrophotometry (2.2.24).

*Comparison*  fluocortolone pivalate CRS.

B. Thin-layer chromatography (2.2.27).

*Solvent mixture*  methanol R, methylene chloride R (1:9 V/V).

*Test solution*  Dissolve 10 mg of the substance to be examined in the solvent mixture and dilute to 10 ml with the solvent mixture.

*Reference solution (a)*  Dissolve 20 mg of fluocortolone pivalate CRS in the solvent mixture and dilute to 20 ml with the solvent mixture.

*Reference solution (b)*  Dissolve 10 mg of norethisterone CRS in reference solution (a) and dilute to 10 ml with reference solution (a).

*Plate*  TLC silica gel F$_{254}$ plate R.

*Mobile phase*  Add a mixture of 1.2 volumes of water R and 8 volumes of methanol R to a mixture of 15 volumes of ether R and 77 volumes of methylene chloride R.

*Application*  5 μl.

*Development*  Over a path of 15 cm.

*Drying*  In air.

*Detection A*  Examine in ultraviolet light at 254 nm.

*Results A*  The principal spot in the chromatogram obtained with the test solution is similar in position and size to the principal spot in the chromatogram obtained with reference solution (a).

*Detection B*  Spray with alcoholic solution of sulphuric acid R. Heat at 120 °C for 10 min or until the spots appear. Allow to cool. Examine in daylight and in ultraviolet light at 365 nm.

*Results B*  The principal spot in the chromatogram obtained with the test solution is similar in position, colour in daylight, fluorescence in ultraviolet light at 365 nm and size to the principal spot in the chromatogram obtained with reference solution (a).

*System suitability*  Reference solution (b):
— the chromatogram shows 2 clearly separated spots.

C. To about 1 mg add 2 ml of a mixture of 2 volumes of glacial acetic acid R and 3 volumes of sulphuric acid R and heat for 1 min on a water-bath. A red colour is produced. Add 5 ml of water R, the colour changes to violet-red.

D. Mix about 5 mg with 45 mg of heavy magnesium oxide R and ignite in a crucible until an almost white residue is obtained (usually less than 5 min). Allow to cool, add 1 ml of water R, 0.05 ml of phenolphthalein solution R1 and about 1 ml of dilute hydrochloric acid R to render the solution colourless. Filter and add to the filtrate a freshly prepared mixture of 0.1 ml of alizarin S solution R and 0.1 ml of zirconyl nitrate solution R. Mix, allow to stand for 5 min and compare the colour of the solution with that of a blank prepared in the same manner. The test solution is yellow and the blank is red.

## TESTS
### Specific optical rotation (2.2.7)
+ 100 to + 105 (dried substance).

Dissolve 0.25 g in dioxan R and dilute to 25.0 ml with the same solvent.

### Related substances
Liquid chromatography (2.2.29).

*Test solution*  Dissolve 10.0 mg of the substance to be examined in acetonitrile R and dilute to 10.0 ml with the same solvent.

*Reference solution (a)*  Dilute 1.0 ml of the test solution to 100.0 ml with acetonitrile R.

*Reference solution (b)*  Dissolve 2 mg of fluocortolone pivalate CRS and 2 mg of prednisolone hexanoate CRS in acetonitrile R, then dilute to 100 ml with the same solvent.

*Column:*
— size: l = 0.25 m, Ø = 4.6 mm;
— stationary phase: octadecylsilyl silica gel for chromatography R (5 μm).

*Mobile phase*  methanol R, acetonitrile R, water R (25:30:32 V/V/V).

*Flow rate*  1.5 ml/min.

*Detection*  Spectrophotometer at 243 nm.

*Injection*  20 μl.

*Run time*  Twice the retention time of fluocortolone pivalate.

*System suitability*  Reference solution (b):
— resolution: minimum 5.0 between the peaks due to fluocortolone pivalate and prednisolone hexanoate.

*Limits:*
— impurities A, B, C, D: for each impurity, not more than the area of the principal peak in the chromatogram obtained with reference solution (a) (1 per cent);
— total: not more than twice the area of the principal peak in the chromatogram obtained with reference solution (a) (2 per cent);

— *disregard limit*: 0.025 times the area of the principal peak in the chromatogram obtained with reference solution (a) (0.025 per cent).

**Loss on drying** (*2.2.32*)

Maximum 1.0 per cent, determined on 1.000 g by drying in an oven at 105 °C.

**Sulphated ash** (*2.4.14*)

Maximum 0.1 per cent, determined on 1.0 g.

**ASSAY**

Dissolve 30.0 mg in *anhydrous ethanol R* and dilute to 100.0 ml with the same solvent. Dilute 5.0 ml of this solution to 100.0 ml with *anhydrous ethanol R*. Measure the absorbance (*2.2.25*) at the absorption maximum at 242 nm.

Calculate the content of $C_{27}H_{37}FO_5$ taking the specific absorbance to be 350.

**STORAGE**

Protected from light.

**IMPURITIES**

*Specified impurities    A, B, C, D.*

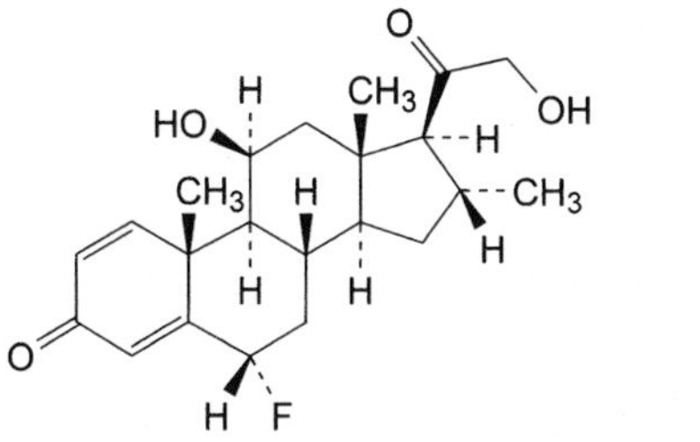

A. 6α-fluoro-11β,21-dihydroxy-16α-methylpregna-1,4-diene-3,20-dione (fluocortolone),

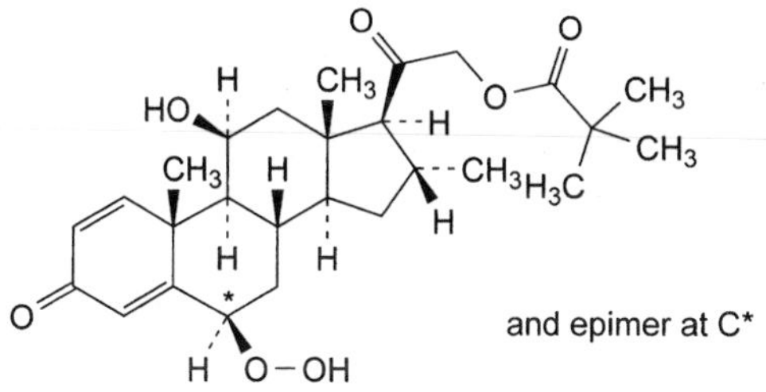

B. 6-hydroperoxy-11β-hydroxy-16α-methyl-3,20-dioxopregna-1,4-dien-21-yl 2,2-dimethylpropanoate,

and epimer at C*

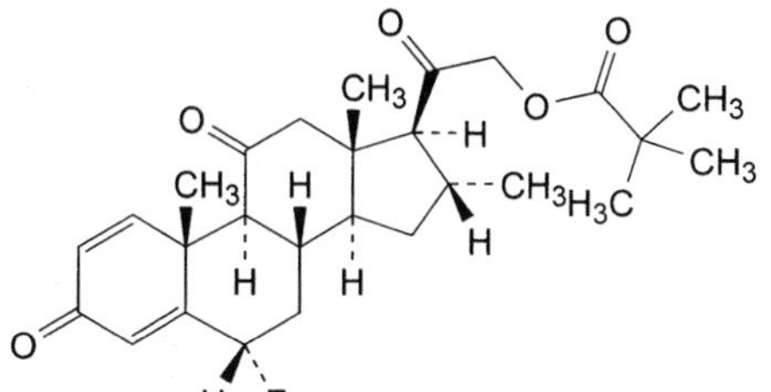

C. 6α-fluoro-16α-methyl-3,11,20-trioxopregna-1,4-dien-21-yl 2,2-dimethylpropanoate,

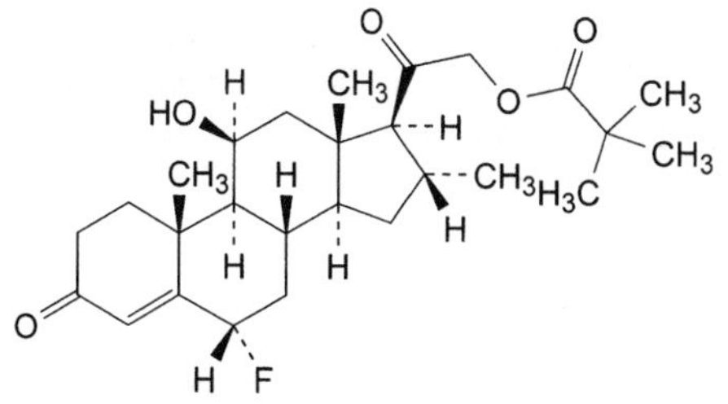

D. 6α-fluoro-11β-hydroxy-16α-methyl-3,20-dioxopregna-4-en-21-yl 2,2-dimethylpropanoate.

*_____ Ph Eur*

# Fluorescein

(*Ph Eur monograph 2348*)

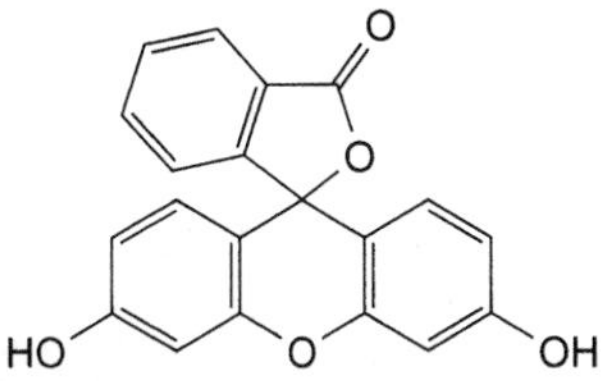

$C_{20}H_{12}O_5$                332.3                *2321-07-5*

**Action and use**

Detection of corneal lesions, retinal angiography and pancreatic function testing.

*Ph Eur* _____

**DEFINITION**

3′,6′-Dihydroxy-3*H*-spiro[isobenzofuran-1,9′-xanthen]-3-one.

**Content**

97.0 per cent to 102.0 per cent (dried substance).

**CHARACTERS**

**Appearance**

Orange-red, fine powder.

**Solubility**

Practically insoluble in water, soluble in hot ethanol (96 per cent). It dissolves in dilute solutions of alkali hydroxides.

**IDENTIFICATION**

*First identification    A, D.*

*Second identification    B, C, D.*

A. Infrared absorption spectrophotometry (*2.2.24*).

*Comparison    fluorescein CRS.*

Dissolve the substance to be examined and the reference substance separately in the minimum volume of *ethanol (96 per cent) R*, evaporate to dryness and record the spectra using the residues.

B. Dilute 0.1 ml of solution S (see Tests) to 10 ml with *water R*. The solution shows a yellowish-green fluorescence. The fluorescence disappears on addition of 0.1 ml of *dilute hydrochloric acid R* and reappears on addition of 0.2 ml of *dilute sodium hydroxide solution R*.

C. The absorption by a piece of filter paper of 0.05 ml of the solution prepared for identification B (before the addition of *dilute hydrochloric acid R*) colours the paper yellow.

On exposing the moist paper to bromine vapour for 1 min and then to ammonia vapour, the colour becomes deep pink.

D. Suspend 0.5 g in 50 ml of *water R* and shake for 10 min. The substance does not completely dissolve.

## TESTS

### Solution S

Suspend 1.0 g in 35.0 ml of *water R* and add dropwise with shaking 4.5 ml of *1 M sodium hydroxide*. Adjust to pH 8.5-9.0 with *1 M sodium hydroxide* and dilute to 50.0 ml with *water R* to obtain a clear solution.

### Appearance of solution

Solution S is clear (*2.2.1*) and orange-yellow with yellowish-green fluorescence.

### Related substances

Liquid chromatography (*2.2.29*).

*Solvent mixture* acetonitrile for chromatography *R*, mobile phase A (30:70 *V/V*).

*Test solution (a)* Disperse 50.0 mg of the substance to be examined in 15.0 ml of *ethanol (96 per cent) R*. Sonicate and dilute to 50.0 ml with the solvent mixture.

*Test solution (b)* Dilute 5.0 ml of test solution (a) to 250.0 ml with the solvent mixture.

*Reference solution (a)* Disperse 50.0 mg of *fluorescein CRS* in 15.0 ml of *ethanol (96 per cent) R*. Sonicate and dilute to 50.0 ml with *water R*. Dilute 5.0 ml of this solution to 250.0 ml with the solvent mixture.

*Reference solution (b)* Dissolve 10.0 mg of *phthalic acid CRS* (impurity B) and 10.0 mg of *resorcinol CRS* (impurity A) in the solvent mixture and dilute to 100.0 ml with the solvent mixture. Dilute 1.0 ml of this solution to 100.0 ml with the solvent mixture.

*Reference solution (c)* Dilute 5.0 ml of test solution (b) to 20.0 ml with the solvent mixture.

*Reference solution (d)* Dilute 10.0 ml of reference solution (c) to 100.0 ml with the solvent mixture.

*Reference solution (e)* Dissolve the contents of a vial of *fluorescein impurity C CRS* in 1 ml of the solvent mixture.

*Column:*
— *size: l* = 0.25 m, Ø = 4.6 mm;
— *stationary phase*: octylsilyl silica gel for chromatography *R3* (5 μm);
— *temperature*: 35 °C.

*Mobile phase:*
— *mobile phase A*: dissolve 0.610 g of *potassium dihydrogen phosphate R* in *water for chromatography R*, adjust to pH 2.0 with *phosphoric acid R* and dilute to 1000.0 ml with *water for chromatography R*;
— *mobile phase B*: acetonitrile for chromatography *R*;

| Time (min) | Mobile phase A (per cent *V/V*) | Mobile phase B (per cent *V/V*) |
|---|---|---|
| 0 - 20 | 85 → 20 | 15 → 80 |
| 20 - 29 | 20 | 80 |
| 29 - 30 | 20 → 85 | 80 → 15 |
| 30 - 40 | 85 | 15 |

*Flow rate* 1.0 ml/min.

*Detection* Spectrophotometer at 220 nm.

*Injection* 20 μl of test solution (a) and reference solutions (b), (c), (d) and (e).

*Identification of impurity C* Use the chromatogram obtained with reference solution (e) to identify the peak due to impurity C.

*Relative retention* With reference to fluorescein (retention time = about 15 min): impurity A = about 0.42; impurity B = about 0.48; impurity C = about 0.86.

*System suitability* Reference solution (b):
— *resolution*: minimum 2.0 between the peaks due to impurities A and B.

*Limits:*
— *correction factor*: for the calculation of content, multiply the peak area of impurity C by 1.9;
— *impurity C*: not more than 1.2 times the area of the principal peak in the chromatogram obtained with reference solution (c) (0.6 per cent);
— *impurities A, B*: for each impurity, not more than the area of the corresponding peak in the chromatogram obtained with reference solution (b) (0.1 per cent);
— *unspecified impurities*: for each impurity, not more than 0.2 times the area of the principal peak in the chromatogram obtained with reference solution (c) (0.10 per cent);
— *sum of impurities other than A, B and C*: not more than 0.4 times the area of the principal peak in the chromatogram obtained with reference solution (c) (0.2 per cent);
— *disregard limit*: the area of the principal peak in the chromatogram obtained with reference solution (d) (0.05 per cent).

### Chlorides (*2.4.4*)

Maximum 0.25 per cent.

To 10.0 ml of solution S add 90.0 ml of *water R* and 3.0 ml of *dilute nitric acid R*, wait for at least 30 min and filter. Dilute 10.0 ml of the filtrate to 15.0 ml with *water R*.

### Loss on drying (*2.2.32*)

Maximum 1.0 per cent, determined on 1.000 g by drying in an oven at 105 °C.

## ASSAY

Liquid chromatography (*2.2.29*) as described in the test for related substances with the following modification.

*Injection* Test solution (b) and reference solution (a).

Calculate the percentage content of $C_{20}H_{12}O_5$ from the declared content of *fluorescein CRS*.

## STORAGE

Protected from light.

## IMPURITIES

*Specified impurities* A, B, C.

A. resorcinol,

B. benzene-1,2-dicarboxylic acid (phthalic acid),

C. 2-(2,4-dihydroxybenzoyl)benzoic acid.

Ph Eur

# Fluorescein Sodium

Soluble Fluorescein

(*Ph Eur monograph 1213*)

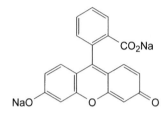

$C_{20}H_{10}Na_2O_5$      376.3      *518-47-8*

## Action and use
Detection of corneal lesions, retinal angiography and pancreatic function testing.

## Preparations
Fluorescein Eye Drops

Fluorescein Injection

Ph Eur

## DEFINITION
Disodium 2-(6-oxido-3-oxo-3*H*-xanthen-9-yl)benzoate.

## Content
95.0 per cent to 103.0 per cent (dried substance).

## CHARACTERS
### Appearance
Orange-red, fine powder, hygroscopic.

### Solubility
Freely soluble in water, soluble in ethanol (96 per cent), practically insoluble in hexane and in methylene chloride.

## IDENTIFICATION
*First identification* B, D.

*Second identification* A, C, D.

A. Dilute 0.1 ml of solution S (see Tests) to 10 ml with *water R*. The solution shows yellowish-green fluorescence. The fluorescence disappears on addition of 0.1 ml of *dilute hydrochloric acid R* and reappears on addition of 0.2 ml of *dilute sodium hydroxide solution R*.

B. Infrared absorption spectrophotometry (*2.2.24*).

*Preparation* Discs.

*Comparison* Ph. Eur. reference spectrum of *fluorescein sodium*.

C. The absorption by a piece of filter paper of 0.05 ml of the solution prepared for identification A (before the addition of *dilute hydrochloric acid R*) colours the paper yellow.

On exposing the moist paper to bromine vapour for 1 min and then to ammonia vapour, the colour becomes deep pink.

D. Ignite 0.1 g in a porcelain crucible. Dissolve the residue in 5 ml of *water R* and filter. 2 ml of the filtrate gives reaction (a) of sodium (*2.3.1*).

## TESTS
### Solution S
Dissolve 1.0 g in *carbon dioxide-free water R* prepared from *distilled water R* and dilute to 50 ml with the same solvent.

### Appearance of solution
Solution S is clear (*2.2.1*) and orange-yellow with yellowish-green fluorescence.

### pH (*2.2.3*)
7.0 to 9.0 for solution S.

### Related substances
Liquid chromatography (*2.2.29*).

*Test solution (a)* Dissolve 0.100 g of the substance to be examined in a mixture of 30 volumes of *acetonitrile R* and 70 volumes of mobile phase A and dilute to 100.0 ml with the same mixture of solvents.

*Test solution (b)* Dilute 5.0 ml of test solution (a) to 250.0 ml with a mixture of 30 volumes of *acetonitrile R* and 70 volumes of mobile phase A.

*Reference solution (a)* Dissolve 55.0 mg of *diacetylfluorescein CRS* in a mixture of 1 ml of *2.5 M sodium hydroxide* and 5 ml of *ethanol (96 per cent) R*, heat on a water-bath for 20 min mixing frequently, cool and dilute to 50.0 ml with *water R*. Dilute 5.0 ml of the solution to 250.0 ml with a mixture of 30 volumes of *acetonitrile R* and 70 volumes of mobile phase A.

*Reference solution (b)* Dissolve 10.0 mg of *phthalic acid R* (impurity B) and 10.0 mg of *resorcinol R* (impurity A) in a mixture of 30 volumes of *acetonitrile R* and 70 volumes of mobile phase A and dilute to 100.0 ml with the same mixture of solvents. Dilute 5.0 ml of the solution to 100.0 ml with a mixture of 30 volumes of *acetonitrile R* and 70 volumes of mobile phase A.

*Reference solution (c)* Dilute 5.0 ml of test solution (b) to 20.0 ml with a mixture of 30 volumes of *acetonitrile R* and 70 volumes of mobile phase A.

*Column:*
— *size*: $l$ = 0.25 m, Ø = 4.6 mm,
— *stationary phase*: octylsilyl silica gel for chromatography R (5 μm),
— *temperature*: 35 °C.

*Mobile phase:*
— *mobile phase A*: dissolve 0.610 g of *potassium dihydrogen phosphate R* in *water R* and dilute to 1000 ml with the same solvent; adjust to pH 2.0 with *phosphoric acid R*;
— *mobile phase B*: acetonitrile for chromatography R;

| Time (min) | Mobile phase A (per cent *V/V*) | Mobile phase B (per cent *V/V*) |
|---|---|---|
| 0 - 20 | 85 → 20 | 15 → 80 |
| 20 - 29 | 20 | 80 |
| 29 - 30 | 20 → 85 | 80 → 15 |
| 30 - 35 | 85 | 15 |

*Flow rate* 1.0 ml/min.

*Detection* Spectrophotometer at 220 nm.

*Injection* 20 μl of test solution (a) and reference solutions (b) and (c).

*Relative retention* With reference to fluorescein (retention time = about 15 min): impurity A = about 0.44; impurity B = about 0.50; impurity C = about 0.87.

*System suitability* Reference solution (b):
— *resolution*: minimum 1.5 between the peaks due to impurity A and impurity B.

*Limits:*
— *correction factor*: for the calculation of content, multiply the peak area of impurity C by 1.6,
— *Impurities A, B*: for each impurity, not more than the area of the corresponding peak in the chromatogram obtained with reference solution (b) (0.5 per cent),
— *impurity C*: not more than the area of the principal peak in the chromatogram obtained with reference solution (c) (0.5 per cent),
— *any other impurity*: for each impurity, not more than 0.2 times the area of the principal peak in the chromatogram obtained with reference solution (c) (0.1 per cent),
— *sum of impurities other than A, B, C*: not more than the area of the principal peak in the chromatogram obtained with reference solution (c) (0.5 per cent),
— *disregard limit*: 0.1 times the area of the principal peak in the chromatogram obtained with reference solution (c) (0.05 per cent).

**Chlorides** *(2.4.4)*
Maximum 0.25 per cent.

To 10 ml of solution S add 90 ml of *water R* and 1 ml of *dilute nitric acid R*, wait for at least 10 min and filter. Dilute 10 ml of the filtrate to 15 ml with *water R*.

**Sulphates** *(2.4.13)*
Maximum 1.0 per cent.

To 5 ml of solution S add 90 ml of *distilled water R*, 2.5 ml of *dilute hydrochloric acid R* and dilute to 100 ml with *distilled water R*. Filter. 15 ml of the filtrate complies with the test.

**Zinc**
Dilute 5 ml of solution S to 10 ml with *water R*. Add 2 ml of *hydrochloric acid R1*, filter and add 0.1 ml of *potassium ferrocyanide solution R*. No turbidity or precipitate is formed immediately.

**Loss on drying** *(2.2.32)*
Maximum 10.0 per cent, determined on 1.000 g by drying in an oven at 105 °C.

**ASSAY**
Liquid chromatography (*2.2.29*) as described in the test for related substances with the following modification.

*Injection* Test solution (b) and reference solution (a).

Calculate the percentage content of $C_{20}H_{10}Na_2O_5$ using the chromatogram obtained with reference solution (a) and the declared content of *diacetylfluorescein CRS*.

1 mg of *diacetylfluorescein CRS* is equivalent to 0.9037 mg of $C_{20}H_{10}Na_2O_5$.

**STORAGE**
In an airtight container, protected from light.

**IMPURITIES**
*Specified impurities   A, B, C.*

A. resorcinol,

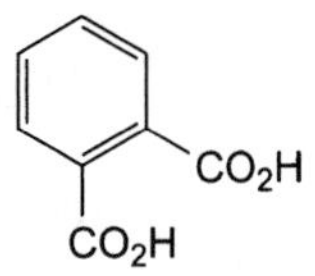

B. benzene-1,2-dicarboxylic acid (phthalic acid),

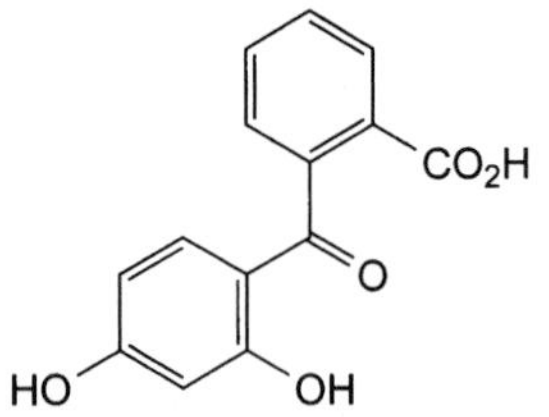

C. 2-(2,4-dihydroxybenzoyl)benzoic acid.

*Ph Eur*

# Fluorometholone

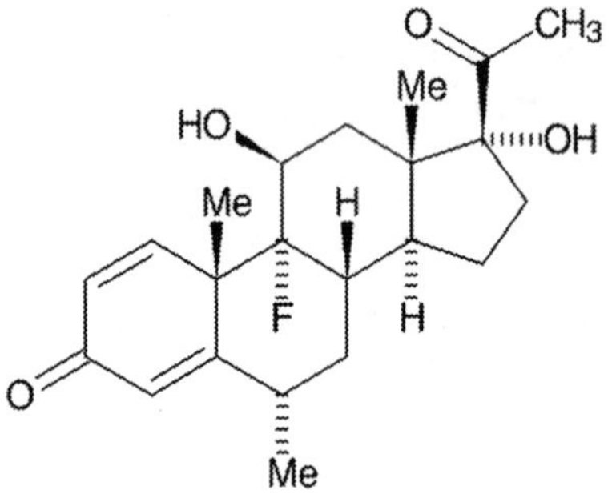

$C_{22}H_{29}FO_4$                 376.5                 426-13-1

**Action and use**
Glucocorticoid.

**Preparation**
Fluorometholone Eye Drops

**DEFINITION**
Fluorometholone is 9α-fluoro-11β,17α-dihydroxy-6α-methylpregna-1,4-diene-3,20-dione. It contains not less than 97.0% and not more than 103.0% of $C_{22}H_{29}FO_4$, calculated with reference to the dried substance.

**CHARACTERISTICS**
A white to yellowish white, crystalline powder. It melts at about 280°, with decomposition.

Practically insoluble in *water*; slightly soluble in *absolute ethanol* and in *ether*.

**IDENTIFICATION**
A. The *infrared absorption spectrum*, Appendix II A, is concordant with the *reference spectrum* of fluorometholone *(RS 152)*.

B. In the Assay, the principal peak in the chromatogram obtained with solution (1) has the same retention time as the principal peak in the chromatogram obtained with solution (2).

## TESTS

**Specific optical rotation**

In a 1% w/v solution in *pyridine*, +52 to +60, Appendix V F, calculated with reference to the dried substance.

**Related substances**

Carry out the method for *liquid chromatography*, Appendix III D, using the following solutions in *methanol*.

(1) 0.010% w/v of the substance being examined.

(2) 0.00005% w/v of the substance being examined.

(3) 0.00005% w/v each of deltamedrane BPCRS and fluorometholone BPCRS.

CHROMATOGRAPHIC CONDITIONS

(a) Use a stainless steel column (30 cm × 3.9 mm) packed with *octadecylsilyl silica gel for chromatography* (10 μm) (μBondapak C18 is suitable).

(b) Use isocratic elution and the mobile phase described below.

(c) Use a flow rate of 2 ml per minute.

(d) Use an ambient column temperature.

(e) Use a detection wavelength of 254 nm.

(f) Inject 20 μl of each solution.

*MOBILE PHASE*

40 volumes of *water* and 60 volumes of *methanol*.

SYSTEM SUITABILITY

The test is not valid unless, in the chromatogram obtained with solution (3), the *resolution factor* between the peaks due to deltamedrane and fluorometholone is at least 1.5.

LIMITS

In the chromatogram obtained with solution (1):

the area of any *secondary peak* is not greater than the area of the principal peak in the chromatogram obtained with solution (2) (0.5%);

the sum of the areas of any *secondary peaks* is not greater than twice the area of the principal peak in the chromatogram obtained with solution (2) (1%).

**Loss on drying**

When dried at 60° at a pressure not exceeding 0.7 kPa for 3 hours, loses not more than 0.5% of its weight. Use 1 g.

**Sulphated ash**

Not more than 0.1%, Appendix IX A.

## ASSAY

Carry out the method for *liquid chromatography*, Appendix III D, using the following solutions in *methanol*.

(1) 0.005% w/v of the substance being examined.

(2) 0.005% w/v of *fluorometholone BPCRS*.

(3) 0.00005% w/v each of *deltamedrane BPCRS* and *fluorometholone BPCRS*.

CHROMATOGRAPHIC CONDITIONS

The chromatographic procedure described under Related substances may be used.

SYSTEM SUITABILITY

The test is not valid unless, in the chromatogram obtained with solution (3), the *resolution factor* between the peaks due to deltamedrane and fluorometholone is at least 1.5.

DETERMINATION OF CONTENT

Calculate the content of $C_{22}H_{29}FO_4$ from the chromatograms obtained and using the declared content of $C_{22}H_{29}FO_4$ in *fluorometholone BPCRS*.

## IMPURITIES

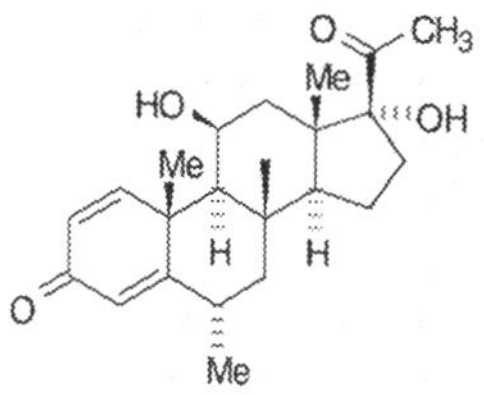

A. 11β,17α-dihydroxy-6α-methylpregna-1,4-diene-3,20-dione *(deltamedrane)*

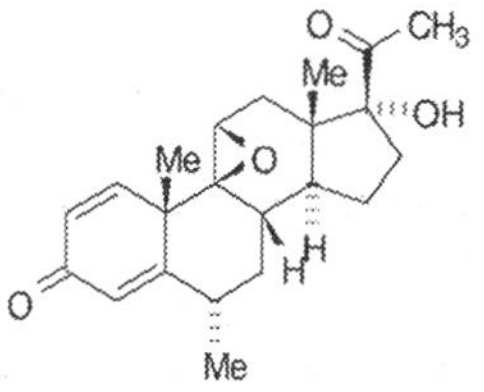

B. 9β,11β-epoxy-17α-hydroxy-6α-methylpregna-1,4-diene-3,20-dione *(epoxymedradiene)*

# Fluorouracil

*(Ph Eur monograph 0611)*

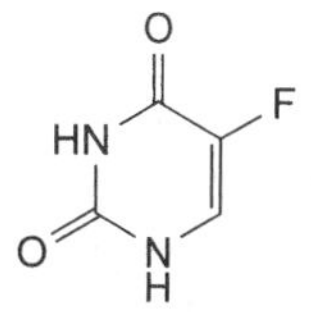

| $C_4H_3FN_2O_2$ | 130.1 | *51-21-8* |
|---|---|---|

**Action and use**

Pyrimidine analogue; cytotoxic.

**Preparations**

Fluorouracil Cream

Fluorouracil Injection

*Ph Eur*

## DEFINITION

5-Fluoropyrimidine-2,4(1*H*,3*H*)-dione.

**Content**

98.5 per cent to 101.0 per cent (dried substance).

## CHARACTERS

**Appearance**

White or almost white, crystalline powder.

**Solubility**

Sparingly soluble in water, slightly soluble in ethanol (96 per cent).

## IDENTIFICATION

Infrared absorption spectrophotometry (*2.2.24*).

*Comparison   fluorouracil CRS.*

## TESTS

**Solution S**

Dissolve 0.5 g in *carbon dioxide-free water R* and dilute to 50 ml with the same solvent.

**Appearance of solution**

Solution S is clear (2.2.1) and not more intensely coloured than reference solution $BY_7$ or $Y_7$ (2.2.2, Method II).

**pH** (2.2.3)

4.5 to 5.0 for solution S.

**Impurities F and G**

Thin-layer chromatography (2.2.27).

*Test solution* Dissolve 0.10 g of the substance to be examined in a mixture of equal volumes of *methanol R* and *water R* and dilute to 10.0 ml with the same mixture of solvents.

*Reference solution (a)* Dissolve 5.0 mg of *fluorouracil impurity F CRS* in a mixture of equal volumes of *methanol R* and *water R* and dilute to 200.0 ml with the same mixture of solvents.

*Reference solution (b)* Dissolve 20.0 mg of *urea R* (impurity G) in *methanol R* and dilute to 10.0 ml with the same solvent. Dilute 1.0 ml of this solution to 100.0 ml with *methanol R*.

*Plate* TLC silica gel $F_{254}$ plate R.

*Mobile phase* methanol R, water R, ethyl acetate R (15:15:70 V/V/V).

*Application* 10 µl.

*Development* Over a path of 2/3 of the plate.

*Drying* In air.

*Detection:*
— impurity F: examine in ultraviolet light at 254 nm;
— impurity G: spray with a mixture of 200 ml of a 10 g/l solution of *dimethylaminobenzaldehyde R* in *anhydrous ethanol R* and 20 ml of *hydrochloric acid R*; dry in an oven at 80 °C for 3-4 min, then examine in daylight (impurity G produces a yellow spot and fluorouracil is not detected by the spray).

*System suitability* The chromatogram shows 2 clearly separated spots after both detections.

*Limits:*
— impurity F: any spot due to impurity F is not more intense than the spot in the chromatogram obtained with reference solution (a) (0.25 per cent);
— impurity G: any spot due to impurity G is not more intense than the spot in the chromatogram obtained with reference solution (b) (0.2 per cent).

**Related substances**

Liquid chromatography (2.2.29). *Carry out the test protected from light.*

*Test solution* Dissolve 50.0 mg of the substance to be examined in the mobile phase and dilute to 50.0 ml with the mobile phase. Dilute 5.0 ml of this solution to 50.0 ml with the mobile phase.

*Reference solution (a)* Dissolve 5.0 mg of *fluorouracil impurity C CRS* in the mobile phase and dilute to 50.0 ml with the mobile phase.

*Reference solution (b)* Dilute 1.0 ml of reference solution (a) to 100.0 ml with the mobile phase. Dilute 1.0 ml of this solution to 10.0 ml with the mobile phase.

*Reference solution (c)* Dissolve 5.0 mg of *fluorouracil impurity A CRS* in the mobile phase and dilute to 50.0 ml with the mobile phase. Dilute 1.0 ml of the solution to 100.0 ml with the mobile phase. Dilute 1.0 ml of this solution to 10.0 ml with the mobile phase.

*Reference solution (d)* Dissolve 5.0 mg of *fluorouracil impurity B CRS* in the mobile phase and dilute to 50.0 ml

with the mobile phase. Dilute 1.0 ml of the solution to 100.0 ml with the mobile phase. Dilute 1.0 ml of this solution to 10.0 ml with the mobile phase.

*Reference solution (e)* Dilute 1.0 ml of the test solution to 100.0 ml with the mobile phase. Dilute 1.0 ml of this solution to 10.0 ml with the mobile phase.

*Reference solution (f)* To 1 ml of reference solution (a) add 1 ml of the test solution and dilute to 10 ml with the mobile phase.

*Reference solution (g)* Dissolve the contents of a vial of *fluorouracil impurity mixture CRS* (containing impurities D and E) in 1.0 ml of the mobile phase.

*Column:*
— size: $l$ = 0.25 m, Ø = 4.6 mm;
— stationary phase: octadecylsilyl silica gel for chromatography R (5 µm).

*Mobile phase* 6.805 g/l solution of *potassium dihydrogen phosphate R* adjusted to pH 5.7 ± 0.1 with 5 M *potassium hydroxide*.

*Flow rate* 1.0 ml/min.

*Detection* Spectrophotometer at 266 nm.

*Injection* 20 µl.

*Run time* 3 times the retention time of fluorouracil.

*Identification of impurities* Use the chromatogram supplied with *fluorouracil impurity mixture CRS* and the chromatogram obtained with reference solution (g) to identify the peaks due to impurities D and E.

*Relative retention* With reference to fluorouracil (retention time = about 6 min): impurity A = about 0.5; impurity B = about 0.7; impurity C = about 0.9; impurity D = about 1.6; impurity E = about 1.9.

*System suitability* Reference solution (f):
— resolution: minimum 2 between the peaks due to impurity C and fluorouracil.

*Limits:*
— correction factors: for the calculation of content, multiply the peak areas of the following impurities by the corresponding correction factor: impurity D = 1.5; impurity E = 1.3;
— impurity A: not more than the area of the corresponding peak in the chromatogram obtained with reference solution (c) (0.1 per cent);
— impurity B: not more than the area of the corresponding peak in the chromatogram obtained with reference solution (d) (0.1 per cent);
— impurity C: not more than the area of the corresponding peak in the chromatogram obtained with reference solution (b) (0.1 per cent);
— impurities D, E: for each impurity, not more than the area of the principal peak in the chromatogram obtained with reference solution (e) (0.1 per cent);
— unspecified impurities: for each impurity, not more than the area of the principal peak in the chromatogram obtained with reference solution (e) (0.10 per cent);
— total: not more than 5 times the area of the principal peak in the chromatogram obtained with reference solution (e) (0.5 per cent);
— disregard limit: 0.5 times the area of the principal peak in the chromatogram obtained with reference solution (e) (0.05 per cent).

**Heavy metals** (2.4.8)

Maximum 20 ppm.

1.0 g complies with test C. Use a platinum crucible. Prepare the reference solution using 2 ml of *lead standard solution (10 ppm Pb) R*.

**Loss on drying** (*2.2.32*)

Maximum 0.5 per cent, determined on 1.000 g by drying *in vacuo* at 80 °C for 4 h.

**Sulphated ash** (*2.4.14*)

Maximum 0.1 per cent, determined on 1.0 g in a platinum crucible.

## ASSAY

Dissolve 0.100 g in 80 ml of *dimethylformamide R*, warming gently. Cool and titrate with *0.1 M tetrabutylammonium hydroxide*, using 0.25 ml of a 10 g/l solution of *thymol blue R* in *dimethylformamide R* as indicator. Carry out a blank titration.

1 ml of *0.1 M tetrabutylammonium hydroxide* is equivalent to 13.01 mg of $C_4H_3FN_2O_2$.

## STORAGE

Protected from light.

## IMPURITIES

*Specified impurities    A, B, C, D, E, F, G.*

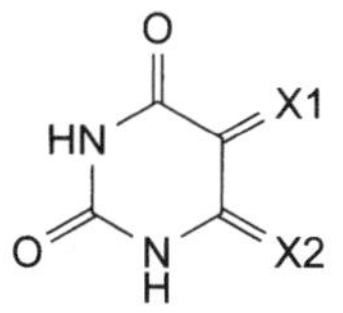

A. X1 = H₂, X2 = O: pyrimidine-2,4,6(1*H*,3*H*,5*H*)-trione (barbituric acid),

B. X1 = O, X2 = H₂: dihydropyrimidine-2,4,5(3*H*)-trione (isobarbituric acid or 5-hydroxyuracil),

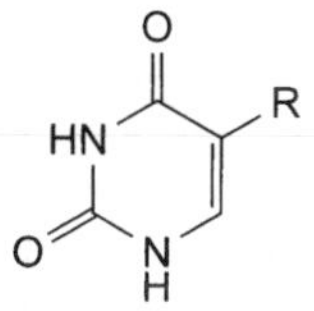

C. R = H: pyrimidine-2,4(1*H*,3*H*)-dione (uracil),

D. R = OCH₃: 5-methoxypyrimidine-2,4(1*H*,3*H*)-dione (5-methoxyuracil),

E. R = Cl: 5-chloropyrimidine-2,4(1*H*,3*H*)-dione (5-chlorouracil),

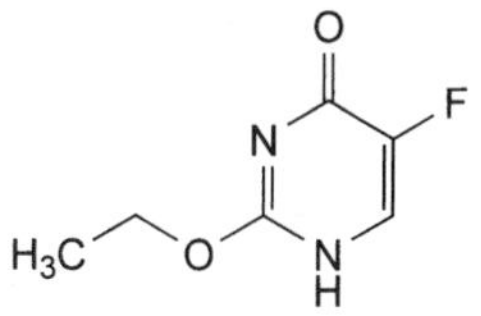

F. 2-ethoxy-5-fluoropyrimidin-4(1*H*)-one (2-ethoxy-5-fluorouracil),

G. urea.

———————————————————— *Ph Eur*

# Fluoxetine Hydrochloride

(*Ph Eur monograph 1104*)

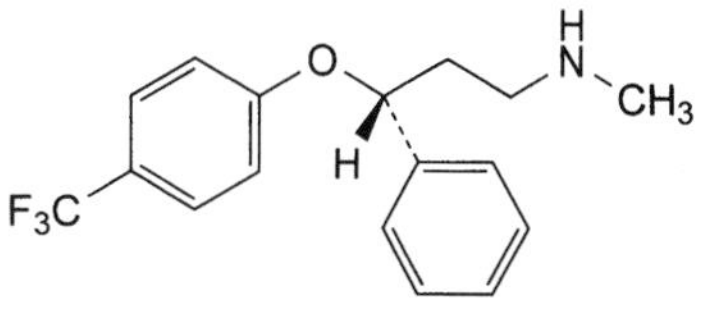

$C_{17}H_{18}F_3NO,HCl$        345.8        *59333-67-4*

**Action and use**

Selective serotonin reuptake inhibitor; antidepressant.

**Preparations**

Fluoxetine Capsules

Fluoxetine Oral Solution

*Ph Eur* ————————————————————

## DEFINITION

(3*RS*)-*N*-Methyl-3-phenyl-3-[4-trifluoromethyl)phenoxy]propan-1-amine hydrochloride.

**Content**

98.0 per cent to 102.0 per cent (anhydrous substance).

## CHARACTERS

**Appearance**

White or almost white, crystalline powder.

**Solubility**

Sparingly soluble in water, freely soluble in methanol, sparingly soluble in methylene chloride.

## IDENTIFICATION

A. Infrared absorption spectrophotometer (*2.2.24*).

*Preparation*  Discs.

*Comparison*  *fluoxetine hydrochloride CRS* .

B. It gives reaction (a) of chlorides (*2.3.1*).

## TESTS

**Solution S**

Dissolve 2.0 g in a mixture of 15 volumes of *water R* and 85 volumes of *methanol R*, then dilute to 100 ml with the same mixture of solvents.

**Appearance of solution**

Solution S is clear (*2.2.1*) and colourless (*2.2.2, Method II*).

**pH** (*2.2.3*)

4.5 to 6.5.

Dissolve 0.20 g in *carbon dioxide-free water R* and dilute to 20 ml with the same solvent.

**Optical rotation** (*2.2.7*)

− 0.05° to + 0.05°, determined on solution S.

**Related substances**

Liquid chromatography (*2.2.29*).

*Test solution (a)*   Dissolve 55.0 mg of the substance to be examined in the mobile phase and dilute to 10.0 ml with the mobile phase.

*Test solution (b)*   Dilute 2.0 ml of test solution (a) to 10.0 ml with the mobile phase.

*Reference solution*   Dissolve 22.0 mg of *fluoxetine hydrochloride CRS* in 10.0 ml of *0.5 M sulphuric acid*. Heat at about 85 °C for 3 h. Allow to cool. The resulting solution contains considerable quantities of impurity A and usually also contains 4-trifluoromethylphenol. To 0.4 ml of this solution add 28.0 mg of *fluoxetine hydrochloride CRS* , about 1 mg of *fluoxetine impurity B CRS* and about 1 mg of *fluoxetine impurity C CRS* , then dilute to 25.0 ml with the mobile phase.

*Column:*
— *size*: $l$ = 0.25 m, Ø = 4.6 mm;
— *stationary phase*: octylsilyl silica gel for chromatography R (5 μm).

*Mobile phase*   Mix 8 volumes of *methanol R*, 30 volumes of *tetrahydrofuran R* and 62 volumes of a solution of *triethylamine R* prepared as follows: to 10 ml of *triethylamine R*, add 980 ml of *water R*, mix and adjust to pH 6.0 with *phosphoric acid R* (about 4.5 ml) and dilute to 1000 ml with *water R*.

*Flow rate*   1 ml/min.

*Detection*   Spectrophotometer at 215 nm.

*Injection*   10 μl.

*Run time*   3 times the retention time of fluoxetine.

*Relative retention*

With reference to fluoxetine: impurity A = about 0.24; impurity B = about 0.27; impurity C = about 0.94.

*System suitability*   Reference solution:
— *retention time*: fluoxetine = 10 min to 18 min; 4-trifluoromethylphenol: maximum 35 min; if no peak due to 4-trifluoromethylphenol is observed, inject a 0.02 per cent solution of *4-trifluoromethylphenol R* in the mobile phase;
— *peak-to-valley ratio*: maximum 1.1, where $H_p$ = height above the baseline of the peak due to impurity C and $H_v$ = height between the top of the peak due to impurity C and the lowest point of the valley between this peak and the peak due to fluoxetine; if necessary, reduce the volume of methanol and increase the volume of the solution of triethylamine in the mobile phase.

*Limit*   Test solution (b):
— *impurity C*: not more than 0.0015 times the area of the principal peak (0.15 per cent).

*Limits*   Test solution (a):
— *impurities A, B*: for each impurity, not more than 0.0125 times the area of the principal peak in the chromatogram obtained with test solution (b) (0.25 per cent);
— *unspecified impurities*: for each impurity, not more than 0.005 times the area of the principal peak in the chromatogram obtained with test solution (b) (0.10 per cent);
— *total*: not more than 0.025 times the area of the principal peak in the chromatogram obtained with test solution (b) (0.5 per cent);
— *disregard limit*: 0.0025 times the area of the principal peak in the chromatogram obtained with test solution (b) (0.05 per cent).

**Acetonitrile**

Gas chromatography (*2.2.28*).

*Test solution*   Dissolve 50 mg of the substance to be examined in *dimethylformamide R* and dilute to 5.0 ml with the same solvent.

*Reference solution*   To 1.0 g of *acetonitrile R*, add *dimethylformamide R*, mix and dilute to 100.0 ml with the same solvent. Dilute 1.0 ml of this solution to 1000.0 ml with *dimethylformamide R*.

*Column:*
— *material*: fused silica;
— *size*: $l$ = 30 m, Ø = 0.53 mm;

— *stationary phase*: *macrogol 20 000 R* (film thickness 1 μm).

*Carrier gas*   helium for chromatography R.

*Flow rate*   10 ml/min.

*Temperature:*

|  | Time (min) | Temperature (°C) |
|---|---|---|
| Column | 0 - 2 | 35 |
|  | 2 - 14.33 | 35 → 220 |
|  | 14.33 - 24.33 | 220 |
| Injection port |  | 250 |
| Detector |  | 250 |

*Detection*   Flame ionisation.

*Injection*   1 μl; inject *dimethylformamide R* as a blank.

In the chromatogram obtained with *dimethylformamide R*, verify that there is no peak with the same retention time as acetonitrile.

*Limit:*
— *acetonitrile*: not more than the area of the corresponding peak in the chromatogram obtained with the reference solution (0.1 per cent).

**Heavy metals** (*2.4.8*)
Maximum 20 ppm.

1.0 g complies with test C. Prepare the reference solution using 2 ml of *lead standard solution (10 ppm Pb) R*.

**Water** (*2.5.12*)
Maximum 0.5 per cent, determined on 1.00 g.

**Sulphated ash** (*2.4.14*)
Maximum 0.1 per cent, determined on 1.0 g.

**ASSAY**

Liquid chromatography (*2.2.29*) as described in the test for related substances with the following modifications.

*Test solution*   Dissolve 55.0 mg of the substance to be examined in the mobile phase and dilute to 50.0 ml with the mobile phase. Dilute 10.0 ml of this solution to 100.0 ml with the mobile phase.

*Reference solution*   Dissolve 55.0 mg of *fluoxetine hydrochloride CRS* in the mobile phase and dilute to 50.0 ml with the mobile phase. Dilute 10.0 ml of this solution to 100.0 ml with the mobile phase.

*Detection*   Spectrophotometer at 227 nm.

*Retention time*   Fluoxetine = 10 min to 18 min; if necessary, adjust the volumes of methanol and of the solution of triethylamine in the mobile phase.

*System suitability*   Reference solution:
— *symmetry factor*: maximum 2.0 calculated at 10 per cent of the height of the peak due to fluoxetine.

Calculate the content of $C_{17}H_{19}ClF_3NO$ from the declared content of *fluoxetine hydrochloride CRS*.

**IMPURITIES**

*Specified impurities*   A, B, C.

and enantiomer

A. R = OH: (1RS)-3-(methylamino)-1-phenylpropan-1-ol,

B. R = H: *N*-methyl-3-phenylpropan-1-amine,

C. (3RS)-N-methyl-3-phenyl-3-[3-(trifluoromethyl)phenoxy]propan-1-amine.

*Ph Eur*

# Flupentixol Decanoate

C₃₃H₄₃F₃N₂O₂S $\quad$ 588.82 $\quad$ *30909-51-4*

**Action and use**
Dopamine receptor antagonist; neuroleptic.

**Preparation**
Flupentixol Injection

## DEFINITION
Flupentixol Decanoate is (Z)-2-{4-[3-(2-trifluoromethylthioxanthen-9-ylidene)propyl]piperazin-1-yl}ethyl decanoate. It contains not less than 98.0% and not more than 101.0% of C₃₃H₄₃F₃N₂O₂S, calculated with reference to the dried substance.

## CHARACTERISTICS
A yellow, viscous oil.

Very slightly soluble in *water*; soluble in *ethanol (96%)*; freely soluble in *ether*.

## IDENTIFICATION
A. The *light absorption*, Appendix II B, in the range 210 to 350 nm of a 0.0015% w/v solution in *ethanol (96%)* exhibits two maxima at 230 nm and 264 nm. The *absorbances* at the maxima are about 0.85 and about 0.35, respectively.

B. The *infrared absorption spectrum*, Appendix II A, is concordant with the *reference spectrum* of flupentixol decanoate *(RS 154)*.

## TESTS
**Heavy metals**
1.0 g complies with *limit test C for heavy metals*, Appendix VII (20 ppm). Prepare the standard using 2 ml of *lead standard solution (10 ppm Pb)*.

**Related substances**
Carry out the method for *liquid chromatography*, Appendix III D, using the following solutions in *acetonitrile*, protected from light. Solution (1) contains 0.25% w/v of the substance being examined. Solution (2) contains 0.000625% w/v of cis-*flupentixol BPCRS*. Solution (3) contains 0.000625% w/v of 2-*trifluoromethylthioxanthone BPCRS*. Solution (4) contains 0.0025% w/v of trans-*flupentixol decanoate dihydrochloride BPCRS*. Solution (5) contains 0.25% w/v of the substance being examined and 0.000625% w/v each of

cis-*flupentixol BPCRS*, 2-*trifluoromethylthioxanthone BPCRS* and 0.0025% w/v of trans-*flupentixol decanoate dihydrochloride BPCRS*.

The chromatographic procedure may be carried out using (a) a stainless steel column (25 cm × 4.6 mm) packed with *octadecylsilyl silica gel for chromatography* (5 μm) (Waters Symmetry C18 is suitable) maintained at a temperature of 40°, (b) as the mobile phase with a flow rate of 1 ml per minute a mixture of 0.1 volume of *orthophosphoric acid*, 25 volumes of a 20 millimole solution of *dioctyl sodium sulphosuccinate* (prepared by dissolving 8.89 g of *dioctyl sodium sulphosuccinate* in 500 ml of *water*, stirring for 6 to 8 hours and diluting to 1000 ml with *water)* and 75 volumes of *ethanol (96%)* and (c) a detection wavelength of 270 nm.

Inject solution (1) and allow the chromatography to proceed for 1.5 times the retention time of the principal peak. Inject 20 μl of each solution. The substances are eluted in the following order: 2-trifluoromethylthioxanthone, cis-flupentixol (free alcohol), flupentixol decanoate and trans-flupentixol decanoate. The test is not valid unless the solution obtained with solution (5) shows clearly separated peaks.

In the chromatogram obtained with solution (1) the areas of any peaks corresponding to cis-flupentixol and 2-trifluoromethylthioxanthone respectively are not greater than the areas of the principal peaks in the chromatograms obtained with solutions (2) and (3) respectively (0.25% each) and the area of any peak corresponding to trans-flupentixol decanoate dihydrochloride is not greater than the area of the principal peak in the chromatogram obtained with solution (4) (1.0%).

**Loss on drying**
When dried at 60° at a pressure of 0.7 kPa for 3 hours, loses not more than 1.0% of its weight. Use 1 g.

**Sulphated ash**
Not more than 0.1%, Appendix IX A.

## ASSAY
Dissolve 0.2 g in 50 ml of *anhydrous acetic acid* and carry out Method I for *non-aqueous titration*, Appendix VIII A, using *crystal violet solution* as indicator. Each ml of 0.1M *perchloric acid VS* is equivalent to 29.44 mg of C₃₃H₄₃F₃N₂O₂S.

## STORAGE
Flupentixol Decanoate should be protected from light and stored at a temperature below -15°.

## IMPURITIES

A. *cis*-flupentixol (free alcohol),

B. 2-trifluoromethylthioxanthone,

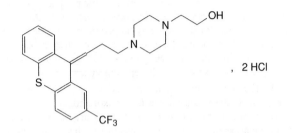

C. *trans*-flupentixol decanoate.

# Flupentixol Hydrochloride

*(Flupentixol Dihydrochloride, Ph Eur monograph 1693)*

$C_{23}H_{25}F_3N_2OS,2HCl$     507.4     *2413-38-9*

## Action and use
Dopamine receptor antagonist; neuroleptic.

*Ph Eur*

## DEFINITION
2-[4-[3-[(*EZ*)-2-(trifluoromethyl)-9*H*-thioxanthen-9-ylidene]propyl]piperazin-1-yl]ethanol dihydrochloride.

## Content
— flupentixol dihydrochloride: 98.0 per cent to 101.5 per cent (dried substance),
— *Z*-isomer: 42.0 per cent to 52.0 per cent.

## CHARACTERS
### Appearance
White or almost white powder.

### Solubility
Very soluble in water, soluble in alcohol, practically insoluble in methylene chloride.

## IDENTIFICATION
*First identification* A, D.

*Second identification* B, C, D.

A. Infrared absorption spectrophotometry (*2.2.24*).

*Comparison* flupentixol dihydrochloride CRS.

B. Thin-layer chromatography (*2.2.27*).

*Test solution* Dissolve 20 mg of the substance to be examined in *methanol R* and dilute to 10 ml with the same solvent.

*Reference solution* Dissolve 20 mg of *flupentixol dihydrochloride CRS* in *methanol R* and dilute to 10 ml with the same solvent.

*Plate* TLC silica gel $F_{254}$ *plate R*.

*Mobile phase* water R, diethylamine R, methyl ethyl ketone R (1:4:95 *V/V/V*).

*Application* 2 μl.

*Development* Twice over a path of 15 cm.

*Drying* In air.

*Detection A* Examine in ultraviolet light at 254 nm.

*Results A* The principal spot in the chromatogram obtained with the test solution is similar in position and size to the principal spot in the chromatogram obtained with the reference solution. Doubling of the spot may be observed in both chromatograms.

*Detection B* Spray with *alcoholic solution of sulphuric acid R*; heat at 110 °C for 5 min and allow to cool; examine in ultraviolet light at 365 nm.

*Results B* The principal spot in the chromatogram obtained with the test solution is similar in position and size to the principal spot in the chromatogram obtained with the reference solution. Doubling of the spot may be observed in both chromatograms.

C. Mix about 5 mg with 45 mg of *heavy magnesium oxide R* and ignite in a crucible until an almost white residue is obtained (usually less than 5 min). Allow to cool, add 1 ml of *water R*, 0.05 ml of *phenolphthalein solution R1* and about 1 ml of *dilute hydrochloric acid R* to render the solution colourless. Filter and add to the filtrate a freshly prepared mixture of 0.1 ml of *alizarin S solution R* and 0.1 ml of *zirconyl nitrate solution R*. Mix, allow to stand for 5 min and compare the colour of the solution with that of a blank prepared in the same manner. The test solution is yellow. The blank is red.

D. It gives reaction (a) of chlorides (*2.3.1*).

## TESTS
### Appearance of solution
The solution is clear (*2.2.1*) and not more intensely coloured than reference solution $GY_6$ (*2.2.2, Method II*).

Dissolve 2.0 g of the substance to be examined in *water R* and dilute to 20 ml with the same solvent.

### pH (*2.2.3*)
2.0 to 3.0.

Dissolve 0.5 g in *carbon dioxide-free water R* and dilute to 50 ml with the same solvent.

### Related substances
Thin-layer chromatography (*2.2.27*). *Carry out the test protected from light and prepare the solutions immediately before use.*

*Test solution (a)* Dissolve 0.40 g of the substance to be examined in *alcohol R* and dilute to 20 ml with the same solvent.

*Test solution (b)* Dilute 2.0 ml of test solution (a) to 20.0 ml with *alcohol R*.

*Reference solution (a)* Dilute 1.0 ml of test solution (b) to 50.0 ml with *alcohol R*.

*Reference solution (b)* Dilute 2.0 ml of reference solution (a) to 20.0 ml with *alcohol R*.

*Reference solution (c)* Dissolve 10 mg of *flupentixol impurity D CRS* in *alcohol R*, add 0.5 ml of test solution (a) and dilute to 20.0 ml with *alcohol R*.

*Plate* TLC silica gel $F_{254}$ *plate R*.

*Mobile phase* diethylamine R, toluene R, ethyl acetate R (10:20:70 *V/V/V*).

*Application* 5 μl.

*Development* In an unsaturated tank over a path of 10 cm.

*Drying* In air.

*Detection* Spray with *alcoholic solution of sulphuric acid R*, heat at 110 °C for 5 min and allow to cool; examine in ultraviolet light at 365 nm. Doubling of the spot due to flupentixol may be observed.

*System suitability*  The chromatogram obtained with reference solution (c) shows 2 clearly separated spots.

*Limits:*

— in the chromatogram obtained with test solution (a): any spots, apart from the principal spot, are not more intense than the spot, or spots in the chromatogram obtained with reference solution (a) (0.2 per cent),

— in the chromatogram obtained with test solution (b): any spots, apart from the principal spot, are not more intense than the spot or spots in the chromatogram obtained with reference solution (b) (0.2 per cent).

**Impurity F**

Liquid chromatography (*2.2.29*). *Carry out the test protected from light and prepare the solutions immediately before use.*

*Test solution*  Dissolve 20.0 mg of the substance to be examined in the mobile phase and dilute to 20.0 ml with the mobile phase.

*Reference solution*  Dissolve 10.0 mg of *flupentixol dihydrochloride CRS* and 10.0 mg of *flupentixol impurity F CRS* in the mobile phase and dilute to 100.0 ml with the mobile phase. Dilute 1.0 ml of the solution to 20.0 ml with the mobile phase.

*Column:*

— *size: l* = 0.125 m, Ø = 4.6 mm,

— *stationary phase: octylsilyl silica gel for chromatography R* (3 μm)

*Mobile phase*  Mix 10 volumes of *acetonitrile R*, 55 volumes of *methanol R* and 35 volumes of a solution containing 8.72 g/l of *potassium dihydrogen phosphate R*, 0.37 g/l of *anhydrous disodium hydrogen phosphate R* and 0.77 g/l of *dodecyltrimethylammonium bromide R*.

*Flow rate*  1.0 ml/min.

*Detection*  Spectrophotometer at 270 nm.

*Injection*  20 μl.

*System suitability*  Reference solution:

— *resolution*: minimum 2.0 between the $2^{nd}$ of the peaks due to impurity F and the $1^{st}$ of the peaks due to flupentixol. Peak splitting may not always occur.

*Limit:*

— *impurity F*: not more than the area of the corresponding peak or peaks in the chromatogram obtained with the reference solution (0.5 per cent).

**Heavy metals** (*2.4.8*)

Maximum 20 ppm.

1.0 g complies with limit test C. Prepare the standard using 2 ml of *lead standard solution (10 ppm Pb) R*.

**Loss on drying** (*2.2.32*)

Maximum 2.0 per cent, determined on 1.000 g by drying in an oven at 105 °C.

**Sulphated ash** (*2.4.14*)

Maximum 0.1 per cent, determined on 1.0 g in a platinum crucible.

**ASSAY**

Flupentixol dihydrochloride . Dissolve 0.200 g in 30 ml of *alcohol R*. Carry out a potentiometric titration (*2.2.20*), using *0.1 M sodium hydroxide*. Read the volume added between the 2 points of inflexion.

1 ml of *0.1 M sodium hydroxide* is equivalent to 50.74 mg of $C_{23}H_{27}Cl_2F_3N_2OS$.

**Z-Isomer**

Liquid chromatography (*2.2.29*).

*Test solution*  Dissolve 20.0 mg of the substance to be examined in the mobile phase and dilute to 50.0 ml with the mobile phase.

*Reference solution*  Dissolve 20.0 mg of *flupentixol dihydrochloride CRS* in the mobile phase and dilute to 50.0 ml with the mobile phase.

*Column:*

— *size: l* = 0.25 m, Ø = 4.0 mm,

— *stationary phase: silica gel for chromatography R* (5 μm).

*Mobile phase*  *water R, concentrated ammonia R, 2-propanol R, heptane R* (2:4:150:850 *V/V/V/V*).

*Flow rate*  1.5 ml/min.

*Detection*  Spectrophotometer at 254 nm.

*Injection*  20 μl.

*System suitability*  Reference solution:

— *resolution*: minimum 3.0 between the peaks due to Z-isomer ($1^{st}$ peak) and to E-isomer ($2^{nd}$ peak).

*Results:*

— calculate the percentage content of Z-isomer taking into account the assigned content of Z-isomer in *flupentixol dihydrochloride CRS* ,

— calculate the ratio of the area of the peak due to the E-isomer to the area of the peak due to the Z-isomer: this ratio is 0.9 to 1.4.

**STORAGE**

Protected from light.

**IMPURITIES**

A. (9RS)-9-[3-(dimethylamino)propyl]-2-(trifluoromethyl)-9H-thioxanthen-9-ol,

B. N,N-dimethyl-3-[(EZ)-2-(trifluoromethyl)-9H-thioxanthen-9-ylidene]propan-1-amine,

C. R = H: 1-[3-[(EZ)-2-(trifluoromethyl)-9H-thioxanthen-9-ylidene]propyl]piperazine,

D. R = CH₂-CH₂-O-CH₂-CH₂-OH: 2-[2-[4-[3-[(*EZ*)-2-(trifluoromethyl)-9*H*-thioxanthen-9-ylidene]propyl]piperazin-1-yl]ethoxy]ethanol,

E. R = CH₂-CH₂-O-CO-CH₃:
2-[4-[3-[(*EZ*)-2-(trifluoromethyl)-9*H*-thioxanthen-9-ylidene]propyl]piperazin-1-yl]ethyl acetate,

and enantiomer

F. 2-[4-[(*EZ*)-3-[(9*RS*)-2-(trifluoromethyl)-9*H*-thioxanthen-9-yl]prop-2-enyl]piperazin-1-yl]ethanol,

G. 2-(trifluoromethyl)-9*H*-thioxanthen-9-one.

*Ph Eur*

# Fluphenazine Decanoate

(*Ph Eur monograph 1014*)

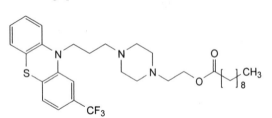

C₃₂H₄₄F₃N₃O₂S        591.8        *5002-47-1*

## Action and use
Dopamine receptor antagonist; neuroleptic.

## Preparation
Fluphenazine Decanoate Injection

*Ph Eur*

## DEFINITION
2-[4-[3-[2-(Trifluoromethyl)-10*H*-phenothiazin-10-yl]propyl]piperazin-1-yl]ethyl decanoate.

## Content
98.5 per cent to 101.5 per cent (dried substance).

## CHARACTERS
### Appearance
Pale yellow, viscous liquid or yellow solid.

### Solubility
Practically insoluble in water, very soluble in ethanol and in methylene chloride, freely soluble in methanol.

## IDENTIFICATION
*First identification*  B, C.

*Second identification*  A, C.

A. Dissolve 50.0 mg in *methanol R* and dilute to 100.0 ml with the same solvent. Dilute 1.0 ml to 50.0 ml with *methanol R*. Examined between 230 nm and 350 nm (*2.2.25*), the solution shows an absorption maximum at 260 nm and a broad absorption maximum at about 310 nm. The specific absorbance at the maximum at 260 nm is 570 to 630.

B. Infrared absorption spectrophotometry (*2.2.24*).

*Preparation*  Apply 50 µl of a 25 g/l solution in *methylene chloride R* to a disc of *potassium bromide R*. Dry the discs at 60 °C for 1 h before use.

*Comparison*  fluphenazine decanoate CRS .

C. Thin-layer chromatography (*2.2.27*).

*Test solution*  Dissolve 10 mg of the substance to be examined in *methanol R* and dilute to 10 ml with the same solvent.

*Reference solution (a)*  Dissolve 10 mg of *fluphenazine decanoate CRS* in *methanol R* and dilute to 10 ml with the same solvent.

*Reference solution (b)*  Dissolve 5 mg of *fluphenazine enantate CRS* in reference solution (a) and dilute to 5 ml with the same solution.

*Plate*  TLC octadecylsilyl silica gel F₂₅₄ plate R.

*Mobile phase*  concentrated ammonia R1, water R, methanol R (1:4:95 *V/V/V*).

*Application*  2 µl.

*Development*  Over a path of 8 cm.

*Detection*  Examine in ultraviolet light at 254 nm.

*System suitability*  The chromatogram obtained with reference solution (b) shows 2 clearly separated spots.

*Results*  The principal spot in the chromatogram obtained with the test solution is similar in position and size to the principal spot in the chromatogram obtained with reference solution (a).

## TESTS
### Related substances
Liquid chromatography (*2.2.29*). *Carry out the test protected from light and prepare the solutions immediately before use.*

*Test solution*  Dissolve 10.0 mg of the substance to be examined in *acetonitrile R* and dilute to 50.0 ml with the same solvent.

*Reference solution (a)*  Dissolve 5 mg of *fluphenazine octanoate CRS* and 5 mg of *fluphenazine enantate CRS* in *acetonitrile R* and dilute to 50 ml with the same solvent.

*Reference solution (b)*  Dilute 5.0 ml of the test solution to 100.0 ml with a mixture of 5 volumes of mobile phase A and 95 volumes of mobile phase B. Dilute 1.0 ml of this solution to 10.0 ml with a mixture of 5 volumes of mobile phase A and 95 volumes of mobile phase B.

*Reference solution (c)*  Dissolve 11.7 mg of *fluphenazine dihydrochloride CRS* and 5.0 mg of *fluphenazine sulphoxide CRS* in a mixture of 5 volumes of *water R* and 95 volumes of *acetonitrile R* and dilute to 100.0 ml with the same mixture of solvents. Dilute 1.0 ml to 50.0 ml with a mixture of 5 volumes of *water R* and 95 volumes of *acetonitrile R*.

*Column:*
— *size: l* = 0.25 m, Ø = 4.6 mm,

— *stationary phase*: *spherical octadecylsilyl silica gel for chromatography R* (5 µm).

*Mobile phase*:
— *mobile phase A*: 10 g/l solution of *ammonium carbonate R* adjusted to pH 7.5 with *dilute hydrochloric acid R*,
— *mobile phase B*: mobile phase A, *acetonitrile R*, *methanol R* (7.5:45:45 *V/V/V*),

| Time (min) | Mobile phase A (per cent *V/V*) | Mobile phase B (per cent *V/V*) |
|---|---|---|
| 0 - 7 | 20 | 80 |
| 7 - 17 | 20 → 0 | 80 → 100 |
| 17 - 80 | 0 | 100 |
| 80 - 81 | 0 → 20 | 100 → 80 |

*Flow rate*   1.0 ml/min.

*Detection*   Spectrophotometer at 260 nm.

*Equilibration*   At least 30 min with the mobile phase at the initial composition.

*Injection*   10 µl.

*Relative retention*   With reference to fluphenazine decanoate (retention time = about 34 min): impurity A = about 0.13; impurity B = about 0.33; impurity C = about 0.76; impurity D = about 0.82.

*System suitability*   Reference solution (a):
— *resolution*: minimum 6 between the peaks due to impurity C and impurity D.

*Limits*:
— *impurity A*: not more than the area of the corresponding peak in the chromatogram obtained with reference solution (c) (0.5 per cent),
— *impurity B*: not more than the area of the corresponding peak in the chromatogram obtained with reference solution (c) (1.0 per cent),
— *any other impurity*: not more than the area of the principal peak in the chromatogram obtained with reference solution (b) (0.5 per cent),
— *total*: not more than 2.0 per cent,
— *disregard limit for any other impurity*: 0.1 times the area of the principal peak in the chromatogram obtained with reference solution (b) (0.05 per cent).

**Heavy metals** (*2.4.8*)
Maximum 20 ppm.

1.0 g complies with limit test C. Prepare the standard using 2 ml of *lead standard solution (10 ppm Pb) R*.

**Loss on drying** (*2.2.32*)
Maximum 1.0 per cent, determined on 1.000 g by drying in an oven at 60 °C at a pressure not exceeding 0.7 kPa for 3 h.

**Sulphated ash** (*2.4.14*)
Maximum 0.1 per cent, determined on 1.0 g in a platinum crucible.

## ASSAY
Dissolve 0.250 g in 30 ml of *glacial acetic acid R*. Using 0.05 ml of *crystal violet solution R* as indicator, titrate with *0.1 M perchloric acid* until the colour changes from violet to green.

1 ml of *0.1 M perchloric acid* is equivalent to 29.59 mg of $C_{32}H_{44}F_3N_3O_2S$.

## STORAGE
Protected from light.

## IMPURITIES

A. X = SO, R = H: fluphenazine *S*-oxide,
B. X = S, R = H: fluphenazine,
C. X = S, R = CO-[CH$_2$]$_5$-CH$_3$: fluphenazine enantate,
D. X = S, R = CO-[CH$_2$]$_6$-CH$_3$: fluphenazine octanoate,
E. X = S, R = CO-[CH$_2$]$_7$-CH$_3$: fluphenazine nonanoate,
F. X = S, R = CO-[CH$_2$]$_9$-CH$_3$: fluphenazine undecanoate,
G. X = S, R = CO-[CH$_2$]$_{10}$-CH$_3$: fluphenazine dodecanoate.

——————————————————— *Ph Eur*

# Fluphenazine Enantate

(*Ph Eur monograph 1015*)

$C_{29}H_{38}F_3N_3O_2S$          549.7          *2746-81-8*

**Action and use**
Dopamine receptor antagonist; neuroleptic.

*Ph Eur* ————————————————————

## DEFINITION
2-[4-[3-[2-(Trifluoromethyl)-10*H*-phenothiazin-10-yl]propyl]piperazin-1-yl]ethyl heptanoate.

**Content**
98.5 per cent to 101.5 per cent (dried substance).

## CHARACTERS
**Appearance**
Pale yellow, viscous liquid or yellow solid.

**Solubility**
Practically insoluble in water, very soluble in ethanol and in methylene chloride, freely soluble in methanol.

## IDENTIFICATION
*First identification*   B, C.

*Second identification*   A, C.

A. Dissolve 50.0 mg in *methanol R* and dilute to 100.0 ml with the same solvent. Dilute 1.0 ml to 50.0 ml with *methanol R*. Examined between 230 nm and 350 nm (*2.2.25*), the solution shows an absorption maximum at 260 nm and a broad absorption maximum at about 310 nm. The specific absorbance at the maximum at 260 nm is 610 to 670.

B. Infrared absorption spectrophotometry (*2.2.24*).

*Preparation* Apply 50 µl of a 25 g/l solution in *methylene chloride R* to a disc of *potassium bromide R*. Dry the discs at 60 °C for 1 h before use.

*Comparison* *fluphenazine enantate CRS* .

C. Thin-layer chromatography (*2.2.27*).

*Test solution* Dissolve 10 mg of the substance to be examined in *methanol R* and dilute to 10 ml with the same solvent.

*Reference solution (a)* Dissolve 10 mg of *fluphenazine enantate CRS* in *methanol R* and dilute to 10 ml with the same solvent.

*Reference solution (b)* Dissolve 5 mg of *fluphenazine decanoate CRS* in reference solution (a) and dilute to 5 ml with the same solution.

*Plate* TLC *octadecylsilyl silica gel F₂₅₄ plate R*.

*Mobile phase* *concentrated ammonia R1, water R, methanol R* (1:4:95 *V/V/V*).

*Application* 2 µl.

*Development* Over a path of 8 cm.

*Detection* Examine in ultraviolet light at 254 nm.

*System suitability* The chromatogram obtained with reference solution (b) shows 2 clearly separated spots.

*Results* The principal spot in the chromatogram obtained with the test solution is similar in position and size to the principal spot in the chromatogram obtained with reference solution (a).

## TESTS

### Related substances

Liquid chromatography (*2.2.29*). *Carry out the test protected from light and prepare the solutions immediately before use.*

*Test solution* Dissolve 10.0 mg of the substance to be examined in *acetonitrile R* and dilute to 50.0 ml with the same solvent.

*Reference solution (a)* Dissolve 5 mg of *fluphenazine octanoate CRS* and 5 mg of *fluphenazine enantate CRS* in *acetonitrile R* and dilute to 50 ml with the same solvent.

*Reference solution (b)* Dilute 5.0 ml of the test solution to 100.0 ml with a mixture of 5 volumes of mobile phase A and 95 volumes of mobile phase B. Dilute 1.0 ml of this solution to 10.0 ml with a mixture of 5 volumes of mobile phase A and 95 volumes of mobile phase B.

*Reference solution (c)* Dissolve 5.0 mg of *fluphenazine sulphoxide CRS* in *acetonitrile R* and dilute to 100.0 ml with the same solvent. Dilute 1.0 ml to 50.0 ml with *acetonitrile R*.

*Column:*
— *size: l* = 0.25 m, Ø = 4.6 mm,
— *stationary phase:* spherical *octadecylsilyl silica gel for chromatography R* (5 µm).

*Mobile phase:*
— *mobile phase A*: 10 g/l solution of *ammonium carbonate R* adjusted to pH 7.5 with *dilute hydrochloric acid R*,
— *mobile phase B*: mobile phase A, *acetonitrile R, methanol R* (7.5:45:45 *V/V/V*),

| Time (min) | Mobile phase A (per cent *V/V*) | Mobile phase B (per cent *V/V*) |
| --- | --- | --- |
| 0 - 7 | 20 | 80 |
| 7 - 17 | 20 → 0 | 80 → 100 |
| 17 - 80 | 0 | 100 |
| 80 - 81 | 0 → 20 | 100 → 80 |

*Flow rate* 1.0 ml/min.

*Detection* Spectrophotometer at 260 nm.

*Equilibration* At least 30 min with the mobile phase at the initial composition.

*Injection* 10 µl.

*Relative retention* With reference to fluphenazine enantate (retention time = about 25 min): impurity A = about 0.2; impurity D = about 1.1.

*System suitability* Reference solution (a):
— *resolution*: minimum 6 between the peaks due to fluphenazine enantate and impurity D.

*Limits:*
— *impurity A*: not more than the area of the principal peak in the chromatogram obtained with reference solution (c) (0.5 per cent),
— *any other impurity*: not more than the area of the principal peak in the chromatogram obtained with reference solution (b) (0.5 per cent),
— *total*: not more than 1.6 per cent,
— *disregard limit for any other impurity*: 0.1 times the area of the principal peak in the chromatogram obtained with reference solution (b) (0.05 per cent).

**Heavy metals** (*2.4.8*)
Maximum 20 ppm.

1.0 g complies with limit test C. Prepare the standard using 2 ml of *lead standard solution (10 ppm Pb) R*.

**Loss on drying** (*2.2.32*)
Maximum 1.0 per cent, determined on 1.000 g by drying in an oven at 60 °C at a pressure not exceeding 0.7 kPa for 3 h.

**Sulphated ash** (*2.4.14*)
Maximum 0.1 per cent, determined on 1.0 g in a platinum crucible.

## ASSAY

Dissolve 0.250 g in 30 ml of *glacial acetic acid R*. Using 0.05 ml of *crystal violet solution R* as indicator titrate with *0.1 M perchloric acid* until the colour changes from violet to green.

1 ml of *0.1 M perchloric acid* is equivalent to 27.49 mg of $C_{29}H_{38}F_3N_3O_2S$.

## STORAGE

Protected from light.

## IMPURITIES

A. X = SO, R = H: fluphenazine *S*-oxide,

B. X = S, R = H: fluphenazine,

C. X = S, R = CO-[CH₂]₈-CH₃: fluphenazine decanoate,

D. X = S, R = CO-[CH₂]₆-CH₃: fluphenazine octanoate,

E. X = S, R = CO-[CH₂]₇-CH₃: fluphenazine nonanoate,

F. X = S, R = CO-[CH₂]₉-CH₃: fluphenazine undecanoate,

G. X = S, R = CO-[CH₂]₁₀-CH₃: fluphenazine dodecanoate.

# Fluphenazine Hydrochloride

Fluphenazine Dihydrochloride

(*Fluphenazine Dihydrochloride, Ph Eur monograph 0904*)

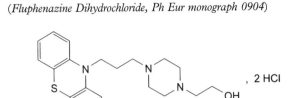

$C_{22}H_{26}F_3N_3OS,2HCl$     510.5     *146-56-5*

## Action and use
Dopamine receptor antagonist; neuroleptic.

## Preparation
Fluphenazine Tablets

*Ph Eur*

## DEFINITION
2-[4-[3-[2-(Trifluoromethyl)-10*H*-phenothiazin-10-yl]propyl]piperazin-1-yl]ethanol dihydrochloride.

## Content
98.5 per cent to 101.5 per cent (dried substance).

## CHARACTERS
### Appearance
White or almost white, crystalline powder.

### Solubility
Freely soluble in water, slightly soluble in ethanol (96 per cent) and in methylene chloride.

## IDENTIFICATION
*First identification*  B, D.

*Second identification*  A, C, D.

A. Ultraviolet and visible absorption spectrophotometry (*2.2.25*).

*Test solution*  Dissolve 50.0 mg in *methanol R* and dilute to 100.0 ml with the same solvent. Dilute 2.0 ml of this solution to 100.0 ml with *methanol R*.

*Spectral range*  230-350 nm.

*Absorption maxima*  At 260 nm and at about 310 nm (broad band).

*Specific absorbance at the absorption maximum at 260 nm*  630 to 700.

B. Infrared absorption spectrophotometry (*2.2.24*).

*Comparison*  fluphenazine dihydrochloride CRS .

C. Thin-layer chromatography (*2.2.27*).

*Test solution*  Dissolve 10 mg of the substance to be examined in *methanol R* and dilute to 10 ml with the same solvent.

*Reference solution (a)*  Dissolve 10 mg of *fluphenazine dihydrochloride CRS* in *methanol R* and dilute to 10 ml with the same solvent.

*Reference solution (b)*  Dissolve 5 mg of *perphenazine CRS* in reference solution (a) and dilute to 5 ml with reference solution (a).

*Plate*  TLC octadecylsilyl silica gel $F_{254}$ plate R.

*Mobile phase*  concentrated ammonia R1, water R, methanol R (1:4:95 *V/V/V*).

*Application*  2 µl.

*Development*  Over 2/3 of the plate.

*Detection*  Examine in ultraviolet light at 254 nm.

*System suitability*  Reference solution (b):
— the chromatogram shows 2 clearly separated principal spots.

*Results*  The principal spot in the chromatogram obtained with the test solution is similar in position and size to the principal spot in the chromatogram obtained with reference solution (a).

D. It gives reaction (a) of chlorides (*2.3.1*).

## TESTS
### pH (*2.2.3*)
1.9 to 2.4.

Dissolve 0.5 g in 10 ml of *water R*.

### Related substances
Liquid chromatography (*2.2.29*). *Carry out the test protected from light and prepare the solutions immediately before use.*

*Test solution*  Dissolve 25.0 mg of the substance to be examined in mobile phase B and dilute to 50.0 ml with mobile phase B.

*Reference solution (a)*  Dilute 1.0 ml of the test solution to 100.0 ml with mobile phase B.

*Reference solution (b)*  Dilute 5.0 ml of reference solution (a) to 25.0 ml with mobile phase B.

*Reference solution (c)*  Dissolve the contents of a vial of *fluphenazine impurity mixture CRS* (containing impurities A, B, C and D) in 1 ml of the test solution.

*Reference solution (d)*  Dissolve 5.0 mg of *fluphenazine sulphoxide CRS* (impurity A) in mobile phase B and dilute to 50.0 ml with mobile phase B. Dilute 1.0 ml of this solution to 100.0 ml with mobile phase B.

*Column:*
— *size: l* = 0.25 m, Ø = 4.6 mm;
— *stationary phase*: spherical octadecylsilyl silica gel for chromatography R (5 µm).

*Mobile phase:*
— *mobile phase A*: 10 g/l solution of *ammonium carbonate R* adjusted to pH 7.5 with *dilute hydrochloric acid R*;
— *mobile phase B*: mobile phase A, *acetonitrile R, methanol R* (7.5:45:45 *V/V/V*);

| Time (min) | Mobile phase A (per cent *V/V*) | Mobile phase B (per cent *V/V*) |
|---|---|---|
| 0 - 7 | 25 | 75 |
| 7 - 17 | 25 → 0 | 75 → 100 |
| 17 - 50 | 0 | 100 |
| 50 - 51 | 0 → 25 | 100 → 75 |

*Flow rate*  1.0 ml/min.

*Detection*  Spectrophotometer at 260 nm and at 274 nm.

*Injection*  10 µl of the test solution and reference solutions (b), (c) and (d).

*Identification of impurities*  Use the chromatogram supplied with *fluphenazine impurity mixture CRS* and the chromatogram obtained with reference solution (c) to identify the peaks due to impurities A, B, C and D.

*Relative retention*  With reference to fluphenazine (retention time = about 14.5 min): impurity A = about 0.3; impurity B = about 0.4; impurity C = about 1.8; impurity D = about 2.2.

*System suitability*  Reference solution (c):

— *resolution*: minimum 2.5 between the peaks due to impurities A and B.

*Limits:*

— *correction factors*: for the calculation of content, multiply the peak areas of the following impurities by the corresponding correction factor: impurity B = 0.3; impurity C = 0.6;

— *impurity A at 274 nm*: not more than the area of the corresponding peak in the chromatogram obtained with reference solution (d) (0.2 per cent);

— *impurity B at 274 nm*: not more than the area of the principal peak in the chromatogram obtained with reference solution (b) (0.2 per cent);

— *impurities C, D at 260 nm*: for each impurity, not more than the area of the principal peak in the chromatogram obtained with reference solution (b) (0.2 per cent);

— *unspecified impurities at 260 nm*: for each impurity, not more than 0.5 times the area of the principal peak in the chromatogram obtained with reference solution (b) (0.10 per cent);

— *sum of the impurities at 260 nm and impurities A and B at 274 nm*: maximum 1.0 per cent;

— *disregard limit at 260 nm*: 0.25 times the area of the principal peak in the chromatogram obtained with reference solution (b) (0.05 per cent).

**Heavy metals** *(2.4.8)*

Maximum 20 ppm.

1.0 g complies with test C. Prepare the reference solution using 2 ml of *lead standard solution (10 ppm Pb) R*.

**Loss on drying** *(2.2.32)*

Maximum 1.0 per cent, determined on 0.500 g by drying in an oven at 65 °C for 3 h.

**Sulphated ash** *(2.4.14)*

Maximum 0.1 per cent, determined on 1.0 g in a platinum crucible.

## ASSAY

*In order to avoid overheating during the titration, mix thoroughly throughout and stop the titration immediately after the end-point has been reached.*

Dissolve 0.220 g in a mixture of 10 ml of *anhydrous formic acid R* and 40 ml of *acetic anhydride R*. Titrate with *0.1 M perchloric acid*, determining the end-point potentiometrically *(2.2.20)*.

1 ml of *0.1 M perchloric acid* is equivalent to 25.52 mg of $C_{22}H_{28}C_{12}F_3N_3OS$.

## STORAGE

Protected from light.

## IMPURITIES

*Specified impurities    A, B, C, D.*

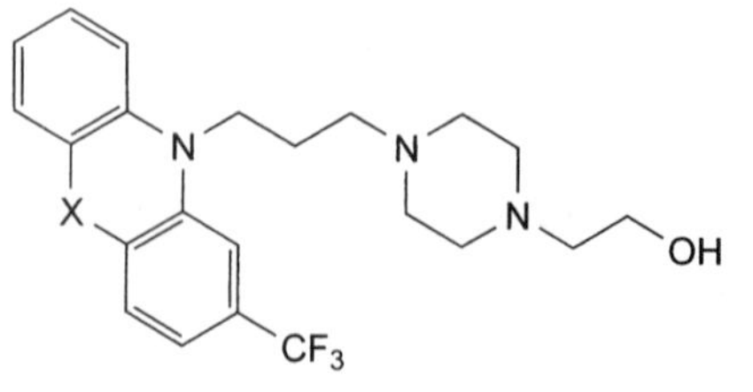

A. X = SO: 2-[4-[3-[5-oxo-2-(trifluoromethyl)-10*H*-5⁴-phenothiazin-10-yl]propyl]piperazin-1-yl]ethanol (fluphenazine *S*-oxide),

B. X = SO₂: 2-[4-[3-[5,5-dioxo-2-(trifluoromethyl)-10*H*-5⁶-phenothiazin-10-yl]propyl]piperazin-1-yl]ethanol (fluphenazine *S,S*-dioxide),

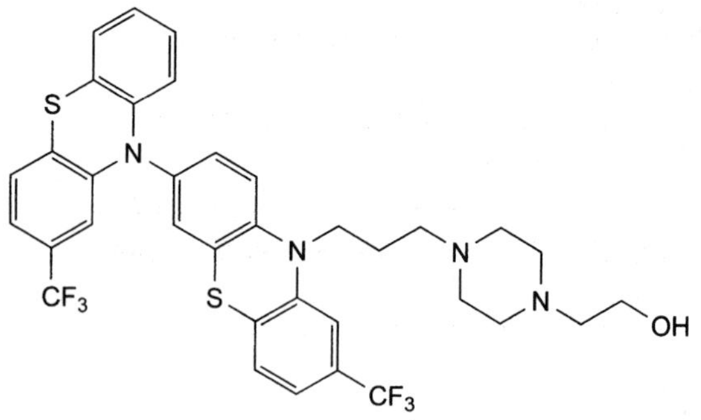

C. 2-[4-[3-[2′,8-bis(trifluoromethyl)-10*H*-3,10′-biphenothiazin-10-yl]propyl]piperazin-1-yl]ethanol,

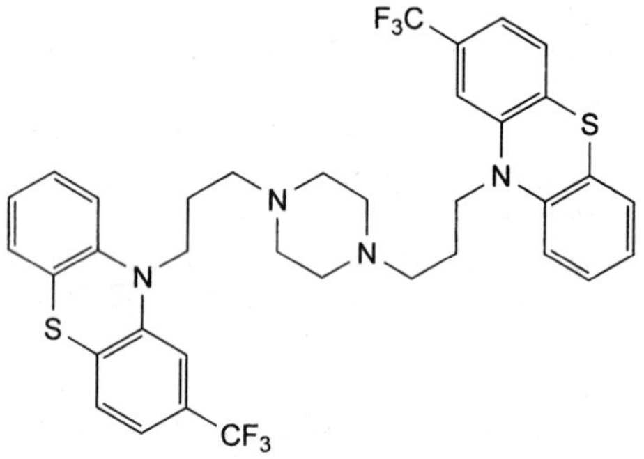

D. 10,10′-[piperazine-1,4-diylbis(propane-3,1-diyl)]bis[2-(trifluoromethyl)-10*H*-phenothiazine].

_____ *Ph Eur*

# Flurazepam Monohydrochloride

*(Ph Eur monograph 0905)*

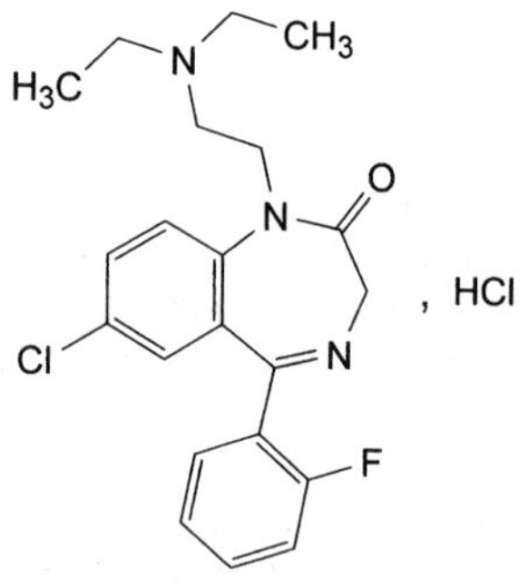

$C_{21}H_{23}ClFN_3O,HCl$          424.3          *36105-20-1*

**Action and use**

Benzodiazepine.

**Preparation**

Flurazepam Capsules

*Ph Eur* _____

## DEFINITION

7-Chloro-1-[2-(diethylamino)ethyl]-5-(2-fluorophenyl)-1,3-dihydro-2*H*-1,4-benzodiazepin-2-one monohydrochloride.

## Content

99.0 per cent to 101.0 per cent (dried substance).

## CHARACTERS

### Appearance

White or almost white, crystalline powder.

### Solubility

Very soluble in water, freely soluble in alcohol.

## IDENTIFICATION

A. Infrared absorption spectrophotometry (2.2.24).

*Comparison* Ph. Eur. *reference spectrum of flurazepam monohydrochloride.*

B. It gives reaction (a) of chlorides (2.3.1).

## TESTS

### pH (2.2.3)

5.0 to 6.0.

Dissolve 0.50 g in *carbon dioxide-free water R* and dilute to 10 ml with the same solvent.

### Related substances

Liquid chromatography (2.2.29). *Prepare the solutions immediately before use.*

*Test solution* Dissolve 50.0 mg of the substance to be examined in the mobile phase and dilute to 50.0 ml with the mobile phase.

*Reference solution (a)* Dilute 1.0 ml of the test solution to 100.0 ml with the mobile phase. Dilute 5.0 ml of this solution to 50.0 ml with the mobile phase.

*Reference solution (b)* Dissolve 5 mg of the substance to be examined and 5 mg of *oxazepam R* in 10 ml of *acetonitrile R* and dilute to 50.0 ml with the mobile phase.

*Column:*
— *size: l* = 0.15 m, Ø = 4.6 mm,
— *stationary phase: base-deactivated octylsilyl silica gel for chromatography R* (5 µm).

*Mobile phase* Mix 350 volumes of *acetonitrile R* and 650 volumes of a 10.5 g/l solution of *potassium dihydrogen phosphate R* and ajust to pH 6.1 with a 40 g/l solution of *sodium hydroxide R.*

*Flow rate* 1.0 ml/min.

*Detection* Spectrophotometer at 239 nm.

*Injection* 20 µl.

*Run time* 6 times the retention time of flurazepam.

*Relative retention* With reference to flurazepam (retention time = about 7 min): impurity C = about 1.5; impurity B = about 1.9; impurity A = about 2.4.

*System suitability* Reference solution (b):
— *resolution*: minimum of 4.5 between the peaks due to flurazepam and to oxazepam.

*Limits:*
— *correction factors*: for the calculation of contents, multiply the peak areas of the following impurities by the corresponding correction factor: impurity B = 0.61; impurity C = 0.65,
— *any impurity*: not more than the area of the principal peak in the chromatogram obtained with reference solution (a) (0.1 per cent),
— *total*: not more than 3 times the area of the principal peak in the chromatogram obtained with reference solution (a) (0.3 per cent),
— *disregard limit*: 0.5 times the area of the principal peak in the chromatogram obtained with reference solution (a) (0.05 per cent).

### Fluorides (2.4.5)

Maximum 500 ppm.

0.10 g complies with the limit test for fluorides.

### Loss on drying (2.2.32)

Maximum 0.5 per cent, determined on 1.000 g by drying in an oven at 105 °C for 4 h.

### Sulphated ash (2.4.14)

Maximum 0.1 per cent, determined on 1.0 g.

## ASSAY

Dissolve 0.350 g in a mixture of 1.0 ml of *0.1 M hydrochloric acid* and 50 ml of *alcohol R*. Carry out a potentiometric titration (2.2.20), using *0.1 M sodium hydroxide*. Read the volume added between the 2 points of inflexion.

1 ml of *0.1 M sodium hydroxide* is equivalent to 42.43 mg of $C_{21}H_{24}Cl_2FN_3O$.

## STORAGE

Protected from light.

## IMPURITIES

A. [5-chloro-2-[[2-(diethylamino)ethyl]amino]phenyl] (2-fluorophenyl)methanone,

B. R = H: 7-chloro-5-(2-fluorophenyl)-1,3-dihydro-2*H*-1,4-benzodiazepin-2-one,

C. R = CHOH-CH₃: 7-chloro-5-(2-fluorophenyl)-1-[(1*RS*)-1-hydroxyethyl]-1,3-dihydro-2*H*-1,4-benzodiazepin-2-one.

*Ph Eur*

# Flurbiprofen

(*Ph Eur monograph 1519*)

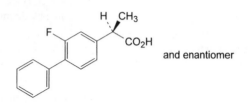

and enantiomer

C$_{15}$H$_{13}$FO$_2$        244.3        *5104-49-4*

## Action and use
Cyclo-oxygenase inhibitor; analgesic; anti-inflammatory.

## Preparations
Flurbiprofen Suppositories

Flurbiprofen Tablets

*Ph Eur* _____

## DEFINITION
(2*RS*)-2-(2-Fluorobiphenyl-4-yl)propanoic acid.

### Content
99.0 per cent to 101.0 per cent (dried substance).

## CHARACTERS

### Appearance
White or almost white, crystalline powder.

### Solubility
Practically insoluble in water, freely soluble in ethanol (96 per cent) and in methylene chloride. It dissolves in aqueous solutions of alkali hydroxides and carbonates.

## IDENTIFICATION
*First identification*   C, D.

*Second identification*   A, B, D.

A. Melting point (*2.2.14*): 114 °C to 117 °C.

B. Ultraviolet and visible absorption spectrophotometry (*2.2.25*).

*Test solution*   Dissolve 0.10 g in *0.1 M sodium hydroxide* and dilute to 100.0 ml with the same alkaline solution. Dilute 1.0 ml of this solution to 100.0 ml with *0.1 M sodium hydroxide*.

*Spectral range*   230-350 nm.

*Absorption maximum*   At 247 nm.

*Specific absorbance at the absorption maximum*   780 to 820.

C. Infrared absorption spectrophotometry (*2.2.24*).

*Comparison*   *flurbiprofen CRS*.

D. Mix about 5 mg with 45 mg of *heavy magnesium oxide R* and ignite in a crucible until an almost white residue is obtained (usually less than 5 min). Allow to cool, add 1 ml of *water R*, 0.05 ml of *phenolphthalein solution R1* and about 1 ml of *dilute hydrochloric acid R* to render the solution colourless. Filter. To a freshly prepared mixture of 0.1 ml of *alizarin S solution R* and 0.1 ml of *zirconyl nitrate solution R* add 1.0 ml of the filtrate. Mix, allow to stand for 5 min and compare the colour of the solution with that of a blank prepared in the same manner. The test solution is yellow and the blank is red.

## TESTS

### Appearance of solution
The solution is clear (*2.2.1*) and colourless (*2.2.2, Method I*).

Dissolve 1.0 g in *methanol R* and dilute to 10 ml with the same solvent.

### Optical rotation (*2.2.7*)
− 0.1° to + 0.1°.

Dissolve 0.50 g in *methanol R* and dilute to 20.0 ml with the same solvent.

### Related substances
Liquid chromatography (*2.2.29*).

*Solvent mixture*   acetonitrile R, water R (45:55 *V/V*).

*Test solution*   Dissolve 0.20 g of the substance to be examined in the solvent mixture and dilute to 100.0 ml with the solvent mixture.

*Reference solution (a)*   Dilute 1.0 ml of the test solution to 50.0 ml with the solvent mixture. Dilute 1.0 ml of this solution to 10.0 ml with the solvent mixture.

*Reference solution (b)*   Dissolve 10.0 mg of *flurbiprofen impurity A CRS* in the solvent mixture and dilute to 100.0 ml with the solvent mixture. Dilute 10.0 ml of this solution to 100.0 ml with the solvent mixture.

*Reference solution (c)*   Dissolve 10 mg of the substance to be examined in the solvent mixture and dilute to 100.0 ml with the solvent mixture. Dilute 1.0 ml of this solution to 10.0 ml with reference solution (b).

*Column:*
— *size: l* = 0.15 m, Ø = 3.9 mm;
— *stationary phase: octadecylsilyl silica gel for chromatography R* (5 μm).

*Mobile phase*   glacial acetic acid R, acetonitrile R, water R (5:35:60 *V/V/V*).

*Flow rate*   1 ml/min.

*Detection*   Spectrophotometer at 254 nm.

*Injection*   10 μl.

*Run time*   Twice the retention time of flurbiprofen.

*System suitability*   Reference solution (c):
— *resolution*: minimum 1.5 between the peaks due to impurity A and flurbiprofen.

*Limits:*
— *impurity A*: not more than the area of the corresponding peak in the chromatogram obtained with reference solution (b) (0.5 per cent);
— *impurities B, C, D, E*: for each impurity, not more than the area of the principal peak in the chromatogram obtained with reference solution (a) (0.2 per cent);
— *sum of impurities other than A*: not more than 5 times the area of the principal peak in the chromatogram obtained with reference solution (a) (1.0 per cent);
— *disregard limit*: 0.1 times the area of the principal peak in the chromatogram obtained with reference solution (a) (0.02 per cent).

### Heavy metals (*2.4.8*)
Maximum 10 ppm.

Dissolve 2.0 g in a mixture of 10 volumes of *water R* and 90 volumes of *methanol R* and dilute to 20 ml with the same mixture of solvents. 12 ml of the solution complies with test B. Prepare the reference solution using lead standard solution (1 ppm Pb) obtained by diluting *lead standard solution (100 ppm Pb) R* with a mixture of 10 volumes of *water R* and 90 volumes of *methanol R*.

### Loss on drying (*2.2.32*)
Maximum 0.5 per cent, determined on 1.000 g by drying at 60 °C at a pressure not exceeding 0.7 kPa for 3 h.

**Sulphated ash** (*2.4.14*)

Maximum 0.1 per cent, determined on 1.0 g in a platinum crucible.

## ASSAY

Dissolve 0.200 g in 50 ml of *ethanol (96 per cent) R*. Titrate with *0.1 M sodium hydroxide*, determining the end-point potentiometrically (*2.2.20*).

1 ml of *0.1 M sodium hydroxide* is equivalent to 24.43 mg of $C_{15}H_{13}FO_2$.

## IMPURITIES

*Specified impurities   A, B, C, D, E.*

A. R = R′ = H: (2RS)-2-(biphenyl-4-yl)propanoic acid,

B. R = $CH(CH_3)$-$CO_2H$, R′ = F:
2-(2-fluorobiphenyl-4-yl)-2,3-dimethylbutanedioic acid,

C. R = OH, R′ = F: (2RS)-2-(2-fluorobiphenyl-4-yl)-2-hydroxypropanoic acid,

D. R = CO-$CH_3$: 1-(2-fluorobiphenyl-4-yl)ethanone,

E. R = $CO_2H$: 2-fluorobiphenyl-4-carboxylic acid.

*Ph Eur*

# Flurbiprofen Sodium

$C_{15}H_{12}FNaO_2,2H_2O$       302.3       *56767-76-1*

**Action and use**

Cyclo-oxygenase inhibitor; analgesic; anti-inflammatory.

**Preparation**

Flurbiprofen Eye Drops

## DEFINITION

Flurbiprofen Sodium is sodium (RS)-2-(2-fluorobiphenyl-4-yl)propionate dihydrate. It contains not less than 98.5% and not more than 101.5% of $C_{15}H_{12}FNaO_2$, calculated with reference to the dried substance.

## CHARACTERISTICS

A white to creamy-white, crystalline powder.

Sparingly soluble in *water*; soluble in *ethanol (96%)*; practically insoluble in *dichloromethane*.

## IDENTIFICATION

A. The *infrared absorption spectrum*, Appendix II A, is concordant with the *reference spectrum* of flurbiprofen sodium (*RS 157*).

B. Heat 0.2 g over a flame until charred and then heat at 600° for 2 hours. The residue yields the reactions characteristic of *sodium salts*, Appendix VI.

## TESTS

**Related substances**

Carry out the method for *liquid chromatography*, Appendix III D, using solutions in a mixture of 25 volumes of *water* and 50 volumes of *methanol* containing (1) 0.10% w/v of the substance being examined, (2) 0.00020% w/v of the substance being examined, (3) 0.00050% w/v of *2-(biphenyl-4-yl)propionic acid BPCRS* and (4) 0.00050% w/v of the substance being examined and 0.00050% w/v of *2-(biphenyl-4-yl)propionic acid BPCRS*.

The chromatographic procedure may be carried out using (a) a stainless steel column (15 cm × 3.9 mm) packed with *octadecylsilyl silica gel for chromatography* (5 μm) (Resolve 5μ is suitable), (b) a mixture of 5 volumes of *glacial acetic acid*, 35 volumes of *acetonitrile* and 60 volumes of *water* as the mobile phase with a flow rate of 1 ml per minute and (c) a detection wavelength of 254 nm. Adjust the sensitivity so that the heights of the principal peaks in the chromatogram obtained with solution (4) are about 40% of full-scale deflection on the chart paper.

The test is not valid unless, in the chromatogram obtained with solution (4), the *resolution factor* between the two principal peaks is at least 1.5.

In the chromatogram obtained with solution (1) the area of any peak corresponding to 2-(biphenyl-4-yl)propionic acid is not greater than the area of the peak in the chromatogram obtained with solution (3) (0.5%), the area of any other *secondary peak* is not greater than the area of the peak in the chromatogram obtained with solution (2) (0.2%) and the sum of the areas of any *secondary peaks* is not greater than five times the area of the peak in the chromatogram obtained with solution (2) (1%).

**Heavy metals**

12 ml of a 20% w/v solution in *methanol* complies with *limit test A for heavy metals*, Appendix VII (10 ppm). Use 10 ml of the solution obtained by diluting 10 ml of *lead standard solution (20 ppm Pb)* to 100 ml with *methanol* to prepare the standard and 10 ml of *methanol* and 2 ml of the solution of the substance being examined to prepare the reagent blank.

**Loss on drying**

11.3% to 12.5% when determined by drying over *phosphorus pentoxide* at 60° at a pressure of 2 kPa for 18 hours. Use 1 g.

## ASSAY

Carry out the method for *liquid chromatography*, Appendix III D, using solutions in a mixture of 25 volumes of *water* and 50 volumes of *methanol* containing (1) 0.015% w/v of the substance being examined, (2) 0.015% w/v of *flurbiprofen sodium BPCRS* and (3) 0.00075% w/v of the substance being examined and 0.00075% w/v of *2-(biphenyl-4-yl)propionic acid BPCRS*.

The chromatographic procedure described under Related substances may be used.

The assay is not valid unless, in the chromatogram obtained with solution (3), the *resolution factor* between the two principal peaks is at least 1.5.

Calculate the content of $C_{15}H_{12}FNaO_2$ in the substance being examined using the declared content of $C_{15}H_{12}FNaO_2$ in *flurbiprofen sodium BPCRS*.

## IMPURITIES

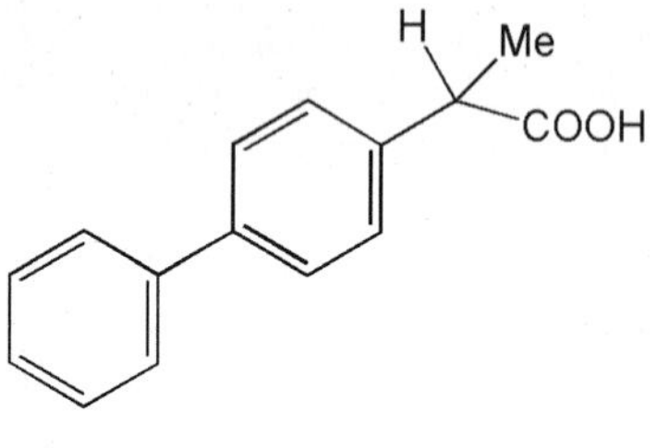

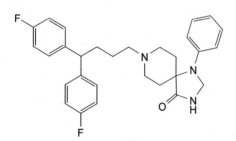

A. 2-(biphenyl-4-yl)propionic acid

# Fluspirilene

*(Ph Eur monograph 1723)*

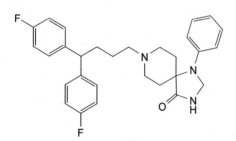

$C_{29}H_{31}F_2N_3O$     475.6     *1841-19-6*

## Action and use
Antipsychotic.

*Ph Eur* _____

## DEFINITION
8-[4,4-bis(4-Fluorophenyl)butyl]-1-phenyl-1,3,8-triazaspiro[4.5]decan-4-one.

## Content
99.0 per cent to 101.0 per cent (dried substance).

## CHARACTERS

### Appearance
White or almost white powder.

### Solubility
Practically insoluble in water, soluble in methylene chloride, slightly soluble in alcohol.

It shows polymorphism (*5.9*).

## IDENTIFICATION
Infrared absorption spectrophotometry (*2.2.24*).

*Preparation*   Discs.

*Comparison*   *fluspirilene CRS*.

If the spectra obtained show differences, dissolve the substance to be examined and the reference substance separately in *methylene chloride R*, gently evaporate to dryness and record new spectra using the residues.

## TESTS

### Appearance of solution
The solution is clear (*2.2.1*) and colourless (*2.2.2, Method II*).

Dissolve 0.25 g in 25 ml of *methylene chloride R*.

### Related substances
Liquid chromatography (*2.2.29*).

*Test solution*   Dissolve 0.100 g of the substance to be examined in *dimethylformamide R* and dilute to 10.0 ml with the same solvent.

*Reference solution (a)*   Dissolve 5.0 mg of *fluspirilene impurity C CRS* in *dimethylformamide R*, add 0.5 ml of the test solution and dilute to 100.0 ml with *dimethylformamide R*.

*Reference solution (b)*   Dilute 1.0 ml of the test solution to 20.0 ml with *dimethylformamide R*. Dilute 1.0 ml of this solution to 25.0 ml with *dimethylformamide R*.

*Column:*
— *size: l* = 0.15 m, Ø = 4.6 mm;
— *stationary phase: octadecylsilyl silica gel for chromatography R* (3 µm).

*Mobile phase A*   13.6 g/l solution of tetrabutylammonium hydrogen sulphate R,

*Mobile phase B*   *acetonitrile R*,

| Time (min) | Mobile phase A (per cent V/V) | Mobile phase B (per cent V/V) |
|---|---|---|
| 0 - 15 | 75 → 70 | 25 → 30 |
| 15 - 20 | 70 | 30 |
| 20 - 22 | 70 → 0 | 30 → 100 |
| 22 - 30 | 0 | 100 |
| 30 - 31 | 0 → 75 | 100 → 25 |
| 31 - 40 | 75 | 25 |

*Flow rate*   1.2 ml/min.

*Detection*   Spectrophotometer at 250 nm.

*Injection*   10 µl.

*Relative retention*   With reference to fluspirilene (retention time = about 15 min): impurity A = about 0.8; impurity B = about 0.93; impurity C = 0.97.

*System suitability*   Reference solution (a):
— *resolution*: minimum 2.2 between the peaks due to impurity C and fluspirilene.

*Limits:*
— *impurities A, B, C*: for each impurity, not more than 1.5 times the area of the principal peak in the chromatogram obtained with reference solution (b) (0.3 per cent);
— *any other impurity*: not more than 0.5 times the area of the principal peak in the chromatogram obtained with reference solution (b) (0.1 per cent);
— *total*: not more than 3 times the area of the principal peak in the chromatogram obtained with reference solution (b) (0.6 per cent);
— *disregard limit*: 0.25 times the area of the principal peak in the chromatogram obtained with reference solution (b) (0.05 per cent).

### Loss on drying (*2.2.32*)
Maximum 0.5 per cent, determined on 1.000 g by drying in an oven at 105 °C for 4 h.

**Sulphated ash** (*2.4.14*)
Maximum 0.1 per cent, determined on 1.0 g in a platinum crucible.

## ASSAY
Dissolve 0.350 g in 50 ml of a mixture of 1 volume of *anhydrous acetic acid R* and 7 volumes of *methyl ethyl ketone R*. Titrate with *0.1 M perchloric acid*, determining the end-point potentiometrically (*2.2.20*). Carry out a blank titration.

1 ml of *0.1 M perchloric acid* is equivalent to 47.56 mg of $C_{29}H_{31}F_2N_3O$.

## STORAGE
Protected from light.

## IMPURITIES
*Specified impurities   A, B, C.*

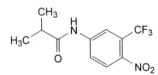

A. R1 = R2 = R3 = H: 8-[(4*RS*)-4-(4-fluorophenyl)-4-phenylbutyl]-1-phenyl-1,3,8-triazaspiro[4.5]decan-4-one,

B. R1 = R3 = H, R2 = F:
8-[(4*RS*)-4-(2-fluorophenyl)-4-(4-fluorophenyl)butyl]-1-phenyl-1,3,8-triazaspiro[4.5]decan-4-one,

C. R1 = CH$_2$OH, R2 = H, R3 = F:
8-[4,4-bis(4-fluorophenyl)butyl]-3-(hydroxymethyl)-1-phenyl-1,3,8-triazaspiro[4.5]decan-4-one.

*_____ Ph Eur*

# Flutamide

(*Ph Eur monograph 1423*)

$$C_{11}H_{11}F_3N_2O_3 \qquad 276.2 \qquad 13311\text{-}84\text{-}7$$

**Action and use**
Antiandrogen.

*Ph Eur* _____

## DEFINITION
2-Methyl-*N*-[4-nitro-3-(trifluoromethyl)phenyl]propanamide.

## Content
97.0 per cent to 103.0 per cent (dried substance).

## CHARACTERS
**Appearance**
Pale yellow, crystalline powder.

**Solubility**
Practically insoluble in water, freely soluble in acetone and in ethanol (96 per cent).

mp: about 112 °C.

## IDENTIFICATION
Infrared absorption spectrophotometry (*2.2.24*).

*Comparison   flutamide CRS.*

## TESTS
**Related substances**
Liquid chromatography (*2.2.29*).

*Test solution*   Dissolve 20.0 mg of the substance to be examined in the mobile phase and dilute to 20.0 ml with the mobile phase.

*Reference solution (a)*   Dissolve 2 mg of *flutamide CRS* and 2 mg of *flutamide impurity C CRS* in the mobile phase, then dilute to 50.0 ml with the mobile phase. Dilute 1.0 ml of this solution to 20.0 ml with the mobile phase.

*Reference solution (b)*   Dilute 1.0 ml of the test solution to 50.0 ml with the mobile phase. Dilute 2.0 ml of this solution to 20.0 ml with the mobile phase.

*Column:*
— *size:* $l = 0.25$ m, $\emptyset = 4.0$ mm;
— *stationary phase:* octadecylsilyl silica gel for chromatography R (5 μm).

*Mobile phase*   acetonitrile R, water R (50:50 *V/V*).

*Flow rate*   0.5 ml/min.

*Detection*   Spectrophotometer at 240 nm.

*Injection*   20 μl.

*Run time*   1.5 times the retention time of flutamide.

*Retention time*   Impurity C = about 14 min; flutamide = about 19 min.

*Relative retention*   With reference to flutamide: impurity C = about 0.72.

*System suitability*   Reference solution (a):
— *resolution:* minimum 10.5 between the peaks due to impurity C and flutamide.

*Limits:*
— *impurity C:* not more than 1.5 times the area of the principal peak in the chromatogram obtained with reference solution (b) (0.3 per cent);
— *impurities A, B, D, E, F:* for each impurity, not more than the area of the principal peak in the chromatogram obtained with reference solution (b) (0.2 per cent);
— *total:* not more than 2.5 times the area of the principal peak in the chromatogram obtained with reference solution (b) (0.5 per cent);
— *disregard limit:* 0.25 times the area of the principal peak in the chromatogram obtained with reference solution (b) (0.05 per cent).

**Heavy metals** (*2.4.8*)
Maximum 20 ppm.

1.0 g complies with test C. Prepare the reference solution using 2 ml of *lead standard solution (10 ppm Pb) R*.

**Loss on drying** (*2.2.32*)
Maximum 0.5 per cent, determined on 1.000 g by drying *in vacuo* at 60 °C for 3 h.

**Sulphated ash** (*2.4.14*)
Maximum 0.1 per cent, determined on 1.0 g.

## ASSAY
Dissolve 25.0 mg in *methanol R* and dilute to 25.0 ml with the same solvent. Dilute 2.0 ml of this solution to 100.0 ml with *methanol R*. Measure the absorbance (*2.2.25*) at the absorption maximum at 295 nm.

Calculate the content of $C_{11}H_{11}F_3N_2O_3$ taking the specific absorbance to be 295.

## STORAGE
Protected from light.

## IMPURITIES
*Specified impurities   A, B, C, D, E, F.*

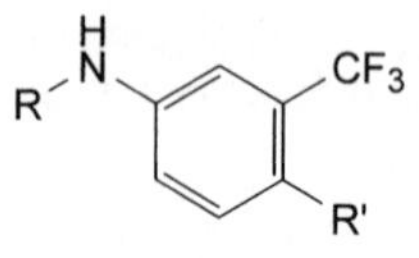

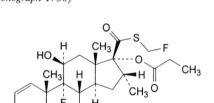

A. R = H, R′ = NO₂: 4-nitro-3-(trifluoromethyl)aniline,

B. R = CO-CH₃, R′ = NO₂:
N-[4-nitro-3-(trifluoromethyl)phenyl]acetamide,

C. R = CO-CH₂-CH₃, R′ = NO₂:
N-[4-nitro-3-(trifluoromethyl)phenyl]propanamide,

D. R = R′ = H: 3-(trifluoromethyl)aniline,

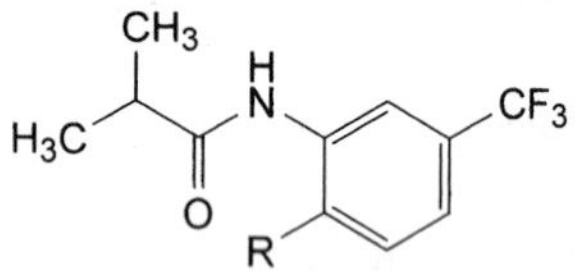

E. R = H: 2-methyl-N-[3-(trifluoromethyl)phenyl]propanamide,

F. R = NO₂: 2-methyl-N-[2-nitro-5-(trifluoromethyl)phenyl]propanamide.

*Ph Eur*

# Fluticasone Propionate

*(Ph Eur monograph 1750)*

$C_{25}H_{31}F_3O_5S$          500.6          *80474-14-2*

## Action and use
Glucocorticoid.

## Preparations
Fluticasone Cream

Futicasone Nasal Drops

Fluticasone Nasal Spray

Fluticasone Ointment

*Ph Eur*

## DEFINITION
6α,9-Difluoro-17-[[(fluoromethyl)sulphanyl]carbonyl]-11β-hydroxy-16α-methyl-3-oxoandrosta-1,4-dien-17α-yl propanoate.

## Content
97.0 per cent to 102.0 per cent (anhydrous substance).

## CHARACTERS
### Appearance
White or almost white powder.

### Solubility
Practically insoluble in water, sparingly soluble in methylene chloride, slightly soluble in alcohol.

## IDENTIFICATION
A. Infrared absorption spectrophotometry (*2.2.24*).

*Comparison   fluticasone propionate CRS.*

B. Examine the chromatograms obtained in the assay.

*Results*   The principal peak in the chromatogram obtained with the test solution is similar in retention time to the principal peak in the chromatogram obtained with reference solution (b).

## TESTS
### Specific optical rotation (*2.2.7*)
+ 32 to + 36 (anhydrous substance).

Dissolve 0.25 g in *methylene chloride R* and dilute to 50.0 ml with the same solvent.

### Related substances
Liquid chromatography (*2.2.29*): use the normalisation procedure.

*Test solution*   Dissolve 20 mg of the substance to be examined in a mixture of equal volumes of mobile phase A and mobile phase B and dilute to 100.0 ml with the same mixture of mobile phases.

*Reference solution (a)*   Dissolve 4 mg of *fluticasone impurity D CRS* in a mixture of equal volumes of mobile phase A and mobile phase B and dilute to 100.0 ml with the same mixture of mobile phases.

*Reference solution (b)*   Dissolve 20 mg of *fluticasone propionate CRS* in a mixture of equal volumes of mobile phase A and mobile phase B, add 1.0 ml of reference solution (a) and dilute to 100.0 ml with a mixture of equal volumes of mobile phase A and mobile phase B.

*Column:*
— size: l = 0.25 m, Ø = 4.6 mm;
— stationary phase: octadecylsilyl silica gel for chromatography R (5 μm);
— temperature: 40 °C.

*Mobile phase A*   A solution containing 0.05 per cent V/V of *phosphoric acid R* and 3.0 per cent V/V of *methanol R* in *acetonitrile R,*

*Mobile phase B*   A solution containing 0.05 per cent V/V of *phosphoric acid R* and 3.0 per cent V/V of *methanol R* in *water R,*

| Time (min) | Mobile phase A (per cent V/V) | Mobile phase B (per cent V/V) |
|---|---|---|
| 0 - 40 | 43 → 55 | 57 → 45 |
| 40 - 60 | 55 → 90 | 45 → 10 |
| 60 - 70 | 90 | 10 |
| 70 - 75 | 90 → 43 | 10 → 57 |

*Flow rate*   1 ml/min.

*Detection*   Spectrophotometer at 239 nm.

*Injection*   50 μl; inject the test solution and reference solution (b).

*Relative retention* With reference to fluticasone propionate (retention time = about 30 min): impurity A = about 0.38; impurity B = about 0.46; impurity C = about 0.76; impurity D = about 0.95; impurity E = about 1.12; impurity F = about 1.18; impurity G = about 1.33; impurity H = about 1.93; impurity I = about 2.01.

*System suitability* Reference solution (b):
— *resolution*: minimum 1.5 between the peaks due to impurity D and to fluticasone propionate.

*Limits:*
— *impurities D, G*: for each impurity, maximum 0.3 per cent;
— *impurities A, B, C, E, F, H, I*: for each impurity, maximum 0.2 per cent;
— *impurity with relative retention at about 1.23*: maximum 0.2 per cent;
— *any other impurity*: maximum 0.1 per cent;
— *total*: maximum 1.2 per cent;
— *disregard limit*: 0.05 per cent.

**Acetone**
Gas chromatography (*2.2.28*).

*Internal standard solution* Dilute 0.5 ml of *tetrahydrofuran R* to 1000 ml with *dimethylformamide R*.

*Test solution* Dissolve 0.50 g of the substance to be examined in the internal standard solution and dilute to 10.0 ml with the same solution.

*Reference solution* Dilute 0.40 g of *acetone R* to 100.0 ml with the internal standard solution. Dilute 1.0 ml to 10.0 ml with the internal standard solution.

*Column:*
— *material*: fused silica;
— *size*: $l$ = 25 m, Ø = 0.53 mm;
— *stationary phase*: cross-linked *macrogol 20 000 R* (film thickness 2 μm).

*Carrier gas* *nitrogen for chromatography R*.

*Flow rate* 5.5 ml/min.

*Temperature:*

| | Time (min) | Temperature (°C) |
|---|---|---|
| Column | 0 - 3.5 | 60 |
| | 3.5 - 7.5 | 60 → 180 |
| | 7.5 - 10.5 | 180 |
| Injection port | | 150 |
| Detector | | 250 |

*Detection* Flame ionisation.

*Injection* 0.1 μl.

*Limit:*
— *acetone*: maximum 1.0 per cent *m/m*.

**Water** (*2.5.12*)
Maximum 0.5 per cent determined on 0.250 g.

Use as solvent a mixture of equal volumes of *chloroform R* and *methanol R*.

**ASSAY**
Liquid chromatography (*2.2.29*).

*Test solution* Dissolve 20.0 mg of the substance to be examined in the mobile phase and dilute to 50.0 ml with the mobile phase. Dilute 1.0 ml to 10.0 ml with the mobile phase.

*Reference solution (a)* Dissolve 20.0 mg of *fluticasone propionate CRS* in the mobile phase and dilute to 50.0 ml with the mobile phase.

*Reference solution (b)* Dilute 1.0 ml of reference solution (a) to 10.0 ml with the mobile phase.

*Reference solution (c)* Dissolve 4.0 mg of *fluticasone impurity D CRS* in the mobile phase and dilute to 50.0 ml with the mobile phase. To 1.0 ml of this solution, add 1.0 ml of reference solution (a) and dilute to 10.0 ml with the mobile phase.

*Column:*
— *size*: $l$ = 0.25 m, Ø = 4.6 mm;
— *stationary phase*: *octadecylsilyl silica gel for chromatography R* (5 μm);
— *temperature*: 40 °C.

*Mobile phase* Mix 15 volumes of *acetonitrile R*, 35 volumes of a 1.15 g/l solution of *ammonium dihydrogen phosphate R* adjusted to pH 3.5 and 50 volumes of *methanol R*.

*Flow rate* 1.5 ml/min.

*Detection* Spectrophotometer at 239 nm.

*Injection* 20 μl; inject the test solution and reference solutions (b) and (c).

*System suitability* Reference solution (c):
— *resolution*: minimum 1.5 between the peaks due to impurity D and to fluticasone propionate.

If necessary, adjust the ratio of acetonitrile to methanol in the mobile phase.

Calculate the percentage content of $C_{25}H_{31}F_3O_5S$ using the chromatograms obtained with the test solution and reference solution (b), and the declared content of *fluticasone propionate CRS*.

**STORAGE**
Protected from light.

**IMPURITIES**
*Specified impurities* *A, B, C, D, E, F, G, H, I*.

A. R1 = R3 = OH, R2 = H, R4 = CH₃: 6α,9-difluoro-11β-hydroxy-16α-methyl-3-oxo-17-(propanoyloxy)androsta-1,4-diene-17β-carboxylic acid,

B. R1 = OH, R2 = H, R3 = S-OH, R4 = CH₃: [[6α,9-difluoro-11β-hydroxy-16α-methyl-3-oxo-17-(propanoyloxy)androsta-1,4-dien-17β-yl]carbonyl]sulphenic acid,

C. R1 = OH, R2 = R4 = H, R3 = S-CH₂-F: 6α,9-difluoro-17-[[(fluoromethyl)sulphanyl]carbonyl]-11β-hydroxy-16α-methyl-3-oxoandrosta-1,4-dien-17α-yl acetate,

D. R1 = OH, R2 = H, R3 = S-CH₃, R4 = CH₃: 6α,9-difluoro-17-[(methylsulphanyl)carbonyl]-11β-hydroxy-16α-methyl-3-oxoandrosta-1,4-dien-17α-yl propanoate,

F. R1 + R2 = O, R3 = S-CH₂-F, R4 = CH₃: 6α,9-difluoro-17-[[(fluoromethyl)sulphanyl]carbonyl]-16α-methyl-3,11-dioxoandrosta-1,4-dien-17α-yl propanoate,

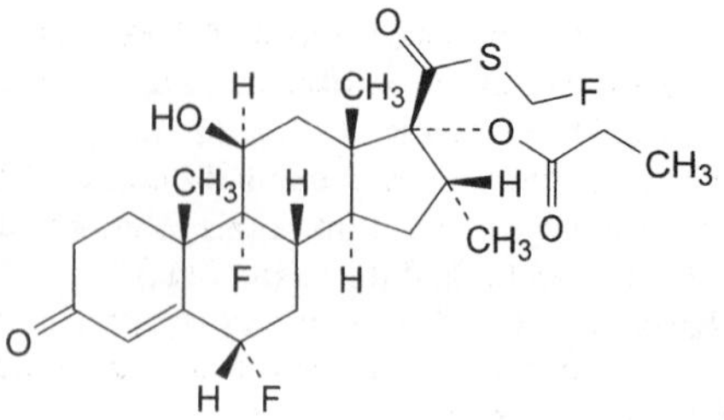

E. 6α,9-difluoro-17-[[(fluoromethyl)sulphanyl]carbonyl]-11β-hydroxy-16α-methyl-3-oxoandrost-4-en-17α-yl propanoate,

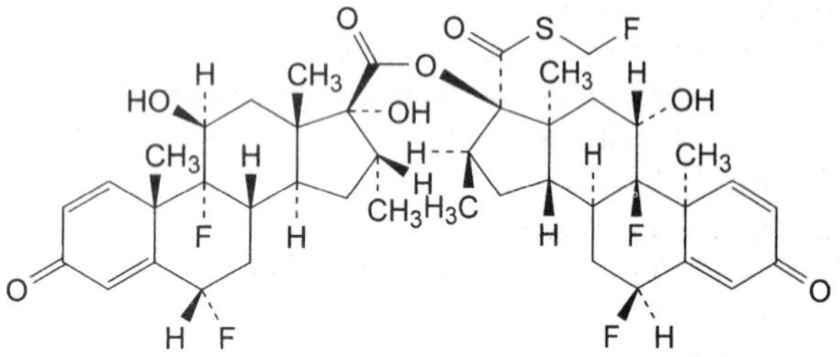

G. 6α,9-difluoro-17-[[(fluoromethyl)sulphanyl]carbonyl]-11β-hydroxy-16α-methyl-3-oxoandrosta-1,4-dien-17α-yl 6α,9-difluoro-11β,17-dihydroxy-16α-methyl-3-oxoandrosta-1,4-diene-17β-carboxylate,

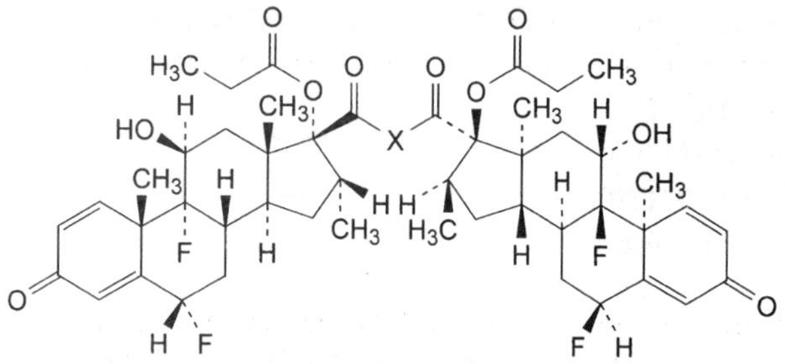

H. X = S-S: 17,17′-(disulphanediyldicarbonyl)bis(6α,9-difluoro-11β-hydroxy-16α-methyl-3-oxoandrosta-1,4-dien-17α-yl) dipropanoate,

I. X = S-S-S: 17,17′-(trisulphanediyldicarbonyl)bis(6α,9-difluoro-11β-hydroxy-16α-methyl-3-oxoandrosta-1,4-dien-17α-yl) dipropanoate.

_____ Ph Eur

# Flutrimazole

(*Ph Eur monograph 1424*)

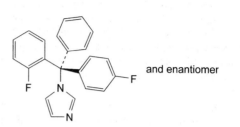

and enantiomer

$C_{22}H_{16}F_2N_2$          346.4          *119006-77-8*

**Action and use**
Antifungal.

*Ph Eur* _____

## DEFINITION
(*RS*)-1-[(2-Fluorophenyl)(4-fluorophenyl)phenylmethyl]-1*H*-imidazole.

## Content
99.0 per cent to 101.0 per cent (dried substance).

## CHARACTERS
**Appearance**
White or almost white powder.

**Solubility**
Practically insoluble in water, freely soluble in tetrahydrofuran, soluble in methanol.

## IDENTIFICATION
*First identification* B.

*Second identification* A, C, D.

A. Melting point (*2.2.14*): 161 °C to 166 °C.

B. Infrared absorption spectrophotometry (*2.2.24*).

*Preparation* Discs.

*Comparison* flutrimazole CRS.

C. Thin-layer chromatography (*2.2.27*).

*Test solution* Dissolve 20 mg of the substance to be examined in *acetone R* and dilute to 10 ml with the same solvent.

*Reference solution (a)* Dissolve 20 mg of *flutrimazole CRS* in *acetone R* and dilute to 10 ml with the same solvent.

*Reference solution (b)* Dissolve 20 mg of *flutrimazole CRS* and 10 mg of *metronidazole benzoate CRS* in *acetone R* and dilute to 10 ml with the same solvent.

*Plate* TLC silica gel F$_{254}$ plate R.

*Pretreatment* Heat the plate at 110 °C for 1 h.

*Mobile phase* 2-propanol R, ethyl acetate R (10:90 *V/V*).

*Application* 10 µl.

*Development* Over 2/3 of the plate.

*Drying* In air.

*Detection* Examine in ultraviolet light at 254 nm.

*System suitability* Reference solution (b):
— the chromatogram shows 2 clearly separated spots.

*Results* The principal spot in the chromatogram obtained with the test solution is similar in position and size to the principal spot in the chromatogram obtained with reference solution (a).

D. Mix about 5 mg with 45 mg of *heavy magnesium oxide R* and ignite in a crucible until an almost white residue is obtained (usually less than 5 min). Allow to cool, add 1 ml of *water R*, 0.05 ml of *phenolphthalein solution R1* and about 1 ml of *dilute hydrochloric acid R* to render the solution colourless. Filter. Add 1.0 ml of the filtrate to a freshly prepared mixture of 0.1 ml of *alizarin S solution R* and 0.1 ml of *zirconyl nitrate solution R*. Mix, allow to stand for 5 min and compare the colour of the solution with that of a blank prepared in the same manner. The test solution is yellow and the blank is red.

## TESTS

### Solution S

Dissolve 1.00 g in *methanol R* and dilute to 50.0 ml with the same solvent.

### Appearance of solution

Solution S is not more opalescent than reference suspension II (*2.2.1*) and not more intensely coloured than reference solution $Y_7$ (*2.2.2, Method II*).

### Optical rotation (*2.2.7*)

− 0.05° to + 0.05°, determined on solution S.

### Related substances

Liquid chromatography (*2.2.29*).

*Test solution*  Dissolve 40.0 mg of the substance to be examined in the mobile phase and dilute to 50.0 ml with the mobile phase.

*Reference solution (a)*  Dissolve 25.0 mg of *imidazole CRS* (impurity A) in the mobile phase and dilute to 50.0 ml with the mobile phase. Dilute 10.0 ml of this solution to 50.0 ml with the mobile phase.

*Reference solution (b)*  Dissolve 30.0 mg of *flutrimazole impurity B CRS* in the mobile phase and dilute to 100.0 ml with the mobile phase.

*Reference solution (c)*  Mix 2.0 ml of reference solution (a) and 2.0 ml of reference solution (b) and dilute to 50.0 ml with the mobile phase.

*Reference solution (d)*  Dilute 10.0 ml of reference solution (c) to 50.0 ml with the mobile phase.

*Reference solution (e)*  Mix 2.0 ml of the test solution and 10.0 ml of reference solution (c) and dilute to 50.0 ml with the mobile phase.

*Reference solution (f)*  Dilute 1.0 ml of the test solution to 100.0 ml with the mobile phase. Dilute 1.0 ml of this solution to 10.0 ml with the mobile phase.

*Column:*
— *size: l* = 0.2 m, Ø = 4.6 mm;
— *stationary phase: octylsilyl silica gel for chromatography R* (5 μm).

*Mobile phase*  0.03 M phosphate buffer solution pH 7.0 R, *acetonitrile R* (40:60 *V/V*).

*Flow rate*  1.3 ml/min.

*Detection*  Spectrophotometer at 220 nm.

*Injection*  20 μl.

*Run time*  2.5 times the retention time of flutrimazole.

*System suitability*  Reference solution (e):
— *resolution*: minimum 2.0 between the peaks due to impurity A (1st peak) and impurity B (2nd peak); minimum 1.5 between the peaks due to impurity B and flutrimazole (3rd peak);
— *symmetry factors*: maximum 2.0 for the peaks due to impurities A and B.

*Limits:*
— *impurity A*: not more than the area of the corresponding peak in the chromatogram obtained with reference solution (d) (0.1 per cent);

— *impurity B*: not more than the area of the corresponding peak in the chromatogram obtained with reference solution (d) (0.3 per cent);
— *unspecified impurities*: for each impurity, not more than the area of the principal peak in the chromatogram obtained with reference solution (f) (0.10 per cent);
— *sum of impurities other than B*: not more than 3 times the area of the principal peak in the chromatogram obtained with reference solution (f) (0.3 per cent);
— *disregard limit*: 0.5 times the area of the principal peak in the chromatogram obtained with reference solution (f) (0.05 per cent).

### Heavy metals (*2.4.8*)

Maximum 10 ppm.

2.0 g complies with test F. Use a platinum crucible. Prepare the reference solution using 2 ml of *lead standard solution (10 ppm Pb) R*.

### Loss on drying (*2.2.32*)

Maximum 0.5 per cent, determined on 1.000 g by drying in an oven at 105 °C.

### Sulphated ash (*2.4.14*)

Maximum 0.1 per cent, determined on 1.0 g in a platinum crucible.

## ASSAY

Dissolve 0.300 g in 50 ml of *anhydrous acetic acid R*. Titrate with *0.1 M perchloric acid*, determining the end-point potentiometrically (*2.2.20*).

1 ml of *0.1 M perchloric acid* is equivalent to 34.64 mg of $C_{22}H_{16}F_2N_2$.

## STORAGE

Protected from light.

## IMPURITIES

*Specified impurities*  A, B.

*Other detectable impurities* (the following substances would, if present at a sufficient level, be detected by one or other of the tests in the monograph. They are limited by the general acceptance criterion for other/unspecified impurities and/or by the general monograph *Substances for pharmaceutical use (2034)*. It is therefore not necessary to identify these impurities for demonstration of compliance. See also *5.10. Control of impurities in substances for pharmaceutical use*) C.

A. imidazole,

and enantiomer

B. R = H:
(*RS*)-(2-fluorophenyl)(4-fluorophenyl)phenylmethanol,

C. R = CH₃:
(*RS*)-(2-fluorophenyl)(4-fluorophenyl) methoxyphenylmethane.

# Fluvastatin Sodium

(Ph Eur monograph 2333)

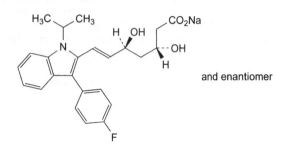

and enantiomer

C₂₄H₂₅FNNaO₄     433.5     93957-55-2

## Action and use
HMG Co-A reductase inhibitor; lipid-regulating drug.

*Ph Eur*

## DEFINITION
Sodium (3RS,5SR,6E)-7-[3-(4-fluorophenyl)-1-
(1-methylethyl)-1H-indol-2-yl]-3,5-dihydroxyhept-6-enoate.

## Content
98.5 per cent to 101.5 per cent (dried substance).

## CHARACTERS
### Appearance
White or almost white, or pale yellow to pale reddish-yellow,
very hygroscopic, crystalline powder.

### Solubility
Soluble in water, freely soluble in methanol, practically
insoluble in acetonitrile.

It shows polymorphism (5.9).

## IDENTIFICATION
A. Infrared absorption spectrophotometry (2.2.24).

*Comparison* fluvastatin sodium CRS.

If the spectra obtained in the solid state show differences,
dissolve the substance to be examined and the reference
substance separately in *methanol R*, evaporate to dryness
and record new spectra using the residues.

B. 0.5 ml of solution S (see Tests) gives reaction (a) of
sodium (2.3.1).

## TESTS
### Solution S
Dissolve 1.0 g in *carbon dioxide-free water R* and dilute to
20.0 ml with the same solvent.

### pH (2.2.3)
8.0 to 10.0 for solution S.

### Related substances
Liquid chromatography (2.2.29). *Carry out the test protected
from light.*

*Test solution* Dissolve 25 mg of the substance to be
examined in 20 ml of mobile phase B and dilute to 50.0 ml
with mobile phase A.

*Reference solution (a)* Dilute 1.0 ml of the test solution to
10.0 ml with mobile phase A. Dilute 1.0 ml of this solution
to 50.0 ml with mobile phase A.

*Reference solution (b)* Dissolve the contents of a vial of
*fluvastatin for system suitability CRS* (containing impurities
A, B and D) in 1.0 ml of a mixture of equal volumes of
mobile phase A and mobile phase B.

## Column:
— size: l = 0.10 m, Ø = 4.6 mm;
— stationary phase: end-capped octadecylsilyl silica gel for
   chromatography R (3 µm);
— temperature: 40 °C.

*Mobile phase:*
— mobile phase A: to 880 ml of *water R* add 20 ml of a
   250 g/l solution of *tetramethylammonium hydroxide R* and
   adjust quickly to pH 7.2 with *phosphoric acid R*; mix with
   100 ml of a mixture of 40 volumes of *acetonitrile R* and
   60 volumes of *methanol R*;
— mobile phase B: to 80 ml of *water R* add 20 ml of a 250 g/l
   solution of *tetramethylammonium hydroxide R* and adjust
   quickly to pH 7.2 with *phosphoric acid R*; mix with 900 ml
   of a mixture of 40 volumes of *acetonitrile R* and
   60 volumes of *methanol R*;

| Time (min) | Mobile phase A (per cent V/V) | Mobile phase B (per cent V/V) |
|---|---|---|
| 0 - 3 | 70 | 30 |
| 3 - 23 | 70 → 10 | 30 → 90 |

*Flow rate* 2.0 ml/min.

*Detection* Spectrophotometer at 305 nm and at 365 nm.

*Injection* 20 µl.

*Identification of impurities* Use the chromatogram supplied
with *fluvastatin for system suitability CRS* and the
chromatogram obtained with reference solution (b) to
identify the peaks due to impurities A, B and D.

*Relative retention* With reference to fluvastatin
(retention time = about 14 min); impurity A = about 1.05;
impurity D = about 1.1; impurity B = about 1.6.

*System suitability* Reference solution (b) at 305 nm:
— peak-to-valley ratio: minimum 5, where $H_p$ = height above
   the baseline of the peak due to impurity A and
   $H_v$ = height above the baseline of the lowest point of the
   curve separating this peak from the peak due to
   fluvastatin.

*Limits:*
— impurity A at 305 nm: not more than 4 times the area of
   the principal peak in the chromatogram obtained with
   reference solution (a) (0.8 per cent);
— impurity B at 305 nm: not more than the area of the
   principal peak in the chromatogram obtained with
   reference solution (a) (0.2 per cent);
— impurity D at 365 nm: not more than 0.75 times the area
   of the principal peak in the chromatogram obtained with
   reference solution (a) at 305 nm (0.15 per cent);
— unspecified impurities at 305 nm: not more than 0.5 times
   the area of the principal peak in the chromatogram
   obtained with reference solution (a) (0.10 per cent);
— sum of impurities at 305 nm: not more than 5 times the
   area of the principal peak in the chromatogram obtained
   with reference solution (a) (1.0 per cent);
— disregard limit at 305 nm: 0.25 times the area of the
   principal peak in the chromatogram obtained with
   reference solution (a) (0.05 per cent).

## Heavy metals (2.4.8)
Maximum 20 ppm.

Dissolve 1.0 g in a mixture of 15 volumes of *water R* and
85 volumes of *methanol R* and dilute to 20 ml with the same
mixture of solvents. 12 ml of the solution complies with
test B. Prepare the reference solution using lead standard
solution (1 ppm Pb) obtained by diluting *lead standard
solution (100 ppm Pb) R* with a mixture of 15 volumes of

*water R* and 85 volumes of *methanol R*. For the evaluation of the results, filter the solutions through a membrane filter (nominal pore size 0.45 μm).

**Loss on drying** (*2.2.32*)
Maximum 4.0 per cent, determined on 1.000 g by drying in an oven at 105 °C.

**ASSAY**
Dissolve 0.325 g in 50 ml of *glacial acetic acid R*. Titrate with *0.1 M perchloric acid*, determining the end-point potentiometrically (*2.2.20*).

1 ml of *0.1 M perchloric acid* is equivalent to 43.35 mg of $C_{24}H_{25}FNNaO_4$.

**STORAGE**
In an airtight container, protected from light.

**IMPURITIES**
*Specified impurities* A, B, D.

*Other detectable impurities* (The following substances would, if present at a sufficient level, be detected by one or other of the tests in the monograph. They are limited by the general acceptance criterion for other/unspecified impurities and/or by the general monograph *Substances for pharmaceutical use (2034)*. It is therefore not necessary to identify these impurities for demonstration of compliance. See also *5.10. Control of impurities in substances for pharmaceutical use*): C, E, F, G.

A. (3RS,5RS,6E)-7-[3-(4-fluorophenyl)-1-(1-methylethyl)-1H-indol-2-yl]-3,5-dihydroxyhept-6-enoic acid,

B. 1,1-dimethylethyl (3R,5S,6E)-7-[3-(4-fluorophenyl)-1-(1-methylethyl)-1H-indol-2-yl]-3,5-dihydroxyhept-6-enoate,

C. (3R,5S,6E)-7-[1-ethyl-3-(4-fluorophenyl)-1H-indol-2-yl]-3,5-dihydroxyhept-6-enoic acid,

D. (6E)-7-[3-(4-fluorophenyl)-1-(1-methylethyl)-1H-indol-2-yl]-3-hydroxy-5-oxohept-6-enoic acid,

E. (6R)-6-[(E)-2-[3-(4-fluorophenyl)-1-(1-methylethyl)-1H-indol-2-yl]ethenyl]-4-hydroxy-5,6-dihydro-2H-pyran-2-one,

F. (4E,6E)-7-[3-(4-fluorophenyl)-1-(1-methylethyl)-1H-indol-2-yl]-3-hydroxyhepta-4,6-dienoic acid,

G. 3-(4-fluorophenyl)-1-(1-methylethyl)-1*H*-indole-2-carbaldehyde.

*Ph Eur*

# Fluvoxamine Maleate

(*Ph Eur monograph 1977*)

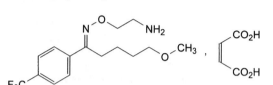

C₁₉H₂₅F₃N₂O₆      434.4      *61718-82-9*

**Action and use**

Selective serotonin reuptake inhibitor; antidepressant.

**Preparation**

Fluvoxamine Tablets

*Ph Eur*

## DEFINITION

2-[[[(1*E*)-5-Methoxy-1-[4-(trifluoromethyl)phenyl]pentylidene]amino]oxy]ethanamine (*Z*)-butenedioate.

## Content

99.0 per cent to 101.0 per cent (dried substance).

## PRODUCTION

The production method must be evaluated to determine the potential for formation of aziridine. Where necessary, a validated test for the substance is carried out or the production method is validated to demonstrate acceptable clearance.

## CHARACTERS

**Appearance**

White or almost white, crystalline powder.

**Solubility**

Sparingly soluble in water, freely soluble in ethanol (96 per cent) and in methanol.

## IDENTIFICATION

Infrared absorption spectrophotometry (*2.2.24*).

*Comparison*   fluvoxamine maleate CRS.

## TESTS

**Related substances**

Liquid chromatography (*2.2.29*). *Prepare the test solution immediately before use.*

*Test solution*   Dissolve 50 mg of the substance to be examined in the mobile phase and dilute to 25 ml with the mobile phase.

*Reference solution (a)*   Dilute 1.0 ml of the test solution to 10.0 ml with the mobile phase. Dilute 1.0 ml of this solution to 100.0 ml with the mobile phase.

*Reference solution (b)*   Dissolve the contents of a vial of *fluvoxamine for system suitability CRS* (containing impurities A, B, C and F) in 1.0 ml of the mobile phase.

*Reference solution (c)*   Dissolve 3.0 mg of *fluvoxamine impurity D CRS* in 5 ml of the mobile phase and dilute to 10.0 ml with the mobile phase. Dilute 1.0 ml of this solution to 100.0 ml with the mobile phase.

*Column:*
— *size: l* = 0.25 m, Ø = 4.6 mm;
— *stationary phase: octylsilyl silica gel for chromatography R* (5 μm).

*Mobile phase*   Mix 370 volumes of *acetonitrile R1* and 630 volumes of a buffer solution containing 1.1 g/l of *potassium dihydrogen phosphate R* and 1.9 g/l of *sodium pentanesulphonate R* in *water R*, previously adjusted to pH 3.0 with *phosphoric acid R*.

*Flow rate*   1.2 ml/min.

*Detection*   Spectrophotometer at 234 nm.

*Injection*   20 μl.

*Run time*   6 times the retention time of fluvoxamine.

*Identification of impurities*   Use the chromatogram supplied with *fluvoxamine for system suitability CRS* and the chromatogram obtained with reference solution (b) to identify the peaks due to impurities A, B, C and F.

*Relative retention*   With reference to fluvoxamine (retention time = about 15 min): maleic acid = about 0.15; impurities F and G = about 0.5; impurity C = about 0.6; impurity B = about 0.8; impurity A = about 2.5; impurity D = about 5.4.

*System suitability*   Reference solution (b):
— *resolution*: minimum 1.5 between the peaks due to impurities F and C.

*Limits:*
— *impurity B*: not more than 5 times the area of the principal peak in the chromatogram obtained with reference solution (a) (0.5 per cent);
— *impurity C*: not more than 3 times the area of the principal peak in the chromatogram obtained with reference solution (a) (0.3 per cent);
— *impurity A*: not more than twice the area of the principal peak in the chromatogram obtained with reference solution (a) (0.2 per cent);
— *impurity D*: not more than the area of the corresponding peak in the chromatogram obtained with reference solution (c) (0.15 per cent);
— *sum of impurities F and G*: not more than 3 times the area of the principal peak in the chromatogram obtained with reference solution (a) (0.3 per cent);
— *unspecified impurities*: for each impurity, not more than the area of the principal peak in the chromatogram obtained with reference solution (a) (0.10 per cent);
— *total*: not more than 10 times the area of the principal peak in the chromatogram obtained with reference solution (a) (1.0 per cent);
— *disregard limit*: 0.5 times the area of the principal peak in the chromatogram obtained with reference solution (a) (0.05 per cent); disregard the peak due to maleic acid.

**Heavy metals** (*2.4.8*)

Maximum 20 ppm.

1.0 g complies with test B. Prepare the reference solution using 2 ml of *lead standard solution (10 ppm Pb) R*.

**Loss on drying** (*2.2.32*)

Maximum 0.5 per cent, determined on 1.000 g by drying *in vacuo* at 80 °C for 2 h.

**Sulphated ash** (*2.4.14*)

Maximum 0.1 per cent, determined on 1.0 g in a platinum crucible.

**ASSAY**

Dissolve 0.350 g in 50 ml of *anhydrous acetic acid R*. Titrate with *0.1 M perchloric acid*, determining the end-point potentiometrically (*2.2.20*).

1 ml of *0.1 M perchloric acid* is equivalent to 43.44 mg of $C_{19}H_{25}F_3N_2O_6$.

**IMPURITIES**

*Specified impurities   A, B, C, D, F, G.*

*Other detectable impurities*   (The following substances would, if present at a sufficient level, be detected by one or other of the tests in the monograph. They are limited by the general acceptance criterion for other/unspecified impurities and/or by the general monograph *Substances for pharmaceutical use (2034)*. It is therefore not necessary to identify these impurities for demonstration of compliance. See also *5.10. Control of impurities in substances for pharmaceutical use*):
*E, I, J.*

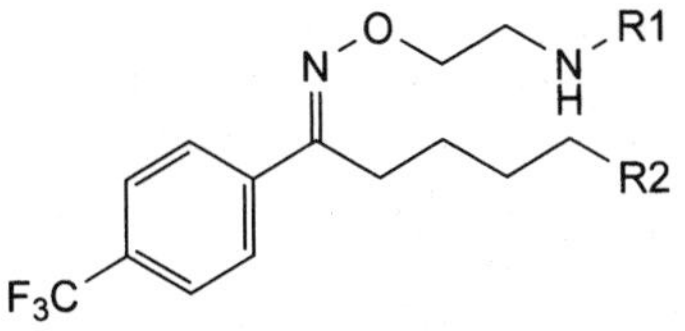

A. R1 = R2 = H: 2-[[[(1*E*)-1-[4-(trifluoromethyl)phenyl]pentylidene]amino]oxy]ethanamine,

F. R1 = CH₂-CH₂-NH₂, R2 = OCH₃: *N*-[2-[[[(1*E*)-5-methoxy-1[4-(trifluoromethyl)phenyl]pentylidene]amino]oxy]ethyl]ethane-1,2-diamine,

G. R1 = H, R2 = OH: (5*E*)-5-[(2-aminoethoxy)imino]-5-[4-(trifluoromethyl)phenyl]pentan-1-ol,

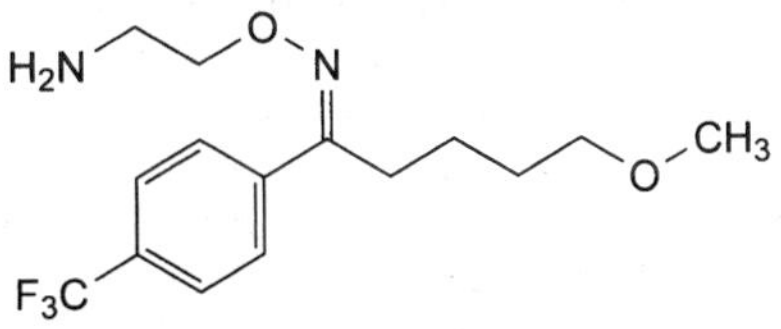

B. 2-[[[(1*Z*)-5-methoxy-1-[4-(trifluoromethyl)phenyl]pentylidene]amino]oxy]ethanamine,

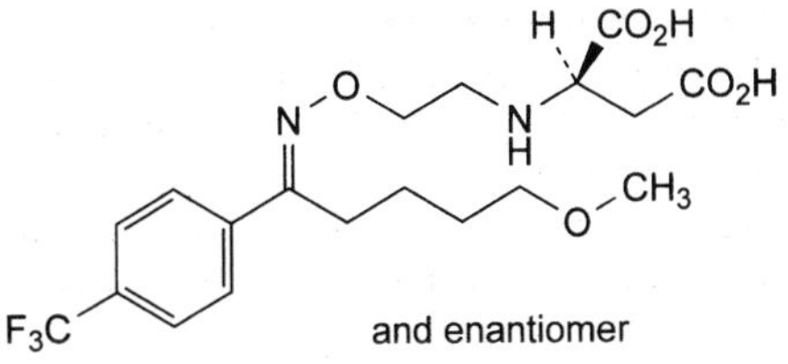

C. (2*RS*)-2-[[2-[[[(1*E*)-5-methoxy-1-[4-(trifluoromethyl)phenyl]pentylidene]amino]oxy]ethyl]amino]butanedioic acid,

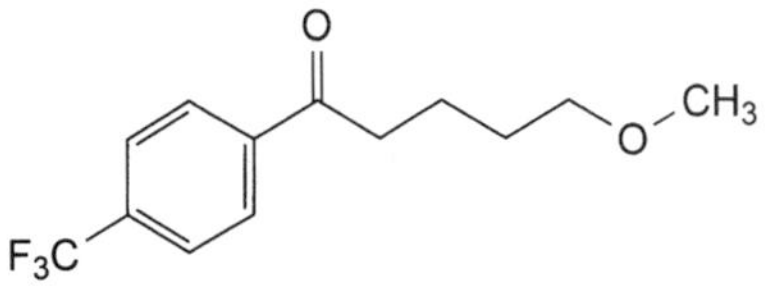

D. 5-methoxy-1-[4-(trifluoromethyl)phenyl]pentan-1-one,

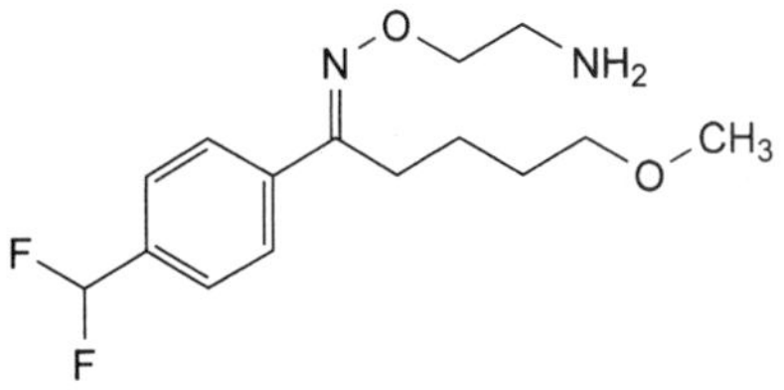

E. 2-[[[(1*E*)-1-[4-(difluoromethyl)phenyl]-5-methoxypentylidene]amino]oxy]ethanamine,

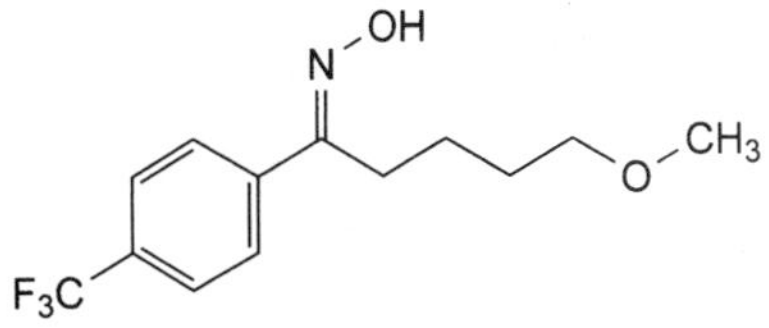

I. (*E*)-*N*-[5-methoxy-1-[4-(trifluoromethyl)phenyl]pentylidene]hydroxylamine,

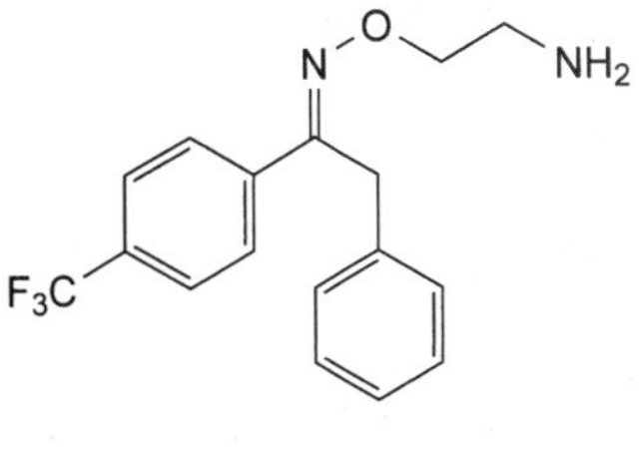

J. 2-[[[(1*E*)-2-phenyl-1-[4-(trifluoromethyl)phenyl]ethylidene]amino]oxy]ethanamine.

_____ *Ph Eur*

# Folic Acid

(*Ph Eur monograph 0067*)

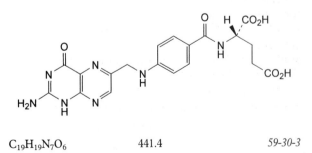

$C_{19}H_{19}N_7O_6$          441.4          *59-30-3*

**Action and use**

Vitamin B component.

**Preparations**

Folic Acid Tablets

Ferrous Fumarate and Folic Acid Tablets

*Ph Eur*

## DEFINITION

(2*S*)-2-[[4-[[(2-Amino-4-oxo-1,4-dihydropteridin-6-yl)methyl]amino]benzoyl]amino]pentanedioic acid.

### Content

96.0 per cent to 102.0 per cent (anhydrous substance).

## CHARACTERS

### Appearance

Yellowish or orange, crystalline powder.

### Solubility

Practically insoluble in water and in most organic solvents. It dissolves in dilute acids and in alkaline solutions.

## IDENTIFICATION

*First identification*   A, B.

*Second identification*   A, C.

A. Specific optical rotation (*2.2.7*): + 18 to + 22 (anhydrous substance).

Dissolve 0.25 g in *0.1 M sodium hydroxide* and dilute to 25.0 ml with the same solvent.

B. Examine the chromatograms obtained in the assay.

*Results*   The principal peak in the chromatogram obtained with the test solution is similar in retention time to the principal peak in the chromatogram obtained with reference solution (a).

C. Thin-layer chromatography (*2.2.27*).

*Test solution*   Dissolve 50 mg of the substance to be examined in a mixture of 2 volumes of *concentrated ammonia R* and 9 volumes of *methanol R* and dilute to 100 ml with the same mixture of solvents.

*Reference solution*   Dissolve 50 mg of *folic acid CRS* in a mixture of 2 volumes of *concentrated ammonia R* and 9 volumes of *methanol R* and dilute to 100 ml with the same mixture of solvents.

*Plate*   TLC *silica gel G plate R*.

*Mobile phase*   concentrated ammonia R, propanol R, ethanol (96 per cent) R (20:20:60 *V/V/V*).

*Application*   2 µl.

*Development*   Over 3/4 of the plate.

*Drying*   In air.

*Detection*   Examine in ultraviolet light at 365 nm.

*Results*   The principal spot in the chromatogram obtained with the test solution is similar in position, fluorescence and size to the principal spot in the chromatogram obtained with the reference solution.

## TESTS

### Related substances

Liquid chromatography (*2.2.29*).

*Test solution*   Dissolve 0.100 g of the substance to be examined in 5 ml of a 28.6 g/l solution of *sodium carbonate R* and dilute to 100.0 ml with the mobile phase. Dilute 2.0 ml of this solution to 10.0 ml with the mobile phase.

*Reference solution (a)*   Dissolve 0.100 g of *folic acid CRS* in 5 ml of a 28.6 g/l solution of *sodium carbonate R* and dilute to 100.0 ml with the mobile phase. Dilute 2.0 ml of this solution to 10.0 ml with the mobile phase.

*Reference solution (b)*   To 20 mg of *pteroic acid R*, add 5 ml of a 28.6 g/l solution of *sodium carbonate R*, dilute to 100.0 ml with the mobile phase and mix until completely dissolved. Mix 1.0 ml of this solution with 1.0 ml of reference solution (a) and dilute to 100.0 ml with the mobile phase.

*Reference solution (c)*   Dilute 2.0 ml of the test solution to 20.0 ml with the mobile phase. Dilute 1.0 ml of this solution to 20.0 ml with the mobile phase.

*Reference solution (d)*   Dissolve 10.0 mg of *N-(4-aminobenzoyl)-L-glutamic acid R* in 1 ml of a 28.6 g/l solution of *sodium carbonate R* and dilute to 100.0 ml with the mobile phase. Dilute 1.0 ml of this solution to 100.0 ml with the mobile phase.

*Reference solution (e)*   To 12.0 mg of *pteroic acid R* , add 1 ml of a 28.6 g/l solution of *sodium carbonate R*, dilute to 100.0 ml with the mobile phase and mix until completely dissolved. Dilute 1.0 ml of this solution to 100.0 ml with the mobile phase.

*Column:*
— size: $l = 0.25$ m, $\varnothing = 4.0$ mm;
— stationary phase: spherical octylsilyl silica gel for chromatography R (5 µm) with a carbon loading of 12.5 per cent, a specific surface of 350 $m^2$/g and a pore size of 10 nm.

*Mobile phase*   Mix 12 volumes of *methanol R* and 88 volumes of a solution containing 11.16 g/l of *potassium dihydrogen phosphate R* and 5.50 g/l of *dipotassium hydrogen phosphate R*.

*Flow rate*   0.6 ml/min.

*Detection*   Spectrophotometer at 280 nm.

*Injection*   5 µl of the test solution and reference solutions (b), (c) (d) and (e).

*Run time*   3 times the retention time of folic acid.

*Relative retention*   With reference to folic acid (retention time = about 8.5 min): impurity A = about 0.5; impurity B = about 0.6; impurity C = about 0.9; impurity E = about 1.27; impurity D = about 1.33; impurity F = about 2.2.

*System suitability*   Reference solution (b):
— resolution: minimum 4.0 between the peaks due to folic acid and impurity D.

*Limits:*
— impurity A: not more than the area of the principal peak in the chromatogram obtained with reference solution (d) (0.5 per cent);
— impurity D: not more than the area of the principal peak in the chromatogram obtained with reference solution (e) (0.6 per cent);
— any other impurity: not more than the area of the principal peak in the chromatogram obtained with reference solution (c) (0.5 per cent);
— Total of other impurities: not more than twice the area of the principal peak in the chromatogram obtained with reference solution (c) (1.0 per cent);
— disregard limit: 0.1 times the area of the principal peak in the chromatogram obtained with reference solution (c) (0.05 per cent).

## Water (*2.5.12*)

5.0 per cent to 8.5 per cent, determined on 0.150 g.

## Sulphated ash (*2.4.14*)

Maximum 0.2 per cent, determined on 1.0 g.

## ASSAY

Liquid chromatography (*2.2.29*) as described in the test for related substances with the following modification.

*Injection*   Test solution and reference solution (a).

**STORAGE**

Protected from light.

**IMPURITIES**

*Specified impurities*  *A, B, C, D, E, F.*

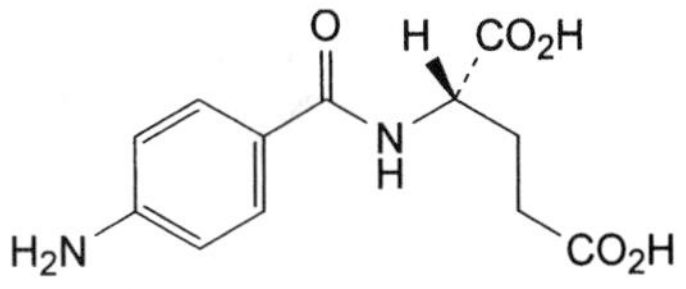

A. (2*S*)-2-[(4-aminobenzoyl)amino]pentanedioic acid (*N*-(4-aminobenzoyl)-L-glutamic acid),

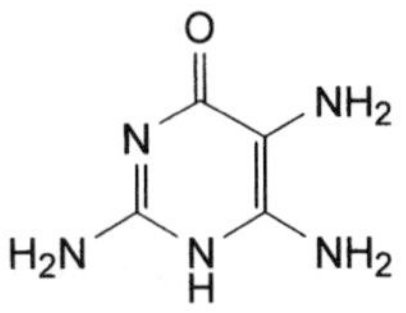

B. 2,5,6-triaminopyrimidin-4(1*H*)-one,

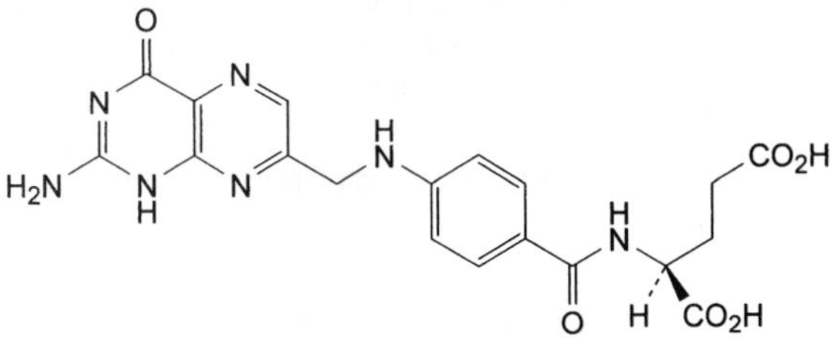

C. (2*S*)-2-[[4-[[(2-amino-4-oxo-1,4-dihydropteridin-7-yl)methyl]amino]benzoyl]amino]pentanedioic acid (isofolic acid),

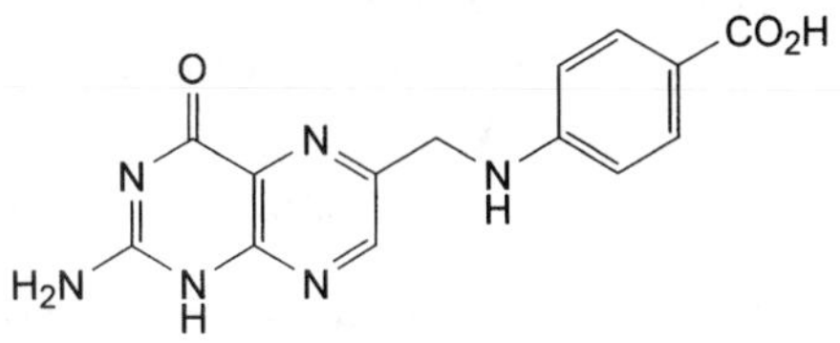

D. 4-[[(2-amino-4-oxo-1,4-dihydropteridin-6-yl)methyl]amino]benzoic acid (pteroic acid),

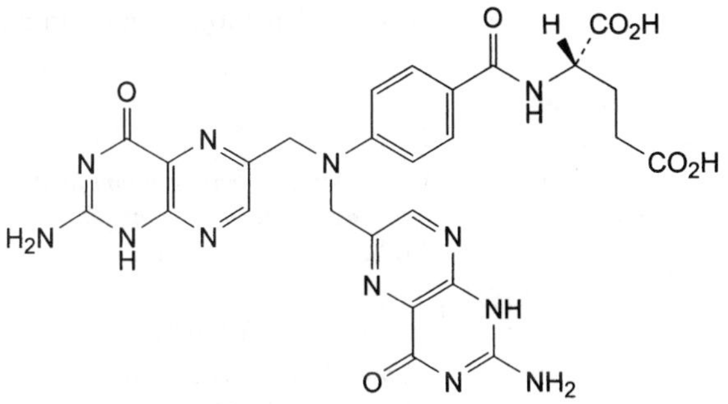

E. (2*S*)-2-[[4-[bis[(2-amino-4-oxo-1,4-dihydropteridin-6-yl)methyl]amino]benzoyl]amino]pentanedioic acid (6-pterinylfolic acid),

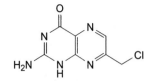

F. 2-amino-7-(chloromethyl)pteridin-4(1*H*)-one.

*Ph Eur*

# Formaldehyde Solution

Formalin

*(Formaldehyde Solution (35 per cent), Ph Eur monograph 0826)*

NOTE: *The name Formalin as a synonym for Formaldehyde Solution may be used freely in many countries, including the United Kingdom, but in other countries exclusive proprietary rights in this name are claimed.*

CH₂O            30.03            *50-00-0*

**Action and use**

When suitably diluted, used in the treatment of warts.

*Ph Eur*

**DEFINITION**

**Content**

34.5 per cent *m/m* to 38.0 per cent *m/m* of formaldehyde (CH₂O; *M*ᵣ 30.03).

It contains methanol as stabiliser.

**CHARACTERS**

**Appearance**

Clear, colourless liquid.

**Solubility**

Miscible with water and with ethanol (96 per cent).

It may be cloudy after storage.

**IDENTIFICATION**

A. Dilute 1 ml of solution S (see Tests) to 10 ml with *water R*. To 0.05 ml of the solution add 1 ml of a 15 g/l solution of *chromotropic acid sodium salt R*, 2 ml of *water R* and 8 ml of *sulphuric acid R*. A violet-blue or violet-red colour develops within 5 min.

B. To 0.1 ml of solution S add 10 ml of *water R*. Add 2 ml of a 10 g/l solution of *phenylhydrazine hydrochloride R*, prepared immediately before use, 1 ml of *potassium ferricyanide solution R* and 5 ml of *hydrochloric acid R*. An intense red colour is formed.

C. Mix 0.5 ml with 2 ml of *water R* and 2 ml of *silver nitrate solution R2* in a test-tube. Add *dilute ammonia R2* until slightly alkaline. Heat on a water-bath. A grey precipitate or a silver mirror is formed.

D. It complies with the limits of the assay.

**TESTS**

**Solution S**

Dilute 10 ml, filtered if necessary, to 50 ml with *carbon dioxide-free water R*.

**Appearance of solution**

Solution S is colourless (*2.2.2, Method II*).

**Acidity**

To 10 ml of solution S add 1 ml of *phenolphthalein solution R*. Not more than 0.4 ml of *0.1 M sodium hydroxide* is required to change the colour of the indicator to red.

**Methanol**

Gas chromatography (*2.2.28*).

*Internal standard solution*  Dilute 10 ml of *ethanol R1* to 100 ml with *water R*.

*Test solution*  To 10.0 ml of the solution to be examined add 10.0 ml of the internal standard solution and dilute to 100.0 ml with *water R*.

*Reference solution*  To 1.0 ml of *methanol R* add 10.0 ml of the internal standard solution and dilute to 100.0 ml with *water R*.

*Column:*
— *material*: glass;
— *size*: l = 1.5-2.0 m, Ø = 2-4 mm;
— *stationary phase*: *ethylvinylbenzene-divinylbenzene copolymer R* (150-180 μm).

*Carrier gas*  *nitrogen for chromatography R*.

*Flow rate*  30-40 ml/min.

*Temperature:*
— *column*: 120 °C;
— *injection port and detector*: 150 °C.

*Detection*  Flame ionisation.

*Injection*  1 μl of the test solution and the reference solution.

*System suitability*  Reference solution:
— *resolution*: minimum 2.0 between the peaks due to methanol and ethanol.

*Limit:*
— *methanol*: 9.0 per cent *V/V* to 15.0 per cent *V/V*.

**Sulphated ash** (*2.4.14*)

Maximum 0.1 per cent, determined on 1.0 g.

**ASSAY**

Into a 100 ml volumetric flask containing 2.5 ml of *water R* and 1 ml of *dilute sodium hydroxide solution R*, introduce 1.000 g of the solution to be examined, shake and dilute to 100.0 ml with *water R*. To 10.0 ml of the solution add 30.0 ml of *0.05 M iodine*. Mix and add 10 ml of *dilute sodium hydroxide solution R*. After 15 min, add 25 ml of dilute *sulphuric acid R* and 2 ml of *starch solution R*. Titrate with *0.1 M sodium thiosulphate*.

1 ml of *0.05 M iodine* is equivalent to 1.501 mg of $CH_2O$.

**STORAGE**

Protected from light, at a temperature of 15 °C to 25 °C.

_____ *Ph Eur*

# Formoterol Fumarate Dihydrate

*(Ph Eur monograph 1724)*

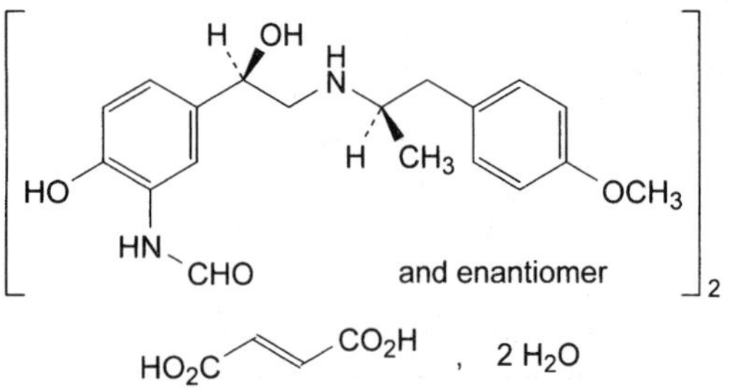

$C_{42}H_{52}N_4O_{12},2H_2O$      841      *43229-80-7*

*(anhydrous)*

**Action and use**

Beta$_2$-adrenoceptor agonist; bronchodilator.

*Ph Eur* _____

**DEFINITION**

*N*-[2-Hydroxy-5-[(1*RS*)-1-hydroxy-2-[[(1*RS*)-2-(4-methoxyphenyl)-1-methylethyl]amino]ethyl]phenyl] formamide (*E*)-butenedioate dihydrate.

**Content**

98.5 per cent to 101.5 per cent (anhydrous substance).

**CHARACTERS**

**Appearance**

White or almost white or slightly yellow powder.

**Solubility**

Slightly soluble in water, soluble in methanol, slightly soluble in 2-propanol, practically insoluble in acetonitrile.

**IDENTIFICATION**

Infrared absorption spectrophotometry (*2.2.24*).

*Comparison*  formoterol fumarate dihydrate CRS .

**TESTS**

**pH** (*2.2.3*)

5.5 to 6.5.

Dissolve 20 mg in *carbon dioxide-free water R* while heating to about 40 °C, allow to cool and dilute to 20 ml with the same solvent.

**Optical rotation** (*2.2.7*)

− 0.10° to + 0.10°.

Dissolve 0.25 g in *methanol R* and dilute to 25.0 ml with the same solvent.

**Related substances**

Liquid chromatography (*2.2.29*).

*Solution A*  Dissolve 6.10 g of *sodium dihydrogen phosphate monohydrate R* and 1.03 g of *disodium hydrogen phosphate dihydrate R* in *water R* and dilute to 1000 ml with the same solvent. The pH is 6.0 ± 0.1.

*Solvent mixture*  *acetonitrile R*, solution A (16:84 *V/V*).

*Test solution*  Dissolve 20.0 mg of the substance to be examined in the solvent mixture and dilute to 100.0 ml with the solvent mixture. *Inject within 4 h of preparation, or within 24 h if stored protected from light at 4 °C.*

*Reference solution (a)*  Dissolve 5 mg of *formoterol fumarate for system suitability CRS* (containing impurities A, B, C, D, E, F and G) in the solvent mixture and dilute to 25.0 ml with the solvent mixture.

*Reference solution (b)* Dilute 1.0 ml of the test solution to 25.0 ml with the solvent mixture. Dilute 1.0 ml of this solution to 20.0 ml with the solvent mixture.

*Column:*
— *size:* $l$ = 0.15 m, Ø = 4.6 mm;
— *stationary phase*: spherical *octylsilyl silica gel for chromatography R3* (5 μm) with a pore size of 8 nm.

*Mobile phase:*
— *mobile phase A: acetonitrile R1;*
— *mobile phase B*: dissolve 3.73 g of *sodium dihydrogen phosphate monohydrate R* and 0.35 g of *phosphoric acid R* in *water R* and dilute to 1000 ml with the same solvent; the pH is 3.1 ± 0.1;

| Time (min) | Mobile phase A (per cent *V/V*) | Mobile phase B (per cent *V/V*) |
|---|---|---|
| 0 - 10 | 16 | 84 |
| 10 - 37 | 16 → 70 | 84 → 30 |
| 37 - 40 | 70 → 16 | 30 → 84 |
| 40 - 55 | 16 | 84 |

*Flow rate* 1.0 ml/min.

*Detection* Spectrophotometer at 214 nm.

*Injection* 20 μl; inject the solvent mixture until a repeatable profile is obtained.

*Identification of impurities* Use the chromatogram obtained with reference solution (a) and the chromatogram supplied with *formoterol for system suitability CRS* to identify the peaks.

*Relative retention* With reference to formoterol (retention time = about 12 min): impurity G = about 0.4; impurity A = about 0.5; impurity B = about 0.7; impurity C = about 1.2; impurity D = about 1.3; impurity E = about 1.8; impurity F = about 2.0; impurity H = about 2.2.

*System suitability* Reference solution (a):
— *resolution*: minimum 1.5 between the peaks due to impurity G and impurity A.
— *peak-to-valley ratio*: minimum 2.5, where $H_p$ = height above the baseline of the peak due to impurity C and $H_v$ = height above the baseline of the lowest point of the curve separating this peak from the peak due to formoterol.

*Limits:*
— *correction factor*: for the calculation of content, multiply the peak area of impurity A by 1.75;
— *impurity A*: not more than 1.5 times the area of the principal peak in the chromatogram obtained with reference solution (b) (0.3 per cent);
— *impurities B, C, D, F*: for each impurity, not more than the area of the principal peak in the chromatogram obtained with reference solution (b) (0.2 per cent);
— *impurity E*: not more than 0.5 times the area of the principal peak in the chromatogram obtained with reference solution (b) (0.1 per cent);
— *unspecified impurities*: for each impurity, not more than 0.5 times the area of the principal peak in the chromatogram obtained with reference solution (b) (0.10 per cent);
— *total*: not more than 2.5 times the area of the principal peak in the chromatogram obtained with reference solution (b) (0.5 per cent);
— *disregard limit*: 0.25 times the area of the principal peak in the chromatogram obtained with reference solution (b) (0.05 per cent).

**Impurity I**
Liquid chromatography (*2.2.29*).

*Test solution* Dissolve 5.0 mg of the substance to be examined in *water R* and dilute to 50.0 ml with the same solvent. Sonicate if necessary.

*Reference solution (a)* Dissolve 5.0 mg of *formoterol for impurity I identification CRS* in *water R* and dilute to 50.0 ml with the same solvent. Sonicate if necessary.

*Reference solution (b)* Dilute 1.0 ml of the test solution to 20.0 ml with *water R*. Dilute 1.0 ml of this solution to 25.0 ml with *water R*.

*Column:*
— *size:* $l$ = 0.15 m, Ø = 4.6 mm;
— *stationary phase*: *octadecyl vinyl polymer for chromatography R.*

*Mobile phase* Mix 12 volumes of *acetonitrile R1* with 88 volumes of a 5.3 g/l solution of *tripotassium phosphate trihydrate R* previously adjusted to pH 12.0 ± 0.1 with a 280 g/l solution of *potassium hydroxide R* or *phosphoric acid R.*

*Flow rate* 0.5 ml/min.

*Detection* Spectrophotometer at 225 nm.

*Injection* 20 μl.

*Elution order* Formoterol, impurity I.

*System suitability* Reference solution (a):
— *peak-to-valley ratio*: minimum 2.5, where $H_p$ = height above the baseline of the peak due to impurity I and $H_v$ = height above the baseline of the lowest point of the curve separating this peak from the peak due to formoterol.

*Limit:*
— *impurity I*: not more than 1.5 times the area of the principal peak in the chromatogram obtained with reference solution (b) (0.3 per cent).

**Water** (*2.5.12*)
4.0 per cent to 5.0 per cent, determined on 0.100 g.

**ASSAY**
Dissolve 0.350 g in 50 ml of *anhydrous acetic acid R*. Titrate with *0.1 M perchloric acid*, determining the end-point potentiometrically (*2.2.20*).

1 ml of *0.1 M perchloric acid* is equivalent to 40.24 mg of $C_{42}H_{52}N_4O_{12}$.

**STORAGE**
Protected from light.

**IMPURITIES**
*Specified impurities A, B, C, D, E, F, I.*

*Other detectable impurities* (the following substances would, if present at a sufficient level, be detected by one or other of the tests in the monograph. They are limited by the general acceptance criterion for other/unspecified impurities and/or by the general monograph *Substances for pharmaceutical use (2034)*. It is therefore not necessary to identify these impurities for demonstration of compliance. See also *5.10*. Control of impurities in substances for pharmaceutical use): *G, H.*

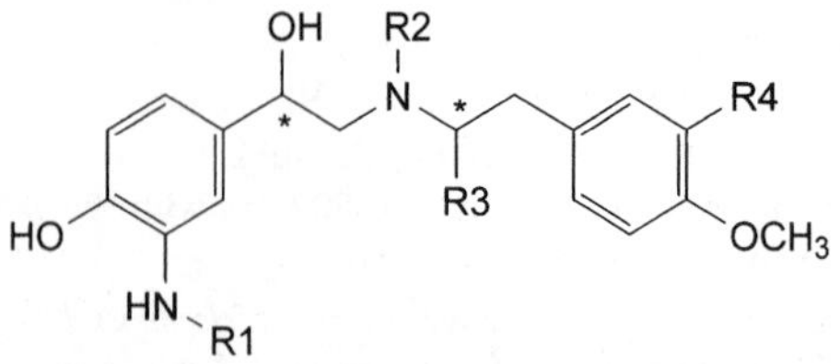

A. R1 = R2 = R4 = H, R3 = CH₃:
1-(3-amino-4-hydroxyphenyl)-2-[[2-(4-methoxyphenyl)-1-methylethyl]amino]ethanol,

B. R1 = CHO, R2 = R3 = R4 = H:
N-[2-hydroxy-5-[(1RS)-1-hydroxy-2-[[2-(4-methoxyphenyl)ethyl]amino]ethyl]phenyl]formamide,

C. R1 = CO-CH₃, R2 = R4 = H, R3 = CH₃:
N-[2-hydroxy-5-[1-hydroxy-2-[[2-(4-methoxyphenyl)-1-methylethyl]amino]ethyl]phenyl]acetamide,

D. R1 = CHO, R2 = R3 = CH₃, R4 = H:
N-[2-hydroxy-5-[1-hydroxy-2-[methyl[2-(4-methoxyphenyl)-1-methylethyl]amino]ethyl]phenyl]formamide,

E. R1 = CHO, R2 = H, R3 = R4 = CH₃:
N-[2-hydroxy-5-[1-hydroxy-2-[[2-(4-methoxy-3-methylphenyl)-1-methylethyl]amino]ethyl]phenyl]formamide,

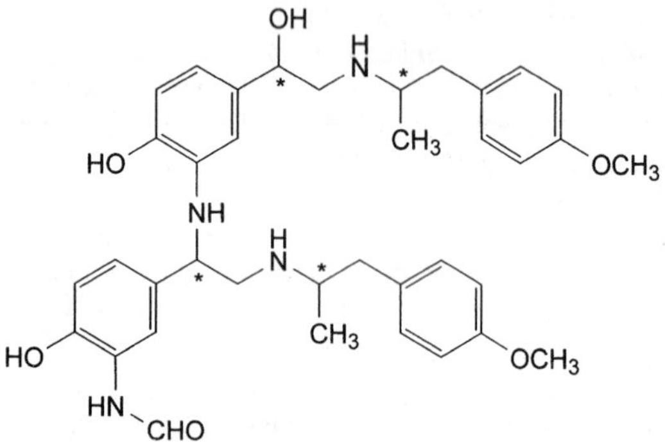

F. N-[2-hydroxy-5-[1-[[2-hydroxy-5-[1-hydroxy-2-[[2-(4-methoxyphenyl)-1-methylethyl]amino]ethyl]phenyl]amino]-2-[[2-(4-methoxyphenyl)-1-methylethyl]amino]ethyl]phenyl]formamide,

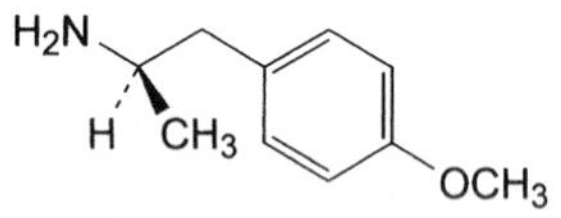

G. (2RS)-1-(4-methoxyphenyl)propan-2-amine,

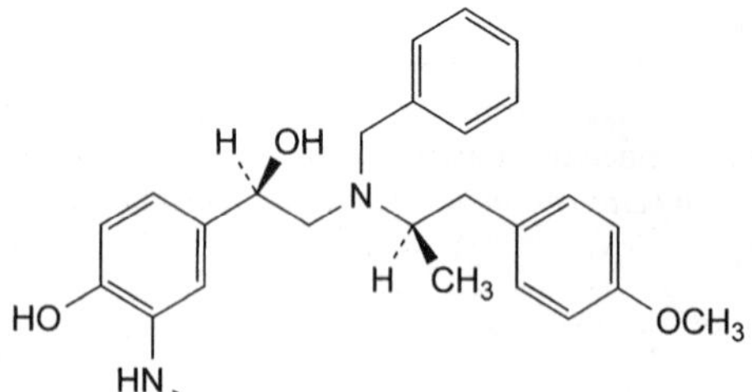

H. N-[5-[(1RS)-2-[benzyl[(1RS)-2-(4-methoxyphenyl)-1-methylethyl]amino]-1-hydroxyethyl]-2-hydroxyphenyl]formamide (monobenzyl analogue),

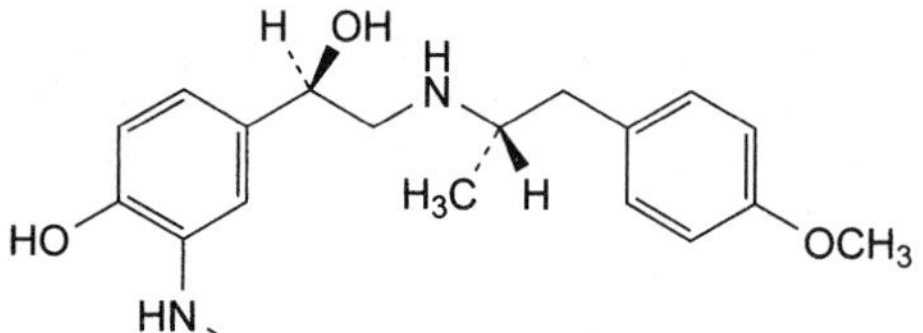

I. N-[2-hydroxy-5-[(1RS)-1-hydroxy-2-[[(1SR)-2-(4-methoxyphenyl)-1-methylethyl]amino]ethyl]phenyl]formamide (diastereoisomer).

*Ph Eur*

# Foscarnet Sodium

(*Foscarnet Sodium Hexahydrate,*
*Ph Eur monograph 1520*)

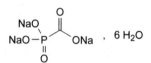

CNa₃O₅P,6H₂O          300.0          *34156-56-4*

**Action and use**
Antiviral (cytomegalovirus).

**Preparation**
Foscarnet Intravenous Infusion

*Ph Eur* _____

## DEFINITION
Trisodium phosphonatoformate hexahydrate.

**Content**
98.5 per cent to 101.0 per cent (dried substance).

## CHARACTERS
**Appearance**
White or almost white, crystalline powder.

**Solubility**
Soluble in water, practically insoluble in ethanol (96 per cent).

## IDENTIFICATION
A. Infrared absorption spectrophotometry (*2.2.24*).

*Comparison*   *foscarnet sodium hexahydrate CRS.*

B. It gives reaction (a) of sodium (*2.3.1*).

## TESTS
**Solution S**
Dissolve 0.5 g in *carbon dioxide-free water R* and dilute to 25 ml with the same solvent.

**Appearance of solution**
Solution S is not more opalescent than reference suspension I (*2.2.1*) and is colourless (*2.2.2, Method II*).

**pH** (*2.2.3*)
9.0 to 11.0 for solution S.

**Impurity D**
Gas chromatography (*2.2.28*).

*Test solution*   Dissolve 0.25 g of the substance to be examined in 9.0 ml of *0.1 M acetic acid* using a magnetic stirrer. Add 1.0 ml of *anhydrous ethanol R* and mix.

*Reference solution* Dissolve 25 mg of *triethyl phosphonoformate R* in *anhydrous ethanol R* and dilute to 100 ml with the same solvent. Dilute 1 ml of this solution to 10 ml with *anhydrous ethanol R*.

*Column:*
— *material*: fused silica;
— *size*: l = 25 m, Ø = 0.31 mm;
— *stationary phase*: poly(dimethyl)(diphenyl)(divinyl)siloxane R (film thickness 0.5 µm).

*Carrier gas* helium for chromatography R.

*Split ratio* 1:20.

*Temperature:*

| | Time (min) | Temperature (°C) |
|---|---|---|
| Column | 0 - 8 | 100 → 180 |
| Injection port | | 200 |
| Detector | | 250 |

*Detection* Flame ionisation.

*Injection* 3 µl

*Limit:*
— *impurity D*: not more than the area of the principal peak in the chromatogram obtained with the reference solution (0.1 per cent).

**Related substances**
Liquid chromatography (2.2.29).

*Test solution* Dissolve 25 mg of the substance to be examined in the mobile phase and dilute to 10.0 ml with the mobile phase.

*Reference solution (a)* Dilute 1.0 ml of the test solution to 50.0 ml with the mobile phase. Dilute 1.0 ml of this solution to 10.0 ml with the mobile phase.

*Reference solution (b)* Dissolve 5.0 mg of *foscarnet impurity B CRS* in the mobile phase, add 2.0 ml of the test solution and dilute to 50.0 ml with the mobile phase.

*Column:*
— *size*: l = 0.10 m, Ø = 4.6 mm;
— *stationary phase*: octadecylsilyl silica gel for chromatography R (3 µm).

*Mobile phase* Dissolve 3.22 g of *sodium sulphate decahydrate R* in *water R*, add 3 ml of *glacial acetic acid R* and 6 ml of a 44.61 g/l solution of *sodium pyrophosphate R* and dilute to 1000 ml with *water R* (solution A); dissolve 3.22 g of *sodium sulphate decahydrate R* in *water R*, add 6.8 g of *sodium acetate R* and 6 ml of a 44.61 g/l solution of *sodium pyrophosphate R* and dilute to 1000 ml with *water R* (solution B). Mix about 700 ml of solution A and about 300 ml of solution B to obtain a solution of pH 4.4. To 1000 ml of this solution, add 0.25 g of *tetrahexylammonium hydrogen sulphate R* and 100 ml of *methanol R*.

*Flow rate* 1.0 ml/min.

*Detection* Spectrophotometer at 230 nm.

*Injection* 20 µl.

*Run time* 2.5 times the retention time of foscarnet.

*System suitability* Reference solution (b):
— *resolution*: minimum 7 between the peaks due to foscarnet and impurity B.

*Limits:*
— *impurities A, B, C*: for each impurity, not more than the area of the principal peak in the chromatogram obtained with reference solution (a) (0.2 per cent);

— *total*: not more than twice the area of the principal peak in the chromatogram obtained with reference solution (a) (0.4 per cent);
— *disregard limit*: 0.2 times the area of the principal peak in the chromatogram obtained with reference solution (a) (0.04 per cent); disregard any peak with a relative retention time less than 0.6.

**Phosphate and phosphate**
Liquid chromatography (2.2.29).

*Test solution* Dissolve 60.0 mg of the substance to be examined in *water R* and dilute to 25.0 ml with the same solvent.

*Reference solution (a)* Dissolve 28 mg of *sodium dihydrogen phosphate monohydrate R* in *water R* and dilute to 100 ml with the same solvent.

*Reference solution (b)* Dissolve 43 mg of *sodium phosphite pentahydrate R* in *water R* and dilute to 100 ml with the same solvent.

*Reference solution (c)* Dilute 1.0 ml of reference solution (a) and 1.0 ml of reference solution (b) to 25 ml with *water R*.

*Reference solution (d)* Dilute 3 ml of reference solution (a) and 3 ml of reference solution (b) to 25 ml with *water R*.

*Column:*
— *size*: l = 0.05 m, Ø = 4.6 mm;
— *stationary phase*: anion exchange resin R.

*Mobile phase* Dissolve 0.102 g of *potassium hydrogen phthalate R* in *water R*, add 2.5 ml of *1 M nitric acid* and dilute to 1000 ml with *water R*.

*Flow rate* 1.4 ml/min.

*Detection* Spectrophotometer at 290 nm (indirect detection).

*Injection* 20 µl of the test solution and reference solutions (c) and (d).

*System suitability* Reference solution (d):
— *resolution*: minimum 2.0 between the peaks due to phosphate (1st peak) and phosphite;
— *signal-to-noise ratio*: minimum 10 for the principal peak.

*Limits:*
— *phosphate*: not more than the area of the corresponding peak in the chromatogram obtained with reference solution (c) (0.3 per cent);
— *phosphite*: not more than the area of the corresponding peak in the chromatogram obtained with reference solution (c) (0.3 per cent).

**Heavy metals**
Maximum 10 ppm.

Dissolve 1.25 g in 12.5 ml of *1 M hydrochloric acid*. Warm on a water-bath for 3 min and cool to room temperature. Transfer to a beaker, adjust to about pH 3.5 with *dilute ammonia R1* and dilute to 25 ml with *water R* (solution A). To 12 ml of solution A, add 2.0 ml of *buffer solution pH 3.5 R*. Rapidly pour the mixture into a test tube containing 1 drop of *sodium sulphide solution R*. The solution is not more intensely coloured than a reference solution prepared simultaneously and in the same manner by pouring a mixture of 5.0 ml of *lead standard solution (1 ppm Pb) R*, 5.0 ml of *water R*, 2.0 ml of solution A and 2.0 ml of *buffer solution pH 3.5 R* into a test tube containing 1 drop of *sodium sulphide solution R*.

**Loss on drying** (2.2.32)
35.0 per cent to 37.0 per cent, determined on 1.000 g by drying in an oven at 150 °C.

**Bacterial endotoxins** *(2.6.14)*
Less than 83.3 IU/g, if intended for use in the manufacture of parenteral preparations without a further appropriate procedure for the removal of bacterial endotoxins.

## ASSAY
Dissolve 0.200 g in 50 ml of *water R*. Titrate with *0.05 M sulphuric acid*, determining the end-point potentiometrically *(2.2.20)* at the 1st point of inflexion.

1 ml of *0.05 M sulphuric acid* is equivalent to 19.20 mg of $CNa_3O_5P$.

## STORAGE
Protected from light.

## IMPURITIES
*Specified impurities    A, B, C, D.*

A. R1 = $OC_2H_5$, R2 = R3 = ONa:
disodium (ethoxycarbonyl)phosphonate,

B. R1 = R2 = ONa, R3 = $OC_2H_5$:
disodium (ethoxyoxydophosphanyl)formate,

C. R1 = R2 = $OC_2H_5$, R3 = ONa:
ethyl sodium (ethoxycarbonyl)phosphonate,

D. R1 = R2 = R3 = $OC_2H_5$:
methyl (diethoxyphosphoryl)formate.

———————————————————————— *Ph Eur*

# Fosfestrol Sodium

$C_{18}H_{18}Na_4O_8P_2,xH_2O$    516.2(anhydrous)    *23519-26-8*

**Action and use**
Estrogen.

**Preparations**
Fosfestrol Injection
Fosfestrol Tablets

## DEFINITION
Fosfestrol Sodium is a hydrate of tetrasodium (*E*)-4,4'-(1,2-diethylvinylene)bis(phenyl orthophosphate). It contains not less than 98.0% and not more than 101.0% of $C_{18}H_{18}Na_4O_8P_2$, calculated with reference to the anhydrous substance.

## CHARACTERISTICS
A white or almost white powder.

Freely soluble in *water*; practically insoluble in *absolute ethanol* and in *ether*.

## IDENTIFICATION
A. The *infrared absorption spectrum*, Appendix II A, is concordant with the *reference spectrum* of fosfestrol sodium *(RS 161)*.

B. Yields the reactions characteristic of *sodium salts*, Appendix VI.

## TESTS
### Acidity or alkalinity
pH of a 5% w/v solution, 7.0 to 9.0, Appendix V L.

To 20 ml of a 2.5% w/v solution, add 3.0 ml of 0.01M *sodium hydroxide VS*. The pH of the resulting solution is not less than 8.8.

### Light absorption
Measure the *absorbance* of a 0.0050% w/v solution in 0.1M *sodium hydroxide* at the maximum at 242 nm, Appendix II B. The A(1%, 1 cm) at the maximum is 280 to 320, calculated with reference to the anhydrous substance.

### Chloride
Dissolve 1.0 g in 10 ml of *water*, add 10 ml of 2M *nitric acid*, filter, wash the precipitate with 25 ml of *water* and dilute the combined filtrate and washings to 100 ml with *water*. 15 ml of the resulting solution complies with the *limit test for chlorides*, Appendix VII (350 ppm).

### Inorganic phosphate
Dissolve 0.5 g in 20 ml of *water*, add 5 ml of 2M *hydrochloric acid* and extract with four 30 ml quantities of *ether*. Discard the ether extracts and heat the aqueous solution on a water bath until any remaining ether has evaporated. Allow to cool, add sufficient *water* to produce 100 ml (solution A) and then add 4 ml of *sulphomolybdic reagent R3*, shake, add 0.1 ml of a mixture of 1 volume of freshly prepared *tin(II) chloride solution* and 9 volumes of 2M *hydrochloric acid*, shake again and examine 20 ml. Any colour produced is not more intense than that of 20 ml of a solution obtained by repeating the operation using a mixture of 5 ml of a 0.01% w/v solution of *potassium dihydrogen orthophosphate* and 95 ml of *water* in place of solution A.

### Related substances
Carry out the method for *thin-layer chromatography*, Appendix III A, using a silica gel 60 $F_{254}$ precoated plate (Merck silica gel 60 $F_{254}$ plates are suitable) and a mixture of 15 volumes each of *pentan-1-ol, triethylamine* and *water* and 55 volumes of *propan-1-ol* as the mobile phase but allowing the solvent front to ascend 10 cm above the line of application. Apply separately to the plate 10 μl of each of three solutions of the substance being examined in *methanol (50%)* containing (1) 2.0% w/v (2) 0.030% w/v and (3) 0.010% w/v. After removal of the plate, allow it to dry in air and examine under *ultraviolet light (254 nm)*. Any *secondary spot* in the chromatogram obtained with solution (1) is not more intense than the spot in the chromatogram obtained with solution (2) (1.5%) and not more than two such spots are more intense than the spot in the chromatogram obtained with solution (3) (0.5%).

### Free diethylstilbestrol
Dissolve a quantity of the substance being examined containing the equivalent of 2 g of anhydrous fosfestrol sodium in 50 ml of *water*, extract with two 20 ml quantities of *dichloromethane* and retain the aqueous phase. Wash the combined dichloromethane extracts with 30 ml of *water* and filter through *anhydrous sodium sulphate*. Extract the water wash with 10 ml of *dichloromethane*, filter the

dichloromethane extract after filtration through *anhydrous sodium sulphate*, add to the original extract and add the aqueous extract to the original aqueous phase. Reserve the aqueous phase for the test for Diethylstilbestrol disodium monophosphate. Evaporate the combined filtrates to dryness on a water bath and dissolve the residue in 20 ml of *absolute ethanol*. To 10 ml of the resulting solution add 10 ml of a solution prepared by dissolving 1 g of *dipotassium hydrogen orthophosphate* in 55 ml of *water*. Transfer a portion of the mixture to a 1-cm closed silica cell, place the cell 10 cm from a 15-watt, short-wave ultraviolet lamp and irradiate for 30 minutes. The *absorbance* of the irradiated solution measured at the maximum at 418 nm, Appendix II B, is not greater than that obtained by repeating the operation using 10 ml of a 0.00150% w/v solution of *diethylstilbestrol BPCRS* in *absolute ethanol*, beginning at the words 'add 10 ml of a solution . . .' (0.015%).

**Diethylstilbestrol disodium monophosphate**

Dilute the combined aqueous phase reserved in the test for Free diethylstilbestrol to 100 ml with *water* (solution A). Prepare a solution containing 0.020% w/v of *diethylstilbestrol BPCRS* in *ethanol (96%)* (solution B). To 2 ml of each solution add 3 ml of *phosphomolybdotungstic reagent*, dilute to 50 ml with a 5% w/v solution of *anhydrous sodium carbonate*, mix thoroughly and allow to stand for 30 minutes; filter the solutions through a polytetrafluoroethylene filter (0.45 μm) and measure the *absorbance*, Appendix II B, at 660 nm using *water* in the reference cell. The *absorbance* of solution A, multiplied by 1.46, is not greater than that obtained for solution B (1%).

**Water**

13.0 to 16.5% w/w, Appendix IX C. Use 0.2 g.

**ASSAY**

Heat 0.2 g in a Kjeldahl flask with 2 ml of *sulphuric acid* and 2.5 ml of *nitric acid* until brown fumes cease to be evolved, allow to cool, add 1 ml of *nitric acid* and heat again. Continue adding *nitric acid* and heating until brown fumes are no longer evolved and the solution is colourless when cold. Heat until dense, white fumes are evolved, cool, transfer the solution to a flask with the aid of 150 ml of *water*, add 50 ml of *citric-molybdic acid solution* and heat slowly to boiling point. Swirling the flask continuously, add 25 ml of *quinoline solution*, at first drop wise and then in a steady stream, heat on a water bath for 5 minutes and cool. Filter, wash the precipitate with *water* until free from acid, transfer the precipitate to a flask with the aid of 100 ml of *water*, add 50 ml of 0.5M *sodium hydroxide VS* and shake until dissolved. Titrate the excess of alkali with 0.5M *hydrochloric acid VS* using *phenolphthalein-thymol blue solution* as indicator. Each ml of 0.5M *sodium hydroxide VS* is equivalent to 4.964 mg of $C_{18}H_{18}Na_4O_8P_2$.

**STORAGE**

Fosfestrol Sodium should be protected from light.

# Fosfomycin Calcium

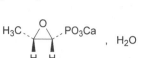

*(Ph Eur monograph 1328)*

$C_3H_5CaO_4P,H_2O$     194.1     *26016-98-8*

**Action and use**

Phosphonic acid derivative; antibacterial.

*Ph Eur*

**DEFINITION**

Calcium (2*R*,3*S*)-(3-methyloxiran-2-yl)phosphonate monohydrate.

Substance produced by certain strains of *Streptomyces fradiae* or obtained by any other means.

**Content**

95.0 per cent to 101.0 per cent (anhydrous substance).

**CHARACTERS**

**Appearance**

White or almost white powder.

**Solubility**

Slightly soluble in water, practically insoluble in acetone, in methanol and in methylene chloride.

**IDENTIFICATION**

*First identification   A, D.*

*Second identification   B, C, D.*

A. Infrared absorption spectrophotometry (*2.2.24*).

*Preparation*   Discs of *potassium bromide R*.

*Comparison*   *Ph. Eur. reference spectrum of fosfomycin calcium.*

B. Dissolve about 0.1 g in 3 ml of a 25 per cent *V/V* solution of *perchloric acid R*. Add 1 ml of *0.1 M sodium periodate* and heat on a water-bath for 30 min. Allow to cool and add 50 ml of *water R*. Neutralise with a saturated solution of *sodium hydrogen carbonate R* and add 1 ml of a freshly prepared 400 g/l solution of *potassium iodide R*. Prepare a blank at the same time and in the same manner. The test solution remains colourless and the blank is orange.

C. To about 8 mg add 2 ml of *water R*, 1 ml of *perchloric acid R* and 2 ml of *0.1 M sodium periodate*. Heat on a water-bath for 10 min and add, without cooling, 1 ml of *ammonium molybdate solution R5* and 1 ml of *aminohydroxynaphthalenesulphonic acid solution R*. Allow to stand for 30 min. A blue colour develops.

D. It gives reaction (a) of calcium (*2.3.1*).

**TESTS**

**pH** (*2.2.3*)

8.1 to 9.6.

Dissolve 20 mg in *carbon dioxide-free water R* and dilute to 20.0 ml with the same solvent.

**Specific optical rotation** (*2.2.7*)

− 11.0 to − 13.0 (anhydrous substance).

Dissolve 2.5 g in a 125 g/l solution of *sodium edetate R* previously adjusted to pH 8.5 with *strong sodium hydroxide solution R*, and dilute to 50.0 ml with the same solution. Measure at 405 nm using a mercury lamp.

**Impurity A**

Maximum 1.5 per cent.

In a glass-stoppered flask, dissolve 0.200 g in 100.0 ml of *water R*. Add 50 ml of *0.5 M phthalate buffer solution pH 6.4 R* and 5.0 ml of *0.005 M sodium periodate*, close and shake. Allow to stand protected from light for 90 min. Add 10 ml of a freshly prepared 400 g/l solution of *potassium iodide R*, close and shake for 2 min. Titrate with *0.0025 M sodium arsenite* until the yellow colour almost disappears. Add 2 ml of *starch solution R* and slowly continue the titration until the colour is completely discharged. Carry out a blank test under the same conditions. Calculate the percentage content of $C_3H_7CaO_5P$ using the following expression:

$$\frac{(n_1 - n_2) \times c \times 97}{m\,(100 - H)} \times 100$$

$m$ = mass of the substance to be examined, in milligrams,
$n_1$ = volume of *0.0025 M sodium arsenite* used in the blank titration,
$n_2$ = volume of *0.0025 M sodium arsenite* used in the titration of the test solution,
$c$ = molarity of the sodium arsenite solution,
$H$ = percentage content of water.

### Chlorides (2.4.4)
Maximum 0.2 per cent.

Dissolve 0.500 g in *water R*, add 2 ml of *nitric acid R* and dilute to 50 ml with the same acid. To 2.5 ml of this solution add 12.5 ml of *water R*.

### Heavy metals (2.4.8)
Maximum 20 ppm.

Dissolve 2.5 g in 6 ml of *glacial acetic acid R* and dilute to 25.0 ml with *water R*. 12 ml of the solution complies with test A. Prepare the reference solution using *lead standard solution (2 ppm Pb) R*.

### Water (2.5.12)
8.5 per cent to 11.5 per cent, determined on 0.250 g. Use as the solvent a mixture of 1 volume of *pyridine R* and 3 volumes of *ethylene glycol R*.

### ASSAY
In a glass-stoppered flask, dissolve 0.120 g in 20.0 ml of *0.1 M sodium periodate*. Add 5 ml of a 50 per cent *V/V* solution of *perchloric acid R* and shake. Heat in a water-bath at 37 °C for 105 min. Add 50 ml of *water R* and immediately adjust to pH 6.4 with a saturated solution of *sodium hydrogen carbonate R*. Add 10 ml of a freshly prepared 400 g/l solution of *potassium iodide R*, close and allow to stand for 2 min. Titrate with *0.1 M sodium arsenite* until the yellow colour almost disappears. Add 2 ml of *starch solution R* and slowly continue the titration until the colour is completely discharged. Carry out a blank test under the same conditions. Calculate the percentage content of $C_3H_5CaO_4P$ using the following expression:

$$\frac{(n_1 - n_2) \times c \times 88 \times 100}{m\,(100 - H)} \times 100 - G$$

$m$ = mass of the substance to be examined, in milligrams,
$n_1$ = volume of *0.1 M sodium arsenite* used in the blank titration,
$n_2$ = volume of *0.1 M sodium arsenite* used in the titration of the test solution,
$c$ = molarity of the sodium arsenite solution,
$G$ = percentage content of impurity A,
$H$ = percentage content of water.

### STORAGE
In an airtight container, protected from light.

### IMPURITIES
*Specified impurities    A.*

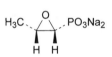

A. calcium (1,2-dihydroxypropyl)phosphonate.

*————————————————————— Ph Eur*

# Fosfomycin Sodium

*(Ph Eur monograph 1329)*

H3C—O—PO3Na2 (H H)

$C_3H_5Na_2O_4P$          182.0          *26016-99-9*

### Action and use
Phosphonic acid derivative; antibacterial.

*Ph Eur* ————————————————

### DEFINITION
Disodium (2*R*,3*S*)-(3-methyloxiran-2-yl)phosphonate.

Substance produced by certain strains of *Streptomyces fradiae* or obtained by any other means.

### Content
95.0 per cent to 101.0 per cent (anhydrous substance).

### CHARACTERS
#### Appearance
White or almost white, very hygroscopic powder.

#### Solubility
Very soluble in water, sparingly soluble in methanol, practically insoluble in ethanol (96 per cent) and in methylene chloride.

### IDENTIFICATION
*First identification    A, D.*

*Second identification    B, C, D.*

A. Infrared absorption spectrophotometry (2.2.24).

*Preparation    Discs of potassium bromide R.*

*Comparison    Ph. Eur. reference spectrum of fosfomycin sodium.*

B. Dissolve about 0.1 g in 3 ml of a 25 per cent *V/V* solution of *perchloric acid R*. Add 1 ml of *0.1 M sodium periodate* and heat on a water-bath for 30 min. Allow to cool and add 50 ml of *water R*. Neutralise with a saturated solution of *sodium hydrogen carbonate R* and add 1 ml of a freshly prepared 400 g/l solution of *potassium iodide R*. Prepare a blank at the same time and in the same manner. The test solution remains colourless and the blank is orange.

C. To about 8 mg add 2 ml of *water R*, 1 ml of *perchloric acid R* and 2 ml of *0.1 M sodium periodate*. Heat on a water-bath for 10 min and add, without cooling, 1 ml of *ammonium molybdate solution R5* and 1 ml of *aminohydroxynaphthalenesulphonic acid solution R*. Allow to stand for 30 min. A blue colour develops.

D. It gives reaction (a) of sodium (*2.3.1*).

## TESTS

### Solution S

Dissolve 5.0 g in *carbon dioxide-free water R* and dilute to 50.0 ml with the same solvent.

### Appearance of solution

Solution S is clear (*2.2.1*) and not more intensely coloured than reference solution $B_9$ (*2.2.2, Method II*).

### pH (*2.2.3*)

9.0 to 10.5.

Dilute 10 ml of solution S to 20 ml with *carbon dioxide-free water R*.

### Specific optical rotation (*2.2.7*)

− 13.0 to − 15.0 (anhydrous substance).

Dissolve 2.5 g in *water R* and dilute to 50.0 ml with the same solvent. Measure at 405 nm using a mercury lamp.

### Impurity A

Maximum 1.0 per cent.

In a glass-stoppered flask, dissolve 0.200 g in 100.0 ml of *water R*. Add 50 ml of *0.5 M phthalate buffer solution pH 6.4 R* and 5.0 ml of *0.005 M sodium periodate*, close and shake. Allow to stand protected from light for 90 min. Add 10 ml of a freshly prepared 400 g/l solution of *potassium iodide R*, close and shake for 2 min. Titrate with *0.0025 M sodium arsenite* until the yellow colour almost disappears. Add 2 ml of *starch solution R* and slowly continue the titration until the colour is completely discharged. Carry out a blank test under the same conditions.

Calculate the percentage content of $C_3H_7Na_2O_5P$ using the following expression:

$$\frac{(n_1 - n_2) \times c \times 100}{m\,(100 - H)} \times 100$$

$m$ = mass of the substance to be examined, in milligrams,
$n_1$ = volume of *0.0025 M sodium arsenite* used in the blank titration,
$n_2$ = volume of *0.0025 M sodium arsenite* used in the titration of the test solution,
$c$ = molarity of the sodium arsenite solution,
$H$ = percentage content of water.

### Heavy metals (*2.4.8*)

Maximum 20 ppm.

12 ml of solution S complies with test A. Prepare the reference solution using *lead standard solution (2 ppm Pb) R*.

### Water (*2.5.12*)

Maximum 1.0 per cent, determined on 0.50 g. Use as the solvent a mixture of 1 volume of *pyridine R* and 3 volumes of *ethylene glycol R*.

### Bacterial endotoxins (*2.6.14*)

Less than 0.083 IU/mg, if intended for use in the manufacture of parenteral dosage forms without a further appropriate procedure for removal of bacterial endotoxins.

## ASSAY

In a glass-stoppered flask, dissolve 0.120 g in 20.0 ml of *0.1 M sodium periodate*. Add 5 ml of a 50 per cent *V/V* solution of *perchloric acid R* and shake. Heat on a water-bath at 37 °C for 105 min. Add 50 ml of *water R* and immediately adjust to pH 6.4 with a saturated solution of *sodium hydrogen carbonate R*. Add 10 ml of a freshly prepared 400 g/l solution of *potassium iodide R*, close and allow to stand for 2 min. Titrate with *0.1 M sodium arsenite* until the yellow colour almost disappears. Add 2 ml of *starch solution R* and slowly continue the titration until the colour is completely discharged. Carry out a blank test under the same conditions.

Calculate the percentage content of $C_3H_5Na_2O_4P$ using the following expression:

$$\frac{(n_1 - n_2) \times c \times 91 \times 100}{m\,(100 - H)} \times 100 - G$$

$m$ = mass of the substance to be examined, in milligrams,
$n_1$ = volume of *0.1 M sodium arsenite* used in the blank titration,
$n_2$ = volume of *0.1 M sodium arsenite* used in the titration of the test solution,
$c$ = molarity of the sodium arsenite solution,
$G$ = percentage content of impurity A,
$H$ = percentage content of water.

## STORAGE

In an airtight container, protected from light. If the substance is sterile, store in a sterile, airtight, tamper-proof container.

## IMPURITIES

*Specified impurities*    A.

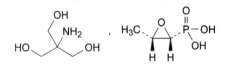

A. disodium (1,2-dihydroxypropyl)phosphonate.

*Ph Eur*

---

# Fosfomycin Trometamol

(*Ph Eur monograph 1425*)

$C_7H_{18}NO_7P$        259.2        78964-85-9

### Action and use

Phosphonic acid derivative; antibacterial.

*Ph Eur*

## DEFINITION

2-Amino-2-(hydroxymethyl)propane-1,3-diol hydrogen (2*R*,3*S*)-(3-methyloxiran-2-yl)phosphonate.

### Content

98.0 per cent to 102.0 per cent (anhydrous substance).

## CHARACTERS

### Appearance

White or almost white, hygroscopic powder.

### Solubility

Very soluble in water, slightly soluble in ethanol (96 per cent) and in methanol, practically insoluble in acetone.

## IDENTIFICATION

*First identification*    A.

*Second identification*    B, C.

A. Infrared absorption spectrophotometry (2.2.24).

*Comparison*   fosfomycin trometamol CRS .

B. Thin-layer chromatography (2.2.27).

*Test solution*   Dissolve 50 mg of the substance to be examined in *water R* and dilute to 10 ml with the same solvent.

*Reference solution*   Dissolve 50 mg of *fosfomycin trometamol CRS* in *water R* and dilute to 10 ml with the same solvent.

*Plate*   cellulose for chromatography R as the coating substance.

*Mobile phase*   concentrated ammonia R, water R, 2-propanol R (10:20:70 V/V/V).

*Application*   10 µl.

*Development*   Over 3/4 of the plate.

*Drying*   In a current of warm air.

*Detection*   Expose to iodine vapour until the spots appear.

*Results*   The principal spot in the chromatogram obtained with the test solution is similar in position, colour and size to the principal spot in the chromatogram obtained with the reference solution.

C. To about 15 mg add 2 ml of *water R*, 1 ml of *perchloric acid R* and 2 ml of *0.1 M sodium periodate*. Heat on a water-bath for 10 min and add, without cooling, 1 ml of *ammonium molybdate solution R5* and 1 ml of *aminohydroxynaphthalenesulphonic acid solution R*. Allow to stand for 30 min. A blue colour develops.

## TESTS

### Solution S

Dissolve 1.00 g in *carbon dioxide-free water R* and dilute to 20.0 ml with the same solvent.

### pH (2.2.3)

3.5 to 5.5 for solution S.

### Specific optical rotation (2.2.7)

− 13.5 to − 12.5 (anhydrous substance), determined on solution S at 365 nm using a mercury lamp.

### Related substances

Liquid chromatography (2.2.29). *Prepare the solutions immediately before use.*

*Test solution*   Dissolve 0.600 g of the substance to be examined in the mobile phase and dilute to 5.0 ml with the mobile phase.

*Reference solution (a)*   Dissolve 0.600 g of *fosfomycin trometamol CRS* in the mobile phase and dilute to 5.0 ml with the mobile phase.

*Reference solution (b)*   Dilute 1.0 ml of the test solution to 100.0 ml with the mobile phase. Dilute 3.0 ml of this solution to 10.0 ml with the mobile phase.

*Reference solution (c)*   Wet 0.3 g of the substance to be examined with 60 µl of *water R* and heat in an oven at 60 °C for 24 h. Dissolve the residue in the mobile phase and dilute to 20.0 ml with the mobile phase (solution A). Dissolve 0.6 g of the substance to be examined in solution A and dilute to 5.0 ml with the same solution (*in situ* degradation to obtain impurities A, B, C and D).

*Blank solution*   The mobile phase.

*Column:*
— *size: l* = 0.25 m, Ø = 4.6 mm,
— *stationary phase: aminopropylsilyl silica gel for chromatography R* (5 µm).

*Mobile phase*   10.89 g/l solution of *potassium dihydrogen phosphate R* in water for chromatography R.

*Flow rate*   1.0 ml/min.

*Detection*   Differential refractometer at 35 °C.

*Injection*   10 µl of the blank solution, the test solution and reference solutions (b) and (c).

*Run time*   Twice the retention time of fosfomycin.

*Relative retention*   With reference to fosfomycin (retention time = about 9 min):
trometamol (2 peaks) = about 0.3; impurity B = about 0.48; impurity C = about 0.54; impurity A = about 0.88; impurity D = about 1.27.

*System suitability*   Reference solution (c):
— *resolution*: minimum 1.5 between the peaks due to impurity A and fosfomycin,
— *peak-to-valley ratio*: minimum 1.5, where $H_p$ = height above the baseline of the peak due to impurity C and $H_v$ = height above the baseline of the lowest point of the curve separating this peak from the peak due to impurity B.

*Limits:*
— *impurities A, B*: for each impurity, not more than the area of the peak due to fosfomycin in the chromatogram obtained with reference solution (b) (0.3 per cent),
— *impurities C, D*: for each impurity, not more than 0.33 times the area of the peak due to fosfomycin in the chromatogram obtained with reference solution (b) (0.1 per cent),
— *unspecified impurities*: for each impurity, not more than 0.33 times the area of the peak due to fosfomycin in the chromatogram obtained with reference solution (b) (0.1 per cent),
— *total*: not more than 1.67 times the area of the peak due to fosfomycin in the chromatogram obtained with reference solution (b) (0.5 per cent);
— *disregard limit*: 0.17 times the area of the peak due to fosfomycin in the chromatogram obtained with reference solution (b) (0.05 per cent); disregard the 2 peaks due to trometamol and any peak due to the blank.

### Phosphates

Maximum 500 ppm.

Dissolve 0.1 g in 3 ml of *dilute nitric acid R* and dilute to 10 ml with *water R*. To 5 ml of this solution add 5 ml of *water R* and 5 ml of *molybdovanadic reagent R*. Shake vigorously. After 5 min, any colour in the test solution is not more intense than that in a standard prepared at the same time in the same manner, using 5 ml of *phosphate standard solution (5 ppm PO₄) R*.

### Heavy metals (2.4.8)

Maximum 10 ppm.

Dissolve 2.0 g in *water R* and dilute to 20 ml with the same solvent. 12 ml of the solution complies with test A. Prepare the reference solution using *lead standard solution (1 ppm Pb) R*.

### Water (2.5.12)

Maximum 0.5 per cent, determined on 0.500 g.

## ASSAY

Liquid chromatography (2.2.29) as described in the test for related substances with the following modification.

*Injection*   5 µl of the test solution and reference solution (a).

Calculate the percentage content of $C_7H_{18}NO_7P$ from the areas of the peaks due to fosfomycin and the declared content of *fosfomycin trometamol CRS* .

## STORAGE

In an airtight container.

## IMPURITIES

*Specified impurities   A, B, C, D.*

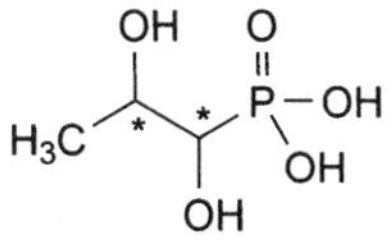

A. (1,2-dihydroxypropyl)phosphonic acid,

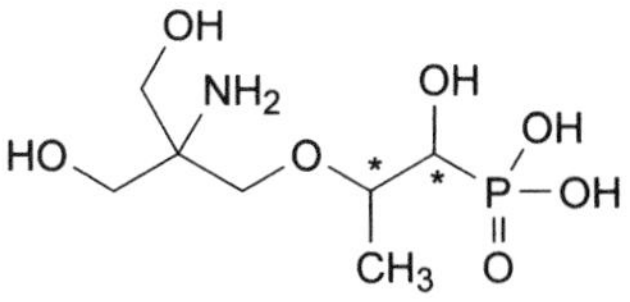

B. [2-[2-amino-3-hydroxy-2-(hydroxymethyl)propoxy]-1-hydroxypropyl]phosphonic acid,

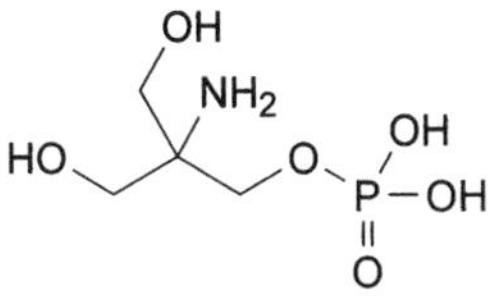

C. 2-amino-3-hydroxy-2-(hydroxymethyl)propyl dihydrogen phosphate (trometamol phosphoric acid monoester),

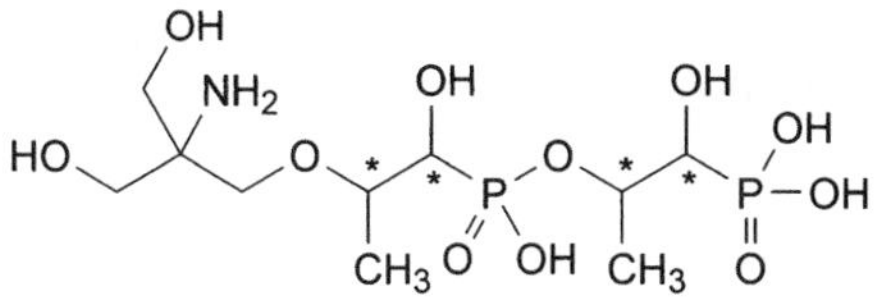

D. [2-[[[2-[2-amino-3-hydroxy-2-(hydroxymethyl)propoxy]-1-hydroxypropyl]hydroxyphosphoryl]oxy]-1-hydroxypropyl]phosphonic acid
(trometamoyloxy fosfomycin dimer).

*Ph Eur*

# Framycetin Sulphate

*(Ph Eur monograph 0180)*

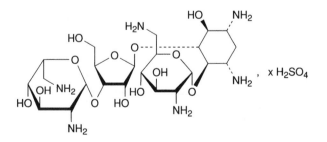

$C_{23}H_{46}N_6O_{13},xH_2SO_4$    615    *4146-30-9*

(base)

## Action and use
Antibacterial.

Ph Eur

## DEFINITION

Sulphate of 2-deoxy-4-*O*-(2,6-diamino-2,6-dideoxy-α-D-glucopyranosyl)-5-*O*-[3-*O*-(2,6-diamino-2,6-dideoxy-β-L-idopyranosyl)-β-D-ribofuranosyl]-D-streptamine (neomycin B).

Substance produced by the growth of selected strains of *Streptomyces fradiae* or *Streptomyces decaris* or obtained by any other means.

## Content
Minimum of 630 IU/mg (dried substance).

## CHARACTERS
### Appearance
White or yellowish-white powder, hygroscopic.

### Solubility
Freely soluble in water, very slightly soluble in alcohol, practically insoluble in acetone.

## IDENTIFICATION
A. Examine the chromatograms obtained in the test for related substances.

*Results:*
— the retention time of the principal peak in the chromatogram obtained with the test solution is approximately the same as that of the principal peak in the chromatogram obtained with reference solution (a),
— it complies with the limit given for impurity C.

B. It gives reaction (a) of sulphates (*2.3.1*).

## TESTS
**pH** (*2.2.3*)
6.0 to 7.0.

Dissolve 0.1 g in *carbon dioxide-free water R* and dilute to 10 ml with the same solvent.

### Specific optical rotation (*2.2.7*)
+ 52.5 to + 55.5 (dried substance).

Dissolve 1.00 g in *water R* and dilute to 10.0 ml with the same solvent

### Related substances
Liquid chromatography (*2.2.29*).

*Test solution*   Dissolve 25.0 mg of the substance to be examined in the mobile phase and dilute to 50.0 ml with the mobile phase.

*Reference solution (a)*   Dissolve the contents of a vial of *framycetin sulphate CRS* in the mobile phase and dilute with the mobile phase to obtain a solution containing 0.5 mg/ml.

*Reference solution (b)*   Dilute 3.0 ml of reference solution (a) to 100.0 ml with the mobile phase.

*Reference solution (c)*   Dilute 1.0 ml of reference solution (a) to 100.0 ml with the mobile phase.

*Reference solution (d*   Dissolve the contents of a vial of *neamine CRS* (corresponding to 0.5 mg) in the mobile phase and dilute to 100.0 ml with the mobile phase.

*Reference solution (e)*   Dissolve 10 mg of *neomycin sulphate CRS* in the mobile phase and dilute to 100.0 ml with the mobile phase.

*Column:*
— *size: l* = 0.25 m, Ø = 4.6 mm,
— *stationary phase: base-deactivated octadecylsilyl silica gel for chromatography R* (5 μm),
— *temperature*: 25 °C.

*Mobile phase*   Mix 20.0 ml of *trifluoroacetic acid R*, 6.0 ml of *carbonate-free sodium hydroxide solution R* and 500 ml of *water R*, allow to equilibrate, dilute to 1000 ml with *water R* and degas.

*Flow rate* 0.7 ml/min.

*Post-column solution* *carbonate-free sodium hydroxide solution R* diluted 1 in 25 previously degassed, which is added pulse-less to the column effluent using a 375 µl polymeric mixing coil.

*Flow rate* 0.5 ml/min.

*Detection* Pulsed amperometric detector with a gold working electrode, a silver-silver chloride reference electrode and a stainless steel auxiliary electrode which is the cell body, held at respectively 0.00 V detection, + 0.80 V oxidation and − 0.60 V reduction potentials, with pulse durations according to the instrument used.

*Injection* 10 µl.

*Run time* 1.5 times the retention time of neomycin B.

*Relative retention* With reference to neomycin B (retention time = about 10 min): impurity A = about 0.65; impurity C = about 0.9; impurity G = about 1.1.

*System suitability:*
— *resolution*: minimum 2.0 between the peaks due to impurity C and to neomycin B in the chromatogram obtained with reference solution (e); if necessary, adjust the volume of the carbonate-free sodium hydroxide solution in the mobile phase,
— *signal-to-noise ratio*: minimum 10 for the principal peak in the chromatogram obtained with reference solution (c).

*Limits:*
— *impurity A*: not more than the area of the principal peak in the chromatogram obtained with reference solution (d) and taking into account the declared content of *neamine CRS* (1.0 per cent),
— *impurity C*: not more than the area of the principal peak in the chromatogram obtained with reference solution (b) (3.0 per cent),
— *total of other impurities*: not more than the area of the principal peak in the chromatogram obtained with reference solution (b) (3.0 per cent),
— *disregard limit*: area of the principal peak in the chromatogram obtained with reference solution (c) (1.0 per cent).

**Sulphate**

27.0 per cent to 31.0 per cent (dried substance).

Dissolve 0.250 g in 100 ml of *water R* and adjust the solution to pH 11 using *concentrated ammonia R*. Add 10.0 ml of *0.1 M barium chloride* and about 0.5 mg of *phthalein purple R*. Titrate with *0.1 M sodium edetate* adding 50 ml of *alcohol R* when the colour of the solution begins to change and continuing the titration until the violet-blue colour disappears.

1 ml of *0.1 M barium chloride* is equivalent to 9.606 mg of $SO_4$.

**Loss on drying** (*2.2.32*)

Maximum 8.0 per cent, determined on 1.000 g by drying at 60 °C over *diphosphorus pentoxide R* at a pressure not exceeding 0.7 kPa for 3 h.

**Sulphated ash** (*2.4.14*)

Maximum 1.0 per cent, determined on 1.0 g.

**Sterility** (*2.6.1*)

If intended for introduction into body cavities without a further appropriate sterilisation procedure, it complies with the test for sterility.

**Bacterial endotoxins** (*2.6.14, Method D*)

Less than 1.3 IU/mg if intended for introduction into body cavities without a further appropriate procedure for the removal of bacterial endotoxins.

**ASSAY**

Carry out the microbiological assay of antibiotics (*2.7.2*). Use *framycetin sulphate CRS* as the reference substance.

**STORAGE**

In an airtight container, protected from light. If the substance is intended for introduction into body cavities, store in a sterile, tamper-proof container.

**IMPURITIES**

A. R1 = H, R$_2$ = NH$_2$: 2-deoxy-4-*O*-(2,6-diamino-2,6-dideoxy-α-D-glucopyranosyl)-D-streptamine (neamine or neomycin A-LP),

B. R1 = CO-CH$_3$, R2 = NH$_2$: 3-*N*-acetyl-2-deoxy-4-*O*-(2,6-diamino-2,6-dideoxy-α-D-glucopyranosyl)-D-streptamine (3-acetylneamine),

D. R1 = H, R2 = OH: 4-*O*-(2-amino-2-deoxy-α-D-glucopyranosyl)-2-deoxy-D-streptamine (paromamine or neomycin D),

C. R1 = CH$_2$-NH$_2$, R2 = R3 = H, R4 = NH$_2$: 2-deoxy-4-*O*-(2,6-diamino-2,6-dideoxy-α-D-glucopyranosyl)-5-*O*-[3-*O*-(2,6-diamino-2,6-dideoxy-α-D-glucopyranosyl)-β-D-ribofuranosyl]-D-streptamine (neomycin C),

E. R1 = R3 = H, R2 = CH$_2$-NH$_2$, R4 = OH: 4-*O*-(2-amino-2-deoxy-α-D-glucopyranosyl)-2-deoxy-5-*O*-[3-*O*-(2,6-diamino-2,6-dideoxy-β-L-idopyranosyl)-β-D-ribofuranosyl]-D-streptamine (paromomycin I or neomycin E),

F. R1 = CH$_2$-NH$_2$, R2 = R3 = H, R4 = OH: 4-*O*-(2-amino-2-deoxy-α-D-glucopyranosyl)-2-deoxy-5-*O*-[3-*O*-(2,6-diamino-2,6-dideoxy-α-D-glucopyranosyl)-β-D-ribofuranosyl]-D-streptamine (paromomycin II or neomycin F),

G. R1 = H, R2 = CH$_2$-NH$_2$, R3 = CO-CH$_3$, R4 = NH$_2$: 3-*N*-acetyl-2-deoxy-4-*O*-(2,6-diamino-2,6-dideoxy-α-D-glucopyranosyl)-5-*O*-[3-*O*-(2,6-diamino-2,6-dideoxy-β-L-idopyranosyl)-β-D-ribofuranosyl]-D-streptamine (neomycin B-LP).

# Fructose

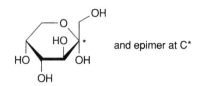

(*Ph Eur monograph 0188*)

and epimer at C*

C₆H₁₂O₆     180.2     57-48-7

$C_6H_{12}O_6$    180.2    57-48-7

**Preparation**

Fructose Intravenous Infusion

*Ph Eur*

### DEFINITION

(–)-D-Arabino-hex-2-ulopyranose.

The substance described in this monograph is not necessarily suitable for parenteral use.

### CHARACTERS

**Appearance**

White or almost white, crystalline powder.

It has a very sweet taste.

**Solubility**

Very soluble in water, soluble in ethanol (96 per cent).

### IDENTIFICATION

A. Thin-layer chromatography (*2.2.27*).

*Solvent mixture*   water *R*, methanol *R* (2:3 *V/V*).

*Test solution*   Dissolve 10 mg of the substance to be examined in the solvent mixture and dilute to 20 ml with the solvent mixture.

*Reference solution (a)*   Dissolve 10 mg of *fructose CRS* in the solvent mixture and dilute to 20 ml with the solvent mixture.

*Reference solution (b)*   Dissolve 10 mg each of *fructose CRS*, *glucose CRS*, *lactose CRS* and *sucrose CRS* in the solvent mixture and dilute to 20 ml with the solvent mixture.

*Plate*   TLC silica gel G plate R.

*Mobile phase*   water *R*, methanol *R*, anhydrous acetic acid *R*, ethylene chloride *R* (10:15:25:50 *V/V/V/V*). Measure the volumes accurately since a slight excess of water produces cloudiness.

*Application*   2 μl; thoroughly dry the starting points.

*Development A*   Over a path of 15 cm.

*Drying A*   In a current of warm air.

*Development B*   Immediately, over a path of 15 cm, after renewing the mobile phase.

*Drying B*   In a current of warm air.

*Detection*   Spray with a solution of 0.5 g of *thymol R* in a mixture of 5 ml of *sulphuric acid R* and 95 ml of *ethanol (96 per cent) R*. Heat at 130 °C for 10 min.

*System suitability*   Reference solution (b):
— the chromatogram shows 4 clearly separated spots.

*Results*   The principal spot in the chromatogram obtained with the test solution is similar in position, colour and size to the principal spot in the chromatogram obtained with reference solution (a).

B. Dissolve 0.1 g in 10 ml of *water R*. Add 3 ml of *cupri-tartaric solution R* and heat. A red precipitate is formed.

C. To 1 ml of solution S (see Tests) add 9 ml of *water R*. To 1 ml of the solution add 5 ml of *hydrochloric acid R* and heat to 70 °C. A brown colour develops.

D. Dissolve 5 g in *water R* and dilute to 10 ml with the same solvent. To 0.5 ml of the solution add 0.2 g of *resorcinol R* and 9 ml of *dilute hydrochloric acid R* and heat on a water-bath for 2 min. A red colour develops.

### TESTS

**Solution S**

Dissolve 10.0 g in *distilled water R* and dilute to 100 ml with the same solvent.

**Appearance of solution**

Dissolve 5.0 g in *water R* and dilute to 10 ml with the same solvent. The solution is clear (*2.2.1*). Add 10 ml of *water R*. The solution is colourless (*2.2.2, Method II*).

**Acidity or alkalinity**

Dissolve 6.0 g in 25 ml of *carbon dioxide-free water R* and add 0.3 ml of *phenolphthalein solution R*. The solution is colourless. Not more than 0.15 ml of *0.1 M sodium hydroxide* is required to change the colour of the indicator to pink.

**Specific optical rotation** (*2.2.7*)

− 91.0 to − 93.5 (anhydrous substance).

Dissolve 10.0 g in 80 ml of *water R*, add 0.2 ml of *dilute ammonia R1*, allow to stand for 30 min and dilute to 100.0 ml with *water R*.

**Foreign sugars**

Dissolve 5.0 g in *water R* and dilute to 10 ml with the same solvent. To 1 ml of the solution add 9 ml of *ethanol (96 per cent) R*. Any opalescence in the solution is not more intense than that in a mixture of 1 ml of the initial solution and 9 ml of *water R*.

**5-Hydroxymethylfurfural and related compounds**

To 5 ml of solution S add 5 ml of *water R*. The absorbance (*2.2.25*) measured at 284 nm is not greater than 0.32.

**Barium**

To 10 ml of solution S add 1 ml of *dilute sulphuric acid R*. When examined immediately and after 1 h, any opalescence in the solution is not more intense than that in a mixture of 1 ml of *distilled water R* and 10 ml of solution S.

**Lead** (*2.4.10*)

Maximum 0.5 ppm.

**Water** (*2.5.12*)

Maximum 0.5 per cent, determined on 1.00 g.

**Sulphated ash**

Maximum 0.1 per cent.

Dissolve 5.0 g in 10 ml of *water R*, add 2 ml of *sulphuric acid R*, evaporate to dryness on a water-bath and ignite to constant mass.

*Ph Eur*

# Furazolidone

C₈H₇N₃O₅     225.2     67-45-8

$C_8H_7N_3O_5$    225.2    67-45-8

**Action and use**

Antiprotozoal; antibacterial.

## DEFINITION

Furazolidone is 3-(5-nitrofurfurylideneamino)oxazolidin-2-one. It contains not less than 97.0% and not more than 103.0% of $C_8H_7N_3O_5$, calculated with reference to the dried substance.

## CHARACTERISTICS

A yellow, crystalline powder.

Very slightly soluble in *water* and in *ethanol (96%)*; practically insoluble in *ether*.

## IDENTIFICATION

A. The *infrared absorption spectrum*, Appendix II A, is concordant with the *reference spectrum* of furazolidone (RS 164).

B. Dissolve 1 mg in 1 ml of *dimethylformamide* and add 0.05 ml of 1M *ethanolic potassium hydroxide*. A deep blue colour is produced.

## TESTS

### Acidity or alkalinity

Shake 1 g for 15 minutes with 100 ml of *carbon dioxide-free water* and filter. The pH of the filtrate is 4.5 to 7.0, Appendix V L.

### Nitrofurfural diacetate

Carry out in subdued light the method for *thin-layer chromatography*, Appendix III A, using *silica gel G* as the coating substance and a mixture of 95 volumes of *toluene* and 5 volumes of *1,4-dioxan* as the mobile phase. Apply separately to the plate 20 μl of solution (1) and 10 μl of solution (2). For solution (1) dissolve 50 mg of the substance being examined in 5 ml of *dimethylformamide* by heating on a water bath for a few minutes, allow to cool and dilute to 10 ml with *acetone*. Solution (2) contains 0.010% w/v solution of *nitrofurfural diacetate BPCRS* in a mixture of equal volumes of *dimethylformamide* and *acetone*. After removal of the plate, heat it at 105° for 5 minutes and spray with a solution prepared by dissolving 0.75 g of *phenylhydrazine hydrochloride* in 10 ml of *ethanol (96%)*, diluting to 50 ml with *water*, adding *activated charcoal*, filtering and then adding 25 ml of *hydrochloric acid* and sufficient *water* to produce 200 ml. Any spot corresponding to nitrofurfural diacetate in the chromatogram obtained with solution (1) is not more intense than the spot in the chromatogram obtained with solution (2).

### Loss on drying

When dried to constant weight at 105°, loses not more than 0.5% of its weight. Use 1 g.

### Sulphated ash

Not more than 0.1%, Appendix IX A.

## ASSAY

Carry out the following procedure protected from light. To 80 mg add 150 ml of *dimethylformamide*, swirl to dissolve and add sufficient *water* to produce 500 ml. Dilute 5 ml to 100 ml with *water* and mix. Measure the *absorbance* of the resulting solution at the maximum at 367 nm, Appendix II B. Calculate the content of $C_8H_7N_3O_5$ taking 750 as the value of A(1%, 1 cm) at the maximum at 367 nm.

## STORAGE

Furazolidone should be protected from light.

# Furosemide

*(Ph Eur monograph 0391)*

$C_{12}H_{11}ClN_2O_5S$  330.7  *54-31-9*

## Action and use

Loop diuretic.

## Preparations

Co-amilofruse Tablets

Furosemide Injection

Furosemide Tablets

*Ph Eur*

## DEFINITION

4-Chloro-2-[(furan-2-ylmethyl)amino]-5-sulphamoylbenzoic acid.

## Content

98.5 per cent to 101.0 per cent (dried substance).

## CHARACTERS

### Appearance

White or almost white, crystalline powder.

### Solubility

Practically insoluble in water, soluble in acetone, sparingly soluble in ethanol (96 per cent), practically insoluble in methylene chloride. It dissolves in dilute solutions of alkali hydroxides.

### mp

About 210 °C, with decomposition.

## IDENTIFICATION

*First identification   B.*

*Second identification   A, C.*

A. Ultraviolet and visible absorption spectrophotometry (2.2.25).

*Test solution*   Dissolve 50 mg in a 4 g/l solution of *sodium hydroxide R* and dilute to 100 ml with the same solution. Dilute 1 ml of this solution to 100 ml with a 4 g/l solution of *sodium hydroxide R*.

*Spectral range*   220-350 nm.

*Absorption maxima*   At 228 nm, 270 nm and 333 nm.

*Absorbance ratio*   $A_{270} / A_{228} = 0.52$ to 0.57.

B. Infrared absorption spectrophotometry (2.2.24).

*Comparison   furosemide CRS .*

C. Dissolve about 25 mg in 10 ml of *ethanol (96 per cent) R*. To 5 ml of this solution add 10 ml of *water R*. To 0.2 ml of the solution add 10 ml of *dilute hydrochloric acid R* and heat under a reflux condenser for 15 min. Allow to cool and add 18 ml of *1 M sodium hydroxide* and 1 ml of a 5 g/l solution of *sodium nitrite R*. Allow to stand for 3 min, add 2 ml of a 25 g/l solution of *sulphamic acid R* and mix. Add 1 ml of a 5 g/l solution of *naphthylethylenediamine dihydrochloride R*. A violet-red colour develops.

## TESTS

### Related substances

Liquid chromatography (2.2.29). *Prepare the solutions immediately before use and protect from light.*

*Test solution* Dissolve 50.0 mg of the substance to be examined in the mobile phase and dilute to 50.0 ml with the mobile phase.

*Reference solution (a)* Dissolve 2.0 mg of *furosemide impurity A CRS* in the mobile phase and dilute to 2.0 ml with the mobile phase.

*Reference solution (b)* Dilute a mixture of 1.0 ml of the test solution and 1.0 ml of reference solution (a) to 20.0 ml with the mobile phase. Dilute 1.0 ml of this solution to 20.0 ml with the mobile phase.

*Column:*
— *size: l* = 0.25 m, Ø = 4.6 mm;
— *stationary phase: octylsilyl silica gel for chromatography R* (5 µm).

*Mobile phase* Dissolve 0.2 g of *potassium dihydrogen phosphate R* and 0.25 g of *cetrimide R* in 70 ml of *water R*; adjust to pH 7.0 with *ammonia R* and add 30 ml of *propanol R.*

*Flow rate* 1 ml/min.

*Detection* Spectrophotometer at 238 nm.

*Injection* 20 µl of the test solution and reference solution (b).

*Run time* 3 times the retention time of furosemide.

*System suitability* Reference solution (b):
— *resolution*: minimum 4 between the peaks due to impurity A (1st peak) and furosemide (2nd peak).

*Limits:*
— *impurities A, B, C, D, E*: for each impurity, not more than the area of the peak due to impurity A in the chromatogram obtained with reference solution (b) (0.25 per cent);
— *total*: not more than twice the area of the peak due to impurity A in the chromatogram obtained with reference solution (b) (0.5 per cent);
— *disregard limit*: 0.1 times the area of the peak due to impurity A in the chromatogram obtained with reference solution (b) (0.025 per cent).

### Chlorides (2.4.4)

Maximum 200 ppm.

To 0.5 g add a mixture of 0.2 ml of *nitric acid R* and 30 ml of *water R* and shake for 5 min. Allow to stand for 15 min and filter.

### Sulphates (2.4.13)

Maximum 300 ppm.

To 1.0 g add a mixture of 0.2 ml of *acetic acid R* and 30 ml of *distilled water R* and shake for 5 min. Allow to stand for 15 min and filter.

### Heavy metals (2.4.8)

Maximum 20 ppm.

1.0 g complies with test C. Prepare the reference solution using 2 ml of *lead standard solution (10 ppm Pb) R.*

### Loss on drying (2.2.32)

Maximum 0.5 per cent, determined on 1.000 g by drying in an oven at 105 °C.

### Sulphated ash (2.4.14)

Maximum 0.1 per cent, determined on 1.0 g.

## ASSAY

Dissolve 0.250 g in 20 ml of *dimethylformamide R*. Titrate with *0.1 M sodium hydroxide* using 0.2 ml of *bromothymol blue solution R2*. Carry out a blank titration.

1 ml of *0.1 M sodium hydroxide* is equivalent to 33.07 mg of $C_{12}H_{11}ClN_2O_5S$.

## STORAGE

Protected from light.

## IMPURITIES

*Specified impurities* A, B, C, D, E.

A. 2-chloro-4-[(furan-2-ylmethyl)amino]-5-sulphamoylbenzoic acid,

B. R1 = Cl, R2 = SO$_2$-NH$_2$:
2,4-dichloro-5-sulphamoylbenzoic acid,

C. R1 = NH$_2$, R2 = SO$_2$-NH$_2$:
2-amino-4-chloro-5-sulphamoylbenzoic acid,

E. R1 = Cl, R2 = H: 2,4-dichlorobenzoic acid,

D. 2,4-bis[(furan-2-ylmethyl)amino]-5-sulphamoylbenzoic acid.

*Ph Eur*

# Fusidic Acid

*(Ph Eur monograph 0798)*

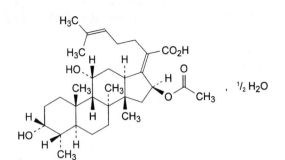

C$_{31}$H$_{48}$O$_6$,½H$_2$O      525.7      6990-06-3

## Action and use
Antibacterial.

## Preparations
Fusidic Acid Cream

Fusidic Acid Eye Drops

Fusidic Acid Oral Suspension

*Ph Eur* _____

## DEFINITION
*ent*-(17Z)-16α-(Acetyloxy)-3β,11β-dihydroxy-4β,8,14-trimethyl-18-nor-5β,10α-cholesta-17(20),24-dien-21-oic acid hemihydrate.

Antimicrobial substance produced by the growth of certain strains of *Fusidium coccineum* or by any other means.

## Content
97.5 per cent to 101.0 per cent (anhydrous substance).

## CHARACTERS

### Appearance
White or almost white, crystalline powder.

### Solubility
Practically insoluble in water, freely soluble in ethanol (96 per cent).

## IDENTIFICATION
A. Infrared absorption spectrophotometry (2.2.24).

*Comparison*  Ph. Eur. reference spectrum of fusidic acid.

B. Thin-layer chromatography (2.2.27).

*Test solution*  Dissolve 20 mg of the substance to be examined in *methanol R* and dilute to 10 ml with the same solvent.

*Reference solution*  Dissolve 24 mg of *diethanolamine fusidate CRS* in *methanol R* and dilute to 10 ml with the same solvent.

*Plate*  TLC silica gel F$_{254}$ plate R.

*Mobile phase*  methanol R, cyclohexane R, glacial acetic acid R, chloroform R (2.5:10:10:80 V/V/V/V).

*Application*  10 µl.

*Development*  Over a path of 15 cm.

*Drying*  In a current of warm air.

*Detection*  Examine in ultraviolet light at 254 nm.

*Results*  The principal spot in the chromatogram obtained with the test solution is similar in position and size to the principal spot in the chromatogram obtained with the reference solution.

## TESTS

### Related substances
Liquid chromatography (2.2.29).

*Test solution*  Dissolve 50 mg of the substance to be examined in the mobile phase and dilute to 10.0 ml with the mobile phase.

*Reference solution (a)*  Dissolve 5 mg of *3-ketofusidic acid CRS* in 5 ml of the mobile phase. To 1.0 ml of this solution add 0.20 ml of the test solution and dilute to 20.0 ml with the mobile phase.

*Reference solution (b)*  Dilute 20 µl of the test solution to 100.0 ml with the mobile phase.

*Column:*
— *size:* l = 0.125-0.15 m, Ø = 4-5 mm;
— *stationary phase:* octadecylsilyl silica gel for chromatography R (5 µm).

*Mobile phase*  methanol R, 10 g/l solution of phosphoric acid R, water R, acetonitrile R (10:20:20:50 V/V/V/V).

*Flow rate*  2 ml/min.

*Detection*  Spectrophotometer at 235 nm.

*Injection*  20 µl.

*Run time*  3.5 times the retention time of fusidic acid.

*System suitability:*
— *resolution:* minimum 2.5 between the peaks due to 3-ketofusidic acid and fusidic acid in the chromatogram obtained with reference solution (a);
— *signal-to-noise ratio:* minimum 3 for the principal peak in the chromatogram obtained with reference solution (b).

*Limits:*
— *total:* not more than twice the area of the peak due to fusidic acid in the chromatogram obtained with reference solution (a) (2.0 per cent);
— *disregard limit:* the area of the principal peak in the chromatogram obtained with reference solution (b) (0.02 per cent).

### Water (2.5.12)
1.4 per cent to 2.0 per cent, determined on 0.50 g.

### Sulphated ash (2.4.14)
Maximum 0.2 per cent, determined on 1.0 g.

## ASSAY
Dissolve 0.500 g in 10 ml of *ethanol (96 per cent) R*. Add 0.5 ml of *phenolphthalein solution R*. Titrate with *0.1 M sodium hydroxide* until a pink colour is obtained.

1 ml of *0.1 M sodium hydroxide* is equivalent to 51.67 mg of C$_{31}$H$_{48}$O$_6$.

## STORAGE
Protected from light, at a temperature of 2 °C to 8 °C.

_____ *Ph Eur*

# Galactose

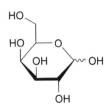

*(Ph Eur monograph 1215)*

$C_6H_{12}O_6$      180.2      59-23-4

*Ph Eur*

## DEFINITION
D-Galactopyranose.

## CHARACTERS

**Appearance**
White or almost white, crystalline or finely granulated powder.

**Solubility**
Freely soluble or soluble in water, very slightly soluble in ethanol (96 per cent).

## IDENTIFICATION
*First identification* A.

*Second identification* B, C.

A. Infrared absorption spectrophotometry (*2.2.24*).

*Preparation* Discs.

*Comparison* galactose CRS.

B. Thin-layer chromatography (*2.2.27*).

*Test solution* Dissolve 10 mg of the substance to be examined in a mixture of 2 volumes of *water R* and 3 volumes of *methanol R* and dilute to 20 ml with the same mixture of solvents.

*Reference solution (a)* Dissolve 10 mg of *galactose CRS* in a mixture of 2 volumes of *water R* and 3 volumes of *methanol R* and dilute to 20 ml with the same mixture of solvents.

*Reference solution (b)* Dissolve 10 mg of *galactose CRS*, 10 mg of *glucose CRS* and 10 mg of *lactose CRS* in a mixture of 2 volumes of *water R* and 3 volumes of *methanol R* and dilute to 20 ml with the same mixture of solvents.

*Plate* Suitable silica gel as the coating substance.

*Mobile phase* water R, propanol R (15:85 *V/V*).

*Application* 2 µl; thoroughly dry the starting points.

*Development* In an unsaturated tank over a path of 15 cm.

*Drying* In a current of warm air.

*Detection* Spray with a solution of 0.5 g of *thymol R* in a mixture of 5 ml of *sulphuric acid R* and 95 ml of *ethanol (96 per cent) R*. Heat in an oven at 130 °C for 10 min.

*System suitability* Reference solution (b):
— the chromatogram shows 3 clearly separated spots.

*Results* The principal spot in the chromatogram obtained with the test solution is similar in position, colour and size to the principal spot in the chromatogram obtained with reference solution (a).

C. Dissolve 0.1 g in 10 ml of *water R*. Add 3 ml of *cupri-tartaric solution R* and heat. An orange or red precipitate is formed.

## TESTS

**Solution S**
Dissolve, with heating in a water-bath at 50 °C, 10.0 g in *carbon dioxide-free water R* prepared from *distilled water R* and dilute to 50 ml with the same solvent.

**Appearance of solution**
Solution S is clear (*2.2.1*) and not more intensely coloured than reference solution $B_8$ (*2.2.2, Method II*).

**Acidity or alkalinity**
To 30 ml of solution S add 0.3 ml of *phenolphthalein solution R*. The solution is colourless. Not more than 1.5 ml of *0.01 M sodium hydroxide* is required to change the colour of the indicator to pink.

**Specific optical rotation** (*2.2.7*)
+ 78.0 to + 81.5 (anhydrous substance).

Dissolve 10.00 g in 80 ml of *water R* and add 0.2 ml of *dilute ammonia R1*. Allow to stand for 30 min and dilute to 100.0 ml with *water R*.

**Barium**
Dilute 5 ml of solution S to 10 ml with *distilled water R*. Add 1 ml of *dilute sulphuric acid R*. When examined immediately and after 1 h, any opalescence in the solution is not more intense than that in a mixture of 5 ml of solution S and 6 ml of *distilled water R*.

**Lead** (*2.4.10*)
Maximum 0.5 ppm.

**Water** (*2.5.12*)
Maximum 1.0 per cent, determined on 1.00 g.

**Sulphated ash**
Maximum 0.1 per cent.

To 5 ml of solution S add 2 ml of *sulphuric acid R*, evaporate to dryness on a water-bath and ignite to constant mass. The residue weighs a maximum of 1 mg.

**Microbial contamination**
TAMC: acceptance criterion $10^2$ CFU/g (*2.6.12*).

*Ph Eur*

# Gallamine Triethiodide

*(Ph Eur monograph 0181)*

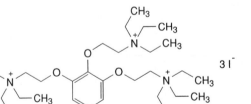

$C_{30}H_{60}I_3N_3O_3$      892      65-29-2

## Action and use
Non-depolarizing neuromuscular blocker.

## Preparation
Gallamine Injection

*Ph Eur*

## DEFINITION
2,2′,2″-[Benzene-1,2,3-triyltris(oxy)]tris(*N,N,N*-triethylethanaminium) triiodide.

**Content**

98.0 per cent to 101.0 per cent (dried substance).

**CHARACTERS**

**Appearance**

White or almost white powder, hygroscopic.

**Solubility**

Very soluble in water, slightly soluble in ethanol (96 per cent), practically insoluble in methylene chloride.

**IDENTIFICATION**

*First identification*   B, D.

*Second identification*   A, C, D.

A. Ultraviolet and visible absorption spectrophotometry (*2.2.25*).

*Test solution*   Dissolve 50 mg in *0.01 M hydrochloric acid* and dilute to 50.0 ml with the same acid. Dilute 1.0 ml of this solution to 100.0 ml with *0.01 M hydrochloric acid*.

*Spectral range*   220-350 nm.

*Absorption maximum*   At 225 nm.

*Specific absorbance at the absorption maximum*   500 to 550.

B. Infrared absorption spectrophotometry (*2.2.24*).

*Comparison*   gallamine triethiodide CRS.

C. To 5 ml of solution S (see Tests) add 1 ml of *potassium tetraiodomercurate solution R*. A yellow precipitate is formed.

D. Dilute 0.5 ml of solution S to 2 ml with *water R*. Add 0.2 ml of *dilute nitric acid R*. The solution gives reaction (a) of iodides (*2.3.1*).

**TESTS**

**Solution S**

Dissolve 0.6 g in *water R* and dilute to 30 ml with the same solvent.

**Appearance of solution**

Solution S is clear (*2.2.1*) and immediately after preparation is not more intensely coloured than reference solution $Y_7$ (*2.2.2, Method II*).

**Acidity or alkalinity**

To 50 ml of *water R* add 0.2 ml of *methyl red solution R*. Add either *0.01 M sulphuric acid* or *0.02 M sodium hydroxide* until an orange-yellow colour is obtained. Add 1.0 g of the substance to be examined and dissolve by shaking. Not more than 0.2 ml of *0.01 M sulphuric acid* or *0.02 M sodium hydroxide* is required to restore the orange-yellow colour.

**Related substances**

Liquid chromatography (*2.2.29*).

*Test solution*   Dissolve 30.0 mg of the substance to be examined in the mobile phase and dilute to 50.0 ml with the mobile phase.

*Reference solution*   Dilute 1.0 ml of the test solution to 100.0 ml with the mobile phase.

*Column:*

— *size: l = 0.25 m, Ø = 4.6 mm;*

— *stationary phase: octadecylsilyl silica gel for chromatography R* (5 µm).

*Mobile phase*   Dissolve 14 g of *sodium perchlorate R* in 850 ml of *phosphate buffer pH 3.0 R* and add 150 ml of *methanol R2*.

*Flow rate*   1 ml/min.

*Detection*   Spectrophotometer at 205 nm.

*Injection*   20 µl.

*Run time*   1.5 times the retention time of triethylgallamine as perchlorate.

*Relative retention* with reference to triethylgallamine as perchlorate (retention time = about 40 min):
impurity A = about 0.45; impurity B = about 0.50;
impurity C = about 0.65; impurity D = about 0.75;
impurity E = about 0.85; impurity F = about 0.90.

*Limits:*

— *impurities A, B, C, D, E, F*: for each impurity, not more than the area of the principal peak in the chromatogram obtained with the reference solution (1 per cent);

— *total*: not more than twice the area of the principal peak in the chromatogram obtained with the reference solution (2 per cent);

— *disregard limit*: disregard the peak due to iodide with a retention time of zero.

**Loss on drying** (*2.2.32*)

Maximum 1.5 per cent, determined on 1.000 g by drying in an oven at 105 °C.

**Sulphated ash** (*2.4.14*)

Maximum 0.1 per cent, determined on 1.0 g.

**ASSAY**

*In order to avoid overheating in the reaction medium, mix thoroughly throughout and stop the titration immediately after the end-point has been reached.*

Dissolve 0.270 g in a mixture of 5.0 ml of *anhydrous formic acid R* and 50.0 ml of *acetic anhydride R*. Titrate with *0.1 M perchloric acid*, determining the end-point potentiometrically (*2.2.20*).

1 ml of *0.1 M perchloric acid* is equivalent to 29.72 mg of $C_{30}H_{60}I_3N_3O_3$.

**STORAGE**

In an airtight container, protected from light.

**IMPURITIES**

*Specified impurities*   A, B, C, D, E, F.

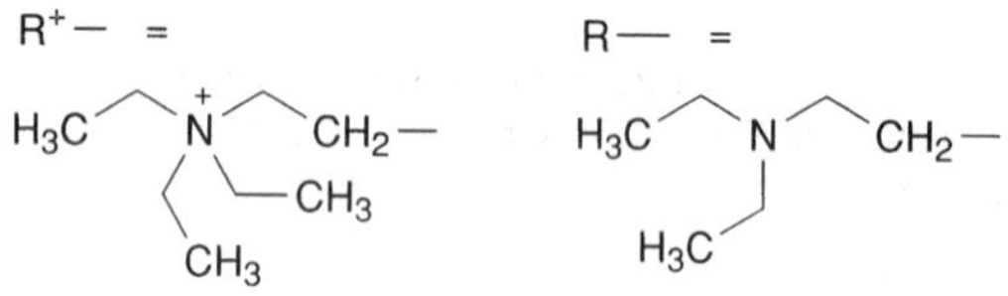

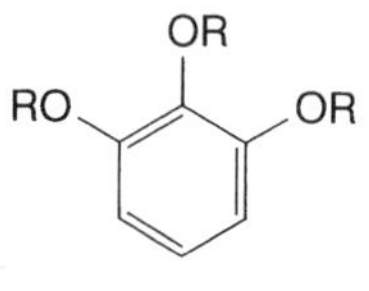

A. 2,2′,2″-[benzene-1,2,3-triyltris(oxy)]tris(*N,N*-diethylethanamine),

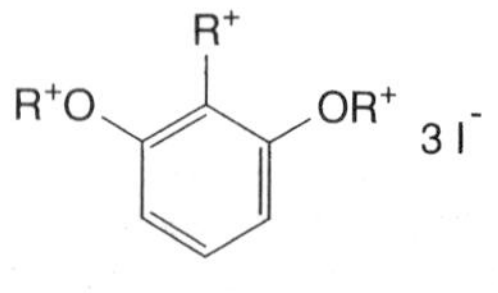

B. 2,2′-[2-[2-(triethylammonio)ethyl]-1,3-phenylenebis(oxy)]bis(*N,N,N*-triethylethanaminium) triiodide,

C. 2,2′-[2-[2-(diethylmethylammonio)ethoxy]-1,3-phenylenebis(oxy)]bis(*N*,*N*,*N*-triethylethanaminium) triiodide,

D. 2,2′-[3-[2-(diethylmethylammonio)ethoxy]-1,2-phenylenebis(oxy)]bis(*N*,*N*,*N*-triethylethanaminium) triiodide,

E. 2,2′-[3-[2-(diethylamino)ethoxy]-1,2-phenylenebis(oxy)]bis(*N*,*N*,*N*-triethylethanaminium) diiodide,

F. 2,2′,2″-[4-[2-(triethylammonio)ethyl]benzene-1,2,3triyltris(oxy)]tris(*N*,*N*,*N*-triethylethanaminium) tetraiodide.

_____ *Ph Eur*

# Gelatin

(*Ph Eur monograph 0330*)

**Action and use**
Excipient.

*Ph Eur* _____

## DEFINITION

Purified protein obtained either by partial acid hydrolysis (type A), partial alkaline hydrolysis (type B) or enzymatic hydrolysis of collagen from animals (including fish and poultry); it may also be a mixture of different types.

The hydrolysis leads to gelling or non-gelling product grades. Both product grades are covered by this monograph.

Gelatin described in this monograph is not suitable for parenteral use or for other special purposes.

## CHARACTERS

### Appearance

Faintly yellow or light yellowish-brown, solid, usually occurring as translucent sheets, shreds, granules or powder.

### Solubility

Practically insoluble in common organic solvents; gelling grades swell in cold water and give on heating a colloidal solution which on cooling forms a more or less firm gel.

The isoelectric point is a relevant quality parameter for use of gelatin in different applications: for type A gelatin it is typically between pH 6.0 and pH 9.5 and for type B gelatin is typically between pH 4.7 and pH 5.6. These ranges cover a variety of different gelatins and for specific applications a narrower tolerance is usually applied.

Different gelatins form aqueous solutions that vary in clarity and colour. For a particular application, a suitable specification for clarity and colour is usually applied.

## IDENTIFICATION

A. To 2 ml of solution S (see Tests) add 0.05 ml of *copper sulphate solution R*. Mix and add 0.5 ml of *dilute sodium hydroxide solution R*. A violet colour is produced.

B. To 0.5 g in a test-tube add 10 ml of *water R*. Allow to stand for 10 min, heat at 60 °C for 15 min and keep the tube upright at 0 °C for 6 h. Invert the tube; the contents immediately flow out for non-gelling grades and do not flow out immediately for gelling grades.

## TESTS

### Solution S

Dissolve 1.00 g in *carbon dioxide-free water R* at about 55 °C, dilute to 100 ml with the same solvent and keep the solution at this temperature to carry out the tests.

**pH** (*2.2.3*)
3.8 to 7.6 for solution S.

**Conductivity** (*2.2.38*)
Maximum 1 mS·cm$^{-1}$, determined on a 1.0 per cent solution at 30 ± 1.0 °C.

**Sulphur dioxide** (*2.5.29*)
Maximum 50 ppm.

**Peroxides**
Maximum 10 ppm, determined using *peroxide test strips R*.

Peroxidase transfers oxygen from peroxides to an organic redox indicator which is converted to a blue oxidation product. The intensity of the colour obtained is proportional to the quantity of peroxide and can be compared with a colour scale provided with the test strips, to determine the peroxide concentration.

*Suitability test* Dip a test strip for 1 s into *hydrogen peroxide standard solution (10 ppm H$_2$O$_2$) R*, such that the reaction zone is properly wetted. Remove the test strip, shake off excess liquid and compare the reaction zone after 15 s with the colour scale provided with the test strips used. The colour must match that of the 10 ppm concentration, otherwise the test is invalid.

*Test* Weigh 20.0 ± 0.1 g of the substance to be tested in a beaker and add 80.0 ± 0.2 ml of *water R*. Stir to moisten all gelatin and allow the sample to stand at room temperature for 1-3 h. Cover the beaker with a watch-glass. Place the beaker for 20 ± 5 min in a water bath at 65 ± 2 °C to dissolve the sample. Stir the contents of the beaker with a glass rod to achieve a homogeneous solution. Dip a test strip for 1 s into the test solution, such that the reaction zone is properly wetted. Remove the test strip, shake off excess liquid and compare the reaction zone after 15 s with the colour scale provided with the test strips used. Multiply the concentration read from the colour scale by a factor of 5 to calculate the concentration in parts per million of peroxide in the test substance.

## Gel strength (Bloom value)

80 to 120 per cent of the labelled nominal value.

The gel strength is expressed as the mass in grams necessary to produce the force which, applied to a plunger 12.7 mm in diameter, makes a depression 4 mm deep in a gel having a concentration of 6.67 per cent *m/m* and matured at 10 °C.

*Apparatus*   Texture analyser or gelometer with:
— a cylindrical piston 12.7 ± 0.1 mm in diameter with a plane pressure surface with a sharp bottom edge,
— a bottle 59 ± 1 mm in internal diameter and 85 mm high.

Adjust the apparatus according to the manufacturer's manual. Settings are: distance 4 mm, test speed 0.5 mm/s.

*Method*   Perform the test in duplicate. Place 7.5 g of the substance to be tested in each bottle. Add 105 ml of *water R*, place a watch-glass over each bottle and allow to stand for 1-4 h. Heat in a water-bath at 65 ± 2 °C for 15 min. While heating, gently stir with a glass rod. Ensure that the solution is uniform and that any condensed water on the inner walls of the bottle is incorporated. Allow to cool at room temperature for 15 min and transfer the bottles to a thermostatically controlled bath at 10.0 ± 0.1 °C, and fitted with a device to ensure that the platform on which the bottles stand is perfectly horizontal. Close the bottles with a rubber stopper and allow to stand for 17 ± 1 h. Remove the sample bottles from the bath and quickly wipe the water from the exterior of the bottle. Centre consecutively the 2 bottles on the platform of the apparatus so that the plunger contacts the sample as nearly at its midpoint as possible and start the measurement. Report the result as the average of the 2 measurements.

## Iron

Maximum 30.0 ppm.

Atomic absorption spectrometry (*2.2.23, Method I*).

*Test solution*   To 5.00 g of the substance to be examined, in a conical flask, add 10 ml of *hydrochloric acid R*. Close the flask and place in a water-bath at 75-80 °C for 2 h. Allow to cool and adjust the content of the flask to 100.0 g with *water R*.

*Reference solutions*   Prepare the reference solutions using *iron standard solution (8 ppm Fe) R*, diluted as necessary with *water R*.

*Wavelength*   248.3 nm.

## Chromium

Maximum 10.0 ppm.

Atomic absorption spectrometry (*2.2.23, Method I*).

*Test solution*   Test solution described in the test for iron.

*Reference solutions*   Prepare the reference solutions using *chromium standard solution (100 ppm Cr) R*, diluted if necessary with *water R*.

*Wavelength*   357.9 nm.

## Zinc

Maximum 30.0 ppm.

Atomic absorption spectrometry (*2.2.23, Method I*).

*Test solution*   Test solution described in the test for iron.

*Reference solutions*   Prepare the reference solutions using *zinc standard solution (10 ppm Zn) R*, diluted if necessary with *water R*.

*Wavelength*   213.9 nm.

## Loss on drying (*2.2.32*)

Maximum 15.0 per cent, determined on 1.000 g, by drying in an oven at 105 °C.

## Microbial contamination

TAMC: acceptance criterion $10^3$ CFU/g (*2.6.12*).

TYMC: acceptance criterion $10^2$ CFU/g (*2.6.12*).

Absence of *Escherichia coli* (*2.6.13*).

Absence of *Salmonella* (*2.6.13*).

## STORAGE

Protect from heat and moisture.

## LABELLING

The label states the gel strength (Bloom value) or that it is a non-gelling grade.

*—————————————— Ph Eur*

# Gemcitabine Hydrochloride

*(Ph Eur monograph 2306)*

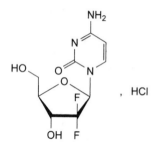

$C_9H_{11}F_2N_3O_4$,HCl          299.7          *122111-03-9*

## Action and use

Pyrimidine analogue; cytotoxic.

*Ph Eur ——————————————*

## DEFINITION

4-Amino-1-(2-deoxy-2,2-difluoro-β-D-*erythro*-pentofuranosyl)pyrimidin-2(1*H*)-one hydrochloride.

## Content

98.0 per cent to 102.0 per cent.

## CHARACTERS

### Appearance

White or almost white powder.

### Solubility

Soluble in water, slightly soluble in methanol, practically insoluble in acetone.

## IDENTIFICATION

A. Infrared absorption spectrophotometry (*2.2.24*).

*Comparison*   gemcitabine hydrochloride CRS .

B. It gives reaction (a) of chlorides (*2.3.1*).

## TESTS

### Solution S

Dissolve 1.00 g in *carbon dioxide-free water R* and dilute to 100.0 ml with the same solvent.

### Appearance of solution

Solution S is clear (*2.2.1*) and not more intensely coloured than reference solution $BY_7$ (*2.2.2, Method II*).

### pH (*2.2.3*)

2.0 to 3.0 for solution S.

### Specific optical rotation (*2.2.7*)

+ 43.0 to + 50.0, determined on solution S.

**Related substances**

Liquid chromatography (*2.2.29*).

*Test solution (a)*   Dissolve 50.0 mg of the substance to be examined in *water R* and dilute to 25.0 ml with the same solvent.

*Test solution (b)*   Dissolve 20.0 mg of the substance to be examined in *water R* and dilute to 200.0 ml with the same solvent.

*Reference solution (a)*   Dissolve 10.0 mg of the substance to be examined and 10.0 mg of *gemcitabine impurity A CRS* in *water R* and dilute to 50.0 ml with the same solvent. Dilute 2.0 ml of this solution to 200.0 ml with *water R*.

*Reference solution (b)*   Dissolve 20.0 mg of *gemcitabine hydrochloride CRS* in *water R* and dilute to 200.0 ml with the same solvent.

*Reference solution (c)*   Place 10 mg of the substance to be examined in a small vial. Add 4 ml of a 168 g/l solution of *potassium hydroxide R* in *methanol R*, sonicate for 5 min then seal with a cap. The mixture may be cloudy. Heat at 55 °C for a minimum of 6 h to produce impurity B. Allow to cool, then transfer the entire contents of the vial to a 100 ml volumetric flask by successively washing with a 1 per cent *V/V* solution of *phosphoric acid R*. Dilute to 100 ml with a 1 per cent *V/V* solution of *phosphoric acid R* and mix.

*Column:*
— *size: l* = 0.25 m, Ø = 4.6 mm;
— *stationary phase*: octylsilyl silica gel for chromatography R (5 μm).

*Mobile phase:*
— *mobile phase A*: 13.8 g/l solution of *sodium dihydrogen phosphate monohydrate R* adjusted to pH 2.5 ± 0.1 with *phosphoric acid R*;
— *mobile phase B*: methanol R;

| Time (min) | Mobile phase A (per cent *V/V*) | Mobile phase B (per cent *V/V*) |
|---|---|---|
| 0 - 8 | 97 | 3 |
| 8 - 13 | 97 → 50 | 3 → 50 |
| 13 - 20 | 50 | 50 |

*Flow rate*   1.2 ml/min.

*Detection*   Spectrophotometer at 275 nm.

*Injection*   20 μl of test solution (a) and reference solutions (a) and (c).

*Relative retention* with reference to gemcitabine (retention time = about 8 min): impurity A = about 0.4; impurity B = about 0.7.

*System suitability*   Reference solution (c):
— *resolution*: minimum 8.0 between the peaks due to impurity B and gemcitabine.

*Limits:*
— *impurity A*: not more than the area of the corresponding peak in the chromatogram obtained with reference solution (a) (0.1 per cent);
— *unspecified impurities*: for each impurity, not more than the area of the peak due to gemcitabine in the chromatogram obtained with reference solution (a) (0.10 per cent);
— *total*: not more than twice the area of the peak due to gemcitabine in the chromatogram obtained with reference solution (a) (0.2 per cent);
— *disregard limit*: 0.5 times the area of the peak due to gemcitabine in the chromatogram obtained with reference solution (a) (0.05 per cent).

**Heavy metals** (*2.4.8*)

Maximum 10 ppm.

Dissolve 1.0 g in *water R* and dilute to 20 ml with the same solvent. 12 ml of the solution complies with test A. Prepare the reference solution using 5 ml of *lead standard solution (1 ppm Pb) R*, 5 ml of *water R* and 2 ml of the aqueous solution to be examined. If necessary, filter the solutions and compare the spots on the membrane filter.

**Sulphated ash** (*2.4.14*)

Maximum 0.1 per cent, determined on 1.0 g in a platinum crucible.

**Bacterial endotoxins** (*2.6.14*)

Less than 0.05 IU/mg, if intended for use in the manufacture of parenteral dosage forms without a further appropriate procedure for the removal of bacterial endotoxins.

## ASSAY

Liquid chromatography (*2.2.29*) as described in the test for related substances with the following modifications.

*Mobile phase*   Mobile phase A.

*Injection*   Test solution (b) and reference solutions (b) and (c).

*Relative retention* with reference to gemcitabine (retention time = about 10 min): impurity B = about 0.5.

*System suitability*   Reference solution (c):
— *resolution*: minimum 8.0 between the peaks due to impurity B and gemcitabine.

Calculate the percentage content of $C_9H_{12}ClF_2N_3O_4$ from the declared content *of gemcitabine hydrochloride CRS*.

## STORAGE

If the substance is sterile, store in a sterile, airtight, tamper-proof container.

## IMPURITIES

*Specified impurities*   *A*.

*Other detectable impurities* (the following substances would, if present at a sufficient level, be detected by one or other of the tests in the monograph. They are limited by the general acceptance criterion for other/unspecified impurities and/or by the general monograph *Substances for pharmaceutical use (2034)*. It is therefore not necessary to identify these impurities for demonstration of compliance. See also *5.10*. *Control of impurities in substances for pharmaceutical use): B*.

A. 4-aminopyrimidin-2(1*H*)-one (cytosine),

B. 4-amino-1-(2-deoxy-2,2-difluoro-α-D-*erythro*-pentofuranosyl)pyrimidin-2(1*H*)-one (gemcitabine α-anomer).

*Ph Eur*

# Gemfibrozil

(*Ph Eur monograph 1694*)

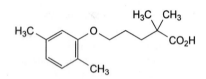

C₁₅H₂₂O₃      250.3      *25812-30-0*

**Action and use**

Fibrate; lipid-regulating drug.

**Preparations**

Gemfibrozil Capsules

Gemfibrozil Tablets

*Ph Eur*

## DEFINITION

5-(2,5-Dimethylphenoxy)-2,2-dimethylpentanoic acid.

**Content**

99.0 per cent to 101.0 per cent (anhydrous substance).

## CHARACTERS

**Appearance**

White or almost white, waxy, crystalline powder.

**Solubility**

Practically insoluble in water, very soluble in methylene chloride, freely soluble in anhydrous ethanol and in methanol.

## IDENTIFICATION

A. Melting point (*2.2.14*): 58 °C to 61 °C.

B. Infrared absorption spectrophotometry (*2.2.24*).

*Comparison* gemfibrozil CRS.

## TESTS

**Related substances**

Liquid chromatography (*2.2.29*).

*Test solution* Dissolve 40 mg of the substance to be examined in mobile phase A and dilute to 10.0 ml with mobile phase A.

*Reference solution (a)* Dissolve the contents of a vial of *gemfibrozil for system suitability CRS* (containing impurities C, D and E) in 2 ml of *acetonitrile R*.

*Reference solution (b)* Dilute 1.0 ml of test solution to 100.0 ml with mobile phase A. Dilute 1.0 ml of this solution to 10.0 ml with mobile phase A.

*Reference solution (c)* Dissolve 5 mg of *2,5-dimethylphenol R* (impurity A) in mobile phase A and dilute to 10 ml with mobile phase A.

*Column:*
— *size: l* = 0.250 m, Ø = 4.0 mm,
— *stationary phase:* end-capped octadecylsilyl silica gel for chromatography *R* (5 μm).

*Mobile phase:*
— *mobile phase A*: dissolve 0.27 g of *potassium dihydrogen phosphate R* in 400 ml of *water R*, adjust to pH 4.0 with *phosphoric acid R* and add 600 ml of *acetonitrile R*;
— *mobile phase B*: *acetonitrile R*;

| Time (min) | Mobile phase A (per cent *V/V*) | Mobile phase B (per cent *V/V*) |
|---|---|---|
| 0 - 5 | 100 | 0 |
| 5 - 20 | 100 → 0 | 0 → 100 |
| 20 - 25 | 0 | 100 |
| 25 - 30 | 0 → 100 | 100 → 0 |
| 30 - 35 | 100 | 0 |

*Flow rate* 1.5 ml/min.

*Detection* Spectrophotometer at 276 nm.

*Injection* 20 μl.

*Identification of impurities* Use the chromatogram supplied with *gemfibrozil for system suitability CRS* and the chromatogram obtained with reference solution (a) to identify the peaks due to impurities C, D and E. Use the chromatogram obtained with reference solution (c) to identify the peak due to impurity A.

*Relative retention* with reference to gemfibrozil (retention time = about 7 min): impurity A = about 0.4; impurity C = about 1.3; impurity D = about 1.5; impurity E = about 1.7; impurity I = about 2.0; impurity H = about 2.9.

*System suitability* Reference solution (a):
— *resolution*: minimum 6.0 between the peaks due to gemfibrozil and impurity C, and minimum 2.0 between the peaks due to impurity D and impurity E.

*Limits:*
— *correction factors*: for the calculations of content multiply the peak areas of the following impurities by the corresponding correction factor: impurity A = 0.5; impurity D = 3.3; impurity E = 0.2; impurity I = 2;
— *impurities E, I*: for each impurity, not more than twice the area of the principal peak in the chromatogram obtained with reference solution (b) (0.2 per cent);
— *impurities A, D, H*: for each impurity, not more than the area of the principal peak in the chromatogram obtained with reference solution (b) (0.1 per cent);
— *unspecified impurities*: for each impurity, not more than the area of the principal peak in the chromatogram obtained with reference solution (b) (0.10 per cent);
— *total*: not more than 5 times the area of the principal peak in the chromatogram obtained with reference solution (b) (0.5 per cent);
— *disregard limit*: 0.5 times the area of the principal peak in the chromatogram obtained with reference solution (b) (0.05 per cent).

**Heavy metals** (*2.4.8*)

Maximum 20 ppm.

1.0 g complies with test F. Prepare the reference solution using 2 ml of *lead standard solution (10 ppm Pb) R*.

**Water** *(2.5.12)*
Maximum 0.25 per cent, determined on 2.000 g.

**Sulphated ash** *(2.4.14)*
Maximum 0.1 per cent, determined on 2.0 g. Allow to stand for 1 h after the first moistening before heating.

**ASSAY**
Dissolve 0.200 g in 25 ml of *methanol R*. Add 25 ml of *water R* and 1 ml of *0.1 M hydrochloric acid*. Carry out a potentiometric titration *(2.2.20)* using *0.1 M sodium hydroxide*. Read the volume added between the 2 points of inflexion.

1 ml of *0.1 M sodium hydroxide* is equivalent to 25.03 mg of $C_{15}H_{22}O_3$.

**STORAGE**
Protected from light.

**IMPURITIES**
*Specified impurities   A, D, E, H, I.*

*Other detectable impurities* (the following substances would, if present at a sufficient level, be detected by one or other of the tests in the monograph. They are limited by the general acceptance criterion for other/unspecified impurities and/or by the general monograph *Substances for pharmaceutical use (2034)*. It is therefore not necessary to identify these impurities for demonstration of compliance. See also *5.10*. *Control of impurities in substances for pharmaceutical use)*: B, C, F, G.

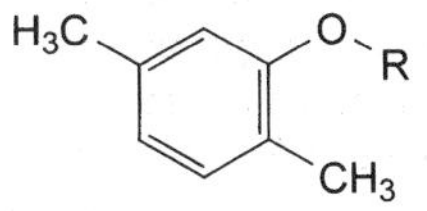

A. R = H: 2,5-dimethylphenol (*p*-xylenol),

C. R = [CH$_2$]$_3$-O-[CH$_2$]2-O-C$_2$H$_5$:
2-[3-(2-ethoxyethoxy)propoxy]-1,4-dimethylbenzene,

F. R = [CH$_2$]$_4$-C$_6$H$_5$:
1,4-dimethyl-2-(4-phenylbutoxy)benzene,

G. R = CH$_2$-CH=CH$_2$:
1,4-dimethyl-2-(prop-2-enyloxy)benzene,

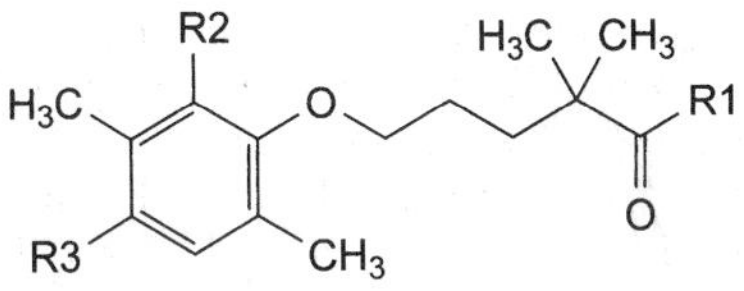

B. R1 = NH$_2$, R2 = R3 = H: 5-(2,5-dimethylphenoxy)-2,2-dimethylpentanamide,

D. R1 = OH, R2 = CH=CH-CH$_3$, R3 = H:
5-[3,6-dimethyl-2-(prop-1-enyl)phenoxy]-2,2-dimethylpentanoic acid,

E. R1 = OH, R2 = H, R3 = CH=CH-CH$_3$:
5-[2,5-dimethyl-4-(prop-1-enyl)phenoxy]-2,2-dimethylpentanoic acid,

I. R1 = OCH$_3$, R2 = R3 = H: methyl 5-(2,5-dimethylphenoxy)-2,2-dimethylpentanoate,

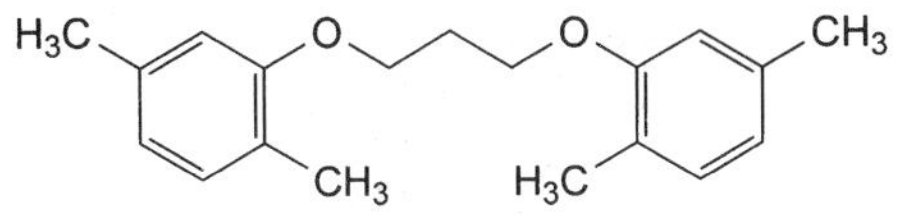

H. 1,3-bis(2,5-dimethylphenoxy)propane.

*Ph Eur*

# Gentamicin Sulphate

*(Ph Eur monograph 0331)*

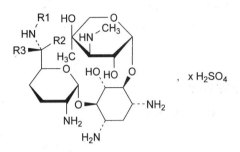

| Gentamicin | Mol. Formula | R1 | R2 | R3 |
|---|---|---|---|---|
| C1 | $C_{21}H_{43}N_5O_7$ | CH$_3$ | CH$_3$ | H |
| C1a | $C_{19}H_{39}N_5O_7$ | H | H | H |
| C2 | $C_{20}H_{41}N_5O_7$ | H | CH$_3$ | H |
| C2a | $C_{20}H_{41}N_5O_7$ | H | H | CH$_3$ |
| C2b | $C_{20}H_{41}N_5O_7$ | CH$_3$ | H | H |

*1405-41-0*

**Action and use**
Aminoglycoside antibacterial.

**Preparations**
Gentamicin Cream
Gentamicin Ear Drops
Gentamicin and Hydrocortisone Acetate Ear Drops
Gentamicin Eye Drops
Gentamicin Injection
Gentamicin Ointment

*Ph Eur*

**DEFINITION**
Mixture of the sulphates of antimicrobial substances produced by *Micromonospora purpurea*, the main components being gentamicins C1, C1a, C2, C2a and C2b.

**Content**
Minimum 590 IU/mg (anhydrous substance).

**CHARACTERS**
**Appearance**
White or almost white, hygroscopic powder.

**Solubility**
Freely soluble in water, practically insoluble in alcohol.

**IDENTIFICATION**
*First identification   C, D.*

*Second identification   A, B, D.*

A. Dissolve about 10 mg in 1 ml of *water R* and add 5 ml of a 400 g/l solution of *sulphuric acid R*. Heat on a water-bath for 100 min, cool and dilute to 25 ml with *water R*.

Examined between 240 nm and 330 nm (2.2.25), the solution shows no absorption maximum.

B. Thin-layer chromatography (2.2.27).

*Test solution*    Dissolve 25 mg of the substance to be examined in *water R* and dilute to 5 ml with the same solvent.

*Reference solution*    Dissolve the contents of a vial of *gentamicin sulphate CRS* in *water R* and dilute to 5 ml with the same solvent.

*Plate*    *TLC silica gel plate R*.

*Mobile phase*    The lower layer of a mixture of equal volumes of *concentrated ammonia R*, *methanol R* and *methylene chloride R*.

*Application*    10 µl.

*Development*    Over 2/3 of the plate.

*Drying*    In air.

*Detection*    Spray with *ninhydrin solution R1* and heat at 110 °C for 5 min.

*Results*    The 3 principal spots in the chromatogram obtained with the test solution are similar in position, colour and size to the 3 principal spots in the chromatogram obtained with the reference solution.

C. Examine the chromatograms obtained in the test for composition.

*Results*    The chromatogram obtained with the test solution shows 5 principal peaks having the same retention times as the 5 principal peaks in the chromatogram obtained with reference solution (a).

D. It gives reaction (a) of sulphates (2.3.1).

**TESTS**

**Solution S**
Dissolve 0.8 g in *carbon dioxide-free water R* and dilute to 20 ml with the same solvent.

**Appearance of solution**
Solution S is clear (2.2.1) and not more intensely coloured than intensity 6 of the range of reference solutions of the most appropriate colour (2.2.2, Method II).

**pH** (2.2.3)
3.5 to 5.5 for solution S.

**Specific optical rotation** (2.2.7)
+ 107 to + 121 (anhydrous substance).

Dissolve 2.5 g in *water R* and dilute to 25.0 ml with the same solvent.

**Composition**
Liquid chromatography (2.2.29): use the normalisation procedure taking into account only the peaks due to gentamicins C1, C1a, C2, C2a and C2b; use the chromatogram supplied with *gentamicin sulphate CRS* to identify the corresponding peaks.

*Test solution*    Dissolve 50 mg of the substance to be examined in the mobile phase and dilute to 100.0 ml with the mobile phase.

*Reference solution (a)*    Dissolve the content of a vial of *gentamicin sulphate CRS* in the mobile phase and dilute with the mobile phase to obtain a solution containing 0.5 mg/ml.

*Reference solution (b)*    Dilute 5.0 ml of reference solution (a) to 100.0 ml with the mobile phase.

*Column:*
— *size*: $l = 0.25$ m, Ø = 4.6 mm,
— *stationary phase*: styrene–divinylbenzene copolymer R (8 µm) with a pore size of 100 nm,

— *temperature*: 55 °C.

*Mobile phase*    A mixture prepared with *carbon dioxide-free water R* containing 60 g/l of *anhydrous sodium sulphate R*, 1.75 g/l of *sodium octanesulphonate R*, 8 ml/l of *tetrahydrofuran R*, 50 ml/l of *0.2 M potassium dihydrogen phosphate R* previously adjusted to pH 3.0 with *dilute phosphoric acid R* and degassed.

*Flow rate*    1.0 ml/min.

*Post-column solution*    A *carbonate-free sodium hydroxide solution R* diluted 1 to 25, previously degassed, which is added pulse-less to the column effluent using a 375 µl polymeric mixing coil.

*Flow rate*    0.3 ml/min.

*Detection*    Pulsed amperometric detector or equivalent with a gold indicator electrode, a silver-silver chloride reference electrode, and a stainless steel auxiliary electrode which is the cell body, held at respectively + 0.05 V detection, + 0.75 V oxidation and − 0.15 V reduction potentials, with pulse durations according to the instrument used.

*Injection*    20 µl.

*Run time*    1.2 times the retention time of gentamicin C1.

*System suitability*    Reference solution (a):
— *peak-to-valley ratio*: minimum 2.0 where $H_p$ = height above the baseline of the peak due to gentamicin C2a, and $H_v$ = height above the baseline of the lowest point of the curve separating this peak from the peak due to gentamicin C2.

*Limits:*
— *gentamicin C1* : 20.0 per cent to 40.0 per cent,
— *gentamicin C1a* : 10.0 per cent to 30.0 per cent,
— *sum of gentamicins C2, C2a, and C2b*: 40.0 per cent to 60.0 per cent,
— *disregard limit*: the area of the peak due to gentamicin C1a in the chromatogram obtained with reference solution (b).

**Related substances**
Liquid chromatography (2.2.29) as described in the test for composition.

*Limits (for related substances eluting before gentamicin C1a):*
— *any impurity*: maximum 3.0 per cent,
— *total*: maximum 10.0 per cent.

**Methanol** (2.4.24, System B)
Maximum 1.0 per cent.

**Sulphate**
32.0 per cent to 35.0 per cent (anhydrous substance).

Dissolve 0.250 g in 100 ml of *distilled water R* and adjust the solution to pH 11 using *concentrated ammonia R*. Add 10.0 ml of *0.1 M barium chloride* and about 0.5 mg of *phthalein purple R*. Titrate with *0.1 M sodium edetate*, adding 50 ml of *alcohol R* when the colour of the solution begins to change and continue the titration until the violet-blue colour disappears.

1 ml of *0.1 M barium chloride* is equivalent to 9.606 mg of $SO_4$.

**Water** (2.5.12)
Maximum 15.0 per cent, determined on 0.300 g.

**Sulphated ash** (2.4.14)
Maximum 1.0 per cent, determined on 0.50 g.

**Bacterial endotoxins** (2.6.14)
Less than 0.71 IU/mg, if intended for use in the manufacture of parenteral dosage forms without a further appropriate procedure for the removal of bacterial endotoxins.

## ASSAY

Carry out the microbiological assay of antibiotics (2.7.2).

## STORAGE

In an airtight container. If the substance is sterile, store in a sterile, airtight, tamper-proof container.

## IMPURITIES

*Specified impurities   A, B, C.*

*Other detectable impurities* (the following substances would, if present at a sufficient level, be detected by one or other of the tests in the monograph. They are limited by the general acceptance criterion for other/unspecified impurities and/or by the general monograph *Substances for pharmaceutical use (2034)*. It is therefore not necessary to identify these impurities for demonstration of compliance. See also *5.10. Control of impurities in substances for pharmaceutical use*) : D, E.

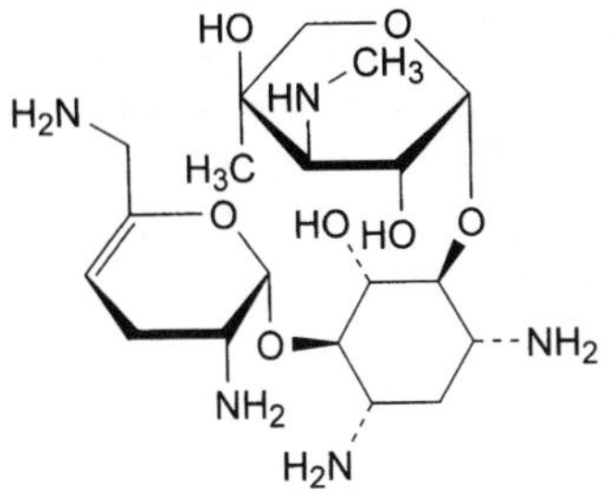

A. 2-deoxy-4-*O*-[3-deoxy-4-*C*-methyl-3-(methylamino)-β-L-arabinopyranosyl]-6-*O*-(2,6-diamino-2,3,4,6-tetradeoxy-α-D-*glycero*-hex-4-enopyranosyl)-L-streptamine (sisomicin),

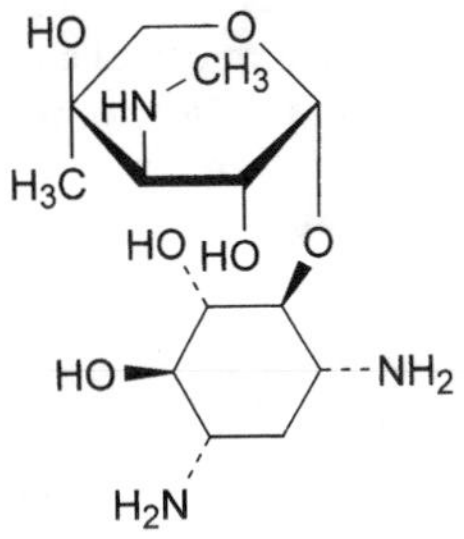

B. 2-deoxy-4-*O*-[3-deoxy-4-*C*-methyl-3-(methylamino)-β-L-arabinopyranosyl]-L-streptamine (garamine),

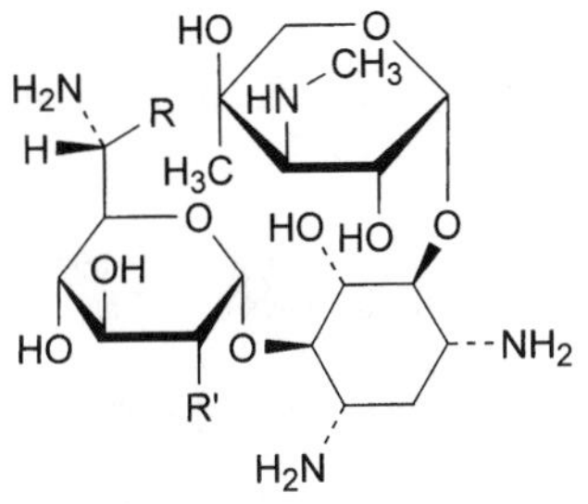

C. R = CH₃, R' = OH: 4-*O*-(6-amino-6,7-dideoxy-D-*glycero*-α-D-*gluco*-heptopyranosyl)-2-deoxy-6-*O*-[3-deoxy-4-*C*-methyl-3-(methylamino)-β-L-arabinopyranosyl]-D-streptamine (gentamicin B ₁),

D. R = H, R' = NH₂: 2-deoxy-4-*O*-[3-deoxy-4-*C*-methyl-3-(methylamino)-β-L-arabinopyranosyl]-6-*O*-(2,6-diamino-2,6-dideoxy-α-D-*gluco*-hexopyranosyl)-L-streptamine,

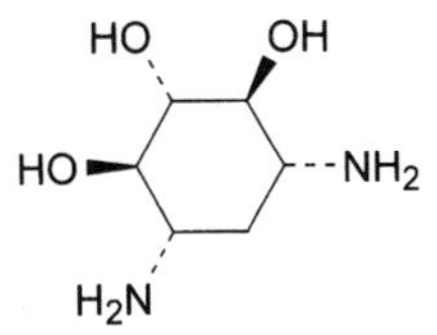

E. 2-deoxystreptamine.

*Ph Eur*

# Gestodene

*(Ph Eur monograph 1726)*

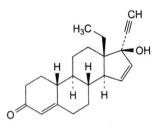

C₂₁H₂₆O₂          310.4          *60282-87-3*

## Action and use

Progestogen.

*Ph Eur*

## DEFINITION

13-Ethyl-17-hydroxy-18,19-dinor-17α-pregna-4,15-dien-20-yn-3-one.

## Content

97.5 per cent to 102.0 per cent (dried substance).

## CHARACTERS

### Appearance

White or yellowish, crystalline powder.

### Solubility

Practically insoluble in water, freely soluble in methylene chloride, soluble in methanol, sparingly soluble in ethanol (96 per cent).

It shows polymorphism (5.9).

## IDENTIFICATION

A. Specific optical rotation (see Tests).

B. Infrared absorption spectrophotometry (2.2.24).

*Comparison   gestodene CRS.*

If the spectra obtained in the solid state show differences, dissolve the substance to be examined and the reference substance separately in *acetone R*, evaporate to dryness and record new spectra using the residues.

## TESTS

### Specific optical rotation (2.2.7)

− 188 to − 198 (dried substance).

Dissolve 0.100 g in *methanol R* and dilute to 10.0 ml with the same solvent.

### Related substances

Liquid chromatography (2.2.29).

*Solvent mixture   acetonitrile R1, water R (50:50 V/V).*

*Test solution (a)* Dissolve 30.0 mg of the substance to be examined in 5 ml of *acetonitrile R1* and dilute to 10.0 ml with *water R.*

*Test solution (b)* Dilute 1.0 ml of test solution (a) to 10.0 ml with the solvent mixture.

*Reference solution (a)* Dissolve 3 mg of *gestodene for system suitability CRS* (containing impurities A, B, C and L) in 0.5 ml of *acetonitrile R1* and dilute to 1.0 ml with *water R.*

*Reference solution (b)* Dilute 1.0 ml of test solution (a) to 100.0 ml with the solvent mixture. Dilute 1.0 ml of this solution to 10.0 ml with the solvent mixture.

*Reference solution (c)* Dissolve 30.0 mg of *gestodene CRS* in 5 ml of *acetonitrile R1* and dilute to 10.0 ml with *water R.* Dilute 1.0 ml of this solution to 10.0 ml with the solvent mixture.

*Reference solution (d)* Dissolve the contents of a vial of *gestodene impurity I CRS* in 1.0 ml of the solvent mixture.

*Column:*
— *size:* $l = 0.15$ m, $\emptyset = 4.6$ mm;
— *stationary phase*: spherical *end-capped octylsilyl silica gel for chromatography R* (3.5 μm).

*Mobile phase:*
— *mobile phase A: water R;*
— *mobile phase B: acetonitrile R1;*

| Time (min) | Mobile phase A (per cent V/V) | Mobile phase B (per cent V/V) |
|---|---|---|
| 0 - 2 | 62 | 38 |
| 2 - 20 | 62 → 58 | 38 → 42 |
| 20 - 24 | 58 → 30 | 42 → 70 |
| 24 - 32 | 30 | 70 |

*Flow rate* 1.0 ml/min.

*Detection* Spectrophotometer at 205 nm and at 254 nm.

*Injection* 10 μl of test solution (a) and reference solutions (a), (b) and (d).

*Identification of impurities* Use the chromatogram supplied with *gestodene for system suitability CRS* and the chromatogram obtained with reference solution (a) to identify the peaks due to impurities A, B, C and L; use the chromatogram obtained with reference solution (d) to identify the peak due to impurity I.

*Relative retention* With reference to gestodene (retention time = about 12.5 min): impurity A = about 0.9; impurity C = about 1.1; impurity I = about 1.2; impurity L = about 1.46; impurity B = about 1.53.

*System suitability* Reference solution (a):
— *resolution*: minimum 2.0 between the peaks due to impurity A and gestodene.

*Limits:*
— *correction factors*: for the calculation of content, multiply the peak areas of the following impurities by the corresponding correction factor: impurity A = 2.2; impurity I = 1.3;
— *impurity A at 254 nm*: not more than 3 times the area of the principal peak in the chromatogram obtained with reference solution (b) (0.3 per cent);
— *impurity B at 205 nm*: not more than twice the area of the principal peak in the chromatogram obtained with reference solution (b) (0.2 per cent);
— *impurity C at 254 nm*: not more than twice the area of the principal peak in the chromatogram obtained with reference solution (b) (0.2 per cent);

— *impurities I, L at 205 nm*: for each impurity, not more than 1.5 times the area of the principal peak in the chromatogram obtained with reference solution (b) (0.15 per cent);
— *unspecified impurities at 254 nm*: for each impurity, not more than the area of the principal peak in the chromatogram obtained with reference solution (b) (0.10 per cent);
— *total at 254 nm*: not more than 5 times the area of the principal peak in the chromatogram obtained with reference solution (b) (0.5 per cent);
— *disregard limit at 254 nm*: 0.5 times the area of the principal peak in the chromatogram obtained with reference solution (b) (0.05 per cent).

**Loss on drying** (2.2.32)
Maximum 0.5 per cent, determined on 1.000 g by drying in an oven at 105 °C for 3 h.

**ASSAY**
Liquid chromatography (2.2.29) as described in the test for related substances with the following modification.

*Injection* Test solution (b) and reference solution (c).

Calculate the percentage content of $C_{21}H_{26}O_2$ from the declared content of *gestodene CRS.*

**IMPURITIES**
*Specified impurities* A, B, C, I, L.

*Other detectable impurities* (The following substances would, if present at a sufficient level, be detected by one or other of the tests in the monograph. They are limited by the general acceptance criterion for other/unspecified impurities and/or by the general monograph *Substances for pharmaceutical use (2034).* It is therefore not necessary to identify these impurities for demonstration of compliance. See also 5.10. Control of impurities in substances for pharmaceutical use):
— *at 205 nm*: G, J, K;
— *at 254 nm*: D, E, F, H.

A. 13-ethyl-17-hydroxy-18,19-dinor-17α-pregna-4,6,15-trien-20-yn-3-one (Δ6-gestodene),

B. 13-ethyl-17-hydroxy-18,19-dinor-17α-pregna-5(10),15-dien-20-yn-3-one (Δ5(10)-gestodene),

C. 13-ethyl-17-hydroxy-2α-(1-hydroxy-1-methylethyl)-18,19-dinor-17α-pregna-4,15-dien-20-yn-3-one (2-isopropanol-gestodene),

H. 13-ethyl-3-ethynyl-18,19-dinor-17α-pregna-3,5,15-trien-20-yn-17-ol (diethynyl-gestodene),

D. 13-ethyl-6β,17-dihydroxy-18,19-dinor-17α-pregna-4,15-dien-20-yn-3-one (6β-hydroxy-gestodene),

I. 13-ethyl-17-hydroxy-5-methoxy-18,19-dinor-5α,17α-pregn-15-en-20-yn-3-one (5-methoxy-gestodene),

E. 13-ethyl-17-hydroxy-18,19-dinor-17α-pregna-4,15-dien-20-yne-3,6-dione (6-keto-gestodene),

J. 13-ethylspiro(18,19-dinor-17α-pregna-5,15-dien-20-yne-3,2′-[1,3]dioxolan)-17-ol and 13-ethylspiro(18,19-dinor-17α-pregna-5(10),15-dien-20-yne-3,2′-[1,3]dioxolan)-17-ol (gestodene ketal),

F. 13-ethyl-17-hydroxy-3-oxo-18,19-dinor-17α-pregn-4-en-20-yn-15α-yl acetate (15α-acetoxy-gestodene),

K. 13-ethyl-3,17-dihydroxy-18,19-dinor-17α-pregna-1,3,5(10),15-tetraen-20-yn-6-one (aromatic 6-keto-gestodene),

G. 13-ethyl-3-methoxy-18,19-dinor-17α-pregna-1,3,5(10),15-tetraen-20-yn-17-ol (A-aromatic-gestodene),

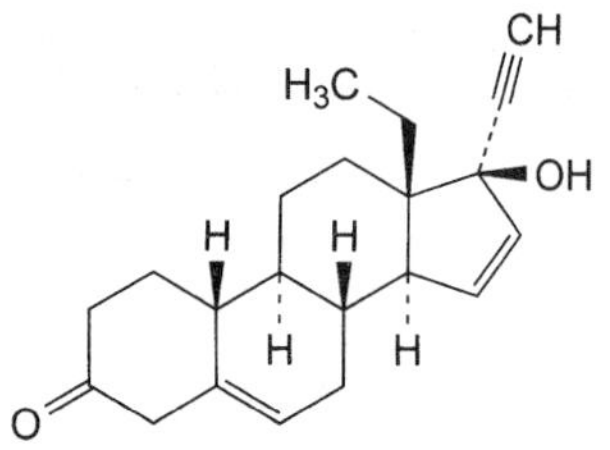

L. 13-ethyl-17-hydroxy-18,19-dinor-17α-pregna-5,15-dien-20-yn-3-one (Δ5(6)-gestodene).

_____ *Ph Eur*

# Glibenclamide

(*Ph Eur monograph 0718*)

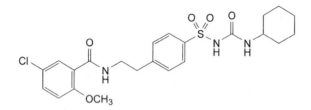

C₂₃H₂₈ClN₃O₅S          494.0          *10238-21-8*

**Action and use**

Inhibition of ATP-dependent potassium channels (sulfonylurea); treatment of diabetes mellitus.

**Preparation**

Glibenclamide Tablets

*Ph Eur* _____

## DEFINITION

1-[[4-[2-[(5-Chloro-2-methoxybenzoyl)amino]ethyl]phenyl]sulphonyl]-3-cyclohexylurea.

## Content

99.0 per cent to 101.0 per cent (dried substance).

## CHARACTERS

**Appearance**

White or almost white, crystalline powder.

**Solubility**

Practically insoluble in water, sparingly soluble in methylene chloride, slightly soluble in alcohol and in methanol.

## IDENTIFICATION

*First identification  A, C.*

*Second identification  A, B, D, E.*

A. Melting point (*2.2.14*): 169 °C to 174 °C.

B. Dissolve 50.0 mg in *methanol R*, with the aid of ultrasound if necessary, and dilute to 50.0 ml with the same solvent. To 10.0 ml of the solution add 1.0 ml of a 103 g/l solution of *hydrochloric acid R* and dilute to 100.0 ml with *methanol R*. Examined between 230 nm and 350 nm (*2.2.25*), the solution shows an absorption maximum at 300 nm and a less intense maximum at 275 nm. The specific absorbances at the maxima are 61 to 65 and 27 to 32, respectively.

C. Infrared absorption spectrophotometry (*2.2.24*).

*Preparation*  Discs of *potassium bromide R*.

*Comparison  glibenclamide CRS* .

If the spectra obtained show differences, moisten separately the substance to be examined and the reference substance with *methanol R*, triturate, dry at 100-105 °C and record the spectra again.

D. Thin-layer chromatography (*2.2.27*).

*Test solution*  Dissolve 10 mg of the substance to be examined in a mixture of equal volumes of *methanol R* and *methylene chloride R* and dilute to 10 ml with the same mixture of solvents.

*Reference solution*  Dissolve 10 mg of *glibenclamide CRS* in a mixture of equal volumes of *methanol R* and *methylene chloride R* and dilute to 10 ml with the same mixture of solvents.

*Plate*  TLC silica gel GF₂₅₄ plate R.

*Mobile phase*  alcohol R, glacial acetic acid R, cyclohexane R, methylene chloride R (5:5:45:45 V/V/V/V).

*Application*  10 μl.

*Development*  Over a path of 10 cm.

*Drying*  In air.

*Detection*  Examine in ultraviolet light at 254 nm.

*Results*  The principal spot in the chromatogram obtained with the test solution is similar in position and size to the principal spot in the chromatogram obtained with the reference solution.

E. Dissolve 20 mg in 2 ml of *sulphuric acid R*. The solution is colourless and shows blue fluorescence in ultraviolet light at 365 nm. Dissolve 0.1 g of *chloral hydrate R* in the solution. Within about 5 min, the colour changes to deep yellow and, after about 20 min, develops a brownish tinge.

## TESTS

**Related substances**

Liquid chromatography (*2.2.29*).

*Test solution*  Dissolve 25.0 mg of the substance to be examined in *methanol R* and dilute to 10.0 ml with the same solvent. Prepare immediately before use.

*Reference solution (a)*  Dissolve 5.0 mg of *glibenclamide impurity A CRS* and 5.0 mg of *glibenclamide impurity B CRS* in *methanol R* and dilute to 100.0 ml with the same solvent. Dilute 5.0 ml of the solution to 20.0 ml with *methanol R*.

*Reference solution (b)*  Dilute 2.0 ml of the test solution to 100.0 ml with *methanol R*. Dilute 5.0 ml of this solution to 50.0 ml with *methanol R*.

*Reference solution (c)*  Dissolve 5 mg of *gliclazide CRS* in *methanol R*, add 2 ml of the test solution and dilute to 100 ml with *methanol R*. Dilute 1 ml of this solution to 10 ml with *methanol R*.

*Column:*

— *size: l* = 0.10 m, Ø = 4.6 mm,

— *stationary phase*: spherical *base-deactivated end-capped octadecylsilyl silica gel for chromatography R* (3 μm),

— *temperature*: 35 °C.

*Mobile phase:*

— *mobile phase A*: mix 20 ml of a 101.8 g/l solution of freshly distilled *triethylamine R* adjusted to pH 3.0 using *phosphoric acid R*, and 50 ml of *acetonitrile R*; dilute to 1000 ml with *water R*,

— *mobile phase B*: mobile phase A, *water R*, *acetonitrile R* (20:65:915 V/V/V),

| Time (min) | Mobile phase A (per cent V/V) | Mobile phase B (per cent V/V) |
|---|---|---|
| 0 - 15 | 45 | 55 |
| 15 - 30 | 45 → 5 | 55 → 95 |
| 30 - 40 | 5 | 95 |
| 40 - 41 | 5 → 45 | 95 → 55 |
| 41 - 55 | 45 | 55 |

*Flow rate*   0.8 ml/min.

*Detection*   Spectrophotometer at 230 nm.

*Injection*   10 µl.

*Relative retention*   With reference to glibenclamide (retention time = about 5 min): impurity A = about 0.5; impurity B = about 0.6.

*System suitability*   Reference solution (c):
— *resolution*: minimum 5.0 between the peaks due to glibenclamide and gliclazide.

*Limits*:
— *impurity A*: not more than the area of the corresponding peak in the chromatogram obtained with reference solution (a) (0.5 per cent),
— *impurity B*: not more than the area of the corresponding peak in the chromatogram obtained with reference solution (a) (0.5 per cent),
— *any other impurity*: not more than the area of the principal peak in the chromatogram obtained with reference solution (b) (0.2 per cent), and not more than 2 such peaks have an area greater than half the area of the principal peak in the chromatogram obtained with reference solution (b) (0.1 per cent),
— *total of other impurities*: not more than 2.5 times the area of the principal peak in the chromatogram obtained with reference solution (b) (0.5 per cent),
— *disregard limit*: 0.25 times the area of the principal peak in the chromatogram obtained with reference solution (b) (0.05 per cent).

**Heavy metals** (*2.4.8*)
Maximum 20 ppm.

1.0 g complies with limit test D. Prepare the standard using 2 ml of *lead standard solution (10 ppm Pb) R*.

**Loss on drying** (*2.2.32*)
Maximum 1.0 per cent, determined on 1.000 g by drying in an oven at 105 °C.

**Sulphated ash** (*2.4.14*)
Maximum 0.1 per cent, determined on 1.0 g.

**ASSAY**
Dissolve 0.400 g with heating in 100 ml of *alcohol R*. Titrate with *0.1 M sodium hydroxide*, using 1.0 ml of *phenolphthalein solution R* as indicator, until a pink colour is obtained.

1 ml of *0.1 M sodium hydroxide* is equivalent to 49.40 mg of $C_{23}H_{28}ClN_3O_5S$.

**IMPURITIES**

A. R = H: 5-chloro-2-methoxy-*N*-[2-(4-sulphamoylphenyl)ethyl]benzamide,

B. R = CO-OCH₃: methyl [[4-[2-[(5-chloro-2-methoxybenzoyl)amino]ethyl]phenyl]sulphonyl]carbamate.

*Ph Eur*

# Gliclazide

(*Ph Eur monograph 1524*)

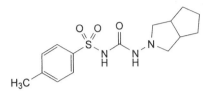

$C_{15}H_{21}N_3O_3S$        323.4        *21187-98-4*

**Action and use**
Inhibition of ATP-dependent potassium channels (sulfonylurea); treatment of diabetes mellitus.

**Preparation**
Gliclazide Tablets

*Ph Eur*

**DEFINITION**
1-(Hexahydrocyclopenta[*c*]pyrrol-2(1*H*)-yl)-3-[(4-methylphenyl)sulphonyl]urea.

**Content**
99.0 per cent to 101.0 per cent (dried substance).

**CHARACTERS**
**Appearance**
White or almost white powder.

**Solubility**
Practically insoluble in water, freely soluble in methylene chloride, sparingly soluble in acetone, slightly soluble in ethanol (96 per cent).

**IDENTIFICATION**
Infrared absorption spectrophotometry (*2.2.24*).

*Preparation*   Discs.

*Comparison*   gliclazide CRS .

**TESTS**
*Related substances*   Liquid chromatography (*2.2.29*). *Prepare the solutions immediately before use.*

*Solvent mixture*   acetonitrile R, water R (45:55 *V/V*).

*Test solution*   Dissolve 50.0 mg of the substance to be examined in 23 ml of *acetonitrile R* and dilute to 50.0 ml with *water R*.

*Reference solution (a)*   Dilute 1.0 ml of the test solution to 100.0 ml with the solvent mixture. Dilute 10.0 ml of this solution to 100.0 ml with the solvent mixture.

*Reference solution (b)*   Dissolve 5 mg of the substance to be examined and 15 mg of *gliclazide impurity F CRS* in 23 ml of *acetonitrile R* and dilute to 50 ml with *water R*. Dilute 1 ml of this solution to 20 ml with the solvent mixture.

*Reference solution (c)*   Dissolve 10.0 mg of *gliclazide impurity F CRS* in 45 ml of *acetonitrile R* and dilute to 100.0 ml with *water R*. Dilute 1.0 ml of this solution to 100.0 ml with the solvent mixture.

*Column:*
— *size: l* = 0.25 m, Ø = 4 mm;

— *stationary phase*: octylsilyl silica gel for chromatography R (5 μm).

*Mobile phase* triethylamine R, trifluoroacetic acid R, acetonitrile R, water R (0.1:0.1:45:55 *V/V/V/V*).

*Flow rate* 0.9 ml/min.

*Detection* Spectrophotometer at 235 nm.

*Injection* 20 μl.

*Run time* Twice the retention time of gliclazide.

*Relative retention* With reference to gliclazide (retention time = about 16 min): impurity F = about 0.9.

*System suitability* Reference solution (b):
— *resolution*: minimum 1.8 between the peaks due to impurity F and gliclazide.

*Limits:*
— *impurity F*: not more than the area of the corresponding peak in the chromatogram obtained with reference solution (c) (0.1 per cent);
— *unspecified impurities*: for each impurity, not more than the area of the principal peak in the chromatogram obtained with reference solution (a) (0.10 per cent);
— *sum of impurities other than F*: not more than twice the area of the principal peak in the chromatogram obtained with reference solution (a) (0.2 per cent);
— *disregard limit*: 0.2 times the area of the principal peak in the chromatogram obtained with reference solution (a) (0.02 per cent).

**Impurity B**

Liquid chromatography (*2.2.29*) as described in the test for related substances with the following modifications.

*Test solution* Dissolve 0.400 g of the substance to be examined in 2.5 ml of *dimethyl sulphoxide R* and dilute to 10.0 ml with *water R*. Stir for 10 min, store at 4 °C for 30 min and filter.

*Reference solution* Dissolve 20.0 mg of *gliclazide impurity B CRS* in *dimethyl sulphoxide R* and dilute to 100.0 ml with the same solvent. To 1.0 ml of the solution, add 12 ml of *dimethyl sulphoxide R* and dilute to 50.0 ml with *water R*. To 1.0 ml of this solution, add 12 ml of *dimethyl sulphoxide R* and dilute to 50.0 ml with *water R*.

*Injection* 50 μl.

*Retention time* Impurity B = about 8 min.

*Limit:*
— *impurity B*: not more than the area of the corresponding peak in the chromatogram obtained with the reference solution (2 ppm).

**Heavy metals** (*2.4.8*)

Maximum 10 ppm.

1.5 g complies with test F. Prepare the reference solution using 1.5 ml of *lead standard solution (10 ppm Pb) R*.

**Loss on drying** (*2.2.32*)

Maximum 0.25 per cent, determined on 1.000 g by drying in an oven at 105 °C for 2 h.

**Sulphated ash** (*2.4.14*)

Maximum 0.1 per cent, determined on 1.0 g.

**ASSAY**

Dissolve 0.250 g in 50 ml of *anhydrous acetic acid R*. Titrate with *0.1 M perchloric acid*, determining the end-point potentiometrically (*2.2.20*).

1 ml of *0.1 M perchloric acid* is equivalent to 32.34 mg of $C_{15}H_{21}N_3O_3S$.

**IMPURITIES**

*Specified impurities* B, F.

*Other detectable impurities* (the following substances would, if present at a sufficient level, be detected by one or other of the tests in the monograph. They are limited by the general acceptance criterion for other/unspecified impurities and/or by the general monograph *Substances for pharmaceutical use (2034)*. It is therefore not necessary to identify these impurities for demonstration of compliance. See also *5.10. Control of impurities in substances for pharmaceutical use*): A, C, D, E, G.

A. R-H: 4-methylbenzenesulphonamide,

B. 2-nitroso-octahydrocyclopenta[*c*]pyrrole,

C. R-CO-O-C₂H₅:
ethyl [(4-methylphenyl)sulphonyl]carbamate,

D. *N*-[(4-methylphenyl)sulphonyl]hexahydrocyclopenta[*c*]pyrrol-2(1*H*)-carboxamide,

E. 1-[(4-methylphenyl)sulphonyl]-3-(3,3a,4,6a-tetrahydrocyclopenta[*c*]pyrrol-2(1*H*)-yl)urea,

F. 1-(hexahydrocyclopenta[*c*]pyrrol-2(1*H*)-yl)-3-[(2-methylphenyl)sulphonyl]urea,

G. *N*-[(4-methylphenyl)sulphonyl]-1,4a,5,6,7,7a-hexahydro-2*H*-cyclopenta[*d*]pyridazine-2-carboxamide.

*———————————————————————— Ph Eur*

# Glimepiride

(*Ph Eur monograph 2223*)

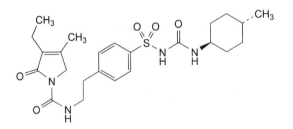

C₂₄H₃₄N₄O₅S     490.6     *93479-97-1*

**Action and use**

Inhibition of ATP-dependent potassium channels (sulfonylurea); treatment of diabetes mellitus.

*Ph Eur _____*

## DEFINITION

1-[[4-[2-(3-Ethyl-4-methyl-2-oxo-3-pyrroline-1-carboxamido)-ethyl]phenyl]sulphonyl]-3-*trans*-(4-methylcyclohexyl)urea.

**Content**

97.0 per cent to 102.0 per cent (anhydrous substance).

## CHARACTERS

**Appearance**

White or almost white powder.

**Solubility**

Practically insoluble in water, soluble in dimethylformamide, slightly soluble in methylene chloride, very slightly soluble in methanol.

It shows polymorphism (*5.9*).

## IDENTIFICATION

Infrared absorption spectrophotometry (*2.2.24*).

*Comparison* glimepiride CRS .

If the spectra obtained in the solid state show differences, dissolve the substance to be examined and the reference substance separately in *dimethylformamide R*, evaporate to dryness and record new spectra using the residues.

## TESTS

**Related substances**

Liquid chromatography (*2.2.29*) *Store the solutions at a temperature not exceeding 12 °C and for not more than 15 h.*

*Solvent mixture* water for chromatography R, acetonitrile for chromatography R (1:4 *V/V*).

*Test solution* Dissolve 20.0 mg of the substance to be examined in the solvent mixture and dilute to 100.0 ml with the solvent mixture.

*Reference solution (a)* Dissolve the contents of a vial of *glimepiride for system suitability CRS* (containing impurities B, C and D) in 2.0 ml of the test solution.

*Reference solution (b)* Dilute 1.0 ml of the test solution to 100.0 ml with the solvent mixture. Dilute 1.0 ml of this solution to 10.0 ml with the solvent mixture.

*Reference solution (c)* Dissolve 20.0 mg of *glimepiride CRS* in the solvent mixture and dilute to 100.0 ml with the solvent mixture.

*Column:*
— *size*: *l* = 0.25 m, Ø = 4 mm,
— *stationary phase*: end-capped octadecylsilyl silica gel for chromatography R (4 µm).

*Mobile phase* Dissolve 0.5 g of *sodium dihydrogen phosphate R* in 500 ml of *water for chromatography R* and adjust to pH 2.5 with *phosphoric acid R*. Add 500 ml of *acetonitrile for chromatography R*.

*Flow rate* 1.0 ml/min.

*Detection* Spectrophotometer at 228 nm.

*Injection* 20 µl of the test solution and reference solutions (a) and (b).

*Run time* 2.5 times the retention time of glimepiride.

*Relative retention* With reference to glimepiride (retention time = about 17 min): impurity B = about 0.2; impurity C = about 0.3; impurity D = about 1.1.

*System suitability* Reference solution (a):
— *resolution*: minimum 4.0 between the peaks due to impurity B and impurity C.

*Limits:*
— *impurity B*: not more than 4 times the area of the principal peak in the chromatogram obtained with reference solution (b) (0.4 per cent),
— *impurity D*: not more than twice the area of the principal peak in the chromatogram obtained with reference solution (b) (0.2 per cent),
— *unspecified impurities*: for each impurity, not more than the area of the principal peak in the chromatogram obtained with reference solution (b) (0.1 per cent),
— *sum of impurities other than B*: not more than 5 times the area of the principal peak in the chromatogram obtained with reference solution (b) (0.5 per cent),
— *disregard limit*: 0.5 times the area of the principal peak in the chromatogram obtained with reference solution (b) (0.05 per cent).

**Impurity A**

Liquid chromatography (*2.2.29*). *Prepare the solutions immediately before use.*

*Test solution* Dissolve 10.0 mg of the substance to be examined in 5 ml of *methylene chloride R* and dilute to 20.0 ml with the mobile phase.

*Reference solution (a)* Dilute 0.8 ml of the test solution to 100.0 ml with the mobile phase.

*Reference solution (b)* Dissolve 2.0 mg of *glimepiride CRS* (containing impurity A) in 1 ml of *methylene chloride R* and dilute to 4.0 ml with the mobile phase.

*Column:*
— *size*: *l* = 0.15 m, Ø = 4 mm,
— *stationary phase*: diol silica gel for chromatography R (5 µm).

*Mobile phase* anhydrous acetic acid R, 2-propanol R, heptane R (1:100:899 *V/V/V*).

*Flow rate* 0.5 ml/min.

*Detection* Spectrophotometer at 228 nm.

*Injection* 10 µl.

*Run time* 1.5 times the retention time of glimepiride.

*Identification of impurities* Use the chromatogram supplied with *glimepiride CRS* and the chromatogram obtained with reference solution (b) to identify the peak due to impurity A.

*Relative retention* With reference to glimepiride (retention time = about 14 min): impurity A = about 0.9.

*System suitability* Reference solution (b):
— *peak-to-valley ratio*: minimum 2.0, where $H_p$ = height above the baseline of the peak due to impurity A and $H_v$ = height above the baseline of the lowest point of the curve separating this peak from the peak due to glimepiride.

*Limit:*
— *impurity* A: not more than the area of the principal peak in the chromatogram obtained with reference solution (a) (0.8 per cent).

**Water** (*2.5.32*)

Maximum 0.5 per cent.

Dissolve 0.250 g in *dimethylformamide R* and dilute to 5.0 ml with the same solvent. Carry out the test on 1.0 ml of solution. Carry out a blank test.

**Sulphated ash** (*2.4.14*)

Maximum 0.1 per cent, determined on 1.0 g.

**ASSAY**

Liquid chromatography (*2.2.29*) as described in the test for related substances with the following modification.

*Injection* Test solution and reference solution (c).

Calculate the percentage content of $C_{24}H_{34}N_4O_5S$ from the areas of the peaks and the declared content of *glimepiride CRS* .

**IMPURITIES**

*Specified impurities* A, B, D.

*Other detectable impurities* (the following substances would, if present at a sufficient level, be detected by one or other of the tests in the monograph. They are limited by the general acceptance criterion for other/unspecified impurities and/or by the general monograph *Substances for pharmaceutical use* (*2034*). It is therefore not necessary to identify these impurities for demonstration of compliance. See also *5.10*.
*Control of impurities in substances for pharmaceutical use)*: C, E, F, G, H, I, J.

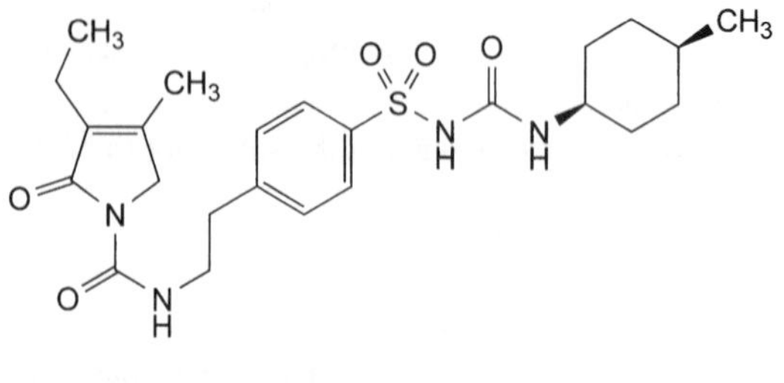

A. 1-[[4-[2-[[(3-ethyl-4-methyl-2-oxo-2,3-dihydro-1*H*-pyrrol-1-yl)carbonyl]amino]ethyl]phenyl]sulphonyl]-3-(*cis*-4-methylcyclohexyl)urea,

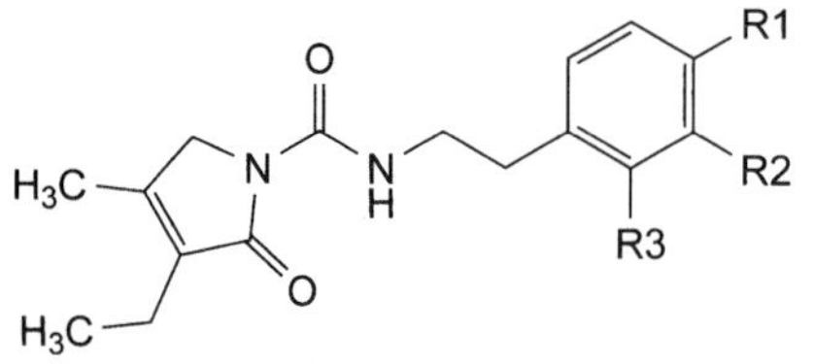

B. R1 = SO2-NH2, R2 = R3 = H: 3-ethyl-4-methyl-2-oxo-*N*-[2-(4-sulphamoylphenyl)ethyl]-2,3-dihydro-1*H*-pyrrole-1-carboxamide,

C. R1 = SO2-NH-CO-OCH3, R2 = R3 = H: methyl [[4-[2-[[(3-ethyl-4-methyl-2-oxo-2,3-dihydro-1*H*-pyrrol-1-yl)carbonyl]amino]ethyl]phenyl]sulphonyl]carbamate,

E. R1 = R3 = H, R2 = SO2-NH2: 3-ethyl-4-methyl-2-oxo-*N*-[2-(3-sulphamoylphenyl)ethyl]-2,3-dihydro-1*H*-pyrrole-1-carboxamide,

F. R1 = R2 = H, R3 = SO2-NH-CO-OCH3: methyl [[2-[2-[[(3-ethyl-4-methyl-2-oxo-2,3-dihydro-1*H*-pyrrol-1-yl)carbonyl]amino]ethyl]phenyl]sulphonyl]carbamate,

G. R1 = SO2-N(CH3)-CO-OCH3, R2 = R3 = H: methyl [[4-[2-[[(3-ethyl-4-methyl-2-oxo-2,3-dihydro-1*H*-pyrrol-1-yl)carbonyl]amino]ethyl]phenyl]sulphonyl]methylcarbamate,

H. R1 = SO2-NH-CO-NH-C6H4-CH3, R2 = R3 = H: 1-[[4-[2-[[(3-ethyl-4-methyl-2-oxo-2,3-dihydro-1*H*-pyrrol-1-yl)carbonyl]amino]ethyl]phenyl]sulphonyl]-3-(4-methylphenyl)urea,

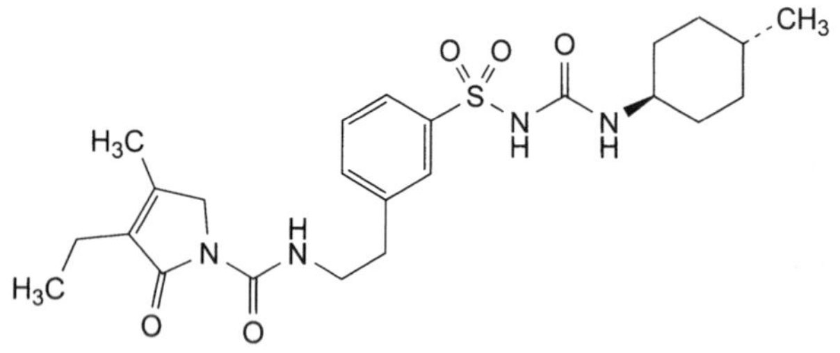

D. 1-[[3-[2-[[(3-ethyl-4-methyl-2-oxo-2,3-dihydro-1*H*-pyrrol-1-yl)carbonyl]amino]ethyl]phenyl]sulphonyl]-3-(*trans*-4-methylcyclohexyl)urea,

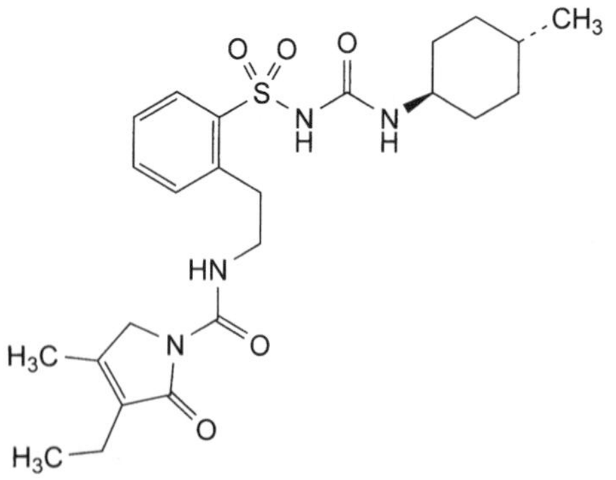

I. 1-[[2-[2-[[(3-ethyl-4-methyl-2-oxo-2,3-dihydro-1*H*-pyrrol-1-yl)carbonyl]amino]ethyl]phenyl]sulphonyl]-3-(*trans*-4-methylcyclohexyl)urea,

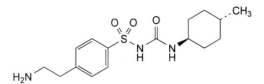

J. 1-[[4-(2-aminoethyl)phenyl]sulphonyl]-3-(*trans*-4-methylcyclohexyl)urea.

*Ph Eur*

# Glipizide

(*Ph Eur monograph 0906*)

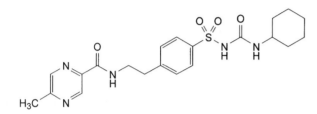

$C_{21}H_{27}N_5O_4S$      445.5      29094-61-9

## Action and use
Inhibition of ATP-dependent potassium channels (sulfonylurea); treatment of diabetes mellitus.

## Preparation
Glipizide Tablets

*Ph Eur*

## DEFINITION
1-Cyclohexyl-3-[[4-[2-[[(5-methylpyrazin-2-yl)carbonyl]amino]ethyl]phenyl]sulphonyl]urea.

## Content
98.0 per cent to 102.0 per cent (dried substance).

## CHARACTERS
### Appearance
White or almost white, crystalline powder.

### Solubility
Practically insoluble in water, very slightly soluble in methylene chloride and in acetone, practically insoluble in ethanol (96 per cent). It dissolves in dilute solutions of alkali hydroxides.

## IDENTIFICATION
*First identification*  B.

*Second identification*  A, C.

A. Ultraviolet and visible absorption spectrophotometry (*2.2.25*).

*Test solution*  Dissolve about 2 mg in *methanol R* and dilute to 100 ml with the same solvent.

*Spectral range*  220-350 nm.

*Absorption maxima*  At 226 nm and 274 nm.

*Absorbance ratio*  $A_{226}/A_{274}$ = 2.0 to 2.4.

B. Infrared absorption spectrophotometry (*2.2.24*).

*Comparison*  glipizide CRS.

C. Thin-layer chromatography (*2.2.27*).

*Test solution*  Dissolve 10 mg of the substance to be examined in a mixture of equal volumes of *methanol R* and

methylene chloride R and dilute to 10 ml with the same mixture of solvents.

*Reference solution*  Dissolve 10 mg of *glipizide CRS* in a mixture of equal volumes of *methanol R* and *methylene chloride R* and dilute to 10 ml with the same mixture of solvents.

*Plate*  TLC silica gel $GF_{254}$ plate R.

*Mobile phase*  *anhydrous formic acid R, ethyl acetate R, methylene chloride R* (25:25:50 *V/V/V*).

*Application*  10 µl.

*Development*  Over 2/3 of the plate.

*Drying*  In air.

*Detection*  Examine in ultraviolet light at 254 nm.

*Results*  The principal spot in the chromatogram obtained with the test solution is similar in position and size to the principal spot in the chromatogram obtained with the reference solution.

## TESTS
### Related substances.
Liquid chromatography (*2.2.29*).

*Test solution*  Place 25 mg of the substance to be examined into a volumetric flask and add 75 ml of the mobile phase. Dissolve using sonication. Dilute to 100.0 ml with the mobile phase.

*Reference solution (a)*  Dilute 1.0 ml of the test solution to 100.0 ml with the mobile phase. Dilute 1.0 ml of this solution to 10.0 ml with the mobile phase.

*Reference solution (b)*  Dissolve 5 mg of *glipizide impurity A CRS* and 5 mg of *glipizide impurity D CRS* in the mobile phase and dilute to 100 ml with the mobile phase.

*Column:*
— *size: l* = 0.15 m, Ø = 4.6 mm,
— *stationary phase*: spherical *end-capped octadecylsilyl silica gel for chromatography R* (5 µm).

*Mobile phase*  Mix 17 volumes of *acetonitrile R* and 83 volumes of a 3.5 g/l solution of *dipotassium hydrogen phosphate R* previously adjusted to pH 8.0 with *phosphoric acid R*.

*Flow rate*  1 ml/min.

*Detection*  Spectrophotometer at 274 nm.

*Injection*  50 µl.

*Run time*  1.5 times the retention time of glipizide.

*Relative retention*  With reference to glipizide (retention time = about 24 min): impurity A = about 0.3; impurity D = about 0.4; impurity E = about 1.1.

*System suitability*  Reference solution (b):
— *resolution*: minimum 2.0 between the peaks due to impurities A and D.

*Limits:*
— *impurity A*: not more 3 times the area of the principal peak in the chromatogram obtained with reference solution (a) (0.3 per cent),
— *impurities D, E*: for each impurity, not more than the area of the principal peak in the chromatogram obtained with reference solution (a) (0.1 per cent),
— *unspecified impurities*: for each impurity, not more than the area of the principal peak in the chromatogram obtained with reference solution (a) (0.1 per cent),
— *total*: not more than 5 times the area of the principal peak in the chromatogram obtained with reference solution (a) (0.5 per cent),

— *disregard limit*: 0.5 times the area of the principal peak in the chromatogram obtained with reference solution (a) (0.05 per cent).

**Impurity B**
Gas chromatography (*2.2.28*).

*Internal standard solution* Dissolve 25 mg of *decane R* in *methylene chloride R* and dilute to 100 ml with the same solvent. Dilute 5 ml of this solution to 100 ml with *methylene chloride R*.

*Test solution (a)* Dissolve 1.0 g of the substance to be examined in 50 ml of a 12 g/l solution of *sodium hydroxide R* and shake with 2 quantities, each of 5.0 ml of *methylene chloride R*. Use the combined lower layers.

*Test solution (b)* Dissolve 1.0 g of the substance to be examined in 50 ml of a 12 g/l solution of *sodium hydroxide R* and shake with 2 quantities, each of 5.0 ml of the internal standard solution. Use the combined lower layers.

*Reference solution* Dissolve 10.0 mg of *cyclohexylamine R* (impurity B) in a 17.5 g/l solution of *hydrochloric acid R* and dilute to 100.0 ml with the same acid. To 1.0 ml of this solution add 50 ml of a 12 g/l solution of *sodium hydroxide R* and shake with 2 quantities, each of 5.0 ml of the internal standard solution. Use the combined lower layers.

*Column:*
— *material*: fused silica,
— *size*: l = 25 m, Ø = 0.32 mm,
— *stationary phase*: poly(dimethyl)(diphenyl)siloxane R (film thickness 0.5 μm).

*Carrier gas* *helium for chromatography R*.

*Flow rate* 1.8 ml/min.

*Split ratio* 1:11.

*Temperature:*

|  | Time (min) | Temperature (°C) |
|---|---|---|
| Column | 0 - 4 | 40 |
|  | 4 - 20 | 40 → 200 |
|  | 20 - 25 | 200 |
| Injection port |  | 250 |
| Detector |  | 270 |

*Detection* Flame ionisation.

*Injection* 1 μl.

*Elution order* Impurity B, decane.

*System suitability:*
— *resolution*: minimum 7 between the peaks due to impurity B and the internal standard in the chromatogram obtained with the reference solution,
— there is no peak with the same retention time as that of the internal standard in the chromatogram obtained with test solution (a).

*Limit:*
— *impurity B*: calculate the ratio (R) of the area of the peak due to impurity B to the area of the peak due to the internal standard from the chromatogram obtained with the reference solution; from the chromatogram obtained with test solution (b), calculate the ratio of the area of any peak due to impurity B to the area of the peak due to the internal standard: this ratio is not greater than R (100 ppm).

**Impurity C**
Liquid chromatography (*2.2.29*).

*Solvent mixture* Mixture of equal volumes of *acetonitrile R* and *water R* previously adjusted to pH 3.5 with *acetic acid R*.

*Test solution* Dissolve 10.0 mg of the substance to be examined in the solvent mixture and dilute to 50.0 ml with the solvent mixture.

*Reference solution* Dissolve 5.0 mg of *glipizide impurity C CRS* in the solvent mixture and dilute to 50.0 ml with the solvent mixture. To 5.0 ml of the solution add 1.0 ml of the test solution and dilute to 100.0 ml with the solvent mixture. Dilute 1.0 ml of this solution to 10.0 ml with the solvent mixture.

*Column:*
— *size*: l = 0.15 m, Ø = 4.6 mm,
— *stationary phase*: spherical *base-deactivated end-capped octadecylsilyl silica gel for chromatography R1* (3 μm).

*Mobile phase* Mix 35 volumes of *acetonitrile R1* and 65 volumes of *water R* previously adjusted to pH 3.5 with *acetic acid R*.

*Flow rate* 1.5 ml/min.

*Detection* Spectrophotometer at 225 nm.

*Injection* 50 μl.

*Run time* Twice the retention time of glipizide.

*Relative retention* With reference to glipizide (retention time = about 6 min): impurity C = about 1.4.

*System suitability* Reference solution:
— *resolution*: minimum 4.0 between the peaks due to glipizide and impurity C,
— *symmetry factor*: maximum 1.2 for the peak due to glipizide.

*Limit:*
— *impurity C*: not more than 0.4 times the area of the corresponding peak in the chromatogram obtained with the reference solution (0.1 per cent).

**Loss on drying** (*2.2.32*)
Maximum 0.5 per cent, determined on 1.000 g by drying in an oven at 105 °C.

**Sulphated ash** (*2.4.14*)
Maximum 0.2 per cent, determined on 1.0 g.

**ASSAY**
Dissolve 0.400 g in 50 ml of *dimethylformamide R*. Add 0.2 ml of *quinaldine red solution R*. Titrate with *0.1 M lithium methoxide* until the colour changes from red to colourless.

1 ml of *0.1 M lithium methoxide* is equivalent to 44.55 mg of $C_{21}H_{27}N_5O_4S$.

**IMPURITIES**
*Specified impurities* *A, B, C, D, E.*

A. R = H, R′ = $CH_3$: 5-methyl-N-[2-(4-sulphamoylphenyl)ethyl]pyrazine-2-carboxamide,

D. R = $CH_3$, R′ = H: 6-methyl-N-[2-(4-sulphamoylphenyl)ethyl]pyrazine-2-carboxamide,

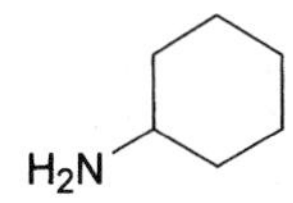

B. cyclohexanamine,

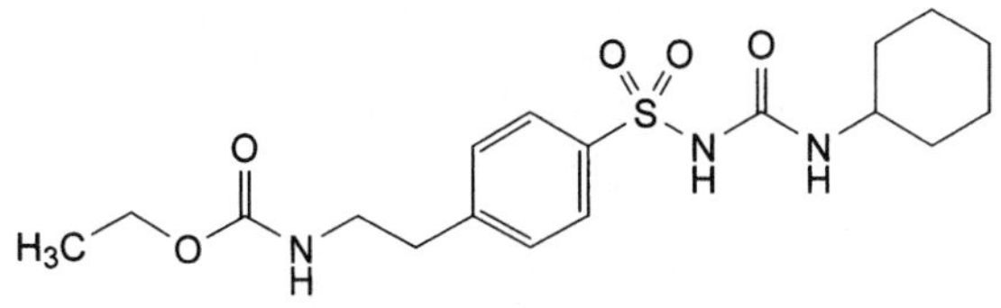

C. ethyl [2-[4-[(cyclohexylcarbamoyl)sulphamoyl]
phenyl]ethyl]carbamate,

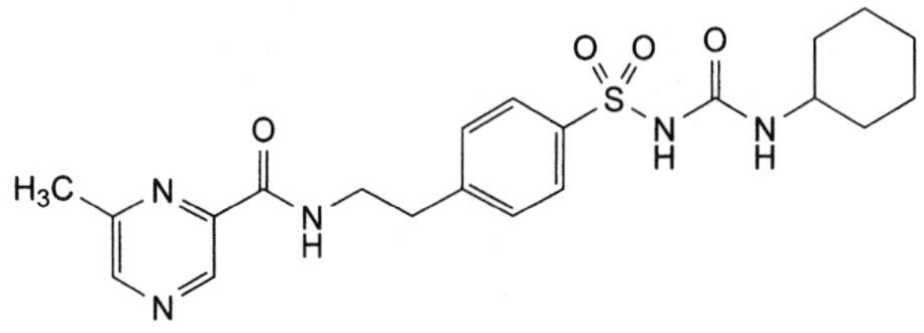

E. 1-cyclohexyl-3-[[4-[2-[[(6-methylpyrazin-2-
yl)carbonyl]amino]ethyl]phenyl]sulphonyl]urea.

*Ph Eur*

# Gliquidone

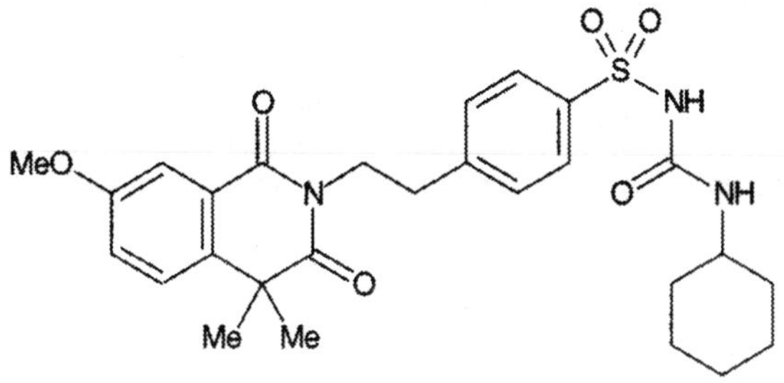

$C_{27}H_{33}N_3O_6S$    527.6    *33342-05-1*

## Action and use

Inhibition of ATP-dependent potassium channels
(sulfonylurea); treatment of diabetes mellitus.

## Preparation

Gliquidone Tablets

## DEFINITION

Gliquidone is 1-cyclohexyl-3-*p*-[2-(3,4-dihydro-7-methoxy-
4,4-dimethyl-1,3-dioxo2(1*H*)-
isoquinolyl)ethyl]phenylsulphonylurea. It contains not less
than 98.5% and not more than 101.5% of $C_{27}H_{33}N_3O_6S$,
calculated with reference to the dried substance.

## CHARACTERISTICS

A white or almost white powder.

Practically insoluble in *water*; slightly soluble in *ethanol (96%)*
and in *methanol*; soluble in *acetone*; freely soluble in
*dimethylformamide*.

## IDENTIFICATION

A. Dissolve 30 mg in 10 ml of *methanol*. Evaporate the
methanol using a rotary evaporator and dry the residue at
a temperature of 50° at a pressure of 2 kPa for 1 hour.
The *infrared absorption spectrum* of the dried residue,
Appendix II A, is concordant with the *reference spectrum* of
gliquidone *(RS 170)*.

B. In the test for Related substances, the principal spot in the
chromatogram obtained with solution (1) corresponds to that
in the chromatogram obtained with solution (2).

## TESTS

### Melting point

176° to 181°, Appendix V A.

### Related substances

Carry out the method for *thin-layer chromatography*,
Appendix III A, using *silica gel 60F* as the coating substance
and a mixture of 5 volumes of *glacial acetic acid*, 5 volumes of
*ethanol (96%)*, 45 volumes of *chloroform* and 45 volumes of
*cyclohexane* as the mobile phase but allowing the solvent front
to ascend 10 cm above the line of application. Apply
separately to the plate 10 µl of each of five solutions in a
mixture of 50 volumes of *dichloromethane* and 50 volumes of
*methanol* containing (1) 1.0% w/v of the substance being
examined, (2) 1.0% w/v of *gliquidone BPCRS*, (3)
0.0030% w/v of *gliquidone BPCRS*, (4) 0.0030% w/v of
*gliquidone sulphonamide BPCRS* and (5) a mixture of
1 volume of solution (3) and 1 volume of solution (4). After
removal of the plate, allow it to dry in air and examine under
*ultraviolet light (254 nm)*. In the chromatogram obtained with
solution (1) any spot corresponding to gliquidone
sulphonamide is not more intense than the spot in the
chromatogram obtained with solution (4) (0.3%) and any
other *secondary spot* is not more intense than the spot in the
chromatogram obtained with solution (3) (0.3%). The test is
not valid unless the chromatogram obtained with solution (5)
shows two clearly separated principal spots.

### Heavy metals

1 g complies with *limit test C for heavy metals*, Appendix VII.
Use 1 ml of *lead standard solution (10 ppm Pb)* to prepare the
standard (10 ppm).

### Loss on drying

When dried to constant weight at 105°, loses not more than
1.0% of its weight. Use 1 g.

### Sulphated ash

Not more than 0.1%, Appendix IX A.

## ASSAY

Dissolve 0.3 g in 70 ml of *dimethylformamide* and immediately
carry out Method II for *non-aqueous titration*,
Appendix VIII A, in an atmosphere of nitrogen using
0.1M *tetrabutylammonium hydroxide VS* as titrant and a
0.3% w/v solution of *thymol blue* as indicator. Each ml of
0.1M *tetrabutylammonium hydroxide VS* is equivalent to
52.76 mg of $C_{27}H_{33}N_3O_6S$.

## IMPURITIES

A. p-[2-(3,4-dihydro-7-methoxy-4,4-dimethyl-1,3-dioxo-2(1H)isoquinolyl)ethyl]benzenesulphonamide
*(gliquidone sulphonamide)*

# Human Glucagon

*(Glucagon, human, Ph Eur monograph 1635)*

H-His−Ser−Gln−Gly−Thr−Phe−Thr−Ser−Asp−Tyr−
                                              10

Ser−Lys−Tyr−Leu−Asp−Ser−Arg−Arg−Ala−Gln−
                                              20

Asp−Phe−Val−Gln−Trp−Leu−Met−Asn−Thr·OH

$C_{153}H_{225}N_{43}O_{49}S$         3483         *16941-32-5*

## Action and use
Hormone; treatment of hypoglycaemia.

*Ph Eur*

## DEFINITION
Polypeptide having the same structure (29 amino acids) as the hormone produced by the α-cells of the human pancreas, which increases the blood-glucose concentration by promoting rapid breakdown of liver glycogen.

## Content
92.5 per cent to 105.0 per cent (anhydrous substance).

## PRODUCTION
Human glucagon is produced by a method based on recombinant DNA (rDNA) technology. During the course of product development it must be demonstrated that the manufacturing process produces a product having a biological activity of not less than 1 IU/mg using a suitable validated bioassay.

## Host-cell-derived proteins
The limit is approved by the competent authority.

## Host-cell- and vector-derived DNA
The limit is approved by the competent authority.

## CHARACTERS
### Appearance
White or almost white powder.

### Solubility
Practically insoluble in water and in most organic solvents. It is soluble in dilute mineral acids and in dilute solutions of alkali hydroxides.

## IDENTIFICATION
A. Peptide mapping. Liquid chromatography (2.2.29).

*Test solution* Prepare a 5 mg/ml solution of the substance to be examined in *0.01 M hydrochloric acid*. Mix 200 μl of this solution with 800 μl of *0.1 M ammonium carbonate buffer solution pH 10.3 R* (diluted stock solution). Prepare a

2 mg/ml solution of α-*chymotrypsin for peptide mapping R* in *0.1 M ammonium carbonate buffer solution pH 10.3 R* and add 25 μl of this solution to the diluted stock solution. Place the solution in a closed vial at 37 °C for 2 h. Remove the vial and stop the reaction immediately by adding 120 μl of *glacial acetic acid R*.

*Reference solution* Prepare a 1 mg/ml solution of *human glucagon CRS* in *0.1 M ammonium carbonate buffer solution pH 10.3 R* (diluted stock solution) and continue as described for the test solution.

*Column:*
— *size*: l = 0.05 m, Ø = 4 mm;
— *stationary phase*: octadecylsilyl silica gel for chromatography R (5 μm ).

*Mobile phase:*
— *mobile phase A*: mix 500 μl of *trifluoroacetic acid R* and 1000 ml of *water R*;
— *mobile phase B*: mix 500 μl of *trifluoroacetic acid R* with 600 ml of *anhydrous ethanol R* and add 400 ml of *water R;*

| Time (min) | Mobile phase A (per cent *V/V*) | Mobile phase B (per cent *V/V*) |
|---|---|---|
| 0 - 35 | 100 → 53 | 0 → 47 |
| 35 - 45 | 53 → 0 | 47 → 100 |
| 45 - 46 | 0 → 100 | 100 → 0 |
| 46 - 75 | 100 | 0 |

*Flow rate* 1.0 ml/min.

*Detection* Spectrophotometer at 215 nm.

*Equilibration* With mobile phase A for at least 15 min.

*Injection* 20 μl.

*Results* The profile of the chromatogram obtained with the test solution corresponds to that of the chromatogram obtained with the reference solution.

B. Examine the chromatograms obtained in the assay.

*Results* The principal peak in the chromatogram obtained with the test solution is similar in retention time to the principal peak in the chromatogram obtained with the reference solution.

## TESTS
### Deamidated glucagon
Liquid chromatography (2.2.29): use the normalisation procedure.

*Test solution* Dissolve the substance to be examined in *0.01 M hydrochloric aci*d to obtain a concentration of 1.0 mg/ml.

*Resolution solution* Dissolve the substance to be examined in *0.1 M hydrochloric acid* to obtain a concentration of 1.0 mg/ml. Incubate in an oven at 60 °C for 2 h. Immediately after degradation, adjust to pH 2.5 with *1 M sodium hydroxide*.

*Column:*
— *material*: glass;
— *size*: l = 0.05 m, Ø = 5 mm;
— *stationary phase*: anion exchange resin R2.

*Mobile phase:*
— *mobile phase A*: mix 1000 ml of *tris-hydrochloride buffer solution pH 8.3 R* and 1000 ml of *anhydrous ethanol R*;
— *mobile phase B*: dissolve 29.2 g of *sodium chloride R* in 1000 ml of *tris-hydrochloride buffer solution pH 8.3 R*; add 1000 ml of *anhydrous ethanol R*;

| Time (min) | Mobile phase A (per cent *V/V*) | Mobile phase B (per cent *V/V*) |
|---|---|---|
| 0 - 4 | 100 | 0 |
| 4 - 30 | 100 → 78 | 0 → 22 |
| 30 - 34 | 78 → 45 | 22 → 55 |
| 34 - 38 | 45 → 20 | 55 → 80 |
| 38 - 40 | 20 → 100 | 80 → 0 |
| 40 - 60 | 100 | 0 |

*Flow rate* 0.6 ml/min.

*Detection* Spectrophotometer at 230 nm.

*Equilibration* With mobile phase A for at least 15 min.

*Injection* 60 µl.

*System suitability* Resolution solution:
— *retention time*: glucagon = about 10 min; 4 deamidated forms: between 15 min and 40 min;
— *resolution*: baseline separation of the 4 deamidated forms and glucagon.

*Limit*:
— *sum of the 4 deamidated forms*: maximum 0.5 per cent, calculated from the peaks eluting between 15 min and 40 min.

**Related proteins**
Liquid chromatography (*2.2.29*): use the normalisation procedure.

*2.8 M urea solution* Dissolve 16.8 g of *urea R* in 100 ml of *water R*.

*Test solution* Dissolve the substance to be examined in *0.01 M hydrochloric acid* to obtain a concentration of 0.5 mg/ml. *Maintain the solution at 2-8 °C.*

*Reference solution* Dissolve the contents of a vial of *human glucagon CRS* in *0.01 M hydrochloric acid* to obtain a concentration of 0.5 mg/ml. *Maintain the solution at 2-8 °C.*

*Resolution solution* Dissolve 10 mg of the substance to be examined in 20 ml of the 2.8 M urea solution. Heat at 50 °C for 2 h. Cool and adjust to pH 2.2 with *1 M hydrochloric acid*. *Maintain the solution at 2-8 °C and use within 2 h, or maintain the solution below − 15 °C and then thaw and filter through a 0.22 µm filter before use.*

*Column*:
— *size*: l = 0.25 m, Ø = 4.6 mm;
— *stationary phase*: octadecylsilyl silica gel for chromatography R (5 µm) with a pore size of 30 nm;
— *temperature*: 45 °C.

*Mobile phase*:
— *mobile phase A*: dissolve 13.6 g of *potassium dihydrogen phosphate R* in 400 ml of *water R*, adjust to pH 2.5 (*2.2.3*) with *phosphoric acid R*, and add 100 ml of *acetonitrile for chromatography R*;
— *mobile phase B*: acetonitrile *for chromatography R*, water R (40:60 *V/V*);

| Time (min) | Mobile phase A (per cent *V/V*) | Mobile phase B (per cent *V/V*) |
|---|---|---|
| 0 - 23 | 57 | 43 |
| 23 - 29 | 57 → 10 | 43 → 90 |
| 29 - 30 | 10 | 90 |
| 30 - 31 | 10 → 57 | 90 → 43 |
| 31 - 75 | 57 | 43 |

*Flow rate* 1.0 ml/min.

*Detection* Spectrophotometer at 214 nm.

*Injection* 50 µl of the test solution and the resolution solution.

*Relative retention* With reference to glucagon (retention time = about 20 min): carbamoylglucagon = about 1.1.

*System suitability* Resolution solution:
— *resolution*: minimum 2.0 between the peaks due to glucagon and carbamoylglucagon.

*Limit*:
— *total*: maximum 2.5 per cent.

**Water** (*2.5.12*)
Maximum 10 per cent, determined on 50 mg.

**Bacterial endotoxins** (*2.6.14*)
Less than 10 IU/mg.

**ASSAY**
Liquid chromatography (*2.2.29*) as described in the test for related proteins with the following modification.

*Injection* Test solution and reference solution.

Calculate the content of human glucagon (C$_{153}$H$_{225}$N$_{43}$O$_{49}$S) from the declared content of C$_{153}$H$_{225}$N$_{43}$O$_{49}$S in *human glucagon CRS* .

**STORAGE**
In an airtight container, protected from light, at a temperature lower than − 15 °C.

*———————————————————— Ph Eur*

# Glucose

(*Glucose Monohydrate, Ph Eur monograph 0178*)

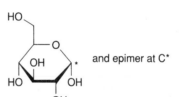

C$_6$H$_{12}$O$_6$,H$_2$O          198.2          5996-10-1

**Preparations**
Glucose Intravenous Infusion

Glucose Irrigation Solution

Oral Rehydration Salts

Potassium Chloride and Glucose Intravenous Infusion

Potassium Chloride, Sodium Chloride and Glucose Intravenous Infusion

Sodium Chloride and Glucose Intravenous Infusion

*Ph Eur* _____

**DEFINITION**
(+)-D-Glucopyranose monohydrate.

**CHARACTERS**

**Appearance**
White or almost white, crystalline powder.

It has a sweet taste.

**Solubility**
Freely soluble in water, sparingly soluble in ethanol (96 per cent).

**IDENTIFICATION**
A. Specific optical rotation (see Tests).

B. Thin-layer chromatography (2.2.27).

*Solvent mixture*    water R, methanol R (2:3 V/V).

*Test solution*    Dissolve 10 mg of the substance to be examined in the solvent mixture and dilute to 20 ml with the solvent mixture.

*Reference solution (a)*    Dissolve 10 mg of *glucose CRS* in the solvent mixture and dilute to 20 ml with the solvent mixture.

*Reference solution (b)*    Dissolve 10 mg each of *fructose CRS, glucose CRS, lactose CRS* and *sucrose CRS* in the solvent mixture and dilute to 20 ml with the solvent mixture.

*Plate*    TLC silica gel G plate R.

*Mobile phase*    water R, methanol R, anhydrous acetic acid R, ethylene chloride R (10:15:25:50 V/V/V/V); measure the volumes accurately since a slight excess of water produces cloudiness.

*Application*    2 μl; thoroughly dry the starting points.

*Development A*    Over a path of 15 cm.

*Drying A*    In a current of warm air.

*Development B*    Immediately, over a path of 15 cm, after renewing the mobile phase.

*Drying B*    In a current of warm air.

*Detection*    Spray with a solution of 0.5 g of *thymol R* in a mixture of 5 ml of *sulphuric acid R* and 95 ml of *ethanol (96 per cent) R*; heat at 130 °C for 10 min.

*System suitability*    Reference solution (b):
— the chromatogram shows 4 clearly separated spots.

*Results*    The principal spot in the chromatogram obtained with the test solution is similar in position, colour and size to the principal spot in the chromatogram obtained with reference solution (a).

C. Dissolve 0.1 g in 10 ml of *water R*. Add 3 ml of *cupri-tartaric solution R* and heat. A red precipitate is formed.

## TESTS

### Solution S

Dissolve 10.0 g in *distilled water R* and dilute to 100 ml with the same solvent.

### Appearance of solution

The solution is clear (2.2.1) and not more intensely coloured than reference solution BY$_7$ (2.2.2, Method II).

Dissolve 10.0 g in 15 ml of *water R*.

### Acidity or alkalinity

Dissolve 6.0 g in 25 ml of *carbon dioxide-free water R* and add 0.3 ml of *phenolphthalein solution R*. The solution is colourless. Not more than 0.15 ml of *0.1 M sodium hydroxide* is required to change the colour of the indicator to pink.

### Specific optical rotation (2.2.7)

+ 52.5 to + 53.3 (anhydrous substance).

Dissolve 10.0 g in 80 ml of *water R*, add 0.2 ml of *dilute ammonia R1*, allow to stand for 30 min and dilute to 100.0 ml with *water R*.

### Foreign sugars, soluble starch, dextrins

Dissolve 1.0 g by boiling in 30 ml of *ethanol (90 per cent V/V) R*. Cool; the appearance of the solution shows no change.

### Sulphites

Maximum 15 ppm, expressed as SO$_2$.

*Test solution*    Dissolve 5.0 g in 40 ml of *water R*, add 2.0 ml of *0.1 M sodium hydroxide* and dilute to 50.0 ml with *water R*. To 10.0 ml of the solution, add 1 ml of a 310 g/l solution of *hydrochloric acid R*, 2.0 ml of *decolorised fuchsin solution R1* and

2.0 ml of a 0.5 per cent V/V solution of *formaldehyde R*. Allow to stand for 30 min.

*Reference solution*    Dissolve 76 mg of *sodium metabisulphite R* in *water R* and dilute to 50.0 ml with the same solvent. Dilute 5.0 ml of this solution to 100.0 ml with *water R*. To 3.0 ml of this solution add 4.0 ml of *0.1 M sodium hydroxide* and dilute to 100.0 ml with *water R*. Immediately add to 10.0 ml of this solution 1 ml of a 310 g/l solution of *hydrochloric acid R*, 2.0 ml of *decolorised fuchsin solution R1* and 2.0 ml of a 0.5 per cent V/V solution of *formaldehyde R*. Allow to stand for 30 min.

Measure the absorbance (2.2.25) of the 2 solutions at the absorption maximum at 583 nm using for both measurements a solution prepared in the same manner using 10.0 ml of *water R* as the compensation liquid. The absorbance of the test solution is not greater than that of the reference solution.

### Chlorides (2.4.4)

Maximum 125 ppm.

Dilute 4 ml of solution S to 15 ml with *water R*.

### Sulphates (2.4.13)

Maximum 200 ppm.

Dilute 7.5 ml of solution S to 15 ml with *distilled water R*.

### Arsenic (2.4.2, Method A)

Maximum 1 ppm, determined on 1.0 g.

### Barium

To 10 ml of solution S add 1 ml of *dilute sulphuric acid R*. When examined immediately and after 1 h, any opalescence in the solution is not more intense than that in a mixture of 1 ml of *distilled water R* and 10 ml of solution S.

### Calcium (2.4.3)

Maximum 200 ppm.

Dilute 5 ml of solution S to 15 ml with *distilled water R*.

### Lead (2.4.10)

Maximum 0.5 ppm.

### Water (2.5.12)

7.0 per cent to 9.5 per cent, determined on 0.50 g.

### Sulphated ash

Maximum 0.1 per cent.

Dissolve 5.0 g in 5 ml of *water R*, add 2 ml of *sulphuric acid R*, evaporate to dryness on a water-bath and ignite to constant mass. If necessary, repeat the heating with *sulphuric acid R*.

### Pyrogens (2.6.8)

If intended for use in the manufacture of large-volume parenteral preparations without a further appropriate procedure for the removal of pyrogens, the competent authority may require that it comply with the test for pyrogens. Inject per kilogram of the rabbit's mass 10 ml of a solution in *water for injections R* containing 55 mg of the substance to be examined per millilitre.

_____ *Ph Eur*

# Anhydrous Glucose

*(Ph Eur monograph 0177)*

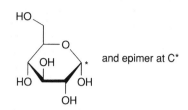

and epimer at C*

C₆H₁₂O₆ 180.2 50-99-7

**Preparations**

Glucose Intravenous Infusion

Glucose Irrigation Solution

Compound Glucose, Sodium Chloride and Sodium Citrate Oral Solution

Oral Rehydration Salts

Potassium Chloride and Glucose Intravenous Infusion

Potassium Chloride, Sodium Chloride and Glucose Intravenous Infusion

Sodium Chloride and Glucose Intravenous Infusion

*Ph Eur* _____

## DEFINITION

(+)-D-Glucopyranose.

## CHARACTERS

**Appearance**

White or almost white, crystalline powder.

It has a sweet taste.

**Solubility**

Freely soluble in water, sparingly soluble in ethanol (96 per cent).

## IDENTIFICATION

A. Specific optical rotation (see Tests).

B. Thin-layer chromatography (2.2.27).

*Solvent mixture* water R, methanol R (2:3 V/V).

*Test solution* Dissolve 10 mg of the substance to be examined in the solvent mixture and dilute to 20 ml with the solvent mixture.

*Reference solution (a)* Dissolve 10 mg of *glucose CRS* in the solvent mixture and dilute to 20 ml with the solvent mixture.

*Reference solution (b)* Dissolve 10 mg each of *fructose CRS*, *glucose CRS*, *lactose CRS* and *sucrose CRS* in the solvent mixture and dilute to 20 ml with the solvent mixture.

*Plate* TLC silica gel G plate R.

*Mobile phase* water R, methanol R, anhydrous acetic acid R, ethylene chloride R (10:15:25:50 V/V/V/V); measure the volumes accurately since a slight excess of water produces cloudiness.

*Application* 2 µl; thoroughly dry the starting points.

*Development A* Over a path of 15 cm.

*Drying A* In a current of warm air.

*Development B* Immediately, over a path of 15 cm, after renewing the mobile phase.

*Drying B* In a current of warm air.

*Detection* Spray with a solution of 0.5 g of *thymol R* in a mixture of 5 ml of *sulphuric acid R* and 95 ml of *ethanol (96 per cent) R*. Heat at 130 °C for 10 min.

*System suitability* Reference solution (b):

— the chromatogram shows 4 clearly separated spots.

*Results* The principal spot in the chromatogram obtained with the test solution is similar in position, colour and size to the principal spot in the chromatogram obtained with reference solution (a).

C. Dissolve 0.1 g in 10 ml of *water R*. Add 3 ml of *cupri-tartaric solution R* and heat. A red precipitate is formed.

## TESTS

**Solution S**

Dissolve 10.0 g in *distilled water R* and dilute to 100 ml with the same solvent.

**Appearance of solution**

The solution is clear (2.2.1) and not more intensely coloured than reference solution BY₇ (2.2.2, Method II).

Dissolve 10.0 g in 15 ml of *water R*.

**Acidity or alkalinity**

Dissolve 6.0 g in 25 ml of *carbon dioxide-free water R* and add 0.3 ml of *phenolphthalein solution R*. The solution is colourless. Not more than 0.15 ml of *0.1 M sodium hydroxide* is required to change the colour of the indicator to pink.

**Specific optical rotation** (2.2.7)

+ 52.5 to + 53.3 (anhydrous substance).

Dissolve 10.0 g in 80 ml of *water R*, add 0.2 ml of *dilute ammonia R1*, allow to stand for 30 min and dilute to 100.0 ml with *water R*.

**Foreign sugars, soluble starch, dextrins**

Dissolve 1.0 g by boiling in 30 ml of *ethanol (90 per cent V/V) R*. Cool; the appearance of the solution shows no change.

**Sulphites**

Maximum 15 ppm, expressed as SO₂.

*Test solution* Dissolve 5.0 g in 40 ml of *water R*, add 2.0 ml of *0.1 M sodium hydroxide* and dilute to 50.0 ml with *water R*. To 10.0 ml of the solution, add 1 ml of a 310 g/l solution of *hydrochloric acid R*, 2.0 ml of *decolorised fuchsin solution R1* and 2.0 ml of a 0.5 per cent V/V solution of *formaldehyde R*. Allow to stand for 30 min.

*Reference solution* Dissolve 76 mg of *sodium metabisulphite R* in *water R* and dilute to 50.0 ml with the same solvent. Dilute 5.0 ml of this solution to 100.0 ml with *water R*. To 3.0 ml of this solution add 4.0 ml of *0.1 M sodium hydroxide* and dilute to 100.0 ml with *water R*. Immediately add to 10.0 ml of this solution 1 ml of a 310 g/l solution of *hydrochloric acid R*, 2.0 ml of *decolorised fuchsin solution R1* and 2.0 ml of a 0.5 per cent V/V solution of *formaldehyde R*. Allow to stand for 30 min.

Measure the absorbance (2.2.25) of the 2 solutions at the absorption maximum at 583 nm using for both measurements a solution prepared in the same manner using 10.0 ml of *water R* as the compensation liquid. The absorbance of the test solution is not greater than that of the reference solution.

**Chlorides** (2.4.4)

Maximum 125 ppm.

Dilute 4 ml of solution S to 15 ml with *water R*.

**Sulphates** (2.4.13)

Maximum 200 ppm.

Dilute 7.5 ml of solution S to 15 ml with *distilled water R*.

**Arsenic** (2.4.2, Method A)

Maximum 1 ppm, determined on 1.0 g.

**Barium**

To 10 ml of solution S add 1 ml of *dilute sulphuric acid R*. When examined immediately and after 1 h, any opalescence in the solution is not more intense than that in a mixture of 1 ml of *distilled water R* and 10 ml of solution S.

**Calcium** (*2.4.3*)

Maximum 200 ppm.

Dilute 5 ml of solution S to 15 ml with *distilled water R*.

**Lead** (*2.4.10*)

Maximum 0.5 ppm.

**Water** (*2.5.12*)

Maximum 1.0 per cent, determined on 0.50 g.

**Sulphated ash**

Maximum 0.1 per cent.

Dissolve 5.0 g in 5 ml of *water R*, add 2 ml of *sulphuric acid R*, evaporate to dryness on a water-bath and ignite to constant mass. If necessary, repeat the heating with *sulphuric acid R*.

**Pyrogens** (*2.6.8*)

If intended for use in the manufacture of large-volume parental preparations without a further appropriate procedure for the removal of pyrogens, the competent authority may require that it comply with the test for pyrogens. Inject per kilogram of the rabbit's mass 10 ml of a solution in *water for injections R* containing 50 mg of the substance to be examined per millilitre.

*———— Ph Eur*

# Liquid Glucose

(*Ph Eur monograph 1330*)

**Action and use**

Excipient.

*Ph Eur ————*

## DEFINITION

Aqueous solution containing a mixture of glucose, oligosaccharides and polysaccharides obtained by hydrolysis of starch.

It contains a minimum of 70.0 per cent dry matter.

The degree of hydrolysis, expressed as dextrose equivalent (DE), is not less than 20 (nominal value).

## CHARACTERS

**Appearance**

Clear, colourless or brown, viscous liquid.

**Solubility**

Miscible with water.

It may partly or totally solidify at room temperature and liquefies again when heated to 50 °C.

## IDENTIFICATION

A. Dissolve 0.1 g in 2.5 ml of *water R* and heat with 2.5 ml of *cupri-tartaric solution R*. A red precipitate is formed.

B. Dip, for 1 s, a suitable stick with a reactive pad containing glucose-oxidase, peroxidase and a hydrogen-donating substance, such as tetramethylbenzidine, in a 5 g/l solution of the substance to be examined. Observe the colour of the reactive pad; within 60 s the colour changes from yellow to green or blue.

C. It is a clear, colourless or brown, viscous liquid, miscible with water. The substance may partly or totally solidify at room temperature and liquefies again when heated to 50 °C.

D. Dextrose equivalent (see Tests).

## TESTS

**Solution S**

Dissolve 25.0 g in *carbon dioxide-free water R* and dilute to 50.0 ml with the same solvent.

**pH** (*2.2.3*)

4.0 to 6.0.

Mix 1 ml of a 223.6 g/l solution of *potassium chloride R* and 30 ml of solution S.

**Sulphur dioxide** (*2.5.29*)

Maximum 20 ppm; maximum 400 ppm if intended for the production of lozenges or pastilles obtained by high boiling techniques, provided that the final product contains maximum 50 ppm of sulphur dioxide.

**Heavy metals** (*2.4.8*)

Maximum 10 ppm.

Dilute 2 ml of solution S to 30 ml with *water R*. The solution complies with test E. Prepare the reference solution using 10 ml of *lead standard solution (1 ppm Pb) R*.

**Loss on drying** (*2.2.32*)

Maximum 30.0 per cent, determined on 1.000 g. Triturate the sample with 3.000 g of *kieselguhr G R*, previously dried at 80 °C under high vacuum for 2 h, and dry at 80 °C under high vacuum for 2 h.

**Sulphated ash** (*2.4.14*)

Maximum 0.5 per cent, determined on 1.0 g.

**Dextrose equivalent (DE)**

Within 10 per cent of the nominal value.

Weigh an amount of the substance to be examined equivalent to 2.85-3.15 g of reducing carbohydrates, calculated as dextrose equivalent, into a 500 ml volumetric flask. Dissolve in *water R* and dilute to 500.0 ml with the same solvent. Transfer the solution to a 50 ml burette. Pipette 25.0 ml of *cupri-tartaric solution R* into a 250 ml flask and add 18.5 ml of the test solution from the burette, mix and add a few glass beads. Place the flask on a hot plate, previously adjusted so that the solution begins to boil after 2 min ± 15 s. Allow to boil for exactly 120 s, add 1 ml of a 1 g/l solution of *methylene blue R* and titrate with the test solution ($V_1$) until the blue colour disappears. Maintain the solution at boiling throughout the titration.

Standardise the cupri-tartaric solution using a 6.00 g/l solution of *glucose R* ($V_0$).

Calculate the dextrose equivalent using the following expression:

$$\frac{300 \times V_0 \times 100}{V_1 \times M \times D}$$

$V_0$ = total volume of glucose standard solution, in millilitres,

$V_1$ = total volume of test solution, in millilitres,

$M$ = mass of the sample, in grams,

$D$ = percentage content of dry matter in the substance.

## LABELLING

The label states the dextrose equivalent (DE) (= nominal value).

*———— Ph Eur*

# Spray-dried Liquid Glucose

(*Glucose, Liquid, Spray-dried,*
*Ph Eur monograph 1525*)

**Action and use**
Excipient.

*Ph Eur*

## DEFINITION

Mixture of glucose, oligosaccharides and polysaccharides, obtained by the partial hydrolysis of starch.

The degree of hydrolysis, expressed as dextrose equivalent (DE), is not less than 20 (nominal value).

## CHARACTERS

**Appearance**
White or almost white, slightly hygroscopic powder or granules.

**Solubility**
Freely soluble in water.

## IDENTIFICATION

A. Dissolve 0.1 g in 2.5 ml of *water R* and heat with 2.5 ml of *cupri-tartaric solution R*. A red precipitate is formed.

B. Dip, for 1 s, a suitable stick with a reactive pad containing glucose-oxidase, peroxidase and a hydrogen-donating substance, such as tetramethylbenzidine, in a 5 g/l solution of the substance to be examined. Observe the colour of the reactive pad; within 60 s the colour changes from yellow to green or blue.

C. It is a powder or granules.

D. Dextrose equivalent (see Tests).

## TESTS

**Solution S**
Dissolve 12.5 g in *carbon dioxide-free water R* and dilute to 50.0 ml with the same solvent.

**pH** (*2.2.3*)
4.0 to 7.0.

Mix 1 ml of a 223.6 g/l solution of *potassium chloride R* and 30 ml of solution S.

**Sulphur dioxide** (*2.5.29*)
Maximum 20 ppm.

**Heavy metals** (*2.4.8*)
Maximum 10 ppm.

Dilute 4 ml of solution S to 30 ml with *water R*. The solution complies with test E. Prepare the reference solution using 10 ml of *lead standard solution (1 ppm Pb) R*.

**Loss on drying** (*2.2.32*)
Maximum 6.0 per cent, determined on 10.00 g by drying in an oven at 105 °C.

**Sulphated ash** (*2.4.14*)
Maximum 0.5 per cent, determined on 1.0 g.

**Dextrose equivalent (DE)**
Within 10 per cent of the nominal value.

Weigh an amount of the substance to be examined equivalent to 2.85-3.15 g of reducing carbohydrates, calculated as dextrose equivalent, into a 500 ml volumetric flask. Dissolve in *water R* and dilute to 500.0 ml with the same solvent. Transfer the solution to a 50 ml burette.

Pipette 25.0 ml of *cupri-tartaric solution R* into a 250 ml flask and add 18.5 ml of the test solution from the burette, mix and add a few glass beads. Place the flask on a hot plate, previously adjusted so that the solution begins to boil after 2 min ± 15 s. Allow to boil for exactly 120 s, add 1 ml of a 1 g/l solution of *methylene blue R* and titrate with the test solution ($V_1$) until the blue colour disappears. Maintain the solution at boiling throughout the titration.

Standardise the cupri-tartaric solution using a 6.00 g/l solution of *glucose R* ($V_0$).

Calculate the dextrose equivalent using the following expression:

$$\frac{300 \times V_0 \times 100}{V_1 \times M \times D}$$

$V_0$ = total volume of glucose standard solution, in millilitres;
$V_1$ = total volume of test solution, in millilitres;
$M$ = mass of the sample, in grams;
$D$ = percentage content of dry matter in the substance.

**Microbial contamination**
TAMC: acceptance criterion $10^3$ CFU/g (*2.6.12*).
TYMC: acceptance criterion $10^2$ CFU/g (*2.6.12*).
Absence of *Escherichia coli* (*2.6.13*).
Absence of *Salmonella* (*2.6.13*).

## LABELLING

The label states the dextrose equivalent (DE) (= nominal value).

## FUNCTIONALITY-RELATED CHARACTERISTICS

*This section provides information on characteristics that are recognised as being relevant control parameters for one or more functions of the substance when used as an excipient (see chapter 5.15). This section is a non-mandatory part of the monograph and it is not necessary to verify the characteristics to demonstrate compliance. Control of these characteristics can however contribute to the quality of a medicinal product by improving the consistency of the manufacturing process and the performance of the medicinal product during use. Where control methods are cited, they are recognised as being suitable for the purpose, but other methods can also be used. Wherever results for a particular characteristic are reported, the control method must be indicated.*

*The following characteristics may be relevant for spray-dried liquid glucose used as filler or binder for wet granulation.*

**Dextrose equivalent** (see Tests).

**Particle-size distribution** (*2.9.31* or *2.9.38*).

*Ph Eur*

# Glutamic Acid

(*Ph Eur monograph 0750*)

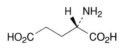

C$_5$H$_9$NO$_4$          147.1          *56-86-0*

**Action and use**
Amino acid.

*Ph Eur*

## DEFINITION

Glutamic acid contains not less than 98.5 per cent and not more than the equivalent of 100.5 per cent of

(2S)-2-aminopentanedioic acid, calculated with reference to the dried substance.

## CHARACTERS

A white or almost white, crystalline powder or colourless crystals, freely soluble in boiling water, slightly soluble in cold water, practically insoluble in acetic acid, in acetone and in alcohol.

## IDENTIFICATION

*First identification* A, B.

*Second identification* A, C, D.

A. It complies with the test for specific optical rotation (see Tests).

B. Examine by infrared absorption spectrophotometry (2.2.24), comparing with the spectrum obtained with *glutamic acid CRS*. Examine the substances prepared as discs. If the spectra obtained show differences, dissolve the substance to be examined and the reference substance separately in the minimum quantity of *water R*, evaporate to dryness at 60 °C and record new spectra using the residues.

C. Examine the chromatograms obtained in the test for ninhydrin-positive substances. The principal spot in the chromatogram obtained with test solution (b) is similar in position, colour and size to the principal spot in the chromatogram obtained with reference solution (a).

D. To 2.0 ml of solution S (see Tests) add 0.1 ml of *phenolphthalein solution R* and 3.0 ml to 3.5 ml of *1 M sodium hydroxide* to change the colour of the indicator to red. Add a mixture of 3 ml of *formaldehyde solution R*, 3 ml of *carbon dioxide-free water R* and 0.1 ml of *phenolphthalein solution R*, to which sufficient *1 M sodium hydroxide* has been added to produce a pink colour. The solution is decolourised. Add *1 M sodium hydroxide* until a red colour is produced. The total volume of *1 M sodium hydroxide* used is 4.0 ml to 4.7 ml.

## TESTS

### Solution S

Dissolve 5.00 g in *1 M hydrochloric acid* with gentle heating, and dilute to 50.0 ml with the same acid.

### Appearance of solution

Solution S is clear (2.2.1) and colourless (*Method II, 2.2.2*).

### Specific optical rotation (2.2.7)

+ 30.5 to + 32.5, determined on solution S and calculated with reference to the dried substance.

### Ninhydrin-positive substances

Examine by thin-layer chromatography (2.2.27), using a *TLC silica gel plate R*.

*Test solution (a)* Dissolve 0.10 g of the substance to be examined in 5 ml of *dilute ammonia R2* and dilute to 10 ml with *water R*.

*Test solution (b)* Dilute 1 ml of test solution (a) to 50 ml with *water R*.

*Reference solution (a)* Dissolve 10 mg of *glutamic acid CRS* in *water R* and dilute to 50 ml with the same solvent.

*Reference solution (b)* Dilute 5 ml of test solution (b) to 20 ml with *water R*.

*Reference solution (c)* Dissolve 10 mg of *glutamic acid CRS* and 10 mg of *aspartic acid CRS* in *water R* and dilute to 25 ml with the same solvent.

Apply to the plate 5 μl of each solution. Dry the plate in a current of air for 15 min. Develop over a path of 15 cm using a mixture of 20 volumes of *glacial acetic acid R*, 20 volumes of *water R* and 60 volumes of *butanol R*. Allow

the plate to dry in air, spray with *ninhydrin solution R* and heat at 100-105 °C for 15 min. Any spot in the chromatogram obtained with test solution (a), apart from the principal spot, is not more intense than the spot in the chromatogram obtained with reference solution (b) (0.5 per cent). The test is not valid unless the chromatogram obtained with reference solution (c) shows 2 clearly separated spots.

### Chlorides (2.4.4)

Dissolve 0.25 g in 3 ml of *dilute nitric acid R* and dilute to 15 ml with *water R*. The solution, to which 1 ml of *water R* is added instead of *dilute nitric acid R*, complies with the limit test for chlorides (200 ppm).

### Sulphates (2.4.13)

Dilute 5 ml of solution S to 15 ml with *distilled water R*. The solution complies with the limit test for sulphates (300 ppm).

### Ammonium (2.4.1)

50 mg complies with limit test B for ammonium (200 ppm). Prepare the standard using 0.1 ml of *ammonium standard solution (100 ppm NH₄) R*.

### Iron (2.4.9)

In a separating funnel, dissolve 1.0 g in 10 ml of *dilute hydrochloric acid R*. Shake with 3 quantities, each of 10 ml, of *methyl isobutyl ketone R1*, shaking for 3 min each time. To the combined organic layers add 10 ml of *water R* and shake for 3 min. The aqueous layer complies with the limit test for iron (10 ppm).

### Heavy metals (2.4.8)

2.0 g complies with limit test D for heavy metals (10 ppm). Prepare the standard using 2 ml of *lead standard solution (10 ppm Pb) R*.

### Loss on drying (2.2.32)

Not more than 0.5 per cent, determined on 1.000 g by drying in an oven at 105 °C.

### Sulphated ash (2.4.14)

Not more than 0.1 per cent, determined on 1.0 g.

## ASSAY

Dissolve 0.130 g in 50 ml of *carbon dioxide-free water R* with gentle heating. Cool. Using 0.1 ml of *bromothymol blue solution R1* as indicator, titrate with *0.1 M sodium hydroxide* until the colour changes from yellow to blue.

1 ml of *0.1 M sodium hydroxide* is equivalent to 14.71 mg of $C_5H_9NO_4$.

## STORAGE

Protected from light.

*Ph Eur*

# Strong Glutaraldehyde Solution

OHC $\diagup\diagdown\diagup$ CHO

| $C_5H_8O_2$ | 100.1 | *111-30-8* |
|---|---|---|
| | | *(anhydrous)* |

## Action and use

Used in treatment of warts.

## Preparation

Glutaraldehyde Solution

## DEFINITION

Strong Glutaraldehyde Solution is an aqueous solution of glutaraldehyde (pentanedial). It contains not less than 47.0% and not more than 53.0% w/w of glutaraldehyde, $C_5H_8O_2$.

## CHARACTERISTICS

A colourless or almost colourless solution.

## IDENTIFICATION

A. Heat 1 ml with 10 ml of a solution containing 1 g of *hydroxylamine hydrochloride* and 2 g of *sodium acetate* in *water* on a water bath for 10 minutes, allow to cool and filter. The *melting point* of the residue, after washing with *water* and drying at 105°, is about 178°, Appendix V A.

B. Add 0.05 ml to 2 ml of *ammoniacal silver nitrate solution* and mix gently for a few minutes. Silver is deposited.

## TESTS

### Acidity

Dilute 10 ml with 10 ml of *carbon dioxide-free water* and titrate with 0.1M *sodium hydroxide VS* using *bromothymol blue solution R3* as indicator. Not more than 5.0 ml of 0.1M *sodium hydroxide VS* is required to change the colour of the solution.

### Clarity and colour of solution

Dilute 1 volume with 4 volumes of *water*. The resulting solution is *clear*, Appendix IV A, and not more intensely coloured than *reference solution $B_6$*, Appendix IV B, Method I.

### Weight per ml

1.126 to 1.134 g, Appendix V G.

## ASSAY

Dissolve 4 g in 100 ml of a 7% w/v solution of *hydroxylamine hydrochloride* previously neutralised to *bromophenol blue solution* with 1M *sodium hydroxide VS* and allow to stand for 30 minutes. Add 20 ml of *petroleum spirit (boiling range, 40° to 60°)* and titrate with 1M *sodium hydroxide VS* until the colour of the aqueous phase matches that of a 7% w/v solution of *hydroxylamine hydrochloride* previously neutralised to *bromophenol blue solution* with 1M *sodium hydroxide VS*. Each ml of 1M *sodium hydroxide VS* is equivalent to 50.05 mg of $C_5H_8O_2$.

## STORAGE

Strong Glutaraldehyde Solution should be stored at a temperature not exceeding 15°.

# Glutathione

*(Ph Eur monograph 1670)*

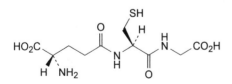

$C_{10}H_{17}N_3O_6S$      307.3      70-18-8

*Ph Eur* _____

## DEFINITION

L-$\gamma$-Glutamyl-L-cysteinylglycine.

Fermentation product.

## Content

98.0 per cent to 101.0 per cent (dried substance).

## CHARACTERS

### Appearance

White or almost white, crystalline powder or colourless crystals.

### Solubility

Freely soluble in water, very slightly soluble in ethanol (96 per cent) and in methylene chloride.

## IDENTIFICATION

A. Specific optical rotation (see Tests).

B. Infrared absorption spectrophotometry (*2.2.24*).

*Comparison*    glutathione CRS.

## TESTS

### Solution S

Dissolve 5.0 g in *distilled water R* and dilute to 50 ml with the same solvent.

### Appearance of solution

Solution S is clear (*2.2.1*) and colourless (*2.2.2, Method II*).

### Specific optical rotation (*2.2.7*)

− 15.5 to − 17.5 (dried substance).

Dissolve 1.0 g in *water R* and dilute to 25.0 ml with the same solvent.

### Related substances

Capillary electrophoresis (*2.2.47*). *Prepare the solutions immediately before use.*

*Internal standard solution (a)*    Dissolve 0.100 g of *phenylalanine R* in the electrolyte solution and dilute to 50.0 ml with the same solution.

*Internal standard solution (b)*    Dilute 10.0 ml of internal standard solution (a) to 100.0 ml with the electrolyte solution.

*Test solution (a)*    Dissolve 0.200 g of the substance to be examined in the electrolyte solution and dilute to 10.0 ml with the same solution.

*Test solution (b)*    Dissolve 0.200 g of the substance to be examined in internal standard solution (b) and dilute to 10.0 ml with the same solution.

*Reference solution (a)*    Dissolve 20.0 mg of the substance to be examined in internal standard solution (a) and dilute to 10.0 ml with the same solution.

*Reference solution (b)*    Dilute 5.0 ml of reference solution (a) to 50.0 ml with the electrolyte solution.

*Reference solution (c)*    Dissolve 0.200 g of the substance to be examined in 5 ml of the electrolyte solution. Add 1.0 ml of internal standard solution (a), 0.5 ml of a 2 mg/ml solution of L-cysteine R (impurity B) in the electrolyte solution, 0.5 ml of a 2 mg/ml solution of oxidised L-glutathione R (impurity C) in the electrolyte solution and 0.5 ml of a 2 mg/ml solution of L-$\gamma$-glutamyl-L-cysteine R (impurity D) in the electrolyte solution. Dilute to 10.0 ml with the electrolyte solution.

*Capillary:*

— *material:* uncoated fused silica;

— *size:* length to the detector cell = 0.5 m; total length = 0.6 m; Ø = 75 µm.

*Temperature*    25 °C.

*Electrolyte solution*    Dissolve 1.50 g of *anhydrous sodium dihydrogen phosphate R* in 230 ml of *water R* and adjust to pH 1.80 with *phosphoric acid R*. Dilute to 250.0 ml with *water R*. Check the pH and, if necessary, adjust with *phosphoric acid R* or *dilute sodium hydroxide solution R*.

*Detection*    Spectrophotometer at 200 nm.

Preconditioning of a new capillary: rinse the new capillary before the first injection with *0.1 M hydrochloric acid* at 138 kPa for 20 min and with *water R* at 138 kPa for 10 min; for complete equilibration, condition the capillary with the electrolyte solution at 350 kPa for 40 min, and subsequently at a voltage of 20 kV for 60 min.

*Preconditioning of the capillary*   Rinse the capillary with the electrolyte solution at 138 kPa for 40 min.

*Between-run rinsing*   Rinse the capillary with *water R* at 138 kPa for 1 min, with *0.1 M sodium hydroxide* at 138 kPa for 2 min, with *water R* at 138 kPa for 1 min, with *0.1 M hydrochloric acid* at 138 kPa for 3 min and with the electrolyte solution at 138 kPa for 10 min.

*Injection*   Test solutions (a) and (b), reference solutions (b) and (c) and the electrolyte solution (blank): under pressure (3.45 kPa) for 5 s.

*Migration*   Apply a voltage of 20 kV.

*Run time*   45 min.

*Relative migration*   With reference to the internal standard (about 14 min): impurity A = about 0.77; impurity B = about 1.04; impurity E = about 1.2; impurity C = about 1.26; impurity D = about 1.3.

*System suitability:*
— *resolution*: minimum 1.5 between the peaks due to the internal standard and impurity B in the chromatogram obtained with reference solution (c); if necessary, increase the pH with *dilute sodium hydroxide solution R*;
— *peak-to-valley ratio*: minimum 2.5, where $H_p$ = height above the baseline of the peak due to impurity D and $H_v$ = height above the baseline of the lowest point of the curve separating this peak from the peak due to glutathione in the chromatogram obtained with reference solution (c); if necessary, lower the pH with *phosphoric acid R*;
— check that in the electropherogram obtained with test solution (a) there is no peak with the same migration time as the internal standard (in such case correct the area of the phenylalanine peak).

*Limits*   Test solution (b):
— *corrected areas*: divide all the peak areas by the corresponding migration times;
— *correction factors*: for the calculation of content, multiply the ratio of time-corrected peak areas of impurity and the internal standard by the corresponding correction factor: impurity B = 3.0; impurity D = 1.4;
— *impurity C:* not more than 1.5 times the ratio of the area of the peak due to glutathione to the area of the peak due to the internal standard in the electropherogram obtained with reference solution (b) (1.5 per cent);
— *impurity D*: not more than the ratio of the area of the peak due to glutathione to the area of the peak due to the internal standard in the electropherogram obtained with reference solution (b) (1.0 per cent);
— *impurities A, B, E*: for each impurity, not more than 0.5 times the ratio of the area of the peak due to glutathione to the area of the peak due to the internal standard in the electropherogram obtained with reference solution (b) (0.5 per cent);
— *any other impurity*: for each impurity, not more than 0.2 times the ratio of the area of the peak due to glutathione to the area of the peak due to the internal standard in the electropherogram obtained with reference solution (b) (0.2 per cent);
— *total*: not more than 2.5 times the ratio of the area of the peak due to glutathione to the area of the peak due to the internal standard in the electropherogram obtained with reference solution (b) (2.5 per cent);
— *disregard limit*: 0.05 times the ratio of the area of the peak due to glutathione to the area of the peak due to the internal standard in the electropherogram obtained with reference solution (b) (0.05 per cent).

**Chlorides** (*2.4.4*)
Maximum 200 ppm.

Dilute 2.5 ml of solution S to 15 ml with *water R*.

**Sulphates** (*2.4.13*)
Maximum 300 ppm.

Dilute 5 ml of solution S to 15 ml with *distilled water R*.

**Ammonium** (*2.4.1, Method B*)
Maximum 200 ppm, determined on 50 mg.

Prepare the standard using 0.1 ml of *ammonium standard solution (100 ppm NH$_4$) R*.

**Iron** (*2.4.9*)
Maximum 10 ppm.

In a separating funnel, dissolve 1.0 g in 10 ml of *dilute hydrochloric acid R*. Shake with 3 quantities, each of 10 ml, of *methyl isobutyl ketone R1*, shaking for 3 min each time. To the combined organic layers, add 10 ml of *water R* and shake for 3 min. The aqueous layer complies with the test.

**Heavy metals** (*2.4.8*)
Maximum 10 ppm.

12 ml of solution S complies with test A. Prepare the reference solution using *lead standard solution (1 ppm Pb) R*.

**Loss on drying** (*2.2.32*)
Maximum 0.5 per cent, determined on 1.000 g by drying in an oven at 105 °C for 3 h.

**Sulphated ash** (*2.4.14*)
Maximum 0.1 per cent, determined on 1.0 g.

**ASSAY**
In a ground-glass-stoppered flask, dissolve 0.500 g of the substance to be examined and 2 g of *potassium iodide R* in 50 ml of *water R*. Cool the solution in iced water and add 10 ml of *hydrochloric acid R1* and 20.0 ml of *0.05 M iodine*. Stopper the flask and allow to stand in the dark for 15 min. Titrate with *0.1 M sodium thiosulphate* using 1 ml of *starch solution R*, added towards the end of the titration, as indicator. Carry out a blank titration.

1 ml of *0.05 M iodine* is equivalent to 30.73 mg of $C_{10}H_{17}N_3O_6S$.

**STORAGE**
Protected from light.

**IMPURITIES**
*Specified impurities*   A, B, C, D, E.

A. L-cysteinylglycine,
B. cysteine,

C. bis(L-γ-glutamyl-L-cysteinylglycine) disulfide (L-glutathione oxidised),

D. L-γ-glutamyl-L-cysteine,

E. unknown structure (product of degradation).

_____ Ph Eur

# Glycerol

Glycerin

(Ph Eur monograph 0496)

C₃H₈O₃        92.1        56-81-5

## Action and use
Lubricant; laxative.

## Preparations
Glycerol Eye Drops

Glycerol Suppositories

_Ph Eur_ _____

## DEFINITION
Propane-1,2,3-triol.

## Content
98.0 per cent _m/m_ to 101.0 per cent _m/m_ (anhydrous substance).

## CHARACTERS
### Aspect
Syrupy liquid, unctuous to the touch, colourless or almost colourless, clear, very hygroscopic.

### Solubility
Miscible with water and with alcohol, slightly soluble in acetone, practically insoluble in fatty oils and in essential oils.

## IDENTIFICATION
_First identification_    A, B.

_Second identification_    A, C, D.

A. It complies with the test for refractive index (see Tests).

B. Infrared absorption spectrophotometry (2.2.24).

_Preparation_    To 5 ml add 1 ml of _water R_ and mix carefully.

_Comparison_    Ph. Eur. reference spectrum of glycerol (85 per cent).

C. Mix 1 ml with 0.5 ml of _nitric acid R_. Superimpose 0.5 ml of _potassium dichromate solution R_. A blue ring develops at the interface of the liquids. Within 10 min, the blue colour does not diffuse into the lower layer.

D. Heat 1 ml with 2 g of _potassium hydrogen sulphate R_ in an evaporating dish. Vapours (acrolein) are evolved which blacken filter paper impregnated with _alkaline potassium tetraiodomercurate solution R_.

## TESTS
### Solution S
Dilute 100.0 g to 200.0 ml with _carbon dioxide-free water R_.

### Appearance of solution
Solution S is clear (2.2.1). Dilute 10 ml of solution S to 25 ml with _water R_. The solution is colourless (2.2.2, Method II).

### Acidity or alkalinity
To 50 ml of solution S add 0.5 ml of _phenolphthalein solution R_. The solution is colourless. Not more than 0.2 ml of _0.1 M sodium hydroxide_ is required to change the colour of the indicator to pink.

### Refractive index (2.2.6)
1.470 to 1.475.

### Aldehydes
Maximum 10 ppm.

Place 7.5 ml of solution S in a ground-glass-stoppered flask and add 7.5 ml of _water R_ and 1.0 ml of _decolorised pararosaniline solution R_. Close the flask and allow to stand for 1 h at a temperature of 25 ± 1 °C. The absorbance (2.2.25) of the solution measured at 552 nm is not greater than that of a standard prepared at the same time and in the same manner using 7.5 ml of _formaldehyde standard solution (5 ppm CH₂O) R_ and 7.5 ml of _water R_. The test is not valid unless the standard is pink.

### Esters
Add 10.0 ml of _0.1 M sodium hydroxide_ to the final solution obtained in the test for acidity or alkalinity. Boil under a reflux condenser for 5 min. Cool. Add 0.5 ml of _phenolphthalein solution R_ and titrate with _0.1 M hydrochloric acid_. Not less than 8.0 ml of _0.1 M hydrochloric acid_ is required to change the colour of the indicator.

### Impurity A and related substances
Gas chromatography (2.2.28).

_Test solution_    Dilute 10.0 ml of solution S to 100.0 ml with _water R_.

_Reference solution (a)_    Dilute 10.0 g of _glycerol R1_ to 20.0 ml with _water R_. Dilute 10.0 ml of the solution to 100.0 ml with _water R_.

_Reference solution (b)_    Dissolve 1.000 g of _diethylene glycol R_ in _water R_ and dilute to 100.0 ml with the same solvent.

_Reference solution (c)_    Dilute 1.0 ml of reference solution (b) to 10.0 ml with reference solution (a). Dilute 1.0 ml of this solution to 20.0 ml with reference solution (a).

_Reference solution (d)_    Mix 1.0 ml of the test solution and 5.0 ml of reference solution (b) and dilute to 100.0 ml with _water R_. Dilute 1.0 ml of this solution to 10.0 ml with _water R_.

_Reference solution (e)_    Dilute 5.0 ml of reference solution (b) to 100.0 ml with _water R_.

_Column:_
— _size: l_ = 30 m, Ø = 0.53 mm,

— *stationary phase*: 6 per cent polycyanopropylphenyl siloxane and 94 per cent of polydimethylsiloxane.

*Carrier gas* *helium for chromatography R.*

*Split ratio* 1:10.

*Linear velocity* 38 cm/s.

*Temperature:*

|  | Time (min) | Temperature (°C) |
|---|---|---|
| Column | 0 | 100 |
|  | 0 - 16 | 100 → 220 |
|  | 16 - 20 | 220 |
| Injection port |  | 220 |
| Detector |  | 250 |

*Detection* Flame ionisation.

*Injection* 0.5 µl.

*Elution order* Impurity A, glycerol.

*System suitability* Reference solution (d):
— *resolution*: minimum 7.0 between the peaks due to impurity A and glycerol.

*Limits:*
— *impurity A*: not more than the area of the corresponding peak in the chromatogram obtained with reference solution (c) (0.1 per cent),
— *any other impurity with a retention time less than the retention time of glycerol*: not more than the area of the peak due to impurity A in the chromatogram obtained with reference solution (c) (0.1 per cent),
— *total of all impurities with retention times greater than the retention time of glycerol*: not more than 5 times the area of the peak due to impurity A in the chromatogram obtained with reference solution (c) (0.5 per cent),
— *disregard limit*: 0.05 times the area of the peak due to impurity A in the chromatogram obtained with reference solution (e) (0.05 per cent).

**Halogenated compounds**
Maximum 35 ppm.

To 10 ml of solution S add 1 ml of *dilute sodium hydroxide solution R*, 5 ml of *water R* and 50 mg of *halogen-free nickel-aluminium alloy R*. Heat on a water-bath for 10 min, allow to cool and filter. Rinse the flask and the filter with *water R* until 25 ml of filtrate is obtained. To 5 ml of the filtrate add 4 ml of *alcohol R*, 2.5 ml of *water R*, 0.5 ml of *nitric acid R* and 0.05 ml of *silver nitrate solution R2* and mix. Allow to stand for 2 min. Any opalescence in the solution is not more intense than that in a standard prepared at the same time by mixing 7.0 ml of *chloride standard solution (5 ppm Cl) R*, 4 ml of *alcohol R*, 0.5 ml of *water R*, 0.5 ml of *nitric acid R* and 0.05 ml of *silver nitrate solution R2*.

**Sugars**
To 10 ml of solution S add 1 ml of *dilute sulphuric acid R* and heat on a water-bath for 5 min. Add 3 ml of *carbonate-free dilute sodium hydroxide solution R* (prepared by the method described for carbonate-free *1 M sodium hydroxide* (4.2.2)), mix and add dropwise 1 ml of freshly prepared *copper sulphate solution R*. The solution is clear and blue. Continue heating on the water-bath for 5 min. The solution remains blue and no precipitate is formed.

**Chlorides** (*2.4.4*)
Maximum 10 ppm.

1 ml of solution S diluted to 15 ml with *water R* complies with the limit test for chlorides. Prepare the standard using 1 ml of *chloride standard solution (5 ppm Cl) R* diluted to 15 ml with *water R*.

**Heavy metals** (*2.4.8*)
Maximum 5 ppm.

Dilute 8 ml of solution S to 20 ml with *water R*. 12 ml of the solution complies with limit test A. Prepare the standard using *lead standard solution (1 ppm Pb) R*.

**Water** (*2.5.12*)
Maximum 2.0 per cent, determined on 1.000 g.

**Sulphated ash** (*2.4.14*)
Maximum 0.01 per cent, determined on 5.0 g after heating to boiling and ignition.

**ASSAY**
Thoroughly mix 0.075 g with 45 ml of *water R*. Add 25.0 ml of a mixture of 1 volume of *0.1 M sulphuric acid* and 20 volumes of *0.1 M sodium periodate*. Allow to stand protected from light for 15 min. Add 5.0 ml of a 500 g/l solution of *ethylene glycol R* and allow to stand protected from light for 20 min. Using 0.5 ml of *phenolphthalein solution R* as indicator, titrate with *0.1 M sodium hydroxide*. Carry out a blank titration.

1 ml of *0.1 M sodium hydroxide* is equivalent to 9.21 mg of $C_3H_8O_3$.

**STORAGE**
In an airtight container.

**IMPURITIES**

A. 2,2'-oxydiethanol (diethylene glycol),

B. ethane-1,2-diol (ethylene glycol),

C. propylene glycol.

_____ *Ph Eur*

# Glycerol (85 per cent)

(*Ph Eur monograph 0497*)

*Ph Eur* _____

**DEFINITION**
Aqueous solution of propane-1,2,3-triol.

**Content**
83.5 per cent *m/m* to 88.5 per cent *m/m* of propane-1,2,3-triol ($C_3H_8O_3$; $M_r$ 92.1).

**CHARACTERS**
**Aspect**
Syrupy liquid, unctuous to the touch, colourless or almost colourless, clear, very hygroscopic.

**Solubility**
Miscible with water and with alcohol, slightly soluble in acetone, practically insoluble in fatty oils and in essential oils.

**IDENTIFICATION**
*First identification* A, B.

*Second identification* A, C, D.

A. It complies with the test for refractive index (see Tests).

B. Infrared absorption spectrophotometry (*2.2.24*).

*Comparison* Ph. Eur. reference spectrum of glycerol *(85 per cent).*

C. Mix 1 ml with 0.5 ml of *nitric acid R.* Superimpose 0.5 ml of *potassium dichromate solution R.* A blue ring develops at the interface of the liquids. Within 10 min, the blue colour does not diffuse into the lower layer.

D. Heat 1 ml with 2 g of *potassium hydrogen sulphate R* in an evaporating dish. Vapours (acrolein) are evolved which blacken filter paper impregnated with *alkaline potassium tetraiodomercurate solution R.*

## TESTS

### Solution S
Dilute 117.6 g to 200.0 ml with *carbon dioxide-free water R.*

### Appearance of solution
Solution S is clear *(2.2.1).* Dilute 10 ml of solution S to 25 ml with *water R.* The solution is colourless *(2.2.2, Method II).*

### Acidity or alkalinity
To 50 ml of solution S add 0.5 ml of *phenolphthalein solution R.* The solution is colourless. Not more than 0.2 ml of *0.1 M sodium hydroxide* is required to change the colour of the indicator to pink.

### Refractive index *(2.2.6)*
1.449 to 1.455.

### Aldehydes
Maximum 10 ppm.

Place 7.5 ml of solution S in a ground-glass-stoppered flask and add 7.5 ml of *water R* and 1.0 ml of *decolorised pararosaniline solution R.* Close the flask and allow to stand for 1 h at a temperature of 25 ± 1 °C. The absorbance *(2.2.25)* of the solution measured at 552 nm is not greater than that of a standard prepared at the same time and in the same manner using 7.5 ml of *formaldehyde standard solution (5 ppm CH₂O) R* and 7.5 ml of *water R.* The test is not valid unless the standard is pink.

### Esters
Add 10.0 ml of *0.1 M sodium hydroxide* to the final solution obtained in the test for acidity or alkalinity. Boil under a reflux condenser for 5 min. Cool. Add 0.5 ml of *phenolphthalein solution R* and titrate with *0.1 M hydrochloric acid.* Not less than 8.0 ml of *0.1 M hydrochloric acid* is required to change the colour of the indicator.

### Impurity A and related substances
Gas chromatography *(2.2.28).*

*Test solution* Dilute 10.0 ml of solution S to 100.0 ml with *water R.*

*Reference solution (a)* Dilute 11.8 g of *glycerol (85 per cent) R1* to 20.0 ml with *water R.* Dilute 10.0 ml of the solution to 100.0 ml with water R.

*Reference solution (b)* Dissolve 1.000 g of *diethylene glycol R* in *water R* and dilute to 100.0 ml with the same solvent.

*Reference solution (c)* Dilute 1.0 ml of reference solution (b) to 10.0 ml with reference solution (a). Dilute 1.0 ml of this solution to 20.0 ml with reference solution (a).

*Reference solution (d)* Mix 1.0 ml of the test solution and 5.0 ml of reference solution (b) and dilute to 100.0 ml with *water R.* Dilute 1.0 ml of this solution to 10.0 ml with *water R.*

*Reference solution (e)* Dilute 5.0 ml of reference solution (b) to 100.0 ml with *water R.*

*Column:*
— *size: l =* 30 m, Ø = 0.53 mm,
— *stationary phase*: 6 per cent polycyanolpropylphenyl siloxane and 94 per cent of polydimethylsiloxane.

*Carrier gas* helium for chromatography R.

*Split ratio* 1:10.

*Linear velocity* 38 cm/s.

*Temperature:*

|  | Time (min) | Temperature (°C) |
|---|---|---|
| Column | 0 | 100 |
|  | 0 - 16 | 100 → 220 |
|  | 16 - 20 | 220 |
| Injection port |  | 220 |
| Detector |  | 250 |

*Detection* Flame ionisation.

*Injection* 0.5 μl.

*Elution order* Impurity A, glycerol.

*System suitability* Reference solution (d):
— *resolution*: minimum 7.0 between the peaks due to impurity A and glycerol.

*Limits:*
— *impurity A*: not more than the area of the corresponding peak in the chromatogram obtained with reference solution (c) (0.1 per cent),
— *any other impurity with a retention time less than the retention time of glycerol*: not more than the area of the peak due to impurity A in the chromatogram obtained with reference solution (c) (0.1 per cent),
— *total of all impurities with retention times greater than the retention time of glycerol*: not more than 5 times the area of the peak due to impurity A in the chromatogram obtained with reference solution (c) (0.5 per cent),
— *disregard limit*: 0.05 times the area of the peak due to impurity A in the chromatogram obtained with reference solution (e) (0.05 per cent).

### Halogenated compounds
Maximum 30 ppm.

To 10 ml of solution S add 1 ml of *dilute sodium hydroxide solution R,* 5 ml of *water R* and 50 mg of *halogen-free nickel-aluminium alloy R.* Heat on a water-bath for 10 min, allow to cool and filter. Rinse the flask and the filter with *water R* until 25 ml of filtrate is obtained. To 5 ml of the filtrate add 4 ml of *alcohol R,* 2.5 ml of *water R,* 0.5 ml of *nitric acid R* and 0.05 ml of *silver nitrate solution R2* and mix. Allow to stand for 2 min. Any opalescence in the solution is not more intense than that in a standard prepared at the same time by mixing 7.0 ml of *chloride standard solution (5 ppm Cl) R,* 4 ml of *alcohol R,* 0.5 ml of *water R,* 0.5 ml of *nitric acid R* and 0.05 ml of *silver nitrate solution R2.*

### Sugars
To 10 ml of solution S add 1 ml of *dilute sulphuric acid R* and heat on a water-bath for 5 min. Add 3 ml of *carbonate-free dilute sodium hydroxide solution R* (prepared by the method described for carbonate-free *1 M sodium hydroxide (4.2.2)),* mix and add dropwise 1 ml of freshly prepared *copper sulphate solution R.* The solution is clear and blue. Continue heating on the water-bath for 5 min. The solution remains blue and no precipitate is formed.

### Chlorides *(2.4.4)*
Maximum 10 ppm.

1 ml of solution S diluted to 15 ml with *water R* complies with the limit test for chlorides. Prepare the standard using

1 ml of *chloride standard solution (5 ppm Cl) R* diluted to 15 ml with *water R*.

**Heavy metals** (*2.4.8*)

Maximum 5 ppm.

Dilute 8 ml of solution S to 20 ml with *water R*. 12 ml of the solution complies with limit test A. Prepare the standard using *lead standard solution (1 ppm Pb) R*.

**Water** (*2.5.12*)

12.0 per cent to 16.0 per cent, determined on 0.200 g.

**Sulphated ash** (*2.4.14*)

Maximum 0.01 per cent, determined on 5.0 g after heating to boiling and ignition.

**ASSAY**

Thoroughly mix 0.075 g with 45 ml of *water R*. Add 25.0 ml of a mixture of 1 volume of *0.1 M sulphuric acid* and 20 volumes of *0.1 M sodium periodate*. Allow to stand protected from light for 15 min. Add 5.0 ml of a 500 g/l solution of *ethylene glycol R* and allow to stand protected from light for 20 min. Using 0.5 ml of *phenolphthalein solution R* as indicator, titrate with *0.1 M sodium hydroxide*. Carry out a blank titration.

1 ml of *0.1 M sodium hydroxide* is equivalent to 9.21 mg of $C_3H_8O_3$.

**STORAGE**

In an airtight container.

**IMPURITIES**

A. 2,2′-oxydiethanol (diethylene glycol),

B. ethane-1,2-diol (ethylene glycol),

C. propylene glycol.

*Ph Eur*

# Glycerol Dibehenate

(*Ph Eur monograph 1427*)

**Action and use**

Excipient.

*Ph Eur*

**DEFINITION**

Mixture of diacylglycerols, mainly dibehenylglycerol, together with variable quantities of mono- and triacylglycerols, obtained by esterification of *glycerol (0496)* with behenic (docosanoic) acid.

**Content:**
— *monoacylglycerols*: 15.0 per cent to 23.0 per cent,
— *diacylglycerols*: 40.0 per cent to 60.0 per cent,
— *triacylglycerols*: 21.0 per cent to 35.0 per cent.

**CHARACTERS**

**Appearance**

Hard, waxy mass or powder or white or almost white, unctuous flakes.

**Solubility**

Practically insoluble in water, soluble in methylene chloride, partly soluble in hot ethanol (96 per cent).

**IDENTIFICATION**

A. Melting point (*2.2.14*): 65 °C to 77 °C.

B. Thin-layer chromatography (*2.2.27*).

*Test solution* Dissolve 1.0 g of the substance to be examined in *toluene R* with gentle heating and dilute to 20 ml with the same solvent.

*Reference solution* Dissolve 1.0 g of *glycerol dibehenate CRS* in *toluene R* with gentle heating and dilute to 20 ml with the same solvent.

*Plate* TLC silica gel plate R.

*Mobile phase* hexane R, ether R (30:70 V/V).

*Application* 10 µl.

*Development* Over a path of 15 cm.

*Drying* In air.

*Detection* Spray with a 0.1 g/l solution of *rhodamine B R* in *ethanol (96 per cent) R*; examine in ultraviolet light at 365 nm.

*Results* The spots in the chromatogram obtained with the test solution are similar in position to the spots in the chromatogram obtained with the reference solution.

C. Composition of fatty acids (see Tests).

**TESTS**

**Acid value** (*2.5.1*)

Maximum 4.0, determined on 1.0 g, using a mixture of equal volumes of *ethanol (96 per cent) R* and *toluene R* as solvent and with gentle heating.

**Iodine value** (*2.5.4, Method A*)

Maximum 3.0.

**Saponification value** (*2.5.6*)

145 to 165.

Carry out the titration with heating.

**Free glycerol**

Maximum 1.0 per cent, determined as described under Assay.

**Composition of fatty acids** (*2.4.22, Method C*)

Raise the temperature of the column to 240 °C and use the mixture of calibrating substances in Table 2.4.22.-3.

*Composition of the fatty acid fraction of the substance:*
— *palmitic acid*: maximum 3.0 per cent;
— *stearic acid*: maximum 5.0 per cent;
— *arachidic acid*: maximum 10.0 per cent;
— *behenic acid*: minimum 83.0 per cent;
— *erucic acid*: maximum 3.0 per cent;
— *lignoceric acid*: maximum 3.0 per cent.

**Nickel** (*2.4.31*)

Maximum 1 ppm.

**Water** (*2.5.12*)

Maximum 1.0 per cent, determined on 1.00 g. Use *pyridine R* as the solvent.

**Total ash** (*2.4.16*)

Maximum 0.1 per cent, determined on 1.00 g.

**ASSAY**

Size-exclusion chromatography (*2.2.30*).

*Stock solution* Place 0.100 g of *glycerol R* in a flask and dilute to 25.0 ml with *tetrahydrofuran R*.

*Test solution* In a 15 ml flask, weigh 0.2 g (*m*) of the substance to be examined. Add 5.0 ml of *tetrahydrofuran R* and shake to dissolve. Heat gently, at about 35 °C. Reweigh the flask and calculate the total mass of solvent and substance (*M*).

*Reference solutions*  Into four 15 ml flasks, introduce respectively 0.25 ml, 0.5 ml, 1.0 ml and 2.5 ml of the stock solution and add 5.0 ml of *tetrahydrofuran R*. Weigh each flask and calculate the concentration of glycerol in milligrams per gram of each reference solution.

*Column:*
— *size*: $l = 0.6$ m, Ø = 7 mm;
— *stationary phase*: *styrene-divinylbenzene copolymer R* (5 µm) with a pore size of 10 nm.

*Mobile phase*  *tetrahydrofuran R*.

*Flow rate*  1 ml/min.

*Detection*  Differential refractive index.

*Injection*  40 µl; when injecting the test solution, maintain the flask at about 35 °C to avoid precipitation.

*Relative retention*  With reference to glycerol (retention time = about 15 min):
triacylglycerols = about 0.73; diacylglycerols = about 0.76; monoacylglycerols = about 0.82.

*Calculations:*
— *free glycerol*: from the calibration curve obtained with the reference solutions, determine the concentration (*C*) in milligrams per gram in the test solution and calculate the percentage content in the substance to be examined using the following expression:

$$\frac{C \times M}{m \times 10}$$

— *monoacylglycerols*: calculate the percentage content of monoacylglycerols using the following expression:

$$A - D$$

*A* = percentage content of monoacylglycerols determined by the normalisation procedure,
*D* = percentage content of free fatty acids.

Calculate the percentage content of free fatty acids using the following expression:

$$\frac{I_A \times 340}{561.1}$$

$I_A$ = acid value.
— *diacylglycerols, triacylglycerols*: determine the percentage content of each by the normalisation procedure.

_____ *Ph Eur*

# Glycerol Distearate

*(Ph Eur monograph 1428)*

★ ★ ★
★      ★
★      ★
★ ★ ★

**Action and use**
Excipient.

*Ph Eur* _____

## DEFINITION
Mixture of diacylglycerols, mainly distearoylglycerol, together with variable quantities of mono- and triacylglycerols. It is obtained by partial glycerolysis of vegetable oils containing triacylglycerols of palmitic (hexadecanoic) or stearic (octadecanoic) acid or by esterification of glycerol with stearic acid. The fatty acids may be of vegetable or animal origin.

**Content:**
— *monoacylglycerols*: 8.0 per cent to 22.0 per cent;
— *diacylglycerols*: 40.0 per cent to 60.0 per cent;
— *triacylglycerols*: 25.0 per cent to 35.0 per cent.

## CHARACTERS
**Appearance**
Hard, waxy mass or powder, or white or almost white, unctuous flakes.

**Solubility**
Practically insoluble in water, soluble in methylene chloride, partly soluble in hot ethanol (96 per cent).

## IDENTIFICATION
*First identification*  C, D.

*Second identification*  A, B.

A. Melting point (*2.2.14*): 50 °C to 60 °C (types I and II), 50 °C to 70 °C (type III).

B. Thin-layer chromatography (*2.2.27*).

*Test solution*  Dissolve 0.5 g of the substance to be examined in *methylene chloride R*, with gentle heating, and dilute to 10 ml with the same solvent.

*Reference solution*  Dissolve 0.5 g of *glycerol distearate CRS* in *methylene chloride R*, with gentle heating, and dilute to 10 ml with the same solvent.

*Plate*  TLC silica gel plate R.

*Mobile phase*  *hexane R*, *ether R* (30:70 *V/V*).

*Application*  10 µl.

*Development*  Over a path of 15 cm.

*Detection*  Spray with a 0.1 g/l solution of *rhodamine B R* in *ethanol (96 per cent) R* and examine in ultraviolet light at 365 nm.

*System suitability*  Reference solution:
— the chromatogram shows 4 clearly separated spots.

*Results*  The spots in the chromatogram obtained with the test solution are similar in position to those in the chromatogram obtained with the reference solution.

C. Composition of fatty acids (see Tests) according to the type stated on the label.

D. It complies with the limits of the assay (diacylglycerol content).

## TESTS
**Acid value** (*2.5.1*)
Maximum 6.0, determined on 1.0 g.

Use a mixture of equal volumes of *ethanol (96 per cent) R* and *toluene R* as solvent and heat gently.

**Iodine value** (*2.5.4, Method A*)
Maximum 3.0.

**Saponification value** (*2.5.6*)
165 to 195, determined on 2.0 g. Carry out the titration with heating.

**Free glycerol**
Maximum 1.0 per cent, determined as described under Assay.

**Composition of fatty acids** (*2.4.22, Method C*)
Use the mixture of calibrating substances in Table 2.4.22.-1.

*Composition of the fatty-acid fraction of the substance:*

| Glycerol distearate | Composition of fatty acids |
|---|---|
| Type I | *Stearic acid*: 40.0 per cent to 60.0 per cent |
| | *Sum of the contents of palmitic and stearic acids*: minimum 90.0 per cent |
| Type II | *Stearic acid*: 60.0 per cent to 80.0 per cent |
| | *Sum of the contents of palmitic and stearic acids*: minimum 90.0 per cent |
| Type III | *Stearic acid*: 80.0 per cent to 99.0 per cent |
| | *Sum of the contents of palmitic and stearic acids*: minimum 96.0 per cent |

**Nickel** (*2.4.31*)
Maximum 1 ppm.

**Water** (*2.5.12*)
Maximum 1.0 per cent, determined on 1.00 g. Use *pyridine R* as the solvent.

**Total ash** (*2.4.16*)
Maximum 0.1 per cent.

## ASSAY

Size-exclusion chromatography (*2.2.30*).

*Test solution*   Into a 15 ml flask, weigh 0.200 g (*m*). Add 5.0 ml of *tetrahydrofuran R* and shake to dissolve. Reweigh the flask and calculate the total mass of solvent and substance (*M*).

*Reference solutions*   Into three 15 ml flasks, respectively weigh 2.0 mg, 5.0 mg and 10.0 mg of *glycerol R* and add 5.0 ml of *tetrahydrofuran R* to each flask. Into a 4th flask, weigh about 2.0 mg of *glycerol R* and add 10.0 ml of *tetrahydrofuran R*. Weigh the flasks again and calculate the concentration of glycerol in milligrams per gram for each reference solution.

*Column:*
— *size*: $l$ = 0.6 m, Ø = 7 mm;
— *stationary phase*: *styrene-divinylbenzene copolymer R* (5 μm) with a pore size of 10 nm.

*Mobile phase*   *tetrahydrofuran R*.

*Flow rate*   1 ml/min.

*Detection*   Differential refractometer.

*Injection*   40 μl.

*Relative retention*   With reference to glycerol (retention time = about 15 min):
triacylglycerols = about 0.75; diacylglycerols = about 0.80; monoacylglycerols = about 0.85.

*Calculations:*
— *free glycerol* : from the calibration curve obtained with the reference solutions, determine the concentration (*C*) in milligrams per gram in the test solution and calculate the percentage content in the substance to be examined using the following expression:

$$\frac{C \times M}{m \times 10}$$

— *mono-, di- and triacylglycerols*: calculate the percentage contents by the normalisation procedure.

## LABELLING

The label states the type of glycerol distearate.

_____ *Ph Eur*

# Glycerol Monocaprylate

(*Ph Eur monograph 2213*)

*Ph Eur* _____

## DEFINITION

Mixture of monoacylglycerols, mainly mono-*O*-octanoylglycerol, containing variable quantities of di- and triacylglycerols, obtained by direct esterification of glycerol with caprylic (octanoic) acid, followed by a distillation step in the case of glycerol monocaprylate (type II).

**Content:**
— *glycerol monocaprylate (type I):*
  — *monoacylglycerols*: 45.0 per cent to 75.0 per cent;
  — *diacylglycerols*: 20.0 per cent to 50.0 per cent;
  — *triacylglycerols*: maximum 10.0 per cent;
— *glycerol monocaprylate (type II):*
  — *monoacylglycerols*: minimum 80.0 per cent;
  — *diacylglycerols*: maximum 20.0 per cent;
  — *triacylglycerols*: maximum 5.0 per cent.

## CHARACTERS

**Appearance**
Colourless or slightly yellow, oily liquid or soft mass.

**Solubility**
Practically insoluble in water, very soluble in ethanol (96 per cent) and freely soluble in methylene chloride.

## IDENTIFICATION

A. Composition of fatty acids (see Tests).

B. It complies with the limits of the assay (monoacylglycerols).

## TESTS

**Acid value** (*2.5.1*)
Maximum 3.0.

**Composition of fatty acids** (*2.4.22, Method C*)
Use the mixture of calibrating substances in Table 2.4.22.-2.

*Composition of the fatty acid fraction of the substance:*
— *caproic acid*: maximum 1.0 per cent;
— *caprylic acid*: minimum 90.0 per cent;
— *capric acid*: maximum 10.0 per cent;
— *lauric acid*: maximum 1.0 per cent;
— *myristic acid*: maximum 0.5 per cent.

**Free glycerol**
Maximum 3.0 per cent.

Dissolve 1.20 g in 25.0 ml of *methylene chloride R*. Heat to about 50 °C then allow to cool. Add 100 ml of *water R*. Shake and add 25.0 ml of periodic *acetic acid solution R*. Shake again and allow to stand for 30 min. Add 40 ml of a 75 g/l solution of *potassium iodide R* and allow to stand for 1 min. Add 1 ml of *starch solution R*. Titrate with *0.1 M sodium thiosulfate* until the aqueous phase becomes colourless. Carry out a blank titration.

1 ml of *0.1 M sodium thiosulfate* is equivalent to 2.3 mg of glycerol.

**Water** (*2.5.12*)
Maximum 1.0 per cent, determined on 1.00 g.

**Total ash** (*2.4.16*)
Maximum 0.5 per cent.

## ASSAY

Gas chromatography (2.2.28)   Use the normalisation procedure.

*Test solution*   To 0.25 g of the substance to be examined, add 5.0 ml of *tetrahydrofuran R* and shake to dissolve.

*Reference solution (a)* To 0.25 g of *glycerol monocaprylate CRS*, add 5.0 ml of *tetrahydrofuran R* and shake to dissolve.

*Reference solution (b)* To 50 mg of *glycerol 1-octanoate R* and 50 mg of *glycerol 1-decanoate R*, add 2.5 ml of *tetrahydrofuran R* and shake to dissolve.

*Column:*
— *size: l* = 10 m, Ø = 0.32 mm;
— *stationary phase: poly(dimethyl)(diphenyl)siloxane R* (film thickness 0.1 μm).

*Carrier gas* helium for chromatography R.

*Flow rate* 2.3 ml/min.

*Split ratio* 1:50.

*Temperature:*

|  | Time (min) | Temperature (°C) |
|---|---|---|
| Column | 0 - 3 | 60 |
|  | 3 - 38 | 60 → 340 |
|  | 38 - 50 | 340 |
| Injection port |  | 350 |
| Detector |  | 370 |

*Detection* Flame ionisation.

*Injection* 1 μl.

*Identification of peaks* Use the chromatogram supplied with *glycerol monocaprylate CRS* and the chromatogram obtained with reference solution (a) to identify the peaks due to mono-, di- and triacylglycerols.

*System suitability* Reference solution (b):
— *resolution:* minimum 5 between the peaks due to glycerol 1-octanoate and glycerol 1-decanoate.

For the calculation of the contents of mono-, di- and triacylglycerols, disregard the peaks with a retention time less than that of the monoacylglycerols, which are due to impurities of the solvent and to the free fatty acids.

Calculate the percentage content of free fatty acids (C) using the following expression:

$$\frac{I_A \times 144}{561.1}$$

$I_A$ = acid value of glycerol monocaprylate.

Calculate the content of mono-, di- and triacylglycerols using the following equations:

$$\text{Monoacylglycerols content} = \frac{X \times (100 - A - B - C)}{100}$$

$$\text{Diacylglycerols content} = \frac{Y \times (100 - A - B - C)}{100}$$

$$\text{Triacylglycerols content} = \frac{Z \times (100 - A - B - C)}{100}$$

$A$ = percentage content of free glycerol (see Tests);
$B$ = percentage content of water;
$X$ = monoacylglycerols content obtained by normalisation;
$Y$ = diacylglycerols content obtained by normalisation;
$Z$ = triacylglycerols content obtained by normalisation.

## LABELLING

The label states the type of glycerol monocaprylate (type I or II).

*Ph Eur*

# Glycerol Monocaprylocaprate

*(Ph Eur monograph 2392)*

*Ph Eur*

## DEFINITION

Mixture of monoacylglycerols, mainly mono-*O*-octanoylglycerol and mono-*O*-decanoylglycerol, containing variable quantities of di- and triacylglycerols, obtained by direct esterification of glycerol with caprylic (octanoic) and capric (decanoic) acids, followed by a distillation step in the case of glycerol monocaprylocaprate (type II).

*Content:*
— *glycerol monocaprylocaprate (type I):*
    — *monoacylglycerols:* 45.0 per cent to 75.0 per cent;
    — *diacylglycerols:* 20.0 per cent to 50.0 per cent;
    — *triacylglycerols:* maximum 10.0 per cent;
— *glycerol monocaprylocaprate (type II):*
    — *monoacylglycerols:* minimum 80.0 per cent;
    — *diacylglycerols:* maximum 20.0 per cent;
    — *triacylglycerols:* maximum 5.0 per cent.

## CHARACTERS

### Appearance

Colourless or slightly yellow, oily liquid or soft mass.

### Solubility

Practically insoluble in water, very soluble in ethanol (96 per cent) and freely soluble in methylene chloride.

## IDENTIFICATION

A. Composition of fatty acids (see Tests).

B. It complies with the limits of the assay (monoacylglycerols).

## TESTS

**Acid value** *(2.5.1)*
Maximum 3.0.

**Composition of fatty acids** *(2.4.22, Method C)*
Use the mixture of calibrating substances in Table 2.4.22.-2.

*Composition of the fatty acid fraction of the substance:*
— *caproic acid:* maximum 3.0 per cent;
— *caprylic acid:* 50.0 per cent to 90.0 per cent;
— *capric acid:* 10.0 per cent to 50.0 per cent;
— *lauric acid:* maximum 3.0 per cent;
— *myristic acid:* maximum 1.0 per cent.

**Free glycerol**
Maximum 3.0 per cent.

Dissolve 1.20 g in 25.0 ml of *methylene chloride R*. Heat to about 50 °C and allow to cool. Add 100 ml of *water R*, shake and add 25.0 ml of *periodic acetic acid solution R*. Shake again and allow to stand for 30 min. Add 40 ml of a 75 g/l solution of *potassium iodide R* and allow to stand for 1 min. Add 1 ml of *starch solution R*. Titrate with *0.1 M sodium thiosulphate* until the aqueous phase becomes colourless. Carry out a blank titration.

1 ml of *0.1 M sodium thiosulphate* is equivalent to 2.3 mg of glycerol.

**Water** *(2.5.12)*
Maximum 0.5 per cent, determined on 1.00 g.

**Total ash** (2.4.16)
Maximum 0.5 per cent.

## ASSAY

*Gas chromatography* (2.2.28)   Use the normalisation procedure.

*Test solution*   To 0.25 g of the substance to be examined, add 5.0 ml of *tetrahydrofuran R* and shake to dissolve.

*Reference solution (a)*   To 0.25 g of *glycerol monocaprylocaprate CRS*, add 5.0 ml of *tetrahydrofuran R* and shake to dissolve.

*Reference solution (b)*   To 50 mg of *glycerol 1-octanoate R* and 50 mg of *glycerol 1-decanoate R*, add 2.5 ml of *tetrahydrofuran R* and shake to dissolve.

*Column:*
— *size: l* = 10 m, Ø = 0.32 mm;
— *stationary phase:* poly(dimethyl)(diphenyl)siloxane R (film thickness 0.1 μm).

*Carrier gas*   helium for chromatography R.

*Flow rate*   2.3 ml/min.

*Split ratio*   1:50.

*Temperature:*

|  | Time (min) | Temperature (°C) |
|---|---|---|
| Column | 0 - 3 | 60 |
|  | 3 - 38 | 60 → 340 |
|  | 38 - 50 | 340 |
| Injection port |  | 350 |
| Detector |  | 370 |

*Detection*   Flame ionisation.

*Injection*   1 μl.

*Identification of peaks*   Use the chromatogram supplied with *glycerol monocaprylocaprate CRS* and the chromatogram obtained with reference solution (a) to identify the peaks due to mono-, di- and triacylglycerols.

*System suitability*   Reference solution (b):
— *resolution*: minimum 5 between the peaks due to glycerol 1-octanoate and glycerol 1-decanoate.

For the calculation of the contents of mono-, di- and triacylglycerols, disregard the peaks with a retention time less than that of the monoacylglycerols, which are due to the impurities of the solvent and to the free fatty acids.

Calculate the percentage content of free fatty acids *(C)* using the following equations:

$$\frac{I_A \times 144}{561.1}$$

$I_A$ = acid value of the glycerol monocaprylocaprate.

Calculate the content of mono-, di- and triacylglycerols using the following equations:

$$\text{Monoacylglycerols content} = \frac{X \times (100 - A - B - C)}{100}$$

$$\text{Diacylglycerols content} = \frac{Y \times (100 - A - B - C)}{100}$$

$$\text{Triacylglycerols content} = \frac{Z \times (100 - A - B - C)}{100}$$

*A* = percentage content of free glycerol (see Tests);
*B* = percentage content of water;
*X* = monoacylglycerols content obtained by normalisation;
*Y* = diacylglycerols content obtained by normalisation;
*Z* = triacylglycerols content obtained by normalisation.

## LABELLING

The labelling states the type of glycerol monocaprylocaprate (type I or II).

*———————— Ph Eur*

# Glycerol Monolinoleate

(*Ph Eur monograph 1429*)

**Action and use**
Excipient.

*Ph Eur*

## DEFINITION

Mixture of monoacylglycerols, mainly mono-oleoyl- and monolinoleoylglycerol, together with variable quantities of di- and triacylglycerols, obtained by partial glycerolysis of vegetable oils mainly containing triacylglycerols of linoleic (*cis,cis*-9,12-octadecadienoic) acid. A suitable antioxidant may be added.

**Content:**
— *monoacylglycerols*: 32.0 per cent to 52.0 per cent;
— *diacylglycerols*: 40.0 per cent to 55.0 per cent;
— *triacylglycerols*: 5.0 per cent to 20.0 per cent.

## CHARACTERS

**Appearance**
Amber, oily liquid which may be partially solidified at room temperature.

**Solubility**
Practically insoluble in water, freely soluble in methylene chloride.

## IDENTIFICATION

A. Iodine value (see Tests).

B. Thin-layer chromatography (2.2.27).

*Test solution*   Dissolve 1.0 g of the substance to be examined in *methylene chloride R* and dilute to 20 ml with the same solvent.

*Reference solution*   Dissolve 1.0 g of *glycerol monolinoleate CRS* in *methylene chloride* R and dilute to 20 ml with the same solvent.

*Plate*   TLC silica gel plate R.

*Mobile phase*   hexane R, ether R (30:70 V/V).

*Application*   10 μl.

*Development*   Over a path of 15 cm.

*Drying*   In air.

*Detection*   Spray with a 0.1 g/l solution of *rhodamine B R* in *ethanol (96 per cent) R* and examine in ultraviolet light at 365 nm.

*Results*   The spots in the chromatogram obtained with the test solution are similar in position to those in the chromatogram obtained with the reference solution.

C. Composition of fatty acids (see Tests).

## TESTS

**Acid value** (*2.5.1*)
Maximum 6.0, determined on 1.0 g.

**Iodine value** (*2.5.4, Method A*)
100 to 140.

**Peroxide value** (*2.5.5, Method A*)
Maximum 12.0, determined on 2.0 g.

**Saponification value** (*2.5.6*)
160 to 180, determined on 2.0 g.

**Free glycerol**
Maximum 6.0 per cent, determined as described in the assay.

**Composition of fatty acids** (*2.4.22, Method C*).
*Composition of the fatty acid fraction of the substance:*
— *palmitic acid*: 4.0 per cent to 20.0 per cent;
— *stearic acid*: maximum 6.0 per cent;
— *oleic acid*: 10.0 per cent to 35.0 per cent;
— *linoleic acid*: minimum 50.0 per cent;
— *linolenic acid*: maximum 2.0 per cent;
— *arachidic acid*: maximum 1.0 per cent;
— *eicosenoic acid*: maximum 1.0 per cent.

**Water** (*2.5.12*)
Maximum 1.0 per cent, determined on 1.00 g. Use as the solvent a mixture of equal volumes of *anhydrous methanol R* and *methylene chloride R*.

**Total ash** (*2.4.16*)
Maximum 0.1 per cent.

## ASSAY

Size-exclusion chromatography (*2.2.30*).

*Test solution* Into a 15 ml flask, weigh about 0.2 g (*m*), to the nearest 0.1 mg. Add 5 ml of *tetrahydrofuran R* and shake to dissolve. Reweigh the flask and calculate the total mass of solvent and substance (*M*).

*Reference solutions* Into four 15 ml flasks, respectively weigh, to the nearest 0.1 mg, about 2.5 mg, 5 mg, 10 mg and 20 mg of *glycerol R*. Add 5 ml of *tetrahydrofuran R* and shake until well mixed. Weigh the flasks again and calculate the concentration of glycerol in milligrams per gram for each reference solution.

*Column:*
— *size: l* = 0.6 m, Ø = 7 mm,
— *stationary phase: styrene-divinylbenzene copolymer R* (5 μm) with a pore size of 10 nm.

*Mobile phase* tetrahydrofuran R.

*Flow rate* 1 ml/min.

*Detection* Differential refractometer.

*Injection* 40 μl.

*Relative retention* With reference to glycerol (retention time = about 15.6 min):
triacylglycerols = about 0.76; diacylglycerols = about 0.80; monoacylglycerols = about 0.86.

*Calculations:*
— *free glycerol* : from the calibration curve obtained with the reference solutions, determine the concentration (*C*) of glycerol in milligrams per gram in the test solution and calculate the percentage content of free glycerol in the substance to be examined using the following expression:

$$\frac{C \times M}{m \times 10}$$

— *mono-, di- and triacylglycerols*: calculate the percentage content of mono-, di- and triacylglycerols using the normalisation procedure.

## STORAGE
In an airtight container, protected from light.

*Ph Eur*

# Glycerol Mono-oleate

(*Ph Eur monograph 1430*)

**Action and use**
Excipient.

*Ph Eur*

## DEFINITION
Mixture of monoacylglycerols, mainly mono-oleoylglycerol, together with variable quantities of di- and triacylglycerols. It is defined by the nominal content of monoacylglycerols and obtained by partial glycerolysis of vegetable oils mainly containing triacylglycerols of oleic (*cis*-9-octadecenoic) acid or by esterification of glycerol by oleic acid, this fatty acid being of vegetable or animal origin. A suitable antioxidant may be added.

**Content**

| | Nominal content of acylglycerol (per cent) | | |
|---|---|---|---|
| | 40 | 60 | 90 |
| Monoacylglycerols | 32.0 - 52.0 | 55.0 - 65.0 | 90.0 - 101.0 |
| Diacylglycerols | 30.0 - 50.0 | 15.0 - 35.0 | < 10.0 |
| Triacylglycerols | 5.0 - 20.0 | 2.0 - 10.0 | < 2.0 |

## CHARACTERS
**Appearance**
Amber, oily liquid which may be partially solidified at room temperature.

**Solubility**
Practically insoluble in water, freely soluble in methylene chloride.

## IDENTIFICATION
A. Iodine value (see Tests).

B. Thin-layer chromatography (*2.2.27*).

*Test solution* Dissolve 1.0 g of the substance to be examined in *methylene chloride R* and dilute to 20 ml with the same solvent.

*Reference solution* Dissolve 1.0 g of *glycerol mono-oleate CRS* in *methylene chloride R* and dilute to 20 ml with the same solvent.

*Plate* TLC silica gel plate R.

*Mobile phase* hexane R, ether R (30:70 V/V).

*Application* 10 μl.

*Development* Over a path of 15 cm.

*Drying* In air.

*Detection* Spray with a 0.1 g/l solution of *rhodamine B R* in *ethanol (96 per cent) R* and examine in ultraviolet light at 365 nm.

*Results* The spots in the chromatogram obtained with the test solution are similar in position to those in the chromatogram obtained with the reference solution.

C. It complies with the limits of the assay (monoacylglycerol content).

## TESTS

**Acid value** (*2.5.1*)
Maximum 6.0, determined on 1.0 g.

**Iodine value** (*2.5.4, Method A*)
65.0 to 95.0.

**Peroxide value** (*2.5.5, Method A*)
Maximum 12.0, determined on 2.0 g.

**Saponification value** (*2.5.6*)
150 to 175, determined on 2.0 g.

**Free glycerol**
Maximum 6.0 per cent, determined as described in the assay.

**Composition of fatty acids** (*2.4.22, Method C*)
*Composition of the fatty acid fraction of the substance:*
— *palmitic acid*: maximum 12.0 per cent,
— *stearic acid*: maximum 6.0 per cent,
— *oleic acid*: minimum 60.0 per cent,
— *linoleic acid*: maximum 35.0 per cent,
— *linolenic acid*: maximum 2.0 per cent,
— *arachidic acid*: maximum 2.0 per cent,
— *eicosenoic acid*: maximum 2.0 per cent.

**Water** (*2.5.12*)
Maximum 1.0 per cent, determined on 1.00 g. Use as the solvent a mixture of equal volumes of *anhydrous methanol R* and *methylene chloride R*.

**Total ash** (*2.4.16*)
Maximum 0.1 per cent.

## ASSAY

Size-exclusion chromatography (*2.2.30*).

*Test solution* Into a 15 ml flask, weigh about 0.2 g (*m*), to the nearest 0.1 mg. Add 5 ml of *tetrahydrofuran R* and shake to dissolve. Reweigh the flask and calculate the total mass of solvent and substance (*M*).

*Reference solutions* Into four 15 ml flasks, respectively weigh, to the nearest 0.1 mg, about 2.5 mg, 5 mg, 10 mg and 20 mg of *glycerol R*. Add 5 ml of *tetrahydrofuran R* and shake until well mixed. Weigh the flasks again and calculate the concentration of glycerol in milligrams per gram for each reference solution.

*Column:*
— *size: l* = 0.6 m, Ø = 7 mm;
— *stationary phase: styrene-divinylbenzene copolymer R* (5 µm) with a pore size of 10 nm.

*Mobile phase* *tetrahydrofuran R.*

*Flow rate* 1 ml/min.

*Detection* Differential refractometer.

*Injection* 40 µl.

*Relative retention* With reference to glycerol (retention time = about 15.6 min):
triacylglycerols = about 0.76; diacylglycerols = about 0.79; monoacylglycerols = about 0.85.

*Calculations:*
— *free glycerol*: from the calibration curve obtained with the reference solutions determine the concentration (*C*) of glycerol in milligrams per gram in the test solution and calculate the percentage content of free glycerol in the substance to be examined using the following expression:

$$\frac{C \times M}{m \times 10}$$

— *mono-, di- and triacylglycerols*: calculate the percentage content of mono-, di- and triacylglycerols using the normalisation procedure.

## STORAGE

In an airtight container, protected from light.

## LABELLING

The label states the nominal content of monoacylglycerol.

*Ph Eur*

# Glycerol Monostearate 40-55

(*Ph Eur monograph 0495*)

31566-31-1

**Action and use**
Excipient.

*Ph Eur*

## DEFINITION

Mixture of monoacylglycerols, mainly monostearoylglycerol, together with variable quantities of di- and triacylglycerols. It is obtained by partial glycerolysis of vegetable oils mainly containing triacylglycerols of palmitic (hexadecanoic) or stearic (octadecanoic) acid or by esterification of glycerol with stearic acid. The fatty acids may be of vegetable or animal origin.

**Content:**
— *monoacylglycerols*: 40.0 per cent to 55.0 per cent;
— *diacylglycerols*: 30.0 per cent to 45.0 per cent;
— *triacylglycerols*: 5.0 per cent to 15.0 per cent.

## CHARACTERS

**Appearance**
Hard, waxy mass or unctuous powder or flakes, white or almost white.

**Solubility**
Practically insoluble in water, soluble in ethanol (96 per cent) at 60 °C.

## IDENTIFICATION

*First identification* C, D.

*Second identification* A, B.

A. Melting point (*2.2.15*): 54 °C to 66 °C.

Introduce the melted substance into the capillary tubes and allow to stand for 24 h in a well-closed container.

B. Thin-layer chromatography (*2.2.27*).

*Test solution* Dissolve 0.5 g of the substance to be examined in *methylene chloride R*, with gentle heating, and dilute to 10 ml with the same solvent.

*Reference solution* Dissolve 0.5 g of *glycerol monostearate 40-55 CRS* in *methylene chloride R*, with gentle heating, and dilute to 10 ml with the same solvent.

*Plate* TLC silica gel plate R.

*Mobile phase* hexane R, ether R (30:70 V/V).

*Application* 10 µl.

*Development* Over a path of 15 cm.

*Detection* Spray with a 0.1 g/l solution of *rhodamine B R* in *ethanol (96 per cent) R* and examine in ultraviolet light at 365 nm.

*Suitability system* Reference solution:
— the chromatogram shows 4 clearly separated spots.

*Results* The spots in the chromatogram obtained with the test solution are similar in position to those in the chromatogram obtained with the reference solution.

C. Composition of fatty acids (see Tests) according to the type stated on the label.

D. It complies with the limits of the assay (monoacylglycerol content).

**TESTS**
**Acid value** (*2.5.1*)
Maximum 3.0, determined on 1.0 g.

Use a mixture of equal volumes of *ethanol (96 per cent) R* and *toluene R* as solvent and heat gently.

**Iodine value** (*2.5.4, Method A*)
Maximum 3.0.

**Saponification value** (*2.5.6*)
158 to 177, determined on 2.0 g. Carry out the titration with heating.

**Free glycerol**
Maximum 6.0 per cent, determined as described under Assay.

**Composition of fatty acids** (*2.4.22, Method C*)
Use the mixture of calibrating substances in Table 2.4.22.-1.
*Composition of the fatty-acid fraction of the substance:*

| Glycerol monostearate 40-55 | Composition of fatty acids |
|---|---|
| Type I | *Stearic acid*: 40.0 per cent to 60.0 per cent |
| | *Sum of the contents of palmitic and stearic acids*: minimum 90.0 per cent |
| Type II | *Stearic acid*: 60.0 per cent to 80.0 per cent |
| | *Sum of the contents of palmitic and stearic acids*: minimum 90.0 per cent |
| Type III | *Stearic acid*: 80.0 per cent to 99.0 per cent |
| | *Sum of the contents of palmitic and stearic acids*: minimum 96.0 per cent |

**Nickel** (*2.4.31*)
Maximum 1 ppm.

**Water** (*2.5.12*)
Maximum 1.0 per cent, determined on 1.00 g. Use *pyridine R* as the solvent and heat gently.

**Total ash** (*2.4.16*)
Maximum 0.1 per cent.

**ASSAY**
Size-exclusion chromatography (*2.2.30*).

*Test solution* Into a 15 ml flask, weigh 0.200 g (*m*). Add 5.0 ml of *tetrahydrofuran R* and shake to dissolve. Reweigh the flask and calculate the total mass of solvent and substance (*M*).

*Reference solutions* Into four 15 ml flasks, respectively weigh 2.5 mg, 5.0 mg, 10.0 mg and 20.0 mg of *glycerol R*, and add 5.0 ml of *tetrahydrofuran R* to each flask. Weigh the flasks again and calculate the concentration of glycerol in milligrams per gram for each reference solution.

*Column:*
— *size*: l = 0.6 m, Ø = 7 mm;
— *stationary phase*: *styrene-divinylbenzene copolymer R* (5 μm) with a pore size of 10 nm.

*Mobile phase* *tetrahydrofuran R*.
*Flow rate* 1 ml/min.
*Detection* Differential refractometer.
*Injection* 40 μl.
*Relative retention* With reference to glycerol (retention time = about 15 min): triacylglycerols = about 0.75; diacylglycerols = about 0.80; monoacylglycerols = about 0.85.
*Calculations:*
— *free glycerol*: from the calibration curve obtained with the reference solutions, determine the concentration (*C*) in milligrams per gram in the test solution and calculate the percentage content in the substance to be examined using the following expression:

$$\frac{C \times M}{m \times 10}$$

— *mono-, di- and triacylglycerols*: calculate the percentage contents by the normalisation procedure.

**LABELLING**
The label states the type of glycerol monostearate 40-55.

*Ph Eur*

# Self-emulsifying Glyceryl Monostearate

Self-emulsifying Monostearin; Self-emulsifying Mono-and Diglycerides of Food Fatty Acids

**Action and use**
Excipient.

**DEFINITION**
Self-emulsifying Glyceryl Monostearate is a mixture consisting principally of mono-, di- and triglycerides of stearic and palmitic acids and of minor proportions of glycerides of other fatty acids; it may also contain free glycerol, free fatty acids and soap. It contains not less than 30.0% of monoglycerides, calculated as $C_{21}H_{42}O_4$, not more than 7.0% of free glycerol, calculated as $C_3H_8O_3$, and not more than 6.0% of soap, calculated as sodium oleate, $C_{18}H_{33}NaO_2$, all calculated with reference to the anhydrous substance.

**CHARACTERISTICS**
A white to cream coloured, hard, waxy solid.

Dispersible in hot *water*; soluble in hot *absolute ethanol*, in hot *liquid paraffin* and, subject to turbidity at concentrations below 20%, in hot vegetable oils.

**TESTS**
**Acid value**
Not more than 6, Appendix X B.

**Iodine value**
Not more than 3 (*iodine monochloride method*), Appendix X E.

**Alkalinity**
Shake 1 g with 20 ml of hot *carbon dioxide-free water* and allow to cool with continuous shaking. The pH of the aqueous layer is 8.0 to 10.0, Appendix V L.

**Heavy metals**
2.0 g complies with *limit test C for heavy metals*, Appendix VII. Use 2 ml of *lead standard solution (10 ppm Pb)* to prepare the standard (10 ppm).

**Water**

Not more than 2.0% w/w, Appendix IX C. Use 0.5 g and a mixture of 10 ml of *anhydrous methanol* and 10 ml of anhydrous *chloroform* as the solvent.

## ASSAY

### For free glycerol

Dissolve 0.4 g in 50 ml of *dichloromethane* in a ground-glass-stoppered separating funnel, cool if necessary, add 25 ml of *water* and shake vigorously for 1 minute; add 0.2 ml of *glacial acetic acid*, if necessary, to break the emulsion. Repeat the extraction a further three times using 25-, 20- and 20- ml quantities of *water* and reserve the dichloromethane solution for the Assay for monoglycerides. Filter the combined aqueous extracts through a filter paper moistened with *water*, wash the filter with two 5 ml quantities of *water* and dilute the combined filtrate and washings to 100 ml with *water*. To 50 ml of this solution add 25 ml of *periodic acetic acid solution*, shaking cautiously, allow to stand at 25° to 30° for 30 minutes and add 100 ml of *water* and 12 ml of *potassium iodide solution*. Titrate with 0.1M *sodium thiosulphate VS* using 1 ml of *starch solution* as indicator. Repeat the determination using 50 ml of *water* in place of the 50 ml of the solution being examined. The difference between the titrations represents the amount of sodium thiosulphate required. Each ml of 0.1M *sodium thiosulphate VS* is equivalent to 2.3 mg of glycerol.

### For monoglycerides

Filter the reserved dichloromethane solution obtained in the Assay for free glycerol through absorbent cotton and wash the separating funnel and the filter with three 5 ml quantities of *dichloromethane*. Dilute the combined filtrate and washings to 100 ml with *dichloromethane* and to 50 ml of the solution add 25 ml of *periodic acetic acid solution*, shaking cautiously. Allow to stand at 25° to 30° for 30 minutes and add 100 ml of *water* and 12 ml of *potassium iodide solution*. Titrate the liberated iodine with 0.1M *sodium thiosulphate VS* using 1 ml of *starch solution* as indicator. Repeat the determination using 50 ml of *dichloromethane* in place of the 50 ml of the solution of the substance being examined. The difference between the titrations represents the amount of sodium thiosulphate required. Each ml of 0.1M *sodium thiosulphate VS* is equivalent to 17.9 mg of 1-monoacylglycerols, calculated as $C_{21}H_{42}O_4$. The quantity of 0.1M *sodium thiosulphate VS* used in the assay is not less than 85% of the quantity of sodium thiosulphate used in the blank assay.

### For soap

Add 10 g to a mixture of 60 ml of *acetone* and 0.15 ml of a 0.5% w/v solution of *bromophenol blue* in a mixture of 20 ml of *ethanol (20%)* and 80 ml of *water*, the solvent having been previously neutralised with 0.1M *hydrochloric acid VS* or 0.1M *sodium hydroxide VS*. Warm gently on a water bath until solution is complete and titrate with 0.1M *hydrochloric acid VS* until the blue colour is discharged. Allow to stand for 20 minutes, warm until any solidified matter has redissolved and, if the blue colour reappears, continue the titration. Each ml of 0.1M *hydrochloric acid VS* is equivalent to 30.45 mg of $C_{18}H_{33}NaO_2$.

# Glyceryl Trinitrate Solution

*(Ph Eur monograph 1331)*

$C_3H_5N_3O_9$    227.1

## Action and use
Vasodilator.

## Preparations
Glyceryl Trinitrate Sublingual Spray

Glyceryl Trinitrate Tablets

Glyceryl Trinitrate Transdermal Patches

When concentrated glyceryl trinitrate solution is demanded, the intention of the purchaser, with respect to the strength expressed, should be ascertained.

*Ph Eur* _____

## DEFINITION
Ethanolic solution of glyceryl trinitrate.

### Content
1 per cent *m/m* to 10 per cent *m/m* of propane-1,2,3-triyl trinitrate and 96.5 per cent to 102.5 per cent of the declared content of glyceryl trinitrate stated on the label.

## CHARACTERS

### Appearance
Clear, colourless or slightly yellow solution.

### Solubility
Miscible with acetone and with anhydrous ethanol.

### Solubility of pure glyceryl trinitrate
Practically insoluble in water, freely soluble in anhydrous ethanol, miscible with acetone.

## IDENTIFICATION
*First identification   A, C.*

*Second identification   B, C.*

*Upon diluting glyceryl trinitrate solution, care must be taken to always use anhydrous ethanol, otherwise droplets of pure glyceryl trinitrate may precipitate from the solution.*

*After examination, the residues and the solutions obtained in both the identification and the test sections must be heated on a water-bath for 5 min with dilute sodium hydroxide solution R.*

A. Infrared absorption spectrophotometry (*2.2.24*).

*Preparation*   Place 50 µl of a solution diluted, if necessary, with *anhydrous ethanol R*, to contain 10 g/l of glyceryl trinitrate, on a disc of *potassium bromide R* and evaporate the solvent *in vacuo*.

*Comparison   Ph. Eur. reference spectrum of glyceryl trinitrate.*

B. Thin-layer chromatography (*2.2.27*).

*Test solution*   Dilute a quantity of the substance to be examined corresponding to 50 mg of glyceryl trinitrate in *acetone R* and dilute to 100 ml with the same solvent.

*Reference solution*   Dilute 0.05 ml of *glyceryl trinitrate solution CRS* to 1 ml with *acetone R*.

*Plate   TLC silica gel G plate R.*

*Mobile phase   ethyl acetate R, toluene R (20:80 V/V).*

*Application   5 µl.*

*Development   Over 2/3 of the plate.*

*Drying*   In air.

*Detection*   Spray with freshly prepared *potassium iodide and starch solution R*; expose to ultraviolet light at 254 nm for 15 min and examine in daylight.

*Results*   The principal spot in the chromatogram obtained with the test solution is similar in position, colour and size to the principal spot in the chromatogram obtained with the reference solution.

C. It complies with the limits of the assay.

## TESTS

*Upon diluting glyceryl trinitrate solution, care must be taken always to use anhydrous ethanol, otherwise droplets of pure glyceryl trinitrate may precipitate from the solution.*

*After examination, the residues and the solutions obtained in both the identification and the test sections must be heated on a water-bath for 5 min with dilute sodium hydroxide solution R.*

### Appearance of solution

If necessary dilute the solution to be examined to a concentration of 10 g/l with *anhydrous ethanol R*. The solution is not more intensely coloured than reference solution $Y_7$ (*2.2.2, Method II*).

### Inorganic nitrates

Thin-layer chromatography (*2.2.27*).

*Test solution*   If necessary dilute the solution to be examined to a concentration of 10 g/l with *anhydrous ethanol R*.

*Reference solution*   Dissolve 5 mg of *potassium nitrate R* in 1 ml of *water R* and dilute to 100 ml with *ethanol (96 per cent) R*.

*Plate*   TLC silica gel plate R.

*Mobile phase*   glacial acetic acid R, acetone R, toluene R (15:30:60 *V/V/V*).

*Application*   10 µl.

*Development*   Over 2/3 of the plate.

*Drying*   In a current of air until the acetic acid is completely removed.

*Detection*   Spray intensively with freshly prepared *potassium iodide and starch solution R*; expose to ultraviolet light at 254 nm for 15 min and examine in daylight.

*Limit:*
— *nitrate ion*: any spot due to the nitrate ion in the chromatogram obtained with the test solution is not more intense than the spot in the chromatogram obtained with the reference solution (0.5 per cent of the content of glyceryl trinitrate calculated as potassium nitrate).

### Related substances

Liquid chromatography (*2.2.29*).

*Test solution*   Dissolve a quantity of the substance to be examined equivalent to 2 mg of glyceryl trinitrate in the mobile phase and dilute to 20.0 ml with the mobile phase.

*Reference solution (a)*   Dissolve 0.10 g of *glyceryl trinitrate solution CRS* and a quantity of *diluted pentaerythrityl tetranitrate CRS* equivalent to 1.0 mg of pentaerythrityl tetranitrate in the mobile phase and dilute to 100.0 ml with the mobile phase. Sonicate and filter if necessary.

*Reference solution (b)*   Dilute 1.0 ml of the test solution to 100.0 ml with the mobile phase.

*Column:*
— *size: l* = 0.25 m, Ø = 4.6 mm;
— *stationary phase*: octadecylsilyl silica gel for chromatography R (5 µm).

*Mobile phase*   acetonitrile R, water R (50:50 *V/V*).

*Flow rate*   1 ml/min.

*Detection*   Spectrophotometer at 210 nm.

*Injection*   20 µl.

*Run time*   3 times the retention time of the principal peak.

*System suitability*   Reference solution (a):
— *resolution*: minimum 2.0 between the peaks due to glyceryl trinitrate and to pentaerythrityl tetranitrate.

*Limits:*
— *any impurity*: not more than the area of the principal peak in the chromatogram obtained with reference solution (b) (1 per cent, expressed as glyceryl trinitrate);
— *total*: not more than 3 times the area of the principal peak in the chromatogram obtained with reference solution (b) (3 per cent, expressed as glyceryl trinitrate);
— *disregard limit*: 0.1 times the area of the principal peak in the chromatogram obtained with reference solution (b) (0.1 per cent).

## ASSAY

*Test solution*   Prepare a solution containing 1.0 mg of glyceryl trinitrate in 250.0 ml of *methanol R*.

*Reference solution*   Dissolve 70.0 mg of *sodium nitrite R* in *methanol R* and dilute to 250.0 ml with the same solvent. Dilute 5.0 ml of the solution to 500.0 ml with *methanol R*.

Into three 50 ml volumetric flasks introduce 10.0 ml of the test solution, 10.0 ml of the reference solution and 10 ml of *methanol R* as a blank. To each flask add 5 ml of *dilute sodium hydroxide solution R*, close the flask, mix and allow to stand at room temperature for 30 min. Add 10 ml of *sulphanilic acid solution R* and 10 ml of *dilute hydrochloric acid R* and mix. After exactly 4 min, add 10 ml of *naphthylethylenediamine dihydrochloride solution R*, dilute to volume with *water R* and mix. After 10 min read the absorbance (*2.2.25*) of the test solution and the reference solution at 540 nm using the blank solution as the compensation liquid.

Calculate the percentage content of glyceryl trinitrate using the following expression:

$$\frac{A_T \times m_S \times C}{A_R \times m_T \times 60.8}$$

$A_T$ = absorption of the test solution;
$m_T$ = mass of the substance to be examined, in milligrams;
$C$  = percentage content of sodium nitrite used as reference;
$A_R$ = absorption of the reference solution;
$m_S$ = mass of sodium nitrite, in milligrams.

## STORAGE

Store the diluted solutions (10 g/l) protected from light, at a temperature of 2 °C to 15 °C.

Store more concentrated solutions protected from light, at a temperature of 15 °C to 20 °C.

## LABELLING

The label states the declared content of glyceryl trinitrate.

## IMPURITIES

A. inorganic nitrates,

and enantiomer

B. R1 = NO$_2$, R2 = R3 = H:
(2RS)-2,3-dihydroxypropyl nitrate,

C. R1 = R3 = H, R2 = NO₂:
2-hydroxy-1-(hydroxymethyl)ethyl nitrate,

D. R1 = R2 = NO₂, R3 = H:
(2RS)-3-hydroxypropane-1,2-diyl dinitrate,

E. R1 = R3 = NO₂, R2 = H:
2-hydroxypropane-1,3-diyl dinitrate.

_____ Ph Eur

# Glycine

(*Ph Eur monograph 0614*)

$$H_2N \diagdown CO_2H$$

C₂H₅NO₂      75.1      56-40-6

**Action and use**
Amino acid used for bladder irrigation during surgery.

**Preparation**
Glycine Irrigation Solution

*Ph Eur* _____

## DEFINITION
2-Aminoacetic acid.

**Content**
98.5 per cent to 101.0 per cent (dried substance).

## CHARACTERS
**Appearance**
White or almost white, crystalline powder.

**Solubility**
Freely soluble in water, very slightly soluble in ethanol
(96 per cent).

It shows polymorphism (*5.9*).

## IDENTIFICATION
*First identification*   A.

*Second identification*   B, C.

A. Infrared absorption spectrophotometry (*2.2.24*).

*Comparison*   glycine CRS.

If the spectra obtained in the solid state show differences,
dissolve the substance to be examined and the reference
substance separately in the minimum volume of *ethanol
(60 per cent V/V) R*, evaporate to dryness and record the
spectra again.

B. Examine the chromatograms obtained in the test for
ninhydrin-positive substances.

*Results*   The principal spot in the chromatogram obtained
with test solution (b) is similar in position, colour and size
to the principal spot in the chromatogram obtained with
reference solution (a).

C. Dissolve 50 mg in 5 ml of *water R*, add 1 ml of *strong
sodium hypochlorite solution R* and boil for 2 min. Add 1 ml
of *hydrochloric acid R* and boil for 4-5 min. Add 2 ml of
*hydrochloric acid R* and 1 ml of a 20 g/l solution of
*resorcinol R*, boil for 1 min and cool. Add 10 ml of *water R*
and mix. To 5 ml of the solution add 6 ml of *dilute sodium
hydroxide solution R*. The solution is violet with greenish-
yellow fluorescence. After a few minutes, the colour becomes
orange and then yellow and an intense fluorescence remains.

## TESTS
**Solution S**
Dissolve 5.0 g in *carbon dioxide-free water R* and dilute to
50 ml with the same solvent.

**Appearance of solution**
Solution S is clear (*2.2.1*) and not more intensely coloured
than reference solution Y₇ (*2.2.2, Method II*).

**pH** (*2.2.3*)
5.9 to 6.4.

Dilute 10 ml of solution S to 20 ml with *carbon dioxide-free
water R*.

**Ninhydrin-positive substances**
Thin-layer chromatography (*2.2.27*).

*Test solution (a)*   Dissolve 0.10 g of the substance to be
examined in *water R* and dilute to 10.0 ml with the same
solvent.

*Test solution (b)*   Dilute 1.0 ml of test solution (a) to 10.0 ml
with *water R*.

*Reference solution (a)*   Dissolve 10 mg of *glycine CRS* in
*water R* and dilute to 10.0 ml with the same solvent.

*Reference solution (b)*   Dilute 1.0 ml of test solution (a) to
200 ml with *water R*.

*Reference solution (c)*   Dissolve 10 mg of *glycine CRS* and
10 mg of *alanine CRS* in *water R* and dilute to 25 ml with
the same solvent.

*Plate*   *cellulose for chromatography R* as the coating substance.

*Mobile phase*   glacial acetic acid R, water R, butanol R
(20:20:60 *V/V/V*).

*Application*   5 µl.

*Development*   Over 2/3 of the plate.

*Drying*   At 80 °C for 30 min.

*Detection*   Spray with *ninhydrin solution R* and dry at
100-105 °C for 15 min.

*System suitability*   The chromatogram obtained with
reference solution (c) shows 2 clearly separated spots.

*Limits*   In the chromatogram obtained with test solution (a):
— *any impurity*: any spots, apart from the principal spot, are
    not more intense than the principal spot in the
    chromatogram obtained with reference solution (b)
    (0.5 per cent).

**Chlorides** (*2.4.4*)
Maximum 75 ppm.

Dissolve 0.67 g in *water R* and dilute to 15 ml with the same
solvent.

**Heavy metals** (*2.4.8*)
Maximum 10 ppm.

12 ml of solution S complies with test A. Prepare the
reference solution using *lead standard solution (1 ppm Pb) R*.

**Loss on drying** (*2.2.32*)
Maximum 0.5 per cent, determined on 1.000 g by drying in
an oven at 105 °C for 2 h.

**Sulphated ash** (*2.4.14*)
Maximum 0.1 per cent, determined on 1.0 g.

## ASSAY
Dissolve 70.0 mg in 3 ml of *anhydrous formic acid R* and add
30 ml of *anhydrous acetic acid R*. Immediately after
dissolution, titrate with *0.1 M perchloric acid*, determining the
end-point potentiometrically (*2.2.20*).

1 ml of *0.1 M perchloric acid* is equivalent to 7.51 mg of $C_2H_5NO_2$.

*Ph Eur*

# Gonadorelin Acetate

(*Ph Eur monograph 0827*)

, $H_3C-CO_2H$

$C_{55}H_{75}N_{17}O_{13}$,$xC_2H_4O_2$     1242     *52699-48-6*

## Action and use

Gonadotropin-releasing hormone; treatment of prostate cancer.

## Preparation

Gonadorelin Injection

*Ph Eur*

## DEFINITION

Gonadorelin acetate is the acetate form of a hypothalamic peptide that stimulates the release of follicle-stimulating hormone and luteinising hormone from the pituitary gland. It contains not less than 95.0 per cent and not more than the equivalent of 102.0 per cent of the peptide $C_{55}H_{75}N_{17}O_{13}$, calculated with reference to the anhydrous, acetic acid-free substance. It is obtained by chemical synthesis.

## CHARACTERS

A white or slightly yellowish powder, soluble in water and in a 1 per cent *V/V* solution of glacial acetic acid, sparingly soluble in methanol.

## IDENTIFICATION

A. Examine the chromatograms obtained in the assay. The retention time and size of the principal peak in the chromatogram obtained with the test solution are approximately the same as those of the principal peak in the chromatogram obtained with reference solution (a).

B. Examine by thin-layer chromatography (*2.2.27*), using a *TLC silica gel G plate R*.

Use the test solution and reference solution (a) prepared under Assay.

Apply to the plate 10 µl of each solution. Develop over a path of 15 cm using a mixture of 6 volumes of *glacial acetic acid R*, 14 volumes of *water R*, 45 volumes of *methanol R* and 60 volumes of *methylene chloride R*. Allow the plate to dry in air for 5 min. At the bottom of a chromatography tank, place an evaporating dish containing a mixture of 10 ml of a 50 g/l solution of *potassium permanganate R* and 3 ml of *hydrochloric acid R*, close the tank and allow to stand. Place the dried plate in the tank and close the tank. Leave the plate in contact with the chlorine vapour for 2 min. Withdraw the plate and place it in a current of cold air until the excess of chlorine is removed and an area of coating below the points of application no longer gives a blue colour with 0.05 ml of *potassium iodide and starch solution R*. Spray with *potassium iodide and starch solution R*. The principal spot in the chromatogram obtained with the test solution corresponds in position and size to the principal spot in the chromatogram obtained with reference solution (a).

## TESTS

### Appearance of solution

A 10 g/l solution is clear (*2.2.1*) and not more intensely coloured than reference solution $Y_5$ (*2.2.2*, *Method II*).

### Specific optical rotation

(*2.2.7*). Dissolve 10.0 mg in 1.0 ml of a 1 per cent *V/V* solution of *glacial acetic acid R*. The specific optical rotation is − 54 to − 66, calculated on the basis of the peptide content as determined in the assay.

### Absorbance (*2.2.25*)

Dissolve 10.0 mg in *water R* and dilute to 100.0 ml with the same solvent. The absorbance, determined at the maximum at 278 nm, corrected to a 10 mg/100 ml solution on the basis of the peptide content determined in the assay, is 0.55 to 0.61.

### Amino acids

Examine by means of an amino-acid analyser. Standardise the apparatus with a mixture containing equimolar amounts of ammonia, glycine and the L-form of the following amino acids:

| | | | |
|---|---|---|---|
| lysine | threonine | alanine | leucine |
| histidine | serine | valine | tyrosine |
| arginine | glutamic acid | methionine | phenylalanine |
| aspartic acid | proline | isoleucine | |

together with half the equimolar amount of L-cystine. For the validation of the method, an appropriate internal standard, such as DL-*norleucine R*, is used.

*Test solution* Place 1.0 mg of the substance to be examined in a rigorously cleaned hard-glass tube 100 mm long and 6 mm in internal diameter. Add a suitable amount of a 50 per cent *V/V* solution of *hydrochloric acid R*. Immerse the tube in a freezing mixture at − 5 °C, reduce the pressure to below 133 Pa and seal. Heat at 110 °C to 115 °C for 16 h. Cool, open the tube, transfer the contents to a 10 ml flask with the aid of five quantities, each of 0.2 ml, of *water R* and evaporate to dryness over *potassium hydroxide R* under reduced pressure. Take up the residue in *water R* and evaporate to dryness over *potassium hydroxide R* under reduced pressure; repeat these operations once. Take up the residue in a buffer solution suitable for the amino-acid analyser used and dilute to a suitable volume with the same buffer solution. Apply a suitable volume to the amino-acid analyser.

Express the content of each amino acid in moles. Calculate the relative proportions of the amino acids, taking one-eighth of the sum of the number of moles of histidine, glutamic acid, leucine, proline, glycine, tyrosine and arginine as equal to one. The values fall within the following limits: serine 0.7 to 1.05; glutamic acid 0.95 to 1.05; proline 0.95 to 1.05; glycine 1.9 to 2.1; leucine 0.9 to 1.1; tyrosine 0.7 to 1.05; histidine 0.95 to 1.05 and arginine 0.95 to 1.05. Lysine and isoleucine are absent; not more than traces of other amino acids are present, with the exception of tryptophan.

### Related substances

Examine by liquid chromatography (*2.2.29*) as described under Assay.

Inject 20 µl of reference solution (b). Adjust the sensitivity of the system so that the height of the principal peak in the chromatogram obtained is at least 50 per cent of the full scale of the recorder.

Inject 20 µl of the test solution. Continue the chromatography for twice the retention time of gonadorelin. In the chromatogram obtained with the test solution: the area of any peak apart from the principal peak, is not greater than

twice the area of the principal peak in the chromatogram
obtained with reference solution (b) (2 per cent); the sum of
the areas of the peaks, apart from the principal peak, is not
greater than 5 times the area of the principal peak in the
chromatogram obtained with reference solution (b)
(5 per cent). Disregard any peak with an area less than
0.05 times that of the principal peak in the chromatogram
obtained with reference solution (b) (0.05 per cent).

**Acetic acid** (2.5.34)

4.0 per cent to 7.5 per cent.

*Test solution*   Dissolve 10.0 mg of the substance to be
examined in a mixture of 5 volumes of mobile phase B and
95 volumes of mobile phase A and dilute to 10.0 ml with the
same mixture of solvents.

**Water** (2.5.12)

Not more than 7.0 per cent, determined on 0.200 g by the
semi-micro determination of water.

**Bacterial endotoxins** (2.6.14)

Less than 70 IU/mg, if intended for use in the manufacture
of parenteral dosage forms without a further appropriate
procedure for the removal of bacterial endotoxins.

## ASSAY

Examine by liquid chromatography (2.2.29).

*Test solution*   Dissolve 5.0 mg of the substance to be
examined in *water R* and dilute to 10.0 ml with the same
solvent.

*Reference solution (a)*   Dissolve the contents of a vial of
*gonadorelin CRS* in *water R* to obtain a concentration of
0.5 mg/ml.

*Reference solution (b)*   Dilute 1.0 ml of the test solution to
100.0 ml with *water R*.

*Reference solution (c)*   Dissolve 2.5 mg of the substance to
be examined in 1 ml of *0.1 M hydrochloric acid* and heat in
a water-bath at 65 °C for 4 h. Add 1 ml of *0.1 M sodium
hydroxide* and dilute to 5.0 ml with *water R*.

The chromatographic procedure may be carried out using:

— a stainless steel column 0.12 m long and 4.0 mm in
  internal diameter packed with *octadecylsilyl silica gel for
  chromatography R* (5 µm),

— as mobile phase at a flow rate of 1.5 ml/min a mixture
  of 13 volumes of *acetonitrile R* and 87 volumes of a
  1.18 per cent *V/V* solution of *phosphoric acid R* (adjusted
  to pH 2.3 with *triethylamine R*),

— as detector a spectrophotometer set at 215 nm.

Inject 20 µl of reference solution (c). The test is not valid
unless the resolution between the first and second peaks is
at least 2.0.

Inject 20 µl of the test solution and 20 µl of reference
solution (a).

Calculate the content of gonadorelin ($C_{55}H_{75}N_{17}O_{13}$) from
the peak areas in the chromatograms obtained with the test
solution and reference solution (a) and the declared content
of $C_{55}H_{75}N_{17}O_{13}$ in *gonadorelin CRS* .

## STORAGE

Store in an airtight container, protected from light at a
temperature of 2 °C to 8 °C. If the substance is sterile, store
in a sterile, airtight, tamper-proof container.

## LABELLING

The label states the mass of peptide in the container.

*Ph Eur*

# Goserelin

*(Ph Eur monograph 1636)*

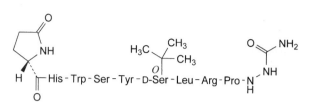

$C_{59}H_{84}N_{18}O_{14}$          1269          *65807-02-5*

### Action and use

Gonadotropin-releasing hormone, gonadorelin analogue;
treatment of prostate cancer.

### Preparation

Goserelin Implants

*Ph Eur*

## DEFINITION

1-Carbamoyl-2-[5-oxo-L-prolyl-L-histidyl-L-tryptophyl-L-seryl-
L-tyrosyl-*O*-(1,1-dimethylethyl)-D-seryl-L-leucyl-L-arginyl-L-
prolyl]diazane.

Synthetic nonapeptide analogue of the hypothalamic
decapeptide, gonadorelin. It is obtained by chemical synthesis
and is available as an acetate.

### Content

94.5 per cent to 103.0 per cent of the peptide $C_{59}H_{84}N_{18}O_{14}$
(anhydrous and acetic-acid free substance).

## CHARACTERS

### Appearance

White or almost white powder.

### Solubility

Soluble in water, freely soluble in glacial acetic acid. It
dissolves in dilute solutions of mineral acids and alkali
hydroxides.

## IDENTIFICATION

A. Nuclear magnetic resonance spectrometry (2.2.33).

*Preparation*   40 mg/ml solution of the substance to be
examined in *deuterium oxide R* adjusted to pH 4.0 with
*deuterated acetic acid R*.

*Results*   The $^{13}$C, proton decoupled NMR spectrum
obtained is qualitatively similar to the *Ph. Eur. reference
spectrum of goserelin*.

B. Examine the chromatograms obtained in the assay.

*Results*   The principal peak in the chromatogram obtained
with the test solution is similar in retention time and size to
the principal peak in the chromatogram obtained with
reference solution (a).

C. Amino acid analysis (2.2.56). For protein hydrolysis use
Method 1 and for analysis use Method 1.

Express the content of each amino acid in moles. Calculate
the relative proportions of the amino acids taking one sixth of
the sum of the number of moles of glutamic acid, histidine,
tyrosine, leucine, arginine, proline as equal to 1. The values
fall within the following limits: glutamic acid, histidine,
tyrosine, leucine, arginine and proline 0.9 to 1.1; serine
1.6 to 2.2. Not more than traces of other amino acids are
present, with the exception of tryptophan.

## TESTS

### Specific optical rotation (2.2.7)

− 52 to − 56 (anhydrous and acetic-acid free substance).
Dissolve the substance to be examined in *water R* to obtain a concentration of 2 mg/ml.

### Related substances

Liquid chromatography (2.2.29).

*Test solution*  Dissolve the substance to be examined in *water R* to obtain a concentration of 1.0 mg/ml.

*Reference solution (a)*  Dissolve the contents of a vial of *goserelin CRS* in *water R* to obtain a concentration of 1.0 mg/ml.

*Reference solution (b)*  Dilute 1.0 ml of the test solution to 100 ml with *water R*.

*Reference solution (c)*  Dilute 1.0 ml of the test solution to 10.0 ml with *water R*.

*Resolution solution (a)*  Dissolve the contents of a vial of *4-D-Ser-goserelin CRS* in *water R* to obtain a concentration of 0.1 mg/ml. Mix equal volumes of this solution and of reference solution (c).

*Resolution solution (b)*  Dissolve the contents of a vial of *goserelin validation mixture CRS* with 1.0 ml of *water R*.

*Column:*
— *size:* $l$ = 0.15 m, Ø = 4.6 mm,
— *stationary phase:* octadecylsilyl amorphous organosilica polymer R (3.5 μm) with a pore size of 12.5 nm,
— *temperature:* 50-55 °C.

*Mobile phase*  trifluoroacetic acid R, acetonitrile for chromatography R, water R (0.5:200:800 *V/V/V*).

*Flow rate*  0.7-1.2 ml/min.

*Detection*  Spectrophotometer at 220 nm.

*Injection*  10 μl of the test solution, reference solution (b) and the resolution solutions.

*Run time*  90 min.

*Relative retention*  With reference to goserelin:
impurity A = about 0.67; impurity C = about 0.78;
impurity B = about 0.79; impurity D = about 0.85;
impurity E = about 0.89; impurity F = about 0.92;
impurity G = about 0.94; impurity H = about 0.98;
impurity I = about 1.43; impurity J = about 1.53;
impurity K = about 1.67; impurity L = about 1.77.

*System suitability:*
— *retention time:* goserelin = 40 min to 50 min in the chromatogram obtained with resolution solution (b); adjust the flow rate of the mobile phase if necessary; if adjusting the flow rate does not result in a correct retention time of the principal peak, change the composition of acetonitrile in the mobile phase to obtain the requested retention time for goserelin;
— *resolution:* minimum 7.0 between the peaks due to impurity A and goserelin in the chromatogram obtained with resolution solution (a);
— *symmetry factor:* 0.8 to 2.5 for the peaks due to impurity A and goserelin in the chromatogram obtained with resolution solution (a);
— the chromatogram obtained with resolution solution (b) is similar to the chromatogram supplied with *goserelin validation mixture CRS*. 2 peaks eluting prior to the principal peak and corresponding to impurity E and impurity G, are clearly visible. 3 peaks eluting after the principal peak are clearly visible.

*Limits:*
— *impurity E:* not more than the area of the principal peak in the chromatogram obtained with reference solution (b) (1.0 per cent),
— *any other impurity:* for each impurity, not more than 0.5 times the area of the principal peak in the chromatogram obtained with reference solution (b) (0.5 per cent),
— *total:* not more than 2.5 times the area of the principal peak in the chromatogram obtained with reference solution (b) (2.5 per cent),
— *disregard limit:* 0.05 times the area of the principal peak in the chromatogram obtained with reference solution (b) (0.05 per cent).

### Acetic acid (2.5.34)

4.5 per cent to 15.0 per cent.

*Test solution*  Dissolve 10.0 mg of the substance to be examined in a mixture of 5 volumes of mobile phase B and 95 volumes of mobile phase A and dilute to 10.0 ml with the same mixture of mobile phases.

### Water (2.5.32)

Maximum 10.0 per cent.

### Bacterial endotoxins (2.6.14)

Less than 16 IU/mg, if intended for use in the manufacture of parenteral dosage forms without a further appropriate procedure for the removal of bacterial endotoxins.

## ASSAY

Liquid chromatography (2.2.29) as described in the test for related substances with the following modifications.

*Injection*  Test solution and reference solution (a).

*Run time*  60 min.

Calculate the content of goserelin ($C_{59}H_{84}N_{18}O_{14}$) using the chromatograms obtained with the test solution and reference solution (a) and the declared content of $C_{59}H_{84}N_{18}O_{14}$ in *goserelin CRS*.

## STORAGE

In an airtight container, protected from light, at a temperature of 2 °C to 8 °C.

## LABELLING

The label states the mass of peptide in the container.

## IMPURITIES

*Specified impurities*  A, B, C, D, E, F, G, H, I, J, K, L.

A. X2 = L-His, X4 = D-Ser, X5 = L-Tyr, X7 = L-Leu, X9 = L-Pro: [4-D-serine]goserelin,

C. X2 = L-His, X4 = L-Ser, X5 = L-Tyr, X7 = L-Leu, X9 = D-Pro: [9-D-proline]goserelin,

F. X2 = L-His, X4 = L-Ser, X5 = D-Tyr, X7 = L-Leu, X9 = L-Pro: [5-D-tyrosine]goserelin,

G. X2 = D-His, X4 = L-Ser, X5 = L-Tyr, X7 = L-Leu, X9 = L-Pro: [2-D-histidine]goserelin,

L. X2 = L-His, X4 = L-Ser, X5 = L-Tyr, X7 = D-Leu, X9 = L-Pro: [7-D-leucine]goserelin,

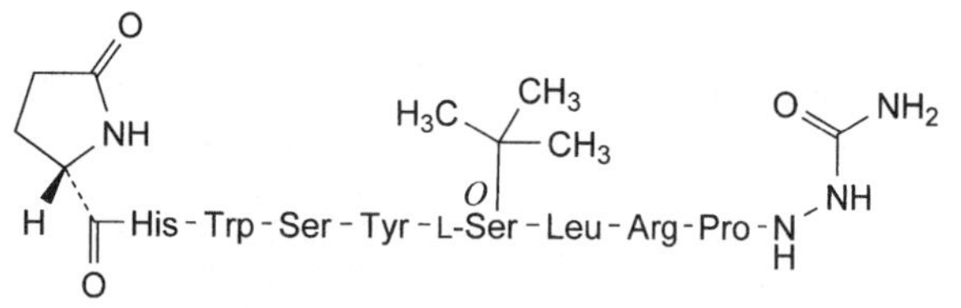

B. [6-[O-(1,1-dimethylethyl)-l-serine]]goserelin,

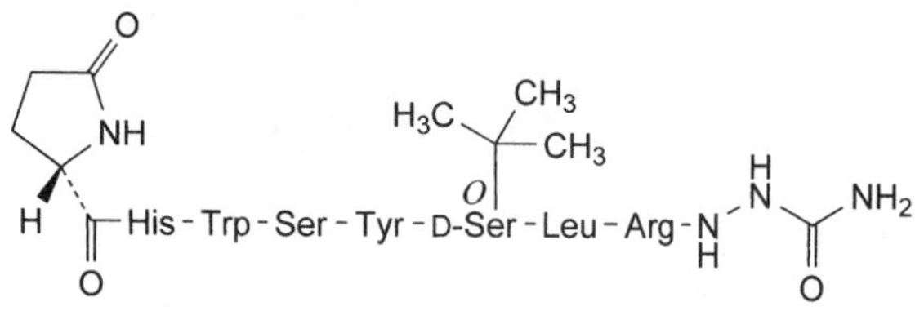

D. 1-carbamoylyl-2-[5-oxo-L-prolyl-L-histidyl-L-tryptophyl-L-seryl-L-tyrosyl-O-(1,1-dimethylethyl)-D-seryl-L-leucyl-L-arginyl]diazane,

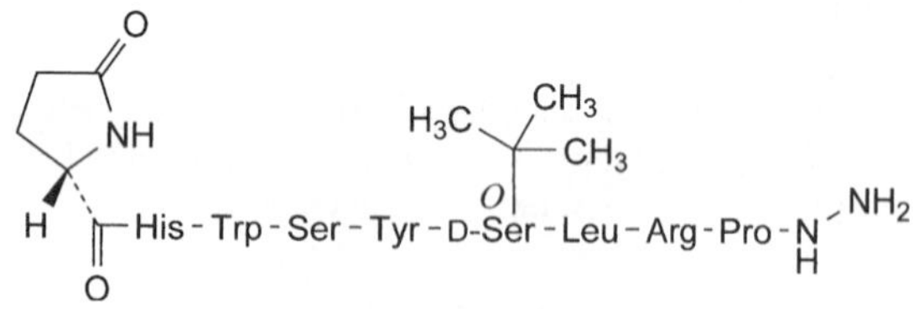

E. 5-oxo-L-prolyl-L-histidyl-L-tryptophyl-L-seryl-L-tyrosyl-O-(1,1-dimethylethyl)-D-seryl-L-leucyl-L-arginyl-L-prolinohydrazide,

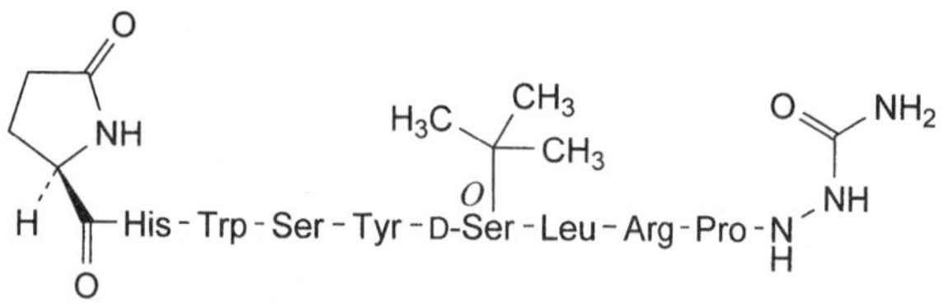

H. [1-(5-oxo-d-proline)]goserelin,

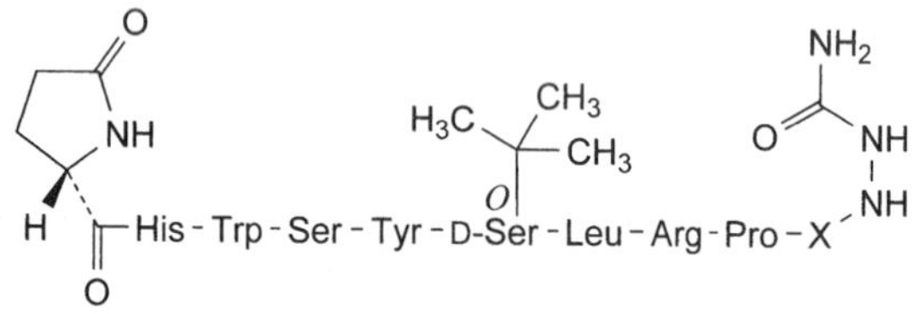

I. X = Pro-Pro: endo-8a,8b-DI-L-proline-goserelin,

J. X = Pro: endo-8a-L-proline-goserelin,

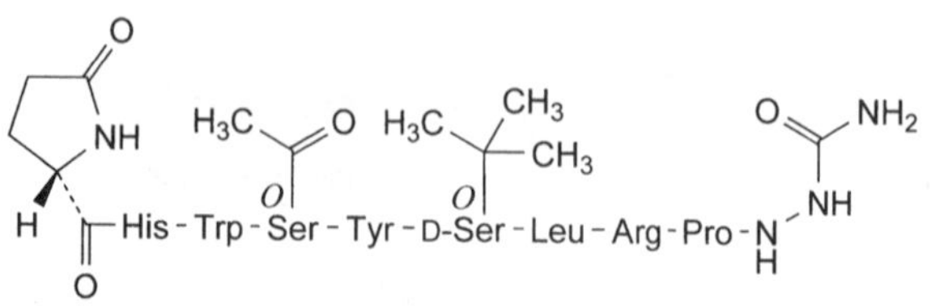

K. $O^4$-acetylgoserelin.

_____ _Ph Eur_

# Gramicidin

(_Ph Eur monograph 0907_)

| Gramicidin | X | Y | Mol. formula | $M_r$ |
|---|---|---|---|---|
| A1 | L-Val | L-Trp | $C_{99}H_{140}N_{20}O_{17}$ | 1882 |
| A2 | L-Ile | L-Trp | $C_{100}H_{142}N_{20}O_{17}$ | 1896 |
| B1 | L-Val | L-Phe | $C_{97}H_{139}N_{19}O_{17}$ | 1843 |
| C1 | L-Val | L-Tyr | $C_{97}H_{139}N_{19}O_{18}$ | 1859 |
| C2 | L-Ile | L-Tyr | $C_{98}H_{141}N_{19}O_{18}$ | 1873 |

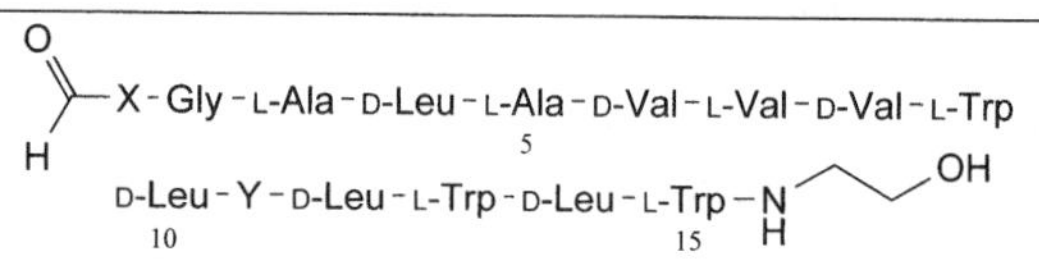

X-Gly-L-Ala-D-Leu-L-Ala-D-Val-L-Val-D-Val-L-Trp
5
D-Leu-Y-D-Leu-L-Trp-D-Leu-L-Trp-N—OH
10                              15

_1405-97-6_

**Action and use**
Polypeptide antibacterial.

_Ph Eur_ _____

## DEFINITION
Gramicidin consists of a family of antimicrobial linear polypeptides, usually obtained by extraction from tyrothricin, the complex isolated from the fermentation broth of _Brevibacillus brevis_ Dubos. The main component is gramicidin A1, together with gramicidins A2, B1, C1 and C2 in particular.

**Content**
Minimum 900 IU/mg (dried substance).

## CHARACTERS
**Appearance**
White or almost white, crystalline powder, slightly hygroscopic.

**Solubility**
Practically insoluble in water, soluble in methanol, sparingly soluble in alcohol.

**mp**
About 230 °C.

## IDENTIFICATION
_First identification   A, C._
_Second identification   A, B._

A. Dissolve 0.100 g in _alcohol R_ and dilute to 100.0 ml with the same solvent. Dilute 5.0 ml of this solution to 100.0 ml with _alcohol R_. Examined between 240 nm and 320 nm (_2.2.25_), the solution shows 2 absorption maxima, at 282 nm and 290 nm, a shoulder at about 275 nm and an absorption minimum at 247 nm. The specific absorbance at the maximum at 282 nm is 105 to 125.

B. Thin-layer chromatography (_2.2.27_).

_Test solution_   Dissolve 5 mg of the substance to be examined in 6.0 ml of _alcohol R_.

_Reference solution (a)_   Dissolve 5 mg of _gramicidin CRS_ in 6.0 ml of _alcohol R_.

_Reference solution (b)_   Dissolve 5 mg of _tyrothricin CRS_ in 6.0 ml of _alcohol R_.

_Plate_   TLC silica gel plate R.

_Mobile phase_   methanol R, butanol R, water R, glacial acetic acid R, butyl acetate R (3:9:15:24:49 V/V/V/V/V).

*Application* 1 μl.

*Development* Over 2/3 of the plate.

*Drying* In air.

*Detection* Dip the plate into *dimethylaminobenzaldehyde solution R2*. Heat at 90 °C until the spots appear.

*System suitability* The chromatogram obtained with reference solution (b) shows 2 clearly separated spots or 2 clearly separated groups of spots.

*Results* The principal spot or group of principal spots in the chromatogram obtained with the test solution is similar in position, colour and size to the principal spot or group of principal spots in the chromatogram obtained with reference solution (a) and to the spot or group of spots with the highest $R_F$ value in the chromatogram obtained with reference solution (b).

C. Examine the chromatograms obtained in the test for composition.

*Results* The 3 principal peaks in the chromatogram obtained with the test solution are similar in retention time to the 3 principal peaks in the chromatogram obtained with reference solution (a).

## TESTS

*Composition* Liquid chromatography (*2.2.29*): use the normalisation procedure.

*Test solution* Dissolve 25 mg of the substance to be examined in 10 ml of *methanol R* and dilute to 25 ml with the mobile phase.

*Reference solution (a)* Dissolve 25 mg of *gramicidin CRS* in 10 ml of *methanol R* and dilute to 25 ml with the mobile phase.

*Reference solution (b)* Dilute 1.0 ml of reference solution (a) to 50.0 ml with the mobile phase. Dilute 1.0 ml of this solution to 10.0 ml with the mobile phase.

*Column:*
— *size: l* = 0.25 m, Ø = 4.6 mm,
— *stationary phase*: base-deactivated end-capped octadecylsilyl silica gel for chromatography R (5 μm),
— *temperature*: 50 °C.

*Mobile phase* water R, methanol R (29:71 V/V).

*Flow rate* 1.0 ml/min.

*Detection* Spectrophotometer at 282 nm.

*Injection* 20 μl.

*Run time* 2.5 times the retention time of gramicidin A1.

*Relative retention* With reference to gramicidin A1 (retention time = about 22 min):
gramicidin C1 = about 0.7; gramicidin C2 = about 0.8; gramicidin A2 = about 1.2; gramicidin B1 = about 1.9.

*System suitability* Reference solution (a):
— *resolution*: minimum 1.5 between the peaks due to gramicidin A1 and gramicidin A2,
— the chromatogram obtained is concordant with the chromatogram supplied with *gramicidin CRS* .

*Composition:*
— *sum of the contents of gramicidins A1, A2, B1, C1 and C2*: minimum 95.0 per cent,
— *ratio of the content of gramicidin A1 to the sum of the contents of gramicidins A1, A2, B1, C1 and C2* : minimum 60.0 per cent,
— *disregard limit*: the area of the peak due to gramicidin A1 in the chromatogram obtained with reference solution (b).

## Related substances

Liquid chromatography (*2.2.29*) as described in the test for composition.

*Limit:*
— *any impurity*: maximum 2.0 per cent and not more than 1 peak is more than 1.0 per cent; disregard the peaks due to gramicidins A1, A2, B1, C1 and C2.

## Loss on drying (*2.2.32*)

Maximum 3.0 per cent, determined on 1.000 g by drying over *diphosphorus pentoxide R* at 60 °C at a pressure not exceeding 0.1 kPa for 3 h.

## Sulphated ash (*2.4.14*)

Maximum 1.0 per cent, determined on 1.0 g.

## ASSAY

Carry out the microbiological assay of antibiotics (*2.7.2*), using the turbidimetric method. Use *gramicidin CRS* as the reference substance.

## STORAGE

In an airtight container, protected from light.

## IMPURITIES

| Impurity | X1 | X4 | X10 | X11 | R |
|----------|------|--------|--------|--------|---------|
| A | L-Val | Met | D-Leu | L-Trp | OH |
| B | L-Val | D-Leu | D-Leu | L-Trp | CH₂-OH |
| C | L-Ile | D-Leu | D-Leu | L-Phe | OH |
| D | L-Val | D-Leu | Met | L-Tyr | OH |
| E | L-Ile | D-Leu | D-Leu | L-Trp | CH₂-OH |

```
O
‖
  C—X1-Gly-L-Ala-X4-L-Ala-D-Val-L-Val-D-Val-L-Trp-
H                         5
      X10-X11-D-Leu-L-Trp-D-Leu-L-Trp-N       R
      10                          15    H
```

A. [4-methionine]gramicidin A1,

B. gramicidin A1 3-hydroxypropyl,

C. gramicidin B2,

D. [10-methionine]gramicidin C1,

E. gramicidin A2 3-hydroxypropyl.

*————————————— Ph Eur*

# Granisetron Hydrochloride

(*Ph Eur monograph 1695*)

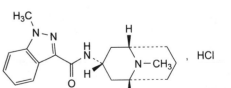

$C_{18}H_{24}N_4O,HCl$      348.9      *107007-99-8*

## Action and use

Serotonin 5HT₃ receptor antagonist; treatment of nausea and vomiting.

*Ph Eur*

## DEFINITION

1-Methyl-*N*-[(1*R*,3*r*,5*S*)-9-methyl-9-azabicyclo[3.3.1]non-3-yl]-1*H*-indazole-3-carboxamide hydrochloride.

## Content

97.0 per cent to 102.0 per cent (dried substance).

## CHARACTERS

### Appearance

White or almost white powder.

### Solubility

Freely soluble in water, sparingly soluble in methylene chloride, slightly soluble in methanol.

## IDENTIFICATION

A. Infrared absorption spectrophotometry (*2.2.24*).

*Comparison* granisetron hydrochloride CRS.

B. It gives reaction (a) of chlorides (*2.3.1*).

## TESTS

### Solution S

Dissolve 0.2 g in *carbon dioxide-free water R* and dilute to 20 ml with the same solvent.

### Appearance of solution

Solution S is clear (*2.2.1*) and colourless (*2.2.2, Method II*).

### pH (*2.2.3*)

4.0 to 6.5 for solution S.

### Impurity E

Thin-layer chromatography (*2.2.27*).

*Solvent mixture* water R, acetonitrile R (20:80 *V/V*).

*Test solution* Dissolve 0.25 g of the substance to be examined in the solvent mixture and dilute to 5 ml with the solvent mixture.

*Reference solution* Dissolve 5.0 mg of *granisetron impurity E CRS* in the solvent mixture and dilute to 20.0 ml with the solvent mixture.

*Plate* TLC silica gel $F_{254}$ plate R.

*Mobile phase* concentrated ammonia R, 2-propanol R, ethyl acetate R (6.5:30:50 *V/V/V*).

*Application* 2 µl.

*Development* Over half of the plate.

*Drying* In air.

*Detection* Expose to iodine vapour for 30 min.

*Limit:*

— *impurity E*: any spot due to impurity E is not more intense than the principal spot in the chromatogram obtained with the reference solution (0.5 per cent).

### Related substances

Liquid chromatography (*2.2.29*). *Carry out the test protected from light.*

*Test solution* Dissolve 50.0 mg of the substance to be examined in the mobile phase and dilute to 50.0 ml with the mobile phase.

*Reference solution (a)* Dilute 1.0 ml of the test solution to 50.0 ml with the mobile phase. Dilute 5.0 ml of this solution to 20.0 ml with the mobile phase.

*Reference solution (b)* Transfer 2 ml of the test solution to a colourless glass vial, stopper and expose the solution either to sunlight for 4 h or under a UV lamp for 16 h (partial degradation of granisetron to impurity C). A degradation of at least about 0.3 per cent of granisetron to impurity C must be obtained as shown by appearance of a corresponding peak in the chromatogram. If not, expose the solution once again to sunlight or under a UV lamp.

*Reference solution (c)* Dissolve 50.0 mg of *granisetron hydrochloride CRS* in the mobile phase and dilute to 50.0 ml with the mobile phase.

*Reference solution (d)* Dissolve the contents of a vial of *granisetron impurity A CRS* in 1 ml of the mobile phase.

*Reference solution (e)* Dissolve the contents of a vial of *granisetron impurity B CRS* in 1 ml of the mobile phase.

*Column:*

— *size*: *l* = 0.25 m, Ø = 4.6 mm;
— *stationary phase*: spherical base-deactivated end-capped octadecylsilyl silica gel for chromatography R (5 µm);
— *temperature*: 40 °C.

*Mobile phase* Dilute 1.6 ml of *phosphoric acid R* to 800 ml with *water R*, add 200 ml of *acetonitrile R* and mix. Add 1.0 ml of *hexylamine R* and mix. Adjust to pH 7.5 ± 0.05 with freshly *distilled triethylamine R* (about 4 ml).

*Flow rate* 1.5 ml/min.

*Detection* Spectrophotometer at 305 nm.

*Injection* 10 µl of the test solution and reference solutions (a), (b), (d) and (e).

*Run time* Twice the retention time of granisetron.

*Relative retention* With reference to granisetron (retention time = about 7 min): impurity D = about 0.4; impurity B = about 0.5; impurity A = about 0.7; impurity C = about 0.8.

*System suitability:*

— *resolution*: minimum 3.5 between the peaks due to impurity C and granisetron in the chromatogram obtained with reference solution (b);
— *symmetry factor*: maximum 2.0 for the peak due to granisetron.

*Limits:*

— *correction factor*: for the calculation of content, multiply the peak area of impurity B by 1.7;
— *impurity B*: not more than the area of the principal peak in the chromatogram obtained with reference solution (a) (0.5 per cent);
— *impurity C*: not more than 0.4 times the area of the principal peak in the chromatogram obtained with reference solution (a) (0.2 per cent);
— *impurity A*: not more than twice the area of the principal peak in the chromatogram obtained with reference solution (a) (1.0 per cent);
— *impurity D*: not more than 0.2 times the area of the principal peak in the chromatogram obtained with reference solution (a) (0.1 per cent);
— *any other impurity*: for each impurity, not more than 0.2 times the area of the principal peak in the chromatogram obtained with reference solution (a) (0.1 per cent);
— *total*: not more than twice the area of the principal peak in the chromatogram obtained with reference solution (a) (1.0 per cent);
— *disregard limit*: 0.1 times the area of the principal peak in the chromatogram obtained with reference solution (a) (0.05 per cent); disregard any peak due to the blank.

## Loss on drying (*2.2.32*)

Maximum 0.5 per cent, determined on 1.000 g by drying in an oven at 105 °C for 4 h.

## Sulphated ash (*2.4.14*)

Maximum 0.1 per cent, determined on 1.0 g.

## ASSAY

Liquid chromatography (*2.2.29*) as described in the test for related substances with the following modification.

*Injection*   Test solution and reference solution (c).

Calculate the percentage content of $C_{18}H_{25}ClN_4O$ using the declared content of *granisetron hydrochloride CRS*.

## IMPURITIES

*Specified impurities   A, B, C, D, E.*

*Other detectable impurities*   (The following substances would, if present at a sufficient level, be detected by one or other of the tests in the monograph. They are limited by the general acceptance criterion for other/unspecified impurities and/or by the general monograph *Substances for pharmaceutical use (2034)*. It is therefore not necessary to identify these impurities for demonstration of compliance. See also *5.10. Control of impurities in substances for pharmaceutical use*): *F, G, H, I*.

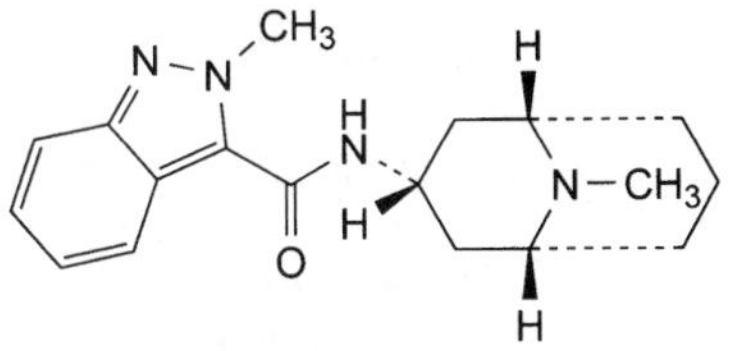

A. 2-methyl-*N*-[(1*R*,3*r*,5*S*)-9-methyl-9-azabicyclo[3.3.1]non-3-yl]-2*H*-indazole-3-carboxamide,

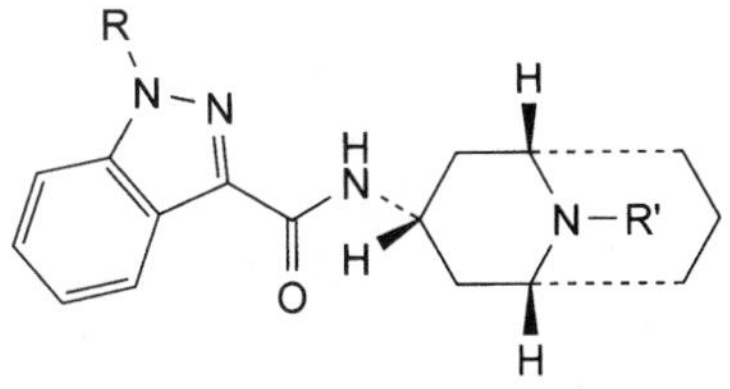

B. R = H, R′ = CH₃: *N*-[(1*R*,3*r*,5*S*)-9-methyl-9-azabicyclo[3.3.1]non-3-yl]-1*H*-indazole-3-carboxamide,
C. R = CH₃, R′ = H: *N*-[(1*R*,3*r*,5*S*)-9-azabicyclo[3.3.1]non-3-yl]-1-methyl-1*H*-indazole-3-carboxamide,

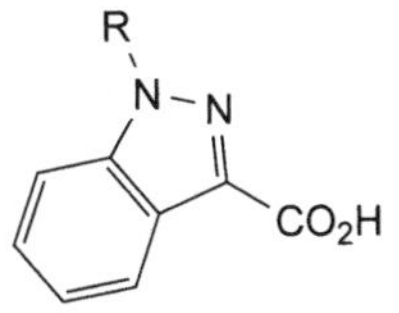

D. R = CH₃: 1-methyl-1*H*-indazole-3-carboxylic acid,
H. R = H: 1*H*-indazole-3-carboxylic acid,

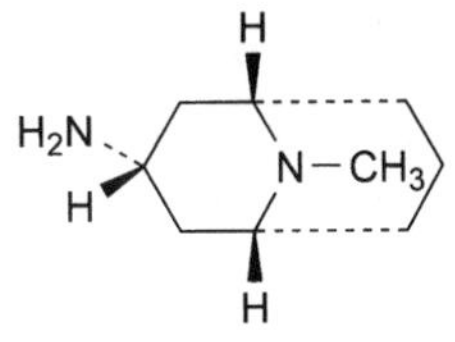

E. (1*R*,3*r*,5*S*)-9-methyl-9-azabicyclo[3.3.1]nonan-3-amine,

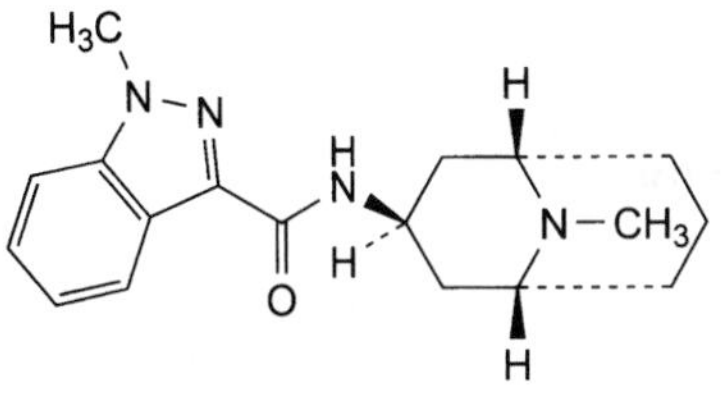

F. 1-methyl-*N*-[(1*R*,3*s*,5*S*)-9-methyl-9-azabicyclo[3.3.1]non-3-yl]-1*H*-indazole-3-carboxamide (*exo*-granisetron),

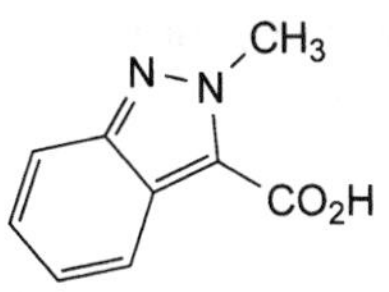

G. 2-methyl-2*H*-indazole-3-carboxylic acid,

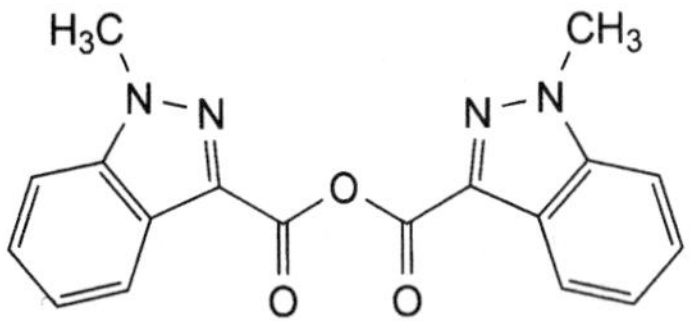

I. 1-methyl-1*H*-indazole-3-carboxylic anhydride.

*Ph Eur*

# Griseofulvin

(*Ph Eur monograph 0182*)

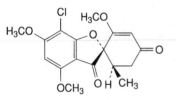

| $C_{17}H_{17}ClO_6$ | 352.8 | *126-07-8* |

**Action and use**
Antibacterial.

**Preparation**
Griseofulvin Tablets

*Ph Eur*

## DEFINITION

(1′*S*,3-6′*R*)-7-Chloro-2′,4,6-trimethoxy-6′-methylspiro[benzofuran-2(3*H*),1′-[2]cyclohexene]-3,4′-dione.

Substance produced by the growth of certain strains of *Penicillium griseofulvum* or obtained by any other means.

**Content**
97.0 per cent to 102.0 per cent (dried substance).

## PRODUCTION

The method of manufacture is validated to demonstrate that the product if tested would comply with the following test.

**Abnormal toxicity**
To each of 5 healthy mice, each weighing 17-22 g, administer orally a suspension of 0.1 g of the substance to be

examined in 0.5-1 ml of *water R*. None of the mice dies within 48 h.

## CHARACTERS

### Appearance

White or yellowish-white, microfine powder, the particles of which generally have a maximum dimension of up to 5 μm, although larger particles that may exceed 30 μm may occasionally be present.

### Solubility

Practically insoluble in water, freely soluble in dimethylformamide and in tetrachloroethane, slightly soluble in anhydrous ethanol and in methanol.

mp: about 220 °C.

## IDENTIFICATION

A. Infrared absorption spectrophotometry (*2.2.24*).

*Comparison*   griseofulvin CRS .

B. Dissolve about 5 mg in 1 ml of *sulphuric acid R* and add about 5 mg of powdered *potassium dichromate R*. A dark red colour develops.

## TESTS

### Appearance of solution

The solution is clear (*2.2.1*) and not more intensely coloured than reference solution $Y_4$ (*2.2.2, Method II*).

Dissolve 0.75 g in *dimethylformamide R* and dilute to 10 ml with the same solvent.

### Acidity

Suspend 0.25 g in 20 ml of *ethanol (96 per cent) R* and add *0.1 ml of phenolphthalein solution R*. Not more than 1.0 ml of *0.02 M sodium hydroxide* is required to change the colour of the indicator.

### Specific optical rotation (*2.2.7*)

+ 354 to + 364 (dried substance).

Dissolve 0.250 g in *dimethylformamide R* and dilute to 25.0 ml with the same solvent.

### Related substances

Gas chromatography (*2.2.28*).

*Internal standard solution*   Dissolve 0.2 g of *diphenylanthracene R* in *acetone R* and dilute to 100.0 ml with the same solvent.

*Test solution (a)*   Dissolve 0.10 g of the substance to be examined in *acetone R* and dilute to 10.0 ml with the same solvent.

*Test solution (b)*   Dissolve 0.10 g of the substance to be examined in *acetone R*, add 1.0 ml of the internal standard solution and dilute to 10.0 ml with *acetone R*.

*Reference solution*   Dissolve 5.0 mg of *griseofulvin CRS* in *acetone R*, add 1.0 ml of the internal standard solution and dilute to 10.0 ml with *acetone R*.

*Column:*
— *material*: glass;
— *size*: *l* = 1 m, Ø = 4 mm;
— *stationary phase*: *diatomaceous earth for gas chromatography R* impregnated with 1 per cent *m/m* of *poly[(cyanopropyl)(methyl)][(phenyl)(methyl)]siloxane R.*

*Carrier gas*   nitrogen for chromatography R.

*Flow rate*   50-60 ml/min.

*Temperature:*
— *column*: 250 °C;
— *injection* port: 270 °C;
— *detector.* 300 °C.

*Detection*   Flame ionisation.

*Run time*   3 times the retention time of griseofulvin.

*Relative retention*   With reference to griseofulvin (retention time = about 11 min): dechloro-griseofulvin = about 0.6; dehydrogriseofulvin = about 1.4.

Calculate the ratio (*R*) of the area of the peak due to griseofulvin to the area of the peak due to the internal standard in the chromatogram obtained with the reference solution.

*Limits:*
— *dechloro-griseofulvin* : calculate the ratio of the area of the peak due to dechloro-griseofulvin to the area of the peak due to the internal standard in the chromatogram obtained with test solution (b): this ratio is not greater than 0.6 *R* (3.0 per cent);
— *dehydrogriseofulvin*: calculate the ratio of the area of the peak due to dehydrogriseofulvin to the area of the peak due to the internal standard in the chromatogram obtained with test solution (b): this ratio is not greater than 0.15 *R* (0.75 per cent).

### Substances soluble in light petroleum

Maximum 0.2 per cent.

Shake 1.0 g with 20 ml of *light petroleum R*. Boil under a reflux condenser for 10 min. Cool, filter and wash with 3 quantities, each of 15 ml, of *light petroleum R*. Combine the filtrate and washings, evaporate to dryness on a water-bath and dry at 100-105 °C for 1 h. The residue weighs not more than 2 mg.

### Loss on drying (*2.2.32*)

Maximum 1.0 per cent, determined on 1.00 g by drying in an oven at 105 °C.

### Sulphated ash (*2.4.14*)

Maximum 0.2 per cent, determined on 1.0 g.

## ASSAY

Dissolve 80.0 mg in *anhydrous ethanol R* and dilute to 200.0 ml with the same solvent. Dilute 2.0 ml of this solution to 100.0 ml with *anhydrous ethanol R*. Measure the absorbance (*2.2.25*) at the absorption maximum at 291 nm.

Calculate the content of $C_{17}H_{17}ClO_6$, taking the specific absorbance to be 686.

*Ph Eur*

# Guaiacol

(*Ph Eur monograph 1978*)

| $C_7H_8O_2$ | 124.1 | 90-05-1 |

*Ph Eur*

## DEFINITION

2-Methoxyphenol.

### Content

97.0 per cent to 102.0 per cent (anhydrous substance).

## CHARACTERS

### Appearance

Crystalline mass or colourless or yellowish liquid, hygroscopic.

**Solubility**

Sparingly soluble in water, very soluble in methylene chloride, freely soluble in ethanol (96 per cent).

**mp**

About 28 °C.

## IDENTIFICATION

*First identification* A.

*Second identification* B.

A. Infrared absorption spectrophotometry (*2.2.24*).

*Comparison* guaiacol CRS.

B. Thin-layer chromatography (*2.2.27*).

*Test solution* Dissolve 0.5 g of the substance to be examined in *methanol R* and dilute to 25 ml with the same solvent.

*Reference solution* Dissolve 0.5 g of *guaiacol CRS* in *methanol R* and dilute to 25 ml with the same solvent.

*Plate* TLC silica gel plate R.

*Mobile phase* anhydrous acetic acid R, methanol R, toluene R (6:14:80 *V/V/V*).

*Application* 5 μl.

*Development* Over 2/3 of the plate.

*Drying* In air.

*Detection* Spray with *ferric chloride solution R1*.

*Results* The principal spot in the chromatogram obtained with the test solution is similar in position, colour and size to the principal spot in the chromatogram obtained with the reference solution.

## TESTS

**Solution S**

Dissolve 1.00 g in *ethanol (96 per cent) R* and dilute to 10.0 ml with the same solvent.

**Appearance of solution**

Solution S is clear (*2.2.1*) and not more intensely coloured than reference solution $BY_6$ (*2.2.2, Method I*).

**Acidity or alkalinity**

To 5.0 ml of solution S, add 10 ml of *carbon dioxide-free water R* and 0.1 ml of *methyl red mixed solution R*. Not more than 0.05 ml of *0.1 M hydrochloric acid* or *0.1 M sodium hydroxide* is required to change the colour of the indicator.

**Impurity A**

Liquid chromatography (*2.2.29*).

*Solvent mixture* phosphoric acid R, water R, methanol R (1:499:500 *V/V/V*).

*Test solution (a)* Dissolve 1.0 g of the substance to be examined in the solvent mixture and dilute to 25.0 ml with the solvent mixture.

*Test solution (b)* Dissolve 20.0 mg of the substance to be examined in the solvent mixture and dilute to 100.0 ml with the solvent mixture.

*Reference solution (a)* Dilute 1.0 ml of test solution (a) to 100.0 ml with the solvent mixture. Dilute 1.0 ml of this solution to 20.0 ml with the solvent mixture.

*Reference solution (b)* Dissolve 0.20 g of *pyrocatechol R* (impurity A) and 0.20 g of *phenol R* (impurity B) in the solvent mixture and dilute to 100 ml with the solvent mixture. Dilute 1 ml of this solution to 10 ml with the solvent mixture.

*Reference solution (c)* Dissolve 20.0 mg of *guaiacol CRS* in the solvent mixture and dilute to 100.0 ml with the solvent mixture.

*Column:*
— size: *l* = 0.15 m, Ø = 4.6 mm;
— stationary phase: *octadecylsilyl silica gel for chromatography R* (5 μm).

*Mobile phase:*
— mobile phase A: *phosphoric acid R, methanol R, water R* (1:150:849 *V/V/V*);
— mobile phase B: *methanol R*;

| Time (min) | Mobile phase A (per cent *V/V*) | Mobile phase B (per cent *V/V*) |
|---|---|---|
| 0 - 28 | 100 | 0 |
| 28 - 30 | 100 → 35 | 0 → 65 |
| 30 - 40 | 35 | 65 |

*Flow rate* 1 ml/min.

*Detection* Spectrophotometer at 270 nm.

*Injection* 20 μl of test solution (a) and reference solutions (a) and (b).

*Retention time* Guaiacol = about 20 min.

*System suitability* Reference solution (b):
— resolution: minimum 5.0 between the peaks due to impurities A (1st peak) and B (2nd peak).

*Limit:*
— impurity A: not more than the area of the principal peak in the chromatogram obtained with reference solution (a) (0.05 per cent).

**Related substances**

Gas chromatography (*2.2.28*): use the normalisation procedure.

*Test solution* Dissolve 1.00 g of the substance to be examined in *acetonitrile R* and dilute to 10.0 ml with the same solvent.

*Reference solution (a)* Dissolve 0.20 g of *phenol R* (impurity B) and 0.40 g of *methyl benzoate R* (impurity E) in *acetonitrile R* and dilute to 50 ml with the same solvent. Dilute 1 ml of this solution to 20 ml with *acetonitrile R*.

*Reference solution (b)* Dilute 0.5 ml of the test solution to 100.0 ml with *acetonitrile R*. Dilute 1.0 ml of this solution to 10.0 ml with *acetonitrile R*.

*Reference solution (c)* Dissolve 10 mg of *veratrole R* (impurity C) in *acetonitrile R* and dilute to 10 ml with the same solvent.

*Column:*
— material: fused silica;
— size: *l* = 25 m, Ø = 0.53 mm;
— stationary phase: *poly(cyanopropyl) (7) (phenyl) (7) (methyl) (86) siloxane R* (film thickness 2 μm).

*Carrier gas* helium for chromatography R.

*Flow rate* 5 ml/min.

*Split ratio* 1:5.

*Temperature:*

| | Time (min) | Temperature (°C) |
|---|---|---|
| Column | 0 - 15 | 90 |
| | 15 - 45 | 90 → 180 |
| Injection port | | 200 |
| Detector | | 220 |

*Detection* Flame ionisation.

*Injection* 1 μl.

*Relative retention* With reference to guaiacol (retention time = about 25 min): impurity E = about 0.88; impurity B = about 0.92; impurity C = about 1.1.

*System suitability* Reference solution (a):
— *resolution*: minimum 2.0 between the peaks due to impurities E (1st peak) and B (2nd peak).

*Limits*:
— *impurity C*: maximum 0.4 per cent;
— *impurity E*: maximum 0.2 per cent;
— *impurity B*: maximum 0.15 per cent;
— *unspecified impurities*: for each impurity, maximum 0.10 per cent;
— *total*: maximum 1.0 per cent;
— *disregard limit*: the area of the principal peak in the chromatogram obtained with reference solution (b) (0.05 per cent).

**Water** *(2.5.12)*
Maximum 0.5 per cent, determined on 2.000 g.

**ASSAY**
Liquid chromatography *(2.2.29)* as described in the test for impurity A with the following modification.

*Injection* Test solution (b) and reference solution (c).

Calculate the percentage content of $C_7H_8O_2$ from the declared content of *guaiacol CRS*.

**STORAGE**
In an airtight container, protected from light.

**IMPURITIES**
*Specified impurities* A, B, C, E.

*Other detectable impurities* (The following substances would, if present at a sufficient level, be detected by one or other of the tests in the monograph. They are limited by the general acceptance criterion for other/unspecified impurities and/or by the general monograph *Substances for pharmaceutical use (2034)*. It is therefore not necessary to identify these impurities for demonstration of compliance. See also *5.10*. *Control of impurities in substances for pharmaceutical use*): D, F, G, H.

A. R1 = R2 = OH: benzene-1,2-diol (pyrocatechol),

B. R1 = OH, R2 = H: phenol,

C. R1 = R2 = OCH₃: 1,2-dimethoxybenzene (veratrole),

E. R1 = CO-O-CH₃, R2 = H: methyl benzoate,

D. R2 = R5 = OCH₃, R3 = R4 = R6 = H: 2,5-dimethoxyphenol,

F. R2 = OCH₃, R3 = R4 = R5 = H, R6 = CH₃: 2-methoxy-6-methylphenol (6-methylguaiacol),

G. R2 = R3 = R5 = R6 = H, R4 = OCH₃: 4-methoxyphenol,

H. R2 = R4 = R5 = R6 = H, R3 = OCH₃: 3-methoxyphenol.

*Ph Eur*

# Guaifenesin

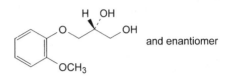

*(Ph Eur monograph 0615)*

and enantiomer

$C_{10}H_{14}O_4$      198.2      *93-14-1*

**Action and use**
Expectorant.

*Ph Eur*

**DEFINITION**
(2*RS*)-3-(2-Methoxyphenoxy)propane-1,2-diol.

**Content**
98.0 per cent to 102.0 per cent (dried substance).

**CHARACTERS**
**Appearance**
White or almost white, crystalline powder.

**Solubility**
Sparingly soluble in water, soluble in alcohol.

**IDENTIFICATION**
*First identification* B.

*Second identification* A, C.

A. Melting point *(2.2.14)*: 79 °C to 83 °C.

B. Infrared absorption spectrophotometry *(2.2.24)*.

*Comparison* guaifenesin CRS .

C. Thin-layer chromatography *(2.2.27)*.

*Test solution* Dissolve 30 mg of the substance to be examined in *methanol R* and dilute to 10 ml with the same solvent.

*Reference solution* Dissolve 30 mg of *guaifenesin CRS* in *methanol R* and dilute to 10 ml with the same solvent.

*Plate* TLC silica gel G plate R.

*Mobile phase* methylene chloride R, propanol R (20:80 *V/V*).

*Application* 5 μl.

*Development* Over 2/3 of the plate.

*Drying* In air.

*Detection* Spray with a mixture of equal volumes of a 10 g/l solution of *potassium ferricyanide R*, a 200 g/l solution of *ferric chloride R* and *alcohol R*.

*Results* The principal spot in the chromatogram obtained with the test solution is similar in position, colour and size to the principal spot in the chromatogram obtained with the reference solution.

**TESTS**
**Solution S**
Dissolve 1.0 g in *carbon dioxide-free water R*, heating gently if necessary, and dilute to 50 ml with the same solvent.

**Appearance of solution**
Solution S is clear *(2.2.1)* and colourless *(2.2.2, Method II)*.

**Acidity or alkalinity**

To 10 ml of solution S add 0.05 ml of *phenolphthalein solution R1*. Not more than 0.1 ml of *0.01 M sodium hydroxide* is required to change the colour of the indicator. To 10 ml of solution S add 0.15 ml of *methyl red solution R*. Not more than 0.1 ml of *0.01 M hydrochloric acid* is required to change the colour of the indicator to red.

**Related substances**

Liquid chromatography (*2.2.29*).

*Test solution*   Dissolve 0.100 g of the substance to be examined in *acetonitrile R* and dilute to 50.0 ml with the same solvent.

*Reference solution (a)*   Dilute 1.0 ml of the test solution to 20.0 ml with *acetonitrile R*. Dilute 1.0 ml of this solution to 10.0 ml with *acetonitrile R*.

*Reference solution (b)*   Dissolve 10.0 mg of *guaiacol R* in *acetonitrile R* and dilute to 50.0 ml with the same solvent. Dilute 0.5 ml of this solution to 50.0 ml with *acetonitrile R*.

*Reference solution (c)*   Dissolve 50.0 mg of *guaiacol R* in *acetonitrile R* and dilute to 50.0 ml with the same solvent. Dilute 5.0 ml of this solution to 10.0 ml with the test solution.

*Column:*
— *size:* $l$ = 0.25 m, Ø = 4.6 mm,
— *stationary phase:* octadecylsilyl silica gel for chromatography R (5 μm).

*Mobile phase:*
— *mobile phase A:* glacial acetic acid R, water R (10:990 *V/V*),
— *mobile phase B:* acetonitrile R,

| Time (min) | Mobile phase A (per cent *V/V*) | Mobile phase B (per cent *V/V*) |
|---|---|---|
| 0 - 32 | 80 → 50 | 20 → 50 |
| 32 - 33 | 50 → 80 | 50 → 20 |
| 33 - 40 | 80 | 20 |

*Flow rate*   1 ml/min.

*Detection*   Spectrophotometer at 276 nm.

*Injection*   10 μl.

*Relative retention*   With reference to guaifenesin (retention time = about 8 min): impurity B = about 0.9; impurity A = about 1.4; impurity C = about 3.1; impurity D = about 3.7.

*System suitability*   Reference solution (c):
— *resolution:* minimum 3.0 between the peaks due to guaifenesin and impurity A.

*Limits:*
— *impurity A:* not more than the area of the principal peak in the chromatogram obtained with reference solution (b) (0.1 per cent),
— *impurity B:* not more than twice the area of the principal peak in the chromatogram obtained with reference solution (a) (1.0 per cent),
— *any other impurity:* not more than the area of the principal peak in the chromatogram obtained with reference solution (a) (0.5 per cent),
— *total (excluding impurity B):* not more than twice the area of the principal peak in the chromatogram obtained with reference solution (a) (1.0 per cent),
— *disregard level:* 0.1 times the area of the principal peak in the chromatogram obtained with reference solution (a) (0.05 per cent).

**Chlorides and monochlorhydrins**

Maximum of 250 ppm.

To 10 ml of solution S add 2 ml of *dilute sodium hydroxide solution R* and heat on a water-bath for 5 min. Cool and add 3 ml of *dilute nitric acid R*. The resulting solution complies with the limit test for chlorides (*2.4.4*).

**Heavy metals** (*2.4.8*)

Maximum of 25 ppm.

Dissolve 2.0 g in a mixture of 1 volume of *water R* and 9 volumes of *alcohol R* and dilute to 25 ml with the same mixture of solvents. 12 ml of the solution complies with limit test B. Prepare the standard using lead standard solution (2 ppm Pb) prepared by diluting *lead standard solution (100 ppm Pb) R* with a mixture of 1 volume of *water R* and 9 volumes of *alcohol R*.

**Loss on drying** (*2.2.32*)

Maximum 0.5 per cent, determined on 1.000 g by drying *in vacuo* at 60 °C for 3 h.

**Sulphated ash** (*2.4.14*)

Maximum 0.1 per cent, determined on 1.0 g.

**ASSAY**

To 0.500 g (*m* g) add 10.0 ml of a freshly prepared mixture of 1 volume of *acetic anhydride R* and 7 volumes of *pyridine R*. Boil under a reflux condenser for 45 min. Cool and add 25 ml of *water R*. Using 0.25 ml of *phenolphthalein solution R* as indicator, titrate with *1 M sodium hydroxide* ($n_1$ ml). Carry out a blank titration ($n_2$ ml).

Calculate the percentage content of $C_{10}H_{14}O_4$ from the expression:

$$\frac{19.82\,(n_2 - n_1)}{2m}$$

**IMPURITIES**

A. R = H: 2-methoxyphenol (guaiacol),

B. R = CH(CH$_2$OH)$_2$: 2-(2-methoxyphenoxy)propane-1,3-diol (B-isomer),

C. 1,1′-oxybis[3-(2-methoxyphenoxy)propan-2-ol] (bisether),

D. 1,3-bis(2-methoxyphenoxy)propan-2-ol.

*Ph Eur*

# Guanethidine Monosulphate

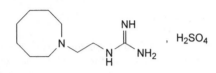

*(Ph Eur monograph 0027)*

$C_{10}H_{22}N_4,H_2SO_4$      296.4      *645-43-2*

## Action and use
Adrenergic neuron blocker.

## Preparation
Guanethidine Tablets

*Ph Eur* _____

## DEFINITION
1-[2-(Hexahydroazocin-1(2*H*)-yl)ethyl]guanidine monosulphate.

## Content
99.0 per cent to 101.0 per cent (dried substance).

## CHARACTERS
### Appearance
Colourless, crystalline powder.

### Solubility
Freely soluble in water, practically insoluble in ethanol (96 per cent).

mp: about 250 °C, with decomposition.

## IDENTIFICATION
A. Dissolve about 25 mg in 25 ml of *water R*, add 20 ml of *picric acid solution R* and filter. The precipitate, washed with *water R* and dried at 100-105 °C, melts *(2.2.14)* at about 154 °C.

B. Dissolve about 25 mg in 5 ml of *water R*. Add 1 ml of *strong sodium hydroxide solution R*, 1 ml of α-*naphthol solution R* and, dropwise with shaking, 0.5 ml of *strong sodium hypochlorite solution R*. A bright pink precipitate is formed and becomes violet-red on standing.

C. It gives the reactions of sulphates *(2.3.1)*.

## TESTS
### Solution S
Dissolve 0.4 g in *carbon dioxide-free water R* and dilute to 20 ml with the same solvent.

### Appearance of solution
Solution S is not more intensely coloured than reference solution $GY_6$ *(2.2.2, Method II)*.

### pH *(2.2.3)*
4.7 to 5.5 for solution S.

### Oxidisable substances
In a conical, ground-glass-stoppered flask, dissolve 1.0 g in 25 ml of *water R* and add 25 ml of *dilute sodium hydroxide solution R*. Allow to stand for 10 min and add 1 g of *potassium bromide R* and 1 ml of *0.0083 M potassium bromate*. Acidify with 30 ml of *dilute hydrochloric acid R*. Mix and allow to stand in the dark for 5 min. Add 2 g of *potassium iodide R* and shake. Allow to stand for 2 min and titrate the liberated iodine with *0.05 M sodium thiosulphate*, using *starch solution R* as indicator. Not less than 0.3 ml of *0.05 M sodium thiosulphate* is required to decolorise the solution.

### Heavy metals *(2.4.8)*
Maximum 10 ppm.

2.0 g complies with test C. Prepare the reference solution using 2 ml of *lead standard solution (10 ppm Pb) R*.

### Loss on drying *(2.2.32)*
Maximum 0.5 per cent, determined on 1.00 g by drying in an oven at 105 °C.

### Sulphated ash *(2.4.14)*
Maximum 0.1 per cent, determined on 1.0 g.

## ASSAY
Dissolve 0.250 g, warming if necessary, in 30 ml of *anhydrous acetic acid R* and add 15 ml of *acetic anhydride R*. Titrate with *0.1 M perchloric acid*, determining the end-point potentiometrically *(2.2.20)*.

1 ml of *0.1 M perchloric acid* is equivalent to 29.64 mg of $C_{10}H_{24}N_4O_4S$.

## STORAGE
Protected from light.

_____ *Ph Eur*

# Guar

*(Ph Eur monograph 1218)*

*Ph Eur* _____

## DEFINITION
Guar is obtained by grinding the endosperms of seeds of *Cyamopsis tetragonolobus* (L.) Taub. It consists mainly of guar galactomannan.

## CHARACTERS
### Appearance
White or almost white powder.

### Solubility
It yields a mucilage of variable viscosity when dissolved in water, practically insoluble in ethanol (96 per cent).

## IDENTIFICATION
A. Examined under a microscope in *glycerol R*, the substance to be examined (125) *(2.9.12)* shows pyriform or ovoid cells, usually isolated, having very thick walls around a central somewhat elongated lumen with granular contents, and smaller polyhedral cells, isolated or in clusters, with thinner walls.

B. In a conical flask place 2 g, add rapidly 45 ml of *water R* and stir vigorously for 30 s. After 5-10 min a stiff gel forms which does not flow when the flask is inverted.

C. Mix a suspension of 0.1 g in 10 ml of *water R* with 1 ml of a 10 g/l solution of *disodium tetraborate R*; the mixture soon gels.

D. Thin-layer chromatography *(2.2.27)*.

*Test solution* To 10 mg in a thick-walled centrifuge test tube add 2 ml of a 100 g/l solution of *trifluoroacetic acid R*, shake vigorously to dissolve the forming gel, stopper the test tube and heat the mixture at 120 °C for 1 h. Centrifuge the hydrolysate, transfer the clear supernatant liquid carefully into a 50 ml flask, add 10 ml of *water R* and evaporate the solution to dryness under reduced pressure. To the resulting clear film add 0.1 ml of *water R* and 0.9 ml of *methanol R*. Centrifuge to separate the amorphous precipitate. Dilute the supernatant liquid, if necessary, to 1 ml with *methanol R*.

*Reference solution* Dissolve 10 mg of *galactose R* and 10 mg of *mannose R* in 2 ml of *water R*, then dilute to 20 ml with *methanol R*.

*Plate*   *TLC silica gel plate R.*

*Mobile phase*   *water R, acetonitrile R* (15:85 *V/V*).

*Application*   5 µl, as bands.

*Development*   Over a path of 15 cm.

*Detection*   Spray with *aminohippuric acid reagent R* and dry at 120 °C for 5 min.

*Results*   The chromatogram obtained with the reference solution shows, in the lower part 2 clearly separated brownish zones due to galactose and mannose in order of increasing $R_F$ value. The chromatogram obtained with the test solution shows 2 zones due to galactose and mannose.

## TESTS

### Tragacanth, sterculia gum, agar, alginates, carrageenan

To a small amount of the substance to be examined add 0.2 ml of freshly prepared *ruthenium red solution R*. Examined under a microscope the cell walls do not stain red.

### Protein

Maximum 8.0 per cent.

Carry out the determination of nitrogen by the method of sulphuric acid digestion (*2.5.9*) using 0.170 g. Multiply the result by 6.25.

### Apparent viscosity (*2.2.10*)

85 per cent to 115 per cent of the value stated on the label.

Moisten a quantity equivalent to 1.00 g of the dried substance with 2.5 ml of *2-propanol R*. While stirring, dilute to 100.0 ml with *water R*. After 1 h, determine the viscosity at 20 °C using a rotating viscometer and a shear rate of 100 s$^{-1}$.

### Loss on drying (*2.2.32*)

Maximum 15.0 per cent, determined on 1.000 g by drying in an oven at 105 °C for 5 h.

### Total ash (*2.4.16*)

Maximum 1.8 per cent.

### Microbial contamination

TAMC: acceptance criterion 10$^4$ CFU/g (*2.6.12*).

TYMC: acceptance criterion 10$^2$ CFU/g (*2.6.12*).

Absence of *Escherichia coli* (*2.6.13*).

Absence of *Salmonella* (*2.6.13*).

## LABELLING

The label states the apparent viscosity in millipascal seconds for a 10 g/l solution.

*Ph Eur*

# Guar Galactomannan

(*Ph Eur monograph 0908*)

### Action and use

Excipient.

*Ph Eur*

## DEFINITION

Guar galactomannan is obtained from the seeds of *Cyamopsis tetragonolobus* (L.) Taub. by grinding of the endosperms and subsequent partial hydrolysis. The main components are polysaccharides composed of D-galactose and D-mannose at molecular ratios of 1:1.4 to 1:2. The molecules consist of a linear main chain of β-(1→4)-glycosidically linked mannopyranoses and single α-(1→6)-glycosidically linked galactopyranoses.

## CHARACTERS

### Appearance

Yellowish-white powder.

### Solubility

Soluble in cold water and in hot water, practically insoluble in organic solvents.

## IDENTIFICATION

A. Mix 5 g of solution S (see Tests) with 0.5 ml of a 10 g/l solution of *disodium tetraborate R*. A gel forms within a short time.

B. Heat 20 g of solution S in a water-bath for 10 min. Allow to cool and adjust to the original mass with *water R*. The solution does not gel.

C. Thin-layer chromatography (*2.2.27*).

*Test solution*   To 10 mg of the substance to be examined in a thick-walled centrifuge tube add 2 ml of a 230 g/l solution of *trifluoroacetic acid R*, shake vigorously to dissolve the forming gel, stopper the tube and heat the mixture at 120 °C for 1 h. Centrifuge the hydrolysate, transfer the clear supernatant liquid carefully into a 50 ml flask, add 10 ml of *water R* and evaporate the solution to dryness under reduced pressure. Take up the residue in 10 ml of *water R* and evaporate again to dryness under reduced pressure. To the resulting clear film, which has no odour of acetic acid, add 0.1 ml of *water R* and 1 ml of *methanol R*. Centrifuge to separate the amorphous precipitate. Dilute the supernatant liquid, if necessary, to 1 ml with *methanol R*.

*Reference solution*   Dissolve 10 mg of *galactose R* and 10 mg of *mannose R* in 2 ml of *water R* and dilute to 10 ml with *methanol R*.

*Plate*   *TLC silica gel G plate R.*

*Mobile phase*   *water R, acetonitrile R* (15:85 *V/V*).

*Application*   5 µl, as bands of 20 mm by 3 mm.

*Development*   Over a path of 15 cm.

*Detection*   Spray with *aminohippuric acid reagent R* and heat at 120 °C for 5 min.

*Results*   The chromatogram obtained with the reference solution shows in the lower part 2 clearly separated brownish zones (galactose and mannose in order of increasing $R_F$ value). The chromatogram obtained with the test solution shows 2 zones due to galactose and mannose.

## TESTS

### Solution S

Moisten 1.0 g with 2 ml of *2-propanol R*. While stirring, dilute to 100 g with *water R* and stir until the substance is uniformly dispersed. Allow to stand for at least 1 h. If the apparent viscosity is below 200 mPa·s, use 3.0 g of substance instead of 1.0 g.

### pH (*2.2.3*)

5.5 to 7.5 for solution S.

### Apparent viscosity (*2.2.10*)

75 per cent to 140 per cent of the value stated on the label.

Moisten a quantity of the substance to be examined equivalent to 2.00 g of the dried substance with 2.5 ml of *2-propanol R* and, while stirring, dilute to 100.0 ml with *water R*. After 1 h, determine the viscosity at 20 °C using a rotating viscometer and a shear rate of 100 s$^{-1}$.

### Insoluble matter

Maximum 7.0 per cent.

In a 250 ml flask disperse, while stirring, 1.50 g in a mixture of 1.6 ml of *sulphuric acid R* and 150 ml of *water R* and weigh. Immerse the flask in a water-bath and heat under a reflux condenser for 6 h. Adjust to the original mass with *water R*. Filter the hot solution through a tared, sintered-glass filter (160) (*2.1.2*). Rinse the filter with hot *water R* and dry at 100-105 °C. The residue weighs a maximum of 105 mg.

### Protein
Maximum 5.0 per cent.

Carry out the determination of nitrogen by sulphuric acid digestion (*2.5.9*), using 0.400 g. Multiply the result by 6.25.

### Tragacanth, sterculia gum, agar, alginates and carrageenan
To a small amount of the substance to be examined, add 0.2 ml of freshly prepared *ruthenium red solution R*. Examined under a microscope, none of the structures are red.

### Loss on drying (*2.2.32*)
Maximum 15.0 per cent, determined on 1.000 g by drying in an oven at 105 °C for 5 h.

### Total ash (*2.4.16*)
Maximum 1.8 per cent, determined on 1.00 g after wetting with 10 ml of *water R*.

### Microbial contamination
TAMC: acceptance criterion $10^3$ CFU/g (*2.6.12*).

TYMC: acceptance criterion $10^2$ CFU/g (*2.6.12*).

Absence of *Escherichia coli* (*2.6.13*).

Absence of *Salmonella* (*2.6.13*).

### LABELLING
The label states the apparent viscosity in millipascal seconds for a 20 g/l solution.

*Ph Eur*

# Halibut-liver Oil

### Action and use
Source of vitamin A.

### Preparation
Halibut-liver Oil Capsules

Halibut-liver Oil may contain up to about 3000 IU of vitamin D activity per g. When a statement is made of the vitamin D content, this is determined by an appropriate method. The method described under Cod-liver Oil (Type A) may be suitable.

### DEFINITION
Halibut-liver Oil is the fixed oil extracted from the fresh, or suitably preserved, liver of the halibut species belonging to the genus *Hippoglossus* and refined. It contains in 1 g not less than 30,000 IU of vitamin A.

### CHARACTERISTICS
A pale to golden yellow liquid; odour and taste, fishy, but not rancid.

Practically insoluble in *ethanol (96%)*; miscible with *ether* and with *petroleum spirit (boiling range, 40° to 60°)*.

### TESTS
#### Acid value
Not more than 2.0, Appendix X B.

#### Iodine value
Not less than 122 (*iodine monochloride method*), Appendix X E.

### Iodine value of glycerides
112 to 150, when determined by the following method. Isolate the unsaponifiable matter as described in Appendix X H, but using 1 g of the oil and evaporating the acetone, drying the residue at 80° in a current of nitrogen and omitting the final titration. Weigh the residue and immediately determine the *iodine value*, Appendix X E, Method B.

Calculate the iodine value of the glycerides from the expression $(100x - Sy)/(100 - S)$, where $x$ is the iodine value of the oil, $y$ is the iodine value of the unsaponifiable matter and $S$ is the percentage of unsaponifiable matter in the oil.

### Saponification value
Not more than 180, Appendix X G.

### Unsaponifiable matter
Not less than 7.0%, Appendix X H.

### Weight per ml
0.915 to 0.925 g, Appendix V G.

### ASSAY
*Carry out the procedure as rapidly as possible, avoiding exposure to actinic light and air, oxidising agents, oxidation catalysts (e.g. copper and iron) and acids.*

Carry out Method A (ultraviolet absorption spectrophotometry) but if method A is found not to be valid, carry out method B (liquid chromatography).

### Method A
To 1 g of the oil being examined in a round-bottomed flask, add 3 ml of a freshly prepared 50% w/w solution of *potassium hydroxide* and 30 ml of *ethanol*, boil under a reflux condenser in a current of *nitrogen* for 30 minutes and cool rapidly. Add 30 ml of *water* and extract with four 50 ml quantities of *ether* and discard the aqueous layer after complete separation of the final extract. Wash the combined ethereal layers with four 50 ml quantities of *water* and evaporate to dryness under a gentle current of *nitrogen* at a temperature not exceeding 30° or in a rotary evaporator at a temperature not exceeding 30° under reduced pressure. Dissolve the residue in sufficient *propan-2-ol R1* to give an expected concentration of vitamin A equivalent to 10 to 15 IU per ml. Measure the *absorbances* of the solution at 300 nm, 310 nm, 325 nm and 334 nm and at the wavelength of maximum absorption, Appendix II B, in a suitable spectrophotometer in 1-cm specially matched cells, using *propan-2-ol R1* in the reference cell.

Calculate the content of vitamin A, as all-*trans*-retinol, in IU per gram from the expression:

$$A_{325} \times \frac{1830}{100m} \times V$$

where $A_{325}$ = absorbance at 325 nm,

$\quad\quad m$ = weight of the oil being examined in grams,

$\quad\quad V$ = total volume of solution containing 10 to 15 IU of vitamin A per ml,

$\quad 1830$ = conversion factor for the specific absorbance of all-*trans*-retinol in International Units.

The above expression can be used only if $A_{325}$ has a value of not greater than $A_{325,\text{corr}}/0.970$ where $A_{325,\text{corr}}$ is the corrected absorbance at 325 nm and is given by the equation:

$$A_{325,\text{corr}} = 6.815 A_{325} - 2.555 A_{310} - 4.260 A_{324}$$

$A$ designates the absorbance at the wavelength indicated by the subscript.

If $A_{325}$ has a value greater than $A_{325,\text{corr}}/0.970$, calculate the content of vitamin A from the expression:

$$A_{325,\text{corr}} \times \frac{1830}{100m} \times V$$

The assay is not valid unless the wavelength of maximum absorption lies between 323 nm and 327 nm and the *absorbance* at 300 nm relative to that at 325 nm is at most 0.73.

**Method B**

Carry out the method for *liquid chromatography*, Appendix III D, using the following solutions. Prepare solution (1) in the following manner. To 2 g of the oil being examined in a round-bottomed flask add 5 ml of a freshly prepared 10% w/v solution of *ascorbic acid* and 10 ml of a freshly prepared 80% w/v solution of *potassium hydroxide* and 100 ml of *ethanol*, boil under a reflux condenser on a water-bath for 15 minutes. Add 100 ml of a 1% w/v solution of *sodium chloride* and cool. Transfer the solution to a 500 ml separating funnel rinsing the round-bottomed flask with about 75 ml of a 1% w/v solution of *sodium chloride* and then with 150 ml of a mixture of equal volumes of *light petroleum R3* and *ether*. Shake for 1 minute and when the layers have separated completely, discard the lower layer and wash the upper layer with 50 ml of a 3% w/v solution of *potassium hydroxide* in a 10% v/v solution of *ethanol* and then with three 50 ml quantities of a 1% w/v solution of *sodium chloride*. Filter the upper layer through 5 g of *anhydrous sodium sulphate* on a fast filter paper into a 250 ml flask suitable for a rotary evaporator. Wash the funnel with 10 ml of fresh extraction mixture, filter and combine the upper layers. Distil them at a temperature not exceeding 30° under reduced pressure (water ejector) and fill with *nitrogen* when evaporation is completed. Alternatively evaporate the solvent under a gentle current of *nitrogen* at a temperature not exceeding 30°. Dissolve the residue in *propan-2-ol*, transfer to a 25 ml graduated flask and dilute to 25 ml with *propan-2-ol*. Gentle heating with the aid of ultrasound may be required. (A large fraction of the white residue is cholesterol.) Solution (2) is a solution of *retinyl acetate EPCRS* in *propan-2-ol R1* containing about 1000 IU per ml of all-*trans*-retinol. The exact concentration of solution (2) is assessed by ultraviolet absorption spectrophotometry, Appendix II B. Dilute the solution with *propan-2-ol R1* to a presumed concentration of 10 to 15 IU per ml and measure the *absorbance* at 326 nm in matched 1-cm cells using *propan-2-ol R1* in the reference cell. Calculate the content of vitamin A in International Units per millilitre of solution (2) from the following expression, taking into account the assigned content of *retinyl acetate EPCRS*:

$$A_{326} \times \frac{1900 \times V_2}{100 \times V_1}$$

where $A_{326}$ = absorbance at 326 nm,
$V_2$ = volume of the diluted solution,
$V_1$ = volume of reference solution (a) used,
1900 = conversion factor for the specific absorbance of *retinyl acetate EPCRS* in International Units.

Prepare solution (3) in the same manner as solution (1) but using 2 ml of solution (2) in place of the oil being examined.

The exact concentration of solution (3) is assessed by ultraviolet absorption spectrophotometry, Appendix II B. Dilute solution (3) with *propan-2-ol R1* to a presumed concentration of 10 to 15 IU per ml of all-*trans*-retinol and measure the *absorbance* at 325 nm in matched 1-cm cells using *propan-2-ol R1* in the reference cell. Calculate the content of all-*trans*-retinol in International Units per millilitre of solution (3) from the expression:

$$A_{325} \times \frac{1830 \times V_4}{100 \times V_3}$$

where $A_{325}$ = absorbance at 325 nm,
$V_3$ = volume of the diluted solution,
$V_4$ = volume of reference solution (b) used,
1830 = conversion factor for the specific absorbance of all-*trans*-retinol in International Units.

The chromatographic procedure may be carried out using (a) a stainless steel column (25 cm × 4.6 mm) packed with *octadecylsilyl silica gel for chromatography* (5 µm to 10 µm), (b) as mobile phase at a flow rate of 1 ml per minute a mixture of 3 volumes of *water* and 97 volumes of *methanol* and (c) as detector a spectrophotometer set at 325 nm.

Inject in triplicate 10 µl of solutions (1) and (3). The retention time of all-*trans*-retinol is 4 to 6 minutes.

The assay is not valid unless (a) the chromatogram obtained with solution (1) shows a peak corresponding to that of all-*trans*-retinol in the chromatogram obtained with solution (3), (b) when using the method of standard additions to solution (1) there is greater than 95% recovery of the added *retinyl acetate EPCRS* and (c) the recovery of all-*trans*-retinol in solution (3) as assessed by direct absorption spectrophotometry is greater than 95%.

Calculate the content of vitamin A using the following expression:

$$A_1 \times \frac{C \times V}{A_2} \times \frac{1}{m}$$

where $A_1$ = area of the peak corresponding to all-*trans*-retinol in the chromatogram obtained with solution (1),
$A_2$ = area of the peak corresponding to all-*trans*-retinol in the chromatogram obtained with solution (3),
$C$ = concentration of *retinyl acetate EPCRS* in solution (2) as assessed before the saponification in IU per ml (1000 IU per ml),
$V$ = volume of solution (2) treated (2 ml),
$m$ = weight of the oil being examined in solution (1) (2 g).

**STORAGE**

Halibut-liver Oil should be kept in a well-filled container and protected from light.

# Halofantrine Hydrochloride

*(Ph Eur monograph 1979)*

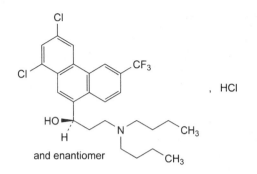

and enantiomer

$C_{26}H_{30}Cl_2F_3NO,HCl$     536.9        36167-63-2

## Action and use
Antiprotozoal (malaria).

*Ph Eur*

## DEFINITION
(1*RS*)-3-(Dibutylamino)-1-[1,3-dichloro-6-(trifluoromethyl)phenanthren-9-yl]propan-1-ol hydrochloride.

## Content
97.5 per cent to 102.0 per cent (dried substance).

## CHARACTERS
### Appearance
White or almost white powder.

### Solubility
Practically insoluble in water, freely soluble in methanol, sparingly soluble in alcohol.

It shows polymorphism (*5.9*).

## IDENTIFICATION
A. Infrared absorption spectrophotometry (*2.2.24*).

*Comparison*   halofantrine hydrochloride CRS.

If the spectra obtained in the solid state show differences, dissolve the substance to be examined and the reference substance separately in *methyl ethyl ketone R*, evaporate to dryness and record new spectra using the residues.

B. It gives reaction (b) of chlorides (*2.3.1*).

## TESTS
### Optical rotation (*2.2.7*)
− 0.10° to + 0.10°.

Dissolve 1.00 g in *alcohol R* and dilute to 100.0 ml with the same solvent.

### Absorbance (*2.2.25*)
Maximum 0.085 at 450 nm.

Dissolve 0.200 g in *methanol R* and dilute to 10.0 ml with the same solvent.

### Related substances
Liquid chromatography (*2.2.29*).

*Test solution (a)*   Dissolve 40.0 mg of the substance to be examined in the mobile phase and dilute to 100.0 ml with the mobile phase.

*Test solution (b)*   Dilute 5.0 ml of test solution (a) to 50.0 ml with the mobile phase.

*Reference solution (a)*   Dissolve 40.0 mg of *halofantrine hydrochloride CRS* in the mobile phase and dilute to 100.0 ml with the mobile phase.

*Reference solution (b)*   Dilute 5.0 ml of reference solution (a) to 50.0 ml with the mobile phase.

*Reference solution (c)*   Dilute 1.0 ml of test solution (a) to 100.0 ml with the mobile phase. Dilute 5.0 ml of the solution to 50.0 ml with the mobile phase.

*Reference solution (d)*   Dissolve 10.0 mg of *halofantrine impurity C CRS* in the mobile phase and dilute to 25 ml with the mobile phase. To 5.0 ml of the solution, add 5.0 ml of reference solution (a) and dilute to 50.0 ml with the mobile phase.

*Column:*
— *size: l* = 0.30 m, Ø = 3.9 mm,
— *stationary phase: octadecylsilyl silica gel for chromatography R* (10 μm) of irregular type, with a specific surface of 330 m²/g, a pore size of 12.5 nm and a carbon loading of 9.8 per cent.

*Mobile phase*   Mix 250 ml of a 2.0 g/l solution of *sodium hydroxide R*, previously adjusted to pH 2.5 with *perchloric acid R* and 750 ml of *acetonitrile R*.

*Flow rate*   1 ml/min.

*Detection*   Spectrophotometer at 260 nm.

*Injection*   20 μl; inject the test solution (a) and reference solutions (c) and (d).

*Run time*   5 times the retention time of halofantrine which is about 6 min.

*System suitability:*
— *resolution*: minimum 3.3 between the peaks due to halofantrine and impurity C in the chromatogram obtained with reference solution (d).

*Limits:*
— *any impurity*: not more than twice the area of the principal peak in the chromatogram obtained with reference solution (c) (0.2 per cent),
— *total*: not more than 5 times the area of the principal peak in the chromatogram obtained with reference solution (c) (0.5 per cent),
— *disregard limit*: 0.5 times the area of the principal peak in the chromatogram obtained with reference solution (c) (0.05 per cent).

### Heavy metals (*2.4.8*)
Maximum 20 ppm.

1.0 g complies with limit test C. Prepare the standard using 2 ml of *lead standard solution (10 ppm Pb) R*.

### Loss on drying (*2.2.32*)
Maximum 0.5 per cent, determined on 1.000 g by drying in an oven at 105 °C for 4 h.

### Sulphated ash (*2.4.14*)
Maximum 0.1 per cent, determined on 1.0 g.

## ASSAY
Liquid chromatography (*2.2.29*) as described in the test for related substances.

*Injection*   Test solution (b) and reference solution (b).

Calculate the percentage content of halofantrine hydrochloride.

## STORAGE
Protected from light.

## IMPURITIES

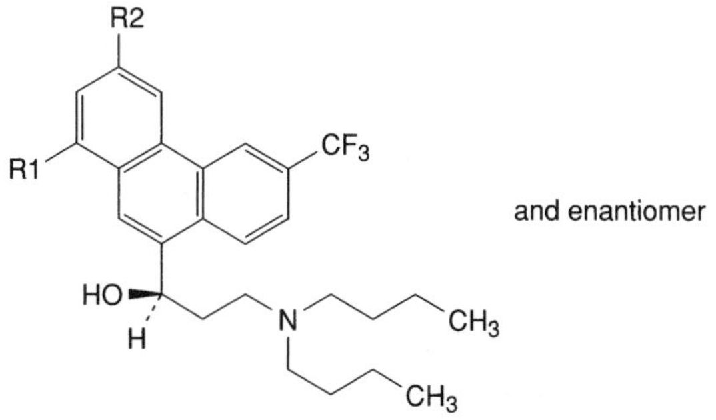

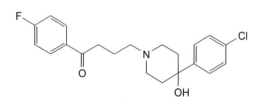

and enantiomer

A. R1 = H, R2 = Cl:
(1*RS*)-1-[3-chloro-6-(trifluoromethyl)phenanthren-9-yl]-3-(dibutylamino)propan-1-ol (1-dechlorohalofantrine),

B. R1 = Cl, R2 = H:
(1*RS*)-1-[1-chloro-6-(trifluoromethyl)phenanthren-9-yl]-3-(dibutylamino)propan-1-ol (3-dechlorohalofantrine),

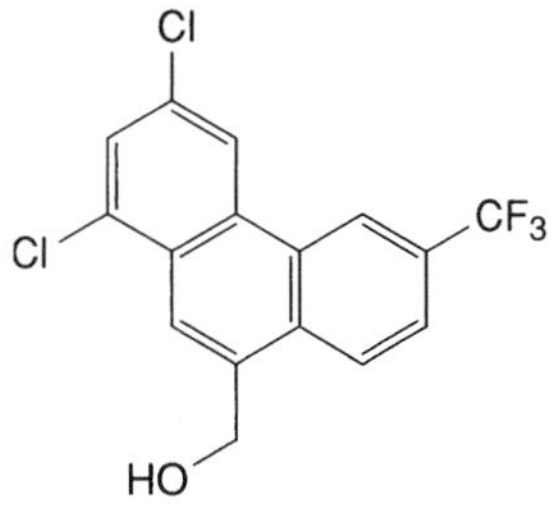

C. [1,3-dichloro-6-(trifluoromethyl)phenanthren-9-yl]methanol.

_____ *Ph Eur*

# Haloperidol

*(Ph Eur monograph 0616)*

C$_{21}$H$_{23}$ClFNO$_2$     375.9     *52-86-8*

### Action and use
Dopamine receptor antagonist; neuroleptic.

### Preparations
Haloperidol Capsules

Haloperidol Injection

Haloperidol Oral Solution

Strong Haloperidol Oral Solution

Haloperidol Tablets

*Ph Eur* _____

## DEFINITION
4-[4-(4-Chlorophenyl)-4-hydroxypiperidin-1-yl]-1-(4-fluorophenyl)butan-1-one.

## Content
99.0 per cent to 101.0 per cent (dried substance).

## CHARACTERS
### Appearance
White or almost white powder.

### Solubility
Practically insoluble in water, slightly soluble in ethanol (96 per cent), in methanol and in methylene chloride.

## IDENTIFICATION
*First identification*   B, E.

*Second identification*   A, C, D, E.

A. Melting point (*2.2.14*): 150 °C to 153 °C.

B. Infrared absorption spectrophotometry (*2.2.24*).

*Preparation*   Discs.

*Comparison*   haloperidol CRS.

C. Thin-layer chromatography (*2.2.27*).

*Test solution*   Dissolve 10 mg of the substance to be examined in *methanol R* and dilute to 10 ml with the same solvent.

*Reference solution (a)*   Dissolve 10 mg of *haloperidol CRS* in *methanol R* and dilute to 10 ml with the same solvent.

*Reference solution (b)*   Dissolve 10 mg of *haloperidol CRS* and 10 mg of *bromperidol CRS* in *methanol R* and dilute to 10 ml with the same solvent.

*Plate*   TLC octadecylsilyl silica gel plate R.

*Mobile phase*   tetrahydrofuran R, methanol R, 58 g/l solution of *sodium chloride R* (10:45:45 *V/V/V*).

*Application*   1 μl.

*Development*   In an unsaturated tank, over a path of 15 cm.

*Drying*   In air.

*Detection*   Examine in ultraviolet light at 254 nm.

*System suitability*   Reference solution (b):
— the chromatogram shows 2 spots which may, however, not be completely separated.

*Results*   The principal spot in the chromatogram obtained with the test solution is similar in position and size to the principal spot in the chromatogram obtained with reference solution (a).

D. Dissolve about 10 mg in 5 ml of *anhydrous ethanol R*. Add 0.5 ml of *dinitrobenzene solution R* and 0.5 ml of *2 M alcoholic potassium hydroxide R*. A violet colour is produced and becomes brownish-red after 20 min.

E. To 0.1 g in a porcelain crucible add 0.5 g of *anhydrous sodium carbonate R*. Heat over an open flame for 10 min. Allow to cool. Take up the residue with 5 ml of *dilute nitric acid R* and filter. To 1 ml of the filtrate add 1 ml of *water R*. The solution gives reaction (a) of chlorides (*2.3.1*).

## TESTS
### Appearance of solution
The solution is clear (*2.2.1*) and not more intensely coloured than reference solution Y$_7$ (*2.2.2, Method II*).

Dissolve 0.2 g in 20 ml of a 1 per cent *V/V* solution of *lactic acid R*.

### Related substances
Liquid chromatography (*2.2.29*). *Prepare the solutions immediately before use and protect from light.*

*Test solution*   Dissolve 0.100 g of the substance to be examined in *methanol R* and dilute to 10.0 ml with the same solvent.

*Reference solution (a)* Dissolve 5.0 mg of *haloperidol CRS* and 2.5 mg of *bromperidol CRS* in *methanol R* and dilute to 50.0 ml with the same solvent.

*Reference solution (b)* Dilute 5.0 ml of the test solution to 100.0 ml with *methanol R*. Dilute 1.0 ml of this solution to 10.0 ml with *methanol R*.

*Column:*
— *size: l* = 0.1 m, Ø = 4.6 mm;
— *stationary phase*: *base-deactivated octadecylsilyl silica gel for chromatography R* (3 μm).

*Mobile phase:*
— *mobile phase A*: 17 g/l solution of *tetrabutylammonium hydrogen sulphate R1*;
— *mobile phase B*: *acetonitrile R*;

| Time (min) | Mobile phase A (per cent *V/V*) | Mobile phase B (per cent *V/V*) |
|---|---|---|
| 0 - 15 | 90 → 50 | 10 → 50 |
| 15 - 20 | 50 | 50 |
| 20 - 25 | 90 | 10 |

*Flow rate* 1.5 ml/min.

*Detection* Spectrophotometer at 230 nm.

*Injection* 10 μl; inject *methanol R* as a blank.

*Retention time* Haloperidol = about 5.5 min; bromperidol = about 6 min.

*System suitability* Reference solution (a):
— *resolution*: minimum 3.0 between the peaks due to haloperidol and bromperidol; if necessary, adjust the concentration of acetonitrile in the mobile phase or adjust the time programme for the linear-gradient elution.

*Limits:*
— *impurities A, B, C, D, E, F*: for each impurity, not more than the area of the principal peak in the chromatogram obtained with reference solution (b) (0.5 per cent);
— *total*: not more than twice the area of the principal peak in the chromatogram obtained with reference solution (b) (1 per cent);
— *disregard limit*: 0.1 times the area of the principal peak in the chromatogram obtained with reference solution (b) (0.05 per cent).

**Loss on drying** (*2.2.32*)
Maximum 0.5 per cent, determined on 1.000 g by drying in an oven at 105 °C.

**Sulphated ash** (*2.4.14*)
Maximum 0.1 per cent, determined on 1.0 g using a platinum crucible.

## ASSAY

Dissolve 0.300 g in 50 ml of a mixture of 1 volume of *anhydrous acetic acid R* and 7 volumes of *methyl ethyl ketone R*. Titrate with *0.1 M perchloric acid*, using 0.2 ml of *naphtholbenzein solution R* as indicator.

1 ml of *0.1 M perchloric acid* is equivalent to 37.59 mg of $C_{21}H_{23}ClFNO_2$.

## STORAGE

Protected from light.

## IMPURITIES

*Specified impurities A, B, C, D, E, F.*

A. R1 = F, R2 = R3 = R4 = H: 1-(4-fluorophenyl)-4-(4-hydroxy-4-phenylpiperidin-1-yl)butan-1-one,

B. R1 = R2 = H, R3 = F, R4 = Cl: 4-[4-(4-chlorophenyl)-4-hydroxypiperidin-1-yl]-1-(2-fluorophenyl)butan-1-one,

C. R1 = F, R2 = $C_2H_5$, R3 = H, R4 = Cl: 4-[4-(4-chlorophenyl)-4-hydroxypiperidin-1-yl]-1-(3-ethyl-4-fluorophenyl)butan-1-one,

D. 4-[4-(4-chlorophenyl)-4-hydroxypiperidin-1-yl]-1-[4-[4-(4-chlorophenyl)-4-hydroxypiperidin-1-yl]phenyl]butan-1-one,

E. R = H, R′ = Cl: 4-[4-(4′-chlorobiphenyl-4-yl)-4-hydroxypiperidin-1-yl]-1-(4-fluorophenyl)butan-1-one,

F. R = Cl, R′ = H: 4-[4-(3′-chlorobiphenyl-4-yl)-4-hydroxypiperidin-1-yl]-1-(4-fluorophenyl)butan-1-one.

*Ph Eur*

# Haloperidol Decanoate

*(Ph Eur monograph 1431)*

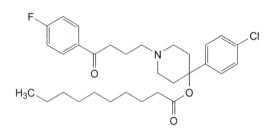

C₃₁H₄₁ClFNO₃    530.1    74050-97-8

## Action and use
Dopamine receptor antagonist; neuroleptic.

*Ph Eur*

## DEFINITION
4-(4-Chlorophenyl)-1-[4-(4-fluorophenyl)-4-oxobutyl]piperidin-4-yl decanoate.

## Content
98.5 per cent to 101.0 per cent (dried substance).

## CHARACTERS
### Appearance
White or almost white powder.

### Solubility
Practically insoluble in water, very soluble in ethanol (96 per cent), in methanol and in methylene chloride.

mp: about 42 °C.

## IDENTIFICATION
A. Infrared absorption spectrophotometry (*2.2.24*).

*Preparation*   Mulls in *liquid paraffin R*.

*Comparison*   haloperidol decanoate CRS.

B. To 0.1 g in a porcelain crucible add 0.5 g of *anhydrous sodium carbonate R*. Heat over an open flame for 10 min. Allow to cool. Take up the residue with 5 ml of *dilute nitric acid R* and filter. To 1 ml of the filtrate add 1 ml of *water R*. The solution gives reaction (a) of chlorides (*2.3.1*).

## TESTS
### Appearance of solution
The solution is clear (*2.2.1*) and not more intensely coloured than reference solution B₅ (*2.2.2, Method II*).

Dissolve 2.0 g in *methylene chloride R* and dilute to 20 ml with the same solvent.

### Related substances
Liquid chromatography (*2.2.29*). *Prepare the solutions immediately before use and protect from light.*

*Test solution*   Dissolve 0.100 g of the substance to be examined in *methanol R* and dilute to 10.0 ml with the same solvent.

*Reference solution (a)*   Dissolve 2.5 mg of *bromperidol decanoate CRS* and 2.5 mg of *haloperidol decanoate CRS* in *methanol R*, then dilute to 50.0 ml with the same solvent.

*Reference solution (b)*   Dilute 5.0 ml of the test solution to 100.0 ml with *methanol R*. Dilute 1.0 ml of this solution to 10.0 ml with *methanol R*.

*Column:*
— *size: l* = 0.1 m, Ø = 4.0 mm;
— *stationary phase: base-deactivated octadecylsilyl silica gel for chromatography R* (3 μm).

*Mobile phase:*
— *mobile phase A*: 27 g/l solution of *tetrabutylammonium hydrogen sulphate R*;
— *mobile phase B*: *acetonitrile R*;

| Time (min) | Mobile phase A (per cent *V/V*) | Mobile phase B (per cent *V/V*) |
|---|---|---|
| 0 - 30 | 80 → 40 | 20 → 60 |
| 30 - 35 | 40 | 60 |
| 35 - 40 | 40 → 80 | 60 → 20 |

*Flow rate*   1.5 ml/min.

*Detection*   Spectrophotometer at 230 nm.

*Equilibration*   With *acetonitrile R* for at least 30 min and then with the mobile phase at the initial composition for at least 5 min.

*Injection*   10 μl; inject *methanol R* as a blank.

*Retention time*   Haloperidol decanoate = about 24 min; bromperidol decanoate = about 24.5 min.

*System suitability*   Reference solution (a):
— *resolution*: minimum 1.5 between the peaks due to haloperidol decanoate and bromperidol decanoate; if necessary, adjust the gradient or the time programme for the linear gradient elution.

*Limits:*
— *impurities A, B, C, D, E, F, G, H, I, J, K*: for each impurity, not more than the area of the principal peak in the chromatogram obtained with reference solution (b) (0.5 per cent);
— *total*: not more than 3 times the area of the principal peak in the chromatogram obtained with reference solution (b) (1.5 per cent);
— *disregard limit*: 0.1 times the area of the principal peak in the chromatogram obtained with reference solution (b) (0.05 per cent).

### Loss on drying (*2.2.32*)
Maximum 0.5 per cent, determined on 1.000 g by drying *in vacuo* at 30 °C.

### Sulphated ash (*2.4.14*)
Maximum 0.1 per cent, determined on 1.0 g in a platinum crucible.

## ASSAY
Dissolve 0.425 g in 50 ml of a mixture of 1 volume of *anhydrous acetic acid R* and 7 volumes of *methyl ethyl ketone R*. Titrate with *0.1 M perchloric acid* using 0.2 ml of *naphtholbenzein solution R* as indicator.

1 ml of *0.1 M perchloric acid* is equivalent to 53.01 mg of C₃₁H₄₁ClFNO₃.

## STORAGE
Protected from light, at a temperature below 25 °C.

## IMPURITIES
*Specified impurities*   *A, B, C, D, E, F, G, H, I, J, K.*

*Other detectable impurities (the following substances would, if present at a sufficient level, be detected by one or other of the tests in the monograph. They are limited by the general acceptance criterion for other/unspecified impurities and/or by the general monograph Substances for pharmaceutical use (2034). It is therefore not necessary to identify these impurities for demonstration of compliance. See also 5.10. Control of impurities in substances for pharmaceutical use): L.*

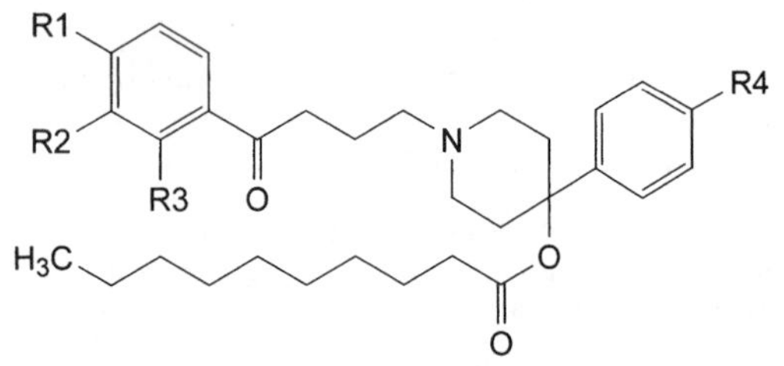

A. R1 = F, R2 = R3 = R4 = H: 1-[4-(4-fluorophenyl)-4-oxobutyl]-4-phenylpiperidin-4-yl decanoate,

B. R1 = R2 = H, R3 = F, R4 = Cl: 4-(4-chlorophenyl)-1-[4-(2-fluorophenyl)-4-oxobutyl]piperidin-4-yl decanoate,

C. R1 = F, R2 = C₂H₅, R3 = H, R4 = Cl: 4-(4-chlorophenyl)-1-[4-(3-ethyl-4-fluorophenyl)-4-oxobutyl]piperidin-4-yl decanoate,

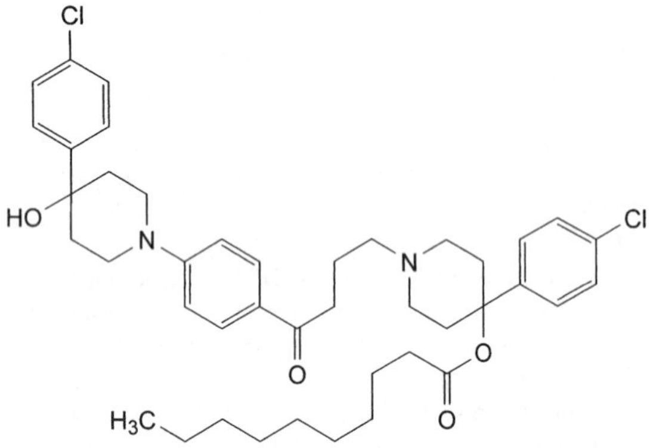

D. 4-(4-chlorophenyl)-1-[4-[4-[4-(4-chlorophenyl)-4-hydroxypiperidin-1-yl]phenyl]-4-oxobutyl]piperidin-4-yl decanoate,

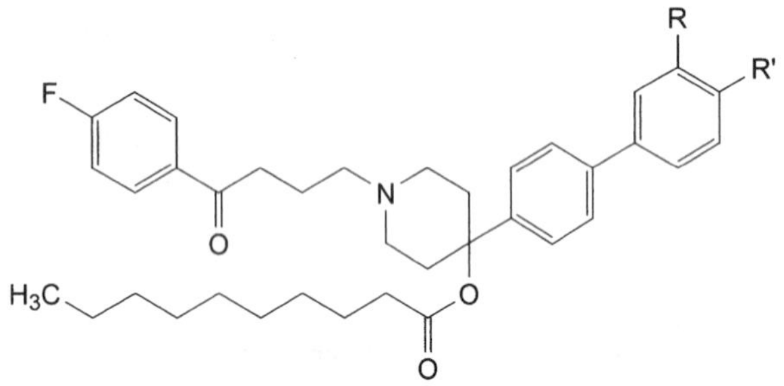

E. R = H, R′ = Cl: 4-(4′-chlorobiphenyl-4-yl)-1-[4-(4-fluorophenyl)-4-oxobutyl]piperidin-4-yl decanoate,

F. R = Cl, R′ = H: 4-(3′-chlorobiphenyl-4-yl)-1-[4-(4-fluorophenyl)-4-oxobutyl]piperidin-4-yl decanoate,

G. haloperidol,

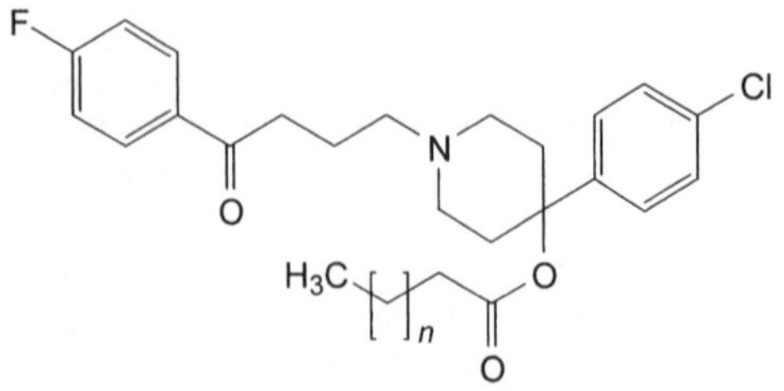

H. n = 5: 4-(4-chlorophenyl)-1-[4-(4-fluorophenyl)-4-oxobutyl]piperidin-4-yl octanoate,

I. n = 6: 4-(4-chlorophenyl)-1-[4-(4-fluorophenyl)-4-oxobutyl]piperidin-4-yl nonanoate,

J. n = 8: 4-(4-chlorophenyl)-1-[4-(4-fluorophenyl)-4-oxobutyl]piperidin-4-yl undecanoate,

K. n = 9: 4-(4-chlorophenyl)-1-[4-(4-fluorophenyl)-4-oxobutyl]piperidin-4-yl dodecanoate,

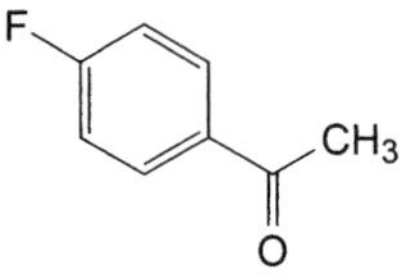

L. 1-(4-fluorophenyl)ethanone.

*Ph Eur*

# Halothane

(*Ph Eur monograph 0393*)

and enantiomer

C₂HBrClF₃          197.4          151-67-7

**Action and use**
General anaesthetic.

*Ph Eur*

## DEFINITION
(*RS*)-2-Bromo-2-chloro-1,1,1-trifluoroethane to which 0.01 per cent *m/m* of thymol has been added.

## CHARACTERS
**Appearance**
Clear, colourless, mobile, heavy, non-flammable liquid.

**Solubility**
Slightly soluble in water, miscible with anhydrous ethanol and with trichloroethylene.

## IDENTIFICATION
*First identification* B.

*Second identification* A, C.

A. Distillation range (see Tests).

B. Infrared absorption spectrophotometry (*2.2.24*).

*Preparation* Examine the substance in a 0.1 mm cell.

*Comparison* Ph. Eur. reference spectrum of halothane.

C. Add 0.1 ml to 2 ml of *2-methyl-2-propanol R* in a test-tube. Add 1 ml of *copper edetate solution R*, 0.5 ml of *concentrated ammonia R* and a mixture of 0.4 ml of *strong hydrogen peroxide solution R* and 1.6 ml of *water R* (solution A). Prepare a blank at the same time (solution B). Place both tubes in a water-bath at 50 °C for 15 min, cool and add 0.3 ml of *glacial acetic acid R*. To 1 ml of each of solutions A and B add 0.5 ml of a mixture of equal volumes of freshly prepared *alizarin S solution R* and *zirconyl nitrate solution R*. Solution A is yellow and solution B is red.

To 1 ml of each of solutions A and B add 1 ml of *buffer solution pH 5.2 R*, 1 ml of *phenol red solution R* diluted 1 to 10 with *water R* and 0.1 ml of *chloramine solution R*. Solution A is bluish-violet and solution B is yellow.

To 2 ml of each of solutions A and B add 0.5 ml of a mixture of 25 volumes of *sulphuric acid R* and 75 volumes of *water R*, 0.5 ml of *acetone R* and 0.2 ml of a 50 g/l solution of *potassium bromate R* and shake. Warm the tubes in a water-bath at 50 °C for 2 min, cool and add 0.5 ml of a mixture of equal volumes of *nitric acid R* and *water R* and 0.5 ml of *silver nitrate solution R2*. Solution A is opalescent and a white precipitate is formed after a few minutes; solution B remains clear.

## TESTS

### Acidity or alkalinity
To 20 ml add 20 ml of *carbon dioxide-free water R*, shake for 3 min and allow to stand. Separate the aqueous layer and add 0.2 ml of *bromocresol purple solution R*. Not more than 0.1 ml of *0.01 M sodium hydroxide* or 0.6 ml of *0.01 M hydrochloric acid* is required to change the colour of the indicator.

### Relative density (2.2.5)
1.872 to 1.877.

### Distillation range (2.2.11)
It distils completely between 49.0 °C and 51.0 °C and 95 per cent distils within a range of 1.0 °C.

### Volatile related substances
Gas chromatography (2.2.28).

*Internal standard    trichlorotrifluoroethane CRS.*

*Test solution (a)    The substance to be examined.*

*Test solution (b)    Dilute 5.0 ml of trichlorotrifluoroethane CRS to 100.0 ml with the substance to be examined. Dilute 1.0 ml of the solution to 100.0 ml with the substance to be examined. Dilute 1.0 ml of this solution to 10.0 ml with the substance to be examined.*

*Column:*
— *size: l = 2.75 m, Ø = 5 mm;*
— *stationary phase: silanised diatomaceous earth for gas chromatography R1 (180-250 μm), the first 1.8 m being impregnated with 30 per cent m/m of macrogol 400 R and the remainder with 30 per cent m/m of dinonyl phthalate R;*
— *temperature: 50 °C.*

*Carrier gas    nitrogen for chromatography R.*

*Flow rate    30 ml/min.*

*Detection    Flame ionisation.*

*Injection    5 μl.*

*Limit    Test solution (b):*
— *total: not than the area of the peak due to the internal standard, corrected if necessary for any impurity with the same retention time as the internal standard (0.005 per cent).*

### Thymol
Gas chromatography (2.2.28).

*Internal standard solution    Dissolve 0.10 g of menthol R in methylene chloride R and dilute to 100.0 ml with the same solvent.*

*Test solution    To 20.0 ml of the substance to be examined add 5.0 ml of the internal standard solution.*

*Reference solution    Dissolve 20.0 mg of thymol R in methylene chloride R and dilute to 100.0 ml with the same solvent. To 20.0 ml of this solution, add 5.0 ml of the internal standard solution.*

*Column:*
— *material: fused silica;*
— *size: l = 15 m, Ø = 0.53 mm;*

— *stationary phase: poly(dimethyl)siloxane R (film thickness 1.5 μm).*

*Carrier gas    nitrogen for chromatography R.*

*Flow rate    15 ml/min.*

*Temperature:*
— *column: 150 °C;*
— *injection port: 170 °C;*
— *detector: 200 °C.*

*Detection    Flame ionisation.*

*Injection    1.0 μl.*

*Limit:*
— *thymol: 0.75 times to 1.15 times the area of the corresponding peak in the chromatogram obtained with the reference solution (0.008 per cent m/m to 0.012 per cent m/m).*

### Bromides and chlorides
To 10 ml add 20 ml of *water R* and shake for 3 min. To 5 ml of the aqueous layer add 5 ml of *water R*, 0.05 ml of *nitric acid R* and 0.2 ml of *silver nitrate solution R1*. The solution is not more opalescent than a mixture of 5 ml of the aqueous layer and 5 ml of *water R*.

### Bromine and chlorine
To 10 ml of the aqueous layer obtained in the test for bromides and chlorides add 1 ml of *potassium iodide and starch solution R*. No blue colour is produced.

### Non-volatile matter
Maximum 20 mg/l.

Evaporate 50 ml to dryness on a water-bath and dry the residue in an oven at 100-105 °C for 2 h. The residue weighs a maximum of 1 mg.

## STORAGE
In an airtight container, protected from light, at a temperature not exceeding 25 °C. The choice of material for the container is made taking into account the particular reactivity of halothane with certain metals.

## IMPURITIES

A. (*E*)-1,1,1,4,4,4-hexafluorobut-2-ene,

B. R = Cl, R′ = H:
(*EZ*)-2-chloro-1,1,1,4,4,4-hexafluorobut-2-ene (*cis* and *trans*),
C. R = R′ = Cl: (*EZ*)-2,3-dichloro-1,1,1,4,4,4-hexafluorobut-2-ene (*cis* and *trans*),

D. (*E*)-2-bromo-1,1,1,4,4,4-hexafluorobut-2-ene,

E. 2-chloro-1,1,1-trifluoroethane,

F. 1,1,2-trichloro-1,2,2-trifluoroethane,

G. 1-bromo-1-chloro-2,2-difluoroethene,

H. R = H: 2,2-dichloro-1,1,1-trifluoroethane,
I. R = Br: 1-bromo-1,1-dichloro-2,2,2-trifluoroethane,

J. 1,2-dichloro-1,1-difluoroethane.

*Ph Eur*

# Helium

*(Ph Eur monograph 2155)*

He          4.00          7440-59-7

*Ph Eur*

## DEFINITION

### Content

Minimum 99.5 per cent *V/V* of He.

This monograph applies to helium obtained by separation from natural gas and intended for medicinal use.

## CHARACTERS

### Appearance

Colourless, inert gas.

## IDENTIFICATION

Examine the chromatograms obtained in the assay. The retention time of the principal peak in the chromatogram obtained with the substance to be examined is approximately the same as that of the principal peak in the chromatogram obtained with the reference gas.

## TESTS

### Methane

Maximum 50.0 ppm *V/V*.

Infrared analyser.

*Gas to be examined* The substance to be examined. It must be filtered to avoid stray light phenomena (3 μm filter).

*Reference gas (a)*   *helium for chromatography R.*

*Reference gas (b)*   Mixture containing 50.0 ppm *V/V* of *methane R* in *helium for chromatography R.*

The infrared analyser generally comprises an infrared source emitting broadband infrared radiation, an optical device, a sample cell, a detector and in some analysers a reference cell. The optical device may be positioned either before or after the sample cell. It consists of one or more optical filters, through which the broadband radiation is passed. The optical device is selected for methane determination. The measurement light beam passes through the sample cell and

may also pass through a reference cell if the analyser integrates such a feature. When methane is present in the sample cell, absorption of energy in the measurement light beam will occur according to the Beer-Lambert law, and this produces a change in the detector signal. This measurement signal is compared to a reference signal to generate an output related to the concentration of methane. The generated signal is linearised in order to determine the methane content.

Calibrate the apparatus and set the sensitivity using reference gases (a) and (b). Measure the methane content in the gas to be examined.

### Oxygen

Maximum 50.0 ppm *V/V*, determined using an oxygen analyser equipped with an electrochemical cell and a detector scale ranging from 0-100 ppm *V/V*.

The gas to be examined passes through a detection cell containing an aqueous solution of an electrolyte, generally potassium hydroxide. The presence of oxygen in the gas to be examined produces a variation in the electric signal recorded at the outlet of the cell that is proportional to the oxygen content.

Calibrate the analyser according to the instructions of the manufacturer. Pass the gas to be examined through the analyser using a suitable pressure regulator and airtight metal tubes and operating at the prescribed flow rates until constant readings are obtained.

### Water *(2.5.28)*

Maximum 67 ppm *V/V*.

## ASSAY

Gas chromatography *(2.2.28)*.

*Gas to be examined* The substance to be examined.

*Reference gas*   *helium for chromatography R.*

*Column:*
— *size: l = 2 m, Ø = 4.5 mm;*
— *stationary phase: molecular sieve for chromatography R* (0.5 nm).

*Carrier gas*   *argon for chromatography R.*

*Flow rate*   60 ml/min.

*Temperature:*
— *column:* 50 °C;
— *detector:* 150 °C.

*Detection*   Thermal conductivity.

*Injection*   0.5 ml.

Inject the reference gas. Adjust the injected volumes and operating conditions so that the height of the peak due to helium in the chromatogram obtained is at least 35 per cent of the full scale of the recorder.

*System suitability*   Reference gas:
— *symmetry factor:* minimum 0.6.

Calculate the content of He in the gas to be examined.

## STORAGE

As compressed gas or liquid at cryogenic temperature, in appropriate containers, complying with the legal regulations.

## IMPURITIES

*Specified impurities*   *A, B, C.*

A. methane,

B. oxygen,

C. water.

*Ph Eur*

# Heparin Calcium

(*Ph Eur monograph 0332*)

**Action and use**
Anticoagulant.

**Preparation**
Heparin Injection

*Ph Eur*

## DEFINITION

Heparin calcium is a preparation containing the calcium salt of a sulphated glycosaminoglycan present in mammalian tissues. On complete hydrolysis, it liberates D-glucosamine, D-glucuronic acid, L-iduronic acid, acetic acid and sulphuric acid. It has the characteristic property of delaying the clotting of freshly shed blood. The potency of heparin calcium intended for parenteral administration is not less than 150 IU/mg, calculated with reference to the dried substance. The potency of heparin calcium not intended for parenteral administration is not less than 120 IU/mg, calculated with reference to the dried substance.

## PRODUCTION

It is prepared either from the lungs of oxen or from the intestinal mucosae of pigs, oxen or sheep. All stages of production and sourcing are subjected to a suitable quality assurance system.

It is produced by methods of manufacturing designed to minimise or eliminate substances lowering blood pressure and to ensure freedom from contamination by over-sulphated glycosaminoglycans.

It complies with the following additional requirements.

**Nuclear magnetic resonance spectrometry** (*2.2.33*)
The $^1$H NMR spectrum obtained with a frequency of at least 300 MHz complies with the specifications approved by the competent authority.

**Capillary electrophoresis** (*2.2.47*)
The electropherogram obtained complies with the specifications approved by the competent authority.

## CHARACTERS

A white or almost white powder, hygroscopic, freely soluble in water.

## IDENTIFICATION

A. It delays the clotting of recalcified citrated sheep plasma (see Assay).

B. Dissolve 0.40 g in *water R* and dilute to 10.0 ml with the same solvent. The specific optical rotation (*2.2.7*) is not less than + 35.

C. Examine by zone electrophoresis (*2.2.31*) using *agarose for electrophoresis R* as the supporting medium. To equilibrate the agarose and as electrolyte solution use a mixture of 50 ml of *glacial acetic acid R* and 800 ml of *water R* adjusted to pH 3 by addition of *lithium hydroxide R* and diluted to 1000.0 ml with *water R*.

*Test solution*   Dissolve 25 mg of the substance to be examined in *water R* and dilute to 10 ml with the same solvent.

*Reference solution*   Dilute *heparin sodium BRP* with an equal volume of *water R*.

Apply separately to the strip 2 μl to 3 μl of each solution. Pass a current of 1 mA to 2 mA per centimetre of strip width at a potential difference of 300 V for about 10 min. Stain the strips using a 1 g/l solution of *toluidine blue R* and remove the

excess by washing. The ratio of the mobility of the principal band or bands in the electropherogram obtained with the test solution to the mobility of the band in the electropherogram obtained with the reference solution is 0.9 to 1.1.

D. It gives the reactions of calcium (*2.3.1*).

## TESTS

**Appearance of solution**
Dissolve a quantity equivalent to 50 000 IU in *water R* and dilute to 10 ml with the same solvent. The solution is clear (*2.2.1*) and not more intensely coloured than degree 5 of the range of reference solutions of the most appropriate colour (*2.2.2, Method II*).

**pH** (*2.2.3*)
Dissolve 0.1 g in *carbon dioxide-free water R* and dilute to 10 ml with the same solvent. The pH of the solution is 5.5 to 8.0.

**Protein and nucleotidic impurities**
Dissolve 40 mg in 10 ml of *water R*. The absorbance (*2.2.25*) measured at 260 nm is not greater than 0.20 and that measured at 280 nm is not greater than 0.15.

**Nitrogen**
Not more than 2.5 per cent, calculated with reference to the dried substance. Carry out the determination of nitrogen by sulphuric acid digestion (*2.5.9*), using 0.100 g.

**Calcium**
9.5 per cent to 11.5 per cent of Ca, calculated with reference to the dried substance. Determine the calcium by complexometric titration (*2.5.11*), using 0.200 g.

**Heavy metals** (*2.4.8*)
0.5 g complies with limit test C for heavy metals (30 ppm). Prepare the reference solution using 1.5 ml of *lead standard solution (10 ppm Pb) R*.

**Loss on drying** (*2.2.32*)
Not more than 8.0 per cent, determined on 1.000 g by drying at 60 °C over *diphosphorus pentoxide R* at a pressure not exceeding 670 Pa for 3 h.

**Sulphated ash** (*2.4.14*)
32 per cent to 40 per cent, determined on 0.20 g and calculated with reference to the dried substance.

**Bacterial endotoxins** (*2.6.14*)
Less than 0.01 IU per IU of heparin, if intended for use in the manufacture of parenteral preparations without a further appropriate procedure for the removal of bacterial endotoxins. The addition of divalent cations may be necessary in order to fulfil the validation criteria.

## ASSAY

Carry out the assay of heparin (*2.7.5*). The estimated potency is not less than 90 per cent and not more than 111 per cent of the stated potency. The confidence limits of the estimated potency (*P* = 0.95) are not less than 80 per cent and not more than 125 per cent of the stated potency.

## STORAGE

Store in an airtight container. If the substance is sterile, store in a sterile, airtight, tamper-proof container.

## LABELLING

The label states:
— the number of International Units per milligram;
— where applicable, that the substance is suitable for use in the manufacture of parenteral preparations.

*Ph Eur*

# Heparin Sodium

*(Ph Eur monograph 0333)*

**Action and use**
Anticoagulant.

**Preparation**
Heparin Injection

*Ph Eur* _____

## DEFINITION

Heparin sodium is a preparation containing the sodium salt of a sulphated glycosaminoglycan present in mammalian tissues. On complete hydrolysis, it liberates D-glucosamine, D-glucuronic acid, L-iduronic acid, acetic acid and sulphuric acid. It has the characteristic property of delaying the clotting of freshly shed blood. The potency of heparin sodium intended for parenteral administration is not less than 150 IU/mg, calculated with reference to the dried substance. The potency of heparin sodium not intended for parenteral administration is not less than 120 IU/mg, calculated with reference to the dried substance.

## PRODUCTION

It is prepared either from the lungs of oxen or from the intestinal mucosae of pigs, oxen or sheep. All stages of production and sourcing are subjected to a suitable quality assurance system.

It is produced by methods of manufacturing designed to minimise or eliminate substances lowering blood pressure and to ensure freedom from contamination by over-sulphated glycosaminoglycans.

It complies with the following additional requirements.

**Nuclear magnetic resonance spectrometry** (*2.2.33*)
The $^1$H NMR spectrum obtained with a frequency of at least 300 MHz complies with the specifications approved by the competent authority.

**Capillary electrophoresis** (*2.2.47*)
The electropherogram obtained complies with the specifications approved by the competent authority.

## CHARACTERS

A white or almost white powder, hygroscopic, freely soluble in water.

## IDENTIFICATION

A. It delays the clotting of recalcified citrated sheep plasma (see Assay).

B. Dissolve 0.40 g in *water R* and dilute to 10.0 ml with the same solvent. The specific optical rotation (*2.2.7*) is not less than + 35.

C. Examine by zone electrophoresis (*2.2.31*) using *agarose for electrophoresis R* as the supporting medium. To equilibrate the agarose and as electrolyte solution use a mixture of 50 ml of *glacial acetic acid R* and 800 ml of *water R* adjusted to pH 3 by addition of *lithium hydroxide R* and diluted to 1000.0 ml with *water R*.

*Test solution*   Dissolve 25 mg of the substance to be examined in *water R* and dilute to 10 ml with the same solvent.

*Reference solution*   Dilute *heparin sodium BRP* with an equal volume of *water R*.

Apply separately to the strip 2 μl to 3 μl of each solution. Pass a current of 1 mA to 2 mA per centimetre of strip width at a potential difference of 300 V for about 10 min. Stain the strips using a 1 g/l solution of *toluidine blue R* and remove the

excess by washing. The ratio of the mobility of the principal band or bands in the electropherogram obtained with the test solution to the mobility of the band in the electropherogram obtained with the reference solution is 0.9 to 1.1.

D. The residue obtained in the test for sulphated ash (see Tests) gives reaction (a) of sodium (*2.3.1*).

## TESTS

**Appearance of solution**
Dissolve a quantity equivalent to 50 000 IU in *water R* and dilute to 10 ml with the same solvent. The solution is clear (*2.2.1*) and not more intensely coloured than intensity 5 of the range of reference solutions of the most appropriate colour (*2.2.2, Method II*).

**pH** (*2.2.3*)
Dissolve 0.1 g in *carbon dioxide-free water R* and dilute to 10 ml with the same solvent. The pH of the solution is 5.5 to 8.0.

**Protein and nucleotidic impurities**
Dissolve 40 mg in 10 ml of *water R*. The absorbance (*2.2.25*) measured at 260 nm is not greater than 0.20 and that measured at 280 nm is not greater than 0.15.

**Nitrogen**
Not more than 2.5 per cent, calculated with reference to the dried substance. Carry out the determination of nitrogen by sulphuric acid digestion (*2.5.9*), using 0.100 g.

**Sodium**
9.5 per cent to 12.5 per cent of Na, calculated with reference to the dried substance and determined by atomic absorption spectrometry (*2.2.23, Method I*).

*Test solution*   Dissolve 50 mg of the substance to be examined in *0.1 M hydrochloric acid* containing 1.27 mg of *caesium chloride R* per millilitre and dilute to 100.0 ml with the same solvent.

*Reference solutions*   Prepare reference solutions containing 25 ppm, 50 ppm and 75 ppm of Na, using *sodium standard solution (200 ppm Na) R* diluted with *0.1 M hydrochloric acid* containing 1.27 mg of *caesium chloride R* per millilitre.

Measure the absorbance at 330.3 nm using a sodium hollow-cathode lamp as the source of radiation and a flame of suitable composition (for example 11 litres of air and 2 litres of acetylene per minute).

**Heavy metals** (*2.4.8*)
0.5 g complies with limit test C for heavy metals (30 ppm). Prepare the reference solution using 1.5 ml of *lead standard solution (10 ppm Pb) R*.

**Loss on drying** (*2.2.32*)
Not more than 8.0 per cent, determined on 1.000 g by drying at 60 °C over *diphosphorus pentoxide R* at a pressure not exceeding 670 Pa for 3 h.

**Sulphated ash** (*2.4.14*)
30 per cent to 43 per cent, determined on 0.20 g and calculated with reference to the dried substance.

**Bacterial endotoxins** (*2.6.14*)
Less than 0.01 IU per IU of heparin, if intended for use in the manufacture of parenteral preparations without a further appropriate procedure for the removal of bacterial endotoxins.

## ASSAY

Carry out the assay of heparin (*2.7.5*). The estimated potency is not less than 90 per cent and not more than 111 per cent of the stated potency. The confidence limits of the estimated potency (*P* = 0.95) are not less than

80 per cent and not more than 125 per cent of the stated potency.

## STORAGE

Store in an airtight container. If the substance is sterile, store in a sterile, airtight, tamper-proof container.

## LABELLING

The label states:
— the number of International Units per milligram;
— where applicable, that the substance is suitable for use in the manufacture of parenteral preparations.

*Ph Eur*

# Low-molecular-weight Heparins

(*Low-molecular-mass Heparins,*
*Ph Eur monograph 0828*)

## Action and use

Anticoagulant.

*Ph Eur*

## DEFINITION

Salts of sulphated glucosaminoglycans having a mass-average relative molecular mass less than 8000 and for which at least 60 per cent of the total mass has a relative molecular mass less than 8000. Low-molecular-mass heparins display different chemical structures at the reducing, or the non-reducing end of the polysaccharide chains.

The potency is not less than 70 IU of anti-factor Xa activity per milligram, calculated with reference to the dried substance. The ratio of anti-factor Xa activity to anti-factor IIa activity, determined as described under Assay, is not less than 1.5.

## PRODUCTION

Low-molecular-mass heparins are obtained by fractionation or depolymerisation of heparin of natural origin that complies with the monograph on *Heparin sodium (0333)* or *Heparin calcium (0332)*, whichever is appropriate, for parenteral use, unless otherwise justified and authorised. For each type of low-molecular-mass heparin the batch-to-batch consistency is ensured by demonstrating, for example, that the mass-average relative molecular mass and the mass percentage within defined relative molecular-mass ranges lower than 8000 are not less than 75 per cent and not more than 125 per cent of the mean value stated as type specification. The same limits apply also to the ratio of anti-factor Xa activity to anti-factor IIa activity.

### Nucleotide and protein impurities of the source material

Dissolve 40 mg of the source material before fractionation in 10 ml of *water R*. The absorbance (*2.2.25*) measured at 260 nm and 280 nm is not greater than 0.20 and 0.15, respectively.

## CHARACTERS

### Appearance

White or almost white powder, hygroscopic.

### Solubility

Freely soluble in water.

## IDENTIFICATION

A. Nuclear magnetic resonance spectrometry (*2.2.33*).

*Preparation*  Dissolve 0.200 g of the substance to be examined in a mixture of 0.2 ml of *deuterium oxide R* and 0.8 ml of *water R*.

*Comparison*  Dissolve 0.200 g of the appropriate specific low-molecular-mass heparin reference standard in a mixture of 0.2 ml of *deuterium oxide R* and 0.8 ml of *water R*.

*Operating conditions*  Use a pulsed (Fourier transform) spectrometer operating at 75 MHz for $^{13}$C. Record the spectra at 40 °C, using cells 5 mm in diameter. Use *deuterated methanol R* as internal reference at $\delta = 50.0$ ppm.

*Results*  The spectrum obtained is similar to the appropriate specific low-molecular-mass heparin reference standard.

B. The ratio of anti-factor Xa activity to anti-factor IIa activity, determined as described under Assay, is not less than 1.5.

C. Size-exclusion chromatography (*2.2.30*).

*Test solution*  Dissolve 20 mg of the substance to be examined in 2 ml of the mobile phase.

*Reference solution*  Dissolve 20 mg of *heparin low-molecular-mass for calibration CRS* in 2 ml of the mobile phase.

*Column:*
— *size: $l = 0.30$ m, $\varnothing = 7.5$ mm;*
— *stationary phase*: appropriate porous silica beads (5 μm) with a fractionation range for proteins of approximately 15 000 to 100 000;
— *number of theoretical plates*: minimum of 20 000 per metre.

*Mobile phase*  28.4 g/l solution of *anhydrous sodium sulphate R* adjusted to pH 5.0 using *dilute sulphuric acid R*.

*Flow rate*  0.5 ml/min.

*Detection*  Differential refractometer.

*Injection*  25 μl.

*Calibration*  For detection, use a differential refractometer (RI) detector connected in series to a ultraviolet spectrophotometer (UV) set at 234 nm such that the UV monitor is connected to the column outlet, and the RI detector to the UV-monitor outlet.

It is necessary to measure the time lapse between the 2 detectors accurately, so that their chromatograms can be aligned correctly. The retention times used in the calibration must be those from the RI detector.

The normalisation factor used to calculate the relative molecular mass from the RI/UV ratio is obtained as follows: calculate the total area under the $UV_{234}$ ($\Sigma UV_{234}$) and the RI ($\Sigma RI$) curves by numerical integration over the range of interest (i.e. excluding salt and solvent peaks at the end of the chromatogram). Calculate the ratio r using the following expression:

$$\frac{\sum RI}{\sum UV_{234}}$$

Calculate the factor $f$ using the following expression:

$$\frac{M_{na}}{r}$$

$M_{na}$ = assigned number-average relative molecular mass of the *Heparin low-molecular-mass for calibration CRS* found in the leaflet supplied with the CRS.

Provided the $UV_{234}$ and the RI responses are aligned, the relative molecular mass $M$ at any point is calculated using the following expression:

$$f\frac{\mathrm{RI}}{\mathrm{UV}_{234}}$$

The resulting table of retention times and relative molecular masses may be used to derive a calibration for the chromatographic system by fitting a suitable mathematical relationship to the data. A polynomial of the $3^{rd}$ degree is recommended. *It must be stressed that the extrapolation of this fitted calibration curve to higher molecular masses is not valid.*

Inject 25 µl of the test solution and record the chromatogram for a period of time, ensuring complete elution of sample and solvent peaks.

The mass-average relative molecular mass is defined by the following expression:

$$\frac{\sum (\mathrm{RI}_i M_i)}{\sum \mathrm{RI}_i}$$

$\mathrm{RI}_i$ = mass of substance eluting in the fraction $i$;
$M_i$ = relative molecular mass corresponding to fraction $i$.

Any low-molecular-mass heparin covered by a specific monograph complies with the requirements for identification C prescribed in the corresponding monograph.

Where no specific monograph exists for the low-molecular-mass heparin to be examined, the mass-average relative molecular mass is not greater than 8000 and at least 60 per cent of the total mass has a relative molecular mass lower than 8000. In addition, the molecular mass parameters (mass-average molecular mass and mass percentages of chains comprised between specified values) correspond to that of the manufacturer's reference preparation.

D. It gives reaction (a) of sodium or the reactions of calcium (as appropriate) (*2.3.1*).

## TESTS

**pH** (*2.2.3*)
5.5 to 8.0.

Dissolve 0.1 g in *carbon dioxide-free water R* and dilute to 10 ml with the same solvent.

**Nitrogen** (*2.5.9*)
1.5 per cent to 2.5 per cent (dried substance).

**Calcium** (*2.5.11*)
9.5 per cent to 11.5 per cent (dried substance), if prepared from heparin complying with the monograph on *Heparin calcium (0332)*. Use 0.200 g.

**Sodium**
9.5 per cent to 12.5 per cent (dried substance), if prepared from heparin complying with the monograph on *Heparin sodium (0333)*.

Atomic absorption spectrometry (*2.2.23, Method I*).

*Test solution* Dissolve 50 mg in *0.1 M hydrochloric acid* containing 1.27 mg of *caesium chloride R* per millilitre and dilute to 100.0 ml with the same solvent.

*Reference solutions* Prepare reference solutions (25 ppm, 50 ppm and 75 ppm) using *sodium standard solution (200 ppm Na) R* diluted with *0.1 M hydrochloric acid* containing 1.27 mg of *caesium chloride R* per millilitre.

*Source* Sodium hollow-cathode lamp.

*Wavelength* 330.3 nm.

*Atomisation device* Flame of suitable composition (for example, 11 litres of air and 2 litres of acetylene per minute).

**Molar ratio of sulphate ions to carboxylate ions** (*2.2.38*)
Minimum 1.8.

*The sample of heparin used in this titration must be free from ionisable impurities, particularly salts.*

Weigh 0.100 g of the substance to be examined taking the necessary measures to avoid the problems linked to hygroscopicity.

Take up into about 20 ml of double-glass-distilled *water R*. Cool to 4 °C and apply 2.0 ml of this solution to a pre-cooled column (approximately 10 × 1 cm), packed with a suitable *cation exchange resin R*. Wash through with double-glass-distilled *water R* into the titration vessel up to a final volume of about 10-15 ml (*the titration vessel must be just large enough to hold the electrodes from the conductivity meter, a small stirrer bar and a fine flexible tube from the outlet of a 2 ml burette*). Stir magnetically. When the conductivity reading is constant, note it and titrate with *0.05 M sodium hydroxide* added in approximately 50 µl portions. Record the burette level and the conductivity meter reading a few seconds after each addition until the end-point is reached.

For each measured figure, calculate the number of milliequivalents of sodium hydroxide added from the volume and the known concentration of the sodium hydroxide solution. Plot on a graph the figures for conductivity (as *y*-axis) against the figures of milliequivalent of sodium hydroxide (as *x*-axis). The graph will have 3, approximately linear sections: an initial steep downward slope, a middle slight rise and a final steep rise. Estimate the best straight lines through these 3 parts of the graph. At the points where the $1^{st}$ and $2^{nd}$ lines intersect, and where the $2^{nd}$ and $3^{rd}$ lines intersect, draw perpendiculars to the *x*-axis to estimate the milliequivalents of sodium hydroxide taken up by the sample at those points. The point where the $1^{st}$ and $2^{nd}$ lines intersect will give the number of milliequivalents of sodium hydroxide taken up by the sulphate groups, and the point where the $2^{nd}$ and $3^{rd}$ lines intersect will give the number of milliequivalents taken up by the sulphate and carboxylate groups together. The difference between the 2 will therefore give the number of milliequivalents taken up by the carboxylate groups.

**Heavy metals** (*2.4.8*)
Maximum 30 ppm.

0.5 g complies with test C. Prepare the reference solution using 1.5 ml of *lead standard solution (10 ppm Pb) R*.

**Loss on drying** (*2.2.32*)
Maximum 10.0 per cent, determined on 1.000 g by drying at 60 °C over *diphosphorus pentoxide R* at a pressure not exceeding 0.67 kPa for 3 h.

**Bacterial endotoxins** (*2.6.14*)
Less than 0.01 IU per International Unit of anti-Xa activity, if intended for use in the manufacture of parenteral dosage forms without a further appropriate procedure for the removal of bacterial endotoxins. The addition of divalent cations may be necessary to fulfil the validation criteria.

## ASSAY

The anticoagulant activity of low-molecular-mass heparins is determined *in vitro* by 2 assays which determine its ability to accelerate the inhibition of factor Xa (anti-Xa assay) and thrombin, factor IIa (anti-IIa assay), by antithrombin III.

The International Units for anti-Xa and anti-IIa activity are the activities contained in a stated amount of the International Standard for low-molecular-mass heparin.

*Heparin low-molecular-mass for assay BRP*, calibrated in International Units by comparison with the International Standard using the 2 assays given below, is used as reference preparation.

## ANTI-FACTOR XA ACTIVITY

### Reference and test solutions

Prepare 4 independent series of 4 dilutions each, of the substance to be examined and of the reference preparation of low-molecular-mass heparin in *tris(hydroxymethyl)aminomethane sodium chloride buffer solution pH 7.4 R*; the concentration range should be within 0.025 IU to 0.2 IU of anti-factor Xa activity per millilitre and the dilutions chosen should give a linear response when results are plotted as absorbance against log concentration.

### Procedure

Label 16 tubes in duplicate: $T_1$, $T_2$, $T_3$, $T_4$ for the dilutions of the substance to be examined and $S_1$, $S_2$, $S_3$, $S_4$ for the dilutions of the reference preparation. To each tube add 50 µl of *antithrombin III solution R1* and 50 µl of the appropriate dilution of the substance to be examined, or the reference preparation. After each addition, mix but do not allow bubbles to form. Treating the tubes in the order $S_1$, $S_2$, $S_3$, $S_4$, $T_1$, $T_2$, $T_3$, $T_4$, $T_1$, $T_2$, $T_3$, $T_4$, $S_1$, $S_2$, $S_3$, $S_4$, allow to equilibrate at 37 °C (water-bath or heating block) for 1 min and add to each tube 100 µl of *bovine factor Xa solution R*. Incubate for exactly 1 min and add 250 µl of *chromogenic substrate R1*. Stop the reaction after exactly 4 min by adding 375 µl of *acetic acid R*. Transfer the mixtures to semi-micro cuvettes and measure the absorbance (*2.2.25*) at 405 nm using a suitable reading device. Determine the blank amidolytic activity at the beginning and at the end of the procedure in a similar manner, using *tris(hydroxymethyl)aminomethane sodium chloride buffer solution pH 7.4 R* instead of the reference and test solutions; the 2 blank values do not differ significantly. Calculate the regression of the absorbance on log concentrations of the solutions of the substance to be examined and of the reference preparation of low-molecular-mass heparins and calculate the potency of the substance to be examined in International Units of anti-factor Xa activity per millilitre using the usual statistical methods for parallel-line assays.

## ANTI-FACTOR IIA ACTIVITY

### Reference and test solutions

Prepare 4 independent series of 4 dilutions each, of the substance to be examined and of the reference preparation of low molecular-mass heparin in *tris(hydroxymethyl)aminomethane sodium chloride buffer solution pH 7.4 R*; the concentration range should be within 0.015 IU to 0.075 IU of anti-factor IIa activity per millilitre and the dilutions chosen should give a linear response when results are plotted as absorbance against log concentration.

### Procedure

Label 16 tubes in duplicate: $T_1$, $T_2$, $T_3$, $T_4$ for the dilutions of the substance to be examined and $S_1$, $S_2$, $S_3$, $S_4$ for the dilutions of the reference preparation. To each tube add 50 µl of *antithrombin III solution R2* and 50 µl of the appropriate dilution of the substance to be examined or the reference preparation. After each addition, mix but do not allow bubbles to form. Treating the tubes in the order $S_1$, $S_2$, $S_3$, $S_4$, $T_1$, $T_2$, $T_3$, $T_4$, $T_1$, $T_2$, $T_3$, $T_4$, $S_1$, $S_2$, $S_3$, $S_4$, allow to equilibrate at 37 °C (water-bath or heating block) for 1 min and add to each tube 100 µl of *human thrombin solution R*. Incubate for exactly 1 min and add 250 µl of *chromogenic substrate R2*. Stop the reaction after exactly 4 min by adding 375 µl of *acetic acid R*. Transfer the mixtures to semi-micro cuvettes and measure the absorbance (*2.2.25*) at 405 nm using a suitable reading device. Determine the blank amidolytic activity at the beginning and at the end of the procedure in a similar manner, using *tris(hydroxymethyl)aminomethane sodium chloride buffer solution pH 7.4 R* instead of the reference and test solutions; the 2 blank values do not differ significantly. Calculate the regression of the absorbance on log concentrations of the solutions of the substance to be examined and of the reference preparation of low-molecular-mass heparins, and calculate the potency of the substance to be examined in International Units of anti-factor IIa activity per millilitre using the usual statistical methods for parallel-line assays.

## LABELLING

The label states:
— the number of International Units of anti-factor Xa activity per milligram;
— the number of International Units of anti-factor IIa activity per milligram;
— the mass-average molecular mass and the percentage of molecules within defined molecular mass ranges;
— where applicable, that the contents are the sodium salt;
— where applicable, that the contents are the calcium salt.

## STORAGE

In an airtight tamper-proof container. If the product is sterile and free of bacterial endotoxins, store in a sterile and apyrogenic container.

*Ph Eur*

# Heptaminol Hydrochloride

(*Ph Eur monograph 1980*)

$C_8H_{19}NO,HCl$      181.7      *543-15-7*

### Action and use

Non-selective phosphodiesterase inhibitor; treatment of reversible airways obstruction.

*Ph Eur*

## DEFINITION

(6*RS*)-6-Amino-2-methylheptan-2-ol hydrochloride.

### Content

99.0 per cent to 101.0 per cent (dried substance).

## CHARACTERS

### Appearance

White or almost white, crystalline powder.

### Solubility

Freely soluble in water, soluble in alcohol, practically insoluble in methylene chloride.

## IDENTIFICATION

*First identification* B, D.

*Second identification* A, C, D.

A. To 1 ml of solution S (see Tests) add 4 ml of *water R* and 2 ml of a 200 g/l solution of *ammonium and cerium nitrate R* in *4 M nitric acid*. An orange-brown colour develops.

B. Infrared absorption spectrophotometry (*2.2.24*).

*Comparison* heptaminol hydrochloride CRS.

C. Examine the chromatograms obtained in the test for related substances.

*Detection* Examine in daylight.

*Results* The principal spot in the chromatogram obtained with test solution (b) is similar in position, colour and size to the principal spot in the chromatogram obtained with reference solution (b).

D. It gives reaction (a) of chlorides (*2.3.1*).

## TESTS

### Solution S
Dissolve 5.0 g in *carbon dioxide-free water R* and dilute to 50 ml with the same solvent.

### Appearance of solution
Solution S is clear (*2.2.1*) and not more intensely coloured than reference solution BY₆ (*2.2.2, Method II*).

### Acidity or alkalinity
To 10 ml of solution S add 0.1 ml of *methyl red solution R* and 0.3 ml of *0.01 M hydrochloric acid*. The solution is red. Add 0.6 ml of *0.01 M sodium hydroxide*. The solution is yellow.

### Related substances
Thin-layer chromatography (*2.2.27*).

*Test solution (a)* Dissolve 0.50 g of the substance to be examined in *methanol R* and dilute to 5.0 ml with the same solvent.

*Test solution (b)* Dilute 1.0 ml of test solution (a) to 10 ml with *methanol R*.

*Reference solution (a)* Dilute 3.0 ml of test solution (a) to 10.0 ml with *methanol R*. Dilute 1.0 ml of this solution to 50.0 ml with *methanol R*.

*Reference solution (b)* Dissolve 0.10 g of *heptaminol hydrochloride CRS* in *methanol R* and dilute to 10 ml with the same solvent.

*Reference solution (c)* Dissolve 10.0 mg of *heptaminol impurity A CRS* in *methanol R* and dilute to 5.0 ml with the same solvent.

*Reference solution (d)* Dilute 1.0 ml of reference solution (c) to 10.0 ml with *methanol R*.

*Reference solution (e)* To 2.5 ml of reference solution (c) add 0.5 ml of test solution (b) and dilute to 5 ml with *methanol R*.

*Plate* TLC silica gel G plate R.

*Mobile phase* concentrated ammonia R, dioxan R, 2-propanol R (10:50:50 *V/V/V*).

*Application* 10 µl; apply test solutions (a) and (b) and reference solutions (a), (b), (d) and (e).

*Development* Over 2/3 of the plate.

*Drying* In air.

*Detection* Expose the plate to iodine vapour for at least 15 h.

*System suitability* The chromatogram obtained with reference solution (e) shows 2 clearly separated principal spots and the chromatogram obtained with reference solution (a) shows a single principal spot.

*Limits* In the chromatogram obtained with test solution (a):
— *impurity A*: any spot corresponding to impurity A is not more intense than the spot in the chromatogram obtained with reference solution (d) (0.2 per cent),
— *any other impurity*: any spot, apart from the principal spot and any spot corresponding to impurity A is not more intense than the spot in the chromatogram obtained with reference solution (a) (0.6 per cent).

### Heavy metals (*2.4.8*)
Maximum 10 ppm.

12 ml of solution S complies with limit test A. Prepare the standard using *lead standard solution (1 ppm Pb) R*.

### Loss on drying (*2.2.32*)
Maximum 0.5 per cent, determined on 1.000 g by drying in an oven at 105 °C for 4 h.

### Sulphated ash (*2.4.14*)
Maximum 0.1 per cent, determined on 1.0 g.

## ASSAY
Dissolve 0.140 g in 50 ml of *alcohol R* and add 5.0 ml of *0.01 M hydrochloric acid*. Carry out a potentiometric titration (*2.2.20*), using *0.1 M sodium hydroxide*. Read the volume added between the 2 points of inflexion.

1 ml of *0.1 M sodium hydroxide* is equivalent to 18.17 mg of $C_8H_{20}ClNO$.

## IMPURITIES

A. (2RS)-6-methylhept-5-en-2-amine.

_____ *Ph Eur*

# Hexachlorophene

$C_{13}H_6Cl_6O_2$ 406.9 70-30-4

### Action and use
Antiseptic.

### Preparation
Hexachlorophene Dusting Powder

## DEFINITION
Hexachlorophene is 2,2-methylenebis(3,4,6-trichlorophenol). It contains not less than 98.0% and not more than 100.5% of $C_{13}H_6Cl_6O_2$, calculated with reference to the dried substance.

## PRODUCTION
A suitable test is carried out to demonstrate that the level of 2,3,7,8-tetrachlorodibenzo-*p*-dioxin present does not exceed 2 ppb.

## CHARACTERISTICS
A white or pale buff, crystalline powder.

Practically insoluble in *water*; very soluble in *acetone*; freely soluble in *ethanol (96%)*. It dissolves in dilute solutions of the alkali hydroxides.

## IDENTIFICATION
The *infrared absorption spectrum*, Appendix II A, is concordant with the *reference spectrum* of hexachlorophene (*RS 174*).

# TESTS

## Chloride

Dissolve 0.50 g in 2 ml of *ethanol (96%)*, dilute to 25 ml with *water* and filter. 5 ml of the clear filtrate diluted to 15 ml with *water* complies with the *limit test for chlorides*, Appendix VII (500 ppm).

## Non-phenolic substances

Dissolve 5 g in 38 ml of *methanol*, add 125 ml of 0.25M *sodium hydroxide* and extract with three 15 ml quantities of n-*pentane*, retaining any foamy interphase with the aqueous layer. Dry the combined extracts over *anhydrous sodium sulphate* and evaporate to dryness at a pressure not exceeding 2 kPa. The residue weighs not more than 37.5 mg when dried to constant weight (0.75%).

## Related substances

Carry out the method for *liquid chromatography*, Appendix III D, using solutions of the substance being examined in *methanol* containing (1) 0.020% w/v and (2) 1.0% w/v.

The chromatographic procedure may be carried out using (a) a stainless steel column (20 cm × 4.6 mm) packed with *octadecylsilyl silica gel for chromatography*, (10 μm) (Spherisorb ODS 1 is suitable), (b) a mixture of 100 volumes of *methanol*, 20 volumes of *water* and 1 volume of *glacial acetic acid* as the mobile phase with a flow rate of 2 ml per minute and (c) a detection wavelength of 300 nm.

Inject 20 μl of solutions (1) and (2). In the chromatogram obtained with solution (2) the sum of the areas of any *secondary peaks* with a retention time not more than 3 times that of the principal peak is not greater than twice the area of the principal peak in the chromatogram obtained with solution (1) (4.0%) and not more than one such peak has an area greater than half of the area of the principal peak in the chromatogram obtained with solution (1) (1.0%).

## Loss on drying

When dried to constant weight at 105°, loses not more than 1.0% of its weight. Use 1 g.

## Sulphated ash

Not more than 0.1%, Appendix IX A.

## ASSAY

Dissolve 1.000 g in 25 ml of *ethanol (96%)* previously adjusted to pH 9.0 and titrate with 0.1M *sodium hydroxide VS* determining the end point potentiometrically. Each ml of 0.1M *sodium hydroxide VS* is equivalent to 40.69 mg of $C_{13}H_6Cl_6O_2$.

## STORAGE

Hexachlorophene should be protected from light.

# Hexamidine Isetionate

(*Hexamidine Diisetionate, Ph Eur monograph 1436*)

$C_{24}H_{38}N_4O_{10}S_2$      607      *659-40-5*

## Action and use

Antiprotozoal.

*Ph Eur*

## DEFINITION

4,4′-(Hexane-1,6-diylbisoxy)dibenzimidamide bis(2-hydroxyethanesulphonate).

## Content

98.5 per cent to 101.5 per cent (dried substance).

## PRODUCTION

The production method must be evaluated to determine the potential for formation of alkyl isetionates, which is particularly likely to occur if the reaction medium contains lower alcohols. Where necessary, the production method is validated to demonstrate that alkyl isetionates are not detectable in the final product.

## CHARACTERS

### Appearance

White or slightly yellow powder, hygroscopic.

### Solubility

Sparingly soluble in water, slightly soluble in ethanol (96 per cent), practically insoluble in methylene chloride.

## IDENTIFICATION

A. Infrared absorption spectrophotometry (*2.2.24*).

*Comparison* hexamidine diisetionate CRS.

B. Dissolve about 40 mg in 5 ml of *water R* and add dropwise with shaking 1 ml of a 100 g/l solution of *sodium chloride R*. Allow to stand for 5 min. An abundant, shimmering white precipitate is slowly formed.

## TESTS

### Appearance of solution

Dissolve 0.50 g in *carbon dioxide-free water R*, heating at about 70 °C and dilute to 10 ml with the same solvent. Allow to cool to room temperature for 10-15 min. The solution is not more opalescent than reference suspension II (*2.2.1*) and not more intensely coloured than intensity 6 of the range of reference solutions of the most appropriate colour (*2.2.2, Method II*).

### Acidity or alkalinity

Dissolve 2.0 g in *water R* heating at about 50 °C and dilute to 20 ml with *water R* heating at about 50 °C. Allow to cool to about 35 °C, add 0.1 ml of *methyl red solution R*. Not more than 0.25 ml of *0.05 M hydrochloric acid* or *0.05 M sodium hydroxide* is required to change the colour of the indicator.

### Related substances

Liquid chromatography (*2.2.29*).

*Test solution* Dissolve 20.0 mg of the substance to be examined in mobile phase A and dilute to 100.0 ml with mobile phase A.

*Reference solution (a)* Dilute 1.0 ml of the test solution to 100.0 ml with mobile phase A.

*Reference solution (b)* Dilute 1.0 ml of reference solution (a) to 10.0 ml with mobile phase A.

*Reference solution (c)* Dissolve 5 mg of the substance to be examined and 5 mg of *pentamidine diisetionate CRS* in mobile phase A and dilute to 100 ml with mobile phase A. Dilute 2 ml of the solution to 5 ml with mobile phase A.

*Column:*
— *size:* $l = 0.25$ m, $\emptyset = 4.6$ mm,
— *stationary phase:* styrene-divinylbenzene copolymer R (8 µm).

*Mobile phase:*
— *mobile phase A:* mix 20 volumes of *acetonitrile R* and 80 volumes of a 6.8 g/l solution of *potassium dihydrogen phosphate R* previously adjusted to pH 3.0 using *phosphoric acid R,*
— *mobile phase B:* mix equal volumes of *acetonitrile R* and of a 6.8 g/l solution of *potassium dihydrogen phosphate R* previously adjusted to pH 3.0 using *phosphoric acid R,*

| Time (min) | Mobile phase A (per cent *V/V*) | Mobile phase B (per cent *V/V*) |
|---|---|---|
| 0 - 30 | 100 → 0 | 0 → 100 |
| 30 - 35 | 0 | 100 |
| 35 - 40 | 0 → 100 | 100 → 0 |

*Flow rate* 1 ml/min.

*Detection* Spectrophotometer at 263 nm.

*Injection* 20 µl.

*Relative retention* With reference to hexamidine (retention time = about 6 min): impurity B = about 1.7; impurity A = about 2.0; impurity C = about 3.7; impurity D = about 4.7.

*System suitability* Reference solution (c):
— *resolution:* minimum 5.0 between the peaks due to hexamidine and pentamidine.

*Limits:*
— *impurity A:* not more than the area of the principal peak in the chromatogram obtained with reference solution (a) (1.0 per cent),
— *impurity B:* not more than 3 times the area of the principal peak in the chromatogram obtained with reference solution (b) (0.3 per cent),
— *impurities C, D:* for each impurity, not more than the area of the principal peak in the chromatogram obtained with reference solution (b) (0.1 per cent),
— *any other impurities:* for each impurity, not more than the area of the principal peak in the chromatogram obtained with reference solution (b) (0.1 per cent),
— *total:* not more than 1.5 times the area of the principal peak in the chromatogram obtained with reference solution (a) (1.5 per cent),
— *disregard limit:* 0.5 times the area of the principal peak in the chromatogram obtained with reference solution (b) (0.05 per cent).

**Loss on drying** (2.2.32)
Maximum 0.5 per cent, determined on 1.000 g by drying in an oven at 105 °C.

**Sulphated ash** (2.4.14)
Maximum 0.1 per cent, determined on 1.0 g.

**ASSAY**
Dissolve 0.250 g in 50 ml of *dimethylformamide R*. Titrate with *0.1 M tetrabutylammonium hydroxide* under a current of *nitrogen R*, determining the end-point potentiometrically (2.2.20).

1 ml of *0.1 M tetrabutylammonium hydroxide* is equivalent to 30.35 mg of $C_{24}H_{38}N_4O_{10}S_2$.

**STORAGE**
In an airtight container.

**IMPURITIES**
*Specified impurities* A, B, C, D.

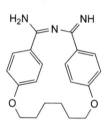

A. X = O, R' = $NH_2$:
4-[[6-(4-carbamimidoylphenoxy)hexyl]oxy]benzamide,
B. X = NH, R' = $OC_2H_5$: ethyl 4-[[6-(4-carbamimidoylphenoxy)hexyl]oxy]benzimidoate,
D. X = O, R' = $OC_2H_5$:
ethyl 4-[[6-(4-carbamimidoylphenoxy)hexyl]oxy]benzoate,

C. 4-imino-9,16-dioxa-3-azatricyclo[15.2.2.2^{5,8}]tricosa-1(19),2,5,7,17,20,22-heptaen-2-amine.

*Ph Eur*

# Hexetidine

*(Ph Eur monograph 1221)*

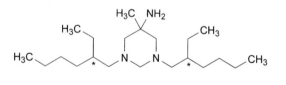

$C_{21}H_{45}N_3$　　　　339.6　　　　*141-94-6*

**Action and use**
Antiseptic.

*Ph Eur*

**DEFINITION**
Hexetidine contains not less than 98.0 per cent and not more than the equivalent of 102.0 per cent of 1,3-bis(2-ethylhexyl)-5-methylhexahydropyrimidin-5-amine.

## CHARACTERS

An oily liquid, colourless or slightly yellow, very slightly soluble in water, very soluble in acetone, in alcohol and in methylene chloride. It dissolves in dilute mineral acids.

## IDENTIFICATION

*First identification   A.*

*Second identification   B, C, D.*

A. Examine by infrared absorption spectrophotometry (*2.2.24*), comparing with the spectrum obtained with *hexetidine CRS*.

B. Examine the chromatograms obtained in the test for related substances. The principal spot in the chromatogram obtained with test solution (b) is similar in position, colour and size to the principal spot in the chromatogram obtained with reference solution (a).

C. To 0.2 ml add 2 ml of *sulphuric acid R* and 2 mg of *chromotropic acid, sodium salt R*. Heat in a water-bath at 60 °C. A violet colour develops.

D. Dissolve 0.2 ml in 1 ml of *methylene chloride R*. Add 0.5 ml of *copper sulphate solution R*, 0.05 ml of *0.25 M alcoholic sulphuric acid R* and 5 ml of *water R*. Shake, then allow to stand. The lower layer becomes deep blue.

## TESTS

### Appearance

The substance to be examined is clear (*2.2.1*)and not more intensely coloured than reference solution $Y_5$ or reference solution $GY_5$ (*2.2.2, Method II*).

### Relative density (*2.2.5*)

0.864 to 0.870.

### Refractive index (*2.2.6*)

1.461 to 1.467.

### Optical rotation (*2.2.7*)

Dissolve 1.0 g in *ethanol R* and dilute to 10.0 ml with the same solvent. The angle of optical rotation is − 0.10° to + 0.10°.

### Absorbance (*2.2.25*)

Dissolve 0.50 g in *heptane R* and dilute to 50.0 ml with the same solvent. At wavelengths from 270 nm to 350 nm, the absorbance of the solution is not greater than 0.1.

### Related substances

Examine by thin-layer chromatography (*2.2.27*), using *silica gel H R* as the coating substance. *Prepare the solutions immediately before use.*

*Test solution (a)*   Dissolve 2.0 g of the substance to be examined in *heptane R* and dilute to 20 ml with the same solvent.

*Test solution (b)*   Dilute 1 ml of test solution (a) to 10 ml with *heptane R*.

*Reference solution (a)*   Dissolve 20 mg of *hexetidine CRS* in *heptane R* and dilute to 2 ml with the same solvent.

*Reference solution (b)*   Dilute 1 ml of test solution (a) to 100 ml with *heptane R*.

*Reference solution (c)*   Dilute 5 ml of reference solution (b) to 10 ml with *heptane R*.

*Reference solution (d)*   Dissolve 10 mg of *dehydrohexetidine CRS* in test solution (a) and dilute to 10 ml with the same solution.

Apply separately to the plate 1 μl of each solution. At the bottom of a chromatography tank, place an evaporating dish containing *concentrated ammonia R1*. Place the dried plate in the tank and close the tank. Leave the plate in contact with the ammonia vapour for 15 min. Withdraw the plate and place it in a current of air to remove the ammonia vapour. Develop over a path of 15 cm using a mixture of 20 volumes of *methanol R* and 80 volumes of *toluene R*. Allow the plate to dry in air. Expose the plate to iodine vapour for 30 min. Any spot in the chromatogram obtained with test solution (a), apart from the principal spot, is not more intense than the spot in the chromatogram obtained with reference solution (b) (1 per cent) and at most two such spots are more intense than the spot in the chromatogram obtained with reference solution (c) (0.5 per cent). The test is not valid unless the chromatogram obtained with reference solution (d) shows two clearly separated spots.

### Heavy metals (*2.4.8*)

Dissolve 2.0 g in a mixture of 15 volumes of *water R* and 85 volumes of *acetone R* and dilute to 20 ml with the same mixture of solvents. 12 ml of the solution complies with limit test B for heavy metals (10 ppm). Prepare the standard using lead standard solution (1 ppm Pb) obtained by diluting *lead standard solution (100 ppm Pb) R* with a mixture of 15 volumes of *water R* and 85 volumes of *acetone R*.

### Sulphated ash (*2.4.14*)

Not more than 0.1 per cent, determined on 1.0 g.

## ASSAY

Dissolve 0.150 g in 80 ml of *anhydrous acetic acid R*. Titrate with *0.1 M perchloric acid*, determining the end-point potentiometrically (*2.2.20*).

1 ml of *0.1 M perchloric acid* is equivalent to 16.98 mg of $C_{21}H_{45}N_3$.

## STORAGE

Store protected from light.

## IMPURITIES

A. 2-ethyl-*N*-[[1-(2-ethylhexyl)-4-methyl-4,5-dihydro-1*H*-imidazol-4-yl]methyl]hexan-1-amine (dehydrohexetidine),

B. $N^1,N^3$-bis(2-ethylhexyl)-2-methylpropane-1,2,3-triamine (triamine),

C. 2,6-bis(2-ethylhexyl)-7a-methylhexahydro-1*H*-imidazo[1,5-*c*]imidazole (hexedine),

D. naphthalene-1,5-disulphonic acid.

# Hexobarbital

*(Ph Eur monograph 0183)*

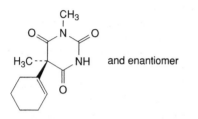

C₁₂H₁₆N₂O₃      236.3      56-29-1

$C_{12}H_{16}N_2O_3$      236.3      56-29-1

## Action and use
Barbiturate.

*Ph Eur* _____

## DEFINITION
Hexobarbital contains not less than 99.0 per cent and not more than the equivalent of 101.0 per cent of (5RS)-5-(cyclohex-1-enyl)-1,5-dimethylpyrimidine-2,4,6(1H,3H,5H)-trione, calculated with reference to the dried substance.

## CHARACTERS
A white or almost white, crystalline powder, very slightly soluble in water, sparingly soluble in alcohol. It forms water-soluble compounds with alkali hydroxides and carbonates and with ammonia.

## IDENTIFICATION
*First identification*  A, B.

*Second identification*  A, C, D.

A. Determine the melting point (2.2.14) of the substance to be examined. Mix equal parts of the substance to be examined and *hexobarbital CRS* and determine the melting point of the mixture. The difference between the melting points (which are about 146 °C) is not greater than 2 °C.

B. Examine by infrared absorption spectrophotometry (2.2.24), comparing with the spectrum obtained with *hexobarbital CRS*.

C. Examine by thin-layer chromatography (2.2.27), using *silica gel GF₂₅₄ R* as the coating substance.

*Test solution*  Dissolve 0.1 g of the substance to be examined in *chloroform R* and dilute to 100 ml with the same solvent.

*Reference solution*  Dissolve 0.1 g of *hexobarbital CRS* in *chloroform R* and dilute to 100 ml with the same solvent.

Apply separately to the plate 10 μl of each solution. Develop over a path of 18 cm using the lower layer of a mixture of 5 volumes of *concentrated ammonia R*, 15 volumes of *alcohol R* and 80 volumes of *chloroform R*. Examine immediately in ultraviolet light at 254 nm. The principal spot in the chromatogram obtained with the test solution is similar in position and size to the principal spot in the chromatogram obtained with the reference solution.

D. To about 10 mg add 1.0 ml of a 10 g/l solution of *vanillin R* in *alcohol R* and 2 ml of a cooled mixture of 1 volume of *water R* and 2 volumes of *sulphuric acid R*. Shake and allow to stand for 5 min. A greenish-yellow colour develops. Heat on a water-bath for 10 min. The colour becomes dark red.

## TESTS
### Appearance of solution
Dissolve 1.0 g in a mixture of 4 ml of *dilute sodium hydroxide solution R* and 6 ml of *water R*. The solution is clear (2.2.1) and not more intensely coloured than reference solution Y₆.(2.2.2, Method II).

### Acidity
Boil 1.0 g with 50 ml of *water R* for 2 min, allow to cool and filter. To 10 ml of the filtrate add 0.15 ml of *methyl red solution R*. The solution is orange-yellow. Not more than 0.1 ml of *0.1 M sodium hydroxide* is required to produce a pure yellow colour.

### Related substances
Examine by thin-layer chromatography (2.2.27), using *silica gel GF₂₅₄ R* as the coating substance.

*Test solution*  Dissolve 1.0 g of the substance to be examined in *chloroform R* and dilute to 100 ml with the same solvent.

*Reference solution*  Dilute 0.5 ml of the test solution to 100 ml with *chloroform R*.

Apply separately to the plate 20 μl of each solution. Develop over a path of 15 cm using the lower layer of a mixture of 5 volumes of *concentrated ammonia R*, 15 volumes of *alcohol R* and 80 volumes of *chloroform R*. Examine immediately in ultraviolet light at 254 nm. Any spot in the chromatogram obtained with the test solution, apart from the principal spot, is not more intense than the spot in the chromatogram obtained with the reference solution (0.5 per cent).

### Loss on drying (2.2.32)
Not more than 0.5 per cent, determined on 1.00 g by drying in an oven at 105 °C.

### Sulphated ash (2.4.14)
Not more than 0.1 per cent, determined on 1.0 g.

## ASSAY
Dissolve 0.200 g in 5 ml of *pyridine R*. Add 0.5 ml of *thymolphthalein solution R* and 10 ml of *silver nitrate solution in pyridine R*. Titrate with *0.1 M ethanolic sodium hydroxide* until a pure blue colour is obtained. Carry out a blank titration.

1 ml of *0.1 M ethanolic sodium hydroxide* is equivalent to 23.63 mg of C₁₂H₁₆N₂O₃.

# Hexylresorcinol

*(Ph Eur monograph 1437)*

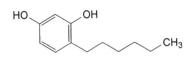

$C_{12}H_{18}O_2$        194.3        *136-77-6*

## Action and use
Antihelminthic.

*Ph Eur*

## DEFINITION
4-Hexylbenzene-1,3-diol.

## Content
98.0 per cent to 101.0 per cent (anhydrous substance).

## CHARACTERS
### Appearance
Colourless, yellowish or reddish, crystalline powder or needles, turning brownish-pink on exposure to light or air.

### Solubility
Very slightly soluble in water, freely soluble in ethanol (96 per cent) and in methylene chloride.

It shows polymorphism (*5.9*).

## IDENTIFICATION
*First identification*   B.

*Second identification*   A, C, D.

A. Melting point (*2.2.14*): 66 °C to 68 °C, melting may occur at about 60 °C, followed by solidification and a second melting between 66 °C and 68 °C.

B. Infrared absorption spectrophotometry (*2.2.24*).

*Comparison*   hexylresorcinol CRS.

If the spectra obtained in the solid state show differences, dissolve the substance to be examined and the reference substance separately *in methanol R*, evaporate to dryness and record new spectra using the residues.

C. Thin-layer chromatography (*2.2.27*).

*Test solution*   Dilute 0.1 ml of solution S (see Tests) to 10 ml with *ethanol (96 per cent) R*.

*Reference solution (a)*   Dissolve 10 mg of *hexylresorcinol CRS* in *ethanol (96 per cent) R* and dilute to 10 ml with the same solvent.

*Reference solution (b)*   Dissolve 10 mg of *hexylresorcinol CRS* and 10 mg of *resorcinol R* in *ethanol (96 per cent) R*, then dilute to 10 ml with the same solvent.

*Plate*   *TLC silica gel G plate R.*

*Mobile phase*   methyl ethyl ketone R, pentane R (50:50 *V/V*).

*Application*   10 µl.

*Development*   Over 2/3 of the plate.

*Drying*   In air for 5 min.

*Detection*   Spray with 3 ml of *anisaldehyde solution R* and heat at 100-105 °C for 5 min.

*System suitability*   Reference solution (b):
— the chromatogram shows 2 clearly separated principal spots.

*Results*   The principal spot in the chromatogram obtained with the test solution is similar in position, colour and size to the principal spot in the chromatogram obtained with reference solution (a).

D. Dissolve 0.1 g in 1 ml of *ethanol (96 per cent) R*. Add one drop of *ferric chloride solution R1*. A green colour is produced. Add *dilute ammonia R1*. The solution becomes brown.

## TESTS
### Solution S
Dissolve 1.0 g in *ethanol (96 per cent) R* and dilute to 10.0 ml with the same solvent.

### Appearance of solution
Solution S is clear (*2.2.1*).

### Acidity
Dissolve 0.5 g in a mixture of 25 ml of *carbon dioxide-free water R* and 25 ml of *ether R* previously neutralised to *phenolphthalein solution R1* and titrate with *0.1 M sodium hydroxide*, shaking vigorously after each addition. Not more than 0.4 ml is required to change the colour of the solution.

### Related substances
Liquid chromatography (*2.2.29*).

*Test solution*   Dissolve 0.1 g of the substance to be examined in the mobile phase and dilute to 10.0 ml with the mobile phase.

*Reference solution (a)*   Dilute 1.0 ml of the test solution to 200.0 ml with the mobile phase.

*Reference solution (b)*   Dissolve 20.0 mg of *phenol R* (impurity A) in the mobile phase and dilute to 100.0 ml with the mobile phase.

*Reference solution (c)*   Dissolve 20.0 mg of *resorcinol R* (impurity B) in the mobile phase and dilute to 100.0 ml with the mobile phase.

*Reference solution (d)*   To 8.0 ml of reference solution (a) add 2.0 ml of reference solution (b), 2.0 ml of reference solution (c) and dilute to 20.0 ml with the mobile phase.

*Column:*
— *size: l* = 0.25 m, Ø = 4.6 mm;
— *stationary phase*: octadecylsilyl silica gel for chromatography R (5 µm).

*Mobile phase*   Mix 25 volumes of a 3.0 g/l solution of *glacial acetic acid R* adjusted to pH 5.9 with *dilute ammonia R1*, and 75 volumes of *methanol R*.

*Flow rate*   1 ml/min.

*Detection*   Spectrophotometer at 281 nm.

*Injection*   20 µl.

*Run time*   Twice the retention time of hexylresorcinol.

*System suitability*   Reference solution (d):
— *resolution*: minimum 5.0 between the peaks due to impurity A (2nd peak) and hexylresorcinol (3rd peak).

*Limits:*
— *impurities A, B*: for each impurity, not more than the area of the corresponding peak in the chromatogram obtained with reference solution (d) (0.2 per cent);
— *any other impurity*: for each impurity, not more than the area of the principal peak in the chromatogram obtained with reference solution (a) (0.5 per cent);
— *total*: not more than twice the area of the principal peak in the chromatogram obtained with reference solution (a) (1 per cent);
— *disregard limit*: 0.1 times the area of the principal peak in the chromatogram obtained with reference solution (a) (0.05 per cent).

### Water (*2.5.12*)
Maximum 0.5 per cent, determined on 1.000 g.

### Sulphated ash (*2.4.14*)
Maximum 0.1 per cent, determined on 1.0 g.

## ASSAY

Dissolve 0.100 g in 10 ml of *methanol R* in a ground-glass-stoppered flask, add 30.0 ml of *0.0167 M potassium bromate* and 2 g of *potassium bromide R*. Shake to dissolve the substance and add 15 ml of *dilute sulphuric acid R*. Stopper the flask, shake and allow to stand in the dark for 15 min, stirring continuously. Add 5 ml of *methylene chloride R* and a solution of 1 g of *potassium iodide R* in 10 ml of *water R*, allow to stand in the dark for 15 min, stirring continuously. Titrate with *0.1 M sodium thiosulphate*, using 1 ml of *starch solution R*, shaking thoroughly. Carry out a blank titration under the same conditions.

1 ml of *0.0167 M potassium bromate* is equivalent to 4.857 mg of $C_{12}H_{18}O_2$.

## STORAGE

In an airtight container, protected from light.

## IMPURITIES

*Specified impurities  A, B.*

A. phenol,

B. resorcinol.

*Ph Eur*

# Histamine Dihydrochloride

(*Ph Eur monograph 0143*)

, 2 HCl

$C_5H_9N_3,2HCl$           184.1           *56-92-8*

*Ph Eur*

## DEFINITION

Histamine dihydrochloride contains not less than 98.5 per cent and not more than the equivalent of 101.0 per cent of 2-(1*H*-imidazol-4-yl)ethanamine dihydrochloride, calculated with reference to the dried substance.

## CHARACTERS

A white or almost white, crystalline powder or colourless crystals, hygroscopic, very soluble in water, soluble in alcohol.

## IDENTIFICATION

*First identification  A, D.*

*Second identification  B, C, D.*

A. Examine by infrared absorption spectrophotometry (*2.2.24*), comparing with the spectrum obtained with *histamine dihydrochloride CRS*. Examine as discs prepared using 1 mg of substance.

B. Examine the chromatograms obtained in the test for histidine. The principal spot in the chromatogram obtained with test solution (b) is similar in position, colour and size to the principal spot in the chromatogram obtained with reference solution (a).

C. Dissolve 0.1 g in 7 ml of *water R* and add 3 ml of a 200 g/l solution of *sodium hydroxide R*. Dissolve 50 mg of *sulphanilic acid R* in a mixture of 0.1 ml of *hydrochloric acid R* and 10 ml of *water R* and add 0.1 ml of *sodium nitrite solution R*. Add the second solution to the first and mix. A red colour is produced.

D. It gives reaction (a) of chlorides (*2.3.1*).

## TESTS
### Solution S

Dissolve 0.5 g in *carbon dioxide-free water R* prepared from *distilled water R* and dilute to 10 ml with the same solvent.

### Appearance of solution

Solution S is clear (*2.2.1*) and not more intensely coloured than reference solution $Y_7$ (*2.2.2, Method II*).

### pH (*2.2.3*)

The pH of solution S is 2.85 to 3.60.

### Histidine

Examine by thin-layer chromatography (*2.2.27*), using a *TLC silica gel G plate R*.

*Test solution (a)*  Dissolve 0.5 g of the substance to be examined in *water R* and dilute to 10 ml with the same solvent.

*Test solution (b)*  Dilute 2 ml of test solution (a) to 10 ml with *water R*.

*Reference solution (a)*  Dissolve 0.1 g of *histamine dihydrochloride CRS* in *water R* and dilute to 10 ml with the same solvent.

*Reference solution (b)*  Dissolve 50 mg of *histidine monohydrochloride R* in *water R* and dilute to 100 ml with the same solvent.

*Reference solution (c)*  Mix 1 ml of test solution (a) and 1 ml of reference solution (b).

Apply to the plate 1 μl of test solution (a), 1 μl of test solution (b), 1 μl of reference solution (a), 1 μl of reference solution (b) and 2 μl of reference solution (c). Develop over a path of 15 cm using a mixture of 5 volumes of *concentrated ammonia R*, 20 volumes of *water R* and 75 volumes of *acetonitrile R*. Dry the plate in a current of air. Repeat the development in the same direction, dry the plate in a current of air and spray with *ninhydrin solution R1*. Heat the plate at 110 °C for 10 min. Any spot corresponding to histidine in the chromatogram obtained with test solution (a) is not more intense than the spot in the chromatogram obtained with reference solution (b) (1 per cent). The test is not valid unless the chromatogram obtained with reference solution (c) shows 2 clearly separated spots.

### Sulphates (*2.4.13*)

3 ml of solution S diluted to 15 ml with *distilled water R* complies with the limit test for sulphates (0.1 per cent).

### Loss on drying (*2.2.32*)

Not more than 0.5 per cent, determined on 0.20 g by drying in an oven at 105 °C.

### Sulphated ash (*2.4.14*)

Not more than 0.1 per cent, determined on 0.5 g.

## ASSAY

Dissolve 0.080 g in a mixture of 5.0 ml of *0.01 M hydrochloric acid* and 50 ml of *alcohol R*. Carry out a potentiometric titration (*2.2.20*), using *0.1 M sodium hydroxide*. Read the volume added between the first and third points of inflexion.

1 ml of *0.1 M sodium hydroxide* is equivalent to 9.203 mg of $C_5H_{11}Cl_2N_3$.

## STORAGE

Store in an airtight container, protected from light.

*Ph Eur*

# Histamine Phosphate

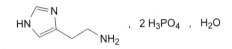

(*Ph Eur monograph 0144*)

C₅H₉N₃,2H₃PO₄,H₂O     325.2     *51-74-1*

*(anhydrous)*

*Ph Eur*

## DEFINITION

Histamine phosphate contains not less than 98.0 per cent and not more than the equivalent of 101.0 per cent of 2-(1*H*-imidazol-4-yl)ethanamine diphosphate, calculated with reference to the anhydrous substance.

## CHARACTERS

Colourless, long prismatic crystals, freely soluble in water, slightly soluble in alcohol.

## IDENTIFICATION

*First identification   A, D.*

*Second identification   B, C, D.*

A. Examine by infrared absorption spectrophotometry (*2.2.24*), comparing with the spectrum obtained with *histamine phosphate CRS*. Examine as discs prepared using 1 mg of substance.

B. Examine the chromatograms obtained in the test for histidine. The principal spot in the chromatogram obtained with test solution (b) is similar in position, colour and size to the principal spot in the chromatogram obtained with reference solution (a).

C. Dissolve 0.1 g in 7 ml of *water R* and add 3 ml of a 200 g/l solution of *sodium hydroxide R*. Dissolve 50 mg of *sulphanilic acid R* in a mixture of 0.1 ml of *hydrochloric acid R* and 10 ml of *water R* and add 0.1 ml of *sodium nitrite solution R*. Add the second solution to the first and mix. A red colour is produced.

D. It gives reaction (a) of phosphates (*2.3.1*).

## TESTS

### Solution S

Dissolve 0.5 g in *carbon dioxide-free water R* prepared from *distilled water R* and dilute to 10 ml with the same solvent.

### Appearance of solution

Solution S is clear (*2.2.1*) and not more intensely coloured than reference solution BY₇ (*2.2.2, Method II*).

### pH (*2.2.3*)

The pH of solution S is 3.75 to 3.95.

### Histidine

Examine by thin-layer chromatography (*2.2.27*), using *silica gel G R* as the coating substance.

*Test solution (a)*   Dissolve 0.5 g of the substance to be examined in *water R* and dilute to 10 ml with the same solvent.

*Test solution (b)*   Dilute 2 ml of test solution (a) to 10 ml with *water R*.

*Reference solution (a)*   Dissolve 0.1 g of *histamine phosphate CRS* in *water R* and dilute to 10 ml with the same solvent.

*Reference solution (b)*   Dissolve 50 mg of *histidine monohydrochloride R* in *water R* and dilute to 100 ml with the same solvent.

*Reference solution (c)*   Mix 1 ml of test solution (a) and 1 ml of reference solution (b).

Apply separately to the plate 1 µl of test solution (a), 1 µl of test solution (b), 1 µl of reference solution (a), 1 µl of reference solution (b) and 2 µl of reference solution (c). Develop over a path of 15 cm using a mixture of 5 volumes of *concentrated ammonia R*, 20 volumes of *water R* and 75 volumes of *acetonitrile R*. Dry the plate in a current of air. Repeat the development in the same direction, dry the plate in a current of air and spray with *ninhydrin solution R1*. Heat at 110 °C for 10 min. Any spot corresponding to histidine in the chromatogram obtained with test solution (a) is not more intense than the spot in the chromatogram obtained with reference solution (b) (1 per cent). The test is not valid unless the chromatogram obtained with reference solution (c) shows 2 clearly separated spots.

### Sulphates (*2.4.13*)

3 ml of solution S diluted to 15 ml with *distilled water R* complies with the limit test for sulphates (0.1 per cent).

### Water (*2.5.12*)

5.0 per cent to 6.2 per cent, determined on 0.30 g by the semi-micro determination of water.

## ASSAY

Dissolve 0.140 g in 5 ml of *anhydrous formic acid R* and add 20 ml of *anhydrous acetic acid R*. Titrate with *0.1 M perchloric acid*, determining the end-point potentiometrically (*2.2.20*). Carry out a blank titration.

1 ml of *0.1 M perchloric acid* is equivalent to 15.36 mg of C₅H₁₅N₃O₈P₂.

## STORAGE

Store protected from light.

*Ph Eur*

# Histidine

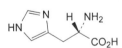

(*Ph Eur monograph 0911*)

C₆H₉N₃O₂     155.2     *71-00-1*

## Action and use

Amino acid.

*Ph Eur*

## DEFINITION

(*S*)-2-Amino-3-(imidazol-4-yl)propanoic acid.

## Content

98.5 per cent to 101.0 per cent (dried substance).

## CHARACTERS

### Appearance

White or almost white, crystalline powder or colourless crystals.

### Solubility

Soluble in water, very slightly soluble in ethanol (96 per cent).

## IDENTIFICATION

*First identification   A, B.*

*Second identification* *A, C, D.*

A. It complies with the test for specific optical rotation (see Tests).

B. Infrared absorption spectrophotometry (*2.2.24*).

*Preparation* Discs.

*Comparison* *histidine CRS.*

If the spectra obtained show differences, dissolve the substance to be examined and the reference substance separately in the minimum volume of *water R*, evaporate to dryness at 60 °C and record new spectra using the residues.

C. Examine the chromatograms obtained in the test for ninhydrin-positive substances. The principal spot in the chromatogram obtained with test solution (b) is similar in position, colour and size to the principal spot in the chromatogram obtained with reference solution (a).

D. Dissolve 0.1 g in 7 ml of *water R* and add 3 ml of a 200 g/l solution of *sodium hydroxide R*. Dissolve 50 mg of *sulphanilic acid R* in a mixture of 0.1 ml of *hydrochloric acid R* and 10 ml of *water R* and add 0.1 ml of *sodium nitrite solution R*. Add the second solution to the first and mix. An orange-red colour develops.

## TESTS

### Solution S

Dissolve 2.5 g in *distilled water R*, heating in a water-bath and dilute to 50 ml with the same solvent.

### Appearance of solution

Solution S is clear (*2.2.1*) and not more intensely coloured than reference solution $BY_7$ (*2.2.2, Method II*).

### Specific optical rotation (*2.2.7*)

+ 11.4 to + 12.4 (dried substance).

Dissolve 2.75 g in 12.0 ml of *hydrochloric acid R1* and dilute to 25.0 ml with *water R*.

### Ninhydrin-positive substances

Thin-layer chromatography (*2.2.27*).

*Test solution (a)* Dissolve 0.10 g of the substance to be examined in *water R* and dilute to 10 ml with the same solvent.

*Test solution (b)* Dilute 1 ml of test solution (a) to 50 ml with *water R*.

*Reference solution (a)* Dissolve 10 mg of *histidine CRS* in *water R* and dilute to 50 ml with the same solvent.

*Reference solution (b)* Dilute 5 ml of test solution (b) to 20 ml with *water R*.

*Reference solution (c)* Dissolve 10 mg of *histidine CRS* and 10 mg of *proline CRS* in *water R* and dilute to 25 ml with the same solvent.

*Plate* TLC silica gel plate R.

*Mobile phase* glacial acetic acid R, water R, butanol R (20:20:60 *V/V/V*).

*Application* 5 μl.

*Development* Over 2/3 of the plate.

*Drying* In air.

*Detection* Spray with *ninhydrin solution R* and heat at 100-105 °C for 15 min.

*System suitability* The chromatogram obtained with reference solution (c) shows 2 clearly separated spots.

*Limits:*

— *any impurity*: any spots in the chromatogram obtained with test solution (a), apart from the principal spot, are not more intense than the spot in the chromatogram obtained with reference solution (b) (0.5 per cent).

### Chlorides (*2.4.4*)

Maximum 200 ppm.

Dilute 5 ml of solution S to 15 ml with *water R..*

### Sulphates (*2.4.13*)

Maximum 300 ppm.

Dilute 10 ml of solution S to 15 ml with *distilled water R..*

### Ammonium (*2.4.1, Method B*)

Maximum 200 ppm, determined on 50 mg.

Prepare the standard using 0.1 ml of *ammonium standard solution (100 ppm NH₄) R*.

### Iron (*2.4.9*)

Maximum 10 ppm.

In a separating funnel, dissolve 1.0 g in 10 ml of *dilute hydrochloric acid R*. Shake with 3 quantities, each of 10 ml, of *methyl isobutyl ketone R1*, shaking for 3 min each time. To the combined organic layers add 10 ml of *water R* and shake for 3 min. The aqueous layer complies with the limit test for iron.

### Heavy metals (*2.4.8*)

Maximum 10 ppm.

Dissolve 2.0 g in a mixture of 3 ml of *dilute hydrochloric acid R* and 15 ml of *water R*, with gentle warming if necessary, and dilute to 20 ml with *water R*. 12 ml of the solution complies with limit test A. Prepare the reference solution using *lead standard solution (1 ppm Pb) R*.

### Loss on drying (*2.2.32*)

Maximum 0.5 per cent, determined on 1.000 g by drying in an oven at 105 °C.

### Sulphated ash (*2.4.14*)

Maximum 0.1 per cent, determined on 1.0 g.

## ASSAY

Dissolve 0.130 g in 50 ml of *water R*. Titrate with *0.1 M hydrochloric acid*, determining the end-point potentiometrically (*2.2.20*).

1 ml of *0.1 M hydrochloric acid* is equivalent to 15.52 mg of $C_6H_9N_3O_2$.

## STORAGE

Protected from light.

*Ph Eur*

# Histidine Hydrochloride Monohydrate

(*Ph Eur monograph 0910*)

$C_6H_9N_3O_2,HCl,H_2O$     209.6     645-35-2
(anhydrous)

### Action and use

Amino acid.

*Ph Eur*

## DEFINITION

Histidine hydrochloride monohydrate contains not less than 98.5 per cent and not more than the equivalent of 101.0 per cent of the hydrochloride of (*S*)-2-amino-3-(imidazol-4-yl)propanoic acid, calculated with reference to the dried substance.

## CHARACTERS
A white or almost white, crystalline powder or colourless crystals, freely soluble in water, slightly soluble in alcohol.

## IDENTIFICATION
*First identification*   A, B, C, F.
*Second identification*   A, B, D, E, F.

A. It complies with the test for specific optical rotation (see Tests).

B. It complies with the test for the pH (see Tests).

C. Examine by infrared absorption spectrophotometry (*2.2.24*), comparing with the spectrum obtained with *histidine hydrochloride monohydrate CRS*. Examine the substances prepared as discs.

D. Examine the chromatograms obtained in the test for ninhydrin-positive substances. The principal spot in the chromatogram obtained with test solution (b) is similar in position, colour and size to the principal spot in the chromatogram obtained with reference solution (a).

E. Dissolve 0.1 g in 7 ml of *water R* and add 3 ml of a 200 g/l solution of *sodium hydroxide R*. Dissolve 50 mg of *sulphanilic acid R* in a mixture of 0.1 ml of *hydrochloric acid R* and 10 ml of *water R* and add 0.1 ml of *sodium nitrite solution R*. Add the second solution to the first and mix. An orange-red colour develops.

F. About 20 mg gives reaction (a) of chlorides (*2.3.1*).

## TESTS
### Solution S
Dissolve 2.5 g in *carbon dioxide-free water R* prepared from *distilled water R* and dilute to 50 ml with the same solvent.

### Appearance of solution
Solution S is clear (*2.2.1*) and not more intensely coloured than reference solution $BY_6$ (*2.2.2, Method II*).

### pH (*2.2.3*)
The pH of solution S is 3.0 to 5.0.

### Specific optical rotation (*2.2.7*)
Dissolve 2.75 g in 12.0 ml of *hydrochloric acid R1* and dilute to 25.0 ml with *water R*. The specific optical rotation is + 9.2 to + 10.6, calculated with reference to the dried substance.

### Ninhydrin-positive substances
Examine by thin-layer chromatography (*2.2.27*), using a *TLC silica gel plate R*.

*Test solution (a)*   Dissolve 0.10 g of the substance to be examined in *water R* and dilute to 10 ml with the same solvent.

*Test solution (b)*   Dilute 1 ml of test solution (a) to 50 ml with *water R*.

*Reference solution (a)*   Dissolve 10 mg of *histidine hydrochloride monohydrate CRS* in *water R* and dilute to 50 ml with the same solvent.

*Reference solution (b)*   Dilute 5 ml of test solution (b) to 20 ml with *water R*.

*Reference solution (c)*   Dissolve 10 mg of *histidine hydrochloride monohydrate CRS* and 10 mg of *proline CRS* in *water R* and dilute to 25 ml with the same solvent.

Apply separately to the plate 5 µl of each solution. Dry the plate in a current of air. Develop over a path of 15 cm using a mixture of 20 volumes of *glacial acetic acid R*, 20 volumes of *water R* and 60 volumes of *butanol R*. Allow the plate to dry in air. Spray with *ninhydrin solution R* and heat at 100 °C to 105 °C for 15 min. Any spot in the chromatogram obtained with test solution (a), apart from the principal spot, is not more intense than the spot in the chromatogram obtained with reference solution (b) (0.5 per cent). The test is not valid unless the chromatogram obtained with reference solution (c) shows two clearly separated principal spots.

### Sulphates (*2.4.13*)
Dilute 10 ml of solution S to 15 ml with *distilled water R*. The solution complies with the limit test for sulphates (300 ppm).

### Ammonium (*2.4.1*)
50 mg complies with limit test B for ammonium (200 ppm). Prepare the standard using 0.1 ml of *ammonium standard solution (100 ppm $NH_4$) R*.

### Iron (*2.4.9*)
In a separating funnel, dissolve 1.0 g in 10 ml of *dilute hydrochloric acid R*. Shake with three quantities, each of 10 ml, of *methyl isobutyl ketone R1*, shaking for 3 min each time. To the combined organic layers add 10 ml of *water R* and shake for 3 min. The aqueous layer complies with the limit test for iron (10 ppm).

### Heavy metals (*2.4.8*)
Dissolve 2.0 g in *water R* and dilute to 20 ml with the same solvent. 12 ml of the solution complies with limit test A for heavy metals (10 ppm). Prepare the standard using *lead standard solution (1 ppm Pb) R*.

### Loss on drying (*2.2.32*)
7.0 per cent to 10.0 per cent, determined on 1.000 g by drying in an oven at 145 °C to 150 °C.

### Sulphated ash (*2.4.14*)
Not more than 0.1 per cent, determined on 1.0 g.

## ASSAY
Dissolve 0.160 g in 50 ml of *carbon dioxide-free water R*. Titrate with *0.1 M sodium hydroxide*, determining the end-point potentiometrically (*2.2.20*).

1 ml of *0.1 M sodium hydroxide* is equivalent to 19.16 mg of $C_6H_{10}ClN_3O_2$.

## STORAGE
Store protected from light.

*Ph Eur*

# Homatropine Hydrobromide
(*Ph Eur monograph 0500*)

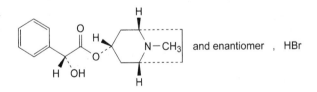

$C_{16}H_{21}NO_3,HBr$          356.3          51-56-9

### Action and use
Anticholinergic.

### Preparation
Homatropine Eye Drops

*Ph Eur*

## DEFINITION
(1R,3r,5S)-8-Methyl-8-azabicyclo[3.2.1]oct-3-yl (2RS)-2-hydroxy-2-phenylacetate hydrobromide.

## Content

99.0 per cent to 101.0 per cent (dried substance).

## CHARACTERS

### Appearance

White or almost white, crystalline powder or colourless crystals.

### Solubility

Freely soluble in water, sparingly soluble in alcohol.

### mp

About 215 °C, with decomposition.

## IDENTIFICATION

*First identification*   A, C.

*Second identification*   B, C.

A. Infrared absorption spectrophotometry (2.2.24).

*Comparison*   homatropine hydrobromide CRS.

B. Dissolve 50 mg in 1 ml of *water R* and add 2 ml of *dilute acetic acid R*. Heat and add 4 ml of *picric acid solution R*. Allow to cool, shaking occasionally. Collect the crystals, wash with 2 quantities, each of 3 ml, of iced *water R* and dry at 100-105 °C. The crystals melt (2.2.14) at 182 °C to 186 °C.

C. It gives reaction (a) of bromides (2.3.1).

## TESTS

### Solution S

Dissolve 1.25 g in *carbon dioxide-free water R* and dilute to 25 ml with the same solvent.

### Appearance of solution

Solution S is clear (2.2.1) and colourless (2.2.2, *Method II*).

### pH (2.2.3)

5.0 to 6.5 for solution S.

### Related substances

Liquid chromatography (2.2.29).

*Test solution*   Dissolve 50.0 mg of the substance to be examined in the mobile phase and dilute to 25.0 ml with the mobile phase.

*Reference solution (a)*   Dilute 5.0 ml of the test solution to 100.0 ml with the mobile phase. Dilute 5.0 ml of this solution to 50.0 ml with the mobile phase.

*Reference solution (b)*   Dilute 5.0 ml of reference solution (a) to 25.0 ml with the mobile phase.

*Reference solution (c)*   Dissolve 5.0 mg of *hyoscine hydrobromide CRS* in the mobile phase and dilute to 50.0 ml with the mobile phase. To 10.0 ml of this solution add 0.5 ml of the test solution and dilute to 100.0 ml with the mobile phase.

*Column:*
— *size: l* = 0.1 m, Ø = 4.6 mm,
— *stationary phase: octadecylsilyl silica gel for chromatography R* (3 μm),
— *temperature:* 40 °C.

*Mobile phase*   Mix 33 volumes of *methanol R2* and 67 volumes of a solution prepared as follows: dissolve 6.8 g of *potassium dihydrogen phosphate R* and 7.0 g of *sodium heptanesulphonate monohydrate R* in 1000 ml of *water R* and adjust to pH 2.7 with a 330 g/l solution of *phosphoric acid R*.

*Flow rate*   1.5 ml/min.

*Detection*   Spectrophotometer at 210 nm.

*Injection*   10 μl.

*Run time*   3 times the retention time of homatropine.

*Relative retention*   With reference to homatropine (retention time = about 6.8 min): impurity C = about 0.2;

impurity A = about 0.9; impurity B = about 1.1; impurity D = about 1.9.

*System suitability*   Reference solution (c):
— *resolution*: minimum 1.5 between the peaks due to homatropine and impurity B,
— *symmetry* factor: maximum 2.5 for the peak due to homatropine.

*Limits:*
— *impurity A*: not more than the area of the principal peak in the chromatogram obtained with reference solution (a) (0.5 per cent),
— *impurities B, C, D*: for each impurity, not more than the area of the principal peak in the chromatogram obtained with reference solution (b) (0.1 per cent),
— *any other impurity*: for each impurity, not more than the area of the principal peak in the chromatogram obtained with reference solution (b) (0.1 per cent),
— *total*: not more than twice the area of the principal peak in the chromatogram obtained with reference solution (a) (1.0 per cent); disregard the peak due to the bromide ion which appears close to the peak due to the solvent,
— *disregard limit*: 0.5 times the area of the principal peak in the chromatogram obtained with reference solution (b) (0.05 per cent).

### Loss on drying (2.2.32)

Maximum 0.5 per cent, determined on 1.000 g by drying in an oven at 105 °C.

### Sulphated ash (2.4.14)

Maximum 0.1 per cent, determined on 1.0 g.

## ASSAY

Dissolve 0.300 g in a mixture of 5.0 ml of *0.01 M hydrochloric acid* and 50 ml of *alcohol R*. Carry out a potentiometric titration (2.2.20), using *0.1 M sodium hydroxide*. Read the volume added between the 2 points of inflexion.

1 ml of *0.1 M sodium hydroxide* is equivalent to 35.63 mg of $C_{16}H_{22}BrNO_3$.

## STORAGE

Protected from light.

## IMPURITIES

*Specified impurities*   A, B, C, D.

A. (1R,3s,5S)-8-methyl-8-azabicyclo[3.2.1]oct-6-en-3-yl (2RS)-2-hydroxy-2-phenylacetate (dehydrohomatropine),

B. hyoscine,

C. (2RS)-2-hydroxy-2-phenylacetic acid (mandelic acid),

D. atropine.

_____ *Ph Eur*

# Homatropine Methylbromide

(*Ph Eur monograph 0720*)

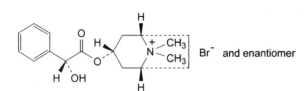

Br⁻ and enantiomer

C₁₇H₂₄BrNO₃      370.3      80-49-9

**Action and use**

Anticholinergic.

*Ph Eur*

## DEFINITION

(1*R*,3*r*,5*S*)-3-[[(2*RS*)-2-hydroxy-2-phenylacetyl]oxy]-8,8-dimethyl-8-azoniabicyclo[3.2.1]octane bromide.

**Content**

98.5 per cent to 101.0 per cent (dried substance).

## CHARACTERS

**Appearance**

White or almost white, crystalline powder or colourless crystals.

**Solubility**

Freely soluble in water, soluble in alcohol.

**mp**

About 190 °C.

## IDENTIFICATION

*First identification*    A, C.

*Second identification*    B, C.

A. Infrared absorption spectrophotometry (*2.2.24*),

*Comparison*    homatropine methylbromide CRS.

B. Dissolve 50 mg in 1 ml of *water R* and add 2 ml of *dilute acetic acid R*. Heat and add 4 ml of *picric acid solution R*. Allow to cool, shaking occasionally. The crystals, washed with 2 quantities, each of 3 ml, of iced *water R* and dried at 100-105 °C melt (*2.2.14*) at 132 °C to 138 °C.

C. It gives reaction (a) of bromides (*2.3.1*).

## TESTS

**Solution S**

Dissolve 1.25 g in *carbon dioxide-free water R* and dilute to 25 ml with the same solvent.

**Appearance of solution**

Solution S is clear (*2.2.1*) and colourless (*2.2.2, Method II*).

**pH** (*2.2.3*)

4.5 to 6.5 for solution S.

**Related substances**

Liquid chromatography (*2.2.29*).

*Solvent mixture*    acetonitrile R, mobile phase A (9:41 *V/V*).

*Test solution*    Dissolve 50.0 mg of the substance to be examined in the solvent mixture and dilute to 25.0 ml with the solvent mixture.

*Reference solution (a)*    Dilute 5.0 ml of the test solution to 100.0 ml with the solvent mixture. Dilute 5.0 ml of the solution to 50.0 ml with the solvent mixture.

*Reference solution (b)*    Dilute 5.0 ml of reference solution (a) to 25.0 ml with the solvent mixture.

*Reference solution (c)*    Dissolve 5.0 mg of *homatropine hydrobromide CRS* in the solvent mixture and dilute to 50.0 ml with the solvent mixture. To 10.0 ml of the solution add 0.5 ml of the test solution and dilute to 100.0 ml with the solvent mixture.

*Column:*
— *size*: l = 0.15 m, Ø = 4.6 mm,
— *stationary phase*: octadecylsilyl silica gel for chromatography R (3 μm),
— *temperature*: 25 °C.

*Mobile phase:*
— *mobile phase A*: dissolve 3.4 g of *potassium dihydrogen phosphate R* and 5.0 g of *sodium heptanesulphonate monohydrate R* in 1000 ml of *water R*, and adjust to pH 3.0 with a 330 g/l solution of *phosphoric acid R*,
— *mobile phase B*: mix 400 ml of mobile phase A and 600 ml of *acetonitrile R*,

| Time (min) | Mobile phase A (per cent *V/V*) | Mobile phase B (per cent *V/V*) |
|---|---|---|
| 0 - 2 | 70 | 30 |
| 2 - 15 | 70 → 30 | 30 → 70 |
| 15 - 20 | 30 → 70 | 70 → 30 |

*Flow rate*    1.4 ml/min.

*Detection*    Spectrophotometer at 210 nm.

*Injection*    10 μl.

*Relative retention*    With reference to homatropine methylbromide (retention time = about 4.8 min): impurity C = about 0.7; impurity A = about 0.9; impurity B = about 1.2; impurity D = about 1.3; impurity E = about 1.4; impurity F = about 1.7.

*System suitability*    Reference solution (c):
— *resolution*: minimum 2.5 between the peaks due to homatropine methylbromide and impurity B,
— *symmetry factor*: maximum 2.5 for the peak due to homatropine methylbromide.

*Limits:*
— *impurities A, B*: for each impurity, not more than the area of the principal peak in the chromatogram obtained with reference solution (a) (0.5 per cent),
— *impurities C, D, E, F*: for each impurity, not more than the area of the principal peak in the chromatogram obtained with reference solution (b) (0.1 per cent),
— *any other impurity*: for each impurity, not more than the area of the principal peak in the chromatogram obtained with reference solution (b) (0.1 per cent),
— *total*: not more than twice the area of the principal peak in the chromatogram obtained with reference solution (a) (1.0 per cent); disregard the peak due to the bromide ion which appears close to the peak due to the solvent,
— *disregard limit*: 0.5 times the area of the principal peak in the chromatogram obtained with reference solution (b) (0.05 per cent).

**Loss on drying** (*2.2.32*)

Maximum 0.5 per cent, determined on 1.000 g by drying in an oven at 105 °C.

**Sulphated ash** (*2.4.14*)

Maximum 0.1 per cent, determined on 1.0 g.

## ASSAY

Dissolve 0.300 g in 10 ml of *water R*. Titrate with *0.1 M silver nitrate*. Determine the end-point potentiometrically (*2.2.20*), using a silver indicator electrode and a silver-silver chloride reference electrode.

1 ml of *0.1 M silver nitrate* is equivalent to 37.03 mg of $C_{17}H_{24}BrNO_3$.

## STORAGE

Protected from light.

## IMPURITIES

*Specified impurities*   A, B, C, D, E, F.

and enantiomer

A. (1R,3s,5S)-3-[[(2RS)-2-hydroxy-2-phenylacetyl]oxy]-8,8-dimethyl-8-azoniabicyclo[3.2.1]oct-6-ene (methyldehydrohomatropine),

B. homatropine,

and enantiomer

C. R = H: (2RS)-2-hydroxy-2-phenylacetic acid (mandelic acid),

F. R = CH₃: methyl (2RS)-2-hydroxy-2-phenylacetate (methyl mandelate),

D. (1R,2R,4S,5S,7s)-7-[[(2S)-3-hydroxy-2-phenylpropanoyl]oxy]-9,9-dimethyl-3-oxa-9-azoniatricyclo[3.3.1.0²,⁴]nonane (methylhyoscine),

E. methylatropine.

*Ph Eur*

# Honey

(*Ph Eur monograph 2051*)

*Ph Eur*

## DEFINITION

Honey is produced by bees (*Apis mellifera* L.) from the nectar of plants or from secretions of living parts of plants which the bees collect, transform by combining with specific substances of their own, deposit, dehydrate, store and leave in the honey comb to ripen and mature.

## PRODUCTION

If the bee has been exposed to treatment to prevent or cure diseases or to any substance intended for preventing, destroying or controlling any pest, unwanted species of plants or animals, appropriate steps are taken to ensure that the levels of residues are as low as possible.

## CHARACTERS

### Appearance

Viscous liquid which may be partly crystalline, almost white to dark brown.

## IDENTIFICATION

Thin-layer chromatography (*2.2.27*).

*Test solution*   Dissolve 0.6 g of the substance to be examined in 50 ml of *ethanol (30 per cent V/V) R*.

*Reference solution*   Dissolve 0.5 g of *fructose R*, 0.5 g of *glucose R* and 0.1 g of *sucrose R* in 100 ml of *ethanol (30 per cent V/V) R*.

*Plate*   TLC *silica gel plate R*.

*Mobile phase*   *Water R*, *acetonitrile R* (13:87 V/V).

*Application*   5 µl as bands.

*Development*   3 times over a path of 15 cm.

*Drying*   In warm air.

*Detection*   Spray with a solution prepared as follows: dissolve 2 g of *diphenylamine R* and 2 ml of *aniline R* in 100 ml of *acetone R*. Add a 850 g/l solution of *phosphoric acid R* until the precipitate formed dissolves again (about 15-20 ml). Examine in daylight after heating at 100-105 °C for 5-10 min.

*Results*   See below the sequence of the zones present in the chromatograms obtained with the reference solution and the test solution. Furthermore, the weak brown zone due to sucrose in the chromatogram obtained with the reference solution may be present in the chromatogram obtained with the test solution. One or more other weak zones may be present in the chromatogram obtained with the test solution.

| Top of the plate | |
|---|---|
| ─── | ─── |
| Fructose: an intense brown zone | An intense brown zone (fructose) |
| Glucose: an intense greyish-blue zone | An intense greyish-blue zone (glucose) |
| | ─── |
| Sucrose: a brown zone | |
| | 2 to 3 brownish-grey zones |
| **Reference solution** | **Test solution** |

## TESTS

### Refractive index (*2.2.6*)

Minimum 1.487 (equivalent to a maximum water content of 20 per cent).

Homogenise 100 g and transfer into a flask. Close tightly and place in a water-bath at 50 ± 0.2 °C until all sugar crystals have dissolved. Cool the solution to 20 °C and rehomogenise. Immediately after rehomogenisation, cover the surface of the refractometer prism evenly with the sample. Determine the refractive index after 2 min if using an Abbe refractometer and after 4 min if using a digital refractometer. Use the average value of 2 determinations.

### Conductivity (*2.2.38*)

Maximum 800 µS·cm⁻¹.

Using the value obtained for the refractive index, determine the water content of the substance to be examined from Table 2051.-1. Using this information, dissolve an amount of the substance to be examined equivalent to 20.0 g of honey dry solids, in *water R* to produce 100.0 ml.

**Optical rotation** (2.2.7)
Maximum + 0.6°.

Using the value obtained for the refractive index, determine the water content of the substance to be examined from Table 2051.-1. Using this information, dissolve an amount of the substance to be examined, equivalent to 20.0 g of honey dry solids, in 50 ml of *water R*. Add 0.2 ml of *concentrated ammonia R* and dilute to 100.0 ml with *water R*. If necessary decolourise the solution with *activated charcoal R*.

Table 2051.-1. – *Relationship of water content of honey to refractive index*

| Water content (per cent *m/m*) | Refractive index at 20 °C |
|---|---|
| 15.0 | 1.4992 |
| 15.2 | 1.4987 |
| 15.4 | 1.4982 |
| 15.6 | 1.4976 |
| 15.8 | 1.4971 |
| 16.0 | 1.4966 |
| 16.2 | 1.4961 |
| 16.4 | 1.4956 |
| 16.6 | 1.4951 |
| 16.8 | 1.4946 |
| 17.0 | 1.4940 |
| 17.2 | 1.4935 |
| 17.4 | 1.4930 |
| 17.6 | 1.4925 |
| 17.8 | 1.4920 |
| 18.0 | 1.4915 |
| 18.2 | 1.4910 |
| 18.4 | 1.4905 |
| 18.6 | 1.4900 |
| 18.8 | 1.4895 |
| 19.0 | 1.4890 |
| 19.2 | 1.4885 |
| 19.4 | 1.4880 |
| 19.6 | 1.4875 |
| 19.8 | 1.4870 |
| 20.0 | 1.4865 |

**5-Hydroxymethylfurfural**
Maximum 80 ppm, calculated on dry solids.

Using the value obtained for the refractive index, determine the water content of the substance to be examined from Table 2051.-1. Using this information, dissolve an amount of the substance to be examined, equivalent to 5.0 g of honey dry solids, in 25 ml of *water R* and transfer to a 50.0 ml volumetric flask with the same solvent. Add 0.5 ml of a 150 g/l solution of *potassium ferrocyanide R* and mix. Add 0.5 ml of a 300 g/l solution of *zinc acetate R*, mix and dilute to 50.0 ml with *water R* (a drop of *anhydrous ethanol R* may be added to avoid foaming). Filter. Transfer 5.0 ml of the filtered solution into each of 2 tubes. To one tube add 5.0 ml of *water R* (test solution). To the other tube add 5.0 ml of a 2.0 g/l solution of *sodium hydrogensulphite R* (reference solution). Determine the absorbance (2.2.25) of the test solution against the reference solution at 284 nm and 336 nm within 60 min. If the absorbance at 284 nm is greater than 0.8, dilute to the same extent the test solution with *water R* and the reference solution with a 2.0 g/l solution of *sodium hydrogensulphite R* so as to obtain an absorbance of less than 0.8.

Calculate the content of 5-hydroxymethylfurfural from the expression:

$$(A_1 - A_2) \times D \times 149.7$$

$A_1$ = absorbance at 284 nm,
$A_2$ = absorbance at 336 nm,
$D$ = dilution factor, where applicable.

**Chlorides** (2.4.4)
Maximum 350 ppm, determined on 15 ml of a 10 g/l solution.

**Sulphates** (2.4.13)
Maximum 250 ppm, determined on 15 ml of a 40 g/l solution.

*—————————— Ph Eur*

# Hyaluronidase

(*Ph Eur monograph 0912*)

**Action and use**
Used to promote absorption of fluid into tissues.

**Preparation**
Hyaluronidase Injection

*Ph Eur —————————————————————*

## DEFINITION
Hyaluronidase is an enzyme extracted from mammalian testes (for example bovine testes) and capable of hydrolysing mucopolysaccharides of the hyaluronic acid type. It contains not less than 300 IU of hyaluronidase activity per milligram, calculated with reference to the dried substance. It may contain a suitable stabiliser.

## PRODUCTION
The animals from which hyaluronidase is derived must fulfil the requirements for the health of animals suitable for human consumption.

## CHARACTERS
A white or yellowish-white, amorphous powder, soluble in water, practically insoluble in acetone and in ethanol.

## IDENTIFICATION
A solution containing the equivalent of 100 IU of hyaluronidase in 1 ml of a 9 g/l solution of *sodium chloride R* depolymerises an equal volume of a 10 g/l solution of *sodium hyaluronate BRP* in 1 min at 20 °C as shown by a pronounced decrease in viscosity. This action is destroyed by heating the hyaluronidase at 100 °C for 30 min.

## TESTS
**Appearance of solution**
Dissolve 0.10 g of the substance to be examined in *water R* and dilute to 10 ml. The solution is clear (2.2.1).

**pH** (2.2.3)
Dissolve 30 mg in 10 ml of *carbon dioxide-free water R*. The pH of the solution is 4.5 to 7.5.

**Loss on drying** *(2.2.32)*

Not more than 5.0 per cent, determined on 0.500 g by drying at 60 °C at a pressure not exceeding 670 Pa for 2 h.

**Bacterial endotoxins** *(2.6.14)*

Less than 0.2 IU per IU of hyaluronidase.

## ASSAY

The activity of hyaluronidase is determined by comparing the rate at which it hydrolyses *sodium hyaluronate BRP* with the rate obtained with the International Standard, or a reference preparation calibrated in International Units, using a slope-ratio assay.

*Substrate solution* To 0.10 g of *sodium hyaluronate BRP* in a 25 ml conical flask add slowly 20.0 ml of *water R* at 4 °C. The rate of addition must be slow enough to allow the substrate particles to swell (about 5 min). Maintain at 4 °C and stir for at least 12 h. Store at 4 °C and use within 4 days.

*For the test solution and the reference solution, prepare the solution and carry out the dilution at 0 °C to 4 °C.*

*Test solution* Dissolve a suitable amount of the substance to be examined in *hyaluronidase diluent R* so as to obtain a solution containing 0.6 ± 0.3 IU of hyaluronidase per millilitre.

*Reference solution* Dissolve a suitable amount of *hyaluronidase BRP* in *hyaluronidase diluent R* so as to obtain a solution containing 0.6 IU of hyaluronidase per millilitre.

In a reaction vessel, mix 1.50 ml of *phosphate buffer solution pH 6.4 R* and 1.0 ml of the substrate solution and equilibrate at 37 ± 0.1 °C. At time $t_1 = 0$ (first chronometer) add 0.50 ml of the test solution containing $E_t$ mg of the enzyme to be examined, mix, measure the viscosity of the solution using a suitable viscometer maintained at 37 ± 0.1 °C and record the outflow time $t_2$ using a second chronometer (graduated in 0.1 second intervals), several times during about 20 min (read on the first chronometer). The following viscometer has been found suitable: Ubbelohde microviscometer (DIN 51 562, Part 2), capillary type MII, viscometer constant about 0.1 mm²/s².

Repeat the procedure using 0.50 ml of the reference solution containing $E_r$ mg of *hyaluronidase BRP*.

Calculate the viscosity ratio from the expression:

$$\eta_r = \frac{k \times t_2}{0.6915}$$

$k$ = the viscometer constant in mm²/s² (indicated on the viscometer);

$t_2$ = the outflow time (in seconds) of the solution;

0.6915 = the kinematic viscosity in mm²/s of the buffer solution at 37 °C.

Since the enzymatic reaction continues during the outflow time measurements, the real reaction time equals $t_1 + t_2/2$, half of the outflow time ($t_2/2$) for which a certain measurement is valid being added to the time $t_1$ at which the measurement is started. Plot $(\ln \eta_r)^{-1}$ as a function of the reaction time ($t_1 + t_2/2$) in seconds. A linear relationship is obtained. Calculate the slope for the substance to be examined ($b_t$) and the reference preparation ($b_r$).

Calculate the specific activity in International Units per milligram from the expression:

$$\frac{b_t}{b_r} \times \frac{E_r}{E_t} \times A$$

$A$ = the specific activity of *hyaluronidase BRP* in International Units per milligram.

Carry out the complete procedure at least three times and calculate the average activity of the substance to be examined.

## STORAGE

Store in an airtight container at a temperature of 2 °C to 8 °C. If the substance is sterile, store in a sterile, tamper-proof container.

## LABELLING

The label states the activity in International Units per milligram.

*Ph Eur*

# Hydralazine Hydrochloride

*(Ph Eur monograph 0829)*

$C_8H_8N_4$,HCl         196.6         *304-20-1*

**Action and use**

Vasodilator; treatment of hypertension.

**Preparations**

Hydralazine Injection

Hydralazine Tablets

*Ph Eur*

## DEFINITION

1-Hydrazinophthalazine hydrochloride.

*Content* 98.5 per cent to 101.0 per cent (dried substance).

## CHARACTERS

*Appearance* White or almost white, crystalline powder.

*Solubility* Soluble in water, slightly soluble in ethanol (96 per cent), very slightly soluble in methylene chloride.

mp: about 275 °C, with decomposition.

## IDENTIFICATION

*First identification* B, E.

*Second identification* A, C, D, E.

A. Ultraviolet and visible absorption spectrophotometry *(2.2.25)*.

*Test solution* Dissolve 50 mg in *water R* and dilute to 100 ml with the same solvent. Dilute 2 ml of this solution to 100 ml with *water R*.

*Spectral range* 220-350 nm.

*Absorption maxima* At 240 nm, 260 nm, 303 nm and 315 nm.

*Absorbance ratio* $A_{240}/A_{303}$ = 2.0 to 2.2.

B. Infrared absorption spectrophotometry *(2.2.24)*.

*Preparation* Discs.

*Comparison* *hydralazine hydrochloride CRS*.

C. Dissolve 0.5 g in a mixture of 8 ml of *dilute hydrochloric acid R* and 100 ml of *water R*. Add 2 ml of *sodium nitrite solution R*, allow to stand for 10 min and filter. The precipitate, washed with *water R* and dried at 100-105 °C, melts (*2.2.14*) at 209 °C to 212 °C.

D. Dissolve about 10 mg in 2 ml of *water R*. Add 2 ml of a 20 g/l solution of *nitrobenzaldehyde R* in *ethanol (96 per cent) R*. An orange precipitate is formed.

E. It gives reaction (a) of chlorides (*2.3.1*).

## TESTS

### Solution S

Dissolve 0.5 g in *carbon dioxide-free water R* and dilute to 25 ml with the same solvent.

### Appearance of solution

The solution is clear (*2.2.1*) and not more intensely coloured than reference solution $GY_6$ (*2.2.2, Method II*).

Dilute 4 ml of solution S to 20 ml with *water R*.

### pH (*2.2.3*)

3.5 to 4.2 for solution S.

### Hydrazine

Thin-layer chromatography (*2.2.27*).

*Test solution* Dissolve 0.12 g of the substance to be examined in 4 ml of *water R* and add 4 ml of a 150 g/l solution of *salicylaldehyde R* in *methanol R* and 0.2 ml of *hydrochloric acid R*. Mix and keep at a temperature not exceeding 25 °C for 2-4 h, until the precipitate formed has sedimented. Add 4 ml of *toluene R*, shake vigorously and centrifuge. Transfer the clear supernatant liquid to a 100 ml separating funnel and shake vigorously, each time for 3 min, with 2 quantities, each of 20 ml, of a 200 g/l solution of *sodium metabisulphite R* and with 2 quantities, each of 50 ml, of *water R*. Separate the upper toluene layer which is the test solution.

*Reference solution (a)* Dissolve 12 mg of *hydrazine sulphate R* in *dilute hydrochloric acid R* and dilute to 100.0 ml with the same acid. Dilute 1.0 ml of this solution to 100.0 ml with *dilute hydrochloric acid R*.

*Reference solution (b)* Prepare the solution at the same time and in the same manner as for the test solution, using 1.0 ml of reference solution (a) and 3 ml of *water R*.

*Plate* TLC silica gel G plate R.

*Mobile phase* ethanol (96 per cent) R, toluene R (10:90 *V/V*).

*Application* 20 μl of the test solution and reference solution (b).

*Development* Over a path of 10 cm.

*Drying* In air.

*Detection* Examine in ultraviolet light at 365 nm.

*Limit:*
— *hydrazine*: any yellow fluorescent spot due to hydrazine is not more intense than the corresponding spot in the chromatogram obtained with reference solution (b) (10 ppm).

### Related substances

Liquid chromatography (*2.2.29*). *The solutions must be injected within one working day.*

*Test solution* Dissolve 25.0 mg of the substance to be examined in the mobile phase and dilute to 50.0 ml with the mobile phase.

*Reference solution (a)* Dilute 1.0 ml of the test solution to 100.0 ml with the mobile phase.

*Reference solution (b)* Dilute 10.0 ml of reference solution (a) to 50.0 ml with the mobile phase.

*Reference solution (c)* Dissolve 25.0 mg of *phthalazine R* in the mobile phase and dilute to 50.0 ml with the mobile phase. Dilute 4.0 ml of this solution to 100.0 ml with the mobile phase.

*Reference solution (d)* Dilute a mixture of 4.0 ml of the test solution and 10.0 ml of reference solution (c) to 100.0 ml with the mobile phase.

*Column:*
— *size: l* = 0.25 m, Ø = 4.6 mm;
— *stationary phase*: nitrile silica gel for chromatography R1 (10 μm).

*Mobile phase*: mix 22 volumes of *acetonitrile R* and 78 volumes of a solution containing 1.44 g/l of *sodium laurilsulfate R* and 0.75 g/l of *tetrabutylammonium bromide R*, then adjust to pH 3.0 with *0.05 M sulphuric acid*.

*Flow rate* 1 ml/min.

*Detection* Spectrophotometer at 230 nm.

*Injection* 20 μl.

*Run time* 3 times the retention time of hydralazine.

*Retention time* hydralazine = about 10 min to 12 min; if necessary, adjust the concentration of acetonitrile in the mobile phase.

*System suitability:*
— the chromatogram obtained with reference solution (d) shows 2 principal peaks;
— *resolution*: minimum 2.5 between the peaks due to hydralazine and phtalazine in the chromatogram obtained with reference solution (d);
— *signal-to-noise ratio*: minimum 3 for the principal peak in the chromatogram obtained with reference solution (b).

*Limit:*
— *any impurity*: for each impurity, not more than the area of the principal peak in the chromatogram obtained with reference solution (b) (0.2 per cent).

### Heavy metals (*2.4.8*)

Maximum 20 ppm.

1.0 g complies with test C. Prepare the reference solution using 2 ml of *lead standard solution (10 ppm Pb) R*.

### Loss on drying (*2.2.32*)

Maximum 0.5 per cent, determined on 1.000 g by drying *in vacuo*.

### Sulphated ash (*2.4.14*)

Maximum 0.1 per cent, determined on 1.0 g.

## ASSAY

Dissolve 80.0 mg in 25 ml of *water R*. Add 35 ml of *hydrochloric acid R* and titrate with *0.05 M potassium iodate*, determining the end-point potentiometrically (*2.2.20*), using a calomel reference electrode and a platinum indicator electrode.

1 ml of *0.05 M potassium iodate* is equivalent to 9.832 mg of $C_8H_9ClN_4$.

## STORAGE

Protected from light.

_____ *Ph Eur*

# Hydrochloric Acid

(*Concentrated Hydrochloric Acid,*
*Ph Eur monograph 0002*)

HCl                  36.46             7647-01-0

**Preparation**
Dilute Hydrochloric Acid

*Ph Eur*

## DEFINITION
### Content
35.0 per cent *m/m* to 39.0 per cent *m/m*.

## CHARACTERS
### Appearance
Clear, colourless, fuming liquid.

### Solubility
Miscible with water.

### Relative density
About 1.18.

## IDENTIFICATION
A. Dilute with *water R*. The solution is strongly acid (*2.2.4*).

B. It gives the reactions of chlorides (*2.3.1*).

C. It complies with the limits of the assay.

## TESTS
### Appearance of solution
To 2 ml add 8 ml of *water R*. The solution is clear (*2.2.1*) and colourless (*2.2.2, Method II*).

### Free chlorine
Maximum 4 ppm.

To 15 ml add 100 ml of *carbon dioxide-free water R*, 1 ml of a 100 g/l solution of *potassium iodide R* and 0.5 ml of *iodide-free starch solution R*. Allow to stand in the dark for 2 min. Any blue colour disappears on the addition of 0.2 ml of *0.01 M sodium thiosulphate*.

### Sulphates (*2.4.13*)
Maximum 20 ppm.

To 6.4 ml add 10 mg of *sodium hydrogen carbonate R* and evaporate to dryness on a water-bath. Dissolve the residue in 15 ml of *distilled water R*.

### Heavy metals (*2.4.8*)
Maximum 2 ppm.

Dissolve the residue obtained in the test for residue on evaporation in 1 ml of *dilute hydrochloric acid R* and dilute to 25 ml with *water R*. Dilute 5 ml of this solution to 20 ml with *water R*. 12 ml of the solution complies with test A. Prepare the reference solution using *lead standard solution (2 ppm Pb) R*.

### Residue on evaporation
Maximum 0.01 per cent.

Evaporate 100.0 g to dryness on a water-bath and dry at 100-105 °C. The residue weighs a maximum of 10 mg.

## ASSAY
Weigh accurately a ground-glass-stoppered flask containing 30 ml of *water R*. Introduce 1.5 ml of the acid to be examined and weigh again. Titrate with *1 M sodium hydroxide*, using *methyl red solution R* as indicator.

1 ml of *1 M sodium hydroxide* is equivalent to 36.46 mg of HCl.

## STORAGE
In a stoppered container made of glass or another inert material, at a temperature not exceeding 30 °C.

*Ph Eur*

# Dilute Hydrochloric Acid

(*Ph Eur monograph 0003*)

*Ph Eur*

## DEFINITION
### Content
9.5 per cent *m/m* to 10.5 per cent *m/m* of HCl ($M_r$ 36.46).

## PREPARATION
To 726 g of *water R* add 274 g of concentrated hydrochloric acid and mix.

## IDENTIFICATION
A. It is strongly acid (*2.2.4*).

B. It gives the reactions of chlorides (*2.3.1*).

C. It complies with the limits of the assay.

## TESTS
### Appearance
It is clear (*2.2.1*) and colourless (*2.2.2, Method II*).

### Free chlorine
Maximum 1 ppm.

To 60 ml add 50 ml of *carbon dioxide-free water R*, 1 ml of a 100 g/l solution of *potassium iodide R* and 0.5 ml of *iodide-free starch solution R*. Allow to stand in the dark for 2 min. Any blue colour disappears on the addition of 0.2 ml of *0.01 M sodium thiosulphate*.

### Sulphates (*2.4.13*)
Maximum 5 ppm.

To 26 ml add 10 mg of *sodium hydrogen carbonate R* and evaporate to dryness on a water-bath. Dissolve the residue in 15 ml of *distilled water R*.

### Heavy metals (*2.4.8*)
Maximum 2 ppm.

Dissolve the residue obtained in the test for residue on evaporation in 1 ml of *dilute hydrochloric acid R* and dilute to 25 ml with *water R*. Dilute 5 ml of this solution to 20 ml with *water R*. 12 ml of the solution complies with test A. Prepare the reference solution using *lead standard solution (2 ppm Pb) R*.

### Residue on evaporation
Maximum 0.01 per cent.

Evaporate 100.0 g to dryness on a water-bath and dry at 100-105 °C. The residue weighs a maximum of 10 mg.

## ASSAY
To 6.00 g add 30 ml of *water R*. Titrate with *1 M sodium hydroxide*, using *methyl red solution R* as indicator.

1 ml of *1 M sodium hydroxide* is equivalent to 36.46 mg of HCl.

*Ph Eur*

# Hydrochlorothiazide

(*Ph Eur monograph 0394*)

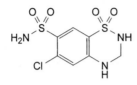

C$_7$H$_8$ClN$_3$O$_4$S$_2$    297.7    58-93-5

## Action and use
Thiazide diuretic.

## Preparations
Co-amilozide Oral Solution

Co-amilozide Tablets

Co-triamterzide Tablets

Hydrochlorothiazide Tablets

*Ph Eur* _____

## DEFINITION
6-Chloro-3,4-dihydro-2*H*-1,2,4-benzothiadiazine-7-sulphonamide 1,1-dioxide.

## Content
98.0 per cent to 102.0 per cent (dried substance).

## CHARACTERS
### Appearance
White or almost white, crystalline powder.

### Solubility
Very slightly soluble in water, soluble in acetone, sparingly soluble in ethanol (96 per cent). It dissolves in dilute solutions of alkali hydroxides.

It shows polymorphism (*5.9*).

## IDENTIFICATION
*First identification* B.

*Second identification* A, C, D.

A. Ultraviolet and visible absorption spectrophotometry (*2.2.25*).

*Test solution* Dissolve 50.0 mg in 10 ml of *0.1 M sodium hydroxide* and dilute to 100.0 ml with *water R*. Dilute 2.0 ml of this solution to 100.0 ml with *0.01 M sodium hydroxide*.

*Spectral range* 250-350 nm.

*Absorption maxima* At 273 nm and 323 nm.

*Absorbance ratio* $A_{273}/A_{323}$ = 5.4 to 5.7.

B. Infrared absorption spectrophotometry (*2.2.24*).

*Comparison* hydrochlorothiazide CRS.

If the spectra obtained in the solid state show differences, dissolve the substance to be examined and the reference substance separately in the minimum volume of *ethanol R1*, evaporate to dryness and record new spectra using the residues.

C. Thin-layer chromatography (*2.2.27*).

*Test solution* Dissolve 50 mg of the substance to be examined in *acetone R* and dilute to 10 ml with the same solvent.

*Reference solution (a)* Dissolve 50 mg of hydrochlorothiazide CRS in *acetone R* and dilute to 10 ml with the same solvent.

*Reference solution (b)* Dissolve 25 mg of *chlorothiazide R* in reference solution (a) and dilute to 5 ml with reference solution (a).

*Plate* TLC silica gel F$_{254}$ *plate R*.

*Mobile phase* ethyl acetate R.

*Application* 2 µl.

*Development* Over a path of 10 cm.

*Drying* In a current of air.

*Detection* Examine in ultraviolet light at 254 nm.

*System suitability* Reference solution (b):
— the chromatogram shows 2 clearly separated spots.

*Results* The principal spot in the chromatogram obtained with the test solution is similar in position and size to the principal spot in the chromatogram obtained with reference solution (a).

D. Gently heat about 1 mg with 2 ml of a freshly prepared 0.5 g/l solution of chromotropic acid, *sodium salt R* in a cooled mixture of 35 volumes of *water R* and 65 volumes of *sulphuric acid R*. A violet colour develops.

## TESTS
### Acidity or alkalinity
Shake 0.5 g of the powdered substance to be examined with 25 ml of *water R* for 2 min and filter. To 10 ml of the filtrate, add 0.2 ml of *0.01 M sodium hydroxide* and 0.15 ml of *methyl red solution R*. The solution is yellow. Not more than 0.4 ml of *0.01 M hydrochloric acid* is required to change the colour of the indicator to red.

### Related substances
Liquid chromatography (*2.2.29*).

*Solvent mixture* Dilute 50.0 ml of a mixture of equal volumes of *acetonitrile R* and *methanol R* to 200.0 ml with *phosphate buffer solution pH 3.2 R1*.

*Test solution* Dissolve 30.0 mg of the substance to be examined in 5 ml of a mixture of equal volumes of *acetonitrile R* and *methanol R*, using sonication if necessary, and dilute to 20.0 ml with *phosphate buffer solution pH 3.2 R1*.

*Reference solution (a)* Dissolve 15 mg of hydrochlorothiazide CRS and 15 mg of chlorothiazide CRS (impurity A) in 25 ml of a mixture of equal volumes of *acetonitrile R* and *methanol R*, using sonication if necessary, and dilute to 100 ml with *phosphate buffer solution pH 3.2 R1*. Dilute 5 ml of this solution to 100 ml with the solvent mixture.

*Reference solution (b)* Dilute 1.0 ml of the test solution to 50.0 ml with the solvent mixture. Dilute 5.0 ml of this solution to 20.0 ml with the solvent mixture.

*Column:*
— size: *l* = 0.1 m, Ø = 4.6 mm;
— stationary phase: *octadecylsilyl silica gel for chromatography R* (3 µm).

*Mobile phase:*
— mobile phase A: to 940 ml of *phosphate buffer solution pH 3.2 R1* add 60.0 ml of *methanol R* and 10.0 ml of *tetrahydrofuran R* and mix;
— mobile phase B: to a mixture of 500 ml of *methanol R* and 500 ml of *phosphate buffer solution pH 3.2 R1* add 50.0 ml of *tetrahydrofuran R* and mix;

| Time (min) | Mobile phase A (per cent V/V) | Mobile phase B (per cent V/V) |
|---|---|---|
| 0 - 17 | 100 → 55 | 0 → 45 |
| 17 - 30 | 55 | 45 |
| 30 - 35 | 55 → 100 | 45 → 0 |
| 35 - 50 | 100 | 0 |

*Flow rate*   0.8 ml/min.

*Detection*   Spectrophotometer at 224 nm.

*Equilibration*   With mobile phase A for at least 20 min.

*Injection*   10 µl; inject the solvent mixture as a blank.

*Retention time*   Impurity A = about 7 min; hydrochlorothiazide = about 8 min.

*System suitability*   Reference solution (a):
— *resolution*: minimum 2.5 between the peaks due to impurity A and hydrochlorothiazide; if necessary, adjust slightly the composition of the mobile phase or the time programme of the linear gradient.

*Limits*:
— *impurities A, B, C*: for each impurity, not more than the area of the principal peak in the chromatogram obtained with reference solution (b) (0.5 per cent);
— *total*: not more than twice the area of the principal peak in the chromatogram obtained with reference solution (b) (1 per cent);
— *disregard limit*: 0.1 times the area of the principal peak in the chromatogram obtained with reference solution (b) (0.05 per cent).

**Chlorides** (*2.4.4*)
Maximum 100 ppm.

Dissolve 1.0 g in 25 ml of *acetone R* and dilute to 30 ml with *water R*. Prepare the standard using 5 ml of *acetone R* containing 15 per cent V/V of *water R* and 10 ml of *chloride standard solution (5 ppm Cl) R*.

**Loss on drying** (*2.2.32*)
Maximum 0.5 per cent, determined on 1.000 g by drying in an oven at 105 °C.

**Sulphated ash** (*2.4.14*)
Maximum 0.1 per cent, determined on 1.0 g.

**ASSAY**
Dissolve 0.120 g in 50 ml of *dimethyl sulphoxide R*. Titrate with *0.1 M tetrabutylammonium hydroxide* in *2-propanol*, determining the end-point potentiometrically (*2.2.20*) at the 2nd point of inflexion. Carry out a blank titration.

1 ml of *0.1 M tetrabutylammonium hydroxide* in *2-propanol* is equivalent to 14.88 mg of $C_7H_8ClN_3O_4S_2$.

**IMPURITIES**
*Specified impurities   A, B, C.*

A. chlorothiazide,

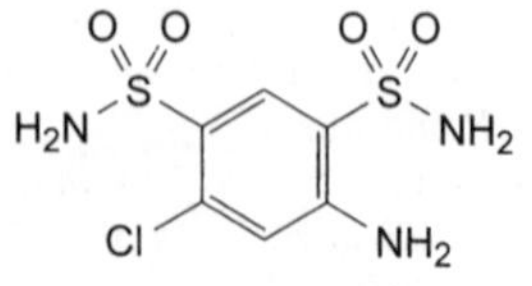

B. 4-amino-6-chlorobenzene-1,3-disulphonamide (salamide),

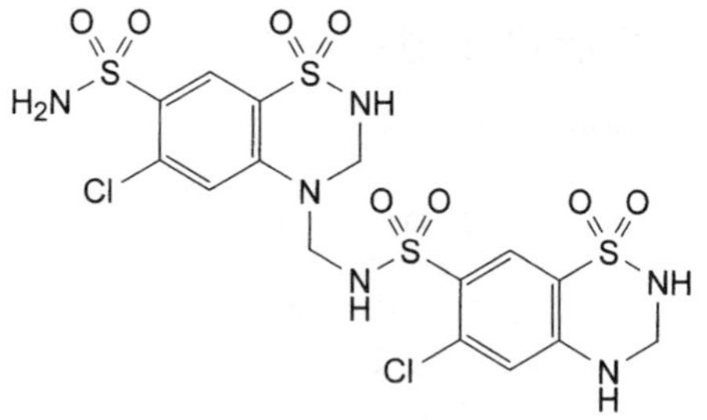

C. 6-chloro-N-[(6-chloro-7-sulphamoyl-2,3-dihydro-4H-1,2,4-benzothiadiazin-4-yl 1,1-dioxide)methyl]-3,4-dihydro-2H-1,2,4-benzothiadiazine-7-sulphonamide 1,1-dioxide.

_____ *Ph Eur*

# Hydrocodone Hydrogen Tartrate Hydrate

(*Hydrocodone Hydrogen Tartrate 2.5-Hydrate, Ph Eur monograph 1784*)

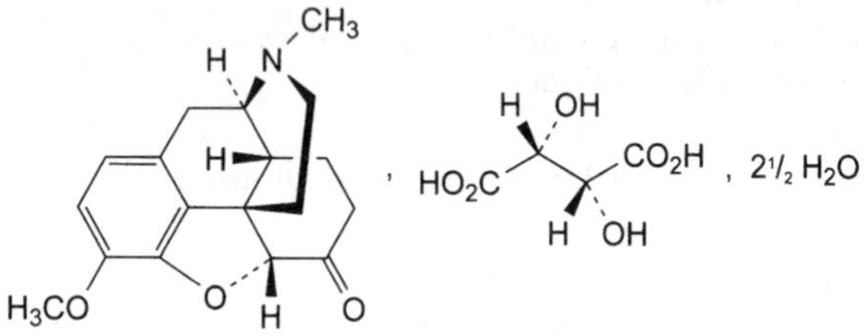

$C_{18}H_{21}NO_3,C_4H_6O_6,2\frac{1}{2}H_2O$   494.5   *34195-34-1*

**Action and use**
Opioid receptor agonist; antitussive.

*Ph Eur* _____

**DEFINITION**
4,5α-Epoxy-3-methoxy-17-methylmorphinan-6-one hydrogen (2R,3R)-2,3-dihydroxybutanedioate 2.5-hydrate.

**Content**
99.0 per cent to 101.0 per cent (anhydrous substance).

**CHARACTERS**

**Appearance**
White or almost white, hygroscopic, crystalline powder.

**Solubility**
Freely soluble or soluble in water, sparingly soluble in ethanol (96 per cent), practically insoluble in cyclohexane.

**IDENTIFICATION**
Infrared absorption spectrophotometry (*2.2.24*).

*Comparison*   hydrocodone hydrogen tartrate 2.5-hydrate CRS.

If the spectra obtained in the solid state show differences, dry the substance to be examined and the reference substance at 105 °C and record new spectra using the residues.

**TESTS**

**Appearance of solution**
The solution is clear (*2.2.1*) and not more intensely coloured than reference solution $Y_5$ (*2.2.2, Method II*).

Dissolve 0.5 g in *water R* and dilute to 10 ml with the same solvent.

**pH** (*2.2.3*)
3.2 to 3.8.

Dissolve 1.0 g in *carbon dioxide-free water R* and dilute to 50.0 ml with the same solvent.

**Specific optical rotation** (2.2.7)
– 87 to – 91 (anhydrous substance).

Dissolve 2.50 g in *carbon dioxide-free water R* and dilute to 50.0 ml with the same solvent.

**Related substances**
Liquid chromatography (2.2.29).

*Test solution* Dissolve 0.100 g of the substance to be examined in mobile phase A and dilute to 10.0 ml with mobile phase A.

*Reference solution (a)* Dissolve 5 mg of *oxycodone hydrochloride CRS* (impurity D) in mobile phase A, add 0.5 ml of the test solution and dilute to 5.0 ml with mobile phase A.

*Reference solution (b)* Dilute 1.0 ml of the test solution to 100.0 ml with mobile phase A. Dilute 1.0 ml of this solution to 10.0 ml with mobile phase A.

*Reference solution (c)* Dissolve 20 mg of *benzophenone CRS* (impurity H) in 50.0 ml of *methanol R*. Dilute 1.0 ml of this solution to 20.0 ml with mobile phase A.

*Reference solution (d)* Dissolve the contents of a vial of *hydrocodone for peak identification CRS* (containing impurities B, C, D, E, F and I) in 1.0 ml of mobile phase A.

*Reference solution (e)* Dissolve 5 mg of *morphine sulphate CRS* (impurity A) in 5 ml of mobile phase A.

*Column:*
— *size: l = 0.25 m, Ø = 4.6 mm;*
— *stationary phase: octadecylsilyl silica gel for chromatography end-capped R (5 µm);*
— *temperature: 40 °C.*

*Mobile phase:*
— *mobile phase A: dissolve 1.08 g of sodium octanesulphonate R in water R, adjust to pH 2.0 with phosphoric acid R and dilute to 1000 ml with water R;*
— *mobile phase B: acetonitrile R;*

| Time (min) | Mobile phase A (per cent V/V) | Mobile phase B (per cent V/V) |
|---|---|---|
| 0 - 15 | 80 | 20 |
| 15 - 30 | 80 → 70 | 20 → 30 |
| 30 - 40 | 70 → 40 | 30 → 60 |
| 40 - 42 | 40 | 60 |
| 42 - 43 | 40 → 80 | 60 → 20 |
| 43 - 52 | 80 | 20 |

*Flow rate* 1.5 ml/min.

*Detection* Spectrophotometer at 283 nm.

*Injection* 10 µl.

*Identification of impurities* Use the chromatogram supplied with *hydrocodone for peak identification CRS* and the chromatogram obtained with reference solution (d) to identify the peaks due to impurities B, C, D, E, F and I; use the chromatogram obtained with reference solution (e) to identify the peak due to impurity A.

*Relative retention* With reference to hydrocodone (retention time = about 14 min): impurity A = about 0.3; impurity K = about 0.43; impurity B = about 0.57; impurity C = about 0.61; impurity D = about 0.9; impurity E = about 1.1; impurity F = about 1.5; impurity I = about 2.0; impurity H = about 2.9.

*System suitability* Reference solution (a):
— *resolution:* minimum 3.0 between the peaks due to impurity D and hydrocodone.

*Limits:*
— *correction factor:* for the calculation of content, multiply the peak area of impurity I by 0.2;
— *impurity I:* not more than the area of the principal peak in the chromatogram obtained with reference solution (b) (0.1 per cent);
— *impurity H:* not more than 0.5 times the area of the corresponding peak in the chromatogram obtained with reference solution (c) (0.1 per cent);
— *impurities A, B, C, D, E, F, K:* for each impurity, not more than twice the area of the principal peak in the chromatogram obtained with reference solution (b) (0.2 per cent);
— *unspecified impurities:* for each impurity, not more than the area of the principal peak in the chromatogram obtained with reference solution (b) (0.10 per cent);
— *total:* not more than 10 times the area of the principal peak in the chromatogram obtained with reference solution (b) (1.0 per cent);
— *disregard limit:* 0.5 times the area of the principal peak in the chromatogram obtained with reference solution (b) (0.05 per cent).

**Water** (2.5.12)
7.0 per cent to 12.0 per cent, determined on 0.100 g.

**Sulphated ash** (2.4.14)
Maximum 0.1 per cent, determined on 1.0 g.

**ASSAY**
Dissolve 0.350 g in 60 ml of *anhydrous acetic acid R*. Titrate with *0.1 M perchloric acid*, determining the end-point potentiometrically (2.2.20).

1 ml of *0.1 M perchloric acid* is equivalent to 44.95 mg of $C_{22}H_{27}NO_9$.

**STORAGE**
In an airtight container, protected from light.

**IMPURITIES**
*Specified impurities* A, B, C, D, E, F, H, I, K.

*Other detectable impurities* (The following substances would, if present at a sufficient level, be detected by one or other of the tests in the monograph. They are limited by the general acceptance criterion for other/unspecified impurities and/or by the general monograph *Substances for pharmaceutical use (2034)*. It is therefore not necessary to identify these impurities for demonstration of compliance. See also 5.10. *Control of impurities in substances for pharmaceutical use*): G, J.

A. R1 = R2 = OH, R3 = H: morphine,

C. R1 = $OCH_3$, R2 = OH, R3 = H: codeine,

E. R1 = $OCH_3$, R2 + R3 = O: 7,8-didehydro-4,5α-epoxy-3-methoxy-17-methylmorphinan-6-one (codeinone),

F. R1 = R2 = $OCH_3$, R3 = H: 7,8-didehydro-4,5α-epoxy-3,6α-dimethoxy-17-methylmorphinan (methylcodeine),

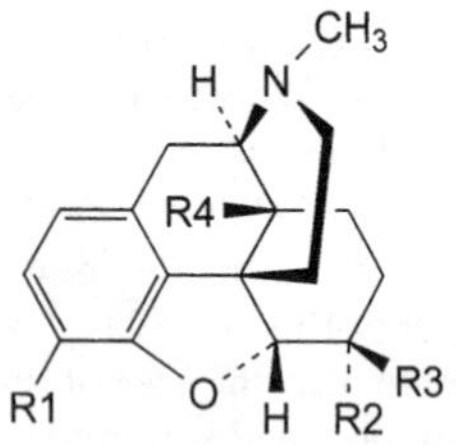

B. R1 = OCH₃, R2 = OH, R3 = R4 = H: 4,5α-epoxy-3-methoxy-17-methylmorphinan-6α-ol (dihydrocodeine),

D. R1 = OCH₃, R2 + R3 = O, R4 = OH: 4,5α-epoxy-14-hydroxy-3-methoxy-17-methylmorphinan-6-one (oxycodone),

K. R1 = OH, R2 + R3 = O, R4 = H: 4,5α-epoxy-3-hydroxy-17-methylmorphinan-6-one,

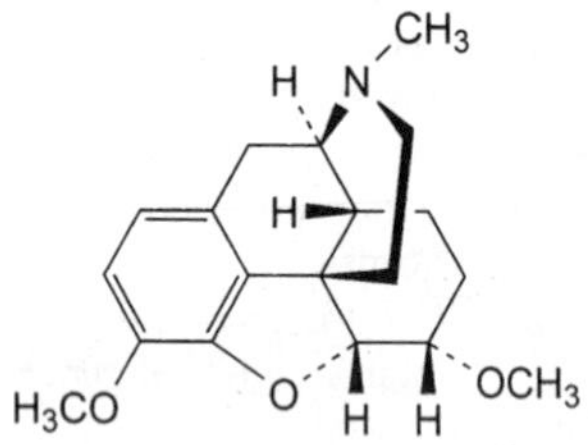

G. 4,5α-epoxy-3,6α-dimethoxy-17-methylmorphinan (tetrahydrothebaine),

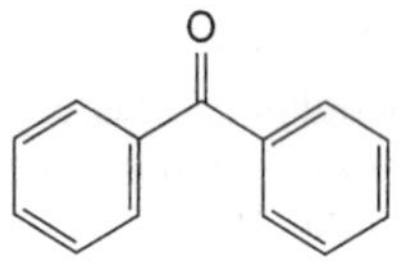

H. diphenylmethanone (benzophenone),

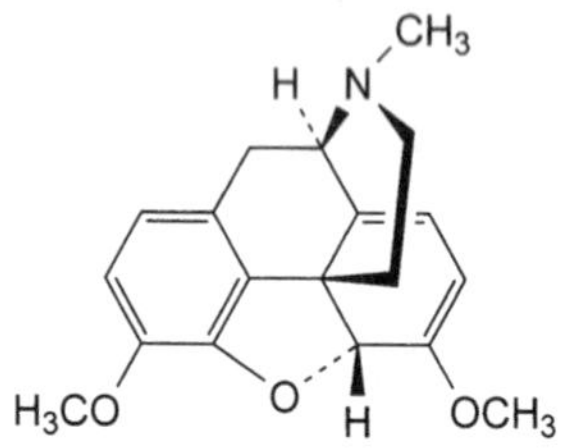

I. 6,7,8,14-tetradehydro-4,5α-epoxy-3,6-dimethoxy-17-methylmorphinan (thebaine),

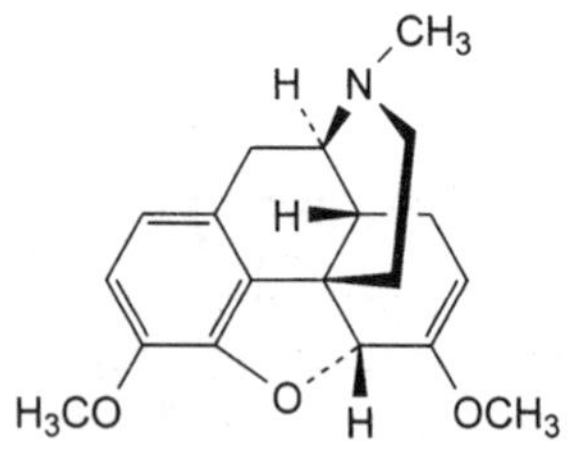

J. 6,7-didehydro-4,5α-epoxy-3,6-dimethoxy-17-methylmorphinan.

*Ph Eur*

# Hydrocortisone

(*Ph Eur monograph 0335*)

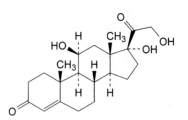

C₂₁H₃₀O₅      362.5      50-23-7

## Action and use
Corticosteroid.

## Preparations
Hydrocortisone Cream
Hydrocortisone and Clioquinol Cream
Hydrocortisone and Neomycin Cream
Hydrocortisone Ointment
Hydrocortisone and Clioquinol Ointment
Miconazole and Hydrocortisone Cream
Miconazole and Hydrocortisone Ointment

*Ph Eur*

## DEFINITION
11β,17,21-Trihydroxypregn-4-ene-3,20-dione.

## Content
97.0 per cent to 103.0 per cent (dried substance).

## CHARACTERS
### Appearance
White or almost white, crystalline powder.

### Solubility
Practically insoluble in water, sparingly soluble in acetone and in ethanol (96 per cent), slightly soluble in methylene chloride.

It shows polymorphism (*5.9*).

## IDENTIFICATION
*First identification A, B.*

*Second identification C, D.*

A. Infrared absorption spectrophotometry (*2.2.24*).

*Comparison hydrocortisone CRS.*

If the spectra obtained in the solid state show differences, dissolve the substance to be examined and the reference substance separately in the minimum volume of *acetone R*, evaporate to dryness on a water-bath and record new spectra using the residues.

B. Liquid chromatography (*2.2.29*) as described in the test for related substances with the following modification.

*Injection* Test solution and reference solution (c).

*Results* The principal peak in the chromatogram obtained with the test solution is similar in retention time and size to the principal peak in the chromatogram obtained with reference solution (c).

C. Thin-layer chromatography (*2.2.27*).

*Solution A* Dissolve 25 mg of the substance to be examined in *methanol R* and dilute to 5 ml with the same solvent.

*Solution B*   Dissolve 25 mg of *hydrocortisone CRS* in *methanol R* and dilute to 5 ml with the same solvent.

*Test solution (a)*   Dilute 2 ml of solution A to 10 ml with *methylene chloride R*.

*Test solution (b)*   Transfer 0.4 ml of solution A to a glass tube 100 mm long and 20 mm in diameter and fitted with a ground-glass stopper or a polytetrafluoroethylene cap. Evaporate the solvent with gentle heating under a stream of *nitrogen R*. Add 2 ml of a 15 per cent *V/V* solution of *glacial acetic acid R* and 50 mg of *sodium bismuthate R*. Stopper the tube and shake the suspension in a mechanical shaker, protected from light, for 1 h. Add 2 ml of a 15 per cent *V/V* solution of *glacial acetic acid R* and filter into a 50 ml separating funnel, washing the filter with 2 quantities, each of 5 ml, of *water R*. Shake the clear filtrate with 10 ml of *methylene chloride R*. Wash the organic layer with 5 ml of *1 M sodium hydroxide* and then with 2 quantities, each of 5 ml, of *water R*. Dry over *anhydrous sodium sulphate R*.

*Reference solution (a)*   Dilute 2 ml of solution B to 10 ml with *methylene chloride R*.

*Reference solution (b)*   Transfer 0.4 ml of solution B to a glass tube 100 mm long and 20 mm in diameter and fitted with a ground-glass stopper or a polytetrafluoroethylene cap. Evaporate the solvent with gentle heating under a stream of *nitrogen R*. Add 2 ml of a 15 per cent *V/V* solution of *glacial acetic acid R* and 50 mg of *sodium bismuthate R*. Stopper the tube and shake the suspension in a mechanical shaker, protected from light, for 1 h. Add 2 ml of a 15 per cent *V/V* solution of *glacial acetic acid R* and filter into a 50 ml separating funnel, washing the filter with 2 quantities, each of 5 ml, of *water R*. Shake the clear filtrate with 10 ml of *methylene chloride R*. Wash the organic layer with 5 ml of *1 M sodium hydroxide* and then with 2 quantities, each of 5 ml, of *water R*. Dry over *anhydrous sodium sulphate R*.

*Plate*   *TLC silica gel F₂₅₄ plate R*.

*Mobile phase A*   Add a mixture of 1.2 volumes of *water R* and 8 volumes of *methanol R* to a mixture of 15 volumes of *ether R* and 77 volumes of *methylene chloride R*.

*Mobile phase B*   *butanol R* saturated with *water R*, *toluene R*, *ether R* (5:15:80 *V/V/V*).

*Application*   5 μl of test solution (a) and reference solution (a), 25 μl of test solution (b) and reference solution (b), applying the latter 2 in small quantities to obtain small spots.

*Development*   Over a path of 15 cm with mobile phase A, and then over a path of 15 cm with mobile phase B.

*Drying*   In air.

*Detection A*   Examine in ultraviolet light at 254 nm.

*Results A*   The principal spot in each of the chromatograms obtained with test solutions (a) and (b) is similar in position and size to the principal spot in the chromatogram obtained with the corresponding reference solution.

*Detection B*   Spray with alcoholic solution of *sulphuric acid R* and heat at 120 °C for 10 min or until the spots appear; allow to cool, and examine in daylight and in ultraviolet light at 365 nm.

*Results B*   The principal spot in each of the chromatograms obtained with test solutions (a) and (b) is similar in position, colour in daylight, fluorescence in ultraviolet light at 365 nm and size to the principal spot in the chromatogram obtained with the corresponding reference solution. The principal spots in the chromatograms obtained with test solution (b) and reference solution (b) have an $R_F$ value distinctly higher than that of the principal spots in the chromatograms obtained with test solution (a) and reference solution (a).

D. Add about 2 mg to 2 ml of *sulphuric acid R* and shake to dissolve. Within 5 min, an intense brownish-red colour develops with a green fluorescence that is particularly intense when examined in ultraviolet light at 365 nm. Add the solution to 10 ml of *water R* and mix. The colour fades and a clear solution remains. The fluorescence in ultraviolet light does not disappear.

## TESTS

**Specific optical rotation** (*2.2.7*)
+ 162 to + 168 (dried substance).

Dissolve 0.200 g in *methanol R*, dilute to 25.0 ml with the same solvent and sonicate for 10 min.

**Related substances**
Liquid chromatography (*2.2.29*).

*Solvent mixture*   *acetonitrile R*, *water R* (40:60 *V/V*).

*Test solution*   Dissolve 20 mg of the substance to be examined in the solvent mixture, dilute to 10.0 ml with the solvent mixture and sonicate for 10 min.

*Reference solution (a)*   Dissolve 4 mg of *prednisolone CRS* (impurity A), 2 mg of *cortisone R* (impurity B), 8 mg of *hydrocortisone acetate CRS* (impurity C) and 6 mg of *Reichstein's substance S R* (impurity F) in 40 ml of *acetonitrile R* and dilute to 100.0 ml with *water R*. Dilute 0.5 ml of this solution to 5.0 ml with the test solution.

*Reference solution (b)*   Dilute 1.0 ml of the test solution to 100.0 ml with the solvent mixture. Dilute 1.0 ml of this solution to 10.0 ml with the solvent mixture.

*Reference solution (c)*   Dissolve 2 mg of *hydrocortisone CRS* in 1.0 ml of the solvent mixture and sonicate for 10 min.

*Reference solution (d)*   Dissolve 2 mg of *hydrocortisone for peak identification CRS* (containing impurities D, E, G, H, I and N) in 1.0 ml of the solvent mixture and sonicate for 10 min.

*Column:*
— *size: l = 0.25 m, Ø = 4.6 mm;*
— *stationary phase: base-deactivated end-capped octadecylsilyl silica gel for chromatography R (5 μm).*

*Mobile phase:*
— *mobile phase A: water R;*
— *mobile phase B: acetonitrile R;*

| Time (min) | Mobile phase A (per cent *V/V*) | Mobile phase B (per cent *V/V*) |
|---|---|---|
| 0 - 18 | 74 | 26 |
| 18 - 32 | 74 → 55 | 26 → 45 |
| 32 - 48 | 55 → 30 | 45 → 70 |

*Flow rate*   0.8 ml/min.

*Detection*   Spectrophotometer at 254 nm.

*Injection*   10 μl of the test solution and reference solutions (a), (b) and (d).

*Identification of impurities*   Use the chromatogram supplied with *hydrocortisone for peak identification CRS* and the chromatogram obtained with reference solution (d) to identify the peaks due to impurities D, E, G, H, I and N; use the chromatogram obtained with reference solution (a) to identify the peaks due to impurities A, B, C and F.

*Relative retention*   With reference to hydrocortisone (retention time = about 24 min): impurity D = about 0.2; impurity H = about 0.3; impurity I = about 0.5; impurity G = about 0.8; impurity E = about 0.86; impurity A = about 0.96; impurity B = about 1.1; impurity F = about 1.4; impurity C = about 1.5; impurity N = about 1.7.

*System suitability* Reference solution (a):
— *peak-to-valley ratio*: minimum 3.0, where $H_p$ = height above the baseline of the peak due to impurity A and $H_v$ = height above the baseline of the lowest point of the curve separating this peak from the peak due to hydrocortisone.

*Limits:*
— *correction factors*: for the calculation of content, multiply the peak areas of the following impurities by the corresponding correction factor: impurity D = 1.8; impurity E = 2.7;
— *impurities C, D, E, I*: for each impurity, not more than 5 times the area of the principal peak in the chromatogram obtained with reference solution (b) (0.5 per cent);
— *impurity F*: not more than 3 times the area of the principal peak in the chromatogram obtained with reference solution (b) (0.3 per cent);
— *impurities A, B, G*: for each impurity, not more than twice the area of the principal peak in the chromatogram obtained with reference solution (b) (0.2 per cent);
— *impurities H, N*: for each impurity, not more than 1.5 times the area of the principal peak in the chromatogram obtained with reference solution (b) (0.15 per cent);
— *unspecified impurities*: for each impurity, not more than the area of the principal peak in the chromatogram obtained with reference solution (b) (0.10 per cent);
— *total*: not more than 20 times the area of the principal peak in the chromatogram obtained with reference solution (b) (2.0 per cent);
— *disregard limit*: 0.5 times the area of the principal peak in the chromatogram obtained with reference solution (b) (0.05 per cent).

**Loss on drying** *(2.2.32)*
Maximum 1.0 per cent, determined on 1.000 g by drying in an oven at 105 °C.

**ASSAY**
Dissolve 0.100 g in *ethanol (96 per cent) R* and dilute to 100.0 ml with the same solvent. Dilute 2.0 ml of this solution to 100.0 ml with *ethanol (96 per cent) R*. Measure the absorbance *(2.2.25)* at the absorption maximum at 241.5 nm.

Calculate the content of $C_{21}H_{30}O_5$ taking the specific absorbance to be 440.

**STORAGE**
Protected from light.

**IMPURITIES**
*Specified impurities*   *A, B, C, D, E, F, G, H, I, N.*

*Other detectable impurities*   (The following substances would, if present at a sufficient level, be detected by one or other of the tests in the monograph. They are limited by the general acceptance criterion for other/unspecified impurities and/or by the general monograph *Substances for pharmaceutical use (2034)*. It is therefore not necessary to identify these impurities for demonstration of compliance. See also *5.10. Control of impurities in substances for pharmaceutical use)*: *J, K, L, M, O.*

A. prednisolone,

B. 17,21-dihydroxypregn-4-ene-3,11,20-trione (cortisone),

C. hydrocortisone acetate (hydrocortisone-21-acetate),

D. R1 = R3 = OH, R2 = R4 = H, R5 = CH₂OH: 6β,11β,17,21-tetrahydroxypregn-4-ene-3,20-dione (6β-hydroxyhydrocortisone),

F. R1 = R2 = R3 = R4 = H, R5 = CH₂OH: 17,21-dihydroxypregn-4-ene-3,20-dione (Reichstein's substance S),

G. R1 = R2 = R4 = H, R3 = OH, R5 = CHO: 11β,17-dihydroxy-3,20-dioxopregn-4-en-21-al (hydrocortisone-21-aldehyde),

H. R1 = R4 = H, R2 = R3 = OH, R5 = CH₂OH: 7α,11β,17,21-tetrahydroxypregn-4-ene-3,20-dione (7α-hydroxyhydrocortisone),

I. R1 = R2 = H, R3 = R4 = OH, R5 = CH₂OH: 11β,14,17,21-tetrahydroxypregn-4-ene-3,20-dione (14α-hydroxyhydrocortisone),

K. R1 = R2 = R3 = R4 = H, R5 = CH₂-O-CO-CH₃: 17-hydroxy-3,20-dioxopregn-4-en-21-yl acetate (Reichstein's substance S-21-acetate),

E. 11β,17,21-trihydroxypregna-4,6-diene-3,20-dione (Δ6-hydrocortisone),

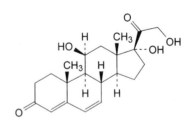

J. R1 = H, R2 = CO-CH₃, R3 = OH: 11β,21-dihydroxy-3,20-dioxopregn-4-en-17-yl acetate (hydrocortisone-17-acetate),

L. R1 = R2 = R3 = H:
11β,17-dihydroxypregn-4-ene-3,20-dione (oxenol),

O. R1 = R3 = OH, R2 = H:
11β,17,19,21-tetrahydroxypregn-4-ene-3,20-dione
(19-hydroxyhydrocortisone),

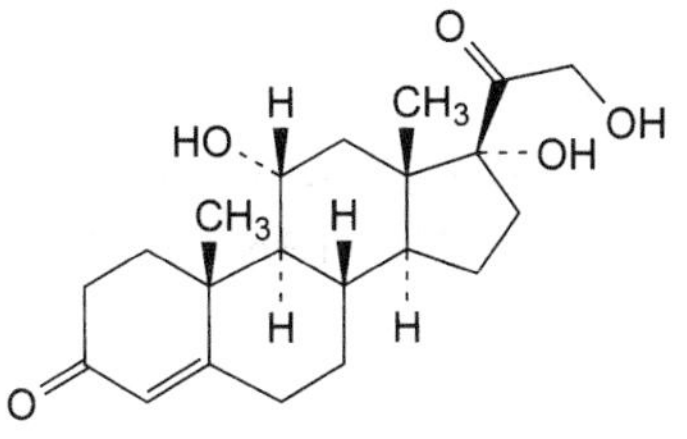

M. 11α,17,21-trihydroxypregn-4-ene-3,20-dione (*epi*-hydrocortisone),

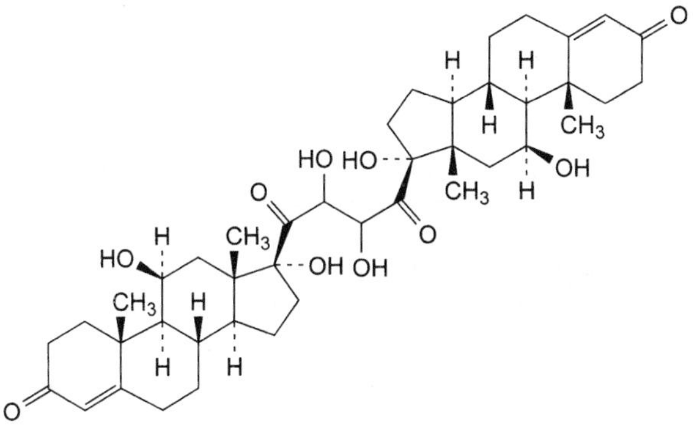

N. 11β,17,21-trihydroxy-21-(11β,17,21-trihydroxy-3,20-dioxopregn-4-en-21-yl)pregn-4-ene-3,20-dione (hydrocortisone dimer).

_____ *Ph Eur*

# Hydrocortisone Acetate

(*Ph Eur monograph 0334*)

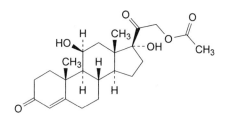

C₂₃H₃₂O₆            404.5            *50-03-3*

**Action and use**
Corticosteroid.

**Preparations**
Gentamicin and Hydrocortisone Acetate Ear Drops
Hydrocortisone Acetate Cream
Hydrocortisone Acetate and Neomycin Ear Drops
Hydrocortisone Acetate and Neomycin Eye Drops
Hydrocortisone Acetate and Neomycin Eye Ointment
Hydrocortisone Acetate Injection
Hydrocortisone Acetate Ointment
Miconazole and Hydrocortisone Acetate Cream

*Ph Eur* _____

**DEFINITION**
11β,17-Dihydroxy-3,20-dioxopregn-4-en-21-yl acetate.

**Content**
97.0 per cent to 103.0 per cent (dried substance).

**CHARACTERS**
**Appearance**
White or almost white, crystalline powder.

**Solubility**
Practically insoluble in water, slightly soluble in anhydrous ethanol and in methylene chloride.

mp: about 220 °C, with decomposition.

**IDENTIFICATION**
*First identification   A, B.*

*Second identification   C, D, E.*

A. Infrared absorption spectrophotometry (*2.2.24*).

*Comparison   hydrocortisone acetate CRS.*

B. Thin-layer chromatography (*2.2.27*).

*Solvent mixture   methanol R, methylene chloride R (1:9 V/V).*

*Test solution   Dissolve 10 mg of the substance to be examined in the solvent mixture and dilute to 10 ml with the solvent mixture.*

*Reference solution (a)   Dissolve 20 mg of hydrocortisone acetate CRS in the solvent mixture and dilute to 20 ml with the solvent mixture.*

*Reference solution (b)   Dissolve 10 mg of cortisone acetate R in reference solution (a) and dilute to 10 ml with reference solution (a).*

*Plate   TLC silica gel F₂₅₄ plate R.*

*Mobile phase   Add a mixture of 1.2 volumes of water R and 8 volumes of methanol R to a mixture of 15 volumes of ether R and 77 volumes of methylene chloride R.*

*Application   5 µl.*

*Development   Over a path of 15 cm.*

*Drying   In air.*

*Detection A   Examine in ultraviolet light at 254 nm.*

*Results A   The principal spot in the chromatogram obtained with the test solution is similar in position and size to the principal spot in the chromatogram obtained with reference solution (a).*

*Detection B   Spray with alcoholic solution of sulphuric acid R. Heat at 120 °C for 10 min or until the spots appear and allow to cool; examine in daylight and in ultraviolet light at 365 nm.*

*Results B   The principal spot in the chromatogram obtained with the test solution is similar in position, colour in daylight, fluorescence in ultraviolet light at 365 nm and size to the principal spot in the chromatogram obtained with reference solution (a).*

*System suitability   Reference solution (b):*
— the chromatogram shows 2 clearly separated spots.

C. Thin-layer chromatography (*2.2.27*).

*Test solution (a)   Dissolve 25 mg of the substance to be examined in methanol R and dilute to 5 ml with the same solvent (solution A). Dilute 2 ml of this solution to 10 ml with methylene chloride R.*

*Test solution (b)   Transfer 2 ml of solution A to a 15 ml glass tube with a ground-glass stopper or a polytetrafluoroethylene cap. Add 10 ml of saturated methanolic potassium hydrogen carbonate solution R and immediately pass a* stream of *nitrogen R* briskly through the solution for 5 min. Stopper the tube. Heat in a water-bath at 45 °C protected from light for 2 h 30 min. Allow to cool.

*Reference solution (a)*   Dissolve 25 mg of *hydrocortisone acetate CRS* in *methanol R* and dilute to 5 ml with the same solvent (solution B). Dilute 2 ml of this solution to 10 ml with *methylene chloride R*.

*Reference solution (b)*   Transfer 2 ml of solution B to a 15 ml glass tube with a ground-glass stopper or a polytetrafluoroethylene cap. Add 10 ml of *saturated methanolic potassium hydrogen carbonate solution R* and immediately pass a stream of *nitrogen R* briskly through the solution for 5 min. Stopper the tube. Heat in a water-bath at 45 °C protected from light for 2 h 30 min. Allow to cool.

*Plate*   *TLC silica gel F$_{254}$ plate R*.

*Mobile phase*   Add a mixture of 1.2 volumes of *water R* and 8 volumes of *methanol R* to a mixture of 15 volumes of *ether R* and 77 volumes of *methylene chloride R*.

*Application*   5 µl.

*Development*   Over a path of 15 cm.

*Drying*   In air.

*Detection A*   Examine in ultraviolet light at 254 nm.

*Results A*   The principal spot in each of the chromatograms obtained with the test solutions is similar in position and size to the principal spot in the chromatogram obtained with the corresponding reference solution.

*Detection B*   Spray with *alcoholic solution of sulphuric acid R* and heat at 120 °C for 10 min or until the spots appear and allow to cool; examine in daylight and in ultraviolet light at 365 nm.

*Results B*   The principal spot in each of the chromatograms obtained with the test solutions is similar in position, colour in daylight, fluorescence in ultraviolet light at 365 nm and size to the principal spot in the chromatogram obtained with the corresponding reference solution. The principal spots in the chromatograms obtained with test solution (b) and reference solution (b) have an $R_F$ value distinctly lower than that of the principal spots in the chromatograms obtained with test solution (a) and reference solution (a).

D. Add about 2 mg to 2 ml of *sulphuric acid R* and shake to dissolve. Within 5 min an intense brownish-red colour develops with a green fluorescence which is particularly intense when viewed in ultraviolet light at 365 nm. Add this solution to 10 ml of *water R* and mix. The colour fades and the fluorescence in ultraviolet light does not disappear.

E. About 10 mg gives the reaction of acetyl (*2.3.1*).

## TESTS

**Specific optical rotation** (*2.2.7*)
+ 158 to + 167 (dried substance).

Dissolve 0.250 g in *dioxan R* and dilute to 25.0 ml with the same solvent.

**Related substances**
Liquid chromatography (*2.2.29*).

*Test solution*   Dissolve 25.0 mg of the substance to be examined in *methanol R* and dilute to 10.0 ml with the same solvent.

*Reference solution (a)*   Dissolve 2 mg of *hydrocortisone acetate CRS* and 2 mg of *cortisone acetate R* in the mobile phase, then dilute to 100.0 ml with the mobile phase.

*Reference solution (b)*   Dilute 1.0 ml of the test solution to 100.0 ml with the mobile phase.

*Column:*
— *size*: $l = 0.25$ m, Ø = 4.6 mm;
— *stationary phase*: *octadecylsilyl silica gel for chromatography R* (5 µm).

*Mobile phase*   In a 1000 ml volumetric flask mix 400 ml of *acetonitrile R* with 550 ml of *water R* and allow to equilibrate; dilute to 1000 ml with *water R* and mix again.

*Flow rate*   1 ml/min.

*Detection*   Spectrophotometer at 254 nm.

*Equilibration*   With the mobile phase for about 30 min.

*Injection*   20 µl.

*Run time*   2.5 times the retention time of hydrocortisone acetate.

*Retention time*   Hydrocortisone acetate = about 10 min; cortisone acetate = about 12 min.

*System suitability*   Reference solution (a):
— *resolution*: minimum 4.2 between the peaks due to hydrocortisone acetate and cortisone acetate; if necessary, adjust the concentration of acetonitrile in the mobile phase.

*Limits:*
— *any impurity*: for each impurity, not more than the area of the principal peak in the chromatogram obtained with reference solution (b) (1.0 per cent), and not more than one such peak has an area greater than 0.5 times the area of the principal peak in the chromatogram obtained with reference solution (b) (0.5 per cent);
— *total*: not more than 1.5 times the area of the principal peak in the chromatogram obtained with reference solution (b) (1.5 per cent);
— *disregard limit*: 0.05 times the area of the principal peak in the chromatogram obtained with reference solution (b) (0.05 per cent).

**Loss on drying** (*2.2.32*)
Maximum 0.5 per cent, determined on 0.500 g by drying in an oven at 105 °C.

## ASSAY

Dissolve 0.100 g in *ethanol (96 per cent) R* and dilute to 100.0 ml with the same solvent. Dilute 2.0 ml of this solution to 100.0 ml with *ethanol (96 per cent) R*. Measure the absorbance (*2.2.25*) at the absorption maximum at 241.5 nm.

Calculate the content of $C_{23}H_{32}O_6$ taking the specific absorbance to be 395.

## STORAGE
Protected from light.

_____ *Ph Eur*

# Hydrocortisone Hydrogen Succinate

(*Ph Eur monograph 0768*)

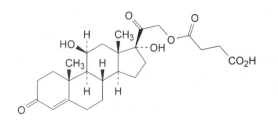

$C_{25}H_{34}O_8$        462.5        2203-97-6

## Action and use
Corticosteroid.

## Preparations
Hydrocortisone Sodium Succinate Injection

Hydrocortisone Oromucosal Tablets

*Ph Eur* _____

## DEFINITION
11β,17-Dihydroxy-3,20-dioxopregn-4-en-21-yl hydrogen butanedioate.

## Content
97.0 per cent to 103.0 per cent (dried substance).

## CHARACTERS
### Appearance
White or almost white, hygroscopic powder.

### Solubility
Practically insoluble in water, freely soluble in acetone and in anhydrous ethanol. It dissolves in dilute solutions of alkali carbonates and alkali hydroxides.

## IDENTIFICATION
*First identification*   A, B.

*Second identification*   C, D.

A. Infrared absorption spectrophotometry (*2.2.24*).

*Preparation*   Dry the substances before use at 100–105 °C for 3 h.

*Comparison*   hydrocortisone hydrogen succinate CRS.

B. Thin-layer chromatography (*2.2.27*).

*Solvent mixture*   methanol R, methylene chloride R (1:9 *V/V*).

*Test solution*   Dissolve 10 mg of the substance to be examined in the solvent mixture and dilute to 10 ml with the solvent mixture.

*Reference solution (a)*   Dissolve 20 mg of *hydrocortisone hydrogen succinate CRS* in the solvent mixture and dilute to 20 ml with the solvent mixture.

*Reference solution (b)*   Dissolve 10 mg of *methylprednisolone hydrogen succinate CRS* in reference solution (a) and dilute to 10 ml with reference solution (a).

*Plate*   TLC silica gel $F_{254}$ plate R.

*Mobile phase*   anhydrous formic acid R, anhydrous ethanol R, methylene chloride R (0.1:1:15 *V/V/V*).

*Application*   5 µl.

*Development*   Over a path of 15 cm.

*Drying*   In air.

*Detection A*   Examine in ultraviolet light at 254 nm.

*Results A*   The principal spot in the chromatogram obtained with the test solution is similar in position and size to the principal spot in the chromatogram obtained with reference solution (a).

*Detection B*   Spray with *alcoholic solution of sulphuric acid R*. Heat at 120 °C for 10 min or until the spots appear. Allow to cool. Examine in daylight and in ultraviolet light at 365 nm.

*Results B*   The principal spot in the chromatogram obtained with the test solution is similar in position, colour in daylight, fluorescence in ultraviolet light at 365 nm and size to the principal spot in the chromatogram obtained with reference solution (a).

*System suitability*   Reference solution (b):
— the chromatogram shows 2 spots which may, however, not be completely separated.

C. Thin-layer chromatography (*2.2.27*).

*Test solution (a)*   Dissolve 25 mg of the substance to be examined in *methanol R* with gentle heating and dilute to 5 ml with the same solvent (solution A). Dilute 2 ml of this solution to 10 ml with *methylene chloride R*.

*Test solution (b)*   Transfer 2 ml of solution A to a 15 ml glass tube with a ground-glass stopper or a polytetrafluoroethylene cap. Add 10 ml of a 0.8 g/l solution of *sodium hydroxide R* in *methanol R* and immediately pass a stream of *nitrogen R* briskly through the solution for 5 min. Stopper the tube. Heat in a water-bath at 45 °C, protected from light, for 30 min. Allow to cool.

*Reference solution (a)*   Dissolve 25 mg of *hydrocortisone hydrogen succinate CRS* in *methanol R* with gentle heating and dilute to 5 ml with the same solvent (solution B). Dilute 2 ml of this solution to 10 ml with *methylene chloride R*.

*Reference solution (b)*   Transfer 2 ml of solution B to a 15 ml glass tube with a ground-glass stopper or a polytetrafluoroethylene cap. Add 10 ml of a 0.8 g/l solution of *sodium hydroxide R* in *methanol R* and immediately pass a stream of *nitrogen R* briskly through the solution for 5 min. Stopper the tube. Heat in a water-bath at 45 °C, protected from light, for 30 min. Allow to cool.

*Plate*   TLC silica gel $F_{254}$ plate R.

*Mobile phase*   Add a mixture of 1.2 volumes of *water R* and 8 volumes of *methanol R* to a mixture of 15 volumes of *ether R* and 77 volumes of *methylene chloride R*.

*Application*   5 µl.

*Developement*   Over a path of 15 cm.

*Drying*   In air.

*Detection A*   Examine in ultraviolet light at 254 nm.

*Results A*   The principal spot in each of the chromatograms obtained with the test solutions is similar in position and size to the principal spot in the chromatogram obtained with the corresponding reference solution.

*Detection B*   Spray with *alcoholic solution of sulphuric acid R*. Heat at 120 °C for 10 min or until the spots appear. Allow to cool. Examine in daylight and in ultraviolet light at 365 nm

*Results B*   The principal spot in each of the chromatograms obtained with the test solutions is similar in position, colour in daylight, fluorescence in ultraviolet light at 365 nm and size to the principal spot in the chromatogram obtained with the corresponding reference solution. The principal spot in each of the chromatograms obtained with test solution (b) and reference solution (b) has an $R_F$ value distinctly higher than that of the principal spot in each of the chromatograms obtained with test solution (a) and reference solution (a).

D. Add about 2 mg to 2 ml of *sulphuric acid R* and shake to dissolve. Within 5 min, an intense brownish-red colour develops with a green fluorescence which is particularly intense when viewed in ultraviolet light at 365 nm. Add this solution to 10 ml of *water R* and mix. The colour fades and a clear solution remains. The fluorescence in ultraviolet light does not disappear.

## TESTS

### Appearance of solution

The solution is clear (*2.2.1*).

Dissolve 0.10 g in 5 ml of *sodium hydrogen carbonate solution R*.

### Specific optical rotation (*2.2.7*)

+ 147 to + 153 (dried substance).

Dissolve 0.250 g in *anhydrous ethanol R* and dilute to 25.0 ml with the same solvent.

### Related substances

Liquid chromatography (*2.2.29*).

*Test solution* Dissolve 25.0 mg of the substance to be examined in a mixture of equal volumes of *acetonitrile R* and *water R* and dilute to 10.0 ml with the same mixture of solvents.

*Reference solution (a)* Dissolve 2 mg of *hydrocortisone hydrogen succinate CRS* and 2 mg of *dexamethasone CRS* in 50 ml of *acetonitrile R*, then dilute to 100.0 ml with *water R*.

*Reference solution (b)* Dilute 1.0 ml of the test solution to 100.0 ml with a mixture of equal volumes of *acetonitrile R* and *water R*.

*Column:*
— *size: l = 0.25 m, Ø = 4.6 mm;*
— *stationary phase: octadecylsilyl silica gel for chromatography R* (5 μm).

*Mobile phase* In a 1000 ml volumetric flask mix 330 ml of *acetonitrile R* with 600 ml of *water R* and 1.0 ml of *phosphoric acid R*, then allow to equilibrate; dilute to 1000 ml with *water R* and mix again.

*Flow rate* 1 ml/min.

*Detection* Spectrophotometer at 254 nm.

*Equilibration* With the mobile phase for about 30 min.

*Injection* 20 μl.

*Run time* Twice the retention time of hydrocortisone hydrogen succinate.

*Retention time* Dexamethasone = about 12.5 min; hydrocortisone hydrogen succinate = about 15 min.

*System suitability* Reference solution (a):
— *resolution*: minimum 5.0 between the peaks due to dexamethasone and hydrocortisone hydrogen succinate; if necessary, adjust the concentration of acetonitrile in the mobile phase.

*Limits:*
— *impurities A, B*: for each impurity, not more than 0.5 times the area of the principal peak in the chromatogram obtained with reference solution (b) (0.5 per cent);
— *total*: not more than 0.75 times the area of the principal peak in the chromatogram obtained with reference solution (b) (0.75 per cent);
— *disregard limit*: 0.05 times the area of the principal peak in the chromatogram obtained with reference solution (b) (0.05 per cent).

### Loss on drying (*2.2.32*)

Maximum 4.0 per cent, determined on 1.000 g by drying in an oven at 105 °C.

### Sulphated ash (*2.4.14*)

Maximum 0.1 per cent, determined on 1.0 g.

## ASSAY

Dissolve 0.100 g in *ethanol (96 per cent) R* and dilute to 100.0 ml with the same solvent. Dilute 2.0 ml of this solution to 100.0 ml with *ethanol (96 per cent) R*. Measure the absorbance (*2.2.25*) at the absorption maximum at 241.5 nm.

Calculate the content of $C_{25}H_{34}O_8$ taking the specific absorbance to be 353.

## STORAGE

In an airtight container, protected from light.

## IMPURITIES

*Specified impurities A, B.*

A. hydrocortisone,

B. hydrocortisone acetate.

_____ *Ph Eur*

# Hydrocortisone Sodium Phosphate

$C_{21}H_{29}Na_2O_8P$     486.4     *6000-74-4*

### Action and use

Corticosteroid.

### Preparations

Hydrocortisone Sodium Phosphate Injection

Hydrocortisone Sodium Phosphate Oral Solution

## DEFINITION

Hydrocortisone Sodium Phosphate is disodium 11β,17α-dihydroxy-3,20-dioxopregn-4-en-21-yl orthophosphate. It contains not less than 96.0% and not more than 103.0% of $C_{21}H_{29}Na_2O_8P$, calculated with reference to the anhydrous substance.

## CHARACTERISTICS

A white or almost white powder; hygroscopic.

Freely soluble in *water*; practically insoluble in *absolute ethanol*.

## IDENTIFICATION

*Test A may be omitted if tests B, C and D are carried out.*
*Tests B and C may be omitted if tests A and D are carried out.*

A. The *infrared absorption spectrum*, Apppendix II A, is concordant with the *reference spectrum* of hydrocortisone sodium phosphate (*RS 386*).

B. Carry out the method for *thin-layer chromatography*, Appendix III A, using *silica gel G* as the coating substance and a freshly prepared mixture of 60 volumes of *butan-1-ol*, 20 volumes of *acetic anhydride* and 20 volumes of *water* as the mobile phase. Apply separately to the plate 2 μl of each of the following solutions. Solution (1) contains 0.25% w/v of the substance being examined in *methanol*. Solution (2) contains 0.25% w/v of *hydrocortisone sodium phosphate BPCRS* in *methanol*. Solution (3) is a mixture of equal volumes of solutions (1) and (2). Solution (4) is a mixture of equal volumes of solution (1) and a 0.25% w/v solution of *betamethasone sodium phosphate BPCRS* in *methanol*. After removal of the plate, allow it to dry in air until the solvent has evaporated, spray with *ethanolic sulphuric acid (20%)*, heat at 120° for 10 minutes and examine under *ultraviolet light (365 nm)*. The principal spot in the chromatogram obtained with solution (1) corresponds to that in the chromatogram obtained with solution (2). The principal spot in the chromatogram obtained with solution (3) appears as a single, compact spot and the chromatogram obtained with solution (4) shows two principal spots with almost identical $R_f$ values.

C. Dissolve 2 mg in 2 ml of *sulphuric acid*. A yellowish green fluorescence is produced immediately (distinction from betamethasone sodium phosphate, dexamethasone sodium phosphate and prednisolone sodium phosphate).

D. Heat gently 40 mg with 2 ml of *sulphuric acid* until white fumes are evolved, add *nitric acid* dropwise until oxidation is complete and cool. Add 2 ml of *water*, heat until white fumes are again evolved, cool, add 10 ml of *water* and neutralise to *litmus paper* with 5M *ammonia*. The resulting solution yields reaction A characteristic of *sodium salts* and reaction B characteristic of *phosphates*, Appendix VI.

## TESTS

### Alkalinity
pH of a 0.5% w/v solution, 7.5 to 9.0, Appendix V L.

### Specific optical rotation
In a 1% w/v solution, +121 to +129, calculated with reference to the anhydrous substance, Appendix V F.

### Inorganic phosphate
Dissolve 25 mg in 10 ml of *water*, add 4 ml of 1M *sulphuric acid*, 1 ml of a 10% w/v solution of *ammonium molybdate* and 2 ml of *methylaminophenol-sulphite reagent* and allow to stand for 15 minutes. Add sufficient *water* to produce 25 ml and allow to stand for a further 15 minutes. The *absorbance* of a 4-cm layer of the resulting solution at 730 nm, Appendix II B, is not more than that of a 4-cm layer of a solution prepared by treating 10 ml of a 0.0036% w/v solution of *potassium dihydrogen orthophosphate* in the same manner, beginning at the words 'add 4 ml . . .'.

### Related substances
Carry out the method for *thin-layer chromatography*, Appendix III A, using *silica gel GF₂₅₄* as the coating substance and a mixture of 77 volumes of *dichloromethane*, 15 volumes of *ether*, 8 volumes of *methanol* and 1.2 volumes of *water* as the mobile phase. Apply separately to the plate 2 μl of each of three solutions in *methanol* containing (1) 1.0% w/v of the substance being examined, (2) 1.0% w/v of *hydrocortisone sodium phosphate BPCRS* and (3) 0.020% w/v of *hydrocortisone BPCRS*. After removal of the plate, allow it to dry in air for 5 minutes and examine under *ultraviolet light (254 nm)*. Any *secondary spot* in the chromatogram obtained with solution (1) is not more intense than the spot in the chromatogram obtained with solution (3) (2%).

### Water
Not more than 10.0%, Appendix IX C. Use 0.4 g.

### ASSAY
Dissolve 0.1 g in sufficient *water* to produce 200 ml. Dilute 5 ml to 100 ml with *water* and measure the *absorbance* of the resulting solution at the maximum at 248 nm, Appendix II B. Calculate the content of $C_{21}H_{29}Na_2O_8P$ taking 333 as the value of A(1%, 1 cm) at the maximum at 248 nm.

### STORAGE
Hydrocortisone Sodium Phosphate should be protected from light.

# Hydroflumethiazide

$C_8H_8F_3N_3O_4S_2$        331.3        *135-09-1*

### Action and use
Thiazide diuretic.

### Preparation
Hydroflumethiazide Tablets

### DEFINITION
Hydroflumethiazide is 3,4-dihydro-6-trifluoromethyl-2*H*-1,2,4-benzothiadiazine-7sulphonamide 1,1-dioxide. It contains not less than 98.0% and not more than 102.0% of $C_8H_8F_3N_3O_4S_2$, calculated with reference to the dried substance.

### CHARACTERISTICS
White or almost white, glistening crystals or crystalline powder.

Practically insoluble in *water*; soluble in *ethanol (96%)*; practically insoluble in *ether*.

### IDENTIFICATION
A. The *infrared absorption spectrum*, Appendix II A, is concordant with the *reference spectrum* of hydroflumethiazide (RS 181).

B. Dissolve 10 mg in 10 ml of 0.1M *sodium hydroxide*, add sufficient *water* to produce 100 ml and dilute 10 ml to 50 ml with 0.01M *sodium hydroxide*. The *light absorption* of the resulting solution, Appendix II B, in the range 230 to 350 nm exhibits two maxima, at 274 nm and 333 nm. The *absorbance* at the maxima is about 0.92 and about 0.19 respectively.

C. Carry out the method for *thin-layer chromatography*, Appendix III A, using *silica gel GF₂₅₄* as the coating substance and *ethyl acetate* as the mobile phase. Apply separately to the plate 5 μl of each of two solutions in *acetone* containing (1) 0.1% w/v of the substance being examined and (2) 0.1% w/v of *hydroflumethiazide BPCRS*. After removal of the plate, dry it in a current of air, examine under *ultraviolet light (254 nm)* and then reveal the spots by

*Method I* and examine again. By each method of visualisation the principal spot in the chromatogram obtained with solution (1) corresponds in colour and intensity to that in the chromatogram obtained with solution (2).

## TESTS
### Related substances
Carry out the method for *thin-layer chromatography*, Appendix III A, using *silica gel G* as the coating substance and *ethyl acetate* as the mobile phase. Apply separately to the plate 10 µl of each of two solutions of the substance being examined in *acetone* containing (1) 1.0% w/v and (2) 0.010% w/v. After removal of the plate, dry it in a current of air and reveal the spots by *Method I*. Any *secondary spot* in the chromatogram obtained with solution (1) is not more intense than the spot in the chromatogram obtained with solution (2).

### Loss on drying
When dried to constant weight at 105°C, loses not more than 0.5% of its weight. Use 1 g.

### Sulphated ash
Not more than 0.1%, Appendix IX A.

## ASSAY
Dissolve 0.3 g in 50 ml of *anhydrous pyridine* and carry out Method II for *non-aqueous titration*, Appendix VIII A, using 0.1M *tetrabutylammonium hydroxide VS* as titrant and determining the end point potentiometrically. Each ml of 0.1M *tetrabutylammonium hydroxide VS* is equivalent to 16.56 mg of $C_8H_8F_3N_3O_4S_2$.

# Hydrogen Peroxide Solution (3 per cent)

Dilute Hydrogen Peroxide Solution
*(Ph Eur monograph 0395)*

### Action and use
Antiseptic; deodorant.

When hydrogen peroxide is prescribed or demanded, Hydrogen Peroxide Solution (6 per cent) shall be dispensed or supplied.

*Ph Eur* _____

## DEFINITION
### Content
2.5 per cent *m/m* to 3.5 per cent *m/m* of $H_2O_2$ ($M_r$ 34.01).

1 volume of hydrogen peroxide solution (3 per cent) corresponds to about 10 times its volume of oxygen. A suitable stabiliser may be added.

## CHARACTERS
### Appearance
Colourless, clear liquid.

## IDENTIFICATION
A. To 2 ml add 0.2 ml of *dilute sulphuric acid R* and 0.2 ml of *0.02 M potassium permanganate*. The solution becomes colourless or slightly pink within 2 min.

B. To 0.5 ml add 1 ml of *dilute sulphuric acid R*, 2 ml of *ether R* and 0.1 ml of *potassium chromate solution R* and shake. The ether layer is blue.

C. It complies with the requirement for the content of $H_2O_2$.

## TESTS
### Acidity
To 10 ml add 20 ml of *water R* and 0.25 ml of *methyl red solution R*. Not less than 0.05 ml and not more than 1.0 ml of *0.1 M sodium hydroxide* is required to change the colour of the indicator.

### Organic stabilisers
Maximum 250 ppm.

Shake 20 ml with 10 ml of *chloroform R* and then with 2 quantities, each of 5 ml, of *chloroform R*. Evaporate the combined chloroform layers under reduced pressure at a temperature not exceeding 25 °C and dry in a desiccator. The residue weighs a maximum of 5 mg.

### Non-volatile residue
Maximum 2 g/l.

Allow 10 ml to stand in a platinum dish until all effervescence has ceased. Evaporate to dryness on a water-bath and dry at 100-105 °C. The residue weighs a maximum of 20 mg.

## ASSAY
Dilute 10.0 g to 100.0 ml with *water R*. To 10.0 ml of this solution add 20 ml of *dilute sulphuric acid R*. Titrate with *0.02 M potassium permanganate* until a pink colour is obtained.

1 ml of *0.02 M potassium permanganate* is equivalent to 1.701 mg of $H_2O_2$ or 0.56 ml of oxygen.

## STORAGE
Protected from light, and if the solution does not contain a stabiliser, at a temperature below 15 °C.

## LABELLING
If the solution contains a stabiliser, the label states that the contents are stabilised. The competent authority may require that the name of the stabiliser be stated on the label.

## CAUTION
It decomposes in contact with oxidisable organic matter and with certain metals and if allowed to become alkaline.

_____ *Ph Eur*

# Hydrogen Peroxide Solution (6 per cent)

Hydrogen Peroxide Solution

### Action and use
Antiseptic; deodorant.

### Preparation
Hydrogen Peroxide Mouthwash

When hydrogen peroxide is prescribed or demanded, Hydrogen Peroxide Solution (6 per cent) shall be dispensed or supplied.

## DEFINITION
Hydrogen Peroxide Solution (6 per cent) is an aqueous solution of hydrogen peroxide containing not less than 5.0% w/v and not more than 7.0% w/v of $H_2O_2$ (34.01), corresponding to about 20 times its volume of available oxygen. It may contain a suitable stabilising agent.

## CHARACTERISTICS

A clear, colourless liquid. It decomposes in contact with oxidisable organic matter and with certain metals and if allowed to become alkaline.

## IDENTIFICATION

A. To 1 ml add 0.2 ml of 1M *sulphuric acid* and 0.25 ml of 0.02M *potassium permanganate*. The solution becomes colourless with evolution of gas.

B. Shake 0.05 ml with 2 ml of 1M *sulphuric acid*, 2 ml of *ether* and 0.05 ml of *potassium chromate solution*. The ether layer is blue.

C. Complies with the requirement for the content of $H_2O_2$.

## TESTS

### Acidity

Dilute 10 ml with 20 ml of *water* and add 0.25 ml of *methyl red solution*. Not less than 0.05 ml and not more than 1.0 ml of 0.1M *sodium hydroxide VS* is required to change the colour of the solution.

### Organic stabilisers

Shake 20 ml with successive quantities of 10, 5 and 5 ml of *chloroform*. Evaporate the combined chloroform extracts at a temperature not exceeding 25° at a pressure of 2 kPa and dry in a desiccator. Any residue weighs not more than 5 mg (250 ppm).

### Non-volatile matter

Place 10 ml in a platinum dish and allow to stand until effervescence has ceased, cooling if necessary. Evaporate the solution on a water bath. Any residue, when dried at 100°C to 105°C, weighs not more than 20 mg (0.2% w/v).

## ASSAY

Dilute 10 ml to 100 ml with *water*. To 10 ml of the resulting solution add 20 ml of 1M *sulphuric acid* and titrate with 0.02M *potassium permanganate VS*. Each ml of 0.02M *potassium permanganate VS* is equivalent to 1.701 mg of $H_2O_2$ or 0.56 ml of oxygen.

## STORAGE

Hydrogen Peroxide Solution (6 per cent) should be protected from light. If the solution does not contain a stabilising agent, it should be stored at a temperature not exceeding 15°C. It should not be stored for long periods.

## LABELLING

The label states, where applicable, that the solution contains a stabilising agent.

# Hydrogen Peroxide Solution (30 per cent)

*(Ph Eur monograph 0396)*

*7722-84-1*

## Action and use

Antiseptic; deodorant.

When hydrogen peroxide is prescribed or demanded, Hydrogen Peroxide Solution (6 per cent) shall be dispensed or supplied.

*Ph Eur*

## DEFINITION

### Content

29.0 per cent *m/m* to 31.0 per cent *m/m* of $H_2O_2$ ($M_r$ 34.01).

1 volume of hydrogen peroxyde solution (30 per cent) corresponds to about 110 times its volume of oxygen. A suitable stabiliser may be added.

## CHARACTERS

### Appearance

Colourless, clear liquid.

## IDENTIFICATION

A. To 1 ml add 0.2 ml of *dilute sulphuric acid R* and 0.25 ml of *0.02 M potassium permanganate*. The solution becomes colourless with evolution of gas.

B. To 0.05 ml add 2 ml of *dilute sulphuric acid R*, 2 ml of *ether R* and 0.05 ml of *potassium chromate solution R* and shake. The ether layer is blue.

C. It complies with the requirement for the content of $H_2O_2$.

## TESTS

### Acidity

To 10 ml add 100 ml of *water R* and 0.25 ml of *methyl red solution R*. Not less than 0.05 ml and not more than 0.5 ml of *0.1 M sodium hydroxide* is required to change the colour of the indicator.

### Organic stabilisers

Maximum 500 ppm.

Shake 20 ml with 10 ml of *chloroform R* and then with 2 quantities, each of 5 ml, of *chloroform R*. Evaporate the combined chloroform layers under reduced pressure at a temperature not exceeding 25 °C and dry in a desiccator. The residue weighs a maximum of 10 mg.

### Non-volatile residue

Maximum 2 g/l.

Allow 10 ml to stand in a platinum dish until all effervescence has ceased, cooling if necessary. Evaporate to dryness on a water-bath and dry at 100-105 °C. The residue weighs a maximum of 20 mg.

## ASSAY

Dilute 1.00 g to 100.0 ml with *water R*. To 10.0 ml of this solution add 20 ml of *dilute sulphuric acid R*. Titrate with *0.02 M potassium permanganate* until a pink colour is obtained.

1 ml of *0.02 M potassium permanganate* is equivalent to 1.701 mg of $H_2O_2$ or 0.56 ml of oxygen.

## STORAGE

Protected from light, and if the solution does not contain a stabiliser, at a temperature below 15 °C.

## LABELLING

If the solution contains a stabiliser, the label states that the contents are stabilised. The competent authority may require that the name of the stabiliser be stated on the label.

## CAUTION

It decomposes vigorously in contact with oxidisable organic matter and with certain metals and if allowed to become alkaline.

*Ph Eur*

# Hydromorphone Hydrochloride

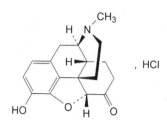

(Ph Eur monograph 2099)

$C_{17}H_{19}NO_3,HCl$    321.8    71-68-1

## Action and use
Opioid receptor agonist; analgesic.

*Ph Eur*

## DEFINITION
4,5α-Epoxy-3-hydroxy-17-methylmorphinan-6-one hydrochloride.

## Content
99.0 per cent to 101.0 per cent (dried substance).

## CHARACTERS
### Appearance
White or almost white, crystalline powder.

### Solubility
Freely soluble in water, very slightly soluble in ethanol (96 per cent), practically insoluble in methylene chloride.

## IDENTIFICATION
A. Infrared absorption spectrophotometry (2.2.24).

*Comparison*    hydromorphone hydrochloride CRS.

B. It gives reaction (a) of chlorides (2.3.1).

## TESTS
### Solution S
Dissolve 1.250 g in *carbon dioxide-free water R* and dilute to 25.0 ml with the same solvent.

### Appearance of solution
Solution S is clear (2.2.1) and not more intensely coloured than reference solution $BY_5$ (2.2.2, Method II).

### Acidity or alkalinity
To 2 ml of solution S add 0.1 ml of *methyl red solution R*. The solution is not yellow. To 2 ml of solution S add 0.05 ml of *bromocresol green solution R*. The solution is not yellow.

### Specific optical rotation (2.2.7)
− 136 to − 140 (dried substance), determined on solution S.

### Related substances
Liquid chromatography (2.2.29).

*Test solution*    Dissolve 0.100 g of the substance to be examined in *water R*, sonicating if necessary and dilute to 100.0 ml with the same solvent.

*Reference solution (a)*    Dilute 1.0 ml of the test solution to 100.0 ml with *water R*. Dilute 1.0 ml of this solution to 10.0 ml with *water R*.

*Reference solution (b)*    To 5 ml of the test solution add 5 mg of *naloxone hydrochloride dihydrate CRS* and dilute to 50 ml with *water R*.

*Column:*
— *size: l* = 0.25 m, Ø = 4.6 mm,

— *stationary phase: base-deactivated end-capped octadecylsilyl silica gel for chromatography R* (5 μm).

*Mobile phase*    Dissolve 18.29 g of *diethylamine R* and 2.88 g of *sodium laurilsulfate R* in *water R* and dilute to 1000 ml with the same solvent. Adjust 800 ml of this solution to pH 3.0 with *phosphoric acid R*. Add 100 ml of *acetonitrile R* and 100 ml of *methanol R*.

*Flow rate*    1 ml/min.

*Detection*    Spectrophotometer at 284 nm.

*Injection*    20 μl.

*Run time*    4 times the retention time of hydromorphone.

*Relative retention* with reference to hydromorphone (retention time = about 9 min): impurity D = about 0.72; impurity B = about 0.77; impurity C = about 0.82; impurity A = about 3.2.

*System suitability*    Reference solution (b):
— *resolution*: minimum 4.0 between the peaks due to hydromorphone and naloxone.

*Limits:*
— *impurity A*: not more than 3 times the area of the principal peak in the chromatogram obtained with reference solution (a) (0.3 per cent),
— *impurities B, C, D*: for each impurity, not more than twice the area of the principal peak in the chromatogram obtained with reference solution (a) (0.2 per cent),
— *any other impurity*: for each impurity, not more than the area of the principal peak in the chromatogram obtained with reference solution (a) (0.1 per cent),
— *total*: not more than 5 times the area of the principal peak in the chromatogram obtained with reference solution (a) (0.5 per cent),
— *disregard limit*: 0.5 times the area of the principal peak in the chromatogram obtained with reference solution (a) (0.05 per cent).

### Loss on drying (2.2.32)
Maximum 0.5 per cent, determined on 1.000 g by drying in an oven at 105 °C.

### Sulphated ash (2.4.14)
Maximum 0.1 per cent, determined on the residue obtained in the test for loss on drying.

## ASSAY
Dissolve 0.250 g in 50 ml of *ethanol (96 per cent) R* and add 5.0 ml of *0.01 M hydrochloric acid*. Carry out a potentiometric titration (2.2.20), using *0.1 M sodium hydroxide*. Read the volume added between the 2 points of inflexion.

1 ml of *0.1 M sodium hydroxide* is equivalent to 32.18 mg of $C_{17}H_{20}ClNO_3$.

## STORAGE
Protected from light.

## IMPURITIES
*Specified impurities*    *A, B, C, D.*

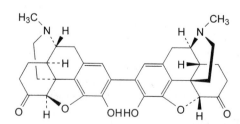

A. 4,5α:4′,5′α-diepoxy-3,3′-dihydroxy-17,17′-dimethyl-2,2′-bimorphinanyl-6,6′-dione (pseudohydromorphone),

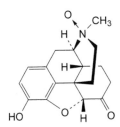

B. 4,5α-epoxy-3-hydroxy-17-methylmorphinan-6-one 17-oxide (hydromorphone *N*-oxide),

C. morphine,

D. 4,5α-epoxy-17-methylmorphinan-3,6α-diol (dihydromorphine).

*Ph Eur*

# Hydrotalcite

Mg$_6$Al$_2$(OH)$_{16}$CO$_3$,4H$_2$O        604.0        *12304-65-3*

## Action and use
Antacid.

## Preparation
Hydrotalcite Tablets

## DEFINITION
Hydrotalcite is a hydrated form of an aluminium magnesium basic carbonate corresponding to the formula Mg$_6$Al$_2$(OH)$_{16}$CO$_3$,4H$_2$O. It contains not less than 15.3% and not more than 18.7% of Al$_2$O$_3$ and not less than 36.0% and not more than 44.0% of MgO. The ratio of the content of Al$_2$O$_3$ to the content of MgO is not less than 0.40 and not more than 0.45.

## CHARACTERISTICS
A white or almost white, free-flowing, granular powder.

Practically insoluble in *water*. It dissolves in dilute mineral acids with slight effervescence.

## IDENTIFICATION
A. Dissolve 1.0 g in 20 ml of 2M *hydrochloric acid*. Effervescence occurs. Add 30 ml of *water*, boil, add 2M *ammonia* until just alkaline to *methyl red solution*, continue boiling for 2 minutes and filter, reserving the filtrate for test B. Wash the precipitate with 50 ml of a hot 2% w/v solution of *ammonium chloride* and dissolve in 15 ml of 2M *hydrochloric acid*. The resulting solution yields the reaction characteristic of *aluminium salts*, Appendix VI.

B. Dilute 1 ml of the filtrate obtained in test A to 10 ml with *water*. The resulting solution yields the reactions characteristic of *magnesium salts*, Appendix VI.

## TESTS
### Alkalinity
pH of a 4% w/v suspension in *carbon dioxide-free water*, 8.0 to 10.0, Appendix V L.

### Neutralising capacity
Mix 0.2 g with a small quantity of *water* to give a smooth paste and gradually add sufficient further quantities of *water* to produce 100 ml. Warm at 37°, add 100 ml of 0.1M *hydrochloric acid VS* previously heated to 37° and stir continuously for 1 hour using a paddle stirrer at a rate of about 200 revolutions per minute, maintaining the temperature at 37°, and titrate with 0.1M *sodium hydroxide VS* to pH 3.5. Subtract the volume of 0.1M *sodium hydroxide VS* from 100 ml to obtain the number of ml of 0.1M *hydrochloric acid VS* required for neutralisation. Not less than 260 ml of 0.1M *hydrochloric acid VS* is required to neutralise 1 g.

### Arsenic
Dissolve 0.33 g in 5 ml of 2M *hydrochloric acid*. The resulting solution complies with the *limit test for arsenic*, Appendix VII (3 ppm).

### Heavy metals
Dissolve 2.7 g in 20 ml of 5M *hydrochloric acid* and 10 ml of *water*, add 0.5 ml of *nitric acid* and boil for 30 seconds. Cool, add 2 g of *ammonium chloride* and 2 g of *ammonium thiocyanate* and extract with three 10 ml quantities of a mixture of equal volumes of *isoamyl alcohol* and *ether*. Add to the aqueous layer 0.1 ml of *phenolphthalein solution* and 13.5M *ammonia* until a pink colour is produced. Cool, add *glacial acetic acid* until the solution is decolorised and add a further 5 ml of *glacial acetic acid*. Filter, if necessary, and dilute the solution to 40 ml with *water*. 12 ml of the resulting solution complies with *limit test A for heavy metals*, Appendix VII. Use *lead standard solution (2 ppm Pb)* to prepare the standard (30 ppm).

### Sodium
Not more than 0.1% of Na when determined by Method II for *atomic emission spectrophotometry*, Appendix II D, measuring at 589 nm. To prepare the test solution dissolve 0.1 g in 4 ml of 5M *hydrochloric acid*, dilute to 200 ml with *water* and use *sodium standard solution (200 ppm Na)*, diluted if necessary with 0.1M *hydrochloric acid*, to prepare the standard solutions.

### Chloride
Dissolve 0.18 g in 10 ml of 2M *nitric acid*, boil, allow to cool and dilute to 100 ml with *water*. To 10 ml add 5 ml of *water*. The resulting solution complies with the *limit test for chlorides*, Appendix VII (0.3%).

### Sulphate
Dissolve 0.14 g in 15 ml of 1M *hydrochloric acid* and dilute to 100 ml with *water*. 15 ml of the resulting solution complies with the *limit test for sulphates*, Appendix VII (0.7%).

### Loss on ignition
When ignited at 800°, loses 40.0 to 50.0% of its weight. Use 1 g.

## ASSAY
### For Al$_2$O$_3$
Dissolve 0.3 g in 2 ml of 7M *hydrochloric acid*, add 250 ml of *water* and 50 ml of 0.05M *disodium edetate VS* and neutralise with 1M *sodium hydroxide* using *methyl red solution* as indicator. Heat the solution on a water bath for 30 minutes and allow to cool. Add 3 g of *hexamine* and titrate the excess of disodium edetate with 0.05M *lead nitrate VS* using *xylenol orange solution* as indicator. Each ml of 0.05M *disodium edetate VS* is equivalent to 2.549 mg of Al$_2$O$_3$.

### For MgO
Dissolve 0.125 g in the minimum volume of 7M *hydrochloric acid*, add 30 ml of *water*, 1 g of *ammonium chloride*, 10 ml of *triethanolamine*, 150 ml of *water* and 5 ml of *ammonia buffer*

pH 10.9 and titrate immediately with 0.05M *disodium edetate VS* using *mordant black 11 solution* as indicator. Each ml of 0.05M *disodium edetate VS* is equivalent to 2.015 mg of MgO.

# Hydroxocobalamin Acetate

(Ph Eur monograph 0913)

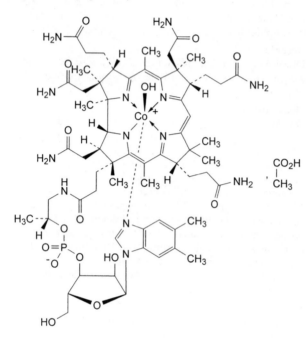

C$_{62}$H$_{89}$CoN$_{13}$O$_{15}$P,C$_2$H$_4$O$_2$   1406          22465-48-1

## Action and use
Vitamin B$_{12}$ analogue.

## Preparation
Hydroxocobalamin Injection

*Ph Eur* _____

## DEFINITION
Coα-[α-(5,6-dimethylbenzimidazolyl)]-Coβ-hydroxocobamide acetate.

## Content
96.0 per cent to 102.0 per cent (dried substance).

This monograph applies to hydroxocobalamin acetate produced by fermentation.

## CHARACTERS
### Appearance
Dark red, crystalline powder or dark red crystals, very hygroscopic.

### Solubility
Soluble in water.

Some decomposition may occur on drying.

## IDENTIFICATION
A. Ultraviolet and visible absorption spectrophotometry (2.2.25).

*Test solution*   Dissolve 2.5 mg in a solution containing 0.8 per cent *V/V* of *glacial acetic acid R* and 10.9 g/l of *sodium acetate R*, then dilute to 100 ml with the same solution.

*Spectral range*   260-610 nm.

*Absorption maxima*   At 274 nm, 351 nm and 525 nm.

*Absorbance ratio:*
— $A_{274}/A_{351}$ = 0.75 to 0.83;
— $A_{525}/A_{351}$ = 0.31 to 0.35.

B. Thin-layer chromatography (2.2.27). *Carry out the test protected from light.*

*Test solution*   Dissolve 2 mg of the substance to be examined in 1 ml of a mixture of equal volumes of *ethanol 96 per cent R* and *water R*.

*Reference solution*   Dissolve 2 mg of *hydroxocobalamin CRS* in 1 ml of a mixture of equal volumes of *ethanol 96 per cent R* and *water R*.

*Plate*   TLC silica gel G plate R.

*Mobile phase*   Dilute ammonia R1, methanol R (25:75 V/V).

*Application*   10 µl.

*Development*   In an unlined tank, over a path of 12 cm.

*Drying*   In air.

*Detection*   Examine in daylight.

*Results*   The principal spot in the chromatogram obtained with the test solution is similar in position, colour and size to the principal spot in the chromatogram obtained with the reference solution.

C. It gives reaction (a) of acetates (2.3.1).

## TESTS
### Related substances
Liquid chromatography (2.2.29). *Use freshly prepared solutions and protect them from bright light.*

*Test solution*   Dissolve 10.0 mg of the substance to be examined in the mobile phase and dilute to 10.0 ml with the mobile phase.

*Reference solution (a)*   Dilute 5.0 ml of the test solution to 100.0 ml with the mobile phase.

*Reference solution (b)*   Dilute 1.0 ml of the test solution to 10.0 ml with the mobile phase. Dilute 1.0 ml of this solution to 100.0 ml with the mobile phase.

*Reference solution (c)*   Dissolve 25 mg of the substance to be examined in 10 ml of *water R*, warming if necessary. Allow to cool and add 1 ml of a 20 g/l solution of *chloramine R* and 0.5 ml of *0.05 M hydrochloric acid*. Dilute this solution to 25 ml with *water R*. Shake and allow to stand for 5 min. Inject immediately.

*Column:*
— size: l = 0.25 m, Ø = 4 mm;
— stationary phase: octylsilyl silica gel for chromatography R (5 µm).

*Mobile phase*   Mix 19.5 volumes of *methanol R* and 80.5 volumes of a solution containing 15 g/l of *citric acid R* and 8.1 g/l of *disodium hydrogen phosphate R*.

*Flow rate*   1.5 ml/min.

*Detection*   Spectrophotometer at 351 nm.

*Injection*   20 µl.

*Run time*   4 times the retention time of hydroxocobalamine.

*System suitability:*
— the chromatogram obtained with reference solution (c) shows 3 principal peaks;
— resolution: minimum 3.0 between each pair of adjacent peaks in the chromatogram obtained with reference solution (c);
— signal-to-noise ratio: minimum 5 for the principal peak in the chromatogram obtained with reference solution (b).

*Limits:*
— *total*: not more than the area of the principal peak in the chromatogram obtained with reference solution (a) (5 per cent);
— *disregard limit*: the area of the principal peak in the chromatogram obtained with reference solution (b) (0.1 per cent).

## Loss on drying (2.2.32)

8.0 per cent to 12.0 per cent, determined on 0.400 g by drying at 105 °C at a pressure not exceeding 0.7 kPa.

## ASSAY

*Protect the solutions from light throughout the assay.* Dissolve 25.0 mg in a solution containing 0.8 per cent *V/V* of *glacial acetic acid R* and 10.9 g/l of *sodium acetate R*, then dilute to 1000.0 ml with the same solution. Measure the absorbance (*2.2.25*) at the absorption maximum at 351 nm.

Calculate the content of $C_{64}H_{93}CoN_{13}O_{17}P$ taking the specific absorbance to be 187.

## STORAGE

In an airtight container, protected from light, at a temperature of 2 °C to 8 °C.

*Ph Eur*

# Hydroxocobalamin Chloride

*(Ph Eur monograph 0914)*

$C_{62}H_{89}CoN_{13}O_{15}P,HCl$     1383     *58288-50-9*

## Action and use

Vitamin $B_{12}$ analogue.

## Preparation

Hydroxocobalamin Injection

*Ph Eur*

## DEFINITION

Coα-[α-(5,6-dimethylbenzimidazolyl)]-Coβ-hydroxocobamide chloride.

Fermentation product.

## Content

96.0 per cent to 102.0 per cent (dried substance).

## CHARACTERS

### Appearance

Dark red crystalline powder or dark red crystals, very hygroscopic.

### Solubility

Soluble in water.

Some decomposition may occur on drying.

## IDENTIFICATION

A. Ultraviolet and visible absorption spectrophotometry (*2.2.25*).

*Test solution* Dissolve 2.5 mg in a solution containing 0.8 per cent *V/V* of *glacial acetic acid R* and 10.9 g/l of *sodium acetate R*, then dilute to 100 ml with the same solution.

*Spectral range* 260-610 nm.

*Absorption maxima* At 274 nm, 351 nm and 525 nm.

*Absorbance ratio:*
— $A_{274}/A_{351} = 0.75$ to 0.83;
— $A_{525}/A_{351} = 0.31$ to 0.35.

B. Thin-layer chromatography (*2.2.27*). *Carry out the identification test protected from light.*

*Test solution* Dissolve 2 mg of the substance to be examined in 1 ml of a mixture of equal volumes of *ethanol 96 per cent R* and *water R*.

*Reference solution* Dissolve 2 mg of *hydroxocobalamin CRS* in 1 ml of a mixture of equal volumes of *ethanol 96 per cent R* and *water R*.

*Plate* TLC silica gel G plate R.

*Mobile phase* dilute ammonia R1, methanol R (25:75 *V/V*).

*Application* 10 μl.

*Development* In an unlined tank, over a path of 12 cm.

*Drying* In air.

*Detection* Examine in daylight.

*Results* The principal spot in the chromatogram obtained with the test solution is similar in position, colour and size to the principal spot in the chromatogram obtained with the reference solution.

C. It gives reaction (a) of chlorides (*2.3.1*).

## TESTS

### Related substances

Liquid chromatography (*2.2.29*). *Use freshly prepared solutions and protect them from bright light.*

*Test solution* Dissolve 10.0 mg of the substance to be examined in the mobile phase and dilute to 10.0 ml with the mobile phase.

*Reference solution (a)* Dilute 5.0 ml of the test solution to 100.0 ml with the mobile phase.

*Reference solution (b)* Dilute 1.0 ml of the test solution to 10.0 ml with the mobile phase. Dilute 1.0 ml of this solution to 100.0 ml with the mobile phase.

*Reference solution (c)* Dissolve 25 mg of the substance to be examined in 10 ml of *water R*, warming if necessary. Allow to cool and add 1 ml of a 20 g/l solution of *chloramine R* and 0.5 ml of *0.05 M hydrochloric acid*. Dilute to 25 ml with *water R*. Shake and allow to stand for 5 min. Inject immediately.

*Column:*
— *size*: l = 0.25 m, Ø = 4 mm;
— *stationary phase*: octylsilyl silica gel for chromatography R (5 μm).

*Mobile phase* Mix 19.5 volumes of *methanol R* and 80.5 volumes of a solution containing 15 g/l of *citric acid R* and 8.1 g/l of *disodium hydrogen phosphate R*.

*Flow rate* 1.5 ml/min.

*Detection* Spectrophotometer at 351 nm.

*Injection* 20 μl.

*Run time* 4 times the retention time of hydroxocobalamin.

*System suitability:*
— the chromatogram obtained with reference solution (c) shows 3 principal peaks;
— *resolution*: minimum 3.0 between each pair of adjacent peaks in the chromatogram obtained with reference solution (c);
— *signal-to-noise ratio*: minimum 5 for the principal peak in the chromatogram obtained with reference solution (b).

*Limits:*
— *total*: not more than the area of the principal peak in the chromatogram obtained with reference solution (a) (5.0 per cent);
— *disregard limit*: the area of the principal peak in the chromatogram obtained with reference solution (b) (0.1 per cent).

**Loss on drying** (*2.2.32*)
8.0 per cent to 12.0 per cent, determined on 0.400 g by drying at 105 °C at a pressure not exceeding 0.7 kPa.

**ASSAY**

*Protect the solutions from light throughout the assay.*

Dissolve 25.0 mg in a solution containing 0.8 per cent *V/V* of *glacial acetic acid R* and 10.9 g/l of *sodium acetate R*, then dilute to 1000.0 ml with the same solution. Measure the absorbance (*2.2.25*) at the absorption maximum at 351 nm.

Calculate the content of $C_{62}H_{90}ClCoN_{13}O_{15}P$ taking the specific absorbance to be 190.

**STORAGE**

In an airtight container protected from light, at a temperature of 2 °C to 8 °C.

———————————————— *Ph Eur*

# Hydroxocobalamin Sulphate

(*Ph Eur monograph 0915*)

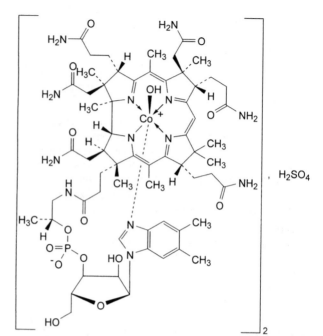

$(C_{62}H_{89}CoN_{13}O_{15}P)_2,H_2SO_4$    2791

**Action and use**
Vitamin $B_{12}$ analogue.

**Preparation**
Hydroxocobalamin Injection

*Ph Eur* ————————————————

**DEFINITION**
Di-(Coα-[α-(5,6-dimethylbenzimidazolyl)]-Coβ-hydroxocobamide) sulphate.

Fermentation product.

**Content**
96.0 per cent to 102.0 per cent (dried substance).

**CHARACTERS**

**Appearance**
Dark red crystalline powder or dark red crystals, very hygroscopic.

**Solubility**
Soluble in water.

Some decomposition may occur on drying.

**IDENTIFICATION**

A. Ultraviolet and visible absorption spectrophotometry (*2.2.25*).

*Test solution* Dissolve 2.5 mg in a solution containing 0.8 per cent *V/V* of *glacial acetic acid R* and 10.9 g/l of *sodium acetate R*, then dilute to 100 ml with the same solution.

*Spectral range* 260-610 nm.

*Absorption maxima* At 274 nm, 351 nm and 525 nm.

*Absorbance ratios:*
— $A_{274}/A_{351} = 0.75$ to 0.83;
— $A_{525}/A_{351} = 0.31$ to 0.35.

B. Thin-layer chromatography (*2.2.27*). *Carry out the test protected from light.*

*Test solution* Dissolve 2 mg of the substance to be examined in 1 ml of a mixture of equal volumes of *ethanol 96 per cent R* and *water R*.

*Reference solution* Dissolve 2 mg of *hydroxocobalamin CRS* in 1 ml of a mixture of equal volumes of *ethanol 96 per cent R* and *water R*.

*Plate* TLC silica gel G plate R.

*Mobile phase* dilute ammonia R1, methanol R (25:75 *V/V*).

*Application* 10 μl.

*Development* In an unlined tank, over a path of 12 cm.

*Drying* In air.

*Detection* Examine in daylight.

*Results* The principal spot in the chromatogram obtained with the test solution is similar in position, colour and size to the principal spot in the chromatogram obtained with the reference solution.

C. It gives reaction (a) of sulphates (*2.3.1*).

## TESTS
**Related substances**
Liquid chromatography (*2.2.29*). *Use freshly prepared solutions and protect them from bright light.*

*Test solution* Dissolve 10.0 mg of the substance to be examined in the mobile phase and dilute to 10.0 ml with the mobile phase.

*Reference solution (a)* Dilute 5.0 ml of the test solution to 100.0 ml with the mobile phase.

*Reference solution (b)* Dilute 1.0 ml of the test solution to 10.0 ml with the mobile phase. Dilute 1.0 ml of this solution to 100.0 ml with the mobile phase.

*Reference solution (c)* Dissolve 25 mg of the substance to be examined in 10 ml of *water R*, warming if necessary. Allow to cool and add 1 ml of a 20 g/l solution of *chloramine R* and 0.5 ml of *0.05 M hydrochloric acid*. Dilute to 25 ml with *water R*. Shake and allow to stand for 5 min. Inject immediately.

*Column:*
— *size: l* = 0.25 m, Ø = 4 mm;
— *stationary phase: octylsilyl silica gel for chromatography R* (5 μm).

*Mobile phase* Mix 19.5 volumes of *methanol R* and 80.5 volumes of a solution containing 15 g/l of *citric acid R* and 8.1 g/l of *disodium hydrogen phosphate R*.

*Flow rate* 1.5 ml/min.

*Detection* Spectrophotometer at 351 nm.

*Injection* 20 μl.

*Run time* 4 times the retention time of hydroxocobalamin.

*System suitability:*
— the chromatogram obtained with reference solution (c) shows 3 principal peaks;
— *resolution*: minimum 3.0 between each pair of adjacent peaks in the chromatogram obtained with reference solution (c);
— *signal-to-noise ratio*: minimum 5 for the principal peak in the chromatogram obtained with reference solution (b).

*Limits:*
— *total*: not more than the area of the principal peak in the chromatogram obtained with reference solution (a) (5.0 per cent);
— *disregard limit*: the area of the principal peak in the chromatogram obtained with reference solution (b) (0.1 per cent).

**Loss on drying** (*2.2.32*)
8.0 per cent to 16.0 per cent, determined on 0.400 g by drying at 105 °C at a pressure not exceeding 0.7 kPa.

## ASSAY
*Protect the solutions from light throughout the assay.*

Dissolve 25.0 mg in a solution containing 0.8 per cent *V/V* of *glacial acetic acid R* and 10.9 g/l of *sodium acetate R* and dilute to 1000.0 ml with the same solution. Measure the absorbance (*2.2.25*) at the absorption maximum at 351 nm.

Calculate the content of $C_{124}H_{180}Co_2N_{26}O_{34}P_2S$ taking the specific absorbance to be 188.

## STORAGE
In an airtight container protected from light, at a temperature of 2 °C to 8 °C.

*Ph Eur*

# Hydroxycarbamide

(*Ph Eur monograph 1616*)

CH$_4$N$_2$O$_2$        76.05        *127-07-1*

**Action and use**
Cytotoxic alkylating drug.

**Preparation**
Hydroxycarbamide Capsules

*Ph Eur*

## DEFINITION
*N*-Hydroxyurea.

**Content**
97.5 per cent to 102.0 per cent (anhydrous substance).

## CHARACTERS
**Appearance**
White or almost white, crystalline powder, hygroscopic.

**Solubility**
Freely soluble in water, practically insoluble in alcohol.

It shows polymorphism (*5.9*).

## IDENTIFICATION
A. Infrared absorption spectrophotometry (*2.2.24*).

*Comparison* hydroxycarbamide CRS.

If the spectra obtained in the solid state show differences dissolve the substance to be examined and the reference substance separately in *alcohol R*, evaporate to dryness and record new spectra using the residues.

B. Examine the chromatograms obtained in the test for urea.

*Results* The principal spot in the chromatogram obtained with the test solution is similar in position and size to the principal spot in the chromatogram obtained with reference solution (c).

## TESTS
**Urea**
Thin-layer chromatography (*2.2.27*).

*Test solution* Dissolve 50 mg of the substance to be examined in *water R* and dilute to 1.0 ml with the same solvent.

*Reference solution (a)* Dissolve 12.5 mg of *urea R* in *water R* and dilute to 50 ml with the same solvent.

*Reference solution (b)* Dissolve 5 mg of the substance to be examined and 5 mg of *urea R* in *water R* and dilute to 20 ml with the same solvent.

*Reference solution (c)* Dissolve 50 mg of *hydroxycarbamide CRS* in *water R* and dilute to 1 ml with the same solvent.

*Plate* TLC silica gel plate R.

*Mobile phase* pyridine R, water R, ethyl acetate R (2:2:10 *V/V/V*).

*Application* 10 μl.

*Development* Over 2/3 of the plate.

*Drying* In air.

*Detection* Spray with a 10 g/l solution of *dimethylaminobenzaldehyde R* in *1 M hydrochloric acid*.

*System suitability* The test is not valid unless the chromatogram obtained with reference solution (b) shows 2 clearly separated spots.

*Limit:*

— *urea*: any spot corresponding to urea in the chromatogram obtained with the test solution is not more intense than the spot in the chromatogram obtained with the reference solution (a) (0.5 per cent).

**Related substances**

Liquid chromatography (2.2.29).

*Test solution (a)* Dissolve 0.100 g of the substance to be examined in the mobile phase and dilute to 10.0 ml with the same mobile phase.

*Test solution (b)* Dilute 5.0 ml of test solution (a) to 50.0 ml with the mobile phase.

*Reference solution (a)* Dissolve 0.100 g of *hydroxylamine hydrochloride R* and 5 mg of the substance to be examined in the mobile phase and dilute to 10.0 ml with the mobile phase. Prepare immediately before use.

*Reference solution (b)* Dilute 0.1 ml of test solution (a) to 100.0 ml with the mobile phase.

*Reference solution (c)* Dissolve 0.100 g of *hydroxycarbamide CRS* in the mobile phase and dilute to 10.0 ml with the same solvent. Dilute 5.0 ml to 50.0 ml with the mobile phase.

*Column:*
— *size:* $l$ = 0.25 m, Ø = 4.6 mm,
— *stationary phase:* octadecylsilyl silica gel for chromatography R (5 μm).

*Mobile phase* methanol R, water R (5:95 *V/V*).

*Flow rate* 0.5 ml/min.

*Detection* Spectrophotometer at 214 nm.

*Injection* 20 μl; inject test solution (a) and reference solutions (a) and (b).

*Run time* 3 times the retention time of hydroxycarbamide which is about 5 min.

*System suitability* Reference solution (a):
— *resolution:* minimum of 1.0 between the peaks due to impurity A and to hydroxycarbamide.

*Limits:*
— *any impurity*: not more than the area of the principal peak in the chromatogram obtained with reference solution (b) (0.1 per cent),
— *total*: not more than 2 times the area of the principal peak in the chromatogram obtained with reference solution (b) (0.2 per cent),
— *disregard limit*: 0.2 times the area of the principal peak in the chromatogram obtained with reference solution (b) (0.02 per cent).

**Chlorides** (2.4.4)

Maximum 50 ppm.

Dissolve 1.0 g in *water R* and dilute to 15 ml with the same solvent. The solution complies with the limit test for chlorides.

**Heavy metals** (2.4.8)

Maximum 10 ppm.

Dissolve 2.0 g in *water R* and dilute to 20 ml with the same solvent. 12 ml of the solution complies with limit test A. Prepare the standard using *lead standard solution (1 ppm Pb) R*.

**Water** (2.5.12)

Maximum 0.5 per cent, determined on 2.00 g.

**Sulphated ash** (2.4.14)

Maximum 0.1 per cent, determined on 1.0 g.

**ASSAY**

Liquid chromatography (2.2.29) as described in the test for related substances.

*Injection* Test solution (b) and reference solution (c).

**STORAGE**

In an airtight container, protected from light.

**IMPURITIES**

A. $H_2N$-OH: hydroxylamine.

_____ *Ph Eur*

# Hydroxychloroquine Sulphate

and enantiomer

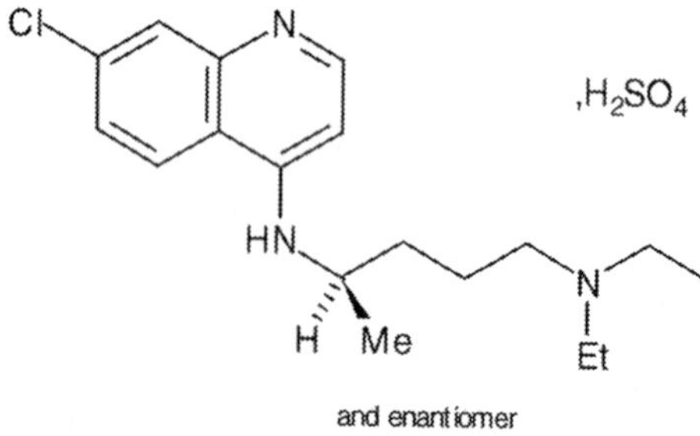

$C_{18}H_{26}ClN_3O,H_2SO_4$       434.0       *747-36-4*

**Action and use**

Antiprotozoal (malaria).

**Preparation**

Hydroxychloroquine Tablets

**DEFINITION**

Hydroxychloroquine Sulphate is (*RS*)-2-*N*-[4-(7-chloro-4-quinolylamino)pentyl]-*N*-ethylaminoethanol sulphate. It contains not less than 98.0% and not more than 100.5% of

$C_{18}H_{26}ClN_3O,H_2SO_4$, calculated with reference to the dried substance.

## CHARACTERISTICS

A white or almost white, crystalline powder.

Freely soluble in *water*; practically insoluble in *ethanol (96%)* and in *ether*.

## IDENTIFICATION

A. Dissolve 0.1 g in 10 ml of *water*, add 2 ml of 2M *sodium hydroxide* and extract with two 20 ml quantities of *dichloromethane*. Wash the dichloromethane extracts with *water*, dry with *anhydrous sodium sulphate*, evaporate to dryness and dissolve the residue in 2 ml of *dichloromethane*. The *infrared absorption spectrum* of the resulting solution, Appendix II A, is concordant with the *reference spectrum* of hydroxychloroquine *(RS 182)*.

B. Yields the reactions characteristic of *sulphates*, Appendix VI.

## TESTS

### Acidity

pH of a 1% w/v solution, 3.5 to 5.5, Appendix V L.

### Clarity and colour of solution

A 10.0% w/v solution is not more than slightly turbid and not more than slightly yellow.

### Lead

Not more than 20 ppm when determined by the following method. Carefully heat 2.0 g for 10 minutes with 8 ml of *water* and 6 ml of *nitric acid* in a Kjeldahl flask. Cool, add 4 ml of *sulphuric acid* and heat until the mixture darkens. Continue heating, with the dropwise addition of *nitric acid*, until the liquid becomes colourless and white fumes of sulphur trioxide are produced. Add 3 ml of *water*, carefully evaporate until white fumes are again produced, cool and dilute to 18 ml with *water*. Add and dissolve 2 g of *citric acid*, make alkaline with 5M *ammonia* and add 1 ml of *potassium cyanide solution PbT*. Transfer to a separating funnel, add 10 ml of *dithizone solution*, shake vigorously and remove the lower layer. Repeat the extraction with two 5 ml quantities of *dithizone solution*. If, after the third extraction, the dichloromethane layer is bright red, continue the extraction with further 5 ml quantities of *dithizone solution* until the colour of the reagent no longer changes to bright red. Wash the combined dichloromethane solutions by shaking with 10 ml of *water* and then extract with two 10 ml quantities of 2M *hydrochloric acid*. Wash the combined acid solutions with 10 ml of *dichloromethane* and discard the dichloromethane. Transfer the solution to a *Nessler cylinder* and make alkaline with 5M *ammonia*. In a second *Nessler cylinder* mix 2 ml of 6M *acetic acid* with 20 ml of 2M *hydrochloric acid*, make alkaline with 5M *ammonia* and add 4 ml of *lead standard solution (10 ppm Pb)*.

Treat the contents of each cylinder as follows. Add 1 ml of *potassium cyanide solution PbT*; the solutions should not be more than faintly opalescent. If the colours of the solutions differ, equalise them by the addition of a few drops of a highly diluted solution of burnt sugar or other non-reactive substance. Dilute to 50 ml with *water*, add 0.1 ml of a solution prepared by dissolving 10 g of *sodium sulphide* in sufficient *water* to produce 100 ml and filtering and mix thoroughly. Compare the colours of the two solutions by a suitable method, such as by light reflected from a white tile through the Nessler cylinders. The colour of the solution in the first cylinder is not more intense than that of the solution in the second cylinder.

### Chloride

Dissolve 0.50 g in 50 ml of *water*. 15 ml of the resulting solution complies with the *limit test for chlorides*, Appendix VII (350 ppm).

### Related substances

Carry out the method for *thin-layer chromatography*, Appendix III A, using the following solutions of the substance being examined in *water*.

(1) 5.0% w/v.

(2) 0.050% w/v.

(3) 0.025% w/v.

CHROMATOGRAPHIC CONDITIONS

(a) Use as the coating *silica gel $F_{254}$*.

(b) Use the mobile phase described below.

(c) Apply 2 µl of each solution.

(d) Develop the plate to 15 cm.

(e) After removal of the plate, dry in air and examine under *ultraviolet light (254 nm)*.

*MOBILE PHASE*

3 volumes of 13.5M *ammonia*, 25 volumes of *water* and 72 volumes of *methanol*.

LIMITS

In the chromatogram obtained with solution (1):
— any *secondary spot* is not more intense than the spot in the chromatogram obtained with solution (2) (1%);
— not more than one such spot is more intense than the spot in the chromatogram obtained with solution (3) (0.5%).

### Loss on drying

When dried to constant weight at 105°, loses not more than 2.0% of its weight. Use 1 g.

### Sulphated ash

Not more than 0.2%, Appendix IX A.

## ASSAY

Dissolve 0.5 g in 10 ml of *water*, add 20 ml of 1M *sodium hydroxide* and extract with four 25 ml quantities of *dichloromethane*. Combine the dichloromethane extracts and evaporate to a volume of about 10 ml. Add 40 ml of *anhydrous acetic acid* and carry out Method I for *non-aqueous titration*, Appendix VIII A, determining the end-point potentiometrically. Each ml of 0.1M *perchloric acid VS* is equivalent to 21.70 mg of $C_{18}H_{26}ClN_3O,H_2SO_4$.

## STORAGE

Hydroxychloroquine Sulphate should be protected from light.

# Hydroxyethyl Salicylate

*(Ph Eur monograph 1225)*

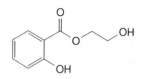

C$_9$H$_{10}$O$_4$        182.2        87-28-5

*Ph Eur*

## DEFINITION

2-Hydroxyethyl 2-hydroxybenzoate.

**Content**

98.0 per cent to 102.0 per cent.

## CHARACTERS

**Appearance**

Oily, colourless or almost colourless liquid, or colourless crystals.

**Solubility**

Sparingly soluble in water, very soluble in acetone and in methylene chloride, freely soluble in alcohol.

**mp**

About 21 °C.

## IDENTIFICATION

*First identification*  A, B.

*Second identification*  A, C, D, E.

A. It complies with the test for refractive index (see Tests).

B. Infrared absorption spectrophotometry (2.2.24).

*Preparation*  Thin films.

*Comparison*  hydroxyethyl salicylate CRS.

C. Examine the chromatograms obtained in the test for related substances.

*Results*  The principal spot in the chromatogram obtained with test solution (b) is similar in position and size to the principal spot in the chromatogram obtained with reference solution (a).

D. To 1 ml of solution S (see Tests), add 1 ml of *water R* and 0.2 ml of *ferric chloride solution R2*. A violet-red colour appears which disappears immediately after the addition of 2 ml of *dilute acetic acid R*. A very faint violet colour may remain.

E. In a test tube 160 mm long, mix 1.0 g with 2.0 g of finely powdered *manganese sulphate R*. Insert 2 cm into the test-tube a strip of filter paper impregnated with a freshly prepared mixture of 1 volume of a 20 per cent *V/V* solution of *diethanolamine R* and 11 volumes of a 50 g/l solution of *sodium nitroprusside R* adjusted to pH 9.8 with *1 M hydrochloric acid*. Heat the test-tube over a naked flame for 1-2 min. The filter paper becomes blue.

## TESTS

**Solution S**

Dissolve 2.5 g in 40 ml of *alcohol R* and dilute to 50 ml with *distilled water R*.

**Appearance of solution**

Solution S is clear (2.2.1) and colourless (2.2.2, *Method II*).

**Acidity or alkalinity**

To 2 ml of solution S add 0.1 ml of *methyl red solution R* and 0.2 ml of *0.01 M sodium hydroxide*. The solution is yellow. Add 0.3 ml of *0.01 M hydrochloric acid*. The solution is red.

**Relative density** *(2.2.5)*

1.252 to 1.257.

**Refractive index** *(2.2.6)*

1.548 to 1.551.

**Related substances**

Thin-layer chromatography (2.2.27).

*Test solution (a)*  Dissolve 0.50 g of the substance to be examined in *methanol R* and dilute to 10 ml with the same solvent.

*Test solution (b)*  Dilute 2 ml of test solution (a) to 50 ml with *methanol R*.

*Reference solution (a)*  Dissolve 50.0 mg of *hydroxyethyl salicylate CRS* in *methanol R* and dilute to 25 ml with the same solvent.

*Reference solution (b)*  Dilute 2.5 ml of test solution (b) to 10 ml with *methanol R*.

*Reference solution (c)*  Dissolve 0.10 g of *ethylene glycol R* in *methanol R* and dilute to 50 ml with the same solvent. Dilute 1.25 ml of the solution to 10 ml with *methanol R*.

*Plate*  TLC silica gel F$_{254}$ plate R.

*Mobile phase*  ethyl acetate R, glacial acetic acid R, cyclohexane R (20:20:60 *V/V/V*).

*Application*  10 μl.

*Development*  Over a path of 15 cm.

*Drying*  In a current of cold air.

*Detection A*  In ultraviolet light at 254 nm.

*Limits A:*

— *Any impurity*: any spot in the chromatogram obtained with test solution (a), apart from the principal spot, is not more intense than the spot in the chromatogram obtained with reference solution (b) (1 per cent).

*Detection B*  Spray the plate with *ammonium vanadate solution R* and heat at 100 °C for 10 min. Allow to cool for 10 min and examine in daylight.

*Limits B*  In the chromatogram obtained with test solution (a):

— *impurity B*: any spot corresponding to impurity B is not more intense than the spot in the chromatogram obtained with reference solution (c) (0.5 per cent),

— *any other impurity*: any spot, apart from the principal spot and any spot corresponding to impurity B is not more intense than the spot in the chromatogram obtained with reference solution (b) (1 per cent).

*System suitability*  The chromatogram obtained with reference solution (c) shows a clearly visible spot.

**Chlorides** *(2.4.4)*

Maximum 100 ppm.

Dilute 10 ml of solution S to 15 ml with *water R*. The solution complies with the limit test for chlorides.

**Sulphates** *(2.4.13)*

Maximum 250 ppm.

Dilute 12 ml of solution S to 15 ml with *distilled water R*. The solution complies with the limit test for sulphates.

**Sulphated ash** *(2.4.14)*

Maximum 0.1 per cent, determined on 1.0 g.

## ASSAY

In a flask with a ground-glass stopper, dissolve 0.125 g in 30 ml of *glacial acetic acid R*. Add 10 ml of *dilute sulphuric acid R*, 1.5 g of *potassium bromide R* and 50.0 ml of *0.0167 M potassium bromate*. Immediately close the flask and allow to stand protected from light for 15 min. Add 1.5 g of *potassium iodide R* immediately after removing the stopper and titrate with *0.1 M sodium thiosulphate*, adding 1 ml of *starch solution R* towards the end of the titration. Carry out a blank titration.

1 ml of *0.0167 M potassium bromate* is equivalent to 4.555 mg of $C_9H_{10}O_4$.

### STORAGE
Protected from light.

### IMPURITIES
A. salicylic acid,

B. ethane-1,2-diol (ethylene glycol).

*Ph*

# Hydroxyethylcellulose

*(Ph Eur monograph 0336)*

9004-62-0

### Action and use
Excipient.

*Ph Eur*

### DEFINITION
Partly *O*-(2-hydroxyethylated) cellulose.

### CHARACTERS
**Appearance**
White, yellowish-white or greyish-white powder or granules.

**Solubility**
Soluble in hot and cold water giving a colloidal solution, practically insoluble in acetone, in ethanol (96 per cent) and in toluene.

### IDENTIFICATION
A. Heat 10 ml of solution S (see Tests) to boiling. The solution remains clear.

B. To 10 ml of solution S add 0.3 ml of *dilute acetic acid R* and 2.5 ml of a 100 g/l solution of *tannic acid R*. A yellowish-white, flocculent precipitate is formed which dissolves in *dilute ammonia R1*.

C. In a test-tube about 160 mm in length, thoroughly mix 1 g with 2 g of finely powdered *manganese sulphate R*. Introduce to a depth of 2 cm into the upper part of the tube a strip of filter paper impregnated with a freshly prepared mixture of 1 volume of a 200 g/l solution of *diethanolamine R* and 11 volumes of a 50 g/l solution of *sodium nitroprusside R*, adjusted to about pH 9.8 with *1 M hydrochloric acid*. Insert the tube 8 cm into a silicone-oil bath and heat at 190-200 °C. The filter paper becomes blue within 10 min. Carry out a blank test.

D. Dissolve 0.2 g completely, without heating, in 15 ml of a 700 g/l solution of *sulphuric acid R*. Pour the solution with stirring into 100 ml of iced *water R* and dilute to 250 ml with iced *water R*. In a test-tube, mix thoroughly while cooling in iced water 1 ml of the solution with 8 ml of *sulphuric acid R*, added dropwise. Heat on a water-bath for exactly 3 min and immediately cool in iced water. While the mixture is cold, carefully add 0.6 ml of *ninhydrin solution R2* and mix well.

Allow to stand at 25 °C. A pink colour is produced immediately and does not become violet within 100 min.

### TESTS
**Solution S**
Disperse a quantity of the substance to be examined equivalent to 1.0 g of the dried substance in 50 ml of *carbon dioxide-free water R*. After 10 min, dilute to 100 ml with *carbon dioxide-free water R* and stir until dissolution is complete.

**pH** *(2.2.3)*
5.5 to 8.5 for solution S.

**Apparent viscosity** *(2.2.10)*
75 per cent to 140 per cent of the value stated on the label.

While stirring, introduce a quantity of the substance to be examined equivalent to 2.00 g of the dried substance into 50 g of *water R*. Dilute to 100.0 g with *water R* and stir until dissolution is complete. Determine the viscosity using a rotating viscometer at 25 °C and at a shear rate of $100\ s^{-1}$ for substances with an expected viscosity up to 100 mPa·s, at a shear rate of $10\ s^{-1}$ for substances with an expected viscosity between 100 mPa·s and 20 000 mPa·s and at a shear rate of $1\ s^{-1}$ for substances with an expected viscosity above 20 000 mPa·s. If it is impossible to obtain a shear rate of exactly $1\ s^{-1}$, $10\ s^{-1}$ or $100\ s^{-1}$ respectively, use a rate slightly higher and a rate slightly lower and interpolate.

**Chlorides** *(2.4.4)*
Maximum 1.0 per cent.

Dilute 1 ml of solution S to 30 ml with *water R*. 15 ml of the solution complies with the limit test for chlorides.

**Nitrates**
Maximum 3.0 per cent (dried substance), if hydroxyethylcellulose has an apparent viscosity of 1000 mPa·s or less and maximum 0.2 per cent (dried substance), if hydroxyethylcellulose has an apparent viscosity of more than 1000 mPa·s.

Determine potentiometrically *(2.2.36, Method I)* using as indicator a nitrate selective electrode and a silver-silver chloride electrode with a 13.2 g/l solution of *ammonium sulphate R* as reference electrolyte.

*Prepare the solutions immediately before use.*

*Buffer solution* To a mixture of 50 ml of *1 M sulphuric acid* and 800 ml of *water R*, add 135 g of *potassium dihydrogen phosphate R* and dilute to 1000 ml with *water R*.

*Buffered water* Dilute 80 ml of buffer solution to 2000 ml with *water R*.

*Nitrate standard solution (500 ppm NO₃)* Dissolve 0.8154 g of *potassium nitrate R* in 500 ml of buffered water and dilute to 1000.0 ml with the same solvent.

*Test solution* Dissolve 0.50 g of the substance to be examined in buffered water and dilute to 100.0 ml with the same solvent.

*Reference solutions* If hydroxyethylcellulose has an apparent viscosity of 1000 mPa·s or less, dilute 10.0 ml, 20.0 ml and 40.0 ml of nitrate standard solution (500 ppm NO₃) to 100.0 ml with buffered water and mix.

If hydroxyethylcellulose has an apparent viscosity of more than 1000 mPa·s, dilute 1.0 ml, 2.0 ml and 4.0 ml of nitrate standard solution (500 ppm NO₃) to 100.0 ml with buffered water and mix.

Carry out the measurements for each solution. Calculate the concentration of nitrates using the calibration curve.

**Glyoxal**

Maximum 20 ppm.

Introduce 1.0 g into a test-tube with a ground-glass stopper and add 10.0 ml of *anhydrous ethanol R*. Stopper the tube and stir mechanically for 30 min. Centrifuge. To 2.0 ml of the supernatant liquid add 5.0 ml of a 4 g/l solution of *methylbenzothiazolone hydrazone hydrochloride R* in an 80 per cent *V/V* solution of *glacial acetic acid R* in *water R*. Shake to homogenise. After 2 h, the solution is not more intensely coloured than a standard prepared at the same time and in the same manner using 2.0 ml of *glyoxal standard solution (2 ppm $C_2H_2O_2$) R* instead of the 2.0 ml of supernatant liquid.

**Ethylene oxide**

Head-space gas chromatography (2.4.25).

*Test preparation*  Place 1.00 g of the substance to be examined in a 5 ml vial (other sizes may be used depending on the operating conditions) and add 1 ml of *water R*. It swells in water but does not dissolve.

*Reference preparation (a)*  Place 1.00 g of the substance to be examined in an identical 5 ml vial. Add 0.1 ml of cooled *ethylene oxide solution R2* and 0.9 ml of *water R*. It swells in water but does not dissolve.

*Reference preparation (b)*  To 0.1 ml of *ethylene oxide solution R2* in a 5 ml vial add 0.1 ml of a freshly prepared 10 mg/l solution of *acetaldehyde R*.

*Close the vials immediately with a butyl rubber membrane stopper, coated with aluminium or polytetrafluoroethylene and secured with an aluminium crimped cap.*

*Limit:*
— ethylene oxide: maximum 1 ppm.

**2-Chloroethanol**

Head-space gas chromatography (2.2.28).

*Test preparation*  To 50 mg of the substance to be examined in a 10 ml vial (other sizes may be used depending on the operating conditions), add 2 µl of *2-propanol R*. Seal the flask and mix.

*Reference preparation (a)*  Dissolve 0.125 g of 2-chloroethanol R and dilute to 50.0 ml with *2-propanol R*. Dilute 1.0 ml of the solution to 10.0 ml with *2-propanol R*.

*Reference preparation (b)*  To 50 mg of the substance to be examined in an identical 10 ml vial, add 2 µl of reference solution (a). Seal the flask and mix.

*Close the vials immediately with a butyl rubber membrane stopper, coated with aluminium or polytetrafluoroethylene and secured with an aluminium crimped cap.*

*Column:*
— *size: l = 50 m, Ø = 0.32 mm,*
— *stationary phase: poly(dimethyl)siloxane R (1.2 µm).*

*Carrier gas*  *helium for chromatography R.*

*Flow rate*  25-35 cm/s.

*Split ratio*  1:10.

*Static head-space conditions which may be used:*
— *equilibration temperature*: 110 °C,
— *equilibration time*: 20 min,
— *temperature of injection system*: 115 °C.

*Temperature:*

| | Time (min) | Temperature (°C) |
|---|---|---|
| Column | 0 - 6 | 60 |
| | 6 - 16 | 60 → 110 |
| | 16 - 31 | 110 → 230 |
| | 31 - 36 | 230 |
| Injection port | | 150 |
| Detector | | 250 |

*Detection*  Flame ionisation.

*Injection*  2 ml.

*Retention time*  2-chloroethanol = about 7.8 min.

*Limit:*
— *2-chloroethanol*: not more than 0.5 times the area of the peak due to 2-chloroethanol in the chromatogram obtained with reference solution (b) (10 ppm).

**Heavy metals** (2.4.8)

Maximum 20 ppm.

1.0 g complies with limit test C. Prepare the reference solution using 2 ml of *lead standard solution (10 ppm Pb) R*.

**Loss on drying** (2.2.32)

Maximum 10.0 per cent, determined on 1.000 g by drying in an oven at 105 °C for 3 h.

**Sulphated ash** (2.4.14)

Maximum 4.0 per cent, determined on 1.0 g.

**LABELLING**

The label states the apparent viscosity, in millipascal seconds for a 2 per cent *m/m* solution.

———————————————————— *Ph Eur*

# Hydroxyethylmethylcellulose

(*Methylhydroxyethylcellulose, Ph Eur monograph 0346*)

**Action and use**
Excipient.

*Ph Eur* ————————————————————

**DEFINITION**

Partly *O*-methylated and *O*-(2-hydroxyethylated) cellulose.

**CHARACTERS**

**Appearance**

White, yellowish-white or greyish-white powder or granules, hygroscopic after drying.

**Solubility**

Practically insoluble in hot water, in acetone, in anhydrous ethanol and in toluene. It dissolves in cold water giving a colloidal solution.

**IDENTIFICATION**

A. Heat 10 ml of solution S (see Tests) in a water-bath while stirring. At a temperature above 50 °C, the solution becomes cloudy or a flocculent precipitate is formed. The solution becomes clear again on cooling.

B. To 10 ml of solution S add 0.3 ml of *dilute acetic acid R* and 2.5 ml of a 100 g/l solution of *tannic acid R*. A yellowish-white flocculent precipitate is formed which dissolves in *dilute ammonia R1*.

C. In a test-tube about 160 mm long, thoroughly mix 1 g with 2 g of finely powdered *manganese sulphate R*. Introduce to a depth of 2 cm into the upper part of the tube a strip of filter paper impregnated with a freshly prepared mixture of 1 volume of a 20 per cent *V/V* solution of *diethanolamine R* and 11 volumes of a 50 g/l solution of *sodium nitroprusside R*, adjusted to about pH 9.8 with *1 M hydrochloric acid*. Insert the tube 8 cm into a silicone-oil bath at 190-200 °C. The filter paper becomes blue within 10 min. Carry out a blank test.

D. Dissolve completely 0.2 g without heating in 15 ml of a 70 per cent *m/m* solution of *sulphuric acid R*. Pour the solution with stirring into 100 ml of iced *water R* and dilute to 250 ml with iced *water R*. In a test-tube, mix thoroughly while cooling in iced water 1 ml of this solution with 8 ml of *sulphuric acid R* added dropwise. Heat in a water-bath for exactly 3 min and immediately cool in iced water. While the mixture is cold, carefully add 0.6 ml of *ninhydrin solution R2* and mix well. Allow to stand at 25 °C. A pink colour is produced immediately and does not become violet within 100 min.

E. Place 1 ml of solution S on a glass plate. After evaporation of the water a thin film is formed.

## TESTS

### Solution S

While stirring, introduce a quantity of the substance to be examined equivalent to 1.0 g of the dried substance into 50 g of *carbon dioxide-free water R* heated to 90 °C. Allow to cool, adjust the mass of the solution to 100 g with *carbon dioxide-free water R* and stir until dissolution is complete.

### Appearance of solution

Solution S is not more opalescent than reference suspension III (*2.2.1*) and not more intensely coloured than reference solution $Y_6$ (*2.2.2, Method II*).

### pH (*2.2.3*)

5.5 to 8.0 for solution S.

### Apparent viscosity (*2.2.10*)

75 per cent to 140 per cent of the value stated on the label.

While stirring, introduce a quantity of the substance to be examined equivalent to 6.00 g of the dried substance into 150 g of *water R* heated to 90 °C. Stir with a propeller-type stirrer for 10 min, place the flask in a bath of iced water, continue the stirring and allow to remain in the bath of iced water for 40 min to ensure that dissolution is complete. Adjust the mass of the solution to 300 g and centrifuge the solution to expel any entrapped air. Adjust the temperature of the solution to 20 ± 0.1 °C. Determine the viscosity with a rotating viscometer at 20 °C and a shear rate of 10 s$^{-1}$.

### Chlorides (*2.4.4*)

Maximum 0.5 per cent.

Dilute 1 ml of solution S to 15 ml with *water R*.

### Heavy metals (*2.4.8*)

Maximum 20 ppm.

1.0 g complies with test C. Prepare the reference solution using 2 ml of *lead standard solution (10 ppm Pb) R*.

### Loss on drying (*2.2.32*)

Maximum 10.0 per cent, determined on 1.000 g by drying in an oven at 105 °C.

### Sulphated ash (*2.4.14*)

Maximum 1.0 per cent, determined on 1.000 g.

LABELLING
The label states the apparent viscosity in millipascal seconds for a 2 per cent *m/m* solution.

*Ph Eur*

# Hydroxypropylbetadex

(*Ph Eur monograph 1804*)

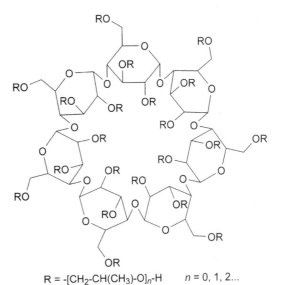

R = -[CH$_2$-CH(CH$_3$)-O]$_n$-H   n = 0, 1, 2...

C$_{42}$H$_{70}$O$_{35}$(C$_3$H$_6$O)$_x$ with x = 7 *MS*

## Action and use

Excipient.

*Ph Eur*

## DEFINITION

Hydroxypropylbetadex (β-cyclodextrin, 2-hydroxypropyl ether) is a partially substituted poly(hydroxypropyl) ether of betadex. The number of hydroxypropyl groups per anhydroglucose unit, expressed as molar substitution (*MS*), is not less than 0.40 and not more than 1.50 and is within 10 per cent of the value stated on the label.

## CHARACTERS

### Appearance

white or almost white, amorphous or crystalline powder.

### Solubility

Freely soluble in water and in propylene glycol.

## IDENTIFICATION

A. Infrared absorption spectrophotometry (*2.2.24*).

*Comparison*   hydroxypropylbetadex CRS.

*Results*   The spectrum obtained with the substance to be examined shows the same absorption bands as the spectrum obtained with *hydroxypropylbetadex CRS*. Due to the difference in the substitution of the substance, the intensity of some absorption bands can vary.

B. Appearance of solution (see Tests).

## TESTS

### Solution S

Dissolve 5.0 g in *carbon dioxide-free water R* prepared from *distilled water R* and dilute to 50.0 ml with the same solvent.

## Appearance of solution

The solution is clear (2.2.1) and colourless (2.2.2, Method II), and remains so after cooling to room temperature.

Dissolve 1.0 g in 2.0 ml of *water R*, with heating.

## Conductivity (2.2.38)

Maximum 200 $\mu$S·cm$^{-1}$.

Measure the conductivity of solution S, while gently stirring with a magnetic stirrer.

## Related substances

Liquid chromatography (2.2.29).

*Test solution*   Dissolve 2.50 g of the substance to be examined in *water R* with heating, cool, and dilute to 25.0 ml with the same solvent.

*Reference solution (a)*   Dissolve 0.15 g of *betadex CRS* and 0.25 g of *propylene glycol R* in *water R* and dilute to 10.0 ml with the same solvent.

*Reference solution (b)*   Dilute 5.0 ml of reference solution (a) to 50.0 ml with *water R*.

*Precolumn:*
— stationary phase: *phenylsilyl silica gel for chromatography R*.

*Column:*
— size: $l$ = 0.30 m, Ø = 3.9 mm;
— stationary phase: *phenylsilyl silica gel for chromatography R*;
— temperature: 40 °C.

*Mobile phase*   *water for chromatography R*.

*Flow rate*   1.5 ml/min.

*Detection*   Differential refractometer, at 40 °C.

*Injection*   20 $\mu$l.

*Run time*   6 times the retention time of impurity A.

*Relative retention*   With reference to impurity B (retention time = about 2.5 min): impurity A = about 4.2; hydroxypropylbetadex = about 6 for the beginning of the elution.

Hydroxypropylbetadex elutes as a very wide peak or several peaks.

*System suitability*   Reference solution (a):
— resolution: minimum 4 between the peaks due to impurities A and B.

*Limits:*
— impurity A: not more than the area of the corresponding peak in the chromatogram obtained with reference solution (b) (1.5 per cent);
— impurity B: not more than the area of the corresponding peak in the chromatogram obtained with reference solution (b) (2.5 per cent);
— any other impurity: for each impurity, not more than 0.04 times the area of the peak due to impurity B in the chromatogram obtained with reference solution (b) (0.1 per cent);
— sum of impurities other than A and B: not more than 0.4 times the area of the peak due to impurity B in the chromatogram obtained with reference solution (b) (1.0 per cent);
— disregard limit: 0.02 times the area of the peak due to impurity B in the chromatogram obtained with reference solution (b) (0.05 per cent); disregard any peak eluting before impurity B or after impurity A.

## Heavy metals (2.4.8)

Maximum 20 ppm.

12 ml of solution S complies with test A. Prepare the reference solution using *lead standard solution (2 ppm Pb) R*.

## Loss on drying (2.2.32)

Maximum 10.0 per cent, determined on 1.000 g by drying in an oven at 120 °C for 2 h.

## Molar substitution

Nuclear magnetic resonance spectrometry (2.2.33).

The molar substitution (*MS*) is calculated from the ratio between the signal from the 3 protons of the methyl group that is part of the hydroxypropyl group and the signal from the proton attached to the C1 carbon (glycosidic proton) of the anhydroglucose units.

Use a Fourier transform nuclear magnetic resonance spectrometer of minimum frequency 250 MHz, suited to record a proton spectrum and to carry out quantitative analysis, at a temperature of at least 25 °C.

Introduce not less than the equivalent of 10.0 mg of the substance to be examined (dried substance) into a 5 mm NMR tube, equipped with a spinner in order to record the spectrum in rotation. Add approximately 0.75 ml of *deuterium oxide R1*. Cap the tube, mix thoroughly and adapt the spinner.

Make the appropriate instrument settings (frequency, gain, digital resolution, sample rotation, shims, probe tuning, resolution/data point, receiver gain etc.) so as to obtain a suitable spectrum for quantitative analysis (good FID (Free Induction Decay), no distortion of the spectrum after Fourier transform and phase corrections). The relaxation delay must be adapted to the pulse angle in order to have sufficient relaxation of the protons concerned between 2 pulses (for example: 10 s for a 90° pulse).

Record the FID, with at least 8 scans, so as to obtain a spectral window comprised, at least, between 0 ppm and 6.2 ppm, referring to the signal of exchangeable protons (solvent) at 4.8 ppm (25 °C).

Make a zero filling of at least 3-fold in size relative to the acquisition data file and transform the FID to the spectrum without any correction of Gaussian broadening factor (GB = 0) and with a line broadening factor not greater than 0.2 (LB $\leq$ 0.2). Call the integration sub-routine after phase corrections and baseline correction between 0.5 ppm and 6.2 ppm.

Measure the peak areas of the doublet from the methyl groups at 1.2 ppm ($A_1$), and of the signals of the glycosidic protons between 5 ppm and 5.4 ppm ($A_2$).

The molar substitution is obtained using the following equation:

$$MS = \frac{A_1}{(3 \times A_2)}$$

$A_1$ = area of the signal due to the 3 protons of the methyl groups that are part of the hydroxypropyl groups;
$A_2$ = area of the signals due to the glycosidic protons.

The degree of substitution is the number of hydroxypropyl groups per molecule of β-cyclodextrin and is obtained by multiplying the *MS* by 7.

## Microbial contamination

If intended for use in the manufacture of parenteral preparations:
— TAMC: acceptance criterion $10^2$ CFU/g (2.6.12).

If not intended for use in the manufacture of parenteral preparations:
— TAMC: acceptance criterion $10^3$ CFU/g (2.6.12);
— TYMC: acceptance criterion $10^2$ CFU/g (2.6.12);

— absence of *Escherichia coli* (*2.6.13*);
— absence of *Salmonella* (*2.6.13*).

**Bacterial endotoxins** (*2.6.14*)
Less than 10 IU/g, if intended for use in the manufacture of parenteral preparations without a further appropriate procedure for the removal of bacterial endotoxins.

**LABELLING**
The label states:
— the molar substitution (*MS*);
— where applicable, that the substance is suitable for use in the manufacture of parenteral preparations.

**IMPURITIES**
A. betadex,

B. propylene glycol.

_____ *Ph Eur*

# Hydroxypropylcellulose

(*Ph Eur monograph 0337*)

9004-64-2

**Action and use**
Excipient.

*Ph Eur* _____

**DEFINITION**
Partly *O*-(2-hydroxypropylated) cellulose.

It may contain maximum 0.6 per cent of silica (SiO$_2$).

**CHARACTERS**
**Appearance**
White or yellowish-white powder or granules, hygroscopic after drying.

**Solubility**
Soluble in cold water, in glacial acetic acid, in anhydrous ethanol, in methanol and in propylene glycol and in a mixture of 10 parts of methanol and 90 parts of methylene chloride giving colloidal solutions, sparingly soluble or slightly soluble in acetone depending on the degree of substitution, practically insoluble in hot water, in ethylene glycol and in toluene.

**IDENTIFICATION**
A. Heat 10 ml of solution S (see Tests) in a water-bath while stirring. At a temperature above 40 °C the solution becomes cloudy or a flocculent precipitate is formed. The solution becomes clear again on cooling.

B. To 10 ml of solution S add 0.3 ml of *dilute acetic acid R* and 2.5 ml of a 100 g/l solution of *tannic acid R*. A yellowish-white flocculent precipitate is formed which dissolves in *dilute ammonia R1*.

C. In a test-tube about 160 mm long, thoroughly mix 1 g with 2 g of finely powdered *manganese sulphate R*. Introduce to a depth of 2 cm into the upper part of the tube a strip of filter paper impregnated with a freshly prepared mixture of 1 volume of a 20 per cent *V/V* solution of *diethanolamine R* and 11 volumes of a 50 g/l solution of *sodium nitroprusside R*, adjusted to about pH 9.8 with *1 M hydrochloric acid*. Insert the tube 8 cm into a silicone-oil bath at 190-200 °C. The filter paper becomes blue within 10 min. Carry out a blank test.

D. Dissolve completely 0.2 g without heating in 15 ml of a 70 per cent *m/m* solution of *sulphuric acid R*. Pour the solution with stirring into 100 ml of iced *water R* and dilute to 250 ml with iced *water R*. In a test-tube, mix thoroughly while cooling in iced water 1 ml of this solution with 8 ml of *sulphuric acid R* added dropwise. Heat in a water-bath for exactly 3 min and immediately cool in iced water. While the mixture is cold, carefully add 0.6 ml of *ninhydrin solution R2* and mix well. Allow to stand at 25 °C. A pink colour is produced immediately and becomes violet within 100 min.

E. Place 1 ml of solution S on a glass plate. After evaporation of the water a thin film is formed.

F. 0.2 g does not dissolve in 10 ml of *toluene R* but dissolves completely in 10 ml of *anhydrous ethanol R*.

**TESTS**
**Solution S**
While stirring, introduce a quantity of the substance to be examined equivalent to 1.0 g of the dried substance into 50 g of *carbon dioxide-free water R* heated to 90 °C. Allow to cool, adjust the mass of the solution to 100 g with *carbon dioxide-free water R* and stir until dissolution is complete.

**Appearance of solution**
Solution S is not more opalescent than reference suspension III (*2.2.1*) and not more intensely coloured than reference solution Y$_6$ (*2.2.2, Method II*).

**pH** (*2.2.3*)
5.0 to 8.5 for solution S.

**Apparent viscosity** (*2.2.10*)
75 per cent to 140 per cent of the value stated on the label.

While stirring, introduce a quantity of the substance to be examined equivalent to 6.00 g of the dried substance into 150 g of *water R* heated to 90 °C. Stir with a propeller-type stirrer for 10 min, place the flask in a bath of iced water, continue the stirring and allow to remain in the bath of iced water for 40 min to ensure that dissolution is complete. Adjust the mass of the solution to 300 g and centrifuge the solution to expel any entrapped air. Adjust the temperature of the solution to 20 ± 0.1 °C. Determine the viscosity with a rotating viscometer at 20 °C and a shear rate of 10 s$^{-1}$.

For a product of low viscosity, use a quantity of the substance to be examined sufficient to prepare a solution of the concentration stated on the label.

**Silica**
Maximum 0.6 per cent.

To the residue obtained in the test for sulphated ash add sufficient *ethanol (96 per cent) R* to moisten the residue completely. Add 6 ml of *hydrofluoric acid R* in small portions. Evaporate to dryness at 95-105 °C, taking care to avoid loss from sputtering. Cool and rinse the wall of the platinum crucible with 6 ml of *hydrofluoric acid R*. Add 0.5 ml of *sulphuric acid R* and evaporate to dryness. Progressively increase the temperature, ignite at 900 ± 50 °C, allow to cool in a desiccator and weigh. The difference between the mass of the residue obtained in the test for sulphated ash and the mass of the final residue is equal to the amount of silica in the substance to be examined.

**Chlorides** (*2.4.4*)
Maximum 0.5 per cent.

Dilute 1 ml of solution S to 15 ml with *water R*.

**Heavy metals** (*2.4.8*)
Maximum 20 ppm.

1.0 g complies with test C. Prepare the reference solution using 2 ml of *lead standard solution (10 ppm Pb) R*.

**Loss on drying** (*2.2.32*)
Maximum 7.0 per cent, determined on 1.000 g by drying in an oven at 105 °C.

**Sulphated ash** (*2.4.14*)
Maximum 1.6 per cent, determined on 1.0 g using a platinum crucible.

## LABELLING
The label states:
— the apparent viscosity in millipascal seconds for a 2 per cent m/m solution,
— for a product of low viscosity, the concentration of the solution to be used and the apparent viscosity in millipascal seconds,
— where applicable, that the substance contains silica.

*———————————————— Ph Eur*

# Hydroxyzine Hydrochloride

(*Ph Eur monograph 0916*)

and enantiomer

C$_{21}$H$_{27}$ClN$_2$O$_2$,2HCl        447.8        *2192-20-3*

**Action and use**
Histamine H$_1$ receptor antagonist.

*Ph Eur _____*

## DEFINITION
(*RS*)-2-[2-[4-[(4-Chlorophenyl)phenylmethyl]piperazin-1-yl]ethoxy]ethanol dihydrochloride.

## Content
99.0 per cent to 101.0 per cent (dried substance).

## CHARACTERS
**Appearance**
White or almost white, hygroscopic, crystalline powder.

**Solubility**
Freely soluble in water and in ethanol (96 per cent), very slightly soluble in acetone.

mp: about 200 °C, with decomposition.

## IDENTIFICATION
*First identification   A, D.*
*Second identification   B, C, D.*

A. Infrared absorption spectrophotometry (*2.2.24*).
*Preparation   Discs.*
*Comparison   hydroxyzine hydrochloride CRS.*

B. Thin-layer chromatography (*2.2.27*).

*Solvent mixture   methanol R, methylene chloride R (50:50 V/V).*

*Test solution   Dissolve 0.50 g of the substance to be examined in the solvent mixture and dilute to 10 ml with the solvent mixture.*

*Reference solution (a)   Dissolve 0.50 g of hydroxyzine hydrochloride CRS in the solvent mixture and dilute to 10 ml with the solvent mixture.*

*Reference solution (b)   Dissolve 0.50 g of meclozine hydrochloride R in the solvent mixture and dilute to 10 ml with the solvent mixture. Dilute 1 ml of this solution to 2 ml with reference solution (a).*

*Plate   TLC silica gel G plate R.*

*Mobile phase   concentrated ammonia R, ethanol (96 per cent) R, toluene R (1:24:75 V/V/V).*

*Application   2 µl.*

*Development   Over a path of 15 cm.*

*Drying   In air.*

*Detection   Spray with potassium iodobismuthate solution R2.*

*System suitability   Reference solution (b):*
— the chromatogram shows 2 clearly separated principal spots.

*Results   The principal spot in the chromatogram obtained with the test solution is similar in position, colour and size to the principal spot in the chromatogram obtained with reference solution (a).*

C. Dissolve 0.1 g in *ethanol (96 per cent) R* and dilute to 15 ml with the same solvent. Add 15 ml of a saturated solution of *picric acid R* in *ethanol (96 per cent) R*. Allow to stand for 15 min. A precipitate is formed. Filter. Recrystallise from *ethanol (96 per cent) R*. Initiate crystallisation, if necessary, by scratching the wall of the tube with a glass rod. The crystals melt (*2.2.14*) at 189 °C to 192 °C.

D. It gives reaction (a) of chlorides (*2.3.1*).

## TESTS
**Solution S**
Dissolve 2.0 g in *water R* and dilute to 20.0 ml with the same solvent.

**Appearance of solution**
Solution S is clear (*2.2.1*) and not more intensely coloured than reference solution Y$_7$ (*2.2.2, Method II*).

**Optical rotation** (*2.2.7*)
– 0.10° to + 0.10°, determined on solution S.

**Related substances**
Liquid chromatography (*2.2.29*).

*Test solution   Dissolve 10.0 mg of the substance to be examined in the mobile phase and dilute to 10.0 ml with the mobile phase.*

*Reference solution (a)   Dissolve 10.0 mg of hydroxyzine hydrochloride CRS in the mobile phase and dilute to 10.0 ml with the mobile phase.*

*Reference solution (b)   Dilute 3.0 ml of the test solution to 200.0 ml with the mobile phase. Dilute 5.0 ml of this solution to 25.0 ml with the mobile phase.*

*Column:*
— *size: l = 0.15 m, Ø = 4.6 mm;*
— *stationary phase: base-deactivated octadecylsilyl silica gel for chromatography R (3 µm).*

*Mobile phase   Dissolve 0.5 g of sodium methanesulphonate R in a mixture of 14 ml of triethylamine R, 300 ml of acetonitrile R and 686 ml of water R, then adjust to pH 2.7 with sulphuric acid R.*

*Flow rate   1 ml/min.*

*Detection   Spectrophotometer at 230 nm.*

*Injection   20 µl.*

*Run time   2.5 times the retention time of hydroxyzine.*

*System suitability   Reference solution (a):*
— *peak-to-valley ratio: minimum 10, where H$_p$ = height above the baseline of the peak immediately before the*

peak due to hydroxyzine and $H_v$ = height above the baseline of the lowest point of the curve separating this peak from the peak due to hydroxyzine.

*Limits:*
— *any impurity*: for each impurity, not more than 1/3 of the area of the principal peak in the chromatogram obtained with reference solution (b) (0.1 per cent);
— *total*: not more than the area of the principal peak in the chromatogram obtained with reference solution (b) (0.3 per cent);
— *disregard limit*: 0.1 times the area of the principal peak in the chromatogram obtained with reference solution (b) (0.03 per cent).

**Heavy metals** (*2.4.8*)
Maximum 10 ppm.

12 ml of solution S complies with test A. Prepare the reference solution using *lead standard solution (1 ppm Pb) R.*

**Loss on drying** (*2.2.32*)
Maximum 5.0 per cent, determined on 1.000 g by drying in an oven at 105 °C.

**Sulphated ash** (*2.4.14*)
Maximum 0.1 per cent, determined on 1.0 g.

**ASSAY**
Dissolve 0.200 g in 10 ml of *anhydrous acetic acid R*. Add 40 ml of *acetic anhydride R*. Titrate with *0.1 M perchloric acid*, determining the end-point potentiometrically (*2.2.20*).

1 ml of *0.1 M perchloric acid* is equivalent to 22.39 mg of $C_{21}H_{29}Cl_3N_2O_2$.

**STORAGE**
In an airtight container, protected from light.

**IMPURITIES**

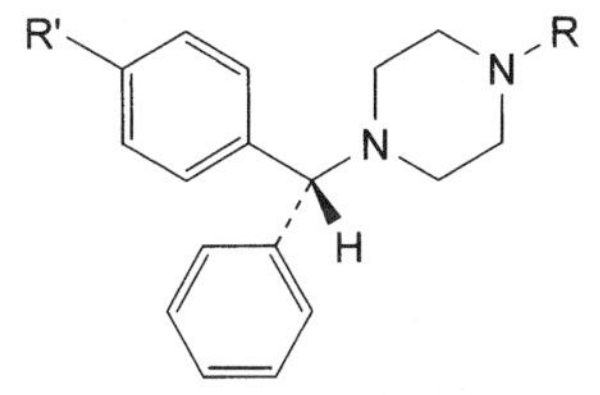

A. R = H, R′ = Cl:
(*RS*)-1-[(4-chlorophenyl)phenylmethyl]piperazine,
B. R = CH₂-CH₂-O-CH₂-CH₂-OH, R′ = H: 2-[2-[4-(diphenylmethyl)piperazin-1-yl]ethoxy]ethanol (decloxizine).

*Ph Eur*

# Hymecromone

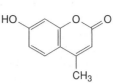

(*Ph Eur monograph 1786*)

$C_{10}H_8O_3$ \qquad 176.2 \qquad *90-33-5*

**Action and use**
Choleretic; antispasmodic.

*Ph Eur*

**DEFINITION**
7-Hydroxy-4-methyl-2*H*-1-benzopyran-2-one.

**Content**
99.0 per cent to 101.0 per cent (dried substance).

**CHARACTERS**
**Appearance**
Almost white crystalline powder.

**Solubility**
Very slightly soluble in water, sparingly soluble in methanol, slightly soluble in methylene chloride. It dissolves in dilute solutions of ammonia.

**IDENTIFICATION**
Infrared absorption spectrophotometry (*2.2.24*).
*Comparison   hymecromone CRS.*

**TESTS**
**Absorbance** (*2.2.25*)
Dissolve 50 mg in 10 ml of *ammonium chloride buffer solution pH 10.4 R* and dilute to 100.0 ml with *water R*. To 1.0 ml of the solution, add 10 ml of *ammonium chloride buffer solution pH 10.4 R* and dilute to 100.0 ml with *water R*. Examined between 200 nm and 400 nm, the solution shows 2 absorption maxima, at 229 nm and 360 nm, and an absorption minimum at 276 nm. The specific absorbance at the maximum at 360 nm is 1020 to 1120.

**Related substances**
Liquid chromatography (*2.2.29*).

*Buffer solution*   To 280 ml of a 1.56 g/l solution of *sodium dihydrogen phosphate R*, add 720 ml of a 3.58 g/l solution of *disodium hydrogen phosphate R*. Adjust to pH 7 with a 100 g/l solution of *phosphoric acid R*.

*Test solution*   Dissolve 10 mg of the substance to be examined in the mobile phase and dilute to 10.0 ml with the mobile phase.

*Reference solution (a)*   Dissolve 20 mg of *hymecromone CRS*, 10 mg of *hymecromone impurity A CRS* and 10 mg of *hymecromone impurity B CRS* in the mobile phase and dilute to 100.0 ml with the mobile phase.

*Reference solution (b)*   Dilute 1.0 ml of reference solution (a) to 200.0 ml with the mobile phase.

*Column:*
— *size: l* = 0.25 m, Ø = 4 mm,
— *stationary phase*: spherical octadecylsilyl silica gel for chromatography R (10 μm).

*Mobile phase   methanol R, buffer solution (465:535 V/V).*

*Flow rate*   1.0 ml/min.

*Detection*   Spectrophotometer at 270 nm.

*Injection*   20 µl.

*Run time*   1.5 times the retention time of hymecromone.

*Relative retention* with reference to hymecromone (retention time = about 6 min): impurity A = about 0.5; impurity B = about 0.7.

*System suitability*   Reference solution (a):
— *resolution*: minimum of 2 between the peaks due to impurity A and to impurity B and minimum of 3 between the peaks due to impurity B and to hymecromone.

*Limits:*
— *impurity A*: not more than the area of the corresponding peak in the chromatogram obtained with reference solution (b) (0.05 per cent),
— *impurity B*: not more than the area of the corresponding peak in the chromatogram obtained with reference solution (b) (0.05 per cent),
— *any other impurity*: not more than the area of the peak due to hymecromone in the chromatogram obtained with reference solution (b) (0.1 per cent),
— *total*: not more than twice the area of the peak due to hymecromone in the chromatogram obtained with reference solution (b) (0.2 per cent),
— *disregard limit*: 0.1 times the area of the peak due to hymecromone in the chromatogram obtained with reference solution (b) (0.01 per cent).

**Heavy metals** (*2.4.8*)

Maximum 10 ppm.

Dissolve 1.5 g in a mixture of 15 volumes of *water R* and 85 volumes of *dimethylformamide R* and dilute to 18 ml with the same mixture of solvents. The solution complies with limit test B. Prepare the standard using a lead standard solution (1 ppm Pb) obtained by diluting *lead standard solution (100 ppm Pb) R* with a mixture of 15 volumes of *water R* and 85 volumes of *dimethylformamide R.*

**Loss on drying** (*2.2.32*)

Maximum 0.5 per cent, determined on 1.000 g by drying in an oven at 105 °C for 4 h.

**Sulphated ash** (*2.4.14*)

Maximum 0.1 per cent, determined on 1.0 g.

**ASSAY**

Dissolve 0.100 g in 80 ml of *2-propanol R*. Titrate with *0.1 M tetrabutylammonium hydroxide in 2-propanol* determining the end-point potentiometrically (*2.2.20*). Carry out a blank titration.

1 ml of *0.1 M tetrabutylammonium hydroxide in 2-propanol* is equivalent to 17.62 mg of $C_{10}H_8O_3$.

**STORAGE**

Protected from light.

**IMPURITIES**

A. resorcinol,

B. 7-hydroxy-2-methyl-4*H*-1-benzopyran-4-one.

———————————————————————————— *Ph Eur*

# Hyoscine

(*Ph Eur monograph 2167*)

$C_{17}H_{21}NO_4$        303.4        *51-34-3*

**Action and use**

Anticholinergic.

*Ph Eur* ————————————————————————

**DEFINITION**

(1*R*,2*R*,4*S*,5*S*,7*s*)-9-Methyl-3-oxa-9-azatricyclo[3.3.1.0²,⁴]non-7-yl (2*S*)-3-hydroxy-2-phenylpropanoate.

**Content**

98.5 per cent to 101.0 per cent (anhydrous substance).

**CHARACTERS**

**Appearance**

White or almost white, crystalline powder or colourless crystals.

**Solubility**

Soluble in water, freely soluble in ethanol (96 per cent).

**mp**

66 °C to 70 °C.

**IDENTIFICATION**

A. Specific optical rotation (see Tests).

B. Infrared absorption spectrophotometry (*2.2.24*).

*Comparison*   hyoscine CRS.

**TESTS**

**Specific optical rotation** (*2.2.7*)

− 33 to − 39 (anhydrous substance).

Dissolve 1.00 g in *dilute hydrochloric acid R* and dilute to 25.0 ml with the same acid.

**Related substances**

Liquid chromatography (2.2.29).

*Test solution*   Dissolve 25.0 mg of the substance to be examined in the mobile phase and dilute to 25.0 ml with the mobile phase.

*Reference solution (a)*   Dilute 1.0 ml of the test solution to 10.0 ml with the mobile phase. Dilute 1.0 ml of this solution to 100.0 ml with the mobile phase.

*Reference solution (b)*   Dissolve 5.0 mg of *hyoscine impurity A CRS* in the mobile phase and dilute to 10.0 ml with the mobile phase.

*Reference solution (c)*   Dilute 5.0 ml of reference solution (b) to 25.0 ml with the mobile phase. Dilute 5.0 ml of this solution to 50.0 ml with the mobile phase.

*Reference solution (d)*   Mix 2.0 ml of reference solution (b) and 1.0 ml of the test solution and dilute to 10.0 ml with the mobile phase.

*Column:*
— *size: l* = 0.125 m, Ø = 4.0 mm;
— *stationary phase: octylsilyl silica gel for chromatography R* (3 µm).

*Mobile phase* Mix 33 volumes of *acetonitrile R* and 67 volumes of a 2.5 g/l solution of *sodium dodecyl sulphate R* previously adjusted to pH 2.5 with a 346 g/l solution of *phosphoric acid R.*

*Flow rate* 1.5 ml/min.

*Detection* Spectrophotometer at 210 nm.

*Injection* 5 µl.

*Run time* 3 times the retention time of hyoscine.

*Relative retention* With reference to hyoscine (retention time = about 5 min): impurity C = about 0.2; impurity A = about 0.9; impurity D = about 1.3; impurity B = about 2.5.

*System suitability* Reference solution (d):
— *resolution*: minimum 1.5 between the peaks due to impurity A and hyoscine.

*Limits:*
— *correction factors*: for the calculation of content, multiply the peak areas of the following impurities by the corresponding correction factor: impurity B = 0.6; impurity C = 0.3;
— *impurity A*: not more than 0.5 times the area of the principal peak in the chromatogram obtained with reference solution (c) (0.5 per cent);
— *impurities B, C, D*: for each impurity, not more than the area of the principal peak in the chromatogram obtained with reference solution (a) (0.1 per cent);
— *any other impurity*: for each impurity, not more than the area of the principal peak in the chromatogram obtained with reference solution (a) (0.1 per cent);
— *total*: not more than 5 times the area of the principal peak in the chromatogram obtained with reference solution (a) (0.5 per cent);
— *disregard limit*: 0.5 times the area of the principal peak in the chromatogram obtained with reference solution (a) (0.05 per cent).

**Water** (*2.5.12*)

Maximum 0.5 per cent, determined on 1.000 g.

**Sulphated ash** (*2.4.14*)

Maximum 0.1 per cent, determined on 1.0 g.

**ASSAY**

Dissolve 0.250 g in 60 ml of *anhydrous acetic acid R.* Titrate with *0.1 M perchloric acid*, determining the end-point potentiometrically (*2.2.20*).

1 ml of *0.1 M perchloric acid* is equivalent to 30.34 mg of $C_{17}H_{21}NO_4$.

**IMPURITIES**

*Specified impurities* A, B, C, D.

A. R1 = $CH_2OH$, R2 = R3 = H: $(1R,2R,4S,5S,7s)$-3-oxa-9-azatricyclo[3.3.1.0²,⁴]non-7-yl (2S)-3-hydroxy-2-phenylpropanoate (norhyoscine),

B. R1 + R2 = $CH_2$, R3 = $CH_3$: $(1R,2R,4S,5S,7s)$-9-methyl-3-oxa-9-azatricyclo[3.3.1.0²,⁴]non-7-yl 2-phenylprop-2-enoate (apohyoscine),

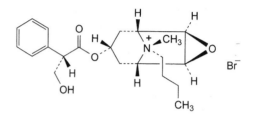

C. (2RS)-3-hydroxy-2-phenylpropanoic acid (DL-tropic acid),

D. hyoscyamine.

*Ph Eur*

# Hyoscine Butylbromide

(*Ph Eur monograph 0737*)

$C_{21}H_{30}BrNO_4$      440.4      *149-64-4*

**Action and use**

Anticholinergic.

**Preparations**

Hyoscine Butylbromide Injection

Hyoscine Butylbromide Tablets

*Ph Eur*

**DEFINITION**

$(1R,2R,4S,5S,7s,9r)$-9-Butyl-7-[[(2S)-3-hydroxy-2-phenylpropanoyl]oxy]-9-methyl-3-oxa-9-azoniatricyclo[3.3.1.0²,⁴]nonane bromide.

**Content**

98.0 per cent to 101.0 per cent (dried substance).

**CHARACTERS**

**Appearance**

White or almost white, crystalline powder.

**Solubility**

Freely soluble in water and in methylene chloride, sparingly soluble in anhydrous ethanol.

**IDENTIFICATION**

*First identification* A, C, F.

*Second identification* A, B, D, E, F.

A. It complies with the test for specific optical rotation (see Tests).

B. Melting point (*2.2.14*): 139 °C to 141 °C.

C. Infrared absorption spectrophotometry (*2.2.24*).

*Comparison* hyoscine butylbromide CRS.

D. To about 1 mg add 0.2 ml of *nitric acid R* and evaporate to dryness on a water-bath. Dissolve the residue in 2 ml of *acetone R* and add 0.1 ml of a 30 g/l solution of *potassium hydroxide R* in *methanol R*. A violet colour develops.

E. To 5 ml of solution S (see Tests) add 2 ml of *dilute sodium hydroxide solution R*. No precipitate is formed.

F. It gives reaction (a) of bromides (*2.3.1*).

## TESTS

### Solution S

Dissolve 1.25 g in *carbon dioxide-free water R* and dilute to 25.0 ml with the same solvent.

### Appearance of solution

Solution S is clear (*2.2.1*) and colourless (*2.2.2, Method II*).

### pH (2.2.3)

5.5 to 6.5 for solution S.

### Specific optical rotation (2.2.7)

− 18 to − 20 (dried substance), determined on solution S.

### Related substances

Liquid chromatography (*2.2.29*).

*Test solution* Dissolve 50.0 mg of the substance to be examined in the mobile phase and dilute to 10.0 ml with the mobile phase.

*Reference solution (a)* Dilute 1.0 ml of the test solution to 50.0 ml with the mobile phase. Dilute 5.0 ml of this solution to 50.0 ml with the mobile phase.

*Reference solution (b)* Dilute 10.0 ml of reference solution (a) to 20.0 ml with the mobile phase.

*Reference solution (c)* Dissolve 5.0 mg of *hyoscine butylbromide impurity E CRS* in the mobile phase, add 1.0 ml of the test solution and dilute to 10.0 ml with the mobile phase. Dilute 5.0 ml of this solution to 50.0 ml with the mobile phase.

*Column:*
— size: $l$ = 0.125 m, Ø = 4.0 mm;
— stationary phase: octylsilyl silica gel for chromatography R (4 μm);
— temperature: 25 ± 1 °C.

*Mobile phase* Dissolve 5.8 g of *sodium dodecyl sulphate R* in a mixture of 410 ml of *acetonitrile R* and 605 ml of a 7.0 g/l solution of *potassium dihydrogen phosphate R* previously adjusted to pH 3.3 with *0.05 M phosphoric acid*.

*Flow rate* 2.0 ml/min.

*Detection* Spectrophotometer at 210 nm.

*Injection* 10 μl.

*Run time* 3.5 times the retention time of butylhyoscine.

*Relative retention* With reference to butylhyoscine (retention time = about 7.0 min): impurity B = about 0.1; impurity A = about 0.36; impurity C = about 0.40; impurity D = about 0.7; impurity E = about 0.8; impurity F = about 0.9; impurity G = about 3.0.

*System suitability* Reference solution (c):
— *resolution*: minimum 1.5 between the peaks due to butylhyoscine and impurity E;
— *symmetry factor*: maximum 2.5 for the peak due to butylhyoscine.

*Limits:*
— *correction factors*: for the calculation of contents, multiply the peak areas of the following impurities by the corresponding correction factor: impurity B = 0.3; impurity G = 0.6;
— *impurity A*: not more than the area of the principal peak in the chromatogram obtained with reference solution (b) (0.1 per cent);
— *impurities B, C, D, E, F, G*: for each impurity, not more than the area of the principal peak in the chromatogram obtained with reference solution (a) (0.2 per cent);
— *any other impurity*: for each impurity, not more than the area of the principal peak in the chromatogram obtained with reference solution (b) (0.1 per cent);

— *total*: not more than twice the area of the principal peak in the chromatogram obtained with reference solution (a) (0.4 per cent); disregard any peak due to the bromide ion which appears close to the solvent peak;
— *disregard limit*: 0.5 times the area of the principal peak in the chromatogram obtained with reference solution (b) (0.05 per cent).

### Loss on drying (2.2.32)

Maximum 2.5 per cent, determined on 0.500 g by drying in an oven at 105 °C.

### Sulphated ash (2.4.14)

Maximum 0.1 per cent, determined on 0.5 g.

## ASSAY

Dissolve 0.400 g in 50 ml of *water R*. Titrate with *0.1 M silver nitrate*, determining the end-point potentiometrically (*2.2.20*) using a silver indicator electrode and a silver-silver chloride reference electrode.

1 ml of *0.1 M silver nitrate* is equivalent to 44.04 mg of $C_{21}H_{30}BrNO_4$.

## IMPURITIES

*Specified impurities* A, B, C, D, E, F, G.

A. hyoscine,

and enantiomer

B. (2RS)-3-hydroxy-2-phenylpropanoic acid (dl-tropic acid),

C. R1 = $CH_2OH$, R2 = H, R3 = R4 = $CH_3$: (1R,2R,4S,5S,7s)-7-[[(2S)-3-hydroxy-2-phenylpropanoyl]oxy]-9,9-dimethyl-3-oxa-9-azoniatricyclo[3.3.1.0$^{2,4}$]nonane (methylhyoscine),

D. R1 = $CH_2OH$, R2 = H, R3 = $CH_3$, R4 = $CH_2$-$CH_2$-$CH_3$: (1R,2R,4S,5S,7s,9r)-7-[[(2S)-3-hydroxy-2-phenylpropanoyl]oxy]-9-methyl-9-propyl-3-oxa-9-azoniatricyclo[3.3.1.0$^{2,4}$]nonane (propylhyoscine),

F. R1 = $CH_2OH$, R2 = H, R3 = $CH_2$-$CH_2$-$CH_2$-$CH_3$, R4 = $CH_3$: (1R,2R,4S,5S,7s,9s)-9-butyl-7-[[(2S)-3-hydroxy-2-phenylpropanoyl]oxy]-9-methyl-3-oxa-9-azoniatricyclo[3.3.1.0$^{2,4}$]nonane (pseudo-isomer),

G. R1 + R2 = $CH_2$ , R3 = $CH_3$, R4 = $CH_2$-$CH_2$-$CH_2$-$CH_3$: (1R,2R,4S,5S,7s,9r)-9-butyl-9-methyl-7-[(2-phenylprop-2-enoyl)oxy]-3-oxa-9-azoniatricyclo[3.3.1.0$^{2,4}$]nonane (apo-N-butylhyoscine);

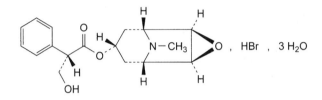

E. (1*R*,2*R*,4*S*,5*S*,7*s*)-9-butyl-3-oxa-9-azatricyclo[3.3.1.0$^{2,4}$]nonan-7-yl (2*S*)-3-hydroxy-2-phenylpropanoate (*N*-butylhyoscine).

_____ *Ph Eur*

# Hyoscine Hydrobromide

★★★
★　★
★　★
★★★

(*Ph Eur monograph 0106*)

C$_{17}$H$_{21}$NO$_4$,HBr,3H$_2$O     438.3         6533-68-2

### Action and use
Anticholinergic.

### Preparations
Hyoscine Eye Drops

Hyoscine Injection

Hyoscine Tablets

*Ph Eur* _____

## DEFINITION
(1*R*,2*R*,4*S*,5*S*,7*s*)-9-Methyl-3-oxa-9-azatricyclo[3.3.1.0$^{2,4}$]non-7-yl (2*S*)-3-hydroxy-2-phenylpropanoate hydrobromide trihydrate.

### Content
99.0 per cent to 101.0 per cent (anhydrous substance).

## CHARACTERS
### Appearance
White or almost white, crystalline powder or colourless crystals, efflorescent.

### Solubility
Freely soluble in water, soluble in ethanol (96 per cent).

## IDENTIFICATION
*First identification*   B, E.

*Second identification*   A, C, D, E.

A. It complies with the test for specific optical rotation (see Tests).

B. Infrared absorption spectrophotometry (*2.2.24*).

*Comparison*   hyoscine hydrobromide CRS.

If the spectra obtained in the solid state show differences, proceed as follows: dissolve 3 mg of the substance to be examined in 1 ml of *ethanol (96 per cent) R* and evaporate to dryness on a water-bath; dissolve the residue in 0.5 ml of *methylene chloride R* and add 0.2 g of *potassium bromide R* and 15 ml of *ether R*; allow to stand for 5 min shaking frequently; decant; dry the residue on a water-bath until the solvents

have evaporated; using the residue prepare a disc and dry at 100-105 °C for 3 h. Repeat the procedure with *hyoscine hydrobromide CRS* and record the spectra.

C. Dissolve about 50 mg in 5 ml of *water R* and add 5 ml of *picric acid solution R* dropwise and with shaking. The precipitate, washed with *water R* and dried at 100-105 °C for 2 h, melts (*2.2.14*) at 188 °C to 193 °C.

D. To about 1 mg add 0.2 ml of *fuming nitric acid R* and evaporate to dryness on a water-bath. Dissolve the residue in 2 ml of *acetone R* and add 0.1 ml of a 30 g/l solution of *potassium hydroxide R* in *methanol R*. A violet colour develops.

E. It gives reaction (a) of bromides (*2.3.1*).

## TESTS
### Solution S
Dissolve 2.50 g in *carbon dioxide-free water R* and dilute to 50.0 ml with the same solvent.

### pH (*2.2.3*)
4.0 to 5.5 for solution S.

### Specific optical rotation (*2.2.7*)
− 24 to − 27 (anhydrous substance), determined on solution S.

### Related substances
Liquid chromatography (*2.2.29*).

*Test solution*   Dissolve 70.0 mg of the substance to be examined in the mobile phase and dilute to 50.0 ml with the mobile phase.

*Reference solution (a)*   Dilute 2.0 ml of the test solution to 100.0 ml with the mobile phase. Dilute 5.0 ml of this solution to 20.0 ml with the mobile phase.

*Reference solution (b)*   Dilute 5.0 ml of reference solution (a) to 25.0 ml with the mobile phase.

*Reference solution (c)*   Dissolve 5.0 mg of *hyoscine hydrobromide impurity B CRS* in the mobile phase, add 5.0 ml of the test solution and dilute to 50.0 ml with the mobile phase. Dilute 1.0 ml of this solution to 10.0 ml with the mobile phase.

*Column:*
— *size: l* = 0.125 m, Ø = 4.0 mm;
— *stationary phase: octylsilyl silica gel for chromatography R* (3 μm);
— *temperature*: 25 ± 1 °C.

*Mobile phase*   Mix 330 ml of *acetonitrile R* with 670 ml of a 2.5 g/l solution of *sodium dodecyl sulphate R* previously adjusted to pH 2.5 with *3 M phosphoric acid*.

*Flow rate*   1.5 ml/min.

*Detection*   Spectrophotometer at 210 nm.

*Injection*   5 μl.

*Run time*   3 times the retention time of hyoscine.

*Relative retention*   With reference to hyoscine (retention time = about 5.0 min): impurity D = about 0.2; impurity B = about 0.9; impurity A = about 1.3; impurity C = about 2.4.

*System suitability*   Reference solution (c):
— *resolution*: minimum 1.5 between the peaks due to impurity B and hyoscine;
— *symmetry factor*: maximum 2.5 for the peak due to hyoscine.

*Limits:*
— *correction factors*: for the calculation of contents, multiply the peak areas of the following impurities by the corresponding correction factor: impurity D = 0.3; impurity C = 0.6;

— *impurity B*: not more than the area of the principal peak in the chromatogram obtained with reference solution (a) (0.5 per cent);

— *impurities A, C, D*: for each impurity, not more than the area of the principal peak in the chromatogram obtained with reference solution (b) (0.1 per cent);

— *any other impurity*: for each impurity, not more than the area of the principal peak in the chromatogram obtained with reference solution (b) (0.1 per cent);

— *total*: not more than 1.4 times the area of the principal peak in the chromatogram obtained with reference solution (a) (0.7 per cent); disregard any peak due to the bromide ion which appears close to the solvent peak;

— *disregard limit*: 0.5 times the area of the principal peak in the chromatogram obtained with reference solution (b) (0.05 per cent).

**Water** (*2.5.12*)

10.0 per cent to 13.0 per cent, determined on 0.20 g.

**Sulphated ash** (*2.4.14*)

Maximum 0.1 per cent, determined on 1.0 g.

**ASSAY**

Dissolve 0.300 g in a mixture of 5.0 ml of *0.01 M hydrochloric acid* and 50 ml of *ethanol (96 per cent) R*. Carry out a potentiometric titration (*2.2.20*), using *0.1 M sodium hydroxide* free from carbonate. Read the volume added between the 2 points of inflexion.

1 ml of *0.1 M sodium hydroxide* is equivalent to 38.43 mg of $C_{17}H_{22}BrNO_4$.

**STORAGE**

In a well-filled, airtight container of small capacity, protected from light.

**IMPURITIES**

Specified impurities

*A, B, C, D.*

A. hyoscyamine,

B. R1 = $CH_2OH$, R2 = R3 = H: (1R,2R,4S,5S,7s)-3-oxa-9-azatricyclo[3.3.1.02,4]non-7-yl (2S)-3-hydroxy-2-phenylpropanoate (norhyoscine),

C. R1 + R2 = $CH_2$, R3 = $CH_3$: (1R,2R,4S,5S,7s)-9-methyl-3-oxa-9-azatricyclo[3.3.1.02,4]non-7-yl 2-phenylprop-2-enoate (apohyoscine),

D. (2RS)-3-hydroxy-2-phenylpropanoic acid (dl-tropic acid).

*Ph Eur*

# Hyoscyamine Sulphate

(*Ph Eur monograph 0501*)

$(C_{17}H_{23}NO_3)_2,H_2SO_4,2H_2O$   713          *6835-16-1*

**Action and use**

Anticholinergic.

*Ph Eur*

**DEFINITION**

Bis[(1R,3r,5S)-8-methyl-8-azabicyclo[3.2.1]oct-3-yl (2S)-3-hydroxy-2-phenylpropanoate] sulphate dihydrate.

**Content**

98.0 per cent to 101.0 per cent (anhydrous substance).

**CHARACTERS**

**Appearance**

White or almost white, crystalline powder or colourless needles.

**Solubility**

Very soluble in water, sparingly soluble or soluble in ethanol (96 per cent).

**IDENTIFICATION**

*First identification   A, B, E.*

*Second identification   C, D, E.*

A. Specific optical rotation (see Tests).

B. Infrared absorption spectrophotometry (*2.2.24*).

*Comparison   hyoscyamine sulphate CRS.*

C. To 0.5 ml of solution S (see Tests) add 2 ml of *dilute acetic acid R* and heat. To the hot solution add 4 ml of *picric acid solution R*. Allow to cool, shaking occasionally. Collect the crystals, wash with 2 quantities, each of 3 ml, of iced *water R* and dry at 100-105 °C. The crystals melt (*2.2.14*) at 164 °C to 168 °C.

D. To about 1 mg add 0.2 ml of *fuming nitric acid R* and evaporate to dryness on a water-bath. Dissolve the residue in 2 ml of *acetone R* and add 0.2 ml of a 30 g/l solution of *potassium hydroxide R* in *methanol R*. A violet colour develops.

E. It gives reaction (a) of sulphates (*2.3.1*).

**TESTS**

**Solution S**

Dissolve 2.50 g in *water R* and dilute to 50.0 ml with the same solvent.

**Appearance of solution**

Solution S is not more intensely coloured than reference solution $BY_6$ (*2.2.2, Method II*).

**pH** (*2.2.3*)

4.5 to 6.2.

Dissolve 0.5 g in *carbon dioxide-free water R* and dilute to 25 ml with the same solvent.

**Specific optical rotation** (*2.2.7*)

− 24 to − 29 (anhydrous substance), determined on solution S.

**Related substances**

Liquid chromatography (2.2.29).

*Test solution* Dissolve 60.0 mg of the substance to be examined in mobile phase A and dilute to 50.0 ml with mobile phase A. Dilute 10.0 ml of the solution to 50.0 ml with mobile phase A.

*Reference solution (a)* Dilute 5.0 ml of the test solution to 100.0 ml with mobile phase A. Dilute 5.0 ml of this solution to 50.0 ml with mobile phase A.

*Reference solution (b)* Dilute 5.0 ml of reference solution (a) to 25.0 ml with mobile phase A.

*Reference solution (c)* Dissolve 5.0 mg of *hyoscyamine impurity E CRS* in the test solution and dilute to 20.0 ml with the test solution. Dilute 5.0 ml of this solution to 25.0 ml with mobile phase A.

*Column:*
— *size: l* = 0.10 m, Ø = 4.6 mm;
— *stationary phase: octadecylsilyl silica gel for chromatography R* (3 μm);
— *temperature:* 25 ± 1 °C.

*Mobile phase:*
— *mobile phase A*: dissolve 3.5 g of *sodium dodecyl sulphate R* in 606 ml of a 7.0 g/l solution of *potassium dihydrogen phosphate R* previously adjusted to pH 3.3 with *0.05 M phosphoric acid* and mix with 320 ml of *acetonitrile R*;
— *mobile phase B: acetonitrile R*;

| Time (min) | Mobile phase A (per cent V/V) | Mobile phase B (per cent V/V) |
|---|---|---|
| 0 - 2.0 | 95 | 5 |
| 2.0 - 20.0 | 95 → 70 | 5 → 30 |
| 20.0 - 20.1 | 70 → 95 | 30 → 5 |
| 20.1 - 25.0 | 95 | 5 |

*Flow rate* 1.0 ml/min.

*Detection* Spectrophotometer at 210 nm.

*Injection* 10 μl.

*Relative retention* With reference to hyoscyamine (retention time = about 10.5 min): impurity A = about 0.2; impurity B = about 0.67; impurity C = about 0.72; impurity D = about 0.8; impurity E = about 0.9; impurity F = about 1.1; impurity G = about 1.8.

*System suitability* Reference solution (c):
— *resolution*: minimum 2.5 between the peaks due to hyoscyamine and impurity E;
— *symmetry factor*: maximum 2.5 for the peak due to hyoscyamine.

*Limits:*
— *correction factors*: for the calculation of contents, multiply the peak areas of the following impurities by the corresponding correction factor: impurity A = 0.3; impurity G = 0.6;
— *impurity E*: not more than 3 times the area of the principal peak in the chromatogram obtained with reference solution (b) (0.3 per cent);
— *impurities A, B, C, D, F, G*: for each impurity, not more than twice the area of the principal peak in the chromatogram obtained with reference solution (b) (0.2 per cent);
— *any other impurity*: for each impurity, not more than the area of the principal peak in the chromatogram obtained with reference solution (b) (0.1 per cent);

— *total*: not more than the area of the principal peak in the chromatogram obtained with reference solution (a) (0.5 per cent);
— *disregard limit*: 0.1 times the area of the principal peak in the chromatogram obtained with reference solution (a) (0.05 per cent).

**Water** (2.5.12)

2.0 per cent to 5.5 per cent, determined on 0.500 g.

**Sulphated ash** (2.4.14)

Maximum 0.1 per cent, determined on 1.0 g.

**ASSAY**

Dissolve 0.500 g in 25 ml of *anhydrous acetic acid R*. Titrate with *0.1 M perchloric acid*, determining the end-point potentiometrically (2.2.20).

1 ml of *0.1 M perchloric acid* is equivalent to 67.7 mg of $C_{34}H_{48}N_2O_{10}S$.

**STORAGE**

In an airtight container, protected from light.

**IMPURITIES**

*Specified impurities    A, B, C, D, E, F, G.*

A. (2RS)-3-hydroxy-2-phenylpropanoic acid (DL-tropic acid),

B. R = OH, R' = H: (1R,3S,5R,6RS)-6-hydroxy-8-methyl-8-azabicyclo[3.2.1]oct-3-yl (2S)-3-hydroxy-2-phenylpropanoate (7-hydroxyhyoscyamine),

C. R = H, R' = OH: (1S,3R,5S,6RS)-6-hydroxy-8-methyl-8-azabicyclo[3.2.1]oct-3-yl (2S)-3-hydroxy-2-phenylpropanoate (6-hydroxyhyoscyamine),

D. hyoscine,

E. R1 = CH₂OH, R2 = R3 = H: (1R,3r,5S)-8-azabicyclo[3.2.1]oct-3-yl (2S)-3-hydroxy-2-phenylpropanoate (norhyoscyamine),

G. R1 + R2 = CH₂, R3 = CH₃: (1R,3r,5S)-8-methyl-8-azabicyclo[3.2.1]oct-3-yl 2-phenylprop-2-enoate (apoatropine),

F. (1R,3r,5S)-8-methyl-8-azabicyclo[3.2.1]oct-3-yl (2R)-2-hydroxy-3-phenylpropanoate (littorine).

*Ph Eur*

# Hypromellose

(*Ph Eur monograph 0348*)

9004-65-3

## Action and use
Artificial tears.

## Preparation
Hypromellose Eye Drops

*Ph Eur*

## DEFINITION
Hydroxypropylmethylcellulose.

Partly *O*-methylated and *O*-(2-hydroxypropylated) cellulose.

## CHARACTERS
### Appearance
White, yellowish-white or greyish-white powder or granules, hygroscopic after drying.

### Solubility
Practically insoluble in hot water, in acetone, in anhydrous ethanol and in toluene. It dissolves in cold water giving a colloidal solution.

## IDENTIFICATION
A. Evenly distribute 1.0 g on the surface of 100 ml of *water R* in a beaker, tapping the top of the beaker, gently if necessary to ensure a uniform layer on the surface. Allow to stand for 1-2 min: the powdered material aggregates on the surface.

B. Evenly distribute 1.0 g into 100 ml of boiling *water R*, and stir the mixture using a magnetic stirrer with a bar 25 mm long: a slurry is formed and the particles do not dissolve. Allow the slurry to cool to 10 °C and stir using a magnetic stirrer: a clear or slightly turbid solution occurs with its thickness dependent on the viscosity grade.

C. To 0.1 ml of the solution obtained in identification B add 9 ml of a 90 per cent *V/V* solution of *sulphuric acid R*, shake, heat on a water-bath for exactly 3 min, immediately cool in an ice-bath, carefully add 0.6 ml of a 20 g/l solution of *ninhydrin R*, shake and allow to stand at 25 °C: a red colour develops at first and changes to purple within 100 min.

D. Place 2-3 ml of the solution obtained in identification B onto a glass slide as a thin film and allow the water to evaporate: a coherent, clear film forms on the glass slide.

E. Add exactly 50 ml of the solution obtained in identification B to exactly 50 ml of *water R* in a beaker. Insert a thermometer into the solution. Stir the solution on a magnetic stirrer/hot plate and begin heating, increasing the temperature at a rate of 2-5 °C per minute. Determine the temperature at which a turbidity increase begins to occur and designate the temperature as the flocculation temperature: the flocculation temperature is higher than 50 °C.

## TESTS
### Solution S
While stirring, introduce a quantity of the substance to be examined equivalent to 1.0 g of the dried substance into 50 g of *carbon dioxide-free water R* heated to 90 °C. Allow to cool, adjust the mass of the solution to 100 g with *carbon dioxide-free water R* and stir until dissolution is complete.

### Appearance of solution
Solution S is not more opalescent than reference suspension III (*2.2.1*) and not more intensely coloured than reference solution $Y_6$ (*2.2.2, Method II*).

### pH (*2.2.3*)
5.0 to 8.0 for the solution prepared as described under Apparent viscosity.

Carry out the test at 20 ± 2 °C and read the indicated pH value after the probe has been immersed for 5 ± 0.5 min.

### Heavy metals (*2.4.8*)
Maximum 20 ppm.

1.0 g complies with test F. Prepare the reference solution using 2 ml of *lead standard solution (10 ppm Pb) R*.

### Loss on drying (*2.2.32*)
Maximum 5.0 per cent, determined on 1.000 g by drying in an oven at 105 °C for 1 h.

### Sulphated ash (*2.4.14*)
Maximum 1.5 per cent, determined on 1.0 g.

## FUNCTIONALITY-RELATED CHARACTERISTICS
*This section provides information on characteristics that are recognised as being relevant control parameters for one or more functions of the substance when used as an excipient (see chapter 5.15). This section is a non-mandatory part of the monograph and it is not necessary to verify the characteristics to demonstrate compliance. Control of these characteristics can however contribute to the quality of a medicinal product by improving the consistency of the manufacturing process and the performance of the medicinal product during use. Where control methods are cited, they are recognised as being suitable for the purpose, but other methods can also be used. Wherever results for a particular characteristic are reported, the control method must be indicated.*

*The following characteristics may be relevant for hypromellose used as binder, viscosity-increasing agent or film former.*

### Apparent viscosity
Minimum 80 per cent and maximum 120 per cent of the nominal value for samples with a viscosity less than 600 mPa·s (Method 1); minimum 75 per cent and maximum 140 per cent of the nominal value for samples with a viscosity of 600 mPa·s or higher (Method 2).

*Method 1, to be applied to samples with a viscosity of less than 600 mPa·s* Weigh accurately a quantity of the substance to be examined equivalent to 4.000 g of the dried substance. Transfer into a wide-mouthed bottle, and adjust the mass to 200.0 g with hot *water R*. Capping the bottle, stir by mechanical means at 400 ± 50 r/min for 10-20 min until the particles are thoroughly dispersed and wetted. Scrape down the insides of the bottle with a spatula if necessary, to ensure that there is no undissolved material on the sides of the bottle, and continue the stirring in a cooling water-bath maintained at a temperature below 10 °C for another 20-40 min. Adjust the solution mass if necessary to 200.0 g using cold *water R*. Centrifuge the solution if necessary to expel any entrapped air bubbles. Using a spatula, remove any foam, if present. Determine the viscosity of this solution using the capillary viscometer method (*2.2.9*) to obtain the kinematic viscosity (*v*). Separately, determine the density (*ρ*)

(2.2.5) of the solution and calculate the dynamic viscosity ($\eta$), as $\eta = \rho v$.

*Method 2, to be applied to samples with a viscosity of 600 mPa·s or higher* Weigh accurately a quantity of the substance to be examined equivalent to 10.00 g of the dried substance. Transfer into a wide-mouthed bottle, and adjust the mass to 500.0 g with hot *water R*. Capping the bottle, stir by mechanical means at $400 \pm 50$ r/min for 10-20 min until the particles are thoroughly dispersed and wetted. Scrape down the insides of the bottle with a spatula if necessary, to ensure that there is no undissolved material on the sides of the bottle, and continue the stirring in a cooling water-bath maintained at a temperature below 10 °C for another 20-40 min. Adjust the solution mass if necessary to 500.0 g using cold *water R*. Centrifuge the solution if necessary to expel any entrapped air bubbles. Using a spatula, remove any foam, if present. Determine the viscosity (2.2.10) of this solution at $20 \pm 0.1$ °C using a rotating viscometer.

*Apparatus* Single-cylinder type spindle viscometer.

*Rotor number, revolution and calculation multiplier* Apply the conditions specified in Table 0348.-1.

Allow the spindle to rotate for 2 min before taking the measurement. Allow a rest period of 2 min between subsequent measurements. Repeat the measurement twice and determine the mean of the 3 readings.

Table 0348.-1.

| Labelled viscosity* (mPa·s) | Rotor number | Revolution (r/min) | Calculation multiplier |
|---|---|---|---|
| 600 to less than 1400 | 3 | 60 | 20 |
| 1400 to less than 3500 | 3 | 12 | 100 |
| 3500 to less than 9500 | 4 | 60 | 100 |
| 9500 to less than 99 500 | 4 | 6 | 1000 |
| 99 500 or more | 4 | 3 | 2000 |

* the nominal viscosity is based on the manufacturer's specifications.

**Degree of substitution**

Gas chromatography (2.2.28).

*Apparatus:*

— *reaction vial*: a 5 ml pressure-tight vial, 50 mm in height, 20 mm in external diameter and 13 mm in internal diameter at the mouth, equipped with a pressure-tight butyl rubber membrane stopper coated with polytetrafluoroethylene and secured with an aluminium crimped cap or another sealing system providing a sufficient air-tightness;

— *heater*: a heating module with a square aluminium block having holes 20 mm in diameter and 32 mm in depth, so that the reaction vials fit; mixing of the contents of the vial is effected using a magnetic stirrer equipped in the heating module or using a reciprocal shaker that performs approximately 100 cycles/min.

*Internal standard solution* 30 g/l solution of *octane R* in *xylene R*.

*Test solution* Weigh 65.0 mg of the substance to be examined, place in a reaction vial, add 0.06-0.10 g of *adipic acid R*, 2.0 ml of the internal standard solution and 2.0 ml of *hydriodic acid R*, immediately cap and seal the vial, and weigh accurately. Mix the contents of the vial continuously for 60 min while heating the block so that the temperature of the contents is maintained at $130 \pm 2$ °C. If a reciprocal shaker or magnetic stirrer cannot be used, shake the vial well by hand at 5-minute intervals during the initial 30 min of the heating time. Allow the vial to cool, and again weigh accurately. If the loss of mass is less than 0.50 per cent of the contents and there is no evidence of a leak, use the upper layer of the mixture as the test solution.

*Reference solution* Place 0.06-0.10 g of *adipic acid R*, 2.0 ml of the internal standard solution and 2.0 ml of *hydriodic acid R* in another reaction vial, cap and seal the vial, and weigh accurately. Add 15-22 µl of *isopropyl iodide R* through the septum with a syringe, weigh accurately, add 45 µl of *methyl iodide R* in the same manner, and weigh accurately. Shake the reaction vial well, and use the upper layer as the reference solution.

*Column:*
— *size: l* = 1.8-3 m, Ø = 3-4 mm;
— *stationary phase: diatomaceous earth for gas chromatography R* impregnated with 10-20 per cent of *poly(dimethyl)(75)(diphenyl)(25)siloxane R* (film thickness 125-150 µm);
— *temperature*: 100 °C.

*Carrier gas helium for chromatography R* (thermal conductivity); *helium for chromatography R* or *nitrogen for chromatography R* (flame ionisation).

*Flow rate* Adjusted so that the retention time of the internal standard is about 10 min.

*Detection* Flame ionisation or thermal conductivity.

*Injection* 1-2 µl.

*System suitability* Reference solution:
— *resolution*: well resolved peaks of methyl iodide (1st peak), isopropyl iodide (2nd peak) and internal standard (3rd peak).

*Calculation:*
— *methoxy and hydroxypropoxy groups*: calculate the ratios ($Q_1$ and $Q_2$) of the areas of the peaks due to methyl iodide and isopropyl iodide to the area of the peak due to the internal standard in the chromatogram obtained with the test solution, and the ratios ($Q_3$ and $Q_4$) of the areas of the peaks due to methyl iodide and isopropyl iodide to the area of the peak due to the internal standard in the chromatogram obtained with the reference solution.

Calculate the percentage content of methoxy groups using the following expression:

$$\frac{Q_1}{Q_3} \times \frac{m_1}{m} \times 21.864$$

Calculate the percentage content of hydroxypropoxy groups using the following expression:

$$\frac{Q_2}{Q_4} \times \frac{m_2}{m} \times 44.17$$

$m_1$ = mass of methyl iodide in the reference solution, in milligrams;

$m_2$ = mass of isopropyl iodide in the reference solution, in milligrams;

$m$ = mass of the sample (dried substance), in milligrams.

| Substitution type | Methoxy (per cent) | Hydroxypropoxy (per cent) |
|---|---|---|
| 1828 | 16.5 to 20.0 | 23.0 to 32.0 |
| 2208 | 19.0 to 24.0 | 4.0 to 12.0 |
| 2906 | 27.0 to 30.0 | 4.0 to 7.5 |
| 2910 | 28.0 to 30.0 | 7.0 to 12.0 |

*The following characteristics may be relevant for hypromellose used as matrix former in prolonged-release tablets.*

**Apparent viscosity**
See test above.

**Degree of substitution**
See test above.

**Molecular mass distribution** (*2.2.30*).

**Particle-size distribution** (*2.9.31* or *2.9.38*).

**Powder flow** (*2.9.36*).

*Ph Eur*

# Hypromellose Phthalate

(*Ph Eur monograph 0347*)

**Action and use**
Artificial tears.

*Ph Eur*

## DEFINITION

Hydroxypropylmethylcellulose phthalate.

Monophthalic acid ester of hypromellose, containing methoxy (-OCH$_3$), 2-hydroxypropoxy (-OCH$_2$CHOHCH$_3$) and phthaloyl (*o*-carboxybenzoyl C$_8$H$_5$O$_3$) groups.

## CHARACTERS
**Appearance**
White or almost white, free-flowing flakes or granular powder.

**Solubility**
Practically insoluble in water, soluble in a mixture of equal volumes of acetone and methanol and in a mixture of equal volumes of methanol and methylene chloride, very slightly soluble in acetone and in toluene, practically insoluble in anhydrous ethanol.

## IDENTIFICATION

Infrared absorption spectrophotometry (*2.2.24*).

*Preparation* Dissolve 40 mg in 1 ml of a mixture of equal volumes of *methanol R* and *methylene chloride R*; spread 2 drops of this solution between 2 sodium chloride plates, then remove one of the plates to evaporate the solvent.

*Comparison* hypromellose phthalate CRS.

## TESTS
**Free phthalic acid**
Liquid chromatography (*2.2.29*).

*Test solution* Dissolve 0.20 g of the substance to be examined in about 50 ml of *acetonitrile R* with the aid of ultrasound. Add 10 ml of *water R*, cool to room temperature, dilute to 100.0 ml with *acetonitrile R* and mix.

*Reference solution* Dissolve 12.5 mg of *phthalic acid R* in 125 ml of *acetonitrile R*. Add 25 ml of *water R*, dilute to 250.0 ml with *acetonitrile R* and mix.

*Column:*
— *size:* $l$ = 0.25 m, Ø = 4.6 mm;
— *stationary phase:* octadecylsilyl silica gel for chromatography R (5-10 µm).

*Mobile phase* acetonitrile R, 1 g/l solution of *trifluoroacetic acid R* (1:9 *V/V*).

*Flow rate* 2.0 ml/min.

*Detection* Spectrophotometer at 235 nm.

*Injection* 10 µl.

*System suitability* Reference solution:
— *repeatability:* maximum relative standard deviation of 1.0 per cent after 2 injections.

*Limit:*
— *phthalic acid:* not more than 0.4 times the area of the corresponding peak in the chromatogram obtained with the reference solution (1.0 per cent).

**Chlorides**
Maximum 0.07 per cent.

Dissolve 1.0 g in 40 ml of *0.2 M sodium hydroxide*, add 0.05 ml of *phenolphthalein solution R* and add *dilute nitric acid R* dropwise, with stirring, until the red colour disappears. Add an additional 20 ml of *dilute nitric acid R* with stirring. Heat on a water-bath with stirring until the gel-like precipitate formed becomes granular. Cool and centrifuge. Separate the liquid phase and wash the residue with 3 quantities, each of 20 ml, of *water R*, separating the washings by centrifugation. Combine the liquid phases, dilute to 200 ml with *water R*, mix and filter. To 50 ml of this solution, add 1 ml of *0.1 M silver nitrate*. The solution is not more opalescent than a standard prepared by mixing 0.5 ml of *0.01 M hydrochloric acid* with 10 ml of *0.2 M sodium hydroxide*, adding 7 ml of *dilute nitric acid R* and 1 ml of *0.1 M silver nitrate*, and diluting to 50 ml with *water R*.

**Heavy metals** (*2.4.8*)
Maximum 10 ppm.

2.0 g complies with test C. Prepare the reference solution using 2 ml of *lead standard solution (10 ppm Pb) R*.

**Water** (*2.5.12*)
Maximum 5.0 per cent, determined on 0.500 g.

**Sulphated ash** (*2.4.14*)
Maximum 0.2 per cent, determined on 1.0 g.

## STORAGE
In an airtight container.

## FUNCTIONALITY-RELATED CHARACTERISTICS

*This section provides information on characteristics that are recognised as being relevant control parameters for one or more functions of the substance when used as an excipient (see chapter 5.15). This section is a non-mandatory part of the monograph and it is not necessary to verify the characteristics to demonstrate compliance. Control of these characteristics can however contribute to the quality of a medicinal product by improving the consistency of the manufacturing process and the performance of the medicinal product during use. Where control methods are cited, they are recognised as being suitable for the purpose, but other methods can also be used. Wherever results for a particular characteristic are reported, the control method must be indicated.*

*The following characteristics may be relevant for hypromellose phthalate used as a gastro-resistant coating agent.*

**Apparent viscosity** (*2.2.9*)

80 per cent to 120 per cent of the nominal value.

Dissolve 10 g, previously dried at 105 °C for 1 h, in 90 g of a mixture of equal masses of *methanol R* and *methylene chloride R* by mixing and shaking.

**Solubility**

0.2 g does not dissolve in *0.1 M hydrochloric acid* but dissolves quickly and completely in 100 ml of *phosphate buffer solution pH 6.8 R* with stirring.

**Phthaloyl groups**

Typically 21.0 per cent to 35.0 per cent (anhydrous substance).

Dissolve 1.000 g in 50 ml of a mixture of 1 volume of *water R*, 2 volumes of *acetone R* and 2 volumes of *ethanol (96 per cent) R*. Add 0.1 ml of *phenolphthalein solution R* and titrate with *0.1 M sodium hydroxide* until a faint pink colour is obtained. Carry out a blank titration.

Calculate the percentage content of phthaloyl groups using the following expression:

$$\frac{149n}{(100-a)\,m} - 1.795S$$

*a* = percentage content of water;

*m* = mass of the substance to be examined, in grams;

*n* = volume of *0.1 M sodium hydroxide* used, in millilitres;

*S* = percentage content of free phthalic acid (see Tests).

_____ *Ph Eur*

# Ibuprofen

(*Ph Eur monograph 0721*)

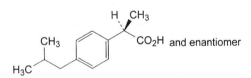

C13H18O2          206.3          *15687-27-1*

$C_{13}H_{18}O_2$

**Action and use**

Cyclo-oxygenase inhibitor; analgesic; anti-inflammatory.

**Preparations**

Ibuprofen Cream

Ibuprofen Gel

Ibuprofen Oral Suspension

Ibuprofen Tablets

Prolonged-release Ibuprofen Capsules

Prolonged-release Ibuprofen Tablets

*Ph Eur* _____

**DEFINITION**

(2*RS*)-2-[4-(2-Methylpropyl)phenyl]propanoic acid.

**Content**

98.5 per cent to 101.0 per cent (dried substance).

**CHARACTERS**

**Appearance**

White or almost white, crystalline powder or colourless crystals.

**Solubility**

Practically insoluble in water, freely soluble in acetone, in methanol and in methylene chloride. It dissolves in dilute solutions of alkali hydroxides and carbonates.

**IDENTIFICATION**

*First identification*   A, C.

*Second identification*   A, B, D.

A. Melting point (*2.2.14*): 75 °C to 78 °C.

B. Ultraviolet and visible absorption spectrophotometry (*2.2.25*).

*Test solution*   Dissolve 50.0 mg in a 4 g/l solution of *sodium hydroxide R* and dilute to 100.0 ml with the same alkaline solution.

*Spectral range*   240-300 nm, using a spectrophotometer with a band width of 1.0 nm and a scan speed of not more than 50 nm/min.

*Absorption maxima*   At 264 nm and 272 nm.

*Shoulder*   At 258 nm.

*Absorbance ratio:*

— $A_{264}$ / $A_{258}$ = 1.20 to 1.30;

— $A_{272}$ / $A_{258}$ = 1.00 to 1.10.

C. Infrared absorption spectrophotometry (*2.2.24*).

*Comparison*   *ibuprofen CRS*.

D. Thin-layer chromatography (*2.2.27*).

*Test solution*   Dissolve 50 mg of the substance to be examined in *methylene chloride R* and dilute to 10 ml with the same solvent.

*Reference solution*   Dissolve 50 mg of *ibuprofen CRS* in *methylene chloride R* and dilute to 10 ml with the same solvent.

*Plate*   *TLC silica gel plate R*.

*Mobile phase*   anhydrous acetic acid R, ethyl acetate R, hexane R (5:24:71 *V/V/V*).

*Application*   5 µl.

*Development*   Over a path of 10 cm.

*Drying*   At 120 °C for 30 min.

*Detection*   Lightly spray with a 10 g/l solution of *potassium permanganate R* in *dilute sulphuric acid R* and heat at 120 °C for 20 min; examine in ultraviolet light at 365 nm.

*Results*   The principal spot in the chromatogram obtained with the test solution is similar in position, colour and size to the principal spot in the chromatogram obtained with the reference solution.

**TESTS**

**Solution S**

Dissolve 2.0 g in *methanol R* and dilute to 20 ml with the same solvent.

**Appearance of solution**

Solution S is clear (*2.2.1*) and colourless (*2.2.2, Method II*).

**Optical rotation** (*2.2.7*)

− 0.05° to + 0.05°.

Dissolve 0.50 g in *methanol R* and dilute to 20.0 ml with the same solvent.

**Related substances**

Liquid chromatography (*2.2.29*).

*Test solution*   Dissolve 20 mg of the substance to be examined in 2 ml of *acetonitrile R1* and dilute to 10.0 ml with mobile phase A.

*Reference solution (a)* Dilute 1.0 ml of the test solution to 100.0 ml with mobile phase A. Dilute 1.0 ml of this solution to 10.0 ml with mobile phase A.

*Reference solution (b)* Dilute 1.0 ml of *ibuprofen impurity B CRS* to 10.0 ml with *acetonitrile R1* (solution A). Dissolve 20 mg of *ibuprofen CRS* in 2 ml of *acetonitrile R1*, add 1.0 ml of solution A and dilute to 10.0 ml with mobile phase A.

*Reference solution (c)* Dissolve the contents of a vial of *ibuprofen for peak identification CRS* (mixture of impurities A, J and N) in 1 ml of *acetonitrile R1* and dilute to 5 ml with mobile phase A.

*Column:*
— *size*: $l$ = 0.15 m, Ø = 4.6 mm;
— *stationary phase*: *octadecylsilyl silica gel for chromatography R* (5 μm).

*Mobile phase:*
— *mobile phase A*: mix 0.5 volumes of *phosphoric acid R*, 340 volumes of *acetonitrile R1* and 600 volumes of *water R*; allow to equilibrate and dilute to 1000 volumes with *water R*;
— *mobile phase B*: *acetonitrile R1*;

| Time (min) | Mobile phase A (per cent *V/V*) | Mobile phase B (per cent *V/V*) |
|---|---|---|
| 0 - 25 | 100 | 0 |
| 25 - 55 | 100 → 15 | 0 → 85 |
| 55 - 70 | 15 | 85 |

*Flow rate* 2 ml/min.

*Detection* Spectrophotometer at 214 nm.

*Injection* 20 μl.

*Identification of impurities* Use the chromatogram supplied with *ibuprofen for peak identification CRS* and the chromatogram obtained with reference solution (c) to identify the peaks due to impurities A, J and N.

*Relative retention* With reference to ibuprofen (retention time = about 16 min): impurity J = about 0.2; impurity N = about 0.3; impurity A = about 0.9; impurity B = about 1.1.

*System suitability* Reference solution (b):
— *peak-to-valley ratio*: minimum 1.5, where $H_p$ = height above the baseline of the peak due to impurity B, and $H_v$ = height above the baseline of the lowest point of the curve separating this peak from the peak due to ibuprofen. If necessary, adjust the concentration of acetonitrile in mobile phase A.

*Limits:*
— *impurities A, J, N*: for each impurity, not more than 1.5 times the area of the principal peak in the chromatogram obtained with reference solution (a) (0.15 per cent);
— *unspecified impurities*: for each impurity, not more than 0.5 times the area of the principal peak in the chromatogram obtained with reference solution (a) (0.05 per cent);
— *total*: not more than twice the area of the principal peak in the chromatogram obtained with reference solution (a) (0.2 per cent);
— *disregard limit*: 0.3 times the area of the principal peak in the chromatogram obtained with reference solution (a) (0.03 per cent).

**Impurity F**

Gas chromatography (*2.2.28*): use the normalisation procedure.

*Methylating solution* Dilute 1 ml of *N,N-dimethylformamide dimethyl acetal R* and 1 ml of *pyridine R* to 10 ml with *ethyl acetate R*.

*Test solution* Weigh about 50.0 mg of the substance to be examined into a sealable vial, dissolve in 1.0 ml of *ethyl acetate R*, add 1 ml of the methylating solution, seal and heat at 100 °C in a block heater for 20 min. Allow to cool. Remove the reagents under a stream of nitrogen at room temperature. Dissolve the residue in 5 ml of *ethyl acetate R*.

*Reference solution (a)* Dissolve 0.5 mg of *ibuprofen impurity F CRS* in *ethyl acetate R* and dilute to 10.0 ml with the same solvent.

*Reference solution (b)* Weigh about 50.0 mg of *ibuprofen CRS* into a sealable vial, dissolve in 1.0 ml of reference solution (a), add 1 ml of the methylating solution, seal and heat at 100 °C in a block heater for 20 min. Allow to cool. Remove the reagents under a stream of nitrogen at room temperature. Dissolve the residue in 5 ml of *ethyl acetate R*.

*Column:*
— *material*: fused silica;
— *size*: $l$ = 25 m, Ø = 0.53 mm;
— *stationary phase*: *macrogol 20 000 R* (film thickness 2 μm).

*Carrier gas* *helium for chromatography R*.

*Flow rate* 5.0 ml/min.

*Temperature:*
— *column*: 150 °C;
— *injection port*: 200 °C;
— *detector*: 250 °C.

*Detection* Flame ionisation.

*Injection* 1 μl of the test solution and reference solution (b).

*Run time* Twice the retention time of ibuprofen.

*System suitability:*
— *relative retention* with reference to ibuprofen (retention time = about 17 min): impurity F = about 1.5.

*Limit:*
— *impurity F*: maximum 0.1 per cent.

**Heavy metals** (*2.4.8*)
Maximum 10 ppm.

12 ml of solution S complies with test B. Prepare the reference solution using lead standard solution (1 ppm Pb) obtained by diluting *lead standard solution (100 ppm Pb) R* with *methanol R*.

**Loss on drying** (*2.2.32*)
Maximum 0.5 per cent, determined on 1.000 g by drying *in vacuo*.

**Sulphated ash** (*2.4.14*)
Maximum 0.1 per cent, determined on 1.0 g.

**ASSAY**

Dissolve 0.450 g in 50 ml of *methanol R*. Add 0.4 ml of *phenolphthalein solution R1*. Titrate with *0.1 M sodium hydroxide* until a red colour is obtained. Carry out a blank titration.

1 ml of *0.1 M sodium hydroxide* is equivalent to 20.63 mg of $C_{13}H_{18}O_2$.

## IMPURITIES

*Specified impurities*  *A, F, J, N.*

*Other detectable impurities* (The following substances would, if present at a sufficient level, be detected by one or other of the tests in the monograph. They are limited by the general acceptance criterion for other/unspecified impurities and/or by the general monograph *Substances for pharmaceutical use (2034)*. It is therefore not necessary to identify these impurities for demonstration of compliance. See also *5.10. Control of impurities in substances for pharmaceutical use)*: *B, C, D, E, G, H, I, K, L, M, O, P, Q, R.*

A. R1 = OH, R2 = CH$_2$-CH(CH$_3$)$_2$, R3 = H:
(2*RS*)-2-[3-(2-methylpropyl)phenyl]propanoic acid,

B. R1 = OH, R2 = H, R3 = [CH$_2$]$_3$-CH$_3$:
(2*RS*)-2-(4-butylphenyl)propanoic acid,

C. R1 = NH2, R2 = H, R3 = CH$_2$-CH(CH$_3$)$_2$:
(2*RS*)-2-[4-(2-methylpropyl)phenyl]propanamide,

D. R1 = OH, R2 = H, R3 = CH$_3$:
(2*RS*)-2-(4-methylphenyl)propanoic acid,

E. 1-[4-(2-methylpropyl)phenyl]ethanone,

F. 3-[4-(2-methylpropyl)phenyl]propanoic acid,

G. (1*RS*,4*RS*)-7-(2-methylpropyl)-1-[4-(2-methylpropyl)phenyl]-1,2,3,4-tetrahydronaphthalene-1,4-dicarboxylic acid,

H. X = O:
(3*RS*)-1,3-bis[4-(2-methylpropyl)phenyl]butan-1-one,

I. X = H$_2$: 1-(2-methylpropyl)-4-[(3*RS*)-3-[4-(2-methylpropyl)phenyl]butyl]benzene,

J. R = CO-CH(CH$_3$)$_2$:
(2*RS*)-2-[4-(2-methylpropanoyl)phenyl]propanoic acid,

N. R = C$_2$H$_5$: (2*RS*)-2-(4-ethylphenyl)propanoic acid,

K. R = CHO: (2*RS*)-2-(4-formylphenyl)propanoic acid,

L. R = CHOH-CH(CH$_3$)$_2$:
2-[4-(1-hydroxy-2-methylpropyl)phenyl]propanoic acid,

O. R = CH(CH$_3$)-C$_2$H$_5$: 2-[4-(1-methylpropyl)phenyl]propanoic acid,

M. R1 = OH, R2 = CH$_3$, R3 = CO$_2$H:
(2*RS*)-2-hydroxy-2-[4-(2-methylpropyl)phenyl]propanoic acid,

P. R1 = H, R2 = CH$_3$, R3 = CH$_2$OH:
(2*RS*)-2-[4-(2-methylpropyl)phenyl]propan-1-ol,

Q. R1 = R2 = H, R3 = CH$_2$OH:
2-[4-(2-methylpropyl)phenyl]ethanol,

R. 1,1'-(ethane-1,1-diyl)-4,4'-(2-methylpropyl)dibenzene.

# Ichthammol

Ammonium Ichthosulphonate

(*Ph Eur monograph 0917*)

## Action and use
Chronic lichenified eczema.

## Preparation
Zinc and Ichthammol Cream

*Ph Eur*

## DEFINITION
Ichthammol is obtained by distillation from certain bituminous schists, sulphonation of the distillate and neutralisation of the product with ammonia.

*Content:*
— *dry matter*: 50.0 per cent *m/m* to 56.0 per cent *m/m*;
— *total ammonia* ($NH_3$; $M_r$ 17.03): 4.5 per cent *m/m* to 7.0 per cent *m/m* (dried substance);
— *organically combined sulphur*: minimum 10.5 per cent *m/m* (dried substance);
— *sulphur in the form of sulphate*: maximum 20.0 per cent *m/m* of the total sulphur.

## CHARACTERS
### Appearance
Dense, blackish-brown liquid.

### Solubility
Miscible with water and with glycerol, slightly soluble in ethanol (96 per cent), in fatty oils and in liquid paraffin. It forms homogeneous mixtures with wool fat and soft paraffin.

## IDENTIFICATION
A. Dissolve 1.5 g in 15 ml of *water R* (solution A). To 2 ml of solution A add 2 ml of *hydrochloric acid R*. A resinous precipitate is formed. Decant the supernatant liquid. The precipitate is partly soluble in *ether R*.

B. 2 ml of solution A, obtained in identification test A, gives the reaction of ammonium salts and salts of volatile bases (*2.3.1*).

C. Evaporate and ignite the mixture of solution A and *dilute sodium hydroxide solution R* obtained in identification test B. Take up the residue with 5 ml of *dilute hydrochloric acid R*. Gas is evolved which turns *lead acetate paper R* brown or black. Filter the solution. The filtrate gives reaction (a) of sulphates (*2.3.1*).

## TESTS
### Acidity or alkalinity
To 10.0 ml of the clear filtrate obtained in the assay of total ammonia add 0.05 ml of *methyl red solution R*. Not more than 0.2 ml of *0.02 M hydrochloric acid* or *0.02 M sodium hydroxide* is required to change the colour of the indicator.

### Relative density (*2.2.5*)
1.040 to 1.085, determined on a mixture of equal volumes of the substance to be examined and *water R*.

### Sulphated ash (*2.4.14*)
Maximum 0.3 per cent, determined on 1.00 g.

## ASSAY
### Dry matter
Weigh 1.000 g in a tared flask containing 2 g of *sand R*, previously dried to constant mass, and a small glass rod. Heat on a water-bath for 2 h with frequent stirring and dry in an oven at 100-105 °C until 2 consecutive weighings do not differ by more than 2.0 mg; the 2$^{nd}$ weighing is carried out after drying again for 1 h.

### Total ammonia
Dissolve 2.50 g in 25 ml of warm *water R*. Rinse the solution into a 250 ml volumetric flask, add 200 ml of *sodium chloride solution R* and dilute to 250.0 ml with *water R*. Filter the solution, discarding the first 20 ml of filtrate. To 100.0 ml of the clear filtrate add 25 ml of *formaldehyde solution R*, neutralised to *phenolphthalein solution R1*. Titrate with *0.1 M sodium hydroxide* until a faint pink colour is obtained.

1 ml of *0.1 M sodium hydroxide* is equivalent to 1.703 mg of $NH_3$.

### Organically combined sulphur
Mix 0.500 g with 4 g of *anhydrous sodium carbonate R* and 3 ml of *methylene chloride R* in a porcelain crucible of about 50 ml capacity, warm and stir until all the methylene chloride has evaporated. Add 10 g of coarsely powdered *copper nitrate R*, mix thoroughly and heat the mixture very gently using a small flame. When the initial reaction has subsided, increase the temperature slightly until most of the material has blackened. Cool, place the crucible in a large beaker, add 20 ml of *hydrochloric acid R* and, when the reaction has ceased, add 100 ml of *water R* and boil until all the copper oxide has dissolved. Filter the solution, add 400 ml of *water R*, heat to boiling and add 20 ml of *barium chloride solution R1*. Allow to stand for 2 h, filter, wash with *water R*, dry and ignite at about 600 ± 50 °C until 2 successive weighings do not differ by more than 0.2 per cent of the mass of the residue.

1 g of residue is equivalent to 0.1374 g of total sulphur.

Calculate the percentage content of total sulphur and subtract the percentage content of sulphur in the form of sulphate.

### Sulphur in the form of sulphate
Dissolve 2.000 g in 100 ml of *water R*, add 2 g of *cupric chloride R* dissolved in 80 ml of *water R* and dilute to 200.0 ml with *water R*. Shake and filter. Heat 100.0 ml of the filtrate almost to boiling, add 1 ml of *hydrochloric acid R* and 5 ml of *barium chloride solution R1* dropwise and heat on a water-bath. Filter, wash the precipitate with *water R*, dry and ignite at about 600 ± 50 °C until 2 successive weighings do not differ by more than 0.2 per cent of the mass of the residue.

1 g of residue is equivalent to 0.1374 g of sulphur present in the form of sulphate.

Calculate the percentage content of sulphur in the form of sulphate.

*Ph Eur*

# Idoxuridine

*(Ph Eur monograph 0669)*

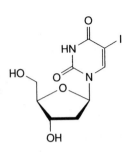

C$_9$H$_{11}$IN$_2$O$_5$      354.1      54-42-2

## Action and use
Pyrimidine nucleoside analogue; antiviral (herpesviruses).

## Preparation
Idoxuridine Eye Drops

*Ph Eur* _____

## DEFINITION
Idoxuridine contains not less than 98.0 per cent and not more than the equivalent of 101.0 per cent of 5-iodo-1-(2-deoxy-β-D-*erythro*-pentofuranosyl)pyrimidine-2,4(1*H*,3*H*)-dione, calculated with reference to the dried substance.

## CHARACTERS
A white or almost white, crystalline powder, slightly soluble in water and in alcohol. It dissolves in dilute solutions of alkali hydroxides.

It melts at about 180 °C, with decomposition.

## IDENTIFICATION
*First identification   A.*

*Second identification   B, C, D.*

A. Examine by infrared absorption spectrophotometry (*2.2.24*), comparing with the spectrum obtained with *idoxuridine CRS*. Examine the substances as discs prepared using 1 mg of the substance to be examined and of the reference substance each in 0.3 g of *potassium bromide R*.

B. Examine the chromatograms obtained in the test for related substances. The principal spot in the chromatogram obtained with test solution (b) is similar in position and size to the principal spot in the chromatogram obtained with reference solution (c).

C. Heat about 5 mg in a test-tube over a naked flame. Violet vapour is evolved.

D. Disperse about 2 mg in 1 ml of *water R* and add 2 ml of *diphenylamine solution R2*. Heat in a water-bath for 10 min. A persistent light-blue colour develops.

## TESTS
### Solution S
Dissolve 0.500 g in *1 M sodium hydroxide* and dilute to 50.0 ml with the same solvent.

### Appearance of solution
Solution S is clear (*2.2.1*) and colourless (*2.2.2, Method II*).

### pH (*2.2.3*)
Dissolve 0.10 g in *carbon dioxide-free water R* and dilute to 100 ml with the same solvent. The pH of the solution is 5.5 to 6.5.

### Specific optical rotation (*2.2.7*)
+ 28 to + 32, determined on solution S and calculated with reference to the dried substance.

### Related substances
Examine by thin-layer chromatography (*2.2.27*), using as coating substance a suitable silica gel with a fluorescent indicator having an optimal intensity at 254 nm.

*Test solution (a)*   Dissolve 0.20 g of the substance to be examined in a mixture of 1 volume of *concentrated ammonia R* and 5 volumes of *methanol R* and dilute to 5 ml with the same mixture of solvents.

*Test solution (b)*   Dilute 1 ml of test solution (a) to 10 ml with a mixture of 1 volume of *concentrated ammonia R* and 5 volumes of *methanol R*.

*Reference solution (a)*   Dissolve 20 mg of *5-iodouracil R*, 20 mg of *2'-deoxyuridine R* and 20 mg of *5-bromo-2'-deoxyuridine R* in a mixture of 1 volume of *concentrated ammonia R* and 5 volumes of *methanol R* and dilute to 100 ml with the same mixture of solvents.

*Reference solution (b)*   Dissolve 0.20 g of the substance to be examined in 5 ml of reference solution (a).

*Reference solution (c)*   Dissolve 20 mg of *idoxuridine CRS* in a mixture of 1 volume of *concentrated ammonia R* and 5 volumes of *methanol R* and dilute to 5 ml with the same mixture of solvents.

*Reference solution (d)*   Dilute 1 ml of test solution (b) to 20 ml with a mixture of 1 volume of *concentrated ammonia R* and 5 volumes of *methanol R*.

Apply separately to the plate 5 µl of each solution. Develop twice over a path of 15 cm using a mixture of 10 volumes of *concentrated ammonia R*, 40 volumes of *chloroform R* and 50 volumes of *2-propanol R*, drying the plate in a current of cold air after each development. Examine in ultraviolet light at 254 nm. In the chromatogram obtained with test solution (a): any spots corresponding to 5-iodouracil, 2'-deoxyuridine and 5-bromo-2'-deoxyuridine are not more intense than the corresponding spots in the chromatogram obtained with reference solution (a) (0.5 per cent); any spot, apart from the principal spot and the spots corresponding to 5-iodouracil, 2'-deoxyuridine and 5-bromo-2'-deoxyuridine, is not more intense than the spot in the chromatogram obtained with reference solution (d) (0.5 per cent). The test is not valid unless the chromatogram obtained with reference solution (b) shows four clearly separated spots.

### Iodide
Dissolve 0.25 g in 25 ml of *0.1 M sodium hydroxide*, add 5 ml of *dilute hydrochloric acid R* and dilute to 50 ml with *water R*. Allow to stand for 10 min and filter. To 25 ml of the filtrate add 5 ml of *dilute hydrogen peroxide solution R* and 10 ml of *chloroform R* and shake. Any pink colour in the organic layer is not more intense than that in a standard prepared at the same time in the same manner using 1 ml of a 0.33 g/l solution of *potassium iodide R* instead of the substance to be examined (0.1 per cent).

### Loss on drying (*2.2.32*)
Not more than 1.0 per cent, determined on 1.000 g by drying *in vacuo* at 60 °C.

### Sulphated ash (*2.4.14*)
Not more than 0.1 per cent, determined on 1.0 g.

## ASSAY
Dissolve 0.3000 g in 20 ml of *dimethylformamide R*. Titrate with *0.1 M tetrabutylammonium hydroxide*, determining the end-point potentiometrically (*2.2.20*).

1 ml of *0.1 M tetrabutylammonium hydroxide* is equivalent to 35.41 mg of $C_9H_{11}IN_2O_5$.

**STORAGE**

Store protected from light.

*Ph Eur*

# Ifosfamide

(*Ph Eur monograph 1529*)

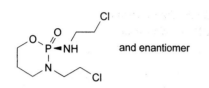

and enantiomer

$C_7H_{15}Cl_2N_2O_2P$          261.1          *3778-73-2*

**Action and use**

Cytotoxic alkylating agent.

**Preparation**

Ifosfamide Injection

*Ph Eur*

**DEFINITION**

Ifosfamide contains not less than 98.0 per cent and not more than the equivalent of 102.0 per cent of (*RS*)-*N*,3-bis(2-chloroethyl)-1,3,2-oxazaphosphinan-2-amine 2-oxide, calculated with reference to the anhydrous substance.

**CHARACTERS**

A white or almost white, fine, crystalline powder, hygroscopic, soluble in water, freely soluble in methylene chloride.

**IDENTIFICATION**

Examine by infrared absorption spectrophotometry (*2.2.24*), comparing with the *Ph. Eur. reference spectrum of ifosfamide*. Examine the substance prepared as a disc.

**TESTS**

**Solution S**

Dissolve 5.0 g in *carbon dioxide-free water R* and dilute to 50.0 ml with the same solvent.

**Appearance of solution**

Solution S is clear (*2.2.1*) and not more intensely coloured than reference solution $Y_7$ (*2.2.2, Method II*).

**Acidity or alkalinity**

Dilute 5 ml of solution S to 50 ml with *carbon dioxide-free water R*. To 10 ml of this solution add 0.1 ml of *methyl red solution R*. Not more than 0.1 ml of *0.01 M hydrochloric acid* is required to change the colour of the indicator to red. To another 10 ml of the solution add 0.1 ml of *phenolphthalein solution R*. Not more than 0.3 ml of *0.01 M sodium hydroxide* is required to change the colour of the indicator to pink.

**Optical rotation** (*2.2.7*).

The angle of optical rotation, determined on solution S, is − 0.10 ° to + 0.10 °.

**Related substances**

A. Examine by thin-layer chromatography (*2.2.27*), using a *TLC silica gel plate R*.

*Test solution*   Dissolve 1.00 g of the substance to be examined in a mixture of equal volumes of *methanol R* and *water R* and dilute to 10 ml with the same mixture of solvents.

*Reference solution (a)*   Dissolve 25 mg of *ifosfamide impurity A CRS* and 25 mg of *chloroethylamine hydrochloride R* (impurity C) in a mixture of equal volumes of *methanol R* and *water R* and dilute to 100 ml with the same mixture of solvents.

*Reference solution (b)*   Dissolve 15 mg of *ifosfamide impurity B CRS* in a mixture of equal volumes of *methanol R* and *water R* and dilute to 100 ml with the same mixture of solvents.

*Reference solution (c)*   Dissolve 5 mg of *ethanolamine R* (impurity D), 20 mg of *ifosfamide impurity A CRS* and 80 mg of *chloroethylamine hydrochloride R* (impurity C) in a mixture of equal volumes of *methanol R* and *water R* and dilute to 100 ml with the same mixture of solvents.

Apply to the plate 10 µl of each solution. Develop over a path of 15 cm using a mixture of 10 volumes of *water R*, 15 volumes of *methanol R*, 25 volumes of *anhydrous acetic acid R* and 50 volumes of *methylene chloride R*. Dry the plate at 115 °C for 45 min. At the bottom of a chromatography tank, place an evaporating dish containing a 3.2 g/l solution of *potassium permanganate R* and add an equal volume of *dilute hydrochloric acid R*, close the tank and allow to stand for 10 min. Place the plate whilst still hot in the tank, avoiding contact of the stationary phase with the solution, and close the tank. Leave the plate in contact with the chlorine vapour for 20 min. Withdraw the plate and place it in a current of cold air until the excess of chlorine is removed (about 20 min) and an area of coating below the points of application does not give a blue colour with a drop of *potassium iodide* and *starch solution R*. Avoid prolonged exposure to cold air. Immerse the plate in a 1 g/l solution of *tetramethylbenzidine R* in *alcohol R* for 5 s. Allow the plate to dry and examine. In the chromatogram obtained with the test solution: any spot corresponding to impurity A or impurity C is not more intense than the corresponding spot in the chromatogram obtained with reference solution (a) (0.25 per cent); any spot corresponding to impurity B is not more intense than the corresponding spot in the chromatogram obtained with reference solution (b) (0.15 per cent); any other spot is not more intense than the principal spot in the chromatogram obtained with reference solution (b) (0.15 per cent). The test is not valid unless the chromatogram obtained with reference solution (c) shows 3 clearly separated spots.

B. Examine by thin-layer chromatography (*2.2.27*), using a *TLC silica gel plate R*.

*Test solution*   Dissolve 0.200 g of the substance to be examined in a mixture of equal volumes of *methanol R* and *methylene chloride R* and dilute to 10 ml with the same mixture of solvents.

*Reference solution (a)*   Dissolve 5 mg of *ifosfamide impurity E CRS* and 5 mg of *ifosfamide impurity F CRS* in a mixture of equal volumes of *methanol R* and *methylene chloride R* and dilute to 100 ml with the same mixture of solvents.

*Reference solution (b)*   Dissolve 10 mg of *ifosfamide impurity E CRS* and 10 mg of *ifosfamide CRS* in a mixture of equal volumes of *methanol R* and *methylene chloride R* and dilute to 100 ml with the same mixture of solvents.

Apply to the plate 5 µl of each solution. Develop over a path of 15 cm using a mixture of 1 volume of *methylene chloride R* and 10 volumes of *acetone R*. Dry the plate at 115 °C for 45 min. Proceed as described in Related substances test A.

Any spot corresponding to impurity E or impurity F in the chromatogram obtained with the test solution is not more intense than the corresponding spot in the chromatogram obtained with reference solution (a) (0.25 per cent). The test is not valid unless the chromatogram obtained with reference solution (b) shows 2 clearly separated spots.

**Chlorides** (*2.4.4*)
Dilute 5 ml of solution S to 15 ml with *water R*. The freshly prepared solution complies with the limit test for chlorides (100 ppm).

**Heavy metals** (*2.4.8*)
12 ml of solution S complies with limit test A for heavy metals (10 ppm). Prepare the standard using *lead standard solution (1 ppm Pb) R*.

**Water** (*2.5.12*)
Not more than 0.5 per cent, determined on 1.00 g by the semi-micro determination of water.

**ASSAY**
Examine by liquid chromatography (*2.2.29*). *Use the solutions within 24 h.*

*Solution A*   Dissolve 50.0 mg of *ethyl parahydroxybenzoate R* in 25 ml of *alcohol R*, dilute to 100.0 ml with *water R* and mix.

*Test solution*   To 0.150 g of the substance to be examined add 10.0 ml of solution A and dilute to 250.0 ml with *water R*.

*Reference solution*   To 15.0 mg of *ifosfamide CRS* add 1.0 ml of solution A and dilute to 25.0 ml with *water R*.

The chromatography may be carried out using:
— a stainless steel column 0.25 m long and 4.6 mm in internal diameter packed with *octadecylsilyl silica gel for chromatography R* (5 μm),
— as mobile phase at a flow rate of 1.5 ml/min a mixture of 30 volumes of *acetonitrile R* and 70 volumes of *water R*,
— as detector a spectrophotometer set at 195 nm.

Inject 1 μl of the reference solution six times. The assay is not valid unless the resolution between the peaks due to ifosfamide and to ethyl parahydroxybenzoate is not less than 6.0 and the relative standard deviation of the peak area for ifosfamide is at most 2.0 per cent.

Inject 1 μl of the test solution. Calculate the percentage content of $C_7H_{15}Cl_2N_2O_2P$ from the area of the corresponding peak in the chromatogram obtained and the declared content of *ifosfamide CRS*.

**STORAGE**
Store in an airtight container.

**IMPURITIES**
*Specified impurities*   A, B, C, E, F.
*Other detectable impurities*   D.

**Related substances test A**

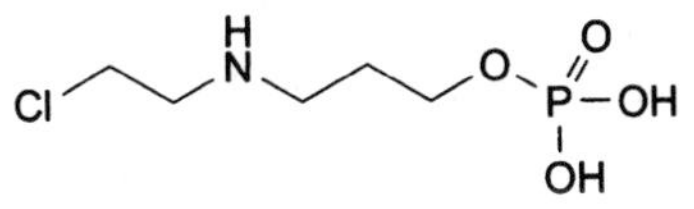

A. 3-[(2-chloroethyl)amino]propyl dihydrogen phosphate,

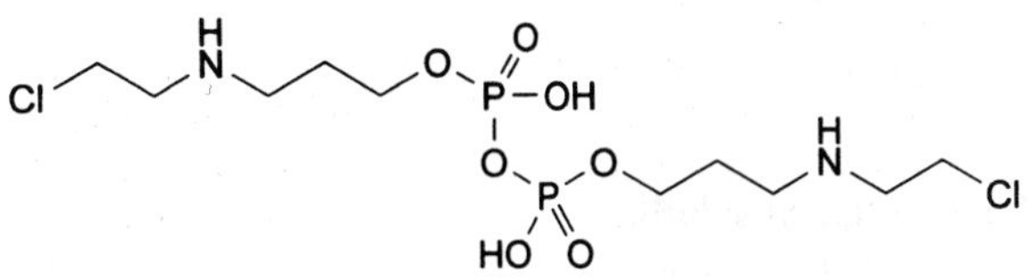

B. bis[3-[(2-chloroethyl)amino]propyl] dihydrogen diphosphate,

C. R = Cl: 2-chloroethanamine,

D. R = OH: 2-aminoethanol.

**Related substances test B**

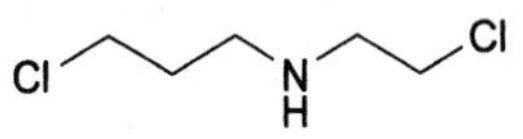

E. 3-chloro-*N*-(2-chloroethyl)propan-1-amine,

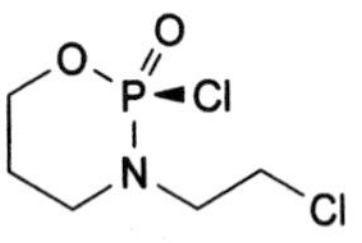

and enantiomer

F. (*RS*)-2-chloro-3-(2-chloroethyl)-1,3,2-oxazaphosphinane 2-oxide.

*Ph Eur*

# Imipenem

(*Ph Eur monograph 1226*)

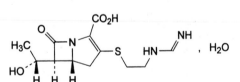

$C_{12}H_{17}N_3O_4S,H_2O$     317.4     *64221-86-9*

**Action and use**
Carbapenem antibacterial.

*Ph Eur*

**DEFINITION**
(5*R*,6*S*)-6-[(*R*)-1-Hydroxyethyl]-3-[[2-[(iminomethyl)amino]-ethyl]sulphanyl]-7-oxo-1-azabicyclo[3.2.0]hept-2-ene-2-carboxylic acid monohydrate.

Semi-synthetic product derived from a fermentation product.

**Content**
98.0 per cent to 102.0 per cent (anhydrous substance).

**CHARACTERS**

**Appearance**
White or almost white or pale yellow powder.

**Solubility**
Sparingly soluble in water, slightly soluble in methanol.

**IDENTIFICATION**
Infrared absorption spectrophotometry (*2.2.24*).

**Comparison**

*imipenem CRS.*

## TESTS

**Appearance of solution**

The solution is not more opalescent than reference suspension II *(2.2.1)* and not more intensely coloured than intensity 6 of the range of the reference solutions of the most appropriate colour *(2.2.2, Method II)*.

Dissolve 0.500 g in *phosphate buffer solution pH 7.0 R3* and dilute to 50 ml with the same solution.

**pH** *(2.2.3)*

4.5 to 7.0.

Dissolve 0.500 g in *carbon dioxide-free water R* and dilute to 100.0 ml with the same solvent.

**Specific optical rotation** *(2.2.7)*

+ 84 to + 89 (anhydrous substance), measured at 25 °C.

Dissolve 0.125 g in *phosphate buffer solution pH 7.0 R3* and dilute to 25.0 ml with the same solution.

**Related substances**

Liquid chromatography *(2.2.29)*. *Keep the solutions in an ice-bath and use within 8 h of preparation.*

*Solvent mixture* Mix 0.7 volumes of *acetonitrile R* and 99.3 volumes of a 0.135 g/l solution of *dipotassium hydrogen phosphate R* adjusted to pH 6.8 with *dilute phosphoric acid R*.

*Test solution* Dissolve 40.0 mg of the substance to be examined in the solvent mixture and dilute to 100.0 ml with the solvent mixture.

*Reference solution (a)* Dissolve 40.0 mg of *imipenem CRS* in the solvent mixture and dilute to 100.0 ml with the solvent mixture.

*Reference solution (b)* Dilute 1.0 ml of the test solution to 100.0 ml with the solvent mixture.

*Reference solution (c)* Heat 20 ml of the test solution, previously adjusted to pH 10 with *sodium hydroxide solution R*, at 80 °C for 5 min (*in situ* preparation of impurity A).

*Column:*
— *size: l* = 0.25 m, Ø = 4.6 mm;
— *stationary phase: octadecylsilyl silica gel for chromatography R* (5 μm).

*Mobile phase* Mix 0.7 volumes of *acetonitrile R* and 99.3 volumes of a 8.7 g/l solution of *dipotassium hydrogen phosphate R* adjusted to pH 7.3 with *dilute phosphoric acid R*.

*Flow rate* 1.0 ml/min.

*Detection* Spectrophotometer at 254 nm.

*Injection* 20 μl of the test solution and reference solutions (b) and (c).

*Run time* Twice the retention time of imipenem.

*Relative retention* with reference to imipenem (retention time = about 9 min): impurity A = about 0.8.

*System suitability* Reference solution (c):
— *resolution*: minimum 3.5 between the peaks due to impurity A and imipenem.

*Limits:*
— *impurity A*: not more than the area of the principal peak in the chromatogram obtained with reference solution (b) (1 per cent);
— *any other impurity*: for each impurity, not more than 0.3 times the area of the principal peak in the chromatogram obtained with reference solution (b) (0.3 per cent);

— *sum of impurities other than A*: not more than the area of the principal peak in the chromatogram obtained with reference solution (b) (1 per cent);
— *disregard limit*: 0.1 times the area of the principal peak in the chromatogram obtained with reference solution (b) (0.1 per cent).

**Water** *(2.5.12)*

5.0 per cent to 8.0 per cent, determined on 0.200 g. Use an iodosulphurous reagent containing imidazole instead of pyridine and a clean container for each determination.

**Sulphated ash** *(2.4.14)*

Maximum 0.2 per cent, determined on 1.0 g.

**Bacterial endotoxins** *(2.6.14)*

Less than 0.17 IU/mg, if intended for use in the manufacture of parenteral dosage forms without a further appropriate procedure for removal of bacterial endotoxins.

## ASSAY

Liquid chromatography *(2.2.29)* as described in the test for related substances with the following modifications.

*Injection* Test solution and reference solution (a).

*System suitability* Reference solution (a):
— *repeatability*: maximum relative standard deviation of 1.0 per cent after 6 injections.

## STORAGE

In an airtight container, at a temperature of 2 °C to 8 °C. If the substance is sterile, store in a sterile, airtight, tamper-proof container.

## IMPURITIES

*Specified impurities* A.

A. (5R,6S)-3-[(2-aminoethyl)sulphanyl]-6-[(R)-1-hydroxyethyl]-7-oxo-1-azabicyclo[3.2.0]hept-2-ene-2-carboxylic acid (thienamycin).

_____ *Ph Eur*

# Imipramine Hydrochloride

*(Ph Eur monograph 0029)*

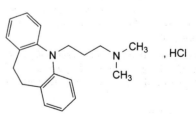

C$_{19}$H$_{24}$N$_2$,HCl          316.9          *113-52-0*

**Action and use**

Monoamine reuptake inhibitor; tricyclic antidepressant.

**Preparation**

Imipramine Tablets

*Ph Eur*

# DEFINITION

3-(10,11-Dihydro-5*H*-dibenzo[*b,f*]azepin-5-yl)-*N,N*-dimethylpropan-1-amine hydrochloride.

## Content

98.5 per cent to 101.0 per cent (dried substance).

# CHARACTERS

## Appearance

White or slightly yellow, crystalline powder.

## Solubility

Freely soluble in water and in ethanol (96 per cent).

# IDENTIFICATION

*First identification*   B, D.

*Second identification*   A, C, D.

A. Melting point (*2.2.14*): 170 °C to 174 °C.

B. Infrared absorption spectrophotometry (*2.2.24*).

*Comparison*   imipramine hydrochloride CRS.

C. Dissolve about 5 mg in 2 ml of *nitric acid R*. An intense blue colour develops.

D. About 20 mg gives reaction (a) of chlorides (*2.3.1*).

# TESTS

## Solution S

To 3.0 g add 20 ml of *carbon dioxide-free water R*, dissolve rapidly by shaking and triturating with a glass rod and dilute to 30 ml with the same solvent.

## Appearance of solution

Solution S is clear (*2.2.1*). Immediately after preparation, dilute solution S with an equal volume of *water R*. This solution is not more intensely coloured than reference solution $BY_6$ (*2.2.2, Method II*).

## pH (*2.2.3*)

3.6 to 5.0 for solution S, measured immediately after preparation.

## Related substances

Liquid chromatography (*2.2.29*).

*Test solution*   Dissolve 50.0 mg of the substance to be examined in the mobile phase and dilute to 50.0 ml with the mobile phase.

*Reference solution (a)*   Dissolve 5.0 mg of *imipramine for system suitability CRS* (containing impurity B) in the mobile phase and dilute to 5.0 ml with the mobile phase.

*Reference solution (b)*   Dilute 1.0 ml of the test solution to 100.0 ml with the mobile phase. Dilute 1.0 ml of this solution to 10.0 ml with the mobile phase.

*Column:*
— *size: l* = 0.15 m, Ø = 4.6 mm;
— *stationary phase: end-capped polar-embedded octadecylsilyl amorphous organosilica polymer R* (5 μm);
— *temperature:* 40 °C.

*Mobile phase*   Mix 40 volumes of *acetonitrile R1* with 60 volumes of a 5.2 g/l solution of *dipotassium hydrogen phosphate R* previously adjusted to pH 7.0 with *phosphoric acid R*.

*Flow rate*   1.0 ml/min.

*Detection*   Spectrophotometer at 220 nm.

*Injection*   10 μl.

*Run time*   2.5 times the retention time of imipramine.

*Relative retention*   With reference to imipramine (retention time = about 7 min): impurity B = about 0.7.

*System suitability*   Reference solution (a):

— *resolution*: minimum 5.0 between the peaks due to impurity B and imipramine.

*Limits:*
— *impurity B*: not more than the area of the corresponding peak in the chromatogram obtained with reference solution (a) (0.1 per cent);
— *unspecified impurities*: for each impurity, not more than the area of the peak due to imipramine in the chromatogram obtained with reference solution (b) (0.10 per cent);
— *total*: not more than 3 times the area of the peak due to imipramine in the chromatogram obtained with reference solution (b) (0.3 per cent);
— *disregard limit*: 0.5 times the area of the peak due to imipramine in the chromatogram obtained with reference solution (b) (0.05 per cent).

## Heavy metals (*2.4.8*)

Maximum 20 ppm.

*Test solution*   Dissolve 0.500 g of the substance to be examined in 20 ml of *water R*.

*Reference solution*   Dilute 10 ml of *lead standard solution (1 ppm Pb) R* to 20 ml with *water R*.

*Blank solution*   20 ml of *water R*.

*Monitor solution*   Dissolve 0.500 g of the substance to be examined in 10 ml of *lead standard solution (1 ppm Pb) R* and dilute to 20 ml of *water R*.

To each solution add 2 ml of *buffer solution pH 3.5 R*. Mix and add to 1.2 ml of *thioacetamide reagent R*. Mix immediately. Filter the solutions through a suitable membrane filter (pore size 0.45 μm). Compare the spots on the filters obtained with the different solutions. The test is invalid if the reference solution and the monitor solution do not show a slight brown colour compared to the blank solution. The substance to be examined complies with the test if the brown colour of the spot resulting from the test solution is not more intense than that of the spot resulting from the reference solution.

## Loss on drying (*2.2.32*)

Maximum 0.5 per cent, determined on 1.000 g by drying in an oven at 105 °C.

## Sulphated ash (*2.4.14*)

Maximum 0.1 per cent, determined on 1.0 g.

# ASSAY

Dissolve 0.250 g in 50 ml of *ethanol (96 per cent) R* and add 5.0 ml of *0.01 M hydrochloric acid*. Carry out a potentiometric titration (*2.2.20*), using *0.1 M sodium hydroxide*. Read the volume added between the 2 points of inflexion.

1 ml of *0.1 M sodium hydroxide* is equivalent to 31.69 mg of $C_{19}H_{25}ClN_2$.

# STORAGE

Protected from light.

## IMPURITIES

*Specified impurities* B.

*Other detectable impurities* (The following substances would, if present at a sufficient level, be detected by one or other of the tests in the monograph. They are limited by the general acceptance criterion for other/unspecified impurities and/or by the general monograph *Substances for pharmaceutical use (2034)*. It is therefore not necessary to identify these impurities for demonstration of compliance. See also *5.10. Control of impurities in substances for pharmaceutical use*): A, C.

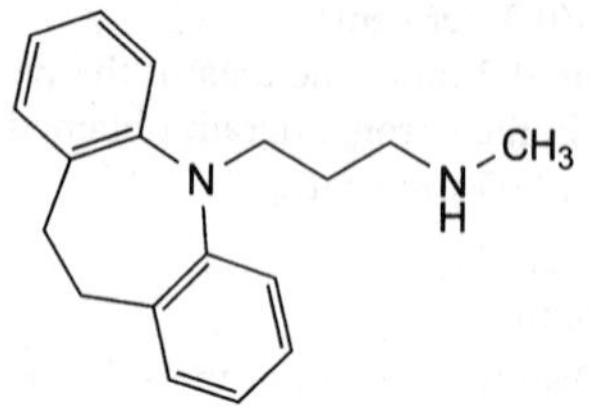

A. 3-(10,11-dihydro-5*H*-dibenzo[*b,f*]azepin-5-yl)-*N*-methylpropan-1-amine (desipramine),

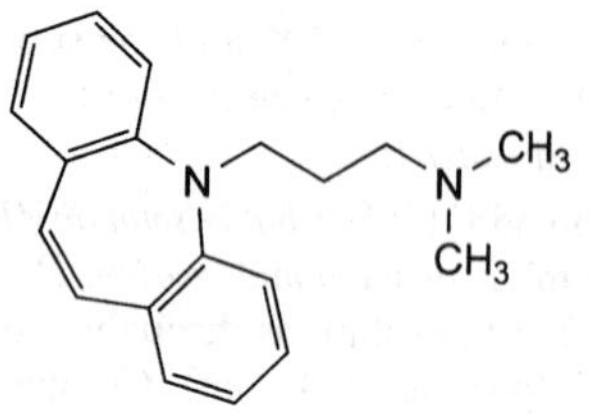

B. 3-(5*H*-dibenzo[*b,f*]azepin-5-yl)-*N,N*-dimethylpropan-1-amine (depramine),

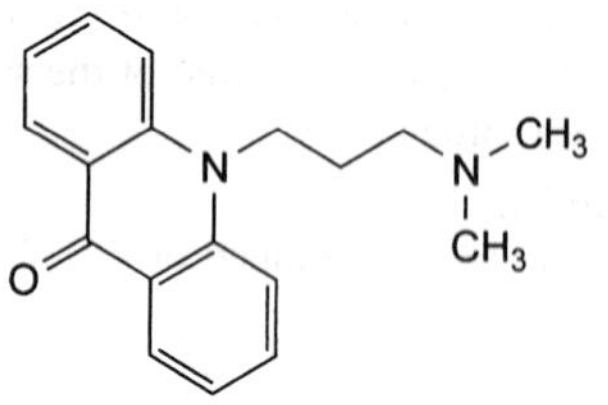

C. 10-[3-(dimethylamino)propyl]acridin-9(10*H*)-one.

_____ *Ph Eur*

# Indapamide

*(Ph Eur monograph 1108)*

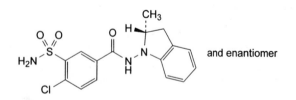

$C_{16}H_{16}ClN_3O_3S$        365.8        *26807-65-8*

**Action and use**
Thiazide-like diuretic.

**Preparation**
Indapamide Tablets

*Ph Eur* _____

## DEFINITION

4-Chloro-*N*-[(2*RS*)-2-methyl-2,3-dihydro-1*H*-indol-1-yl]-3-sulphamoylbenzamide.

## Content

98.0 per cent to 102.0 per cent (anhydrous substance).

## CHARACTERS

**Appearance**

White or almost white powder.

**Solubility**

Practically insoluble in water, soluble in ethanol (96 per cent).

## IDENTIFICATION

*First identification* B.

*Second identification* A, C.

A. Ultraviolet and visible absorption spectrophotometry (2.2.25).

*Test solution* Dissolve 50.0 mg in *ethanol (96 per cent) R* and dilute to 100.0 ml with the same solvent. Dilute 2.0 ml of this solution to 100.0 ml with *ethanol (96 per cent) R*.

*Spectral range* 220-350 nm.

*Absorption maximum* At 242 nm.

*Shoulders* At 279 nm and 287 nm.

*Specific absorbance at the absorption maximum* 590 to 630.

B. Infrared absorption spectrophotometry (2.2.24).

*Preparation* Discs of *potassium bromide R*.

*Comparison* indapamide CRS.

C. Thin-layer chromatography (2.2.27).

*Test solution* Dissolve 20 mg of the substance to be examined in *ethanol (96 per cent) R* and dilute to 10 ml with the same solvent.

*Reference solution (a)* Dissolve 20 mg of *indapamide CRS* in ethanol (96 per cent) R and dilute to 10 ml with the same solvent.

*Reference solution (b)* Dissolve 10 mg *of indometacin R* in 5 ml of reference solution (a) and dilute to 10 ml with *ethanol (96 per cent) R*.

*Plate* TLC silica gel $GF_{254}$ plate R.

*Mobile phase* glacial acetic acid R, acetone R, toluene R (1:20:79 *V/V/V*).

*Application* 10 µl.

*Development* Over a path of 15 cm.

*Drying* In air.

*Detection* Examine in ultraviolet light at 254 nm.

*System suitability*

Reference solution (b):

— the chromatogram shows 2 clearly separated spots.

*Results* The principal spot in the chromatogram obtained with the test solution is similar in position and size to the principal spot in the chromatogram obtained with reference solution (a).

## TESTS

**Optical rotation** *(2.2.7)*

− 0.02 ° to + 0.02 °.

Dissolve 0.250 g in *anhydrous ethanol R* and dilute to 25.0 ml with the same solvent.

**Related substances**

Liquid chromatography (2.2.29). *Carry out the test protected from light and prepare the solutions immediately before use or maintain them at 4 °C.*

*Test solution* Dissolve 20.0 mg of the substance to be examined in 7 ml of a mixture of equal volumes of *acetonitrile R* and *methanol R* and dilute to 20.0 ml with a 0.2 g/l solution of *sodium edetate R*.

*Reference solution (a)* Dissolve 3.0 mg of *indapamide impurity B CRS* in 3.5 ml of a mixture of equal volumes of *acetonitrile R* and *methanol R* and dilute to 10.0 ml with a 0.2 g/l solution of *sodium edetate R*. To 1.0 ml of this solution, add 35 ml of a mixture of equal volumes of *acetonitrile R* and *methanol R* and dilute to 100.0 ml with a 0.2 g/l solution of *sodium edetate R*.

*Reference solution (b)* Dilute 1.0 ml of the test solution to 50.0 ml with a mixture of 17.5 volumes of *acetonitrile R*, 17.5 volumes of *methanol R* and 65 volumes of a 0.2 g/l solution of *sodium edetate R*. Dilute 1.0 ml of this solution to 20.0 ml with a mixture of 17.5 volumes of *acetonitrile R*, 17.5 volumes of *methanol R* and 65 volumes of a 0.2 g/l solution of *sodium edetate R*.

*Reference solution (c)* Dissolve 20.0 mg of *indapamide CRS* in 7 ml of a mixture of equal volumes of *acetonitrile R* and *methanol R* and dilute to 20.0 ml with a 0.2 g/l solution of *sodium edetate R*.

*Reference solution (d)* Dissolve 25.0 mg of *indapamide CRS* and 45.0 mg of *methylnitrosoindoline CRS* (impurity A) in 17.5 ml of a mixture of equal volumes of *acetonitrile R* and *methanol R* and dilute to 50.0 ml with a 0.2 g/l solution of *sodium edetate R*.

*Column:*
— *size*: $l$ = 0.20 m, Ø = 4.6 mm;
— *stationary phase: octadecylsilyl silica gel for chromatography R* (5 μm);
— *temperature*: 40 °C.

*Mobile phase* glacial acetic acid *R*, acetonitrile *R*, methanol *R*, 0.2 g/l solution of *sodium edetate R* (0.1:17.5:17.5:65 *V/V/V/V*).

*Flow rate* 2 ml/min.

*Detection* Spectrophotometer at 254 nm.

*Injection* 10 μl.

*Run time* 2.5 times the retention time of indapamide.

*Retention time* Indapamide = about 11 min.

*System suitability:*
— *resolution*: minimum 4.0 between the peaks due to indapamide and impurity A in the chromatogram obtained with reference solution (d);
— *signal-to-noise ratio*: minimum 6 for the principal peak in the chromatogram obtained with reference solution (b).

*Limits:*
— *impurity B*: not more than the area of the principal peak in the chromatogram obtained with reference solution (a) (0.3 per cent);
— *unspecified impurities*: for each impurity, not more than the area of the principal peak in the chromatogram obtained with reference solution (b) (0.10 per cent);
— *total*: not more than 5 times the area of the principal peak in the chromatogram obtained with reference solution (b) (0.5 per cent);
— *disregard limit*: 0.5 times the area of the principal peak in the chromatogram obtained with reference solution (b) (0.05 per cent).

**Impurity A**

Liquid chromatography (2.2.29). *Carry out the test protected from light.*

*Test solution* Dissolve 25.0 mg of the substance to be examined in 1 ml of *acetonitrile R* and dilute to 10.0 ml with *water R*. Shake for 15 min. Allow to stand at 4 °C for 1 h and filter.

*Reference solution* Dissolve 25.0 mg of the substance to be examined in 1.0 ml of a 0.125 mg/l solution of *methylnitrosoindoline CRS* (impurity A) in *acetonitrile R* and dilute to 10.0 ml with *water R*. Shake for 15 min. Allow to stand at 4 °C for 1 h and filter.

*Column:*
— *size*: $l$ = 0.15 m, Ø = 4.6 mm;
— *stationary phase: octadecylsilyl silica gel for chromatography R* (5 μm);
— *temperature*: 30 °C.

*Mobile phase* Mix 7 volumes of *acetonitrile R*, 20 volumes of *tetrahydrofuran R* and 73 volumes of a 1.5 g/l solution of *triethylamine R* adjusted to pH 2.8 with *phosphoric acid R*.

*Flow rate* 1.4 ml/min.

*Detection* Spectrophotometer at 305 nm.

*Injection* 0.1 ml.

*System suitability* Reference solution:
— *signal-to-noise ratio*: minimum 3 for the peak due to impurity A appearing just before the peak due to indapamide;
— *peak-to-valley-ratio*: minimum 6.7, where $H_p$ = height above the baseline of the peak due to impurity A and $H_v$ = height above the baseline of the lowest point of the curve separating this peak from the peak due to indapamide.

*Limit:*
— *impurity A*: not more than the difference between the areas of the peaks due to impurity A in the chromatograms obtained with the reference solution and the test solution (5 ppm).

**Heavy metals** (2.4.8)

Maximum 10 ppm.

2.0 g complies with test C. Prepare the reference solution using 2 ml of *lead standard solution (10 ppm Pb) R*.

**Water** (2.5.12)

Maximum 3.0 per cent, determined on 0.100 g.

**Sulphated ash** (2.4.14)

Maximum 0.1 per cent, determined on 1.0 g.

**ASSAY**

Liquid chromatography (2.2.29) as described in the test for related substances with the following modifications.

*Injection* The test solution and reference solution (c).

*System suitability* Reference solution (c)
— *repeatability*: maximum relative standard deviation of 1.0 per cent after 6 injections; if necessary, adjust the integrator parameters.

Calculate the percentage content of $C_{16}H_{16}ClN_3O_3S$ from the declared content of *indapamide CRS*.

**STORAGE**

Protected from light.

## IMPURITIES

*Specified impurities   A, B.*

A. (2RS)-2-methyl-1-nitroso-2,3-dihydro-1H-indole,

B. 4-chloro-N-(2-methyl-1H-indol-1-yl]-3-sulphamoylbenzamide.

*———————————————————— Ph Eur*

# Indinavir Sulphate

*(Ph Eur monograph 2214)*

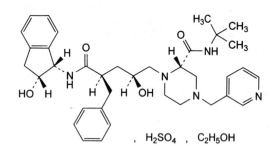

, H<sub>2</sub>SO<sub>4</sub> , C<sub>2</sub>H<sub>5</sub>OH

$C_{36}H_{47}N_5O_4,H_2SO_4,C_2H_6O$    758         *157810-81-6*

## Action and use
Protease inhibitor; antiviral (HIV).

*Ph Eur ———————————————————————————*

## DEFINITION
(2S)-1-[(2S,4R)-4-Benzyl-2-hydroxy-5-[[(1S,2R)-2-hydroxy-2,3-dihydro-1H-inden-1-yl]amino]-5-oxopentyl]-N-(1,1-dimethylethyl)-4-(pyridin-3-ylmethyl)piperazine-2-carboxamide sulphate ethanolate.

## Content
98.0 per cent to 102.0 per cent (anhydrous and ethanol-free substance).

## PRODUCTION
A test for enantiomeric purity is carried out unless it has been demonstrated that the manufacturing process is enantioselective for the substance.

## CHARACTERS
### Appearance
White or almost white, hygroscopic powder.

### Solubility
Freely soluble in water, soluble in methanol, practically insoluble in heptane.

## IDENTIFICATION
A. Specific optical rotation (2.2.7): + 122 to + 129 (anhydrous and ethanol-free substance), determined at 365 nm and at 25 °C.

Dissolve 0.500 g in *water R* and dilute to 50.0 ml with the same solvent.

B. Infrared absorption spectrophotometry (2.2.24).

*Comparison   Ph. Eur. reference spectrum of indinavir sulphate.*

C. It gives reaction (a) of sulphates (2.3.1).

D. It complies with the test for ethanol (see Tests).

## TESTS
### Related substances
Liquid chromatography (2.2.29).

*Solution A*   Thoroughly mix equal volumes of mobile phase A and *acetonitrile R1*.

*Test solution*   Dissolve 50.0 mg of the substance to be examined in solution A and dilute to 100.0 ml with the same solution.

*Reference solution (a)*   Dissolve 4 mg of *indinavir for system suitability CRS* (containing impurities B, C and E) in solution A and dilute to 10 ml with the same solution.

*Reference solution (b)*   Dilute 1.0 ml of the test solution to 100.0 ml with solution A. Dilute 1.0 ml of this solution to 10.0 ml with solution A.

*Reference solution (c)*   Dissolve 5.0 mg of *cis-aminoindanol R* (impurity A) in solution A and dilute to 10.0 ml with the same solution. Dilute 1.0 ml of the solution to 100.0 ml with solution A. Dilute 1.0 ml of this solution to 10.0 ml with solution A.

*Reference solution (d)*   To 30 mg of the substance to be examined add 0.25 ml of *2 M hydrochloric acid R* and allow to stand at room temperature for 1 h. Dilute to 100 ml with a mixture of 2 volumes of *acetonitrile R1* and 3 volumes of mobile phase A and mix (*in situ* degradation to obtain impurity D).

*Column:*
— *size:* l = 0.25 m, Ø = 4.6 mm;
— *stationary phase:* octadecylsilyl silica gel for chromatography R (5 µm).

*Mobile phase:*
— *mobile phase A:* solution containing 0.27 g/l of *potassium dihydrogen phosphate R* and 1.40 g/l of *dipotassium hydrogen phosphate R*; filter and degas;
— *mobile phase B: acetonitrile R1*;

| Time (min) | Mobile phase A (per cent V/V) | Mobile phase B (per cent V/V) |
|---|---|---|
| 0 - 5 | 80 | 20 |
| 5 - 40 | 80 → 30 | 20 → 70 |
| 40 - 45 | 30 | 70 |
| 45 - 47 | 30 → 80 | 70 → 20 |
| 47 - 52 | 80 | 20 |

*Flow rate*   1.0 ml/min.

*Detection*   Spectrophotometer at 220 nm.

*Injection*   20 µl.

*Identification of impurities*   Use the chromatogram supplied with *indinavir for system suitability CRS* and the chromatogram obtained with reference solution (a) to identify the peaks due to impurities B, C and E; use the chromatogram obtained with reference solution (d) to identify the peak due to impurity D.

*Relative retention*   With reference to indinavir
(retention time = about 25 min): impurity A = about 0.2;
impurity B = about 0.8; impurity C = about 0.98;
impurity D = about 1.1; impurity E = about 1.3.

*System suitability*   Reference solution (a):
— *resolution*: minimum 1.8 between the peaks due to
   impurity C and indinavir.

*Limits:*
— *correction factor*: for the calculation of content, multiply the
   peak area of impurity D by 1.8;
— *impurity A*: not more than the area of the principal peak
   in the chromatogram obtained with reference solution (c)
   (0.1 per cent);
— *impurity D*: not more than twice the area of the principal
   peak in the chromatogram obtained with reference
   solution (b) (0.2 per cent);
— *impurities B, C, E*: for each impurity, not more than the
   area of the principal peak in the chromatogram obtained
   with reference solution (b) (0.1 per cent);
— *unspecified impurities*: for each impurity, not more than
   0.5 times the area of the principal peak in the
   chromatogram obtained with reference solution (b)
   (0.05 per cent);
— *total*: not more than 5 times the area of the principal peak
   in the chromatogram obtained with reference solution (b)
   (0.5 per cent);
— *disregard limit*: 0.3 times the area of the principal peak in
   the chromatogram obtained with reference solution (b)
   (0.03 per cent).

**Ethanol**
Gas chromatography (*2.2.28*).

*Internal standard solution*   Dilute 1.0 ml of *propanol R* to
200.0 ml with *water R*.

*Test solution*   Dissolve 0.400 g of the substance to be
examined in 50.0 ml of *water R*, add 8.0 ml of the internal
standard solution and dilute to 100.0 ml with *water R*.

*Reference solution*   Dilute 1.0 ml of *anhydrous ethanol R* to
200.0 ml. Dilute 2.0 ml of this solution and 2.0 ml of the
internal standard solution to 25.0 ml with *water R*.

*Column:*
— *material*: fused silica;
— *size: l* = 30 m, Ø = 0.53 mm;
— *stationary phase: macrogol 20 000 R* (film thickness
   1.0 µm).

*Carrier gas*   *helium for chromatography R*.

*Flow rate*   10 ml/min.

*Split ratio*   1:10.

*Temperature:*
— *column*: 35 °C;
— *injection port*: 140 °C;
— *detector*: 220 °C.

*Detection*   Flame ionisation.

*Injection*   1.0 µl.

*System suitability*   Reference solution:
— *retention time*: ethanol = 2 min to 4 min;
— *resolution*: minimum 5.0 between the peaks due to
   ethanol and propanol.

Calculate the percentage content of ethanol taking the
density (*2.2.5*) to be 0.790 g/ml.

*Limit:*
— *ethanol*: 5.0 per cent to 8.0 per cent (*m/m*).

**Heavy metals** (*2.4.8*)
Maximum 10 ppm.

Dissolve 2.0 g in *water R* and dilute to 20 ml with the same
solvent. 12 ml of the solution complies with test A. Prepare
the reference solution using *lead standard solution
(1 ppm Pb) R*.

**Water** (*2.5.12*)
Maximum 1.5 per cent, determined on 0.500 g.

**Sulphated ash** (*2.4.14*)
Maximum 0.1 per cent, determined on 1.0 g.

**ASSAY**
Liquid chromatography (*2.2.29*).

*Solution B*   Add 20 ml of *dibutylammonium phosphate for ion-
pairing R* to 1000 ml of *water R*. Adjust to pH 6.5 with *1 M
sodium hydroxide*.

*Test solution*   Dissolve 60.0 mg of the substance to be
examined in the mobile phase and dilute to 100.0 ml with
the mobile phase.

*Reference solution*   Dissolve 50.0 mg of *indinavir CRS* in the
mobile phase and dilute to 100.0 ml with the mobile phase.

*Column:*
— *size: l* = 0.25 m, Ø = 4.6 mm;
— *stationary phase: base-deactivated octylsilyl silica gel for
   chromatography R* (5 µm);
— *temperature*: 40 °C.

*Mobile phase*   *acetonitrile R, solution B* (45:55 *V/V*).

*Flow rate*   1.0 ml/min.

*Detection*   Spectrophotometer at 260 nm.

*Injection*   10 µl.

*Run time*   Twice the retention time of indinavir.

*Retention time*   Indinavir = about 10 min.

Calculate the percentage content of $C_{36}H_{49}N_5O_8S$ using the
declared content of *indinavir CRS* and multiplying by a
correction factor of 1.1598.

**STORAGE**
In an airtight container, protected from light.

**IMPURITIES**
*Specified impurities*   *A, B, C, D, E.*

*Other detectable impurities*   (The following substances would,
if present at a sufficient level, be detected by one or other of
the tests in the monograph. They are limited by the general
acceptance criterion for other/unspecified impurities and/or
by the general monograph *Substances for pharmaceutical use
(2034)*. It is therefore not necessary to identify these
impurities for demonstration of compliance. See also *5.10.
Control of impurities in substances for pharmaceutical use): F.*

A. (1*S*,2*R*)-1-amino-2,3-dihydro-1*H*-inden-2-ol
(*cis*-aminoindanol),

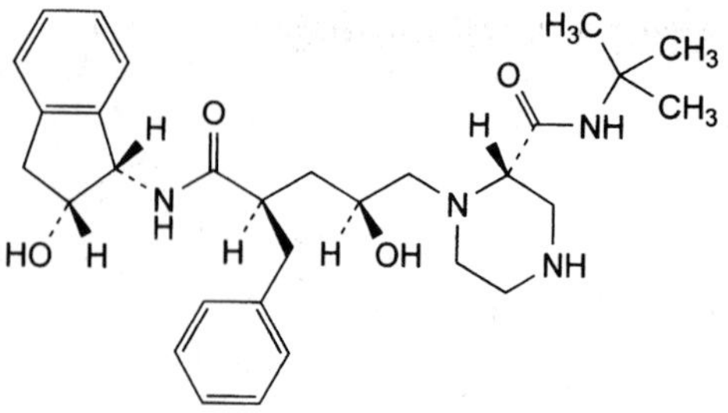

B. (2S)-1-[(2S,4R)-4-benzyl-2-hydroxy-5-[[(1S,2R)-2-hydroxy-2,3-dihydro-1H-inden-1-yl]amino]-5-oxopentyl]-N-(1,1-dimethylethyl)piperazine-2-carboxamide,

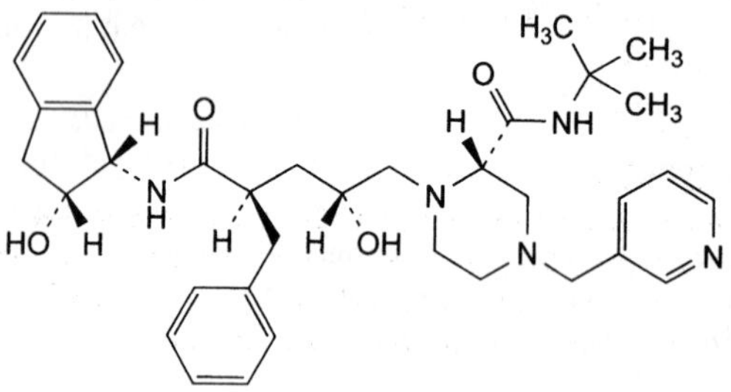

C. (2S)-1-[(2R,4R)-4-benzyl-2-hydroxy-5-[[(1S,2R)-2-hydroxy-2,3-dihydro-1H-inden-1-yl]amino]-5-oxopentyl]-N-(1,1-dimethylethyl)-4-(pyridin-3-ylmethyl)piperazine-2-carboxamide,

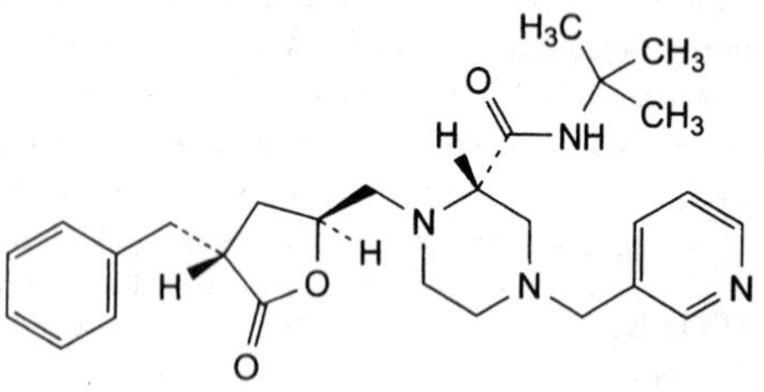

D. (3R,5S)-3-benzyl-5-[[(2S)-2-[(1,1-dimethylethyl)carbamoyl]-4-(pyridin-3-ylmethyl)piperazin-1-yl]methyl]-4,5-dihydrofuran-2(3H)-one,

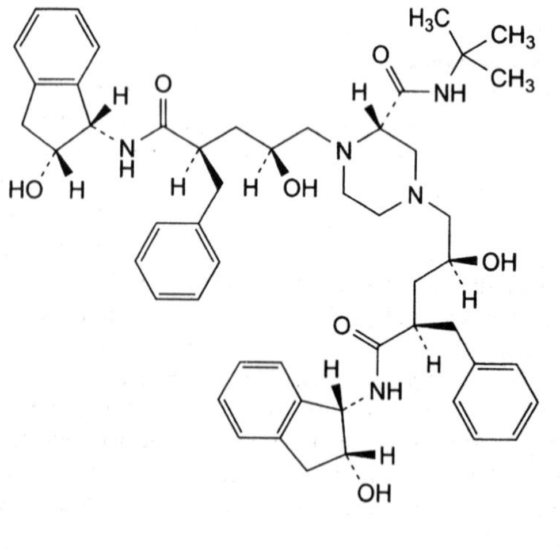

E. (2S)-1,4-bis[(2S,4R)-4-benzyl-2-hydroxy-5-[[(1S,2R)-2-hydroxy-2,3-dihydro-1H-inden-1-yl]amino]-5-oxopentyl]-N-(1,1-dimethylethyl)piperazine-2-carboxamide,

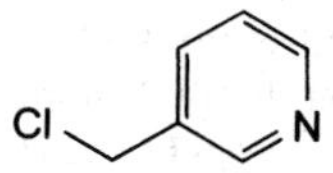

F. 3-(chloromethyl)pyridine (nicotinyl chloride).

_____ Ph Eur

# Indometacin

(*Ph Eur monograph 0092*)

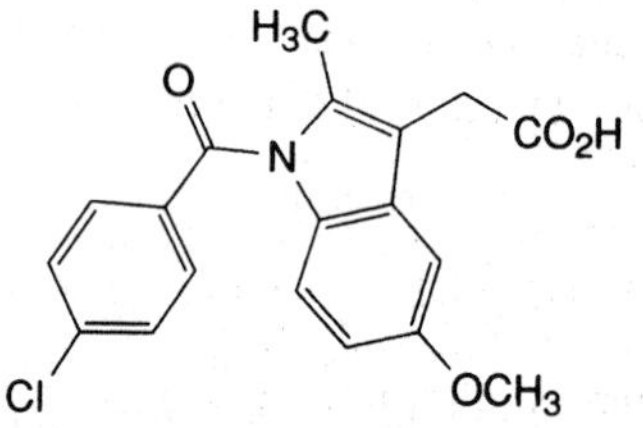

C19H16ClNO4      357.8      *53-86-1*

**Action and use**

Cyclo-oxygenase inhibitor; analgesic; anti-inflammatory.

**Preparations**

Indometacin Capsules

Indometacin Suppositories

Ph Eur _____

**DEFINITION**

Indometacin contains not less than 98.5 per cent and not more than the equivalent of 100.5 per cent of [1-(4-chlorobenzoyl)-5-methoxy-2-methylindol-3-yl]acetic acid, calculated with reference to the dried substance.

**CHARACTERS**

A white or yellow, crystalline powder, practically insoluble in water, sparingly soluble in alcohol.

**IDENTIFICATION**

*First identification*    A, C.

*Second identification*    A, B, D, E.

A. Melting point (*2.2.14*): 158 °C to 162 °C.

B. Dissolve 25 mg in a mixture of 1 volume of *1 M hydrochloric acid* and 9 volumes of *methanol R* and dilute to 100.0 ml with the same mixture of solvents. Dilute 10.0 ml of the solution to 100.0 ml with a mixture of 1 volume of *1 M hydrochloric acid* and 9 volumes of *methanol R*. Examined between 300 nm and 350 nm (*2.2.25*), the solution shows an absorption maximum at 318 nm. The specific absorbance at the maximum is 170 to 190.

C. Examine by infrared absorption spectrophotometry (*2.2.24*), comparing with the spectrum obtained with *indometacin CRS*. Examine the substances in the solid state without recrystallisation.

D. Dissolve 0.1 g in 10 ml of *alcohol R*, heating slightly if necessary. To 0.1 ml of the solution add 2 ml of a freshly prepared mixture of 1 volume of a 250 g/l solution of *hydroxylamine hydrochloride R* and 3 volumes of *dilute sodium hydroxide solution R*. Add 2 ml of *dilute hydrochloric acid R* and 1 ml of *ferric chloride solution R2* and mix. A violet-pink colour develops.

E. To 0.5 ml of the solution in alcohol prepared in identification test D, add 0.5 ml of *dimethylaminobenzaldehyde solution R2.* A precipitate is formed that dissolves on shaking. Heat on a water-bath. A bluish-green colour is produced. Continue to heat for 5 min and cool in iced water for 2 min. A precipitate is formed and the colour changes to light greyish-green. Add 3 ml of *alcohol R.* The solution is clear and violet-pink in colour.

## TESTS

### Related substances

Examine by thin-layer chromatography (*2.2.27*), using *silica gel HF$_{254}$ R* as the coating substance. Prepare the slurry using a 46.8 g/l solution of *sodium dihydrogen phosphate R.*

*Test solution*   Dissolve 0.2 g of the substance to be examined in *methanol R* and dilute to 10 ml with the same solvent. Prepare immediately before use.

*Reference solution*   Dilute 1 ml of the test solution to 200 ml with *methanol R.*

Apply separately to the plate 10 µl of each solution. Develop over a path of 15 cm using a mixture of 30 volumes of *light petroleum R* and 70 volumes of *ether R.* Allow the plate to dry in air and examine in ultraviolet light at 254 nm. Any spot in the chromatogram obtained with the test solution, apart from the principal spot, is not more intense than the spot in the chromatogram obtained with the reference solution (0.5 per cent).

### Heavy metals (*2.4.8*)

2.0 g complies with limit test C for heavy metals (20 ppm). Prepare the standard using 4 ml of *lead standard solution (10 ppm Pb) R.*

### Loss on drying (*2.2.32*)

Not more than 0.5 per cent, determined on 1.000 g by drying in an oven at 105 °C.

### Sulphated ash (*2.4.14*)

Not more than 0.1 per cent, determined on 1.0 g.

## ASSAY

Dissolve 0.300 g in 75 ml of *acetone R,* through which *nitrogen R,* free from carbon dioxide, has been passed for 15 min. Maintain a constant stream of nitrogen through the solution. Add 0.1 ml of *phenolphthalein solution R.* Titrate with *0.1 M sodium hydroxide.* Carry out a blank titration.

1 ml of *0.1 M sodium hydroxide* is equivalent to 35.78 mg of $C_{19}H_{16}ClNO_4$.

## STORAGE

Store protected from light.

## IMPURITIES

A. 4-chlorobenzoic acid.

*Ph Eur*

# Indoramin Hydrochloride

$C_{22}H_{25}N_3O,HCl$          383.9          *33124-53-7*

### Action and use

Alpha$_1$-adrenoceptor antagonist.

### Preparation

Indoramin Tablets

## DEFINITION

Indoramin Hydrochloride is *N*-1-[2-(indol-3-yl)ethyl]-4-piperidylbenzamide hydrochloride. It contains not less than 98.5% and not more than 100.5% of $C_{22}H_{25}N_3O,HCl$, calculated with reference to the dried substance.

## CHARACTERISTICS

A white or almost white powder. It exhibits polymorphism.

Slightly soluble in *water*; sparingly soluble in *ethanol (96%)*; soluble in *methanol*; very slightly soluble in *ether*.

## IDENTIFICATION

A. The *light absorption,* Appendix II B, in the range 230 to 350 nm of a 0.0045% w/v solution in *ethanol (96%)* exhibits three maxima, at 273, 280 and 290 nm. The *absorbances* at the maxima are about 0.76, 0.77 and 0.64, respectively.

B. Dissolve 50 mg in 30 ml of *water,* make the solution alkaline by the addition of 5M *ammonia* and shake with 50 ml of *dichloromethane.* Dry the dichloromethane layer with *anhydrous sodium sulphate,* filter and evaporate the filtrate to dryness using a rotary evaporator. The *infrared absorption spectrum* of the residue, Appendix II A, is concordant with the *reference spectrum* of indoramin (*RS 188*).

C. Yields reaction A characteristic of *chlorides,* Appendix VI.

## TESTS

### Acidity

pH of a 2% w/v suspension in *water,* 4.0 to 5.5, Appendix V L.

### Related substances

Carry out the method for *thin-layer chromatography,* Appendix III A, using a *silica gel F$_{254}$* precoated plate (Merck silica gel 60 F$_{254}$ plates are suitable) and a mixture of 1 volume of 18M *ammonia,* 20 volumes of *absolute ethanol* and 79 volumes of *toluene* as the mobile phase. Apply separately to the plate 10 µl of each of three solutions of the substance being examined in *ethanol (96%)* containing (1) 1.0% w/v, (2) 0.0050% w/v and (3) 0.0010% w/v. After removal of the plate, allow it to dry in a current of warm air and examine under *ultraviolet light (254 nm)*. Any *secondary spot* in the chromatogram obtained with solution (1) is not more intense than the spot in the chromatogram obtained with solution (2) (0.5%) and not more than one such spot is more intense than the spot in the chromatogram obtained with solution (3) (0.1%).

### Loss on drying

When dried at 100° to 105° for 4 hours, loses not more than 0.5% of its weight. Use 1 g.

**Sulphated ash**

Not more than 0.1%, Appendix IX A.

## ASSAY

Dissolve 0.2 g in 30 ml of *anhydrous acetic acid*, add 6 ml of *acetic anhydride* and 6 ml of *mercury(II) acetate* solution. Titrate with 0.1M *perchloric acid VS* determining the end point potentiometrically. Each ml of 0.1M *perchloric acid VS* is equivalent to 38.39 mg of $C_{22}H_{25}N_3O,HCl$.

## STORAGE

Indoramin Hydrochloride should be protected from light.

## IMPURITIES

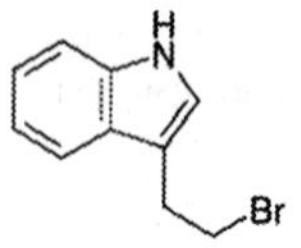

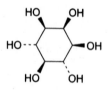

A. 3-(2-bromoethyl)indole

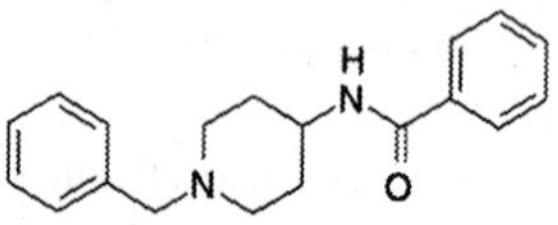

B. *N*-(1-benzyl-4-piperidyl)benzamide

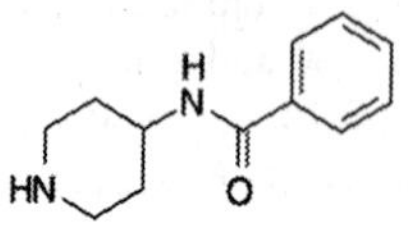

C. *N*-(4-piperidyl)benzamide

## *myo*-Inositol

(*Ph Eur monograph 1805*)

$C_6H_{12}O_6$          180.2          87-89-8

## Action and use

Vasodilator.

*Ph Eur* _____

## DEFINITION

Cyclohexane-1,2,3,5/4,6-hexol.

## Content

97.0 per cent to 102.0 per cent (anhydrous substance).

## CHARACTERS

**Appearance**

White or almost white, crystalline powder.

**Solubility**

Very soluble in water, practically insoluble in ethanol (96 per cent).

## IDENTIFICATION

A. Infrared absorption spectrophotometry (*2.2.24*).

*Comparison*   *myo*-inositol CRS.

B. Examine the chromatograms obtained in the assay.

*Results*   The principal peak in the chromatogram obtained with the test solution is similar in retention time and size to the principal peak in the chromatogram obtained with reference solution (a).

## TESTS

**Solution S**

Dissolve 10.0 g in *distilled water R* and dilute to 100.0 ml with the same solvent.

**Appearance of solution**

Solution S is clear (*2.2.1*) and colourless (*2.2.2, Method II*).

**Conductivity** (*2.2.38*)

Maximum 30 $\mu S \cdot cm^{-1}$.

Dissolve 10.0 g in *carbon dioxide-free water R* prepared from *distilled water R*, with gentle warming if necessary, and dilute to 50.0 ml with the same solvent. Measure the conductivity of the solution while gently stirring with a magnetic stirrer.

**Related substances**

Liquid chromatography (*2.2.29*).

*Test solution*   Dissolve 0.500 g of the substance to be examined in *water R* and dilute to 10.0 ml with the same solvent.

*Reference solution (a)*   Dissolve 0.500 g of *myo*-inositol CRS in *water R* and dilute to 10.0 ml with the same solvent.

*Reference solution (b)*   Dilute 2.0 ml of the test solution to 100.0 ml with *water R*. Dilute 5.0 ml of this solution to 100.0 ml with *water R*.

*Reference solution (c)*   Dissolve 0.5 g of *myo*-inositol R and 0.5 g of *mannitol R* in *water R* and dilute to 10 ml with the same solvent.

*Column:*
— *size: l* = 0.3 m, Ø = 7.8 mm;
— *stationary phase: strong cation exchange resin (calcium form) R* (9 μm);
— *temperature:* 85 °C.

*Mobile phase   water R.*

*Flow rate*   0.5 ml/min.

*Detection*   Refractometer maintained at a constant temperature (at about 30-35 °C for example).

*Injection*   20 μl of the test solution and reference solutions (b) and (c).

*Run time*   Twice the retention time of *myo*-inositol.

*Relative retention* with reference to *myo*-inositol (retention time = about 17.5 min): impurity A = about 1.3; impurity B = about 1.4.

*System suitability*   Reference solution (c):
— *resolution*: minimum 4 between the peaks due to *myo*-inositol and impurity A.

*Limits:*
— *impurities A, B*: for each impurity, not more than 3 times the area of the principal peak in the chromatogram obtained with reference solution (b) (0.3 per cent);
— *unspecified impurities*: for each impurity, not more than the area of the principal peak in the chromatogram obtained with reference solution (b) (0.10 per cent);

— *total*: not more than 10 times the area of the principal peak in the chromatogram obtained with reference solution (b) (1.0 per cent);

— *disregard limit*: 0.5 times the area of the principal peak in the chromatogram obtained with reference solution (b) (0.05 per cent).

### Barium
To 10 ml of solution S add 1 ml of *dilute sulphuric acid R*. When examined immediately, and after 1 h, any opalescence in the solution is not more intense than that in a mixture of 1 ml of *distilled water R* and 10 ml of solution S.

### Lead (2.4.10)
Maximum 0.5 ppm.

Prepare the test solution by dissolving 20.0 g of the substance to be examined in 100 ml of *water R*, heating if necessary, and diluting to 200.0 ml with *dilute acetic acid R*.

### Water (2.5.12)
Maximum 0.5 per cent, determined on 1.00 g.

### ASSAY
Liquid chromatography (2.2.29) as described in the test for related substances with the following modification.

*Injection*   Test solution and reference solution (a).

Calculate the percentage content of $C_6H_{12}O_6$ from the declared content of *myo-inositol CRS*.

### IMPURITIES
*Specified impurities   A, B.*

A. mannitol,

B. glycerol.

_____ *Ph Eur*

# Inositol Nicotinate

$C_{42}H_{30}N_6O_{12}$        810.7        *6556-11-2*

### Action and use
Vasodilator.

### Preparation
Inositol Nicotinate Tablets

### DEFINITION
Inositol Nicotinate is *myo*-inositol hexanicotinate. It contains not less than 98.0% and not more than 101.0% of $C_{42}H_{30}N_6O_{12}$, calculated with reference to the dried substance.

### CHARACTERISTICS
A white or almost white powder.

Practically insoluble in *water*, practically insoluble in *acetone*, in *ethanol (96%)* and in *ether*. It dissolves in dilute mineral acids.

## IDENTIFICATION
The *infrared absorption spectrum*, Appendix II A, is concordant with the *reference spectrum* of inositol nicotinate *(RS 190)*.

## TESTS
### Clarity and colour of solution
A 5.0% w/v solution in 0.5M *sulphuric acid* is *clear*, Appendix IV A, and not more intensely coloured than *reference solution BY₆*, Appendix IV B, Method II.

### Heavy metals
2.0 g complies with *limit test C for heavy metals*, Appendix VII. Use 2 ml of *lead standard solution (10 ppm Pb)* to prepare the standard (10 ppm).

### Chloride
Dissolve 0.14 g in a sufficient quantity of 2M *nitric acid* and dilute to 16 ml with *water*. The resulting solution complies with the *limit test for chlorides*, Appendix VII, beginning at the words 'pour the mixture as a single addition...' (350 ppm).

### Free nicotinic acid
To 1 g add 75 ml of *water*, shake for 15 minutes and titrate with 0.02M *sodium hydroxide VS* using *phenolphthalein solution R1* as indicator. Not more than 0.8 ml of 0.02M *sodium hydroxide VS* is required to produce the first pink colour.

### Related substances
Carry out the method for *thin-layer chromatography*, Appendix III A, using a plate 200 mm × 200 mm in size and *silica gel GF₂₅₄* as the coating substance. For the first development use a mixture of 90 volumes of *chloroform* and 10 volumes of *methanol* as the mobile phase. Apply to the bottom right-hand corner of the plate 5 µl of solution (1) containing 5.0% w/v of the substance being examined in a mixture of 9 volumes of *chloroform* and 1 volume of *methanol* and develop over a path of 12 cm. After removal of the plate, allow it to dry in air and turn the plate through 90° in a clockwise direction. Apply separately to the bottom right-hand corner of the plate, and to the right of the solvent front, 5 µl of each of two solutions of the substance being examined in a mixture of 9 volumes of *chloroform* and 1 volume of *methanol* containing (2) 0.075% w/v and (3) 0.050% w/v. For the second development use a mixture of 50 volumes of *ethyl acetate* and 5 volumes each of *glacial acetic acid*, *ethanol (96%)* and *water* as the mobile phase. After removal of the plate, allow it to dry in air and examine under *ultraviolet light (254 nm)*. In the chromatogram obtained with solution (1) any *secondary spot* is not more intense than the spot in the chromatogram obtained with solution (2) (1.5%) and not more than one such spot is more intense than the spot in the chromatogram obtained with solution (3) (1%).

### Acetone
Prepare a 0.020% v/v solution of *butan-2-one* (internal standard) in *dimethylformamide* (solution A). Carry out the method for *gas chromatography*, Appendix III B, using the following solutions. Solution (1) contains 0.020% v/v of *acetone* in solution A. For solution (2) add 5 ml of *dimethylformamide* to 0.20 g of the substance being examined contained in a suitable vessel, stopper securely, suspend in a water bath until solution is complete and allow to cool. Prepare solution (3) in the same manner as solution (2) but using 5 ml of solution A in place of the dimethylformamide.

The chromatographic procedure may be carried out using a glass column (1.5 m × 4 mm) packed with *acid-washed, silanised diatomaceous support* coated with 10% w/w of polyethylene glycol 1000 and maintained at 60°.

In the chromatogram obtained with solution (3) the ratio of the area of any peak corresponding to acetone to the area of the peak due to the internal standard is not greater than the corresponding ratio in the chromatogram obtained with solution (1).

**Loss on drying**

When dried to constant weight at 105°, loses not more than 0.5% of its weight. Use 1 g.

**Sulphated ash**

Not more than 0.1%, Appendix IX A.

**ASSAY**

Carry out Method I for *non-aqueous titration*, Appendix VIII A, using 0.2 g and *1-naphtholbenzein solution* as indicator. Each ml of 0.1M *perchloric acid VS* is equivalent to 13.51 mg of $C_{42}H_{30}N_6O_{12}$.

# Insulin Aspart

(*Ph Eur monograph 2084*)

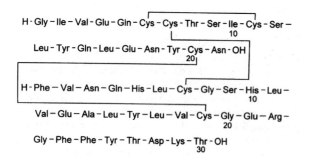

$C_{256}H_{381}N_{65}O_{79}S_6$　　5826　　*116094-23-6*

**Action and use**

Hormone; treatment of diabetes mellitus.

*Ph Eur* ___

## DEFINITION

$28^B$-L-Aspartate insulin (human).

Insulin aspart is a 2-chain peptide containing 51 amino acids. The A-chain is composed of 21 amino acids and the B-chain is composed of 30 amino acids. It is identical in primary structure to human insulin, except that it has aspartic acid instead of proline at position 28 of the B-chain. As in human insulin, insulin aspart contains 2 interchain disulphide bonds and 1 intrachain disulphide bond.

## Content

90.0 per cent to 104.0 per cent of insulin aspart $C_{256}H_{381}N_{65}O_{79}S_6$ plus A21Asp insulin aspart, B3Asp insulin aspart, B3isoAsp insulin aspart and B28isoAsp insulin aspart (dried substance).

By convention, for the purpose of labelling insulin aspart preparations, 0.0350 mg of insulin aspart is equivalent to 1 unit.

## PRODUCTION

Insulin aspart is produced by a method based on recombinant DNA (rDNA) technology under conditions designed to minimise the degree of microbial contamination.

*Prior to release the following tests are carried out on each batch of the final bulk product, unless exemption has been granted by the competent authority.*

**Host-cell-derived proteins**

The limit is approved by the competent authority.

**Single-chain precursor**

The limit is approved by the competent authority. Use a suitably sensitive method.

## CHARACTERS

**Appearance**

White or almost white powder.

**Solubility**

Practically insoluble in ethanol (96 per cent), in methanol and in aqueous solutions with a pH around 5.1. In aqueous solutions below pH 3.5 or above pH 6.5, the solubility is greater than or equal to 25 mg/ml.

## IDENTIFICATION

A. Examine the chromatograms obtained in the assay.

*Results*　The principal peak in the chromatogram obtained with the test solution is similar in retention time to the principal peak in the chromatogram obtained with reference solution (a).

B. Peptide mapping (*2.2.55*).

*SELECTIVE CLEAVAGE OF THE PEPTIDE BONDS*

*Test solution*　Prepare a 2.0 mg/ml solution of the substance to be examined in *0.01 M hydrochloric acid* and transfer 25 µl of this solution to a clean tube. Add 100 µl of *HEPES buffer solution pH 7.5 R* and 20 µl of a 1 mg/ml solution of *Staphylococcus aureus strain V8 protease R*. Cap the tube and incubate at 25 °C for 6 h. Stop the reaction by adding 145 µl of *sulphate buffer solution pH 2.0 R*.

*Reference solution*　Prepare at the same time and in the same manner as for the test solution, but using *insulin aspart CRS* instead of the substance to be examined.

*CHROMATOGRAPHIC SEPARATION*

Liquid chromatography (*2.2.29*).

*Column*:
— *size*: $l = 0.10$ m, $\varnothing = 4.6$ mm,
— *stationary phase*: octadecylsilyl silica gel for chromatography R (3 µm) with a pore size of 8 nm,
— *temperature*: 40 °C.

*Mobile phase*:
— *mobile phase A*: mix 100 ml of *acetonitrile for chromatography R*, 200 ml of *sulphate buffer solution pH 2.0 R* and 700 ml of *water R*; filter and degas;
— *mobile phase B*: mix 200 ml of *sulphate buffer solution pH 2.0 R*, 400 ml of *acetonitrile for chromatography R* and 400 ml of *water R*; filter and degas;

| Time (min) | Mobile phase A (per cent V/V) | Mobile phase B (per cent V/V) |
|---|---|---|
| 0 - 60 | 90 → 30 | 10 → 70 |
| 60 - 65 | 30 → 0 | 70 → 100 |
| 65 - 70 | 0 | 100 |

*Flow rate*　1 ml/min.

*Detection*　Spectrophotometer at 214 nm.

*Equilibration*　At initial conditions for at least 15 min. Carry out a blank run using the above-mentioned gradient.

*Injection*　50 µl.

*System suitability*:
— the chromatograms obtained with the test solution and the reference solution are qualitatively similar to the chromatogram of insulin aspart digest supplied with *insulin aspart CRS*,

— in the chromatogram obtained with the reference solution, identify the peaks due to digest fragments I, II and III:

*Symmetry factor*   Maximum 1.5, for the peaks due to fragments II and III,

*Resolution*   Minimum 8.0, between the peaks due to fragments II and III.

*Results*   The profile of the chromatogram obtained with the test solution corresponds to that of the chromatogram obtained with the reference solution.

*NOTE: the retention times of fragments I, II and IV are the same as for human insulin. The retention time of fragment III differs from human insulin due to substitution of proline by aspartic acid.*

## TESTS

### Impurities with molecular masses greater than that of insulin aspart

Size-exclusion chromatography (*2.2.30*): use the normalisation procedure.

*Test solution*   Prepare a solution containing 4 mg/ml of the substance to be examined in *0.01 M hydrochloric acid*. Maintain the solution at 2-8 °C and use within 48 h.

*Resolution solution*   Use a solution of insulin (about 4 mg/ml), containing more than 0.4 per cent of high molecular mass proteins. An injectable insulin preparation, whether a solution or a suspension, that has been clarified with a sufficient amount of *6 M hydrochloric acid R*, containing the indicated percentage of high molecular mass proteins, or a solution prepared from insulin, dissolved in *0.01 M hydrochloric acid* may be used. Insulin containing the indicated percentage of high molecular mass proteins may be prepared by allowing insulin powder to stand at room temperature for about 10 days. Maintain the solution at 2-8 °C and use within 7 days.

*Column:*
— *size*: $l$ = 0.3 m, Ø = 7.8 mm,
— *stationary phase*: *hydrophilic silica gel for chromatography R* (5-10 μm) with a pore size of 12-12.5 nm, of a grade suitable for the separation of insulin monomer from dimer and polymers.

*Mobile phase*   Mix 15 volumes of *glacial acetic acid R*, 20 volumes of *acetonitrile for chromatography R* and 65 volumes of a 1.0 g/l solution of *arginine R*; filter and degas.

*Flow rate*   0.5 ml/min.

*Detection*   Spectrophotometer at 276 nm.

*Equilibration*   At least 3 injections of the resolution solution; the column is equilibrated when repeatable results are obtained from 2 subsequent injections.

*Injection*   100 μl.

*Run time*   About 35 min.

*Retention time*   Insulin aspart polymers = 13-17 min; insulin aspart dimer = about 17.5 min; insulin aspart monomer = about 20 min; salts = about 22 min.

*System suitability*   Resolution solution:
— *peak-to-valley ratio*: minimum 2.0, where $H_p$ = height above the baseline of the peak due to the dimer and $H_v$ = height above the baseline of the lowest point of the curve separating this peak from the peak due to the monomer.

*Limits*   The sum of the areas of the peaks with a retention time less than that of the principal peak is not more than 0.5 per cent of the total area of the peaks. Disregard any peak with a retention time greater than that of the peak due to insulin aspart monomer.

### Related proteins

Liquid chromatography (*2.2.29*) as described under Assay: use the normalisation procedure.

*Limits:*
— *B28isoAsp insulin aspart*: maximum 1.0 per cent,
— *total of the peaks due to A21Asp insulin aspart, B3Asp insulin aspart and B3isoAsp insulin aspart*: maximum 2.0 per cent,
— *total of other impurities*: maximum 1.5 per cent.

### Loss on drying (*2.2.32*)

Maximum 10.0 per cent, determined on 0.200 g by drying in an oven at 105 °C for 24 h.

### Sulphated ash (*2.4.14*)

Maximum 6.0 per cent, determined on 0.200 g (dried substance).

### Bacterial endotoxins (*2.6.14*)

Less than 10 IU/mg, if intended for use in the manufacture of parenteral dosage forms without a further appropriate procedure for the removal of bacterial endotoxins.

## ASSAY

Liquid chromatography (*2.2.29*).

*Test solution*   Dissolve the substance to be examined in *0.01 M hydrochloric acid* to obtain a concentration of 4.0 mg/ml. Maintain the solution at 2-8 °C and use within 24 h.

*Reference solution*   Dissolve the contents of a vial of *insulin aspart CRS* in *0.01 M hydrochloric acid* to obtain a concentration of 4.0 mg/ml. Maintain the solution at 2-8 °C and use within 48 h.

*Resolution solution*   Use an appropriate solution with a content of B3Asp insulin aspart and A21Asp insulin aspart of not less than 1 per cent. This may be achieved by storing reference solution at room temperature for about 1-3 days. Maintain the solution at 2-8 °C and use within 72 h.

*Column:*
— *size*: $l$ = 0.25 m, Ø = 4 mm,
— *stationary phase*: *octadecylsilyl silica gel for chromatography R* (5 μm),
— *temperature*: 40 °C.

*Mobile phase:*
— *mobile phase A*: dissolve 142.0 g of *anhydrous sodium sulphate R* in *water R*; add 13.5 ml of *phosphoric acid R* and dilute to 5000 ml with *water R*; adjust to pH 3.6, if necessary, with *strong sodium hydroxide solution R*; filter and degas; mix 9 volumes of the solution with 1 volume of *acetonitrile for chromatography R*; filter and degas;
— *mobile phase B*: mix equal volumes of *water R* and *acetonitrile for chromatography R*; filter and degas;

| Time (min) | Mobile phase A (per cent *V/V*) | Mobile phase B (per cent *V/V*) |
|---|---|---|
| 0 - 35 | 58 | 42 |
| 35 - 40 | 58 → 20 | 42 → 80 |
| 40 - 45 | 20 | 80 |
| 45 - 46 | 20 → 58 | 80 → 42 |
| 46 - 60 | 58 | 42 |

*Flow rate*   1 ml/min.

*Detection*   Spectrophotometer at 214 nm.

*Injection*   10 μl.

*Relative retention* with reference to insulin aspart (retention time = 20-24 min): B28isoAsp insulin aspart = about 0.9; B3Asp insulin aspart plus A21Asp insulin aspart (generally coeluted) = about 1.3; B3isoAsp insulin aspart = about 1.5.

*System suitability* Resolution solution:
— *resolution*: minimum 2.0 between the peak due to insulin aspart and the peak due to A21Asp insulin aspart and to B3Asp insulin aspart.

Calculate the content of insulin aspart $C_{256}H_{381}N_{65}O_{79}S_6$, plus B28isoAsp insulin aspart, A21Asp insulin aspart, B3Asp insulin aspart and B3isoAsp insulin aspart using the areas of the corresponding peaks in the chromatograms obtained with the test solution and reference solution and the declared content of insulin aspart plus B28isoAsp insulin aspart, A21Asp insulin aspart, B3Asp insulin aspart and B3isoAsp insulin aspart in *insulin aspart CRS*.

## STORAGE

In an airtight container, protected from light, at or below − 18 °C until released by the manufacturer. When thawed, insulin aspart is stored at 5 ± 3 °C and used for manufacturing preparations within a short period of time. To avoid absorption of humidity from the air during weighing, insulin aspart must be at room temperature before opening the container.

*Ph Eur*

# Bovine Insulin

*(Ph Eur monograph 1637)*

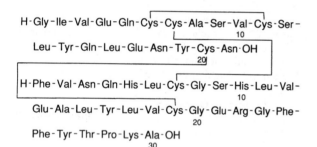

$C_{254}H_{377}N_{65}O_{75}S_6$          5734          *11070-73-8*

**Action and use**
Hormone; treatment of diabetes mellitus.

**Preparation**
Insulin Preparations

*Ph Eur*

## DEFINITION

Bovine insulin is the natural antidiabetic principle obtained from beef pancreas and purified.

**Content:**
— *sum of bovine insulin ($C_{254}H_{377}N_{65}O_{75}S_6$) and A21 desamido bovine insulin*: 93.0 per cent to 105.0 per cent (dried subtance).

By convention, for the purpose of labelling insulin preparations, 0.0342 mg of bovine insulin is equivalent to 1 IU of insulin.

## PRODUCTION

The animals from which bovine insulin is derived must fulfil the requirements for the health of animals suitable for human consumption.

## CHARACTERS

**Appearance**
White or almost white powder.

**Solubility**
Practically insoluble in water and in ethanol. It dissolves in dilute mineral acids and with decomposition in dilute solutions of alkali hydroxides.

## IDENTIFICATION

A. Examine the chromatograms obtained in the assay.

*Results* The retention time of the principal peak in the chromatogram obtained with the test solution corresponds to that of the principal peak in the chromatogram obtained with reference solution (c).

B. Peptide mapping.

*Test solution* Prepare a 2.0 mg/ml solution of the substance to be examined in *0.01 M hydrochloric acid* and transfer 500 µl of this solution to a clean tube. Add 2.0 ml of *HEPES buffer solution pH 7.5 R* and 400 µl of a 1 mg/ml solution of *Staphylococcus aureus strain V8 protease R*. Cap the tube and incubate at 25 °C for 6 h. Stop the reaction by adding 2.9 ml of *sulphate buffer solution pH 2.0 R*.

*Reference solution* Prepare at the same time and in the same manner as for the test solution but using *bovine insulin CRS* instead of the substance to be examined.

Examine the digests by liquid chromatography (2.2.29).
*Column:*
— *size*: l = 0.10 m, Ø = 4.6 mm;
— *stationary phase*: octadecylsilyl silica gel for chromatography R (3 µm);
— *temperature*: 40 °C.

*Mobile phase:*
— *mobile phase A*: mix 100 ml of *acetonitrile for chromatography R*, 700 ml of *water R* and 200 ml of *sulphate buffer solution pH 2.0 R*; filter and degas;
— *mobile phase B*: mix 400 ml of *acetonitrile for chromatography R*, 400 ml of *water R* and 200 ml of *sulphate buffer solution pH 2.0 R*; filter and degas;

| Time (min) | Mobile phase A (per cent V/V) | Mobile phase B (per cent V/V) |
|---|---|---|
| 0 - 60 | 90 → 30 | 10 → 70 |
| 60 - 65 | 30 → 0 | 70 → 100 |
| 65 - 70 | 0 | 100 |

*Flow rate* 1 ml/min.

*Detection* Spectrophotometer at 214 nm.

*Equilibration* At initial conditions for at least 15 min. Carry out a blank run using the above-mentioned gradient.

*Injection* 50 µl.

*System suitability* The chromatograms obtained with the test solution and the reference solution are qualitatively similar to the chromatogram of bovine insulin digest supplied with *bovine insulin CRS*. In the chromatogram obtained with the reference solution, identify the peaks due to digest fragments I, II and III. The symmetry factor of the peaks due to fragments II and III is not greater than 1.5, and the resolution between the 2 peaks is at least 1.9.

*Results* The profile of the chromatogram obtained with the test solution corresponds to that of the chromatogram obtained with the reference solution.

*NOTE: The retention time of fragment I is the same for porcine insulin and for human insulin. The retention times of fragments II and IV are the same for all insulins. The retention time of fragment III is the same for bovine insulin and for porcine insulin.*

## TESTS

### Impurities with molecular masses greater than that of insulin

Size-exclusion chromatography (*2.2.30*): use the normalisation procedure. *Maintain the solutions at 2-10 °C and use within 7 days. If an automatic injector is used, maintain the temperature at 2-10 °C.*

*Test solution* Dissolve 4 mg of the substance to be examined in 1.0 ml of *0.01 M hydrochloric acid.*

*Resolution solution* Use a solution of insulin (approximately 4 mg/ml), containing more than 0.4 per cent of high molecular mass proteins. An injectable insulin preparation, whether a solution or a suspension, that has been clarified with a sufficient amount of *6 M hydrochloric acid R*, containing the indicated percentage of high molecular mass proteins, or a solution prepared from insulin, dissolved in *0.01 M hydrochloric acid*, may be used. Insulin containing the indicated percentage of high molecular mass proteins may be prepared by allowing insulin powder to stand at room temperature for about 10 days.

*Column:*
— *size*: $l = 0.3$ m, $\emptyset$ = at least 7.5 mm;
— *stationary phase*: *hydrophilic silica gel for chromatography R* (5-10 μm), of a grade suitable for the separation of insulin monomer from dimer and polymers.

*Mobile phase* Mix of 15 volumes of *glacial acetic acid R*, 20 volumes of *acetonitrile R* and 65 volumes of a 1.0 g/l solution of *arginine R*; filter and degas.

*Flow rate* 0.5 ml/min.

*Detection* Spectrophotometer at 276 nm.

*Equilibration* Before using a new column for chromatographic analysis, equilibrate by repeated injections of an insulin solution containing high molecular mass proteins. This can be done by at least 3 injections of the resolution solution. The column is equilibrated when repeatable results are obtained from 2 subsequent injections.

*Injection* 100 μl.

*Run time* About 35 min.

*Retention times* Polymeric insulin complexes = 13 min to 17 min; covalent insulin dimer = about 17.5 min; insulin monomer = about 20 min; salts = about 22 min.

*System suitability* Resolution solution:
— *peak-to-valley ratio*: minimum 2.0, where $H_p$ = height above the baseline of the peak due to the dimer and $H_v$ = height above the baseline of the lowest point of the curve separating this peak from the peak due to the monomer.

*Limits* The sum of the areas of any peaks with a retention time less than that of the principal peak is not greater than 1.0 per cent of the total area of the peaks; disregard any peak with a retention time greater than that of the insulin peak.

*Related proteins* Liquid chromatography (*2.2.29*) as described under Assay, following the elution conditions as described in the table below.

| Time (min) | Mobile phase A (per cent *V/V*) | Mobile phase B (per cent *V/V*) |
|---|---|---|
| 0 - 30 | 42 | 58 |
| 30 - 44 | 42 → 11 | 58 → 89 |
| 44 - 50 | 11 | 89 |

*Maintain the solutions at 2-10 °C and use within 24 h.* Perform a system suitability test (resolution, linearity) as described under Assay. If necessary, the relative proportions of the mobile phases may be adjusted to ensure complete elution of A21 desamido porcine insulin before commencement of the gradient. The profile of the gradient may also be adjusted to ensure complete elution of all insulin related impurities.

Inject 20 μl of reference solution (c) and 20 μl of the test solution. If necessary, adjust the injection volume to between 10 μl and 20 μl in accordance with the results obtained in the test for linearity as described under Assay. Record the chromatograms for approximately 50 min. In the chromatogram obtained with reference solution (c), A21 desamido bovine insulin appears as a small peak after the principal peak and has a relative retention of about 1.3 with reference to the principal peak. In the chromatogram obtained with the test solution, the area of the peak due to A21 desamido bovine insulin is not greater than 3.0 per cent of the total area of the peaks; the sum of the areas of all the peaks, apart from those due to bovine insulin and A21 desamido bovine insulin, is not greater than 3.0 per cent of the total area of the peaks.

### Bovine proinsulin-like immunoreactivity (PLI)

Maximum 10 ppm (dried substance).

Use a suitably sensitive immunochemical method (*2.7.1*) such as radio-immunoassay, using the International Reference Reagent for bovine proinsulin to calibrate the method.

### Zinc

Maximum 1.0 per cent (dried substance).

Atomic absorption spectrometry (*2.2.23, Method I*).

*Test solution* Dissolve 50.0 mg of the substance to be examined in *0.01 M hydrochloric acid* and dilute to 25.0 ml with the same acid. Dilute if necessary to a suitable concentration (for example, 0.4 μg to 1.6 μg of Zn per millilitre) with *0.01 M hydrochloric acid.*

*Reference solutions* Use solutions containing 0.40 μg, 0.80 μg, 1.00 μg, 1.20 μg and 1.60 μg of Zn per millilitre, freshly prepared by diluting *zinc standard solution (5 mg/ml Zn) R* with *0.01 M hydrochloric acid.*

*Source* Zinc hollow-cathode lamp.

*Wavelength* 213.9 nm.

*Flame* Air-acetylene flame of suitable composition (for example, 11 litres of air and 2 litres of acetylene per minute).

### Loss on drying (*2.2.32*)

Maximum 10.0 per cent, determined on 0.200 g by drying in an oven at 105 °C for 24 h.

### Sulphated ash (*2.4.14*)

Maximum 2.5 per cent (dried substance), determined on 0.200 g.

### Bacterial endotoxins (*2.6.14*)

Less than 10 IU/mg, if intended for use in the manufacture of parenteral dosage forms without a further appropriate procedure for the removal of bacterial endotoxins.

## ASSAY

Liquid chromatography (*2.2.29*).

*Test solution* Dissolve a suitable amount of the substance to be examined in *0.01 M hydrochloric acid* to obtain a concentration of 4.0 mg/ml.

*Reference solution (a)* Dissolve the contents of a vial of *human insulin CRS* in *0.01 M hydrochloric acid* to obtain a concentration of 4.0 mg/ml.

*Reference solution (b)*  Dissolve the contents of a vial of *porcine insulin CRS* in *0.01 M hydrochloric acid* to obtain a concentration of 4.0 mg/ml.

*Reference solution (c)*  Dissolve the contents of a vial of *bovine insulin CRS* in *0.01 M hydrochloric acid* to obtain a concentration of 4.0 mg/ml.

*Reference solution (d)*  Dilute 1.0 ml of reference solution (c) to 10.0 ml with *0.01 M hydrochloric acid*.

*Resolution solution*  Mix 1.0 ml of reference solution (a) and 1.0 ml of reference solution (b).

Maintain the solutions at 2-10 °C and use within 48 h. If an automatic injector is used, maintain the temperature at 2-10 °C.

*Column:*
— *size*: $l = 0.25$ m, $\emptyset = 4.6$ mm;
— *stationary phase: octadecylsilyl silica gel for chromatography R* (5 μm);
— *temperature*: 40 °C.

*Mobile phase*  Mix 42 volumes of mobile phase A and 58 volumes of mobile phase B, adjusting the composition of the mixture if necessary.

Prepare and maintain the following solutions at a temperature of at least 20 °C:
— *mobile phase A*: dissolve 28.4 g of *anhydrous sodium sulphate R* in *water R* and dilute to 1000 ml with the same solvent; add 2.7 ml of *phosphoric acid R;* adjust to pH 2.3, if necessary, with *ethanolamine R;* filter and degas;
— *mobile phase B*: mix 550 ml of mobile phase A with 450 ml of *acetonitrile R*. Warm the solution to a temperature of at least 20 °C in order to avoid precipitation (mixing of mobile phase A with acetonitrile is endothermic); filter and degas.

*Flow rate*  1 ml/min.

*Detection*  Spectrophotometer at 214 nm.

*System suitability:*
— *resolution*: inject 20 μl of the resolution solution and 20 μl of reference solution (b). Record the chromatogram of the resolution solution until the peak corresponding to the principal peak in the chromatogram obtained with reference solution (b) is clearly visible. In the chromatogram obtained with the resolution solution, identify the peaks due to porcine insulin and human insulin. The test is not valid unless the resolution between the peaks corresponding to human insulin and porcine insulin is at least 1.2. If necessary, adjust the concentration of acetonitrile in the mobile phase until this resolution is achieved;
— *linearity*: inject 20 μl each of reference solutions (c) and (d). The test is not valid unless the area of the principal peak in the chromatogram obtained with reference solution (c) is 10 ± 0.5 times the area of the principal peak in the chromatogram obtained with reference solution (d). If this test fails, adjust the injection volume to between 10 μl and 20 μl, in order that the responses are within the linearity range of the detector.

*Injection*  20 μl of the test solution.

Calculate the content of bovine insulin $C_{254}H_{377}N_{65}O_{75}S_6$ plus A21 desamido bovine insulin from the area of the principal peak and the area of the peak corresponding to A21 desamido bovine insulin in the chromatograms obtained with the test solution and reference solution (c) and the declared content of bovine insulin plus A21 desamido bovine insulin in *bovine insulin CRS*.

**STORAGE**

In an airtight container, protected from light, at − 20 °C until released by the manufacturer. When thawed, insulin may be stored at 5 ± 3 °C and used for manufacturing preparations within a short period of time. To avoid absorption of humidity from the air during weighing, the insulin must be at room temperature.

*Ph Eur*

# Human Insulin

*(Ph Eur monograph 0838)*

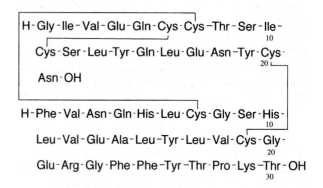

$C_{257}H_{383}N_{65}O_{77}S_6$          5808          *11061-68-0*

**Action and use**
Hormone; treatment of diabetes mellitus.

**Preparations**
Insulin Preparations

*Ph Eur*

**DEFINITION**
Human insulin is a 2-chain peptide having the structure of the antidiabetic hormone produced by the human pancreas.

**Content**
95.0 per cent to 105.0 per cent of human insulin $C_{257}H_{383}N_{65}O_{77}S_6$ plus A21 desamido human insulin (dried substance).

By convention, for the purpose of labelling insulin preparations, 0.0347 mg of human insulin is equivalent to 1 IU of insulin.

**PRODUCTION**
Human insulin is produced either by enzymatic modification and suitable purification of insulin obtained from the pancreas of the pig or by a method based on recombinant DNA (rDNA) technology.

Human insulin is produced under conditions designed to minimise the degree of microbial contamination.

*For human insulin produced by enzymatic modification of insulin obtained from the pancreas of the pig, the manufacturing process is validated to demonstrate removal of any residual proteolytic activity. The competent authority may require additional tests.*

*For human insulin produced by a method based on rDNA technology, prior to release the following tests are carried out on each batch of the final bulk product, unless exemption has been granted by the competent authority.*

**Host-cell-derived proteins**
The limit is approved by the competent authority.

## Single chain precursor

The limit is approved by the competent authority. Use a suitably sensitive method.

## CHARACTERS

### Appearance

White or almost white powder.

### Solubility

Practically insoluble in water and in ethanol (96 per cent). It dissolves in dilute mineral acids and with decomposition in dilute solutions of alkali hydroxides.

## IDENTIFICATION

A. Examine the chromatograms obtained in the assay.

*Results*   The principal peak in the chromatogram obtained with the test solution is similar in retention time to the principal peak in the chromatogram obtained with reference solution (a).

B. Peptide mapping (2.2.55).

### SELECTIVE CLEAVAGE OF THE PEPTIDE BONDS

*Test solution*   Prepare a 2.0 mg/ml solution of the substance to be examined in *0.01 M hydrochloric acid* and transfer 500 µl of this solution to a clean tube. Add 2.0 ml of *HEPES buffer solution pH 7.5 R* and 400 µl of a 1 mg/ml solution of *Staphylococcus aureus strain V8 protease R*. Cap the tube and incubate at 25 °C for 6 h. Stop the reaction by adding 2.9 ml of *sulphate buffer solution pH 2.0 R*.

*Reference solution*   Prepare at the same time and in the same manner as for the test solution but using *human insulin CRS* instead of the substance to be examined.

### CHROMATOGRAPHIC SEPARATON

Liquid chromatography (2.2.29).

*Column:*
— size: *l* = 0.10 m, Ø = 4.6 mm,
— stationary phase: *octadecylsilyl silica gel for chromatography R* (3 µm) with a pore size of 8 nm,
— temperature: 40 °C.

*Mobile phase:*
— mobile phase A: mix 100 ml of *acetonitrile for chromatography R*, 200 ml of *sulphate buffer solution pH 2.0 R* and 700 ml of *water R*; filter and degas;
— mobile phase B: mix 200 ml of *sulphate buffer solution pH 2.0 R*, 400 ml of *acetonitrile for chromatography R* and 400 ml of *water R*; filter and degas;

| Time (min) | Mobile phase A (per cent *V/V*) | Mobile phase B (per cent *V/V*) |
|---|---|---|
| 0 - 60 | 90 → 30 | 10 → 70 |
| 60 - 65 | 30 → 0 | 70 → 100 |
| 65 - 70 | 0 | 100 |

*Flow rate*   1 ml/min.

*Detection*   Spectrophotometer at 214 nm.

*Equilibration*   At initial conditions for at least 15 min. Carry out a blank run using the above-mentioned gradient.

*Injection*   50 µl.

*System suitability:*
— the chromatograms obtained with the test solution and the reference solution are qualitatively similar to the chromatogram of human insulin digest supplied with *human insulin CRS*,
— in the chromatogram obtained with the reference solution, identify the peaks due to digest fragments I, II and III:

*Symmetry factor*   Maximum 1.5 for the peaks due to fragments II and III,

*Resolution*   Minimum 3.4 between the peaks due to fragments II and III.

*Results*   The profile of the chromatogram obtained with the test solution corresponds to that of the chromatogram obtained with the reference solution.

*NOTE: the retention time of fragment I is the same for porcine insulin and for human insulin. The retention times of fragments II and IV are the same for all insulins. The retention time of fragment III is the same for bovine insulin and for porcine insulin.*

## TESTS

### Impurities with molecular masses greater than that of insulin

Size-exclusion chromatography (2.2.30): use the normalisation procedure.

*Test solution*   Prepare a solution containing 4 mg/ml of the substance to be examined in *0.01 M hydrochloric acid.*

*Resolution solution*   Use a solution of insulin (about 4 mg/ml), containing more than 0.4 per cent of high molecular mass proteins. An injectable insulin preparation, whether a solution or a suspension, that has been clarified with a sufficient amount of *6 M hydrochloric acid R*, containing the indicated percentage of high molecular mass proteins, or a solution prepared from insulin, dissolved in *0.01 M hydrochloric acid*, may be used. Insulin containing the indicated percentage of high molecular mass proteins may be prepared by allowing insulin powder to stand at room temperature for about 10 days.

Maintain the solutions at 2-8 °C and use within 7 days. If an automatic injector is used, maintain the temperature at 2-8 °C.

*Column:*
— size: *l* = 0.3 m, Ø = minimum 7.5 mm,
— stationary phase: *hydrophilic silica gel for chromatography R* (5-10 µm) with a pore size of 12-12.5 nm, of a grade suitable for the separation of insulin monomer from dimer and polymers.

*Mobile phase*   Mix 15 volumes of *glacial acetic acid R*, 20 volumes of *acetonitrile R* and 65 volumes of a 1.0 g/l solution of *arginine R*; filter and degas.

*Flow rate*   0.5 ml/min.

*Detection*   Spectrophotometer at 276 nm.

*Equilibration*   Before using a new column for chromatographic analysis, equilibrate by repeated injections of an insulin solution containing high molecular mass proteins. This can be done by at least 3 injections of the resolution solution. The column is equilibrated when repeatable results are obtained from 2 subsequent injections.

*Injection*   100 µl.

*Run time*   About 35 min.

*Retention time*   Polymeric insulin complexes = 13-17 min; covalent insulin dimer = about 17.5 min; insulin monomer = about 20 min; salts = about 22 min.

*System suitability*

Resolution solution:
— *peak-to-valley ratio*: minimum 2.0, where $H_p$ = height above the baseline of the peak due to the dimer and $H_v$ = height above the baseline of the lowest point of the curve separating this peak from the peak due to the monomer.

*Limits*   The sum of the areas of any peaks with a retention time less than that of the principal peak is not greater than

1.0 per cent of the total area of the peaks. Disregard any peak with a retention time greater than that of the peak due to insulin.

### Related proteins

Liquid chromatography (2.2.29) as described under Assay, following the elution conditions as described below:

| Time (min) | Mobile phase A (per cent V/V) | Mobile phase B (per cent V/V) |
|---|---|---|
| 0 - 30 | 42 | 58 |
| 30 - 44 | 42 → 11 | 58 → 89 |
| 44 - 50 | 11 | 89 |

Maintain the solutions at 2-8 °C and use within 24 h. Perform a system suitability test (resolution, linearity) as described in the assay. If necessary, the relative proportions of the mobile phases may be adjusted to ensure complete elution of A21 desamido porcine insulin before commencement of the gradient. The profile of the gradient may also be adjusted to ensure complete elution of all insulin related impurities.

Inject 20 µl of reference solution (a), 20 µl of reference solution (b), 20 µl of reference solution (c) and 20 µl of the test solution. If necessary, adjust the injection volume to a volume between 10 µl and 20 µl in accordance with the results obtained in the test for linearity as described in the assay. Record the chromatograms for approximately 50 min. In the chromatogram obtained with reference solution (a), A21 desamido human insulin appears as a small peak after the principal peak and has a retention time of about 1.3 relative to the principal peak. In the chromatogram obtained with the test solution, the area of the peak due to A21 desamido human insulin is not greater than 2.0 per cent of the total area of the peaks; the sum of the areas of all peaks, apart from those due to human insulin and that due to A21 desamido human insulin, is not greater than 2.0 per cent of the total area of the peaks. For semisynthetic human insulin only: in the chromatogram obtained with the test solution, the area of any peak corresponding to the principal peak in the chromatogram obtained with reference solution (b) is not greater than the area of the corresponding peak in the chromatogram obtained with reference solution (c) (1.0 per cent of porcine insulin in human insulin).

*The following test applies only to human insulin produced by enzymatic modification of porcine insulin.*

### Proinsulin-like immunoreactivity (PLI)

Maximum 10 ppm, calculated with reference to the dried substance and determined by a suitably sensitive immunochemical method (2.7.1) such as radio-immunoassay. Use the International Reference Reagent for porcine proinsulin to calibrate the method.

### Zinc

Maximum 1.0 per cent (dried substance).

Atomic absorption spectrometry (2.2.23, Method I).

### Test solution

Dissolve 50.0 mg of the substance to be examined in *0.01 M hydrochloric acid* and dilute to 25.0 ml with the same acid. Dilute if necessary to a suitable concentration (for example, 0.4-1.6 µg of Zn per millilitre) with *0.01 M hydrochloric acid*.

### Reference solutions

Use solutions containing 0.40 µg, 0.80 µg, 1.00 µg, 1.20 µg and 1.60 µg of Zn per millilitre, freshly prepared by diluting

*zinc standard solution (5 mg/ml Zn) R* with *0.01 M hydrochloric acid*.

### Source

Zinc hollow-cathode lamp.

### Wavelength

213.9 nm.

*Atomisation device*: air-acetylene flame of suitable composition (for example, 11 litres of air and 2 litres of acetylene per minute).

### Loss on drying (2.2.32)

Maximum 10.0 per cent, determined on 0.200 g by drying in an oven at 105 °C for 24 h.

### Sulphated ash (2.4.14)

Maximum 2.5 per cent, determined on 0.200 g (dried substance).

### Bacterial endotoxins (2.6.14)

Less than 10 IU/mg, if intended for use in the manufacture of parenteral dosage forms without a further appropriate procedure for removal of bacterial endotoxins.

### ASSAY

Liquid chromatography (2.2.29).

*Test solution*   Dissolve 40.0 mg of the substance to be examined in *0.01 M hydrochloric acid* and dilute to 10.0 ml with the same solvent.

*Reference solution (a)*   Dissolve the contents of a vial of *human insulin CRS* in *0.01 M hydrochloric acid* to obtain a concentration of 4.0 mg/ml.

*Reference solution (b)*   Dissolve the contents of a vial of *porcine insulin CRS* in *0.01 M hydrochloric acid* to obtain a concentration of 4.0 mg/ml.

*Reference solution (c)*   Dilute 1.0 ml of reference solution (b) to 50.0 ml with *0.01 M hydrochloric acid*. To 1.0 ml of this solution add 1.0 ml of reference solution (a).

*Reference solution (d)*   Dilute 1.0 ml of reference solution (a) to 10.0 ml with *0.01 M hydrochloric acid*.

*Resolution solution*   Mix 1.0 ml of reference solution (a) and 1.0 ml of reference solution (b).

Maintain the solutions at 2-8 °C and use within 48 h. If an automatic injector is used, maintain at 2-8 °C.

*Column:*
— size: $l = 0.25$ , $\varnothing = 4.6$ mm,
— stationary phase: octadecylsilyl silica gel for chromatography R (5 µm),
— temperature: 40 °C.

*Mobile phase*   Mix 42 volumes of mobile phase A and 58 volumes of mobile phase B, adjusting the composition of the mixture if necessary.

Prepare and maintain the following solutions at a temperature of at least 20 °C:
— mobile phase A: dissolve 28.4 g of *anhydrous sodium sulphate R* in *water R* and dilute to 1000 ml with the same solvent; add 2.7 ml of *phosphoric acid R*; adjust to pH 2.3, if necessary, with *ethanolamine R*; filter and degas;
— mobile phase B: mix 550 ml of mobile phase A with 450 ml of *acetonitrile R*. Warm the solution to a temperature of at least 20 °C in order to avoid precipitation (mixing of mobile phase A with acetonitrile is endothermic); filter and degas.

*Flow rate*   1 ml/min.

*Detection*   Spectrophotometer at 214 nm.

*System suitability:*
— *resolution*: inject 20 μl of the resolution solution and 20 μl of reference solution (b). Record the chromatogram of the resolution solution until the peak corresponding to the principal peak in the chromatogram obtained with reference solution (b) is clearly visible. In the chromatogram obtained with the resolution solution, identify the peaks due to porcine insulin and human insulin. The test is not valid unless the resolution between the peaks due to human insulin and porcine insulin is at least 1.2. If necessary, adjust the concentration of acetonitrile in the mobile phase until this resolution is achieved.
— *linearity*: inject 20 μl each of reference solutions (a) and (d). The test is not valid unless the area of the principal peak in the chromatogram obtained with reference solution (a) is 10 ± 0.5 times the area of the principal peak in the chromatogram obtained with reference solution (d). If this test fails, adjust the injection volume to between 10 μl and 20 μl, in order that the responses are within the linearity range of the detector.

*Injection* 20 μl of the test solution and reference solution (a).

Calculate the content of human insulin $C_{257}H_{383}N_{65}O_{77}S_6$ plus A21 desamido human insulin using the areas of the corresponding peaks in the chromatograms obtained with the test solution and reference solution (a) and the declared content of human insulin plus A21 desamido human insulin in *human insulin CRS*.

## STORAGE
In an airtight container, protected from light, at − 18 °C or below, until released by the manufacturer. When thawed, insulin is stored at 5 ± 3 °C and used for manufacturing preparations within a short period of time. To avoid absorption of humidity from the air during weighing, the insulin must be at room temperature.

## LABELLING
The label states whether the substance is produced by enzymatic modification of porcine insulin or by rDNA technology.

_____ *Ph Eur*

# Insulin Lispro

*(Ph Eur monograph 2085)*

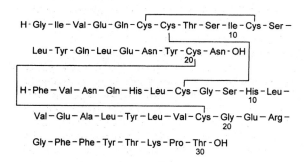

$C_{257}H_{383}N_{65}O_{77}S_6$          5808          *133107-64-9*

## Action and use
Hormone; treatment of diabetes mellitus.

*Ph Eur* _____

## DEFINITION
28$^B$-L-Lysine-29$^B$-L-proline insulin (human).

Insulin lispro is a 2-chain peptide containing 51 amino acids. The A-chain is composed of 21 amino acids and the B-chain is composed of 30 amino acids. It is identical in primary structure to human insulin, only differing in amino acid sequence at positions 28 and 29 of the B-chain. Human insulin is Pro(B28), Lys(B29), whereas insulin lispro is Lys(B28), Pro(B29). As in human insulin, insulin lispro contains 2 interchain disulphide bonds and 1 intrachain disulphide bond.

## Content
94.0 per cent to 104.0 per cent (dried substance).

By convention, for the purpose of labelling insulin lispro preparations, 0.0347 mg of insulin lispro is equivalent to 1 unit.

## PRODUCTION
Insulin lispro is produced by a method based on recombinant DNA (rDNA) technology under conditions designed to minimise the degree of microbial contamination.

*Prior to release the following tests are carried out on each batch of final bulk product, unless exemption has been granted by the competent authority.*

### Host-cell-derived proteins
The limit is approved by the competent authority.

### Single-chain precursor
The limit is approved by the competent authority. Use a suitably sensitive method.

## CHARACTERS
### Appearance
White or almost white powder.

### Solubility
Practically insoluble in water and in ethanol (96 per cent). It dissolves in dilute mineral acids and with decomposition in dilute solutions of alkali hydroxides.

## IDENTIFICATION
A. Examine the chromatograms obtained in the assay.

*Results* The principal peak in the chromatogram obtained with the test solution is similar in retention time to the principal peak in the chromatogram obtained with the reference solution.

B. Peptide mapping (*2.2.55*).

*SELECTIVE CLEAVAGE OF THE PEPTIDE BONDS*

*Test solution* Prepare a 2.0 mg/ml solution of the substance to be examined in *0.01 M hydrochloric acid* and transfer 500 μl of this solution to a clean tube. Add 2.0 ml of *HEPES buffer solution pH 7.5 R* and 400 μl of a 1 mg/ml solution of *Staphylococcus aureus strain V8 protease R*. Cap the tube and incubate at 25 °C for 6 h. Stop the reaction by adding 2.9 ml of *sulphate buffer solution pH 2.0 R*.

*Reference solution* Prepare at the same time and in the same manner as for the test solution but using *insulin lispro CRS* instead of the substance to be examined.

*CHROMATOGRAPIC SEPARATION*

Liquid chromatography (*2.2.29*).

*Column:*
— *size*: *l* = 0.10 m, Ø = 4.6 mm,
— *stationary phase*: *octadecylsilyl silica gel for chromatography R* (3 μm) with a pore size of 8 nm,
— *temperature*: 40 °C.

*Mobile phase:*
— *mobile phase A*: mix 100 ml of *acetonitrile for chromatography R*, 200 ml of *sulphate buffer solution pH 2.0 R* and 700 ml of *water R*; filter and degas;
— *mobile phase B*: mix 200 ml of *sulphate buffer solution pH 2.0 R*, 400 ml of *acetonitrile for chromatography R* and 400 ml of *water R*; filter and degas;

| Time (min) | Mobile phase A (per cent *V/V*) | Mobile phase B (per cent *V/V*) |
|---|---|---|
| 0 - 60 | 90 → 30 | 10 → 70 |
| 60 - 65 | 30 → 0 | 70 → 100 |
| 65 - 70 | 0 | 100 |

*Flow rate* 1 ml/min.

*Detection* Spectrophotometer at 214 nm.

*Equilibration* At initial conditions for at least 15 min. Carry out a blank run using the above-mentioned gradient.

*Injection* 50 μl.

*System suitability:*
— the chromatograms obtained with the test solution and the reference solution are qualitatively similar to the chromatogram of insulin lispro digest supplied with *insulin lispro CRS*,
— in the chromatogram obtained with the reference solution, identify the peaks due to digest fragments I, II and III.

*Symmetry factor* Maximum 1.5 for the peaks due to fragments II and III,

*Resolution* Minimum 8.0 between the peaks due to fragments II and III.

*Results* The profile of the chromatogram obtained with the test solution corresponds to that of the chromatogram obtained with the reference solution.

*NOTE: the retention times of fragments I, II and IV are the same as for human insulin. The retention time of fragment III differs from human insulin due to differences in sequence at positions 28 and 29 of the B-chain.*

## TESTS

**Impurities with molecular masses greater than that of insulin lispro**
Size-exclusion chromatography (*2.2.30*): use the normalisation procedure.

*Test solution* Prepare a solution containing 4 mg/ml of the substance to be examined in *0.01 M hydrochloric acid*. Maintain the solution at 2-8 °C and use within 48 h.

*Resolution solution* Use a solution of insulin (about 4 mg/ml), containing more than 0.4 per cent of high molecular mass proteins. An injectable insulin preparation, whether a solution or a suspension, that has been clarified with a sufficient amount of *6 M hydrochloric acid R*, containing the indicated percentage of high molecular mass proteins, or a solution prepared from insulin, dissolved in *0.01 M hydrochloric acid*, may be used. Insulin containing the indicated percentage of high molecular mass proteins may be prepared by allowing insulin powder to stand at room temperature for about 10 days. Maintain the solution at 2-8 °C and use within 8 days.

*Column:*
— *size*: *l* = 0.30 m, Ø = 7.8 mm,
— *stationary phase: hydrophilic silica gel for chromatography R* (5-10 μm) with a pore size of 12-12.5 nm, of a grade suitable for the separation of insulin monomer from dimer and polymers.

*Mobile phase* Mix 15 volumes of *glacial acetic acid R*, 20 volumes of *acetonitrile for chromatography R* and 65 volumes of a 1.0 g/l *solution of arginine R*; filter and degas.

*Flow rate* 0.5 ml/min.

*Detection* Spectrophotometer at 276 nm.

*Equilibration* At least 3 injections of the resolution solution; the column is equilibrated when repeatable results are obtained for 2 subsequent injections.

*Injection* 100 μl.

*Run time* About 35 min.

*Retention time* Insulin lispro polymers = 13-17 min; insulin lispro dimer = about 17.5 min; insulin lispro monomer = about 20 min; salts = about 22 min.

*System suitability* Resolution solution:
— *peak-to-valley ratio*: minimum 2.0, where $H_p$ = height above the baseline of the peak due to the dimer and $H_v$ = height above the baseline of the lowest point of the curve separating this peak from the peak due to the monomer,
— *symmetry factor*: maximum 2.0 for the peak due to insulin lispro.

*Limits* The sum of the areas of the peaks with a retention time less than that of the principal peak is not more than 0.25 per cent of the total area of the peaks. Disregard any peak with a retention time greater than that of the peak due to insulin lispro monomer.

**Related proteins**
Liquid chromatography (*2.2.29*): use the normalisation procedure.

*Test solution* Dissolve 3.5 mg of the substance to be examined in 1.0 ml of *0.01 M hydrochloric acid*. Maintain the solution at 2-8 °C and use within 56 h.

*Resolution solution* Dissolve 3.5 mg of the substance to be examined in 1.0 ml of *0.01 M hydrochloric acid*. Allow to stand at room temperature to obtain a solution containing between 0.8 per cent and 11 per cent of A21 desamido insulin lispro.

*Column:*
— *size*: *l* = 0.25 m, Ø = 4.6 mm,
— *stationary phase: octadecylsilyl silica gel for chromatography R* (5 μm) with a pore size of 30 nm,
— *temperature*: 40 °C.

*Mobile phase:*
— *mobile phase A*: mix 82 volumes of a 28.4 g/l solution of *anhydrous sodium sulphate R* adjusted to pH 2.3 with *phosphoric acid R* and 18 volumes of *acetonitrile for chromatography R*; filter and degas;
— *mobile phase B*: mix equal volumes of a 28.4 g/l solution of *anhydrous sodium sulphate R* adjusted to pH 2.3 with *phosphoric acid R* and *acetonitrile for chromatography R*; filter and degas;

| Time (min) | Mobile phase A (per cent *V/V*) | Mobile phase B (per cent *V/V*) |
|---|---|---|
| 0 - 60 | 81 | 19 |
| 60 - 83 | 81 → 51 | 19 → 49 |
| 83 - 84 | 51 → 81 | 49 → 19 |
| 84 - 94 | 81 | 19 |

*Flow rate* 1 ml/min.

*Detection* Spectrophotometer at 214 nm.

*Injection* 20 μl.

*Retention time*   Adjust the mobile phase composition to obtain a retention time of about 41 min for insulin lispro; A21 desamido insulin lispro elutes near the start of the gradient elution.

*System suitability*   Resolution solution:
— *resolution*: minimum 1.5 between the 1st peak (insulin lispro) and the 2nd peak (A21 desamido insulin lispro),
— *symmetry factor*: maximum 2.0 for the peak due to insulin lispro.

*Limits:*
— *A21 desamido insulin lispro*: maximum 1.0 per cent,
— *any other impurity*: maximum 0.50 per cent,
— *total (excluding A21)*: maximum 2.0 per cent.

**Zinc**

Maximum 1.0 per cent (dried substance).

Atomic absorption spectrometry (*2.2.23, Method I*).

*Test solution*   Dissolve at least 50 mg of the substance to be examined in *0.01 M hydrochloric acid* and dilute to 25 ml with the same acid. Dilute if necessary to a suitable concentration (for example 0.4-0.6 μg of Zn per millilitre) with *0.01 M hydrochloric acid*.

*Reference solutions*   Use solutions of concentrations which bracket the expected zinc concentration of the samples, for example, 0.2-0.8 μg of Zn per millilitre, freshly prepared by diluting *zinc standard solution (5 mg/ml Zn) R* with *0.01 M hydrochloric acid*.

*Source*   Zinc hollow-cathode lamp.

*Wavelength*   213.9 nm.

*Atomisation device*   Air-acetylene flame of suitable composition (for example, 11 litres of air and 2 litres of acetylene per minute).

**Loss on drying** (*2.2.32*)

Maximum 10.0 per cent, determined on 0.200 g by drying in an oven at 105 °C for 16 h.

**Sulphated ash** (*2.4.14*)

Maximum 2.5 per cent, determined on 0.200 g (dried substance).

**Bacterial endotoxins** (*2.6.14, Method D*)

Less than 10 IU/mg, if intended for use in the manufacture of parenteral dosage forms without a further appropriate procedure for the removal of bacterial endotoxins.

**ASSAY**

Liquid chromatography (*2.2.29*).

*Test solution*   Dissolve the substance to be examined in *0.01 M hydrochloric acid* to obtain a concentration of 0.8 mg/ml. Maintain the solution at 2-8 °C and use within 48 h.

*Reference solution*   Dissolve the contents of a vial *of insulin lispro CRS* in *0.01 M hydrochloric acid* to obtain a concentration of 0.8 mg/ml. Maintain the solution at 2-8 °C and use within 48 h.

*Resolution solution*   Dissolve about 10 mg of the substance to be examined in 10 ml of *0.01 M hydrochloric acid*. Allow to stand at room temperature to obtain a solution containing between 0.8 per cent and 11 per cent of A21 desamido insulin lispro. Maintain the solution at 2-8 °C and use within 14 days.

*Column:*
— *size*: $l$ = 0.10 m, Ø = 4.6 mm,
— *stationary phase*: octadecylsilyl silica gel for chromatography R (3 μm) with a pore size of 8 nm,
— *temperature*: 40 °C.

*Mobile phase*   Mix 745 volumes of a 28.4 g/l solution of *anhydrous sodium sulphate R* adjusted to pH 2.3 with *phosphoric acid R* and 255 volumes of *acetonitrile for chromatography R*; filter and degas.

*Flow rate*   0.8 ml/min.

*Detection*   Spectrophotometer at 214 nm.

*Injection*   20 μl.

*Retention time*   Insulin lispro = about 24 min.

*System suitability:*
— *resolution*: minimum 1.8 between the 1st peak (insulin lispro) and the 2nd peak (A21 desamido insulin lispro), in the chromatogram obtained with the resolution solution,
— *repeatability*: maximum relative standard deviation of 1.1 per cent after 3 injections of the reference solution.

Calculate the content of insulin lispro $C_{257}H_{383}N_{65}O_{77}S_6$ using the chromatograms obtained with the test solution and the reference solution and the declared content of $C_{257}H_{383}N_{65}O_{77}S_6$ in *insulin lispro CRS*.

**STORAGE**

In an airtight container, protected from light, at or below − 18 °C. When thawed, insulin lispro is stored and weighed under conditions defined by the manufacturer to maintain the quality attributes of the drug substance and is used for manufacturing preparations within a short period of time. To avoid absorption of humidity from the air during weighing, insulin lispro must be at room temperature before opening the container.

*_____ Ph Eur*

# Porcine Insulin

(*Ph Eur monograph 1638*)

H‑Gly‑Ile‑Val‑Glu‑Gln‑Cys‑Cys‑Thr‑Ser‑Ile‑Cys‑Ser‑
                                      10
Leu‑Tyr‑Gln‑Leu‑Glu‑Asn‑Tyr‑Cys‑Asn‑OH
                              20
H‑Phe‑Val‑Asn‑Gln‑His‑Leu‑Cys‑Gly‑Ser‑His‑Leu‑Val‑
                                      10
Glu‑Ala‑Leu‑Tyr‑Leu‑Val‑Cys‑Gly‑Glu‑Arg‑Gly‑Phe‑
                              20
Phe‑Tyr‑Thr‑Pro‑Lys‑Ala‑OH
                    30

$C_{256}H_{381}N_{65}O_{76}S_6$       5778       *12584-58-6*

**Action and use**

Hormone; treatment of diabetes mellitus.

**Preparations**

Insulin Preparations

*Ph Eur _____*

**DEFINITION**

Porcine insulin is the natural antidiabetic principle obtained from pork pancreas and purified.

**Content:**
— *sum of porcine insulin ($C_{256}H_{381}N_{65}O_{76}S_6$) and A21 desamido porcine insulin*: 95.0 per cent to 105.0 per cent (dried substance).

By convention, for the purpose of labelling insulin preparations, 0.0345 mg of porcine insulin is equivalent to 1 IU of insulin.

## PRODUCTION

The animals from which porcine insulin is derived must fulfil the requirements for the health of animals suitable for human consumption.

## CHARACTERS

### Appearance

White or almost white powder.

### Solubility

Practically insoluble in water and in ethanol. It dissolves in dilute mineral acids and with decomposition in dilute solutions of alkali hydroxides.

## IDENTIFICATION

A. Examine the chromatograms obtained in the assay.

*Results* The retention time of the principal peak in the chromatogram obtained with the test solution corresponds to that of the principal peak in the chromatogram obtained with reference solution (b).

B. Peptide mapping.

*Test solution* Prepare a 2.0 mg/ml solution of the substance to be examined in *0.01 M hydrochloric acid* and transfer 500 µl of this solution to a clean tube. Add 2.0 ml of *HEPES buffer solution pH 7.5 R* and 400 µl of a 1 mg/ml solution of *Staphylococcus aureus strain V8 protease R*. Cap the tube and incubate at 25 °C for 6 h. Stop the reaction by adding 2.9 ml of *sulphate buffer solution pH 2.0 R*.

*Reference solution* Prepare at the same time and in the same manner as for the test solution but using *porcine insulin CRS* instead of the substance to be examined.

Examine the digests by liquid chromatography (*2.2.29*).

*Column:*
— *size*: *l* = 0.10 m, Ø = 4.6 mm;
— *stationary phase*: *octadecylsilyl silica gel for chromatography R (3 µm)*;
— *temperature*: 40 °C.

*Mobile phase:*
— *mobile phase A*: mix 100 ml of *acetonitrile for chromatography R*, 700 ml of *water R* and 200 ml of *sulphate buffer solution pH 2.0 R*; filter and degas;
— *mobile phase B*: mix 400 ml of *acetonitrile for chromatography R*, 400 ml of *water R* and 200 ml of *sulphate buffer solution pH 2.0 R*; filter and degas;

| Time (min) | Mobile phase A (per cent *V/V*) | Mobile phase B (per cent *V/V*) |
|---|---|---|
| 0 - 60 | 90 → 30 | 10 → 70 |
| 60 - 65 | 30 → 0 | 70 → 100 |
| 65 - 70 | 0 | 100 |

*Flow rate* 1 ml/min.

*Detection* Spectrophotometer at 214 nm.

*Equilibration* At initial conditions for at least 15 min. Carry out a blank run using the above-mentioned gradient.

*Injection* 50 µl.

*System suitability* The chromatograms obtained with the test solution and the reference solution are qualitatively similar to the chromatogram of porcine insulin digest supplied with *porcine insulin CRS*. In the chromatogram obtained with the reference solution, identify the peaks due to digest fragments I and III. The symmetry factor of the peaks due to

fragments II and III is not greater than 1.5, and the resolution between the 2 peaks is at least 1.9.

*Results* The profile of the chromatogram obtained with the test solution corresponds to that of the chromatogram obtained with the reference solution.

*NOTE: the retention time of fragment I is the same for porcine insulin and for human insulin. The retention times of fragments II and IV are the same for all insulins. The retention time of fragment III is the same for bovine insulin and for porcine insulin.*

## TESTS

### Impurities with molecular masses greater than that of insulin

Size-exclusion chromatography (*2.2.30*): use the normalisation procedure. *Maintain the solutions at 2-10 °C and use within 7 days. If an automatic injector is used, maintain the temperature at 2-10 °C.*

*Test solution* Dissolve 4 mg of the substance to be examined in 1.0 ml of *0.01 M hydrochloric acid.*

*Resolution solution* Use a solution of insulin (approximately 4 mg/ml), containing more than 0.4 per cent of high molecular mass proteins. An injectable insulin preparation, whether a solution or a suspension, that has been clarified with a sufficient amount of *6 M hydrochloric acid R*, containing the indicated percentage of high molecular mass proteins, or a solution prepared from insulin, dissolved in *0.01 M hydrochloric acid*, may be used. Insulin containing the indicated percentage of high molecular mass proteins may be prepared by allowing insulin powder to stand at room temperature for about 10 days.

*Column:*
— *size*: *l* = 0.3 m, Ø = at least 7.5 mm;
— *stationary phase*: *hydrophilic silica gel for chromatography R (5-10 µm)*, of a grade suitable for the separation of insulin monomer from dimer and polymers.

*Mobile phase* Mix 15 volumes of *glacial acetic acid R*, 20 volumes of *acetonitrile R* and 65 volumes of a 1.0 g/l solution of *arginine R*; filter and degas.

*Flow rate* 0.5 ml/min.

*Detection* Spectrophotometer at 276 nm.

*Equilibration* Before using a new column for chromatographic analysis, equilibrate by repeated injections of an insulin solution containing high molecular mass proteins. This can be done by at least 3 injections of the resolution solution. The column is equilibrated when repeatable results are obtained from 2 subsequent injections.

*Injection* 100 µl.

*Run time* About 35 min.

*Retention times* Polymeric insulin complexes = 13 min to 17 min; covalent insulin dimer = about 17.5 min; insulin monomer = about 20 min; salts = about 22 min.

*System suitability* Resolution solution:
— *peak-to-valley ratio*: minimum 2.0, where $H_p$ = height above the baseline of the peak due to the dimer and $H_v$ = height above the baseline of the lowest point of the curve separating this peak from the peak due to the monomer.

*Limits* The sum of the areas of any peaks with a retention time less than that of the principal peak is not greater than 1.0 per cent of the total area of the peaks; disregard any peak with a retention time greater than that of the insulin peak.

**Related proteins**

Liquid chromatography (2.2.29) as described under Assay, following the elution conditions as described in the table below.

| Time (min) | Mobile phase A (per cent V/V) | Mobile phase B (per cent V/V) |
|---|---|---|
| 0 - 30 | 42 | 58 |
| 30 - 44 | 42 → 11 | 58 → 89 |
| 44 - 50 | 11 | 89 |

*Maintain the solutions at 2-10 °C and use within 24 h.*
Perform a system suitability test (resolution, linearity) as described under Assay. If necessary, the relative proportions of the mobile phases may be adjusted to ensure complete elution of A21 desamido porcine insulin before commencement of the gradient. The profile of the gradient may also be adjusted to ensure complete elution of all insulin related impurities.

Inject 20 µl of reference solution (b) and 20 µl of the test solution. If necessary, adjust the injection volume to between 10 µl and 20 µl in accordance with the results obtained in the test for linearity as described under Assay. Record the chromatograms for approximately 50 min. In the chromatogram obtained with reference solution (b), A21 desamido porcine insulin appears as a small peak after the principal peak and has a relative retention of about 1.3 with reference to the principal peak. In the chromatogram obtained with the test solution, the area of the peak due to A21 desamido porcine insulin is not greater than 2.0 per cent of the total area of the peaks; the sum of the areas of all the peaks, apart from those due to porcine insulin and A21 desamido porcine insulin, is not greater than 2.0 per cent of the total area of the peaks.

**Porcine proinsulin-like immunoreactivity (PLI)**

Maximum 10 ppm (dried substance).

Use a suitably sensitive immunochemical method (2.7.1) such as radio-immunoassay, using the International Reference Reagent for porcine proinsulin to calibrate the method.

**Zinc**

Maximum 1.0 per cent (dried substance).

Atomic absorption spectrometry (2.2.23, Method I).

*Test solution* Dissolve 50.0 mg of the substance to be examined in *0.01 M hydrochloric acid* and dilute to 25.0 ml with the same acid. Dilute if necessary to a suitable concentration (for example, 0.4 µg to 1.6 µg of Zn per millilitre) with *0.01 M hydrochloric acid.*

*Reference solutions* Use solutions containing 0.40 µg, 0.80 µg, 1.00 µg, 1.20 µg and 1.60 µg of Zn per millilitre, freshly prepared by diluting *zinc standard solution (5 mg/ml Zn) R* with *0.01 M hydrochloric acid.*

*Source* Zinc hollow-cathode lamp.

*Wavelength* 213.9 nm.

*Flame* Air-acetylene flame of suitable composition (for example, 11 litres of air and 2 litres of acetylene per minute).

**Loss on drying** (2.2.32)

Maximum 10.0 per cent, determined on 0.200 g by drying in an oven at 105 °C for 24 h.

**Sulphated ash** (2.4.14)

Maximum 2.5 per cent (dried substance), determined on 0.200 g.

**Bacterial endotoxins** (2.6.14)

Less than 10 IU/mg, if intended for use in the manufacture of parenteral dosage forms without a further appropriate procedure for the removal of bacterial endotoxins.

**ASSAY**

Liquid chromatography (2.2.29).

*Test solution* Dissolve 40.0 mg of the substance to be examined in *0.01 M hydrochloric acid* and dilute to 10.0 ml with the same solvent.

*Reference solution (a)* Dissolve the contents of a vial of *human insulin CRS* in *0.01 M hydrochloric acid* to obtain a concentration of 4.0 mg/ml.

*Reference solution (b)* Dissolve the contents of a vial of *porcine insulin CRS* in *0.01 M hydrochloric acid* to obtain a concentration of 4.0 mg/ml.

*Reference solution (c)* Dilute 1.0 ml of reference solution (b) to 10.0 ml with *0.01 M hydrochloric acid.*

*Resolution solution* Mix 1.0 ml of reference solution (a) and 1.0 ml of reference solution (b).

Maintain the solutions at 2-10 °C and use within 48 h. If an automatic injector is used, maintain the temperature at 2-10 °C.

*Column:*
— size: $l = 0.25$ , Ø = 4.6 mm;
— *stationary phase: octadecylsilyl silica gel for chromatography R* (5 µm);
— *temperature*: 40 °C.

*Mobile phase* Mix 42 volumes of mobile phase A and 58 volumes of mobile phase B, adjusting the composition of the mixture if necessary.

Prepare and maintain the following solutions at a temperature of at least 20 °C:
— *mobile phase A*: dissolve 28.4 g of *anhydrous sodium sulphate R* in *water R* and dilute to 1000 ml with the same solvent; add 2.7 ml of *phosphoric acid R*; adjust to pH 2.3, if necessary, with *ethanolamine R;* filter and degas;
— *mobile phase B*: mix 550 ml of mobile phase A with 450 ml of *acetonitrile R*. Warm the solution to a temperature of at least 20 °C in order to avoid precipitation (mixing of mobile phase A with acetonitrile is endothermic); filter and degas.

*Flow rate:* 1 ml/min.

*Detection* Spectrophotometer at 214 nm.

*System suitability:*
— *resolution*: inject 20 µl of the resolution solution and 20 µl of reference solution (b). Record the chromatogram of the resolution solution until the peak corresponding to the principal peak in the chromatogram obtained with reference solution (b) is clearly visible. In the chromatogram obtained with the resolution solution, identify the peaks due to porcine insulin and human insulin. The test is not valid unless the resolution between the peaks corresponding to human insulin and porcine insulin is at least 1.2. If necessary, adjust the concentration of acetonitrile in the mobile phase until this resolution is achieved.
— *linearity*: inject 20 µl each of reference solutions (b) and (c). The test is not valid unless the area of the principal peak in the chromatogram obtained with reference solution (b) is 10 ± 0.5 times the area of the principal peak in the chromatogram obtained with reference solution (c). If this test fails, adjust the injection volume to between 10 µl and 20 µl, in order that the responses are within the linearity range of the detector.

*Injection* 20 µl of the test solution.

Calculate the content of porcine insulin $C_{256}H_{381}N_{65}O_{76}S_6$ plus A21 desamido porcine insulin from the area of the principal peak and the area of the peak corresponding to A21 desamido porcine insulin in the chromatograms obtained with the test solution and reference solution (b) and the declared content of porcine insulin plus A21 desamido porcine insulin in *porcine insulin CRS*.

## STORAGE

In an airtight container, protected from light, at $-20\,°C$ until released by the manufacturer. When thawed, insulin may be stored at $5 \pm 3\,°C$ and used for manufacturing preparations within a short period of time. To avoid absorption of humidity from the air during weighing, the insulin must be at room temperature.

_____ *Ph Eur*

# Interferon Alfa-2 Concentrated Solution

*(Ph Eur monograph 1110)*

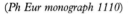

```
CDLPQTHSLG   SRRTLMLLAQ   MRX₁ISLFSCL   KDRHDFGFPQ
EEFGNQFQKA   ETIPVLHEMI   QQIFNLFSTK   DSSAAWDETL
LDKFYTELYQ   QLNDLEACVI   QGVGVTETPL   MKEDSILAVR
KYFQRITLYL   KEKKYSPCAW   EVVRAEIMRS   FSLSTNLQES
LRSKE
```

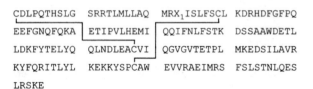

alfa-2a: $C_{860}H_{1353}N_{227}O_{255}S_9$   19,241   *76543-85-9*

alfa-2b: $C_{860}H_{1353}N_{229}O_{255}S_9$   19,269   *99210-65-8*

**Action and use**
Cytokine.

*Ph Eur* _____

## DEFINITION

Interferon alfa-2 concentrated solution is a solution of a protein that is produced according to the information coded by the alfa-2 sub-species of interferon alfa gene and that exerts non-specific antiviral activity, at least in homologous cells, through cellular metabolic processes involving synthesis of both ribonucleic acid and protein. Interferon alfa-2 concentrated solution also exerts antiproliferative activity. Different types of alfa-2 interferon, varying in the amino acid residue at position 23, are designated by a letter in lower case.

| Designation | Residue at position 23 ($X_1$) |
|---|---|
| alfa-2a | Lys |
| alfa-2b | Arg |

This monograph applies to interferon alfa-2a and -2b concentrated solutions.

The potency of interferon alfa-2 concentrated solution is not less than $1.4 \times 10^8$ IU per milligram of protein. Interferon alfa-2 concentrated solution contains not less than $2 \times 10^8$ IU of interferon alfa-2 per millilitre.

## PRODUCTION

Interferon alfa-2 concentrated solution is produced by a method based on recombinant DNA (rDNA) technology using bacteria as host cells. It is produced under conditions designed to minimise microbial contamination of the product.

Interferon alfa-2 concentrated solution complies with the following additional requirements.

**Host-cell-derived proteins**
The limit is approved by the competent authority.

**Host-cell- or vector-derived DNA**
The limit is approved by the competent authority.

## CHARACTERS

A clear, colourless or slightly yellowish liquid.

## IDENTIFICATION

A. It shows the expected biological activity (see Assay).

B. Examine by isoelectric focusing.

*Test solution* Dilute the preparation to be examined with *water R* to a protein concentration of 1 mg/ml.

*Reference solution* Prepare a 1 mg/ml solution of the appropriate *interferon alfa-2 CRS* in *water R*.

*Isoelectric point calibration solution pI range 3.0 to 10.0.* Prepare and use according to the manufacturer's instructions.

Use a suitable apparatus connected with a recirculating temperature controlled water-bath set at 10 °C and gels for isoelectric focusing with a pH gradient from 3.5 to 9.5. Operate the apparatus in accordance with the manufacturer's instructions. Use as the anode solution *phosphoric acid R* (98 g/l $H_3PO_4$) and as the cathode solution *1 M sodium hydroxide*. Samples are applied to the gel by filter papers. Place sample application filters on the gel close to the cathode.

Apply 15 µl of the test solution and 15 µl of the reference solution. Start the isoelectric focusing at 1500 V and 50 mA. Turn off the power after 30 min, remove the application filters and reconnect the power supply for 1 h. Keep the power constant during the focusing process. After focusing, immerse the gel in a suitable volume of a solution containing 115 g/l of *trichloroacetic acid R* and 34.5 g/l of *sulphosalicylic acid R* in *water R* and agitate the container gently for 60 min. Transfer the gel to a mixture of 32 volumes of *glacial acetic acid R*, 100 volumes of *anhydrous ethanol R* and 268 volumes of *water R*, and soak for 5 min. Immerse the gel for 10 min in a staining solution prewarmed to 60 °C in which 1.2 g/l of *acid blue 83 R* has been added to the previous mixture of glacial acetic acid, ethanol and water. Wash the gel in several containers with the previous mixture of glacial acetic acid, ethanol and water and keep the gel in this mixture until the background is clear (12 h to 24 h). After adequate destaining, soak the gel for 1 h in a 10 per cent $V/V$ solution of *glycerol R* in the previous mixture of glacial acetic acid, ethanol and water.

The principal bands of the electropherogram obtained with the test solution correspond in position to the principal bands of the electropherogram obtained with the reference solution. Plot the migration distances of the isoelectric point markers versus their isoelectric points and determine the isoelectric points of the principal components of the test solution and the reference solution. They do not differ by more than 0.2 pI units. The test is not valid unless the isoelectric point markers are distributed along the entire length of the gel and the isoelectric points of the principal bands in the electropherogram obtained with the reference solution are between 5.8 and 6.3.

C. Examine the electropherograms obtained under reducing conditions in the test for impurities of molecular masses differing from that of interferon alfa-2. The principal band in the electropherogram obtained with test solution (a) corresponds in position to the principal band in the electropherogram obtained with reference solution (a).

D. Examine by peptide mapping.

*Test solution*  Dilute the preparation to be examined in *water R* to a protein concentration of 1.5 mg/ml. Transfer 25 µl to a polypropylene or glass tube of 1.5 ml capacity. Add 1.6 µl of *1 M phosphate buffer solution pH 8.0 R*, 2.8 µl of a freshly prepared 1.0 mg/ml solution of *trypsin for peptide mapping R* in *water R* and 3.6 µl of *water R* and mix vigorously. Cap the tube and place it in a water-bath at 37 °C for 18 h, then add 100 µl of a 573 g/l solution of *guanidine hydrochloride R* and mix well. Add 7 µl of 154.2 g/l solution of *dithiothreitol R* and mix well. Place the capped tube in boiling water for 1 min. Cool to room temperature.

*Reference solution*  Prepare at the same time and in the same manner as for the test solution but use a 1.5 mg/ml solution of the appropriate *interferon alfa-2 CRS* in *water R*.

Examine by liquid chromatography (*2.2.29*).

The chromatographic procedure may be carried out using:
— a stainless steel column 0.10 m long and 4.6 mm in internal diameter packed with *octadecylsilyl silica gel for chromatography R* (5 µm) with a pore size of 30 nm,
— as mobile phase at a flow rate of 1.0 ml/min:

*Mobile phase A*  Dilute 1 ml of *trifluoroacetic acid R* to 1000 ml with *water R*,

*Mobile phase B*  To 100 ml of *water R* add 1 ml of *trifluoroacetic acid R* and dilute to 1000 ml with *acetonitrile for chromatography R*,

| Time (min) | Mobile phase A (per cent *V/V*) | Mobile phase B (per cent *V/V*) | Comment |
|---|---|---|---|
| 0 - 8 | 100 | 0 | isocratic |
| 8 - 68 | 100 → 40 | 0 → 60 | linear gradient |
| 68 - 72 | 40 | 60 | isocratic |
| 72 - 75 | 40 → 100 | 60 → 0 | linear gradient |
| 75 - 80 | 100 | 0 | re-equilibration |

— as detector a spectrophotometer set at 214 nm,

maintaining the temperature of the column at 30 °C.

Equilibrate the column with mobile phase A for at least 15 min.

Inject 100 µl of the test solution and 100 µl of the reference solution. The test is not valid unless the chromatogram obtained with each solution is qualitatively similar to the chromatogram of interferon alfa-2 digest supplied with the appropriate *interferon alfa-2 CRS*. The profile of the chromatogram obtained with the test solution corresponds to that of the chromatogram obtained with the reference solution.

**TESTS**

**Impurities of molecular masses differing from that of interferon alfa-2**

Examine by SDS polyacrylamide gel electrophoresis (*2.2.31*). The test is performed under both reducing and non-reducing conditions, using resolving gels of 14 per cent acrylamide and silver staining as the detection method.

*Sample buffer (non-reducing conditions)*  Mix equal volumes of *water R* and *concentrated SDS PAGE sample buffer R*.

*Sample buffer (reducing conditions)*  Mix equal volumes of *water R* and *concentrated SDS PAGE sample buffer for reducing conditions R* containing 2-mercaptoethanol as the reducing agent.

*Test solution (a)*  Dilute the preparation to be examined in sample buffer to a protein concentration of 0.5 mg/ml.

*Test solution (b)*  Dilute 0.20 ml of test solution (a) to 1 ml with sample buffer.

*Reference solution (a)*  Prepare a 0.625 mg/ml solution of the appropriate *interferon alfa-2 CRS* in sample buffer.

*Reference solution (b)*  Dilute 0.20 ml of reference solution (a) to 1 ml with sample buffer.

*Reference solution (c)*  Dilute 0.20 ml of reference solution (b) to 1 ml with sample buffer.

*Reference solution (d)*  Dilute 0.20 ml of reference solution (c) to 1 ml with sample buffer.

*Reference solution (e)*  Dilute 0.20 ml of reference solution (d) to 1 ml with sample buffer.

*Reference solution (f)*  Use a solution of molecular mass standards suitable for calibrating SDS-PAGE gels in the range 15 kDa to 67 kDa.

Place test and reference solutions, contained in covered test-tubes, on a water-bath for 2 min.

Apply 10 µl of reference solution (f) and 50 µl of each of the other solutions to the stacking gel wells. Perform the electrophoresis under the conditions recommended by the manufacturer of the equipment. Detect proteins in the gel by silver staining.

The test is not valid unless: the validation criteria are met (*2.2.31*); a band is seen in the electropherogram obtained with reference solution (e); and a gradation of intensity of staining is seen in the electropherograms obtained, respectively, with test solution (a) and test solution (b) and with reference solutions (a) to (e).

The electropherogram obtained with test solution (a) under reducing conditions may show, in addition to the principal band, less intense bands with molecular masses lower than the principal band. No such band is more intense than the principal band in the electropherogram obtained with reference solution (d) (1.0 per cent) and not more than 3 such bands are more intense than the principal band in the electropherogram obtained with reference solution (e) (0.2 per cent).

The electropherogram obtained with test solution (a) under non-reducing conditions may show, in addition to the principal band, less intense bands with molecular masses higher than the principal band. No such band is more intense than the principal band in the electropherogram obtained with reference solution (d) (1.0 per cent) and not more than 3 such bands are more intense than the principal band in the electropherogram obtained with reference solution (e) (0.2 per cent).

**Related proteins**

Examine by liquid chromatography (*2.2.29*).

*Test solution*  Dilute the preparation to be examined with *water R* to a protein concentration of 1 mg/ml.

*0.25 per cent m/m hydrogen peroxide solution.*  Dilute *dilute hydrogen peroxide solution R* in *water R* in order to obtain a 0.25 per cent m/m solution.

*Reference solution*  To a volume of the test solution, add a suitable volume of 0.25 per cent *m/m* hydrogen peroxide solution to give a final hydrogen peroxide concentration of 0.005 per cent *m/m*, and allow to stand at room temperature for 1 h, or for the length of time that will generate about 5 per cent oxidised interferon. Add 12.5 mg of *L-methionine R* per millilitre of solution. Allow to stand at room temperature for 1 h. Store the solutions for not longer than 24 h at a temperature of 2-8 °C.

The chromatographic procedure may be carried out using:
— a stainless steel column 0.25 m long and 4.6 mm in internal diameter packed with *octadecylsilyl silica gel for chromatography R* (5 µm) with a pore size of 30 nm,
— as mobile phase at a flow rate of 1.0 ml/min:

*Mobile phase A*  To 700 ml of *water R* add 2 ml of *trifluoroacetic acid R* and 300 ml of *acetonitrile for chromatography R*,

*Mobile phase B*  To 200 ml of *water R* add 2 ml of *trifluoroacetic acid R* and 800 ml of *acetonitrile for chromatography R*,

| Time (min) | Mobile phase A (per cent *V/V*) | Mobile phase B (per cent *V/V*) | Comment |
|---|---|---|---|
| 0 - 1 | 72 | 28 | isocratic |
| 1 - 5 | 72 → 67 | 28 → 33 | linear gradient |
| 5 - 20 | 67 → 63 | 33 → 37 | linear gradient |
| 20 - 30 | 63 → 57 | 37 → 43 | linear gradient |
| 30 - 40 | 57 → 40 | 43 → 60 | linear gradient |
| 40 - 42 | 40 | 60 | isocratic |
| 42 - 50 | 40 → 72 | 60 → 28 | linear gradient |
| 50 - 60 | 72 | 28 | re-equilibration |

— as detector a spectrophotometer set at 210 nm.

Equilibrate the column with the mobile phases in the initial gradient ratio for at least 15 min. Inject 50 µl of each solution.

In the chromatograms obtained, interferon alfa-2 elutes at a retention time of about 20 min. In the chromatogram obtained with the reference solution a peak related to oxidised interferon appears at a retention time of about 0.9 relative to the principal peak. The test is not valid unless the resolution between the peaks corresponding to oxidised interferon and interferon is at least 1.0. Consider only the peaks whose retention time is 0.7 to 1.4 relative to that of the principal peak. In the chromatogram obtained with the test solution, the area of any peak, apart from the principal peak, is not greater than 3.0 per cent of the total area of all of the peaks. The sum of the areas of any peaks other than the principal peak is not greater than 5.0 per cent of the total area of all of the peaks.

**Bacterial endotoxins** (*2.6.14*)
Less than 100 IU in the volume that contains 1.0 mg of protein.

## ASSAY
### Protein

*Test solution*  Dilute the preparation to be examined with *water R* to obtain a concentration of about 0.5 mg/ml of interferon alfa-2.

*Reference solutions*  Prepare a stock solution of 0.5 mg/ml of *bovine albumin R*. Prepare 8 dilutions of the stock solution containing between 3 µg/ml and 30 µg/ml of *bovine albumin R*.

Prepare 30-fold and 50-fold dilutions of the test solution. Add 1.25 ml of a mixture prepared the same day by combining 2.0 ml of a 20 g/l solution of *copper sulphate R* in

*water R*, 2.0 ml of a 40 g/l solution of *sodium tartrate R* in *water R* and 96.0 ml of a 40 g/l solution of *sodium carbonate R* in *0.2 M sodium hydroxide* to test-tubes containing 1.5 ml of *water R* (blank), 1.5 ml of the different dilutions of the test solution or 1.5 ml of the reference solutions. Mix after each addition. After approximately 10 min, add to each test-tube 0.25 ml of a mixture of equal volumes of *water R* and *phosphomolybdotungstic reagent R*. Mix after each addition. After approximately 30 min, measure the absorbance (*2.2.25*) of each solution at 750 nm using the blank as the compensation liquid. Draw a calibration curve from the absorbances of the 8 reference solutions and the corresponding protein contents and read from the curve the content of protein in the test solution.

### Potency

The potency of interferon alfa-2 is estimated by comparing its effect to protect cells against a viral cytopathic effect with the same effect of the appropriate International Standard of human recombinant interferon alfa-2 or of a reference preparation calibrated in International Units.

The International Unit is the activity contained in a stated amount of the appropriate International Standard. The equivalence in International Units of the International Standard is stated by the World Health Organisation.

Carry out the assay by a suitable method, based on the following design.

Use, in standard culture conditions, an established cell line sensitive to the cytopathic effect of a suitable virus (a human diploid fibroblast cell line, free of microbial contamination, responsive to interferon and sensitive to encephalomyocarditis virus, is suitable).

The following cell cultures and virus have been shown to be suitable: MDBK cells (ATCC No. CCL22), or Mouse L cells (NCTC clone 929; ATCC No. CCL 1) as the cell culture and vesicular stomatitis virus VSV, Indiana strain (ATCC No. VR-158) as the infective agent; or A-549 cells (ATCC No. CCL-185) responsive to interferon as the cell culture, and encephalomyocarditis virus (ATCC No. VR-129B) as the infective agent.

Incubate in at least 4 series, cells with 3 or more different concentrations of the preparation to be examined and the reference preparation in a microtitre plate and include in each series appropriate controls of untreated cells. Choose the concentrations of the preparations such that the lowest concentration produces some protection and the largest concentration produces less than maximal protection against the viral cytopathic effect. Add at a suitable time the cytopathic virus to all wells with the exception of a sufficient number of wells in all series, which are left with uninfected control cells. Determine the cytopathic effect of virus quantitatively with a suitable method. Calculate the potency of the preparation to be examined by the usual statistical methods for a parallel line assay.

The estimated potency is not less than 80 per cent and not more than 125 per cent of the stated potency. The confidence limits of the estimated potency (*P* = 0.95) are not less than 64 per cent and not more than 156 per cent of the stated potency.

## STORAGE
Store in an airtight container, protected from light, at or below − 20 °C.

## LABELLING
The label states:
— the type of interferon (alfa-2a or alfa-2b),

— the type of production.

*Ph Eur*

# Interferon Beta-1a Concentrated Solution

*(Ph Eur monograph 1639)*

```
MSYNLLGFLQ  RSSNFQCQKL  LWQLNGRLEY  CLKDRMNFDI
PEEIKQLQQF  QKEDAALTIY  EMLQNIFAIF  RQDSSSTGWN*
ETIVENLLAN  VYHQINHLKT  VLEEKLEKED  FTRGKLMSSL
HLKRYYGRIL  HYLKAKEYSH  CAWTIVRVEI  LRNFYFINRL
TGYLRN
```

\* glycosylation site

$C_{908}H_{1406}N_{246}O_{252}S_7$     22,500

## Action and use
Cytokine.

*Ph Eur*

## DEFINITION
Solution of a glycosylated protein having the same amino acid sequence and disulphide bridge and a similar glycosylation pattern as interferon beta produced by human diploid fibroblasts in response to viral infections and various other inducers. It exerts antiviral, antiproliferative and immunomodulatory activity.

### Content
Minimum 0.20 mg of protein per millilitre.

### Potency
Minimum $1.5 \times 10^8$ IU per milligram of protein.

It may contain buffer salts.

## PRODUCTION
Interferon beta-1a concentrated solution is produced by a method based on recombinant DNA (rDNA) technology, using mammalian cells in culture.

Prior to release, the following tests are carried out on each batch of the final bulk product, unless exemption has been granted by the competent authority.

### Host-cell-derived proteins
The limit is approved by the competent authority.

### Host-cell or vector-derived DNA
The limit is approved by the competent authority.

### N-terminal truncated forms
Examination for specific *N*-terminal truncated forms should be performed using a suitable technique such as *N*-terminal sequence determination. The limits are approved by the competent authority.

### Dimer and related substances of higher molecular mass
Not more than the amount approved by the competent authority, using an appropriate validated liquid chromatography method.

## CHARACTERS
### Appearance
Clear or slightly opalescent, colourless or slightly yellowish liquid.

## IDENTIFICATION
A. It shows the expected biological activity (see Assay).

B. Isoform distribution. Mass spectrometry *(2.2.43)*.

*Introduction of the sample*   Direct inflow of a desalted preparation to be examined or liquid chromatography-mass spectrometry combination.

*Mode of ionisation*   Electrospray.

*Signal acquisition*   Complete spectrum mode from 1100 to 2400.

*Calibration*   Use myoglobin in the *m/z* range of 600-2400; set the instrument within validated instrumental settings and analyse the sample; the deviation of the measured mass does not exceed 0.02 per cent of the reported mass.

*Interpretation of results*   A typical spectrum consists of 6 major glycoforms (A to F), which differ in their degree of sialylation and/or antennarity type as shown in Table 1639.-1.

Table 1639.-1.

| MS peak | Glycoform* | Expected $M_r$ | Sialylation level |
|---------|-----------|----------------|-------------------|
| A | 2A2S1F | 22 375 | Disialylated |
| B | 2A1S1F | 22 084 | Monosialylated |
| C | 3A2S1F and/or 2A2S1F + 1 HexNacHex repeat | 22 739 | Disialylated |
| D | 3A3S1F | 23 031 | Trisialylated |
| E | 4A3S1F and/or 3A3S1F + 1 HexNacHex repeat | 23 400 | Trisialylated |
| F | 2A0S1F | 21 793 | Non-sialylated |

\* 2A = biantennary complex type oligosaccharide; 3A = triantennary complex type oligosaccharide; 4A = tetraantennary complex type oligosaccharide; 0S = non-sialylated; 1S = monosialylated; 2S = disialylated; 3S = trisialylated; 1F = fucosylated.

*Results*   The mass spectrum obtained with the preparation to be examined corresponds, with respect to the 6 major peaks, to the mass spectrum obtained with *interferon beta-1a CRS*.

C. Peptide mapping *(2.2.55)* and liquid chromatography *(2.2.29)*.

*Test solution*   Add 5 µl of a 242 g/l solution of *tris(hydroxymethyl)aminomethane R* and a volume of the preparation to be examined containing 20 µg of protein to a polypropylene tube of 0.5 ml capacity. Add 4 µl of a 1 mg/ml solution of *endoprotease LysC R* in *0.05 M tris-hydrochloride buffer solution pH 9.0 R*. Mix gently and incubate at 30 °C for 2 h. Add 10 µl of a 15.4 g/l solution of *dithiothreitol R*. Dilute the solution with the same volume of a 573 g/l solution of *guanidine hydrochloride R*. Incubate at 4 °C for 3-4 h.

*Reference solution*   Prepare at the same time and in the same manner as for the test solution but using *interferon beta-1a CRS* instead of the preparation to be examined.

*Precolumn:*
— *size:* l = 0.02 m, Ø = 2.1 mm;
— *stationary phase*: spherical *octadecylsilyl silica gel for chromatography R* (5 µm) with a pore size of 30 nm.

*Column:*
— *size:* l = 0.25 m, Ø = 2.1 mm;
— *stationary phase*: spherical *octadecylsilyl silica gel for chromatography R* (5 µm) with a pore size of 30 nm.

*Mobile phase:*
— *mobile phase A*: dilute 1 ml of *trifluoroacetic acid R* to 1000 ml with *water R*;
— *mobile phase B*: dilute 1 ml of *trifluoroacetic acid R* in 700 ml of *acetonitrile for chromatography R*, then dilute to 1000 ml with *water R*;

| Time (min) | Mobile phase A (per cent *V/V*) | Mobile phase B (per cent *V/V*) |
|---|---|---|
| 0 - 30 | 100 → 64 | 0 → 36 |
| 30 - 45 | 64 → 55 | 36 → 45 |
| 45 - 50 | 55 → 40 | 45 → 60 |
| 50 - 70 | 40 → 0 | 60 → 100 |
| 70 - 83 | 0 | 100 |
| 83 - 85 | 0 → 100 | 100 → 0 |

*Flow rate*   0.2 ml/min.

*Detection*   Spectrophotometer at 214 nm.

*Injection*   Volume that contains 20 μg of digested protein.

*System suitability*   The chromatogram obtained with the reference solution is qualitatively similar to the chromatogram of interferon beta-1a digest supplied with *interferon beta-1a CRS*.

*Results*   The profile of the chromatogram obtained with the test solution corresponds to that of the chromatogram obtained with the reference solution.

## TESTS

### Impurities of molecular masses differing from that of interferon beta-1a

Polyacrylamide gel electrophoresis (*2.2.31*) under reducing conditions.

*Resolving gel*   12 per cent acrylamide.

*Concentrated sample buffer*   *Concentrated SDS-PAGE sample buffer for reducing conditions R* containing 2-mercaptoethanol as the reducing agent.

*Sample buffer*   Mixture of equal volumes of *concentrated SDS-PAGE sample buffer for reducing conditions R* and *water R*.

*Test solution (a)*   Concentrate the preparation to be examined using a suitable method to obtain a protein concentration of 1.5 mg/ml.

*Test solution (b)*   Mixture of equal volumes of test solution (a) and the concentrated sample buffer.

*Test solution (c)*   Dilute test solution (a) to obtain a protein concentration of 0.6 mg/ml. Mix equal volumes of this solution and the concentrated sample buffer.

*Test solution (d)*   Mix 8 μl of test solution (c) and 40 μl of the sample buffer.

*Test solution (e)*   Mix 15 μl of test solution (d) and 35 μl of the sample buffer.

*Test solution (f)*   Mix 18 μl of test solution (e) and 18 μl of the sample buffer.

*Test solution (g)*   Mix 12 μl of test solution (f) and 12 μl of the sample buffer.

*Reference solution (a)*   Solution of relative molecular mass markers suitable for calibrating SDS-PAGE gels in the range of 15-67 kDa. Dissolve in the sample buffer.

*Reference solution (b)*   0.75 mg/ml solution of *interferon beta-1a CRS* in sample buffer.

*Sample treatment*   Boil for 3 min.

*Application*   20 μl of test solutions (b) to (g) and reference solutions (a) and (b).

*Detection*   Coomassie staining, carried out as follows: immerse the gel in *Coomassie staining solution R1* at 33-37 °C for 90 min with gentle shaking, then remove the staining solution; destain the gel with a large excess of a mixture of 1 volume of *glacial acetic acid R*, 1 volume of *2-propanol R* and 8 volumes of *water R*.

*Apparent molecular masses*   Interferon beta-1a = about 23 000; underglycosylated interferon beta-1a = about 21 000; deglycosylated interferon beta-1a = about 20 000; interferon beta-1a dimer = about 46 000.

*Identification of bands*   Use the electropherogram provided with *interferon beta-1a CRS*.

*System suitability:*
— the validation criteria are met (*2.2.31*);
— a band is seen in the electropherogram obtained with test solution (g);
— a gradation of intensity of staining is seen in the electropherograms obtained with test solutions (b) to (g).

*Limits:*
— in the electropherogram obtained with test solution (c), the band corresponding to underglycosylated interferon beta-1a is not more intense than the principal band in the electropherogram obtained with test solution (e) (5 per cent);
— in the electropherogram obtained with test solution (b), the band corresponding to deglycosylated interferon beta-1a is not more intense than the principal band in the electropherogram obtained with test solution (e) (2 per cent); any other band corresponding to an impurity of a molecular mass lower than that of interferon beta-1a, apart from the band corresponding to underglycosylated interferon beta-1a is not more intense than the principal band in the electropherogram obtained with test solution (f) (1 per cent).

### Oxidised interferon beta-1a

Maximum 6 per cent.

Use the chromatogram obtained with the test solution in identification C. Locate the peaks due to the peptide fragment comprising amino acids 34-45 and its oxidised form using the chromatogram of oxidised interferon beta-1a digest supplied with *interferon beta-1a CRS*.

Calculate the percentage of oxidation of interferon beta-1a using the following expression:

$$\frac{A_{34-45ox}}{A_{34-45} + A_{34-45ox}} \times 100$$

$A_{34-45ox}$ = area of the peak corresponding to the oxidised peptide fragment 34-45;

$A_{34-45}$ = area of the peak corresponding to the peptide fragment 34-45.

### Bacterial endotoxins (*2.6.14*)

Less than 0.7 IU in the volume that contains $1 \times 10^6$ IU of interferon beta-1a, if intended for use in the manufacture of parenteral preparations without a further appropriate procedure for removal of bacterial endotoxins.

## ASSAY

### Protein

Liquid chromatography (*2.2.29*). Prepare 3 independent dilutions for each solution.

*Test solution*  Dilute the preparation to be examined to obtain a concentration of 100 µg/ml.

*Reference solution*  Dissolve the contents of a vial of *interferon beta-1a CRS* to obtain a concentration of 100 µg/ml.

*Precolumn:*
— *size: l* = 0.02 m, Ø = 2.1 mm;
— *stationary phase: butylsilyl silica gel for chromatography R* (5 µm) with a pore size of 30 nm.

*Column:*
— *size: l* = 0.25 m, Ø = 2.1 mm;
— *stationary phase: butylsilyl silica gel for chromatography R* (5 µm) with a pore size of 30 nm.

*Mobile phase:*
— *mobile phase A*: 0.1 per cent *V/V* solution of *trifluoroacetic acid R*;
— *mobile phase B*: to 300 ml of *water R*, add 1 ml of *trifluoroacetic acid R* and dilute to 1000 ml with *acetonitrile for chromatography R*;

| Time (min) | Mobile phase A (per cent *V/V*) | Mobile phase B (per cent *V/V*) |
|---|---|---|
| 0 - 20 | 100 → 0 | 0 → 100 |
| 20 - 25 | 0 | 100 |
| 25 - 26 | 0 → 100 | 100 → 0 |
| 26 - 40 | 100 | 0 |

*Flow rate*  0.2 ml/min.

*Detection*  Spectrophotometer at 214 nm.

*Injection*  50 µl.

*Retention time*  Interferon beta-1a = about 20 min.

*System suitability*  Reference solution:
— *symmetry factor*: 0.8 to 2.0 for the peak due to interferon beta-1a;
— *repeatability*: maximum relative standard deviation of 3.0 per cent between the peak areas obtained after injection of the 3 independent dilutions.

Calculate the content of interferon beta-1a ($C_{908}H_{1406}N_{246}O_{252}S_7$) from the declared content of $C_{908}H_{1406}N_{246}O_{252}S_7$ in *interferon beta-1a CRS*.

### Potency

The potency of interferon beta-1a is estimated by comparing its ability to protect cells against a viral cytopathic effect with the same ability of the appropriate International Standard of human recombinant interferon beta-1a or of a reference preparation calibrated in International Units.

The International Unit is the activity contained in a stated amount of the appropriate International Standard. The equivalence in International Units of the International Standard is stated by the World Health Organisation.

Carry out the assay using a suitable method, based on the following design.

Use, in standard culture conditions, an established cell line sensitive to the cytopathic effect of a suitable virus and responsive to interferon. The cell cultures and viruses that have been shown to be suitable include the following:
— WISH cells (ATCC No. CCL-25) and vesicular stomatitis virus VSV, Indiana strain (ATCC No. VR-158) as infective agent;

— A549 cells (ATCC No. CCL-185) and encephalomyocarditis virus EMC (ATCC No. VR-129B) as infective agent.

Incubate in at least 4 series, cells with 3 or more different concentrations of the preparation to be examined and the reference preparation in a microtitre plate and include in each series appropriate controls of untreated cells. Choose the concentrations of the preparations such that the lowest concentration produces some protection and the largest concentration produces less than maximal protection against the viral cytopathic effect. Add at a suitable time the cytopathic virus to all wells with the exception of a sufficient number of wells in all series, which are left with uninfected control cells. Determine the cytopathic effect of the virus quantitatively with a suitable method. Calculate the potency of the preparation to be examined by the usual statistical methods (for example, *5.3*).

The estimated potency is not less than 80 per cent and not more than 125 per cent of the stated potency. The confidence limits ($P = 0.95$) are not less than 64 per cent and not more than 156 per cent of the estimated potency.

## STORAGE

In an airtight container, protected from light, at a temperature below − 70 °C. If the substance is sterile, store in a sterile, airtight, tamper-proof container.

## LABELLING

The label states:
— the interferon beta-1a content, in milligrams per millilitre;
— the antiviral activity, in International Units per millilitre;
— where applicable, that the substance is suitable for use in the manufacture of parenteral preparations.

*Ph Eur*

# Interferon Gamma-1b Concentrated Solution

(*Ph Eur monograph 1440*)

$C_{734}H_{1166}N_{204}O_{216}S_5$     16,465     *98059-61-1*

### Action and use
Cytokine.

*Ph Eur*

## DEFINITION

Interferon gamma-1b concentrated solution is a solution of the *N*-terminal methionyl form of interferon gamma, a protein which is produced and secreted by human antigen-stimulated T lymphocytes in response to viral infections and various other inducers. It has specific immunomodulatory properties, such as potent phagocyte-activating effects. The protein consists of non-covalent dimers of two identical monomers. The formula of the monomer is as follows:

```
                                                        M
QDPYVKEAEN   LKKYFNAGHS   DVADNGTLFL   GILKNWKEES

DRKIMQSQIV   SFYFKLFKNF   KDDQSIQKSV   ETIKEDMNVK

FFNSNKKKRD   DFEKLTNYSV   TDLNVQRKAI   HELIQVMAEL

SPAAKTGKRK   RSQMLFRGR
```

The potency of interferon gamma-1b is not less than $20 \times 10^6$ IU per milligram of protein. Interferon gamma-1b concentrated solution contains not less than $30 \times 10^6$ IU of interferon gamma-1b per millilitre.

## PRODUCTION

Interferon gamma-1b concentrated solution is produced by a method based on recombinant DNA technology, using bacteria as host-cells. It is produced under conditions designed to minimise microbial contamination.

Interferon gamma-1b concentrated solution complies with the following additional requirements.

### Host-cell derived proteins

The limit is approved by the competent authority.

### Host-cell- and vector-derived DNA

The limit is approved by the competent authority.

## CHARACTERS

A clear, colourless or slightly yellowish liquid.

## IDENTIFICATION

A. It shows the expected biological activity when tested as prescribed in the assay.

B. Examine the electropherograms obtained in the test for impurities of molecular masses differing from that of interferon gamma-1b. The principal bands in the electropherogram obtained with the test solution correspond in position to the principal bands in the electropherogram obtained with reference solution (a).

C. Examine by peptide mapping.

*Solution A* Prepare a solution containing 1.2 g/l of *tris(hydroxymethyl)aminomethane R*, 8.2 g/l of *anhydrous sodium acetate R*, 0.02 g/l of *calcium chloride R* and adjust to pH 8.3 (*2.2.3*) with *dilute acetic acid R*. Add *polysorbate 20 R* to a concentration of 0.1 per cent *V/V*.

*Test solution* Desalt a volume of the preparation to be examined containing 1 mg of protein by a suitable procedure. For example, filter in a microcentrifuge tube and reconstitute with 500 μl of solution A. Add 10 μl of a freshly prepared 1 mg/ml solution of *trypsin for peptide mapping R* in *water R* and mix gently by inversion. Incubate at 30 °C to 37 °C for 24 h, add 100 μl of *phosphoric acid R* per millilitre of digested sample and mix by inversion.

*Reference solution* Dilute *interferon gamma-1b CRS* in *water R* to obtain a concentration of 1 mg/ml. Prepare as for the test solution, ensuring that all procedures are carried out simultaneously and under identical conditions.

Examine by liquid chromatography (*2.2.29*).

The chromatographic procedure may be carried out using:
— a stainless steel column, 0.15 m long and 4.6 mm in internal diameter packed with *octadecylsilyl silica gel for chromatography R* (10 μm),
— as mobile phase at a flow rate of 1.0 ml/min:

*Mobile phase A (0.05 M sodium phosphate buffer solution pH 3.3)* Solution I: Dissolve 7.80 g of *sodium dihydrogen phosphate R* in *water R* and dilute to 1000.0 ml with the same solvent. Solution II: dilute 0.33 ml of *phosphoric acid R* to 100.0 ml with *water R*. Mix 920 ml of solution I and 80 ml of solution II. Adjust the pH (*2.2.3*) if necessary,

*Mobile phase B* *Acetonitrile for chromatography R*,

With the following elution conditions (if necessary, the gradient may be modified to improve the separation of the digest):

| Time (min) | Mobile phase A (per cent *V/V*) | Mobile phase B (per cent *V/V*) |
|---|---|---|
| 0 - 30 | 100 → 80 | 0 → 20 |
| 30 - 50 | 80 → 60 | 20 → 40 |
| 50 - 51 | 60 → 30 | 40 → 70 |
| 51 - 59 | 30 | 70 |
| 59 - 60 | 30 → 100 | 70 → 0 |

— as detector a spectrophotometer set at 214 nm, maintaining the temperature of the column at 40 °C.

Equilibrate the column for at least 15 min at the initial elution composition. Carry out a blank run using the above-mentioned gradient.

Inject 100 μl of the test solution and 100 μl of the reference solution. The test is not valid unless the chromatogram obtained with each solution is qualitatively similar to the chromatogram of interferon gamma-1b digest supplied with *interferon gamma-1b CRS*. The profile of the chromatogram obtained with the test solution corresponds to that of the chromatogram obtained with the reference solution.

D. Examine by *N*-terminal sequence analysis.

Use an automated solid-phase sequencer, operated in accordance with the manufacturer's instructions.

Equilibrate by a suitable procedure the equivalent of 100 μg of interferon gamma-1b in a 10 g/l solution of *ammonium hydrogen carbonate R*, pH 9.0.

Identify the phenylthiohydantoin (PTH)-amino acids released at each sequencing cycle by reverse-phase liquid chromatography. The procedure may be carried out using the column and reagents recommended by the manufacturer of the sequencing equipment for the separation of PTH-amino acids.

The separation procedure is calibrated using:
— the mixture of PTH-amino acids provided by the manufacturer, with the gradient conditions adjusted as indicated to achieve optimum resolution of all amino acids,
— a sample from a blank sequencing cycle, obtained as recommended by the equipment manufacturer.

The first fifteen amino acids are:

Met-Gln-Asp-Pro-Tyr-Val-Lys-Glu-Ala-Glu-Asn-Leu-Lys-Lys-Tyr.

## TESTS

### Appearance

The preparation to be examined is clear (*2.2.1*) and not more intensely coloured than reference solution $Y_7$ (*2.2.2, Method II*).

### pH (*2.2.3*)

The pH of the preparation to be examined is 4.5 to 5.5.

### Covalent dimers and oligomers

Not greater than 2 per cent, determined by size-exclusion chromatography (*2.2.30*).

*Test solution* Dilute the preparation to be examined with the mobile phase to a protein concentration of 0.1 mg/ml.

*Reference solution (a)* Dilute *interferon gamma-1b CRS* with the mobile phase to a protein concentration of 0.1 mg/ml.

*Reference solution (b)* Prepare a mixture of the following molecular mass standards: bovine albumin, ovalbumin, trypsinogen, lysozyme, at a concentration of 0.1 mg/ml to 0.2 mg/ml for each standard.

The chromatographic procedure may be carried out using:

— a stainless steel column 0.3 m long and 7.8 mm in internal diameter packed with *hydrophilic silica gel for chromatography R*, of a grade suitable for fractionation of globular proteins in the molecular weight range of 10 000 to 500 000 (5 μm),

— as mobile phase at a flow rate of 1.0 ml/min a mixture prepared as follows (0.2 M sodium phosphate buffer solution pH 6.8). Solution I: dissolve 31.2 g of *sodium dihydrogen phosphate R* and 1.0 g of *sodium dodecyl sulphate R* in *water R* and dilute to 1000.0 ml with the same solvent. Solution II: dissolve 28.4 g of *anhydrous disodium hydrogen phosphate R* and 1.0 g of *sodium dodecyl sulphate R* in *water R* and dilute to 1000.0 ml with the same solvent. Mix 450 ml of solution I and 550 ml of solution II. Adjust the pH (*2.2.3*) if necessary,

— as detector a spectrophotometer set at 210 nm to 214 nm.

Inject 200 μl of each solution. The test is not valid unless: the molecular mass standards in reference solution (b) are well separated; the retention time of the principal peak in the chromatogram obtained with reference solution (a) is between the retention time of trypsinogen and lysozyme in the chromatogram obtained with reference solution (b).

Compare the chromatograms obtained with the test solution and with reference solution (a). There are no additional shoulders or peaks in the chromatogram obtained with the test solution compared with the chromatogram obtained with reference solution (a).

Calculate the percentage content of covalent dimers and oligomers.

**Monomer and aggregates**

Examine by size-exclusion chromatography (*2.2.30*). The content of monomer and aggregates is not greater than 2 per cent.

*Solution A*    Prepare a solution of the following composition: 0.59 g/l of *succinic acid R* and 40 g/l of *mannitol R*, adjusted to pH 5.0 (*2.2.3*) with *sodium hydroxide solution R*.

*Test solution*    Dilute the preparation to be examined with solution A to a protein concentration of 1 mg/ml.

*Reference solution*    Dilute *interferon gamma-1b CRS* with solution A to a protein concentration of 1 mg/ml.

*Resolution solution*    Prepare 500 μl of a mixture consisting of 0.04 mg/ml of *bovine albumin R* and 0.2 mg/ml of *interferon gamma-1b CRS* in solution A. Use this solution within 24 h of preparation.

The chromatographic procedure may be carried out using:

— a stainless steel column 0.3 m long and 7.8 mm in internal diameter packed with *hydrophilic silica gel for chromatography R*, of a grade suitable for fractionation of globular proteins in the molecular weight range of 10 000 - 300 000 (5 μm),

— as mobile phase at a flow rate of 0.8 ml/min a 89.5 g/l solution of *potassium chloride R* (1.2 M),

— as detector a spectrophotometer set at 214 nm.

Inject 20 μl of the resolution solution. In the chromatogram obtained, the retention time of the principal peak, corresponding to the native interferon gamma-1b dimer, is about 10 min. bovine albumin elutes at a relative retention time of about 0.85, relative to the main peak. The test is not valid unless the resolution between the peaks corresponding to bovine albumin and interferon gamma-1b is at least 1.5.

Inject 20 μl of the test solution and 20 μl of the reference solution. The chromatograms obtained show principal peaks with identical retention times. Calculate the percentage

content of monomer and aggregates from the peak area of the monomer peak and of peaks which elute prior to the native interferon gamma-1b peak in the chromatogram obtained with the test solution, by the normalisation procedure, disregarding any peak due to the solvent.

**Deamidated and oxidised forms and heterodimers**

Examine by liquid chromatography (*2.2.29*). The content of deamidated and oxidised forms is not greater than 10 per cent. The content of heterodimers is not greater than 3 per cent.

*Test solution*    Dilute the preparation to be examined with *water R* to a protein concentration of 1 mg/ml.

*Reference solution*    Dilute *interferon gamma-1b CRS* with *water R* to a protein concentration of 1 mg/ml.

*Resolution solution*    Use *interferon gamma-1b validation solution CRS*.

The chromatographic procedure may be carried out using:

— a stainless steel column 0.075 m long and 7.5 mm in internal diameter packed with an appropriate hydrophilic polymethacrylate, strong cation exchange gel (10 μm, 100 nm),

— as mobile phase at a flow rate of 1.2 ml/min:

*Mobile phase A (0.05 M ammonium acetate buffer pH 6.5)* A 3.86 g/l solution of *ammonium acetate R*, adjusted to pH 6.5 with *dilute acetic acid R*,

*Mobile phase B (1.2 M ammonium acetate buffer pH 6.5)* A 92.5 g/l solution of *ammonium acetate R*, adjusted to pH 6.5 with *dilute acetic acid R*,

With the following elution conditions (if necessary, the slope of the gradient may be modified to improve the separation).

| Time (min) | Mobile phase A (per cent V/V) | Mobile phase B (per cent V/V) |
|---|---|---|
| 0 - 1 | 100 | 0 |
| 2 - 30 | 100 → 0 | 0 → 100 |
| 31 - 35 | 0 | 100 |
| 36 - 37 | 0 → 100 | 100 → 0 |
| 38 - 47 | 100 | 0 |

— as detector a spectrophotometer set at 280 nm, maintaining the temperature of the column at 35 °C.

Inject 25 μl of the resolution solution. In the chromatogram obtained, the retention time of the principal peak is about 26 min. Deamidated and oxidised forms co-elute at a relative retention time of about 0.95, relative to the principal peak. The test is not valid unless the resolution, defined by the ratio of the height of the peak corresponding to the deamidated and oxidised forms to the height above the baseline of the valley separating the two peaks, is at least 1.2.

Inject 25 μl of the test solution and 25 μl of the reference solution. The chromatograms obtained show principal peaks with identical retention times. Calculate the percentage content of deamidated and oxidised interferon gamma-1b as a percentage of the area of the main peak. Heterodimers have relative retention times of 0.7 and 0.85 relative to the main peak. Calculate the percentage of heterodimers as a percentage of the sum of the areas of all peaks.

**Impurities of molecular masses differing from that of interferon gamma-1b**

Examine by polyacrylamide gel electrophoresis (*2.2.31*). The test is performed under both reducing and non-reducing conditions, using resolving gels of 15 per cent acrylamide and silver staining as the detection method.

*Sample buffer (non-reducing conditions)* Dissolve 3.78 g of *tris(hydroxymethyl)aminomethane R*, 10.0 g of *sodium dodecyl sulphate R* and 0.100 g of *bromophenol blue R* in *water R*. Add 50.0 ml of *glycerol R* and dilute to 80 ml with *water R*. Adjust the pH (*2.2.3*) to 6.8 with *hydrochloric acid R* and dilute to 100 ml with *water R*.

*Sample buffer (reducing conditions)* Dissolve 3.78 g of *tris(hydroxymethyl)aminomethane R*, 10.0 g of *sodium dodecyl sulphate R* and 0.100 g of *bromophenol blue R* in *water R*. Add 50.0 ml of *glycerol R* and dilute to 80 ml with *water R*. Adjust the pH (*2.2.3*) to 6.8 with *hydrochloric acid R* and dilute to 100 ml with *water R*. Immediately before use, add *dithiothreitol R* to a final concentration of 250 mM.

*Test solution* Dilute the preparation to be examined in *water R* to a protein concentration of 1 mg/ml. Dilute 150 µl of the solution with 38 µl of sample buffer.

*Reference solution (a)* Prepare in the same manner as for the test solution, but using *interferon gamma-1b CRS* instead of the preparation to be examined.

*Reference solution (b) (5 ng control)* Mix 50 µl of a 0.01 mg/ml solution of *bovine albumin R* with 2000 µl of *water R* and 450 µl of sample buffer.

*Reference solution (c) (2 ng control)* Mix 20 µl of a 0.01 mg/ml solution of *bovine albumin R* with 2000 µl of *water R* and 450 µl of sample buffer.

*Reference solution (d)* Use a solution of molecular mass standards suitable for calibrating SDS-polyacrylamide gels in the range of 10 kDa to 70 kDa.

Leave each solution, contained in a test tube, at ambient temperature for 15 min, then store on ice.

Apply 25 µl of each solution to the stacking gel wells. Perform the electrophoresis under the conditions recommended by the manufacturer of the equipment. Detect proteins in the gel by silver staining.

The test is not valid unless: the validation criteria are met (*2.2.31*); a band is seen in the electropherograms obtained with reference solutions (b) and (c).

The principal band in the electropherogram obtained with the test solution is similar in intensity to the principal band in the electropherogram obtained with reference solution (a). In the electropherogram obtained with the test solution, no significant bands are observed that are not present in the electropherogram obtained with reference solution (a) (0.01 per cent). A significant band is defined as any band whose intensity is greater than or equal to that of the band in the electropherogram obtained with reference solution (c).

**Norleucine**

Not more than 0.2 mole of norleucine per mole of interferon gamma-1b, determined by amino acid analysis.

*Test solution* Add 2.5 ml of the preparation to be examined onto a column suitable for the desalting of proteins previously equilibrated with 25 ml of a 10 per cent *V/V* solution of *acetic acid R*. Elute the sample with another 2.5 ml of a 10 per cent *V/V* solution of *acetic acid R*. Determine the protein content by measuring the absorbance of this solution as described under Protein, in the Assay section. Pipette a volume containing the equivalent of 100 µg of interferon gamma-1b into each of three reaction vials. Evaporate to dryness under reduced pressure.

Perform the hydrolysis of the three samples as follows. Add to each reaction vial 200 µl of a 50 per cent *V/V* solution of

*hydrochloric acid R* containing 1 per cent *V/V* of *phenol R*, evacuate the samples, purge with nitrogen and hydrolyse in the gas phase. Heat the reaction vials at 110 °C for 22 h. After hydrolysis evaporate to dryness under reduced pressure.

Perform the derivatisation of the samples as follows. Prepare immediately before use a mixture consisting of two volumes of *ethanol R*, one volume of *water R* and one volume of *triethylamine R*. Add 50 µl of this solution to each reaction vial and shake lightly. Evaporate to dryness under reduced pressure. Add to each vial 50 µl of a mixture consisting of 7 volumes of *ethanol R*, one volume of *water R*, one volume of *triethylamine R* and one volume of *phenyl isothiocyanate R*. Shake lightly and allow to stand at room temperature for about 15 min. Evaporate to dryness under reduced pressure. Reconstitute the samples in 250 µl of mobile phase A.

*Norleucine stock solution* Prepare a 250 nmol/ml solution of DL-*norleucine R* in *0.01 M hydrochloric acid. This solution may be kept for two months at 4 °C.*

*Leucine stock solution* Prepare a 250 nmol/ml solution of *leucine R* in *0.01 M hydrochloric acid. This solution may be kept at 4 °C for two months.*

*Reference solution* Mix 10 µl of norleucine stock solution with 100 µl of leucine stock solution in each of the three reaction vials. Evaporate to dryness under reduced pressure. Perform the derivatisation of the samples as described for the preparation of the test solution.

Examine by liquid chromatography (*2.2.29*).

The chromatographic procedure may be carried out using:
— a stainless steel column 0.15 m long and 3.9 mm in diameter packed with *octadecylsilyl silica gel for chromatography R* (4 µm),
— as mobile phase at a flow rate of 1.0 ml/min:

*Mobile phase A* Mix 70 volumes of a 19 g/l solution of *sodium acetate R* containing 0.05 per cent *V/V* of *triethylamine R* and adjusted to pH 6.4 with *dilute acetic acid R* and 30 volumes of mobile phase B,

*Mobile phase B* Mix 40 volumes of *water R* and 60 volumes of *acetonitrile R*,

| Time (min) | Mobile phase A (per cent *V/V*) | Mobile phase B (per cent *V/V*) | Comment |
|---|---|---|---|
| 0 - 7 | 100 | 0 | isocratic |
| 7 - 7.1 | 100 → 0 | 0 → 100 | linear gradient |
| 7.1 - 10 | 0 | 100 | washing step |
| 10 - 10.1 | 0 → 100 | 100 → 0 | linear gradient |
| 10.1 - 15 | 100 | 0 | re-equilibration |

— as detector a spectrophotometer set at 254 nm, maintaining the temperature of the column at 43 °C.

Inject 50 µl of each solution.

In the chromatograms obtained with the test solution, identify the peaks corresponding to leucine and norleucine. The retention time of norleucine is 6.2 min to 7 min.

Calculate the content of norleucine (in moles of norleucine per mole of interferon gamma-1b) from the peak areas of leucine and norleucine in the chromatograms obtained with the reference and test solutions, considering that there are 10 moles of leucine per mole of interferon gamma-1b.

**Bacterial endotoxins** (*2.6.14*)

Less than 5 IU in the volume that contains $20 \times 10^6$ IU of interferon gamma-1b.

## ASSAY

**Protein** (*2.2.25*)

Dilute the substance to be examined in *water R* to obtain a concentration of 1 mg/ml. Record the absorbance spectrum between 220 nm and 340 nm. Measure the value at the absorbance maximum of 280 nm, after correction for any light scattering due to turbidity measured at 316 nm. Calculate the concentration of interferon gamma-1b using a specific absorbance value of 7.5.

**Potency**

The potency of interferon gamma-1b is estimated by evaluating the increase of the expression of human-leukocyte-antigen-DR (HLA-DR) due to the interferon gamma-1b present in test solutions during cultivation of the cells, and comparing this increase with the same effect of the appropriate International Standard of human recombinant interferon gamma or of a reference preparation calibrated in International Units.

The International Unit is the activity contained in a stated amount of the appropriate International Standard. The equivalence in International Units of the International Standard is stated by the World Health Organisation.

Carry out the assay by a suitable method, based on the following design.

Use COLO 205 cells under standard culture conditions. Trypsinise a 3- to 5-day-old flask of COLO 205 cells and prepare a cell suspension at a concentration of $1.0 \times 10^6$ cells/ml.

Add 100 µl of the dilution medium to all wells of a 96-well microtitre plate. Add an additional 100 µl of this solution to the wells designed for the blanks. Add 100 µl of each solution to be tested onto the plate and carry out a series of twofold dilution steps in order to obtain a standard curve. Then add 100 µl of the cell suspension to all wells and incubate the plate under appropriate conditions for cell cultivation.

After cultivation remove the growth medium and wash and fix cells to the plate. Add an antibody able to detect HLA-DR expressed due to the presence of interferon gamma-1b and incubate under appropriate conditions. After washing the plate, incubate with an antibody conjugated to a marker enzyme which is able to detect the anti-HLA-DR antibody. After this incubation step, wash the plate and add an appropriate substrate solution. Stop the reaction. Measure the absorbance of the solution and calculate the potency of the preparation to be examined by the usual statistical methods.

The estimated specific activity is not less than 80 per cent and not more than 125 per cent of the stated potency. The confidence limits ($P = 0.95$) are not less than 70 per cent and not more than 140 per cent of the estimated potency.

## STORAGE

Store in an airtight container, protected from light and at a temperature of $-70\,^\circ\text{C}$.

*Ph Eur*

# Inulin

## Action and use

Diagnostic agent used in the determination of renal function (glomerular filtration rate).

**Preparation**

Inulin Injection

## DEFINITION

Inulin consists of polysaccharide granules obtained from the tubers of *Dahlia variabilis*, *Helianthus tuberosus* and other genera of the family Compositae.

## CHARACTERISTICS

A white, amorphous, granular powder; hygroscopic.

*Microscopical*   When mounted in *absolute ethanol*, appears as large, very irregular, angular masses, whole or fragmented, with occasional smaller, spherical to ovoid particles.

Slightly soluble in *water*; freely soluble in hot *water*; slightly soluble in organic solvents.

## IDENTIFICATION

A. Carry out the method for *thin-layer chromatography*, Appendix III A, using a suspension of *silica gel G* in a 0.3% w/v solution of *sodium acetate* to coat the plate, but spreading a layer 0.5 mm thick. Use a mixture of 70 volumes of *glacial acetic acid*, 60 volumes of *chloroform* and 10 volumes of *water* as the mobile phase. Apply separately to the plate 1 µl of each of three solutions in *water* containing (1) 2.5% w/v of the substance being examined, prepared using heat, (2) 2.5% w/v of the substance being examined and 10% w/v of *oxalic acid*, prepared by boiling for 10 minutes and cooling, and (3) 2.5% w/v of D-*fructose* and 0.1% w/v of D-*glucose monohydrate*. Develop the chromatograms in a continuous elution tank for about 4 hours. After removal of the plate, evaporate the solvent in a current of warm air and spray with a solution in *acetone* containing 1% v/v of *diphenylamine*, 1% v/v of *aniline* and 1% v/v of *orthophosphoric acid* and heat for 10 minutes at 130°. The two principal spots in the chromatogram obtained with solution (2) correspond to those in the chromatogram obtained with solution (3). The spot in the chromatogram obtained with solution (1) remains on the line of application.

B. Dissolve 10 mg in 2 ml of hot *water*, add 3 ml of a 0.15% w/v solution of *resorcinol* in *ethanol (96%)* followed by 3 ml of *hydrochloric acid*, mix and heat at 80°. A red colour is produced.

C. Boil 5 ml of a 10% w/v solution for 2 minutes with 0.5 ml of *hydrochloric acid*, cool and neutralise to *litmus paper* with 5M *sodium hydroxide*. Add 0.5 ml of *cupri-tartaric solution R1* and heat. A red precipitate is produced.

## TESTS

**Acidity**

Dissolve 5 g in 50 ml of freshly boiled *water* and titrate with 0.1M *sodium hydroxide VS* using *phenolphthalein solution R1* as indicator. Not more than 0.20 ml is required to change the colour of the solution to pink.

**Clarity and colour of solution**

A 10.0% w/v solution in hot *water* is *clear*, Appendix IV A, and *colourless*, Appendix IV B, Method I.

**Specific optical rotation**

In a 2% w/v solution, prepared using heat, $-36.5$ to $-40.5$, calculated with reference to the dried substance, Appendix V F.

**Arsenic**

1.0 g dissolved in 25 ml of hot *water* complies with the *limit test for arsenic*, Appendix VII (1 ppm).

**Calcium**

Dissolve 1.0 g in 10 ml of hot *water*, place the solution in a water bath at 40°, add 0.5 ml of a 2.5% w/v solution of *ammonium oxalate* and allow to stand for 15 minutes. Any turbidity produced is not greater than that obtained by treating 10 ml of a 0.010% w/v solution of *calcium chloride* in the same manner (270 ppm).

**Lead**

Dissolve 2.5 g in 20 ml of hot *water* and transfer to a separating funnel with the aid of 5 ml of *water*. Add 2.5 ml of *hydrochloric acid* and shake for 5 minutes. Add 0.25 ml of *bromothymol blue solution R3* and sufficient 13.5M *ammonia* to produce a full blue colour and add 1.5 ml in excess. Add 1 ml of a 25% w/v solution of *citric acid* previously adjusted to pH 11 with 13.5M *ammonia* (ammonium citrate solution), 1 ml of *potassium cyanide solution PbT* and sufficient of a 0.002% w/v solution of *dithizone* in *chloroform* until, on shaking, the chloroform layer becomes purple or blue. Separate the chloroform layer, add to the aqueous layer 2 ml of the dithizone solution, shake and separate the chloroform layer. To the combined chloroform solutions add 10 ml of a 1% v/v solution of *nitric acid*, shake until the chloroform layer becomes green, allow to separate and discard the chloroform layer. To the aqueous layer add 0.2 ml of the ammonium citrate solution, 0.25 ml of 13.5M *ammonia*, 0.2 ml of *potassium cyanide solution PbT* and sufficient of the dithizone solution until, on shaking, the chloroform layer becomes purple or blue. Transfer the contents of the separating funnel to a stoppered tube. Repeat the operations without the substance being examined and using the same quantities of the reagents. To the tube containing the reference solution add *lead standard solution (10 ppm Pb)* dropwise until, on shaking, the colour of the chloroform layer matches that of the chloroform layer obtained from the substance being examined. Not more than 0.5 ml of *lead standard solution (10 ppm Pb)* is required (2 ppm).

**Chloride**

Dissolve 2.0 g in hot *water*, cool and dilute to 100 ml with *water*. 15 ml of the resulting solution complies with the *limit test for chlorides*, Appendix VII (170 ppm).

**Oxalate**

Dissolve 1.0 g in 10 ml of hot *water*, place the solution in a water bath at 40°, add 0.5 ml of a 7% w/v solution of *calcium chloride* and allow to stand for 15 minutes. Any turbidity produced is not greater than that obtained by treating 10 ml of a 0.003% w/v solution of *oxalic acid* in the same manner.

**Sulphate**

Dissolve 2.3 g in 20 ml of hot *water*, cool, add 2 ml of 2M *hydrochloric acid* and dilute to 45 ml with *water*. The solution complies with the *limit test for sulphates*, Appendix VII (200 ppm).

**Reducing sugars**

Heat 10 ml of *cupri-tartaric solution R1* and titrate with a 10% w/v solution of the substance being examined, adding a few ml at a time and boiling for 10 to 15 seconds between each addition. When the solution becomes greenish yellow, add 0.25 ml of a 1% w/v solution of *methylene blue* and continue the titration until the solution becomes orange. Repeat the operation using a 0.20% w/v solution of D-*fructose* in place of the solution of the substance being examined. The volume of the fructose solution required is not greater than that of the solution of the substance being examined.

**Loss on drying**

When dried to constant weight at 105°, loses not more than 10.0% of its weight. Use 1 g.

**Sulphated ash**

Not more than 0.1%, Appendix IX A.

# Iodine

(*Ph Eur monograph 0031*)

$I_2$                    253.8                    7553-56-2

**Action and use**

Antiseptic; antithyroid.

**Preparations**

Alcoholic Iodine Solution

Aqueous Iodine Oral Solution

*Ph Eur* _____

**DEFINITION**

**Content**

99.5 per cent to 100.5 per cent of I.

**CHARACTERS**

**Appearance**

Greyish-violet, brittle plates or fine crystals with a metallic sheen.

**Solubility**

Very slightly soluble in water, very soluble in concentrated solutions of iodides, soluble in ethanol (96 per cent), slightly soluble in glycerol.

It volatilises slowly at room temperature.

**IDENTIFICATION**

A. Heat a few fragments in a test-tube. Violet vapour is evolved and a bluish-black crystalline sublimate is formed.

B. To a saturated solution add *starch solution R*. A blue colour is produced. Heat until decolourised. On cooling, the colour reappears.

**TESTS**

**Solution S**

Triturate 3.0 g with 20 ml of *water R*, filter, wash the filter with *water R* and dilute the filtrate to 30 ml with the same solvent. To the solution add 1 g of *zinc powder R*. When the solution is decolourised, filter, wash the filter with *water R* and dilute to 40 ml with the same solvent.

**Bromides and chlorides**

Maximum 250 ppm.

To 10 ml of solution S add 3 ml of *ammonia R* and 6 ml of *silver nitrate solution R2*. Filter, wash the filter with *water R* and dilute the filtrate to 20 ml with the same solvent. To 10 ml of the solution add 1.5 ml of *nitric acid R*. After 1 min, any opalescence in the solution is not more intense than that in a standard prepared at the same time by mixing 10.75 ml of *water R*, 0.25 ml of *0.01 M hydrochloric acid*, 0.2 ml of *dilute nitric acid R* and 0.3 ml of *silver nitrate solution R2*.

**Non-volatile substances**

Maximum 0.1 per cent.

Heat 1.00 g in a porcelain dish on a water-bath until the iodine has volatilised. Dry the residue at 100-105 °C. The residue weighs a maximum of 1 mg.

## ASSAY

Introduce 0.200 g into a flask containing 1 g of *potassium iodide R* and 2 ml of *water R* and add 1 ml of *dilute acetic acid R*. When dissolution is complete, add 50 ml *of water R* and titrate with *0.1 M sodium thiosulphate*, using *starch solution R* as indicator.

1 ml of *0.1 M sodium thiosulphate* is equivalent to 12.69 mg of I.

_____ *Ph Eur*

# Iohexol

(*Ph Eur monograph 1114*)

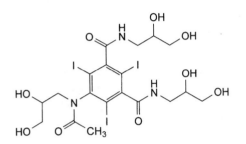

C₁₉H₂₆I₃N₃O₉ 821 66108-95-0

$C_{19}H_{26}I_3N_3O_9$      821      66108-95-0

### Action and use
Iodinated contrast medium.

*Ph Eur* _____

## DEFINITION

5-[Acetyl(2,3-dihydroxypropyl)amino]-*N*,*N'*-bis(2,3-dihydroxypropyl)-2,4,6-triiodobenzene-1,3-dicarboxamide.

The substance is a mixture of diastereoisomers and atropisomers.

### Content

98.0 per cent to 101.0 per cent (anhydrous substance).

## CHARACTERS

### Appearance
White or greyish-white, hygroscopic powder.

### Solubility
Very soluble in water, freely soluble in methanol, practically insoluble in methylene chloride.

## IDENTIFICATION

A. Infrared absorption spectrophotometry (*2.2.24*).

*Comparison* iohexol CRS.

B. Examine the chromatograms obtained in test A for related substances (see Tests).

*Results* The principal peaks in the chromatogram obtained with reference solution (b) are similar in retention time and size to the peaks due to iohexol in the chromatogram obtained with reference solution (a).

## TESTS

### Solution S
Dissolve 5.0 g in *water R* and dilute to 50.0 ml with the same solvent.

### Appearance of solution
Solution S is clear (*2.2.1*) and not more intensely coloured than reference solution Y₇ (*2.2.2, Method II*).

## Related substances

A. Liquid chromatography (*2.2.29*).

*NOTE: iohexol gives rise to 2 non-resolved peaks in the chromatogram due to endo-exo isomerism. In addition, a small peak (also due to iohexol) usually appears at the leading edge of the 1ˢᵗ principal peak. This small peak has a retention time about 1.2 min less than the 1ˢᵗ principal peak.*

*Test solution* Dissolve 0.150 g of the substance to be examined in *water R* and dilute to 100.0 ml with the same solvent.

*Reference solution (a)* Dissolve 15.0 mg of *iohexol CRS* and 15.0 mg of *iohexol impurity A CRS* in a mixture of 1-2 drops of *dilute sodium hydroxide solution R* and 10 ml of *water R* and dilute to 100.0 ml with w*ater R*. Dilute 1.0 ml of this solution to 10.0 ml with *water R*.

*Reference solution (b)* Dilute 1.0 ml of the test solution to 100.0 ml with *water R*.

*Reference solution (c)* Dissolve 5.0 mg of *iohexol for peak identification CRS* (containing impurities B, C, D and E) in *water R* and dilute to 5.0 ml with the same solvent.

*Blank solution* water R.

*Column:*
— *size: l = 0.25 m, Ø = 4.6 mm,*
— *stationary phase: octadecylsilyl silica gel for chromatography R* (5 μm).

*Mobile phase:*
— *mobile phase A: water R*;
— *mobile phase B: acetonitrile R*;

| Time (min) | Mobile phase A (per cent V/V) | Mobile phase B (per cent V/V) |
|---|---|---|
| 0 - 60 | 99 → 87 | 1 → 13 |
| 60 - 65 | 87 → 99 | 13 → 1 |

*Flow rate* 1 ml/min.

*Detection* Spectrophotometer at 254 nm.

*Equilibration* At the initial eluent composition for at least 10 min.

*Injection* 10 μl.

*Retention times* Impurity A and impurity H = about 17 min; iohexol (peaks corresponding to *endo-exo* isomerism) = about 20 min.

*System suitability* Reference solution (a):
— *resolution*: minimum 5.0 between the peak due to impurity A and the 2ⁿᵈ and greater peak due to iohexol.

*Limits:*
— *sum of impurities B, C, D and E* (relative retention with reference to the 2nd and greater peak due to iohexol between 1.1 and 1.4): not more than 0.6 times the total area of the principal peaks in the chromatogram obtained with reference solution (b) (0.6 per cent); use the chromatogram obtained with reference solution (c) to identify the corresponding peaks;
— *sum of impurities A and H*: not more than 0.5 times the total area of the principal peaks in the chromatogram obtained with reference solution (b) (0.5 per cent);
— *impurities M, N, O, P, Q*: for each impurity, not more than 0.1 times the total area of the principal peaks in the chromatogram obtained with reference solution (b) (0.1 per cent);
— *any other impurity*: for each impurity, not more than 0.1 times the total area of the principal peaks in the chromatogram obtained with reference solution (b) (0.1 per cent);

— *total*: not more than 1.5 times the total area of the principal peaks in the chromatogram obtained with reference solution (b) (1.5 per cent);

— *disregard limit*: 0.03 times the total area of the principal peaks in the chromatogram obtained with reference solution (b) (0.03 per cent); disregard any peak observed with the blank.

B. Thin-layer chromatography (*2.2.27*).

*Test solution*   Dissolve 1.0 g of the substance to be examined in *water R* and dilute to 10.0 ml with the same solvent.

*Reference solution (a)*   Dissolve 50 mg of *iohexol impurity J CRS* and 50 mg of *iohexol CRS* in *water R* and dilute to 10.0 ml with the same solvent.

*Reference solution (b)*   Dilute 1.0 ml of the test solution to 10.0 ml with *water R*. Dilute 1.0 ml of this solution to 50.0 ml with *water R*.

*Plate*   *TLC silica gel F$_{254}$ plate R*.

*Preconditioning*   Wash the plate with the mobile phase, dry at room temperature for 30 min, then at 90 °C for 1 h.

*Mobile phase*   *Concentrated ammonia R*, *methanol R*, *2-propanol R*, *acetone R* (16:16:28:40 *V/V/V/V*).

*Application*   10 µl.

*Development*   Over half of the plate.

*Drying*   In air.

*Detection*   Examine in ultraviolet light at 254 nm.

*System suitability*   Reference solution (a):
— the chromatogram shows 2 clearly separated spots.

*Limits*:
— *any impurity*: any spot in the chromatogram obtained with the test solution, apart from the principal spot, is not more intense than the spot in the chromatogram obtained with reference solution (b) (0.2 per cent).

**3-Chloropropane-1,2-diol**

Gas chromatography (*2.2.28*).

*Test solution*   Dissolve 1.0 g of the substance to be examined in 1.0 ml of *water R*. Shake with 4 quantities, each of 2 ml, of *methyl acetate R*. Dry the combined upper layers over *anhydrous sodium sulphate R*. Filter and concentrate to about 0.7 ml using a warm water bath at 60 °C and a stream of nitrogen and dilute to 1.0 ml with *methyl acetate R*.

*Reference solution*   Dissolve 0.25 g of *3-chloropropane-1,2-diol R* in 100.0 ml of *methyl acetate R*. Dilute 1.0 ml of this solution with 100.0 ml of *methyl acetate R*.

*Column*:
— *material*: fused silica,
— *size*: l = 25 m, Ø = 0.33 mm,
— *stationary phase*: polymethylphenylsiloxane R (film thickness 1 µm).

*Carrier gas*   *helium for chromatography R*.

*Flow rate*   1 ml/min.

*Temperature*:

|  | Time (min) | Temperature (°C) |
|---|---|---|
| Column | 0 - 2 | 80 |
|  | 2 - 8 | 80 → 170 |
|  | 8 - 10 | 170 |
| Injection port |  | 230 |
| Detector |  | 250 |

*Detection*   Flame ionisation.

*Injection*   2 µl (splitless for 30 s).

*System suitability*   Reference solution:
— *retention time*: 3-chloropropane-1,2-diol = about 8 min.

*Limit*:
— *3-chloropropane-1,2-diol*: not more than the area of the principal peak in the chromatogram obtained with the reference solution (25 ppm).

**Free aromatic amine**

Maximum 500 ppm.

*Test solution*   Transfer 0.200 g of the substance to be examined to a 25 ml volumetric flask and dissolve in 15.0 ml of *water R*.

*Reference solution*   Dissolve 5.0 mg of *iohexol impurity J CRS* in *water R* and dilute to 5.0 ml with *water R*. Dilute 1.0 ml of this solution to 100.0 ml with *water R*. Mix 10.0 ml of this solution with 5.0 ml of *water R* in a 25 ml volumetric flask.

*Blank solution*   Transfer 15.0 ml of *water R* to a 25 ml volumetric flask.

*In conducting the following steps, keep the flasks in iced water and protected as much as possible from light until all of the reagents have been added.*

Place the 3 flasks containing respectively the test solution, the reference solution and the blank solution in iced water, protected from light, for 5 min. Add 1.5 ml of *hydrochloric acid R1* and mix by swirling. Add 1.0 ml of a 20 g/l solution of *sodium nitrite R*, mix and allow to stand for 4 min. Add 1.0 ml of a 40 g/l solution of *sulphamic acid R*, swirl gently until gas liberation has ceased and allow to stand for 1 min. (*CAUTION: considerable pressure is produced*). Add 1.0 ml of a freshly prepared 3 g/l solution of *naphthylethylenediamine dihydrochloride R* in a mixture of 30 volumes of *water R* and 70 volumes of *propylene glycol R* and mix. Remove the flasks from the iced water, dilute to 25.0 ml with *water R*, mix and allow to stand for 5 min. Simultaneously determine the absorbance (*2.2.25*) at 495 nm of the solutions obtained from the test solution and the reference solution in 5 cm cells, using the blank as the compensation liquid. The absorbance of the test solution is not greater than that of the reference solution.

**Iodide:**

Maximum 10 ppm.

Dissolve 6.000 g in *water R* and dilute to 20 ml with the same solvent. Add 2.0 ml of *0.001 M potassium iodide*. Titrate with *0.001 M silver nitrate*. Determine the end-point potentiometrically (*2.2.20*), using a silver indicator electrode and an appropriate reference electrode. Subtract the volume of titrant corresponding to the 2.0 ml of *0.001 M potassium iodide*, determined by titrating a blank to which is added 2.0 ml of *0.001 M potassium iodide* and use the residual value to calculate the iodide content.

1 ml of *0.001 M silver nitrate* is equivalent to 126.9 µg of I−.

**Ionic compounds** (*2.2.38*)

Maximum 0.01 per cent *m/m* calculated as sodium chloride.

*Rinse all glassware with distilled water R 5 times before use.*

*Test solution*   Dissolve 1.0 g of the substance to be examined in *water R* and dilute to 50.0 ml with the same solvent.

*Reference solution*   Dissolve 20.0 mg of *sodium chloride R* in *water R* and dilute to 100.0 ml with the same solvent. Dilute 1.0 ml of this solution to 100.0 ml with *water R*.

Measure the conductivity of the test solution and the reference solution using a suitable conductivity meter. The conductivity of the test solution is not greater than that of the reference solution.

**Heavy metals** (*2.4.8*)

Maximum 10 ppm.

12 ml of solution S complies with limit test A. Prepare the reference solution using *lead standard solution (1 ppm Pb) R*.

**Water** (*2.5.12*)

Maximum 4.0 per cent, determined on 1.00 g.

## ASSAY

To 0.500 g in a 125 ml round-bottomed flask add 25 ml of a 50 g/l solution of *sodium hydroxide R*, 0.5 g of *zinc powder R* and a few glass beads. Boil under a reflux condenser for 30 min. Allow to cool and rinse the condenser with 20 ml of *water R*, adding the rinsings to the flask. Filter through a sintered-glass filter (*2.1.2*) and wash the filter with several quantities of *water R*. Collect the filtrate and washings. Add 5 ml of *glacial acetic acid R* and titrate immediately with *0.1 M silver nitrate*. Determine the end-point potentiometrically (*2.2.20*).

1 ml of *0.1 M silver nitrate* is equivalent to 27.37 mg of $C_{19}H_{26}I_3N_3O_9$.

## STORAGE

In an airtight container, protected from light and moisture.

## IMPURITIES

*Specified impurities   A, B, C, D, E, F, G, H, I, J, K, L, M, N, O, P, Q.*

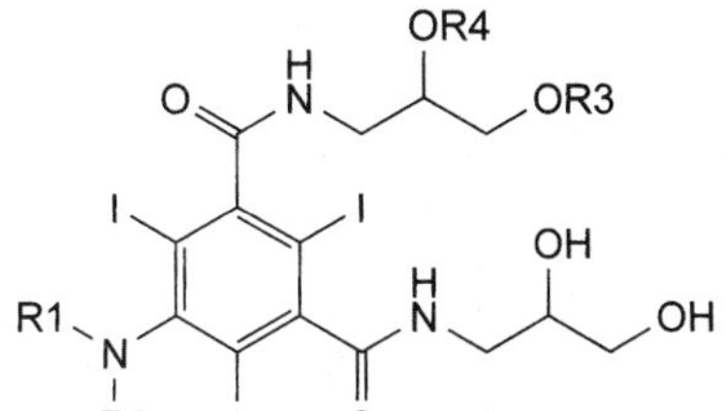

A. R1 = CO-CH₃, R2 = R3 = R4 = H: 5-(acetylamino)-*N,N'*-bis(2,3-dihydroxypropyl)-2,4,6-triiodobenzene-1,3-dicarboxamide,

J. R1 = R2 = R3 = R4 = H: 5-amino-*N,N'*-bis(2,3-dihydroxypropyl)-2,4,6-triiodobenzene-1,3-dicarboxamide,

P. R1 = R2 = CO-CH₃, R3 = CH₂-CHOH-CH₂OH, R4 = H: 5-(diacetylamino)-*N*-[3-(2,3-dihydroxypropoxy)-2-hydroxypropyl]-*N'*-(2,3-dihydroxypropyl)-2,4,6-triiodobenzene-1,3-dicarboxamide,

Q. R1 = R2 = CO-CH₃, R3 = H, R4 = CH₂-CHOH-CH₂OH: 5-(diacetylamino)-*N*-[2-(2,3-dihydroxypropoxy)-3-hydroxypropyl]-*N'*-(2,3-dihydroxypropyl)-2,4,6-triiodobenzene-1,3-dicarboxamide,

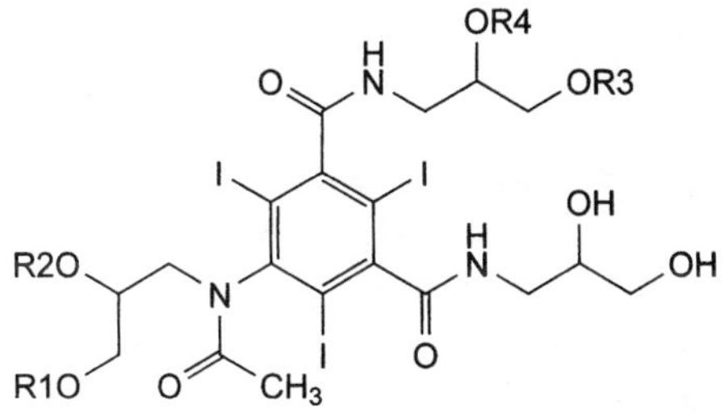

B. R1 = CH₂-CHOH-CH₂OH, R2 = R3 = R4 = H: 5-[acetyl[3-(2,3-dihydroxypropoxy)-2-hydroxypropyl]amino]-*N,N'*-bis(2,3-dihydroxypropyl)-2,4,6-triiodobenzene-1,3-dicarboxamide,

C. R2 = CH₂-CHOH-CH₂OH, R1 = R3 = R4 = H: 5-[acetyl[2-(2,3-dihydroxypropoxy)-3-hydroxypropyl]amino]-*N,N'*-bis(2,3-dihydroxypropyl)-2,4,6-triiodobenzene-1,3-dicarboxamide,

D. R3 = CH₂-CHOH-CH₂OH, R1 = R2 = R4 = H: 5-[acetyl(2,3-dihydroxypropyl)amino]-*N*-[3-(2,3-dihydroxypropoxy)-2-hydroxypropyl]-*N'*-(2,3-dihydroxypropyl)-2,4,6-triiodobenzene-1,3-dicarboxamide,

E. R4 = CH₂-CHOH-CH₂OH, R1 = R2 = R3 = H: 5-[acetyl(2,3-dihydroxypropyl)amino]-*N*-[2-(2,3-dihydroxypropoxy)-3-hydroxypropyl]-*N'*-(2,3-dihydroxypropyl)-2,4,6-triiodobenzene-1,3-dicarboxamide,

N. R4 = CO-CH₃, R1 = R2 = R3 = H: 5-[acetyl(2,3-dihydroxypropyl)amino]-*N*-[2-(acetyloxy)-3-hydroxypropyl]-*N'*-(2,3-dihydroxypropyl)-2,4,6-triiodobenzene-1,3-dicarboxamide,

O. R3 = CO-CH₃, R1 = R2 = R4 = H: 5-[acetyl(2,3-dihydroxypropyl)amino]-*N*-[3-(acetyloxy)-2-hydroxypropyl]-*N'*-(2,3-dihydroxypropyl)-2,4,6-triiodobenzene-1,3-dicarboxamide,@

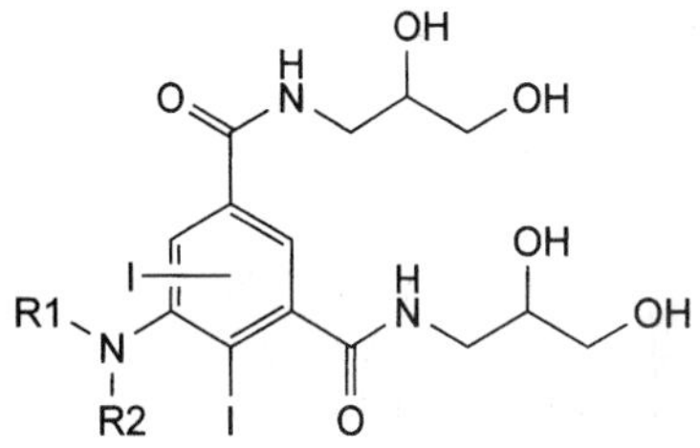

F. R1 = R2 = H: 5-amino-*N,N'*-bis(2,3-dihydroxypropyl)diiodobenzene-1,3-dicarboxamide,

G. R1 = H, R2 = CO-CH₃: 5-(acetylamino)-*N,N'*-bis(2,3-dihydroxypropyl)diiodobenzene-1,3-dicarboxamide,

H. R1 = CH₂-CHOH-CH₂OH, R2 = CO-CH₃: 5-[acetyl(2,3-dihydroxypropyl)amino]-*N,N'*-bis(2,3-dihydroxypropyl)diiodobenzene-1,3-dicarboxamide,

M. R1 = CH₂-CHOH-CH₂OH, R2 = H: *N,N'*-bis(2,3-dihydroxypropyl)-5-[(2,3-dihydroxypropyl)amino]diiodobenzene-1,3-dicarboxamide,

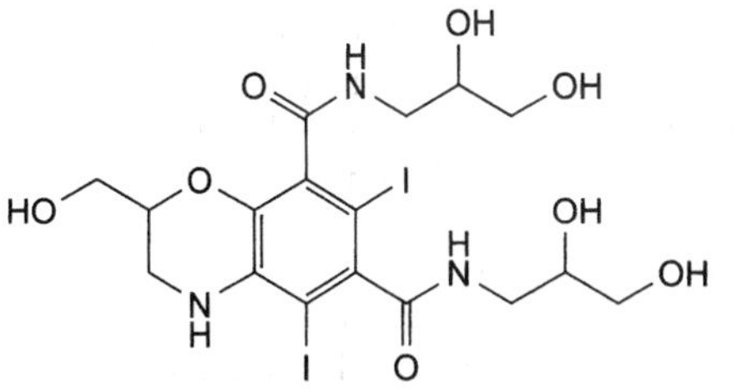

I. *N,N'*-bis(2,3-dihydroxypropyl)-2-(hydroxymethyl)-5,7-diiodo-3,4-dihydro-2H-1,4-benzoxazine-6,8-dicarboxamide,

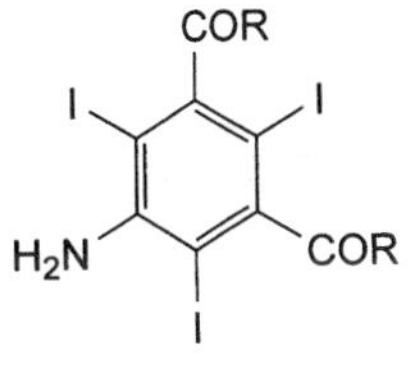

K. R = OH: 5-amino-2,4,6-triiodobenzene-1,3-dicarboxylic acid,

L. R = Cl: 5-amino-2,4,6-triiodobenzene-1,3-dicarbonyl dichloride.

# Iopamidol

*(Ph Eur monograph 1115)*

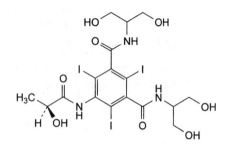

C$_{17}$H$_{22}$I$_3$N$_3$O$_8$      777      60166-93-0

## Action and use

Iodinated contrast medium.

*Ph Eur* _____

## DEFINITION

*N,N'*-Bis[2-hydroxy-1-(hydroxymethyl)ethyl]-5-[[(2*S*)-2-hydroxypropanoyl]amino]-2,4,6-triiodobenzene-1,3-dicarboxamide.

## Content

98.5 per cent to 101.0 per cent (dried substance).

## CHARACTERS

### Appearance

White or almost white powder.

### Solubility

Freely soluble in water, very slightly soluble in methanol, practically insoluble in ethanol (96 per cent) and in methylene chloride.

## IDENTIFICATION

A. Infrared absorption spectrophotometry (*2.2.24*).

*Comparison*   iopamidol CRS.

B. It complies with the test for loss on drying (see Tests).

C. It complies with the test for specific optical rotation (see Tests).

## TESTS

### Appearance of solution

The solution is clear (*2.2.1*) and colourless (*2.2.2, Method II*).

Dissolve 1 g in *water R* and dilute to 50 ml with the same solvent.

### Acidity or alkalinity

Dissolve 10.0 g in *carbon dioxide-free water R* and dilute to 100 ml with the same solvent. Not more than 0.75 ml of *0.01 M hydrochloric acid* or 1.4 ml of *0.01 M sodium hydroxide* is required to adjust to pH 7.0 (*2.2.3*).

### Specific optical rotation (*2.2.7*)

− 4.6 to − 5.2 (dried substance), determined at 436 nm.

Dissolve 10.0 g, with heating if necessary, in *water R* and dilute to 25.0 ml with the same solvent.

### Related substances

Liquid chromatography (*2.2.29*).

*Test solution*   Dissolve 0.50 g of the substance to be examined in *water R* and dilute to 50.0 ml with the same solvent.

*Reference solution (a)*   Dissolve 5.0 mg of *iopamidol impurity H CRS* in *water R* and dilute to 100.0 ml with the same solvent.

*Reference solution (b)*   Dilute 2.0 ml of the test solution to 20.0 ml with *water R*. Dilute 1.0 ml of this solution to 50.0 ml with *water R*.

*Reference solution (c)*   Add 0.1 ml of the test solution to 20 ml of reference solution (a) and dilute to 50 ml with *water R*.

*Column*:

2 columns coupled in series,
— *size*: *l* = 0.25 m, Ø = 4.6 mm,
— *stationary phase*: *phenylsilyl silica gel for chromatography R* (5 μm),
— *temperature*: 60 °C.

*Mobile phase*:
— mobile phase A: *water R*,
— mobile phase B: *acetonitrile R*, *water R* (50:50 *V/V*),

| Time (min) | Mobile phase A (per cent *V/V*) | Mobile phase B (per cent *V/V*) |
|---|---|---|
| 0 - 18 | 100 | 0 |
| 18 - 40 | 100 - 62 | 0 - 38 |
| 40 - 45 | 62 - 50 | 38 - 50 |
| 45 - 50 | 50 - 100 | 50 - 0 |
| 50 - 60 | 100 | 0 |

*Flow rate*   2.0 ml/min.

*Detection*   Spectrophotometer at 240 nm.

*Injection*   20 μl.

*Relative retention* with reference to iopamidol (retention time = about 14.6 min): impurity D = about 0.1; impurity B = about 0.6; impurities I and H = about 0.9; impurity G = about 1.1; impurity K = about 1.2; impurity C = about 1.3; impurity J = about 1.5; impurity A = about 1.8; impurity E = about 2.2; impurity F = about 2.3.

*System suitability*   Reference solution (c):
— *resolution*: minimum 2.0 between the peaks due to impurity H and iopamidol.

*Limits*:
— *sum of impurities H and I*: not more than the area of the principal peak in the chromatogram obtained with reference solution (a) (0.5 per cent),
— *impurities A, B, C, D, E, F, G, J, K*: for each impurity, not more than 0.5 times the area of the principal peak in the chromatogram obtained with reference solution (b) (0.1 per cent),
— *any other impurity*: for each impurity, not more than 0.5 times the area of the principal peak in the chromatogram obtained with reference solution (b) (0.1 per cent),
— *sum of impurities other than H and I*: not more than the area of the principal peak in the chromatogram obtained with reference solution (b) (0.2 per cent),
— *disregard limit*: 0.05 times the area of the principal peak in the chromatogram obtained with reference solution (b) (0.01 per cent).

### Free aromatic amines

Maximum 200 ppm.

*Keep the solutions and reagents in iced water, protected from bright light.*

*Test solution*   In a 25 ml volumetric flask, dissolve 0.500 g of the substance to be examined in 20.0 ml of *water R*.

*Reference solution*   In a 25 ml volumetric flask, mix 4.0 ml of a 25.0 mg/l solution of *iopamidol impurity A CRS* with 16.0 ml of *water R*.

*Blank solution*   Place 20.0 ml of *water R* in a 25 ml volumetric flask.

Place the flasks in iced water, protected from light, for 5 min. Add *1.0 ml of hydrochloric acid R* to each flask, mix and allow to stand for 5 min. Add 1.0 ml of a 20 g/l solution of *sodium nitrite R* prepared immediately before use, mix and allow to stand for 5 min. Add 1.0 ml of a 120 g/l solution of *ammonium sulphamate R*, swirl gently until gas liberation has ceased, and allow to stand for 5 min. *(CAUTION: considerable pressure is produced)*. Add 1.0 ml of a freshly prepared 1 g/l solution of *naphthylethylenediamine dihydrochloride R* and mix. Remove the flasks from the iced water and allow to stand for 10 min. Dilute to 25.0 ml with *water R* and mix. Measure immediately the absorbance *(2.2.25)* at 500 nm of the solutions obtained from the test solution and the reference solution using, as the compensation liquid, the solution obtained from the blank solution.

The absorbance of the test solution is not greater than that of the reference solution.

**Free iodine**

Maximum 10 ppm.

Dissolve 2.0 g in 25 ml of *water R* in a ground-glass stoppered centrifuge tube. Add 5 ml of *toluene R* and 5 ml of *diluted sulphuric acid R*. Shake and centrifuge. Any red colour of the upper layer is not more intense than that of the upper phase obtained in the same way from 22 ml of *water R*, 2 ml of *iodide standard solution (10 ppm I) R*, 5 ml of *dilute sulphuric acid R*, 1 ml of *concentrated hydrogen peroxide solution R* and 5 ml of *toluene R*.

**Iodide**

Maximum 10 ppm.

Dissolve 6.000 g in *water R* and dilute to 20 ml with the same solvent. Add 2.0 ml of *0.001 M potassium iodide*. Carry out a potentiometric titration (*2.2.20*) with *0.001 M silver nitrate* using a silver indicator electrode and an appropriate reference electrode. Subtract the volume of titrant corresponding to the 2.0 ml of *0.001 M potassium iodide*, determined by titrating a blank to which is added 2.0 ml of *0.001 M potassium iodide* and use the residual value to calculate the iodide content.

1 ml of *0.001 M silver nitrate* is equivalent to 126.9 μg of iodide.

**Heavy metals** (*2.4.8*)

Maximum 10 ppm.

2.0 g complies with limit test C. Prepare the reference solution using 2 ml of *lead standard solution (10 ppm Pb) R*.

**Loss on drying** (*2.2.32*)

Maximum 0.5 per cent, determined on 1.000 g by drying in an oven at 105 °C.

**Sulphated ash** (*2.4.14*)

Maximum 0.1 per cent, determined on 1.0 g.

**Bacterial endotoxins** (*2.6.14*)

Less than 1.4 IU/g, if intended for use in the manufacture of parenteral dosage forms without a further appropriate procedure for the removal of bacterial endotoxins.

**ASSAY**

To 0.300 g in a 250 ml round-bottomed flask add 5 ml of *strong sodium hydroxide solution R*, 20 ml of *water R*, 1 g of *zinc powder R* and a few glass beads. Boil under a reflux condenser for 30 min. Allow to cool and rinse the condenser with 20 ml of *water R*, adding the rinsings to the flask. Filter through a sintered-glass filter (*2.1.2*) and wash the filter with several quantities of *water R*. Collect the filtrate and washings. Add 5 ml of *glacial acetic acid R* and titrate immediately with *0.1 M silver nitrate*. Determine the end-point potentiometrically (*2.2.20*) using a suitable electrode system such as silver-silver chloride.

1 ml of *0.1 M silver nitrate* is equivalent to 25.90 mg of $C_{17}H_{22}I_3N_3O_8$.

**STORAGE**

Protected from light. If the substance is sterile, store in a sterile, airtight, tamper-proof container.

**IMPURITIES**

*Specified impurities*   A, B, C, D, E, F, G, H, I, J, K.

A. R1 = NH-CH(CH$_2$OH)$_2$, R2 = H:
5-amino-*N,N'*-bis[2-hydroxy-1-(hydroxymethyl)ethyl]-2,4,6-triiodobenzene-1,3-dicarboxamide,

B. R1 = NH-CH(CH$_2$OH)$_2$, R2 = CO-CH$_2$OH:
5-[(hydroxyacetyl)amino]-*N,N'*-bis[2-hydroxy-1-(hydroxymethyl)ethyl]-2,4,6-triiodobenzene-1,3-dicarboxamide,

C. R1 = NH-CH(CH$_2$OH)$_2$, R2 = CO-CH$_3$:
5-(acetylamino)-*N,N'*-bis[2-hydroxy-1-(hydroxymethyl)ethyl]-2,4,6-triiodobenzene-1,3-dicarboxamide,

D. R1 = OH, R2 = CO-CHOH-CH$_3$: 3-[[2-hydroxy-1-(hydroxymethyl)ethyl]carbamoyl]-5-[[(2*S*)-2-hydroxypropanoyl]amino]-2,4,6-triiodobenzoic acid,

E. R1 = NH-CH(CH$_2$OH)$_2$, R2 = CO-CH(CH$_3$)-O-CO-CH$_3$: (1*S*)-2-[[3,5-bis[[2-hydroxy-1-(hydroxymethyl)ethyl]carbamoyl]-2,4,6-triiodophenyl]amino]-1-methyl-2-oxoethyl acetate,

F. R1 = N(CH$_3$)$_2$, R2 = CO-CHOH-CH$_3$:
*N'*-[2-hydroxy-1-(hydroxymethyl)ethyl]-5-[[(2*S*)-2-hydroxypropanoyl]amino]-2,4,6-triiodo-*N,N*-dimethylbenzene-1,3-dicarboxamide,

G. R1 = NH-CH$_2$-CHOH-CH$_2$OH, R2 = CO-CHOH-CH$_3$: *N*-(2,3-dihydroxypropyl)-*N'*-[2-hydroxy-1-(hydroxymethyl)ethyl]-5-[[(2*S*)-2-hydroxypropanoyl]amino]-2,4,6-triiodobenzene-1,3-dicarboxamide,

J. R1 = NH-CH$_2$-CH$_2$OH, R2 = CO-CHOH-CH$_3$: *N*-(2-hydroxyethyl)-*N'*-[2-hydroxy-1-(hydroxymethyl)ethyl]-5-[[(2*S*)-2-hydroxypropanoyl]amino]-2,4,6-triiodobenzene-1,3-dicarboxamide,

H. R1 = I, R2 = Cl: 4-chloro-N,N'-bis[2-hydroxy-1-(hydroxymethyl)ethyl]-5-[[(2S)-2-hydroxypropanoyl]amino]-2,6-diiodobenzene-1,3-dicarboxamide,

I. R1 = Cl, R2 = I: 2-chloro-N,N'-bis[2-hydroxy-1-(hydroxymethyl)ethyl]-5-[[(2S)-2-hydroxypropanoyl]amino]-4,6-diiodobenzene-1,3-dicarboxamide,

K. R1 = I, R2 = H: N,N'-bis[2-hydroxy-1-(hydroxymethyl)ethyl]-5-[[(2S)-2-hydroxypropanoyl]amino]-2,4-diiodobenzene-1,3-dicarboxamide.

_____ *Ph Eur*

# Iopanoic Acid

*(Ph Eur monograph 0700)*

C₁₁H₁₂I₃NO₂      571      96-83-3

$C_{11}H_{12}I_3NO_2 \quad 571 \quad 96\text{-}83\text{-}3$

## Action and use
Iodinated contrast medium.

## Preparation
Iopanoic Acid Tablets

*Ph Eur* _____

## DEFINITION
Iopanoic acid contains not less than 98.5 per cent and not more than the equivalent of 101.0 per cent of (RS)-2-(3-amino-2,4,6-tri-iodobenzyl)butanoic acid, calculated with reference to the dried substance.

## CHARACTERS
A white or yellowish-white powder, practically insoluble in water, soluble in ethanol and in methanol. It dissolves in dilute solutions of alkali hydroxides.

## IDENTIFICATION
*First identification*   B.

*Second identification*   A, C, D.

A. Melting point (2.2.14): about 155 °C, with decomposition.

B. Examine by infrared absorption spectrophotometry (2.2.24), comparing with the spectrum obtained with *iopanoic acid CRS*.

C. Examine the chromatograms obtained in the test for related substances (see Tests). Spray the plate with a 1 g/l solution of *4-dimethylaminocinnamaldehyde R* in a mixture of 1 volume of *hydrochloric acid R* and 99 volumes of *alcohol R*. The principal spot in the chromatogram obtained with test

solution (b) is similar in position, colour and size to the principal spot in the chromatogram obtained with reference solution (a).

D. Heat 50 mg carefully in a small porcelain dish over a flame. Violet vapour is evolved.

## TESTS
### Appearance of solution
Dissolve 1.0 g in *1 M sodium hydroxide* and dilute to 20 ml with the same solvent. The solution is clear (2.2.1) and not more intensely coloured than reference solution Y₃ (2.2.2, *Method II*).

### Related substances
Examine by thin-layer chromatography (2.2.27), using *silica gel GF₂₅₄ R* as the coating substance.

*Test solution (a)*   Dissolve 1.0 g of the substance to be examined in a mixture of 3 volumes of *ammonia R* and 97 volumes of *methanol R* and dilute to 10 ml with the same mixture of solvents.

*Test solution (b)*   Dilute 1 ml of test solution (a) to 10 ml with a mixture of 3 volumes of *ammonia R* and 97 volumes of *methanol R*.

*Reference solution (a)*   Dissolve 50 mg of *iopanoic acid CRS* in a mixture of 3 volumes of *ammonia R* and 97 volumes of *methanol R* and dilute to 5 ml with the same mixture of solvents.

*Reference solution (b)*   Dilute 1 ml of test solution (b) to 50 ml with a mixture of 3 volumes of *ammonia R* and 97 volumes of *methanol R*.

Apply separately to the plate 5 µl of each solution. Develop over a path of 10 cm using a mixture of 10 volumes of *concentrated ammonia R*, 20 volumes of *methanol R*, 20 volumes of *toluene R* and 50 volumes of *dioxan R*. Examine in ultraviolet light at 254 nm. Any spot in the chromatogram obtained with test solution (a), apart from the principal spot, is not more intense than the spot in the chromatogram obtained with reference solution (b) (0.2 per cent).

### Halides
To 0.46 g add 10 ml of *nitric acid R* and 15 ml of *water R*. Shake for 5 min and filter. 15 ml of the filtrate complies with the limit test for chlorides (2.4.4) (180 ppm, expressed as chloride).

### Loss on drying (2.2.32)
Not more than 0.5 per cent, determined on 1.000 g by drying in an oven at 105 °C for 1 h.

### Sulphated ash (2.4.14)
Not more than 0.1 per cent, determined on 1.0 g.

## ASSAY
To 0.150 g in a 250 ml round-bottomed flask add 5 ml of *strong sodium hydroxide solution R*, 20 ml of *water R*, 1 g of *zinc powder R* and a few glass beads. Boil under a reflux condenser for 60 min. Allow to cool and rinse the condenser with 20 ml of *water R*, adding the rinsings to the flask. Filter through a sintered-glass filter (2.1.2) and wash the filter with several quantities of *water R*. Collect the filtrate and washings. Add 40 ml of *dilute sulphuric acid R* and titrate immediately with *0.1 M silver nitrate*. Determine the end-point potentiometrically (2.2.20), using a suitable electrode system such as silver-mercurous sulphate.

1 ml of *0.1 M silver nitrate* is equivalent to 19.03 mg of C₁₁H₁₂I₃NO₂.

**STORAGE**

Store protected from light.

Ph Eur

# Iopromide

(Ph Eur monograph 1753 )

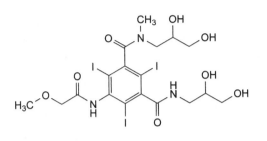

C$_{18}$H$_{24}$I$_3$N$_3$O$_8$      791.0      73334-07-3

**Action and use**

Iodinated contrast medium.

Ph Eur

**DEFINITION**

N,N'-Bis(2,3-dihydroxypropyl)-2,4,6-triiodo-5-[(methoxyacetyl)amino]-N-methylbenzene-1,3-dicarboxamide.

Mixture of diastereoisomers and atropisomers.

**Content**

97.0 per cent to 102.0 per cent (anhydrous substance).

**CHARACTERS**

**Appearance**

White or slightly yellowish powder.

**Solubility**

Freely soluble in water and in dimethyl sulphoxide, practically insoluble in ethanol (96 per cent) and in acetone.

**IDENTIFICATION**

Infrared absorption spectrophotometry (2.2.24).

Comparison iopromide CRS.

**TESTS**

**Appearance of solution**

The solution is clear (2.2.1) and not more intensely coloured than reference solutions BY$_6$, B$_6$ and Y$_6$ (2.2.2, Method I).

Dissolve 16.5 g in 20 ml of carbon dioxide-free water R while heating on a water-bath at a temperature not exceeding 70 °C. Allow to cool to room temperature.

**Conductivity (2.2.38)**

Maximum 50 μS·cm$^{-1}$.

Dissolve 1.000 g in water R and dilute to 50.0 ml with the same solvent.

**Impurity A and related primary aromatic amines**

Maximum 0.01 per cent.

Protect the solutions from light throughout the test. All given times are critical for the test results. The test solution, reference solution and blank solution must be processed in parallel.

Test solution Dissolve 0.500 g of the substance to be examined in 20.0 ml of water R in a 25 ml volumetric flask.

Reference solution Dissolve the contents of a vial of iopromide impurity A CRS in 5.0 ml of water R. Transfer 2.0 ml of this solution to a 25 ml volumetric flask and add 18.0 ml of water R.

Blank solution Place 20.0 ml of water R in a 25 ml volumetric flask.

Cool the test solution, reference solution and blank solution in a bath of iced water for 5 min. Add 1.0 ml of hydrochloric acid R1 to each solution and cool again for 5 min in a bath of iced water. Add 1.0 ml of a 20 g/l solution of sodium nitrite R, shake vigorously and cool for another 5 min in a bath of iced water. To each solution add 0.50 ml of an 80 g/l solution of sulphamic acid R. Over the next 5 min, shake vigorously several times, raising the stoppers to vent the gas that evolves. Afterwards, add to each solution 1.0 ml of a 1 g/l solution of naphthylethylenediamine dihydrochloride R in a mixture of 300 volumes of water R and 700 volumes of propylene glycol R, shake, allow to cool to room temperature for 10 min and dilute to 25.0 ml with water R. Degas the solutions in an ultrasonic bath for 1 min and measure the absorbance (2.2.25) of the test solution and the reference solution at 495 nm against the blank, within 5 min. The test is not valid unless the absorbance of the reference solution is at least 0.08. The absorbance of the test solution is not greater than the absorbance of the reference solution.

**Impurity B**

Liquid chromatography (2.2.29).

Solvent mixture methanol R, water R (50:50 V/V).

Test solution Dissolve 40.0 mg of the substance to be examined in the solvent mixture and dilute to 25.0 ml with the solvent mixture.

Reference solution (a) Dissolve 40.0 mg of iopromide CRS in the solvent mixture and dilute to 25.0 ml with the solvent mixture.

Reference solution (b) Introduce several millilitres of reference solution (a) into a vial sealed with a crimp-top. Heat at 121 °C for 15 min.

Reference solution (c) Dilute 1.5 ml of the test solution to 100.0 ml with the solvent mixture.

Column:
— size: l = 0.25 m, Ø = 4.6 mm;
— stationary phase: end-capped octadecylsilyl silica gel for chromatography R (5 μm);
— temperature: 20 °C.

Mobile phase Mix 6 g of chloroform R with 59 g of methanol R. Add 900 g of water for chromatography R in small portions to the chloroform/methanol mixture and stir for at least 2 h to obtain a homogeneous solution.

Flow rate 1.2 ml/min.

Detection Spectrophotometer at 254 nm.

Injection 10 μl of the test solution and reference solutions (a) and (c).

Run time 50 min.

Identification of impurities Use the chromatogram supplied with iopromide CRS and the chromatogram obtained with reference solution (a) to identify the peaks due to impurity B isomers Y$_1$ and Y$_2$.

Relative retention With reference to iopromide isomer Z$_2$ (retention time = about 34 min):
impurity B isomer Y$_1$ = about 0.28;
impurity B isomer Y$_2$ = about 0.31.

System suitability Reference solution (a):
— the chromatogram obtained shows 2 peaks due to impurity B isomers Y$_1$ and Y$_2$.

*Limit:*
— *sum of impurity B isomers $Y_1$ and $Y_2$:* not more than the sum of the areas of the 2 principal peaks due to the iopromide in the chromatogram obtained with reference solution (c) (1.5 per cent).

**Related substances**

Thin-layer chromatography (*2.2.27*).

*Solvent mixture*   methanol R, water R (50:50 *V/V*).

*Test solution*   Dissolve 1.0 g of the substance to be examined in the solvent mixture and dilute to 10.0 ml with the solvent mixture.

*Reference solution (a)*   Dilute 1.0 ml of the test solution to 100.0 ml with the solvent mixture.

*Reference solution (b)*   Dilute 5.0 ml of reference solution (a) to 10.0 ml with the solvent mixture.

*Reference solution (c)*   Dilute 2.0 ml of reference solution (a) to 10.0 ml with the solvent mixture.

*Reference solution (d)*   Dilute 1.0 ml of reference solution (a) to 10.0 ml with the solvent mixture.

*Reference solution (e)*   Dissolve the contents of a vial of *iopromide for system suitability 1 CRS* (containing impurities B and E) in 50 µl of the solvent mixture.

*Reference solution (f)*   Dissolve the contents of a vial of *iopromide for system suitability 2 CRS* (containing impurities B, C, D and F) in 50 µl of the solvent mixture.

*Plates*   TLC silica gel $F_{254}$ plate R (2 plates).

A. *Mobile phase:* concentrated ammonia R, water R, dioxan R (4:15:85 *V/V/V*).

*Application*   2 µl of the test solution and reference solutions (b), (d) and (e).

*Development*   Over 3/4 of the plate.

*Drying*   In a current of air, until complete evaporation of the solvents, then at 120 °C for 30 min.

*Detection*   Examine immediately in ultraviolet light at 254 nm; expose to ultraviolet light for 2-5 min until the principal spots appear clearly as yellow spots, then spray with *ferric chloride-ferricyanide-arsenite reagent R* and examine immediately in daylight.

*Retardation factors*   Impurity B = about 0.26; iopromide = about 0.34; impurity E = about 0.41.

*System suitability*   Reference solution (e):
— the chromatogram shows 3 clearly separated spots.

*Limits:*
— *impurity E:* any spot due to impurity E is not more intense than the principal spot in the chromatogram obtained with reference solution (b) (0.5 per cent);
— *unspecified impurities:* any other spot is not more intense than the principal spot in the chromatogram obtained with reference solution (d) (0.10 per cent); disregard any spot due to impurity B.

B. *Mobile phase:* anhydrous formic acid R, water R, methanol R, chloroform R (2:6:32:62 *V/V/V/V*).

*Application*   2 µl of the test solution and reference solutions (a), (b) ,(c), (d) and (f).

*Development*   Over 3/4 of the plate.

*Drying*   In a current of air, until complete evaporation of the solvents, then at 120 °C for 30 min.

*Detection*   Examine immediately in ultraviolet light at 254 nm; expose to an ammonia vapour for 30 min, dry in a current of air for 10 min, then expose to ultraviolet light for 2-5 min until the principal spots appear clearly as yellow spots, then spray with *ferric chloride-ferricyanide-arsenite reagent R* and examine immediately in daylight.

*Retardation factors*   Impurity C = about 0.23; impurity D = about 0.29; impurity B = about 0.36; iopromide = about 0.43; impurity F = about 0.71.

*System suitability*   Reference solution (f):
— the chromatogram shows 5 clearly separated spots.

*Limits:*
— *impurity D:* any spot due to impurity D is not more intense than the principal spot in the chromatogram obtained with reference solution (a) (1.0 per cent);
— *impurity C:* any spot due to impurity C is not more intense than the principal spot in the chromatogram obtained with reference solution (b) (0.5 per cent);
— *impurity F:* any spot due to impurity F is not more intense than the principal spot in the chromatogram obtained with reference solution (c) (0.2 per cent);
— *unspecified impurities:* any other spot is not more intense than the principal spot in the chromatogram obtained with reference solution (d) (0.10 per cent); disregard any spot due to impurity B.

**Isomer distribution**

Liquid chromatography (*2.2.29*) as described in the test for impurity B with the following modifications.

Calculate the percentage content of the isomer groups with reference to the total area of all the peaks due to the 4 iopromide isomers, using the chromatogram obtained with the test solution.

*Limits:*
— *sum of iopromide isomers $E_1$ and $Z_1$:* 40.0 per cent to 51.0 per cent;
— *sum of iopromide isomers $E_2$ and $Z_2$:* 49.0 per cent to 60.0 per cent.

**Free iodine**

Dissolve 2.0 g in 20 ml of *water R* in a glass-stoppered test tube. Add 2 ml of *dilute sulphuric acid R* and 2 ml of *toluene R*, close and shake vigorously. The upper layer remains colourless (*2.2.2, Method II*).

**Iodide**

Maximum 2 ppm.

Dissolve 10.0 g in 50 ml of *carbon dioxide-free water R*. Adjust to pH 3-4 adding about 0.15 ml of *0.1 M sulphuric acid*. Titrate with *0.001 M silver nitrate*. Determine the end-point potentiometrically (*2.2.20*) using a combined metal electrode. Not more than 0.15 ml of *0.001 M silver nitrate* is required to reach the end-point.

**Heavy metals** (*2.4.8*)

Maximum 10 ppm.

Dissolve 2.0 g in *water R* and dilute to 20 ml with the same solvent. 12 ml of the solution complies with test A. Prepare the reference solution using *lead standard solution (1 ppm Pb) R*.

**Water** (*2.5.12*)

Maximum 1.5 per cent, determined on 1.00 g.

**Sulphated ash** (*2.4.14*)

Maximum 0.1 per cent, determined on 1.0 g.

**Bacterial endotoxins** (*2.6.14*)

Less than 1.0 IU/g.

**ASSAY**

Liquid chromatography (*2.2.29*) as described in the test for impurity B with the following modifications.

*Injection*   Test solution and reference solutions (a) and (b).

*Identification of the isomers* The 2 principal peaks in the chromatogram obtained with reference solution (a) are due to iopromide isomers $Z_1$ and $Z_2$. The 2 peaks that have an increased size in the chromatogram obtained with reference solution (b) in comparison to the chromatogram obtained with reference solution (a), are due to iopromide isomers $E_1$ and $E_2$.

*Relative retention* With reference to iopromide isomer $Z_2$ (retention time = about 34 min):

iopromide isomer $E_1$ = about 0.70;

iopromide isomer $E_2$ = about 0.75;

iopromide isomer $Z_1$ = about 0.85.

*System suitability* Reference solution (a):

— *resolution*: minimum 2.0 between the peaks due to iopromide isomers $Z_1$ and $Z_2$.

Calculate the percentage content of iopromide from the declared content of *iopromide CRS* and from the sum of the areas of all of the peaks due to isomer groups E and Z.

## STORAGE

Protected from light.

## IMPURITIES

*Specified impurities*  A, B, C, D, E, F.

*Other detectable impurities* (The following substances would, if present at a sufficient level, be detected by one or other of the tests in the monograph. They are limited by the general acceptance criterion for other/unspecified impurities and/or by the general monograph *Substances for pharmaceutical use (2034)*. It is therefore not necessary to identify these impurities for demonstration of compliance. See also 5.10. *Control of impurities in substances for pharmaceutical use*): G, H.

A. R = H: 5-amino-*N,N'*-bis(2,3-dihydroxypropyl)-2,4,6-triiodo-*N*-methylbenzene-1,3-dicarboxamide,

B. R = CO-CH₃: 5-(acetylamino)-*N,N'*-bis(2,3-dihydroxypropyl)-2,4,6-triiodo-*N*-methylbenzene-1,3-dicarboxamide,

C. R = CO-CH₂OH: *N,N'*-bis(2,3-dihydroxypropyl)-5-[(hydroxyacetyl)amino]-2,4,6-triiodo-*N*-methylbenzene-1,3-dicarboxamide,

D. *N*-(2,3-dihydroxypropyl)-*N'*-[3-[[3-[(2,3-dihydroxypropyl)carbamoyl]-5-[(2,3-dihydroxypropyl)methylcarbamoyl]-2,4,6-triiodophenyl](methoxyacetyl)amino]-2-hydroxypropyl]-2,4,6-triiodo-5-[(methoxyacetyl)amino]-*N*-methylbenzene-1,3-dicarboxamide,

E. 3-[[3-[(2,3-dihydroxypropyl)carbamoyl]-2,4,6-triiodo-5-[(methoxyacetyl)amino]benzoyl]methylamino]-2-hydroxypropyl 3-[(2,3-dihydroxypropyl)carbamoyl]-2,4,6-triiodo-5-[(methoxyacetyl)amino]benzoate,

F. *N'*-(2,3-dihydroxypropyl)-*N*-[[2-(hydroxymethyl)-2-methyl-1,3-dioxolan-4-yl]methyl]-2,4,6-triiodo-5-[(methoxyacetyl)amino]-*N*-methylbenzene-1,3-dicarboxamide,

G. *N'*-(2-chloro-3-hydroxypropyl)-*N*-(2,3-dihydroxypropyl)-2,4,6-triiodo-5-[(methoxyacetyl)amino]-*N*-methylbenzene-1,3-dicarboxamide,

H. 3-[(2,3-dihydroxypropyl)carbamoyl]-2,4,6-triiodo-5-[(methoxyacetyl)amino]benzoic acid.

*_____ Ph Eur*

# Iotalamic Acid

(*Ph Eur monograph 0751*)

$C_{11}H_9I_3N_2O_4$      614      *2276-90-6*

## Action and use

Iodinated contrast medium.

*Ph Eur* _____

## DEFINITION

Iotalamic acid contains not less than 98.5 per cent and not more than the equivalent of 101.0 per cent of 3-(acetylamino)-2,4,6-tri-iodo-5-(methylcarbamoyl)benzoic acid, calculated with reference to the dried substance.

## CHARACTERS

A white or almost white powder, slightly soluble in water and in alcohol. It dissolves in dilute solutions of alkali hydroxides.

## IDENTIFICATION

*First identification*   A.

*Second identification*   B, C.

A. Examine by infrared absorption spectrophotometry (*2.2.24*), comparing with the spectrum obtained with *iotalamic acid CRS*.

B. Examine by thin-layer chromatography (*2.2.27*), using a *TLC silica gel GF₂₅₄ plate R*.

*Test solution*   Dissolve 50 mg of the substance to be examined in *methanol R* containing 3 per cent *V/V* of *ammonia R* and dilute to 5 ml with the same solvent.

*Reference solution*   Dissolve 50 mg of *iotalamic acid CRS* in *methanol R* containing 3 per cent *V/V* of *ammonia R* and dilute to 5 ml with the same solvent.

Apply separately to the plate 5 µl of each solution. Develop over a path of 15 cm using a mixture of 20 volumes of *anhydrous formic acid R*, 25 volumes of *methyl ethyl ketone R* and 60 volumes of *toluene R*. Allow the plate to dry until the solvents have evaporated and examine in ultraviolet light at 254 nm. The principal spot in the chromatogram obtained with the test solution is similar in position and size to the principal spot in the chromatogram obtained with the reference solution.

C. Heat 50 mg gently in a small porcelain dish over a flame. Violet vapour is evolved.

## TESTS

### Appearance of solution

Dissolve 1.0 g in *1 M sodium hydroxide* and dilute to 20 ml with the same solvent. The solution is clear (*2.2.1*) and colourless (*2.2.2, Method II*).

### Related substances

Examine by thin-layer chromatography (*2.2.27*), using a *TLC silica gel GF₂₅₄ plate R*.

*Test solution*   Dissolve 1.0 g of the substance to be examined in *methanol R* containing 3 per cent *V/V* of *ammonia R* and dilute to 10 ml with the same solvent.

*Reference solution (a)*   Dilute 1 ml of the test solution to 50 ml with *water R*. Dilute 1 ml of the solution to 10 ml with *water R*.

*Reference solution (b)*   Dissolve 1 mg of *iotalamic acid impurity A CRS* in 5 ml of reference solution (a).

Apply to the plate 5 µl of each solution. Develop over a path of 10 cm using a mixture of 1 volume of *glacial acetic acid R*, 1 volume of *anhydrous formic acid R*, 1 volume of *methanol R*, 5 volumes of *ether R* and 10 volumes of *methylene chloride R*. Allow the plate to dry until the solvents have evaporated. Examine in ultraviolet light at 254 nm. Any spot in the chromatogram obtained with the test solution, apart from the principal spot, is not more intense than the spot in the chromatogram obtained with reference solution (a) (0.2 per cent). The test is not valid unless the chromatogram obtained with reference solution (b) shows two clearly separated principal spots.

### Halides

Dissolve 0.55 g in a mixture of 4 ml of *dilute sodium hydroxide solution R* and 15 ml of *water R*. Add 6 ml of *dilute nitric acid R* and filter. 15 ml of the filtrate complies with the limit test for chlorides (*2.4.4*) (150 ppm, expressed as chloride).

### Impurity A

Not more than 0.05 per cent *m/m* determined by absorption spectrophotometry (*2.2.25*).

*Test solution*   Transfer 0.500 g of the substance to be examined to a 50 ml volumetric flask, add 14 ml of *water R*, shake and add 1 ml of *dilute sodium hydroxide solution R*.

*Reference solution*   Prepare the reference solution by mixing 10.0 ml of a 8.5 g/l solution of *sodium hydroxide R* containing 25 µg/ml of *iotalamic acid impurity A CRS* with 5 ml of *water R* in a 50 ml volumetric flask.

*Blank solution*   Transfer 14 ml of *water R* and 1 ml of *dilute sodium hydroxide solution R* to a 50 ml volumetric flask.

*In conducting the following steps, keep the flasks in iced water and protected as far as possible from light until all of the reagents have been added.*

Place all three of the flasks containing the test solution, the reference solution and the blank solution in iced water, protected from light. Add 5 ml of a 5 g/l solution of *sodium nitrite R* and 12 ml of *dilute hydrochloric acid R*. Shake gently and allow to stand for exactly 2 min after adding the hydrochloric acid. Add 10 ml of a 20 g/l solution of *ammonium sulphamate R*. Allow to stand for 5 min shaking frequently *(CAUTION: considerable pressure is produced)*, and add 0.15 ml of a 100 g/l solution of α-*naphthol R* in *alcohol R*. Shake and allow to stand for 5 min. Add 3.5 ml of *buffer solution pH 10.9 R*, mix and dilute to 50.0 ml with *water R*. Concomitantly and within 20 min determine the absorbance at 485 nm of the solutions obtained from the test solution and the reference solution in 5 cm cells, using the blank as the compensation liquid.

Calculate the content of impurity A.

### Iodide

Not more than 20 ppm, determined by potentiometric titration *(2.2.20)*. Dissolve 6.000 g in 20 ml of *1 M sodium hydroxide*, add 10 ml of *water R* and adjust to pH 4.5 to 5.5 with *acetic acid R*. Add 2.0 ml of *0.001 M potassium iodide*. Titrate with *0.001 M silver nitrate* using a silver indicator electrode and an appropriate reference electrode. Subtract the volume of titrant corresponding to the 2.0 ml of *0.001 M potassium iodide*, determined by titrating a blank to which is added 2.0 ml of *0.001 M potassium iodide* and use the residual value to calculate the iodide content.

1 ml of *0.001 M silver nitrate* is equivalent to 126.9 μg of iodide.

### Heavy metals *(2.4.8)*

Dissolve 2.0 g in 4 ml of *dilute sodium hydroxide solution R* and dilute to 20 ml with *water R*. 12 ml of this solution complies with limit test A for heavy metals (20 ppm). Prepare the standard using *lead standard solution (2 ppm Pb) R*.

### Loss on drying *(2.2.32)*

Not more than 0.5 per cent, determined on 0.300 g by drying in an oven at 105 °C.

### Sulphated ash *(2.4.14)*

Not more than 0.1 per cent, determined on 1.0 g.

### ASSAY

To 0.150 g in a 250 ml round-bottomed flask add 5 ml of *strong sodium hydroxide solution R*, 20 ml of *water R*, 1 g of *zinc powder R* and a few glass beads. Boil under a reflux condenser for 30 min. Allow to cool and rinse the condenser with 20 ml of *water R*, adding the rinsings to the flask. Filter through a sintered-glass filter *(2.1.2)* and wash the filter with several quantities of *water R*. Collect the filtrate and washings. Add 40 ml of *dilute sulphuric acid R* and titrate immediately with *0.1 M silver nitrate*. Determine the end-point potentiometrically *(2.2.20)*, using a suitable electrode system such as silver-mercurous sulphate.

1 ml of *0.1 M silver nitrate* is equivalent to 20.47 mg of $C_{11}H_9I_3N_2O_4$.

### STORAGE

Store protected from light.

### IMPURITIES

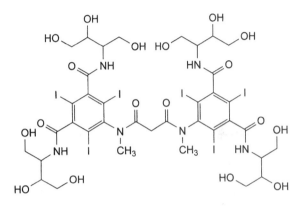

A. 3-amino-2,4,6-triiodo-5-(methylcarbamoyl)benzoic acid.

*Ph Eur*

# Iotrolan

*(Ph Eur monograph 1754)*

$C_{37}H_{48}I_6N_6O_{18}$       1626       *79770-24-4*

### Action and use

Iodinated contrast medium.

*Ph Eur*

### DEFINITION

Mixture of stereoisomers of 5,5′-[propanedioylbis(methylimino)]bis[N,N′-bis[2,3-dihydroxy-1-(hydroxymethyl)propyl]2,4,6-triiodobenzene-1,3-dicarboxamide].

### Content

98.0 per cent to 102.0 per cent (anhydrous substance).

### CHARACTERS

#### Appearance

White or yellowish-white powder, hygroscopic.

#### Solubility

Very soluble in water, freely soluble in dimethyl sulphoxide, practically insoluble in ethanol (96 per cent).

### IDENTIFICATION

Infrared absorption spectrophotometry *(2.2.24)*.

*Comparison*    iotrolan CRS.

### TESTS

#### Appearance of solution

The solution is clear *(2.2.1)* and not more intensely coloured than reference solution $BY_6$ *(2.2.2, Method II)*.

Dissolve 18.0 g in *carbon dioxide-free water R* and dilute to 20.0 ml with the same solvent.

#### Conductivity *(2.2.28)*

Maximum 25 μS·cm$^{-1}$.

Dissolve 1.000 g in *water R* and dilute to 50.0 ml with the same solvent.

**Primary aromatic amines**

*Protect the solutions from light throughout the test. All given times are critical for the test results. The test solution, the reference solution and the blank solution must be processed in parallel.*

*Test solution*   Dissolve 0.500 g of the substance to be examined in 20.0 ml of *water R* in a 25 ml volumetric flask.

*Reference solution*   Dissolve 5.0 mg of *iopamidol impurity A CRS* in *water R* and dilute to 20.0 ml with the same solvent. Transfer 1.0 ml of this solution to a 25 ml volumetric flask and add 19.0 ml of *water R*.

*Blank solution*   Place 20.0 ml of *water R* in a 25 ml volumetric flask.

*Procedure*   Cool the test solution, reference solution and blank solution in a bath of iced water for 5 min. Add 1.0 ml of *hydrochloric acid R1* to each solution and cool again for 5 min in a bath of iced water. Add 1.0 ml of a 20 g/l solution of *sodium nitrite R*, shake vigorously and cool for another 5 min in a bath of iced water. To each solution add 0.50 ml of an 80 g/l solution of *sulphamic acid R*. Over the next 5 min, shake vigorously several times, raising the stoppers to vent the gas that evolves. Afterwards add to each solution 1.0 ml of a 1 g/l solution of *naphthylethylenediamine dihydrochloride R* in a mixture of 300 volumes of *water R* and 700 volumes of *propylene glycol R*, shake, allow to cool to room temperature for 10 min and dilute to 25.0 ml with *water R*. Degas the solutions in an ultrasonic bath for 1 min and measure the absorbance (*2.2.25*) of the test solution and the reference solution at 495 nm against the blank, within 5 min.

*System suitability:*
— *absorbance of the reference solution*: minimum 0.40.

*Limit:*
— *absorbance of the test solution*: not more than the absorbance of the reference solution (0.05 per cent).

**Related substances**

Thin-layer chromatography (*2.2.27*). *Prepare the solutions immediately before use.*

*Test solution*   Dissolve 1.0 g of the substance to be examined in a mixture of equal volumes of *methanol R* and *water R* and dilute to 10.0 ml with the same mixture of solvents.

*Reference solution (a)*   Dilute 1.0 ml of the test solution to 200.0 ml with a mixture of equal volumes of *methanol R* and *water R*.

*Reference solution (b)*   Dilute 2.0 ml of reference solution (a) to 10.0 ml with a mixture of equal volumes of *methanol R* and *water R*.

*Reference solution (c)*   Dissolve the contents of a vial of *iotrolan for system suitability CRS* (containing about 0.05 per cent of each of impurities A and B) in 50 μl of a mixture of equal volumes of *methanol R* and *water R*.

*Plate*   TLC silica gel $F_{254}$ plate R.

*Pretreatment*   Over 3/4 of the plate with *methylene chloride R*.

*Mobile phase*   concentrated ammonia R, water R, dioxan R (4:20:80 *V/V/V*).

*Application*   2 μl.

*Development*   Over 3/4 of the plate.

*Drying*   In a current of air until the solvents have evaporated.

*Detection*   Examine in ultraviolet light at 254 nm. Expose the plate to the ultraviolet light for 2–5 min until the principal spots appear clearly as yellow spots. Spray with *ferric chloride-ferricyanide-arsenite reagent R* and examine in daylight.

*$R_F$ values*   Iotrolan = about 0.25; impurity A = about 0.4; impurity B = about 0.5.

*System suitability*   Reference solution (c):
— the chromatogram shows 3 clearly separated spots.

*Limits:*
— *impurities A, B*: any spot due to impurity A or B is not more intense than the principal spot in the chromatogram obtained with reference solution (a) (0.5 per cent);
— *unspecified impurities*: any other spot is not more intense than the principal spot in the chromatogram obtained with reference solution (b) (0.10 per cent).

**Isomer distribution**

Liquid chromatography (*2.2.29*) as described under Assay. Use the normalisation procedure.

*Identification of peaks*   Use the chromatogram supplied with *iotrolan CRS* and the chromatogram obtained with the reference solution to identify the peaks due to the 3 isomer groups.

Calculate the percentage content of each of the isomer groups G1, G2 and G3, with reference to the total area of all of the peaks due to the 3 isomer groups, using the chromatogram obtained with the test solution.

*Limits:*
— *isomer group G1*: 53.0 per cent to 70.0 per cent;
— *isomer group G2*: 3.0 per cent to 11.0 per cent;
— *isomer group G3*: 25.0 per cent to 39.0 per cent.

**Free iodine**

Dissolve 0.20 g in 1 ml of *water R* in a glass-stoppered test tube. Add 4 ml of a 370 g/l solution of *sulphuric acid R* and 5 ml of *toluene R*, close and shake vigorously. The upper layer remains colourless (*2.2.2, Method II*).

**Iodide**

Maximum 20 ppm.

Dissolve 10.0 g in 50 ml of *carbon dioxide-free water R*. Adjust to pH 3–4 adding about 0.15 ml of *dilute sulphuric acid R*. Titrate with *0.001 M silver nitrate*, determining the end-point potentiometrically (*2.2.20*). Not more than 1.5 ml of *0.001 M silver nitrate* is required to reach the end-point.

**Heavy metals** (*2.4.8*)

Maximum 10 ppm.

Dissolve 2.0 g in w*ater R* and dilute to 20 ml with the same solvent. 12 ml of the solution complies with test A. Prepare the reference solution using *lead standard solution (1 ppm Pb) R*.

**Water** (*2.5.12*)

Maximum 3.5 per cent, determined on 0.250 g.

**Sulphated ash** (*2.4.14*)

Maximum 0.1 per cent, determined on 1.0 g.

**Bacterial endotoxins** (*2.6.14*)

Less than 0.7 IU/g.

**ASSAY**

Liquid chromatography (*2.2.29*).

*Test solution*   Dissolve 40.0 mg of the substance to be examined in *water R* and dilute to 25.0 ml with the same solvent.

*Reference solution*   Dissolve 40.0 mg of *iotrolan CRS* in *water R* and dilute to 25.0 ml with the same solvent.

*Column:*
— *size*: $l = 0.25$ m, $\emptyset = 4.6$ mm;

— *stationary phase: end-capped octadecylsilyl silica gel for chromatography R (5 μm)*;
— *temperature*: 40 °C.

*Mobile phase* methanol R, water for chromatography R (10:90 V/V).

*Flow rate* 0.5 ml/min.

*Detection* Spectrophotometer at 254 nm.

*Injection* 10 μl.

*Run time* 40 min.

*Retention time* Isomer group G1 = about 8 min to 12 min; isomer group G2 = about 15 min to 22 min; isomer group G3 = about 22 min to 32 min.

*System suitability* Reference solution:
— the chromatogram obtained is similar to the chromatogram supplied with *iotrolan CRS*.

Calculate the percentage content of iotrolan from the total area of all of the peaks of the 3 isomer groups G1, G2 and G3 and the declared content of *iotrolan CRS*.

## STORAGE
In an airtight container, protected from light.

## IMPURITIES
*Specified impurities* A, B.

*Other detectable impurities* (the following substances would, if present at a sufficient level, be detected by one or other of the tests in the monograph. They are limited by the general acceptance criterion for other/unspecified impurities and/or by the general monograph *Substances for pharmaceutical use (2034)*. It is therefore not necessary to identify these impurities for demonstration of compliance. See also *5.10. Control of impurities in substances for pharmaceutical use)*:
C, D, E, F, G, H, I, J.

A. *N,N'*-bis[2,3-dihydroxy-1-(hydroxymethyl)propyl]-5-[[3-[[3-[[2,3-dihydroxy-1-(hydroxymethyl)propyl]carbamoyl]-5-[(6-hydroxy-2,2-dimethyl-1,3-dioxepan-5-yl)carbamoyl]-2,4,6-triiodophenyl]methylamino]-3-oxopropanoyl]methylamino]-2,4,6-triiodobenzene-1,3-dicarboxamide,

B. R = CO-CH₃: 5-(acetylmethylamino)-*N,N'*-bis[2,3-dihydroxy-1-(hydroxymethyl)propyl]-2,4,6-triiodobenzene-1,3-dicarboxamide,

C. R = CO-CH₂-CO₂H: 3-[[3,5-bis[[2,3-dihydroxy-1-(hydroxymethyl)propyl]carbamoyl]-2,4,6-triiodophenyl]methylamino]-3-oxopropanoic acid,

E. R = H: *N,N'*-bis[2,3-dihydroxy-1-(hydroxymethyl)propyl]-2,4,6-triiodo-5-(methylamino)benzene-1,3-dicarboxamide,

D. 3-[[3-[[3,5-bis[[2,3-dihydroxy-1-(hydroxymethyl)propyl]carbamoyl]-2,4,6-triiodophenyl]methylamino]-3-oxopropanoyl]methylamino]-5-[[2,3-dihydroxy-1-(hydroxymethyl)propyl]carbamoyl]-2,4,6-triiodobenzoic acid,

F. R = OH: 5,5'-[propanedioylbis(methylimino)]bis[2,4,6-triiodobenzene-1,3-dicarboxylic] acid,

G. R = Cl: 5,5'-[propanedioylbis(methylimino)]bis[2,4,6-triiodobenzene-1,3-dicarbonyl] tetrachloride,

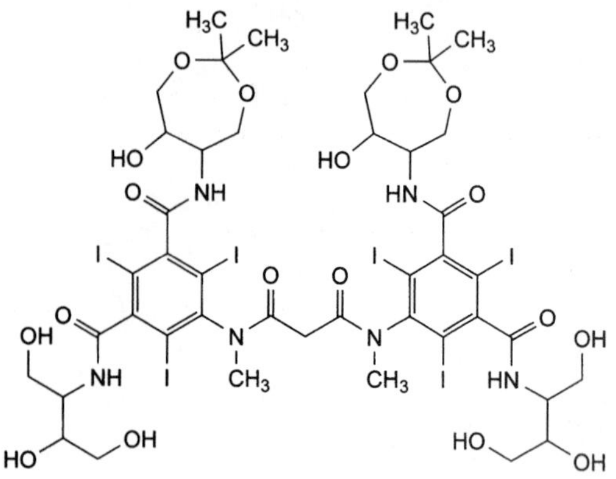

H. 5,5′-[propanedioylbis(methylimino)]bis[*N*-[2,3-dihydroxy-1-(hydroxymethyl)propyl]-*N*′-(6-hydroxy-2,2-dimethyl-1,3-dioxepan-5-yl)-2,4,6-triiodobenzene-1,3-dicarboxamide],

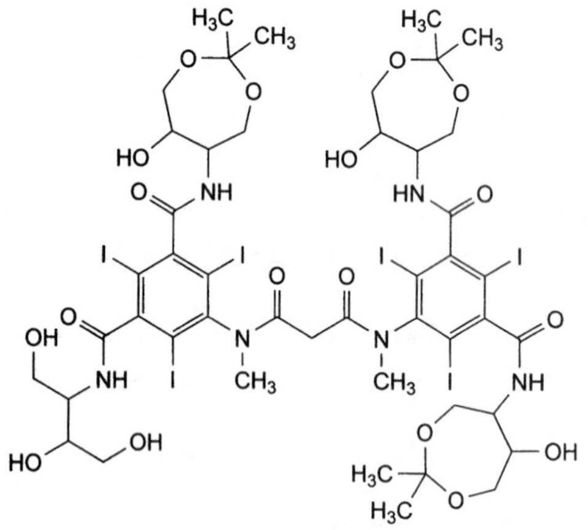

I. 5-[[3-[[3-[[2,3-dihydroxy-1-(hydroxymethyl)propyl]carbamoyl]-5-[(6-hydroxy-2,2-dimethyl-1,3-dioxepan-5-yl)carbamoyl]-2,4,6-triiodophenyl]methylamino]-3-oxopropanoyl]methylamino]-*N*,*N*′-bis(6-hydroxy-2,2-dimethyl-1,3-dioxepan-5-yl)-2,4,6-triiodobenzene-1,3-dicarboxamide,

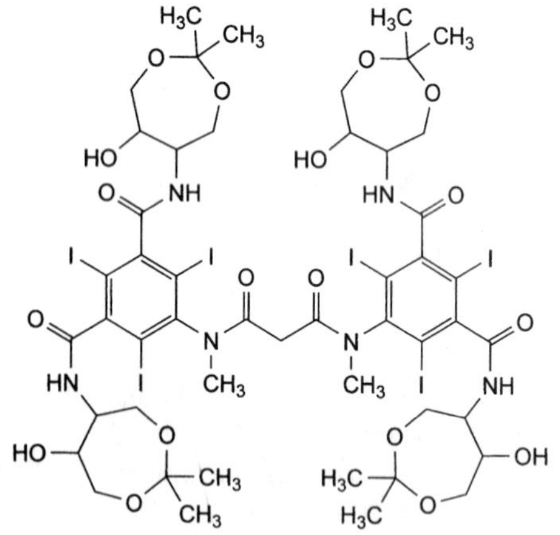

J. 5,5′-[propanedioylbis(methylimino)]bis[*N*,*N*′-bis(6-hydroxy-2,2-dimethyl-1,3-dioxepan-5-yl)-2,4,6-triiodobenzene-1,3-dicarboxamide].

*Ph Eur*

# Ioxaglic Acid

*(Ph Eur monograph 2009)*

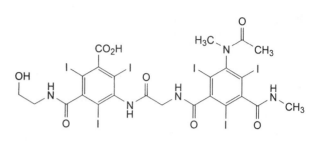

C$_{24}$H$_{21}$I$_6$N$_5$O$_8$          1269          *59017-64-0*

**Action and use**

Iodinated contrast medium.

*Ph Eur*

## DEFINITION

3-[[[[3-(Acetylmethylamino)-2,4,6-triiodo-5-(methylcarbamoyl)benzoyl]amino]acetyl]amino]-5-[(2-hydroxyethyl)carbamoyl]-2,4,6-triiodobenzoic acid.

**Content**

98.5 per cent to 101.5 per cent (anhydrous substance).

## CHARACTERS

**Appearance**

White or almost white powder, hygroscopic.

**Solubility**

Very slightly soluble in water, slightly soluble in alcohol, very slightly soluble in methylene chloride. It dissolves in dilute solutions of alkali hydroxides.

## IDENTIFICATION

Infrared absorption spectrophotometry *(2.2.24)*.

*Comparison*   ioxaglic acid CRS.

## TESTS

**Appearance of solution**

The solution is clear *(2.2.1)*.

Dissolve 1.0 g in a 40 g/l solution of *sodium hydroxide R* and dilute to 20 ml with the same solution.

**Absorbance** *(2.2.25)*

Maximum 0.18, calculated for a solution containing 40 per cent of *anhydrous ioxaglic acid*.

Dissolve 10.0 g in about 8 ml of a 40 g/l solution of *sodium hydroxide R*. Adjust to pH 7.2-7.6 with a 40 g/l solution of *sodium hydroxide R* or *1 M hydrochloric acid*. Dilute to 25 ml with *water R*. Filter using a filter of 0.45 μm pore size. Measure the absorbance at 450 nm using *water R* as the compensation liquid.

**Related substances**

Liquid chromatography *(2.2.29)*: use the normalisation procedure.

*Test solution*   Dissolve 0.10 g of the substance to be examined in about 40 ml of a mixture of 5 volumes of *acetonitrile R* and 95 volumes of *water R*. Add 0.5 ml ± 0.1 ml of a 4 g/l solution of *sodium hydroxide R* and dilute to 50.0 ml with a mixture of 5 volumes of *acetonitrile R* and 95 volumes of *water R*. Shake until dissolution is complete (using ultrasound, if necessary).

*Reference solution (a)*   Dissolve 0.10 g of *ioxaglic acid CRS* in about 40 ml of a mixture of 5 volumes of *acetonitrile R* and 95 volumes of *water R*. Add 0.5 ml ± 0.1 ml of a 4 g/l solution of *sodium hydroxide R* and dilute to 50.0 ml with a mixture of 5 volumes of *acetonitrile R* and 95 volumes of *water R*. Shake until dissolution is complete (using ultrasound, if necessary).

*Reference solution (b)*  Dissolve 5 mg of *ioxaglic acid impurity A CRS* in a mixture of 5 volumes of *acetonitrile R* and 95 volumes of *water R* and dilute to 50.0 ml with the same mixture of solvents. Dilute 1.0 ml of the solution to 50.0 ml with a mixture of 5 volumes of *acetonitrile R* and 95 volumes of *water R*.

*Column*:
— *size*: l = 0.25 m, Ø = 4.6 mm,
— *stationary phase*: spherical end-capped *octylsilyl silica gel for chromatography R* (5 μm) with a specific surface area of not less than 335 m$^2$/g, a pore size of 10 nm and a carbon loading of not less than 12 per cent,
— *temperature*: 25 °C.

*Mobile phase*:
— *mobile phase A*: 136 mg/l solution of *potassium dihydrogen phosphate R* adjusted to pH 3.0 with *phosphoric acid R*,
— *mobile phase B*: *acetonitrile R*,

| Time (min) | Mobile phase A (per cent *V/V*) | Mobile phase B (per cent *V/V*) |
|---|---|---|
| 0 - 5 | 95 → 90 | 5 → 10 |
| 5 - 40 | 90 | 10 |
| 40 - 85 | 90 → 70 | 10 → 30 |
| 85 - 115 | 70 | 30 |
| 115 - 120 | 70 → 50 | 30 → 50 |
| 120 - 125 | 50 | 50 |
| 125 - 130 | 50 → 95 | 50 → 5 |
| 130 - 140 | 95 | 5 |

*Flow rate*  0.8 ml/min.

*Detection*  Spectrophotometer at 242 nm.

*Injection*  10 μl.

*System suitability*:
— *retention time*: ioxaglic acid = about 65 min (reference solution (a)), impurity A = about 22 min (reference solution (b)),
— the chromatogram obtained with reference solution (a) is similar to the chromatogram provided with *ioxaglic acid CRS*,
— *peak-to-valley ratio*: minimum 1.3, where $H_p$ = height above the baseline of the peak due to impurity C and $H_v$ = height above the baseline of the lowest point of the curve separating this peak from the peak due to ioxaglic acid in the chromatogram obtained with reference solution (a).

*Limit*  Locate the impurities by comparison with the chromatogram provided with *ioxaglic acid CRS*.
— *impurity A*: not more than 0.1 per cent,
— *impurity B*: not more than 0.3 per cent,
— *impurity C*: not more than 0.3 per cent,
— *impurity E*: not more than 0.7 per cent,
— *impurity F*: not more than 0.4 per cent,
— *impurity D (sum of the peaks D1, D2, D3 and D4)*: not more than 0.7 per cent,
— *any other impurity*: not more than 0.2 per cent,
— *total*: not more than 2 per cent,
— *disregard limit*: 0.05 per cent; disregard any peak appearing at a retention time greater than 125 min.

**Iodides**

Maximum 50 ppm.

Disperse 10.0 g in 50 ml of *water R*. Add 8 ml of *1 M sodium hydroxide*. After dissolution and homogenisation, add 1.0 ml of *glacial acetic acid R*. Immediately titrate with *0.001 M silver nitrate*, determining the end-point potentiometrically (2.2.20), using a silver indicator electrode and a suitable reference electrode.

1 ml of *0.001 M silver nitrate* is equivalent to 0.1269 mg of iodides.

**Heavy metals** (2.4.8)
Maximum 10 ppm.

Dissolve 2.0 g in 4 ml of a 40 g/l solution of *sodium hydroxide R* and dilute to 20 ml with *water R*. 12 ml of the solution complies with limit test A. Prepare the standard using 1 ml of *lead standard solution (10 ppm Pb) R*.

**Water** (2.5.12)
Maximum 5.0 per cent, determined on 0.100 g.

**Sulphated ash** (2.4.14)
Maximum 0.1 per cent, determined on 1.0 g.

**ASSAY**

In a round-bottomed flask, place 0.100 g of the substance to be examined, add 5 ml of *strong sodium hydroxide solution R*, 20 ml of *water R*, 1 g of *zinc powder R* and a few glass beads. Fit the flask with a reflux condenser and boil for 30 min. Cool and rinse the condenser with 20 ml of *water R*. Add the rinsing liquid to the contents of the flask. Filter, wash the filter 3 times with 15 ml of *water R* and add the washings to the filtrate. Add 40 ml of *dilute sulphuric acid R* and titrate immediately with *0.05 M silver nitrate*. Determine the end-point potentiometrically (2.2.20), using a suitable electrode combination such as the silver/mercurous sulphate system.

1 ml of *0.05 M silver nitrate* is equivalent to 10.58 mg of $C_{24}H_{21}I_6N_5O_8$.

**STORAGE**

In an airtight container, protected from light.

**IMPURITIES**

A. Ar-NH$_2$: 3-amino-5-[(2-hydroxyethyl)carbamoyl]-2,4,6-triiodobenzoic acid,

B. 3-[[[[3-(acetylmethylamino)-2,6-diiodo-5-(methylcarbamoyl)benzoyl]amino]acetyl]amino]-5-[(2-hydroxyethyl)carbamoyl]-2,4,6-triiodobenzoic acid,

C. specified impurity whose structure is unknown,

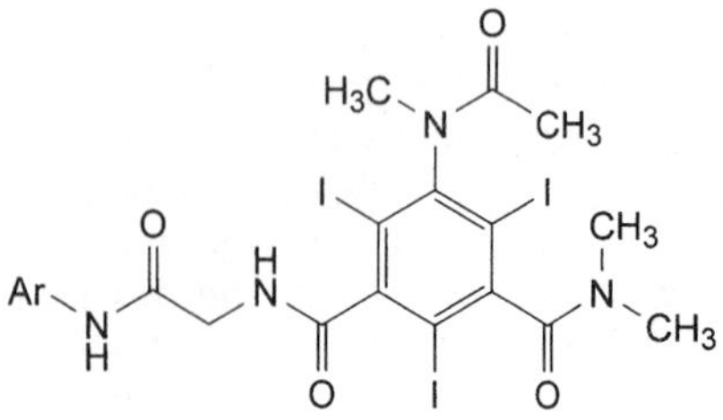

D. D1, D2, D3 and D4:
3-[[[[3-(acetylmethylamino)-5-(dimethylcarbamoyl)-2,4,6-triiodobenzoyl]amino]acetyl]amino]-5-[(2-hydroxyethyl)carbamoyl]-2,4,6-triiodobenzoic acid,

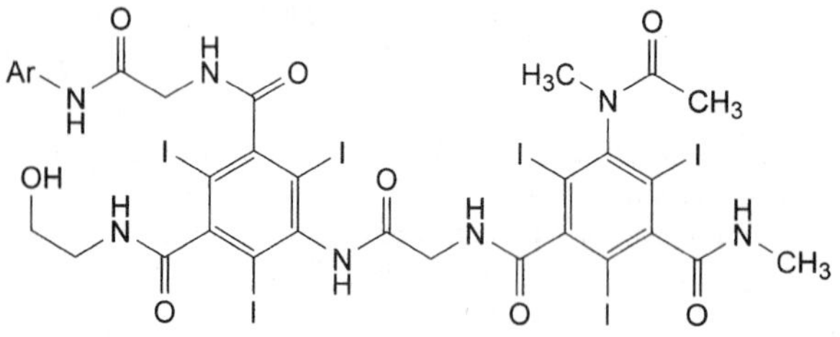

E. 3-[[[[3-[[[[3-(acetylmethylamino)-2,4,6-triiodo-5-(methylcarbamoyl)benzoyl]amino]acetyl]amino]-5-[(2-hydroxyethyl)carbamoyl]-2,4,6-triiodobenzoyl]amino]acetyl]amino]-5-[(2-hydroxyethyl)carbamoyl]-2,4,6-triiodobenzoic acid,

F. specified impurity whose structure is unknown,

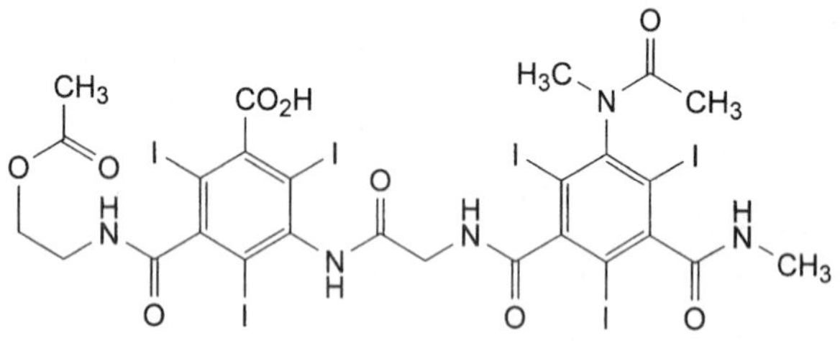

G. 3-[[[[3-(acetylmethylamino)-2,4,6-triiodo-5-(methylcarbamoyl)benzoyl]amino]acetyl]amino]-5-[[2-(acetyloxy)ethyl]carbamoyl]-2,4,6-triiodobenzoic acid,

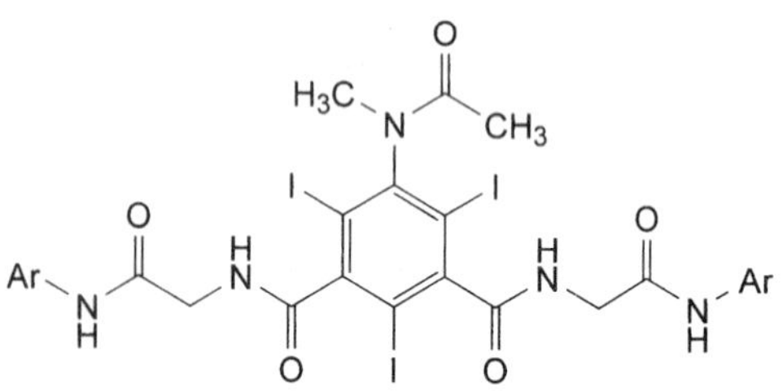

H. 3,3'-[[5-(acetylmethylamino)-2,4,6-triiodo-1,3-phenylene]bis(carbonyliminomethylenecarbonylimino)]bis[5-[(2-hydroxyethyl)carbamoyl]-2,4,6-triiodobenzoic] acid.

*Ph Eur*

# Ipratropium Bromide

*(Ph Eur monograph 0919)*

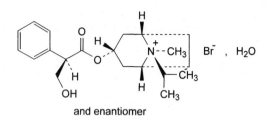

and enantiomer

$C_{20}H_{30}BrNO_3,H_2O$     430.4     *66985-17-9*

## Action and use
Anticholinergic (antimuscarinic) bronchodilator.

## Preparations
Ipratropium Nebuliser Solution
Ipratropium Powder for Inhalation
Ipratropium Pressurised Inhalation

*Ph Eur*

## DEFINITION
(1R,3r,5S,8r)-3-[[(2RS)-3-Hydroxy-2-phenylpropanoyl]oxy]-8-methyl-8-(1-methylethyl)-8-azoniabicyclo[3.2.1]octane bromide monohydrate.

## Content
99.0 per cent to 100.5 per cent (anhydrous substance).

## CHARACTERS
### Appearance
White or almost white, crystalline powder.

### Solubility
Soluble in water, freely soluble in methanol, slightly soluble in ethanol (96 per cent).

mp: about 230 °C, with decomposition.

## IDENTIFICATION
*First identification* A, E.

*Second identification* B, C, D, E.

A. Infrared absorption spectrophotometry (*2.2.24*).

*Comparison* ipratropium bromide CRS.

B. Examine the chromatograms obtained in the test for impurity A.

*Results* The principal spot in the chromatogram obtained with the test solution is similar in position, colour and size to the principal spot in the chromatogram obtained with reference solution (a).

C. To 5 ml of solution S (see Tests), add 2 ml of *dilute sodium hydroxide solution R*. No precipitate is formed.

D. To about 1 mg add 0.2 ml of *nitric acid R* and evaporate to dryness on a water-bath. Dissolve the residue in 2 ml of *acetone R* and add 0.1 ml of a 30 g/l solution of *potassium hydroxide R* in *methanol R*. A violet colour develops.

E. It gives reaction (a) of bromides (*2.3.1*).

## TESTS
### Solution S
Dissolve 0.50 g in *carbon dioxide-free water R* and dilute to 50.0 ml with the same solvent.

### Appearance of solution
Solution S is clear (*2.2.1*) and not more intensely coloured than reference solution $GY_7$ (*2.2.2, Method II*).

**pH** (*2.2.3*)

5.0 to 7.5 for solution S.

**Impurity A**

Thin-layer chromatography (*2.2.27*).

*Test solution*  Dissolve 20 mg of the substance to be examined in *methanol R* and dilute to 1.0 ml with the same solvent.

*Reference solution (a)*  Dissolve 20 mg of *ipratropium bromide CRS* in *methanol R* and dilute to 1.0 ml with the same solvent.

*Reference solution (b)*  Dissolve 20 mg of *methylatropine bromide CRS* in 1.0 ml of reference solution (a).

*Reference solution (c)*  Dissolve 5 mg of *ipratropium impurity A CRS* in 100.0 ml of *methanol R*. Dilute 2.0 ml of the solution to 5.0 ml with *methanol R*.

*Plate*  TLC silica gel plate R (2-10 μm).

*Mobile phase*  anhydrous formic acid R, water R, ethanol (96 per cent) R, methylene chloride R (1:3:18:18 V/V/V/V).

*Application*  1 μl.

*Development*  Over a path of 6 cm.

*Drying*  At 60 °C for 15 min.

*Detection*  Spray with *potassium iodobismuthate solution R*, allow the plate to dry in air, spray with a 50 g/l solution of *sodium nitrite R* and protect immediately with a sheet of glass.

*System suitability*  The chromatogram obtained with reference solution (b) shows 2 clearly separated principal spots.

*Limit:*

— *impurity A*: any spot due to impurity A is not more intense than the principal spot in the chromatogram obtained with reference solution (c) (0.1 per cent).

**Related substances**

Liquid chromatography (*2.2.29*).

*Test solution*  Dissolve 0.200 g of the substance to be examined in the mobile phase and dilute to 20.0 ml with the mobile phase.

*Reference solution (a)*  Dissolve 10.0 mg of *ipratropium bromide CRS* in the mobile phase and dilute to 20.0 ml with the mobile phase. Dilute 1.0 ml of the solution to 50.0 ml with the mobile phase.

*Reference solution (b)*  Dissolve 5 mg of *ipratropium bromide CRS* and 5 mg of *ipratropium impurity B CRS* in 1 ml of *methanol R* and dilute to 25.0 ml with the mobile phase. Dilute 1.0 ml of the solution to 20.0 ml with the mobile phase.

*Column:*

— *size*: l = 0.15 m, Ø = 3.9 mm;
— *stationary phase*: octadecylsilyl silica gel for chromatography R (5 μm);
— *temperature*: 30 °C.

*Mobile phase*  Dissolve 12.4 g of *sodium dihydrogen phosphate R* and 1.7 g of *tetrapropylammonium chloride R* in 870 ml of *water R*; adjust to pH 5.5 with a 180 g/l solution of *disodium hydrogen phosphate R* and add 130 ml of *methanol R*.

*Flow rate*  1.5 ml/min.

*Detection*  Spectrophotometer at 220 nm.

*Injection*  5 μl.

*Run time*  6 times the retention time of ipratropium.

*Relative retention*  With reference to ipratropium (retention time = about 4.9 min): impurity C = about 0.7;

impurity B = about 1.2; impurity D = about 1.8; impurity E = about 2.3; impurity F = about 5.1.

*System suitability*  Reference solution (b):

— *resolution*: minimum 3.0 between the peaks due to impurity B and ipratropium;
— *symmetry factor*: maximum 2.5 for the principal peak.

*Limits:*

— *correction factors*: for the calculation of content, multiply the peak areas of the following impurities by the corresponding correction factor: impurity C = 0.3; impurity D = 0.2; impurity F = 0.5;
— *impurity D*: not more than 0.5 times the area of the principal peak in the chromatogram obtained with reference solution (a) (0.05 per cent);
— *impurities B, C*: for each impurity, not more than the area of the principal peak in the chromatogram obtained with reference solution (a) (0.1 per cent);
— *unspecified impurities*: for each impurity, not more than the area of the principal peak in the chromatogram obtained with reference solution (a) (0.10 per cent);
— *total*: not more than 2.5 times the area of the principal peak in the chromatogram obtained with reference solution (a) (0.25 per cent);
— *disregard limit*: one-third of the area of the principal peak in the chromatogram obtained with reference solution (a) (0.03 per cent); disregard the peak due to the bromide ion.

**Water** (*2.5.12*)

3.9 per cent to 4.4 per cent, determined on 0.50 g.

**Sulphated ash** (*2.4.14*)

Maximum 0.1 per cent, determined on 1.0 g.

**ASSAY**

Dissolve 0.350 g in 50 ml of *water R* and add 3 ml of *dilute nitric acid R*. Titrate with *0.1 M silver nitrate*, determining the end-point potentiometrically (*2.2.20*).

1 ml of *0.1 M silver nitrate* is equivalent to 41.24 mg of $C_{20}H_{30}BrNO_3$.

**IMPURITIES**

*Specified impurities*  A, B, C, D.

*Other detectable impurities* (the following substances would, if present at a sufficient level, be detected by one or other of the tests in the monograph. They are limited by the general acceptance criterion for other/unspecified impurities and/or by the general monograph *Substances for pharmaceutical use (2034)*. It is therefore not necessary to identify these impurities for demonstration of compliance. See also *5.10*. *Control of impurities in substances for pharmaceutical use*): E, F.

A. (1R,3r,5S,8r)-3-hydroxy-8-methyl-8-(1-methylethyl)-8-azoniabicyclo[3.2.1]octane,

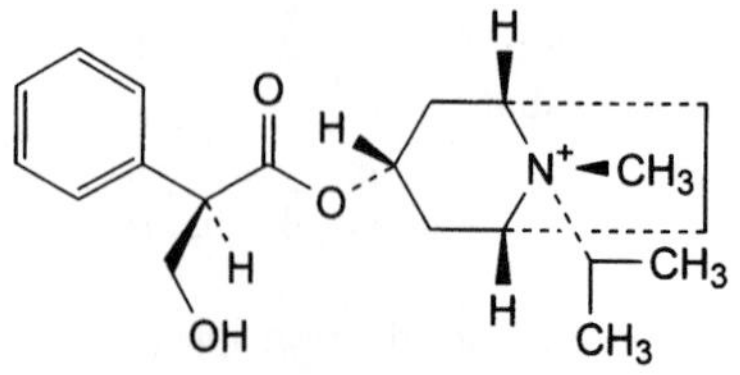

B. (1R,3r,5S,8s)-3-[[(2RS)-3-hydroxy-2-phenylpropanoyl]oxy]-8-methyl-8-(1-methylethyl)-8-azoniabicyclo[3.2.1]octane,

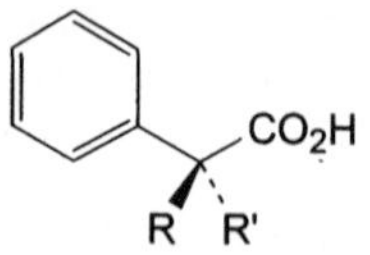

and enantiomer

C. R = CH₂-OH, R′ = H:
(2RS)-3-hydroxy-2-phenylpropanoic acid (DL-tropic acid),
D. R + R′ = CH₂: 2-phenylpropenoic acid (atropic acid),

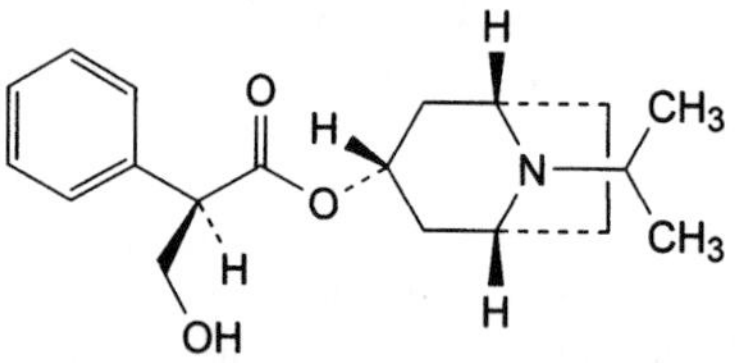

and enantiomer

E. (1R,3r,5S)-8-(1-methylethyl)-8-azabicyclo[3.2.1]oct-3-yl (2RS)-3-hydroxy-2-phenylpropanoate,

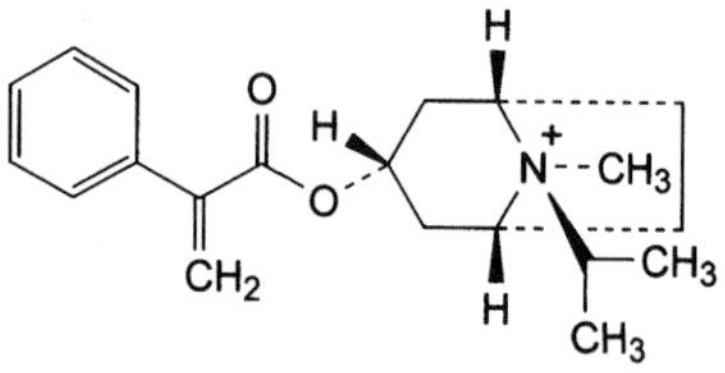

and enantiomer

F. (1R,3r,5S,8r)-8-methyl-8-(1-methylethyl)-3-[(2-phenylpropenoyl)oxy]-8-azoniabicyclo[3.2.1]octane.

_____ Ph Eur

# Isoconazole

(Ph Eur monograph 1018)

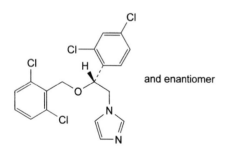

and enantiomer

$C_{18}H_{14}Cl_4N_2O$        416.1        27523-40-6

**Action and use**
Antifungal.

Ph Eur _____

## DEFINITION
1-[(2RS)-2-[(2,6-Dichlorobenzyl)oxy]-2-(2,4-dichlorophenyl)ethyl]-1H-imidazole.

## Content
99.0 per cent to 101.0 per cent (dried substance).

## CHARACTERS
### Appearance
White or almost white powder.

### Solubility
Practically insoluble in water, very soluble in methanol, freely soluble in ethanol (96 per cent).

## IDENTIFICATION
*First identification*   A, B.

*Second identification*   A, C, D.

A. Melting point (2.2.14): 111 °C to 115 °C.

B. Infrared absorption spectrophotometry (2.2.24).

*Preparation*   Discs.

*Comparison*   isoconazole CRS.

C. Thin-layer chromatography (2.2.27).

*Test solution*   Dissolve 30 mg of the substance to be examined in *methanol R* and dilute to 5 ml with the same solvent.

*Reference solution (a)*   Dissolve 30 mg of isoconazole CRS in *methanol R* and dilute to 5 ml with the same solvent.

*Reference solution (b)*   Dissolve 30 mg of isoconazole CRS and 30 mg of econazole nitrate CRS in *methanol R*, then dilute to 5 ml with the same solvent.

*Plate*   TLC octadecylsilyl silica gel plate R.

*Mobile phase*   ammonium acetate solution R, dioxan R, methanol R (20:40:40 V/V/V).

*Application*   5 µl.

*Development*   Over a path of 15 cm.

*Drying*   In a current of warm air for 15 min.

*Detection*   Expose to iodine vapour until the spots appear and examine in daylight.

*System suitability*   Reference solution (b):
— the chromatogram shows 2 clearly separated spots.

*Results*   The principal spot in the chromatogram obtained with the test solution is similar in position, colour and size to the principal spot in the chromatogram obtained with reference solution (a).

D. To about 30 mg in a porcelain crucible add 0.3 g of *anhydrous sodium carbonate R*. Heat over an open flame for 10 min. Allow to cool. Take up the residue with 5 ml of *dilute nitric acid R* and filter. To 1 ml of the filtrate add 1 ml of *water R*. The solution gives reaction (a) of chlorides (2.3.1).

## TESTS
### Solution S
Dissolve 0.20 g in *methanol R* and dilute to 20.0 ml with the same solvent.

### Appearance of solution
Solution S is clear (2.2.1) and not more intensely coloured than reference solution $Y_6$ (2.2.2, Method II).

### Optical rotation (2.2.7)
− 0.10° to + 0.10°, determined on solution S.

### Related substances
Liquid chromatography (2.2.29).

*Test solution*   Dissolve 0.100 g of the substance to be examined in 3.2 ml of *methanol R*. Add 3.0 ml of *acetonitrile R* and dilute to 10.0 ml with a solution of *ammonium acetate R* (6.0 g in 380 ml of *water R*).

*Reference solution (a)* Dissolve 2.5 mg of *isoconazole CRS* and 2.5 mg of *econazole nitrate CRS* in the mobile phase, then dilute to 100.0 ml with the mobile phase.

*Reference solution (b)* Dilute 1.0 ml of the test solution to 100.0 ml with the mobile phase. Dilute 5.0 ml of this solution to 20.0 ml with the mobile phase.

*Column:*
— *size*: l = 0.1 m, Ø = 4.6 mm;
— *stationary phase: octadecylsilyl silica gel for chromatography R* (3 μm).

*Mobile phase* Dissolve 6.0 g of *ammonium acetate R* in a mixture of 300 ml of *acetonitrile R*, 320 ml of *methanol R* and 380 ml of *water R*.

*Flow rate* 2 ml/min.

*Detection* Spectrophotometer at 235 nm.

*Equilibration* With the mobile phase for about 30 min.

*Injection* 10 μl.

*Run time* 1.5 times the retention time of isoconazole.

*Retention time* econazole = about 10 min; isoconazole = about 14 min.

*System suitability* Reference solution (a):
— *resolution*: minimum 5.0 between the peaks due to econazole and isoconazole; if necessary, adjust the composition of the mobile phase.

*Limits:*
— *impurities B, C, D*: for each impurity, not more than the area of the principal peak in the chromatogram obtained with reference solution (b) (0.25 per cent);
— *total*: not more than twice the area of the principal peak in the chromatogram obtained with reference solution (b) (0.5 per cent);
— *disregard limit*: 0.2 times the area of the principal peak in the chromatogram obtained with reference solution (b) (0.05 per cent).

**Loss on drying** (*2.2.32*)
Maximum 0.5 per cent, determined on 1.000 g by drying in an oven at 105 °C for 2 h.

**Sulphated ash** (*2.4.14*)
Maximum 0.1 per cent, determined on 1.0 g.

**ASSAY**
Dissolve 0.300 g in 50 ml of a mixture of 1 volume of *anhydrous acetic acid R* and 7 volumes of *methyl ethyl ketone R*. Using 0.2 ml of *naphtholbenzein solution R* as indicator, titrate with *0.1 M perchloric acid* until the colour changes from orange-yellow to green.

1 ml of *0.1 M perchloric acid* is equivalent to 41.61 mg of $C_{18}H_{14}Cl_4N_2O$.

**STORAGE**
Protected from light.

**IMPURITIES**
*Specified impurities B, C, D.*
A. deleted,

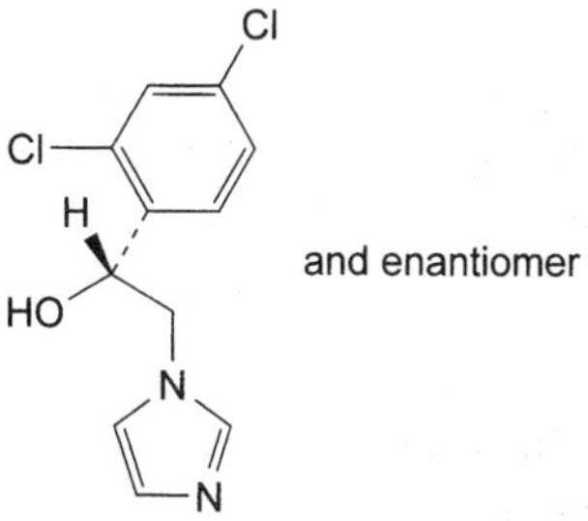

B. (1*RS*)-1-(2,4-dichlorophenyl)-2-(1*H*-imidazol-1-yl)ethanol,

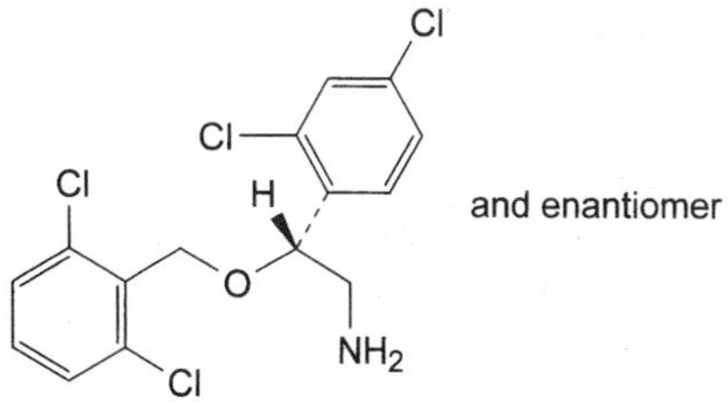

C. (2*RS*)-2-[(2,6-dichlorobenzyl)oxy]-2-(2,4-dichlorophenyl)ethanamine,

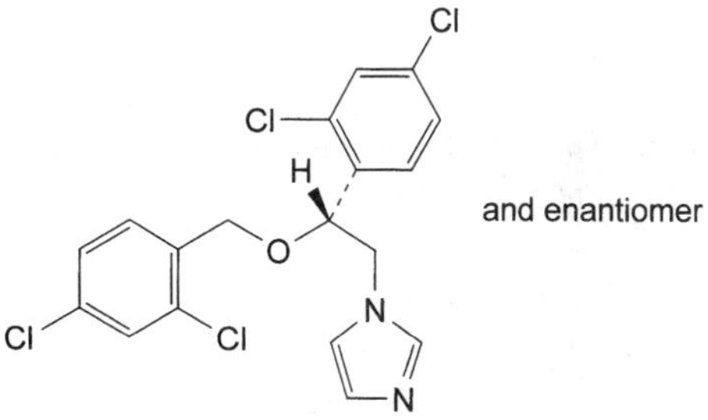

D. 1-[(2*RS*)-2-[(2,4-dichlorobenzyl)oxy]-2-(2,4-dichlorophenyl)ethyl]-1*H*-imidazole.

*Ph Eur*

# Isoconazole Nitrate

(*Ph Eur monograph 1017*)

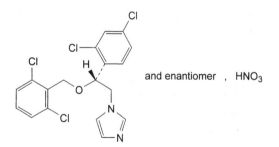

$C_{18}H_{14}Cl_4N_2O,HNO_3$     479.1     *40036-10-0*

**Action and use**
Antifungal.

**Preparation**
Isoconazole Pessaries

*Ph Eur*

**DEFINITION**
1-[(2*RS*)-2-[(2,6-Dichlorobenzyl)oxy]-2-(2,4-dichlorophenyl)ethyl]-1*H*-imidazole nitrate.

**Content**

99.0 per cent to 101.0 per cent (dried substance).

## CHARACTERS

**Appearance**

White or almost white powder.

**Solubility**

Very slightly soluble in water, soluble in methanol, slightly soluble in ethanol (96 per cent).

## IDENTIFICATION

*First identification*   A, B.

*Second identification*   A, C, D.

A. Melting point (*2.2.14*) 178 °C to 182 °C.

B. Infrared absorption spectrophotometry (*2.2.24*).

*Preparation*   Discs.

*Comparison*   isoconazole nitrate CRS.

C. Thin-layer chromatography (*2.2.27*).

*Test solution*   Dissolve 30 mg of the substance to be examined in *methanol R* and dilute to 5 ml with the same solvent.

*Reference solution (a)*   Dissolve 30 mg of *isoconazole nitrate CRS* in *methanol R* and dilute to 5 ml with the same solvent.

*Reference solution (b)*   Dissolve 30 mg of *isoconazole nitrate CRS* and 30 mg of *econazole nitrate CRS* in *methanol R*, then dilute to 5 ml with the same solvent.

*Plate*   TLC octadecylsilyl silica gel plate R.

*Mobile phase*   ammonium acetate solution R, dioxan R, methanol R (20:40:40 V/V/V).

*Application*   5 µl.

*Development*   Over a path of 15 cm.

*Drying*   In a current of warm air for 15 min.

*Detection*   Expose to iodine vapour until the spots appear and examine in daylight.

*System suitability*   Reference solution (b):
— the chromatogram shows 2 clearly separated spots.

*Results*   The principal spot in the chromatogram obtained with the test solution is similar in position, colour and size to the principal spot in the chromatogram obtained with reference solution (a).

D. It gives the reaction of nitrates (*2.3.1*).

## TESTS

**Solution S**

Dissolve 0.20 g in *methanol R* and dilute to 20.0 ml with the same solvent.

**Appearance of solution**

Solution S is clear (*2.2.1*) and not more intensely coloured than reference solution Y$_7$ (*2.2.2, Method II*).

**Optical rotation** (*2.2.7*)

− 0.10° to + 0.10°, determined on solution S.

**Related substances**

Liquid chromatography (*2.2.29*).

*Test solution*   Dissolve 0.100 g of the substance to be examined in the mobile phase and dilute to 10.0 ml with the mobile phase.

*Reference solution (a)*   Dissolve 2.5 mg of *isoconazole nitrate CRS* and 2.5 mg of *econazole nitrate CRS* in the mobile phase, then dilute to 100.0 ml with the mobile phase.

*Reference solution (b)*   Dilute 1.0 ml of the test solution to 100.0 ml with the mobile phase. Dilute 5.0 ml of this solution to 20.0 ml with the mobile phase.

*Column:*
— *size*: $l$ = 0.1 m, Ø = 4.6 mm;
— *stationary phase*: octadecylsilyl silica gel for chromatography R (3 µm).

*Mobile phase*   Dissolve 6.0 g of *ammonium acetate R* in a mixture of 300 ml of *acetonitrile R*, 320 ml of *methanol R* and 380 ml of *water R*.

*Flow rate*   2 ml/min.

*Detection*   Spectrophotometer at 235 nm.

*Equilibration*   With the mobile phase for about 30 min.

*Injection*   10 µl.

*Run time*   1.5 times the retention time of *isoconazole*.

*Retention time*   econazole = about 10 min; isoconazole = about 14 min.

*System suitability*   Reference solution (a):
— *resolution*: minimum 5.0 between the peaks due to econazole and isoconazole; if necessary, adjust the composition of the mobile phase.

*Limits:*
— *impurities A, B, C*: for each impurity, not more than the area of the principal peak in the chromatogram obtained with reference solution (b) (0.25 per cent);
— *total*: not more than twice the area of the principal peak in the chromatogram obtained with reference solution (b) (0.5 per cent);
— *disregard limit*: 0.2 times the area of the principal peak in the chromatogram obtained with reference solution (b) (0.05 per cent); disregard the peak due to the nitrate ion.

**Loss on drying** (*2.2.32*)

Maximum 0.5 per cent, determined on 1.000 g by drying in an oven at 105 °C for 2 h.

**Sulphated ash** (*2.4.14*)

Maximum 0.1 per cent, determined on 1.0 g.

## ASSAY

Dissolve 0.350 g in 75 ml of a mixture of 1 volume of *anhydrous acetic acid R* and 7 volumes of *methyl ethyl ketone R*. Titrate with *0.1 M perchloric acid*, determining the end-point potentiometrically (*2.2.20*).

1 ml of *0.1 M perchloric acid* is equivalent to 47.91 mg of $C_{18}H_{15}Cl_4N_3O_4$.

## STORAGE

Protected from light.

## IMPURITIES

*Specified impurities   A, B, C.*

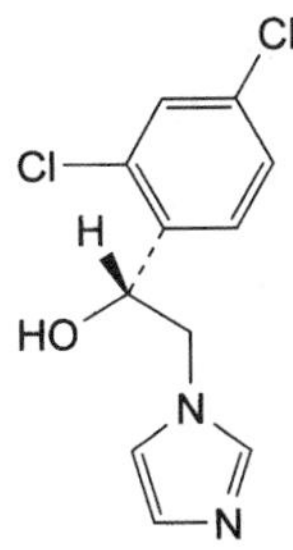

A. (1*RS*)-1-(2,4-dichlorophenyl)-2-(1*H*-imidazol-1-yl)ethanol,

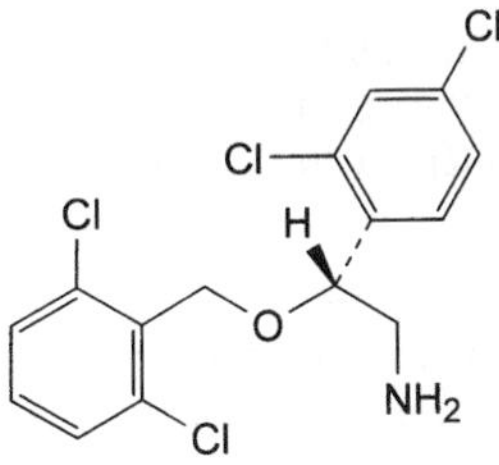

B. (2*RS*)-2-[(2,6-dichlorobenzyl)oxy]-2-(2,4-dichlorophenyl)ethanamine,

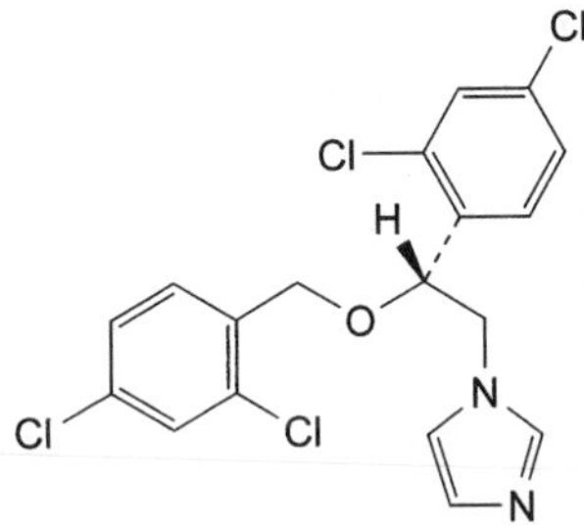

C. 1-[(2*RS*)-2-[(2,4-dichlorobenzyl)oxy]-2-(2,4-dichlorophenyl)ethyl]-1*H*-imidazole.

_____ *Ph Eur*

# Isoflurane

(*Ph Eur monograph 1673*)

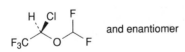

C₃H₂ClF₅O        184.5        *26675-46-7*

$C_3H_2ClF_5O$        184.5        *26675-46-7*

## Action and use
General anaesthetic.

*Ph Eur* _____

## DEFINITION
(2*RS*)-2-Chloro-2-(difluoromethoxy)-1,1,1-trifluoroethane.

## CHARACTERS
### Appearance
Clear, colourless, mobile, heavy liquid.

### Solubility
Practically insoluble in water, miscible with ethanol and trichloroethylene.

bp: about 48 °C.

It is non-flammable.

## IDENTIFICATION
Infrared absorption spectrophotometry (*2.2.24*).

*Preparation*   Examine the substance in the gaseous state.

*Comparison*   *Ph. Eur. reference spectrum of isoflurane.*

## TESTS
### Acidity or alkalinity
To 20 ml add 20 ml of *carbon dioxide-free water R*, shake for 3 min and allow to stand. Collect the upper layer and add 0.2 ml of *bromocresol purple solution R*. Not more than 0.1 ml of *0.01 M sodium hydroxide* or 0.6 ml of *0.01 M hydrochloric acid* is required to change the colour of the indicator.

### Related substances
Gas chromatography (*2.2.28*).

*Test solution*   The substance to be examined.

*Reference solution*   To 80 ml of *ethanol R*, add 1.0 ml of the substance to be examined and 1.0 ml of *acetone R*, avoiding loss by evaporation. Dilute to 100.0 ml with *ethanol R*. Dilute 1.0 ml of the solution to 100.0 ml with *ethanol R*.

*Column:*
— *material*: fused silica,
— *size*: *l* = 30 m, Ø = 0.32 mm,
— *stationary phase*: *macrogol 20 000 R* (film thickness 0.25 µm).

*Carrier gas*   *helium for chromatography R.*

*Flow rate*   1.0 ml/min.

*Split ratio*   1:25.

*Temperature:*
— *column*: 35 °C,
— *injection port*: 150 °C,
— *detector*: 250 °C.

*Detection*   Flame ionisation.

*Injection*   1.0 µl of each solution and 1.0 µl of *ethanol R* as a blank.

*Run time*   Until elution of the ethanol peak in the chromatogram obtained with the reference solution.

*Relative retention* with reference to isoflurane (retention time = about 3.8 min): acetone = about 0.75.

*System suitability*   Reference solution:
— *resolution*: minimum of 5 between the peaks due to acetone and to isoflurane,
— *repeatability*: maximum relative standard deviation 15.0 per cent for the peak due to isoflurane after 3 injections.

*Limits:*
— *acetone*: not more than the area of the corresponding peak in the chromatogram obtained with the reference solution (0.01 per cent),
— *any other impurity*: not more than the area of the peak due to isoflurane in the chromatogram obtained with the reference solution (0.01 per cent),
— *total*: not more than 3 times the area of the peak due to isoflurane in the chromatogram obtained with the reference solution (0.03 per cent),
— *disregard limit*: 0.1 times the area of the peak due to isoflurane in the chromatogram obtained with the reference solution (0.001 per cent).

**Chlorides** (*2.4.4*)
Maximum 10 ppm.

To 10 ml add 10 ml *of 0.01 M sodium hydroxide* and shake for 3 min. To 5 ml of the upper layer add 10 ml of *water R*. The solution complies with the limit test for chlorides.

**Fluorides**
Maximum 10 ppm.

Determine by potentiometry (*2.2.36, Method I*) using a fluoride-selective indicator-electrode and a silver-silver chloride reference electrode.

*Test solution* To 10.0 ml in a separating funnel, add 10 ml of a mixture of 30.0 ml of *dilute ammonia R2* and 70.0 ml of *distilled water R*. Shake for 1 min and collect the upper layer. Repeat this extraction procedure twice collecting the upper layer each time. Adjust the combined upper layers to pH 5.2 using *dilute hydrochloric acid R*. Add 5.0 ml of *fluoride standard solution (1 ppm F) R* and dilute to 50.0 ml with *distilled water R*. To 20.0 ml of the solution add 20.0 ml of *total-ionic-strength-adjustment buffer R* and dilute to 50.0 ml with *distilled water R*.

*Reference solutions* To each of 5.0 ml, 4.0 ml, 3.0 ml, 2.0 ml and 1.0 ml of *fluoride standard solution (10 ppm F) R* add 20.0 ml of *total-ionic-strength-adjustment buffer R* and dilute to 50.0 ml with *distilled water R*.

Carry out the measurements on 20 ml of each solution. Calculate the concentration of fluorides using the calibration curve, taking into account the addition of fluoride to the test solution.

**Non-volatile matter**
Maximum 200 mg/l.

Evaporate 10.0 ml to dryness with the aid of a stream of cold air and dry the residue at 50 °C for 2 h. The residue weighs a maximum of 2.0 mg.

**Water** (*2.5.12*)
Maximum 1.0 mg/ml, determined on 10.0 ml.

**STORAGE**
In an airtight container, protected from light.

**IMPURITIES**

A. R1 = H, R2 = Cl:
2-(chlorodifluoromethoxy)-1,1,1-trifluoroethane,

B. R1 = R2 = H: 2-(difluoromethoxy)-1,1,1-trifluoroethane,

C. R1 = R2 = Cl: (2*RS*)-2-chloro-2-(chlorodifluoromethoxy)-1,1,1-trifluoroethane,

D. R = H: 1,1-dichloro-1-(difluoromethoxy)-2,2,2-trifluoroethane,

E. R = Cl: 1,1-dichloro-1-(chlorodifluoromethoxy)-2,2,2-trifluoroethane,

F. acetone.

*Ph Eur*

# Isoleucine

*(Ph Eur monograph 0770)*

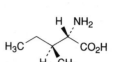

$C_6H_{13}NO_2$      131.2      73-32-5

**Action and use**
Amino acid.

*Ph Eur*

**DEFINITION**
Isoleucine contains not less than 98.5 per cent and not more than the equivalent of 101.0 per cent of (2*S*,3*S*)-2-amino-3-methylpentanoic acid, calculated with reference to the dried substance.

**CHARACTERS**
White or almost white, crystalline powder or flakes, sparingly soluble in water, slightly soluble in alcohol. It dissolves in dilute mineral acids and in dilute solutions of alkali hydroxides.

**IDENTIFICATION**
*First identification* A, C.

*Second identification* A, B, D.

A. It complies with the test for specific optical rotation (see Tests).

B. Dissolve 0.5 g in *water R* and dilute to 25 ml with the same solvent. The solution is dextrorotatory.

C. Examine by infrared absorption spectrophotometry (*2.2.24*), comparing with the spectrum obtained with *isoleucine CRS*. Examine the substances prepared as discs.

D. Examine the chromatograms obtained in the test for ninhydrin-positive substances. The principal spot in the chromatogram obtained with test solution (b) is similar in position, colour and size to the principal spot in the chromatogram obtained with reference solution (a).

**TESTS**
**Appearance of solution**
Dissolve 0.5 g in *1 M hydrochloric acid* and dilute to 10 ml with the same acid. The solution is clear (*2.2.1*) and not more intensely coloured than reference solution $BY_6$ (*2.2.2, Method II*).

**Specific optical rotation** (*2.2.7*)
Dissolve 1.00 g in *hydrochloric acid R1* and dilute to 25.0 ml with the same acid. The specific optical rotation is + 40.0 to + 43.0, calculated with reference to the dried substance.

**Ninhydrin-positive substances**
Examine by thin-layer chromatography (*2.2.27*), using a *TLC silica gel plate R*.

*Test solution (a)* Dissolve 0.10 g of the substance to be examined in *0.1 M hydrochloric acid* and dilute to 10 ml with the same acid.

*Test solution (b)* Dilute 1 ml of test solution (a) to 50 ml with *water R*.

*Reference solution (a)* Dissolve 10 mg of *isoleucine CRS* in *0.1 M hydrochloric acid* and dilute to 50 ml with the same acid.

*Reference solution (b)*   Dilute 5 ml of test solution (b) to 20 ml with *water R*.

*Reference solution (c)*   Dissolve 10 mg of *isoleucine CRS* and 10 mg of *valine CRS* in *0.1 M hydrochloric acid* and dilute to 25 ml with the same acid.

Apply separately to the plate 5 μl of each solution. Develop over a path of 15 cm using a mixture of 20 volumes of *glacial acetic acid R*, 20 volumes of *water R* and 60 volumes of *butanol R*. Allow the plate to dry in air, spray with *ninhydrin solution R* and heat at 100-105 °C for 15 min. Any spot in the chromatogram obtained with test solution (a), apart from the principal spot, is not more intense than the spot in the chromatogram obtained with reference solution (b) (0.5 per cent). The test is not valid unless the chromatogram obtained with reference solution (c) shows 2 clearly separated spots.

**Chlorides** *(2.4.4)*
Dissolve 0.25 g in *water R* and dilute to 15 ml with the same solvent. The solution complies with the limit test for chlorides (200 ppm).

**Sulphates** *(2.4.13)*
Dissolve 0.5 g in 3 ml of *dilute hydrochloric acid R* and dilute to 15 ml with *distilled water R*. The solution complies with the limit test for sulphates (300 ppm).

**Ammonium** *(2.4.1)*
50 mg complies with limit test B for ammonium (200 ppm). Prepare the standard using 0.1 ml of *ammonium standard solution (100 ppm NH₄) R*.

**Iron** *(2.4.9)*
In a separating funnel, dissolve 1.0 g in 10 ml of *dilute hydrochloric acid R*. Shake with 3 quantities, each of 10 ml, of *methyl isobutyl ketone R1*, shaking for 3 min each time. To the combined organic layers add 10 ml of *water R* and shake for 3 min. The aqueous layer complies with the limit test for iron (10 ppm).

**Heavy metals** *(2.4.8)*
2.0 g complies with limit test D for heavy metals (10 ppm). Prepare the standard using 2 ml of *lead standard solution (10 ppm Pb) R*.

**Loss on drying** *(2.2.32)*
Not more than 0.5 per cent, determined on 1.000 g by drying in an oven at 105 °C.

**Sulphated ash** *(2.4.14)*
Not more than 0.1 per cent, determined on 1.0 g.

**ASSAY**
Dissolve 0.100 g in 3 ml of *anhydrous formic acid R*. Add 30 ml of *anhydrous acetic acid R*. Using 0.1 ml of *naphtholbenzein solution R* as indicator, titrate with *0.1 M perchloric acid* until the colour changes from brownish-yellow to green.

1 ml of *0.1 M perchloric acid* is equivalent to 13.12 mg of $C_6H_{13}NO_2$.

**STORAGE**
Store protected from light.

_____ *Ph Eur*

# Isomalt

*(Ph Eur monograph 1531)*

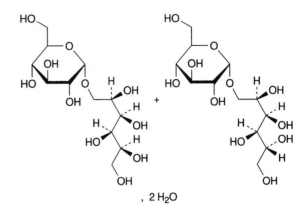

| | |
|---|---|
| $C_{12}H_{24}O_{11}$ | 344.3 |
| $C_{12}H_{24}O_{11},2H_2O$ | 380.3 |

**Action and use**
Sweetening agent.

*Ph Eur* _____

## DEFINITION
Mixture of 6-*O*-α-D-glucopyranosyl-D-glucitol (6-*O*-α-D-glucopyranosyl-D-sorbitol; 1,6-GPS) and 1-*O*-α-D-glucopyranosyl-D-mannitol (1,1-GPM).

**Content**
98.0 per cent to 102.0 per cent for the mixture of 1,6-GPS and 1,1-GPM and neither of the 2 components is less than 3.0 per cent (anhydrous substance).

## CHARACTERS
**Appearance**
White or almost white powder or granules.

**Solubility**
Freely soluble in water, practically insoluble in anhydrous ethanol.

## IDENTIFICATION
*First identification   A.*

*Second identification   B, C.*

A. Examine the chromatograms obtained in the assay.

*Results*   The 2 principal peaks in the chromatogram obtained with the test solution are similar in retention time to the 2 principal peaks in the chromatogram obtained with reference solution (a).

B. Thin-layer chromatography *(2.2.27)*.

*Test solution*   Dissolve 50 mg of the substance to be examined in *water R* and dilute to 10 ml with the same solvent.

*Reference solution*   Dissolve 50 mg of *isomalt CRS* in *water R* and dilute to 10 ml with the same solvent.

*Plate*   TLC silica gel $F_{254}$ plate R.

*Mobile phase*   acetic acid R, propionic acid R, water R, ethyl acetate R, pyridine R (5:5:10:50:50 *V/V/V/V/V*).

*Application*   1 μl; thoroughly dry the starting points in warm air.

*Development*   Over a path of 10 cm.

*Drying*   In a current of warm air.

*Detection* Dip for 3 s in a 1 g/l solution of *sodium periodate R* and dry in a current of hot air; dip for 3 s in a mixture of 1 volume of *acetic acid R*, 1 volume of *anisaldehyde* R, 5 volumes of *sulphuric acid R* and 90 volumes of *anhydrous ethanol R*; dry in a current of hot air until coloured spots become visible; the background colour may be brightened in warm steam; examine in daylight.

*Results* The chromatogram obtained with the reference solution shows 2 blue-grey spots with $R_F$ values of about 0.13 (1,6-GPS) and 0.16 (1,1-GPM). The chromatogram obtained with the test solution shows principal spots similar in position and colour to the principal spots in the chromatogram obtained with the reference solution.

C. To 3 ml of a freshly prepared 100 g/l solution of *pyrocatechol R* add 6 ml of *sulphuric acid R* while cooling in iced water. To 3 ml of the cooled mixture add 0.3 ml of a 100 g/l solution of the substance to be examined. Heat gently over a naked flame for about 30 s. A pink colour develops.

## TESTS

### Conductivity (*2.2.38*)
Maximum 20 $\mu$S·cm$^{-1}$.

Dissolve 20.0 g in *carbon dioxide-free water R* prepared from *distilled water R* and dilute to 100.0 ml with the same solvent. Measure the conductivity of the solution while gently stirring with a magnetic stirrer.

### Reducing sugars
Maximum 0.3 per cent, expressed as glucose equivalent.

Dissolve 3.3 g in 10 ml of *water R* with the aid of gentle heat. Cool and add 20 ml of *cupri-citric solution R* and a few glass beads. Heat so that the boiling begins after 4 min and maintain boiling for 3 min. Cool rapidly and add 100 ml of a 2.4 per cent *V/V* solution of *glacial acetic acid R* and 20.0 ml of *0.025 M iodine*. With continuous shaking, add 25 ml of a mixture of 6 volumes of *hydrochloric acid R* and 94 volumes of *water R*. When the precipitate has dissolved, titrate the excess of iodine with *0.05 M sodium thiosulphate* using 1 ml of *starch solution R* as indicator, added towards the end of the titration. Not less than 12.8 ml of *0.05 M sodium thiosulphate* is required.

### Related products
Liquid chromatography (*2.2.29*).

*Test solution* Dissolve 1.00 g of the substance to be examined in 20 ml of *water R* and dilute to 50.0 ml with the same solvent.

*Reference solution (a)* Dissolve 1.00 g of *isomalt CRS* in 20 ml of *water R* and dilute to 50.0 ml with the same solvent.

*Reference solution (b)* Dissolve 10.0 mg of *sorbitol CRS* (impurity C) and 10.0 mg of *mannitol CRS* (impurity B) in 20 ml of *water R* and dilute to 100.0 ml with the same solvent.

*Precolumn:*
— *size*: $l$ = 30 mm, $\varnothing$ = 4.6 mm;
— *stationary phase: strong cation-exchange resin (calcium form) R* (9 $\mu$m);
— *temperature*: 80 $\pm$ 1 °C.

*Column:*
— *size*: $l$ = 0.3 m, $\varnothing$ = 7.8 mm;
— *stationary phase: strong cation-exchange resin (calcium form) R* (9 $\mu$m);
— *temperature*: 80 $\pm$ 1 °C.

*Mobile phase* degassed *water R*.

*Flow rate* 0.5 ml/min.

*Detection* Differential refractometer maintained at a constant temperature.

*Injection* 20 $\mu$l of the test solution and reference solution (b).

*Run time* Until impurity C is completely eluted (about 25 min).

*Relative retention* with reference to 1,1-GPM (retention time = about 12.3 min): impurity A = about 0.8; 1,6-GPS = about 1.2; impurity B = about 1.6; impurity C = about 2.0.

*Limits:*
— *impurities B, C*: for each impurity, not more than the area of the corresponding peak in the chromatogram obtained with reference solution (b) (0.5 per cent);
— *any other impurity*: for each impurity, not more than the area of the peak due to impurity C in the chromatogram obtained with reference solution (b) (0.5 per cent);
— *total*: not more than 4 times the area of the peak due to impurity C in the chromatogram obtained with reference solution (b) (2 per cent);
— *disregard limit*: 0.2 times the area of the peak due to impurity C in the chromatogram obtained with reference solution (b) (0.1 per cent).

### Lead (*2.4.10*)
Maximum 0.5 ppm.

### Nickel (*2.4.15*)
Maximum 1 ppm.

### Water (*2.5.12*)
Maximum 7.0 per cent, determined on 0.3 g. As solvent, use a mixture of 20 ml of *anhydrous methanol R* and 20 ml of *formamide R* at 50 $\pm$ 5 °C.

## ASSAY

Liquid chromatography (*2.2.29*) as described in the test for related products with the following modification.

*Injection* Test solution and reference solution (a).

Calculate the percentage content of isomalt (1,1-GPM and 1,6-GPS) from the declared content of 1,1-GPM and 1,6-GPS in *isomalt CRS*.

## LABELLING

The label states the percentage content of 1,6-GPS and 1,1-GPM.

## IMPURITIES

*Specified impurities* B, C.

*Other detectable impurities* (the following substances would, if present at a sufficient level, be detected by one or other of the tests in the monograph. They are limited by the general acceptance criterion for other/unspecified impurities and/or by the general monograph *Substances for pharmaceutical use* (*2034*). It is therefore not necessary to identify these impurities for demonstration of compliance. See also *5.10*. Control of impurities in substances for pharmaceutical use): A, D.

A. 6-*O*-α-D-glucopyranosyl-β-D-*arabino*-hex-2-ulofuranose (isomaltulose),

B. mannitol,

C. sorbitol,

and epimer at C*

D. 1-*O*-α-D-glucopyranosyl-D-*arabino*-hex-2-ulofuranose (trehalulose).

*Ph Eur*

# Isometheptene Mucate

and enantiomer

$(C_9H_{19}N)_2, C_6H_{10}O_8$          492.7          *7492-31-1*

## Action and use
Adrenoceptor agonist.

## DEFINITION
Isometheptene Mucate is (*RS*)-1,5-dimethylhex-4-enyl(methyl)amine *galacto*-2,3,4,5-tetrahydroxyadipate. It contains not less than 98.5% and not more than 100.5% of $(C_9H_{19}N)_2, C_6H_{10}O_8$, calculated with reference to the dried substance.

## CHARACTERISTICS
A white, crystalline powder.

Very soluble in *water*; slightly soluble in *absolute ethanol*; practically insoluble in *ether*.

## IDENTIFICATION
A. Dissolve 0.2 g in 10 ml of *water*, make the solution alkaline with 2M *sodium hydroxide*, extract with 20 ml of dichloromethane, dry the dichloromethane layer over *anhydrous sodium sulphate*, filter and evaporate to dryness at a pressure of 2 kPa. The *infrared absorption spectrum* of the residue, Appendix II A, is concordant with the *reference spectrum* of isometheptene *(RS 195)*.

B. Prepare a 5.0% w/v solution of the substance being examined in *carbon-dioxide free water* (solution A) and acidify 10 ml with 6M *hydrochloric acid*, scratch the side of the tube with a glass rod to initiate crystallisation, filter, wash the precipitate with *water* and dry at 105° for 10 minutes. The *infrared absorption spectrum* of the residue, Appendix II A, is concordant with the *reference spectrum* of mucic acid *(RS 377)*.

## TESTS
### Acidity
pH of solution A, 5.4 to 6.6, Appendix V L.

### Clarity and colour of solution
Solution A is *clear*, Appendix IV A, and *colourless*, Appendix IV B, Method II.

### Related substances
Dissolve 20 mg of *linalool* (internal standard) in sufficient *dichloromethane* to produce 100 ml (solution B). Carry out the method for *gas chromatography*, Appendix III B, using the following solutions. For solution (1) add 1 ml of 5M *sodium hydroxide* to 5 ml of a 0.050% w/v solution of the substance being examined, extract with 10 ml of solution B followed by 10 ml of *dichloromethane*, combine the dichloromethane layers and filter through *anhydrous sodium sulphate*. For solution (2) dissolve 0.5 g of the substance being examined in 5 ml of *water*, add 1 ml of 5M *sodium hydroxide*, extract with two 10 ml quantities of *dichloromethane*, combine the dichloromethane layers and filter through *anhydrous sodium sulphate*. Prepare solution (3) in the same manner as solution (2) but using 10 ml of solution B and 10 ml of *dichloromethane* in place of the two 10 ml quantities of *dichloromethane*. For solution (4) dissolve 10 mg of *1,5-dimethylhexyl(methyl)amine BPCRS* and 10 mg of *2-methyl-6-methylaminoheptan-2-ol BPCRS* in 50 ml of *dichloromethane*. For solution (5) dissolve 5 mg of the substance being examined and 5 mg of *linalool* in 25 ml of solution (4) and filter, if necessary.

The chromatographic procedure may be carried out using a glass column (1.5 m × 4 mm) packed with *acid-washed, silanised diatomaceous support* (100 to 120 mesh) (Chromosorb W-HP is suitable) coated with 10% w/w of polyethylene glycol (Carbowax 20M is suitable) and 5% w/w of *potassium hydroxide* at a temperature increased from 80° to 140° at a rate of 4° per minute and then maintained at 140° for 10 minutes or the time required for the emergence of the peak due to 2-methyl-6-methylaminoheptan-2-ol and with the inlet port at 190°, the detector at 200° and a flow rate of 40 ml per minute for the carrier gas.

The test is not valid unless the chromatogram obtained with solution (5) resembles the reference chromatogram provided with *1,5-dimethylhexyl(methyl)amine BPCRS* and *2-methyl-6-methylaminoheptan-2-ol BPCRS*.

Calculate the ratio (*a*) of the area of the peak due to isometheptene to that of the peak due to the internal standard in the chromatogram obtained with solution (1). In the chromatogram obtained with solution (3) the ratio of the area of any peak corresponding to 1,5-dimethylhexyl-(methyl)amine to the area of the peak due to the internal standard is not greater than 2*a*, the ratio of the area of any other *secondary peak* to the area of the peak due to the internal standard is not greater than *a* and the ratio of the sum of the areas of any secondary peaks to the area of the peak due to the internal standard is not greater than 3a.

**Loss on drying**

When dried to constant weight over *phosphorus pentoxide* at 60° at a pressure not exceeding 0.7 kPa, loses not more than 0.5% of its weight. Use 1 g.

**Sulphated ash**

Not more than 0.1%, Appendix IX A.

**ASSAY**

Dissolve 0.2 g in 25 ml of *water* and add 20 ml of 0.0167M *potassium bromate VS*, 10 ml of a 10% w/v solution of *potassium bromide* and 8 ml of *hydrochloric acid*. Allow to stand for 5 minutes in a stoppered flask, add 10 ml of *dilute potassium iodide solution*, allow to stand for 5 minutes and titrate the resulting solution with 0.1M *sodium thiosulphate VS* using *starch solution* as indicator. Repeat the procedure using 25 ml of *water* in place of the solution of the substance being examined. The difference between the titrations represents the amount of sodium thiosulphate required. Each ml of 0.0167M *potassium bromate VS* is equivalent to 12.32 mg of $(C_9H_{19}N)_2,C_6H_{10}O_8$.

**STORAGE**

Isometheptene Mucate should be kept in an airtight container and protected from light.

**IMPURITIES**

Me—⟍⟋⟍⟋—NHMe
        |
        Me

A. 1,5-dimethylhexyl(methyl)amine,

Me—⟍⟋⟍⟋—OH
        |
        Me

B. 2-methylheptan-6-ol,

Me—⟍⟋⟍⟋—OH
        ‖
        Me

C. 2-methylhept-2-en-6-ol,

Me—⟍⟋⟍⟋—O
        ‖
        Me

D. 2-methylhept-2-en-6-one,

Me—⟍⟋⟍⟋—NHMe
        |       |
        Me     OH

E. 2-methyl-6-methylaminoheptan-2-ol.

# Isoniazid

*(Ph Eur monograph 0146)*

$C_6H_7N_3O$  137.1  54-85-3

**Action and use**

Antituberculosis drug.

**Preparations**

Isoniazid Injection

Isoniazid Tablets

*Ph Eur* _____

**DEFINITION**

Isoniazid contains not less than 99.0 per cent and not more than the equivalent of 101.0 per cent of pyridine-4-carbohydrazide, calculated with reference to the dried substance.

**CHARACTERS**

A white or almost white, crystalline powder or colourless crystals, freely soluble in water, sparingly soluble in alcohol.

**IDENTIFICATION**

*First identification  A, B.*

*Second identification  A, C.*

A. Melting point (*2.2.14*): 170 °C to 174 °C.

B. Examine by infrared absorption spectrophotometry (*2.2.24*), comparing with the spectrum obtained with *isoniazid CRS*.

C. Dissolve 0.1 g in 2 ml of *water R* and add 10 ml of a warm 10 g/l solution of *vanillin R*. Allow to stand and scratch the wall of the test tube with a glass rod. A yellow precipitate is formed, which, after recrystallisation from 5 ml of *alcohol (70 per cent V/V) R* and drying at 100 °C to 105 °C, melts (*2.2.14*) at 226 °C to 231 °C.

**TESTS**

**Solution S**

Dissolve 2.5 g in *carbon dioxide-free water R* and dilute to 50 ml with the same solvent.

**Appearance of solution**

Solution S is clear (*2.2.1*) and not more intensely coloured than reference solution $BY_7$ (*2.2.2, Method II*).

**pH** (*2.2.3*)

The pH of solution S is 6.0 to 8.0.

**Hydrazine and related substances**

Examine by thin-layer chromatography (*2.2.27*), using *silica gel GF_{254} R* as the coating substance.

*Test solution*  Dissolve 1.0 g of the substance to be examined in a mixture of equal volumes of *acetone R* and *water R* and dilute to 10.0 ml with the same mixture of solvents.

*Reference solution*  Dissolve 50.0 mg of *hydrazine sulphate R* in 50 ml of *water R* and dilute to 100.0 ml with *acetone R*. To 10.0 ml of this solution add 0.2 ml of the test solution and dilute to 100.0 ml with a mixture of equal volumes of *acetone R* and *water R*.

Apply separately to the plate 5 µl of each solution and develop over a path of 15 cm using a mixture of 10 volumes of *water R*, 20 volumes of *acetone R*, 20 volumes of *methanol R* and 50 volumes of *ethyl acetate R*. Allow the plate to dry in air and examine in ultraviolet light at 254 nm. Any spot in the chromatogram obtained with the test solution, apart from the principal spot, is not more intense than the spot in the chromatogram obtained with the reference solution (0.2 per cent). Spray the plate with *dimethylaminobenzaldehyde solution R1*. Examine in daylight. An additional spot, corresponding to hydrazine, appears in the chromatogram obtained with the reference solution. Any corresponding spot in the chromatogram obtained with the test solution is not more intense than the spot corresponding to hydrazine in the chromatogram obtained with the reference solution (0.05 per cent).

**Heavy metals** *(2.4.8)*
2.0 g complies with limit test C for heavy metals (10 ppm). Prepare the standard using 2 ml of *lead standard solution (10 ppm Pb) R*.

**Loss on drying** *(2.2.32)*
Not more than 0.5 per cent, determined on 1.00 g by drying in an oven at 105 °C.

**Sulphated ash** *(2.4.14)*
Not more than 0.1 per cent, determined on 1.0 g.

**ASSAY**
Dissolve 0.250 g in *water R* and dilute to 100.0 ml with the same solvent. To 20.0 ml of the solution add 100 ml of *water R*, 20 ml of *hydrochloric acid R*, 0.2 g of *potassium bromide R* and 0.05 ml of *methyl red solution R*. Titrate dropwise with *0.0167 M potassium bromate*, shaking continuously, until the red colour disappears.

1 ml of *0.0167 M potassium bromate* is equivalent to 3.429 mg of $C_6H_7N_3O$.

*Ph Eur*

# Isoprenaline Hydrochloride

*(Ph Eur monograph 1332)*

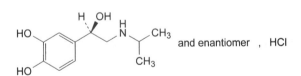

and enantiomer , HCl

$C_{11}H_{17}NO_3$,HCl $\qquad$ 247.7 $\qquad$ *51-30-9*

**Action and use**
Adrenoceptor agonist.

**Preparation**
Isoprenaline Injection

*Ph Eur*

**DEFINITION**
(1*RS*)-1-(3,4-Dihydroxyphenyl)-2-[(1-methylethyl)amino]ethanol hydrochloride.

**Content**
98.0 per cent to 101.5 per cent (dried substance).

**CHARACTERS**
**Appearance**
White or almost white, crystalline powder.

**Solubility**
Freely soluble in water, sparingly soluble in ethanol (96 per cent), practically insoluble in methylene chloride.

**IDENTIFICATION**
*First identification* B, C, E.

*Second identification* A, C, D, E.

A. Melting point *(2.2.14)*: 165 °C to 170 °C, with decomposition.

B. Infrared absorption spectrophotometry *(2.2.24)*.

*Preparation* Discs.

*Comparison* isoprenaline hydrochloride CRS.

C. Optical rotation (see Tests).

D. To 0.1 ml of solution S (see Tests) add 0.05 ml of *ferric chloride solution R1* and 0.9 ml of *water R*. A green colour is produced. Add dropwise *sodium hydrogen carbonate solution R*. The colour becomes blue then red.

E. To 0.5 ml of solution S add 1.5 ml of *water R*. The solution gives reaction (a) of chlorides *(2.3.1)*.

**TESTS**
*Prepare the solutions immediately before use.*

**Solution S**
Dissolve 2.5 g in *carbon dioxide-free water R* and dilute to 25.0 ml with the same solvent.

**Appearance of solution**
Solution S is clear *(2.2.1)* and not more intensely coloured than reference solution $B_7$ or $BY_7$ *(2.2.2, Method II)*.

**pH** *(2.2.3)*
4.3 to 5.5.

Mix 5 ml of solution S and 5 ml of *carbon dioxide-free water R*.

**Optical rotation** *(2.2.7)*
− 0.10 ° to + 0.10 °, determined on solution S.

**Related substances**
Liquid chromatography *(2.2.29)*.

*Test solution (a)* Dissolve 50.0 mg of the substance to be examined in the mobile phase and dilute to 10.0 ml with the mobile phase.

*Test solution (b)* Dilute 0.5 ml of test solution (a) to 100.0 ml with the mobile phase.

*Reference solution (a)* Dissolve 2.5 mg of *isoprenaline hydrochloride CRS* in the mobile phase and dilute to 100.0 ml with the mobile phase.

*Reference solution (b)* Dissolve 2.5 mg of *orciprenaline sulphate CRS* in the mobile phase and dilute to 100.0 ml with the mobile phase.

*Reference solution (c)* To 1.0 ml of test solution (b) add 1.0 ml of reference solution (b) and dilute to 20.0 ml with the mobile phase.

*Column:*
— *size: l* = 0.125 m, Ø = 4.0 mm;
— *stationary phase: octadecylsilyl silica gel for chromatography R* (5 μm).

*Mobile phase* *methanol R*, 11.5 g/l solution of *phosphoric acid R* (5:95 *V/V*).

*Flow rate* 1.0 ml/min.

*Detection* Spectrophotometer at 280 nm.

*Injection* 20 μl of test solution (a) and reference solutions (a) and (c).

*Run time* 7 times the retention time of isoprenaline.

*Retention time* Isoprenaline = about 3 min; if necessary, adjust the concentration of methanol in the mobile phase.

*System suitability* Reference solution (c):
— *resolution*: minimum 3 between the peaks due to isoprenaline and orciprenaline;
— *signal-to-noise ratio*: minimum 3 for the peak due to isoprenaline.

*Limits:*
— *impurity A*: not more than the area of the principal peak in the chromatogram obtained with reference solution (a) (0.5 per cent);
— *total*: not more than twice the area of the principal peak in the chromatogram obtained with reference solution (a) (1 per cent);
— *disregard limit*: 0.05 times the area of the principal peak in the chromatogram obtained with reference solution (a) (0.025 per cent).

### Loss on drying *(2.2.32)*
Maximum 1.0 per cent, determined on 1.000 g by drying *in vacuo* at 15-25 °C for 4 h.

### Sulphated ash *(2.4.14)*
Maximum 0.1 per cent, determined on 1.0 g.

### ASSAY
*In order to avoid overheating in the reaction medium, mix thoroughly throughout and stop the titration immediately after the end-point has been reached.*

Dissolve 0.150 g in 10 ml of *anhydrous formic acid R* and add 50 ml of *acetic anhydride R*. Titrate with *0.1 M perchloric acid*, determining the end-point potentiometrically *(2.2.20)*.

1 ml of *0.1 M perchloric acid* is equivalent to 24.77 mg of $C_{11}H_{18}ClNO_3$.

### STORAGE
In an airtight container, protected from light.

### IMPURITIES
*Specified impurities* A.

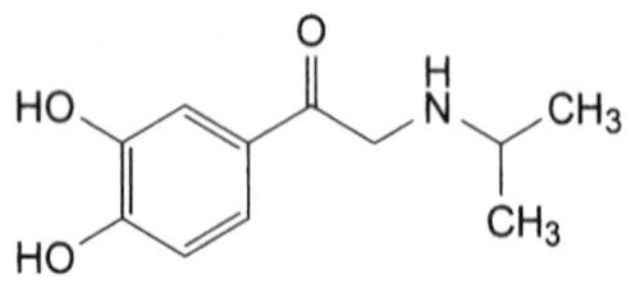

A. 1-(3,4-dihydroxyphenyl)-2-[(1-methylethyl)amino]ethanone.

_____ *Ph Eur*

# Isoprenaline Sulphate

*(Ph Eur monograph 0502)*

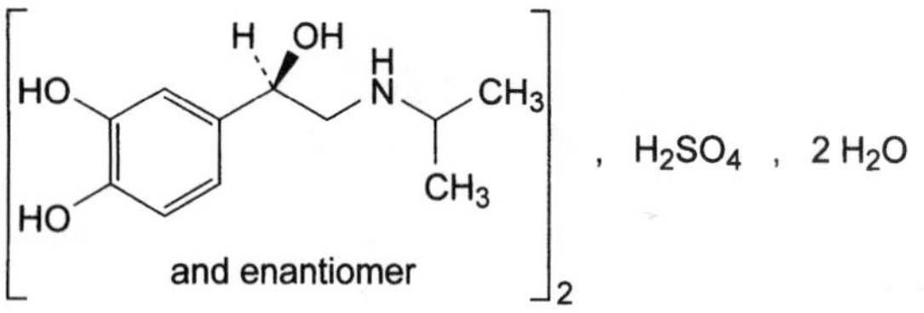

$C_{11}H_{17}NO_3,H_2SO_4,2H_2O$    556.6    *6700-39-6*

### Action and use
Adrenoceptor agonist.

*Ph Eur* _____

### DEFINITION
Bis[(1*RS*)-1-(3,4-dihydroxyphenyl)-2-[(1-methylethyl)amino]ethanol] sulphate dihydrate.

### Content
98.0 per cent to 102.0 per cent (anhydrous substance).

### CHARACTERS
**Appearance**
White or almost white, crystalline powder.

**Solubility**
Freely soluble in water, very slightly soluble in ethanol (96 per cent).

**mp**
About 128 °C, with decomposition.

### IDENTIFICATION
*First identification* A, D.

*Second identification* B, C, D.

A. Infrared absorption spectrophotometry *(2.2.24)*.

Dissolve 0.5 g in 1.5 ml of *water R* and add 3.5 ml of *2-propanol R*. Scratch the wall of the tube with a glass rod to initiate crystallisation. Collect the crystals and dry *in vacuo* at 60 °C over *diphosphorus pentoxide R*.

*Comparison* Repeat the operations using 0.5 g of *isoprenaline sulphate CRS*.

B. To 0.1 ml of solution S (see Tests) add 0.9 ml of *water R* and 0.05 ml of *ferric chloride solution R1*. A green colour is produced. Add dropwise *sodium hydrogen carbonate solution R*. The colour becomes blue and then red.

C. Dilute 1 ml of solution S to 10 ml with *water R* and add 0.25 ml of *silver nitrate solution R1*. A shining, grey, fine precipitate is formed within 10 min and the solution becomes pink.

D. Solution S gives reaction (a) of sulphates *(2.3.1)*.

### TESTS
**Solution S**
Dissolve 5.0 g in *carbon dioxide-free water R* and dilute to 50 ml with the same solvent. Use within 2 h of preparation.

**Appearance of solution**
Solution S is clear *(2.2.1)* and not more intensely coloured than reference solution $Y_6$ *(2.2.2, Method II)*.

**pH** *(2.2.3)*
4.3 to 5.5.

Dilute 5 ml of solution S to 10 ml with *carbon dioxide-free water R*.

**Isoprenalone**

The absorbance (*2.2.25*) is not greater than 0.20 at 310 nm.

Dissolve 0.20 g in *0.005 M sulphuric acid* and dilute to 100.0 ml with the same acid.

**Water** (*2.5.12*)

5.0 per cent to 7.5 per cent, determined on 0.200 g.

**Sulphated ash** (*2.4.14*)

Maximum 0.1 per cent, determined on 1.0 g.

## ASSAY

Dissolve 0.400 g in 20 ml of *anhydrous acetic acid R*, warming gently if necessary and add 20 ml of *methyl isobutyl ketone R*. Titrate with *0.1 M perchloric acid* determining the end-point potentiometrically (*2.2.20*).

1 ml of *0.1 M perchloric acid* is equivalent to 52.06 mg of $C_{22}H_{36}N_2O_{10}S$.

## STORAGE

In an airtight container, protected from light.

*————————————————— Ph Eur*

# Isopropyl Alcohol

(*Ph Eur monograph 0970*)

$C_3H_8O$  60.1  *67-63-0*

*Ph Eur ———————————————*

## DEFINITION

Propan-2-ol.

## CHARACTERS

**Appearance**

Clear, colourless liquid.

**Solubility**

Miscible with water and with alcohol.

## IDENTIFICATION

A. Relative density (*2.2.5*): 0.785 to 0.789.

B. Refractive index (*2.2.6*): 1.376 to 1.379.

C. To 1 ml add 2 ml of *potassium dichromate solution R* and 1 ml of *dilute sulphuric acid R*. Boil. Vapour is produced which changes the colour of a piece of filter paper impregnated with *nitrobenzaldehyde solution R* to green. Moisten the filter paper with *dilute hydrochloric acid R*. The colour changes to blue.

## TESTS

**Appearance**

The substance to be examined is clear (*2.2.1*) and colourless (*2.2.2, Method II*). Dilute 1 ml to 20 ml with *water R*. After 5 min, the solution is clear (*2.2.1*).

**Acidity or alkalinity**

Gently boil 25 ml for 5 min. Add 25 ml of *carbon dioxide-free water R* and allow to cool protected from carbon dioxide in the air. Add 0.1 ml of *phenolphthalein solution R*. The solution is colourless. Not more than 0.6 ml of *0.01 M sodium hydroxide* is required to change the colour of the indicator to pale pink.

**Absorbance** (*2.2.25*)

Maximum 0.30 at 230 nm, 0.10 at 250 nm, 0.03 at 270 nm, 0.02 at 290 nm and 0.01 at 310 nm.

The absorbance is measured between 230 nm and 310 nm using *water R* as the compensation liquid. The absorption curve is smooth.

**Benzene and related substances**

Gas chromatography (*2.2.28*).

*Test solution (a)*   The substance to be examined.

*Test solution (b)*   Dilute 1.0 ml of *2-butanol R1* to 50.0 ml with test solution (a). Dilute 5.0 ml of the solution to 100.0 ml with test solution (a).

*Reference solution (a)*   Dilute 0.5 ml of *2-butanol R1* and 0.5 ml of *propanol R* to 50.0 ml with test solution (a). Dilute 5.0 ml of the solution to 50.0 ml with test solution (a).

*Reference solution (b)*   Dilute 100 µl of *benzene R* to 100.0 ml with test solution (a). Dilute 0.20 ml of the solution to 100.0 ml with test solution (a).

*Column:*

— *material*: fused silica,

— *size*: $l$ = 30 m, Ø = 0.32 mm,

— *stationary phase*: poly[(cyanopropyl)(phenyl)][dimethyl]siloxane R (film thickness 1.8 µm).

*Carrier gas   helium for chromatography R.*

*Auxiliary gas   nitrogen for chromatography R* or *helium for chromatography R.*

*Linear velocity*   35 cm/s.

*Split ratio*   1:5.

*Temperature:*

|  | Time (min) | Temperature (°C) |
|---|---|---|
| Column | 0 - 12 | 40 |
|  | 12 - 32 | 40 → 240 |
|  | 32 - 42 | 240 |
| Injection port |  | 280 |
| Detector |  | 280 |

*Detection*   Flame ionisation.

*Injection*   1 µl.

*Retention time*   benzene = about 10 min.

*System suitability*   Reference solution (a):

— *resolution*: minimum of 10 between the first peak (propanol) and the second peak (2-butanol).

*Limits*

— *benzene* (test solution (a)): not more than half of the area of the corresponding peak in the chromatogram obtained with reference solution (b) (2 ppm), after the sensitivity has been adjusted so that the height of the peak due to benzene in the chromatogram obtained with reference solution (b) represents at least 10 per cent of the full scale of the recorder.

— *total of impurities apart from 2-butanol* (test solution (b)): not more than 3 times the area of the peak due to 2-butanol in the chromatogram obtained with test solution (b) (0.3 per cent), after the sensitivity has been adjusted so that the height of the 2 peaks following the principal peak in the chromatogram obtained with reference solution (a) represents at least 50 per cent of the full scale of the recorder.

## Peroxides

In a 12 ml test-tube with a ground-glass stopper and a diameter of about 15 mm, introduce 8 ml of *potassium iodide and starch solution R.* Fill completely with the substance to be examined. Shake vigorously and allow to stand protected from light for 30 min. No colour develops.

## Non-volatile substances

Maximum 20 ppm.

Evaporate 100 g to dryness on a water-bath *after having verified that it complies with the test for peroxides* and dry in an oven at 100-105 °C. The residue weighs a maximum of 2 mg.

## Water (2.5.12)

Maximum 0.5 per cent, determined on 5.0 g.

## STORAGE

Protected from light.

## IMPURITIES

A. acetone,

B. benzene,

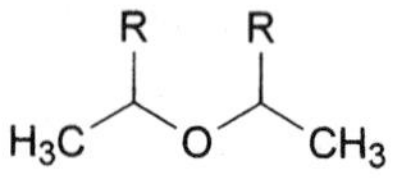

C. $R = CH_3$: 2-(1-methylethoxy)propane (diisopropyl ether),

D. $R = H$: ethoxyethane (diethyl ether),

E. $CH_3$-OH: methanol,

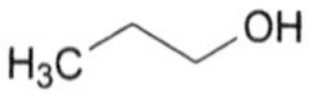

F. propan-1-ol (*n*-propanol).

*Ph Eur* ──────────

# Isopropyl Myristate

(*Ph Eur monograph 0725*)

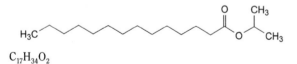

$C_{17}H_{34}O_2$

| $C_{17}H_{34}O_2$ | 270.5 | *110-27-0* |

## Action and use

Excipient.

*Ph Eur* ──────────

## DEFINITION

1-Methylethyl tetradecanoate together with variable amounts of other fatty acid isopropyl esters.

## Content

Minimum 90.0 per cent of $C_{17}H_{34}O_2$.

## CHARACTERS

### Appearance

Clear, colourless, oily liquid.

### Solubility

Immiscible with water, miscible with ethanol (96 per cent), with methylene chloride, with fatty oils and with liquid paraffin.

### Relative density

About 0.853.

## IDENTIFICATION

*First identification   B.*

*Second identification   A, C.*

A. It complies with the test for saponification value (see Tests).

B. Examine the chromatograms obtained in the assay.

*Results*   The principal peak in the chromatogram obtained with the test solution is similar in retention time to the principal peak in the chromatogram obtained with the reference solution.

C. Superpose 2 ml of a 1 g/l solution in *ethanol (96 per cent) R* on a freshly prepared solution of 20 mg of *dimethylaminobenzaldehyde R* in 2 ml of *sulphuric acid R*. After 2 min, a yellowish-red colour appears at the junction of the 2 liquids and gradually becomes red.

## TESTS

### Appearance of solution

The solution is clear (*2.2.1*) and not more intensely coloured than reference solution $Y_7$ (*2.2.2, Method II*).

Dissolve 2.0 g in *methanol R* and dilute to 20 ml with the same solvent.

### Refractive index (2.2.6)

1.434 to 1.437.

### Viscosity (2.2.9)

5 mPa·s to 6 mPa·s.

### Acid value (2.5.1)

Maximum 1.0.

### Iodine value (2.5.4)

Maximum 1.0.

### Saponification value (2.5.6)

202 to 212.

### Water (2.5.12)

Maximum 0.1 per cent, determined on 5.0 g.

### Total ash (2.4.16)

Maximum 0.1 per cent, determined on 1.0 g.

## ASSAY

Gas chromatography (*2.2.28*).

*Internal standard solution*   Dissolve 50.0 mg of *tricosane R* in *heptane R* and dilute to 250.0 ml with the same solvent.

*Test solution*   Dissolve 20.0 mg of the substance to be examined in the internal standard solution and dilute to 100.0 ml with the same solution.

*Reference solution*   Dissolve 20.0 mg of *isopropyl tetradecanoate CRS* in the internal standard solution and dilute to 100.0 ml with the same solution.

*Column:*

— *material*: fused silica,

— *size*: l = 50 m, Ø = 0.2 mm,

— *stationary phase*: *poly(cyanopropyl)siloxane R* (film thickness 0.2 μm).

*Carrier gas   helium for chromatography R.*

*Flow rate*   1 ml/min.

*Split ratio*   1:40.

*Temperature:*

|  | Time (min) | Temperature (°C) |
|---|---|---|
| Column | 0 - 6 | 125 → 185 |
|  | 6 - 16 | 185 |
| Injection port |  | 250 |
| Detector |  | 250 |

*Detection*   Flame ionisation.

*Injection*   2 µl.

Calculate the percentage content of $C_{17}H_{34}O_2$ in the substance to be examined.

**STORAGE**

Protected from light.

————————————————————— *Ph Eur*

# Isopropyl Palmitate

*(Ph Eur monograph 0839)*

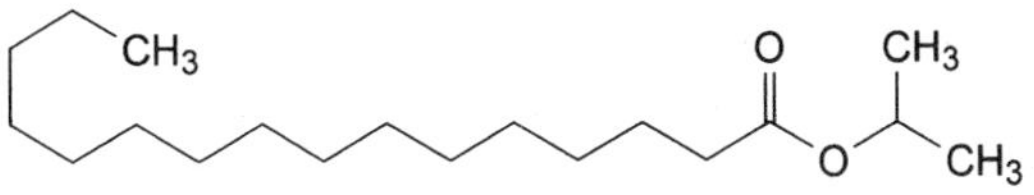

| $C_{19}H_{38}O_2$ | 298.5 | *142-91-6* |

**Action and use**

Excipient.

*Ph Eur* ————————————————————————

**DEFINITION**

1-Methylethyl hexadecanoate together with varying amounts of other fatty acid isopropyl esters.

**Content**

Minimum 90.0 per cent of $C_{19}H_{38}O_2$.

**CHARACTERS**

**Appearance**

Clear, colourless, oily liquid.

**Solubility**

Immiscible with water, miscible with ethanol (96 per cent), with methylene chloride, with fatty oils and with liquid paraffin.

**Relative density**

About 0.854.

**IDENTIFICATION**

*First identification   B.*

*Second identification   A, C.*

A. It complies with the test for saponification value (see Tests).

B. Examine the chromatograms obtained in the assay.

*Results*   The principal peak in the chromatogram obtained with the test solution is similar in retention time to the principal peak in the chromatogram obtained with the reference solution.

C. Superpose 2 ml of a 1 g/l solution in *ethanol (96 per cent) R* on a freshly prepared solution of 20 mg of

dimethylaminobenzaldehyde *R* in 2 ml of *sulphuric acid R*. After 2 min, a yellowish-red colour appears at the junction of the 2 liquids which gradually becomes red.

**TESTS**

**Appearance of solution**

The solution is clear (*2.2.1*) and not more intensely coloured than reference solution $Y_7$ (*2.2.2, Method II*).

Dissolve 2.0 g in *methanol R* and dilute to 20 ml with the same solvent.

**Refractive index** (*2.2.6*)

1.436 to 1.440.

**Viscosity** (*2.2.9*)

5 mPa·s to 10 mPa·s.

**Acid value** (*2.5.1*)

Maximum 1.0.

**Iodine value** (*2.5.4*)

Maximum 1.0.

**Saponification value** (*2.5.6*)

183 to 193.

**Water** (*2.5.12*)

Maximum 0.1 per cent, determined on 5.0 g.

**Total ash** (*2.4.16*)

Maximum 0.1 per cent, determined on 1.0 g.

**ASSAY**

Gas chromatography (*2.2.28*).

*Internal standard solution*   Dissolve 50.0 mg of *tricosane R* in *heptane R* and dilute to 250.0 ml with the same solvent.

*Test solution*   Dissolve 20.0 mg of the substance to be examined in the internal standard solution and dilute to 100.0 ml with the same solution.

*Reference solution*   Dissolve 20.0 mg of *isopropyl hexadecanoate CRS* in the internal standard solution and dilute to 100.0 ml with the same solution.

*Column:*

— *material:* fused silica,

— *size:* $l$ = 50 m, Ø = 0.2 mm,

— *stationary phase:* poly(cyanopropyl)siloxane *R* (film thickness 0.2 µm).

*Carrier gas*   helium for chromatography *R*.

*Flow rate*   1 ml/min.

*Split ratio*   1:40.

*Temperature:*

|  | Time (min) | Temperature (°C) |
|---|---|---|
| Column | 0 - 6 | 125 → 185 |
|  | 6 - 16 | 185 |
| Injection port |  | 250 |
| Detector |  | 250 |

*Detection*   Flame ionisation.

*Injection*   2 µl.

Calculate the percentage content of $C_{19}H_{38}O_2$ in the substance to be examined.

**STORAGE**

Protected from light.

————————————————————— *Ph Eur*

# Diluted Isosorbide Dinitrate

*(Ph Eur monograph 1117)*

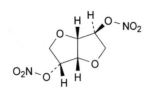

C₆H₈N₂O₈          236.1          87-33-2

$C_6H_8N_2O_8$          236.1          87-33-2

## Action and use

Nitric acid analogue; treatment of angina pectoris.

## Preparation

Isosorbide Dinitrate Tablets

*Ph Eur* ⎯⎯⎯⎯⎯⎯⎯⎯⎯⎯⎯⎯⎯⎯⎯⎯⎯⎯

## DEFINITION

Dry mixture of isosorbide dinitrate and *Lactose monohydrate (0187)* or *Mannitol (0559)*.

## Content

95.0 per cent *m/m* to 105.0 per cent *m/m* of the content of 1,4:3,6-dianhydro-D-glucitol 2,5-dinitrate stated on the label.

*CAUTION: undiluted isosorbide dinitrate may explode if subjected to percussion or excessive heat. Appropriate precautions must be taken and only very small quantities handled.*

## CHARACTERS

### Appearance

Undiluted isosorbide dinitrate is a fine, white or almost white, crystalline powder.

### Solubility

Undiluted isosorbide dinitrate is very slightly soluble in water, very soluble in acetone, sparingly soluble in ethanol (96 per cent).

The solubility of the diluted product depends on the diluent and its concentration.

## IDENTIFICATION

*First identification  A, C, D.*

*Second identification  B, C, D.*

A. Infrared absorption spectrophotometry (2.2.24).

*Preparation*  Discs prepared with the residue obtained in identification test D.

*Comparison  isosorbide dinitrate CRS.*

B. Thin-layer chromatography (2.2.27).

*Test solution*  Shake a quantity of the substance to be examined corresponding to 10 mg of isosorbide dinitrate with 10 ml of *ethanol (96 per cent) R* for 5 min and filter.

*Reference solution*  Shake a quantity of *isosorbide dinitrate CRS* corresponding to 10 mg of isosorbide dinitrate with 10 ml of *ethanol (96 per cent) R* for 5 min and filter.

*Plate  TLC silica gel G plate R.*

*Mobile phase  methanol R, methylene chloride R (5:95 V/V).*

*Application  10 µl.*

*Development  Over a path of 15 cm.*

*Drying  In a current of air.*

*Detection*  Spray with freshly prepared *potassium iodide* and *starch solution R*; expose to ultraviolet light at 254 nm for 15 min and examine in daylight.

*Results*  The principal spot in the chromatogram obtained with the test solution is similar in position, colour and size to the principal spot in the chromatogram obtained with the reference solution.

C. Thin-layer chromatography (2.2.27).

*Test solution*  Shake a quantity of the substance to be examined corresponding to 0.10 g of lactose or mannitol with 10 ml of *water R*. Filter if necessary.

*Reference solution (a)*  Dissolve 0.10 g of *lactose R* in *water R* and dilute to 10 ml with the same solvent.

*Reference solution (b)*  Dissolve 0.10 g of *mannitol R* in *water R* and dilute to 10 ml with the same solvent.

*Reference solution (c)*  Mix equal volumes of reference solutions (a) and (b).

*Plate  TLC silica gel G plate R.*

*Mobile phase  water R, methanol R, anhydrous acetic acid R, ethylene chloride R (10:15:25:50 V/V/V/V);* measure the volumes accurately since a slight excess of water produces cloudiness.

*Application*  1 µl; thoroughly dry the starting points.

*Development A*  Over a path of 15 cm.

*Drying A*  In a current of warm air.

*Development B*  Immediately, over a path of 15 cm, after renewing the mobile phase.

*Drying B*  In a current of warm air.

*Detection*  Spray with *4-aminobenzoic acid solution R*, dry in a current of cold air until the acetone is removed, then heat at 100 °C for 15 min; allow to cool, spray with a 2 g/l solution of *sodium periodate R*, dry in a current of cold air, and heat at 100 °C for 15 min.

*System suitability*  Reference solution (c):
— the chromatogram shows 2 clearly separated spots.

*Results*  The principal spot in the chromatogram obtained with the test solution is similar in position, colour and size to the principal spot in the chromatogram obtained with reference solution (a) for lactose or to the principal spot in the chromatogram obtained with reference solution (b) for mannitol.

D. Shake a quantity of the substance to be examined corresponding to 25 mg of isosorbide dinitrate with 10 ml of *acetone R* for 5 min. Filter, evaporate to dryness at a temperature below 40 °C and dry the residue over *diphosphorus pentoxide R* at a pressure of 0.7 kPa for 16 h. The melting point (2.2.14) of the residue is 69 °C to 72 °C.

## TESTS

### Impurity A

Thin-layer chromatography (2.2.27).

*Test solution*  Shake a quantity of the substance to be examined corresponding to 0.10 g of isosorbide dinitrate with 5 ml of *ethanol (96 per cent) R* and filter.

*Reference solution*  Dissolve 10 mg of *potassium nitrate R* in 1 ml of *water R* and dilute to 100 ml with *ethanol (96 per cent) R.*

*Plate  TLC silica gel plate R.*

*Mobile phase  glacial acetic acid R, acetone R, toluene R (15:30:60 V/V/V).*

*Application  10 µl.*

*Development  Over a path of 15 cm.*

*Drying*  In a current of air until the acetic acid is completely removed.

*Detection* Spray copiously with freshly prepared *potassium iodide and starch solution R*; expose to ultraviolet light at 254 nm for 15 min and examine in daylight.

*Limit:*

— *impurity A*: any spot due to impurity A is not more intense than the principal spot in the chromatogram obtained with the reference solution (0.5 per cent, calculated as potassium nitrate).

**Impurities B and C**

Liquid chromatography (*2.2.29*).

*Test solution (a)* Sonicate a quantity of the substance to be examined corresponding to 25.0 mg of isosorbide dinitrate with 20 ml of the mobile phase for 15 min and dilute to 25.0 ml with the mobile phase. Filter the solution through a suitable membrane filter.

*Test solution (b)* Dilute 1.0 ml of test solution (a) to 10.0 ml with the mobile phase.

*Reference solution (a)* Sonicate a quantity of *isosorbide dinitrate CRS* corresponding to 25.0 mg of *isosorbide dinitrate CRS* with 20 ml of the mobile phase for 15 min and dilute to 25.0 ml with the mobile phase. Filter the solution through a suitable membrane filter.

*Reference solution (b)* Dilute 1.0 ml of reference solution (a) to 10.0 ml with the mobile phase.

*Reference solution (c)* Dissolve 10.0 mg of *isosorbide 2-nitrate CRS* (impurity B) in the mobile phase and dilute to 10.0 ml with the mobile phase. Dilute 0.1 ml of this solution to 20.0 ml with the mobile phase.

*Reference solution (d)* Dissolve 10.0 mg of *isosorbide mononitrate CRS* (impurity C) in the mobile phase and dilute to 10.0 ml with the mobile phase. Dilute 0.1 ml of this solution to 20.0 ml with the mobile phase.

*Reference solution (e)* Dissolve 5 mg of *isosorbide 2-nitrate CRS* (impurity B) in the mobile phase and dilute to 10 ml with the mobile phase. To 1 ml of this solution add 0.5 ml of reference solution (a) and dilute to 10 ml with the mobile phase.

*Column:*

— *size*: $l$ = 0.25 m, Ø = 4.6 mm;
— *stationary phase*: aminopropylmethylsilyl silica gel for chromatography R (10 µm).

*Mobile phase* anhydrous ethanol R, trimethylpentane R (15:85 *V/V*).

*Flow rate* 1 ml/min.

*Detection* Spectrophotometer at 210-215 nm.

*Injection* 10 µl of test solution (a) and reference solutions (c), (d) and (e).

*Retention time* Isosorbide dinitrate = about 5 min; impurity B = about 8 min; impurity C = about 11 min.

*System suitability* Reference solution (e):

— *resolution*: minimum 6.0 between the peaks due to isosorbide dinitrate and impurity B.

*Limits:*

— *impurity B*: not more than the area of the principal peak in the chromatogram obtained with reference solution (c) (0.5 per cent);
— *impurity C*: not more than the area of the principal peak in the chromatogram obtained with reference solution (d) (0.5 per cent).

**ASSAY**

Liquid chromatography (*2.2.29*) as described in the test for impurities B and C with the following modifications.

*Detection* Spectrophotometer at 230 nm.

*Injection* 20 µl of test solution (b) and reference solution (b).

If the areas of the peaks from 2 successive injections of reference solution (b) do not agree to within 1.0 per cent, then inject a further 4 times and calculate, for the 6 injections, the relative standard deviation.

*System suitability* Reference solution (b):

— *repeatability*: maximum relative standard deviation of 2.0 per cent after 6 injections.

Calculate the content of isosorbide dinitrate as a percentage of the declared content.

**STORAGE**

Protected from light.

**LABELLING**

The label states the percentage content of isosorbide dinitrate.

**IMPURITIES**

*Specified impurities* A, B, C.

A. inorganic nitrates,

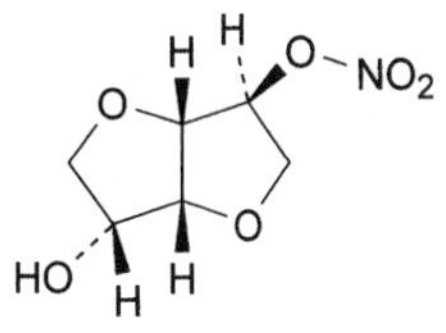

B. isosorbide 2-nitrate,

C. isosorbide mononitrate (isosorbide 5-nitrate).

_____ *Ph Eur*

# Diluted Isosorbide Mononitrate

(*Ph Eur monograph 1118*)

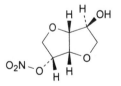

$C_6H_9NO_6$        191.1        *16051-77-7*

**Action and use**

Nitric acid analogue; treatment of angina pectoris.

**Preparations**

Isosorbide Mononitrate Tablets

Prolonged-release Isosorbide Mononitrate Tablets

*Ph Eur* _____

**DEFINITION**

Dry mixture of isosorbide mononitrate and *Lactose monohydrate (0187)* or *Mannitol (0559)*.

**Content**

95.0 per cent *m/m* to 105.0 per cent *m/m* of the content of 1,4:3,6-dianhydro-D-glucitol 5-nitrate stated on the label.

## CHARACTERS

### Appearance

Undiluted isosorbide mononitrate is a white or almost white, crystalline powder.

### Solubility

Undiluted isosorbide mononitrate is freely soluble in water, in acetone, in ethanol (96 per cent) and in methylene chloride.

The solubility of the diluted product depends on the diluent and its concentration.

## IDENTIFICATION

*First identification* A, C, D.

*Second identification* B, C, D.

A. Infrared absorption spectrophotometry (*2.2.24*).

*Preparation* Discs prepared with the residue obtained in identification test D.

*Comparison* isosorbide mononitrate CRS.

B. Thin-layer chromatography (*2.2.27*).

*Test solution* Shake a quantity of the substance to be examined corresponding to 10 mg of isosorbide mononitrate with 10 ml of *ethanol (96 per cent) R* for 5 min and filter.

*Reference solution* Dissolve 10 mg of *isosorbide mononitrate CRS* in *ethanol (96 per cent) R* and dilute to 10 ml with the same solvent.

*Plate* TLC *silica gel G plate R*.

*Mobile phase* methanol R, methylene chloride R (5:95 V/V).

*Application* 10 μl.

*Development* Over a path of 15 cm.

*Drying* In a current of air.

*Detection* Spray with freshly prepared *potassium iodide and starch solution R*. Expose to ultraviolet light at 254 nm for 15 min and examine in daylight.

*Results* The principal spot in the chromatogram obtained with the test solution is similar in position, colour and size to the principal spot in the chromatogram obtained with the reference solution.

C. Thin-layer chromatography (*2.2.27*).

*Test solution* Shake a quantity of the substance to be examined corresponding to 0.10 g of lactose or mannitol with 10 ml of *water R*; filter if necessary.

*Reference solution (a)* Dissolve 0.10 g of *lactose R* in *water R* and dilute to 10 ml with the same solvent.

*Reference solution (b)* Dissolve 0.10 g of *mannitol R* in *water R* and dilute to 10 ml with the same solvent.

*Reference solution (c)* Mix equal volumes of reference solutions (a) and (b).

*Plate* TLC *silica gel G plate R*.

*Mobile phase* water R, methanol R, anhydrous acetic acid R, ethylene chloride R (10:15:25:50 V/V/V/V); measure the volumes accurately since a slight excess of water produces cloudiness.

*Application* 1 μl; thoroughly dry the starting points.

*Development A* Over a path of 15 cm.

*Drying A* In a current of warm air.

*Development B* Immediately, over a path of 15 cm, after renewing the mobile phase.

*Drying B* In a current of warm air.

*Detection* Spray with *4-aminobenzoic acid solution R* and dry in a current of cold air until the acetone is removed; heat at 100 °C for 15 min and allow to cool; spray with a 2 g/l

solution of *sodium periodate R* and dry in a current of cold air; heat at 100 °C for 15 min.

*System suitability* Reference solution (c):
— the chromatogram shows 2 clearly separated spots.

*Results* The principal spot in the chromatogram obtained with the test solution is similar in position, colour and size to the principal spot in the chromatogram obtained with reference solution (a) for lactose or to the principal spot in the chromatogram obtained with reference solution (b) for mannitol.

D. Shake a quantity of the substance to be examined corresponding to 25 mg of isosorbide mononitrate with 10 ml of *acetone R* for 5 min. Filter, evaporate to dryness at a temperature below 40 °C and dry the residue over *diphosphorus pentoxide R* at a pressure of 0.7 kPa for 16 h. The melting point (*2.2.14*) of the residue is 89 °C to 91 °C.

## TESTS

### Impurity A

Thin-layer chromatography (*2.2.27*).

*Test solution* Shake a quantity of the substance to be examined corresponding to 0.10 g of isosorbide mononitrate with 5 ml of *ethanol (96 per cent) R* and filter.

*Reference solution* Dissolve 10 mg of *potassium nitrate R* in 1 ml of *water R* and dilute to 100 ml with *ethanol (96 per cent) R*.

*Plate* TLC *silica gel plate R*.

*Mobile phase* glacial acetic acid R, acetone R, toluene R (15:30:60 V/V/V).

*Application* 10 μl.

*Development* Over a path of 15 cm.

*Drying* In a current of air until the acetic acid is completely removed.

*Detection* Spray copiously with freshly prepared *potassium iodide and starch solution R*; expose to ultraviolet light at 254 nm for 15 min and examine in daylight.

*Limit:*
— *impurity A*: any spot due to impurity A is not more intense than the principal spot in the chromatogram obtained with the reference solution (0.5 per cent, calculated as potassium nitrate).

### Impurities B and C

Liquid chromatography (*2.2.29*).

*Test solution (a)* Sonicate a quantity of the substance to be examined corresponding to 25.0 mg of isosorbide mononitrate with 20 ml of the mobile phase for 15 min and dilute to 25.0 ml with the mobile phase. Filter the solution through a suitable membrane filter.

*Test solution (b)* Dilute 1.0 ml of test solution (a) to 10.0 ml with the mobile phase.

*Reference solution (a)* Dissolve 25.0 mg of *isosorbide mononitrate CRS* in the mobile phase and dilute to 25.0 ml with the mobile phase. Dilute 1.0 ml of this solution to 10.0 ml with the mobile phase.

*Reference solution (b)* Dissolve 10.0 mg of *isosorbide-2-nitrate CRS* (impurity C) in the mobile phase and dilute to 10.0 ml with the mobile phase. Dilute 0.1 ml of this solution to 20.0 ml with the mobile phase.

*Reference solution (c)* Sonicate a quantity of *isosorbide dinitrate CRS* (impurity B) corresponding to 10.0 mg of isosorbide dinitrate in 15 ml of the mobile phase for 15 min and dilute to 20.0 ml with the mobile phase. Filter the solution through a suitable membrane filter. Dilute 0.1 ml of this solution to 10.0 ml with the mobile phase.

*Reference solution (d)* Dissolve 5 mg of *isosorbide mononitrate CRS* and 5 mg of *isosorbide-2-nitrate CRS* (impurity C) in the mobile phase and dilute to 10 ml with the mobile phase. Dilute 1 ml of this solution to 10 ml with the mobile phase.

*Column:*
— *size*: *l* = 0.25 m, Ø = 4.6 mm;
— *stationary phase*: *aminopropylmethylsilyl silica gel for chromatography R* (10 μm).

*Mobile phase* *anhydrous ethanol R, trimethylpentane R* (15:85 *V/V*).

*Flow rate* 1 ml/min.

*Detection* Spectrophotometer at 210-215 nm.

*Injection* 10 μl of test solution (a) and reference solutions (b), (c) and (d).

*Retention time* Impurity B = about 5 min; impurity C = about 8 min; isosorbide 5-nitrate = about 11 min.

*System suitability* Reference solution (d):
— *resolution*: minimum 4.0 between the peaks due to impurity C and isosorbide 5-nitrate.

*Limits:*
— *impurity B*: not more than the area of the principal peak in the chromatogram obtained with reference solution (c) (0.5 per cent);
— *impurity C:* not more than the area of the principal peak in the chromatogram obtained with reference solution (b) (0.5 per cent).

## ASSAY

Liquid chromatography (*2.2.29*) as described in the test for impurities B and C with the following modifications.

*Detection* Spectrophotometer at 230 nm.

*Injection* 20 μl of test solution (b) and reference solution (a).

If the areas of the peaks from 2 successive injections of reference solution (a) do not agree to within 1.0 per cent, then inject a further 4 times and calculate, for the 6 injections, the relative standard deviation.

*System suitability* Reference solution (a):
— *repeatability*: maximum relative standard deviation of 2.0 per cent after 6 injections.

Calculate the content of isosorbide mononitrate as a percentage of the declared content.

## STORAGE

Protected from light.

## LABELLING

The label states the percentage content of isosorbide mononitrate.

## IMPURITIES

*Specified impurities* *A, B, C.*

A. inorganic nitrates,

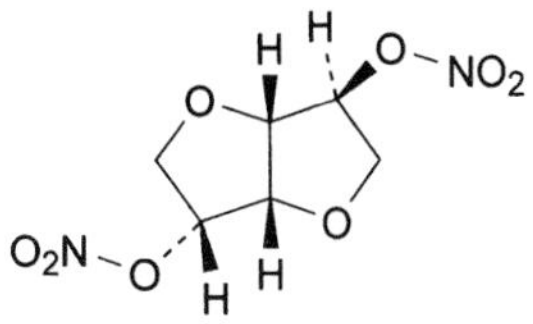

B. isosorbide dinitrate,

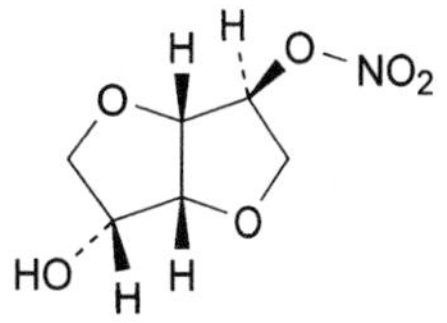

C. isosorbide 2-nitrate.

*Ph Eur*

# Isotretinoin

(*Ph Eur monograph 1019*)

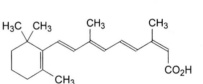

C$_{20}$H$_{28}$O$_2$        300.4        4759-48-2

## Action and use

Vitamin A analogue (retinoid); treatment of acne.

## Preparations

Isotretinoin Capsules

Isotretinoin Gel

*Ph Eur*

## DEFINITION

Isotretinoin contains not less than 98.0 per cent and not more than the equivalent of 102.0 per cent of (2Z,4E,6E,8E)-3,7-dimethyl-9-(2,6,6-trimethylcyclohex-1-enyl)nona-2,4,6,8-tetraenoic acid, calculated with reference to the dried substance.

## CHARACTERS

A yellow or light-orange, crystalline powder, practically insoluble in water, soluble in methylene chloride, slightly soluble in alcohol. It is sensitive to air, heat and light, especially in solution.

*Carry out all operations as rapidly as possible and avoid exposure to actinic light; use freshly prepared solutions.*

## IDENTIFICATION

*First identification* *A, B.*

*Second identification* *A, C, D.*

A. Dissolve 75.0 mg in 5 ml of *methylene chloride R* and dilute immediately to 100.0 ml with acidified 2-propanol (prepared by diluting 1 ml of *0.01 M hydrochloric acid* to 1000 ml with *2-propanol R*). Dilute 5.0 ml of this solution to 100.0 ml with the acidified 2-propanol (solution A). Dilute 5.0 ml of solution A to 50.0 ml with the acidified 2-propanol. Examined between 300 nm and 400 nm

(2.2.25), the solution shows an absorption maximum at 354 nm. The specific absorbance at the maximum is 1290 to 1420.

B. Examine by infrared absorption spectrophotometry (2.2.24), comparing with the spectrum obtained with *isotretinoin CRS*. Examine the substances prepared as discs.

C. Examine by thin-layer chromatography (2.2.27), using a *TLC silica gel GF₂₅₄ plate R*.

*Test solution*   Dissolve 10 mg of the substance to be examined in *methylene chloride R* and dilute to 10 ml with the same solvent.

*Reference solution (a)*   Dissolve 10 mg of *isotretinoin CRS* in *methylene chloride R* and dilute to 10 ml with the same solvent.

*Reference solution (b)*   Dissolve 10 mg of *isotretinoin CRS* and 10 mg of *tretinoin CRS* in *methylene chloride R* and dilute to 10 ml with the same solvent.

Apply separately to the plate 5 μl of each solution. Develop over a path of 15 cm using a mixture of 2 volumes of *glacial acetic acid R*, 4 volumes of *acetone R*, 40 volumes of *peroxide-free ether R* and 54 volumes of *cyclohexane R*. Allow the plate to dry in air and examine in ultraviolet light at 254 nm. The principal spot in the chromatogram obtained with the test solution is similar in position and size to the principal spot in the chromatogram obtained with reference solution (a). The test is not valid unless the chromatogram obtained with reference solution (b) shows two clearly separated principal spots.

D. Dissolve about 5 mg in 2 ml of *antimony trichloride solution R*. An intense red colour develops and later becomes violet.

**TESTS**

**Related substances**

Examine by liquid chromatography (2.2.29).

*Test solution*   Dissolve 0.100 g of the substance to be examined in *methanol R* and dilute to 50.0 ml with the same solvent.

*Reference solution (a)*   Dissolve 10.0 mg of *tretinoin CRS* in *methanol R* and dilute to 10.0 ml with the same solvent.

*Reference solution (b)*   Dilute 1.0 ml of reference solution (a) to 25.0 ml with *methanol R*.

*Reference solution (c)*   Mix 1.0 ml of reference solution (a) with 0.5 ml of the test solution and dilute to 25.0 ml with *methanol R*.

*Reference solution (d)*   Dilute 0.5 ml of the test solution to 100.0 ml with *methanol R*.

The chromatographic procedure may be carried out using:
— a stainless steel column 0.15 m long and 4.6 mm in internal diameter packed with *octadecylsilyl silica gel for chromatography R* (3 μm),
— as mobile phase at a flow rate of 1.0 ml/min a mixture of 5 volumes of *glacial acetic acid R*, 225 volumes of *water R* and 770 volumes of *methanol R*.
— as detector a spectrophotometer set at 355 nm.

Inject separately 10 μl of each of reference solutions (b), (c) and (d) and of the test solution. Adjust the sensitivity of the detector so that the height of the principal peak in the chromatogram obtained with reference solution (b) is not less than 70 per cent of the full scale of the recorder. The test is not valid unless the resolution between the peaks due to isotretinoin and tretinoin in the chromatogram obtained with reference solution (c) is at least 2.0. In the chromatogram obtained with the test solution: the area of any peak due to

tretinoin is not greater than the area of the principal peak in the chromatogram obtained with reference solution (b) (2.0 per cent); the sum of the areas of any peaks, apart from the principal peak and any peak due to tretinoin, is not greater than the area of the principal peak in the chromatogram obtained with reference solution (d) (0.5 per cent).

**Heavy metals** (2.4.8)

0.5 g complies with limit test D for heavy metals (20 ppm). Prepare the standard using 1 ml of *lead standard solution (10 ppm Pb) R*.

**Loss on drying** (2.2.32)

Not more than 0.5 per cent, determined on 1.000 g by drying *in vacuo* for 16 h.

**Sulphated ash** (2.4.14)

Not more than 0.1 per cent, determined on 1.0 g.

**ASSAY**

Dissolve 0.200 g in 70 ml of *acetone R*. Titrate with *0.1 M tetrabutylammonium hydroxide* determining the end-point potentiometrically (2.2.20).

1 ml of *0.1 M tetrabutylammonium hydroxide* is equivalent to 30.04 mg of $C_{20}H_{28}O_2$.

**STORAGE**

Store in an airtight container, protected from light, at a temperature not exceeding 25 °C.

It is recommended that the contents of an opened container be used as soon as possible and any unused part be protected by an atmosphere of an inert gas.

**IMPURITIES**

A. tretinoin,

B. R = CO₂H, R′ = H: (2Z,4E,6Z,8E)-3,7-dimethyl-9-(2,6,6-trimethylcyclohex-1-enyl)nona-2,4,6,8-tetraenoic acid (9,13-di-*cis*-retinoic acid),

D. R = H, R′ = CO₂H: (2E,4E,6Z,8E)-3,7-dimethyl-9-(2,6,6-trimethylcyclohex-1-enyl)nona-2,4,6,8-tetraenoic acid (9-*cis*-retinoic acid),

C. (2Z,4Z,6E,8E)-3,7-dimethyl-9-(2,6,6-trimethylcyclohex-1-enyl)nona-2,4,6,8-tetraenoic acid (11,13-di-*cis*-retinoic acid),

E. oxidation products of isotretinoin.

*Ph Eur*

# Isoxsuprine Hydrochloride

(*Ph Eur monograph 1119*)

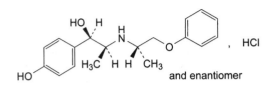

and enantiomer

$C_{18}H_{23}NO_3,HCl$      337.8      *579-56-6*

**Action and use**

Beta$_2$-adrenoceptor agonist.

*Ph Eur*

## DEFINITION

(1*RS*,2*SR*)-1-(4-Hydroxyphenyl)-2-[[(1*SR*)-1-methyl-2-phenoxyethyl]amino]propan-1-ol hydrochloride.

**Content**

99.0 per cent to 101.0 per cent (dried substance).

## CHARACTERS

**Appearance**

White or almost white, crystalline powder.

**Solubility**

Sparingly soluble in water and in ethanol (96 per cent), practically insoluble in methylene chloride.

**mp**

About 205 °C, with decomposition.

## IDENTIFICATION

*First identification*  B, E.

*Second identification*  A, C, D, E.

A. Ultraviolet and visible absorption spectrophotometry (*2.2.25*).

*Test solution*  Dissolve 50.0 mg in *0.1 M hydrochloric acid* and dilute to 50.0 ml with the same acid. Dilute 10.0 ml of this solution to 100.0 ml with *0.1 M hydrochloric acid*.

*Spectral range*  230-350 nm.

*Absorption maxima*  At 269 nm and 275 nm.

*Resolution (2.2.25)*  Minimum 1.7 for the absorbance ratio.

*Specific absorbance at the absorption maxima:*

— at 269 nm: 71 to 74;

— at 275 nm: 70 to 73.

B. Infrared absorption spectrophotometry (*2.2.24*).

*Preparation*  Discs.

*Comparison*  isoxsuprine hydrochloride CRS.

If the spectra obtained show differences, dissolve 50 mg of the substance to be examined and of the reference substance separately in 2 ml of *methanol R*, add 15 ml of *methylene chloride R*, evaporate to dryness and record new spectra using the residues.

C. Thin-layer chromatography (*2.2.27*).

*Test solution*  Dissolve 20 mg of the substance to be examined in *methanol R* and dilute to 10 ml with the same solvent.

*Reference solution*  Dissolve 20 mg of *isoxsuprine hydrochloride CRS* in *methanol R* and dilute to 10 ml with the same solvent.

*Plate*  TLC silica gel G plate R.

*Mobile phase*  concentrated ammonia R, methanol R, methylene chloride R (0.25:15:85 *V/V/V*).

*Application*  10 μl.

*Development*  Over a path of 12 cm.

*Drying*  In a current of warm air.

*Detection*  Spray with a 10 g/l solution of *potassium permanganate R*.

*Results*  The principal spot in the chromatogram obtained with the test solution is similar in position, colour and size to the principal spot in the chromatogram obtained with the reference solution.

D. To 1 ml of solution S (see Tests) add 0.05 ml of *copper sulphate solution R* and 0.5 ml of *strong sodium hydroxide solution R*. The solution becomes blue. Add 1 ml of *ether R* and shake. Allow to separate. The upper layer remains colourless.

E. 2 ml of solution S gives reaction (a) of chlorides (*2.3.1*).

## TESTS

**Solution S**

Dissolve 0.50 g, with gentle heating if necessary, in *carbon dioxide-free water R*, cool and dilute to 50.0 ml with the same solvent.

**Appearance of solution**

Solution S is clear (*2.2.1*) and colourless (*2.2.2, Method II*).

**pH** (*2.2.3*)

4.5 to 6.0 for solution S.

**Optical rotation** (*2.2.7*)

− 0.05 ° to + 0.05 °, determined on solution S.

**Phenones**

Maximum 1.0 per cent, calculated as impurity B.

Dissolve 10.0 mg in *water R* and dilute to 100.0 ml with the same solvent. The absorbance (*2.2.25*) of the solution measured at the absorption maximum at 310 nm is not greater than 0.10.

**Related substances**

Gas chromatography (*2.2.28*). *Prepare the solutions immediately before use.*

*Internal standard solution (a)*  Dissolve 0.1 g of *hexacosane R* in *trimethylpentane R* and dilute to 20 ml with the same solvent.

*Internal standard solution (b)*  Dilute 1 ml of internal standard solution (a) to 50 ml with *trimethylpentane R*.

*Test solution*  To 10.0 mg of the substance to be examined, add 0.5 ml of *N-trimethylsilylimidazole R*. Heat to 65 °C for 10 min. Allow to cool, then add 2.0 ml of the internal standard solution (b) and 2.0 ml of *water R*. Shake. Use the upper layer.

*Reference solution (a)*  To 10.0 mg of the substance to be examined, add 0.5 ml of *N-trimethylsilylimidazole R*. Heat to 65 °C for 10 min. Allow to cool, then add 2.0 ml of the internal standard solution (a) and 2.0 ml of *water R*. Shake. Dilute 1.0 ml of the upper layer to 50.0 ml with *trimethylpentane R*.

*Reference solution (b)*  To 10.0 mg of the substance to be examined, add 0.5 ml of *N-trimethylsilylimidazole R*. Heat to 65 °C for 10 min. Allow to cool, then add 2.0 ml of *trimethylpentane R* and 2.0 ml of *water R*. Shake. Use the upper layer.

*Column:*

— *material: glass;*

— *size: l* = 1.5 m, Ø = 4 mm;

— *stationary phase*: *silanised diatomaceous earth for gas chromatography R* (125-135 μm) impregnated with 3 per cent *m/m* of *poly(dimethyl)siloxane R*.

*Carrier gas*  *nitrogen for chromatography R*.

*Flow rate*  30 ml/min.

*Temperature:*

|  | Time (min) | Temperature (°C) |
|---|---|---|
| Column | 0 - 25 | 195 |
|  | 25 - 29 | 195 → 215 |
|  | 29 - 39 | 215 |
| Injection port |  | 225 |
| Detector |  | 225 |

*Detection*  Flame ionisation.

*Injection*  1 μl.

*Elution order*  Isoxsuprine, hexacosane.

*System suitability:*

— *resolution*: minimum 5.0 between the peaks due to isoxsurpine and hexacosane in the chromatogram obtained with reference solution (a);

— in the chromatogram obtained with reference solution (b), there is no peak with the same retention time as the internal standard.

*Limit:*

— *total*: calculate the ratio (*R*) of the area of the peak due to the trimethylsilyl derivative of isoxsuprine to the area of the peak due to the internal standard from the chromatogram obtained with reference solution (a); from the chromatogram obtained with the test solution, calculate the ratio of the sum of the areas of any peaks, apart from the principal peak and the peak due to the internal standard, to the area of the peak due to the internal standard: this ratio is not greater than *R* (2.0 per cent).

**Heavy metals** (*2.4.8*)

Maximum 20 ppm.

1.0 g complies with test C. Prepare the reference solution using 2 ml of *lead standard solution (10 ppm Pb) R*.

**Loss on drying** (*2.2.32*)

Maximum 0.5 per cent, determined on 1.000 g by drying in an oven at 105 °C.

**Sulphated ash** (*2.4.14*)

Maximum 0.1 per cent, determined on 1.0 g.

**ASSAY**

Dissolve 0.250 g in 80 ml of *ethanol (96 per cent) R* and add 1.0 ml of *0.1 M hydrochloric acid*. Carry out a potentiometric titration (*2.2.20*), using *0.1 M sodium hydroxide*. Read the volume added between the 2 points of inflexion.

1 ml of *0.1 M sodium hydroxide* is equivalent to 33.78 mg of $C_{18}H_{24}ClNO_3$.

**STORAGE**

Protected from light.

**IMPURITIES**

*Specified impurities*  B.

*Other detectable impurities*  (the following substances would, if present at a sufficient level, be detected by one or other of the tests in the monograph. They are limited by the general acceptance criterion for other/unspecified impurities and/or by the general monograph *Substances for pharmaceutical use* (*2034*). It is therefore not necessary to identify these impurities for demonstration of compliance. See also *5.10. Control of impurities in substances for pharmaceutical use*): A.

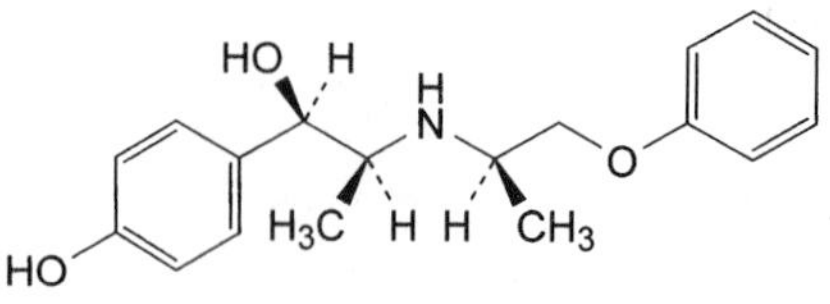

A. (1*RS*,2*SR*)-1-(4-hydroxyphenyl)-2-[[(1*RS*)-1-methyl-2-phenoxyethyl]amino]propan-1-ol,

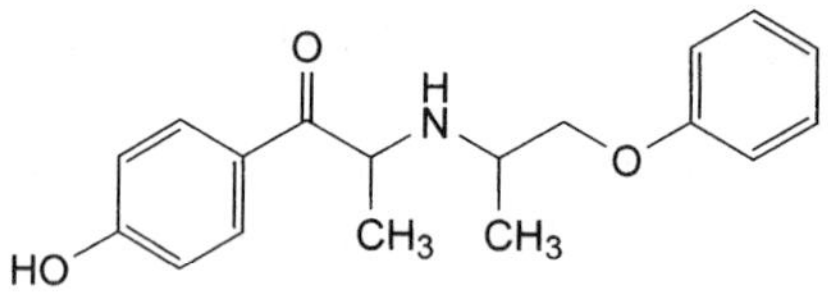

B. 1-(4-hydroxyphenyl)-2-[(1-methyl-2-phenoxyethyl)amino]propan-1-one.

*Ph Eur*

# Isradipine

*(Ph Eur monograph 2110)*

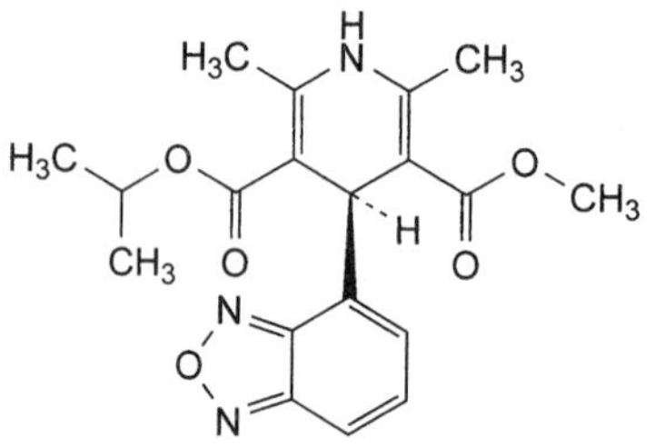

$C_{19}H_{21}N_3O_5$    371.4    *75695-93-1*

**Action and use**

Calcium channel blocker.

**Preparation**

Isradipine Tablets

*Ph Eur*

**DEFINITION**

Methyl 1-methylethyl (4*RS*)-4-(2,1,3-benzoxadiazol-4-yl)-2,6-dimethyl-1,4-dihydropyridine-3,5-dicarboxylate.

**Content**

97.0 per cent to 102.0 per cent (dried substance).

**CHARACTERS**

**Appearance**

Yellow, crystalline powder.

**Solubility**

Practically insoluble in water, freely soluble in acetone, soluble in methanol.

**mp**

About 168 °C.

## IDENTIFICATION

Infrared absorption spectrophotometry (*2.2.24*).

*Comparison*   isradipine CRS.

## TESTS

**Related substances**

Liquid chromatography (*2.2.29*).

*Test solution (a)*   Dissolve 50.0 mg of the substance to be examined in 1 ml of *methanol R*, using an ultrasonic bath if necessary, and dilute to 25.0 ml with the mobile phase.

*Test solution (b)*   Dissolve 50.0 mg of the substance to be examined in 2 ml of *methanol R* and dilute to 250.0 ml with the mobile phase.

*Reference solution (a)*   Dilute 1.0 ml of test solution (a) to 100.0 ml with the mobile phase. Dilute 1.0 ml of this solution to 10.0 ml with the mobile phase.

*Reference solution (b)*   Dissolve 2 mg of the substance to be examined and 2 mg of *isradipine impurity D CRS* in the mobile phase and dilute to 10.0 ml with the mobile phase. Dilute 1.0 ml of this solution to 10.0 ml with the mobile phase.

*Reference solution (c)*   Dissolve 50.0 mg of *isradipine CRS* in 2 ml of *methanol R* and dilute to 250.0 ml with the mobile phase.

*Column:*
— *size: l* = 0.10 m, Ø = 4.6 mm,
— *stationary phase: octadecylsilyl silica gel for chromatography R* (5 µm).

*Mobile phase*   acetonitrile R, tetrahydrofuran R, water R (125:270:625 *V/V/V*).

*Flow rate*   1.2 ml/min.

*Detection*   Spectrophotometer at 230 nm.

*Injection*   20 µl of test solution (a) and reference solutions (a) and (b).

*Run time*   5 times the retention time of isradipine.

*Identification of impurities*   Use the chromatogram supplied with *isradipine CRS* to identify the peaks due to impurities A and B.

*Relative retention*   with reference to isradipine (retention time = about 7 min): impurity A = about 0.8; impurity D = about 0.9; impurity B = about 1.8.

*System suitability*   Reference solution (b):
— *resolution*: minimum 2.0 between the peaks due to isradipine and impurity D.

*Limits:*
— *correction factor*: for the calculation of content, multiply the peak area of impurity D by 1.4;
— *impurity A*: not more than twice the area of the principal peak in the chromatogram obtained with reference solution (a) (0.2 per cent);
— *impurity B*: not more than 8 times the area of the principal peak in the chromatogram obtained with reference solution (a) (0.8 per cent);
— *impurity D*: not more than the area of the principal peak in the chromatogram obtained with reference solution (a) (0.1 per cent);

— *any other impurity*: for each impurity, not more than the area of the principal peak in the chromatogram obtained with reference solution (a) (0.1 per cent);
— *total*: not more than 10 times the area of the principal peak in the chromatogram obtained with reference solution (a) (1.0 per cent);
— *disregard limit*: 0.5 times the area of the principal peak in the chromatogram obtained with reference solution (a) (0.05 per cent).

**Loss on drying** (*2.2.32*)

Maximum 0.2 per cent, determined on 1.000 g by drying in an oven at 105 °C for 4 h.

**Sulphated ash** (*2.4.14*)

Maximum 0.1 per cent, determined on 1.0 g.

## ASSAY

Liquid chromatography (*2.2.29*) as described in the test for related substances with the following modifications.

*Detection*   Spectrophotometer at 326 nm.

*Injection*   Test solution (b) and reference solution (c).

*Run time*   Twice the retention time of isradipine.

Calculate the percentage content of isradipine from the areas of the peaks and the declared content of *isradipine CRS*.

## STORAGE

Protected from light.

## IMPURITIES

*Specified impurities*   A, B, D.

*Other detectable impurities*   (the following substances would, if present at a sufficient level, be detected by one or other of the tests in the monograph. They are limited by the general acceptance criterion for other/unspecified impurities and/or by the general monograph *Substances for pharmaceutical use* (*2034*). It is therefore not necessary to identify these impurities for demonstration of compliance. See also *5.10*. *Control of impurities in substances for pharmaceutical use*): C, E.

A. R = C₂H₅, R' = CH₃: ethyl methyl (4*RS*)-4-(2,1,3-benzoxadiazol-4-yl)-2,6-dimethyl-1,4-dihydropyridine-3,5-dicarboxylate,

B. R = R' = CH(CH₃)₂: bis(1-methylethyl) (4*RS*)-4-(2,1,3-benzoxadiazol-4-yl)-2,6-dimethyl-1,4-dihydropyridine-3,5-dicarboxylate,

C. R = R' = CH₃: dimethyl (4*RS*)-4-(2,1,3-benzoxadiazol-4-yl)-2,6-dimethyl-1,4-dihydropyridine-3,5-dicarboxylate,

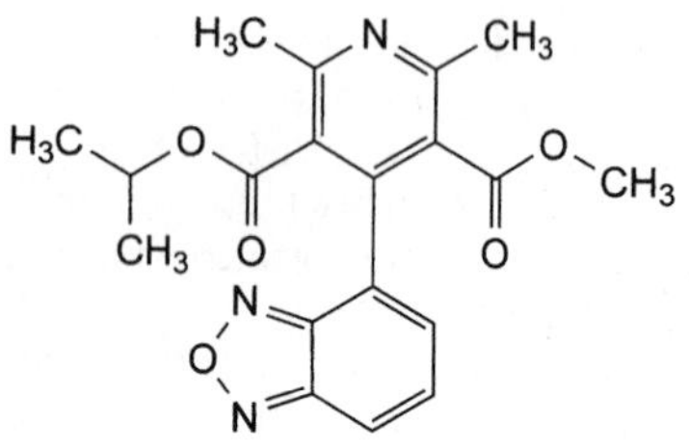

D. methyl 1-methylethyl 4-(2,1,3-benzoxadiazol-4-yl)-2,6-dimethylpyridine-3,5-dicarboxylate,

its (Z) isomer and their enantiomers

R = CH₃, R' = CH(CH₃)₂
and
R = CH(CH₃)₂, R' = CH₃

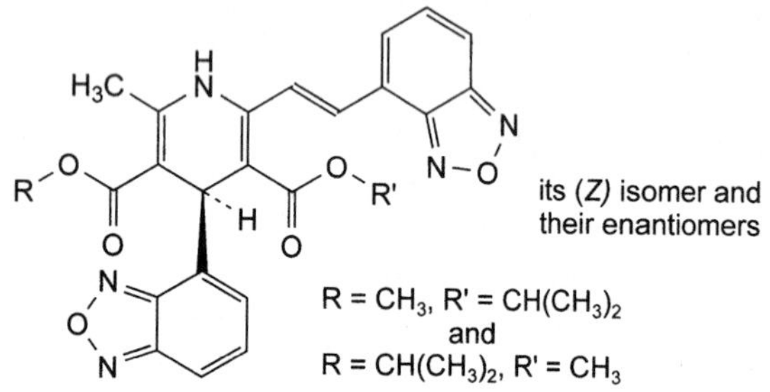

E. methyl 1-methylethyl (4RS)-4-(2,1,3-benzoxadiazol-4-yl)-2-[(EZ)-2-(2,1,3-benzoxadiazol-4-yl)ethenyl]-6-methyl-1,4-dihydropyridine-3,5-dicarboxylate.

_____ Ph Eur

# Itraconazole

(Ph Eur monograph 1335)

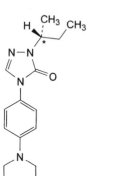

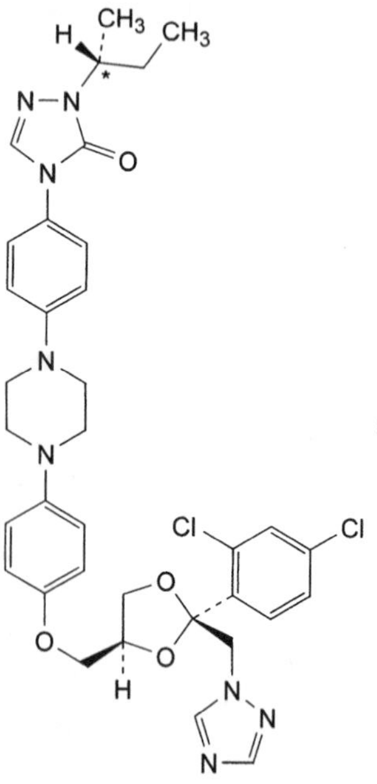

its epimer at C*

and their enantiomers

C₃₅H₃₈Cl₂N₈O₄     706     84625-61-6

**Action and use**
Antifungal.

Ph Eur

## DEFINITION
4-[4-[4-[4-[[cis-2-(2,4-Dichlorophenyl)-2-(1H-1,2,4-triazol-1-ylmethyl)-1,3-dioxolan-4-yl]methoxy]phenyl]piperazin-1-yl]phenyl]-2-[(1RS)-1-methylpropyl]-2,4-dihydro-3H-1,2,4-triazol-3-one.

### Content
99.0 per cent to 101.0 per cent (dried substance).

## CHARACTERS
### Appearance
White or almost white powder.

### Solubility
Practically insoluble in water, freely soluble in methylene chloride, very slightly soluble in ethanol (96 per cent).

## IDENTIFICATION
Infrared spectrophotometry (2.2.24).

Comparison   itraconazole CRS.

## TESTS
### Solution S
Dissolve 2.0 g in methylene chloride R and dilute to 20.0 ml with the same solvent.

### Appearance of solution
Solution S is clear (2.2.1) and not more intensely coloured than reference solution R₆ or B₆ (2.2.2, Method II).

### Related substances
Liquid chromatography (2.2.29). Prepare the solutions immediately before use.

Test solution   Dissolve 0.100 g of the substance to be examined in methanolic hydrochloric acid R and dilute to 10.0 ml with the same solvent.

Reference solution (a)   Dilute 1.0 ml of the test solution to 100.0 ml with methanolic hydrochloric acid R. Dilute 1.0 ml of this solution to 10.0 ml with methanolic hydrochloric acid R.

Reference solution (b)   Dissolve 10 mg of itraconazole for system suitability CRS (containing impurities B, C, D, E, F and G) in 1.0 ml of methanolic hydrochloric acid R.

Column:
— size: l = 0.10 m, Ø = 4.6 mm;
— stationary phase: base-deactivated end-capped octadecylsilyl silica gel for chromatography R (3 μm);
— temperature: 30 °C.

Mobile phase:
— mobile phase A: 27.2 g/l solution of tetrabutylammonium hydrogen sulphate R1;
— mobile phase B: acetonitrile R1;

| Time (min) | Mobile phase A (per cent V/V) | Mobile phase B (per cent V/V) |
|---|---|---|
| 0 - 2 | 80 | 20 |
| 2 - 22 | 80 → 50 | 20 → 50 |
| 22 - 27 | 50 | 50 |

Flow rate   1.5 ml/min.

Detection   Spectrophotometer at 225 nm.

Injection   10 μl.

Identification of impurities   Use the chromatogram supplied with itraconazole for system suitability CRS and the chromatogram obtained with reference solution (b) to identify the peaks due to impurities B, C, D, E, F and G.

*Relative retention*  With reference to itraconazole (retention time = about 14 min): impurity B = about 0.7; impurities C and D = about 0.8; impurity E = about 0.9; impurity F = about 1.05; impurity G = about 1.3.

*System suitability*  Reference solution (b):
— *peak-to-valley ratio*: minimum 1.5, where $H_p$ = height above the baseline of the peak due to impurity F and $H_v$ = height above the baseline of the lowest point of the curve separating this peak from the peak due to itraconazole.

*Limits:*
— *impurities B, G*: for each impurity, not more than 3 times the area of the principal peak in the chromatogram obtained with reference solution (a) (0.3 per cent);
— *impurity E*: not more than twice the area of the principal peak in the chromatogram obtained with reference solution (a) (0.2 per cent);
— *sum of impurities C and D*: not more than 3 times the area of the principal peak in the chromatogram obtained with reference solution (a) (0.3 per cent);
— *unspecified impurities*: for each impurity, not more than the area of the principal peak in the chromatogram obtained with reference solution (a) (0.10 per cent);
— *total*: not more than 8 times the area of the principal peak in the chromatogram obtained with reference solution (a) (0.8 per cent);
— *disregard limit*: 0.5 times the area of the principal peak in the chromatogram obtained with reference solution (a) (0.05 per cent).

**Loss on drying** (2.2.32)
Maximum 0.5 per cent, determined on 1.000 g by drying in an oven at 105 °C for 4 h.

**Sulphated ash** (2.4.14)
Maximum 0.1 per cent, determined on 1.0 g.

**ASSAY**
Dissolve 0.300 g in 70 ml of a mixture of 1 volume of *anhydrous acetic acid R* and 7 volumes of *methyl ethyl ketone R* by vigorous stirring for at least 10 min. Titrate with *0.1 M perchloric acid*, determining the end-point potentiometrically at the second point of inflexion (2.2.20).

1 ml of *0.1 M perchloric acid* is equivalent to 35.3 mg of $C_{35}H_{38}Cl_2N_8O_4$.

**STORAGE**
Protected from light.

**IMPURITIES**
*Specified impurities*  B, C, D, E, G.

*Other detectable impurities*  (The following substances would, if present at a sufficient level, be detected by one or other of the tests in the monograph. They are limited by the general acceptance criterion for other/unspecified impurities and/or by the general monograph *Substances for pharmaceutical use (2034)*. It is therefore not necessary to identify these impurities for demonstration of compliance. See also 5.10. *Control of impurities in substances for pharmaceutical use*): A, F.

A. 4-[4-[4-(4-methoxyphenyl)piperazin-1-yl]phenyl]-2-[(1*RS*)-1-methylpropyl]-2,4-dihydro-3*H*-1,2,4-triazol-3-one,

B. 4-[4-[4-[4-[[*cis*-2-(2,4-dichlorophenyl)-2-(4*H*-1,2,4-triazol-4-ylmethyl)-1,3-dioxolan-4-yl]methoxy]phenyl]piperazin-1-yl]phenyl]-2-[(1*RS*)-1-methylpropyl]-2,4-dihydro-3*H*-1,2,4-triazol-3-one,

C. 4-[4-[4-[4-[[*cis*-2-(2,4-dichlorophenyl)-2-(1*H*-1,2,4-triazol-1-ylmethyl)-1,3-dioxolan-4-yl]methoxy]phenyl]piperazin-1-yl]phenyl]-2-propyl-2,4-dihydro-3*H*-1,2,4-triazol-3-one,

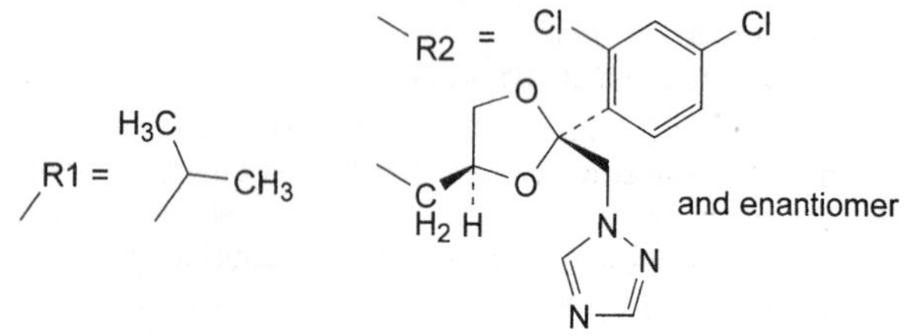

R1 = (isopropyl group)

R2 = (2,4-dichlorophenyl dioxolane triazole group) and enantiomer

D. 4-[4-[4-[4-[[*cis*-2-(2,4-dichlorophenyl)-2-(1*H*-1,2,4-triazol-1-ylmethyl)-1,3-dioxolan-4-yl]methoxy]phenyl]piperazin-1-yl]phenyl]-2-(1-methylethyl)-2,4-dihydro-3*H*-1,2,4-triazol-3-one,

R1 = (sec-butyl group) and enantiomer

R2 = (2,4-dichlorophenyl dioxolane triazole group) and enantiomer

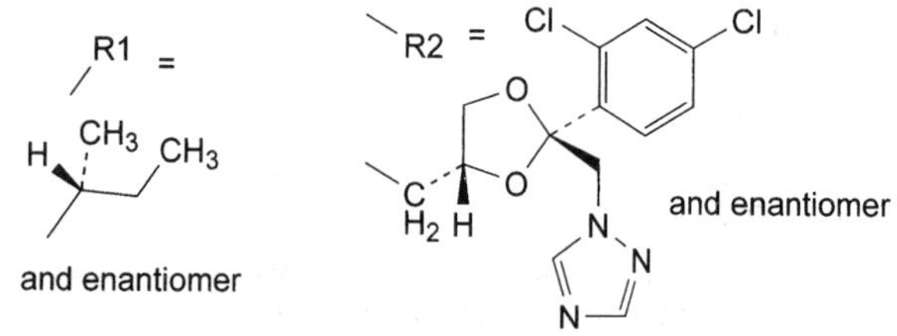

E. 4-[4-[4-[4-[[*trans*-2-(2,4-dichlorophenyl)-2-(1*H*-1,2,4-triazol-1-ylmethyl)-1,3-dioxolan-4-yl]methoxy]phenyl]piperazin-1-yl]phenyl]-2-[(1*RS*)-1-methylpropyl]-2,4-dihydro-3*H*-1,2,4-triazol-3-one,

R1 = (butyl group)

R2 = (2,4-dichlorophenyl dioxolane triazole group) and enantiomer

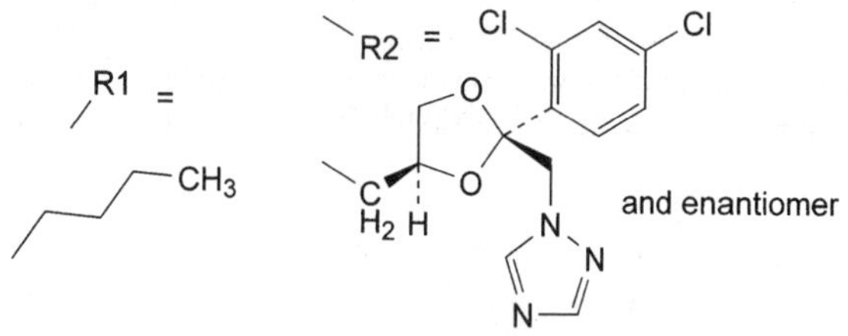

F. 2-butyl-4-[4-[4-[4-[[*cis*-2-(2,4-dichlorophenyl)-2-(1*H*-1,2,4-triazol-1-ylmethyl)-1,3-dioxolan-4-yl]methoxy]phenyl]piperazin-1-yl]phenyl]-2,4-dihydro-3*H*-1,2,4-triazol-3-one,

R1 = R2 = (2,4-dichlorophenyl dioxolane triazole group) and enantiomer

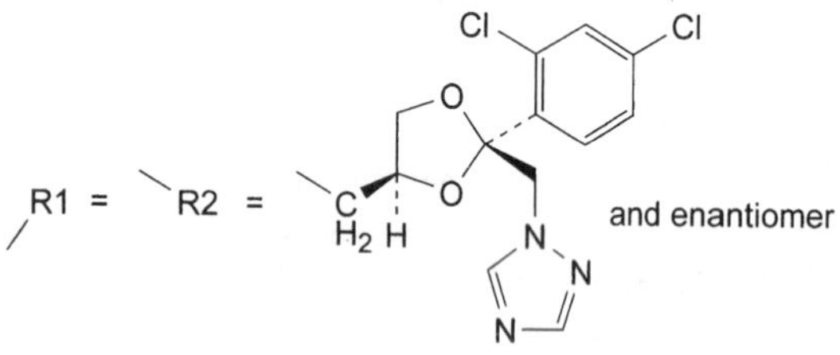

G. 4-[4-[4-[4-[[*cis*-2-(2,4-dichlorophenyl)-2-(1*H*-1,2,4-triazol-1-ylmethyl)-1,3-dioxolan-4-yl]methoxy]phenyl]piperazin-1-yl]phenyl]-2-[[*cis*-2-(2,4-dichlorophenyl)-2-(1*H*-1,2,4-triazol-1-ylmethyl)-1,3-dioxolan-4-yl]methyl]-2,4-dihydro-3*H*-1,2,4-triazol-3-one.

*Ph Eur*

# Ivermectin

*(Ph Eur monograph 1336)*

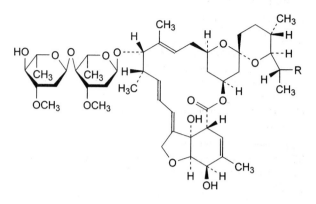

| Component | R | Molecular formula | $M_r$ |
|---|---|---|---|
| $H_2B_{1a}$ | $CH_2$-$CH_3$ | $C_{48}H_{74}O_{14}$ | 875 |
| $H_2B_{1b}$ | $CH_3$ | $C_{47}H_{72}O_{14}$ | 861 |

*70161-11-4* (ivermectin $B_{1a}$)

*70209-81-3* (ivermectin $B_{1b}$)

**Action and use**

Antihelminthic.

*Ph Eur*

## DEFINITION

Mixture of
(2a*E*,4*E*,5′*S*,6*S*,6′*R*,7*S*,8*E*,11*R*,13*R*,15*S*,17a*R*,20*R*,20a*R*,20b*S*)-7-[[2,6-dideoxy-4-*O*-(2,6-dideoxy-3-*O*-methyl-α-L-*arabino*-hexopyranosyl)-3-*O*-methyl-α-L-*arabino*-hexopyranosyl]oxy]-20,20b-dihydroxy-5′,6,8,19-tetramethyl-6′-[(1*S*)-1-methylpropyl]-3′,4′,5′,6,6′,7,10,11,14,15,17a,20,20a,20b-tetradecahydrospiro[11,15-methano-2*H*,13*H*,17*H*-furo[4,3,2-*pq*][2,6]benzodioxacyclooctadecene-13,2′-[2*H*]pyran]-17-one (or 5-*O*-demethyl-22,23-dihydroavermectin A$_{1a}$) (component $H_2B_{1a}$) and (2a*E*,4*E*,5′*S*,6*S*,6′*R*,7*S*,8*E*,11*R*,13*R*,15*S*,17a*R*,20*R*,20a*R*,20b*S*)-7-[[2,6-dideoxy-4-*O*-(2,6-dideoxy-3-*O*-methyl-α-L-*arabino*-hexopyranosyl)-3-*O*-methyl-α-L-*arabino*-hexopyranosyl]oxy]-20,20b-dihydroxy-5′,6,8,19-tetramethyl-6′-(1-methylethyl)-3′,4′,5′,6,6′,7,10,11,14,15,17a,20,20a,20b-tetradecahydrospiro[11,15-methano-2*H*,13*H*,17*H*-furo[4,3,2-*pq*][2,6]benzodioxacyclooctadecene-13,2′-[2*H*]pyran]-17-one (or 5-*O*-demethyl-25-de(1-methylpropyl)-25-(1-methylethyl)-22,23-dihydroavermectin A$_{1a}$) (component $H_2B_{1b}$).

Semi-synthetic product derived from a fermentation product.

**Content:**

— ivermectin ($H_2B_{1a}$ + $H_2B_{1b}$): 95.0 per cent to 102.0 per cent (anhydrous substance);

— ratio $H_2B_{1a}$/($H_2B_{1a}$ + $H_2B_{1b}$) (areas by liquid chromatography): minimum 90.0 per cent.

## CHARACTERS

**Appearance**

White or yellowish-white, crystalline powder, slightly hygroscopic.

**Solubility**

Practically insoluble in water, freely soluble in methylene chloride, soluble in alcohol.

## IDENTIFICATION

A. Infrared absorption spectrophotometry (*2.2.24*).

*Comparison*   ivermectin CRS.

B. Examine the chromatograms obtained in the assay.

*Results*   The retention times and sizes of the 2 principal peaks in the chromatogram obtained with the test solution are similar to those of the 2 principal peaks in the chromatogram obtained with reference solution (a).

## TESTS

### Appearance of solution

The solution is clear (*2.2.1*) and not more intensely coloured than reference solution BY$_7$ (*2.2.2, Method II*).

Dissolve 1.0 g in 50 ml of *toluene R*.

### Specific optical rotation (*2.2.7*)

− 17 to − 20 (anhydrous substance).

Dissolve 0.250 g in *methanol R* and dilute to 10.0 ml with the same solvent.

### Related substances

Liquid chromatography (*2.2.29*).

*Test solution*   Dissolve 40.0 mg of the substance to be examined in *methanol R* and dilute to 50.0 ml with the same solvent.

*Reference solution (a)*   Dissolve 40.0 mg of *ivermectin CRS* in *methanol R* and dilute to 50.0 ml with the same solvent.

*Reference solution (b)*   Dilute 1.0 ml of reference solution (a) to 100.0 ml with *methanol R*.

*Reference solution (c)*   Dilute 5.0 ml of reference solution (b) to 100.0 ml with *methanol R*.

*Column:*
— size: $l = 0.25$ m, $\emptyset = 4.6$ mm;
— stationary phase: octadecylsilyl silica gel for chromatography R (5 μm).

*Mobile phase*   water R, methanol R, acetonitrile R (15:34:51 *V/V/V*).

*Flow rate*   1 ml/min.

*Detection*   Spectrophotometer at 254 nm.

*Injection*   20 μl.

*System suitability:*
— resolution: minimum of 3.0 between the first peak (component H$_2$B$_{1b}$) and the second peak (component H$_2$B$_{1a}$) in the chromatogram obtained with reference solution (a);
— signal-to-noise ratio: minimum of 10 for the principal peak in the chromatogram obtained with reference solution (c);
— symmetry factor: maximum of 2.5 for the principal peak in the chromatogram obtained with reference solution (a).

*Limits:*
— impurity with a relative retention of 1.3 to 1.5 with reference to the principal peak: not more than 2.5 times the area of the principal peak in the chromatogram obtained with reference solution (b) (2.5 per cent);
— any other impurity (apart from the 2 principal peaks): not more than the area of the principal peak in the chromatogram obtained with reference solution (b) (1 per cent);
— total: not more than 5 times the area of the principal peak in the chromatogram obtained with reference solution (b) (5 per cent);

— disregard limit: area of the principal peak in the chromatogram obtained with reference solution (c) (0.05 per cent).

### Ethanol and formamide

Gas chromatography (*2.2.28*).

*Internal standard solution*   Dilute 0.5 ml of *propanol R* to 100 ml with *water R*.

*Test solution*   In a centrifuge tube, dissolve 0.120 g of the substance to be examined in 2.0 ml of *m-xylene R* (if necessary heat in a water-bath at 40-50 °C). Add 2.0 ml of *water R*, mix thoroughly and centrifuge. Remove the upper layer and extract it with 2.0 ml of *water R*. Discard the upper layer and combine the aqueous layers. Add 1.0 ml of the internal standard solution. Centrifuge and discard any remaining *m*-xylene.

*Reference solution (a)*   Dilute 3.0 g of *ethanol R* to 100.0 ml with *water R*.

*Reference solution (b)*   Dilute 1.0 g of *formamide R* to 100.0 ml with *water R*.

*Reference solution (c)*   Dilute 5.0 ml of reference solution (a) and 5.0 ml of reference solution (b) to 50.0 ml with *water R*. Introduce 2.0 ml of this solution into a centrifuge tube, add 2.0 ml of *m-xylene R*, mix thoroughly and centrifuge. Remove the upper layer and extract it with 2.0 ml of *water R*. Discard the upper layer and combine the aqueous layers. Add 1.0 ml of the internal standard solution. Centrifuge and discard any remaining *m*-xylene.

*Reference solution (d)*   Dilute 10.0 ml of reference solution (a) and 10.0 ml of reference solution (b) to 50.0 ml with *water R*. Treat as prescribed for reference solution (c) (from "Introduce 2.0 ml of this solution...").

*Column:*
— material: fused silica;
— size: $l = 30$ m, $\emptyset = 0.53$ mm;
— stationary phase: macrogol 20 000 R (film thickness 1 μm).

*Carrier gas*   helium for chromatography R.

*Flow rate*   7.5 ml/min.

*Split ratio*   1:10.

*Temperature:*

|  | Time (min) | Temperature (°C) |
|---|---|---|
| Column | 0 - 2 | 50 → 80 |
|  | 2 - 8 | 80 → 240 |
| Injection port |  | 220 |
| Detector |  | 280 |

*Detection*   Flame ionisation.

*Injection*   1 μl; inject the test solution and reference solutions (c) and (d).

*Limits:*
— ethanol: maximum 5.0 per cent;
— formamide: maximum 3.0 per cent.

### Heavy metals (*2.4.8*)

Maximum 20 ppm.

1.0 g complies with limit test C. Prepare the standard using 2 ml of *lead standard solution (10 ppm Pb) R*.

### Water (*2.5.12*)

Maximum 1.0 per cent, determined on 0.50 g.

### Sulphated ash (*2.4.14*)

Maximum 0.1 per cent, determined on 1.0 g.

## ASSAY

Liquid chromatography (*2.2.29*) as described in the test for related substances.

*Injection*  20 µl; inject the test solution and reference solution (a).

Calculate the percentage contents of ivermectin ($H_2B_{1a}$ + $H_2B_{1b}$) and the ratio $H_2B_{1a}$/($H_2B_{1a}$ + $H_2B_{1b}$) using the declared contents of *ivermectin CRS*.

## STORAGE

In an airtight container.

## IMPURITIES

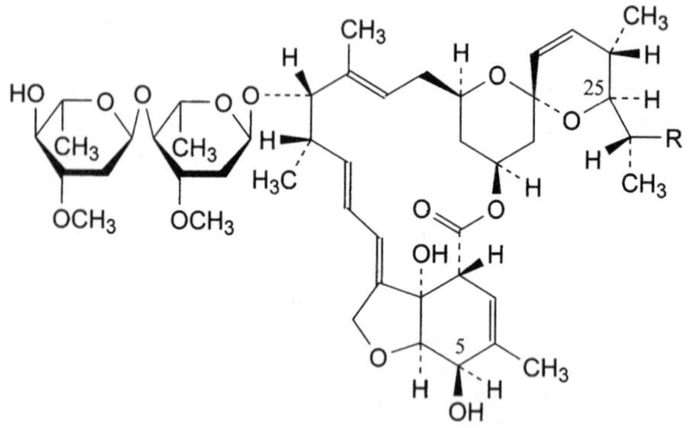

A. R = $C_2H_5$: 5-*O*-demethylavermectin $A_{1a}$ (avermectin $B_{1a}$),

B. R = $CH_3$: 5-*O*-demethyl-25-de(1-methylpropyl)-25-(1-methylethyl)avermectin $A_{1a}$ (avermectin $B_{1b}$),

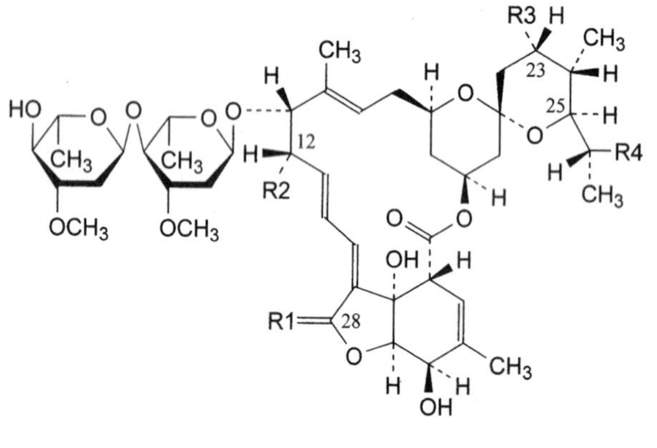

C. R1 = $H_2$, R2 = $CH_3$, R3 = OH, R4 = $C_2H_5$: (23*S*)-5-*O*-demethyl-23-hydroxy-22,23-dihydroavermectin $A_{1a}$ (avermectin $B_{2a}$),

D. R1 = O, R2 = $CH_3$, R3 = H, R4 = $C_2H_5$: 5-*O*-demethyl-28-oxo-22,23-dihydroavermectin $A_{1a}$ (28-oxo$H_2B_{1a}$),

E. R1 = $H_2$, R2 = $C_2H_5$, R3 = H, R4 = $C_2H_5$: 5-*O*,12-didemethyl-12-ethyl-22,23-dihydroavermectin $A_{1a}$ (12-demethyl-12-ethyl-$H_2B_{1a}$),

F. R1 = $H_2$, R2 = $C_2H_5$, R3 = H, R4 = $CH_3$: 5-*O*,12-didemethyl-25-de(1-methylpropyl)-12-ethyl-25-(1-methylethyl)-22,23-dihydroavermectin $A_{1a}$ (12-demethyl-12-ethyl-$H_2B_{1b}$),

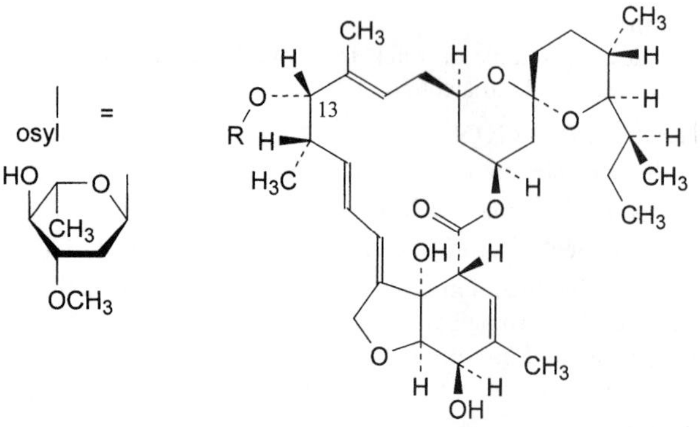

```
osyl  =
```

G. R = H: (6*R*,13*S*,25*R*)-5-*O*-demethyl-28-deoxy-6,28-epoxy-13-hydroxy-25-[(1*S*)-1-methylpropyl]milbemycin B ($H_2B_{1a}$ aglycone),

H. R = osyl: 4'-*O*-de(2,6-dideoxy-3-*O*-methyl-α-L-*arabino*-hexopyranosyl)-5-*O*-demethyl-22,23-dihydroavermectin $A_{1a}$,

and epimer at C*

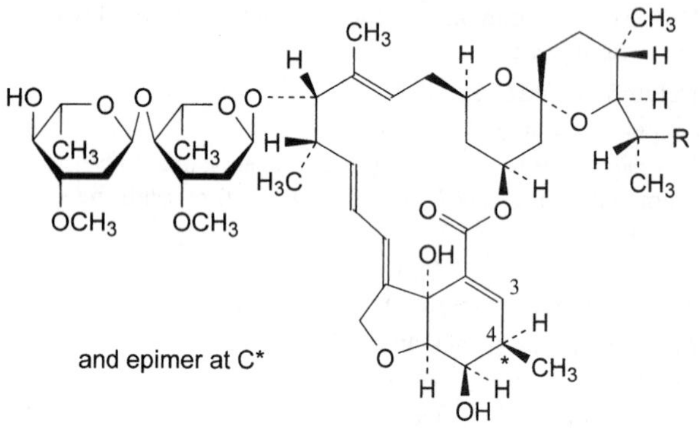

I. R = $C_2H_5$: 2,3-didehydro-5-*O*-demethyl-3,4,22,23-tetrahydroavermectin $A_{1a}$ ($\Delta^{2,3}$ $H_2B_{1a}$),

J. R = $CH_3$: 2,3-didehydro-5-*O*-demethyl-25-de(1-methylpropyl)-25-(1-methylethyl)-3,4,22,23-tetrahydroavermectin $A_{1a}$ ($\Delta^{2,3}$ $H_2B_{1b}$),

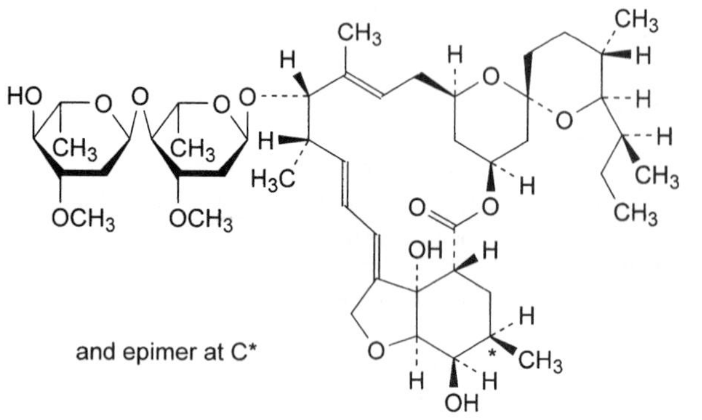

and epimer at C*

K. (4*R*) and (4*S*)-5-*O*-demethyl-3,4,22,23-tetrahydroavermectin $A_{1a}$ ($H_4B_{1a}$ isomers).

Ph Eur